LITERAL STANDARD VERSION (LSV)
of
THE HOLY BIBLE
First Edition

CONTAINING THE OLD AND NEW TESTAMENTS

Copyright © 2020 by Covenant Press of the
Covenant Christian Coalition
www.ccc.one | www.lsvbible.com

Presented To
By

THE NAMES AND ORDER OF THE BOOKS OF THE HOLY BIBLE

The Books of the Old Testament

GENESIS 17	ECCLESIASTES 525
EXODUS 61	SONG OF SONGS 532
LEVITICUS 98	ISAIAH 536
NUMBERS 125	JEREMIAH 578
DEUTERONOMY 163	LAMENTATIONS 628
JOSHUA 195	EZEKIEL 633
JUDGES 217	DANIEL 678
RUTH 239	HOSEA 692
1 SAMUEL 242	JOEL 698
2 SAMUEL 271	AMOS 701
1 KINGS 295	OBADIAH 706
2 KINGS 323	JONAH 707
1 CHRONICLES 350	MICAH 709
2 CHRONICLES 374	NAHUM 713
EZRA 405	HABAKKUK 715
NEHEMIAH 414	ZEPHANIAH 717
ESTHER 427	HAGGAI 719
JOB 434	ZECHARIAH 721
PSALMS 455	MALACHI 729
PROVERBS 507	

The Books of the New Testament

MATTHEW 735	1 TIMOTHY 915
MARK 763	2 TIMOTHY 918
LUKE 781	TITUS 921
JOHN 812	PHILEMON 923
ACTS 835	HEBREWS 924
ROMANS 865	JAMES 933
1 CORINTHIANS 877	1 PETER 936
2 CORINTHIANS 888	2 PETER 940
GALATIANS 896	1 JOHN 943
EPHESIANS 900	2 JOHN 946
PHILIPPIANS 904	3 JOHN 947
COLOSSIANS 907	JUDE 948
1 THESSALONIANS 910	REVELATION 949
2 THESSALONIANS 913	

PREFACE

Many have undertaken translation of the sacred Hebrew, Aramaic, and Greek writings—known collectively as *The Holy Bible*—into English, with varying degrees of success. The word *Bible* comes from the Greek βιβλία, the plural form of βιβλίον ("book" or "scroll"). Thus, the Holy Books or Holy Scrolls are the protocanonical collection of God-breathed writings central to Judeo-Christian belief. Christians regard the original autographic manuscripts to be directly inspired by God, inerrant ("without error"), and infallible ("without fault"; i.e., incapable of fallacy). The absolute truth of God revealed therein is the basis for the Protestant/Evangelical doctrine of Sola Scriptura ("by Scripture alone")—the fundamental belief that God's word stands alone as the ultimate arbiter of religious, spiritual, and historical truth because that knowledge which is directly revealed by God to mankind is perfect and without flaw. All beliefs and theories regarding origins and religion are only true insofar as they agree with Scripture, and are false inasmuch as they disagree.

While Christians recognize the infallibility of the autographs, there is also necessary recognition that the original writings have been lost to history. What we now possess are manuscript copies or copies of copies of the originals. Some of these copies were made shortly after the originals and others were written many decades later. To complicate matters, there are distinct manuscript versions and text-types of the Old and New Testaments with minor discrepancies. For the Old Testament we must consider the distinctives between various manuscript versions such as the Masoretic Text (MT), Septuagint (LXX), Samaritan Pentateuch (SP), and Dead Sea Scrolls (DSS). And for the New Testament, translators compare the Alexandrian, Western, and Byzantine text-types.

The goal of any good translation is to produce a readable text that preserves the original autographic meaning and comes as close as possible to translating, word-for-word, manuscripts that accurately represent the original writings. It's with this goal in mind that the Literal Standard Version (LSV) was written—a modern, yet literal English translation based upon the most prolific texts: the Masoretic Text (MT) for the Old Testament and the Textus Receptus (TR) and Majority Text (M) for the New. However, in certain, specific instances other manuscript versions and text-types are used where the evidence seems incontrovertible (e.g., the LXX and DSS in the Hebrew and Aramaic; the Alexandrian in the Greek).

While many may at first feel disoriented by the cacophony of textual questions, it should be stated with utmost certainty that one of the *many* things that sets The Holy Bible apart as the unique and divinely inspired word of God is that the manuscript evidence for it is simply overwhelming. No other ancient text, religious or otherwise, has as much manuscript support as The Holy Bible. There are literally tens of thousands of papyri fragments, external citations, and complete copies of ancient manuscripts in the original languages and though there are minor variations, the texts, across all versions, are largely identical. Recent discoveries, such as the Dead Sea Scrolls, add further weight to the authenticity of the Scriptures and the accuracy of the translation-base from which we translate to English.

Distinctive features of the Literal Standard Version of The Holy Bible:

- A modern, literal, word-for-word (formal equivalence) English translation of the Holy Scriptures utilizing English word rearrangement when necessitated for readability. The LSV is the most literal translation of The Holy Bible, with significant improvement over previous literal translations, including Robert Young's excellent Young's Literal Translation.

- Preservation of verb tenses wherever possible.

- Utilization of the transliterated Tetragrammaton in the Old Testament. All uppercase L<small>ORD</small> is used in the New Testament when a reference to Y<small>HWH</small> is likely.

- Generally consistent approach to formal equivalence translation; most English translations use a broad set of words when translating a single Greek or Hebrew word based on context. We are striving to only use varying words when the context demands it.

- Removal of many Hebrew and Greek transliterations; remember, *transliterations* are generally not *translations*.

- Unlike most translations, justified typographic alignment consistent with the style of the original Hebrew, Aramaic, and Greek biblical autographs. The ancient caesura mark is used for easy readability of poetic literature such as the Psalms.

- Inclusion of the verses found in older English translations such as the King James Version (KJV) that are not found in many modern translations; and inclusion of the alternative LXX Genesis chronology set next to the MT. These are contained within bolded double brackets for distinction.

- Capitalized pronouns and other nounal forms when referring to God, Christ, or the Holy Spirit. References to the Messenger of the L<small>ORD</small> are also capitalized when the subject appears to be a clear reference to God or the Messiah (as found in translations such as the NKJV).

Why should we trust in The Holy Bible over other religious, historical, and scientific texts?

The Holy Bible is the complete account of God's revelation to mankind, telling the whole story of history from beginning to end. We can know with absolute certainty that the Bible is true because the Bible is God-breathed. In its original Hebrew, Aramaic, and Greek manuscripts it is inerrant and infallible. The true God spoke true words to fallible human beings (cf. 2 Tim. 3: 16–17 and 2 Pet. 1: 20–21). Enabled by the Holy Spirit, they were moved to accurately record God's message. But, understandably, that answer will not satisfy the skeptic. There are at least six key arguments that powerfully vouch for the Bible's unique authenticity:

1. Every claim in the Bible that can be demonstrably tested has been verified. In other words, if we presently possess some scientific know-how, archaeological discovery, or corroborating text that can directly test a specific claim from the Bible, the claim has been verified. As a matter of fact, this truth has been a great source of humiliation for secular historians over the past several decades as discovery after discovery has proven the Bible true even after historians had said "it just can't be." Whether it be the fallen walls of Jericho, the reign of King Hezekiah, or even the existence of a Jewish temple, every bit of physical evidence that has turned up to answer the Bible's claims has proven the Bible true.

2. There are more ancient manuscripts of the Bible than any other ancient text. Furthermore, the discovery of the Dead Sea Scrolls in 1946/47 dealt a significant defeat to the theory of that generation's textual critics. They taught that the Old Testament was composed much later than Jews and Christians believed and had undergone a significant evolution in content. Not only did the Dead Sea Scrolls disprove that claim, showing that the Old Testament we have today is equivalent to the one used by Christ and His disciples, but they also provided rock-solid evidence that numerous prophecies about Jesus Christ were written before He was born.

3. The Bible contains self-verifying mathematical and thematic codes underlying the text. In recent years scholars have discovered numerous number patterns in the text in various books such as Genesis and the synoptic gospels, that would be impossible for humans to have developed on their own. There are similar thematic codes that testify to the Bible's divine origins.

4. Despite having been written over a period of 1,600 years by 40 different authors, the Bible forms a single metanarrative. It forms a continuous story with a clear beginning, ending, climax, protagonist, antagonist and complex, repeating themes that recur in almost every book. Yet its authors' lives were separated by many centuries, occurring on three different continents and in several different ancient cultures. This incredible collection of history, poetry, prophecy, and letters forms a single, overarching story from beginning to end. The protagonist and antagonist show up at the beginning of the story, continue their parts throughout, and reach a climactic moment, culminating with a final showdown at the very end. Dozens of themes, symbols, and patterns recur through the entire text, from Genesis to Revelation. No other religious text can boast of such miraculous development.

5. The Bible forms a doctrinal hologram. Typical religious texts are one or two-dimensional. If you take out a passage from the text the religion is fundamentally altered—removing key doctrines. It is like a painting on a canvas—mar a section of the picture and you can no longer see the whole. Strangely, the Bible is different. From a doctrinal perspective it forms something analogous to a three-dimensional hologram. You can remove any piece of a hologram, move to a different viewing angle and still see the whole. Doctrines revealed in the Bible are spread out across the entire book, like an interconnected web. This is strong evidence that the book's underlying author intended His message to get through even if someone tampered with the text. This complex web or layering is hinted at in Isaiah 28: "...precept upon precept, line upon line, here a little, there a little."

6. Prophecy is unique to the Bible and is its watermark of authenticity. Other religious texts contain "prophecy," but unique to the Bible are very specific prophecies that can be demonstrably proven to have been written before the events occurred. Isaiah 53 is an important example. Written some 700 years before Jesus Christ was born, it correctly prophesied that He would come from humble origins, die as a substitutionary sacrifice for our sins, be buried in a rich man's tomb, rise to life again, and be glorified. There are hundreds of other such prophecies.

INTRODUCTION TO THE LSV

The Literal Standard Version of The Holy Bible is a major revision of Young's Literal Translation (YLT). It maintains many of Robert Young's great contributions to the field of Bible translation and research. The relationship of the LSV to Young's Literal Translation is similar to that of the English Standard Version (ESV) to the Revised Standard Version or the New King James Version (NKJV) and Modern English Version (MEV) to the KJV. Young's Literal Translation was the most literal translation of The Holy Bible ever made into English up to this point for three key reasons: 1. Preservation of verb tenses, 2. Consistent word-for-word translation, and 3. General preservation of word order.

The LSV maintains the first two rules while having more flexibility with the third, which actually results in a more literal end-result. To understand why, you must first understand the nature of language. Language is a series of written and/or spoken words that convey meaning. Words *and* meaning are inherent to the definition of language. Furthermore, words have meaning by themselves, but also when structured together. A word by itself contains meaning but has no context. As grand an undertaking as the YLT was, it suffered from overdependence on word order at the expense of readability. This begs the question: if word order is maintained, but a sentence is unreadable, is a translation truly made? Languages not only differ in alphabet, but also in word order and sentence structure. For instance, in the Latin languages "I love you" would be structured "You I love." In the Germanic family it would be the former. In more complicated sentences, the differing word order can result in unintelligible translation if the word order is maintained. Since context and sentence structure are as vital to translation as capturing the proper meaning of each word, the translators of the LSV have used these three key principles in translation: 1. Preservation of verb tenses, 2. Consistent word-for-word translation, and 3. Preservation of word order when readability is unimpacted, but revised word order when necessary for readability.

The use of these three principles in combination with other LSV peculiarities *discussed below* has resulted in the most literal translation of The Holy Bible into modern English, as well as the most distinctive.

Another translation, *why?*

There have been a slew of new English translations in the past half-century, which may cause some to wonder why the need for another. The translators agree with the premise that different translations can serve different demographics and different reading levels to maximize exposure to God's word. In this sense, the LSV is not a competitor to other excellent translations, but is complimentary. As the most literal modern English translation, the LSV is an excellent resource for deep and thoughtful Bible study and research, essentially an interlinear in terms of word-for-word translation, but arranged with English sentence structure. At the same time, some newer translations and revisions are twisting the Holy Scriptures in order to appease a postmodern, progressive, and secular readership. The LSV is a line in the sand against such perversion. Let God's word speak on its own terms. The LSV has been translated to improve upon what has come before and to ensure that God's word in English is passed along to the next generation.

The Name of God

One of the first things a reader may notice about the LSV is the use of the transliterated Tetragrammaton ("YHWH") instead of "LORD." This decision was made on the premise that God did in fact reveal His Name as YHWH to the Israelites of antiquity and many Scriptures emphasize the importance and sacredness of His Name. Replacing His actual Name with an English title does disservice to the Name and to the many Scriptures that emphasize the Name. At the same time, an impersonal title such as "LORD" may cause the reader to view an ever-present and very personal God impersonally. We want the reader to recognize that God has indeed given us His Name and we must respect His decision. Moreover, while a handful of translations use a pronounceable name, we thought it best to recognize that none of these names are universally accepted in scholarship and the original unpointed Hebrew did not provide us with the vowels. *Yahweh*, *Yehovah*, and others, are mere suggestions based on differing bodies of research. While "Yahweh" or something of very similar pronunciation seems the most likely, or at least as close as we may come at the present time, we have chosen to use the transliterated Tetragrammaton because it is more than likely accurate, represents the original unpointed Name, and leaves it to the reader to respectfully and thoughtfully pronounce the Name according to the research they are more personally persuaded by. At the same time, we have opted to retain many Anglicized names, including the Name of God's Son, *Jesus*. Our reasons are threefold: *first*, it is already a name and not a title; *second*, the Name is in near-universal use in the English-speaking world; and *third*, it is a close transliteration of the original Greek *Iesous*.

Justified typographic alignment, the caesura mark, and other formatting peculiarities

The LSV may be the only English translation of The Holy Bible entirely formatted with justified typographic alignment throughout. This same format is maintained in poetic literature. While some readers may prefer paragraph breaks in narrative and line breaks in poetic portions for the purpose of readability, it was the decision of the translators to mimic the style of the original Hebrew, Aramaic, and Greek autographs in presenting God's word as a continuous text block. This decision wasn't arbitrary. In formatting the text this way, the LSV sets itself against the modern push for more and more formatting within the text, in favor of simplicity. Furthermore, the modern trend even extended to differentiating the words of Christ in red letters, as if God's word should be divided in such a way. The LSV is the polar opposite, regarding the entirety of Scripture as God-breathed, with its different genres of literature resting on a level playing field.

In summary, this formatting decision was made to mimic the style of the original autographs, elevate the entirety of Scripture as God-breathed, exclude the possibility of formatting passages in a way contrary to the author's intended delivery, and finally: it was made for ease of sharing in an era where digital reading is as common as reading from paper. Whether it be a printed copy, an eBook, an app, or some other format, the LSV is the easiest translation to copy and share ever made. In addition, justified typographic alignment throughout reduces the overall length of the printed and digital editions by a substantial margin, offering considerable cost savings to publishers and distributors seeking to get God's word into as many hands as possible.

Like alignment, the LSV adopts a more ancient approach to handle quotations. Recent translations continue the trend of deeply-nested quotation marks, which many readers find confusing. The original biblical autographs contained no punctuation denoting the opening or closing of a quotation, whereas many modern translations use alternating double quotes (" ") and single quotes (' ') to nest quotes two, three, or even four levels deep. The LSV utilizes a middle approach between modern translations and the older English translations like the KJV, which didn't use quotation marks at all. The LSV uses double quotes to denote the outermost quotation within a single chapter (similar to recent translations), and a capitalized opening word of a nested quote (similar to the King James Version). This lends itself to a simpler, more elegant, and easier-to-follow text.

For ease of readability, the LSV includes the double pipe ("‖") *caesura mark* to separate phrases within poetic portions of Scripture. The caesura mark was extensively used this way in ancient Greek, Latin, and English poetry. Verse numbers, periods, colons, semicolons, question marks, exclamation marks, and em dashes generally stand in for caesura marks in these passages if they are followed by a capital letter.

Finally, clarifying, interpolated words are placed in unbolded brackets ("[ ]") to make clear that they do not form part of the original Hebrew, Aramaic, and Greek text. Bolded double brackets ("[[ ]]") are reserved for identifying words, phrases, and passages whose inclusion in the original text is disputed.

Definite articles and prepositions

The greatest flexibility in translation can be found in regard to definite articles and prepositions. The LSV is generally more literal with definite articles than the YLT. Definite articles are often surrounded by brackets when they are missing from the original text (although not always—when the use of the definite article in English is demanded). When the definite article's usage is flexible, the LSV generally defers to the original text in its absence or inclusion.

While the LSV doesn't use a single word to consistently translate each preposition, the LSV does strive to maintain consistency in semantic range (in other words, a certain set of English prepositions are matched to each Bible language preposition, and the consistency is maintained wherever possible). This consistency results in the LSV being equally literal and readable.

Church, repentance, baptism, and *age*

The LSV chooses a literal translation even for "theologically loaded" words like ἐκκλησία (LSV: "assembly"), μετάνοια (LSV: "conversion"), βάπτισμα (LSV: "immersion"), and עוֹלָם and αἰών (LSV: "age" or "continuous," depending on the context). These decisions were not made to disparage the common translations and were not made lightly. They were made to give the reader the best sense of what the original words mean in English, without the use of words that are the result of centuries of theological tradition. The frequent translation of metanoia as "repentance" has been particularly troubling to scholars who emphasize the fundamental differences in their etymology and meaning, with the original Greek word referring to persuasion, conversion, or a change of mind or belief.

THE GOOD NEWS OF SALVATION

> In accordance with the Scriptures, Christ the Messiah, the Son of the living God, became human, incarnate in the person of Jesus of Nazareth, lived a morally perfect and sinless life, died for our sins on the Cross as a substitutionary sacrifice, was buried in a tomb, and was raised bodily from the dead on the third day. Everyone who hears and accepts this message of salvation, believing in their heart that God raised the Christ from the dead, will be pardoned of all their sins, given the gift of the Holy Spirit, and granted everlasting life with God. Salvation is found in Christ alone by grace alone through faith alone and not by works.

KEY SCRIPTURES

God, Creator and source of all things	Gen. 1:1
Man created in the image of God	Gen. 1:27
Man given dominion over the earth	Gen. 1:28
God completes creation in six days	Gen. 1:31–2:1 (cf. Ex. 20:11)
The seventh day is the Sabbath	Gen. 2:2
Marriage, the union of one man and one woman	Gen. 2:24
Man disobeys God's single commandment and falls into sin	Gen. 3 (cf. Rom. 5:12)
God promises a human Redeemer	Gen. 3:15
God destroys the ancient, evil world with a flood	Gen. 6–7
The earth is replenished through Noah and his family	Gen. 8–10
God scatters mankind and creates different languages	Gen. 11
Abraham, the father of Israel	Gen. 12:1–4
Abraham's faith counted as righteousness	Gen. 15:6
God's covenant established with Isaac and not Ishmael	Gen. 17:18–19
Isaac's son Jacob becomes Israel	Gen. 32:27–28
God reveals that His Name is YHWH	Ex. 3:13–15
The Israelites escape slavery in Egypt and receive the Law	Ex. 12:31–42; 19–24
God gives the Holy Land to the Israelites	Josh. 1:1–6
God's own Son to rule all nations from Zion	Ps. 2
The coming Redeemer will die as an atoning sacrifice for our sins	Isa. 53
Jesus Christ, the Son of God, born of a virgin, is revealed	Mt. 1:1–2:6; Lk. 1:26–2:52
Jesus reveals that salvation is only found in Him	Jn. 14:6 (cf. Acts 4:12)
Jesus gives His life as an atoning sacrifice for our sins	Mt. 27:11–56; Jn. 18:28–37
Jesus is buried in a rich man's tomb	Mt. 27:57–61; Jn. 19:38–42
Jesus is resurrected from the dead and appears to many	Mt. 28:1–15; Lk. 24:1–49; Jn. 20
Jesus reveals the Trinity	Mt. 28:19 (cf. Lk. 3:22; Jn. 14:26; 15:26; Acts 2:33; 2 Cor. 13:14)
Jesus ascends into Heaven	Mk. 16:19; Lk. 24:50–53; Acts 1:6–9
Jesus will return to the same place He left	Acts 1:10–11 (cf. Zech. 14:1–5)
The Holy Spirit is given to the Church on Pentecost	Acts 2:1–4 (cf. Acts 1:1–5)
The Early Church is filled with zeal and love for one another	Acts 2:42–47
The Church is the mystical Body of Christ, made of many members	1 Cor. 12:12–27
The Gospel explicitly defined	1 Cor. 15:1–8
Believers will be resurrected to inherit eternal life	1 Cor. 15:50–58 (cf. Jn. 3:1–36; 5:24)
Everyone is wicked and in need of Jesus	Rom. 3:9–20, 23; Isa. 64:6; Jas. 3:2
Salvation is through faith alone	Rom. 3:21–5:21; Gal. 2:15–5:6; Eph. 2:8–9
Believers called to live holy lives	1 Thess. 4:1–12
Believers will be taken to Heaven by Jesus	Jn. 14:1–4; 1 Thess. 4:16–18
Jesus defeats the Devil and rules all nations	Rev. 12:7–10; 19:11–16
Jesus judges all men and unbelievers are destroyed	Rev. 20:11–15
A new heaven, new earth, and New Jerusalem	Rev. 21:1–27 (cf. Isa. 65:17; 2 Pet. 3:13)
Jesus is coming soon, invitation to believe	Rev. 22

THE OLD TESTAMENT

GENESIS

1 In [the] beginning God created the heavens and the earth, **2** and the earth was formless and void, and darkness [was] on the face of the deep, and the Spirit of God [was] fluttering on the face of the waters, **3** and God says, "Let light be"; and light is. **4** And God sees that the light [is] good, and God separates between the light and the darkness, **5** and God calls the light "Day," and the darkness He has called "Night"; and there is an evening, and there is a morning—day one. **6** And God says, "Let an expanse be in the midst of the waters, and let it be separating between waters and waters." **7** And God makes the expanse, and it separates between the waters which [are] under the expanse, and the waters which [are] above the expanse: and it is so. **8** And God calls the expanse "Heavens"; and there is an evening, and there is a morning—[the] second day. **9** And God says, "Let the waters under the heavens be collected to one place, and let the dry land be seen": and it is so. **10** And God calls the dry land "Earth," and the collection of the waters He has called "Seas"; and God sees that [it is] good. **11** And God says, "Let the earth yield tender grass, herb sowing seed, fruit-tree (whose seed [is] in itself) making fruit after its kind, on the earth": and it is so. **12** And the earth brings forth tender grass, herb sowing seed after its kind, and tree making fruit (whose seed [is] in itself) after its kind; and God sees that [it is] good; **13** and there is an evening, and there is a morning—[the] third day. **14** And God says, "Let luminaries be in the expanse of the heavens, to make a separation between the day and the night, then they have been for signs, and for appointed times, and for days and years, **15** and they have been for luminaries in the expanse of the heavens to give light on the earth": and it is so. **16** And God makes the two great luminaries, the great luminary for the rule of the day, and the small luminary—and the stars—for the rule of the night; **17** and God gives them in the expanse of the heavens to give light on the earth, **18** and to rule over day and over night, and to make a separation between the light and the darkness; and God sees that [it is] good; **19** and there is an evening, and there is a morning—[the] fourth day. **20** And God says, "Let the waters teem with the teeming living creature, and let [the] bird fly above the earth on the face of the expanse of the heavens." **21** And God creates the great dragons, and every living creature that is creeping, which the waters have teemed with, after their kind, and every bird with wing, after its kind, and God sees that [it is] good. **22** And God blesses them, saying, "Be fruitful, and multiply, and fill the waters in the seas, and let the bird multiply in the earth": **23** and there is an evening, and there is a morning—[the] fifth day. **24** And God says, "Let the earth bring forth the living creature after its kind, livestock and creeping thing, and beast of the earth after its kind": and it is so. **25** And God makes the beast of the earth after its kind, and the livestock after their kind, and every creeping thing of the ground after its kind, and God sees that [it is] good. **26** And God says, "Let Us make man in Our image, according to Our likeness, and let them rule over [the] fish of the sea, and over [the] bird of the heavens, and over livestock, and over all the earth, and over every creeping thing that is creeping on the earth." **27** And God creates the man in His image; in the image of God He created him, a male and a female He created them. **28** And God blesses them, and God says to them, "Be fruitful, and multiply, and fill the earth, and subdue it, and rule over [the] fish of the sea, and over [the] bird of the heavens, and over every living thing that is creeping on the earth." **29** And God says, "Behold, I have given to you every herb sowing seed, which [is] on the face of all the earth, and every tree in which [is] the fruit of a tree sowing seed, to you it is for food; **30** and to every beast of the earth, and to every bird of the heavens, and to every creeping thing on the earth, in which [is] breath of life, every green herb [is] for food": and it is so. **31** And God sees all that He has done, and behold, [it is] very good; and there is an evening, and there is a morning—the sixth day.

2 And the heavens and the earth are completed, and all their host; **2** and God completes by the seventh day His work which He has made, and ceases by the seventh day from all His work which He has made. **3** And God blesses the seventh day, and sanctifies it, for in it He has ceased from all His work which God had created for making. **4** These [are] the generations of the heavens and of the earth in their being created, in the day of YHWH God's making the earth and the heavens; **5** and no shrub of the field is yet in the earth, and no herb of the field yet sprouts, for YHWH God has not rained on the earth, and there is not a man to serve the ground, **6** and a mist goes up from the earth, and has watered the whole face of the ground. **7** And YHWH God forms the man—dust from the ground, and breathes into his nostrils breath of life, and the man becomes a living creature. **8** And YHWH God plants a garden in Eden, at the east, and He sets there the man whom He has formed; **9** and YHWH God causes to sprout from the ground every tree desirable for appearance, and good for food, and the Tree of Life in the midst of the garden, and the Tree of the Knowledge of Good and Evil. **10** And a river is going out from Eden to water the garden, and from there it is parted, and has become four chief [rivers]; **11** the name of the first [is] Pison, it [is] that which is surrounding the whole land of Havilah where the gold [is], **12** and the gold of that land [is] good; the bdellium and the shoham stone [are] there; **13** and the name of the second river [is] Gihon, it [is] that which is surrounding the whole land of Cush; **14** and the name of the third river [is] Hiddekel, it [is] that which is going east of Asshur; and the fourth river is the Euphrates. **15** And YHWH God takes the man, and causes him to rest in the Garden of Eden, to serve it and to keep it. **16** And YHWH God lays a charge on the man, saying, "From every tree of the garden eating you eat; **17** but from the Tree of the Knowledge of Good and Evil, you do not eat from it, for in the day of your eating from it—dying you die." **18** And YHWH God says, "[It is] not good for the man to be alone; I make him a helper as his counterpart." **19** And YHWH God forms from the ground every beast of the field, and every bird of the heavens, and brings [them] to the man, to see what he calls it; and whatever the man calls a living creature, that [is] its name. **20** And the man calls names to all the livestock, and to bird of the heavens, and to every beast of the field; but for man a helper has not been found as his counterpart. **21** And YHWH God causes a deep sleep to fall on the man, and he sleeps, and He takes one of his ribs, and closes up flesh in its stead. **22** And YHWH God builds up the rib which He has taken out of the man into a woman, and brings her to the man; **23** and the man says, "This at last! Bone of my bone, and flesh of my flesh!" For this is called Woman, for this has been taken from Man; **24** therefore a man leaves his father and his mother, and has cleaved to his wife, and they have become one flesh. **25** And both of them are naked, the man and his wife, and they are not ashamed of themselves.

3 And the serpent has been cunning above every beast of the field which YHWH God has made, and he says to the woman, "Is it true that God has said, You do not eat from every tree of the garden?" **2** And the woman says to the serpent, "From the fruit of the trees of the garden we eat, **3** but from the fruit of the tree which [is] in the midst of the garden, God has said, You do not eat of it, nor touch it, lest you die." **4** And the serpent says to the woman, "Dying, you do not die, **5** for God knows that in the day of your eating of it—your eyes have been opened, and you have been as God, knowing good and evil." **6** And the woman sees that the tree [is] good for food, and that it [is] pleasant to the eyes, and the tree is desirable to make [one] wise, and she takes from its fruit and eats, and also gives [some] to her husband with her, and he eats; **7** and the eyes of them both are opened, and they know that they [are] naked, and they sew fig-leaves, and make girdles for themselves. **8** And they hear the sound of YHWH God walking up and down in the garden at the breeze of the day, and the man and his wife hide themselves from the face of YHWH God in the midst of the trees of the garden. **9** And YHWH God calls to the man and says to him, "Where [are] you?" **10** And he says, "I have heard Your sound in the garden, and I am afraid, for I am naked, and I hide myself." **11** And He says, "Who has declared to you that you [are] naked? Have you eaten from the tree of which I have commanded you not to eat?" **12** And the man says, "The woman whom You placed with me—she has given to me from the tree, and I eat." **13** And

GENESIS

Y<small>HWH</small> God says to the woman, "What [is] this you have done?" And the woman says, "The serpent has caused me to forget, and I eat." **14** And Y<small>HWH</small> God says to the serpent, "Because you have done this, cursed [are] you above all the livestock, and above every beast of the field: on your belly you go, and dust you eat, [for] all days of your life; **15** and I put enmity between you and the woman, and between your seed and her Seed; He bruises your head, and you bruise His heel." **16** To the woman He said, "Multiplying I multiply your sorrow and your conception; you will bear children in sorrow, and your desire [is] toward your Man [[or husband]], and He [[or he]] will rule over you." **17** And to the man He said, "Because you have listened to the voice of your wife, and eat from the tree concerning which I have charged you, saying, You do not eat of it, cursed [is] the ground on your account; in sorrow you eat of it [for] all days of your life, **18** and it brings forth thorn and bramble for you, and you have eaten the herb of the field; **19** by the sweat of your face you eat bread until your return to the ground, for you have been taken out of it, for dust you [are], and to dust you return." **20** And the man calls his wife's name Eve, for she has been mother of all living. **21** And Y<small>HWH</small> God makes coats of skin [for] the man and his wife, and clothes them. **22** And Y<small>HWH</small> God says, "Behold, the man was as one of Us, as to the knowledge of good and evil; and now, lest he send forth his hand, and has also taken from the Tree of Life, and eaten, and lived for all time." **23** Y<small>HWH</small> God sends him forth from the Garden of Eden to serve the ground from which he has been taken; **24** indeed, He casts out the man, and causes the cherubim to dwell at the east of the Garden of Eden with the sword of flame whirling around to guard the way of the Tree of Life.

4 And the man knew his wife Eve, and she conceives and bears Cain, and says, "I have acquired a man by Y<small>HWH</small>"; **2** and she adds to bear his brother, even Abel. And Abel is feeding a flock, and Cain has been servant of the ground. **3** And it comes to pass at the end of days that Cain brings from the fruit of the ground a present to Y<small>HWH</small>; **4** and Abel, he has brought, he also, from the female firstlings of his flock, and from their fat ones; and Y<small>HWH</small> looks to Abel and to his present, **5** and to Cain and to his present He has not looked; and it is very displeasing to Cain, and his countenance is fallen. **6** And Y<small>HWH</small> says to Cain, "Why do you have displeasure? And why has your countenance fallen? **7** Is there not, if you do well, acceptance? And if you do not do well, sin [[or a sin-offering]] is lying at the opening, and its [[or His]] desire [is] for you, and you rule over it [[or by Him]]." **8** And Cain says to his brother Abel, [["Let us go into the field";]] and it comes to pass in their being in the field, that Cain rises up against his brother Abel, and slays him. **9** And Y<small>HWH</small> says to Cain, "Where [is] your brother Abel?" And he says, "I have not known; am I my brother's keeper?" **10** And He says, "What have you done? The voice of your brother's blood is crying to Me from the ground; **11** and now, cursed [are] you from the ground, which has opened her mouth to receive the blood of your brother from your hand; **12** when you till the ground, it will not add to give its strength to you—a wanderer, even a trembling one, you are in the earth." **13** And Cain says to Y<small>HWH</small>, "My punishment is too great than to bear; **14** behold, You have driven me today from off the face of the ground, and from Your face I am hid; and I have been a wanderer, even a trembling one, in the earth, and it has been—everyone finding me will slay me." **15** And Y<small>HWH</small> says to him, "Therefore, of any slayer of Cain it is required sevenfold"; and Y<small>HWH</small> sets to Cain a token that none finding him will slay him. **16** And Cain goes out from before Y<small>HWH</small>, and dwells in the land, moving about east of Eden; **17** and Cain knows his wife, and she conceives, and bears Enoch; and he is building a city, and he calls the name of the city, according to the name of his son—Enoch. **18** And born to Enoch is Irad; and Irad has begotten Mehujael; and Mehujael has begotten Methusael; and Methusael has begotten Lamech. **19** And Lamech takes to himself two wives, the name of the first Adah, and the name of the second Zillah. **20** And Adah bears Jabal, he has been father of those inhabiting tents and [having] purchased livestock; **21** and the name of his brother [is] Jubal, he has been father of everyone handling harp and pipe. **22** And Zillah, she also bears Tubal-Cain, an instructor of every craftsman in bronze and iron; and a sister of Tubal-Cain

[is] Naamah. **23** And Lamech says to his wives: "Adah and Zillah, hear my voice; Wives of Lamech, give ear [to] my saying: For I have slain a man for my wound, ‖ Even a young man for my hurt; **24** For sevenfold is required for Cain, ‖ And for Lamech seventy-sevenfold." **25** And Adam again knows his wife, and she bears a son, and calls his name Seth, "for God has appointed for me another seed instead of Abel": for Cain had slain him. **26** And to Seth, to him also a son has been born, and he calls his name Enos; then a beginning was made of preaching in the Name of YHWH.

5 This [is] an account of the generations of Adam. In the day of God's creating man, in the likeness of God He has made him; **2** a male and a female He has created them, and He blesses them, and calls their name Man, in the day of their being created. **3** And Adam lives one hundred and thirty years [[*or* two hundred and thirty years]], and begets [a son] in his likeness, according to his image, and calls his name Seth. **4** And the days of Adam after his begetting Seth are eight hundred years [[*or* seven hundred years]], and he begets sons and daughters. **5** And all the days of Adam which he lived are nine hundred and thirty years, and he dies. **6** And Seth lives one hundred and five years [[*or* two hundred and five years]], and begets Enos. **7** And Seth lives after his begetting Enos eight hundred and seven years [[*or* seven hundred and seven years]], and begets sons and daughters. **8** And all the days of Seth are nine hundred and twelve years, and he dies. **9** And Enos lives ninety years [[*or* one hundred and ninety years]], and begets Cainan. **10** And Enos lives after his begetting Cainan eight hundred and fifteen years [[*or* seven hundred and fifteen years]], and begets sons and daughters. **11** And all the days of Enos are nine hundred and five years, and he dies. **12** And Cainan lives seventy years [[*or* one hundred and seventy years]], and begets Mahalaleel. **13** And Cainan lives after his begetting Mahalaleel eight hundred and forty years [[*or* seven hundred and forty years]], and begets sons and daughters. **14** And all the days of Cainan are nine hundred and ten years, and he dies. **15** And Mahalaleel lives sixty-five years [[*or* one hundred and sixty-five years]], and begets Jared. **16** And Mahalaleel lives after his begetting Jared eight hundred and thirty years [[*or* seven hundred and thirty years]], and begets sons and daughters. **17** And all the days of Mahalaleel are eight hundred and ninety-five years, and he dies. **18** And Jared lives one hundred and sixty-two years, and begets Enoch. **19** And Jared lives after his begetting Enoch eight hundred years, and begets sons and daughters. **20** And all the days of Jared are nine hundred and sixty-two years, and he dies. **21** And Enoch lives sixty-five years [[*or* one hundred and sixty-five years]], and begets Methuselah. **22** And Enoch habitually walks with God after his begetting Methuselah three hundred years [[*or* two hundred years]], and begets sons and daughters. **23** And all the days of Enoch are three hundred and sixty-five years. **24** And Enoch habitually walks with God, and he is not, for God has taken him. **25** And Methuselah lives one hundred and eighty-seven years, and begets Lamech. **26** And Methuselah lives after his begetting Lamech seven hundred and eighty-two years, and begets sons and daughters. **27** And all the days of Methuselah are nine hundred and sixty-nine years, and he dies. **28** And Lamech lives one hundred and eighty-two years [[*or* one hundred and eighty-eight years]], and begets a son, **29** and calls his name Noah, saying, "This [one] comforts us concerning our work, and concerning the labor of our hands, because of the ground which YHWH has cursed." **30** And Lamech lives after his begetting Noah five hundred and ninety-five years [[*or* five hundred and sixty-five years]], and begets sons and daughters. **31** And all the days of Lamech are seven hundred and seventy-seven years [[*or* seven hundred and fifty-three years]], and he dies. **32** And Noah is a son of five hundred years, and Noah begets Shem, Ham, and Japheth.

6 And it comes to pass that mankind has begun to multiply on the face of the ground, and daughters have been born to them, **2** and the sons of God see that they, the daughters of men, [are] beautiful, and they take women for themselves of all whom they have chosen. **3** And YHWH says, "My Spirit does not strive in man for all time, for indeed, he [is] flesh, but his days have been one hundred and twenty years." **4** The giants were in the earth in

GENESIS

those days, and even afterward, when sons of God come in to the daughters of men, and they have borne to them those who [were] the mighty from of old, the men of renown. **5** And YHWH sees that the wickedness of man [is] abundant in the earth, and every imagination of the thoughts of his heart [is] only evil every day; **6** and YHWH regrets that He has made man in the earth, and He grieves Himself—to His heart. **7** And YHWH says, "I wipe away man whom I have created from off the face of the ground, from man to beast, to creeping thing, and to bird of the heavens, for I have regretted that I have made them." **8** And Noah found grace in the eyes of YHWH. **9** These [are] the generations of Noah: Noah [is] a righteous man; he has been perfect among his generations; Noah has habitually walked with God. **10** And Noah begets three sons: Shem, Ham, and Japheth. **11** And the earth is corrupt before God, and the earth is filled [with] violence. **12** And God sees the earth, and behold, it has been corrupted, for all flesh has corrupted its way on the earth. **13** And God said to Noah, "An end of all flesh has come before Me, for the earth has been full of violence from their presence; and behold, I am destroying them with the earth. **14** Make an ark of gopher-wood for yourself; you make rooms within the Ark, and you have covered it from inside and from outside with pitch; **15** and this [is] how you do it: three hundred cubits [is] the length of the Ark, fifty cubits its breadth, and thirty cubits its height; **16** you make a window for the Ark, and you finish it to a cubit from above; and you put the opening of the Ark in its side; you make it [with] lower, second, and third [stories]. **17** And I, behold, I am bringing in the flood of waters on the earth, to destroy from under the heavens all flesh in which [is] a living spirit; all that [is] in the earth expires. **18** And I have established My covenant with you, and you have come into the Ark—you, and your sons, and your wife, and your son's wives with you; **19** and of all that lives, of all flesh, you bring two from every [kind] into the Ark, to keep alive with you; they are male and female. **20** From the bird after its kind, and from the livestock after its kind, [and] from every creeping thing of the ground after its kind, two of every [kind] they come to you, to keep alive. **21** And you, take for yourself from all food that is eaten; and you have gathered [it] to yourself, and it has been for you and for them for food." **22** And Noah does according to all that God has commanded him; so he has done.

7 And YHWH says to Noah, "Come, you and all your house, into the Ark, for I have seen you [are] righteous before Me in this generation; **2** you take seven pairs from all the clean beasts to yourself, a male and its female; and of the beasts which are not clean—two, a male and its female; **3** also, seven pairs from [each] bird of the heavens, a male and a female, to keep alive seed on the face of all the earth; **4** for after seven more days I am sending rain on the earth [for] forty days and forty nights, and have wiped away all the substance that I have made from off the face of the ground." **5** And Noah does according to all that YHWH has commanded him. **6** And Noah [is] a son of six hundred years, and the flood of waters has been on the earth. **7** And Noah goes—and his sons, and his wife, and his sons' wives with him—into the Ark, out of the presence of the waters of the flood; **8** from the clean beast, and from the beast that [is] not clean, and from the bird, and of everything that is creeping on the ground, **9** they have come to Noah two by two into the Ark, a male and a female, as God has commanded Noah. **10** And it comes to pass, after seven days, that waters of the flood have been on the earth. **11** In the six hundredth year of the life of Noah, in the second month, on the seventeenth day of the month, on this day all [the] fountains of the great deep have been broken up, and the network of the heavens has been opened, **12** and the shower is on the earth [for] forty days and forty nights. **13** On this very same day Noah, and Shem, and Ham, and Japheth, sons of Noah, and Noah's wife, and the three wives of his sons with them, went into the Ark— **14** they, and every living creature after its kind, and every beast after its kind, and every creeping thing that is creeping on the earth after its kind, and every bird after its kind (every bird, every wing). **15** And they come to Noah, into the Ark, two by two of all the flesh in which [is] a living spirit; **16** and they that are coming in, male and female of all flesh, have come in as God has commanded him, and YHWH closes [it] for him. **17** And the flood is on the earth [for] forty days, and the waters multiply and lift up the Ark, and it is raised up from off the earth; **18** and the waters are mighty and multiply exceedingly on the earth; and the Ark goes on the face of the waters. **19** And the waters have been very, very mighty on the earth, and all the high mountains are covered which [are] under the whole heavens; **20** the waters prevailed from above the mountains, and cover [them] fifteen cubits; **21** and all flesh expires that is moving on the earth, among bird, and among livestock, and among beast, and among every teeming thing which is teeming on the earth, and all mankind; **22** all in whose nostrils [is] breath of a living spirit—of all that [is] in the dry land—have died. **23** And all the substance that is on the face of the ground is wiped away—from man to beast, to creeping thing, and to bird of the heavens; indeed, they are wiped away from the earth, and only Noah is left, and those who [are] with him in the Ark; **24** and the waters are mighty on the earth [for] one hundred and fifty days.

8 And God remembers Noah, and every living thing, and all the livestock which [are] with him in the Ark, and God causes a wind to pass over the earth, and the waters subside, **2** and the fountains of the deep and the network of the heavens are closed, and the shower is restrained from the heavens. **3** And the waters return from off the earth, going on and returning; and the waters are lacking at the end of one hundred and fifty days. **4** And the Ark rests, in the seventh month, on the seventeenth day of the month, on mountains of Ararat; **5** and the waters have been going and decreasing until the tenth month; in the tenth [month], on the first of the month, the heads of the mountains appeared. **6** And it comes to pass, at the end of forty days, that Noah opens the window of the Ark which he made, **7** and he sends forth the raven, and it goes out, going out and turning back until the drying of the waters from off the earth. **8** And he sends forth the dove from him to see whether the waters have been lightened from off the face of the ground, **9** and the dove has not found rest for the sole of her foot, and she turns back to him, to the Ark, for waters [are] on the face of all the earth, and he puts out his hand, and takes her, and brings her in to him, into the Ark. **10** And he stays yet seven more days, and adds to send forth the dove from the Ark; **11** and the dove comes to him at evening, and behold, an olive leaf [is] torn off in her mouth; and Noah knows that the waters have been lightened from off the earth. **12** And he stays yet seven more days, and sends forth the dove, and it did not add to return to him anymore. **13** And it comes to pass in the six hundredth and first year, in the first [month], on the first of the month, the waters have been dried from off the earth; and Noah turns aside the covering of the Ark, and looks, and behold, the face of the ground has been dried. **14** And in the second month, on the twenty-seventh day of the month, the earth has become dry. **15** And God speaks to Noah, saying, "Go out from the Ark, you, and your wife, and your sons, and your sons' wives with you; **16** every living thing that [is] with you, of all flesh, among bird, and among livestock, and among every creeping thing which is creeping on the earth, bring out with you; **17** and they have teemed in the earth, and been fruitful, and have multiplied on the earth." **18** And Noah goes out, and his sons, and his wife, and his sons' wives with him; **19** every beast, every creeping thing, and every bird; every creeping thing on the earth, after their families, have gone out from the Ark. **20** And Noah builds an altar to Yhwh, and takes from every clean beast and from every clean bird, and causes burnt-offerings to ascend on the altar; **21** and Yhwh smells the refreshing fragrance, and Yhwh says to His heart, "I do not continue to disfavor the ground because of man anymore, though the imagination of the heart of man [is] evil from his youth; and I do not continue to strike all living anymore, as I have done; **22** during all [the] days of the earth, seed-time and harvest, and cold and heat, and summer and winter, and day and night never cease."

9 And God blesses Noah and his sons, and says to them, "Be fruitful, and multiply, and fill the earth; **2** and your fear and your dread is on every beast of the earth, and on every bird of the heavens, on all that creeps on the ground, and on all fishes of the sea—into your hand they have been given. **3** Every creeping thing that is alive, to you it is for food; as the green herb I have given to you the whole; **4** only flesh in its life—

GENESIS

its blood—you do not eat. **5** And only your blood for your lives do I require; from the hand of every living thing I require it, and from the hand of man, from the hand of every man's brother I require the life of man; **6** whoever sheds man's blood, by man is his blood shed: for in the image of God has He made man. **7** And you, be fruitful and multiply, teem in the earth, and multiply in it." **8** And God speaks to Noah, and to his sons with him, saying, **9** "And I, behold, I am establishing My covenant with you, and with your seed after you, **10** and with every living creature which [is] with you, among bird, among livestock, and among every beast of the earth with you, from all who are going out of the Ark—to every beast of the earth. **11** And I have established My covenant with you, and all flesh is not cut off anymore by waters of a flood, and there is not a flood to destroy the earth anymore." **12** And God says, "This is a token of the covenant which I am giving between Me and you, and every living creature that [is] with you, to continuous generations; **13** My bow I have given in the cloud, and it has been for a token of a covenant between Me and the earth; **14** and it has come to pass (in My sending a cloud over the earth) that the bow has been seen in the cloud, **15** and I have remembered My covenant which is between Me and you, and every living creature among all flesh, and the waters no longer become a flood to destroy all flesh; **16** and the bow has been in the cloud, and I have seen it—to remember the perpetual covenant between God and every living creature among all flesh which [is] on the earth." **17** And God says to Noah, "This [is] a token of the covenant which I have established between Me and all flesh that [is] on the earth." **18** And the sons of Noah who are going out of the Ark are Shem, and Ham, and Japheth; and Ham is father of Canaan. **19** These three [are] sons of Noah, and from these has all the earth been overspread. **20** And Noah remains a man of the ground, and plants a vineyard, **21** and drinks of the wine, and is drunken, and uncovers himself in the midst of the tent. **22** And Ham, father of Canaan, sees the nakedness of his father, and declares to his two brothers outside. **23** And Shem takes—Japheth also—the garment, and they place on the shoulder of them both, and go backward, and cover the nakedness of their father; and their faces [are] backward, and their father's nakedness they have not seen. **24** And Noah awakens from his wine, and knows that which his young son has done to him, **25** and says: "Cursed [is] Canaan, ‖ Servant of servants he is to his brothers." **26** And he says: "Blessed of my God YHWH [is] Shem, ‖ And Canaan is servant to him. **27** God gives beauty to Japheth, ‖ And he dwells in tents of Shem, ‖ And Canaan is servant to him." **28** And Noah lives after the flood three hundred and fifty years; **29** and all the days of Noah are nine hundred and fifty years, and he dies.

10 And these [are] the generations of the sons of Noah, Shem, Ham, and Japheth: and sons are born to them after the flood. **2** Sons of Japheth [are] Gomer, and Magog, and Madai, and Javan, and Tubal, and Meshech, and Tiras. **3** And sons of Gomer [are] Ashkenaz, and Riphath, and Togarmah. **4** And sons of Javan [are] Elishah, and Tarshish, Kittim, and Dodanim. **5** By these the islands of the nations have been parted in their lands, each by his tongue, by their families, in their nations. **6** And sons of Ham [are] Cush, and Mitzraim, and Phut, and Canaan. **7** And sons of Cush [are] Seba, and Havilah, and Sabtah, and Raamah, and Sabtechah; and sons of Raamah [are] Sheba and Dedan. **8** And Cush has begotten Nimrod; **9** he has begun to be a hero in the land; he has been a hero in hunting before YHWH; therefore it is said, "As Nimrod the hero [in] hunting before YHWH." **10** And the first part of his kingdom is Babel, and Erech, and Accad, and Calneh, in the land of Shinar; **11** from that land he has gone out to Asshur, and builds Nineveh, even the broad places of the city, and Calah, **12** and Resen, between Nineveh and Calah; it [is] the great city. **13** And Mitzraim has begotten the Ludim, and the Anamim, and the Lehabim, and the Naphtuhim, **14** and the Pathrusim, and the Casluhim (from where have come out Philistim), and the Caphtorim. **15** And Canaan has begotten Sidon his firstborn, and Heth, **16** and the Jebusite, and the Amorite, and the Girgashite, **17** and the Hivite, and the Arkite, and the Sinite, **18** and the Arvadite, and the Zemarite, and the Hamathite; and afterward the families of the Canaanite have been scattered. **19** And the border of the Canaanite is from

Sidon, [in] your coming toward Gerar, to Gaza; [in] your coming toward Sodom, and Gomorrah, and Admah, and Zeboim, to Lasha. **20** These [are] sons of Ham, by their families, by their tongues, in their lands, in their nations. **21** As for Shem, father of all sons of Eber, the older brother of Japheth, he has also begotten. **22** Sons of Shem [are] Elam, and Asshur, and Arphaxad, and Lud, and Aram. **23** And sons of Aram [are] Uz, and Hul, and Gether, and Mash. **24** And Arphaxad has begotten Salah, and Salah has begotten Eber. **25** And two sons have been born to Eber; the name of the first [is] Peleg (for in his days the earth has been divided), and his brother's name [is] Joktan. **26** And Joktan has begotten Almodad, and Sheleph, and Hazarmaveth, and Jerah, **27** and Hadoram, and Uzal, and Diklah, **28** and Obal, and Abimael, and Sheba, **29** and Ophir, and Havilah, and Jobab; all these [are] sons of Joktan; **30** and their dwelling is from Mesha, [in] your coming toward Sephar, a mountain of the east. **31** These [are] sons of Shem, by their families, by their tongues, in their lands, by their nations. **32** These [are] families of the sons of Noah, by their generations, in their nations, and by these the nations have been parted in the earth after the flood.

11 And the whole earth is of one language, and of the same words, **2** and it comes to pass, in their journeying from the east, that they find a valley in the land of Shinar and dwell there; **3** and they each say to his neighbor, "Give help, let us make bricks, and burn [them] thoroughly": and the brick is to them for stone, and the bitumen has been to them for mortar. **4** And they say, "Give help, let us build for ourselves a city and tower with its head in the heavens, and make for ourselves a name, lest we be scattered over the face of all the earth." **5** And YHWH comes down to see the city and the tower which the sons of men have built; **6** and YHWH says, "Behold, the people [is] one, and one language [is] to them all, and this it has dreamed of doing; and now, nothing is restrained from them of that which they have purposed to do. **7** Give help, let us go down there and confuse their language, so that a man will not understand the language of his companion." **8** And YHWH scatters them from there over the face of all the earth, and they cease to build the city; **9** therefore [one] has called its name Babel, for there YHWH has confused the language of all the earth, and from there YHWH has scattered them over the face of all the earth. **10** These [are] the generations of Shem: Shem [is] a son of one hundred years, and begets Arphaxad two years after the flood. **11** And Shem lives after his begetting Arphaxad five hundred years, and begets sons and daughters. **12** And Arphaxad has lived thirty-five years [[*or* one hundred and thirty-five years]], and begets Salah. **13** And Arphaxad lives after his begetting Salah four hundred and three years [[*or* four hundred and thirty years]], and begets sons and daughters. **14** And Salah has lived thirty years [[*or* one hundred and thirty years]], and begets Eber. **15** And Salah lives after his begetting Eber four hundred and three years [[*or* three hundred and thirty years]], and begets sons and daughters. **16** And Eber lives thirty-four years [[*or* one hundred and thirty-four years]], and begets Peleg. **17** And Eber lives after his begetting Peleg four hundred and thirty years [[*or* three hundred and seventy years]], and begets sons and daughters. **18** And Peleg lives thirty years [[*or* one hundred and thirty years]], and begets Reu. **19** And Peleg lives after his begetting Reu two hundred and nine years, and begets sons and daughters. **20** And Reu lives thirty-two years [[*or* one hundred and thirty-two years]], and begets Serug. **21** And Reu lives after his begetting Serug two hundred and seven years, and begets sons and daughters. **22** And Serug lives thirty years [[*or* one hundred and thirty years]], and begets Nahor. **23** And Serug lives after his begetting Nahor two hundred years, and begets sons and daughters. **24** And Nahor lives twenty-nine years [[*or* seventy-nine years]], and begets Terah. **25** And Nahor lives after his begetting Terah one hundred and nineteen years [[*or* one hundred and twenty-nine years]], and begets sons and daughters. **26** And Terah lives seventy years, and begets Abram, Nahor, and Haran. **27** And these [are] the generations of Terah: Terah has begotten Abram, Nahor, and Haran; and Haran has begotten Lot; **28** and Haran dies in the presence of Terah his father, in the land of his birth, in Ur of the Chaldees. **29** And Abram and Nahor take to themselves wives; the name of Abram's wife [is] Sarai, and the name of Nahor's wife [is] Milcah,

GENESIS

daughter of Haran, father of Milcah, and father of Iscah. **30** And Sarai is barren—she has no child. **31** And Terah takes his son Abram, and Lot, son of Haran, his son's son, and his daughter-in-law Sarai, wife of his son Abram, and they go out with them from Ur of the Chaldees, to go toward the land of Canaan; and they come to Haran, and dwell there. **32** And the days of Terah are two hundred and five years, and Terah dies in Haran.

12 And YHWH says to Abram, "Go for yourself, from your land, and from your family, and from the house of your father, to the land which I show you. **2** And I make you become a great nation, and bless you, and make your name great; and be a blessing. **3** And I bless those blessing you, and I curse him who is cursing you, and all families of the ground have been blessed in you." **4** And Abram goes on, as YHWH has spoken to him, and Lot goes with him, and Abram [is] a son of seventy-five years in his going out from Haran. **5** And Abram takes his wife Sarai, and his brother's son Lot, and all their substance that they have gained, and the persons that they have obtained in Haran; and they go out to go toward the land of Canaan; and they come to the land of Canaan. **6** And Abram passes over into the land, to the place of Shechem, to the oak of Moreh; and the Canaanite [is] then in the land. **7** And YHWH appears to Abram and says, "To your seed I give this land"; and there he builds an altar to YHWH, who has appeared to him. **8** And he removes from there toward a mountain at the east of Beth-El, and stretches out the tent (Beth-El at the west, and Hai at the east), and he builds an altar to YHWH there, and preaches in the Name of YHWH. **9** And Abram journeys, going on and journeying toward the south. **10** And there is a famine in the land, and Abram goes down toward Egypt to sojourn there, for the famine [is] grievous in the land; **11** and it comes to pass as he has drawn near to enter Egypt, that he says to his wife Sarai, "Now behold, I have known that you [are] a woman of beautiful appearance; **12** and it has come to pass that the Egyptians see you, and they have said, This [is] his wife; and they have slain me, and you they keep alive: **13** please say you [are] my sister, so that it is well with me because of you, and my soul has lived for your sake." **14** And it comes to pass, at the entering of Abram into Egypt, that the Egyptians see the woman that she [is] exceedingly beautiful; **15** and princes of Pharaoh see her, and praise her to Pharaoh, and the woman is taken [to] Pharaoh's house; **16** and to Abram he has done good because of her, and he has sheep and oxen, and male donkeys, and menservants, and handmaids, and female donkeys, and camels. **17** And YHWH plagues Pharaoh and his house—great plagues—for the matter of Sarai, Abram's wife. **18** And Pharaoh calls for Abram and says, "What [is] this you have done to me? Why have you not declared to me that she [is] your wife? **19** Why have you said, She [is] my sister, and I take her to myself for a wife? And now, behold, your wife, take and go." **20** And Pharaoh charges men concerning him, and they send him away, and his wife, and all that he has.

13 And Abram goes up from Egypt (he and his wife, and all that he has, and Lot with him) toward the south; **2** and Abram [is] exceedingly wealthy in livestock, in silver, and in gold. **3** And he goes on his journeys from the south, even to Bethel, to the place where his tent had been at the commencement, between Bethel and Hai— **4** to the place of the altar which he made there at the first, and there Abram preaches in the Name of YHWH. **5** And also to Lot, who is going with Abram, there has been sheep and oxen and tents; **6** and the land has not permitted them to dwell together, for their substance has been much, and they have not been able to dwell together; **7** and there is a strife between those feeding Abram's livestock and those feeding Lot's livestock; and the Canaanite and the Perizzite [are] then dwelling in the land. **8** And Abram says to Lot, "Please let there not be strife between me and you, and between my shepherds and your shepherds, for we [are] men—brothers. **9** Is not all the land before you? Please be parted from me; if to the left, then I to the right; and if to the right, then I to the left." **10** And Lot lifts up his eyes, and sees the whole circuit of the Jordan that it [is] all a watered country (before YHWH's destroying Sodom and Gomorrah, as YHWH's garden, as the land of Egypt), in your coming toward Zoar, **11** and Lot chooses for himself the whole circuit of the

Jordan; and Lot journeys from the east, and they are parted—a man from his companion; **12** Abram has dwelt in the land of Canaan, and Lot has dwelt in the cities of the circuit, and moves [his] tent to Sodom; **13** and the men of Sodom [are] evil, and sinners before YHWH exceedingly. **14** And YHWH said to Abram, after Lot's being parted from him, "Now lift up your eyes and look from the place where you [are], northward, and southward, and eastward, and westward; **15** for the whole of the land which you are seeing, I give it to you and to your Seed for all time. **16** And I have set your seed as dust of the earth, so that, if one is able to number the dust of the earth, even your seed is numbered; **17** rise, go up and down through the land, to its length, and to its breadth, for to you I give it." **18** And Abram moves [his] tent, and comes, and dwells among the oaks of Mamre, which [are] in Hebron, and builds there an altar to YHWH.

14 And it comes to pass in the days of Amraphel king of Shinar, Arioch king of Ellasar, Chedorlaomer king of Elam, and Tidal king of nations, **2** they have made war with Bera king of Sodom, and with Birsha king of Gomorrah, Shinab king of Admah, and Shemeber king of Zeboim, and the king of Bela, which [is] Zoar. **3** All these have been joined together to the Valley of Siddim, which [is] the Salt Sea; **4** [for] twelve years they served Chedorlaomer, and the thirteenth year they rebelled. **5** And in the fourteenth year came Chedorlaomer, and the kings who [are] with him, and they strike the Rephaim in Ashteroth Karnaim, and the Zuzim in Ham, and the Emim in Shaveh Kiriathaim, **6** and the Horites in their Mount Seir, to El-Paran, which [is] by the wilderness; **7** and they turn back and come to En-Mishpat, which [is] Kadesh, and strike the whole field of the Amalekite, and also the Amorite who is dwelling in Hazezon-Tamar. **8** And the king of Sodom goes out, and the king of Gomorrah, and the king of Admah, and the king of Zeboim, and the king of Bela, which [is] Zoar; and they set in array [for] battle with them in the Valley of Siddim, **9** with Chedorlaomer king of Elam, and Tidal king of nations, and Amraphel king of Shinar, and Arioch king of Ellasar; four kings with the five. **10** And the Valley of Siddim [is] full of bitumen-pits; and the kings of Sodom and Gomorrah flee, and fall there, and those left have fled to the mountain. **11** And they take the whole substance of Sodom and Gomorrah, and the whole of their food, and go away; **12** and they take Lot, Abram's brother's son (seeing he is dwelling in Sodom), and his substance, and go away. **13** And one who is escaping comes and declares to Abram the Hebrew, and he is dwelling among the oaks of Mamre the Amorite, brother of Eshcol, and brother of Aner, and they [are] Abram's allies. **14** And Abram hears that his brother has been taken captive, and he draws out his trained servants, three hundred and eighteen, and pursues to Dan. **15** And he divides himself against them by night, he and his servants, and strikes them, and pursues them to Hobah, which [is] at the left of Damascus; **16** and he brings back the whole of the substance, and he has also brought back his brother Lot and his substance, and also the women and the people. **17** And the king of Sodom goes out to meet him (after his turning back from the striking of Chedorlaomer, and of the kings who [are] with him), to the Valley of Shaveh, which [is] the king's valley. **18** And Melchizedek king of Salem has brought out bread and wine, and he [is] priest of God Most High; **19** and he blesses him and says, "Blessed [is] Abram to God Most High, possessing the heavens and earth; **20** and blessed [is] God Most High, who has delivered your adversaries into your hand"; and he gives to him a tenth of all. **21** And the king of Sodom says to Abram, "Give to me the persons, and take the substance to yourself," **22** and Abram says to the king of Sodom, "I have lifted up my hand to YHWH, God Most High, possessing the heavens and earth— **23** from a thread even to a shoe-strap I do not take of anything which you have, that you do not say, I have made Abram rich; **24** save only that which the young men have eaten, and the portion of the men who have gone with me—Aner, Eshcol, and Mamre—they take their portion."

15 After these things the word of YHWH has been to Abram in a vision, saying, "Do not fear, Abram, I [am] a shield to you, your reward [is] exceedingly great." **2** And Abram says, "Lord YHWH, what do You give to me, and I am going childless?

GENESIS

And an acquired son in my house is Demmesek Eliezer." **3** And Abram says, "Behold, to me You have not given seed, and behold, a servant will be my heir." **4** And behold, the word of Y<small>HWH</small> [is] to him, saying, "This [one] will not be your heir; but he who comes out from your bowels, he will be your heir"; **5** and He brings him out outside and says, "Now look attentively toward the heavens and count the stars, if you are able to count them"; and He says to him, "Thus is your seed." **6** And he has believed in Y<small>HWH</small>, and He reckons it to him—righteousness. **7** And He says to him, "I [am] Y<small>HWH</small> who brought you out from Ur of the Chaldees, to give to you this land to possess it"; **8** and he says, "Lord Y<small>HWH</small>, whereby do I know that I possess it?" **9** And He says to him, "Take for Me a heifer of three years, and a female goat of three years, and a ram of three years, and a turtle-dove, and a young bird"; **10** and he takes all these to Him, and separates them in the midst, and puts each piece opposite its fellow, but the bird he has not divided; **11** and the ravenous birds come down on the carcasses, and Abram causes them to turn back. **12** And the sun is about to go in, and deep sleep has fallen on Abram, and behold, a terror of great darkness is falling on him; **13** and He says to Abram, "knowing—know that your seed is a sojourner in a land not theirs, and they have served them, and they have afflicted them four hundred years, **14** and the nation also whom they serve I judge, and after this they go out with great substance; **15** and you come to your fathers in peace; you are buried in a good old age; **16** and the fourth generation turns back here, for the iniquity of the Amorite is not yet complete." **17** And it comes to pass—the sun has gone in, and thick darkness has been and behold, a furnace of smoke, and a lamp of fire, which has passed over between those pieces. **18** In that day has Y<small>HWH</small> made with Abram a covenant, saying, "To your seed I have given this land, from the River of Egypt to the great river, the Euphrates River, **19** with the Kenite, and the Kenizzite, and the Kadmonite, **20** and the Hittite, and the Perizzite, and the Rephaim, **21** and the Amorite, and the Canaanite, and the Girgashite, and the Jebusite."

16 And Sarai, Abram's wife, has not borne to him, and she has a handmaid, an Egyptian, and her name [is] Hagar; **2** and Sarai says to Abram, "Now behold, Y<small>HWH</small> has restrained me from bearing, please go in to my handmaid; perhaps I am built up from her"; and Abram listens to the voice of Sarai. **3** And Sarai, Abram's wife, takes Hagar the Egyptian, her handmaid, at the end of the tenth year of Abram's dwelling in the land of Canaan, and gives her to her husband Abram—to him for a wife, **4** and he goes in to Hagar, and she conceives, and she sees that she has conceived, and her mistress is lightly esteemed in her eyes. **5** And Sarai says to Abram, "My violence [is] for you; I have given my handmaid into your bosom, and she sees that she has conceived, and I am lightly esteemed in her eyes; Y<small>HWH</small> judges between me and you." **6** And Abram says to Sarai, "Behold, your handmaid [is] in your hand, do to her that which is good in your eyes"; and Sarai afflicted her, and she flees from her presence. **7** And the Messenger of Y<small>HWH</small> finds her by the fountain of water in the wilderness, by the fountain in the way [to] Shur, **8** and He says, "Hagar, Sarai's handmaid, from where have you come, and to where do you go?" And she says, "From the presence of Sarai, my mistress, I am fleeing." **9** And the Messenger of Y<small>HWH</small> says to her, "Return to your mistress, and humble yourself under her hands"; **10** and the Messenger of Y<small>HWH</small> says to her, "Multiplying I multiply your seed, and it is not numbered from multitude"; **11** and the Messenger of Y<small>HWH</small> says to her, "Behold you [are] conceiving, and bearing a son, and have called his name Ishmael, for Y<small>HWH</small> has listened to your affliction; **12** and he is a wild-donkey man, his hand against everyone, and everyone's hand against him—and before the face of all his brothers he dwells." **13** And she calls the Name of Y<small>HWH</small> who is speaking to her, "You [are], O God, my beholder"; for she said, "Even here have I looked behind my beholder?" **14** Therefore has one called the well, "The well of the Living One, my beholder"; behold, between Kadesh and Bered. **15** And Hagar bears a son to Abram; and Abram calls the name of his son, whom Hagar has borne, Ishmael; **16** and Abram [is] a son of eighty-six years in Hagar's bearing Ishmael to Abram.

GENESIS

17 And Abram is a son of ninety-nine years, and YHWH appears to Abram, and says to him, "I [am] God Almighty, habitually walk before Me, and be perfect; **2** and I give My covenant between Me and you, and multiply you very exceedingly." **3** And Abram falls on his face, and God speaks with him, saying, **4** "I—behold, My covenant [is] with you, and you have become father of a multitude of nations; **5** and your name is no longer called Abram, but your name has been Abraham, for father of a multitude of nations have I made you; **6** and I have made you exceedingly fruitful, and made you become nations, and kings go out from you. **7** And I have established My covenant between Me and you, and your seed after you, throughout their generations, for a perpetual covenant, to become God to you, and to your seed after you; **8** and I have given to you, and to your seed after you, the land of your sojournings, the whole land of Canaan, for a continuous possession, and I have become their God." **9** And God says to Abraham, "And you keep My covenant, you and your seed after you, throughout their generations; **10** this [is] My covenant which you keep between Me and you, and your seed after you: every male of you [is] to be circumcised; **11** and you have circumcised the flesh of your foreskin, and it has become a token of a covenant between Me and you. **12** And a son of eight days is circumcised by you; every male throughout your generations, born in the house, or bought with money from any son of a stranger, who is not of your seed; **13** he is certainly circumcised who [is] born in your house, or bought with your money; and My covenant has become in your flesh a perpetual covenant; **14** and an uncircumcised one, a male, the flesh of whose foreskin is not circumcised, indeed, that person has been cut off from his people; My covenant he has broken." **15** And God says to Abraham, "Sarai your wife—you do not call her name Sarai, for Sarah [is] her name; **16** and I have blessed her, and have also given to you a son from her; and I have blessed her, and she has become nations—kings of peoples are from her." **17** And Abraham falls on his face, and laughs, and says in his heart, "Is one born to the son of one hundred years? Or does Sarah—daughter of ninety years—bear?" **18** And Abraham says to God, "O that Ishmael may live before You"; **19** and God says, "Your wife Sarah is certainly bearing a son to you, and you have called his name Isaac, and I have established My covenant with him, for a perpetual covenant, to his seed after him. **20** As for Ishmael, I have heard you; behold, I have blessed him, and made him fruitful, and multiplied him, very exceedingly; twelve princes does he beget, and I have made him become a great nation; **21** and My covenant I establish with Isaac, whom Sarah does bear to you at this appointed time in the next year"; **22** and He finishes speaking with him, and God goes up from Abraham. **23** And Abraham takes his son Ishmael, and all those born in his house, and all those bought with his money—every male among the men of Abraham's house and circumcises the flesh of their foreskin, in this very same day, as God has spoken with him. **24** And Abraham [is] a son of ninety-nine years in the flesh of his foreskin being circumcised; **25** and his son Ishmael [is] a son of thirteen years in the flesh of his foreskin being circumcised; **26** in this very same day Abraham has been circumcised, and his son Ishmael; **27** and all the men of his house—born in the house, and bought with money from the son of a stranger—have been circumcised with him.

18 And YHWH appears to him among the oaks of Mamre, and he is sitting at the opening of the tent, about the heat of the day; **2** and he lifts up his eyes and looks, and behold, three men standing by him, and he sees, and runs to meet them from the opening of the tent, and bows himself toward the earth, **3** and he says, "My Lord, if now I have found grace in Your eyes, please do not pass on from Your servant; **4** please let a little water be accepted, and wash Your feet, and recline under the tree; **5** and I bring a piece of bread, and support Your heart; afterward pass on, for therefore You have passed over to Your servant"; and they say, "So may you do as you have spoken." **6** And Abraham hurries toward the tent, to Sarah, and says, "Hurry three measures of flour-meal, knead, and make cakes"; **7** and Abraham ran to the herd, and takes a son of the herd, tender and good, and gives to the young man, and he hurries to prepare it; **8** and he takes butter and milk, and the son

GENESIS

of the herd which he has prepared, and sets before them; and he is standing by them under the tree, and they eat. **9** And they say to him, "Where [is] Sarah your wife?" And he says, "Behold—in the tent"; **10** and He says, "Returning I return to you, about the time of life, and behold, to Sarah your wife a son." And Sarah is listening at the opening of the tent, which is behind him; **11** and Abraham and Sarah [are] aged, entering into days—the way of women has ceased to be to Sarah; **12** and Sarah laughs in her heart, saying, "After I have waxed old have I had pleasure? My lord [is] also old!" **13** And YHWH says to Abraham, "Why [is] this? Sarah has laughed, saying, Is it really true—I bear—and I am aged? **14** Is anything too wonderful for YHWH? At the appointed time I return to you, about the time of life, and Sarah has a son." **15** And Sarah denies, saying, "I did not laugh"; for she has been afraid; and He says, "No, but you did laugh." **16** And the men rise from there, and look on the face of Sodom, and Abraham is going with them to send them away; **17** and YHWH said, "Am I concealing from Abraham that which I am doing, **18** and Abraham certainly becomes a great and mighty nation, and blessed in him have been all nations of the earth? **19** For I have known him, that he commands his children, and his house after him (and they have kept the way of YHWH), to do righteousness and judgment, that YHWH may bring on Abraham that which He has spoken concerning him." **20** And YHWH says, "The cry of Sodom and Gomorrah—because great; and their sin—because exceedingly grievous: **21** I go down now, and see whether according to its cry which is coming to Me they have done completely—and if not—I know"; **22** and the men turn from there, and go toward Sodom; and Abraham is yet standing before YHWH. **23** And Abraham draws near and says, "Do You also consume righteous with wicked? **24** Perhaps there are fifty righteous in the midst of the city; do You also consume, and not bear with the place for the sake of the fifty righteous who [are] in its midst? **25** Far be it from You to do according to this thing, to put to death the righteous with the wicked; that it has been—as the righteous so the wicked—far be it from You; does the Judge of all the earth not do justice?" **26** And YHWH says, "If I find in Sodom fifty righteous in the midst of the city, then have I borne with all the place for their sake." **27** And Abraham answers and says, "Now behold, I have willed to speak to the Lord, and I [am] dust and ashes; **28** perhaps there are lacking five of the fifty righteous—do You destroy for five the whole of the city?" And He says, "I do not destroy [it], if I find there forty-five." **29** And he adds again to speak to Him and says, "Perhaps there are found there forty?" And He says, "I do not do [it], because of the forty." **30** And he says, "Please let it not be displeasing to the Lord, and I speak: perhaps there are found there thirty?" And He says, "I do not do [it], if I find there thirty." **31** And he says, "Now behold, I have willed to speak to the Lord: perhaps there are found there twenty?" And He says, "I do not destroy [it], because of the twenty." **32** And he says, "Please let it not be displeasing to the Lord, and I speak only this time: perhaps there are found there ten?" And He says, "I do not destroy [it], because of the ten." **33** And YHWH goes on, when He has finished speaking to Abraham, and Abraham has turned back to his place.

19 And two of the messengers come toward Sodom at evening, and Lot is sitting at the gate of Sodom, and Lot sees, and rises to meet them, and bows himself—face to the earth, **2** and he says, "Now behold, my lords, please turn aside to the house of your servant, and lodge, and wash your feet—then you have risen early and gone on your way"; and they say, "No, but we lodge in the broad place." **3** And he presses on them greatly, and they turn aside to him, and come into his house; and he makes a banquet for them, and has baked unleavened things; and they eat. **4** Before they lie down, the men of the city—men of Sodom—have surrounded the house, from young even to aged, all the people from the extremity; **5** and they call to Lot and say to him, "Where [are] the men who have come to you tonight? Bring them out to us, and we know them." **6** And Lot goes out to them, to the opening, and the door has shut behind him, **7** and says, "Please, my brothers, do not do evil; **8** now behold, I have two daughters who have not known anyone; please let me bring them out to you, and do to them as [is] good in your eyes; only do nothing to these men, for therefore they have come in within the shadow of my roof." **9** And they say, "Come near here"; they also say, "This one has come to sojourn, and he certainly judges! Now, we do evil to you more than [to] them"; and they press against the man, against Lot greatly, and come near to break the door. **10** And the men put forth their hand, and bring in Lot to them, into the house, and have shut the door; **11** and the men who [are] at the opening of the house they have struck with blindness, from small even to great, and they weary themselves to find the opening. **12** And the men say to Lot, "Whom have you here still? Son-in-law, your sons also, and your daughters, and all whom you have in the city, bring out from this place; **13** for we are destroying this place, for their cry has been great [before] the face of YHWH, and YHWH does send us to destroy it." **14** And Lot goes out and speaks to his sons-in-law, those taking his daughters, and says, "Rise, go out from this place, for YHWH is destroying the city"; and he is as [one] mocking in the eyes of his sons-in-law. **15** And when the dawn has ascended, then the messengers press on Lot, saying, "Rise, take your wife, and your two daughters who are found present, lest you are consumed in the iniquity of the city." **16** And he lingers, and the men lay hold on his hand, and on the hand of his wife, and on the hand of his two daughters, through the mercy of YHWH to him, and they bring him out, and cause him to rest outside the city. **17** And it comes to pass, when he has brought them outside, that he says, "Escape for your life; do not look behind you, nor stand in all the circuit; escape to the mountain, lest you are consumed." **18** And Lot says to them, "Oh not [so], my lord; **19** now behold, your servant has found grace in your eyes, and you make great your kindness which you have done with me by saving my life, and I am unable to escape to the mountain, lest the evil cleave [to] me and I have died; **20** now behold, this city [is] near to flee there, and it [is] little; please let me escape there (is it not little?) that my soul may live." **21** And he says to him, "Behold, I have also accepted your face for this thing, without overthrowing the city [for] which you have spoken; **22** hurry, escape there, for I am not able to do anything until your entering there"; therefore he calls the name of the city Zoar.

23 The sun has gone out on the earth, and Lot has entered into Zoar, **24** and YHWH has rained on Sodom and on Gomorrah brimstone and fire from YHWH, from the heavens; **25** and He overthrows these cities, and all the circuit, and all the inhabitants of the cities, and that which is shooting up from the ground. **26** And his wife looks from behind him, and she becomes a pillar of salt! **27** And Abraham rises early in the morning to the place where he has stood [before] the face of YHWH; **28** and he looks on the face of Sodom and Gomorrah, and on all the face of the land of the circuit, and sees, and behold, the smoke of the land went up as smoke of the furnace. **29** And it comes to pass, in God's destroying the cities of the circuit, that God remembers Abraham, and sends Lot out of the midst of the overthrow in the overthrowing of the cities in which Lot dwelt. **30** And Lot goes up out of Zoar, and dwells in the mountain, and his two daughters with him, for he has been afraid of dwelling in Zoar, and he dwells in a cave, he and his two daughters. **31** And the firstborn says to the younger, "Our father [is] old, and there is not a man in the earth to come in to us, as [is] the way of all the earth; **32** come, we cause our father to drink wine, and lie with him, and preserve a seed from our father." **33** And they cause their father to drink wine on that night; and the firstborn goes in and lies with her father, and he has not known in her lying down or in her rising up. **34** And it comes to pass, on the next day, that the firstborn says to the younger, "Behold, I have lain with my father last night: we also cause him to drink wine tonight, then go in, lie with him, and we preserve a seed from our father." **35** And they cause their father to drink wine on that night also, and the younger rises and lies with him, and he has not known in her lying down or in her rising up. **36** And the two daughters of Lot conceive from their father, **37** and the firstborn bears a son and calls his name Moab: he [is] father of Moab to this day. **38** As for the younger, she has also born a son and calls his name Ben-Ammi: he [is] father of the sons of Ammon to this day.

20 And Abraham journeys from there toward the land of the south, and dwells between Kadesh and Shur, and sojourns in Gerar; **2** and Abraham says

GENESIS

concerning his wife Sarah, "She is my sister"; and Abimelech king of Gerar sends and takes Sarah. **3** And God comes to Abimelech in a dream of the night and says to him, "Behold, you [are] a dead man, because of the woman whom you have taken—and she married to a husband." **4** And Abimelech has not drawn near to her, and he says, "Lord, do you also slay a righteous nation? **5** Has he not himself said to me, She [is] my sister! And she, even she herself, said, He [is] my brother; in the integrity of my heart, and in the innocence of my hands, I have done this." **6** And God says to him in the dream, "Indeed, I have known that in the integrity of your heart you have done this, and I withhold you, even I, from sinning against Me, therefore I have not permitted you to come against her; **7** and now send back the man's wife, for he [is] inspired, and he prays for you, and you live; and if you do not send back, know that dying you die, you and all that you have." **8** And Abimelech rises early in the morning, and calls for all his servants, and speaks all these words in their ears; and the men fear exceedingly; **9** and Abimelech calls for Abraham and says to him, "What have you done to us? And what have I sinned against you, that you have brought on me, and on my kingdom, a great sin? Works which are not done you have done with me." **10** Abimelech also says to Abraham, "What have you seen that you have done this thing?" **11** And Abraham says, "Because I said, Surely the fear of God is not in this place, and they have slain me for the sake of my wife; **12** and also, she is truly my sister, daughter of my father, only not daughter of my mother, and she becomes my wife; **13** and it comes to pass, when God has caused me to wander from my father's house, that I say to her, This [is] your kindness which you do with me: at every place to where we come, say of me, He [is] my brother." **14** And Abimelech takes sheep and oxen, and servants and handmaids, and gives to Abraham, and sends back his wife Sarah to him; **15** and Abimelech says, "Behold, my land [is] before you, where it is good in your eyes, dwell"; **16** and to Sarah he has said, "Behold, I have given one thousand pieces of silver to your brother; behold, it is to you a covering of eyes, to all who are with you"; and by all this she is reasoned with. **17** And Abraham prays to God, and God heals Abimelech and his wife, and his handmaids, and they bear: **18** for YHWH restraining had restrained every womb of the house of Abimelech, because of Sarah, Abraham's wife.

21 And YHWH has looked after Sarah as He has said, and YHWH does to Sarah as He has spoken; **2** and Sarah conceives, and bears a son to Abraham, to his old age, at the appointed time that God has spoken of with him; **3** and Abraham calls the name of his son who is born to him, whom Sarah has borne to him—Isaac; **4** and Abraham circumcises his son Isaac, [being] a son of eight days, as God has commanded him. **5** And Abraham [is] a son of one hundred years in his son Isaac being born to him, **6** and Sarah says, "God has made laughter for me; everyone who is hearing laughs for me." **7** She also says, "Who has said to Abraham, Sarah has suckled sons, that I have born a son for his old age?" **8** And the boy grows, and is weaned, and Abraham makes a great banquet in the day of Isaac's being weaned; **9** and Sarah sees the son of Hagar the Egyptian, whom she has borne to Abraham, mocking, **10** and she says to Abraham, "Cast out this handmaid and her son; for the son of this handmaid has no possession with my son—with Isaac." **11** And the thing is very wrong in the eyes of Abraham, for his son's sake; **12** and God says to Abraham, "Let it not be wrong in your eyes because of the youth, and because of your handmaid: all that Sarah says to you—listen to her voice, for in Isaac is a seed called to you. **13** As for the son of the handmaid also, for a nation I set him, because he [is] your seed." **14** And Abraham rises early in the morning, and takes bread, and a bottle of water, and gives to Hagar (placing [it] on her shoulder), also the boy, and sends her out; and she goes on, and goes astray in the wilderness of Beer-Sheba; **15** and the water is consumed from the bottle, and she places the boy under one of the shrubs. **16** And she goes and sits by herself opposite [him], far off, about a bow-shot, for she said, "Do not let me look on the death of the boy"; and she sits opposite [him], and lifts up her voice, and weeps. **17** And God hears the voice of the youth; and the messenger of God calls to Hagar from the heavens and says to her, "What to you, Hagar? Do not fear; for God has listened to the voice of the youth where he

[is]; **18** rise, lift up the youth, and lay hold on him with your hand, for I set him for a great nation." **19** And God opens her eyes, and she sees a well of water, and she goes and fills the bottle [with] water, and causes the youth to drink; **20** and God is with the youth, and he grows, and dwells in the wilderness, and is an archer; **21** and he dwells in the wilderness of Paran, and his mother takes for him a wife from the land of Egypt. **22** And it comes to pass at that time that Abimelech speaks—Phichol also, head of his host—to Abraham, saying, "God [is] with you in all that you are doing; **23** and now, swear to me by God here: you do not lie to me, or to my continuator, or to my successor; according to the kindness which I have done with you—do with me, and with the land in which you have sojourned." **24** And Abraham says, "I swear." **25** And Abraham reasoned with Abimelech concerning the matter of a well of water which Abimelech's servants have violently taken away, **26** and Abimelech says, "I have not known who has done this thing, and even you did not declare to me, and I also, I have not heard except today." **27** And Abraham takes sheep and oxen, and gives to Abimelech, and they make, both of them, a covenant; **28** and Abraham sets seven lambs of the flock by themselves. **29** And Abimelech says to Abraham, "What [are] they—these seven lambs which you have set by themselves?" **30** And he says, "For—the seven lambs you accept from my hand, so that it becomes a witness for me that I have dug this well"; **31** therefore he has called that place "Beer-Sheba," for both of them have sworn there. **32** And they make a covenant in Beer-Sheba, and Abimelech rises—Phichol also, head of his host—and they return to the land of the Philistines; **33** and [Abraham] plants a tamarisk in Beer-Sheba, and preaches there in the Name of Y<small>HWH</small>, the perpetual God; **34** and Abraham sojourns in the land of the Philistines many days.

22 And it comes to pass after these things that God has tried Abraham and says to him, "Abraham"; and he says, "Here I [am]." **2** And He says, "Now take your son, your only one, whom you have loved, even Isaac, and go for yourself to the land of Moriah, and cause him to ascend there for a burnt-offering on one of the mountains of which I speak to you." **3** And Abraham rises early in the morning, and saddles his donkey, and takes two of his young men with him, and his son Isaac, and he cleaves the wood of the burnt-offering, and rises and goes to the place of which God has spoken to him. **4** On the third day—Abraham lifts up his eyes, and sees the place from afar; **5** and Abraham says to his young men, "Remain by yourselves here with the donkey, and I and the youth go over there and worship, and return to you." **6** And Abraham takes the wood of the burnt-offering, and places on his son Isaac, and he takes in his hand the fire, and the knife; and they go on both of them together. **7** And Isaac speaks to his father Abraham and says, "My father," and he says, "Here I [am], my son." And he says, "Behold, the fire and the wood, and where the lamb for a burnt-offering?" **8** And Abraham says, "God provides for Himself the lamb for a burnt-offering, my son"; and they go on both of them together. **9** And they come to the place of which God has spoken to him, and there Abraham builds the altar, and arranges the wood, and binds his son Isaac, and places him on the altar above the wood; **10** and Abraham puts forth his hand, and takes the knife—to slaughter his son. **11** And the Messenger of Y<small>HWH</small> calls to him from the heavens and says, "Abraham, Abraham"; and he says, "Here I [am]"; **12** and He says, "Do not put forth your hand to the youth, nor do anything to him, for now I have known that you are fearing God, and have not withheld your son, your only one, from Me." **13** And Abraham lifts up his eyes, and looks, and behold, a ram behind, seized in a thicket by its horns; and Abraham goes, and takes the ram, and causes it to ascend for a burnt-offering instead of his son; **14** and Abraham calls the name of that place "Y<small>HWH</small>-Jireh," because it is said this day in the mountain, "Y<small>HWH</small> provides." **15** And the Messenger of Y<small>HWH</small> calls to Abraham a second time from the heavens, **16** and says, "I have sworn by Myself—a declaration of Y<small>HWH</small>—that because you have done this thing, and have not withheld your son, your only one, **17** that blessing I bless you, and multiplying I multiply your seed as stars of the heavens, and as sand which [is] on the seashore; and your Seed possesses the gate of His enemies; **18** and all nations of the earth have blessed

GENESIS

themselves in your Seed, because you have listened to My voice." **19** And Abraham turns back to his young men, and they rise and go together to Beer-Sheba; and Abraham dwells in Beer-Sheba. **20** And it comes to pass after these things that it is declared to Abraham, saying, "Behold, Milcah has borne, even she, sons to your brother Nahor: **21** his firstborn Huz, and his brother Buz; and Kemuel father of Aram, **22** and Chesed, and Hazo, and Pildash, and Jidlaph, and Bethuel; **23** and Bethuel has begotten Rebekah"; Milcah has borne these eight to Nahor, Abraham's brother; **24** and his concubine, whose name [is] Reumah, she also has borne Tebah, and Gaham, and Tahash, and Maachah.

23 And the life of Sarah is one hundred and twenty-seven years—years of the life of Sarah; **2** and Sarah dies in Kirjath-Arba, which [is] Hebron, in the land of Canaan, and Abraham goes to mourn for Sarah, and to lament her. **3** And Abraham rises up from the presence of his dead, and speaks to the sons of Heth, saying, **4** "A sojourner and a settler I [am] with you; give to me a possession of a burying-place with you, and I bury my dead from before me." **5** And the sons of Heth answer Abraham, saying to him, **6** "Hear us, my lord; a prince of God [are] you in our midst; in the choice of our burying-places bury your dead: none of our burying-places do we withhold from you, from burying your dead." **7** And Abraham rises and bows himself to the people of the land, to the sons of Heth, **8** and he speaks with them, saying, "If it is your desire to bury my dead from before me, hear me, and meet for me with Ephron, son of Zoar; **9** and he gives to me the cave of Machpelah, which he has, which [is] in the extremity of his field; for full money does he give it to me, in your midst, for a possession of a burying-place." **10** And Ephron is sitting in the midst of the sons of Heth, and Ephron the Hittite answers Abraham in the ears of the sons of Heth, of all those entering the gate of his city, saying, **11** "No, my lord, hear me: the field I have given to you, and the cave that [is] in it, to you I have given it; before the eyes of the sons of my people I have given it to you—bury your dead." **12** And Abraham bows himself before the people of the land, **13** and speaks to Ephron in the ears of the people of the land, saying, "Only—if you would hear me—I have given the money of the field—accept from me, and I bury my dead there." **14** And Ephron answers Abraham, saying to him, **15** "My lord, hear me: the land—four hundred shekels of silver; between me and you, what [is] it? Bury your dead." **16** And Abraham listens to Ephron, and Abraham weighs to Ephron the silver which he has spoken of in the ears of the sons of Heth, four hundred silver shekels, passing with the merchant. **17** And established are the field of Ephron, which [is] in Machpelah, which [is] before Mamre, the field and the cave which [is] in it, and all the trees which [are] in the field, which [are] around all its border, **18** to Abraham by purchase, before the eyes of the sons of Heth, among all entering the gate of his city. **19** And after this Abraham has buried his wife Sarah at the cave of the field of Machpelah before Mamre (which [is] Hebron), in the land of Canaan; **20** and established are the field, and the cave which [is] in it, to Abraham for a possession of a burying-place, from the sons of Heth.

24 And Abraham [is] old, he has entered into days, and YHWH has blessed Abraham in all [things]; **2** and Abraham says to his servant, the eldest of his house, who is ruling over all that he has, "Please put your hand under my thigh, **3** and I cause you to swear by YHWH, God of the heavens and God of the earth, that you do not take a wife for my son from the daughters of the Canaanite, in the midst of whom I am dwelling; **4** but to my land and to my family you go, and have taken a wife for my son, for Isaac." **5** And the servant says to him, "It may be the woman is not willing to come after me to this land; do I at all cause your son to return to the land from where you came out?" **6** And Abraham says to him, "Take heed to yourself lest you cause my son to return there; **7** YHWH, God of the heavens, who has taken me from the house of my father, and from the land of my birth, and who has spoken to me, and who has sworn to me, saying, To your seed I give this land, He sends His messenger before you, and you have taken a wife for my son from there; **8** and if the woman is not willing to come after you, then you have been acquitted from this my oath: only you do not cause my son to return there." **9** And the servant puts his hand

GENESIS

under the thigh of Abraham his lord, and swears to him concerning this matter. **10** And the servant takes ten camels of the camels of his lord and goes, also of all the goods of his lord in his hand, and he rises, and goes to Aram-Naharaim, to the city of Nahor; **11** and he causes the camels to kneel at the outside of the city, at the well of water, at evening, at the time of the coming out of the women who draw water. **12** And he says, "YHWH, God of my lord Abraham, please cause to meet before me this day—(and do kindness with my lord Abraham; **13** behold, I am standing by the fountain of water, and daughters of the men of the city are coming out to draw water; **14** and it has been, the young person to whom I say, Please incline your pitcher and I drink, and she has said, Drink, and I also water your camels)—her [whom] You have decided for Your servant, for Isaac; and by it I know that You have done kindness with my lord." **15** And it comes to pass, before he has finished speaking, that behold, Rebekah (who was born to Bethuel, son of Milcah, wife of Nahor, brother of Abraham) is coming out, and her pitcher on her shoulder, **16** and the young person [is] of very good appearance, a virgin, and a man has not known her; and she goes down to the fountain, and fills her pitcher, and comes up. **17** And the servant runs to meet her and says, "Please let me swallow a little water from your pitcher"; **18** and she says, "Drink, my lord"; and she hurries, and lets down her pitcher on her hand, and gives him drink. **19** And she finishes giving him drink and says, "Also for your camels I draw until they have finished drinking"; **20** and she hurries, and empties her pitcher into the drinking-trough, and runs again to the well to draw, and draws for all his camels. **21** And the man, wondering at her, remains silent, to know whether YHWH has made his way prosperous or not. **22** And it comes to pass, when the camels have finished drinking, that the man takes a golden ring (whose weight [is] a bekah), and two bracelets for her hands (whose weight [is] ten [bekahs] of gold), **23** and says, "Whose daughter [are] you? Please declare to me, is the house of your father a place for us to lodge in?" **24** And she says to him, "I [am] daughter of Bethuel, son of Milcah, whom she has borne to Nahor." **25** She also says to him, "Both straw and provender [are] abundant with us, also a place to lodge in." **26** And the man bows, and pays respect to YHWH, **27** and says, "Blessed [is] YHWH, God of my lord Abraham, who has not left off His kindness and His truth with my lord—I [being] in the way, YHWH has led me to the house of my lord's brothers." **28** And the young person runs, and declares to the house of her mother according to these words. **29** And Rebekah has a brother, and his name [is] Laban, and Laban runs to the man who [is] outside, to the fountain; **30** indeed, it comes to pass, when he sees the ring, and the bracelets on the hands of his sister, and when he hears the words of his sister Rebekah, saying, "Thus has the man spoken to me," that he comes to the man, and behold, he is standing by the camels by the fountain. **31** And he says, "Come in, O blessed one of YHWH! Why do you stand outside—and I have prepared the house and place for the camels?" **32** And he brings in the man into the house, and looses the camels, and gives straw and provender for the camels, and water to wash his feet, and the feet of the men who [are] with him: **33** and sets before him to eat; but he says, "I do not eat until I have spoken my word"; and he says, "Speak." **34** And he says, "I [am] Abraham's servant; **35** and YHWH has blessed my lord exceedingly, and he is great; and He gives to him flock, and herd, and silver, and gold, and menservants, and maidservants, and camels, and donkeys; **36** and Sarah, my lord's wife, bears a son to my lord, after she has been aged, and he gives to him all that he has. **37** And my lord causes me to swear, saying, You do not take a wife to my son from the daughters of the Canaanite, in whose land I am dwelling. **38** If not—to the house of my father you go, and to my family, and you have taken a wife for my son. **39** And I say to my lord, It may be the woman does not come after me; **40** and he says to me, YHWH, before whom I have habitually walked, sends His messenger with you, and has prospered your way, and you have taken a wife for my son from my family, and from the house of my father; **41** then you are acquitted from my oath, when you come to my family; and if they do not give [one] to you, then you have been acquitted from my oath. **42** And I come to the fountain today, and I say, YHWH, God of my lord Abraham, now if You are making prosperous my way in which I am going—

GENESIS

43 (behold, I am standing by the fountain of water), then the virgin is coming out to draw, and I have said to her, Please let me drink a little water from your pitcher, 44 and she has said to me, Both drink, and I also draw for your camels—she is the woman whom YHWH has decided for my lord's son. 45 Before I finish speaking to my heart, then behold, Rebekah is coming out, and her pitcher [is] on her shoulder, and she goes down to the fountain and draws; and I say to her, Please let me drink, 46 and she hurries and lets down her pitcher from off her and says, Drink, and I also water your camels; and I drink, and she has also watered the camels. 47 And I ask her, and say, Whose daughter [are] you? And she says, Daughter of Bethuel, son of Nahor, whom Milcah has borne to him, and I put the ring on her nose, and the bracelets on her hands, 48 and I bow, and pay respect before YHWH, and I bless YHWH, God of my lord Abraham, who has led me in the true way to receive the daughter of my lord's brother for his son. 49 And now, if you are dealing kindly and truly with my lord, declare to me; and if not, declare to me; and I turn to the right or to the left." 50 And Laban answers—Bethuel also—and they say, "The thing has gone out from YHWH; we are not able to speak to you bad or good; 51 behold, Rebekah [is] before you, take and go, and she is a wife to your lord's son, as YHWH has spoken." 52 And it comes to pass, when the servant of Abraham has heard their words, that he bows himself toward the earth before YHWH; 53 and the servant takes out vessels of silver, and vessels of gold, and garments, and gives to Rebekah; precious things also he has given to her brother and to her mother. 54 And they eat and drink, he and the men who [are] with him, and lodge all night; and they rise in the morning, and he says, "Send me to my lord"; 55 and her brother says—her mother also, "Let the young person abide with us a week or ten days, afterward she goes." 56 And he says to them, "Do not delay me, seeing YHWH has prospered my way; send me away, and I go to my lord"; 57 and they say, "Let us call for the young person, and inquire of her mouth"; 58 and they call for Rebekah, and say to her, "Do you go with this man?" And she says, "I go." 59 And they send away their sister Rebekah, and her nurse, and Abraham's servant, and his men; 60 and they bless Rebekah, and say to her, "You [are] our sister; become thousands of myriads, and your seed possesses the gate of those hating it." 61 And Rebekah and her young women arise, and ride on the camels, and go after the man; and the servant takes Rebekah and goes. 62 And Isaac has come in from the entrance of the Well of the Living One, my Beholder; and he is dwelling in the land of the south, 63 and Isaac goes out to meditate in the field, at the turning of the evening, and he lifts up his eyes, and looks, and behold, camels are coming. 64 And Rebekah lifts up her eyes, and sees Isaac, and comes down off the camel; 65 and she says to the servant, "Who [is] this man who is walking in the field to meet us?" And the servant says, "It [is] my lord"; and she takes the veil, and covers herself. 66 And the servant recounts to Isaac all the things that he has done, 67 and Isaac brings her into the tent of his mother Sarah, and he takes Rebekah, and she becomes his wife, and he loves her, and Isaac is comforted after [the death of] his mother.

25

And Abraham adds and takes a wife, and her name [is] Keturah; 2 and she bears to him Zimran, and Jokshan, and Medan, and Midian, and Ishbak, and Shuah. 3 And Jokshan has begotten Sheba and Dedan; and the sons of Dedan were Asshurim, and Letushim, and Leummim; 4 and the sons of Midian [are] Ephah, and Epher, and Enoch, and Abidah, and Eldaah: all these [are] sons of Keturah. 5 And Abraham gives all that he has to Isaac; 6 and to the sons of the concubines whom Abraham has, Abraham has given gifts, and sends them away from his son Isaac (in his being yet alive) eastward, to the east country. 7 And these [are] the days of the years of the life of Abraham, which he lived, one hundred and seventy-five years; 8 and Abraham expires, and dies in a good old age, aged and satisfied, and is gathered to his people. 9 And his sons Isaac and Ishmael bury him at the cave of Machpelah, at the field of Ephron, son of Zoar the Hittite, which [is] before Mamre— 10 the field which Abraham bought from the sons of Heth—there Abraham has been buried, and his wife Sarah. 11 And it comes to pass after the death of Abraham, that God blesses his son Isaac; and Isaac dwells by the Well of the

Living One, my Beholder. **12** And these [are] the generations of Ishmael, Abraham's son, whom Hagar the Egyptian, Sarah's handmaid, has borne to Abraham; **13** and these [are] the names of the sons of Ishmael, by their names, according to their births: firstborn of Ishmael, Nebajoth; and Kedar, and Adbeel, and Mibsam, **14** and Mishma, and Dumah, and Massa, **15** Hadar, and Tema, Jetur, Naphish, and Kedemah: **16** these are sons of Ishmael, and these [are] their names, by their villages, and by their towers; twelve princes according to their peoples. **17** And these [are] the years of the life of Ishmael, one hundred and thirty-seven years; and he expires, and dies, and is gathered to his people; **18** and they dwell from Havilah to Shur, which [is] before Egypt, in [your] going toward Asshur; in the presence of all his brothers has he fallen. **19** And these [are] the generations of Isaac, Abraham's son: Abraham has begotten Isaac; **20** and Isaac is a son of forty years in his taking Rebekah, daughter of Bethuel the Aramean, from Padan-Aram, sister of Laban the Aramean, to him for a wife. **21** And Isaac makes plea to YHWH before his wife, for she [is] barren: and YHWH accepts his plea, and his wife Rebekah conceives, **22** and the children struggle together within her, and she says, "If [it is] right—why [am] I thus?" And she goes to seek YHWH. **23** And YHWH says to her, "Two nations [are] in your womb, and two peoples from your bowels are parted; and the [one] people is stronger than the [other] people; and the older serves the younger." **24** And her days to bear are fulfilled, and behold, twins [are] in her womb; **25** and the first comes out all red as a hairy robe, and they call his name Esau; **26** and afterward his brother has come out, and his hand is taking hold on Esau's heel, and one calls his name Jacob; and Isaac [is] a son of sixty years in her bearing them. **27** And the youths grew, and Esau is a man acquainted [with] hunting, a man of the field; and Jacob [is] a plain man, inhabiting tents; **28** and Isaac loves Esau, for [his] game [is] in his mouth; and Rebekah is loving Jacob. **29** And Jacob boils stew, and Esau comes in from the field, and he [is] weary; **30** and Esau says to Jacob, "Please let me eat some of this red-red thing, for I [am] weary"; therefore [one] has called his name Edom; **31** and Jacob says, "Sell your birthright to me today." **32** And Esau says, "Behold, I am going to die, and what is this to me—a birthright?" **33** And Jacob says, "Swear to me today": and he swears to him, and sells his birthright to Jacob; **34** and Jacob has given bread and stew of lentils to Esau, and he eats, and drinks, and rises, and goes; and Esau despises the birthright.

26 And there is a famine in the land, besides the first famine which was in the days of Abraham, and Isaac goes to Abimelech king of the Philistines, to Gerar. **2** And YHWH appears to him and says, "Do not go down toward Egypt, dwell in the land concerning which I speak to you, **3** sojourn in this land, and I am with you, and bless you, for to you and to your seed I give all these lands, and I have established the oath which I have sworn to your father Abraham; **4** and I have multiplied your seed as stars of the heavens, and I have given to your seed all these lands; and all nations of the earth have blessed themselves in your Seed; **5** because that Abraham has listened to My voice, and keeps My charge, My commands, My statutes, and My laws." **6** And Isaac dwells in Gerar; **7** and men of the place ask him of his wife, and he says, "She [is] my sister": for he has been afraid to say, "My wife—lest the men of the place kill me for Rebekah, for she [is] of good appearance." **8** And it comes to pass, when the days have been prolonged to him there, that Abimelech king of the Philistines looks through the window, and sees, and behold, Isaac is playing with his wife Rebekah. **9** And Abimelech calls for Isaac and says, "Behold, she [is] surely your wife; and how could you have said, She [is] my sister?" And Isaac says to him, "Because I said, Lest I die for her." **10** And Abimelech says, "What [is] this you have done to us? As a little thing one of the people had lain with your wife, and you had brought on us guilt"; **11** and Abimelech commands all the people, saying, "He who comes against this man or against his wife, dying does die." **12** And Isaac sows in that land, and finds in that year a hundredfold, and YHWH blesses him; **13** and the man is great, and goes on, going on and becoming great, until he has been very great, **14** and he has possession of a flock, and possession of a herd, and an abundant service; and the Philistines envy him, **15** and all the wells which his father's servants dug in the days of his father Abraham, the Philistines have stopped them, and fill them with dust. **16** And Abimelech says to Isaac, "Go from us; for you have become much mightier than we"; **17** and Isaac goes from there, and encamps in the Valley of Gerar, and dwells there; **18** and Isaac turns back, and digs the wells of water which they dug in the days of his father Abraham, which the Philistines have stopped after the death of Abraham, and he calls to them names according to the names which his father called them. **19** And Isaac's servants dig in the valley, and find there a well of living water, **20** and shepherds of Gerar strive with shepherds of Isaac, saying, "The water [is] ours"; and he calls the name of the well "Strife," because they have striven habitually with him; **21** and they dig another well, and they strive also for it, and he calls its name "Hatred." **22** And he removes from there, and digs another well, and they have not striven for it, and he calls its name "Enlargements," and says, "For—now has YHWH given enlargement to us, and we have been fruitful in the land." **23** And he goes up from there [to] Beer-Sheba, **24** and YHWH appears to him during that night and says, "I [am] the God of your father Abraham, do not fear, for I [am] with you, and have blessed you, and have multiplied your seed, because of My servant Abraham"; **25** and he builds there an altar, and preaches in the Name of YHWH, and stretches out there his tent, and there Isaac's servants dig a well. **26** And Abimelech has gone to him from Gerar, and Ahuzzath his friend, and Phichol head of his host; **27** and Isaac says to them, "Why have you come to me, and you have hated me, and you send me away from you?" **28** And they say, "We have certainly seen that YHWH has been with you, and we say, Now let there be an oath between us, between us and you, and let us make a covenant with you; **29** do no evil with us, as we have not touched you, and as we have only done good with you, and send you away in peace; you [are] now blessed of YHWH." **30** And he makes a banquet for them, and they eat and drink, **31** and rise early in the morning, and swear to one another, and Isaac sends them away, and they go from him in peace. **32** And it comes to pass during that day that Isaac's servants come and declare to him concerning the circumstances of the well which they have dug, and say to him, "We have found water"; **33** and he calls it Shebah, [oath,] therefore the name of the city [is] Beer-Sheba, [Well of the Oath,] to this day. **34** And Esau is a son of forty years, and he takes a wife, Judith, daughter of Beeri the Hittite, and Bashemath, daughter of Elon the Hittite, **35** and they are a bitterness of spirit to Isaac and to Rebekah.

27 And it comes to pass that Isaac [is] aged, and his eyes are too dim for seeing, and he calls [for] his older son Esau and says to him, "My son"; and he says to him, "Here I [am]." **2** And he says, "Now behold, I have become aged, I have not known the day of my death; **3** and now, please take up your instruments, your quiver, and your bow, and go out to the field, and hunt provision for me, **4** and make tasteful things for me, [such] as I have loved, and bring [them] to me, and I eat, so that my soul blesses you before I die." **5** And Rebekah is listening while Isaac is speaking to his son Esau; and Esau goes to the field to hunt game—to bring in; **6** and Rebekah has spoken to her son Jacob, saying, "Behold, I have heard your father speaking to your brother Esau, saying, **7** Bring game for me, and make tasteful things for me, and I eat, and bless you before YHWH before my death. **8** And now, my son, listen to my voice, to that which I am commanding you: **9** Now go to the flock, and take for me two good kids of the goats from there, and I make them tasteful things for your father, [such] as he has loved; **10** and you have taken [them] to your father, and he has eaten, so that his soul blesses you before his death." **11** And Jacob says to his mother Rebekah, "Behold, my brother Esau [is] a hairy man, and I [am] a smooth man, **12** it may be my father feels me, and I have been in his eyes as a deceiver, and have brought on me disapproval, and not a blessing"; **13** and his mother says to him, "On me your disapproval, my son; only listen to my voice, and go, take for me." **14** And he goes, and takes, and brings to his mother, and his mother makes tasteful things, [such] as his father has loved; **15** and Rebekah takes the desirable garments of Esau her older son, which [are] with her in the house, and puts them on Jacob her younger son; **16** and she has put the skins

GENESIS

of the kids of the goats on his hands, and on the smooth of his neck, **17** and she gives the tasteful things, and the bread which she has made, into the hand of her son Jacob. **18** And he comes to his father and says, "My father"; and he says, "Here I [am]; who [are] you, my son?" **19** And Jacob says to his father, "I [am] Esau your firstborn; I have done as you have spoken to me; please rise, sit and eat of my game, so that your soul blesses me." **20** And Isaac says to his son, "What [is] this you have hurried to find, my son?" And he says, "That which your God YHWH has caused to come before me." **21** And Isaac says to Jacob, "Please come near, and I feel you, my son, whether you [are] he, my son Esau, or not." **22** And Jacob comes near to his father Isaac, and he feels him, and says, "The voice [is] the voice of Jacob, and the hands hands of Esau." **23** And he has not discerned him, for his hands have been hairy, as the hands of his brother Esau, and he blesses him, **24** and says, "You are he—my son Esau?" And he says, "I [am]." **25** And he says, "Bring [it] near to me, and I eat of my son's game, so that my soul blesses you"; and he brings [it] near to him, and he eats; and he brings wine to him, and he drinks. **26** And his father Isaac says to him, "Please come near and kiss me, my son"; **27** and he comes near, and kisses him, and he smells the fragrance of his garments, and blesses him, and says, "See, the fragrance of my son [is] as the fragrance of a field which YHWH has blessed; **28** and God gives to you of the dew of the heavens, and of the fatness of the earth, and abundance of grain and wine; **29** peoples serve you, and nations bow themselves to you, be mighty over your brothers, and the sons of your mother bow themselves to you; those who curse you [are] cursed, and those who bless you [are] blessed." **30** And it comes to pass, as Isaac has finished blessing Jacob, and Jacob is only just going out from the presence of his father Isaac, that his brother Esau has come in from his hunting; **31** and he also makes tasteful things, and brings to his father, and says to his father, "Let my father arise, and eat of his son's game, so that your soul blesses me." **32** And his father Isaac says to him, "Who [are] you?" And he says, "I [am] your son, your firstborn, Esau"; **33** and Isaac trembles a very great trembling and says, "Who, now, [is] he who has provided game, and brings to me, and I eat of all before you come in, and I bless him? Indeed, he is blessed." **34** When Esau hears the words of his father, then he cries a very great and bitter cry, and says to his father, "Bless me, me also, O my father"; **35** and he says, "Your brother has come with subtlety, and takes your blessing." **36** And he says, "Is it because he whose name is called Jacob takes me by the heel these two times? He has taken my birthright; and behold, now he has taken my blessing"; he also says, "Have you not kept back a blessing for me?" **37** And Isaac answers and says to Esau, "Behold, a mighty one have I set him over you, and all his brothers have I given to him for servants, and [with] grain and wine have I sustained him; and for you now, what will I do, my son?" **38** And Esau says to his father, "One blessing have you my father? Bless me, me also, O my father"; and Esau lifts up his voice, and weeps. **39** And his father Isaac answers and says to him, "Behold, of the fatness of the earth is your dwelling, and of the dew of the heavens from above; **40** and by your sword you live, and your brother serves you; and it has come to pass, when you rule, that you have broken his yoke from off your neck." **41** And Esau hates Jacob, because of the blessing with which his father blessed him, and Esau says in his heart, "The days of mourning [for] my father draw near, and I slay my brother Jacob." **42** And the words of Esau her older son are declared to Rebekah, and she sends and calls for Jacob her younger son, and says to him, "Behold, your brother Esau is comforting himself in regard to you—to slay you; **43** and now, my son, listen to my voice, and rise, flee for yourself to my brother Laban, to Haran, **44** and you have dwelt with him some days, until your brother's fury turns back, **45** until your brother's anger turns back from you, and he has forgotten that which you have done to him, and I have sent and taken you from there; why am I bereaved even of you both the same day?" **46** And Rebekah says to Isaac, "I have been disgusted with my life because of the presence of the daughters of Heth; if Jacob takes a wife of the daughters of Heth, like these—from the daughters of the land—why do I live?"

28 And Isaac calls to Jacob, and blesses him, and commands him, and says to him, "You must not take a wife of the daughters of Canaan; **2** rise, go to Padan-Aram, to the house of your mother's father Bethuel, and take for yourself a wife from there, from the daughters of your mother's brother Laban; **3** and God Almighty bless you, and make you fruitful, and multiply you, and you have become an assembly of peoples; **4** and He gives to you the blessing of Abraham, to you and to your seed with you, to cause you to possess the land of your sojournings, which God gave to Abraham." **5** And Isaac sends Jacob away, and he goes to Padan-Aram, to Laban, son of Bethuel the Aramean, brother of Rebekah, mother of Jacob and Esau. **6** And Esau sees that Isaac has blessed Jacob, and has sent him to Padan-Aram to take to himself from there a wife—in his blessing him that he lays a charge on him, saying, You must not take a wife from the daughters of Canaan— **7** that Jacob listens to his father and to his mother, and goes to Padan-Aram— **8** and Esau sees that the daughters of Canaan are evil in the eyes of his father Isaac, **9** and Esau goes to Ishmael, and takes Mahalath, daughter of Ishmael, Abraham's son, sister of Nebajoth, to his wives, to himself, for a wife. **10** And Jacob goes out from Beer-Sheba, and goes toward Haran, **11** and he touches at a [certain] place, and lodges there, for the sun has gone in, and he takes of the stones of the place, and makes [them] his pillows, and lies down in that place. **12** And he dreams, and behold, a ladder set up on the earth, and its head is touching the heavens; and behold, messengers of God are going up and coming down by it; **13** and behold, YHWH is standing on it, and He says, "I [am] YHWH, God of your father Abraham, and God of Isaac; the land on which you are lying, to you I give it, and to your seed; **14** and your seed has been as the dust of the land, and you have broken forth westward, and eastward, and northward, and southward, and all families of the ground have been blessed in you and in your seed. **15** And behold, I [am] with you, and have kept you wherever you go, and have caused you to return to this ground; for I do not leave you until I have surely done that which I have spoken to you." **16** And Jacob awakens out of his sleep and says, "Surely YHWH is in this place, and I did not know"; **17** and he fears and says, "How fearful [is] this place; this is nothing but a house of God, and this a gate of the heavens." **18** And Jacob rises early in the morning, and takes the stone which he has made his pillows, and makes it a standing pillar, and pours oil on its top, **19** and he calls the name of that place Bethel, [house of God,] and yet, Luz [is] the name of the city at the first. **20** And Jacob vows a vow, saying, "Seeing God is with me, and has kept me in this way which I am going, and has given to me bread to eat, and a garment to put on— **21** when I have turned back in peace to the house of my father, and YHWH has become my God, **22** then this stone which I have made a standing pillar is a house of God, and all that You give to me—tithing I tithe to You."

29 And Jacob lifts up his feet, and goes toward the land of the sons of the east; **2** and he looks, and behold, a well in the field, and behold, there [are] three droves of a flock crouching by it, for they water the droves from that well, and the great stone [is] on the mouth of the well. **3** (When all the droves have been gathered there, and they have rolled the stone from off the mouth of the well, and have watered the flock, then they have turned back the stone on the mouth of the well to its place.) **4** And Jacob says to them, "My brothers, where [are] you from?" And they say, "We [are] from Haran." **5** And he says to them, "Have you known Laban, son of Nahor?" And they say, "We have known." **6** And he says to them, "Does he have peace?" And they say, "Peace; and behold, his daughter Rachel is coming with the flock." **7** And he says, "Behold, the day [is] still great, [it is] not time for the livestock to be gathered; water the flock, and go, delight yourselves." **8** And they say, "We are not able, until all the droves be gathered together, and they have rolled away the stone from the mouth of the well, and we have watered the flock." **9** He is yet speaking with them, and Rachel has come with the flock which her father has, for she [is] shepherdess; **10** and it comes to pass, when Jacob has seen Rachel, daughter of his mother's brother Laban, and the flock of his mother's brother Laban, that Jacob comes near and rolls the stone from off the mouth of the well, and waters the flock of his mother's brother Laban. **11** And Jacob kisses Rachel, and lifts up his voice, and weeps, **12** and Jacob declares to Rachel that

GENESIS

he [is] her father's brother, and that he [is] Rebekah's son, and she runs and declares [it] to her father. **13** And it comes to pass, when Laban hears the report of his sister's son Jacob, that he runs to meet him, and embraces him, and kisses him, and brings him into his house; and he recounts to Laban all these things, **14** and Laban says to him, "You [are] surely my bone and my flesh"; and he dwells with him a month of days. **15** And Laban says to Jacob, "Is it because you [are] my brother that you have served me for nothing? Declare to me what your hire [is]." **16** And Laban has two daughters, the name of the older [is] Leah, and the name of the younger Rachel, **17** and the eyes of Leah [are] tender, and Rachel has been beautiful of form and beautiful of appearance. **18** And Jacob loves Rachel and says, "I serve you seven years for Rachel your younger daughter": **19** and Laban says, "It is better for me to give her to you than to give her to another man; dwell with me"; **20** and Jacob serves for Rachel seven years; and they are in his eyes as some days, because of his loving her. **21** And Jacob says to Laban, "Give up my wife, for my days have been fulfilled, and I go in to her"; **22** and Laban gathers all the men of the place, and makes a banquet. **23** And it comes to pass in the evening, that he takes his daughter Leah, and brings her to him, and he goes in to her; **24** and Laban gives his maidservant Zilpah to her, to his daughter Leah, [for] a maidservant. **25** And it comes to pass in the morning, that behold, it [is] Leah; and he says to Laban, "What [is] this you have done to me? Have I not served with you for Rachel? And why have you deceived me?" **26** And Laban says, "It is not done so in our place, to give the younger before the firstborn; **27** fulfill the period of seven [for] this one, and we also give to you this one, for the service which you serve with me yet seven other years." **28** And Jacob does so, and fulfills the period of seven [for] this one, and he gives his daughter Rachel to him for a wife for him; **29** and Laban gives his maidservant Bilhah to his daughter Rachel for a maidservant for her. **30** And he also goes in to Rachel, and he also loves Rachel more than Leah; and he serves with him yet seven other years. **31** And YHWH sees that Leah [is] the hated one, and He opens her womb, and Rachel [is] barren; **32** and Leah conceives, and bears a son, and calls his name Reuben, for she said, "Because YHWH has looked on my affliction; because now does my husband love me." **33** And she conceives again, and bears a son, and says, "Because YHWH has heard that I [am] the hated one, He also gives to me even this [one]"; and she calls his name Simeon. **34** And she conceives again and bears a son, and says, "Now [is] the time, my husband is joined to me, because I have born to him three sons," therefore has [one] called his name Levi. **35** And she conceives again and bears a son, and this time says, "I praise YHWH"; therefore has she called his name Judah; and she ceases from bearing.

30 And Rachel sees that she has not borne to Jacob, and Rachel is envious of her sister, and says to Jacob, "Give me sons, and if there is none—I die." **2** And Jacob's anger burns against Rachel, and he says, "Am I in stead of God who has withheld from you the fruit of the womb?" **3** And she says, "Behold, my handmaid Bilhah, go in to her, and she bears on my knees, and I am built up, even I, from her"; **4** and she gives Bilhah her maidservant to him for a wife, and Jacob goes in to her; **5** and Bilhah conceives, and bears a son to Jacob, **6** and Rachel says, "God has decided for me, and has also listened to my voice, and gives a son to me"; therefore she has called his name Dan. **7** And Bilhah, Rachel's maidservant, conceives again, and bears a second son to Jacob, **8** and Rachel says, "With wrestlings of God I have wrestled with my sister, indeed, I have prevailed"; and she calls his name Napthali. **9** And Leah sees that she has ceased from bearing, and she takes Zilpah her maidservant, and gives her to Jacob for a wife; **10** and Zilpah, Leah's maidservant, bears a son to Jacob, **11** and Leah says, "A troop is coming"; and she calls his name Gad. **12** And Zilpah, Leah's maidservant, bears a second son to Jacob, **13** and Leah says, "Because of my happiness, for daughters have pronounced me blessed"; and she calls his name Asher. **14** And Reuben goes in the days of wheat-harvest, and finds love-apples in the field, and brings them to his mother Leah, and Rachel says to Leah, "Please give to me of the love-apples of your son." **15** And she says to her, "Is your taking my husband a little thing, that you have also taken the love-apples of my son?" And Rachel says, "He therefore lies with you tonight, for your son's love-apples." **16** And Jacob comes in from the field at evening; and Leah goes to meet him and says, "You come in to me, for [in] hiring I have hired you with my son's love-apples"; and he lies with her during that night. **17** And God listens to Leah, and she conceives, and bears a son to Jacob, a fifth, **18** and Leah says, "God has given my hire, because I have given my maidservant to my husband"; and she calls his name Issachar. **19** And Leah conceives again, and she bears a sixth son to Jacob, **20** and Leah says, "God has endowed me—a good dowry; this time my husband dwells with me, for I have borne six sons to him"; and she calls his name Zebulun; **21** and afterward she has borne a daughter, and calls her name Dinah. **22** And God remembers Rachel, and God listens to her, and opens her womb, **23** and she conceives and bears a son, and says, "God has gathered up my reproach"; **24** and she calls his name Joseph, saying, "Yhwh is adding to me another son." **25** And it comes to pass, when Rachel has borne Joseph, that Jacob says to Laban, "Send me away, and I go to my place, and to my land; **26** give up my wives and my children, for whom I have served you, and I go; for you have known my service which I have served you." **27** And Laban says to him, "Now if I have found grace in your eyes—I have observed diligently that Yhwh blesses me for your sake." **28** He also says, "Define your hire to me, and I give." **29** And he says to him, "You have known that which I have served you [in], and that which your substance was with me; **30** for [it is] little which you have had at my appearance, and it breaks forth into a multitude, and Yhwh blesses you at my coming; and now, when do I make, I also, for my own house?" **31** And he says, "What do I give to you?" And Jacob says, "You do not give me anything; if you do this thing for me, I turn back; I have delight; I watch your flock; **32** I pass through all your flock today to turn aside every speckled and spotted sheep from there, and every brown sheep among the lambs, and speckled and spotted among the goats—and it has been my hire; **33** and my righteousness has answered for me in the day to come, when it comes in for my hire before your face—everyone which is not speckled and spotted among [my] goats, and brown among [my] lambs—it is stolen with me." **34** And Laban says, "Behold, O that it were according to your word"; **35** and he turns aside during that day the striped and the spotted male goats, and all the speckled and the spotted female goats, everyone that [has] white in it, and every brown one among the lambs, and he gives into the hand of his sons, **36** and sets a journey of three days between himself and Jacob; and Jacob is feeding the rest of the flock of Laban. **37** And Jacob takes to himself a rod of fresh poplar and almond and plane-tree, and peels in them white peelings, making bare the white that [is] on the rods, **38** and sets up the rods which he has peeled in the gutters in the watering troughs (where the flock comes to drink), in front of the flock, that they may conceive in their coming to drink; **39** and the flocks conceive at the rods, and the flock bears striped, speckled, and spotted ones. **40** And Jacob has parted the lambs, and he puts the face of the flock toward the striped, also all the brown in the flock of Laban, and he sets his own droves by themselves, and has not set them near Laban's flock. **41** And it has come to pass, whenever the strong ones of the flock conceive, that Jacob sets the rods before the eyes of the flock in the gutters, to cause them to conceive by the rods, **42** and when the flock is feeble, he does not set [them]; and the feeble ones have been Laban's, and the strong ones Jacob's. **43** And the man increases very exceedingly, and has many flocks, and maidservants, and menservants, and camels, and donkeys.

31 And he hears the words of Laban's sons, saying, "Jacob has taken all that our father has; indeed, from that which our father has, he has made all this glory"; **2** and Jacob sees the face of Laban, and behold, it is not with him as before. **3** And Yhwh says to Jacob, "Return to the land of your fathers, and to your family, and I am with you." **4** And Jacob sends and calls for Rachel and for Leah to the field to his flock; **5** and says to them, "I am beholding your father's face—that it is not toward me as before, and the God of my father has been with me, **6** and you have known that with all my power I have served your father, **7** and your father has played on me, and has changed my hire ten times; and God has not permitted him to do evil with me. **8** If he says thus: The speckled are your hire, then all the flock bore speckled ones; and if he says thus: The striped are your hire, then all the flock bore striped; **9** and God takes away the substance of your father, and gives to me. **10** And it comes to pass at the time of the flock conceiving, that I lift up my eyes and see in a dream, and behold, the male goats, which are going up on the flock, [are] striped, speckled, and spotted; **11** and the Messenger of God says to me in the dream, Jacob, and I say, Here I [am]. **12** And He says, Now lift up your eyes and see [that] all the male goats which are going up on the flock [are] striped, speckled, and spotted, for I have seen all that Laban is doing to you; **13** I [am] the God of Bethel where you have anointed a standing pillar, where you have vowed a vow to me; now, arise, go out from this land, and return to the land of your birth." **14** And Rachel answers—Leah also—and says to him, "Have we yet a portion and inheritance in the house of our father? **15** Have we not been reckoned strangers to him? For he has sold us, and he also utterly consumes our money; **16** for all the wealth which God has taken away from our father, it [is] ours, and our children's; and now, all that God has said to you—do." **17** And Jacob rises, and lifts up his sons and his wives on the camels, **18** and leads all his livestock, and all his substance which he has acquired, the livestock of his getting, which he has acquired in Padan-Aram, to go to his father Isaac, to the land of Canaan. **19** And Laban has gone to shear his flock, and Rachel steals the teraphim which her father has; **20** and Jacob deceives the heart of Laban the Aramean, because he has not declared to him that he is fleeing; **21** and he flees, he and all that he has, and rises, and passes over the River, and sets his face [toward] the Mount of Gilead. **22** And it is told to Laban on the third day that Jacob has fled, **23** and he takes his brothers with him, and pursues after him a journey of seven days, and overtakes him in the Mount of Gilead. **24** And God comes to Laban the Aramean in a dream of the night and says to him, "Take heed to yourself lest you speak with Jacob from good to evil." **25** And Laban overtakes Jacob; and Jacob has fixed his tent in the mountain; and Laban with his brothers have fixed [theirs] in the Mount of Gilead. **26** And Laban says to Jacob, "What have you done that you deceive my heart, and lead away my daughters as captives of the sword? **27** Why have you hidden yourself to flee, and deceive me, and have not declared to me, and I send you away with joy and with songs, with tambourine and with harp, **28** and have not permitted me to kiss my sons and my daughters? Now you have acted foolishly in doing [so]; **29** my hand is to God to do evil with you, but the God of your father last night has spoken to me, saying, Take heed to yourself from speaking with Jacob from good to evil. **30** And now, you have certainly gone, because you have been very desirous for the house of your father; why have you stolen my gods?" **31** And Jacob answers and says to Laban, "Because I was afraid, for I said, Lest you violently take away your daughters from me; **32** with whomsoever you find your gods—he must not live; before our brothers discern for yourself what [is] with me, and take to yourself": and Jacob has not known that Rachel has stolen them. **33** And Laban goes into the tent of Jacob, and into the tent of Leah, and into the tent of the two handmaidens, and has not found; and he goes out from the tent of Leah, and goes into the tent of Rachel. **34** And Rachel has taken the teraphim, and puts them in the furniture of the camel, and sits on them; and Laban feels all the tent, and has not found; **35** and she says to her father, "Let it not be displeasing in the eyes of my lord that I am not able to rise at your presence, for the way of women [is] on me"; and he searches, and has not found the teraphim. **36** And it is displeasing to Jacob, and he strives with Laban; and Jacob answers and says to Laban, "What [is] my transgression? What my sin, that you have burned after me? **37** For you have felt all my vessels: what have you found of all the vessels of your house? Set here before my brothers, and your brothers, and they decide between us both. **38** These twenty years I [am] with you: your ewes and your female goats have not miscarried, and the rams of your flock I have not eaten; **39** the torn I have not brought to you—I repay it—from my hand you seek it; I have been deceived by day, and I have been deceived by night; **40** I have been [thus]: drought has consumed me in the day, and frost by night, and my sleep wanders from my eyes. **41** This [is] to me twenty years in your house: I have served you fourteen years for your two

GENESIS

daughters, and six years for your flock; and you change my hire ten times; **42** unless the God of my father, the God of Abraham, and the Fear of Isaac, had been for me, surely now you had sent me away empty; God has seen my affliction and the labor of my hands, and reproves last night." **43** And Laban answers and says to Jacob, "The daughters [are] my daughters, and the sons my sons, and the flock my flock, and all that you are seeing [is] mine; and to my daughters—what do I to these today, or to their sons whom they have born? **44** And now, come, let us make a covenant, I and you, and it has been for a witness between me and you." **45** And Jacob takes a stone, and lifts it up [for] a standing pillar; **46** and Jacob says to his brothers, "Gather stones," and they take stones, and make a heap; and they eat there on the heap; **47** and Laban calls it Jegar-Sahadutha; and Jacob has called it Galeed. **48** And Laban says, "This heap [is] witness between me and you today"; therefore has he called its name Galeed; **49** Mizpah also, for he said, "YHWH watches between me and you, for we are hidden from one another; **50** if you afflict my daughters, or take wives beside my daughters—there is no man with us—see, God [is] witness between me and you." **51** And Laban says to Jacob, "Behold, this heap, and behold, the standing pillar which I have cast between me and you; **52** this heap [is] witness, and the standing pillar [is] witness, that I do not pass over this heap to you, and that you do not pass over this heap and this standing pillar to me—for evil; **53** the God of Abraham and the God of Nahor, judges between us—the God of their father," and Jacob swears by the Fear of his father Isaac. **54** And Jacob sacrifices a sacrifice on the mountain, and calls to his brothers to eat bread, and they eat bread, and lodge on the mountain; **55** and Laban rises early in the morning, and kisses his sons and his daughters, and blesses them; and Laban goes on, and turns back to his place.

32 And Jacob has gone on his way, and messengers of God come on him; **2** and Jacob says, when he has seen them, "This [is] the camp of God"; and he calls the name of that place "Two Camps." **3** And Jacob sends messengers before him to his brother Esau, toward the land of Seir, the field of Edom, **4** and commands them, saying, "Thus you say to my lord, to Esau, Thus said your servant Jacob: I have sojourned with Laban, and I linger until now; **5** and I have ox, and donkey, flock, and manservant, and maidservant, and I send to declare to my lord, to find grace in his eyes." **6** And the messengers return to Jacob, saying, "We came to your brother, to Esau, and he is also coming to meet you, and four hundred men with him"; **7** and Jacob fears exceedingly, and is distressed, and he divides the people who [are] with him, and the flock, and the herd, and the camels, into two camps, **8** and says, "If Esau comes to one camp, and has struck it—then the camp which is left has been for an escape." **9** And Jacob says, "God of my father Abraham and God of my father Isaac, YHWH who says to me, Return to your land and to your family, and I do good with you: **10** I have been unworthy of all the kind acts and of all the truth which You have done with your servant—for with my staff I passed over this Jordan, and now I have become two camps. **11** Please deliver me from the hand of my brother, from the hand of Esau: for I am fearing him, lest he come and has struck me—mother beside sons; **12** and You have said, I certainly do good with you, and have set your seed as the sand of the sea, which is not numbered because of the multitude." **13** And he lodges there during that night, and takes from that which is coming into his hand, a present for his brother Esau: **14** female goats two hundred, and male goats twenty, ewes two hundred, and rams twenty, **15** suckling camels and their young ones thirty, cows forty, and bullocks ten, female donkeys twenty, and foals ten; **16** and he gives into the hand of his servants every drove by itself, and says to his servants, "Pass over before me, and a space you put between drove and drove." **17** And he commands the first, saying, "When my brother Esau meets you, and has asked you, saying, Whose [are] you? And to where do you go? And whose [are] these before you? **18** Then you have said, Your servant Jacob's: it [is] a present sent to my lord, to Esau; and behold, he also [is] behind us." **19** And he commands also the second, also the third, also all who are going after the droves, saying, "According to this manner do you speak to Esau in your finding him, **20** and you have also said, Behold, your servant Jacob [is] behind us"; for he said, "I pacify his face with the present which is going before me, and afterward I see his face; it may be he lifts up my face"; **21** and the present passes over before his face, and he has lodged during that night in the camp. **22** And he rises in that night, and takes his two wives, and his two maidservants, and his eleven children, and passes over the passage of Jabbok; **23** and he takes them, and causes them to pass over the brook, and he causes that which he has to pass over. **24** And Jacob is left alone, and One wrestles with him until the ascending of the dawn; **25** and He sees that He is not able for him, and He comes against the hollow of his thigh, and the hollow of Jacob's thigh is disjointed in his wrestling with Him; **26** and He says, "Send Me away, for the dawn has ascended": and he says, "I do not send You away, except You have blessed me." **27** And He says to him, "What [is] your name?" And he says, "Jacob." **28** And He says, "Your name is no longer called Jacob, but Israel; for you have reigned with God and with men, and prevail." **29** And Jacob asks and says, "Please declare Your Name"; and He says, "Why [is] this, you ask for My Name?" And He blesses him there. **30** And Jacob calls the name of the place Peniel: "For I have seen God face to face, and my life is delivered"; **31** and the sun rises on him when he has passed over Penuel, and he is halting on his thigh; **32** therefore the sons of Israel do not eat the sinew which shrank, which [is] on the hollow of the thigh, to this day, because He came against the hollow of Jacob's thigh, against the sinew which shrank.

33 And Jacob lifts up his eyes, and looks, and behold, Esau is coming, and with him four hundred men; and he divides the children to Leah, and to Rachel, and to the two maidservants; **2** and he sets the maidservants and their children first, and Leah and her children behind, and Rachel and Joseph last. **3** And he himself passed over before them, and bows himself to the earth seven times, until his drawing near to his brother, **4** and Esau runs to meet him, and embraces him, and falls on his neck, and kisses him, and they weep; **5** and he lifts up his eyes, and sees the women and the children, and says, "What [are] these to you?" And he says, "The children with whom God has favored your servant." **6** And the maidservants draw near, they and their children, and bow themselves; **7** and Leah also draws near, and her children, and they bow themselves; and afterward Joseph has drawn near with Rachel, and they bow themselves. **8** And he says, "What to you [is] all this camp which I have met?" And he says, "To find grace in the eyes of my lord." **9** And Esau says, "I have abundance, my brother, that which you have, let it be for yourself." **10** And Jacob says, "No, please, now if I have found grace in your eyes, then you have received my present from my hand, because that I have seen your face, as the seeing of the face of God, and you are pleased with me; **11** please receive my blessing which is brought to you, because God has favored me, and because I have all [things]"; and he presses on him, and he receives [it], **12** and says, "Let us journey and go on, and I go on before you." **13** And he says to him, "My lord knows that the children [are] tender, and the suckling flock and the herd [are] with me; when they have beaten them one day, then all the flock has died. **14** Please let my lord pass over before his servant, and I lead on gently, according to the foot of the work which [is] before me, and to the foot of the children, until I come to my lord, to Seir." **15** And Esau says, "Please let me place with you some of the people who [are] with me"; and he said, "Why [is] this? I find grace in the eyes of my lord." **16** And Esau turns back on that day on his way to Seir; **17** and Jacob has journeyed to Succoth, and builds a house for himself, and has made shelters for his livestock, therefore he has called the name of the place Succoth. **18** And Jacob comes safe [to the] city of Shechem, which [is] in the land of Canaan, in his coming from Padan-Aram, and encamps before the city, **19** and he buys the portion of the field where he has stretched out his tent, from the hand of the sons of Hamor, father of Shechem, for one hundred kesitah; **20** and he sets up there an altar, and proclaims at it God—the God of Israel.

34 And Dinah, daughter of Leah, whom she has borne to Jacob, goes out to look on the daughters of the land, **2** and Shechem, son of Hamor the Hivite, a prince of the land, sees her, and takes her, and lies with her, and humbles her; **3** and his soul cleaves to Dinah, daughter of Jacob, and he loves the young person, and

GENESIS

speaks to the heart of the young person. **4** And Shechem speaks to his father Hamor, saying, "Take for me this girl for a wife." **5** And Jacob has heard that he has defiled his daughter Dinah, and his sons were with his livestock in the field, and Jacob kept silent until their coming. **6** And Hamor, father of Shechem, goes out to Jacob to speak with him; **7** and the sons of Jacob came in from the field when they heard, and the men grieve themselves, and it [is] very displeasing to them, for folly he has done against Israel, to lie with the daughter of Jacob—and so it is not done. **8** And Hamor speaks with them, saying, "Shechem, my son, his soul has cleaved to your daughter; please give her to him for a wife, **9** and join in marriage with us; you give your daughters to us, and you take our daughters for yourselves, **10** and you dwell with us, and the land is before you; dwell and trade [in] it, and have possessions in it." **11** And Shechem says to her father and to her brothers, "Let me find grace in your eyes, and that which you say to me, I give; **12** multiply on me dowry and gift exceedingly, and I give as you say to me, and give to me the young person for a wife." **13** And the sons of Jacob answer Shechem and his father Hamor deceitfully, and they speak (because he defiled their sister Dinah), **14** and say to them, "We are not able to do this thing, to give our sister to one who has a foreskin, for it [is] a reproach to us. **15** Only for this we consent to you: if you are as we, to have every male of you circumcised, **16** then we have given our daughters to you, and we take your daughters for ourselves, and we have dwelt with you, and have become one people; **17** and if you do not listen to us to be circumcised, then we have taken our daughter, and have gone." **18** And their words are good in the eyes of Hamor, and in the eyes of Shechem, Hamor's son; **19** and the young man did not delay to do the thing, for he had delight in Jacob's daughter, and he is honorable above all the house of his father. **20** And Hamor comes—his son Shechem also—to the gate of their city, and they speak to the men of their city, saying, **21** "These men are peaceable with us; then let them dwell in the land, and trade [in] it; and the land, behold, [is] wide before them; their daughters let us take to ourselves for wives, and our daughters give to them. **22** Only for this do the men consent to us, to dwell with us, to become one people, in every male of us being circumcised, as they are circumcised; **23** their livestock, and their substance, and all their beasts—are they not ours? Only let us consent to them, and they dwell with us." **24** And to Hamor, and to his son Shechem, do all those going out of the gate of his city listen, and every male is circumcised, all those going out of the gate of his city. **25** And it comes to pass, on the third day, in their being pained, that two of the sons of Jacob, Simeon and Levi, Dinah's brothers, take each his sword, and come in against the city confidently, and slay every male; **26** and Hamor, and his son Shechem, they have slain by the mouth of the sword, and they take Dinah out of Shechem's house, and go out. **27** Jacob's sons have come in on the wounded, and they spoil the city, because they had defiled their sister; **28** their flock and their herd, and their donkeys, and that which [is] in the city, and that which [is] in the field, have they taken; **29** and all their wealth, and all their infants, and their wives they have taken captive, and they spoil also all that [is] in the house. **30** And Jacob says to Simeon and to Levi, "You have troubled me, by causing me to stink among the inhabitants of the land, among the Canaanite, and among the Perizzite: and I [am] few in number, and they have been gathered against me, and have struck me, and I have been destroyed, I and my house." **31** And they say, "Does he make our sister as a harlot?"

35 And God says to Jacob, "Rise, go up to Bethel, and dwell there, and make there an altar to God, who appeared to you in your fleeing from the face of your brother Esau." **2** And Jacob says to his household, and to all who [are] with him, "Turn aside the gods of the stranger which [are] in your midst, and cleanse yourselves, and change your garments; **3** and we rise, and go up to Bethel, and I make there an altar to God, who is answering me in the day of my tribulation, and is with me in the way that I have gone." **4** And they give to Jacob all the gods of the stranger that [are] in their hand, and the rings that [are] in their ears, and Jacob hides them under the oak which [is] by Shechem; **5** and they journey, and the terror of God is on the cities which [are] around them, and they have not pursued after the sons of Jacob. **6** And Jacob comes to Luz which [is] in the land of Canaan (it [is] Bethel), he and all the people who [are] with him, **7** and he builds there an altar, and proclaims at the place the God of Bethel: for there had God been revealed to him, in his fleeing from the face of his brother. **8** And Deborah, Rebekah's nurse, dies, and she is buried at the lower part of Bethel, under the oak, and he calls its name "Oak of Weeping." **9** And God appears to Jacob again, in his coming from Padan-Aram, and blesses him; **10** and God says to him, "Your name [is] Jacob: your name is no longer called Jacob, but Israel is your name"; and He calls his name Israel. **11** And God says to him, "I [am] God Almighty; be fruitful and multiply, a nation and an assembly of nations is from you, and kings from your loins go out; **12** and the land which I have given to Abraham and to Isaac—to you I give it, indeed to your seed after you I give the land." **13** And God goes up from him, in the place where He has spoken with him. **14** And Jacob sets up a standing pillar in the place where He has spoken with him, a standing pillar of stone, and he pours on it an oblation, and he pours on it oil; **15** and Jacob calls the name of the place where God spoke with him Bethel. **16** And they journey from Bethel, and there is yet a distance of land before entering Ephratha, and Rachel bears, and is sharply pained in her bearing; **17** and it comes to pass, in her being sharply pained in her bearing, that the midwife says to her, "Do not fear, for this also [is] a son for you." **18** And it comes to pass in the going out of her soul (for she died), that she calls his name Ben-Oni; and his father called him Benjamin; **19** and Rachel dies, and is buried in the way to Ephratha, which [is] Beth-Lehem, **20** and Jacob sets up a standing pillar over her grave; which [is] the standing pillar of Rachel's grave to this day. **21** And Israel journeys, and stretches out his tent beyond the Tower of Edar; **22** and it comes to pass in Israel's dwelling in that land, that Reuben goes, and lies with his father's concubine Bilhah; and Israel hears. **23** And the sons of Jacob are twelve. Sons of Leah: Jacob's firstborn Reuben, and Simeon, and Levi, and Judah, and Issachar, and Zebulun. **24** Sons of Rachel: Joseph and Benjamin. **25** And sons of Bilhah, Rachel's maidservant: Dan and Naphtali. **26** And sons of Zilpah, Leah's maidservant: Gad and Asher. These [are] sons of Jacob, who have been born to him in Padan-Aram. **27** And Jacob comes to his father Isaac, at Mamre, the city of Arba (which [is] Hebron), where Abraham and Isaac have sojourned. **28** And the days of Isaac are one hundred and eighty years, **29** and Isaac expires; and dies, and is gathered to his people, aged and satisfied with days; and his sons Esau and Jacob bury him.

36 And these [are] the generations of Esau, who [is] Edom. **2** Esau has taken his wives from the daughters of Canaan: Adah daughter of Elon the Hittite, and Aholibamah daughter of Anah, daughter of Zibeon the Hivite, **3** and Bashemath daughter of Ishmael, sister of Nebajoth. **4** And Adah bears to Esau, Eliphaz; and Bashemath has borne Reuel; **5** and Aholibamah has borne Jeush, and Jaalam, and Korah. These [are] sons of Esau, who were born to him in the land of Canaan. **6** And Esau takes his wives, and his sons, and his daughters, and all the persons of his house, and his livestock, and all his beasts, and all his substance which he has acquired in the land of Canaan, and goes into the country from the face of his brother Jacob; **7** for their substance was more abundant than to dwell together, and the land of their sojournings was not able to bear them because of their livestock; **8** and Esau dwells in Mount Seir: Esau is Edom. **9** And these [are] the generations of Esau, father of Edom, in Mount Seir. **10** These [are] the names of the sons of Esau: Eliphaz son of Adah, wife of Esau; Reuel son of Bashemath, wife of Esau. **11** And the sons of Eliphaz are Teman, Omar, Zepho, and Gatam, and Kenaz; **12** and Timnath has been concubine to Eliphaz son of Esau, and she bears to Eliphaz, Amalek; these [are] sons of Adah wife of Esau. **13** And these [are] sons of Reuel: Nahath and Zerah, Shammah and Mizzah; these were sons of Bashemath wife of Esau. **14** And these have been the sons of Aholibamah daughter of Anah, daughter of Zibeon, wife of Esau; and she bears to Esau, Jeush and Jaalam and Korah. **15** These [are] chiefs of the sons of Esau: sons of Eliphaz, firstborn of Esau: Chief Teman, Chief Omar, Chief Zepho, Chief Kenaz, **16** Chief Korah, Chief Gatam, Chief Amalek; these [are] chiefs of

GENESIS

Eliphaz, in the land of Edom; these [are] sons of Adah. **17** And these [are] sons of Reuel son of Esau: Chief Nahath, Chief Zerah, Chief Shammah, Chief Mizzah; these [are] chiefs of Reuel, in the land of Edom; these [are] sons of Bashemath wife of Esau. **18** And these [are] sons of Aholibamah wife of Esau: Chief Jeush, Chief Jaalam, Chief Korah; these [are] chiefs of Aholibamah daughter of Anah, wife of Esau. **19** These [are] sons of Esau (who [is] Edom), and these their chiefs. **20** These [are] sons of Seir the Horite, the inhabitants of the land: Lotan, and Shobal, and Zibeon, and Anah, **21** and Dishon, and Ezer, and Dishan; these [are] chiefs of the Horites, sons of Seir, in the land of Edom. **22** And the sons of Lotan are Hori and Heman; and a sister of Lotan [is] Timna. **23** And these [are] sons of Shobal: Alvan and Manahath, and Ebal, Shepho and Onam. **24** And these [are] sons of Zibeon, both Ajah and Anah: it [is] Anah that has found the Imim in the wilderness, in his feeding the donkeys of his father Zibeon. **25** And these [are] sons of Anah: Dishon, and Aholibamah daughter of Anah. **26** And these [are] sons of Dishon: Hemdan, and Eshban, and Ithran, and Cheran. **27** These [are] sons of Ezer: Bilhan, and Zaavan, and Akan. **28** These [are] sons of Dishan: Uz and Aran. **29** These [are] chiefs of the Horite: Chief Lotan, Chief Shobal, Chief Zibeon, Chief Anah, **30** Chief Dishon, Chief Ezer, Chief Dishan: these [are] chiefs of the Horite in reference to their chiefs in the land of Seir. **31** And these [are] the kings who have reigned in the land of Edom before the reigning of a king over the sons of Israel. **32** And Bela son of Beor reigns in Edom, and the name of his city [is] Dinhabah; **33** and Bela dies, and Jobab son of Zerah from Bozrah reigns in his stead; **34** and Jobab dies, and Husham from the land of the Temanite reigns in his stead. **35** And Husham dies, and Hadad son of Bedad reigns in his stead (who strikes Midian in the field of Moab), and the name of his city [is] Avith; **36** and Hadad dies, and Samlah of Masrekah reigns in his stead; **37** and Samlah dies, and Saul from Rehoboth of the River reigns in his stead; **38** and Saul dies, and Ba'al-hanan son of Achbor reigns in his stead; **39** and Ba'al-hanan son of Achbor dies, and Hadar reigns in his stead, and the name of his city [is] Pau; and his wife's name [is] Mehetabel daughter of Matred, daughter of Me-zahab. **40** And these [are] the names of the chiefs of Esau, according to their families, according to their places, by their names: Chief Timnah, Chief Alvah, Chief Jetheth, **41** Chief Aholibamah, Chief Elah, Chief Pinon, **42** Chief Kenaz, Chief Teman, Chief Mibzar, **43** Chief Magdiel, Chief Iram: these [are] chiefs of Edom, in reference to their dwellings, in the land of their possession; he [is] Esau father of Edom.

37 And Jacob dwells in the land of his father's sojournings—in the land of Canaan. **2** These [are] the generations of Jacob: Joseph, a son of seventeen years, has been enjoying himself with his brothers among the flock (and he [is] a youth), with the sons of Bilhah, and with the sons of Zilpah, his father's wives, and Joseph brings in an account of their evil to their father. **3** And Israel has loved Joseph more than any of his sons, for he [is] a son of his old age, and has made for him a long coat; **4** and his brothers see that their father has loved him more than any of his brothers, and they hate him, and have not been able to speak [to] him peaceably. **5** And Joseph dreams a dream, and declares to his brothers, and they add still more to hate him. **6** And he says to them, "Please hear this dream which I have dreamed: **7** that, behold, we are binding bundles in the midst of the field, and behold, my bundle has arisen, and has also stood up, and behold, your bundles are all around, and they bow themselves to my bundle." **8** And his brothers say to him, "Do you certainly reign over us? Do you certainly rule over us?" And they add still more to hate him, for his dreams, and for his words. **9** And he dreams yet another dream, and recounts it to his brothers, and says, "Behold, I have dreamed a dream again, and behold, the sun and the moon, and eleven stars, are bowing themselves to me." **10** And he recounts to his father, and to his brothers; and his father pushes against him, and says to him, "What [is] this dream which you have dreamed? Do we certainly come, I, and your mother, and your brothers—to bow ourselves to you, to the earth?" **11** And his brothers are zealous against him, and his father has watched the matter. **12** And his brothers go to feed the flock of their father in Shechem, **13** and Israel says to

Joseph, "Are your brothers not feeding in Shechem? Come, and I send you to them"; and he says to him, "Here I [am]"; **14** and he says to him, "Now go see the peace of your brothers, and the peace of the flock, and bring me back word"; and he sends him from the Valley of Hebron, and he comes to Shechem. **15** And a man finds him, and behold, he is wandering in the field, and the man asks him, saying, "What do you seek?" **16** And he says, "I am seeking my brothers, please declare to me where they are feeding." **17** And the man says, "They have journeyed from this, for I have heard some saying, Let us go to Dothan," and Joseph goes after his brothers, and finds them in Dothan. **18** And they see him from afar, even before he draws near to them, and they conspire against him to put him to death. **19** And they say to one another, "Behold, this man of the dreams comes; **20** and now, come, and we slay him, and cast him into one of the pits, and have said, An evil beast has devoured him; and we see what his dreams are." **21** And Reuben hears, and delivers him out of their hand, and says, "Let us not strike the life"; **22** and Reuben says to them, "Shed no blood; cast him into this pit which [is] in the wilderness, and do not put forth a hand on him," in order to deliver him out of their hand, to bring him back to his father. **23** And it comes to pass, when Joseph has come to his brothers, that they strip Joseph of his coat, the long coat which [is] on him, **24** and take him and cast him into the pit, and the pit [is] empty, there is no water in it. **25** And they sit down to eat bread, and they lift up their eyes, and look, and behold, a caravan of Ishmaelites coming from Gilead, and their camels carrying spices, and balm, and myrrh, going to take [them] down to Egypt. **26** And Judah says to his brothers, "What gain when we slay our brother, and have concealed his blood? **27** Come, and we sell him to the Ishmaelites, and our hands are not on him, for he [is] our brother—our flesh"; and his brothers listen. **28** And Midianite merchantmen pass by and they draw out and bring up Joseph out of the pit, and sell Joseph to the Ishmaelites for twenty pieces of silver, and they bring Joseph into Egypt. **29** And Reuben returns to the pit, and behold, Joseph is not in the pit, and he tears his garments, **30** and he returns to his brothers and says, "The boy is not, and I—to where am I going?" **31** And they take the coat of Joseph, and slaughter a kid of the goats, and dip the coat in the blood, **32** and send the long coat, and they bring [it] to their father, and say, "We have found this; please discern whether it [is] your son's coat or not." **33** And he discerns it and says, "My son's coat! An evil beast has devoured him; torn—Joseph is torn!" **34** And Jacob tears his raiment, and puts sackcloth on his loins, and becomes a mourner for his son many days, **35** and all his sons and all his daughters rise to comfort him, and he refuses to comfort himself, and says, "For I go down to my son mourning, to Sheol," and his father weeps for him. **36** And the Midianites have sold him to Egypt, to Potiphar, a eunuch of Pharaoh, head of the executioners.

38 And it comes to pass, at that time, that Judah goes down from his brothers, and turns aside to a man, an Adullamite, whose name [is] Hirah; **2** and Judah sees there the daughter of a man, a Canaanite, whose name [is] Shuah, and takes her, and goes in to her. **3** And she conceives, and bears a son, and he calls his name Er; **4** and she conceives again, and bears a son, and calls his name Onan; **5** and she adds again, and bears a son, and calls his name Shelah; and he was in Chezib in her bearing him. **6** And Judah takes a wife for Er, his firstborn, and her name [is] Tamar; **7** and Er, Judah's firstborn, is evil in the eyes of YHWH, and YHWH puts him to death. **8** And Judah says to Onan, "Go in to the wife of your brother, and marry her, and raise up seed to your brother"; **9** and Onan knows that the seed is not [reckoned] his; and it has come to pass, if he has gone in to his brother's wife, that he has destroyed [it] to the earth, so as not to give seed to his brother; **10** and that which he has done is evil in the eyes of YHWH, and He puts him also to death. **11** And Judah says to his daughter-in-law Tamar, "Abide [as] a widow at your father's house, until my son Shelah grows up"; for he said, "Lest he die—even he—like his brothers"; and Tamar goes and dwells at her father's house. **12** And the days are multiplied, and the daughter of Shuah, Judah's wife, dies; and Judah is comforted, and goes up to his sheep-shearers, he and Hirah his friend the Adullamite, to Timnath. **13** And it is declared to Tamar, saying, "Behold, your husband's father is going up to Timnath to shear his flock"; **14** and she turns aside the garments of her widowhood from off her, and covers herself with a veil, and wraps herself up, and sits in the opening of Enayim, which [is] by the way to Timnath, for she has seen that Shelah has grown up, and she has not been given to him for a wife. **15** And Judah sees her, and reckons her for a harlot, for she has covered her face, **16** and he turns aside to her by the way and says, "Please come, let me come in to you," for he has not known that she [is] his daughter-in-law; and she says, "What do you give to me, that you may come in to me?" **17** And he says, "I send a kid of the goats from the flock." And she says, "Do you give a pledge until you send [it]?" **18** And he says, "What [is] the pledge that I give to you?" And she says, "Your seal, and your ribbon, and your staff which [is] in your hand"; and he gives to her, and goes in to her, and she conceives to him; **19** and she rises, and goes, and turns aside her veil from off her, and puts on the garments of her widowhood. **20** And Judah sends the kid of the goats by the hand of his friend the Adullamite, to receive the pledge from the hand of the woman, and he has not found her. **21** And he asks the men of her place, saying, "Where [is] the separated one—she in Enayim, by the way?" And they say, "There has not been in this [place] a separated one." **22** And he turns back to Judah and says, "I have not found her; and the men of the place also have said, There has not been in this [place] a separated one," **23** and Judah says, "Let her take to herself, lest we become despised; behold, I sent this kid, and you have not found her." **24** And it comes to pass about three months [after], that it is declared to Judah, saying, "Your daughter-in-law Tamar has committed fornication; and also, behold, she has conceived by fornication": and Judah says, "Bring her out—and she is burned." **25** She is brought out, and she has sent to her husband's father, saying, "To a man whose these [are], I [am] pregnant"; and she says, "Please discern whose these [are]—the seal, and the ribbons, and the staff." **26** And Judah discerns and says, "She has been more righteous than I, because that I did not give her to my son Shelah"; and he has not added to know her again. **27** And it comes to pass in the time of her bearing, that behold, twins [are] in her womb; **28** and it comes to pass in her bearing, that [one] gives out a hand, and the midwife takes and binds on his hand a scarlet thread, saying, "This has come out first." **29** And it comes to pass as he draws back his hand, that behold, his brother has come out, and she says, "What! You have broken forth—the breach [is] on you"; and he calls his name Perez; **30** and afterward his brother has come out, on whose hand [is] the scarlet thread, and he calls his name Zerah.

39 And Joseph has been brought down to Egypt, and Potiphar, a eunuch of Pharaoh, head of the executioners, an Egyptian man, buys him out of the hands of the Ishmaelites who have brought him there. **2** And YHWH is with Joseph, and he is a prosperous man, and he is in the house of his lord the Egyptian, **3** and his lord sees that YHWH is with him, and all that he is doing YHWH is causing to prosper in his hand, **4** and Joseph finds grace in his eyes and serves him, and he appoints him over his house, and all that he has he has given into his hand. **5** And it comes to pass from the time that he has appointed him over his house, and over all that he has, that YHWH blesses the house of the Egyptian for Joseph's sake, and the blessing of YHWH is on all that he has, in the house, and in the field; **6** and he leaves all that he has in the hand of Joseph, and he has not known anything that he has, except the bread which he is eating. And Joseph is of a handsome form, and of a handsome appearance. **7** And it comes to pass after these things, that his lord's wife lifts up her eyes to Joseph and says, "Lie with me"; **8** and he refuses and says to his lord's wife, "Behold, my lord has not known what [is] with me in the house, and all that he has he has given into my hand; **9** none is greater in this house than I, and he has not withheld from me anything, except you, because you [are] his wife; and how will I do this great evil? Then I have sinned against God." **10** And it comes to pass at her speaking to Joseph day [by] day, that he has not listened to her, to lie near her, to be with her; **11** and it comes to pass about this day, that he goes into the house to do his work, and there is none of the men of the house there in the house, **12** and she catches him by his garment, saying, "Lie with me"; and he leaves his garment in her hand, and flees, and goes outside. **13** And it comes to pass, when she sees that he has left his garment in her hand, and flees outside, **14** that she calls for the men of her house, and speaks to them, saying, "See, he has brought a man to us, a Hebrew, to play with us; he has come in to me, to lie with me, and I call with a loud voice, **15** and it comes to pass, when he hears that I have lifted up my voice and call, that he leaves his garment near me, and flees, and goes outside." **16** And she places his garment near her, until the coming in of his lord to his house. **17** And she speaks to him according to these words, saying, "The Hebrew servant whom you have brought to us, has come in to me to play with me; **18** and it comes to pass, when I lift my voice and call, that he leaves his garment near me, and flees outside." **19** And it comes to pass, when his lord hears the words of his wife, which she has spoken to him, saying, "According to these things has your servant done to me," that his anger burns; **20** and Joseph's lord takes him, and puts him to the round-house, a place where the king's prisoners [are] bound; and he is there in the round-house. **21** And YHWH is with Joseph, and stretches out kindness to him, and puts his grace in the eyes of the chief of the round-house; **22** and the chief of the round-house gives into the hand of Joseph all the prisoners who [are] in the round-house, and of all that they are doing there, he has been doer; **23** the chief of the round-house does not see anything under his hand, because YHWH [is] with him, and that which he is doing YHWH is causing to prosper.

40 And it comes to pass, after these things—the butler of the king of Egypt and the baker have sinned against their lord, against the king of Egypt; **2** and Pharaoh is angry against his two eunuchs, against the chief of the butlers, and against the chief of the bakers, **3** and puts them in confinement in the house of the chief of the executioners, into the round-house, the place where Joseph [is] a prisoner, **4** and the chief of the executioners charges Joseph with them, and he serves them; and they are in confinement [for some] days. **5** And they dream a dream both of them, each his dream in one night, each according to the interpretation of his dream, the butler and the baker whom the king of Egypt has, who [are] prisoners in the round-house. **6** And Joseph comes to them in the morning, and sees them, and behold, they [are] morose; **7** and he asks Pharaoh's eunuchs who [are] with him in confinement in the house of his lord, saying, "Why [are] your faces sad today?" **8** And they say to him, "We have dreamed a dream, and there is no interpreter of it"; and Joseph says to them, "Are interpretations not with God? Please recount to me." **9** And the chief of the butlers recounts his dream to Joseph and says to him, "In my dream, then behold, a vine [is] before me! **10** And in the vine [are] three branches, and it [is] as it were flourishing; gone up has its blossom, its clusters have ripened grapes; **11** and Pharaoh's cup [is] in my hand, and I take the grapes and press them into the cup of Pharaoh, and I give the cup into the hand of Pharaoh." **12** And Joseph says to him, "This [is] its interpretation: the three branches are three days; **13** yet, within three days Pharaoh lifts up your head, and has put you back on your station, and you have given the cup of Pharaoh into his hand, according to the former custom when you were his butler. **14** Surely if you have remembered me with you, when it is well with you, and have please done kindness with me, and have made mention of me to Pharaoh, then you have brought me out from this house, **15** for I was really stolen from the land of the Hebrews; and here also I have done nothing that they have put me in the pit [for]." **16** And the chief of the bakers sees that he has interpreted good, and he says to Joseph, "I also [am] in a dream, and behold, three baskets of white bread [are] on my head, **17** and in the highest basket [are] of all [kinds] of Pharaoh's food, work of a baker; and the birds are eating them out of the basket, from off my head." **18** And Joseph answers and says, "This [is] its interpretation: the three baskets are three days; **19** yet, within three days Pharaoh lifts up your head from off you, and has hanged you on a tree, and the birds have eaten your flesh from off you." **20** And it comes to pass, on the third day, Pharaoh's birthday, that he makes a banquet to all his servants, and lifts up the head of the chief of the butlers, and the head of the chief of the bakers among his servants, **21** and he puts back the chief of the butlers to his butlership, and he gives the cup into the hand of Pharaoh; **22** and the chief of the bakers he has hanged, as

GENESIS

Joseph has interpreted to them; **23** and the chief of the butlers has not remembered Joseph, but forgets him.

41 And it comes to pass, at the end of two years of days that Pharaoh is dreaming, and behold, he is standing by the River, **2** and behold, from the River coming up are seven cows, of beautiful appearance, and fat [in] flesh, and they feed among the reeds; **3** and behold, seven other cows are coming up after them out of the River, of bad appearance, and lean [in] flesh, and they stand near the cows on the edge of the River, **4** and the cows of bad appearance and lean [in] flesh eat up the seven cows of beautiful appearance, and fat—and Pharaoh awakens. **5** And he sleeps, and dreams a second time, and behold, seven ears are coming up on one stalk, fat and good, **6** and behold, seven ears, thin, and blasted with an east wind, are springing up after them; **7** and the thin ears swallow the seven fat and full ears—and Pharaoh awakens, and behold, a dream. **8** And it comes to pass in the morning, that his spirit is moved, and he sends and calls all the enchanters of Egypt, and all its wise men, and Pharaoh recounts to them his dream, and there is no interpreter of them to Pharaoh. **9** And the chief of the butlers speaks with Pharaoh, saying, "I mention my sin this day: **10** Pharaoh has been angry against his servants, and puts me in confinement in the house of the chief of the executioners, me and the chief of the bakers; **11** and we dream a dream in one night, I and he, each according to the interpretation of his dream we have dreamed. **12** And there [is] with us a youth, a Hebrew, servant to the chief of the executioners, and we recount to him, and he interprets to us our dreams, [to] each according to his dream has he interpreted, **13** and it comes to pass, as he has interpreted to us so it has been, me he put back on my station, and him he hanged." **14** And Pharaoh sends and calls Joseph, and they cause him to run out of the pit, and he shaves, and changes his garments, and comes to Pharaoh. **15** And Pharaoh says to Joseph, "I have dreamed a dream, and there is no interpreter of it, and I have heard concerning you, saying, You understand a dream to interpret it," **16** and Joseph answers Pharaoh, saying, "Without me—God answers Pharaoh with peace." **17** And Pharaoh speaks to Joseph: "In my dream, behold, I am standing by the edge of the River, **18** and behold, out of the River coming up are seven cows, fat [in] flesh, and of beautiful form, and they feed among the reeds; **19** and behold, seven other cows are coming up after them, thin, and of very bad form, and lean [in] flesh; I have not seen like these in all the land of Egypt for badness. **20** And the lean and the bad cows eat up the first seven fat cows, **21** and they come in to their midst, and it has not been known that they have come in to their midst, and their appearance [is] bad as at the commencement; and I awake. **22** And I see in my dream, and behold, seven ears are coming up on one stalk, full and good; **23** and behold, seven ears, withered, thin, blasted with an east wind, are springing up after them; **24** and the thin ears swallow the seven good ears; and I tell [it] to the enchanters, and there is none declaring [it] to me." **25** And Joseph says to Pharaoh, "The dream of Pharaoh is one: that which God is doing he has declared to Pharaoh; **26** the seven good cows are seven years, and the seven good ears are seven years, the dream is one; **27** and the seven thin and bad cows which are coming up after them are seven years, and the seven empty ears, blasted with an east wind, are seven years of famine; **28** this [is] the thing which I have spoken to Pharaoh: God has shown Pharaoh what He is doing. **29** Behold, seven years are coming of great abundance in all the land of Egypt, **30** and seven years of famine have arisen after them, and all the plenty is forgotten in the land of Egypt, and the famine has finished the land, **31** and the plenty is not known in the land because of that famine afterward, for it [is] very grievous. **32** And because of the repeating of the dream to Pharaoh twice, surely the thing is established by God, and God is hurrying to do it. **33** And now, let Pharaoh provide a man, intelligent and wise, and set him over the land of Egypt; **34** let Pharaoh make and appoint overseers over the land, and receive a fifth of the land of Egypt in the seven years of plenty, **35** and they gather all the food of these good years that are coming, and heap up grain under the hand of Pharaoh—food in the cities; and they have kept [it], **36** and the food has been for a store for the land, for the seven years of famine which are in the land of Egypt; and the land is cut off by the famine."

GENESIS

37 And the thing is good in the eyes of Pharaoh, and in the eyes of all his servants, **38** and Pharaoh says to his servants, "Do we find like this, a man in whom the Spirit of God [is]?" **39** And Pharaoh says to Joseph, "After God's causing you to know all this, there is none intelligent and wise as you; **40** you are over my house, and at your mouth do all my people kiss; only in the throne I am greater than you." **41** And Pharaoh says to Joseph, "See, I have put you over all the land of Egypt." **42** And Pharaoh turns aside his seal-ring from off his hand, and puts it on the hand of Joseph, and clothes him [with] garments of fine linen, and places a chain of gold on his neck, **43** and causes him to ride in the second chariot which he has, and they proclaim before him, "Bow the knee!" And [he] set him over all the land of Egypt. **44** And Pharaoh says to Joseph, "I [am] Pharaoh, and without you a man does not lift up his hand and his foot in all the land of Egypt"; **45** and Pharaoh calls Joseph's name Zaphnath-Paaneah, and he gives to him Asenath daughter of Poti-Pherah, priest of On, for a wife, and Joseph goes out over the land of Egypt. **46** And Joseph [is] a son of thirty years in his standing before Pharaoh king of Egypt, and Joseph goes out from the presence of Pharaoh, and passes over through all the land of Egypt; **47** and the land makes in the seven years of plenty by handfuls. **48** And he gathers all the food of the seven years which have been in the land of Egypt, and puts food in the cities; the food of the field which [is] around [each] city has he put in its midst; **49** and Joseph gathers grain as sand of the sea, multiplying exceedingly, until he has ceased to number, for there is no number. **50** And to Joseph were born two sons before the year of famine comes, whom Asenath daughter of Poti-Pherah, priest of On, has borne to him, **51** and Joseph calls the name of the firstborn Manasseh: "For God has made me to forget all my labor, and all the house of my father"; **52** and the name of the second he has called Ephraim: "For God has caused me to be fruitful in the land of my affliction." **53** And the seven years of plenty are completed which have been in the land of Egypt, **54** and the seven years of famine begin to come, as Joseph said, and famine is in all the lands, but in all the land of Egypt has been bread; **55** and all the land of Egypt is famished, and the people cry to Pharaoh for bread, and Pharaoh says to all the Egyptians, "Go to Joseph; that which he says to you—do." **56** And the famine has been over all the face of the land, and Joseph opens all [places] which have [grain] in them, and sells to the Egyptians; and the famine is severe in the land of Egypt, **57** and all the earth has come to Egypt, to buy, to Joseph, for the famine was severe in all the earth.

42 And Jacob sees that there is grain in Egypt, and Jacob says to his sons, "Why do you look at each other?" **2** He also says, "Behold, I have heard that there is grain in Egypt, go down there, and buy for us from there, and we live and do not die"; **3** and the ten brothers of Joseph go down to buy grain in Egypt, **4** and Benjamin, Joseph's brother, Jacob has not sent with his brothers, for he said, "Lest harm meet him." **5** And the sons of Israel come to buy in the midst of those coming, for the famine has been in the land of Canaan, **6** and Joseph is the ruler over the land, he who is selling to all the people of the land, and Joseph's brothers come and bow themselves to him—face to the earth. **7** And Joseph sees his brothers, and discerns them, and makes himself strange to them, and speaks sharp things with them, and says to them, "From where have you come?" And they say, "From the land of Canaan—to buy food." **8** And Joseph discerns his brothers, but they have not discerned him, **9** and Joseph remembers the dreams which he dreamed of them and says to them, "You [are] spies; you have come to see the nakedness of the land." **10** And they say to him, "No, my lord, but your servants have come to buy food; **11** we [are] all of us sons of one man, we [are] right men; your servants have not been spies"; **12** and he says to them, "No, but you have come to see the nakedness of the land"; **13** and they say, "Your servants [are] twelve brothers; we [are] sons of one man in the land of Canaan, and behold, the young one [is] with our father today, and one is not." **14** And Joseph says to them, "This [is] that which I have spoken to you, saying, You [are] spies, **15** by this you are proved: [as] Pharaoh lives, if you go out from this—except by your young brother coming here; **16** send one of you, and let him bring your brother, and you, remain bound, and let your words be proved,

GENESIS

whether truth be with you: and if not, [as] Pharaoh lives, surely you [are] spies"; **17** and he gathers them into confinement [for] three days. **18** And Joseph says to them on the third day, "Do this and live; I fear God! **19** If you [are] right men, let one of your brothers be bound in the house of your confinement, and you, go, carry in grain [for] the famine of your houses, **20** and you bring your young brother to me, and your words are established, and you do not die"; and they do so. **21** And they say to one another, "Truly we [are] guilty concerning our brother, because we saw the distress of his soul, in his making supplication to us, and we did not listen: therefore this distress has come on us." **22** And Reuben answers them, saying, "Did I not speak to you, saying, Do not sin against the boy? And you did not listen; and his blood also, behold, it is required." **23** And they have not known that Joseph understands, for the interpreter [is] between them; **24** and he turns around from them, and weeps, and turns back to them, and speaks to them, and takes Simeon from them, and binds him before their eyes. **25** And Joseph commands, and they fill their vessels [with] grain, also to put back the money of each of them into his sack, and to give to them provision for the way; and one does to them so. **26** And they lift up their grain on their donkeys, and go from there, **27** and the one opens his sack to give provender to his donkey at a lodging-place, and he sees his money, and behold, it [is] in the mouth of his bag, **28** and he says to his brothers, "My money has been put back, and also, behold, in my bag": and their heart goes out, and they tremble, to one another saying, "What [is] this God has done to us!" **29** And they come to their father Jacob, to the land of Canaan, and they declare to him all the things meeting them, saying, **30** "The man, the lord of the land, has spoken with us sharp things, and makes us as spies of the land; **31** and we say to him, We [are] right men, we have not been spies, **32** we [are] twelve brothers, sons of our father, one is not, and the young one [is] today with our father in the land of Canaan. **33** And the man, the lord of the land, says to us, By this I know that you [are] right men—leave one of your brothers with me, and take [for] the famine of your houses and go, **34** and bring your young brother to me, and I know that you [are] not spies, but you [are] right men; I give your brother to you, and you trade with the land." **35** And it comes to pass, they are emptying their sacks, and behold, the bundle of each man's silver [is] in his sack, and they see their bundles of silver, they and their father, and are afraid; **36** and their father Jacob says to them, "You have bereaved me; Joseph is not, and Simeon is not, and Benjamin you take—all these [things] have been against me." **37** And Reuben speaks to his father, saying, "You put to death my two sons, if I do not bring him to you; give him into my hand, and I bring him back to you"; **38** and he says, "My son does not go down with you, for his brother [is] dead, and he by himself is left; when harm has met him in the way in which you go, then you have brought down my grey hairs in sorrow to Sheol."

43 And the famine [is] severe in the land; **2** and it comes to pass, when they have finished eating the grain which they brought from Egypt, that their father says to them, "Return, buy for us a little food." **3** And Judah speaks to him, saying, "The man protesting protested to us, saying, You do not see my face without your brother [being] with you; **4** if you are sending our brother with us, we go down, and buy for you food, **5** and if you are not sending—we do not go down, for the man said to us, You do not see my face without your brother [being] with you." **6** And Israel says, "Why did you do evil to me, by declaring to the man that you had yet a brother?" **7** And they say, "The man asked diligently concerning us, and concerning our family, saying, Is your father yet alive? Have you a brother? And we declare to him according to the tenor of these things; do we certainly know that he will say, Bring down your brother?" **8** And Judah says to his father Israel, "Send the youth with me, and we arise, and go, and live, and do not die, both we, and you, and our infants. **9** I am guarantor [for] him, from my hand you require him; if I have not brought him to you, and set him before you—then I have sinned against you all the days; **10** for if we had not lingered, surely now we had returned these two times." **11** And their father Israel says to them, "If so, now, do this: take of the praised thing of the land in your vessels, and take down to the man a present, a little balm, and a little honey,

53

spices and myrrh, nuts and almonds; **12** and double money take in your hand, even the money which is brought back in the mouth of your bags, you take back in your hand, it may be it [is] an oversight. **13** And take your brother, and rise, return to the man; **14** and God Almighty give to you mercies before the man, so that he has sent to you your other brother and Benjamin; and I, when I am bereaved—I am bereaved." **15** And the men take this present, double money also they have taken in their hand, and Benjamin; and they rise, and go down to Egypt, and stand before Joseph; **16** and Joseph sees Benjamin with them and says to him who [is] over his house, "Bring the men into the house, and slaughter an animal, and make ready, for the men eat with me at noon." **17** And the man does as Joseph has said, and the man brings in the men into the house of Joseph, **18** and the men are afraid because they have been brought into the house of Joseph, and they say, "For the matter of the money which was put back in our bags at the commencement are we brought in—to roll himself on us, and to throw himself on us, and to take us for servants—our donkeys also." **19** And they come near to the man who [is] over the house of Joseph, and speak to him at the opening of the house, **20** and say, "O my lord, we really come down at the commencement to buy food; **21** and it comes to pass, when we have come to the lodging-place, and open our bags, that behold, each one's money [is] in the mouth of his bag, our money in its weight, and we bring it back in our hand; **22** and other money have we brought down in our hand to buy food; we have not known who put our money in our bags." **23** And he says, "Peace to you, do not fear: your God and the God of your father has given to you hidden treasure in your bags, your money came to me"; and he brings out Simeon to them. **24** And the man brings in the men into Joseph's house, and gives water, and they wash their feet; and he gives provender for their donkeys, **25** and they prepare the present until the coming of Joseph at noon, for they have heard that there they eat bread. **26** And Joseph comes into the house, and they bring to him the present which [is] in their hand, into the house, and bow themselves to him, to the earth; **27** and he asks of them of peace and says, "Is your father well? The aged man of whom you have spoken, is he yet alive?" **28** And they say, "Your servant our father [is] well, he is yet alive"; and they bow, and pay respect. **29** And he lifts up his eyes and sees his brother Benjamin, his mother's son, and says, "Is this your young brother, of whom you have spoken to me?" And he says, "God favor you, my son." **30** And Joseph hurries, for his bowels have been moved for his brother, and he seeks to weep, and enters the inner chamber, and weeps there; **31** and he washes his face, and goes out, and refrains himself, and says, "Place bread." **32** And they place for him by himself, and for them by themselves, and for the Egyptians who are eating with him by themselves: for the Egyptians are unable to eat bread with the Hebrews, for it [is] an abomination to the Egyptians. **33** And they sit before him, the firstborn according to his birthright, and the young one according to his youth, and the men wonder one at another; **34** and he lifts up gifts from before him to them, and the gift of Benjamin is five hands more than the gifts of all of them; and they drink, indeed, they drink abundantly with him.

44 And he commands him who [is] over his house, saying, "Fill the bags of the men [with] food, as they are able to carry, and put the money of each in the mouth of his bag; **2** and my cup, the silver cup, you put in the mouth of the bag of the young one, and his grain-money"; and he does according to the word of Joseph which he has spoken. **3** The morning is bright, and the men have been sent away, they and their donkeys— **4** they have gone out of the city—they have not gone far off—and Joseph has said to him who [is] over his house, "Rise, pursue after the men; and you have overtaken them, and you have said to them: Why have you repaid evil for good? **5** Is this not that with which my lord drinks? And he observes diligently with it; you have done evil [in] that which you have done." **6** And he overtakes them, and speaks to them these words, **7** and they say to him, "Why does my lord speak according to these words? Far be it from your servants to do according to this word; **8** behold, the money which we found in the mouth of our bags we brought back to you from the land of Canaan, and how do we steal from the

GENESIS

house of your lord silver or gold? **9** With whomsoever of your servants it is found, he has died, and we also are to my lord for servants." **10** And he says, "Now also, according to your words, so it [is]; he with whom it is found becomes my servant, and you are acquitted"; **11** and they hurry and take down each his bag to the earth, and each opens his bag; **12** and he searches—at the eldest he has begun, and at the youngest he has completed—and the cup is found in the bag of Benjamin; **13** and they tear their garments, and each loads his donkey, and they return to the city. **14** And Judah and his brothers come to the house of Joseph, and he is yet there, and they fall to the earth before him; **15** and Joseph says to them, "What [is] this deed that you have done? Have you not known that a man like me diligently observes?" **16** And Judah says, "What do we say to my lord? What do we speak? And how do we justify ourselves? God has found out the iniquity of your servants; behold, we [are] servants to my lord, both we, and he in whose hand the cup has been found"; **17** and he says, "Far be it from me to do this; the man in whose hand the cup has been found, he becomes my servant; and you, go up in peace to your father." **18** And Judah comes near to him and says, "O my lord, please let your servant speak a word in the ears of my lord, and do not let your anger burn against your servant—for you are as Pharaoh. **19** My lord has asked his servants, saying, Do you have a father or brother? **20** And we say to my lord, We have a father, an aged one, and a child of old age, a little one; and his brother died, and he is left alone of his mother, and his father has loved him. **21** And you say to your servants, Bring him down to me, and I set my eye on him; **22** and we say to my lord, The youth is not able to leave his father, when he has left his father, then he has died; **23** and you say to your servants, If your young brother does not come down with you, you do not add to see my face. **24** And it comes to pass, that we have come up to your servant my father, that we declare to him the words of my lord; **25** and our father says, Return, buy for us a little food, **26** and we say, We are not able to go down; if our young brother is with us, then we have gone down; for we are not able to see the man's face, and our young brother not with us. **27** And your servant my father says to us, You have known that my wife bore two to me, **28** and one goes out from me, and I say, Surely he is torn—torn! And I have not seen him since; **29** when you have taken also this from my presence, and harm has met him, then you have brought down my grey hairs with evil to Sheol. **30** And now, at my coming to your servant my father, and the youth not with us (and his soul is bound up in his soul), **31** then it has come to pass, when he sees that the youth is not, that he has died, and your servants have brought down the grey hairs of your servant our father with sorrow to Sheol; **32** for your servant obtained the youth by guarantee to my father, saying, If I do not bring him to you—then I have sinned against my father all the days. **33** And now, please let your servant abide instead of the youth [as] a servant to my lord, and the youth goes up with his brothers, **34** for how do I go up to my father, and the youth not with me? Lest I look on the evil which finds my father."

45 And Joseph has not been able to refrain himself before all those standing by him, and he calls, "Put out every man from me"; and no man has stood with him when Joseph makes himself known to his brothers, **2** and he gives forth his voice in weeping, and the Egyptians hear, and the house of Pharaoh hears. **3** And Joseph says to his brothers, "I [am] Joseph, is my father yet alive?" And his brothers have not been able to answer him, for they have been troubled at his presence. **4** And Joseph says to his brothers, "Please come near to me," and they come near; and he says, "I [am] your brother Joseph, whom you sold into Egypt; **5** and now, do not be grieved, nor let it be displeasing in your eyes that you sold me here, for God has sent me before you to preserve life. **6** Because these two years the famine [is] in the heart of the land, and yet five years [remain in] which there is neither plowing nor harvest; **7** and God sends me before you, to place a remnant of you in the land, and to give life to you by a great escape; **8** and now, you have not sent me here, but God, and He sets me for a father to Pharaoh, and for lord to all his house, and ruler over all the land of Egypt. **9** Hurry, and go up to my father, then you have said to him, Thus said your son Joseph: God has set me for lord to all Egypt; come down to me, do not stay, **10** and you have dwelt in the land of Goshen, and been near to me, you and your sons, and your son's sons, and your flock, and your herd, and all that you have, **11** and I have nourished you there—for yet [are] five years of famine—lest you become poor, you and your household, and all that you have. **12** And behold, your eyes are seeing, and the eyes of my brother Benjamin, that [it is] my mouth which is speaking to you; **13** and you have declared to my father all my glory in Egypt, and all that you have seen, and you have hurried, and have brought down my father here." **14** And he falls on the neck of his brother Benjamin, and weeps, and Benjamin has wept on his neck; **15** and he kisses all his brothers, and weeps over them; and afterward his brothers have spoken with him. **16** And the sound has been heard in the house of Pharaoh, saying, "The brothers of Joseph have come"; and it is good in the eyes of Pharaoh, and in the eyes of his servants, **17** and Pharaoh says to Joseph, "Say to your brothers, This you do: load your beasts, and go, enter the land of Canaan, **18** and take your father, and your households, and come to me, and I give to you the good of the land of Egypt, and you eat the fat of the land. **19** Indeed, you have been commanded: this you do, take for yourselves out of the land of Egypt, wagons for your infants, and for your wives, and you have brought your father, and come; **20** and your eye has no pity on your vessels, for the good of all the land of Egypt [is] yours." **21** And the sons of Israel do so, and Joseph gives wagons to them by the command of Pharaoh, and he gives to them provision for the way; **22** to all of them has he given—to each changes of garments, and to Benjamin he has given three hundred pieces of silver, and five changes of garments; **23** and to his father he has sent thus: ten donkeys carrying of the good things of Egypt, and ten female donkeys carrying grain and bread, even food for his father for the way. **24** And he sends his brothers away, and they go; and he says to them, "Do not be angry in the way." **25** And they go up out of Egypt, and come to the land of Canaan, to their father Jacob, **26** and they declare to him, saying, "Joseph [is] yet alive," and that he [is] ruler over all the land of Egypt; and his heart ceases, for he has not given credence to them. **27** And they speak to him all the words of Joseph, which he has spoken to them, and he sees the wagons which Joseph has sent to carry him away, and the spirit of their father Jacob lives; **28** and Israel says, "Enough! My son Joseph [is] yet alive; I go and see him before I die."

46 And Israel journeys, and all that he has, and comes to Beer-Sheba, and sacrifices sacrifices to the God of his father Isaac; **2** and God speaks to Israel in visions of the night and says, "Jacob, Jacob"; and he says, "Here I [am]." **3** And He says, "I [am] God, God of your father, do not be afraid of going down to Egypt, for I set you there for a great nation; **4** I go down with you to Egypt, and I also certainly bring you up, and Joseph puts his hand on your eyes." **5** And Jacob rises from Beer-Sheba, and the sons of Israel carry away their father Jacob, and their infants, and their wives, in the wagons which Pharaoh has sent to carry him, **6** and they take their livestock, and their goods which they have acquired in the land of Canaan, and come into Egypt—Jacob, and all his seed with him, **7** his sons, and his sons' sons with him, his daughters, and his sons' daughters, indeed, all his seed he brought with him into Egypt. **8** And these [are] the names of the sons of Israel who are coming into Egypt: Jacob and his sons, Jacob's firstborn, Reuben. **9** And sons of Reuben: Enoch, and Phallu, and Hezron, and Carmi. **10** And sons of Simeon: Jemuel, and Jamin, and Ohad, and Jachin, and Zohar, and Shaul son of the Canaanite. **11** And sons of Levi: Gershon, Kohath, and Merari. **12** And sons of Judah: Er, and Onan, and Shelah, and Perez, and Zerah (and Er and Onan die in the land of Canaan). And sons of Perez are Hezron and Hamul. **13** And sons of Issachar: Tola, and Phuvah, and Job, and Shimron. **14** And sons of Zebulun: Sered, and Elon, and Jahleel. **15** These [are] sons of Leah whom she bore to Jacob in Padan-Aram, and his daughter Dinah; all the persons of his sons and his daughters [are] thirty-three. **16** And sons of Gad: Ziphion, and Haggi, Shuni, and Ezbon, Eri, and Arodi, and Areli. **17** And sons of Asher: Jimnah, and Ishuah, and Isui, and Beriah, and their sister Serah. And sons of Beriah: Heber and Malchiel. **18** These [are] sons of Zilpah, whom Laban gave to his daughter Leah, and she bears these to Jacob—sixteen persons. **19** Sons of Rachel, Jacob's wife: Joseph and Benjamin. **20** And born to Joseph in the

GENESIS

land of Egypt (whom Asenath daughter of Poti-Pherah, priest of On, has borne to him) [are] Manasseh and Ephraim. **21** And sons of Benjamin: Belah, and Becher, and Ashbel, Gera, and Naaman, Ehi, and Rosh, Muppim, and Huppim, and Ard. **22** These [are] sons of Rachel, who were born to Jacob; all the persons [are] fourteen. **23** And sons of Dan: Hushim. **24** And sons of Naphtali: Jahzeel, and Guni, and Jezer, and Shillem. **25** These [are] sons of Bilhah, whom Laban gave to his daughter Rachel; and she bears these to Jacob—all the persons [are] seven. **26** All the persons who are coming to Jacob to Egypt, coming out of his thigh, apart from the wives of Jacob's sons, all the persons [are] sixty-six. **27** And the sons of Joseph who have been born to him in Egypt [are] two persons. All the persons of the house of Jacob who are coming into Egypt [are] seventy. **28** And Judah he has sent before him to Joseph, to direct before him to Goshen, and they come into the land of Goshen; **29** and Joseph harnesses his chariot, and goes up to meet his father Israel, to Goshen, and appears to him, and falls on his neck, and weeps on his neck again; **30** and Israel says to Joseph, "Let me die this time, after my seeing your face, for you [are] yet alive." **31** And Joseph says to his brothers, and to the house of his father, "I go up, and declare to Pharaoh, and say to him, My brothers, and the house of my father who [are] in the land of Canaan have come to me; **32** and the men [are] feeders of a flock, for they have been men of livestock; and their flock, and their herd, and all that they have, they have brought. **33** And it has come to pass, when Pharaoh calls for you and has said, What [are] your works? **34** That you have said, Your servants have been men of livestock from our youth, even until now, both we and our fathers, in order that you may dwell in the land of Goshen, for the abomination of the Egyptians is everyone feeding a flock."

47 And Joseph comes and declares [it] to Pharaoh, and says, "My father, and my brothers, and their flock, and their herd, and all they have, have come from the land of Canaan, and behold, they [are] in the land of Goshen." **2** And out of his brothers he has taken five men, and sets them before Pharaoh; **3** and Pharaoh says to his brothers, "What [are] your works?" And they say to Pharaoh, "Your servants [are] feeders of a flock, both we and our fathers"; **4** and they say to Pharaoh, "We have come to sojourn in the land, for there is no pasture for the flock which your servants have, for the famine in the land of Canaan [is] grievous; and now, please let your servants dwell in the land of Goshen." **5** And Pharaoh speaks to Joseph, saying, "Your father and your brothers have come to you: **6** the land of Egypt is before you; cause your father and your brothers to dwell in the best of the land—they dwell in the land of Goshen, and if you have known, and there are among them men of ability, then you have set them [as] heads over the livestock I have." **7** And Joseph brings in his father Jacob, and causes him to stand before Pharaoh; and Jacob blesses Pharaoh. **8** And Pharaoh says to Jacob, "How many [are] the days of the years of your life?" **9** And Jacob says to Pharaoh, "The days of the years of my sojournings [are] one hundred and thirty years; few and evil have been the days of the years of my life, and they have not reached the days of the years of the life of my fathers, in the days of their sojournings." **10** And Jacob blesses Pharaoh, and goes out from before Pharaoh. **11** And Joseph settles his father and his brothers, and gives a possession to them in the land of Egypt, in the best of the land, in the land of Rameses, as Pharaoh commanded; **12** and Joseph nourishes his father, and his brothers, and all the house of his father [with] bread, according to the mouth of the infants. **13** And there is no bread in all the land, for the famine [is] very grievous, and the land of Egypt and the land of Canaan are feeble because of the famine; **14** and Joseph gathers all the silver that is found in the land of Egypt and in the land of Canaan, for the grain that they are buying, and Joseph brings the silver into the house of Pharaoh. **15** And the silver is consumed out of the land of Egypt and out of the land of Canaan, and all the Egyptians come to Joseph, saying, "Give bread to us—why do we die before you, though the money has ceased?" **16** And Joseph says, "Give your livestock; and I give to you for your livestock, if the money has ceased." **17** And they bring in their livestock to Joseph, and Joseph gives to them bread, for the horses, and for the livestock of the flock, and for the livestock of the herd, and for the donkeys; and he tends them with bread, for all their livestock, during that year. **18** And that year is finished, and they come to him on the second year, and say to him, "We do not hide from my lord, that since the money has been finished, and possession of the livestock [is] to my lord, there has not been left before my lord except our bodies, and our ground; **19** why do we die before your eyes, both we and our ground? Buy us and our ground for bread, and we and our ground are servants to Pharaoh; and give seed, and we live, and do not die, and the ground is not desolate." **20** And Joseph buys all the ground of Egypt for Pharaoh, for the Egyptians have each sold his field, for the famine has been severe on them, and the land becomes Pharaoh's; **21** as for the people, he has removed them to cities from the [one] end of the border of Egypt even to its [other] end. **22** Only the ground of the priests he has not bought, for the priests have a portion from Pharaoh, and they have eaten their portion which Pharaoh has given to them, therefore they have not sold their ground. **23** And Joseph says to the people, "Behold, I have bought you today and your ground for Pharaoh; behold, seed for you, and you have sown the ground, **24** and it has come to pass in the increases, that you have given a fifth to Pharaoh, and four of the parts are for yourselves, for seed of the field, and for your food, and for those who [are] in your houses, and for food for your infants." **25** And they say, "You have revived us; we find grace in the eyes of my lord, and have been servants to Pharaoh"; **26** and Joseph sets it for a statute to this day, concerning the ground of Egypt, [that] Pharaoh has a fifth; only the ground of the priests alone has not become Pharaoh's. **27** And Israel dwells in the land of Egypt, in the land of Goshen, and they have possession in it, and are fruitful, and multiply exceedingly; **28** and Jacob lives in the land of Egypt seventeen years, and the days of Jacob, the years of his life, are one hundred and forty-seven years. **29** And the days of Israel are near to die, and he calls for his son, for Joseph, and says to him, "Now if I have found grace in your eyes, please put your hand under my thigh, and you have done kindness and truth with me; please do not bury me in Egypt, **30** and I have lain with my fathers, and you have carried me out of Egypt, and buried me in their burying-place." And he says, "I do according to your word"; **31** and he says, "Swear to me"; and he swears to him, and Israel bows himself on the head of the bed.

48

And it comes to pass, after these things, that [one] says to Joseph, "Behold, your father is sick"; and he takes his two sons with him, Manasseh and Ephraim. **2** And [one] declares [it] to Jacob and says, "Behold, your son Joseph is coming to you"; and Israel strengthens himself, and sits on the bed. **3** And Jacob says to Joseph, "God Almighty has appeared to me, in Luz, in the land of Canaan, and blesses me, **4** and says to me, Behold, I am making you fruitful, and have multiplied you, and given you for an assembly of peoples, and given this land to your seed after you, a continuous possession. **5** And now, your two sons, who are born to you in the land of Egypt, before my coming to you to Egypt, they [are] mine; Ephraim and Manasseh, as Reuben and Simeon, they are mine; **6** and your family which you have begotten after them are yours; by the name of their brothers they are called in their inheritance. **7** And I—in my coming in from Padan-[Aram] Rachel has died by me in the land of Canaan, in the way, while yet a distance of land to enter Ephrata, and I bury her there in the way of Ephrata, which [is] Beth-Lehem." **8** And Israel sees the sons of Joseph and says, "Who [are] these?" **9** And Joseph says to his father, "They [are] my sons, whom God has given to me in this [place]"; and he says, "Please bring them to me, and I bless them." **10** And the eyes of Israel have been heavy from age—he is unable to see; and he brings them near to him, and he kisses them and cleaves to them; **11** and Israel says to Joseph, "I had not thought [possible] to see your face, and behold, God has also showed me your seed." **12** And Joseph brings them out from between his knees, and bows himself on his face to the earth; **13** and Joseph takes them both, Ephraim in his right hand toward Israel's left, and Manasseh in his left toward Israel's right, and brings [them] near to him. **14** And Israel puts out his right hand and places [it] on the head of Ephraim, who [is] the younger, and his left hand on the head of Manasseh; he has guided his hands wisely, for Manasseh [is] the firstborn. **15** And he blesses Joseph and says, "God, before whom my fathers

Abraham and Isaac habitually walked: God who is feeding me from my being to this day: **16** the Messenger who is redeeming me from all evil blesses the youths, and my name is called on them, and the name of my fathers Abraham and Isaac; and they increase into a multitude in the midst of the land." **17** And Joseph sees that his father sets his right hand on the head of Ephraim, and it is wrong in his eyes, and he supports the hand of his father to turn it aside from off the head of Ephraim to the head of Manasseh; **18** and Joseph says to his father, "Not so, my father, for this [is] the firstborn; set your right hand on his head." **19** And his father refuses and says, "I have known, my son, I have known; he also becomes a people, and he also is great, and yet, his young brother is greater than he, and his seed is the fullness of the nations"; **20** and he blesses them in that day, saying, "By you does Israel bless, saying, God set you as Ephraim and as Manasseh"; and he sets Ephraim before Manasseh. **21** And Israel says to Joseph, "Behold, I am dying, and God has been with you, and has brought you back to the land of your fathers; **22** and I have given to you one portion above your brothers, which I have taken out of the hand of the Amorite by my sword and by my bow."

49 And Jacob calls to his sons and says, "Be gathered together, and I declare to you that which happens with you in the latter end of the days. **2** Be assembled, and hear, sons of Jacob, ‖ And listen to your father Israel. **3** Reuben! You [are] my firstborn, ‖ My power, and beginning of my strength, ‖ The abundance of exaltation, ‖ And the abundance of strength; **4** Unstable as water, you are not abundant; For you have gone up your father's bed; Then you have defiled [it]: He went up my couch! **5** Simeon and Levi [are] brothers! Instruments of violence—their espousals! **6** Into their secret, do not come, O my soul! Do not be united to their assembly, O my glory; For in their anger they slew a man, ‖ And in their self-will eradicated a prince. **7** Cursed [is] their anger, for [it is] fierce, ‖ And their wrath, for [it is] sharp; I divide them in Jacob, ‖ And I scatter them in Israel. **8** Judah! Your brothers praise you! Your hand [is] on the neck of your enemies, ‖ Sons of your father bow themselves to you. **9** A lion's whelp [is] Judah, ‖ For prey, my son, you have gone up; He has bent, he has crouched as a lion, ‖ And as a lioness; who causes him to arise? **10** The scepter does not turn aside from Judah, ‖ And a lawgiver from between his feet, ‖ Until his Seed comes; And His [is] the obedience of peoples. **11** Binding to the vine his donkey, ‖ And to the choice vine the colt of his donkey, ‖ He has washed in wine his clothing, ‖ And in the blood of grapes his covering; **12** Red [are] eyes with wine, ‖ And white [are] teeth with milk! **13** Zebulun dwells at a haven of the seas, ‖ And he [is] for a haven of ships; And his side [is] to Sidon. **14** Issachar [is] a strong donkey, ‖ Crouching between the two folds; **15** And he sees rest, that [it is] good, ‖ And the land, that [it is] pleasant, ‖ And he inclines his shoulder to bear, ‖ And is a servant for tribute. **16** Dan judges his people, ‖ As one of the tribes of Israel; **17** Dan is a serpent by the way, a viper by the path, ‖ Which is biting the horse's heels, ‖ And its rider falls backward. **18** For Your salvation I have waited, YHWH! **19** Gad! A troop assaults him, ‖ But he assaults last. **20** Out of Asher his bread [is] fat; And he gives delicacies of a king. **21** Naphtali [is] a doe sent away, ‖ Who is giving beautiful young ones. **22** Joseph [is] a fruitful son; A fruitful son by a fountain, ‖ Daughters step over the wall; **23** And embitter him indeed, they have striven, ‖ Indeed, archers hate him; **24** And his bow abides in strength, ‖ And strengthened are the arms of his hands ‖ By the hands of the Mighty One of Jacob, ‖ From where is a shepherd, a son of Israel. **25** By the God of your father who helps you, ‖ And the Mighty One who blesses you, ‖ Blessings of the heavens from above, ‖ Blessings of the deep lying under, ‖ Blessings of breasts and womb— **26** Your father's blessings have been mighty ‖ Above the blessings of my progenitors, ‖ To the limit of the perpetual heights ‖ They are for the head of Joseph, ‖ And for the crown of the one ‖ Separate [from] his brothers. **27** Benjamin! A wolf tears; In the morning he eats prey, ‖ And at evening he apportions spoil." **28** All these [are] the twelve tribes of Israel, and this [is] that which their father has spoken to them, and he blesses them; each according to his blessing he has blessed them. **29** And he commands them and says to them, "I am being gathered to my people; bury me by my fathers, at the cave which [is] in the field of Ephron the Hittite; **30** in the cave which [is] in the field of Machpelah, which [is] on the front of Mamre, in the land of Canaan, which Abraham bought with the field from Ephron the Hittite for a possession of a burying-place; **31** (there they buried Abraham and his wife Sarah; there they buried Isaac and his wife Rebekah; and there I buried Leah); **32** the purchase of the field and of the cave which [is] in it, [is] from sons of Heth." **33** And Jacob finishes commanding his sons, and gathers up his feet to the bed, and expires, and is gathered to his people.

50 And Joseph falls on his father's face, and weeps over him, and kisses him; **2** and Joseph commands his servants, the physicians, to embalm his father, and the physicians embalm Israel; **3** and they fulfill for him forty days, for so they fulfill the days of the embalmed, and the Egyptians weep for him seventy days. **4** And the days of his weeping pass away, and Joseph speaks to the house of Pharaoh, saying, "Now if I have found grace in your eyes, please speak in the ears of Pharaoh, saying, **5** My father caused me to swear, saying, Behold, I am dying; in my burying-place which I have prepared for myself in the land of Canaan, there you bury me; and now, please let me go up and bury my father, then I return"; **6** and Pharaoh says, "Go up and bury your father, as he caused you to swear." **7** And Joseph goes up to bury his father, and all [the] servants of Pharaoh go up with him, [the] elderly of his house, and all [the] elderly of the land of Egypt, **8** and all the house of Joseph, and his brothers, and the house of his father; only their infants, and their flock, and their herd, have they left in the land of Goshen; **9** and there go up with him both chariot and horsemen, and the camp is very great. **10** And they come to the threshing-floor of Atad, which [is] beyond the Jordan, and they lament there, a lamentation great and very grievous; and he makes for his father a mourning seven days, **11** and the inhabitant of the land, the Canaanite, sees the mourning in the threshing-floor of Atad and says, "A grievous mourning [is] this to the Egyptians"; therefore [one] has called its name "The mourning of the Egyptians," which [is] beyond the Jordan. **12** And his sons do to him so as he commanded them, **13** and his sons carry him away to the land of Canaan, and bury him in the cave of the field of Machpelah, which Abraham bought with the field for a possession of a burying-place, from Ephron the Hittite, on the front of Mamre. **14** And Joseph turns back to Egypt, he and his brothers, and all who are going up with him to bury his father, after his burying his father. **15** And the brothers of Joseph see that their father is dead, and say, "Perhaps Joseph hates us, and certainly returns to us all the evil which we did with him." **16** And they give a charge for Joseph, saying, "Your father commanded before his death, saying, **17** Thus you say to Joseph: Ah, now, please bear with the transgression of your brothers and their sin, for they have done you evil; and now, please bear with the transgression of the servants of the God of your father"; and Joseph weeps in their speaking to him. **18** And his brothers also go and fall before him, and say, "Behold, we [are] to you for servants." **19** And Joseph says to them, "Do not fear, for [am] I in the place of God? **20** As for you, you devised evil against me, [but] God devised it for good, in order to do as [at] this day, to keep alive a numerous people; **21** and now, do not fear: I nourish you and your infants"; and he comforts them, and speaks to their heart. **22** And Joseph dwells in Egypt, he and the house of his father, and Joseph lives one hundred and ten years, **23** and Joseph looks on Ephraim's sons of a third [generation]; sons also of Machir, son of Manasseh, have been born on the knees of Joseph. **24** And Joseph says to his brothers, "I am dying, and God certainly inspects you, and has caused you to go up from this land, to the land which He has sworn to Abraham, to Isaac, and to Jacob." **25** And Joseph causes the sons of Israel to swear, saying, "God certainly inspects you, and you have brought up my bones from this [place]." **26** And Joseph dies, a son of one hundred and ten years, and they embalm him, and he is put into a coffin in Egypt.

EXODUS

1 And these [are] the names of the sons of Israel who are coming into Egypt; each man and his household have come with Jacob: **2** Reuben, Simeon, Levi, and Judah, **3** Issachar, Zebulun, and Benjamin, **4** Dan, and Naphtali, Gad, and Asher. **5** And all the persons coming out of the thigh of Jacob are seventy persons; as for Joseph, he was in Egypt. **6** And Joseph dies, and all his brothers, and all that generation; **7** and the sons of Israel have been fruitful, and they teem, and multiply, and are very, very mighty, and the land is filled with them. **8** And there rises a new king over Egypt, who has not known Joseph, **9** and he says to his people, "Behold, the people of the sons of Israel [are] more numerous and mighty than we. **10** Give help! Let us act wisely concerning it, lest it multiply, and it has come to pass, when war happens, that it has been joined, even it, to those hating us, and has fought against us, and has gone up out of the land." **11** And they set princes of tribute over it, so as to afflict it with their burdens, and it builds the store-cities of Pithom and Rameses for Pharaoh; **12** and as they afflict it, so it multiplies, and so it breaks forth, and they are distressed because of the sons of Israel; **13** and the Egyptians cause the sons of Israel to serve with rigor, **14** and make their lives bitter in hard service, in clay, and in brick, and in every [kind] of service in the field; all their service in which they have served [is] with rigor. **15** And the king of Egypt speaks to the midwives, the Hebrewesses (of whom the name of the first [is] Shiphrah, and the name of the second Puah), **16** and says, "When you cause the Hebrew women to bear, and have looked on the children, if it [is] a son, then you have put him to death; and if it [is] a daughter, then she has lived." **17** And the midwives fear God, and have not done as the king of Egypt has spoken to them, and they keep the boys alive; **18** and the king of Egypt calls for the midwives and says to them, "Why have you done this thing, and keep the boys alive?" **19** And the midwives say to Pharaoh, "Because the Hebrew women [are] not as the Egyptian women, for they [are] lively; before the midwife comes to them—they have borne!" **20** And God does good to the midwives, and the people multiply, and are very mighty; **21** and it comes to pass, because the midwives have feared God, that He makes households for them; **22** and Pharaoh lays a charge on all his people, saying, "Every son who is born—you cast him into the River, and every daughter you keep alive."

2 And there goes a man of the house of Levi, and he takes the daughter of Levi, **2** and the woman conceives, and bears a son, and she sees him, that he [is] beautiful, and she hides him [for] three months, **3** and she has not been able to hide him anymore, and she takes an ark of rushes for him, and covers it with bitumen and with pitch, and puts the boy in it, and puts [it] in the weeds by the edge of the River; **4** and his sister stations herself far off, to know what is done to him. **5** And a daughter of Pharaoh comes down to bathe at the River, and her girls are walking by the side of the River, and she sees the ark in the midst of the weeds, and sends her handmaid, and she takes it, **6** and opens, and sees him—the boy, and behold, a child weeping! And she has pity on him and says, "This is [one] of the Hebrews' children." **7** And his sister says to the daughter of Pharaoh, "Do I go? When I have called a suckling woman of the Hebrews for you, then she suckles the boy for you"; **8** and the daughter of Pharaoh says to her, "Go"; and the virgin goes, and calls the mother of the boy, **9** and the daughter of Pharaoh says to her, "Take this boy away, and suckle him for me, and I give your hire"; and the woman takes the boy, and suckles him. **10** And the boy grows, and she brings him to the daughter of Pharaoh, and he is to her for a son, and she calls his name Moses, and says, "Because I have drawn him from the water." **11** And it comes to pass, in those days, that Moses is grown, and he goes out to his brothers, and looks on their burdens, and sees a man, an Egyptian, striking a man, a Hebrew, [one] of his brothers, **12** and he turns here and there, and sees that there is no man, and strikes the Egyptian, and hides him in the sand. **13** And he goes out on the second day, and behold, two men, Hebrews, are striving, and he says to

EXODUS

the wrongdoer, "Why do you strike your neighbor?" **14** And he says, "Who set you for a head and judge over us? Are you saying [it] to slay me as you have slain the Egyptian?" And Moses fears and says, "Surely the thing has been known." **15** And Pharaoh hears of this thing, and seeks to slay Moses, and Moses flees from the face of Pharaoh, and dwells in the land of Midian, and dwells by the well. **16** And to a priest of Midian [are] seven daughters, and they come and draw, and fill the troughs to water the flock of their father, **17** and the shepherds come and drive them away, and Moses arises, and saves them, and waters their flock. **18** And they come to their father Reuel, and he says, "Why have you hurried to come in today?" **19** And they say, "A man, an Egyptian, has delivered us out of the hand of the shepherds, and has also diligently drawn for us, and waters the flock"; **20** and he says to his daughters, "And where [is] he? Why [is] this [that] you left the man? Call for him, and he eats bread." **21** And Moses is willing to dwell with the man, and he gives his daughter Zipporah to Moses, **22** and she bears a son, and he calls his name Gershom, for he said, "I have been a sojourner in a strange land." **23** And it comes to pass during these many days, that the king of Egypt dies, and the sons of Israel sigh because of the service, and cry, and their cry goes up to God, because of the service; **24** and God hears their groaning, and God remembers His covenant with Abraham, with Isaac, and with Jacob; **25** and God sees the sons of Israel, and God knows.

3 And Moses has been feeding the flock of his father-in-law Jethro, priest of Midian, and he leads the flock behind the wilderness, and comes to the mountain of God, to Horeb; **2** and the Messenger of YHWH appears to him in a flame of fire, out of the midst of the bush, and he sees, and behold, the bush is burning with fire, and the bush is not consumed. **3** And Moses says, "Now I turn aside and see this great appearance. Why is the bush not burned?" **4** And YHWH sees that he has turned aside to see, and God calls to him out of the midst of the bush and says, "Moses! Moses!" And he says, "Here I [am]." **5** And He says, "Do not come near here. Cast your shoes from off your feet, for the place on which you are standing is holy ground." **6** He also says, "I [am] the God of your father, God of Abraham, God of Isaac, and God of Jacob"; and Moses hides his face, for he is afraid to look toward God. **7** And YHWH says, "I have certainly seen the affliction of My people who [are] in Egypt, and I have heard their cry because of its exactors, for I have known its pains; **8** and I go down to deliver it out of the hand of the Egyptians, and to cause it to go up out of the land to a land good and broad, to a land flowing with milk and honey—to the place of the Canaanite, and the Hittite, and the Amorite, and the Perizzite, and the Hivite, and the Jebusite. **9** And now, behold, the cry of the sons of Israel has come to Me, and I have also seen the oppression with which the Egyptians are oppressing them, **10** and now, come, and I send you to Pharaoh; and bring out My people, the sons of Israel, from Egypt." **11** And Moses says to God, "Who [am] I, that I go to Pharaoh, and that I bring out the sons of Israel from Egypt?" **12** And He says, "Because I am with you, and this [is] the sign to you that I have sent you: in your bringing out the people from Egypt—you serve God on this mountain." **13** And Moses says to God, "Behold, I am coming to the sons of Israel, and have said to them, The God of your fathers has sent me to you, and they have said to me, What [is] His Name? What do I say to them?" **14** And God says to Moses, "I AM THAT WHICH I AM." He also says, "Thus you say to the sons of Israel: I AM has sent me to you." **15** And God says again to Moses, "Thus you say to the sons of Israel: YHWH, God of your fathers, God of Abraham, God of Isaac, and God of Jacob, has sent me to you; this [is] My Name for all time, and this [is] My memorial, to generation [and] generation. **16** Go, and you have gathered the elderly of Israel, and have said to them: YHWH, God of your fathers, has appeared to me, God of Abraham, Isaac, and Jacob, saying, I have certainly inspected you, and that which is done to you in Egypt; **17** and I say [that] I bring you up out of the affliction of Egypt to the land of the Canaanite, and the Hittite, and the Amorite, and the Perizzite, and the Hivite, and the Jebusite, to a land flowing [with] milk and honey. **18** And they have listened to your voice, and you have entered, you and [the] elderly of Israel, to the king of Egypt, and you have said to him: YHWH,

God of the Hebrews, has met with us; and now, please let us go a journey of three days into the wilderness, and we sacrifice to our God YHWH. **19** And I have known that the king of Egypt does not permit you to go, unless by a strong hand, **20** and I have put forth My hand, and have struck Egypt with all My wonders, which I do in its midst—and afterward he sends you away. **21** And I have given the grace of this people in the eyes of the Egyptians, and it has come to pass, when you go, you do not go empty; **22** and [every] woman has asked from her neighbor, and from her who is sojourning in her house, [for] vessels of silver, and vessels of gold, and garments, and you have put [them] on your sons and on your daughters, and have spoiled the Egyptians."

4 And Moses answers and says, "And if they do not give credence to me, nor listen to my voice, and say, YHWH has not appeared to you?" **2** And YHWH says to him, "What [is] this in your hand?" And he says, "A rod"; **3** and He says, "Cast it to the earth"; and he casts it to the earth, and it becomes a serpent—and Moses flees from its presence. **4** And YHWH says to Moses, "Put forth your hand, and lay hold on the tail of it"; and he puts forth his hand, and lays hold on it, and it becomes a rod in his hand— **5** "so that they believe that YHWH, God of their fathers, has appeared to you, God of Abraham, God of Isaac, and God of Jacob." **6** And YHWH says to him again, "Now put your hand into your bosom"; and he puts his hand into his bosom, and he brings it out, and behold, his hand [is] leprous as snow; **7** and He says, "Put your hand back into your bosom"; and he puts his hand back into his bosom, and he brings it out from his bosom, and behold, it has turned back as his flesh— **8** "and it has come to pass, if they do not give credence to you, and do not listen to the voice of the first sign, that they have given credence to the voice of the latter sign. **9** And it has come to pass, if they do not give credence even to these two signs, nor listen to your voice, that you have taken of the waters of the River, and have poured [it] on the dry land, and the waters which you take from the River have been, indeed, they have become blood on the dry land." **10** And Moses says to YHWH, "O my Lord, I [am] not a man of words, either yesterday, or before, or since Your speaking to Your servant, for I [am] slow of mouth, and slow of tongue." **11** And YHWH says to him, "Who appointed a mouth for man? Or who appoints the mute, or deaf, or open, or blind? Is it not I, YHWH? **12** And now, go, and I am with your mouth, and have directed you that which you speak"; **13** and he says, "O my Lord, please send by the hand [of another that] You send." **14** And the anger of YHWH burns against Moses, and He says, "Is Aaron the Levite not your brother? I have known that he speaks well, and also, behold, he is coming out to meet you; when he has seen you, then he has rejoiced in his heart, **15** and you have spoken to him, and have set the words in his mouth, and I am with your mouth, and with his mouth, and have directed you that which you do; **16** and he, he has spoken to the people for you, and it has come to pass, he is to you for a mouth, and you are to him for God; **17** and you take this rod in your hand, with which you do the signs." **18** And Moses goes and turns back to his father-in-law Jethro, and says to him, "Please let me go, and I return to my brothers who [are] in Egypt, and I see whether they are yet alive." And Jethro says to Moses, "Go in peace." **19** And YHWH says to Moses in Midian, "Go, return to Egypt, for all the men who seek your life have died"; **20** and Moses takes his wife, and his sons, and causes them to ride on the donkey, and turns back to the land of Egypt, and Moses takes the rod of God in his hand. **21** And YHWH says to Moses, "In your going to return to Egypt, see—all the wonders which I have put in your hand—that you have done them before Pharaoh, and I strengthen his heart, and he does not send the people away; **22** and you have said to Pharaoh, Thus said YHWH: My son, My firstborn [is] Israel, **23** and I say to you, send My son away, and he serves Me; and [if] you refuse to send him away, behold, I am slaying your son, your firstborn." **24** And it comes to pass in the way, in a lodging place, that YHWH meets him, and seeks to put him to death; **25** and Zipporah takes a flint, and cuts off the foreskin of her son, and causes [it] to touch his feet, and says, "You [are] surely a bridegroom of blood to me"; **26** and He desists from him. Then she said, "A bridegroom of blood," in reference to the circumcision. **27** And YHWH says to Aaron, "Go into the wilderness to meet Moses"; and he goes, and meets him on the mountain of God, and kisses him, **28** and Moses declares to Aaron all the words of YHWH with which He has sent him, and all the signs with which He has charged him. **29** And Moses goes—Aaron also—and they gather all the elderly of the sons of Israel, **30** and Aaron speaks all the words which YHWH has spoken to Moses, and does the signs before the eyes of the people; **31** and the people believe when they hear that YHWH has looked after the sons of Israel, and that He has seen their affliction; and they bow and pay respect.

5 And afterward Moses and Aaron have entered, and they say to Pharaoh, "Thus said YHWH, God of Israel: Send My people away, and they keep a celebration for Me in the wilderness"; **2** and Pharaoh says, "Who [is] YHWH, that I listen to His voice to send Israel away? I have not known YHWH, and I also do not send Israel away." **3** And they say, "The God of the Hebrews has met with us; please let us go a journey of three days into the wilderness, and we sacrifice to our God YHWH, lest He meet us with pestilence or with sword." **4** And the king of Egypt says to them, "Why, Moses and Aaron, do you free the people from its works? Go to your burdens." **5** Pharaoh also says, "Behold, the people of the land [are] numerous now, and you have caused them to cease from their burdens!" **6** And on that day Pharaoh commands the exactors among the people and its authorities, saying, **7** "You do not add to give straw to the people for the making of the bricks as before—they go and have gathered straw for themselves; **8** and you put on them the proper quantity of the bricks which they are making before, you do not diminish from it, for they are remiss, therefore they are crying, saying, Let us go, let us sacrifice to our God; **9** let the service be heavy on the men, and let them work at it, and not be dazzled by lying words." **10** And the exactors of the people, and its authorities, go out, and speak to the people, saying, "Thus said Pharaoh: I do not give you straw, **11** you—go, take straw for yourselves where you can find [it], for there is nothing diminished of your service." **12** And the people are scattered over all the land of Egypt, to gather stubble for straw, **13** and the exactors are making haste, saying, "Complete your works, the matter of a day in its day, as when there is straw." **14** And the authorities of the sons of Israel, whom the exactors of Pharaoh have placed over them, are beaten, saying, "Why have you not completed your portion in making brick as before, both yesterday and today?" **15** And the authorities of the sons of Israel come in and cry to Pharaoh, saying, "Why do you do thus to your servants? **16** Straw is not given to your servants, and they are saying to us, Make bricks, and behold, your servants are struck—and your people have sinned." **17** And he says, "Remiss—you are remiss, therefore you are saying, Let us go, let us sacrifice to YHWH; **18** and now, go, serve; and straw is not given to you, and you give the [required] measure of bricks." **19** And the authorities of the sons of Israel see them in affliction, saying, "You do not diminish from your bricks; the matter of a day in its day." **20** And they meet Moses and Aaron standing to meet them in their coming out from Pharaoh, **21** and say to them, "YHWH look on you, and judge, because you have caused our fragrance to stink in the eyes of Pharaoh, and in the eyes of his servants—to give a sword into their hand to slay us." **22** And Moses turns back to YHWH and says, "Lord, why have You done evil to this people? Why [is] this [that] You have sent me? **23** And since I have come to Pharaoh to speak in Your Name, he has done evil to this people, and You have not delivered Your people at all."

6 And YHWH says to Moses, "Now you see that which I do to Pharaoh, for with a strong hand he sends them away, indeed, with a strong hand he casts them out of his land." **2** And God speaks to Moses and says to him, "I [am] YHWH, **3** and I appear to Abraham, to Isaac, and to Jacob, as God Almighty; as for My Name YHWH, I have not been known to them; **4** and I have also established My covenant with them, to give the land of Canaan to them, the land of their sojournings, wherein they have sojourned; **5** and I have also heard the groaning of the sons of Israel, whom the Egyptians are causing to serve, and I remember My covenant. **6** Therefore say to the sons of Israel: I [am] YHWH, and I have brought you out from under the burdens of the Egyptians, and have delivered you from their service, and have redeemed you by an outstretched arm, and by great

EXODUS

judgments, **7** and have taken you to Myself for a people, and I have been to you for God, and you have known that I [am] your God YHWH, who is bringing you out from under the burdens of the Egyptians; **8** and I have brought you to the land which I have lifted up My hand to give it to Abraham, to Isaac, and to Jacob, and have given it to you—a possession; I [am] YHWH." **9** And Moses speaks so to the sons of Israel, and they did not listen to Moses, for anguish of spirit, and for harsh service. **10** And YHWH speaks to Moses, saying, **11** "Go in, speak to Pharaoh king of Egypt, and he sends the sons of Israel out of his land"; **12** and Moses speaks before YHWH, saying, "Behold, the sons of Israel have not listened to me, and how does Pharaoh hear me, and I of uncircumcised lips?" **13** And YHWH speaks to Moses and to Aaron, and charges them for the sons of Israel, and for Pharaoh king of Egypt, to bring out the sons of Israel from the land of Egypt. **14** These [are] heads of the house of their fathers. Sons of Reuben firstborn of Israel: Enoch, and Phallu, Hezron, and Carmi; these [are] families of Reuben. **15** And sons of Simeon: Jemuel, and Jamin, and Ohad, and Jachin, and Zohar, and Shaul, son of the Canaanite; these [are] families of Simeon. **16** And these [are] the names of the sons of Levi, as to their births: Gershon, and Kohath, and Merari; and the years of the life of Levi [are] one hundred and thirty-seven years. **17** The sons of Gershon: Libni and Shimi, as to their families. **18** And the sons of Kohath: Amram, and Izhar, and Hebron, and Uzziel; and the years of the life of Kohath [are] one hundred and thirty-three years. **19** And the sons of Merari: Mahli and Mushi; these [are] families of Levi, as to their births. **20** And Amram takes his aunt Jochebed to himself for a wife, and she bears Aaron and Moses to him; and the years of the life of Amram [are] one hundred and thirty-seven years. **21** And sons of Izhar: Korah, and Nepheg, and Zichri. **22** And sons of Uzziel: Mishael, and Elzaphan, and Sithri. **23** And Aaron takes Elisheba daughter of Amminadab, sister of Naashon, to himself for a wife, and she bears to him Nadab, and Abihu, Eleazar, and Ithamar. **24** And sons of Korah: Assir, and Elkanah, and Abiasaph; these [are] families of the Korahite. **25** And Eleazar, Aaron's son, has taken to himself [one] of the daughters of Putiel for a wife for himself, and she bears Phinehas to him; these [are] heads of the fathers of the Levites, as to their families. **26** This [is] Aaron—and Moses—to whom YHWH said, "Bring out the sons of Israel from the land of Egypt, by their hosts"; **27** these are they who are speaking to Pharaoh king of Egypt, to bring out the sons of Israel from Egypt, this [is] Moses—and Aaron. **28** And it comes to pass in the day of YHWH's speaking to Moses in the land of Egypt, **29** that YHWH speaks to Moses, saying, "I [am] YHWH, speak to Pharaoh king of Egypt all that I am speaking to you." **30** And Moses says before YHWH, "Behold, I [am] of uncircumcised lips, and how does Pharaoh listen to me?"

7 And YHWH says to Moses, "See, I have given you [as] a god to Pharaoh, and your brother Aaron is your prophet; **2** you speak all that I command you, and your brother Aaron speaks to Pharaoh, and he has sent the sons of Israel out of his land. **3** And I harden the heart of Pharaoh, and have multiplied My signs and My wonders in the land of Egypt, **4** and Pharaoh does not listen, and I have put My hand on Egypt, and have brought out My hosts, My people, the sons of Israel, from the land of Egypt by great judgments; **5** and the Egyptians have known that I [am] YHWH, in My stretching out My hand against Egypt; and I have brought out the sons of Israel from their midst." **6** And Moses does—Aaron also—as YHWH commanded them; so have they done; **7** and Moses [is] a son of eighty years, and Aaron [is] a son of eighty-three years, in their speaking to Pharaoh. **8** And YHWH speaks to Moses and to Aaron, saying, **9** "When Pharaoh speaks to you, saying, Give a wonder for yourselves; then you have said to Aaron, Take your rod and cast [it] before Pharaoh—it becomes a dragon." **10** And Moses goes in—Aaron also—to Pharaoh, and they do so as YHWH has commanded; and Aaron casts his rod before Pharaoh and before his servants, and it becomes a dragon. **11** And Pharaoh also calls for wise men and for sorcerers; and the enchanters of Egypt, they also, with their [enchanting] flames, do so, **12** and they each cast down his rod, and they become dragons, and the rod of Aaron swallows their rods; **13** and the heart of Pharaoh is strong, and he has not listened to them, as YHWH has spoken. **14** And YHWH says to Moses, "The heart of Pharaoh has been hard, he has refused to send the people away; **15** go to Pharaoh in the morning, behold, he is going out to the water, and you have stood to meet him by the edge of the River, and the rod which was turned to a serpent you take in your hand, **16** and you have said to him: YHWH, God of the Hebrews, has sent me to you, saying, Send My people away, and they serve Me in the wilderness; and behold, you have not listened until now. **17** Thus said YHWH: By this you know that I [am] YHWH; behold, I am striking with the rod which [is] in my hand, on the waters which [are] in the River, and they have been turned to blood, **18** and the fish that [are] in the River die, and the River has stunk, and the Egyptians have been wearied of drinking waters from the River." **19** And YHWH says to Moses, "Say to Aaron, Take your rod, and stretch out your hand against the waters of Egypt, against their streams, against their rivers, and against their ponds, and against all their collections of waters; and they are blood—and there has been blood in all the land of Egypt, both in [vessels of] wood, and in [those of] stone." **20** And Moses and Aaron do so, as YHWH has commanded, and he lifts up [his hand] with the rod, and strikes the waters which [are] in the River, before the eyes of Pharaoh and before the eyes of his servants, and all the waters which [are] in the River are turned to blood, **21** and the fish which [is] in the River has died, and the River stinks, and the Egyptians have not been able to drink water from the River; and the blood is in all the land of Egypt. **22** And the enchanters of Egypt do so with their secrets, and the heart of Pharaoh is strong, and he has not listened to them, as YHWH has spoken, **23** and Pharaoh turns and goes into his house, and has not set his heart even to this; **24** and all the Egyptians seek water all around the River to drink, for they have not been able to drink of the waters of the River. **25** And seven days are completed after YHWH's striking the River.

8 And YHWH says to Moses, "Go to Pharaoh, and you have said to him, Thus said YHWH: Send My people away, and they serve Me; **2** and if you are refusing to send [them] away, behold, I am striking all your border with frogs; **3** and the River has teemed [with] frogs, and they have gone up and gone into your house, and into the inner-chamber of your bed, and on your couch, and into the house of your servants, and among your people, and into your ovens, and into your kneading-troughs; **4** indeed, on you, and on your people, and on all your servants the frogs go up." **5** And YHWH says to Moses, "Say to Aaron, Stretch out your hand, with your rod, against the streams, against the rivers, and against the ponds, and cause the frogs to come up against the land of Egypt." **6** And Aaron stretches out his hand against the waters of Egypt, and the frog comes up, and covers the land of Egypt; **7** and the enchanters do so with their secrets, and cause the frogs to come up against the land of Egypt. **8** And Pharaoh calls for Moses and for Aaron and says, "Make supplication to YHWH, that he may turn aside the frogs from me, and from my people, and I send the people away, and they sacrifice to YHWH." **9** And Moses says to Pharaoh, "Beautify yourself over me; when do I make supplication for you, and for your servants, and for your people, to cut off the frogs from you and from your houses—only in the River they remain?" **10** And he says, "Tomorrow." And he says, "According to your word [it is], so that you know that there is none like our God YHWH, **11** and the frogs have turned aside from you, and from your houses, and from your servants, and from your people; only in the River they remain." **12** And Moses—Aaron also—goes out from Pharaoh, and Moses cries to YHWH concerning the matter of the frogs which He has set on Pharaoh; **13** and YHWH does according to the word of Moses, and the frogs die out of the houses, out of the courts, and out of the fields, **14** and they heap them up together, and the land stinks. **15** And Pharaoh sees that there has been a respite, and he has hardened his heart, and has not listened to them, as YHWH has spoken. **16** And YHWH says to Moses, "Say to Aaron, Stretch out your rod, and strike the dust of the land, and it has become gnats in all the land of Egypt." **17** And they do so, and Aaron stretches out his hand with his rod, and strikes the dust of the land, and the gnats are on man and on beast; all the dust of the land has been gnats in all the land of Egypt. **18** And the enchanters do so with their secrets, to bring out the gnats, and they

EXODUS

have not been able, and the gnats are on man and on beast; **19** and the enchanters say to Pharaoh, "It [is] the finger of God"; and the heart of Pharaoh is strong, and he has not listened to them, as YHWH has spoken. **20** And YHWH says to Moses, "Rise early in the morning, and station yourself before Pharaoh, behold, he is going out to the waters, and you have said to him, Thus said YHWH: Send My people away, and they serve Me; **21** for if you are not sending My people away, behold, I am sending against you, and against your servants, and against your people, and against your houses, the beetle, and the houses of the Egyptians have been full of the beetle, and also the ground on which they are. **22** And I have separated in that day the land of Goshen, in which My people are staying, that the beetle is not there, so that you know that I [am] YHWH in the midst of the land, **23** and I have put a division between My people and your people; this sign is tomorrow." **24** And YHWH does so, and the grievous beetle enters the house of Pharaoh, and the house of his servants, and in all the land of Egypt the land is corrupted from the presence of the beetle. **25** And Pharaoh calls to Moses and to Aaron and says, "Go, sacrifice to your God in the land"; **26** and Moses says, "[It is] not right to do so—for us to sacrifice the abomination of the Egyptians to our God YHWH; behold, we sacrifice the abomination of the Egyptians before their eyes—and they do not stone us! **27** We go a journey of three days into the wilderness and have sacrificed to our God YHWH as He says to us." **28** And Pharaoh says, "I send you away, and you have sacrificed to your God YHWH in the wilderness, only do not go very far off; make supplication for me"; **29** and Moses says, "Behold, I am going out from you, and have made supplication to YHWH, and tomorrow the beetle has turned aside from Pharaoh, from his servants, and from his people; only, do not let Pharaoh add to deceive in not sending the people away to sacrifice to YHWH." **30** And Moses goes out from Pharaoh, and makes supplication to YHWH, **31** and YHWH does according to the word of Moses, and turns aside the beetle from Pharaoh, from his servants, and from his people—there has not been one left; **32** and Pharaoh also hardens his heart at this time, and has not sent the people away.

9 And YHWH says to Moses, "Go to Pharaoh, and you have spoken to him, Thus said YHWH, God of the Hebrews: Send My people away, and they serve Me, **2** for if you are refusing to send [them] away, and are still keeping hold on them, **3** behold, the hand of YHWH is on your livestock which [are] in the field, on horses, on donkeys, on camels, on herd, and on flock—a very grievous pestilence. **4** And YHWH has separated between the livestock of Israel and the livestock of Egypt, and there does not die a thing of all the sons of Israel; **5** and YHWH sets an appointed time, saying, Tomorrow YHWH does this thing in the land." **6** And YHWH does this thing on the next day, and all the livestock of Egypt die, and of the livestock of the sons of Israel not one has died; **7** and Pharaoh sends, and behold, not even one of the livestock of Israel has died, and the heart of Pharaoh is hard, and he has not sent the people away. **8** And YHWH says to Moses and to Aaron, "Take for yourselves the fullness of your handfuls—soot of a furnace, and Moses has sprinkled it toward the heavens, before the eyes of Pharaoh, **9** and it has become small dust over all the land of Egypt, and it has become on man and on livestock a boil breaking forth [with] blisters in all the land of Egypt." **10** And they take the soot of the furnace, and stand before Pharaoh, and Moses sprinkles it toward the heavens, and it is a boil [with] blisters breaking forth on man and on beast; **11** and the enchanters have not been able to stand before Moses because of the boil, for the boil has been on the enchanters, and on all the Egyptians. **12** And YHWH strengthens the heart of Pharaoh, and he has not listened to them, as YHWH has spoken to Moses. **13** And YHWH says to Moses, "Rise early in the morning, and station yourself before Pharaoh, and you have said to him, Thus said YHWH, God of the Hebrews: Send My people away, and they serve Me, **14** for at this time I am sending all My plagues to your heart, and on your servants, and on your people, so that you know that there is none like Me in all the earth, **15** for now I have put forth My hand, and I strike you, and your people, with pestilence, and you are hidden from the earth. **16** And yet for this I have caused you to stand, so as to show you My power, and for the sake of declaring My Name in all the earth; **17** still you are exalting

EXODUS

yourself against My people—so as not to send them away; **18** behold, I am raining very grievous hail about [this] time tomorrow, such as has not been in Egypt from the day of its founding and until now. **19** And now, send, strengthen your livestock and all that you have in the field; every man and beast which is found in the field, and is not gathered into the house— the hail has come down on them, and they have died." **20** He who is fearing the word of YHWH among the servants of Pharaoh has caused his servants and his livestock to flee to the houses; **21** and he who has not set his heart to the word of YHWH leaves his servants and his livestock in the field. **22** And YHWH says to Moses, "Stretch forth your hand toward the heavens, and there is hail in all the land of Egypt, on man, and on beast, and on every herb of the field in the land of Egypt." **23** And Moses stretches out his rod toward the heavens, and YHWH has given voices and hail, and fire goes toward the earth, and YHWH rains hail on the land of Egypt, **24** and there is hail, and fire catching itself in the midst of the hail, very grievous, such as has not been in all the land of Egypt since it has become a nation. **25** And the hail strikes all that [is] in the field in all the land of Egypt, from man even to beast, and the hail has struck every herb of the field, and it has broken every tree of the field; **26** only in the land of Goshen, where the sons of Israel [are], there has been no hail. **27** And Pharaoh sends, and calls for Moses and for Aaron, and says to them, "I have sinned this time—YHWH [is] the righteous, and I and my people [are] the wicked, **28** make supplication to YHWH, and plead that there be no voices of God and hail, and I send you away, and you do not add to remain." **29** And Moses says to him, "At my going out of the city, I spread my palms to YHWH—the voices cease, and there is no more hail, so that you know that the earth [is] YHWH's; **30** but you and your servants—I have known that you are not yet afraid of the face of YHWH God." **31** And the flax and the barley have been struck, for the barley [is] budding, and the flax forming flowers, **32** and the wheat and the rye have not been struck, for they are late. **33** And Moses goes out from Pharaoh, [from] the city, and spreads his hands to YHWH, and the voices and the hail cease, and rain has not been poured out to the earth; **34** and Pharaoh sees that the rain has ceased, and the hail and the voices, and he continues to sin, and hardens his heart, he and his servants; **35** and the heart of Pharaoh is strong, and he has not sent the sons of Israel away, as YHWH has spoken by the hand of Moses.

10 And YHWH says to Moses, "Go to Pharaoh, for I have declared his heart hard, and the heart of his servants, so that I set these signs of Mine in their midst, **2** and so that you recount in the ears of your son, and of your son's son, that which I have done in Egypt, and My signs which I have set among them, and you have known that I [am] YHWH." **3** And Moses comes in— Aaron also—to Pharaoh, and they say to him, "Thus said YHWH, God of the Hebrews: Until when have you refused to be humbled at My presence? Send My people away, and they serve Me, **4** for if you are refusing to send My people away, behold, tomorrow I am bringing in the locust into your border, **5** and it has covered the eye of the land, and none is able to see the land, and it has eaten the remnant of that which is escaped, which is left to you from the hail, and it has eaten every tree which is springing out of the field for you; **6** and they have filled your houses, and the houses of all your servants, and the houses of all the Egyptians, which neither your fathers nor your father's fathers have seen, since the day of their being on the ground to this day." And he turns and goes out from Pharaoh. **7** And the servants of Pharaoh say to him, "Until when does this [one] become a snare to us? Send the men away, and they serve their God YHWH; do you not yet know that Egypt has perished?" **8** And Moses is brought back—Aaron also—to Pharaoh, and he says to them, "Go, serve your God YHWH, but who—who [are] those going?" **9** And Moses says, "With our young ones, and with our aged ones, we go, with our sons, and with our daughters, with our flock, and our herd, we go, for we have a festival to YHWH." **10** And he says to them, "Be it so, YHWH [is] with you when I send you and your infants away; see—for evil [is] before your faces. **11** Not so! Go now, you who [are] men, and serve YHWH, for that you are seeking"; and [one] casts them out from the presence of Pharaoh. **12** And YHWH says to Moses, "Stretch out your

EXODUS

hand against the land of Egypt for the locust, and it goes up against the land of Egypt, and eats every herb of the land—all that the hail has left." **13** And Moses stretches out his rod against the land of Egypt, and YHWH has led an east wind over the land all that day, and all the night; the morning has been, and the east wind has lifted up the locust. **14** And the locust goes up against all the land of Egypt, and rests in all the border of Egypt—very grievous: before it there has not been such a locust as it, and after it there is none such; **15** and it covers the eye of all the land, and the land is darkened; and it eats every herb of the land, and all the fruit of the trees which the hail has left, and there has not been left any green thing in the trees, or in the herb of the field, in all the land of Egypt. **16** And Pharaoh hurries to call for Moses and for Aaron and says, "I have sinned against your God YHWH, and against you, **17** and now, please bear with my sin, only this time, and make supplication to your God YHWH, that He may turn aside from off me only this death." **18** And he goes out from Pharaoh, and makes supplication to YHWH, **19** and YHWH turns a very strong sea wind, and it lifts up the locust, and blows it into the Red Sea—there has not been left one locust in all the border of Egypt; **20** and YHWH strengthens the heart of Pharaoh, and he has not sent the sons of Israel away. **21** And YHWH says to Moses, "Stretch out your hand toward the heavens, and there is darkness over the land of Egypt, and the darkness is felt." **22** And Moses stretches out his hand toward the heavens, and there is darkness—thick darkness in all the land of Egypt [for] three days; **23** they have not seen one another, and none has risen from his place [for] three days; but there has been light for all the sons of Israel in their dwellings. **24** And Pharaoh calls to Moses and says, "Go, serve YHWH, only your flock and your herd are stayed, your infants also go with you"; **25** and Moses says, "You also give sacrifices and burnt-offerings in our hand, and we have prepared for our God YHWH; **26** and also our livestock go with us—there is not left a hoof, for we take from it to serve our God YHWH; and we do not know how we serve YHWH until our going there." **27** And YHWH strengthens the heart of Pharaoh, and he has not been willing to send them away; **28** and Pharaoh says to him, "Go from me, take heed to yourself, do not add to see my face, for in the day you see my face you die"; **29** and Moses says, "You have spoken correctly, I do not add to see your face anymore."

11 And YHWH says to Moses, "One more plague I bring in on Pharaoh and on Egypt, afterward he sends you away from this; when he is sending you away, he surely casts you out from this [place] altogether; **2** now speak in the ears of the people, and they ask—each man from his neighbor, and each woman from her neighbor—[for] vessels of silver and vessels of gold." **3** And YHWH gives the grace of the people in the eyes of the Egyptians; also the man Moses [is] very great in the land of Egypt, in the eyes of the servants of Pharaoh, and in the eyes of the people. **4** And Moses says, "Thus said YHWH: About midnight I am going out into the midst of Egypt, **5** and every firstborn in the land of Egypt has died, from the firstborn of Pharaoh who is sitting on his throne, to the firstborn of the maidservant who [is] behind the millstones, and all the firstborn of beasts; **6** and there has been a great cry in all the land of Egypt, such as there has not been, and such as there is not again; **7** and against all the sons of Israel a dog does not sharpen its tongue, from man even to beast, so that you know that YHWH makes a separation between the Egyptians and Israel. **8** And all these servants of yours have come down to me, and bowed themselves to me, saying, Go out, you and all the people who [are] at your feet; and afterward I go out"; and he goes out from Pharaoh in the heat of anger. **9** And YHWH says to Moses, "Pharaoh does not listen to you, so as to multiply My wonders in the land of Egypt"; **10** and Moses and Aaron have done all these wonders before Pharaoh, and YHWH strengthens Pharaoh's heart, and he has not sent the sons of Israel out of his land.

12 And YHWH speaks to Moses and to Aaron in the land of Egypt, saying, **2** "This month [is] the chief of months to you—it [is] the first of the months of the year to you; **3** speak to all the congregation of Israel, saying, In the tenth of this month they take to themselves, each man, a lamb for the house of the fathers, a lamb for a house. **4** And if the household is too few for

EXODUS

a lamb, then he has taken, he and his neighbor who is near to his house, for the number of persons, each according to his eating you count for the lamb. **5** A lamb, a perfect one, a male, a son of a year, let [it] be to you; you take [it] from the sheep or from the goats. **6** And it has become a charge to you, until the fourteenth day of this month, and the whole assembly of the congregation of Israel has slaughtered it between the evenings; **7** and they have taken of the blood, and have put [it] on the two doorposts, and on the lintel over the houses in which they eat it. **8** And they have eaten the flesh in this night, a roast with fire; they eat it with unleavened things and bitters; **9** you do not eat of it raw, or boiled in water at all, but a roast with fire, its head with its legs, and with its innards; **10** and you do not leave of it until morning, and that which is remaining of it until morning you burn with fire. **11** And thus you eat it: your loins girded, your sandals on your feet, and your staff in your hand, and you have eaten it in haste; it is YHWH's Passover, **12** and I have passed over through the land of Egypt during this night, and have struck every firstborn in the land of Egypt, from man even to beast, and I do judgments on all the gods of Egypt; I [am] YHWH. **13** And the blood has become a sign for you on the houses where you [are], and I have seen the blood, and have passed over you, and a plague is not on you for destruction in My striking in the land of Egypt. **14** And this day has become a memorial to you, and you have kept it [for] a celebration to YHWH throughout your generations—a continuous statute; you keep it [for] a celebration. **15** Seven days you eat unleavened things; only—in the first day you cause leaven to cease out of your houses; for anyone eating anything fermented from the first day until the seventh day, indeed, that person has been cut off from Israel. **16** And in the first day [is] a holy convocation, and in the seventh day you have a holy convocation; any work is not done in them, only that which is eaten by any person—it alone is done by you, **17** and you have observed the Unleavened Things, for in this very day I have brought out your hosts from the land of Egypt, and you have observed this day throughout your generations—a continuous statute. **18** In the first [month], on the fourteenth day of the month, in the evening, you eat unleavened things until the twenty-first day of the month, at evening; **19** seven days leaven is not found in your houses, for anyone eating anything fermented—that person has been cut off from the congregation of Israel, among the sojourners or among the natives of the land; **20** you do not eat anything fermented—in all your dwellings you eat [only] unleavened things." **21** And Moses calls for all [the] elderly of Israel and says to them, "Draw out and take for yourselves [from] the flock, for your families, and slaughter the Passover-sacrifice; **22** and you have taken a bunch of hyssop, and have dipped [it] in the blood which [is] in the basin, and have struck [it] on the lintel, and on the two doorposts, from the blood which [is] in the basin, and you, you do not go out—each from the opening of his house—until morning. **23** And YHWH has passed on to strike the Egyptians, and has seen the blood on the lintel, and on the two doorposts, and YHWH has passed over the opening, and does not permit the destruction to come into your houses to strike. **24** And you have observed this thing for a statute to you and to your sons for all time; **25** and it has been, when you come to the land which YHWH gives to you as He has spoken, that you have kept this service; **26** and it has come to pass, when your sons say to you, What [is] this service you have? **27** That you have said, It [is] a sacrifice of Passover to YHWH, who passed over the houses of the sons of Israel in Egypt, in His striking the Egyptians, and our houses He delivered." **28** And the people bow and pay respect, and the sons of Israel go and do as YHWH commanded Moses and Aaron; so they have done. **29** And it comes to pass, at midnight, that YHWH has struck every firstborn in the land of Egypt, from the firstborn of Pharaoh who is sitting on his throne, to the firstborn of the captive who [is] in the prison-house, and every firstborn of beasts. **30** And Pharaoh rises by night, he and all his servants, and all the Egyptians, and there is a great cry in Egypt, for there is not a house where there is not [one] dead, **31** and he calls for Moses and for Aaron by night and says, "Rise, go out from the midst of my people, both you and the sons of Israel, and go, serve YHWH according to your word; **32** take both your flock and your herd as you have spoken, and go; then you have also blessed me." **33** And the

Egyptians are urgent on the people, hastening to send them away out of the land, for they said, "We are all dead"; **34** and the people take up their dough before it is fermented, their kneading-troughs [are] bound up in their garments on their shoulder. **35** And the sons of Israel have done according to the word of Moses, and they ask for vessels of silver and vessels of gold, and garments, from the Egyptians; **36** and YHWH has given the grace of the people in the eyes of the Egyptians, and they cause them to ask, and they spoil the Egyptians. **37** And the sons of Israel journey from Rameses to Succoth, about six hundred thousand men on foot, apart from infants; **38** and a great rabble has also gone up with them, and flock and herd—very much livestock. **39** And they bake unleavened cakes with the dough which they have brought out from Egypt, for it has not fermented; for they have been cast out of Egypt, and have not been able to delay, and also they have not made provision for themselves. **40** And the dwelling of the sons of Israel [in] which they have dwelt in Egypt [is] four hundred and thirty years; **41** and it comes to pass, at the end of four hundred and thirty years—indeed, it comes to pass on this very same day—all the hosts of YHWH have gone out from the land of Egypt. **42** It [is] a night of watchings to YHWH, to bring them out from the land of Egypt; it [is] this night of watchings to YHWH to all the sons of Israel throughout their generations. **43** And YHWH says to Moses and Aaron, "This [is] a statute of the Passover; any son of a stranger does not eat of it; **44** and any man's servant, the purchase of money, when you have circumcised him—then he eats of it; **45** a settler or hired servant does not eat of it; **46** it is eaten in one house, you do not carry out of the house [any] of the flesh outside, and you do not break a bone of it; **47** all the congregation of Israel keeps it. **48** And when a sojourner sojourns with you, and has made a Passover to YHWH, every male of his [is] to be circumcised, and then he comes near to keep it, and he has been as a native of the land, but any uncircumcised one does not eat of it; **49** one law is to a native, and to a sojourner who is sojourning in your midst." **50** And all the sons of Israel do as YHWH commanded Moses and Aaron; so they have done. **51** And it comes to pass on this very same day, YHWH has brought out the sons of Israel from the land of Egypt by their hosts.

13 And YHWH speaks to Moses, saying, **2** "Sanctify to Me every firstborn, opening any womb among the sons of Israel, among man and among beast; it [is] Mine." **3** And Moses says to the people, "Remember this day [in] which you have gone out from Egypt, from the house of servants, for by strength of hand YHWH has brought you out from this, and anything fermented is not eaten; **4** you are going out today, in the month of Abib. **5** And it has been, when YHWH brings you to the land of the Canaanite, and of the Hittite, and of the Amorite, and of the Hivite, and of the Jebusite, which He has sworn to your fathers to give to you, a land flowing with milk and honey, that you have done this service in this month. **6** Seven days you eat unleavened things, and in the seventh day [is] a celebration to YHWH; **7** unleavened things are eaten the seven days, and anything fermented is not seen with you; indeed, leaven is not seen with you in all your border. **8** And you have declared to your son in that day, saying, [It is] because of what YHWH did to me, in my going out from Egypt, **9** and it has been to you for a sign on your hand, and for a memorial between your eyes, so that the Law of YHWH is in your mouth, for by a strong hand YHWH has brought you out from Egypt; **10** and you have kept this statute at its appointed time from days to days. **11** And it has been, when YHWH brings you to the land of the Canaanite as He has sworn to you and to your fathers, and has given it to you, **12** that you have caused everyone opening a womb to pass over to YHWH, and every firstling—the increase of beasts which you have: the males [are] YHWH's. **13** And every firstling of a donkey you ransom with a lamb, and if you do not ransom [it], then you have beheaded it; and you ransom every firstborn of man among your sons. **14** And it has been, when your son asks you hereafter, saying, What [is] this? That you have said to him, By strength of hand YHWH has brought us out from Egypt, from a house of servants; **15** indeed, it comes to pass, when Pharaoh has been pained to send us away, that YHWH slays every firstborn in the land of Egypt, from the firstborn of man even to

EXODUS

the firstborn of beast; therefore I am sacrificing to Y<small>HWH</small> all opening a womb who [are] males, and I ransom every firstborn of my sons; **16** and it has been for a token on your hand, and for frontlets between your eyes, for by strength of hand Y<small>HWH</small> has brought us out of Egypt." **17** And it comes to pass in Pharaoh's sending the people away, that God has not led them the way of the land of the Philistines, for it [is] near; for God said, "Lest the people sigh in their seeing war, and have turned back toward Egypt"; **18** and God turns around the people the way of the wilderness of the Red Sea, and the sons of Israel have gone up by fifties from the land of Egypt. **19** And Moses takes the bones of Joseph with him, for he certainly caused the sons of Israel to swear, saying, "God certainly inspects you, and you have brought up my bones from this [place] with you." **20** And they journey from Succoth, and encamp in Etham at the extremity of the wilderness, **21** and Y<small>HWH</small> is going before them by day in a pillar of a cloud, to lead them in the way, and by night in a pillar of fire, to give light to them, to go by day and by night; **22** He does not remove the pillar of the cloud by day, and the pillar of the fire by night, [from] before the people.

14 And Y<small>HWH</small> speaks to Moses, saying, **2** "Speak to the sons of Israel, and they turn back and encamp before Pi-Hahiroth, between Migdol and the sea, before Ba'al-Zephon; you encamp in front of it by the sea, **3** and Pharaoh has said of the sons of Israel, They are entangled in the land, the wilderness has shut on them; **4** and I have strengthened the heart of Pharaoh, and he has pursued after them, and I am honored by Pharaoh, and by all his force, and the Egyptians have known that I [am] Y<small>HWH</small>"; and they do so. **5** And it is declared to the king of Egypt that the people have fled, and the heart of Pharaoh and of his servants is turned against the people, and they say, "What [is] this we have done, that we have sent Israel away from our service?" **6** And he harnesses his chariot, and he has taken his people with him, **7** and he takes six hundred chosen chariots, even all the chariots of Egypt, and captains over them all; **8** and Y<small>HWH</small> strengthens the heart of Pharaoh king of Egypt, and he pursues after the sons of Israel, and the sons of Israel are going out with a high hand, **9** and the Egyptians pursue after them, and all the chariot horses of Pharaoh, and his horsemen, and his force, overtake them, encamping by the sea, by Pi-Hahiroth, before Ba'al-Zephon. **10** And Pharaoh has drawn near, and the sons of Israel lift up their eyes, and behold, the Egyptians are journeying after them, and they fear exceedingly, and the sons of Israel cry to Y<small>HWH</small>. **11** And they say to Moses, "Because there are no graves in Egypt, have you taken us away to die in a wilderness? What is this you have done to us—to bring us out from Egypt? **12** Is this not the word which we spoke to you in Egypt, saying, Cease from us, and we serve the Egyptians; for [it is] better for us to serve the Egyptians than to die in a wilderness?" **13** And Moses says to the people, "Do not fear, station yourselves, and see the salvation of Y<small>HWH</small>, which He does for you today; for as you have seen the Egyptians today, you add no more to see them for all time; **14** Y<small>HWH</small> fights for you, and you keep silent." **15** And Y<small>HWH</small> says to Moses, "Why do you cry to Me? Speak to the sons of Israel, and they journey; **16** and you, lift up your rod, and stretch out your hand toward the sea, and cleave it, and the sons of Israel go into the midst of the sea on dry land. **17** And I—behold, I am strengthening the heart of the Egyptians, and they go in after them, and I am honored by Pharaoh, and by all his force, by his chariots, and by his horsemen; **18** and the Egyptians have known that I [am] Y<small>HWH</small>, in My being honored by Pharaoh, by his chariots, and by his horsemen." **19** And the Messenger of God, who is going before the camp of Israel, journeys and goes at their rear; and the pillar of the cloud journeys from their front, and stands at their rear, **20** and comes in between the camp of the Egyptians and the camp of Israel, and the cloud and the darkness are, and he enlightens the night, and the one has not drawn near to the other all the night. **21** And Moses stretches out his hand toward the sea, and Y<small>HWH</small> causes the sea to go on by a strong east wind all the night, and makes the sea become dry ground, and the waters are cleaved, **22** and the sons of Israel go into the midst of the sea on dry land, and the waters [are] a wall to them, on their right and on their left. **23** And the Egyptians pursue, and go in

EXODUS

after them (all the horses of Pharaoh, his chariots, and his horsemen) into the midst of the sea, **24** and it comes to pass, in the morning watch, that YHWH looks to the camp of the Egyptians through the pillar of fire and of the cloud, and troubles the camp of the Egyptians, **25** and turns aside the wheels of their chariots, and they lead them with difficulty, and the Egyptians say, "Let us flee from the face of Israel, for YHWH is fighting for them against the Egyptians." **26** And YHWH says to Moses, "Stretch out your hand toward the sea, and the waters turn back on the Egyptians, on their chariots, and on their horsemen." **27** And Moses stretches out his hand toward the sea, and the sea turns back, at the turning of the morning, to its perennial flow, and the Egyptians are fleeing at its coming, and YHWH shakes off the Egyptians in the midst of the sea, **28** and the waters turn back, and cover the chariots and the horsemen, even all the force of Pharaoh, who are coming in after them into the sea—there has not been left even one of them. **29** And the sons of Israel have gone on dry land in the midst of the sea, and the waters [are] a wall to them, on their right and on their left; **30** and YHWH saves Israel out of the hand of the Egyptians in that day, and Israel sees the Egyptians dead on the seashore, **31** and Israel sees the great hand with which YHWH has worked against the Egyptians, and the people fear YHWH, and remain steadfast in YHWH, and in His servant Moses.

15 Then Moses sings—and the sons of Israel—this song to YHWH, and they speak, saying, "I sing to YHWH, ‖ For triumphing He has triumphed; The horse and its rider He has thrown into the sea. **2** My strength and song is YAH, ‖ And He is become my salvation: This [is] my God, and I glorify Him; God of my father, and I exalt Him. **3** YHWH [is] a man of battle; YHWH [is] His Name. **4** Chariots of Pharaoh and his force ‖ He has cast into the sea; And the choice of his captains ‖ Have sunk in the Red Sea! **5** The depths cover them; They went down into the depths as a stone. **6** Your right hand, O YHWH, ‖ Has become honorable in power; Your right hand, O YHWH, ‖ Crushes an enemy. **7** And in the abundance of Your excellence ‖ You throw down Your withstanders, ‖ You send forth Your wrath—It consumes them as stubble. **8** And by the wind of Your anger ‖ Waters have been heaped together; Flowings have stood as a heap; Depths have been congealed ‖ In the heart of a sea. **9** The enemy said, I pursue, I overtake; I apportion spoil; My soul is filled with them; I draw out my sword; My hand destroys them— **10** You have blown with Your wind ‖ The sea has covered them; They sank as lead in mighty waters. **11** Who [is] like You among the gods, O YHWH? Who [is] like You—honorable in holiness—Fearful in praises—doing wonders? **12** You have stretched out Your right hand—Earth swallows them! **13** You have led forth in Your kindness ‖ The people whom You have redeemed. You have led on in Your strength ‖ To Your holy habitation. **14** Peoples have heard, they are troubled; Pain has seized inhabitants of Philistia. **15** Then chiefs of Edom have been troubled; Mighty ones of Moab—Trembling seizes them! All inhabitants of Canaan have melted! **16** Terror and dread fall on them; By the greatness of Your arm ‖ They are still as a stone, ‖ Until Your people pass over, O YHWH; Until the people pass over ‖ Whom You have purchased. **17** You bring them in, and plant them ‖ In a mountain of Your inheritance, ‖ A fixed place for Your dwelling You have made, O YHWH; A sanctuary, O Lord, Your hands have established; **18** YHWH reigns—[for] all time and forever!" **19** For the horse of Pharaoh has gone in with his chariots and with his horsemen into the sea, and YHWH turns back the waters of the sea on them, and the sons of Israel have gone on dry land in the midst of the sea. **20** And Miriam the inspired one, sister of Aaron, takes the timbrel in her hand, and all the women go out after her, with timbrels and with choruses; **21** and Miriam answers to them: "Sing to YHWH, ‖ For triumphing He has triumphed; The horse and its rider He has thrown into the sea!" **22** And Moses causes Israel to journey from the Red Sea, and they go out to the wilderness of Shur, and they go three days in the wilderness, and have not found water, **23** and they come to Marah, and have not been able to drink the waters of Marah, for they [are] bitter; therefore [one] has called its name Marah. **24** And the people murmur against Moses, saying, "What do we drink?" **25** And he cries to YHWH, and YHWH shows him a tree, and he casts [it] into the waters, and the waters become sweet. He has made a statute for them there, and an ordinance, and He has tried them there, **26** and He says, "If you really listen to the voice of your God YHWH, and do that which is right in His eyes, and have listened to His commands, and kept all His statutes, none of the sickness which I laid on the Egyptians do I lay on you, for I, YHWH, am healing you." **27** And they come to Elim, and there [are] twelve fountains of water, and seventy palm trees; and they encamp there by the waters.

16 And they journey from Elim, and all the congregation of the sons of Israel come to the wilderness of Sin, which [is] between Elim and Sinai, on the fifteenth day of the second month of their going out from the land of Egypt. **2** And all the congregation of the sons of Israel murmur against Moses and against Aaron in the wilderness; **3** and the sons of Israel say to them, "Oh that we had died by the hand of YHWH in the land of Egypt, in our sitting by the flesh-pot, in our eating bread to satiety—for you have brought us out to this wilderness to put all this assembly to death with hunger." **4** And YHWH says to Moses, "Behold, I am raining bread from the heavens for you—and the people have gone out and gathered the matter of a day in its day—so that I try them whether they walk in My law or not; **5** and it has been on the sixth day, that they have prepared that which they bring in, and it has been double above that which they gather day [by] day." **6** And Moses says—Aaron also—to all the sons of Israel, "Evening—and you have known that YHWH has brought you out from the land of Egypt; **7** and morning—and you have seen the glory of YHWH, in His hearing your murmurings against YHWH, and what [are] we, that you murmur against us?" **8** And Moses says, "In YHWH's giving to you flesh to eat in the evening, and bread in the morning to satiety—in YHWH's hearing your murmurings, which you are murmuring against Him, and what [are] we? Your murmurings [are] not against us, but against YHWH." **9** And Moses says to Aaron, "Say to all the congregation of the sons of Israel, Come near before YHWH, for He has heard your murmurings"; **10** and it comes to pass, when Aaron is speaking to all the congregation of the sons of Israel, that they turn toward the wilderness, and behold, the glory of YHWH is seen in the cloud. **11** And YHWH speaks to Moses, saying, **12** "I have heard the murmurings of the sons of Israel; speak to them, saying, Between the evenings you eat flesh, and in the morning you are satisfied [with] bread, and you have known that I [am] your God YHWH." **13** And it comes to pass in the evening, that the quail comes up, and covers the camp, and in the morning there has been the lying of dew around the camp, **14** and the lying of the dew goes up, and behold, on the face of the wilderness [is] a thin, bare thing, thin as hoarfrost on the earth. **15** And the sons of Israel see, and say to one another, "What [is] it?" For they have not known what it [is]; and Moses says to them, "It [is] the bread which YHWH has given to you for food. **16** This [is] the thing which YHWH has commanded: Gather of it, each according to his eating, an omer for the counted head; and the number of your persons, take, each, for those in his tent." **17** And the sons of Israel do so, and they gather, he who is [gathering] much, and he who is [gathering] little; **18** and they measure with an omer, and he who is [gathering] much has nothing over, and he who is [gathering] little has no lack, each according to his eating they have gathered. **19** And Moses says to them, "Let no man leave of it until morning"; **20** and they have not listened to Moses, and some of them leave of it until morning, and it brings up worms and stinks; and Moses is angry with them. **21** And they gather it morning by morning, each according to his eating; when the sun has been warm, then it has melted. **22** And it comes to pass on the sixth day, they have gathered a second bread, two omers for one, and all the princes of the congregation come in, and declare [it] to Moses. **23** And he says to them, "It [is] that which YHWH has spoken: A rest—a holy Sabbath to YHWH—[is] tomorrow; that which you bake, bake; and that which you boil, boil; and all that is remaining, let [it] rest for yourselves for preservation until the morning." **24** And they let it rest until the morning, as Moses has commanded, and it has not stunk, and a worm has not been in it. **25** And Moses says, "Eat it today, for today [is] a Sabbath to YHWH; today you do not find it in the field: **26** six days you gather it, and in the seventh day—the Sabbath—there is none in it." **27** And it

EXODUS

comes to pass on the seventh day, some of the people have gone out to gather, and have not found. **28** And YHWH says to Moses, "How long have you refused to keep My commands and My laws? **29** See, because YHWH has given the Sabbath to you, therefore He is giving to you on the sixth day bread of two days; each abide [in] his place, no one goes out from his place on the seventh day." **30** And the people rest on the seventh day, **31** and the house of Israel calls its name Manna, and it [is] as white coriander seed; and its taste [is] as a cake with honey. **32** And Moses says, "This [is] the thing which YHWH has commanded: Fill the omer with it, for a charge for your generations, so that they see the bread which I have caused you to eat in the wilderness, in My bringing you out from the land of Egypt." **33** And Moses says to Aaron, "Take one pot, and put the fullness of the omer of manna [in] there, and let it rest before YHWH, for a charge for your generations"; **34** as YHWH has given command to Moses, so Aaron lets it rest before the Testimony, for a charge. **35** And the sons of Israel have eaten the manna [for] forty years, until their coming to the land to be inhabited; they have eaten the manna until their coming to the extremity of the land of Canaan. **36** And the omer is a tenth of the ephah.

17 And all the congregation of the sons of Israel journey from the wilderness of Sin, on their journeys, by the command of YHWH, and encamp in Rephidim, and there is no water for the people to drink; **2** and the people strive with Moses, and say, "Give us water, and we drink." And Moses says to them, "Why do you strive with me? Why do you try YHWH?" **3** And the people thirst for water there, and the people murmur against Moses, and say, "Why [is] this [that] you have brought us up out of Egypt to put us to death, also our sons and our livestock, with thirst?" **4** And Moses cries to YHWH, saying, "What do I do to this people? Yet a little, and they have stoned me." **5** And YHWH says to Moses, "Pass over before the people, and take with you from [the] elderly of Israel, and take your rod in your hand, with which you have struck the River, and you have gone. **6** Behold, I am standing before you there on the rock in Horeb, and you have struck on the rock, and waters have come out from it, and the people have drunk." And Moses does so before the eyes of [the] elderly of Israel, **7** and he calls the name of the place Massah, and Meribah, because of the strife of the sons of Israel, and because of their trying YHWH, saying, "Is YHWH in our midst or not?" **8** And Amalek comes, and fights with Israel in Rephidim, **9** and Moses says to Joshua, "Choose men for us, and go out, fight with Amalek: tomorrow I am standing on the top of the hill, and the rod of God in my hand." **10** And Joshua does as Moses has said to him, to fight with Amalek, and Moses, Aaron, and Hur have gone up [to] the top of the height; **11** and it has come to pass, when Moses lifts up his hand, that Israel has been mighty, and when he lets his hands rest, that Amalek has been mighty. **12** And the hands of Moses [are] heavy, and they take a stone and set [it] under him, and he sits on it, and Aaron and Hur have taken hold on his hands, one on this [side] and one on that [side]; and his hands are steadfast until the going in of the sun; **13** and Joshua weakens Amalek and his people by the mouth of the sword. **14** And YHWH says to Moses, "Write this, a memorial in a Scroll, and set [it] in the ears of Joshua, that I utterly wipe away the remembrance of Amalek from under the heavens"; **15** and Moses builds an altar, and calls its name YHWH-Nissi, **16** and says, "Because a hand [is] on the throne of YAH, war [is] to YHWH with Amalek from generation [to] generation."

18 And Jethro priest of Midian, father-in-law of Moses, hears all that God has done for Moses and for His people Israel, that YHWH has brought out Israel from Egypt, **2** and Jethro, father-in-law of Moses, takes Zipporah, wife of Moses, after her parting, **3** and her two sons, of whom the name of one [is] Gershom, for he said, "I have been a sojourner in a strange land"; **4** and the name of the other [is] Eliezer, for, "The God of my father [is] for my help, and He delivers me from the sword of Pharaoh." **5** And Jethro, father-in-law of Moses, comes, and his sons, and his wife, to Moses, to the wilderness where he is encamping—the mountain of God; **6** and he says to Moses, "I, your father-in-law Jethro, am coming to you, and your wife, and her two sons with her." **7** And Moses goes out to meet his father-in-law, and bows himself, and kisses him, and they ask

EXODUS

of one another of welfare, and come into the tent; **8** and Moses recounts to his father-in-law all that YHWH has done to Pharaoh, and to the Egyptians, on account of Israel, all the travail which has found them in the way, and [how] YHWH delivers them. **9** And Jethro rejoices for all the good which YHWH has done to Israel, whom He has delivered from the hand of the Egyptians; **10** and Jethro says, "Blessed [is] YHWH, who has delivered you from the hand of the Egyptians, and from the hand of Pharaoh—who has delivered this people from under the hand of the Egyptians; **11** now I have known that YHWH [is] greater than all the gods, for in the thing they have acted proudly—[He is] above them!" **12** And Jethro, father-in-law of Moses, takes a burnt-offering and sacrifices [it] for God; and Aaron comes in, and all [the] elderly of Israel, to eat bread with the father-in-law of Moses, before God. **13** And it comes to pass on the next day, that Moses sits to judge the people, and the people stand before Moses from the morning to the evening; **14** and the father-in-law of Moses sees all that he is doing for the people and says, "What [is] this thing which you are doing for the people? Why are you sitting by yourself, and all the people standing by you from morning until evening?" **15** And Moses says to his father-in-law, "Because the people come to me to seek God; **16** when they have a matter, it has come to me, and I have judged between a man and his neighbor, and made known the statutes of God, and His laws." **17** And the father-in-law of Moses says to him, "The thing which you are doing [is] not good; **18** you surely wear away, both you, and this people which [is] with you, for the thing is too heavy for you, you are not able to do it by yourself. **19** Now listen to my voice, I counsel you, and God is with you: be for the people before God, and you have brought in the things to God; **20** and you have warned them [concerning] the statutes and the laws, and have made known to them the way in which they go, and the work which they do. **21** And you provide out of all the people men of ability, fearing God, men of truth, hating dishonest gain, and have placed [these] over them [for] heads of thousands, heads of hundreds, heads of fifties, and heads of tens, **22** and they have judged the people at all times; and it has come to pass, they bring every great matter to you, and they judge every small matter themselves; and lighten it from off yourself, and they have borne with you. **23** If you do this thing, and God has commanded you, then you have been able to stand, and all this people also goes to its place in peace." **24** And Moses listens to the voice of his father-in-law, and does all that he said, **25** and Moses chooses men of ability out of all Israel, and makes them chiefs over the people [for] heads of thousands, heads of hundreds, heads of fifties, and heads of tens, **26** and they have judged the people at all times; they bring the hard matter to Moses, and they judge every small matter themselves. **27** And Moses sends his father-in-law away, and he goes away to his own land.

19 In the third month of the going out of the sons of Israel from the land of Egypt, in this day they have come into the wilderness of Sinai, **2** and they journey from Rephidim, and enter the wilderness of Sinai, and encamp in the wilderness; and Israel encamps there before the mountain. **3** And Moses has gone up to God, and YHWH calls to him out of the mountain, saying, "Thus you say to the house of Jacob, and declare to the sons of Israel: **4** You have seen that which I have done to the Egyptians, and [how] I carry you on eagles' wings and bring you to Myself. **5** And now, if you really listen to My voice, then you have kept My covenant, and have been a special treasure to Me more than all the peoples, for all the earth [is] Mine; **6** and you are to Me a kingdom of priests and a holy nation: these [are] the words which you speak to the sons of Israel." **7** And Moses comes, and calls for [the] elderly of the people, and sets before them all these words which YHWH has commanded him; **8** and all the people answer together and say, "All that YHWH has spoken we do"; and Moses returns the words of the people to YHWH. **9** And YHWH says to Moses, "Behold, I am coming to you in the thickness of the cloud, so that the people hear in My speaking with you, and also believe in you for all time"; and Moses declares the words of the people to YHWH. **10** And YHWH says to Moses, "Go to the people and you have sanctified them today and tomorrow, and they have washed their garments, **11** and have been prepared for the third day; for on the third

EXODUS

day Y<small>HWH</small> comes down on Mount Sinai before the eyes of all the people. **12** And you have made a border [for] the people all around, saying, Take heed to yourselves, going up into the mountain or coming against its extremity; whoever is coming against the mountain is certainly put to death; **13** a hand does not come against him, for he is certainly stoned or shot through, whether beast or man—it does not live; in the prolonging of the ram's horn they go up into the mountain." **14** And Moses comes down from the mountain to the people, and sanctifies the people, and they wash their garments; **15** and he says to the people, "Be prepared for the third day, do not come near to a woman." **16** And it comes to pass, on the third day, while it is morning, that there are voices, and lightnings, and a heavy cloud on the mountain, and the sound of a very strong horn; and all the people who [are] in the camp tremble. **17** And Moses brings out the people from the camp to meet God, and they station themselves at the lower part of the mountain, **18** and Mount Sinai [is] wholly [in] smoke from the presence of Y<small>HWH</small>, who has come down on it in fire, and its smoke goes up as smoke of the furnace, and the whole mountain trembles exceedingly; **19** and the sound of the horn is going on, and [is] very strong; Moses speaks, and God answers him with a voice. **20** And Y<small>HWH</small> comes down on Mount Sinai, to the top of the mountain, and Y<small>HWH</small> calls for Moses to the top of the mountain, and Moses goes up. **21** And Y<small>HWH</small> says to Moses, "Go down, protest to the people, lest they break through to Y<small>HWH</small> to see, and many of them have fallen; **22** and also the priests who are coming near to Y<small>HWH</small> sanctify themselves, lest Y<small>HWH</small> break forth on them." **23** And Moses says to Y<small>HWH</small>, "The people [are] unable to come up to Mount Sinai, for You have protested to us, saying, Make a border [for] the mountain, then you have sanctified it." **24** And Y<small>HWH</small> says to him, "Go, descend, then you have come up, you and Aaron with you; and the priests and the people do not break through to come up to Y<small>HWH</small>, lest He break forth on them." **25** And Moses goes down to the people and speaks to them.

20 And God speaks all these words, saying, **2** "I [am] your God Y<small>HWH</small>, who has brought you out of the land of Egypt, out of a house of servants. **3** You have no other Gods before Me. **4** You do not make a carved image for yourself, or any likeness which [is] in the heavens above, or which [is] in the earth beneath, or which [is] in the waters under the earth. **5** You do not bow yourself to them, nor serve them: for I, your God Y<small>HWH</small>, [am] a zealous God, charging iniquity of fathers on sons, on a third and on a fourth [generation] of those hating Me, **6** and doing kindness to thousands, of those loving Me and keeping My commands. **7** You do not take up the Name of your God Y<small>HWH</small> for a vain thing, for Y<small>HWH</small> does not acquit him who takes up His Name for a vain thing. **8** Remember the Sabbath day to sanctify it; **9** six days you labor and have done all your work, **10** and the seventh day [is] a Sabbath to your God Y<small>HWH</small>; you do not do any work, you, and your son, and your daughter, your manservant, and your handmaid, and your livestock, and your sojourner who is within your gates— **11** for [in] six days Y<small>HWH</small> has made the heavens and the earth, the sea, and all that [is] in them, and rests in the seventh day; therefore Y<small>HWH</small> has blessed the Sabbath day and sanctifies it. **12** Honor your father and your mother, so that your days are prolonged on the ground which your God Y<small>HWH</small> is giving to you. **13** You do not murder. **14** You do not commit adultery. **15** You do not steal. **16** You do not answer [with] a false testimony against your neighbor. **17** You do not desire the house of your neighbor, you do not desire the wife of your neighbor, or his manservant, or his handmaid, or his ox, or his donkey, or anything which [is] your neighbor's." **18** And all the people are seeing the voices, and the flames, and the sound of the horn, and the mountain smoking; and the people see, and move, and stand far off, **19** and say to Moses, "Speak with us, and we hear, and do not let God speak with us, lest we die." **20** And Moses says to the people, "Do not fear, for God has come to try you, and in order that His fear may be before your faces—that you do not sin." **21** And the people stand far off, and Moses has drawn near to the thick darkness where God [is]. **22** And Y<small>HWH</small> says to Moses, "Thus you say to the sons of Israel: You have seen that I have spoken with you from the heavens; **23** you do not make gods of silver and gods of gold [to be] with Me—you do not make [any idol] for yourselves. **24** You make an altar of earth for Me, and you have sacrificed on it your burnt-offerings and your peace-offerings, your flock and your herd; in every place where I cause My Name to be remembered I come to you, and have blessed you. **25** And if you make an altar of stones for Me, you do not build them of hewn work; when you have waved your tool over it, then you defile it; **26** neither do you go up by steps on My altar, that your nakedness is not revealed on it.

21 And these [are] the judgments which you set before them: **2** When you buy a Hebrew servant, he serves [for] six years, and in the seventh he goes out as a freeman for nothing; **3** if he comes in by himself, he goes out by himself; if he [is] owner of a wife, then his wife has gone out with him; **4** if his lord gives a wife to him, and she has borne sons or daughters to him—the wife and her children are her lord's, and he goes out by himself. **5** And if the servant really says: I have loved my lord, my wife, and my sons—I do not go out free, **6** then his lord has brought him near to God, and has brought him near to the door, or to the doorpost, and his lord has bored his ear with an awl, and he has served him for all time. **7** And when a man sells his daughter for a handmaid, she does not go out according to the going out of the menservants; **8** if [it is] evil in the eyes of her lord, so that he has not betrothed her, then he has let her be ransomed; he has no power to sell her to a strange people, in his dealing treacherously with her. **9** And if he betroths her to his son, he does to her according to the right of daughters. **10** If he takes another [woman] for him, he does not withdraw her food, her covering, and her habitation; **11** and if he does not do these three for her, then she has gone out for nothing, without money. **12** He who strikes a man so that he has died is certainly put to death; **13** as for him who has not laid wait, but God has brought [him] to his hand, I have even set a place for you to where he flees. **14** And when a man presumes against his neighbor to slay him with subtlety, you take him from My altar to die. **15** And he who strikes his father or his mother is certainly put to death. **16** And he who steals a man, and has sold him, and he has been found in his hand, is certainly put to death. **17** And he who is reviling his father or his mother is certainly put to death. **18** And when men contend, and a man has struck his neighbor with a stone, or with the fist, and he does not die, but has fallen on the bed; **19** if he rises, and has gone up and down outside on his staff, then the striker has been acquitted; he only gives [for] his cessation, and he is thoroughly healed. **20** And when a man strikes his manservant or his handmaid with a rod, and he has died under his hand—he is certainly avenged; **21** only if he remains a day, or two days, he is not avenged, for he [is] his money. **22** And when men strive, and have struck a pregnant woman, and her children have come out, and there is no harm [to them], he is certainly fined as the husband of the woman lays on him, and he has given through the judges; **23** and if there is harm [to them], then you have given life for life, **24** eye for eye, tooth for tooth, hand for hand, foot for foot, **25** burning for burning, wound for wound, stripe for stripe. **26** And when a man strikes the eye of his manservant, or the eye of his handmaid, and has destroyed it, he sends him away as a freeman for his eye; **27** and if he knocks out a tooth of his manservant or a tooth of his handmaid, he sends him away as a freeman for his tooth. **28** And when an ox gores man or woman, and they have died, the ox is certainly stoned, and his flesh is not eaten, and the owner of the ox [is] acquitted; **29** and if the ox is [one] accustomed to gore before, and it has been testified to its owner, and he does not watch it, and it has put to death a man or woman, the ox is stoned, and its owner is also put to death. **30** If atonement is laid on him, then he has given the ransom of his life, according to all that is laid on him; **31** whether it gores a son or gores a daughter, according to this judgment it is done to him. **32** If the ox gores a manservant or a handmaid, he gives thirty silver shekels to their lord, and the ox is stoned. **33** And when a man opens a pit, or when a man digs a pit, and does not cover it, and an ox or donkey has fallen [in] there— **34** the owner of the pit repays, he gives back money to its owner, and the dead is his. **35** And when a man's ox strikes the ox of his neighbor and it has died, then they have sold the living ox, and halved its money, and they also halve the dead one;

36 or, [if] it has been known that the ox is [one] accustomed to gore before, and its owner does not watch it, he certainly repays ox for ox, and the dead is his.

22 When a man steals an ox or sheep, and has slaughtered it or sold it, he repays [with] five of the herd for the ox, and four of the flock for the sheep. **2** If in the breaking through, the thief is found, and he has been struck and has died, there is no blood for him; **3** if the sun has risen on him, blood [is] for him, he certainly repays; if he has nothing, then he has been sold for his theft; **4** if the theft is certainly found alive in his hand, whether ox, or donkey, or sheep—he repays double. **5** When a man depastures a field or vineyard, and has sent out his beast, and it has pastured in the field of another, he repays [with] the best of his field, and the best of his vineyard. **6** When fire goes forth and has found thorns, and a stack, or the standing grain, or the field has been consumed, he who causes the burning certainly repays. **7** When a man gives silver or vessels to his neighbor to keep, and it has been stolen out of the man's house; if the thief is found, he repays double. **8** If the thief is not found, then the master of the house has been brought near to God [to see] whether he has not put forth his hand against the work of his neighbor. **9** For every matter of transgression, for ox, for donkey, for sheep, for raiment, for any lost thing of which it is said that it is his, the matter of them both comes to God; he whom God condemns repays double to his neighbor. **10** When a man gives to his neighbor a donkey, or ox, or sheep, or any beast to keep, and it has died, or has been hurt, or taken captive, [with] none seeing— **11** an oath of YHWH is between them both, that he has not put forth his hand against the work of his neighbor, and its owner has accepted, and he does not repay; **12** but if it is certainly stolen from him, he repays to its owner; **13** if it is certainly torn, he brings it in [as] a witness; he does not repay the torn thing. **14** And when a man asks for [anything] from his neighbor, and it has been hurt or has died—its owner not being with it—he certainly repays; **15** if its owner [is] with it, he does not repay—if it [is] a hired thing, it has come for its hire. **16** And when a man entices a virgin who [is] not betrothed, and has lain with her, he certainly endows her to himself for a wife; **17** if her father utterly refuses to give her to him, he weighs out money according to the dowry of virgins. **18** You do not keep a witch alive. **19** Whoever lies with a beast is certainly put to death. **20** He who is sacrificing to a god, except to YHWH alone, is devoted. **21** And you do not oppress a sojourner, nor crush him, for you have been sojourners in the land of Egypt. **22** You do not afflict any widow or orphan; **23** if you really afflict him, surely if he cries to Me at all, I certainly hear his cry; **24** and My anger has burned, and I have slain you by the sword, and your wives have been widows, and your sons orphans. **25** If you lend money [to] My poor people [who are] with you, you are not as a usurer to him; you do not lay usury on him; **26** if you take the garment of your neighbor in pledge at all, you return it to him during the going in of the sun: **27** for it is his only covering, it [is] his garment for his skin; wherein does he lie down? And it has come to pass, when he cries to Me, that I have heard, for I [am] gracious. **28** You do not revile God, and you do not curse a prince among your people. **29** You do not delay your fullness and your liquids; you give the firstborn of your sons to Me; **30** so you do to your ox [and] to your sheep; it is with its mother [for] seven days, on the eighth day you give it to Me. **31** And you are holy men to Me, and you do not eat flesh torn in the field, you cast it to a dog.

23 You do not lift up a vain report; you do not put your hand with a wicked man to be a violent witness. **2** You are not after many to [do] evil, nor do you testify concerning a strife, to turn aside after many to cause [others] to turn aside; **3** and you do not honor a poor man in his strife. **4** When you meet your enemy's ox or his donkey going astray, you certainly turn it back to him; **5** when you see the donkey of him who is hating you crouching under its burden, then you have ceased from leaving [it] to it—you certainly leave [it] with him. **6** You do not turn aside the judgment of your poor in his strife; **7** you keep far off from a false matter, and you do not slay an innocent and righteous man; for I do not justify a wicked man. **8** And you do not take a bribe, for the bribe binds the open-[eyed] and perverts the words of the righteous. **9** And you do not oppress a sojourner, since you have known the soul of the sojourner, for you have been sojourners in the land of Egypt. **10** And [for] six years you sow your land and have gathered its increase; **11** and [in] the seventh you release it, and have left it, and the needy of your people have eaten, and the beast of the field eats their remainder; so you do to your vineyard [and] to your olive-yard. **12** Six days you do your work, and on the seventh day you rest, so that your ox and your donkey rest, and the son of your handmaid and the sojourner is refreshed; **13** and in all that which I have said to you—take heed; and you do not mention the name of other gods; it is not heard on your mouth. **14** You keep a celebration to Me three times in a year: **15** you keep the Celebration of Unleavened Things (you eat unleavened things [for] seven days as I have commanded you, at the time appointed [in] the month of Abib; for in it you have come forth out of Egypt, and you do not appear [in] My presence empty); **16** and the Celebration of Harvest, the first-fruits of your works which you sow in the field; and the Celebration of the Ingathering in the outgoing of the year, in your gathering your works out of the field. **17** Three times in a year all your males appear before [the] face of the Lord YHWH. **18** You do not sacrifice the blood of My sacrifice on a fermented thing, and the fat of My festival does not remain until morning; **19** the beginning of the first-fruits of your ground you bring into the house of your God YHWH; you do not boil a kid in its mother's milk. **20** Behold, I am sending a Messenger before you to keep you in the way, and to bring you to the place which I have prepared; **21** be watchful because of His presence, and listen to His voice, do not rebel against Him, for He does not bear with your transgression, for My Name [is] in His heart; **22** for if you listen diligently to His voice, and have done all that which I speak, then I have been at enmity with your enemies, and have distressed those distressing you. **23** For My Messenger goes before you, and has brought you to the Amorite, and the Hittite, and the Perizzite, and the Canaanite, the Hivite, and the Jebusite, and I have cut them off. **24** You do not bow yourself to their gods, nor serve them, nor do according to their doings, but utterly devote them, and thoroughly break their standing pillars. **25** And you have served your God YHWH, and He has blessed your bread and your water, and I have turned aside sickness from your heart; **26** there is not a miscarrying and barren one in your land; I fulfill the number of your days. **27** I send My terror before you, and I have put to death all the people among whom you come, and I have given the neck of all your enemies to you. **28** And I have sent the hornet before you, and it has cast out the Hivite, the Canaanite, and the Hittite from before you; **29** I do not cast them out from before you in one year, lest the land be a desolation, and the beast of the field has multiplied against you; **30** I cast them out little [by] little from before you, until you are fruitful, and have inherited the land. **31** And I have set your border from the Red Sea, even to the sea of the Philistines, and from the wilderness to the River; for I give the inhabitants of the land into your hand, and you have cast them out from before you. **32** You do not make a covenant with them and with their gods; **33** they do not dwell in your land, lest they cause you to sin against Me when you serve their gods, when it becomes a snare to you."

24 And He said to Moses, "Come up to YHWH, you, and Aaron, Nadab, and Abihu, and seventy from [the] elderly of Israel, and you have bowed yourselves far off"; **2** and Moses has drawn near to YHWH by himself; and they do not draw near, and the people do not go up with him. **3** And Moses comes in, and recounts to the people all the words of YHWH, and all the judgments, and all the people answer [with] one voice, and say, "All the words which YHWH has spoken we do." **4** And Moses writes all the words of YHWH, and rises early in the morning, and builds an altar under the hill, and twelve standing pillars for the twelve tribes of Israel; **5** and he sends the youths of the sons of Israel, and they cause burnt-offerings to ascend, and sacrifice sacrifices of peace-offerings to YHWH—calves. **6** And Moses takes half of the blood and puts [it] in basins, and he has sprinkled half of the blood on the altar; **7** and he takes the Scroll of the Covenant, and proclaims [it] in the ears of the people, and they say, "All that which YHWH has spoken we do, and we obey." **8** And Moses takes the blood and sprinkles [it] on the people, and says, "Behold, the blood of the covenant which YHWH has made with you, concerning all these things." **9** And Moses goes up, Aaron also, Nadab and Abihu, and seventy from [the] elderly of Israel, **10** and they see the God of Israel, and under His feet [is] as the work of a pavement of sapphire, and as the substance of the heavens for purity; **11** and He has not put forth His hand to those of the sons of Israel who are near, and they see God, and eat and drink. **12** And YHWH says to Moses, "Come up to Me [on] the mountain and be there, and I give to you the tablets of stone, and the Law, and the command, which I have written to direct them." **13** And Moses rises—his minister Joshua also—and Moses goes up to the mountain of God; **14** and he has said to the elderly, "Abide for us in this [place] until we return to you, and behold, Aaron and Hur [are] with you—he who has matters comes near to them." **15** And Moses goes up to the mountain, and the cloud covers the mountain; **16** and the glory of YHWH dwells on Mount Sinai, and the cloud covers it [for] six days, and He calls to Moses on the seventh day from the midst of the cloud. **17** And the appearance of the glory of YHWH [is] as a consuming fire on the top of the mountain, before the eyes of the sons of Israel; **18** and Moses goes into the midst of the cloud, and goes up to the mountain, and Moses is on the mountain forty days and forty nights.

25 And YHWH speaks to Moses, saying, **2** "Speak to the sons of Israel, and they take a raised-offering for Me; you take My raised-offering from every man whose heart impels him. **3** And this [is] the raised-offering which you take from them: gold, and silver, and bronze, **4** and blue, and purple, and scarlet, and linen, and goats' [hair], **5** and rams' skins made red, and tachashim skins, and shittim wood, **6** oil for the light, spices for the anointing oil, and for the incense of the spices, **7** shoham stones, and stones for setting for an ephod, and for a breastplate. **8** And they have made a sanctuary for Me, and I have dwelt in their midst; **9** according to all that which I am showing you, the pattern of the Dwelling Place, and the pattern of all its vessels, even so you make [it]. **10** And they have made an ark of shittim wood; two cubits and a half its length, and a cubit and a half its breadth, and a cubit and a half its height; **11** and you have overlaid it [with] pure gold, you overlay it inside and outside, and you have made a ring of gold on it all around. **12** And you have cast four rings of gold for it, and have put [them] on its four feet, even two rings on its one side, and two rings on its second side; **13** and you have made poles of shittim wood, and have overlaid them [with] gold, **14** and have brought the poles into the rings on the sides of the Ark, to carry the Ark by them; **15** the poles are in the rings of the Ark, they are not turned aside from it; **16** and you have put the Testimony which I give to you into the Ark. **17** And you have made a propitiatory covering of pure gold, two cubits and a half its length, and a cubit and a half its breadth; **18** and you have made two cherubim of gold; you make them beaten work at the two ends of the propitiatory covering; **19** and make one cherub at the end on this [side] and one cherub at the end on that [side]; at the propitiatory covering you make the cherubim on its two ends. **20** And the cherubim have been spreading out wings on high, covering over the propitiatory covering with their wings, and their faces [are] toward one another—the faces of the cherubim are toward the propitiatory covering. **21** And you have put the propitiatory covering on the Ark above, and you put the Testimony which I give to you into the Ark; **22** and I have met with you there, and have spoken with you from off the propitiatory covering (from between the two cherubim, which [are] on the Ark of the Testimony) all that which I command you concerning the sons of Israel. **23** And you have made a table of shittim wood, two cubits its length, and a cubit its breadth, and a cubit and a half its height, **24** and have overlaid it [with] pure gold, and have made a crown of gold for it all around, **25** and have made a border of a handbreadth for it all around, and have made a crown of gold for its border all around. **26** And you have made four rings of gold for it, and have put the rings on the four corners, which [are] at its four feet; **27** close by the border are the rings for places for poles to carry the table; **28** and you have made the poles of shittim wood, and have overlaid them with gold, and the table has been carried with them; **29** and you have made its dishes, and its bowls, and its covers, and its cups, with which they pour out; you make them of pure gold; **30** and you have put Bread of the Presentation on the table before Me continually. **31** And you have made a lampstand of pure gold; the lampstand is made of beaten work; its base, and its branch, its calyxes, its knobs, and its flowers are of the same; **32** and six branches are coming out of its sides, three branches of the lampstand out of the first side, and three branches of the lampstand out of the second side; **33** three calyxes made like almonds in one branch, a knob and a flower, and three calyxes made like almonds in one branch, a knob and a flower—so for the six branches which are coming out from the lampstand. **34** And in the lampstand [are] four calyxes made like almonds, its knobs and its flowers; **35** and a knob under two branches of the same, and a knob under two branches of the same, and a knob under two branches of the same, for the six branches which are coming out of the lampstand; **36** their knobs and their branches are of the same, all of it one beaten work of pure gold; **37** and you have made its seven lamps, and [one] has caused its lamps to go up, and it has given light over [and] beyond its front. **38** And its snuffers and its snuff dishes [are] of pure gold; **39** he makes it of a talent of pure gold, with all these vessels. **40** Now see and make [them] by their pattern which you are shown on the mountain."

26 "And you make the Dwelling Place [with] ten curtains of twined linen, and blue, and purple, and scarlet; [with] cherubim, the work of a designer, you make them; **2** the length of the one curtain [is] twenty-eight by the cubit, and the breadth of the one curtain [is] four by the cubit, one measure [is] for all the curtains; **3** five of the curtains are joining to one another, and five curtains are joining to one another. **4** And you have made loops of blue on the edge of the first curtain, at the end in the joining; and so you make in the edge of the outermost curtain, in the joining of the second. **5** You make fifty loops in the first curtain, and you make fifty loops in the edge of the curtain which [is] in the joining of the second, causing the loops to take hold to one another; **6** and you have made fifty hooks of gold, and have joined the curtains to one another by the hooks, and the Dwelling Place has been one. **7** And you have made curtains of goats' [hair] for a tent over the Dwelling Place; you make eleven curtains: **8** the length of one curtain [is] thirty by the cubit, and the breadth of one curtain [is] four by the cubit; one measure [is] for the eleven curtains; **9** and you have joined the five curtains apart, and the six curtains apart, and have doubled the six curtains at the front of the tent. **10** And you have made fifty loops on the edge of the first curtain, the outermost in the joining, and fifty loops on the edge of the curtain which is joining the second; **11** and you have made fifty hooks of bronze, and have brought in the hooks into the loops, and have joined the tent, and it has been one. **12** And the excess remaining in the curtains of the tent—the half of the curtain which is remaining—has spread over the back part of the Dwelling Place; **13** and the cubit on this [side], and the cubit on that [side], in the remaining [part] of the length of the curtains of the tent, is spread out over the sides of the Dwelling Place, on this [side] and on that [side], to cover it; **14** and you have made a covering for the tent of rams' skins made red, and a covering of tachashim skins above. **15** And you have made the boards for the Dwelling Place of shittim wood, standing up; **16** ten cubits [is] the length of the board, and a cubit and a half the breadth of one board; **17** two handles [are] to one board, joined to one another; so you make for all the boards of the Dwelling Place; **18** and you have made the boards of the Dwelling Place—twenty boards for the south side southward; **19** and you make forty sockets of silver under the twenty boards, two sockets under one board for its two handles, and two sockets under the other board for its two handles. **20** And for the second side of the Dwelling Place, for the north side, [are] twenty boards, **21** and their forty sockets of silver, two sockets under one board, and two sockets under another board. **22** And for the sides of the Dwelling Place westward, you make six boards. **23** And you make two boards for the corners of the Dwelling Place in the two sides. **24** And they are pairs beneath, and together they are pairs above its head to one ring; so is it for them both, they are for the two corners. **25** And they have been eight boards, and their sockets of silver [are] sixteen sockets, two sockets under one board, and two sockets under another board. **26** And you have made bars of

EXODUS

shittim wood: five for the boards of the first side of the Dwelling Place, **27** and five bars for the boards of the second side of the Dwelling Place, and five bars for the boards of the side of the Dwelling Place at the two sides, westward; **28** and one has caused the middle bar in the midst of the boards to reach from end to end; **29** and you overlay the boards [with] gold, and you make their rings of gold [for] places for bars, and have overlaid their bars with gold; **30** and you have raised up the Dwelling Place according to its fashion which you have been shown on the mountain. **31** And you have made a veil of blue, and purple, and scarlet, and twined linen, the work of a designer; he makes it [with] cherubim; **32** and you have put it on four pillars of shittim wood, overlaid [with] gold, their pegs [are] of gold, on four sockets of silver. **33** And you have put the veil under the hooks, and have brought in the Ark of the Testimony there within the veil; and the veil has made a separation for you between the holy and the Holy of Holies. **34** And you have put the propitiatory covering on the Ark of the Testimony in the Holy of Holies. **35** And you have set the table at the outside of the veil, and the lampstand opposite the table on the side of the Dwelling Place southward, and you put the table on the north side. **36** And you have made a covering for the opening of the tent of blue, and purple, and scarlet, and twined linen, the work of an embroiderer; **37** and you have made five pillars of shittim [wood] for the covering, and have overlaid them [with] gold, their pegs [are] of gold, and you have cast five sockets of bronze for them."

27 "And you have made the altar of shittim wood, five cubits the length, and five cubits the breadth—the altar is square—and three cubits [is] its height. **2** And you have made its horns on its four corners, its horns are of the same, and you have overlaid it [with] bronze. **3** And you have made its pots to remove its ashes, and its shovels, and its bowls, and its forks, and its fire-pans, even all its vessels you make of bronze. **4** And you have made a grate of network of bronze for it, and have made four rings of bronze on the net on its four extremities, **5** and have put it under the rim of the altar beneath, and the net has been up to the middle of the altar. **6** And you have made poles for the altar, poles of shittim wood, and have overlaid them [with] bronze. **7** And the poles have been brought into the rings, and the poles have been on the two sides of the altar in carrying it. **8** You make it hollow [with] boards; as it has been showed [to] you on the mountain, so do they make [it]. **9** And you have made the court of the Dwelling Place: for the south side southward, hangings for the court of twined linen, the length of the first side [is] one hundred by the cubit, **10** and its twenty pillars and their twenty sockets [are] of bronze, the pegs of the pillars and their fillets [are] of silver; **11** and so for the north side in length, hangings of one hundred [cubits] in length, and its twenty pillars and their twenty sockets [are] of bronze, the pegs of the pillars and their fillets [are] of silver. **12** And [for] the breadth of the court at the west side [are] hangings of fifty cubits, their pillars ten, and their sockets ten. **13** And the breadth of the court at the east side, eastward, [is] fifty cubits. **14** And the hangings at the side [are] fifteen cubits, their pillars three, and their sockets three. **15** And at the second side [are] hangings of fifteen [cubits], their pillars three, and their sockets three. **16** And for the gate of the court [is] a covering of twenty cubits of blue, and purple, and scarlet, and twined linen, the work of an embroiderer; their pillars four, their sockets four. **17** All the pillars of the court all around [are] filleted [with] silver, their pegs [are] silver, and their sockets bronze. **18** The length of the court [is] one hundred by the cubit, and the breadth fifty by fifty, and the height five cubits, of twined linen, and their sockets [are] bronze; **19** for all the vessels of the Dwelling Place, in all its service, and all its pins, and all the pins of the court, [are] bronze. **20** And you command the sons of Israel, and they bring pure oil of beaten olive to you for the light, to cause the lamp to go up continually. **21** In the Tent of Meeting, at the outside of the veil, which [is] over the Testimony, Aaron—his sons also—arrange it from evening until morning before YHWH. [It is] a continuous statute for their generations, from the sons of Israel."

28 "And you, bring your brother Aaron near to you, and his sons with him, from the midst of the sons of Israel, for his being priest to Me, [even] Aaron, Nadab,

EXODUS

and Abihu, Eleazar, and Ithamar, sons of Aaron; **2** and you have made holy garments for your brother Aaron, for glory and for beauty; **3** and you speak to all the wise of heart, whom I have filled [with] a spirit of wisdom, and they have made the garments of Aaron to sanctify him for his being priest to Me. **4** And these [are] the garments which they make: a breastplate, and an ephod, and an upper robe, and an embroidered coat, a turban, and a girdle; indeed, they have made holy garments for your brother Aaron, and for his sons, for his being priest to Me. **5** And they take the gold, and the blue, and the purple, and the scarlet, and the linen, **6** and have made the ephod of gold, blue, and purple, and scarlet, and twined linen, the work of a designer; **7** it has two shoulders joining at its two ends, and it is joined. **8** And the girdle of his ephod which [is] on him, according to its work, is of the same, of gold, blue, and purple, and scarlet, and twined linen. **9** And you have taken the two shoham stones, and have engraved the names of the sons of Israel on them; **10** six of their names on the first stone, and the names of the remaining six on the second stone, according to their births; **11** the work of an engraver of stone, [as] engravings of a signet—you engrave the names of the sons of Israel on the two stones; encompassing, you make them [with] filigrees of gold. **12** And you have set the two stones on the shoulders of the ephod—stones of memorial to the sons of Israel—and Aaron has borne their names before YHWH, on his two shoulders, for a memorial. **13** And you have made filigrees of gold, **14** and you make them [with] two chains of pure gold [as] wreathed work, work of thick bands, and you have put the thick chains on the filigrees. **15** And you have made a breastplate of judgment, the work of a designer; you make it according to the work of the ephod; you make it of gold, blue, and purple, and scarlet, and twined linen; **16** it is square, doubled, a span its length, and a span its breadth. **17** And you have set settings of stone in it, four rows of stone: a row of sardius, topaz, and carbuncle [is] the first row; **18** and the second row [is] emerald, sapphire, and diamond; **19** and the third row [is] opal, agate, and amethyst; **20** and the fourth row [is] beryl, and onyx, and jasper; they are embroidered with gold in their settings, **21** and the stones are according to the names of the sons of Israel, twelve according to their names, [as] engravings of a signet, each with his name; they are for the twelve tribes. **22** And you have made wreathed chains on the breastplate, [the] work of thick bands of pure gold; **23** and you have made two rings of gold on the breastplate, and have put the two rings on the two ends of the breastplate; **24** and you have put the two thick bands of gold on the two rings at the ends of the breastplate; **25** and you put the two ends of the two thick bands on the two filigrees, and you have put [them] on the shoulders of the ephod toward the front of its face. **26** And you have made two rings of gold, and have set them on the two ends of the breastplate, on its border, which [is] toward the side of the ephod within it; **27** and you have made two rings of gold, and have put them on the two shoulders of the ephod, from beneath, in front of its face, close by its joining, above the girdle of the ephod, **28** and they bind the breastplate by its rings to the rings of the ephod with a ribbon of blue, to be above the girdle of the ephod, and the breastplate is not loosed from the ephod. **29** And Aaron has borne the names of the sons of Israel in the breastplate of judgment, on his heart, in his going into the holy place, for a memorial before YHWH continually. **30** And you have put the Lights and the Perfections into the breastplate of judgment, and they have been on the heart of Aaron, in his going in before YHWH, and Aaron has borne the judgment of the sons of Israel on his heart before YHWH continually. **31** And you have made the upper robe of the ephod completely of blue, **32** and the opening for his head has been in its midst; there is a border for its opening all around—the work of a weaver—[and] there is as the opening of a [linen] habergeon for it; it is not torn. **33** And you have made on its hem pomegranates of blue, and purple, and scarlet, on its hem all around, and bells of gold in their midst all around; **34** a bell of gold and a pomegranate [and] a bell of gold and a pomegranate [are] on the hems of the upper robe all around. **35** And it has been on Aaron to minister in, and its sound has been heard in his coming into the holy place before YHWH, and in his going out, and he does not die. **36** And you have made a flower of pure gold, and have engraved

84

engravings of a signet on it: Holy to YHWH; **37** and you have put it on a blue ribbon, and it has been on the turban—it is toward the front of the face of the turban; **38** and it has been on the forehead of Aaron, and Aaron has borne the iniquity of the holy things which the sons of Israel hallow, even all their holy gifts; and it has been on his forehead continually for a pleasing thing for them before YHWH. **39** And you have embroidered the coat of linen, and have made a turban of linen, and you make a girdle—the work of an embroiderer. **40** And you make coats for the sons of Aaron, and you have made girdles for them, and you make caps for them, for glory and for beauty; **41** and you have clothed your brother Aaron with them, and his sons with him, and have anointed them, and have consecrated their hand, and have sanctified them, and they have been priests to Me. **42** And make linen trousers for them to cover the naked flesh; they are from the loins even to the thighs; **43** and they have been on Aaron and on his sons in their going into the Tent of Meeting, or in their drawing near to the altar to minister in the holy place, and they do not bear iniquity nor have they died; [it is] a continuous statute to him and to his seed after him."

29 "And this [is] the thing which you do to them, to hallow them, for being priests to Me: take one bullock, a son of the herd, and two rams, perfect ones, **2** and unleavened bread, and unleavened cakes anointed with oil; you make them of fine wheat flour, **3** and you have put them on one basket, and have brought them near in the basket, also the bullock and the two rams. **4** And you bring Aaron and his sons near to the opening of the Tent of Meeting, and have bathed them with water; **5** and you have taken the garments, and have clothed Aaron with the coat, and the upper robe of the ephod, and the ephod, and the breastplate, and have girded him with the girdle of the ephod, **6** and have set the turban on his head, and have put the holy crown on the turban, **7** and have taken the anointing oil, and have poured [it] on his head, and have anointed him. **8** And you bring his sons near, and have clothed them [with] coats, **9** and have girded them [with] a girdle (Aaron and his sons), and have bound caps on them; and the priesthood has been theirs by a continuous statute, and you have consecrated the hand of Aaron, and the hand of his sons, **10** and have brought the bullock near before the Tent of Meeting, and Aaron has laid—his sons also—their hands on the head of the bullock. **11** And you have slaughtered the bullock before YHWH, at the opening of the Tent of Meeting, **12** and have taken of the blood of the bullock, and have put [it] on the horns of the altar with your finger, and you pour out all the blood at the foundation of the altar; **13** and you have taken all the fat which is covering the innards, and the redundance on the liver, and the two kidneys, and the fat which [is] on them, and have made incense on the altar; **14** and the flesh of the bullock, and his skin, and his dung, you burn with fire at the outside of the camp; it [is] a sin-offering. **15** And you take the first ram, and Aaron and his sons have laid their hands on the head of the ram, **16** and you have slaughtered the ram, and have taken its blood, and have sprinkled [it] around the altar, **17** and you cut the ram into its pieces, and have washed its innards, and its legs, and have put [them] on its pieces, and on its head; **18** and you have made incense with the whole ram on the altar. It [is] a burnt-offering to YHWH, a refreshing fragrance; it [is] a fire-offering to YHWH. **19** And you have taken the second ram, and Aaron has laid—his sons also—their hands on the head of the ram, **20** and you have slaughtered the ram, and have taken of its blood, and have put [it] on the tip of the right ear of Aaron, and on the tip of the right ear of his sons, and on the thumb of their right hand, and on the great toe of their right foot, and have sprinkled the blood around the altar; **21** and you have taken of the blood which [is] on the altar, and of the anointing oil, and have sprinkled [it] on Aaron, and on his garments, and on his sons, and on the garments of his sons with him, and he has been hallowed, he and his garments, and his sons, and the garments of his sons with him. **22** And you have taken from the ram the fat, and the fat tail, and the fat which is covering the innards, and the redundance on the liver, and the two kidneys, and the fat which [is] on them, and the right leg, for it [is] a ram of consecration, **23** and one round cake of bread, and one cake of oiled bread, and one thin cake out of the basket of the unleavened things which [is] before YHWH; **24** and you have set the whole on the hands of Aaron, and on the hands of his sons, and have waved them [for] a wave-offering before YHWH; **25** and you have taken them out of their hand, and have made incense on the altar beside the burnt-offering, for refreshing fragrance before YHWH; it [is] a fire-offering to YHWH. **26** And you have taken the breast from the ram of the consecration which [is] for Aaron, and have waved it [for] a wave-offering before YHWH, and it has become your portion; **27** and you have sanctified the breast of the wave-offering, and the leg of the raised-offering, which has been waved, and which has been lifted up from the ram of the consecration, of that which [is] for Aaron, and of that which [is] for his sons; **28** and it has been for Aaron and for his sons, by a continuous statute from the sons of Israel, for it [is] a raised-offering; and it is a raised-offering from the sons of Israel, from the sacrifices of their peace-offerings—their raised-offering to YHWH. **29** And the holy garments which are Aaron's are for his sons after him, to be anointed in them and to consecrate their hand in them; **30** [for] seven days the priest in his stead (of his sons) puts them on when he goes into the Tent of Meeting to minister in the holy place. **31** And you take the ram of the consecration and have boiled its flesh in the holy place; **32** and Aaron has eaten—his sons also—the flesh of the ram, and the bread which [is] in the basket, at the opening of the Tent of Meeting; **33** and they have eaten those things by which there is atonement to consecrate their hand, to sanctify them; and a stranger does not eat [them], for they [are] holy; **34** and if there is left of the flesh of the consecration or of the bread until the morning, then you have burned that which is left with fire; it is not eaten, for it [is] holy. **35** And you have done thus to Aaron and to his sons, according to all that I have commanded you; [for] seven days you consecrate their hand; **36** and a bullock, a sin-offering, you prepare daily for the atonements, and you have atoned for the altar in your making atonement on it, and have anointed it to sanctify it; **37** [for] seven days you make atonement for the altar, and have sanctified it, and the altar has been most holy; all that is coming against the altar is holy. **38** And this [is] that which you prepare on the altar: two lambs, sons of a year, daily continually; **39** you prepare the first lamb in the morning, and you prepare the second lamb between the evenings; **40** and a tenth part of fine flour mixed with a fourth part of a hin of beaten oil, and a fourth part of a hin of wine [for] a drink-offering, [is] for the first lamb. **41** And you prepare the second lamb between the evenings; according to the present of the morning, and according to its drink-offering, you prepare for it, for refreshing fragrance, a fire-offering to YHWH— **42** a continual burnt-offering for your generations [at] the opening of the Tent of Meeting before YHWH, to where I meet with you to speak to you there, **43** and I have met with the sons of Israel there, and it has been sanctified by My glory. **44** And I have sanctified the Tent of Meeting and the altar, and I sanctify Aaron and his sons for being priests to Me, **45** and I have dwelt in the midst of the sons of Israel, and have become their God, **46** and they have known that I [am] their God YHWH, who has brought them out of the land of Egypt, that I may dwell in their midst; I [am] their God YHWH."

30 "And you have made an altar [for] making incense; you make it of shittim wood; **2** a cubit its length and a cubit its breadth (it is square), and two cubits its height; its horns [are] of the same. **3** And you have overlaid it with pure gold—its top, and around its sides, and its horns; and you have made a crown of gold for it all around; **4** and you make two rings of gold for it, under its crown on its two ribs; you make [them] on its two sides, and they have become places for poles to carry it with them. **5** And you have made the poles of shittim wood, and have overlaid them with gold; **6** and you have put it before the veil, which [is] by the Ark of the Testimony, before the propitiatory covering which [is] over the Testimony, where I meet with you. **7** And Aaron has made incense on it, incense of spices, morning by morning; in his making the lamps right, he makes incense [on] it, **8** and in Aaron's causing the lamps to go up between the evenings, he makes incense [on] it; [it is] a continual incense before YHWH throughout your generations. **9** You do not cause strange incense to go up on it—and burnt-offering and present; and you do not pour out a drink-offering on it; **10** and Aaron has made atonement on its horns once in a year, by the blood of the sin-offering of atonements; once in a year he makes atonement for it, throughout your generations; it [is] most holy to YHWH." **11** And YHWH speaks to Moses, saying, **12** "When you take up the census of the sons of Israel for their numbers, then they have each given an atonement [for] his soul to YHWH in their being numbered, and there is no plague among them in their being numbered. **13** This they give, everyone passing over to those numbered, half a shekel, by the shekel of the holy place (the shekel [is] twenty gerahs); half a shekel [is] the raised-offering to YHWH; **14** everyone passing over to those numbered, from a son of twenty years and upwards, gives the raised-offering of YHWH; **15** the rich do not multiply, and the poor do not diminish from the half-shekel, to give the raised-offering of YHWH, to make atonement for your souls. **16** And you have taken the atonement-money from the sons of Israel, and have given it for the service of the Tent of Meeting; and it has been to the sons of Israel for a memorial before YHWH, to make atonement for your souls." **17** And YHWH speaks to Moses, saying, **18** "And you have made a laver of bronze (and its base of bronze), for washing; and you have put it between the Tent of Meeting and the altar, and have put water [in] there, **19** and Aaron and his sons have washed their hands and their feet from it; **20** they wash [with] water in their going into the Tent of Meeting, and do not die; or in their drawing near to the altar to minister, to make incense [as] a fire-offering to YHWH, **21** then they have washed their hands and their feet, and they do not die, and it has been a continuous statute to them, to him and to his seed, throughout their generations." **22** And YHWH speaks to Moses, saying, **23** "And you, take [these] principal spices for yourself: five hundred [shekels] of liquid myrrh, and the half of that—two hundred and fifty [shekels]—of spice-cinnamon, and two hundred and fifty [shekels] of spice-cane, **24** and five hundred [shekels] of cassia, by the shekel of the holy place, and a hin of olive oil; **25** and you have made it a holy anointing oil, a compound mixture, work of a compounder; it is a holy anointing oil. **26** And with it you have anointed the Tent of Meeting, and the Ark of the Testimony, **27** and the table and all its vessels, and the lampstand and its vessels, and the altar of incense, **28** and the altar of burnt-offering and all its vessels, and the laver and its base; **29** and you have sanctified them, and they have been most holy; all that is coming against them is holy; **30** and you anoint Aaron and his sons, and have sanctified them for being priests to Me. **31** And you speak to the sons of Israel, saying, This is a holy anointing oil to Me, throughout your generations; **32** it is not poured on [the] flesh of man, and you make nothing [else] like it in its proportion; it [is] holy—it is holy to you; **33** a man who compounds [any] like it, or who puts of it on a stranger, has even been cut off from his people." **34** And YHWH says to Moses, "Take to yourself spices—stacte, and onycha, and galbanum—spices and pure frankincense; they are part for part; **35** and you have made it an incense, a compound, work of a compounder, salted, pure, holy; **36** and you have beaten [some] of it small, and have put of it before the Testimony in the Tent of Meeting, to where I meet with you; it is most holy to you. **37** As for the incense which you make, you do not make [any] for yourselves in its proportion; it is holy to you for YHWH; **38** a man who makes [any] like it—to be refreshed by it—has even been cut off from his people."

31 And YHWH speaks to Moses, saying, **2** "See, I have called by name Bezaleel, son of Uri, son of Hur, of the tribe of Judah, **3** and I fill him [with] the Spirit of God, in wisdom, and in understanding, and in knowledge, and in all work, **4** to devise inventions to work in gold, and in silver, and in bronze, **5** and in a carving of stone for settings, and in a carving of wood to work in all work. **6** And I, behold, have given with him Aholiab, son of Ahisamach, of the tribe of Dan, and I have given wisdom in the heart of every wise-hearted one, and they have made all that which I have commanded you. **7** The Tent of Meeting, and the Ark of Testimony, and the propitiatory covering which [is] on it, and all the vessels of the tent, **8** and the table and its vessels, and the pure lampstand and all its vessels, and the altar of the incense, **9** and the altar of the burnt-offering and all its vessels, and the laver and its base, **10** and the colored garments, and the holy garments for Aaron the priest, and the garments of his sons, for acting as priests in; **11** and the anointing oil, and the incense of the spices for the holy place; according to all that I have commanded you—they do." **12** And YHWH speaks to Moses, saying, **13** "And you, speak to the sons of Israel, saying, Surely you keep My Sabbaths, for it [is] a sign between Me and you throughout your generations, to know that I, YHWH, am sanctifying you; **14** and you have kept the Sabbath, for it [is] holy to you, he who is defiling it is certainly put to death—for any who does work in it—that person has even been cut off from the midst of his people. **15** [For] six days work is done, and in the seventh day [is] a Sabbath of holy rest to YHWH; any who does work in the Sabbath day is certainly put to death, **16** and the sons of Israel have observed the Sabbath; to keep the Sabbath throughout their generations [is] a perpetual covenant— **17** it [is] a sign between Me and the sons of Israel for all time; for [in] six days YHWH made the heavens and the earth, and in the seventh day He has ceased and is refreshed." **18** And He gives to Moses, when He finishes speaking with him in Mount Sinai, two tablets of the Testimony, tablets of stone, written by the finger of God.

32 And the people see that Moses is delaying to come down from the mountain, and the people assemble against Aaron, and say to him, "Rise, make gods for us, who go before us, for this Moses—the man who brought us up out of the land of Egypt—we have not known what has happened to him." **2** And Aaron says to them, "Break off the rings of gold which [are] in the ears of your wives, your sons, and your daughters, and bring [them] to me"; **3** and all the people break off the rings of gold which [are] in their ears, and bring [them] to Aaron, **4** and he receives [it] from their hand, and fashions it with an engraving tool, and makes it [into] a molten calf, and they say, "These [are] your gods, O Israel, who brought you up out of the land of Egypt!" **5** And Aaron sees, and builds an altar before it, and Aaron calls, and says, "A festival to YHWH—tomorrow"; **6** and they rise early on the next day, and cause burnt-offerings to ascend, and bring peace-offerings near; and the people sit down to eat and to drink, and rise up to play. **7** And YHWH says to Moses, "Go, descend, for your people whom you have brought up out of the land of Egypt have done corruptly, **8** they have quickly turned aside from the way that I have commanded them; they have made a molten calf for themselves, and bow themselves to it, and sacrifice to it, and say, These [are] your gods, O Israel, who brought you up out of the land of Egypt!" **9** And YHWH says to Moses, "I have seen this people, and behold, it [is] a stiff-necked people; **10** and now, leave Me alone, and My anger burns against them, and I consume them, and I make you become a great nation." **11** And Moses appeases the face of his God YHWH and says, "Why, O YHWH, does Your anger burn against Your people, whom You have brought forth out of the land of Egypt with great power and with a strong hand? **12** Why do the Egyptians speak, saying, He brought them out in calamity to slay them among mountains, and to consume them from off the face of the ground? Turn back from the heat of Your anger, and relent from this calamity against Your people. **13** Be mindful of Abraham, of Isaac, and of Israel, Your servants, to whom You have sworn by Yourself, and to whom You speak: I multiply your seed as stars of the heavens, and all this land, as I have said, I give to your seed, and they have inherited [it] for all time"; **14** and YHWH relents from the evil which He has spoken of doing to His people. **15** And Moses turns, and goes down from the mountain, and the two tablets of the Testimony [are] in his hand, tablets written on both their sides; they [are] written on this [side] and on that [side]; **16** and the tablets are the work of God, and the writing is the writing of God, engraved on the tablets. **17** And Joshua hears the voice of the people in their shouting and says to Moses, "A noise of battle in the camp!" **18** And he says, "It is not the voice of the crying of might, nor is it the voice of the crying of weakness—I am hearing a voice of singing." **19** And it comes to pass, when he has drawn near to the camp, that he sees the calf, and the dancing, and the anger of Moses burns, and he casts the tablets out of his hands, and breaks them below the mountain; **20** and he takes the calf which they have made, and burns [it] with fire, and grinds [it] until [it is] small, and scatters [it] on the face of the waters, and causes the sons of Israel to drink. **21** And Moses says to Aaron, "What has

EXODUS

this people done to you, that you have brought in a great sin on it?" **22** And Aaron says, "Do not let the anger of my lord burn; you have known the people, that it [is beset] with evil; **23** and they say to me, Make gods for us, who go before us, for this Moses—the man who brought us up out of the land of Egypt—we have not known what has happened to him; **24** and I say to them, Whoever has gold, let them break [it] off, and they give [it] to me, and I cast it into the fire, and this calf comes out." **25** And Moses sees the people, that it [is] unbridled, for Aaron has made it unbridled for contempt among its withstanders, **26** and Moses stands in the gate of the camp and says, "Who [is] for YHWH? [Come] to me!" And all the sons of Levi are gathered to him; **27** and he says to them, "Thus said YHWH, God of Israel: Each put his sword by his thigh, pass over and turn back from gate to gate through the camp, and each slay his brother, and each his friend, and each his relation." **28** And the sons of Levi do according to the word of Moses, and there falls of the people on that day about three thousand men, **29** and Moses says, "Consecrate your hand to YHWH today, for a man [is] against his son, and against his brother, so as to bring a blessing on you today." **30** And it comes to pass, on the next day, that Moses says to the people, "You have sinned a great sin, and now I go up to YHWH, perhaps I can atone for your sin." **31** And Moses turns back to YHWH and says, "Ah, now this people has sinned a great sin, that they make a god of gold for themselves; **32** and now, if You take away their sin—and if not—please blot me out of Your scroll which You have written." **33** And YHWH says to Moses, "Whoever has sinned against Me—I blot him out of My scroll; **34** and now, go, lead the people wherever I have spoken to you of; behold, My Messenger goes before you, and in the day of my charging—then I have charged their sin on them." **35** And YHWH plagues the people because they made the calf which Aaron made.

33 And YHWH speaks to Moses, "Go, ascend from this [place], you and the people, whom you have brought up out of the land of Egypt, to the land which I have sworn to Abraham, to Isaac, and to Jacob, saying, I give it to your seed. **2** And I have sent a Messenger before you, and have cast out the Canaanite, the Amorite, and the Hittite, and the Perizzite, the Hivite, and the Jebusite. **3** [Go up] to a land flowing with milk and honey, for I do not go up in your midst, for you [are] a stiff-necked people—lest I consume you in the way." **4** And the people hear this sad thing, and mourn; and none puts his ornaments on him. **5** And YHWH says to Moses, "Say to the sons of Israel: You [are] a stiff-necked people; [in] one moment I could come up into your midst and could have consumed you; and now, put down your ornaments from off you, and I know what I do to you"; **6** and the sons of Israel take off their ornaments at Mount Horeb. **7** And Moses takes the tent, and has stretched it out at the outside of the camp, far off from the camp, and has called it, "Tent of Meeting"; and it has come to pass, everyone seeking YHWH goes out to the Tent of Meeting, which [is] at the outside of the camp. **8** And it has come to pass, at the going out of Moses to the tent, all the people rise, and have stood, each at the opening of his tent, and have looked expectingly after Moses, until his going into the tent. **9** And it has come to pass, at the going in of Moses to the tent, the pillar of the cloud comes down, and has stood at the opening of the tent, and He has spoken with Moses; **10** and all the people have seen the pillar of the cloud standing at the opening of the tent, and all the people have risen and bowed themselves, each at the opening of his tent. **11** And YHWH has spoken to Moses face to face, as a man speaks to his friend; and he has turned back to the camp, and his minister Joshua, son of Nun, a youth, does not depart out of the tent. **12** And Moses says to YHWH, "See, You are saying to me, Bring up this people, and You have not caused me to know whom You send with me; and You have said, I have known you by name, and you have also found grace in My eyes. **13** And now, if, please, I have found grace in Your eyes, please cause me to know Your way, and I know You, so that I find grace in Your eyes, and consider that this nation [is] Your people"; **14** and He says, "My presence goes, and I have given rest to you." **15** And he says to Him, "If Your presence is not going—do not take us up from this [place]; **16** and in what is it known now, that I have found grace in Your eyes—I and Your people—is it not in Your going with us? And we have been distinguished—I and Your people—from all the people who [are] on the face of the ground." **17** And Y<small>HWH</small> says to Moses, "Even this thing which you have spoken I do; for you have found grace in My eyes, and I know you by name." **18** And he says, "Please show me Your glory"; **19** and He says, "I cause all My goodness to pass before your face, and have called concerning the Name of Y<small>HWH</small> before you, and favored him whom I favor, and loved him whom I love." **20** He also says, "You are unable to see My face, for man does not see Me and live"; **21** Y<small>HWH</small> also says, "Behold, a place [is] by Me, and you have stood on the rock, **22** and it has come to pass, in the passing by of My glory, that I have set you in a cleft of the rock, and spread out My hands over you until My passing by, **23** and I have turned aside My hands, and you have seen My back parts, and My face is not seen."

34 And Y<small>HWH</small> says to Moses, "Hew for yourself two tablets of stone like the first, and I have written on the tablets the words which were on the first tablets which you have broken; **2** and be prepared at morning, and you have come up in the morning to Mount Sinai, and have stood before Me there, on the top of the mountain, **3** and no man comes up with you, and also no man is seen in all the mountain, also the flock and the herd do not feed toward the front of that mountain." **4** And he hews two tablets of stone like the first, and Moses rises early in the morning, and goes up to Mount Sinai as Y<small>HWH</small> commanded him, and takes [the] two tablets of stone in his hand. **5** And Y<small>HWH</small> comes down in a cloud, and stations Himself with him there, and calls in the Name of Y<small>HWH</small>, **6** and Y<small>HWH</small> passes over before his face, and calls: "Y<small>HWH</small>, Y<small>HWH</small> God, merciful and gracious, slow to anger, and abundant in kindness and truth, **7** keeping kindness for thousands, taking away iniquity, and transgression, and sin, and not entirely acquitting, charging iniquity of fathers on sons and on sons' sons, on a third and on a fourth [generation]." **8** And Moses hurries, and bows to the earth, and pays respect, **9** and says, "Now if I have found grace in Your eyes, O my Lord, please let my Lord go in our midst (for it [is] a stiff-necked people), and you have forgiven our iniquity and our sin, and have inherited us." **10** And He says, "Behold, I am making a covenant. I do wonders before all your people, which have not been done in all the earth, or in any nation, and all the people in whose midst you [are in] have seen the work of Y<small>HWH</small>, for it [is] fearful—that which I am doing with you. **11** Observe for yourself that which I am commanding you today. Behold, I am casting out from before you the Amorite, and the Canaanite, and the Hittite, and the Perizzite, and the Hivite, and the Jebusite; **12** take heed to yourself lest you make a covenant with the inhabitant of the land into which you are going, lest it become a snare in your midst; **13** for you break down their altars, and you shatter their standing pillars, and you cut down its Asherim; **14** for you do not bow yourselves to another god—for Y<small>HWH</small>, whose Name [is] Zealous, is a zealous God. **15** Lest you make a covenant with the inhabitant of the land, and they have gone whoring after their gods, and have sacrificed to their gods, and [one] has called to you, and you have eaten of his sacrifice, **16** and you have taken of their daughters for your sons, and their daughters have gone whoring after their gods, and have caused your sons to go whoring after their gods; **17** you do not make a molten god for yourself. **18** You keep the Celebration of Unleavened Things; [for] seven days you eat unleavened things, as I have commanded you, at an appointed time, [in] the month of Abib: for in the month of Abib you came out from Egypt. **19** All opening a womb [are] Mine, and every firstling of your livestock born a male, [whether] ox or sheep; **20** and you ransom the firstling of a donkey with a lamb; and if you do not ransom, then you have beheaded it; you ransom every firstborn of your sons, and they do not appear before Me empty. **21** [For] six days you work, and on the seventh day you rest; in plowing-time and in harvest you rest. **22** And you observe [the] Celebration of Weeks for yourself, of [the] first-fruits of wheat-harvest; and the Celebration of Ingathering at the revolution of the year. **23** Three times in a year all your males appear before the Lord Y<small>HWH</small>, God of Israel; **24** for I dispossess nations from before you, and have enlarged your border, and no man desires your land in your going up to appear before your God Y<small>HWH</small> three times in a year. **25** You do not slaughter the blood of My sacrifice with a fermented thing; and the sacrifice of the Celebration of the Passover does not remain until morning. **26** You bring the first of the first-fruits of the land into the house of your God YHWH. You do not boil a kid in its mother's milk." **27** And YHWH says to Moses, "Write these words for yourself, for I have made a covenant with you and with Israel according to the tenor of these words." **28** And he is there with YHWH forty days and forty nights; he has not eaten bread, and he has not drunk water; and he writes on the tablets the matters of the covenant—the Ten Commandments. **29** And it comes to pass, when Moses is coming down from Mount Sinai (and the two tablets of the Testimony [are] in the hand of Moses in his coming down from the mountain), that Moses has not known that the skin of his face has shone in His speaking with him, **30** and Aaron sees—all the sons of Israel also—Moses, and behold, the skin of his face has shone, and they are afraid of coming near to him. **31** And Moses calls to them, and Aaron and all the princes in the congregation return to him, and Moses speaks to them; **32** and afterward all the sons of Israel have come near, and he charges them with all that YHWH has spoken with him in Mount Sinai. **33** And Moses finishes speaking with them, and puts a veil on his face; **34** and in the going in of Moses before YHWH to speak with Him, he turns aside the veil until his coming out; and he has come out and has spoken to the sons of Israel that which he is commanded; **35** and the sons of Israel have seen the face of Moses, that the skin of the face of Moses has shone, and Moses has put back the veil on his face until his going in to speak with Him.

35 And Moses assembles all the congregation of the sons of Israel and says to them, "These [are] the things which YHWH has commanded—to do them: **2** [For] six days work is done, and on the seventh day there is a holy [day] for you, a Sabbath of rest to YHWH; any who does work in it is put to death; **3** you do not burn a fire in any of your dwellings on the Sabbath day." **4** And Moses speaks to all the congregation of the sons of Israel, saying, "This [is] the thing which YHWH has commanded, saying, **5** Take a raised-offering for YHWH from among you; everyone whose heart [is] willing brings it [as] the raised-offering of YHWH: gold, and silver, and bronze, **6** and blue, and purple, and scarlet, and linen, and goats' [hair], **7** and rams' skins made red, and tachashim skins, and shittim wood, **8** and oil for the light, and spices for the anointing oil, and for the spice-incense, **9** and shoham stones, and stones for settings, for an ephod, and for a breastplate. **10** And all the wise-hearted among you come in, and make all that YHWH has commanded: **11** the Dwelling Place, its tent, and its covering, its hooks, and its boards, its bars, its pillars, and its sockets, **12** the Ark and its poles, the propitiatory covering, and the veil of the covering, **13** the table and its poles, and all its vessels, and the Bread of the Presentation, **14** and the lampstand for the light, and its vessels, and its lamps, and the oil for the light, **15** and the altar of incense, and its poles, and the anointing oil, and the spice-incense, and the covering of the opening at the opening of the Dwelling Place, **16** the altar of burnt-offering and the bronze grate which it has, its poles, and all its vessels, the laver and its base, **17** the hangings of the court, its pillars, and their sockets, and the covering of the gate of the court, **18** the pins of the Dwelling Place, and the pins of the court, and their cords, **19** the colored garments, to do service in the holy place, the holy garments for Aaron the priest, and the garments of his sons to act as priest in." **20** And all the congregation of the sons of Israel go out from the presence of Moses, **21** and they come in—every man whom his heart has lifted up, and everyone whom his spirit has made willing—they have brought in the raised-offering of YHWH for the work of the Tent of Meeting, and for all its service, and for the holy garments. **22** And they come in—the men with the women—every willing-hearted one—they have brought in nose-ring, and earring, and seal-ring, and necklace, all golden goods, even everyone who has waved a wave-offering of gold to YHWH. **23** And every man with whom has been found blue, and purple, and scarlet, and linen, and goats' [hair], and rams' skins made red, and tachashim skins, have brought [them] in; **24** everyone lifting up a raised-offering of silver and bronze has brought in the raised-offering of YHWH; and everyone with whom has been found shittim wood for any work of the service brought [it] in. **25** And every wise-hearted woman has spun with her hands, and they bring in yarn—of the blue, and the purple, [and] the scarlet—and the linen; **26** and all the women whose heart has lifted them up in wisdom, have spun the goats' [hair]. **27** And the princes have brought in the shoham stones, and the stones for settings, for the ephod, and for the breastplate, **28** and the spices, and the oil for the light, and for the anointing oil, and for the spice-incense; **29** every man and woman of the sons of Israel (whom their heart has made willing to bring in for all the work which YHWH commanded to be done by the hand of Moses) brought in a willing-offering to YHWH. **30** And Moses says to the sons of Israel, "See, YHWH has called Bezaleel, son of Uri, son of Hur, of the tribe of Judah, by name, **31** and He fills him [with] the Spirit of God, in wisdom, in understanding, and in knowledge, and in all work, **32** even to devise inventions to work in gold, and in silver, and in bronze, **33** and in a carving of stones for settings, and in a carving of wood to work in any work of design. **34** And He has put [it] in his heart to direct, he and Aholiab, son of Ahisamach, of the tribe of Dan; **35** He has filled them with wisdom of heart to do every work, of engraver, and designer, and embroiderer (in blue, and in purple, in scarlet, and in linen), and weaver, who does any work, and of designers of designs."

36 And Bezaleel, and Aholiab, and every wise-hearted man, in whom YHWH has given wisdom and understanding to know to do every work of the service of the holy place, have done according to all that YHWH commanded. **2** And Moses calls to Bezaleel, and to Aholiab, and to every wise-hearted man in whose heart YHWH has given wisdom, everyone whom his heart lifted up, to come near to the work to do it. **3** And they take from before Moses all the raised-offering which the sons of Israel have brought in for the work of the service of the holy place to do it; and still they have brought to him a willing-offering morning by morning. **4** And all the wise men, who are doing all the work of the holy place, each come from his work which they are doing, **5** and speak to Moses, saying, "The people are multiplying to bring in more than sufficient for the service of the work which YHWH commanded [us] to do." **6** And Moses commands, and they cause a voice to pass over through the camp, saying, "Do not let man or woman make anymore work for the raised-offering of the holy place"; and the people are restrained from bringing, **7** and the work has been sufficient for them, for all the work, to do it, and to leave. **8** And all the wise-hearted ones among the doers of the work make the Dwelling Place; he has made them [with] ten curtains of twined linen, and blue, and purple, and scarlet, [with] cherubim, the work of a designer. **9** The length of one curtain [is] twenty-eight by the cubit, and the breadth of one curtain [is] four by the cubit; one measure [is] for all the curtains. **10** And he joins the five curtains to one another, and the [other] five curtains he has joined to one another; **11** and he makes loops of blue on the edge of one curtain, at the end, in the joining; so he has made in the edge of the outmost curtain, in the joining of the second; **12** he has made fifty loops in the first curtain, and he has made fifty loops in the end of the curtain which [is] in the joining of the second; the loops are taking hold on one another. **13** And he makes fifty hooks of gold, and joins the curtains to one another by the hooks, and the Dwelling Place is one. **14** And he makes curtains of goats' [hair] for a tent over the Dwelling Place; eleven curtains he has made them; **15** the length of one curtain [is] thirty by the cubit, and the breadth of one curtain [is] four cubits; one measure [is] for the eleven curtains; **16** and he joins the five curtains apart, and the six curtains apart. **17** And he makes fifty loops on the outer edge of the curtain, in the joining; and he has made fifty loops on the edge of the curtain which is joining the second; **18** and he makes fifty hooks of bronze to join the tent—to be one; **19** and he makes a covering for the tent of rams' skins made red, and a covering of tachashim skins above. **20** And he makes the boards for the Dwelling Place of shittim wood, standing up; **21** ten cubits [is] the length of the [one] board, and a cubit and a half the breadth of the [one] board; **22** two handles [are] to one board, joined to one another; so he has made for all the boards of the Dwelling Place. **23** And he makes the boards for the Dwelling Place; twenty boards for the south side southward; **24** and he has made forty sockets of silver under the twenty boards: two sockets under one board for its two handles, and two sockets under the other board for its two handles. **25** And for the second side of the Dwelling Place, for the north side, he has made twenty boards, **26** and their forty sockets of silver: two sockets under one board, and two sockets under the other board; **27** and for the sides of the Dwelling Place westward, he has made six boards; **28** and he has made two boards for the corners of the Dwelling Place, in the two sides; **29** and they have been twins below, and together they are twins at its head, at one ring; so he has done to both of them at the two corners; **30** and there have been eight boards; and their sockets of silver [are] sixteen sockets, two sockets under one board. **31** And he makes bars of shittim wood: five for the boards of the first side of the Dwelling Place, **32** and five bars for the boards of the second side of the Dwelling Place, and five bars for the boards of the Dwelling Place, for the sides westward; **33** and he makes the middle bar to enter into the midst of the boards from end to end; **34** and he has overlaid the boards with gold, and he has made their rings of gold, places for bars, and he overlays the bars with gold. **35** And he makes the veil of blue, and purple, and scarlet, and twined linen; he has made it [with] cherubim—the work of a designer; **36** and he makes four pillars of shittim [wood] for it, and overlays them with gold; their pegs [are] of gold; and he casts four sockets of silver for them. **37** And he makes a covering for the opening of the tent, of blue, and purple, and scarlet, and twined linen, the work of an embroiderer, **38** also its five pillars, and their pegs; and he overlaid their tops and their fillets [with] gold, and their five sockets [are] bronze.

37And Bezaleel makes the Ark of shittim wood; two cubits and a half its length, and a cubit and a half its breadth, and a cubit and a half its height; **2** and he overlays it with pure gold inside and outside, and makes a wreath of gold for it all around; **3** and he casts four rings of gold for it on its four feet, even two rings on its one side, and two rings on its second side; **4** and he makes poles of shittim wood, and overlays them with gold, **5** and he brings in the poles into the rings, by the sides of the Ark, to carry the Ark. **6** And he makes a propitiatory covering of pure gold, two cubits and a half its length, and a cubit and a half its breadth; **7** and he makes two cherubim of gold; he has made them of beaten work at the two ends of the propitiatory covering— **8** one cherub at the end on this [side] and one cherub at the end on that [side]; he has made the cherubim from [above] the propitiatory covering, at its two ends; **9** and the cherubim are spreading out wings on high, covering over the propitiatory covering with their wings, and their faces [are] toward one another; the faces of the cherubim have been toward the propitiatory covering. **10** And he makes the table of shittim wood; two cubits its length, and a cubit its breadth, and a cubit and a half its height, **11** and overlays it with pure gold, and makes a wreath of gold for it all around. **12** And he makes a border for it of a handbreadth around, and makes a wreath of gold around for its border; **13** and he casts four rings of gold for it, and puts the rings on the four corners which [are] at its four feet; **14** the rings have been close by the border, places for poles to carry the table. **15** And he makes the poles of shittim wood, and overlays them with gold, to carry the table; **16** and he makes the vessels which [are] on the table, its dishes, and its bowls, and its cups, and the cups by which they pour out, of pure gold. **17** And he makes the lampstand of pure gold; he has made the lampstand of beaten work, its base, and its branch, its calyxes, its knobs, and its flowers, have been of the same; **18** and six branches are coming out of its sides, three branches of the lampstand out of its one side, and three branches of the lampstand out of its second side; **19** three calyxes, made like almonds, in one branch, a knob and a flower; and three calyxes, made like almonds, in another branch, a knob and a flower; so for the six branches which are coming out of the lampstand. **20** And in the lampstand [are] four calyxes, made like almonds, its knobs, and its flowers, **21** and a knob under the two branches of the same, and a knob under the two branches of the same, and a knob under the two branches of the same, [are] for the six branches which are coming out of it; **22** their knobs and their branches have been of the same; all of it one beaten work of pure gold. **23** And he makes its seven lamps, and its snuffers, and its snuff-dishes, of pure gold; **24** he has made it of a

EXODUS

talent of pure gold, and with all its vessels. **25** And he makes the incense-altar of shittim wood; a cubit its length, and a cubit its breadth (square), and two cubits its height; its horns have been of the same; **26** and he overlays it with pure gold, around its top and its sides, and its horns; and he makes a wreath of gold for it all around; **27** and he has made two rings of gold for it under its wreath, at its two corners, at its two sides, for places for poles to carry it with them. **28** And he makes the poles of shittim wood, and overlays them with gold; **29** and he makes the holy anointing oil, and the pure spice-incense—work of a compounder.

38 And he makes the altar of burnt-offering of shittim wood; five cubits its length, and five cubits its breadth (square), and three cubits its height; **2** and he makes its horns on its four corners; its horns have been of the same; and he overlays it with bronze; **3** and he makes all the vessels of the altar, the pots, and the shovels, and the sprinkling-pans, the forks, and the fire-pans; he has made all its vessels of bronze. **4** And he makes a bronze grate of network for the altar, under its rim beneath, to its midst; **5** and he casts four rings for the four ends of the bronze grate—places for bars; **6** and he makes the poles of shittim wood, and overlays them with bronze; **7** and he brings in the poles into the rings on the sides of the altar, to carry it with them; he made it hollow [with] boards. **8** And he makes the laver of bronze, and its base of bronze, with the mirrors of the women assembling, who have assembled at the opening of the Tent of Meeting. **9** And he makes the court: at the south side southward, the hangings of the court of twined linen, one hundred by the cubit, **10** their pillars [are] twenty, and their bronze sockets twenty, the pegs of the pillars and their fillets [are] silver; **11** and at the north side, one hundred by the cubit, their pillars [are] twenty, and their sockets of bronze twenty; the pegs of the pillars and their fillets [are] silver; **12** and at the west side [are] hangings, fifty by the cubit; their pillars [are] ten, and their sockets ten; the pegs of the pillars and their fillets [are] silver; **13** and at the east side eastward, fifty cubits. **14** The hangings on the side [are] fifteen cubits, their pillars three, and their sockets three, **15** and at the second side at the gate of the court, on this [side] and on that [side]—hangings of fifteen cubits, their pillars three, and their sockets three; **16** all the hangings of the court around [are] of twined linen, **17** and the sockets for the pillars of bronze, the pegs of the pillars and their fillets of silver, and the overlaying of their tops of silver, and all the pillars of the court are filleted with silver. **18** And the covering of the gate of the court [is] the work of an embroiderer, of blue, and purple, and scarlet, and twined linen; and twenty cubits [is] the length, and the height with the breadth [is] five cubits, corresponding to the hangings of the court; **19** and their pillars [are] four, and their sockets of bronze four, their pegs [are] of silver, and the overlaying of their tops and their fillets [are] of silver; **20** and all the pins for the Dwelling Place, and for the court all around, [are] of bronze. **21** These are the numberings of the Dwelling Place (the Dwelling Place of Testimony), which has been numbered by the command of Moses, the service of the Levites, by the hand of Ithamar son of Aaron the priest. **22** And Bezaleel son of Uri, son of Hur, of the tribe of Judah, has made all that YHWH commanded Moses; **23** and with him [is] Aholiab son of Ahisamach, of the tribe of Dan, an engraver, and designer and embroiderer in blue, and in purple, and in scarlet, and in linen. **24** All the gold which is prepared for the work in all the work of the holy place (and it is the gold of the wave-offering) [is] twenty-nine talents, and seven hundred and thirty shekels, by the shekel of the holy place. **25** And the silver of those numbered of the congregation [is] one hundred talents, and one thousand and seven hundred and seventy-five shekels, by the shekel of the holy place; **26** a bekah for the counted head (half a shekel, by the shekel of the holy place), for everyone who is passing over to those numbered, from a son of twenty years and upwards, for six hundred thousand and three thousand and five hundred and fifty. **27** And one hundred talents of silver are for casting the sockets of the holy place, and the sockets of the veil; one hundred sockets for the hundred talents, a talent for a socket; **28** and [from] the one thousand and seven hundred and seventy-five [shekels] he has made pegs for the pillars, and overlaid their tops, and filleted them. **29** And the bronze of the wave-offering [is] seventy talents, and two thousand and four hundred shekels; **30** and he makes with it the sockets of the opening of the Tent of Meeting, and the bronze altar, and the bronze grate which it has, and all the vessels of the altar, **31** and the sockets of the court all around, and the sockets of the gate of the court, and all the pins of the Dwelling Place, and all the pins of the court all around.

39 And of the blue, and the purple, and the scarlet, they made colored garments, to minister in the holy place; and they make the holy garments which [are] for Aaron, as YHWH has commanded Moses. **2** And he makes the ephod, of gold, blue, and purple, and scarlet, and twined linen, **3** and they expand the plates of gold, and have cut off wires to work in the midst of the blue, and in the midst of the purple, and in the midst of the scarlet, and in the midst of the linen—the work of a designer; **4** they have made shoulder-pieces for it, joining; it is joined at its two ends. **5** And the girdle of his ephod which [is] on it is of the same, according to its work, of gold, blue, and purple, and scarlet, and twined linen, as YHWH has commanded Moses. **6** And they prepare the shoham stones, set [with] filigrees of gold, engraved with engravings of a signet—the names of the sons of Israel on [them]; **7** and he sets them on the shoulders of the ephod—stones of memorial for the sons of Israel, as YHWH has commanded Moses. **8** And he makes the breastplate, the work of a designer, like the work of the ephod, of gold, blue, and purple, and scarlet, and twined linen; **9** it has been square; they have made the breastplate double, a span its length, and a span its breadth, doubled. **10** And they fill four rows of stones in it: a row of a sardius, a topaz, and a carbuncle [is] the first row; **11** and the second row an emerald, a sapphire, and a diamond; **12** and the third row an opal, an agate, and an amethyst; **13** and the fourth row a beryl, an onyx, and a jasper—set [with] filigrees of gold in their settings. **14** And the stones, according to the names of the sons of Israel, are twelve, according to their names, engravings of a signet, each according to his name, for the twelve tribes. **15** And they make wreathed chains on the breastplate, [the] work of thick bands of pure gold; **16** and they make two filigrees of gold, and two rings of gold, and put the two rings on the two ends of the breastplate, **17** and they put the two thick bands of gold on the two rings on the ends of the breastplate; **18** and they have put the two ends of the two thick bands on the two filigrees, and they put them on the shoulders of the ephod, toward the front of its face. **19** And they make two rings of gold, and set [them] on the two ends of the breastplate, on its border, which [is] on the side of the ephod within; **20** and they make two rings of gold, and put them on the two shoulders of the ephod below, in front of its front, close by its joining, above the girdle of the ephod; **21** and they bind the breastplate by its rings to the rings of the ephod, with a ribbon of blue, to be above the girdle of the ephod, and the breastplate is not loosed from off the ephod, as YHWH has commanded Moses. **22** And he makes the upper robe of the ephod, the work of a weaver, completely of blue; **23** and the opening of the upper robe [is] in its midst, as the opening of a [linen] habergeon, [with] a border for its opening all around; it is not torn; **24** and they make on the hems of the upper robe pomegranates of blue, and purple, and scarlet, twined. **25** And they make bells of pure gold, and put the bells in the midst of the pomegranates, on the hems of the upper robe, all around, in the midst of the pomegranates; **26** a bell and a pomegranate [and] a bell and a pomegranate [are] on the hems of the upper robe all around, to minister in, as YHWH has commanded Moses. **27** And they make the coats of linen, the work of a weaver, for Aaron and for his sons, **28** and the turban of linen, and the beautiful caps of linen, and the linen trousers, of twined linen, **29** and the girdle of twined linen, and blue, and purple, and scarlet, the work of an embroiderer, as YHWH has commanded Moses. **30** And they make the flower of the holy crown of pure gold, and write a writing on it, engravings of a signet: "Holy to YHWH"; **31** and they put a ribbon of blue on it, to put [it] on the turban above, as YHWH has commanded Moses. **32** And all the service of the Dwelling Place of the Tent of Meeting is completed; and the sons of Israel do according to all that YHWH has commanded Moses; so they have done. **33** And they bring in the Dwelling Place to Moses, the tent, and all its vessels, its hooks, its boards, its bars, and its pillars, and its sockets; **34** and the covering of rams' skins, which are made red, and the covering of tachashim skins, and the veil of the covering; **35** the Ark of the Testimony and its poles, and the propitiatory covering; **36** the table, all its vessels, and the Bread of the Presentation; **37** the pure lampstand, its lamps, the lamps of arrangement, and all its vessels, and the oil for the light. **38** And the golden altar, and the anointing oil, and the spice-incense, and the covering of the opening of the tent; **39** the bronze altar and the bronze grate which it has, its poles, and all its vessels, the laver and its base; **40** the hangings of the court, its pillars, and its sockets; and the covering for the gate of the court, its cords, and its pins; and all the vessels of the service of the Dwelling Place, for the Tent of Meeting; **41** the colored clothes to minister in the holy place, the holy garments for Aaron the priest, and the garments of his sons, to act as priest in. **42** According to all that YHWH has commanded Moses, so the sons of Israel have done all the service; **43** and Moses sees all the work, and behold, they have done it as YHWH has commanded; so they have done. And Moses blesses them.

40 And YHWH speaks to Moses, saying, **2** "On the first day of the month, in the first month, you raise up the Dwelling Place of the Tent of Meeting, **3** and have set the Ark of the Testimony [in] there, and have covered over the Ark with the veil, **4** and have brought in the table, and set its arrangement in order, and have brought in the lampstand, and caused its lamps to go up. **5** And you have put the golden altar for incense before the Ark of the Testimony, and have put the covering of the opening to the Dwelling Place, **6** and have put the altar of the burnt-offering before the opening of the Dwelling Place of the Tent of Meeting, **7** and have put the laver between the Tent of Meeting and the altar, and have put water [in] there. **8** And you have set the court all around, and have placed the covering of the gate of the court, **9** and have taken the anointing oil, and anointed the Dwelling Place, and all that [is] in it, and hallowed it, and all its vessels, and it has been holy; **10** and you have anointed the altar of the burnt-offering, and all its vessels, and sanctified the altar, and the altar has been most holy; **11** and you have anointed the laver and its base, and sanctified it. **12** And you have brought Aaron and his sons near to the opening of the Tent of Meeting, and have bathed them with water; **13** and you have clothed Aaron with the holy garments, and anointed him, and sanctified him, and he has acted as priest to Me. **14** And you bring his sons near, and have clothed them with coats, **15** and anointed them as you have anointed their father, and they have acted as priests to Me, and their anointing has been to them for a continuous priesthood throughout their generations." **16** And Moses does according to all that YHWH has commanded him; so he has done. **17** And it comes to pass, in the first month, in the second year, on the first of the month, the Dwelling Place has been raised up; **18** and Moses raises up the Dwelling Place, and sets its sockets, and places its boards, and places its bars, and raises its pillars, **19** and spreads the tent over the Dwelling Place, and puts the covering of the tent on it above, as YHWH has commanded Moses. **20** And he takes and puts the Testimony into the Ark, and sets the poles on the Ark, and puts the propitiatory covering on the Ark above; **21** and brings the Ark into the Dwelling Place, and places the veil of the covering, and covers over the Ark of the Testimony, as YHWH has commanded Moses. **22** And he puts the table in the Tent of Meeting, on the side of the Dwelling Place northward, at the outside of the veil, **23** and sets in order the arrangement of bread on it, before YHWH, as YHWH has commanded Moses. **24** And he puts the lampstand in the Tent of Meeting, opposite the table, on the side of the Dwelling Place southward, **25** and causes the lamps to go up before YHWH, as YHWH has commanded Moses. **26** And he sets the golden altar in the Tent of Meeting, before the veil, **27** and makes incense on it—spice-incense—as YHWH has commanded Moses. **28** And he sets the covering [at] the opening of the Dwelling Place, **29** and he has set the altar of the burnt-offering [at] the opening of the Dwelling Place of the Tent of Meeting, and causes the burnt-offering to go up on it, and the present, as YHWH has commanded Moses. **30** And he puts the laver between the Tent of Meeting and the altar, and puts water [in] there for washing, **31** and Moses and Aaron and his sons have washed their hands and their feet at the same; **32** in their going into the Tent of Meeting, and in their drawing near to the altar, they wash, as YHWH has commanded Moses. **33** And he raises up the court all around the Dwelling Place, and around the altar, and places the covering of the gate of the court; and Moses completes the work. **34** And the cloud covers the Tent of Meeting, and the glory of YHWH has filled the Dwelling Place; **35** and Moses has not been able to go into the Tent of Meeting, for the cloud has dwelt on it, and the glory of YHWH has filled the Dwelling Place. **36** And in the going up of the cloud from off the Dwelling Place the sons of Israel journey in all their journeys; **37** and if the cloud does not go up then they do not journey, until the day of its going up. **38** For the cloud of YHWH [is] on the Dwelling Place by day, and fire is in it by night, before the eyes of all the house of Israel in all their journeys.

LEVITICUS

1 And YHWH calls to Moses, and speaks to him out of the Tent of Meeting, saying, **2** "Speak to the sons of Israel, and you have said to them: Any man of you, when he brings an offering near to YHWH out of the livestock—out of the herd or out of the flock—you bring your offering near. **3** If his offering [is] a burnt-offering out of the herd, he brings a male near, a perfect one, to the opening of the Tent of Meeting; he brings it near at his pleasure before YHWH; **4** and he has laid his hand on the head of the burnt-offering, and it has been accepted for him to make atonement for him; **5** and he has slaughtered the son of the herd before YHWH; and sons of Aaron, the priests, have brought the blood near, and sprinkled the blood around the altar, which [is] at the opening of the Tent of Meeting. **6** And he has stripped the burnt-offering, and has cut it into its pieces; **7** and the sons of Aaron the priest have put fire on the altar, and arranged wood on the fire; **8** and sons of Aaron, the priests, have arranged the pieces, with the head and the fat, on the wood, which [is] on the fire, which [is] on the altar; **9** and he washes its innards and its legs with water; and the priest has made incense with the whole on the altar, a burnt-offering, a fire-offering of refreshing fragrance to YHWH. **10** And if his offering [is] out of the flock—out of the sheep or out of the goats—he brings a male near, a perfect one, for a burnt-offering, **11** and he has slaughtered it by the side of the altar northward, before YHWH; and sons of Aaron, the priests, have sprinkled its blood around the altar; **12** and he has cut it into its pieces, and its head and its fat, and the priest has arranged them on the wood, which [is] on the fire, which [is] on the altar; **13** and he washes the innards and the legs with water, and the priest has brought the whole near, and has made incense on the altar; it [is] a burnt-offering, a fire-offering of refreshing fragrance to YHWH. **14** And if his offering [is] a burnt-offering out of the bird to YHWH, then he has brought his offering near out of the turtle-doves or out of the young pigeons, **15** and the priest has brought it near to the altar, and has wrung off its head, and has made incense on the altar, and its blood has been wrung out by the side of the altar; **16** and he has turned aside its crop with its feathers, and has cast it near the altar, eastward, to the place of ashes; **17** and he has cleaved it with its wings (he does not separate [it]), and the priest has made it an incense on the altar, on the wood, which [is] on the fire; it [is] a burnt-offering, a fire-offering of refreshing fragrance to YHWH."

2 "And when a person brings an offering near, a present to YHWH, [and] his offering is of flour, then he has poured oil on it, and has put frankincense on it; **2** and he has brought it to the sons of Aaron, the priests, and one [of the priests] has taken from there the fullness of his hand of its flour and of its oil, besides all its frankincense, and the priest has made incense with its memorial on the altar, a fire-offering of refreshing fragrance to YHWH; **3** and the remnant of the present [is] for Aaron and for his sons, most holy, of the fire-offerings of YHWH. **4** And when you bring an offering near, a present baked in an oven, [it is of] unleavened cakes of flour mixed with oil, or thin unleavened cakes anointed with oil. **5** And if your offering [is] a present [made] on the griddle, it is of flour, mixed with oil, unleavened; **6** divide it into parts, and you have poured oil on it; it [is] a present. **7** And if your offering [is] a present [made] on the frying-pan, it is made of flour with oil, **8** and you have brought in the present which is made of these to YHWH, and [one] has brought it near to the priest, and he has brought it near to the altar, **9** and the priest has lifted up from the present its memorial, and has made incense on the altar, a fire-offering of refreshing fragrance to YHWH; **10** and the remnant of the present [is] for Aaron and for his sons, most holy, of the fire-offerings of YHWH. **11** No present which you bring near to YHWH is made fermented, for you do not make incense [as] a fire-offering to YHWH with any leaven or any honey. **12** An offering of first-[fruits]—you bring them near to YHWH, but they do not go up on the altar for refreshing fragrance. **13** And every offering—your present—you season with salt, and you do not let the salt of the covenant of your God cease from your present; you bring salt near with all your offerings. **14** And if you bring a present of first-fruits near to YHWH, you bring the present of your first-fruits near of green ears, roasted with fire, beaten out [grain] of a fruitful field, **15** and you have put oil on it, and laid frankincense on it, [for] it [is] a present; **16** and the priest has made incense with its memorial from its beaten out [grain], and from its oil, besides all its frankincense, [as] a fire-offering to YHWH."

3 "And if his offering [is] a sacrifice of peace-offerings, if he is bringing near out of the herd, whether male or female, he brings a perfect one near before YHWH, **2** and he has laid his hand on the head of his offering, and has slaughtered it at the opening of the Tent of Meeting, and sons of Aaron, the priests, have sprinkled the blood around the altar. **3** And he has brought near from the sacrifice of the peace-offerings a fire-offering to YHWH, the fat which is covering the innards, and all the fat which [is] on the innards, **4** and the two kidneys, and the fat which [is] on them, which [is] on the flanks, and the redundance on the liver above the kidneys—he turns it aside, **5** and sons of Aaron have made it an incense on the altar, on the burnt-offering which [is] on the wood, which [is] on the fire, [as] a fire-offering of refreshing fragrance to YHWH. **6** And if his offering [is] out of the flock for a sacrifice of peace-offerings to YHWH, male or female, he brings a perfect one near; **7** if he is bringing a sheep near [for] his offering, then he has brought it near before YHWH, **8** and has laid his hand on the head of his offering, and has slaughtered it before the Tent of Meeting, and sons of Aaron have sprinkled its blood around the altar. **9** And he has brought near from the sacrifice of the peace-offerings a fire-offering to YHWH, its fat, the whole fat tail close by the bone—he turns it aside, and the fat which is covering the innards, and all the fat which [is] on the innards, **10** and the two kidneys, and the fat which [is] on them, which [is] on the flanks, and the redundance on the liver above the kidneys—he turns it aside, **11** and the priest has made it an incense on the altar [as] bread of a fire-offering to YHWH. **12** And if his offering [is] a goat, then he has brought it near before YHWH, **13** and has laid his hand on its head, and has slaughtered it before the Tent of Meeting, and sons of Aaron have sprinkled its blood around the altar; **14** and he has brought his offering near from it, a fire-offering to YHWH, the fat which is covering the innards, and all the fat which [is] on the innards, **15** and the two kidneys, and the fat which [is] on them, which [is] on the flanks, and the redundance on the liver above the kidneys—he turns it aside, **16** and the priest has made them an incense on the altar [as] bread of a fire-offering, for refreshing fragrance; all the fat [is] YHWH's. **17** [This is] a continuous statute throughout your generations in all your dwellings: you do not eat any fat or any blood."

4 And YHWH speaks to Moses, saying, **2** "Speak to the sons of Israel, saying, When a person sins through ignorance against any of the commands of YHWH [regarding things] which are not to be done, and has done [something] against one of these— **3** if the priest who is anointed sins according to the guilt of the people, then he has brought near for his sin which he has sinned a bullock, a son of the herd, a perfect one, to YHWH, for a sin-offering, **4** and he has brought in the bullock to the opening of the Tent of Meeting before YHWH, and has laid his hand on the head of the bullock, and has slaughtered the bullock before YHWH. **5** And the priest who is anointed has taken of the blood of the bullock, and has brought it into the Tent of Meeting, **6** and the priest has dipped his finger in the blood, and sprinkled of the blood seven times before YHWH, at the front of the veil of the holy place; **7** and the priest has put of the blood on the horns of the altar of spice-incense before YHWH, which [is] in the Tent of Meeting, and he pours out all the blood of the bullock at the foundation of the altar of the burnt-offering, which [is] at the opening of the Tent of Meeting. **8** And he lifts up from it all the fat of the bullock of the sin-offering, the fat which is covering over the innards, and all the fat which [is] on the innards, **9** and the two kidneys, and the fat which [is] on them, which [is] on the flanks, and the redundance on the liver above the kidneys—he turns it aside, **10** as it is lifted up from the ox of the sacrifice of the peace-offerings; and the priest has made them an incense on the altar of the burnt-offering.

LEVITICUS

11 And the skin of the bullock, and all its flesh, with its head, and with its legs, and its innards, and its dung— **12** he has even brought out the whole bullock to the outside of the camp, to a clean place, to the place of the pouring out of the ashes, and he has burned it on the wood with fire; it is burned beside the place of the pouring out of the ashes. **13** And if all the congregation of Israel errs ignorantly, and the thing has been hidden from the eyes of the assembly, and they have done [something against] one of all the commands of YHWH [regarding things] which are not to be done, and have been guilty; **14** when the sin which they have sinned concerning it has been known, then the assembly has brought a bullock near, a son of the herd, for a sin-offering, and they have brought it in before the Tent of Meeting; **15** and the elderly of the congregation have laid their hands on the head of the bullock, before YHWH, and [one] has slaughtered the bullock before YHWH. **16** And the priest who is anointed has brought in of the blood of the bullock to the Tent of Meeting, **17** and the priest has dipped his finger in the blood, and has sprinkled seven times before YHWH at the front of the veil, **18** and he puts [some] of the blood on the horns of the altar which [is] before YHWH, which [is] in the Tent of Meeting; and he pours out all the blood at the foundation of the altar of the burnt-offering, which [is] at the opening of the Tent of Meeting; **19** and he lifts up all its fat from it, and has made incense on the altar. **20** And he has done to the bullock as he has done to the bullock of the sin-offering, so he does to it; and the priest has made atonement for them, and it has been forgiven them; **21** and he has brought out the bullock to the outside of the camp, and has burned it as he has burned the first bullock; it [is] a sin-offering of the assembly. **22** When a prince sins, and has done [something against] one of all the commands of his God YHWH [regarding things] which are not to be done, through ignorance, and has been guilty, **23** or his sin wherein he has sinned has been made known to him, then he has brought in his offering, a kid of the goats, a male, a perfect one, **24** and he has laid his hand on the head of the goat, and has slaughtered it in the place where he slaughters the burnt-offering before YHWH; it [is] a sin-offering. **25** And the priest has taken of the blood of the sin-offering with his finger, and has put [it] on the horns of the altar of the burnt-offering, and he pours out its blood at the foundation of the altar of the burnt-offering, **26** and he makes incense on the altar with all its fat, as the fat of the sacrifice of the peace-offerings; and the priest has made atonement for him because of his sin, and it has been forgiven him. **27** And if any person of the people of the land sins through ignorance, by his doing [something against] one of the commands of YHWH [regarding things] which are not to be done, and has been guilty, **28** or his sin which he has sinned has been made known to him, then he has brought in his offering, a kid of the goats, a perfect one, a female, for his sin which he has sinned, **29** and he has laid his hand on the head of the sin-offering, and has slaughtered the sin-offering in the place of the burnt-offering. **30** And the priest has taken of its blood with his finger, and has put [it] on the horns of the altar of the burnt-offering, and he pours out all its blood at the foundation of the altar, **31** and he turns aside all its fat, as the fat has been turned aside from off the sacrifice of the peace-offerings, and the priest has made incense on the altar for refreshing fragrance to YHWH; and the priest has made atonement for him, and it has been forgiven him. **32** And if he brings in a sheep [for] his offering, a female for a sin-offering, he brings in a perfect one, **33** and he has laid his hand on the head of the sin-offering, and has slaughtered it for a sin-offering in the place where he slaughters the burnt-offering. **34** And the priest has taken of the blood of the sin-offering with his finger, and has put [it] on the horns of the altar of the burnt-offering, and he pours out all its blood at the foundation of the altar, **35** and he turns aside all its fat, as the fat of the sheep is turned aside from the sacrifice of the peace-offerings, and the priest has made them an incense on the altar, according to the fire-offerings of YHWH, and the priest has made atonement for him, for his sin which he has sinned, and it has been forgiven him."

5 "And when a person sins, and has heard the voice of an oath, and he [is] witness, or has seen, or has known—if he does not declare [it], then he has borne his iniquity. **2** Or when a person comes against anything unclean, or against a carcass of an unclean beast, or against a carcass of unclean livestock, or against a carcass of an unclean teeming creature, and it has been hidden from him, then he [is] unclean and guilty; **3** or when he comes against [the] uncleanness of man, even any of his uncleanness whereby he is unclean, and it has been hidden from him, and he has known, then he has been guilty. **4** Or when a person swears, speaking wrongfully with the lips to do evil, or to do good, even anything which man speaks wrongfully with an oath, and it has been hid from him—when he has known then he has been guilty of one of these; **5** and it has been when he is guilty of one of these, that he has confessed concerning that which he has sinned, **6** and has brought in his guilt-offering to Y<small>HWH</small> for his sin which he has sinned, a female out of the flock, a lamb, or a kid of the goats, for a sin-offering, and the priest has made atonement for him because of his sin. **7** And if his hand does not reach to the sufficiency of a lamb, then he has brought in his guilt-offering—he who has sinned—two turtle-doves or two young pigeons to Y<small>HWH</small>, one for a sin-offering and one for a burnt-offering; **8** and he has brought them to the priest, and has brought near that which [is] for a sin-offering first, and has wrung off its head from its neck, and does not separate [it], **9** and he has sprinkled of the blood of the sin-offering on the side of the altar, and that which is left of the blood is wrung out at the foundation of the altar; it [is] a sin-offering. **10** And he makes the second a burnt-offering, according to the ordinance, and the priest has made atonement for him because of his sin which he has sinned, and it has been forgiven him. **11** And if his hand does not reach to two turtle-doves, or to two young pigeons, then he has brought in his offering—he who has sinned—a tenth of an ephah of flour for a sin-offering; he puts no oil on it, nor does he put frankincense on it, for it [is] a sin-offering, **12** and he has brought it to the priest, and the priest has taken a handful from it of the fullness of his hand—its memorial—and has made incense on the altar, according to the fire-offerings of Y<small>HWH</small>; it [is] a sin-offering. **13** And the priest has made atonement for him, for his sin which he has sinned against one of these, and it has been forgiven him, and [the remnant] has been for the priest, like the present." **14** And Y<small>HWH</small> speaks to Moses, saying, **15** "When a person commits a trespass, and has sinned through ignorance against the holy things of Y<small>HWH</small>, then he has brought in his guilt-offering to Y<small>HWH</small>, a ram, a perfect one, out of the flock, at your valuation [in] silver—shekels by the shekel of the holy place—for a guilt-offering. **16** And that which he has sinned against the holy thing he repays, and is adding to it its fifth, and has given it to the priest, and the priest makes atonement for him with the ram of the guilt-offering, and it has been forgiven him. **17** And when any person sins, and has done [something against] one of all the commands of Y<small>HWH</small> [regarding things] which are not to be done, and has not known, then he has been guilty, and has borne his iniquity. **18** Then he has brought in a ram, a perfect one, out of the flock, at your valuation, for a guilt-offering, to the priest; and the priest has made atonement for him, for his ignorance in which he has erred and he has not known, and it has been forgiven him; **19** it [is] a guilt-offering; he has certainly been guilty before Y<small>HWH</small>."

6 And Y<small>HWH</small> speaks to Moses, saying, **2** "When any person sins, and has committed a trespass against Y<small>HWH</small>, and has lied to his fellow concerning a deposit, or concerning fellowship, or concerning violent robbery, or has oppressed his fellow; **3** or has found a lost thing, and has lied concerning it, and has sworn to a falsehood, concerning one of all [these] which man does, sinning in them: **4** then it has been, when he sins and has been guilty, that he has returned the plunder which he has violently taken away, or the thing which he has gotten by oppression, or the deposit which has been deposited with him, or the lost thing which he has found; **5** or all that concerning which he swears falsely, he has even repaid it in its principal, and he is adding to it its fifth; he gives it to him whose it [is] in the day of his guilt-offering. **6** And he brings his guilt-offering to Y<small>HWH</small>, a ram, a perfect one, out of the flock, at your valuation, for a guilt-offering, to the priest, **7** and the priest has made atonement for him before Y<small>HWH</small>, and it has been forgiven him, concerning one thing of all that he does, by being guilty therein." **8** And Y<small>HWH</small> speaks to Moses, saying, **9** "Command Aaron and his sons, saying, This [is] a law of the burnt-offering: the burnt-offering on [the] burning pile [remains] on the altar all the night until the morning, and the fire of the altar is burning on it. **10** And the priest has put on his long robe of fine linen, and he puts his fine linen trousers on his flesh, and has lifted up the ashes which the fire consumes with the burnt-offering on the altar, and has put them near the altar; **11** and he has stripped off his garments, and has put on other garments, and has brought out the ashes to the outside of the camp, to a clean place. **12** And the fire on the altar is burning on it, it is not quenched, and the priest has burned wood on it morning by morning, and has arranged the burnt-offering on it, and has made incense on it [with] the fat of the peace-offerings; **13** fire is continually burning on the altar, it is not quenched. **14** And this [is] a law of the present: sons of Aaron have brought it near before YHWH to the front of the altar, **15** and [one] has lifted up of it with his hand from the flour of the present, and from its oil, and all the frankincense which [is] on the present, and has made incense on the altar of refreshing fragrance—its memorial to YHWH. **16** And Aaron and his sons eat the remnant of it; it is eaten [with] unleavened things in a holy place—they eat it in the court of the Tent of Meeting. **17** It is not baked [with] anything fermented; I have given it [for] their portion out of My fire-offerings; it [is] most holy, like the sin-offering, and like the guilt-offering. **18** Every male among the sons of Aaron eats it—a continuous statute throughout your generations, out of the fire-offerings of YHWH. All that comes against them is holy." **19** And YHWH speaks to Moses, saying, **20** "This [is] an offering of Aaron and of his sons, which they bring near to YHWH in the day of his being anointed: a tenth of the ephah of flour [for] a continual present, half of it in the morning, and half of it in the evening; **21** it is made on a griddle with oil—you bring it in stirred; you bring baked pieces of the present near [for] a refreshing fragrance to YHWH. **22** And the priest who is anointed in his stead, from among his sons, makes it; [it is] a continuous statute of YHWH; it is completely burned as incense; **23** and every present of a priest is a whole burnt-offering; it is not eaten." **24** And YHWH speaks to Moses, saying, **25** "Speak to Aaron and to his sons, saying, This [is] a law of the sin-offering: in the place where the burnt-offering is slaughtered, the sin-offering is slaughtered before YHWH; it [is] most holy. **26** The priest who is making atonement with it eats it; it is eaten in a holy place, in the court of the Tent of Meeting; **27** all that comes against its flesh is holy, and when [any] of its blood is sprinkled on the garment, that on which it is sprinkled you wash in the holy place; **28** and an earthen vessel in which it is boiled is broken, and if it is boiled in a bronze vessel, then it is scoured and rinsed with water. **29** Every male among the priests eats it—it [is] most holy; **30** and no sin-offering, [any] of whose blood is brought into the Tent of Meeting to make atonement in the holy place, is eaten; it is burned with fire."

7 "And this [is] a law of the guilt-offering: it [is] most holy; **2** in the place where they slaughter the burnt-offering they slaughter the guilt-offering, and he sprinkles its blood on the altar all around, **3** and he brings near all its fat from it, the fat tail, and the fat which is covering the innards, **4** and the two kidneys, and the fat which [is] on them, which [is] on the flanks, and the redundance on the liver above the kidneys—he turns it aside; **5** and the priest has made them an incense on the altar, a fire-offering to YHWH; it [is] a guilt-offering. **6** Every male among the priests eats it; it is eaten in a holy place—it [is] most holy; **7** as [is] a sin-offering, so [is] a guilt-offering; one law [is] for them; the priest who makes atonement by it—it is his. **8** And the priest who is bringing any man's burnt-offering near, the skin of the burnt-offering which he has brought near, it is the priest's, his own; **9** and every present which is baked in an oven, and all done in a frying-pan, and on a griddle, [is] the priest's who is bringing it near; it is his; **10** and every present, mixed with oil or dry, is for all the sons of Aaron—one as another. **11** And this [is] a law of the sacrifice of the peace-offerings which [one] brings near to YHWH: **12** if he brings it near for a thank-offering, then he has brought near with the sacrifice of thank-offering unleavened cakes mixed with oil, and thin unleavened cakes anointed with oil, and of stirred flour cakes mixed with oil; **13** besides the cakes, he brings fermented bread near [with] his offering, besides the sacrifice of thank-offering of his peace-offerings; **14** and he has brought near from it one [cake] from every offering [as] a raised-offering to YHWH for the priest who is sprinkling the blood of the peace-offerings; it is for him; **15** as for the flesh of the sacrifice of the thank-offering of his peace-offerings, it is eaten in the day of his offering; he does not leave of it until morning. **16** And if the sacrifice of his offering [is] a vow or free-will offering, it is eaten in the day of his bringing his sacrifice near; and on the next day the remnant of it is also eaten; **17** and the remnant of the flesh of the sacrifice is burned with fire on the third day; **18** and if any of the flesh of the sacrifice of his peace-offerings is eaten at all on the third day, it is not pleasing; it is not reckoned for him who is bringing it near; it is an abomination, and the person who is eating of it bears his iniquity. **19** And the flesh which comes against any unclean thing is not eaten; it is burned with fire; as for the flesh, every clean one eats of the flesh; **20** and the person who eats of the flesh of the sacrifice of the peace-offerings which [are] YHWH's, and his uncleanness [is] on him, indeed, that person has been cut off from his people. **21** And when a person comes against anything unclean, of the uncleanness of man, or of the uncleanness of beasts, or of any unclean teeming creature, and has eaten of the flesh of the sacrifice of the peace-offerings which [are] YHWH's, indeed, that person has been cut off from his people." **22** And YHWH speaks to Moses, saying, **23** "Speak to the sons of Israel, saying, You do not eat any fat of ox, and sheep, and goat; **24** and the fat of a carcass, and the fat of a torn thing, is prepared for any work, but you certainly do not eat it; **25** for whoever eats the fat of the beast, of which [one] brings near [as] a fire-offering to YHWH, indeed, the person who eats [it] has been cut off from his people. **26** And you do not eat any blood in all your dwellings, of bird, or of beast; **27** any person who eats any blood, indeed, that person has been cut off from his people." **28** And YHWH speaks to Moses, saying, **29** "Speak to the sons of Israel, saying, He who is bringing the sacrifice of his peace-offerings near to YHWH brings in his offering to YHWH from the sacrifice of his peace-offerings; **30** his own hands bring in the fire-offerings of YHWH; the fat beside the breast—he brings it in with the breast to wave it [as] a wave-offering before YHWH. **31** And the priest has made incense with the fat on the altar, and the breast has been Aaron's and his sons; **32** and you give the right leg to the priest [as] a raised-offering of the sacrifices of your peace-offerings; **33** he from the sons of Aaron who is bringing the blood of the peace-offerings and the fat near—the right leg is for a portion for him. **34** For I have taken the breast of the wave-offering and the leg of the raised-offering from the sons of Israel, from the sacrifices of their peace-offerings, and I give them to Aaron the priest, and to his sons, by a continuous statute, from the sons of Israel." **35** This [is] an anointed portion [for] Aaron, and an anointed portion [for] his sons out of the fire-offerings of YHWH, in the day he has brought them near to act as priest of YHWH, **36** which YHWH has commanded to give to them from the sons of Israel, in the day of His anointing them—a continuous statute throughout their generations. **37** This [is] the law for burnt-offering, for present, and for sin-offering, and for guilt-offering, and for consecrations, and for a sacrifice of the peace-offerings, **38** which YHWH has commanded Moses in Mount Sinai, in the day of His commanding the sons of Israel to bring their offerings near to YHWH, in the wilderness of Sinai.

8 And YHWH speaks to Moses, saying, **2** "Take Aaron and his sons with him, and the garments, and the anointing oil, and the bullock of the sin-offering, and the two rams, and the basket of unleavened things, **3** and assemble all the congregation to the opening of the Tent of Meeting." **4** And Moses does as YHWH has commanded him, and the congregation is assembled to the opening of the Tent of Meeting, **5** and Moses says to the congregation, "This [is] the thing which YHWH has commanded to do." **6** And Moses brings Aaron and his sons near, and bathes them with water, **7** and puts the coat on him, and girds him with the girdle, and clothes him with the upper robe, and puts the ephod on him, and girds him with the girdle of the ephod, and binds [it] to him with it, **8** and puts the breastplate on him, and puts the Lights and the Perfections into the breastplate, **9** and puts the turban on his head, and puts the golden flower of the holy crown on the turban, toward the front of its face, as YHWH has commanded Moses. **10** And Moses takes the anointing oil, and anoints the Dwelling Place, and all that [is] in it, and sanctifies them; **11** and he sprinkles of it on the altar seven times, and anoints the altar, and all its vessels, and the laver, and its base, to sanctify them; **12** and he pours of the anointing oil on the head of Aaron, and anoints him to sanctify him. **13** And Moses brings the sons of Aaron near, and clothes them [with] coats, and girds them [with] girdles, and binds caps to them, as YHWH has commanded Moses. **14** And he brings the bullock of the sin-offering near, and Aaron lays—his sons also—their hands on the head of the bullock of the sin-offering, **15** and [one] slaughters, and Moses takes the blood, and puts [it] around the horns of the altar with his finger, and cleanses the altar, and he has poured out the blood at the foundation of the altar, and sanctifies it, to make atonement on it. **16** And he takes all the fat that [is] on the innards, and the redundance on the liver, and the two kidneys, and their fat, and Moses makes incense on the altar, **17** and the bullock, and its skin, and its flesh, and its dung, he has burned with fire, at the outside of the camp, as YHWH has commanded Moses. **18** And he brings the ram of the burnt-offering near, and Aaron and his sons lay their hands on the head of the ram, **19** and [one] slaughters, and Moses sprinkles the blood around the altar; **20** and he has cut the ram into its pieces, and Moses makes incense with the head, and the pieces, and the fat, **21** and he has washed the innards and the legs with water, and Moses makes incense with the whole ram on the altar; it [is] a burnt-offering for refreshing fragrance; it [is] a fire-offering to YHWH, as YHWH has commanded Moses. **22** And he brings the second ram near, a ram of the consecrations, and Aaron and his sons lay their hands on the head of the ram, **23** and [one] slaughters, and Moses takes of its blood, and puts [it] on the tip of the right ear of Aaron, and on the thumb of his right hand, and on the great toe of his right foot; **24** and he brings the sons of Aaron near, and Moses puts of the blood on the tip of their right ear, and on the thumb of their right hand, and on the great toe of their right foot. And Moses sprinkles the blood around the altar, **25** and takes the fat, and the fat tail, and all the fat that [is] on the innards, and the redundance on the liver, and the two kidneys, and their fat, and the right leg; **26** and out of the basket of unleavened things, which [is] before YHWH, he has taken one unleavened cake, and one cake of oiled bread, and one thin cake, and puts [them] on the fat, and on the right leg; **27** and he puts the whole on the hands of Aaron, and on the hands of his sons, and waves them [as] a wave-offering before YHWH. **28** And Moses takes them from off their hands, and makes incense on the altar, on the burnt-offering—they [are] consecrations for refreshing fragrance; it [is] a fire-offering to YHWH; **29** and Moses takes the breast, and waves it [as] a wave-offering before YHWH; it has been for Moses for a portion of the ram of the consecrations, as YHWH has commanded Moses. **30** And Moses takes of the anointing oil, and of the blood which [is] on the altar, and sprinkles [them] on Aaron, on his garments, and on his sons, and on the garments of his sons with him, and he sanctifies Aaron, his garments, and his sons, and the garments of his sons with him. **31** And Moses says to Aaron and to his sons, "Boil the flesh at the opening of the Tent of Meeting, and there you eat it and the bread which [is] in the basket of the consecrations, as I have commanded, saying, Aaron and his sons eat it. **32** And the remnant of the flesh and of the bread you burn with fire; **33** and you do not go out from the opening of the Tent of Meeting [for] seven days, until the day of the fullness, the days of your consecration—for seven days he consecrates your hand; **34** as he has done on this day, YHWH has commanded to do, to make atonement for you; **35** and you abide at the opening of the Tent of Meeting by day and by night [for] seven days, and you have kept the charge of YHWH, and do not die, for so I have been commanded." **36** And Aaron does—his sons also—all the things which YHWH has commanded by the hand of Moses.

9 And it comes to pass on the eighth day, Moses has called for Aaron and for his sons, and for [the] elderly of Israel, **2** and he says to Aaron, "Take a calf for yourself, a son of the herd, for a sin-offering, and a ram for a burnt-offering, perfect ones, and bring [them] near before YHWH. **3** And you

LEVITICUS

speak to the sons of Israel, saying, Take a kid of the goats for a sin-offering, and a calf, and a lamb, sons of a year, perfect ones, for a burnt-offering, **4** and a bullock and a ram for peace-offerings, to sacrifice before YHWH, and a present mixed with oil; for today YHWH has appeared to you." **5** And they take that which Moses has commanded to the front of the Tent of Meeting, and all the congregation draws near and stands before YHWH; **6** and Moses says, "This [is] the thing which YHWH has commanded; do [it], and the glory of YHWH appears to you." **7** And Moses says to Aaron, "Draw near to the altar, and make your sin-offering, and your burnt-offering, and make atonement for yourself, and for the people, and make the offering of the people, and make atonement for them, as YHWH has commanded." **8** And Aaron draws near to the altar, and slaughters the calf of the sin-offering, which [is] for himself; **9** and the sons of Aaron bring the blood near to him, and he dips his finger in the blood, and puts [it] on the horns of the altar, and he has poured out the blood at the foundation of the altar; **10** and the fat, and the kidneys, and the redundance of the liver, of the sin-offering, he has made incense on the altar, as YHWH has commanded Moses; **11** and he has burned the flesh and the skin with fire, at the outside of the camp. **12** And he slaughters the burnt-offering, and the sons of Aaron have presented the blood to him, and he sprinkles it around the altar; **13** and they have presented the burnt-offering to him, by its pieces, and the head, and he makes incense on the altar; **14** and he washes the innards and the legs, and makes incense for the burnt-offering on the altar. **15** And he brings the offering of the people near, and takes the goat of the sin-offering which [is] for the people, and slaughters it, and makes it a sin-offering, like the first; **16** and he brings the burnt-offering near, and makes it, according to the ordinance; **17** and he brings the present near, and fills his palm with it, and makes incense on the altar, apart from the burnt-offering of the morning. **18** And he slaughters the bullock and the ram, a sacrifice of the peace-offerings, which [are] for the people, and sons of Aaron present the blood to him (and he sprinkles it around the altar), **19** and the fat of the bullock, and of the ram, the fat tail, and the covering [of the innards], and the kidneys, and the redundance on the liver, **20** and they set the fat on the breasts, and he makes incense with the fat on the altar; **21** and Aaron has waved the breasts and the right leg [as] a wave-offering before YHWH, as He has commanded Moses. **22** And Aaron lifts up his hand toward the people, and blesses them, and comes down from making the sin-offering, and the burnt-offering, and the peace-offerings. **23** And Moses goes in—Aaron also—to the Tent of Meeting, and they come out, and bless the people, and the glory of YHWH appears to all the people; **24** and fire comes out from before YHWH, and consumes the burnt-offering and the fat on the altar; and all the people see, and cry aloud, and fall on their faces.

10 And the sons of Aaron, Nadab and Abihu, each take his censer, and put fire in them, and put incense on it, and bring strange fire near before YHWH, which He has not commanded them; **2** and fire goes out from before YHWH and consumes them, and they die before YHWH. **3** And Moses says to Aaron, "It [is] that which YHWH has spoken, saying, By those drawing near to Me I am sanctified, and in the face of all the people I am honored"; and Aaron is silent. **4** And Moses calls to Mishael and to Elzaphan, sons of Uzziel, uncle of Aaron, and says to them, "Come near, carry your brothers from the front of the holy place to the outside of the camp"; **5** and they come near, and carry them in their coats to the outside of the camp, as Moses has spoken. **6** And Moses says to Aaron and his sons, to Eleazar and to Ithamar, "You do not uncover your heads, and you do not tear your garments, that you do not die, and He is angry on all the congregation; as for your brothers, the whole house of Israel, they lament the burning which YHWH has kindled; **7** and you do not go out from the opening of the Tent of Meeting, lest you die, for the anointing oil of YHWH [is] on you"; and they do according to the word of Moses. **8** And YHWH speaks to Aaron, saying, **9** "You do not drink wine and strong drink, you and your sons with you, in your going into the Tent of Meeting, and you do not die—a continuous statute throughout your generations, **10** so as to make a separation between the holy and the common, and between the unclean and the

LEVITICUS

pure; **11** and to teach the sons of Israel all the statutes which YHWH has spoken to them by the hand of Moses." **12** And Moses speaks to Aaron and his sons, to Eleazar and to Ithamar, who are left, "Take the present that is left from the fire-offerings of YHWH, and eat it unleavened near the altar, for it [is] most holy, **13** and you have eaten it in the holy place, for it [is] your portion, and the portion of your sons, from the fire-offerings of YHWH; for so I have been commanded. **14** And you eat the breast of the wave-offering and the leg of the raised-offering in a clean place, you, and your sons, and your daughters with you; they have been given for your portion and the portion of your sons, out of the sacrifices of peace-offerings of the sons of Israel; **15** the leg of the raised-offering, and breast of the wave-offering, besides fire-offerings of the fat, they bring in to wave [as] a wave-offering before YHWH, and it has been to you, and to your sons with you, by a continuous statute, as YHWH has commanded." **16** And Moses has diligently sought the goat of the sin-offering, and behold, it is burned, and he is angry against Eleazar and against Ithamar, sons of Aaron, who are left, saying, **17** "Why have you not eaten the sin-offering in the holy place, for it [is] most holy—and He has given it to you to take away the iniquity of the congregation, to make atonement for them before YHWH? **18** Behold, its blood has not been brought into the holy place within; eating you eat it in the holy place, as I have commanded." **19** And Aaron speaks to Moses, "Behold, today they have brought their sin-offering and their burnt-offering near before YHWH; and [things] like these meet me, yet I have eaten a sin-offering today; is it good in the eyes of YHWH?" **20** And Moses listens, and it is good in his eyes.

11 And YHWH speaks to Moses and to Aaron, saying to them, **2** "Speak to the sons of Israel, saying, This [is] the beast which you eat out of all the beasts which [are] on the earth: **3** any dividing a hoof, and cleaving the cleft of the hooves, bringing up the cud, among the beasts—you eat it. **4** Only, this you do not eat, of those bringing up the cud, and of those dividing the hoof: the camel, though it is bringing up the cud, yet the hoof is not dividing—it [is] unclean to you; **5** and the hyrax, though it is bringing up the cud, yet the hoof is not divided—it [is] unclean to you; **6** and the hare, though it is bringing up the cud, yet the hoof has not divided—it [is] unclean to you; **7** and the sow, though it is dividing the hoof, and cleaving the cleft of the hoof, yet it does not bring up the cud—it [is] unclean to you. **8** You do not eat of their flesh, and you do not come against their carcass—they [are] unclean to you. **9** This you eat of all which [are] in the waters: anything that has fins and scales in the waters, in the seas, and in the brooks, them you eat; **10** and anything that does not have fins and scales in the seas, and in the brooks, of any teeming creature of the waters, and of any creature which lives, which [is] in the waters—they [are] an abomination to you; **11** indeed, they are an abomination to you; you do not eat of their flesh, and you detest their carcass. **12** Anything that does not have fins and scales in the waters—it [is] an abomination to you. **13** And these you detest of the bird—they are not eaten, they [are] an abomination: the eagle, and the bearded vulture, and the osprey, **14** and the kite, and the falcon after its kind, **15** every raven after its kind, **16** and the ostrich, and the nightjar [[or male ostrich]], and the seagull, and the hawk after its kind, **17** and the little owl, and the cormorant, and the great owl, **18** and the waterhen, and the pelican, and the Egyptian vulture, **19** and the stork, the heron after its kind, and the hoopoe, and the bat. **20** Every teeming creature which is flying, which is going on four [legs]—it [is] an abomination to you. **21** Only, this you eat of any teeming thing which is flying, which is going on four, which has legs above its feet, to move with them on the earth; **22** these of them you eat: the locust after its kind, and the bald locust after its kind, and the cricket after its kind, and the grasshopper after its kind; **23** and every teeming thing which is flying, which has four feet—it [is] an abomination to you. **24** And you are made unclean by these; anyone who is coming against their carcass is unclean until the evening; **25** and anyone who is lifting up of their carcass washes his garments, and has been unclean until the evening— **26** even every beast which is dividing the hoof, and is not cloven-footed, and is not bringing up the cud—they [are] unclean to you; anyone who is coming against them is unclean. **27** And anything

LEVITICUS

going on its paws, among all the beasts which are going on four—they [are] unclean to you; anyone who is coming against their carcass is unclean until the evening; **28** and he who is lifting up their carcass washes his garments, and has been unclean until the evening—they [are] unclean to you. **29** And this [is] the unclean to you among the teeming things which are teeming on the earth: the weasel, and the muroid, and the tortoise [[*or* large lizard]] after its kind, **30** and the gecko [[*or* ferret]], and the chameleon, and the lizard, and the snail, and the mole; **31** these [are] the unclean to you among all which are teeming; anyone who is coming against them in their death is unclean until the evening. **32** And anything on which anyone of them falls, in their death, is unclean, of any vessel of wood or garment or skin or sack, any vessel in which work is done is brought into water, and has been unclean until the evening, then it has been clean; **33** and any earthen vessel, into the midst of which [any] one of them falls, all that [is] in its midst is unclean, and you break it. **34** Of all the food which is eaten, that on which comes [such] water, is unclean, and all drink which is drunk in any [such] vessel is unclean; **35** and anything on which [any] of their carcass falls is unclean; oven or double pots, it is broken down, they [are] unclean, indeed, they are unclean to you. **36** Only, a fountain or pit, a collection of water, is clean, but that which is coming against their carcass is unclean; **37** and when [any] of their carcass falls on any sown seed which is sown—it [is] clean; **38** and when water is put on the seed, and [any] of its carcass has fallen on it—it [is] unclean to you. **39** And when any of the beasts which are for food for you dies, he who is coming against its carcass is unclean until the evening; **40** and he who is eating of its carcass washes his garments, and has been unclean until the evening; and he who is lifting up its carcass washes his garments, and has been unclean until the evening. **41** And every teeming thing which is teeming on the earth is an abomination, it is not eaten; **42** anything going on the belly, and any going on four, to every multiplier of feet, to every teeming thing which is teeming on the earth—you do not eat them, for they [are] an abomination; **43** you do not make yourselves abominable with any teeming thing which is teeming, nor do you make yourselves unclean with them, so that you have been unclean with them. **44** For I [am] your God Y<small>HWH</small>, and you have sanctified yourselves, and you have been holy, for I [am] holy; and you do not defile your persons with any teeming thing which is creeping on the earth; **45** for I [am] Y<small>HWH</small> who am bringing you up out of the land of Egypt to become your God; and you have been holy, for I [am] holy. **46** This [is] a law of the beasts, and of the bird, and of every living creature which is moving in the waters, and of every creature which is teeming on the earth, **47** to make separation between the unclean and the pure, and between the beast that is eaten, and the beast that is not eaten."

12 And Y<small>HWH</small> speaks to Moses, saying, **2** "Speak to the sons of Israel, saying, A woman when she gives seed, and has borne a male, then she has been unclean [for] seven days; she is unclean according to the days of separation for her sickness; **3** and in the eighth day the flesh of his foreskin is circumcised; **4** and she abides in the blood of her cleansing [for] thirty-three days; she does not come against any holy thing, and she does not go into the sanctuary, until the fullness of the days of her cleansing. **5** And if she bears a female, then she has been unclean [for] two weeks, as in her separation; and she abides by the blood of her cleansing [for] sixty-six days. **6** And in the fullness of the days of her cleansing for son or for daughter she brings in a lamb, a son of a year, for a burnt-offering, and a young pigeon or a turtle-dove for a sin-offering, to the opening of the Tent of Meeting, to the priest; **7** and he has brought it near before Y<small>HWH</small>, and has made atonement for her, and she has been cleansed from the fountain of her blood; this [is] the law of her who is bearing, in regard to a male or to a female. **8** And if her hand does not find the sufficiency of a sheep, then she has taken two turtle-doves or two young pigeons, one for a burnt-offering and one for a sin-offering, and the priest has made atonement for her, and she has been cleansed."

13 And Y<small>HWH</small> speaks to Moses and to Aaron, saying, **2** "When a man has a rising, or scab, or bright spot in the skin of his flesh, and it has become a leprous

LEVITICUS

plague in the skin of his flesh, then he has been brought to Aaron the priest, or to one of his sons the priests; **3** and the priest has seen the plague in the skin of the flesh, and the hair in the plague has turned white, and the appearance of the plague [is] deeper than the skin of his flesh—it [is] a plague of leprosy, and the priest has seen him, and has pronounced him unclean. **4** And if the bright spot is white in the skin of his flesh, and its appearance is not deeper than the skin, and its hair has not turned white, then the priest has shut up [him who has] the plague [for] seven days. **5** And the priest has seen him on the seventh day, and behold, the plague has stood in his eyes, the plague has not spread in the skin, and the priest has shut him up [for] a second seven days. **6** And the priest has seen him on the second seventh day, and behold, the plague has faded, and the plague has not spread in the skin, and the priest has pronounced him clean; it [is] a scab, and he has washed his garments, and has been clean. **7** And if the scab spreads greatly in the skin, after his being seen by the priest for his cleansing, then he has been seen a second time by the priest; **8** and the priest has seen, and behold, the scab has spread in the skin, and the priest has pronounced him unclean; it [is] leprosy. **9** When a plague of leprosy is in a man, then he has been brought to the priest, **10** and the priest has seen, and behold, a white rising in the skin, and it has turned the hair white, and a quickening of raw flesh [is] in the rising— **11** it [is] an old leprosy in the skin of his flesh, and the priest has pronounced him unclean; he does not shut him up, for he [is] unclean. **12** And if the leprosy breaks out greatly in the skin, and the leprosy has covered all the skin of [him who has] the plague, from his head even to his feet, to all that appears to the eyes of the priest, **13** then the priest has seen, and behold, the leprosy has covered all his flesh, and he has pronounced [him who has] the plague clean; it has all turned white; he [is] clean. **14** And in the day of raw flesh being seen in him, he is unclean; **15** and the priest has seen the raw flesh, and has pronounced him unclean; the raw flesh is unclean—it [is] leprosy. **16** Or when the raw flesh turns back, and has been turned to white, then he has come to the priest, **17** and the priest has seen him, and behold, the plague has been turned to white, and the priest has pronounced clean [him who has] the plague; he [is] clean. **18** And when flesh has in it, in its skin, an ulcer, and it has been healed, **19** and there has been in the place of the ulcer a white rising, or a bright white spot, reddish, then it has been seen by the priest, **20** and the priest has seen, and behold, its appearance [is] lower than the skin, and its hair has turned white, and the priest has pronounced him unclean; it [is] a plague of leprosy—it has broken out in an ulcer. **21** And if the priest sees it, and behold, there is no white hair in it, and it is not lower than the skin, and has faded, then the priest has shut him up [for] seven days; **22** and if it spreads greatly in the skin, then the priest has pronounced him unclean—it [is] a plague; **23** and if the bright spot stays in its place—it has not spread—it [is] an inflammation of the ulcer; and the priest has pronounced him clean. **24** Or when flesh has a fiery burning in its skin, and the quickening of the burning, the bright white spot, has been reddish or white, **25** and the priest has seen it, and behold, the hair has turned white in the bright spot, and its appearance [is] deeper than the skin, it [is] leprosy; it has broken out in the burning, and the priest has pronounced him unclean; it [is] a plague of leprosy. **26** And if the priest sees it, and behold, there is no white hair on the bright spot, and it is not lower than the skin, and it has faded, then the priest has shut him up [for] seven days; **27** and the priest has seen him on the seventh day, [and] if it spreads greatly in the skin, then the priest has pronounced him unclean; it [is] a plague of leprosy. **28** And if the bright spot stays in its place, it has not spread in the skin, and has faded; it [is] a rising of the burning, and the priest has pronounced him clean; for it [is] inflammation of the burning. **29** And when a man (or a woman) has a plague in him, in the head or in the beard, **30** then the priest has seen the plague, and behold, its appearance is deeper than the skin, and a thin, shining hair [is] in it, and the priest has pronounced him unclean; it [is] a scale—it [is] a leprosy of the head or of the beard. **31** And when the priest sees the scaly plague, and behold, its appearance is not deeper than the skin, and there is no black hair in it, then the priest has shut up [him who has] the scaly plague [for] seven days. **32** And the priest has seen the plague on the seventh day, and behold, the scale has not spread, and a shining hair has not been in it,

LEVITICUS

and the appearance of the scale is not deeper than the skin, **33** then he has shaved himself, but he does not shave the scale; and the priest has shut up [him who has] the scale [for] a second seven days. **34** And the priest has seen the scale on the seventh day, and behold, the scale has not spread in the skin, and its appearance is not deeper than the skin, and the priest has pronounced him clean, and he has washed his garments, and has been clean. **35** And if the scale spreads greatly in the skin after his cleansing, **36** and the priest has seen him, and behold, the scale has spread in the skin, the priest does not seek for the shining hair—he is unclean; **37** and if in his eyes the scale has stayed, and black hair has sprung up in it, the scale has been healed—he [is] clean—and the priest has pronounced him clean. **38** And when a man or woman has bright spots in the skin of their flesh, white bright spots, **39** and the priest has seen, and behold, white [and] faded bright spots [are] in the skin of their flesh—it [is] a freckled spot broken out in the skin; he [is] clean. **40** And when a man's head [is] polished, he [is] bald; he [is] clean; **41** and if his head is polished from the corner of his face, he [is] bald of the forehead; he [is] clean. **42** And when there is in the bald back of the head, or in the bald forehead, a reddish-white plague, it [is] a leprosy breaking out in the bald back of the head, or in the bald forehead; **43** and the priest has seen him, and behold, the rising of the reddish-white plague in the bald back of the head, or in the bald forehead, [is] as the appearance of leprosy, in the skin of the flesh, **44** he [is] a leprous man—he [is] unclean; the priest pronounces him utterly unclean; his plague [is] in his head. **45** As for the leper in whom [is] the plague, his garments are torn, and his head is uncovered, and he covers over the upper lip, and he calls, Unclean! Unclean! **46** He is unclean all the days that the plague [is] in him; he [is] unclean. He dwells alone; his dwelling [is] at the outside of the camp. **47** And when there is a plague of leprosy in any garment—in a garment of wool, or in a garment of linen, **48** or in the warp, or in the woof, of linen or of wool, or in a skin, or in any work of skin— **49** and the plague has been greenish or reddish in the garment, or in the skin, or in the warp, or in the woof, or in any vessel of skin, it [is] a plague of leprosy, and it has been shown [to] the priest. **50** And the priest has seen the plague, and has shut up [that which has] the plague [for] seven days; **51** and he has seen the plague on the seventh day, and the plague has spread in the garment, or in the warp, or in the woof, or in the skin, of all that is made of skin for work, the plague [is] a fretting leprosy; it [is] unclean. **52** And he has burned the garment, or the warp, or the woof, in wool or in linen, or any vessel of skin in which the plague is; for it [is] a fretting leprosy; it is burned with fire. **53** And if the priest sees, and behold, the plague has not spread in the garment, or in the warp, or in the woof, or in any vessel of skin, **54** then the priest has commanded, and they have washed that in which the plague [is], and he has shut it up [for] a second seven days. **55** And the priest has seen [that which has] the plague after it has been washed, and behold, the plague has not changed its aspect, and the plague has not spread—it [is] unclean; you burn it with fire; it [is] a fretting in its back-part or in its front-part. **56** And if the priest has seen, and behold, the plague has faded after it has been washed, then he has torn it out of the garment, or out of the skin, or out of the warp, or out of the woof; **57** and if it is still seen in the garment, or in the warp, or in the woof, or in any vessel of skin, it [is] a fretting; you burn it with fire—that in which the plague [is]. **58** And the garment, or the warp, or the woof, or any vessel of skin which you wash when the plague has turned aside from them, then it has been washed a second time, and has been clean. **59** This [is] the law of a plague of leprosy [in] a garment of wool or of linen, or of the warp or of the woof, or of any vessel of skin, to pronounce it clean or to pronounce it unclean."

14 And YHWH speaks to Moses, saying, **2** "This is a law of the leper, in the day of his cleansing, that he has been brought to the priest, **3** and the priest has gone out to the outside of the camp, and the priest has seen, and behold, the plague of leprosy has ceased from the leper, **4** and the priest has commanded, and he has taken for him who is to be cleansed, two clean living birds, and cedar wood, and scarlet, and hyssop. **5** And the priest has commanded, and he has slaughtered one bird on an earthen vessel, over running water; **6** [as for] the living bird, he takes it, and the cedar wood, and the scarlet, and the hyssop, and has dipped them and the living bird in the blood of the slaughtered bird, over the running water, **7** and he has sprinkled on him who is to be cleansed from the leprosy seven times, and has pronounced him clean, and has sent out the living bird over the face of the field. **8** And he who is to be cleansed has washed his garments, and has shaved all his hair, and has bathed with water, and has been clean, and afterward he comes into the camp, and has dwelt at the outside of his tent [for] seven days. **9** And it has been, on the seventh day—he shaves all his hair, his head, and his beard, and his eyebrows, even all his hair he shaves, and he has washed his garments, and has bathed his flesh with water, and has been clean. **10** And on the eighth day he takes two lambs, perfect ones, and one ewe-lamb, daughter of a year, a perfect one, and three-tenth parts of flour [for] a present, mixed with oil, and one log of oil. **11** And the priest who is cleansing has caused the man who is to be cleansed to stand with them before YHWH, at the opening of the Tent of Meeting, **12** and the priest has taken one male lamb, and has brought it near for a guilt-offering, also the log of oil, and has waved them [as] a wave-offering before YHWH. **13** And he has slaughtered the lamb in the place where he slaughters the sin-offering and the burnt-offering, in the holy place; for like the sin-offering, the guilt-offering is for the priest; it [is] most holy. **14** And the priest has taken of the blood of the guilt-offering, and the priest has put [it] on the tip of the right ear of him who is to be cleansed, and on the thumb of his right hand, and on the great toe of his right foot; **15** and the priest has taken of the log of oil, and has poured [it] on the left palm of the priest, **16** and the priest has dipped his right finger in the oil which [is] on his left palm, and has sprinkled of the oil with his finger seven times before YHWH. **17** And of the remainder of the oil which [is] on his palm, the priest puts [it] on the tip of the right ear of him who is to be cleansed, and on the thumb of his right hand, and on the great toe of his right foot, on the blood of the guilt-offering; **18** and the remnant of the oil which [is] on the palm of the priest, he puts [it] on the head of him who is to be cleansed, and the priest has made atonement for him before YHWH. **19** And the priest has made the sin-offering, and has made atonement for him who is to be cleansed from his uncleanness, and afterward he slaughters the burnt-offering; **20** and the priest has caused the burnt-offering to ascend, also the present, on the altar, and the priest has made atonement for him, and he has been clean. **21** And if he [is] poor, and his hand is not reaching [these things], then he has taken one lamb [for] a guilt-offering, for a wave-offering, to make atonement for him, and one-tenth part of flour mixed with oil for a present, and a log of oil, **22** and two turtle-doves, or two young pigeons, which his hand reaches to, and one has been a sin-offering and one a burnt-offering; **23** and he has brought them in on the eighth day for his cleansing to the priest, to the opening of the Tent of Meeting, before YHWH. **24** And the priest has taken the lamb of the guilt-offering, and the log of oil, and the priest has waved them [as] a wave-offering before YHWH; **25** and he has slaughtered the lamb of the guilt-offering, and the priest has taken of the blood of the guilt-offering, and has put [it] on the tip of the right ear of him who is to be cleansed, and on the thumb of his right hand, and on the great toe of his right foot; **26** and the priest pours of the oil on the left palm of the priest; **27** and the priest has sprinkled with his right finger of the oil which [is] on his left palm, seven times before YHWH. **28** And the priest has put of the oil which [is] on his palm, on the tip of the right ear of him who is to be cleansed, and on the thumb of his right hand, and on the great toe of his right foot, on the place of the blood of the guilt-offering; **29** and he puts the remnant of the oil which [is] on the palm of the priest on the head of him who is to be cleansed, to make atonement for him, before YHWH. **30** And he has made one of the turtle-doves or of the young pigeons (from that which his hand reaches to, **31** [even] that which his hand reaches to), one a sin-offering and one a burnt-offering, besides the present, and the priest has made atonement for him who is to be cleansed before YHWH. **32** This [is] a law of him in whom [is] a plague of leprosy, whose hand does not reach to his cleansing." **33** And YHWH speaks to Moses and to Aaron, saying, **34** "When you come into the land of Canaan, which I am giving to you for a possession, and I have put a plague of leprosy in a house [in] the land of

LEVITICUS

your possession, **35** then he whose the house [is] has come in and declared [it] to the priest, saying, Some plague has appeared to me in the house; **36** and the priest has commanded, and they have prepared the house before the priest comes in to see the plague (that all which [is] in the house is not unclean), and afterward the priest comes in to see the house; **37** and he has seen the plague, and behold, the plague [is] in the walls of the house, hollow streaks, greenish or reddish, and their appearance [is] lower than the wall, **38** and the priest has gone out of the house to the opening of the house, and has shut up the house [for] seven days. **39** And the priest has turned back on the seventh day, and has seen, and behold, the plague has spread in the walls of the house, **40** and the priest has commanded, and they have drawn out the stones in which the plague [is], and have cast them to the outside of the city, to an unclean place; **41** and he causes the house to be scraped all around inside, and they have poured out the clay which they have scraped off, at the outside of the city, at an unclean place; **42** and they have taken other stones, and brought [them] to the place of the stones, and he takes other clay and has coated the house. **43** And if the plague returns, and has broken out in the house, after he has drawn out the stones, and after the scraping of the house, and after the coating, **44** then the priest has come in and seen, and behold, the plague has spread in the house; it [is] a fretting leprosy in the house; it [is] unclean. **45** And he has broken down the house, its stones, and its wood, and all the clay of the house, and he has brought [them] forth to the outside of the city, to an unclean place. **46** And he who is going into the house all the days he has shut it up, is unclean until the evening; **47** and he who is lying in the house washes his garments; and he who is eating in the house washes his garments. **48** And if the priest certainly comes in, and has seen, and behold, the plague has not spread in the house after the coating of the house, then the priest has pronounced the house clean, for the plague has been healed. **49** And he has taken two birds, and cedar wood, and scarlet, and hyssop for the cleansing of the house; **50** and he has slaughtered one bird on an earthen vessel, over running water; **51** and he has taken the cedar wood, and the hyssop, and the scarlet, and the living bird, and has dipped them in the blood of the slaughtered bird, and in the running water, and has sprinkled against the house seven times. **52** And he has cleansed the house with the blood of the bird, and with the running water, and with the living bird, and with the cedar wood, and with the hyssop, and with the scarlet; **53** and he has sent the living bird away to the outside of the city to the face of the field, and has made atonement for the house, and it has been clean. **54** This [is] the law for every plague of the leprosy and for scale, **55** and for leprosy of a garment, and of a house, **56** and for a rising, and for a scab, and for a bright spot— **57** to direct in the day of being unclean, and in the day of being clean; this [is] the law of the leprosy."

15 And YHWH speaks to Moses and to Aaron, saying, **2** "Speak to the sons of Israel, and you have said to them: When there is discharging out of the flesh of any man, he [is] unclean [from] his discharge; **3** and this is his uncleanness in his discharge—his flesh has run with his discharge, or his flesh has stopped from his discharge; it [is] his uncleanness. **4** Every bed on which he who has the discharging lies is unclean, and every vessel on which he sits is unclean; **5** and anyone who comes against his bed washes his garments, and has bathed with water, and been unclean until the evening. **6** And he who is sitting on the vessel on which he sits who has the discharging, washes his garments, and has bathed with water, and been unclean until the evening. **7** And he who is coming against the flesh of him who has the discharging, washes his garments, and has bathed with water, and been unclean until the evening. **8** And when he who has the discharging spits on him who is clean, then he has washed his garments, and has bathed with water, and been unclean until the evening. **9** And all the saddle on which he who has the discharging rides is unclean; **10** and anyone who is coming against anything which is under him is unclean until the evening, and he who is carrying them washes his garments, and has bathed with water, and been unclean until the evening. **11** And anyone against whom he who has the discharging comes (and has not rinsed his hands with water) has even washed his garments, and bathed with water, and been unclean until the evening. **12** And the earthen vessel which he who has the discharging comes against is broken; and every wooden vessel is rinsed with water. **13** And when he who has the discharging is clean from his discharge, then he has numbered seven days for himself for his cleansing, and has washed his garments, and has bathed his flesh with running water, and been clean. **14** And on the eighth day he takes two turtle-doves or two young pigeons for himself, and has come in before YHWH to the opening of the Tent of Meeting, and has given them to the priest; **15** and the priest has made them, one a sin-offering and one a burnt-offering; and the priest has made atonement for him before YHWH, because of his discharge. **16** And when a man's seed [from] intercourse goes out from him, then he has bathed all his flesh with water, and been unclean until the evening. **17** And any garment, or any skin on which there is seed [from] intercourse, has also been washed with water, and been unclean until the evening. **18** And a woman with whom a man lies with seed [from] intercourse, they also have bathed with water, and been unclean until the evening. **19** And when a woman has discharging—blood is her discharge in her flesh—she is in her separation [for] seven days, and anyone who is coming against her is unclean until the evening. **20** And anything on which she lies in her separation is unclean, and anything on which she sits is unclean; **21** and anyone who is coming against her bed washes his garments, and has bathed with water, and been unclean until the evening. **22** And anyone who is coming against any vessel on which she sits washes his garments, and has washed with water, and been unclean until the evening. **23** And if it [is] on the bed, or on the vessel on which she is sitting, in his coming against it, he is unclean until the evening. **24** And if a man really lies with her, and her separation is on him, then he has been unclean [for] seven days, and all the bed on which he lies is unclean. **25** And when a woman's discharge of blood flows many days within the time of her separation, or when it flows over her separation—all the days of the discharge of her uncleanness are as the days of her separation; she [is] unclean. **26** Every bed on which she lies all the days of her discharge is as the bed of her separation to her, and every vessel on which she sits is unclean as the uncleanness of her separation; **27** and anyone who is coming against them is unclean, and has washed his garments, and has bathed with water, and been unclean until the evening. **28** And if she has been clean from her discharge, then she has numbered seven days for herself, and afterward she is clean; **29** and on the eighth day she takes two turtle-doves or two young pigeons for herself, and has brought them to the priest, to the opening of the Tent of Meeting; **30** and the priest has made one a sin-offering and one a burnt-offering, and the priest has made atonement for her before YHWH, because of the discharge of her uncleanness. **31** And you have separated the sons of Israel from their uncleanness, and they do not die in their uncleanness, in their defiling My Dwelling Place which [is] in their midst. **32** This [is] the law of him who has the discharging, and of him whose seed [from] intercourse goes out from him, to become unclean with it, **33** and of her who is sick in her separation, and of him who has the discharging (his discharge, of the male or of the female), and of a man who lies with an unclean woman."

16 And YHWH speaks to Moses after the death of the two sons of Aaron, in their drawing near before YHWH, and they die; **2** indeed, YHWH says to Moses, "Speak to your brother Aaron, and he does not come in at all times to the holy place within the veil, to the front of the propitiatory covering, which [is] on the Ark, and he does not die, for I am seen in a cloud on the propitiatory covering. **3** With this Aaron comes into the holy place: with a bullock, a son of the herd, for a sin-offering, and a ram for a burnt-offering; **4** he puts on a holy linen coat, and linen trousers are on his flesh, and he girds himself with a linen girdle, and he wraps himself up with a linen turban; they [are] holy garments; and he has bathed his flesh with water and put them on. **5** And from the congregation of the sons of Israel he takes two kids of the goats for a sin-offering and one ram for a burnt-offering; **6** and Aaron has brought the bullock of the sin-offering near, which is his own, and has made atonement for himself and for his house; **7** and he has taken the two goats, and has caused them to stand before YHWH, at the opening of the Tent of Meeting. **8** And Aaron has given lots over the two goats, one lot for YHWH and one lot for a goat of departure; **9** and Aaron has brought the goat near, on which the lot for YHWH has gone up, and has made it a sin-offering. **10** And the goat on which the lot for a goat of departure has gone up is caused to stand living before YHWH to make atonement by it, to send it away for a goat of departure into the wilderness. **11** And Aaron has brought the bullock of the sin-offering near, which is his own, and has made atonement for himself and for his house, and has slaughtered the bullock of the sin-offering which [is] his own, **12** and has taken the fullness of the censer of burning coals of fire from off the altar, from before YHWH, and the fullness of his hands of thin spice-incense, and has brought [it] within the veil; **13** and he has put the incense on the fire before YHWH, and the cloud of the incense has covered the propitiatory covering which [is] on the Testimony, and he does not die. **14** And he has taken of the blood of the bullock, and has sprinkled with his finger on the front of the propitiatory covering eastward; even at the front of the propitiatory covering he sprinkles seven times of the blood with his finger. **15** And he has slaughtered the goat of the sin-offering which [is] the people's, and has brought in its blood to the inside of the veil, and has done with its blood as he has done with the blood of the bullock, and has sprinkled it on the propitiatory covering, and at the front of the propitiatory covering, **16** and he has made atonement for the holy place because of the uncleanness of the sons of Israel, and because of their transgressions in all their sins; and so he does for the Tent of Meeting which is dwelling with them in the midst of their uncleannesses. **17** And no man is in the Tent of Meeting in his going in to make atonement in the holy place, until his coming out; and he has made atonement for himself, and for his house, and for all the assembly of Israel. **18** And he has gone out to the altar which [is] before YHWH, and has made atonement for it; and he has taken of the blood of the bullock and of the blood of the goat, and has put [it] around the horns of the altar; **19** and he has sprinkled on it of the blood with his finger seven times, and has cleansed it, and has hallowed it from the uncleannesses of the sons of Israel. **20** And he has ceased from making atonement [for] the holy place, and the Tent of Meeting, and the altar, and has brought the living goat near; **21** and Aaron has laid his two hands on the head of the living goat, and has confessed over it all the iniquities of the sons of Israel, and all their transgressions in all their sins, and has put them on the head of the goat, and has sent [it] away by the hand of a ready man into the wilderness; **22** and the goat has borne on himself all their iniquities to a land of separation. And he has sent the goat away into the wilderness, **23** and Aaron has come into the Tent of Meeting, and has stripped off the linen garments which he had put on in his going into the holy place, and has placed them there; **24** and he has bathed his flesh with water in the holy place, and has put on his garments, and has come out, and has made his burnt-offering, and the burnt-offering of the people, and has made atonement for himself and for the people; **25** and with the fat of the sin-offering he makes incense on the altar. **26** And he who is sending the goat away for a goat of departure washes his garments, and has bathed his flesh with water, and afterward he comes into the camp. **27** And the bullock of the sin-offering and the goat of the sin-offering, whose blood has been brought in to make atonement in the holy place, [one] brings out to the outside of the camp, and they have burned their skins, and their flesh, and their dung with fire; **28** and he who is burning them washes his garments, and has bathed his flesh with water, and afterward he comes into the camp. **29** And it has been for a continuous statute to you, in the seventh month, on the tenth of the month, you humble yourselves, and do no work—the native and the sojourner who is sojourning in your midst; **30** for on this day he makes atonement for you, to cleanse you; you are clean from all your sins before YHWH; **31** it [is] a Sabbath of rest for you, and you have humbled yourselves—a continuous statute. **32** And the priest whom he anoints, and whose hand he consecrates to act as priest instead of his father, has made atonement, and has put on the linen garments, the holy garments; **33** and he has made atonement [for] the holy sanctuary; and [for] the Tent of Meeting, even [for] the altar he makes atonement; indeed, he makes atonement for the priests and for all the people of the assembly. **34** And this has

LEVITICUS

been for a continuous statute to you, to make atonement for the sons of Israel, because of all their sins, once in a year"; and he does as YHWH has commanded Moses.

17 And YHWH speaks to Moses, saying, **2** "Speak to Aaron and to his sons, and to all the sons of Israel; and you have said to them: This [is] the thing which YHWH has commanded, saying, **3** Any man of the house of Israel who slaughters ox, or lamb, or goat in the camp, or who slaughters [it] at the outside of the camp, **4** and has not brought it in to the opening of the Tent of Meeting to bring an offering near to YHWH before the Dwelling Place of YHWH, blood is reckoned to that man—he has shed blood—and that man has been cut off from the midst of his people; **5** so that the sons of Israel bring in their sacrifices which they are sacrificing on the face of the field, indeed, they have brought them to YHWH, to the opening of the Tent of Meeting, to the priest, and they have sacrificed sacrifices of peace-offerings to YHWH with them. **6** And the priest has sprinkled the blood on the altar of YHWH, at the opening of the Tent of Meeting, and has made incense with the fat for refreshing fragrance to YHWH; **7** and they do not sacrifice their sacrifices anymore to the goat [idols] after which they are going whoring; this is a continuous statute to them, throughout their generations. **8** And you say to them: Any man of the house of Israel, or of the sojourners who sojourns in your midst, who causes burnt-offering or sacrifice to ascend, **9** and does not bring it in to the opening of the Tent of Meeting to make it to YHWH—that man has been cut off from his people. **10** And any man of the house of Israel, or of the sojourners who is sojourning in your midst, who eats any blood, I have even set My face against the person who is eating the blood, and have cut him off from the midst of his people; **11** for the life of the flesh is in the blood, and I have given it to you on the altar, to make atonement for your souls; for it [is] the blood which makes atonement for the soul. **12** Therefore I have said to the sons of Israel: No person among you eats blood, and the sojourner who is sojourning in your midst does not eat blood; **13** and any man of the sons of Israel, or of the sojourners who is sojourning in your midst, who hunts game, beast or bird, which is eaten—has even poured out its blood and covered it with dust; **14** for [it is] the life of all flesh, its blood is for its life; and I say to the sons of Israel: You do not eat [the] blood of any flesh, for the life of all flesh is its blood; anyone eating it is cut off. **15** And any person who eats a carcass or torn thing, among natives or among sojourners, has washed his garments and bathed with water, and been unclean until the evening—then he has been clean; **16** and if he does not wash, and does not bathe his flesh—then he has borne his iniquity."

18 And YHWH speaks to Moses, saying, **2** "Speak to the sons of Israel, and you have said to them: I [am] your God YHWH; **3** you do not do according to the work of the land of Egypt in which you have dwelt, and you do not do according to the work of the land of Canaan to where I am bringing you in, and you do not walk in their statutes. **4** You do My judgments and you keep My statutes, to walk in them; I [am] your God YHWH. **5** And you have kept My statutes and My judgments which man does and lives in them; I [am] YHWH. **6** None of you draws near to any relation of his flesh to uncover nakedness; I [am] YHWH. **7** You do not uncover the nakedness of your father and the nakedness of your mother, she [is] your mother; you do not uncover her nakedness. **8** You do not uncover the nakedness of the wife of your father; it [is] the nakedness of your father. **9** The nakedness of your sister, daughter of your father, or daughter of your mother, born at home or born outside—you do not uncover their nakedness. **10** The nakedness of your son's daughter, or of your daughter's daughter—you do not uncover their nakedness; for theirs [is] your nakedness. **11** The nakedness of a daughter of your father's wife, begotten of your father, she [is] your sister—you do not uncover her nakedness. **12** You do not uncover the nakedness of a sister of your father; she [is] a relation of your father. **13** You do not uncover the nakedness of your mother's sister, for she [is] your mother's relation. **14** You do not uncover the nakedness of your father's brother; you do not draw near to his wife; she [is] your aunt. **15** You do not uncover the nakedness of your daughter-in-law; she [is] your son's wife; you do not uncover her nakedness.

16 You do not uncover the nakedness of your brother's wife; it [is] your brother's nakedness. **17** You do not uncover the nakedness of a woman and her daughter, nor do you take her son's daughter and her daughter's daughter, to uncover her nakedness; they [are] her relations; it [is] wickedness. **18** And you do not take a woman [in addition] to her sister, to be an adversary, to uncover her nakedness beside her, in her life. **19** And you do not draw near to a woman in the separation of her uncleanness to uncover her nakedness. **20** And you do not give your seed [from] intercourse to the wife of your fellow, to become unclean with her. **21** And you do not give from your seed to pass over to the Molech, nor do you defile the Name of your God; I [am] YHWH. **22** And you do not lie with a male as one lies with a woman; it [is] an abomination. **23** And you do not commit your intercourse with any beast, to become unclean with it; and a woman does not stand before a beast to mate with it; it [is] perversion. **24** Do not defile yourselves with all these, for with all these the nations have been defiled which I am sending away from before you; **25** and the land is defiled, and I charge its iniquity on it, and the land vomits out its inhabitants. **26** And you have kept My statutes and My judgments, and do not do [any] of all these abominations, the native and the sojourner who is sojourning in your midst, **27** for the men of the land who [are] before you have done all these abominations and the land is defiled, **28** and the land does not vomit you out in your defiling it, as it has vomited out the nation which [is] before you; **29** for anyone who does [any] of all these abominations— even the persons who are doing [so]—have been cut off from the midst of their people; **30** and you have kept My charge, so as not to do [any] of the abominable statutes which have been done before you, and you do not defile yourselves with them; I [am] your God YHWH."

19 And YHWH speaks to Moses, saying, **2** "Speak to all the congregation of the sons of Israel, and you have said to them: You are holy, because I, your God YHWH, [am] holy. **3** You each fear his mother and his father, and you keep My Sabbaths; I [am] your God YHWH. **4** You do not turn to the idols, and you do not make a molten god for yourselves; I [am] your God YHWH. **5** And when you sacrifice a sacrifice of peace-offerings to YHWH, you sacrifice it at your pleasure; **6** it is eaten in the day of your sacrificing [it], and on the next day, and that which is left to the third day is burned with fire, **7** and if it is really eaten on the third day, it [is] an abomination, it is not pleasing, **8** and he who is eating it bears his iniquity, for he has defiled the holy thing of YHWH, and that person has been cut off from his people. **9** And in your reaping the harvest of your land you do not completely reap the corner of your field, and you do not gather the gleaning of your harvest, **10** and you do not glean your vineyard, even the omitted part of your vineyard you do not gather, you leave them for the poor and for the sojourner; I [am] your God YHWH. **11** You do not steal, nor feign, nor lie—each against his fellow. **12** And you do not swear by My Name for falsehood, or you have defiled the Name of your God; I [am] YHWH. **13** You do not oppress your neighbor, nor take plunder; the wages of the hired worker do not remain with you until morning. **14** You do not revile the deaf; and you do not put a stumbling block before the blind; and you have been afraid of your God; I [am] YHWH. **15** You do not do perversity in judgment; you do not lift up the face of the poor, nor honor the face of the great; you judge your fellow in righteousness. **16** You do not go slandering among your people; you do not stand against the blood of your neighbor; I [am] YHWH. **17** You do not hate your brother in your heart; you certainly reprove your fellow, and do not permit sin on him. **18** You do not take vengeance, nor watch the sons of your people; and you have had love for your neighbor as yourself; I [am] YHWH. **19** You keep My statutes. You do not cause your livestock to mate [with] two kinds; you do not sow your field with two kinds; and a garment of two kinds, mixed material, does not go up on you. **20** And when a man lies with a woman with seed [from] intercourse, and she [is] a maidservant, betrothed to a man, and not really ransomed, or freedom has not been given to her, there is an investigation; they are not put to death, for she [is] not free. **21** And he has brought in his guilt-offering to YHWH, to the opening of the Tent of Meeting, a ram [for] a guilt-offering, **22** and the priest has made atonement for him with the ram of the guilt-offering before YHWH, for his sin which he has sinned, and it has been forgiven him because of his sin which he has sinned. **23** And when you come into the land and have planted all [kinds] of trees [for] food, then you have reckoned its fruit as uncircumcised, it is uncircumcised to you [for] three years, it is not eaten, **24** and in the fourth year all its fruit is holy—praises for YHWH. **25** And in the fifth year you eat its fruit—to add to you its increase; I [am] your God YHWH. **26** You do not eat with the blood. You do not enchant, nor observe clouds. **27** You do not round the corner of your head, nor destroy the corner of your beard. **28** And you do not put a cutting for the soul in your flesh; and a writing, a cross-mark, you do not put on yourself; I [am] YHWH. **29** You do not defile your daughter to cause her to go whoring, that the land does not go whoring, and the land has been full of wickedness. **30** You keep My Sabbaths and you revere My sanctuary; I [am] YHWH. **31** You do not turn to those having familiar spirits, and you do not seek for wizards, to become unclean by them; I [am] your God YHWH. **32** You rise up at the presence of grey hairs, and you have honored the presence of an old man, and have been afraid of your God; I [am] YHWH. **33** And when a sojourner sojourns with you in your land, you do not oppress him; **34** the sojourner who is sojourning with you is to you as a native among you, and you have had love for him as for yourself, for you have been sojourners in the land of Egypt; I [am] your God YHWH. **35** You do not do perversity in the judgment, in the measure, in the weight, and in the liquid measure; **36** you have righteous balances, righteous weights, a righteous ephah, and a righteous hin; I [am] your God YHWH, who has brought you out from the land of Egypt; **37** and you have observed all my statutes, and all my judgments, and have done them; I [am] YHWH."

20 And YHWH speaks to Moses, saying, **2** "And you say to the sons of Israel: Any man of the sons of Israel, and of the sojourners who is sojourning in Israel, who gives to the Molech from his seed, is certainly put to death; the people of the land stone him with stone; **3** and I set My face against that man, and have cut him off from the midst of his people, for he has given to the Molech from his seed, so as to defile My sanctuary, and to defile My holy Name. **4** And if the people of the land really hide their eyes from that man, in his giving to the Molech from his seed, so as not to put him to death, **5** then I have set My face against that man and against his family, and have cut him off, and all who are going whoring after him, even going whoring after the Molech, from the midst of their people. **6** And the person who turns to those having familiar spirits, and to the wizards, to go whoring after them, I have even set My face against that person, and cut him off from the midst of his people. **7** And you have sanctified yourselves, and you have been holy, for I [am] your God YHWH; **8** and you have kept My statutes and have done them; I [am] YHWH, sanctifying you. **9** For any man who reviles his father and his mother is certainly put to death; he has reviled his father and his mother: his blood [is] on him. **10** And a man who commits adultery with a man's wife—who commits adultery with the wife of his neighbor—the adulterer and the adulteress are surely put to death. **11** And a man who lies with his father's wife—he has uncovered the nakedness of his father—both of them are certainly put to death; their blood [is] on them. **12** And a man who lies with his daughter-in-law—both of them are certainly put to death; they have done perversion; their blood [is] on them. **13** And a man who lies with a male as one lies with a woman—both of them have done an abomination; they are certainly put to death; their blood [is] on them. **14** And a man who takes the woman and her mother—it [is] wickedness; they burn him and them with fire, and there is no wickedness in your midst. **15** And a man who commits his intercourse with a beast is certainly put to death, and you slay the beast. **16** And a woman who draws near to any beast to mate with it—you have even slain the woman and the beast; they are certainly put to death; their blood [is] on them. **17** And a man who takes his sister, a daughter of his father or daughter of his mother, and he has seen her nakedness, and she sees his nakedness—it is a shame; and they have been cut off before the eyes of the sons of their people; he has uncovered the nakedness of his sister; he bears his iniquity. **18** And a man who lies with a sick woman and has uncovered her nakedness, her fountain he has made bare, and she has uncovered the fountain of her blood—even both of them have been cut off from the midst of their people. **19** And you do not uncover the nakedness of your mother's sister and your father's sister, because his relation he has made bare; they bear their iniquity. **20** And a man who lies with his aunt, he has uncovered the nakedness of his uncle; they bear their sin; they die childless. **21** And a man who takes his brother's wife—it [is] impurity; he has uncovered the nakedness of his brother; they are childless. **22** And you have kept all My statutes and all My judgments, and have done them, and the land does not vomit you out to where I am bringing you in to dwell in it; **23** and you do not walk in the statutes of the nation which I am sending away from before you, for they have done all these, and I am wearied with them. **24** And I say to you, You possess their ground, and I give it to you to possess it—a land flowing with milk and honey. I [am] your God YHWH, who has separated you from the peoples. **25** And you have made separation between the pure beasts and the unclean, and between the unclean bird and the pure, and you do not make yourselves abominable by beast or by bird, or by anything which creeps [on] the ground which I have separated to you for unclean. **26** And you have been holy to Me, for I, YHWH, [am] holy; and I separate you from the peoples to become Mine. **27** And a man or woman, when there is a familiar spirit in them, or who [are] wizards, are certainly put to death; they stone them with stone; their blood [is] on them."

21 And YHWH says to Moses, "Speak to the priests, sons of Aaron, and you have said to them: No one defiles himself for a [dead] person among his people, **2** except for his relation who [is] near to him: for his mother, and for his father, and for his son, and for his daughter, and for his brother, **3** and for his sister, the virgin, who is near to him, who has not been to a man; he is defiled for her. **4** A master [priest] does not defile himself among his people— to defile himself; **5** they do not make baldness on their head, and they do not shave the corner of their beard, and they do not make a cutting in their flesh; **6** they are holy to their God, and they do not defile the Name of their God, for the fire-offerings of YHWH, bread of their God, they are bringing near, and have been holy. **7** They do not take a woman of harlotry, or defiled, and they do not take a woman cast out from her husband, for he [is] holy to his God; **8** and you have sanctified him, for he is bringing the bread of your God near. He is holy to you, for I, YHWH, sanctifying you, [am] holy. **9** And when a daughter of any priest defiles herself by going whoring— she is defiling her father; she is burned with fire. **10** And the high priest of his brothers, on whose head the anointing oil is poured, and who has consecrated his hand to put on the garments, does not uncover his head, nor tear his garments, **11** nor does he come beside any dead person; he does not defile himself for his father and for his mother; **12** nor does he go out from the sanctuary, nor does he defile the sanctuary of his God, for the separation of the anointing oil of his God [is] on him; I [am] YHWH. **13** And he takes a wife in her virginity, **14** a widow, or cast out, or defiled, [or] a harlot—these he does not take, but he takes a virgin of his own people [for] a wife, **15** and he does not defile his seed among his people; for I [am] YHWH, sanctifying him." **16** And YHWH speaks to Moses, saying, **17** "Speak to Aaron, saying, No man of your seed throughout their generations in whom there is blemish draws near to bring the bread of his God near, **18** for no man in whom [is] a blemish draws near: a man blind, or lame, or disfigured, or deformed, **19** or a man in whom there is a breach in the foot, or a breach in the hand, **20** or hunchbacked, or a dwarf, or [with] a defect in his eye, or [with] an itch, or [with] a scab, or [with] a broken testicle. **21** No man in whom is blemish (of the seed of Aaron the priest) comes near to bring the fire-offerings of YHWH near; blemish [is] in him; he does not come near to bring the bread of his God near. **22** Bread of his God—from the most holy things and from the holy things—he eats; **23** only, he does not come toward the veil, and he does not draw near to the altar; for blemish [is] in him; and he does not defile My sanctuaries; for I [am] YHWH, sanctifying them." **24** And Moses speaks to Aaron, and to his sons, and to all the sons of Israel.

22 And YHWH speaks to Moses, saying, **2** "Speak to Aaron and to his sons, and they are separated from the holy things

LEVITICUS

of the sons of Israel, and they do not defile My holy Name in what they are hallowing to Me; I [am] YHWH. **3** Say to them: Throughout your generations, any man who draws near, out of all your seed, to the holy things which the sons of Israel sanctify to YHWH, and his uncleanness [is] on him—indeed, that person has been cut off from before My face; I [am] YHWH. **4** Any man of the seed of Aaron, and he is leprous or has discharging—he does not eat of the holy things until he is clean; and he who is coming against any uncleanness of a person, or a man whose seed [from] intercourse goes out from him, **5** or a man who comes against any teeming thing which is unclean to him, or against a man who is unclean to him, even any of his uncleanness— **6** the person who comes against it has even been unclean until the evening, and does not eat of the holy things, but has bathed his flesh with water, **7** and the sun has gone in, and he has been clean, and afterward he eats of the holy things, for it [is] his food; **8** he does not eat a carcass or torn thing, to become unclean with it; I [am] YHWH. **9** And they have kept My charge, and bear no sin for it, that they have died for it when they defile it; I [am] YHWH sanctifying them. **10** And no stranger eats of the holy thing; a settler [with] a priest and a hired worker does not eat of the holy thing; **11** but when a priest buys a person, the purchase of his money, he eats of it, also one born in his house; they eat of his bread. **12** And a priest's daughter, when she is a strange man's, she does not eat of the raised-offering of the holy things; **13** but a priest's daughter, when she is a widow, or cast out, and has no seed, and has turned back to the house of her father, as [in] her youth, she eats of her father's bread; but no stranger eats of it. **14** And when a man eats of a holy thing through ignorance, then he has added its fifth part to it, and has given [it] to the priest, with the holy thing; **15** and they do not defile the holy things of the sons of Israel—that which they lift up to YHWH, **16** or have caused them to bear the iniquity of the guilt-offering in their eating their holy things; for I [am] YHWH, sanctifying them." **17** And YHWH speaks to Moses, saying, **18** "Speak to Aaron, and to his sons, and to all the sons of Israel, and you have said to them: Any man of the house of Israel, or of the sojourners in Israel, who brings his offering near, of all his vows, or of all his willing offerings which they bring near to YHWH for a burnt-offering— **19** [you bring near] at your pleasure a perfect one, a male of the herd, of the sheep or of the goats; **20** nothing in which [is] blemish do you bring near, for it is not for a pleasing thing for you. **21** And when a man brings a sacrifice of peace-offerings near to YHWH, to complete a special vow, or for a willing-offering, of the herd or of the flock, it is perfect for a pleasing thing: no blemish is in it. **22** Blind, or broken, or maimed, or [having] an oozing sore [[or a defect of the eye]], or itch, or scab—you do not bring these near to YHWH, and you do not make a fire-offering from them on the altar to YHWH. **23** As for an ox or sheep [that] is deformed or stunted—you make it a willing-offering, but it is not pleasing for a vow. **24** As for bruised, or beaten, or torn, or cut—you do not bring [it] near to YHWH; and in your land you do not do it. **25** And you do not bring the bread of your God near from the hand of a son of a stranger, from any of these, for their corruption [is] in them; blemish [is] in them; they are not pleasing for you." **26** And YHWH speaks to Moses, saying, **27** "When ox, or lamb, or goat is born, and it has been under its mother [for] seven days, then from the eighth day and from now on, it is pleasing for an offering, a fire-offering to YHWH; **28** but an ox or sheep—you do not slaughter it and its young one in one day. **29** And when you sacrifice a sacrifice of thanksgiving to YHWH, you sacrifice at your pleasure; **30** it is eaten on that day—you do not leave of it until morning; I [am] YHWH. **31** And you have kept my commands and have done them; I [am] YHWH; **32** and you do not defile My holy Name, and I have been hallowed in the midst of the sons of Israel; I [am] YHWH, sanctifying you, **33** who am bringing you up out of the land of Egypt, to become your God; I [am] YHWH."

23 And YHWH speaks to Moses, saying, **2** "Speak to the sons of Israel, and you have said to them: Appointed times of YHWH, which you proclaim [as] holy convocations, these [are] My appointed times. **3** [For] six days work is done, and in the seventh day [is] a Sabbath of rest, a holy convocation; you do no work; it [is] a Sabbath to YHWH in all your dwellings.

LEVITICUS

4 These [are] appointed times of YHWH, holy convocations, which you proclaim in their appointed times: **5** in the first month, on the fourteenth of the month, between the evenings, [is] the Passover to YHWH; **6** and on the fifteenth day of this month [is] the Celebration of Unleavened Things to YHWH; [for] seven days you eat unleavened things; **7** on the first day you have a holy convocation, you do no servile work; **8** and you have brought a fire-offering near to YHWH [for] seven days; in the seventh day [is] a holy convocation; you do no servile work." **9** And YHWH speaks to Moses, saying, **10** "Speak to the sons of Israel, and you have said to them: When you come into the land which I am giving to you, and have reaped its harvest, and have brought in the sheaf, the beginning of your harvest to the priest, **11** then he has waved the sheaf before YHWH for your acceptance; on the next day of the Sabbath the priest waves it. **12** And you have prepared a lamb, a perfect one, a son of a year, in the day of your waving the sheaf for a burnt-offering to YHWH, **13** and its present [is] two-tenth parts of flour mixed with oil, a fire-offering to YHWH, a refreshing fragrance, and its drink-offering [is] a fourth of the hin of wine. **14** And you do not eat bread and roasted grain and full ears until this very day, until your bringing in the offering of your God—a continuous statute throughout your generations, in all your dwellings. **15** And you have numbered for yourselves from the day after the Sabbath, from the day of your bringing in the sheaf of the wave-offering: they are seven perfect Sabbaths; **16** you number fifty days to the day after the seventh Sabbath, and you have brought a new present near to YHWH; **17** you bring in two [loaves] of bread out of your dwellings [for] a wave-offering; they are of two-tenth parts of flour; they are baked [with] yeast—first-[fruits] to YHWH. **18** And you have brought near, besides the bread, seven lambs, perfect ones, sons of a year, and one bullock, a son of the herd, and two rams; they are a burnt-offering to YHWH, with their present and their drink-offerings, a fire-offering of refreshing fragrance to YHWH. **19** And you have prepared one kid of the goats for a sin-offering, and two lambs, sons of a year, for a sacrifice of peace-offerings, **20** and the priest has waved them, besides the bread of the first-[fruits], [as] a wave-offering before YHWH, besides the two lambs; they are holy to YHWH for the priest; **21** and you have proclaimed in this very day [that] it is a holy convocation for yourselves, you do no servile work—a continuous statute in all your dwellings, throughout your generations. **22** And in your reaping the harvest of your land you do not complete the corner of your field in your reaping, and you do not gather the gleaning of your harvest, you leave them for the poor and for the sojourner; I [am] your God YHWH." **23** And YHWH speaks to Moses, saying, **24** "Speak to the sons of Israel, saying, In the seventh month, on the first of the month, you have a Sabbath, a memorial of shouting, a holy convocation; **25** you do no servile work, and you have brought a fire-offering near to YHWH." **26** And YHWH speaks to Moses, saying, **27** "Only—on the tenth of this seventh month is the Day of Atonements; you have a holy convocation, and you have humbled yourselves, and have brought a fire-offering near to YHWH; **28** and you do no work in this very day, for it is a day of atonements, to make atonement for you, before your God YHWH. **29** For any person who is not humbled in this very day has even been cut off from his people; **30** and any person who does any work in this very day, I have even destroyed that person from the midst of his people; **31** you do no work—a continuous statute throughout your generations in all your dwellings. **32** It [is] a Sabbath of rest for yourselves, and you have humbled yourselves in the ninth of the month at evening; you keep your Sabbath from evening until evening." **33** And YHWH speaks to Moses, saying, **34** "Speak to the sons of Israel, saying, In the fifteenth day of this seventh month [is the] Celebration of Shelters [for] seven days to YHWH; **35** the first day [is] a holy convocation, you do no servile work; **36** [for] seven days you bring a fire-offering near to YHWH, on the eighth day you have a holy convocation, and you have brought a fire-offering near to YHWH; it [is] a restraint, you do no servile work. **37** These [are] appointed times of YHWH, which you proclaim [as] holy convocations, to bring a fire-offering near to YHWH, a burnt-offering, and a present, a sacrifice, and drink-offerings, a thing of a day in its day, **38** apart from the Sabbaths of YHWH, and apart from your gifts, and apart from all your vows, and apart from all your willing-offerings, which you give to YHWH. **39** Only—on the fifteenth day of the seventh month, in your gathering the increase of the land, you keep the celebration of YHWH [for] seven days; on the first day [is] a Sabbath, and on the eighth day a Sabbath; **40** and you have taken for yourselves on the first day the fruit of beautiful trees, branches of palms, and boughs of thick trees, and willows of a brook, and have rejoiced before your God YHWH [for] seven days. **41** And you have kept it [as] a celebration to YHWH, seven days in a year—a continuous statute throughout your generations; in the seventh month you keep it [as] a celebration. **42** You dwell in shelters [for] seven days; all who are natives in Israel dwell in shelters, **43** so that your generations know that I caused the sons of Israel to dwell in shelters in My bringing them out of the land of Egypt; I [am] your God YHWH." **44** And Moses speaks to the sons of Israel [concerning] the appointed times of YHWH.

24 And YHWH speaks to Moses, saying, **2** "Command the sons of Israel, and they bring pure oil of beaten olive to you for the lamp, to cause a light to go up continually; **3** Aaron arranges it at the outside of the veil of the Testimony, in the Tent of Meeting, from evening until morning before YHWH continually—a continuous statute throughout your generations; **4** he arranges the lights on the pure lampstand before YHWH continually. **5** And you have taken flour, and have baked twelve cakes with it, two-tenth parts are in one cake, **6** and you have set them [in] two rows (six in the row) on the pure table before YHWH, **7** and you have put pure frankincense on the row, and it has been with the bread for a memorial, a fire-offering to YHWH. **8** On each Sabbath day he arranges it before YHWH continually, from the sons of Israel—a perpetual covenant; **9** and it has been for Aaron and for his sons, and they have eaten it in the holy place, for it [is] most holy to him, from the fire-offerings of YHWH—a continuous statute." **10** And a son of an Israeli woman goes out (and he [is] son of an Egyptian man) in the midst of the sons of Israel, and the son of the Israeli woman and a man of Israel strive in the camp, **11** and the son of the Israeli woman execrates the Name and reviles; and they bring him to Moses; and his mother's name [is] Shelomith daughter of Dibri, of the tribe of Dan; **12** and he causes him to rest in confinement —to explain to them by the mouth of YHWH. **13** And YHWH speaks to Moses, saying, **14** "Bring out the reviler to the outside of the camp; and all those hearing have laid their hands on his head, and all the congregation has stoned him. **15** And you speak to the sons of Israel, saying, When any man reviles his God—then he has borne his sin; **16** and he who is execrating the Name of YHWH is certainly put to death; all the congregation certainly casts stones at him; as a sojourner so a native, in his execrating the Name, he is put to death. **17** And when a man strikes any soul of man, he is certainly put to death. **18** And he who strikes a beast repays it, body for body. **19** And when a man puts a blemish in his fellow, as he has done so it is done to him; **20** breach for breach, eye for eye, tooth for tooth; as he puts a blemish in a man so it is done in him. **21** And he who strikes a beast repays it, and he who strikes [the life of] man is put to death. **22** One judgment is for you; as a sojourner so is a native; for I [am] your God YHWH." **23** And Moses speaks to the sons of Israel, and they bring out the reviler to the outside of the camp, and stone him [with] stone; and the sons of Israel have done as YHWH has commanded Moses.

25 And YHWH speaks to Moses, in Mount Sinai, saying, **2** "Speak to the sons of Israel, and you have said to them: When you come into the land which I am giving to you, then the land has kept a Sabbath to YHWH. **3** [For] six years you sow your field, and [for] six years you prune your vineyard, and have gathered its increase, **4** and in the seventh year is a Sabbath of rest for the land, a Sabbath to YHWH; you do not sow your field, and you do not prune your vineyard; **5** you do not reap the spontaneous growth of your harvest, and you do not gather the grapes of your separated thing; it is a year of rest for the land. **6** And the Sabbath [increase] of the land has been for you for food, to you, and to your manservant, and to your handmaid, and to your hired worker, and to your settler, who are sojourning with you; **7** and for your livestock, and for the beast

LEVITICUS

which [is] in your land, is all its increase for [them] to eat. 8 And you have numbered seven Sabbaths of years for yourself, seven times seven years, and the days of the seven Sabbaths of years have been forty-nine years for you, 9 and you have caused a horn of shouting to pass over in the seventh month, on the tenth of the month; in the Day of Atonements you cause a horn to pass over through all your land; 10 and you have hallowed the year, the fiftieth year; and you have proclaimed liberty in the land to all its inhabitants; it is a Jubilee for you; and you have turned back each to his possession; indeed, you return each to his family. 11 It [is] a Jubilee, the fiftieth year, it is a year for you; you do not sow, nor reap its spontaneous growth, nor gather its separated things; 12 for it [is] a Jubilee—it is holy to you; you eat its increase from the field; 13 you return each to his possession in this Year of the Jubilee. 14 And when you sell anything to your fellow, or buy from the hand of your fellow, you do not oppress one another; 15 you buy from your fellow by the number of years after the Jubilee; he sells to you by the number of the years of increase; 16 you multiply its price according to the multitude of the years, and you diminish its price according to the fewness of the years; for [it is] a number of increases [that] he is selling to you; 17 and you do not oppress one another, and you have been afraid of your God; for I [am] your God YHWH. 18 And you have done My statutes, and you keep My judgments, and have done them, and you have dwelt on the land confidently, 19 and the land has given its fruit, and you have eaten to satiety, and have dwelt confidently on it. 20 And when you say, What do we eat in the seventh year, behold, do we not sow, nor gather our increase? 21 Then I have commanded My blessing on you in the sixth year, and it has made the increase for three years; 22 and you have sown [in] the eighth year, and have eaten of the old increase; you eat the old until the ninth year, until the coming in of its increase. 23 And the land is not sold—to extinction, for the land [is] Mine, for you [are] sojourners and settlers with Me; 24 and in all the land of your possession you give a redemption for the land. 25 When your brother becomes poor, and has sold his possession, then his redeemer who is near to him has come, and has redeemed the sold thing of his brother; 26 and when a man has no redeemer, and his own hand has attained [means], and he has found [it] as sufficient [for] its redemption, 27 then he has reckoned the years of its sale, and has given back that which is over to the man to whom he sold [it], and he has returned to his possession. 28 And if his hand has not found sufficiency to give back to him, then his sold thing has been in the hand of him who buys it until the Year of Jubilee; and it has gone out in the Jubilee, and he has returned to his possession. 29 And when a man sells a dwelling-house [in] a walled city, then his right of redemption has been until the completion of a year from its selling; his right of redemption is [during these] days; 30 and if it is not redeemed to him until the fullness of a perfect year, then the house which [is] in a walled city has been established to extinction to him buying it, throughout his generations; it does not go out in the Jubilee. 31 And a house of the villages which have no surrounding wall is reckoned on the field of the country; there is redemption for it, and it goes out in the Jubilee. 32 As for cities of the Levites—houses of the cities of their possession—continuous redemption is for the Levites; 33 as for him who redeems from the Levites, then the sale of a house (and [in] the city of his possession) has gone out in the Jubilee, for the houses of the cities of the Levites are their possession in the midst of the sons of Israel. 34 And a field, a outskirt of their cities, is not sold; for it [is] a continuous possession for them. 35 And when your brother has become poor, and his hand has failed with you, then you have kept hold on him, sojourner and settler, and he has lived with you; 36 you take no usury or increase from him; and you have been afraid of your God; and your brother has lived with you; 37 you do not give your money to him in usury, and you do not give your food for increase. 38 I [am] your God YHWH, who has brought you out of the land of Egypt to give the land of Canaan to you, to become your God. 39 And when your brother becomes poor with you, and he has been sold to you, you do not lay servile service on him; 40 he is as a hired worker [and] as a settler with you; he serves with you until the Year of the Jubilee— 41 then he has gone out from you, he and his sons with him, and has turned back to his family; and he turns back to the possession of his fathers. **42** For they [are] My servants, whom I have brought out from the land of Egypt: they are not sold [with] the sale of a servant; **43** you do not rule over him with rigor, and you have been afraid of your God. **44** And your manservant and your handmaid whom you have [are] from the nations who [are] around you; you buy manservant and handmaid from them, **45** and also from the sons of the settlers who are sojourning with you, you buy from them, and from their families who [are] with you, which they have begotten in your land, and they have been to you for a possession; **46** and you have taken them for an inheritance for your sons after you, to inherit [for] a possession; you lay service on them for all time, but on your brothers, the sons of Israel, each with his brother—you do not rule over him with rigor. **47** And when the hand of a sojourner or settler with you attains [riches], and your brother with him has become poor, and he has been sold to a sojourner, a settler with you, or to the root of the family of a sojourner, **48** after he has been sold, there is a right of redemption for him; one of his brothers redeems him, **49** or his uncle or a son of his uncle redeems him, or any of the relations of his flesh, of his family, redeems him, or [if] his own hand has attained [means] then he has been redeemed. **50** And he has reckoned with his buyer from the year of his being sold to him until the Year of Jubilee, and the money of his sale has been by the number of years; it is with him as the days of a hired worker. **51** If many years still [remain], he gives back his redemption [money] according to them, from the money of his purchase. **52** And if few are left of the years until the Year of Jubilee, then he has reckoned with him [and] he gives back his redemption [money] according to his years; **53** as a hired worker, year by year, he is with him, and he does not rule him with rigor before your eyes. **54** And if he is not redeemed in these [years], then he has gone out in the Year of Jubilee, he and his sons with him. **55** For the sons of Israel [are] servants to Me; they [are] My servants whom I have brought out of the land of Egypt; I [am] your God Y<small>HWH</small>."

26 "You do not make idols for yourselves; and you do not set up carved image or standing image for yourselves; and you do not put a stone of imagery in your land, to bow yourselves to it; for I [am] your God Y<small>HWH</small>. **2** You keep My Sabbaths and you revere My sanctuary; I [am] Y<small>HWH</small>. **3** If you walk in My statutes, and you keep My commands, and have done them, **4** then I have given your rains in their season, and the land has given her produce, and the tree of the field gives its fruit; **5** and the threshing has reached to you, [and] the gathering, and the gathering reaches the sowing-[time]; and you have eaten your bread to satiety, and have dwelt confidently in your land. **6** And I have given peace in the land, and you have lain down, and there is none causing trembling; and I have caused evil beasts to cease out of the land, and the sword does not pass over into your land. **7** And you have pursued your enemies, and they have fallen before you by the sword; **8** and five of you have pursued one hundred, and one hundred of you pursue a myriad; and your enemies have fallen before you by the sword. **9** And I have turned to you, and have made you fruitful, and have multiplied you, and have established My covenant with you; **10** and you have eaten old [store], and you bring out the old because of the new. **11** And I have given My Dwelling Place in your midst, and My soul does not loathe you; **12** and I have habitually walked in your midst, and have become your God, and you become My people; **13** I [am] your God Y<small>HWH</small>, who has brought you out of the land of the Egyptians, from being their servants; and I break the bars of your yoke and cause you to go erect. **14** And if you do not listen to Me and do not do all these commands, **15** and if you kick at My statutes, and if your soul loathes My judgments, so as not to do all My commands—to your breaking My covenant— **16** I also do this to you: I have even appointed trouble over you, the consumption, and the burning fever, consuming eyes, and causing pain of soul; and you have sowed your seed in vain, and your enemies have eaten it; **17** and I have set My face against you, and you have been struck before your enemies; and those hating you have ruled over you, and you have fled when there is none pursuing you. **18** And if up to these you [still] do not listen to Me—then I have added to discipline you sevenfold for your sins; **19** and I have

LEVITICUS

broken the pride of your strength, and have made your heavens as iron, and your earth as bronze; **20** and your strength has been consumed in vain, and your land does not give her produce, and the tree of the land does not give its fruit. **21** And if you walk with Me [in] opposition, and are not willing to listen to Me, then I have added to you a plague sevenfold, according to your sins, **22** and sent the beast of the field against you, and it has bereaved you; and I have cut off your livestock, and have made you few, and your ways have been desolate. **23** And if by these you are not instructed by Me, and have walked with Me [in] opposition, **24** then I have walked—I also—with you in opposition, and have struck you, even I, sevenfold for your sins; **25** and I have brought in a sword on you, executing the vengeance of a covenant; and you have been gathered to your cities, and I have sent pestilence into your midst, and you have been given into the hand of an enemy. **26** In My breaking your staff of bread, then ten women have baked your bread in one oven, and have given back your bread by weight; and you have eaten and are not satisfied. **27** And if for this you do not listen to Me, and have walked with Me in opposition, **28** then I have walked with you in the fury of opposition, and have disciplined you, even I, sevenfold for your sins. **29** And you have eaten [the] flesh of your sons; and you eat [the] flesh of your daughters. **30** And I have destroyed your high places, and cut down your images, and have put your carcasses on the carcasses of your idols, and My soul has loathed you; **31** and I have made your cities a ruin, and have made your sanctuaries desolate, and I do not smell your refreshing fragrance; **32** and I have made the land desolate, and your enemies who are dwelling in it have been astonished at it. **33** And I scatter you among nations, and have drawn out a sword after you, and your land has been a desolation, and your cities are a ruin. **34** Then the land enjoys its Sabbaths all the days of the desolation—and you [are] in the land of your enemies; then the land rests, and has enjoyed its Sabbaths; **35** it rests all the days of the desolation [for] that which it has not rested in your Sabbaths, in your dwelling on it. **36** And those who are left of you—I have also brought a faintness into their heart in the lands of their enemies, and the sound of a leaf driven away has pursued them, and they have fled [as in] flight from a sword—and they have fallen, and there is none pursuing. **37** And they have stumbled on one another, as from the face of a sword, and there is none pursuing, and you have no standing before your enemies, **38** and you have perished among the nations, and the land of your enemies has consumed you. **39** And those who are left of you—they consume away in their iniquity, in the lands of your enemies; and also in the iniquities of their fathers, they consume away with them. **40** And [if] they have confessed their iniquity and the iniquity of their fathers, in their trespass which they have trespassed against Me, and also that they have walked with Me in opposition, **41** when I also walk in opposition to them, and have brought them into the land of their enemies—if then their uncircumcised heart is humbled, and then they accept the punishment of their iniquity— **42** then I have remembered My covenant [with] Jacob, and also My covenant [with] Isaac, and also My covenant [with] Abraham I remember, and I remember the land. **43** And the land is left by them, and enjoys its Sabbaths, in the desolation without them, and they accept the punishment of their iniquity, because, even because, they have kicked against My judgments, and their soul has loathed My statutes, **44** and also even this, in their being in the land of their enemies, I have not rejected them, nor have I loathed them, to consume them, to break My covenant with them; for I [am] their God YHWH— **45** then I have remembered for them the covenant of the ancestors, whom I brought forth out of the land of Egypt before the eyes of the nations to become their God; I [am] YHWH." **46** These [are] the statutes, and the judgments, and the laws, which YHWH has given between Him and the sons of Israel in Mount Sinai, by the hand of Moses.

27 And YHWH speaks to Moses, saying, **2** "Speak to the sons of Israel, and you have said to them: When a man makes a special vow in your valuation of persons to YHWH, **3** then your valuation has been of the male from a son of twenty years even to a son of sixty years, and your valuation has been fifty shekels of silver by the shekel of the holy place. **4** And if it [is] a female, then your valuation has been thirty shekels; **5** and if from a son of five years even to a son of twenty years, then your valuation of the male has been twenty shekels, and for the female, ten shekels; **6** and if from a son of a month even to a son of five years, then your valuation of the male has been five shekels of silver, and for the female your valuation [is] three shekels of silver; **7** and if from a son of sixty years and above, if a male, then your valuation has been fifteen shekels, and for a female, ten shekels. **8** And if he is poorer than your valuation, then he has presented himself before the priest, and the priest has valued him; according to that which the hand of him who is vowing reaches, the priest values him. **9** And if [it is] a beast of which they bring near [as] an offering to YHWH, all that [one] gives of it to YHWH is holy; **10** he does not change it nor exchange it, a good for a bad, or a bad for a good; and if he really exchanges beast for beast, then it has been [holy] and its exchange is holy. **11** And if [it is] any unclean beast of which they do not bring near [as] an offering to YHWH, then he has presented the beast before the priest, **12** and the priest has valued it, whether good or bad; according to your valuation, O priest, so it is; **13** and if he really redeems it, then he has added its fifth to your valuation. **14** And when a man sanctifies his house [as] a holy thing to YHWH, then the priest has valued it, whether good or bad; as the priest values it so it stands; **15** and if he who is sanctifying redeems his house, then he has added a fifth of the money of your valuation to it, and it has become his. **16** And if a man sanctifies to YHWH from a field of his possession, then your valuation has been according to its seed—a homer of barley-seed at fifty shekels of silver; **17** if he sanctifies his field from the Year of the Jubilee, according to your valuation it stands; **18** and if he sanctifies his field after the Jubilee, then the priest has reckoned the money to him according to the years which are left, to the Year of the Jubilee, and it has been diminished from your valuation. **19** And if he really redeems the field—he who is sanctifying it—then he has added a fifth of the money of your valuation to it, and it has been established to him; **20** and if he does not redeem the field, or if he has sold the field to another man, it is not redeemed anymore; **21** and the field has been, in its going out in the Jubilee, holy to YHWH as a field which is devoted; his possession is for the priest. **22** And if he sanctifies a field of his purchase to YHWH, which [is] not of the fields of his possession, **23** then the priest has reckoned to him the amount of your valuation up to the Year of Jubilee, and he has given your valuation in that day [as] a holy thing to YHWH; **24** in the Year of the Jubilee the field returns to him from whom he bought it, to him who [has] the possession of the land. **25** And all your valuation is by the shekel of the holy place: the shekel is twenty gerahs. **26** Only, a firstling which is YHWH's firstling among beasts—no man sanctifies it, whether ox or sheep; it [is] YHWH's. **27** And if [from] among the unclean beast, then he has ransomed [it] at your valuation, and he has added its fifth to it; and if it is not redeemed, then it has been sold at your valuation. **28** Only, no devoted thing which a man devotes to YHWH of all that he has, of man, and beast, and of the field of his possession, is sold or redeemed; every devoted thing is most holy to YHWH. **29** No devoted thing, which is devoted of man, is ransomed, it is surely put to death. **30** And all tithe of the land, of the seed of the land, of the fruit of the tree, is YHWH's; [it is] holy to YHWH. **31** And if a man really redeems [any] of his tithe, he adds its fifth to it. **32** And all the tithe of the herd and of the flock—all that passes by under the rod—the tenth is holy to YHWH; **33** he does not inquire between good and bad, nor does he exchange it; and if he really exchanges it, then it has been [holy] and its exchange is holy; it is not redeemed." **34** These [are] the commands which YHWH has commanded Moses for the sons of Israel in Mount Sinai.

NUMBERS

1 And Y<small>HWH</small> speaks to Moses in the wilderness of Sinai, in the Tent of Meeting, on the first of the second month, in the second year of their going out of the land of Egypt, saying, **2** "Take a census of all the congregation of the sons of Israel by their families, by the house of their fathers, in the number of names—every male by their counted heads; **3** from a son of twenty years and upward, everyone going out to the host in Israel, you number them by their hosts, you and Aaron; **4** and with you there is a man for a tribe, each is a head of the house of his fathers. **5** And these [are] the names of the men who stand with you: for Reuben, Elizur son of Shedeur; **6** for Simeon, Shelumiel son of Zurishaddai; **7** for Judah, Nahshon son of Amminadab; **8** for Issachar, Nathaneel son of Zuar; **9** for Zebulun, Eliab son of Helon; **10** for the sons of Joseph: for Ephraim, Elishama son of Ammihud; for Manasseh, Gamaliel son of Pedahzur; **11** for Benjamin, Abidan son of Gideoni; **12** for Dan, Ahiezer son of Ammishaddai; **13** for Asher, Pagiel son of Ocran; **14** for Gad, Eliasaph son of Deuel; **15** for Naphtali, Ahira son of Enan." **16** These [are] those called of the congregation, princes of the tribes of their fathers; they [are] heads of the thousands of Israel. **17** And Moses takes—Aaron also—these men, who were defined by name, **18** and they assembled all the congregation on the first of the second month, and they declare their births, by their families, by the house of their fathers, in the number of names from a son of twenty years and upward, by their counted heads, **19** as Y<small>HWH</small> has commanded Moses; and he numbers them in the wilderness of Sinai. **20** And the sons of Reuben, Israel's firstborn—their births, by their families, by the house of their fathers, in the number of names, by their counted heads, every male from a son of twenty years and upward, everyone going out to the host— **21** their numbered ones, for the tribe of Reuben, are forty-six thousand and five hundred. **22** Of the sons of Simeon—their births, by their families, by the house of their fathers, its numbered ones in the number of names, by their counted heads, every male from a son of twenty years and upward, everyone going out to the host— **23** their numbered ones, for the tribe of Simeon, [are] fifty-nine thousand and three hundred. **24** Of the sons of Gad—their births, by their families, by the house of their fathers, in the number of names, from a son of twenty years and upward, everyone going out to the host— **25** their numbered ones, for the tribe of Gad, [are] forty-five thousand and six hundred and fifty. **26** Of the sons of Judah—their births, by their families, by the house of their fathers, in the number of names, from a son of twenty years and upward, everyone going out to the host— **27** their numbered ones, for the tribe of Judah, [are] seventy-four thousand and six hundred. **28** Of the sons of Issachar—their births, by their families, by the house of their fathers, in the number of names, from a son of twenty years and upward, everyone going out to the host— **29** their numbered ones, for the tribe of Issachar, [are] fifty-four thousand and four hundred. **30** Of the sons of Zebulun—their births, by their families, by the house of their fathers, in the number of names, from a son of twenty years and upward, everyone going out to the host— **31** their numbered ones, for the tribe of Zebulun, [are] fifty-seven thousand and four hundred. **32** Of the sons of Joseph: of the sons of Ephraim—their births, by their families, by the house of their fathers, in the number of names, from a son of twenty years and upward, everyone going out to the host— **33** their numbered ones, for the tribe of Ephraim, [are] forty thousand and five hundred. **34** Of the sons of Manasseh—their births, by their families, by the house of their fathers, in the number of names, from a son of twenty years and upward, everyone going out to the host— **35** their numbered ones, for the tribe of Manasseh, [are] thirty-two thousand and two hundred. **36** Of the sons of Benjamin—their births, by their families, by the house of their fathers, in the number of names, from a son of twenty years and upward, everyone going out to the host— **37** their numbered ones, for the tribe of Benjamin, [are] thirty-five thousand and four hundred. **38** Of the sons of Dan—their births, by their families, by the house of their fathers, in the number of names, from a son of twenty years and upward, everyone going out to the host— **39** their numbered ones, for the tribe of Dan, [are] sixty-two thousand and seven hundred. **40** Of the sons of Asher—their births, by their families, by the house of their fathers, in the number of names, from a son of twenty years and upward, everyone going out to the host— **41** their numbered ones, for the tribe of Asher, [are] forty-one thousand and five hundred. **42** Of the sons of Naphtali—their births, by their families, by the house of their fathers, in the number of names, from a son of twenty years and upward, everyone going out to the host— **43** their numbered ones, for the tribe of Naphtali, [are] fifty-three thousand and four hundred. **44** These [are] those numbered, whom Moses numbered—Aaron also—and the princes of Israel, twelve men, each one has been [the representative] for the house of his fathers. **45** And they are, all those numbered of the sons of Israel, by the house of their fathers, from a son of twenty years and upward, everyone going out to the host in Israel, **46** indeed, all those numbered are six hundred thousand and three thousand and five hundred and fifty. **47** And the Levites, for the tribe of their fathers, have not numbered themselves in their midst, **48** seeing YHWH speaks to Moses, saying, **49** "Only the tribe of Levi you do not number, and you do not take up their census in the midst of the sons of Israel; **50** and you, appoint the Levites over the Dwelling Place of the Testimony, and over all its vessels, and over all that it has; they carry the Dwelling Place, and all its vessels, and they serve it; and they encamp around the Dwelling Place. **51** And in the journeying of the Dwelling Place, the Levites take it down, and in the encamping of the Dwelling Place, the Levites raise it up; and the stranger who is coming near is put to death." **52** And the sons of Israel have encamped, each by his camp, and each by his standard, by their hosts; **53** and the Levites encamp around the Dwelling Place of the Testimony; and there is no wrath on the congregation of the sons of Israel, and the Levites have kept the charge of the Dwelling Place of the Testimony. **54** And the sons of Israel do according to all that YHWH has commanded Moses; so they have done.

2 And YHWH speaks to Moses and to Aaron, saying, **2** "The sons of Israel encamp, each by his standard, with ensigns of the house of their fathers; they encamp around, from in sight of the Tent of Meeting." **3** And those encamping eastward toward the sun-rising [are] of the standard of the camp of Judah, by their hosts; and the prince of the sons of Judah [is] Nahshon, son of Amminadab; **4** and his host, and their numbered ones, [are] seventy-four thousand and six hundred. **5** And those encamping by him [are] of the tribe of Issachar; and the prince of the sons of Issachar [is] Nethaneel son of Zuar; **6** and his host, and its numbered ones, [are] fifty-four thousand and four hundred. **7** The tribe of Zebulun [is with them]; and the prince of the sons of Zebulun [is] Eliab son of Helon; **8** and his host, and its numbered ones, [are] fifty-seven thousand and four hundred. **9** All those numbered of the camp of Judah [are] one hundred thousand and eighty thousand and six thousand and four hundred, by their hosts; they journey first. **10** The standard of the camp of Reuben [is] southward, by their hosts; and the prince of the sons of Reuben [is] Elizur son of Shedeur; **11** and his host, and its numbered ones, [are] forty-six thousand and five hundred. **12** And those encamping by him [are of] the tribe of Simeon; and the prince of the sons of Simeon [is] Shelumiel son of Zurishaddai; **13** and his host, and their numbered ones, [are] fifty-nine thousand and three hundred. **14** And the tribe of Gad [is with him]; and the prince of the sons of Gad [is] Eliasaph son of Reuel; **15** and his host, and their numbered ones, [are] forty-five thousand and six hundred and fifty. **16** All those numbered of the camp of Reuben [are] one hundred thousand and fifty-one thousand and four hundred and fifty, by their hosts; and they journey second. **17** And the Tent of Meeting has journeyed [with] the camp of the Levites in the middle of the camps; as they encamp so they journey, each at his station by their standards. **18** The standard of the camp of Ephraim, by their hosts, [is] westward; and the prince of the sons of Ephraim [is] Elishama son of Ammihud; **19** and his host, and their numbered ones, [are] forty thousand and five hundred. **20** And by him [is] the tribe of Manasseh; and the prince of the sons of Manasseh [is] Gamaliel son of Pedahzur; **21** and his host, and their numbered ones, [are] thirty-two thousand and two hundred. **22** And the tribe of Benjamin [is with them]; and the prince of the sons of Benjamin [is] Abidan son of Gideoni; **23** and his host, and their numbered ones, [are] thirty-five thousand and four hundred. **24** All those numbered of the camp of Ephraim [are] one hundred thousand and eight thousand and one hundred, by their hosts; and they journey third. **25** The standard of the camp of Dan [is] northward, by their hosts; and the prince of the sons of Dan [is] Ahiezer son of Ammishaddai; **26** and his host, and their numbered ones, [are] sixty-two thousand and seven hundred. **27** And those encamping by him [are of] the tribe of Asher; and the prince of the sons of Asher [is] Pagiel son of Ocran; **28** and his host, and their numbered ones, [are] forty-one thousand and five hundred. **29** And the tribe of Naphtali [is with them]; and the prince of the sons of Naphtali [is] Ahira son of Enan; **30** and his host, and their numbered ones, [are] fifty-three thousand and four hundred. **31** All those numbered of the camp of Dan [are] one hundred thousand and fifty-seven thousand and six hundred; they journey at the rear by their standards. **32** These [are] those numbered of the sons of Israel by the house of their fathers; all those numbered of the camps by their hosts [are] six hundred thousand and three thousand and five hundred and fifty. **33** And the Levites have not numbered themselves in the midst of the sons of Israel, as YHWH has commanded Moses. **34** And the sons of Israel do according to all that YHWH has commanded Moses; so they have encamped by their standards, and so they have journeyed, each by his families, by the house of his fathers.

3 And these [are] the generations of Aaron and Moses, in the day of YHWH's speaking with Moses in Mount Sinai. **2** And these [are] the names of the sons of Aaron: the firstborn Nadab, and Abihu, Eleazar, and Ithamar; **3** these [are] the names of the sons of Aaron, the anointed priests, whose hand he has consecrated for acting as priest. **4** And Nadab dies—Abihu also—before YHWH, in their bringing strange fire near before YHWH, in the wilderness of Sinai, and they did not have sons; and Eleazar—Ithamar also—acts as priest in the presence of their father Aaron. **5** And YHWH speaks to Moses, saying, **6** "Bring the tribe of Levi near, and you have caused it to stand before Aaron the priest, and they have served him, **7** and kept his charge, and the charge of all the congregation before the Tent of Meeting, to do the service of the Dwelling Place; **8** and they have kept all the vessels of the Tent of Meeting, and the charge of the sons of Israel, to do the service of the Dwelling Place; **9** and you have given the Levites to Aaron and to his sons; they are surely given to him out of the sons of Israel. **10** And you appoint Aaron and his sons, and they have kept their priesthood, and the stranger who comes near is put to death." **11** And YHWH speaks to Moses, saying, **12** "And I, behold, have taken the Levites from the midst of the sons of Israel instead of every firstborn opening a womb among the sons of Israel, and the Levites have been Mine; **13** for every firstborn [is] Mine, in the day of My striking every firstborn in the land of Egypt I have sanctified to Myself every firstborn in Israel, from man to beast; they are Mine; I [am] YHWH." **14** And YHWH speaks to Moses in the wilderness of Sinai, saying, **15** "Number the sons of Levi by the house of their fathers, by their families; every male from a son of a month and upward—you number them." **16** And Moses numbers them according to the command of YHWH, as he has been commanded. **17** And these are the sons of Levi by their names: Gershon, and Kohath, and Merari. **18** And these [are] the names of the sons of Gershon by their families: Libni and Shimei. **19** And the sons of Kohath by their families: Amram, and Izhar, Hebron, and Uzziel. **20** And the sons of Merari by their families: Mahli and Mushi; these are the families of the Levites, by the house of their fathers. **21** Of Gershon—the family of the Libnite and the family of the Shimite; these are the families of the Gershonite. **22** Their numbered ones, in number, every male from a son of a month and upward, their numbered ones [are] seven thousand and five hundred. **23** The families of the Gershonite encamp westward behind the Dwelling Place. **24** And the prince of a father's house for the Gershonite [is] Eliasaph son of Lael. **25** And the charge of the sons of Gershon in the Tent of Meeting [is] the Dwelling Place, and the tent, its

NUMBERS

covering, and the veil at the opening of the Tent of Meeting, **26** and the hangings of the court, and the veil at the opening of the court, which [is] by the Dwelling Place and by the altar all around, and its cords, to all its service. **27** And of Kohath—the family of the Amramite, and the family of the Izharite, and the family of the Hebronite, and the family of the Uzzielite; these are families of the Kohathite. **28** In number, all the males, from a son of a month and upward, [are] eight thousand and six hundred, keeping the charge of the holy place. **29** The families of the sons of Kohath encamp southward by the side of the Dwelling Place. **30** And the prince of a father's house for the families of the Kohathite [is] Elizaphan son of Uzziel. **31** And their charge [is] the Ark, and the table, and the lampstand, and the altars, and the vessels of the holy place with which they serve, and the veil, and all its service. **32** And Eleazar son of Aaron the priest [is] the prince of the princes of the Levites, [with] the oversight of the keepers of the charge of the holy place. **33** Of Merari—the family of the Mahlite and the family of the Mushite; these [are] the families of Merari. **34** And their numbered ones, in number, all the males from a son of a month and upward, [are] six thousand and two hundred. **35** And the prince of a father's house for the families of Merari [is] Zuriel son of Abihail; they encamp northward by the side of the Dwelling Place. **36** And the oversight [and] charge of the sons of Merari [are] the boards of the Dwelling Place, and its bars, and its pillars, and its sockets, and all its vessels, and all its service, **37** and the pillars of the court all around, and their sockets, and their pins, and their cords. **38** And those encamping before the Dwelling Place eastward, before the Tent of Meeting, at the east, [are] Moses and Aaron, and his sons, keeping the charge of the sanctuary for the charge of the sons of Israel, and the stranger who comes near is put to death. **39** All those numbered of the Levites whom Moses numbered—Aaron also—by the command of YHWH, by their families, every male from a son of a month and upward, [are] twenty-two thousand. **40** And YHWH says to Moses, "Number every firstborn male of the sons of Israel from a son of a month and upward, and take up the number of their names; **41** and you have taken the Levites for Me (I [am] YHWH), instead of every firstborn among the sons of Israel, and the livestock of the Levites instead of every firstling among the livestock of the sons of Israel." **42** And Moses numbers, as YHWH has commanded him, all the firstborn among the sons of Israel. **43** And every firstborn male, by the number of names, from a son of a month and upward, of their numbered ones, are twenty-two thousand two hundred and seventy-three. **44** And YHWH speaks to Moses, saying, **45** "Take the Levites instead of every firstborn among the sons of Israel, and the livestock of the Levites instead of their livestock; and the Levites have been Mine; I [am] YHWH. **46** And [from] those ransomed of the two hundred and seventy-three of the firstborn of the sons of Israel, who are more than the Levites, **47** you have even taken five shekels apiece by the counted head—you take by the shekel of the holy place; the shekel [is] twenty gerahs; **48** and you have given the money to Aaron and to his sons, whereby those over and above are ransomed." **49** And Moses takes the ransom money from those over and above those ransomed by the Levites; **50** he has taken the money from the firstborn of the sons of Israel—one thousand and three hundred and sixty-five, by the shekel of the holy place; **51** and Moses gives the money of those ransomed to Aaron and to his sons, according to the command of YHWH, as YHWH has commanded Moses.

4 And YHWH speaks to Moses and to Aaron, saying, **2** "Take a census of the sons of Kohath from the midst of the sons of Levi, by their families, by the house of their fathers; **3** from a son of thirty years and upward, even until a son of fifty years, everyone going in to the host, to do work in the Tent of Meeting. **4** This [is] the service of the sons of Kohath in the Tent of Meeting [for] the most holy things: **5** when Aaron and his sons have come in, in the journeying of the camp, and have taken down the veil of the hanging, and have covered the Ark of the Testimony with it, **6** then they have put a covering of tachash skin on it, and have spread a garment completely of blue above, and have placed its poles. **7** And they spread a garment of blue over the table of the presence, and have put the dishes, and the spoons, and the bowls, and the cups of the drink-offering

NUMBERS

on it, and the bread of continuity is on it, **8** and they have spread a garment of scarlet over them, and have covered it with a covering of tachash skin, and have placed its poles, **9** and have taken a garment of blue, and have covered the lampstand of the lamp, and its lights, and its snuffers, and its snuff-dishes, and all its oil vessels with which they minister to it; **10** and they have put it and all its vessels into a covering of tachash skin, and have put [it] on the bar. **11** And they spread a garment of blue over the golden altar, and have covered it with a covering of tachash skin, and have placed its poles, **12** and have taken all the vessels of ministry with which they minister in the holy place, and have put [them] into a garment of blue, and have covered them with a covering of tachash skin, and have put [them] on the bar, **13** and have removed the ashes of the altar, and have spread a garment of purple over it, **14** and have put on it all its vessels with which they minister on it—the censers, the hooks, and the shovels, and the bowls, all the vessels of the altar—and have spread a covering of tachash skin on it, and have placed its poles. **15** And Aaron has finished—his sons also—covering the holy place, and all the vessels of the holy place, in the journeying of the camp, and afterward the sons of Kohath come in to carry [it], and they do not come to the holy thing, lest they have died; these [things are] the burden of the sons of Kohath in the Tent of Meeting. **16** And the oversight of Eleazar, son of Aaron the priest, [is] the oil of the lamp, and the spice-incense, and the present of continuity, and the anointing oil, the oversight of all the Dwelling Place and of all that [is] in it, in the sanctuary and in its vessels." **17** And YHWH speaks to Moses and to Aaron, saying, **18** "You do not cut off the tribe of the families of the Kohathite from the midst of the Levites; **19** but do this for them, and they have lived and do not die in their drawing near [to] the Holy of Holies: Aaron and his sons go in, and have set them, each man to his service, and to his burden, **20** and they do not go in to see when the holy thing is swallowed, lest they have died." **21** And YHWH speaks to Moses, saying, **22** "Also take a census of the sons of Gershon by the house of their fathers, by their families; **23** from a son of thirty years and upward, until a son of fifty years, you number them—everyone who is going in to serve the host, to do the service in the Tent of Meeting. **24** This [is] the service of the families of the Gershonite, to serve and for burden: **25** and they have carried the curtains of the Dwelling Place, and the Tent of Meeting, its covering, and the covering of the tachash [skin] which [is] on it above, and the veil at the opening of the Tent of Meeting, **26** and the hangings of the court, and the veil at the opening of the gate of the court which [is] by the Dwelling Place, and by the altar all around, and their cords, and all the vessels of their service, and all that is made for them—and they have served. **27** By the command of Aaron and his sons is all the service of the sons of the Gershonite, in all their burden and in all their service; and you have laid a charge on them concerning the charge of all their burden. **28** This [is] the service of the families of the sons of the Gershonite in the Tent of Meeting; and their charge [is] under the hand of Ithamar son of Aaron the priest. **29** The sons of Merari, by their families, by the house of their fathers—you number them; **30** from a son of thirty years and upward even to a son of fifty years, you number them—everyone who is going in to the host, to do the service of the Tent of Meeting. **31** And this [is] the charge of their burden, of all their service in the Tent of Meeting: the boards of the Dwelling Place, and its bars, and its pillars, and its sockets, **32** and the pillars of the court all around, and their sockets, and their pins, and their cords, of all their vessels, and of all their service; and you number the vessels of the charge of their burden by name. **33** This [is] the service of the families of the sons of Merari, for all their service, in the Tent of Meeting, by the hand of Ithamar son of Aaron the priest." **34** And Moses numbers—Aaron also, and the princes of the congregation—the sons of the Kohathite, by their families, and by the house of their fathers, **35** from a son of thirty years and upward even to a son of fifty years, everyone who is going in to the host, for service in the Tent of Meeting, **36** and their numbered ones, by their families, are two thousand seven hundred and fifty. **37** These [are] those numbered of the families of the Kohathite, everyone who is serving in the Tent of Meeting, whom Moses and Aaron numbered by the command of YHWH, by the hand of Moses. **38** And those numbered of the sons of

NUMBERS

Gershon, by their families, and by the house of their fathers, **39** from a son of thirty years and upward even to a son of fifty years, everyone who is going in to the host, for service in the Tent of Meeting, **40** even their numbered ones, by their families, by the house of their fathers, are two thousand and six hundred and thirty. **41** These [are] those numbered of the families of the sons of Gershon, everyone who is serving in the Tent of Meeting, whom Moses and Aaron numbered by the command of YHWH. **42** And those numbered of the families of the sons of Merari, by their families, by the house of their fathers, **43** from a son of thirty years and upward even to a son of fifty years, everyone who is going in to the host, for service in the Tent of Meeting, **44** even their numbered ones, by their families, are three thousand and two hundred. **45** These [are] those numbered of the families of the sons of Merari, whom Moses and Aaron numbered by the command of YHWH, by the hand of Moses. **46** All those numbered, whom Moses numbered—Aaron also, and the princes of Israel—of the Levites, by their families, and by the house of their fathers, **47** from a son of thirty years and upward even to a son of fifty years, everyone who is going in to do the work of the service, even the service of burden in the Tent of Meeting, **48** even their numbered ones are eight thousand and five hundred and eighty; **49** he has numbered them by the command of YHWH, by the hand of Moses, each man by his service, and by his burden, with his numbered ones, as YHWH has commanded Moses.

5 And YHWH speaks to Moses, saying, **2** "Command the sons of Israel, and they send out of the camp every leper, and everyone with discharging, and everyone defiled by a body; **3** you send out from male even to female; you send them to the outside of the camp and they do not defile their camps in the midst of which I dwell." **4** And the sons of Israel do so, and they send them out to the outside of the camp; as YHWH has spoken to Moses so the sons of Israel have done. **5** And YHWH speaks to Moses, saying, **6** "Speak to the sons of Israel: Man or woman, when they do any of the sins of man, by committing a trespass against YHWH, and that person [is] guilty, **7** and they have confessed their sin which they have done, then he has restored his guilt in its principal, and is adding its fifth to it, and has given [it] to him in reference to whom he has been guilty. **8** And if the man has no redeemer to restore the guilt to, the guilt which is restored [is] to YHWH for the priest, apart from the ram of the atonements, whereby he makes atonement for him. **9** And every raised-offering of all the holy things of the sons of Israel, which they bring near to the priest, becomes his; **10** and any man's hallowed things become his; that which any man gives to the priest becomes his." **11** And YHWH speaks to Moses, saying, **12** "Speak to the sons of Israel, and you have said to them: When any man's wife turns aside, and has committed a trespass against him, **13** and a man has lain with her [with] the seed [from] intercourse, and it has been hid from the eyes of her husband, and concealed, and she has been defiled, and there is no witness against her, and she has not been caught, **14** and a spirit of jealousy has passed over him, and he has been jealous [for] his wife, and she has been defiled—or a spirit of jealousy has passed over him, and he has been jealous [for] his wife, and she has not been defiled— **15** then the man has brought in his wife to the priest, and he has brought in her offering for her—a tenth of the ephah of barley meal; he does not pour oil on it, nor does he put frankincense on it, for it [is] a present of jealousy, a present of memorial, causing remembrance of iniquity. **16** And the priest has brought her near, and has caused her to stand before YHWH, **17** and the priest has taken holy water in an earthen vessel, and the priest takes of the dust which is on the floor of the Dwelling Place, and has put [it] into the water, **18** and the priest has caused the woman to stand before YHWH, and has uncovered the woman's head, and has given the present of the memorial into her hands (it [is] a present of jealousy), and the bitter waters which cause the curse are in the hand of the priest. **19** And the priest has caused her to swear, and has said to the woman, If no man has lain with you, and if you have not turned aside [to] uncleanness under your husband, be free from these bitter waters which cause the curse; **20** and you, if you have turned aside under your husband, and if you have been defiled, and a man commits his intercourse with you besides your

NUMBERS

husband— **21** then the priest has caused the woman to swear with an oath of execration, and the priest has said to the woman— YHWH gives you for an execration and for a curse in the midst of your people, in YHWH's giving your thigh to fall and your belly to swell, **22** and these waters which cause the curse have gone into your bowels to cause the belly to swell and the thigh to fall; and the woman has said, Amen, Amen. **23** And the priest has written these execrations in a scroll, and has blotted [them] out with the bitter waters, **24** and has caused the woman to drink the bitter waters which cause the curse, and the waters which cause the curse have entered into her for bitter things. **25** And the priest has taken the present of jealousy out of the hand of the woman, and has waved the present before YHWH, and has brought it near to the altar; **26** and the priest has taken a handful of the present, its memorial, and has made incense on the altar, and afterward causes the woman to drink the water; **27** indeed, he has caused her to drink the water, and it has come to pass, if she has been defiled and commits a trespass against her husband, that the waters which cause the curse have gone into her for bitter things, and her belly has swelled, and her thigh has fallen, and the woman has become an execration in the midst of her people. **28** And if the woman has not been defiled, and is clean, then she has been acquitted, and has been sown [with] seed. **29** This [is] the law of jealousies when a wife turns aside under her husband and has been defiled, **30** or when a spirit of jealousy passes over a man and he has been jealous of his wife, then he has caused the woman to stand before YHWH, and the priest has done to her all this law, **31** and the man has been acquitted from iniquity, and that woman bears her iniquity."

6 And YHWH speaks to Moses, saying, **2** "Speak to the sons of Israel, and you have said to them: When a man or woman does extraordinarily by vowing a vow of a Nazarite, to be separate to YHWH, **3** he keeps separate from wine and strong drink; he does not drink vinegar of wine and vinegar of strong drink, and he does not drink any juice of grapes, and he does not eat moist or dry grapes; **4** all [the] days of his separation he does not eat of anything which is made of the wine-vine, from kernels even to husk. **5** All [the] days of the vow of his separation a razor does not pass over his head; he is holy until the fullness of the days [in] which he separates himself to YHWH; the upper part of the hair of his head has grown up. **6** All [the] days of his keeping separate to YHWH, he does not go near a dead person; **7** for his father, or for his mother, for his brother, or for his sister—he does not become unclean for them at their death, for the separation of his God [is] on his head; **8** all [the] days of his separation he [is] holy to YHWH. **9** And when the dead dies beside him in an instant, suddenly, and he has defiled the head of his separation, then he has shaved his head in the day of his cleansing; on the seventh day he shaves it, **10** and on the eighth day he brings in two turtle-doves or two young pigeons to the priest, to the opening of the Tent of Meeting, **11** and the priest has prepared one for a sin-offering and one for a burnt-offering, and has made atonement for him because of that which he has sinned by the body, and he has hallowed his head on that day; **12** and he has separated to YHWH the days of his separation, and he has brought in a lamb, a son of a year, for a guilt-offering, and the former days are fallen, for his separation has been defiled. **13** And this [is] the law of the Nazarite: in the day of the fullness of the days of his separation, he is brought to the opening of the Tent of Meeting, **14** and he has brought his offering near to YHWH—one male lamb, a son of a year, a perfect one, for a burnt-offering, and one female lamb, a daughter of a year, a perfect one, for a sin-offering, and one ram, a perfect one, for peace-offerings, **15** and a basket of unleavened things of flour, cakes mixed with oil, and thin cakes of unleavened things anointed with oil, and their present, and their drink-offerings. **16** And the priest has brought [them] near before YHWH, and has made his sin-offering and his burnt-offering; **17** and he makes the ram [as] a sacrifice of peace-offerings to YHWH, besides the basket of unleavened things; and the priest has made its present and its drink-offering. **18** And the Nazarite has shaved (at the opening of the Tent of Meeting) the head of his separation, and has taken the hair of the head of his separation, and has put [it] on the fire which [is] under the sacrifice of the peace-offerings. **19** And the priest has taken the boiled shoulder from the ram, and one unleavened cake out of the basket, and one thin unleavened cake, and has put [them] on the palms of the Nazarite after his shaving [the hair of] his separation; **20** and the priest has waved them [as] a wave-offering before YHWH; it [is] holy to the priest, besides the breast of the wave-offering, and besides the leg of the raised-offering; and afterward the Nazarite drinks wine. **21** This [is] the law of the Nazarite who vows his offering to YHWH for his separation, apart from that which his hand attains; according to his vow which he vows so he does by the law of his separation." **22** And YHWH speaks to Moses, saying, **23** "Speak to Aaron and to his sons, saying, Thus you bless the sons of Israel, saying to them: **24** YHWH bless you and keep you; **25** YHWH cause His face to shine on you, ‖ And favor you; **26** YHWH lift up His countenance on you, ‖ And appoint for you—peace. **27** And they have put My Name on the sons of Israel, and I bless them."

7 And it comes to pass on the day [when] Moses [was] finishing to set up the Dwelling Place, that he anoints it, and sanctifies it, and all its vessels, and the altar, and all its vessels, and he anoints them, and sanctifies them, **2** and the princes of Israel (heads of the house of their fathers, they [are] princes of the tribes, they who are standing over those numbered) bring near, **3** indeed, they bring their offering before YHWH of six covered wagons and twelve oxen—a wagon for two of the princes, and an ox for one—and they bring them near before the Dwelling Place. **4** And YHWH speaks to Moses, saying, **5** "Receive [these] from them, and they have been [used] for doing the service of the Tent of Meeting, and you have given them to the Levites, each according to his service." **6** And Moses takes the wagons and the oxen, and gives them to the Levites. **7** He has given the two wagons and the four oxen to the sons of Gershon, according to their service, **8** and he has given the four wagons and the eight oxen to the sons of Merari, according to their service, by the hand of Ithamar son of Aaron the priest, **9** but he has not given [any] to the sons of Kohath, for the service of the holy place [is] on them, [which] they carry on the shoulder. **10** And the princes bring the dedication of the altar near in the day of its being anointed, indeed, the princes bring their offering near before the altar. **11** And YHWH says to Moses, "One prince a day, one prince a day—they bring their offering near for the dedication of the altar." **12** And he who is bringing his offering near on the first day is Nahshon son of Amminadab, of the tribe of Judah. **13** And his offering [is] one silver dish, its weight one hundred and thirty [shekels], [and] one silver bowl of seventy shekels, by the shekel of the holy place, both of them full of flour mixed with oil for a present; **14** one golden spoon of ten [shekels], full of incense; **15** one bullock, a son of the herd, one ram, one lamb, a son of a year, for a burnt-offering; **16** one kid of the goats for a sin-offering; **17** and for a sacrifice of the peace-offerings: two oxen, five rams, five male goats, five lambs, sons of a year; this [is] the offering of Nahshon son of Amminadab. **18** On the second day Nethaneel son of Zuar, prince of Issachar, has brought [an offering] near. **19** He has brought his offering near: one silver dish, its weight one hundred and thirty [shekels], [and] one silver bowl of seventy shekels, by the shekel of the holy place, both of them full of flour mixed with oil for a present; **20** one golden spoon of ten [shekels], full of incense; **21** one bullock, a son of the herd, one ram, one lamb, a son of a year, for a burnt-offering; **22** one kid of the goats for a sin-offering; **23** and for a sacrifice of the peace-offerings: two oxen, five rams, five male goats, five lambs, sons of a year; this [is] the offering of Nethaneel son of Zuar. **24** On the third day, Eliab son of Helon, prince of the sons of Zebulun— **25** his offering [is] one silver dish, its weight one hundred and thirty [shekels], [and] one silver bowl of seventy shekels, by the shekel of the holy place, both of them full of flour mixed with oil for a present; **26** one golden spoon of ten [shekels], full of incense; **27** one bullock, a son of the herd, one ram, one lamb, a son of a year, for a burnt-offering; **28** one kid of the goats for a sin-offering; **29** and for a sacrifice of the peace-offerings: two oxen, five rams, five male goats, five lambs, sons of a year; this [is] the offering of Eliab son of Helon. **30** On the fourth day, Elizur son of Shedeur, prince of the sons of Reuben— **31** his offering [is] one silver dish, its weight one hundred and thirty [shekels], [and] one silver bowl of seventy shekels, by

NUMBERS

the shekel of the holy place, both of them full of flour mixed with oil for a present; 32 one golden spoon of ten [shekels], full of incense; 33 one bullock, a son of the herd, one ram, one lamb, a son of a year, for a burnt-offering; 34 one kid of the goats for a sin-offering; 35 and for a sacrifice of the peace-offerings: two oxen, five rams, five male goats, five lambs, sons of a year; this [is] the offering of Elizur son of Shedeur. 36 On the fifth day, Shelumiel son of Zurishaddai, prince of the sons of Simeon— 37 his offering [is] one silver dish, its weight one hundred and thirty [shekels], [and] one silver bowl of seventy shekels, by the shekel of the holy place, both of them full of flour mixed with oil for a present; 38 one golden spoon of ten [shekels], full of incense; 39 one bullock, a son of the herd, one ram, one lamb, a son of a year, for a burnt-offering; 40 one kid of the goats for a sin-offering; 41 and for a sacrifice of the peace-offerings: two oxen, five rams, five male goats, five lambs, sons of a year; this [is] the offering of Shelumiel son of Zurishaddai. 42 On the sixth day, Eliasaph son of Deuel, prince of the sons of Gad— 43 his offering [is] one silver dish, its weight one hundred and thirty [shekels], [and] one silver bowl of seventy shekels, by the shekel of the holy place, both of them full of flour mixed with oil for a present; 44 one golden spoon of ten [shekels], full of incense; 45 one bullock, a son of the herd, one ram, one lamb, a son of a year, for a burnt-offering; 46 one kid of the goats for a sin-offering; 47 and for a sacrifice of the peace-offerings: two oxen, five rams, five male goats, five lambs, sons of a year; this [is] the offering of Eliasaph son of Deuel. 48 On the seventh day, Elishama son of Ammihud, prince of the sons of Ephraim— 49 his offering [is] one silver dish, its weight one hundred and thirty [shekels], [and] one silver bowl of seventy shekels, by the shekel of the holy place, both of them full of flour mixed with oil for a present; 50 one golden spoon of ten [shekels], full of incense; 51 one bullock, a son of the herd, one ram, one lamb, a son of a year, for a burnt-offering; 52 one kid of the goats for a sin-offering; 53 and for a sacrifice of the peace-offerings: two oxen, five rams, five male goats, five lambs, sons of a year; this [is] the offering of Elishama son of Ammihud. 54 On the eighth day, Gamaliel son of Pedahzur, prince of the sons of Manasseh— 55 his offering [is] one silver dish, its weight one hundred and thirty [shekels], [and] one silver bowl of seventy shekels, by the shekel of the holy place, both of them full of flour mixed with oil for a present; 56 one golden spoon of ten [shekels], full of incense; 57 one bullock, a son of the herd, one ram, one lamb, a son of a year, for a burnt-offering; 58 one kid of the goats for a sin-offering; 59 and for a sacrifice of the peace-offerings: two oxen, five rams, five male goats, five lambs, sons of a year; this [is] the offering of Gamaliel son of Pedahzur. 60 On the ninth day, Abidan son of Gideoni, prince of the sons of Benjamin— 61 his offering [is] one silver dish, its weight one hundred and thirty [shekels], [and] one silver bowl of seventy shekels, by the shekel of the holy place, both of them full of flour mixed with oil for a present; 62 one golden spoon of ten [shekels], full of incense; 63 one bullock, a son of the herd, one ram, one lamb, a son of a year, for a burnt-offering; 64 one kid of the goats for a sin-offering: 65 and for a sacrifice of the peace-offerings: two oxen, five rams, five male goats, five lambs, sons of a year; this [is] the offering of Abidan son of Gideoni. 66 On the tenth day, Ahiezer son of Ammishaddai, prince of the sons of Dan— 67 his offering [is] one silver dish, its weight one hundred and thirty [shekels], [and] one silver bowl of seventy shekels, by the shekel of the holy place, both of them full of flour mixed with oil for a present; 68 one golden spoon of ten [shekels], full of incense; 69 one bullock, a son of the herd, one ram, one lamb, a son of a year, for a burnt-offering; 70 one kid of the goats for a sin-offering; 71 and for a sacrifice of the peace-offerings: two oxen, five rams, five male goats, five lambs, sons of a year; this [is] the offering of Ahiezer son of Ammishaddai. 72 On the eleventh day, Pagiel son of Ocran, prince of the sons of Asher— 73 his offering [is] one silver dish, its weight one hundred and thirty [shekels], [and] one silver bowl of seventy shekels, by the shekel of the holy place, both of them full of flour mixed with oil for a present; 74 one golden spoon of ten [shekels], full of incense; 75 one bullock, a son of the herd, one ram, one lamb, a son of a year, for a burnt-offering; 76 one kid of the goats for a sin-offering; 77 and for a sacrifice of the peace-offerings: two oxen, five rams, five male goats, five lambs, sons of a year; this [is] the offering of Pagiel son of Ocran. **78** On the twelfth day, Ahira son of Enan, prince of the sons of Naphtali— **79** his offering [is] one silver dish, its weight one hundred and thirty [shekels], [and] one silver bowl of seventy shekels, by the shekel of the holy place, both of them full of flour mixed with oil for a present; **80** one golden spoon of ten [shekels], full of incense; **81** one bullock, a son of the herd, one ram, one lamb, a son of a year, for a burnt-offering; **82** one kid of the goats for a sin-offering; **83** and for a sacrifice of the peace-offerings: two oxen, five rams, five male goats, five lambs, sons of a year; this [is] the offering of Ahira son of Enan. **84** This [is] the dedication of the altar, in the day of its being anointed by the princes of Israel: twelve silver dishes, twelve silver bowls, twelve golden spoons; **85** each silver dish [is] one hundred and thirty [shekels], and each bowl seventy; all the silver of the vessels [is] two thousand and four hundred [shekels], by the shekel of the holy place; **86** twelve golden spoons full of incense, ten [shekels] each spoon, by the shekel of the holy place; all the gold of the spoons [is] one hundred and twenty [shekels]; **87** all the oxen for burnt-offering [are] twelve bullocks; twelve rams, twelve lambs, sons of a year, and their present, and twelve kids of the goats for sin-offering; **88** and all the oxen for the sacrifice of the peace-offerings [are] twenty-four bullocks; sixty rams, sixty male goats, sixty lambs, sons of a year; this is the dedication of the altar in the day of its being anointed. **89** And in the entering of Moses into the Tent of Meeting to speak with Him, indeed, he hears the voice speaking to him from off the propitiatory covering which [is] on the Ark of the Testimony, from between the two cherubim; and He speaks to him.

8 And YHWH speaks to Moses, saying, **2** "Speak to Aaron, and you have said to him: In your causing the lights to go up, the seven lights give light toward the front of the face of the lampstand." **3** And Aaron does so; he has caused its lights to go up toward the front of the face of the lampstand, as YHWH has commanded Moses. **4** And this [is] the work of the lampstand: beaten work of gold; from its thigh to its flower it [is] beaten work; as the appearance which YHWH showed Moses, so he has made the lampstand. **5** And YHWH speaks to Moses, saying, **6** "Take the Levites from the midst of the sons of Israel, and you have cleansed them. **7** And thus you do to them to cleanse them: sprinkle waters of atonement on them, and they have caused a razor to pass over all their flesh, and have washed their garments, and cleansed themselves, **8** and have taken a bullock, a son of the herd, and its present, flour mixed with oil, and you take a second bullock, a son of the herd, for a sin-offering; **9** and you have brought the Levites near before the Tent of Meeting, and you have assembled all the congregation of the sons of Israel, **10** and you have brought the Levites near before YHWH, and the sons of Israel have laid their hands on the Levites, **11** and Aaron has waved the Levites [as] a wave-offering before YHWH, from the sons of Israel, and they have been [consecrated] for doing the service of YHWH. **12** And the Levites lay their hands on the head of the bullocks, and make one a sin-offering and one a burnt-offering to YHWH, to atone for the Levites. **13** And you have caused the Levites to stand before Aaron, and before his sons, and have waved them [as] a wave-offering to YHWH; **14** and you have separated the Levites from the midst of the sons of Israel, and the Levites have become Mine; **15** and afterward the Levites come in to serve the Tent of Meeting, and you have cleansed them, and have waved them [as] a wave-offering. **16** For they are certainly given to Me out of the midst of the sons of Israel, instead of him who opens any womb—the firstborn of all; I have taken them for Myself from the sons of Israel; **17** for every firstborn among the sons of Israel [is] Mine, among man and among beast; in the day of My striking every firstborn in the land of Egypt I sanctified them for Myself; **18** and I take the Levites instead of every firstborn among the sons of Israel. **19** And I give the Levites [as] gifts to Aaron and to his sons, from the midst of the sons of Israel, to do the service of the sons of Israel in the Tent of Meeting, and to make atonement for the sons of Israel, and there is no plague among the sons of Israel in the sons of Israel drawing near to the holy place." **20** And Moses does—Aaron also, and all the congregation of the sons of Israel—to the Levites according to all that YHWH has commanded Moses concerning the

Levites; so the sons of Israel have done to them. **21** And the Levites cleanse themselves, and wash their garments, and Aaron waves them [as] a wave-offering before YHWH, and Aaron makes atonement for them to cleanse them, **22** and afterward the Levites have gone in to do their service in the Tent of Meeting, before Aaron and before his sons; as YHWH has commanded Moses concerning the Levites, so they have done to them. **23** And YHWH speaks to Moses, saying, **24** "This [is] who [is] for the Levites: from a son of twenty-five years and upward he goes in to serve the host in the service of the Tent of Meeting, **25** and from a son of fifty years he returns from the host of the service, and does not serve anymore, **26** and he has ministered with his brothers in the Tent of Meeting, to keep the charge, and does not do service; thus you do to the Levites concerning their charge."

9 And YHWH speaks to Moses, in the wilderness of Sinai, in the second year of their going out of the land of Egypt, in the first month, saying, **2** "Also, the sons of Israel prepare the Passover in its appointed time; **3** in the fourteenth day of this month between the evenings you prepare it in its appointed time; you prepare it according to all its statutes and according to all its ordinances." **4** And Moses speaks to the sons of Israel to prepare the Passover, **5** and they prepare the Passover in the first [month], on the fourteenth day of the month, between the evenings, in the wilderness of Sinai; according to all that YHWH has commanded Moses, so the sons of Israel have done. **6** And there are men who have been defiled by the body of a man, and they have not been able to prepare the Passover on that day, and they come near before Moses and before Aaron on that day, **7** and those men say to him, "We are defiled by the body of a man; why are we withheld so as not to bring the offering of YHWH near in its appointed time, in the midst of the sons of Israel?" **8** And Moses says to them, "Stand, and I hear what YHWH has commanded concerning you." **9** And YHWH speaks to Moses, saying, **10** "Speak to the sons of Israel, saying, Though any man is unclean by a body or in a distant journey (of you or of your generations), he has still prepared a Passover to YHWH; **11** they prepare it in the second month, on the fourteenth day, between the evenings; they eat it with unleavened and bitter things; **12** they do not leave of [it] until morning; and they do not break a bone in it; they prepare it according to all the statute of the Passover. **13** And the man who is clean, and has not been on a journey, and has ceased to prepare the Passover, indeed, that person has been cut off from his people; because he has not brought the offering of YHWH near in its appointed time, that man bears his sin. **14** And when a sojourner sojourns with you, then he has prepared a Passover to YHWH—according to the statute of the Passover and according to its ordinance, so he does; one statute is for you, indeed, for a sojourner and for a native of the land."

15 And in the day of the raising up of the Dwelling Place, the cloud has covered the Dwelling Place, even the Tent of the Testimony; and in the evening there is as an appearance of fire on the Dwelling Place until morning; **16** so it is continually; the cloud covers it, also the appearance of fire by night. **17** And according to the going up of the cloud from off the tent, then afterward the sons of Israel journey; and in the place where the cloud dwells, there the sons of Israel encamp; **18** by the command of YHWH the sons of Israel journey, and by the command of YHWH they encamp; all the days that the cloud dwells over the Dwelling Place they encamp. **19** And in the cloud prolonging itself over the Dwelling Place many days, then the sons of Israel have kept the charge of YHWH, and do not journey. **20** And so when the cloud is over the Dwelling Place [for] a number of days: by the command of YHWH they encamp, and by the command of YHWH they journey. **21** And so when the cloud is from evening until morning, when the cloud has gone up in the morning, then they have journeyed; whether by day or by night, when the cloud has gone up, then they have journeyed. **22** Whether two days, or a month, or days, in the cloud prolonging itself over the Dwelling Place, to dwell over it, the sons of Israel encamp and do not journey; and in its being lifted up they journey. **23** By the command of YHWH they encamp, and by the command of YHWH they journey; they have kept the charge of YHWH, by the command of YHWH in the hand of Moses.

NUMBERS

10 And Y<small>HWH</small> speaks to Moses, saying, 2 "Make two trumpets of silver for yourself; you make them of beaten work, and they have been for you for the convocation of the congregation, and for the journeying of the camps; 3 and they have blown with them, and all the congregation has assembled to you at the opening of the Tent of Meeting. 4 And if they blow with one, then the princes, heads of the thousands of Israel, have assembled to you; 5 and you have blown—a shout, and the camps which are encamping eastward have journeyed. 6 And you have blown—a second shout, and the camps which are encamping southward have journeyed; they blow a shout for their journeys. 7 And in the assembling of the assembly you blow, and do not shout; 8 and sons of Aaron, the priests, blow with the trumpets; and they have been for a continuous statute to you throughout your generations. 9 And when you go into battle in your land against the adversary who is distressing you, then you have shouted with the trumpets, and you have been remembered before your God Y<small>HWH</small>, and you have been saved from your enemies. 10 And in the day of your gladness, and in your appointed times, and in the beginnings of your months, you have also blown with the trumpets over your burnt-offerings, and over the sacrifices of your peace-offerings, and they have been for a memorial to you before your God; I [am] your God Y<small>HWH</small>." 11 And it comes to pass, in the second year, in the second month, on the twentieth of the month, the cloud has gone up from off the Dwelling Place of the Testimony, 12 and the sons of Israel journey in their journeys from the wilderness of Sinai, and the cloud dwells in the wilderness of Paran; 13 and they journey at first by the command of Y<small>HWH</small> in the hand of Moses. 14 And the standard of the camp of the sons of Judah journeys in the first [place], by their hosts, and over its host [is] Nahshon son of Amminadab. 15 And over the host of the tribe of the sons of Issachar [is] Nathaneel son of Zuar. 16 And over the host of the tribe of the sons of Zebulun [is] Eliab son of Helon. 17 And the Dwelling Place has been taken down, and the sons of Gershon and the sons of Merari have journeyed, carrying the Dwelling Place. 18 And the standard of the camp of Reuben has journeyed, by their hosts, and over its host [is] Elizur son of Shedeur. 19 And over the host of the tribe of the sons of Simeon [is] Shelumiel son of Zurishaddai. 20 And over the host of the tribe of the sons of Gad [is] Eliasaph son of Deuel. 21 And the Kohathites have journeyed, carrying the Dwelling Place, and the [others] have raised up the Dwelling Place until their coming in. 22 And the standard of the camp of the sons of Ephraim has journeyed, by their hosts, and over its host [is] Elishama son of Ammihud. 23 And over the host of the tribe of the sons of Manasseh [is] Gamalial son of Pedahzur. 24 And over the host of the tribe of the sons of Benjamin [is] Abidan son of Gideoni. 25 And the standard of the camp of the sons of Dan has journeyed (rearward to all the camps), by their hosts, and over its host [is] Ahiezer son of Ammishaddai. 26 And over the host of the tribe of the sons of Asher [is] Pagiel son of Ocran. 27 And over the host of the tribe of the sons of Naphtali [is] Ahira son of Enan. 28 These [are] the journeys of the sons of Israel by their hosts when they journey. 29 And Moses says to Hobab son of Raguel the Midianite, father-in-law of Moses, "We are journeying to the place of which Y<small>HWH</small> has said, I give it to you; go with us, and we have done good to you, for Y<small>HWH</small> has spoken good concerning Israel." 30 And he says to him, "I do not go; but I go to my land and to my family." 31 And he says, "Please do not forsake us, because you have known our encamping in the wilderness, and you have been to us for eyes; 32 and it has come to pass, when you go with us—indeed, it has come to pass—that good which Y<small>HWH</small> does kindly with us, we have done it kindly to you." 33 And they journey from the mountain of Y<small>HWH</small> a journey of three days; and the Ark of the Covenant of Y<small>HWH</small> is journeying before them [for] the journey of three days, to spy out a resting place for them; 34 and the cloud of Y<small>HWH</small> [is] on them by day, in their journeying from the camp. 35 And it comes to pass in the journeying of the Ark, that Moses says, "Rise, O Y<small>HWH</small>, and Your enemies are scattered, and those hating You flee from Your presence." 36 And in its resting he says, "Return, O Y<small>HWH</small>, [to] the myriads, the thousands of Israel."

11 And the people are evil, as those sighing habitually in the ears of

NUMBERS

YHWH, and YHWH hears, and His anger burns, and the fire of YHWH burns among them, and consumes in the extremity of the camp. **2** And the people cry to Moses, and Moses prays to YHWH, and the fire is quenched; **3** and he calls the name of that place Taberah, for the fire of YHWH has "burned" among them. **4** And the rabble who [are] in its midst have lusted greatly, and the sons of Israel also turn back and weep, and say, "Who gives us flesh? **5** We have remembered the fish which we eat in Egypt for nothing, the cucumbers, and the melons, and the leeks, and the onions, and the garlic; **6** and now our soul [is] dry, there is not anything, except the manna, before our eyes." **7** And the manna is as coriander seed, and its aspect as the aspect of bdellium; **8** the people have turned aside and gathered [it], and ground [it] with millstones, or beat [it] in a mortar, and boiled [it] in a pan, and made it cakes, and its taste has been as the taste of the moisture of oil. **9** And in the descending of the dew on the camp by night, the manna descends on it. **10** And Moses hears the people weeping by its families, each at the opening of his tent, and the anger of YHWH burns exceedingly, and in the eyes of Moses [it is] evil. **11** And Moses says to YHWH, "Why have You done evil to Your servant? And why have I not found grace in Your eyes—to put the burden of all this people on me? **12** I—have I conceived all this people? I—have I begotten it, that You say to me, Carry it in your bosom, as the one supporting carries the nursing suckling, to the ground which You have sworn to its fathers? **13** From where do I have flesh to give to all this people? For they weep to me, saying, Give flesh to us, and we eat. **14** I am not able—I alone—to bear all this people, for [it is] too heavy for me; **15** and if thus You are doing to me—please slay me; slay, if I have found grace in your eyes, and do not let me look on my affliction." **16** And YHWH says to Moses, "Gather to Me seventy men from [the] elderly of Israel, whom you have known that they are [the] elderly of the people, and its authorities; and you have taken them to the Tent of Meeting, and they have stationed themselves there with you, **17** and I have come down and spoken with you there, and have kept back of the Spirit which [is] on you, and have put [that One] on them, and they have borne some of the burden of the people with you, and you do not bear [it] alone. **18** And you say to the people: Sanctify yourselves for tomorrow, and you have eaten flesh, for you have wept in the ears of YHWH, saying, Who gives us flesh? For we [had] good in Egypt; and YHWH has given flesh to you, and you have eaten. **19** You do not eat one day, nor two days, nor five days, nor ten days, nor twenty days, **20** [but] even to a month of days, until it comes out from your nostrils, and it has become an abomination to you, because that you have loathed YHWH, who [is] in your midst, and weep before Him, saying, Why is this [that] we have come out of Egypt!" **21** And Moses says, "Six hundred thousand footmen [are] the people in whose midst I [dwell]; and You, You have said, I give flesh to them, and they have eaten [for] a month of days! **22** Is flock and herd slaughtered for them, that one has found [enough] for them? Are all the fishes of the sea gathered for them, that one has found [enough] for them?" **23** And YHWH says to Moses, "Has the hand of YHWH become short? Now you see whether My word meets you or not." **24** And Moses goes out, and speaks the words of YHWH to the people, and gathers seventy men from [the] elderly of the people, and causes them to stand around the tent, **25** and YHWH comes down in the cloud, and speaks to him, and keeps back of the Spirit which [is] on him, and puts [that One] on the seventy elderly men; and it comes to pass at the resting of the Spirit on them, that they prophesy, and they have never done [so] again. **26** And two of the men are left in the camp, the name of the first [is] Eldad and the name of the second Medad, and the spirit rests on them (and they are among those written, but they have not gone out to the tent), and they prophesy in the camp; **27** and the young man runs, and declares [it] to Moses, and says, "Eldad and Medad are prophesying in the camp." **28** And Joshua son of Nun, minister of Moses, [one] of his young men, answers and says, "My lord Moses, restrain them." **29** And Moses says to him, "Are you zealous for me? O that all YHWH's people were prophets! That YHWH would put His Spirit on them!" **30** And Moses is gathered to the camp, he and [the] elderly of Israel. **31** And a spirit has journeyed from YHWH, and cuts off quails from the sea, and leaves [them] by the camp, as a day's journey here and as a day's journey there, around the camp, and about two cubits above the face of the land. **32** And the people rise all that day, and all the night, and all the day after, and gather the quails—he who has least has gathered ten homers—and they spread them out for themselves around the camp. **33** The flesh is yet between their teeth—it is not yet cut off—and the anger of YHWH has burned among the people, and YHWH strikes [with] a very great striking among the people; **34** and [one] calls the name of that place Kibroth-Hattaavah, for there they have buried the people who lust. **35** From Kibroth-Hattaavah the people have journeyed to Hazeroth, and they are in Hazeroth.

12 And Miriam speaks—Aaron also—against Moses concerning the circumstance of the Cushite woman whom he had taken, for he had taken a Cushite woman; **2** and they say, "Has YHWH only spoken by Moses? Has he not also spoken by us?" And YHWH hears. **3** And the man Moses [is] very humble, more than any of the men who [are] on the face of the ground. **4** And YHWH suddenly says to Moses, and to Aaron, and to Miriam, "Come out, you three, to the Tent of Meeting"; and those three come out. **5** And YHWH comes down in the pillar of the cloud, and stands at the opening of the tent, and calls Aaron and Miriam, and both of them come out. **6** And He says, "Now hear My words: If your prophet is of YHWH, ‖ I make Myself known to him in a vision; I speak with him in a dream. **7** Not so My servant Moses; He [is] steadfast in all My house. **8** I speak with him mouth to mouth, ‖ Even [by] an appearance, and not in riddles; And he beholds the form of YHWH attentively. Now why have you not been afraid ‖ To speak against My servant—against Moses?" **9** And the anger of YHWH burns against them, and He goes on, **10** and the cloud has turned aside from off the tent, and behold, Miriam [is] leprous as snow; and Aaron turns to Miriam, and behold, leprous! **11** And Aaron says to Moses, "O my lord, please do not lay [this] sin on us [in] which we have been foolish, and [in] which we have sinned; **12** please do not let her be as [one] dead, when in his coming out from the womb of his mother—the half of his flesh is consumed." **13** And Moses cries to YHWH, saying, "O God, please give healing to her! Please!" **14** And YHWH says to Moses, "But [if] her father had but spat in her face—is she not ashamed [for] seven days? She is shut out [for] seven days at the outside of the camp, and afterward she is gathered." **15** And Miriam is shut out at the outside of the camp [for] seven days, and the people have not journeyed until Miriam is gathered; **16** and afterward the people have journeyed from Hazeroth, and they encamp in the wilderness of Paran.

13 And YHWH speaks to Moses, saying, **2** "Send men for yourself, and they spy out the land of Canaan, which I am giving to the sons of Israel; one man—you send one man for the tribe of his fathers, everyone a prince among them." **3** And Moses sends them from the wilderness of Paran by the command of YHWH; all of them [are] men, [and] they are heads of the sons of Israel, **4** and these [are] their names: for the tribe of Reuben, Shammua son of Zaccur; **5** for the tribe of Simeon, Shaphat son of Hori; **6** for the tribe of Judah, Caleb son of Jephunneh; **7** for the tribe of Issachar, Igal son of Joseph; **8** for the tribe of Ephraim, Oshea son of Nun; **9** for the tribe of Benjamin, Palti son of Raphu; **10** for the tribe of Zebulun, Gaddiel son of Sodi; **11** for the tribe of Joseph (for the tribe of Manasseh), Gaddi son of Susi; **12** for the tribe of Dan, Ammiel son of Gemalli; **13** for the tribe of Asher, Sethur son of Michael; **14** for the tribe of Naphtali, Nahbi son of Vopshi; **15** for the tribe of Gad, Geuel son of Machi. **16** These [are] the names of the men whom Moses has sent to spy out the land; and Moses calls Hoshea son of Nun, Joshua. **17** And Moses sends them to spy out the land of Canaan and says to them, "Go up this [way] into the south, and you have gone up the mountain, **18** and have seen the land, what it [is], and the people which is dwelling on it, whether it [is] strong or feeble, [and] whether it [is] few or many; **19** and what the land [is] in which it is dwelling, whether it [is] good or bad; and what [are] the cities in which it is dwelling, whether in camps or in fortresses. **20** And what the land [is], whether it [is] fat or lean; whether there is wood in it or not; and you have strengthened yourselves, and have taken of the fruit of the land"; now the days [are] days of the first-fruits of grapes. **21** And they go up and spy out the land, from the wilderness of Zin to Rehob at the going in to Hamath; **22** and they go up by the south, and come to Hebron, and there [are] Ahiman, Sheshai, and Talmai, children of Anak (and Hebron was built seven years before Zoan in Egypt), **23** and they come to the Brook of Eshcol, and cut down a branch and one cluster of grapes there, and they carry it on a staff by two, also [some] of the pomegranates, and of the figs. **24** That place has been called the Brook of Eshcol, because of the cluster which the sons of Israel cut from there. **25** And they return from spying out the land at the end of forty days. **26** And they go and come to Moses, and to Aaron, and to all the congregation of the sons of Israel, to the wilderness of Paran, to Kadesh; and they bring them and all the congregation back word, and show them the fruit of the land. **27** And they recount to him, and say, "We came to the land to where you have sent us, and it is indeed flowing with milk and honey—and this [is] its fruit; **28** only, surely the people which is dwelling in the land [is] strong; and the cities are fortified [and] very great; and we have also seen children of Anak there. **29** Amalek is dwelling in the land of the south, and the Hittite, and the Jebusite, and the Amorite are dwelling in the hill country, and the Canaanite is dwelling by the sea, and by the side of the Jordan." **30** And Caleb stills the people concerning Moses and says, "Let us certainly go up—and we have possessed it; for we are thoroughly able to [do] it." **31** And the men who have gone up with him said, "We are not able to go up against the people, for it [is] stronger than we"; **32** and they bring out an evil account of the land which they have spied out to the sons of Israel, saying, "The land into which we passed over to spy it out is a land eating up its inhabitants; and all the people whom we saw in its midst [are] men of stature; **33** and there we saw the giants, sons of Anak, of the giants; and we are as grasshoppers in our own eyes—and so we were in their eyes."

14 And all the congregation lifts up, and they give forth their voice, and the people weep during that night; **2** and all the sons of Israel murmur against Moses and against Aaron, and all the congregation says to them, "O that we had died in the land of Egypt, or in this wilderness, O that we had died! **3** And why is YHWH bringing us to this land to fall by the sword, [that] our wives and our infants become a prey? Is it not good for us to return to Egypt?" **4** And they say to one another, "Let us appoint a head and return to Egypt." **5** And Moses falls—Aaron also—on their faces, before all the assembly of the congregation of the sons of Israel. **6** And Joshua son of Nun and Caleb son of Jephunneh, of those spying out the land, have torn their garments, **7** and they speak to all the congregation of the sons of Israel, saying, "The land into which we have passed over to spy it out [is] a very, very good land; **8** if YHWH has delighted in us, then He has brought us into this land, and has given it to us, a land which is flowing with milk and honey; **9** only, do not rebel against YHWH: and you, do not fear the people of the land, for they [are] our bread; their defense has turned aside from off them, and YHWH [is] with us; do not fear them." **10** And all the congregation says to stone them with stones, and the glory of YHWH has appeared in the Tent of Meeting to all the sons of Israel. **11** And YHWH says to Moses, "Until when does this people despise Me? And until when do they not believe in Me, for all the signs which I have done in its midst? **12** I strike it with pestilence, and dispossess it, and make you become a nation greater and mightier than it." **13** And Moses says to YHWH, "Then the Egyptians have heard! For with Your power You have brought up this people out of their midst, **14** and they have said [it] to the inhabitant of this land, they have heard that You, YHWH, [are] in the midst of this people, that You are seen eye to eye—O YHWH, and Your cloud is standing over them—and in a pillar of cloud You are going before them by day, and in a pillar of fire by night. **15** And You have put to death this people as one man, and the nations who have heard Your fame have spoken, saying, **16** From YHWH's want of ability to bring in this people to the land which He has sworn to them, He slaughters them in the wilderness. **17** And now, please let the power of my Lord be great, as You have spoken, saying, **18** YHWH [is] slow to anger and of great kindness, bearing away iniquity and transgression, and not entirely acquitting, charging iniquity of fathers on sons, on a third and on a fourth [generation]— **19** please forgive the iniquity of this people, according to the greatness of Your kindness, and as You have borne with this people from Egypt, even until now." **20** And YHWH says, "I have forgiven according to your word, **21** but nevertheless, as I live, indeed, the whole earth is filled [with] the glory of YHWH, **22** for all the men who are seeing My glory and My signs which I have done in Egypt and in the wilderness, and try Me these ten times, and have not listened to My voice— **23** they do not see the land which I have sworn to their fathers, indeed, none of those despising Me see it; **24** but My servant Caleb, because there has been another spirit with him, and he is fully after Me—I have brought him into the land to where he has entered, and his seed possesses it. **25** And the Amalekite and the Canaanite are dwelling in the valley; tomorrow turn and journey for yourselves into the wilderness—the way of the Red Sea." **26** And YHWH speaks to Moses and to Aaron, saying, **27** "Until when [do I bear] with this evil congregation—they who are murmuring against Me? The murmurings of the sons of Israel, which they are murmuring against Me, I have heard; **28** say to them: As I live—a declaration of YHWH—if, as you have spoken in My ears, do I not do so to you? **29** Your carcasses fall in this wilderness, even all your numbered ones, to all your number, from a son of twenty years and upward, who have murmured against Me; **30** you do not come into the land [for] which I have lifted up My hand to cause you to dwell in it, except Caleb son of Jephunneh and Joshua son of Nun. **31** As for your infants—of whom you have said, They become a spoil—I have even brought them in, and they have known the land which you have kicked against; **32** as for you—your carcasses fall in this wilderness, **33** and your sons are shepherding in the wilderness [for] forty years, and have borne your whoredoms until your carcasses are consumed in the wilderness; **34** by the number of the days [in] which you spied out the land, forty days—a day for a year, a day for a year— you bear your iniquities [for] forty years, and you have known My opposition; **35** I, YHWH, have spoken; if, nonetheless, I do this to all this evil congregation who are meeting against Me—they are consumed in this wilderness, and there they die." **36** Then the men whom Moses has sent to spy out the land, [who] then return and cause all the congregation to murmur against him by bringing out an evil account concerning the land, **37** even the men bringing out an evil account of the land, they die by the plague before YHWH; **38** and Joshua son of Nun and Caleb son of Jephunneh have lived, of those men who go to spy out the land. **39** And Moses speaks these words to all the sons of Israel, and the people mourn exceedingly, **40** and they rise early in the morning, and go up to the top of the mountain, saying, "Here we [are], and we have come up to the place which YHWH has spoken of, for we have sinned." **41** And Moses says, "Why [is] this [that] you are transgressing the command of YHWH? For it does not prosper; **42** do not go up, for YHWH is not in your midst, and you are not struck before your enemies; **43** for the Amalekite and the Canaanite [are] there before you, and you have fallen by the sword, because that you have turned back from after YHWH, and YHWH is not with you." **44** And they presume to go up to the top of the mountain, but the Ark of the Covenant of YHWH, and Moses, have not departed out of the midst of the camp. **45** And the Amalekite and the Canaanite who are dwelling in that mountain come down and strike them, and beat them down to Hormah.

15 And YHWH speaks to Moses, saying, **2** "Speak to the sons of Israel, and you have said to them: When you come into the land of your dwellings, which I am giving to you, **3** then you have prepared a fire-offering to YHWH, a burnt-offering or a sacrifice, for separating a vow or freewill offering, or in your appointed things, to make a refreshing fragrance to YHWH, out of the herd or out of the flock. **4** And he who is bringing his offering near to YHWH has brought a present near of a tenth part of flour mixed with a fourth of the hin of oil; **5** and you prepare a fourth of the hin of wine for a drink-offering, with the burnt-offering or for the sacrifice, for one lamb; **6** or for a ram you prepare a present of two-tenth parts of flour mixed with a third of the hin of oil; **7** and you bring a third part of the hin of wine near for a drink-offering—a refreshing fragrance to YHWH. **8** And when you make a son of the herd a burnt-offering, or a sacrifice for separating a vow, or peace-offerings to YHWH, **9** then he has brought near for the son of the herd a present of three-tenth parts of flour mixed with a half of the hin of oil; **10** and you bring a half of the hin of wine near for a drink-offering, [for] a fire-offering of refreshing fragrance to YHWH; **11** thus it is done for one ox, or for one ram, or for a lamb of the sheep or of the goats. **12** According to the number that you prepare, so you do to each, according to their number; **13** every native does thus with these, for bringing a fire-offering near of refreshing fragrance to YHWH; **14** and when a sojourner sojourns with you, or whoever [is] in your midst throughout your generations, and he has made a fire-offering of refreshing fragrance to YHWH, as you do so he does. **15** One statute is for you of the congregation and for the sojourner who is sojourning, a continuous statute throughout your generations: as you [are] so is the sojourner before YHWH; **16** one law and one ordinance is for you and for the sojourner who is sojourning with you." **17** And YHWH speaks to Moses, saying, **18** "Speak to the sons of Israel, and you have said to them: In your coming into the land to where I am bringing you in, **19** then it has been, in your eating of the bread of the land, you raise up a raised-offering to YHWH; **20** you raise up a cake of the first of your dough [as] a raised-offering; as the raised-offering of a threshing-floor, so you raise it up. **21** You give to YHWH from the first of your dough [as] a raised-offering throughout your generations. **22** And when you err, and do not do all these commands which YHWH has spoken to Moses— **23** the whole that YHWH has charged on you by the hand of Moses, from the day that YHWH has commanded and from now on, throughout your generations— **24** then it has been, if from the eyes of the congregation it has been done through ignorance, that all the congregation has prepared one bullock, a son of the herd, for a burnt-offering, for refreshing fragrance to YHWH, and its present, and its drink-offering, according to the ordinance, and one kid of the goats for a sin-offering. **25** And the priest has made atonement for all the congregation of the sons of Israel, and it has been forgiven them, for it [is] ignorance, and they have brought in their offering, a fire-offering to YHWH, and their sin-offering before YHWH for their ignorance; **26** and it has been forgiven to all the congregation of the sons of Israel and to the sojourner who is sojourning in their midst, for that all the people [did it] through ignorance. **27** And if one person sins through ignorance, then he has brought a female goat near, daughter of a year, for a sin-offering; **28** and the priest has made atonement for the person who is erring, in his sinning through ignorance before YHWH, by making atonement for him, and it has been forgiven him; **29** one law is for yourselves—for the native among the sons of Israel and for the sojourner who is sojourning in their midst—for him who is doing [anything] through ignorance. **30** And the person who does [evil] with a high hand—of the native or of the sojourner—he is reviling YHWH, and that person has been cut off from the midst of his people; **31** because he despised the word of YHWH and has broken His command, that person is certainly cut off; his iniquity [is] on him." **32** And the sons of Israel are in the wilderness, and they find a man gathering wood on the Sabbath day, **33** and those finding him gathering wood bring him near to Moses, and to Aaron, and to all the congregation, **34** and they place him in confinement, for it [is] not explained what is [to be] done to him. **35** And YHWH says to Moses, "The man is certainly put to death [by] all the congregation stoning him with stones at the outside of the camp." **36** And all the congregation brings him out to the outside of the camp and stone him with stones, and he dies, as YHWH has commanded Moses. **37** And YHWH speaks to Moses, saying, **38** "Speak to the sons of Israel, and you have commanded to them, and they have made fringes on the skirts of their garments for themselves, throughout their generations, and they have put a ribbon of blue on the fringe of the skirt, **39** and it has been to you for a fringe, and you have seen it, and have remembered all the commands of YHWH, and have done them, and you do not search after your heart and after your eyes, after which you are going whoring, **40** so that you remember and have done all My commands, and you have been holy to your God. **41** I [am] your God YHWH, who has brought you out from the land of Egypt to become your God; I [am] your God YHWH."

NUMBERS

16 And Korah, son of Izhar, son of Kohath, son of Levi, takes both Dathan and Abiram sons of Eliab, and On son of Peleth, sons of Reuben, **2** and they rise up before Moses with men of the sons of Israel, two hundred and fifty princes of the congregation, called of the convention, men of renown, **3** and they are assembled against Moses and against Aaron, and say to them, "Enough of you! For all the congregation—all of them [are] holy, and YHWH [is] in their midst; and why do you lift yourselves up above the assembly of YHWH?" **4** And Moses hears, and falls on his face, **5** and he speaks to Korah and to all his congregation, saying, "Indeed, [in the] morning YHWH may cause [you] to know those who are His and him who is holy, and has brought [him] near to Him; even him whom He fixes on He brings near to Him. **6** Do this: take censers for yourselves—Korah and all his company— **7** and put fire in them and put incense on them before YHWH tomorrow, and it has been, the man whom YHWH chooses, he [is] the holy one—enough of you, sons of Levi!" **8** And Moses says to Korah, "Now hear, sons of Levi; **9** is it little to you that the God of Israel has separated you from the congregation of Israel to bring you near to Himself, to do the service of the Dwelling Place of YHWH, and to stand before the congregation to serve them? **10** Indeed, He brings you near, and all your brothers, the sons of Levi, with you—and you have also sought the priesthood! **11** Therefore, you and all your congregation are meeting against YHWH; and Aaron, what [is] he, that you murmur against him?" **12** And Moses sends to call for Dathan and for Abiram, sons of Eliab, and they say, "We do not come up! **13** Is it little that you have brought us up out of a land flowing with milk and honey, to put us to death in a wilderness, that you also certainly make yourself prince over us? **14** Indeed, you have not brought us into a land flowing with milk and honey, nor do you give an inheritance of field and vineyard to us; do you pick out the eyes of these men? We do not come up!" **15** And it is very displeasing to Moses, and he says to YHWH, "Do not turn to their present; I have not taken one donkey from them, nor have I afflicted one of them." **16** And Moses says to Korah, "You and all your congregation, be [present] before YHWH—you, and they, and Aaron—tomorrow; **17** and let each take his censer and you have put incense on them, and each has brought his censer near before YHWH—two hundred and fifty censers; indeed, you and Aaron, each [with] his censer." **18** And they each take his censer, and put fire on them, and lay incense on them, and they stand at the opening of the Tent of Meeting with Moses and Aaron. **19** And Korah assembles all the congregation against them at the opening of the Tent of Meeting, and the glory of YHWH is seen by all the congregation. **20** And YHWH speaks to Moses and to Aaron, saying, **21** "Be separated from the midst of this congregation, and I consume them in a moment"; **22** and they fall on their faces, and say, "God, God of the spirits of all flesh—one man sins, and are You angry against all the congregation?" **23** And YHWH speaks to Moses, saying, **24** "Speak to the congregation, saying, Go up from around the dwelling place of Korah, Dathan, and Abiram." **25** And Moses rises, and goes to Dathan and Abiram, and [the] elderly of Israel go after him, **26** and he speaks to the congregation, saying, "Now turn aside from the tents of these wicked men, and do not come against anything that they have, lest you are consumed in all their sins." **27** And they go up from the dwelling place of Korah, Dathan, and Abiram, from all around, and Dathan and Abiram have come out, standing at the opening of their tents, with their wives, and their sons, and their infants. **28** And Moses says, "By this you know that YHWH has sent me to do all these works, that [they are] not from my own heart; **29** if these die according to the death of all men, or the charge of all men is charged on them, YHWH has not sent me; **30** but if YHWH does a strange thing, and the ground has opened her mouth and swallowed them and all that they have, and they have gone down alive to Sheol, then you have known that these men have despised YHWH." **31** And it comes to pass at his finishing speaking all these words, that the ground which [is] under them cleaves, **32** and the earth opens her mouth and swallows them, and their houses, and all the men who [are] for Korah, and all the goods, **33** and they go down—they and all that they have—alive to Sheol, and the earth closes over them, and they perish from the midst of the assembly; **34** and all

NUMBERS

Israel who [are] around them have fled at their voice, for they said, "Lest the earth swallow us"; **35** and fire has come out from YHWH and consumes the two hundred and fifty men bringing the incense near. **36** And YHWH speaks to Moses, saying, **37** "Say to Eleazar son of Aaron the priest to lift up the censers from the midst of the burning and scatter the fire away, for they have been hallowed. **38** [As for] the censers of these sinners against their own souls, indeed, they have made them [into] spread-out plates [for] a covering for the altar, for they have brought them near before YHWH, and they are hallowed; and they become a sign to the sons of Israel." **39** And Eleazar the priest takes the bronze censers which they who are burned had brought near, and they spread them out [for] a covering for the altar— **40** a memorial to the sons of Israel, so that a stranger who is not of the seed of Aaron does not draw near to make incense before YHWH, and is not as Korah and as his congregation, as YHWH has spoken by the hand of Moses to him. **41** And on the next day all the congregation of the sons of Israel murmurs against Moses and against Aaron, saying, "You have put the people of YHWH to death." **42** And it comes to pass, in the congregation being assembled against Moses and against Aaron, that they turn toward the Tent of Meeting, and behold, the cloud has covered it and the glory of YHWH is seen; **43** and Moses comes—Aaron also—to the front of the Tent of Meeting. **44** And YHWH speaks to Moses, saying, **45** "Get up from the midst of this congregation, and I consume them in a moment"; and they fall on their faces, **46** and Moses says to Aaron, "Take the censer and put fire on it from off the altar, and place incense, and go quickly to the congregation and make atonement for them, for the wrath has gone out from the presence of YHWH—the plague has begun." **47** And Aaron takes [it] as Moses has spoken, and runs to the midst of the assembly, and behold, the plague has begun among the people; and he gives the incense, and makes atonement for the people, **48** and stands between the dead and the living, and the plague is restrained; **49** and those who die by the plague are fourteen thousand and seven hundred, apart from those who die for the matter of Korah; **50** and Aaron turns back to Moses, to the opening of the Tent of Meeting, and the plague has been restrained.

17 And YHWH speaks to Moses, saying, **2** "Speak to the sons of Israel, and take a rod from each of them, for a father's house, from all their princes, for the house of their fathers—twelve rods; you write the name of each on his rod, **3** and you write Aaron's name on the tribe of Levi; for one rod [is] for the head of their fathers' house. **4** And you have placed them in the Tent of Meeting before the Testimony, where I meet with you. **5** And it has come to pass, the man's rod on whom I fix flourishes, and I have caused the murmurings of the sons of Israel, which they are murmuring against you, to cease from off Me." **6** And Moses speaks to the sons of Israel, and all their princes give to him one rod for a prince, one rod for a prince, for their fathers' house—twelve rods; and the rod of Aaron [is] in the midst of their rods; **7** and Moses places the rods before YHWH in the Tent of the Testimony. **8** And it comes to pass, on the next day, that Moses goes into the Tent of the Testimony, and behold, the rod of Aaron has flourished for the house of Levi, and brings out a bud, and blossoms [with] a blossom, and produces almonds; **9** and Moses brings out all the rods from before YHWH to all the sons of Israel, and they look, and each takes his rod. **10** And YHWH says to Moses, "Put back the rod of Aaron before the Testimony, for a charge, for a sign to the sons of rebellion, and you remove their murmurings from off Me, and they do not die"; **11** and Moses does as YHWH has commanded him; so he has done. **12** And the sons of Israel speak to Moses, saying, "Behold, we have expired, we have perished, all of us have perished! **13** Any who is at all drawing near to the Dwelling Place of YHWH dies; have we not been consumed—to expire?"

18 And YHWH says to Aaron, "You, and your sons, and the house of your father with you, bear the iniquity of the sanctuary; and you and your sons with you bear the iniquity of your priesthood; **2** and also your brothers, the tribe of Levi, the tribe of your father, bring near with you, and they are joined to you, and serve you, even you and your sons with you, before the Tent of the Testimony. **3** And they have kept your charge, and the charge of all the tent; only, they do not come near to the vessels of the holy place and to the altar, and they do not die, either they or you; **4** and they have been joined to you and have kept the charge of the Tent of Meeting for all the service of the tent; and a stranger does not come near to you; **5** and you have kept the charge of the holy place and the charge of the altar, and there is no more wrath against the sons of Israel. **6** And I, behold, have taken your brothers the Levites from the midst of the sons of Israel; they are a gift given to you by YHWH to do the service of the Tent of Meeting; **7** and you and your sons with you keep your priesthood for everything of the altar and within the veil, and you have served; I make your priesthood a gift [for] service; and the stranger who is coming near is put to death." **8** And YHWH speaks to Aaron: "And I, behold, have given to you the charge of My raised-offerings, of all the hallowed things of the sons of Israel—I have given them to you and to your sons for the anointing, by a continuous statute. **9** This is yours from the most holy things, from the fire: all their offering, of all their present, and of all their sin-offering, and of all their guilt-offering, which they give back to Me, is most holy to you and to your sons; **10** you eat it among the most holy things; every male eats it; it is holy to you. **11** And this [is] yours: the raised-offering of their gift, with all the wave-offerings of the sons of Israel; I have given them to you, and to your sons, and to your daughters with you, by a continuous statute; every clean one in your house eats it; **12** all the best of the oil, and all the best of the new wine, and wheat—their first-[fruits] which they give to YHWH—I have given them to you. **13** The first-fruits of all that [is] in their land, which they bring to YHWH, are yours; every clean one in your house eats it; **14** every devoted thing in Israel is yours; **15** everyone opening a womb of all flesh which they bring near to YHWH, among man and among beast, is yours; only, you certainly ransom the firstborn of man, and you ransom the firstling of the unclean beast. **16** And their ransomed ones from a son of a month, you ransom with your valuation [for] five shekels of silver, by the shekel of the holy place; it [is] twenty gerahs. **17** Only, the firstling of a cow, or the firstling of a sheep, or the firstling of a goat, you do not ransom, they [are] holy: you sprinkle their blood on the altar, and you make incense of their fat [as] a fire-offering of refreshing fragrance to YHWH; **18** and their flesh is yours, as the breast of the wave-offering and as the right leg are yours. **19** All the raised-offerings of the holy things, which the sons of Israel lift up to YHWH, I have given to you, and to your sons, and to your daughters with you, by a continuous statute—a covenant of salt; it [is] continuous before YHWH to you and to your seed with you." **20** And YHWH says to Aaron, "You do not inherit in their land, and you do not have a portion in their midst: I [am] your portion and your inheritance in the midst of the sons of Israel; **21** and to the sons of Levi, behold, have given all the tenth in Israel for inheritance in exchange for their service which they are serving—the service of the Tent of Meeting. **22** And the sons of Israel no longer come near to the Tent of Meeting, to bear sin, to die, **23** and the Levites have done the service of the Tent of Meeting, and they bear their iniquity; [it is] a continuous statute throughout your generations that they have no inheritance in the midst of the sons of Israel; **24** but the tithe of the sons of Israel which they lift up to YHWH, a raised-offering, I have given to the Levites for inheritance; therefore I have said of them, They have no inheritance in the midst of the sons of Israel." **25** And YHWH speaks to Moses, saying, **26** "And you speak to the Levites, and you have said to them: When you take the tithe from the sons of Israel which I have given to you from them for your inheritance, then you have lifted up the raised-offering of YHWH from it, a tithe of the tithe; **27** and your raised-offering has been reckoned to you as grain from the threshing-floor and as the fullness from the wine-vat; **28** so you lift up—you also—the raised-offering of YHWH from all your tithes which you receive from the sons of Israel; and you have given the raised-offering of YHWH from it to Aaron the priest; **29** out of all your gifts you lift up every raised-offering of YHWH, out of all its fat—its hallowed part—out of it. **30** And you have said to them: In your lifting up its fat out of it, then it has been reckoned to the Levites as increase of a threshing-floor and as increase of a wine-vat; **31** and you have eaten it in every place, you and your

NUMBERS

households, for it [is] your hire in exchange for your service in the Tent of Meeting; **32** and you bear no sin for it in your lifting up its fat out of it, but you do not defile the holy things of the sons of Israel, and you do not die."

19 And Y<small>HWH</small> speaks to Moses and to Aaron, saying, **2** "This [is] a statute of the law which Y<small>HWH</small> has commanded, saying, Speak to the sons of Israel, and they bring a red cow to you, a perfect one, in which there is no blemish, on which no yoke has gone up; **3** and you have given it to Eleazar the priest, and he has brought it out to the outside of the camp, and has slaughtered it before him. **4** And Eleazar the priest has taken of its blood with his finger, and has sprinkled [it] toward the front of the face of the Tent of Meeting from its blood seven times; **5** and [one] has burned the cow before his eyes; her skin, and her flesh, and her blood, besides her dung, he burns; **6** and the priest has taken cedar wood, and hyssop, and scarlet, and has cast [them] into the midst of the burning of the cow; **7** and the priest has washed his garments, and has bathed his flesh with water, and afterward comes into the camp, and the priest is unclean until the evening; **8** and he who is burning it washes his garments with water, and has bathed his flesh with water, and is unclean until the evening. **9** And a clean man has gathered the ashes of the cow, and has placed [them] at the outside of the camp in a clean place, and it has become a charge for the congregation of the sons of Israel for waters of separation—it [is for] sin; **10** and he who is gathering the ashes of the heifer has washed his garments and is unclean until the evening; and it has been to the sons of Israel and to the sojourner who is sojourning in their midst for a continuous statute. **11** He who is coming against the dead body of any man is unclean [for] seven days; **12** he cleanses himself for it on the third day and on the seventh day, [and] he is clean; and if he does not cleanse himself on the third day and on the seventh day, he is not clean. **13** Anyone who is coming against the dead, against the body of man who dies, and does not cleanse himself, he has defiled the Dwelling Place of Y<small>HWH</small>, and that person has been cut off from Israel, for water of separation is not sprinkled on him; he is unclean; his uncleanness [is] still on him. **14** This [is] the law when a man dies in a tent: everyone who is coming into the tent and all that [is] in the tent are unclean [for] seven days; **15** and every open vessel which has no covering of thread on it is unclean. **16** And everyone on the face of the field who comes against the pierced of a sword, or against the dead, or against a bone of man, or against a grave, is unclean [for] seven days; **17** and for the unclean person they have taken from the ashes of the burning of the [cow], and he has put running water over it into a vessel; **18** and a clean person has taken hyssop, and has dipped [it] in water, and has sprinkled [it] on the tent, and on all the vessels, and on the persons who have been there, and on him who is coming against a bone, or against one pierced, or against the dead, or against a grave. **19** And the clean has sprinkled [it] on the unclean on the third day and on the seventh day, and has cleansed him on the seventh day, and he has washed his garments, and has bathed with water, and has been clean in the evening. **20** And the man who is unclean and does not cleanse himself, indeed, that person has been cut off from the midst of the assembly; for he has defiled the sanctuary of Y<small>HWH</small>; water of separation is not sprinkled on him; he [is] unclean. **21** And it has been for a continuous statute to them, that he who is sprinkling the water of separation washes his garments, and he who is coming against the water of separation is unclean until the evening, **22** and all against which the unclean person comes is unclean, and the person who is coming against [it] is unclean until the evening."

20 And the sons of Israel, all the congregation, come [into] the wilderness of Zin in the first month, and the people abide in Kadesh; and Miriam dies there and is buried there. **2** And there has been no water for the congregation, and they are assembled against Moses and against Aaron, **3** and the people strive with Moses and speak, saying, "And oh that we had expired when our brothers expired before Y<small>HWH</small>! **4** And why have you brought in the assembly of Y<small>HWH</small> to this wilderness to die there, we and our beasts? **5** And why have you brought us up out of Egypt to bring us to this evil place? [It is] not a place of seed, and fig, and vine, and pomegranate; and there is no water to drink." **6** And Moses and Aaron go in from the presence of the assembly to the opening of the Tent of Meeting and fall on their faces, and the glory of YHWH is seen by them. **7** And YHWH speaks to Moses, saying, **8** "Take the rod and assemble the congregation—you and your brother Aaron—and you have spoken to the rock before their eyes, and it has given its water, and you have brought out water to them from the rock, and have watered the congregation and their beasts." **9** And Moses takes the rod from before YHWH as He has commanded him, **10** and Moses and Aaron assemble the assembly to the front of the rock, and he says to them, "Now hear, O rebels, do we bring out water to you from this rock?" **11** And Moses lifts up his hand and strikes the rock with his rod twice; and much water comes out, and the congregation drinks, and their beasts [drink]. **12** And YHWH says to Moses and to Aaron, "Because you have not believed in Me to sanctify Me before the eyes of the sons of Israel, therefore you do not bring in this assembly to the land which I have given to them." **13** These [are] the waters of Meribah, because the sons of Israel have "striven" with YHWH, and He is sanctified among them. **14** And Moses sends messengers from Kadesh to the king of Edom, "Thus said your brother Israel: You have known all the travail which has found us, **15** that our fathers go down to Egypt, and we dwell in Egypt [for] many days, and the Egyptians do evil to us and to our fathers; **16** then we cry to YHWH, and He hears our voice, and sends a Messenger, and is bringing us out of Egypt; and behold, we [are] in Kadesh, a city [in] the extremity of your border. **17** Please let us pass over through your land; we do not pass over through a field or through a vineyard, nor do we drink waters of a well; we go the way of the king, we do not turn aside [to] the right or left until we pass over your border." **18** And Edom says to him, "You do not pass over through me, lest I come out to meet you with the sword." **19** And the sons of Israel say to him, "We go in the highway, and if we drink of your waters—I and my livestock—then I have given their price; only, let me pass over on my feet, nothing [more]." **20** And he says, "You do not pass over"; and Edom comes out to meet him with many people and with a strong hand; **21** and Edom refuses to permit Israel to pass over through his border, and Israel turns aside from off him. **22** And the sons of Israel, all the congregation, journey from Kadesh and come to Mount Hor, **23** and YHWH speaks to Moses and to Aaron in Mount Hor, on the border of the land of Edom, saying, **24** "Aaron is gathered to his people, for he does not go into the land which I have given to the sons of Israel, because that you provoked My mouth at the waters of Meribah. **25** Take Aaron and his son Eleazar, and cause them to go up Mount Hor, **26** and strip Aaron of his garments, and you have clothed his son Eleazar [with] them, and Aaron is gathered, and dies there." **27** And Moses does as YHWH has commanded, and they go up to Mount Hor before the eyes of all the congregation, **28** and Moses strips Aaron of his garments, and clothes his son Eleazar with them, and Aaron dies there on the top of the mountain; and Moses comes down— Eleazar also—from the mountain, **29** and all the congregation sees that Aaron has expired, and all the house of Israel laments Aaron [for] thirty days.

21 And the Canaanite, king of Arad, dwelling in the south, hears that Israel has come the way of the Atharim, and he fights against Israel, and takes [some] of them captive. **2** And Israel vows a vow to YHWH and says, "If You certainly give this people into my hand, then I have devoted their cities"; **3** and YHWH listens to the voice of Israel and gives up the Canaanite, and he devotes them and their cities, and calls the name of the place Hormah. **4** And they journey from Mount Hor, the way of the Red Sea, to go around the land of Edom, and the soul of the people is short in the way, **5** and the people speak against God and against Moses, "Why have you brought us up out of Egypt to die in a wilderness? For there is no bread, and there is no water, and our soul has been weary of this light bread." **6** And YHWH sends the burning serpents among the people, and they bite the people, and many people of Israel die; **7** and the people come to Moses and say, "We have sinned, for we have spoken against YHWH and against you; pray to YHWH that He turns the serpent aside from us"; and Moses prays in behalf of the people. **8** And YHWH says to

Moses, "Make a burning [serpent] for yourself, and set it on an ensign; and it has been, everyone who is bitten and has seen it—he has lived." **9** And Moses makes a serpent of bronze, and sets it on the ensign, and it has been, if the serpent has bitten any man, and he has looked expectingly to the serpent of bronze—he has lived. **10** And the sons of Israel journey and encamp in Oboth. **11** And they journey from Oboth and encamp in Ije-Abarim, in the wilderness that [is] on the front of Moab, at the rising of the sun. **12** From there they have journeyed and encamp in the Valley of Zared. **13** From there they have journeyed and encamp beyond Arnon, which [is] in the wilderness which is coming out of the border of the Amorite, for Arnon [is] the border of Moab, between Moab and the Amorite; **14** therefore it is said in [the] scroll of the Wars of YHWH: "Waheb in Suphah, || And the brooks of Arnon; **15** And the spring of the brooks, || Which turned aside to the dwelling of Ar, || And has leaned to the border of Moab." **16** And from there [they journeyed] to Beer; it [is] the well [concerning] which YHWH said to Moses, "Gather the people, and I give water to them." **17** Then Israel sings this song: "Spring up, O well, || Let all answer to it! **18** A well—princes have dug it, || Nobles of the people have prepared it, || With the lawgiver, with their staffs." And from the wilderness [they journeyed] to Mattanah, **19** and from Mattanah to Nahaliel, and from Nahaliel to Bamoth, **20** and from Bamoth, in the valley which [is] in the field of Moab, [to] the top of Pisgah, which has looked on the front of the wilderness. **21** And Israel sends messengers to Sihon king of the Amorite, saying, **22** "Let me pass through your land, we do not turn aside into a field or into a vineyard; we do not drink waters of a well; we go in the king's way until we pass over your border." **23** And Sihon has not permitted Israel to pass through his border, and Sihon gathers all his people, and comes out to meet Israel in the wilderness, and comes to Jahaz, and fights against Israel. **24** And Israel strikes him by the mouth of the sword, and possesses his land from Arnon to Jabbok—to the sons of Ammon; for the border of the sons of Ammon [is] strong. **25** And Israel takes all these cities, and Israel dwells in all the cities of the Amorite, in Heshbon and in all its villages; **26** for Heshbon is a city of Sihon king of the Amorite, and he has fought against the former king of Moab, and takes all his land out of his hand as far as Arnon; **27** therefore those using allegories say: "Enter Heshbon, || Let the city of Sihon be built and ready, **28** For fire has gone out from Heshbon, || A flame from the city of Sihon, || It has consumed Ar of Moab, || Owners of the high places of Arnon. **29** Woe to you, O Moab, || You have perished, O people of Chemosh! He has given his sons [as] fugitives, || And his daughters into captivity, || To Sihon king of the Amorite! **30** And we shoot them; Heshbon has perished as far as Dibon, || And we make desolate as far as Nophah, || Which [is] as far as Medeba." **31** And Israel dwells in the land of the Amorite, **32** and Moses sends to spy out Jaazer, and they capture its villages, and dispossess the Amorite who [is] there, **33** and turn and go up the way of Bashan, and Og king of Bashan comes out to meet them, he and all his people, to battle [at] Edrei. **34** And YHWH says to Moses, "Do not fear him, for into your hand I have given him, and all his people, and his land, and you have done to him as you have done to Sihon king of the Amorite, who is dwelling in Heshbon." **35** And they strike him, and his sons, and all his people, until he has no remnant left to him, and they possess his land.

22 And the sons of Israel journey and encamp in the plains of Moab beyond the Jordan, [by] Jericho. **2** And Balak son of Zippor sees all that Israel has done to the Amorite, **3** and Moab is exceedingly afraid of the presence of the people, for it [is] numerous; and Moab is distressed by the presence of the sons of Israel, **4** and Moab says to [the] elderly of Midian, "Now the assembly licks up all that is around us, as the ox licks up the green thing of the field." And Balak son of Zippor [is] king of Moab at that time, **5** and he sends messengers to Balaam son of Beor, to Pethor, which [is] by the River of the land of the sons of his people, to call for him, saying, "Behold, a people has come out of Egypt; behold, it has covered the eye of the land, and it is abiding in front of me; **6** and now, come, please curse this people for me, for it [is] mightier than I. It may be I prevail, [and] we strike it, and I cast it out from the land; for I have known that which

NUMBERS

you bless is blessed, and that which you curse is cursed." **7** And [the] elderly of Moab and [the] elderly of Midian go with divinations in their hand, and they come to Balaam and speak the words of Balak to him, **8** and he says to them, "Lodge here tonight, and I have brought you back word, as YHWH speaks to me"; and the princes of Moab abide with Balaam. **9** And God comes to Balaam and says, "Who [are] these men with you?" **10** And Balaam says to God, "Balak, son of Zippor, king of Moab, has sent to me: **11** Behold, the people that is coming out from Egypt and covers the eye of the land—now come, pierce it for me; it may be I am able to fight against it and have cast it out"; **12** and God says to Balaam, "You do not go with them; you do not curse the people, for it [is] blessed." **13** And Balaam rises in the morning and says to the princes of Balak, "Go to your land, for YHWH is refusing to permit me to go with you"; **14** and the princes of Moab rise, and come to Balak, and say, "Balaam is refusing to come with us." **15** And Balak adds yet to send princes, more numerous and honored than these, **16** and they come to Balaam and say to him, "Thus said Balak son of Zippor: Please do not be withheld from coming to me, **17** for I honor you very greatly, and all that you say to me I do; and come, please pierce this people for me." **18** And Balaam answers and says to the servants of Balak, "If Balak gives to me the fullness of his house of silver and gold, I am not able to pass over the command of my God YHWH, to do a little or a great thing; **19** and now, please abide in this [place], you also, tonight, then I know what YHWH is adding to speak with me." **20** And God comes to Balaam by night and says to him, "If the men have come to call for you, rise, go with them, and only the thing which I speak to you—do it." **21** And Balaam rises in the morning, and saddles his donkey, and goes with the princes of Moab, **22** and the anger of God burns because he is going, and the Messenger of YHWH stations Himself in the way for an adversary to him, and he is riding on his donkey, and two of his servants [are] with him, **23** and the donkey sees the Messenger of YHWH standing in the way with His drawn sword in His hand, and the donkey turns aside out of the way and goes into a field, and Balaam strikes the donkey to turn it aside into the way. **24** And the Messenger of YHWH stands in a narrow path of the vineyards, [with] a wall on this [side] and a wall on that [side], **25** and the donkey sees the Messenger of YHWH, and is pressed to the wall, and presses Balaam's foot to the wall, and he adds to strike her; **26** and the Messenger of YHWH adds to pass over, and stands in a narrow place where there is no way to turn aside [to] the right or left, **27** and the donkey sees the Messenger of YHWH, and crouches under Balaam, and the anger of Balaam burns, and he strikes the donkey with a staff. **28** And YHWH opens the mouth of the donkey, and she says to Balaam, "What have I done to you that you have struck me these three times?" **29** And Balaam says to the donkey, "Because you have rolled yourself against me; oh that there were a sword in my hand, for now I had slain you"; **30** and the donkey says to Balaam, "Am I not your donkey on which you have ridden since [I became] yours, even to this day? Have I at all been accustomed to do thus to you?" And he says, "No." **31** And YHWH uncovers the eyes of Balaam, and he sees the Messenger of YHWH standing in the way with His drawn sword in His hand, and he bows and pays respect, to his face; **32** and the Messenger of YHWH says to him, "Why have you struck your donkey these three times? Behold, I have come out for an adversary, for [your] way has been perverse before Me, **33** and the donkey sees Me and turns aside at My presence these three times; unless she had turned aside from My presence, surely I had also slain you now, and kept her alive." **34** And Balaam says to the Messenger of YHWH, "I have sinned, for I did not know that You [are] standing to meet me in the way; and now, if [it is] evil in Your eyes, I turn back by myself." **35** And the Messenger of YHWH says to Balaam, "Go with the men; and only the word which I speak to you—it you speak"; and Balaam goes with the princes of Balak. **36** And Balak hears that Balaam has come, and goes out to meet him, to a city of Moab, which [is] on the border of Arnon, which [is] in the extremity of the border; **37** and Balak says to Balaam, "Did I not diligently send to you to call for you? Why did you not come to me? Am I not truly able to honor you?" **38** And Balaam says to Balak, "Behold, I have come to you; now, am I able to speak anything at all? The word which God sets

NUMBERS

in my mouth—it I speak." **39** And Balaam goes with Balak, and they come to Kirjath-Huzoth, **40** and Balak sacrifices oxen and sheep, and sends [some] to Balaam and to the princes who [are] with him; **41** and it comes to pass in the morning, that Balak takes Balaam and causes him to go up [to] the high places of Ba'al, and he sees the extremity of the people from there.

23 And Balaam says to Balak, "Build seven altars for me in this [place], and prepare seven bullocks and seven rams for me in this [place]." **2** And Balak does as Balaam has spoken, and Balak—Balaam also—offers a bullock and a ram on the altar, **3** and Balaam says to Balak, "Station yourself by your burnt-offering and I go on, it may be YHWH comes to meet me, and the thing which He shows me I have declared to you"; and he goes [to] a high place. **4** And God comes to Balaam, and he says to Him, "I have arranged the seven altars, and I offer a bullock and a ram on the altar"; **5** and YHWH puts a word in the mouth of Balaam and says, "Return to Balak, and thus you speak." **6** And he returns to him, and behold, he is standing by his burnt-offering, he and all the princes of Moab. **7** And he takes up his allegory and says: "Balak king of Moab leads me from Aram; From mountains of the east. Come—curse Jacob for me, ‖ And come—be indignant [with] Israel. **8** How do I pierce [when] God has not pierced? And how am I indignant [when] YHWH has not been indignant? **9** For from the top of rocks I see him, ‖ And from heights I behold him; Behold a people! He dwells alone, ‖ And does not reckon himself among nations. **10** Who has counted the dust of Jacob, ‖ And the number of the fourth of Israel? Let me die the death of upright ones, ‖ And let my last end be like his!" **11** And Balak says to Balaam, "What have you done to me? I have taken you to pierce my enemies, and behold, you have certainly blessed"; **12** and he answers and says, "That which YHWH puts in my mouth—do I not take heed to speak it?" **13** And Balak says to him, "Come! Come to another place with me, from where you see it—you see only its extremity, and you do not see all of it, and pierce it for me there"; **14** and he takes him [to] the field of Zophim, to the top of Pisgah, and builds seven altars, and offers a bullock and a ram on the altar. **15** And he says to Balak, "Station yourself here by your burnt-offering, and I meet [Him] there"; **16** and YHWH comes to Balaam, and sets a word in his mouth, and says, "Return to Balak, and thus you speak." **17** And he comes to him, and behold, he is standing by his burnt-offering, and the princes of Moab [are] with him, and Balak says to him: "What has YHWH spoken?" **18** And he takes up his allegory and says: "Rise, Balak, and hear; Give ear to me, son of Zippor! **19** God [is] not a man—and lies, ‖ And a son of man—and relents! Has He said—and He does not do [it]? And spoken—and He does not confirm it? **20** Behold, I have received [only] to bless; Indeed, He blesses, and I cannot reverse it. **21** He has not beheld iniquity in Jacob, ‖ Nor has He seen perverseness in Israel; His God YHWH [is] with him, ‖ And a shout of a king [is] in him. **22** God is bringing them out from Egypt, ‖ As the swiftness of a wild ox for him; **23** For no enchantment [is] against Jacob, ‖ Nor divination against Israel; At the time it is said of Jacob and Israel, ‖ O what God has worked! **24** Behold, the people rises as a lioness, ‖ And he lifts himself up as a lion; He does not lie down until he eats prey, ‖ And drinks blood of pierced ones." **25** And Balak says to Balaam, "Neither pierce it at all, nor bless it at all"; **26** and Balaam answers and says to Balak, "Have I not spoken to you, saying, All that YHWH speaks—I do it?" **27** And Balak says to Balaam, "Please come, I take you to another place; it may be it is right in the eyes of God to pierce it for me from there." **28** And Balak takes Balaam to the top of Peor, which is looking on the front of the wilderness, **29** and Balaam says to Balak, "Build seven altars for me in this [place], and prepare seven bullocks and seven rams for me in this [place]"; **30** and Balak does as Balaam said, and he offers a bullock and a ram on an altar.

24 And Balaam sees that [it is] good in the eyes of YHWH to bless Israel, and he has not gone as time by time to seek enchantments, and he sets his face toward the wilderness; **2** and Balaam lifts up his eyes, and sees Israel dwelling by its tribes, and the Spirit of God is on him, **3** and he takes up his allegory and says: "An affirmation of Balaam son of Beor, ‖ And an affirmation of the man whose eyes are shut, **4** An affirmation of him who is hearing sayings of God, ‖ Who sees a vision of the Almighty, ‖ Falling—and eyes uncovered: **5** How good have been your tents, O Jacob, ‖ Your dwelling places, O Israel; **6** They have been stretched out as valleys, ‖ As gardens by a river; As aloes YHWH has planted, ‖ As cedars by waters; **7** He makes water flow from his buckets, ‖ And his seed [is] in many waters; And his King [is] higher than Gog [[*or* Agag]], ‖ And his kingdom is exalted. **8** God is bringing him out of Egypt, ‖ As the swiftness of a wild ox for him, ‖ He eats up nations—his adversaries, ‖ And he breaks their bones, ‖ And he strikes [with] his arrows. **9** He has bent, he has lain down as a lion, ‖ And as a lioness, who raises him up? He who is blessing you [is] blessed, ‖ And he who is cursing you [is] cursed." **10** And the anger of Balak burns against Balaam, and he strikes his hands; and Balak says to Balaam, "I called you to pierce my enemies, and behold, you have certainly blessed these three times; **11** and now, flee for yourself to your place; I have said, I greatly honor you, and behold, YHWH has kept you back from honor." **12** And Balaam says to Balak, "Did I not also speak to your messengers whom you have sent to me, saying, **13** If Balak gives to me the fullness of his house of silver and gold, I am not able to pass over the command of YHWH, to do good or evil of my own heart; that which YHWH speaks—it I speak? **14** And now, behold, I am going to my people; come, I counsel you [concerning] that which this people does to your people in the latter end of the days." **15** And he takes up his allegory and says: "An affirmation of Balaam son of Beor, ‖ And an affirmation of the man whose eyes [are] shut; **16** An affirmation of him who is hearing sayings of God, ‖ And knowing knowledge of the Most High; He sees a vision of the Almighty, ‖ Falling—and eyes uncovered: **17** I see Him, but not now; I behold Him, but not near; A star has proceeded from Jacob, ‖ And a scepter has risen from Israel, ‖ And has struck corners of Moab, ‖ And has destroyed all sons of Seth. **18** And Edom has been a possession, ‖ And Seir has been a possession [for] his enemies, ‖ And Israel is doing valiantly; **19** And [One] rules out of Jacob, ‖ And has destroyed a remnant from the city." **20** And he sees Amalek, and takes up his allegory, and says: "Amalek [is] first [among] nations, ‖ But his latter end—destruction forever." **21** And he sees the Kenite, and takes up his allegory, and says: "Your dwelling [is] enduring, ‖ And your nest is being set in a rock, **22** But the Kenite is for a burning; Until when does Asshur keep you captive?" **23** And he takes up his allegory and says: "Woe! Who lives when God does this? **24** But ships [come] from the side of Chittim, ‖ And they have humbled Asshur, ‖ And they have humbled Eber, ‖ But it is also perishing forever." **25** And Balaam rises, and goes, and turns back to his place, and Balak has also gone on his way.

25 And Israel dwells in Shittim, and the people begin to go whoring to daughters of Moab, **2** and they call for the people to the sacrifices of their gods, and the people eat and bow themselves to their gods, **3** and Israel is joined to Ba'al-Peor, and the anger of YHWH burns against Israel. **4** And YHWH says to Moses, "Take all the chiefs of the people and hang them before YHWH in sight of the sun; and the fierceness of the anger of YHWH turns back from Israel." **5** And Moses says to [the] judges of Israel, "Each slays his men who are joined to Ba'al-Peor." **6** And behold, a man of the sons of Israel has come, and brings a Midianitess to his brothers before the eyes of Moses and before the eyes of all the congregation of the sons of Israel, who are weeping at the opening of the Tent of Meeting; **7** and Phinehas, son of Eleazar, son of Aaron the priest, sees, and rises from the midst of the congregation, and takes a javelin in his hand, **8** and goes in after the man of Israel to the hollow place, and pierces them both, the man of Israel and the woman—to her belly, and the plague is restrained from the sons of Israel; **9** and the dead by the plague are twenty-four thousand. **10** And YHWH speaks to Moses, saying, **11** "Phinehas, son of Eleazar, son of Aaron the priest, has turned back My fury from the sons of Israel by his being zealous with My zeal in their midst, and I have not consumed the sons of Israel in My zeal. **12** Therefore say, Behold, I am giving My covenant of peace to him, **13** and it has been to him and to his seed after him [for] a covenant of a continuous priesthood, because that he has been zealous for his God, and makes atonement for the sons of

Israel." **14** And the name of the man of Israel who is struck, who has been struck with the Midianitess, [is] Zimri son of Salu, prince of the house of a father of the Simeonite; **15** and the name of the woman who is struck, the Midianitess, [is] Cozbi daughter of Zur; he [is] head of peoples of a father's house in Midian. **16** And YHWH speaks to Moses, saying, **17** "Distress the Midianites, and you have struck them, **18** for they are adversaries to you with their frauds, [with] which they have acted fraudulently to you, concerning the matter of Peor and concerning the matter of Cozbi, daughter of a prince of Midian, their sister, who is struck in the day of the plague for the matter of Peor."

26 And it comes to pass, after the plague, that YHWH speaks to Moses and to Eleazar son of Aaron the priest, saying, **2** "Take a census of all the congregation of the sons of Israel, from a son of twenty years and upward, by the house of their fathers, everyone going out to the host in Israel." **3** And Moses speaks—Eleazar the priest also—with them in the plains of Moab by the Jordan, [near] Jericho, saying, **4** "From a son of twenty years and upward," as YHWH has commanded Moses and the sons of Israel who are coming out from the land of Egypt. **5** Reuben, firstborn of Israel—sons of Reuben: of Enoch [is] the family of the Enochite; of Pallu the family of the Palluite; **6** of Hezron the family of the Hezronite; of Carmi the family of the Carmite. **7** These [are] families of the Reubenite, and their numbered ones are forty-three thousand and seven hundred and thirty. **8** And the son of Pallu [is] Eliab; **9** and the sons of Eliab [are] Nemuel, and Dathan, and Abiram; this [is that] Dathan and Abiram, called ones of the congregation, who have striven against Moses and against Aaron in the congregation of Korah, in their striving against YHWH, **10** and the earth opens her mouth, and swallows them and Korah, in the death of the congregation, in the fire consuming the two hundred and fifty men, and they become a sign; **11** but the sons of Korah did not die. **12** Sons of Simeon by their families: of Nemuel [is] the family of the Nemuelite; of Jamin the family of the Jaminite; of Jachin the family of the Jachinite; **13** of Zerah the family of the Zerahite; of Shaul the family of the Shaulite. **14** These [are] families of the Simeonite—twenty-two thousand and two hundred. **15** Sons of Gad by their families: of Zephon [is] the family of the Zephonite; of Haggi the family of the Haggite; of Shuni the family of the Shunite; **16** of Ozni the family of the Oznite; of Eri the family of the Erite: **17** of Arod the family of the Arodite; of Areli the family of the Arelite. **18** These [are] families of the sons of Gad by their numbered ones—forty thousand and five hundred. **19** Sons of Judah [are] Er and Onan; and Er dies—Onan also—in the land of Canaan. **20** And sons of Judah by their families are: of Shelah the family of the Shelanite; of Perez the family of the Perezite; of Zerah the family of the Zerahite; **21** and sons of Perez are: of Hezron the family of the Hezronite; of Hamul the family of the Hamulite. **22** These [are] families of Judah by their numbered ones—seventy-six thousand and five hundred. **23** Sons of Issachar by their families: of Tola [is] the family of the Tolaite; of Pua the family of the Punite; **24** of Jashub the family of the Jashubite; of Shimron the family of the Shimronite. **25** These [are] families of Issachar by their numbered ones—sixty-four thousand and three hundred. **26** Sons of Zebulun by their families: of Sered [is] the family of the Sardite; of Elon the family of the Elonite; of Jahleel the family of the Jahleelite. **27** These [are] families of the Zebulunite by their numbered ones—sixty thousand and five hundred. **28** Sons of Joseph by their families [are] Manasseh and Ephraim. **29** Sons of Manasseh: of Machir [is] the family of the Machirite; and Machir has begotten Gilead; of Gilead [is] the family of the Gileadite. **30** These [are] sons of Gilead: of Jeezer [is] the family of the Jeezerite; of Helek the family of the Helekite; **31** and of Asriel the family of the Asrielite; and of Shechem the family of the Shechemite; **32** and of Shemida the family of the Shemidaite; and of Hepher the family of the Hepherite. **33** And Zelophehad son of Hepher had no sons, but [only] daughters, and the names of the daughters of Zelophehad [are] Mahlah, and Noah, Hoglah, Milcah, and Tirzah. **34** These [are] families of Manasseh, and their numbered ones [are] fifty-two thousand and seven hundred. **35** These [are] sons of Ephraim by their families: of

Shuthelah [is] the family of the Shuthelhite; of Becher the family of the Bachrite; of Tahan the family of the Tahanite. **36** And these [are] sons of Shuthelah: of Eran the family of the Eranite. **37** These [are] families of the sons of Ephraim by their numbered ones—thirty-two thousand and five hundred. These [are] sons of Joseph by their families. **38** Sons of Benjamin by their families: of Bela [is] the family of the Belaite; of Ashbel the family of the Ashbelite; of Ahiram the family of the Ahiramite; **39** of Shupham the family of the Shuphamite; of Hupham the family of the Huphamite. **40** And sons of Bela are Ard and Naaman: [of Ard is] the family of the Ardite; of Naaman the family of the Naamite. **41** These [are] sons of Benjamin by their families, and their numbered ones [are] forty-five thousand and six hundred. **42** These [are] sons of Dan by their families: of Shuham [is] the family of the Shuhamite; these [are] families of Dan by their families; **43** all the families of the Shuhamite by their numbered ones—sixty-four thousand and four hundred. **44** Sons of Asher by their families: of Jimna [is] the family of the Jimnite; of Jesui the family of the Jesuite; of Beriah the family of the Beriite. **45** Of sons of Beriah: of Heber [is] the family of the Heberite; of Malchiel the family of the Malchielite. **46** And the name of the daughter of Asher [is] Sarah. **47** These [are] families of the sons of Asher by their numbered ones—fifty-three thousand and four hundred. **48** Sons of Naphtali by their families: of Jahzeel [is] the family of the Jahzeelite; of Guni the family of the Gunite; **49** of Jezer the family of the Jezerite; of Shillem the family of the Shillemite. **50** These [are] families of Naphtali by their families, and their numbered ones [are] forty-five thousand and four hundred. **51** These [are] numbered ones of the sons of Israel—six hundred thousand and one thousand seven hundred and thirty. **52** And YHWH speaks to Moses, saying, **53** "The land is apportioned to these by inheritance, by the number of names; **54** to the many you increase their inheritance, and to the few you diminish their inheritance; each is given his inheritance according to his numbered ones. **55** Surely the land is apportioned by lot; they inherit by the names of the tribes of their fathers; **56** their inheritance is apportioned according to the lot between many and few." **57** And these [are] numbered ones of the Levite by their families: of Gershon [is] the family of the Gershonite; of Kohath the family of the Kohathite; of Merari the family of the Merarite. **58** These [are] families of the Levite: the family of the Libnite, the family of the Hebronite, the family of the Mahlite, the family of the Mushite, the family of the Korathite. And Kohath has begotten Amram, **59** and the name of Amram's wife is Jochebed, daughter of Levi, whom has been born to Levi in Egypt; and she bears to Amram Aaron, and Moses, and their sister Miriam. **60** And born to Aaron [are] Nadab, and Abihu, Eleazar, and Ithamar; **61** and Nadab dies—Abihu also—in their bringing strange fire near before YHWH. **62** And their numbered ones are twenty-three thousand, every male from a son of a month and upwards, for they have not numbered themselves in the midst of the sons of Israel, because an inheritance has not been given to them in the midst of the sons of Israel. **63** These [are] those numbered by Moses and Eleazar the priest, who have numbered the sons of Israel in the plains of Moab by the Jordan, [near] Jericho; **64** and among these there has not been a man of those numbered by Moses and Aaron the priest, who numbered the sons of Israel in the wilderness of Sinai, **65** for YHWH said of them, "They certainly die in the wilderness"; and there has not been left a man of them, except Caleb son of Jephunneh and Joshua son of Nun.

27 And daughters of Zelophehad son of Hepher, son of Gilead, son of Machir, son of Manasseh, of the families of Manasseh son of Joseph, draw near—and these [are] the names of his daughters: Mahlah, Noah, and Hoglah, and Milcah, and Tirzah— **2** and stand before Moses, and before Eleazar the priest, and before the princes, and all the congregation, at the opening of the Tent of Meeting, saying, **3** "Our father died in the wilderness, and he was not in the midst of the congregation who were gathered together against YHWH in the congregation of Korah, but he died for his own sin, and had no sons; **4** why is the name of our father withdrawn from the midst of his family because he has no son? Give a possession to us in the midst of the brothers of our father"; **5** and Moses brings their cause near before YHWH. **6** And YHWH speaks to Moses, saying, **7** "The daughters of Zelophehad are speaking correctly; you certainly give to them a possession of an inheritance in the midst of their father's brothers, and have caused the inheritance of their father to pass over to them. **8** And you speak to the sons of Israel, saying, When a man dies and has no son, then you have caused his inheritance to pass over to his daughter; **9** and if he has no daughter, then you have given his inheritance to his brothers; **10** and if he has no brothers, then you have given his inheritance to his father's brothers; **11** and if his father has no brothers, then you have given his inheritance to his relation who is near to him of his family, and he has possessed it"; and it has been to the sons of Israel for a statute of judgment, as YHWH has commanded Moses. **12** And YHWH says to Moses, "Go up to this Mount Abarim, and see the land which I have given to the sons of Israel; **13** and you have seen it, and you have been gathered to your people, also you, as your brother Aaron has been gathered, **14** because you provoked My mouth in the wilderness of Zin, in the strife of the congregation—to sanctify Me at the waters before their eyes"; they [are] the waters of Meribah, in Kadesh, in the wilderness of Zin. **15** And Moses speaks to YHWH, saying, **16** "YHWH, God of the spirits of all flesh, appoint a man over the congregation, **17** who goes out before them, and who comes in before them, and who takes them out, and who brings them in, and the congregation of YHWH is not as sheep which have no shepherd." **18** And YHWH says to Moses, "Take Joshua son of Nun to yourself, a man in whom [is] the Spirit, and you have laid your hand on him, **19** and have caused him to stand before Eleazar the priest and before all the congregation, and have charged him before their eyes, **20** and have put of your splendor on him, so that all the congregation of the sons of Israel listens. **21** And he stands before Eleazar the priest, and he has inquired before YHWH for him by the judgment of the Lights; at his word they go out, and at his word they come in, he and all the sons of Israel with him—even all the congregation." **22** And Moses does as YHWH has commanded him, and takes Joshua and causes him to stand before Eleazar the priest and before all the congregation, **23** and lays his hands on him and charges him, as YHWH has spoken by the hand of Moses.

28 And YHWH speaks to Moses, saying, **2** "Command the sons of Israel, and you have said to them: My offering, My bread for My fire-offerings, My refreshing fragrance, you take heed to bring near to Me in its appointed time. **3** And you have said to them: This [is] the fire-offering which you bring near to YHWH: two lambs, sons of a year, perfect ones, daily, [for] a continual burnt-offering; **4** you prepare the first lamb in the morning, and you prepare the second lamb between the evenings; **5** and a tenth of the ephah of flour for a present mixed with a fourth of the hin of beaten oil; **6** [it is] a continual burnt-offering, which was made in Mount Sinai for refreshing fragrance, [for] a fire-offering to YHWH. **7** And its drink-offering [is] a fourth of the hin for one lamb; pour out a drink-offering of strong drink to YHWH in the holy place. **8** And you prepare the second lamb between the evenings; as the present of the morning and as its drink-offering, you prepare [it as] a fire-offering of refreshing fragrance to YHWH. **9** And on the Sabbath day, two lambs, sons of a year, perfect ones, and two-tenth parts of flour, a present mixed with oil, and its drink-offering— **10** the burnt-offering of the Sabbath in its Sabbath, besides the continual burnt-offering and its drink-offering. **11** And in the beginnings of your months you bring a burnt-offering near to YHWH: two bullocks, sons of the herd, and one ram, seven lambs, sons of a year, perfect ones; **12** and three-tenth parts of flour, a present mixed with oil, for one bullock, and two-tenth parts of flour, a present mixed with oil, for one ram; **13** and a tenth—a tenth part of flour, a present mixed with oil, for one lamb, [for] a burnt-offering, a refreshing fragrance, a fire-offering to YHWH; **14** and their drink-offerings are a half of the hin for a bullock, and a third of the hin for a ram, and a fourth of the hin for a lamb, of wine; this [is] the burnt-offering of every month for the months of the year. **15** And one kid of the goats is prepared for a sin-offering to YHWH, besides the continual burnt-offering and its drink-offering. **16** And in the first month, on the fourteenth day of the month, [is] the Passover to YHWH; **17** and in the fifteenth day of this month [is] a festival; [for] seven days unleavened bread is eaten. **18** In the first day [is] a holy convocation; you do no servile work; **19** and you have brought a fire-offering near, a burnt-offering to YHWH: two bullocks, sons of the herd, and one ram, and seven lambs, sons of a year, they are perfect ones for you; **20** and their present of flour mixed with oil—you prepare three-tenth parts for a bullock and two-tenth parts for a ram; **21** you prepare a tenth—a tenth part for one lamb, for the seven lambs, **22** and one goat [for] a sin-offering, to make atonement for you. **23** Apart from the burnt-offering of the morning, which [is] for the continual burnt-offering, you prepare these; **24** like these you prepare bread of a fire-offering daily [for] seven days, a refreshing fragrance to YHWH; it is prepared besides the continual burnt-offering and its drink-offering. **25** And on the seventh day you have a holy convocation; you do no servile work. **26** And on the day of the first-fruits, in your bringing a new present near to YHWH, in your weeks, you have a holy convocation; you do no servile work. **27** And you have brought a burnt-offering near for refreshing fragrance to YHWH: two bullocks, sons of the herd, one ram, seven lambs, sons of a year, **28** and their present, flour mixed with oil, three-tenth parts for one bullock, two-tenth parts for one ram, **29** a tenth—a tenth part for one lamb, for the seven lambs; **30** one kid of the goats to make atonement for you; **31** apart from the continual burnt-offering and its present, you prepare [them] and their drink-offerings; they are perfect ones for you."

29 "And in the seventh month, on the first of the month, you have a holy convocation; you do no servile work; it is a day of shouting to you; **2** and you have prepared a burnt-offering for refreshing fragrance to YHWH: one bullock, a son of the herd, one ram, seven lambs, sons of a year, perfect ones; **3** and their present of flour mixed with oil: three-tenth parts for the bullock, two-tenth parts for the ram, **4** and one-tenth part for one lamb, for the seven lambs; **5** and one kid of the goats [for] a sin-offering, to make atonement for you; **6** apart from the burnt-offering of the month and its present, and the continual burnt-offering and its present, and their drink-offerings, according to their ordinance, for refreshing fragrance, a fire-offering to YHWH. **7** And on the tenth of this seventh month you have a holy convocation, and you have humbled your souls; you do no work; **8** and you have brought a burnt-offering near to YHWH, a refreshing fragrance: one bullock, a son of the herd, one ram, seven lambs, sons of a year; they are perfect ones for you; **9** and their present of flour mixed with oil: three-tenth parts for the bullock, two-tenth parts for one ram, **10** a tenth—a tenth part for one lamb, for the seven lambs, **11** one kid of the goats [for] a sin-offering, apart from the sin-offering of the atonements, and the continual burnt-offering and its present, and their drink-offerings. **12** And on the fifteenth day of the seventh month you have a holy convocation; you do no servile work; and you have celebrated a festival to YHWH [for] seven days, **13** and have brought a burnt-offering near, a fire-offering of refreshing fragrance, to YHWH: thirteen bullocks, sons of the herd, two rams, fourteen lambs, sons of a year; they are perfect ones; **14** and their present of flour mixed with oil: three-tenth parts for one bullock, for the thirteen bullocks, two-tenth parts for one ram, for the two rams, **15** and a tenth—a tenth part for one lamb, for the fourteen lambs; **16** and one kid of the goats [for] a sin-offering, apart from continual burnt-offering, its present, and its drink-offering. **17** And on the second day: twelve bullocks, sons of the herd, two rams, fourteen lambs, sons of a year, perfect ones; **18** and their present and their drink-offerings for the bullocks, for the rams, and for the sheep, in their number, according to the ordinance; **19** and one kid of the goats [for] a sin-offering, apart from the continual burnt-offering, and its present, and their drink-offerings. **20** And on the third day: eleven bullocks, two rams, fourteen lambs, sons of a year, perfect ones; **21** and their present and their drink-offerings for the bullocks, for the rams, and for the lambs, in their number, according to the ordinance; **22** and one goat [for] a sin-offering, apart from the continual burnt-offering, and its present, and its drink-offering. **23** And on the fourth day: ten bullocks, two rams, fourteen lambs, sons of a year, perfect ones; **24** their present and their drink-offerings for the bullocks, for the rams, and for the lambs, in their number, according to the ordinance; **25** and one kid of the goats [for] a sin-offering, apart from the continual burnt-offering, its present, and its drink-offering. **26** And on the fifth day: nine bullocks, two rams, fourteen lambs, sons of a year, perfect ones; **27** and their present and their drink-offerings for the bullocks, for the rams, and for the lambs, in their number, according to the ordinance; **28** and one goat [for] a sin-offering, apart from the continual burnt-offering, and its present, and its drink-offering. **29** And on the sixth day: eight bullocks, two rams, fourteen lambs, sons of a year, perfect ones; **30** and their present and their drink-offerings for the bullocks, for the rams, and for the lambs, in their number, according to the ordinance; **31** and one goat [for] a sin-offering, apart from the continual burnt-offering, its present, and its drink-offering. **32** And on the seventh day: seven bullocks, two rams, fourteen lambs, sons of a year, perfect ones; **33** and their present and their drink-offerings for the bullocks, for the rams, and for the lambs, in their number, according to the ordinance; **34** and one goat [for] a sin-offering, apart from the continual burnt-offering, its present, and its drink-offering. **35** On the eighth day you have a restraint; you do no servile work; **36** and you have brought a burnt-offering near, a fire-offering of refreshing fragrance, to YHWH: one bullock, one ram, seven lambs, sons of a year, perfect ones; **37** their present and their drink-offerings for the bullock, for the ram, and for the lambs, in their number, according to the ordinance; **38** and one goat [for] a sin-offering, apart from the continual burnt-offering, and its present, and its drink-offering. **39** You prepare these to YHWH in your appointed times—apart from your vows and your free-will offerings—for your burnt-offerings, and for your presents, and for your drink-offerings, and for your peace-offerings." **40** And Moses speaks to the sons of Israel according to all that YHWH has commanded Moses.

30 And Moses speaks to the heads of the tribes of the sons of Israel, saying, "This [is] the thing which YHWH has commanded: **2** When a man vows a vow to YHWH, or has sworn an oath to bind a bond on his soul, he does not defile his word; he does according to all that is going out from his mouth. **3** And when a woman vows a vow to YHWH, and has bound a bond in the house of her father in her youth, **4** and her father has heard her vow and her bond which she has bound on her soul, and her father has kept silent to her, then all her vows have been established, and every bond which she has bound on her soul is established. **5** And if her father has disallowed her in the day of his hearing, none of her vows and her bonds which she has bound on her soul are established, and YHWH is propitious to her, for her father has disallowed her. **6** And if she is having a husband, and her vows [are] on her, or a wrongful utterance [on] her lips which she has bound on her soul, **7** and her husband has heard, and in the day of his hearing he has kept silent to her, then her vows have been established, and her bonds which she has bound on her soul are established. **8** And if in the day of her husband's hearing he disallows her, then he has broken her vow which [is] on her, and the wrongful utterance of her lips which she has bound on her soul, and YHWH is propitious to her. **9** As for the vow of a widow or cast-out woman, all that she has bound on her soul is established on her. **10** And if she has vowed [in] the house of her husband, or has bound a bond on her soul with an oath, **11** and her husband has heard, and has kept silent to her—he has not disallowed her—then all her vows have been established, and every bond which she has bound on her soul is established. **12** And if her husband certainly breaks them in the day of his hearing, none of the outgoing of her lips concerning her vows, or concerning the bond of her soul, is established—her husband has broken them—and YHWH is propitious to her. **13** Every vow and every oath—a bond to humble a soul—her husband establishes it, or her husband breaks it; **14** and if her husband certainly keeps silent to her from day to day, then he has established all her vows or all her bonds which [are] on her; he has established them, for he has kept silent to her in the day of his hearing; **15** and if he indeed breaks them after his hearing, then he has borne her iniquity." **16** These [are] the statutes which YHWH has commanded Moses between a man and his wife, between a father and his daughter, in her youth, [in] the house of her father.

NUMBERS

31 And Y<small>HWH</small> speaks to Moses, saying, **2** "Execute the vengeance of the sons of Israel against the Midianites—afterward you are gathered to your people." **3** And Moses speaks to the people, saying, "Arm men from [among] you for the war, and they are against Midian, to put the vengeance of Y<small>HWH</small> on Midian; **4** one thousand for a tribe—you send one thousand for a tribe, of all the tribes of Israel, to the war." **5** And there are given out of the thousands of Israel one thousand for a tribe—twelve thousand armed ones [for] war; **6** and Moses sends them, one thousand for a tribe, to the war; [he sent] them and Phinehas son of Eleazar the priest to the war, with the holy vessels and the trumpets of shouting in his hand. **7** And they war against Midian, as Y<small>HWH</small> has commanded Moses, and slay every male; **8** and they have slain the kings of Midian besides their pierced ones: Evi, and Rekem, and Zur, and Hur, and Reba—five kings of Midian; and they have slain Balaam son of Beor with the sword. **9** And the sons of Israel take the women of Midian and their infants captive; and they have plundered all their livestock, and all their substance, and all their wealth; **10** and they have burned all their cities, with their habitations, and all their towers, with fire. **11** And they take all the spoil and all the prey, among man and among beast; **12** and they bring in the captives, and the prey, and the spoil to Moses, and to Eleazar the priest, and to the congregation of the sons of Israel, to the camp, to the plains of Moab, which [are] by the Jordan, [near] Jericho. **13** And Moses, and Eleazar the priest, and all the princes of the congregation, go out to meet them, to the outside of the camp, **14** and Moses is angry against the inspectors of the force, chiefs of the thousands, and chiefs of the hundreds, who are coming in from the warfare of battle. **15** And Moses says to them, "Have you kept every female alive? **16** Behold, they have been to the sons of Israel, through the word of Balaam, to cause a trespass against Y<small>HWH</small> in the matter of Peor, and the plague is in the congregation of Y<small>HWH</small>. **17** And now, slay every male among the infants, indeed, slay every woman knowing a man by the lying of a male; **18** and all the infants among the women who have not known the lying of a male you have kept alive for yourselves.

19 And you, encamp at the outside of the camp [for] seven days; any who has slain a person, and any who has come against a pierced one, cleanse yourselves on the third day and on the seventh day—you and your captives; **20** and every garment, and every skin vessel, and every work of goats' [hair], and every wooden vessel, you yourselves cleanse." **21** And Eleazar the priest says to the men of war who go to battle, "This [is] the statute of the law which Y<small>HWH</small> has commanded Moses: **22** only the gold, and the silver, the bronze, the iron, the tin, and the lead, **23** everything which may go into fire, you cause to pass over through fire, and it has been clean; it is surely cleansed with the water of separation; and all that may not go into fire, you cause to pass over through water; **24** and you have washed your garments on the seventh day and have been clean, and afterward you come into the camp." **25** And Y<small>HWH</small> speaks to Moses, saying, **26** "Take up the sum of the prey of the captives, among man and among beast, you, and Eleazar the priest, and the heads of the fathers of the congregation; **27** and you have halved the prey between those handling the battle, who go out to the war, and all the congregation; **28** and you have raised a tribute to Y<small>HWH</small> from the men of battle, who go out to the war, one body out of five hundred, of man, and of the herd, and of the donkeys, and of the flock; **29** you take from their half and have given [it] to Eleazar the priest [as] a raised-offering of Y<small>HWH</small>. **30** And from the sons of Israel's half you take one possession out of fifty, of man, of the herd, of the donkeys, and of the flock, of all the livestock, and you have given them to the Levites keeping the charge of the Dwelling Place of Y<small>HWH</small>." **31** And Moses does—Eleazar the priest also—as Y<small>HWH</small> has commanded Moses. **32** And the prey, the remainder of the spoil which the people of the host have spoiled, is six hundred thousand and seventy thousand and five thousand of the flock; **33** and seventy-two thousand of the herd; **34** and sixty-one thousand donkeys; **35** and of mankind—of the women who have not known the lying of a male—all the persons [are] thirty-two thousand. **36** And the half, the portion of those who go out into the war, is [in] number three hundred thousand and thirty thousand and seven thousand and five hundred of the flock.

NUMBERS

37 And the tribute to YHWH of the sheep is six hundred seventy-five; **38** and the herd [is] thirty-six thousand, and their tribute to YHWH [is] seventy-two; **39** and the donkeys [are] thirty thousand and five hundred, and their tribute to YHWH [is] sixty-one; **40** and of mankind [are] sixteen thousand, and their tribute to YHWH [is] thirty-two persons. **41** And Moses gives the tribute—YHWH's raised-offering—to Eleazar the priest, as YHWH has commanded Moses. **42** And of the sons of Israel's half, which Moses halved from the men who war— **43** and the congregation's half is three hundred thousand and thirty thousand [and] seven thousand and five hundred of the flock; **44** and thirty-six thousand of the herd; **45** and thirty thousand and five hundred donkeys; **46** and sixteen thousand of mankind— **47** Moses takes from the sons of Israel's half one possession from the fifty, of man and of beast, and gives them to the Levites keeping the charge of the Dwelling Place of YHWH, as YHWH has commanded Moses. **48** And the inspectors whom the thousands of the host have (heads of the thousands and heads of the hundreds), draw near to Moses, **49** and they say to Moses, "Your servants have taken up the sum of the men of war who [are] with us, and not a man of us has been missed; **50** and we bring YHWH's offering near, each of that which he has found of vessels of gold—chain, and bracelet, seal-ring, [ear]-ring, and bead—to make atonement for ourselves before YHWH." **51** And Moses receives—Eleazar the priest also—the gold from them, every vessel of workmanship; **52** and all the gold of the raised-offering which they have lifted up to YHWH is sixteen thousand seven hundred and fifty shekels, from heads of the thousands and from heads of the hundreds; **53** (the men of the host have each taken spoil for himself); **54** and Moses takes—Eleazar the priest also—the gold from the heads of the thousands and of the hundreds, and they bring it into the Tent of Meeting [as] a memorial for the sons of Israel before YHWH.

32 And much livestock has [belonged] to the sons of Reuben and to the sons of Gad—very many; and they see the land of Jazer and the land of Gilead, and behold, the place [is] a place [for] livestock; **2** and the sons of Gad and the sons of Reuben come in and speak to Moses, and to Eleazar the priest, and to the princes of the congregation, saying, **3** "Ataroth, and Dibon, and Jazer, and Nimrah, and Heshbon, and Elealeh, and Shebam, and Nebo, and Beon, **4** the land which YHWH has struck before the congregation of Israel, is a land for livestock, and your servants have livestock." **5** And they say, "If we have found grace in your eyes, let this land be given to your servants for a possession; cause us not to pass over the Jordan." **6** And Moses says to the sons of Gad and to the sons of Reuben, "Do your brothers go to the battle, and you—do you sit here? **7** And why discourage the heart of the sons of Israel from passing over to the land which YHWH has given to them? **8** Thus your fathers did in my sending them from Kadesh-Barnea to see the land; **9** and they go up to the Valley of Eshcol, and see the land, and discourage the heart of the sons of Israel so as not to go into the land which YHWH has given to them; **10** and the anger of YHWH burns in that day, and He swears, saying, **11** They do not see—the men who are coming up out of Egypt from a son of twenty years and upward—the ground which I have sworn to Abraham, to Isaac, and to Jacob, for they have not been fully after Me, **12** except Caleb son of Jephunneh the Kenezite and Joshua son of Nun, for they have been fully after YHWH; **13** and the anger of YHWH burns against Israel, and He causes them to wander in the wilderness [for] forty years, until the consumption of all the generation which is doing evil in the eyes of YHWH. **14** And behold, you have risen in the stead of your fathers, an increase of sinful men, to add yet to the fury of the anger of YHWH toward Israel; **15** when you turn back from after Him, then He has added yet to leave him in the wilderness, and you have done corruptly to all this people." **16** And they come near to him and say, "We build folds for the flock here for our livestock, and cities for our infants; **17** but we are armed, hastening before the sons of Israel until we have brought them to their place; and our infants have dwelt in the cities of defense because of the inhabitants of the land; **18** we do not return to our houses until the sons of Israel have each inherited his inheritance, **19** for we do not inherit with them across the Jordan and beyond, for our

NUMBERS

inheritance has come to us beyond the Jordan at the [sun]-rising." **20** And Moses says to them, "If you do this thing, if you are armed before YHWH for battle, **21** and every armed one of you has passed over the Jordan before YHWH, until His dispossessing His enemies from before Him, **22** and the land has been subdued before YHWH, then afterward you return, and have been acquitted by YHWH and by Israel, and this land has been to you for a possession before YHWH. **23** And if you do not do so, behold, you have sinned against YHWH, and know that your sin finds you; **24** build for yourselves cities for your infants and folds for your flock, and that which is going out from your mouth you do." **25** And the sons of Gad and the sons of Reuben speak to Moses, saying, "Your servants do as my lord is commanding; **26** our infants, our wives, our livestock, and all our beasts, are there in cities of Gilead, **27** and your servants pass over, every armed one of the host, before YHWH, to battle, as my lord is saying." **28** And Moses commands Eleazar the priest, and Joshua son of Nun, and the heads of the fathers of the tribes of the sons of Israel concerning them; **29** and Moses says to them, "If the sons of Gad and the sons of Reuben pass over the Jordan with you, everyone armed for battle, before YHWH, and the land has been subdued before you, then you have given the land of Gilead to them for a possession; **30** and if they do not pass over armed with you, then they have possessions in your midst in the land of Canaan." **31** And the sons of Gad and the sons of Reuben answer, saying, "That which YHWH has spoken to your servants, so we do; **32** we pass over armed before YHWH [to] the land of Canaan, and with us [is] the possession of our inheritance beyond the Jordan." **33** And Moses gives to them—to the sons of Gad, and to the sons of Reuben, and to the half of the tribe of Manasseh son of Joseph—the kingdom of Sihon king of the Amorite and the kingdom of Og king of Bashan, the land by its cities, in the borders, the cities of the surrounding land. **34** And the sons of Gad build Dihon, and Ataroth, and Aroer, **35** and Atroth, Shophan, and Jaazer, and Jogbehah, **36** and Beth-Nimrah, and Beth-Haran, cities of defense, and sheepfolds. **37** And the sons of Reuben have built Heshbon, and Elealeh, and Kirjathaim, **38** and Nebo, and Ba'al-Meon (changed in name), and Shibmah, and they call the names of the cities which they have built by [these] names. **39** And sons of Machir son of Manasseh go to Gilead, and capture it, and dispossess the Amorite who [is] in it; **40** and Moses gives Gilead to Machir son of Manasseh, and he dwells in it. **41** And Jair son of Manasseh has gone and captures their towns, and calls them "Towns of Jair"; **42** and Nobah has gone and captures Kenath and its villages, and calls it Nobah, by his own name.

33 These [are] the journeys of the sons of Israel who have come out of the land of Egypt, by their hosts, by the hand of Moses and Aaron; **2** and Moses writes their outgoings, by their journeys, by the command of YHWH; and these [are] their journeys, by their outgoings: **3** And they journey from Rameses in the first month, on the fifteenth day of the first month; from the day after the Passover the sons of Israel have gone out with a high hand before the eyes of all the Egyptians— **4** and the Egyptians are burying those whom YHWH has struck among them, every firstborn, and YHWH has done judgments on their gods. **5** And the sons of Israel journey from Rameses and encamp in Succoth. **6** And they journey from Succoth and encamp in Etham, which [is] in the extremity of the wilderness. **7** And they journey from Etham and turn back over Pi-Hahiroth, which [is] on the front of Ba'al-Zephon, and they encamp before Migdol. **8** And they journey from Pi-Hahiroth, and pass over through the midst of the sea into the wilderness, and go a journey of three days in the wilderness of Etham, and encamp in Marah. **9** And they journey from Marah and come to Elim, and twelve fountains of waters and seventy palm trees [are] in Elim, and they encamp there. **10** And they journey from Elim and encamp by the Red Sea. **11** And they journey from the Red Sea and encamp in the wilderness of Sin. **12** And they journey from the wilderness of Sin and encamp in Dophkah. **13** And they journey from Dophkah and encamp in Alush. **14** And they journey from Alush and encamp in Rephidim; and there was no water there for the people to drink. **15** And they journey from Rephidim and encamp in the wilderness of Sinai. **16** And they journey from the wilderness of Sinai and encamp in Kibroth-Hattaavah. **17** And they journey from Kibroth-Hattaavah and encamp in Hazeroth. **18** And they journey from Hazeroth and encamp in Rithmah. **19** And they journey from Rithmah and encamp in Rimmon-Parez. **20** And they journey from Rimmon-Parez and encamp in Libnah. **21** And they journey from Libnah and encamp in Rissah. **22** And they journey from Rissah and encamp in Kehelathah. **23** And they journey from Kehelathah and encamp in Mount Shapher. **24** And they journey from Mount Shapher and encamp in Haradah. **25** And they journey from Haradah and encamp in Makheloth. **26** And they journey from Makheloth and encamp in Tahath. **27** And they journey from Tahath and encamp in Tarah. **28** And they journey from Tarah and encamp in Mithcah. **29** And they journey from Mithcah and encamp in Hashmonah. **30** And they journey from Hashmonah and encamp in Moseroth. **31** And they journey from Moseroth and encamp in Bene-Jaakan. **32** And they journey from Bene-Jaakan and encamp at Hor-Hagidgad. **33** And they journey from Hor-Hagidgad and encamp in Jotbathah. **34** And they journey from Jotbathah and encamp in Ebronah. **35** And they journey from Ebronah and encamp in Ezion-Gaber. **36** And they journey from Ezion-Gaber and encamp in the wilderness of Zin, which [is] Kadesh. **37** And they journey from Kadesh and encamp in Mount Hor, in the extremity of the land of Edom. **38** And Aaron the priest goes up to Mount Hor by the command of YHWH, and dies there in the fortieth year of the going out of the sons of Israel from the land of Egypt, in the fifth month, on the first of the month; **39** and Aaron [is] a son of one hundred and twenty-three years in his dying on Mount Hor. **40** And the Canaanite, king of Arad, who is dwelling in the south in the land of Canaan, hears of the coming of the sons of Israel. **41** And they journey from Mount Hor and encamp in Zalmonah. **42** And they journey from Zalmonah and encamp in Punon. **43** And they journey from Punon and encamp in Oboth. **44** And they journey from Oboth and encamp in Ije-Abarim, in the border of Moab. **45** And they journey from Iim and encamp in Dibon-Gad. **46** And they journey from Dibon-Gad and encamp in Almon-Diblathaim. **47** And they journey from Almon-Diblathaim and encamp in the mountains of Abarim, before Nebo. **48** And they journey from the mountains of Abarim and encamp in the plains of Moab by the Jordan, [near] Jericho. **49** And they encamp by the Jordan, from Beth-Jeshimoth as far as Abel-Shittim in the plains of Moab. **50** And YHWH speaks to Moses in the plains of Moab by the Jordan, [near] Jericho, saying, **51** "Speak to the sons of Israel, and you have said to them: When you are passing over the Jordan to the land of Canaan, **52** then you have dispossessed all the inhabitants of the land from before you, and have destroyed all their imagery, indeed, you destroy all their molten images, and you lay waste [to] all their high places, **53** and you have possessed the land and dwelt in it, for I have given the land to you to possess it. **54** And you have inherited the land by lot, by your families; to the many you increase their inheritance, and to the few you diminish their inheritance; to where the lot goes out to him, it is his; you inherit by the tribes of your fathers. **55** And if you do not dispossess the inhabitants of the land from before you, then it has been [that] those whom you let remain of them [are] for pricks in your eyes and for thorns in your sides, and they have distressed you on the land in which you are dwelling, **56** and it has come to pass, as I thought to do to them, I do to you."

34 And YHWH speaks to Moses, saying, **2** "Command the sons of Israel, and you have said to them: When you are coming into the land of Canaan—this [is] the land which falls to you by inheritance, the land of Canaan, by its borders— **3** then the south quarter has been to you from the wilderness of Zin, by the sides of Edom, indeed, the south border has been to you from the extremity of the Salt Sea eastward; **4** and the border has turned around to you from the south to the ascent of Akrabbim, and has passed on to Zin, and its outgoings have been from the south to Kadesh-Barnea, and it has gone out at Hazar-Addar, and has passed on to Azmon; **5** and the border has turned around from Azmon to the Brook of Egypt, and its outgoings have been at the sea. **6** As for the west border, even the Great Sea has been a border to you; this is the west border to you. **7** And this is the north border to you:

from the Great Sea you mark out for yourselves Mount Hor; **8** from Mount Hor you mark out to go to Hamath, and the outgoings of the border have been to Zedad; **9** and the border has gone out to Ziphron, and its outgoings have been at Hazar-Enan; this is the north border to you. **10** And you have marked out for yourselves for the border eastward, from Hazar-Enan to Shepham; **11** and the border has gone down from Shepham to Riblah, on the east of Ain, and the border has gone down, and has struck against the shoulder of the Sea of Chinnereth eastward; **12** and the border has gone down to the Jordan, and its outgoings have been at the Salt Sea; this is the land for you by its borders all around."

13 And Moses commands the sons of Israel, saying, "This [is] the land which you inherit by lot, which YHWH has commanded to give to the nine tribes and the half of the tribe; **14** for the tribe of the sons of Reuben, by the house of their fathers, and the tribe of the children of Gad, by the house of their fathers, have received [their inheritance]; and [those of] the half of the tribe of Manasseh have received their inheritance; **15** the two tribes and the half of the tribe have received their inheritance beyond the Jordan, [near] Jericho, eastward, at the [sun]-rising." **16** And YHWH speaks to Moses, saying, **17** "These [are] the names of the men who give the inheritance of the land to you: Eleazar the priest and Joshua son of Nun. **18** And one prince—you take one prince from a tribe to give the land by inheritance. **19** And these [are] the names of the men: of the tribe of Judah, Caleb son of Jephunneh; **20** and of the tribe of the sons of Simeon, Shemuel son of Aminihud; **21** of the tribe of Benjamin, Elidad son of Chislon; **22** and a prince of the tribe of the sons of Dan, Bukki son of Jogli; **23** of the sons of Joseph, a prince of the tribe of the sons of Manasseh, Hanniel son of Ephod; **24** and a prince of the tribe of the sons of Ephraim, Kemuel son of Shiphtan; **25** and a prince of the tribe of the sons of Zebulun, Elizaphan son of Parnach; **26** and a prince of the tribe of the sons of Issachar, Paltiel son of Azzan; **27** and a prince of the tribe of the sons of Asher, Ahihud son of Shelomi; **28** and a prince of the tribe of the sons of Naphtali, Pedahel son of Ammihud." **29** These [are] those whom YHWH has commanded to give the sons of Israel inheritance in the land of Canaan.

35 And YHWH speaks to Moses in the plains of Moab by the Jordan, [near] Jericho, saying, **2** "Command the sons of Israel, and they have given to the Levites cities to inhabit from the inheritance of their possession; you also give [the] outskirt around them, of the cities, to the Levites. **3** And the cities have been for them to inhabit, and their outskirts are for their livestock, and for their goods, and for all their beasts. **4** And the outskirts of the cities which you give to the Levites [are], from the wall of the city and outside, one thousand cubits around. **5** And you have measured from the outside of the city: the east quarter—two thousand by the cubit, and the south quarter—two thousand by the cubit, and the west quarter—two thousand by the cubit, and the north quarter—two thousand by the cubit; and the city [is] in the midst; this is the outskirts of the cities to them. **6** And the cities which you give to the Levites [are] the six cities of refuge, which you give for the fleeing there of the manslayer, and besides them you give forty-two cities; **7** all the cities which you give to the Levites [are] forty-eight cities, them and their outskirts. **8** And the cities which you give [are] from the possession of the sons of Israel; from the many you multiply, and from the few you diminish; each, according to his inheritance which they inherit, gives to the Levites from his cities." **9** And YHWH speaks to Moses, saying, **10** "Speak to the sons of Israel, and you have said to them: When you are passing over the Jordan to the land of Canaan, **11** and have prepared cities for yourselves—they are cities of refuge to you—then a manslayer, striking a person through ignorance, has fled there, **12** and the cities have been for a refuge to you from the redeemer, and the manslayer does not die until his standing before the congregation for judgment. **13** As for the cities which you give, six [are] cities of refuge to you; **14** three of the cities you give from beyond the Jordan, and three of the cities you give in the land of Canaan; they are cities of refuge. **15** For sons of Israel, and for a sojourner, and for a settler in their midst, are these six cities for a refuge, for the fleeing there of anyone striking a person through ignorance. **16** And if he has struck him with an

NUMBERS

instrument of iron, and he dies, he [is] a murderer: the murderer is certainly put to death. **17** And if he has struck him with a stone [in] the hand, with which he could die, and he dies, he [is] a murderer: the murderer is certainly put to death. **18** Or [if] he has struck him with a wooden instrument [in] the hand, with which he could die, and he dies, he [is] a murderer: the murderer is certainly put to death. **19** The redeemer of blood puts the murderer to death himself; in his coming against him he puts him to death. **20** And if he pushes him in hatred, or has cast [anything] at him by lying in wait, and he dies, **21** or he has struck him with his hand in enmity, and he dies, the striker is certainly put to death; he [is] a murderer; the redeemer of blood puts the murderer to death in his coming against him. **22** And if, in an instant, without enmity, he has pushed him, or has cast any instrument at him without lying in wait, **23** or with any stone with which he could die, without seeing, indeed, causes [it] to fall on him, and he dies, and he [is] not his enemy, nor seeking his evil, **24** then the congregation has judged between the striker and the redeemer of blood by these judgments. **25** And the congregation has delivered the manslayer out of the hand of the redeemer of blood, and the congregation has caused him to return to the city of his refuge, to where he has fled, and he has dwelt in it until the death of the chief priest who has been anointed with the holy oil. **26** And if the manslayer indeed goes out [from] the border of the city of his refuge to where he flees, **27** and the redeemer of blood has found him at the outside of the border of the city of his refuge, and the redeemer of blood has slain the manslayer, blood [is] not [reckoned] to him; **28** for he dwells in the city of his refuge until the death of the chief priest; and after the death of the chief priest the manslayer turns back to the city of his possession. **29** And these things have been for a statute of judgment to you throughout your generations, in all your dwellings. **30** Whoever strikes a person, by the mouth of witnesses [one] slays the murderer; and one witness does not testify against a person to cause [him] to die. **31** And you take no atonement for the life of a murderer who [is] condemned to die, for he is certainly put to death; **32** and you take no atonement for him [who had] to flee to the city of his refuge, to return to dwell in the land, until the death of the priest. **33** And you do not profane the land which you [are] in, for blood profanes the land; as for the land, it is not pardoned for blood which is shed in it except by the blood of him who sheds it; **34** and you do not defile the land in which you are dwelling, in the midst of which I dwell, for I, YHWH, dwell in the midst of the sons of Israel."

36 And the heads of the fathers of the families of the sons of Gilead, son of Machir, son of Manasseh, of the families of the sons of Joseph, come near and speak before Moses and before the princes, heads of the fathers of the sons of Israel, **2** and say, "YHWH commanded my lord to give the land for inheritance by lot to the sons of Israel, and my lord has been commanded by YHWH to give the inheritance of our brother Zelophehad to his daughters. **3** Now [if] they have been [given] to one from the sons of the [other] tribes of the sons of Israel for wives, and their inheritance has been withdrawn from the inheritance of our fathers, and has been added to the inheritance of the tribe which is theirs, and it is withdrawn from the lot of our inheritance, **4** and if it is the Jubilee of the sons of Israel, then their inheritance has been added to the inheritance of the tribe which is theirs, and their inheritance is withdrawn from the inheritance of the tribe of our fathers." **5** And Moses commands the sons of Israel by the command of YHWH, saying, "The tribe of the sons of Joseph is speaking correctly; **6** this [is] the thing which YHWH has commanded concerning the daughters of Zelophehad, saying, To those good in their eyes let them be for wives; only, let them be for wives to a family of the tribe of their fathers; **7** and the inheritance of the sons of Israel does not turn around from tribe to tribe; for each of the sons of Israel cleaves to the inheritance of the tribe of his fathers. **8** And every daughter possessing an inheritance from the tribes of the sons of Israel is for a wife to one from the family of the tribe of her father, so that the sons of Israel each possess the inheritance of his fathers, **9** and the inheritance does not turn around from [one] tribe to another tribe; for each of the tribes of the sons of Israel cleaves to his inheritance." **10** As YHWH has commanded Moses, so the daughters of Zelophehad have done, **11** and Mahlah, Tirzah, and Hoglah, and Milcah, and Noah, daughters of Zelophehad, are for wives to the sons of their fathers' brothers; **12** they have been for wives [to men] from the families of the sons of Manasseh, son of Joseph, and their inheritance is with the tribe of the family of their father. **13** These [are] the commands and the judgments which YHWH has commanded by the hand of Moses concerning the sons of Israel, in the plains of Moab by the Jordan, [near] Jericho.

DEUTERONOMY

1 These [are] the words which Moses has spoken to all Israel beyond the Jordan in the wilderness, in the plain opposite Suph, between Paran, and Tophel, and Laban, and Hazeroth, and Di-Zahab. **2** [It takes] eleven days [to go] from Horeb, the way of Mount Seir, to Kadesh-Barnea. **3** And it comes to pass in the fortieth year, in the eleventh month, on the first of the month, Moses has spoken to the sons of Israel according to all that YHWH has commanded him concerning them, **4** after his striking Sihon king of the Amorite who is dwelling in Heshbon, and Og king of Bashan who is dwelling in Ashtaroth in Edrei. **5** Beyond the Jordan, in the land of Moab, Moses has begun to explain this law, saying, **6** "Our God YHWH has spoken to us in Horeb, saying, For you dwell at this mountain long enough; **7** turn and journey for yourselves, and go to the mountain of the Amorite, and to all its neighboring places in the plain, in the hill-country, and in the low country, and in the south, and in the haven of the sea, the land of the Canaanite, and of Lebanon, as far as the great river, the Euphrates River; **8** see, I have set the land before you; go in and possess the land which YHWH has sworn to your fathers, to Abraham, to Isaac, and to Jacob, to give to them and to their seed after them. **9** And I speak to you at that time, saying, I am not able to bear you by myself; **10** your God YHWH has multiplied you, and behold, today you [are] as the stars of the heavens for multitude; **11** YHWH, God of your fathers, is adding to you, as you [are], one thousand times, and blesses you as He has spoken to you. **12** How do I bear your pressure, and your burden, and your strife by myself? **13** Provide wise and understanding men for yourselves that are known to your tribes, and I set them for your heads; **14** and you answer me and say, The thing which you have spoken [is] good to do. **15** And I take the heads of your tribes, wise men that are known, and I appoint them [as] heads over you, princes of thousands, and princes of hundreds, and princes of fifties, and princes of tens, and authorities for your tribes. **16** And I command your judges at that time, saying, Listen between your brothers—then you have judged [in] righteousness between a man, and his brother, and his sojourner; **17** you do not discern faces in judgment; you hear the little as well as the great; you are not afraid of the face of any, for the judgment is God's, and the thing which is too hard for you, you bring near to me, and I have heard it. **18** And I command you at that time all the things which you do. **19** And we journey from Horeb, and go [through] all that great and fearful wilderness which you have seen, the way of the hill-country of the Amorite, as our God YHWH has commanded us, and we come to Kadesh-Barnea. **20** And I say to you, You have come to the hill-country of the Amorite, which our God YHWH is giving to us; **21** see, your God YHWH has set the land before you; go up, possess, as YHWH, God of your fathers, has spoken to you; do not fear, nor be frightened. **22** And you come near to me, all of you, and say, Let us send men before us, and they search the land for us, and they bring us back word [concerning] the way in which we go up into it, and the cities to which we come in; **23** and the thing is good in my eyes, and I take twelve men from you, one man for the tribe. **24** And they turn and go up to the hill-country, and come to the Valley of Eshcol, and spy it out, **25** and they take in their hand from the fruit of the land, and bring [it] down to us, and bring us back word, and say, The land is good which our God YHWH is giving to us. **26** And you have not been willing to go up, and you provoke the mouth of your God YHWH, **27** and murmur in your tents, and say, In YHWH's hating us He has brought us out of the land of Egypt, to give us into the hand of the Amorite—to destroy us; **28** to where are we going up? Our brothers have melted our heart, saying, [The] people [are] greater and taller than we; [the] cities [are] great and fortified up to the heavens, and we have also seen sons of Anakim there. **29** And I say to you, Do not be terrified, nor be afraid of them; **30** your God YHWH, who is going before you—He fights for you, according to all that He has done with you in Egypt before your eyes, **31** and in the wilderness where you have seen that your God YHWH has carried you, as a man carries his son, in all the way which you have gone until your coming to this place. **32** And in this thing you are not steadfast in your God YHWH, **33** who is going before you in the way to search out for you a place for your encamping, in fire by night, to show you in the way in which you go, and in a cloud by day. **34** And YHWH hears the voice of your words, and is angry, and swears, saying, **35** Not one of these men of this evil generation sees the good land which I have sworn to give to your fathers, **36** except Caleb son of Jephunneh—he sees it, and to him I give the land on which he has trodden, and to his sons, because that he has been fully after YHWH. **37** Moreover, YHWH has been angry with me for your sake, saying, Indeed, you do not go in there; **38** Joshua son of Nun, who is standing before you, he goes in there; strengthen him, for he causes Israel to inherit [it]. **39** And your infants, of whom you have said, They are for a prey, and your sons who today have not known good and evil, they go in there, and I give it to them, and they possess it; **40** but you, turn and journey for yourselves toward the wilderness, the way of the Red Sea. **41** And you answer and say to me, We have sinned against YHWH; we go up and we have fought, according to all that which our God YHWH has commanded us; and you each gird on his weapons of war, and you are ready to go up into the hill-country; **42** and YHWH says to me, Say to them, You do not go up, nor fight, for I am not in your midst, and you are not struck before your enemies. **43** And I speak to you, and you have not listened, and provoke the mouth of YHWH, and act proudly, and go up into the hill-country; **44** and the Amorite who is dwelling in that hill-country comes out to meet you, and they pursue you as the bees do, and strike you in Seir, even to Hormah. **45** And you return and weep before YHWH, and YHWH has not listened to your voice, nor has He given ear to you; **46** and you dwell in Kadesh [for] many days, according to the days which you had dwelt."

2 "And we turn and journey into the wilderness, the way of the Red Sea, as YHWH has spoken to me, and we go around Mount Seir [for] many days. **2** And YHWH speaks to me, saying, **3** For you go around this mountain long enough; turn for yourselves northward. **4** And the people command you, saying, You are passing over into the border of your brothers, sons of Esau, who are dwelling in Seir, and they are afraid of you; and you have been very watchful; **5** you do not strive with them, for I do not give [any] of their land to you— even the treading of the sole of a foot; I have given Mount Seir to Esau for a possession. **6** You buy food from them with money, and have eaten; and you also buy water from them with money, and have drunk. **7** For your God YHWH has blessed you in all the work of your hands; He has known your walking in this great wilderness these forty years; your God YHWH [is] with you; you have not lacked anything. **8** And we pass by from our brothers, sons of Esau, who are dwelling in Seir, by the way of the plain, by Elath and by Ezion-Gaber, and we turn and pass over the way of the wilderness of Moab; **9** and YHWH says to me, Do not distress Moab, nor stir yourself up against them [in] battle, for I do not give [any] of their land to you [for] a possession; for I have given Ar to the sons of Lot [for] a possession. **10** The Emim have formerly dwelt in it, a people great, and numerous, and tall as the Anakim; **11** they are reckoned [as] Rephaim, they also, as the Anakim; and the Moabites call them Emim. **12** And the Horim have formerly dwelt in Seir, but the sons of Esau dispossess them, and destroy them from before them, and dwell in their stead, as Israel has done to the land of his possession which YHWH has given to them. **13** Now rise and pass over the Brook of Zered for yourselves; and we pass over the Brook of Zered. **14** And the days which we have walked from Kadesh-Barnea until we have passed over the Brook of Zered [are] thirty-eight years, until the consumption of all the generation of the men of battle from the midst of the camp, as YHWH has sworn to them; **15** and indeed the hand of YHWH has been against them, to destroy them from the midst of the camp until they are consumed. **16** And it comes to pass, when all the men of battle have finished dying from the midst of the people, **17** that YHWH speaks to me, saying, **18** Today you are passing over the border of Moab, even Ar, **19** and [when] you have come near the sons of Ammon, you do not distress them, nor stir yourself up against them, for I do not give [any] of the land of the sons of Ammon to you [for] a possession; for I have given it

DEUTERONOMY

to the sons of Lot [for] a possession. **20** It is reckoned [as] a land of Rephaim, even it; Rephaim formerly dwelt in it, and the Ammonites call them Zamzummim, **21** a people great, and numerous, and tall as the Anakim, and YHWH destroys them before them, and they dispossess them, and dwell in their stead, **22** as He has done for the sons of Esau who are dwelling in Seir, when He destroyed the Horim from before them, and they dispossess them, and dwell in their stead to this day. **23** As for the Avim who are dwelling in villages as far as Gaza, the Caphtorim—who are coming out from Caphtor—have destroyed them, and dwell in their stead. **24** Rise, journey, and pass over the Brook of Arnon; see, I have given into your hand Sihon king of Heshbon, the Amorite, and his land; begin to possess [it], and stir yourself up against him [in] battle. **25** This [is] the day I begin to put your dread and your fear on the face of the peoples under the whole heavens, who hear your fame, and have trembled and been pained because of you. **26** And I send messengers from the wilderness of Kedemoth to Sihon king of Heshbon, [with] words of peace, saying, **27** Let me pass over through your land; in the way—in the way I go, I do not turn aside [to the] right or left. **28** You sell me food for money, and I have eaten; and you give to me water for money, and I have drunk; only, let me pass over on my feet, **29** as the sons of Esau who are dwelling in Seir and the Moabites who are dwelling in Ar have done for me, until I pass over the Jordan to the land which our God YHWH is giving to us. **30** And Sihon king of Heshbon has not been willing to let us pass over by him, for your God YHWH has hardened his spirit and strengthened his heart, so as to give him into your hand as at this day. **31** And YHWH says to me, See, I have begun to give Sihon and his land before your faces; begin to possess—to possess his land. **32** And Sihon comes out to meet us, he and all his people, to the battle at Jahaz; **33** and our God YHWH gives him before our faces, and we strike him, and his sons, and all his people; **34** and we capture all his cities at that time, and devote the whole city—men, and the women, and the infants; we have not left a remnant; **35** only, we have spoiled the livestock for ourselves, and the spoil of the cities which we have captured. **36** From Aroer, which [is] by the edge of the Brook of Arnon, and the city which [is] by the brook, even to Gilead, there has not been a city which [is] too high for us; our God YHWH has given the whole before our faces. **37** Only, you have not drawn near to the land of the sons of Ammon—any part of the Brook of Jabbok, and cities of the hill-country, and anything which our God YHWH has [not] commanded."

3 "And we turn and go up the way to Bashan, and Og king of Bashan comes out to meet us, he and all his people, to the battle [at] Edrei. **2** And YHWH says to me, Do not fear him, for I have given him, and all his people, and his land into your hand, and you have done to him as you have done to Sihon king of the Amorite who is dwelling in Heshbon. **3** And our God YHWH indeed gives Og king of Bashan and all his people into our hands, and we strike him until there has been no remnant left to him; **4** and we capture all his cities at that time; there has not been a city which we have not taken from them—sixty cities, all the region of Argob, the kingdom of Og in Bashan. **5** All these [are] cities fortified with high walls, double gates, and bar, apart from very many cities of the open place; **6** and we devote them, as we have done to Sihon king of Heshbon, devoting [the] men, the women, and the infants of every city; **7** and all the livestock, and the spoil of the cities, we have spoiled for ourselves. **8** And at that time we take the land out of the hand of the two kings of the Amorite, which is beyond the Jordan, from the Brook of Arnon to Mount Hermon **9** (Sidonians call Hermon Sirion, and the Amorites call it Senir), **10** all the cities of the plain, and all Gilead, and all Bashan, as far as Salchah and Edrei, cities of the kingdom of Og in Bashan. **11** For only Og king of Bashan had been left of the remnant of the Rephaim; behold, his bedstead [is] a bedstead of iron. Is it not in Rabbath of the sons of Ammon? Its length [is] nine cubits and its breadth [is] four cubits, by the cubit of a man. **12** And this land, [which] we had possessed at that time, from Aroer, which [is] by the Brook of Arnon, and the half of Mount Gilead and its cities, I have given to the Reubenite and to the Gadite; **13** and the rest of Gilead and all Bashan, the kingdom of Og, I have given to the half tribe of Manasseh; all the region of Argob, with all Bashan—it is called the land of [the]

Rephaim. **14** Jair son of Manasseh has taken all the region of Argob, as far as the border of Geshuri and Maachathi ([namely] Bashan), and calls them by his own name, Havoth-Jair, to this day. **15** And I have given Gilead to Machir. **16** And to the Reubenite and to the Gadite I have given from Gilead even to the Brook of Arnon, the middle of the valley and the border, even to the Brook of Jabbok, the border of the sons of Ammon, **17** and the plain, and the Jordan, and the border, from Chinnereth even to the Sea of the Plain (the Salt Sea), under the Springs of Pisgah, at the [sun]-rising. **18** And at that time I command you, saying, Your God YHWH has given this land to you to possess it; you pass over armed before your brothers the sons of Israel, all the sons of might. **19** Only your wives, and your infants, and your livestock—I have known that you have much livestock—dwell in your cities which I have given to you, **20** until YHWH gives rest to your brothers like yourselves, and they also have possessed the land which your God YHWH is giving to them beyond the Jordan; then you have each turned back to his possession which I have given to you. **21** And I have commanded Joshua at that time, saying, Your eyes are seeing all that which your God YHWH has done to these two kings—so YHWH does to all the kingdoms to where you are passing over; **22** do not fear them, for your God YHWH—He is fighting for you. **23** And to YHWH I beg for grace at that time, saying, **24** Lord YHWH, You have begun to show Your servant Your greatness and Your strong hand; for who [is] a god in the heavens or in earth who does according to Your works and according to Your might? **25** Please let me pass over and see the good land which [is] beyond the Jordan, this good hill-country, and Lebanon. **26** And YHWH shows Himself angry with me for your sake, and has not listened to me, and YHWH says to me, Enough of you; do not add to speak to Me about this thing anymore; **27** go up [to] the top of Pisgah, and lift up your eyes westward, and northward, and southward, and eastward, and see with your eyes, for you do not pass over this Jordan; **28** and charge Joshua, and strengthen him, and harden him, for he passes over before this people, and he causes them to inherit the land which you see. **29** And we dwell in a valley opposite Beth-Peor."

4 "And now, O Israel, listen to the statutes and to the judgments which I am teaching you to do, so that you live, and have gone in, and possessed the land which YHWH God of your fathers is giving to you. **2** You do not add to the word which I am commanding you, nor diminish from it, to keep the commands of your God YHWH which I am commanding you. **3** Your eyes are seeing that which YHWH has done in Ba'al-Peor, for every man who has gone after Ba'al-Peor, your God YHWH has destroyed him from your midst; **4** and you who are cleaving to your God YHWH [are] alive today—all of you. **5** See, I have taught you statutes and judgments, as my God YHWH has commanded me, to do so in the midst of the land to where you are going in to possess it; **6** and you have kept and done [them] (for it [is] your wisdom and your understanding) before the eyes of the peoples who hear all these statutes, and they have said, Surely a people wise and understanding [is] this great nation. **7** For which [is] the great nation that has God [so] near to it, as our God YHWH, in all we have called to Him? **8** And which [is] the great nation which has righteous statutes and judgments according to all this law which I am setting before you today? **9** Only, take heed to yourself, and watch your soul exceedingly, lest you forget the things which your eyes have seen, and lest they turn aside from your heart all [the] days of your life; and you have made them known to your sons and to your sons' sons. **10** [Never forget] the day when you have stood before your God YHWH in Horeb, in YHWH's saying to me, Assemble the people to Me, and I cause them to hear My words, so that they learn to fear Me all the days that they are alive on the ground, and they teach their sons; **11** and you draw near and stand under the mountain, and the mountain is burning with fire to the heart of the heavens, [with] darkness, cloud, and thick darkness, **12** and YHWH speaks to you out of the midst of the fire; you are hearing a voice of words, but you are seeing no likeness, only a voice; **13** and He declares His covenant to you, which He has commanded you to do, the Ten Commandments, and He writes them on two tablets of stone. **14** And YHWH has

DEUTERONOMY

commanded me at that time to teach you statutes and judgments, for your doing them in the land to where you are passing over to possess it. **15** And you have been very watchful of your souls, for you have not seen any likeness in the day of YHWH's speaking to you in Horeb out of the midst of the fire, **16** lest you do corruptly, and have made for yourselves a carved image, a likeness of any figure: a form of male or female, **17** a form of any beast which [is] in the earth, a form of any winged bird which flies in the heavens, **18** a form of any creeping thing on the ground, a form of any fish which [is] in the waters below the earth. **19** And lest you lift up your eyes to the heavens, and have seen the sun, and the moon, and the stars, all the host of the heavens, and have been drawn away, and have bowed yourself to them and served them, which your God YHWH has apportioned to all the peoples under all the heavens. **20** And YHWH has taken you, and He is bringing you out from the iron furnace, from Egypt, to be to Him for a people, an inheritance, as [at] this day. **21** And YHWH has showed Himself angry with me because of your words, and swears to my not passing over the Jordan, and to my not going into the good land which your God YHWH is giving to you [for] an inheritance; **22** for I am dying in this land; I am not passing over the Jordan, but you are passing over and have possessed this good land. **23** Take heed to yourselves lest you forget the covenant of your God YHWH which He has made with you, and have made a carved image for yourselves, a likeness of anything [concerning] which your God YHWH has charged you; **24** for your God YHWH is a consuming fire—a zealous God. **25** When you beget sons and sons' sons, and you have become old in the land, and have done corruptly, and have made a carved image, a likeness of anything, and have done evil in the eyes of YHWH to provoke Him to anger, **26** I have caused the heavens and the earth to testify against you this day, that you perish utterly quickly from off the land to where you are passing over the Jordan to possess it; you do not prolong days on it, but are utterly destroyed; **27** and YHWH has scattered you among the peoples, and you have been left few in number among the nations to where YHWH leads you, **28** and you have served gods there, work of man's hands, wood and stone, which do not see, nor hear, nor eat, nor smell. **29** And you have sought your God YHWH from there, and have found [Him] when you seek Him with all your heart and with all your soul. **30** In the distress of yours, when all these things have found you in the latter end of the days, and you have turned back to your God YHWH and have listened to His voice— **31** for your God YHWH [is] a merciful God—He does not fail you, nor destroy you, nor forget the covenant of your fathers which He has sworn to them. **32** For ask now of the former days which have been before you, from the day that God created man on the earth, and from the [one] end of the heavens even to the [other] end of the heavens, whether there has been as this great thing, or [if anything] has been heard like it. **33** Has a people heard the voice of God speaking out of the midst of the fire, as you have heard, you—and live? **34** Or has God tried to go in to take a nation for Himself from the midst of a nation, by trials, by signs, and by wonders, and by war, and by a strong hand, and by an outstretched arm, and by great terrors, according to all that your God YHWH has done to you in Egypt before your eyes? **35** You—you have been shown [it], to know that He, YHWH, [is] God; there is none else besides Him. **36** He has caused you to hear His voice from the heavens, to instruct you; and on earth He has showed you His great fire, and you have heard His words out of the midst of the fire. **37** And because that He has loved your fathers, He also fixes on their seed after them, and brings you out in His presence, by His great power, from Egypt, **38** to dispossess nations greater and stronger than you from your presence, to bring you in to give their land to you [for] an inheritance, as [at] this day. **39** And you have known today, and have turned [it] back to your heart, that He, YHWH, [is] God in the heavens above and on the earth below—there is none else; **40** and you have kept His statutes and His commands which I am commanding you today, so that it is well for you, and for your sons after you, and so that you prolong days on the ground which your God YHWH is giving to you—all the days." **41** Then Moses separates three cities beyond the Jordan, toward the sun-rising, **42** for the fleeing there of the manslayer who slays his neighbor unknowingly, and he is not hating him before, and he has fled to one of these cities and he has lived: **43** Bezer in the wilderness, in the land of the plain, for the Reubenite; and Ramoth in Gilead for the Gadite; and Golan in Bashan for the Manassite. **44** And this [is] the law which Moses has set before the sons of Israel; **45** these [are] the testimonies, and the statutes, and the judgments, which Moses has spoken to the sons of Israel in their coming out of Egypt, **46** beyond the Jordan, in the valley opposite Beth-Peor, in the land of Sihon, king of the Amorite, who is dwelling in Heshbon, whom Moses and the sons of Israel have struck in their coming out of Egypt; **47** and they possess his land and the land of Og king of Bashan, two kings of the Amorite who [are] beyond the Jordan, [toward] the sun-rising, **48** from Aroer, which [is] by the edge of the Brook of Arnon, even to Mount Zion, which [is] Hermon— **49** and all the plain beyond the Jordan eastward, even to the Sea of the Plain, below the Springs of Pisgah.

5 And Moses calls to all Israel and says to them, "Hear, O Israel, the statutes and the judgments which I am speaking in your ears today, and you have learned them and have observed to do them. **2** Our God YHWH made a covenant with us in Horeb; **3** YHWH has not made this covenant with our fathers, but with us, we—these here— all of us living today. **4** YHWH has spoken with you face to face on the mountain, out of the midst of the fire; **5** I am standing between YHWH and you, at that time, to declare the word of YHWH to you, for you have been afraid from the presence of the fire, and you have not gone up into the mountain; for [He] says: **6** I, YHWH, [am] your God who has brought you out from the land of Egypt, from a house of servants. **7** You have no other gods in My presence. **8** You do not make a carved image for yourself, any likeness which [is] in the heavens above, or which [is] in the earth beneath, or which [is] in the waters under the earth. **9** You do not bow yourself to them, nor serve them: for I, your God YHWH, [am] a zealous God, charging iniquity of fathers on sons, and on a third and on a fourth [generation] of those hating Me, **10** and doing kindness to thousands, of those loving Me and of those keeping My commands. **11** You do not take up the Name of your God YHWH for a vain thing, for YHWH does not acquit him who takes up His Name for a vain thing. **12** Observe the Sabbath day to sanctify it, as your God YHWH has commanded you; **13** six days you labor and have done all your work, **14** and the seventh day [is] a Sabbath to your God YHWH; you do not do any work, you, and your son, and your daughter, and your manservant, and your handmaid, and your ox, and your donkey, and all your livestock, and your sojourner who [is] within your gates, so that your manservant and your handmaid rest like yourself. **15** And you have remembered that you have been a servant in the land of Egypt, and your God YHWH brings you out from there by a strong hand and by an outstretched arm; therefore your God YHWH has commanded you to keep the Sabbath day. **16** Honor your father and your mother, as your God YHWH has commanded you, so that your days are prolonged, and so that it is well with you on the ground which your God YHWH is giving to you. **17** You do not murder. **18** You do not commit adultery. **19** You do not steal. **20** You do not answer [with] a false testimony against your neighbor. **21** You do not desire your neighbor's wife, nor do you covet your neighbor's house, his field, and his manservant, and his handmaid, his ox, and his donkey, and anything which [is] your neighbor's. **22** YHWH has spoken these words to all your assembly in the mountain, out of the midst of the fire, [and] of the cloud, and of the thick darkness, [with] a great voice; and He has not added; and He writes them on two tablets of stone and gives them to me. **23** And it comes to pass, as you hear the voice out of the midst of the darkness and of the mountain burning with fire, that you come near to me, all [the] heads of your tribes and your elderly, **24** and say, Behold, our God YHWH has showed us His glory and His greatness; and we have heard His voice out of the midst of the fire; this day we have seen that God speaks with man— and he has lived. **25** And now, why do we die? For this great fire consumes us if we add to hear the voice of our God YHWH anymore—then we have died. **26** For who of all flesh [is] he who has heard the voice of the living God speaking out of the midst of the fire like us, and lives? **27** Draw near and hear all that which our God YHWH says, and you, you speak to us all that

DEUTERONOMY

which our God Y<small>HWH</small> speaks to you, and we have listened and done it. **28** And Y<small>HWH</small> hears the voice of your words in your speaking to me, and Y<small>HWH</small> says to me, I have heard the voice of the words of this people which they have spoken to you; they have done well [in] all that they have spoken. **29** O that their heart had been thus to them, to fear Me and to keep My commands [for] all the days, that it may be well with them and with their sons for all time! **30** Go, say to them, Return for yourselves, to your tents; **31** and you, stand here with Me, and let Me speak to you all the command, and the statutes, and the judgments which you teach them, and they have done [them] in the land which I am giving to them to possess it. **32** And you have observed to do as your God Y<small>HWH</small> has commanded you, you do not turn aside [to] the right or left; **33** in all the way which your God Y<small>HWH</small> has commanded you—walk, so that you live, and [it is] well with you, and you have prolonged days in the land which you possess."

6 "And this [is] the command, the statutes and the judgments which your God Y<small>HWH</small> has commanded to teach you to do in the land which you are passing over there to possess it, **2** so that you fear your God Y<small>HWH</small>, to keep all His statutes and His commands which I am commanding you, you, and your son, and your son's son, all [the] days of your life, and so that your days are prolonged. **3** And you have heard, O Israel, and observed to do [them], that it may be well with you, and that you may multiply exceedingly, as Y<small>HWH</small>, God of your fathers, has spoken to you, [in] the land flowing with milk and honey. **4** Hear, O Israel: Our God Y<small>HWH</small>—Y<small>HWH</small> [is] one! **5** And you have loved your God Y<small>HWH</small> with all your heart, and with all your soul, and with all your might. **6** And these words which I am commanding you today have been on your heart, **7** and you have repeated them to your sons, and spoken of them in your sitting in your house, and in your walking in the way, and in your lying down, and in your rising up, **8** and have bound them for a sign on your hand, and they have been for frontlets between your eyes, **9** and you have written them on doorposts of your house and on your gates. **10** And it has been, when your God Y<small>HWH</small> brings you into the land which He has sworn to your fathers, to Abraham, to Isaac, and to Jacob, to give to you great and good cities which you have not built, **11** and houses full of all good things which you have not filled, and wells dug which you have not dug, vineyards and oliveyards which you have not planted, that you have eaten and been satisfied. **12** Take heed to yourself lest you forget Y<small>HWH</small> who has brought you out of the land of Egypt, out of a house of servants. **13** You fear your God Y<small>HWH</small>, and you serve Him, and you swear by His Name. **14** You do not go after other gods, of the gods of the peoples who [are] around you, **15** for your God Y<small>HWH</small> [is] a zealous God in your midst—lest the anger of your God Y<small>HWH</small> burns against you, and He has destroyed you from off the face of the ground. **16** You do not try your God Y<small>HWH</small> as you tried [Him] in Massah. **17** You diligently keep the commands of your God Y<small>HWH</small>, and His testimonies and His statutes which He has commanded you, **18** and you have done that which is right and good in the eyes of Y<small>HWH</small>, so that it is well with you, and you have gone in and possessed the good land which Y<small>HWH</small> has sworn to your fathers, **19** to drive away all your enemies from your presence, as Y<small>HWH</small> has spoken. **20** When your son asks you hereafter, saying, What [are] the testimonies, and the statutes, and the judgments which our God Y<small>HWH</small> has commanded you? **21** Then you have said to your son, We have been servants of Pharaoh in Egypt, and Y<small>HWH</small> brings us out of Egypt by a high hand; **22** and Y<small>HWH</small> gives signs and wonders, great and severe, on Egypt, on Pharaoh, and on all his house, before our eyes; **23** and He has brought us out from there, in order to bring us in, to give to us the land which He had sworn to our fathers. **24** And Y<small>HWH</small> commands us to do all these statutes, to fear our God Y<small>HWH</small>, for good to ourselves [for] all the days, to keep us alive, as [at] this day; **25** and it is righteousness for us when we observe to do all this command before our God Y<small>HWH</small>, as He has commanded us."

7 "When your God Y<small>HWH</small> brings you into the land to where you are going in to possess it, and He has cast out many nations from your presence, the Hittite, and the Girgashite, and the Amorite, and the Canaanite, and the Perizzite, and the Hivite, and the Jebusite, seven nations

DEUTERONOMY

more numerous and mighty than you, **2** and your God Y<small>HWH</small> has given them before you, then you have struck them—you utterly devote them—you do not make a covenant with them, nor do you favor them. **3** And you do not join in marriage with them; you do not give your daughter to his son, and you do not take his daughter to your son, **4** for he turns aside your son from after Me, and they have served other gods; and the anger of Y<small>HWH</small> has burned against you and has destroyed you quickly. **5** But thus you do to them: you break down their altars, and you shatter their standing pillars, and you cut down their Asherim, and you burn their carved images with fire. **6** For you [are] a holy people to your God Y<small>HWH</small>; your God Y<small>HWH</small> has fixed on you, to be to Him for a peculiar people, out of all the peoples who [are] on the face of the ground. **7** Y<small>HWH</small> has delighted in you and fixes on you, not because of your being more numerous than any of the peoples, for you [are] the least of all the peoples, **8** but because of Y<small>HWH</small>'s loving you, and because of His keeping the oath which He has sworn to your fathers; Y<small>HWH</small> has brought you out by a strong hand, and ransoms you from a house of servants, from the hand of Pharaoh king of Egypt. **9** And you have known that He, your God Y<small>HWH</small>, [is] God, the faithful God keeping the covenant and the kindness with those loving Him and with those keeping His commands, for one thousand generations, **10** and repaying to those hating Him to their face, to destroy them; He does not delay to him who is hating Him, He repays [it] to him to his face. **11** And you have kept the command, and the statutes, and the judgments, which I am commanding you today to do them. **12** And it has been, because you hear these judgments, and have kept and done them, that your God Y<small>HWH</small> has kept the covenant and the kindness with you which He has sworn to your fathers, **13** and has loved you, and blessed you, and multiplied you, and has blessed the fruit of your womb, and the fruit of your ground, your grain, and your new wine, and your oil, the increase of your oxen, and the wealth of your flock, on the ground which He has sworn to your fathers to give to you. **14** Blessed are you above all the peoples; there is not a barren man or a barren woman in you—nor among your livestock; **15** and Y<small>HWH</small> has turned aside every sickness from you, and none of the evil diseases of Egypt (which you have known) does He put on you, and He has put them on all hating you. **16** And you have consumed all the peoples whom your God Y<small>HWH</small> is giving to you; your eye has no pity on them, and you do not serve their gods, for it [is] a snare to you. **17** When you say in your heart, These nations [are] more numerous than I, how am I able to dispossess them? **18** You are not afraid of them; you surely remember that which your God Y<small>HWH</small> has done to Pharaoh and to all of Egypt, **19** the great trials which your eyes have seen, and the signs, and the wonders, and the strong hand, and the outstretched arm, with which your God Y<small>HWH</small> has brought you out; so does your God Y<small>HWH</small> do to all the peoples of whose presence you are afraid. **20** And your God Y<small>HWH</small> also sends the locust among them, until the destruction of those who are left, even those who are hidden from your presence; **21** you are not terrified by their presence, for your God Y<small>HWH</small> [is] in your midst, a God great and fearful. **22** And your God Y<small>HWH</small> has cast out these nations from your presence little [by] little (you are not able to consume them quickly, lest the beast of the field multiplies against you), **23** and your God Y<small>HWH</small> has given them before you, and confused them [with] a great destruction until their being destroyed; **24** and He has given their kings into your hand, and you have destroyed their name from under the heavens; no man stations himself in your presence until you have destroyed them. **25** You burn the carved images of their gods with fire; you do not desire the silver and gold on them, nor have you taken [it] for yourself, lest you are snared by it, for it [is] an abomination [to] your God Y<small>HWH</small>; **26** and you do not bring in an abomination to your house, or you have been devoted like it—you utterly detest it and you utterly abhor it; for it [is] devoted."

8 "All the command which I am commanding you today you observe to do, so that you live, and have multiplied, and gone in, and possessed the land which Y<small>HWH</small> has sworn to your fathers; **2** and you have remembered all the way which your God Y<small>HWH</small> has caused you to go these forty years in the wilderness, in order to humble you to try you, to know that which

DEUTERONOMY

[is] in your heart, whether you keep His commands or not. **3** And He humbles you, and causes you to hunger, and causes you to eat the manna (which you have not known, even your fathers have not known), in order to cause you to know that man does not live by bread alone, but man lives by everything proceeding [from] the mouth of Yhwh. **4** Your raiment has not worn out from off you, and your foot has not swelled these forty years, **5** and you have known with your heart that as a man disciplines his son, your God Yhwh is disciplining you, **6** and you have kept the commands of your God Yhwh, to walk in His ways and to fear Him. **7** For your God Yhwh is bringing you into a good land, a land of brooks of waters, of fountains, and of depths coming out in valley and in mountain; **8** a land of wheat, and barley, and vine, and fig, and pomegranate; a land of oil olive and honey; **9** a land in which you eat bread without scarcity—you do not lack anything in it; a land whose stones [are] iron, and you dig bronze out of its mountains. **10** And you have eaten and been satisfied, and have blessed your God Yhwh on the good land which he has given to you. **11** Take heed to yourself lest you forget your God Yhwh so as not to keep His commands, and His judgments, and His statutes which I am commanding you today; **12** lest you eat and have been satisfied, and build good houses and have inhabited [them], **13** and your herd and your flock are multiplied, and silver and gold are multiplied to you, and all that is yours is multiplied, **14** and your heart has been high, and you have forgotten your God Yhwh who is bringing you out of the land of Egypt, out of a house of servants; **15** who is causing you to go in the great and the terrible wilderness [with] burning serpent, and scorpion, and thirst—where there is no water; who is bringing out waters to you from the flinty rock; **16** who is causing you to eat manna in the wilderness, which your fathers have not known, in order to humble you, and in order to try you, to do you good in your latter end; **17** and you have said in your heart, My power and the might of my hand have made this wealth for me. **18** And you have remembered your God Yhwh, for it [is] He who is giving power to you to make wealth, in order to establish His covenant which He has sworn to your fathers, as [at] this day. **19** And it has been, if you really forget your God Yhwh, and have gone after other gods, and served them, and bowed yourself to them, I have testified against you today that you utterly perish. **20** As the nations whom Yhwh is destroying from your presence, so you perish, because you do not listen to the voice of your God Yhwh."

9 "Hear, O Israel: You are passing over the Jordan today to go in to possess nations greater and mightier than yourself, cities great and fortified up to the heavens, **2** a people great and tall, sons of Anakim, whom you have known, and [of whom] you have heard: Who stations himself before sons of Anak? **3** And you have known today that your God Yhwh [is] He who is passing over before you [as] a consuming fire; He destroys them, and He humbles them before you, and you have dispossessed them, and destroyed them quickly, as Yhwh has spoken to you. **4** You do not speak in your heart (in your God Yhwh's driving them away from before you), saying, In my righteousness Yhwh has brought me in to possess this land; but in Yhwh dispossessing these nations from your presence, [it is because of] their being wicked. **5** [It is] not in your righteousness and in the uprightness of your heart [that] you are going in to possess their land, but in Yhwh dispossessing these nations from your presence, [it is because of] their being wicked, and in order to establish the word which Yhwh has sworn to your fathers, to Abraham, to Isaac, and to Jacob; **6** and you have known that [it is] not in your righteousness [that] your God Yhwh is giving this good land to you to possess it, for you [are] a people stiff of neck. **7** Remember [and] do not forget that [with] which you have made your God Yhwh angry in the wilderness; from the day that you have come out of the land of Egypt until your coming to this place, you have been rebellious against Yhwh; **8** even in Horeb you have made Yhwh angry, and Yhwh shows Himself angry against you—to destroy you. **9** In my going up into the mountain to receive the tablets of stone (tablets of the covenant which Yhwh has made with you), then I abide on the mountain forty days and forty nights; I have not eaten bread and I have not drunk water; **10** and Yhwh gives to me the two

DEUTERONOMY

tablets of stone written with the finger of God, and on them [is] according to all the words which YHWH has spoken with you on the mountain, out of the midst of the fire, in the day of the assembly. **11** And it comes to pass, at the end of forty days and forty nights, YHWH has given the two tablets of stone to me—tablets of the covenant. **12** Then YHWH says to me, Rise, go down, hurry from here, for your people whom you have brought out of Egypt have done corruptly; they have quickly turned aside from the way which I have commanded them—they have made a molten thing for themselves! **13** And YHWH speaks to me, saying, I have seen this people, and behold, it [is] a people stiff of neck. **14** Desist from Me, and I destroy them, and blot out their name from under the heavens, and I make you become a nation more mighty and numerous than it. **15** And I turn and come down from the mountain, and the mountain is burning with fire, and the two tablets of the covenant [are] on my two hands, **16** and I see, and behold, you have sinned against your God YHWH; you have made a molten calf for yourselves; you have quickly turned aside from the way which YHWH has commanded you. **17** And I lay hold on the two tablets, and cast them out of my two hands, and break them before your eyes, **18** and I throw myself before YHWH, as at first, [for] forty days and forty nights; I have not eaten bread and I have not drunk water, because of all your sins which you have sinned by doing evil in the eyes of YHWH, to make Him angry. **19** For I have been afraid because of the anger and the fury with which YHWH has been angry against you, to destroy you; and YHWH also listens to me at this time. **20** And YHWH has showed Himself very angry with Aaron, to destroy him, and I also pray for Aaron at that time. **21** And I have taken your sin, the calf which you have made, and I burn it with fire, and beat it, grinding well until it [is] small as dust, and I cast its dust into the brook which is going down out of the mountain. **22** And in Taberah, and in Massah, and in Kibroth-Hattaavah, you have been making YHWH angry; **23** also in YHWH's sending you from Kadesh-Barnea, saying, Go up and possess the land which I have given to you; then you provoke the mouth of your God YHWH, and have not given credence to Him, nor listened to His voice. **24** You have been rebellious against YHWH from the day of my knowing you. **25** And I throw myself before YHWH—the forty days and the forty nights when I had thrown myself—because YHWH has commanded to destroy you; **26** and I pray to YHWH, and say, Lord YHWH, do not destroy Your people and Your inheritance whom You have ransomed in Your greatness, whom You have brought out of Egypt with a strong hand; **27** be mindful of Your servants, of Abraham, of Isaac, and of Jacob; do not turn to the stiffness of this people, and to its wickedness, and to its sin, **28** lest the land from which You have brought us out says, Because of YHWH's want of ability to bring them into the land of which He has spoken to them, and because of His hating them, He brought them out to put them to death in the wilderness. **29** And they [are] Your people and Your inheritance, whom You have brought out by Your great power and by Your outstretched arm!"

10 "At that time YHWH has said to me, Hew two tablets of stone for yourself like the first, and come up to Me into the mountain, and you have made an ark of wood for yourself, **2** and I write on the tablets the words which were on the first tablets, which you have broken, and you have placed them in the Ark. **3** And I make an ark of shittim wood, and hew two tablets of stone like the first, and go up to the mountain with the two tablets in my hand. **4** And He writes on the tablets according to the first writing, the Ten Commandments, which YHWH has spoken to you in the mountain, out of the midst of the fire, in the day of the assembly, and YHWH gives them to me, **5** and I turn and come down from the mountain, and put the tablets in the Ark which I had made, and they are there, as YHWH commanded me. **6** And the sons of Israel have journeyed from Beeroth of the sons of Jaakan to Mosera; Aaron died there, and he is buried there, and his son Eleazar acts as priest in his stead. **7** From there they journeyed to Gudgodah, and from Gudgodah to Jotbathah, a land of brooks of water. **8** At that time YHWH has separated the tribe of Levi to carry the Ark of the Covenant of YHWH, to stand before YHWH, to serve Him, and to bless in His Name to this day; **9** therefore there has not been a portion and inheritance for Levi with his brothers; YHWH Himself [is] his inheritance, as your God YHWH has spoken to him. **10** And I have stood in the mountain, as the former days, [for] forty days and forty nights, and YHWH also listens to me at that time; YHWH has not willed to destroy you. **11** And YHWH says to me, Rise, go to journey before the people, and they go in and possess the land which I have sworn to their fathers to give to them. **12** And now, O Israel, what is your God YHWH asking from you, except to fear your God YHWH, to walk in all His ways, and to love Him, and to serve your God YHWH with all your heart and with all your soul, **13** to keep the commands of YHWH, and His statutes which I am commanding you today, for good for you? **14** Behold, the heavens, even the heavens of the heavens, [belong] to your God YHWH, [as does] the earth and all that [is] in it. **15** Only, YHWH has delighted in your fathers, to love them, and He fixes on their seed after them—on you, out of all the peoples, as [at] this day. **16** And you have circumcised the foreskin of your heart, and you do not harden your neck anymore. **17** For He, your God YHWH, [is] God of the gods and Lord of the lords—the great, the mighty, and the fearful God, who does not accept by appearances, nor takes a bribe; **18** He is doing the judgment of fatherless and widow, and loving the sojourner, to give bread and raiment to him. **19** And you have loved the sojourner, for you were sojourners in the land of Egypt. **20** You fear your God YHWH, you serve Him, and you cleave to Him, and you swear by His Name. **21** He [is] your praise, and He [is] your God, who has done these great and fearful [things] with you which your eyes have seen. **22** Your fathers went down to Egypt with seventy persons, and now your God YHWH has made you as [the] stars of the heavens for multitude."

11 "And you have loved your God YHWH, and kept His charge, and His statutes, and His judgments, and His commands, [for] all the days; **2** and you have known today—for it is not your sons who have not known and who have not seen the discipline of your God YHWH, His greatness, His strong hand, and His outstretched arm; **3** and His signs and His doings which He has done in the midst of Egypt, to Pharaoh king of Egypt and to all his land; **4** and that which He has done to the force of Egypt, to its horses, and to its chariot, when He has caused the waters of the Red Sea to flow against their faces in their pursuing after them, and YHWH destroys them, to this day; **5** and that which He has done to you in the wilderness until your coming to this place; **6** and that which He has done to Dathan and to Abiram, sons of Eliab, sons of Reuben, when the earth has opened her mouth and swallows them, and their houses, and their tents, and all that lives which is at their feet, in the midst of all Israel— **7** but [it is] your eyes which are seeing all the great work of YHWH which He has done. **8** And you have kept all the command which I am commanding you today, so that you are strong, and have gone in, and possessed the land to where you are passing over to possess it, **9** and so that you prolong days on the ground which YHWH has sworn to your fathers to give to them and to their seed—a land flowing with milk and honey. **10** For the land to where you are going in to possess it is not as the land of Egypt from where you have come out, where you sow your seed and have watered with your foot, as a garden of the green herb; **11** but the land to where you are passing over to possess it [is] a land of hills and valleys—it drinks water of the rain of the heavens— **12** a land which your God YHWH is searching; the eyes of your God YHWH [are] continually on it, from the beginning of the year even to the latter end of the year. **13** And it has been, if you listen diligently to My commands which I am commanding you today, to love your God YHWH, and to serve Him with all your heart and with all your soul, **14** then I have given the rain of your land in its season—autumn rain and spring rain—and you have gathered your grain, and your new wine, and your oil, **15** and I have given herbs in your field for your livestock, and you have eaten and been satisfied. **16** Take heed to yourselves lest your heart be enticed, and you have turned aside, and served other gods, and bowed yourselves to them, **17** and the anger of YHWH has burned against you, and He has restrained the heavens and there is no rain, and the ground does not give her increase, and you have perished quickly from off the good land which YHWH is giving to you. **18** And you have placed these words of mine on your heart and on your soul, and have bound them for a sign on your hand, and they have been for frontlets between your eyes; **19** and you have taught them to your sons by speaking of them in your sitting in your house, and in your going in the way, and in your lying down, and in your rising up, **20** and have written them on the doorposts of your house and on your gates, **21** so that your days are multiplied, and the days of your sons, on the ground which YHWH has sworn to your fathers to give to them, as the days of the heavens above the earth. **22** For if you diligently keep all this command which I am commanding you to do—to love your God YHWH, to walk in all His ways, and to cleave to Him— **23** then YHWH has dispossessed all these nations from before you, and you have possessed nations greater and mightier than you. **24** Every place on which the sole of your foot treads is yours: from the wilderness and Lebanon, from the river, the Euphrates River, even to the Western Sea, is your border. **25** No man stations himself in your presence; your God YHWH puts your dread and your fear on the face of all the land on which you tread, as He has spoken to you. **26** See, today I am setting before you a blessing and a reviling: **27** the blessing when you listen to the commands of your God YHWH which I am commanding you today; **28** and the reviling if you do not listen to the commands of your God YHWH, and have turned aside from the way which I am commanding you today, to go after other gods which you have not known. **29** And it has been, when your God YHWH brings you into the land to where you are going in to possess it, that you have given the blessing on Mount Gerizim and the reviling on Mount Ebal; **30** are they not beyond the Jordan, behind the way of the going in of the sun, in the land of the Canaanite who is dwelling in the plain opposite Gilgal, near the oaks of Moreh? **31** For you are passing over the Jordan to go in to possess the land which your God YHWH is giving to you; and you have possessed it, and dwelt in it, **32** and observed to do all the statutes and the judgments which I am setting before you today."

12 "These [are] the statutes and the judgments which you observe to do in the land which YHWH, God of your fathers, has given to you to possess it, all the days that you are living on the ground. **2** You utterly destroy all the places where the nations which you are dispossessing served their gods, on the high mountains, and on the heights, and under every green tree; **3** and you have broken down their altars, and shattered their standing pillars, and you burn their Asherim with fire, and you cut down carved images of their gods, and have destroyed their name out of that place. **4** You do not do so to your God YHWH; **5** rather—that you seek after the place which your God YHWH chooses out of all your tribes to put His Name there, for His Dwelling Place, and you have entered there, **6** and have brought in there your burnt-offerings, and your sacrifices, and your tithes, and the raised-offering of your hand, and your vows, and your free-will offerings, and the firstlings of your herd and of your flock; **7** and you have eaten there before your God YHWH, and have rejoiced in every putting forth of your hand, you and your households, with which your God YHWH has blessed you. **8** You do not do according to all that we are doing here today—each [doing] anything that is right in his own eyes— **9** for until now you have not come to the rest and to the inheritance which your God YHWH is giving to you. **10** When you have passed over the Jordan, and have dwelt in the land which your God YHWH is causing you to inherit, and He has given rest to you from all your surrounding enemies, and you have dwelt confidently, **11** then it has been, the place on which your God YHWH fixes to cause His Name to dwell there, there you bring in all that which I am commanding you: your burnt-offerings, and your sacrifices, your tithes, and the raised-offering of your hand, and all the choice of your vows which you vow to YHWH. **12** And you have rejoiced before your God YHWH, you, and your sons, and your daughters, and your menservants, and your handmaids, and the Levite who [is] within your gates, for he has no part and inheritance with you. **13** Take heed to yourself lest you cause your burnt-offerings to ascend in any place which you see; **14** rather—that in the place which YHWH chooses in one of your tribes, there you cause your burnt-offerings to ascend, and there you do all that which I am commanding you. **15** Nevertheless, you slaughter anything of the desire of your

DEUTERONOMY

soul, and have eaten [its] flesh according to the blessing of your God YHWH which He has given to you in all your gates; the unclean and the clean eat it, as [if] the roe and as [if] the deer. **16** Only, you do not eat the blood—you pour it on the earth as water; **17** you are not able to eat within your gates the tithe of your grain, and of your new wine, and your oil, and the firstlings of your herd and of your flock, and any of your vows which you vow, and your free-will offerings, and a raised-offering of your hand; **18** but you eat it before your God YHWH in the place which your God YHWH fixes on, you, and your son, and your daughter, and your manservant, and your handmaid, and the Levite who [is] within your gates, and you have rejoiced before your God YHWH in every putting forth of your hand; **19** take heed to yourself lest you forsake the Levite [for] all your days on your ground. **20** When your God YHWH enlarges your border, as He has spoken to you, and you have said, Let me eat flesh—for your soul desires to eat flesh—you eat flesh of all the desire of your soul. **21** When the place is far from you [in] which your God YHWH chooses to put His Name there, then you have sacrificed from your herd and from your flock which YHWH has given to you, as I have commanded you, and have eaten within your gates, of all the desire of your soul; **22** only, as the roe and the deer is eaten, so do you eat it; the unclean and the clean alike eat it. **23** Only, be sure not to eat the blood, for the blood [is] the life, and you do not eat the life with the flesh; **24** you do not eat it—you pour it on the earth as water; **25** you do not eat it, in order that it may be well with you and with your sons after you when you do that which [is] right in the eyes of YHWH. **26** Only, your holy things which you have, and your vows, you take up, and have gone to the place which YHWH chooses, **27** and you have made your burnt-offerings—the flesh and the blood—on the altar of your God YHWH; and the blood of your sacrifices is poured out by the altar of your God YHWH, and you eat the flesh. **28** Observe, and you have obeyed all these words which I am commanding you, in order that it may be well with you and with your sons after you for all time, when you do that which [is] good and right in the eyes of your God YHWH. **29** When your God YHWH cuts off the nations—to where you are going in to possess them—from your presence, and you have possessed them, and have dwelt in their land— **30** take heed to yourself lest you are ensnared after them, after their being destroyed out of your presence, and lest you inquire about their gods, saying, How do these nations serve their gods, that I also do so? **31** You do not do so to your God YHWH; for every abomination that YHWH has hated they have done for their gods, for they even burn their sons and their daughters with fire for their gods. **32** The whole thing which I am commanding you, you observe to do it; you do not add to it, nor diminish from it."

13 "When a prophet or a dreamer of a dream arises in your midst, and he has given a sign or wonder to you, **2** and the sign and the wonder has come to pass, which he has spoken of to you, saying, Let us go after other gods (which you have not known) and serve them, **3** you do not listen to the words of that prophet or to that dreamer of the dream, for your God YHWH is trying you to know whether you are loving your God YHWH with all your heart and with all your soul; **4** you walk after your God YHWH, and you fear Him, and you keep His commands, and you listen to His voice, and you serve Him, and you cleave to Him. **5** And that prophet or that dreamer of the dream is put to death, for he has spoken apostasy against your God YHWH (who is bringing you out of the land of Egypt, and has ransomed you out of a house of servants), to drive you out of the way in which your God YHWH has commanded you to walk, and you have put away evil from your midst. **6** When your brother, son of your mother, or your son, or your daughter, or the wife of your bosom, or your friend who [is] as your own soul, moves you in secret, saying, Let us go and serve other gods (which you have not known, you and your fathers, **7** of the gods of the peoples who [are] around you, who are near to you, or who are far off from you, from the end of the earth even to the [other] end of the earth), **8** you do not consent to him, nor listen to him, nor does your eye have pity on him, nor do you spare, nor do you cover him over. **9** But you surely kill him; your hand is on him in the first place to put him to death, and the hand of all the people last; **10** and you have stoned him with stones and he has died, for he has sought to drive you away from your God YHWH, who is bringing you out of the land of Egypt, out of a house of servants; **11** and all Israel hears and fears, and does not add to do like this evil thing in your midst. **12** When you hear [someone] in one of your cities, which your God YHWH is giving to you to dwell there, saying, **13** Men, sons of worthlessness, have gone out of your midst, and they force away the inhabitants of their city, saying, Let us go and serve other gods (which you have not known), **14** then you have inquired, and searched, and asked diligently, and behold, [if] truth, the thing is established; this abomination has been done in your midst— **15** you surely strike the inhabitants of that city by the mouth of the sword, devoting it and all that [is] in it, even its livestock, by the mouth of the sword. **16** And you gather all its spoil into the midst of its broad place, and have completely burned the city and all its spoil with fire for your God YHWH, and it has been a continuous heap, it is not built anymore; **17** and nothing from any of that [which is] devoted stays in your hand, so that YHWH turns back from the fierceness of His anger, and has given mercies to you, and loved you, and multiplied you, as He has sworn to your fathers, **18** because you listen to the voice of your God YHWH, to keep all his commands which I am commanding you today, to do that which [is] right in the eyes of your God YHWH."

14 "You [are] sons of your God YHWH; you do not cut yourselves, nor make baldness between your eyes for the dead; **2** for you [are] a holy people to your God YHWH, and YHWH has fixed on you to be to Him for a people, a peculiar treasure, out of all the peoples who [are] on the face of the ground. **3** You do not eat any abomination; **4** this [is] the beast which you eat: ox, lamb of the sheep, or kid of the goats, **5** deer, and roe, and fallow deer, and wild goat, and ibex, and antelope, and zemer; **6** and every beast dividing the hoof, and cleaving the cleft into two hooves, bringing up the cud, among the beasts— you eat it. **7** Only, this you do not eat, of those bringing up the cud, and of those dividing the cloven hoof: the camel, and the hare, and the hyrax, for they are bringing up the cud, but the hoof has not divided—they [are] unclean to you; **8** and the sow, for it is dividing the hoof, and not [bringing] up the cud—it [is] unclean to you; you do not eat of their flesh, and you do not come against their carcass. **9** This you eat of all which [are] in the waters: anything that has fins and scales you eat; **10** and anything which does not have fins and scales you do not eat—it [is] unclean to you. **11** Any clean bird you eat; **12** and these [are] they of which you do not eat: the eagle, and the bearded vulture, and the osprey, **13** and the kite, and the falcon, and the vulture after its kind, **14** and every raven after its kind; **15** and the ostrich, and the nightjar [[or male ostrich]], and the seagull, and the hawk after its kind; **16** the little owl, and the great owl, and the waterhen, **17** and the pelican, and the Egyptian vulture, and the cormorant, **18** and the stork, and the heron after its kind, and the hoopoe, and the bat. **19** And every teeming thing which is flying—it [is] unclean to you; they are not eaten; **20** any clean bird you eat. **21** You do not eat of any carcass; you give it to the sojourner who [is] within your gates, and he has eaten it; or sell [it] to a stranger; for you [are] a holy people to your God YHWH. You do not boil a kid in its mother's milk. **22** You certainly tithe all the increase of your seed which the field is bringing forth year by year; **23** and you have eaten before your God YHWH, in the place where He chooses to cause His Name to dwell, the tithe of your grain, of your new wine, and of your oil, and the firstlings of your herd, and of your flock, so that you learn to fear your God YHWH [for] all the days. **24** And when the way is too much for you, that you are not able to carry it—when the place is too far off from you which your God YHWH chooses to put His Name there, when your God YHWH blesses you— **25** then you have given [it] in money, and have bound up the money in your hand, and gone to the place on which your God YHWH fixes; **26** and you have given the money for anything which your soul desires, for oxen, and for sheep, and for wine, and for strong drink, and for anything which your soul asks for, and you have eaten before your God YHWH there, and you have rejoiced, you and your house. **27** As for the Levite who [is] within your gates, you do not forsake him, for he has no portion and inheritance with you. **28** At the end of three years you bring out all the tithe of your increase in that year, and have placed [it] within your gates; **29** and the Levite has come in—for he has no part and inheritance with you—and the sojourner, and the fatherless, and the widow, who [are] within your gates, and they have eaten, and been satisfied, so that your God YHWH blesses you in all the work of your hand which you do."

15 "At the end of seven years you make a release, **2** and this [is] the matter of the release: every owner of a loan [is] to release his hand which he lifts up against his neighbor, he does not exact of his neighbor and of his brother, but has proclaimed a release to YHWH; **3** of the stranger you may exact, but that which is yours with your brother your hand releases, **4** except there is an end [when] no poor [are] with you; for YHWH greatly blesses you in the land which your God YHWH is giving to you [for] an inheritance to possess it, **5** only if you listen diligently to the voice of your God YHWH, to observe to do all this command which I am commanding you today. **6** For your God YHWH has blessed you as He has spoken to you; and you have lent [to] many nations, but you have not borrowed; and you have ruled over many nations, but they do not rule over you. **7** When there is with you any poor of one of your brothers, in one of your cities, in your land which your God YHWH is giving to you, you do not harden your heart, nor shut your hand from your needy brother; **8** for you certainly open your hand to him, and certainly lend him sufficiency for his lack which he lacks. **9** Take heed to yourself lest there be a worthless word in your heart, saying, The seventh year [is] near, the year of release; and your eye is evil against your needy brother, and you do not give to him, and he has called to YHWH concerning you, and it has been sin in you; **10** you certainly give to him, and your heart is not sad in your giving to him, for because of this thing your God YHWH blesses you in all your works and in every putting forth of your hand; **11** because the poor does not cease out of the land, therefore I am commanding you, saying, You certainly open your hand to your brother, to your poor and to your needy one in your land. **12** When your brother is sold to you, a Hebrew or a Hebrewess, and he has served you [for] six years, then in the seventh year you send him away free from you. **13** And when you send him away free from you, you do not send him away empty; **14** you certainly adorn him from your flock, and from your threshing-floor, and from your wine-vat; you give to him [from] that which your God YHWH has blessed you [with], **15** and you have remembered that you have been a servant in the land of Egypt, and your God YHWH ransoms you; therefore I am commanding you this thing today. **16** And it has been, when he says to you, I do not go out from you, because he has loved you and your house, because [it is] good for him with you, **17** then you have taken the awl, and have put [it] through his ear, and through the door, and he has been a perpetual servant to you; and you also do so to your handmaid. **18** It is not hard in your eyes in your sending him away free from you; for [his worth has been] double the hire of a hired worker [when] he has served you six years; and your God YHWH has blessed you in all that you do. **19** Every firstling that is born in your herd and in your flock—you sanctify the male to your God YHWH; you do not work with the firstling of your ox, nor shear the firstling of your flock; **20** you eat it before your God YHWH year by year, in the place which YHWH chooses, you and your house. **21** And when there is a blemish in it, [or it is] lame or blind, [or has] any evil blemish, you do not sacrifice it to your God YHWH; **22** you eat it within your gates, the unclean and the clean alike, as the roe and as the deer. **23** Only, you do not eat its blood—you pour it on the earth as water."

16 "Observe the month of Abib, and you have made a Passover to your God YHWH, for in the month of Abib your God YHWH has brought you out of Egypt by night; **2** and you have sacrificed a Passover to your God YHWH, of the flock and of the herd, in the place which YHWH chooses to cause His Name to dwell there. **3** You do not eat any fermented thing with it; [for] seven days you eat unleavened things with it, bread of affliction (for you have come out of the land of Egypt in haste), so that you remember the day of your coming out of the land of Egypt all [the] days of your life; **4** and leaven is not seen with you in all your border [for] seven days, and there does not remain [any] of the flesh which you sacrifice at evening on the first day until morning. **5** You are not able

DEUTERONOMY

to sacrifice the Passover within any of your gates which your God YHWH is giving to you, **6** except at the place which your God YHWH chooses to cause His Name to dwell—there you sacrifice the Passover in the evening, at the going in of the sun, the season of your coming out of Egypt; **7** and you have cooked and eaten in the place on which your God YHWH fixes, and have turned in the morning and gone to your tents; **8** [for] six days you eat unleavened things, and on the seventh day [is] a restraint to your God YHWH; you do no work. **9** You number seven weeks for yourself; you begin to number seven weeks from the beginning of the sickle among the standing grain, **10** and you have observed the Celebration of Weeks to your God YHWH, a tribute of a free-will offering of your hand, which you give as your God YHWH blesses you. **11** And you have rejoiced before your God YHWH, you, and your son, and your daughter, and your manservant, and your handmaid, and the Levite who [is] within your gates, and the sojourner, and the fatherless, and the widow, who [are] in your midst, in the place which your God YHWH chooses to cause His Name to dwell there, **12** and you have remembered that you have been a servant in Egypt, and have observed and done these statutes. **13** You observe the Celebration of Shelters for yourself [for] seven days, in your ingathering of your threshing-floor and of your wine-vat; **14** and you have rejoiced in your celebration, you, and your son, and your daughter, and your manservant, and your handmaid, and the Levite, and the sojourner, and the fatherless, and the widow, who [are] within your gates. **15** [For] seven days you celebrate before your God YHWH in the place which YHWH chooses, for your God YHWH blesses you in all your increase and in every work of your hands, and you have been only rejoicing. **16** Three times in a year all of your males appear before your God YHWH in the place which He chooses: in the Celebration of Unleavened Things, and in the Celebration of Weeks, and in the Celebration of Shelters; and they do not appear before YHWH empty; **17** each [gives] according to the gift of his hand, according to the blessing of your God YHWH, which He has given to you. **18** You set for yourself judges and authorities within all your gates which your God YHWH is giving to you, for your tribes; and they have judged the people [with] a righteous judgment. **19** You do not turn aside judgment; you do not discern faces, nor take a bribe, for the bribe blinds the eyes of the wise and perverts the words of the righteous. **20** Righteousness—you pursue righteousness, so that you live and have possessed the land which your God YHWH is giving to you. **21** You do not plant an Asherah of any trees for yourself near the altar of your God YHWH, which you make for yourself, **22** and you do not raise up any standing image for yourself which your God YHWH is hating."

17 "You do not sacrifice to your God YHWH ox or sheep in which there is a blemish—any bad thing; for it [is] an abomination [to] your God YHWH. **2** When there is found in your midst, in one of your cities which your God YHWH is giving to you, a man or a woman who does evil in the eyes of your God YHWH by transgressing His covenant, **3** and he goes and serves other gods, and bows himself to them, and to the sun, or to the moon, or to any of the host of the heavens, which I have not commanded, **4** and it has been declared to you, and you have heard, and have searched diligently, and behold, [if] truth, the thing is established; this abomination has been done in Israel— **5** then you have brought out that man or that woman who has done this evil thing, to your gates—the man or the woman—and you have stoned them with stones, and they have died. **6** By the mouth of two witnesses or three witnesses is he who is being put to death put to death; he is not put to death by the mouth of one witness; **7** the hand of the witnesses is on him in the first place to put him to death, and the hand of all the people last; and you have put away evil out of your midst. **8** When anything is too hard for you for judgment, between blood and blood, between plea and plea, and between stroke and stroke—matters of strife within your gates—then you have risen and gone up to the place on which your God YHWH fixes, **9** and have come to the priests, the Levites, and to the judge who is in those days, and have inquired, and they have declared the word of judgment to you, **10** and you have done according to the tenor of the word which they declare to you ([they] of that

DEUTERONOMY

place which YHWH chooses); and you have observed to do according to all that they direct you. **11** According to the tenor of the law which they direct you, and according to the judgment which they say to you, you do; you do not turn aside from the word which they declare to you [to] the right or left. **12** And the man who acts with presumption, so as not to listen to the priest (who is standing to serve your God YHWH there), or to the judge, even that man has died, and you have put away evil from Israel, **13** and all the people hear and fear, and do not presume anymore. **14** When you come into the land which your God YHWH is giving to you, and have possessed it, and dwelt in it, and you have said, Let me set a king over me like all the nations which [are] around me— **15** you certainly set a king over you on whom YHWH fixes; you set a king over you from the midst of your brothers; you are not able to set a stranger over you, who is not your brother. **16** Only, he does not multiply horses for himself, nor cause the people to return to Egypt, so as to multiply horses, seeing YHWH has said to you, You do not add to return in this way anymore. **17** And he does not multiply wives for himself, and his heart does not turn aside, and he does not exceedingly multiply silver and gold for himself. **18** And it has been, when he sits on the throne of his kingdom, that he has written a copy of this law for himself, on a scroll, from [that] before the priests, the Levites, **19** and it has been with him, and he has read in it all [the] days of his life, so that he learns to fear his God YHWH, to keep all the words of this law and these statutes—to do them, **20** so that his heart is not high above his brothers, and so as not to turn aside from the command [to] the right or left, so that he prolongs days over his kingdom, he and his sons in the midst of Israel."

18 "There is not for the priests, the Levites—all the tribe of Levi—a portion and inheritance with Israel; they eat fire-offerings of YHWH, even His inheritance, **2** and he has no inheritance in the midst of his brothers; YHWH Himself [is] his inheritance, as He has spoken to him. **3** And this is the priest's right from the people, from those sacrificing a sacrifice, whether ox or sheep, he has even given to the priest the leg, and the two cheeks, and the stomach; **4** you give to him the first of your grain, of your new wine, and of your oil, and the first of the fleece of your flock; **5** for your God YHWH has fixed on him, out of all your tribes, to stand to serve in the Name of YHWH—him and his sons continually. **6** And when the Levite comes from one of your cities, out of all Israel where he has sojourned, and has come with all the desire of his soul to the place which YHWH chooses, **7** then he has ministered in the Name of his God YHWH like all his brothers, the Levites, who are standing there before YHWH. **8** They eat portion like portion, apart from his sold things from the fathers. **9** When you are coming into the land which your God YHWH is giving to you, you do not learn to do according to the abominations of those nations. **10** There is not found in you one causing his son and his daughter to pass over into fire, a user of divinations, an observer of clouds, and an enchanter, and a sorcerer, **11** and a charmer, and one inquiring from a familiar spirit, and a wizard, and one seeking to the dead. **12** For everyone doing these [is] an abomination [to] YHWH, and because of these abominations your God YHWH is dispossessing them from your presence. **13** You must be perfect with your God YHWH, **14** for these nations whom you are possessing listen to observers of clouds and to diviners; but you—your God YHWH has not permitted you so. **15** Your God YHWH raises up for you a Prophet like me out of your midst, out of your brothers—you must listen to Him, **16** according to all that you asked from your God YHWH in Horeb, in the day of the assembly, saying, Do not let me add to hear the voice of my God YHWH, and do not let me see this great fire anymore, and I do not die; **17** and YHWH says to me, They have done well [in] what they have spoken; **18** I raise up for them a Prophet like you out of the midst of their brothers, and I have given My words in His mouth, and He has spoken to them all that which I command Him; **19** and it has been [that] the man who does not listen to My words which He speaks in My Name, I require [it] of him. **20** Only, the prophet who presumes to speak a word in My Name, which I have not commanded him to speak, and who speaks in the name of other gods, indeed, that prophet has died. **21** And when you say in your heart, How do we know the word which YHWH has not spoken? **22** That which the prophet speaks in the Name of YHWH, and the thing is not, and does not come—it [is] the word which YHWH has not spoken; the prophet has spoken it in presumption; you are not afraid of him."

19 "When your God YHWH cuts off the nations whose land your God YHWH is giving to you, and you have dispossessed them, and dwelt in their cities and in their houses, **2** you separate three cities for yourself in the midst of your land which your God YHWH is giving to you to possess it. **3** You prepare the way for yourself, and have divided into three parts the border of your land which your God YHWH causes you to inherit, and it has been for the fleeing there of every manslayer. **4** And this [is] the matter of the manslayer who flees there, and has lived: he who strikes his neighbor unknowingly, and is not hating him before— **5** even he who comes into a forest with his neighbor to hew wood, and his hand has driven with an axe to cut the tree, and the iron has slipped from the wood, and has met his neighbor, and he has died—he flees to one of these cities, and has lived, **6** lest the redeemer of blood pursue after the manslayer when his heart is hot and has overtaken him, because the way is great, and has struck his life, and he has no sentence of death, for he is not hating him before; **7** therefore I am commanding you, saying, You separate three cities for yourself. **8** And if your God YHWH enlarges your border, as He has sworn to your fathers, and has given to you all the land which He has spoken to give to your fathers— **9** when you keep all this command to do it, which I am commanding you today, to love your God YHWH and to walk in His ways [for] all the days—then you have added three more cities for yourself to these three; **10** and [do this] lest innocent blood is shed in the midst of your land which your God YHWH is giving to you [for] an inheritance, and there has been blood on you. **11** And when a man is hating his neighbor, and has lain in wait for him, and risen against him, and struck his life, and he has died, then he has fled to one of these cities, **12** and [the] elderly of his city have sent and taken him from there, and given him into the hand of the redeemer of blood, and he has died; **13** your eye has no pity on him, and you have put away the innocent blood from Israel, and it is well with you. **14** You do not remove a border of your neighbor, which they of former times have made, in your inheritance, which you inherit in the land which your God YHWH is giving to you to possess it. **15** One witness does not rise against a man for any iniquity and for any sin, in any sin which he sins; by the mouth of two witnesses or by the mouth of three witnesses is a thing established. **16** When a violent witness rises against a man to testify against him apostasy, **17** then both of the men who have the strife have stood before YHWH, before the priests and the judges who are in those days, **18** and the judges have searched diligently, and behold, the witness [is] a false witness who has testified a falsehood against his brother, **19** then you have done to him as he devised to do to his brother, and you have put away evil out of your midst, **20** and those who are left hear and fear, and do not add to do according to this evil thing in your midst anymore. **21** And your eye does not pity—life for life, eye for eye, tooth for tooth, hand for hand, foot for foot."

20 "When you go out to battle against your enemy, and have seen horse and chariot—a people more numerous than you—you are not afraid of them, for your God YHWH [is] with you, who is bringing you up out of the land of Egypt; **2** and it has been, in your drawing near to the battle, that the priest has come near, and spoken to the people, **3** and said to them, Hear, O Israel: You are drawing near today to battle against your enemies, do not let your hearts be tender, do not fear, nor make haste, nor be terrified at their presence, **4** for your God YHWH [is] He who is going with you, to fight for you with your enemies—to save you. **5** And the authorities have spoken to the people, saying, Who [is] the man that has built a new house and has not dedicated it? Let him go and return to his house, lest he die in battle and another man dedicate it. **6** And who [is] the man that has planted a vineyard and has not made it common? Let him go and return to his house, lest he die in battle, and another man make it common. **7** And who [is] the man that has betrothed a woman and has not taken her? Let him go and return to his house, lest he die in battle, and another man take her. **8** And the authorities have added to speak to the people and said, Who [is] the man

DEUTERONOMY

that is afraid and tender of heart? Let him go and return to his house, and the heart of his brothers does not melt like his heart. **9** And it has come to pass, as the authorities finish to speak to the people, that they have appointed princes of the hosts at the head of the people. **10** When you draw near to a city to fight against it, then you have called to it for peace, **11** and it has been, if it answers you [with] peace, and has opened to you, then it has come to pass, all the people who are found in it are for tributaries to you, and have served you. **12** And if it does not make peace with you, and has made war with you, then you have laid siege against it, **13** and your God YHWH has given it into your hand, and you have struck every male of it by the mouth of the sword. **14** Only, the women, and the infants, and the livestock, and all that is in the city, all its spoil, you seize for yourself, and you have eaten the spoil of your enemies which your God YHWH has given to you. **15** So you do to all the cities which are very far off from you, which are not of the cities of these nations. **16** Only, of the cities of these peoples which your God YHWH is giving to you [for] an inheritance, you do not keep alive any [that are] breathing; **17** for you certainly devote the Hittite, and the Amorite, the Canaanite, and the Perizzite, the Hivite, and the Jebusite, as your God YHWH has commanded you, **18** so that they do not teach you to do according to all their abominations which they have done for their gods, and you have sinned against your God YHWH. **19** When you lay siege to a city [for] many days to fight against it, to capture it, you do not destroy its trees to force an axe against them, for you eat of them, and you do not cut them down—for the tree of the field [is] man's—to go in at your presence in the siege. **20** Only, the tree of which you know that it [is] not a fruit-tree, you destroy it, and have cut [it] down, and have built a bulwark against the city which is making war with you until you have subdued it."

21 "When one is found slain, fallen in a field on the ground which your God YHWH is giving to you to possess it, [and] it is not known who has struck him, **2** then your elderly and yours [of those] judging have gone out and measured to the cities which [are] around the slain one, **3** and it has been, the city which [is] near to the slain one, even [the] elderly of that city have taken a heifer of the herd, which has not been worked with, which has not drawn in a yoke, **4** and [the] elderly of that city have brought down the heifer to a hard valley, which is not tilled nor sown, and have beheaded the heifer there in the valley. **5** And the priests, sons of Levi, have come near—for your God YHWH has fixed on them to serve Him and to bless in the Name of YHWH, and by their mouth is every strife and every stroke— **6** and all [the] elderly of that city, who are near to the slain one, wash their hands over the heifer which is beheaded in the valley, **7** and they have answered and said, Our hands have not shed this blood, and our eyes have not seen— **8** receive atonement for Your people Israel, whom You have ransomed, O YHWH, and do not permit innocent blood in the midst of Your people Israel; and the blood has been pardoned to them, **9** and you put away the innocent blood out of your midst, for you do that which [is] right in the eyes of YHWH. **10** When you go out to battle against your enemies, and your God YHWH has given them into your hand, and you have taken captive its captivity, **11** and have seen a woman of beautiful form in the captivity, and have delighted in her, and have taken [her] to yourself for a wife, **12** then you have brought her into the midst of your household, and she has shaved her head, and prepared her nails, **13** and turned aside the raiment of her captivity from off her, and has dwelt in your house, and lamented her father and her mother [for] a month of days, and afterward you go in to her and have married her, and she has been to you for a wife. **14** And it has been, if you have not delighted in her, that you have sent her away at her desire, and surely you do not sell her for money; you do not tyrannize over her, because that you have humbled her. **15** When a man has two wives, one loved and the other hated, and they have borne sons to him (the loved one and the hated one), and the firstborn son has been to the hated one, **16** then it has been, in the day of his causing his sons to inherit that which he has, he is not able to declare firstborn the son of the loved one, in the face of the son of the hated one—the firstborn. **17** But the firstborn, son of the hated one, he acknowledges, to give to him a double portion of all that is found with him, for he [is] the beginning of his strength; to him [is] the right of the firstborn. **18** When a man has a son apostatizing and being rebellious—he is not listening to the voice of his father and to the voice of his mother, and they have disciplined him, and he does not listen to them— **19** then his father and his mother have laid hold on him, and they have brought him out to [the] elderly of his city, and to the gate of his place, **20** and have said to [the] elderly of his city, Our son—this one—is apostatizing and being rebellious; he is not listening to our voice—a glutton and drunkard. **21** Then all the men of his city have stoned him with stones and he has died, and you have put away the evil out of your midst, and all Israel hears and fears. **22** And when there is a sin in a man [with] a judgment of death, and he has been put to death, and you have hanged him on a tree, **23** his corpse does not remain on the tree, for you certainly bury him in the day—for he who is hanged [becomes] a curse of God—and you do not defile your ground which your God YHWH is giving to you [for] an inheritance."

22 "You do not see the ox of your brother or his sheep driven away, and have hidden yourself from them, you certainly turn them back to your brother; **2** and if your brother [is] not near to you, and you have not known him, then you have removed it to the midst of your house, and it has been with you until your brother seeks it, and you have given it back to him; **3** and so you do to his donkey, and so you do to his garment, and so you do to any lost thing of your brother's, which is lost by him, and you have found it; you are not able to hide yourself. **4** You do not see the donkey of your brother, or his ox, falling in the way, and have hid yourself from them; you certainly raise [them] up for him. **5** Anything of a man is not on a woman, nor does a man put on the garment of a woman, for anyone doing these [is] an abomination [to] your God YHWH. **6** When a bird's nest comes before you in the way, in any tree, or on the earth, [with] brood or eggs, and the mother is sitting on the brood or on the eggs, you do not take the mother with the young ones; **7** you certainly send the mother away, and take the young ones for yourself, so that it is well with you and you have prolonged days. **8** When you build a new house, then you have made a parapet for your roof, and you do not put blood on your house when one falls from it. **9** You do not sow your vineyard [with] two kinds [of seed], lest the fullness of the seed which you sow and the increase of the vineyard be separated. **10** You do not plow with an ox and with a donkey together. **11** You do not put on mixed material, wool and linens together. **12** You make fringes for yourself on the four skirts of your covering with which you cover [yourself]. **13** When a man takes a wife, and has gone in to her, and hated her, **14** and laid evil deeds of words against her, and brought out an evil name against her, and said, I have taken this woman, and I draw near to her, and I have not found proofs of virginity in her; **15** then the father of the girl, and her mother, have taken and brought out the girl's proofs of virginity to [the] elderly of the city in the gate, **16** and the father of the girl has said to the elderly, I have given my daughter to this man for a wife, and he hates her; **17** and behold, he has laid evil deeds of words, saying, I have not found proofs of virginity for your daughter—and these [are] the proofs of virginity of my daughter! And they have spread out the garment before [the] elderly of the city. **18** And [the] elderly of that city have taken the man, and discipline him, **19** and fined him one hundred pieces of silver, and given [them] to the father of the girl, because he has brought out an evil name on a virgin of Israel; and she is to him for a wife—he is not able to send her away [for] all his days. **20** And if this thing has been truth—proofs of virginity have not been found for the girl— **21** then they have brought out the girl to the opening of her father's house, and the men of her city have stoned her with stones and she has died, for she has done folly in Israel, to go whoring [in] her father's house; and you have put away evil out of your midst. **22** When a man is found lying with a woman married to a husband, then both of them have died—the man who is lying with the woman, and the woman; and you have put away evil out of Israel. **23** When there is a girl, a virgin, betrothed to a man, and a man has found her in a city and lain with her, **24** then you have brought them both out to the gate of that city, and stoned them with stones, and they have died: the girl, because that she has not cried

DEUTERONOMY

in a city; and the man, because that he has humbled his neighbor's wife; and you have put away evil out of your midst. **25** And if the man finds the girl who is betrothed in a field, and the man has laid hold on her, and lain with her, then the man who has lain with her has died alone; **26** and you do not do anything to the girl—the girl has no deadly sin; for as a man rises against his neighbor and has murdered him, [taking] a life, so [is] this thing; **27** for he found her in a field, [and when] she has cried—the girl who is betrothed—then she has no savior. **28** When a man finds a girl, a virgin who is not betrothed, and has caught her, and lain with her, and they have been found, **29** then the man who is lying with her has given fifty pieces of silver to the father of the girl, and she is to him for a wife; because that he has humbled her, he is not able to send her away [for] all his days. **30** A man does not take his father's wife, nor uncover his father's skirt."

23 "No one wounded, bruised, or cut in the genitals enters into the assembly of YHWH; **2** a bastard does not enter into the assembly of YHWH; even a tenth generation of him does not enter into the assembly of YHWH. **3** An Ammonite and a Moabite do not enter into the assembly of YHWH; even a tenth generation of them do not enter into the assembly of YHWH—for all time, **4** because that they have not come before you with bread and with water in the way, in your coming out from Egypt, and because he has hired against you Balaam son of Beor, of Pethor of Aram-Naharaim, to revile you; **5** and your God YHWH has not been willing to listen to Balaam, and your God YHWH turns the reviling to a blessing for you, because your God YHWH has loved you; **6** you do not seek their peace and their good all your days—for all time. **7** You do not detest an Edomite, for he [is] your brother; you do not detest an Egyptian, for you have been a sojourner in his land; **8** sons who are begotten of them, a third generation of them, enter into the assembly of YHWH. **9** When a camp goes out against your enemies, then you have kept from every evil thing. **10** When there is a man who is not clean in you, from an accident at night, then he has gone out to the outside of the camp; he does not come into the midst of the camp; **11** and it has been, at the turning of the evening, he bathes with water, and at the going in of the sun he comes into the midst of the camp. **12** And you have a station at the outside of the camp, and you have gone out there outside; **13** and you have a peg on your staff, and it has been, in your sitting outside, that you have dug with it, and turned back, and covered your filth. **14** For your God YHWH is walking up and down in the midst of your camp, to deliver you and to give your enemies before you, and your camp has been holy, and He does not see the nakedness of anything in you, and has turned back from after you. **15** You do not shut up a servant to his lord, who escapes to you from his lord; **16** he dwells with you in your midst, in the place which he chooses within one of your gates, where it is pleasing to him; you do not oppress him. **17** There is not a whore among the daughters of Israel, nor is there a whoremonger among the sons of Israel; **18** you do not bring the wage of a whore or the price of a dog into the house of your God YHWH for any vow; for even both of them [are] an abomination [to] your God YHWH. **19** You do not lend in usury to your brother—usury of money, usury of food, usury of anything which is lent on usury. **20** You may lend in usury to a stranger, but you do not lend in usury to your brother, so that your God YHWH blesses you in every putting forth of your hand on the land to where you go in to possess it. **21** When you vow a vow to your God YHWH, you do not delay to complete it; for your God YHWH certainly requires it from you, lest it has been sin in you. **22** And when you refrain to vow, it is not sin in you. **23** You keep and have done the utterance of your lips, as you have vowed to your God YHWH, a free-will offering which you have spoken with your mouth. **24** When you come into the vineyard of your neighbor, then you have eaten grapes according to your desire, your sufficiency, but you do not put [any] into your vessel. **25** When you come in among the standing grain of your neighbor, then you have plucked the ears with your hand, but you do not wave a sickle over the standing grain of your neighbor."

24 "When a man takes a wife and has married her, and it has been, if she does not find grace in his eyes (for he has found nakedness in her of anything), then he has written a writing of divorce for her, and given [it] into her hand, and sent her out of his house; **2** when she has gone out of his house, and has gone and been another man's, **3** and the latter man has hated her, and written a writing of divorce for her, and given [it] into her hand, and sent her out of his house, or when the latter man dies, who has taken her to himself for a wife, **4** her former husband who sent her away is not able to return to take her to be to him for a wife, after that she has become defiled; for it [is] an abomination before YHWH, and you do not cause the land to sin which your God YHWH is giving to you [for] an inheritance. **5** When a man takes a new wife, he does not go out into the host, and [one] does not pass over to him for anything; he is free at his own house [for] one year, and his wife, whom he has taken, he has made glad. **6** No one takes millstones and rider in pledge, for it [is one's] life he is taking in pledge. **7** When a man is found stealing a person from his brothers, from the sons of Israel, and has tyrannized over him and sold him, then that thief has died, and you have put away evil out of your midst. **8** Take heed in the plague of leprosy, to watch greatly, and to do according to all that the priests, the Levites, teach you; you observe to do as I have commanded them; **9** remember that which your God YHWH has done to Miriam in the way, in your coming out of Egypt. **10** When you lift up a debt of anything on your brother, you do not go into his house to obtain his pledge; **11** you stand at the outside, and the man on whom you are lifting [it] up is bringing out the pledge to you at the outside. **12** And if he is a poor man, you do not lie down with his pledge; **13** you certainly give back the pledge to him at the going in of the sun, and he has lain down in his own raiment and has blessed you; and it is righteousness to you before your God YHWH. **14** You do not oppress a hired worker, poor and needy, of your brothers or of your sojourner who is in your land within your gates; **15** you give his hire in his day, and the sun does not go in on it, for he [is] poor, and he is supporting his life on it, lest he cries against you to YHWH, and it has been sin in you. **16** Fathers are not put to death for sons, and sons are not put to death for fathers—they are each put to death for his own sin. **17** You do not turn aside the judgment of a fatherless sojourner, nor take the garment of a widow in pledge; **18** and you have remembered that you have been a servant in Egypt, and your God YHWH ransoms you from there; therefore I am commanding you to do this thing. **19** When you reap your harvest in your field, and have forgotten a sheaf in a field, you do not return to take it; it is for the sojourner, for the fatherless, and for the widow, so that your God YHWH blesses you in all the work of your hands. **20** When you beat your olive, you do not examine the branch behind you; it is for the sojourner, for the fatherless, and for the widow. **21** When you cut your vineyard, you do not glean behind you; it is for the sojourner, for the fatherless, and for the widow; **22** and you have remembered that you have been a servant in the land of Egypt; therefore I am commanding you to do this thing."

25 "When there is a strife between men, and they have come near to the judgment, and they have judged, and declared righteous the righteous, and declared wrong the wrongdoer, **2** then it has come to pass, if the wrongdoer is to be struck, that the judge has caused him to fall down, and [one] has struck him in his presence, according to the sufficiency of his wrongdoing, by number; **3** he strikes him forty [times]; he is not adding, lest he is adding to strike him above these many stripes, and your brother be lightly esteemed in your eyes. **4** You do not muzzle an ox in its threshing. **5** When brothers dwell together, and one of them has died and has no son, the wife of the dead is not given to a strange man; her husband's brother goes in to her, and has taken her to him for a wife, and performs the duty of her husband's brother; **6** and it has been, the firstborn which she bears rises for the name of his dead brother, and his name is not wiped away out of Israel. **7** And if the man does not delight to take his brother's wife, then his brother's wife has gone up to the gate, to the elderly, and said, My husband's brother is refusing to raise up a name for his brother in Israel; he has not been willing to perform the duty of my husband's brother; **8** and [the] elderly of his city have called for him, and spoken to him, and he has stood and said, I have no desire to take her. **9** Then his brother's wife has drawn near to him before the eyes of the elderly, and drawn his shoe from off his foot, and spat in his face, and answered and said, Thus it is done to the man who does not build up the house of his brother; **10** and his name has been called in Israel, The house of him whose shoe is drawn off. **11** When men strive together with one another, and the wife of one has drawn near to deliver her husband out of the hand of his striker, and has put forth her hand, and laid hold on his private parts, **12** then you have cut off her hand; your eye does not spare. **13** You do not have [both] a great stone and a small stone in your bag. **14** You do not have a great ephah and a small ephah in your house. **15** You have a complete and just stone, [and] you have a complete and just ephah, so that they prolong your days on the ground which your God YHWH is giving to you; **16** for anyone doing these things, anyone doing iniquity, [is] an abomination [to] your God YHWH. **17** Remember that which Amalek has done to you in the way in your going out from Egypt, **18** that he has met you in the way, and strikes among you all those feeble behind you (when you [were] weary and fatigued), and is not fearing God. **19** And it has been, in your God YHWH giving rest to you from all your surrounding enemies, in the land which your God YHWH is giving to you [for] an inheritance to possess it, you blot out the remembrance of Amalek from under the heavens—you do not forget."

26 "And it has been, when you come into the land which your God YHWH is giving to you [for] an inheritance, and you have possessed it and dwelt in it, **2** that you have taken from the first of all the fruits of the ground, which you bring in out of your land which your God YHWH is giving to you, and have put [it] in a basket, and gone to the place which your God YHWH chooses to cause His Name to dwell there. **3** And you have come to the priest who is in those days, and have said to him, I have declared to your God YHWH today that I have come into the land which YHWH has sworn to our fathers to give to us; **4** and the priest has taken the basket out of your hand and placed it before the altar of your God YHWH. **5** And you have answered and said before your God YHWH, My father [is] a perishing Aramean! And he goes down to Egypt, and sojourns there with few men, and becomes a great, mighty, and populous nation there; **6** and the Egyptians do us evil, and afflict us, and put hard service on us; **7** and we cry to YHWH, God of our fathers, and YHWH hears our voice, and sees our affliction, and our labor, and our oppression; **8** and YHWH brings us out from Egypt by a strong hand, and by an outstretched arm, and by great fear, and by signs, and by wonders, **9** and He brings us to this place, and gives this land to us—a land flowing with milk and honey. **10** And now, behold, I have brought in the first of the fruits of the ground which you have given to me, O YHWH. (And you have placed it before your God YHWH, and bowed yourself before your God YHWH, **11** and rejoiced in all the good which your God YHWH has given to you and to your house—you, and the Levite, and the sojourner who [is] in your midst.) **12** When you complete to tithe all the tithe of your increase in the third year, the year of the tithe, then you have given to the Levite, to the sojourner, to the fatherless, and to the widow, and they have eaten within your gates and been satisfied, **13** and you have said before your God YHWH, I have put away the separated thing out of the house, and have also given it to the Levite, and to the sojourner, and to the orphan, and to the widow, according to all Your command which You have commanded me; I have not passed over from Your commands, nor have I forgotten. **14** I have not eaten of it in my affliction, nor have I put away of it for uncleanness, nor have I given of it for the dead; I have listened to the voice of my God YHWH; I have done according to all that You have commanded me; **15** look from Your holy habitation, from the heavens, and bless Your people Israel and the ground which You have given to us, as You have sworn to our fathers—a land flowing [with] milk and honey. **16** This day your God YHWH is commanding you to do these statutes and judgments; and you have listened and done them with all your heart and with all your soul. **17** Today you have proclaimed YHWH to be to you for God, that [you are] to walk in His ways, and to keep His statutes, and His commands, and His judgments, and to listen to His voice. **18** And today YHWH has proclaimed you to be to Him for a people, a peculiar treasure, as He has spoken to you, that [you are] to keep all His commands, **19** so as to make you highest above all the nations whom He has made for a praise, and for a name, and for beauty, and for your being a holy people to your God YHWH, as He has spoken."

27 And Moses and [the] elderly of Israel command the people, saying, "Keep all the command which I am commanding you today; **2** and it has been, in the day that you pass over the Jordan to the land which your God YHWH is giving to you, that you have raised up great stones for yourself, and plastered them with plaster, **3** and written on them all the words of this law in your passing over, so that you go into the land which your God YHWH is giving to you—a land flowing with milk and honey, as YHWH, God of your fathers, has spoken to you. **4** And it has been, in your passing over the Jordan, you raise up these stones which I am commanding you today, in Mount Ebal, and you have plastered them with plaster, **5** and built an altar there to your God YHWH, an altar of stones; you do not wave iron over them. **6** You build the altar of your God YHWH [with] complete stones, and have caused burnt-offerings to ascend on it to your God YHWH, **7** and sacrificed peace-offerings, and eaten there, and rejoiced before your God YHWH, **8** and written on the stones all the words of this law, well engraved." **9** And Moses speaks—the priests, the Levites, also—to all Israel, saying, "Keep silent and hear, O Israel: This day you have become a people for your God YHWH; **10** and you have listened to the voice of your God YHWH, and done His commands and His statutes which I am commanding you today." **11** And Moses commands the people on that day, saying, **12** "These stand on Mount Gerizzim to bless the people, in your passing over the Jordan: Simeon, and Levi, and Judah, and Issachar, and Joseph, and Benjamin. **13** And these stand, for the reviling, on Mount Ebal: Reuben, Gad, and Asher, and Zebulun, Dan, and Naphtali." **14** And the Levites have answered and said to every man of Israel [with] a loud voice: **15** "Cursed [is] the man who makes a carved and molten image, an abomination [to] YHWH, work of the hands of a craftsman, and has put [it] in a secret place." And all the people have answered and said, "Amen." **16** "Cursed [is] he who is making light of his father and his mother." And all the people have said, "Amen." **17** "Cursed [is] he who is removing his neighbor's border." And all the people have said, "Amen." **18** "Cursed [is] he who is causing the blind to err in the way." And all the people have said, "Amen." **19** "Cursed [is] he who is turning aside the judgment of fatherless, sojourner, and widow." And all the people have said, "Amen." **20** "Cursed [is] he who is lying with his father's wife, for he has uncovered his father's skirt." And all the people have said, "Amen." **21** "Cursed [is] he who is lying with any beast." And all the people have said, "Amen." **22** "Cursed [is] he who is lying with his sister, daughter of his father or daughter of his mother." And all the people have said, "Amen." **23** "Cursed [is] he who is lying with his mother-in-law." And all the people have said, "Amen." **24** "Cursed [is] he who is striking his neighbor in secret." And all the people have said, "Amen." **25** "Cursed [is] he who is taking a bribe to strike a person, innocent blood." And all the people have said, "Amen." **26** "Cursed [is] he who does not establish the words of this law, to do them." And all the people have said, "Amen."

28 "And it has been, if you listen diligently to the voice of your God YHWH, to observe to do all His commands which I am commanding you today, that your God YHWH has made you highest above all the nations of the earth, **2** and all these blessings have come on you and overtaken you, because you listen to the voice of your God YHWH: **3** Blessed [are] you in the city, and blessed [are] you in the field. **4** Blessed [is] the fruit of your womb, and the fruit of your ground, and the fruit of your livestock, the increase of your oxen, and the wealth of your flock. **5** Blessed [is] your basket and your kneading-trough. **6** Blessed [are] you in your coming in, and blessed [are] you in your going out. **7** YHWH makes your enemies, who are rising up against you, to be struck before your face; in one way they come out to you, and in seven ways they flee before you. **8** YHWH commands the blessing with you in your storehouses, and in every putting forth of your hand, and has blessed you in the land which your God YHWH is giving to you. **9** YHWH establishes you to Himself for a holy people, as He has sworn to you, when you keep the commands of your God YHWH and have walked in His ways; **10** and all the

DEUTERONOMY

peoples of the land have seen that the Name of YHWH is called by you, and they have been afraid of you. **11** And YHWH has made you abundant in good, in the fruit of the womb, and in the fruit of your livestock, and in the fruit of your ground, on the ground which YHWH has sworn to your fathers to give to you. **12** YHWH opens his good treasure to you—the heavens—to give the rain of your land in its season, and to bless all the work of your hand, and you have lent to many nations, and you do not borrow. **13** And YHWH has set you for head and not for tail; and you have been only above, and are not beneath, for you listen to the commands of your God YHWH, which I am commanding you today, to keep and to do, **14** and you do not turn aside from all the words which I am commanding you today [to] the right or left, to go after other gods, to serve them. **15** And it has been, if you do not listen to the voice of your God YHWH, to observe to do all His commands and His statutes which I am commanding you today, that all these revilings have come on you and overtaken you: **16** Cursed [are] you in the city, and cursed [are] you in the field. **17** Cursed [is] your basket and your kneading-trough. **18** Cursed [is] the fruit of your body, and the fruit of your land, the increase of your oxen, and the wealth of your flock. **19** Cursed [are] you in your coming in, and cursed [are] you in your going out. **20** YHWH sends the curse, the trouble, and the rebuke on you, in every putting forth of your hand which you do, until you are destroyed, and until you perish quickly, because of the evil of your doings [by] which you have forsaken Me. **21** YHWH causes the pestilence to cleave to you until He consumes you from off the ground to where you are going in to possess it. **22** YHWH strikes you with consumption, and with fever, and with inflammation, and with extreme burning, and with sword, and with blasting, and with mildew, and they have pursued you until you perish **23** And your heavens which [are] over your head have been bronze, and the earth which [is] under you iron; **24** YHWH gives dust and ashes [for] the rain of your land; it comes down on you from the heavens until you are destroyed. **25** YHWH makes you struck before your enemies; in one way you go out to them, and in seven ways you flee before them, and you have been for a trembling to all kingdoms of the earth; **26** and your carcass has been for food for every bird of the heavens and for the beast of the earth, and there is none causing [them] to tremble. **27** YHWH strikes you with the ulcer of Egypt, and with lumps, and with scurvy, and with itch, of which you are not able to be healed. **28** YHWH strikes you with madness, and with blindness, and with astonishment of heart; **29** and you have been groping at noon, as the blind gropes in darkness; and you do not cause your ways to prosper; and you have been only oppressed and plundered [for] all the days, and there is no savior. **30** You betroth a woman, and another man lies with her; you build a house, and do not dwell in it; you plant a vineyard, and do not make it common; **31** your ox [is] slaughtered before your eyes, and you do not eat of it; your donkey [is] violently taken away from before you, and it is not given back to you; your sheep [are] given to your enemies, and there is no savior for you. **32** Your sons and your daughters [are] given to another people, and your eyes are looking and consumed for them all the day, but your hand is not to God! **33** A people whom you have not known eat the fruit of your ground and all your labor; and you have been only oppressed and bruised [for] all the days; **34** and you have been mad because of the sight of your eyes which you see. **35** YHWH strikes you with a severe ulcer on the knees and on the legs (of which you are not able to be healed), from the sole of your foot even to your crown. **36** YHWH causes you and your king whom you raise up over you to go to a nation which you have not known, you and your fathers, and you have served other gods there—wood and stone; **37** and you have been for an astonishment, for an allegory, and for a byword among all the peoples to where YHWH leads you. **38** You take much seed out into the field, and you gather little in, for the locust consumes it; **39** you plant vineyards and have labored, but you do not drink wine, nor gather [grapes], for the worm consumes it; **40** olives are yours in all your border, but you do not pour out oil, for your olive falls off. **41** You beget sons and daughters, but they are not with you, for they go into captivity; **42** the locust possesses all your trees and the fruit of your ground; **43** the sojourner who [is] in your midst goes up very high above you, and you go down very low; **44** he lends [to] you, and you do not lend [to] him; he is for head and you are for tail. **45** And all these curses have come on you, and pursued you, and overtaken you, until you are destroyed, because you have not listened to the voice of your God Yhwh, to keep His commands and His statutes which he has commanded you; **46** and they have been on you for a sign and for a wonder, also on your seed—for all time. **47** Because that you have not served your God Yhwh with joy and with gladness of heart, because of the abundance of all things— **48** you have served your enemies, whom Yhwh sends against you, in hunger, and in thirst, and in nakedness, and in lack of all things; and He has put a yoke of iron on your neck until He has destroyed you. **49** Yhwh lifts up a nation against you from afar, from the end of the earth—it flies as the eagle—a nation whose tongue you have not heard, **50** a nation of fierce countenance, which does not accept the face of the aged and does not favor the young; **51** and it has eaten the fruit of your livestock and the fruit of your ground, until you are destroyed; which does not leave to you grain, new wine, and oil, the increase of your oxen, and the wealth of your flock, until it has destroyed you. **52** And it has laid siege to you in all your gates until your walls come down—the high and the fortified ones in which you are trusting, in all your land; indeed, it has laid siege to you in all your gates, in all your land which your God Yhwh has given to you. **53** And you have eaten the fruit of your body, [the] flesh of your sons and your daughters (whom your God Yhwh has given to you), in the siege and in the constriction with which your enemies constrict you. **54** The man who is tender in you, and who [is] very delicate—his eye is evil against his brother, and against the wife of his bosom, and against the remnant of his sons whom he leaves, **55** against giving to one of them of the flesh of his sons whom he eats, because he has nothing left for himself in the siege and in the constriction with which your enemy constricts you in all your gates. **56** The tender woman in you, and the delicate, who has not tried the sole of her foot to place on the ground because of delicateness and because of tenderness—her eye is evil against the husband of her bosom, and against her son, and against her daughter, **57** and against her seed which comes out from between her feet, even against her sons whom she bears, for she eats them in secret, in the lacking of everything, in the siege and in the constriction with which your enemy constricts you within your gates. **58** If you do not observe to do all the words of this law which are written in this scroll, to fear this honored and fearful Name—your God Yhwh— **59** then Yhwh has made your strokes extraordinary, and the strokes [against] your seed [are] great strokes that are persisting and severe sicknesses that are persisting. **60** And He has brought back all the diseases of Egypt on you, from the presence of which you have been afraid, and they have cleaved to you. **61** Also every sickness and every stroke which is not written in the scroll of this law—Yhwh causes them to go up on you until you are destroyed, **62** and you have been left with few men, whereas that you would have been as stars of the heavens for multitude, for you have not listened to the voice of your God Yhwh. **63** And it has been, as Yhwh has rejoiced over you to do you good and to multiply you, so Yhwh rejoices over you to destroy you and to lay you waste; and you have been pulled away from off the ground to where you are going in to possess it; **64** and Yhwh has scattered you among all the peoples, from the end of the earth even to the [other] end of the earth; and you have served other gods there which you have not known, you and your fathers—wood and stone. **65** And you do not rest among those nations, indeed, there is no resting place for the sole of your foot, and Yhwh has given to you a trembling heart, and failing of eyes, and grief of soul there; **66** and your life has been hanging in suspense before you, and you have been afraid by night and by day, and you do not have assurance in your life; **67** in the morning you say, O that it were evening! And in the evening you say, O that it were morning! (From the fear of your heart, with which you are afraid, and from the sight of your eyes which you see.) **68** And Yhwh has brought you back to Egypt in ships, by the way of which I said to you, You do not add to see it anymore; and you have sold yourselves to your enemies there, for menservants and for maidservants, and there is no buyer."

29 These [are] the words of the covenant which Yhwh has commanded

DEUTERONOMY

Moses to make with the sons of Israel in the land of Moab, apart from the covenant which He made with them in Horeb. **2** And Moses calls to all Israel and says to them, "You have seen all that which YHWH has done before your eyes in the land of Egypt, to Pharaoh, and to all his servants, and to all his land— **3** the great trials which your eyes have seen, the signs, and those great wonders. **4** And YHWH has not given to you a heart to know, and eyes to see, and ears to hear, until this day. **5** And I cause you to go in a wilderness [for] forty years; your garments have not been consumed from off you, and your shoe has not worn away from off your foot; **6** you have not eaten bread, and you have not drunk wine and strong drink, so that you know that I [am] your God YHWH. **7** And you come to this place, and Sihon king of Heshbon—also Og king of Bashan—comes out to meet us to battle, and we strike them, **8** and take their land, and give it for an inheritance to the Reubenite, and to the Gadite, and to the half of the tribe of the Manassite; **9** and you have kept the words of this covenant and done them, so that you cause all that you do to prosper. **10** You are standing today, all of you, before your God YHWH: your heads, your tribes, your elderly, and your authorities, every man of Israel, **11** your infants, your wives, and your sojourner who [is] in the midst of your camps, from the hewer of your wood to the drawer of your water, **12** for your passing over into the covenant of your God YHWH, and into His oath which your God YHWH is making with you today, **13** in order to establish you to Himself for a people today, and He Himself is your God, as He has spoken to you, and as He has sworn to your fathers, to Abraham, to Isaac, and to Jacob. **14** And I am not making this covenant and this oath with you alone, **15** but with him who is here with us, standing before our God YHWH today, and with him who is not here with us today, **16** for you have known how you dwelt in the land of Egypt, and how we passed by through the midst of the nations which you have passed by; **17** and you see their abominations, and their idols of wood and stone, silver and gold, which [are] with them, **18** lest there be among you a man or woman, or family or tribe, whose heart is turning from our God YHWH today, to go to serve the gods of those nations, lest there be in you a root bearing the fruit of gall and wormwood; **19** and it has been, in his hearing the words of this oath, that he has blessed himself in his heart, saying, I have peace, though I go on in the stubbornness of my heart—in order to sweep away the watered with the thirsty. **20** YHWH is not willing to be propitious to him, for then the anger of YHWH smokes, also His zeal, against that man, and all the oath which is written in this scroll has lain down on him, and YHWH has blotted out his name from under the heavens, **21** and YHWH has separated him for calamity out of all the tribes of Israel, according to all the oaths of the covenant which is written in this Scroll of the Law. **22** And the latter generation of your sons who rise after you, and the stranger who comes in from a far-off land, have said, when they have seen the strokes of that land and its sicknesses which YHWH has sent into it: **23** The whole land is burned [with] brimstone and salt, it is not sown, nor does it shoot up, nor does any herb go up on it there, like the overthrow of Sodom and Gomorrah, Admah and Zeboim, which YHWH overturned in His anger and in His fury. **24** Indeed, all the nations have said, Why has YHWH done thus to this land? Why the heat of this great anger? **25** And they have said, Because that they have forsaken the covenant of YHWH, God of their fathers, which He made with them in His bringing them out of the land of Egypt, **26** and they go and serve other gods, and bow themselves to them—gods which they have not known, and which He has not apportioned to them; **27** and the anger of YHWH burns against that land, to bring in on it all the reviling that is written in this scroll, **28** and YHWH plucks them from off their ground in anger, and in fury, and in great wrath, and casts them into another land, as [at] this day. **29** The things hidden [belong] to our God YHWH, and the things revealed [belong] to us and to our sons for all time, to do all the words of this law."

30 "And it has been, when all these things come on you, the blessing and the reviling, which I have set before you, and you have brought [them] back to your heart among all the nations to where your God YHWH has driven you away, **2** and have turned back to your God YHWH and listened to His voice, according to all that I am commanding you today, you and your

DEUTERONOMY

sons, with all your heart and with all your soul— **3** then your God Y<small>HWH</small> has turned back [to] your captivity and pitied you, indeed, He has turned back and gathered you out of all the peoples to where your God Y<small>HWH</small> has scattered you. **4** If your outcast is in the extremity of the heavens, your God Y<small>HWH</small> gathers you from there and He takes you from there; **5** and your God Y<small>HWH</small> has brought you into the land which your fathers have possessed, and you have inherited it, and He has done you good, and multiplied you above your fathers. **6** And your God Y<small>HWH</small> has circumcised your heart and the heart of your seed, to love your God Y<small>HWH</small> with all your heart and with all your soul, for the sake of your life; **7** and your God Y<small>HWH</small> has put all this oath on your enemies and on those hating you, who have pursued you. **8** And you turn back, and have listened to the voice of Y<small>HWH</small>, and have done all His commands which I am commanding you today; **9** and your God Y<small>HWH</small> has made you abundant in every work of your hand, in the fruit of your body, and in the fruit of your livestock, and in the fruit of your ground, for good; for Y<small>HWH</small> turns back to rejoice over you for good, as He rejoiced over your fathers, **10** for you listen to the voice of your God Y<small>HWH</small>, to keep His commands and His statutes which are written in the scroll of this law, for you turn back to your God Y<small>HWH</small> with all your heart and with all your soul. **11** For this command which I am commanding you today, it is not too wonderful for you, nor [is] it far off. **12** It is not in the heavens, saying, Who goes up into the heavens for us, and takes it for us, and causes us to hear it, that we may do it? **13** And it [is] not beyond the sea, saying, Who passes over beyond the sea for us, and takes it for us, and causes us to hear it, that we may do it? **14** For the word is very near to you, in your mouth, and in your heart—to do it. **15** See, today I have set before you life and good, and death and evil, **16** in that today I am commanding you to love your God Y<small>HWH</small>, to walk in His ways, and to keep His commands, and His statutes, and His judgments; and you have lived and multiplied, and your God Y<small>HWH</small> has blessed you in the land to where you are going in to possess it. **17** And if your heart turns away, and you do not listen, and have been drawn away, and have bowed yourself to other gods and served them, **18** I have declared to you this day that you certainly perish, you do not prolong days on the ground which you are passing over the Jordan to go in there to possess it. **19** I have caused the heavens and the earth to testify against you today—I have set before you life and death, the blessing and the reviling, and you have fixed on life, so that you live, you and your seed, **20** to love your God Y<small>HWH</small>, to listen to His voice, and to cleave to Him (for He [is] your life and the length of your days), to dwell on the ground which Y<small>HWH</small> has sworn to your fathers, to Abraham, to Isaac, and to Jacob, to give to them."

31 And Moses goes and speaks these words to all Israel, **2** and he says to them, "I [am] a son of one hundred and twenty years today; I am not able to go out and to come in anymore, and Y<small>HWH</small> has said to me, You do not pass over this Jordan. **3** Your God Y<small>HWH</small>—He is passing over before you; He destroys these nations from before you, and you have possessed them; Joshua—he is passing over before you, as Y<small>HWH</small> has spoken. **4** And Y<small>HWH</small> has done to them as he has done to Sihon and to Og, kings of the Amorite, and to their land, whom He destroyed. **5** And Y<small>HWH</small> has given them before your face, and you have done to them according to all the command which I have commanded you; **6** be strong and courageous, do not fear, nor be terrified because of them, for your God Y<small>HWH</small> [is] He who is going with you; He does not fail you nor forsake you." **7** And Moses calls for Joshua and says to him before the eyes of all Israel, "Be strong and courageous, for you go in with this people to the land which Y<small>HWH</small> has sworn to their fathers to give to them, and you cause them to inherit it; **8** and Y<small>HWH</small> [is] He who is going before you, He Himself is with you; He does not fail you nor forsake you; do not fear, nor be frightened." **9** And Moses writes this law and gives it to the priests (sons of Levi, those carrying the Ark of the Covenant of Y<small>HWH</small>), and to all [the] elderly of Israel, **10** and Moses commands them, saying, "At the end of seven years, in the appointed time, the year of release, in the Celebration of Shelters, **11** in the coming in of all Israel to see the face of Y<small>HWH</small> in the place which He chooses, you proclaim this law before all Israel in their

DEUTERONOMY

ears. **12** Assemble the people, the men, and the women, and the infants, and your sojourner who [is] within your gates, so that they hear, and so that they learn, and have feared your God YHWH, and observed to do all the words of this law; **13** and their sons, who have not known, hear and have learned to fear your God YHWH [for] all the days which you are living on the ground to where you are passing over the Jordan to possess it." **14** And YHWH says to Moses, "Behold, your days have drawn near to die; call Joshua, and station yourselves in the Tent of Meeting, and I charge him"; and Moses goes—Joshua also—and they station themselves in the Tent of Meeting, **15** and YHWH is seen in the tent in a pillar of a cloud; and the pillar of the cloud stands at the opening of the tent. **16** And YHWH says to Moses, "Behold, you are lying down with your fathers, and this people has risen and gone whoring after the gods of the stranger of the land, into the midst of which it has entered, and it has forsaken Me and broken My covenant which I made with it; **17** and My anger has burned against it in that day, and I have forsaken them, and hidden My face from them, and it has been for consumption, and many evils and distresses have found it, and it has said in that day, [Is] it not because my God is not in my midst that these evils have found me? **18** And I certainly hide My face in that day for all the evil which it has done, for it has turned to other gods. **19** And now, write this song for yourselves, and teach it [to] the sons of Israel; put it in their mouths, so that this song is to Me for a witness against the sons of Israel. **20** When I bring them to the ground flowing with milk and honey, which I have sworn to their fathers, and they have eaten, and been satisfied, and been fat, and have turned to other gods, and they have served them, and despised Me, and broken My covenant, **21** then it has been, when many evils and distresses meet it, that this song has testified to its face for a witness; for it is not forgotten out of the mouth of its seed, for I have known its imagining which it is doing today, before I bring them into the land of which I have sworn." **22** And Moses writes this song on that day, and teaches it [to] the sons of Israel. **23** Then He commands Joshua son of Nun, and says, "Be strong and courageous, for you bring in the sons of Israel to the land which I have sworn to them, and I am with you." **24** And it comes to pass, when Moses finishes to write the words of this law on a scroll, until their completion, **25** that Moses commands the Levites carrying the Ark of the Covenant of YHWH, saying, **26** "Take this Scroll of the Law, and you have set it on the side of the Ark of the Covenant of your God YHWH, and it has been against you for a witness there; **27** for I have known your rebellion and your stiff neck; behold, in my being yet alive with you today, you have been rebelling against YHWH, and surely also after my death. **28** Assemble to me all the elderly of your tribes, and your authorities, and I speak these words in their ears, and cause the heavens and the earth to testify against them, **29** for I have known that you act very corruptly after my death, and have turned aside from the way which I commanded you, and evil has met you in the latter end of the days, because you do evil in the eyes of YHWH, to make Him angry with the work of your hands." **30** And Moses speaks the words of this song in the ears of all the assembly of Israel, until their completion:

32 "Give ear, O heavens, and I speak; And you hear, O earth, sayings of my mouth! **2** My doctrine drops as rain; My sayings flow as dew; As storms on the tender grass, ‖ And as showers on the herb, **3** For I proclaim the Name of YHWH; Ascribe greatness to our God! **4** The Rock—His work [is] perfect, ‖ For all His ways [are] just; God of steadfastness, and without iniquity; Righteous and upright [is] He. **5** It has done corruptly to Him; Their blemish is not of His sons, ‖ A generation perverse and crooked! **6** Do you act thus to YHWH, ‖ O people foolish and not wise? Is He not your Father—He who bought you? He made you, and establishes you. **7** Remember days of old—Understand the years of many generations—Ask your father, and he tells you; Your elderly, and they say to you: **8** In the Most High causing nations to inherit, ‖ In His separating sons of Adam—He sets up the borders of the peoples ‖ By the number of the sons of God [[or sons of Israel]]. **9** For YHWH's portion [is] His people, ‖ Jacob [is] the line of His inheritance. **10** He finds him in a land—a desert, ‖ And in a void—a howling wilderness, ‖ He turns him around—He causes him to understand—He keeps him

DEUTERONOMY

as the apple of His eye. **11** As an eagle wakes up its nest, ‖ Flutters over its young ones, ‖ Spreads its wings [and] takes them, ‖ Carries them on its pinions— **12** YHWH alone leads him, ‖ And there is no strange god with him. **13** He makes him ride on high places of earth, ‖ And he eats increase of the fields, ‖ And He makes him suck honey from a rock, ‖ And oil out of the flint of a rock; **14** Butter of the herd, and milk of the flock, ‖ With fat of lambs, and rams of sons of Bashan, ‖ And male goats, with fat of kidneys of wheat; And of the blood of the grape you drink wine! **15** And Yeshurun waxes fat, and kicks: You have been fat, you have been thick, ‖ You have been covered. And he leaves God who made him, ‖ And dishonors the Rock of his salvation. **16** They make Him zealous with strangers, ‖ They make Him angry with abominations. **17** They sacrifice to the demons, not God, ‖ To gods they have not known, ‖ New ones—they came from the vicinity; Your fathers have not feared them! **18** You forget the Rock that begot you, ‖ And neglect God who forms you. **19** And YHWH sees and despises—For the provocation of His sons and His daughters. **20** And He says: I hide My face from them, ‖ I see what their latter end [is]; For they [are] a contrary generation, ‖ Sons in whom is no steadfastness. **21** They have made Me jealous by [what is] not God, ‖ They made Me angry by their vanities; And I make them jealous by [what is] not a people, ‖ I make them angry by a foolish nation. **22** For a fire has been kindled in My anger, ‖ And it burns to the lowest [part] of Sheol, ‖ And consumes earth and its increase, ‖ And sets on fire [the] foundations of mountains. **23** I heap calamities on them, ‖ I consume My arrows on them. **24** Exhausted by famine, ‖ And consumed by heat and bitter destruction—I also send the teeth of beasts on them, ‖ With poison of fearful things of the dust. **25** The sword destroys from outside, ‖ And out of the inner-chambers—terror, ‖ Both youth and virgin, ‖ Suckling with man of grey hair. **26** I have said: I blow them away, ‖ I cause their remembrance to cease from man; **27** If I do not fear the anger of an enemy, ‖ Lest their adversaries know—Lest they say, Our hand is high, ‖ And YHWH has not worked all this. **28** For they [are] a nation lost to counsels, ‖ And there is no understanding in them. **29** If only they were wise, ‖ They would deal wisely [with] this, ‖ They would attend to their latter end! **30** How does one pursue a thousand, ‖ And two cause a myriad to flee, ‖ If not that their Rock has sold them, ‖ And YHWH has shut them up? **31** For their rock [is] not as our Rock ‖ (And our enemies [are] judges!) **32** For their vine [is] of the vine of Sodom, ‖ And of the fields of Gomorrah; Their grapes [are] grapes of gall—They have bitter clusters; **33** The poison of dragons [is] their wine ‖ And the fierce venom of cobras. **34** Is it not laid up with Me? Sealed among My treasures? **35** Vengeance and retribution [are] Mine, ‖ At the due time— their foot slides; For near is a day of their calamity, ‖ And things prepared for them have hastened. **36** For YHWH judges His people, ‖ And gives comfort over His servants. For He sees the going away of power, ‖ And none is restrained and left. **37** And He has said, Where [are] their gods—The rock in which they trusted? **38** Who eat the fat of their sacrifices, ‖ [And] drink the wine of their drink-offering? Let them arise and help you, ‖ Let it be a hiding place for you! **39** See, now, that I [am] He, ‖ And there is no god besides Me; I put to death and I keep alive; I have struck and I heal; And there is not a deliverer from My hand, **40** For I lift up My hand to the heavens, ‖ And have said, I live for all time! **41** If I have sharpened the brightness of My sword, ‖ And My hand lays hold on judgment, ‖ I return vengeance to My adversaries, ‖ And to those hating Me—I repay! **42** I make My arrows drunk with blood, ‖ And My sword devours flesh, ‖ From the blood of the pierced and captive, ‖ From the head of the leaders of the enemy. **43** Sing, O nations, [with] His people, ‖ For He avenges the blood of His servants, ‖ And He turns back vengeance on His adversaries, ‖ And has pardoned His land [and] His people." **44** And Moses comes and speaks all the words of this song in the ears of the people, he and Hoshea son of Nun; **45** and Moses finishes to speak all these words to all Israel, **46** and says to them, "Set your heart to all the words which I am testifying against you today, that you command your sons to observe to do all the words of this law, **47** for it [is] not a vain thing for you, for it [is] your life, and by this thing you prolong days on the ground to where you are passing over the Jordan to possess it." **48** And YHWH speaks

DEUTERONOMY

to Moses on this very same day, saying, **49** "Go up to this Mount Abarim, Mount Nebo, which [is] in the land of Moab, which [is] on the front of Jericho, and see the land of Canaan which I am giving to the sons of Israel for a possession; **50** and die on the mountain to where you are going up, and be gathered to your people, as your brother Aaron has died on Mount Hor and is gathered to his people; **51** because you trespassed against Me in the midst of the sons of Israel at the waters of Meribath-Kadesh, the wilderness of Zin, because you did not sanctify Me in the midst of the sons of Israel. **52** Indeed, you see the land before [you], but you do not go in there to the land which I am giving to the sons of Israel."

33 And this [is] the blessing [with] which Moses the man of God blessed the sons of Israel before his death, **2** and he says: "YHWH has come from Sinai, ‖ And has risen from Seir for them; He has shone from Mount Paran, ‖ And has come [with] myriads of holy ones; At His right hand [came] a fiery law [[*or* a flaming fire]] for them. **3** Indeed, He [is] loving the peoples; All His holy ones [are] in Your hand, ‖ And they sat down at Your foot, ‖ [Each] lifts up Your words. **4** Moses has commanded a law for us, ‖ A possession of the assembly of Jacob. **5** And He is King in Yeshurun, ‖ In the heads of the people gathering together, ‖ The tribes of Israel! **6** Let Reuben live, and not die, ‖ And let his men be an [incalculable] number. **7** And this [is] for Judah, and he says: Hear, O YHWH, the voice of Judah, ‖ And You bring him in to his people; His hand has striven for him, ‖ And You are a help from his adversaries. **8** And of Levi he said: Your Perfections and your Lights [are] for your pious one, ‖ Whom You have tried in Massah, ‖ You strive with him at the waters of Meribah; **9** Who is saying of his father and his mother, ‖ I have not seen him; And he has not discerned his brothers, ‖ And he has not known his sons; For they have observed Your saying, ‖ And they keep Your covenant. **10** They teach Your judgments to Jacob, ‖ And Your law to Israel; They put incense in Your nose, ‖ And whole burnt-offering on Your altar. **11** Bless, O YHWH, his strength, ‖ And accept the work of his hands, ‖ Strike the loins of his withstanders, ‖ And of those hating him— that they do not rise! **12** Of Benjamin he said: The beloved of YHWH dwells confidently by Him, ‖ Covering him over every day; Indeed, he dwells between His shoulders. **13** And of Joseph he said: His land [is] blessed [by] YHWH, ‖ By a precious thing of the heavens, ‖ By dew, and by the deep crouching beneath, **14** And by a precious thing—fruits of the sun, ‖ And by a precious thing—cast forth by the months, **15** And by a chief thing—of the ancient mountains, ‖ And by a precious thing—of the continuous heights, **16** And by a precious thing—of earth and its fullness, ‖ And the good pleasure of Him who is dwelling in the bush; Let it come for the head of Joseph, ‖ And for the crown of him [who is] separate from his brothers. **17** His splendor [is] a firstling of his ox, ‖ And his horns [are] horns of a wild ox; With them he pushes the peoples ‖ Altogether to the ends of the earth; And they [are] the myriads of Ephraim, ‖ And they [are] the thousands of Manasseh. **18** And of Zebulun he said: Rejoice, O Zebulun, in your going out, ‖ And, O Issachar, in your tents; **19** They call peoples [to] the mountain, ‖ There they sacrifice righteous sacrifices; For they suck up the abundance of the seas, ‖ And hidden things hidden in the sand. **20** And of Gad he said: Blessed is he who is enlarging Gad, ‖ He dwells as a lioness, ‖ And has torn the arm—also the crown! **21** And he provides the first part for himself, ‖ For there the portion of the lawgiver is covered, ‖ And he comes [with] the heads of the people; He has done the righteousness of YHWH, ‖ And His judgments with Israel. **22** And of Dan he said: Dan [is] a lion's whelp; He leaps from Bashan. **23** And of Naphtali he said: O Naphtali, satisfied with pleasure, ‖ And full of the blessing of YHWH, ‖ Possess [the] west and [the] south. **24** And of Asher he said: Asher [is] blessed with sons, ‖ Let him be accepted by his brothers, ‖ And dipping his foot in oil. **25** Iron and bronze [are] your shoes, ‖ And as your days—your strength. **26** [There is] none like the God of Yeshurun, ‖ Riding the heavens to your help, ‖ And in His excellence the skies. **27** The eternal God [is] a habitation, ‖ And beneath [are] continuous arms. And He casts out the enemy from your presence and says, Destroy! **28** And Israel dwells [in] confidence alone; The eye of Jacob [is] to a land of grain and wine; Also His heavens drop down dew. **29** O your blessedness, O

Israel! Who is like you? A people saved by YHWH, ‖ The shield of your help, ‖ And He who [is] the sword of your excellence! And your enemies are subdued for you, ‖ And you tread on their high places."

34 And Moses goes up from the plains of Moab to Mount Nebo, the top of Pisgah, which [is] on the front of Jericho, and YHWH shows him all the land—Gilead to Dan, **2** and all Naphtali, and the land of Ephraim, and Manasseh, and all the land of Judah to the Western Sea, **3** and the south, and the circuit of the Valley of Jericho, the city of palms, to Zoar. **4** And YHWH says to him, "This [is] the land which I have sworn to Abraham, to Isaac, and to Jacob, saying, I give it to your seed; I have caused you to see with your eyes, but you do not pass over there." **5** And Moses, servant of the Lord, dies there in the land of Moab, according to the command of YHWH; **6** and He buries him in a valley in the land of Moab, opposite Beth-Peor, and no man has known his burying place to this day. **7** And Moses [is] a son of one hundred and twenty years when he dies; his eye has not become dim, nor has his moisture fled. **8** And the sons of Israel lament Moses in the plains of Moab [for] thirty days; and the days of weeping [and] mourning for Moses are completed. **9** And Joshua son of Nun is full of the spirit of wisdom, for Moses had laid his hands on him, and the sons of Israel listen to him, and do as YHWH commanded Moses. **10** And there has not arisen a prophet in Israel like Moses anymore, whom YHWH has known face to face, **11** in reference to all the signs and the wonders which YHWH sent him to do in the land of Egypt, to Pharaoh, and to all his servants, and to all his land, **12** and in reference to all the strong hand and to all the great fear which Moses did before the eyes of all Israel.

JOSHUA

1 And it comes to pass after the death of Moses, servant of YHWH, that YHWH speaks to Joshua son of Nun, minister of Moses, saying, **2** "My servant Moses is dead, and now, rise, pass over this Jordan, you and all this people, to the land which I am giving to them, to the sons of Israel. **3** Every place on which the sole of your foot treads, I have given it to you, as I have spoken to Moses. **4** From this wilderness and Lebanon, and to the great river, the Euphrates River, all the land of the Hittites, and to the Great Sea—the going in of the sun—is your border. **5** No man stations himself before you all [the] days of your life; as I have been with Moses, I am with you, I do not fail you, nor forsake you; **6** be strong and courageous, for you cause this people to inherit the land which I have sworn to their fathers to give to them. **7** Only, be strong and very courageous, to observe to do according to all the Law which Moses My servant commanded you; you do not turn aside from it right or left, so that you act wisely in every [place] to where you go; **8** the scroll of this Law does not depart out of your mouth, and you have meditated in it by day and by night, so that you observe to do according to all that is written in it, for then you cause your way to prosper, and then you act wisely. **9** Have I not commanded you? Be strong and courageous; do not be terrified nor frightened, for your God YHWH [is] with you in every [place] to where you go." **10** And Joshua commands the authorities of the people, saying, **11** "Pass over into the midst of the camp, and command the people, saying, Prepare provision for yourselves, for within three days you are passing over this Jordan, to go in to possess the land which your God YHWH is giving to you to possess it." **12** And to the Reubenite, and to the Gadite, and to the half of the tribe of Manasseh, Joshua has spoken, saying, **13** "Remember the word which Moses, servant of YHWH, commanded you, saying, Your God YHWH is giving rest to you, and He has given this land to you; **14** your wives, your infants, and your substance, abide in the land which Moses has given to you beyond the Jordan, and you pass over by fifties, before your brothers, all the mighty men of valor, and have helped them, **15** until YHWH gives rest to your brothers as to yourselves, and they have possessed, even they, the land which your God YHWH is giving to them; then you have turned back to the land of your possession, and have possessed it, which Moses, servant of YHWH, has given to you beyond the Jordan, [at] the sun-rising." **16** And they answer Joshua, saying, "All that you have commanded us we do; and to every [place] to where you send us, we go; **17** according to all that we listened to [from] Moses, so we listen to you; surely your God YHWH is with you as He has been with Moses. **18** Any man who provokes your mouth, and does not hear your words, in all that you command him, is put to death; only, be strong and courageous."

2 And Joshua son of Nun silently sends two men, spies, from Shittim, saying, "Go, see the land—and Jericho"; and they go and come into the house of a woman, a harlot, and her name [is] Rahab, and they lie down there. **2** And it is told to the king of Jericho, saying, "Behold, men have come in here tonight, from the sons of Israel, to search the land." **3** And the king of Jericho sends to Rahab, saying, "Bring out the men who are coming to you, who have come into your house, for they have come to search the entirety of the land." **4** And the woman takes the two men, and hides them, and says thus: "The men came to me, and I have not known where they [are] from; **5** and it comes to pass—the gate is to [be] shut—in the dark, and the men have gone out; I have not known to where the men have gone; pursue, hurry after them, for you overtake them"; **6** and she has caused them to go up on the roof, and hides them with the flax wood, which is arranged for her on the roof. **7** And the men have pursued after them the way of the Jordan, by the fords, and they have shut the gate afterward when the pursuers have gone out after them. **8** And before they lie down, she has gone up to them on the roof, **9** and she says to the men, "I have known that YHWH has given the land to you, and that your terror has fallen on us, and that all the inhabitants of the land have melted at your presence. **10** For we have heard how YHWH dried up the waters of the Red Sea at your presence, in your going out of Egypt, and that which you have done to the two kings of the Amorite who [are] beyond the Jordan; to Sihon and to Og whom you devoted. **11** And we hear, and our heart melts, and there has not stood anymore spirit in [any] man from your presence, for He, your God YHWH, [is] God in the heavens above and on the earth below. **12** And now, please swear to me by YHWH—because I have done kindness with you—that you have done, even you, kindness with the house of my father, and have given a true token to me, **13** and have kept alive my father, and my mother, and my brothers, and my sisters, and all that they have, and have delivered our souls from death." **14** And the men say to her, "Our soul to die for yours; if you do not declare this—our matter, then it has been, in YHWH's giving this land to us, that we have done kindness and truth with you." **15** And she causes them to go down by a rope through the window, for her house [is] in the side of the wall, and she [is] dwelling in the wall; **16** and she says to them, "Go to the mountain, lest the pursuers come on you; and you have been hidden there three days until the turning back of the pursuers, and afterward you go on your way." **17** And the men say to her, "We are acquitted of this, your oath, which you have caused us to swear: **18** behold, we are coming into the land, bind this line of scarlet thread to the window by which you have caused us to go down, and gather your father, and your mother, and your brothers, and all the house of your father to you, to the house; **19** and it has been, anyone who goes out from the doors of your house outside, his blood [is] on his head, and we are innocent; and anyone who is with you in the house, his blood [is] on our head, if a hand is on him; **20** and if you declare this—our matter, then we have been acquitted from your oath which you have caused us to swear." **21** And she says, "According to your words, so it [is]"; and she sends them away, and they go; and she binds the scarlet line to the window. **22** And they go, and come to the mountain, and abide there three days until the pursuers have turned back; and the pursuers seek in all the way, and have not found. **23** And the two men turn back, and come down from the hill, and pass over, and come to Joshua son of Nun, and recount to him all that has come on them; **24** and they say to Joshua, "Surely YHWH has given all the land into our hand; and also, all the inhabitants of the land have melted at our presence."

3 And Joshua rises early in the morning, and they journey from Shittim, and come to the Jordan, he and all the sons of Israel, and they lodge there before they pass over. **2** And it comes to pass, at the end of three days, that the authorities pass over into the midst of the camp, **3** and command the people, saying, "When you see the Ark of the Covenant of your God YHWH, and the priests, the Levites, carrying it, then you journey from your place, and have gone after it; **4** only, a distance is between you and it, about two thousand cubits by measure; you do not come near to it, so that you know the way in which you go, for you have not passed over in the way before." **5** And Joshua says to the people, "Sanctify yourselves, for tomorrow YHWH does wonders in your midst." **6** And Joshua speaks to the priests, saying, "Take up the Ark of the Covenant, and pass over before the people"; and they take up the Ark of the Covenant, and go before the people. **7** And YHWH says to Joshua, "This day I begin to make you great in the eyes of all Israel, so that they know that as I was with Moses I am with you; **8** and you, command the priests carrying the Ark of the Covenant, saying, When you come to the extremity of the waters of the Jordan, stand in the Jordan." **9** And Joshua says to the sons of Israel, "Come near here, and hear the words of your God YHWH"; **10** and Joshua says, "By this you know that the living God [is] in your midst, and He certainly dispossesses from before you the Canaanite, and the Hittite, and the Hivite, and the Perizzite, and the Girgashite, and the Amorite, and the Jebusite: **11** behold, the Ark of the Covenant of the Lord of all the earth is passing over before you into the Jordan; **12** and now, take for yourselves twelve men out of the tribes of Israel, one man—one man for a tribe; **13** and it has been, at the resting of the soles of the feet of the priests carrying the Ark of YHWH, Lord of all the earth, in the waters of the Jordan, the waters of the Jordan are cut off—the waters which are coming down from above—and they stand—one heap."

JOSHUA

14 And it comes to pass, in the journeying of the people from their tents to pass over the Jordan, and of the priests carrying the Ark of the Covenant before the people, **15** and at those carrying the Ark coming to the Jordan, and the feet of the priests carrying the Ark have been dipped in the extremity of the waters (and the Jordan is full over all its banks all the days of harvest)— **16** that the waters stand; those coming down from above have risen—one heap, very far above Adam, the city which [is] at the side of Zaretan; and those going down by the Sea of the Plain (the Salt Sea), have been completely cut off; and the people have passed through opposite Jericho; **17** and the priests carrying the Ark of the Covenant of YHWH stand on dry ground in the midst of the Jordan—established, and all Israel are passing over on dry ground until all the nation has completed to pass over the Jordan.

4 And it comes to pass, when all the nation has completed to pass over the Jordan, that YHWH speaks to Joshua, saying, **2** "Take for yourselves twelve men out of the people, one man—one man out of a tribe; **3** and command them, saying, Take up for yourselves from this [place], from the midst of the Jordan, from the established standing-place of the feet of the priests, twelve stones, and you have removed them over with you, and placed them in the lodging-place in which you lodge tonight." **4** And Joshua calls to the twelve men whom he prepared out of the sons of Israel, one man—one man out of a tribe; **5** and Joshua says to them, "Pass over before the Ark of your God YHWH into the midst of the Jordan, and each of you lift up one stone on his shoulder, according to the number of the tribes of the sons of Israel, **6** so that this is a sign in your midst when your children ask hereafter, saying, What [are] these stones to you? **7** That you have said to them, Because the waters of the Jordan were cut off, at the presence of the Ark of the Covenant of YHWH; in its passing over into the Jordan the waters of the Jordan were cut off; and these stones have been for a memorial to the sons of Israel for all time." **8** And the sons of Israel do so as Joshua commanded, and take up twelve stones out of the midst of the Jordan, as YHWH has spoken to Joshua, according to the number of the tribes of the sons of Israel, and remove them over with them to the lodging-place, and place them there, **9** even the twelve stones Joshua has raised up out of the midst of the Jordan, the place of the standing of the feet of the priests carrying the Ark of the Covenant, and they are there to this day. **10** And the priests carrying the Ark are standing in the midst of the Jordan until the completion of the whole thing which YHWH commanded Joshua to speak to the people, according to all that Moses commanded Joshua, and the people hurry and pass over. **11** And it comes to pass, when all the people have completed to pass over, that the Ark of YHWH passes over, and the priests, in the presence of the people; **12** and the sons of Reuben, and the sons of Gad, and the half of the tribe of Manasseh, pass over, by fifties, before the sons of Israel, as Moses had spoken to them; **13** about forty thousand, armed ones of the host, passed over before YHWH for battle, to the plains of Jericho. **14** On that day YHWH has made Joshua great in the eyes of all Israel, and they fear him, as they feared Moses, all [the] days of his life. **15** And YHWH speaks to Joshua, saying, **16** "Command the priests carrying the Ark of the Testimony, and they come up out of the Jordan." **17** And Joshua commands the priests, saying, "Come up out of the Jordan." **18** And it comes to pass, in the coming up of the priests carrying the Ark of the Covenant of YHWH out of the midst of the Jordan—the soles of the feet of the priests have been drawn up into the dry ground—and the waters of the Jordan return to their place, and go over all its banks as before. **19** And the people have come up out of the Jordan on the tenth of the first month, and encamp in Gilgal, in the extremity east of Jericho; **20** and these twelve stones, which they have taken out of the Jordan, Joshua has raised up in Gilgal. **21** And he speaks to the sons of Israel, saying, "When your sons ask their fathers hereafter, saying, What [are] these stones? **22** Then you have caused your sons to know, saying, Israel passed over this Jordan on dry land; **23** because your God YHWH dried up the waters of the Jordan at your presence, until your passing over, as your God YHWH did to the Red Sea which He dried up at our presence until our passing over; **24** so that all the people of the land know the hand of YHWH—that it [is]

JOSHUA

strong, so that you have feared your God YHWH [for] all the days."

5 And it comes to pass, when all the kings of the Amorite which [are] beyond the Jordan, toward the sea, and all the kings of the Canaanite which [are] by the sea, hear how that YHWH has dried up the waters of the Jordan at the presence of the sons of Israel until their passing over, that their heart is melted, and there has not been anymore spirit in them because of the presence of the sons of Israel. **2** At that time YHWH said to Joshua, "Make knives of flint for yourself, and return, circumcise the sons of Israel a second time"; **3** and Joshua makes knives of flint for himself, and circumcises the sons of Israel at the height of the foreskins. **4** And this [is] the thing [for] which Joshua circumcises [them]: all the people who are coming out of Egypt, who are males, all the men of war have died in the wilderness, in the way, in their coming out of Egypt, **5** for all the people who are coming out were circumcised, and all the people who [are] born in the wilderness, in the way, in their coming out from Egypt, they have not circumcised; **6** for forty years the sons of Israel have gone in the wilderness, until all the nation of the men of war who are coming out of Egypt, who did not listen to the voice of YHWH, to whom YHWH has sworn not to show them the land which YHWH swore to their fathers to give to us, a land flowing with milk and honey, are consumed; **7** and He raised up their sons in their stead, Joshua has circumcised them, for they have been uncircumcised, for they have not circumcised them in the way. **8** And it comes to pass, when all the nation has completed to be circumcised, that they abide in their places in the camp until their recovering; **9** and YHWH says to Joshua, "Today I have rolled the reproach of Egypt from off you"; and [one] calls the name of that place Gilgal to this day. **10** And the sons of Israel encamp in Gilgal, and make the Passover on the fourteenth day of the month, at evening, in the plains of Jericho; **11** and they eat of the old grain of the land on the next day of the Passover, unleavened things and roasted [grain], on this very same day; **12** and the manna ceases on the next day in their eating of the old grain of the land, and there has been no more manna for [the] sons of Israel, and they eat of the increase of the land of Canaan in that year. **13** And it comes to pass in Joshua's being by Jericho, that he lifts up his eyes, and looks, and behold, [there is] one standing in front of him, and his drawn sword [is] in his hand, and Joshua goes to him, and says to him, "Are you for us or for our adversaries?" **14** And He says, "No, for I [am] Prince of YHWH's host; now I have come"; and Joshua falls on his face to the earth, and pays respect, and says to Him, "What is my Lord speaking to His servant?" **15** And the Prince of YHWH's host says to Joshua, "Cast off your shoe from off your foot, for the place on which you are standing is holy"; and Joshua does so.

6 And Jericho shuts itself up, and is shut up, because of the presence of the sons of Israel—none going out, and none coming in. **2** And YHWH says to Joshua, "See, I have given Jericho and its king into your hand—mighty men of valor, **3** and you have surrounded the city—all the men of battle—going around the city once; thus you do [for] six days; **4** and seven priests carry seven horns of the rams before the Ark, and on the seventh day you go around the city seven times, and the priests blow with the horns, **5** and it has been, in the prolonging of the horn of the ram, in your hearing the voice of the horn, all the people shout [with] a great shout, and the wall of the city has fallen under it, and the people have gone up, each straight before him." **6** And Joshua son of Nun calls to the priests and says to them, "Carry the Ark of the Covenant, and seven priests carry seven horns of the rams before the Ark of YHWH"; **7** and He said to the people, "Pass over, and go around the city, and he who is armed passes over before the Ark of YHWH." **8** And it comes to pass, when Joshua speaks to the people, that the seven priests carrying seven horns of the rams before YHWH have passed over and blown with the horns, and the Ark of the Covenant of YHWH is going after them; **9** and he who is armed is going before the priests blowing the horns, and he who is gathering up is going after the Ark, going on and blowing with the horns; **10** and Joshua has commanded the people, saying, "Do not shout, nor cause your voice to be heard, nor does a word go out from your mouth, until the day of my saying to you, Shout! Then

JOSHUA

you have shouted." **11** And the Ark of YHWH goes around the city, going around once, and they come into the camp, and lodge in the camp. **12** And Joshua rises early in the morning, and the priests carry the Ark of YHWH, **13** and seven priests carrying seven horns of the rams before the Ark of YHWH are walking, going on, and they have blown with the horns—and he who is armed is going before them, and he who is gathering up is going behind the Ark of YHWH—going on and blowing with the horns. **14** And they go around the city once on the second day, and return to the camp; thus they have done [for] six days. **15** And it comes to pass, on the seventh day, that they rise early, at the ascending of the dawn, and go around the city, according to this manner, seven times; (only on that day have they gone around the city seven times); **16** and it comes to pass, at the seventh time, the priests have blown with the horns, and Joshua says to the people, "Shout! For YHWH has given the city to you; **17** and the city has been devoted, it and all that [is] in it, to YHWH; only Rahab the harlot lives, she and all who [are] with her in the house, for she hid the messengers whom we sent; **18** and surely you have kept from the devoted thing, lest you devote [yourselves], and have taken from the devoted thing, and have made the camp of Israel become a devoted thing, and have troubled it; **19** and all the silver and gold, and vessels of bronze and iron—it [is] holy to YHWH; it comes into the treasury of YHWH." **20** And the people shout, and blow with the horns, and it comes to pass, when the people hear the voice of the horn, that the people shout [with] a great shout, and the wall falls under it, and the people goes up into the city, each straight before him, and they capture the city; **21** and they devote all that [is] in the city, from man even to woman, from young even to aged, even to ox, and sheep, and donkey, by the mouth of the sword. **22** And Joshua said to the two men who are spying out the land, "Go into the house of the woman, the harlot, and bring out the woman from there, and all whom she has, as you have sworn to her." **23** And the young men, those spying, go in and bring out Rahab, and her father, and her mother, and her brothers, and all whom she has; indeed, they have brought out all her relatives, and place them at the outside of the camp of Israel. **24** And they have burned the city with fire, and all that [is] in it; only, the silver and the gold, and the vessels of bronze, and of iron, they have given [to] the treasury of the house of YHWH; **25** and Rahab the harlot, and the house of her father, and all whom she has, Joshua has kept alive; and she dwells in the midst of Israel to this day, for she hid the messengers whom Joshua sent to spy out Jericho. **26** And Joshua adjures [them] at that time, saying, "Cursed [is] the man before YHWH who raises up and has built this city, [even] Jericho; he lays its foundation in his firstborn, and he sets up its doors in his youngest." **27** And YHWH is with Joshua, and his fame is in all the land.

7 And the sons of Israel commit a trespass in the devoted thing, and Achan, son of Carmi, son of Zabdi, son of Zerah, of the tribe of Judah, takes from the devoted thing, and the anger of YHWH burns against the sons of Israel. **2** And Joshua sends men from Jericho to Ai, which [is] near Beth-Aven, on the east of Bethel, and speaks to them, saying, "Go up and spy out the land"; and the men go up and spy Ai, **3** and they return to Joshua, and say to him, "Do not let all the people go up; let about two thousand men, or about three thousand men, go up, and they strike Ai; do not cause all the people to labor there; for they [are] few." **4** So about three thousand men of the people go up from there, and they flee before the men of Ai, **5** and the men of Ai strike about thirty-six men from them, and pursue them before the gate to Shebarim, and they strike them in Morad; and the heart of the people is melted, and becomes water. **6** And Joshua tears his garments, and falls on his face to the earth before the Ark of YHWH until the evening, he and [the] elderly of Israel, and they cause dust to go up on their head. **7** And Joshua says, "Aah! Lord YHWH, why have You caused this people to pass over the Jordan at all, to give us into the hand of the Amorite to destroy us? And oh that we had been willing—and we dwell beyond the Jordan! **8** Oh, Lord, what do I say, after that Israel has turned the neck before its enemies? **9** And the Canaanite and all the inhabitants of the land hear, and have come around against us, and cut off our name from the earth; and what do You do for Your great Name?" **10** And YHWH says to Joshua, "Rise, for you—why this—[that]

JOSHUA

you [are] falling on your face? **11** Israel has sinned, and they have also transgressed My covenant which I commanded them, and also taken of the devoted thing, and also stolen, and also deceived, and also put [it] among their vessels, **12** and the sons of Israel have not been able to stand before their enemies; they turn the neck before their enemies, for they have become a devoted thing; I do not add to be with you—if you do not destroy the devoted thing from your midst. **13** Rise, sanctify the people, and you have said, Sanctify yourselves for tomorrow; for thus said YHWH, God of Israel: A devoted thing [is] in your midst, O Israel, you are not able to stand before your enemies until your turning aside the devoted thing from your midst; **14** and you have been brought near in the morning by your tribes, and it has been [that] the tribe which YHWH captures draws near by families, and the family which YHWH captures draws near by households, and the household which YHWH captures draws near by men; **15** and it has been, he who is captured with the devoted thing is burned with fire, he and all that he has, because he has transgressed the covenant of YHWH, and because he has done folly in Israel." **16** And Joshua rises early in the morning, and brings Israel near by its tribes, and the tribe of Judah is captured; **17** and he brings the family of Judah near, and he captures the family of the Zerahite; and he brings the family of the Zerahite near by men, and Zabdi is captured; **18** and he brings his household near by men, and Achan—son of Carmi, son of Zabdi, son of Zerah, of the tribe of Judah—is captured. **19** And Joshua says to Achan, "My son, please give glory to YHWH, God of Israel, and give thanks to Him, and now declare to me what you have done—do not hide [it] from me." **20** And Achan answers Joshua and says, "Truly I have sinned against YHWH, God of Israel, and I have done thus and thus; **21** and I see among the spoil a good robe of Shinar, and two hundred shekels of silver, and one wedge of gold, whose weight [is] fifty shekels, and I desire them, and take them; and behold, they [are] hid in the earth, in the midst of my tent, and the silver [is] under it." **22** And Joshua sends messengers, and they run to the tent, and behold, it is hidden in his tent, and the silver [is] under it; **23** and they take them out of the midst of the tent, and bring them to Joshua, and to all the sons of Israel, and pour them out before YHWH. **24** And Joshua takes Achan son of Zerah, and the silver, and the robe, and the wedge of gold, and his sons, and his daughters, and his ox, and his donkey, and his flock, and his tent, and all that he has, and all Israel with him, and they brought them up [to] the Valley of Achor. **25** And Joshua says, "Why have you troubled us? YHWH troubles you this day!" And all Israel cast stone at him, and they burn them with fire, and they stone them with stones, **26** and they raise up a great heap of stones over him to this day, and YHWH turns back from the heat of His anger, therefore [one] has called the name of that place "Valley of Achor" until this day.

8 And YHWH says to Joshua, "Do not fear, nor be frightened, take with you all the people of war, and rise, go up to Ai; see, I have given into your hand the king of Ai, and his people, and his city, and his land, **2** and you have done to Ai and to her king as you have done to Jericho and to her king; only spoil its spoil and its livestock for yourselves; for you set an ambush for the city at its rear." **3** And Joshua rises, and all the people of war, to go up to Ai, and Joshua chooses thirty thousand men, mighty men of valor, and sends them away by night, **4** and commands them, saying, "See, you are ones lying in wait against the city, at the rear of the city, you do not go very far off from the city, and all of you have been prepared, **5** and I and all the people who [are] with me draw near to the city, and it has come to pass, when they come out to meet us as at the first, and we have fled before them, **6** and they have come out after us until we have drawn them out of the city, for they say, They are fleeing before us as at the first, and we have fled before them, **7** and you rise from the ambush, and have occupied the city, and your God YHWH has given it into your hand; **8** and it has been, when you capture the city, you burn the city with fire, you do according to the word of YHWH, see, I have commanded you." **9** And Joshua sends them away, and they go to the ambush, and abide between Bethel and Ai, on the west of Ai; and Joshua lodges on that night in the midst of the people. **10** And Joshua rises early in the morning, and inspects the people, and goes up, he and [the] elderly of

JOSHUA

Israel, before the people to Ai; **11** and all the people of war who [are] with him have gone up, and draw near and come in before the city, and encamp on the north of Ai; and the valley [is] between him and Ai. **12** And he takes about five thousand men, and sets them [for] an ambush between Bethel and Ai, on the west of the city; **13** and they set the people, all the camp which [is] on the north of the city, and its rear on the west of the city, and that night Joshua goes on into the midst of the valley. **14** And it comes to pass, when the king of Ai sees [it], that he hurries, and rises early, and the men of the city go out to meet Israel for battle, he and all his people, at the appointed time, at the front of the plain, and he has not known that an ambush [is] against him, on the rear of the city. **15** And Joshua and all Israel [seem] struck before them, and flee the way of the wilderness, **16** and all the people who [are] in the city are called to pursue after them, and they pursue after Joshua, and are drawn away out of the city, **17** and there has not been a man left in Ai and Bethel who has not gone out after Israel, and they leave the city open, and pursue after Israel. **18** And YHWH says to Joshua, "Stretch out with the javelin which [is] in your hand toward Ai, for I give it into your hand"; and Joshua stretches out with the javelin which [is] in his hand toward the city, **19** and the ambush has risen [with] haste, out of its place, and they run at the stretching out of his hand, and go into the city, and capture it, and hurry, and burn the city with fire. **20** And the men of Ai look behind them, and see, and behold, the smoke of the city has gone up to the heavens, and there has not been power in them to flee here and there—and the people who are fleeing to the wilderness have turned against the pursuer— **21** and Joshua and all Israel have seen that the ambush has captured the city, and that the smoke of the city has gone up, and they turn back and strike the men of Ai; **22** and these have come out from the city to meet them, and they are in the midst of Israel, some on this [side], and some on that [side], and they strike them until he has not left a remnant and escaped one to them; **23** and they have caught the king of Ai alive, and bring him near to Joshua. **24** And it comes to pass, at Israel's finishing to slay all the inhabitants of Ai in the field, in the wilderness in which they pursued them (and all of them fall by the mouth of the sword until their consumption), that all of Israel turns back to Ai, and strikes it by the mouth of the sword; **25** and all who fall during the day, of men and of women, are twelve thousand—all men of Ai. **26** And Joshua has not brought back his hand which he stretched out with the javelin until he has devoted all the inhabitants of Ai; **27** only the livestock and the spoil of that city has Israel spoiled for themselves, according to the word of YHWH which He commanded Joshua. **28** And Joshua burns Ai, and makes it a continuous heap—a desolation to this day; **29** and he has hanged the king of Ai on the tree until evening, and at the going in of the sun Joshua has commanded, and they take down his carcass from the tree, and cast it to the opening of the gate of the city, and raise a great heap of stones over it until this day. **30** Then Joshua builds an altar to YHWH, God of Israel, in Mount Ebal, **31** as Moses, servant of YHWH, commanded the sons of Israel, as it is written in the Scroll of the Law of Moses—an altar of whole stones, over which he has not waved iron—and they cause burnt-offerings to go up on it to YHWH, and sacrifice peace-offerings; **32** and he writes there on the stones a copy of the Law of Moses, which he has written in the presence of the sons of Israel. **33** And all Israel, and its elderly, and authorities, and his judges, are standing on this [side] and on that [side] of the Ark, before the priests, the Levites, carrying the Ark of the Covenant of YHWH, the sojourner as well as the native, half of them in front of Mount Gerizim, and the half of them in front of Mount Ebal, as Moses servant of YHWH had commanded to bless the people of Israel at the first. **34** And afterward he has proclaimed all the words of the Law, the blessing and the reviling, according to all that is written in the Scroll of the Law; **35** there has not been a thing of all that Moses commanded which Joshua has not proclaimed before all the assembly of Israel, and the women, and the infants, and the sojourner who is going in their midst.

9 And it comes to pass, when all the kings who [are] beyond the Jordan, in the hill-country, and in the low-country, and in every haven of the Great Sea, toward Lebanon, the Hittite, and the Amorite, the Canaanite, the Perizzite, the Hivite, and the

JOSHUA

Jebusite, hear— **2** that they gather themselves together to fight with Joshua, and with Israel—[with] one mouth. **3** And the inhabitants of Gibeon have heard that which Joshua has done to Jericho and to Ai, **4** and they work, even they, with subtlety, and go, and feign to be ambassadors, and take old sacks for their donkeys, and wine-bottles, old, and split, and bound up, **5** and sandals, old and patched, on their feet, and old garments on them, and all the bread of their provision is dry—it was crumbs. **6** And they go to Joshua, to the camp at Gilgal, and say to him, and to the men of Israel, "We have come from a far-off land, and now, make a covenant with us"; **7** and the men of Israel say to the Hivite, "It may be [that] you are dwelling in our midst, so how do we make a covenant with you?" **8** And they say to Joshua, "We [are] your servants." And Joshua says to them, "Who [are] you? And where do you come from?" **9** And they say to him, "Your servants have come from a very far-off land, for the Name of your God YHWH, for we have heard His fame, and all that He has done in Egypt, **10** and all that He has done to the two kings of the Amorite who [are] beyond the Jordan, to Sihon king of Heshbon, and to Og king of Bashan, who [is] in Ashtaroth. **11** And our elderly, and all the inhabitants of our land speak to us, saying, Take provision in your hand for the way, and go to meet them, and you have said to them: We [are] your servants, and now, make a covenant with us; **12** this bread of ours—we provided ourselves with it hot out of our houses, on the day of our coming out to go to you, and now, behold, it is dry, and has been crumbs; **13** and these [are] the wine-bottles which we filled, new, and behold, they have split; and these, our garments and our sandals, have become old, from the exceeding greatness of the way." **14** And the men take of their provision, and have not asked the mouth of YHWH; **15** and Joshua makes peace with them, and makes a covenant with them, to keep them alive; and the princes of the congregation swear to them. **16** And it comes to pass, that at the end of three days after they have made a covenant with them, that they hear that they [are] their neighbors—that they are dwelling in their midst. **17** And the sons of Israel journey and come to their cities on the third day— and their cities [are] Gibeon, and Chephirah, and Beeroth, and Kirjath-Jearim— **18** and the sons of Israel have not struck them, for the princes of the congregation have sworn to them by YHWH, God of Israel, and all the congregation murmur against the princes. **19** And all the princes say to all the congregation, "We have sworn to them by YHWH, God of Israel; and now, we are not able to come against them; **20** we do this to them, and have kept them alive, and wrath is not on us, because of the oath which we have sworn to them." **21** And the princes say to them, "They live, and are hewers of wood and drawers of water for all the congregation, as the princes spoke to them." **22** And Joshua calls for them, and speaks to them, saying, "Why have you deceived us, saying, We are very far from you, yet you [are] dwelling in our midst? **23** And now you are cursed, and none of you is cut off [from being] a servant, even hewers of wood and drawers of water, for the house of my God." **24** And they answer Joshua and say, "Because it was certainly declared to your servants that your God YHWH commanded His servant Moses to give all the land to you, and to destroy all the inhabitants of the land from before you; and we fear greatly for ourselves because of you, and we do this thing; **25** and now, behold, we [are] in your hand, as [it is] good, and as [it is] right in your eyes to do to us— do." **26** And he does to them so, and delivers them from the hand of the sons of Israel, and they have not slain them; **27** and on that day Joshua makes them hewers of wood and drawers of water for the congregation, and for the altar of YHWH, to this day, at the place which He chooses.

10 And it comes to pass, when Adoni-Zedek king of Jerusalem hears that Joshua has captured Ai, and devotes it (as he had done to Jericho and to her king so he has done to Ai and to her king), and that the inhabitants of Gibeon have made peace with Israel, and are in their midst— **2** that they are greatly afraid, because Gibeon [is] a great city, as one of the royal cities, and because it [is] greater than Ai, and all its men [are] heroes. **3** And Adoni-Zedek king of Jerusalem sends to Hoham king of Hebron, and to Piram king of Jarmuth, and to Japhia king of Lachish, and to Debir king of Eglon, saying, **4** "Come up to me, and help me, and we strike Gibeon, for it

JOSHUA

has made peace with Joshua, and with the sons of Israel." **5** And five kings of the Amorite (the king of Jerusalem, the king of Hebron, the king of Jarmuth, the king of Lachish, the king of Eglon) are gathered together, and go up, they and all their camps, and encamp against Gibeon, and fight against it. **6** And the men of Gibeon send to Joshua, to the camp at Gilgal, saying, "Do not let your hand cease from your servants; come up to us [with] haste, and give safety to us, and help us; for all the kings of the Amorite, dwelling in the hill-country, have been assembled against us." **7** And Joshua goes up from Gilgal, he, and all the people of war with him, even all the mighty men of valor. **8** And YHWH says to Joshua, "Do not be afraid of them, for I have given them into your hand, there does not stand a man of them in your presence." **9** And Joshua comes to them suddenly (all the night he has gone up from Gilgal), **10** and YHWH crushes them before Israel, and strikes them [with] a great striking at Gibeon, and pursues them the way of the ascent of Beth-Horon, and strikes them to Azekah, and to Makkedah. **11** And it comes to pass, in their fleeing from the face of Israel—they [are] in the descent of Beth-Horon—and YHWH has cast great stones on them out of the heavens, to Azekah, and they die; more are they who have died by the hailstones than they whom the sons of Israel have slain by the sword. **12** Then Joshua speaks to YHWH in the day of YHWH's giving up the Amorites before the sons of Israel, and he says before the eyes of Israel, "Sun—stand still in Gibeon; and moon—in the Valley of Ajalon"; **13** and the sun stands still, and the moon has stood—until the nation takes vengeance [on] its enemies; is it not written on the Scroll of the Upright, "and the sun stands in the midst of the heavens, and has not hurried to go in—as a perfect day?" **14** And there has not been like that day before it or after it, for YHWH's listening to the voice of a man; for YHWH is fighting for Israel. **15** And Joshua turns back, and all Israel with him, to the camp at Gilgal. **16** And these five kings flee, and are hidden in a cave at Makkedah, **17** and it is declared to Joshua, saying, "The five kings have been found hidden in a cave at Makkedah." **18** And Joshua says, "Roll great stones to the mouth of the cave, and appoint men over it to watch them; **19** and you, do not stand, pursue after your enemies, and you have struck them from the rear; do not permit them to go into their cities, for your God YHWH has given them into your hand." **20** And it comes to pass, when Joshua and the sons of Israel finish to strike them [with] a very great striking until they are consumed, and the remnant who have remained of them go into the fortified cities, **21** that all the people return to the camp, to Joshua, [at] Makkedah, in peace; none moved his tongue sharply against the sons of Israel. **22** And Joshua says, "Open the mouth of the cave, and bring out to me these five kings from the cave"; **23** and they do so, and bring out to him these five kings from the cave: the king of Jerusalem, the king of Hebron, the king of Jarmuth, the king of Lachish, the king of Eglon. **24** And it comes to pass, when they bring out these kings to Joshua, that Joshua calls to every man of Israel, and says to the captains of the men of war, who have gone with him, "Draw near, set your feet on the necks of these kings"; and they draw near, and set their feet on their necks. **25** And Joshua says to them, "Do not fear, nor be frightened; be strong and courageous; for thus does YHWH do to all your enemies with whom you are fighting"; **26** and Joshua strikes them afterward, and puts them to death, and hangs them on five trees; and they are hanging on the trees until the evening. **27** And it comes to pass, at the time of the going in of the sun, Joshua has commanded, and they take them down from off the trees, and cast them into the cave where they had been hid, and put great stones on the mouth of the cave until this very day. **28** And Joshua has captured Makkedah on that day, and he strikes it by the mouth of the sword, and he has devoted its king, them and every person who [is] in it—he has not left a remnant; and he does to the king of Makkedah as he did to the king of Jericho. **29** And Joshua passes over, and all Israel with him, from Makkedah [to] Libnah, and fights with Libnah; **30** and YHWH also gives it into the hand of Israel, and its king, and [Joshua] strikes it by the mouth of the sword, and every person who [is] in it—he does not leave a remnant in it; and he does to its king as he did to the king of Jericho. **31** And Joshua passes over, and all Israel with him, from Libnah to Lachish, and encamps against it, and fights against it. **32** And YHWH gives Lachish into the hand of Israel, and [Joshua] captures it on the second day, and strikes it by the mouth of the sword, and every person who [is] in it, according to all that he did to Libnah. **33** Then Horam king of Gezer has come up to help Lachish, and Joshua strikes him and his people, until he has not left a remnant to him. **34** And Joshua passes over, and all Israel with him, from Lachish to Eglon, and they encamp against it, and fight against it, **35** and capture it on that day, and strike it by the mouth of the sword, and every person who [is] in it he has devoted on that day, according to all that he did to Lachish. **36** And Joshua goes up, and all Israel with him, from Eglon to Hebron, and they fight against it, **37** and capture it, and strike it by the mouth of the sword, and its king, and all its cities, and every person who [is] in it—he has not left a remnant—according to all that he did to Eglon—and devotes it, and every person who [is] in it. **38** And Joshua turns back, and all Israel with him, to Debir, and fights against it, **39** and captures it, and its king, and all its cities, and they strike them by the mouth of the sword, and devote every person who [is] in it—he has not left a remnant; as he did to Hebron so he did to Debir, and to its king, and as he did to Libnah, and to its king. **40** And Joshua strikes all the land of the hill-country, and of the south, and of the low-country, and of the springs, and all their kings—he has not left a remnant, and he has devoted all that breathe, as Y<small>HWH</small>, God of Israel, commanded. **41** And Joshua strikes them from Kadesh-Barnea, even to Gaza, and all the land of Goshen, even to Gibeon; **42** and Joshua has captured all these kings and their land [at] one time, for Y<small>HWH</small>, God of Israel, is fighting for Israel. **43** And Joshua turns back, and all Israel with him, to the camp at Gilgal.

11 And it comes to pass, when Jabin king of Hazor hears, that he sends to Jobab king of Madon, and to the king of Shimron, and to the king of Achshaph, **2** and to the kings who [are] on the north in the hill-country, and in the plain south of Chinneroth, and in the low country, and in the elevations of Dor, on the west, **3** [to] the Canaanite on the east, and on the west, and the Amorite, and the Hittite, and the Perizzite, and the Jebusite in the hill-country, and the Hivite under Hermon, in the land of Mizpeh— **4** and they go out, they and all their camps with them, a people numerous, as the sand which [is] on the seashore for multitude, and [with] very many horse and charioteer; **5** and all these kings are met together, and they come and encamp together at the waters of Merom, to fight with Israel. **6** And Y<small>HWH</small> says to Joshua, "Do not be afraid of their presence, for about this time tomorrow I am giving all of them slain before Israel; hamstring their horses, and burn their chariots with fire." **7** And Joshua comes, and all the people of war with him, against them by the waters of Merom, and they suddenly fall on them; **8** and Y<small>HWH</small> gives them into the hand of Israel, and they strike them and pursue them to the great Sidon, and to Misrephoth-Maim, and to the Valley of Mizpeh eastward, and they strike them, until he has not left a remnant to them; **9** and Joshua does to them as Y<small>HWH</small> commanded to him; he has hamstrung their horses, and burned their chariots with fire. **10** And Joshua turns back at that time, and captures Hazor, and he has struck its king by the sword; for Hazor [was] formerly head of all these kingdoms; **11** and they strike every person who [is] in it by the mouth of the sword; he has devoted—he has not left anyone breathing, and he has burned Hazor with fire; **12** and all the cities of these kings, and all their kings, Joshua has captured, and he strikes them by the mouth of the sword; he devoted them, as Moses, servant of Y<small>HWH</small>, commanded. **13** Only, all the cities which are standing by their hill, Israel has not burned them—except Joshua has burned Hazor, only; **14** and all the spoil of these cities, and the livestock, the sons of Israel have spoiled for themselves; only, they have struck every man by the mouth of the sword, until their destroying them; they have not left anyone breathing. **15** As Y<small>HWH</small> commanded His servant Moses, so Moses commanded Joshua, and so Joshua has done; he has not turned aside a thing of all that Y<small>HWH</small> commanded Moses. **16** And Joshua takes all this land: the hill-country, and all the south, and all the land of Goshen, and the low country, and the plain, even the hill-country of Israel and its low lands, **17** from the Mount of Halak, which is going up [to] Seir, and to Ba'al-Gad, in the Valley of Lebanon, under Mount Hermon; and he has captured all their kings, and he strikes them, and puts them to death. **18** Joshua has made war with all these kings [for] many days; **19** there has not been a city which made peace with the sons of Israel except the Hivite, inhabitants of Gibeon; they have taken the whole in battle; **20** for it has been from Y<small>HWH</small> to strengthen their heart, to meet in battle with Israel, in order to devote them, so that they have no grace, but in order to destroy them, as Y<small>HWH</small> commanded Moses. **21** And Joshua comes at that time, and cuts off the Anakim from the hill-country, from Hebron, from Debir, from Anab, and from all the hill-country of Judah, and from all the hill-country of Israel; Joshua has devoted them with their cities. **22** There has not been Anakim left in the land of the sons of Israel; only in Gaza, in Gath, and in Ashdod, were they left. **23** And Joshua takes the whole of the land, according to all that Y<small>HWH</small> has spoken to Moses, and Joshua gives it for an inheritance to Israel according to their divisions, by their tribes; and the land has rest from war.

12 And these [are] kings of the land whom the sons of Israel have struck, and possess their land beyond the Jordan, at the sun-rising, from the Brook of Arnon to Mount Hermon, and all the plain eastward: **2** Sihon, king of the Amorite, who is dwelling in Heshbon, ruling from Aroer which [is] on the border of the Brook of Arnon, and the middle of the brook, and half of Gilead, and to the Brook of Jabok, the border of the sons of Ammon; **3** and the plain to the Sea of Chinneroth eastward, and to the Sea of the Plain (the Salt Sea) eastward, the way to Beth-Jeshimoth, and from the south under the Springs of Pisgah. **4** And the border of Og king of Bashan (of the remnant of the Rephaim), who is dwelling in Ashtaroth and in Edrei, **5** and ruling in Mount Hermon, and in Salcah, and in all Bashan, to the border of the Geshurite, and the Maachathite, and the half of Gilead, the border of Sihon king of Heshbon. **6** Moses, servant of Y<small>HWH</small>, and the sons of Israel have struck them, and Moses, servant of Y<small>HWH</small>, gives it—a possession to the Reubenite, and to the Gadite, and to the half of the tribe of Manasseh. **7** And these [are] kings of the land whom Joshua and the sons of Israel have struck beyond the Jordan westward, from Ba‘al-Gad, in the Valley of Lebanon, and to the Mount of Halak, which is going up to Seir; and Joshua gives it to the tribes of Israel—a possession according to their divisions; **8** in the hill-country, and in the low country, and in the plain, and in the springs, and in the wilderness, and in the south; the Hittite, the Amorite, and the Canaanite, the Perizzite, the Hivite, and the Jebusite: **9** the king of Jericho, one; the king of Ai, which [is] beside Bethel, one; **10** the king of Jerusalem, one; the king of Hebron, one; **11** the king of Jarmuth, one; the king of Lachish, one; **12** the king of Eglon, one; the king of Gezer, one; **13** the king of Debir, one; the king of Geder, one; **14** the king of Hormah, one; the king of Arad, one; **15** the king of Libnah, one; the king of Adullam, one; **16** the king of Mekkedah, one; the king of Beth-El, one; **17** the king of Tappuah, one; the king of Hepher, one; **18** the king of Aphek, one; the king of Lasharon, one; **19** the king of Madon, one; the king of Hazor, one; **20** the king of Shimron-Meron, one; the king of Achshaph, one; **21** the king of Taanach, one; the king of Megiddo, one; **22** the king of Kedesh, one; the king of Jokneam of Carmel, one; **23** the king of Dor, at the elevation of Dor, one; the king of the nations of Gilgal, one; **24** the king of Tirzah, one; all the kings [are] thirty-one.

13 And Joshua is old, entering into days, and Y<small>HWH</small> says to him, "You have become aged, you have entered into days; as for the land, very much has been left to possess. **2** This [is] the land that is left: all the circuits of the Philistines, and all Geshuri, **3** from Sihor which [is] on the front of Egypt, and to the border of Ekron northward (it is reckoned to the Canaanite), five princes of the Philistines, the Gazathite, and the Ashdothite, the Eshkalonite, the Gittite, and the Ekronite, also the Avim; **4** from the south, all the land of the Canaanite, and Mearah, which [is] to the Sidonians, to Aphek, to the border of the Amorite; **5** and the land of the Giblite, and all Lebanon, at the sun-rising, from Ba‘al-Gad under Mount Hermon, to the going in to Hamath: **6** all the inhabitants of the hill-country, from Lebanon to Misrephoth-Maim, all the Sidonians: I dispossess them before the sons of Israel; only, cause it to fall to Israel for an inheritance, as I have commanded you. **7** And now, apportion this land for an inheritance to the nine tribes, and half of

JOSHUA

the tribe of Manasseh." **8** With [the other half], the Reubenite and the Gadite have received their inheritance, which Moses has given to them beyond the Jordan eastward, as Moses servant of YHWH has given to them; **9** from Aroer, which [is] on the edge of the Brook of Arnon, and the city which [is] in the midst of the brook, and all the plain of Medeba to Dihon, **10** and all the cities of Sihon king of the Amorite, who reigned in Heshbon, to the border of the sons of Ammon, **11** and Gilead, and the border of the Geshurite, and of the Maachathite, and all Mount Hermon, and all Bashan to Salcah; **12** all the kingdom of Og in Bashan, who reigned in Ashtaroth and in Edrei; he was left of the remnant of the Rephaim, and Moses strikes them, and dispossesses them; **13** and the sons of Israel did not dispossess the Geshurite, and the Maachathite; and Geshur and Maachath dwell in the midst of Israel to this day. **14** Only, he has not given an inheritance to the tribe of Levi; fire-offerings of YHWH, God of Israel, [are] its inheritance, as He has spoken to it. **15** And Moses gives to the tribe of the sons of Reuben, for their families; **16** and the border is to them from Aroer, which [is] on the edge of the Brook of Arnon, and the city which [is] in the midst of the brook, and all the plain by Medeba, **17** Heshbon, and all its cities which [are] in the plain, Dibon, and Bamoth-Ba'al, and Beth-Ba'al-Meon, **18** and Jahazah, and Kedemoth, and Mephaath, **19** and Kirjathaim, and Sibmah, and Zareth-Shahar, on the mountain of the valley, **20** and Beth-Peor, and the Springs of Pisgah, and Beth-Jeshimoth, **21** and all the cities of the plain, and all the kingdom of Sihon king of the Amorite, who reigned in Heshbon, whom Moses struck, with the princes of Midian, Evi, and Rekem, and Zur, and Hur, and Reba, princes of Sihon, inhabitants of the land. **22** And the sons of Israel have slain Balaam, son of Beor, the diviner, with the sword, among their wounded ones. **23** And the border of the sons of Reuben is the Jordan, and [its] border; this [is] the inheritance of the sons of Reuben, for their families, the cities and their villages. **24** And Moses gives to the tribe of Gad, to the sons of Gad, for their families; **25** and the border to them is Jazer, and all the cities of Gilead, and half of the land of the sons of Ammon, to Aroer which [is] on the front of Rabbah, **26** and from Heshbon to Ramath-Mispeh, and Betonim, and from Mahanaim to the border of Debir, **27** and in the valley, Beth-Aram, and Beth-Nimrah, and Succoth, and Zaphon, the rest of the kingdom of Sihon king of Heshbon, the Jordan and [its] border, to the extremity of the Sea of Chinnereth, beyond the Jordan eastward. **28** This [is] the inheritance of the sons of Gad, for their families, the cities and their villages. **29** And Moses gives to the half-tribe of Manasseh; and it is to the half-tribe of the sons of Manasseh, for their families. **30** And their border is from Mahanaim, all Bashan, all the kingdom of Og king of Bashan, and all the small towns of Jair, which [are] in Bashan—sixty cities; **31** and half of Gilead, and Ashteroth, and Edrei, cities of the kingdom of Og in Bashan, [are] to the sons of Machir, son of Manasseh, to the half of the sons of Machir, for their families. **32** These [are] they whom Moses caused to inherit in the plains of Moab beyond the Jordan, [by] Jericho, eastward; **33** and Moses did not give an inheritance to the tribe of Levi; YHWH, God of Israel, Himself, [is] their inheritance, as He has spoken to them.

14 And these [are] they of the sons of Israel who inherited in the land of Canaan, whom Eleazar the priest, and Joshua son of Nun, and the heads of the fathers of the tribes of the sons of Israel, caused to inherit; **2** their inheritance [is] by lot, as YHWH commanded by the hand of Moses, for the nine tribes and the half-tribe; **3** for Moses has given the inheritance of two of the tribes, and of half of the tribe, beyond the Jordan, and he has not given an inheritance to the Levites in their midst; **4** for the sons of Joseph have been two tribes, Manasseh and Ephraim, and they have not given a portion to the Levites in the land, except cities to dwell in, and their outskirts for their livestock, and for their possessions; **5** as YHWH commanded Moses, so the sons of Israel have done, and they apportion the land. **6** And the sons of Judah come near to Joshua in Gilgal, and Caleb son of Jephunneh the Kenezzite says to him, "You have known the word that YHWH has spoken to Moses, the man of God, concerning me and concerning you in Kadesh-Barnea: **7** I [was] a son of forty years in Moses, servant of YHWH, sending me from Kadesh-Barnea, to spy out the

JOSHUA

land, and I bring him back word as with my heart; **8** and my brothers who have gone up with me have caused the heart of the people to melt, and I have been fully after my God YHWH; **9** and Moses swears in that day, saying, Nevertheless—the land on which your foot has trodden, it is to you for an inheritance, and to your sons—for all time, for you have been fully after my God YHWH. **10** And now, behold, YHWH has kept me alive, as He has spoken, these forty-five years, since YHWH spoke this word to Moses when Israel went in the wilderness; and now, behold, I [am] a son of eighty-five years today; **11** yet today I [am] strong as in the day of Moses' sending me; as my power [was] then, so [is] my power now, for battle, and to go out, and to come in. **12** And now, give this hill-country to me, of which YHWH spoke in that day, for you heard in that day, for Anakim [are] there, and great, fortified cities; if [it] so be [that] YHWH [is] with me, then I have dispossessed them, as YHWH has spoken." **13** And Joshua blesses him, and gives Hebron to Caleb son of Jephunneh for an inheritance, **14** therefore Hebron has been to Caleb son of Jephunneh the Kenezzite for an inheritance to this day, because that he was fully after YHWH, God of Israel; **15** and the name of Hebron [was] formerly Kirjath-Arba (the man [was] the greatest among the Anakim); and the land has rest from war.

15 And the lot for the tribe of the sons of Judah, for their families, is to the border of Edom; the wilderness of Zin southward, at the extremity of the south; **2** and to them the south border is at the extremity of the Salt Sea, from the bay which is looking southward; **3** and it has gone out to the south to Maaleh-Akrabbim, and passed over to Zin, and gone up on the south to Kadesh-Barnea, and passed over [to] Hezron, and gone up to Adar, and turned around to Karkaa, **4** and passed over [to] Azmon, and gone out [at] the Brook of Egypt, and the outgoings of the border have been at the sea; this is the south border to you. **5** And the east border [is] the Salt Sea, to the extremity of the Jordan, and the border at the north quarter [is] from the bay of the sea, at the extremity of the Jordan; **6** and the border has gone up [to] Beth-Hoglah, and passed over on the north of Beth-Arabah, and the border has gone up [to] the stone of Bohan son of Reuben: **7** and the border has gone up toward Debir from the Valley of Achor, and northward looking to Gilgal, which [is] opposite the ascent of Adummim, which [is] on the south of the brook, and the border has passed over to the waters of En-Shemesh, and its outgoings have been to En-Rogel; **8** and the border has gone up the Valley of the Son of Hinnom, to the side of the Jebusite on the south (it [is] Jerusalem), and the border has gone up to the top of the hill-country which [is] on the front of the Valley of Hinnom westward, which [is] in the extremity of the Valley of the Rephaim northward; **9** and the border has been marked out, from the top of the hill-country to the fountain of the waters of Nephtoah, and has gone out to the cities of Mount Ephron, and the border has been marked out [to] Ba'alah (it [is] Kirjath-Jearim); **10** and the border has gone around from Ba'alah westward, to Mount Seir, and passed over to the side of Mount Jearim (it [is] Chesalon), on the north, and gone down [to] Beth-Shemesh, and passed over to Timnah; **11** and the border has gone out to the side of Ekron northward, and the border has been marked out [to] Shicron, and has passed over to Mount Ba'alah, and gone out [to] Jabneel; and the outgoings of the border have been at the sea. **12** And the west border [is] to the Great Sea, and [its] border; this [is] the border of the sons of Judah all around for their families. **13** And to Caleb son of Jephunneh he has given a portion in the midst of the sons of Judah, according to the command of YHWH to Joshua, [even] the city of Arba, father of Anak—it [is] Hebron. **14** And Caleb is dispossessing there the three sons of Anak: Sheshai, and Ahiman, and Talmai, children of Anak, **15** and he goes up there to the inhabitants of Debir; and the name of Debir [was] formerly Kirjath-Sepher. **16** And Caleb says, "He who strikes Kirjath-Sephar, and has captured it—I have given my daughter Achsah to him for a wife." **17** And Othniel son of Kenaz, brother of Caleb, captures it, and he gives his daughter Achsah to him for a wife. **18** And it comes to pass, in her coming in, that she persuades him to ask [for] a field from her father, and she comes down off the donkey, and Caleb says to her, "What do you [want]?" **19** And she says, "Give a blessing to me; when you have given me

JOSHUA

the land of the south, then you have given springs of waters to me"; and he gives the upper springs and the lower springs to her. **20** This [is] the inheritance of the tribe of the sons of Judah, for their families. **21** And the cities at the extremity of the tribe of the sons of Judah are to the border of Edom in the south, Kabzeel, and Eder, and Jagur, **22** and Kinah, and Dimonah, and Adadah, **23** and Kedesh, and Hazor, and Ithnan, **24** Ziph, and Telem, and Bealoth, **25** and Hazor, Hadattah, and Kerioth, Hezron (it [is] Hazor), **26** Amam, and Shema, and Moladah, **27** and Hazar-Gaddah, and Heshmon, and Beth-Palet, **28** and Hazar-Shual, and Beer-Sheba, and Bizjothjah, **29** Ba'alah, and Iim, and Azem, **30** and Eltolad, and Chesil, and Hormah, **31** and Ziklag, and Madmannah, and Sansannah, **32** and Lebaoth, and Shilhim, and Ain, and Rimmon; all the cities [are] twenty-nine, and their villages. **33** In the low country: Eshtaol, and Zoreah, and Ashnah, **34** and Zanoah, and En-Gannim, Tappuah, and Enam, **35** Jarmuth, and Adullam, Socoh, and Azekah, **36** and Sharaim, and Adithaim, and Gederah, and Gederothaim; fourteen cities and their villages. **37** Zenan, and Hadashah, and Migdal-Gad, **38** and Dilean, and Mizpeh, and Joktheel, **39** Lachish, and Bozkath, and Eglon, **40** and Cabbon, and Lahmam, and Kithlish, **41** and Gederoth, Beth-Dagon, and Naamah, and Makkedah; sixteen cities and their villages. **42** Libnah, and Ether, and Ashan, **43** and Jiphtah, and Ashnah, and Nezib, **44** and Keilah, and Achzib, and Mareshah; nine cities and their villages. **45** Ekron and its towns and its villages, **46** from Ekron and westward, all that [are] by the side of Ashdod, and their villages. **47** Ashdod, its towns and its villages, Gaza, its towns and its villages, to the Brook of Egypt, and the Great Sea, and [its] border. **48** And in the hill-country: Shamir, and Jattir, and Socoh, **49** and Dannah, and Kirjath-Sannah (it [is] Debir), **50** and Anab, and Eshtemoh, and Anim, **51** and Goshen, and Holon, and Giloh; eleven cities and their villages. **52** Arab, and Dumah, and Eshean, **53** and Janum, and Beth-Tappuah, and Aphekah, **54** and Humtah, and Kirjath-Arba (it [is] Hebron), and Zior; nine cities and their villages. **55** Maon, Carmel, and Ziph, and Juttah, **56** and Jezreel, and Jokdeam, and Zanoah, **57** Cain, Gibeah, and Timnah; ten cities and their villages.

58 Halhul, Beth-Zur, and Gedor, **59** and Maarath, and Beth-Anoth, and Eltekon; six cities and their villages. **60** Kirjath-Ba'al (it [is] Kirjath-Jearim), and Rabbah; two cities and their villages. **61** In the wilderness: Beth-Arabah, Middin, and Secacah, **62** and Nibshan, and the City of Salt, and En-Gedi; six cities and their villages. **63** As for the Jebusites, inhabitants of Jerusalem, the sons of Judah have not been able to dispossess them, and the Jebusite dwells with the sons of Judah in Jerusalem to this day.

16 And the lot for the sons of Joseph goes out from Jordan [by] Jericho, to the waters of Jericho on the east, to the wilderness going up from Jericho in the hill-country of Beth-El, **2** and has gone out from Beth-El to Luz, and passed over to the border of Archi [to] Ataroth, **3** and gone down westward to the border of Japhleti, to the border of the lower Beth-Horon, and to Gezer, and its outgoings have been at the sea. **4** And the sons of Joseph—Manasseh and Ephraim—inherit. **5** And the border of the sons of Ephraim is by their families; and the border of their inheritance is on the east, Atroth-Addar to the upper Beth-Horon; **6** and the border has gone out at the sea, to Michmethah on the north, and the border has gone around eastward [to] Taanath-Shiloh, and passed over it eastward to Janohah, **7** and gone down from Janohah [to] Ataroth, and to Naarath, and touched against Jericho, and gone out at the Jordan. **8** From Tappuah the border goes westward to the Brook of Kanah, and its outgoings have been at the sea: this [is] the inheritance of the tribe of the sons of Ephraim, for their families. **9** And the separate cities of the sons of Ephraim [are] in the midst of the inheritance of the sons of Manasseh, all the cities and their villages; **10** and they have not dispossessed the Canaanite who is dwelling in Gezer, and the Canaanite dwells in the midst of Ephraim to this day, and is for forced labor—serving.

17 And the lot is for the tribe of Manasseh (for he [is] firstborn of Joseph), for Machir firstborn of Manasseh, father of Gilead, for he has been a man of war, and his are Gilead and Bashan. **2** And there is [a lot] for the sons of Manasseh who are left, for their families; for the sons of

JOSHUA

Abiezer, and for the sons of Helek, and for the sons of Asriel, and for the sons of Shechem, and for the sons of Hepher, and for the sons of Shemida; these [are] the children of Manasseh son of Joseph—the males—by their families. **3** As for Zelophehad, son of Hepher, son of Gilead, son of Machir, son of Manasseh, he has no children except daughters, and these [are] the names of his daughters: Mahlah, and Noah, Hoglah, Milcah, and Tirzah, **4** and they draw near before Eleazar the priest, and before Joshua son of Nun, and before the princes, saying, "YHWH commanded Moses to give an inheritance to us in the midst of our brothers"; and he gives to them, at the command of YHWH, an inheritance in the midst of the brothers of their father. **5** And ten portions fall [to] Manasseh, apart from the land of Gilead and Bashan, which [are] beyond the Jordan; **6** for the daughters of Manasseh have inherited an inheritance in the midst of his sons, and the land of Gilead has been for the sons of Manasseh who are left. **7** And the border of Manasseh is from Asher to Michmethah, which [is] on the front of Shechem, and the border has gone on to the right, to the inhabitants of En-Tappuah. **8** The land of Tappuah has been for Manasseh, and Tappuah to the border of Manasseh for the sons of Ephraim. **9** And the border has come down [to] the Brook of Kanah, southward of the brook; these cities of Ephraim [are] in the midst of the cities of Manasseh, and the border of Manasseh [is] on the north of the brook, and its outgoings are at the sea. **10** Southward [is] for Ephraim and northward for Manasseh, and the sea is his border, and in Asher they meet on the north, and in Issachar on the east. **11** And in Issachar and in Asher, Manasseh has Beth-Shean and its towns, and Ibleam and its towns, and the inhabitants of Dor and its towns, and the inhabitants of En-Dor and its towns, and the inhabitants of Taanach and its towns, and the inhabitants of Megiddo and its towns—three counties. **12** And the sons of Manasseh have not been able to occupy these cities, and the Canaanite is desirous to dwell in this land, **13** and it comes to pass, when the sons of Israel have been strong, that they put the Canaanite to forced labor, and have not utterly dispossessed him. **14** And the sons of Joseph speak with Joshua, saying, "Why have you given an inheritance to me—one lot and one portion, and I [am] a numerous people? YHWH has blessed me until now." **15** And Joshua says to them, "If you [are] a numerous people, go up to the forest for yourself, then you have created [a place] for yourself there in the land of the Perizzite and of the Rephaim, when Mount Ephraim has been narrow for you." **16** And the sons of Joseph say, "The mountain is not enough for us, and a chariot of iron [is] with every Canaanite who is dwelling in the land of the valley—to him who [is] in Beth-Shean and its towns, and to him who [is] in the Valley of Jezreel." **17** And Joshua speaks to the house of Joseph, to Ephraim and to Manasseh, saying, "You [are] a numerous people, and have great power; you do not have [only] one lot, **18** because the mountain is yours; because it [is] a forest—you have created it, and its outgoings have been yours; because you dispossess the Canaanite, though it has chariots of iron—though it [is] strong."

18 And all the congregation of the sons of Israel is assembled [at] Shiloh, and they cause the Tent of Meeting to dwell there, and the land has been subdued before them. **2** And there are seven tribes left among the sons of Israel who have not shared their inheritance, **3** and Joshua says to the sons of Israel, "Until when are you remiss to go in to possess the land which He, YHWH, God of your fathers, has given to you? **4** Give three men from you for [each] tribe, and I send them, and they rise and go up and down through the land, and describe it according to their inheritance, and come to me, **5** and they have divided it into seven portions—Judah stays by its border on the south, and the house of Joseph stays by their border on the north—**6** and you describe the land [in] seven portions, and have brought [it] to me here, and I have cast a lot for you here before our God YHWH; **7** for there is no portion for the Levites in your midst, for the priesthood of YHWH [is] their inheritance, and Gad, and Reuben, and half of the tribe of Manasseh received their inheritance beyond the Jordan eastward, which Moses, servant of YHWH, gave to them." **8** And the men rise and go; and Joshua commands those who are going to describe the land, saying, "Go, and walk up and down through the land, and describe it, and return to me, and here I

JOSHUA

cast a lot for you before YHWH in Shiloh." **9** And the men go, and pass over through the land, and describe it by cities, in seven portions, on a scroll, and they come to Joshua, to the camp [at] Shiloh. **10** And Joshua casts a lot for them in Shiloh before YHWH, and there Joshua apportions the land to the sons of Israel, according to their divisions. **11** And a lot goes up [for] the tribe of the sons of Benjamin, for their families; and the border of their lot goes out between the sons of Judah and the sons of Joseph. **12** And the border is for them at the north side from the Jordan, and the border has gone up to the side of Jericho on the north, and gone up through the hill-country westward, and its outgoings have been at the wilderness of Beth-Aven; **13** and the border has gone over there to Luz, to the side of Luz (it [is] Beth-El) southward, and the border has gone down [to] Atroth-Addar, by the hill that [is] on the south of the lower Beth-Horon; **14** and the border has been marked out, and has gone around to the corner of the sea southward, from the hill which [is] at the front of Beth-Horon southward, and its outgoings have been to Kirjath-Ba'al (it [is] Kirjath-Jearim), a city of the sons of Judah: this [is] the west quarter. **15** And the south quarter [is] from the end of Kirjath-Jearim, and the border has gone out westward, and has gone out to the fountain of the waters of Nephtoah; **16** and the border has come down to the extremity of the hill which [is] on the front of the Valley of the Son of Hinnom, which [is] in the Valley of the Rephaim northward, and has gone down the Valley of Hinnom to the side of Jebusi southward, and gone down [to] En-Rogel, **17** and has been marked out on the north, and gone out to En-Shemesh, and gone out to Geliloth, which [is] opposite the ascent of Adummim, and gone down [to] the stone of Bohan son of Reuben, **18** and passed over to the side in front of the Arabah northward, and gone down to Arabah; **19** and the border has passed over to the side of Beth-Hoglah northward, and the outgoings of the border have been to the north bay of the Salt Sea, to the south extremity of the Jordan; this [is] the south border; **20** and the Jordan borders it at the east quarter; this [is] the inheritance of the sons of Benjamin, by its borders all around, for their families. **21** And the cities for the tribe of the sons of Benjamin, for their families, have been Jericho, and Beth-Hoglah, and the Valley of Keziz, **22** and Beth-Arabah, Zemaraim, and Beth-El, **23** and Avim, and Parah, and Ophrah, **24** and Chephar-Haammonai, and Ophni, and Gaba; twelve cities and their villages. **25** Gibeon, and Ramah, and Beeroth, **26** and Mizpeh, and Chephirah, and Mozah, **27** and Rekem, and Irpeel, and Taralah, **28** and Zelah, Eleph, and Jebusi (it [is] Jerusalem), Gibeath, Kirjath; fourteen cities and their villages. This [is] the inheritance of the sons of Benjamin, for their families.

19 And the second lot goes out for Simeon, for the tribe of the sons of Simeon, for their families; and their inheritance is in the midst of the inheritance of the sons of Judah, **2** and they have in their inheritance Beer-Sheba, and Sheba, and Moladah, **3** and Hazar-Shual, and Balah, and Azem, **4** and Eltolad, and Bethul, and Hormah, **5** and Ziklag, and Beth-Marcaboth, and Hazar-Susah, **6** and Beth-Lebaoth, and Sharuhen; thirteen cities and their villages. **7** Ain, Remmon, and Ether, and Ashan; four cities and their villages; **8** also all the villages which [are] around these cities, to Ba'alath-Beer, Ramoth of the south. This [is] the inheritance of the tribe of the sons of Simeon, for their families; **9** out of the portion of the sons of Judah [is] the inheritance of the sons of Simeon, for the portion of the sons of Judah has been too much for them, and the sons of Simeon inherit in the midst of their inheritance. **10** And the third lot goes up for the sons of Zebulun, for their families; and the border of their inheritance is to Sarid, **11** and their border has gone up toward the sea, and Maralah, and come against Dabbasheth, and come to the brook which [is] on the front of Jokneam, **12** and turned back from Sarid eastward, at the sun-rising, by the border of Chisloth-Tabor, and gone out to Daberath, and gone up to Japhia, **13** and there it has passed over eastward, to the east, to Gittah-Hepher, [to] Ittah-Kazin, and gone out [to] Rimmon-Methoar to Neah; **14** and the border has gone around it, from the north to Hannathon; and its outgoings have been [in] the Valley of Jiphthah-El, **15** and Kattath, and Nahallal, and Shimron, and Idalah, and Beth-Lehem; twelve cities and their villages.

JOSHUA

16 This [is] the inheritance of the sons of Zebulun, for their families, these cities and their villages. **17** The fourth lot has gone out for Issachar, for the sons of Issachar, for their families; **18** and their border is [at] Jezreel, and Chesulloth, and Shunem, **19** and Haphraim, and Shihon, and Anaharath, **20** and Rabbith, and Kishion, and Abez, **21** and Remeth, and En-Gannim, and En-Haddah, and Beth-Pazzez; **22** and the border has touched against Tabor, and Shahazimah, and Beth-Shemesh, and the outgoings of their border have been [at] the Jordan; sixteen cities and their villages. **23** This [is] the inheritance of the tribe of the sons of Issachar, for their families, the cities and their villages. **24** And the fifth lot goes out for the tribe of the sons of Asher, for their families; **25** and their border is Helkath, and Hali, and Beten, and Achshaph, **26** and Alammelech, and Amad, and Misheal; and it touches against Carmel westward, and against Shihor-Libnath; **27** and has turned back, at the sun-rising, [to] Beth-Dagon, and come against Zebulun, and against the Valley of Jiphthah-El toward the north of Beth-Emek, and Neiel, and has gone out to Cabul on the left, **28** and Hebron, and Rehob, and Hammon, and Kanah, to great Sidon; **29** and the border has turned back to Ramah, and to the fortified city Tyre; and the border has turned back to Hosah, and its outgoings are at the sea, from the coast to Achzib, **30** and Ummah, and Aphek, and Rehob; twenty-two cities and their villages. **31** This [is] the inheritance of the tribe of the sons of Asher, for their families, these cities and their villages. **32** The sixth lot has gone out for the sons of Naphtali—for the sons of Naphtali, for their families; **33** and their border is from Heleph, from Allon in Zaanannim, and Adami, Nekeb, and Jabneel, to Lakkum, and its outgoings are [at] the Jordan; **34** and the border has turned back westward [to] Aznoth-Tabor, and gone out there to Hukkok, and touched against Zebulun on the south, and it has touched against Asher on the west, and against Judah [at] the Jordan, at the sun-rising; **35** and the cities of defense [are] Ziddim, Zer, and Hammath, Rakkath, and Chinnereth, **36** and Adamah, and Ramah, and Hazor, **37** and Kedesh, and Edrei, and En-Hazor, **38** and Iron, and Migdal-El, Horem, and Beth-Anath, and Beth-Shemesh; nineteen cities and their villages. **39** This [is] the inheritance of the tribe of the sons of Naphtali, for their families, the cities and their villages. **40** The seventh lot has gone out for the tribe of the sons of Dan, for their families; **41** and the border of their inheritance is Zorah, and Eshtaol, and Ir-Shemesh, **42** and Shalabbin, and Aijalon, and Jethlah, **43** and Elon, and Thimnathah, and Ekron, **44** and Eltekeh, and Gibbethon, and Ba'alath, **45** and Jehud, and Bene-Barak, and Gath-Rimmon, **46** and Me-Jarkon, and Rakkon, with the border in front of Joppa. **47** And the border of the sons of Dan goes out from them, and the sons of Dan go up and fight with Leshem, and capture it, and strike it by the mouth of the sword, and possess it, and dwell in it, and call Leshem, Dan, according to the name of their father Dan. **48** This [is] the inheritance of the tribe of the sons of Dan, for their families, these cities and their villages. **49** And they finish to give the land in inheritance, by its borders, and the sons of Israel give an inheritance to Joshua son of Nun in their midst; **50** by the command of YHWH they have given to him the city which he asked for, Timnath-Serah, in the hill-country of Ephraim, and he builds the city and dwells in it. **51** These [are] the inheritances which Eleazar the priest, and Joshua son of Nun, and the heads of the fathers of the tribes of the sons of Israel, have caused to inherit by lot, in Shiloh, before YHWH, at the opening of the Tent of Meeting; and they finish to apportion the land.

20 And YHWH speaks to Joshua, saying, **2** "Speak to the sons of Israel, saying, Give cities of refuge for yourselves, as I have spoken to you by the hand of Moses, **3** for the fleeing there of a manslayer striking life through ignorance, without knowledge; and they have been for a refuge to you from the redeemer of blood. **4** When [one] has fled to one of these cities, and has stood [at] the opening of the gate of the city, and has spoken his matter in the ears of [the] elderly of that city, then they have gathered him into the city to them, and have given a place to him, and he has dwelt with them. **5** And when the redeemer of blood pursues after him, then they do not shut up the manslayer into his hand, for he has struck his neighbor without knowledge, and is not hating him until now; **6** and he has dwelt in that city until

JOSHUA

his standing before the congregation for judgment, until the death of the chief priest who is in those days—then the manslayer turns back and has come to his city, and to his house, to the city from where he fled." **7** And they sanctify Kedesh in Galilee, in the hill-country of Naphtali, and Shechem in the hill-country of Ephraim, and Kirjath-Arba (it [is] Hebron), in the hill-country of Judah; **8** and beyond the Jordan, [at] Jericho eastward, they have given Bezer in the wilderness, in the plain, out of the tribe of Reuben, and Ramoth in Gilead out of the tribe of Gad, and Golan in Bashan out of the tribe of Manasseh. **9** These have been cities of meeting for all the sons of Israel, and for a sojourner who is sojourning in their midst, for the fleeing there of anyone striking life through ignorance, and he does not die by the hand of the redeemer of blood until his standing before the congregation.

21 And the heads of the fathers of the Levites draw near to Eleazar the priest, and to Joshua son of Nun, and to the heads of the fathers of the tribes of the sons of Israel, **2** and they speak to them in Shiloh, in the land of Canaan, saying, "YHWH commanded by the hand of Moses to give to us cities to dwell in, and their outskirts for our livestock." **3** And the sons of Israel give to the Levites, out of their inheritance, at the command of YHWH, these cities and their outskirts: **4** and the lot goes out for the families of the Kohathite, and there are for the sons of Aaron the priest (of the Levites), out of the tribe of Judah, and out of the tribe of Simeon, and out of the tribe of Benjamin, thirteen cities by lot, **5** and for the sons of Kohath who are left, out of the families of the tribe of Ephraim, and out of the tribe of Dan, and out of the half-tribe of Manasseh, ten cities by lot. **6** And for the sons of Gershon, out of the families of the tribe of Issachar, and out of the tribe of Asher, and out of the tribe of Naphtali, and out of the half-tribe of Manasseh in Bashan, [are] thirteen cities by lot. **7** For the sons of Merari, for their families, out of the tribe of Reuben, and out of the tribe of Gad, and out of the tribe of Zebulun, [are] twelve cities. **8** And the sons of Israel give these cities and their outskirts to the Levites, as YHWH commanded by the hand of Moses, by lot. **9** And they give out of the tribe of the sons of Judah, and out of the tribe of the sons of Simeon, these cities which are called by name; **10** and they are for the sons of Aaron, of the families of the Kohathite, of the sons of Levi, for the first lot has been theirs; **11** and they give to them the city of Arba father of Anak (it [is] Hebron), in the hill-country of Judah, and its outskirts around it; **12** and they have given the field of the city and its villages to Caleb son of Jephunneh for his possession. **13** And to the sons of Aaron the priest they have given the city of refuge [for] the manslayer, Hebron and its outskirts, and Libnah and its outskirts, **14** and Jattir and its outskirts, and Eshtemoa and its outskirts, **15** and Holon and its outskirts, and Debir and its outskirts, **16** and Ain and its outskirts, and Juttah and its outskirts, Beth-Shemesh and its outskirts; nine cities out of these two tribes. **17** And out of the tribe of Benjamin, Gibeon and its outskirts, Geba and its outskirts, **18** Anathoth and its outskirts, and Almon and its outskirts—four cities; **19** all the cities of the sons of Aaron the priests, [are] thirteen cities and their outskirts. **20** And for the families of the sons of Kohath, the Levites, who are left of the sons of Kohath, even the cities of their lot are of the tribe of Ephraim; **21** and they give to them the city of refuge [for] the manslayer, Shechem and its outskirts, in the hill-country of Ephraim, and Gezer and its outskirts, **22** and Kibzaim and its outskirts, and Beth-Horon and its outskirts—four cities. **23** And out of the tribe of Dan, Eltekeh and its outskirts, Gibbethon and its outskirts, **24** Aijalon and its outskirts, Gath-Rimmon and its outskirts—four cities. **25** And out of the half-tribe of Manasseh, Taanach and its outskirts, and Gath-Rimmon and its outskirts—two cities; **26** all the cities [are] ten and their outskirts, for the families of the sons of Kohath who are left. **27** And for the sons of Gershon, of the families of the Levites, out of the half-tribe of Manasseh, the city of refuge [for] the manslayer, Golan in Bashan and its outskirts, and Beeshterah and its outskirts—two cities. **28** And out of the tribe of Issachar, Kishon and its outskirts, Dabarath and its outskirts, **29** Jarmuth and its outskirts, En-Gannim and its outskirts—four cities. **30** And out of the tribe of Asher, Mishal and its outskirts, Abdon and its outskirts, **31** Helkath and its outskirts, and Rehob and its outskirts—four cities. **32** And out of the tribe of

JOSHUA

Naphtali, the city of refuge [for] the manslayer, Kedesh in Galilee and its outskirts, and Hammoth-Dor and its outskirts, and Kartan and its outskirts—three cities; **33** all the cities of the Gershonite, for their families, [are] thirteen cities and their outskirts. **34** And for the families of the sons of Merari, the Levites, who are left, [are,] out of the tribe of Zebulun, Jokneam and its outskirts, Kartah and its outskirts, **35** Dimnah and its outskirts, Nahalal and its outskirts—four cities. **36** And out of the tribe of Reuben, Bezer and its outskirts, and Jahazah and its outskirts, **37** Kedemoth and its outskirts, and Mephaath and its outskirts—four cities. **38** And out of the tribe of Gad, the city of refuge [for] the manslayer, Ramoth in Gilead and its outskirts, and Mahanaim and its outskirts, **39** Heshbon and its outskirts, Jazer and its outskirts—four cities [in] all. **40** All the cities for the sons of Merari, for their families, who are left of the families of the Levites—their lot is twelve cities. **41** All the cities of the Levites in the midst of the possession of the sons of Israel [are] forty-eight cities, and their outskirts. **42** These cities are each city and its outskirts around it; so to all these cities. **43** And YHWH gives to Israel the whole of the land which He has sworn to give to their fathers, and they possess it, and dwell in it; **44** and YHWH gives rest to them all around, according to all that which He has sworn to their fathers, and there has not stood a man in their presence of all their enemies, YHWH has given the whole of their enemies into their hand; **45** there has not fallen a thing of all the good thing which YHWH spoke to the house of Israel—the whole has come.

22 Then Joshua calls for the Reubenite, and for the Gadite, and for the half-tribe of Manasseh, **2** and says to them, "You have kept the whole of that which Moses, servant of YHWH, commanded you, and you listen to my voice, to all that I have commanded you; **3** you have not left your brothers these many days to this day, and have kept the charge—the command of your God YHWH. **4** And now, your God YHWH has given rest to your brothers, as He spoke to them; and now, turn, and go for yourselves to your tents, to the land of your possession, which Moses, servant of YHWH, has given to you beyond the Jordan. **5** Only, be very watchful to do the command and the Law which Moses, servant of YHWH, commanded you, to love your God YHWH, and to walk in all His ways, and to keep His commands, and to cleave to Him, and to serve Him, with all your heart, and with all your soul." **6** And Joshua blesses them, and sends them away, and they go to their tents. **7** And to the half-tribe of Manasseh Moses has given, in Bashan, and to its [other] half Joshua has given with their brothers beyond the Jordan westward; and also when Joshua has sent them away to their tents, then he blesses them, **8** and speaks to them, saying, "Turn back to your tents with great riches, and with very much livestock, with silver, and with gold, and with bronze, and with iron, and with very much raiment; divide the spoil of your enemies with your brothers." **9** And the sons of Reuben, and the sons of Gad, and the half-tribe of Manasseh, turn back and go from the sons of Israel out of Shiloh, which [is] in the land of Canaan, to go to the land of Gilead, to the land of their possession, in which they have possession, according to the command of YHWH, by the hand of Moses; **10** and they come to the districts of the Jordan, which [are] in the land of Canaan, and the sons of Reuben, and the sons of Gad, and the half-tribe of Manasseh, build an altar there by the Jordan—a great altar in appearance. **11** And the sons of Israel hear, saying, "Behold, the sons of Reuben, and the sons of Gad, and the half-tribe of Manasseh, have built the altar at the frontier of the land of Canaan, in the districts of the Jordan, at the passage of the sons of Israel." **12** And the sons of Israel hear, and all the congregation of the sons of Israel is assembled at Shiloh, to go up against them to war; **13** and the sons of Israel send to the sons of Reuben, and to the sons of Gad, and to the half-tribe of Manasseh—to the land of Gilead—Phinehas son of Eleazar the priest, **14** and ten princes with him, one prince—one prince for a house of a father, for all the tribes of Israel, and each of them a head of a house of their fathers, for the thousands of Israel. **15** And they come to the sons of Reuben, and to the sons of Gad, and to the half-tribe of Manasseh, to the land of Gilead, and speak with them, saying, **16** "Thus said all the congregation of YHWH: What [is] this trespass which you have trespassed against the God of Israel, to turn back today from after YHWH, by your building an altar for yourselves, for your rebelling today against YHWH? **17** Is the iniquity of Peor little to us, from which we have not been cleansed until this day—and the plague is in the congregation of YHWH, **18** that you turn back today from after YHWH? And it has been [that] you rebel against YHWH today, and tomorrow He is angry against all the congregation of Israel. **19** And surely, if the land of your possession is unclean, pass over for yourselves to the land of the possession of YHWH, where the Dwelling Place of YHWH has dwelt, and have possession in our midst; and do not rebel against YHWH, and do not rebel against us, by your building an altar for yourselves, besides the altar of our God YHWH. **20** Did Achan son of Zerah not commit a trespass in the devoted thing, and there was wrath on all the congregation of Israel? And he alone did not expire in his iniquity." **21** And the sons of Reuben, and the sons of Gad, and the half-tribe of Manasseh, answer and speak with the heads of the thousands of Israel: **22** "The God of gods—YHWH, the God of gods—YHWH, He is knowing, and Israel—he knows, if [we are] in rebellion, and if in trespass against YHWH, do not save us this day! **23** [If we] are building an altar for ourselves to turn back from after YHWH, and if to cause burnt-offering and present to go up on it, and if to make peace-offerings on it—YHWH Himself requires [it]. **24** And nevertheless, we have done it from fear of [this] thing, saying, Hereafter your sons speak to our sons, saying, And what have you to [do with] YHWH God of Israel? **25** For YHWH has put a border between us and you, O sons of Reuben, and sons of Gad—Jordan; you have no portion in YHWH—and your sons have caused our sons to cease, not to fear YHWH. **26** And we say, Now let us prepare to build the altar for ourselves—not for burnt-offering, nor for sacrifice— **27** but it [is] a witness between us and you, and between our generations after us, to do the service of YHWH before Him with our burnt-offerings, and with our sacrifices, and with our peace-offerings, and your sons do not say hereafter to our sons, You have no portion in YHWH. **28** And we say, And it has been, when they say [so] to us, and to our generations hereafter, that we have said, See the pattern of the altar of YHWH, which our fathers made—not for burnt-offering nor for sacrifice—but it [is] a witness between us and you. **29** Far be it from us to rebel against YHWH, and to turn back from after YHWH today, to build an altar for burnt-offering, for present, and for sacrifice, apart from the altar of our God YHWH, which [is] before His Dwelling Place." **30** And Phinehas the priest, and the princes of the congregation, and the heads of the thousands of Israel, who [are] with him, hear the words which the sons of Reuben, and the sons of Gad, and the sons of Manasseh have spoken, and it is good in their eyes. **31** And Phinehas son of Eleazar the priest says to the sons of Reuben, and to the sons of Gad, and to the sons of Manasseh, "Today we have known that YHWH [is] in our midst, because you have not committed this trespass against YHWH—then you have delivered the sons of Israel out of the hand of YHWH." **32** And Phinehas son of Eleazar the priest, and the princes, turn back from the sons of Reuben, and from the sons of Gad, out of the land of Gilead, to the land of Canaan, to the sons of Israel, and bring them back word; **33** and the thing is good in the eyes of the sons of Israel, and the sons of Israel bless God, and have not spoken to go up against them to war, to destroy the land which the sons of Reuben, and the sons of Gad, are dwelling in. **34** And the sons of Reuben and the sons of Gad proclaim concerning the altar, that, "[It is] a witness between us that YHWH [is] God."

23 And it comes to pass, many days after that YHWH has given rest to Israel from all their surrounding enemies, that Joshua is old, entering into days, **2** and Joshua calls for all Israel, for his elderly, and for his heads, and for his judges, and for his authorities, and says to them, "I have become old; I have entered into days; **3** and you have seen all that your God YHWH has done to all these nations because of you, for your God YHWH [is] He who is fighting for you; **4** see, I have caused these nations who are left to fall to you for an inheritance to your tribes, from the Jordan (and all the nations which I cut off), and the Great Sea [at] the [setting] sun. **5** As for your God YHWH, He thrusts them from your presence, and has dispossessed them from before you, and you have possessed their land, as your God YHWH has spoken to you, **6** and you have been very strong to keep and to do the whole that is written in the Scroll of the Law of Moses, so as not to turn aside from it right or left, **7** so as not to go in among these nations, these who are left with you; and you do not make mention of the name of their gods, nor do you swear, nor do you serve them, nor do you bow yourselves to them; **8** but you cleave to your God YHWH, as you have done until this day. **9** And YHWH is dispossessing great and mighty nations from before you; as for you, none has stood in your presence until this day; **10** one man of you pursues a thousand, for your God YHWH [is] He who is fighting for you, as He has spoken to you; **11** and you have been very watchful for yourselves to love your God YHWH. **12** But—if you turn back at all and have cleaved to the remnant of these nations, these who are left with you, and intermarried with them, and gone in to them, and they to you, **13** certainly know that your God YHWH is not continuing to dispossess these nations from before you, and they have been to you for a trap, and for a snare, and for a scourge, in your sides, and for thorns in your eyes, until you perish from off this good ground which your God YHWH has given to you. **14** And behold, I am going, today, in the way of all the earth, and you have known—with all your heart, and with all your soul—that there has not fallen one thing of all the good things which your God YHWH has spoken concerning you; the whole have come to you; there has not failed of it one thing. **15** And it has been, as there has come on you all the good thing which your God YHWH has spoken to you, so YHWH brings on you the whole of the evil thing, until His destroying you from off this good ground which your God YHWH has given to you; **16** in your transgressing the covenant of your God YHWH which He commanded you, and you have gone and served other gods, and bowed yourselves to them, then the anger of YHWH has burned against you, and you have perished quickly from off the good land which He has given to you."

24 And Joshua gathers all the tribes of Israel to Shechem, and calls for [the] elderly of Israel, and for his heads, and for his judges, and for his authorities, and they station themselves before God. **2** And Joshua says to all the people, "Thus said YHWH, God of Israel: Beyond the River your fathers have dwelt of old—Terah father of Abraham and father of Nachor—and they serve other gods; **3** and I take your father Abraham from beyond the River, and cause him to go through all the land of Canaan, and multiply his seed, and give Isaac to him. **4** And I give Jacob and Esau to Isaac; and I give Mount Seir to Esau, to possess it; and Jacob and his sons have gone down to Egypt. **5** And I send Moses and Aaron, and plague Egypt, as I have done in its midst, and afterward I have brought you out. **6** And I bring out your fathers from Egypt, and you go to the sea, and the Egyptians pursue after your fathers, with chariot and with horsemen, to the Red Sea; **7** and they cry to YHWH, and He sets thick darkness between you and the Egyptians, and brings the sea over him, and covers them, and your eyes see that which I have done in Egypt; and you dwell in a wilderness [for] many days. **8** And I bring you into the land of the Amorite who is dwelling beyond the Jordan, and they fight with you, and I give them into your hand, and you possess their land, and I destroy them out of your presence. **9** And Balak son of Zippor, king of Moab, rises and fights against Israel, and sends and calls for Balaam son of Beor, to revile you, **10** and I have not been willing to listen to Balaam, and he greatly blesses you, and I deliver you out of his hand. **11** And you pass over the Jordan, and come to Jericho, and the possessors of Jericho fight against you—the Amorite, and the Perizzite, and the Canaanite, and the Hittite, and the Girgashite, the Hivite, and the Jebusite—and I give them into your hand. **12** And I send the hornet before you, and it casts them out from your presence—two kings of the Amorite—not by your sword, nor by your bow. **13** And I give a land to you for which you have not labored, and cities which you have not built, and you dwell in them; you are eating of vineyards and olive-yards which you have not planted. **14** And now, fear YHWH, and serve Him, in perfection and in truth, and turn aside the gods which your fathers served beyond the River, and in Egypt, and serve YHWH; **15** and if [it is] wrong in your eyes to serve YHWH—choose for yourselves today whom you serve—whether the gods whom your fathers served, which [are] beyond the River, or the gods of the Amorite in whose land you are dwelling; but me and my house—we serve YHWH." **16** And the people answer and say, "Far be it from us to forsake YHWH, to serve other gods; **17** for our God YHWH [is] He who is bringing us and our fathers up out of the land of Egypt, out of a house of servants, and who has done these great signs before our eyes, and keeps us in all the way in which we have gone, and among all the peoples through whose midst we passed; **18** and YHWH casts out the whole of the peoples, even the Amorite inhabiting the land, from our presence; we also serve YHWH, for He [is] our God." **19** And Joshua says to the people, "You are not able to serve YHWH, for He [is] a most holy God; He [is] a zealous God; He does not bear with your transgression and with your sins. **20** When you forsake YHWH, and have served gods of a stranger, then He has turned back and done harm to you, and consumed you, after that He has done good to you." **21** And the people say to Joshua, "No, but we serve YHWH!" **22** And Joshua says to the people, "You are witnesses against yourselves, that you have chosen YHWH for yourselves, to serve Him," and they say, "Witnesses!" **23** "And now, turn aside the gods of the stranger which [are] in your midst, and incline your heart to YHWH, God of Israel." **24** And the people say to Joshua, "We serve our God YHWH, and we listen to His voice." **25** And Joshua makes a covenant with the people on that day, and lays a statute and an ordinance on it, in Shechem. **26** And Joshua writes these words in the Scroll of the Law of God, and takes a great stone, and raises it up there under the oak which [is] in the sanctuary of YHWH. **27** And Joshua says to all the people, "Behold, this stone is for a witness against us, for it has heard all the sayings of YHWH which He has spoken with us, and it has been for a witness against you, lest you lie against your God." **28** And Joshua sends the people away, each to his inheritance. **29** And it comes to pass, after these things, that Joshua son of Nun, servant of YHWH, dies, a son of one hundred and ten years, **30** and they bury him in the border of his inheritance, in Timnath-Serah, which [is] in the hill-country of Ephraim, on the north of the hill of Gaash. **31** And Israel serves YHWH all [the] days of Joshua, and all [the] days of the elderly who prolonged days after Joshua, and who knew all the work of YHWH which He did to Israel. **32** And the bones of Joseph, which the sons of Israel brought up out of Egypt, they buried in Shechem, in the portion of the field which Jacob bought from the sons of Hamor father of Shechem, with one hundred kesitah; and they are for an inheritance to the sons of Joseph. **33** And Eleazar son of Aaron died, and they bury him in a hill of his son Phinehas, which was given to him in the hill-country of Ephraim.

JUDGES

1 And it comes to pass after the death of Joshua, that the sons of Israel ask of YHWH, saying, "Who goes up for us to the Canaanite, at the commencement, to fight against it?" **2** And YHWH says, "Judah goes up; behold, I have given the land into his hand." **3** And Judah says to his brother Simeon, "Go up with me into my lot, and we fight against the Canaanite—and I have gone, even I, with you into your lot"; and Simeon goes with him. **4** And Judah goes up, and YHWH gives the Canaanite and the Perizzite into their hand, and they strike them in Bezek—ten thousand men; **5** and they find Adoni-Bezek in Bezek, and fight against him, and strike the Canaanite and the Perizzite. **6** And Adoni-Bezek flees, and they pursue after him, and seize him, and cut off his thumbs and his great toes, **7** and Adoni-Bezek says, "Seventy kings—their thumbs and their great toes cut off—have been gathering under my table; as I have done so God has repaid to me"; and they bring him to Jerusalem, and he dies there. **8** And the sons of Judah fight against Jerusalem, and capture it, and strike it by the mouth of the sword, and they have sent the city into fire; **9** and afterward the sons of Judah have gone down to fight against the Canaanite inhabiting the hill-country, and the south, and the low country; **10** and Judah goes to the Canaanite who is dwelling in Hebron (and the name of Hebron [was] formerly Kirjath-Arba), and they strike Sheshai, and Ahiman, and Talmai. **11** And he goes there to the inhabitants of Debir (and the name of Debir [was] formerly Kirjath-Sepher), **12** and Caleb says, "He who strikes Kirjath-Sepher and has captured it—then I have given my daughter Achsah to him for a wife." **13** And Othniel son of Kenaz, younger brother of Caleb, captures it, and he gives his daughter Achsah to him for a wife. **14** And it comes to pass in her coming in, that she persuades him to ask from her father the field, and she comes down off the donkey, and Caleb says to her, "What do you [want]?" **15** And she says to him, "Give a blessing to me; when you have given me the south land—then you have given springs of water to me"; and Caleb gives the upper springs and the lower springs to her. **16** And the sons of the Kenite, father-in-law of Moses, have gone up out of the city of palms with the sons of Judah [to] the wilderness of Judah, which [is] in the south of Arad, and they go and dwell with the people. **17** And Judah goes with his brother Simeon, and they strike the Canaanite inhabiting Zephath, and devote it; and [one] calls the name of the city Hormah. **18** And Judah captures Gaza and its border, and Askelon and its border, and Ekron and its border; **19** and YHWH is with Judah, and he occupies the hill-country, but not to dispossess the inhabitants of the valley, for they have chariots of iron. **20** And they give Hebron to Caleb, as Moses has spoken, and he dispossesses the three sons of Anak there. **21** And the sons of Benjamin have not dispossessed the Jebusite inhabiting Jerusalem; and the Jebusite dwells with the sons of Benjamin, in Jerusalem, until this day. **22** And the house of Joseph goes up—even they—to Beth-El, and YHWH [is] with them; **23** and the house of Joseph causes [men] to spy out Beth-El (and the name of the city [was] formerly Luz), **24** and the watchers see a man coming out from the city, and say to him, "Please show us the entrance of the city, and we have done kindness with you." **25** And he shows them the entrance of the city, and they strike the city by the mouth of the sword, and they have sent the man and all his family away; **26** and the man goes to the land of the Hittites, and builds a city, and calls its name Luz—it [is] its name to this day. **27** And Manasseh has not occupied Beth-Shean and its towns, and Taanach and its towns, and the inhabitants of Dor and its towns, and the inhabitants of Iblaim and its towns, and the inhabitants of Megiddo and its towns, and the Canaanite is desirous to dwell in that land; **28** and it comes to pass, when Israel has been strong, that he sets the Canaanite to forced labor, and has not utterly dispossessed it. **29** And Ephraim has not dispossessed the Canaanite who is dwelling in Gezer, and the Canaanite dwells in its midst, in Gezer. **30** Zebulun has not dispossessed the inhabitants of Kitron, and the inhabitants of Nahalol, and the Canaanite dwells in its midst, and they become forced labor. **31** Asher has not

JUDGES

dispossessed the inhabitants of Accho, and the inhabitants of Sidon, and Ahlab, and Achzib, and Helbah, and Aphik, and Rehob; **32** and the Asherite dwells in the midst of the Canaanite, the inhabitants of the land, for it has not dispossessed them. **33** Naphtali has not dispossessed the inhabitants of Beth-Shemesh, and the inhabitants of Beth-Anath, and he dwells in the midst of the Canaanite, the inhabitants of the land; and the inhabitants of Beth-Shemesh and of Beth-Anath were for forced labor for them. **34** And the Amorites press the sons of Dan to the mountain, for they have not permitted them to go down to the valley; **35** and the Amorite is desirous to dwell in Mount Heres, in Aijalon, and in Shaalbim, and the hand of the house of Joseph is heavy, and they are for forced labor; **36** and the border of the Amorite [is] from the ascent of Akrabbim, from the rock and upward.

2 And the Messenger of YHWH goes up from Gilgal to Bochim, **2** and says, "I cause you to come up out of Egypt, and bring you into the land which I have sworn to your fathers, and say, I do not break My covenant with you for all time; and you make no covenant with the inhabitants of this land—you break down their altars; and you have not listened to My voice—what [is] this you have done? **3** And I have also said, I do not cast them out from your presence, and they have been for adversaries to you, and their gods are for a snare to you." **4** And it comes to pass, when the Messenger of YHWH speaks these words to all the sons of Israel, that the people lift up their voice and weep, **5** and they call the name of that place Bochim, and sacrifice to YHWH there. **6** And Joshua sends the people away, and the sons of Israel go, each to his inheritance, to possess the land; **7** and the people serve YHWH all [the] days of Joshua, and all [the] days of [the] elderly who prolonged days after Joshua, who saw all the great work of YHWH which He did to Israel. **8** And Joshua son of Nun, servant of YHWH, dies, a son of one hundred and ten years, **9** and they bury him in the border of his inheritance, in Timnath-Heres, in the hill-country of Ephraim, on the north of Mount Gaash; **10** and all that generation have also been gathered to their fathers, and another generation rises after them who have not known YHWH, and even the work which He has done to Israel. **11** And the sons of Israel do evil in the eyes of YHWH, and serve the Ba'alim, **12** and forsake YHWH, God of their fathers, who brings them out from the land of Egypt, and go after other gods (of the gods of the peoples who [are] around them), and bow themselves to them, and provoke YHWH, **13** indeed, they forsake YHWH, and do service to Ba'al and to Ashtaroth. **14** And the anger of YHWH burns against Israel, and He gives them into the hand of spoilers, and they spoil them, and He sells them into the hand of their surrounding enemies, and they have not been able to stand before their enemies anymore; **15** in every [place] where they have gone out, the hand of YHWH has been against them for calamity, as YHWH has spoken, and as YHWH has sworn to them, and they are greatly distressed. **16** And YHWH raises up judges, and they save them from the hand of their spoilers; **17** and they have also not listened to their judges, but have gone whoring after other gods, and bow themselves to them; they have turned aside [with] haste out of the way [in] which their fathers walked to obey the commands of YHWH—they have not done so. **18** And when YHWH raised up judges for them—then YHWH was with the judge, and saved them out of the hand of their enemies all [the] days of the judge; for YHWH sighs, because of their groaning from the presence of their oppressors, and of those thrusting them away. **19** And it has come to pass, when the judge dies—they turn back and have done corruptly above their fathers, to go after other gods, to serve them, and to bow themselves to them; they have not fallen from their doings, and from their stiff way. **20** And the anger of YHWH burns against Israel, and He says, "Because that this nation has transgressed My covenant which I commanded their fathers, and have not listened to My voice— **21** I also do not continue to dispossess any from before them of the nations which Joshua has left when he dies, **22** in order to try Israel by them, whether they are keeping the way of YHWH, to go in it, as their fathers kept [it], or not." **23** And YHWH leaves these nations, so as not to dispossess them quickly, and did not give them into the hand of Joshua.

JUDGES

3 And these [are] the nations which YHWH left, to try Israel by them, all who have not known all the wars of Canaan; **2** (only for the sake of the generations of the sons of Israel knowing, to teach them war, only those who formerly have not known them)— **3** five princes of the Philistines, and all the Canaanite, and the Zidonian, and the Hivite inhabiting Mount Lebanon, from Mount Ba'al-Hermon to the entering in of Hamath; **4** and they are to prove Israel by them, to know whether they obey the commands of YHWH that He commanded their fathers by the hand of Moses. **5** And the sons of Israel have dwelt in the midst of the Canaanite, the Hittite, and the Amorite, and the Perizzite, and the Hivite, and the Jebusite, **6** and take their daughters to them for wives, and have given their daughters to their sons, and they serve their gods; **7** and the sons of Israel do evil in the eyes of YHWH, and forget their God YHWH, and serve the Ba'alim and the Asheroth. **8** And the anger of YHWH burns against Israel, and He sells them into the hand of Chushan-Rishathaim king of Aram-Naharaim, and the sons of Israel serve Chushan-Rishathaim eight years; **9** and the sons of Israel cry to YHWH, and YHWH raises a savior to the sons of Israel, and he saves them—Othniel son of Kenaz, Caleb's younger brother; **10** and the Spirit of YHWH is on him, and he judges Israel, and goes out to battle, and YHWH gives Chushan-Rishathaim king of Aram into his hand, and his hand is strong against Chushan-Rishathaim; **11** and the land rests forty years. And Othniel son of Kenaz dies, **12** and the sons of Israel add to do evil in the eyes of YHWH; and YHWH strengthens Eglon king of Moab against Israel, because that they have done evil in the eyes of YHWH; **13** and he gathers the sons of Ammon and Amalek to himself, and goes and strikes Israel, and they possess the city of palms; **14** and the sons of Israel serve Eglon king of Moab eighteen years. **15** And the sons of Israel cry to YHWH, and YHWH raises a savior to them, Ehud son of Gera, a Benjamite (a man [with] his right hand bound), and the sons of Israel send a present by his hand to Eglon king of Moab; **16** and Ehud makes a sword for himself, and it has two mouths (its length [is] a cubit), and he girds it under his long robe on his right thigh; **17** and he brings the present near to Eglon king of Moab, and Eglon [is] a very fat man. **18** And it comes to pass, when he has finished to bring the present near, that he sends the people carrying the present away, **19** and he himself has turned back from the carved images which [are] at Gilgal and says, "I have a secret word for you, O king"; and he says, "Hush!" And all those standing by him go out from him. **20** And Ehud has come to him, and he is sitting in the cool upper chamber which he has for himself, and Ehud says, "I have a word of God for you"; and he rises from off the throne; **21** and Ehud puts forth his left hand, and takes the sword from off his right thigh, and thrusts it into his belly; **22** and the hilt also goes in after the blade, and the fat shuts on the blade, that he has not drawn the sword out of his belly, and he goes out [through] the antechamber [[or and the dung came out]]. **23** And Ehud goes out at the porch, and shuts the doors of the upper chamber on him, and has bolted [it]; **24** and he has gone out, and his servants have come in, and look, and behold, the doors of the upper chamber are bolted, and they say, "He is surely covering his feet, [relieving himself,] in the cool inner chamber." **25** And they stay until confounded, and behold, he is not opening the doors of the upper chamber, and they take the key, and open, and behold, their lord is fallen to the earth—dead. **26** And Ehud escaped during their lingering, and has passed by the images, and escapes to Seirath. **27** And it comes to pass, in his coming in, that he blows with a horn in the hill-country of Ephraim, and the sons of Israel go down with him from the hill-country, and he before them; **28** and he says to them, "Pursue after me, for YHWH has given your enemies, the Moabites, into your hand"; and they go down after him, and capture the passages of the Jordan toward Moab, and have not permitted a man to pass over. **29** And they strike Moab at that time, about ten thousand men, all robust, and everyone a man of valor, and no man has escaped, **30** and Moab is humbled in that day under the hand of Israel; and the land rests [for] eighty years. **31** And after him has been Shamgar son of Anath, and he strikes the Philistines—six hundred men—with an ox-goad, and he also saves Israel.

4 And the sons of Israel add to do evil in the eyes of YHWH when Ehud is dead,

2 and YHWH sells them into the hand of Jabin king of Canaan, who has reigned in Hazor, and Sisera [is] the head of his host, and he is dwelling in Harosheth of the nations; **3** and the sons of Israel cry to YHWH, for he has nine hundred chariots of iron, and he has oppressed the sons of Israel mightily [for] twenty years. **4** And Deborah, a woman, a prophetess, wife of Lapidoth, she is judging Israel at that time, **5** and she is dwelling under the palm-tree of Deborah, between Ramah and Beth-El, in the hill-country of Ephraim, and the sons of Israel go up to her for judgment. **6** And she sends and calls for Barak son of Abinoam, out of Kedesh-Naphtali, and says to him, "Has YHWH, God of Israel, not commanded? Go, and you have drawn toward Mount Tabor, and have taken with you ten thousand men, out of the sons of Naphtali, and out of the sons of Zebulun, **7** and I have drawn to you, to the Brook of Kishon, Sisera, head of the host of Jabin, and his chariot, and his multitude, and have given him into your hand." **8** And Barak says to her, "If you go with me, then I have gone; and if you do not go with me, I do not go"; **9** and she says, "I certainly go with you; only, surely your glory is not on the way which you are going, for YHWH sells Sisera into the hand of a woman"; and Deborah rises and goes with Barak to Kedesh. **10** And Barak calls Zebulun and Naphtali to Kedesh, and he goes up—ten thousand men [are] at his feet—and Deborah goes up with him. **11** And Heber the Kenite has been separated from the Kenite, from the sons of Hobab father-in-law of Moses, and he stretches out his tent to the oak in Zaanaim, which [is] by Kedesh. **12** And they declare to Sisera that Barak son of Abinoam has gone up to Mount Tabor, **13** and Sisera calls all his chariots, nine hundred chariots of iron, and all the people who [are] with him, from Harosheth of the nations, to the Brook of Kishon. **14** And Deborah says to Barak, "Rise, for this [is] the day in which YHWH has given Sisera into your hand; has YHWH not gone out before you?" And Barak goes down from Mount Tabor, and ten thousand men after him. **15** And YHWH destroys Sisera, and all the chariots, and all the camp, by the mouth of the sword, before Barak, and Sisera comes down from off the chariot, and flees on his feet. **16** And Barak has pursued after the chariots and after the camp, to Harosheth of the nations, and all the camp of Sisera falls by the mouth of the sword—there has not been left even one. **17** And Sisera has fled on his feet to the tent of Jael wife of Heber the Kenite, for [there is] peace between Jabin king of Hazor and the house of Heber the Kenite; **18** and Jael goes out to meet Sisera and says to him, "Turn aside, my lord, turn aside to me, do not fear"; and he turns aside to her, into the tent, and she covers him with a mantle. **19** And he says to her, "Please give me a little water to drink, for I am thirsty"; and she opens the bottle of milk, and gives him to drink, and covers him. **20** And he says to her, "Stand at the opening of the tent, and it has been, if any comes in, and has asked you and said, Is there a man here? That you have said, There is not." **21** And Jael wife of Heber takes the pin of the tent, and takes the hammer in her hand, and goes to him gently, and strikes the pin into his temples, and it fastens in the earth—and he has been fast asleep, and is weary—and he dies. **22** And behold, Barak is pursuing Sisera, and Jael comes out to meet him, and says to him, "Come, and I show you the man whom you are seeking"; and he comes to her, and behold, Sisera is fallen—dead, and the pin [is] in his temples. **23** And God humbles Jabin king of Canaan before the sons of Israel on that day, **24** and the hand of the sons of Israel goes, going on and becoming hard on Jabin king of Canaan, until they have cut off Jabin king of Canaan.

5 And Deborah sings—also Barak son of Abinoam—on that day, saying, **2** "For freeing leaders in Israel, ‖ For a people willingly offering themselves, ‖ Bless YHWH. **3** Hear, you kings; give ear, you princes, ‖ I sing to YHWH, ‖ I sing praise to YHWH, God of Israel. **4** YHWH, in Your going forth out of Seir, ‖ In Your stepping out of the field of Edom, ‖ The earth trembled and the heavens dropped, ‖ And thick clouds dropped water. **5** Hills flowed from the face of YHWH, ‖ This one—Sinai—From the face of YHWH, God of Israel. **6** In the days of Shamgar son of Anath—In the days of Jael—The ways have ceased, ‖ And those going in the paths go [in] crooked ways. **7** Villages ceased in Israel—they ceased, ‖ Until I arose—Deborah, ‖ That I arose, a mother in Israel. **8** He chooses new gods, ‖ Then war [is] at the gates! A shield is not seen—and a spear ‖ Among forty thousand in Israel. **9** My heart [is] to the lawgivers of Israel, ‖ Who are offering themselves willingly among the people, ‖ Bless YHWH! **10** Riders on white donkeys—Sitters on a long robe—And walkers by the way—meditate! **11** By the voice of shouters ‖ Between the places of drawing water, ‖ There they give out righteous acts of YHWH, ‖ Righteous acts of His villages in Israel, ‖ Then the people of YHWH have gone down to the gates. **12** Awake, awake, Deborah; Awake, awake, utter a song; Rise, Barak, and take your captivity captive, ‖ Son of Abinoam. **13** Then him who is left of the majestic ones He caused to rule the people of YHWH, ‖ He caused me to rule among the mighty. **14** From Ephraim [are] those whose root [is] in Amalek, ‖ After you, Benjamin, among your peoples, ‖ From Machir lawgivers came down, ‖ And from Zebulun those drawing with the reed of a writer. **15** And princes in Issachar [are] with Deborah, ‖ Indeed, Issachar [is] right with Barak, ‖ Into the valley he was sent on his feet. In the divisions of Reuben, ‖ The decrees of heart [are] great! **16** Why have you abided between the boundaries, ‖ To hear lowings of herds? For the divisions of Reuben, ‖ The searchings of heart [are] great! **17** Gilead dwelt beyond the Jordan, ‖ And why does Dan sojourn [in] ships? Asher has abided at the haven of the seas, ‖ And dwells by his creeks. **18** Zebulun [is] a people who exposed its soul to death, ‖ Naphtali also—on high places of the field. **19** Kings came—they fought; Then kings of Canaan fought, ‖ In Taanach, by the waters of Megiddo; They did not take gain of money! **20** They fought from the heavens: The stars fought with Sisera from their highways. **21** The Brook of Kishon swept them away, ‖ The most ancient brook—the Brook of Kishon. You tread down strength, O my soul! **22** Then the horse-heels were broken, ‖ By gallopings—gallopings of its mighty ones. **23** Curse Meroz, said a messenger of YHWH, ‖ Cursing, curse its inhabitants! For they did not come to the help of YHWH, ‖ To the help of YHWH among the mighty! **24** Above women is Jael, ‖ The wife of Heber the Kenite, ‖ She is blessed above women in the tent. **25** He asked for water—she gave milk; She brought butter near in a lordly dish. **26** She sends forth her hand to the pin, ‖ And her right hand to the laborers' hammer, ‖ And she hammered Sisera—she struck his head, ‖ Indeed, she struck, and it passed through his temple. **27** He bowed between her feet—He fell, he lay down; He bowed between her feet, he fell; Where he bowed, there he fell—destroyed. **28** She has looked out through the window—Indeed, she cries out—the mother of Sisera, ‖ Through the lattice: Why is his chariot delaying to come? Why have the steps of his chariot tarried? **29** The wise ones, her princesses, answer her, ‖ Indeed, she returns her sayings to herself: **30** Do they not find? They apportion spoil, ‖ A female—two females—for every head, ‖ Spoil of finger-work for Sisera, ‖ Spoil of embroidered finger-work, ‖ Finger-work—a pair of embroidered things, ‖ For the necks of the spoil! **31** So do all Your enemies perish, O YHWH, ‖ And those loving Him [are] ‖ As the going out of the sun in its might!" And the land rests [for] forty years.

6 And the sons of Israel do evil in the eyes of YHWH, and YHWH gives them into the hand of Midian [for] seven years, **2** and the hand of Midian is strong against Israel, [so] the sons of Israel have made for themselves the nooks which [are] in the mountains, and the caves, and the strongholds [to hide] from the presence of Midian. **3** And it has been, if Israel has sowed, that Midian has come up, and Amalek, and the sons of the east, indeed, they have come up against him, **4** and encamp against them, and destroy the increase of the land until your entering Gaza; and they leave no sustenance in Israel, either sheep, or ox, or donkey; **5** for they and their livestock come up, with their tents; they come in as the fullness of the locust for multitude, and of them and of their livestock there is no number, and they come into the land to destroy it. **6** And Israel is very weak from the presence of Midian, and the sons of Israel cry to YHWH. **7** And it comes to pass, when the sons of Israel have cried to YHWH concerning Midian, **8** that YHWH sends a man, a prophet, to the sons of Israel, and he says to them, "Thus said YHWH, God of Israel: I have brought you up out of Egypt, and I bring you out from a house of servants, **9** and I deliver you out of the hand of the Egyptians, and out of the hand of all your

JUDGES

oppressors, and I cast them out from your presence, and I give their land to you, **10** and I say to you, I [am] your God YHWH, you do not fear the gods of the Amorite in whose land you are dwelling—and you have not listened to My voice." **11** And the Messenger of YHWH comes and sits under the oak which [is] in Ophrah, which [is] to Joash the Abi-Ezrite, and his son Gideon is beating out wheat in the winepress, to remove [it] from the presence of the Midianites; **12** and the Messenger of YHWH appears to him and says to him, "YHWH [is] with you, O mighty man of valor." **13** And Gideon says to Him, "O my Lord, [if] YHWH is indeed with us, then why has all this found us? And where [are] all His wonders which our fathers recounted to us, saying, Has YHWH not brought us up out of Egypt? And now YHWH has left us, and gives us into the hand of Midian." **14** And YHWH turns to him and says, "Go in this—your power; and you have saved Israel out of the hand of Midian—have I not sent you?" **15** And he says to Him, "O my Lord, with what do I save Israel? Behold, my chief [is] weak in Manasseh, and I [am] the least in the house of my father." **16** And YHWH says to him, "Because I am with you—you have struck the Midianites as one man." **17** And he says to Him, "Now if I have found grace in Your eyes, then You have done a sign for me that You are speaking with me. **18** Please do not move from here until my coming to You, and I have brought out my present, and put it before You"; and He says, "I abide until your return." **19** And Gideon has gone in, and prepares a kid of the goats, and an ephah of flour [worth] of unleavened things; he has put the flesh in a basket, and he has put the broth in a pot, and he brings [them] out to Him, to the place of the oak, and brings [them] near. **20** And the Messenger of God says to him, "Take the flesh and the unleavened things, and place [them] on this rock—and pour out the broth"; and he does so. **21** And the Messenger of YHWH puts forth the end of the staff which [is] in His hand, and comes against the flesh, and against the unleavened things, and the fire goes up out of the rock and consumes the flesh and the unleavened things—and the Messenger of YHWH has gone from his eyes. **22** And Gideon sees that He [is] the Messenger of YHWH, and Gideon says, "Aah, Lord YHWH! For so I have looked on the Messenger of YHWH face to face!" **23** And YHWH says to him, "Peace to you; do not fear; you do not die." **24** And Gideon builds an altar to YHWH there, and calls it YHWH-Shalom, it [is] yet in Ophrah of the Abi-Ezrites to this day. **25** And it comes to pass, on that night, that YHWH says to him, "Take the young ox which your father has, and the second bullock of seven years, and you have thrown down the altar of Ba'al which your father has, and cut down the Asherah which [is] by it, **26** and you have built an altar to your God YHWH on the top of this stronghold, by the arrangement, and have taken the second bullock, and caused a burnt-offering to ascend with the wood of the Asherah which you cut down." **27** And Gideon takes ten men of his servants, and does as YHWH has spoken to him, and it comes to pass, because he has been afraid of the house of his father, and the men of the city, to do [it] by day, that he does [it] by night. **28** And the men of the city rise early in the morning, and behold, the altar of Ba'al has been broken down, and the Asherah which is by it has been cut down, and the second bullock has been offered on the altar which is built. **29** And they say to one another, "Who has done this thing?" And they inquire and seek, and they say, "Gideon son of Joash has done this thing." **30** And the men of the city say to Joash, "Bring out your son, and he dies, because he has broken down the altar of Ba'al, and because he has cut down the Asherah which [is] by it." **31** And Joash says to all who have stood against him, "You, do you plead for Ba'al? You—do you save him? He who pleads for him is put to death during the morning; if he [is] a god he pleads against him himself, because he has broken down his altar." **32** And he calls him, on that day, Jerubba'al, saying, "The Ba'al pleads against him, because he has broken down his altar." **33** And all Midian and Amalek and the sons of the east have been gathered together, and pass over, and encamp in the Valley of Jezreel, **34** and the Spirit of YHWH has clothed Gideon, and he blows with a horn, and Abi-Ezer is called after him; **35** and he has sent messengers into all Manasseh, and it is also called after him; and he has sent messengers into Asher, and into Zebulun, and into Naphtali, and they come up to meet them. **36** And Gideon says to God, "If You are Savior of

Israel by my hand, as You have spoken, 37 behold, I am placing the fleece of wool in the threshing-floor: if dew is only on the fleece, and dryness on all the earth—then I have known that You save Israel by my hand, as You have spoken"; 38 and it is so, and he rises early on the next day, and presses the fleece, and wrings dew out of the fleece—the fullness of the bowl of waters. 39 And Gideon says to God, "Do not let Your anger burn against me, and I only speak this time; please let me try only this time with the fleece—please let there be only dryness on the fleece, and let there be dew on all the earth." 40 And God does so on that night, and there is only dryness on the fleece, and there has been dew on all the earth.

7 And Jerubba'al (he [is] Gideon) rises early, and all the people who [are] with him, and they encamp by the well of Harod, and the camp of Midian has been on the south of him, on the height of Moreh, in the valley. 2 And YHWH says to Gideon, "The people who [are] with you [are] too many for My giving Midian into their hand, lest Israel beautify itself against Me, saying, My hand has given salvation to me; 3 and now, please call in the ears of the people, saying, Whoever [is] afraid and trembling, let him turn back and go early from Mount Gilead"; and there return twenty-two thousand of the people, and ten thousand have been left. 4 And YHWH says to Gideon, "The people [are] yet too many; bring them down to the water, and I refine him for you there; and it has been, he of whom I say to you, This goes with you—he goes with you; and any of whom I say to you, This does not go with you—he does not go." 5 And he brings the people down to the water, and YHWH says to Gideon, "Everyone who laps of the water with his tongue as the dog laps—you set him apart; also everyone who bows on his knees to drink." 6 And the number of those lapping with their hand to their mouth is three hundred men, and all the rest of the people have bowed down on their knees to drink water. 7 And YHWH says to Gideon, "I save you by the three hundred men who are lapping, and have given Midian into your hand, and all the people go, each to his place." 8 And the people take the provision in their hand, and their horns, and he has sent every man of Israel away, each to his tents; and he has kept hold on the three hundred men, and the camp of Midian has been by him at the lower part of the valley. 9 And it comes to pass, on that night, that YHWH says to him, "Rise, go down into the camp, for I have given it into your hand; 10 and if you are afraid to go down—go down, you and your young man Phurah, to the camp, 11 and you have heard what they speak, and afterward your hands are strengthened, and you have gone down against the camp." And he goes down, he and his young man Phurah, to the extremity of the fifties who [are] in the camp; 12 and Midian, and Amalek, and all the sons of the east are lying in the valley, as the locust for multitude, and of their camels there is no number, as sand which [is] on the seashore for multitude. 13 And Gideon comes in, and behold, a man is recounting a dream to his companion, and says, "Behold, I have dreamed a dream, and behold, a cake of barley-bread is turning itself over into the camp of Midian, and it comes to the tent, and strikes it, and it falls, and turns it upwards, and the tent has fallen." 14 And his companion answers and says, "This is nothing except the sword of Gideon son of Joash, a man of Israel; God has given Midian and all the camp into his hand." 15 And it comes to pass, when Gideon hears the narration of the dream and its interpretation, that he bows himself, and turns back to the camp of Israel, and says, "Rise, for YHWH has given the camp of Midian into your hand." 16 And he divides the three hundred men [into] three detachments, and puts horns into the hand of all of them, and empty pitchers, and lamps within the pitchers. 17 And he says to them, "Look at me, and thus do; and behold, I am coming into the extremity of the camp—and it has been—as I do so you do; 18 and I have blown with a horn—I and all who [are] with me, and you have blown with horns, even you, around all the camp, and have said, For YHWH and for Gideon!" 19 And Gideon comes—and the hundred men who [are] with him—into the extremity of the camp, [at] the beginning of the middle watch (they had just posted watchmen), and they blow with horns—also dashing in pieces the pitchers which [are] in their hand; 20 and the three detachments blow with horns, and break the pitchers, and keep hold with their left hand on the lamps, and with their right

hand on the horns to blow, and they cry, "The sword of YHWH and of Gideon!" **21** And they each stand in his place, around the camp, and all the camp runs, and they shout, and flee; **22** and the three hundred blow the horns, and YHWH sets the sword of each against his companion, even through all the camp; and the camp flees to Beth-Shittah, at Zererath, to the border of Abel-Meholah, by Tabbath. **23** And the men of Israel are called from Naphtali, and from Asher, and from all Manasseh, and pursue after Midian. **24** And Gideon has sent messengers into all the hill-country of Ephraim, saying, "Come down to meet Midian, and capture the waters from them as far as Beth-Barah, and the Jordan"; and every man of Ephraim is called, and they capture the waters as far as Beth-Barah, and the Jordan, **25** and they capture two of the heads of Midian, Oreb and Zeeb, and slay Oreb at the rock of Oreb, and they have slain Zeeb at the wine-vat of Zeeb, and they pursue into Midian; and they have brought the heads of Oreb and Zeeb to Gideon beyond the Jordan.

8 And the men of Ephraim say to him, "What [is] this thing you have done to us—not to call for us when you went to fight with Midian?" And they strive with him severely; **2** and he says to them, "What have I now done like you? Are the gleanings of Ephraim not better than the harvest of Abi-Ezer? **3** God has given the heads of Midian, Oreb and Zeeb, into your hand; and what have I been able to do like you?" Then their temper desisted from off him in his speaking this thing. **4** And Gideon comes to the Jordan, passing over, he and the three hundred men who [are] with him—wearied, yet pursuing— **5** and he says to the men of Succoth, "Please give cakes of bread to the people who [are] at my feet, for they [are] wearied, and I am pursuing after Zebah and Zalmunna, kings of Midian." **6** And the heads of Succoth say, "Is the hand of Zebah and Zalmunna now in your hand, that we give bread to your host?" **7** And Gideon says, "Therefore—in YHWH's giving Zebah and Zalmunna into my hand—I have threshed your flesh with the thorns of the wilderness, and with the threshing instruments." **8** And he goes up there [to] Penuel, and speaks to them thus; and the men of Penuel answer him as the men of Succoth answered. **9** And he also speaks to the men of Penuel, saying, "In my turning back in peace, I break down this tower." **10** And Zebah and Zalmunna [are] in Karkor, and their camps with them, about fifteen thousand, all who are left of all the camp of the sons of the east; and those falling [are] one hundred and twenty thousand men, drawing sword. **11** And Gideon goes up the way of those who dwell in tents, on the east of Nobah and Jogbehah, and strikes the camp, and the camp was confident; **12** and Zebab and Zalmunna flee, and he pursues after them, and captures the two kings of Midian, Zebah and Zalmunna, and he has caused all the camp to tremble. **13** And Gideon son of Joash turns back from the battle, at the going up of the sun, **14** and captures a young man of the men of Succoth, and asks him, and he describes to him the heads of Succoth, and its elderly—seventy-seven men. **15** And he comes to the men of Succoth and says, "Behold Zebah and Zalmunna, with whom you reproached me, saying, Is the hand of Zebah and Zalmunna now in your hand that we give bread to your men who [are] wearied?" **16** And he takes the elderly of the city, and [the] thorns of the wilderness, and the threshing instruments, and teaches the men of Succoth by them, **17** and he has broken down the Tower of Penuel, and slays the men of the city. **18** And he says to Zebah and to Zalmunna, "What manner of men [were they] whom you slew in Tabor?" And they say, "As you—so they, [each] one as the form of the king's sons." **19** And he says, "They [were] my brothers—sons of my mother; YHWH lives, if you had kept them alive—I would not kill you." **20** And he says to his firstborn Jether, "Rise, slay them"; and the young man has not drawn his sword, for he has been afraid, for he [is] yet a youth. **21** And Zebah and Zalmunna say, "Rise and fall on us; for as the man—his might"; and Gideon rises, and slays Zebah and Zalmunna, and takes the crescents which [are] on the necks of their camels. **22** And the men of Israel say to Gideon, "Rule over us, both you, and your son, and your son's son, for you have saved us from the hand of Midian." **23** And Gideon says to them, "I do not rule over you, nor does my son rule over you; YHWH rules over you." **24** And Gideon says to them, "Let me ask a petition of you, and each give to me the ring of his prey, for they have rings of gold, for they [are] Ishmaelites." **25** And they say, "We certainly give"; and they spread out the garment, and each casts the ring of his prey there; **26** and the weight of the rings of gold which he asked for is one thousand and seven hundred [shekels] of gold, apart from the crescents, and the pendants, and the purple garments, which [are] on the kings of Midian, and apart from the chains which [are] on the necks of their camels, **27** and Gideon makes it into an ephod, and sets it up in his city, in Ophrah, and all Israel go whoring after it there, and it is for a snare to Gideon and to his house. **28** And Midian is humbled before the sons of Israel, and have not added to lift up their head; and the land rests [for] forty years in the days of Gideon. **29** And Jerubba'al son of Joash goes and dwells in his own house, **30** and there have been seventy sons of Gideon, coming out of his loin, for he had many wives; **31** and his concubine, who [is] in Shechem, has borne to him—even she—a son, and he appoints his name Abimelech. **32** And Gideon son of Joash dies, in a good old age, and is buried in the burying-place of his father Joash, in Ophrah of the Abi-Ezrite. **33** And it comes to pass, when Gideon [is] dead, that the sons of Israel turn back and go whoring after the Ba'alim, and set Ba'al-Berith over them for a god; **34** and the sons of Israel have not remembered their God YHWH, who is delivering them out of the hand of all their surrounding enemies, **35** neither have they done kindness with the house of Jerubba'al—Gideon—according to all the good which he did with Israel.

9 And Abimelech son of Jerubba'al goes to Shechem, to his mother's brothers, and speaks to them, and to all the family of the house of his mother's father, saying, **2** "Now speak in the ears of all the masters of Shechem, Which [is] good for you—seventy men ruling over you (all the sons of Jerubba'al), or one man ruling over you? And you have remembered that I [am] your bone and your flesh." **3** And his mother's brothers speak concerning him, in the ears of all the masters of Shechem, all these words, and their heart inclines after Abimelech, for they said, "He [is] our brother"; **4** and they give seventy [pieces] of silver out of the house of Ba'al-Berith to him, and Abimelech hires vain and unstable men with them, and they go after him; **5** and he goes into the house of his father at Ophrah, and slays his brothers, sons of Jerubba'al, seventy men, on one stone; and Jotham, youngest son of Jerubba'al, is left, for he was hidden. **6** And all the masters of Shechem are gathered together, and all the house of Millo, and come and cause Abimelech to reign for king at the oak of the camp which [is] in Shechem; **7** and they declare [it] to Jotham, and he goes and stands on the top of Mount Gerizim, and lifts up his voice, and calls, and says to them, "Listen to me, O masters of Shechem, and God listens to you: **8** The trees have diligently gone to anoint a king over them, and they say to the olive, Reign over us. **9** And the olive says to them, Have I ceased from my fatness, by which they honor gods and men, that I have gone to stagger over the trees? **10** And the trees say to the fig, Come, reign over us. **11** And the fig says to them, Have I ceased from my sweetness, and my good increase, that I have gone to stagger over the trees? **12** And the trees say to the vine, Come, reign over us. **13** And the vine says to them, Have I ceased from my new wine, which is making gods and men glad, that I have gone to stagger over the trees? **14** And all the trees say to the bramble, Come, reign over us. **15** And the bramble says to the trees, If in truth you are anointing me for king over you, come, take refuge in my shadow; and if not—fire comes out from the bramble, and devours the cedars of Lebanon. **16** And now, if you have acted in truth and in sincerity when you make Abimelech king; and if you have done good with Jerubba'al, and with his house; and if you have done to him according to the deed of his hands— **17** because my father has fought for you, and casts his life away from [him], and delivers you from the hand of Midian; **18** and you have risen against the house of my father today, and slay his sons, seventy men, on one stone, and cause Abimelech son of his handmaid to reign over the masters of Shechem, because he [is] your brother— **19** indeed, if in truth and in sincerity you have acted with Jerubba'al and with his house this day, rejoice in Abimelech, and he rejoices—even he—in you; **20** and if not—fire comes out from Abimelech and devours the masters of Shechem and the house of

Millo, and fire comes out from the masters of Shechem and from the house of Millo, and devours Abimelech." 21 And Jotham hurries, and flees, and goes to Beer, and dwells there, from the face of his brother Abimelech. 22 And Abimelech is prince over Israel [for] three years, 23 and God sends an evil spirit between Abimelech and the masters of Shechem, and the masters of Shechem deal treacherously with Abimelech, 24 for [the] coming in of [the] violence [against] seventy sons of Jerubba'al, and to place their blood on their brother Abimelech, who slew them, and on the masters of Shechem, who strengthened his hands to slay his brothers. 25 And the masters of Shechem set ambushes for him on the top of the hills, and rob everyone who passes over by them in the way, and it is declared to Abimelech. 26 And Gaal son of Ebed comes—also his brothers—and they pass over into Shechem, and the masters of Shechem trust in him, 27 and go out into the field, and gather their vineyards, and tread, and make praises, and go into the house of their god, and eat and drink, and revile Abimelech. 28 And Gaal son of Ebed says, "Who [is] Abimelech, and who [is] Shechem, that we serve him? Is [he] not son of Jerubba'al? And his commander Zebul? The men of Hamor father of Shechem serve you, and why do we serve him—we? 29 And oh that this people were in my hand—then I turn Abimelech aside"; and he says to Abimelech, "Increase your host, and come out." 30 And Zebul, prince of the city, hears the words of Gaal son of Ebed, and his anger burns, 31 and he sends messengers to Abimelech deceitfully, saying, "Behold, Gaal son of Ebed and his brothers are coming into Shechem, and behold, they are fortifying the city against you; 32 and now, rise by night, you and the people who [are] with you, and lay wait in the field, 33 and it has been, in the morning, about the rising of the sun, you rise early, and have pushed against the city; and behold, he and the people who [are] with him are going out to you—and you have done to him as your hand finds." 34 And Abimelech rises, and all the people who [are] with him, by night, and they lay wait against Shechem—four detachments; 35 and Gaal son of Ebed goes out, and stands at the opening of the gate of the city, and Abimelech rises—also the people who [are] with him—from the ambush, 36 and Gaal sees the people and says to Zebul, "Behold, people are coming down from the top of the hills"; and Zebul says to him, "You are seeing the shadow of the hills like men." 37 And Gaal adds yet to speak and says, "Behold, people are coming down from the high part of the land, and another detachment is coming by the way of the oak of Meonenim." 38 And Zebul says to him, "Where [is] your mouth now, in that you say, Who [is] Abimelech that we serve him? Is this not the people against which you have kicked? Please go out now and fight against it." 39 And Gaal goes out before the masters of Shechem, and fights against Abimelech, 40 and Abimelech pursues him, and he flees from his presence, and many fall wounded—to the opening of the gate. 41 And Abimelech abides in Arumah, and Zebul casts out Gaal and his brothers from dwelling in Shechem. 42 And it comes to pass, on the next day, that the people go out to the field, and they declare [it] to Abimelech, 43 and he takes the people, and divides them into three detachments, and lays wait in a field, and looks, and behold, the people are coming out from the city, and he rises against them, and strikes them. 44 And Abimelech and the detachments who [are] with him have pushed on, and stand at the opening of the gate of the city, and the two detachments have pushed against all who are in the field, and strike them, 45 and Abimelech has fought against the city all that day, and captures the city, and has slain the people who [are] in it, and he breaks down the city, and sows it [with] salt. 46 And all the masters of the Tower of Shechem hear, and go into the high place of the house of the god Berith, 47 and it is declared to Abimelech that all the masters of the Tower of Shechem have gathered themselves together, 48 and Abimelech goes up to Mount Zalmon, he and all the people who [are] with him, and Abimelech takes the great axe in his hand, and cuts off a bough of the trees, and lifts it up, and sets [it] on his shoulder, and says to the people who [are] with him, "What you have seen me do—hurry, do as I [have done]." 49 And every one of the people cuts down his bough and goes after Abimelech, and sets [them] at the high place, and burns the high place with fire by these, and also all the men of the Tower of Shechem die—about one thousand men and women. 50 And

Abimelech goes to Thebez, and encamps against Thebez, and captures it, **51** and a strong tower has been in the midst of the city, and all the men and the women flee there, and all the masters of the city, and they shut [it] behind them, and go up on the roof of the tower. **52** And Abimelech comes to the tower, and fights against it, and draws near to the opening of the tower to burn it with fire, **53** and a certain woman casts a piece of a millstone on the head of Abimelech, and breaks his skull, **54** and he calls quickly to the young man carrying his weapons and says to him, "Draw your sword, and you have put me to death, lest they say of me—A woman slew him"; and his young man pierced him through, and he dies. **55** And the men of Israel see that Abimelech [is] dead, and each one goes to his place; **56** and God turns back the evil of Abimelech which he did to his father to slay his seventy brothers; **57** and God has returned all the evil of the men of Shechem on their [own] head, and the cursing of Jotham son of Jerubba'al comes to them.

10 And there rises after Abimelech, to save Israel, Tola son of Puah, son of Dodo, a man of Issachar, and he is dwelling in Shamir, in the hill-country of Ephraim, **2** and he judges Israel [for] twenty-three years, and he dies, and is buried in Shamir. **3** And there rises Jair the Gileadite after him, and he judges Israel [for] twenty-two years, **4** and he has thirty sons riding on thirty donkey-colts, and they have thirty cities (they call them Havoth-Jair to this day), which [are] in the land of Gilead; **5** and Jair dies, and is buried in Kamon. **6** And the sons of Israel add to do evil in the eyes of YHWH, and serve the Ba'alim, and Ashtaroth, and the gods of Aram, and the gods of Sidon, and the gods of Moab, and the gods of the sons of Ammon, and the gods of the Philistines, and forsake YHWH, and have not served Him; **7** and the anger of YHWH burns against Israel, and He sells them into the hand of the Philistines, and into the hand of the sons of Ammon, **8** and they crush and oppress the sons of Israel in that year; [and for] eighteen years—all the sons of Israel [who] are beyond the Jordan, in the land of the Amorite, which [is] in Gilead. **9** And the sons of Ammon pass over the Jordan to also fight against Judah, and against Benjamin, and against the house of Ephraim, and Israel has great distress. **10** And the sons of Israel cry to YHWH, saying, "We have sinned against You, because we have even forsaken our God, and serve the Ba'alim." **11** And YHWH says to the sons of Israel, "[Have I] not [saved you] from the Egyptians, and from the Amorite, from the sons of Ammon, and from the Philistines? **12** And the Zidonians, and Amalek, and Maon have oppressed you, and you cry to Me, and I save you out of their hand; **13** and you have forsaken Me, and serve other gods, therefore I do not add to save you. **14** Go and cry to the gods on which you have fixed; they save you in the time of your tribulation." **15** And the sons of Israel say to YHWH, "We have sinned, do to us according to all that is good in Your eyes; only please deliver us this day." **16** And they turn aside the gods of the stranger out of their midst, and serve YHWH, and His soul is grieved with the misery of Israel. **17** And the sons of Ammon are called together, and encamp in Gilead, and the sons of Israel are gathered together, and encamp in Mizpah. **18** And the people—heads of Gilead—say to one another, "Who [is] the man that begins to fight against the sons of Ammon? He is for head to all inhabitants of Gilead."

11 And Jephthah the Gileadite has been a mighty man of valor, and he [is the] son of a harlot woman; and Gilead begets Jephthah, **2** and the wife of Gilead bears sons to him, and the wife's sons grow up and cast Jephthah out, and say to him, "You do not inherit in the house of our father; for you [are the] son of another woman." **3** And Jephthah flees from the face of his brothers, and dwells in the land of Tob; and vain men gather themselves together to Jephthah, and they go out with him. **4** And it comes to pass, after a time, that the sons of Ammon fight with Israel, **5** and it comes to pass, when the sons of Ammon have fought with Israel, that [the] elderly of Gilead go to take Jephthah from the land of Tob; **6** and they say to Jephthah, "Come, and you have been for a captain to us, and we fight against the sons of Ammon." **7** And Jephthah says to [the] elderly of Gilead, "Have you not hated me? And you cast me out from the house of my father, and why have you come to me now when you are in distress?" **8** And [the] elderly of Gilead say to Jephthah, "Therefore, now, we have turned back to you; and you have gone with us, and have fought against the sons of Ammon, and you have been for head to us—to all the inhabitants of Gilead." **9** And Jephthah says to [the] elderly of Gilead, "If you are taking me back to fight against the sons of Ammon, and YHWH has given them before me—am I for a head to you?" **10** And [the] elderly of Gilead say to Jephthah, "YHWH is listening between us—if we do not do so according to your word." **11** And Jephthah goes with [the] elderly of Gilead, and the people set him over them for head and for captain, and Jephthah speaks all his words before YHWH in Mizpeh. **12** And Jephthah sends messengers to the king of the sons of Ammon, saying, "What [is this] to me and to you, that you have come to me, to fight in my land?" **13** And the king of the sons of Ammon says to the messengers of Jephthah, "Because Israel took my land in his coming up out of Egypt, from Arnon, and to the Jabbok, and to the Jordan; and now, restore them in peace." **14** And Jephthah adds yet and sends messengers to the king of the sons of Ammon, **15** and says to him, "Thus said Jephthah: Israel did not take the land of Moab, and the land of the sons of Ammon, **16** for in their coming up out of Egypt, Israel goes in the wilderness to the Red Sea, and comes to Kadesh, **17** and Israel sends messengers to the king of Edom, saying, Please let me pass over through your land, and the king of Edom did not listen; and [Israel] has also sent to the king of Moab, and he has not been willing; and Israel abides in Kadesh, **18** and he goes through the wilderness, and goes around the land of Edom and the land of Moab, and comes in at the rising of the sun of the land of Moab, and they encamp beyond Arnon, and have not come into the border of Moab, for Arnon [is] the border of Moab. **19** And Israel sends messengers to Sihon, king of the Amorite, king of Heshbon, and Israel says to him, Please let us pass over through your land, to my place, **20** and Sihon has not trusted Israel to pass over through his border, and Sihon gathers all his people, and they encamp in Jahaz, and fight with Israel; **21** and YHWH, God of Israel, gives Sihon and all his people into the hand of Israel, and they strike them, and Israel possesses all the land of the Amorite, the inhabitant of that land, **22** and they possess all the border of the Amorite from Arnon, and to the Jabbok, and from the wilderness, and to the Jordan. **23** And now, YHWH, God of Israel, has dispossessed the Amorite from the presence of His people Israel, and you would possess it! **24** That which your god Chemosh causes you to possess—do you not possess it? And all that which our God YHWH has dispossessed from our presence—we possess it. **25** And now, [are] you at all better than Balak son of Zippor, king of Moab? Did he strive with Israel at all? Did he fight against them at all? **26** In Israel's dwelling in Heshbon and in its towns, and in Aroer and in its towns, and in all the cities which [are] by the sides of Arnon [for] three hundred years—and why have you not delivered them in that time? **27** And I have not sinned against you, and you are doing evil with me—to fight against me. YHWH, the Judge, judges between the sons of Israel and the sons of Ammon today." **28** And the king of the sons of Ammon has not listened to the words of Jephthah which he sent to him, **29** and the Spirit of YHWH is on Jephthah, and he passes over Gilead and Manasseh, and passes over Mizpeh of Gilead, and he has passed over from Mizpeh of Gilead to the sons of Ammon. **30** And Jephthah vows a vow to YHWH and says, "If You give the sons of Ammon into my hand at all— **31** then it has been, that which comes out from the doors of my house at all to meet me in my turning back in peace from the sons of Ammon—it has been for YHWH, or I have offered up a burnt-offering for it." **32** And Jephthah passes over to the sons of Ammon to fight against them, and YHWH gives them into his hand, **33** and he strikes them from Aroer, and to [where] you are going in to Minnith—twenty cities—and to the meadow of the vineyards, [with] a very great striking; and the sons of Ammon are humbled at the presence of the sons of Israel. **34** And Jephthah comes into Mizpeh, to his house, and behold, his daughter is coming out to meet him with timbrels, and with choruses, and except her alone, he has no son or daughter. **35** And it comes to pass, when he sees her, that he tears his garments and says, "Aah! My daughter, you have caused me to bend greatly, and you have been among those troubling me; and I have opened my mouth to YHWH, and I am not able to turn back." **36** And she says to him, "My father, you have opened your mouth to YHWH, do to me as it has gone out from your mouth, after that YHWH has done vengeance for you on your enemies, on the sons of Ammon." **37** And she says to her father, "Let this thing be done to me; desist from me [for] two months, and I go on, and have gone down on the hills, and I weep for my virginity—I and my friends." **38** And he says, "Go"; and he sends her away [for] two months, and she goes, she and her friends, and she weeps for her virginity on the hills; **39** and it comes to pass at the end of two months that she turns back to her father, and he does to her his vow which he has vowed, and she did not know a man; and it is a statute in Israel: **40** from time to time the daughters of Israel go to talk to the daughter of Jephthah the Gileadite, four days in a year.

12 And the men of Ephraim are called together, and pass over northward, and say to Jephthah, "Why have you passed over to fight against the sons of Ammon, and have not called on us to go with you? We burn your house with fire over you." **2** And Jephthah says to them, "I have been a man of great strife (I and my people) with the sons of Ammon, and I call you, and you have not saved me out of their hand, **3** and I see that you are not a savior, and I put my life in my hand, and pass over to the sons of Ammon, and YHWH gives them into my hand—and why have you come up to me this day to fight against me?" **4** And Jephthah gathered all the men of Gilead, and fights with Ephraim, and the men of Gilead strike Ephraim, because they said, "You Gileadites [are] fugitives of Ephraim, in the midst of Ephraim—in the midst of Manasseh." **5** And Gilead captures the passages of the Jordan to Ephraim, and it has been, when [any of] the fugitives of Ephraim say, "Let me pass over," and the men of Gilead say to him, "[Are] you an Ephraimite?" And he says, "No"; **6** that they say to him, "Now say, Shibboleth"; and he says, "Sibboleth," and is not prepared to speak right—and they seize him, and slaughter him at the passages of the Jordan, and there fall at that time, of Ephraim, forty-two chiefs. **7** And Jephthah judged Israel [for] six years, and Jephthah the Gileadite dies, and is buried in [one of] the cities of Gilead. **8** And after him Ibzan of Beth-Lehem judges Israel, **9** and he has thirty sons, and thirty daughters he gave away [in marriage], and thirty daughters he brought in from outside for his sons; and he judges Israel [for] seven years. **10** And Ibzan dies, and is buried in Beth-Lehem. **11** And after him Elon the Zebulunite judges Israel, and he judges Israel [for] ten years, **12** and Elon the Zebulunite dies, and is buried in Aijalon, in the land of Zebulun. **13** And after him, Abdon son of Hillel, the Pirathonite, judges Israel, **14** and he has forty sons, and thirty grandsons, riding on seventy donkey-colts, and he judges Israel [for] eight years. **15** And Abdon son of Hillel, the Pirathonite, dies, and is buried in Pirathon, in the land of Ephraim, in the hill-country of the Amalekite.

13 And the sons of Israel add to do evil in the eyes of YHWH, and YHWH gives them into the hand of the Philistines [for] forty years. **2** And there is a certain man of Zorah, of the family of the Danite, and his name [is] Manoah, his wife [is] barren, and has not borne; **3** and the Messenger of YHWH appears to the woman and says to her, "Now behold, you [are] barren and have not borne; when you have conceived, then you have borne a son. **4** And now, please take heed and do not drink wine and strong drink, and do not eat any unclean thing, **5** for behold, you are conceiving and bearing a son, and a razor does not go up on his head, for the youth is a Nazarite to God from the womb, and he begins to save Israel out of the hand of the Philistines." **6** And the woman comes and speaks to her husband, saying, "A Man of God has come to me, and His appearance [is] as the appearance of the Messenger of God, very fearful, and I have not asked Him where He [is] from, and he has not declared His Name to me; **7** and He says to me, Behold, you are pregnant, and bearing a son, and now do not drink wine and strong drink, and do not eat any unclean thing, for the youth is a Nazarite to God from the womb until the day of his death." **8** And Manoah makes plea to YHWH and says, "O my Lord, the Man of God whom You sent, please let Him come in again to us, and direct us what we do to the youth who is born." **9** And God listens to the voice of Manoah, and the Messenger of God comes again to the woman, and she [is] sitting in a field, and her husband Manoah is not with her, **10** and the woman hurries, and runs, and declares [it] to her husband, and says to him, "Behold, He has appeared to me—the Man who came on [that] day to me." **11** And Manoah rises, and goes after his wife, and comes to the Man, and says to Him, "Are you the Man who spoke to the woman?" And He says, "I [am]." **12** And Manoah says, "Now let Your words come to pass; what is the custom of the youth—and his work?" **13** And the Messenger of Y<small>HWH</small> says to Manoah, "Of all that I said to the woman let her take heed; **14** she does not eat of anything which comes out from the wine-vine, and she does not drink wine and strong drink, and she does not eat any unclean thing; she observes all that I have commanded her." **15** And Manoah says to the Messenger of Y<small>HWH</small>, "Please let us detain You, and we prepare a kid of the goats before You." **16** And the Messenger of Y<small>HWH</small> says to Manoah, "If you detain Me—I do not eat of your bread; and if you prepare a burnt-offering—offer it to Y<small>HWH</small>"; for Manoah has not known that He [is] the Messenger of Y<small>HWH</small>. **17** And Manoah says to the Messenger of Y<small>HWH</small>, "What [is] Your Name? When Your words come to pass, then we have honored You." **18** And the Messenger of Y<small>HWH</small> says to him, "Why do you ask this, My Name, since it [is] incomprehensible?" **19** And Manoah takes the kid of the goats, and the present, and offers on the rock to Y<small>HWH</small>, and He is doing wonderfully, and Manoah and his wife are looking on, **20** and it comes to pass, in the going up of the flame from off the altar toward the heavens, that the Messenger of Y<small>HWH</small> goes up in the flame of the altar, and Manoah and his wife are looking on, and they fall on their faces to the earth, **21** and the Messenger of Y<small>HWH</small> has not added again to appear to Manoah, and to his wife, then Manoah has known that He [is] the Messenger of Y<small>HWH</small>. **22** And Manoah says to his wife, "We certainly die, for we have seen God." **23** And his wife says to him, "If Y<small>HWH</small> were desirous to put us to death, He had not received burnt-offering and present from our hands, nor showed us all these things, nor caused us to hear [anything] like this as [at this] time." **24** And the woman bears a son, and calls his name Samson, and the youth grows, and Y<small>HWH</small> blesses him, **25** and the Spirit of Y<small>HWH</small> begins to move him in the camp of Dan, between Zorah and Eshtaol.

14 And Samson goes down to Timnath, and sees a woman in Timnath of the daughters of the Philistines, **2** and comes up and declares [it] to his father and to his mother, and says, "I have seen a woman in Timnath, of the daughters of the Philistines; and now, take her for me for a wife." **3** And his father says to him—also his mother, "Is there no woman among the daughters of your brothers, and among all my people, that you are going to take a woman from the uncircumcised Philistines?" And Samson says to his father, "Take her for me, for she is right in my eyes." **4** And his father and his mother have not known that it [is] from Y<small>HWH</small>, that He is seeking a meeting of the Philistines; and the Philistines are ruling over Israel at that time. **5** And Samson goes down—also his father and his mother, to Timnath, and they come to the vineyards of Timnath, and behold, a lion's whelp roars at meeting him, **6** and the Spirit of Y<small>HWH</small> prospers over him, and he tears it as the tearing of a kid, and there is nothing in his hand, and he has not declared to his father and to his mother that which he has done. **7** And he goes down and speaks to the woman, and she is right in the eyes of Samson; **8** and he turns back after [some] days to take her, and turns aside to see the carcass of the lion, and behold, a swarm of bees [are] in the body of the lion—and honey. **9** And he takes it down on to his hands, and goes on, going and eating; and he goes to his father, and to his mother, and gives to them, and they eat, and he has not declared to them that he took down the honey from the body of the lion. **10** And his father goes down to the woman, and Samson makes a banquet there, for so the young men does; **11** and it comes to pass, when they see him, that they take thirty companions, and they are with him. **12** And Samson says to them, "Now let me put forth a riddle to you; if you certainly declare it to me [in] the seven days of the banquet, and have found [it] out, then I have given thirty linen shirts and thirty changes of garments to you; **13** and if you are not able to declare [it] to me, then you have given thirty linen shirts and thirty changes of garments to me." And they say to him, "Put forth your riddle, and we hear it!" **14** And he says to them: "Out of the

JUDGES

eater came forth something to eat, ‖ And out of the strong came forth [something] sweet"; and they were not able to declare the riddle [in] three days. **15** And it comes to pass, on the seventh day, that they say to Samson's wife, "Entice your husband, that he declare the riddle to us, lest we burn you and the house of your father with fire; have you not called for us [here] to rob us?" **16** And Samson's wife weeps for it and says, "You have only hated me, and have not loved me; you have put forth the riddle to the sons of my people, but have not declared it to me"; and he says to her, "Behold, I have not declared [it] to my father and to my mother—and I declare [it] to you?" **17** And she weeps for it the seven days [in] which their banquet has been, and it comes to pass on the seventh day that he declares [it] to her, for she has distressed him; and she declares the riddle to the sons of her people. **18** And the men of the city say to him on the seventh day, before the sun goes in: "What [is] sweeter than honey? And what [is] stronger than a lion?" And he says to them: "Unless you had plowed with my heifer, ‖ You had not found out my riddle." **19** And the Spirit of YHWH prospers over him, and he goes down to Ashkelon, and strikes down thirty of their men, and takes their armor, and gives the changes to those declaring the riddle; and his anger burns, and he goes up to the house of his father; **20** and Samson's wife becomes his companion's, who had attended to him.

15 And it comes to pass after [some] days, in the days of wheat-harvest, that Samson looks after his wife, with a kid of the goats, and says, "I go in to my wife, to the inner chamber"; and her father has not permitted him to go in, **2** and her father says, "I certainly said that you surely hated her, and I give her to your companion; is her younger sister not better than she? Please let her be to you instead of her." **3** And Samson says of them, "I am more innocent this time than the Philistines, though I am doing evil with them." **4** And Samson goes and catches three hundred foxes, and takes torches, and turns tail to tail, and puts a torch between the two tails, in the midst, **5** and kindles fire in the torches, and sends [them] out into the standing grain of the Philistines, and burns [it] from heap even to standing grain, even to vineyard [and] olive-yard. **6** And the Philistines say, "Who has done this?" And they say, "Samson, son-in-law of the Timnite, because he has taken away his wife, and gives her to his companion"; and the Philistines go up, and burn her and her father with fire. **7** And Samson says to them, "Though you do thus, nevertheless I am avenged on you, and afterward I cease!" **8** And he strikes them hip and thigh [with] a great striking, and goes down and dwells in the cleft of the rock of Etam. **9** And the Philistines go up, and encamp in Judah, and are spread out in Lehi, **10** and the men of Judah say, "Why have you come up against us?" And they say, "We have come up to bind Samson, to do to him as he has done to us." **11** And three thousand men of Judah go down to the cleft of the rock of Etam, and say to Samson, "Have you now known that the Philistines are rulers over us? And what [is] this you have done to us?" And he says to them, "As they did to me, so I did to them." **12** And they say to him, "We have come down to bind you—to give you into the hand of the Philistines." And Samson says to them, "Swear to me, lest you fall on me yourselves." **13** And they speak to him, saying, "No, but we certainly bind you, and have given you into their hand, and we certainly do not put you to death"; and they bind him with two thick bands, new ones, and bring him up from the rock. **14** He has come to Lehi—and the Philistines have shouted at meeting him—and the Spirit of YHWH prospers over him, and the thick bands which [are] on his arms are as flax which they burn with fire, and his bands are melted from off his hands, **15** and he finds a fresh jawbone of a donkey, and puts forth his hand and takes it, and strikes down one thousand men with it. **16** And Samson says, "With the jawbone of a donkey, heap on heaps—I have struck down one thousand men with the jawbone of a donkey!" **17** And it comes to pass, when he finishes speaking, that he casts away the jawbone out of his hand, and calls that place Ramath-Lehi; **18** and he thirsts exceedingly, and calls to YHWH, and says, "You have given this great salvation by the hand of Your servant; and now, I die with thirst, and have fallen into the hand of the uncircumcised." **19** And God cleaves the hollow place which [is] in Lehi, and waters come out of it, and he drinks, and his spirit comes back, and he revives; therefore [one] has called its name "The fountain of him who is calling," which [is] in Lehi to this day. **20** And he judges Israel in the days of the Philistines [for] twenty years.

16 And Samson goes to Gaza, and sees a woman there, a harlot, and goes in to her; **2** [it is told] to the Gazathites, saying, "Samson has come in here"; and they go around and lay wait for him all the night at the gate of the city, and keep themselves silent all the night, saying, "Until the morning light—then we have slain him." **3** And Samson lies down until the middle of the night, and rises in the middle of the night, and lays hold on the doors of the gate of the city, and on the two side-posts, and removes them with the bar, and puts [them] on his shoulders, and takes them up to the top of the hill, which [is] on the front of Hebron. **4** And it comes to pass afterward that he loves a woman in the Valley of Sorek, and her name [is] Delilah, **5** and the princes of the Philistines come up to her, and say to her, "Entice him, and see wherein his great power [is], and wherein we are able for him—and we have bound him to afflict him, and each one of us gives eleven hundred pieces of silver to you." **6** And Delilah says to Samson, "Please declare to me wherein your great power [is], and with what you are bound, to afflict you." **7** And Samson says to her, "If they bind me with seven green cords which have not been dried, then I have been weak, and have been as one of mankind." **8** And the princes of the Philistines bring up to her seven green cords which have not been dried, and she binds him with them. **9** And the ambush is abiding with her in an inner chamber, and she says to him, "Philistines [are] on you, Samson!" And he breaks the cords as a thread of tow is broken in its touching fire, and his power has not been known. **10** And Delilah says to Samson, "Behold, you have played on me, and speak lies to me; now, please declare to me with what you are bound." **11** And he says to her, "If they certainly bind me with thick bands, new ones, by which work has not been done, then I have been weak, and have been as one of mankind." **12** And Delilah takes thick bands, new ones, and binds him with them, and says to him, "Philistines [are] on you, Samson!" And the ambush is abiding in an inner chamber, and he breaks them from off his arms as a thread. **13** And Delilah says to Samson, "Until now you have played on me, and speak lies to me; declare to me with what you are bound." And he says to her, "If you weave the seven locks of my head with the web." **14** And she fixes [it] with the pin and says to him, "Philistines [are] on you, Samson!" And he awakens out of his sleep, and pulls out the pin of the loom, and with the web. **15** And she says to him, "How do you say, I have loved you, and your heart is not with me? These three times you have played on me, and have not declared to me wherein your great power [is]." **16** And it comes to pass, because she distressed him with her words all the days, and urges him, and his soul is grieved to death, **17** that he declares all his heart to her, and says to her, "A razor has not gone up on my head, for I [am] a Nazarite to God from the womb of my mother; if I have been shaven, then my power has turned aside from me, and I have been weak, and have been as all of mankind." **18** And Delilah sees that he has declared all his heart to her, and she sends and calls for the princes of the Philistines, saying, "Come up this time, for he has declared all his heart to me"; and the princes of the Philistines have come up to her, and bring up the money in their hand. **19** And she makes him sleep on her knees, and calls for a man, and shaves the seven locks of his head, and begins to afflict him, and his power turns aside from off him; **20** and she says, "Philistines [are] on you, Samson!" And he awakens out of his sleep and says, "I go out as time by time, and shake free"; but he has not known that YHWH has turned aside from off him. **21** And the Philistines seize him, and pick out his eyes, and bring him down to Gaza, and bind him with two bronze chains; and he is grinding in the prison-house. **22** And the hair of his head begins to shoot up when he has been shaven, **23** and the princes of the Philistines have been gathered together to sacrifice a great sacrifice to their god Dagon, and to rejoice; and they say, "Our god has given our enemy Samson into our hand." **24** And the people see him, and praise their god, for they said, "Our god has given into our hand our enemy, and he who is laying waste to our land, and who multiplied our wounded." **25** And it comes to pass, when their heart [is] glad, that they say, "Call for Samson, and he entertains for us"; and they call for Samson out of the prison-house, and he entertains their faces, and they cause him to stand between the pillars. **26** And Samson says to the young man who is keeping hold on his hand, "Let me also feel the pillars on which the house is established, and I lean on them." **27** And the house has been full of the men and the women, and all the princes of the Philistines [are] there, and about three thousand men and women [are] on the roof, who are watching Samson entertain. **28** And Samson calls to YHWH and says, "Lord YHWH, please remember me and please strengthen me only this time, O God; and I am avenged—vengeance at once—because of my two eyes, on the Philistines." **29** And Samson turns aside [to] the two middle pillars, on which the house is established, and on which it is supported, [to] one with his right hand and one with his left; **30** and Samson says, "Let me die with the Philistines," and he inclines himself powerfully, and the house falls on the princes, and on all the people who [are] in it, and the dead whom he has put to death in his death are more than those whom he put to death in his life. **31** And his brothers come down, and all the house of his father, and lift him up, and bring him up, and bury him between Zorah and Eshtaol, in the burying-place of his father Manoah; and he has judged Israel [for] twenty years.

17 And there is a man of the hill-country of Ephraim, and his name [is] Micah, **2** and he says to his mother, "The eleven hundred pieces of silver which have been taken of yours, and [of which] you have sworn, and also spoken in my ears; behold, the silver [is] with me, I have taken it"; and his mother says, "Blessed [is] my son of YHWH." **3** And he gives back the eleven hundred pieces of silver to his mother, and his mother says, "I had certainly sanctified the silver to YHWH, from my hand, for my son, to make a carved image, and a molten image; and now, I give it back to you." **4** And he gives back the money to his mother, and his mother takes two hundred pieces of silver, and gives them to a refiner, and he makes them a carved image, and a molten image, and it is in the house of Micah. **5** As for the man Micah, he has a house of gods, and he makes an ephod, and teraphim, and consecrates the hand of one of his sons, and he is for a priest to him; **6** in those days there is no king in Israel, each does that which is right in his own eyes. **7** And there is a young man of Beth-Lehem-Judah, of the family of Judah, and he [is] a Levite, and he [is] a sojourner there. **8** And the man goes out of the city, out of Beth-Lehem-Judah, to sojourn where he finds, and comes to the hill-country of Ephraim, to the house of Micah, to work his way. **9** And Micah says to him, "Where do you come from?" And he says to him, "I [am] a Levite of Beth-Lehem-Judah, and I am going to sojourn where I find." **10** And Micah says to him, "Dwell with me, and be for a father and for a priest to me, and I give ten pieces of silver to you for the days, and a suit of garments, and your sustenance"; and the Levite goes [in]. **11** And the Levite is willing to dwell with the man, and the young man is to him as one of his sons. **12** And Micah consecrates the hand of the Levite, and the young man is for a priest to him, and he is in the house of Micah, **13** and Micah says, "Now I have known that YHWH does good to me, for the Levite has been for a priest to me."

18 In those days there is no king in Israel, and in those days the tribe of the Danite is seeking an inheritance to inhabit for itself, for [that] has not fallen to it to that day in the midst of the tribes of Israel by inheritance. **2** And the sons of Dan send, out of their family, five of their men—men, sons of valor—from Zorah, and from Eshtaol, to traverse the land, and to search it, and they say to them, "Go, search the land"; and they come into the hill-country of Ephraim, to the house of Micah, and lodge there. **3** They [are] with the household of Micah, and they have discerned the voice of the young man, the Levite, and turn aside there, and say to him, "Who has brought you here? And what are you doing in this [place]? And why are you here?" **4** And he says to them, "Thus and thus has Micah done to me; and he hires me, and I am for a priest to him." **5** And they say to him, "Please ask of God, and we know whether our way on which we are going is prosperous." **6** And the priest says to them, "Go in peace; before YHWH [is] your way in which you go." **7** And the five men go, and come to Laish, and see the people which [is] in its midst, dwelling confidently, according to the custom of

JUDGES

Zidonians, quiet and confident; and there is none putting to shame in the land in [any] thing, possessing restraint, and they [are] far off from the Zidonians, and have no word with [any] man. **8** And they come to their brothers at Zorah and Eshtaol, and their brothers say to them, "What [did] you [find]?" **9** And they say, "Rise, and we go up against them, for we have seen the land, and behold—very good; and you are keeping silent! Do not be slothful to go—to enter to possess the land. **10** When you go, you come to a confident people, and the land [is] large on both hands, for God has given it into your hand, a place where there is no lack of anything which [is] in the land." **11** And there journey there, of the family of the Danite, from Zorah, and from Eshtaol, six hundred men girded with weapons of war. **12** And they go up and encamp in Kirjath-Jearim, in Judah, therefore they have called that place, "Camp of Dan," until this day; behold, behind Kirjath-Jearim. **13** And they pass over there [to] the hill-country of Ephraim, and come to the house of Micah. **14** And the five men, those going to traverse the land of Laish, answer and say to their brothers, "Have you known that in these houses there is an ephod, and teraphim, and carved image, and molten image? And now, know what you do." **15** And they turn aside there, and come to the house of the young man, the Levite, the house of Micah, and ask of him of welfare— **16** (and the six hundred men girded with their weapons of war, who [are] of the sons of Dan, are standing at the opening of the gate)— **17** indeed, the five men, those going to traverse the land, go up—they have come in there—they have taken the carved image, and the ephod, and the teraphim, and the molten image—and the priest is standing at the opening of the gate, and the six hundred men who are girded with weapons of war— **18** indeed, these have entered the house of Micah, and take the carved image, the ephod, and the teraphim, and the molten image; and the priest says to them, "What are you doing?" **19** And they say to him, "Keep silent, lay your hand on your mouth, and go with us, and be for a father and for a priest to us: is it better your being a priest for the house of one man, or your being priest for a tribe and for a family in Israel?" **20** And the heart of the priest is glad, and he takes the ephod, and the teraphim, and the carved image, and goes into the midst of the people, **21** and they turn and go, and put the infants, and the livestock, and the baggage, before them. **22** They have been far off from the house of Micah—and the men who [are] in the houses which [are] near the house of Micah have been called together, and overtake the sons of Dan, **23** and call to the sons of Dan, and they turn their faces around, and say to Micah, "What [is this] to you that you have been called together?" **24** And he says, "You have taken my gods which I made, and the priest, and you go; and what more do I [have]? And what [is] this you say to me, What [is this] to you?" **25** And the sons of Dan say to him, "Do not let your voice be heard with us, lest men bitter in soul fall on you, and you have gathered your life, and the life of your household"; **26** and the sons of Dan go on their way, and Micah sees that they are stronger than he, and turns, and goes back to his house. **27** And they have taken that which Micah had made, and the priest whom he had, and come in against Laish, against a people quiet and confident, and strike them by the mouth of the sword, and have burned the city with fire, **28** and there is no deliverer, for it [is] far off from Sidon, and they have no word with [any] man, and it [is] in the valley which [is] by Beth-Rehob; and they build the city, and dwell in it, **29** and call the name of the city Dan, by the name of their father Dan, who was born to Israel; and yet Laish [is] the name of the city at the first. **30** And the sons of Dan raise up the carved image for themselves, and Jonathan son of Gershom, son of Manasseh, he and his sons have been priests for the tribe of the Danite, until the day of the expulsion of [the people] of the land. **31** And they appoint for themselves the carved image of Micah, which he had made, all the days of the house of God being in Shiloh.

19 And it comes to pass in those days, when there is no king in Israel, that there is a man, a Levite, a sojourner in the sides of the hill-country of Ephraim, and he takes a wife for himself, a concubine, out of Beth-Lehem-Judah; **2** and his concubine commits whoredom against him, and she goes from him to the house of her father, to Beth-Lehem-Judah, and is there four months of days. **3** And her husband rises

JUDGES

and goes after her, to speak to her heart, to bring her back, and his young man [is] with him, and a couple of donkeys; and she brings him into the house of her father, and the father of the young woman sees him, and rejoices to meet him. **4** And his father-in-law keeps hold on him, father of the young woman, and he abides with him three days, and they eat and drink, and lodge there. **5** And it comes to pass, on the fourth day, that they rise early in the morning, and he rises to go, and the father of the young woman says to his son-in-law, "Support your heart with a morsel of bread, and afterward you go on." **6** And both of them sit, and eat and drink together, and the father of the young woman says to the man, "Please be willing and lodge all night, and let your heart be glad." **7** And the man rises to go, and his father-in-law presses on him, and he turns back and lodges there. **8** And he rises early in the morning, on the fifth day, to go, and the father of the young woman says, "Please support your heart"; and they have tarried until the turning of the day, and both of them eat. **9** And the man rises to go, he, and his concubine, and his young man, but his father-in-law, father of the young woman, says to him, "Now behold, the day has fallen toward evening, please lodge all night; behold, the declining of the day! Lodge here and let your heart be glad—and you have risen early tomorrow for your journey, and you have gone to your tent." **10** And the man has not been willing to lodge all night, and he rises, and goes, and comes in until [he is] opposite Jebus (it [is] Jerusalem), and a couple of saddled donkeys [are] with him; and his concubine [is] with him. **11** They [are] near Jebus, and the day has greatly gone down, and the young man says to his lord, "Please come, and we turn aside to this city of the Jebusite and lodge in it." **12** And his lord says to him, "Let us not turn aside to the city of a stranger, that is not of the sons of Israel there, but we have passed over to Gibeah." **13** And he says to his young man, "Come, and we draw near to one of the places, and have lodged in Gibeah, or in Ramah." **14** And they pass over, and go on, and the sun goes in on them near Gibeah, which is of Benjamin; **15** and they turn aside there to go in to lodge in Gibeah, and he goes in and sits in a broad place of the city, and there is no man gathering them into the house to lodge. **16** And behold, an old man has come from his work from the field in the evening, and the man [is] of the hill-country of Ephraim, and he [is] a sojourner in Gibeah, and the men of the place [are] Benjamites. **17** And he lifts up his eyes, and sees the man, the traveler, in a broad place of the city, and the old man says, "To where do you go? And where do you come from?" **18** And he says to him, "We are passing over from Beth-Lehem-Judah to the sides of the hill-country of Ephraim—I [am] from there, and I go to Beth-Lehem-Judah; and I am going to the house of YHWH, and there is no man gathering me into the house, **19** and there is both straw and provender for our donkeys, and there is also bread and wine for me, and for your handmaid, and for the young man with your servants; there is no lack of anything." **20** And the old man says, "Peace to you; only, all your lack [is] on me, but do not lodge in the broad place." **21** And he brings him into his house, and mixes [food] for the donkeys, and they wash their feet, and eat and drink. **22** They are making their heart glad, and behold, men of the city, men—sons of worthlessness—have gone around the house, beating on the door, and they speak to the old man, the master of the house, saying, "Bring out the man who has come into your house, and we know him." **23** And the man, the master of the house, goes out to them and says to them, "No, my brothers, please do not do evil after that this man has come into my house; do not do this folly; **24** behold, my daughter, the virgin, and his concubine, please let me bring them out and you humble them, and do that which is good in your eyes to them, and do not do this foolish thing to this man." **25** And the men have not been willing to listen to him, and the man takes hold on his concubine and brings [her] out to them outside, and they know her and roll themselves on her all the night until the morning, and they send her away in the ascending of the dawn; **26** and the woman comes in at the turning of the morning, and falls at the opening of the man's house where her lord [is], until the light. **27** And her lord rises in the morning, and opens the doors of the house, and goes out to go on his way, and behold, the woman, his concubine, is fallen at the opening of the house, and her hands [are] on the threshold,

28 and he says to her, "Rise, and we go"; but there is no answering, and he takes her on the donkey, and the man rises and goes to his place, **29** and comes into his house, and takes the knife, and lays hold on his concubine, and cuts her in pieces to her bones—into twelve pieces, and sends her into all the border of Israel. **30** And it has come to pass, everyone who sees has said, "There has not been—indeed, there has not been seen [anything] like this, from the day of the coming up of the sons of Israel out of the land of Egypt until this day; set your [heart] on it, take counsel, and speak."

20 And all the sons of Israel go out, and the congregation is assembled as one man, from Dan even to Beer-Sheba, and the land of Gilead, to YHWH, at Mizpeh. **2** And the chiefs of all the people, of all the tribes of Israel, station themselves in the assembly of the people of God, four hundred thousand footmen drawing sword. **3** And the sons of Benjamin hear that the sons of Israel have gone up to Mizpeh. And the sons of Israel say, "Speak! How has this evil been?" **4** And the man, the Levite, husband of the woman who has been murdered, answers and says, "My concubine and I went into Gibeah, which [is] of Benjamin, to lodge; **5** and the masters of Gibeah rise against me—and they go around the house against me by night—they thought to slay me, and they have humbled my concubine, and she dies; **6** and I lay hold on my concubine, and cut her in pieces, and send her into all the country of the inheritance of Israel; for they have done wickedness and folly in Israel; **7** behold, you [are] all sons of Israel; give for yourselves a word and counsel here." **8** And all the people rise as one man, saying, "None of us goes to his tent, and none of us turns aside to his house; **9** and now, this [is] the thing which we do to Gibeah: [we go up] against it by lot! **10** And we have taken ten men of one hundred, of all the tribes of Israel, and one hundred of a thousand, and a thousand of a myriad, to receive provision for the people, to do, at their coming to Gibeah of Benjamin, according to all the folly which it has done in Israel." **11** And every man of Israel is gathered to the city, as one man—companions. **12** And the tribes of Israel send men among all the tribes of Benjamin, saying, "What [is] this evil which has been among you? **13** And now, give up the men—sons of worthlessness—which [are] in Gibeah, and we put them to death, and we put away evil from Israel." And [the sons of] Benjamin have not been willing to listen to the voice of their brothers, the sons of Israel; **14** and the sons of Benjamin are gathered out of the cities to Gibeah, to go out to battle with the sons of Israel. **15** And the sons of Benjamin number themselves on that day; out of the cities [are] twenty-six thousand men drawing sword, apart from the inhabitants of Gibeah, [who] numbered themselves, seven hundred chosen men; **16** among all this people [are] seven hundred chosen men, their right hand bound, each of these slinging with a stone at the hair, and he does not err. **17** And the men of Israel numbered themselves, apart from Benjamin, four hundred thousand men, drawing sword, each of these a man of war. **18** And they rise and go up to Beth-El, and ask of God, and the sons of Israel say, "Who goes up for us at the commencement to battle with the sons of Benjamin?" And YHWH says, "Judah—at the commencement." **19** And the sons of Israel rise in the morning, and encamp against Gibeah, **20** and the men of Israel go out to battle with Benjamin, and the men of Israel set themselves in array [for] battle with them, against Gibeah, **21** and the sons of Benjamin come out from Gibeah, and destroy twenty-two thousand men in Israel on that day—to the earth. **22** And the people, the men of Israel, strengthen themselves, and add to set in array [for] battle in the place where they arranged themselves on the first day. **23** And the sons of Israel go up and weep before YHWH until the evening, and ask of YHWH, saying, "Do I add to draw near to battle with the sons of my brother Benjamin?" And YHWH says, "Go up against him." **24** And the sons of Israel draw near to the sons of Benjamin on the second day, **25** and Benjamin comes out to meet them from Gibeah on the second day, and destroy eighteen thousand men among the sons of Israel again—to the earth; all these are drawing sword. **26** And all the sons of Israel go up, even all the people, and come to Beth-El, and weep, and sit there before YHWH, and fast on that day until the evening, and cause burnt-offerings and peace-offerings to ascend before YHWH. **27** And the sons of Israel ask of YHWH—and the Ark of the Covenant of God [is] there in those days, **28** and Phinehas son of Eleazar, son of Aaron, is standing before it in those days, saying, "Do I add to go out to battle again with the sons of my brother Benjamin, or do I cease?" And YHWH says, "Go up, for tomorrow I give him into your hand." **29** And Israel sets ones lying in wait against Gibeah, all around, **30** and the sons of Israel go up against the sons of Benjamin on the third day, and arrange themselves against Gibeah, as time by time. **31** And the sons of Benjamin come out to meet the people; they have been drawn away out of the city, and begin to strike [some] of the people—wounded as time by time—in the highways (of which one is going up to Beth-El, and the other to Gibeah in the field), [are] about thirty men of Israel. **32** And the sons of Benjamin say, "They are struck before us as at the beginning"; but the sons of Israel said, "Let us flee, and draw them away out of the city, to the highways." **33** And all the men of Israel have risen from their place, and arrange themselves at Ba'al-Tamar, and the ambush of Israel is coming forth out of its place, out of the meadow of Gibeah. **34** And they come in from the front against Gibeah—ten thousand chosen men out of all Israel—and the battle [is] grievous, and they have not known that the calamity is reaching toward them. **35** And YHWH strikes Benjamin before Israel, and the sons of Israel destroy in Benjamin, on that day, twenty-five thousand and one hundred men; all these [are] drawing sword. **36** And the sons of Benjamin see that they have been struck—and the men of Israel give place to Benjamin, for they have trusted in the ambush which they had set against Gibeah, **37** and the ambush has hurried, and pushes against Gibeah, and the ambush draws itself out, and strikes the whole of the city by the mouth of the sword. **38** And the appointed sign of the men of Israel with the ambush was their causing a great volume of smoke to go up from the city. **39** And the men of Israel turn in battle, and Benjamin has begun to strike the wounded among the men of Israel, about thirty men, for they said, "Surely they are utterly struck before us, as [at] the first battle"; **40** but the volume has begun to go up from the city—a pillar of smoke—and Benjamin turns behind, and behold, the perfection of the city has gone up toward the heavens. **41** And the men of Israel have turned, and the men of Benjamin are troubled, for they have seen that the calamity has struck against them— **42** and they turn before the men of Israel to the way of the wilderness, and the battle has followed them; and those who [are] from the cities are destroying them in their midst; **43** they have surrounded the Benjamites—they have pursued them—they have trodden them down with ease as far as the front of Gibeah, at the sun-rising. **44** And eighteen thousand men of Benjamin fall—all these [were] men of valor; **45** and they turn and flee toward the wilderness, to the rock of Rimmon; and they glean five thousand of their men in the highways, and follow after them to Gidom, and strike two thousand [more] of their men. **46** And all those falling of Benjamin are twenty-five thousand men drawing sword, on that day—all these [were] men of valor; **47** but six hundred men turn and flee into the wilderness, to the rock of Rimmon, and they dwell in the rock of Rimmon four months. **48** And the men of Israel have turned back to the sons of Benjamin, and strike them by the mouth of the sword out of the city—men even to livestock, even to all that is found; they have also sent all the cities which are found into the fire.

21 And the men of Israel have sworn in Mizpeh, saying, "None of us gives his daughter to Benjamin for a wife." **2** And the people come to Beth-El, and sit there until the evening before God, and lift up their voice, and weep [with] a great weeping, **3** and say, "Why, O YHWH, God of Israel, has this been in Israel today?" **4** And it comes to pass on the next day, that the people rise early, and build an altar there, and cause burnt-offerings and peace-offerings to ascend. **5** And the sons of Israel say, "Who [is] he that has not come up in the assembly to YHWH out of all the tribes of Israel?" For the great oath has been concerning him who has not come up to YHWH to Mizpeh, saying, "He is surely put to death." **6** And the sons of Israel sigh concerning their brother Benjamin, and say, "Today there has been one tribe cut off from Israel, **7** what do we do for them—for those who are left—for wives, since we have sworn by YHWH not to give to them from our daughters for wives?" **8** And they say, "Who is [that] one out of the tribes of Israel who has not come up to YHWH to Mizpeh?" And behold, none has come to the camp from Jabesh-Gilead—to the assembly. **9** And the people numbered themselves, and behold, there is no man from the inhabitants of Jabesh-Gilead. **10** And the congregation sends twelve thousand men of the sons of valor there, and commands them, saying, "Go—and you have struck the inhabitants of Jabesh-Gilead by the mouth of the sword, even the women and the infants. **11** And this [is] the thing which you do; every male, and every woman knowing the lying of a male, you devote." **12** And they find four hundred young women, virgins, out of the inhabitants of Jabesh-Gilead, who have not known man by the lying of a male, and they bring them to the camp at Shiloh, which [is] in the land of Canaan. **13** And all the congregation sends [word] and speaks to the sons of Benjamin who [are] in the rock of Rimmon, and proclaims peace to them; **14** and Benjamin turns back at that time, and they give to them the women whom they have kept alive of the women of Jabesh-Gilead, and they have not found for [all of] them so. **15** And the people sighed concerning Benjamin, for YHWH had made a breach among the tribes of Israel. **16** And [the] elderly of the congregation say, "What do we do to the remnant for wives—for the women have been destroyed out of Benjamin?" **17** And they say, "A possession of an escaped party [is] to Benjamin, and a tribe is not blotted out from Israel; **18** and we are not able to give wives to them out of our daughters, for the sons of Israel have sworn, saying, Cursed [is] he who is giving a wife to Benjamin." **19** And they say, "Behold, a festival of YHWH [is] in Shiloh, from time to time, which [is] on the north of Beth-El, at the rising of the sun, by the highway which is going up from Beth-El to Shechem, and on the south of Lebonah." **20** And they command the sons of Benjamin, saying, "Go—and you have laid wait in the vineyards, **21** and have seen, and behold, if the daughters of Shiloh come out to dance in dances—then you have gone out from the vineyards, and each caught his wife out of the daughters of Shiloh for yourselves, and have gone to the land of Benjamin; **22** and it has been, when their fathers or their brothers come in to plead to us, that we have said to them, Favor us [by] them, for we have not each taken his wife in battle, for you have not given [wives] to them at this time, [so] you are [not] guilty." **23** And the sons of Benjamin do so, and take women according to their number, out of the dancers whom they have seized; and they go, and return to their inheritance, and build the cities, and dwell in them. **24** And the sons of Israel go up and down there at that time, each to his tribe, and to his family; and they each go out there to his inheritance. **25** In those days there is no king in Israel; each does that which is right in his own eyes.

RUTH

1 And it comes to pass, in [the] days [when] the ones judging judge, that there is a famine in the land, and there goes a man from Beth-Lehem-Judah to sojourn in the fields of Moab, he, and his wife, and his two sons. **2** And the name of the man [is] Elimelech, and the name of his wife Naomi, and the name of his two sons Mahlon and Chilion, Ephraimites from Beth-Lehem-Judah; and they come into the fields of Moab, and are there. **3** And Elimelech husband of Naomi dies, and she is left, she and her two sons; **4** and they take to them wives, Moabitesses: the name of the first [is] Orpah, and the name of the second Ruth; and they dwell there about ten years. **5** And they die also, both of them—Mahlon and Chilion—and the woman is left of her two children and of her husband. **6** And she rises, and she and her daughters-in-law, and turns back from the fields of Moab, for she has heard in the fields of Moab that God has looked after His people—to give to them bread. **7** And she goes out from the place where she has been, and her two daughters-in-law with her, and they go in the way to return to the land of Judah. **8** And Naomi says to her two daughters-in-law, "Go, return, each to the house of her mother; YHWH does with you kindness as you have done with the dead, and with me; **9** YHWH grants to you, and you find rest each in the house of her husband"; and she kisses them, and they lift up their voice and weep. **10** And they say to her, "Surely with you we go back to your people." **11** And Naomi says, "Turn back, my daughters; why do you go with me? Are there yet to me sons in my bowels that they have been to you for husbands? **12** Turn back, my daughters, go, for I am too aged to be to a husband; though I had said, There is for me hope, also, I have been tonight to a husband, and also I have borne sons: **13** do you wait for them until they grow up? Do you shut yourselves up for them, not to be to a husband? No, my daughters, for more bitter to me than to you, for the hand of YHWH has gone out against me." **14** And they lift up their voice, and weep again, and Orpah kisses her mother-in-law, and Ruth has cleaved to her. **15** And she says, "Behold, your sister-in-law has turned back to her people, and to her god, turn back after your sister-in-law." **16** And Ruth says, "Do not urge me to leave you—to turn back from after you; for to where you go I go, and where you lodge I lodge; your people [is] my people, and your God my God. **17** Where you die I die, and there I am buried; thus does YHWH to me, and thus He adds—for death itself parts between me and you." **18** And she sees that she is strengthening herself to go with her, and she ceases to speak to her; **19** and the two of them go until their coming to Beth-Lehem; and it comes to pass at their coming to Beth-Lehem, that all the city is moved at them, and they say, "Is this Naomi?" **20** And she says to them, "Do not call me Naomi; call me Mara, for the Almighty has dealt very bitterly to me, **21** I went out full, and YHWH has brought me back empty, why do you call me Naomi, and YHWH has testified against me, and the Almighty has done evil to me?" **22** And Naomi turns back, and Ruth the Moabitess, her daughter-in-law, with her, who has turned back from the fields of Moab, and they have come to Beth-Lehem at the commencement of barley-harvest.

2 And Naomi has an acquaintance of her husband's, a man mighty in wealth, of the family of Elimelech, and his name [is] Boaz. **2** And Ruth the Moabitess says to Naomi, "Please let me go into the field, and I gather among the ears of grain after him in whose eyes I find grace"; and she says to her, "Go, my daughter." **3** And she goes and comes and gathers in a field after the reapers, and her chance happens—the portion of the field is Boaz's who [is] of the family of Elimelech. **4** And behold, Boaz has come from Beth-Lehem, and says to the reapers, "YHWH [is] with you"; and they say to him, "YHWH blesses you." **5** And Boaz says to his young man who is set over the reapers, "Whose [is] this young person?" **6** And the young man who is set over the reapers answers and says, "A young woman—Moabitess—she [is], who came back with Naomi from the fields of Moab, **7** and she says, Please let me glean and I have gathered among the sheaves after the reapers; and she comes and

RUTH

remains since the morning and until now; she sat in the house a little [while]." **8** And Boaz says to Ruth, "Have you not heard, my daughter? Do not go to glean in another field, and also, do not pass over from here, and thus you cleave to my young women: **9** your eyes [are] on the field which they reap, and you have gone after them; have I not charged the young men not to touch you? When you are thirsty then you have gone to the vessels, and have drunk from that which the young men draw." **10** And she falls on her face, and bows herself to the earth, and says to him, "Why have I found grace in your eyes, to discern me, and I a stranger?" **11** And Boaz answers and says to her, "It has been thoroughly declared to me all that you have done with your mother-in-law, after the death of your husband, and you leave your father, and your mother, and the land of your birth, and come to a people which you have not known before. **12** YHWH repays your work, and your reward is complete from YHWH, God of Israel, under whose wings you have come to take refuge." **13** And she says, "Let me find grace in your eyes, my lord, because you have comforted me, and because you have spoken to the heart of your maidservant, and I am not as one of your maidservants." **14** And Boaz says to her, "At meal-time come near here, and you have eaten of the bread, and dipped your morsel in the vinegar." And she sits at the side of the reapers, and he reaches to her roasted grain, and she eats, and is satisfied, and leaves. **15** And she rises to glean, and Boaz charges his young men, saying, "Even between the sheaves she gleans, and you do not cause her to blush; **16** and also you surely cast to her of the handfuls—and have left, and she has gleaned, and you do not push against her." **17** And she gleans in the field until the evening, and beats out that which she has gleaned, and it is about an ephah of barley; **18** and she takes [it] up, and goes into the city, and her mother-in-law sees that which she has gleaned, and she brings out and gives to her that which she left from her satiety. **19** And her mother-in-law says to her, "Where have you gleaned today? And where have you worked? May he who is discerning you be blessed." And she declares to her mother-in-law with whom she has worked, and says, "The name of the man with whom I have worked today [is] Boaz." **20** And Naomi says to her daughter-in-law, "Blessed [is] he of YHWH who has not forsaken His kindness with the living and with the dead"; and Naomi says to her, "The man is a relation of ours; he [is] of our redeemers." **21** And Ruth the Moabitess says, "Also he surely said to me, Near the young people whom I have you cleave until they have completed the whole of the harvest which I have." **22** And Naomi says to her daughter-in-law Ruth, "Good, my daughter, that you go out with his young women, and they do not come against you in another field." **23** And she cleaves to the young women of Boaz to glean, until the completion of the barley-harvest, and of the wheat-harvest, and she dwells with her mother-in-law.

3 And her mother-in-law Naomi says to her, "My daughter, do I not seek rest for you, that it may be well with you? **2** And now, is not Boaz of our acquaintance, with whose young women you have been? Behold, he is winnowing the threshing-floor of barley tonight, **3** and you have bathed, and anointed yourself, and put your garments on you, and gone down to the threshing-floor; do not let yourself be known to the man until he completes to eat and to drink; **4** and it comes to pass, when he lies down, that you have known the place where he lies down, and have gone in, and uncovered his feet, and lain down—and he declares to you that which you do." **5** And she says to her, "All that you say—I do." **6** And she goes down [to] the threshing-floor, and does according to all that her mother-in-law commanded her **7** And Boaz eats and drinks, and his heart is glad; and he goes in to lie down at the end of the heap; and she comes in gently, and uncovers his feet, and lies down. **8** And it comes to pass, at the middle of the night, that the man trembles, and turns himself, and behold, a woman is lying at his feet. **9** And he says, "Who [are] you?" And she says, "I [am] Ruth your handmaid, and you have spread your skirt over your handmaid, for you [are] a redeemer." **10** And he says, "Blessed [are] you of YHWH, my daughter; you have dealt more kindly at the latter end than at the beginning—not to go after the young men, either poor or rich. **11** And now, my daughter, do not fear, all that you say I do to you, for all the gate of my people knows that you [are] a virtuous woman.

12 And now, surely, true, that I [am] a redeemer, but also there is a redeemer nearer than I. **13** Lodge tonight, and it has been in the morning, if he redeems you, well: he redeems; and if he does not delight to redeem you, then I have redeemed you—I; YHWH lives! Lie down until the morning." **14** And she lies down at his feet until the morning, and rises before one discerns another; and he says, "Let it not be known that the woman has come into the floor." **15** And he says, "Give the covering which [is] on you, and keep hold on it"; and she keeps hold on it, and he measures six [measures] of barley, and lays [it] on her; and he goes into the city. **16** And she comes to her mother-in-law, and she says, "Who [are] you, my daughter?" And she declares to her all that the man has done to her. **17** And she says, "These six [measures] of barley he has given to me, for he said, You do not go in empty to your mother-in-law." **18** And she says, "Sit still, my daughter, until you know how the matter falls, for the man does not rest except he has completed the matter today."

4 And Boaz has gone up to the gate, and sits there, and behold, the redeemer is passing by of whom Boaz had spoken, and he says, "Turn aside, sit down here, such a one, such a one"; and he turns aside and sits down. **2** And he takes ten men from [the] elderly of the city, and says, "Sit down here"; and they sit down. **3** And he says to the redeemer, "A portion of the field which [is] to our brother, to Elimelech, has Naomi sold, who has come back from the fields of Moab; **4** and I said, I uncover your ear, saying, Buy before the inhabitants and before [the] elderly of my people; if you redeem—redeem, and if none redeems—declare [it] to me and I know, for there is none except you to redeem, and I after you." And he says, "I redeem [it]." **5** And Boaz says, "In the day of your buying the field from the hand of Naomi, then from Ruth the Moabitess, wife of the dead, you have bought [it], to raise up the name of the dead over his inheritance." **6** And the redeemer says, "I am not able to redeem [it] for myself, lest I destroy my inheritance; redeem for yourself—you—my right of redemption, for I am not able to redeem." **7** And this [is] formerly in Israel for redemption and for exchanging, to establish anything: a man has drawn off his sandal, and given [it] to his neighbor, and this [is] the Testimony in Israel. **8** And the redeemer says to Boaz, "Buy [it] for yourself," and draws off his sandal. **9** And Boaz says to the elderly, and [to] all the people, "You [are] witnesses today that I have bought all that [belonged] to Elimelech, and all that [belonged] to Chilion and Mahlon, from the hand of Naomi; **10** and also Ruth the Moabitess, wife of Mahlon, I have bought to myself for a wife, to raise up the name of the dead over his inheritance; and the name of the dead is not cut off from among his brothers, and from the gate of his place; witnesses you [are] today." **11** And all the people who [are] in the gate say—also the elderly, "Witnesses! YHWH makes the woman who is coming to your house as Rachel and as Leah, both of whom built the house of Israel; and you do virtuously in Ephrathah, and proclaim the name in Beth-Lehem; **12** and let your house be as the house of Perez (whom Tamar bore to Judah), of the seed which YHWH gives to you of this young woman." **13** And Boaz takes Ruth, and she becomes his wife, and he goes in to her, and YHWH gives conception to her, and she bears a son. **14** And the women say to Naomi, "Blessed [is] YHWH who has not let a redeemer cease to you today, and his name is proclaimed in Israel, **15** and he has been to you for a restorer of life, and for a nourisher of your old age, for your daughter-in-law who has loved you—who is better to you than seven sons—has borne him." **16** And Naomi takes the boy, and lays him in her bosom, and is to him for a nurse; **17** and the neighboring women give a name to him, saying, "There has been a son born to Naomi," and they call his name Obed; he [is] father of Jesse, father of David. **18** And these are generations of Perez: Perez begot Hezron, **19** and Hezron begot Ram, and Ram begot Amminidab, **20** and Amminidab begot Nahshon, and Nahshon begot Salmon, **21** and Salmon begot Boaz, and Boaz begot Obed, **22** and Obed begot Jesse, and Jesse begot David.

1 SAMUEL

1 And there is a certain man of Ramathaim-Zophim, of the hill-country of Ephraim, and his name [is] Elkanah, son of Jeroham, son of Elihu, son of Tohu, son of Zuph, an Ephraimite, **2** and he has two wives, the name of the first [is] Hannah, and the name of the second Peninnah, and Peninnah has children, and Hannah has no children. **3** And that man has gone up out of his city from time to time, to bow himself, and to sacrifice, before YHWH of Hosts, in Shiloh, and there [are] two sons of Eli, Hophni and Phinehas, priests of YHWH. **4** And the day comes, and Elkanah sacrifices, and he has given portions to his wife Peninnah, and to all her sons and her daughters, **5** and he gives a certain portion to Hannah—double, for he has loved Hannah, and YHWH has shut her womb; **6** and her rival has also provoked her greatly, so as to make her tremble, for YHWH has shut up her womb. **7** And so is done year by year, from the time of her going up into the house of YHWH, so she provokes her, and she weeps, and does not eat. **8** And her husband Elkanah says to her, "Hannah, why do you weep? And why do you not eat? And why is your heart afflicted? Am I not better to you than ten sons?" **9** And Hannah rises after eating in Shiloh, and after drinking, and Eli the priest is sitting on the throne by the doorpost of the temple of YHWH. **10** And she is bitter in soul, and prays to YHWH, and weeps greatly, **11** and vows a vow, and says, "YHWH of Hosts, if You certainly look on the affliction of Your handmaid, and have remembered me, and do not forget Your handmaid, and have given to Your handmaid seed of men—then I have given him to YHWH all [the] days of his life, and a razor does not go up on his head." **12** And it has been, when she multiplied praying before YHWH, that Eli is watching her mouth, **13** and Hannah, she is speaking over her heart—only her lips are moving, and her voice is not heard, and Eli reckons her to be drunken. **14** And Eli says to her, "Until when are you drunken? Turn aside your wine from you." **15** And Hannah answers and says, "No, my lord, I [am] a woman sharply pained in spirit, and I have not drunk wine and strong drink, and I pour out my soul before YHWH; **16** do not put your handmaid before a daughter of worthlessness, for from the abundance of my meditation, and of my provocation, I have spoken until now." **17** And Eli answers and says, "Go in peace, and the God of Israel gives your petition which you have asked of Him." **18** And she says, "Let your handmaid find grace in your eyes"; and the woman goes on her way, and eats, and her face has not been [downcast] for herself anymore. **19** And they rise early in the morning, and bow themselves before YHWH, and turn back, and come to their house in Ramah, and Elkanah knows his wife Hannah, and YHWH remembers her; **20** and it comes to pass, at the revolution of the days, that Hannah conceives, and bears a son, and calls his name Samuel, for, "I have asked for him from YHWH." **21** And the man Elkanah goes up, and all his house, to sacrifice to YHWH the sacrifice of the days, and his vow. **22** And Hannah has not gone up, for she said to her husband, "Until the youth is weaned—then I have brought him in, and he has appeared before the face of YHWH, and dwelt there for all time." **23** And her husband Elkanah says to her, "Do that which is good in your eyes; abide until your weaning him; only, let YHWH establish His word"; and the woman abides and suckles her son until she has weaned him, **24** and she causes him to go up with her when she has weaned him, with three bullocks, and one ephah of flour, and a bottle of wine, and she brings him into the house of YHWH at Shiloh, and the youth [is but] a youth. **25** And they slaughter the bullock, and bring in the youth to Eli, **26** and she says, "O my lord, your soul lives! My lord, I [am] the woman who stood with you in this [place], to pray to YHWH; **27** I prayed for this youth, and YHWH gives to me my petition which I asked of Him; **28** and I also have called him to YHWH, all the days that he has lived—he is called to YHWH"; and he bows himself there before YHWH.

2 And Hannah prays and says: "My heart has exulted in YHWH, ‖ My horn has been high in YHWH, ‖ My mouth has been large over my enemies, ‖ For I have

1 SAMUEL

rejoiced in Your salvation. **2** There is none holy like YHWH, ‖ For there is none except You, ‖ And there is no rock like our God. **3** You do not multiply—you speak haughtily—The old saying goes out from your mouth, ‖ For YHWH [is] a God of knowledge, ‖ And actions are weighed by Him. **4** Bows of the mighty are broken, ‖ And the stumbling have girded on strength. **5** The satiated hired themselves for bread, ‖ And the hungry have ceased. While the barren has borne seven, ‖ And she abounding with sons has languished. **6** YHWH puts to death, and keeps alive, ‖ He brings down to Sheol, and brings up. **7** YHWH dispossesses, and He makes rich, ‖ He makes low, indeed, He makes high. **8** He raises the poor from the dust, ‖ He lifts up the needy from a dunghill, ‖ To cause [them] to sit with nobles, ‖ Indeed, He causes them to inherit a throne of glory, ‖ For the fixtures of earth [are] of YHWH, ‖ And He sets the habitable world on them. **9** He keeps the feet of His saints, ‖ And the wicked are silent in darkness, ‖ For man does not become mighty by power. **10** YHWH—His adversaries are broken down, ‖ He thunders against them in the heavens: YHWH judges the ends of the earth, ‖ And gives strength to His king, ‖ And exalts the horn of His anointed." **11** And Elkanah goes to Ramath, to his house, and the youth has been serving YHWH [in] the presence of Eli the priest; **12** and the sons of Eli [are] sons of worthlessness, they have not known YHWH. **13** And the custom of the priests with the people [is that when] any man is sacrificing a sacrifice, then the servant of the priest has come in when the flesh is boiling, and [with] the hook of three teeth in his hand, **14** and has struck [it] into the pan, or kettle, or cauldron, or pot; all that the hook brings up the priest takes for himself; thus they do to all Israel who are coming in there in Shiloh. **15** Also, before they make incense with the fat, then the priest's servant has come in and said to the man who is sacrificing, "Give flesh to roast for the priest, and he does not take boiled flesh from you, but raw"; **16** and the man says to him, "Let them surely make incense with the fat according to the [custom] today, then take to yourself as your soul desires"; and he has said to him, "Surely you give now; and if not—I have taken by strength." **17** And the sin of the young men is very great [in] the presence of YHWH, for the men have despised the offering of YHWH. **18** And Samuel is ministering [in] the presence of YHWH, a youth girt [with] an ephod of linen; **19** and his mother makes a small upper coat for him, and she has brought it up to him from time to time, in her coming up with her husband to sacrifice the sacrifice of the time. **20** And Eli blessed Elkanah and his wife, and said, "YHWH appoints seed of this woman for you, for the petition which she asked for YHWH"; and they have gone to their place. **21** When YHWH has looked after Hannah, then she conceives and bears three sons and two daughters; and the youth Samuel grows up with YHWH. **22** And Eli [is] very old, and has heard all that his sons do to all Israel, and how that they lie with the women who are assembling [at] the opening of the Tent of Meeting, **23** and he says to them, "Why do you do things like these? For I am hearing of your evil words from all the people—these! **24** No, my sons; for the report which I am hearing is not good, causing the people of YHWH to transgress. **25** If a man sins against a man, then God has judged him; but if a man sins against YHWH, who prays for him?" And they do not listen to the voice of their father, though YHWH has delighted to put them to death. **26** And the youth Samuel is going on and growing up, and [is] good with both YHWH, and also with men. **27** And a man of God comes to Eli and says to him, "Thus said YHWH: Was I really revealed to the house of your father in their being in Egypt, before Pharaoh's house, **28** even to choose him out of all the tribes of Israel for a priest for Myself, to go up on My altar, to make incense, to bear an ephod before Me, and I give to the house of your father all the fire-offerings of the sons of Israel? **29** Why do you kick at My sacrifice and at My offering, which I commanded [in] My habitation, and honor your sons above Me, to make yourselves fat from the first part of every offering of Israel, of My people? **30** Therefore—a declaration of YHWH, God of Israel—I certainly said, Your house and the house of your father walk up and down before Me for all time; and now—a declaration of YHWH—Far be it from Me! For he who is honoring Me, I honor, and those despising Me, are lightly esteemed. **31** Behold, days [are] coming, and I have cut off your arm, and the arm of

1 SAMUEL

the house of your father, that an old man is not in your house; **32** and you have beheld an adversary [in My] habitation, in all that He does good with Israel, and there is not an old man in your house all the days. **33** And the man of yours I do not cut off from My altar—[My purpose is] to consume your eyes, and to grieve your soul; and all the increase of men [in] your house die; **34** and this [is] the sign to you that comes to your two sons, to Hophni and Phinehas—in one day both of them die; **35** and I have raised up a steadfast priest for Myself; he does as in My heart and in My soul; and I have built a steadfast house for him, and he has walked up and down before My anointed all the days; **36** and it has been, everyone who is left in your house comes to bow himself to him for a wage of silver and a cake of bread, and has said, Please admit me to one of the priest's offices, to eat a morsel of bread."

3 And the youth Samuel is serving YHWH before Eli, and the word of YHWH has been precious in those days—there is no vision breaking forth. **2** And it comes to pass, at that time, that Eli is lying down in his place, and his eyes have begun [to be] faded—he is not able to see. **3** And the lamp of God is not yet extinguished, and Samuel is lying down in the temple of YHWH, where the Ark of God [is], **4** and YHWH calls to Samuel, and he says, "Here I [am]." **5** And he runs to Eli and says, "Here I [am], for you have called for me"; and he says, "I did not call; turn back, lie down"; and he goes and lies down. **6** And YHWH adds to call Samuel again, and Samuel rises and goes to Eli, and says, "Here I [am], for you have called for me"; and he says, "I have not called, my son; turn back, lie down." **7** And Samuel has not yet known YHWH, and the word of YHWH is not yet revealed to him. **8** And YHWH adds to call Samuel the third time, and he rises and goes to Eli, and says, "Here I [am], for you have called for me"; and Eli understands that YHWH is calling to the youth. **9** And Eli says to Samuel, "Go, lie down, and it has been, if He calls to you, that you have said, Speak, YHWH, for Your servant is hearing"; and Samuel goes and lies down in his place. **10** And YHWH comes, and stations Himself, and calls as time by time, "Samuel, Samuel"; and Samuel says, "Speak, for Your servant is hearing." **11** And YHWH says to Samuel, "Behold, I am doing a thing in Israel, at which the two ears of everyone hearing it tingle. **12** In that day I establish to Eli all that I have spoken to his house, beginning and completing; **13** and I have declared to him that I am judging his house for all time, for the iniquity which he has known, for his sons are making themselves vile, and he has not restrained them, **14** and therefore I have sworn to the house of Eli: the iniquity of the house of Eli is not atoned for, by sacrifice, and by offering—for all time." **15** And Samuel lies until the morning, and opens the doors of the house of YHWH, and Samuel is afraid of declaring the vision to Eli. **16** And Eli calls Samuel and says, "Samuel, my son"; and he says, "Here I [am]." **17** And he says, "What [is] the word which He has spoken to you? Please do not hide it from me; so God does to you, and so does He add, if you hide from me a word of all the words that He has spoken to you." **18** And Samuel declares to him the whole of the words, and has not hid from him; and he says, "It [is] YHWH; that which is good in His eyes He does." **19** And Samuel grows up, and YHWH has been with him, and has not let any of his words fall to the earth; **20** and all Israel knows, from Dan even to Beer-Sheba, that Samuel is established for a prophet to YHWH. **21** And YHWH adds to appear in Shiloh, for YHWH has been revealed to Samuel, in Shiloh, by the word of YHWH.

4 And the word of Samuel is to all Israel, and Israel goes out to meet the Philistines for battle, and they encamp by Eben-Ezer, and the Philistines have encamped in Aphek, **2** and the Philistines set themselves in array to meet Israel, and the battle spreads itself, and Israel is struck before the Philistines, and they strike among the ranks in the field about four thousand men. **3** And the people come into the camp, and [the] elderly of Israel say, "Why has YHWH struck us today before the Philistines? We take the Ark of the Covenant of YHWH from Shiloh to ourselves, and it comes into our midst, and He saves us out of the hand of our enemies." **4** And the people send to Shiloh, and they take from there the Ark of the Covenant of YHWH of Hosts, inhabiting the cherubim, and there [are] two sons of Eli with the Ark of the Covenant of God,

Hophni and Phinehas. **5** And it comes to pass, at the coming in of the Ark of the Covenant of YHWH to the camp, that all Israel shouts [with] a great shout, and the earth is moved. **6** And the Philistines hear the noise of the shouting, and say, "What [is] the noise of this great shout in the camp of the Hebrews?" And they perceive that the Ark of YHWH has come into the camp. **7** And the Philistines are afraid, for they said, "God has come into the camp"; and they say, "Woe to us, for there has been nothing like this before. **8** Woe to us, who delivers us out of the hand of these majestic gods? These [are] the gods who are striking the Egyptians with every plague in the wilderness. **9** Strengthen yourselves, and become men, O Philistines, lest you do service to Hebrews, as they have done to you—then you have become men, and have fought." **10** And the Philistines fight, and Israel is struck, and they each flee to his tents, and the slaughter is very great, and thirty thousand footmen of Israel fall; **11** and the Ark of God has been taken, and the two sons of Eli, Hophni and Phinehas, have died. **12** And a man of Benjamin runs out of the ranks, and comes into Shiloh, on that day, and his long robes [are] torn, and earth [is] on his head; **13** and he comes in, and behold, Eli is sitting on the throne by the side of the way, watching, for his heart has been trembling for the Ark of God, and the man has come into the city and declares [it], and all the city cries out. **14** And Eli hears the noise of the cry and says, "What [is] the noise of this tumult?" And the man hurried, and comes in, and tells Eli. **15** And Eli is a son of ninety-eight years, and his eyes have stood, and he has not been able to see. **16** And the man says to Eli, "I [am] he who has come out of the ranks, and I have fled out of the ranks today"; and he says, "What has been the matter, my son?" **17** And he who is bearing tidings answers and says, "Israel has fled before the Philistines, and also a great slaughter has been among the people, and also your two sons have died—Hophni and Phinehas—and the Ark of God has been captured." **18** And it comes to pass, at his mentioning the Ark of God, that he falls backward from off the throne, by the side of the gate, and his neck is broken, and he dies, for the man [is] old and heavy, and he has judged Israel [for] forty years. **19** And his daughter-in-law, wife of Phinehas, [is] pregnant, about to bear, and she hears the report of the taking of the Ark of God, that her father-in-law and her husband have died, and she bows, and bears, for her pains have turned on her. **20** And at the time of her death, the women who are standing by her say, "Do not fear, for you have borne a son," she has not answered, nor set her heart [to it]; **21** and she calls the youth Ichabod, saying, "Glory has removed from Israel," because of the taking of the Ark of God, and because of her father-in-law and her husband. **22** And she says, "Glory has removed from Israel, for the Ark of God has been taken."

5 And the Philistines have taken the Ark of God, and bring it in from Eben-Ezer to Ashdod, **2** and the Philistines take the Ark of God and bring it into the house of Dagon, and set it near Dagon. **3** And the Ashdodites rise early on the next day, and behold, Dagon is fallen on its face to the earth, before the Ark of YHWH; and they take Dagon, and put it back in its place. **4** And they rise early in the morning on the next day, and behold, Dagon is fallen on its face to the earth, before the Ark of YHWH, and the head of Dagon, and the two palms of its hands are cut off at the threshold, only Dagon's [body] has been left of him; **5** therefore the priests of Dagon, and all those coming into the house of Dagon, do not tread on the threshold of Dagon, in Ashdod, until this day. **6** And the hand of YHWH is heavy on the Ashdodites, and He makes them desolate, and strikes them with lumps, Ashdod and its borders. **7** And the men of Ashdod see that [it is] so, and have said, "The Ark of the God of Israel does not abide with us, for His hand has been hard on us, and on our god Dagon." **8** And they send and gather all the princes of the Philistines to them, and say, "What do we do to the Ark of the God of Israel?" And they say, "Let the Ark of the God of Israel be brought around to Gath"; and they bring around the Ark of the God of Israel; **9** and it comes to pass after they have brought it around, that the hand of YHWH is against the city—a very great destruction; and He strikes the men of the city, from small and to great; and lumps break forth on them. **10** And they send the Ark of God to Ekron, and it comes to pass, at the coming in of the Ark of God to Ekron, that the Ekronites cry out, saying, "They have brought around the

1 SAMUEL

Ark of the God of Israel to us, to put us and our people to death." **11** And they send and gather all the princes of the Philistines, and say, "Send the Ark of the God of Israel away, and it turns back to its place, and it does not put us and our people to death"; for there has been a deadly destruction throughout all the city, the hand of God has been very heavy there, **12** and the men who have not died have been struck with lumps, and the cry of the city goes up into the heavens.

6 And the Ark of YHWH is in the field of the Philistines [for] seven months, **2** and the Philistines call for priests and for diviners, saying, "What do we do to the Ark of YHWH? Let us know with what we send it to its place." **3** And they say, "If you are sending the Ark of the God of Israel away, you do not send it away empty; for you certainly send back a guilt-offering to Him; then you are healed, and it has been known to you why His hand does not turn aside from you." **4** And they say, "What [is] the guilt-offering which we send back to Him?" And they say, "The number of the princes of the Philistines—five golden lumps, and five golden muroids—for one plague [is] to you all, and to your princes, **5** and you have made images of your lumps, and images of your muroids that are corrupting the land, and have given glory to the God of Israel; it may be [that] He lightens His hand from off you, and from off your gods, and from off your land; **6** and why do you harden your heart as the Egyptians and Pharaoh hardened their heart? Do they not—when He has rolled Himself on them—send them away, and they go? **7** And now, take and make one new cart, and two suckling cows, on which a yoke has not gone up, and you have bound the cows in the cart, and caused their young ones to turn back from after them to the house, **8** and you have taken the Ark of YHWH, and put it on the cart, and the vessels of gold which you have returned to Him—a guilt-offering—you put in a coffer on its side, and have sent it away, and it has gone; **9** and you have seen if it goes up the way of its own border, to Beth-Shemesh— He has done this great evil to us; and if not, then we have known that His hand has not come against us; it has been an accident to us." **10** And the men do so, and take two suckling cows, and bind them in the cart, and they shut up their young ones in the house; **11** and they place the Ark of YHWH on the cart, and the coffer, and the golden muroids, and the images of their lumps. **12** And the cows go straight in the way, on the way to Beth-Shemesh, they have gone in one highway, going and lowing, and have not turned aside right or left; and the princes of the Philistines are going after them to the border of Beth-Shemesh. **13** And the Beth-Shemeshites are reaping their wheat-harvest in the valley, and they lift up their eyes, and see the Ark, and rejoice to see [it]. **14** And the cart has come into the field of Joshua the Beth-Shemeshite, and stands there, and there [is] a great stone, and they cleave the wood of the cart, and they have caused the cows to ascend [as] a burnt-offering to YHWH. **15** And the Levites have taken down the Ark of YHWH, and the coffer which [is] with it, in which [are] the vessels of gold, and place [them] on the great stone; and the men of Beth-Shemesh have caused burnt-offerings to ascend and sacrifice sacrifices in that day to YHWH; **16** and the five princes of the Philistines have seen [it], and return [to] Ekron, on that day. **17** And these [are] the golden lumps which the Philistines have sent back—a guilt-offering to YHWH: one for Ashdod, one for Gaza, one for Ashkelon, one for Gath, one for Ekron; **18** and the golden muroids—the number of all the cities of the Philistines, for the five princes, from the fortified city even to a village of the open place, and to the great stone [[or great meadow]] on which they placed the Ark of YHWH—[are] in the field of Joshua the Beth-Shemeshite to this day. **19** And He strikes among the men of Beth-Shemesh, for they looked into the Ark of YHWH, indeed, He strikes seventy men [out] of fifty thousand men [[or fifty thousand and seventy men]] among the people; and the people mourn, because YHWH struck among the people [with] a great striking. **20** And the men of Beth-Shemesh say, "Who is able to stand before YHWH, this holy God? And to whom does He go up from us?" **21** And they send messengers to the inhabitants of Kirjath-Jearim, saying, "The Philistines have sent back the Ark of YHWH; come down, take it up with you."

7 And the men of Kirjath-Jearim come and bring up the Ark of YHWH, and

1 SAMUEL

bring it into the house of Abinadab, in the height, and they have sanctified his son Eleazar to keep the Ark of YHWH. **2** And it comes to pass, from the day of the dwelling of the Ark in Kirjath-Jearim, that the days are multiplied—indeed, they are twenty years—and all the house of Israel wails after YHWH. **3** And Samuel speaks to all the house of Israel, saying, "If you are turning back to YHWH with all your heart—turn aside the gods of the stranger from your midst, and Ashtaroth; and prepare your heart for YHWH, and serve Him only, and He delivers you out of the hand of the Philistines." **4** And the sons of Israel turn aside the Ba'alim and Ashtaroth, and serve YHWH alone; **5** and Samuel says, "Gather all Israel to Mizpeh, and I pray to YHWH for you." **6** And they are gathered to Mizpeh, and draw water, and pour out before YHWH, and fast on that day, and say there, "We have sinned against YHWH"; and Samuel judges the sons of Israel in Mizpeh. **7** And the Philistines hear that the sons of Israel have gathered themselves to Mizpeh; and the princes of the Philistines go up against Israel, and the sons of Israel hear, and are afraid of the presence of the Philistines. **8** And the sons of Israel say to Samuel, "Do not keep silent for us from crying to our God YHWH, and He saves us out of the hand of the Philistines." **9** And Samuel takes a fat lamb, and causes it to go up—a whole burnt-offering to YHWH; and Samuel cries to YHWH for Israel, and YHWH answers him; **10** and Samuel is causing the burnt-offering to go up—and the Philistines have drawn near to battle against Israel—and YHWH thunders with a great noise, on that day, on the Philistines, and troubles them, and they are struck before Israel. **11** And the men of Israel go out from Mizpeh, and pursue the Philistines, and strike them to the place of Beth-Car. **12** And Samuel takes a stone, and sets [it] between Mizpeh and Shen, and calls its name Eben-Ezer, saying, "Until now YHWH has helped us." **13** And the Philistines are humbled, and have not added anymore to come into the border of Israel, and the hand of YHWH is on the Philistines all the days of Samuel. **14** And the cities which the Philistines have taken from Israel are restored to Israel—from Ekron even to Gath—and Israel has delivered their border out of the hand of the Philistines; and there is peace between Israel and the Amorite. **15** And Samuel judges Israel all the days of his life, **16** and he has gone from year to year, and gone around Beth-El, and Gilgal, and Mizpeh, and judged Israel [in] all these places; **17** and his returning [is] to Ramath, for his house [is] there, and he has judged Israel there, and he builds an altar to YHWH there.

8 And it comes to pass, when Samuel [is] aged, that he makes his sons judges over Israel. **2** And the name of his firstborn son is Joel, and the name of his second Abiah, judges in Beer-Sheba: **3** and his sons have not walked in his ways, and turn aside after the dishonest gain, and take a bribe, and turn aside judgment. **4** And all [the] elderly of Israel gather themselves together, and come to Samuel at Ramath, **5** and say to him, "Behold, you have become aged, and your sons have not walked in your ways; now, appoint a king to us, to judge us, like all the nations." **6** And the thing is evil in the eyes of Samuel when they have said, "Give a king to us, to judge us"; and Samuel prays to YHWH. **7** And YHWH says to Samuel, "Listen to the voice of the people, to all that they say to you, for they have not rejected you, but they have rejected Me from reigning over them. **8** According to all the works that they have done from the day of My bringing them up out of Egypt, even to this day, when they forsake Me, and serve other gods—so they are also doing to you. **9** And now, listen to their voice; only, surely you certainly protest to them, and have declared to them the custom of the king who reigns over them." **10** And Samuel speaks all the words of YHWH to the people who are asking [for] a king from him, **11** and says, "This is the custom of the king who reigns over you: he takes your sons, and has appointed for himself among his chariots, and among his horsemen, and they have run before his chariots; **12** also to appoint for himself heads of thousands, and heads of fifties; also to plow his plowing, and to reap his reaping; and to make instruments of his war, and instruments of his charioteer. **13** And he takes your daughters for perfumers, and for cooks, and for bakers; **14** and your fields, and your vineyards, and your olive-yards—he takes the best, and has given to his servants. **15** And he tithes your seed and your vineyards, and has given to his eunuchs, and to his servants.

1 SAMUEL

16 And your menservants and your maidservants, and the best of your young men and your donkeys, he takes, and has prepared for his own work; **17** he tithes your flock, and you are for servants to him. **18** And you have cried out in that day because of the king whom you have chosen for yourselves, and YHWH does not answer you in that day." **19** And the people refuse to listen to the voice of Samuel, and say, "No, but a king is over us, **20** and we have been, even we, like all the nations; and our king has judged us, and gone out before us, and fought our battles." **21** And Samuel hears all the words of the people, and speaks them in the ears of YHWH; **22** and YHWH says to Samuel, "Listen to their voice, and you have caused a king to reign over them." And Samuel says to the men of Israel, "Go, each man, to his city."

9 And there is a man of Benjamin, and his name [is] Kish, son of Abiel, son of Zeror, son of Bechorath, son of Aphiah, a Benjamite, a mighty man of valor, **2** and he has a son, and his name [is] Saul, a choice youth and handsome, and there is not a man among the sons of Israel more handsome than he—from his shoulder and upward, higher than any of the people. **3** And the donkeys of Kish, father of Saul, are lost, and Kish says to his son Saul, "Now take one of the young men with you, and rise, go, seek the donkeys." **4** And he passes over through the hill-country of Ephraim, and passes over through the land of Shalisha, and they have not found [them]; and they pass over through the land of Shaalim, and they are not; and he passes over through the land of Benjamin, and they have not found [them]. **5** They have come to the land of Zuph, and Saul has said to his young man who [is] with him, "Come, and we return, lest my father leave off from the donkeys, and has been sorrowful for us." **6** And he says to him, "Now behold, a man of God [is] in this city, and the man is honored; all that he speaks certainly comes; now, we go there, it may be he declares to us our way on which we have gone." **7** And Saul says to his young man, "And behold, we go, and what do we bring to the man? For the bread has gone from our vessels, and there is no present to bring to the man of God—what [is] with us?" **8** And the young man adds to answer Saul and says, "Behold, there is found a fourth of a shekel of silver with me: and I have given to the man of God, and he has declared our way to us." **9** Formerly in Israel, thus said the man in his going to seek God: "Come and we go to the seer." For the "prophet" of today is formerly called "the seer." **10** And Saul says to his young man, "Your word [is] good; come, we go"; and they go to the city where the man of God [is]. **11** They are going up in the ascent of the city, and have found young women going out to draw water, and say to them, "Is the seer in this [place]?" **12** And they answer them and say, "He is; behold, before you! Hurry, now, for he has come to the city today, for the people [have] a sacrifice today in a high place. **13** At your going into the city so you find him, before he goes up to the high place to eat; for the people do not eat until his coming, for he blesses the sacrifice; afterward, they who are called eat, and now, go up, for you should find him at this time." **14** And they go up to the city; they are coming into the midst of the city, and behold, Samuel is coming out to meet them, to go up to the high place; **15** and YHWH had uncovered the ear of Samuel one day before the coming of Saul, saying, **16** "At this time tomorrow, I send to you a man out of the land of Benjamin—and you have anointed him for leader over My people Israel, and he has saved My people out of the hand of the Philistines; for I have seen My people, for its cry has come to Me." **17** When Samuel has seen Saul, then YHWH has answered him, "Behold, the man of whom I have spoken to you; this [one] restrains My people." **18** And Saul draws near to Samuel in the midst of the gate and says, "Please declare to me where this seer's house [is]." **19** And Samuel answers Saul and says, "I [am] the seer; go up before me into the high place, and you have eaten with me today, and I have sent you away in the morning, and all that [is] in your heart I declare to you. **20** And as for the donkeys which are lost from you [for] three days as of today, do not set your heart to them, for they have been found; and to whom [is] all the desire of Israel? Is it not to you and to all your father's house?" **21** And Saul answers and says, "Am I not a Benjamite—of the smallest of the tribes of Israel? And my family the least of all the families of the tribe of Benjamin? And why have you spoken to me according to this word?"

22 And Samuel takes Saul, and his young man, and brings them into the chamber, and gives a place to them at the head of those called; and they [are] about thirty men. **23** And Samuel says to the cook, "Give the portion which I gave to you, of which I said to you, Set it by you." **24** (And the cook lifts up the leg, and that which [is] on it, and sets [it] before Saul), and he says, "Behold, that which is left; [it] is set before your face—eat, for it is kept for you for this appointed time, [at my] saying, I have called the people"; and Saul eats with Samuel on that day. **25** And they come down from the high place to the city, and he speaks with Saul on the roof. **26** And they rise early, and it comes to pass, at the ascending of the dawn, that Samuel calls to Saul, on the roof, saying, "Rise, and I send you away"; and Saul rises, and they go out, both of them—he and Samuel, outside. **27** They are going down in the extremity of the city, and Samuel has said to Saul, "Say to the young man that he should pass on before us (and he passes on), and you, stand at this time, and I cause you to hear the word of God."

10 And Samuel takes the vial of the oil, and pours [it] on his head, and kisses him, and says, "Is it not because YHWH has appointed you over His inheritance for leader? **2** In your going from me today—then you have found two men by the grave of Rachel, in the border of Benjamin, at Zelzah, and they have said to you, The donkeys have been found which you have gone to seek; and behold, your father has left the matter of the donkeys, and has sorrowed for you, saying, What do I do for my son? **3** And you have passed on there, and beyond, and have come to the oak of Tabor, and three men going up to God to Beth-El have found you there, one carrying three kids, and one carrying three cakes of bread, and one carrying a bottle of wine, **4** and they have asked of your welfare, and given two loaves to you, and you have received from their hand. **5** Afterward you come to the hill of God, where the garrison of the Philistines [is], and it comes to pass, at your coming in there to the city, that you have met a band of prophets coming down from the high place, and before them stringed instrument, and tambourine, and pipe, and harp, and they are prophesying; **6** and the Spirit of YHWH has prospered over you, and you have prophesied with them, and have turned into a [new] man; **7** and it has been, when these signs come to you—do for yourself as your hand finds, for God [is] with you. **8** And you have gone down before me to Gilgal, and behold, I am going down to you, to cause burnt-offerings to ascend, to sacrifice sacrifices of peace-offerings; you wait [for] seven days until my coming to you, and I have made known to you that which you do." **9** And it has been, at his turning his shoulder to go from Samuel, that God turns to him another heart, and all these signs come on that day, **10** and they come in there to the height, and behold, a band of prophets [is there] to meet him, and the Spirit of God prospers over him, and he prophesies in their midst. **11** And it comes to pass, all knowing him before, see, and behold, he has prophesied with prophets, and the people say to one another, "What [is] this [that] has happened to the son of Kish? Is Saul also among the prophets?" **12** And a man there answers and says, "And who [is] their father?" Therefore it has been for an allegory, "Is Saul also among the prophets?" **13** And he ceases from prophesying, and comes to the high place, **14** and the uncle of Saul says to him, and to his young man, "To where did you go?" And he says, "To seek the donkeys; and we see that they are not, and we come to Samuel." **15** And the uncle of Saul says, "Please declare to me what Samuel said to you." **16** And Saul says to his uncle, "He certainly declared to us that the donkeys were found"; and of the matter of the kingdom he has not declared to him that which Samuel said. **17** And Samuel calls the people to YHWH to Mizpeh, **18** and says to the sons of Israel, "Thus said YHWH, God of Israel: I have brought up Israel out of Egypt, and I deliver you out of the hand of the Egyptians, and out of the hand of all the kingdoms who are oppressing you; **19** and you have rejected your God today, who [is] Himself your Savior out of all your evils and your distresses, and you say, No, but you set a king over us; and now, station yourselves before YHWH, by your tribes, and by your thousands." **20** And Samuel brings all the tribes of Israel near, and the tribe of Benjamin is captured, **21** and he brings the tribe of Benjamin near by its families, and the family of Matri is captured, and Saul son of Kish is captured,

ered; and they seek him, and he has not been found. **22** And they ask again of Y<small>HWH</small>, "Has the man come here yet?" And Y<small>HWH</small> says, "Behold, he has been hidden near the vessels." **23** And they run and bring him there, and he stationed himself in the midst of the people, and he is higher than any of the people from his shoulder and upward. **24** And Samuel says to all the people, "Have you seen him on whom Y<small>HWH</small> has fixed, for there is none like him among all the people?" And all the people shout, and say, "Let the king live!" **25** And Samuel speaks to the people the right of the kingdom, and writes in a scroll, and places [it] before Y<small>HWH</small>; and Samuel sends all the people away, each to his house. **26** And Saul has also gone to his house, to Gibeah, and the force goes with him whose heart God has touched; **27** and the sons of worthlessness have said, "How can this one save us?" And they despise him, and have not brought a present to him; and he is as one being deaf.

11 And Nahash the Ammonite comes up, and encamps against Jabesh-Gilead, and all the men of Jabesh say to Nahash, "Make a covenant with us, and we serve you." **2** And Nahash the Ammonite says to them, "For this I cut [a covenant] with you, in picking out every right eye of yours—and I have set it [for] a reproach on all Israel." **3** And [the] elderly of Jabesh say to him, "Leave us alone [for] seven days, and we send messengers into all the border of Israel: and if there is none saving us—then we have come out to you." **4** And the messengers come to Gibeah of Saul, and speak the words in the ears of the people, and all the people lift up their voice and weep; **5** and behold, Saul has come out of the field after the herd, and Saul says, "What [is that] to the people, that they weep?" And they recount the words of the men of Jabesh to him. **6** And the Spirit of God prospers over Saul, in his hearing these words, and his anger burns greatly, **7** and he takes a couple of oxen, and cuts them in pieces, and sends [them] through all the border of Israel, by the hand of the messengers, saying, "He who is not coming out after Saul and after Samuel—thus it is done to his oxen"; and the fear of Y<small>HWH</small> falls on the people, and they come out as one man. **8** And he inspects them in Bezek, and the sons of Israel are three hundred thousand, and the men of Judah thirty thousand. **9** And they say to the messengers who are coming, "Thus you say to the men of Jabesh-Gilead: Tomorrow you have safety—by the heat of the sun"; and the messengers come and declare [it] to the men of Jabesh, and they rejoice; **10** and the men of Jabesh say [to the Ammonites], "Tomorrow we come out to you, and you have done to us according to all that [is] good in your eyes." **11** And it comes to pass, on the next day, that Saul puts the people in three detachments, and they come into the midst of the camp in the morning-watch, and strike Ammon until the heat of the day; and it comes to pass that those left are scattered, and there have not been left two of them together. **12** And the people say to Samuel, "Who is he that says, Saul reigns over us? Give up the men, and we put them to death." **13** And Saul says, "There is no man put to death on this day, for today Y<small>HWH</small> has worked salvation in Israel." **14** And Samuel says to the people, "Come and we go to Gilgal, and renew the kingdom there"; **15** and all the people go to Gilgal, and cause Saul to reign there before Y<small>HWH</small> in Gilgal, and sacrifice sacrifices of peace-offerings there before Y<small>HWH</small>, and Saul rejoices there—and all the men of Israel—very greatly.

12 And Samuel says to all Israel, "Behold, I have listened to your voice, to all that you said to me, and I cause a king to reign over you, **2** and now, behold, the king is habitually walking before you, and I have become aged and gray-headed, and my sons, behold, they [are] with you, and I have habitually walked before you from my youth until this day. **3** Behold, here I [am]; testify against me before Y<small>HWH</small>, and before His anointed; whose ox have I taken, and whose donkey have I taken, and whom have I oppressed; whom have I bruised, and of whose hand have I taken a ransom, and hide my eyes with it? And I restore [it] to you." **4** And they say, "You have not oppressed us, nor have you crushed us, nor have you taken anything from the hand of anyone." **5** And he says to them, "Y<small>HWH</small> [is] a witness against you, and His anointed [is] a witness this day, that you have not found anything in my hand"; and they say, "A witness." **6** And Samuel says to the people, "Y<small>HWH</small> [is] He who made Moses and Aaron, and who brought up your fathers out of the land of Egypt! **7** And now, station yourselves, and I judge you before YHWH, with all the righteous acts of YHWH, which He did with you, and with your fathers. **8** When Jacob has come to Egypt, and your fathers cry to YHWH, then YHWH sends Moses and Aaron, and they bring out your fathers from Egypt, and cause them to dwell in this place, **9** and they forget their God YHWH, and He sells them into the hand of Sisera, head of the host of Hazor, and into the hand of the Philistines, and into the hand of the king of Moab, and they fight against them, **10** and they cry to YHWH, and say, We have sinned, because we have forsaken YHWH, and serve the Ba'alim, and Ashtaroth, and now, deliver us out of the hand of our enemies, and we serve You. **11** And YHWH sends Jerubba'al, and Bedan, and Jephthah, and Samuel, and delivers you out of the hand of your surrounding enemies, and you dwell confidently. **12** And you see that Nahash king of the sons of Ammon has come against you, and you say to me, No, but a king reigns over us; and your God YHWH [is] your king! **13** And now, behold the king whom you have chosen—whom you have asked for! And behold, YHWH has placed a king over you. **14** If you fear YHWH, and have served Him, and listened to His voice, then you do not provoke the mouth of YHWH, and you have been—both you and the king who has reigned over you—after your God YHWH. **15** And if you do not listen to the voice of YHWH—then you have provoked the mouth of YHWH, and the hand of YHWH has been against you, and against your fathers. **16** Also now, station yourselves and see this great thing which YHWH is doing before your eyes; **17** is it not wheat-harvest today? I call to YHWH, and He gives voices and rain; and know and see that your evil is great which you have done in the eyes of YHWH, to ask [for] a king for yourselves." **18** And Samuel calls to YHWH, and YHWH gives voices and rain on that day, and all the people greatly fear YHWH and Samuel; **19** and all the people say to Samuel, "Pray for your servants to your God YHWH, and we do not die, for we have added evil to all our sins to ask [for] a king for ourselves." **20** And Samuel says to the people, "Do not fear; you have done all this evil; only, do not turn aside from after YHWH—and you have served YHWH with all your heart, **21** and you do not turn aside after the vain things which do not profit nor deliver, for they [are] vain, **22** for YHWH does not leave His people, on account of His great Name; for YHWH has been pleased to make you for a people to Him. **23** I, also, far be it from me to sin against YHWH, by ceasing to pray for you, and I have directed you in the good and upright way; **24** only, fear YHWH, and you have served Him in truth with all your heart, for see that which He has made great with you; **25** and if you really do evil, both you and your king are consumed."

13 Saul [is] a son of [[thirty]] years in his reigning, and he has reigned over Israel [forty]-two years, **2** then Saul chooses for himself three thousand [men] out of Israel; and two thousand are with Saul in Michmash, and in the hill-country of Beth-El; and one thousand have been with Jonathan in Gibeah of Benjamin; and he has sent each one of the remnant of the people to his tents. **3** And Jonathan strikes the garrison of the Philistines which [is] in Geba, and the Philistines hear, and Saul has blown with a horn through all the land, saying, "Let the Hebrews hear." **4** And all Israel have heard, saying, "Saul has struck the garrison of the Philistines," and also, "Israel has been abhorred by the Philistines"; and the people are called after Saul to Gilgal. **5** And the Philistines have been gathered to fight with Israel; thirty thousand chariots, and six thousand horsemen, and a people as the sand which [is] on the seashore for multitude; and they come up and encamp in Michmash, east of Beth-Aven. **6** And the men of Israel have seen that they are distressed, that the people have been oppressed, and the people hide themselves in caves, and in thickets, and in rocks, and in high places, and in pits. **7** And Hebrews have passed over the Jordan to the land of Gad and Gilead; and Saul [is] yet in Gilgal, and all the people have trembled after him. **8** And he waits seven days, according to the appointment with Samuel, and Samuel has not come to Gilgal, and the people are scattered from off him. **9** And Saul says, "Bring the burnt-offering and the peace-offerings near to me"; and he causes the burnt-offering to ascend. **10** And it comes to pass at his completing to cause the burnt-offering to ascend, that behold, Samuel has come, and Saul goes out to meet him, to bless him; **11** and Samuel says, "What have you done?" And Saul says, "Because I saw that the people were scattered from off me, and you had not come at the appointment of the days, and the Philistines are gathered to Michmash, **12** and I say, Now the Philistines come down to me to Gilgal, and I have not appeased the face of Y<small>HWH</small>; and I force myself, and cause the burnt-offering to ascend." **13** And Samuel says to Saul, "You have been foolish; you have not kept the command of your God Y<small>HWH</small>, which He commanded you, for now Y<small>HWH</small> had established your kingdom over Israel for all time; **14** and now, your kingdom does not stand, Y<small>HWH</small> has sought [for] a man for Himself according to His own heart, and Y<small>HWH</small> charges him for leader over His people, for you have not kept that which Y<small>HWH</small> commanded you." **15** And Samuel rises, and goes up from Gilgal to Gibeah of Benjamin; and Saul inspects the people who are found with him, about six hundred men, **16** and Saul, and his son Jonathan, and the people who are found with them, are abiding in Gibeah of Benjamin, and the Philistines have encamped in Michmash. **17** And the destroyer goes out from the camp of the Philistines—three detachments: one detachment turns to the way of Ophrah, to the land of Shual, **18** and one detachment turns the way of Beth-Horon, and one detachment turns the way of the border which is looking on the Valley of the Zeboim, toward the wilderness. **19** And a craftsman is not found in all the land of Israel, for the Philistines said, "Lest the Hebrews make sword or spear"; **20** and all Israel goes down to the Philistines, to each sharpen his plowshare, and his coulter, and his axe, and his mattock; **21** and there has been the file for mattocks, and for coulters, and for three-pronged rakes, and for the axes, and to set up the goads. **22** And it has been, in the day of battle, that there has not been found a sword and spear in the hand of any of the people who [are] with Saul and with Jonathan—but it is found with Saul and with his son Jonathan. **23** And the station of the Philistines goes out to the passage of Michmash.

14 And the day comes that Jonathan son of Saul says to the young man carrying his weapons, "Come, and we pass over to the station of the Philistines, which [is] on the other side of this"; and he has not declared [it] to his father. **2** And Saul is abiding at the extremity of Gibeah, under the pomegranate which [is] in Migron, and the people who [are] with him [are] about six hundred men, **3** and Ahiah, son of Ahitub, brother of Ichabod, son of Phinehas son of Eli priest of Y<small>HWH</small> in Shiloh, [was] bearing an ephod; and the people did not know that Jonathan has gone. **4** And between the passages where Jonathan sought to pass over to the station of the Philistines [is] the edge of a rock on one side, and the edge of a rock on the other side, and the name of one is Bozez, and the name of the other Seneh. **5** One edge [is] fixed on the north in front of Michmash, and the one on the south in front of Gibeah. **6** And Jonathan says to the young man carrying his weapons, "Come, and we pass over to the station of these uncircumcised; it may be Y<small>HWH</small> works for us, for there is no restraint to Y<small>HWH</small> to save by many or by few." **7** And the bearer of his weapons says to him, "Do all that [is] in your heart; turn for yourself; behold, I [am] with you, as your own heart." **8** And Jonathan says, "Behold, we are passing over to the men, and are revealed to them; **9** if they thus say to us, Stand still until we have come to you, then we have stood in our place, and do not go up to them; **10** and if they thus say, Come up against us, then we have gone up, for Y<small>HWH</small> has given them into our hand, and this [is] the sign to us." **11** And both of them are revealed to the station of the Philistines, and the Philistines say, "Behold, Hebrews are coming out of the holes where they have hid themselves." **12** And the men of the station answer Jonathan, and the bearer of his weapons, and say, "Come up to us, and we cause you to know something." And Jonathan says to the bearer of his weapons, "Come up after me, for Y<small>HWH</small> has given them into the hand of Israel." **13** And Jonathan goes up on his hands, and on his feet, and the bearer of his weapons after him; and they fall before Jonathan, and the bearer of his weapons is putting [them] to death after him. **14** And the first striking which Jonathan and the bearer of his weapons have struck is of about twenty men, in about half a furrow of a yoke of a field, **15** and there is a trembling in the camp, in the field, and among all the people, the station and the destroyers have

1 SAMUEL

trembled—even they, and the earth shakes, and it becomes a trembling of God. **16** And the watchmen of Saul in Gibeah of Benjamin see, and behold, the multitude has melted away, and it goes on, and is beaten down. **17** And Saul says to the people who [are] with him, "Now inspect and see; who has gone from us?" And they inspect, and behold, Jonathan and the bearer of his weapons are not. **18** And Saul says to Ahiah, "Bring the Ark of God near"; for the Ark of God has been with the sons of Israel on that day. **19** And it comes to pass, while Saul spoke to the priest, that the noise which [is] in the camp of the Philistines goes on, going on and becoming great, and Saul says to the priest, "Remove your hand." **20** And Saul is called, and all the people who [are] with him, and they come to the battle, and behold, the sword of each has been against his neighbor—a very great destruction. **21** And the Hebrews [who] have been with the Philistines before the day prior, who had gone up with them into the camp, have turned around, even they, to be with Israel who [are] with Saul and Jonathan, **22** and all the men of Israel, who are hiding themselves in the hill-country of Ephraim, have heard that the Philistines have fled, and they pursue—even they—after them in battle. **23** And YHWH saves Israel on that day, and the battle has passed over to Beth-Aven. **24** And the men of Israel have been distressed on that day, and Saul adjures the people, saying, "Cursed [is] the man who eats food until the evening, and I have been avenged of my enemies"; and none of the people have tasted food. **25** And all [those of] the land have come into a forest, and there is honey on the face of the field; **26** and the people come into the forest, and behold, the honey dropped, and none is moving his hand to his mouth, for the people feared the oath. **27** And Jonathan has not heard of his father's adjuring the people, and puts forth the end of the rod, which [is] in his hand, and dips it in the honeycomb, and brings back his hand to his mouth—and his eyes see! **28** And a man of the people answers and says, "Your father certainly adjured the people, saying, Cursed [is] the man who eats food today; and the people are weary." **29** And Jonathan says, "My father has troubled the land; now see that my eyes have become bright because I tasted a little of this honey. **30** How much more if the people had well eaten today of the spoil of its enemies which it has found, for now the striking has not been great among the Philistines." **31** And they strike on that day among the Philistines from Michmash to Aijalon, and the people are very weary, **32** and the people make toward the spoil, and take sheep, and oxen, and sons of the herd, and slaughter on the earth, and the people eat with the blood. **33** And they declare to Saul, saying, "Behold, the people are sinning against YHWH, to eat with the blood." And he says, "You have dealt treacherously, roll a great stone to me today." **34** And Saul says, "Be scattered among the people, and you have said to them: Each bring his ox to me, and each his sheep; and you have slain [them] in this place, and eaten, and you do not sin against YHWH to eat with the blood." And all the people bring [them]—each one [with] his ox in his hand, that night—and slaughter [them] there. **35** And Saul builds an altar to YHWH; with it he has begun to build altars to YHWH. **36** And Saul says, "Let us go down after the Philistines by night, and we prey on them until the morning light, and do not leave a man of them." And they say, "Do all that is good in your eyes." And the priest says, "Let us draw near to God here." **37** And Saul asks of God, "Do I go down after the Philistines? Do You give them into the hand of Israel?" And He has not answered him on that day. **38** And Saul says, "Everyone draw near here, the chiefs of the people, and know and see in what this sin has been today; **39** for YHWH lives, who is saving Israel: surely if it is in my son Jonathan, surely he certainly dies"; and none is answering him out of all the people. **40** And he says to all Israel, "You are on one side, and I and my son Jonathan are on another side"; and the people say to Saul, "Do that which is good in your eyes." **41** And Saul says to YHWH, God of Israel, "Give perfection"; and Jonathan and Saul are captured, and the people went out. **42** And Saul says, "Cast between me and my son Jonathan"; and Jonathan is captured. **43** And Saul says to Jonathan, "Declare to me, what have you done?" And Jonathan declares to him and says, "I certainly tasted a little honey with the end of the rod that [is] in my hand; behold, I die!" **44** And Saul says, "Thus God does, and thus does He add, for you certainly die, Jonathan." **45** And the people say to Saul, "Does Jonathan die who worked this great salvation in Israel? Certainly not! YHWH lives, if there falls to the earth [even one] hair from his head, for with God he has worked this day"; and the people rescue Jonathan, and he has not died. **46** And Saul goes up from after the Philistines, and the Philistines have gone to their place; **47** and Saul captured the kingdom over Israel, and he fights all around against all his enemies, against Moab, and against the sons of Ammon, and against Edom, and against the kings of Zobah, and against the Philistines, and wherever he turns he distresses [them]. **48** And he makes a force, and strikes Amalek, and delivers Israel out of the hand of its spoiler. **49** And the sons of Saul are Jonathan, and Ishui, and Melchi-Shua; as for the name of his two daughters, the name of the firstborn [is] Merab, and the name of the younger Michal; **50** and the name of the wife of Saul [is] Ahinoam, daughter of Ahimaaz; and the name of the head of his host [is] Abner son of Ner, uncle of Saul; **51** and Kish [is] the father of Saul, and Ner, the father of Abner, [is] the son of Ahiel. **52** And the war is severe against the Philistines all the days of Saul; when Saul has seen any mighty man, and any son of valor, then he gathers him to himself.

15 And Samuel says to Saul, "YHWH sent me to anoint you for king over His people, over Israel; and now, listen to the voice of the words of YHWH. **2** Thus said YHWH of Hosts: I have looked after that which Amalek did to Israel, that which he laid for him in the way in his going up out of Egypt. **3** Now go, and you have struck Amalek, and devoted all that he has, and you have no pity on him, and have put to death from man to woman, from infant to suckling, from ox to sheep, from camel to donkey." **4** And Saul summons the people, and inspects them in Telaim, two hundred thousand footmen, and ten thousand [are] men of Judah. **5** And Saul comes to a city of Amalek, and lays wait in a valley; **6** and Saul says to the Kenite, "Go, turn aside, go down from the midst of Amalek, lest I consume you with it, and you did kindness with all the sons of Israel, in their going up out of Egypt"; and the Kenite turns aside from the midst of Amalek. **7** And Saul strikes Amalek from Havilah [to] your going to Shur, which [is] on the front of Egypt, **8** and he catches Agag king of Amalek alive, and he has devoted all the people by the mouth of the sword; **9** and Saul has pity—also the people—on Agag, and on the best of the flock, and of the herd, and of the seconds, and on the lambs, and on all that [is] good, and have not been willing to devote them; and all the work, despised and wasted—it they devoted. **10** And the word of YHWH is to Samuel, saying, **11** "I have regretted that I caused Saul to reign for king, for he has turned back from after Me, and he has not performed My words"; and it is displeasing to Samuel, and he cries to YHWH all the night. **12** And Samuel rises early to meet Saul in the morning, and it is declared to Samuel, saying, "Saul has come to Carmel, and behold, he is setting up a monument to himself, and goes around, and passes over, and goes down to Gilgal." **13** And Samuel comes to Saul, and Saul says to him, "Blessed [are] you of YHWH; I have performed the word of YHWH." **14** And Samuel says, "And what [is] the noise of this flock in my ears—and the noise of the herd which I am hearing?" **15** And Saul says, "They have brought them from Amalek, because the people had pity on the best of the flock, and of the herd, in order to sacrifice to your God YHWH, and we have devoted the remnant." **16** And Samuel says to Saul, "Desist, and I declare to you that which YHWH has spoken to me tonight"; and he says to him, "Speak." **17** And Samuel says, "Are you not, if you [are] little in your own eyes, head of the tribes of Israel? And YHWH anoints you for king over Israel, **18** and YHWH sends you in the way, and says, Go, and you have devoted the sinners, the Amalekite, and fought against them until they are consumed; **19** and why have you not listened to the voice of YHWH—and fly to the spoil, and do evil in the eyes of YHWH?" **20** And Saul says to Samuel, "Because—I have listened to the voice of YHWH, and I go in the way which YHWH has sent me, and bring in Agag king of Amalek, and I have devoted Amalek; **21** and the people take of the spoil of the flock and herd, the first part of the devoted thing, for sacrifice to your God YHWH in Gilgal." **22** And Samuel says, "Has YHWH had delight in burnt-offerings and sacrifices as [in] listening to the voice of YHWH? Behold, listening is better than sacrifice; to give attention than fat of rams; **23** for rebellion [is as] a sin of divination, and stubbornness [is as] iniquity and teraphim; because you have rejected the word of YHWH, He also rejects you from [being] king." **24** And Saul says to Samuel, "I have sinned, for I passed over the command of YHWH, and your words; because I have feared the people, I also listen to their voice; **25** and now, please bear with my sin, and return with me, and I bow myself to YHWH." **26** And Samuel says to Saul, "I do not return with you; for you have rejected the word of YHWH, and YHWH rejects you from being king over Israel." **27** And Samuel turns around to go, and he lays hold on the skirt of his upper robe—and it is torn! **28** And Samuel says to him, "YHWH has torn the kingdom of Israel from you today, and given it to your neighbor who is better than you; **29** and also, the Preeminence of Israel does not lie nor relent, for He [is] not a man that He should relent." **30** And he says, "I have sinned; now please honor me before [the] elderly of my people and before Israel, and return with me; and I have bowed myself to your God YHWH." **31** And Samuel turns back after Saul, and Saul bows himself to YHWH; **32** and Samuel says, "Bring Agag king of Amalek to me," and Agag comes to him daintily, and Agag says, "Surely the bitterness of death has turned aside." **33** And Samuel says, "As your sword bereaved women—so is your mother bereaved above women"; and Samuel hews Agag in pieces before YHWH in Gilgal. **34** And Samuel goes to Ramath, and Saul has gone to his house—to Gibeah of Saul. **35** And Samuel has not added to see Saul until the day of his death, for Samuel mourned for Saul, and YHWH regretted that He had caused Saul to reign over Israel.

16 And YHWH says to Samuel, "Until when are you mourning for Saul, and I have rejected him from reigning over Israel? Fill your horn with oil and go, I send you to Jesse the Beth-Lehemite, for I have seen among his sons a king for Myself." **2** And Samuel says, "How do I go? When Saul has heard, then he has slain me." And YHWH says, "You take a heifer of the herd in your hand, and have said, I have come to sacrifice to YHWH; **3** and you have called for Jesse in the sacrifice, and I cause you to know that which you do, and you have anointed for Me him of whom I speak to you." **4** And Samuel does that which YHWH has spoken, and comes to Beth-Lehem, and [the] elderly of the city tremble to meet him, and [one] says, "Is your coming peace?" **5** And he says, "Peace; I have come to sacrifice to YHWH, sanctify yourselves, and you have come in with me to the sacrifice"; and he sanctifies Jesse and his sons, and calls them to the sacrifice. **6** And it comes to pass, in their coming in, that he sees Eliab and says, "Surely His anointed [is] here before YHWH." **7** And YHWH says to Samuel, "Do not look at his appearance, and at the height of his stature, for I have rejected him; for [it is] not as man sees—for man looks at the eyes, and YHWH looks at the heart." **8** And Jesse calls to Abinadab, and causes him to pass by before Samuel; and he says, "Indeed, YHWH has not fixed on this [one]." **9** And Jesse causes Shammah to pass by, and he says, "Indeed, YHWH has not fixed on this [one]." **10** And Jesse causes seven of his sons to pass by before Samuel, and Samuel says to Jesse, "YHWH has not fixed on these." **11** And Samuel says to Jesse, "Are the young men finished?" And he says, "Yet the youngest has been left; and behold, he delights himself among the flock"; and Samuel says to Jesse, "Send and take him, for we do not turn around until his coming in here." **12** And he sends, and brings him in, and he [is] ruddy, with beautiful eyes, and of good appearance; and YHWH says, "Rise, anoint him, for this [is] he." **13** And Samuel takes the horn of oil, and anoints him in the midst of his brothers, and the Spirit of YHWH prospers over David from that day and onward; and Samuel rises and goes to Ramath. **14** And the Spirit of YHWH turned aside from Saul, and a spirit of sadness from YHWH terrified him; **15** and the servants of Saul say to him, "Now behold, a spirit of sadness [from] God is terrifying you; **16** now let our lord command your servants before you [that] they seek a skillful man playing on a harp, and it has come to pass, in the spirit of sadness [from] God being on you, that he has played with his hand and [it is] well with you." **17** And Saul says to his servants, "Now provide for me a man playing well—then you have brought [him] to me." **18** And one of the servants answers and says, "Behold, I have seen a son of Jesse the Beth-Lehemite, skillful in playing, and

1 SAMUEL

a mighty, virtuous man, and a man of battle, and intelligent in word, and a man of form, and YHWH [is] with him." **19** And Saul sends messengers to Jesse and says, "Send to me your son David, who [is] with the flock." **20** And Jesse takes a donkey, bread, and a bottle of wine, and one kid of the goats, and sends [them] by the hand of his son David to Saul. **21** And David comes to Saul, and stands before him, and he loves him greatly; and he is a bearer of his weapons. **22** And Saul sends to Jesse, saying, "Please let David stand before me, for he has found grace in my eyes." **23** And it has come to pass, in the spirit of [sadness from] God being on Saul, that David has taken the harp, and played with his hand, and Saul has refreshment and gladness, and the spirit of sadness has turned aside from off him.

17 And the Philistines gather their camps to battle, and are gathered to Shochoh, which [is] to Judah, and encamp between Shochoh and Azekah, in Ephes-Dammim; **2** and Saul and the men of Israel have been gathered, and encamp by the Valley of Elah, and set in array [for] battle to meet the Philistines. **3** And the Philistines are standing on the mountain on this [side], and Israel is standing on the mountain on that [side], and the valley [is] between them. **4** And a man goes out, the champion from the camps of the Philistines, his name [is] Goliath, from Gath; his height [is] six cubits and a span [[*or* four cubits and a span]], **5** and a helmet of bronze [is] on his head, and he is clothed [with] a scaled coat of mail, and the weight of the coat of mail [is] five thousand shekels of bronze, **6** and a frontlet of bronze [is] on his feet, and a javelin of bronze between his shoulders, **7** and the wood of his spear [is] like a weavers' beam, and the flame of his spear [is] six hundred shekels of iron, and the bearer of the buckler is going before him. **8** And he stands and calls to the ranks of Israel, and says to them, "Why do you come out to set in array for battle? [Am] I not the Philistine, and you the servants of Saul? Choose a man for yourselves, and let him come down to me; **9** if he is able to fight with me, and has struck me, then we have been for servants to you; and if I prevail against him, and have struck him, then you have been for servants to us, and have served us." **10** And the Philistine says, "I have reproached the ranks of Israel this day; give a man to me and we fight together!" **11** And Saul hears—and all Israel—these words of the Philistine, and they are broken down and greatly afraid. **12** And David [is] son of this Ephraimite of Beth-Lehem-Judah, whose name [is] Jesse, and he has eight sons, and the man has become aged among men in the days of Saul; **13** and the three eldest sons of Jesse go, they have gone after Saul to battle; and the name of his three sons who have gone into battle [are] Eliab the firstborn, and his second Abinadab, and the third Shammah. **14** And David is the youngest, and the three eldest have gone after Saul, **15** and David is going and returning from Saul, to feed the flock of his father at Beth-Lehem. **16** And the Philistine draws near, morning and evening, and stations himself [for] forty days. **17** And Jesse says to his son David, "Now take an ephah of this roasted [grain] and these ten loaves for your brothers, and run to the camp to your brothers; **18** and take these ten cuttings of the cheese to the head of the one thousand, and inspect your brothers for welfare, and receive their pledge." **19** And Saul, and they, and all the men of Israel, [are] in the Valley of Elah, fighting with the Philistines. **20** And David rises early in the morning, and leaves the flock to a keeper, and lifts up, and goes, as Jesse commanded him, and he comes to the path, and to the force which is going out to the rank, and they have shouted for battle; **21** and Israel and the Philistines set in array rank to meet rank. **22** And David lets down the goods from off him on the hand of a keeper of the goods, and runs into the rank, and comes and asks of his brothers of [their] welfare. **23** And he is speaking with them, and behold, a man, the champion, is coming up, his name [is] Goliath the Philistine, from Gath, out of the ranks of the Philistines, and he speaks according to those words, and David hears; **24** and all the men of Israel, when they see the man, flee from his presence, and are greatly afraid. **25** And the men of Israel say, "Have you seen this man who is coming up? For he is coming up to reproach Israel, and it has been—the man who strikes him, the king enriches him with great riches, and he gives his daughter to him, and makes his father's house free in Israel." **26** And David speaks to the men who are standing by him, saying, "What is done to the man who strikes this Philistine, and has turned aside reproach from Israel? For who [is] this uncircumcised Philistine that he has reproached the ranks of the living God?" **27** And the people speak to him according to this word, saying, "Thus it is done to the man who strikes him." **28** And Eliab, his eldest brother, hears when he speaks to the men, and the anger of Eliab burns against David, and he says, "Why [is] this—[that] you have come down? And to whom have you left those few sheep in the wilderness? I have known your pride, and the evil of your heart—for you have come down to see the battle." **29** And David says, "What have I done now? Is it not a word?" **30** And he turns around from him to another, and says according to this word, and the people return him word as the first word. **31** And the words which David has spoken are heard, and they declare [them] before Saul, and he receives him; **32** and David says to Saul, "Let no man's heart fall because of him, your servant goes, and has fought with this Philistine." **33** And Saul says to David, "You are not able to go to this Philistine, to fight with him, for you [are] a youth, and he [has been] a man of war from his youth." **34** And David says to Saul, "Your servant has been a shepherd among the sheep for his father, and the lion has come—and the bear—and has taken away a sheep out of the drove, **35** and I have gone out after him, and struck him, and delivered [it] out of his mouth, and he rises against me, and I have taken hold on his beard, and struck him, and put him to death. **36** Your servant has struck both the lion and the bear, and this uncircumcised Philistine has been as one of them, for he has reproached the ranks of the living God." **37** And David says, "YHWH, who delivered me out of the paw of the lion, and out of the paw of the bear, He delivers me from the hand of this Philistine." And Saul says to David, "Go, and YHWH is with you." **38** And Saul clothes David with his long robe, and has put a helmet of bronze on his head, and clothes him with a coat of mail. **39** And David girded his sword above his long robe, and begins to go, for he has not tried [it]; and David says to Saul, "I am not able to go with these, for I had not tried"; and David turns them aside from off him. **40** And he takes his staff in his hand, and chooses five smooth stones for himself from the brook, and puts them in the shepherds' vessel that he has, even in the leather pouch, and his sling [is] in his hand, and he draws near to the Philistine. **41** And the Philistine goes on, going and drawing near to David, and the man carrying the buckler [is] before him, **42** and the Philistine looks attentively, and sees David, and despises him, for he was a youth, and ruddy, with a handsome appearance. **43** And the Philistine says to David, "Am I a dog that you are coming to me with sticks?" And the Philistine reviles David by his gods, **44** and the Philistine says to David, "Come to me, and I give your flesh to the bird of the heavens, and to the beast of the field." **45** And David says to the Philistine, "You are coming to me with sword, and with spear, and with buckler, and I am coming to you in the Name of YHWH of Hosts, God of the ranks of Israel, which you have reproached! **46** This day YHWH shuts you up into my hand—and I have struck you, and turned aside your head from off you, and given the carcass of the camp of the Philistines this day to the bird of the heavens, and to the beast of the earth, and all the earth knows that God is for Israel! **47** And all this assembly knows that YHWH does not save by sword and by spear, for the battle [is] YHWH's, and He has given you into our hand." **48** And it has come to pass, that the Philistine has risen, and goes, and draws near to meet David, and David hurries and runs to the rank to meet the Philistine, **49** and David puts forth his hand into the vessel, and takes a stone from there, and slings, and strikes the Philistine on his forehead, and the stone sinks into his forehead, and he falls on his face to the earth. **50** And David is stronger than the Philistine with a sling and with a stone, and strikes the Philistine, and puts him to death, and there is no sword in the hand of David, **51** and David runs and stands over the Philistine, and takes his sword, and draws it out of its sheath, and puts him to death, and cuts off his head with it; and the Philistines see that their hero [is] dead, and flee. **52** And the men of Israel rise—also Judah—and shout, and pursue the Philistines until you enter the valley, and to the gates of Ekron, and the wounded of the Philistines fall in the way of Shaaraim, even to Gath, and to Ekron, **53** and the sons of Israel return from burning after the Philistines, and spoil their camps. **54** And

David takes the head of the Philistine, and brings it to Jerusalem, and he has put his weapons in his own tent. **55** And when Saul sees David going out to meet the Philistine, he has said to Abner, head of the host, "Whose son [is] this—the youth, Abner?" And Abner says, "Your soul lives, O king, I have not known." **56** And the king says, "Ask whose son this [is]—the young man." **57** And when David turns back from striking the Philistine, then Abner takes him and brings him in before Saul, and the head of the Philistine [is] in his hand; **58** and Saul says to him, "Whose son [are] you, O youth?" And David says, "Son of your servant Jesse, the Beth-Lehemite."

18 And it comes to pass, when he finishes to speak to Saul, that the soul of Jonathan has been bound to the soul of David, and Jonathan loves him as his own soul. **2** And Saul takes him on that day, and has not permitted him to return to the house of his father. **3** And Jonathan makes—David also—a covenant, because he loves him as his own soul, **4** and Jonathan strips himself of the upper robe which [is] on him, and gives it to David, and his long robe, even to his sword, and to his bow, and to his girdle. **5** And David goes out wherever Saul sends him; he acted wisely, and Saul sets him over the men of war, and it is good in the eyes of all the people, and also in the eyes of the servants of Saul. **6** And it comes to pass, in their coming in, in David's returning from striking the Philistine, that the women come out from all the cities of Israel to sing—also the dancers—to meet Saul the king, with tambourines, with joy, and with three-stringed instruments; **7** and the women answer—those playing, and say, "Saul has struck among his thousands, ‖ And David among his myriads." **8** And it is exceedingly displeasing to Saul, and this thing is evil in his eyes, and he says, "They have given myriads to David, and they have given the thousands to me, and what more [is there] for him but the kingdom?" **9** And Saul is eyeing David from that day and from then on. **10** And it comes to pass, on the next day, that the spirit of sadness [from] God prospers over Saul, and he prophesies in the midst of the house, and David is playing with his hand, as [he did] day by day, and the javelin [is] in the hand of Saul, **11** and Saul casts the javelin and says, "I strike through David, even through the wall"; and David turns around out of his presence twice. **12** And Saul is afraid of the presence of David, for YHWH has been with him, and He has turned aside from Saul; **13** and Saul turns him aside from him, and appoints him to himself [for] head of one thousand, and he goes out and comes in, before the people. **14** And David is acting wisely in all his ways, and YHWH [is] with him, **15** and Saul sees that he is acting very wisely, and is afraid of him, **16** and all Israel and Judah love David when he is going out and coming in before them. **17** And Saul says to David, "Behold, my elder daughter Merab—I give her to you for a wife; only, be for a son of valor to me, and fight the battles of YHWH"; and Saul said, "Do not let my hand be on him, but let the hand of the Philistines be on him." **18** And David says to Saul, "Who [am] I? And what [is] my life—the family of my father in Israel—that I am son-in-law of the king?" **19** And it comes to pass, at the time of the giving of Merab daughter of Saul to David, that she has been given to Adriel the Meholathite for a wife. **20** And Michal daughter of Saul loves David, and they declare [it] to Saul, and the thing is right in his eyes, **21** and Saul says, "I give her to him, and she is for a snare to him, and the hand of the Philistines is on him"; and Saul says to David, "By the second—you become my son-in-law today." **22** And Saul commands his servants, "Speak to David gently, saying, Behold, the king has delighted in you, and all his servants have loved you, and now, be son-in-law of the king." **23** And the servants of Saul speak these words in the ears of David, and David says, "Is it a light thing in your eyes to be son-in-law of the king—and I a poor man, and lightly esteemed?" **24** And the servants of Saul declare [it] to him, saying, "David has spoken according to these words." **25** And Saul says, "Thus you say to David, There is no delight for the king in dowry, but in one hundred foreskins of the Philistines—to be avenged on the enemies of the king"; and Saul thought to cause David to fall by the hand of the Philistines. **26** And his servants declare these words to David, and the thing is right in the eyes of David, to be son-in-law of the king; and the days have not been full, **27** and David rises and goes, he and his men, and strikes two hundred men among the Philistines, and David brings in their foreskins, and they set them before the king, to be son-in-law of the king; and Saul gives his daughter Michal to him for a wife. **28** And Saul sees and knows that YHWH [is] with David, and Michal daughter of Saul has loved him, **29** and Saul adds to be afraid of the presence of David still; and Saul is an enemy of David [for] all the days. **30** And the princes of the Philistines come out, and it comes to pass from the time of their coming out, David has acted more wisely than any of the servants of Saul, and his name is very precious.

19 And Saul speaks to his son Jonathan, and to all his servants, to put David to death, **2** and Jonathan son of Saul delighted in David exceedingly, and Jonathan declares [it] to David, saying, "My father Saul is seeking to put you to death, and now, please take heed in the morning, and you have abided in a secret place and been hidden, **3** and I go out, and have stood by the side of my father in the field where you [are], and I speak of you to my father, and have seen what [is coming], and have declared [it] to you." **4** And Jonathan speaks good of David to his father Saul and says to him, "Do not let the king sin against his servant, against David, because he has not sinned against you, and because his works [are] very good for you; **5** indeed, he puts his life in his hand, and strikes the Philistine, and YHWH works a great salvation for all Israel; you have seen, and rejoice, and why do you sin against innocent blood, to put David to death for nothing?" **6** And Saul listens to the voice of Jonathan, and Saul swears, "YHWH lives—he does not die." **7** And Jonathan calls for David, and Jonathan declares all these words to him, and Jonathan brings in David to Saul, and he is before him as before. **8** And there adds to be war, and David goes out and fights against the Philistines, and strikes among them [with] a great striking, and they flee from his face. **9** And a spirit of sadness [from] YHWH is to Saul, and he is sitting in his house, and his javelin [is] in his hand, and David is playing with the hand, **10** and Saul seeks to strike with the javelin through David, and through the wall, and he frees himself from the presence of Saul, and he strikes the javelin through the wall; and David has fled and escapes during that night. **11** And Saul sends messengers to the house of David to watch him, and to put him to death in the morning; and his wife Michal declares [it] to David, saying, "If you are not delivering your life tonight—tomorrow you are put to death." **12** And Michal causes David to go down through the window, and he goes on, and flees, and escapes; **13** and Michal takes the teraphim, and lays [it] on the bed, and she has put the mattress of goats' [hair for] his pillows, and covers [it] with a garment. **14** And Saul sends messengers to take David, and she says, "He [is] sick." **15** And Saul sends the messengers to see David, saying, "Bring him up in the bed to me in order to put him to death." **16** And the messengers come in, and behold, the teraphim [are] on the bed, and the mattress of goats' [hair for] his pillows. **17** And Saul says to Michal, "Why have you thus deceived me—that you send my enemy away, and he escapes?" And Michal says to Saul, "He said to me, Send me away. Why do I put you to death?" **18** And David has fled, and escapes, and comes to Samuel at Ramath, and declares to him all that Saul has done to him, and he goes, he and Samuel, and they dwell in Naioth. **19** And it is declared to Saul, saying, "Behold, David [is] in Naioth in Ramah." **20** And Saul sends messengers to take David, and they see the assembly of the prophets prophesying, and Samuel standing, set over them, and the Spirit of God is on Saul's messengers, and they prophesy—they also. **21** And they declare [it] to Saul, and he sends other messengers, and they prophesy—they also; and Saul adds and sends messengers a third time, and they prophesy—they also. **22** And he goes, he also—to Ramath, and comes to the great well which [is] in Sechu, and asks and says, "Where [are] Samuel and David?" And [one] says, "Behold, in Naioth in Ramah." **23** And he goes there—to Naioth in Ramah, and the Spirit of God is on him also; and he goes, going on, and he prophesies until his coming to Naioth in Ramah, **24** and he strips off—he also—his garments, and prophesies—he also—before Samuel, and falls down naked all that day and all the night; therefore they say, "Is Saul also among the prophets?"

20 And David flees from Naioth in Ramah, and comes, and says before Jonathan, "What have I done? What [is] my iniquity? And what [is] my sin before your

1 SAMUEL

father, that he is seeking my life?" **2** And he says to him, "Far be it! You do not die; behold, my father does not do anything great or small and does not uncover my ear; and why does my father hide this thing from me? This [thing] is not." **3** And David swears again and says, "Your father has certainly known that I have found grace in your eyes, and he says, Do not let Jonathan know this, lest he is grieved; and yet, YHWH lives, and your soul lives, but—as a step between me and death." **4** And Jonathan says to David, "What does your soul [desire]? Command and I do it for you." **5** And David says to Jonathan, "Behold, the new moon [is] tomorrow; and I certainly sit with the king to eat; and you have sent me away, and I have been hidden in a field until the third evening; **6** if your father looks after me at all, then you have said, David earnestly asked of me to run to his city of Beth-Lehem, for there [is] a sacrifice of the days for all the family. **7** If thus he says: Good; [there is] peace for your servant; and if it is very displeasing to him—know that the evil has been determined by him; **8** and you have done kindness to your servant, for you have brought your servant into a covenant of YHWH with you—and if there is iniquity in me, put me to death yourself; for why [is] this [that] you bring me to your father?" **9** And Jonathan says, "Far be it from you! For I certainly do not know that the evil has been determined by my father to come on you, and I do not declare it to you." **10** And David says to Jonathan, "Who declares [it] to me? Or what [if] your father answers you sharply?" **11** And Jonathan says to David, "Come, and we go out into the field"; and both of them go out into the field. **12** And Jonathan says to David, "YHWH, God of Israel, [is my witness]—when I search out my father about [this] time tomorrow [or] the third [day], and behold, [there is] good toward David, and I do not then send to you, and have uncovered your ear— **13** thus YHWH does to Jonathan, and thus He adds; when the evil concerning you is good to my father, then I have uncovered your ear, and sent you away, and you have gone in peace, and YHWH is with you, as he was with my father; **14** and not only while I am alive do you do the kindness of YHWH with me, and I do not die, **15** but you do not cut off your kindness from my house for all time, nor in YHWH's cutting off the enemies of David, each one from off the face of the ground." **16** So Jonathan cuts [a covenant] with the house of David, and YHWH has sought [it] from the hand of the enemies of David; **17** and Jonathan adds to cause David to swear, because he loves him, for he has loved him [as] the love [for] his own soul. **18** And Jonathan says to him, "Tomorrow [is] the new moon, and you have been looked after, for your seat is looked after; **19** and on the third day you certainly come down, and have come to the place where you were hidden in the day of the work, and have remained near the stone of Ezel. **20** And I shoot three of the arrows at the side, sending out at a mark for myself; **21** and behold, I send the youth, [saying], Go, find the arrows. If I say to the youth at all, Behold, the arrows [are] on this side of you—take them and come, for [there is] peace for you, and there is no [adverse] word—[as] YHWH lives. **22** And if thus I say to the young man, Behold, the arrows [are] beyond you—go, for YHWH has sent you away; **23** as for the thing which you and I have spoken, behold, YHWH [is] between me and you for all time." **24** And David is hidden in the field, and it is the new moon, and the king sits down by the food to eat, **25** and the king sits on his seat, as time by time, on a seat by the wall, and Jonathan rises, and Abner sits at the side of Saul, and David's place is looked after. **26** And Saul has not spoken anything on that day, for he said, "It [is] an accident; he is not clean—surely not clean." **27** And it comes to pass on the second day of the new moon, that David's place is looked after, and Saul says to his son Jonathan, "Why has the son of Jesse not come in, either yesterday or today, to the food?" **28** And Jonathan answers Saul, "David has earnestly asked [permission] from me [to go] to Beth-Lehem, **29** and he says, Please send me away, for we have a family sacrifice in the city, and my brother has given command to me himself, and now, if I have found grace in your eyes, please let me go away and see my brothers; therefore he has not come to the table of the king." **30** And the anger of Saul burns against Jonathan, and he says to him, "Son of a perverse [woman] of rebellion! Have I not known that you are fixing on the son of Jesse to your own shame, and to the shame of the nakedness of your mother? **31** For all the days that the son of Jesse lives on the

1 SAMUEL

ground you are not established, you and your kingdom; and now, send and bring him to me, for he [is] a son of death." **32** And Jonathan answers his father Saul and says to him, "Why is he put to death? What has he done?" **33** And Saul casts the javelin at him to strike him, and Jonathan knows that it has been determined by his father to put David to death. **34** And Jonathan rises from the table in the heat of anger, and has not eaten food on the second day of the new moon, for he has been grieved for David, for his father put him to shame. **35** And it comes to pass in the morning, that Jonathan goes out into the field for the appointment with David, and a little youth [is] with him. **36** And he says to his youth, "Now run, find the arrows which I am shooting"; the youth is running, and he has shot the arrow, causing [it] to pass over him. **37** And the youth comes to the place of the arrow which Jonathan has shot, and Jonathan calls after the youth, and says, "Is the arrow not beyond you?" **38** And Jonathan calls after the youth, "Speed, hurry, do not stand"; and Jonathan's youth gathers the arrows, and comes to his lord. **39** And the youth has not known anything, only Jonathan and David knew the word. **40** And Jonathan gives his weapons to the youth whom he has and says to him, "Go, carry into the city." **41** The youth has gone, and David has risen from Ezel, at the south, and falls on his face to the earth, and bows himself three times, and they kiss one another, and they weep with one another, until David exerted himself; **42** and Jonathan says to David, "Go in peace, in that we have sworn—the two of us—in the Name of YHWH, saying, YHWH is between me and you, and between my seed and your seed—for all time"; and he rises and goes; and Jonathan has gone into the city.

21 And David comes to Nob, to Ahimelech the priest, and Ahimelech trembles at meeting David and says to him, "Why [are] you alone, and no man [is] with you?" **2** And David says to Ahimelech the priest, "The king has commanded me [on] a matter, and he says to me, Let no man know anything of the matter about which I send you, and which I have commanded you; and [my] young men know [to go] to such and such a place. **3** And now, what is there under your hand? Give five loaves into my hand, or that which is found." **4** And the priest answers David and says, "There is no common bread under my hand, but there is holy bread; if only the youths have been kept from women." **5** And David answers the priest and says to him, "Surely, if women have been restrained from us as before in my going out, then the vessels of the young men are holy, and it [is] a common way; and also, surely it is sanctified today in the vessel." **6** And the priest gives the holy thing to him, for there was no bread there except the Bread of the Presentation, which is turned aside from the presence of YHWH to put hot bread [there] in the day of its being taken away. **7** And there [is] a man of the servants of Saul detained before YHWH on that day, and his name [is] Doeg the Edomite, chief of the shepherds whom Saul has. **8** And David says to Ahimelech, "And is there not spear or sword here under your hand? For I have taken neither my sword nor my vessels in my hand, for the matter of the king was urgent." **9** And the priest says, "The sword of Goliath the Philistine, whom you struck in the Valley of Elah, behold, it is wrapped in a garment behind the ephod, if you take it to yourself, take; for there is none other except it in this [place]." And David says, "There is none like it—give it to me." **10** And David rises and flees on that day from the face of Saul, and comes to Achish king of Gath; **11** and the servants of Achish say to him, "Is this not David, the king of the land? Is it not of this one [that] they sing in dances, saying, Saul struck among his thousands, and David among his myriads?" **12** And David lays these words in his heart, and is exceedingly afraid of the face of Achish king of Gath, **13** and changes his behavior before their eyes, and feigns himself mad in their hand, and scribbles on the doors of the gate, and lets down his spittle to his beard. **14** And Achish says to his servants, "Behold, you see a man acting as a madman; why do you bring him to me? **15** Am I lacking madmen, that you have brought in this one to act as a madman before me? Does this one come into my house?"

22 And David goes from there, and escapes to the cave of Adullam, and his brothers hear, and all the house of his father, and they go down to him there;

1 SAMUEL

2 and every man in distress gathers themselves to him, and every man who has an exactor, and every man bitter in soul, and he is for head over them, and there are about four hundred men with him. **3** And David goes from there to Mizpeh of Moab and says to the king of Moab, "Please let my father and my mother come out with you, until I know what God does for me"; **4** and he leads them before the king of Moab, and they dwell with him all the days of David's being in the fortress. **5** And the prophet Gad says to David, "You do not abide in a fortress, go, and you have entered the land of Judah for yourself"; and David goes and enters the forest of Hareth. **6** And Saul hears that David has become known, and the men who [are] with him, and Saul is abiding in Gibeah, under the grove in Ramah, and his spear [is] in his hand, and all his servants [are] standing by him. **7** And Saul says to his servants who are standing by him, "Now hear, sons of Benjamin; does the son of Jesse also give fields and vineyards to all of you? Does he appoint all of you [to be] heads of thousands and heads of hundreds? **8** For all of you have conspired against me, and there is none uncovering my ear about my son's cutting [a covenant] with the son of Jesse, and there is none of you grieving for me, and uncovering my ear, that my son has raised up my servant against me, to lie in wait as [at] this day." **9** And Doeg the Edomite answers, who is set over the servants of Saul, and says, "I have seen the son of Jesse coming to Nob, to Ahimelech son of Ahitub, **10** and he inquires of YHWH for him, and has given provision to him, and has given the sword of Goliath the Philistine to him." **11** And the king sends to call Ahimelech son of Ahitub, the priest, and all the house of his father, the priests, who [are] in Nob, and all of them come to the king; **12** and Saul says, "Now hear, son of Ahitub"; and he says, "Here I [am], my lord." **13** And Saul says to him, "Why have you conspired against me, you and the son of Jesse, by your giving bread and a sword to him, and to inquire of God for him, to rise against me, to lie in wait, as [at] this day?" **14** And Ahimelech answers the king and says, "And who among all your servants [is] as David—faithful, and son-in-law of the king, and has turned aside to your council, and is honored in your house? **15** Today have I begun to inquire of God for him? Far be it from me! Do not let the king lay anything against his servant, against any of the house of my father, for your servant has known nothing of all this, little or much." **16** And the king says, "You surely die, Ahimelech, you and all the house of your father." **17** And the king says to the runners, those standing by him, "Turn around, and put the priests of YHWH to death, because their hand [is] also with David, and because they have known that he is fleeing, and have not uncovered my ear"; and the servants of the king have not been willing to put forth their hand to come against the priests of YHWH. **18** And the king says to Doeg, "Turn around, and come against the priests"; and Doeg the Edomite turns around, and comes against the priests himself, and in that day puts to death eighty-five men bearing a linen ephod, **19** and Nob, the city of the priests, he has struck by the mouth of the sword, from man and to woman, from infant and to suckling, and ox, and donkey, and sheep, by the mouth of the sword. **20** And one son of Ahimelech, son of Ahitub, escapes, and his name [is] Abiathar, and he flees after David, **21** and Abiathar declares to David that Saul has slain the priests of YHWH. **22** And David says to Abiathar, "I have known on that day when Doeg the Edomite [is] there, that he certainly declares [it] to Saul; I have brought [it] around to every person of the house of your father; **23** dwell with me; do not fear; for he who seeks my life seeks your life; for you [are my] charge with me."

23 And they declare to David, saying, "Behold, the Philistines are fighting against Keilah, and they are spoiling the threshing-floors." **2** And David inquires of YHWH, saying, "Do I go? And have I struck among these Philistines?" And YHWH says to David, "Go, and you have struck among the Philistines, and saved Keilah." **3** And David's men say to him, "Behold, we here in Judah are afraid; and how much more when we go to Keilah, to the ranks of the Philistines?" **4** And David adds again to inquire of YHWH, and YHWH answers him and says, "Rise, go down to Keilah, for I am giving the Philistines into your hand." **5** And David goes, and his men, to Keilah, and fights with the Philistines, and leads away their livestock, and strikes among them [with] a great striking, and David

1 SAMUEL

saves the inhabitants of Keilah. **6** And it comes to pass, in the fleeing of Abiathar son of Ahimelech to David, to Keilah, an ephod came down in his hand. **7** And it is declared to Saul that David has come to Keilah, and Saul says, "God has made him known for my hand, for he has been shut in, to enter into a city of doors and bar." **8** And Saul summons all the people to the battle, to go down to Keilah, to lay siege to David and to his men. **9** And David knows that Saul is devising the evil against him and says to Abiathar the priest, "Bring the ephod near." **10** And David says, "YHWH, God of Israel, Your servant has certainly heard that Saul is seeking to come to Keilah, to destroy the city on my account. **11** Do the possessors of Keilah shut me up into his hand? Does Saul come down as Your servant has heard? YHWH, God of Israel, please declare [it] to Your servant." And YHWH says, "He comes down." **12** And David says, "Do the possessors of Keilah shut up me and my men into the hand of Saul?" And YHWH says, "They shut [you] up." **13** And David rises—and his men—about six hundred men, and they go out from Keilah, and go up and down where they go up and down; and it has been declared to Saul that David has escaped from Keilah, and he ceases to go out. **14** And David abides in the wilderness, in fortresses, and abides in the hill-country, in the wilderness of Ziph; and Saul seeks him [for] all the days, and God has not given him into his hand. **15** And David sees that Saul has come out to seek his life, and David [is] in the wilderness of Ziph, in a forest. **16** And Jonathan son of Saul rises, and goes to David [in the] forest, and strengthens his hand in God, **17** and says to him, "Do not fear, for the hand of my father Saul does not find you, and you reign over Israel, and I am to you for second, and also so knows my father Saul." **18** And both of them make a covenant before YHWH; and David abides in the forest, and Jonathan has gone to his house. **19** And the Ziphites go up to Saul at Gibeah, saying, "Is David not hiding himself with us in fortresses, in the forest, in the height of Hachilah, which [is] on the south of the desolate place? **20** And now, by all the desire of your soul, O king, to come down, come down, and ours [is] to shut him up into the hand of the king." **21** And Saul says, "Blessed [are] you of YHWH, for you have pity on me; **22** now go prepare yet, and know and see his place where his foot is; who has seen him there? For [one] has said to me, He is very cunning. **23** And see and know of all the hiding places where he hides himself, and you have turned back prepared to me, and I have gone with you, and it has been, if he is in the land, that I have searched him out through all the thousands of Judah." **24** And they rise and go to Ziph before Saul, and David and his men [are] in the wilderness of Maon, in the plain, at the south of the desolate place. **25** And Saul and his men go to seek, and they declare [it] to David, and he goes down the rock, and abides in the wilderness of Maon; and Saul hears, and pursues after David [to] the wilderness of Maon. **26** And Saul goes on this side of the mountain, and David and his men on that side of the mountain, and David is hurried to go from the face of Saul, and Saul and his men are surrounding David and his men, to catch them. **27** And a messenger has come to Saul, saying, "Hurry, and come, for the Philistines have pushed against the land." **28** And Saul turns back from pursuing after David, and goes to meet the Philistines, therefore they have called that place "The Rock of Divisions." **29** And David goes up there, and abides in fortresses [at] En-gedi.

24 And it comes to pass, when Saul has turned back from after the Philistines, that they declare to him, saying, "Behold, David [is] in the wilderness of En-gedi." **2** And Saul takes three thousand chosen men out of all Israel, and goes to seek David and his men, on the front of the rocks of the wild goats, **3** and he comes to folds of the flock, on the way, and there [is] a cave, and Saul goes in to cover his feet; and David and his men are abiding in the sides of the cave. **4** And the men of David say to him, "Behold, the day of which YHWH said to you, Behold, I am giving your enemy into your hand, and you have done to him as it is good in your eyes"; and David rises and cuts off the skirt of the upper robe which [is] on Saul with stealth. **5** And it comes to pass afterward that the heart of David strikes him, because that he has cut off the skirt which [is] on Saul, **6** and he says to his men, "Far be it from me, by YHWH; I do not do this thing to my lord—to the anointed of YHWH—to put forth my hand against him, for he [is] the anointed of Y{HWH}." **7** And David subdues his men by words, and has not permitted them to rise against Saul; and Saul has risen from the cave, and goes on the way; **8** and David rises afterward, and goes out from the cave, and calls after Saul, saying, "My lord, O king!" And Saul looks attentively behind him, and David bows—face to the earth—and pays respect. **9** And David says to Saul, "Why do you hear the words of man, saying, Behold, David is seeking your calamity? **10** Behold, this day your eyes have seen how that Y{HWH} has given you into my hand today in the cave; and [one] said to slay you, and [my eye] has pity on you, and I say, I do not put forth my hand against my lord, for he [is] the anointed of Y{HWH}. **11** And my father, see, indeed see the skirt of your upper robe in my hand; for by cutting off the skirt of your upper robe, and I have not slain you, know and see that there is not evil and transgression in my hand, and I have not sinned against you, and you are hunting my soul to take it! **12** Y{HWH} judges between me and you, and Y{HWH} has avenged me of you, and my hand is not on you; **13** as the allegory of the ancients says, Wickedness goes out from the wicked, and my hand is not on you. **14** After whom has the king of Israel come out? After whom are you pursuing? After a dead dog! After one flea! **15** And Y{HWH} has been for judge, and has judged between me and you, indeed, He sees and pleads my cause, and delivers me out of your hand." **16** And it comes to pass, when David completes to speak these words to Saul, that Saul says, "Is this your voice, my son David?" And Saul lifts up his voice, and weeps. **17** And he says to David, "You [are] more righteous than I; for you have done me good, and I have done you evil; **18** and you have declared today how that you have done good with me, how that Y{HWH} shut me up into your hand, and you did not slay me, **19** and that a man finds his enemy, and has sent him away in a good manner; and Y{HWH} repays you good for that which you did to me this day. **20** And now, behold, I have known that you certainly reign, and the kingdom of Israel has stood in your hand; **21** and now, swear to me by Y{HWH} [that] you do not cut off my seed after me, nor do you destroy my name from the house of my father." **22** And David swears to Saul, and Saul goes to his house, and David and his men have gone up to the fortress.

25 And Samuel dies, and all Israel is gathered, and mourns for him, and buries him in his house, in Ramah; and David rises and goes down to the wilderness of Paran. **2** And [there is] a man in Maon, and his work [is] in Carmel; and the man [is] very great, and he has three thousand sheep and one thousand goats; and he is shearing his flock in Carmel. **3** And the name of the man [is] Nabal, and the name of his wife [is] Abigail, and the woman [is] of good understanding, and of beautiful form, and the man [is] hard and evil [in his] doings; and he [is] a Calebite. **4** And David hears in the wilderness that Nabal is shearing his flock, **5** and David sends ten young men, and David says to the young men, "Go up to Carmel, and you have come to Nabal, and asked of him in my name of welfare, **6** and said thus to the living: And peace to you, and peace to your house, and peace to all that you have! **7** And now, I have heard that you have shearers; now, the shepherds whom you have have been with us, we have not put them to shame, nor has anything been looked after by them, all the days of their being in Carmel. **8** Ask your young men, and they declare [it] to you, and the young men find grace in your eyes, for we have come on a good day; please give that which your hand finds to your servants and to your son, to David." **9** And the young men of David come in, and speak to Nabal according to all these words, in the name of David—and rest. **10** And Nabal answers the servants of David and says, "Who [is] David, and who [is] the son of Jesse? Have servants been multiplied today who are each breaking away from his master? **11** And have I taken my bread, and my water, and my flesh, which I slaughtered for my shearers, and have given [it] to men whom I have not known where they [are] from?" **12** And the young men of David turn on their way, and turn back, and come in, and declare to him according to all these words. **13** And David says to his men, "Each gird on his sword"; and they each gird on his sword, and David also girds on his sword, and about four hundred men go up after David, and two hundred have remained by the vessels. **14** And one young man of the youths has declared [it] to

Abigail wife of Nabal, saying, "Behold, David has sent messengers out of the wilderness to bless our lord, and he flies on them; **15** and the men [are] very good to us, and have not put us to shame, and we have not looked after anything all the days we have gone up and down with them, in our being in the field; **16** they have been a wall to us both by night and by day, all the days of our being with them, feeding the flock. **17** And now, know and consider what you do; for evil has been determined against our lord, and against all his house, and he [is] too much a son of worthlessness to be spoken to." **18** And Abigail hurries, and takes two hundred loaves, and two bottles of wine, and five sheep, prepared, and five measures of roasted grain, and one hundred bunches of raisins, and two hundred bunches of figs, and sets [them] on the donkeys. **19** And she says to her young men, "Pass over before me; behold, I am coming after you"; and she has not declared [it] to her husband Nabal; **20** and it has come to pass, she is riding on the donkey and is coming down in the secret part of the hill-country, and behold, David and his men are coming down to meet her, and she meets them. **21** And David said, "Surely in vain I have kept all that this [one] has in the wilderness, and nothing has been looked after of all that he has, and he turns back to me evil for good; **22** thus God does to the enemies of David, and thus He adds, if I leave of all that he has until the morning light—of those sitting on the wall." **23** And Abigail sees David, and hurries and comes down from off the donkey, and falls on her face before David, and bows herself to the earth, **24** and falls at his feet and says, "On me, my lord, the iniquity; and please let your handmaid speak in your ear, and hear the words of your handmaid. **25** Please do not let my lord set his heart to this man of worthlessness, on Nabal, for as his name [is] so [is] he; Nabal [is] his name, and folly [is] with him; and I, your handmaid, did not see the young men of my lord whom you sent; **26** and now, my lord, YHWH lives, and your soul lives, in that YHWH has withheld you from coming in with blood, and to save your hand from yourself—now let your enemies be as Nabal, even those seeking evil toward my lord. **27** And now, this blessing which your maidservant has brought to my lord—it has been given to the young men who are going up and down at the feet of my lord. **28** Please bear with the transgression of your handmaid, for YHWH certainly makes a steadfast house for my lord; for my lord has fought the battles of YHWH, and evil is not found in you [all] your days. **29** And man rises to pursue you and to seek your soul, and the soul of my lord has been bound in the bundle of life with your God YHWH; as for the soul of your enemies, He slings them out in the midst of the hollow of the sling. **30** And it has been, when YHWH does to my lord according to all the good which He has spoken concerning you, and appointed you for leader over Israel, **31** that this is not to you for a stumbling-block, and for an offense of heart to my lord—either to shed blood for nothing, or my lord's restraining himself; and YHWH has done good to my lord, and you have remembered your handmaid." **32** And David says to Abigail, "Blessed [is] YHWH, God of Israel, who has sent you to meet me this day, **33** and blessed [is] your discretion, and blessed [are] you in that you have restrained me this day from coming in with blood, and to restrain my hand to myself. **34** And yet, YHWH lives, God of Israel, who has kept me back from doing evil with you, for unless you had hurried, and come to meet me, surely there had not been left to Nabal until the morning light, of those sitting on the wall." **35** And David receives from her hand that which she has brought to him, and he has said to her, "Go up in peace to your house; see, I have listened to your voice, and accept your face." **36** And Abigail comes to Nabal, and behold, he has a banquet in his house, like a banquet of the king, and the heart of Nabal [is] glad within him, and he [is] drunk to excess, and she has not declared anything to him, little or much, until the morning light. **37** And it comes to pass in the morning, when the wine is gone out from Nabal, that his wife declares these things to him, and his heart dies within him, and he has been as a stone. **38** And it comes to pass [in] about ten days, that YHWH strikes Nabal and he dies, **39** and David hears that Nabal [is] dead and says, "Blessed [is] YHWH who has pleaded the cause of my reproach from the hand of Nabal, and His servant has kept back from evil, and YHWH has turned back the wickedness of Nabal on his own head"; and David sends and speaks with Abigail, to take her to himself for a wife. **40** And the servants of David come to Abigail at Carmel, and speak to her, saying, "David has sent us to you to take you to himself for a wife." **41** And she rises and bows herself—face to the earth—and says, "Behold, your handmaid [is] for a maidservant to wash the feet of the servants of my lord." **42** And Abigail hurries and rises, and rides on the donkey; and [there are] five of her young women who are going at her feet; and she goes after the messengers of David, and is to him for a wife. **43** And David has taken Ahinoam from Jezreel, and they are—even both of them—for wives to him; **44** and Saul gave his daughter Michal, David's wife, to Phalti son of Laish, who [is] of Gallim.

26 And the Ziphites come to Saul at Gibeah, saying, "Is David not hiding himself in the height of Hachilah, on the front of the desert?" **2** And Saul rises, and goes down to the wilderness of Ziph, and with him [are] three thousand men, chosen ones of Israel, to seek David in the wilderness of Ziph. **3** And Saul encamps in the height of Hachilah, which [is] on the front of the desert, by the way, and David is abiding in the wilderness, and he sees that Saul has come into the wilderness after him; **4** and David sends spies, and knows that Saul has come to Nachon, **5** and David rises, and comes to the place where Saul has encamped, and David sees the place where Saul has lain, and Abner son of Ner, head of his host, and Saul is lying in the path, and the people are encamping around him. **6** And David answers and says to Ahimelech the Hittite, and to Abishai son of Zeruiah, brother of Joab, saying, "Who goes down with me to Saul, to the camp?" And Abishai says, "I go down with you." **7** And David comes—and Abishai—by night to the people, and behold, Saul is lying sleeping in the path, and his spear is pressed into the earth by his pillow, and Abner and the people are lying around him. **8** And Abishai says to David, "God has shut up your enemy into your hand today; and now, please let me strike him with [the] spear, even into the earth, at once—and not repeat [it] to him." **9** And David says to Abishai, "Do not destroy him; for who has put forth his hand against the anointed of YHWH and been acquitted?" **10** And David says, "YHWH lives; except YHWH strikes him, or his day comes that he has died, or he goes down into battle and has been consumed— **11** far be it from me, by YHWH, from putting forth my hand against the anointed of YHWH; and now, please take the spear which [is] by his pillow, and the jug of water, and we go away." **12** And David takes the spear, and the jug of water by the pillow of Saul, and they go away, and there is none seeing, and there is none knowing, and there is none awaking, for all of them are sleeping, for a deep sleep [from] YHWH has fallen on them. **13** And David passes over to the other side, and stands on the top of the hill far off—great [is] the place between them; **14** and David calls to the people, and to Abner son of Ner, saying, "Do you not answer, Abner?" And Abner answers and says, "Who [are] you [who] have called to the king?" **15** And David says to Abner, "Are you not a man? And who [is] like you in Israel? But why have you not watched over your lord the king? For one of the people had come in to destroy the king, your lord. **16** This thing which you have done is not good; YHWH lives, but you [are] sons of death, in that you have not watched over your lord, over the anointed of YHWH; and now, see where the king's spear [is], and the jug of water which [is] by his pillow." **17** And Saul discerns the voice of David and says, "Is this your voice, my son David?" And David says, "My voice, my lord, O king!" **18** And he says, "Why [is] this—my lord is pursuing after his servant? For what have I done, and what evil [is] in my hand? **19** And now, please let my lord the king hear the words of his servant: if YHWH has moved you against me, let Him accept a present; but if [merely] the sons of men, they [are] cursed before YHWH, for today they have cast me out from being admitted into the inheritance of YHWH, saying, Go, serve other gods. **20** And now, do not let my blood fall to the earth before the face of YHWH, for the king of Israel has come out to seek one flea, as [one] pursues the partridge in mountains." **21** And Saul says, "I have sinned; return, my son David, for I do evil to you no more, because that my soul has been precious in your eyes this day; behold, I have acted foolishly, and err very greatly." **22** And David answers and says, "Behold, the king's spear; and let one of the young men pass over, and receive it; **23** and YHWH turns each back to his righteousness and his faithfulness, in that

1 SAMUEL

YHWH has given you into [my] hand today, and I have not been willing to put forth my hand against the anointed of YHWH, **24** and behold, as your soul has been great in my eyes this day, so is my soul great in the eyes of YHWH, and He delivers me out of all distress." **25** And Saul says to David, "Blessed [are] you, my son David, also working you work, and also prevailing you prevail." And David goes on his way, and Saul has turned back to his place.

27 And David says to his heart, "Now I am consumed by the hand of Saul one day; there is nothing better for me than that I diligently escape to the land of the Philistines, and Saul has been despairing of me—of seeking me anymore in all the border of Israel, and I have escaped out of his hand." **2** And David rises, and passes over, he and six hundred men who [are] with him, to Achish son of Maoch king of Gath; **3** and David dwells with Achish in Gath, he and his men, each one with his household, [even] David and his two wives, Ahinoam the Jezreelitess, and Abigail wife of Nabal the Carmelitess. **4** And it is declared to Saul that David has fled to Gath, and he has not added to seek him anymore. **5** And David says to Achish, "Now if I have found grace in your eyes, they give a place to me in one of the cities of the field, and I dwell there, indeed, why does your servant dwell in the royal city with you?" **6** And Achish gives Ziklag to him in that day, therefore Ziklag has been for the kings of Judah until this day. **7** And the number of the days which David has dwelt in the field of the Philistines [is one year] of days and four months; **8** and David and his men go up, and they push toward the Geshurite, and the Gerizite, and the Amalekite (for they are inhabitants of the land from of old), as you come to Shur and to the land of Egypt, **9** and David has struck the land, and does not keep alive man and woman, and has taken sheep, and oxen, and donkeys, and camels, and garments, and turns back, and comes to Achish. **10** And Achish says, "To where have you pushed today?" And David says, "Against the south of Judah, and against the south of the Jerahmeelite, and to the south of the Kenite." **11** David keeps alive neither man nor woman, to bring in [word] to Gath, saying, "Lest they declare [it] against us, saying, Thus David has done, and thus [is] his custom all the days that he has dwelt in the fields of the Philistines." **12** And Achish believes in David, saying, "He has made himself utterly abhorred among his people in Israel, and has been for a perpetual servant to me."

28 And it comes to pass in those days, that the Philistines gather their camps for the war, to fight against Israel, and Achish says to David, "You certainly know that you go out with me into the camp, you and your men." **2** And David says to Achish, "Therefore you know that which your servant does." And Achish says to David, "Therefore I appoint you keeper of my head [for] all the days." **3** And Samuel has died, and all Israel mourns for him, and buries him in Ramah, even in his city, and Saul has turned aside those having familiar spirits, and the wizards, out of the land. **4** And the Philistines are gathered, and come in, and encamp in Shunem, and Saul gathers all Israel, and they encamp in Gilboa, **5** and Saul sees the camp of the Philistines, and fears, and his heart trembles greatly, **6** and Saul inquires of YHWH, and YHWH has not answered him, either by the dreams, or by the Lights, or by the prophets. **7** And Saul says to his servants, "Seek a woman for me possessing a familiar spirit, and I go to her, and inquire of her"; and his servants say to him, "Behold, a woman possessing a familiar spirit [is] in En-dor." **8** And Saul disguises himself and puts on other garments, and goes, he and two of the men with him, and they come to the woman by night, and he says, "Please divine to me by the familiar spirit, and cause him whom I say to you to come up to me." **9** And the woman says to him, "Behold, you have known that which Saul has done, that he has cut off those having familiar spirits, and the wizards, out of the land; and why are you laying a snare for my soul—to put me to death?" **10** And Saul swears to her by YHWH, saying, "YHWH lives, punishment does not meet you for this thing." **11** And the woman says, "Whom do I bring up to you?" And he says, "Bring up Samuel to me." **12** And the woman sees Samuel, and cries with a loud voice, and the woman speaks to Saul, saying, "Why have you deceived me? For you [are] Saul!" **13** And the king says to her, "Do not fear; for what have you seen?" And the woman says to

1 SAMUEL

Saul, "I have seen gods coming up out of the earth." **14** And he says to her, "What [is] his form?" And she says, "An aged man is coming up, and he [is] covered with an upper robe"; and Saul knows that he [is] Samuel, and bows—face to her earth—and pays respect. **15** And Samuel says to Saul, "Why have you troubled me, to bring me up?" And Saul says, "I have great distress, and the Philistines are fighting against me, God has turned aside from me, and has not answered me anymore, either by the hand of the prophets, or by dreams; and I call for you to let me know what I [should] do." **16** And Samuel says, "And why do you ask me, and YHWH has turned aside from you, and is your enemy? **17** And YHWH does for Himself as He has spoken by my hand, and YHWH tears the kingdom out of your hand, and gives it to your neighbor—to David. **18** Because you have not listened to the voice of YHWH, nor did the fierceness of His anger on Amalek—therefore YHWH has done this thing to you this day; **19** indeed, YHWH also gives Israel into the hand of the Philistines with you, and tomorrow you and your sons [are] with me; YHWH also gives the camp of Israel into the hand of the Philistines." **20** And Saul hurries and falls—the fullness of his stature—to the earth, and fears greatly because of the words of Samuel; also power was not in him, for he had not eaten bread all the day, and all the night. **21** And the woman comes to Saul, and sees that he has been greatly troubled, and says to him, "Behold, your maidservant has listened to your voice, and I put my soul in my hand, and I obey your words which you have spoken to me; **22** and now, please listen, you also, to the voice of your maidservant, and I set a morsel of bread before you; and eat, and there is power in you when you go in the way." **23** And he refuses and says, "I do not eat"; and his servants urge him on, and also the woman, and he listens to their voice, and rises from the earth, and sits on the bed. **24** And the woman has a calf of the stall in the house, and she hurries and slaughters it, and takes flour, and kneads, and bakes it [into] unleavened things, **25** and brings [them] near before Saul, and before his servants, and they eat, and rise, and go on during that night.

29 And the Philistines gather all their camps to Aphek, and Israel is encamping at a fountain which [is] in Jezreel, **2** and the princes of the Philistines are passing on by hundreds, and by thousands, and David and his men are passing on in the rear with Achish. **3** And the heads of the Philistines say, "What [are] these Hebrews?" And Achish says to the heads of the Philistines, "Is this not David, servant of Saul king of Israel, who has been with me these days or these years, and I have not found anything in him [wrong] from the day of his falling away until this day?" **4** And the heads of the Philistines are angry against him, and the heads of the Philistines say to him, "Send back the man, and he turns back to his place to where you have appointed him, and does not go down with us into battle, and is not for an adversary to us in battle; and with what does this one reconcile himself to his lord—is it not with the heads of those men? **5** Is this not David, of whom they answer in choruses, saying, Saul has struck among his thousands, and David among his myriads?" **6** And Achish calls to David and says to him, "YHWH lives, surely you [are] upright, and good in my eyes is your going out, and your coming in with me in the camp, for I have not found evil in you from the day of your coming to me until this day; but you are not good in the eyes of the princes; **7** and now, return, and go in peace, and you do no evil in the eyes of the princes of the Philistines." **8** And David says to Achish, "But what have I done? And what have you found in your servant from the day that I have been before you until this day—that I do not go in and have fought against the enemies of my lord the king?" **9** And Achish answers and says to David, "I have known that you [are] good in my eyes as a messenger of God; only, the princes of the Philistines have said, He does not go up with us into battle; **10** and now, rise early in the morning—and the servants of your lord who have come with you. When you have risen early in the morning, and have light, then go." **11** And David rises early, he and his men, to go in the morning, to return to the land of the Philistines, and the Philistines have gone up to Jezreel.

30 And it comes to pass, in the coming in of David and his men to Ziklag on the third day, that the Amalekites have pushed toward the south, and to Ziklag, and

1 SAMUEL

strike Ziklag, and burn it with fire, **2** and they take the women who [are] in it captive; they have not put anyone to death from small to great, and they lead [them] away, and go on their way. **3** And David comes in—and his men—to the city, and behold, [it is] burned with fire, and their wives, and their sons, and their daughters have been taken captive. **4** And David lifts up—and the people who [are] with him—their voice and weep, until they have no power to weep. **5** And the two wives of David have been taken captive, Ahinoam the Jezreelitess, and Abigail wife of Nabal the Carmelite; **6** and David has great distress, for the people have said to stone him, for the soul of all the people has been bitter, each for his sons and for his daughters; and David strengthens himself in his God YHWH. **7** And David says to Abiathar the priest, son of Ahimelech, "Please bring the ephod near to me"; and Abiathar brings the ephod near to David, **8** and David inquires of YHWH, saying, "I pursue after this troop—do I overtake it?" And He says to him, "Pursue, for you certainly overtake, and certainly deliver." **9** And David goes on, he and six hundred men who [are] with him, and they come to the Brook of Besor, and those left have stood still, **10** and David pursues, he and four hundred men (and two hundred men stand still who have been too faint to pass over the Brook of Besor), **11** and they find a man, an Egyptian, in the field, and take him to David, and give bread to him, and he eats, and they cause him to drink water, **12** and give to him a piece of a bunch of dried figs, and two bunches of raisins, and he eats, and his spirit returns to him, for he has not eaten bread nor drunk water [for] three days and three nights. **13** And David says to him, "Whose [are] you? And where [are] you from?" And he says, "I [am] an Egyptian youth, servant to a man, an Amalekite, and my lord forsakes me, for I have been sick [for] three days, **14** we pushed [to] the south of the Cherethite, and against that which [is] to Judah, and against the south of Caleb, and we burned Ziklag with fire." **15** And David says to him, "Do you bring me down to this troop?" And he says, "Swear to me by God [that] you do not put me to death, nor do you shut me up into the hand of my lord, and I bring you down to this troop." **16** And he brings him down, and behold, they are spread out over the face of all the earth, eating, and drinking, and celebrating, with all the great spoil which they have taken out of the land of the Philistines, and out of the land of Judah. **17** And David strikes them from the twilight even to the evening of the next day, and there has not escaped of them a man, except four hundred young men who have ridden on the camels and flee. **18** And David delivers all that the Amalekites have taken; David has also delivered his two wives. **19** And nothing of theirs has lacked, from small to great, and to sons and daughters, and from the spoil, even to all that they had taken to themselves, David has brought back the whole, **20** and David takes the whole of the flock and of the herd [that] they have led on before these livestock, and they say, "This [is] David's spoil." **21** And David comes to the two hundred men who were too faint to go after David, and whom they cause to abide at the Brook of Besor, and they go out to meet David, and to meet the people who [are] with him, and David approaches the people, and asks of them of welfare. **22** And every bad and worthless man, of the men who have gone with David, answers, indeed, they say, "Because that they have not gone with us we do not give to them of the spoil which we have delivered, except each his wife and his children, and they lead away and go." **23** And David says, "You do not do so, my brothers, with that which YHWH has given to us, and He preserves us, and gives the troop which comes against us into our hand; **24** and who listens to you in this thing? For as the portion of him who was brought down into battle, so also [is] the portion of him who is abiding by the vessels—they share alike." **25** And it comes to pass from that day and forward, that he appoints it for a statute and for an ordinance for Israel to this day. **26** And David comes to Ziklag, and sends of the spoil to [the] elderly of Judah, to his friends, saying, "Behold, a blessing for you of the spoil of the enemies of YHWH," **27** to those in Beth-El, and to those in South Ramoth, and to those in Jattir, **28** and to those in Aroer, and to those in Siphmoth, and to those in Eshtemoa, **29** and to those in Rachal, and to those in the cities of the Jerahmeelites, and to those in the cities of the Kenites, **30** and to those in Hormah, and to those in Chor-Ashan, and to those in Athach, **31** and to those in Hebron, and to

1 SAMUEL

all the places where David—he and his men—had gone up and down.

31 And the Philistines are fighting against Israel, and the men of Israel flee from the face of the Philistines, and fall wounded in Mount Gilboa, **2** and the Philistines follow Saul and his sons, and the Philistines strike Jonathan, and Abinadab, and Malchishua, the sons of Saul. **3** And the battle is hard against Saul, and the archers find him—men with bow—and he is greatly pained by the archers; **4** and Saul says to the bearer of his weapons, "Draw your sword, and pierce me with it, lest they come—these uncircumcised—and have pierced me, and rolled themselves on me"; and the bearer of his weapons has not been willing, for he is greatly afraid, and Saul takes the sword, and falls on it. **5** And the bearer of his weapons sees that Saul [is] dead, and he falls—he also—on his sword, and dies with him; **6** and Saul dies, and three of his sons, and the bearer of his weapons, also all his men, together on that day. **7** And they see—the men of Israel, who [are] beyond the valley, and who [are] beyond the Jordan—that the men of Israel have fled, and that Saul and his sons have died, and they forsake the cities and flee, and Philistines come in, and dwell in them. **8** And it comes to pass on the next day, that the Philistines come to strip the wounded, and they find Saul and his three sons fallen on Mount Gilboa, **9** and they cut off his head, and strip off his weapons, and send [them] into the land of the surrounding Philistines, to proclaim tidings [in] the house of their idols, and [among] the people; **10** and they place his weapons [in] the house of Ashtaroth, and they have fixed his body on the wall of Beth-Shan. **11** And they hear regarding it—the inhabitants of Jabesh-Gilead—that which the Philistines have done to Saul, **12** and all the men of valor arise, and go all the night, and take the body of Saul, and the bodies of his sons, from the wall of Beth-Shan, and come to Jabesh, and burn them there, **13** and they take their bones, and bury [them] under the tamarisk in Jabesh, and fast seven days.

2 SAMUEL

1 And it comes to pass after the death of Saul, that David has returned from striking the Amalekite, and David dwells in Ziklag [for] two days, **2** and it comes to pass, on the third day, that behold, a man has come in out of the camp from Saul, and his garments [are] torn, and earth [is] on his head; and it comes to pass in his coming to David, that he falls to the earth and pays respect. **3** And David says to him, "Where do you come from?" And he says to him, "I have escaped out of the camp of Israel." **4** And David says to him, "What has been the matter? Please declare [it] to me." And he says, "That the people have fled from the battle, and also a multitude of the people have fallen, and they die; and also Saul and his son Jonathan have died." **5** And David says to the youth who is declaring [it] to him, "How have you known that Saul and his son Jonathan [are] dead?" **6** And the youth who is declaring [it] to him says, "I happened to meet in Mount Gilboa, and behold, Saul is leaning on his spear; and behold, the chariots and those possessing horses have followed him; **7** and he turns behind him, and sees me, and calls to me, and I say, Here I [am]. **8** And he says to me, Who [are] you? And I say to him, I [am] an Amalekite. **9** And he says to me, Please stand over me and put me to death, for the arrow has seized me, for all my soul [is] still in me. **10** And I stand over him, and put him to death, for I knew that he does not live after his falling, and I take the crown which [is] on his head, and the bracelet which [is] on his arm, and bring them to my lord here." **11** And David takes hold on his garments, and tears them, and also all the men who [are] with him, **12** and they mourn, and weep, and fast until the evening, for Saul, and for his son Jonathan, and for the people of YHWH, and for the house of Israel, because they have fallen by the sword. **13** And David says to the youth who is declaring [it] to him, "Where [are] you from?" And he says, "I [am] the son of a sojourner, an Amalekite." **14** And David says to him, "How were you not afraid to put forth your hand to destroy the anointed of YHWH?" **15** And David calls to one of the youths and says, "Draw near—fall on him"; and he strikes him, and he dies; **16** and David says to him, "Your blood [is] on your own head, for your mouth has testified against you, saying, I put to death the anointed of YHWH." **17** And David laments with this lamentation over Saul, and over his son Jonathan; **18** and he says to teach the sons of Judah "The Bow"; behold, it is written on the Scroll of the Upright: **19** "The beauty of Israel ‖ [Is] wounded on your high places; How the mighty have fallen! **20** Do not declare [it] in Gath, ‖ Do not proclaim the tidings in the streets of Ashkelon, ‖ Lest they rejoice—The daughters of the Philistines, ‖ Lest they exult—The daughters of the uncircumcised! **21** Mountains of Gilboa! No dew nor rain be on you, ‖ And fields of raised-offerings! For there has become loathsome ‖ The shield of the mighty, ‖ The shield of Saul—without the anointed with oil. **22** From the blood of the wounded, ‖ From the fat of the mighty, ‖ The bow of Jonathan ‖ Has not turned backward; And the sword of Saul does not return empty. **23** Saul and Jonathan! They are loved and pleasant in their lives, ‖ And in their death they have not been parted. They have been lighter than eagles, ‖ They have been mightier than lions! **24** Daughters of Israel! Weep for Saul, ‖ Who is clothing you [in] scarlet with delights. Who is lifting up ornaments of gold on your clothing. **25** How the mighty have fallen ‖ In the midst of the battle! Jonathan [was] wounded on your high places! **26** I am in distress for you, my brother Jonathan, ‖ You were very pleasant to me; Your love was wonderful to me, ‖ Above the love of women! **27** How the mighty have fallen, ‖ Indeed, the weapons of war perish!"

2 And it comes to pass afterward, that David inquires of YHWH, saying, "Do I go up into one of the cities of Judah?" And YHWH says to him, "Go up." And David says, "To where do I go up?" And He says, "To Hebron." **2** And David goes up there, and also his two wives, Ahinoam the Jezreelitess, and Abigail wife of Nabal the Carmelite; **3** and David has brought up his men who [are] with him—a man and his household—and they dwell in the cities of Hebron. **4** And the men of Judah come, and anoint David there for king over the house of Judah; and they declare to David, saying, "The men of Jabesh-Gilead [are] they who buried Saul." **5** And David sends messengers to the men of Jabesh-Gilead and says to them, "Blessed [are] you of YHWH, in that you have done this kindness with your lord, with Saul, that you bury him. **6** And now YHWH does kindness and truth with you, and I also do this good with you because you have done this thing; **7** and now your hands are strong, and be for sons of valor, for your lord Saul [is] dead, and the house of Judah has also anointed me for king over them." **8** And Abner, son of Ner, head of the host which Saul has, has taken Ish-Bosheth, son of Saul, and causes him to pass over to Mahanaim, **9** and causes him to reign over Gilead, and over the Ashurite, and over Jezreel, and over Ephraim, and over Benjamin, and over Israel—all of it. **10** Ish-Bosheth son of Saul [is] a son of forty years in his reigning over Israel, and he has reigned [for] two years; only the house of Judah has been after David. **11** And the number of the days that David has been king in Hebron, over the house of Judah, is seven years and six months. **12** And Abner son of Ner goes out, and servants of Ish-Bosheth son of Saul, from Mahanaim to Gibeon. **13** And Joab son of Zeruiah, and servants of David, have gone out, and they meet by the pool of Gibeon together, and sit down, these by the pool on this [side], and these by the pool on that [side]. **14** And Abner says to Joab, "Now let the youths rise and they play before us"; and Joab says, "Let them rise." **15** And they rise and pass over, in number twelve of Benjamin, even of Ish-Bosheth son of Saul, and twelve of the servants of David. **16** And they each lay hold on the head of his companion, and his sword [is] in the side of his companion, and they fall together, and [one] calls that place Helkath-Hazzurim, which [is] in Gibeon, **17** and the battle is very hard on that day, and Abner is struck, and the men of Israel, before the servants of David. **18** And there are three sons of Zeruiah there: Joab, and Abishai, and Asahel; and Asahel [is] light on his feet, as one of the roes which [are] in the field, **19** and Asahel pursues after Abner, and has not turned aside to go to the right or to the left, from after Abner. **20** And Abner looks behind him and says, "Are you he—Asahel?" And he says, "I [am]." **21** And Abner says to him, "Turn aside to your right hand or to your left, and seize one of the youths for yourself, and take his armor for yourself"; and Asahel has not been willing to turn aside from after him. **22** And Abner adds again, saying to Asahel, "Turn aside from after me, why do I strike you to the earth? And how do I lift up my face to your brother Joab?" **23** And he refuses to turn aside, and Abner strikes him with the back part of the spear to the fifth [rib], and the spear comes out from behind him, and he falls there, and dies under it; and it comes to pass, everyone who has come to the place where Asahel has fallen and dies—they stand still. **24** And Joab and Abishai pursue after Abner, and the sun has gone in, and they have come to the height of Ammah, which [is] on the front of Giah, the way of the wilderness of Gibeon. **25** And the sons of Benjamin gather themselves together after Abner, and become one troop, and stand on the top of a certain height, **26** and Abner calls to Joab and says, "Does the sword consume forever? Have you not known that it is bitterness in the latter end? And until when do you not say to the people to turn back from after their brothers?" **27** And Joab says, "God lives! For unless you had spoken, surely then from the morning each of the people had gone up from after his brother." **28** And Joab blows with a horn, and all the people stand still, and no longer pursue after Israel, nor have they added to fight anymore. **29** And Abner and his men have gone through the plain all that night, and pass over the Jordan, and go on [through] all Bithron, and come to Mahanaim. **30** And Joab has turned back from after Abner, and gathers all the people, and there are lacking of the servants of David nineteen men, and Asahel; **31** and the servants of David have struck of Benjamin, even among the men of Abner, three hundred and sixty men—they died. **32** And they lift up Asahel, and bury him in the burying-place of his father, which [is] in Beth-Lehem, and they go all the night—Joab and his men—and [dawn's light] shines on them in Hebron.

3 And the war is long between the house of Saul and the house of David, and David is going on and [is] strong, and the house of Saul is going on and [is] weak. **2** And there are sons born to David in

Hebron, and his firstborn is Amnon, of Ahinoam the Jezreelitess, 3 and his second [is] Chileab, of Abigail wife of Nabal the Carmelite, and the third [is] Absalom son of Maacah daughter of Talmai king of Geshur, 4 and the fourth [is] Adonijah son of Haggith, and the fifth [is] Shephatiah son of Abital, 5 and the sixth [is] Ithream, of Eglah wife of David; these have been born to David in Hebron. 6 And it comes to pass, in the war being between the house of Saul and the house of David, that Abner has been strengthening himself in the house of Saul, 7 and Saul has a concubine, and her name [is] Rizpah daughter of Aiah, and [Ish-Bosheth] says to Abner, "Why have you gone in to the concubine of my father?" 8 And it is exceedingly displeasing to Abner, because of the words of Ish-Bosheth, and he says, "[Am] I the head of a dog—that in reference to Judah, today I do kindness with the house of your father Saul, to his brothers, and to his friends, and have not delivered you into the hand of David—that you charge against me iniquity concerning the woman today? 9 Thus God does to Abner, and thus He adds to him, surely as YHWH has sworn to David—surely so I do to him: 10 to cause the kingdom to pass over from the house of Saul, and to raise up the throne of David over Israel, and over Judah, from Dan even to Beer-Sheba." 11 And he is not able to return a word [to] Abner anymore, because of his fearing him. 12 And Abner sends messengers to David for himself, saying, "Whose [is] the land?" [And] saying, "Make your covenant with me, and behold, my hand [is] with you, to bring around all Israel to you." 13 And [David] says, "Good—I make a covenant with you; only, one thing I am asking of you, that is, you do not see my face, except [that] you first bring in Michal daughter of Saul in your coming in to see my face." 14 And David sends messengers to Ish-Bosheth son of Saul, saying, "Give up my wife Michal, whom I betrothed to myself with one hundred foreskins of the Philistines." 15 And Ish-Bosheth sends, and takes her from a man, from Phaltiel son of Laish, 16 and her husband goes with her, going on and weeping behind her, to Bahurim, and Abner says to him, "Go, return"; and he turns back. 17 And the word of Abner was with [the] elderly of Israel, saying, "Thus far you have been seeking David for king over you, 18 and now, do [it], for YHWH has spoken of David saying, [It is] by the hand of my servant David to save My people Israel out of the hand of the Philistines, and out of the hand of all their enemies." 19 And Abner also speaks in the ears of Benjamin, and Abner also goes to speak in the ears of David in Hebron all that [is] good in the eyes of Israel, and in the eyes of all the house of Benjamin, 20 and Abner comes to David, to Hebron, and twenty men [are] with him, and David makes a banquet for Abner and for the men who [are] with him. 21 And Abner says to David, "I arise, and go, and gather the whole of Israel to my lord the king, and they make a covenant with you, and you have reigned over all that your soul desires"; and David sends Abner away, and he goes in peace. 22 And behold, the servants of David, and Joab, have come from the troop, and have brought much spoil with them, and Abner is not with David in Hebron, for he has sent him away, and he goes in peace; 23 and Joab and all the host that [were] with him have come, and they declare to Joab, saying, "Abner son of Ner has come to the king, and he sends him away, and he goes in peace." 24 And Joab comes to the king and says, "What have you done? Behold, Abner has come to you! Why [is] this—you have sent him away, and he is really gone? 25 You have known Abner son of Ner, that he came to deceive you, and to know your going out and your coming in, and to know all that you are doing." 26 And Joab goes out from David, and sends messengers after Abner, and they bring him back from the well of Sirah, and David did not know. 27 And Abner turns back to Hebron, and Joab turns him aside to the midst of the gate to speak with him quietly, and strikes him there in the fifth [rib]—and he dies—for the blood of his brother Asahel. 28 And David hears afterward and says, "My kingdom and I [are] acquitted by YHWH for all time, from the blood of Abner son of Ner; 29 it stays on the head of Joab, and on all the house of his father, and there is not cut off from the house of Joab one who has discharging, and leprous, and laying hold on a staff, and falling by a sword, and lacking bread." 30 And Joab and his brother Abishai slew Abner because that he put their brother Asahel to death in Gibeon, in battle. 31 And David says to Joab, and to

2 SAMUEL

all the people who [are] with him, "Tear your garments, and gird on sackcloth, and mourn before Abner"; and King David is going after the bier. **32** And they bury Abner in Hebron, and the king lifts up his voice, and weeps at the grave of Abner, and all the people weep; **33** and the king laments for Abner and says, "Does Abner die as the death of a fool? **34** Your hands not bound, ‖ And your feet not brought near to chains! You have fallen as one falling before sons of evil!" And all the people add to weep over him. **35** And all the people come to cause David to eat bread while yet day, and David swears, saying, "Thus God does to me, and thus He adds, for—before the going in of the sun, I taste no bread or any other thing." **36** And all the people have discerned [it], and it is good in their eyes, as all that the king has done is good in the eyes of all the people; **37** and all the people know, even all Israel, in that day, that it has not been from the king—to put Abner son of Ner to death. **38** And the king says to his servants, "Do you not know that a prince and a great one has fallen this day in Israel? **39** And today I [am] tender, and an anointed king: and these men, sons of Zeruiah, [are] too hard for me; YHWH repays to the doer of the evil according to his evil."

4 And the son of Saul hears that Abner [is] dead in Hebron, and his hands are feeble, and all of Israel has been troubled. **2** And two men, heads of troops, have been [to] the son of Saul, the name of the first [is] Baanah, and the name of the second Rechab, sons of Rimmon the Beerothite, of the sons of Benjamin, for Beeroth is also reckoned to Benjamin, **3** and the Beerothites flee to Gittaim, and are sojourners there to this day. **4** And to Jonathan son of Saul [is] a son—lame; he was a son of five years at the coming in of the rumor of [the death of] Saul and Jonathan, out of Jezreel, and his nurse lifts him up, and flees, and it comes to pass in her hastening to flee, that he falls, and becomes lame, and his name [is] Mephibosheth. **5** And the sons of Rimmon the Beerothite, Rechab and Baanah, go, and come in at the heat of the day to the house of Ish-Bosheth, and he is lying down—the lying down of noon; **6** and they have come there, to the midst of the house, taking wheat, and they strike him to the fifth [rib], and Rechab and his brother Baanah have escaped; **7** indeed, they come into the house, and he is lying on his bed, in the inner part of his bed-chamber, and they strike him, and put him to death, and turn his head aside, and they take his head, and go the way of the plain all the night, **8** and bring in the head of Ish-Bosheth to David in Hebron, and say to the king, "Behold, the head of Ish-Bosheth, son of Saul, your enemy, who sought your life; and YHWH gives vengeance to my lord the king this day, of Saul and of his seed." **9** And David answers Rechab and his brother Baanah, sons of Rimmon the Beerothite, and says to them, "YHWH lives, who has redeemed my soul out of all adversity, **10** when one is declaring to me, saying, Behold, Saul is dead, and he was as a bearer of tidings in his own eyes, then I take hold on him, and slay him in Ziklag, instead of my giving to him [for] the tidings. **11** Also—when wicked men have slain the righteous man in his own house, on his bed; and now, do I not require his blood from your hand, and have taken you away from the earth?" **12** And David commands the young men, and they slay them, and cut off their hands and their feet, and hang [them] over the pool in Hebron, and they have taken the head of Ish-Bosheth, and bury [it] in the burying-place of Abner in Hebron.

5 And all the tribes of Israel come to David, to Hebron, and speak, saying, "Behold, we [are] your bone and your flesh; **2** also thus far, in Saul's being king over us, you have been he who is bringing out and bringing in Israel, and YHWH says to you, You feed My people Israel, and you are for leader over Israel." **3** And all [the] elderly of Israel come to the king, to Hebron, and King David makes a covenant with them in Hebron before YHWH, and they anoint David for king over Israel. **4** A son of thirty years [is] David in his being king; he has reigned [for] forty years; **5** he reigned over Judah in Hebron [for] seven years and six months, and in Jerusalem he reigned [for] thirty-three years, over all Israel and Judah. **6** And the king goes, and his men, to Jerusalem, to the Jebusite, the inhabitant of the land, and they speak to David, saying, "You do not come in here, except [that] you turn aside the blind and the lame," saying, "David does not come in here." **7** And David captures the fortress of Zion, it [is] the City of David. **8** And on that day David says, "Anyone striking the Jebusite, let him go up by the watercourse (and the lame and the blind—the hated of David's soul)." Therefore they say, "The blind and lame—he does not come into the house." **9** And David dwells in the fortress, and calls it the City of David, and David builds all around, from Millo and inward, **10** and David goes, going on and becoming great, and YHWH, God of Hosts, [is] with him. **11** And Hiram king of Tyre sends messengers to David, and cedar-trees, and craftsmen of wood, and craftsmen of stone, for walls, and they build a house for David, **12** and David knows that YHWH has established him for king over Israel, and that He has lifted up his kingdom, because of His people Israel. **13** And again David takes concubines and wives out of Jerusalem, after his coming from Hebron, and again there are born to David sons and daughters. **14** And these [are] the names of those born to him in Jerusalem: Shammuah, and Shobab, and Nathan, and Solomon, **15** and Ibhar, and Elishua, and Nepheg, and Japhia, **16** and Elishama, and Eliada, and Eliphalet. **17** And the Philistines hear that they have anointed David for king over Israel, and all the Philistines come up to seek David, and David hears, and goes down to the fortress, **18** and the Philistines have come, and are spread out in the Valley of Rephaim. **19** And David asks of YHWH, saying, "Do I go up to the Philistines? Do You give them into my hand?" And YHWH says to David, "Go up, for I certainly give the Philistines into your hand." **20** And David comes to Ba'al-Perazim, and David strikes them there, and says, "YHWH has broken forth [on] my enemies before me, as the breaking forth of waters"; therefore he has called the name of that place Ba'al-Perazim. **21** And they forsake their idols there, and David and his men lift them up. **22** And the Philistines add again to come up, and are spread out in the Valley of Rephaim, **23** and David asks of YHWH, and He says, "You do not go up, turn around to their rear, and you have come to them from the front [[or in front]] of the mulberries, **24** and it comes to pass, in your hearing the sound of a stepping in the tops of the mulberries, then you move sharply, for then YHWH has gone out before you to strike in the camp of the Philistines." **25** And David does so, as YHWH commanded him, and strikes the Philistines from Geba to your coming to Gazer.

6 And again David gathered every chosen one in Israel—thirty thousand, **2** and David rises and goes, and all the people who [are] with him, from Ba'ale-Judah, to bring up the Ark of God from there, whose name has been called—the Name of YHWH of Hosts, inhabiting the cherubim—on it. **3** And they cause the Ark of God to ride on a new cart, and lift it up from the house of Abinadab, which [is] in the height, and Uzzah and Ahio sons of Abinadab are leading the new cart; **4** and they lift it up from the house of Abinadab, which [is] in the height, with the Ark of God, and Ahio is going before the Ark, **5** and David and all the house of Israel are playing before YHWH, with all kinds of [instruments] of fir-wood, even with harps, and with psalteries, and with timbrels, and with horns, and with cymbals. **6** And they come to the threshing-floor of Nachon, and Uzzah puts forth [his hand] to the Ark of God, and lays hold on it, for they released the oxen; **7** and the anger of YHWH burns against Uzzah, and God strikes him there for the error, and he dies there by the Ark of God. **8** And it is displeasing to David, because that YHWH has broken forth a breach on Uzzah, and [one] calls that place Perez-Uzzah to this day; **9** and David fears YHWH on that day and says, "How does the Ark of YHWH come to me?" **10** And David has not been willing to turn aside the Ark of YHWH to himself, to the City of David, and David turns it aside to the house of Obed-Edom the Gittite, **11** and the Ark of YHWH inhabits the house of Obed-Edom the Gittite [for] three months, and YHWH blesses Obed-Edom and all his house. **12** And it is declared to King David, saying, "YHWH has blessed the house of Obed-Edom, and all that he has, because of the Ark of God"; and David goes and brings up the Ark of God from the house of Obed-Edom to the City of David with joy. **13** And it comes to pass, when those carrying the Ark of YHWH have stepped six steps, that he sacrifices an ox and a fatling. **14** And David is dancing with all [his] strength before YHWH, and David is girded with a linen ephod, **15** and David and all the house

2 SAMUEL

of Israel are bringing up the Ark of YHWH with shouting, and with the voice of a horn, **16** and it has come to pass, the Ark of YHWH has come into the City of David, and Michal daughter of Saul has looked through the window and sees King David moving and dancing before YHWH, and she despises him in her heart. **17** And they bring in the Ark of YHWH, and set it up in its place, in the midst of the tent which David has spread out for it, and David causes burnt-offerings and peace-offerings to ascend before YHWH. **18** And David finishes from causing the burnt-offering and the peace-offerings to ascend, and blesses the people in the Name of YHWH of Hosts, **19** and he apportions to all the people, to all the multitude of Israel, from man and to woman, to each, one cake of bread, and one eshpar, and one ashisha, and all the people go, each to his house. **20** And David turns back to bless his house, and Michal daughter of Saul goes out to meet David and says, "How honorable was the king of Israel today, who was uncovered today before the eyes of the handmaids of his servants, as one of the vain ones is openly uncovered!" **21** And David says to Michal, "Before YHWH, who fixed on me above your father, and above all his house, to appoint me leader over the people of YHWH, and over Israel—indeed, I played before YHWH; **22** and I have been more vile than this, and have been low in my eyes, and with the handmaids whom you have spoken of, I am honored with them." **23** As for Michal daughter of Saul, she had no child until the day of her death.

7 And it comes to pass, when the king sat in his house, and YHWH has given rest to him all around, from all his enemies, **2** that the king says to Nathan the prophet, "Now see, I am dwelling in a house of cedars, but the Ark of God is dwelling in the midst of the curtain." **3** And Nathan says to the king, "All that [is] in your heart—go, do, for YHWH [is] with you." **4** And it comes to pass in that night, that the word of YHWH is to Nathan, saying, **5** "Go, and you have said to My servant, to David, Thus said YHWH: Do you build for Me a house for My dwelling in? **6** For I have not dwelt in a house even from the day of My bringing up the sons of Israel out of Egypt, even to this day, and am walking up and down in a tent and in a dwelling place. **7** During all [the time] that I have walked up and down among all the sons of Israel, have I spoken a word with one of the tribes of Israel, which I commanded to feed my people Israel, saying, Why have you not built a house of cedars for Me? **8** And now, thus you say to My servant, to David, Thus said YHWH of Hosts: I have taken you from the pasture, from after the flock, to be leader over My people, over Israel; **9** and I am with you wherever you have gone, and I cut off all your enemies from your presence, and have made a great name for you, as the name of the great ones who [are] in the earth, **10** and I have appointed a place for My people, for Israel, and have planted it, and it has dwelt in its place, and it is not troubled anymore, and the sons of perverseness do not add to afflict it anymore, as in the beginning, **11** even from the day that I appointed judges over My people Israel; and I have given rest to you from all your enemies, and YHWH has declared to you that YHWH makes a house for you. **12** When your days are full, and you have lain with your fathers, then I have raised up your seed after you which goes out from your bowels, and have established his kingdom; **13** he builds a house for My Name, and I have established the throne of his kingdom for all time. **14** I am to him for a father, and he is to Me for a son; whom in his dealing perversely I have even reproved with a rod of men, and with strokes of the sons of Adam, **15** and My kindness does not turn aside from him, as I turned it aside from Saul, whom I turned aside from before you, **16** and your house and your kingdom [are] steadfast before you for all time, your throne is established for all time." **17** According to all these words, and according to all this vision, so spoke Nathan to David. **18** And King David comes in and sits before YHWH, and says, "Who [am] I, Lord YHWH? And what [is] my house, that You have brought me here? **19** And yet this [is] little in Your eyes, Lord YHWH, and You also speak concerning the house of Your servant far off; and this [is] the law of the man, Lord YHWH. **20** And what does David add more to speak to You? And You, You have known Your servant, Lord YHWH. **21** Because of Your word, and according to Your heart, You have done all this greatness, to cause Your servant to know [it]. **22** Therefore You have been great, YHWH God, for there is none like You, and there is no God except You, according to all that we have heard with our ears. **23** And who [is] as Your people, as Israel—one nation in the earth, whom God has gone to redeem for a people for Himself, and to make for Himself a name—and to do for Yourself the greatness—even fearful things for Your land, at the presence of Your people, whom You have redeemed for Yourself out of Egypt—[among the] nations and their gods? **24** Indeed, You establish Your people Israel for Yourself, for a people for Yourself for all time, and You, YHWH, have been to them for God. **25** And now, YHWH God, the word which You have spoken concerning Your servant, and concerning his house, establish for all time, and do as You have spoken. **26** And Your Name is great for all time, saying, YHWH of Hosts [is] God over Israel, and the house of Your servant David is established before You, **27** for You, YHWH of Hosts, God of Israel, have uncovered the ear of Your servant, saying, I build a house for you, therefore Your servant has found his heart to pray this prayer to You. **28** And now, Lord YHWH, You [are] God Himself, and Your words are truth, and You speak this goodness to Your servant, **29** and now, begin and bless the house of Your servant, to be before You for all time, for You, Lord YHWH, have spoken, and by Your blessing the house of Your servant is blessed for all time."

8 And it comes to pass afterward that David strikes the Philistines, and humbles them, and David takes the bridle of the metropolis out of the hand of the Philistines. **2** And he strikes Moab, and measures them with a line, causing them to lie down on the earth, and he measures two lines to put to death, and the fullness of the line to keep alive, and the Moabites are for servants to David, bearers of a present. **3** And David strikes Hadadezer son of Rehob, king of Zobah, in his going to bring back his power by the River [Euphrates]; **4** and David captures from him one thousand and seven hundred horsemen, and twenty thousand footmen, and David utterly destroys the whole of the charioteers; he leaves only one hundred of their charioteers. **5** And Aram of Damascus comes to give help to Hadadezer king of Zobah, and David strikes twenty-two thousand men of Aram; **6** and David puts garrisons in Aram of Damascus, and Aram is for a servant to David, carrying a present; and YHWH saves David wherever he has gone; **7** and David takes the shields of gold which were on the servants of Hadadezer, and brings them to Jerusalem; **8** and from Betah, and from Berothai, cities of Hadadezer, King David has taken very much bronze. **9** And Toi king of Hamath hears that David has struck all the force of Hadadezer, **10** and Toi sends his son Joram to King David to ask of him of welfare, and to bless him (because that he has fought against Hadadezer, and strikes him, for Hadadezer had been a man of wars [with] Toi), and in his hand have been vessels of silver, and vessels of gold, and vessels of bronze, **11** also King David sanctified them to YHWH, with the silver and the gold which he sanctified of all the nations which he subdued: **12** of Aram, and of Moab, and of the sons of Ammon, and of the Philistines, and of Amalek, and of the spoil of Hadadezer son of Rehob king of Zobah. **13** And David makes a name in his turning back from his striking Aram in the Valley of Salt—eighteen thousand; **14** and he puts garrisons in Edom—he has put garrisons in all of Edom, and all Edom are servants to David; and YHWH saves David wherever he has gone. **15** And David reigns over all Israel, and David is doing judgment and righteousness to all his people, **16** and Joab son of Zeruiah [is] over the host, and Jehoshaphat son of Ahilud [is] remembrancer, **17** and Zadok son of Ahitub, and Ahimelech son of Abiathar, [are] priests, and Seraiah [is] scribe, **18** and Benaiah son of Jehoiada [is over] both the Cherethite and the Pelethite, and the sons of David have been ministers.

9 And David says, "Is there yet any left of the house of Saul, and I do with him kindness because of Jonathan?" **2** And the house of Saul has a servant, and his name [is] Ziba, and they call for him to David; and the king says to him, "Are you Ziba?" And he says, "Your servant." **3** And the king says, "Is there not yet a man of the house of Saul, and I do with him the kindness of God?" And Ziba says to the king, "Jonathan has yet a son—lame." **4** And the king says to him, "Where [is] he?" And Ziba says to the king, "Behold, he [is] in the house of Machir, son of Ammiel, in Behold-Debar." **5** And King David sends, and takes him out of the house of Machir son of Ammiel, of Behold-Debar, **6** and Mephibosheth son of Jonathan, son of Saul, comes to David, and falls on his face, and pays respect, and David says, "Mephibosheth"; and he says, "Behold, your servant." **7** And David says to him, "Do not be afraid; for I certainly do with you kindness because of your father Jonathan, and have given back to you all the field of your father Saul, and you continually eat bread at my table." **8** And he bows himself and says, "What [is] your servant, that you have turned to the dead dog—such as I?" **9** And the king calls to Ziba servant of Saul and says to him, "All that was of Saul and of all his house, I have given to the son of your lord, **10** and you have served the land for him, you and your sons, and your servants, and have brought in, and there has been bread for the son of your lord, and he has eaten it; and Mephibosheth, son of your lord, continually eats bread at my table"; and Ziba has fifteen sons and twenty servants. **11** And Ziba says to the king, "According to all that my lord the king commands his servant, so your servant does." "As for Mephibosheth," [says the king,] "he is eating at my table as one of the sons of the king." **12** And Mephibosheth has a young son, and his name [is] Micha, and everyone dwelling in the house of Ziba [are] servants to Mephibosheth. **13** And Mephibosheth is dwelling in Jerusalem, for he is continually eating at the table of the king, and he [is] lame [in] his two feet.

10 And it comes to pass afterward, that the king of the sons of Ammon dies, and his son Hanun reigns in his stead, **2** and David says, "I do kindness with Hanun son of Nahash, as his father did kindness with me"; and David sends to comfort him by the hand of his servants concerning his father, and the servants of David come into the land of the sons of Ammon. **3** And the heads of the sons of Ammon say to their lord Hanun, "Is David honoring your father in your eyes because he has sent comforters to you? For has David not sent his servants to you to search the city, and to spy it, and to overthrow it?" **4** And Hanun takes the servants of David, and shaves off the half of their beard, and cuts off their long robes in the midst—to their buttocks, and sends them away; **5** and they declare [it] to David, and he sends to meet them, for the men have been greatly ashamed, and the king says, "Abide in Jericho until your beard springs up—then you have returned." **6** And the sons of Ammon see that they have been abhorred by David, and the sons of Ammon send and hire Aram of Beth-Rehob, and Aram of Zoba, twenty thousand footmen, and the king of Maacah [with] one thousand men, and Ish-Tob [with] twelve thousand men; **7** and David hears, and sends Joab, and all the host—the mighty men. **8** And the sons of Ammon come out, and set in array [for] battle, at the opening of the gate, and Aram of Zoba, and Rehob, and Ish-Tob, and Maacah, [are] by themselves in the field; **9** and Joab sees that the front of the battle has been to him before and behind, and he chooses [out] of all the chosen in Israel, and sets in array to meet Aram, **10** and he has given the rest of the people into the hand of his brother Abishai, and sets in array to meet the sons of Ammon. **11** And he says, "If Aram is stronger than I, then you have been for salvation to me, and if the sons of Ammon are stronger than you, then I have come to give salvation to you; **12** be strong and strengthen yourself for our people, and for the cities of our God, and YHWH does that which is good in His eyes." **13** And Joab draws near, and the people who [are] with him, to battle against Aram, and they flee from his presence; **14** and the sons of Ammon have seen that Aram has fled, and they flee from the presence of Abishai, and go into the city; and Joab turns back from the sons of Ammon, and comes to Jerusalem. **15** And Aram sees that it is struck before Israel, and they are gathered together; **16** and Hadadezer sends, and brings out Aram which [is] beyond the River, and they come to Helam, and Shobach, head of the host of Hadadezer, [is] before them. **17** And it is declared to David, and he gathers all Israel, and passes over the Jordan, and comes to Helam, and Aram sets itself in array to meet David, and they fight with him; **18** and Aram flees from the presence of Israel, and David slays seven hundred charioteers and forty thousand horsemen of Aram, and he has struck Shobach, [the] head of its host, and he dies there. **19** And all the kings—servants of Hadadezer—see that they have been struck before Israel, and make peace with Israel, and serve them; and Aram is afraid to help the sons of Ammon anymore.

11 And it comes to pass, at the revolution of the year—at the time of the going out of the messengers—that David sends Joab, and his servants with him, and all Israel, and they destroy the sons of Ammon, and lay siege against Rabbah, but David is dwelling in Jerusalem. **2** And it comes to pass, at evening-time, that David rises from off his bed, and walks up and down on the roof of the king's house, and sees a woman bathing from the roof, and the woman [is] of very good appearance, **3** and David sends and inquires about the woman, and [someone] says, "Is this not Bathsheba, daughter of Eliam, wife of Uriah the Hittite?" **4** And David sends messengers, and takes her, and she comes to him, and he lies with her—and she is purifying herself from her uncleanness—and she turns back to her house; **5** and the woman conceives, and sends, and declares [it] to David, and says, "I [am] conceiving." **6** And David sends to Joab, [saying], "Send Uriah the Hittite to me," and Joab sends Uriah to David; **7** and Uriah comes to him, and David asks of the prosperity of Joab, and of the prosperity of the people, and of the prosperity of the war. **8** And David says to Uriah, "Go down to your house, and wash your feet"; and Uriah goes out of the king's house, and there goes out a gift from the king after him, **9** and Uriah lies down at the opening of the king's house, with all the servants of his lord, and has not gone down to his house. **10** And they declare [it] to David, saying, "Uriah has not gone down to his house"; and David says to Uriah, "Have you not come from a journey? Why have you not gone down to your house?" **11** And Uriah says to David, "The ark, and Israel, and Judah, are abiding in shelters, and my lord Joab, and the servants of my lord, are encamping on the face of the field; and should I go to my house to eat and to drink, and to lie with my wife? [By] your life and the life of your soul—if I do this thing." **12** And David says to Uriah, "Also abide in this [place] today, and tomorrow I send you away"; and Uriah abides in Jerusalem on that day and on the next day, **13** and David calls for him, and he eats before him, and drinks, and he causes him to drink, and he goes out in the evening to lie on his bed with the servants of his lord, and he has not gone down to his house. **14** And it comes to pass in the morning that David writes a letter to Joab and sends [it] by the hand of Uriah; **15** and he writes in the letter, saying, "Place Uriah in front of the face of the most severe battle, and you have turned back from after him, and he has been struck, and has died." **16** And it comes to pass in Joab's watching of the city, that he appoints Uriah to the place where he knew that valiant men [were]; **17** and the men of the city go out and fight with Joab, and [some] of the people, from the servants of David, fall; and Uriah the Hittite also dies. **18** And Joab sends and declares to David all the matters of the war, **19** and commands the messenger, saying, "At your finishing all the matters of the war to speak to the king, **20** then, it has been, if the king's fury ascends, and he has said to you, Why did you draw near to the city to fight? Did you not know that they shoot from off the wall? **21** Who struck Abimelech son of Jerubbesheth? Did a woman not cast a piece of a rider from the wall on him, and he dies in Thebez? Why did you draw near to the wall? That you have said, Also—your servant Uriah the Hittite is dead." **22** And the messenger goes, and comes in, and declares to David all that with which Joab sent him, **23** and the messenger says to David, "Surely the men have been mighty against us, and come out to us into the field, and we are on them to the opening of the gate, **24** and those shooting shoot at your servants from off the wall, and [some] of the servants of the king are dead, and also, your servant Uriah the Hittite is dead." **25** And David says to the messenger, "Thus you say to Joab, Do not let this thing be evil in your eyes; for thus and thus the sword devours; strengthen your warfare against the city, and throw it down; so you strengthen him." **26** And the wife of Uriah hears that her husband Uriah [is] dead, and laments for her lord; **27** and the mourning passes by, and David sends and gathers her to his house, and she is to him for a wife, and bears a son to him; and the thing which David has done is evil in the eyes of YHWH.

12 And YHWH sends Nathan to David, and he comes to him, and says to him: "Two men have been in one city, one rich and one poor. **2** The rich has very many flocks and herds, **3** but the poor one has nothing, except one little ewe-lamb which he has bought and keeps alive. And it grows up together with him and with his sons. It eats of his morsel, and it drinks from his cup, and it lies in his bosom, and it is as a daughter to him. **4** And a traveler comes to the rich man, and he spares to take from his own flock, and from his own herd, to prepare for the traveling [man] who has come to him; and he takes the ewe-lamb of the poor man and prepares it for the man who has come to him." **5** And the anger of David burns against the man exceedingly, and he says to Nathan, "YHWH lives, surely the man who is doing this [is] a son of death, **6** and [for] the ewe-lamb he repays fourfold, because that he has done this thing, and because that he had no pity." **7** And Nathan says to David, "You [are] the man! Thus said YHWH, God of Israel: I anointed you for king over Israel, and I delivered you out of the hand of Saul; **8** and I give to you the house of your lord, and the wives of your lord, into your bosom, and I give the house of Israel and Judah to you; and if [that is] too little, then I add such and such [things] to you. **9** Why have you despised the word of YHWH, to do evil in His eyes? You have struck Uriah the Hittite by the sword, and you have taken his wife for a wife for yourself, and you have slain him by the sword of the sons of Ammon. **10** And now, the sword does not turn aside from your house for all time, because you have despised Me, and take the wife of Uriah the Hittite to be for a wife for yourself; **11** thus said YHWH: Behold, I am raising up calamity against you, out of your [own] house, and have taken your wives before your eyes, and given [them] to your neighbor, and he has lain with your wives before the eyes of this sun; **12** for you have done [it] in secret, and I do this thing before all Israel, and before the sun." **13** And David says to Nathan, "I have sinned against YHWH." And Nathan says to David, "Also—YHWH has caused your sin to pass away; you do not die; **14** only, because you have caused the enemies of YHWH to greatly despise by this thing, also—the son who is born to you surely dies." **15** And Nathan goes to his house, and YHWH strikes the boy, whom the wife of Uriah has borne to David, and it is incurable; **16** and David seeks God for the youth, and David keeps a fast, and has gone in and lodged, and lain on the earth. **17** And [the] elderly of his house rise against him, to raise him up from the earth, and he has not been willing, nor has he eaten bread with them; **18** and it comes to pass on the seventh day, that the boy dies, and the servants of David fear to declare to him that the boy is dead, for they said, "Behold, in the boy being alive we spoke to him, and he did not listen to our voice; and how do we say to him, The boy is dead? Then he has done evil." **19** And David sees that his servants are whispering, and David understands that the boy is dead, and David says to his servants, "Is the boy dead?" And they say, "Dead." **20** And David rises from the earth, and bathes and anoints [himself], and changes his raiment, and comes into the house of YHWH, and bows himself, and comes to his house, and asks and they place bread for him, and he eats. **21** And his servants say to him, "What [is] this thing you have done? Because of the living boy you have fasted and you weep, and when the boy is dead you have risen and eat bread." **22** And he says, "While the boy is alive I have fasted and I weep, for I said, Who knows [if] YHWH pities me and the boy has lived? **23** And now, he has died, why [is] this—I fast? Am I able to bring him back again? I am going to him, and he does not return to me." **24** And David comforts his wife Bathsheba, and goes in to her, and lies with her, and she bears a son, and he calls his name Solomon; and YHWH has loved him, **25** and sends by the hand of Nathan the prophet, and calls his name Jedidiah, because of YHWH. **26** And Joab fights against Rabbah of the sons of Ammon, and captures the royal city, **27** and Joab sends messengers to David and says, "I have fought against Rabbah—I have also captured the city of waters; **28** and now, gather the rest of the people, and encamp against the city, and capture it, lest I capture the city, and my name has been called on it." **29** And David gathers all the people, and goes to Rabbah, and fights against it, and captures it; **30** and he takes the crown of their king from off his head, and its weight [is] a talent of gold, and precious stones, and it is on the head of David; and he has brought out the spoil of the city—very much; **31** and he has brought out the people who [are] in it, and sets [them] to the saw, and to cutting instruments of iron, and to axes of iron, and has caused them to pass over into the brick-kiln; and so he does to all the cities of the sons of Ammon; and David turns back, and all the people, to Jerusalem.

13 And it comes to pass afterward that Absalom son of David has a beautiful sister, and her name [is] Tamar, and Amnon son of David loves her. **2** And Amnon has distress—even to become sick, because of his sister Tamar, for she [is] a virgin, and it is hard in the eyes of Amnon to do anything to her. **3** And Amnon has a friend, and his name [is] Jonadab, son of Shimeah, David's brother, and Jonadab [is] a very wise man, **4** and says to him, "Why [are] you thus lean, O king's son, morning by morning? Do you not declare [it] to me?" And Amnon says to him, "Tamar—sister of my brother Absalom—I am loving." **5** And Jonadab says to him, "Lie down on your bed, and feign yourself sick, and your father has come in to see you, and you have said to him: Please let my sister Tamar come in and give me bread to eat; and she has made the food before my eyes so that I see [it], and have eaten from her hand." **6** And Amnon lies down, and feigns himself sick, and the king comes in to see him, and Amnon says to the king, "Please let my sister Tamar come, and she makes two cakes before my eyes, and I eat from her hand." **7** And David sends to Tamar, to the house, saying, "Now go to the house of your brother Amnon and make food for him." **8** And Tamar goes to the house of her brother Amnon, and he is lying down, and she takes the dough, and kneads, and makes cakes before his eyes, and cooks the cakes, **9** and takes the frying-pan, and pours out before him, and he refuses to eat, and Amnon says, "Have everyone go out from me"; and everyone goes out from him. **10** And Amnon says to Tamar, "Bring the food into the inner chamber, and I eat from your hand"; and Tamar takes the cakes that she has made and brings [them] to her brother Amnon [in] the inner chamber, **11** and she brings [them] near to him to eat, and he lays hold on her, and says to her, "Come, lie with me, my sister." **12** And she says to him, "No, my brother, do not humble me, for it is not done so in Israel; do not do this folly. **13** And I—to where do I cause my reproach to go? And you are as one of the fools in Israel; and now, please speak to the king; for he does not withhold me from you." **14** And he has not been willing to listen to her voice, and is stronger than she, and humbles her, and lies with her. **15** And Amnon hates her—a very great hatred—that greater [is] the hatred with which he has hated her than the love with which he loved her, and Amnon says to her, "Rise, go." **16** And she says to him, "Because of the circumstances this evil is greater than the other that you have done with me—to send me away"; and he has not been willing to listen to her, **17** and calls his young man, his servant, and says, "Now send this one away from me outside, and bolt the door after her." **18** And a long coat [is] on her, for such upper robes daughters of the king who [are] virgins put on—and his servant takes her outside, and has bolted the door after her. **19** And Tamar takes ashes for her head, and has torn the long coat that [is] on her, and puts her hand on her head, and goes, going on and crying; **20** and her brother Absalom says to her, "Has your brother Amnon been with you? And now, my sister, keep silent, he [is] your brother; do not set your heart to this thing"; and Tamar dwells—but desolate—in the house of her brother Absalom. **21** And King David has heard all these things, and it is very displeasing to him; **22** and Absalom has not spoken with Amnon either evil or good, for Absalom is hating Amnon, because that he humbled his sister Tamar. **23** And it comes to pass, after two years of days, that Absalom has shearers in Ba'al-Hazor, which [is] near Ephraim, and Absalom calls for all the sons of the king. **24** And Absalom comes to the king and says, "Now behold, your servant has shearers, please let the king go—and his servants—with your servant." **25** And the king says to Absalom, "No, my son, please let us not all go, and we are not too heavy on you"; and he presses on him, and he has not been willing to go, and he blesses him. **26** And Absalom says, "If not, please let my brother Amnon go with us"; and the king says to him, "Why does he go with you?" **27** And Absalom urges for him, and he sends Amnon and all the sons of the king with him. **28** And Absalom commands his young men, saying, "Now see, when the heart of Amnon [is] glad with wine, and I have said to you, Strike Amnon, that you have put him to death; do not fear; is it not because I have commanded you? Be strong, indeed, become sons of valor."

29 And the young men of Absalom do to Amnon as Absalom commanded, and all the sons of the king rise, and they ride, each on his mule, and flee. **30** And it comes to pass—they [are] in the way—and the report has come to David, saying, "Absalom has struck all the sons of the king, and there is not left [even] one of them"; **31** and the king rises, and tears his garments, and lies on the earth, and all his servants are standing by [with] torn garments. **32** And Jonadab son of Shimeah, David's brother, answers and says, "Do not let my lord say, The whole of the young men, the sons of the king, they have put to death; for Amnon alone [is] dead, for it has been appointed by the command of Absalom from the day of his humbling his sister Tamar; **33** and now, do not let my lord the king lay the word to his heart, saying, All the sons of the king have died, for Amnon alone [is] dead." **34** And Absalom flees, and the young man who is watching lifts up his eyes and looks, and behold, many people are coming by the way behind him, on the side of the hill. **35** And Jonadab says to the king, "Behold, the sons of the king have come; as the word of your servant, so it has been." **36** And it comes to pass at his finishing to speak, that behold, the sons of the king have come, and they lift up their voice, and weep, and also the king and all his servants have wept—a very great weeping. **37** And Absalom has fled, and goes to Talmai, son of Ammihud, king of Geshur, and [David] mourns for his son all the days. **38** And Absalom has fled, and goes to Geshur, and is there [for] three years; **39** and King David determines to go out to Absalom, for he has been comforted for Amnon, for [he is] dead.

14 And Joab son of Zeruial knows that the heart of the king [is] on Absalom, **2** and Joab sends to Tekoah, and takes a wise woman from there, and says to her, "Please feign yourself a mourner, and now put on garments of mourning, and do not anoint yourself with oil, and you have been as a woman mourning for the dead [for] these many days, **3** and you have gone to the king, and spoken to him, according to this word"; and Joab puts the words into her mouth. **4** And the woman of Tekoah speaks to the king, and falls on her face to the earth, and pays respect, and says, "Save, O king." **5** And the king says to her, "What do you [want]?" And she says, "I [am] truly a widow woman, and my husband dies, **6** and your maidservant has two sons; and both of them strive in a field, and there is no deliverer between them, and one strikes the other, and puts him to death; **7** and behold, the whole family has risen against your maidservant, and say, Give up him who strikes his brother, and we put him to death for the life of his brother whom he has slain, and we also destroy the heir; and they have quenched my coal which is left—so as not to set a name and remnant on the face of the ground for my husband." **8** And the king says to the woman, "Go to your house, and I give charge concerning you." **9** And the woman of Tekoah says to the king, "On me, my lord, O king, [is] the iniquity, and on the house of my father; and the king and his throne [are] innocent." **10** And the king says, "He who speaks to you, and you have brought him to me, then he does not add to come against you anymore." **11** And she says, "Please let the king remember by your God YHWH, that the redeemer of blood does not add to destroy, and they do not destroy my son"; and he says, "YHWH lives; if there falls [even one] hair of your son to the earth." **12** And the woman says, "Please let your maidservant speak a word to my lord the king"; and he says, "Speak." **13** And the woman says, "And why have you thought thus concerning the people of God? Indeed, the king is speaking this thing as a guilty one, in that the king has not brought back his outcast; **14** for we surely die, and [are] as water which is running down to the earth, which is not gathered, and God does not accept a person, and has devised plans in that the outcast is not outcast by Him. **15** And now that I have come to speak this word to my lord the king, [it is] because the people made me afraid, and your maidservant says, Please let me speak to the king; it may be the king does the word of his handmaid, **16** for the king listens to deliver his handmaid out of the paw of the man [seeking] to destroy me and my son together out of the inheritance of God, **17** and your maidservant says, Please let the word of my lord the king be for ease; for as a messenger of God so [is] my lord the king, to understand the good and the evil; and your God YHWH is with you." **18** And the king answers and says to the woman, "Please do not hide from me

2 SAMUEL

the thing that I am asking you"; and the woman says, "Please let my lord the king speak." **19** And the king says, "Is the hand of Joab with you in all this?" And the woman answers and says, "Your soul lives, my lord, O king, none [turn] to the right or to the left from all that my lord the king has spoken; for your servant Joab commanded me, and he put all these words in the mouth of your maidservant. **20** Your servant Joab has done this thing in order to bring around the appearance of the thing, and my lord [is] wise, according to the wisdom of a messenger of God, to know all that [is] in the land." **21** And the king says to Joab, "Now behold, you have done this thing; and go, bring back the young man Absalom." **22** And Joab falls on his face to the earth, and pays respect, and blesses the king, and Joab says, "Today your servant has known that I have found grace in your eyes, my lord, O king, in that the king has done the word of his servant." **23** And Joab rises and goes to Geshur, and brings in Absalom to Jerusalem, **24** and the king says, "Let him turn around to his house, and he does not see my face." And Absalom turns around to his house, and he has not seen the face of the king. **25** And there was no man [so] beautiful in all Israel like Absalom, to praise greatly; from the sole of his foot even to his crown there was no blemish in him; **26** and in his shaving his head—and it has been at the end of year by year that he shaves [it], for it [is] heavy on him, and he has shaved it—he has even weighed out the hair of his head—two hundred shekels by the king's weight. **27** And there are born to Absalom three sons and one daughter, and her name [is] Tamar; she was a woman of beautiful appearance. **28** And Absalom dwells in Jerusalem [for] two years of days, and he has not seen the face of the king; **29** and Absalom sends to Joab, to send him to the king, and he has not been willing to come to him; and he sends again a second time, and he has not been willing to come. **30** And he says to his servants, "See, the portion of Joab [is] by the side of mine, and he has barley there; go and burn it with fire"; and the servants of Absalom burn the portion with fire. **31** And Joab rises and comes to Absalom in the house, and says to him, "Why have your servants burned the portion that I have with fire?" **32** And Absalom says to Joab, "Behold, I sent to you, saying, Come here, and I send you to the king to say, Why have I come in from Geshur? [It was] good for me while I [was] there—and now, let me see the king's face, and if there is iniquity in me then you have put me to death." **33** And Joab comes to the king, and declares [it] to him, and he calls to Absalom, and he comes to the king, and bows himself to him, on his face, to the earth, before the king, and the king gives a kiss to Absalom.

15 And it comes to pass afterward that Absalom prepares a chariot and horses for himself, and fifty men are running before him; **2** and Absalom has risen early, and stood by the side of the way of the gate, and it comes to pass, every man who has a pleading to come to the king for judgment, that Absalom calls to him and says, "Of what city [are] you?" And he says, "Your servant [is] of one of the tribes of Israel." **3** And Absalom says to him, "See, your matters [are] good and straightforward—and there is none listening to you from the king." **4** And Absalom says, "Who makes me judge in the land, that every man who has a plea and judgment comes to me? Then I have declared him righteous." **5** And it has come to pass, in the drawing near of anyone to bow himself to him, that he has put forth his hand, and laid hold on him, and given a kiss to him; **6** and Absalom does according to this thing to all Israel who come in for judgment to the king, and Absalom steals the heart of the men of Israel. **7** And it comes to pass, at the end of forty years, that Absalom says to the king, "Please let me go, and I complete my vow that I vowed to YHWH in Hebron, **8** for your servant has vowed a vow in my dwelling in Geshur, in Aram, saying, If YHWH certainly brings me back to Jerusalem, then I have served YHWH." **9** And the king says to him, "Go in peace"; and he rises and goes to Hebron, **10** and Absalom sends spies through all the tribes of Israel, saying, "At your hearing the voice of the horn, then you have said, Absalom has reigned in Hebron." **11** And two hundred men have gone with Absalom out of Jerusalem, invited ones, and they are going in their simplicity, and have not known anything; **12** and Absalom sends Ahithophel the Gilonite, a counselor of David, out of his city, out of Gilo, in his sacrificing sacrifices; and the conspiracy is

2 SAMUEL

strong, and the people are going and increasing with Absalom. **13** And he who is declaring tidings comes to David, saying, "The heart of the men of Israel has been after Absalom." **14** And David says to all his servants who [are] with him in Jerusalem, "Rise, and we flee, for we have no escape from the face of Absalom; hurry to go, lest he hurries, and has overtaken us, and forced evil on us, and struck the city by the mouth of the sword." **15** And the servants of the king say to the king, "According to all that my lord the king chooses—behold, your servants do." **16** And the king goes out, and all his household at his feet, and the king leaves ten women—concubines—to keep the house. **17** And the king goes out, and all the people at his feet, and they stand still at the farthest off house. **18** And all his servants are passing on at his side, and all the Cherethite, and all the Pelethite, and all the Gittites, six hundred men who came at his feet from Gath, are passing on at the front of the king. **19** And the king says to Ittai the Gittite, "Why do you go—you also—with us? Return and abide with the king, for you [are] a stranger, and also an exile, you—to your place. **20** Your coming in [was only] yesterday, and should I move you to go with us today, since I am going over [to] where [I do not know where] I am going? Return, and take your brothers back. Kindness and truth [be] with you." **21** And Ittai answers the king and says, "YHWH lives, and my lord the king lives, surely in the place where my lord the king is—if for death, if for life, surely your servant is there." **22** And David says to Ittai, "Go and pass over"; and Ittai the Gittite passes over, and all his men, and all the infants who [are] with him. **23** And all the land is weeping [with] a great voice, and all the people are passing over; and the king is passing over through the Brook of Kidron, and all the people are passing over on the front of the way of the wilderness; **24** and behold, also Zadok, and all the Levites with him, are carrying the Ark of the Covenant of God, and they make the Ark of God firm, and Abiathar goes up, until the completion of all the people to pass over out of the city. **25** And the king says to Zadok, "Take back the Ark of God to the city; if I find grace in the eyes of YHWH, then He has brought me back, and shown me it and His habitation; **26** and if thus He says, I have not delighted in you; here I [am], He does to me as [is] good in His eyes." **27** And the king says to Zadok the priest, "Are you a seer? Return to the city in peace, and your son Ahimaaz, and Jonathan son of Abiathar, your two sons with you; **28** see, I am lingering in the plains of the wilderness until the coming in of a word from you to declare to me." **29** And Zadok takes back—and Abiathar—the Ark of God to Jerusalem, and they abide there. **30** And David is going up in the ascent of the [Mount of] Olives, going up and weeping, and he has the head covered, and he is going barefooted, and all the people who [are] with him have each covered his head, and have gone up, going up and weeping; **31** and David declared, saying, "Ahithophel [is] among the conspirators with Absalom"; and David says, "Please make the counsel of Ahithophel foolish, O YHWH." **32** And it comes to pass, David has come to the top, where he bows himself to God, and behold, Hushai the Archite [is there] to meet him, [with] his coat torn, and earth on his head; **33** and David says to him, "If you have passed on with me then you have been for a burden on me, **34** and if you return to the city and have said to Absalom, I am your servant, O king; I [am] also servant of your father until now, and presently, I [am] also your servant; then you have made void the counsel of Ahithophel for me; **35** and are Zadok and Abiathar the priests not with you there? And it has been, the whole of the matter that you hear from the house of the king you declare to Zadok and to Abiathar the priests. **36** Behold, their two sons [are] there with them: Ahimaaz to Zadok, and Jonathan to Abiathar, and you have sent to me by their hand anything that you hear." **37** And Hushai, David's friend, comes to the city, and Absalom comes to Jerusalem.

16 And David has passed on a little from the top, and behold, Ziba, servant of Mephibosheth, [is there] to meet him, and a couple of donkeys [are] saddled, and on them [are] two hundred loaves, and one hundred bunches of raisins, and one hundred of summer-fruit, and a bottle of wine. **2** And the king says to Ziba, "What [are] these to you?" And Ziba says, "The donkeys for the household of the king to ride on, and the bread and the summer-fruit for the young men to eat, and the wine for the wearied to drink in the wilderness."

3 And the king says, "And where [is] the son of your lord?" And Ziba says to the king, "Behold, he is abiding in Jerusalem, for he said, Today the house of Israel gives back the kingdom of my father to me." **4** And the king says to Ziba, "Behold, all that Mephibosheth has [is] for you"; and Ziba says, "I have bowed myself—I find grace in your eyes, my lord, O king." **5** And King David has come to Bahurim, and behold, a man there is coming out, of the family of the house of Saul, and his name [is] Shimei, son of Gera, he comes out, coming out and reviling; **6** and he stones David with stones, and all the servants of King David, and all the people, and all the mighty men on his right and on his left. **7** And thus said Shimei in his reviling: "Go out, go out, O man of blood, and man of worthlessness! **8** YHWH has turned back on you all the blood of the house of Saul, in whose stead you have reigned, and YHWH gives the kingdom into the hand of your son Absalom; and behold, you [are] in your evil, for you [are] a man of blood." **9** And Abishai son of Zeruiah says to the king, "Why does this dead dog revile my lord the king? Please let me pass over and I turn aside his head." **10** And the king says, "And what do I [have to do] with you, O sons of Zeruiah? For let him revile; even because YHWH has said to him, Revile David; and who says, Why have You done so?" **11** And David says to Abishai, and to all his servants, "Behold, my son who came out of my bowels is seeking my life, and also surely now the Benjamite; leave him alone, and let him revile, for YHWH has commanded [so] to him; **12** it may be YHWH looks on my affliction, and YHWH has turned back good to me for his reviling this day." **13** And David goes with his men in the way, and Shimei is going at the side of the hill opposite him, going on, and he reviles, and stones with stones close by him, and has dusted with dust. **14** And the king comes in, and all the people who [are] with him, wearied, and they are refreshed there. **15** And Absalom and all the people, the men of Israel, have come to Jerusalem, and Ahithophel with him, **16** and it comes to pass, when Hushai the Archite, David's friend, has come to Absalom, that Hushai says to Absalom, "Let the king live! Let the king live!" **17** And Absalom says to Hushai, "[Is] this your kindness with your friend? Why have you not gone with your friend?" **18** And Hushai says to Absalom, "No, for he whom YHWH has chosen, and this people, even all the men of Israel, I am his, and I abide with him; **19** and secondly, for whom do I labor? Is it not before his son? As I served before your father, so I am before you." **20** And Absalom says to Ahithophel, "Give counsel for yourself [for] what we do." **21** And Ahithophel says to Absalom, "Go in to the concubines of your father, whom he left to keep the house, and all Israel has heard that you have been abhorred by your father, and the hands of all who [are] with you have been strong." **22** And they spread out the tent for Absalom on the roof, and Absalom goes in to the concubines of his father before the eyes of all Israel. **23** And the counsel of Ahithophel which he counseled in those days [is] as [when] one inquires at the word of God; so [is] all the counsel of Ahithophel both to David and to Absalom.

17 And Ahithophel said to Absalom, "Please let me choose twelve thousand men, and I arise and pursue after David tonight, **2** and come on him, and he [will be] weary and feeble-handed, and I have caused him to tremble, and all the people who [are] with him have fled, and I have struck the king by himself, **3** and I bring back all the people to you—as the turning back of the whole [except] the man whom you are seeking—[then] all the people are [at] peace." **4** And the word is right in the eyes of Absalom, and in the eyes of all [the] elderly of Israel. **5** And Absalom says, "Now call for Hushai the Archite also, and we hear what [is] in his mouth—even he." **6** And Hushai comes to Absalom, and Absalom speaks to him, saying, "According to this word Ahithophel has spoken; do we do his word? If not, you—speak." **7** And Hushai says to Absalom, "The counsel that Ahithophel has counseled [is] not good at this time." **8** And Hushai says, "You have known your father and his men, that they [are] heroes, and they are bitter in soul as a bereaved bear in a field, and your father [is] a man of war, and does not lodge with the people; **9** behold, now, he is hidden in one of the pits, or in one of the places, and it has been at the falling among them at the commencement, that the hearer has heard and said, There has been a slaughter among the people who [are] after Absalom; **10** and he also, the son of valor, whose heart [is] as the heart of the lion, utterly melts, for all Israel knows that your father is a hero, and those with him [are] sons of valor. **11** So that I have counseled: let all Israel be diligently gathered to you, from Dan even to Beer-Sheba, as the sand that [is] by the sea for multitude, and you yourself are going in the midst; **12** and we have come to him in one of the places where he is found, and we [are] on him as the dew falls on the ground, and there has not been left of him and of all the men who [are] with him even one. **13** And if he is gathered to a city, then they have caused all Israel to carry ropes to that city, and we have drawn it to the brook until there has not even been found a stone there." **14** And Absalom says—and all the men of Israel, "The counsel of Hushai the Archite [is] better than the counsel of Ahithophel"; and YHWH willed to make void the good counsel of Ahithophel for the sake of YHWH's bringing the calamity to Absalom. **15** And Hushai says to Zadok and to Abiathar the priests, "Thus and thus Ahithophel has counseled Absalom and the elderly of Israel, and thus and thus I have counseled; **16** and now, send quickly, and declare [it] to David, saying, Do not lodge in the plains of the wilderness tonight, and also, certainly pass over, lest there is a swallowing up of the king and of all the people who are with him." **17** And Jonathan and Ahimaaz are standing at En-Rogel, and the maidservant has gone and declared [it] to them—and they go and have declared [it] to King David—for they are not able to be seen to go into the city. **18** And a youth sees them, and declares [it] to Absalom; and both of them go on quickly, and come to the house of a man in Bahurim, and he has a well in his court, and they go down there, **19** and the woman takes and spreads the covering over the face of the well, and spreads the ground grain on it, and the thing has not been known. **20** And the servants of Absalom come to the woman at the house, and say, "Where [are] Ahimaaz and Jonathan?" And the woman says to them, "They passed over the brook of water"; and they seek, and have not found, and return to Jerusalem. **21** And it comes to pass, after their going on, that they come up out of the well, and go and declare [it] to King David, and say to David, "Rise, and pass over the waters quickly, for thus has Ahithophel counseled against you." **22** And David rises, and all the people who [are] with him, and they pass over the Jordan, until the morning light, until not one has been lacking who has not passed over the Jordan. **23** And Ahithophel has seen that his counsel was not done, and he saddles the donkey, and rises and goes to his house, to his city, and gives charge to his household, and strangles himself, and dies, and he is buried in the burying-place of his father. **24** And David came to Mahanaim, and Absalom passed over the Jordan, he and all the men of Israel with him; **25** and Absalom has set Amasa over the host instead of Joab, and Amasa [is] a man's son whose name is Ithra the Israeli who has gone in to Abigail, daughter of Nahash, sister of Zeruiah, mother of Joab; **26** and Israel encamps with Absalom [in] the land of Gilead. **27** And it comes to pass at the coming in of David to Mahanaim, that Shobi son of Nahash, from Rabbah of the sons of Ammon, and Machir son of Ammiel, from Behold-Debar, and Barzillai the Gileadite, from Rogelim, **28** [have brought] bed, and basin, and earthen vessel, and wheat, and barley, and flour, and roasted [grain], and beans, and lentiles, and roasted [pulse], **29** and honey, and butter, and sheep, and cheese of cows; they have brought [these] near for David, and for the people who [are] with him to eat, for they said, "Your people [are] hungry, and weary, and thirsty, in the wilderness."

18 And David inspects the people who [are] with him, and sets over them heads of thousands and heads of hundreds, **2** and David sends the third of the people by the hand of Joab, and the third by the hand of Abishai, son of Zeruiah, brother of Joab, and the third by the hand of Ittai the Gittite, and the king says to the people, "I certainly go out—I also—with you." **3** And the people say, "You do not go out, for if we utterly flee, they do not set [their] heart on us; and if half of us die, they do not set [their] heart to us—for [you are] now like ten thousand of us; and now, [it is] better that you are for a helper to us from the city." **4** And the king says to them, "That which is good in your eyes I do"; and the king stands at the side of the gate, and all the people have gone out by hundreds and by thousands, **5** and the king charges Joab, and Abishai, and Ittai, saying, "[Deal]

2 SAMUEL

gently—for me, for the youth, for Absalom"; and all the people heard in the king's charging all the heads concerning Absalom. **6** And the people go out into the field to meet Israel, and the battle is in a forest of Ephraim; **7** and the people of Israel are struck there before the servants of David, and the striking there is great on that day—twenty thousand; **8** and the battle there is scattered over the face of all the land, and the forest multiplies to devour among the people more than those whom the sword has devoured in that day. **9** And Absalom meets before the servants of David, and Absalom is riding on the mule, and the mule comes in under an entangled bough of the great oak, and his head takes hold on the oak, and he is placed between the heavens and the earth, and the mule that [is] under him has passed on. **10** And one man sees, and declares [it] to Joab, and says, "Behold, I saw Absalom hanging in an oak." **11** And Joab says to the man who is declaring [it] to him, "And behold, you have seen—and why did you not strike him there to the earth—and [it would be] on me to give to you ten pieces of silver and one girdle?" **12** And the man says to Joab, "Indeed, though I am weighing on my hand one thousand pieces of silver, I do not put forth my hand to the son of the king; for in our ears the king has charged you, and Abishai, and Ittai, saying, Observe who [is] against the youth—against Absalom; **13** or I had done a vain thing against my soul, and no matter is hid from the king, and you would station yourself opposite from [me]." **14** And Joab says, "[It is] not right [that] I linger before you"; and he takes three darts in his hand, and strikes them into the heart of Absalom, while he [is] alive, in the midst of the oak. **15** And they go around—ten youths carrying weapons of Joab—and strike Absalom, and put him to death. **16** And Joab blows with a horn, and the people turn back from pursuing after Israel, for Joab has kept back the people; **17** and they take Absalom and cast him into the great pit in the forest, and set up a very great heap of stones over him, and all Israel has fled—each to his tent. **18** And Absalom has taken, and sets up for himself in his life, the standing-pillar that [is] in the king's valley, for he said, "I have no son to cause my name to be remembered"; and he calls the standing-pillar by his own name, and it is called "The Monument of Absalom" to this day. **19** And Ahimaaz son of Zadok said, "Please let me run, and I bear the king tidings, for YHWH has delivered him out of the hand of his enemies"; **20** and Joab says to him, "You are not a man of tidings this day, but you have borne tidings on another day, and this day you do not bear tidings, because the king's son [is] dead." **21** And Joab says to Cushi, "Go, declare to the king that which you have seen"; and Cushi bows himself to Joab, and runs. **22** And Ahimaaz son of Zadok adds again and says to Joab, "And whatever it is, please let me run, I also, after the Cushite." And Joab says, "Why [is] this—you are running, my son, and [there are] no tidings found from you?" **23** "And whatever happens," he said, "let me run." And he says to him, "Run"; and Ahimaaz runs the way of the circuit, and passes by the Cushite. **24** And David is sitting between the two gates, and the watchman goes to the roof of the gate, to the wall, and lifts up his eyes, and looks, and behold, a man running by himself. **25** And the watchman calls, and declares [it] to the king, and the king says, "If [he is] by himself, tidings [are] in his mouth"; and he comes, coming on and drawing near. **26** And the watchman sees another man running, and the watchman calls to the gatekeeper, and says, "Behold, a man running by himself"; and the king says, "This one is also bearing tidings." **27** And the watchman says, "I see the running of the first as the running of Ahimaaz son of Zadok." And the king says, "This [is] a good man, and he comes with good tidings." **28** And Ahimaaz calls and says to the king, "Peace"; and he bows himself to the king, on his face, to the earth, and says, "Blessed [is] your God YHWH who has shut up the men who lifted up their hand against my lord the king." **29** And the king says, "Peace to the youth—for Absalom?" And Ahimaaz says, "I saw the great multitude, at the sending away of the servant of the king, even your servant [by] Joab, and I have not known what [it is]." **30** And the king says, "Turn around, station yourself here"; and he turns around and stands still. **31** And behold, the Cushite has come, and the Cushite says, "Let tidings be proclaimed, my lord, O king; for today YHWH has delivered you out of the hand of all those rising up against you." **32** And the king says to the Cushite, "Peace to the youth—for Absalom?" And the Cushite says, "Let them be—as the youth—the enemies of my lord the king, and all who have risen up against you for evil." **33** And the king trembles, and goes up on the upper chamber of the gate, and weeps, and thus he has said in his going, "My son Absalom! My son! My son Absalom! Oh that I had died for you, Absalom, my son, my son!"

19 And it is declared to Joab, "Behold, the king is weeping and mourning for Absalom"; **2** and the salvation on that day becomes mourning to all the people, for the people have heard on that day, saying, "The king has been grieved for his son." **3** And the people steals away, on that day, to go into the city, as the people steal away, who are ashamed, in their fleeing in battle; **4** and the king has covered his face, indeed, the king cries [with] a loud voice, "My son Absalom! Absalom, my son, my son!" **5** And Joab comes into the house to the king and says, "Today you have put to shame the faces of all your servants, those delivering your life today, and the life of your sons, and of your daughters, and the life of your wives, and the life of your concubines, **6** to love your enemies, and to hate those loving you, for today you have declared that you have no princes and servants, for today I have known that if Absalom [were] alive, and all of us dead today, that then it were right in your eyes. **7** And now, rise, go out and speak to the heart of your servants, for I have sworn by YHWH, that [if] you are not going out—there does not lodge a man with you tonight; and this [is] worse for you than all the evil that has come on you from your youth until now." **8** And the king rises, and sits in the gate, and they have declared to all the people, saying, "Behold, the king is sitting in the gate"; and all the people come in before the king, and Israel has fled, each to his tents. **9** And it comes to pass, all the people are contending through all the tribes of Israel, saying, "The king delivered us out of the hand of our enemies, indeed, he himself delivered us out of the hand of the Philistines, and now he has fled out of the land because of Absalom, **10** and Absalom whom we anointed over us [is] dead in battle, and now, why are you silent—to bring back the king?" **11** And King David sent to Zadok and to Abiathar the priests, saying, "Speak to [the] elderly of Judah, saying, Why are you last to bring back the king to his house, since the word of all Israel has come to the king, to his house; **12** you [are] my brothers, you [are] my bone and my flesh, and why are you last to bring back the king? **13** And say to Amasa, Are you not my bone and my flesh? Thus God does to me, and thus He adds, if you are not head of the host before me instead of Joab [for] all the days." **14** And he inclines the heart of all the men of Judah as one man, and they send to the king, "Return, you and all your servants." **15** And the king turns back, and comes to the Jordan, and Judah has come to Gilgal, to go to meet the king, to bring the king over the Jordan, **16** and Shimei son of Gera, the Benjamite, who [is] from Bahurim, hurries, and comes down with the men of Judah, to meet King David, **17** and one thousand men [are] with him from Benjamin, and Ziba servant of the house of Saul, and his fifteen sons and his twenty servants with him, and they have gone prosperously over the Jordan before the king. **18** And the ferry-boat has passed over to carry over the household of the king, and to do that which [is] good in his eyes, and Shimei son of Gera has fallen before the king in his passing over into the Jordan, **19** and he says to the king, "Do not let my lord impute iniquity to me; neither remember that which your servant did perversely in the day that my lord the king went out from Jerusalem—for the king to set [it] to his heart; **20** for your servant has known that I have sinned; and behold, I have come today, first of all the house of Joseph, to go down to meet my lord the king." **21** And Abishai son of Zeruiah answers and says, "Is Shimei not put to death for this—because he reviled the anointed of YHWH?" **22** And David says, "And what do I [have to do] with you, O sons of Zeruiah, that today you are for an adversary to me? Is any man put to death in Israel today? For have I not known that today I [am] king over Israel?" **23** And the king says to Shimei, "You do not die"; and the king swears to him. **24** And Mephibosheth son of Saul has come down to meet the king—and he did not prepare his feet, nor did he prepare his upper lip, indeed, he did not wash his garments, even from the day of the going away of the king, until the day that he came in peace— **25** and it comes to pass, when he has come to Jerusalem to meet the king, that the king says to him, "Why did you not go with me, Mephibosheth?" **26** And he says, "My lord, O king, my servant deceived me, for your servant said, I saddle the donkey for myself, and ride on it, and go with the king, for your servant [is] lame; **27** and he utters slander against your servant to my lord the king, and my lord the king [is] as a messenger of God; and do that which is good in your eyes, **28** for all the house of my father have been nothing except men of death before my lord the king, and you set your servant among those eating at your table, and what right do I have anymore—even to cry anymore to the king?" **29** And the king says to him, "Why do you speak anymore of your matters? I have said, You and Ziba—share the field." **30** And Mephibosheth says to the king, "Indeed, let him take the whole, after that my lord the king has come in peace to his house." **31** And Barzillai the Gileadite has gone down from Rogelim, and passes over the Jordan with the king, to send him away over the Jordan; **32** and Barzillai [is] very aged, a son of eighty years, and he has sustained the king in his abiding in Mahanaim, for he [is] a very great man; **33** and the king says to Barzillai, "Pass over with me, and I have sustained you in Jerusalem with me." **34** And Barzillai says to the king, "How many [are] the days of the years of my life, that I go up with the king to Jerusalem? **35** I [am] a son of eighty years today; do I know between good and evil? Does your servant taste that which I am eating, and that which I drink? Do I listen anymore to the voice of male and female singers? And why is your servant for a burden to my lord the king anymore? **36** As a little thing, your servant passes over the Jordan with the king, and why does the king repay me this repayment? **37** Please let your servant turn back again, and I die in my own city, near the burying-place of my father and of my mother—and behold, your servant Chimham, let him pass over with my lord the king, and do to him that which [is] good in your eyes." **38** And the king says, "Chimham goes over with me, and I do to him that which [is] good in your eyes, indeed, all that you fix on me I do to you." **39** And all the people pass over the Jordan, and the king has passed over, and the king gives a kiss to Barzillai, and blesses him, and he turns back to his place. **40** And the king passes over to Gilgal, and Chimham has passed over with him, and all the people of Judah, and they bring over the king, and also the half of the people of Israel. **41** And behold, all the men of Israel are coming to the king, and they say to the king, "Why have our brothers, the men of Judah, stolen you—and they bring the king and his household over the Jordan, and all the men of David with him?" **42** And all the men of Judah answer against the men of Israel, "Because the king [is] near to us, and why [is] this [that] you are displeased about this matter? Have we eaten of the king's [substance] at all? Has he lifted up a gift to us?" **43** And the men of Israel answer the men of Judah, and say, "We have ten parts in the king, and also more than you in David; and why have you lightly esteemed us, that our word has not been first to bring back our king?" And the word of the men of Judah is sharper than the word of the men of Israel.

20 And there happened to be a man of worthlessness there, and his name [is] Sheba, son of Bichri, a Benjamite, and he blows with a horn and says, "We have no portion in David, and we have no inheritance in the son of Jesse; each [goes] to his tents, O Israel." **2** And every man of Israel goes up from after David, after Sheba son of Bichri, and the men of Judah have cleaved to their king, from the Jordan even to Jerusalem. **3** And David comes to his house at Jerusalem. And the king takes the ten women-concubines whom he had left to keep the house, and puts them in a house of ward and sustains them, and he has not gone in to them, and they are shut up to the day of their death, living in widowhood. **4** And the king says to Amasa, "Call the men of Judah for me [within] three days, and you, stand here," **5** and Amasa goes to call Judah, and tarries beyond the appointed time that he had appointed him; **6** and David says to Abishai, "Now Sheba son of Bichri does evil to us more than Absalom; you, take the servants of your lord, and pursue after him, lest he has found fortified cities for himself, and delivered himself [from] our eye." **7** And the men of Joab go out after him, and the Cherethite, and the Pelethite, and all the mighty men, and they go out from Jerusalem to pursue after Sheba son of Bichri; **8** they [are] near the great stone that [is] in Gibeon, and Amasa has gone before them, and Joab [is] girded; he has put his long robe on him, and on it a girdle—a sword [is] fastened on his loins in its sheath; and he has gone out, and it falls. **9** And Joab says to Amasa, "Are you [in] peace, my brother?" And the right hand of Joab lays hold on the beard of Amasa to give a kiss to him; **10** and Amasa has not been watchful of the sword that [is] in the hand of Joab, and he strikes him with it to the fifth [rib], and sheds out his bowels to the earth, and he has not repeated [it] to him, and he dies; and Joab and his brother Abishai have pursued after Sheba son of Bichri. **11** And a man has stood by him, of the young men of Joab, and says, "He who has delight in Joab, and he who [is] for David—after Joab!" **12** And Amasa is rolling himself in blood, in the midst of the highway, and the man sees that all the people have stood still, and he brings around Amasa out of the highway to the field, and casts a garment over him when he has seen that everyone who has come by him has stood still. **13** When he has been removed out of the highway, every man has passed on after Joab, to pursue after Sheba son of Bichri. **14** And he passes over through all the tribes of Israel to Abel, and to Beth-Maachah, and to all the Berites, and they are assembled, and also go in after him, **15** and they go in and lay siege against him, in Abel of Beth-Maachah, and cast up a mound against the city, and it stands in a trench, and all the people who are [are] with Joab are destroying, to cause the wall to fall. **16** And a wise woman calls out of the city, "Hear! Hear! Please say to Joab, Come near here, and I speak to you." **17** And he comes near to her, and the woman says, "Are you Joab?" And he says, "I [am]." And she says to him, "Hear the words of your handmaid"; and he says, "I am hearing." **18** And she speaks, saying, "They spoke often in former times, saying, Let them diligently inquire at Abel, and so they finished. **19** I [am] of the peaceable, faithful ones of Israel; you are seeking to destroy a city and mother in Israel; why do you swallow up the inheritance of YHWH?" **20** And Joab answers and says, "Far be it—far be it from me; I do not swallow up nor destroy. **21** The matter [is] not so; for a man of the hill-country of Ephraim—Sheba son of Bichri [is] his name—has lifted up his hand against the king, against David; give him up by himself, and I go away from the city." And the woman says to Joab, "Behold, his head is cast to you over the wall." **22** And the woman comes to all the people in her wisdom, and they cut off the head of Sheba son of Bichri, and cast [it] to Joab, and he blows with a horn, and they are scattered from the city, each [goes] to his tents, and Joab has turned back to Jerusalem to the king. **23** And Joab [is] over all the host of Israel, and Benaiah son of Jehoiada [is] over the Cherethite, and over the Pelethite, **24** and Adoram [is] over the tribute, and Jehoshaphat son of Ahilud [is] the remembrancer, **25** and Sheva [is] scribe, and Zadok and Abiathar [are] priests, **26** and also, Ira the Jairite has been minister to David.

21 And there is a famine in the days of David [for] three years, year after year, and David seeks the face of YHWH, and YHWH says, "[This is] for Saul and for the bloody house, because that he put the Gibeonites to death." **2** And the king calls for the Gibeonites and says to them—as for the Gibeonites, they [are] not of the sons of Israel, but of the remnant of the Amorite, and the sons of Israel had sworn to them, and Saul seeks to strike them in his zeal for the sons of Israel and Judah— **3** indeed, David says to the Gibeonites, "What do I do for you? And with what do I make atonement? And bless the inheritance of YHWH." **4** And the Gibeonites say to him, "We have no silver and gold by Saul and by his house, and we have no man to put to death in Israel"; and he says, "What you are saying I do to you." **5** And they say to the king, "The man who consumed us, and who devised against us—we have been destroyed from stationing ourselves in all the border of Israel— **6** let there be given to us seven men of his sons, and we have hanged them before YHWH, in the height of Saul, the chosen of YHWH." And the king says, "I give"; **7** and the king has pity on Mephibosheth son of Jonathan, son of Saul, because of the oath of YHWH that [is] between them, between David and Jonathan son of Saul; **8** and the king takes the two sons of Rizpah daughter of Aiah, whom she bore to Saul, Armoni and Mephibosheth, and the five sons of Michal daughter of Saul whom she bore to Adriel son of Barzillai the Meholathite, **9** and gives them into the hand of the Gibeonites, and they hang them in the hill before

YHWH; and the seven fall together, and they have been put to death in the days of harvest, in the first [days], the commencement of barley-harvest. **10** And Rizpah daughter of Aiah takes the sackcloth, and stretches it out for herself on the rock, from the commencement of harvest until water has been poured out on them from the heavens, and has not permitted a bird of the heavens to rest on them by day, or the beast of the field by night. **11** And it is declared to David that which Rizpah daughter of Aiah, concubine of Saul, has done, **12** and David goes and takes the bones of Saul, and the bones of his son Jonathan, from the possessors of Jabesh-Gilead, who had stolen them from the broad place of Beth-Shan, where the Philistines hanged them, in the day of the Philistines striking Saul in Gilboa; **13** and he brings up there the bones of Saul, and the bones of his son Jonathan, and they gather the bones of those hanged, **14** and bury the bones of Saul and of his son Jonathan in the land of Benjamin, in Zelah, in the burying-place of his father Kish, and do all that the king commanded, and God accepts the plea for the land afterward. **15** And again the Philistines have war with Israel, and David goes down, and his servants with him, and they fight with the Philistines; and David is weary, **16** and Ishbi-Benob, who [is] among the children of the giant—the weight of his spear [is] three hundred [shekels in] weight of bronze, and he is girded with a new one—speaks of striking David, **17** and Abishai son of Zeruiah gives help to him, and strikes the Philistine, and puts him to death; then the men of David swear to him, saying, "You do not go out with us to battle again, nor quench the lamp of Israel." **18** And it comes to pass afterward that the battle is again in Gob with the Philistines. Then Sibbechai the Hushathite has struck Saph, who [is] among the children of the giant. **19** And the battle is again in Gob with the Philistines, and Elhanan son of Jaare-Oregim, the Beth-Lehemite, strikes [a brother of] Goliath the Gittite, and the wood of his spear [is] like a weavers' beam. **20** And the battle is again in Gath, and there is a man of [great] stature, and the fingers of his hands [are] six, and the toes of his feet [are] six—twenty-four in number, and he has also been born to the giant, **21** and he reproaches Israel, and Jonathan son of Shimeah, David's brother, strikes him; **22** these four have been born to the giant in Gath, and they fall by the hand of David, and by the hand of his servants.

22 And David speaks the words of this song to YHWH in the day YHWH has delivered him out of the hand of all his enemies, and out of the hand of Saul, **2** and he says: "YHWH [is] my rock, ‖ And my bulwark, and a deliverer to me, **3** My God [is] my rock—I take refuge in Him; My shield, and the horn of my salvation, ‖ My high tower, and my refuge! My Savior, You save me from violence! **4** I call on YHWH, [who is worthy] to be praised: And I am saved from my enemies. **5** When the breakers of death surrounded me, ‖ The streams of the worthless terrify me, **6** The cords of Sheol have surrounded me, ‖ The snares of death have been before me. **7** In my adversity I call on YHWH, ‖ And I call to my God, ‖ And He hears my voice from His temple, ‖ And my cry [is] in His ears, **8** And the earth shakes and trembles, ‖ Foundations of the heavens are troubled, ‖ And are shaken, for He has wrath! **9** Smoke has gone up by His nostrils, ‖ And fire devours from His mouth; Brands have been kindled by it. **10** And He inclines the heavens and comes down, ‖ And thick darkness [is] under His feet. **11** And He rides on a cherub and flies, ‖ And is seen on the wings of the wind. **12** And He sets darkness around Him [for His] dwelling places, ‖ Darkness of waters [and] thick clouds of the skies. **13** From the brightness before Him ‖ Brands of fire were kindled! **14** YHWH thunders from the heavens, ‖ And the Most High gives forth His voice. **15** And He sends forth arrows, and scatters them; Lightning, and troubles them; **16** And the streams of the sea are seen, ‖ [The] foundations of the world are revealed, ‖ By the rebuke of YHWH, ‖ From the breath of the spirit of His anger. **17** He sends from above—He takes me, ‖ He draws me out of many waters. **18** He delivers me from my strong enemy, ‖ From those hating me, ‖ For they were stronger than me. **19** They are before me in a day of my calamity, ‖ And YHWH is my support, **20** And He brings me out to a large place, ‖ He draws me out for He delighted in me. **21** YHWH repays me, ‖ According to my righteousness, ‖ According to the cleanness of my hands, He returns to me. **22** For I have kept the ways of YHWH, ‖ And have not done wickedly against my God. **23** For all His judgments [are] before me, ‖ As for His statutes, I do not turn from them. **24** And I am perfect before Him, ‖ And I keep myself from my iniquity. **25** And YHWH returns to me, ‖ According to my righteousness, ‖ According to my cleanness before His eyes. **26** With the kind You show Yourself kind, ‖ With the perfect man You show Yourself perfect, **27** With the pure You show Yourself pure, ‖ And with the perverse You show Yourself a wrestler. **28** And You save the poor people, ‖ But Your eyes on the high cause [them] to fall. **29** For You [are] my lamp, O YHWH, ‖ And YHWH lightens my darkness. **30** For by You I run [against] a troop, ‖ By my God I leap a wall. **31** God—His way [is] perfect, ‖ The saying of YHWH is tried, ‖ He [is] a shield to all those trusting in Him. **32** For who is God except YHWH? And who [is the] Rock except our God? **33** God—my bulwark, [my] strength, ‖ And He makes my way perfect; **34** Making my feet like does, ‖ And causes me to stand on my high places, **35** Teaching my hands for battle, ‖ And a bow of bronze was brought down by my arms, **36** And You give the shield of Your salvation to me, ‖ And Your lowliness makes me great. **37** You enlarge my step under me, ‖ And my ankles have not slipped. **38** I pursue my enemies and destroy them, ‖ And I do not turn until they are consumed. **39** And I consume them, and strike them, ‖ And they do not rise, and fall under my feet. **40** And You gird me [with] strength for battle, ‖ You cause my withstanders to bow under me. **41** And my enemies—You give to me the neck, ‖ Those hating me—and I cut them off. **42** They look, and there is no savior; To YHWH, and He has not answered them. **43** And I beat them as dust of the earth, ‖ As mire of the streets I beat them small—I spread them out! **44** And You deliver me ‖ From the strivings of my people, ‖ You place me for a head of nations; A people I have not known serve me. **45** Sons of a stranger feign obedience to me, ‖ At the hearing of the ear they listen to me. **46** Sons of a stranger fade away, ‖ And gird themselves by their close places. **47** YHWH lives, and blessed [is] my Rock, ‖ And exalted is my God—The Rock of my salvation. **48** God—who is giving vengeance to me, ‖ And bringing down peoples under me, **49** And bringing me forth from my enemies, ‖ Indeed, You raise me up above my withstanders. You deliver me from a man of violence. **50** Therefore I confess You, O YHWH, among nations, ‖ And I sing praise to Your Name. **51** Magnifying the salvations of His king, ‖ And doing loving-kindness to His anointed, ‖ To David, and to his seed—for all time!"

23 And these [are] the last words of David: "A declaration of David son of Jesse, ‖ And a declaration of the man raised up—Concerning the anointed of the God of Jacob, ‖ And the sweetness of the songs of Israel: **2** The Spirit of YHWH has spoken by me, ‖ And His word [is] on my tongue. **3** He said—the God of Israel—to me, ‖ He spoke—the Rock of Israel: He who is ruling over man [is] righteous, ‖ He is ruling in the fear of God. **4** And he rises as the light of morning, ‖ A morning sun [with] no clouds! By the shining, by the rain, ‖ Tender grass of the earth! **5** For though my house [is] not so with God; So He made a perpetual covenant with me, ‖ Arranged in all things, and kept; For all my salvation, and all desire, ‖ For He has not caused [it] to spring up. **6** As for the worthless—All of them [are] driven away as a thorn, ‖ For they are not taken away by hand; **7** And the man who comes against them ‖ Is filled with iron and the staff of a spear, ‖ And they are utterly burned with fire ‖ In the cessation." **8** These [are] the names of the mighty ones whom David has: sitting in the seat [is] the Tachmonite, head of the captains—he [is] Adino, who hardened himself against eight hundred—wounded at one time. **9** And after him [is] Eleazar son of Dodo, son of Ahohi, of the three mighty men with David; in their exposing themselves among the Philistines—they have been gathered there to battle, and the men of Israel go up—**10** he has arisen, and strikes among the Philistines until his hand has been weary, and his hand cleaves to the sword, and YHWH works a great salvation on that day, and the people turn back after him only to strip off. **11** And after him [is] Shammah son of Agee the Hararite, and the Philistines are gathered into a company, and there is a portion of the field full of lentils there, and the people have fled from the presence of the Philistines, **12** and he stations himself in the midst of the portion, and delivers it, and strikes the Philistines, and YHWH works a great salvation. **13** And three of the thirty heads go down and come to the harvest, to David, to the cave of Adullam, and the company of the Philistines are encamping in the Valley of Rephaim, **14** and David [is] then in a fortress, and the station of the Philistines [is] then in Beth-Lehem, **15** and David longs and says, "Who gives me a drink of the water of the well of Beth-Lehem, which [is] by the gate?" **16** And the three mighty ones cleave through the camp of the Philistines, and draw water out of the well of Beth-Lehem, which [is] by the gate, and take [it] up, and bring [it] to David; and he was not willing to drink it, and pours it out to YHWH, **17** and says, "Far be it from me, O YHWH, to do this; is it the blood of the men who are going with their lives?" And he was not willing to drink it; the three mighty ones did these [things]. **18** And Abishai brother of Joab, son of Zeruiah, he [is] head of three, and he is lifting up his spear against three hundred—wounded, and he has a name among three. **19** Is he not the honored of the three? And he becomes their head; and he has not come to the [first] three. **20** And Benaiah son of Jehoiada (son of a man of valor, great in deeds from Kabzeel), has struck two lion-like men of Moab, and he has gone down and struck the lion in the midst of the pit in a day of snow. **21** And he has struck the Egyptian man, a man of appearance, and a spear [is] in the hand of the Egyptian, and he goes down to him with a rod, and takes the spear violently away out of the hand of the Egyptian, and slays him with his own spear. **22** Benaiah son of Jehoiada has done these [things], and has a name among the three mighty ones. **23** He is honored more than the thirty, but he did not come to the three; and David sets him over his guard. **24** Asahel brother of Joab [is] of the thirty; Elhanan son of Dodo of Beth-Lehem, **25** Shammah the Harodite, Elika the Harodite, **26** Helez the Paltite, Ira son of Ikkesh the Tekoite, **27** Abiezer the Annethothite, Mebunnai the Hushathite, **28** Zalmon the Ahohite, Maharai the Netophathite, **29** Heleb son of Baanah the Netophathite, Ittai son of Ribai from Gibeah of the sons of Benjamin, **30** Benaiah the Pirathonite, Hiddai of the brooks of Gaash, **31** Abi-Albon the Arbathite, Azmaveth the Barhumite, **32** Eliahba the Shaalbonite, of the sons of Jashen, Jonathan, **33** Shammah the Hararite, Ahiam son of Sharar the Hararite, **34** Eliphelet son of Ahasbai, son of the Maachathite, Eliam son of Ahithophel the Gilonite, **35** Hezrai the Carmelite, Paarai the Arbite, **36** Igal son of Nathan from Zobah, Bani the Gadite, **37** Zelek the Ammonite, Naharai the Beerothite, bearer of the weapons of Joab son of Zeruiah, **38** Ira the Ithrite, Gareb the Ithrite, **39** Uriah the Hittite: thirty-seven in all.

24 And the anger of YHWH adds to burn against Israel, and [an adversary] moves David about them, saying, "Go, number Israel and Judah." **2** And the king says to Joab, head of the host that [is] with him, "Now go to and fro through all the tribes of Israel, from Dan even to Beer-Sheba, and inspect the people; then I have known the number of the people." **3** And Joab says to the king, "Indeed, your God YHWH adds to the people, as they are, one hundred times, and the eyes of my lord the king are seeing; and my lord the king, why is he desirous of this thing?" **4** And the word of the king is severe toward Joab, and against the heads of the force, and Joab goes out, and the heads of the force, [from] before the king to inspect the people, even Israel; **5** and they pass over the Jordan, and encamp in Aroer, on the right of the city that [is] in the midst of the Brook of Gad, and to Jazer, **6** and they come to Gilead, and to the land of Tahtim-Hodshi, and they come to Dan-Jaan, and around to Sidon, **7** and they come to the fortress of Tyre, and all the cities of the Hivite, and of the Canaanite, and go out to the south of Judah, to Beer-Sheba. **8** And they go to and fro through all the land, and come in to Jerusalem at the end of nine months and twenty days, **9** and Joab gives the account of the inspection of the people to the king, and Israel is eight hundred thousand men of valor, drawing sword, and the men of Judah five hundred thousand men. **10** And the heart of David strikes him, after that he has numbered the people, and David says to YHWH, "I have greatly sinned in that which I have done, and now, O YHWH, please cause the iniquity of Your servant to pass away, for I have acted very foolishly." **11** And David rises in the morning, and the word of YHWH has been to Gad the prophet, seer of David, saying, **12** "Go, and you have spoken to David, Thus said YHWH: I am lifting up three [choices] for you, choose one of them, and I do [it] to you." **13** And Gad comes to David, and declares [it] to him, and says to him, "Does seven years of famine come to you in your land? Or are you fleeing before your adversary [for] three months—and he is pursuing you? Or is there pestilence [for] three days in your land? Now, know and see what word I take back to Him sending me." **14** And David says to Gad, "I have great distress; please let us fall into the hand of YHWH, for His mercies [are] many, but do not let me fall into the hand of man." **15** And YHWH gives a pestilence on Israel from the morning even to the time appointed, and there dies of the people, from Dan even to Beer-Sheba, seventy thousand men, **16** and the messenger puts forth his hand to Jerusalem to destroy it, and YHWH sighs concerning the calamity, and says to the messenger who is destroying among the people, "Enough, now, cease your hand"; and the messenger of YHWH was near the threshing-floor of Araunah the Jebusite. **17** And David speaks to YHWH when he sees the messenger who is striking among the people, and says, "Behold, I have sinned, indeed, I have done perversely; and these—the flock—what have they done? Please let Your hand be on me and on the house of my father." **18** And Gad comes to David on that day and says to him, "Go up, raise an altar to YHWH in the threshing-floor of Araunah the Jebusite"; **19** and David goes up, according to the word of Gad, as YHWH commanded. **20** And Araunah looks, and sees the king and his servants passing over to him, and Araunah goes out and bows himself to the king [with] his face to the earth. **21** And Araunah says, "Why has my lord the king come to his servant?" And David says, "To buy the threshing-floor from you, to build an altar to YHWH, and the plague is restrained from the people." **22** And Araunah says to David, "Let my lord the king take [it] and cause that which is good in his eyes to ascend; see, [here are] the oxen for a burnt-offering, and the threshing instruments, and the instruments of the oxen, for wood"; **23** Araunah has given the whole [as] a king to a king; and Araunah says to the king, "Your God YHWH accepts you." **24** And the king says to Araunah, "No, for I surely buy from you for a price, and I do not cause burnt-offerings to ascend to my God YHWH for nothing"; and David buys the threshing-floor and the oxen for fifty shekels of silver, **25** and David builds an altar to YHWH there, and causes burnt-offerings and peace-offerings to ascend, and YHWH accepts the plea for the land, and the plague is restrained from Israel.

1 KINGS

1 And King David [is] old, entering into days, and they cover him with garments, and he has no heat, **2** and his servants say to him, "Let them seek [for] a young woman, a virgin, for my lord the king, and she has stood before the king, and is a companion to him, and has lain in your bosom, and my lord the king has heat." **3** And they seek [for] a beautiful young woman in all the border of Israel, and find Abishag the Shunammite, and bring her to the king, **4** and the young woman [is] very, very beautiful, and she is a companion to the king, and serves him, and the king has not known her. **5** And Adonijah son of Haggith is lifting himself up, saying, "I reign"; and he prepares for himself a chariot and horsemen, and fifty men running before him, **6** and his father has not grieved him [all] his days, saying, "Why have you done this?" And he also [is] of a very good form, and [his mother] bore him after Absalom. **7** And his words are with Joab son of Zeruiah, and with Abiathar the priest, and they help after Adonijah; **8** and Zadok the priest, and Benaiah son of Jehoiada, and Nathan the prophet, and Shimei, and Rei, and the mighty ones whom David has, have not been with Adonijah. **9** And Adonijah sacrifices sheep and oxen and fatlings near the stone of Zoheleth that [is] by En-Rogel, and calls all his brothers, sons of the king, and for all the men of Judah, servants of the king; **10** and he has not called Nathan the prophet, and Benaiah, and the mighty ones, and his brother Solomon. **11** And Nathan speaks to Bathsheba, mother of Solomon, saying, "Have you not heard that Adonijah son of Haggith has reigned, and our lord David has not known? **12** And now, come, please let me counsel you, and deliver your life and the life of your son Solomon; **13** go and enter in to King David, and you have said to him: Have you not, my lord, O king, sworn to your handmaid, saying, Surely your son Solomon reigns after me, and he sits on my throne? And why has Adonijah reigned? **14** Behold, you are yet speaking there with the king, and I come in after you, and have completed your words." **15** And Bathsheba comes in to the king, [into] the inner chamber, and the king [is] very aged, and Abishag the Shunammite is serving the king; **16** and Bathsheba bows and pays respect to the king, and the king says, "What do you [want]?" **17** And she says to him, "My lord, you have sworn by your God YHWH to your handmaid, [saying], Surely your son Solomon reigns after me, and he sits on my throne; **18** and now, behold, Adonijah has reigned, and now, my lord, O king, you have not known; **19** and he sacrifices ox, and fatling, and sheep in abundance, and calls for all the sons of the king, and for Abiathar the priest, and for Joab head of the host—and he has not called for your servant Solomon. **20** And you, my lord, O king, the eyes of all Israel [are] on you, to declare to them who sit on the throne of my lord the king after him; **21** and it has been, when my lord the king lies with his fathers, that I have been, I and my son Solomon—[reckoned] sinners." **22** And behold, she is yet speaking with the king, and Nathan the prophet has come in; **23** and they declare to the king, saying, "Behold, Nathan the prophet"; and he comes in before the king, and bows himself to the king, on his face to the earth. **24** And Nathan says, "My lord, O king, you have said, Adonijah reigns after me, and he sits on my throne; **25** for he has gone down today, and sacrifices ox, and fatling, and sheep, in abundance, and calls for all the sons of the king, and for the heads of the host, and for Abiathar the priest, and behold, they are eating and drinking before him, and they say, Let King Adonijah live! **26** But he has not called for me, your servant, and for Zadok the priest, and for Benaiah, son of Jehoiada, and for your servant Solomon; **27** if this thing has been from my lord the king, then you have not caused your servant to know who sits on the throne of my lord the king after him." **28** And King David answers and says, "Call for Bathsheba for me"; and she comes in before the king, and stands before the king. **29** And the king swears and says, "YHWH lives, who has redeemed my soul out of all adversity; **30** surely as I swore to you by YHWH, God of Israel, saying, Surely your son Solomon reigns after me, and he sits on my throne in my stead; surely so I do this day." **31** And Bathsheba bows—face to the

1 KINGS

earth—and pays respect to the king, and says, "Let my lord, King David, live for all time." **32** And King David says, "Call for Zadok the priest, and for Nathan the prophet, and for Benaiah son of Jehoiada for me"; and they come in before the king. **33** And the king says to them, "Take the servants of your lord with you, and you have caused my son Solomon to ride on my own mule, and caused him to go down to Gihon, **34** and Zadok the priest has anointed him there—and Nathan the prophet—for king over Israel, and you have blown with a horn and said, Let King Solomon live; **35** and you have come up after him, and he has come in and has sat on my throne, and he reigns in my stead, and I have appointed him to be leader over Israel, and over Judah." **36** And Benaiah son of Jehoiada answers the king and says, "Amen! So does YHWH, God of my lord the king, say; **37** as YHWH has been with my lord the king, so is He with Solomon, and makes his throne greater than the throne of my lord King David." **38** And Zadok the priest goes down, and Nathan the prophet, and Benaiah son of Jehoiada, and the Cherethite, and the Pelethite, and they cause Solomon to ride on the mule of King David, and cause him to go to Gihon, **39** and Zadok the priest takes the horn of oil out of the tent, and anoints Solomon, and they blow with a horn, and all the people say, "Let King Solomon live." **40** And all the people come up after him, and the people are piping with pipes, and rejoicing [with] great joy, and the earth splits with their voice. **41** And Adonijah hears, and all those called who [are] with him, and they have finished to eat, and Joab hears the noise of the horn and says, "Why [is] the noise of the city roaring?" **42** He is yet speaking, and behold, Jonathan son of Abiathar the priest has come in, and Adonijah says, "Come in, for you [are] a man of valor, and you bear good tidings." **43** And Jonathan answers and says to Adonijah, "Truly our lord King David has caused Solomon to reign, **44** and the king sends with him Zadok the priest, and Nathan the prophet, and Benaiah son of Jehoiada, and the Cherethite, and the Pelethite, and they cause him to ride on the king's mule, **45** and they anoint him—Zadok the priest and Nathan the prophet—for king in Gihon, and have come up there rejoicing, and the city is moved; it [is] the noise that you have heard. **46** And also Solomon has sat on the throne of the kingdom, **47** and also the servants of the king have come into bless our lord King David, saying, Your God makes the name of Solomon better than your name, and his throne greater than your throne; and the king bows himself on the bed, **48** and also thus the king has said, Blessed [is] YHWH, God of Israel, who has given [one] sitting on my throne today, and my eyes are seeing." **49** And they tremble, and rise—all those called who [are] for Adonijah—and go, each on his way; **50** and Adonijah fears because of Solomon, and rises, and goes, and lays hold on the horns of the altar. **51** And it is declared to Solomon, saying, "Behold, Adonijah fears King Solomon, and behold, he has laid hold on the horns of the altar, saying, Let King Solomon swear to me as today—he does not put his servant to death by the sword." **52** And Solomon says, "If he becomes a virtuous man—there does not fall [even one] hair of his to the earth, and if evil is found in him—then he has died." **53** And King Solomon sends, and they bring him down from off the altar, and he comes in and bows himself to King Solomon, and Solomon says to him, "Go to your house."

2 And the days of David to die draw near, and he charges his son Solomon, saying, **2** "I am going in the way of all the earth, and you have been strong, and become a man, **3** and you have kept the charge of your God YHWH, to walk in His ways, to keep His statutes, His commands, and His judgments, and His testimonies, as it is written in the Law of Moses, so that you do wisely [in] all that you do, and wherever you turn, **4** so that YHWH establishes His word which He spoke to me, saying, If your sons observe their way to walk before Me in truth, with all their heart, and with all their soul; saying, A man of yours is never cut off from the throne of Israel. **5** And also, you have known that which he did to me—Joab son of Zeruiah—that which he did to two heads of the hosts of Israel, to Abner son of Ner, and to Amasa son of Jether—that he slays them, and makes the blood of war in peace, and puts the blood of war in his girdle, that [is] on his loins, and in his sandals that [are] on his feet; **6** and you have done according to your wisdom, and do not let his old age go down in peace to Sheol. **7** And you do kindness to the sons of Barzillai the Gileadite, and they have been among those eating at your table, for so they drew near to me in my fleeing from the face of your brother Absalom. **8** And behold, Shimei son of Gera, the Benjamite of Bahurim, [is] with you, and he reviled me—a grievous reviling—in the day of my going to Mahanaim; and he has come down to meet me at the Jordan, and I swear to him by YHWH, saying, I do not put you to death by the sword; **9** and now, do not acquit him, for you [are] a wise man, and you have known that which you do to him, and have brought down his old age with blood to Sheol." **10** And David lies down with his fathers, and is buried in the City of David, **11** and the days that David has reigned over Israel [are] forty years; he has reigned seven years in Hebron, and he has reigned thirty-three years in Jerusalem. **12** And Solomon has sat on the throne of his father David, and his kingdom is established greatly, **13** and Adonijah son of Haggith comes to Bathsheba, mother of Solomon, and she says, "Is your coming peace?" And he says, "Peace." **14** And he says, "I have a word for you," and she says, "Speak." **15** And he says, "You have known that the kingdom was mine, and all Israel had set their faces toward me for reigning, and the kingdom is turned around, and is my brother's, for it was his from YHWH; **16** and now, I am asking one petition of you—do not turn back my face"; and she says to him, "Speak." **17** And he says, "Please speak to Solomon the king, for he does not turn back your face, and he gives Abishag the Shunammite to me for a wife." **18** And Bathsheba says, "Good; I speak to the king for you." **19** And Bathsheba comes to King Solomon to speak to him for Adonijah, and the king rises to meet her, and bows himself to her, and sits on his throne, and places a throne for the mother of the king, and she sits at his right hand. **20** And she says, "I ask one small petition of you, do not turn back my face"; and the king says to her, "Ask, my mother, for I do not turn back your face." **21** And she says, "Let Abishag the Shunammite be given to your brother Adonijah for a wife." **22** And King Solomon answers and says to his mother, "And why are you asking [for] Abishag the Shunammite for Adonijah? Also ask [for] the kingdom for him—for he [is] my elder brother—even for him, and for Abiathar the priest, and for Joab son of Zeruiah." **23** And King Solomon swears by YHWH, saying, "Thus God does to me, and thus He adds—surely Adonijah has spoken this word against his [own] soul; **24** and now, YHWH lives, who has established me, and causes me to sit on the throne of my father David, and who has made a house for me as He spoke—surely Adonijah is put to death today." **25** And King Solomon sends by the hand of Benaiah son of Jehoiada, and he falls on him, and he dies. **26** And the king said to Abiathar the priest, "Go to Anathoth, to your fields; for you [are] a man of death, but I do not put you to death in this day, because you have carried the Ark of Lord YHWH before my father David, and because you were afflicted in all that my father was afflicted in." **27** And Solomon casts out Abiathar from being priest of YHWH, to fulfill the word of YHWH which He spoke concerning the house of Eli in Shiloh. **28** And the report has come to Joab—for Joab has turned aside after Adonijah, though he did not turn aside after Absalom—and Joab flees to the tent of YHWH, and lays hold on the horns of the altar. **29** And it is declared to King Solomon that Joab has fled to the tent of YHWH, and behold, [is] near the altar; and Solomon sends Benaiah son of Jehoiada, saying, "Go, fall on him." **30** And Benaiah comes into the tent of YHWH and says to him, "Thus said the king: Come out"; and he says, "No, but I die here." And Benaiah brings back word [to] the king, saying, "Thus spoke Joab, indeed, thus he answered me." **31** And the king says to him, "Do as he has spoken, and fall on him, and you have buried him, and turned aside the causeless blood which Joab shed from off me, and from off the house of my father; **32** and YHWH has turned back his blood on his own head, [on him] who has fallen on two men more righteous and better than he, and slays them with the sword—and my father David did not know—Abner son of Ner, head of the host of Israel, and Amasa son of Jether, head of the host of Judah; **33** indeed, their blood has turned back on the head of Joab, and on the head of his seed for all time; and for David, and for his seed, and for his house, and for his throne, there is peace for all time, from YHWH." **34** And Benaiah son of Jehoiada goes up and falls on him, and puts

1 KINGS

him to death, and he is buried in his own house in the wilderness, **35** and the king puts Benaiah son of Jehoiada over the host in his stead, and the king has put Zadok the priest in the stead of Abiathar. **36** And the king sends and calls for Shimei, and says to him, "Build a house for yourself in Jerusalem, and you have dwelt there, and do not go out [from] there anywhere; **37** and it has been, in the day of your going out, and you have passed over the Brook of Kidron, you certainly know that you surely die—your blood is on your head." **38** And Shimei says to the king, "The word [is] good; as my lord the king has spoken so your servant does"; and Shimei dwells in Jerusalem many days. **39** And it comes to pass, at the end of three years, that two of the servants of Shimei flee to Achish son of Maachah, king of Gath, and they declare to Shimei, saying, "Behold, your servants [are] in Gath"; **40** and Shimei rises, and saddles his donkey, and goes to Gath, to Achish, to seek his servants, and Shimei goes and brings his servants from Gath. **41** And it is declared to Solomon that Shimei has gone from Jerusalem to Gath, and returns, **42** and the king sends and calls for Shimei, and says to him, "Have I not caused you to swear by YHWH—and I testify against you, saying, In the day of your going out, and you have gone anywhere, you certainly know that you surely die; and you say to me, The word I have heard [is] good? **43** And why have you not kept the oath of YHWH, and the charge that I charged on you?" **44** And the king says to Shimei, "You have known all the evil that your heart has known, which you did to my father David, and YHWH has turned back your evil on your head, **45** and King Solomon [is] blessed, and the throne of David is established before YHWH for all time." **46** And the king charges Benaiah son of Jehoiada, and he goes out and falls on him, and he dies, and the kingdom is established in the hand of Solomon.

3 And Solomon joins in marriage with Pharaoh king of Egypt, and takes the daughter of Pharaoh, and brings her to the City of David, until he completes to build his own house, and the house of YHWH, and the wall of Jerusalem all around. **2** Only, the people are sacrificing in high places, for there has not been built a house for the Name of YHWH until those days. **3** And Solomon loves YHWH, to walk in the statutes of his father David—only, he is sacrificing and making incense in high places— **4** and the king goes to Gibeon, to sacrifice there, for it [is] the great high place; Solomon causes one thousand burnt-offerings to ascend on that altar. **5** YHWH has appeared to Solomon in Gibeon, in a dream of the night, and God says, "Ask—what do I give to you?" **6** And Solomon says, "You have done with Your servant, my father David, great kindness, as he walked before You in truth and in righteousness, and in uprightness of heart with You, and You keep this great kindness for him, and give to him a son sitting on his throne, as [at] this day. **7** And now, O YHWH my God, You have caused Your servant to reign instead of my father David; and I [am] a little child, I do not know [how] to go out and to come in; **8** and Your servant [is] in the midst of your people, whom You have chosen, a people numerous, that is not numbered nor counted for multitude, **9** and You have given an understanding heart to Your servant, to judge Your people, to discern between good and evil; for who is able to judge this great people of Yours?" **10** And the thing is good in the eyes of the Lord, that Solomon has asked this thing, **11** and God says to him, "Because that you have asked for this thing, and have not asked for many days for yourself, nor asked for riches for yourself, nor asked for the life of your enemies, and have asked for discernment for yourself to understand judgment, **12** behold, I have done according to your words; behold, I have given a wise and understanding heart to you, that there has not been [one] like you before you, and after you there does not arise [one] like you; **13** and also, that which you have not asked for I have given to you, both riches and honor, that there has not been a man like you among the kings [for] all your days; **14** and if you walk in My ways to keep My statutes, and My commands, as your father David walked, then I have prolonged your days." **15** And Solomon awakens, and behold, [it was] a dream; and he comes to Jerusalem, and stands before the Ark of the Covenant of YHWH, and causes burnt-offerings to ascend, and makes peace-offerings, and he makes a banquet for all his servants. **16** Then two women, harlots, come to the king, and they stand before him, **17** and the first woman says, "O my lord, this woman and I are dwelling in one house, and I bring forth with her, in the house; **18** and it comes to pass on the third day of my bringing forth, that this woman also brings forth, and we [are] together, there is no stranger with us in the house, except the two of us, in the house. **19** And the son of this woman dies at night, because she has lain on him, **20** and she rises in the middle of the night, and takes my son from beside me—and your handmaid is asleep—and lays him in her bosom, and she has laid her dead son in my bosom; **21** and I rise in the morning to suckle my son, and behold, [he is] dead; and I consider in the morning concerning it, and behold, it was not my son whom I bore." **22** And the other woman says, "No, but my son [is] the living, and your son the dead"; and this [one] says, "No, but your son [is] the dead, and my son the living." And they speak before the king. **23** And the king says, "This [one] says, This [is] my son, the living, and your son [is] the dead; and that [one] says, No, but your son [is] the dead, and my son the living." **24** And the king says, "Take a sword for me"; and they bring the sword before the king, **25** and the king says, "Cut the living child into two, and give half to one, and half to the other." **26** And the woman whose son [is] the living one says to the king (for her bowels yearned over her son), indeed, she says, "O my lord, give the living child to her, and do not put him to death at all"; and this [one] says, "Let him be neither mine or yours—cut [him]." **27** And the king answers and says, "Give the living child to her [who wants him], and do not put him to death at all; she [is] his mother." **28** And all [in] Israel hear of the judgment that the king has judged, and fear because of the king, for they have seen that the wisdom of God [is] in his heart to do judgment.

4 And King Solomon is king over all Israel, **2** and these [are] the heads whom he has: Azariah son of Zadok [is] the priest; **3** Elihoreph and Ahiah sons of Shisha [are] scribes; Jehoshaphat son of Ahilud [is] remembrancer; **4** and Benaiah son of Jehoiada [is] over the host; and Zadok and Abiathar [are] priests; **5** and Azariah son of Nathan [is] over the officers; and Zabud son of Nathan [is] minister, friend of the king; **6** and Ahishar [is] over the household, and Adoniram son of Abda [is] over the tribute. **7** And Solomon has twelve officers over all Israel, and they have sustained the king and his household—a month in the year is on each one for sustenance; **8** and these [are] their names: Ben-Hur in the hill-country of Ephraim; **9** Ben-Dekar in Makaz, and Shaalbim, and Beth-Shemesh, and Elon-Beth-Hanan; **10** Ben-Hesed, in Aruboth, has Sochoh and all the land of Hepher; **11** Ben-Abinadab [has] all the elevation of Dor; Taphath daughter of Solomon became his wife; **12** Baana Ben-Ahilud [has] Taanach and Megiddo, and all Beth-Shean, which [is] by Zartanah beneath Jezreel, from Beth-Shean to Abel-Meholah, to beyond Jokneam; **13** Ben-Geber, in Ramoth-Gilead, has the small towns of Jair son of Manasseh, which [are] in Gilead; he has a portion of Argob that [is] in Bashan—sixty great cities [with] wall and bronze bar; **14** Ahinadab son of Iddo [has] Mahanaim; **15** Ahimaaz [is] in Naphtali; he also has taken Basemath daughter of Solomon for a wife; **16** Baanah Ben-Hushai [is] in Asher, and in Aloth; **17** Jehoshaphat Ben-Paruah [is] in Issachar; **18** Shimei Ben-Elah [is] in Benjamin; **19** Geber Ben-Uri [is] in the land of Gilead, the land of Sihon king of the Amorite, and of Og king of Bashan: and [he is] the one officer who [is] in the land. **20** Judah and Israel [are] many, as the sand that [is] by the sea for multitude, eating and drinking and rejoicing. **21** And Solomon has been ruling over all the kingdoms, from the River [to] the land of the Philistines and to the border of Egypt: they are bringing a present near, and serving Solomon, all [the] days of his life. **22** And the provision of Solomon for one day is thirty cors of flour, and sixty cors of meal, **23** ten fat oxen, and twenty feeding oxen, and one hundred sheep, apart from deer, and roe, and fallow-deer, and fatted beasts of the stalls, **24** for he is ruling over all beyond the river, from Tiphsah and to Gaza, over all the kings beyond the River, and he has peace from all his surrounding servants. **25** And Judah dwells—and Israel—in confidence, each under his vine, and under his fig tree, from Dan even to Beer-Sheba, all the days of Solomon. **26** And Solomon has forty thousand stalls of horses for his chariots, and twelve thousand horsemen. **27** And these officers have sustained King

1 KINGS

Solomon and everyone drawing near to the table of King Solomon, each [in] his month; they let nothing be lacking. **28** And the barley and the straw, for horses and for dromedaries, they bring to the place where they are, each according to his ordinance. **29** And God gives very much wisdom and understanding to Solomon, and breadth of heart, as the sand that [is] on the edge of the sea; **30** and the wisdom of Solomon is greater than the wisdom of any of the sons of the east, and [greater] than all the wisdom of Egypt; **31** and he is wiser than all men, [wiser] than Ethan the Ezrahite, and Heman, and Chalcol, and Darda, sons of Mahol, and his name is in all the surrounding nations. **32** And he speaks three thousand allegories, and his songs [are] one thousand and five; **33** and he speaks concerning the trees, from the cedar that [is] in Lebanon, even to the hyssop that is coming out in the wall, and he speaks concerning the livestock, and concerning the bird, and concerning the creeping things, and concerning the fishes, **34** and there come out [those] of all the peoples to hear the wisdom of Solomon, from all kings of the earth who have heard of his wisdom.

5 And Hiram king of Tyre sends his servants to Solomon, for he heard that they had anointed him for king instead of his father, for Hiram was loving toward David all the days; **2** and Solomon sends to Hiram, saying, **3** "You have known my father David, that he has not been able to build a house for the Name of his God YHWH, because of the wars that have been all around him, until YHWH's putting them under the soles of his feet. **4** And now, my God YHWH has given rest to me all around, there is no adversary nor evil occurrence, **5** and behold, I am saying to build a house for the Name of my God YHWH, as YHWH spoke to my father David, saying, Your son whom I appoint in your stead on your throne, he builds the house for My Name. **6** And now, command, and they cut down cedars for me out of Lebanon, and my servants are with your servants, and I give the hire of your servants to you according to all that you say, for you have known that there is not a man among us acquainted with cutting wood, like the Sidonians." **7** And it comes to pass at Hiram's hearing the words of Solomon, that he rejoices exceedingly and says, "Blessed [is] YHWH today, who has given to David a wise son over this numerous people." **8** And Hiram sends to Solomon, saying, "I have heard that which you have sent to me, I do all your desire concerning cedar-wood and fir-wood; **9** my servants bring [them] down from Lebanon to the sea, and I make them floats in the sea to the place that you send to me, and I have spread them out there; and you take [them] up, and you execute my desire, to give the food [for] my house." **10** And Hiram is giving cedar-trees and fir-trees to Solomon—all his desire, **11** and Solomon has given twenty thousand cors of wheat to Hiram, [the] food for his house, and twenty cors of beaten oil; thus Solomon gives to Hiram year by year. **12** And YHWH has given wisdom to Solomon as He spoke to him, and there is peace between Hiram and Solomon, and both of them make a covenant. **13** And King Solomon lifts up a tribute out of all Israel, and the tribute is thirty thousand men, **14** and he sends them to Lebanon, ten thousand a month, by changes; they are in Lebanon [for] a month [and] two months in their own house; and Adoniram [is] over the tribute. **15** And King Solomon has seventy thousand bearing burdens, and eighty thousand hewing in the mountain, **16** apart from the three thousand and three hundred heads of the officers of Solomon who [are] over the work—those ruling over the people who are working in the business. **17** And the king commands, and they bring great stones, precious stones, [and] hewn stones, to lay the foundation of the house; **18** and the builders of Solomon, and the builders of Hiram, and the Giblites hew [them], and prepare the wood and the stones to build the house.

6 And it comes to pass, in the four hundred and eightieth year of the going out of the sons of Israel from the land of Egypt, in the fourth year—in the month of Ziv, it [is] the second month—of the reigning of Solomon over Israel, that he builds the house for YHWH. **2** As for the house that King Solomon has built for YHWH, its length [is] sixty cubits, and its breadth twenty, and its height thirty cubits. **3** As for the porch on the front of the temple of the house, its length [is] twenty cubits on the front of the breadth of the house; its breadth [is] ten by the cubit on the front of

1 KINGS

the house; **4** and he makes frames of narrowing windows for the house. **5** And he builds a couch against the wall of the house all around, [even] the walls of the house all around, of the temple and of the oracle, and makes sides all around. **6** The lowest couch, its breadth [is] five by the cubit; and the middle, its breadth [is] six by the cubit; and the third, its breadth [is] seven by the cubit, for he has put withdrawings of the house all around outside—not to lay hold on the walls of the house. **7** And the house, in its being built, has been built of perfect stone [that was] brought; and hammer and the axe—any instrument of iron—was not heard in the house in its being built. **8** The opening of the middle side [is] at the right shoulder of the house, and with windings they go up on the middle one, and from the middle one to the third. **9** And he builds the house, and completes it, and covers the house [with] beams and rows of cedars. **10** And he builds the couch against all the house, its breadth [is] five cubits, and it takes hold of the house by cedar-wood. **11** And the word of YHWH is to Solomon, saying, **12** "This house that you are building—if you walk in My statutes, and do My judgments, indeed, have done all My commands, to walk in them, then I have established My word with you, which I spoke to your father David, **13** and have dwelt in the midst of the sons of Israel, and do not forsake My people Israel." **14** And Solomon builds the house and completes it; **15** and he builds the walls of the house within with beams of cedar, from the floor of the house to the walls of the ceiling; he has overlaid the inside with wood, and covers the floor of the house with ribs of fir. **16** And he builds the twenty cubits on the sides of the house with ribs of cedar, from the floor to the walls; and he builds for it within, for the oracle, for the Holy of Holies. **17** And [this area of] the house was forty by the cubit; it [is the area of] the temple before My face. **18** And the cedar for the house within [is] carvings of knobs and openings of flowers; the whole [is] cedar, there is not a stone seen. **19** And he has prepared the oracle in the midst of the house within, to put the Ark of the Covenant of YHWH there. **20** And before the oracle [is] twenty cubits in length, and twenty cubits in breadth, and its height [is] twenty cubits; and he overlays it with gold refined, and overlays the altar with cedar. **21** And Solomon overlays the house within with gold refined, and causes [it] to pass over in chains of gold before the oracle, and overlays it with gold. **22** And he has overlaid the whole of the house with gold, until the completion of all the house; and the whole of the altar that the oracle has, he has overlaid with gold. **23** And he makes two cherubim of the oil-tree within the oracle; their height [is] ten cubits; **24** and the first wing of the cherub [is] five cubits, and the second wing of the cherub five cubits—ten cubits from the ends of his wings even to the ends of his wings; **25** and the second cherub [is] ten by the cubit; one measure and one form [are] of the two cherubim, **26** the height of the first cherub [is] ten by the cubit, and so [is] the second cherub; **27** and he sets the cherubim in the midst of the inner house, and they spread out the wings of the cherubim, and a wing of the first comes against the wall, and a wing of the second cherub is coming against the second wall, and their wings [stretched] into the midst of the house, coming wing against wing; **28** and he overlays the cherubim with gold, **29** and he has carved all around the walls of the house with engravings of carvings, cherubim, and palm trees, and openings of flowers, inside and outside. **30** And he has overlaid the floor of the house with gold, inside and outside; **31** as for the opening of the oracle, he made doors of the oil-tree; the lintel [and] doorposts [are] a fifth [of the wall]. **32** And the two doors [are] of the oil-tree, and he has carved on them carvings of cherubim, and palm-trees, and openings of flowers, and overlaid with gold, and he causes the gold to go down on the cherubim and on the palm-trees. **33** And so he has made for the opening of the temple, doorposts of the oil-tree, from the fourth [of the wall]. **34** And the two doors [are] of fir-tree, the two sides of the first door are revolving, and the two hangings of the second door are revolving. **35** And he has carved cherubim, and palms, and openings of flowers, and overlaid the carved work with straightened gold. **36** And he builds the inner court, three rows of hewn work, and a row of beams of cedar. **37** In the fourth year the house of YHWH has been founded, in the month of Ziv, **38** and in the eleventh year, in the month of Bul (the eighth month), the house has been finished

1 KINGS

in all its matters, and in all its ordinances, and he builds it [in] seven years.

7 And Solomon has built his own house [in] thirteen years, and he finishes all his house. **2** And he builds the House of the Forest of Lebanon; its length [is] one hundred cubits, and its breadth fifty cubits, and its height thirty cubits, on four rows of cedar pillars, and cedar-beams on the pillars; **3** and [it is] covered with cedar above, on the sides that [are] on the forty-five pillars, fifteen in the row. **4** And frames [are] in three rows, and window [is] toward window three times. **5** And all the openings and the doorposts [are of] square frame; and window [is] toward window three times. **6** And he has made the porch of the pillars; its length fifty cubits, and its breadth thirty cubits, and the porch [is] before them, and pillars and a thick place [are] before them. **7** And the porch of the throne where he judges—the porch of judgment—he has made, and [it is] covered with cedar from the floor to the floor. **8** As for his house where he dwells, the other court [is] within the porch—it has been as this work; and he makes a house for the daughter of Pharaoh—whom Solomon has taken—like this porch. **9** All these [are] of precious stones, according to the measures of hewn work, sawn with a saw, inside and outside, even from the foundation to the coping, and at the outside, to the great court. **10** And the foundation [is] of precious stones, great stones, stones of ten cubits, and stones of eight cubits; **11** and precious stones [are] above, according to the measures of hewn work, and cedar; **12** and the great court around [is] three rows of hewn work, and a row of cedar-beams, even for the inner court of the house of YHWH, and for the porch of the house. **13** And King Solomon sends and takes Hiram out of Tyre— **14** he [is the] son of a woman, a widow, of the tribe of Naphtali, and his father [is] a man of Tyre, a worker in bronze, and he is filled with the wisdom and the understanding, and the knowledge to do all work in bronze—and he comes to King Solomon, and does all his work. **15** And he forms the two pillars of bronze; eighteen cubits [is] the height of the first pillar, and a cord of twelve cubits goes around the second pillar. **16** And he has made two chapiters to put on the tops of the pillars, cast in bronze; five cubits the height of the first capital, and five cubits the height of the second capital. **17** Nets of network, wreaths of chain-work [are] for the chapiters that [are] on the top of the pillars, seven for the first capital, and seven for the second capital. **18** And he makes the pillars, and two rows around on the one network, to cover the chapiters that [are] on the top, with the pomegranates, and so he has made for the second capital. **19** And the chapiters that [are] on the top of the pillars [are] of lily-work in the porch, four cubits; **20** and the chapiters on the two pillars also [have pomegranates] above, close by the protuberance that [is] beside the net; and the pomegranates [are] two hundred, in rows around on the second capital. **21** And he raises up the pillars for the porch of the temple, and he raises up the right pillar, and calls its name Jachin, and he raises up the left pillar, and calls its name Boaz; **22** and on the top of the pillars [is] lily-work; and the work of the pillars [is] completed. **23** And he makes the molten sea, ten by the cubit from its edge to its edge; [it is] round all about, and its height [is] five by the cubit, and a line of thirty by the cubit surrounds it around; **24** and knobs beneath its brim around are going around it, ten by the cubit, going around the sea; the knobs [are] in two rows, cast in its being cast. **25** It is standing on twelve oxen, three facing the north, and three facing the west, and three facing the south, and three facing the east, and the sea [is] on them above, and all their back parts [are] inward. **26** And its thickness [is] a handbreadth, and its edge [is] as the work of the edge of a cup, [as] flowers of lilies; it contains two thousand baths. **27** And he makes the ten bases of bronze; the length of the one base [is] four by the cubit, and its breadth [is] four by the cubit, and its height [is] three by the cubit. **28** And this [is] the work of the base: they have borders, and the borders [are] between the joinings; **29** and on the borders that [are] between the joinings [are] lions, oxen, and cherubim, and on the joinings a base above, and beneath the lions and the oxen [are] additions—sloping work. **30** And four wheels of bronze [are] for the one base, and axles of bronze; and its four corners have shoulders—the molten shoulders [are] under the laver, beside each addition. **31** And its mouth within the capital and above [is] by the cubit, and its mouth [is] round, the work of the base, a cubit and half

1 KINGS

a cubit; and also on its mouth [are] carvings and their borders, square, not round. **32** And the four wheels [are] under the borders, and the spokes of the wheels [are] in the base, and the height of the one wheel [is] a cubit and half a cubit. **33** And the work of the wheels [is] as the work of the wheel of a chariot, their spokes, and their axles, and their felloes, and their naves; the whole [is] molten. **34** And four shoulders [are] for the four corners of the one base; its shoulders [are] out of the base. **35** And in the top of the base [is] the half of a cubit in the height all around; and on the top of the base its spokes and its borders [are] of the same. **36** And he engraves on the tablets of its spokes, and on its borders, cherubim, lions, and palm-trees, according to the void space of each, and additions all around. **37** Thus he has made the ten bases; they all have one casting, one measure, one form. **38** And he makes ten lavers of bronze; the one laver contains forty baths [and] the one laver [is] four by the cubit; one laver on the one base [is] for [each of] the ten bases; **39** and he puts the five bases on the right side of the house, and five on the left side of the house, and he has put the sea on the right side of the house eastward—from toward the south. **40** And Hiram makes the lavers, and the shovels, and the bowls; and Hiram completes to do all the work that he made for King Solomon, [for] the house of YHWH: **41** two pillars, and bowls of the chapiters that [are] on the top of the two pillars, and the two nets to cover the two bowls of the chapiters that [are] on the top of the pillars; **42** and the four hundred pomegranates for the two nets (two rows of pomegranates for the one net to cover the two bowls of the chapiters that [are] on the front of the pillars); **43** and the ten bases, and the ten lavers on the bases; **44** and the one sea, the twelve oxen under the sea, **45** and the pots, and the shovels, and the bowls; and all these vessels, that Hiram has made for King Solomon [for] the house of YHWH, [are] of polished bronze. **46** The king has cast them in the circuit of the Jordan, in the thick soil of the ground, between Succoth and Zarthan. **47** And Solomon places the whole of the vessels; because of the very great abundance, the weight of the bronze has not been searched out. **48** And Solomon makes all the vessels that [are] in the house of YHWH: the altar of gold, and the table of gold (on which [is] the Bread of the Presentation), **49** and the lampstands, five on the right, and five on the left, before the oracle, of refined gold, and the flowers, and the lamps, and the tongs, of gold, **50** and the basins, and the snuffers, and the bowls, and the spoons, and the censers, of refined gold, and the hinges for the doors of the inner-house, for the Holy of Holies, for the doors of the house of the temple, of gold. **51** And it is complete—all the work that King Solomon has made [for] the house of YHWH, and Solomon brings in the sanctified things of his father David; he has put the silver, and the gold, and the vessels in the treasuries of the house of YHWH.

8 Then Solomon assembles the elderly of Israel, and all the heads of the tribes, princes of the fathers of the sons of Israel, to King Solomon, to Jerusalem, to bring up the Ark of the Covenant of YHWH from the City of David—it [is] Zion; **2** and all the men of Israel are assembled to King Solomon, in the month of Ethanim, in the festival (the seventh month). **3** And all [the] elderly of Israel come in, and the priests lift up the Ark, **4** and bring up the Ark of YHWH, and the Tent of Meeting, and all the holy vessels that [are] in the tent, indeed, the priests and the Levites bring them up. **5** And King Solomon and all the congregation of Israel who are assembled to him [are] with him before the Ark, sacrificing sheep and oxen, that are not counted nor numbered for multitude. **6** And the priests bring in the Ark of the Covenant of YHWH to its place, to the oracle of the house, to the Holy of Holies, to the place of the wings of the cherubim; **7** for the cherubim are spreading forth two wings to the place of the Ark, and the cherubim cover over the Ark, and over its poles from above; **8** and they lengthen the poles, and the heads of the poles are seen from the holy [place] on the front of the oracle, and are not seen outside, and they are there to this day. **9** There is nothing in the Ark, only the two tablets of stone which Moses put there in Horeb when YHWH covenanted with the sons of Israel in their going out of the land of Egypt. **10** And it comes to pass, in the going out of the priests from the holy [place], that the cloud has filled the house of YHWH, **11** and the priests have not been able to stand to minister because of the cloud, for the glory of YHWH has filled the house of YHWH. **12** Then Solomon said, "YHWH has said [He is] to dwell in thick darkness; **13** I have surely built a house of habitation for You; a fixed place for Your abiding for all ages." **14** And the king turns his face around, and blesses the whole assembly of Israel; and all the assembly of Israel is standing. **15** And he says, "Blessed [is] YHWH, God of Israel, who spoke by His mouth with my father David, and by His hand has fulfilled [it], saying, **16** From the day that I brought out My people, even Israel, from Egypt, I have not fixed on a city out of all the tribes of Israel, to build a house for My Name being there; and I fix on David to be over My people Israel. **17** And it is with the heart of my father David to build a house for the Name of YHWH, God of Israel, **18** and YHWH says to my father David, Because that it has been with your heart to build a house for My Name, you have done well that it has been with your heart; **19** only, you do not build the house, but your son who is coming out from your loins, he builds the house for My Name. **20** And YHWH establishes His word which He spoke, and I am risen up instead of my father David, and I sit on the throne of Israel, as YHWH spoke, and build the house for the Name of YHWH, God of Israel, **21** and I set a place for the Ark there, where the covenant of YHWH [is], which He made with our fathers in His bringing them out from the land of Egypt." **22** And Solomon stands before the altar of YHWH, in front of all the assembly of Israel, and spreads his hands toward the heavens, **23** and says, "YHWH, God of Israel, there is not a God like You, in the heavens above and on the earth below, keeping the covenant and the kindness for Your servants, those walking before You with all their heart, **24** which You have kept for Your servant, my father David, that which You spoke to him; indeed, You speak with Your mouth, and with Your hand have fulfilled [it], as [at] this day. **25** And now, YHWH, God of Israel, keep for Your servant, my father David, that which You spoke to him, saying, A man of yours is never cut off from before My face, sitting on the throne of Israel—only, if your sons watch their way, to walk before Me as you have walked before Me. **26** And now, O God of Israel, please let Your word be established which You have spoken to Your servant, my father David. **27** But is it true [that] God dwells on the earth? Behold, the heavens and the heavens of the heavens cannot contain You, how much less this house which I have built! **28** Then You have turned to the prayer of Your servant, and to his supplication, O YHWH my God, to listen to the cry and to the prayer which Your servant is praying before You today, **29** for Your eyes being open toward this house night and day, toward the place of which You have said, My Name is there; to listen to the prayer which Your servant prays toward this place. **30** Then You have listened to the supplication of Your servant, and of Your people Israel, which they pray toward this place; indeed, You listen in the place of Your dwelling, in the heavens—and You have listened, and have forgiven, **31** that which a man sins against his neighbor, and he has lifted up an oath on him to cause him to swear, and the oath has come in before Your altar in this house, **32** then You hear in the heavens, and have done, and have judged Your servants, to declare wicked the wicked, to put his way on his [own] head, and to declare righteous the righteous, to give him according to his righteousness. **33** In Your people Israel being struck before an enemy, because they sin against You, and they have turned back to You, and have confessed Your Name, and prayed, and made supplication to You in this house, **34** then you hear in the heavens, and have forgiven the sin of Your people Israel, and brought them back to the ground that You gave to their fathers. **35** In the heavens being restrained, and there is no rain, because they sin against You, and they have prayed toward this place, and confessed Your Name, and turn back from their sin, for You afflict them, **36** then You hear in the heavens, and have forgiven the sin of Your servants, and of Your people Israel, for You direct them [to] the good way in which they go, and have given rain on Your land which You have given to Your people for inheritance. **37** Famine—when it is in the land; pestilence—when it is [in the land]; blasting, mildew, locust; caterpillar—when it is [in the land]; when its enemy has distressed it in the land [in] its gates, any plague, any sickness— **38** any prayer, any supplication that [is] of any man of all Your people Israel, each who knows the plague of his own heart, and has spread his hands toward this house, **39** then

You hear in the heavens, the settled place of Your dwelling, and have forgiven, and have done, and have given to each according to all his ways, whose heart You know (for You have known—You alone—the heart of all the sons of man), **40** so that they fear You all the days that they are living on the face of the ground that You have given to our fathers. **41** And also, to the stranger who is not of Your people Israel, and has come from a far-off land for Your Name's sake— **42** for they hear of Your great Name, and of Your strong hand, and of Your outstretched arm—and he has come in and prayed toward this house, **43** You hear in the heavens, the settled place of Your dwelling, and have done according to all that the stranger calls to You for, in order that all the peoples of the earth may know Your Name, to fear You like Your people Israel, and to know that Your Name has been called on this house which I have built. **44** When Your people go out to battle against its enemy, in the way that You send them, and they have prayed to YHWH [in] the way of the city which you have fixed on, and of the house which I have built for Your Name, **45** then You have heard their prayer and their supplication in the heavens, and have maintained their cause. **46** When they sin against You (for there is not a man who does not sin), and You have been angry with them, and have given them up before an enemy, and they have taken captive their captivity to the land of the enemy far off or near; **47** and they have turned [it] back to their heart in the land to where they have been taken captive, and have turned back, and made supplication to You in the land of their captors, saying, We have sinned and done perversely—we have done wickedly; **48** indeed, they have turned back to You with all their heart and with all their soul, in the land of their enemies who have taken them captive, and have prayed to You [in] the way of their land, which You gave to their fathers, the city which You have chosen, and the house which I have built for Your Name: **49** then You have heard in the heavens, the settled place of Your dwelling, their prayer and their supplication, and have maintained their cause, **50** and have forgiven Your people who have sinned against You, even all their transgressions which they have transgressed against You, and have given them mercies before their captors, and they have had mercy [on] them— **51** for they [are] Your people and Your inheritance, whom You brought out of Egypt, out of the midst of the furnace of iron— **52** for Your eyes being open to the supplication of Your servant, and to the supplication of Your people Israel, to listen to them in all they call to You for; **53** for You have separated them to Yourself for an inheritance, out of all the peoples of the earth, as You spoke by the hand of Your servant Moses, in Your bringing out our fathers from Egypt, O Lord YHWH." **54** And it comes to pass, at Solomon's finishing to pray to YHWH all this prayer and supplication, he has risen from before the altar of YHWH, from bending on his knees and [having] his hands spread out to the heavens, **55** and he stands and blesses all the assembly of Israel [with] a loud voice, saying, **56** "Blessed [is] YHWH who has given rest to His people Israel, according to all that He has spoken; not [even] one word has fallen of all His good word, which He spoke by the hand of His servant Moses. **57** Our God YHWH is with us as He has been with our fathers; He does not forsake us nor leave us; **58** to incline our heart to Himself, to walk in all His ways, and to keep His commands, and His statutes, and His judgments, which He commanded our fathers; **59** and these, my words, with which I have made supplication before YHWH, are near to our God YHWH by day and by night, to maintain the cause of His servant, and the cause of His people Israel, the matter of a day in its day, **60** that all the peoples of the earth may know that He, YHWH, [is] God; there is none else; **61** and your heart has been perfect with our God YHWH, to walk in His statutes, and to keep His commands, as [at] this day." **62** And the king and all Israel with him are sacrificing a sacrifice before YHWH; **63** and Solomon sacrifices the sacrifice of peace-offerings, which he has sacrificed to YHWH: twenty-two thousand oxen and one hundred and twenty thousand sheep; and the king and all the sons of Israel dedicate the house of YHWH. **64** On that day the king has sanctified the middle of the court that [is] before the house of YHWH, for he has made the burnt-offering, and the present, and the fat of the peace-offerings there; for the altar of bronze that [is] before YHWH [is] too small to contain the burnt-offering, and the present, and the fat of the peace-offerings. **65** And Solomon makes, at that time, the festival—and all Israel with him, a great assembly from the entering in of Hamath to the Brook of Egypt—before our God YHWH, [for] seven days and seven [more] days—fourteen days. **66** On the eighth day he has sent the people away, and they bless the king, and go to their tents, rejoicing and glad of heart for all the good that YHWH has done to His servant David, and to His people Israel.

9 And it comes to pass, at Solomon's finishing to build the house of YHWH, and the house of the king, and all the desire of Solomon that he delighted to do, **2** that YHWH appears to Solomon a second time, as He appeared to him in Gibeon, **3** and YHWH says to him, "I have heard your prayer and your supplication with which you have made supplication before Me; I have hallowed this house that you have built to put My Name there for all time, and My eyes and My heart have been there [for] all the days. **4** And you—if you walk before Me as your father David walked, in simplicity of heart, and in uprightness, to do according to all that I have commanded you, [and] you keep My statutes and My judgments, **5** then I have established the throne of your kingdom over Israel for all time, as I spoke to your father David, saying, A man of yours is never cut off from [being] on the throne of Israel. **6** If you at all turn back—you and your sons—from after Me, and do not keep My commands [and] My statutes that I have set before you, and have gone and served other gods, and bowed yourselves to them, **7** then I have cut off Israel from the face of the ground that I have given to them, and the house that I have hallowed for My Name I send away from My presence, and Israel has been for an allegory and for a byword among all the peoples; **8** as for this house [that] is high, everyone passing by it is astonished, and has hissed, and they have said, Why has YHWH done this to this land and to this house? **9** And they have said, Because that they have forsaken their God YHWH, who brought out their fathers from the land of Egypt, and they lay hold on other gods, and bow themselves to them and serve them; therefore YHWH has brought all this calamity on them." **10** And it comes to pass, at the end of twenty years, that Solomon has built the two houses, the house of YHWH, and the house of the king. **11** Hiram king of Tyre has assisted Solomon with cedar-trees, and with fir-trees, and with gold, according to all his desire; then King Solomon gives to Hiram twenty cities in the land of Galilee. **12** And Hiram comes out from Tyre to see the cities that Solomon has given to him, and they have not been right in his eyes, **13** and he says, "What [are] these cities that you have given to me, my brother?" And one calls them the land of Cabul to this day. **14** And Hiram sends one hundred and twenty talents of gold to the king. **15** And this [is] the matter of the tribute that King Solomon has lifted up, to build the house of YHWH, and his own house, and Millo, and the wall of Jerusalem, and Hazor, and Megiddo, and Gezer **16** (Pharaoh king of Egypt has gone up and captures Gezer, and burns it with fire, and he has slain the Canaanite who is dwelling in the city, and gives it [as] presents to his daughter, wife of Solomon). **17** And Solomon builds Gezer, and the lower Beth-Horon, **18** and Ba'alath, and Tadmor in the wilderness, in the land, **19** and all the cities of stores that King Solomon has, and the cities of the chariots, and the cities of the horsemen, and the desire of Solomon that he desired to build in Jerusalem, and in Lebanon, and in all the land of his dominion. **20** The whole of the people that is left of the Amorite, the Hittite, the Perizzite, the Hivite, and the Jebusite, who [are] not of the sons of Israel— **21** their sons who are left behind them in the land, whom the sons of Israel have not been able to devote—he has even lifted up a tribute of service [on] them to this day. **22** And Solomon has not appointed a servant out of the sons of Israel, for they [are] the men of war, and his servants, and his heads, and his captains, and the heads of his chariots, and his horsemen. **23** These [are] the five hundred and fifty heads of the officers who [are] over the work of Solomon, those ruling among the people who are laboring in the work. **24** Only, the daughter of Pharaoh went up out of the City of David to her house that [Solomon] built for her; then he built Millo. **25** And Solomon caused burnt-offerings and peace-offerings to ascend three times in a year on the altar that he built for YHWH, and he burned it as incense with that which [is] before YHWH, and finished the house. **26** And King Solomon has made a navy in Ezion-Geber, that is beside Eloth, on the edge of the Sea of Suph, in the land of Edom. **27** And Hiram sends his servants in the navy, shipmen knowing the sea, with servants of Solomon, **28** and they come to Ophir, and take four hundred and twenty talents of gold from there, and bring [it] to King Solomon.

10 And the queen of Sheba is hearing of the fame of Solomon concerning the Name of Y<small>HWH</small>, and comes to try him with enigmas, **2** and she comes to Jerusalem, with a very great company, camels carrying spices, and very much gold, and precious stone, and she comes to Solomon, and speaks to him all that has been with her heart. **3** And Solomon declares to her all her matters—there has not been a thing hid from the king that he has not declared to her. **4** And the queen of Sheba sees all the wisdom of Solomon, and the house that he built, **5** and the food of his table, and the sitting of his servants, and the standing of his ministers, and their clothing, and his butlers, and his burnt-offering that he causes to ascend in the house of Y<small>HWH</small>, and there has not been anymore spirit in her. **6** And she says to the king, "The word that I heard in my land has been true concerning your matters and your wisdom; **7** and I gave no credence to the words until I have come, and my eyes see, and behold, not [even] half was declared to me; you have added wisdom and goodness to the report that I heard. **8** O the blessedness of your men, O the blessedness of your servants—these—who are standing before you continually, who are hearing your wisdom! **9** Your God Y<small>HWH</small> is blessed, who delighted in you, to put you on the throne of Israel; in Y<small>HWH</small>'s loving Israel for all time He sets you for king, to do judgment and righteousness." **10** And she gives to the king one hundred and twenty talents of gold, and very many spices, and precious stone; there never again came in abundance like that spice that the queen of Sheba gave to King Solomon. **11** And also, the navy of Hiram that bore gold from Ophir, brought in very much almug-trees and precious stone from Ophir; **12** and the king makes the almug-trees a support for the house of Y<small>HWH</small>, and for the house of the king, and harps and psalteries for singers; there have not come such almug-trees, nor have there been seen [such] to this day. **13** And King Solomon gave to the queen of Sheba all her desire that she asked, apart from that which he gave to her as a memorial of King Solomon, and she turns and goes to her land, she and her servants. **14** And the weight of the gold that has come to Solomon in one year is six hundred sixty-six talents of gold, **15** apart from [that of] the tourists, and of the traffic of the merchants, and of all the kings of Arabia, and of the governors of the land. **16** And King Solomon makes two hundred bucklers of alloyed gold—six hundred [shekels] of gold go up on the one buckler; **17** and three hundred shields of alloyed gold—three pounds of gold go up on the one shield; and the king puts them [in] the House of the Forest of Lebanon. **18** And the king makes a great throne of ivory, and overlays it with refined gold; **19** the throne has six steps, and a round top [is] to the throne behind it, and hands [are] on this [side] and on that, to the place of the sitting, and two lions are standing near the hands, **20** and twelve lions are standing there on the six steps, on this [side] and on that; it has not been made so for any kingdom. **21** And all the drinking vessels of King Solomon [are] of gold, and all the vessels of the House of the Forest of Lebanon [are] of refined gold—there are none of silver; it was not reckoned in the days of Solomon for anything, **22** for the king has a navy of Tarshish at sea with a navy of Hiram; once in three years the navy of Tarshish comes, carrying gold, and silver, ivory, and apes, and peacocks [[*or* monkeys]]. **23** And King Solomon is greater than any of the kings of the earth for riches and for wisdom, **24** and all the earth is seeking the presence of Solomon, to hear his wisdom that God has put into his heart, **25** and they are each bringing his present, vessels of silver, and vessels of gold, and garments, and armor, and spices, horses, and mules, the matter of a year in a year. **26** And Solomon gathers chariots, and horsemen, and he has one thousand and four hundred chariots, and twelve thousand horsemen, and he places them in the cities of the chariot, and with the king in Jerusalem. **27** And the king makes the silver in Jerusalem as stones, and he has made the cedars as the sycamores that [are] in the low country, for abundance. **28** And the outgoing of the

1 KINGS

horses that King Solomon has [is] from Egypt, and from Keveh; merchants of the king take from Keveh at a price; **29** and a chariot comes up and comes out of Egypt for six hundred pieces of silver, and a horse for one hundred and fifty, and so for all the kings of the Hittites, and for the kings of Aram; they bring out by their hand.

11 And King Solomon has loved many strange women, and the daughter of Pharaoh, females of Moab, Ammon, Edom, Sidon, [and] of the Hittites, **2** of the nations of which YHWH said to the sons of Israel, "You do not go in to them, and they do not go in to you; surely they turn aside your heart after their gods"; Solomon has cleaved to them for love. **3** And he has seven hundred wives, princesses, and three hundred concubines; and his wives turn aside his heart. **4** And it comes to pass, at the time of Solomon's old age, his wives have turned aside his heart after other gods, and his heart has not been perfect with his God YHWH, like the heart of his father David. **5** And Solomon goes after Ashtoreth goddess of the Zidonians, and after Milcom the abomination of the Ammonites; **6** and Solomon does evil in the eyes of YHWH, and has not been fully after YHWH, like his father David. **7** Then Solomon builds a high place for Chemosh the abomination of Moab, in the hill that [is] on the front of Jerusalem, and for Molech the abomination of the sons of Ammon; **8** and so he has done for all his strange women, who are perfuming and sacrificing to their gods. **9** And YHWH shows Himself angry with Solomon, for his heart has turned aside from YHWH, God of Israel, who had appeared to him twice, **10** and given a charge to him concerning this thing, not to go after other gods; and he has not kept that which YHWH commanded, **11** and YHWH says to Solomon, "Because that this has been with you, and you have not kept My covenant and My statutes that I charged on you, I surely tear the kingdom from you, and have given it to your servant. **12** Only, I do not do it in your days, for the sake of your father David; I tear it out of the hand of your son; **13** only, I do not tear away all of the kingdom; I give one tribe to your son, for the sake of My servant David, and for the sake of Jerusalem that I have chosen." **14** And YHWH raises up an adversary against Solomon, Hadad the Edomite; he [is] of the seed of the king in Edom; **15** and it comes to pass, in David's being with Edom, in the going up of Joab head of the host to bury the slain, that he strikes every male in Edom— **16** for six months Joab abided there, and all Israel, until the cutting off of every male in Edom— **17** and Hadad flees, he and certain Edomites, of the servants of his father, with him, to go to Egypt, and Hadad [is] a little youth, **18** and they rise out of Midian, and come into Paran, and take men with them out of Paran, and come into Egypt, to Pharaoh king of Egypt, and he gives a house to him, and has commanded bread for him, and has given land to him. **19** And Hadad finds grace in the eyes of Pharaoh exceedingly, and he gives to him a wife, the sister of his own wife, sister of Tahpenes the mistress; **20** and the sister of Tahpenes bears to him his son Genubath, and Tahpenes weans him within the house of Pharaoh, and Genubath is in the house of Pharaoh in the midst of the sons of Pharaoh. **21** And Hadad has heard in Egypt that David has lain with his fathers, and that Joab head of the host is dead, and Hadad says to Pharaoh, "Send me away, and I go to my land." **22** And Pharaoh says to him, "But what are you lacking with me, that behold, you are seeking to go to your own land?" And he says, "Nothing, but you certainly send me away." **23** And God raises an adversary against him, Rezon son of Eliadah, who has fled from Hadadezer king of Zobah, his lord, **24** and gathers men to himself, and is head of a troop in David's slaying them, and they go to Damascus, and dwell in it, and reign in Damascus; **25** and he is an adversary against Israel all the days of Solomon (besides the evil that Hadad [did]), and he cuts off in Israel, and reigns over Aram. **26** And Jeroboam son of Nebat, an Ephraimite of Zereda—the name of whose mother [is] Zeruah, a widow woman—servant to Solomon, he also lifts up a hand against the king; **27** and this [is] the thing [for] which he lifted up a hand against the king: Solomon built Millo—he shut up the breach of the city of his father David, **28** and the man Jeroboam [is] mighty in valor, and Solomon sees that the young man is doing business, and appoints him over all the burden of the house of Joseph. **29** And it comes to pass, at that time, that Jeroboam has gone out from

1 KINGS

Jerusalem, and Ahijah the Shilonite, the prophet, finds him in the way, and he is covering himself with a new garment; and both of them [are] by themselves in a field, **30** and Ahijah lays hold on the new garment that [is] on him, and tears it [into] twelve pieces, **31** and says to Jeroboam, "Take ten pieces for yourself, for thus said YHWH, God of Israel: Behold, I am tearing the kingdom out of the hand of Solomon, and have given the ten tribes to you, **32** but he has the one tribe for My servant David's sake, and for Jerusalem's sake, the city which I have fixed on, out of all the tribes of Israel, **33** because they have forsaken Me, and bow themselves to Ashtoreth, goddess of the Zidonians, to Chemosh god of Moab, and to Milcom god of the sons of Ammon, and have not walked in My ways, to do that which [is] right in My eyes, and My statutes and My judgments, like his father David. **34** And I do not take the whole of the kingdom out of his hand, for I make him prince all [the] days of his life, for the sake of My servant David whom I chose, who kept My commands and My statutes; **35** and I have taken the kingdom out of the hand of his son, and given it to you—the ten tribes; **36** and to his son I give one tribe, for there being a lamp before Me for My servant David in Jerusalem [for] all the days, the city that I have chosen for Myself to put My Name there. **37** And I take you, and you have reigned over all that your soul desires, and you have been king over Israel; **38** and it has been, if you hear all that I command you, and have walked in My ways, and done that which is right in My eyes, to keep My statutes and My commands, as My servant David did, that I have been with you, and have built a steadfast house for you, as I built for David, and have given Israel to you, **39** and I humble the seed of David for this; only, not [for] all the days." **40** And Solomon seeks to put Jeroboam to death, and Jeroboam rises and flees to Egypt, to Shishak king of Egypt, and he is in Egypt until the death of Solomon. **41** And the rest of the matters of Solomon, and all that he did, and his wisdom, are they not written on the scroll of the matters of Solomon? **42** And the days that Solomon has reigned in Jerusalem over all Israel [are] forty years, **43** and Solomon lies with his fathers, and is buried in the city of his father David, and his son Rehoboam reigns in his stead.

12 And Rehoboam goes to Shechem, for all Israel has come to Shechem to make him king. **2** And it comes to pass, at Jeroboam son of Nebat's hearing (and he [is] yet in Egypt where he has fled from the presence of Solomon the king, and Jeroboam dwells in Egypt), **3** that they send and call for him; and they come—Jeroboam and all the assembly of Israel—and speak to Rehoboam, saying, **4** "Your father hardened our yoke, and you, now, lighten [some] of the hard service of your father, and his heavy yoke that he put on us, and we serve you." **5** And he says to them, "Yet go [for] three days, and come back to me"; and the people go. **6** And King Rehoboam consults with the elderly who have been standing in the presence of his father Solomon, in his being alive, saying, "How are you counseling to answer this people?" **7** And they speak to him, saying, "If, today, you are a servant of this people, and have served them, and answered them, and spoken good words to them, then they have been servants to you [for] all the days." **8** And he forsakes the counsel of the elderly which they counseled him, and consults with the boys who have grown up with him, who are standing before him; **9** and he says to them, "What are you counseling, and we answer this people, who have spoken to me, saying, Lighten [some] of the yoke that your father put on us?" **10** And they speak to him—the boys who had grown up with him—saying, "Thus you say to this people who have spoken to you, saying, Your father made our yoke heavy, and you, make [it] light on us; thus you speak to them, My little [finger] is thicker than the loins of my father; **11** and now, my father laid a heavy yoke on you, and I add to your yoke; my father disciplined you with whips, and I discipline you with scorpions." **12** And they come—Jeroboam and all the people—to Rehoboam, on the third day, as the king had spoken, saying, "Come back to me on the third day." **13** And the king answers the people sharply, and forsakes the counsel of the elderly which they counseled him, **14** and speaks to them, according to the counsel of the boys, saying, "My father made your yoke heavy, and I add to your yoke; my father disciplined you with whips, and I discipline you with scorpions"; **15** and the king did not listen to the people, for the revolution was from

YHWH, in order to establish His word that YHWH spoke by the hand of Ahijah the Shilonite to Jeroboam son of Nebat. **16** And all Israel sees that the king has not listened to them, and the people send the king back word, saying, "What portion do we have in David? Indeed, there is no inheritance in the son of Jesse; [return] to your tents, O Israel; now see your house, O David!" And Israel goes to its tents. **17** As for the sons of Israel, those dwelling in the cities of Judah—Rehoboam reigns over them. **18** And King Rehoboam sends Adoram who [is] over the tribute, and all Israel casts stones at him, and he dies; and King Rehoboam has strengthened himself to go up into a chariot to flee to Jerusalem; **19** and Israel transgresses against the house of David to this day. **20** And it comes to pass, at all Israel hearing that Jeroboam has returned, that they send and call him to the congregation, and cause him to reign over all Israel; none has been after the house of David except the tribe of Judah alone. **21** And Rehoboam comes to Jerusalem, and assembles all the house of Judah and the tribe of Benjamin, one hundred and eighty thousand chosen warriors, to fight with the house of Israel, to bring back the kingdom to Rehoboam son of Solomon. **22** And the word of God is to Shemaiah a man of God, saying, **23** "Speak to Rehoboam son of Solomon, king of Judah, and to all the house of Judah and Benjamin, and the rest of the people, saying, **24** Thus said YHWH: You do not go up nor fight with your brothers the sons of Israel; let each return to his house, for this thing has been from Me"; and they hear the word of YHWH, and turn back to go according to the word of YHWH. **25** And Jeroboam builds Shechem in the hill-country of Ephraim, and dwells in it, and goes out there, and builds Penuel; **26** and Jeroboam says in his heart, "Now the kingdom turns back to the house of David— **27** if this people goes up to make sacrifices in the house of YHWH in Jerusalem, then the heart of this people has turned back to their lord, to Rehoboam king of Judah, and they have slain me, and turned back to Rehoboam king of Judah." **28** And the king takes counsel, and makes two calves of gold, and says to them, "Enough of you from going up to Jerusalem; behold, your gods, O Israel, which brought you up out of the land of Egypt." **29** And he sets the one in Beth-El, and the other he has put in Dan, **30** and this thing becomes a sin, and the people go before the one—to Dan. **31** And he makes the house of high places, and makes priests from the extremities of the people, who were not of the sons of Levi; **32** and Jeroboam makes a festival in the eighth month, on the fifteenth day of the month, like the festival that [is] in Judah, and he offers on the altar—so he did in Beth-El—to sacrifice to the calves which he made, and he has appointed in Beth-El the priests of the high places that he made. **33** And he offers up on the altar that he made in Beth-El, on the fifteenth day of the eighth month, in the month that he devised from his own heart, and he makes a festival for the sons of Israel, and offers on the altar—to make incense.

13 And behold, a man of God has come from Judah, by the word of YHWH, to Beth-El, and Jeroboam is standing by the altar—to make incense; **2** and he calls against the altar, by the word of YHWH, and says, "Altar! Altar! Thus said YHWH: Behold, a son is born to the house of David—Josiah [is] his name—and he has sacrificed on you the priests of the high places who are making incense on you, and bones of man are burned on you." **3** And he has given a sign on that day, saying, "This [is] the sign that YHWH has spoken, Behold, the altar is torn, and the ashes that [are] on it [are] poured forth." **4** And it comes to pass, at the king's hearing the word of the man of God that he calls against the altar in Beth-El, that Jeroboam puts forth his hand from off the altar, saying, "Catch him"; and his hand that he has put forth against him is dried up, and he is not able to bring it back to himself, **5** and the altar is torn, and the ashes [are] poured forth from the altar, according to the sign that the man of God had given by the word of YHWH. **6** And the king answers and says to the man of God, "Please appease the face of your God YHWH, and pray for me, and my hand comes back to me"; and the man of God appeases the face of YHWH, and the hand of the king comes back to him, and it is as at the beginning. **7** And the king speaks to the man of God, "Come in with me to the house, and refresh yourself, and I give a gift to you." **8** And the man of God says to the king, "If you give to me the half of your house, I do not go in with you, nor do I eat bread, nor do I drink water, in this place; **9** for so He commanded me by the word of YHWH, saying, You do not eat bread nor drink water, nor return in the way that you have come." **10** And he goes on in another way, and has not turned back in the way in which he came in to Beth-El. **11** And a certain aged prophet is dwelling in Beth-El, and his son comes and recounts to him every deed that the man of God has done today in Beth-El, the words that he has spoken to the king—indeed, they recount them to their father. **12** And their father says to them, "Where [is] this—the way he has gone?" And his sons see the way that the man of God who came from Judah has gone. **13** And he says to his sons, "Saddle the donkey for me," and they saddle the donkey for him, and he rides on it, **14** and goes after the man of God, and finds him sitting under the oak, and says to him, "Are you the man of God who has come from Judah?" And he says, "I [am]." **15** And he says to him, "Come with me to the house and eat bread." **16** And he says, "I am not able to return with you, and to go in with you, nor do I eat bread or drink water with you in this place, **17** for [there is] a word to me by the word of YHWH, You do not eat bread nor drink water there [and] you do not return to go in the way in which you came." **18** And he says to him, "I [am] also a prophet like you, and a messenger spoke to me by the word of YHWH, saying, Bring him back with you to your house, and he eats bread and drinks water." He has lied to him. **19** And he turns back with him, and eats bread in his house, and drinks water. **20** And it comes to pass—they are sitting at the table—and [there] is a word of YHWH to the prophet who brought him back, **21** and he calls to the man of God who came from Judah, saying, "Thus said YHWH: Because that you have provoked the mouth of YHWH, and have not kept the command that your God YHWH charged you, **22** and turn back and eat bread and drink water in the place of which He said to you, You do not eat bread nor drink water—your carcass does not come into the burying-place of your fathers." **23** And it comes to pass, after his eating bread, and after his drinking, that he saddles the donkey for him, for the prophet whom he had brought back, **24** and he goes, and a lion finds him in the way, and puts him to death, and his carcass is cast in the way, and the donkey is standing near it, and the lion is standing near the carcass. **25** And behold, men are passing by, and see the carcass cast in the way, and the lion standing near the carcass, and they come and speak [of it] in the city in which the old prophet is dwelling. **26** And the prophet who brought him back out of the way hears and says, "It [is] the man of God who provoked the mouth of YHWH, and YHWH gives him to the lion, and it destroys him, and puts him to death, according to the word of YHWH that he spoke to him." **27** And he speaks to his sons saying, "Saddle the donkey for me," and they saddle [it]. **28** And he goes and finds his carcass cast in the way, and the donkey and the lion are standing near the carcass—the lion has not eaten the carcass nor destroyed the donkey. **29** And the prophet takes up the carcass of the man of God, and places it on the donkey, and brings it back, and the old prophet comes to the city to mourn and to bury him, **30** and he places his carcass in his own grave, and they mourn for him, "Oh, my brother!" **31** And it comes to pass, after his burying him, that he speaks to his sons, saying, "At my death—you have buried me in the burying-place in which the man of God is buried; place my bones near his bones; **32** for the word certainly comes to pass that he called by the word of YHWH concerning the altar which [is in] Beth-El, and concerning all the houses of the high places that [are] in cities of Samaria." **33** After this thing Jeroboam has not turned from his evil way, and turns back, and makes priests of high places from the extremities of the people; he who is desirous—he consecrates his hand, and he is of the priests of the high places. **34** And in this thing is the sin of the house of Jeroboam, even to cut [it] off, and to destroy [it] from off the face of the ground.

14 At that time Abijah son of Jeroboam was sick, **2** and Jeroboam says to his wife, "Now rise and change yourself, and they do not know that you [are the] wife of Jeroboam, and you have gone to Shiloh; behold, Ahijah the prophet [is] there; he spoke to me of [being] king over this people; **3** and you have taken in your hand ten loaves, and crumbs, and a bottle of honey, and have gone to him; he declares to you what becomes of the youth." **4** And the wife of Jeroboam does so, and rises, and goes to Shiloh, and enters the house of Ahijah, and Ahijah is not able to see, for his eyes have stood because of his age. **5** And YHWH said to Ahijah, "Behold, the wife of Jeroboam is coming to seek a word from you concerning her son, for he is sick; thus and thus you speak to her, and it comes to pass at her coming in, that she is making herself strange." **6** And it comes to pass, at Ahijah's hearing the sound of her feet [as] she came to the opening, that he says, "Come in, wife of Jeroboam, why is this [that] you are making yourself strange? And I am sent to you [with] a sharp thing. **7** Go, say to Jeroboam, Thus said YHWH, God of Israel: Because that I have made you high out of the midst of the people, and appoint you leader over my people Israel, **8** and tear the kingdom from the house of David, and give it to you—and you have not been as My servant David who kept My commands, and who walked after Me with all his heart, to only do that which [is] right in My eyes, **9** and you do evil above all who have been before you, and go, and make other gods and molten images for yourself to provoke Me to anger, and you have cast Me behind your back— **10** therefore, behold, I am bringing calamity to the house of Jeroboam, and have cut off to Jeroboam those sitting on the wall—shut up and left—in Israel, and have put away the posterity of the house of Jeroboam, as one puts away the dung until its consumption; **11** the dogs eat him who dies of Jeroboam in a city, and birds of the heavens eat him who dies in a field, for YHWH has spoken. **12** And you, rise, go to your house; in the going in of your feet to the city, the boy has died; **13** and all Israel has mourned for him, and buried him, for this one—by himself—of Jeroboam comes to a grave, because there has been found in him a good thing toward YHWH, God of Israel, in the house of Jeroboam. **14** And YHWH has raised up for Himself a king over Israel who cuts off the house of Jeroboam this day—and what? Even now! **15** And YHWH has struck Israel as the reed is moved by the waters, and has plucked Israel from off this good ground that He gave to their fathers, and scattered them beyond the River, because that they made their Asherim, provoking YHWH to anger; **16** and He gives up Israel because of the sins of Jeroboam that he sinned, and that he caused Israel to sin." **17** And the wife of Jeroboam rises, and goes, and comes to Tirzah; she has come to the threshold of the house, and the youth dies; **18** and they bury him, and all Israel mourns for him, according to the word of YHWH that he spoke by the hand of His servant Ahijah the prophet. **19** And the rest of the matters of Jeroboam, how he fought, and how he reigned, behold, they are written on the scroll of the Chronicles of the Kings of Israel. **20** And the days that Jeroboam reigned [are] twenty-two years, and he lies with his fathers, and his son Nadab reigns in his stead. **21** And Rehoboam son of Solomon has reigned in Judah; Rehoboam [is] a son of forty-one years in his reigning, and he has reigned seventeen years in Jerusalem, the city that YHWH chose to set His Name there, out of all the tribes of Israel, and the name of his mother [is] Naamah the Ammonitess. **22** And Judah does evil in the eyes of YHWH, and they make Him zealous above all that their fathers did by their sins that they have sinned. **23** And they build—they also—for themselves high places, and standing-pillars, and Asherim, on every high height, and under every green tree; **24** and a whoremonger has also been in the land; they have done according to all the abominations of the nations that YHWH dispossessed from the presence of the sons of Israel. **25** And it comes to pass, in the fifth year of King Rehoboam, Shishak king of Egypt has gone up against Jerusalem, **26** and he takes the treasures of the house of YHWH, and the treasures of the house of the king, indeed, he has taken the whole; and he takes all the shields of gold that Solomon made. **27** And King Rehoboam makes shields of bronze in their stead, and has made [them] a charge on the hand of the heads of the runners, those keeping the opening of the house of the king, **28** and it comes to pass, from the going in of the king to the house of YHWH, the runners carry them, and have brought them back to the chamber of the runners. **29** And the rest of the matters of Rehoboam and all that he did, are they not written on the scroll of the Chronicles of the Kings of Judah? **30** And there has been war between Rehoboam and Jeroboam [for] all the days; **31** and Rehoboam lies with his fathers, and is buried with his fathers in the City of David, and the name of his mother [is] Naamah the Ammonitess, and his son Abijam reigns in his stead.

1 KINGS

15 And in the eighteenth year of King Jeroboam son of Nebat, Abijam has reigned over Judah; **2** he has reigned three years in Jerusalem, and the name of his mother [is] Maachah daughter of Abishalom; **3** and he walks in all the sins of his father that he did before him, and his heart has not been perfect with his God YHWH, as the heart of his father David; **4** but for David's sake his God YHWH has given to him a lamp in Jerusalem, to raise up his son after him, and to establish Jerusalem, **5** in that David did that which [is] right in the eyes of YHWH, and did not turn aside from all that He commanded him all [the] days of his life—except in the matter of Uriah the Hittite; **6** and there has been war between Rehoboam and Jeroboam all the days of his life. **7** And the rest of the matters of Abijam and all that he did, are they not written on the scroll of the Chronicles of the Kings of Judah? And there has been war between Abijam and Jeroboam; **8** and Abijam lies with his fathers, and they bury him in the City of David, and his son Asa reigns in his stead. **9** And in the twentieth year of Jeroboam king of Israel, Asa has reigned over Judah, **10** and he has reigned forty-one years in Jerusalem, and the name of his mother [is] Maachah daughter of Abishalom. **11** And Asa does that which [is] right in the eyes of YHWH, like his father David, **12** and removes the whoremongers out of the land, and turns aside all the idols that his fathers made; **13** and also his mother Maachah—he turns her aside from being mistress, in that she made a horrible thing for an Asherah, and Asa cuts down her horrible thing, and burns [it] by the Brook of Kidron; **14** but the high places have not been removed; only, the heart of Asa has been perfect with YHWH [for] all his days, **15** and he brings in the sanctified things of his father, and his own sanctified things, to the house of YHWH: silver, and gold, and vessels. **16** And there has been war between Asa and Baasha king of Israel [for] all their days, **17** and Baasha king of Israel goes up against Judah, and builds Ramah, not to permit anyone going out and coming in to Asa king of Judah. **18** And Asa takes all the silver and the gold that are left in the treasures of the house of YHWH, and the treasures of the house of the king, and gives them into the hand of his servants, and King Asa sends them to Ben-Hadad, son of Tabrimmon, son of Hezion king of Aram, who is dwelling in Damascus, saying, **19** "A covenant [is] between me and you, between my father and your father; behold, I have sent a reward of silver and gold to you; go, break your covenant with Baasha king of Israel, and he goes up from off me." **20** And Ben-Hadad listens to King Asa, and sends the heads of the forces that he has against cities of Israel, and strikes Ijon, and Dan, and Abel-Beth-Maachah, and all Chinneroth, besides all the land of Naphtali; **21** and it comes to pass at Baasha's hearing, that he ceases from building Ramah, and dwells in Tirzah. **22** And King Asa has summoned all Judah—there is none exempt—and they lift up the stones of Ramah, and its wood, that Baasha has built, and King Asa builds with them Geba of Benjamin, and Mizpah. **23** And the rest of all the matters of Asa, and all his might, and all that he did, and the cities that he built, are they not written on the scroll of the Chronicles of the Kings of Judah? Only, at the time of his old age he was diseased in his feet; **24** and Asa lies with his fathers, and is buried with his fathers in the city of his father David, and his son Jehoshaphat reigns in his stead. **25** And Nadab son of Jeroboam has reigned over Israel, in the second year of Asa king of Judah, and he reigns over Israel two years, **26** and does evil in the eyes of YHWH, and goes in the way of his father, and in his sin that he made Israel to sin. **27** And Baasha son of Ahijah, of the house of Issachar, conspires against him, and Baasha strikes him in Gibbethon, which [belonged] to the Philistines—and Nadab and all Israel are laying siege against Gibbethon— **28** indeed, Baasha puts him to death in the third year of Asa king of Judah, and reigns in his stead. **29** And it comes to pass, at his reigning, he has struck the whole house of Jeroboam, he has not left any breathing to Jeroboam until his destroying him, according to the word of YHWH, that He spoke by the hand of His servant Ahijah the Shilonite, **30** because of the sins of Jeroboam that he sinned, and that he caused Israel to sin, by his provocation with which he provoked YHWH, God of Israel, to anger. **31** And the rest of the matters of Nadab and all that he did, are they not written on the scroll of the Chronicles of the Kings of Israel? **32** And there has been war between Asa and

Baasha king of Israel [for] all their days. **33** In the third year of Asa king of Judah, Baasha son of Ahijah has reigned over all Israel in Tirzah, twenty-four years, **34** and he does evil in the eyes of YHWH, and walks in the way of Jeroboam, and in his sin that he caused Israel to sin.

16 And a word of YHWH is to Jehu son of Hanani, against Baasha, saying, **2** "Because that I have raised you up out of the dust, and appoint you leader over My people Israel, and you walk in the way of Jeroboam, and cause My people Israel to sin—to provoke Me to anger with their sins; **3** behold, I am putting away the posterity of Baasha, even the posterity of his house, and have given up your house as the house of Jeroboam son of Nebat; **4** the dogs eat him who dies of Baasha in a city, and [the] bird of the heavens eats him who dies of his in a field." **5** And the rest of the matters of Baasha, and that which he did, and his might, are they not written on the scroll of the Chronicles of the Kings of Israel? **6** And Baasha lies with his fathers, and is buried in Tirzah, and his son Elah reigns in his stead. **7** And also by the hand of Jehu son of Hanani the prophet a word of YHWH has been concerning Baasha, and concerning his house, and concerning all the evil that he did in the eyes of YHWH to provoke Him to anger with the work of his hands, to be like the house of Jeroboam, and concerning that for which he struck him. **8** In the twenty-sixth year of Asa king of Judah, Elah son of Baasha has reigned over Israel in Tirzah, two years; **9** and his servant Zimri conspires against him (head of the half of the chariots) and he [is] in Tirzah drinking—a drunkard in the house of Arza, who [is] over the house in Tirzah. **10** And Zimri comes in and strikes him, and puts him to death, in the twenty-seventh year of Asa king of Judah, and reigns in his stead; **11** and it comes to pass in his reigning, at his sitting on his throne, he has struck the whole house of Baasha; he has not left to him any sitting on the wall, and of his redeemers, and of his friends. **12** And Zimri destroys the whole house of Baasha, according to the word of YHWH that He spoke concerning Baasha, by the hand of Jehu the prophet, **13** concerning all the sins of Baasha, and the sins of his son Elah, that they sinned, and that they caused Israel to sin to provoke YHWH, God of Israel, with their vanities. **14** And the rest of the matters of Elah and all that he did, are they not written on the scroll of the Chronicles of the Kings of Israel? **15** In the twenty-seventh year of Asa king of Judah, Zimri has reigned seven days in Tirzah; and the people are encamping against Gibbethon, which [belonged] to the Philistines; **16** and the people who are encamping hear, saying, "Zimri has conspired, and also has struck the king"; and all Israel causes Omri head of the host to reign over Israel on that day in the camp. **17** And Omri goes up, and all Israel with him, from Gibbethon, and they lay siege to Tirzah. **18** And it comes to pass, at Zimri's seeing that the city has been captured, that he comes into a high place of the house of the king, and burns the house of the king over himself with fire, and he dies, **19** for his sins that he sinned, to do evil in the eyes of YHWH, to walk in the way of Jeroboam, and in his sin that he did, to cause Israel to sin; **20** and the rest of the matters of Zimri and his conspiracy that he made, are they not written on the scroll of the Chronicles of the Kings of Israel? **21** Then the sons of Israel are parted into halves; half of the people have been after Tibni son of Ginath to cause him to reign, and the [other] half after Omri; **22** and the people that are after Omri are stronger than the people that are after Tibni son of Ginath, and Tibni dies, and Omri reigns. **23** In the thirty-first year of Asa king of Judah, Omri has reigned over Israel twelve years; he has reigned in Tirzah six years, **24** and he buys the Mount of Samaria from Shemer with two talents of silver, and builds [on] the mountain, and calls the name of the city that he has built by the name of Shemer, lord of the hill—Samaria. **25** And Omri does evil in the eyes of YHWH, and does evil above all who [are] before him, **26** and walks in all the way of Jeroboam son of Nebat, and in his sin that he caused Israel to sin, to provoke YHWH, God of Israel, with their vanities. **27** And the rest of the matters of Omri that he did and his might that he exercised, are they not written on the scroll of the Chronicles of the Kings of Israel? **28** And Omri lies with his fathers, and is buried in Samaria, and his son Ahab reigns in his stead. **29** And Ahab son of Omri has reigned over Israel in the thirty-eighth year of Asa king of Judah, and Ahab son of Omri reigns over Israel in Samaria twenty-two years, **30** and

1 KINGS

Ahab son of Omri does evil in the eyes of YHWH above all who [are] before him. **31** And it comes to pass, as if it had been trivial—his walking in the sins of Jeroboam son of Nebat—that he takes a wife, Jezebel daughter of Ethba'al, king of the Zidonians, and goes and serves Ba'al, and bows himself to it, **32** and raises up an altar for Ba'al in the house of the Ba'al, which he built in Samaria; **33** and Ahab makes the Asherah, and Ahab adds to do so as to provoke YHWH, God of Israel, above all the kings of Israel who have been before him. **34** In his days Hiel the Beth-Elite has built Jericho; he laid its foundation with Abiram his firstborn, and he set up its doors with Segub his youngest, according to the word of YHWH that He spoke by the hand of Joshua son of Nun.

17 And Elijah the Tishbite, of the inhabitants of Gilead, says to Ahab, "YHWH, God of Israel, lives, before whom I have stood, there is not dew and rain these years, except according to my word." **2** And the word of YHWH is to him, saying, **3** "Go from this [place]; and you have turned for yourself eastward, and been hidden by the Brook of Cherith that [is] on the front of the Jordan, **4** and it has been [that] you drink from the brook, and I have commanded the ravens to sustain you there." **5** And he goes and does according to the word of YHWH, indeed, he goes and dwells by the Brook of Cherith, that [is] on the front of the Jordan, **6** and the ravens are bringing bread and flesh to him in the morning, and bread and flesh in the evening, and he drinks from the brook. **7** And it comes to pass, at the end of [the] days, that the brook dries up, for there has been no rain in the land, **8** and the word of YHWH is to him, saying, **9** "Rise, go to Zarephath, that [belongs] to Sidon, and you have dwelt there; behold, I have commanded a widow woman to sustain you there." **10** And he rises, and goes to Zarephath, and comes to the opening of the city, and behold, there [is] a widow woman gathering sticks, and he calls to her and says, "Please bring a little water to me in a vessel, and I drink." **11** And she goes to bring [it], and he calls to her and says, "Please bring a morsel of bread to me in your hand." **12** And she says, "Your God YHWH lives, I do not have a cake, but the fullness of the hand of meal in a pitcher, and a little oil in a dish; and behold, I am gathering two sticks, and have gone in and prepared it for myself, and for my son, and we have eaten it—and died." **13** And Elijah says to her, "Do not fear, go, do according to your word, only make a little cake for me there, in the first place, and you have brought [it] out to me; and for you and for your son make [it] last; **14** for thus said YHWH, God of Israel: The pitcher of meal is not consumed, and the dish of oil is not lacking, until the day of YHWH's giving a shower on the face of the ground." **15** And she goes, and does according to the word of Elijah, and she eats, she and he and her household [for many] days; **16** the pitcher of meal was not consumed, and the dish of oil did not lack, according to the word of YHWH that He spoke by the hand of Elijah. **17** And it comes to pass, after these things, the son of the woman, mistress of the house, has been sick, and his sickness is very severe until no breath has been left in him. **18** And she says to Elijah, "What [is this] to me and to you, O man of God? You have come to me to cause my iniquity to be remembered, and to put my son to death!" **19** And he says to her, "Give your son to me"; and he takes him out of her bosom, and takes him up to the upper chamber where he is abiding, and lays him on his own bed, **20** and cries to YHWH and says, "My God YHWH, have You also brought calamity on the widow with whom I am sojourning, to put her son to death?" **21** And he stretches himself out on the boy three times, and calls to YHWH and says, "O YHWH my God, please let the soul of this boy return into his midst"; **22** and YHWH listens to the voice of Elijah, and the soul of the boy turns back into his midst, and he lives. **23** And Elijah takes the boy, and brings him down from the upper chamber of the house, and gives him to his mother, and Elijah says, "See, your son lives!" **24** And the woman says to Elijah, "Now [by] this I have known that you [are] a man of God, and the word of YHWH in your mouth [is] truth."

18 And the days are many, and the word of YHWH has been to Elijah in the third year, saying, "Go, appear to Ahab, and I give rain on the face of the ground"; **2** and Elijah goes to appear to Ahab. And the famine is severe in Samaria, **3** and Ahab calls to Obadiah, who [is] over the house—and Obadiah has been fearing YHWH greatly, **4** and it comes to pass, in Jezebel's cutting off the prophets of YHWH, that Obadiah takes one hundred prophets, and hides them, fifty men in a cave, and has sustained them with bread and water— **5** and Ahab says to Obadiah, "Go through the land, to all fountains of waters, and to all the brooks, perhaps we find hay, and keep alive horse and mule, and do not cut off any of the livestock." **6** And they apportion the land to themselves, to pass over into it; Ahab has gone in one way by himself, and Obadiah has gone in another way by himself; **7** and Obadiah [is] in the way, and behold, Elijah [is there] to meet him; and he discerns him, and falls on his face and says, "Are you he—my lord Elijah?" **8** And he says to him, "I [am]; go, say to your lord, Behold, Elijah." **9** And he says, "What have I sinned, that you are giving your servant into the hand of Ahab—to put me to death? **10** Your God YHWH lives, if there is a nation and kingdom to where my lord has not sent to seek [for] you; and they said, He is not, then he caused the kingdom and the nation to swear, that it does not find you; **11** and now, you are saying, Go, say to your lord, Behold, Elijah; **12** and it has been, I go from you, and the Spirit of YHWH lifts you up to where I do not know, and I have come to declare to Ahab, and he does not find you, and he has slain me; and your servant is fearing YHWH from my youth. **13** Has it not been declared to my lord that which I have done in Jezebel's slaying the prophets of YHWH, that I hide one hundred men of the prophets of YHWH, fifty by fifty in a cave, and sustained them with bread and water? **14** And now you are saying, Go, say to my lord, Behold, Elijah—and he has slain me!" **15** And Elijah says, "YHWH of Hosts lives, before whom I have stood, surely I appear to him today." **16** Obadiah goes to meet Ahab, and declares [it] to him, and Ahab goes to meet Elijah. **17** [And it] comes to pass at Ahab's seeing Elijah that Ahab says to him, "Are you he—the troubler of Israel?" **18** And he says, "I have not troubled Israel, but you and the house of your father, in your forsaking the commands of YHWH, and you go after the Ba'alim; **19** and now, send, gather all Israel to me, to the Mount of Carmel, and the four hundred and fifty prophets of Ba'al, and the four hundred prophets of Asherah who are eating at the table of Jezebel." **20** And Ahab sends among all the sons of Israel, and gathers the prophets to the Mount of Carmel; **21** and Elijah comes near to all the people and says, "Until when are you leaping on the two branches? If YHWH [is] God, go after Him; and if Ba'al, go after him"; and the people have not answered him a word. **22** And Elijah says to the people, "I have been left, by myself, a prophet of YHWH; and the prophets of Ba'al [are] four hundred and fifty men; **23** and let them give two bullocks to us, and they choose one bullock for themselves, and cut it in pieces, and place [it] on the wood, and place no fire; and I prepare the other bullock, and have put [it] on the wood, and I do not place fire— **24** and you have called in the name of your god, and I call in the Name of YHWH, and it has been, the god who answers by fire—He [is] the God." And all the people answer and say, "The word [is] good." **25** And Elijah says to the prophets of Ba'al, "Choose one bullock for yourselves, and prepare [it] first, for you [are] the multitude, and call in the name of your god, and place no fire." **26** And they take the bullock that [one] gave to them, and prepare [it], and call in the name of Ba'al from the morning even until the noon, saying, "O Ba'al, answer us!" And there is no voice, and there is none answering; and they leap on the altar that one had made. **27** And it comes to pass, at noon, that Elijah mocks at them and says, "Call with a loud voice, for he [is] a god, for he is meditating, or pursuing, or on a journey; it may be he is asleep, and awakes." **28** And they call with a loud voice, and cut themselves, according to their ordinance, with swords and with spears, until a flowing of blood [is] on them; **29** and it comes to pass, at the passing by of the noon, that they feign themselves prophets until the going up of the present, and there is no voice, and there is none answering, and there is none attending. **30** And Elijah says to all the people, "Come near to me"; and all the people come near to him, and he repairs the altar of YHWH that is broken down; **31** and Elijah takes twelve stones, according to the number of the tribes of the sons of Jacob, to whom the word of YHWH was, saying, "Israel is your name"; **32** and he builds an altar with the stones, in the Name of YHWH, and makes a trench, as about the space of

1 KINGS

two measures of seed, around the altar. **33** And he arranges the wood, and cuts the bullock in pieces, and places [it] on the wood, and says, "Fill four pitchers of water, and pour [them] on the burnt-offering, and on the wood"; **34** and he says, "Do [it] a second time"; and they do [it] a second time; and he says, "Do [it] a third time"; and they do [it] a third time; **35** and the water goes around the altar, and he has also filled the trench with water. **36** And it comes to pass, at the going up of the [evening] present, that Elijah the prophet comes near and says, "YHWH, God of Abraham, Isaac, and Israel, let it be known today that You [are] God in Israel, and that I, Your servant, have done the whole of these things by Your word; **37** answer me, O YHWH, answer me, and this people [then] knows that You [are] YHWH God; and You have turned their heart backward." **38** And a fire falls [from] YHWH, and consumes the burnt-offering, and the wood, and the stones, and the dust, and it has licked up the water that [is] in the trench. **39** And all the people see, and fall on their faces, and say, "YHWH, He [is] the God! YHWH, He [is] the God!" **40** And Elijah says to them, "Catch the prophets of Ba'al; do not let a man escape from them"; and they catch them, and Elijah brings them down to the Brook of Kishon, and slaughters them there. **41** And Elijah says to Ahab, "Go up, eat and drink, because of the sound of the noise of the shower." **42** And Ahab goes up to eat, and to drink, and Elijah has gone up to the top of Carmel, and he stretches himself out on the earth, and he places his face between his knees, **43** and says to his young man, "Now go up, look attentively [toward] the way of the sea"; and he goes up and looks attentively, and says, "There is nothing"; and he says, "Turn back," seven times. **44** And it comes to pass, at the seventh, that he says, "Behold, a little thickness as the palm of a man is coming up out of the sea." And he says, "Go up, say to Ahab, Bind and go down, and the shower does not restrain you." **45** And it comes to pass, in the meantime, that the heavens have become black—thick clouds and wind—and the shower is great; and Ahab rides, and goes to Jezreel, **46** and the hand of YHWH has been on Elijah, and he girds up his loins, and runs before Ahab, until your entering Jezreel.

19 And Ahab declares to Jezebel all that Elijah did, and all of how he slew all the prophets by the sword, **2** and Jezebel sends a messenger to Elijah, saying, "Thus the gods do, and thus do they add—surely about this time tomorrow, I make your life as the life of one of them." **3** And he fears, and rises, and goes for his life, and comes to Beer-Sheba, that [is] Judah's, and leaves his young man there, **4** and he himself has gone a day's journey into the wilderness, and comes and sits under a certain broom tree, and desires his soul to die, and says, "Enough, now, O YHWH, take my soul, for I [am] not better than my fathers." **5** And he lies down and sleeps under a certain broom tree, and behold, a messenger is reaching toward him and says to him, "Rise, eat"; **6** and he looks attentively, and behold, at his bolster [is] a cake [on] burning stones, and a dish of water, and he eats, and drinks, and turns, and lies down. **7** And the messenger of YHWH turns back a second time, and is reaching toward him, and says, "Rise, eat, for the way is too great for you"; **8** and he rises, and eats, and drinks, and goes in the power of that food [for] forty days and forty nights, to the mountain of God—Horeb. **9** And he comes in there, to the cave, and lodges there, and behold, the word of YHWH [is] to him, and says to him, "What are you [doing] here, Elijah?" **10** And he says, "I have been very zealous for YHWH, God of Hosts, for the sons of Israel have forsaken Your covenant—they have thrown down Your altars, and they have slain Your prophets by the sword, and I am left, I, by myself, and they seek my life—to take it." **11** And He says, "Go out, and you have stood on the mountain before YHWH." And behold, YHWH is passing by, and a wind—great and strong—is tearing mountains, and shattering rocks before YHWH, [but] YHWH [is] not in the wind; and after the wind [is] a shaking, [but] YHWH [is] not in the shaking; **12** and after the shaking [is] a fire, [but] YHWH [is] not in the fire; and after the fire [is] a voice [like] a small whisper; **13** and it comes to pass, at Elijah's hearing [it], that he wraps his face in his robe, and goes out, and stands at the opening of the cave, and behold, a voice [speaks] to him, and it says, "What are you [doing] here, Elijah?" **14** And he says, "I have been very zealous for YHWH, God of Hosts; for the sons of Israel have forsaken Your covenant, they have thrown down

Your altars, and they have slain Your prophets by the sword, and I am left, I, by myself, and they seek my life—to take it." **15** And YHWH says to him, "Go, return on your way to the wilderness of Damascus, and you have gone in, and anointed Hazael for king over Aram, **16** and you anoint Jehu son of Nimshi for king over Israel, and you anoint Elisha son of Shaphat, of Abel-Meholah, for prophet in your stead. **17** And it has been, he who has escaped from the sword of Hazael, Jehu puts to death, and he who has escaped from the sword of Jehu, Elisha puts to death; **18** and I have left in Israel seven thousand—all the knees that have not bowed to Ba'al, and every mouth that has not kissed him." **19** And he goes there, and finds Elisha son of Shaphat, and he is plowing; twelve yoke [are] before him, and he [is] with the twelfth; and Elijah passes over to him, and casts his robe at him, **20** and he forsakes the ox, and runs after Elijah, and says, "Please let me give a kiss to my father and to my mother, and I go after you." And he says to him, "Go, turn back, for what have I done to you?" **21** And he turns back from after him, and takes the yoke of the ox, and sacrifices it, and with [the] instruments of the ox he has boiled its flesh, and gives to the people, and they eat, and he rises, and goes after Elijah, and serves him.

20 And Ben-Hadad king of Aram has gathered all his force, and thirty-two kings [are] with him, and horse and chariot, and he goes up and lays siege against Samaria, and fights with it, **2** and sends messengers to Ahab king of Israel, to the city, **3** and says to him, "Thus said Ben-Hadad: Your silver and your gold are mine, and your wives and your sons—the best—are mine." **4** And the king of Israel answers and says, "According to your word, my lord, O king: I [am] yours, and all that I have." **5** And the messengers turn back and say, "Thus spoke Ben-Hadad, saying, Surely I sent to you, saying, Your silver, and your gold, and your wives, and your sons, you give to me; **6** for if, at this time tomorrow, I send my servants to you, then they have searched your house, and the houses of your servants, and it has been [that] every desirable thing of your eyes they place in their hand, and have taken [them] away." **7** And the king of Israel calls to all [the] elderly of the land and says, "Please know and see that this [one] is seeking evil, for he sent to me for my wives, and for my sons, and for my silver, and for my gold, and I did not withhold from him." **8** And all the elderly and all the people say to him, "Do not listen, nor consent." **9** And he says to the messengers of Ben-Hadad, "Say to my lord the king, All that you sent to your servant for at the first I do, and this thing I am not able to do"; and the messengers go and take him back word. **10** And Ben-Hadad sends to him and says, "Thus the gods do to me, and thus do they add, if the dust of Samaria suffice for handfuls for all the people who [are] at my feet." **11** And the king of Israel answers and says, "Speak: Do not let him who is girding on boast himself as him who is loosing [his armor]." **12** And it comes to pass at the hearing of this word—and he is drinking, he and the kings, in the shelters—that he says to his servants, "Set yourselves"; and they set themselves against the city. **13** And behold, a certain prophet has come near to Ahab king of Israel and says, "Thus said YHWH: Have you seen all this great multitude? Behold, I am giving it into your hand today, and you have known that I [am] YHWH." **14** And Ahab says, "By whom?" And he says, "Thus said YHWH: By the young men of the heads of the provinces"; and he says, "Who directs the battle?" And he says, "You." **15** And he inspects the young men of the heads of the provinces, and they are two hundred and thirty-two, and after them he has mustered all the people, all the sons of Israel—seven thousand, **16** and they go out at noon, and Ben-Hadad is drinking—drunk in the shelters, he and the kings, the thirty-two kings helping him. **17** And the young men of the heads of the provinces go out at the first, and Ben-Hadad sends, and they declare to him, saying, "Men have come out of Samaria." **18** And he says, "If they have come out for peace, catch them alive; and if they have come out for battle, catch them alive." **19** And these have gone out of the city—the young men of the heads of the provinces—and the force that [is] after them, **20** and each strikes his man, and Aram flees, and Israel pursues them, and Ben-Hadad king of Aram escapes on a horse—and the horsemen; **21** and the king of Israel goes out, and strikes the horses, and the charioteers, and has struck among the Arameans a great striking. **22** And the prophet comes near to the king of Israel and says to him, "Go, strengthen yourself, and know and see that which you do, for at the turn of the year the king of Aram is coming up against you." **23** And the servants of the king of Aram said to him, "Their gods [are] gods of hills, therefore they were stronger than us; and yet, we fight with them in the plain—are we not stronger than they? **24** And this thing you do: turn aside each of the kings out of his place, and set captains in their stead; **25** and you, number for yourself a force as the force that is fallen from you, and horse for horse, and chariot for chariot, and we fight with them in the plain; are we not stronger than they?" And he listens to their voice, and does so. **26** And it comes to pass at the turn of the year, that Ben-Hadad inspects the Arameans, and goes up to Aphek, to battle with Israel, **27** and the sons of Israel have been inspected, and supported, and go to meet them, and the sons of Israel encamp before them, like two flocks of goats, and the Arameans have filled the land. **28** And a man of God comes near, and speaks to the king of Israel and says, "Thus said YHWH: Because that the Arameans have said, YHWH [is] God of [the] hills, but He [is] not God of [the] valleys—I have given the whole of this great multitude into your hand, and you have known that I [am] YHWH." **29** And they encamp opposite one another [for] seven days, and it comes to pass on the seventh day, that the battle draws near, and the sons of Israel strike one hundred thousand footmen of Aram in one day. **30** And those left flee to Aphek, into the city, and the wall falls on twenty-seven chief men who are left, and Ben-Hadad has fled, and comes into the city, into the innermost part. **31** And his servants say to him, "Now behold, we have heard that the kings of the house of Israel—that they are kind kings; please let us put sackcloth on our loins and ropes on our heads, and we go out to the king of Israel; it may be he keeps you alive." **32** And they gird sackcloth on their loins, and ropes [are] on their heads, and they come to the king of Israel, and say, "Your servant Ben-Hadad has said, Please let me live"; and he says, "Is he still alive? He [is] my brother." **33** And the men observe diligently, and hurry, and catch [the word] from him, and say, "Your brother Ben-Hadad"; and he says, "Go in, bring him"; and Ben-Hadad comes out to him, and he causes him to come up on the chariot. **34** And he says to him, "The cities that my father took from your father, I give back, and you make streets for yourself in Damascus, as my father did in Samaria; and I, with a covenant, send you away"; and he makes a covenant with him, and sends him away. **35** And a certain man of the sons of the prophets said to his neighbor by the word of YHWH, "Please strike me"; and the man refuses to strike him, **36** and he says to him, "Because that you have not listened to the voice of YHWH, behold, you are going from me, and the lion has struck you"; and he goes from him, and the lion finds him, and strikes him. **37** And he finds another man and says, "Please strike me"; and the man strikes him, striking and wounding, **38** and the prophet goes and stands for the king on the way, and disguises himself with ashes on his eyes. **39** And it comes to pass—the king is passing by—that he has cried to the king and says, "Your servant went out into the midst of the battle, and behold, a man has turned aside and brings a man to me, and says, Keep this man; if he is at all missing, then your life has been for his life, or you weigh out a talent of silver; **40** and it comes to pass, your servant is working here and there, and he is not!" And the king of Israel says to him, "Your judgment [is] right; you have determined [it]." **41** And he hurries and turns aside the ashes from off his eyes, and the king of Israel discerns him, that he [is] of the prophets, **42** and he says to him, "Thus said YHWH: Because you have sent away the man I devoted, out of [your] hand, even your life has been for his life, and your people for his people"; **43** and the king of Israel goes to his house, sulky and angry, and comes to Samaria.

21 And it comes to pass after these things, a vineyard has been to Naboth the Jezreelite, that [is] in Jezreel, near the palace of Ahab king of Samaria, **2** and Ahab speaks to Naboth, saying, "Give your vineyard to me, and it is for a garden of green herbs for me, for it [is] near by my house, and I give to you a better vineyard than it in its stead; if [this is] good in your eyes, I give to you its price [in] silver." **3** And Naboth says to Ahab, "Far be it from me, by YHWH, my giving the inheritance of my fathers to you"; **4** and Ahab comes to his house, sulky and angry,

1 KINGS

because of the word that Naboth the Jezreelite has spoken to him when he says, "I do not give the inheritance of my fathers to you," and he lies down on his bed, and turns around his face, and has not eaten bread. **5** And his wife Jezebel comes to him, and speaks to him, "Why [is] this [that] your spirit [is] sulky, and you are not eating bread?" **6** And he says to her, "Because I speak to Naboth the Jezreelite, and say to him, Give your vineyard to me for money, or if you desire, I give a vineyard to you in its stead; and he says, I do not give my vineyard to you." **7** And his wife Jezebel says to him, "You now execute rule over Israel! Rise, eat bread, and let your heart be glad—I give the vineyard of Naboth the Jezreelite to you." **8** And she writes letters in the name of Ahab, and seals with his seal, and sends the letters to the elderly and to the nobles who are in his city, those dwelling with Naboth, **9** and she writes in the letters, saying, "Proclaim a fast, and cause Naboth to sit at the head of the people, **10** and cause two men—sons of worthlessness—to sit opposite him, and they testify of him, saying, You have blessed [[or cursed]] God and [the] king; and they have brought him out, and stoned him, and he dies." **11** And the men of his city, the elderly and the nobles who are dwelling in his city, do as Jezebel has sent to them, as written in the letters that she sent to them, **12** they have proclaimed a fast, and caused Naboth to sit at the head of the people, **13** and two men—sons of worthlessness—come in, and sit opposite him, and the men of worthlessness testify of him, even Naboth, before the people, saying, "Naboth blessed [[or cursed]] God and [the] king"; and they take him out to the outside of the city, and stone him with stones, and he dies; **14** and they send to Jezebel, saying, "Naboth was stoned, and is dead." **15** And it comes to pass, at Jezebel's hearing that Naboth has been stoned, and is dead, that Jezebel says to Ahab, "Rise, possess the vineyard of Naboth the Jezreelite, that he refused to give to you for money, for Naboth is not alive but dead." **16** And it comes to pass, at Ahab's hearing that Naboth is dead, that Ahab rises to go down to the vineyard of Naboth the Jezreelite, to possess it. **17** And the word of YHWH is to Elijah the Tishbite, saying, **18** "Rise, go down to meet Ahab king of Israel, who [is] in Samaria— behold, in the vineyard of Naboth, to where he has gone down to possess it, **19** and you have spoken to him, saying, Thus said YHWH: Have you murdered, and also possessed? And you have spoken to him, saying, Thus said YHWH: In the place where the dogs licked the blood of Naboth, the dogs lick your blood, even yours." **20** And Ahab says to Elijah, "Have you found me, O my enemy?" And he says, "I have found—because of your selling yourself to do evil in the eyes of YHWH; **21** behold, I am bringing calamity on you, and have taken away your posterity, and cut off from Ahab those sitting on the wall, and restrained, and left, in Israel, **22** and given up your house like the house of Jeroboam son of Nebat, and like the house of Baasha son of Ahijah, for the provocation with which you have provoked [Me], and cause Israel to sin. **23** And YHWH has also spoken of Jezebel, saying, The dogs eat Jezebel in the bulwark of Jezreel; **24** the dogs eat him who dies of Ahab in a city, and [the] bird of the heavens eats him who dies in a field; **25** surely there has been none like Ahab, who sold himself to do evil in the eyes of YHWH, whom his wife Jezebel has moved, **26** and he does very abominably to go after the idols, according to all that the Amorite did whom YHWH dispossessed from the presence of the sons of Israel." **27** And it comes to pass, at Ahab's hearing these words, that he tears his garments, and puts sackcloth on his flesh, and fasts, and lies in sackcloth, and goes gently. **28** And the word of YHWH is to Elijah the Tishbite, saying, **29** "Have you seen that Ahab has been humbled before Me? Because that he has been humbled before Me, I do not bring in the calamity in his days; I bring in the calamity on his house in the days of his son."

22 And they sit still three years; there is no war between Aram and Israel. **2** And it comes to pass in the third year, that Jehoshaphat king of Judah comes down to the king of Israel, **3** and the king of Israel says to his servants, "Have you not known that Ramoth-Gilead [is] ours? And we are keeping silent from taking it out of the hand of the king of Aram!" **4** And he says to Jehoshaphat, "Do you go with me to battle [against] Ramoth-Gilead?" And Jehoshaphat says to the king of Israel, "As I am, so [are] you; as my people, so your people; as my horses, so your horses." **5** And Jehoshaphat says to the king of Israel, "Please seek the word of YHWH today"; **6** and the king of Israel gathers the prophets, about four hundred men, and says to them, "Do I go to battle against Ramoth-Gilead, or do I refrain?" And they say, "Go up, and the Lord gives [it] into the hand of the king." **7** And Jehoshaphat says, "[Is there] not a prophet of YHWH still here that we may seek from him?" **8** And the king of Israel says to Jehoshaphat, "Yet one man [remains] to seek YHWH from him, and I have hated him, for he does not prophesy good concerning me, but evil—Micaiah son of Imlah"; and Jehoshaphat says, "Do not let the king say so." **9** And the king of Israel calls to a certain eunuch and says, "Hurry along Micaiah son of Imlah." **10** And the king of Israel and Jehoshaphat king of Judah are sitting, each on his throne, clothed with garments, in a threshing-floor, at the opening of the Gate of Samaria, and all the prophets are prophesying before them. **11** And Zedekiah son of Chenaanah makes horns of iron for himself and says, "Thus said YHWH: By these you push the Arameans until they are consumed"; **12** and all the prophets are prophesying so, saying, "Go up to Ramoth-Gilead, and prosper, and YHWH has given [it] into the hand of the king." **13** And the messenger who has gone to call Micaiah has spoken to him, saying, "Now behold, the words of the prophets, with one mouth, [are] good toward the king; please let your word be as the word of one of them—and you have spoken good." **14** And Micaiah says, "YHWH lives; surely that which YHWH says to me—it I speak." **15** And he comes to the king, and the king says to him, "Micaiah, do we go to Ramoth-Gilead, to battle, or do we refrain?" And he says to him, "Go up, and prosper, and YHWH has given [it] into the hand of the king." **16** And the king says to him, "How many times am I adjuring you that you speak nothing to me but truth in the Name of YHWH?" **17** And he says, "I have seen all Israel scattered on the hills as sheep that have no shepherd, and YHWH says, These have no master; let them return—each to his house in peace." **18** And the king of Israel says to Jehoshaphat, "Have I not said to you, He does not prophesy of me good, but evil?" **19** And he says, "Therefore, hear a word of YHWH! I have seen YHWH sitting on His throne, and all the host of the heavens standing by Him, on His right and on His left; **20** and YHWH says, Who entices Ahab, and he goes up and falls in Ramoth-Gilead? And this one says thus, and that one is saying thus. **21** And the spirit goes out and stands before YHWH, and says, I entice him; and YHWH says to him, By what? **22** And he says, I go out, and have been a spirit of falsehood in the mouth of all his prophets; and He says, You entice, and also you are able; go out and do so. **23** And now, behold, YHWH has put a spirit of falsehood in the mouth of all these prophets of yours, and YHWH has spoken calamity concerning you." **24** And Zedekiah son of Chenaanah draws near and strikes Micaiah on the cheek, and says, "Where [is] this [that] the spirit [from] YHWH has passed over from me to speak with you?" **25** And Micaiah says, "Behold, you are seeing on that day when you go into the innermost chamber to be hidden." **26** And the king of Israel says, "Take Micaiah, and turn him back to Amon head of the city, and to Joash son of the king, **27** and you have said, Thus said the king: Place this one in the house of restraint, and cause him to eat bread of oppression, and water of oppression, until my coming in peace." **28** And Micaiah says, "If you return in peace at all, YHWH has not spoken by me"; and he says, "Hear, O peoples, all of them." **29** And the king of Israel goes up—and Jehoshaphat king of Judah—to Ramoth-Gilead. **30** And the king of Israel says to Jehoshaphat to disguise himself, and to go into battle, "And you, put on your garments." And the king of Israel disguises himself, and goes into battle. **31** And the king of Aram commanded the thirty-two heads of the charioteers whom he has, saying, "You do not fight with small or with great, but with the king of Israel by himself." **32** And it comes to pass, at the heads of the charioteers seeing Jehoshaphat, that they said, "He [is] surely the king of Israel!" And they turn aside to him to fight, and Jehoshaphat cries out, **33** and it comes to pass, at the heads of the charioteers seeing that he [is] not the king of Israel, that they turn back from after him. **34** And a man has drawn with a bow in his simplicity, and strikes the king of Israel between the joinings and the coat of mail, and he says to his charioteer, "Turn your hand, and take me out from the camp, for I have become sick." **35** And the battle increases on that day, and the king has been caused to stand in the chariot, in front of Aram, and he dies in the evening, and the blood of the wound runs out to the midst of the chariot, **36** and he causes the cry to pass over through the camp, at the going in of the sun, saying, "Each to his city, and each to his land!" **37** And the king dies, and comes into Samaria, and they bury the king in Samaria; **38** and [one] rinses the chariot by the pool of Samaria, and the dogs lick his blood when they had washed the armor, according to the word of YHWH that He spoke. **39** And the rest of the matters of Ahab, and all that he did, and the house of ivory that he built, and all the cities that he built, are they not written on the scroll of the Chronicles of the Kings of Israel? **40** And Ahab lies with his fathers, and his son Ahaziah reigns in his stead. **41** And Jehoshaphat son of Asa has reigned over Judah in the fourth year of Ahab king of Israel, **42** Jehoshaphat [is] a son of thirty-five years in his reigning, and he has reigned twenty-five years in Jerusalem, and the name of his mother [is] Azubah daughter of Shilhi. **43** And he walks in all the way of his father Asa, he has not turned aside from it, to do that which [is] right in the eyes of YHWH; only, the high places have not been removed—the people are still sacrificing and making incense in high places. **44** And Jehoshaphat makes peace with the king of Israel; **45** and the rest of the matters of Jehoshaphat, and his might that he exercised, and with which he fought, are they not written on the scroll of the Chronicles of the Kings of Judah? **46** And the remnant of the whoremongers who were left in the days of his father Asa he took away out of the land; **47** and there is no king in Edom; he set up a king. **48** Jehoshaphat made ships of Tarshish to go to Ophir for gold, and they did not go, for the ships were broken in Ezion-Geber. **49** Then Ahaziah son of Ahab said to Jehoshaphat, "Let my servants go with your servants in the ships"; and Jehoshaphat was not willing. **50** And Jehoshaphat lies with his fathers, and is buried with his fathers in the city of his father David, and his son Jehoram reigns in his stead. **51** Ahaziah son of Ahab has reigned over Israel in Samaria in the seventeenth year of Jehoshaphat king of Judah, and reigns over Israel two years, **52** and does evil in the eyes of YHWH, and walks in the way of his father, and in the way of his mother, and in the way of Jeroboam son of Nebat who caused Israel to sin, **53** and serves the Ba'al, and bows himself to it, and provokes YHWH, God of Israel, according to all that his father had done.

2 KINGS

1 And Moab transgresses against Israel after the death of Ahab, **2** and Ahaziah falls through the lattice in his upper chamber that [is] in Samaria, and is sick, and sends messengers, and says to them, "Go, inquire of Ba'al-Zebub god of Ekron if I recover from this sickness." **3** And a messenger of YHWH has spoken to Elijah the Tishbite, "Rise, go up to meet the messengers of the king of Samaria, and speak to them, Is it because there is not a God in Israel—you are going to inquire of Ba'al-Zebub god of Ekron? **4** And therefore, thus said YHWH: The bed to where you have gone up, you do not come down from it, for you certainly die"; and Elijah goes on. **5** And the messengers return to him, and he says to them, "What [is] this—you have turned back!" **6** And they say to him, "A man has come up to meet us and says to us, Go, return to the king who sent you, and you have said to him, Thus said YHWH: Is it because there is not a God in Israel—you are sending to inquire of Ba'al-Zebub god of Ekron? Therefore, the bed to where you have gone up, you do not come down from it, for you certainly die." **7** And he says to them, "What [is] the fashion of the man who has come up to meet you, and speaks these words to you?" **8** And they say to him, "A hairy man, and a girdle of skin girt around his loins"; and he says, "He [is] Elijah the Tishbite." **9** And he sends to him a head of fifty and his fifty, and he goes up to him (and behold, he is sitting on the top of the hill), and he speaks to him, "O man of God, the king has spoken, Come down." **10** And Elijah answers and speaks to the head of the fifty, "And if I [am] a man of God, fire comes down from the heavens and consumes you and your fifty"; and fire comes down from the heavens and consumes him and his fifty. **11** And he turns and sends to him another head of fifty and his fifty, and he answers and speaks to him, "O man of God, thus said the king: Hurry, come down." **12** And Elijah answers and speaks to them, "If I [am] a man of God, fire comes down from the heavens and consumes you and your fifty"; and fire of God comes down from the heavens and consumes him and his fifty. **13** And he turns and sends a third head of fifty and his fifty, and the third head of fifty goes up, and comes in, and bows on his knees before Elijah, and makes supplication to him, and speaks to him, "O man of God, please let my soul and the soul of your servants—these fifty—be precious in your eyes. **14** Behold, fire has come down from the heavens and consumes the two heads of the former fifties and their fifties; and now, let my soul be precious in your eyes." **15** And a messenger of YHWH speaks to Elijah, "Go down with him, do not be afraid of him"; and he rises and goes down with him to the king, **16** and speaks to him, "Thus said YHWH: Because that you have sent messengers to inquire of Ba'al-Zebub god of Ekron—is it because there is not a God in Israel to inquire of His word? Therefore, the bed to where you have gone up—you do not come down from it, for you certainly die." **17** And he dies, according to the word of YHWH that Elijah spoke, and Jehoram reigns in his stead, in the second year of Jehoram son of Jehoshaphat king of Judah, for he had no son. **18** And the rest of the matters of Ahaziah that he did, are they not written on the scroll of the Chronicles of the Kings of Israel?

2 And it comes to pass, at YHWH's taking up Elijah to the heavens in a whirlwind, that Elijah goes, and Elisha, from Gilgal, **2** and Elijah says to Elisha, "Please abide here, for YHWH has sent me to Beth-El"; and Elisha says, "YHWH lives, and your soul lives, if I leave you"; and they go down to Beth-El. **3** And sons of the prophets who [are] in Beth-El come out to Elisha, and say to him, "Have you known that today YHWH is taking your lord from your head?" And he says, "I also have known—keep silent." **4** And Elijah says to him, "Elisha, please abide here, for YHWH has sent me to Jericho"; and he says, "YHWH lives, and your soul lives, if I leave you"; and they come to Jericho. **5** And sons of the prophets who [are] in Jericho come near to Elisha, and say to him, "Have you known that today YHWH is taking your lord from your head?" And he says, "I also have known—keep silent." **6** And Elijah says to him, "Please abide here, for YHWH has sent me to the Jordan"; and he says, "YHWH lives, and your soul lives, if I leave you"; and both of them go on— **7** and fifty men of the sons of the prophets have gone on, and stand opposite [them] far off—and both of them have stood by the Jordan. **8** And Elijah takes his robe, and wraps [it] together, and strikes the waters, and they are halved, here and there, and both of them pass over on dry land. **9** And it comes to pass, at their passing over, that Elijah has said to Elisha, "Ask what I do for you before I am taken from you." And Elisha says, "Indeed, please let there be a double portion of your spirit to me"; **10** and he says, "You have asked a hard thing; if you see me taken from you, it is to you so; and if not, it is not." **11** And it comes to pass, they are going, going on and speaking, and behold, a chariot of fire and horses of fire [appear], and they separate between them both, and Elijah goes up to the heavens in a whirlwind. **12** And Elisha is seeing, and he is crying, "My father! My father! The chariot of Israel and its horsemen!" And he has not seen him again; and he takes hold on his garments and tears them into two pieces. **13** And he takes up the robe of Elijah that fell from off him, and turns back and stands on the edge of the Jordan, **14** and he takes the robe of Elijah that fell from off him, and strikes the waters, and says, "Where [is] YHWH, God of Elijah—even He?" And he strikes the waters, and they are halved, here and there, and Elisha passes over. **15** And they see him—the sons of the prophets who [are] in Jericho—from opposite [them], and they say, "The spirit of Elijah has rested on Elisha"; and they come to meet him, and bow themselves to him to the earth, **16** and say to him, "Now behold, there are fifty men with your servants, sons of valor: please let them go, and they seek your lord, lest the Spirit of YHWH has taken him up, and casts him on one of the hills or into one of the valleys"; and he says, "You do not send." **17** And they press on him, until he is ashamed, and he says, "Send"; and they send fifty men, and they seek three days, and have not found him; **18** and they return to him—and he is abiding in Jericho—and he says to them, "Did I not say to you, Do not go?" **19** And the men of the city say to Elisha, "Now behold, the site of the city [is] good, as my lord sees, and the waters [are] bad, and the earth sterile." **20** And he says, "Bring a new dish to me, and place salt there"; and they bring [it] to him, **21** and he goes out to the source of the waters, and casts salt there, and says, "Thus said YHWH: I have given healing to these waters; there is not anymore death and sterility there." **22** And the waters are healed to this day, according to the word of Elisha that he spoke. **23** And he goes up from there to Beth-El, and he is going up in the way, and little youths have come out from the city, and scoff at him, and say to him, "Go up, bald-head! Go up, bald-head!" **24** And he looks behind him, and sees them, and declares them vile in the Name of YHWH, and two bears come out of the forest and ripped apart forty-two of the boys. **25** And he goes from there to the hill of Carmel, and from there he has turned back to Samaria.

3 And Jehoram son of Ahab has reigned over Israel, in Samaria, in the eighteenth year of Jehoshaphat king of Judah, and he reigns twelve years, **2** and does evil in the eyes of YHWH, only not like his father, and like his mother, and he turns aside the standing-pillar of Ba‘al that his father made; **3** surely he has cleaved to the sins of Jeroboam son of Nebat that he caused Israel to sin; he has not turned aside from it. **4** And Mesha king of Moab was a sheep-master, and he rendered to the king of Israel one hundred thousand lambs and one hundred thousand rams, [with] wool, **5** and it comes to pass at the death of Ahab, that the king of Moab transgresses against the king of Israel. **6** And King Jehoram goes out from Samaria in that day, and inspects all Israel, **7** and goes and sends to Jehoshaphat king of Judah, saying, "The king of Moab has transgressed against me; do you go with me to Moab for battle?" And he says, "I go up, as I, so you; as my people, so your people; as my horses, so your horses." **8** And he says, "Where [is] this—the way we go up?" And he says, "The way of the wilderness of Edom." **9** And the king of Israel goes, and the king of Judah, and the king of Edom, and they turn around the way seven days, and there has been no water for the camp, and for the livestock that [are] at their feet, **10** and the king of Israel says, "Aah! For YHWH has called for these three kings to give them into the hand of Moab." **11** And

2 KINGS

Jehoshaphat says, "Is there not a prophet of YHWH here, and we seek YHWH by him?" And one of the servants of the king of Israel answers and says, "Here [is] Elisha son of Shaphat, who poured water on the hands of Elijah." **12** And Jehoshaphat says, "The word of YHWH is with him"; and the king of Israel goes down to him, and Jehoshaphat, and the king of Edom. **13** And Elisha says to the king of Israel, "And what do I [have to do] with you? Go to the prophets of your father, and to the prophets of your mother"; and the king of Israel says to him, "No, for YHWH has called for these three kings to give them into the hand of Moab." **14** And Elisha says, "YHWH of Hosts lives, before whom I have stood; for unless I am lifting up the face of Jehoshaphat king of Judah, I do not look to you, nor see you; **15** and now, bring a musician to me"; and it has been, at the playing of the musician, that the hand of YHWH is on him, **16** and he says, "Thus said YHWH: Make this valley ditches—ditches; **17** for thus said YHWH: You do not see wind, nor do you see rain, and that valley is full of water, and you have drunk—you, and your livestock, and your beasts. **18** And this has been light in the eyes of YHWH, and he has given Moab into your hand, **19** and you have struck every fortified city, and every choice city, and you cause every good tree to fall, and you stop all fountains of waters, and you mar every good portion with stones." **20** And it comes to pass in the morning, at the ascending of the [morning] present, that behold, waters are coming in from the way of Edom, and the land is filled with the waters, **21** and all of Moab has heard that the kings have come up to fight against them, and they are called together, from everyone girding on a girdle and upward, and they stand by the border. **22** And they rise early in the morning, and the sun has shone on the waters, and the Moabites see, from opposite [them], [that] the waters [are] red as blood, **23** and say, "This [is] blood; the kings have been surely destroyed, and they each strike his neighbor; and now for spoil, Moab!" **24** And they come to the camp of Israel, and Israel rises, and strikes the Moabites, and they flee from their face; and they enter into Moab, so as to strike Moab, **25** and they break down the cities, and they each cast his stone [on] every good portion, and have filled it, and they stop every fountain of water, and they cause every good tree to fall—until one had left its stones in Kir-Haraseth, and the slingers go around and strike it. **26** And the king of Moab sees that the battle has been too strong for him, and he takes with him seven hundred men drawing sword, to cleave through to the king of Edom, and they have not been able, **27** and he takes his son, the firstborn who reigns in his stead, and causes him to ascend [as] a burnt-offering on the wall, and there is great wrath against Israel, and they journey from off him, and return to the land.

4 And a certain woman of the wives of the sons of the prophets has cried to Elisha, saying, "Your servant, my husband, is dead, and you have known that your servant was fearing YHWH, and the lender has come to take my two children to himself for servants." **2** And Elisha says to her, "What do I do for you? Declare to me, what do you have in the house?" And she says, "Your maidservant has nothing in the house except a pot of oil." **3** And he says, "Go, ask [for] vessels for yourself from outside, from all your neighbors—empty vessels—let [them] not be few; **4** and you have entered, and have shut the door on you, and on your sons, and have poured it into all these vessels, and the full ones you remove." **5** And she goes from him, and shuts the door on her, and on her sons; they are bringing [them] near to her, and she is pouring [it] out, **6** and it comes to pass, at the filling of the vessels, that she says to her son, "Bring another vessel near to me," and he says to her, "There is not another vessel"; and the oil stays. **7** And she comes and declares [it] to the man of God, and he says, "Go, sell the oil, and repay your loan; and you [and] your sons live off the rest." **8** And the day comes that Elisha passes over to Shunem, and there [is] a great woman, and she lays hold on him to eat bread, and it comes to pass, at the time of his passing over, he turns aside there to eat bread, **9** and she says to her husband, "Now behold, I have known that he is a holy man of God, passing over by us continually; **10** please let us make a little upper chamber of the wall, and we set for him there a bed, and a table, and a high seat, and a lampstand; and it has been, in his coming to us, he turns aside there." **11** And the day comes that he comes in there, and turns

2 KINGS

aside to the upper chamber, and lies there, **12** and he says to his young man Gehazi, "Call for this Shunammite"; and he calls for her, and she stands before him. **13** And he says to him, "Now say to her, Behold, you have troubled yourself concerning us with all this trouble; what can [I] do for you? Is it to speak for you to the king, or to the head of the host?" And she says, "I am dwelling in the midst of my people." **14** And he says, "And what can [I] do for her?" And Gehazi says, "Truly she has no son, and her husband [is] aged." **15** And he says, "Call for her"; and he calls for her, and she stands at the opening, **16** and he says, "At this season, according to the time of life, you are embracing a son"; and she says, "No, my lord, O man of God, do not lie to your maidservant." **17** And the woman conceives and bears a son, at this season, according to the time of life that Elisha spoke of to her. **18** And the boy grows, and the day comes that he goes out to his father, to the reapers, **19** and he says to his father, "My head, my head"; and he says to the young man, "Carry him to his mother"; **20** and he carries him, and brings him to his mother, and he sits on her knees until the noon, and dies. **21** And she goes up, and lays him on the bed of the man of God, and shuts [the door] on him, and goes out, **22** and calls to her husband and says, "Please send one of the young men and one of the donkeys to me, and I run to the man of God, and return." **23** And he says, "Why are you going to him today? [It is] neither new moon nor Sabbath!" And she says, "Peace [to you]!" **24** And she saddles the donkey and says to her young man, "Lead, and go, do not restrain riding for me, except I have commanded [so] to you." **25** And she goes, and comes to the man of God, to the hill of Carmel, and it comes to pass, at the man of God's seeing her from within view, that he says to his young man Gehazi, "Behold, this Shunammite; **26** now please run to meet her, and say to her, Is there peace to you? Is there peace to your husband? Is there peace to the boy?" And she says, "Peace." **27** And she comes to the man of God, to the hill, and lays hold on his feet, and Gehazi comes near to thrust her away, and the man of God says, "Leave her alone, for her soul [is] bitter to her, and YHWH has hidden [it] from me, and has not declared [it] to me." **28** And she says, "Did I ask for a son from my lord? Did I not say, Do not deceive me?" **29** And he says to Gehazi, "Gird up your loins, and take my staff in your hand, and go; when you meet a man, you do not greet him; and when a man greets you, you do not answer him; and you have laid my staff on the face of the youth." **30** And the mother of the youth says, "YHWH lives, and your soul lives—if I leave you"; and he rises and goes after her. **31** And Gehazi has passed on before them, and lays the staff on the face of the youth, and there is no voice, and there is no attention, and he turns back to meet him, and declares to him, saying, "The youth has not awoken." **32** And Elisha comes into the house, and behold, the youth is dead, laid on his bed, **33** and he goes in and shuts the door on them both, and prays to YHWH. **34** And he goes up, and lies down on the boy, and puts his mouth on his mouth, and his eyes on his eyes, and his hands on his hands, and stretches himself on him, and the flesh of the boy becomes warm; **35** and he turns back and walks in the house, once here and once there, and goes up and stretches himself on him, and the youth sneezes until seven times, and the youth opens his eyes. **36** And he calls to Gehazi and says, "Call to this Shunammite"; and he calls her, and she comes to him, and he says, "Lift up your son." **37** And she goes in, and falls at his feet, and bows herself to the earth, and lifts up her son, and goes out. **38** And Elisha has turned back to Gilgal, and the famine [is] in the land, and the sons of the prophets are sitting before him, and he says to his young man, "Set on the great pot, and boil stew for the sons of the prophets." **39** And one goes out to the field to gather herbs, and finds a vine of the field, and gathers gourds of the field from it—the fullness of his garment—and comes in and splits [them] into the pot of stew, for they did not know [them]; **40** and they pour out for the men to eat, and it comes to pass at their eating of the stew, that they have cried out, and say, "Death [is] in the pot, O man of God!" And they have not been able to eat. **41** And he says, "Then bring a meal"; and he casts into the pot and says, "Pour out for the people, and they eat"; and there was no bad thing in the pot. **42** And a man has come from Ba'al-Shalishah, and brings to the man of God bread of first-fruits, twenty loaves of barley, and full ears of grain in its husk, and he says, "Give to the people, and they eat." **43** And his minister says, "How do I give this before one hundred men?" And he says, "Give to the people, and they eat, for thus said YHWH: Eat and leave"; **44** and he gives before them, and they eat and leave, according to the word of YHWH.

5And Naaman, head of the host of the king of Aram, was a great man before his lord, and accepted of face, for YHWH had given salvation to Aram by him, and the man was mighty in valor, [but] leprous. **2** And the Arameans have gone out [by] troops, and they take a little girl captive out of the land of Israel, and she is before the wife of Naaman, **3** and she says to her mistress, "O that my lord [were] before the prophet who [is] in Samaria; then he recovers him from his leprosy." **4** And [one] goes in and declares [it] to his lord, saying, "Thus and thus the girl who [is] from the land of Israel has spoken." **5** And the king of Aram says, "Go, enter, and I send a letter to the king of Israel"; and he goes and takes in his hand ten talents of silver, and six thousand [pieces] of gold, and ten changes of garments. **6** And he brings in the letter to the king of Israel, saying, "And now, at the coming in of this letter to you, behold, I have sent my servant Naaman to you, and you have recovered him from his leprosy." **7** And it comes to pass, at the king of Israel's reading the letter, that he tears his garments and says, "Am I God, to put to death and to keep alive, that this [one] is sending to me to recover a man from his leprosy? For surely know now, and see, for he is presenting himself to me." **8** And it comes to pass, at Elisha the man of God's hearing that the king of Israel has torn his garments, that he sends to the king, saying, "Why have you torn your garments? Please let him come to me, and he knows that there is a prophet in Israel." **9** And Naaman comes, with his horses and with his chariot, and stands at the opening of the house for Elisha; **10** and Elisha sends a messenger to him, saying, "Go, and you have washed seven times in the Jordan, and your flesh turns back to you—and be clean." **11** And Naaman is angry, and goes on and says, "Behold, I said, He certainly comes out to me, and has stood and called in the Name of his God YHWH, and waved his hand over the place, and recovered the leper. **12** Are not Abana and Pharpar, rivers of Damascus, better than all the waters of Israel? Do I not wash in them and I have been clean?" And he turns and goes on in fury. **13** And his servants come near, and speak to him, and say, "My father, the prophet had spoken a great thing to you—do you not do [it]? And surely, when he has said to you, Wash, and be clean." **14** And he goes down and dips in the Jordan seven times, according to the word of the man of God, and his flesh turns back as the flesh of a little youth, and is clean. **15** And he turns back to the man of God, he and all his camp, and comes in, and stands before him, and says, "Now behold, I have known that there is not a God in all the earth except in Israel; and now, please take a blessing from your servant." **16** And he says, "YHWH lives, before whom I have stood—if I take [it]"; and he presses on him to take, and he refuses. **17** And Naaman says, "If not, please let a couple of mules' burden of earth be given to your servant, for your servant makes no more burnt-offering and sacrifice to other gods, but [only sacrifices] to YHWH. **18** For in this thing may YHWH be propitious to your servant, in the coming in of my lord into the house of Rimmon to bow himself there, and he was supported by my hand, and I bowed myself [in] the house of Rimmon; for my bowing myself in the house of Rimmon, may YHWH now be propitious to your servant in this thing." **19** And he says to him, "Go in peace." And he goes from him a distance of land, **20** and Gehazi, servant of Elisha the man of God, says, "Behold, my lord has spared this Aramean Naaman, not to receive from his hand that which he brought; for YHWH lives; if I have run after him, then I have taken something from him." **21** And Gehazi pursues after Naaman, and Naaman sees one running after him, and comes down off the chariot to meet him, and says, "Is there peace?" **22** And he says, "Peace; my lord has sent me, saying, Behold, now, this, two young men of the sons of the prophets have come to me from the hill-country of Ephraim; please give a talent of silver and two changes of garments to them." **23** And Naaman says, "Be pleased, take two talents"; and he urges him, and binds two talents of silver in two purses, and two changes of garments, and gives [them] to two of his young men, and they carry [them] before him; **24** and he comes to the high place, and takes [them] out of their hand, and lays [them] up in the house, and sends the men away, and they go. **25** And he has come in, and stands by his lord, and Elisha says to him, "From where—Gehazi?" And he says, "Your servant did not go here or there." **26** And he says to him, "My heart did not go when the man turned from off his chariot to meet you; is it a time to take silver, and to take garments, and olives, and vines, and flock, and herd, and menservants, and maidservants? **27** Indeed, the leprosy of Naaman cleaves to you and to your seed for all time"; and he goes out from before him—leprous as snow.

6 And sons of the prophet say to Elisha, "Now behold, the place where we are dwelling before you is too narrow for us; **2** please let us go to the Jordan, and we each take one beam from there, and we make a place there for ourselves to dwell there"; and he says, "Go." **3** And the one says, "Please be willing, and go with your servants"; and he says, "I go." **4** And he goes with them, and they come to the Jordan, and cut down the trees, **5** and it comes to pass, the one is felling the beam, and the iron [ax head] has fallen into the water, and he cries and says, "Aah! My lord, for it was borrowed!" **6** And the man of God says, "To where has it fallen?" And he shows him the place, and he cuts a stick, and casts [it] there, and causes the iron to swim, **7** and says, "Raise [it] up for yourself"; and he puts forth his hand and takes it. **8** And the king of Aram has been fighting against Israel, and takes counsel with his servants, saying, "At such and such a place [is] my encamping." **9** And the man of God sends to the king of Israel, saying, "Take heed of passing by this place, for the Arameans are coming down there"; **10** and the king of Israel sends to the place of which the man of God spoke to him, and warned him, and he is preserved there not [just] once and not [just] twice. **11** And the heart of the king of Aram is tossed about concerning this thing, and he calls to his servants and says to them, "Do you not declare to me who of us [is] for the king of Israel?" **12** And one of his servants says, "No, my lord, O king, for Elisha the prophet, who [is] in Israel, declares to the king of Israel the words that you speak in the inner part of your bed-chamber." **13** And he says, "Go and see where he [is], and I send and take him"; and it is declared to him, saying, "Behold—in Dothan." **14** And he sends horses and chariot, and a heavy force there, and they come in by night, and go around against the city. **15** And the servant of the man of God rises early, and goes out, and behold, a force is surrounding the city, and horse and chariot, and his young man says to him, "Aah! My lord, how do we do?" **16** And he says, "Do not fear, for more [are] they who [are] with us than they who [are] with them." **17** And Elisha prays and says, "Y<small>HWH</small>, please open his eyes, and he sees"; and Y<small>HWH</small> opens the eyes of the young man, and he sees, and behold, the hill is full of horses and chariots of fire around Elisha. **18** And they come down to it, and Elisha prays to Y<small>HWH</small> and says, "Please strike this nation with blindness"; and He strikes them with blindness, according to the word of Elisha. **19** And Elisha says to them, "This [is] not the way, nor [is] this the city; come after me, and I lead you to the man whom you seek"; and he leads them to Samaria. **20** And it comes to pass, at their coming to Samaria, that Elisha says, "Y<small>HWH</small>, open the eyes of these, and they see"; and Y<small>HWH</small> opens their eyes, and they see, and behold, [they are] in the midst of Samaria! **21** And the king of Israel says to Elisha at his seeing them, "My father, do I strike, do I strike?" **22** And he says, "You do not strike; are you striking those whom you have taken captive with your sword and with your bow? Set bread and water before them, and they eat, and drink, and go to their lord." **23** And he prepares great provision for them, and they eat and drink, and he sends them away, and they go to their lord: and troops of Aram have not added to come into the land of Israel anymore. **24** And it comes to pass afterward, that Ben-Hadad king of Aram gathers all his camp, and goes up, and lays siege to Samaria, **25** and there is a great famine in Samaria, and behold, they are laying siege to it, until the head of a donkey is at eighty pieces of silver, and a forth of the cab of dove's dung at five pieces of silver. **26** And it comes to pass, the king of Israel is passing by on the wall, and a woman has cried to him, saying, "Save, my lord, O king." **27** And he says, "Y<small>HWH</small> does not save you—from where do I save you? Out of the threshing-floor or out of the wine-vat?" **28** And the king says to her, "What is [troubling] you?" And she says,

"This woman said to me, Give your son, and we eat him today, and we eat my son tomorrow; **29** and we boil my son and eat him, and I say to her on the next day, Give your son, and we eat him; and she hides her son." **30** And it comes to pass, at the king's hearing the words of the woman, that he tears his garments, and he is passing by on the wall, and the people see, and behold, the sackcloth [is] within on his flesh. **31** And he says, "Thus God does to me and thus He adds, if the head of Elisha son of Shaphat remains on him this day." **32** And Elisha is sitting in his house, and the elderly are sitting with him, and [the king] sends a man from before him; before the messenger comes to him, even he himself said to the elderly, "Have you seen that this son of the murderer has sent [him] to turn aside my head? See, at the coming in of the messenger, shut the door, and you have held him fast at the door, is not the sound of the feet of his lord behind him?" **33** He is yet speaking with them, and behold, the messenger is coming down to him, and he says, "Behold, this [is] the calamity from YHWH; why do I wait for YHWH anymore?"

7 And Elisha says, "Hear a word of YHWH! Thus said YHWH: About this time tomorrow, a measure of fine flour [is] at a shekel, and two measures of barley at a shekel, in the Gate of Samaria." **2** And the captain whom the king has, by whose hand he has been supported, answers the man of God and says, "Behold, YHWH is making windows in the heavens—will this thing be?" And he says, "Behold, you are seeing it with your eyes, and you do not eat thereof." **3** And four men have been leprous at the opening of the gate, and they say to one another, "Why are we sitting here until we have died? **4** If we have said, We go into the city, then the famine [is] in the city and we have died there; and if we have sat here, then we have died; and now, come and we go down to the camp of Aram; if they keep us alive, we live, and if they put us to death—we have died." **5** And they rise in the twilight, to go to the camp of Aram, and they come to the extremity of the camp of Aram, and behold, there is not a man there, **6** seeing YHWH has caused the camp of Aram to hear a noise of chariot and a noise of horse—a noise of great force, and they say to one another, "Behold, the king of Israel has hired against us the kings of the Hittites, and the kings of Egypt, to come against us." **7** And they rise and flee in the twilight, and forsake their tents, and their horses, and their donkeys—the camp as it [is]—and flee for their life. **8** And these lepers come to the extremity of the camp, and come into one tent, and eat, and drink, and lift up silver, and gold, and garments from there, and go and hide; and they turn back and go into another tent, and lift up from there, and go and hide. **9** And they say to one another, "We are not doing right this day; it [is] a day of tidings, and we are keeping silent; and we have waited until the morning light, then punishment has found us; and now, come and we go in and declare [it] to the house of the king." **10** And they come in, and call to the gatekeeper of the city, and declare for themselves, saying, "We have come to the camp of Aram, and behold, there is no man or sound of man there, but the bound horse, and the bound donkey, and tents as they [are]." **11** And he calls the gatekeepers, and they declare [it] to the house of the king within. **12** And the king rises by night and says to his servants, "Now let me declare to you that which the Arameans have done to us; they have known that we are famished, and they go out from the camp to be hidden in the field, saying, When they come out from the city, then we catch them alive, and we enter into the city." **13** And one of his servants answers and says, "Then please let them take five of the horses that are left, that have been left in it—behold, they [are] as all the multitude of Israel who have been left in it; behold, they are as all the multitude of Israel who have been consumed—and we send and see." **14** And they take two chariot-horses, and the king sends [them] after the camp of Aram, saying, "Go, and see." **15** And they go after them to the Jordan, and behold, all the way is full of garments and vessels that the Arameans have cast away in their haste, and the messengers return and declare [it] to the king. **16** And the people go out and spoil the camp of Aram, and there is a measure of fine flour at a shekel, and two measures of barley at a shekel, according to the word of YHWH. **17** And the king has appointed the captain, by whose hand he is supported, over the gate, and the people tread him down in the gate, and he dies, as the man of God spoke, which he spoke in

2 KINGS

the coming down of the king to him, **18** indeed, it comes to pass, according to the speaking of the man of God to the king, saying, "Two measures of barley at a shekel, and a measure of fine flour at a shekel are, at this time tomorrow, in the Gate of Samaria"; **19** and the captain answers the man of God and says, "And behold, YHWH is making windows in the heavens—will this thing be?" And he says, "Behold, you are seeing it with your eyes, and you do not eat thereof"; **20** and it comes to him so, and the people tread him down in the gate, and he dies.

8 And Elisha spoke to the woman whose son he had revived, saying, "Rise and go, you and your household, and sojourn where you sojourn, for YHWH has called for a famine, and also, it is coming to the land [for] seven years." **2** And the woman rises, and does according to the word of the man of God, and goes, she and her household, and sojourns in the land of the Philistines [for] seven years. **3** And it comes to pass, at the end of seven years, that the woman turns back from the land of the Philistines, and goes out to cry to the king for her house and for her field. **4** And the king is speaking to Gehazi, servant of the man of God, saying, "Please recount to me the whole of the great things that Elisha has done." **5** And it comes to pass, he is recounting to the king how he had revived the dead, and behold, the woman whose son he had revived is crying to the king for her house and for her field, and Gehazi says, "My lord, O king, this [is] the woman, and this [is] her son, whom Elisha revived." **6** And the king inquires of the woman, and she recounts to him, and the king appoints a certain eunuch to her, saying, "Give back all that she has, and all the increase of the field from the day of her leaving the land even until now." **7** And Elisha comes to Damascus, and Ben-Hadad king of Aram is sick, and it is declared to him, saying, "The man of God has come here." **8** And the king says to Hazael, "Take a present in your hand, and go to meet the man of God, and you have sought YHWH by him, saying, Do I revive from this sickness?" **9** And Hazael goes to meet him, and takes a present in his hand, even of every good thing of Damascus, a burden of forty camels, and he comes in and stands before him, and says, "Your son Ben-Hadad, king of Aram, has sent me to you, saying, Do I revive from this sickness?" **10** And Elisha says to him, "Go, say, You certainly do not revive, seeing [that] YHWH has showed me that he surely dies." **11** And he sets his face, indeed, he sets [it] until he is ashamed, and the man of God weeps. **12** And Hazael says, "Why is my lord weeping?" And he says, "Because I have known the evil that you do to the sons of Israel—you send their fortifications into fire, and you slay their young men with sword, and you dash their sucklings to pieces, and you rip up their pregnant women." **13** And Hazael says, "But what [is] your servant—the dog, that he does this great thing?" And Elisha says, "YHWH has showed me you—king of Aram." **14** And he goes from Elisha, and comes to his lord, and he says to him, "What did Elisha say to you?" And he says, "He said to me, You certainly recover." **15** And it comes to pass on the next day, that he takes the coarse cloth, and dips [it] in water, and spreads [it] on his face, and he dies, and Hazael reigns in his stead. **16** And in the fifth year of Joram son of Ahab, king of Israel—and Jehoshaphat [is] king of Judah—Jehoram son of Jehoshaphat, king of Judah, has reigned; **17** he was a son of thirty-two years in his reigning, and he has reigned eight years in Jerusalem. **18** And he walks in the way of the kings of Israel, as the house of Ahab did, for a daughter of Ahab was to him for a wife, and he does evil in the eyes of YHWH, **19** and YHWH was not willing to destroy Judah, for the sake of His servant David, as He said to him, to give a lamp to him—to his sons [for] all the days. **20** In his days Edom has revolted from under the hand of Judah, and they cause a king to reign over them, **21** and Joram passes over to Zair, and all the chariots with him, and he himself has risen by night, and strikes Edom that is coming around to him, and the heads of the chariots, and the people flee to their tents; **22** and Edom revolts from under the hand of Judah until this day; then Libnah revolts at that time. **23** And the rest of the matters of Joram and all that he did, are they not written on the scroll of the Chronicles of the Kings of Judah? **24** And Joram lies with his fathers, and is buried with his fathers in the City of David, and his son Ahaziah reigns in his stead. **25** In the twelfth year of Joram son of Ahab, king of Israel, Ahaziah son of Jehoram, king of Judah, has reigned;

2 KINGS

26 Ahaziah [is] a son of twenty-two years in his reigning, and he has reigned one year in Jerusalem, and the name of his mother [is] Athaliah daughter of Omri, king of Israel, **27** and he walks in the way of the house of Ahab, and does evil in the eyes of YHWH, like the house of Ahab, for he [is] son-in-law of the house of Ahab. **28** And he goes with Joram son of Ahab to battle with Hazael king of Aram in Ramoth-Gilead, and the Arameans strike Joram, **29** and Joram the king turns back to be healed in Jezreel of the wounds with which the Arameans strike him in Ramah, in his fighting with Hazael king of Aram, and Ahaziah son of Jehoram, king of Judah, has gone down to see Joram son of Ahab in Jezreel, for he is sick.

9 And Elisha the prophet has called to one of the sons of the prophets and says to him, "Gird up your loins, and take this vial of oil in your hand, and go to Ramoth-Gilead, **2** and you have gone in there, and see Jehu son of Jehoshaphat, son of Nimshi, there, and you have gone in, and caused him to rise out of the midst of his brothers, and brought him into the inner part of an inner-chamber, **3** and taken the vial of oil, and poured [it] on his head, and said, Thus said YHWH: I have anointed you for king to Israel; and you have opened the door, and fled, and do not wait." **4** And the young man goes—the young man the prophet—to Ramoth-Gilead, **5** and comes in, and behold, chiefs of the force are sitting, and he says, "I have a word for you, O chief!" And Jehu says, "To which of all of us?" And he says, "To you, O chief." **6** And he rises and comes into the house, and he pours the oil on his head, and says to him, "Thus said YHWH, God of Israel: I have anointed you for king to the people of YHWH, to Israel, **7** and you have struck the house of your lord Ahab, and I have required the blood of My servants the prophets, and the blood of all the servants of YHWH, from the hand of Jezebel; **8** and all the house of Ahab has perished, and I have cut off from Ahab those sitting on the wall, and restrained, and left, in Israel, **9** and I have given up the house of Ahab like the house of Jeroboam son of Nebat, and as the house of Baasha son of Ahijah, **10** and dogs eat Jezebel in the portion of Jezreel, and there is none burying"; and he opens the door and flees. **11** And Jehu has gone out to the servants of his lord, and [one] says to him, "Is there peace? Why did this madman come to you?" And he says to them, "You have known the man and his talk." **12** And they say, "False! Declare to us now"; and he says, "He spoke thus and thus to me, saying, Thus said YHWH: I have anointed you for king to Israel." **13** And they hurry—each [one]—and take his garment, and put [it] under him at the top of the stairs, and blow with a horn, and say, "Jehu has reigned!" **14** And Jehu son of Jehoshaphat, son of Nimshi, conspires against Joram. And Joram was keeping in Ramoth-Gilead, he and all Israel, from the presence of Hazael king of Aram, **15** and King Joram turns back to be healed in Jezreel, of the wounds with which the Arameans strike him in his fighting with Hazael king of Aram. And Jehu says, "If it is your mind, do not let an escaped one go out from the city, to go to declare [it] in Jezreel." **16** And Jehu rides, and goes to Jezreel, for Joram is lying there, and Ahaziah king of Judah has gone down to see Joram. **17** And the watchman is standing on the tower in Jezreel, and sees the company of Jehu in his coming, and says, "I see a company"; and Joram says, "Take a rider and send [him] to meet them, and let him say, Is there peace?" **18** And the rider on the horse goes to meet him and says, "Thus said the king: Is there peace?" And Jehu says, "And what is peace to you? Turn around behind me." And the watchman declares, saying, "The messenger came to them, and he has not returned." **19** And he sends a second rider on a horse, and he comes to them and says, "Thus said the king: Is there peace?" And Jehu says, "And what is peace to you? Turn around behind me." **20** And the watchman declares, saying, "He came to them, and he has not returned, and the driving [is] like the driving of Jehu son of Nimshi, for he drives with madness." **21** And Jehoram says, "Harness"; and his chariot is harnessed, and Jehoram king of Israel goes out, and Ahaziah king of Judah, each in his chariot, and they go out to meet Jehu, and find him in the portion of Naboth the Jezreelite. **22** And it comes to pass, at Jehoram's seeing Jehu, that he says, "Is there peace, Jehu?" And he says, "What [is] the peace, while the whoredoms of your mother Jezebel, and her witchcrafts, are many?" **23** And Jehoram turns his hands and flees, and says to Ahaziah, "Deceit, O Ahaziah!" **24** And Jehu has filled his hand with a bow, and strikes Jehoram between his arms, and the arrow goes out from his heart, and he bows down in his chariot. **25** And [Jehu] says to his captain Bidkar, "Lift up, cast him into the portion of the field of Naboth the Jezreelite—for remember, you and I were riding together after his father Ahab, and YHWH lifted this burden on him: **26** Have I not seen the blood of Naboth and the blood of his sons last night—a declaration of YHWH—indeed, I have repaid to you in this portion—a declaration of YHWH—and now, lift up, cast him into the portion, according to the word of YHWH." **27** And Ahaziah king of Judah has seen, and flees the way of the garden-house, and Jehu pursues after him, and says, "Strike him—also him—in the chariot," in the going up to Gur, that [is] Ibleam, and he flees to Megiddo, and dies there, **28** and his servants carry him to Jerusalem in a chariot, and bury him in his burying-place with his fathers in the City of David. **29** And in the eleventh year of Joram son of Ahab, Ahaziah reigned over Judah. **30** And Jehu comes to Jezreel, and Jezebel has heard, and puts her eyes in paint and beautifies her head, and looks out through the window. **31** And Jehu has come into the gate, and she says, "Was there peace [for] Zimri—slayer of his lord?" **32** And he lifts up his face to the window and says, "Who [is] with me? Who?" And two [or] three eunuchs look out to him; **33** and he says, "Let her go"; and they let her go, and [some] of her blood is sprinkled on the wall, and on the horses, and he treads her down. **34** And he comes in, and eats, and drinks, and says, "Now look after this cursed one and bury her, for she [is] a king's daughter." **35** And they go to bury her, and have not found [anything] of her except the skull, and the feet, and the palms of the hands. **36** And they turn back, and declare [it] to him, and he says, "It [is] the word of YHWH that He spoke by the hand of this servant, Elijah the Tishbite, saying, In the portion of Jezreel the dogs eat the flesh of Jezebel, **37** and the carcass of Jezebel has been as dung on the face of the field in the portion of Jezreel, that they do not say, This [is] Jezebel."

10 And Ahab has seventy sons in Samaria, and Jehu writes letters, and sends [them] to Samaria, to the heads of Jezreel, the elderly, and to those supporting Ahab, saying, **2** "And now, at the coming in of this letter to you, and sons of your lord [are] with you, and the chariots and the horses, and a fortified city, and the armor, [are] with you, **3** that you have seen the best and the most upright of the sons of your lord, and have set [him] on the throne of his father, and fight for the house of your lord." **4** And they fear very greatly, and say, "Behold, the two kings have not stood before him, and how do we stand—we?" **5** And he who [is] over the house, and he who [is] over the city, and the elderly, and those supporting, send to Jehu, saying, "We [are] your servants, and all that you say to us we do; we do not make anyone king—do that which [is] good in your eyes." **6** And he writes a letter to them a second time, saying, "If you [are] for me, and are listening to my voice, take the heads of the men—the sons of your lord, and come to me about this time tomorrow, to Jezreel"; and the sons of the king [are] seventy men, with the great ones of the city—those bringing them up. **7** And it comes to pass, at the coming in of the letter to them, that they take the sons of the king, and slaughter seventy men, and put their heads in baskets, and send [them] to him at Jezreel, **8** and the messenger comes in, and declares [it] to him, saying, "They have brought in the heads of the sons of the king," and he says, "Make them two heaps at the opening of the gate until the morning." **9** And it comes to pass in the morning, that he goes out, and stands, and says to all the people, "You are righteous; behold, I have conspired against my lord, and slay him—and who struck all these? **10** Now you know that nothing falls of the word of YHWH to the earth that YHWH spoke against the house of Ahab, and YHWH has done that which He spoke by the hand of His servant Elijah." **11** And Jehu strikes all those left to the house of Ahab in Jezreel, and all his great men, and his acquaintances, and his priests, until he has not left a remnant to him. **12** And he rises, and comes in and goes to Samaria; he [is] at the shepherds' shearing-house in the way, **13** and Jehu has found the brothers of Ahaziah king of Judah and says, "Who [are] you?" And they say, "We [are] brothers of Ahaziah, and we go down to greet the sons of the king and the sons of the mistress." **14** And he says, "Catch them alive"; and they catch them alive, and slaughter them at the pit of the shearing-house, forty-two men, and he has not left [even one] man of them. **15** And he goes there, and finds Jehonadab son of Rechab to meet him, and blesses him, and says to him, "Is your heart right, as my heart [is] with your heart?" And Jehonadab says, "It is." "Then it is; give your hand"; and he gives his hand, and he causes him to come up into the chariot to him, **16** and says, "Come with me, and look on my zeal for YHWH"; and they cause him to ride in his chariot. **17** And he comes to Samaria, and strikes all those left to Ahab in Samaria, until his destroying him, according to the word of YHWH that He spoke to Elisha. **18** And Jehu gathers the whole of the people and says to them, "Ahab served Ba'al a little—Jehu serves him much: **19** and now, all the prophets of Ba'al, all his servants, and all his priests, call to me; do not let a man be lacking, for I have a great sacrifice for Ba'al; everyone who is lacking—he does not live"; and Jehu has done [it] in subtlety, in order to destroy the servants of Ba'al. **20** And Jehu says, "Sanctify a restraint for Ba'al"; and they proclaim [it]. **21** And Jehu sends into all Israel, and all the servants of Ba'al come in, and there has not been left a man who has not come in; and they come into the house of Ba'al, and the house of Ba'al is full—mouth to mouth. **22** And he says to him who [is] over the wardrobe, "Bring out clothing for all those serving Ba'al"; and he brings out the clothing to them. **23** And Jehu goes in—and Jehonadab son of Rechab—to the house of Ba'al, and says to the servants of Ba'al, "Search and see, lest there be [any] from the servants of YHWH here with you—but [only] the servants of Ba'al by themselves." **24** And they come in to make sacrifices and burnt-offerings, and Jehu has set eighty men for himself in an out-place, and says, "The man who lets [any] of the men whom I am bringing into your hand escape—his soul for his soul." **25** And it comes to pass, at his finishing to make the burnt-offering, that Jehu says to the runners and to the captains, "Go in, strike them, let none come out"; and they strike them by the mouth of the sword, and the runners and the captains cast [them] out; and they go to the city, to the house of Ba'al, **26** and bring out the standing-pillars of the house of Ba'al, and burn them, **27** and break down the standing-pillar of Ba'al, and break down the house of Ba'al, and appoint it for a latrine to this day. **28** And Jehu destroys Ba'al out of Israel, **29** only [not]—the sins of Jeroboam son of Nebat, that he caused Israel to sin, Jehu has not turned aside from after them—the calves of gold that [are] at Beth-El and in Dan. **30** And YHWH says to Jehu, "Because that you have done well, to do that which [is] right in My eyes—according to all that [is] in My heart you have done to the house of Ahab—the sons of the fourth [generation] sit on the throne of Israel for you." **31** And Jehu has not taken heed to walk in the Law of YHWH, God of Israel, with all his heart; he has not turned aside from the sins of Jeroboam that he caused Israel to sin. **32** In those days YHWH has begun to cut off [some] in Israel, and Hazael strikes them in all the border of Israel, **33** from the Jordan, at the sun-rising: the whole land of Gilead, of the Gadite, and the Reubenite, and the Manassite (from Aroer, that [is] by the Brook of Arnon), even Gilead and Bashan. **34** And the rest of the matters of Jehu, and all that he did, and all his might, are they not written on the scroll of the Chronicles of the Kings of Israel? **35** And Jehu lies with his fathers, and they bury him in Samaria, and his son Jehoahaz reigns in his stead. **36** And the days that Jehu has reigned over Israel in Samaria [are] twenty-eight years.

11 And Athaliah [is] mother of Ahaziah, and she has seen that her son [is] dead, and she rises, and destroys all the seed of the kingdom; **2** and Jehosheba daughter of king Joram, sister of Ahaziah, takes Joash son of Ahaziah, and steals him out of the midst of the sons of the king who are put to death, him and his nurse, in the inner part of the bed-chambers, and they hide him from the presence of Athaliah, and he has not been put to death, **3** and he is with her, in the house of YHWH, hiding himself, six years, and Athaliah is reigning over the land. **4** And in the seventh year Jehoiada has sent and takes the heads of the hundreds, of the executioners and of the runners, and brings them to him, into the house of YHWH, and makes a covenant with them, and causes them to swear in the house of YHWH, and shows them the son of the king, **5** and commands them, saying, "This [is] the thing that you do; the third of you [are] going in on the Sabbath, and keepers of the charge of the house of the king, **6** and the third [is] at the Gate of Sur, and the third at the gate behind the runners, and you have kept the charge of the house pulled down; **7** and two parts of you, all going out on the Sabbath—they have kept the charge of the house of YHWH about the king, **8** and you have surrounded the king all around, each with his weapons in his hand, and he who is coming to the ranges is put to death; and be with the king in his going out and in his coming in." **9** And the heads of the hundreds do according to all that Jehoiada the priest commanded, and take—each [one]—his men going in on the Sabbath, with those going out on the Sabbath, and come to Jehoiada the priest, **10** and the priest gives to the heads of the hundreds the spears and the shields that King David had, that [are] in the house of YHWH. **11** And the runners stand, each with his weapons in his hand, from the right shoulder of the house to the left shoulder of the house, by the altar and by the house, by the king all around; **12** and he brings out the son of the king, and puts the crown on him, and the Testimony, and they make him king, and anoint him, and strike the hand, and say, "Let the king live." **13** And Athaliah hears the voice of the runners [and] of the people, and she comes to the people [in] the house of YHWH, **14** and looks, and behold, the king is standing by the pillar, according to the ordinance, and the heads and the trumpets [are] by the king, and all the people of the land are rejoicing and blowing with trumpets, and Athaliah tears her garments, and calls, "Conspiracy! Conspiracy!" **15** And Jehoiada the priest commands the heads of the hundreds, inspectors of the force, and says to them, "Bring her out to the outside of the ranges, and him who is going after her, put to death by the sword": for the priest had said, "Do not let her be put to death in the house of YHWH." **16** And they make sides for her, and she enters the way of the entering in of the horses to the house of the king, and is put to death there. **17** And Jehoiada makes the covenant between YHWH and the king and the people, to be for a people to YHWH, and between the king and the people. **18** And all the people of the land go to the house of Ba'al, and break it down; they have thoroughly broken its altars and its images, and they have slain Mattan priest of Ba'al before the altars; and the priest sets inspectors over the house of YHWH, **19** and takes the heads of the hundreds, and the executioners, and the runners, and all the people of the land, and they bring down the king from the house of YHWH, and come by the way of the gate of the runners, to the house of the king, and he sits on the throne of the kings. **20** And all the people of the land rejoice, and the city [is] quiet, and they have put Athaliah to death by the sword in the house of the king; **21** Jehoash is a son of seven years in his reigning.

12 In the seventh year of Jehu, Jehoash has reigned, and he has reigned forty years in Jerusalem, and the name of his mother [is] Zibiah of Beer-Sheba, **2** and Jehoash does that which is right in the eyes of YHWH all his days in which Jehoiada the priest directed him, **3** only, the high places have not been removed—the people are still sacrificing and making incense in high places. **4** And Jehoash says to the priests, "All the money of the sanctified things that is brought into the house of YHWH, the money of him who is passing over, the money of each of the souls—his valuation, all the money that goes up on the heart of a man to bring into the house of YHWH, **5** the priests take to themselves, each from his acquaintance, and they strengthen the breach of the house in all [places] there where a breach is found." **6** And it comes to pass, in the twenty-third year of King Jehoash, the priests have not strengthened the breach of the house, **7** and King Jehoash calls to Jehoiada the priest, and to the priests, and says to them, "Why are you not strengthening the breach of the house? And now, receive no money from your acquaintances, but give it for the breach of the house." **8** And the priests do not consent to receive money from the people, nor to strengthen the breach of the house, **9** and Jehoiada the priest takes a chest, and pierces a hole in its lid, and puts it near the altar, on the right side, as one comes into the house of YHWH, and the priests keeping the threshold have put all the money there that is brought into the house of YHWH. **10** And it comes to pass, at their seeing that the money [is] abundant in the chest, that there goes up a scribe of the king, and of the high priest, and they bind [it] up, and count the money that is found [in] the house of YHWH, **11** and have given the weighed money into the hands of those doing the work, those inspecting the house of YHWH, and they bring it out to those working in the wood, and to builders who are working in the house of YHWH, **12** and to those [repairing] the wall, and to hewers of stone, and to buy wood and hewn stones to strengthen the breach of the house of YHWH, and for all that goes out on the house, to strengthen it. **13** Only, there is not made for the house of YHWH basins of silver, snuffers, bowls, trumpets, any vessel of gold, and vessel of silver, out of the money that is brought into the house of YHWH; **14** for they give it to those doing the work, and they have strengthened the house of YHWH with it, **15** and they do not reckon with the men into whose hand they give the money to give to those doing the work, for they are dealing in faithfulness. **16** The money of a trespass-offering and the money of sin-offerings is not brought into the house of YHWH—it is for the priests. **17** Then Hazael king of Aram goes up and fights against Gath, and captures it, and Hazael sets his face to go up against Jerusalem; **18** and Jehoash king of Judah takes all the sanctified things that Jehoshaphat, and Jehoram, and Ahaziah, his fathers, kings of Judah, had sanctified, and his own sanctified things, and all the gold that is found in the treasures of the house of YHWH and of the house of the king, and sends [them] to Hazael king of Aram, and he goes up from off Jerusalem. **19** And the rest of the matters of Joash and all that he did, are they not written on the scroll of the Chronicles of the Kings of Judah? **20** And his servants rise, and make a conspiracy, and strike Joash in the house of Millo, that is going down to Silla. **21** Indeed, Jozachar son of Shimeath, and Jehozabad son of Shemer, his servants, have struck him, and he dies, and they bury him with his fathers in the City of David, and his son Amaziah reigns in his stead.

13 In the twenty-third year of Joash son of Ahaziah, king of Judah, Jehoahaz son of Jehu has reigned over Israel in Samaria, seventeen years, **2** and he does evil in the eyes of YHWH, and goes after the sins of Jeroboam son of Nebat, that he caused Israel to sin—he did not turn aside from it, **3** and the anger of YHWH burns against Israel, and He gives them into the hand of Hazael king of Aram, and into the hand of Ben-Hadad son of Hazael, all the days. **4** And Jehoahaz appeases the face of YHWH, and YHWH listens to him, for He has seen the oppression of Israel, for the king of Aram has oppressed them— **5** and YHWH gives a savior to Israel, and they go out from under the hand of Aram, and the sons of Israel dwell in their tents as before; **6** only, they have not turned aside from the sins of the house of Jeroboam that he caused Israel to sin, therein they walked, and also, the Asherah has remained in Samaria— **7** for he did not leave to Jehoahaz of the people except fifty horsemen, and ten chariots, and ten thousand footmen, for the king of Aram has destroyed them, and makes them as dust for threshing. **8** And the rest of the matters of Jehoahaz, and all that he did, and his might, are they not written on the scroll of the Chronicles of the Kings of Israel? **9** And Jehoahaz lies with his fathers, and they bury him in Samaria, and his son Joash reigns in his stead. **10** In the thirty-seventh year of Joash king of Judah, Jehoash son of Jehoahaz has reigned over Israel in Samaria, sixteen years, **11** and he does evil in the eyes of YHWH, he has not turned aside from all the sins of Jeroboam son of Nebat that he caused Israel to sin, therein he walked. **12** And the rest of the matters of Joash, and all that he did, and his might with which he fought with Amaziah king of Judah, are they not written on the scroll of the Chronicles of the Kings of Israel? **13** And Joash lies with his fathers, and Jeroboam has sat on his throne, and Joash is buried in Samaria with the kings of Israel. **14** And Elisha has been sick with his sickness in which he dies, and Joash king of Israel comes down to him and weeps on his face, and says, "My father, my father, the chariot of Israel, and its horsemen." **15** And Elisha says to him, "Take bow and arrows": and he takes bow and arrows for himself. **16** And he says to the king of Israel, "Place your hand on the bow"; and he places his hand, and Elisha puts his hands on the hands of the king, **17** and says, "Open the window eastward"; and he opens, and Elisha says, "Shoot," and he shoots; and he says, "An arrow of salvation from YHWH, and an arrow of salvation against Aram, and you have struck Aram, in Aphek, until consuming." **18** And he says, "Take the arrows," and he takes; and he says to the king of Israel, "Strike to the earth"; and he strikes three times, and stays. **19** And the man of God is angry against him and says, "By striking five or six times then you had struck Aram until consuming; but now you [only] strike Aram three times." **20** And Elisha dies, and they bury him, and troops of Moab come into the land at the coming in of the year, **21** and it comes to pass, they are burying a man, and behold, they have seen the troop, and cast the man into the grave of Elisha, and the man goes and comes against the bones of Elisha, and lives, and rises on his feet. **22** And Hazael king of Aram has oppressed Israel all the days of Jehoahaz, **23** and YHWH favors them, and pities them, and turns to them for the sake of His covenant with Abraham, Isaac, and Jacob, and has not been willing to destroy them, nor to cast them from His presence as yet. **24** And Hazael king of Aram dies, and his son Ben-Hadad reigns in his stead, **25** and Jehoash son of Jehoahaz turns and takes the cities out of the hand of Ben-Hadad son of Hazael that he had taken out of the hand of his father Jehoahaz in war; Joash has struck him three times, and he brings back the cities of Israel.

14 In the second year of Joash son of Jehoahaz, king of Israel, Amaziah son of Joash, king of Judah, has reigned; **2** he was a son of twenty-five years in his reigning, and he has reigned twenty-nine years in Jerusalem, and the name of his mother [is] Jehoaddan of Jerusalem, **3** and he does that which [is] right in the eyes of YHWH, only not like his father David; he has done according to all that his father Joash did, **4** only, the high places have not been removed—the people are still sacrificing and making incense in high places. **5** And it comes to pass, when the kingdom has been strong in his hand, that he strikes his servants, those striking his father the king, **6** and the sons of those striking [him] he has not put to death, as it is written in the Scroll of the Law of Moses that YHWH commanded, saying, "Fathers are not put to death for sons, and sons are not put to death for fathers, but each is put to death for his own sin." **7** He has struck ten thousand of Edom in the Valley of Salt, and seized Selah in war, and [one] calls its name Joktheel to this day, **8** then Amaziah has sent messengers to Jehoash son of Jehoahaz, son of Jehu, king of Israel, saying, "Come, we look one another in the face." **9** And Jehoash king of Israel sends to Amaziah king of Judah, saying, "The thorn that [is] in Lebanon has sent to the cedar that [is] in Lebanon, saying, Give your daughter to my son for a wife; and a beast of the field that [is] in Lebanon passes by, and treads down the thorn. **10** You have certainly struck Edom, and your heart has lifted you up; be honored, and abide in your house; and why do you stir yourself up in evil, that you have fallen, you and Judah with you?" **11** And Amaziah has not listened, and Jehoash king of Israel goes up, and they look one another in the face, he and Amaziah king of Judah, in Beth-Shemesh, that [is] Judah's, **12** and Judah is struck before Israel, and they each flee to his tent. **13** And Jehoash king of Israel caught Amaziah king of Judah, son of Jehoash, son of Ahaziah, in Beth-Shemesh, and they come to Jerusalem, and he bursts through the wall of Jerusalem, at the Gate of Ephraim to the Corner Gate, four hundred cubits, **14** and has taken all the gold and the silver, and all the vessels that are found in the house of YHWH, and in the treasures of the house of the king, and the sons of the pledges, and turns back to Samaria. **15** And the rest of the matters of Jehoash that he did, and his might, and how he fought with Amaziah king of Judah, are they not written on the scroll of the Chronicles of the Kings of Israel? **16** And Jehoash lies with his fathers, and is buried in Samaria with the kings of Israel, and his son Jeroboam reigns in his stead. **17** And Amaziah son of Joash, king of Judah, lives after the death of Jehoash son of Jehoahaz, king of Israel, fifteen years, **18** and the rest of the matters of Amaziah, are they not written on the scroll of the Chronicles of the Kings of Judah? **19** And they make a conspiracy against him in Jerusalem, and he flees to Lachish, and they send after him to Lachish, and put him to death there, **20** and lift him up on the horses, and he is buried in Jerusalem with his fathers in the City of David. **21** And all the people of Judah take Azariah, and he [is] a son of sixteen years, and cause him to reign instead of his father Amaziah; **22** he has built Elath, and brings it back to Judah, after the lying of the king with his fathers. **23** In the fifteenth year of Amaziah son of Joash, king of Judah, Jeroboam son of Joash, king of Israel, has reigned in Samaria, forty-one years, **24** and he does evil in the eyes of YHWH; he has not turned aside from all the sins of Jeroboam son of Nebat that he caused Israel to sin. **25** He has brought back the border of Israel, from the entering in of Hamath to the sea of the desert, according to the word of YHWH, God of Israel, that He spoke by the hand of His servant Jonah son of Amittai the prophet, who [is] of Gath-Hepher, **26** for YHWH has seen the very bitter affliction of Israel, and there is none restrained, and there is none left, and there is no helper for Israel; **27** and YHWH has not spoken to blot out the name of Israel from under the heavens, and saves them by the hand of Jeroboam son of Joash. **28** And the rest of the matters of Jeroboam, and all that he did, and his might with which he fought, and with which he brought back Damascus, and Hamath of Judah, into Israel, are they not written on the scroll of the Chronicles of the Kings of Israel? **29** And Jeroboam lies with his fathers, with the kings of Israel, and his son Zechariah reigns in his stead.

15 In the twenty-seventh year of Jeroboam king of Israel, Azariah son of Amaziah, king of Judah, has reigned; **2** he was a son of sixteen years in his reigning, and he has reigned fifty-two years in Jerusalem, and the name of his mother [is] Jecholiah of Jerusalem, **3** and he does that which [is] right in the eyes of YHWH, according to all that his father Amaziah did, **4** only, the high places have not been removed—the people are still sacrificing and making incense in high places. **5** And YHWH strikes the king, and he is a leper to the day of his death, and he dwells in a separate house, and Jotham son of the king [is] over the house, judging the people of the land. **6** And the rest of the matters of Azariah and all that he did, are they not written on the scroll of the Chronicles of the Kings of Judah? **7** And Azariah lies with his fathers, and they bury him with his fathers in the city of David, and his son Jotham reigns in his stead. **8** In the thirty-eighth year of Azariah king of Judah, Zechariah son of Jeroboam has reigned over Israel in Samaria, six months, **9** and he does evil in the eyes of YHWH as his fathers did; he has not turned aside from the sins of Jeroboam son of Nebat that he caused Israel to sin. **10** And Shallum son of Jabesh conspires against him, and strikes him before the people, and puts him to death, and reigns in his stead. **11** And the rest of the matters of Zechariah, behold, they are written on the scroll of the Chronicles of the Kings of Israel. **12** It [is] the word of YHWH that He spoke to Jehu, saying, "Sons of the fourth [generation] sit on the throne of Israel for you"; and it is so. **13** Shallum son of Jabesh has reigned in the thirty-ninth year of Uzziah king of Judah, and he reigns a month of days in Samaria; **14** and Menahem son of Gadi goes up from Tirzah and comes to Samaria, and strikes Shallum son of Jabesh in Samaria, and puts him to death, and reigns in his stead. **15** And the rest of the matters of Shallum and his conspiracy that he made, behold, they are written on the scroll of the Chronicles of the Kings of Israel. **16** Then Menahem strikes Tiphsah, and all who [are] in it, and its borders from Tirzah, for it did not open [to him], and he strikes [it], [and] he has ripped up all its pregnant women. **17** In the thirty-ninth year of Azariah king of Judah, Menahem son of Gadi has reigned over Israel in Samaria, ten years. **18** And he does evil in the eyes of YHWH; he has not turned aside from the sins of Jeroboam son of Nebat that he caused Israel to sin, all his days. **19** Pul king of Asshur has come against the land, and Menahem gives one thousand talents of silver to Pul, for his hand being with him to strengthen the kingdom in his hand. **20** And Menahem brings out the silver [from] Israel, [from] all the mighty men of wealth, to give to the king of Asshur, fifty shekels of silver for each one, and the king of Asshur turns back and has not stayed there in the land. **21** And the rest of the matters of Menahem and all that he did, are they not written on the scroll of the Chronicles of the Kings of Israel? **22** And Menahem lies with his fathers, and his son Pekahiah reigns in his stead. **23** In the fiftieth year of Azariah king of Judah, Pekahiah son of Menahem has reigned over Israel in Samaria, two years, **24** and he does evil in the eyes of YHWH; he has not turned aside from the sins of Jeroboam son of Nebat that he caused Israel to sin. **25** And Pekah son of Remaliah, his captain, conspires against him, and strikes him in Samaria, in the high place of the house of the king with Argob and Arieh; and fifty men of the sons of the Gileadites [were] with him, and he puts him to death, and reigns in his stead. **26** And the rest of the matters of Pekahiah and all that he did, behold, they are written on the scroll of the Chronicles of the Kings of Israel. **27** In the fifty-second year of Azariah king of Judah, Pekah son of Remaliah has reigned over Israel in Samaria, twenty years, **28** and he does evil in the eyes of YHWH, he has not turned aside from the sins of Jeroboam son of Nebat that he caused Israel to sin. **29** In the days of Pekah king of Israel, Tiglath-Pileser king of Asshur has come, and takes Ijon, and Abel-Beth-Maachah, and Janoah, and Kedesh, and Hazor, and Gilead, and Galilee, all the land of Naphtali, and removes them to Asshur. **30** And Hoshea son of Elah makes a conspiracy against Pekah son of Remaliah, and strikes him, and puts him to death, and reigns in his stead, in the twentieth year of Jotham son of Uzziah. **31** And the rest of the matters of Pekah and all that he did, behold, they are written on the scroll of the Chronicles of the Kings of Israel. **32** In the second year of Pekah son of Remaliah, king of Israel, Jotham son of Uzziah, king of Judah, has reigned. **33** He was a son of twenty-five years in his reigning, and he has reigned sixteen years in Jerusalem, and the name of his mother [is] Jerusha daughter of Zadok, **34** and he does that which [is] right in the eyes of YHWH; he has done according to all that his father Uzziah did. **35** Only, the high places have not been removed—the people are still sacrificing and making incense in high places; he has built the high gate of the house of YHWH. **36** And the rest of the matters of Jotham and all that he did, are they not written on the scroll of the Chronicles of the Kings of Judah? **37** In those days YHWH has begun to send Rezin king of Amram and Pekah son of Remaliah against Judah. **38** And Jotham lies with his fathers, and is buried with his fathers in the city of his father David, and his son Ahaz reigns in his stead.

16 In the seventeenth year of Pekah son of Remaliah, Ahaz son of Jotham, king of Judah, has reigned. **2** Ahaz [is] a son of twenty years in his reigning, and he has reigned sixteen years in Jerusalem, and he has not done that which [is] right in the eyes of his God YHWH, like his father David, **3** and he walks in the way of the kings of Israel, and he has also caused his son to pass over into fire, according to the abominations of the nations that YHWH dispossessed from the presence of the sons of Israel, **4** and he sacrifices and makes incense in high places, and on the heights, and under every green tree. **5** Then Rezin king of Aram, and Pekah son of Remaliah, king of Israel, go up to Jerusalem, to battle, and they lay siege to Ahaz, and they have not been able to fight. **6** At that time Rezin king of Aram has brought back Elath to Aram, and casts out the Jews from Elath, and the Arameans have come to Elath, and dwell there to this day. **7** And Ahaz sends messengers to Tiglath-Pileser king of Asshur, saying, "I [am] your servant and your son; come up and save me out of the hand of the king of Aram, and out of the hand of the king of Israel, who are rising up against me." **8** And Ahaz takes the silver and the gold that is found in the house of YHWH, and in the treasures of the house of the king, and sends to the king of Asshur [as] a bribe. **9** And the king of Asshur listens to him, and the king of Asshur goes up to Damascus, and seizes it, and removes [the people of] it to Kir, and he has put Rezin to death. **10** And King Ahaz goes to meet Tiglath-Pileser king of Asshur [at] Damascus, and sees the altar that [is] in Damascus, and King Ahaz sends to Urijah the priest the likeness of the altar, and its pattern, according to all its work, **11** and Urijah the priest builds the altar according to all that King Ahaz has sent from Damascus; so Urijah the priest did until the coming in of King Ahaz from Damascus. **12** And the king comes in from Damascus, and the king sees the altar, and the king draws near on the altar, and offers on it, **13** and burns his burnt-offering and his present as incense, and pours out his drink-offering, and sprinkles the blood of the peace-offerings that he has, on the altar. **14** As for the altar of bronze that [is] before YHWH—he brings [it] near from the front of the house, from between the altar and the house of YHWH, and puts it on the side of the altar, northward. **15** And King Ahaz commands him—Urijah the priest—saying, "On the great altar burn as incense the burnt-offering of the morning, and the present of the evening, and the burnt-offering of the king, and his present, and the burnt-offering of all the people of the land, and their present, and their drink-offerings; and all the blood of the burnt-offering, and all the blood of the sacrifice, you sprinkle on it, and the altar of bronze is for me to inquire [by]." **16** And Urijah the priest does according to all that King Ahaz commanded. **17** And King Ahaz cuts off the borders of the bases, and turns aside the laver from off them, and he has taken down the sea from off the bronze oxen that [are] under it, and puts it on a pavement of stones. **18** And the covered place for the Sabbath that they built in the house, and the entrance of the king outside, he turned [from] the house of YHWH, because of the king of Asshur. **19** And the rest of the matters of Ahaz that he did, are they not written on the scroll of the Chronicles of the Kings of Judah? **20** And Ahaz lies with his fathers, and is buried with his fathers in the City of David, and his son Hezekiah reigns in his stead.

17 In the twelfth year of Ahaz king of Judah, Hoshea son of Elah has reigned over Israel in Samaria, nine years, **2** and he does evil in the eyes of YHWH, only, not as the kings of Israel who were before him; **3** Shalmaneser king of Asshur came up against him, and Hoshea is a servant to him, and renders a present to him. **4** And the king of Asshur finds in Hoshea a conspiracy, in that he has sent messengers to So king of Egypt, and has not caused a present to go up to the king of Asshur, as year by year, and the king of Asshur restrains him, and binds him in a house of restraint. **5** And the king of Asshur goes up into all the land, and he goes up to Samaria, and lays siege against it [for] three years; **6** in the ninth year of Hoshea, the king of Asshur has captured Samaria, and removes Israel to Asshur, and causes them to dwell in Halah, and in Habor, [by] the river Gozan, and [in] the cities of the Medes. **7** And it comes to pass, because the sons of Israel have sinned against their God YHWH—who brings them up out of the land of Egypt, from under the hand of Pharaoh king of Egypt—and fear other gods, **8** and walk in the statutes of the nations that YHWH dispossessed from the presence of the sons of Israel, and of the kings of Israel that they made; **9** and the sons of Israel covertly do things that [are] not right against their God YHWH, and build high places for themselves in all their cities, from a tower of the watchers to the fortified city, **10** and set up standing-pillars and Asherim for themselves on every high height, and under every green tree, **11** and make incense there in all high places, like the nations that YHWH removed from their presence, and do evil things to provoke YHWH, **12** and serve the idols, of which YHWH said to them, "You do not do this thing." **13** And YHWH testifies against Israel, and against Judah, by the hand of every prophet, and every seer, saying, "Turn back from your evil ways, and keep My commands, My statutes, according to all the Law that I commanded your fathers, and that I sent to you by the hand of My servants the prophets"; **14** and they have not listened, and harden their neck, like the neck of their fathers, who did not remain steadfast in their God YHWH, **15** and reject His statutes and His covenant that He made with their fathers, and His testimonies that He testified against them, and go after the vain thing, and become vain, and after the nations that are around them, of whom YHWH commanded them not to do like them. **16** And they forsake all the commands of their God YHWH, and make a molten image for themselves—two calves, and make an Asherah, and bow themselves to all the host of the heavens, and serve Ba'al, **17** and cause their sons and their daughters to pass over through fire, and divine divinations, and use enchantments, and sell themselves to do evil in the eyes of YHWH, to provoke Him. **18** And YHWH shows Himself very angry against Israel, and turns them aside from His presence; none has been left, only the tribe of Judah by itself. **19** Also Judah has not kept the commands of their God YHWH, and they walk in the statutes of Israel that they had made. **20** And YHWH kicks against all the seed of Israel, and afflicts them, and gives them into the hand of spoilers, until He has cast them out of His presence, **21** for He has torn Israel from the house of David, and they make Jeroboam son of Nebat king, and Jeroboam drives Israel from after YHWH, and has caused them to sin a great sin, **22** and the sons of Israel walk in all the sins of Jeroboam that he did, they have not turned aside from them, **23** until YHWH has turned

2 KINGS

Israel aside from His presence, as He spoke by the hand of all His servants the prophets, and Israel is removed from off its land to Asshur, to this day. **24** And the king of Asshur brings in [people] from Babylon and from Cutha, and from Ava, and from Hamath, and Sepharvaim, and causes [them] to dwell in the cities of Samaria instead of the sons of Israel, and they possess Samaria, and dwell in its cities; **25** and it comes to pass, at the commencement of their dwelling there, they have not feared YHWH, and YHWH sends the lions among them, and they are destroying among them. **26** And they speak to the king of Asshur, saying, "The nations that you have removed and place in the cities of Samaria have not known the custom of the God of the land, and He sends the lions among them, and behold, they are destroying them, as they do not know the custom of the God of the land." **27** And the king of Asshur commands, saying, "Cause one of the priests to go there whom you removed from there, and they go and dwell there, and he teaches them the custom of the God of the land." **28** And one of the priests whom they removed from Samaria comes in, and dwells in Beth-El, and he is teaching them how they fear YHWH, **29** and each nation is making its gods, and they place [them] in the houses of the high places that the Samaritans have made—each nation in their cities where they are dwelling. **30** And the men of Babylon have made Succoth-Benoth, and the men of Cuth have made Nergal, and the men of Hamath have made Ashima, **31** and the Avites have made Nibhaz and Tartak, and the Sepharvites are burning their sons with fire to Adrammelech and Anammelech, gods of Sepharvim. **32** And they are fearing YHWH, and make for themselves from their extremities priests of high places, and they are working for them in the house of the high places. **33** They are fearing YHWH, and they are serving their gods, according to the custom of the nations from where they removed them. **34** To this day they are doing according to the former customs—they are not fearing YHWH, and are not doing according to their statutes, and according to their ordinances, and according to the Law, and according to the command, that YHWH commanded the sons of Jacob whose name He made Israel, **35** and YHWH makes a covenant with them and charges them, saying, "You do not fear other gods, nor bow yourselves to them, nor serve them, nor sacrifice to them, **36** but YHWH who brought you up out of the land of Egypt with great power, and with an outstretched arm, Him you fear, and to Him you bow yourselves, and to Him you sacrifice; **37** and the statutes, and the judgments, and the Law, and the command, that He wrote for you, you observe to do all the days, and you do not fear other gods; **38** and you do not forget the covenant that I have made with you, and you do not fear other gods; **39** but you fear your God YHWH, and He delivers you out of the hand of all your enemies"; **40** and they have not listened, but they are doing according to their former custom, **41** and these nations are fearing YHWH, and they have served their carved images, both their sons and their sons' sons; as their fathers did, they are doing to this day.

18 And it comes to pass, in the third year of Hoshea son of Elah, king of Israel, Hezekiah son of Ahaz, king of Judah, has reigned; **2** he was a son of twenty-five years in his reigning, and he has reigned twenty-nine years in Jerusalem, and the name of his mother [is] Abi daughter of Zechariah. **3** And he does that which [is] right in the eyes of YHWH, according to all that his father David did, **4** he has turned aside the high places, and broken in pieces the standing-pillars, and cut down the Asherah, and beaten down the bronze serpent that Moses made, for up to these days the sons of Israel were making incense to it, and he calls it "a piece of bronze." **5** In YHWH, God of Israel, he has trusted, and after him there has not been like him among all the kings of Judah, nor [among any] who were before him; **6** and he cleaves to YHWH, he has not turned aside from after Him, and keeps His commands that YHWH commanded Moses. **7** And YHWH has been with him; in every place where he goes out he acts wisely, and he rebels against the king of Asshur, and has not served him; **8** he has struck the Philistines, even to Gaza and its borders, from a tower of watchers to the fortified city. **9** And it comes to pass, in the fourth year of King Hezekiah—it [is] the seventh year of Hoshea son of Elah, king of Israel—Shalmaneser king of Asshur has

2 KINGS

come up against Samaria and lays siege to it, **10** and they capture it at the end of three years; in the sixth year of Hezekiah—it [is] the ninth year of Hoshea king of Israel—Samaria has been captured, **11** and the king of Asshur removes Israel to Asshur, and placed them in Halah, and in Habor [by] the river Gozan, and [in] cities of the Medes, **12** because that they have not listened to the voice of their God YHWH, and transgress His covenant—all that He commanded Moses, servant of YHWH—indeed, they have not listened nor done [it]. **13** And in the fourteenth year of King Hezekiah, Sennacherib king of Asshur has come up against all the fortified cities of Judah, and seizes them, **14** and Hezekiah king of Judah sends to the king of Asshur at Lachish, saying, "I have sinned, turn back from off me; that which you put on me I bear"; and the king of Asshur lays on Hezekiah king of Judah three hundred talents of silver and thirty talents of gold, **15** and Hezekiah gives all the silver that is found in the house of YHWH and in the treasures of the house of the king; **16** at that time Hezekiah has cut off the doors of the temple of YHWH, and the pillars that Hezekiah king of Judah had overlaid, and gives them to the king of Asshur. **17** And the king of Asshur sends Tartan, and the chief of the eunuchs, and the chief of the butlers, from Lachish, to King Hezekiah, with a heavy force, to Jerusalem, and they go up and come to Jerusalem, and they go up, and come in and stand by the conduit of the upper pool that [is] in the highway of the fuller's field. **18** And they call to the king, and Eliakim son of Hilkiah, who [is] over the house, and Shebna the scribe, and Joah son of Asaph, the remembrancer, go out to them. **19** And the chief of the butlers says to them, "Now say to Hezekiah, Thus said the great king, the king of Asshur: What [is] this confidence in which you have confided? **20** You have said: Only a word of the lips! Counsel and might [are] for battle; now, on whom have you trusted that you have rebelled against me? **21** Now behold, you have trusted for yourself on the staff of this broken reed, on Egypt; which a man leans on, and it has gone into his hand and pierced it! So [is] Pharaoh king of Egypt to all those trusting on him. **22** And when you say to me, We have trusted in our God YHWH, is it not He whose high places and whose altars Hezekiah has turned aside, and says to Judah and to Jerusalem, You bow yourselves before this altar in Jerusalem? **23** And now, please give a pledge for yourself to my lord the king of Asshur, and I give two thousand horses to you, if you are able to give riders for yourself on them. **24** And how do you turn back the face of one captain of the least of the servants of my lord, that you trust for yourself on Egypt for chariot and for horsemen? **25** Have I now come up without YHWH against this place to destroy it? YHWH said to me, Go up against this land, and you have destroyed it." **26** And Eliakim son of Hilkiah says—and Shebna and Joah—to the chief of the butlers, "Please speak to your servants [in] Aramaic, for we are understanding, but do not speak with us [in] Jewish, in the ears of the people who [are] on the wall." **27** And the chief of the butlers says to them, "For your lord, and to you, has my lord sent me to speak these words? Is it not for the men—those sitting on the wall—to eat their own dung and to drink their own water, with you?" **28** And the chief of the butlers stands and calls with a great voice [in] Jewish, and speaks and says, "Hear a word of the great king, the king of Asshur— **29** thus said the king: Do not let Hezekiah lift you up, for he is not able to deliver you out of his hand; **30** and do not let Hezekiah make you trust in YHWH, saying, YHWH certainly delivers us, and this city is not given into the hand of the king of Asshur. **31** Do not listen to Hezekiah, for thus said the king of Asshur: Make a blessing with me, and come out to me, and each eat of his vine, and each [eat] of his fig tree, and each drink the waters of his own well, **32** until my coming in, and I have taken you to a land like your own land, a land of grain and new wine, a land of bread and vineyards, a land of olive oil, and honey; and live, and do not die; and do not listen to Hezekiah when he persuades you, saying, YHWH delivers us. **33** Have each of the gods of the nations ever delivered his land out of the hand of the king of Asshur? **34** Where [are] the gods of Hamath and Arpad? Where [are] the gods of Sepharvaim, Hena, and Ivvah, that they have delivered Samaria out of my hand? **35** Who [are they] among all the gods of the lands that have delivered their land out of my hand, that YHWH delivers Jerusalem out of my hand?" **36** And the people have kept silent, and have not answered him a word, for the command of the king is, saying, "Do not answer him." **37** And Eliakim son of Hilkiah, who [is] over the house, comes in, and Shebna the scribe, and Joah son of Asaph, the remembrancer, to Hezekiah, with torn garments, and they declare to him the words of the chief of the butlers.

19 And it comes to pass, at King Hezekiah's hearing, that he tears his garments, and covers himself with sackcloth, and enters the house of YHWH, **2** and sends Eliakim, who [is] over the house, and Shebna the scribe, and the elderly of the priests, covering themselves with sackcloth, to Isaiah the prophet, son of Amoz, **3** and they say to him, "Thus said Hezekiah: This day [is] a day of distress, and rebuke, and despising; for sons have come to the birth, and there is not power to bring forth. **4** It may be your God YHWH hears all the words of the chief of the butlers with which the king of Asshur his lord has sent him to reproach the living God, and has decided concerning the words that your God YHWH has heard, and you have lifted up prayer for the remnant that is found." **5** And the servants of King Hezekiah come to Isaiah, **6** and Isaiah says to them, "Thus you say to your lord, Thus said YHWH: Do not be afraid because of the words that you have heard, with which the servants of the king of Asshur have reviled Me. **7** Behold, I am giving a spirit in him, and he has heard a report, and has turned back to his land, and I have caused him to fall by the sword in his land." **8** And the chief of the butlers turns back and finds the king of Asshur fighting against Libnah, for he has heard that he has journeyed from Lachish. **9** And he hears concerning Tirhakah king of Cush, saying, "Behold, he has come out to fight with you"; and he turns and sends messengers to Hezekiah, saying, **10** "Thus you speak to Hezekiah king of Judah, saying, Do not let your God in whom you are trusting lift you up, saying, Jerusalem is not given into the hand of the king of Asshur. **11** Behold, you have heard that which the kings of Asshur have done to all the lands—to devote them; and are you delivered? **12** Did the gods of the nations deliver them whom my fathers destroyed—Gozan, and Haran, and Rezeph, and the sons of Eden, who [are] in Thelassar? **13** Where [is] the king of Hamath, and the king of Arpad, and the king of the city of Sepharvaim, Hena, and Ivvah?" **14** And Hezekiah takes the letters out of the hand of the messengers and reads them, and goes up to the house of YHWH, and Hezekiah spreads it before YHWH. **15** And Hezekiah prays before YHWH and says, "O YHWH, God of Israel, inhabiting the cherubim, You [are] God Himself—You alone—to all the kingdoms of the earth: You have made the heavens and the earth. **16** Incline, O YHWH, Your ear, and hear; open, O YHWH, Your eyes, and see; and hear the words of Sennacherib with which he has sent him to reproach the living God. **17** Truly, O YHWH, kings of Asshur have laid waste the nations and their land, **18** and have put their gods into fire, for they [are] no gods, but work of the hands of man, wood and stone, and destroy them. **19** And now, O our God YHWH, please save us out of his hand, and all kingdoms of the earth know that You [are] YHWH God—You alone." **20** And Isaiah son of Amoz sends to Hezekiah, saying, "Thus said YHWH, God of Israel: That which you have prayed to Me concerning Sennacherib king of Asshur I have heard; **21** this [is] the word that YHWH spoke concerning him: Trampled on you—laughed at you ‖ Has the virgin daughter of Zion; Shaken the head behind you ‖ Has the daughter of Jerusalem! **22** Whom have you reproached and reviled? And against whom lifted up a voice? Indeed, you lift up your eyes on high—Against the Holy One of Israel! **23** By the hand of your messengers ‖ You have reproached the Lord, and say, ‖ In the multitude of my chariots I have come up to a high place of mountains—The sides of Lebanon, ‖ And I cut down the height of its cedars, ‖ The choice of its firs, ‖ And I enter the lodging of its extremity, ‖ The forest of its Carmel. **24** I have dug, and drunk strange waters, ‖ And I dry up with the sole of my steps ‖ All floods of a bulwark. **25** Have you not heard from afar [that] I made it, ‖ From days of old that I formed it? Now I have brought it in, ‖ And it becomes a desolation, ‖ Ruinous heaps [are] fortified cities, **26** And their inhabitants [are] feeble-handed, ‖ They were broken down, and are dried up, ‖ They have been the herb of the field, ‖ And the greenness of the tender grass, ‖ Grass of the roofs, ‖ And blasted grain—before it has risen up! **27** And your sitting down, and your going out, ‖ And your coming in, I have known, ‖ And your anger toward Me; **28** Because of your anger toward Me, ‖ And your noise—it came up into My ears, ‖ I have put My hook in your nose, ‖ And My bridle in your lips, ‖ And have caused you to turn back ‖ In the way in which you came. **29** And this [is] the sign to you, ‖ Food of the year [is] the spontaneous growth, ‖ And in the second year the self-produced, ‖ And in the third year you sow, and reap, ‖ And plant vineyards, and eat their fruits. **30** And it has continued—The escaped of the house of Judah ‖ That has been left—to take root beneath, ‖ And has made fruit upward. **31** For a remnant goes out from Jerusalem, ‖ And an escape from Mount Zion; The zeal of YHWH [of Hosts] does this. **32** Therefore, thus said YHWH, ‖ Concerning the king of Asshur: He does not come into this city, ‖ Nor does he shoot an arrow there, ‖ Nor does he come before it with shield, ‖ Nor does he pour out a mound against it. **33** In the way that he comes in—In it he turns back, ‖ And to this city he does not come in, ‖ A declaration of YHWH— **34** And I have covered over this city, ‖ To save it for My own sake, ‖ And for the sake of My servant David." **35** And it comes to pass, in that night, that a messenger of YHWH goes out, and strikes one hundred eighty-five thousand in the camp of Asshur, and they rise early in the morning, and behold, all of them [are] dead corpses. **36** And Sennacherib king of Asshur journeys, and goes, and turns back, and dwells in Nineveh; **37** and it comes to pass, he is bowing himself in the house of his god Nisroch, and [his sons] Adramelech and Sharezar have struck him with the sword, and they have escaped to the land of Ararat, and his son Esar-Haddon reigns in his stead.

20 In those days Hezekiah has been sick to death, and Isaiah son of Amoz the prophet comes to him and says to him, "Thus said YHWH: Give a charge to your house, for you are dying, and do not live." **2** And he turns around his face to the wall, and prays to YHWH, saying, **3** "Ah, now, O YHWH, please remember how I have habitually walked before You in truth and with a perfect heart, and I have done that which [is] good in Your eyes"; and Hezekiah weeps [with] a great weeping. **4** And it comes to pass, [when] Isaiah has not [yet] gone out to the middle court, that the word of YHWH has been to him, saying, **5** "Return, and you have said to Hezekiah, leader of My people, Thus said YHWH, God of your father David: I have heard your prayer, I have seen your tear, behold, I give healing to you. On the third day you go up to the house of YHWH; **6** and I have added fifteen years to your days, and I deliver you and this city out of the hand of the king of Asshur, and have covered over this city for My own sake, and for the sake of My servant David." **7** And Isaiah says, "Take a cake of figs"; and they take and lay [it] on the boil, and he revives. **8** And Hezekiah says to Isaiah, "What [is] the sign that YHWH gives healing to me, that I have gone up to the house of YHWH on the third day?" **9** And Isaiah says, "This [is] the sign to you from YHWH, that YHWH does the thing that He has spoken—[will] the shadow have gone on ten degrees, or does it turn back ten degrees?" **10** And Hezekiah says, "It has been light for the shadow to incline ten degrees; no, but let the shadow turn backward ten degrees." **11** And Isaiah the prophet calls to YHWH, and He brings back the shadow by the degrees that it had gone down in the degrees of Ahaz—backward ten degrees. **12** At that time Berodach-Baladan son of Baladan, king of Babylon, has sent letters and a present to Hezekiah, for he heard that Hezekiah had been sick; **13** and Hezekiah listens to them, and shows them all the house of his treasury, the silver, and the gold, and the spices, and the good ointment, and all the house of his vessels, and all that has been found in his treasuries; there has not been a thing that Hezekiah has not showed them in his house and in all his dominion. **14** And Isaiah the prophet comes to King Hezekiah and says to him, "What did these men say? And from where do they come to you?" And Hezekiah says, "They have come from a far-off land—from Babylon." **15** And he says, "What did they see in your house?" And Hezekiah says, "They saw all that [is] in my house; there has not been a thing that I have not showed them among my treasures." **16** And Isaiah says to Hezekiah, "Hear a word of YHWH: **17** Behold, days are coming, and all that [is] in your house, and [all] that your father has treasured up until this day, has been carried to Babylon; there is not a thing left, said

YHWH; **18** and of your sons who go out from you, whom you beget, they take away, and they have been eunuchs in the palace of the king of Babylon." **19** And Hezekiah says to Isaiah, "The word of YHWH that you have spoken [is] good"; and he says, "Why not, if there is peace and truth in my days?" **20** And the rest of the matters of Hezekiah, and all his might, and how he made the pool, and the conduit, and brings in the waters to the city, are they not written on the scroll of the Chronicles of the Kings of Judah? **21** And Hezekiah lies with his fathers, and his son Manasseh reigns in his stead.

21 Manasseh [is] a son of twelve years in his reigning, and he has reigned fifty-five years in Jerusalem, and the name of his mother [is] Hephzi-Bah; **2** and he does evil in the eyes of YHWH, according to the abominations of the nations that YHWH dispossessed from the presence of the sons of Israel, **3** and he turns and builds the high places that his father Hezekiah destroyed, and raises altars for Ba'al, and makes an Asherah, as Ahab king of Israel did, and bows himself to all the host of the heavens, and serves them. **4** And he has built altars in the house of YHWH, of which YHWH said, "In Jerusalem I put My Name." **5** And he builds altars to all the host of the heavens in the two courts of the house of YHWH; **6** and he has caused his son to pass through fire, and observed clouds, and used enchantment, and dealt with a familiar spirit and wizards; he has multiplied to do evil in the eyes of YHWH—to provoke to anger. **7** And he sets the carved image of the Asherah that he made in the house of which YHWH said to David and to his son Solomon, "In this house, and in Jerusalem, that I have chosen out of all the tribes of Israel, I put My Name for all time; **8** and I do not add to cause the foot of Israel to move from the ground that I gave to their fathers, only, if they observe to do according to all that I commanded them, and to all the Law that My servant Moses commanded them." **9** And they have not listened, and Manasseh causes them to err, to do evil above the nations that YHWH destroyed from the presence of the sons of Israel. **10** And YHWH speaks by the hand of his servants the prophets, saying, **11** "Because that Manasseh king of Judah has done these abominations—he has done evil above all that the Amorites have done who [are] before him, and also causes Judah to sin by his idols— **12** therefore, thus said YHWH, God of Israel: Behold, I am bringing in calamity on Jerusalem and Judah, that whoever hears of it, his two ears tingle. **13** And I have stretched out the line of Samaria over Jerusalem, and the plummet of the house of Ahab, and wiped Jerusalem as one wipes the dish—he has wiped, and has turned [it] on its face. **14** And I have left the remnant of My inheritance, and given them into the hand of their enemies, and they have been for a prey and for a spoil to all their enemies, **15** because that they have done evil in My eyes, and are provoking Me to anger from the day that their fathers came out of Egypt, even to this day." **16** And also, Manasseh has shed very much innocent blood, until he has filled Jerusalem mouth to mouth, apart from his sin that he has caused Judah to sin, to do evil in the eyes of YHWH. **17** And the rest of the matters of Manasseh, and all that he did, and his sin that he sinned, are they not written on the scroll of the Chronicles of the Kings of Judah? **18** And Manasseh lies with his fathers, and is buried in the garden of his house, in the garden of Uzza, and his son Amon reigns in his stead. **19** Amon [is] a son of twenty-two years in his reigning, and he has reigned two years in Jerusalem, and the name of his mother [is] Meshullemeth daughter of Haruz of Jotbah, **20** and he does evil in the eyes of YHWH, as his father Manasseh did, **21** and walks in all the way that his father walked in, and serves the idols that his father served, and bows himself to them, **22** and forsakes YHWH, God of his fathers, and has not walked in the way of YHWH. **23** And the servants of Amon conspire against him, and put the king to death in his own house, **24** and the people of the land strike all those conspiring against King Amon, and the people of the land cause his son Josiah to reign in his stead. **25** And the rest of the matters of Amon that he did, are they not written on the scroll of the Chronicles of the Kings of Judah? **26** And [one] buries him in his burying-place in the garden of Uzza, and his son Josiah reigns in his stead.

22 Josiah [is] a son of eight years in his reigning, and he has reigned thirty-one years in Jerusalem, and the name of his mother [is] Jedidah daughter of Adaiah of Boskath, **2** and he does that which is right in the eyes of Y<small>HWH</small>, and walks in all the way of his father David, and has not turned aside [to] the right or left. **3** And it comes to pass, in the eighteenth year of King Josiah, the king has sent Shaphan son of Azaliah, son of Meshullam, the scribe, to the house of Y<small>HWH</small>, saying, **4** "Go up to Hilkiah the high priest, and he completes the silver that is brought into the house of Y<small>HWH</small>, that the keepers of the threshold have gathered from the people, **5** and they give it into the hand of those doing the work, the overseers, in the house of Y<small>HWH</small>, and they give it to those doing the work, that [are] in the house of Y<small>HWH</small>, to strengthen the breach of the house, **6** to craftsmen, and to builders, and [to repairers of] the wall, and to buy wood and hewn stones to strengthen the house; **7** only, the silver that is given into their hand is not reckoned with them, for they are dealing in faithfulness." **8** And Hilkiah the high priest says to Shaphan the scribe, "I have found [the] Scroll of the Law in the house of Y<small>HWH</small>"; and Hilkiah gives the scroll to Shaphan, and he reads it. **9** And Shaphan the scribe comes to the king, and brings the king back word, and says, "Your servants have poured out the silver that has been found in the house, and give it into the hand of those doing the work, the inspectors, in the house of Y<small>HWH</small>." **10** And Shaphan the scribe declares to the king, saying, "Hilkiah the priest has given a scroll to me"; and Shaphan reads it before the king. **11** And it comes to pass, at the king's hearing the words of the Scroll of the Law, that he tears his garments, **12** and the king commands Hilkiah the priest, and Ahikam son of Shaphan, and Achbor son of Michaiah, and Shaphan the scribe, and Asahiah servant of the king, saying, **13** "Go, seek Y<small>HWH</small> for me, and for the people, and for all Judah, concerning the words of this scroll that is found, for great [is] the fury of Y<small>HWH</small> that is kindled against us, because that our fathers have not listened to the words of this scroll, to do according to all that is written for us." **14** And Hilkiah the priest goes, and Ahikam, and Achbor, and Shaphan, and Asahiah, to Huldah the prophetess, wife of Shallum, son of Tikvah, son of Harhas, keeper of the garments, and she is dwelling in Jerusalem in the second [quarter], and they speak to her. **15** And she says to them, "Thus said Y<small>HWH</small>, God of Israel: Say to the man who has sent you to me, **16** Thus said Y<small>HWH</small>: Behold, I am bringing in calamity to this place and on its inhabitants, all the words of the scroll that the king of Judah has read, **17** because that they have forsaken Me, and make incense to other gods, so as to provoke Me to anger with every work of their hands, and My wrath has been kindled against this place, and it is not quenched. **18** And to the king of Judah, who is sending you to seek Y<small>HWH</small>, thus you say to him, Thus said Y<small>HWH</small>, God of Israel: The words that you have heard— **19** because your heart [is] tender, and you are humbled because of Y<small>HWH</small>, in your hearing that which I have spoken against this place, and against its inhabitants, to be for a desolation, and for a reviling, and you tear your garments and weep before Me— I also have heard—a declaration of Y<small>HWH</small>— **20** therefore, behold, I am gathering you to your fathers, and you have been gathered to your grave in peace, and your eyes do not look on any of the calamity that I am bringing in on this place"; and they bring the king back word.

23 And the king sends, and they gather all [the] elderly of Judah and Jerusalem to him, **2** and the king goes up to the house of Y<small>HWH</small>, and every man of Judah, and all the inhabitants of Jerusalem, with him, and the priests, and the prophets, and all the people, from small to great, and he reads in their ears all the words of the Scroll of the Covenant that is found in the house of Y<small>HWH</small>. **3** And the king stands by the pillar, and makes the covenant before Y<small>HWH</small>, to walk after Y<small>HWH</small>, and to keep His commands, and His testimonies, and His statutes, with all the heart, and with all the soul, to establish the words of this covenant that are written on this scroll, and all the people stand in the covenant. **4** And the king commands Hilkiah the high priest, and the priests of the second order, and the keepers of the threshold, to bring out from the temple of Y<small>HWH</small> all the vessels that are made for Ba'al, and for the Asherah, and for all the host of the heavens, and he burns them at the outside of Jerusalem, in the fields of Kidron, and has carried their ashes to Beth-El. **5** And he has caused to cease the idolatrous priests whom the kings of Judah have appointed (and they make incense in high places, in cities of Judah and outskirts of Jerusalem), and those making incense to Ba'al, to the sun, and to the moon, and to the twelve signs, and to all the host of the heavens. **6** And he brings out the Asherah from the house of YHWH to the outside of Jerusalem, to the Brook of Kidron, and burns it at the Brook of Kidron, and beats it small to dust, and casts its dust on the grave of the sons of the people. **7** And he breaks down the houses of the whoremongers that [are] in the house of YHWH, where the women are weaving houses for the Asherah. **8** And he brings in all the priests out of the cities of Judah, and defiles the high places where the priests have made incense, from Geba to Beer-Sheba, and has broken down the high places of the gates that [are] at the opening of the Gate of Joshua, head of the city, that [is] on a man's left hand at the gate of the city; **9** only, the priests of the high places do not come up to the altar of YHWH in Jerusalem, but they have eaten unleavened things in the midst of their brothers. **10** And he has defiled Topheth that [is] in the Valley of the Son of Hinnom, so that no man causes his son and his daughter to pass over through fire to Molech. **11** And he causes to cease the horses that the kings of Judah have given to the sun from the entering in of the house of YHWH, by the chamber of Nathan-Melech the eunuch, that [is] in the outskirts; and he has burned the chariots of the sun with fire. **12** And the altars that [are] on the top of the upper chamber of Ahaz, that the kings of Judah made, and the altars that Manasseh made in the two courts of the house of YHWH, the king has broken down, and removes from there, and has cast their dust into the Brook of Kidron. **13** And the high places that [are] on the front of Jerusalem, that [are] on the right of the Mount of Corruption, that Solomon king of Israel had built to Ashtoreth, abomination of the Zidonians, and Chemosh, abomination of Moab, and to Milcom, abomination of the sons of Ammon, the king has defiled. **14** And he has broken the standing-pillars in pieces, and cuts down the Asherim, and fills their place with bones of men; **15** and also the altar that [is] in Beth-El, the high place that Jeroboam son of Nebat made, by which he made Israel sin, both that altar and the high place he has broken down, and burns the high place—he has beat it small to dust, and has burned the Asherah. **16** And Josiah turns, and sees the graves that [are] there on the mountain, and sends and takes the bones out of the graves, and burns [them] on the altar, and defiles it, according to the word of YHWH that the man of God proclaimed, who proclaimed these things. **17** And he says, "What [is] this sign that I see?" And the men of the city say to him, "The grave of the man of God who has come from Judah, and proclaims these things that you have done concerning the altar of Beth-El." **18** And he says, "Leave him alone, let no man touch his bones"; and they let his bones escape with the bones of the prophet who came out of Samaria. **19** And also all the houses of the high places that [are] in the cities of Samaria, that the kings of Israel made to provoke to anger, Josiah has turned aside, and does to them according to all the deeds that he did in Beth-El. **20** And he slays all the priests of the high places who [are] there by the altars, and burns the bones of man on them, and turns back to Jerusalem. **21** And the king commands the whole of the people, saying, "Make a Passover to your God YHWH, as it is written on this scroll of the covenant." **22** Surely there has not been made like this Passover from the days of the ones judging who judged Israel, even all the days of the kings of Israel, and of the kings of Judah; **23** but in the eighteenth year of King Josiah, this Passover has been made to YHWH in Jerusalem. **24** And also, those having familiar spirits, and the wizards, and the teraphim, and the idols, and all the abominations that were seen in the land of Judah, and in Jerusalem, Josiah has put away, in order to establish the words of the Law that are written on the scroll that Hilkiah the priest has found in the house of YHWH. **25** And like him there has not been before him a king who turned back to YHWH with all his heart, and with all his soul, and with all his might, according to all the Law of Moses, and after him there has none risen like him. **26** Only, YHWH has not turned back from the fierceness of His great anger with which His anger burned against Judah, because of all the provocations with which Manasseh provoked him, **27** and YHWH says, "I also turn Judah aside from my presence, as I turned Israel aside, and I have rejected this city that I have chosen—Jerusalem, and the house of which I said, My Name is there."

28 And the rest of the matters of Josiah and all that he did, are they not written on the scroll of the Chronicles of the Kings of Judah? **29** In his days Pharaoh Necho king of Egypt has come up against the king of Asshur, by the Euphrates River, and King Josiah goes out to meet him, and [Pharaoh Necho] puts him to death in Megiddo when he sees him. **30** And his servants cause him to ride dying from Megiddo, and bring him to Jerusalem, and bury him in his own grave, and the people of the land take Jehoahaz son of Josiah, and anoint him, and cause him to reign instead of his father. **31** Jehoahaz [is] a son of twenty-three years in his reigning, and he has reigned three months in Jerusalem, and the name of his mother [is] Hamutal daughter of Jeremiah of Libnah, **32** and he does evil in the eyes of YHWH, according to all that his fathers did, **33** and Pharaoh Necho binds him in Riblah, in the land of Hamath, from reigning in Jerusalem, and he puts a fine on the land—one hundred talents of silver, and a talent of gold. **34** And Pharaoh Necho causes Eliakim son of Josiah to reign instead of his father Josiah, and turns his name to Jehoiakim, and he has taken Jehoahaz away, and he comes to Egypt, and dies there. **35** And Jehoiakim has given the silver and the gold to Pharaoh; only he valued the land to give the silver by the command of Pharaoh; from each, according to his valuation, he exacted the silver and the gold, from the people of the land, to give to Pharaoh Necho. **36** Jehoiakim [is] a son of twenty-five years in his reigning, and he has reigned eleven years in Jerusalem, and the name of his mother [is] Zebudah daughter of Pedaiah of Rumah, **37** and he does evil in the eyes of YHWH, according to all that his fathers did.

24 In his days Nebuchadnezzar king of Babylon has come up, and Jehoiakim is a servant to him [for] three years; and he turns and rebels against him, **2** and YHWH sends against him the troops of the Chaldeans, and the troops of Aram, and the troops of Moab, and the troops of the sons of Ammon, and He sends them against Judah to destroy it, according to the word of YHWH that He spoke by the hand of His servants the prophets; **3** only, by the command of YHWH it has been against Judah to turn [them] aside from His presence, for the sins of Manasseh, according to all that he did, **4** and also the innocent blood that he has shed, and he fills Jerusalem with innocent blood, and YHWH was not willing to forgive. **5** And the rest of the matters of Jehoiakim and all that he did, are they not written on the scroll of the Chronicles of the Kings of Judah? **6** And Jehoiakim lies with his fathers, and his son Jehoiachin reigns in his stead. **7** And the king of Egypt has not added anymore to go out from his own land, for the king of Babylon has taken, from the Brook of Egypt to the Euphrates River, all that had been to the king of Egypt. **8** Jehoiachin [is] a son of eighteen years in his reigning, and he has reigned three months in Jerusalem, and the name of his mother [is] Nehushta daughter of Elnathan of Jerusalem, **9** and he does evil in the eyes of YHWH, according to all that his fathers did. **10** At that time servants of Nebuchadnezzar king of Babylon have come up to Jerusalem, and the city goes into siege, **11** and Nebuchadnezzar king of Babylon comes against the city, and his servants are laying siege to it, **12** and Jehoiachin king of Judah goes out to the king of Babylon, he, and his mother, and his servants, and his chiefs, and his eunuchs, and the king of Babylon takes him in the eighth year of his reign, **13** and brings out from there all the treasures of the house of YHWH, and the treasures of the house of the king, and cuts in pieces all the vessels of gold that Solomon king of Israel made in the temple of YHWH, as YHWH had spoken. **14** And he has removed all Jerusalem, and all the chiefs, and all the mighty men of valor—ten thousand [is] the expulsion—and every craftsman and smith; none has been left except the poor of the people of the land. **15** And he removes Jehoiachin to Babylon, and the mother of the king, and the wives of the king, and his eunuchs, and the mighty ones of the land—he has caused a removal to go from Jerusalem to Babylon, **16** and all the men of valor, seven thousand, and the craftsmen and the smiths, one thousand, the whole [are] mighty men, warriors; and the king of Babylon brings them in a captivity to Babylon. **17** And the king of Babylon causes his father's brother Mattaniah to reign in his stead, and turns his name to Zedekiah. **18** Zedekiah [is] a son of twenty-one years in his reigning, and he has reigned eleven years in Jerusalem, and the name of his mother [is]

Hamutal daughter of Jeremiah of Libnah, **19** and he does evil in the eyes of YHWH according to all that Jehoiakim did, **20** for by the anger of YHWH it has been against Jerusalem and against Judah, until He [finally] cast them out from His presence. And Zedekiah rebels against the king of Babylon.

25 And it comes to pass, in the ninth year of his reign, in the tenth month, on the tenth of the month, Nebuchadnezzar king of Babylon has come, he and all his force, against Jerusalem, and encamps against it, and builds a surrounding fortification against it. **2** And the city enters into siege until the eleventh year of King Zedekiah. **3** On the ninth of the month, when the famine is severe in the city, then there has not been bread for the people of the land. **4** And the city is broken up, and all the men of war [go] by night the way of the gate, between the two walls that [are] by the garden of the king, and the Chaldeans [are] against the city all around, and [the king] goes the way of the plain. **5** And the force of the Chaldeans pursue after the king, and overtake him in the plains of Jericho, and all his force have been scattered from him; **6** and they seize the king, and bring him up to the king of Babylon, to Riblah, and they speak judgment with him. **7** And they have slaughtered the sons of Zedekiah before his eyes, and he has blinded the eyes of Zedekiah, and binds him with bronze chains, and they bring him to Babylon. **8** And in the fifth month, on the seventh of the month (it [is] the nineteenth year of King Nebuchadnezzar king of Babylon), Nebuzaradan chief of the executioners, servant of the king of Babylon, has come to Jerusalem, **9** and he burns the house of YHWH, and the house of the king, and all the houses of Jerusalem, indeed, he has burned every great house with fire; **10** and all the forces of the Chaldeans, who [are] with the chief of the executioners, have broken down the walls of Jerusalem all around. **11** And the rest of the people, those left in the city, and those falling who have fallen to the king of Babylon, and the rest of the multitude, Nebuzaradan chief of the executioners has removed; **12** and of the poor of the land the chief of the executioners has left for vinedressers and for farmers. **13** And the pillars of bronze that [are] in the house of YHWH, and the bases, and the sea of bronze, that [is] in the house of YHWH, the Chaldeans have broken in pieces, and carry away their bronze to Babylon. **14** And the pots, and the shovels, and the snuffers, and the spoons, and all the vessels of bronze with which they minister, they have taken; **15** and the fire-pans, and the bowls that [are] wholly of silver, the chief of the executioners has taken. **16** The two pillars, the one sea, and the bases that Solomon made for the house of YHWH, there was no weighing of the bronze of all these vessels; **17** eighteen cubits [is] the height of the one pillar, and the capital on it [is] of bronze, and the height of the capital [is] three cubits, and the net and the pomegranates [are] on the capital all around—the whole [is] of bronze; and the second pillar has like these, with the net. **18** And the chief of the executioners takes Seraiah the head priest, and Zephaniah the second priest, and the three keepers of the threshold; **19** and he has taken out of the city a certain eunuch who is appointed over the men of war, and five men of those seeing the king's face who have been found in the city, and the head scribe of the host who musters the people of the land, and sixty men of the people of the land who are found in the city; **20** and Nebuzaradan chief of the executioners takes them, and causes them to go to the king of Babylon, to Libnah, **21** and the king of Babylon strikes them, and puts them to death in Riblah, in the land of Hamath, and he removes Judah from off its land. **22** And the people that are left in the land of Judah whom Nebuchadnezzar king of Babylon has left—he appoints Gedaliah son of Ahikam, son of Shaphan, over them. **23** And all the heads of the forces hear—they and the men—that the king of Babylon has appointed Gedaliah, and they come to Gedaliah, to Mizpah, even Ishmael son of Nethaniah, and Johanan son of Kareah, and Seraiah son of Tanhumeth the Netophathite, and Jaazaniah son of the Maachathite—they and their men; **24** and Gedaliah swears to them and to their men, and says to them, "Do not be afraid of the servants of the Chaldeans, dwell in the land and serve the king of Babylon, and it is good for you." **25** And it comes to pass, in the seventh month, Ishmael son of Nathaniah has come, son of Elishama of the seed of the kingdom, and ten men with him, and they strike Gedaliah, and he dies, and the Jews and the Chaldeans who have been with him in Mizpah. **26** And all the people rise, from small even to great, and the heads of the forces, and come to Egypt, for they have been afraid of the presence of the Chaldeans. **27** And it comes to pass, in the thirty-seventh year of the expulsion of Jehoiachin king of Judah, in the twelfth month, on the twenty-seventh of the month, Evil-Merodach king of Babylon has lifted up, in the year of his reigning, the head of Jehoiachin king of Judah, out of the house of restraint, **28** and speaks good things with him and puts his throne above the throne of the kings who [are] with him in Babylon, **29** and has changed the garments of his restraint, and he has eaten bread continually before him all [the] days of his life, **30** and his allowance—a continual allowance—has been given to him from the king, the matter of a day in its day, all [the] days of his life.

1 CHRONICLES

1 Adam, Seth, Enosh, **2** Kenan, Mahalaleel, Jered, **3** Enoch, Methuselah, Lamech, **4** Noah, Shem, Ham, and Japheth. **5** Sons of Japheth: Gomer and Magog, and Madai, and Javan, and Tubal, and Meshech, and Tiras. **6** And sons of Gomer: Ashchenaz, and Riphath, and Togarmah. **7** And sons of Javan: Elisha, and Tarshishah, Kittim, and Dodanim. **8** Sons of Ham: Cush, and Mizraim, Put, and Canaan. **9** And sons of Cush: Seba and Havilah, and Sabta, and Raamah, and Sabtecka. And sons of Raamah: Sheba and Dedan. **10** And Cush begot Nimrod: he began to be a mighty one in the land. **11** And Mizraim begot the Ludim, and the Anamim, and the Lehabim, and the Naphtuhim, **12** and the Pathrusim, and the Casluhim (from whom the Philistim came out), and the Caphtorim. **13** And Canaan begot Sidon his firstborn, and Heth, **14** and the Jebusite, and the Amorite, and the Girgashite, **15** and the Hivite, and the Arkite, and the Sinite, **16** and the Arvadite, and the Zemarite, and the Hamathite. **17** Sons of Shem: Elam and Asshur, and Arphaxad, and Lud, and Aram, and Uz, and Hul, and Gether, and Meshech. **18** And Arphaxad begot Shelah, and Shelah begot Eber. **19** And two sons have been born to Eber, the name of the first [is] Peleg, for in his days the earth has been divided, and the name of his brother is Joktan. **20** And Joktan begot Almodad, and Sheleph, and Hazarmaveth, and Jerah, **21** and Hadoram, and Uzal, and Diklah, **22** and Ebal, and Abimael, and Sheba, **23** and Ophir, and Havilah, and Jobab; all these [are] sons of Joktan. **24** Shem, Arphaxad, Shelah, **25** Eber, Peleg, Reu, **26** Serug, Nahor, Terah, **27** Abram—he [is] Abraham. **28** Sons of Abraham: Isaac and Ishmael. **29** These [are] their generations: [the] firstborn of Ishmael [was] Nebaioth, then Kedar, and Adheel, and Mibsam, **30** Mishma, and Dumah, Massa, Hadad, and Tema, **31** Jetur, Naphish, and Kedema. These are sons of Ishmael. **32** And sons of Keturah, Abraham's concubine: she bore Zimran, and Jokshan, and Medan, and Midian, and Ishbak, and Shuah. And sons of Jokshan: Sheba and Dedan. **33** And sons of Midian: Ephah and Epher, and Enoch, and Abida, and Eldaah; all these [are] sons of Keturah. **34** And Abraham begets Isaac. Sons of Isaac: Esau and Israel. **35** Sons of Esau: Eliphaz, Reuel, and Jeush, and Jaalam, and Korah. **36** Sons of Eliphaz: Teman, and Omar, Zephi, and Gatam, Kenaz, and Timna, and Amalek. **37** Sons of Reuel: Nahath, Zerah, Shammah, and Mizzah. **38** And sons of Seir: Lotan, and Shobal, and Zibeon, and Anah, and Dishon, and Ezar, and Dishan. **39** And sons of Lotan: Hori and Homam, and sister of Lotan [is] Timna. **40** Sons of Shobal: Alian, and Manahath, and Ebal, Shephi, and Onam. And sons of Zideon: Aiah and Anah. **41** The sons of Anah: Dishon. And sons of Dishon: Amram, and Eshban, and Ithran, and Cheran. **42** Sons of Ezer: Bilhan, and Zavan, Jakan. Sons of Dishan: Uz and Aran. **43** And these [are] the kings who reigned in the land of Edom before the reigning of a king of the sons of Israel: Bela son of Beor, and the name of his city [is] Dinhabah. **44** And Bela dies, and Jobab son of Zerah from Bozrali reigns in his stead; **45** and Jobab dies, and Husham from the land of the Temanite reigns in his stead; **46** and Husham dies, and Hadad son of Bedad reigns in his stead (who strikes Midian in the field of Moab) and the name of his city [is] Avith; **47** and Hadad dies, and Samlah from Masrekah reigns in his stead; **48** and Samlah dies, and Shaul from Rehoboth of the River reigns in his stead; **49** and Shaul dies, and Ba'al-Hanan son of Achbor reigns in his stead; **50** and Ba'al-Hanan dies, and Hadad reigns in his stead, and the name of his city [is] Pai, and the name of his wife [is] Mehetabel daughter of Matred, daughter of Me-Zahab; Hadad also dies. **51** And chiefs of Edom are: Chief Timnah, Chief Aliah, Chief Jetheth, **52** Chief Aholibamah, Chief Elah, Chief Pinon, **53** Chief Kenaz, Chief Teman, Chief Mibzar, **54** Chief Magdiel, Chief Iram. These [are] chiefs of Edom.

2 These [are] sons of Israel: Reuben, Simeon, Levi, and Judah, Issachar, and Zebulun, **2** Dan, Joseph, and Benjamin, Naphtali, Gad, and Asher. **3** Sons of Judah: Er, and Onan, and Shelah, three have been born to him of a daughter of Shua the

1 CHRONICLES

Canaanitess. And Er, firstborn of Judah, is evil in the eyes of YHWH, and He puts him to death. **4** And his daughter-in-law Tamar has borne Perez and Zerah to him. All the sons of Judah [are] five. **5** Sons of Perez: Hezron, and Hamul. **6** And sons of Zerah: Zimri, and Ethan, and Heman, and Calcol, and Dara; all of them five. **7** And sons of Carmi: Achar, troubler of Israel, who trespassed in the devoted thing. **8** And sons of Ethan: Azariah. **9** And sons of Hezron who were born to him: Jerahmeel, and Ram, and Chelubai. **10** And Ram begot Amminadab, and Amminadab begot Nahshon, prince of the sons of Judah; **11** and Nahshon begot Salma, and Salma begot Boaz, **12** and Boaz begot Obed, and Obed begot Jesse; **13** and Jesse begot his firstborn Eliab, and Abinadab the second, and Shimea the third, **14** Nethaneel the fourth, Raddai the fifth, **15** Ozem the sixth, David the seventh, **16** and their sisters Zeruiah and Abigail. And sons of Zeruiah: Abishai, and Joab, and Asah-El—three. **17** And Abigail has borne Amasa, and the father of Amasa [is] Jether the Ishmaelite. **18** And Caleb son of Hezron has begotten Azubah, Isshah, and Jerioth; and these [are] her sons: Jesher, and Shobab, and Ardon. **19** And Azubah dies, and Caleb takes Ephrath to himself, and she bears Hur to him. **20** And Hur begot Uri, and Uri begot Bezaleel. **21** And afterward Hezron has gone in to a daughter of Machir father of Gilead, and he has taken her, and he [is] a son of sixty years, and she bears Segub to him. **22** And Segub begot Jair, and he has twenty-three cities in the land of Gilead, **23** and he takes Geshur and Aram, the small villages of Jair, from them, with Kenath and its small towns, sixty cities—all these [belonged to] the sons of Machir father of Gilead. **24** And after the death of Hezron in Caleb-Ephrath, then the wife of Hezron, Abijah, even bears to him Asshur, father of Tekoa. **25** And sons of Jerahmeel, firstborn of Hezron, are: the firstborn Ram, and Bunah, and Oren, and Ozem, Ahijah. **26** And Jerahmeel has another wife, and her name [is] Atarah, she [is] mother of Onam. **27** And sons of Ram, firstborn of Jerahmeel, are Maaz, and Jamin, and Eker. **28** And sons of Onam are Shammai and Jada. And sons of Shammai: Nadab and Abishur. **29** And the name of the wife of Abishur [is] Abihail, and she bears Ahban and Molid to him. **30** And sons of Nadab: Seled and Appaim; and Seled dies without sons. **31** And sons of Appaim: Ishi. And sons of Ishi: Sheshan. And sons of Sheshan: Ahlai. **32** And sons of Jada, brother of Shammai: Jether and Jonathan; and Jether dies without sons. **33** And sons of Jonathan: Peleth and Zaza. These were sons of Jerahmeel. **34** And Sheshan had no sons, but daughters, and Sheshan has a servant, an Egyptian, and his name [is] Jarha, **35** and Sheshan gives his daughter to his servant Jarha for a wife, and she bears Attai to him; **36** and Attai begot Nathan, and Nathan begot Zabad, **37** and Zabad begot Ephlal, and Ephlal begot Obed, **38** and Obed begot Jehu, **39** and Jehu begot Azariah, and Azariah begot Helez, and Helez begot Eleasah, **40** and Eleasah begot Sismai, and Sismai begot Shallum, **41** and Shallum begot Jekamiah, and Jekamiah begot Elishama. **42** And sons of Caleb brother of Jerahmeel: Mesha his firstborn, he [is] father of Ziph; and sons of Mareshah: Abi-Hebron. **43** And sons of Hebron: Korah, and Tappuah, and Rekem, and Shema. **44** And Shema begot Raham father of Jorkoam, and Rekem begot Shammai. **45** And a son of Shammai [is] Maon, and Maon [is] father of Beth-Zur. **46** And Ephah concubine of Caleb bore Haran, and Moza, and Gazez; and Haran begot Gazez. **47** And sons of Jahdai: Regem, and Jotham, and Geshem, and Pelet, and Ephah, and Shaaph. **48** The concubine of Caleb, Maachah, bore Sheber and Tirhanah; **49** and she bears Shaaph father of Madmannah, Sheva father of Machbenah, and father of Gibea; and a daughter of Caleb [is] Achsa. **50** These were sons of Caleb son of Hur, firstborn of Ephrathah: Shobal father of Kirjath-Jearim, **51** Salma father of Beth-Lehem, Hareph father of Beth-Gader. **52** And there are sons to Shobal father of Kirjath-Jearim: Haroeh, half of the Menuhothite; **53** and the families of Kirjath-Jearim: the Ithrite, and the Puhite, and the Shumathite, and the Mishraite. The Zorathite and the Eshtaolite went out from these. **54** Sons of Salma: Beth-Lehem, and the Netophathite, Atroth, Beth-Joab, and half of the Menuhothite, the Zorite; **55** and the families of the scribes, the inhabitants of Jabez: Tirathites, Shimeathites, Suchathites. They [are] the Kenites, those coming of Hammath father of the house of Rechab.

1 CHRONICLES

3 And these were sons of David, who were born to him in Hebron: the firstborn Amnon, of Ahinoam the Jezreelitess; second Daniel, of Abigail the Carmelitess; **2** the third Absalom, son of Maachah daughter of Talmai king of Geshur; the fourth Adonijah, son of Haggith; **3** the fifth Shephatiah, of Abital; the sixth Ithream, of his wife Eglah. **4** Six have been borne to him in Hebron, and he reigns seven years and six months there, and he has reigned thirty-three years in Jerusalem. **5** And these were born to him in Jerusalem: Shimea, and Shobab, and Nathan, and Solomon—four, of Bathsheba daughter of Ammiel. **6** Also Ibhar, and Elishama, and Eliphelet, **7** and Nogah, and Nepheg, and Japhia, **8** and Elishama, and Eliada, and Eliphelet—nine. **9** All [are] sons of David, apart from sons of the concubines, and their sister Tamar. **10** And the son of Solomon [is] Rehoboam, Abijah his son, Asa his son, Jehoshaphat his son, **11** Joram his son, Ahaziah his son, Joash his son, **12** Amaziah his son, Azariah his son, Jotham his son, **13** Ahaz his son, Hezekiah his son, Manasseh his son, **14** Amon his son, Josiah his son. **15** And sons of Josiah: the firstborn Johanan, the second Jehoiakim, the third Zedekiah, the fourth Shallum. **16** And sons of Jehoiakim: Jeconiah his son, Zedekiah his son. **17** And sons of Jeconiah: Assir; Salathiel his son; **18** also Malchiram and Pedaiah, and Shenazzar, Jecamiah, Hoshama, and Nedabiah. **19** And sons of Pedaiah: Zerubbabel and Shimei. And sons of Zerubbabel: Meshullam, and Hananiah, and their sister Shelomith, **20** and Hashubah, and Ohel, and Berechiah, and Hasadiah, Jushab-Hesed—five. **21** And sons of Hananiah: Pelatiah, and Jesaiah, sons of Rephaiah, sons of Arnan, sons of Obadiah, sons of Shechaniah. **22** And sons of Shechaniah: Shemaiah; and sons of Shemaiah: Hattush, and Igeal, and Bariah, and Neariah, and Shaphat—six. **23** And sons of Neariah: Elioenai, and Hezekiah, and Azrikam—three. **24** And sons of Elioenai: Hodaiah, and Eliashib, and Pelaiah, and Akkub, and Johanan, and Delaiah, and Anani—seven.

4 Sons of Judah: Perez, Hezron, and Carmi, and Hur, and Shobal. **2** And Reaiah son of Shobal begot Jahath, and Jahath begot Ahumai and Lahad; these [are] families of the Zorathite. **3** And these [are] of the father of Etam: Jezreel, and Ishma, and Idbash; and the name of their sister [is] Hazzelelponi; **4** and Penuel [is] father of Gedor, and Ezer father of Hushah. These [are] sons of Hur, firstborn of Ephratah, father of Beth-Lehem. **5** And to Ashhur father of Tekoa were two wives, Helah and Naarah; **6** and Naarah bears to him Ahuzzam, and Hepher, and Temeni, and Haahashtari: these [are] sons of Naarah. **7** And sons of Helah: Zereth, and Zohar, and Ethnan. **8** And Coz begot Anub, and Zobebah, and the families of Aharhel son of Harum. **9** And Jabez is honored above his brothers, and his mother called his name Jabez, saying, "Because I have brought forth with grief." **10** And Jabez calls to the God of Israel, saying, "If blessing You bless me, then You have made my border great, and Your hand has been with me, and You have kept [me] from evil—not to grieve me"; and God brings in that which he asked. **11** And Chelub brother of Shuah begot Mehir; he [is] father of Eshton. **12** And Eshton begot Beth-Rapha, and Paseah, and Tehinnah father of Ir-Nahash; these [are] men of Rechah. **13** And sons of Kenaz: Othniel and Seraiah; and sons of Othniel: Hathath. **14** And Meonothai begot Ophrah, and Seraiah begot Joab father of the Valley of the Craftsmen, for they were craftsmen. **15** And sons of Caleb son of Jephunneh: Iru, Elah, and Naam; and sons of Elah: even Kenaz. **16** And sons of Jehaleleel: Ziph and Ziphah, Tiria, and Asareel. **17** And sons of Ezra: Jether, and Mered, and Epher, and Jalon. And she bears Miriam, and Shammai, and Ishbah father of Eshtemoa. **18** And his wife Jehudijah bore Jered father of Gedor, and Heber father of Socho, and Jekuthiel father of Zanoah. And these [are] sons of Bithiah daughter of Pharaoh, whom Mered took, **19** and sons of the wife of Hodiah sister of Naham: Abi-Keilah the Garmite, and Eshtemoa the Maachathite. **20** And sons of Shimon: Amnon, and Rinnah, Ben-Hanon, and Tilon; and sons of Ishi: Zoheth, and Ben-Zoheth. **21** Sons of Shelah son of Judah: Er father of Lecah, and Laadah father of Mareshah, and the families of the house of the service of fine linen, of the house of Ashbea; **22** and Jokim, and the men of Chozeba, and Joash, and Saraph, who ruled over Moab and Jashubi-Lehem;

and these things [are] ancient. **23** They [are] the potters and inhabitants of Netaim and Gedera; they dwelt there with the king in his work. **24** Sons of Simeon: Nemuel, and Jamin, Jarib, Zerah, Shaul; **25** Shallum his son, Mibsam his son, Mishma his son. **26** And sons of Mishma: Hammuel his son, Zacchur his son, Shimei his son. **27** And to Shimei [are] sixteen sons and six daughters, and to his brothers there are not many sons, and none of their families have multiplied as much as the sons of Judah. **28** And they dwell in Beer-Sheba, and Moladah, and Hazar-Shaul, **29** and in Bilhah, and in Ezem, and in Tolad, **30** and in Bethuel, and in Hormah, and in Ziklag, **31** and in Beth-Marcaboth, and in Hazar-Susim, and in Beth-Birei, and in Shaarim; these [are] their cities until the reigning of David. **32** And their villages [are] Etam, and Ain, Rimmon, and Tochen, and Ashan—five cities, **33** and all their villages that [are] around these cities to Ba'al; these [are] their dwellings, and they have their genealogy: **34** even Meshobab, and Jamlech, and Joshah son of Amaziah, **35** and Joel, and Jehu son of Josibiah, son of Seraiah, son of Asiel, **36** and Elioenai, and Jaakobah, and Jeshohaiah, and Asaiah, and Adiel, and Jesimiel, and Benaiah, **37** and Ziza son of Shiphi, son of Allon, son of Jedaiah, son of Shimri, son of Shemaiah. **38** These who are coming in by name [are] princes in their families, and the house of their fathers has broken forth into a multitude; **39** and they go to the entrance of Gedor, to the east of the valley, to seek pasture for their flock, **40** and they find pasture, fat and good, and the land broad of sides, and quiet, and safe, for those dwelling there before are of Ham. **41** And these who are written by name come in the days of Hezekiah king of Judah, and strike their tents, and the habitations that have been found there, and devote them to destruction to this day, and dwell in their stead, because pasture for their flock [is] there. **42** And of them, of the sons of Simeon, five hundred men have gone to Mount Seir, and Pelatiah, and Neariah, and Rephaiah, and Uzziel, sons of Ishi, at their head, **43** and they strike the remnant of those escaped of Amalek, and dwell there to this day.

5 As for sons of Reuben, firstborn of Israel—for he [is] the firstborn, and on account of his profaning the bed of his father his birthright has been given to the sons of Joseph son of Israel, and [he is] not to be reckoned by genealogy for the birthright, **2** for Judah has been mighty over his brother, and for leader above him, and the birthright [is] to Joseph— **3** sons of Reuben, firstborn of Israel: Enoch, and Pallu, Hezron, and Carmi. **4** Sons of Joel: Shemaiah his son, Gog his son, Shimei his son, **5** Micah his son, Reaiah his son, Ba'al his son, **6** Beerah his son, whom Tilgath-Pilneser king of Asshur removed; he [is] prince of the Reubenite. **7** And his brothers, by their families, in the genealogy of their generations, [are] heads: Jeiel, and Zechariah, **8** and Bela son of Azaz, son of Shema, son of Joel—he is dwelling in Aroer, even to Nebo and Ba'al-Meon; **9** and he dwelt at the east even to the entering in of the wilderness, even from the Euphrates River, for their livestock were multiplied in the land of Gilead. **10** And they have made war with the Hagarites in the days of Saul, who fall by their hand, and they dwell in their tents over all the face of the east of Gilead. **11** And the sons of Gad have dwelt opposite them in the land of Bashan to Salcah: **12** Joel the head, and Shapham the second, and Jaanai and Shaphat in Bashan; **13** and their brothers of the house of their fathers [are] Michael, and Meshullam, and Sheba, and Jorai, and Jachan, and Zia, and Heber—seven. **14** These [are] sons of Abihail son of Huri, son of Jaroah, son of Gilead, son of Michael, son of Jeshishai, son of Jahdo, son of Buz; **15** Ahi son of Abdiel, son of Guni, [is] head of the house of their fathers; **16** and they dwell in Gilead in Bashan, and in her small towns, and in all outskirts of Sharon, on their outskirts; **17** all of them reckoned themselves by genealogy in the days of Jotham king of Judah, and in the days of Jeroboam king of Israel. **18** Sons of Reuben, and the Gadite, and the half of the tribe of Manasseh, of sons of valor, men carrying shield and sword, and treading bow, and taught in battle, [are] forty-four thousand and seven hundred and sixty, going out to the host. **19** And they make war with the Hagarites, and Jetur, and Naphish, and Nodab, **20** and they are helped against them, and the Hagarites are given into their hand, and all who [are] with them, for they cried to God in battle, and He received their plea, because they trusted

1 CHRONICLES

in Him. **21** And they take their livestock captive—fifty thousand of their camels, and two hundred and fifty thousand sheep, and two thousand donkeys, and one hundred thousand of mankind; **22** for many have fallen pierced, for the battle [is] of God; and they dwell in their stead until the expulsion. **23** And the sons of the half of the tribe of Manasseh dwelt in the land, from Bashan to Ba'al-Hermon, and Senir, and Mount Hermon; they have multiplied. **24** And these [are] heads of the house of their fathers: even Epher, and Ishi, and Eliel, and Azriel, and Jeremiah, and Hodaviah, and Jahdiel, men mighty in valor, men of renown, heads of the house of their fathers. **25** And they trespass against the God of their fathers, and go whoring after the gods of the peoples of the land whom God destroyed from their presence; **26** and the God of Israel stirs up the spirit of Pul king of Asshur, and the spirit of Tilgath-Pilneser king of Asshur, and he removes them—even the Reubenite, and the Gadite, and the half of the tribe of Manasseh—and brings them to Halah, and Habor, and Hara, and the River of Gozan to this day.

6 Sons of Levi: Gershon, Kohath, and Merari. **2** And the sons of Kohath: Amram, Izhar, and Hebron, and Uzziel. **3** And sons of Amram: Aaron, and Moses, and [his daughter] Miriam. And sons of Aaron: Nadab, and Abihu, Eleazar, and Ithamar. **4** Eleazar begot Phinehas, Phinehas begot Abishua, **5** and Abishua begot Bukki, and Bukki begot Uzzi, **6** and Uzzi begot Zerahiah, and Zerahiah begot Meraioth, **7** Meraioth begot Amariah, and Amariah begot Ahitub, **8** and Ahitub begot Zadok, and Zadok begot Ahimaaz, **9** and Ahimaaz begot Azariah, and Azariah begot Johanan, **10** and Johanan begot Azariah—him who acted as priest in the house that Solomon built in Jerusalem. **11** And Azariah begets Amariah, and Amariah begot Ahitub, **12** and Ahitub begot Zadok, and Zadok begot Shallum, **13** and Shallum begot Hilkiah, and Hilkiah begot Azariah, **14** and Azariah begot Seraiah, and Seraiah begot Jehozadak; **15** and Jehozadak has gone in YHWH's removing Judah and Jerusalem by the hand of Nebuchadnezzar. **16** Sons of Levi: Gershom, Kohath, and Merari. **17** And these [are] names of sons of Gershom: Libni and Shimei. **18** And sons of Kohath: Amram, and Izhar, and Hebron, and Uzziel. **19** Sons of Merari; Mahli and Mushi. And these [are] families of the Levite according to their fathers; **20** of Gershom: Libni his son, Jahath his son, Zimmah his son, **21** Joah his son, Iddo his son, Zerah his son, Jeaterai his son. **22** Sons of Kohath: Amminadab his son, Korah his son, Assir his son, **23** Elkanah his son, and Ebiasaph his son, and Assir his son, **24** Tahath his son, Uriel his son, Uzziah his son, and Shaul his son. **25** And sons of Elkanah: Amasai and Ahimoth. **26** Elkanah—sons of Elkanah: Zophai his son, and Nahath his son, **27** Eliab his son, Jeroham his son, Elkanah his son. **28** And sons of Samuel: the firstborn Vashni, and the second Abijah. **29** Sons of Merari: Mahli, Libni his son, Shimei his son, Uzzah his son, **30** Shimea his son, Haggiah his son, Asaiah his son. **31** And these [are] they whom David stationed over the parts of the song of the house of YHWH, from the resting of the Ark, **32** and they are ministering before the Dwelling Place of the Tent of Meeting, in song, until the building by Solomon of the house of YHWH in Jerusalem; and they stand according to their ordinance over their service. **33** And these [are] those standing, and their sons, of the sons of the Kohathite: Heman the singer, son of Joel, son of Shemuel, **34** son of Elkanah, son of Jeroham, son of Eliel, son of Toah, **35** son of Zuph, son of Elkanah, son of Mahath, son of Amasai, **36** son of Elkanah, son of Joel, son of Azariah, son of Zephaniah, **37** son of Tahath, son of Assir, son of Ebiasaph, son of Korah, **38** son of Izhar, son of Kohath, son of Levi, son of Israel. **39** And his brother Asaph, who is standing on his right—Asaph, son of Berachiah, son of Shimea, **40** son of Michael, son of Baaseiah, son of Malchiah, **41** son of Ethni, son of Zerah, son of Adaiah, **42** son of Ethan, son of Zimmah, son of Shimei, **43** son of Jahath, son of Gershom, son of Levi. **44** And sons of Merari, their brothers, on the left: Ethan son of Kishi, son of Abdi, son of Malluch, **45** son of Hashabiah, son of Amaziah, son of Hilkiah, **46** son of Amzi, son of Bani, son of Shamer, **47** son of Mahli, son of Mushi, son of Merari, son of Levi. **48** And their brothers the Levites are put to all the service of the Dwelling Place of the house of God. **49** And Aaron and his sons are making incense on the altar of the burnt-offering, and on the altar of the incense, for all the work of the Holy of Holies, and to make atonement for Israel, according to all that Moses servant of God commanded. **50** And these [are] sons of Aaron: Eleazar his son, Phinehas his son, Abishua his son, **51** Bukki his son, Uzzi his son, Zerahiah his son, **52** Meraioth his son, Amariah his son, Ahitub his son, **53** Zadok his son, Ahimaaz his son. **54** And these [are] their dwellings, throughout their towers, in their borders, of the sons of Aaron, of the family of the Kohathite, for the lot was theirs; **55** and they give to them Hebron in the land of Judah and its outskirts around it; **56** and they gave the field of the city and its villages to Caleb son of Jephunneh. **57** And they gave the cities of refuge to the sons of Aaron: Hebron, and Libnah and its outskirts, and Jattir, and Eshtemoa and its outskirts, **58** and Hilen and its outskirts, Debir and its outskirts, **59** and Ashan and its outskirts, and Beth-Shemesh and its outskirts. **60** And from the tribe of Benjamin: Geba and its outskirts, and Allemeth and its outskirts, and Anathoth and its outskirts. All their cities [are] thirteen cities among their families. **61** And to the sons of Kohath, those left of the family of the tribe, from the half of the tribe, the half of Manasseh, by lot, [are] ten cities. **62** And to the sons of Gershom, for their families, from the tribe of Issachar, and from the tribe of Asher, and from the tribe of Naphtali, and from the tribe of Manasseh in Bashan, [are] thirteen cities. **63** To the sons of Merari, for their families, from the tribe of Reuben, and from the tribe of Gad, and from the tribe of Zebulun, by lot, [are] twelve cities. **64** And the sons of Israel give the cities and their outskirts to the Levites. **65** And they give by lot from the tribe of the sons of Judah, and from the tribe of the sons of Simeon, and from the tribe of the sons of Benjamin, these cities which they call by name; **66** and some of the families of the sons of Kohath have cities of their border from the tribe of Ephraim; **67** and they give the cities of refuge to them: Shechem and its outskirts in the hill-country of Ephraim, and Gezer and its outskirts, **68** and Jokmeam and its outskirts, and Beth-Horan and its outskirts, **69** and Aijalon and its outskirts, and Gath-Rimmon and its outskirts; **70** and from the half tribe of Manasseh: Aner and its outskirts, and Bileam and its outskirts, for the family of the sons of Kohath who are left. **71** To the sons of Gershom from the family of the half of the tribe of Manasseh: Golan in Bashan and its outskirts, and Ashtaroth and its outskirts; **72** and from the tribe of Issachar: Kedesh and its outskirts, Daberath and its outskirts, **73** and Ramoth and its outskirts, and Anem and its outskirts; **74** and from the tribe of Asher: Mashal and its outskirts, and Abdon and its outskirts, **75** and Hukok and its outskirts, and Rehob and its outskirts; **76** and from the tribe of Naphtali: Kedesh in Galilee and its outskirts, and Hammon and its outskirts, and Kirjathaim and its outskirts. **77** To the sons of Merari who are left, from the tribe of Zebulun: Rimmon and its outskirts, Tabor and its outskirts; **78** and from beyond the Jordan by Jericho, at the east of the Jordan, from the tribe of Reuben: Bezer in the wilderness and its outskirts, and Jahzah and its outskirts, **79** and Kedemoth and its outskirts, and Mephaath and its outskirts; **80** and from the tribe of Gad: Ramoth in Gilead and its outskirts, and Mahanaim and its outskirts, **81** and Heshbon and its outskirts, and Jazer and its outskirts.

7 And sons of Issachar: Tola, and Puah, Jashub, and Shimron—four. **2** And sons of Tola: Uzzi, and Rephaiah, and Jeriel, and Jahmai, and Jibsam, and Shemuel, heads of the house of their fathers, [even] of Tola, mighty men of valor in their generations; their number in the days of David [is] twenty-two thousand and six hundred. **3** And sons of Uzzi: Izrahiah; and sons of Izrahiah: Michael, and Obadiah, and Joel, Ishiah, Hamishah—all of them heads. **4** And beside them, by their generations, of the house of their fathers, [are] thirty-six thousand troops of the host of battle, for they multiplied wives and sons; **5** and their brothers of all the families of Issachar, mighty men of valor, listed by their genealogy, [are] eighty-seven thousand for the whole. **6** Of Benjamin: Bela, and Becher, and Jediael—three. **7** And sons of Bela: Ezbon, and Uzzi, and Uzziel, and Jerimoth, and Iri—five; heads of a house of fathers, mighty men of valor, with their genealogy, twenty-two thousand and thirty-four. **8** And sons of Becher: Zemirah, and Joash, and Eliezar, and Elioenai, and Omri, and Jerimoth, and Abijah, and Anathoth, and Alameth. All

1 CHRONICLES

these [are] sons of Becher, **9** with their genealogy, after their generations, heads of a house of their fathers, mighty men of valor, twenty thousand and two hundred. **10** And sons of Jediael: Bilhan; and sons of Bilhan: Jeush, and Benjamin, and Ehud, and Chenaanah, and Zethan, and Tarshish, and Ahishahar. **11** All these [are] sons of Jediael, even heads of the fathers, mighty in valor, seventeen thousand and two hundred going out to the host for battle. **12** And Shuppim and Huppim [are] sons of Ir, [and] Hushim [is] the son of Aher. **13** Sons of Naphtali: Jahziel, and Guni, and Jezer, and Shallum, sons of Bilhah. **14** Sons of Manasseh: Ashriel, whom Jaladah his Aramean concubine bore, with Machir father of Gilead. **15** And Machir took wives for Huppim and for Shuppim, and the name of the first [is] Maachah, and the name of the second Zelophehad, and Zelophehad has daughters. **16** And Maachah wife of Machir bears a son and calls his name Peresh, and the name of his brother [is] Sheresh, and his sons [are] Ulam and Rakem. **17** And son of Ulam: Bedan. These [are] sons of Gilead son of Machir, son of Manasseh. **18** And his sister Hammolecheth bore Ishhod, and Abiezer, and Mahalah. **19** And the sons of Shemida are Ahian, and Shechem, and Likhi, and Aniam. **20** And sons of Ephraim: Shuthelah, and Bered his son, and Tahath his son, and Eladah his son, and Tahath his son, **21** and Zabad his son, and Shuthelah his son, and Ezer, and Elead; and men of Gath who are born in the land have slain them because they came down to take their livestock. **22** And their father Ephraim mourns many days, and his brothers come to comfort him, **23** and he goes in to his wife, and she conceives and bears a son, and he calls his name Beriah, because his house had been in calamity— **24** and his daughter [is] Sherah, and she builds Beth-Horon, the lower and the upper, and Uzzen-Sherah— **25** Rephah [is] his son, and Resheph, and Telah his son, and Tahan his son, **26** Laadan his son, Ammihud his son, Elishama his son, **27** Nun his son, Joshua his son. **28** And their possession and their dwellings [are] Beth-El and its small towns, and Naaran to the east, and Gezer and its small towns to the west, and Shechem and its small towns, as far as Gaza and its small towns; **29** and by the parts of the sons of Manasseh [are] Beth-Shean and its small towns, Taanach and its small towns, Megiddo and its small towns, Dor and its small towns; the sons of Joseph, son of Israel, dwelt in these. **30** Son of Asher: Imnah, and Ishve, and Ishvi, and Beriah, and their sister Serah. **31** And sons of Beriah: Heber and Malchiel—he [is] father of Birzavith. **32** And Heber begot Japhlet, and Shomer, and Hotham, and their sister Shua. **33** And sons of Japhlet: Pasach, and Bimhal, and Ashvath; these [are] sons of Japhlet. **34** And sons of Shamer: Ahi, and Rohgah, Jehubbah, and Aram. **35** And [each] son of his brother Helem: Zophah, and Imna, and Shelesh, and Amal. **36** Sons of Zophah: Suah, and Harnepher, and Shual, and Beri, and Imrah, **37** Bezer, and Hod, and Shamma, and Shilshah, and Ithran, and Beera. **38** And sons of Jether: Jephunneh, and Pispah, and Ara. **39** And sons of Ulla: Arah, and Hanniel, and Rezia. **40** All these [are] sons of Asher, heads of the house of the fathers, chosen ones, mighty in valor, heads of the princes, with their genealogy, for the host, for battle, their number [is] twenty-six thousand men.

8 And Benjamin begot Bela his firstborn, Ashbel the second, and Aharah the third, **2** Nohah the fourth, and Rapha the fifth. **3** And there are sons to Bela: Addar, and Gera, **4** and Abihud, and Abishua, and Naaman, and Ahoah, **5** and Gera, and Shephuphan, and Huram. **6** And these [are] sons of Ehud—they are heads of fathers to the inhabitants of Geba, and they remove them to Manahath: **7** even Naaman, and Ahiah, and Gera, who removed them and begot Uzza and Ahihud. **8** And Shaharaim begot in the field of Moab after his sending them away; Hushim and Baara [are] his wives. **9** And he begets of his wife Hodesh: Jobab, and Zibia, and Mesha, and Malcham, **10** and Jeuz, and Shachiah, and Mirmah. These [are] his sons, heads of fathers. **11** And of Hushim he begot Ahitub and Elpaal. **12** And sons of Elpaal: Eber, and Misheam, and Shamer (he built Ono and Lod and its small towns), **13** and Beriah and Shema (they [are] the heads of fathers to the inhabitants of Aijalon—they caused the inhabitants of Gath to flee), **14** and Ahio, Shashak, and Jeremoth, **15** and Zebadiah, and Arad, and Ader, **16** and Michael, and Ispah, and Joha, sons of Beriah, **17** and Zebadiah, and Meshullam,

1 CHRONICLES

and Hezeki, and Heber, **18** and Ishmerai, and Jezliah, and Jobab, sons of Elpaal; **19** and Jakim, and Zichri, and Zabdi, **20** and Elienai, and Zillethai, and Eliel, **21** and Adaiah, and Beraiah, and Shimrath, sons of Shimei; **22** and Ishpan, and Heber, and Eliel, **23** and Abdon, and Zichri, and Hanan, **24** and Hananiah, and Elam, and Antothijah, **25** and Iphedeiah, and Penuel, sons of Shashak; **26** and Shamsherai, and Shehariah, and Athaliah, **27** and Jaareshiah, and Eliah, and Zichri, sons of Jeroham. **28** These [are] heads of fathers, by their generations, [the] heads. These dwelt in Jerusalem. **29** And the father of Gibeon has dwelt in Gibeon, and the name of his wife [is] Maachah; **30** and his son, the firstborn, [is] Abdon, and Zur, and Kish, and Ba'al, and Nadab, **31** and Gedor, and Ahio, and Zacher; **32** and Mikloth begot Shimeah. And they also dwelt opposite their brothers—with their brothers in Jerusalem. **33** And Ner begot Kish, and Kish begot Saul, and Saul begot Jonathan, and Malchi-Shua, and Abinadab, and Esh-Ba'al. **34** And a son of Jonathan [is] Merib-Ba'al, and Merib-Ba'al begot Micah; **35** and sons of Micah: Pithon, and Melech, and Tarea, and Ahaz: **36** and Ahaz begot Jehoadah, and Jehoadah begot Alemeth, and Azmaveth, and Zimri; and Zimri begot Moza, **37** and Moza begot Binea, Raphah his son, Eleasah his son, Azel his son. **38** And to Azel [are] six sons, and these [are] their names: Azrikam, Bocheru, and Ishmael, and Sheariah, and Obadiah, and Hanan. All these [are] sons of Azel. **39** And sons of his brother Eshek: Ulam his firstborn, Jehush the second, and Eliphelet the third. **40** And the sons of Ulam are men mighty in valor, treading bow, and multiplying sons and son's sons—one hundred and fifty. All these [are] of the sons of Benjamin.

9 And all [those of] Israel have reckoned themselves by genealogy, and behold, they are written on the scroll of the kings of Israel and Judah—they were removed to Babylon for their trespass. **2** And the first inhabitants, who [are] in their possession, in their cities, of Israel, [are] the priests, the Levites, and the Nethinim. **3** And those who dwelt in Jerusalem of the sons of Judah, and of the sons of Benjamin, and of the sons of Ephraim and Manasseh: **4** Uthai son of Ammihud, son of Omri, son of Imri, son of Bani, of the sons of Perez, son of Judah. **5** And of the Shilonite: Asaiah the firstborn, and his sons. **6** And of the sons of Zerah: Jeuel, and their brothers—six hundred and ninety. **7** And of the sons of Benjamin: Sallu son of Meshullam, son of Hodaviah, son of Hassenuah, **8** and Ibneiah son of Jeroham, and Elah son of Uzzi, son of Michri, and Meshullam son of Shephatiah, son of Reuel, son of Ibnijah. **9** And their brothers, according to their generations, [are] nine hundred and fifty-six. All these [are] men, heads of fathers, according to the house of their fathers. **10** And of the priests: Jedaiah, and Jehoiarib, and Jachin, **11** and Azariah son of Hilkiah, son of Meshullam, son of Zadok, son of Meraioth, son of Ahitub, leader in the house of God; **12** and Adaiah son of Jeroham, son of Pashhur, son of Malchijah, and Maasai son of Adiel, son of Jahzerah, son of Meshullam, son of Meshillemith, son of Immer. **13** And their brothers, heads of the house of their fathers, [are] one thousand and seven hundred and sixty, mighty in valor, for the work of the service of the house of God. **14** And of the Levites: Shemaiah son of Hashshub, son of Azrikam, son of Hashabiah, of the sons of Merari; **15** and Bakbakkar, Heresh, and Galal, and Mattaniah son of Micah, son of Zichri, son of Asaph; **16** and Obadiah son of Shemariah, son of Galal, son of Jeduthun, and Berechiah, son of Asa, son of Elkanah, who is dwelling in the villages of the Netophathite. **17** And the gatekeepers [are] Shallum, and Akkub, and Talmon, and Ahiman, and their brothers—Shallum [is] the head; **18** and until now they [are] at the gate of the king eastward; they [are] the gatekeepers for the companies of the sons of Levi. **19** And Shallum son of Kore, son of Ebiasaph, son of Korah, and his brothers, of the house of his father, the Korahites, [are] over the work of the service, keepers of the thresholds of the tent, and their fathers [are] over the camp of YHWH, keepers of the entrance; **20** and Phinehas son of Eleazar has been leader over them formerly; YHWH [is] with him. **21** Zechariah son of Meshelemiah [is] gatekeeper at the opening of the Tent of Meeting. **22** All of those who are chosen for gatekeepers at the thresholds [are] two hundred and twelve; they [are] in their villages, by their genealogy; they whom

David and Samuel the seer appointed in their office. **23** And they and their sons [are] over the gates of the house of YHWH, even of the house of the tent, by watches. **24** The gatekeepers are at [the] four sides: east, west, north, and south. **25** And their brothers in their villages [are] to come in with these for seven days from time to time. **26** For the four chiefs of the gatekeepers in office, they are Levites, and they have been over the chambers, and over the treasuries of the house of God, **27** and they lodge around the house of God, for the watch [is] on them, and they [are] over the opening, even morning by morning. **28** And [some] of them [are] over the vessels of service, for they bring them in by number, and by number they take them out. **29** And [some] of them are appointed over the vessels, even over all the vessels of the holy place, and over the fine flour, and the wine, and the oil, and the frankincense, and the spices. **30** And [some] of the sons of the priests are mixing the mixture for spices. **31** And Mattithiah of the Levites (he [is] the firstborn to Shallum the Korahite), [is] in office over the work of the pans. **32** And of the sons of the Kohathite, [some] of their brothers [are] over the bread of the arrangement, to prepare [it] Sabbath by Sabbath. **33** And these who sing, heads of fathers of the Levites, in the chambers, [are] free, for [they are] over them in the work by day and by night. **34** These heads of the fathers of the Levites [are] heads throughout their generations. These have dwelt in Jerusalem. **35** And the father of Gibeon, Jehiel, has dwelt in Gibeon, and the name of his wife [is] Maachah; **36** and his son, the firstborn, [is] Abdon, and Zur, and Kish, and Ba'al, and Ner, and Nadab, **37** and Gedor, and Ahio, and Zechariah, and Mikloth. **38** And Mikloth begot Shimeam, and they have also dwelt opposite their brothers—with their brothers in Jerusalem. **39** And Ner begot Kish, and Kish begot Saul, and Saul begot Jonathan, and Malchi-Shua, and Abinadab, and Esh-Ba'al. **40** And a son of Jonathan [is] Merib-Ba'al, and Merib-Ba'al begot Micah. **41** And sons of Micah: Pithon, and Melech, and Tahrea, **42** and Ahaz—he begot Jaarah, and Jaarah begot Alemeth, and Azmaveth, and Zimri, and Zimri begot Moza, **43** and Moza begot Binea, and Rephaiah his son, Eleasah his son, Azel his son. **44** And to Azel [are] six sons, and these [are] their names: Azrikam, Bocheru, and Ishmael, and Sheariah, and Obadiah, and Hanan; these [are] sons of Azel.

10 And the Philistines have fought with Israel, and the men of Israel flee from the face of the Philistines, and fall wounded in Mount Gilboa, **2** and the Philistines pursue after Saul, and after his sons, and the Philistines strike Jonathan, and Abinadab, and Malchi-Shua, sons of Saul. **3** And the battle [is] heavy on Saul, and those shooting with the bow find him, and he is wounded by those shooting, **4** and Saul says to the bearer of his weapons, "Draw your sword and pierce me with it, lest these uncircumcised come and have abused me." And the bearer of his weapons has not been willing, for he fears exceedingly, and Saul takes the sword, and falls on it; **5** and the bearer of his weapons sees that Saul [is] dead, and falls, he also, on the sword, and dies; **6** and Saul dies, and his three sons, and all his house—they died together. **7** And all the men of Israel who [are] in the valley see that they have fled and that Saul and his sons have died, and they forsake their cities and flee, and the Philistines come and dwell in them. **8** And it comes to pass, on the next day, that the Philistines come to strip the wounded, and find Saul and his sons fallen in Mount Gilboa, **9** and strip him, and carry away his head and his weapons, and send [them] into the land of the surrounding Philistines to proclaim tidings [to] their idols and the people; **10** and they put his weapons in the house of their gods, and have fixed his skull in the house of Dagon. **11** And all Jabesh-Gilead hears of all that the Philistines have done to Saul, **12** and all the men of valor rise and carry away the body of Saul, and the bodies of his sons, and bring them to Jabesh, and bury their bones under the oak in Jabesh, and fast seven days. **13** And Saul dies because of his trespass that he trespassed against YHWH, against the word of YHWH that he did not keep, and also for asking to inquire of a familiar spirit; **14** and he did not inquire of YHWH, and He puts him to death, and turns around the kingdom to David son of Jesse.

11 And all Israel is gathered to David at Hebron, saying, "Behold, we [are] your bone and your flesh; **2** even in time

1 CHRONICLES

past, even in Saul's being king, it is you who are taking out and bringing in Israel, and your God YHWH says to you: You feed My people Israel, and you are leader over My people Israel." **3** And all [the] elderly of Israel come to the king at Hebron, and David makes a covenant with them in Hebron before YHWH, and they anoint David for king over Israel, according to the word of YHWH by the hand of Samuel. **4** And David goes, and all Israel, to Jerusalem—it [is] Jebus—and the Jebusite [is] there, the inhabitants of the land. **5** And the inhabitants of Jebus say to David, "You do not come in here"; and David captures the fortress of Zion—it [is] the City of David. **6** And David says, "Whoever strikes the Jebusite first becomes head and prince"; and Joab son of Zeruiah goes up first and becomes head. **7** And David dwells in the fortress, therefore they have called it the City of David; **8** and he builds the city all around, from Millo, and to the circumference, and Joab restores the rest of the city. **9** And David goes, going on and becoming great, and YHWH of Hosts [is] with him. **10** And these [are] heads of the mighty ones whom David has, who are strengthening themselves with him in his kingdom, with all Israel, to cause him to reign, according to the word of YHWH, over Israel. **11** And this [is] an account of the mighty ones whom David has: Jashobeam son of a Hachmonite [is] head of the thirty; he is lifting up his spear against three hundred—wounded, at one time. **12** And after him [is] Eleazar son of Dodo the Ahohite, he [is] among the three mighty; **13** he has been with David in Pas-Dammim, and the Philistines have been gathered there to battle, and a portion of the field is full of barley, and the people have fled from the face of the Philistines, **14** and they station themselves in the midst of the portion, and deliver it, and strike the Philistines, and YHWH saves [with] a great salvation. **15** And three of the thirty heads go down on the rock to David, to the cave of Adullam, and the host of the Philistines is encamping in the Valley of Rephaim, **16** and David [is] then in the fortress, and the station of the Philistines [is] then in Beth-Lehem, **17** and David longs and says, "Who gives me water to drink from the well of Beth-Lehem that [is] at the gate!" **18** And the three break through the camp of the Philistines, and draw water from the well of Beth-Lehem that [is] at the gate, and carry and bring [it] to David, and David has not been willing to drink it, and pours it out to YHWH, **19** and says, "Far be it from me, by my God, to do this; do I drink the blood of these men with their lives? For with their lives they have brought it"; and he was not willing to drink it; these [things] the three mighty ones did. **20** And Abishai brother of Joab, he has been head of the three: and he is lifting up his spear against three hundred—wounded, and has a name among three. **21** Of the three he is more honored than the [other] two, and becomes their head; but he has not come to the [first] three. **22** Benaiah son of Jehoiada, son of a man of valor, of great deeds, from Kabzeel: he has struck the two lion-like Moabites, and he has gone down and struck the lion in the midst of the pit, in the day of snow. **23** And he has struck the man, the Egyptian, a man of [great] measure—five by the cubit—and in the hand of the Egyptian [is] a spear like a weavers' beam, and he goes down to him with a rod, and violently takes away the spear out of the hand of the Egyptian, and slays him with his own spear. **24** These [things] Benaiah son of Jehoiada has done, and has a name among the three mighty ones. **25** Of the thirty, behold, he [is] honored, but he has not come to the [first] three, and David sets him over his guard. **26** And the mighty ones of the forces [are] Asahel brother of Joab, Elhanan son of Dodo of Beth-Lehem, **27** Shammoth the Harorite, Helez the Pelonite, **28** Ira son of Ikkesh the Tekoite, Abi-Ezer the Annethothite, **29** Sibbecai the Hushathite, Ilai the Ahohite, **30** Maharai the Netophathite, Heled son of Baanah the Netophathite, **31** Ithai son of Ribai of Gibeah, of the sons of Benjamin, Benaiah the Pirathonite, **32** Hurai of the brooks of Gaash, Abiel the Arbathite, **33** Azmaveth the Baharumite, Eliahba the Shaalbonite, **34** the sons of Hashem the Gizonite, Jonathan son of Shage the Hararite, **35** Ahiam son of Sacar the Hararite, Eliphal son of Ur, **36** Hepher the Mecherathite, Ahijah the Pelonite, **37** Hezor the Carmelite, Naarai son of Ezbai, **38** Joel brother of Nathan, Mibhar son of Haggeri, **39** Zelek the Ammonite, Naharai the Berothite, bearer of the weapons of Joab son of Zeruiah, **40** Ira the Ithrite, Gareb the Ithrite, **41** Uriah the Hittite, Zabad son of Ahlai, **42** Adina son of Shiza the

1 CHRONICLES

Reubenite, head of the Reubenites, and thirty by him, **43** Hanan son of Maachah, and Joshaphat the Mithnite, **44** Uzzia the Ashterathite, Shama and Jehiel sons of Hothan the Aroerite, **45** Jediael son of Shimri, and his brother Joha the Tizite, **46** Eliel the Mahavite, and Jeribai, and Joshaviah, sons of Elnaam, and Ithmah the Moabite, **47** Eliel, and Obed, and Jaasiel the Mesobaite.

12 And these [are] those coming to David at Ziklag, while shut up because of Saul son of Kish, and they [are] among the mighty ones, helping the battle, **2** armed with bow, right and left handed, with stones, and with arrows, with bows, of the brothers of Saul, of Benjamin. **3** The head [is] Ahiezer, and Joash, sons of Shemaab the Gibeathite, and Jeziel, and Pelet, sons of Azmaveth, and Berachah, and Jehu the Antothite, **4** and Ishmaiah the Gibeonite, a mighty one among the thirty, and over the thirty, and Jeremiah, and Jahaziel, and Johanan, and Josabad the Gederathite. **5** Eluzai, and Jerimoth, and Bealiah, and Shemariah, and Shephatiah the Haruphite; **6** Elkanah, and Jesiah, and Azareel, and Joezer, and Jashobeam the Korahites, **7** and Joelah, and Zebadiah, sons of Jeroham of Gedor. **8** And of the Gadite there have been separated to David, to the fortress, to the wilderness, mighty men of valor, men of the host for battle, setting in array buckler and spear, and their faces [are as] the face of the lion, and as roes on the mountains for speed: **9** Ezer the head, Obadiah the second, Eliab the third, **10** Mishmannah the fourth, Jeremiah the fifth, **11** Attai the sixth, Eliel the seventh, **12** Johanan the eighth, Elzabad the ninth, **13** Jeremiah the tenth, Machbannai the eleventh. **14** These [are] of the sons of Gad, heads of the host; the least [is] one of one hundred, and the greatest, of one thousand; **15** these [are] they who have passed over the Jordan in the first month—and it is full over all its banks—and cause all [those in] the valley to flee to the east and to the west. **16** And [some] from the sons of Benjamin and Judah came to David at the stronghold, **17** and David goes out before them, and answers and says to them, "If you have come to me for peace, to help me, I have a heart to unite with you; and if to betray me to my adversaries—without violence in my hands—the God of our fathers sees and reproves." **18** And the Spirit has clothed Amasai, head of the captains: "To you, O David, and with you, O son of Jesse—peace! Peace to you, and peace to your helper, for your God has helped you"; and David receives them, and puts them among the heads of the troop. **19** And [some] from Manasseh have defected to David in his coming with the Philistines against Israel to battle—and they did not help them, for by counsel the princes of the Philistines sent him away, saying, "He defects with our heads to his master Saul." **20** In his going to Ziglag there have fallen to him from Manasseh: Adnah, and Jozabad, and Jediael, and Michael, and Jozabad, and Elihu, and Zillthai, heads of the thousands who [are] of Manasseh; **21** and they have helped with David over the troop, for all of them [are] mighty men of valor, and they are captains in the host, **22** for at that time, day by day, they come to David to help him, until it is a great camp, like a camp of God. **23** And these [are] the numbers of the head, of the armed men of the host; they have come to David at Hebron to turn around the kingdom of Saul to him, according to the mouth of YHWH. **24** The sons of Judah, carrying buckler and spear, [are] six thousand and eight hundred, armed ones of the host. **25** Of the sons of Simeon, mighty men of valor for the host, [are] seven thousand and one hundred. **26** Of the sons of Levi [are] four thousand and six hundred; **27** and Jehoiada [is] the leader of the Aaronite, and with him [are] three thousand and seven hundred, **28** and Zadok, a young man, a mighty man of valor, and of the house of his father [are] twenty-two heads. **29** And of the sons of Benjamin, brothers of Saul, [are] three thousand, and until now their greater part are keeping the charge of the house of Saul. **30** And of the sons of Ephraim [are] twenty thousand and eight hundred, mighty men of valor, men of renown, according to the house of their fathers. **31** And of the half of the tribe of Manasseh [are] eighteen thousand, who have been defined by name, to come to cause David to reign. **32** And of the sons of Issachar, having understanding for the times, to know what Israel should do; their heads [are] two hundred, and all their brothers [are] at their command. **33** Of Zebulun, going forth to the host, arranging battle with all instruments of battle, [are] fifty thousand, and keeping rank without a double heart. **34** And of Naphtali, one thousand heads, and with them, with buckler and spear, [are] thirty-seven thousand. **35** And of the Danite, arranging battle, [are] twenty-eight thousand and six hundred. **36** And of Asher, going forth to the host, to arrange battle, [are] forty thousand. **37** And from beyond the Jordan, of the Reubenite, and of the Gadite, and of the half of the tribe of Manasseh, with all instruments of the host for battle, [are] one hundred and twenty thousand. **38** All these [are] men of war, keeping rank—they have come to Hebron with a perfect heart, to cause David to reign over all Israel, and also all the rest of Israel [are] of one heart, to cause David to reign, **39** and they are there, with David, three days, eating and drinking, for their brothers have prepared for them. **40** And also those near to them—to Issachar, and Zebulun, and Naphtali—are bringing in bread on donkeys, and on camels, and on mules, and on oxen—food of fine flour, fig-cakes and grape-cakes, and wine, and oil, and oxen, and sheep, in abundance, for joy [is] in Israel.

13 And David consults with the heads of the thousands and of the hundreds, [and] with every leader, **2** and David says to all the assembly of Israel, "If it is good to you, and it has broken forth from our God YHWH—we send to our brothers, those left in all the lands of Israel, and the priests and the Levites with them in the cities of their outskirts, and they are gathered to us, **3** and we bring around the Ark of our God to us, for we did not seek Him in the days of Saul." **4** And all the assembly says to do so, for the thing is right in the eyes of all the people. **5** And David assembles all Israel from Shihor of Egypt even to the entering in of Hamath, to bring in the Ark of God from Kirjath-Jearim, **6** and David goes up, and all Israel, to Ba'alah, to Kirjath-Jearim that [belongs] to Judah, to bring up from there the Ark of God, YHWH, inhabiting the cherubim, where the Name is called on. **7** And they place the Ark of God on a new cart from the house of Abinadab, and Uzza and Ahio are leading the cart, **8** and David and all Israel are playing before God, with all strength, and with songs, and with harps, and with psalteries, and with timbrels, and with cymbals, and with trumpets. **9** And they come to the threshing-floor of Chidon, and Uzza puts forth his hand to seize the Ark, for the oxen were released, **10** and the anger of YHWH is kindled against Uzza, and He strikes him, because that he has put forth his hand on the Ark, and he dies there before God. **11** And it is displeasing to David, because YHWH has made a breach on Uzza, and one calls that place "Breach of Uzza" to this day. **12** And David fears God on that day, saying, "How do I bring the Ark of God to me?" **13** And David has not turned aside the Ark to himself, to the City of David, and turns it aside to the house of Obed-Edom the Gittite. **14** And the Ark of God dwells with the household of Obed-Edom, in his house, three months, and YHWH blesses the house of Obed-Edom, and all that he has.

14 And Huram king of Tyre sends messengers to David, and cedar-wood, and craftsmen of walls, and craftsmen of wood, to build a house for him. **2** And David knows that YHWH has established him for king over Israel, because of the lifting up on high of his kingdom, for the sake of His people Israel. **3** And David takes wives again in Jerusalem, and David begets sons and daughters again; **4** and these [are] the names of the children whom he has in Jerusalem: Shammua, and Shobab, Nathan, and Solomon, **5** and Ibhar, and Elishua, and Elpalet, **6** and Nogah, and Nepheg, and Japhia, **7** and Elishama, and Beeliada, and Eliphalet. **8** And the Philistines hear that David has been anointed for king over all Israel, and all the Philistines go up to seek David, and David hears, and goes out before them. **9** And the Philistines have come, and rush into the Valley of Rephaim, **10** and David asks of God, saying, "Do I go up against the Philistines—and have You given them into my hand?" And YHWH says to him, "Go up, and I have given them into your hand." **11** And they go up into Ba'al-Perazim, and David strikes them there, and David says, "God has broken up my enemies by my hand, like the breaking up of waters"; therefore they have called the name of that place Ba'al-Perazim. **12** And they leave their gods there, and David commands, and they are burned with fire. **13** And the Philistines add again, and rush into the valley, **14** and David asks again of God, and God says to him, "Do not go up after them, turn around from them, and you have come to them from the front [[*or* in front]] of the mulberries; **15** and it comes to pass, when you hear the sound of the stepping at the heads of the mulberries, then you go out into battle, for God has gone out before you to strike the camp of the Philistines." **16** And David does as God commanded him, and they strike the camp of the Philistines from Gibeon even to Gazer; **17** and the name of David goes out into all the lands, and YHWH has put his fear on all the nations.

15 And he makes houses for himself in the City of David, and prepares a place for the Ark of God, and stretches out a tent for it. **2** Then David said, "None [are] to carry the Ark of God, except the Levites, for YHWH has fixed on them to carry the Ark of God and to serve Him for all time." **3** And David assembles all Israel to Jerusalem, to bring up the Ark of YHWH to its place that he had prepared for it. **4** And David gathers the sons of Aaron and the Levites— **5** of sons of Kohath: Uriel the chief and one hundred and twenty of his brothers; **6** of sons of Merari: Asaiah the chief and two hundred and twenty of his brothers; **7** of sons of Gershom: Joel the chief and one hundred and thirty of his brothers; **8** of sons of Elizaphan: Shemaiah the chief and two hundred of his brothers; **9** of sons of Hebron: Eliel the chief and eighty of his brothers; **10** of sons of Uzziel: Amminadab the chief and one hundred and twelve of his brothers. **11** And David calls to Zadok and to Abiathar the priests, and to the Levites, to Uriel, Asaiah, and Joel, Shemaiah, and Eliel, and Amminadab, **12** and says to them, "You [are] heads of the fathers of the Levites; sanctify yourselves, you and your brothers, and you have brought up the Ark of YHWH, God of Israel, to [the place] I have prepared for it; **13** because you [did] not [do it] at the first, our God YHWH made a breach on us, because we did not seek Him according to the ordinance." **14** And the priests and the Levites sanctify themselves to bring up the Ark of YHWH, God of Israel; **15** and sons of the Levites carry the Ark of God, as Moses commanded, according to the word of YHWH, above them with poles on their shoulder. **16** And David says to the heads of the Levites to appoint their brothers the singers, with instruments of song, psalteries, and harps, and cymbals, sounding, to lift up with the voice for joy. **17** And the Levites appoint Heman son of Joel, and of his brothers, Asaph son of Berechiah, and of the sons of Merari their brothers, Ethan son of Kushaiah; **18** and with them their brothers, the seconds [in rank]: Zechariah, Ben, and Jaaziel, and Shemiramoth, and Jehiel, and Unni, Eliab, and Benaiah, and Maaseiah, and Mattithiah, and Elipheleh, and Mikneiah; and Obed-Edom and Jeiel the gatekeepers; **19** and the singers, Heman, Asaph, and Ethan, [are] to sound with cymbals of bronze; **20** and Zechariah, and Aziel, and Shemiramoth, and Jeheil, and Unni, and Eliab, and Maaseiah, and Benaiah, with psalteries over the girls' [voices], **21** and Mattithiah, and Elipheleh, and Mikneiah, and Obed-Edom, and Jeiel, and Azaziah, to oversee with harps on the eighth. **22** And Chenaniah, head of the Levites, [is] over the burden; he instructs about the burden, for he [is] intelligent. **23** And Berechiah and Elkanah [are] gatekeepers for the Ark. **24** And Shebaniah, and Joshaphat, and Nethaneel, and Amasai, and Zechariah, and Benaiah, and Eliezer the priests, are blowing with trumpets before the Ark of God; and Obed-Edom and Jehiah [are] gatekeepers for the Ark. **25** And it is David, and [the] elderly of Israel, and the heads of the thousands, who are going to bring up the Ark of the Covenant of YHWH from the house of Obed-Edom with joy; **26** and it comes to pass, in God's helping the Levites carrying the Ark of the Covenant of YHWH, that they sacrifice seven bullocks and seven rams. **27** And David is wrapped in an upper robe of fine linen, and all the Levites who are carrying the Ark, and the singers, and Chenaniah head of the burden of the singers; and an Ephod of linen [is] on David. **28** And all of Israel is bringing up the Ark of the Covenant of YHWH with shouting, and with the sound of a horn, and with trumpets, and with cymbals, sounding with psalteries and harps, **29** and it comes to pass, the Ark of the Covenant of YHWH is entering into the City of David, and Michal daughter of Saul is looking through the window, and sees King David dancing and playing, and despises him in her heart.

16 And they bring in the Ark of God, and set it up in the midst of the tent that David has stretched out for it, and they bring burnt-offerings and peace-offerings near before God; **2** and David ceases from offering the burnt-offering and the peace-offerings, and blesses the people in the Name of YHWH, **3** and gives a portion to every man of Israel, both man and woman: to each a cake of bread, and a measure of wine, and a grape-cake. **4** And he puts before the Ark of YHWH, those ministering from the Levites, even to make mention of, and to thank, and to give praise to YHWH, God of Israel: **5** Asaph the head, and his second Zechariah; Jeiel, and Shemiramoth, and Jehiel, and Mattithiah, and Eliab, and Benaiah, and Obed-Edom, and Jeiel, with instruments of psalteries, and with harps; and Asaph is sounding with cymbals; **6** and Benaiah and Jahaziel the priests [are] continually [sounding] with trumpets before the Ark of the Covenant of God. **7** On that day, at that time, David has given at the beginning to give thanks to YHWH by the hand of Asaph and his brothers: **8** "Give thanks to YHWH, call on His Name, ‖ Make His doings known among the peoples. **9** Sing to Him, sing psalms to Him, ‖ Meditate on all His wonders. **10** Boast yourselves in His Holy Name, ‖ The heart of those seeking YHWH rejoices. **11** Seek YHWH and His strength, ‖ Seek His face continually. **12** Remember His wonders that He did, ‖ His signs, and the judgments of His mouth, **13** O seed of Israel, His servant, ‖ O sons of Jacob, His chosen ones! **14** He [is] our God YHWH, ‖ His judgments [are] in all the earth. **15** Remember His covenant for all time, ‖ The word He commanded—To one thousand generations, **16** Which He has made with Abraham, ‖ And His oath—to Isaac, **17** And He establishes it to Jacob for a statute, ‖ To Israel [for] a perpetual covenant, **18** Saying, To you I give the land of Canaan, ‖ The portion of your inheritance, **19** When you were few in number, ‖ As a little thing, and sojourners in it. **20** And they go up and down, ‖ From nation to nation, ‖ And from a kingdom to another people. **21** He has not permitted any to oppress them, ‖ And reproves kings on their account: **22** Do not come against My anointed ones, ‖ And do no evil against My prophets. **23** Sing to YHWH, all the earth, ‖ Proclaim His salvation from day to day. **24** Recount His glory among nations, ‖ His wonders among all the peoples. **25** For great [is] YHWH, and greatly praised, ‖ And He [is] fearful above all gods. **26** For all gods of the peoples [are] nothing, ‖ And YHWH has made the heavens. **27** Splendor and majesty [are] before Him, ‖ Strength and joy [are] in His place. **28** Ascribe to YHWH, you families of peoples, ‖ Ascribe to YHWH glory and strength. **29** Ascribe to YHWH the glory of His Name, ‖ Lift up a present, and come before Him. Bow yourselves to YHWH, ‖ In the beauty of holiness. **30** Be pained before Him, all the earth; Also, the world is established, ‖ It is not moved! **31** The heavens rejoice, and the earth is glad, ‖ And they say among nations, YHWH has reigned! **32** The sea roars, and its fullness, ‖ The field exults, and all that [is] in it, **33** Then trees of the forest sing, ‖ From the presence of YHWH, ‖ For He has come to judge the earth! **34** Give thanks to YHWH, for [He is] good, ‖ For His kindness [is] for all time, **35** And say, Save us, O God of our salvation, ‖ And gather us, and deliver us from the nations, ‖ To give thanks to Your Holy Name, ‖ To triumph in Your praise. **36** Blessed [is] YHWH, God of Israel, ‖ From age to age"; And all the people say, "Amen," and have given praise to YHWH. **37** And he leaves there [those] of Asaph and of his brothers, before the Ark of the Covenant of YHWH, to minister before the Ark continually, according to the matter of a day in its day; **38** both Obed-Edom and their sixty-eight brothers, and Obed-Edom son of Jeduthun, and Hosah, for gatekeepers; **39** and Zadok the priest, and his brothers the priests, before the Dwelling Place of YHWH, in a high place that [is] in Gibeon, **40** to cause burnt-offerings to ascend continually to YHWH on the altar of burnt-offering, morning and evening, and for all that is written in the Law of YHWH that He charged on Israel. **41** And with them [are] Heman and Jeduthun, and the rest of those chosen, who were defined by name, to give thanks to YHWH, for His kindness [is] for all time; **42** and with them—Heman and Jeduthun—[are] trumpets and cymbals for those sounding, and instruments of the song of God, and the sons of Jeduthun [are] at the gate. **43** And all the people go, each to his house, and David turns around to bless his house.

17 And it comes to pass as David sat in his house, that David says to Nathan the prophet, "Behold, I am dwelling in a house of cedars, and the Ark of the

1 CHRONICLES

Covenant of YHWH [is] under curtains"; **2** and Nathan says to David, "All that [is] in your heart do, for God [is] with you." **3** And it comes to pass on that night that a word of God is to Nathan, saying, **4** "Go, and you have said to My servant David, Thus said YHWH: You do not build for Me the house to dwell in. **5** For I have not dwelt in a house from the day that I brought up Israel until this day, and I am [going] from tent to tent, and from the Dwelling Place. **6** Wherever I have walked up and down among all Israel, have I spoken a word with one of [the] judges of Israel, whom I commanded to feed My people, saying, Why have you not built a house of cedars for Me? **7** And now, thus you say to My servant, to David, Thus said YHWH of Hosts: I have taken you from the habitation, from after the sheep, to be leader over My people Israel, **8** and I am with you wherever you have walked, and I cut off all your enemies from your presence, and have made a name for you like the name of the great ones who [are] in the earth. **9** And I have prepared a place for My people Israel, and planted it, and it has dwelt in its place, and is not troubled anymore, and the sons of perverseness do not add to wear it out as at first, **10** indeed, even from the days that I appointed judges over My people Israel. And I have humbled all your enemies, and I declare to you that YHWH builds a house for you. **11** And it has come to pass, when your days have been fulfilled to go with your fathers, that I have raised up your seed after you, who is of your sons, and I have established his kingdom; **12** he builds a house for Me, and I have established his throne for all time; **13** I am to him for a father, and he is to Me for a son, and I do not turn aside My kindness from him as I turned it aside from him who was before you, **14** and I have established him in My house, and in My kingdom for all time, and his throne is established for all time." **15** According to all these words, and according to all this vision, so spoke Nathan to David. **16** And David the king comes in and sits before YHWH, and says, "Who [am] I, O YHWH God, and what [is] my house, that You have brought me here? **17** And this is small in Your eyes, O God, and You speak concerning the house of Your servant far off, and have seen me as a type of the man who is on high, O YHWH God! **18** What more does David add to You for the honor of Your servant; and You have known Your servant. **19** O YHWH, for Your servant's sake, and according to Your own heart You have done all this greatness, to make known all these great things. **20** O YHWH, there is none like You, and there is no god except You, according to all that we have heard with our ears. **21** And who [is] as Your people Israel, one nation in the earth whom God has gone to ransom to Himself for a people, to make a great and fearful name for Yourself, to cast out nations from the presence of Your people whom You have ransomed out of Egypt? **22** Indeed, You appoint Your people Israel to Yourself for a people for all time, and You, O YHWH, have been to them for God. **23** And now, O YHWH, let the word that You have spoken concerning Your servant, and concerning his house, be steadfast for all time, and do as You have spoken; **24** and let it be steadfast, and Your Name is great for all time, saying, YHWH of Hosts, God of Israel, [is] God to Israel, and the house of Your servant David is established before You; **25** for You, O my God, have uncovered the ear of Your servant—to build a house for him, therefore Your servant has found [desire] to pray before You. **26** And now, YHWH, You [are] God Himself, and You speak this goodness concerning Your servant; **27** and now, You have been pleased to bless the house of Your servant, to be before You for all time; for You, O YHWH, have blessed, and it is blessed for all time."

18 And it comes to pass after this, that David strikes the Philistines, and humbles them, and takes Gath and its small towns out of the hand of the Philistines; **2** and he strikes Moab, and the Moabites are servants to David, bringing a present. **3** And David strikes Hadarezer king of Zobah, at Hamath, in his going to establish his power by the Euphrates River, **4** and David captures from him one thousand chariots, and seven thousand horsemen, and twenty thousand footmen, and David utterly destroys all the chariots, and leaves of them [only] one hundred chariots. **5** And Aram of Damascus comes to give help to Hadarezer king of Zobah, and David strikes twenty-two thousand men in Aram, **6** and David puts [garrisons] in Aram of Damascus, and the Arameans are for servants to David, carrying a present, and YHWH gives salvation to David wherever he has gone. **7** And David takes the shields of gold that have been on the servants of Hadarezer, and brings them to Jerusalem; **8** and from Tibhath, and from Chun, cities of Hadarezer, David has taken very much bronze; with it Solomon has made the bronze sea, and the pillars, and the vessels of bronze. **9** And Tou king of Hamath hears that David has struck the whole force of Hadarezer king of Zobah, **10** and he sends his son Hadoram to King David, to ask of him of peace, and to bless him, because that he has fought against Hadarezer and strikes him (for Hadarezer had been a man of wars with Tou); and [with him were] all kinds of vessels, of gold, and silver, and bronze; **11** King David has also sanctified them to YHWH with the silver and the gold that he has taken from all the nations, from Edom, and from Moab, and from the sons of Ammon, and from the Philistines, and from Amalek. **12** And Abishai son of Zeruiah has struck Edom in the Valley of Salt—eighteen thousand, **13** and he puts garrisons in Edom, and all the Edomites are servants to David; and YHWH saves David wherever he has gone. **14** And David reigns over all Israel, and he is doing judgment and righteousness to all his people, **15** and Joab son of Zeruiah [is] over the host, and Jehoshaphat son of Ahilud [is] remembrancer, **16** and Zadok son of Ahitub and Abimelech son of Abiathar [are] priests, and Shavsha [is] scribe, **17** and Benaiah son of Jehoiada [is] over the Cherethite and the Pelethite, and the chief sons of David [are] at the hand of the king.

19 And it comes to pass after this, that Nahash king of the sons of Ammon dies, and his son reigns in his stead, **2** and David says, "I do kindness with Hanun son of Nahash, for his father did kindness with me"; and David sends messengers to comfort him concerning his father. And the servants of David come to the land of the sons of Ammon, to Hanun, to comfort him, **3** and the heads of the sons of Ammon say to Hanun, "Is David honoring your father in your eyes because he has sent comforters to you? Have his servants not come to you in order to search, and to overthrow, and to spy out the land?" **4** And Hanun takes the servants of David and shaves them, and cuts their long robes in the midst, to the buttocks, and sends them away. **5** And [some] go and declare to David concerning the men, and he sends to meet them—for the men have been greatly ashamed—and the king says, "Dwell in Jericho until your beard is grown, then you have returned." **6** And the sons of Ammon see that they have made themselves abhorred by David, and Hanun and the sons of Ammon send one thousand talents of silver, to hire for themselves, from Aram-Naharaim, and from Aram-Maachah, and from Zobah, chariots and horsemen; **7** and they hire for themselves thirty-two thousand chariots, and the king of Maachah and his people, and they come in and encamp before Medeba, and the sons of Ammon have been gathered out of their cities, and come to the battle. **8** And David hears, and sends Joab, and all the host of the mighty men, **9** and the sons of Ammon come out and set in array [for] battle at the opening of the city, and the kings who have come [are] by themselves in the field. **10** And Joab sees that the front of the battle has been to him, before and behind, and he chooses out of all the choice in Israel, and sets in array to meet Aram, **11** and he has given the remnant of the people into the hand of his brother Abishai, and they set in array to meet the sons of Ammon. **12** And he says, "If Aram is stronger than me, then you have been for salvation to me; and if the sons of Ammon are stronger than you, then I have saved you; **13** be strong, and we strengthen ourselves, for our people, and for the cities of our God, and YHWH does that which is good in His eyes." **14** And Joab draws near, and the people who [are] with him, before Aram to battle, and they flee from his face; **15** and the sons of Ammon have seen that Aram has fled, and they flee—they also—from the face of his brother Abishai, and go into the city. And Joab comes to Jerusalem. **16** And Aram sees that they have been struck before Israel, and send messengers, and bring out Aram that [is] beyond the River, and Shophach head of the host of Hadarezer [is] before them. **17** And it is declared to David, and he gathers all Israel, and passes over the Jordan, and comes to them, and sets in array against them; indeed, David sets in array [for] battle to meet Aram, and they fight with him; **18** and Aram flees from the face of Israel, and David slays seven thousand charioteers and forty thousand footmen of Aram, and he has put Shophach head of the host to death. **19** And the servants of Hadarezer see that they have been struck before Israel, and they make peace with David and serve him, and Aram has not been willing to help the sons of Ammon anymore.

20 And it comes to pass, at the time of the turn of the year—at the time of the going out of the messengers—that Joab leads out the force of the host, and destroys the land of the sons of Ammon, and comes in and besieges Rabbah—David is abiding in Jerusalem—and Joab strikes Rabbah, and breaks it down. **2** And David takes the crown of their king from off his head, and finds it [to be] a talent of gold [in] weight, and [with] precious stone in it, and it is on the head of David; and he has brought out very much spoil of the city, **3** and he has brought out the people who [are] in it, and sets [them] to the saw, and to cutting instruments of iron, and to axes; and thus David does to all cities of the sons of Ammon, and David turns back—and all the people—to Jerusalem. **4** And it comes to pass after this, that war remains in Gezer with the Philistines; then Sibbechai the Hushathite has struck Sippai, of the children of the giant, and they are humbled. **5** And there is war with the Philistines again, and Elhanan son of Jair strikes Lahmi, brother of Goliath the Gittite, the wood of whose spear [is] like a weavers' beam. **6** And there is war in Gath again, and there is a man of [great] measure, and his fingers and his toes [are] six and six—twenty-four [total], and he has also been born to the giant. **7** And he reproaches Israel, and Jonathan son of Shimea, brother of David, strikes him. **8** These were born to the giant in Gath, and they fall by the hand of David, and by the hand of his servants.

21 Then Satan stands up against Israel, and persuades David to number Israel, **2** and David says to Joab and to the heads of the people, "Go, number Israel from Beer-Sheba even to Dan, and bring [the account] to me, and I know their number." **3** And Joab says, "YHWH adds to His people as they are one hundred times; are they not, my lord, O king, all of them for servants to my lord? Why does my lord seek this? Why is he for a cause of guilt to Israel?" **4** And the word of the king [is] severe against Joab, and Joab goes out, and goes up and down in all Israel, and comes to Jerusalem. **5** And Joab gives the account of the numbering of the people to David, and all Israel is one million and one hundred thousand, each drawing sword, and Judah [is] four hundred and seventy thousand, each drawing sword. **6** And he has not numbered Levi and Benjamin in their midst, for the word of the king was abominable with Joab. **7** And it is evil in the eyes of God concerning this thing, and He strikes Israel, **8** and David says to God, "I have sinned exceedingly in that I have done this thing; and now, please cause the iniquity of Your servant to pass away, for I have acted very foolishly." **9** And YHWH speaks to Gad, seer of David, saying, **10** "Go, and you have spoken to David, saying, Thus said YHWH: I am extending three [choices] to you; choose one of these for yourself, and I do [it] to you." **11** And Gad comes to David and says to him, "Thus said YHWH: Take for yourself—**12** either famine for three years, or three months to be consumed from the face of your adversaries (even [for] the sword of your enemies to overtake), or three days of the sword of YHWH (even pestilence in the land, and a messenger of YHWH destroying in all the border of Israel); and now, see; what word do I return to Him who is sending me?" **13** And David says to Gad, "I am greatly distressed, please let me fall into the hand of YHWH, for His mercies [are] very many, and do not let me fall into the hand of man." **14** And YHWH gives a pestilence in Israel, and there falls from Israel seventy thousand men, **15** and God sends a messenger to Jerusalem to destroy it, and as he is destroying, YHWH has seen, and is comforted concerning the calamity, and says to the messenger who [is] destroying, "Enough now, cease your hand." And the messenger of YHWH is standing by the threshing-floor of Ornan the Jebusite, **16** and David lifts up his eyes, and sees the messenger of YHWH standing between the earth and the heavens, and his sword [is] drawn in his hand, stretched out over Jerusalem, and David falls, and the elderly, covered with sackcloth, on their faces. **17** And David says to God, "Did I not command to number the people? Indeed, it [is] I who have sinned, and done great evil: and these, the flock, what did they do? O YHWH, my God, please let Your hand be on me, and on the house of my father, and not on Your people—to be plagued." **18** And the messenger of YHWH commanded to Gad to say to David, "Surely David goes up to raise an altar to YHWH in the threshing-floor of Ornan the Jebusite." **19** And David goes up by the word of Gad, that he spoke in the Name of YHWH. **20** And Ornan turns back and sees the messenger, and his four sons [are] with him hiding themselves, and Ornan is threshing wheat. **21** And David comes to Ornan, and Ornan looks attentively and sees David, and goes out from the threshing-floor, and bows himself to David—face to the earth. **22** And David says to Ornan, "Give the place of the threshing-floor to me, and I build an altar to YHWH in it; give it to me for full price, and the plague is restrained from the people." **23** And Ornan says to David, "Take [it] to yourself, and my lord the king does that which is good in his eyes; see, I have given the oxen for burnt-offerings, and the threshing instruments for wood, and the wheat for a present; I have given the whole." **24** And King David says to Ornan, "No, for I surely buy [it] for full price; for I do not lift up that which is yours to YHWH, so as to offer a burnt-offering without cost." **25** And David gives to Ornan six hundred shekels of gold [in] weight for the place; **26** and David builds an altar to YHWH there, and offers burnt-offerings and peace-offerings, and calls to YHWH, and He answers him from the heavens with fire on the altar of the burnt-offering. **27** And YHWH speaks to the messenger, and he turns back his sword to its sheath. **28** At that time, when David sees that YHWH has answered him in the threshing-floor of Ornan the Jebusite, then he sacrifices there; **29** and the Dwelling Place of YHWH that Moses made in the wilderness, and the altar of the burnt-offering, [are] at that time at a high place in Gibeon; **30** and David is not able to go before it to seek God, for he has been afraid because of the sword of the messenger of YHWH.

22 And David says, "This is the house of YHWH God, and this [is] the altar for burnt-offering for Israel." **2** And David says to gather the sojourners who [are] in the land of Israel, and appoints hewers to hew hewn-stones to build a house of God. **3** And David has prepared iron in abundance for nails for leaves of the gates and for couplings, and bronze in abundance—there is no weighing, **4** and cedar-trees without number, for the Zidonians and the Tyrians brought in cedar-trees in abundance to David. **5** And David says, "My son Solomon [is] a youth and tender, and the house to be built for YHWH [is] to be made exceedingly great, for renown and for beauty to all the lands; now let me prepare for it"; and David prepares in abundance before his death. **6** And he calls for his son Solomon, and charges him to build a house for YHWH, God of Israel, **7** and David says to his son Solomon, "As for me, it has been with my heart to build a house for the Name of my God YHWH, **8** and the word of YHWH [is] against me, saying, You have shed blood in abundance, and you have made great wars; you do not build a house for My Name, for you have shed much blood to the earth before Me. **9** Behold, a son is born to you; he is a man of rest, and I have given rest to him from all his surrounding enemies, for Solomon is his name, and I give peace and quietness to Israel in his days; **10** he builds a house for My Name, and he is to Me for a son, and I [am] to him for a father, and I have established the throne of his kingdom over Israel for all time. **11** Now my son, YHWH is with you, and you have prospered, and have built the house of your God YHWH, as He spoke concerning you. **12** Only, may YHWH give wisdom and understanding to you, and charge you concerning Israel, even to keep the Law of your God YHWH; **13** then you prosper, if you observe to do the statutes and the judgments that YHWH charged Moses with concerning Israel; be strong and courageous; do not fear, nor be cast down. **14** And behold, in my affliction I have prepared for the house of YHWH one hundred thousand talents of gold, and one million talents of silver; and of bronze and of iron there is no weighing, for it has been in abundance; and I have prepared wood and stones, and you add to them. **15** And with you in abundance [are] workmen, hewers and craftsmen of stone and of wood, and every skillful man for every work. **16** Of the gold, of the silver, and of the bronze, and of the iron, there is no number; arise and do, and YHWH is with you." **17** And David gives charge to all heads of Israel to give help to his son

1 CHRONICLES

Solomon, [saying], **18** "Is your God YHWH not with you? Indeed, He has given rest to you all around, for He has given the inhabitants of the land into my hand, and the land has been subdued before His people. **19** Now give your heart and your soul to seek for your God YHWH, and rise and build the sanctuary of YHWH God, to bring in the Ark of the Covenant of YHWH, and the holy vessels of God, to the house that is built for the Name of YHWH."

23 And David was old and satisfied with days, and he causes his son Solomon to reign over Israel, **2** and gathers all the heads of Israel, and the priests, and the Levites; **3** and the Levites are numbered from a son of thirty years and upward, and their number, for their counted heads, is of thirty-eight thousand mighty men. **4** Of these, twenty-four thousand [are] to preside over the work of the house of YHWH, and six thousand officers and judges, **5** and four thousand gatekeepers, and four thousand giving praise to YHWH, "with instruments that I made for praising," [says David.] **6** And David distributes them into divisions of the sons of Levi—of Gershon, Kohath, and Merari. **7** Of the Gershonite: Laadan and Shimei. **8** Sons of Laadan: the head [is] Jehiel, and Zetham, and Joel—three. **9** Sons of Shimei: Shelomith, and Haziel, and Haran—three; these [are] heads of the fathers of Laadan. **10** And sons of Shimei: Jahath, Zina, and Jeush, and Beriah; these [are] the four sons of Shimei. **11** And Jahath is the head, and Zizah the second, and Jeush and Beriah have not multiplied sons, and they become the house of a father by one numbering. **12** Sons of Kohath: Amram, Izhar, Hebron, and Uzziel—four. **13** Sons of Amram: Aaron and Moses; and Aaron is separated for his sanctifying the Holy of Holies, he and his sons, for all time, to make incense before YHWH, to serve Him, and to bless in His Name for all time. **14** As for Moses, the man of God, his sons are called after the tribe of Levi. **15** Sons of Moses: Gershom and Eliezer. **16** Sons of Gershom: Shebuel the head. **17** And sons of Eliezer are Rehabiah the head, and Eliezer had no other sons, and the sons of Rehabiah have multiplied exceedingly. **18** Sons of Izhar: Shelomith the head. **19** Sons of Hebron: Jeriah the head, Amariah the second, Jahaziel the third, and Jekameam the fourth. **20** Sons of Uzziel: Micah the head, and Ishshiah the second. **21** Sons of Merari: Mahli and Mushi; sons of Mahli: Eleazar and Kish. **22** And Eleazar dies, and he had no sons, but daughters, and their brothers, sons of Kish, take them. **23** Sons of Mushi: Mahli, and Eder, and Jerimoth—three. **24** These [are] sons of Levi, by the house of their fathers, heads of the fathers, by their appointments, in the number of names, by their counted heads, doing the work for the service of the house of YHWH, from a son of twenty years and upward, **25** for David said, "YHWH, God of Israel, has given rest to His people, and He dwells in Jerusalem for all time"; **26** and also of the Levites, "None [are] to carry the Dwelling Place and all its vessels for its service"; **27** for by the last words of David they [took] the number of the sons of Levi from a son of twenty years and upward, **28** for their station [is] at the side of the sons of Aaron, for the service of the house of YHWH, over the courts, and over the chambers, and over the cleansing of every holy thing, and the work of the service of the house of God, **29** and for the bread of the arrangement, and for fine flour for present, and for the thin unleavened cakes, and for [the work of] the pan, and for that which is stirred, and for all [liquid] measure and [solid] measure; **30** and to stand, morning by morning, to give thanks, and to give praise to YHWH, and so at evening; **31** and for all the burnt-offerings—burnt-offerings to YHWH for Sabbaths, for new moons, and for appointed times, by number, according to the ordinance on them continually, before YHWH. **32** And they have kept the charge of the Tent of Meeting, and the charge of the holy place, and the charge of their brothers, the sons of Aaron, for the service of the house of YHWH.

24 And [these are] their divisions, of the sons of Aaron. [The] sons of Aaron [are] Nadab, and Abihu, Eleazar, and Ithamar. **2** And Nadab dies—and Abihu—in the presence of their father, and they had no sons, and Eleazar and Ithamar act as priests. **3** And David distributes them—and Zadok of the sons of Eleazar, and Ahimelech of the sons of Ithamar—according to their office in their service; **4** and there are found of the sons of Eleazar more for heads of the mighty men than of the sons of Ithamar; and they distribute them. Of the sons of Eleazar, heads for [each] house of [their] fathers—sixteen; and of the sons of Ithamar, for [each] house of their fathers—eight. **5** And they distribute them by lots, with one another, for they have been princes of the holy place and princes of God, from the sons of Eleazar and from the sons of Ithamar. **6** And Shemaiah son of Nethaneel the scribe, of the Levites, writes them before the king, and the princes, and Zadok the priest, and Ahimelech son of Abiathar, and heads of the fathers for priests and for Levites, one house of a father being taken possession of for Eleazar and one being taken possession of for Ithamar. **7** And the first lot goes out for Jehoiarib, for Jedaiah the second, **8** for Harim the third, for Seorim the fourth, **9** for Malchijah the fifth, for Mijamin the sixth, **10** for Hakkoz the seventh, for Abijah the eighth, **11** for Jeshuah the ninth, for Shecaniah the tenth, **12** for Eliashib the eleventh, for Jakim the twelfth, **13** for Huppah the thirteenth, for Jeshebeab the fourteenth, **14** for Bilgah the fifteenth, for Immer the sixteenth, **15** for Hezir the seventeenth, for Aphses the eighteenth, **16** for Pethahiah the nineteenth, for Jehezekel the twentieth, **17** for Jachin the twenty-first, for Gamul the twenty-second, **18** for Delaiah the twenty-third, for Maaziah the twenty-fourth. **19** These [are] their appointments for their service, to come into the house of YHWH, according to their ordinance by the hand of their father Aaron, as YHWH God of Israel commanded them. **20** And of the sons of Levi who are left—of sons of Amram: Shubael; of sons of Shubael: Jehdeiah. **21** Of Rehabiah, of sons of Rehabiah: the head Ishshiah. **22** Of the Izharite: Shelomoth; of sons of Shelomoth: Jahath. **23** And sons of Jeriah: Amariah the second, Jahaziel the third, Jekameam the fourth. **24** Sons of Uzziel: Michah; of sons of Michah: Shamir. **25** Ishshiah [is] a brother of Michah; of sons of Ishshiah: Zechariah; **26** sons of Merari: Mahli and Mushi; sons of Jaaziah: Beno; **27** sons of Merari, of Jaaziah: Beno, and Shoham, and Zaccur, and Ibri. **28** Of Mahli: Eleazar, who had no sons; **29** of Kish, sons of Kish: Jerahmeel. **30** And sons of Mushi [are] Mahli, and Eder, and Jerimoth; these [are] sons of the Levites, for the house of their fathers, **31** and they also cast lots just as their brothers, the sons of Aaron, before David the king, and Zadok, and Ahimelech, and heads of the fathers for priests and for Levites; the chief father just as his younger brother.

25 And David and the heads of the host separate for service, of the sons of Asaph, and Heman, and Jeduthun, who are prophesying with harps, with psalteries, and with cymbals; and the number of the workmen is according to their service. **2** Of sons of Asaph: Zaccur, and Joseph, and Nethaniah, and Asharelah; sons of Asaph [are] by the side of Asaph, who is prophesying by the side of the king. **3** Of Jeduthun, sons of Jeduthun: Gedaliah, and Zeri, and Jeshaiah, [and Shimei, and] Hashabiah, and Mattithiah, six, by the side of their father Jeduthun; he is prophesying with a harp, for giving of thanks and of praise for YHWH. **4** Of Heman, sons of Heman: Bukkiah, Mattaniah, Uzziel, Shebuel, and Jerimoth, Hananiah, Hanani, Eliathah, Giddalti, and Romamti-Ezer, Joshbekashah, Mallothi, Hothir, Mahazioth; **5** all these [are] sons of Heman, seer of the king in the things of God, to lift up a horn; and God gives fourteen sons and three daughters to Heman. **6** All these [are] by the side of their father in the song of the house of YHWH, with cymbals, psalteries, and harps, for the service of the house of God; by the side of the king [are] Asaph, and Jeduthun, and Heman. **7** And their number, with their brothers taught in the song of YHWH—all who are intelligent—[is] two hundred and eighty-eight. **8** And they cause lots to fall, charge next to [charge], the small as well as the great, the intelligent with the learner. **9** And the first lot goes out for Asaph to Joseph; the second, Gedaliah—him, and his brothers and his sons—twelve; **10** the third, Zaccur, his sons and his brothers—twelve; **11** the fourth to Izri, his sons and his brothers—twelve; **12** the fifth, Nethaniah, his sons and his brothers—twelve; **13** the sixth, Bukkiah, his sons and his brothers—twelve; **14** the seventh, Jesharelah, his sons and his brothers—twelve; **15** the eighth, Jeshaiah, his sons and his brothers—twelve; **16** the ninth, Mattaniah, his sons and his brothers—twelve; **17** the tenth, Shimei, his sons and his brothers—twelve; **18** eleventh, Azareel, his sons and his brothers—twelve; **19** the twelfth to Hashabiah, his sons and his brothers—

twelve; **20** for the thirteenth, Shubael, his sons and his brothers—twelve; **21** for the fourteenth, Mattithiah, his sons and his brothers—twelve; **22** for the fifteenth to Jeremoth, his sons and his brothers—twelve; **23** the sixteenth to Hananiah, his sons and his brothers—twelve; **24** the seventeenth to Joshbekashah, his sons and his brothers—twelve; **25** the eighteenth to Hanani, his sons and his brothers—twelve; **26** the nineteenth to Mallothi, his sons and his brothers—twelve; **27** the twentieth to Eliathah, his sons and his brothers—twelve; **28** the twenty-first to Hothir, his sons and his brothers—twelve; **29** the twenty-second to Giddalti, his sons and his brothers—twelve; **30** the twenty-third to Mahazioth, his sons and his brothers—twelve; **31** the twenty-fourth to Romamti-Ezer, his sons and his brothers—twelve.

26 For the divisions of the gatekeepers, of the Korahites: Meshelemiah son of Kore, of the sons of Asaph; **2** and sons of Meshelemiah: Zechariah the firstborn, Jediael the second, Zebadiah the third, Jathniel the fourth, **3** Elam the fifth, Jehohanan the sixth, Elioenai the seventh. **4** And moreover, sons of Obed-Edom: Shemaiah the firstborn, Jehozabad the second, Joah the third, and Sacar the fourth, and Nethaneel the fifth, **5** Ammiel the sixth, Issachar the seventh, Peullethai the eighth, for God has blessed him. **6** And sons have been born to his son Shemaiah, who are ruling throughout the house of their father, for they [are] mighty men of valor. **7** Sons of Shemaiah: Othni, and Rephael, and Obed, [and] Elzabad; his brothers Elihu and Semachiah [are] sons of valor. **8** All these [are] of the sons of Obed-Edom; they, and their sons, and their brothers, men of valor with might for service—sixty-two of Obed-Edom. **9** And sons and brothers of Meshelemiah, sons of valor—eighteen; **10** and of Hosah, of the sons of Merari, [are these] sons: Shimri the head (though he was not firstborn, yet his father sets him for head), **11** Hilkiah the second, Tebaliah the third, Zechariah the fourth; all the sons and brothers of Hosah—thirteen. **12** For these [are] the divisions of the gatekeepers, of the heads of the mighty ones, [with] charges just as their brothers, to minister in the house of YHWH, **13** and they cause lots to fall, the small as well as the great, according to the house of their fathers, for every gate. **14** And the lot falls eastward to Shelemiah; and [for] his son Zechariah, a counselor with understanding, they cause lots to fall, and his lot goes out northward; **15** to Obed-Edom southward, and to his sons, the house of the gatherings; **16** to Shuppim and to Hosah to the west, with Shallecheth Gate, in the highway, the ascent, watch next to watch; **17** to the east [are] six Levites, to the north [are] four each day, to the south [are] four each day, and for the gatherings, two by two; **18** at Parbar, to the west, [are] four at the highway, two at Parbar. **19** These are the divisions of the gatekeepers, of the sons of the Korahite, and of the sons of Merari. **20** And of the Levites, Ahijah [is] over the treasures of the house of God, even for the treasures of the holy things. **21** Sons of Laadan, sons of the Gershonite, of Laadan, heads of the fathers of Laadan the Gershonite: Jehieli. **22** Sons of Jehieli: Zetham and his brother Joel, over the treasures of the house of YHWH. **23** Of the Amramite, of the Izharite, of the Hebronite, of [the] Uzzielite— **24** and Shebuel son of Gershom, son of Moses, [is] president over the treasures. **25** And his brothers, of Eliezer: Rehabiah his son, and Jeshaiah his son, and Joram his son, and Zichri his son, and Shelomith his son. **26** This Shelomith and his brothers [are] over all the treasures of the holy things that David the king, and heads of the fathers, even heads of thousands, and of hundreds, and heads of the host, sanctified; **27** from the battles and from the spoil, they sanctified to strengthen the house of YHWH; **28** and all that Samuel the seer, and Saul son of Kish, and Abner son of Ner, and Joab son of Zeruiah sanctified, everyone sanctifying [anything—it is] by the side of Shelomith and his brothers. **29** Of the Izharite, Chenaniah and his sons [are] for the outward work over Israel, for officers and for judges. **30** Of the Hebronite, Hashabiah and his brothers, one thousand and seven hundred sons of valor, [are] over the inspection of Israel, beyond the Jordan westward, for all the work of YHWH, and for the service of the king. **31** Of the Hebronite, Jerijah [is] the head of the Hebronite, according to the generations of his fathers. In the fortieth year of the reign of David they have been sought out, and there are found among them mighty men of valor, in Jazer of Gilead— **32** and ers, two thousand and seven ...ons of valor, [are] heads of the ......s, and King David appoints them over the Reubenite, and the Gadite, and the half of the tribe of the Manassite, for every matter of God and matter of the king.

27 And the sons of Israel, after their number, heads of the fathers, and princes of the thousands and of the hundreds, and their officers, those serving the king in any matter of the divisions, that are coming in and going out month by month throughout all months of the year, [are] twenty-four thousand in each division. **2** Over the first division for the first month [is] Jashobeam son of Zabdiel, and twenty-four thousand [are] on his division; **3** [he was] of the sons of Perez, [and] the head of all princes of the hosts for the first month. **4** And over the division of the second month [is] Dodai the Ahohite, and Mikloth [is] also president of his division, and twenty-four thousand [are] on his division. **5** Head of the third host, for the third month, [is] Benaiah son of Jehoiada, the head priest, and twenty-four thousand [are] on his division. **6** This Benaiah [is] a mighty one of the thirty, and over the thirty, and his son Ammizabad [is in] his division. **7** The fourth, for the fourth month, [is] Asahel brother of Joab, and his son Zebadiah after him, and twenty-four thousand [are] on his division. **8** The fifth, for the fifth month, [is] the prince Shamhuth the Izrahite, and twenty-four thousand [are] on his division. **9** The sixth, for the sixth month, [is] Ira son of Ikkesh the Tekoite, and twenty-four thousand [are] on his division. **10** The seventh, for the seventh month, [is] Helez the Pelonite, of the sons of Ephraim, and twenty-four thousand [are] on his division. **11** The eighth, for the eighth month, [is] Sibbecai the Hushathite, of the Zerahite, and twenty-four thousand [are] on his division. **12** The ninth, for the ninth month, [is] Abiezer the Antothite, of the Benjamite, and twenty-four thousand [are] on his division. **13** The tenth, for the tenth month, [is] Maharai the Netophathite, of the Zerahite, and twenty-four thousand [are] on his division. **14** Eleventh, for the eleventh month, [is] Benaiah the Pirathonite, of the sons of Ephraim, and twenty-four thousand [are] on his division. **15** The twelfth, for the twelfth month, [is] Heldai the Netophathite, of Othniel, and twenty-four thousand [are] on his division. **16** And over the tribes of Israel: the leader of the Reubenite [is] Eliezer son of Zichri; of the Simeonite, Shephatiah son of Maachah; **17** of the Levite, Hashabiah son of Kemuel; of the Aaronite, Zadok; **18** of Judah, Elihu, of the brothers of David; of Issachar, Omri son of Michael; **19** of Zebulun, Ishmaiah son of Obadiah; of Naphtali, Jerimoth son of Azriel; **20** of the sons of Ephraim, Hoshea son of Azaziah; of the half of the tribe of Manasseh, Joel son of Pedaiah; **21** of the half of Manasseh in Gilead, Iddo son of Zechariah; of Benjamin, Jaasiel son of Abner; of Dan, Azareel son of Jeroham. **22** These [are the] heads of the tribes of Israel. **23** But David has not taken up their number from a son of twenty years and under, for YHWH had said [He would] multiply Israel as the stars of the heavens. **24** Joab son of Zeruiah has begun to number, but has not finished; and there is wrath against Israel for this, and the number has not gone up in the account of the Chronicles of King David. **25** And Azmaveth son of Adiel [is] over the treasures of the king; and Jonathan son of Uzziah [is] over the treasures in the field, in the cities, and in the villages, and in the towers; **26** and Ezri son of Chelub [is] over workmen of the field for the service of the ground; **27** and Shimei the Ramathite [is] over the vineyards; and Zabdi the Shiphmite [is] over what [is] in the vineyards for the treasures of wine; **28** and Ba'al-Hanan the Gederite [is] over the olives and the sycamores that [are] in the low country; and Joash [is] over the treasures of oil; **29** and Shitrai the Sharonite [is] over the herds that are feeding in Sharon; and Shaphat son of Adlai [is] over the herds in the valleys; **30** and Obil the Ishmaelite [is] over the camels; and Jehdeiah the Meronothite [is] over the donkeys; **31** and Jaziz the Hagerite [is] over the flock; all these [are] heads of the substance that King David has. **32** And Jonathan, David's uncle, [is] counselor, a man of understanding, [and] he is also a scribe; and Jehiel son of Hachmoni [is] with the sons of the king; **33** and Ahithophel [is] counselor to the king; and Hushai the Archite [is] the friend of the king; **34** and after Ahithophel [is] Jehoiada son of Benaiah, and Abiathar; and the head of the host of the king [is] Joab.

1 CHRONICLES

28 And David assembles all the heads of Israel, heads of the tribes, and heads of the divisions who are serving the king, and heads of the thousands, and heads of the hundreds, and heads of all the substance and possessions of the king, and of his sons, with the officers and the mighty ones, and of every mighty man of valor—to Jerusalem. **2** And David the king rises on his feet and says, "Hear me, my brothers and my people, I [had it] with my heart to build a house of rest for the Ark of the Covenant of YHWH, and for the footstool of our God, and I prepared to build, **3** and God has said to me, You do not build a house for My Name, for you [are] a man of wars, and you have shed blood. **4** And YHWH, God of Israel, fixes on me out of all the house of my father to be for king over Israel for all time, for He has fixed on Judah for a leader, and in the house of Judah, the house of my father, and among the sons of my father, He has been pleased with me to make [me] king over all Israel; **5** and out of all my sons—for YHWH has given many sons to me—He also fixes on my son Solomon, to sit on the throne of the kingdom of YHWH over Israel, **6** and says to me, Your son Solomon builds My house and My courts, for I have fixed on him [to be] to Me for a son, and I am to him for a father. **7** And I have established his kingdom for all time, if he is strong to do My commands and My judgments, as at this day. **8** And now, before the eyes of all Israel, the assembly of YHWH, and in the ears of our God, keep and seek all the commands of your God YHWH, so that you possess this good land, and have caused your sons to inherit after you for all time. **9** And you, my son Solomon, know the God of your father, and serve Him with a perfect heart and with a willing mind, for YHWH is seeking all hearts, and He is understanding every imagination of the thoughts; if you seek Him, He is found by you, and if you forsake Him, He casts you off forever. **10** See, now, for YHWH has fixed on you to build a house for a sanctuary; be strong, and do." **11** And David gives to his son Solomon the pattern of the porch, and of its houses, and of its treasures, and of its upper chambers, and of its innermost chambers, and of the house of the atonement; **12** and the pattern of all that has been with him by the Spirit, for the courts of the house of YHWH, and for all the surrounding chambers, for the treasures of the house of God, and for the treasures of the things sacrificed; **13** and for the divisions of the priests and of the Levites, and for all the work of the service of the house of YHWH, and for all vessels of service of the house of YHWH, **14** even gold by weight, for [things of] gold, for all instruments of every service; for all instruments of silver by weight, for all instruments of every service; **15** and [by] weight for the lampstands of gold, and their lamps of gold, by weight [for] lampstand and lampstand, and its lamps; and for the lampstands of silver, by weight for a lampstand and its lamps, according to the service of lampstand and lampstand; **16** and the gold [by] weight for tables of the arrangement, for table and table, and silver for the tables of silver; **17** and the forks, and the bowls, and the cups of pure gold, and for the basins of gold, by weight for basin and basin, and for the basins of silver, by weight for basin and basin, **18** and for the altar of incense, refined gold by weight, and for the pattern of the chariot of the cherubim of gold, spreading and covering over the Ark of the Covenant of YHWH. **19** The whole [is] in writing from the hand of YHWH, "He caused me to understand all the work of the pattern," [said David.] **20** And David says to his son Solomon, "Be strong and courageous, and do; do not fear nor be frightened, for YHWH God, my God, [is] with you; He does not fail you, nor forsake you, to the completion of all the work of the service of the house of YHWH. **21** And behold, divisions of the priests and of the Levites [are] for all the service of the house of God; and with you in all work [is] every willing one with wisdom, for every service; and the heads and all the people [are] according to all your words."

29 And David the king says to all the assembly, "My son Solomon—the one on whom God has fixed—[is] young and tender, and the work [is] great, for the palace is not for man, but for YHWH God; **2** and with all my power I have prepared for the house of my God, the gold for [things of] gold, and the silver for [things of] silver, and the bronze for [things of] bronze, the iron for [things of] iron, and the wood for [things of] wood, shoham stones, and settings, and stones of painting and of diverse colors, and all [kinds of] precious stone, and stones of white marble, in

1 CHRONICLES

... again, because of my ... house of my God, the ... e—a peculiar treasure of ... —I have given for the house ... en over and above all I have ... the holy house: **4** three thous... ents of gold, of the gold of Ophir, and seven thousand talents of refined silver, to overlay the walls of the houses, **5** even gold for [things of] gold, and silver for [things of] silver, and for all the work by the hand of craftsmen; and who [is] he that is offering to willingly consecrate his hand to YHWH today?" **6** And the heads of the fathers, and the heads of the tribes of Israel, and the heads of the thousands, and of the hundreds, and of the heads of the work of the king, offer willingly. **7** And they give for the service of the house of God five thousand talents and ten thousand drams of gold, and ten thousand talents of silver, and eighteen thousand talents of bronze, and one hundred thousand talents of iron; **8** and he with whom stones are found has given [them] to the treasury of the house of YHWH, by the hand of Jehiel the Gershonite. **9** And the people rejoice because of their offering willingly, for with a perfect heart they have offered willingly to YHWH; and David the king has also rejoiced [with] great joy. **10** And David blesses YHWH before the eyes of all the assembly, and David says, "Blessed [are] You, YHWH, God of Israel, our Father, from age even to age. **11** To You, O YHWH, [is] the greatness, and the might, and the beauty, and the victory, and the splendor, because of all in the heavens and in the earth; to You, O YHWH, [is] the kingdom, and He who is lifting up Himself over all for head; **12** and the riches, and the honor [are] from before You, and You are ruling over all, and in Your hand [is] power and might, and [it is] in Your hand to make great and to give strength to all. **13** And now, our God, we are giving thanks to You, and giving praise to Your beautiful Name; **14** indeed, because who [am] I, and who [are] my people, that we retain power to offer thus willingly? But the whole [is] from You, and we have given to You out of Your [own] hand; **15** for we [are] sojourners and settlers before You, like all our fathers; our days on the land [are] as a shadow, and there is none abiding. **16** O our God YHWH, all this store [with] which we have prepared to build a house for You, for Your Holy Name, [is] out of Your [own] hand, and the whole [is] of You. **17** And I have known, my God, that You are trying the heart, and desire uprightness; I, in the uprightness of my heart, have willingly offered all these; and now, I have seen Your people who are found here with joy to offer willingly to You. **18** O YHWH, God of Abraham, Isaac, and Israel, our fathers, keep this for all time for the imagination of the thoughts of the heart of Your people, and prepare their heart for You; **19** and give a perfect heart to my son Solomon, to keep Your commands, Your testimonies, and Your statutes, and to do the whole, even to build the palace [for] which I have prepared." **20** And David says to all the assembly, "Now bless your God YHWH"; and all the assembly blesses YHWH, God of their fathers, and bows and pays respect to YHWH and to the king. **21** And they sacrifice sacrifices to YHWH, and cause burnt-offerings to ascend to YHWH on that next day: one thousand bullocks, one thousand rams, one thousand lambs, and their oblations, and sacrifices in abundance for all Israel. **22** And they eat and drink before YHWH on that day with great joy, and cause Solomon son of David to reign a second time, and anoint [him] before YHWH for leader, and Zadok for priest. **23** And Solomon sits on the throne of YHWH for king instead of his father David, and prospers, and all of Israel listens to him, **24** and all the heads, and the mighty men, and also all the sons of King David have given a hand under Solomon the king; **25** and YHWH makes Solomon exceedingly great before the eyes of all Israel, and puts on him the splendor of the kingdom that has not been on any king over Israel before him. **26** And David son of Jesse has reigned over all Israel, **27** and the days that he has reigned over Israel [are] forty years; he reigned in Hebron seven years, and he reigned in Jerusalem thirty-three; **28** and he dies in a good old age, satisfied with days, riches, and honor, and his son Solomon reigns in his stead. **29** And the matters of David the king, the first and the last, behold, they are written beside the matters of Samuel the seer, and beside the matters of Nathan the prophet, and beside the matters of Gad the seer, **30** with all his reign, and his might, and the times that went over him, and over Israel, and over all kingdoms of the lands.

2 CHRONICLES

1 And Solomon son of David strengthens himself over his kingdom, and his God YHWH [is] with him, and makes him exceedingly great. **2** And Solomon says to all Israel, to heads of the thousands, and of the hundreds, and to the ones judging, and to every honorable one of all Israel, heads of the fathers, **3** and they go—Solomon, and all the assembly with him—to the high place that [is] in Gibeon, for God's Tent of Meeting has been there, that Moses, servant of YHWH, made in the wilderness, **4** but David had the Ark of God brought up from Kirjath-Jearim to the [place] David had prepared for it, for he stretched out a tent for it in Jerusalem; **5** and the altar of bronze that Bezaleel son of Uri, son of Hur made, he put before the Dwelling Place of YHWH; and Solomon and the assembly seek Him [there]. **6** And Solomon goes up there, on the altar of bronze, before YHWH, that [is] at the Tent of Meeting, and causes one thousand burnt-offerings to ascend on it. **7** In that night God has appeared to Solomon and says to him, "Ask—what do I give to you?" **8** And Solomon says to God, "You have done great kindness with my father David, and have caused me to reign in his stead. **9** Now, O YHWH God, Your word with my father David is steadfast, for You have caused me to reign over a people [as] numerous as the dust of the earth; **10** now, give wisdom and knowledge to me, and I go out before this people, and I come in, for who judges this—Your great people?" **11** And God says to Solomon, "Because that this has been with your heart, and you have not asked for riches, wealth, and honor, and the life of those hating you, and also have not asked for many days, and ask for wisdom and knowledge for yourself, so that you judge My people over which I have caused you to reign— **12** the wisdom and the knowledge is given to you, and riches and wealth and honor I [also] give to you, that there has not been so to the kings who [are] before you, and after you it is not so." **13** And Solomon comes in to Jerusalem [from] the high place that [is] in Gibeon, from before the Tent of Meeting, and reigns over Israel, **14** and Solomon gathers chariots and horsemen, and he has one thousand and four hundred chariots, and twelve thousand horsemen, and he places them in the cities of the chariots, and with the king in Jerusalem. **15** And the king makes the silver and the gold in Jerusalem as stones, and the cedars he made as sycamores that [are] in the low country, for abundance. **16** And the source of the horses that [are] for Solomon [is] from Egypt and from Keva; merchants of the king take [them] from Keva at a price, **17** and they come up, and bring out a chariot from Egypt for six hundred pieces of silver, and a horse for one hundred and fifty, and so for all the kings of the Hittites and the kings of Aram—they bring [them] out by their hand.

2 And Solomon says to build a house for the Name of YHWH, and a house for his kingdom, **2** and Solomon numbers seventy thousand men bearing burden, and eighty thousand men hewing in the mountain, and three thousand and six hundred overseers over them. **3** And Solomon sends to Huram king of Tyre, saying, "When you have dealt with my father David, then you send cedars to him to build a house for him to dwell in; **4** behold, I am building a house for the Name of my God YHWH, to sanctify [it] to Him, to make incense before Him, incense of spices, and a continual arrangement, and burnt-offerings at morning and at evening, at Sabbaths, and at new moons, and at appointed times of our God YHWH; this [is] on Israel for all time. **5** And the house that I am building [is] great, for our God [is] greater than all gods; **6** and who retains strength to build a house for Him, since the heavens, even the heavens of the heavens, do not contain Him? And who [am] I that I build a house for Him, except to make incense before Him? **7** And now, send a wise man to me to work in gold, and in silver, and in bronze, and in iron, and in purple, and crimson, and blue, and knowing to engrave engravings with the wise men who [are] with me in Judah and in Jerusalem, whom my father David prepared; **8** and send to me cedar-trees, firs, and algums from Lebanon, for I have known that your servants know to cut down trees of Lebanon, and behold, my servants [are] with your servants, **9** even to prepare trees in abundance for me, for the house that I am building [is] great and wonderful. **10** And behold, I have given to your servants, to hewers, to those cutting the trees, twenty thousand cors of beaten wheat, and twenty thousand cors of barley, and twenty thousand baths of wine, and twenty thousand baths of oil." **11** And Huram king of Tyre answers in writing, and sends [it] to Solomon: "In the love of YHWH for His people, He has set you [as] king over them." **12** And Huram says, "Blessed [is] YHWH, God of Israel, who made the heavens and the earth, who has given a wise son to David the king, knowing wisdom and understanding, who builds a house for YHWH, and a house for his kingdom. **13** And now, I have sent a wise man having understanding, of [my] father Huram **14** (son of a woman of the daughters of Dan, and his father a man of Tyre), knowing to work in gold, and in silver, in bronze, in iron, in stones, and in wood, in purple, in blue, and in fine linen, and in crimson, and to engrave any engraving, and to devise any invention that is given to him, with your wise men, and the wise men of my lord, your father David. **15** And now, the wheat, and the barley, the oil, and the wine, as my lord said, let him send to his servants, **16** and we cut trees out of Lebanon, according to all your need, and bring them to you—floats by sea, to Joppa, and you take them up to Jerusalem." **17** And Solomon numbers all the men, the sojourners who [are] in the land of Israel, after the numbering with which his father David numbered them, and they are found [to be] one hundred and fifty thousand and three thousand and six hundred; **18** and he makes from them seventy thousand burden-bearers, and eighty thousand hewers in the mountain, and three thousand and six hundred overseers, to cause the people to work.

3 And Solomon begins to build the house of YHWH in Jerusalem, on the mount of Moriah where He appeared to his father David, in the place that David had prepared, in the threshing-floor of Ornan the Jebusite, **2** and he begins to build in the second [day], in the second month, in the fourth year of his reign. **3** And [in] these Solomon has been instructed to build the house of God: the length [in] cubits by the former measure [is] sixty cubits, and the breadth twenty cubits. **4** As for the porch that [is] on the front, the length [is] by the front of the breadth of the house—twenty cubits, and the height one hundred and twenty [[*or* twenty]], and he overlays it within with pure gold. **5** And he has covered the large house with fir-trees, and he covers it with fine gold, and causes palms and chains to ascend on it, **6** and he overlays the house with precious stone for beauty, and the gold [is] gold of Parvaim, **7** and he covers the house, the beams, the thresholds, and its walls, and its doors, with gold, and has engraved cherubim on the walls. **8** And he makes the most holy house: its length by the front of the breadth of the house—twenty cubits, and its breadth twenty cubits, and he covers it with six hundred talents of fine gold; **9** and the weight of the nails [is] fifty shekels of gold, and he has covered the upper chambers with gold. **10** And he makes two cherubim in the most holy house, image work, and he overlays them with gold; **11** as for the wings of the cherubim, their length [is] twenty cubits, the wing of the one [is] five cubits, touching the wall of the house, and the other wing [is] five cubits, touching the wing of the other cherub. **12** And the wing of the other cherub [is] five cubits touching the wall of the house, and the other wing [is] five cubits, adhering to the wing of the other cherub. **13** The wings of these cherubim are spreading forth twenty cubits, and they are standing on their feet and their faces [are] inward. **14** And he makes the veil of blue, and purple, and crimson, and fine linen, and causes cherubim to go up on it. **15** And he makes two pillars at the front of the house, thirty-five cubits in length, and the ornament that [is] on their heads [is] five cubits. **16** And he makes chains in the oracle, and puts [them] on the heads of the pillars, and makes one hundred pomegranates, and puts [them] on the chains. **17** And he raises up the pillars on the front of the temple, one on the right and one on the left, and calls the name of that on the right Jachin, and the name of that on the left Boaz.

4 And he makes an altar of bronze: twenty cubits its length, and twenty cubits its breadth, and ten cubits its height. **2** And he makes the molten sea; ten by the cubit, from its edge to its edge, round in encompassment, and its height [is] five by the cubit, and a line of thirty by the cubit surrounds it around. **3** And the likeness of oxen [is] under it, encompassing it all around, ten to the cubit, surrounding the sea around; two rows of oxen are cast in its being cast. **4** It is standing on twelve oxen, three facing the north, and three facing the west, and three facing the south, and three facing the east, and the sea [is] on them above, and all their back parts [are] within. **5** And its thickness [is] a handbreadth, and its lip as the work of the lip of a cup flowered with lilies; holding [within]—it contains three thousand baths. **6** And he makes ten lavers, and puts five on the right, and five on the left, to wash with them; they purge the work of the burnt-offering with them; and the sea [is] for priests to wash with. **7** And he makes the ten lampstands of gold, according to their ordinance, and places [them] in the temple, five on the right, and five on the left. **8** And he makes ten tables, and places [them] in the temple, five on the right, and five on the left; and he makes one hundred bowls of gold. **9** And he makes the court of the priests, and the great court, and doors for the court, and he has overlaid their doors with bronze. **10** And he has placed the sea on the right shoulder eastward, from toward the south. **11** And Huram makes the pots, and the shovels, and the bowls, and Huram finishes to make the work that he made for King Solomon in the house of God; **12** two pillars, and the bowls, and the crowns on the heads of the two pillars, and the two networks to cover the two bowls of the crowns that [are] on the heads of the pillars; **13** and the four hundred pomegranates for the two networks, two rows of pomegranates for the one network, to cover the two bowls of the crowns that [are] on the front of the pillars. **14** And he has made the bases; and he has made the lavers on the bases; **15** the one sea, and the twelve oxen under it, **16** and the pots, and the shovels, and the forks, and all their vessels, his father Huram has made for King Solomon, for the house of YHWH, of bronze purified. **17** The king has cast them in the circuit of the Jordan, in the thick soil of the ground, between Succoth and Zeredathah. **18** And Solomon makes all these vessels in great abundance, that the weight of the bronze has not been searched out. **19** And Solomon makes all the vessels that [are for] the house of God, and the altar of gold, and the tables, and on them [is] Bread of the Presentation; **20** and the lampstands, and their lamps, for their burning according to the ordinance, before the oracle, of gold refined; **21** and the flowers, and the lamps, and the tongs of gold—it [is] the perfection of gold; **22** and the snuffers, and the bowls, and the spoons, and the censers, of gold refined, and the opening of the house, its innermost doors to the Holy of Holies, and the doors of the house to the temple, of gold.

5 And all the work that Solomon made for the house of YHWH is finished, and Solomon brings in the sanctified things of his father David, and the silver, and the gold, and all the vessels he has put among the treasures of the house of God. **2** Then Solomon assembles the elderly of Israel, and all the heads of the tribes, princes of the fathers of the sons of Israel, to Jerusalem, to bring up the Ark of the Covenant of YHWH from the City of David—it [is] Zion. **3** And all the men of Israel are assembled to the king in the celebration—it [is] the seventh month; **4** and all [the] elderly of Israel come in, and the Levites lift up the Ark, **5** and they bring up the Ark, and the Tent of Meeting, and all the holy vessels that [are] in the tent; the priests, the Levites, have brought them up; **6** and King Solomon and all the congregation of Israel who are convened to him before the Ark are sacrificing sheep and oxen that are not counted nor numbered from multitude. **7** And the priests bring in the Ark of the Covenant of YHWH to its place, to the oracle of the house, to the Holy of Holies, to the place of the wings of the cherubim; **8** and the cherubim are spreading out wings over the place of the Ark, and the cherubim cover over the Ark, and over its poles, from above; **9** and they lengthen the poles, and the heads of the poles are seen out of the Ark on the front of the oracle, and they are not seen outside; and it is there to this day. **10** There is nothing in the Ark but the two tablets that Moses gave in Horeb, where YHWH covenanted with the sons of Israel, in their going out from Egypt. **11** And it comes to pass, in the going out of the priests from the holy place—for all the priests who are present have sanctified themselves, there is none to watch by divisions, **12** and the Levites, the singers, to all of them, to Asaph, to Heman, to

2 CHRONICLES

Jeduthun, and to their sons, and to their brothers, clothed in white linen, with cymbals, and with psalteries, and harps, are standing on the east of the altar, and with them one hundred and twenty priests blowing with trumpets— **13** indeed, it comes to pass, trumpeters and singers [are] as one, to sound [with] one voice—to praise and to give thanks to YHWH, and at the lifting up of the sound with trumpets, and with cymbals, and with instruments of song, and at giving praise to YHWH, [saying], "For [He is] good, for His kindness [is] for all time," that the house is filled with a cloud—the house of YHWH, **14** and the priests have not been able to stand to minister from the presence of the cloud, for the glory of YHWH has filled the house of God.

6 Then Solomon said, "YHWH said [He would] dwell in thick darkness, **2** and I have built a house of habitation for You, and a fixed place for Your dwelling for all ages." **3** And the king turns around his face, and blesses the whole assembly of Israel, and the whole assembly of Israel is standing, **4** and he says, "Blessed [is] YHWH, God of Israel, who has spoken with His mouth with my father David, and with His hands has fulfilled [it], saying, **5** From the day that I brought out My people from the land of Egypt, I have not fixed on a city out of any of the tribes of Israel to build a house for my name being there, and I have not fixed on a man to be leader over My people Israel; **6** and I fix on Jerusalem for My Name being there, and I fix on David to be over My people Israel. **7** And it is with the heart of my father David to build a house for the Name of YHWH God of Israel, **8** and YHWH says to my father David, Because that it has been with your heart to build a house for My Name, you have done well that it has been with your heart, **9** but you do not build the house, for your son who comes forth out from your loins, he builds the house for My Name. **10** And YHWH establishes His word that He spoke, and I rise up in the stead of my father David, and sit on the throne of Israel, as YHWH spoke, and I build the house for the Name of YHWH, God of Israel, **11** and I place the Ark there, where the covenant of YHWH [is] that He made with the sons of Israel." **12** And he stands before the altar of YHWH, in front of all the assembly of Israel, and spreads out his hand— **13** for Solomon has made a scaffold of bronze, and puts it in the midst of the court, five cubits its length, and five cubits its breadth, and three cubits its height, and he stands on it, and kneels on his knees in front of all the assembly of Israel, and spreads forth his hands toward the heavens— **14** and says, "O YHWH God of Israel, there is not like You a god in the heavens and in the earth, keeping the covenant and the kindness for Your servants who are walking before You with all their heart; **15** who has kept for Your servant, my father David, that which You spoke to him; indeed, You speak with Your mouth, and with Your hand have fulfilled [it], as at this day. **16** And now, O YHWH, God of Israel, keep for Your servant, my father David, that which You spoke to him, saying, A man of yours is never cut off from before My face, sitting on the throne of Israel—only, if your sons watch their way to walk in My law, as you have walked before Me. **17** And now, O YHWH, God of Israel, let Your word be steadfast that You have spoken to Your servant, to David. **18** For is it true [that] God dwells with man on the earth? Behold, the heavens, and the heavens of the heavens, do not contain You, how much less this house that I have built? **19** And You have turned to the prayer of Your servant, and to his supplication, O YHWH my God, to listen to the cry and to the prayer that Your servant is praying before You, **20** for Your eyes being open toward this house by day and by night, toward the place that You have said to put Your Name there, to listen to the prayer that Your servant prays toward this place. **21** And You have listened to the supplications of Your servant, and of Your people Israel, that they pray toward this place, and You hear from the place of Your dwelling, from the heavens, and have listened, and forgiven. **22** If a man sins against his neighbor, and he has lifted up an oath on him to cause him to swear, and the oath has come in before Your altar in this house— **23** then You hear from the heavens, and have done, and have judged Your servants, to give back to the wicked, to put his way on his head, and to declare righteous the righteous, to give to him according to his righteousness. **24** And if Your people Israel is struck before an enemy because they sin against You, and they have turned back and confessed Your

2 CHRONICLES

Name, and prayed and made supplication before You in this house— **25** then You hear from the heavens and have forgiven the sin of Your people Israel, and caused them to return to the ground that You have given to them, and to their fathers. **26** In the heavens being restrained and there is no rain because they sin against You, and they have prayed toward this place and confessed Your Name, [and] they turn back from their sin because You afflict them— **27** then You hear in the heavens, and have forgiven the sin of Your servants, and of Your people Israel, because You direct them to the good way in which they walk, and have given rain on Your land that You have given to Your people for an inheritance. **28** Famine, when it is in the land, [and] pestilence, when it is [in the land], blasting and mildew, locust and caterpillar, when they are [in the land], when its enemies have distressed it in the land—its gates, any plague and any sickness; **29** any prayer, any supplication that is for any man, and for all Your people Israel, when they each know his own plague, and his own pain, and he has spread out his hands toward this house— **30** then You hear from the heavens, the settled place of Your dwelling, and have forgiven, and have given to each according to all his ways (because You know his heart, for You alone have known the heart of the sons of men), **31** so that they fear You, to walk in Your ways, all the days that they are living on the face of the ground that You have given to our fathers. **32** And also, to the stranger who is not of Your people Israel, and he has come from a far-off land for the sake of Your great Name, and Your strong hand, and Your outstretched arm, and they have come in and prayed toward this house— **33** then You hear from the heavens, from the settled place of Your dwelling, and have done according to all that the stranger calls to You for, so that all the peoples of the earth know Your Name, so as to fear You, as Your people Israel, and to know that Your Name is called on this house that I have built. **34** When Your people go out to battle against its enemies in the way that You send them, and they have prayed to You [in] the way of this city that You have fixed on, and the house that I have built for Your Name— **35** then You have heard their prayer and their supplication from the heavens, and have maintained their cause. **36** When they sin against You—for there is not a man who does not sin—and You have been angry with them, and have given them before an enemy, and their captors have taken them captive to a land far off or near; **37** and they have turned [it] back to their heart in the land to where they have been taken captive, and have turned back and made supplication to You in the land of their captivity, saying, We have sinned, we have done perversely, and have done wickedly; **38** indeed, they have turned back to You with all their heart, and with all their soul, in the land of their captivity, to where they have taken them captive, and they have prayed [in] the way of their land that You have given to their fathers, and of the city that You have chosen, and of the house that I have built for Your Name— **39** then You have heard from the heavens, from the settled place of Your dwelling, their prayer and their supplications, and have maintained their cause, and forgiven Your people who have sinned against You. **40** Now my God, I implore You, let Your eyes be open and Your ears attentive to the prayer of this place. **41** And now, rise, O YHWH God, to Your rest, You and the Ark of Your strength; Your priests, O YHWH God, are clothed with salvation, and Your saints rejoice in the goodness. **42** O YHWH God, do not turn back the face of Your anointed, be mindful of the kind acts of Your servant David."

7 And at Solomon's finishing to pray, then the fire has come down from the heavens and consumes the burnt-offering and the sacrifices, and the glory of YHWH has filled the house, **2** and the priests have not been able to go into the house of YHWH, because the glory of YHWH has filled the house of YHWH. **3** And all the sons of Israel are looking on the descending of the fire, and the glory of YHWH on the house, and they bow—faces to the earth—on the pavement, and pay respect, and give thanks to YHWH, [saying], "For [He is] good, for His kindness [is] for all time!" **4** And the king and all the people are sacrificing a sacrifice before YHWH, **5** and King Solomon sacrifices the sacrifice: twenty-two thousand of the herd and one hundred and twenty thousand of the flock; and the king and all the people dedicate the house of God. **6** And the priests are standing over their charges, and the Levites with instruments of the song of YHWH that David the king made, to give thanks to YHWH, for His kindness [is] for all time, in David's praising by their hand—and the priests are blowing trumpets opposite them, and all of Israel is standing. **7** And Solomon sanctifies the middle of the court that [is] before the house of YHWH, for he has made the burnt-offerings and the fat of the peace-offerings there, for the altar of bronze that Solomon made has not been able to contain the burnt-offering, and the present, and the fat. **8** And Solomon makes the celebration at that time [for] seven days, and all Israel with him—a very great assembly—from the entering in of Hamath to the Brook of Egypt. **9** And they make a restraint on the eighth day, because they have made the dedication of the altar [for] seven days, and the celebration [for] seven days. **10** And on the twenty-third day of the seventh month he has sent the people to their tents, rejoicing, and glad in heart, for the goodness that YHWH has done to David, and to Solomon, and to His people Israel. **11** And Solomon finishes the house of YHWH, and the house of the king; and all that has come on the heart of Solomon to do in the house of YHWH, and in his own house, he has caused to prosper. **12** And YHWH appears to Solomon by night and says to him, "I have heard your prayer, and have fixed on this place for Myself for a house of sacrifice. **13** If I restrain the heavens and there is no rain, and if I lay charge on the locust to consume the land, and if I send pestilence among My people— **14** and My people on whom My Name is called are humbled, and pray, and seek My face, and turn back from their evil ways, then I hear from the heavens, and forgive their sin, and heal their land. **15** Now My eyes are open and My ears attentive to the prayer of this place; **16** and now, I have chosen and sanctified this house for My Name being there for all time; indeed, My eyes and My heart have been there [for] all the days. **17** And you, if you walk before Me as your father David walked, even to do according to all that I have commanded you, and keep My statutes and My judgments— **18** then I have established the throne of your kingdom, as I covenanted with your father David, saying, A man of yours is never cut off [from] ruling in Israel; **19** and if you turn back—you—and have forsaken My statutes and My commands that I have placed before you, and have gone and served other gods, and bowed yourselves to them—then I have plucked them from off My ground that I have given to them, **20** and this house that I have sanctified for My Name, I cast from before My face, and make it for a proverb and for a byword among all the peoples. **21** And this house that has been high is an astonishment to everyone passing by it, and he has said, Why has YHWH done thus to this land and to this house? **22** And they have said, Because that they have forsaken YHWH, God of their fathers, who brought them out from the land of Egypt, and lay hold on other gods, and bow themselves to them, and serve them, therefore He has brought all this calamity on them."

8 And it comes to pass at the end of twenty years that Solomon has built the house of YHWH and his own house. **2** As for the cities that Huram has given to Solomon, Solomon has built them, and he causes the sons of Israel to dwell there. **3** And Solomon goes to Hamath-Zobah, and lays hold on it; **4** and he builds Tadmor in the wilderness, and all the cities of store that he has built in Hamath. **5** And he builds Beth-Horon the upper, and Beth-Horon the lower—cities of defense, with walls, double gates, and bar— **6** and Ba'alath, and all the cities of store that Solomon had, and all the cities of the chariot, and the cities of the horsemen, and all the desire of Solomon that he desired to build in Jerusalem, and in Lebanon, and in all the land of his dominion. **7** All the people who are left of the Hittite, and the Amorite, and the Perizzite, and the Hivite, and the Jebusite, who are not of Israel— **8** of their sons who have been left after them in the land, whom the sons of Israel did not consume—Solomon lifts up a tribute to this day. **9** And Solomon has made none of the sons of Israel servants for his work, but they [are] men of war, and heads of his captains, and heads of his charioteers, and of his horsemen; **10** and these [are] heads of the officers whom King Solomon has, two hundred and fifty who are rulers among the people. **11** And Solomon has brought up the daughter of Pharaoh from the City of David to the house that he built for her, for he said, "My wife does not dwell in the

2 CHRONICLES

house of David king of Israel, for they are holy to whom the Ark of YHWH has come." **12** Then Solomon has caused burnt-offerings to ascend to YHWH on the altar of YHWH that he built before the porch, **13** even by the matter of a day in its day, to cause to ascend according to the command of Moses, on Sabbaths, and on new moons, and on appointed times, three times in a year—in the Celebration of Unleavened Things, and in the Celebration of Weeks, and in the Celebration of Shelters. **14** And he establishes, according to the ordinance of his father David, the divisions of the priests over their service, and of the Levites over their charges, to praise and to minister before the priests, according to the matter of a day in its day, and the gatekeepers in their divisions at every gate, for so [is] the command of David the man of God. **15** And they have not turned aside [from] the command of the king concerning the priests and the Levites, in reference to any matter, and to the treasures. **16** And all the work of Solomon is prepared until the day of the foundation of the house of YHWH, and until its completion; the house of YHWH is perfect. **17** Then Solomon has gone to Ezion-Geber, and to Elath, on the border of the sea, in the land of Edom; **18** and Huram sends to him, by the hand of his servants, ships and servants knowing the sea, and they go with servants of Solomon to Ophir, and take four hundred and fifty talents of gold from there, and bring it to King Solomon.

9 And the queen of Sheba has heard of the fame of Solomon, and comes to Jerusalem to try Solomon with acute sayings, with a very great company, and camels carrying spices and gold in abundance, and precious stone; and she comes to Solomon, and speaks with him all that has been with her heart, **2** and Solomon declares all her matters to her, and there has not been hid a thing from Solomon that he has not declared to her. **3** And the queen of Sheba sees the wisdom of Solomon, and the house that he has built, **4** and the food of his table, and the sitting of his servants, and the standing of his ministers, and their clothing, and his stewards, and their clothing, and his burnt-offering that he offered up in the house of YHWH, and there has not been anymore spirit in her. **5** And she says to the king, "The word [is] true that I heard in my land concerning your matters and concerning your wisdom, **6** and I have given no credence to their words until I have come and my eyes see, and behold, there has not been declared to me the half of the abundance of your wisdom—you have added to the report that I heard. **7** O the blessedness of your men, and the blessedness of your servants—these—who are standing before you continually, and hearing your wisdom. **8** Let your God YHWH be blessed who has delighted in you to put you on His throne for king for your God YHWH; in the love of your God to Israel, to establish it for all time, He has put you over them for king, to do judgment and righteousness." **9** And she gives to the king one hundred and twenty talents of gold, and spices in great abundance, and precious stone; and there has not been any such spice as the queen of Sheba has given to King Solomon. **10** And also, servants of Huram, and servants of Solomon, who brought in gold from Ophir, have brought in algum-trees and precious stone. **11** And the king makes the algum-trees [into] staircases for the house of YHWH, and for the house of the king, and harps and psalteries for singers; and there have been none seen like these before in the land of Judah. **12** And King Solomon has given to the queen of Sheba all her desire that she asked, apart from that which she had brought to the king, and she turns and goes to her land, she and her servants. **13** And the weight of the gold that is coming to Solomon in one year is six hundred and sixty-six talents of gold, **14** apart from [what] the tourists and the merchants are bringing in; and all the kings of Arabia, and the governors of the land, are bringing in gold and silver to Solomon. **15** And King Solomon makes two hundred bucklers of alloyed gold—he causes six hundred [shekels] of alloyed gold to go up on the one buckler; **16** and three hundred shields of alloyed gold—he causes three hundred [shekels] of gold to go up on the one shield, and the king puts them in the House of the Forest of Lebanon. **17** And the king makes a great throne of ivory, and overlays it with pure gold; **18** and six steps [are] to the throne, and a footstool of gold, [and] they are fastened to the throne; and [places for] hands [are] on this [side] and on that [side] on the place of the sitting, and two lions are standing near the hands, **19** and twelve lions are standing there on the six steps on this [side] and on that [side]: it has not been made so for any kingdom. **20** And all the drinking vessels of King Solomon [are] of gold, and all the vessels of the House of the Forest of Lebanon [are] of refined gold—silver is not reckoned in the days of Solomon for anything; **21** for ships of the king are going to Tarshish with servants of Huram: once in three years the ships of Tarshish come carrying gold, and silver, ivory, apes, and peacocks [[*or* monkeys]]. **22** And King Solomon becomes greater than any of the kings of the earth for riches and wisdom; **23** and all the kings of the earth are seeking the presence of Solomon to hear his wisdom that God has put in his heart, **24** and they are each bringing in his present, vessels of silver, and vessels of gold, and garments, harness, and spices, horses, and mules, a rate year by year. **25** And there are four thousand stalls for horses and chariots, and twelve thousand horsemen for Solomon, and he placed them in cities of the chariot, and with the king in Jerusalem. **26** And he is ruling over all the kings from the River even to the land of the Philistines, and to the border of Egypt. **27** And the king makes the silver in Jerusalem as stones, and he has made the cedars as sycamores that [are] in the low country, for abundance, **28** and they are bringing out horses from Egypt to Solomon, and from all the lands. **29** And the rest of the matters of Solomon, the first and the last, are they not written beside the matters of Nathan the prophet, and beside the prophecy of Ahijah the Shilonite, and with the visions of Iddo the seer concerning Jeroboam son of Nebat? **30** And Solomon reigns in Jerusalem over all Israel [for] forty years, **31** and Solomon lies with his fathers, and they bury him in the city of his father David, and his son Rehoboam reigns in his stead.

10 And Rehoboam goes to Shechem, for all of Israel has come [to] Shechem to cause him to reign. **2** And it comes to pass, at Jeroboam son of Nebat—who [is] in Egypt because he has fled from the face of Solomon the king—hearing, that Jeroboam turns back out of Egypt; **3** and they send and call for him, and Jeroboam comes in, and all of Israel, and they speak to Rehoboam, saying, **4** "Your father made our yoke sharp, and now, make light [some] of the sharp service of your father, and [some] of his heavy yoke that he put on us, and we serve you." **5** And he says to them, "Yet three days—then return to me"; and the people go. **6** And King Rehoboam consults with the aged men who have been standing before his father Solomon in his being alive, saying, "How are you counseling to answer this people?" **7** And they speak to him, saying, "If you become good to this people, and have been pleased with them, and spoken to them good words, then they have been servants to you [for] all the days." **8** And he forsakes the counsel of the aged men that they counseled him, and consults with the boys who have grown up with him, those standing before him, **9** and he says to them, "What are you counseling, and we answer this people that have spoken to me, saying, Make light [some] of the yoke that your father put on us?" **10** And the boys who have grown up with him speak with him, saying, "Thus you say to the people who have spoken to you, saying, Your father made our yoke heavy, and you, make light [some] of our yoke; thus you say to them, My little finger is thicker than the loins of my father; **11** and now, my father laid a heavy yoke on you, and I add to your yoke; my father disciplined you with whips, and I—with scorpions." **12** And Jeroboam comes in, and all the people, to Rehoboam on the third day, as the king spoke, saying, "Return to me on the third day." **13** And the king answers them sharply, and King Rehoboam forsakes the counsel of the aged men, **14** and speaks to them according to the counsel of the boys, saying, "My father made your yoke heavy, and I add to it; my father disciplined you with whips, and I—with scorpions." **15** And the king has not listened to the people, for the revolution has been from God, for the sake of YHWH's establishing His word that He spoke by the hand of Abijah the Shilonite to Jeroboam son of Nebat. **16** And all Israel have seen that the king has not listened to them, and the people send back [word to] the king, saying, "What portion do we have in David? Indeed, there is no inheritance in a son of Jesse; [go], each to your tents, O Israel! Now see your house, O David!" And all [in] Israel go to their tents. **17** As for the sons of Israel who are dwelling in the cities of Judah—Rehoboam reigns over them. **18** And King Rehoboam sends

Hadoram, who [is] over the tribute, and the sons of Israel cast stones at him, and he dies; and King Rehoboam has strengthened himself to go up into a chariot to flee to Jerusalem; **19** and Israel transgresses against the house of David to this day.

11 And Rehoboam comes to Jerusalem, and assembles the house of Judah and Benjamin—one hundred and eighty thousand chosen warriors—to fight with Israel, to bring back the kingdom to Rehoboam. **2** And a word of YHWH is to Shemaiah, a man of God, saying, **3** "Speak to Rehoboam son of Solomon king of Judah, and to all Israel in Judah and Benjamin, saying, **4** Thus said YHWH: You do not go up nor fight with your brothers! Let each return to his house, for this thing has been from Me"; and they hear the words of YHWH, and turn back from going against Jeroboam. **5** And Rehoboam dwells in Jerusalem, and builds cities for a bulwark in Judah, **6** indeed, he builds Beth-Lehem, and Etam, and Tekoa, **7** and Beth-Zur, and Shocho, and Adullam, **8** and Gath, and Mareshah, and Ziph, **9** and Adoraim, and Lachish, and Azekah, **10** and Zorah, and Aijalon, and Hebron, that [are] in Judah and in Benjamin, cities of bulwarks. **11** And he strengthens the bulwarks, and puts leaders in them, and treasures of food, and oil, and wine, **12** and in each and every city [he puts] bucklers and spears, and strengthens them very greatly; and he has Judah and Benjamin. **13** And the priests and the Levites that [are] in all Israel have stationed themselves by him, out of all their border, **14** for the Levites have left their outskirts and their possession, and they come to Judah and to Jerusalem, for Jeroboam and his sons have cast them off from acting as priests for YHWH, **15** and he establishes for himself priests for high places, and for goat [idols] and for calf [idols] that he made. **16** And after them, out of all the tribes of Israel, those giving their heart to seek YHWH, God of Israel, have come to Jerusalem to sacrifice to YHWH, God of their father. **17** And they strengthen the kingdom of Judah, and strengthen Rehoboam son of Solomon, for three years, because they walked in the way of David and Solomon for three years. **18** And Rehoboam takes a wife for himself, Mahalath, child of Jerimoth son of David, [and of] Abigail daughter of Eliab son of Jesse. **19** And she bears sons to him: Jeush, and Shamaria, and Zaham. **20** And after her he has taken Maachah daughter of Absalom, and she bears to him Abijah, and Attai, and Ziza, and Shelomith. **21** And Rehoboam loves Maachah daughter of Absalom above all his wives and his concubines—for he has taken eighteen wives and sixty concubines—and he begets twenty-eight sons and sixty daughters. **22** And Rehoboam appoints Abijah son of Maachah for head, for leader among his brothers, for to cause him to reign. **23** And he has understanding, and disperses from all his sons to all lands of Judah and Benjamin, to all cities of the bulwarks, and gives provision in abundance to them; and he asks for a multitude of wives [for them].

12 And it comes to pass, at the establishing of the kingdom of Rehoboam, and at his strengthening himself, he has forsaken the Law of YHWH, and all Israel with him. **2** And it comes to pass, in the fifth year of King Rehoboam, Shishak king of Egypt has come up against Jerusalem—because they trespassed against YHWH— **3** with one thousand and two hundred chariots, and with sixty thousand horsemen, and there is no number to the people who have come with him out of Egypt—Lubim, Sukkiim, and Cushim— **4** and he captures the cities of the bulwarks that [are] of Judah, and comes to Jerusalem. **5** And Shemaiah the prophet has come to Rehoboam and the heads of Judah who have been gathered to Jerusalem [to escape] from the presence of Shishak, and says to them, "Thus said YHWH: You have forsaken Me, and also, I have left you in the hand of Shishak"; **6** and the heads of Israel are humbled—and the king—and they say, "YHWH [is] righteous." **7** And when YHWH sees that they have been humbled, a word of YHWH has been [sent] to Shemaiah, saying, "They have been humbled; I do not destroy them, and I have given to them as a little thing for an escape, and I do not pour out My fury in Jerusalem by the hand of Shishak; **8** but they become servants to him, and they know My service, and the service of the kingdoms of the lands." **9** And Shishak king of Egypt comes up against Jerusalem, and takes the treasures of the house of

YHWH and the treasures of the house of the king—he has taken the whole—and he takes the shields of gold that Solomon had made; **10** and King Rehoboam makes shields of bronze in their stead, and has given [them] a charge on the hand of the heads of the runners who are keeping the opening of the house of the king; **11** and it comes to pass, from the time of the going in of the king to the house of YHWH, the runners have come in and lifted them up, and brought them back to the chamber of the runners. **12** And in his being humbled, the wrath of YHWH has turned back from him, so as not to destroy to completion; and also, there have been good things in Judah. **13** And King Rehoboam strengthens himself in Jerusalem and reigns; for Rehoboam [is] a son of forty-two years in his reigning, and he has reigned seventeen years in Jerusalem, the city that YHWH has chosen to put His Name there, out of all the tribes of Israel, and the name of his mother [is] Naamah the Ammonitess, **14** and he does evil, for he has not prepared his heart to seek YHWH. **15** And the matters of Rehoboam, the first and the last, are they not written among the matters of Shemaiah the prophet, and of Iddo the seer, concerning genealogy? And the wars of Rehoboam and Jeroboam [are for] all the days; **16** and Rehoboam lies with his fathers, and is buried in the City of David, and his son Abijah reigns in his stead.

13 In the eighteenth year of King Jeroboam, Abijah reigns over Judah; **2** he has reigned three years in Jerusalem (and the name of his mother [is] Michaiah daughter of Uriel, from Gibeah), and there has been war between Abijah and Jeroboam. **3** And Abijah directs the war with a force of mighty men of war, four hundred thousand chosen men, and Jeroboam has set in array [for] battle with him, with eight hundred thousand chosen men, mighty men of valor. **4** And Abijah rises up on the hill of Zemaraim that [is] in the hill-country of Ephraim, and says, "Hear me, Jeroboam and all Israel! **5** Is it not for you to know that YHWH, God of Israel, has given the kingdom over Israel to David for all time, to him and to his sons—a covenant of salt? **6** And Jeroboam, son of Nebat, servant of Solomon son of David, rises up and rebels against his lord! **7** And vain men are gathered to him, sons of worthlessness, and they strengthen themselves against Rehoboam son of Solomon, and Rehoboam was a youth, and tender of heart, and has not strengthened himself against them. **8** And now you are saying to strengthen yourselves before the kingdom of YHWH in the hand of the sons of David, and you [are] a numerous multitude, and calves of gold [are] with you that Jeroboam has made for you for gods. **9** Have you not cast out the priests of YHWH, the sons of Aaron, and the Levites, and make priests for yourselves like the peoples of the lands? Everyone who has come to fill his hand with a bullock, a son of the herd, and seven rams, even he has been a priest for [those which are] not gods! **10** As for us, YHWH [is] our God, and we have not forsaken Him, and priests are ministering to YHWH, sons of Aaron and the Levites, in the work, **11** and are making incense to YHWH, burnt-offerings morning by morning, and evening by evening, and incense of spices, and the arrangement of bread [is] on the pure table, and the lampstand of gold, and its lamps, to burn evening by evening, for we are keeping the charge of our God YHWH, and you have forsaken Him. **12** And behold, with us—at [our] head—[is] God, and His priests and trumpets of shouting to shout against you; O sons of Israel, do not fight with YHWH, God of your fathers, for you do not prosper." **13** And Jeroboam has brought around the ambush to come in from behind them, and they are before Judah, and the ambush [is] behind them. **14** And Judah turns, and behold, the battle [is] against them, before and behind, and they cry to YHWH, and the priests are blowing with trumpets, **15** and the men of Judah shout; and it comes to pass, at the shouting of the men of Judah, that God has struck Jeroboam and all Israel before Abijah and Judah. **16** And the sons of Israel flee from the face of Judah, and God gives them into their hand, **17** and Abijah and his people strike among them a great striking, and five hundred thousand chosen men of Israel fall wounded. **18** And the sons of Israel are humbled at that time, and the sons of Judah are strong, for they have leaned on YHWH, God of their fathers. **19** And Abijah pursues after Jeroboam and captures cities from him: Beth-El and its small towns, and Jeshanah and its small towns, and Ephraim

2 CHRONICLES

and its small towns. **20** And Jeroboam has not retained power anymore in the days of Abijah, and YHWH strikes him, and he dies. **21** And Abijah strengthens himself, and takes fourteen wives for himself, and begets twenty-two sons and sixteen daughters; **22** and the rest of the matters of Abijah, and his ways, and his words, are written in the commentary of the prophet Iddo.

14 And Abijah lies with his fathers, and they bury him in the City of David, and his son Asa reigns in his stead. In his days the land was quiet [for] ten years. **2** And Asa does that which is good and that which is right in the eyes of his God YHWH, **3** and turns aside the altars of the stranger, and the high places, and breaks the standing-pillars, and cuts down the Asherim, **4** and commands to Judah to seek YHWH, God of their fathers, and to do the Law and the command; **5** and he turns aside the high places and the images out of all cities of Judah, and the kingdom is quiet before him. **6** And he builds cities of bulwarks in Judah, for the land has quiet; and there is no war with him in these years, because YHWH has given rest to him. **7** And he says to Judah, "Let us build these cities, and surround [them] with wall, and towers, double gates, and bars, while the land [is] before us, because we have sought our God YHWH, we have sought, and He gives rest to us all around"; and they build and prosper. **8** And Asa has a force of three hundred thousand from Judah carrying buckler and spear, and two hundred and eighty thousand from Benjamin carrying shield and treading bow; all these [are] mighty men of valor. **9** And Zerah the Cushite comes out to them with a force of one million [men] and three hundred chariots, and he comes to Mareshah, **10** and Asa goes out before him, and they set in array [for] battle in the Valley of Zephathah at Mareshah. **11** And Asa calls to his God YHWH and says, "YHWH, it is nothing for You to help, between the mighty and those who have no power; help us, O YHWH, our God, for we have leaned on You, and in Your Name we have come against this multitude; O YHWH, You [are] our God; do not let mortal man prevail against You!" **12** And YHWH strikes the Cushim before Asa and before Judah, and the Cushim flee, **13** and Asa and the people who [are] with him pursue them even to Gerar, and there falls [many] from the Cushim, for they have no preserving, because they have been broken before YHWH and before His camp; and [those of Judah] carry away very much spoil, **14** and strike all the cities around Gerar, for a fear of YHWH has been on them, and they spoil all the cities, for abundant spoil has been in them; **15** and they have also struck tents of livestock, and they capture sheep in abundance, and camels, and return to Jerusalem.

15 And the Spirit of God has been on Azariah son of Oded, **2** and he goes out before Asa and says to him, "Hear me, Asa, and all Judah and Benjamin; YHWH [is] with you—in your being with Him, and if you seek Him, He is found by you, and if you forsake Him, He forsakes you; **3** and many days [are] to Israel without [the] true God, and without a teaching priest, and without law, **4** and it turns back in its distress to YHWH, God of Israel, and they seek Him, and He is found by them, **5** and in those times there is no peace for him who is going out, and for him who is coming in, for many troubles [are] on all the inhabitants of the lands, **6** and they have been beaten down, nation by nation, and city by city, for God has troubled them with every adversity; **7** and you, be strong, and do not let your hands be feeble, for there is a reward for your work." **8** And at Asa's hearing these words, and the prophecy of Oded the prophet, he has strengthened himself, and causes the abominations to pass away out of all the land of Judah and Benjamin, and out of the cities that he has captured from the hill-country of Ephraim, and renews the altar of YHWH that [is] before the porch of YHWH, **9** and gathers all Judah and Benjamin, and the sojourners with them out of Ephraim, and Manasseh, and out of Simeon—for they have defected to him from Israel in abundance, in their seeing that his God YHWH [is] with him. **10** And they are gathered to Jerusalem in the third month of the fifteenth year of the reign of Asa, **11** and sacrifice to YHWH on that day from the spoil they have brought in—seven hundred oxen and seven thousand sheep, **12** and they enter into a covenant to seek YHWH, God of their fathers, with all their heart and with all their soul, **13** and everyone who does not seek for YHWH, God of Israel, is put to death, from small to great, from man to woman. **14** And they swear to YHWH with a loud voice, and with shouting, and with trumpets, and with horns, **15** and all Judah rejoices concerning the oath, for they have sworn with all their heart, and they have sought Him with all their goodwill, and He is found by them, and YHWH gives rest to them all around. **16** And also Maachah, mother of Asa the king—he has removed her from [being] mistress, in that she has made for an Asherah a horrible thing, and Asa cuts down her horrible thing, and beats [it] small, and burns [it] by the Brook of Kidron: **17** yet the high places have not been removed from Israel; only, the heart of Asa has been perfect all his days. **18** And he brings in the sanctified things of his father, and his own sanctified things, to the house of God: silver, and gold, and vessels. **19** And war has not been until the thirty-fifth year of the reign of Asa.

16 In the thirty-sixth year of the reign of Asa, Baasha king of Israel has come up against Judah, and builds Ramah, so as not to permit any going out and coming in to Asa king of Judah. **2** And Asa brings out silver and gold from the treasures of the house of YHWH and of the house of the king, and sends [them] to Ben-Hadad king of Aram, who is dwelling in Damascus, saying, **3** "A covenant [is] between me and you, and between my father and your father, behold, I have sent silver and gold to you; go, break your covenant with Baasha king of Israel, and he goes up from off me." **4** And Ben-Hadad listens to King Asa, and sends the heads of the forces that he has to cities of Israel, and they strike Ijon, and Dan, and Abel-Maim, and all the stores, cities of Naphtali. **5** And it comes to pass, at Baasha's hearing, that he ceases from building Ramah, and lets his work rest; **6** and Asa the king has taken all Judah, and they carry away the stones of Ramah and its wood that Baasha has built [with], and he builds Geba and Mizpah with them. **7** And at that time Hanani the seer has come to Asa king of Judah and says to him, "Because of your leaning on the king of Aram, and you have not leaned on your God YHWH, therefore the force of the king of Aram has escaped from your hand. **8** Did the Cushim and the Lubim not become a very great force for multitude, for chariot, and for horsemen? And in your leaning on YHWH He gave them into your hand, **9** for YHWH—His eyes go to and fro in all the earth, to show Himself strong [for] a people whose heart [is] perfect toward Him; you have been foolish concerning this, because from now on there are wars with you." **10** And Asa is angry at the seer, and puts him [in] the house of stocks, for [he is] in a rage with him for this; and Asa oppresses [some] of the people at that time. **11** And behold, the matters of Asa, the first and the last, behold, they are written on the scroll of the kings of Judah and Israel. **12** And Asa is diseased—in the thirty-ninth year of his reign—in his feet, until his disease is excessive; and also in his disease he has not sought YHWH, but among physicians. **13** And Asa lies with his fathers, and dies in the forty-first year of his reign, **14** and they bury him in [one of] his graves that he had prepared for himself in the City of David, and they cause him to lie on a bed that [one] has filled [with] spices, and various kinds of mixtures, with perfumed work; and they burn a very great burning for him.

17 And his son Jehoshaphat reigns in his stead, and he strengthens himself against Israel, **2** and puts a force in all the fortified cities of Judah, and puts garrisons in the land of Judah, and in the cities of Ephraim that his father Asa had captured. **3** And YHWH is with Jehoshaphat, for he has walked in the first ways of his father David, and has not sought for the Ba'alim, **4** for he has sought for the God of his father, and he has walked in His commands, and not according to the work of Israel. **5** And YHWH establishes the kingdom in his hand, and all Judah gives a present to Jehoshaphat, and he has riches and honor in abundance, **6** and his heart is high in the ways of YHWH, and again he has turned aside the high places and the Asherim out of Judah. **7** And in the third year of his reign he has sent for his heads, for Ben-Hail, and for Obadiah, and for Zechariah, and for Nethaneel, and for Michaiah, to teach in cities of Judah; **8** and with them the Levites: Shemaiah, and Nethaniah, and Zebadiah, and Asahel, and Shemiramoth, and Jonathan, and Adonijah, and Tobijath, and Tob-Adonijah—the Levites; and with them Elishama and Jehoram, the priests. **9** And they teach in Judah, and the Scroll of the Law of YHWH [is] with them, and they go around into all cities of Judah, and teach among the people. **10** And there is a fear of YHWH on all kingdoms of the lands that [are] around Judah, and they have not fought with Jehoshaphat; **11** and [some] from the Philistines are bringing a present to Jehoshaphat, and silver [as] tribute; also, the Arabians are bringing to him a flock of seven thousand and seven hundred rams, and seven thousand and seven hundred male goats. **12** And Jehoshaphat is going on and becoming very great, and he builds palaces and cities of store in Judah, **13** and he has much work in cities of Judah; and men of war, mighty men of valor, [are] in Jerusalem. **14** And these [are] their numbers, for the house of their fathers—of Judah, heads of thousands: Adnah the head, and with him three hundred thousand mighty men of valor; **15** and at his hand [is] Jehohanan the head, and with him two hundred and eighty thousand; **16** and at his hand [is] Amasiah son of Zichri, who is willingly offering himself to YHWH, and with him two hundred thousand mighty men of valor. **17** And of Benjamin, mighty men of valor: Eliada, and with him two hundred thousand armed with bow and shield; **18** and at his hand [is] Jehozabad, and with him one hundred and eighty thousand armed ones of the host. **19** These [are] those serving the king, apart from those whom the king put in the fortress cities in all of Judah.

18 And Jehoshaphat has riches and honor in abundance, and joins affinity to Ahab, **2** and goes down at the end of [certain] years to Samaria to [visit] Ahab, and Ahab sacrifices sheep and oxen in abundance for him and for the people who [are] with him, and persuades him to go up to Ramoth-Gilead. **3** And Ahab king of Israel says to Jehoshaphat king of Judah, "Do you go with me [to] Ramoth-Gilead?" And he says to him, "As I—so you, and as your people—my people, and [we go] with you into the battle." **4** And Jehoshaphat says to the king of Israel, "Please seek the word of YHWH this day." **5** And the king of Israel gathers the prophets, four hundred men, and says to them, "Do we go to Ramoth-Gilead to battle, or do I refrain?" And they say, "Go up, and God gives [it] into the hand of the king." **6** And Jehoshaphat says, "[Is there] not still a prophet of YHWH here, and we seek from him?" **7** And the king of Israel says to Jehoshaphat, "[There is] still one man to seek YHWH from him, and I have hated him, for he is not prophesying of good concerning me, but of evil [for] all his days, he [is] Micaiah son of Imlah"; and Jehoshaphat says, "Do not let the king say so." **8** And the king of Israel calls to a certain officer and says, "Hurry Micaiah son of Imlah." **9** And the king of Israel and Jehoshaphat king of Judah are sitting, each on his throne, clothed with garments, and they are sitting in a threshing-floor at the opening of the Gate of Samaria, and all the prophets are prophesying before them. **10** And Zedekiah son of Chenaanah makes horns of iron for himself and says, "Thus said YHWH: **11** With these you push Aram until you have consumed them." And all the prophets are prophesying so, saying, "Go up [to] Ramath-Gilead and prosper, and YHWH has given [it] into the hand of the king." **12** And the messenger who has gone to call for Micaiah has spoken to him, saying, "Behold, the words of the prophets [as] one mouth [are] good toward the king, and please let your word be like one of theirs: and you have spoken good." **13** And Micaiah says "YHWH lives, surely that which my God says, I speak it." **14** And he comes to the king, and the king says to him, "Micaiah, do we go to Ramoth-Gilead to battle, or do I refrain?" And he says, "Go up, and prosper, and they are given into your hand." **15** And the king says to him, "How many times am I adjuring you that you speak to me only truth in the Name of YHWH?" **16** And he says, "I have seen all Israel scattered on the mountains, as sheep that have no shepherd, and YHWH says, There are no masters for these, they each return to his house in peace." **17** And the king of Israel says to Jehoshaphat, "Did I not say to you [that] he does not prophesy good concerning me, but rather of evil?" **18** And [Micaiah] says, "Therefore, hear a word of YHWH: I have seen YHWH sitting on His throne, and all the host of the heavens standing on His right and His left; **19** and YHWH says, Who entices Ahab king of Israel, and he goes up and falls in Ramoth-Gilead? And this speaker says thus, and that speaker thus. **20** And the spirit goes out, and stands before YHWH, and says, I entice him; and YHWH says to him, With what? **21** And he says, I go out, and have become a spirit of falsehood in the mouth of all his prophets. And He says, You entice, and also, you are able; go out and do so. **22** And now, behold, YHWH has put a spirit of falsehood in the mouth of these prophets of yours, and YHWH has spoken calamity concerning you." **23** And Zedekiah son of Chenaanah comes near and strikes Micaiah on the cheek, and says, "Where [is] this—the way the spirit [from] YHWH passed over from me to speak with you?" **24** And Micaiah says, "Behold, you see in that day that you enter into the innermost chamber to be hidden." **25** And the king of Israel says, "Take Micaiah, and turn him back to Amon head of the city, and to Joash son of the king, **26** and you have said, Thus said the king: Put this [one] in the house of restraint, and cause him to eat bread of oppression, and water of oppression, until my return in peace." **27** And Micaiah says, "If you certainly return in peace, YHWH has not spoken by me"; and he says, "Hear, O peoples, all of them!" **28** And the king of Israel goes up—and Jehoshaphat king of Judah—to Ramoth-Gilead; **29** and the king of Israel says to Jehoshaphat to disguise himself, and to go into battle, "And you, put on your garments." And the king of Israel disguises himself, and they go into battle. **30** And the king of Aram has commanded the heads of the charioteers whom he has, saying, "You do not fight with small or with great, except with the king of Israel by himself." **31** And it comes to pass at the heads of the charioteers seeing Jehoshaphat, that they have said, "He is the king of Israel," and they turn around against him to fight, and Jehoshaphat cries out, and YHWH has helped him, and God entices them from him; **32** indeed, it comes to pass, at the heads of the charioteers seeing that it has not been the king of Israel—they turn back from after him. **33** And a man has drawn with a bow in his simplicity, and strikes the king of Israel between the joinings and the coat of mail, and he says to the charioteer, "Turn your hand, and you have brought me out of the camp, for I have become [gravely] sick." **34** And the battle increases on that day, and the king of Israel has been propped up in the chariot in front of Aram until the evening, and he dies at the time of the going in of the sun.

19 And Jehoshaphat king of Judah turns back to his house in peace, to Jerusalem, **2** and Jehu son of Hanani the seer goes out to his presence and says to King Jehoshaphat, "Do you love to give help to the wicked and to those hating YHWH? And for this, wrath [is] against you from before YHWH, **3** but good things have been found with you, for you have put away the Asheroth out of the land, and have prepared your heart to seek God." **4** And Jehoshaphat dwells in Jerusalem, and he turns back and goes out among the people from Beer-Sheba to the hill-country of Ephraim, and brings them back to YHWH, God of their fathers. **5** And he establishes judges in the land, in all the fortified cities of Judah, for every city, **6** and says to the ones judging, "See what you are doing—for you do not judge for man, but for YHWH, who [is] with you in the matter of judgment; **7** and now, let fear of YHWH be on you, observe and do, for there is not perverseness with our God YHWH, and favoring by appearance, and taking of a bribe." **8** And also in Jerusalem, Jehoshaphat has appointed the Levites, and of the priests, and of the heads of the fathers of Israel, for the judgment of YHWH, and for strife; and they return to Jerusalem, **9** and he lays a charge on them, saying, "Thus do you do in the fear of YHWH, in faithfulness, and with a perfect heart, **10** and any strife that comes to you of your brothers who are dwelling in their cities, between blood and blood, between law and command, statutes, and judgments, then you have warned them and they do not become guilty before YHWH, and wrath has not been on you and on your brothers; thus do you do, and you are not guilty. **11** And behold, Amariah the head priest [is] over you for every matter of YHWH, and Zebadiah son of Ishmael, the leader of the house of Judah, [is] for every matter of the king, and the Levites [are] officers before you; be strong and do, and YHWH is with the good."

20 And it comes to pass after this, the sons of Moab have come in, and the sons of Ammon, and with them of the peoples, to battle against Jehoshaphat. **2** And [some] come in and declare [it] to Jehoshaphat, saying, "A great multitude has come against you from beyond the sea, from Aram, and behold, they [are] in Hazezon-Tamar—it [is] En-Gedi." **3** And Jehoshaphat fears, and sets his face to seek for YHWH, and proclaims a fast over all Judah; **4** and Judah is gathered to inquire of YHWH; also, from all the cities of Judah they have come to seek YHWH. **5** And Jehoshaphat stands in the assembly of Judah and Jerusalem, in the house of YHWH, at the front of the new court, **6** and says, "O YHWH, God of our fathers, are You not God in the heavens? Indeed, You are ruling over all kingdoms of the nations, and power and might [are] in Your hand, and there is none with You to station himself. **7** Are You not our God? You have dispossessed the inhabitants of this land from before Your people Israel, and give it to the seed of Your friend Abraham for all time, **8** and they dwell in it, and build a sanctuary in it for You, for Your Name, saying, **9** If evil comes on us—sword, judgment, and pestilence, and famine—we stand before this house, and before You, for Your Name [is] in this house, and cry to You out of our distress, and You hear and save. **10** And now, behold, sons of Ammon, and Moab, and Mount Seir, whom You did not grant to Israel to go in against in their coming out of the land of Egypt, for they turned aside from off them and did not destroy them, **11** and behold, they are repaying to us—to come to drive us out of Your possession that You have caused us to possess. **12** O our God, do You not execute judgment on them? For there is no power in us before this great multitude that has come against us, and we do not know what we do, but our eyes [are] on You." **13** And all Judah is standing before YHWH, also their infants, their wives, and their sons. **14** And the Spirit of YHWH has been on Jahaziel, son of Zechariah, son of Benaiah, son of Jeiel, son of Mattaniah, the Levite, of the sons of Asaph, in the midst of the assembly, **15** and he says, "Attend, all Judah, and you inhabitants of Jerusalem, and O King Jehoshaphat, Thus said YHWH to you: You do not fear, nor be afraid of the face of this great multitude, for the battle [is] not for you, but for God. **16** Tomorrow, go down against them, behold, they are coming up by the ascent of Ziz, and you have found them in the end of the valley, the front of the wilderness of Jeruel. **17** [It is] not for you to fight in this; station yourselves, stand, and see the salvation of YHWH with you, O Judah and Jerusalem—do not be afraid nor fear—tomorrow go out before them, and YHWH [is] with you." **18** And Jehoshaphat bows—face to the earth—and all Judah and the inhabitants of Jerusalem have fallen before YHWH, to bow themselves to YHWH. **19** And the Levites, of the sons of the Kohathites, and of the sons of the Korahites, rise to give praise to YHWH, God of Israel, with a loud voice on high. **20** And they rise early in the morning, and go out to the wilderness of Tekoa, and in their going out Jehoshaphat has stood and says, "Hear me, O Judah and inhabitants of Jerusalem, remain steadfast in your God YHWH, and be steadfast; remain steadfast in His prophets and prosper." **21** And he takes counsel with the people, and appoints singers for YHWH, and those giving praise for the honor of holiness, in the going out before the armed [men], and saying, "Give thanks to YHWH, for His kindness [is] for all time." **22** And at the time they have begun with singing and praise, YHWH has put ambushes against the sons of Ammon, Moab, and Mount Seir, who are coming in to Judah, and they are struck, **23** and the sons of Ammon stand up, and Moab, against the inhabitants of Mount Seir, to devote and to destroy, and at their finishing with the inhabitants of Seir, they helped, a man against his neighbor, to destroy. **24** And Judah has come to the watchtower in the wilderness, and they look toward the multitude, and behold, they [are] carcasses fallen to the earth, and none [had] an escape, **25** and Jehoshaphat comes in, and his people, to seize their spoil, and they find among them, in abundance, both goods and carcasses, and desirable vessels, and they take spoil for themselves without prohibition, and they are seizing the spoil [for] three days, for it [is] abundant. **26** And on the fourth day they have been assembled at the Valley of Blessing, for there they blessed YHWH: therefore they have called the name of that place, "Valley of Blessing," to this day. **27** And they return, every man of Judah and Jerusalem, and Jehoshaphat at their head, to go back to Jerusalem with joy, for YHWH has made them rejoice over their enemies. **28** And they come to Jerusalem with psalteries, and with harps, and with trumpets, to the house of YHWH. **29** And there is a fear of God on all kingdoms of the lands in their hearing that YHWH has fought with the enemies of Israel, **30** and the kingdom of Jehoshaphat is quiet, and his God gives rest to him all around.

2 CHRONICLES

31 And Jehoshaphat reigns over Judah, a son of thirty-five years in his reigning, and he has reigned twenty-five years in Jerusalem, and the name of his mother [is] Azubah daughter of Shilhi. **32** And he walks in the way of his father Asa, and has not turned aside from it, to do that which is right in the eyes of YHWH. **33** Only, the high places have not been removed, and still the people have not prepared their heart for the God of their fathers. **34** And the rest of the matters of Jehoshaphat, the first and the last, behold, they are written among the matters of Jehu son of Hanani, who has been mentioned on the scroll of the kings of Israel. **35** And after this Jehoshaphat king of Judah has joined himself with Ahaziah king of Israel (he did wickedly in doing [this]), **36** and he joins him with himself to make ships to go to Tarshish, and they make ships in Ezion-Geber, **37** and Eliezer son of Dodavah, of Mareshah, prophesies against Jehoshaphat, saying, "For your joining yourself with Ahaziah, YHWH has broken up your works"; and the ships are broken, and have not retained [power] to go to Tarshish.

21 And Jehoshaphat lies with his fathers, and is buried with his fathers in the City of David, and his son Jehoram reigns in his stead. **2** And he has brothers, sons of Jehoshaphat: Azariah, and Jehiel, and Zechariah, and Azariah, and Michael, and Shephatiah; all these [are] sons of Jehoshaphat king of Israel, **3** and their father gives to them many gifts of silver and of gold, and of precious things, with fortified cities in Judah, and he has given the kingdom to Jehoram, for he [is] the firstborn. **4** And Jehoram rises up over the kingdom of his father, and strengthens himself, and slays all his brothers with the sword, and also of the heads of Israel. **5** Jehoram [is] a son of thirty-two years in his reigning, and he has reigned eight years in Jerusalem, **6** and he walks in the way of the kings of Israel, as the house of Ahab did, for a daughter of Ahab has been to him for a wife, and he does evil in the eyes of YHWH, **7** and YHWH has not been willing to destroy the house of David, for the sake of the covenant that He made with David, and as He had said to give a lamp to him and to his sons [for] all the days. **8** In his days Edom has revolted from under the hand of Judah, and they cause a king to reign over them; **9** and Jehoram passes over with his heads, and all the chariots with him, and it comes to pass, he has risen by night and strikes the Edomites who are coming around against him, and the princes of the chariots, **10** and Edom revolts from under the hand of Judah to this day; then Libnah revolts at that time from under his hand, because he has forsaken YHWH, God of his fathers; **11** also, he has made high places on the mountains of Judah, and causes the inhabitants of Jerusalem to commit whoredom, and compels Judah. **12** And a writing from Elijah the prophet comes to him, saying, "Thus said YHWH, God of your father David: Because that you have not walked in the ways of your father Jehoshaphat, and in the ways of Asa king of Judah, **13** and you walk in the way of the kings of Israel, and cause Judah and the inhabitants of Jerusalem to commit whoredom like the whoredoms of the house of Ahab, and also your brothers, the house of your father, who are better than yourself, you have slain; **14** behold, YHWH is striking [with] a great striking among your people, and among your sons, and among your wives, and among all your goods— **15** and you, with many sicknesses, with disease of your bowels, until your bowels come out by the sickness, day by day." **16** And YHWH wakes up against Jehoram the spirit of the Philistines and of the Arabians, who [are] beside the Cushim, **17** and they come up into Judah, and break into it, and take captive all the substance that is found at the house of the king, and also his sons, and his wives, and there has not been left to him a son except Jehoahaz the youngest of his sons. **18** And after all this YHWH has plagued him in his bowels by a disease for which there is no healing, **19** and it comes to pass, from days to days, and at the time of the going out of the end of two years, his bowels have gone out with his sickness, and he dies of severe diseases, and his people have not made for him a burning like the burning of his fathers. **20** He was a son of thirty-two [years] in his reigning, and he has reigned eight years in Jerusalem, and he goes without desire, and they bury him in the City of David, and not in the graves of the kings.

22 And the inhabitants of Jerusalem cause his youngest son Ahaziah to reign in his stead (for the troop had slain all

2 CHRONICLES

the chiefly that came in with the Arabians to the camp), and Ahaziah son of Jehoram, king of Judah, reigns. **2** Ahaziah [is] a son of twenty-two years in his reigning, and he has reigned one year in Jerusalem, and the name of his mother [is] Athaliah daughter of Omri; **3** he has also walked in the ways of the house of Ahab, for his mother has been his counselor to do wickedly. **4** And he does evil in the eyes of YHWH, like the house of Ahab, for they have been his counselors, after the death of his father, for destruction to him. **5** Also, he has walked in their counsel, and goes with Jehoram son of Ahab, king of Israel, to battle against Hazael king of Aram in Ramoth-Gilead, and they of Ramah strike Joram; **6** and he turns back to be healed in Jezreel because of the wounds with which they had struck him in Ramah, in his fighting with Hazael king of Aram. And Azariah son of Jehoram, king of Judah, has gone down to see Jehoram son of Ahab in Jezreel, for he [is] sick; **7** and to come to Joram has been from God [for] the destruction of Ahaziah; and in his coming he has gone out with Jehoram to Jehu son of Nimshi, whom YHWH anointed to cut off the house of Ahab. **8** And it comes to pass, in Jehu's executing judgment with the house of Ahab, that he finds the heads of Judah and sons of the brothers of Ahaziah, ministers of Ahaziah, and slays them. **9** And he seeks Ahaziah, and they capture him (and he is hiding himself in Samaria), and bring him to Jehu, and put him to death, and bury him, for they said, "He [is] son of Jehoshaphat, who sought YHWH with all his heart"; and there is none of the house of Ahaziah to retain power for the kingdom. **10** And Athaliah mother of Ahaziah has seen that her son is dead, and she rises and destroys the whole seed of the kingdom of the house of Judah. **11** And Jehoshabeath daughter of the king takes Joash son of Ahaziah, and steals him from the midst of the sons of the king who are put to death, and puts him and his nurse into the inner part of the bedchambers, and Jehoshabeath daughter of King Jehoram, wife of Jehoiada the priest, because she has been sister of Ahaziah, hides him from the face of Athaliah, and she has not put him to death. **12** And he is with them in the house of God hiding himself [for] six years, and Athaliah is reigning over the land.

23 And in the seventh year Jehoiada has strengthened himself, and takes the heads of the hundreds, even Azariah son of Jeroham, and Ishmael son of Jehohanan, and Azariah son of Obed, and Maaseiah son of Adaiah, and Elishaphat son of Zichri, into the covenant with him. **2** And they go around in Judah, and gather the Levites out of all the cities of Judah, and heads of the fathers of Israel, and come to Jerusalem, **3** and all the assembly make a covenant in the house of God with the king, and he says to them, "Behold, the son of the king reigns, as YHWH spoke concerning the sons of David. **4** This [is] the thing that you do: the third of you, going in on the Sabbath, of the priests, and of the Levites, [are] for gatekeepers of the thresholds, **5** and the third [are] at the house of the king, and the third at the Foundation Gate, and all the people [are] in the courts of the house of YHWH. **6** And none enter the house of YHWH except the priests, and those ministering of the Levites (they go in for they [are] holy), and all the people keep the watch of YHWH; **7** and the Levites have surrounded the king all around, each with his weapon in his hand, and he who has gone into the house is put to death; and be with the king in his coming in and in his going out." **8** And the Levites and all Judah do according to all that Jehoiada the priest has commanded, and each takes his men going in on the Sabbath, with those going out on the Sabbath, for Jehoiada the priest has not let away the divisions. **9** And Jehoiada the priest gives to the heads of the hundreds the spears, and the shields, and the bucklers that [are] King David's, that [are] in the house of God; **10** and he stations the whole of the people, and each [with] his dart in his hand, from the right shoulder of the house to the left shoulder of the house, at the altar, and at the house, by the king, all around. **11** And they bring out the son of the king, and put the crown on him, and [give him] the Testimony, and cause him to reign; and Jehoiada and his sons anoint him, and say, "Let the king live!" **12** And Athaliah hears the voice of the people who are running, and who are praising the king, and she comes to the people [in] the house of YHWH, **13** and sees, and behold, the king is standing by his pillar in the entrance, and the heads, and the trumpets [are] by the king, and all the people of the land rejoicing and shouting with trumpets, and the singers with instruments of song, and the teachers, to praise, and Athaliah tears her garments and says, "Conspiracy! Conspiracy!" **14** And Jehoiada the priest brings out the heads of the hundreds, inspectors of the force, and says to them, "Take her out from within the rows, and he who has gone after her is put to death by the sword"; for the priest said, "Do not put her to death [in] the house of YHWH." **15** And they make sides for her, and she comes to the entrance of the Horse Gate at the house of the king, and they put her to death there. **16** And Jehoiada makes a covenant between him, and between all the people, and between the king, to be for a people to YHWH; **17** and all the people enter the house of Baʻal, and break it down, indeed, they have broken his altars and his images, and they have slain Mattan priest of Baʻal before the altars. **18** And Jehoiada puts the offices of the house of YHWH into the hand of the priests, the Levites, whom David had apportioned over the house of YHWH, to cause the burnt-offerings of YHWH to ascend, as written in the Law of Moses, with joy, and with singing, by the hands of David; **19** and he stations the gatekeepers over the gates of the house of YHWH, and the unclean in anything do not go in. **20** And he takes the heads of the hundreds, and the majestic ones, and the rulers among the people, and all the people of the land, and brings down the king from the house of YHWH, and they come in through the high gate to the house of the king, and cause the king to sit on the throne of the kingdom. **21** And all the people of the land rejoice, and the city has been quiet, and they have put Athaliah to death by the sword.

24 Joash [is] a son of seven years in his reigning, and he has reigned forty years in Jerusalem, and the name of his mother [is] Zibiah of Beer-Sheba. **2** And Joash does that which is right in the eyes of YHWH all the days of Jehoiada the priest. **3** And Jehoiada takes two wives for him, and he begets sons and daughters. **4** And it comes to pass after this, it has been with the heart of Joash to renew the house of YHWH, **5** and he gathers the priests and the Levites, and says to them, "Go out to the cities of Judah, and gather money from all Israel to strengthen the house of your God sufficiently year by year, and you, hurry to the matter"; and the Levites have not hurried. **6** And the king calls for Jehoiada the head and says to him, "Why have you not required of the Levites to bring in out of Judah and out of Jerusalem the tribute of Moses, servant of YHWH, and of the assembly of Israel, for the Tent of the Testimony? **7** For sons of Athaliah, the wicked one, have broken up the house of God, and also, they have prepared all the holy things of the house of YHWH for Baʻalim." **8** And the king commands, and they make one chest, and put it at the gate of the house of YHWH outside, **9** and give an intimation in Judah and in Jerusalem to bring to YHWH the tribute of Moses, servant of God, [laid] on Israel in the wilderness. **10** And all the heads, and all the people rejoice, and they bring in, and cast into the chest, to completion. **11** And it comes to pass, at the time one brings in the chest for the inspection of the king by the hand of the Levites, and at their seeing that the money [is] abundant, that a scribe of the king has come in, and an officer of the head-priest, and they empty the chest, and take it up and turn it back to its place; thus they have done day by day, and gather money in abundance. **12** And the king and Jehoiada give it to the doers of the work of the service of the house of YHWH, and they are hiring hewers and craftsmen to renew the house of YHWH, and also—to craftsmen in iron and bronze to strengthen the house of YHWH. **13** And those doing the business work, and there goes up lengthening to the work by their hand, and they establish the house of God by its proper measure, and strengthen it. **14** And at their completing [it], they have brought in the rest of the money before the king and Jehoiada, and they make [with] it vessels for the house of YHWH, vessels of serving, and of offering up, and spoons, even vessels of gold and silver; and they are causing burnt-offerings to ascend in the house of YHWH continually, all the days of Jehoiada. **15** And Jehoiada is aged and satisfied with days, and dies—a son of one hundred and thirty years in his death, **16** and they bury him in the City of David with the kings, for he has done good in Israel, and with God and his house. **17** And after the death of Jehoiada, heads of Judah have come in, and bow themselves to the king; then the king has listened to them, **18** and they forsake the house of YHWH, God of their fathers, and serve the Asherim and the idols, and there is wrath on Judah and Jerusalem for this guilt of theirs. **19** And He sends among them prophets, to bring them back to YHWH, and they testify against them, and they have not given ear; **20** and the Spirit of God has clothed Zechariah son of Jehoiada the priest, and he stands above the people, and says to them, "Thus said God: Why are you transgressing the commands of YHWH, and do not prosper? Because you have forsaken YHWH, He forsakes you." **21** And they conspire against him, and stone him [with] stone by the command of the king, in the court of the house of YHWH, **22** and Joash the king has not remembered the kindness that his father Jehoiada did with him, and slays his son, and in his death he said, "YHWH sees and requires." **23** And it comes to pass, at the turn of the year, the force of Aram has come up against him, and they come to Judah and Jerusalem, and destroy all the heads of the people from the people, and they have sent all their spoil to the king of Damascus, **24** for with few men the force of Aram has come in, and YHWH has given into their hand a mighty force for multitude, because they have forsaken YHWH, God of their fathers; and they have executed judgments with Joash. **25** And in their going from him—for they left him with many diseases—his servants themselves have conspired against him for the blood of the sons of Jehoiada the priest, and slay him on his bed, and he dies; and they bury him in the City of David, and have not buried him in the graves of the kings. **26** And these [are] those conspiring against him: Zabad son of Shimeath the Ammonitess, and Jehozabad son of Shimrith the Moabitess. **27** As for his sons, and the greatness of the burden on him, and the foundation of the house of God, behold, they are written on the commentary of the scroll of the Kings; and his son Amaziah reigns in his stead.

25 Amaziah [was] a son of twenty-five years [when] he has reigned, and he has reigned twenty-nine years in Jerusalem, and the name of his mother [is] Jehoaddan of Jerusalem, **2** and he does that which is right in the eyes of YHWH—only, not with a perfect heart. **3** And it comes to pass, when the kingdom has been strong on him, that he slays his servants, those striking his father the king, **4** and he has not put their sons to death, but [did] as is written in the Law, in the Scroll of Moses, whom YHWH commanded, saying, "Fathers do not die for sons, and sons do not die for fathers, but they each die for his own sin." **5** And Amaziah gathers Judah and appoints them according to the house of the fathers, for heads of the thousands and for heads of the hundreds, for all Judah and Benjamin; and he inspects them from a son of twenty years and upward, and finds them [to be] three hundred thousand chosen ones, going forth to the host, holding spear and buckler. **6** And he hires out of Israel one hundred thousand mighty men of valor, with one hundred talents of silver; **7** and a man of God has come to him, saying, "O king, the host of Israel does not go with you; for YHWH is not with Israel—all the sons of Ephraim; **8** but if you are going, do [it], be strong for battle, God causes you to stumble before an enemy, for there is power in God to help, and to cause to stumble." **9** And Amaziah says to the man of God, "But what to do about the hundred talents that I have given to the troop of Israel?" And the man of God says, "YHWH has more to give to you than this." **10** And Amaziah separates them, of the troop that has come to him from Ephraim, to go to their own place; and their anger burns mightily against Judah, and they return to their place in the heat of anger. **11** And Amaziah has strengthened himself, and leads his people, and goes to the Valley of Salt, and strikes ten thousand of the sons of Seir. **12** And the sons of Judah have taken captive ten thousand alive, and they bring them to the top of the rock, and cast them from the top of the rock, and all of them have been broken. **13** And the sons of the troop that Amaziah has sent back from going with him to battle—they rush against cities of Judah, from Samaria even to Beth-Horon, and strike three thousand of them, and seize much prey. **14** And it comes to pass after the coming in of Amaziah from striking the Edomites, that he brings in the gods of the sons of Seir, and establishes them for gods for himself, and bows himself before them, and he makes incense to them. **15** And the anger of YHWH burns against Amaziah, and He sends a prophet to him, and he says to him, "Why have you sought the gods of the people that have not delivered their people out of your hand?" **16** And it comes

2 CHRONICLES

to pass, in his speaking to him, that he says to him, "Have we appointed you for a counselor to the king? For you [must] cease; why do they strike you?" And the prophet ceases and says, "I have known that God has counseled to destroy you, because you have done this and have not listened to my counsel." **17** And Amaziah king of Judah takes counsel, and sends to Joash son of Jehoahaz, son of Jehu, king of Israel, saying, **18** "Come, we look one another in the face." And Joash king of Israel sends to Amaziah king of Judah, saying, "The thorn that [is] in Lebanon has sent to the cedar that [is] in Lebanon, saying, Give your daughter to my son for a wife; and a beast of the field that [is] in Lebanon passes by and treads down the thorn. **19** You have said, Behold, I have struck Edom; and your heart has lifted you up to boast; now, abide in your house, why do you stir yourself up in evil, that you have fallen, you and Judah with you?" **20** And Amaziah has not listened, for it [is] from God in order to give them into [their] hand, because they have sought the gods of Edom; **21** and Joash king of Israel goes up, and they look one another in the face, he and Amaziah king of Judah, in Beth-Shemesh, that [is] Judah's, **22** and Judah is struck before Israel, and they flee—each to his tents. **23** And Joash king of Israel has caught Amaziah king of Judah, son of Joash, son of Jehoahaz, in Beth-Shemesh, and brings him to Jerusalem, and breaks down in the wall of Jerusalem from the Gate of Ephraim to the Corner Gate—four hundred cubits, **24** and [takes] all the gold, and the silver, and all the vessels that are found in the house of God with Obed-Edom, and the treasures of the house of the king, and the sons of the pledges, and turns back to Samaria. **25** And Amaziah son of Joash, king of Judah, lives after the death of Joash son of Jehoahaz, king of Israel, fifteen years; **26** and the rest of the matters of Amaziah, the first and the last, behold, are they not written on the scrolls of the kings of Judah and Israel? **27** And from the time that Amaziah has turned aside from after YHWH—they make a conspiracy against him in Jerusalem, and he flees to Lachish, and they send after him to Lachish, and put him to death there, **28** and lift him up on the horses, and bury him with his fathers in the city of Judah.

26 And all the people of Judah take Uzziah (and he [is] a son of sixteen years), and cause him to reign instead of his father Amaziah. **2** He has built Eloth, and restores it to Judah after the king's lying with his fathers. **3** Uzziah [is] a son of sixteen years in his reigning, and he has reigned fifty-two years in Jerusalem, and the name of his mother [is] Jecholiah of Jerusalem. **4** And he does that which is right in the eyes of YHWH, according to all that his father Amaziah did, **5** and he is as one seeking God in the days of Zechariah who has understanding in visions of God: and in the days of his seeking YHWH, God has caused him to prosper. **6** And he goes forth and fights with the Philistines, and breaks down the wall of Gath, and the wall of Jabneh, and the wall of Ashdod, and builds cities [around] Ashdod, and among the Philistines. **7** And God helps him against the Philistines, and against the Arabians who are dwelling in Gur-Ba'al and the Mehunim. **8** And the Ammonites give a present to Uzziah, and his name goes to the entering in of Egypt, for he strengthened himself greatly. **9** And Uzziah builds towers in Jerusalem, by the Corner Gate, and by the Valley Gate, and by the angle, and strengthens them; **10** and he builds towers in the wilderness, and digs many wells, for he had much livestock, both in the low country and in the plain, farmers and vinedressers in the mountains, and in Carmel; for he was a lover of the ground. **11** And Uzziah has a force making war, going forth to the host, by troops, in the number of their reckoning by the hand of Jeiel the scribe and Masseiah the officer, by the hand of Hananiah [one] of the heads of the king. **12** The whole number of heads of the fathers of the mighty men of valor [is] two thousand and six hundred; **13** and by their hand [is] the force of the host—three hundred thousand and seven thousand and five hundred warriors, with mighty power to give help to the king against the enemy. **14** And Uzziah prepares for them, for all the host, shields, and spears, and helmets, and coats of mail, and bows, even to stones of the slings. **15** And he makes inventions in Jerusalem—a device of an inventor—to be on the towers, and on the corners, to shoot with arrows and with great stones, and his name goes out to a distance, for he has been wonderfully helped until he has been strong. **16** And at his being strong his heart has been high to destruction, and he trespasses against his God YHWH, and goes into the temple of YHWH to make incense on the altar of incense. **17** And Azariah the priest goes in after him, and with him eighty priests of YHWH, sons of valor, **18** and they stand up against Uzziah the king, and say to him, "[It is] not for you, O Uzziah, to make incense to YHWH, but for priests, sons of Aaron, who are sanctified to make incense; go forth from the sanctuary, for you have trespassed, indeed, for you [will] not [have] honor from YHWH God." **19** And Uzziah is angry, and in his hand [is] a censer to make incense, and in his being angry with the priests—the leprosy has risen in his forehead, before the priests, in the house of YHWH, from beside the altar of incense. **20** And Azariah the head priest looks toward him, and all the priests, and behold, he [is] leprous in his forehead, and they hurry him there, and also he himself has hurried to go out, for YHWH has plagued him. **21** And Uzziah the king is a leper to the day of his death, and inhabits a separate house—a leper, for he has been cut off from the house of YHWH, and his son Jotham [is] over the house of the king, judging the people of the land. **22** And the rest of the matters of Uzziah, the first and the last, Isaiah son of Amoz the prophet has written; **23** and Uzziah lies with his fathers, and they bury him with his fathers in the field of the burying-place that the kings have, for they said, "He [is] a leper"; and his son Jotham reigns in his stead.

27 Jotham [is] a son of twenty-five years in his reigning, and he has reigned sixteen years in Jerusalem, and the name of his mother [is] Jerushah daughter of Zadok. **2** And he does that which is right in the eyes of YHWH, according to all that his father Uzziah did; only, he has not come into the temple of YHWH; and again the people are doing corruptly. **3** He has built the Upper Gate of the house of YHWH, and in the wall of Ophel he has built abundantly; **4** and he has built cities in the hill-country of Judah, and he has built palaces and towers in the forests. **5** And he has fought with the king of the sons of Ammon, and prevails over them, and the sons of Ammon give to him in that year one hundred talents of silver, and ten thousand cors of wheat, and ten thousand of barley; the sons of Ammon have returned this to him both in the second year and in the third. **6** And Jotham strengthens himself, for he has prepared his ways before his God YHWH. **7** And the rest of the matters of Jotham, and all his battles, and his ways, behold, they are written on the scroll of the kings of Israel and Judah. **8** He was a son of twenty-five years in his reigning, and he has reigned sixteen years in Jerusalem; **9** and Jotham lies with his fathers, and they bury him in the City of David, and his son Ahaz reigns in his stead.

28 Ahaz [is] a son of twenty years in his reigning, and he has reigned sixteen years in Jerusalem, and he has not done that which is right in the eyes of YHWH, as his father David, **2** and walks in the ways of the kings of Israel, and has also made molten images for Ba'alim, **3** and has made incense himself in the Valley of the Son of Hinnom, and burns his sons with fire according to the abominations of the nations that YHWH dispossessed from the presence of the sons of Israel, **4** and sacrifices and makes incense in high places, and on the heights, and under every green tree. **5** And his God YHWH gives him into the hand of the king of Aram, and they strike him, and take captive a great captivity from him, and bring [them] to Damascus, and he has also been given into the hand of the king of Israel, and he strikes him [with] a great striking. **6** And Pekah son of Remaliah slays one hundred and twenty thousand in Judah in one day (the whole [are] sons of valor), because of their forsaking YHWH, God of their fathers. **7** And Zichri, a mighty one of Ephraim, slays Maaseiah son of the king, and Azrikam leader of the house, and Elkanah second to the king. **8** And the sons of Israel take captive of their brothers: two hundred thousand wives, sons, and daughters; and they have also seized much spoil from them, and they bring in the spoil to Samaria. **9** And there has been a prophet of YHWH there (Oded [is] his name), and he goes out before the host that has come to Samaria, and says to them, "Behold, in the fury of YHWH, God of your fathers, against Judah, He has given them into your hand, and you slay among them in rage—it has come to the heavens; **10** and now you are saying to subdue sons of Judah and Jerusalem for menservants and for maidservants for yourselves; but are there

2 CHRONICLES

not causes of guilt with you before your God YHWH? **11** And now, hear me, and send back the captives whom you have taken captive of your brothers, for the heat of the anger of YHWH [is] on you." **12** And certain of the heads of the sons of Ephraim (Azariah son of Johanan, Berechiah son of Meshillemoth, and Jehizkiah son of Shallum, and Amasa son of Hadlai), rise up against those coming in from the host, **13** and say to them, "You do not bring in the captives here, for guilt against YHWH [is already] on us, you are saying to add to our sin and to our guilt. For abundant [is] the guilt we have, and the fierceness of anger on Israel." **14** And the armed men leave the captives and the prey before the heads and all the assembly; **15** and the men who have been expressed by name rise and take hold on the captives, and they have clothed all their naked ones from the spoil, indeed, they clothe them, and shoe them, and cause them to eat and drink, and anoint them, and lead them on donkeys, even every feeble one, and bring them to Jericho, the city of palms, near their brothers, and return to Samaria. **16** At that time King Ahaz has sent to the king of Asshur to give help to him; **17** and again the Edomites have come, and strike in Judah, and take captive a captivity. **18** And the Philistines have rushed against the cities of the low country, and of the south of Judah, and capture Beth-Shemesh, and Aijalon, and Gederoth, and Shocho and its villages, and Timnah and its villages, and Gimzo and its villages, and dwell there, **19** for YHWH has humbled Judah because of Ahaz king of Israel, for he made free with Judah, even to commit a trespass against YHWH. **20** And Tilgath-Pilneser king of Asshur comes to him, and does distress him, and has not strengthened him, **21** though Ahaz has taken a portion [out] of the house of YHWH, and [out] of the house of the king, and of the princes, and gives to the king of Asshur, yet it is no help to him. **22** And in the time of his distress—he adds to trespass against YHWH (this King Ahaz), **23** and he sacrifices to the gods of Damascus [which were] those striking him, and says, "Because the gods of the kings of Aram are helping them, I sacrifice to them, and they help me," and they have been to him to cause him to stumble, and to all Israel. **24** And Ahaz gathers the vessels of the house of God, and cuts in pieces the vessels of the house of God, and shuts the doors of the house of YHWH, and makes altars for himself in every corner in Jerusalem. **25** And in each and every city of Judah he has made high places to make incense to other gods, and provokes YHWH, God of his fathers. **26** And the rest of his matters, and all his ways, the first and the last, behold, they are written on the scroll of the kings of Judah and Israel. **27** And Ahaz lies with his fathers, and they bury him in the city, in Jerusalem, but have not brought him to the graves of the kings of Israel, and his son Hezekiah reigns in his stead.

29 Hezekiah [was] a son of twenty-five years [when] he has reigned, and he has reigned twenty-nine years in Jerusalem, and the name of his mother [is] Abijah daughter of Zechariah; **2** and he does that which is right in the eyes of YHWH, according to all that his father David did. **3** He, in the first year of his reign, in the first month, has opened the doors of the house of YHWH, and strengthens them, **4** and brings in the priests and the Levites, and gathers them to the broad place to the east. **5** And he says to them, "Hear me, O Levites, now sanctify yourselves, and sanctify the house of YHWH, God of your fathers, and bring out the impurity from the holy place, **6** for our fathers have trespassed, and done that which is evil in the eyes of our God YHWH, and forsake him, and turn around their faces from the Dwelling Place of YHWH, and give the neck. **7** They have also shut the doors of the porch, and quench the lamps, and they have not made incense, and have not caused burnt-offering to ascend in the holy place to the God of Israel, **8** and the wrath of YHWH is on Judah and Jerusalem, and He gives them for a trembling, for an astonishment, and for a hissing, as you are seeing with your eyes. **9** And behold, our fathers have fallen by the sword, and our sons, and our daughters, and our wives [are] in captivity for this. **10** Now [it is] with my heart to make a covenant before YHWH, God of Israel, and the fierceness of His anger turns back from us. **11** My sons, do not be at rest now, for YHWH has fixed on you to stand before Him, to serve Him, and to be ministering and making incense to Him." **12** And the Levites rise—Mahath son of Amasai, and

Joel son of Azariah, of the sons of the Kohathite; and of the sons of Merari: Kish son of Abdi, and Azariah son of Jehalelel; and of the Gershonite: Joah son of Zimmah, and Eden son of Joah; **13** and of the sons of Elizaphan: Shimri and Jeiel; and of the sons of Asaph: Zechariah and Mattaniah; **14** and of the sons of Heman: Jehiel and Shimei; and of the sons of Jeduthun: Shemaiah and Uzziel— **15** and they gather their brothers, and sanctify themselves, and come in, according to the command of the king in the matters of YHWH, to cleanse the house of YHWH, **16** and the priests come into the inner part of the house of YHWH to cleanse [it], and bring out all the uncleanness that they have found in the temple of YHWH to the court of the house of YHWH, and the Levites receive [it], to take [it] out to the Brook of Kidron outside. **17** And they begin to sanctify on the first of the first month, and on the eighth day of the month they have come to the porch of YHWH, and they sanctify the house of YHWH in eight days, and on the sixteenth day of the first month they have finished. **18** And they come in to Hezekiah the king within, and say, "We have cleansed all the house of YHWH, and the altar of the burnt-offering, and all its vessels, and the table of the arrangement, and all its vessels, **19** and all the vessels that King Ahaz cast away in his reign—in his trespass—we have prepared and sanctified, and behold, they [are] before the altar of YHWH." **20** And Hezekiah the king rises early, and gathers the heads of the city, and goes up to the house of YHWH; **21** and they bring in seven bullocks, and seven rams, and seven lambs, and seven young male goats, for a sin-offering for the kingdom, and for the sanctuary, and for Judah; and he commands to sons of Aaron, the priests, to cause [them] to ascend on the altar of YHWH. **22** And they slaughter the oxen, and the priests receive the blood, and sprinkle on the altar; and they slaughter the rams, and sprinkle the blood on the altar; and they slaughter the lambs, and sprinkle the blood on the altar; **23** and they bring the male goats of the sin-offering near before the king and the assembly, and they lay their hands on them; **24** and the priests slaughter them, and make a sin-offering with their blood on the altar, to make atonement for all Israel, that "For all Israel," said the king, "[is] the burnt-offering and the sin-offering." **25** And he appoints the Levites in the house of YHWH with cymbals, with psalteries, and with harps, by the command of David, and of Gad, seer of the king, and of Nathan the prophet, for the command [is] by the hand of YHWH, by the hand of His prophets; **26** and the Levites stand with the instruments of David, and the priests with the trumpets. **27** And Hezekiah commands to cause the burnt-offering to ascend on the altar; and at the time the burnt-offering began, the song of YHWH began, and the trumpets, and with [the] hands of [the] instruments of David king of Israel. **28** And all the assembly are worshiping, and the singers singing, and the trumpeters blowing; the whole [is] until the completion of the burnt-offering. **29** And at the completion of the offering up, the king and all those found with him have bowed, and pay respect. **30** And Hezekiah the king commands—and the princes—to the Levites [to cause them] to give praise to YHWH in the words of David, and of Asaph the seer, and they praise—to joy, and they bow, and pay respect. **31** And Hezekiah answers and says, "Now you have filled your hand for YHWH, come near, and bring in sacrifices and thank-offerings to the house of YHWH"; and the assembly brings in sacrifices and thank-offerings, and every willing-hearted one—burnt-offerings. **32** And the number of the burnt-offerings that the assembly has brought in is seventy oxen, one hundred rams, [and] two hundred lambs; for all these [are] a burnt-offering to YHWH. **33** And the sanctified things [are] six hundred oxen and three thousand sheep. **34** Only, the priests have become few, and have not been able to strip the whole of the burnt-offerings, and their brothers the Levites strengthen them until the completion of the work, and until the priests sanctify themselves, for the Levites [are] more upright of heart to sanctify themselves than the priests. **35** And also, burnt-offerings [are] in abundance, with fat of the peace-offerings, and with oblations for the burnt-offering; and the service of the house of YHWH is established, **36** and Hezekiah and all the people rejoice because of God's giving preparation to the people, for the thing has been suddenly.

30 And Hezekiah sends to all Israel and Judah, and he has also written letters to Ephraim and Manasseh, [to cause them] to come to the house of YHWH in Jerusalem, to make a Passover to YHWH, God of Israel. **2** And the king takes counsel, and his heads, and all the assembly in Jerusalem, to make the Passover in the second month, **3** for they have not been able to make it at that time, for the priests have not sanctified themselves sufficiently, and the people have not been gathered to Jerusalem. **4** And the thing is right in the eyes of the king, and in the eyes of all the assembly, **5** and they establish the thing, to cause an intimation to pass over into all Israel, from Beer-Sheba even to Dan, to come to make a Passover to YHWH, God of Israel, in Jerusalem; for they had not done as it is written for a long time. **6** And the runners go with letters from the hand of the king and his heads into all Israel and Judah, even according to the command of the king, saying, "O sons of Israel, turn back to YHWH, God of Abraham, Isaac, and Israel, and He turns back to the escaped part that is left of you from the hand of the kings of Asshur; **7** and do not be like your fathers and like your brothers, who trespassed against YHWH, God of their fathers, and He gives them to desolation, as you see. **8** Now do not harden your neck like your fathers, give a hand to YHWH, and come into His sanctuary that He has sanctified for all time, and serve your God YHWH, and the fierceness of His anger turns back from you; **9** for in your turning back to YHWH, your brothers and your sons have mercies before their captors, even to return to this land, for your God YHWH [is] gracious and merciful, and He does not turn aside the face from you if you turn back to Him." **10** And the runners are passing over from city to city in the land of Ephraim and Manasseh, even to Zebulun, but they are laughing at them and mocking at them, **11** only, certain from Asher, and Manasseh, and from Zebulun, have been humbled, and come to Jerusalem. **12** Also, in Judah the hand of God has been to give one heart to them to do the command of the king and of the heads in the matter of YHWH; **13** and many people are gathered to Jerusalem to make the Celebration of Unleavened Things in the second month— a mighty assembly for multitude. **14** And they arise and turn aside the altars that [are] in Jerusalem, and they have turned aside all the incense altars, and cast [them] into the Brook of Kidron; **15** and they slaughter the Passover-offering on the fourteenth of the second month, and the priests and the Levites have been ashamed, and sanctify themselves, and bring in burnt-offerings to the house of YHWH. **16** And they stand on their station according to their ordinance, according to the Law of Moses the man of God; the priests are sprinkling the blood out of the hand of the Levites, **17** for many [are] in the assembly who have not sanctified themselves, and the Levites [are] over the slaughtering of the Passover-offerings for everyone not clean, to sanctify [him] to YHWH: **18** for a multitude of the people, many from Ephraim, and Manasseh, Issachar, and Zebulun, have not been cleansed, but have eaten the Passover otherwise than it is written; but Hezekiah prayed for them, saying, "YHWH, who [is] good, receives atonement for everyone **19** who has prepared his heart to seek God—YHWH, God of his fathers—yet not according to the cleansing of the holy place"; **20** and YHWH listens to Hezekiah and heals the people. **21** And the sons of Israel, those found in Jerusalem, make the Celebration of Unleavened Things [for] seven days with great joy; and the Levites and the priests are giving praise to YHWH day by day with instruments of praise before YHWH. **22** And Hezekiah speaks to the heart of all the Levites, those giving good understanding concerning YHWH, and they eat the appointed thing [for] seven days; sacrificing sacrifices of peace-offerings, and making confession to YHWH, God of their fathers. **23** And all the assembly take counsel to keep [it] another seven days, and they keep [it for] seven days [with] joy; **24** for Hezekiah king of Judah has presented one thousand bullocks and seven thousand sheep to the assembly; and the heads have presented one thousand bullocks and ten thousand sheep to the assembly; and priests sanctify themselves in abundance. **25** And all the assembly of Judah rejoices, and the priests, and the Levites, and all the assembly, those coming in from Israel, and the sojourners—those coming in from the land of Israel and those dwelling in Judah, **26** and there is great joy in Jerusalem; for from the days of Solomon son of David, king of Israel, there is not like this in Jerusalem, **27** and the priests, the Levites, rise and bless the people, and their

2 CHRONICLES

voice is heard, and their prayer comes into His holy habitation in the heavens.

31 And at the completion of all this, all [those of] Israel who are found present have gone out to the cities of Judah, and break the standing-pillars, and cut down the Asherim, and break down the high places and the altars, out of all Judah and Benjamin, and in Ephraim and Manasseh, even to completion, and all the sons of Israel return, each to his possession, to their cities. **2** And Hezekiah appoints the divisions of the priests and of the Levites, by their divisions, each according to his service, of the priests and of the Levites, for burnt-offering and for peace-offerings, to minister and to give thanks, and to give praise in the gates of the camps of YHWH. **3** And a portion of the king, from his substance, [is] for burnt-offerings, for burnt-offerings of the morning and of the evening, and the burnt-offerings of Sabbaths, and of new moons, and of appointed times, as it is written in the Law of YHWH. **4** And he commands to the people, to the inhabitants of Jerusalem, to give the portion of the priests and of the Levites, so that they are strengthened in the Law of YHWH; **5** and at the spreading forth of the thing, the sons of Israel have multiplied the first-fruit of grain, new wine, and oil, and honey, and of all the increase of the field, and they have brought in the tithe of the whole in abundance. **6** And the sons of Israel and Judah, those dwelling in cities of Judah, have also brought in a tithe of herd and flock, and a tithe of the holy things that are sanctified to their God YHWH, and they set [them in] heaps of heaps. **7** In the third month they have begun to lay the foundation of the heaps, and in the seventh month they have finished. **8** And Hezekiah and the heads come in and see the heaps, and bless YHWH and His people Israel, **9** and Hezekiah inquires at the priests and the Levites concerning the heaps, **10** and Azariah the head priest, of the house of Zadok, speaks to him and says, "From the beginning of the bringing of the raised-offering to the house of YHWH, [there is enough] to eat, and to be satisfied, and to leave abundantly, for YHWH has blessed His people, and that left [is] this store." **11** And Hezekiah commands to prepare chambers in the house of YHWH, and they prepare, **12** and they bring in the raised-offering, and the tithe, and the holy things faithfully; and over them is a leader, Conaniah the Levite, and his brother Shimei [is] second; **13** and Jehiel, and Azaziah, and Nahath, and Asahel, and Jerimoth, and Jozabad, and Eliel, and Ismachiah, and Mahath, and Benaiah, [are] inspectors under the hand of Conaniah and his brother Shimei, by the appointment of Hezekiah the king, and Azariah leader of the house of God. **14** And Kore son of Imnah the Levite, the gatekeeper at the east, [is] over the willing-offerings of God, to give the raised-offering of YHWH, and the most holy things. **15** And by his hand [are] Eden, and Miniamin, and Jeshua, and Shemaiah, Amariah, and Shechaniah, in cities of the priests, faithfully to give to their brothers in divisions, as the great so the small, **16** apart from their genealogy, to males from a son of three years and upward, to everyone who has gone into the house of YHWH, by the matter of a day in its day, for their service in their charges, according to their divisions; **17** and the genealogy of the priests by the house of their fathers, and of the Levites, from a son of twenty years and upward, in their charges, in their divisions; **18** and to the genealogy among all their infants, their wives, and their sons, and their daughters to all the congregation, for in their faithfulness they sanctify themselves in holiness. **19** And for sons of Aaron, the priests, in the fields of the outskirt of their cities, in each and every city, [are] men who have been defined by name, to give portions to every male among the priests, and to everyone who reckoned himself by genealogy among the Levites. **20** And Hezekiah does thus in all Judah, and does that which is good, and that which is right, and that which is true, before his God YHWH; **21** and in every work that he has begun for the service of the house of God, and for the Law, and for the command, to seek for his God with all his heart, he has worked and prospered.

32 After these things and this truth, Sennacherib king of Asshur has come, indeed, he comes to Judah, and encamps against the cities of the bulwarks, and says to break into them himself. **2** And Hezekiah sees that Sennacherib has come, and his face [is] to the battle against Jerusalem, **3** and he takes counsel with his heads and his mighty ones, to stop the waters of the fountains that [are] at the outside of the city—and they help him, **4** and many people are gathered, and they stop all the fountains and the brook that is rushing into the midst of the land, saying, "Why do the kings of Asshur come, and have found much water?" **5** And he strengthens himself, and builds the whole of the wall that is broken, and causes [it] to ascend to the towers, and at the outside of the wall [builds] another, and strengthens Millo [in] the City of David, and makes darts in abundance, and shields. **6** And he puts heads of war over the people, and gathers them to him, to the broad place of a gate of the city, and speaks to their heart, saying, **7** "Be strong and courageous, do not be afraid, nor be cast down from the face of the king of Asshur, and from the face of all the multitude that [is] with him, for with us [are] more than with him. **8** With him [is] an arm of flesh, but with us [is] our God YHWH to help us and to fight our battles"; and the people are supported by the words of Hezekiah king of Judah. **9** After this Sennacherib king of Asshur has sent his servants to Jerusalem—and he [is] by Lachish, and all his power with him—against Hezekiah king of Judah and against all Judah who [are] in Jerusalem, saying, **10** "Thus said Sennacherib king of Asshur: On what are you trusting and abiding in the bulwark in Jerusalem? **11** Is Hezekiah not persuading you to give you up to die by famine and by thirst, saying, Our God YHWH delivers us from the hand of the king of Asshur? **12** Has Hezekiah himself not turned aside His high places and His altars, and speaks to Judah and to Jerusalem, saying, You bow yourselves before one altar and you make incense on it? **13** Do you not know what I have done—I and my fathers—to all peoples of the lands? Were the gods of the nations of the lands at all able to deliver their land out of my hand? **14** Who among all the gods of these nations whom my fathers have devoted to destruction [is] he who has been able to deliver his people out of my hand, that your God is able to deliver you out of my hand? **15** And now, do not let Hezekiah lift you up, nor persuade you thus, nor give credence to him, for no god of any nation and kingdom is able to deliver his people from my hand and from the hand of my fathers: also, surely your God does not deliver you from my hand!" **16** And again his servants have spoken against YHWH God and against His servant Hezekiah, **17** and he has written letters to give reproach to YHWH, God of Israel, and to speak against Him, saying, "As the gods of the nations of the lands that have not delivered their people from my hand, so the God of Hezekiah does not deliver His people from my hand." **18** And they call with a great voice [in] Jewish against the people of Jerusalem who [are] on the wall, to frighten them and to trouble them, that they may capture the city, **19** and they speak against the God of Jerusalem as against the gods of the peoples of the land—work of the hands of man. **20** And Hezekiah the king prays, and Isaiah son of Amoz the prophet, concerning this, and they cry to the heavens, **21** and YHWH sends a messenger and cuts off every mighty man of valor—both leader and head—in the camp of the king of Asshur, and he turns back with shame of face to his land and enters the house of his god, and those coming out of his bowels have caused him to fall there by the sword. **22** And YHWH saves Hezekiah and the inhabitants of Jerusalem from the hand of Sennacherib king of Asshur and from the hand of all, and He leads them around; **23** and many are bringing in an offering to YHWH, to Jerusalem, and precious things to Hezekiah king of Judah, and he is lifted up before the eyes of all the nations after this. **24** In those days Hezekiah has been sick even to death, and he prays to YHWH, and He speaks to him and has appointed a wonder for him; **25** and Hezekiah has not returned according to the deed [done] to him, for his heart has been lofty, and there is wrath on him and on Judah and Jerusalem; **26** and Hezekiah is humbled for the loftiness of his heart, he and the inhabitants of Jerusalem, and the wrath of YHWH has not come on them in the days of Hezekiah. **27** And Hezekiah has very much riches and honor, and he has made treasures for himself of silver, and of gold, and of precious stone, and of spices, and of shields, and of all [kinds] of desirable vessels, **28** and storehouses for the increase of grain, and new wine, and oil, and stalls for all kinds of livestock, and herds for stalls; **29** and he has made cities for himself, and possessions of flocks and herds in abundance, for God has given very much substance to him. **30** And Hezekiah himself has stopped the upper source of the waters of Gihon, and directs them beneath to the west of the City of David, and Hezekiah prospers in all his work; **31** and so with the ambassadors of the heads of Babylon, those sending to him to inquire of the wonder that has been in the land, God has left him to try him, to know all in his heart. **32** And the rest of the matters of Hezekiah and his kind acts, behold, they are written in the vision of Isaiah son of Amoz the prophet, on the scroll of the kings of Judah and Israel. **33** And Hezekiah lies with his fathers, and they bury him in the highest of the graves of the sons of David, and all Judah and the inhabitants of Jerusalem have done honor to him at his death, and his son Manasseh reigns in his stead.

33 Manasseh is a son of twelve years in his reigning, and he has reigned fifty-five years in Jerusalem; **2** and he does evil in the eyes of YHWH, like the abominations of the nations that YHWH dispossessed from the presence of the sons of Israel, **3** and he turns and builds the high places that his father Hezekiah has broken down, and raises altars for Ba'alim, and makes Asherim, and bows himself to all the host of the heavens, and serves them. **4** And he has built altars in the house of YHWH of which YHWH had said, "My Name is in Jerusalem for all time." **5** And he builds altars for all the host of the heavens in the two courts of the house of YHWH. **6** And he has caused his sons to pass over through fire in the Valley of the Son of Hinnom, and observed clouds and used enchantments and witchcraft, and dealt with a familiar spirit, and a wizard; he has multiplied to do evil in the eyes of YHWH, to provoke him to anger. **7** And he places the carved image of the idol that he made in the house of God, of which God said to David, and to his son Solomon, "In this house, and in Jerusalem that I have chosen out of all the tribes of Israel, I put My Name for all time, **8** and I do not add to turn aside the foot of Israel from off the ground that I appointed to your fathers, only, if they watch to do all that I have commanded them—to all the Law, and the statutes, and the ordinances by the hand of Moses." **9** And Manasseh causes Judah and the inhabitants of Jerusalem to err, to do evil above the nations that YHWH destroyed from the presence of the sons of Israel. **10** And YHWH speaks to Manasseh and to his people, and they have not attended, **11** and YHWH brings in against them the heads of the host that the king of Asshur has, and they capture Manasseh among the thickets, and bind him with bronze chains, and cause him to go to Babylon. **12** And when he is in distress he has appeased the face of his God YHWH, and is exceedingly humbled before the God of his fathers, **13** and prays to Him, and He accepts his plea, and hears his supplication, and brings him back to Jerusalem, to his kingdom, and Manasseh knows that He, YHWH, [is] God. **14** And after this he has built an outer wall for the City of David, on the west of Gihon, in the valley, and at the entering in at the Fish Gate, and it has gone around to the tower, and he makes it exceedingly high, and he puts heads of the force in all the cities of the bulwarks in Judah. **15** And he turns aside the gods of the stranger, and the idol, out of the house of YHWH, and all the altars that he had built on the mountain of the house of YHWH and in Jerusalem, and casts [them] to the outside of the city. **16** And he builds the altar of YHWH, and sacrifices on it sacrifices of peace-offerings and thank-offering, and commands to Judah to serve YHWH, God of Israel; **17** but still the people are sacrificing in high places, only—to their God YHWH. **18** And the rest of the matters of Manasseh, and his prayer to his God, and the matters of the seers, those speaking to him in the Name of YHWH, God of Israel, behold, they are [on the scroll of] the matters of the kings of Israel; **19** and his prayer, and his plea, and all his sin, and his trespass, and the places in which he had built high places, and established the Asherim and the carved images before his being humbled, behold, they are written beside the matters of Hozai. **20** And Manasseh lies with his fathers, and they bury him in his own house, and his son Amon reigns in his stead. **21** Amon [is] a son of twenty-two years in his reigning, and he has reigned two years in Jerusalem, **22** and he does evil in the eyes of YHWH, as his father Manasseh did, and Amon has sacrificed to all the carved images that his father Manasseh had made, and serves them, **23** and has not been humbled before YHWH, like the humbling of his father

Manasseh, for Amon himself has multiplied guilt. **24** And his servants conspire against him and put him to death in his own house, **25** and the people of the land strike all those conspiring against King Amon, and the people of the land cause his son Josiah to reign in his stead.

34 Josiah [is] a son of eight years in his reigning, and he has reigned thirty-one years in Jerusalem, **2** and he does that which is right in the eyes of YHWH, and walks in the ways of his father David, and has not turned aside [to] the right or left. **3** And in the eighth year of his reign (and he [is] yet a youth), he has begun to seek for the God of his father David, and in the twelfth year he has begun to cleanse Judah and Jerusalem from the high places, and the Asherim, and the carved images, and the molten images. **4** And they break down the altars of the Ba'alim before him, and he has cut down the images that [are] on high above them, and the Asherim, and the carved images, and the molten images, he has broken and beaten small, and strews [them] on the surface of the graves of those sacrificing to them, **5** and he has burned the bones of the priests on their altars, and cleanses Judah and Jerusalem, **6** and in the cities of Manasseh, and Ephraim, and Simeon, even to Naphtali, with their tools, all around. **7** And he breaks down the altars and the Asherim, and he has beaten down the carved images very small, and he has cut down all the images in all the land of Israel, and turns back to Jerusalem. **8** And in the eighteenth year of his reign, to purify the land and the house, he has sent Shaphan son of Azaliah, and Maaseiah head of the city, and Joah son of Johaz the remembrancer, to strengthen the house of his God YHWH. **9** And they come to Hilkiah the high priest, and they give the money that is brought into the house of God, that the Levites, keeping the threshold, have gathered from the hand of Manasseh, and Ephraim, and from all the remnant of Israel, and from all Judah, and Benjamin, and the inhabitants of Jerusalem, **10** and they give [it] into the hand of the workmen, those appointed over the house of YHWH, and they give it [to] the workmen who are working in the house of YHWH, to repair and to strengthen the house; **11** and they give [it] to craftsmen and to builders to buy hewn stones, and wood for couplings and for beams [for] the houses that the kings of Judah had destroyed. **12** And the men are working faithfully in the business, and over them are appointed Jahath and Obadiah, the Levites, of the sons of Merari, and Zechariah and Meshullam, of the sons of the Kohathite, to overlook; and of the Levites, everyone understanding about instruments of song, **13** and over the burden-bearers, and overseers of everyone doing work for every service; and of the Levites [are] scribes, and officers, and gatekeepers. **14** And in their bringing out the money that is brought into the house of YHWH, Hilkiah the priest has found the Scroll of the Law of YHWH by the hand of Moses, **15** and Hilkiah answers and says to Shaphan the scribe, "I have found [the] Scroll of the Law in the house of YHWH"; and Hilkiah gives the scroll to Shaphan, **16** and Shaphan brings in the scroll to the king, and brings the king back word again, saying, "All that has been given into the hand of your servants they are doing, **17** and they pour out the money that is found in the house of YHWH, and give it into the hand of those appointed and into the hands of those doing the work." **18** And Shaphan the scribe declares [it] to the king, saying, "Hilkiah the priest has given a scroll to me"; and Shaphan reads in it before the king. **19** And it comes to pass, at the king's hearing the words of the Law, that he tears his garments, **20** and the king commands Hilkiah, and Ahikam son of Shaphan, and Abdon son of Micah, and Shaphan the scribe, and Asaiah, servant of the king, saying, **21** "Go, seek YHWH for me, and for him who is left in Israel and in Judah, concerning the words of the scroll that is found, for great [is] the fury of YHWH that is poured on us, because that our fathers did not keep the word of YHWH to do according to all that is written on this scroll." **22** And Hilkiah goes, and they of the king, to Huldah the prophetess, wife of Shallum son of Tikvath, son of Hasrah, keeper of the garments, and she is dwelling in Jerusalem in the Second [Quarter], and they speak to her thus. **23** And she says to them, "Thus said YHWH, God of Israel: Say to the man who has sent you to me, **24** Thus said YHWH: Behold, I am bringing in calamity on this place and on its inhabitants, all the execrations that are written on the scroll that they read before the king of Judah, **25** because that they have forsaken Me, and make incense to other gods, so as to provoke Me with all the works of their hands, and My fury is poured out on this place, and it is not quenched. **26** And to the king of Judah who is sending you to inquire of YHWH, thus you say to him, Thus said YHWH God of Israel, whose words you have heard: **27** Because your heart [is] tender, and you are humbled before God in your hearing His words concerning this place and concerning its inhabitants, and are humbled before Me, and tear your garments, and weep before Me, indeed, I have also heard [you]—a declaration of YHWH. **28** Behold, I am gathering you to your fathers, and you have been gathered to your graves in peace, and your eyes do not look on all the calamity that I am bringing on this place and on its inhabitants"; and they bring the king back word. **29** And the king sends and gathers all the elderly of Judah and Jerusalem, **30** and the king goes up to the house of YHWH, and [to] every man of Judah, and the inhabitants of Jerusalem, and the priests, and the Levites, even all the people, from great even to small, and he reads in their ears all the words of the scroll of the covenant that is found in the house of YHWH. **31** And the king stands on his station, and makes the covenant before YHWH to walk after YHWH, and to keep His commands, and His testimonies, and His statutes, with all his heart and with all his soul, to do the words of the covenant that are written on this scroll. **32** And he presents everyone who is found in Jerusalem and Benjamin, and the inhabitants of Jerusalem do according to the covenant of God, the God of their fathers. **33** And Josiah turns aside all the abominations out of all the lands that the sons of Israel have, and causes everyone who is found in Israel to serve, to serve their God YHWH; all his days they did not turn aside from after YHWH, God of their fathers.

35 And Josiah makes a Passover to YHWH in Jerusalem, and they slaughter the Passover-offering on the fourteenth of the first month, **2** and he stations the priests over their charges, and strengthens them for the service of the house of YHWH, **3** and says to the Levites who are teaching all Israel, who are sanctified to YHWH, "Put the holy Ark in the house that Solomon son of David, king of Israel, built; it is not a burden on the shoulder to you. Now serve your God YHWH and His people Israel, **4** and prepare, by the house of your fathers, according to your divisions, by the writing of David king of Israel, and by the writing of his son Solomon, **5** and stand in the holy place, by the divisions of the house of the fathers of your brothers, sons of the people, and the portion of the house of a father of the Levites, **6** and slaughter the Passover-offering and sanctify yourselves, and prepare for your brothers, to do according to the word of YHWH by the hand of Moses." **7** And Josiah lifts up to the sons of the people a flock of lambs and young goats, the whole for Passover-offerings, for everyone who is found, to the number of thirty thousand, and three thousand oxen: these [are] from the substance of the king. **8** And his heads, for a willing-offering to the people, to the priests and to the Levites, have lifted up; Hilkiah, and Zechariah, and Jehiel, leaders in the house of God, have given two thousand and six hundred to the priests for Passover-offerings, and three hundred oxen; **9** and Conaniah, and Shemaiah, and Nethaneel, his brothers, and Hashabiah, and Jeiel, and Jozabad, heads of the Levites, have lifted up five thousand to the Levites for Passover-offerings, and five hundred oxen. **10** And the service is prepared, and the priests stand on their station, and the Levites on their divisions, according to the command of the king, **11** and they slaughter the Passover-offering, and the priests sprinkle out of their hand, and the Levites are stripping [them]; **12** and they turn aside the burnt-offering to put them by the divisions of the house of the fathers of the sons of the people, to bring near to YHWH, as it is written in the scroll of Moses—and so for the oxen. **13** And they cook the Passover with fire according to the ordinance, and they have cooked the sanctified things in pots, and in kettles, and in pans—for all the sons of the people. **14** And afterward they have prepared for themselves and for the priests; for the priests, sons of Aaron, [are] occupied] in the offering up of the burnt-offering and of the fat until night; and the Levites have prepared for themselves and for the priests, sons of Aaron. **15** And the singers, sons of Asaph, [are] on their station according to the command of David, and Asaph, and Heman, and Jeduthun seer of the king, and the gatekeepers [are] at every gate; it is not for them to turn aside from off their service, for their brothers the Levites have prepared for them. **16** And all the service of YHWH is prepared on that day to keep the Passover and to cause burnt-offering to ascend on the altar of YHWH, according to the command of King Josiah. **17** And the sons of Israel who are found make the Passover at that time, and the Celebration of Unleavened Things, [for] seven days. **18** And there has not been made a Passover like it in Israel from the days of Samuel the prophet, and none of the kings of Israel made such a Passover as Josiah has made, and the priests, and the Levites, and all Judah and Israel who are found, and the inhabitants of Jerusalem. **19** In the eighteenth year of the reign of Josiah this Passover has been made. **20** After all this, when Josiah has prepared the house, Necho king of Egypt has come up to fight against Carchemish by the Euphrates, and Josiah goes forth to meet him; **21** and he sends messengers to him, saying, "And what do I [have to do] with you, O king of Judah? I do not come against you today, but to the house with which I have war, and God commanded to hurry me; cease for yourself from God who [is] with me, and He does not destroy you." **22** And Josiah has not turned around his face from him, but has disguised himself to fight against him, and has not listened to the words of Necho, from the mouth of God, and comes to fight in the Valley of Megiddo; **23** and the archers shoot at King Josiah, and the king says to his servants, "Remove me, for I have become very sick." **24** And his servants remove him from the chariot, and cause him to ride on the second chariot that he has, and cause him to go to Jerusalem, and he dies, and is buried in the graves of his fathers, and all Judah and Jerusalem are mourning for Josiah, **25** and Jeremiah laments for Josiah, and all the male and female singers speak in their lamentations of Josiah to this day, and set them for a statute on Israel, and behold, they are written beside the Lamentations. **26** And the rest of the matters of Josiah and his kind acts, according as it is written in the Law of YHWH, **27** even his matters, the first and the last, behold, they are written on the scroll of the kings of Israel and Judah.

36 And the people of the land take Jehoahaz son of Josiah and cause him to reign instead of his father in Jerusalem. **2** Jehoahaz [is] a son of twenty-three years in his reigning, and he has reigned three months in Jerusalem, **3** and the king of Egypt turns him aside in Jerusalem, and fines the land one hundred talents of silver, and a talent of gold; **4** and the king of Egypt causes his brother Eliakim to reign over Judah and Jerusalem, and turns his name to Jehoiakim; and Necho has taken his brother Jehoahaz and brings him to Egypt. **5** Jehoiakim [is] a son of twenty-five years in his reigning, and he has reigned eleven years in Jerusalem, and he does evil in the eyes of his God YHWH; **6** Nebuchadnezzar king of Babylon has come up against him, and binds him in bronze chains to take him away to Babylon. **7** And Nebuchadnezzar has brought from the vessels of the house of YHWH to Babylon, and puts them in his temple in Babylon. **8** And the rest of the matters of Jehoiakim, and his abominations that he has done, and that which is found against him, behold, they are written on the scroll of the kings of Israel and Judah, and his son Jehoiachin reigns in his stead. **9** Jehoiachin [is] a son of eight years in his reigning, and he has reigned three months and ten days in Jerusalem, and he does evil in the eyes of YHWH; **10** and at the turn of the year King Nebuchadnezzar has sent and brings him to Babylon with the desirable vessels of the house of YHWH, and causes his brother Zedekiah to reign over Judah and Jerusalem. **11** Zedekiah [is] a son of twenty-one years in his reigning, and he has reigned eleven years in Jerusalem; **12** and he does evil in the eyes of his God YHWH, he has not been humbled before Jeremiah the prophet [speaking] from the mouth of YHWH; **13** and he has also rebelled against King Nebuchadnezzar who had caused him to swear by God, and he hardens his neck and strengthens his heart against turning back to YHWH, God of Israel. **14** Also, all the heads of the priests and the people have multiplied to commit a trespass according to all the abominations of the nations, and they defile the house of YHWH that He has sanctified in Jerusalem. **15** And YHWH,

God of their fathers, sends to them by the hand of His messengers—rising early and sending—for He has had pity on His people and on His habitation, **16** but they are mocking at the messengers of God, and despising His words, and acting deceitfully with His prophets, until the going up of the fury of YHWH against His people—until there is no healing. **17** And He causes the king of the Chaldeans to go up against them, and he slays their chosen ones by the sword in the house of their sanctuary, and has had no pity on young man and virgin, old man and very aged—He has given the whole into his hand. **18** And all the vessels of the house of God, the great and the small, and the treasures of the house of YHWH, and the treasures of the king and of his princes—he has brought the whole to Babylon. **19** And they burn the house of God, and break down the wall of Jerusalem, and they have burned all its palaces with fire, and all its desirable vessels—to destruction. **20** And he removes those left of the sword to Babylon, and they are to him and to his sons for servants, until the reigning of the kingdom of Persia, **21** to fulfill the word of YHWH in the mouth of Jeremiah, until the land has enjoyed its Sabbaths; all the days of the desolation it kept Sabbath—to the fullness of seventy years. **22** And in the first year of Cyrus king of Persia, at the completion of the word of YHWH in the mouth of Jeremiah, YHWH has awoken the spirit of Cyrus king of Persia, and he causes an intimation to pass over into all his kingdom, and also in writing, saying, **23** "Thus said Cyrus king of Persia: YHWH, God of the heavens, has given all kingdoms of the earth to me, and He has laid a charge on me to build a house for Him in Jerusalem which [is] in Judah; who is among you of all His people? His God YHWH [is] with him, and he goes up!"

EZRA

1 And in the first year of Cyrus king of Persia, at the completion of the word of YHWH from the mouth of Jeremiah, has YHWH awoken the spirit of Cyrus king of Persia, and he causes an intimation to pass over into all his kingdom, and also in writing, saying, 2 "Thus said Cyrus king of Persia: YHWH, God of the heavens, has given all kingdoms of the earth to me, and He has laid a charge on me to build a house for Him in Jerusalem, that [is] in Judah; 3 who [is] among you of all His people? His God is with him, and he goes up to Jerusalem, that [is] in Judah, and builds the house of YHWH, God of Israel (He [alone is] God), that [is] in Jerusalem. 4 And everyone who is left, of any of the places where he [is] a sojourner, the men of his place assist him with silver, and with gold, and with goods, and with beasts, along with a free-will offering for the house of God, that [is] in Jerusalem." 5 And heads of the fathers of Judah and Benjamin rise, and the priests and the Levites, even everyone whose spirit God has awoken, to go up to build the house of YHWH, that [is] in Jerusalem; 6 and all those around them have strengthened [them] with their hands, with vessels of silver, with gold, with goods, and with beasts, and with precious things, apart from all that has been offered willingly. 7 And King Cyrus has brought out the vessels of the house of YHWH that Nebuchadnezzar has brought out of Jerusalem, and puts them in the house of his gods; 8 indeed, Cyrus king of Persia brings them out by the hand of Mithredath the treasurer, and numbers them to Sheshbazzar the prince of Judah. 9 And this [is] their number: dishes of gold thirty, dishes of silver one thousand, knives twenty-nine, 10 basins of gold thirty, basins of silver (seconds) four hundred and ten, other vessels one thousand. 11 All the vessels of gold and of silver [are] five thousand and four hundred; the whole has Sheshbazzar brought up with the going up of the expulsion from Babylon to Jerusalem.

2 And these [are] sons of the province who are going up—of the captives of the expulsion that Nebuchadnezzar king of Babylon removed to Babylon, and they return to Jerusalem and Judah, each to his city— 2 who have come in with Zerubbabel, Jeshua, Nehemiah, Seraiah, Reelaiah, Mordecai, Bilshan, Mispar, Bigvai, Rehum, Baanah. The number of the men of the people of Israel: 3 sons of Parosh, two thousand one hundred seventy-two; 4 sons of Shephatiah, three hundred seventy-two; 5 sons of Arah, seven hundred seventy-five; 6 sons of Pahath-Moab, of the sons of Jeshua [and] Joab, two thousand eight hundred and twelve; 7 sons of Elam, one thousand two hundred fifty-four; 8 sons of Zattu, nine hundred and forty-five; 9 sons of Zaccai, seven hundred and sixty; 10 sons of Bani, six hundred forty-two; 11 sons of Bebai, six hundred twenty-three; 12 sons of Azgad, one thousand two hundred twenty-two; 13 sons of Adonikam, six hundred sixty-six; 14 sons of Bigvai, two thousand fifty-six; 15 sons of Adin, four hundred fifty-four; 16 sons of Ater of Hezekiah, ninety-eight; 17 sons of Bezai, three hundred twenty-three; 18 sons of Jorah, one hundred and twelve; 19 sons of Hashum, two hundred twenty-three; 20 sons of Gibbar, ninety-five; 21 sons of Beth-Lehem, one hundred twenty-three; 22 men of Netophah, fifty-six; 23 men of Anathoth, one hundred twenty-eight; 24 sons of Azmaveth, forty-two; 25 sons of Kirjath-Arim, Chephirah, and Beeroth, seven hundred and forty-three; 26 sons of Ramah and Gaba, six hundred twenty-one; 27 men of Michmas, one hundred twenty-two; 28 men of Beth-El and Ai, two hundred twenty-three; 29 sons of Nebo, fifty-two; 30 sons of Magbish, one hundred fifty-six; 31 sons of another Elam, one thousand two hundred fifty-four; 32 sons of Harim, three hundred and twenty; 33 sons of Lod, Hadid, and Ono, seven hundred twenty-five; 34 sons of Jericho, three hundred forty-five; 35 sons of Senaah, three thousand and six hundred and thirty. 36 The priests: sons of Jedaiah, of the house of Jeshua, nine hundred seventy-three; 37 sons of Immer, one thousand fifty-two; 38 sons of Pashhur, one thousand two hundred forty-seven; 39 sons of Harim, one thousand and

seventeen. **40** The Levites: sons of Jeshua and Kadmiel, of the sons of Hodaviah, seventy-four. **41** The singers: sons of Asaph, one hundred twenty-eight. **42** Sons of the gatekeepers: sons of Shallum, sons of Ater, sons of Talmon, sons of Akkub, sons of Hatita, sons of Shobai, the whole [are] one hundred thirty-nine. **43** The Nethinim: sons of Ziha, sons of Hasupha, sons of Tabbaoth, **44** sons of Keros, sons of Siaha, sons of Padon, **45** sons of Lebanah, sons of Hagabah, sons of Akkub, **46** sons of Hagab, sons of Shalmai, sons of Hanan, **47** sons of Giddel, sons of Gahar, sons of Reaiah, **48** sons of Rezin, sons of Nekoda, sons of Gazzam, **49** sons of Uzza, sons of Paseah, sons of Besai, **50** sons of Asnah, sons of Mehunim, sons of Nephusim, **51** sons of Bakbuk, sons of Hakupha, sons of Harhur, **52** sons of Bazluth, sons of Mehida, sons of Harsha, **53** sons of Barkos, sons of Sisera, sons of Thamah, **54** sons of Neziah, sons of Hatipha. **55** Sons of the servants of Solomon: sons of Sotai, sons of Sophereth, sons of Peruda, **56** sons of Jaalah, sons of Darkon, sons of Giddel, **57** sons of Shephatiah, sons of Hattil, sons of Pochereth of Zebaim, sons of Ami. **58** All the Nethinim, and the sons of the servants of Solomon [are] three hundred ninety-two. **59** And these [are] those going up from Tel-Melah, Tel-Harsa, Cherub, Addan, Immer, and they have not been able to declare the house of their fathers, and their seed, whether they [are] of Israel: **60** sons of Delaiah, sons of Tobiah, sons of Nekoda, six hundred fifty-two. **61** And of the sons of the priests: sons of Habaiah, sons of Koz, sons of Barzillai (who took a wife from the daughters of Barzillai the Gileadite, and is called by their name); **62** these have sought their register among those reckoning themselves by genealogy, and they have not been found, and they are redeemed from the priesthood, **63** and the Tirshatha says to them that they do not eat of the most holy things until the standing up of a priest with [the] Lights and with [the] Perfections. **64** All the assembly together [is] forty-two thousand three hundred sixty, **65** apart from their servants and their handmaids; these [are] seven thousand three hundred thirty-seven: and of them [are] two hundred male and female singers. **66** Their horses [are] seven hundred thirty-six, their mules, two hundred forty-five, **67** their camels, four hundred thirty-five, donkeys, six thousand seven hundred and twenty. **68** And some of the heads of the fathers in their coming to the house of YHWH that [is] in Jerusalem, have offered willingly for the house of God, to establish it on its base; **69** according to their power they have given to the treasure of the work; of gold, sixty-one thousand drams, and of silver, five thousand pounds, and of priests' coats, one hundred. **70** And the priests dwell, and the Levites, and of the people, and the singers, and the gatekeepers, and the Nethinim, in their cities; even all Israel in their cities.

3 And the seventh month comes, and the sons of Israel [are] in the cities, and the people are gathered, as one man, to Jerusalem. **2** And Jeshua son of Jozadak rises, and his brothers the priests, and Zerubbabel son of Shealtiel, and his brothers, and they build the altar of the God of Israel, to cause to ascend on it burnt-offerings, as it is written in the Law of Moses, the man of God. **3** And they establish the altar on its bases, because of the fear on them of the peoples of the lands, and he causes burnt-offerings to ascend on it to YHWH, burnt-offerings for the morning and for the evening. **4** And they make the Celebration of the Shelters as it is written, and the burnt-offering of the day daily in number according to the ordinance, the matter of a day in its day; **5** and after this a continual burnt-offering, and for new moons, and for all appointed times of YHWH that are sanctified; and for everyone who is willingly offering a willing-offering to YHWH. **6** From the first day of the seventh month they have begun to cause burnt-offerings to ascend to YHWH, and the temple of YHWH has not been founded, **7** and they give money to hewers and to craftsmen, and food, and drink, and oil to Zidonians and to Tyrians, to bring in cedar-trees from Lebanon to the Sea of Joppa, according to the permission of Cyrus king of Persia concerning them. **8** And in the second year of their coming to the house of God, to Jerusalem, in the second month, began Zerubbabel son of Shealtiel, and Jeshua son of Jozadak, and the remnant of their brothers the priests and the Levites, and all those coming from the captivity to Jerusalem, and they appoint the Levites from a son of twenty years and

EZRA

upward, to overlook the work of the house of YHWH. **9** And Jeshua stands, [and] his sons, and his brothers, Kadmiel and his sons, sons of Judah together, to overlook those doing the work in the house of God; the sons of Henadad, [and] their sons and their brothers the Levites. **10** And those building have founded the temple of YHWH, and they appoint the priests, clothed, with trumpets, and the Levites, sons of Asaph, with cymbals, to praise YHWH, by means of [the instruments of] David king of Israel. **11** And they respond in praising and in giving thanks to YHWH, "For [He is] good, for His kindness [is] for all time over Israel!" And all the people have shouted [with] a great shout in giving praise to YHWH, because the house of YHWH has been founded. **12** And many of the priests, and the Levites, and the heads of the fathers, the aged men who had seen the first house—in this house being founded before their eyes—are weeping with a loud voice, and many with a shout, in joy, lifting up the voice; **13** and the people are not discerning the noise of the shout of joy from the noise of the weeping of the people, for the people are shouting [with] a great shout, and the noise has been heard to a distance.

4 And adversaries of Judah and Benjamin hear that the sons of the captivity are building a temple to YHWH, God of Israel, **2** and they draw near to Zerubbabel, and to heads of the fathers, and say to them, "Let us build with you; for, like you, we seek to your God, and we are not sacrificing since the days of Esar-Haddon king of Asshur, who brought us up here." **3** And Zerubbabel says to them, also Jeshua, and the rest of the heads of the fathers of Israel, "Not for you, and for us, to build a house to our God; but we ourselves together build to YHWH God of Israel, as King Cyrus, king of Persia, commanded us." **4** And it comes to pass, the people of the land are making the hands of the people of Judah feeble, and troubling them in building, **5** and are hiring against them counselors to make void their counsel all the days of Cyrus king of Persia, even until the reign of Darius king of Persia. **6** And in the reign of Ahasuerus, in the commencement of his reign, they have written an accusation against the inhabitants of Judah and Jerusalem; **7** and in the days of Artaxerxes have Bishlam, Mithredath, Tabeel, and the rest of his companions written to Artaxerxes king of Persia, and the writing of the letter is written in Aramaic, and interpreted in Aramaic. **8** Rehum counselor, and Shimshai scribe have written a letter concerning Jerusalem to Artaxerxes the king, thus: **9** Then Rehum counselor, and Shimshai scribe, and the rest of their companions, Dinaites, and Apharsathchites, Tarpelites, Apharsites, Archevites, Babylonians, Susanchites (who are Elamites), **10** and the rest of the nations that the great and honorable Asnapper removed and set in the city of Samaria, and the rest beyond the river, and at such a time: **11** This [is] a copy of a letter that they have sent to him, to Artaxerxes the king: "Your servants, men beyond the river, and at such a time; **12** be it known to the king, that the Jews who have come up from you to us, have come to Jerusalem, the rebellious and base city they are building, and the walls they have finished, and the foundations they join. **13** Now let it be known to the king, that if this city is built and the walls finished, that they do not give toll, tribute, and custom; and at length it causes loss [to] the kings. **14** Now because that the salt of the palace [is] our salt, and we have no patience to see the nakedness of the king, therefore we have sent and made known to the king; **15** so that he seeks in the scroll of the records of your fathers, and you find in the scroll of the records, and know, that this city [is] a rebellious city, and causing loss [to] kings and provinces, and makers of sedition [are] in its midst from the days of old, therefore this city has been ruined. **16** We are making known to the king that, if this city be built and the walls finished, by this means you have no portion beyond the river." **17** The king has sent an answer to Rehum counselor, and Shimshai scribe, and the rest of their companions who are dwelling in Samaria, and the rest beyond the river, "Peace, and at such a time: **18** The letter that you sent to us, explained, has been read before me, **19** and by me a decree has been made, and they sought, and have found that this city is lifting up itself against kings from the days of old, and rebellion and sedition is made in it, **20** and mighty kings have been over Jerusalem, even rulers over all beyond the river, and toll, tribute, and custom is given to them. **21** Now make a

EZRA

decree to cause these men to cease, and this city is not built, until a decree is made by me. **22** And beware of negligence in doing this; why does the hurt become great to the loss of the kings?" **23** Then from the time that a copy of the letter of King Artaxerxes is read before Rehum, and Shimshai the scribe, and their companions, they have gone in haste to Jerusalem, to the Jews, and caused them to cease by force and strength; **24** then ceased the service of the house of God that [is] in Jerusalem, and it ceased until the second year of the reign of Darius king of Persia.

5 And the prophets have prophesied (Haggai the prophet, and Zechariah son of Iddo) to the Jews who [are] in Judah and in Jerusalem, in the Name of the God of Israel—to them. **2** Then Zerubbabel son of Shealtiel, and Jeshua son of Jozadak, have risen, and begun to build the house of God, that [is] in Jerusalem, and with them are the prophets of God supporting them. **3** At that time have come to them Tatnai, governor beyond the river, and Shethar-Boznai, and their companions, and thus they are saying to them, "Who has made for you a decree to build this house, and to finish this wall?" **4** Then we have said thus to them, "What [are] the names of the men who are building this building?" **5** And the eye of their God has been on [the] elders of [the] Jews, and they have not caused them to cease until [the] matter goes to Darius, and then they send back a letter concerning this thing. **6** The copy of a letter that Tatnai, governor beyond the river, has sent, and Shethar-Boznai and his companions, the Apharsachites who [are] beyond the river, to Darius the king. **7** A letter they have sent to him, and thus is it written in it: **8** "To Darius the king, all peace! Be it known to the king that we have gone to the province of Judah, to the great house of God, and it is built [with] rolled stones, and wood is placed in the walls, and this work is done speedily, and prospering in their hand. **9** Then we have asked of these elders, thus we have said to them, Who has made for you a decree to build this house, and to finish this wall? **10** And also their names we have asked of them, to let you know, that we might write the names of the men who [are] at their head. **11** And thus they have returned us word, saying, We [are] servants of the God of the heavens and earth, and are building the house that was built many years before this, that a great king of Israel built and finished: **12** but after that our fathers made the God of the heavens angry, he gave them into the hand of Nebuchadnezzar king of Babylon the Chaldean, and this house he destroyed, and the people he removed to Babylon; **13** but in the first year of Cyrus king of Babylon, Cyrus the king made a decree to build this house of God, **14** and also, the vessels of the house of God, of gold and silver, that Nebuchadnezzar had taken forth out of the temple that [is] in Jerusalem, and brought them to the temple of Babylon, them has Cyrus the king brought forth out of the temple of Babylon, and they have been given to [one], Sheshbazzar [is] his name, whom he made governor, **15** and said to him, Lift up these vessels, go, put them down in the temple that [is] in Jerusalem, and the house of God is built on its place. **16** Then this Sheshbazzar has come—he has laid the foundations of the house of God that [is] in Jerusalem, and from there even until now it has been building, and is not finished. **17** And now, if it is good to the king, let a search be made in the treasure-house of the king, that [is] there in Babylon, whether it be that there was a decree made by Cyrus the king to build this house of God in Jerusalem, and the will of the king concerning this thing he sends to us."

6 Then Darius the king made a decree, and they sought in the house of the scrolls of the treasuries placed there in Babylon, **2** and there has been found at Achmetha, in a palace that [is] in the province of Media, a scroll, and a record thus written within it [is]: **3** "In the first year of Cyrus the king, Cyrus the king has made a decree concerning the house of God in Jerusalem: let the house be built in the place where they are sacrificing sacrifices, and its foundations strongly laid; its height sixty cubits, its breadth sixty cubits; **4** three rows of rolled stones, and a row of new wood, and let the outlay be given out of the king's house. **5** And also, the vessels of the house of God, of gold and silver, that Nebuchadnezzar took forth out of the temple that [is] in Jerusalem, and brought to Babylon, let be given back, and go to the temple that [is] in Jerusalem, [each] to its place, and put [them] down in the house of God. **6** Now Tatnai, governor beyond the

EZRA

river, Shethar-Boznai, and their companions, the Apharsachites, who [are] beyond the river, be far from here; **7** let alone the work of this house of God, let the governor of the Jews, and [the] elders of the Jews, build this house of God on its place. **8** And a decree is made by me concerning that which you do with [the] elders of these Jews to build this house of God, that of [the] riches of [the] king, that [are] of [the] tribute beyond [the] river, let the outlay be given speedily to these men, that they do not cease; **9** and what they are needing—both young bullocks, and rams, and lambs for burnt-offerings to the God of the heavens, wheat, salt, wine, and oil according to the saying of the priests who [are] in Jerusalem—let be given to them day by day without fail, **10** that they are bringing sweet savors near to the God of the heavens, and praying for the life of the king, and of his sons. **11** And a decree is made by me, that anyone who changes this thing, let wood be pulled down from his house, and being raised up, let him be struck on it, and let his house be made a dunghill for this. **12** And God, who caused His Name to dwell there, casts down any king and people that puts forth his hand to change, to destroy this house of God that [is] in Jerusalem; I Darius have made a decree; let it be done speedily." **13** Then Tatnai, governor beyond the river, Shethar-Boznai, and their companions, according to that which Darius the king has sent, so they have done speedily; **14** and [the] elders of [the] Jews are building and prospering through [the] prophecy of Haggai [the] prophet, and Zechariah son of Iddo, and they have built and finished by [the] decree of [the] God of Israel, and by [the] decree of Cyrus, and Darius, and Artaxerxes king of Persia. **15** And this house has gone out until the third day of the month Adar, that is [in] the sixth year of the reign of Darius the king. **16** And the sons of Israel have made, [and] the priests, and the Levites, and the rest of the sons of the captivity, a dedication of this house of God with joy, **17** and have brought near for the dedication of this house of God: one hundred bullocks, two hundred rams, four hundred lambs; and twelve young male goats for a sin-offering for all Israel according to the number of the tribes of Israel; **18** and they have established the priests in their divisions, and the Levites in their courses, over the service of God that [is] in Jerusalem, as it is written in the scroll of Moses. **19** And the sons of the captivity make the Passover on the fourteenth of the first month, **20** for the priests and the Levites have been purified together—all of them [are] pure—and they slaughter the Passover for all the sons of the captivity, and for their brothers the priests, and for themselves. **21** And the sons of Israel, those returning from the captivity, and everyone who is separated from the uncleanness of the nations of the land to them, to seek to YHWH, God of Israel, eat, **22** and they make the Celebration of Unleavened Things seven days with joy, for YHWH made them to rejoice, and turned around the heart of the king of Asshur to them, to strengthen their hands in the work of the house of God, the God of Israel.

7 And after these things, in the reign of Artaxerxes king of Persia, Ezra son of Seraiah, son of Azariah, son of Hilkiah, **2** son of Shallum, son of Zadok, son of Ahitub, **3** son of Amariah, son of Azariah, son of Meraioth, **4** son of Zerahiah, son of Uzzi, son of Bukki, **5** son of Abishua, son of Phinehas, son of Eleazar, son of Aaron the head priest; **6** Ezra himself has come up from Babylon, and he [is] a scribe ready in the Law of Moses, that YHWH God of Israel gave, and the king gives to him—according to the hand of his God YHWH on him—all his request. **7** And there go up of the sons of Israel, and of the priests, and the Levites, and the singers, and the gatekeepers, and the Nethinim, to Jerusalem, in the seventh year of Artaxerxes the king. **8** And he comes to Jerusalem in the fifth month, that [is in] the seventh year of the king, **9** for on the first of the month he has founded the ascent from Babylon, and on the first of the fifth month he has come to Jerusalem, according to the good hand of his God on him, **10** for Ezra has prepared his heart to seek the Law of YHWH, and to do, and to teach in Israel statute and judgment. **11** And this [is] a copy of the letter that King Artaxerxes gave to Ezra the priest, the scribe, a scribe of the words of the commands of YHWH, and of His statutes on Israel: **12** "Artaxerxes, king of kings, to Ezra the priest, a perfect scribe of the Law of the God of the heavens, and at such a time: **13** By me has been made a decree that

EZRA

everyone who is willing, in my kingdom, of the people of Israel and of its priests and Levites, to go to Jerusalem with you, go; **14** because that from the king and his seven counselors you are sent, to inquire concerning Judah and concerning Jerusalem, with the Law of God that [is] in your hand, **15** and to carry silver and gold that the king and his counselors willingly offered to the God of Israel, whose dwelling place [is] in Jerusalem, **16** and all the silver and gold that you find in all the province of Babylon, with the free-will offerings of the people, and of the priests, offering willingly, for the house of their God that [is] in Jerusalem, **17** therefore you speedily buy with this money, bullocks, rams, lambs, and their presents, and their drink-offerings, and bring them near to the altar of the house of your God that [is] in Jerusalem, **18** and that which to you and to your brothers is good to do with the rest of the silver and gold, according to the will of your God you do. **19** And the vessels that are given to you, for the service of the house of your God, make perfect before the God of Jerusalem; **20** and the rest of the necessary things of the house of your God, that it falls to you to give, you give from the treasure-house of the king. **21** And by me—I Artaxerxes the king—is made a decree to all treasurers who [are] beyond the river, that all that Ezra the priest, scribe of the Law of the God of the heavens, asks of you, be done speedily: **22** To silver one hundred talents, and to wheat one hundred cors, and to wine one hundred baths, and to oil one hundred baths, and salt without reckoning; **23** all that [is] by the decree of the God of the heavens, let be done diligently for the house of the God of the heavens; for why is there wrath against the kingdom of the king and his sons? **24** And to you we are making known, that on any of the priests and Levites, singers, gatekeepers, Nethinim, and servants of the house of God, tribute and custom there is no authority to lift up. **25** And you, Ezra, according to the wisdom of your God, that [is] in your hand, appoint magistrates—even judges who may be judging—judging all the people who are beyond the river, to all knowing the Law of your God, and he who has not known, you cause to know; **26** and any who does not do the Law of your God, and the law of the king, judgment is done speedily on him, whether to death, or to banishment, or to confiscation of riches, and to bonds." **27** Blessed [is] YHWH, God of our fathers, who has given such a thing as this in the heart of the king, to beautify the house of YHWH that [is] in Jerusalem, **28** and to me has stretched out kindness before the king and his counselors, and before all the mighty heads of the king: and I have strengthened myself as the hand of my God YHWH [is] on me, and I gather out of Israel heads to go up with me.

8 And these [are] heads of their fathers, and the genealogy of those going up with me, in the reign of Artaxerxes the king, from Babylon. **2** From the sons of Phinehas: Gershom; from the sons of Ithamar: Daniel; from the sons of David: Hattush; **3** from the sons of Shechaniah, from the sons of Pharosh: Zechariah, and with him, reckoning themselves by genealogy, of males one hundred and fifty. **4** From the sons of Pahath-Moab: Elihoenai son of Zerahiah, and with him two hundred who are males. **5** From the sons of Shechaniah: the son of Jahaziel, and with him three hundred who are males. **6** And from the sons of Adin: Ebed son of Jonathan, and with him fifty who are males. **7** And from the sons of Elam: Jeshaiah son of Athaliah, and with him seventy who are males. **8** And from the sons of Shephatiah: Zebadiah son of Michael, and with him eighty who are males. **9** From the sons of Joab: Obadiah son of Jehiel, and with him two hundred and eighteen who are males. **10** And from the sons of Shelomith, the son of Josiphiah, and with him one hundred and sixty who are males. **11** And from the sons of Bebai: Zechariah son of Bebai, and with him twenty-eight who are males. **12** And from the sons of Azgad: Johanan son of Hakkatan, and with him one hundred and ten who are males. **13** And from the younger sons of Adonikam—and these [are] their names—Eliphelet, Jeiel, and Shemaiah, and with them sixty who are males. **14** And from the sons of Bigvai, Uthai and Zabbud, and with them seventy who are males. **15** And I gather them to the river that is going to Ahava, and we encamp there three days; and I consider about the people, and about the priests, and of the sons of Levi I have found none there; **16** and I send for Eliezer, for Ariel, for

Shemaiah, and for Elnathan, and for Jarib, and for Elnathan, and for Nathan, and for Zechariah, and for Meshullam, heads, and for Joiarib, and for Elnathan, men of understanding; **17** and I charge them for Iddo the head, in the place Casiphia, and put in their mouth words to speak to Iddo, [and] his brothers the Nethinim, in the place Casiphia, to bring to us servants for the house of our God. **18** And they bring to us, according to the good hand of our God on us, a man of understanding, of the sons of Mahli, son of Levi, son of Israel, and Sherebiah, and his sons, and his brothers, eighteen; **19** and Hashabiah, and with him Jeshaiah, of the sons of Merari, his brothers, and their sons, twenty; **20** and from the Nethinim, whom David and the heads gave for the service of the Levites, two hundred and twenty Nethinim, all of them defined by name. **21** And I proclaim there a fast, by the river Ahava, to afflict ourselves before our God, to seek from Him a right way for us, and for our infants, and for all our substance, **22** for I was ashamed to ask from the king a force and horsemen to help us because of the enemy in the way, for we spoke to the king, saying, "The hand of our God [is] on all seeking Him for good, and His strength and His wrath [is] on all forsaking Him." **23** And we fast, and seek from our God for this, and He accepts our plea. **24** And I separate from the heads of the priests, twelve, even Sherebiah, Hashabiah, and with them of their brothers ten, **25** and I weigh to them the silver, and the gold, and the vessels, a raised-offering of the house of our God, that the king, and his counselors, and his heads, and all Israel—those present—lifted up; **26** and I weigh to their hand six hundred and fifty talents of silver, and one hundred talents of vessels of silver, one hundred talents of gold, **27** and twenty basins of gold, of one thousand drams, and two vessels of good shining bronze, desirable as gold. **28** And I say to them, "You [are] holy to YHWH, and the vessels [are] holy, and the silver and the gold [are] a willing-offering to YHWH, God of your fathers; **29** watch, and keep, until you weigh before the heads of the priests, and of the Levites, and the heads of the fathers of Israel, in Jerusalem, in the chambers of the house of YHWH." **30** And the priests and the Levites took the weight of the silver, and of the gold, and of the vessels, to bring to Jerusalem to the house of our God. **31** And we journey from the river Ahava, on the twelfth of the first month, to go to Jerusalem, and the hand of our God has been on us, and He delivers us from the hand of the enemy and the one lying in wait by the way; **32** and we come to Jerusalem, and dwell there three days. **33** And on the fourth day has been weighed the silver, and the gold, and the vessels, in the house of our God, to the hand of Meremoth son of Uriah the priest, and with him Eleazar son of Phinehas, and with them Jozabad son of Jeshua, and Noadiah son of Binnui, the Levites: **34** by number, by weight of everyone, and all the weight is written at that time. **35** Those coming in of the captives—sons of the expulsion—have brought burnt-offerings near to the God of Israel: twelve bullocks for all Israel, ninety-six rams, seventy-seven lambs, twelve young male goats for a sin-offering—the whole a burnt-offering to YHWH; **36** and they give the laws of the king to the lieutenants of the king and the governors beyond the river, and they have lifted up the people and the house of God.

9 And at the completion of these things, the heads have drawn near to me, saying, "The people of Israel, and the priests, and the Levites, have not been separated from the peoples of the lands, as to their abominations, even the Canaanite, the Hittite, the Perizzite, the Jebusite, the Ammonite, the Moabite, the Egyptian, and the Amorite, **2** for they have taken of their daughters to them, and to their sons, and the holy seed have mingled themselves among the peoples of the lands, and the hand of the heads and of the seconds have been first in this trespass." **3** And at my hearing this word, I have torn my garment and my upper robe, and pluck out of the hair of my head, and of my beard, and sit astonished, **4** and to me are gathered everyone trembling at the words of the God of Israel, because of the trespass of the expulsion, and I am sitting astonished until the present of the evening. **5** And at the present of the evening I have risen from my affliction, and at my tearing my garment and my upper robe, then I bow down on my knees, and spread out my hands to my God YHWH, **6** and say, "O my God, I have been ashamed, and have blushed to lift up, O my God, my face to You, for our iniquities have increased over the head, and our guilt has become great to the heavens. **7** From the days of our fathers we [are] in great guilt to this day, and in our iniquities we have been given—we, our kings, our priests—into the hand of the kings of the lands, with sword, with captivity, and with spoiling, and with shame of face, as [at] this day. **8** And now, as a small moment grace has been from our God YHWH, to leave an escape for us, and to give to us a nail in His holy place, by our God's enlightening our eyes, and by giving us a little quickening in our servitude; **9** for we [are] servants, and in our servitude our God has not forsaken us, and stretches out to us kindness before the kings of Persia, to give to us a quickening to lift up the house of our God, and to cause its ruins to cease, and to give to us a wall in Judah and in Jerusalem. **10** And now, what do we say, O our God, after this? For we have forsaken Your commands, **11** that You have commanded by the hands of Your servants the prophets, saying, The land into which you are going to possess it, [is] a land of impurity, by the impurity of the people of the lands, by their abominations with which they have filled it—from mouth to mouth—by their uncleanness; **12** and now, your daughters you do not give to their sons, and their daughters you do not take to your sons, and you do not seek their peace, and their good—for all time, so that you are strong, and have eaten the good of the land, and given possession to your sons for all time. **13** And after all that has come on us for our evil works, and for our great guilt (for You, O our God, have kept back of the rod from our iniquities, and have given to us an escape like this), **14** do we turn back to break Your commands, and to join ourselves in marriage with the people of these abominations? Are You not angry against us—even to consumption—until there is no remnant and escaped part? **15** O YHWH, God of Israel, You [are] righteous, for we have been left an escape, as [it is] this day; behold, we [are] before You in our guilt, for there is none to stand before You concerning this."

10 And at Ezra's praying, and at his making confession, weeping and casting himself down before the house of God, there have been gathered to him out of Israel a very great assembly—men and women and children—for the people have wept, multiplying weeping. **2** And Shechaniah son of Jehiel, of the sons of Elam, answers and says to Ezra, "We have trespassed against our God, and we settle strange women of the peoples of the land; and now there is hope for Israel concerning this, **3** and now, let us make a covenant with our God, to cause all the women to go out, and that which is born of them, by the counsel of the Lord, and of those trembling at the command of our God, and according to law it is done; **4** rise, for on you [is] the matter, and we [are] with you; be strong, and do." **5** And Ezra rises, and causes the heads of the priests, the Levites, and all Israel, to swear to do according to this word—and they swear. **6** And Ezra rises from before the house of God, and goes to the chamber of Jehohanan son of Eliashib; indeed, he goes there, bread he has not eaten, and water he has not drunk, for he is mourning because of the trespass of the expulsion. **7** And they cause a voice to pass over into Judah and Jerusalem, to all sons of the expulsion, to be gathered to Jerusalem, **8** and everyone who does not come in by the third day, according to the counsel of the heads and the elderly, all his substance is devoted, and himself separated from the assembly of the expulsion. **9** And all the men of Judah and Benjamin are gathered to Jerusalem by the third day, it [is] the ninth month, on the twentieth of the month, and all the people sit in the broad place of the house of God, trembling on account of the matter and of the showers. **10** And Ezra the priest rises and says to them, "You have trespassed, and you settle strange women, to add to the guilt of Israel; **11** and now, make confession to YHWH, God of your fathers, and do His good pleasure, and be separated from the peoples of the land, and from the strange women." **12** And all the assembly answers and says [with] a great voice, "Right; according to your word—on us to do; **13** but the people [are] many, and [it is] the time of showers, and there is no power to stand outside, and the work [is] not for one day, nor for two, for we have multiplied to transgress in this thing. **14** Please let our heads of all the assembly stand; and all who [are] in our cities, who have settled strange wives, come in at [the] appointed times, and with them [the] elderly of city and city, and judges in it, until the turning back of the fury of the wrath of our God from us, for this thing." **15** Only Jonathan son of Asahel, and Jahaziah son of Tikvah, stood against this, and Meshullam, and Shabbethai the Levite, helped them. **16** And the sons of the expulsion do so, and Ezra the priest, [and] men, heads of the fathers, for the house of their fathers, are separated, even all of them by name, and they sit on the first day of the tenth month, to examine the matter; **17** and they finish with all the men who have settled strange women to the first day of the first month. **18** And there are found of the sons of the priests that have settled strange women: of the sons of Jeshua son of Jozadak, and his brothers, Maaseiah, and Eliezer, and Jarib, and Gedaliah; **19** and they give their hand to send out their wives, and being guilty, a ram of the flock for their guilt. **20** And of the sons of Immer: Hanani and Zebadiah; **21** and of the sons of Harim: Maaseiah, and Elijah, and Shemaiah, and Jehiel, and Uzziah; **22** and of the sons of Pashhur: Elioenai, Maaseiah, Ishmael, Nethaneel, Jozabad, and Elasah. **23** And of the Levites: Jozabad, and Shimei, and Kelaiah (he [is] Kelita), Pethahiah, Judah, and Eliezer. **24** And of the singers: Eliashib. And of the gatekeepers: Shallum, and Telem, and Uri. **25** And of Israel: of the sons of Parosh: Ramiah, and Jeziah, and Malchijah, and Miamin, and Eleazar, and Malchijah, and Benaiah. **26** And of the sons of Elam: Mattaniah, Zechariah, and Jehiel, and Abdi, and Jeremoth, and Elijah. **27** And of the sons of Zattu: Elioenai, Eliashib, Mattaniah, and Jeremoth, and Zabad, and Aziza. **28** And of the sons of Bebai: Jehohanan, Hananiah, Zabbai, Athlai. **29** And of the sons of Bani: Meshullam, Malluch, and Adaiah, Jashub, and Sheal, and Ramoth. **30** And of the sons of Pahath-Moab: Adna, and Chelal, Benaiah, Maaseiah, Mattaniah, Bezaleel, and Binnui, and Manasseh. **31** And of the sons of Harim: Eliezer, Ishijah, Malchiah, Shemaiah, Shimeon, **32** Benjamin, Malluch, Shemariah. **33** Of the sons of Hashum: Mattenai, Mattathah, Zabad, Eliphelet, Jeremai, Manasseh, Shimei. **34** Of the sons of Bani: Maadai, Amram, and Uel, **35** Benaiah, Bedeiah, Cheluhu, **36** Vaniah, Meremoth, Eliashib, **37** Mattaniah, Mattenai, and Jaasau, **38** and Bani, and Binnui, Shimei, **39** and Shelemiah, and Nathan, and Adaiah, **40** Machnadbai, Shashai, Sharai, **41** Azareel, and Shelemiah, Shemariah, **42** Shallum, Amariah, Joseph. **43** Of the sons of Nebo: Jeiel, Mattithiah, Zabad, Zebina, Jadau, and Joel, Benaiah; **44** all these have taken strange women, and there are of them women who adopt sons.

NEHEMIAH

1 Words of Nehemiah son of Hachaliah. And it comes to pass, in the month of Chisleu, the twentieth year, and I have been in Shushan the palace, **2** and Hanani, one of my brothers, he and men of Judah come in, and I ask them concerning the Jews, the escaped part that have been left of the captivity, and concerning Jerusalem; **3** and they say to me, "Those left, who have been left of the captivity there in the province, [are] in great evil, and in reproach, and the wall of Jerusalem is broken down, and its gates have been burned with fire." **4** And it comes to pass, at my hearing these words, I have sat down, and I weep and mourn [for] days, and I am fasting and praying before the God of the heavens. **5** And I say, "Ah, now, O YHWH, God of the heavens, God, the great and the fearful, keeping the covenant and kindness for those loving Him, and for those keeping His commands, **6** please let Your ear be attentive and Your eyes open, to listen to the prayer of Your servant, that I am praying before You today, by day and by night, concerning the sons of Israel, Your servants, and confessing concerning the sins of the sons of Israel, that we have sinned against You; indeed, I and the house of my father have sinned; **7** we have acted very corruptly against You, and have not kept the commands, and the statutes, and the judgments, that You commanded Your servant Moses. **8** Please remember the word that You commanded Your servant Moses, saying, You trespass—I scatter you among peoples; **9** and you have turned back to Me, and kept My commands, and done them—if your outcast is in the end of the heavens, there I gather them, and have brought them to the place that I have chosen to cause My Name to dwell there. **10** And they [are] Your servants, and Your people, whom You have ransomed by Your great power, and by Your strong hand. **11** Ah, now, O Lord, please let Your ear be attentive to the prayer of Your servant, and to the prayer of Your servants, those delighting to fear Your Name; and please give prosperity to Your servant today, and give him for mercies before this man"; and I have been butler to the king.

2 And it comes to pass, in the month of Nisan, the twentieth year of Artaxerxes the king, wine [is] before him, and I lift up the wine, and give to the king, and I had not been sad before him; **2** and the king says to me, "Why [is] your face sad, and you not sick? This is nothing except sadness of heart"; and I fear very much, **3** and say to the king, "Let the king live for all time! Why should my face not be sad, when the city, the place of the graves of my fathers, [is] a desolation, and its gates have been consumed with fire?" **4** And the king says to me, "For what are you seeking?" And I pray to the God of the heavens, **5** and say to the king, "If [it is] good to the king, and if your servant is pleasing before you, that you send me to Judah, to the city of the graves of my fathers, and I have built it." **6** And the king says to me (and the queen is sitting near him), "How long is your journey? And when do you return?" And it is good before the king, and he sends me away, and I set to him a time. **7** And I say to the king, "If [it is] good to the king, let letters be given to me for the governors beyond the River, that they let me pass over until I come to Judah: **8** and a letter to Asaph, keeper of the paradise that the king has, that he give to me trees for beams [for] the gates of the palace that the house has, and for the wall of the city, and for the house into which I enter"; and the king gives to me, according to the good hand of my God on me. **9** And I come to the governors beyond the River, and give to them the letters of the king; and the king sends with me heads of a force, and horsemen; **10** and Sanballat the Horonite hears, and Tobiah the servant, the Ammonite, and it is evil to them—a great evil—that a man has come to seek good for the sons of Israel. **11** And I come to Jerusalem, and I am there three days, **12** and I rise by night, I and a few men with me, and have not declared to a man what my God is giving to my heart to do for Jerusalem, and there is no beast with me except the beast on which I am riding. **13** And I go out through the Valley Gate by night, and to the front of the Dragon Fountain, and to the Refuse Gate, and I am inspecting the walls of Jerusalem, that are broken down, and its gates consumed with fire. **14** And I pass over to the Fountain Gate, and to the King's Pool, and there is no place for the beast under me to pass over, **15** and I am going up through the brook by night, and am inspecting the wall, and turn back, and come in through the Valley Gate, and turn back. **16** And the prefects have not known to where I have gone, and what I am doing; and to the Jews, and to the priests, and to the nobles, and to the prefects, and to the rest of those doing the work, until now I have not declared [it]; **17** and I say to them, "You are seeing the evil that we are in, in that Jerusalem [is] desolate, and its gates have been burned with fire; come and we build the wall of Jerusalem, and we are not a reproach anymore." **18** And I declare to them the hand of my God that is good on me, and also the words of the king that he said to me, and they say, "Let us rise, and we have built"; and they strengthen their hands for good. **19** And Sanballat the Horonite hears, and Tobiah the servant, the Ammonite, and Geshem the Arabian, and they mock at us, and despise us, and say, "What [is] this thing that you are doing? Are you rebelling against the king?" **20** And I return them word, and say to them, "The God of the heavens—He gives prosperity to us, and we His servants rise and have built; and to you there is no portion, and right, and memorial in Jerusalem."

3 And Eliashib the high priest rises, and his brothers the priests, and they build the Sheep Gate; they have sanctified it, and set up its doors, even to the Tower of Meah they have sanctified it, to the Tower of Hananeel; **2** and by his hand men of Jericho have built; and by their hand Zaccur son of Imri has built; **3** and sons of Hassenaah have built the Fish Gate; they have walled it, and set up its doors, its locks, and its bars. **4** And by their hand Merimoth son of Urijah, son of Koz, has strengthened; and by his hand Meshullam son of Berechiah, son of Meshezabeel, has strengthened; and by his hand Zadok son of Baana has strengthened; **5** and by his hand the Tekoites have strengthened, and their majestic ones have not brought in their neck to the service of their Lord. **6** And Jehoiada son of Paseah and Meshullam son of Besodeiah have strengthened the Old Gate; they have walled it, and set up its doors, and its locks, and its bars. **7** And by their hand Melatiah the Gibeonite has strengthened, and Jadon the Meronothite, men of Gibeon and of Mizpah, [belonging] to the throne of the governor beyond the River. **8** By his hand Uzziel son of Harhaiah of the refiners has strengthened; and by his hand Hananiah son of [one of] the compounders has strengthened; and they leave Jerusalem to the broad wall. **9** And by their hand Rephaiah son of Hur, head of the half of the district of Jerusalem, has strengthened. **10** And by their hand Jedaiah son of Harumaph has strengthened, and opposite his own house; and by his hand Hattush son of Hashabniah has strengthened. **11** A second measure Malchijah son of Harim has strengthened, and Hashub son of Pahath-Moab, even the Tower of the Furnaces. **12** And by his hand Shallum son of Halohesh, head of the half of the district of Jerusalem, has strengthened, he and his daughters. **13** Hanun has strengthened the Valley Gate, and the inhabitants of Zanoah; they have built it, and set up its doors, its locks, and its bars, and one thousand cubits in the wall to the Refuse Gate. **14** And Malchijah son of Rechab, head of the district of Beth-Haccerem, has strengthened the Refuse Gate; he builds it, and sets up its doors, its locks, and its bars. **15** And Shallum son of Col-Hozeh, head of the district of Mizpah, has strengthened the Fountain Gate: he builds it, and covers it, and sets up its doors, its locks, and its bars, and the wall of the pool of Siloah, to the garden of the king, and to the steps that are going down from the City of David. **16** After him Nehemiah son of Azbuk, head of the half of the district of Beth-Zur, has strengthened to opposite the graves of David, and to the pool that is made, and to the house of the mighty ones. **17** After him the Levites have strengthened, [and] Rehum son of Bani; by his hand Hashabiah, head of the half of the district of Keilah, has strengthened for his district. **18** After him their brothers have strengthened, [and] Bavvai son of Henadad, head of the half of the district of Keilah. **19** And Ezer son of Jeshua, head of Mizpah, strengthens, by his hand, a second measure, from in front of the ascent of the armory at the angle. **20** After him Baruch son of Zabbai has hurried to strengthen a second measure from the angle to the opening of the house of Eliashib the high priest. **21** After him Meremoth son of Urijah, son of Koz, has strengthened a second measure, from the opening of the house of Eliashib even to the completion of the house of Eliashib. **22** And after him the priests, men of the circuit, have strengthened. **23** After them Benjamin has strengthened, and Hashub, opposite their house; after him Azariah son of Maaseiah, son of Ananiah, has strengthened near his house. **24** After him Binnui son of Henadad has strengthened a second measure, from the house of Azariah to the angle, and to the corner. **25** Palal son of Uzai [strengthened] from opposite the angle, and the tower that is going out from the upper house of the king that [is] at the court of the prison; after him Pedaiah son of Parosh [strengthened]. **26** And the Nethinim have been dwelling in Ophel, to opposite the Water Gate at the east, and the tower that goes out. **27** After him the Tekoites have strengthened a second measure, from opposite the great tower that goes out, and to the wall of Ophel. **28** From above the Horse Gate the priests have strengthened, each opposite his house. **29** After them Zadok son of Immer has strengthened opposite his house; and after him Shemaiah son of Shechaniah, keeper of the East Gate, has strengthened. **30** After him Hananiah son of Shelemiah has strengthened, and Hanun the sixth son of Zalaph, a second measure; after him Meshullam son of Berechiah has strengthened opposite his chamber. **31** After him Malchijah son of the refiner has strengthened, to the house of the Nethinim, and of the merchants, opposite the Miphkad Gate, and to the ascent of the corner. **32** And between the ascent of the corner and the Sheep Gate, the refiners and the merchants have strengthened.

4 And it comes to pass, when Sanballat has heard that we are building the wall, that it is displeasing to him, and he is very angry and mocks at the Jews, **2** and says before his brothers and the force of Samaria, indeed, he says, "What [are] the weak Jews doing? Are they left to themselves? Do they sacrifice? Do they complete in a day? Do they revive the stones out of the heaps of the rubbish—and they are burned?" **3** And Tobiah the Ammonite [is] by him and says, "Also, that which they are building—if a fox goes up, then it has broken down their stone wall." **4** Hear, O our God, for we have been despised; and return their reproach on their own head, and give them for a spoil in a land of captivity; **5** and do not cover over their iniquity, and do not let their sin be blotted out from before You, for they have provoked [You] to anger in front of those building. **6** And we build the wall, and all the wall is joined—to its half, and the people have a heart to work. **7** And it comes to pass, when Sanballat has heard, and Tobiah, and the Arabians, and the Ammonites, and the Ashdodites, that lengthening has gone up to the walls of Jerusalem, that the breeches have begun to be stopped, then it is very displeasing to them, **8** and they conspire, all of them together, to come to fight against Jerusalem, and to do to it injury. **9** And we pray to our God, and appoint a watch against them, by day and by night, because of them. **10** And Judah says, "The power of the burden-bearers has become feeble, and the rubbish [is] abundant, and we are not able to build on the wall." **11** And our adversaries say, "They do not know, nor see, until we come into their midst, and have slain them, and caused the work to cease." **12** And it comes to pass, when the Jews have come who are dwelling near them, that they say to us ten times from all the places to where you return—[they are] against us. **13** And I appoint at the lowest of the places, at the back of the wall, in the clear places, indeed, I appoint the people, by their families, with their swords, their spears, and their bows. **14** And I see, and rise up, and say to the nobles, and to the prefects, and to the rest of the people, "Do not be afraid of them; remember the Lord, the great and the fearful, and fight for your brothers, your sons, and your daughters, your wives, and your houses." **15** And it comes to pass, when our enemies have heard that it has been known to us, and God frustrates their counsel, and we return, all of us, to the wall, each to his work; **16** indeed, it comes to pass, from that day, half of my servants are working in the business, and half of them are keeping hold of both the spears, the shields, and the bows, and the coats of mail; and the heads [are] behind all the house of Judah. **17** The builders on the wall, and the bearers of the burden, those loading, [each] with one of his hands is working in the business, and one is laying hold of the missile. **18** And the builders [are] each with his sword, girded on his loins, and building, and he who is blowing with a horn [is] beside me. **19** And I say to the nobles, and to the prefects, and to the rest of the people, "The work is abundant, and large, and we are separated on the wall, far off from one another; **20** in the place that you hear the voice of the horn there you are gathered to us; our God fights for us." **21** And we are working in the business, and half of them are keeping hold of the spears, from the going up of the dawn until the coming forth of the stars. **22** Also, at that time I said to the people, "Let each lodge with his servant in the midst of Jerusalem, and they have been a watch for us by night, and [for] the work by day": **23** and there are none—I, and my brothers, and my servants, the men of the watch who [are] after me—there are none of us putting off our garments, each [has] his vessel of water.

5 And there is a great cry of the people and their wives, concerning their brothers the Jews, **2** indeed, there are [those] who are saying, "Our sons, and our daughters, we—are many, and we receive grain, and eat, and live." **3** And there are [those] who are saying, "Our fields, and our vineyards, and our houses, we are pledging, and we receive grain for the famine." **4** And there are [those] who are saying, "We have borrowed money for the tribute of the king, [on] our fields, and our vineyards; **5** and now, as the flesh of our brothers [is] our flesh, as their sons [are] our sons, and behold, we are subduing our sons and our daughters for servants, and there are [those] of our daughters subdued, and our hand has no might, and our fields and our vineyards [are] to others." **6** And it is very displeasing to me when I have heard their cry and these words, **7** and my heart reigns over me, and I strive with the nobles, and with the prefects, and say to them, "You are exacting usury on one another"; and I set against them a great assembly, **8** and say to them, "We have acquired our brothers the Jews, those sold to the nations, according to the ability that [is] in us, and you also sell your brothers, and they have been sold to us!" And they are silent, and have not found a word. **9** And I say, "The thing that you are doing [is] not good; do you not walk in the fear of our God, because of the reproach of the nations our enemies? **10** And also, I, my brothers, and my servants, are exacting silver and grain on them; please let us leave off this usury. **11** Please give back to them, as today, their fields, their vineyards, their olive-yards, and their houses, and the hundredth [part] of the money, and of the grain, of the new wine, and of the oil, that you are exacting of them." **12** And they say, "We give back, and we seek nothing from them; so we do as you are saying." And I call the priests, and cause them to swear to do according to this thing; **13** also, I have shaken my lap, and I say, "Thus God shakes out every man from his house and from his labor who does not perform this thing; indeed, thus is he shaken out and empty"; and all the assembly says, "Amen," and praises YHWH; and the people do according to this thing. **14** Also, from the day that he appointed me to be their governor in the land of Judah, from the twentieth year even to the thirty-second year of Artaxerxes the king—twelve years—I, and my brothers, have not eaten the bread of the governor: **15** the former governors who [are] before me have made themselves heavy on the people, and take of them in bread and wine, besides forty shekels in silver; also, their servants have ruled over the people—and I have not done so, because of the fear of God. **16** And also, in the work of this wall I have done mightily, even a field we have not bought, and all my servants are gathered there for the work; **17** and of the Jews, and of the prefects, one hundred and fifty men, and those coming to us of the nations that [are] around us, [are] at my table; **18** and that which has been prepared for one day [is] one ox, six fat sheep, also birds have been prepared for me, and once in ten days of all wines abundantly, and with this, the bread of the governor I have not sought, for heavy is the service on this people. **19** Remember for me, O my God, for good, all that I have done for this people.

6 And it comes to pass, when it has been heard by Sanballat, and Tobiah, and by Geshem the Arabian, and by the rest of our enemies, that I have built the wall, and there has not been left in it a breach (also, until that time I had not set up the doors in the gates), **2** that Sanballat sends, also Geshem, to me, saying, "Come and we meet together in the villages, in the Valley of Ono"; and they are thinking to do to me evil. **3** And I send to them messengers, saying, "A great work I am doing, and I am not able to come down; why does the work cease when I let it alone, and have come down to you?" **4** And they send to me, according to this word, four times, and I return them [word] according to this word. **5** And Sanballat sends to me, according to this word, a fifth time, his servant, and an open letter in his hand; **6** it is written in it, "Among the nations it has been heard, and Gashmu is saying: You and the Jews are thinking to rebel, therefore you are building the wall, and you have been to them for a king—according to these words! **7** And also, you have appointed prophets to call for you in Jerusalem, saying, A king [is] in Judah, and now it is heard by the king according to these words; and now come, and we take counsel together." **8** And I send to him, saying, "It has not been according to these words that you are saying, for from your own heart you are devising them"; **9** for all of them are making us afraid, saying, "Their hands are too feeble for the work, and it is not done"; and now, strengthen my hands. **10** And I have entered the house of Shemaiah son of Delaiah, son of Mehetabeel—and he is restrained—and he says, "Let us meet at the house of God, at the inside of the temple, and we shut the doors of the temple, for they are coming to slay you—indeed, by night they are coming to slay you." **11** And I say, "A man such as I—does he flee? And who as I, that goes into the temple, and lives? I do not go in." **12** And I discern, and behold, God has not sent him, for in the prophecy he has spoken to me both Tobiah and Sanballat hired him, **13** so that he [is] a hired worker, that I may fear and do so, and I had sinned, and it had been to them for an evil name that they may reproach me. **14** Be mindful, O my God, of Tobiah, and of Sanballat, according to these his works, and also, of Noadiah the prophetess, and of the rest of the prophets who have been making me afraid. **15** And the wall is completed in the twenty-fifth of Elul, on the fifty-second day; **16** and it comes to pass, when all our enemies have heard, and all the nations who are all around us see, that they fall greatly in their own eyes, and know that by our God has this work been done. **17** Also, in those days the nobles of Judah are multiplying their letters going to Tobiah, and those of Tobiah are coming to them; **18** for many in Judah are sworn to him, for he [is] son-in-law to Shechaniah son of Arah, and his son Jehohanan has taken the daughter of Meshullam son of Berechiah; **19** also, they have been speaking of his good deeds before me, and they have been taking my words out to him; Tobiah has sent letters to make me afraid.

7 And it comes to pass, when the wall has been built, that I set up the doors, and the gatekeepers are appointed, and the singers, and the Levites, **2** and I charge my brother Hanani, and Hananiah head of the palace, concerning Jerusalem—for he [is] as a man of truth, and fearing God above many— **3** and I say to them, "Do not let the gates of Jerusalem be opened until the heat of the sun, and while they are standing by let them shut the doors, and fasten, and appoint guards of the inhabitants of Jerusalem, each at his watch, and each in front of his house." **4** And the city [is] broad on both sides, and great, and the people [are] few in its midst, and there are no houses built; **5** and my God puts it to my heart, and I gather the nobles, and the prefects, and the people, for the genealogy, and I find a scroll of the genealogy of those coming up at the beginning, and I find written in it: **6** These [are] sons of the province, those coming up of the captives of the expulsion that Nebuchadnezzar king of Babylon removed—and they return to Jerusalem and to Judah, each to his city— **7** who are coming in with Zerubbabel, Jeshua, Nehemiah, Azariah, Raamiah, Nahamani, Mordecai, Bilshan, Mispereth, Bigvai, Nehum, Baanah. The number of the men of the people of Israel: **8** sons of Parosh, two thousand one hundred and seventy-two; **9** sons of Shephatiah, three hundred seventy-two; **10** sons of Arah, six hundred fifty-two; **11** sons of Pahath-Moab, of the sons of Jeshua and Joab, two thousand and eight hundred [and] eighteen; **12** sons of Elam, one thousand two hundred fifty-four; **13** sons of Zattu, eight hundred forty-five; **14** sons of Zaccai, seven hundred and sixty; **15** sons of Binnui, six hundred forty-eight; **16** sons of Bebai, six hundred twenty-eight; **17** sons of Azgad, two thousand three hundred twenty-two; **18** sons of Adonikam, six hundred sixty-

NEHEMIAH

seven; **19** sons of Bigvai, two thousand sixty-seven; **20** sons of Adin, six hundred fifty-five; **21** sons of Ater of Hezekiah, ninety-eight; **22** sons of Hashum, three hundred twenty-eight; **23** sons of Bezai, three hundred twenty-four; **24** sons of Hariph, one hundred [and] twelve; **25** sons of Gibeon, ninety-five; **26** men of Beth-Lehem and Netophah, one hundred eighty-eight; **27** men of Anathoth, one hundred twenty-eight; **28** men of Beth-Azmaveth, forty-two; **29** men of Kirjath-Jearim, Chephirah, and Beeroth, seven hundred forty-three; **30** men of Ramah and Gaba, six hundred twenty-one; **31** men of Michmas, one hundred and twenty-two; **32** men of Bethel and Ai, one hundred twenty-three; **33** men of the other Nebo, fifty-two; **34** sons of the other Elam, one thousand two hundred fifty-four; **35** sons of Harim, three hundred and twenty; **36** sons of Jericho, three hundred forty-five; **37** sons of Lod, Hadid, and Ono, seven hundred and twenty-one; **38** sons of Senaah, three thousand nine hundred and thirty. **39** The priests: sons of Jedaiah, of the house of Jeshua, nine hundred seventy-three; **40** sons of Immer, one thousand fifty-two; **41** sons of Pashur, one thousand two hundred forty-seven; **42** sons of Harim, one thousand and seventeen. **43** The Levites: sons of Jeshua, of Kadmiel, of sons of Hodevah, seventy-four. **44** The singers: sons of Asaph, one hundred forty-eight. **45** The gatekeepers: sons of Shallum, sons of Ater, sons of Talmon, sons of Akkub, sons of Hatita, sons of Shobai: one hundred thirty-eight. **46** The Nethinim: sons of Ziha, sons of Hasupha, sons of Tabbaoth, **47** sons of Keros, sons of Sia, sons of Padon, **48** sons of Lebanah, sons of Hagaba, sons of Shalmai, **49** sons of Hanan, sons of Giddel, sons of Gahar, **50** sons of Reaiah, sons of Rezin, sons of Nekoda, **51** sons of Gazzam, sons of Uzza, sons of Phaseah, **52** sons of Bezai, sons of Meunim, sons of Nephishesim, **53** sons of Bakbuk, sons of Hakupha, sons of Harhur, **54** sons of Bazlith, sons of Mehida, sons of Harsha, **55** sons of Barkos, sons of Sisera, sons of Tamah, **56** sons of Neziah, sons of Hatipha. **57** Sons of the servants of Solomon: sons of Sotai, sons of Sophereth, sons of Perida, **58** sons of Jaala, sons of Darkon, sons of Giddel, **59** sons of Shephatiah, sons of Hattil, sons of Pochereth of Zebaim, sons of Amon. **60** All the Nethinim and the sons of the servants of Solomon [are] three hundred ninety-two. **61** And these [are] those coming up from Tel-Melah, Tel-Harsha, Cherub, Addon, and Immer—and they have not been able to declare the house of their fathers, and their seed, whether they [are] of Israel— **62** sons of Delaiah, sons of Tobiah, sons of Nekoda, six hundred forty-two. **63** And of the priests: sons of Habaiah, sons of Koz, sons of Barzillai (who has taken a wife from the daughters of Barzillai the Gileadite, and is called by their name). **64** These have sought their register among those reckoning themselves by genealogy, and it has not been found, and they are redeemed from the priesthood, **65** and the Tirshatha says to them that they do not eat of the most holy things until the standing up of the priest with [the] Lights and Perfections. **66** All the assembly together [is] forty-two thousand three hundred and sixty, **67** apart from their servants and their handmaids—these [are] seven thousand three hundred thirty-seven; and of them [are] male and female singers, two hundred forty-five. **68** Their horses [are] seven hundred thirty-six; their mules, two hundred [and] forty-five; **69** camels, four hundred thirty-five; donkeys, six thousand seven hundred and twenty. **70** And from the extremity of the heads of the fathers they have given to the work; the Tirshatha has given to the treasure, one thousand drams of gold, fifty bowls, five hundred and thirty priests' coats. **71** And of the heads of the fathers they have given to the treasure of the work, twenty thousand drams of gold, and two thousand and two hundred pounds of silver. **72** And that which the rest of the people have given [is] twenty thousand drams of gold, and two thousand pounds of silver, and sixty-seven priests' coats. **73** And they dwell—the priests, and the Levites, and the gatekeepers, and the singers, and [some] of the people, and the Nethinim, and all Israel—in their cities, and the seventh month comes, and the sons of Israel [are] in their cities.

8 And all the people are gathered as one man to the broad place that [is] before the Water Gate, and they say to Ezra the scribe to bring the Scroll of the Law of Moses, that YHWH commanded Israel. **2** And Ezra the priest brings the Law before

NEHEMIAH

the assembly, both of men and women, and everyone intelligent to hear, on the first day of the seventh month, 3 and he reads in it before the broad place that [is] before the Water Gate, from the light until the middle of the day, in front of the men, and the women, and those intelligent, and the ears of all the people [are] toward the Scroll of the Law. 4 And Ezra the scribe stands on a tower of wood that they made for the purpose, and Mattithiah stands near him, and Shema, and Anaiah, and Urijah, and Hilkiah, and Maaseiah, on his right; and on his left Pedaiah, and Mishael, and Malchijah, and Hashum, and Hashbaddana, Zechariah, Meshullam. 5 And Ezra opens the scroll before the eyes of all the people—for he has been above all the people—and at his opening [it] all the people have stood up, 6 and Ezra blesses YHWH, the great God, and all the people answer, "Amen, Amen," with lifting up of their hands, and they bow and pay respect to YHWH—faces to the earth. 7 And Jeshua, and Bani, and Sherebiah, Jamin, Akkub, Shabbethai, Hodijah, Maaseiah, Kelita, Azariah, Jozabad, Hanan, Pelaiah, and the Levites, giving the people understanding in the Law, and the people, [are] on their station, 8 and they read in the Scroll, in the Law of God, explaining—so as to give the meaning, and they give understanding to the convocation. 9 And Nehemiah—he [is] the Tirshatha—says (and Ezra the priest, the scribe, and the Levites who are instructing the people) to all the people, "Today is holy to your God YHWH, do not mourn, nor weep": for all the people are weeping at their hearing the words of the Law. 10 And he says to them, "Go, eat fat things, and drink sweet things, and send portions to him for whom nothing is prepared, for today [is] holy to our Lord, and do not be grieved, for the joy of YHWH is your strength." 11 And the Levites are keeping all the people silent, saying, "Be silent, for today [is] holy, and do not be grieved." 12 And all the people go to eat, and to drink, and to send portions, and to make great joy, because they have understood concerning the words that they made known to them. 13 And on the second day have been gathered heads of the fathers of all the people, the priests, and the Levites, to Ezra the scribe, even to act wisely concerning the words of the Law. 14 And they find written in the Law that YHWH commanded by the hand of Moses, that the sons of Israel dwell in shelters in the celebration, in the seventh month, 15 and that they proclaim and cause to pass over all their cities (and in Jerusalem), saying, "Go out to the mountain, and bring leaves of the olive, and leaves of the oil tree, and leaves of the myrtle, and leaves of the palms, and leaves of thick trees, to make shelters as it is written." 16 And the people go out, and bring in, and make for themselves shelters, each on his roof, and in their courts, and in the courts of the house of God, and in the broad place of the Water Gate, and in the broad place of the Gate of Ephraim. 17 And they make—all the assembly of the captives of the captivity—shelters, and they sit in shelters; for the sons of Israel had not done, from the days of Jeshua son of Nun, so to that day, and there is very great joy. 18 And he reads in the Scroll of the Law of God day by day, from the first day until the last day, and they make a celebration seven days, and on the eighth day a restraint, according to the ordinance.

9 And in the twenty-fourth day of this month the sons of Israel have been gathered with fasting, and with sackcloth, and earth on them; 2 and the seed of Israel are separated from all sons of a stranger, and stand and confess concerning their sins, and the iniquities of their fathers, 3 and rise up on their station, and read in the Scroll of the Law of their God YHWH a fourth of the day, and a fourth they are confessing and bowing themselves to their God YHWH. 4 And there stand up on the ascent, of the Levites, Jeshua, and Bani, Kadmiel, Shebaniah, Bunni, Sherebiah, Bani, Chenani, and they cry with a loud voice to their God YHWH. 5 And the Levites say, [even] Jeshua, and Kadmiel, Bani, Hashabniah, Sherebiah, Hodijah, Shebaniah, Pethahiah, "Rise, bless your God YHWH, ‖ From age to age, ‖ And they bless the Name of Your glory ‖ That [is] exalted above all blessing and praise. 6 You [are] He, O YHWH, Yourself—You have made the heavens, ‖ The heavens of the heavens, and all their host, ‖ The earth and all that [are] on it, ‖ The seas and all that [are] in them, ‖ And You are keeping all of them alive, ‖ And the host of the heavens are bowing themselves to You. 7 You [are] He, O YHWH God, ‖ Who fixed on

NEHEMIAH

Abraham, ‖ And brought him out from Ur of the Chaldeans, ‖ And made his name Abraham, **8** And found his heart steadfast before You, ‖ So as to make with him the covenant, ‖ To give the land of the Canaanite, ‖ The Hittite, the Amorite, and the Perizzite, and the Jebusite, and the Girgashite, ‖ To give [it] to his seed. And You establish Your words, ‖ For You [are] righteous, **9** And see the affliction of our fathers in Egypt, ‖ And their cry have heard by the Sea of Suph, **10** And give signs and wonders on Pharaoh, ‖ And on all his servants, ‖ And on all the people of his land, ‖ For You have known that they have acted proudly against them, ‖ And You make to Yourself a name as [at] this day. **11** And You have cleaved the sea before them, ‖ And they pass over into the midst of the sea on the dry land, ‖ And their pursuers You have cast into the depths, ‖ As a stone, into the strong waters. **12** And by a pillar of cloud You have led them by day, ‖ And by a pillar of fire by night, ‖ To lighten to them the way in which they go. **13** And on Mount Sinai You have come down, ‖ Even to speak with them from the heavens, ‖ And You give to them right judgments, ‖ And true laws, good statutes and commands. **14** And Your holy Sabbath You have made known to them, ‖ And commands, and statutes, and law, ‖ You have commanded for them, ‖ By the hand of Your servant Moses; **15** And bread from the heavens You have given to them for their hunger, ‖ And water from a rock have brought out to them for their thirst, ‖ And say to them to go in to possess the land ‖ That You have lifted up Your hand to give to them. **16** And they and our fathers have acted proudly, ‖ And harden their neck, ‖ And have not listened to Your commands, **17** Indeed, they refuse to listen, ‖ And have not remembered Your wonders that You have done with them, ‖ And harden their neck and appoint a head, ‖ To turn back to their service, in their rebellion; And You [are] a God of pardons, ‖ Gracious, and merciful, long-suffering, and abundant in kindness, ‖ And have not forsaken them. **18** Also, when they have made to themselves a molten calf, ‖ And say, This [is] your god ‖ That brought you up out of Egypt, ‖ And do great despisings, **19** and You, in Your abundant mercies, ‖ Have not forsaken them in the wilderness—The pillar of the cloud has not turned aside from off them by day, ‖ To lead them in the way, ‖ And the pillar of the fire by night, ‖ To give light to them and the way in which they go. **20** And Your good Spirit You have given, ‖ To cause them to act wisely; And Your manna You have not withheld from their mouth, ‖ And water You have given to them for their thirst, **21** And forty years You have nourished them in a wilderness; They have not lacked; Their garments have not worn out, ‖ And their feet have not swelled. **22** And You give to them kingdoms, and peoples, ‖ And apportion them to the corner, ‖ And they possess the land of Sihon, ‖ And the land of the king of Heshbon, ‖ And the land of Og king of Bashan. **23** And You have multiplied their sons as the stars of the heavens, ‖ And bring them into the land ‖ That You have said to their fathers to go in to possess. **24** And the sons come in, and possess the land, ‖ And You humble the inhabitants of the land—the Canaanites—before them, ‖ And give them into their hand, and their kings, ‖ And the peoples of the land, ‖ To do with them according to their pleasure. **25** And they capture fortified cities, and fat ground, ‖ And possess houses full of all good, ‖ Dug-wells, vineyards, and olive-yards, ‖ And fruit-trees in abundance, ‖ And they eat, and are satisfied, ‖ And become fat, ‖ And delight themselves in Your great goodness. **26** And they are disobedient, ‖ And rebel against You, ‖ And cast Your law behind their back, ‖ And Your prophets they have slain, ‖ Who testified against them, ‖ To bring them back to You, ‖ And they do great despisings, **27** And You give them into the hand of their adversaries, ‖ And they distress them, ‖ And in the time of their distress they cry to You, ‖ And You, from the heavens, hear, ‖ And according to Your abundant mercies, ‖ Give saviors to them, ‖ And they save them out of the hand of their adversaries. **28** And when they have rest, ‖ They turn back to do evil before You, ‖ And You leave them in the hand of their enemies, ‖ And they rule over them; And they return, and call You, ‖ And You hear from the heavens, ‖ And deliver them many times, ‖ According to Your mercies, **29** And testify against them, ‖ To bring them back to Your law; And they have acted proudly, ‖ And have not listened to Your commands, ‖ And against Your judgments have sinned—Which man does and has lived in them—And they give a stubborn shoulder,

‖ And have hardened their neck, ‖ And have not listened. **30** And You draw over them many years, ‖ And testify against them by Your Spirit, ‖ By the hand of Your prophets, ‖ And they have not given ear, ‖ And You give them into the hand of peoples of the lands, **31** and in Your abundant mercies ‖ You have not made them a consumption, ‖ Nor have forsaken them; For a God, gracious and merciful, [are] You. **32** And now, O our God—God, the great, the mighty, ‖ And the fearful, ‖ Keeping the covenant and the kindness— Do not let all the travail that has found us be little before You, ‖ For our kings, for our heads, and for our priests, ‖ And for our prophets, and for our fathers, ‖ And for all Your people, ‖ From the days of the kings of Asshur to this day; **33** And You [are] righteous concerning all that has come on us, ‖ For You have done truth, ‖ And we have done wickedly; **34** And our kings, our heads, ‖ Our priests, and our fathers, ‖ Have not done Your law, ‖ Nor attended to Your commands, ‖ And to Your testimonies, ‖ That You have testified against them; **35** And they, in their kingdom, ‖ And in Your abundant goodness, ‖ That You have given to them, ‖ And in the land, the large and the fat, ‖ That You have set before them, ‖ Have not served You, ‖ Nor turned back from their evil doings. **36** Behold, we—today—[are] servants, ‖ And the land that You have given to our fathers, ‖ To eat its fruit and its good, ‖ Behold, we [are] servants on it, **37** And its increase it is multiplying to the kings ‖ Whom You have set over us ‖ In our sins; And over our bodies they are ruling, ‖ And over our livestock, ‖ According to their pleasure, ‖ And we [are] in great distress. **38** And for all this we are making a steadfast covenant, ‖ And are writing, ‖ And over him who is sealed ‖ [Are] our heads, our Levites, [and] our priests."

10 And over those sealed [are] Nehemiah the Tirshatha, son of Hachaliah, and Zidkijah, **2** Seraiah, Azariah, Jeremiah, **3** Pashhur, Amariah, Malchijah, **4** Huttush, Shebaniah, Malluch, **5** Harim, Meremoth, Obadiah, **6** Daniel, Ginnethon, Baruch, **7** Meshullam, Abijah, Mijamin, **8** Maaziah, Bilgai, Shemaiah; these [are] the priests. **9** And the Levites: both Jeshua son of Azaniah, Binnui of the sons of Henadad, Kadmiel; **10** and their brothers: Shebaniah, Hodijah, Kelita, Pelaiah, Hanan, **11** Micha, Rehob, Hashabiah, **12** Zaccur, Sherebiah, Shebaniah, **13** Hodijah, Bani, Beninu. **14** Heads of the people: Parosh, Pahath-Moab, Elam, Zatthu, Bani, **15** Bunni, Azgad, Bebai, **16** Adonijah, Bigvai, Adin, **17** Ater, Hizkijah, Azzur, **18** Hodijah, Hashum, Bezai, **19** Hariph, Anathoth, Nebai, **20** Magpiash, Meshullam, Hezir, **21** Meshezabeel, Zadok, Jaddua, **22** Pelatiah, Hanan, Anaiah, **23** Hoshea, Hananiah, Hashub, **24** Hallohesh, Pilha, Shobek, **25** Rehum, Hashabnah, Maaseiah, **26** and Ahijah, Hanan, Anan, **27** Malluch, Harim, Baanah. **28** And the rest of the people, the priests, the Levites, the gatekeepers, the singers, the Nethinim, and everyone who has been separated from the peoples of the lands to the Law of God, their wives, their sons, and their daughters, every knowing intelligent one, **29** are laying hold on their brothers, their majestic ones, and coming into an execration and an oath, to walk in the Law of God, that was given by the hand of Moses, servant of God, and to observe and to do all the commands of YHWH our Lord, and His judgments, and His statutes; **30** and that we do not give our daughters to the peoples of the land, and we do not take their daughters to our sons; **31** and the peoples of the land who are bringing in the wares and any grain on the Sabbath day to sell, we do not receive of them on the Sabbath, and on a holy day, and we leave the seventh year, and usury on every hand. **32** And we have appointed for ourselves commands, to put on ourselves the third of a shekel in a year, for the service of the house of our God, **33** for bread of the arrangement, and the continual present, and the continual burnt-offering of the Sabbaths, of the new moons, for appointed times, and for holy things, and for sin-offerings, to make atonement for Israel, even all the work of the house of our God. **34** And we have caused the lots to fall for the offering of wood, [among] the priests, the Levites, and the people, to bring into the house of our God, by the house of our fathers, at times appointed, year by year, to burn on the altar of our God YHWH, as it is written in the Law, **35** and to bring in the first-fruits of our ground, and the first-fruits of all fruit of every tree, year by year, to the house of YHWH, **36** and the firstlings of our sons, and of our livestock, as it is written in the Law, and the firstlings of our herds and our flocks, to bring into the house of our God, to the priests who are ministering in the house of our God. **37** And the beginning of our dough, and our raised-offerings, and the fruit of every tree, of new wine, and of oil, we bring to the priests, into the chambers of the house of our God, and the tithe of our ground to the Levites; and they—the Levites—have the tithes in all the cities of our tillage; **38** and the priest, son of Aaron, has been with the Levites in the tithing of the Levites, and the Levites bring up the tithe of the tithe to the house of our God to the chambers, to the treasure-house; **39** for they bring to the chambers—the sons of Israel and the sons of Levi—the raised-offering of the grain, the new wine, and the oil, and there [are] vessels of the sanctuary, and the priests, those ministering, and the gatekeepers, and the singers, and we do not forsake the house of our God.

11 And the heads of the people dwell in Jerusalem, and the rest of the people have caused lots to fall to bring in one out of ten to dwell in Jerusalem the holy city, and nine parts in the cities, **2** and the people give a blessing to all the men who are offering themselves willingly to dwell in Jerusalem. **3** And these [are] heads of the province who have dwelt in Jerusalem, and in cities of Judah, they have dwelt each in his possession in their cities; Israel, the priests, and the Levites, and the Nethinim, and the sons of the servants of Solomon. **4** And in Jerusalem have dwelt of the sons of Judah, and of the sons of Benjamin. Of the sons of Judah: Athaiah son of Uzziah, son of Zechariah, son of Amariah, son of Shephatiah, son of Mahalaleel, of the sons of Perez; **5** and Masseiah son of Baruch, son of Col-Hozeh, son of Hazaiah, son of Adaiah, son of Joiarib, son of Zechariah, son of Shiloni; **6** all the sons of Perez who are dwelling in Jerusalem [are] four hundred sixty-eight, men of valor. **7** And these [are] sons of Benjamin: Sallu son of Meshullam, son of Joed, son of Pedaiah, son of Kolaiah, son of Maaseiah, son of Ithiel, son of Jesaiah; **8** and after him Gabbai, Sallai, nine hundred twenty-eight. **9** And Joel son of Zichri [is] inspector over them, and Judah son of Senuah [is] over the city—second. **10** Of the priests: Jedaiah son of Joiarib, Jachin, **11** Seraiah son of Hilkiah, son of Meshullam, son of Zadok, son of Meraioth, son of Ahitub, leader of the house of God, **12** and their brothers doing the work of the house [are] eight hundred twenty-two; and Adaiah son of Jeroham, son of Pelaliah, son of Amzi, son of Zechariah, son of Pashhur, son of Malchiah, **13** and his brothers, heads of fathers, two hundred forty-two; and Amashsai son of Azareel, son of Ahazai, son of Meshillemoth, son of Immer, **14** and their brothers, one hundred twenty-eight mighty men of valor; and an inspector over them [is] Zabdiel, son of [one of] the great men. **15** And of the Levites: Shemaiah son of Hashub, son of Azrikam, son of Hashabiah, son of Bunni, **16** and Shabbethai, and Jozabad, [are] over the outward work of the house of God, of the heads of the Levites, **17** and Mattaniah son of Micha, son of Zabdi, son of Asaph, [is] head—at the commencement he gives thanks in prayer; and Bakbukiah [is] second among his brothers, and Abda son of Shammua, son of Galal, son of Jeduthun. **18** All the Levites, in the holy city, [are] two hundred eighty-four. **19** And the gatekeepers, Akkub, Talmon, and their brothers, those watching at the gates, [are] one hundred seventy-two. **20** And the rest of Israel, of the priests, of the Levites, [are] in all cities of Judah, each in his inheritance; **21** and the Nethinim are dwelling in Ophel, and Ziha and Gishpa [are] over the Nethinim. **22** And the overseer of the Levites in Jerusalem [is] Uzzi son of Bani, son of Hashabiah, son of Mattaniah, son of Micha—of the sons of Asaph, the singers [who are] for the front of the work of the house of God, **23** for the command of the king [is] on them, and support [is] for the singers, a matter of a day in its day. **24** And Pethahiah son of Meshezabeel, of the sons of Zerah, son of Judah, [is] by the hand of the king, for every matter of the people. **25** And at the villages with their fields, of the sons of Judah there have dwelt, in Kirjath-Arba and its small towns, and in Dibon and its small towns, and in Jekabzeel and its villages, **26** and in Jeshua, and in Moladah, and in Beth-Phelet, **27** and in Hazar-Shaul, and in Beer-Sheba and its small towns, **28** and in Ziklag, and in Mekonah and in its small towns, **29** and in En-Rimmon, and in Zareah, and in Jarmuth, **30** Zanoah, Adullam, and their villages, Lachish and its fields,

NEHEMIAH

Azekah and its small towns; and they encamp from Beer-Sheba to the Valley of Hinnom. 31 And sons of Benjamin [are] at Geba, Michmash, and Aija, and Beth-El, and its small towns, 32 Anathoth, Nob, Ananiah, 33 Hazor, Ramah, Gittaim, 34 Hadid, Zeboim, Neballat, 35 Lod, and Ono, the Valley of the Craftsmen. 36 And of the Levites, the divisions of Judah [are] for Benjamin.

12 And these [are] the priests and the Levites who came up with Zerubbabel son of Shealtiel, and Jeshua: Seraiah, Jeremiah, Ezra, 2 Amariah, Malluch, Hattush, 3 Shechaniah, Rehum, Meremoth, 4 Iddo, Ginnethoi, Abijah, 5 Miamin, Maadiah, Bilgah, 6 Shemaiah, and Joiarib, Jedaiah, 7 Sallu, Amok, Hilkiah, Jedaiah; these [are] heads of the priests and of their brothers in the days of Jeshua. 8 And the Levites: Jeshua, Binnui, Kadmiel, Sherebiah, Judah, Mattaniah, he [is] over the thanksgiving, and his brothers, 9 and Bakbukiah and Unni, their brothers, [are] opposite them in charges. 10 And Jeshua has begotten Joiakim, and Joiakim has begotten Eliashib, and Eliashib has begotten Joiada, 11 and Joiada has begotten Jonathan, and Jonathan has begotten Jaddua. 12 And in the days of Joiakim have been priests, heads of the fathers: of Seraiah, Meraiah; of Jeremiah, Hananiah; 13 of Ezra, Meshullam; of Amariah, Jehohanan; 14 of Melicu, Jonathan; of Shebaniah, Joseph; 15 of Harim, Adna; of Meraioth, Helkai; 16 of Iddo, Zechariah; of Ginnethon, Meshullam; 17 of Abijah, Zichri; of Miniamin; of Moadiah, Piltai; 18 of Bilgah, Shammua; of Shemaiah, Jonathan; 19 and of Joiarib, Mattenai; of Jedaiah, Uzzi; 20 of Sallai, Kallai; of Amok, Eber; 21 of Hilkiah, Hashabiah; of Jedaiah, Nethaneel. 22 The Levites, in the days of Eliashib, Joiada, and Johanan, and Jaddua, are written, heads of fathers, and of the priests, in the kingdom of Darius the Persian. 23 Sons of Levi, heads of the fathers, are written on the scroll of the Chronicles even until the days of Johanan son of Eliashib; 24 and heads of the Levites: Hashabiah, Sherebiah, and Jeshua son of Kadmiel, and their brothers, [are] opposite them, to give praise, to give thanks, by command of David the man of God, charge close by charge. 25 Mattaniah, and Bakbukiah, Obadiah, Meshullam, Talmon, Akkub, [are] gatekeepers, keeping watch in the gatherings of the gates. 26 These [are] in the days of Joiakim son of Jeshua, son of Jozadak, and in the days of Nehemiah the governor, and of Ezra the priest, the scribe. 27 And at the dedication of the wall of Jerusalem they sought the Levites out of all their places, to bring them to Jerusalem, to make the dedication even with gladness, and with thanksgivings, and with singing, [with] cymbals, psalteries, and with harps; 28 and sons of the singers are gathered together even from the circuit around Jerusalem, and from the villages of Netophathi, 29 and from the house of Gilgal, and from fields of Geba and Azmaveth, the singers have built for villages for themselves around Jerusalem; 30 and the priests and the Levites are cleansed, and they cleanse the people, and the gates, and the wall. 31 And I bring up the heads of Judah on the wall, and appoint two great thanksgiving companies and processions. At the right, on the wall, to the Refuse Gate; 32 and after them goes Hoshaiah, and half of the heads of Judah, 33 and Azariah, Ezra, and Meshullam, 34 Judah, and Benjamin, and Shemaiah, and Jeremiah; 35 and of the sons of the priests with trumpets, Zechariah son of Jonathan, son of Shemaiah, son of Mattaniah, son of Michaiah, son of Zaccur, son of Asaph, 36 and his brothers Shemaiah, and Azarael, Milalai, Gilalai, Maai, Nethaneel, and Judah, Hanani, with instruments of song of David the man of God, and Ezra the scribe [is] before them; 37 and by the Fountain Gate and in front of them, they have gone up by the steps of the City of David, at the going up of the wall beyond the house of David, and to the Water Gate eastward. 38 And the second thanksgiving company that is going opposite, and I after it, and half of the people on the wall from beyond the Tower of the Furnaces and to the broad wall, 39 and from beyond the Gate of Ephraim, and by the Old Gate, and by the Fish Gate, and the Tower of Hananeel, and the Tower of Meah, and to the Sheep Gate—and they have stood at the Prison Gate. 40 And the two thanksgiving companies stand in the house of God, and I and half of the prefects with me, 41 and the priests, Eliakim, Maaseiah, Miniamin, Michaiah, Elioenai, Zechariah, Hananiah, with trumpets,

NEHEMIAH

42 and Masseiah, and Shemaiah, and Eleazar, and Uzzi, and Jehohanan, and Malchijah, and Elam, and Ezer, and the singers sound, and Jezrahiah the inspector; **43** and they sacrifice on that day great sacrifices and rejoice, for God has made them rejoice [with] great joy, and also, the women and the children have rejoiced, and the joy of Jerusalem is heard—to a distance. **44** And certain are appointed on that day over the chambers for treasures, for raised-offerings, for first-fruits, and for tithes, to gather into them out of the fields of the cities the portions of the law for priests, and for Levites, for the joy of Judah [is] over the priests, and over the Levites, who are standing up. **45** And the singers and the gatekeepers keep the charge of their God, even the charge of the cleansing—according to the command of David [and] his son Solomon, **46** for in the days of David and Asaph of old [were] heads of the singers, and a song of praise and thanksgiving to God. **47** And all Israel in the days of Zerubbabel, and in the days of Nehemiah, are giving the portions of the singers, and of the gatekeepers, the matter of a day in its day, and are sanctifying to the Levites, and the Levites are sanctifying to the sons of Aaron.

13 On that day there was read in the scroll of Moses, in the ears of the people, and it has been found written in it that an Ammonite and Moabite does not come into the assembly of God for all time, **2** because they have not come before the sons of Israel with bread and with water, and hire against them Balaam to revile them, and our God turns the reviling into a blessing. **3** And it comes to pass, at their hearing the Law, that they separate all the mixed people from Israel. **4** And before this Eliashib the priest, appointed over chambers of the house of our God, [is] a relation of Tobiah, **5** and he makes for him a great chamber, and there they were formerly putting the present, the frankincense, and the vessels, and the tithe of the grain, the new wine, and the oil—the commanded thing of the Levites, and the singers, and the gatekeepers—and the raised-offering of the priests. **6** And during all this I was not in Jerusalem, for in the thirty-second year of Artaxerxes king of Babylon I came to the king, and at the end of days I have asked of the king, **7** and I come to Jerusalem, and understand concerning the evil that Eliashib has done for Tobiah, to make to him a chamber in the courts of the house of God, **8** and it is very displeasing to me, and I cast all the vessels of the house of Tobiah outside, out of the chamber, **9** and I command, and they cleanse the chambers, and I bring back there the vessels of the house of God with the present and the frankincense. **10** And I know that the portions of the Levites have not been given, and they flee each to his field—the Levites and the singers, doing the work. **11** And I strive with the prefects, and say, "Why has the house of God been forsaken?" And I gather them, and set them on their station; **12** and all Judah has brought in the tithe of the grain, and of the new wine, and of the oil, to the treasuries. **13** And I appoint treasurers over the treasuries, Shelemiah the priest, and Zadok the scribe, and Pedaiah of the Levites; and by their hand [is] Hanan son of Zaccur, son of Mattaniah, for they have been reckoned steadfast, and on them [it is] to give a portion to their brothers. **14** Be mindful of me, O my God, for this, and do not blot out my kind acts that I have done, for the house of my God, and for its charges. **15** In those days I have seen in Judah those treading wine-vats on Sabbath, and bringing in the sheaves, and loading on the donkeys, and also, wine, grapes, and figs, and every burden, indeed, they are bringing into Jerusalem on the Sabbath day, and I testify in the day of their selling provision. **16** And the Tyrians have dwelt in it, bringing in fish, and every ware, and selling on Sabbath to the sons of Judah and in Jerusalem. **17** And I strive with the nobles of Judah, and say to them, "What [is] this evil thing that you are doing, and defiling the Sabbath day? **18** Thus did not your fathers do? And our God brings in on us all this evil, and on this city, and you are adding fierceness on Israel, to defile the Sabbath." **19** And it comes to pass, when the gates of Jerusalem have been dark before the Sabbath, that I command, and the doors are shut, and I command that they do not open them until after the Sabbath; and of my servants I have stationed at the gates; there does not come in a burden on the Sabbath day. **20** And they lodge—the merchants and sellers of all ware—at the outside of Jerusalem, once or twice, **21** and I testify against them, and say to them,

"Why are you lodging in front of the wall? If you repeat [it], I put forth a hand on you"; from that time they have not come in on the Sabbath. **22** And I command to the Levites that they be cleansed, and coming in, keeping the gates, to sanctify the Sabbath day. Also, this, remember for me, O my God, and have pity on me, according to the abundance of Your kindness. **23** Also, in those days, I have seen the Jews [who] have settled women of Ashdod, of Ammon, of Moab. **24** And of their sons, half are speaking Ashdoditish—and are not knowing to speak Jewish—and according to the language of people and people. **25** And I strive with them, and declare them vile, and strike certain of them, and pluck off their hair, and cause them to swear by God, "You do not give your daughters to their sons, nor do you take of their daughters to your sons, and to yourselves. **26** By these did not Solomon king of Israel sin? And among the many nations there was no king like him, and he was beloved by his God, and God makes him king over all Israel—even him [whom] the strange women caused to sin. **27** And do we listen to you to do all this great evil, to trespass against our God, to settle strange women?" **28** And [one] of the sons of Joiada son of Eliashib the high priest, [is] son-in-law to Sanballat the Horonite, and I cause him to flee from off me. **29** Be mindful of them, O my God, for the redeemed of the priesthood, and the covenant of the priesthood, and of the Levites. **30** And I have cleansed them from every stranger, and appoint charges to priests and to Levites, each in his work, **31** and for the wood-offering at appointed times, and for first-fruits. Be mindful of me, O my God, for good.

ESTHER

1 And it comes to pass, in the days of Ahasuerus—he [is] Ahasuerus who is reigning from Hodu even to Cush, one hundred twenty-seven provinces— **2** in those days, at the sitting of King Ahasuerus on the throne of his kingdom, that [is] in Shushan the palace, **3** in the third year of his reign, he has made a banquet to all his heads and his servants; of the force of Persia and Media, the chiefs and heads of the provinces [are] before him, **4** in his showing the wealth of the glory of his kingdom, and the glory of the beauty of his greatness, many days—one hundred eighty days. **5** And at the fullness of these days the king has made a banquet to all the people who are found in Shushan the palace, from great even to small, [for] seven days, in the court of the garden of the house of the king— **6** white linen, white cotton, and blue, fastened with cords of fine linen and purple on rings of silver, and pillars of marble, couches of gold, and of silver, on a pavement of smaragdus, and white marble, and mother-of-pearl, and black marble— **7** and the giving of drink in vessels of gold, and the vessels [are] various vessels, and the royal wine [is] abundant, as a memorial of the king. **8** And the drinking [is] according to law, none is pressing, for so the king has appointed for every chief one of his house, to do according to the pleasure of man and man. **9** Also Vashti the queen has made a banquet for women, in the royal house that King Ahasuerus has. **10** On the seventh day, as the heart of the king is glad with wine, he has commanded to Mehuman, Biztha, Harbona, Bigtha, and Abagtha, Zethar, and Carcas, the seven eunuchs who are ministering in the presence of King Ahasuerus, **11** to bring in Vashti the queen before the king, with a royal crown, to show the peoples and the heads her beauty, for she [is] of good appearance, **12** and the queen Vashti refuses to come in at the word of the king that [is] by the hand of the eunuchs, and the king is very angry, and his fury has burned in him. **13** And the king says to wise men, knowing the times—for so [is] the word of the king before all knowing law and judgment, **14** and he who is near to him [is] Carshena, Shethar, Admatha, Tarshish, Meres, Marsena, Memucan, seven heads of Persia and Media seeing the face of the king, who are sitting first in the kingdom— **15** "According to law, what should [I] do with Queen Vashti, because that she has not done the saying of King Ahasuerus by the hand of the eunuchs?" **16** And Memucan says before the king and the heads, "Queen Vashti has not done perversely against the king by himself, but against all the heads, and against all the peoples that [are] in all provinces of King Ahasuerus; **17** for the word of the queen goes forth to all the women, to render their husbands contemptible in their eyes, in their saying, King Ahasuerus commanded to bring in Vashti the queen before him, and she did not come; **18** indeed, this day princesses of Persia and Media, who have heard the word of the queen, say [so] to all heads of the king, even according to the sufficiency of contempt and wrath. **19** If to the king [it be] good, there goes forth a royal word from before him, and it is written with the laws of Persia and Media, and does not pass away, that Vashti does not come in before King Ahasuerus, and the king gives her royalty to her companion who [is] better than she; **20** and the sentence of the king that he makes has been heard in all his kingdom—for it [is] great—and all the wives give honor to their husbands, from great even to small." **21** And the thing is good in the eyes of the king, and of the princes, and the king does according to the word of Memucan, **22** and sends letters to all provinces of the king, to province and province according to its writing, and to people and people according to its tongue, for every man being head in his own house—and speaking according to the language of his people.

2 After these things, at the ceasing of the fury of King Ahasuerus, he has remembered Vashti, and that which she did, and that which has been decreed concerning her; **2** and servants of the king, his ministers, say, "Let them seek for the king young women, virgins, of good appearance, **3** and the king appoints inspectors in all provinces of his kingdom,

ESTHER

and they gather every young woman—virgin, of good appearance—to Shushan the palace, to the house of the women, to the hand of Hegai eunuch of the king, keeper of the women, and to give their purifications, **4** and the young woman who is good in the eyes of the king reigns instead of Vashti"; and the thing is good in the eyes of the king, and he does so. **5** A man, a Jew, there has been in Shushan the palace, and his name [is] Mordecai son of Jair, son of Shimei, son of Kish, a Benjamite— **6** who had been removed from Jerusalem with the expulsion that was removed with Jeconiah king of Judah, whom Nebuchadnezzar king of Babylon removed— **7** and he is supporting Hadassah—she [is] Esther—daughter of his uncle, for she has neither father nor mother, and the young woman [is] of beautiful form, and of good appearance, and at the death of her father and her mother Mordecai has taken her to himself for a daughter. **8** And it comes to pass, in the word of the king, even his law, being heard, and in many young women being gathered to Shushan the palace, to the hand of Hegai, that Esther is taken to the house of the king, to the hand of Hegai, keeper of the women, **9** and the young woman is good in his eyes, and she receives kindness before him, and he hurries her purifications and her portions—to give to her, and the seven young women who are provided—to give to her, from the house of the king, and he changes her and her young women to a good [place in] the house of the women. **10** Esther has not declared her people, and her family, for Mordecai has laid a charge on her that she does not declare [it]; **11** and during every day Mordecai is walking up and down before the court of the house of the women to know the welfare of Esther, and what is done with her. **12** And in the drawing near of the turn of each young woman to come in to King Ahasuerus, at the end of there being to her—according to the law of the women—twelve months, for so they fulfill the days of their purifications; six months with oil of myrrh, and six months with perfumes, and with the purifications of women, **13** and with this the young woman has come in to the king, all that she says is given to her to go in with her out of the house of the women to the house of the king; **14** in the evening she has gone in, and in the morning she has turned back to the second house of the women, to the hand of Shaashgaz eunuch of the king, keeper of the concubines; she does not come in anymore to the king except the king has delighted in her, and she has been called by name. **15** And in the drawing near of the turn of Esther—daughter of Abihail, uncle of Mordecai, whom he had taken to himself for a daughter—to come in to the king, she has not sought a thing except that which Hegai eunuch of the king, keeper of the women, says, and Esther is receiving grace in the eyes of all seeing her. **16** And Esther is taken to King Ahasuerus, to his royal house, in the tenth month—it [is] the month of Tebeth—in the seventh year of his reign, **17** and the king loves Esther above all the women, and she receives grace and kindness before him above all the virgins, and he sets a royal crown on her head, and causes her to reign instead of Vashti, **18** and the king makes a great banquet to all his heads and his servants—the banquet of Esther—and has made a release to the provinces, and gives gifts as a memorial of the king. **19** And in the virgins being gathered a second time, then Mordecai is sitting in the gate of the king; **20** Esther is not declaring her family and her people, as Mordecai has laid a charge on her, and the saying of Mordecai Esther is doing as when she was truly with him. **21** In those days, when Mordecai is sitting in the gate of the king, has Bigthan been angry, and Teresh (two of the eunuchs of the king, the keepers of the threshold), and they seek to put forth a hand on King Ahasuerus, **22** and the thing is known to Mordecai, and he declares [it] to Esther the queen, and Esther speaks to the king in the name of Mordecai, **23** and the thing is sought out, and found, and both of them are hanged on a tree, and it is written in the scroll of the Chronicles before the king.

3 After these things has King Ahasuerus exalted Haman son of Hammedatha the Agagite, and lifts him up, and sets his throne above all the heads who [are] with him, **2** and all servants of the king, who [are] in the gate of the king, are bowing and doing homage to Haman, for so the king has commanded for him; and Mordecai does not bow nor pay respect. **3** And the servants of the king, who [are] in the gate of the king, say to Mordecai, "Why [are] you transgressing the command of the king?"

ESTHER

4 And it comes to pass, in their speaking to him, day by day, and he has not listened to them, that they declare [it] to Haman, to see whether the words of Mordecai stand, for he has declared to them that he [is] a Jew. **5** And Haman sees that Mordecai is not bowing and doing homage to him, and Haman is full of fury, **6** and it is contemptible in his eyes to put forth a hand on Mordecai by himself, for they have declared to him the people of Mordecai, and Haman seeks to destroy all the Jews who [are] in all the kingdom of Ahasuerus—the people of Mordecai. **7** In the first month—it [is] the month of Nisan—in the twelfth year of King Ahasuerus, has one caused to fall Pur (that [is] the lot) before Haman, from day to day, and from month to month, [to] the twelfth, it [is] the month of Adar. **8** And Haman says to King Ahasuerus, "There is one people scattered and separated among the peoples, in all provinces of your kingdom, and their laws [are] diverse from all people, and the laws of the king they are not doing, and for the king it is not profitable to permit them; **9** if to the king [it be] good, let it be written to destroy them, and ten thousand talents of silver I weigh into the hands of those doing the work, to bring [it] into the treasuries of the king." **10** And the king turns aside his signet from off his hand, and gives it to Haman son of Hammedatha the Agagite, adversary of the Jews; **11** and the king says to Haman, "The silver is given to you, and the people, to do with it as [it is] good in your eyes." **12** And scribes of the king are called, on the first month, on the thirteenth day of it, and it is written according to all that Haman has commanded, to lieutenants of the king, and to the governors who [are] over province and province, and to the heads of people and people, province and province, according to its writing, and people and people according to its tongue, in the name of King Ahasuerus it has been written and sealed with the signet of the king, **13** and letters to be sent by the hand of the runners to all provinces of the king, to cut off, to slay, and to destroy all the Jews, from young even to old, infant and women, on one day, on the thirteenth of the twelfth month—it [is] the month of Adar—and to seize their spoil, **14** a copy of the writing to be made law in each and every province is revealed to all the peoples, to be ready for this day. **15** The runners have gone forth, hurried by the word of the king, and the law has been given in Shushan the palace, and the king and Haman have sat down to drink, and the city Shushan is perplexed.

4 And Mordecai has known all that has been done, and Mordecai tears his garments, and puts on sackcloth and ashes, and goes forth into the midst of the city and cries—a cry loud and bitter, **2** and he comes to the front of the gate of the king, but none is to come to the gate of the king with a sackcloth-garment. **3** And in each and every province, the place where the word of the king, even his law, is coming, the Jews have a great mourning, and fasting, and weeping, and lamenting: sackcloth and ashes are spread for many. **4** And young women of Esther come in and her eunuchs, and declare [it] to her, and the queen is exceedingly pained, and sends garments to clothe Mordecai, and to turn aside his sackcloth from off him, and he has not received [them]. **5** And Esther calls to Hatach, of the eunuchs of the king, whom he has stationed before her, and gives him a charge for Mordecai, to know what this [is], and why this [is]. **6** And Hatach goes out to Mordecai, to a broad place of the city, that [is] before the gate of the king, **7** and Mordecai declares to him all that has met him, and the explanation of the money that Haman said to weigh to the treasuries of the king for the Jews, to destroy them, **8** and the copy of the writing of the law that had been given in Shushan to destroy them he has given to him, to show Esther, and to declare [it] to her, and to lay a charge on her to go in to the king, to make supplication to him, and to seek from before him, for her people. **9** And Hatach comes in and declares to Esther the words of Mordecai, **10** and Esther speaks to Hatach, and charges him for Mordecai: **11** "All servants of the king, and people of the provinces of the king, know that any man and woman who comes to the king, into the inner court, who is not called—one law of his [is] to put [them] to death, apart from him to whom the king holds out the golden scepter, then he has lived; and I have not been called to come in to the king these thirty days." **12** And they declare to Mordecai the words of Esther, **13** and Mordecai commands to send back to Esther: "Do not think in your soul to be

ESTHER

delivered [in] the house of the king, more than all the Jews, **14** but if you keep entirely silent at this time, respite and deliverance remains to the Jews from another place, and you and the house of your fathers are destroyed; and who knows whether for a time like this you have come to the kingdom?" **15** And Esther commands to send back to Mordecai: **16** "Go, gather all the Jews who are found in Shushan, and fast for me, and do not eat nor drink three days, by night and by day; also I and my young women fast likewise, and so I go in to the king, that [is] not according to law, and when I have perished—I have perished." **17** And Mordecai passes on, and does according to all that Esther has charged on him.

5 And it comes to pass on the third day, that Esther puts on royalty, and stands in the inner-court of the house of the king in front of the house of the king, and the king is sitting on his royal throne, in the royal-house, opposite the opening of the house, **2** and it comes to pass, at the king's seeing Esther the queen standing in the court, she has received grace in his eyes, and the king holds out to Esther the golden scepter that [is] in his hand, and Esther draws near, and touches the top of the scepter. **3** And the king says to her, "What do you [want], Esther, O queen? And what [is] your request? To the half of the kingdom—and it is given to you." **4** And Esther says, "If to the king [it be] good, the king comes in, and Haman, today, to the banquet that I have made for him"; **5** and the king says, "Hurry Haman—to do the word of Esther"; and the king comes in, and Haman, to the banquet that Esther has made. **6** And the king says to Esther, during the banquet of wine, "What [is] your petition? And it is given to you; and what [is] your request? To the half of the kingdom—and it is done." **7** And Esther answers and says, "My petition and my request [is]: **8** if I have found grace in the eyes of the king, and if to the king [it be] good, to give my petition, and to perform my request, the king comes, and Haman, to the banquet that I make for them, and tomorrow I do according to the word of the king." **9** And Haman goes forth on that day rejoicing and glad in heart, and at Haman's seeing Mordecai in the gate of the king, and he has not risen nor moved for him, then is Haman full of fury against Mordecai. **10** And Haman forces himself, and comes into his house, and sends, and brings in his friends, and his wife Zeresh, **11** and Haman recounts to them the glory of his wealth, and the abundance of his sons, and all that with which the king made him great, and with which he lifted him up above the heads and servants of the king. **12** And Haman says, "Indeed, Esther the queen brought none in with the king, to the feast that she made, except myself, and also for tomorrow I am called to her, with the king, **13** and all this is not profitable to me, during all the time that I am seeing Mordecai the Jew sitting in the gate of the king." **14** And his wife Zeresh says to him, and all his friends, "Let them prepare a tree, in height fifty cubits, and in the morning speak to the king, and they hang Mordecai on it, and go in with the king to the banquet rejoicing"; and the thing is good before Haman, and he prepares the tree.

6 On that night the sleep of the king has fled away, and he commands to bring in the scroll of memorials of the chronicles, and they are read before the king, **2** and it is found written that Mordecai had declared concerning Bigthana and Teresh, two of the eunuchs of the king, of the keepers of the threshold, who sought to put forth a hand on King Ahasuerus. **3** And the king says, "What honor and greatness has been done to Mordecai for this?" And the servants of the king, his ministers, say, "Nothing has been done with him." **4** And the king says, "Who [is] in the court?" And Haman has come into the outer court of the house of the king, to say to the king to hang Mordecai on the tree that he had prepared for him. **5** And the servants of the king say to him, "Behold, Haman is standing in the court"; and the king says, "Let him come in." **6** And Haman comes in, and the king says to him, "What should [I] do with the man in whose honor the king has delighted?" And Haman says in his heart, "To whom does the king delight to do honor more than myself?" **7** And Haman says to the king, "The man in whose honor the king has delighted, **8** let them bring in royal clothing that the king has put on himself, and a horse on which the king has ridden, and that the royal crown be put on his head, **9** and to give the clothing and the horse into the hand of a man of the heads of the king, the chiefs, and they have clothed the man in whose honor the king has delighted, and caused him to ride on the horse in a broad place of the city, and called before him: Thus it is done to the man in whose honor the king has delighted." **10** And the king says to Haman, "Hurry, take the clothing and the horse, as you have spoken, and do so to Mordecai the Jew, who is sitting in the gate of the king; there does not fall a thing of all that you have spoken." **11** And Haman takes the clothing, and the horse, and clothed Mordecai, and causes him to ride in a broad place of the city, and calls before him, "Thus it is done to the man in whose glory the king has delighted." **12** And Mordecai turns back to the gate of the king, and Haman has been hurried to his house mourning, and with covered head, **13** and Haman recounts to his wife Zeresh, and to all his friends, all that has met him, and his wise men and his wife Zeresh say to him, "If Mordecai [is] of the seed of the Jews, before whom you have begun to fall, you are not able for him, but certainly fall before him." **14** They are yet speaking with him, and eunuchs of the king have come, and hurry to bring in Haman to the banquet that Esther has made.

7 And the king comes in, and Haman, to drink with Esther the queen, **2** and the king says to Esther also on the second day, during the banquet of wine, "What [is] your petition, Esther, O queen? And it is given to you; and what [is] your request? To the half of the kingdom—and it is done." **3** And Esther the queen answers and says, "If I have found grace in your eyes, O king, and if to the king [it be] good, let my life be given to me at my petition, and my people at my request; **4** for we have been sold, I and my people, to cut off, to slay, and to destroy; and if for menservants and for maidservants we had been sold I had kept silent—but the adversity is not equal to the loss of the king." **5** And King Ahasuerus says, indeed, he says to Esther the queen, "Who [is] he—this one? And where [is] this one whose heart has filled him to do so?" **6** And Esther says, "The man—adversary and enemy—[is] this wicked Haman"; and Haman has been afraid at the presence of the king and of the queen. **7** And the king has risen, in his fury, from the banquet of wine, to the garden of the house, and Haman has remained to seek for his life from Esther the queen, for he has seen that evil has been determined against him by the king. **8** And the king has turned back out of the garden of the house to the house of the banquet of wine, and Haman is falling on the couch on which Esther [is], and the king says, "Also to subdue the queen with me in the house?" The word has gone out from the mouth of the king, and the face of Haman they have covered. **9** And Harbonah, one of the eunuchs, says before the king, "Also behold, the tree that Haman made for Mordecai, who spoke good for the king, is standing in the house of Haman, in height fifty cubits"; and the king says, "Hang him on it." **10** And they hang Haman on the tree that he had prepared for Mordecai, and the fury of the king has lain down.

8 On that day has King Ahasuerus given to Esther the queen the house of Haman, adversary of the Jews, and Mordecai has come in before the king, for Esther has declared what he [is] to her, **2** and the king turns aside his signet, that he has caused to pass away from Haman, and gives it to Mordecai, and Esther sets Mordecai over the house of Haman. **3** And Esther adds, and speaks before the king, and falls before his feet, and weeps, and makes supplication to him, to cause the evil of Haman the Agagite to pass away, and his scheme that he had devised against the Jews; **4** and the king holds out to Esther the golden scepter, and Esther rises, and stands before the king, **5** and says, "If to the king [it be] good, and if I have found grace before him, and the thing has been right before the king, and I [am] good in his eyes, let it be written to bring back the letters—a scheme of Haman son of Hammedatha the Agagite—that he wrote to destroy the Jews who [are] in all provinces of the king, **6** for how do I endure when I have looked on the evil that finds my people? And how do I endure when I have looked on the destruction of my family?" **7** And King Ahasuerus says to Esther the queen, and to Mordecai the Jew, "Behold, the house of Haman I have given to Esther, and him they have hanged on the tree, because that he put forth his hand on the Jews, **8** and you, write for the Jews, as [it is] good in your eyes, in the name of the king, and seal with the signet of the king—for the writing that is written in the name of the king, and

ESTHER

sealed with the signet of the king, there is none to turn back." **9** And the scribes of the king are called, at that time, in the third month—it [is] the month of Sivan—in the twenty-third [day] of it, and it is written, according to all that Mordecai has commanded, to the Jews, and to the lieutenants, and the governors, and the heads of the provinces, that [are] from Hodu even to Cush, one hundred twenty-seven provinces—province and province according to its writing, and people and people according to its tongue, and to the Jews according to their writing, and according to their tongue. **10** And he writes in the name of King Ahasuerus, and seals with the signet of the king, and sends letters by the hand of the runners with horses, riders of the dromedary, the mules, the young mares, **11** that the king has given to the Jews who [are] in each and every city, to be assembled, and to stand for their life, to cut off, to slay, and to destroy the whole force of the people and province who are distressing them, infants and women, and their spoil to seize. **12** In one day, in all the provinces of King Ahasuerus, on the thirteenth of the twelfth month—it [is] the month of Adar— **13** a copy of the writing to be made law in each and every province is revealed to all the peoples, and for the Jews being ready at this day to be avenged of their enemies. **14** The runners, riding on the dromedary, [and] the mules, have gone out, hurried and pressed by the word of the king, and the law has been given in Shushan the palace. **15** And Mordecai went out from before the king, in royal clothing of blue and white, and a great crown of gold, and a garment of fine linen and purple, and the city of Shushan has rejoiced and been glad; **16** to the Jews has been light, and gladness, and joy, and honor, **17** and in each and every province, and in each and every city, the place where the word of the king, even his law, is coming, gladness and joy [are] to the Jews, a banquet, and a good day; and many of the peoples of the land are becoming Jews, for a fear of the Jews has fallen on them.

9 And in the twelfth month—it [is] the month of Adar—on the thirteenth day of it, in which the word of the king, even his law, has come to be done, in the day that the enemies of the Jews had hoped to rule over them, and it is turned that the Jews rule over those hating them— **2** the Jews have been assembled in their cities, in all provinces of King Ahasuerus, to put forth a hand on those seeking their evil, and no man has stood in their presence, for their fear has fallen on all the peoples. **3** And all heads of the provinces, and the lieutenants, and the governors, and those doing the work that the king has, are lifting up the Jews, for a fear of Mordecai has fallen on them; **4** for great [is] Mordecai in the house of the king, and his fame is going into all the provinces, for the man Mordecai is going on and becoming great. **5** And the Jews strike among all their enemies—a striking of the sword, and slaughter, and destruction—and do with those hating them according to their pleasure, **6** and in Shushan the palace the Jews have slain and destroyed five hundred men; **7** and Parshandatha, and Dalphon, and Aspatha, **8** and Poratha, and Adalia, and Aridatha, **9** and Parmashta, and Arisai, and Aridai, and Vajezatha, **10** ten sons of Haman son of Hammedatha, adversary of the Jews, they have slain, and on the prey they have not put forth their hand. **11** On that day has come the number of the slain in Shushan the palace before the king, **12** and the king says to Esther the queen, "In Shushan the palace the Jews have slain and destroyed five hundred men, and the ten sons of Haman; in the rest of the provinces of the king what have they done? And what [is] your petition? And it is given to you; and what your request again? And it is done." **13** And Esther says, "If [it is] good to the king, let it also be given tomorrow, to the Jews who [are] in Shushan, to do according to the law of today; and the ten sons of Haman they hang on the tree." **14** And the king commands [for it] to be done so; and a law is given in Shushan, and they have hanged the ten sons of Haman. **15** And the Jews who [are] in Shushan are also assembled on the fourteenth day of the month of Adar, and they slay three hundred men in Shushan, and they have not put forth their hand on the prey. **16** And the rest of the Jews, who [are] in the provinces of the king, have been assembled, even to stand for their life, and to rest from their enemies, and to slay seventy-five thousand among those hating them, and they have not put forth their hand on the prey; **17** on the thirteenth day of the month of Adar, even to rest on the fourteenth of it, and to

ESTHER

make it a day of banquet and of joy. **18** And the Jews who [are] in Shushan have been assembled, on the thirteenth day of it, and on the fourteenth of it, even to rest on the fifteenth of it, and to make it a day of banquet and of joy. **19** Therefore the Jews of the open places, who are dwelling in cities of the open places, are making the fourteenth day of the month of Adar—joy and banquet, and a good day, of sending portions to one another. **20** And Mordecai writes these things, and sends letters to all the Jews who [are] in all provinces of King Ahasuerus, who are near and who are far off, **21** to establish on them, to be keeping the fourteenth day of the month of Adar, and the fifteenth day of it, in every year and year, **22** as days on which the Jews have rested from their enemies, and the month that has been turned to them from sorrow to joy, and from mourning to a good day, to make them days of banquet and of joy, and of sending portions to one another, and gifts to the needy. **23** And the Jews have received that which they had begun to do, and that which Mordecai has written to them, **24** because Haman son of Hammedatha the Agagite, adversary of all the Jews, had devised concerning the Jews to destroy them, and had caused to fall Pur—that [is] the lot—to crush them and to destroy them; **25** and in her coming in before the king, he commanded with the letter, "Let his evil scheme that he devised against the Jews return on his own head," and they have hanged him and his sons on the tree, **26** therefore they have called these days Purim—by the name of the lot—therefore, because of all the words of this letter, and what they have seen concerning this, and what has come to them, **27** the Jews have established and received on them, and on their seed, and on all those joined to them, and it does not pass away, to be keeping these two days according to their writing, and according to their season, in every year and year; **28** and these days are remembered and kept in every generation and generation, family and family, province and province, and city and city, and these days of Purim do not pass away from the midst of the Jews, and their memorial is not ended from their seed. **29** And Esther the queen, daughter of Abihail, writes, and Mordecai the Jew, with all might, to establish this second letter of Purim, **30** and he sends letters to all the Jews, to the one hundred twenty-seven provinces of the kingdom of Ahasuerus—words of peace and truth— **31** to establish these days of Purim, in their seasons, as Mordecai the Jew has established on them, and Esther the queen, and as they had established on themselves, and on their seed—matters of the fastings, and of their cry. **32** And a saying of Esther has established these matters of Purim, and it is written in the Scroll.

10 And King Ahasuerus sets a tribute on the land and the islands of the sea; **2** and all the work of his strength, and his might, and the explanation of the greatness of Mordecai with which the king made him great, are they not written on the scroll of the Chronicles of Media and Persia? **3** For Mordecai the Jew [is] second to King Ahasuerus, and a great man of the Jews, and accepted of the multitude of his brothers, seeking good for his people, and speaking peace to all his seed.

JOB

1 There has been a man in the land of Uz—his name Job—and that man has been perfect and upright—both fearing God, and turning aside from evil. **2** And seven sons and three daughters are borne to him, **3** and his substance is seven thousand sheep, and three thousand camels, and five hundred pairs of oxen, and five hundred female donkeys, and a very abundant service; and that man is greater than any of the sons of the east. **4** And his sons have gone and made a banquet—the house of each [in] his day—and have sent and called to their three sisters to eat and to drink with them; **5** and it comes to pass, when they have gone around the days of the banquet, that Job sends and sanctifies them, and has risen early in the morning, and caused burnt-offerings to ascend—the number of them all—for Job said, "Perhaps my sons have sinned, yet blessed God in their heart." Thus Job does all the days. **6** And the day is, that sons of God come to station themselves by YHWH, and there also comes Satan in their midst. **7** And YHWH says to Satan, "Where do you come from?" And Satan answers YHWH and says, "From going to and fro in the land, and from walking up and down on it." **8** And YHWH says to Satan, "Have you set your heart against My servant Job because there is none like him in the land, a man perfect and upright, fearing God, and turning aside from evil?" **9** And Satan answers YHWH and says, "Is Job fearing God for nothing? **10** Have You not made a hedge for him, and for his house, and for all that he has—all around? **11** You have blessed the work of his hands, and his substance has spread in the land, and yet, put forth Your hand now, and strike against anything that he has—if not, he blesses You to Your face!" **12** And YHWH says to Satan, "Behold, all that he has [is] in your hand, only do not put forth your hand to him." And Satan goes out from the presence of YHWH. **13** And the day is, that his sons and his daughters are eating and drinking wine in the house of their brother, the firstborn. **14** And a messenger has come to Job and says, "The oxen have been plowing, and the female donkeys feeding by their sides, **15** and Sheba falls, and takes them, and they have struck the young men by the mouth of the sword, and I have escaped—only I alone—to declare [it] to you." **16** While this [one] is speaking another has also come and says, "Fire of God has fallen from the heavens, and burns among the flock, and among the young men, and consumes them, and I have escaped—only I alone—to declare [it] to you." **17** While this [one] is speaking another also has come and says, "Chaldeans made three heads, and rush on the camels, and take them, and they have struck the young men by the mouth of the sword, and I have escaped—only I alone—to declare [it] to you." **18** While this [one] is speaking another has also come and says, "Your sons and your daughters are eating, and drinking wine, in the house of their brother, the firstborn. **19** And behold, a great wind has come from over the wilderness, and strikes against the four corners of the house, and it falls on the young men, and they are dead, and I have escaped—only I alone—to declare [it] to you." **20** And Job rises, and tears his robe, and shaves his head, and falls to the earth, and pays respect, **21** and he says, "I came forth naked from the womb of my mother, ‖ And naked I return there. YHWH has given and YHWH has taken; Let the Name of YHWH be blessed." **22** In all this Job has not sinned, nor given folly to God.

2 And the day is, that sons of God come to station themselves by YHWH, and there also comes Satan in their midst to station himself by YHWH. **2** And YHWH says to Satan, "From where have you come?" And Satan answers YHWH and says, "From going to and fro in the land, and from walking up and down in it." **3** And YHWH says to Satan, "Have you set your heart to My servant Job because there is none like him in the land, a man perfect and upright, fearing God and turning aside from evil? And still he is keeping hold on his integrity, and you move Me against him to swallow him up for nothing!" **4** And Satan answers YHWH and says, "A skin for a skin, and all that a man has he gives for his life. **5** Yet, put forth Your hand now, and strike to his bone and to his flesh—if not, he blesses You to Your face!" **6** And YHWH says to

JOB

Satan, "Behold, he [is] in your hand; only take care of his life." **7** And Satan goes forth from the presence of YHWH, and strikes Job with a severe ulcer from the sole of his foot to his crown. **8** And he takes to him a potsherd to scrape himself with it, and he is sitting in the midst of the ashes. **9** And his wife says to him, "You are still keeping hold on your integrity: bless God and die." **10** And he says to her, "As one of the foolish women speaks, you speak; indeed, do we receive the good from God, and we do not receive the bad?" In all this Job has not sinned with his lips. **11** And three of the friends of Job hear of all this evil that has come on him, and they each come in from his place—Eliphaz the Temanite, and Bildad the Shuhite, and Zophar the Naamathite—and they have met together to come to bemoan him, and to comfort him; **12** and they lift up their eyes from afar and have not discerned him, and they lift up their voice and weep, and each tears his robe, and sprinkle dust on their heads—heavenward. **13** And they sit with him on the earth seven days and seven nights, and there is none speaking to him a word when they have seen that the pain has been very great.

3 After this Job has opened his mouth, and reviles his day. **2** And Job answers and says: **3** "Let the day perish in which I am born, ‖ And the night that has said: A man-child has been conceived. **4** That day—let it be darkness, ‖ Do not let God require it from above, ‖ Nor let light shine on it. **5** Let darkness and death-shade redeem it, ‖ Let a cloud dwell on it, ‖ Let them terrify it as the most bitter of days. **6** That night—let thick darkness take it, ‖ Let it not be united to days of the year, ‖ Let it not come into the number of months. **7** Behold! That night— let it be barren, ‖ Let no singing come into it. **8** Let the cursers of day mark it, ‖ Who are ready to wake up Leviathan. **9** Let the stars of its twilight be dark, ‖ Let it wait for light, and there is none, ‖ And let it not look on the eyelids of the dawn. **10** Because it has not shut the doors ‖ Of the womb that was mine! And hide misery from my eyes. **11** Why do I not die from the womb? I have come forth from the belly and gasp! **12** Why have knees been before me? And what [are] breasts, that I suck? **13** For now, I have lain down, and am quiet, I have slept—then there is rest to me, **14** With kings and counselors of earth, ‖ These building ruins for themselves. **15** Or with princes—they have gold, ‖ They are filling their houses [with] silver. **16** (Or I am not as a hidden abortion, ‖ As infants—they have not seen light.) **17** There the wicked have ceased troubling, ‖ And there the wearied rest in power. **18** Together prisoners have been at ease, ‖ They have not heard the voice of an exactor, **19** Small and great [are] the same there. And a servant [is] free from his lord. **20** Why does He give light to the miserable, and life to the bitter soul? **21** Who are waiting for death, and it is not, ‖ And they seek it above hid treasures. **22** Who are glad—to joy, ‖ They rejoice when they find a grave. **23** To a man whose way has been hidden, ‖ And whom God shuts up? **24** For before my food, my sighing comes, ‖ And my roarings [are] poured out as waters. **25** For I feared a fear and it meets me, ‖ And what I was afraid of comes to me. **26** I was not safe—nor was I quiet—Nor was I at rest—and trouble comes!"

4 And Eliphaz the Temanite answers and says: **2** "Has one tried a word with you? You are weary! And who is able to keep in words? **3** Behold, you have instructed many, ‖ And feeble hands you make strong. **4** Your words raise up the stumbling one, ‖ And you strengthen bowing knees. **5** But now, it comes to you, ‖ And you are weary; It strikes to you, and you are troubled. **6** Is your reverence not your confidence? Your hope—the perfection of your ways? **7** Now remember, ‖ Who, being innocent, has perished? And where have the upright been cut off? **8** As I have seen—plowers of iniquity, ‖ And sowers of misery, reap it! **9** From the breath of God they perish, ‖ And from the spirit of His anger [are] consumed. **10** The roaring of a lion, ‖ And the voice of a fierce lion, ‖ And teeth of young lions have been broken. **11** An old lion is perishing without prey, ‖ And the whelps of the lioness separate. **12** And a thing is secretly brought to me, ‖ And my ear receives a little of it. **13** In thoughts from visions of the night, ‖ In the falling of deep sleep on men, **14** Fear has met me, and trembling, ‖ And the multitude of my bones caused to fear. **15** And a spirit passes before my face, ‖ The hair of my flesh stands up; **16** It stands, and I do not discern its aspect, ‖ A likeness [is] before my eyes, ‖ Silence!

JOB

And I hear a voice: **17** Is mortal man more righteous than God? Is a man cleaner than his Maker? **18** Behold, He puts no credence in His servants, ‖ Nor sets praise in His messengers, **19** Also—the inhabitants of houses of clay ‖ (Whose foundation [is] in the dust, ‖ They bruise them before a moth). **20** From morning to evening are beaten down, ‖ Without any regarding, they perish forever. **21** Has their excellence not been removed with them? They die, and not in wisdom!"

5 "Pray, call, is there any to answer you? And to which of the holy ones do you turn? **2** For provocation slays the perverse, ‖ And envy puts to death the simple, **3** I have seen the perverse taking root, ‖ And I mark his habitation straight away, **4** His sons are far from safety, ‖ And they are bruised in the gate, ‖ And there is no deliverer. **5** Whose harvest the hungry eat, ‖ And even take it from the thorns, ‖ And the designing swallowed their wealth. **6** For sorrow does not come forth from the dust, ‖ Nor does misery spring up from the ground. **7** For man is born to misery, ‖ And the sparks go high to fly. **8** Yet I inquire for God, ‖ And for God I give my word, **9** Doing great things, and there is no searching. Wonderful, until there is no numbering. **10** Who is giving rain on the face of the land, ‖ And is sending waters on the out-places. **11** To set the low on a high place, ‖ And the mourners have been high [in] safety. **12** Making void thoughts of the cunning, ‖ And their hands do not execute wisdom. **13** Capturing the wise in their subtlety, ‖ And the counsel of wrestling ones was hurried, **14** By day they meet darkness, ‖ And as night—they grope at noon. **15** He saves the needy from the sword in their mouth, ‖ And from a strong hand, **16** And there is hope for the poor, ‖ And perverseness has shut her mouth. **17** Behold, the blessedness of mortal man, ‖ God reproves him: And do not despise the discipline of the Mighty, **18** For He pains, and He binds up, ‖ He strikes, and His hands heal. **19** In six distresses He delivers you, ‖ And in seven evil does not strike on you. **20** In famine He has redeemed you from death, ‖ And in battle from the hands of the sword. **21** When the tongue scourges you are hid, ‖ And you are not afraid of destruction, ‖ When it comes. **22** At destruction and at hunger you mock, ‖ And of the beast of the earth, ‖ You are not afraid. **23** (For with sons of the field [is] your covenant, ‖ And the beast of the field ‖ Has been at peace with you.) **24** And you have known that your tent [is] peace, ‖ And inspected your habitation, and do not err, **25** And have known that your seed [is] numerous, ‖ And your offspring as the herb of the earth; **26** You come in full age to the grave, ‖ As the going up of a stalk in its season. **27** Behold, this—we searched it out—it [is] right, listen; And you, know for yourself!"

6 And Job answers and says: **2** "O that my provocation were thoroughly weighed, ‖ And my calamity in balances ‖ They would lift up together! **3** For now it is heavier than the sands of the sea, ‖ Therefore my words have been rash. **4** For arrows of the Mighty [are] with me, ‖ Whose poison is drinking up my spirit. Terrors of God array themselves [for] me! **5** Does a wild donkey bray over tender grass? Does an ox low over his provender? **6** Is an insipid thing eaten without salt? Is there sense in the drivel of dreams? **7** My soul is refusing to touch! They [are] as my sickening food. **8** O that my request may come, ‖ That God may grant my hope! **9** That God would please—and bruise me, ‖ Loose His hand and cut me off! **10** And yet it is my comfort ‖ (And I exult in pain—He does not spare), ‖ That I have not hidden ‖ The sayings of the Holy One. **11** What [is] my power that I should hope? And what [is] my end that I should prolong my life? **12** Is my strength the strength of stones? Is my flesh bronze? **13** Is my help not with me, ‖ And substance driven from me? **14** To a despiser of his friends [is] shame, ‖ And the fear of the Mighty he forsakes. **15** My brothers have deceived as a brook, ‖ As a stream of brooks they pass away. **16** That are black because of ice, ‖ By them snow hides itself. **17** By the time they are warm they have been cut off, ‖ By its being hot they have been ‖ Extinguished from their place. **18** The paths turn aside of their way, ‖ They ascend into emptiness, and are lost. **19** Passengers of Tema looked expectingly, ‖ Travelers of Sheba hoped for them. **20** They were ashamed that one has trusted, ‖ They have come to it and are confounded. **21** Surely now you have become the same! You see a downfall, and are afraid. **22** Is it because I said, Give to me? And, By your power

JOB

bribe for me? **23** And, Deliver me from the hand of an adversary? And, Ransom me from the hand of terrible ones? **24** Show me, and I keep silent, ‖ And what I have erred, let me understand. **25** How powerful have been upright sayings, ‖ And what reproof from you reproves? **26** For reproof—do you reckon words? For wind—sayings of the desperate? **27** You cause anger to fall on the fatherless, ‖ And are strange to your friend. **28** And now, please, look on me, ‖ Even to your face do I lie? **29** Please turn back, let it not be perverseness, ‖ Indeed, turn back again— my righteousness [is] in it. **30** Is there perverseness in my tongue? Does my palate not discern calamity?"

7 "Is there not warfare to man on earth? And his days as the days of a hired worker? **2** As a servant desires the shadow, ‖ And as a hired worker expects his wage, **3** So I have been caused to inherit months of vanity, ‖ And they numbered nights of misery to me. **4** If I lay down, then I have said, When do I rise, ‖ And evening has been measured? And I have been full of tossings until dawn. **5** My flesh has been clothed [with] worms, ‖ And a clod of dust, ‖ My skin has been shriveled and is loathsome, **6** My days swifter than a loom, ‖ And they are consumed without hope. **7** Remember that my life [is] a breath, ‖ My eye does not turn back to see good. **8** The eye of my beholder does not behold me. Your eyes [are] on me—and I am not. **9** A cloud has been consumed, and it goes, ‖ So he who is going down to Sheol does not come up. **10** He does not turn to his house again, ‖ Nor does his place discern him again. **11** Also I do not withhold my mouth—I speak in the distress of my spirit, I talk in the bitterness of my soul. **12** Am I a sea [monster], or a dragon, ‖ That You set a watch over me? **13** When I said, My bed comforts me, ‖ In my talking He takes away my couch. **14** And You have frightened me with dreams, ‖ And You terrify me from visions, **15** And my soul chooses strangling, ‖ Death rather than my bones. **16** I have wasted away—I do not live for all time. Cease from me, for my days [are] vanity. **17** What [is] man that You magnify him? And that You set Your heart to him? **18** And inspect him in the mornings, ‖ [And] in the evenings try him? **19** How long do You not look from me? You do not desist until I swallow my spittle. **20** I have sinned, what do I do to You, ‖ O watcher of man? Why have You set me for a mark to You, ‖ And I am for a burden to myself—and what? **21** You do not take away my transgression, ‖ And [do not] cause my iniquity to pass away, ‖ Because now, I lie down in dust, ‖ And You have sought me— and I am not!"

8 And Bildad the Shuhite answers and says: **2** "Until when do you speak these things? And a strong wind—sayings of your mouth? **3** Does God pervert judgment? And does the Mighty One pervert justice? **4** If your sons have sinned before Him, ‖ And He sends them away, ‖ By the hand of their transgression, **5** If you seek for God early, ‖ And make supplication to the Mighty, **6** If you [are] pure and upright, ‖ Surely now He wakes for you, ‖ And has completed ‖ The habitation of your righteousness. **7** And your beginning has been small, ‖ And your latter end is very great. **8** For inquire, please, of a former generation, ‖ And prepare for a search of their fathers, **9** For we [are] of yesterday, and we do not know, ‖ For our days [are] a shadow on earth. **10** Do they not show you—speak to you, ‖ And from their heart bring forth words? **11** Does a rush rise without a marsh? A reed increase without water? **12** While it [is] in its budding—uncropped, ‖ Even before any herb it withers. **13** So [are] the paths of all forgetting God, ‖ And the hope of the profane perishes, **14** Whose confidence is loathsome, ‖ And the house of a spider his trust. **15** He leans on his house—and it does not stand, ‖ He takes hold on it—and it does not abide. **16** He [is] green before the sun, ‖ And over his garden his branch goes out. **17** His roots are wrapped by a heap, ‖ He looks for a house of stones. **18** If [one] destroys him from his place, ‖ Then it has feigned concerning him, ‖ I have not seen you! **19** Behold, this [is] the joy of His way, ‖ And from the dust others spring up. **20** Behold, God does not reject the perfect, ‖ Nor takes hold on the hand of evildoers. **21** While He fills your mouth with laughter, ‖ And your lips with shouting, **22** Those hating you put on shame, ‖ And the tent of the wicked is not!"

9 And Job answers and says: **2** "Truly I have known that [it is] so, ‖ But how is

JOB

man righteous with God? **3** If he delights to strive with Him—He does not answer him one of a thousand. **4** Wise in heart and strong in power—Who has hardened toward Him and is at peace? **5** Who is removing mountains, ‖ And they have not known, ‖ Who has overturned them in His anger. **6** Who is shaking earth from its place, ‖ And its pillars move themselves. **7** Who is commanding to the sun, and it does not rise, ‖ And the stars He seals up. **8** Stretching out the heavens by Himself, ‖ And treading on the heights of the sea, **9** Making the Great Bear, Orion, and the Pleiades, ‖ And the inner chambers of the south. **10** Doing great things until there is no searching, ‖ And wonderful, until there is no numbering. **11** Behold, He goes over by me, and I do not see, ‖ And He passes on, and I do not attend to it. **12** Behold, He snatches away, who brings it back? Who says to Him, What [are] You doing? **13** God does not turn back His anger, ‖ Proud helpers have bowed under Him. **14** How much less do I answer Him? Choose out my words with Him? **15** Whom, though I were righteous, I do not answer, ‖ For my judgment I make supplication. **16** Though I had called and He answers me, I do not believe that He gives ear [to] my voice. **17** Because He bruises me with a storm, ‖ And has multiplied my wounds for nothing. **18** He does not permit me to refresh my spirit, ‖ But fills me with bitter things. **19** If of power, behold, the Strong One; And if of judgment—who convenes me? **20** If I am righteous, my mouth declares me wicked; [If] I am perfect, it declares me perverse. **21** I am perfect; I do not know my soul, I despise my life. **22** It is the same thing, therefore I said, ‖ He is consuming the perfect and the wicked. **23** If a scourge puts to death suddenly, He laughs at the trial of the innocent. **24** Earth has been given ‖ Into the hand of the wicked. He covers the faces of her judges, ‖ If not—where, who [is] he? **25** My days have been swifter than a runner, ‖ They have fled, they have not seen good, **26** They have passed on with ships of reed, ‖ As an eagle darts on food. **27** Though I say, I forget my talking, ‖ I forsake my corner, and I brighten up! **28** I have been afraid of all my griefs, ‖ I have known that You do not acquit me. **29** I become wicked; why [is] this? I labor [in] vain. **30** If I have washed myself with snow-water, ‖ And purified my hands with soap, **31** Then You dip me in corruption, ‖ And my garments have detested me. **32** But if a man like myself—I answer Him, ‖ We come together into judgment. **33** If there were a mediator between us, ‖ He places his hand on us both. **34** He turns aside His rod from off me, ‖ And His terror does not make me afraid, **35** I speak, and do not fear Him, but I am not right with myself."

10 "My soul has been weary of my life, I leave off my talking to myself, I speak in the bitterness of my soul. **2** I say to God, Do not condemn me, ‖ Let me know why You strive [with] me. **3** Is it good for You that You oppress? That You despise the labor of Your hands, ‖ And shine on the counsel of the wicked? **4** Do you have eyes of flesh? Do You see as man sees? **5** [Are] Your days as the days of man? Your years as the days of a man? **6** That You inquire for my iniquity, ‖ And seek for my sin? **7** For You know that I am not wicked, ‖ And there is no deliverer from Your hand. **8** Your hands have taken pains about me, ‖ And they make me together all around, ‖ And You swallow me up! **9** Please remember ‖ That You have made me as clay, ‖ And You bring me back to dust. **10** Do You not pour me out as milk? And curdle me as cheese? **11** Skin and flesh You put on me, ‖ And fence me with bones and sinews. **12** Life and kindness You have done with me. And Your inspection has preserved my spirit. **13** And these You have laid up in Your heart, I have known that this [is] with You. **14** If I sinned, then You have observed me, ‖ And do not acquit me from my iniquity, **15** If I have done wickedly—woe to me, ‖ And righteously—I do not lift up my head, ‖ Full of shame—then see my affliction, **16** And it rises—as a lion You hunt me. And You turn back—You show Yourself wonderful in me. **17** You renew Your witnesses against me, and multiply Your anger with me, ‖ Changes and warfare [are] with me. **18** And why from the womb ‖ Have You brought me forth? I expire, and the eye does not see me. **19** I am as [if] I had not been, ‖ I am brought from the belly to the grave, **20** Are my days not few? Cease then, and put from me, ‖ And I brighten up a little, **21** Before I go, and do not return, ‖ To a land of darkness and death-shade, **22** A land of obscurity as thick darkness, ‖ Death-shade—and no order, ‖ And the shining [is] as thick darkness."

11 And Zophar the Naamathite answers and says: **2** "Is a multitude of words not answered? And is a man of lips justified? **3** Your boastings make men keep silent, ‖ You scorn, and none is causing blushing! **4** And you say, My discourse [is] pure, ‖ And I have been clean in Your eyes. **5** And yet, O that God had spoken! And opens His lips with you. **6** And declares to you secrets of wisdom, for counsel has foldings. And know that God forgets of your iniquity for you. **7** Do you find out God by searching? To perfection find out the Mighty One? **8** Heights of the heavens—what [can] you do? Deeper than Sheol—what [can] you know? **9** Its measure [is] longer than earth, and broader than the sea. **10** If He passes on, and shuts up, and assembles, ‖ Who then reverses it? **11** For He has known men of vanity, ‖ And He sees iniquity, ‖ And one does not consider [it]! **12** And empty man is bold, ‖ And man is born [as] the colt of a wild donkey. **13** If you have prepared your heart, ‖ And have spread out your hands to Him, **14** If iniquity [is] in your hand, put it far off, ‖ And do not let perverseness dwell in your tents. **15** For then you lift up your face from blemish, ‖ And you have been firm, and do not fear. **16** For you forget misery, ‖ As waters passed away you remember. **17** And age rises above the noon, ‖ You fly—you are as the morning. **18** And you have trusted because there is hope, ‖ And searched—in confidence you lie down, **19** And you have rested, ‖ And none is causing trembling, ‖ And many have begged [at] your face; **20** And the eyes of the wicked are consumed, ‖ And refuge has perished from them, ‖ And their hope [is] a breathing out of soul!"

12 And Job answers and says: **2** "Truly—you [are] the people, and wisdom dies with you. **3** I also have a heart like you, I am not fallen more than you, ‖ And with whom is there not like these? **4** I am a laughter to his friend: He calls to God, and He answers him, ‖ A laughter [is] the perfect righteous one. **5** A torch—despised in the thoughts of the secure ‖ Is prepared for those sliding with the feet. **6** The tents of spoilers are at peace, ‖ And those provoking God have confidence, ‖ Into whose hand God has brought. **7** And yet, now ask [one of] the beasts, ‖ And it shows you, ‖ And a bird of the heavens, ‖ And it declares to you. **8** Or talk to the earth, and it shows you, ‖ And fishes of the sea recount to you: **9** Who has not known in all these, ‖ That the hand of Y$_{HWH}$ has done this? **10** In whose hand [is] the breath of every living thing, ‖ And the spirit of all flesh of man. **11** Does the ear not try words? And the palate taste food for itself? **12** With the very aged [is] wisdom, ‖ And [with] length of days [is] understanding. **13** With Him [are] wisdom and might, ‖ To Him [are] counsel and understanding. **14** Behold, He breaks down, and it is not built up, ‖ He shuts against a man, ‖ And it is not opened. **15** Behold, He keeps in the waters, and they are dried up, ‖ And He sends them forth, ‖ And they overturn the land. **16** With Him [are] strength and wisdom, ‖ His the deceived and deceiver. **17** Causing counselors to go away [as] a spoil, ‖ Indeed, He makes fools of judges. **18** He has opened the bands of kings, ‖ And He binds a girdle on their loins. **19** Causing ministers to go away [as] a spoil ‖ And strong ones He overthrows. **20** Turning aside the lip of the steadfast, ‖ And the reason of the aged He takes away. **21** Pouring contempt on princes, ‖ And the girdle of the mighty He made feeble. **22** Removing deep things out of darkness, ‖ And He brings out to light death-shade. **23** Magnifying the nations, and He destroys them, ‖ Spreading out the nations, and He quiets them. **24** Turning aside the heart ‖ Of the heads of the people of the land, ‖ And He causes them to wander ‖ In vacancy—no way! **25** They feel darkness, and not light, ‖ He causes them to wander as a drunkard."

13 "Behold, my eye has seen all, ‖ My ear has heard, and it attends to it. **2** According to your knowledge I have known—also I. I am not more fallen than you. **3** Yet I speak for the Mighty One, ‖ And I delight to argue for God. **4** And yet, you [are] forgers of falsehood, ‖ Physicians of nothing—all of you, **5** O that you would keep perfectly silent, ‖ And it would be to you for wisdom. **6** Please hear my argument, ‖ And attend to the pleadings of my lips, **7** Do you speak perverseness for God? And do you speak deceit for Him? **8** Do you accept His face, if you strive for God? **9** Is [it] good that He searches you, ‖

JOB

If, as one mocks at a man, you mock at Him? **10** He surely reproves you, if you accept faces in secret. **11** Does His excellence not terrify you? And His dread fall on you? **12** Your remembrances [are] allegories of ashes, ‖ For high places of clay [are] your heights. **13** Keep silent from me, and I speak, ‖ And pass over me what will. **14** Why do I take my flesh in my teeth? And my soul put in my hand? **15** Behold, He slays me—I do not wait! Only, I argue my ways to His face. **16** Also—He [is] to me for salvation, ‖ For the profane do not come before Him. **17** Hear my word diligently, ‖ And my declaration with your ears. **18** Now behold, I have set the cause in order, ‖ I have known that I am righteous. **19** Who [is] he that strives with me? For now I keep silent and gasp. **20** Only two things, O God, do with me, ‖ Then I am not hidden from Your face: **21** Put Your hand far off from me, ‖ And do not let Your terror terrify me. **22** And You call, and I answer, ‖ Or—I speak, and You answer me. **23** How many iniquities and sins do I have? Let me know my transgression and my sin. **24** Why do You hide Your face? And reckon me for an enemy to You? **25** Do You terrify a leaf driven away? And do You pursue the dry stubble? **26** For You write bitter things against me, ‖ And cause me to possess iniquities of my youth, **27** And you put my feet in the stocks, ‖ And observe all my paths—You set a print on the roots of my feet, **28** And he, as a rotten thing, wears away, ‖ A moth has consumed him as a garment."

14 "Man, born of woman! Of few days, and full of trouble! **2** As a flower he has gone forth, and is cut off, ‖ And he flees as a shadow and does not stand. **3** Also—on this You have opened Your eyes, and bring me into judgment with You. **4** Who gives a clean thing out of an unclean? Not one. **5** If his days are determined, ‖ The number of his months [are] with You, ‖ You have made his limit, ‖ And he does not pass over; **6** Look away from off him that he may cease, ‖ Until he enjoy as a hired worker his day. **7** For there is hope for a tree, if it is cut down, ‖ That it changes again, ‖ That its tender branch does not cease. **8** If its root becomes old in the earth, ‖ And its stem dies in the dust, **9** From the fragrance of water it flourishes, ‖ And has made a crop as a plant. **10** And a man dies, and becomes weak, ‖ And man expires, and where [is] he? **11** Waters have gone away from a sea, ‖ And a river becomes waste and dry. **12** And man has lain down, and does not rise, ‖ Until the wearing out of the heavens they do not awaken, ‖ Nor are roused from their sleep. **13** O that You would conceal me in Sheol, ‖ Hide me until the turning of Your anger, ‖ Set a limit for me, and remember me. **14** If a man dies—does he revive? All [the] days of my warfare I wait, until my change comes. **15** You call, and I answer You; To the work of Your hands You have desire. **16** But now, You number my steps, ‖ You do not watch over my sin. **17** My transgression [is] sealed up in a bag, and You sew up my iniquity. **18** And yet, a falling mountain wastes away, and a rock is removed from its place. **19** Waters have worn away stones, ‖ Their outpourings wash away the dust of earth, ‖ And You have destroyed the hope of man. **20** You prevail [over] him forever, and he goes, ‖ He is changing his countenance, ‖ And You send him away. **21** His sons are honored, and he does not know; And they are little, and he does not attend to them. **22** Only—his flesh is pained for him, ‖ And his soul mourns for him."

15 And Eliphaz the Temanite answers and says: **2** "Does a wise man answer [with] vain knowledge? And fill his belly [with] an east wind? **3** To reason with a word not useful? And speeches—no profit in them? **4** Indeed, you make reverence void, and diminish meditation before God. **5** For your mouth teaches your iniquity, ‖ And you choose the tongue of the cunning. **6** Your mouth declares you wicked, and not I, ‖ And your lips testify against you. **7** Are you the first man born? And were you formed before the heights? **8** Do you hear of the secret counsel of God? And withdraw wisdom to you? **9** What have you known, and we do not know? [What] do you understand, and it is not with us? **10** Both the gray-headed ‖ And the very aged [are] among us—Greater than your father [in] days. **11** Are the comforts of God too few for you? And a gentle word [is] with you, **12** Why does your heart take you away? And why are your eyes high? **13** Do you turn your spirit against God? And have brought out words from your mouth: **14** What [is] man that he is pure, ‖ And that he is righteous, one born of woman? **15** Behold, He puts no credence in His holy ones, ‖ And the heavens have not been pure in His eyes. **16** Also—surely abominable and filthy ‖ Is man drinking perverseness as water. **17** I show you—listen to me—And this I have seen and declare, **18** Which the wise declare—And have not hid—from their fathers. **19** To them alone was the land given, ‖ And a stranger did not pass over into their midst: **20** All [the] days of the wicked he is paining himself, ‖ And few years have been laid up for the terrible one. **21** A fearful voice [is] in his ears, ‖ In peace a destroyer comes to him. **22** He does not believe to return from darkness, ‖ And he watches for the sword. **23** He is wandering for bread: Where [is] it? He has known that ready at his hand ‖ Is a day of darkness. **24** Adversity and distress terrify him, ‖ They prevail over him as a king ready for a boaster. **25** For he stretched out his hand against God, ‖ And against the Mighty he makes himself mighty. **26** He runs to Him with a neck, ‖ With thick bosses of his shields. **27** For he has covered his face with his fat, ‖ And makes vigor over [his] confidence. **28** And he inhabits cities cut off, houses not dwelt in, ‖ That have been ready to become heaps. **29** He is not rich, nor does his wealth rise, ‖ Nor does he stretch out their continuance on earth. **30** He does not turn aside from darkness, ‖ A flame dries up his tender branch, ‖ And he turns aside at the breath of His mouth! **31** Do not let him put credence in vanity, ‖ He has been deceived, ‖ For vanity is his exchange. **32** It is not completed in his day, ‖ And his bending branch is not green. **33** He shakes off his unripe fruit as a vine, ‖ And casts off his blossom as an olive. **34** For the company of the profane [is] barren, ‖ And fire has consumed tents of bribery. **35** To conceive misery, and to bear iniquity, ‖ Even their heart prepares deceit."

16 And Job answers and says: **2** "I have heard many such things, ‖ Miserable comforters [are] you all. **3** Is there an end to words of wind? Or what emboldens you that you answer? **4** I also, like you, might speak, ‖ If your soul were in my soul's stead. I might join against you with words, ‖ And nod at you with my head. **5** I might harden you with my mouth, ‖ And the moving of my lips might be sparing. **6** If I speak, my pain is not restrained, ‖ And I cease—what goes from me? **7** Only, now, it has wearied me; You have desolated all my company, **8** And You loathe me, ‖ For it has been a witness, ‖ And my failure rises up against me, ‖ It testifies in my face. **9** His anger has torn, and He hates me, ‖ He has gnashed at me with His teeth, ‖ My adversary sharpens His eyes for me. **10** They have gaped on me with their mouth, ‖ In reproach they have struck my cheeks, ‖ Together they set themselves against me. **11** God shuts me up to the perverse, ‖ And turns me over to the hands of the wicked. **12** I have been at ease, and He breaks me, ‖ And He has laid hold on my neck, ‖ And He breaks me in pieces, ‖ And He raises me to Him for a mark. **13** His archers go around against me. He split my reins, and does not spare, ‖ He pours out my gall to the earth. **14** He breaks me—breach on breach, ‖ He runs on me as a mighty one. **15** I have sewed sackcloth on my skin, ‖ And have rolled my horn in the dust. **16** My face is foul with weeping, ‖ And on my eyelids [is] death-shade. **17** Not for violence in my hands, ‖ And my prayer [is] pure. **18** O earth, do not cover my blood! And let there not be a place for my cry. **19** Also, now, behold, my witness [is] in the heavens, ‖ And my testifier in the high places. **20** My interpreter [is] my friend, ‖ My eye has dropped to God; **21** And He reasons for a man with God, ‖ As a son of man for his friend. **22** When a few years come, ‖ Then I go [on] the path of no return."

17 "My spirit has been destroyed, ‖ My days extinguished—graves [are] for me. **2** If not—mockeries [are] with me. And my eye lodges in their provocations. **3** Now place my pledge with You; Who is he that strikes hand with me? **4** For You have hidden their heart from understanding, ‖ Therefore You do not exalt them. **5** For a portion he shows friendship, ‖ And the eyes of his sons are consumed. **6** And He set me up for a proverb of the peoples, ‖ And I am a wonder before them. **7** And my eye is dim from sorrow, ‖ And my members—all of them—as a shadow. **8** The upright are astonished at this, and the innocent stirs himself up against the profane. **9** And the righteous lays hold [on] his way, ‖ And the clean of hands adds strength. **10** But please return and come in, all of you, ‖ And I do not find a wise man among you. **11** My days have passed by, ‖ My plans have been broken off, ‖ The possessions of my heart! **12** They appoint night for day, ‖ Light [is] near because of darkness. **13** If I wait—Sheol [is] my house, ‖ In darkness I have spread out my bed. **14** To corruption I have called: You [are] my father. To the worm: My mother and my sister. **15** And where [is] my hope now? Indeed, my hope, who beholds it? **16** You go down [to] the parts of Sheol, ‖ If we may rest together on the dust."

18 And Bildad the Shuhite answers and says: **2** "When do you set an end to words? Consider, and afterward we speak. **3** Why have we been reckoned as livestock? We have been defiled in your eyes! **4** He is tearing himself in his anger. Is earth forsaken for your sake? And is a rock removed from its place? **5** Also, the light of the wicked is extinguished. And there does not shine a spark of his fire. **6** The light has been dark in his tent, ‖ And his lamp over him is extinguished. **7** The steps of his strength are restricted, ‖ And his own counsel casts him down. **8** For he is sent into a net by his own feet, ‖ And he habitually walks on a snare. **9** A trap seizes on the heel, ‖ The designing prevails over him. **10** His cord is hidden in the earth, ‖ And his trap on the path. **11** Terrors have terrified him all around, ‖ And they have scattered him—at his feet. **12** His sorrow is hungry, ‖ And calamity is ready at his side. **13** It consumes the parts of his skin, ‖ Death's firstborn consumes his parts. **14** His confidence is drawn from his tent, ‖ And it causes him to step to the king of terrors. **15** It dwells in his tent—out of his provender, ‖ Sulfur is scattered over his habitation. **16** From beneath his roots are dried up, ‖ And from above his crop is cut off. **17** His memorial has perished from the land, ‖ And he has no name on the street. **18** They thrust him from light to darkness, ‖ And cast him out from the habitable earth. **19** He has no continuator, ‖ Nor successor among his people, ‖ And none is remaining in his dwellings. **20** At this day, those [in the] west have been astonished, ‖ And those [in the] east have taken fright. **21** Only these [are] dwelling places of the perverse, ‖ And this [is] the place God has not known."

19 And Job answers and says: **2** "Until when do you afflict my soul, ‖ And bruise me with words? **3** These ten times you put me to shame, you do not blush. You make yourselves strange to me— **4** And also—truly, I have erred, ‖ My error remains with me. **5** If, truly, you magnify yourselves over me, ‖ And decide my reproach against me; **6** Know now, that God turned me upside down, ‖ And has set around His net against me, **7** Behold, I cry out—violence, and am not answered, I cry aloud, and there is no judgment. **8** He hedged up my way, and I do not pass over, ‖ And He places darkness on my paths. **9** He has stripped my honor from off me, ‖ And He turns the crown from my head. **10** He breaks me down all around, and I go, ‖ And removes my hope like a tree. **11** And He kindles His anger against me, ‖ And reckons me to Him as His adversaries. **12** His troops come in together, ‖ And they raise up their way against me, ‖ And encamp around my tent. **13** He has put my brothers far off from me, ‖ And my acquaintances have surely been estranged from me. **14** My neighbors have ceased ‖ And my familiar friends have forgotten me, **15** Sojourners of my house and my maids, ‖ Reckon me for a stranger; I have been an alien in their eyes. **16** I have called to my servant, ‖ And he does not answer, ‖ With my mouth I make supplication to him. **17** My spirit is strange to my wife, ‖ And my favors to the sons of my [mother's] womb. **18** Also sucklings have despised me, I rise, and they speak against me. **19** All the men of my counsel detest me, ‖ And those I have loved, ‖ Have been turned against me. **20** To my skin and to my flesh ‖ My bone has cleaved, ‖ And I deliver myself with the skin of my teeth. **21** Pity me, pity me, you my friends, ‖ For the hand of God has struck against me. **22** Why do you pursue me as God? And are not satisfied with my flesh? **23** Who grants now, that my words may be written? Who grants that they may be inscribed in a scroll? **24** With a pen of iron and lead— They may be hewn in a rock forever. **25** That—I have known my Redeemer, ‖ The Living and the Last, ‖ For He raises the dust. **26** And after my skin has surrounded this [body], ‖ Then from my flesh I see God— **27** Whom I see on my side, ‖ And my eyes have beheld, and not a stranger, ‖ My reins have been consumed in my

JOB

bosom. **28** But you say, Why do we pursue after him? And the root of the matter has been found in me. **29** Be afraid because of the sword, ‖ For the punishments of the sword [are] furious, ‖ That you may know that [there is] a judgment."

20 And Zophar the Naamathite answers and says: **2** "Therefore my thoughts cause me to answer, ‖ And because of my sensations in me. **3** I hear the discipline of my shame, ‖ And the spirit of my understanding causes me to answer: **4** Have you known this from antiquity? Since the placing of man on earth? **5** That the singing of the wicked [is] short, ‖ And the joy of the profane for a moment, **6** Though his excellence goes up to the heavens, ‖ He strikes his head against a cloud— **7** He perishes as his own dung forever, ‖ His beholders say, Where [is] he? **8** He flees as a dream, and they do not find him, ‖ And he is driven away as a vision of the night, **9** The eye has not seen him, and does not add. And his place does not behold him again. **10** His sons oppress the poor, ‖ And his hands give back his wealth. **11** His bones have been full of his youth, and it lies down with him on the dust. **12** Though he sweetens evil in his mouth, hides it under his tongue, **13** has pity on it, and does not forsake it, and keeps it back in the midst of his palate, **14** his food is turned in his bowels, the bitterness of cobras [is] in his heart. **15** He has swallowed wealth, and vomits it. God drives it out from his belly. **16** He sucks [the] gall of cobras, the tongue of a viper slays him. **17** He does not look on streams, ‖ Flowing of brooks of honey and butter. **18** He is giving back [what] he labored for, and does not consume [it]; As a bulwark [is] his exchange, and he does not exult. **19** For he oppressed—he forsook the poor, ‖ He has taken a house away violently, ‖ And he does not build it. **20** For he has not known ease in his belly. With his desirable thing he does not deliver himself. **21** There is not a remnant to his food, ‖ Therefore his good does not stay. **22** In the fullness of his sufficiency he is constricted. Every perverse hand meets him. **23** It comes to pass, at the filling of his belly, ‖ He sends forth against him ‖ The fierceness of His anger, ‖ Indeed, He rains on him in his eating. **24** He flees from an iron weapon, ‖ A bow of bronze passes through him. **25** One has drawn, ‖ And it comes out from the body, ‖ And a glittering weapon proceeds from his gall. Terrors [are] on him. **26** All darkness is hid for his treasures, ‖ A fire not blown consumes him, ‖ The remnant is broken in his tent. **27** The heavens reveal his iniquity, ‖ And earth is raising itself against him. **28** The increase of his house is removed, ‖ Poured forth in a day of His anger. **29** This [is] the portion of a wicked man from God. And an inheritance appointed him by God."

21 And Job answers and says: **2** "Hear my word diligently, ‖ And this is your consolation. **3** Bear with me, and I speak, ‖ And after my speaking—you may deride. **4** [Is] my complaint [against] man? And if [so], why may my temper not become short? **5** Turn to me, and be astonished, ‖ And put hand to mouth. **6** Indeed, if I have remembered, then I have been troubled. And my flesh has taken fright. **7** Why do the wicked live? They have become old, ‖ Indeed, they have been mighty in wealth. **8** Their seed is established, ‖ Before their face with them, ‖ And their offspring before their eyes. **9** Their houses [are] peace without fear, ‖ Nor [is] a rod of God on them. **10** His bullock breeds without fail. His cow brings forth safely, and does not miscarry. **11** They send forth their sucklings as a flock, ‖ And their children skip, **12** They lift [themselves] up at timbrel and harp, ‖ And rejoice at the sound of a pipe. **13** They wear out their days in good, ‖ And in a moment go down [to] Sheol. **14** And they say to God, Turn aside from us, ‖ And the knowledge of Your ways ‖ We have not desired. **15** What [is] the Mighty One that we serve Him? And what do we profit when we meet with Him? **16** Behold, their good [is] not in their hand ‖ (The counsel of the wicked ‖ Has been far from me). **17** How often is the lamp of the wicked extinguished, ‖ And their calamity comes on them? He apportions pangs in His anger. **18** They are as straw before wind, ‖ And as chaff a windstorm has stolen away, **19** God lays up for his sons his sorrow, ‖ He gives repayment to him—and he knows. **20** His own eyes see his destruction, ‖ And he drinks of the wrath of the Mighty. **21** For what [is] his delight in his house after him, ‖ And the number of his months cut off? **22** Does [one] teach knowledge to God, ‖ Since He judges [those] on high? **23** This [one] dies in his

JOB

perfect strength, ‖ Wholly at ease and quiet. **24** His breasts have been full of milk, ‖ And marrow moistens his bones. **25** And this [one] dies with a bitter soul, ‖ And has not eaten with gladness. **26** Together they lie down on the dust, ‖ And the worm covers them over. **27** Behold, I have known your thoughts, ‖ And the schemes against me you do wrongfully. **28** For you say, Where [is] the house of the noble? And where the tent—the dwelling places of the wicked? **29** Have you not asked those passing by the way? And do you not know their signs? **30** That the wicked is spared to a day of calamity. They are brought to a day of wrath. **31** Who declares his way to his face? And [for] that which he has done, ‖ Who gives repayment to him? **32** And he is brought to the graves, ‖ And a watch is kept over the heap. **33** The clods of the valley have been sweet to him, ‖ And he draws every man after him, ‖ And there is no numbering before him. **34** And how do you comfort me [with] vanity, ‖ And trespass has been left in your answers?"

22 And Eliphaz the Temanite answers and says: **2** "Is a man profitable to God, ‖ Because a wise man is profitable to himself? **3** Is it a delight to the Mighty One ‖ That you are righteous? Is it gain, ‖ That you make your ways perfect? **4** Because of your reverence ‖ Does He reason [with] you? He enters with you into judgment: **5** Is your wickedness not abundant? And there is no end to your iniquities. **6** For you take a pledge of your brother for nothing, ‖ And you strip off the garments of the naked. **7** You do not cause the weary to drink water, ‖ And you withhold bread from the hungry. **8** As for the man of arm—he has the earth, ‖ And the accepted of face—he dwells in it. **9** You have sent widows away empty, ‖ And the arms of the fatherless are bruised. **10** Therefore snares [are] all around you, ‖ And sudden fear troubles you. **11** Or darkness—you do not see, ‖ And abundance of waters covers you. **12** Is God not high [in] the heavens? And see the summit of the stars, ‖ That they are high. **13** And you have said, How has God known? Does He judge through thickness? **14** Thick clouds [are] a secret place to Him, ‖ And He does not see, ‖ And He habitually walks [above] the circle of the heavens. **15** Do you observe the path of the age, ‖ That men of iniquity have trodden, **16** Who have been cut down unexpectedly? A flood is poured out on their foundation. **17** Those saying to God, Turn aside from us, ‖ And what does the Mighty One do to them? **18** And He has filled their houses [with] good (And the counsel of the wicked ‖ Has been far from me). **19** The righteous see and they rejoice, ‖ And the innocent mocks at them: **20** Surely our substance has not been cut off, ‖ And fire has consumed their excellence. **21** Now acquaint yourself with Him, and be at peace, ‖ Thereby your increase [is] good. **22** Please receive a law from His mouth, ‖ And set His sayings in your heart. **23** If you return to the Mighty you are built up, ‖ You put iniquity far from your tents. **24** So as to set a defense on the dust, ‖ And a covering on a rock of the valleys. **25** And the Mighty has been your defense, ‖ And silver [is] strength to you. **26** For then you delight yourself on the Mighty, ‖ And lift up your face to God, **27** You make supplication to Him, ‖ And He hears you, ‖ And you complete your vows. **28** And you decree a saying, ‖ And it is established to you, ‖ And light has shone on your ways. **29** For they have made low, ‖ And you say, Lift up. And He saves the bowed down of eyes. **30** He delivers the one [who is] not innocent, ‖ Indeed, he has been delivered ‖ By the cleanness of your hands."

23 And Job answers and says: **2** "Also—today my complaint [is] bitter, ‖ My hand has been heavy because of my sighing. **3** O that I had known—and I find Him, ‖ I come to His seat, **4** I arrange the cause before Him, ‖ And fill my mouth [with] arguments. **5** I know the words He answers me, ‖ And understand what He says to me. **6** Does He strive with me in the abundance of power? No! Surely He puts [it] in me. **7** There the upright reason with Him, ‖ And I escape from mine who is judging—forever. **8** Behold, I go forward—and He is not, ‖ And backward—and I do not perceive Him. **9** [To] the left in His working—and I do not see, ‖ He is covered [on] the right, and I do not behold. **10** For He has known the way with me, ‖ He has tried me—I go forth as gold. **11** My foot has laid hold on His step, ‖ I have kept His way, and do not turn aside, **12** The command of His lips, and I do not depart. I have laid up above my allotted portion ‖ The sayings of His mouth. **13** And He [is] in

JOB

one [mind], ‖ And who turns Him back? And His soul has desired—and He does [it]. **14** For He completes my portion, ‖ And many such things [are] with Him. **15** Therefore, I am troubled at His presence, I consider, and am afraid of Him. **16** And God has made my heart soft, ‖ And the Mighty has troubled me. **17** For I have not been cut off before darkness, ‖ And before me He covered thick darkness."

24 "For this reason from the Mighty One ‖ Times have not been hidden, ‖ And those knowing Him have not seen His days. **2** They reach the borders, ‖ They have taken a drove away violently, ‖ Indeed, they do evil. **3** They lead away the donkey of the fatherless, ‖ They take in pledge the ox of the widow, **4** They turn aside the needy from the way, ‖ Together have hid the poor of the earth. **5** Behold, wild donkeys in a wilderness, ‖ They have gone out about their work, ‖ Seeking early for prey, ‖ A mixture for himself—food for young ones. **6** They reap his provender in a field, ‖ And they glean the vineyard of the wicked. **7** They cause the naked to lodge without clothing. And there is no covering in the cold. **8** From the inundation of hills they are wet, ‖ And without a refuge—have embraced a rock. **9** They take away violently ‖ The orphan from the breast, ‖ And they lay a pledge on the poor. **10** Naked, they have gone without clothing, ‖ And hungry—have taken away a sheaf. **11** They make oil between their walls, ‖ They have trodden winepresses, and thirst. **12** Men groan because of enmity, ‖ And the soul of pierced ones cries, ‖ And God does not give praise. **13** They have been those rebelling against light, ‖ They have not discerned His ways, ‖ Nor abided in His paths. **14** The murderer rises at the light, ‖ He slays the poor and needy, ‖ And in the night he is as a thief. **15** And the eye of an adulterer ‖ Has observed the twilight, ‖ Saying, No eye beholds me. And he puts the face in secret. **16** He has dug in the darkness—houses; By day they shut themselves up, ‖ They have not known light. **17** When together, morning [is] death-shade to them, ‖ When he discerns the terrors of death-shade. **18** He [is] light on the face of the waters, ‖ Their portion is vilified in the earth, ‖ He does not turn the way of vineyards. **19** Drought—also heat—consume snow-waters, ‖ Sheol— [those who] have sinned. **20** The womb forgets him, ‖ The worm sweetens [on] him, ‖ He is remembered no more, ‖ And wickedness is broken as a tree. **21** Treating evil the barren [who] does not bear, ‖ And he does no good [to] the widow, **22** And [God] has drawn the mighty by His power, ‖ He rises, and none believes in life. **23** He gives to him confidence, and he is supported, ‖ And His eyes [are] on their ways. **24** They were high [for] a little, and they are not, ‖ And they have been brought low. They are shut up as all [others], ‖ And cut off as the head of an ear of grain. **25** And if not now, who proves me a liar, ‖ And makes my word of nothing?"

25 And Bildad the Shuhite answers and says: **2** "The rule and fear [are] with Him, ‖ Making peace in His high places. **3** Is their [any] number to His troops? And on whom does His light not arise? **4** And what? Is man righteous with God? And what? Is he pure—born of a woman? **5** Behold—to the moon, and it does not shine, ‖ And stars have not been pure in His eyes. **6** How much less man—a grub, ‖ And the son of man—a worm!"

26 And Job answers and says: **2** "How you have helped the powerless, ‖ Saved an arm not strong! **3** How you have given counsel to the unwise, ‖ And made known wise plans in abundance. **4** With whom have you declared words? And whose breath came forth from you? **5** The Rephaim are formed, ‖ Also their inhabitants beneath the waters. **6** Sheol [is] naked before Him, ‖ And there is no covering to destruction. **7** Stretching out the north over desolation, ‖ Hanging the earth on nothing, **8** Binding up the waters in His thick clouds, ‖ And the cloud is not burst under them. **9** Taking hold of the face of the throne, ‖ Spreading His cloud over it. **10** He has placed a limit on the waters, ‖ To the boundary of light with darkness. **11** Pillars of the heavens tremble, ‖ And they wonder because of His rebuke. **12** By His power He has quieted the sea, ‖ And by His understanding struck the proud. **13** He beautified the heavens by His Spirit, ‖ His hand has formed the fleeing serpent. **14** Behold, these [are] the borders of His way, and how little a matter is heard of Him, and who understands the thunder of His might?"

JOB

27 And Job adds to lift up his allegory and says: **2** "God lives! He turned aside my judgment, ‖ And the Mighty—He made my soul bitter. **3** For all the while my breath [is] in me, ‖ And the wind of God in my nostrils. **4** My lips do not speak perverseness, ‖ And my tongue does not utter deceit. **5** Defilement to me—if I justify you, ‖ Until I expire I do not turn aside my integrity from me. **6** On my righteousness I have laid hold, ‖ And I do not let it go, ‖ My heart does not reproach me while I live. **7** My enemy is as the wicked, ‖ And my withstander as the perverse. **8** For what [is] the hope of the profane, ‖ When He cuts off? When God casts off his soul? **9** [Does] God hear his cry, ‖ When distress comes on him? **10** Does he delight himself on the Mighty? Call God at all times? **11** I show you by the hand of God, ‖ That which [is] with the Mighty I do not hide. **12** Behold, you—all of you—have seen, ‖ And why [is] this—you are altogether vain? **13** This [is] the portion of wicked man with God, ‖ And the inheritance of terrible ones ‖ They receive from the Mighty. **14** If his sons multiply—a sword [is] for them. And his offspring [are] not satisfied [with] bread. **15** His remnant are buried in death, ‖ And his widows do not weep. **16** If he heaps up silver as dust, ‖ And prepares clothing as clay, **17** He prepares—and the righteous puts [it] on, ‖ And the innocent apportions the silver. **18** He has built his house as a moth, ‖ And as a shelter a watchman has made. **19** He lies down rich, and he is not gathered, ‖ He has opened his eyes, and he is not. **20** Terrors overtake him as waters, ‖ By night a whirlwind has stolen him away. **21** An east wind takes him up, and he goes, ‖ And it frightens him from his place, **22** And it casts at him, and does not spare, ‖ He diligently flees from its hand. **23** It claps its hands at him, ‖ And it hisses at him from his place."

28 "Surely there is a source for silver, ‖ And a place for the gold they refine; **2** Iron is taken from the dust, ‖ And bronze [from] the firm stone. **3** He has set an end to darkness, ‖ And he is searching to all perfection, ‖ A stone of darkness and death-shade. **4** A stream has broken out from a sojourner, ‖ Those forgotten of the foot, ‖ They were low, they wandered from man. **5** The earth! Bread comes forth from it, ‖ And its under-part is turned like fire. **6** A place of the sapphire [are] its stones, ‖ And it has dust of gold. **7** A path—a ravenous bird has not known it, ‖ Nor has an eye of the falcon scorched it, **8** Nor have the sons of pride trodden it, ‖ The fierce lion has not passed over it. **9** He sent forth his hand against the flint, ‖ He overturned mountains from the root. **10** Among rocks, he has cleaved brooks, ‖ And his eye has seen every precious thing. **11** He has bound overflowing rivers, ‖ And the hidden thing brings out [to] light. **12** And the wisdom—from where is it found? And where [is] this, the place of understanding? **13** Man has not known its arrangement, ‖ Nor is it found in the land of the living. **14** The deep has said, It [is] not in me, ‖ And the sea has said, It is not with me. **15** Gold is not given for it, ‖ Nor is silver weighed—its price. **16** It is not valued with pure gold of Ophir, ‖ With precious onyx and sapphire, **17** Gold and crystal do not equal it, ‖ Nor [is] its exchange a vessel of fine gold. **18** Corals and pearl are not remembered, ‖ The acquisition of wisdom [is] above rubies. **19** The topaz of Cush does not equal it, ‖ It is not valued with pure gold. **20** And the wisdom—from where does it come? And where [is] this, the place of understanding? **21** It has been hid from the eyes of all living. And from the bird of the heavens ‖ It has been hidden. **22** Destruction and death have said: With our ears we have heard its fame. **23** God has understood its way, ‖ And He has known its place. **24** For He looks to the ends of the earth, ‖ He sees under the whole heavens, **25** To make a weight for the wind, ‖ And He meted out the waters in measure. **26** In His making for the rain a limit, ‖ And a way for the brightness of the voices, **27** Then He has seen and declares it, ‖ He has prepared it, and also searched it out, **28** And He says to man: Behold, fear of the Lord, that [is] wisdom, ‖ And to turn from evil [is] understanding."

29 And Job adds to lift up his allegory and says: **2** "Who makes me as [in] months past, ‖ As [in] the days of God's preserving me? **3** In His causing His lamp to shine on my head, ‖ By His light I walk [through] darkness. **4** As I have been in days of my maturity, ‖ And the counsel of God on my tent. **5** When yet the Mighty One [is] with me. Around me—my young ones, **6** When washing my goings with butter, ‖ And the firm rock [is] with me—streams of oil. **7** When I go out to the gate by the city, ‖ In a broad place I prepare my seat. **8** Youths have seen me, and they have been hidden, ‖ And the aged have risen—they stood up. **9** Princes have kept in words, ‖ And they place a hand on their mouth. **10** The voice of leaders has been hidden, ‖ And their tongue has cleaved to the palate. **11** For the ear heard, and declares me blessed, ‖ And the eye has seen, and testifies [to] me. **12** For I deliver the afflicted who is crying, ‖ And the fatherless who has no helper. **13** The blessing of the perishing comes on me, ‖ And I cause the heart of the widow to sing. **14** I have put on righteousness, and it clothes me, ‖ My justice as a robe and a crown. **15** I have been eyes to the blind, ‖ And I [am] feet to the lame. **16** I [am] a father to the needy, ‖ And the cause I have not known I search out. **17** And I break the jaw-teeth of the perverse, ‖ And from his teeth I cast away prey. **18** And I say, I expire with my nest, ‖ And I multiply days as the sand. **19** My root is open to the waters, ‖ And dew lodges on my branch. **20** My glory [is] fresh with me, ‖ And my bow is renewed in my hand. **21** They have listened to me, ‖ Indeed, they wait, and are silent for my counsel. **22** After my word they do not change, ‖ And my speech drops on them, **23** And they wait for me as [for] rain, ‖ And they have opened wide their mouth ‖ [As] for the spring rain. **24** I laugh at them—they give no credence, ‖ And do not cause the light of my face to fall. **25** I choose their way, and sit [as] head, ‖ And I dwell as a king in a troop, ‖ When he comforts mourners."

30 "And now, laughed at me, ‖ Have the younger in days than I, ‖ Whose fathers I have loathed to set ‖ With the dogs of my flock. **2** Also—the power of their hands, why [is it] to me? On them old age has perished. **3** With want and with harsh famine, ‖ They are gnawing a dry place [in] the recent night, ‖ [In] desolation and ruin, **4** Those cropping mallows near a shrub, ‖ And their food [is] root of broom trees. **5** They are cast out from the midst ‖ (They shout against them as a thief), **6** To dwell in a frightful place of valleys, ‖ Holes of earth and clefts. **7** They groan among shrubs, ‖ They are gathered together under nettles. **8** Sons of folly—even sons without name, ‖ They have been struck from the land. **9** And now, I have been their song, ‖ And I am to them for a byword. **10** They have detested me, ‖ They have kept far from me, ‖ And from before me have not spared to spit. **11** Because He loosed His cord and afflicts me, ‖ And the bridle from before me, ‖ They have cast away. **12** A brood arises on the right hand, ‖ They have cast away my feet, ‖ And they raise up against me, ‖ Their paths of calamity. **13** They have broken down my path, ‖ They profit by my calamity: He has no helper. **14** They come as a wide breach, ‖ Under the desolation have rolled themselves. **15** He has turned terrors against me, ‖ It pursues my abundance as the wind, ‖ And as a thick cloud, ‖ My safety has passed away. **16** And now, in me my soul pours itself out, ‖ Days of affliction seize me. **17** [At] night my bone has been pierced in me, ‖ And my gnawing [pain] does not lie down. **18** By the abundance of power, ‖ Is my clothing changed, ‖ As the mouth of my coat it girds me. **19** Casting me into mire, ‖ And I have become like dust and ashes. **20** I cry to You, ‖ And You do not answer me, I have stood, and You consider me. **21** You are turned to be fierce to me, ‖ With the strength of Your hand, ‖ You oppress me. **22** You lift me up, ‖ You cause me to ride on the wind, ‖ And You melt—You level me. **23** For I have known You bring me back [to] death, ‖ And [to] the house appointed for all living. **24** Surely not against the heap ‖ Does He send forth the hand, ‖ Though they have safety in its ruin. **25** Did I not weep for him whose day is hard? My soul has grieved for the needy. **26** When I expected good, then comes evil, ‖ And I wait for light, and darkness comes. **27** My bowels have boiled, and have not ceased, ‖ Days of affliction have gone before me. **28** I have gone mourning without the sun, ‖ I have risen, I cry in an assembly. **29** I have been a brother to dragons, ‖ And a companion to daughters of the ostrich. **30** My skin has been black on me, ‖ And my bone has burned from heat, **31** And my harp becomes mourning, ‖ And my pipe the sound of weeping."

31 "I made a covenant for my eyes, ‖ And how do I attend to a virgin? **2** And what [is] the portion of God from above? And the inheritance of the Mighty from the heights? **3** Is not calamity to the perverse? And strangeness to workers of iniquity? **4** Does He not see my ways, ‖ And number all my steps? **5** If I have walked with vanity, ‖ And my foot hurries to deceit, **6** He weighs me in righteous balances, ‖ And God knows my integrity. **7** If my step turns aside from the way, ‖ And my heart has gone after my eyes, ‖ And blemish has cleaved to my hands, **8** Let me sow—and another eat, ‖ And let my products be rooted out. **9** If my heart has been enticed by a woman, ‖ And I laid wait by the opening of my neighbor, **10** Let my wife grind to another, ‖ And let others bend over her. **11** For it [is] a wicked thing, and a judicial iniquity; **12** For it [is] a fire, it consumes to destruction, ‖ And takes root among all my increase, **13** If I despise the cause of my manservant, ‖ And of my handmaid, ‖ In their contending with me, **14** Then what do I do when God arises? And when He inspects, ‖ What do I answer Him? **15** Did He that made me in the womb not make him? Indeed, One prepares us in the womb. **16** If I withhold the poor from pleasure, ‖ And consume the eyes of the widow, **17** And I eat my morsel by myself, ‖ And the orphan has nothing [to] eat of it, **18** (But from my youth ‖ He grew up with me as [with] a father, ‖ And from the belly of my mother I am led), **19** If I see [any] perishing without clothing, ‖ And there is no covering for the needy, **20** If his loins have not blessed me, ‖ And from the fleece of my sheep ‖ He does not warm himself, **21** If I have waved my hand at the fatherless, ‖ When I see [him] in the gate of my court, **22** Let my shoulder fall from its blade, ‖ And the bone from my arm be broken. **23** For calamity [from] God [is] a dread to me, ‖ And because of His excellence I am not able. **24** If I have made gold my confidence, ‖ And to the pure gold have said, My trust; **25** If I rejoice because my wealth [is] great, ‖ And because my hand has found abundance, **26** If I see the light when it shines, ‖ And the precious moon walking, **27** And my heart is enticed in secret, ‖ And my hand kisses my mouth, **28** It also [is] a judicial iniquity, ‖ For I had lied to God above. **29** If I rejoice at the ruin of my hater, ‖ And stirred up myself when evil found him, **30** Indeed, I have not permitted my mouth to sin, ‖ To ask with an oath his life. **31** If not, say, O men of my tent: O that we had of his flesh, we are not satisfied. **32** A stranger does not lodge in the street, ‖ I open my doors to the traveler. **33** If I have covered my transgressions as Adam, ‖ To hide my iniquity in my bosom, **34** Because I fear a great multitude, ‖ And the contempt of families frightens me, ‖ Then I am silent, I do not go out of the opening. **35** Who gives to me a hearing? Behold, my mark. The Mighty One answers me, ‖ And my adversary has written a bill. **36** If not—on my shoulder I take it up, ‖ I bind it [as] a crown on myself. **37** The number of my steps I tell Him, ‖ As a leader I approach Him. **38** If my land cries out against me, ‖ And together its furrows weep, **39** If I consumed its strength without money, ‖ And the life of its possessors, I have caused to breathe out, **40** Instead of wheat let a thorn go forth, ‖ And instead of barley a useless weed!" The words of Job are finished.

32 And these three men cease from answering Job, for he [is] righteous in his own eyes, **2** and the anger of Elihu son of Barachel the Buzite burns, of the family of Ram; his anger has burned against Job, because of his justifying himself more than God; **3** and his anger has burned against his three friends, because that they have not found an answer, and condemn Job. **4** And Elihu has waited earnestly beside Job with words, for they are older than he in days. **5** And Elihu sees that there is no answer in the mouth of the three men, and his anger burns. **6** And Elihu son of Barachel the Buzite answers and says: "I [am] young in days, and you [are] aged; Therefore I have feared, ‖ And am afraid of showing you my opinion. **7** I said, Days speak, ‖ And a multitude of years teach wisdom. **8** Surely a spirit is in man, ‖ And the breath of the Mighty One ‖ Causes them to understand. **9** The multitude are not wise, ‖ Nor do the aged understand judgment. **10** Therefore I have said: Listen to me, I show my opinion—even I. **11** Behold, I have waited for your words, I give ear to your reasons, ‖ Until you search out sayings. **12** And to you I attend, ‖ And behold, there is no reasoner for Job, ‖ [Or] answerer of his sayings among you. **13** Lest you say, We have found wisdom, ‖ God thrusts him away, not man. **14** And he has not set words in array for me, ‖ And I do not answer him with your sayings. **15** (They have broken down, ‖ They have not answered again, ‖ They removed words from themselves. **16** And I have waited, but they do not speak, ‖ For they have stood still, ‖ They have not answered anymore.) **17** I answer, even I—my share, ‖ I show my opinion—even I. **18** For I have been full of words, ‖ The spirit of my breast has distressed me, **19** Behold, my breast [is] as wine not opened, ‖ It is broken up like new bottles. **20** I speak, and there is refreshment to me, ‖ I open my lips and answer. **21** Please do not let me accept the face of any, ‖ Nor give flattering titles to man, **22** For I have not known to give flattering titles, ‖ My Maker takes me away in a little."

33 "And yet, please, O Job, ‖ Hear my speech and give ear [to] all my words. **2** Now behold, I have opened my mouth, ‖ My tongue has spoken in the palate. **3** Of the uprightness of my heart [are] my sayings, ‖ And my lips have clearly spoken knowledge. **4** The Spirit of God has made me, ‖ And the breath of the Mighty quickens me. **5** If you are able—answer me, ‖ Set in array before me—station yourself. **6** Behold, I [am], according to your word, for God, ‖ I have also been formed from the clay. **7** Behold, my terror does not frighten you, ‖ And my burden on you is not heavy. **8** Surely you have spoken in my ears, ‖ And the sounds of words I hear: **9** I [am] pure, without transgression, ‖ I [am] innocent, and I have no iniquity. **10** Behold, He develops hindrances against me, ‖ He reckons me for an enemy to Him, **11** He puts my feet in the stocks, ‖ He watches all my paths. **12** Behold, you have not been righteous [in] this, ‖ I answer you, that God is greater than man. **13** Why have you striven against Him, ‖ When [for] all His matters He does not answer? **14** For once God speaks, and twice (he does not behold it), **15** In a dream—a vision of night, ‖ In the falling of deep sleep on men, ‖ In slumberings on a bed. **16** Then He uncovers the ear of men, ‖ And seals for their instruction, **17** To turn aside man [from] doing, ‖ And He conceals pride from man. **18** He keeps back his soul from corruption, ‖ And his life from passing away by a dart. **19** And he has been reproved ‖ With pain on his bed, ‖ And the strife of his bones [is] enduring. **20** And his life has nauseated bread, ‖ And his soul desirable food. **21** His flesh is consumed from being seen, ‖ And his bones are high, they were not seen! **22** And his soul draws near to the pit, ‖ And his life to those causing death. **23** If there is a messenger by him, ‖ An interpreter—one of a thousand, ‖ To declare for man his uprightness, **24** Then He favors him and says, ‖ Ransom him from going down to the pit, ‖ I have found an atonement. **25** Fresher [is] his flesh than a child's, ‖ He returns to the days of his youth. **26** He makes supplication to God, ‖ And He accepts him. And he sees His face with shouting, ‖ And He returns to man His righteousness. **27** [Then] he looks on men and says, ‖ I sinned, and I have perverted uprightness, ‖ And it has not been profitable to me. **28** He has ransomed my soul ‖ From going over into the pit, ‖ And my life looks on the light. **29** Behold, God works all these, ‖ Twice, [even] three times with man, **30** To bring back his soul from the pit, ‖ To be enlightened with the light of the living. **31** Attend, O Job, listen to me, ‖ Keep silent, and I speak. **32** If there are words—answer me, ‖ Speak, for I have a desire to justify you. **33** If there are not—listen to me, ‖ Keep silent, and I teach you wisdom."

34 And Elihu answers and says: **2** "Hear, O wise men, my words, ‖ And, O knowing ones, give ear to me. **3** For the ear tries words, ‖ And the palate tastes to eat. **4** Let us choose judgment for ourselves, ‖ Let us know among ourselves what [is] good. **5** For Job has said, I have been righteous, ‖ And God has turned aside my right, **6** Against my right do I lie? My arrow [is] mortal—without transgression. **7** Who [is] a man like Job? He drinks scoffing like water, **8** And he has traveled for company ‖ With workers of iniquity, ‖ So as to go with men of wickedness. **9** For he has said, It does not profit a man ‖ When he delights himself with God. **10** Therefore, O men of heart, listen to me; Far be it from God to do wickedness, ‖ And [from] the Mighty to do perverseness, **11** For He repays the work of man to him, ‖ And according to the path of each He causes him to find. **12** Indeed, truly, God does not do wickedly, ‖ And the Mighty does not pervert judgment. **13** Who has inspected for Himself the earth? And who has placed all the habitable world? **14** If He sets His heart on him, ‖ [If] He gathers His Spirit and His breath to Himself, **15** All flesh expires together, ‖ And man returns to dust. **16** And if [there is] understanding,

JOB

hear this, ‖ Give ear to the voice of my words. **17** Indeed, does one hating justice govern? Or do you condemn the Most Just? **18** Who has said to a king, Worthless, ‖ To princes, Wicked? **19** That has not accepted the person of princes, ‖ Nor has known the rich before the poor, ‖ For all of them [are] a work of His hands. **20** [In] a moment they die, ‖ And at midnight people shake, ‖ And they pass away, ‖ And they remove the mighty without hand. **21** For His eyes [are] on the ways of each, ‖ And He sees all his steps. **22** There is no darkness nor death-shade, ‖ For workers of iniquity to be hidden there; **23** For He does not permit man anymore, ‖ To go to God in judgment, **24** He breaks the mighty—no searching! And He appoints others in their stead. **25** Therefore He knows their works, ‖ And He has overturned by night, ‖ And they are bruised. **26** As wicked He has struck them, ‖ In the place of beholders. **27** Because that against right ‖ They have turned aside from after Him, ‖ And have considered none of His ways, **28** To cause to come to Him ‖ The cry of the poor, ‖ And He hears the cry of the afflicted. **29** And He gives rest, and who makes wrong? And hides the face, and who beholds it? And in reference to a nation and to a man, ‖ [It is] the same. **30** From the reigning of a profane man, ‖ From the snares of a people; **31** For has any said to God: I have taken away, ‖ I do not do corruptly, **32** Besides [that which] I see, You show me, ‖ If I have done iniquity—I do not add? **33** Does He repay by you, that you have refused—That you choose, and not I? And what you have known, speak. **34** Let men of heart say to me, ‖ And a wise man is listening to me: **35** Job—he does not speak with knowledge, ‖ And his words [are] not with wisdom. **36** My Father! Let Job be tried—to victory, ‖ Because of answers for men of iniquity, **37** For he adds to his sin, ‖ He vomits transgression among us, ‖ And multiplies his sayings to God."

35 And Elihu answers and says: **2** "Have you reckoned this for judgment [when] you have said, ‖ My righteousness [is] more than God's? **3** For you say, What does it profit You? What do I profit from my sin? **4** I return words, and your friends with you, **5** Behold attentively the heavens—and see, ‖ And behold the clouds, ‖ They have been higher than you. **6** If you have sinned, what do you do against Him? And your transgressions have been multiplied, ‖ What do you do to Him? **7** If you have been righteous, ‖ What do you give to Him? Or what does He receive from your hand? **8** For a man like yourself [is] your wickedness, ‖ And for a son of man your righteousness. **9** Because of the multitude of oppressions ‖ They cause to cry out, ‖ They cry because of the arm of the mighty. **10** And none said, Where [is] God my Maker? Giving songs in the night, **11** Teaching us more than the beasts of the earth, ‖ Indeed, He makes us wiser than the bird of the heavens. **12** There they cry, and He does not answer, ‖ Because of the pride of evildoers. **13** Surely God does not hear vanity, ‖ And the Mighty does not behold it. **14** Indeed, though you say you do not behold Him, ‖ Judgment [is] before Him, and stays for Him. **15** And now, because there is not, ‖ He has appointed His anger, ‖ And He has not known in great extremity. **16** And Job opens his mouth [with] vanity, ‖ He multiplies words without knowledge."

36 And Elihu adds and says: **2** "Honor me a little, and I show you, ‖ That yet for God [are] words. **3** I lift up my knowledge from afar, ‖ And I ascribe righteousness to my Maker. **4** For my words [are] truly not false, ‖ The perfect in knowledge [is] with you. **5** Behold, God [is] mighty, and does not despise, ‖ Mighty [in] power [and] heart. **6** He does not revive the wicked, ‖ And appoints the judgment of the poor; **7** He does not withdraw His eyes from the righteous, ‖ And [from] kings on the throne, ‖ And causes them to sit forever, and they are high, **8** And if prisoners in chains ‖ They are captured with cords of affliction, **9** Then He declares to them their work, ‖ And their transgressions, ‖ Because they have become mighty, **10** And He uncovers their ear for instruction, ‖ And commands that they turn back from iniquity. **11** If they hear and serve, ‖ They complete their days in good, ‖ And their years in pleasantness. **12** And if they do not listen, ‖ They pass away by the dart, ‖ And expire without knowledge. **13** And the profane in heart set the face, ‖ They do not cry when He has bound them. **14** Their soul dies in youth, ‖ And their life among the defiled. **15** He draws out the afflicted in his affliction, ‖ And uncovers their ear in oppression. **16** And He also moved you from a narrow place ‖ [To] a broad place—

no constriction under it, ‖ And the sitting beyond of your table has been full of fatness. **17** And you have fulfilled the judgment of the wicked, ‖ Judgment and justice are upheld because of fury, **18** Lest He move you with a stroke, ‖ And the abundance of an atonement not turn you aside. **19** Does He value your riches? He has gold, and all the forces of power. **20** Do not desire the night, ‖ For the going up of peoples in their stead. **21** Take heed—do not turn to iniquity, ‖ For you have fixed on this ‖ Rather than [on] affliction. **22** Behold, God sits on high by His power, ‖ Who [is] like Him—a teacher? **23** Who has appointed to Him His way? And who said, You have done iniquity? **24** Remember that you magnify His work ‖ That men have beheld. **25** All men have looked on it, ‖ Man looks attentively from afar. **26** Behold, God [is] high, ‖ And we do not know the number of His years, ‖ Indeed, there [is] no searching. **27** When He diminishes droppings of the waters, ‖ They refine rain according to its vapor, **28** Which clouds drop, ‖ They distill on man abundantly. **29** Indeed, do [any] understand ‖ The spreadings out of a cloud? The noises of His dwelling place? **30** Behold, He has spread His light over it, ‖ And He has covered the roots of the sea, **31** For He judges peoples by them, ‖ He gives food in abundance. **32** By two palms He has covered the light, ‖ And lays a charge over it in meeting, **33** His shout shows it, ‖ The livestock also, the rising [storm]."

37 "Also, my heart trembles at this, ‖ And it moves from its place. **2** Listen diligently to the trembling of His voice, ‖ Indeed, the sound goes forth from His mouth. **3** He directs it under the whole heavens, ‖ And its light [is] over the skirts of the earth. **4** A voice roars after it—He thunders with the voice of His excellence, ‖ And He does not hold them back, ‖ When His voice is heard. **5** God thunders with His voice wonderfully, ‖ Doing great things and we do not know. **6** For He says to snow: Be [on] the earth. And the small rain and great rain of His power. **7** Into the hand of every man he seals, ‖ For the knowledge by all men of His work. **8** And the beast enters into [its] lair, ‖ And it continues in its habitations. **9** From the inner chamber comes a windstorm, ‖ And from scatterings winds—cold, **10** From the breath of God is frost given, ‖ And the breadth of waters is constricted, **11** Indeed, by filling He presses out a cloud, [and] His light scatters a cloud. **12** And it is turning itself around by His counsels, ‖ For their doing all He commands them, ‖ On the face of the habitable earth. **13** Whether for a rod, or for His land, ‖ Or for kindness—He causes it to come. **14** Hear this, O Job, ‖ Stand and consider the wonders of God. **15** Do you know when God places them, ‖ And caused the light of His cloud to shine? **16** Do you know the balancings of a cloud? The wonders of the Perfect in knowledge? **17** How your garments [are] warm, ‖ In the quieting of the earth from the south? **18** You have made an expanse with Him ‖ For the clouds—strong as a hard mirror! **19** Let us know what we say to Him, ‖ We do not set in array because of darkness. **20** Is it declared to Him that I speak? If a man has spoken, surely he is swallowed up. **21** And now, they have not seen the light, ‖ It [is] bright in the clouds, ‖ And the wind has passed by and cleanses them. **22** It comes from the golden north, ‖ Fearful splendor [is] beside God. **23** The Mighty! We have not found Him out, ‖ High in power and judgment, ‖ He does not answer! And abundant in righteousness, **24** Therefore men fear Him, ‖ He does not see any of the wise of heart."

38 And YHWH answers Job out of the whirlwind and says: **2** "Who [is] this—darkening counsel, ‖ By words without knowledge? **3** Now gird your loins as a man, ‖ And I ask you, and you cause Me to know. **4** Where were you when I founded the earth? Declare, if you have known understanding. **5** Who placed its measures—if you know? Or who has stretched out a line on it? **6** On what have its sockets been sunk? Or who has cast its cornerstone— **7** In the singing together of [the] stars of morning, ‖ When all [the] sons of God shout for joy? **8** And He shuts up the sea with doors, ‖ In its coming forth, it goes out from the womb. **9** In My making a cloud its clothing, ‖ And thick darkness its swaddling band, **10** And I measure My statute over it, ‖ And place bar and doors, **11** And say, To here you come, and no more, ‖ And a command is placed ‖ On the pride of your billows. **12** Have you commanded morning since your days? Do you cause the dawn to know its place?

13 To take hold on the skirts of the earth, ‖ And the wicked are shaken out of it, **14** It turns itself as clay of a seal ‖ And they station themselves as clothed. **15** And their light is withheld from the wicked, ‖ And the arm lifted up is broken. **16** Have you come to springs of the sea? And in searching the deep ‖ Have you walked up and down? **17** Were the gates of death revealed to you? And do you see the gates of death-shade? **18** You have understanding, ‖ Even to the broad places of earth! Declare—if you have known it all. **19** Where [is] this—the way light dwells? And darkness, where [is] this—its place? **20** That you take it to its boundary, ‖ And that you understand the paths of its house. **21** You have known— for then you are born, ‖ And the number of your days [are] many! **22** Have you come to the treasure of snow? Indeed, do you see the treasures of hail, **23** That I have kept back for a time of distress, ‖ For a day of conflict and battle? **24** Where [is] this, the way light is apportioned? It scatters an east wind over the earth. **25** Who has divided a conduit for the flood? And a way for the lightning of the voices? **26** To cause [it] to rain on a land [with] no man, ‖ A wilderness [with] no man in it. **27** To satisfy a desolate and ruined place, ‖ And to cause to shoot up ‖ The produce of the tender grass? **28** Does the rain have a father? Or who has begotten the drops of dew? **29** From whose belly came forth the ice? And the hoarfrost of the heavens, ‖ Who has begotten it? **30** Waters are hidden as a stone, ‖ And the face of the deep is captured. **31** Do you bind the chains of the Pleiades? Or do you open the cords of Orion? **32** Do you bring out the twelve signs in [their] season? And do you comfort the Great Bear over her sons? **33** Have you known the statutes of the heavens? Or do you appoint ‖ Its dominion in the earth? **34** Do you lift up your voice to the cloud, ‖ And abundance of water covers you? **35** Do you send out lightnings, and they go ‖ And say to you, Behold us? **36** Who has put wisdom in the inward parts? Or who has given understanding to the covered part? **37** Who numbers the clouds by wisdom? And the bottles of the heavens, ‖ Who causes to lie down, **38** In the hardening of dust into hardness, ‖ And clods cleave together? **39** Do you hunt prey for a lion? And fulfill the desire of young lions? **40** When they bow down in dens—Abide in a thicket for a covert? **41** Who prepares for a raven his provision, ‖ When his young ones cry to God? They wander without food."

39 "Have you known the time of ‖ The bearing of the wild goats of the rock? Do you mark the bringing forth of does? **2** Do you number the months they fulfill? And have you known the time of their bringing forth? **3** They bow down, ‖ They bring forth their young ones safely, ‖ They cast forth their pangs. **4** Their young ones are safe, ‖ They grow up in the field, they have gone out, ‖ And have not returned to them. **5** Who has sent forth the wild donkey free? Indeed, who opened the bands of the wild donkey? **6** Whose house I have made the wilderness, ‖ And his dwellings the barren land, **7** He laughs at the multitude of a city, ‖ He does not hear the cries of an exactor. **8** The range of mountains [is] his pasture, ‖ And he seeks after every green thing. **9** Is a wild ox willing to serve you? Does he lodge by your crib? **10** Do you bind a wild ox in a furrow [with] his thick band? Does he harrow valleys after you? **11** Do you trust in him because his power [is] great? And do you leave your labor to him? **12** Do you trust in him ‖ That he brings back your seed, ‖ And gathers [it to] your threshing-floor? **13** [The] wing of the crying ostriches exults, but as a pinion and feather of a stork? **14** For she leaves her eggs on the earth, ‖ And she warms them on the dust, **15** And she forgets that a foot may press it, ‖ And a beast of the field treads it down. **16** It has hardened her young ones without her, ‖ Her labor [is] in vain, without fear. **17** For God has caused her to forget wisdom, ‖ And He has not given a portion ‖ To her in understanding; **18** At the time she lifts herself up on high, ‖ She laughs at the horse and his rider. **19** Do you give might to the horse? Do you clothe his neck [with] a mane? **20** Do you cause him to rush as a locust? The splendor of his snorting [is] terrible. **21** They dig in a valley, and he rejoices in power, ‖ He goes forth to meet the armor. **22** He laughs at fear, and is not frightened, ‖ And he does not turn back from the face of the sword. **23** Quiver rattles against him, ‖ The flame of a spear, and a javelin. **24** He swallows the ground with trembling and rage, ‖ And does not remain steadfast ‖ Because of the sound of a horn. **25** Among the horns he says, Aha, ‖ And from afar he smells battle, ‖ Roaring of princes and shouting. **26** By your understanding does a hawk fly? Does he spread his wings to the south? **27** At your command does an eagle go up high? Or lift up his nest? **28** He inhabits a rock, ‖ Indeed, he lodges on the tooth of a rock, and fortress. **29** From there he has sought food, ‖ His eyes look attentively to a far-off place, **30** And his brood sucks up blood, ‖ And where the pierced [are]—there [is] he!"

40 And YHWH answers Job and says: **2** "Is the striver with the Mighty instructed? The reprover of God, let him answer it." **3** And Job answers YHWH and says: **4** "Behold, I have been vile, ‖ What do I return to You? I have placed my hand on my mouth. **5** I have spoken once, and I do not answer, ‖ And twice, and I do not add." **6** And YHWH answers Job out of the whirlwind and says: **7** "Now gird your loins as a man, ‖ I ask you, and you cause Me to know. **8** Do you also make My judgment void? Do you condemn Me, ‖ That you may be righteous? **9** And do you have an arm like God? And do you thunder with a voice like His? **10** Now put on excellence and loftiness, ‖ Indeed, put on splendor and beauty. **11** Scatter abroad the wrath of your anger, ‖ And see every proud one, and make him low. **12** See every proud one—humble him, ‖ And tread down the wicked in their place. **13** Hide them in the dust together, ‖ Bind their faces in secret. **14** And even I praise you, ‖ For your right hand gives salvation to you. **15** Now behold, behemoth, ‖ That I made with you: He eats grass as an ox. **16** Now behold, his power [is] in his loins, ‖ And his strength in the muscles of his belly. **17** He bends his tail as a cedar, ‖ The sinews of his thighs are wrapped together, **18** His bones [are] tubes of bronze, ‖ His bones [are] as a bar of iron. **19** He [is] a beginning of the ways of God, ‖ His Maker [alone] brings His sword near; **20** For mountains bear food for him, ‖ And all the beasts of the field play there. **21** He lies down under shades, ‖ In a secret place of reed and marsh. **22** Shades cover him, [with] their shadow, ‖ Willows of the brook cover him. **23** Behold, a flood oppresses—he does not hurry, ‖ He is confident though Jordan ‖ Comes forth to his mouth. **24** Does [one] take him by his eyes? ‖ Does [one] pierce the nose with snares?"

41 "Do you draw leviathan with a hook? And do you let down his tongue with a rope? **2** Do you put a reed in his nose? And pierce his jaw with a thorn? **3** Does he multiply supplications to you? Does he speak tender things to you? **4** Does he make a covenant with you? Do you take him for a perpetual servant? **5** Do you play with him as a bird? And do you bind him for your girls? **6** (Companions feast on him, ‖ They divide him among the merchants!) **7** Do you fill his skin with barbed irons? And his head with fish-spears? **8** Place your hand on him, ‖ Remember the battle—do not add! **9** Behold, the hope of him is found a liar, ‖ Also, is one not cast down at his appearance? **10** None so fierce that he awakes him, ‖ And who [is] he [who] stations himself before Me? **11** Who has brought before Me and I repay? Under the whole heavens it [is] Mine. **12** I do not keep silent concerning his parts, ‖ And the matter of might, ‖ And the grace of his arrangement. **13** Who has uncovered the face of his clothing? Who enters within his double bridle? **14** Who has opened the doors of his face? Around his teeth [are] terrible. **15** A pride—strong ones of shields, ‖ Shut up—a close seal. **16** They draw near to one another, ‖ And air does not enter between them. **17** They adhere to one another, ‖ They stick together and are not separated. **18** His sneezings cause light to shine, ‖ And his eyes [are] as the eyelids of the dawn. **19** Flames go out of his mouth, sparks of fire escape. **20** Smoke goes forth out of his nostrils, ‖ As a blown pot and reeds. **21** His breath sets coals on fire, ‖ And a flame goes forth from his mouth. **22** Strength lodges in his neck, ‖ And grief exults before him. **23** The flakes of his flesh have adhered—Firm on him—it is not moved. **24** His heart [is] firm as a stone, ‖ Indeed, firm as the lower piece. **25** The mighty are afraid at his rising, ‖ From his breakings they keep themselves free. **26** The sword of his overtaker does not stand, ‖ Spear, dart, and breastplate. **27** He reckons iron as straw, bronze as rotten wood. **28** The son of the bow does not cause him to flee, ‖ Stones of the sling are turned into stubble by him. **29** Darts have been reckoned as stubble, ‖ And he laughs at the shaking of a javelin. **30** Sharp points of clay [are] under him, ‖ He spreads gold on the mire. **31** He causes the deep to boil as a pot, ‖ He makes the sea as a pot of

JOB

ointment. **32** He causes a path to shine after him, ‖ One thinks the deep to be hoary. **33** There is not on the earth his like, ‖ That is made without terror. **34** He sees every high thing, ‖ He [is] king over all sons of pride."

42 And Job answers Y<small>HWH</small> and says: **2** "You have known that [for] all things You are able, ‖ And no purpose is withheld from You. **3** [You said], Who [is] this hiding counsel without knowledge? Therefore, I have declared, and do not understand, ‖ Too wonderful for me, and I do not know. **4** Please hear, and I speak; [You said], I ask you, and you cause Me to know. **5** By the hearing of the ear I heard You, ‖ And now my eye has seen You. **6** Therefore I loathe [it], ‖ And I have sighed on dust and ashes." **7** And it comes to pass after Y<small>HWH</small>'s speaking these words to Job, that Y<small>HWH</small> says to Eliphaz the Temanite, "My anger has burned against you and against your two friends, because you have not spoken correctly concerning Me, like My servant Job. **8** And now, take seven bullocks and seven rams for yourselves, and go to My servant Job, and you have caused a burnt-offering to ascend for yourselves; and Job My servant prays for you, for surely I accept his face, so as not to do folly with you, because you have not spoken correctly concerning Me, like My servant Job." **9** And they go—Eliphaz the Temanite, and Bildad the Shuhite, Zophar the Naamathite—and do as Y<small>HWH</small> has spoken to them; and Y<small>HWH</small> accepts the face of Job. **10** And Y<small>HWH</small> has turned [to] the captivity of Job in his praying for his friends, and Y<small>HWH</small> adds [to] all that Job has—to double. **11** And all his brothers come to him, and all his sisters, and all his former acquaintances, and they eat bread with him in his house, and bemoan him, and comfort him concerning all the calamity that Y<small>HWH</small> had brought on him, and they each gave to him one kesitah, and each one ring of gold. **12** And Y<small>HWH</small> has blessed the latter end of Job more than his beginning, and he has fourteen thousand of a flock, and six thousand camels, and one thousand pairs of oxen, and one thousand female donkeys. **13** And he has seven sons and three daughters; **14** and he calls the name of the first Jemima, and the name of the second Kezia, and the name of the third Keren-Happuch. **15** And there have not been found women [as] beautiful as the daughters of Job in all the land, and their father gives to them an inheritance in the midst of their brothers. **16** And Job lives after this one hundred and forty years, and sees his sons, and his sons' sons, four generations; **17** and Job dies, aged and satisfied [with] days.

PSALMS

1 O the blessedness of that one, ‖ Who has not walked in the counsel of the wicked, ‖ And has not stood in the way of sinners, ‖ And has not sat in the seat of scorners; **2** But his delight [is] in the Law of YHWH, ‖ And in His law he meditates by day and by night: **3** And he has been as a tree, ‖ Planted by streams of water, ‖ That gives its fruit in its season, ‖ And its leaf does not wither, ‖ And all that he does he causes to prosper. **4** Not so the wicked: But [they are] as chaff that wind drives away! **5** Therefore the wicked do not rise in judgment, ‖ Nor sinners in the congregation of the righteous, **6** For YHWH is knowing the way of the righteous, ‖ And the way of the wicked is lost!

2 Why have nations assembled tumultuously? And peoples meditate vanity? **2** Kings of the earth station themselves, and princes have been united together, against YHWH, and against His Messiah: **3** "Let us draw off Their cords, ‖ And cast Their thick bands from us." **4** He who is sitting in the heavens laughs, ‖ The Lord mocks at them. **5** Then He speaks to them in His anger, and in His wrath He troubles them: **6** "And I have anointed My King, ‖ On Zion—My holy hill." **7** I declare concerning a statute: YHWH said to me, "You [are] My Son, today I have brought You forth. **8** Ask of Me and I give nations [as] Your inheritance, ‖ And the ends of the earth [for] Your possession. **9** You rule them with a scepter of iron, ‖ You crush them as a vessel of a potter." **10** And now, O kings, act wisely, ‖ Be instructed, O judges of earth, **11** Serve YHWH with fear, ‖ And rejoice with trembling. **12** Kiss the Chosen One [[*or* Son]], lest He is angry, ‖ And you perish [from] the way, ‖ When His anger burns but a little, ‖ O the blessedness of all trusting in Him!

3 A PSALM OF DAVID, IN HIS FLEEING FROM THE FACE OF HIS SON ABSALOM. YHWH, how my distresses have multiplied! Many are rising up against me. **2** Many are saying of my soul, "There is no salvation for him in God." Selah. **3** And You, O YHWH, [are] a shield for me, ‖ My glory, and lifter up of my head. **4** My voice [is] to YHWH: I call and He answers me from His holy hill, Selah. **5** I have lain down, and I sleep, ‖ I have awoken, for YHWH sustains me. **6** I am not afraid of myriads of people, ‖ That they have set against me all around. **7** Rise, O YHWH! Save me, my God! For You have struck all my enemies [on] the cheek. You have broken the teeth of the wicked. **8** This salvation [is] of YHWH; Your blessing [is] on Your people! Selah.

4 TO THE OVERSEER. WITH STRINGED INSTRUMENTS. A PSALM OF DAVID. In my calling answer me, ‖ O God of my righteousness. In adversity You gave enlargement to me; Favor me, and hear my prayer. **2** Sons of men! Until when [is] my glory for shame? You love a vain thing, you seek a lie. Selah. **3** And know that YHWH ‖ Has separated a saintly one to Himself. YHWH hears in my calling to Him. **4** "Tremble, and do not sin"; Say [thus] in your heart on your bed, ‖ And be silent. Selah. **5** Sacrifice sacrifices of righteousness, ‖ And trust in YHWH. **6** Many are saying, "Who shows us good?" Lift on us the light of Your face, O YHWH, **7** You have given joy in my heart, ‖ From the time their grain and their wine ‖ Have been multiplied. **8** Together I lie down and sleep in peace, ‖ For You, O YHWH, alone, ‖ Cause me to dwell in confidence!

5 TO THE OVERSEER. [BLOWN] INTO THE PIPES. A PSALM OF DAVID. Hear my sayings, O YHWH, ‖ Consider my meditation. **2** Be attentive to the voice of my cry, ‖ My King and my God, ‖ For I pray to You habitually. **3** YHWH, [in] the morning You hear my voice, ‖ [In] the morning I set in array for You, ‖ And I look out [expectantly]. **4** For You [are] not a God desiring wickedness, ‖ Evil does not inhabit You. **5** The boastful do not station themselves before Your eyes: You have hated all working iniquity. **6** You destroy those speaking lies, ‖ YHWH detests a man of blood and deceit. **7** And I, in the abundance of Your kindness, ‖ I enter Your house, ‖ I bow myself toward Your holy temple in Your fear. **8** O YHWH, lead me in Your righteousness, ‖ Because of those observing me, ‖ Make Your way straight

PSALMS

before me, **9** For there is no stability in their mouth. Their heart [is] mischiefs, ∥ Their throat [is] an open grave, ∥ They make their tongue smooth. **10** Declare them guilty, O God, ∥ Let them fall from their own counsels, ∥ In the abundance of their transgressions ∥ Drive them away, ∥ Because they have been rebellious against You. **11** And all trusting in You rejoice, ∥ They sing for all time, and You cover them over, ∥ And those loving Your Name exult in You. **12** For You bless the righteous, O YHWH, ∥ Surrounding him with favor as a buckler!

6 TO THE OVERSEER. WITH STRINGED INSTRUMENTS, ON THE EIGHTH. A PSALM OF DAVID. O YHWH, do not reprove me in Your anger, ∥ Nor discipline me in Your fury. **2** Favor me, O YHWH, for I [am] weak, ∥ Heal me, O YHWH, ∥ For my bones have been troubled, **3** And my soul has been troubled greatly, ∥ And You, O YHWH, until when? **4** Turn back, O YHWH, draw out my soul, ∥ Save me for Your kindness' sake. **5** For in death there is no memorial of You, ∥ In Sheol, who gives thanks to You? **6** I have been weary with my sighing, ∥ I meditate [on] my bed through all the night, ∥ I dissolve my couch with my tear. **7** My eye is old from provocation, ∥ It is old because of all my adversaries, **8** Turn from me all you workers of iniquity, ∥ For YHWH heard the voice of my weeping, **9** YHWH has heard my supplication, ∥ YHWH receives my prayer. **10** All my enemies are greatly ashamed and troubled, ∥ They turn back—ashamed [in] a moment!

7 A SHIGGAION OF DAVID, THAT HE SUNG TO YHWH CONCERNING THE WORDS OF CUSH, A BENJAMITE. O YHWH, my God, in You I have trusted, ∥ Save me from all my pursuers, and deliver me. **2** Lest he tear my soul as a lion, ∥ Tearing, and there is no deliverer. **3** O YHWH, my God, if I have done this, ∥ If there is iniquity in my hands, **4** If I have done my well-wisher evil, ∥ And draw my adversary without cause, **5** [Then] an enemy pursues my soul, and overtakes, ∥ And treads down my life to the earth, ∥ And places my glory in the dust. Selah. **6** Rise, O YHWH, in Your anger, ∥ Be lifted up at the wrath of my adversaries, ∥ And awake Yourself for me. You have commanded judgment: **7** And a congregation of peoples surround You, ∥ And over it turn back on high. **8** YHWH judges the peoples; Judge me, O YHWH, ∥ According to my righteousness, ∥ And according to my integrity [that is] on me. **9** Please let the evil of the wicked be ended, ∥ And establish the righteous, ∥ And a trier of hearts and reins is the righteous God. **10** My shield [is] on God, ∥ Savior of the upright in heart! **11** God [is] judging right, ∥ And He is not angry at all times. **12** If [one] does not turn, ∥ He sharpens His sword, ∥ He has bent His bow [and] He prepares it, **13** Indeed, He has prepared for Himself ∥ Instruments of death, ∥ He makes His arrows for burning pursuers. **14** Behold, he travails [with] iniquity, ∥ And he has conceived perverseness, ∥ And has brought forth falsehood. **15** He has prepared a pit, and he digs it, ∥ And he falls into a ditch he makes. **16** His perverseness returns on his head, ∥ And his violence comes down on his crown. **17** I thank YHWH, ∥ According to His righteousness, ∥ And I praise the Name of YHWH Most High!

8 TO THE OVERSEER. ON THE GITTITH. A PSALM OF DAVID. YHWH, our Lord, ∥ How majestic [is] Your Name in all the earth, ∥ Who have set Your splendor on the heavens! **2** From the mouths of infants and sucklings ∥ You have founded strength, ∥ Because of Your adversaries, ∥ To still an enemy and a self-avenger. **3** For I see Your heavens, a work of Your fingers, ∥ [The] moon and stars that You established. **4** What [is] man that You remember him? The son of man that You inspect him? **5** You make him a little lower than the gods [[*or* God]], ∥ And surround him with glory and majesty. **6** You cause him to rule ∥ Over the works of Your hands, ∥ You have placed all under his feet. **7** Sheep and oxen, all of them, ∥ And also beasts of the field, **8** Bird of the heavens, and fish of the sea, ∥ Passing through the paths of the seas! **9** YHWH, our Lord, ∥ How majestic [is] Your Name in all the earth!

9 TO THE OVERSEER. [SET] ON "DEATH OF THE SON." A PSALM OF DAVID. I confess, O YHWH, with all my heart, ∥ I recount all Your wonders, **2** I rejoice and exult in You, ∥ I praise Your Name, O Most High. **3** In my enemies turning backward, ∥ They stumble and perish from Your face. **4** For You have done my judgment and my right. You have sat on a throne, ‖ Judging [with] righteousness. **5** You have rebuked nations, ‖ You have destroyed the wicked, ‖ You have blotted out their name for all time and forever. **6** The enemy—[your] destructions have been completed forever, ‖ As for cities you have plucked up, ‖ Their memorial has perished with them. **7** And YHWH abides for all time, ‖ He is preparing His throne for judgment. **8** And He judges the world in righteousness, ‖ He judges the peoples in uprightness. **9** And YHWH is a tower for the bruised, ‖ A tower for times of adversity. **10** They trust in You who know Your Name, ‖ For You have not forsaken those seeking You, O YHWH. **11** Sing praise to YHWH, inhabiting Zion, ‖ Declare His acts among the peoples, **12** For He who is seeking for blood ‖ Has remembered them, ‖ He has not forgotten the cry of the afflicted. **13** Favor me, O YHWH, ‖ See my affliction by those hating me, ‖ You who lift me up from the gates of death, **14** So that I recount all Your praise, ‖ In the gates of the daughter of Zion. I rejoice on Your salvation. **15** Nations have sunk in a pit they made, ‖ Their foot has been captured in a net that they hid. **16** YHWH has been known, ‖ He has done judgment; By a work of his hands ‖ The wicked has been snared. Meditation. Selah. **17** The wicked turn back to Sheol, ‖ All nations forgetting God. **18** For the needy is not forgotten forever, ‖ [Nor] the hope of the humble lost for all time. **19** Rise, O YHWH, do not let man be strong, ‖ Let nations be judged before Your face. **20** Appoint them to fear, O YHWH, ‖ Let nations know they [are] men! Selah.

10 Why, YHWH, do You stand at a distance? Do You hide in times of adversity? **2** Through the pride of the wicked, ‖ Is the poor inflamed, ‖ They are caught in schemes that they devised. **3** Because the wicked has boasted ‖ Of the desire of his soul, ‖ And he has blessed a dishonest gainer, ‖ He has despised YHWH. **4** The wicked does not inquire according to the height of his face. "There is no God!" [are] all his schemes. **5** His ways writhe at all times, ‖ Your judgments [are] on high before him, ‖ All his adversaries—he puffs at them. **6** He has said in his heart, "I am not moved, ‖ [And am] not in calamity to generation and generation." **7** His mouth is full of oaths, ‖ And deceits, and fraud: Under his tongue [is] perverseness and iniquity, **8** He sits in an ambush of the villages, ‖ He slays the innocent in secret places. His eyes secretly watch for the afflicted, **9** He lies in wait in a secret place, as a lion in a covert. He lies in wait to catch the poor, ‖ He catches the poor, drawing him into his net. **10** He is bruised—he bows down, ‖ The afflicted has fallen by his mighty ones. **11** He said in his heart, "God has forgotten, ‖ He has hid His face, ‖ He has never seen." **12** Arise, O YHWH! O God, lift up Your hand! Do not forget the humble. **13** Why has the wicked despised God? He has said in his heart, "It is not required." **14** You have seen, ‖ For You behold perverseness and anger; By giving into Your hand, ‖ The afflicted leave [it] on You, ‖ You have been a helper of the fatherless. **15** Break the arm of the wicked and the evil, ‖ Seek out his wickedness, find none; **16** YHWH [is] King for all time and forever, ‖ The nations have perished out of His land! **17** You have heard the desire of the humble, O YHWH. You prepare their heart; You cause Your ear to attend, **18** To judge the fatherless and bruised: He adds no more to oppress—man of the earth!

11 TO THE OVERSEER. BY DAVID. In YHWH I trusted, how do you say to my soul, "They moved to your mountain [as] the bird?" **2** For behold, the wicked bend a bow, ‖ They have prepared their arrow on the string, ‖ To shoot in darkness at the upright in heart. **3** When the foundations are destroyed, ‖ The righteous—what has he done? **4** YHWH [is] in His holy temple: YHWH—His throne [is] in the heavens. His eyes see—His eyelids try the sons of men. **5** YHWH tries the righteous. And the wicked and the lover of violence, ‖ His soul has hated, **6** He pours on the wicked snares, fire, and brimstone, ‖ And a horrible wind [is] the portion of their cup. **7** For YHWH [is] righteous, ‖ He has loved righteousness, ‖ His countenance sees the upright!

12 TO THE OVERSEER. ON THE EIGHTH. A PSALM OF DAVID. Save, YHWH, for the saintly has failed, ‖ For the steadfast have ceased ‖ From the sons of men: **2** They each speak vanity with his neighbor, ‖ Lip of flattery! With heart and heart they speak. **3** YHWH cuts off all lips of flattery, ‖ A tongue speaking great things, **4** Who said, "By our tongue we do

PSALMS

mightily: Our lips [are] our own; who [is] lord over us?" **5** Because of the spoiling of the poor, ‖ Because of the groaning of the needy, ‖ Now I arise, says YHWH, ‖ I set in safety [him who] breathes for it. **6** Sayings of YHWH [are] pure sayings—Silver tried in a furnace of earth, refined sevenfold. **7** You, O YHWH, preserve them, ‖ You keep us from this generation for all time. **8** The wicked walk around continually, ‖ According as vileness is exalted by sons of men!

13 TO THE OVERSEER. A PSALM OF DAVID. Until when, O YHWH, ‖ Do You forget me forever? Until when do You hide Your face from me? **2** Until when do I set counsels in my soul, ‖ [With] sorrow in my heart daily? Until when is my enemy exalted over me? **3** Look attentively; Answer me, O YHWH, my God, ‖ Enlighten my eyes, lest I sleep in death, **4** Lest my enemy say, "I overcame him," ‖ My adversaries rejoice when I am moved. **5** And I have trusted in Your kindness, ‖ My heart rejoices in Your salvation. **6** I sing to YHWH, ‖ For He has conferred benefits on me!

14 TO THE OVERSEER. BY DAVID. A fool has said in his heart, "There is no God"; They have done corruptly, ‖ They have done abominable actions, ‖ There is not a doer of good. **2** YHWH has looked from the heavens on the sons of men, ‖ To see if there is a wise one—seeking God. **3** The whole have turned aside, ‖ Together they have been filthy: There is not a doer of good, not even one. **4** Have all working iniquity not known? Those consuming my people have eaten bread, ‖ They have not called YHWH. **5** They have feared a fear there, ‖ For God [is] in the generation of the righteous. **6** You cause the counsel of the poor to stink, ‖ Because YHWH [is] his refuge. **7** "Who gives the salvation of Israel from Zion?" When YHWH turns back ‖ [To] a captivity of His people, ‖ Jacob rejoices—Israel is glad!

15 A PSALM OF DAVID. YHWH, who sojourns in Your tent? Who dwells in Your holy hill? **2** He who is walking uprightly, ‖ And working righteousness, ‖ And speaking truth in his heart. **3** He has not slandered by his tongue, ‖ He has not done evil to his friend; And he has not lifted up reproach ‖ Against his neighbor. **4** A rejected one [is] despised in his eyes, ‖ And he honors those fearing YHWH. He has sworn to endure evil, and does not change; **5** He has not given his silver in usury, ‖ And has not taken a bribe against the innocent; Whoever is doing these is not moved for all time!

16 A MIKTAM OF DAVID. Preserve me, O God, for I trusted in You. **2** You have said to YHWH, "You [are] my Lord"; My goodness [is] not above You; **3** For the holy ones who [are] in the land, ‖ And the honorable, all my delight [is] in them. **4** Their griefs are multiplied, [who] have hurried backward; I do not pour out their drink-offerings of blood, ‖ Nor do I take up their names on my lips. **5** YHWH [is] the portion of my share, and of my cup, ‖ You uphold my lot. **6** Lines have fallen to me in pleasant places, ‖ Indeed, a beautiful inheritance [is] for me. **7** I bless YHWH who has counseled me; Also [in] the nights my reins instruct me. **8** I placed YHWH before me continually, ‖ Because [He is] at my right hand I am not moved. **9** Therefore my heart has been glad, ‖ And my glory rejoices, ‖ Also my flesh dwells confidently: **10** For You do not leave my soul to Sheol, ‖ Nor give your Holy One to see corruption. **11** You cause me to know the path of life; In Your presence [is] fullness of joys, ‖ Pleasant things [are] by Your right hand forever!

17 A PRAYER OF DAVID. Hear, O YHWH, righteousness, attend my cry, ‖ Give ear [to] my prayer, without lips of deceit. **2** My judgment goes out from before You; Your eyes see uprightly. **3** You have proved my heart, ‖ You have inspected by night, ‖ You have tried me, You find nothing; My thoughts do not pass over my mouth. **4** As for doings of man, ‖ Through a word of Your lips I have observed ‖ The paths of a destroyer; **5** To uphold my goings in Your paths, ‖ My steps have not slipped. **6** I called You, for You answer me, ‖ O God, incline Your ear to me, hear my speech. **7** Separate Your kindness wonderfully, O Savior of the confiding, ‖ By Your right hand, from withstanders. **8** Keep me as the apple, the daughter of the eye; Hide me in the shadow of Your wings, **9** From the face of the wicked who spoiled me, ‖ [From] my enemies in soul who go around against me. **10** They have closed up their fat, ‖ Their mouths have spoken with pride: **11** "Our steps have now surrounded [him]"; They set their eyes to turn aside in the land. **12** His likeness as a lion desirous to tear, ‖ As a young lion dwelling in secret places. **13** Arise, O YHWH, go before his face, ‖ Cause him to bend. Deliver my soul from the wicked, Your sword, **14** From men, Your hand, O YHWH, ‖ From men of the world, their portion [is] in life, ‖ And [with] Your hidden things You fill their belly, ‖ They are satisfied [with] sons, ‖ And have left their abundance to their sucklings. **15** I—in righteousness, ‖ I see Your face; I am satisfied, in awaking, [with] Your form!

18 To the Overseer. By a servant of YHWH, by David, who has spoken to YHWH the words of this song in the day YHWH delivered him from the hand of all his enemies, and from the hand of Saul, and he says: I love You, O YHWH, my strength. **2** YHWH [is] my rock, and my bulwark, ‖ And my deliverer, ‖ My God [is] my rock, ‖ I trust in Him: My shield, and the horn of my salvation, ‖ My high tower. **3** I call on YHWH, the Praised One, ‖ And I am saved from my enemies. **4** Cords of death have surrounded me, ‖ And streams of the worthless make me afraid. **5** Cords of Sheol have surrounded me, ‖ Snares of death have been before me. **6** In my adversity I call YHWH, ‖ And I cry to my God. He hears my voice from His temple, ‖ And My cry comes into His ears before Him. **7** And the earth shakes and trembles, ‖ And foundations of hills are troubled, ‖ And they shake—because He has wrath. **8** Smoke has gone up from His nostrils, ‖ And fire from His mouth consumes, ‖ Coals have been kindled by it. **9** And He inclines the heavens, and comes down, ‖ And thick darkness [is] under His feet. **10** And He rides on a cherub, and flies, ‖ And He flies on wings of wind. **11** He makes darkness His secret place, ‖ Around Him His dwelling place, ‖ Darkness of waters, thick clouds of the skies. **12** From the brightness before Him His thick clouds have passed on, ‖ Hail and coals of fire. **13** And YHWH thunders in the heavens, ‖ And the Most High gives forth His voice, ‖ Hail and coals of fire. **14** And He sends His arrows and scatters them, ‖ And much lightning, and crushes them. **15** And the streams of waters are seen, ‖ And foundations of the earth are revealed, ‖ From Your rebuke, O YHWH, ‖ From the breath of the wind of Your anger. **16** He sends from above—He takes me, ‖ He draws me out of many waters. **17** He delivers me from my strong enemy, ‖ And from those hating me, ‖ For they have been stronger than I. **18** They go before me in a day of my calamity ‖ And YHWH is for a support to me. **19** And He brings me forth to a large place, ‖ He draws me out, because He delighted in me. **20** YHWH repays me ‖ According to my righteousness, ‖ According to the cleanness of my hands, ‖ He returns to me. **21** For I have kept the ways of YHWH, ‖ And have not done wickedly against my God. **22** For all His judgments [are] before me, ‖ And I do not turn His statutes from me. **23** And I am perfect with Him, ‖ And I keep myself from my iniquity. **24** And YHWH returns to me, ‖ According to my righteousness, ‖ According to the cleanness of my hands, ‖ Before His eyes. **25** With the kind You show Yourself kind, ‖ With a perfect man You show Yourself perfect. **26** With the pure You show Yourself pure, ‖ And with the perverse You show Yourself a wrestler, **27** For You save a poor people, ‖ And cause the eyes of the high to fall. **28** For You light my lamp, ‖ My God YHWH enlightens my darkness. **29** For by You I run [against] a troop! And by my God I leap a wall. **30** God—perfect [is] His way, ‖ The saying of YHWH is tried, ‖ He [is] a shield to all those trusting in Him. **31** For who [is] God besides YHWH? And who [is] a rock except our God? **32** God—who is girding me [with] strength, ‖ And He makes my way perfect. **33** Making my feet like does, ‖ And on my high places causes me to stand. **34** Teaching my hands for battle, ‖ And a bow of bronze was brought down by my arms. **35** And You give to me the shield of Your salvation, ‖ And Your right hand supports me, ‖ And Your lowliness makes me great. **36** You enlarge my step under me, ‖ And my ankles have not slipped. **37** I pursue my enemies, and overtake them, ‖ And do not turn back until they are consumed. **38** I strike them, and they are not able to rise, ‖ They fall under my feet, **39** And You gird me [with] strength for battle, ‖ You cause my withstanders to bow under me. **40** As for my enemies—You have given to me the neck, ‖ As for those hating me—I cut them off. **41** They cry, and there is no savior, ‖ On YHWH, and He does not answer them. **42** And I beat them as dust before wind, ‖ I empty them out as mire of the streets. **43** You deliver me ‖ From the strivings of the people, ‖ You place me for a head of nations, ‖ A people I have not known serve me. **44** At the hearing of the ear they listen to me, ‖ Sons of a stranger feign obedience to me, **45** Sons of a stranger fade away, ‖ And are slain out of their close places. **46** YHWH lives—and blessed [is] my rock, ‖ And exalted is the God of my salvation. **47** God—who is giving vengeance to me, ‖ And He subdues peoples under me, **48** My deliverer from my enemies, ‖ You raise me above my withstanders, ‖ Deliver me from a man of violence. **49** Therefore I confess You among nations, O YHWH, ‖ And I sing praise to Your Name, **50** Magnifying the salvation of His king, ‖ And doing kindness to His anointed, ‖ To David, and to his seed—for all time!

19 TO THE OVERSEER. A PSALM OF DAVID. The heavens [are] recounting the glory of God, ‖ And the expanse [is] declaring the work of His hands. **2** Day to day utters speech, ‖ And night to night shows knowledge. **3** There is no speech, and there are no words. Their voice has not been heard. **4** Their line has gone forth into all the earth, ‖ And their sayings to the end of the world, ‖ In them He placed a tent for the sun, **5** And he, as a bridegroom, goes out from his covering, ‖ He rejoices as a mighty one ‖ To run the path. **6** From the end of the heavens [is] his going out, ‖ And his revolution [is] to their ends, ‖ And nothing is hid from his heat. **7** The law of YHWH [is] perfect, refreshing the soul, ‖ The testimonies of YHWH [are] steadfast, ‖ Making the simple wise, **8** The precepts of YHWH [are] upright, ‖ Rejoicing the heart, ‖ The command of YHWH [is] pure, enlightening the eyes, **9** The fear of YHWH [is] clean, standing for all time, ‖ The judgments of YHWH [are] true, ‖ They have been righteous—together. **10** They are more desirable than gold, ‖ Indeed, than much fine gold; and sweeter than honey, ‖ Even liquid honey of the comb. **11** Also—Your servant is warned by them, "In keeping them [is] a great reward." **12** [His] errors—who understands? Declare me innocent from hidden ones, **13** Also—keep back Your servant from presumptuous ones, ‖ Do not let them rule over me, ‖ Then I am perfect, ‖ And declared innocent of much transgression. **14** Let the sayings of my mouth, ‖ And the meditation of my heart, ‖ Be for a pleasing thing before You, ‖ O YHWH, my rock, and my redeemer!

20 TO THE OVERSEER. A PSALM OF DAVID. YHWH answers you, ‖ In a day of adversity, ‖ The Name of the God of Jacob sets you on high, **2** He sends your help from the sanctuary, ‖ And supports you from Zion, **3** He remembers all your presents, ‖ And reduces your burnt-offering to ashes. Selah. **4** He gives to you according to your heart, ‖ And fulfills all your counsel. **5** We sing of Your salvation, ‖ And in the Name of our God set up a banner. YHWH fulfills all your requests. **6** Now I have known ‖ That YHWH has saved His anointed, ‖ He answers him from His holy heavens, ‖ With the saving might of His right hand. **7** Some of chariots, and some of horses, ‖ And we of the Name of our God YHWH ‖ Make mention. **8** They have bowed and have fallen, ‖ And we have risen and station ourselves upright. **9** O YHWH, save the king, ‖ He answers us in the day we call!

21 TO THE OVERSEER. A PSALM OF DAVID. YHWH, the king is joyful in Your strength, ‖ How greatly he rejoices in Your salvation. **2** You gave the desire of his heart to him, ‖ And You have not withheld the request of his lips. Selah. **3** For You put blessings of goodness before him, ‖ You set a crown of fine gold on his head. **4** He has asked for life from You, ‖ You have given length of days to him, ‖ For all time and forever. **5** Great [is] his glory in Your salvation, ‖ You place splendor and majesty on him. **6** For You make him blessings forever, ‖ You cause him to rejoice with joy, ‖ By Your countenance. **7** For the king is trusting in YHWH, ‖ And in the kindness of the Most High he is not moved. **8** Your hand comes to all Your enemies, ‖ Your right hand finds Your haters. **9** You make them as a furnace of fire, ‖ At the time of Your presence. YHWH swallows them in His anger, ‖ And fire devours them. **10** You destroy their fruit from earth, ‖ And their seed from the sons of men. **11** For they stretched out evil against You, ‖ They devised a wicked scheme, they do not prevail, **12** For You make them turn their back, ‖ When You prepare Your strings against their faces. **13** Be exalted, O YHWH, in Your strength, ‖ We sing and we praise Your might!

22 TO THE OVERSEER. [SET] ON "DOE OF THE MORNING." A PSALM OF DAVID. My God, My God, why have You forsaken Me? Far from My salvation, ‖ The words of My roaring? **2** My God, I call by day, and You do not answer, ‖ And by night, and am not silent. **3** And You [are] holy, ‖ Sitting—the Praise of Israel. **4** In You our fathers trusted; They trusted, and You deliver them. **5** To You they cried, and were delivered, ‖ In You they trusted, and were not disappointed. **6** And I [am] a worm, and no man, ‖ A reproach of man, and despised of the people. **7** All beholding Me mock at Me, ‖ They make free with the lip—shake the head, **8** "Roll to YHWH, He delivers Him, ‖ He delivers Him, for He delighted in Him." **9** For You [are] He bringing Me forth from the womb, ‖ Causing Me to trust, ‖ On the breasts of My mother. **10** On You I have been cast from the womb, ‖ From the belly of My mother You [are] My God. **11** Do not be far from Me, ‖ For adversity is near, for there is no helper. **12** Many bulls have surrounded Me, ‖ Mighty ones of Bashan have surrounded Me, **13** They have opened their mouth against Me, ‖ A lion tearing and roaring. **14** I have been poured out as waters, ‖ And all my bones have separated themselves, ‖ My heart has been like wax, ‖ It is melted in the midst of My bowels. **15** My power is dried up as an earthen vessel, ‖ And My tongue is cleaving to My jaws. **16** And You appoint Me to the dust of death, ‖ For dogs have surrounded Me, ‖ A company of evildoers has surrounded Me, ‖ Piercing My hands and My feet. **17** I count all My bones—they look expectingly, ‖ They look on Me, **18** They apportion My garments to themselves, ‖ And they cause a lot to fall for My clothing. **19** And You, O YHWH, do not be far off, ‖ O My strength, hurry to help Me. **20** Deliver My soul from the sword, ‖ My only one from the paw of a dog. **21** Save Me from the mouth of a lion ‖ And You have answered Me from the horns of the high places! **22** I declare Your Name to My brothers, ‖ In the midst of the assembly I praise You. **23** You who fear YHWH, praise Him, ‖ All the seed of Jacob, honor Him, ‖ And be afraid of Him, all you seed of Israel. **24** For He has not despised, nor detested, ‖ The affliction of the afflicted, ‖ Nor has He hidden His face from Him, ‖ And in His crying to Him He hears. **25** Of You My praise [is] in the great assembly. I complete My vows before His fearers. **26** The humble eat and are satisfied, ‖ Those seeking Him praise YHWH, ‖ Your heart lives forever. **27** Remember and return to YHWH, ‖ Do all the ends of the earth, ‖ And bow themselves before You, ‖ Do all families of the nations, **28** For to YHWH [is] the kingdom, ‖ And He is ruling among nations. **29** And the fat ones of earth have eaten, ‖ And they bow themselves, ‖ All going down to dust bow before Him, ‖ And he [who] has not revived his soul. **30** A seed serves Him, ‖ It is declared of the Lord to the generation. **31** They come and declare His righteousness, ‖ To a people that is born, that He has made!

23 A PSALM OF DAVID. YHWH [is] my shepherd, I do not lack, **2** He causes me to lie down in pastures of tender grass, ‖ He leads me by quiet waters. **3** He refreshes my soul, ‖ He leads me in paths of righteousness ‖ For His Name's sake; **4** Also—when I walk in a valley of death-shade, ‖ I fear no evil, for You [are] with me, ‖ Your rod and Your staff—they comfort me. **5** You arrange a table before me, ‖ In front of my adversaries, ‖ You have anointed my head with oil, ‖ My cup is full! **6** Surely goodness and kindness pursue me ‖ All the days of my life, ‖ And my dwelling [is] in the house of YHWH, ‖ For [the] length of [my] days!

24 A PSALM OF DAVID. To YHWH [is] the earth and its fullness, ‖ The world and the inhabitants in it. **2** For He has founded it on the seas, ‖ And He establishes it on the floods. **3** Who goes up into the hill of YHWH? And who rises up in His holy place? **4** The clean of hands, and pure of heart, ‖ Who has not lifted up his soul to vanity, ‖ Nor has sworn to deceit. **5** He carries away a blessing from YHWH, ‖ Righteousness from the God of his salvation. **6** This [is] a generation of those seeking Him. Seeking Your face, O Jacob! Selah. **7** Lift up your heads, O gates! And be lifted up, O perpetual doors! And the King of Glory comes in! **8** Who [is] this—"the King of Glory?" YHWH—strong and

PSALMS

mighty, ‖ YHWH, the mighty in battle. **9** Lift up your heads, O gates! And be lifted up, O perpetual doors! And the King of Glory comes in! **10** Who [is] He—this "King of Glory?" YHWH of hosts—He [is] the King of Glory! Selah.

25 BY DAVID. [ALEPH-BET] To You, O YHWH, I lift up my soul. **2** My God, in You I have trusted, ‖ Do not let me be ashamed, ‖ Do not let my enemies exult over me. **3** Also let none waiting on You be ashamed, ‖ Let the treacherous dealers without cause be ashamed. **4** Your ways, O YHWH, cause me to know, ‖ You teach me Your paths. **5** Cause me to tread in Your truth, and teach me, ‖ For You [are] the God of my salvation, ‖ Near You I have waited all the day. **6** Remember Your mercies, O YHWH, ‖ And Your kindnesses, for they [are] from the age. **7** Sins of my youth, and my transgressions, ‖ Do not remember. According to Your kindness be mindful of me, ‖ For Your goodness' sake, O YHWH. **8** Good and upright [is] YHWH, ‖ Therefore He directs sinners in the way. **9** He causes the humble to tread in judgment, ‖ And teaches the humble His way. **10** All the paths of YHWH [are] kindness and truth, ‖ To those keeping His covenant, ‖ And His testimonies. **11** For Your Name's sake, O YHWH, ‖ You have pardoned my iniquity, for it [is] great. **12** Who [is] this—the man fearing YHWH? He directs him in the way He chooses. **13** His soul remains in good, ‖ And his seed possesses the land. **14** The secret of YHWH [is] for those fearing Him, ‖ And His covenant—to cause them to know. **15** My eyes [are] continually to YHWH, ‖ For He brings my feet out from a net. **16** Turn to me, and favor me, ‖ For I [am] lonely and afflicted. **17** The distresses of my heart have enlarged themselves, ‖ Bring me out from my distresses. **18** See my affliction and my misery, ‖ And bear with all my sins. **19** See my enemies, for they have been many, ‖ And they have hated me with violent hatred. **20** Keep my soul, and deliver me, ‖ Do not let me be ashamed, for I trusted in You. **21** Integrity and uprightness keep me, ‖ For I have waited [on] You. **22** Redeem Israel, O God, from all his distresses!

26 BY DAVID. Judge me, O YHWH, for I have walked in my integrity, ‖ And I have trusted in YHWH, ‖ I do not slide. **2** Try me, O YHWH, and prove me, ‖ My reins and my heart [are] purified, **3** For Your kindness [is] before my eyes, ‖ And I have habitually walked in Your truth. **4** I have not sat with vain men, ‖ And I do not enter with pretenders. **5** I have hated the assembly of evildoers, ‖ And I do not sit with the wicked. **6** I wash my hands in innocence, ‖ And I go around Your altar, O YHWH. **7** To sound with a voice of confession, ‖ And to recount all Your wonders. **8** YHWH, I have loved the habitation of Your house, ‖ And the place of the Dwelling Place of Your glory. **9** Do not gather my soul with sinners, ‖ And my life with men of blood, **10** In whose hand [is] a wicked scheme, ‖ And their right hand [is] full of bribes. **11** And I walk in my integrity, ‖ Redeem me, and favor me. **12** My foot has stood in uprightness, ‖ In assemblies I bless YHWH!

27 BY DAVID. YHWH [is] my light and my salvation, ‖ Whom do I fear? YHWH [is] the strength of my life, ‖ Of whom am I afraid? **2** When evildoers come near to me to eat my flesh, ‖ My adversaries and my enemies to me, ‖ They have stumbled and fallen. **3** Though a host encamps against me, ‖ My heart does not fear, ‖ Though war rises up against me, ‖ In this I [am] confident. **4** One [thing] I asked of YHWH—it I seek: My dwelling in the house of YHWH, ‖ All the days of my life, ‖ To look on the pleasantness of YHWH, ‖ And to inquire in His temple. **5** For He hides me in a dwelling place in the day of evil, ‖ He hides me in a secret place of His tent, ‖ He raises me up on a rock. **6** And now my head is lifted up, ‖ Above my enemies—my surrounders, ‖ And I sacrifice in His tent sacrifices of shouting, ‖ I sing, indeed, I sing praise to YHWH. **7** Hear, O YHWH, my voice—I call, ‖ And favor me, and answer me. **8** My heart said to You, "They sought my face, ‖ Your face, O YHWH, I seek." **9** Do not hide Your face from me, ‖ Do not turn Your servant aside in anger, ‖ You have been my help. Do not leave me, nor forsake me, ‖ O God of my salvation. **10** When my father and my mother ‖ Have forsaken me, then YHWH gathers me. **11** Show me, O YHWH, Your way, ‖ And lead me in a path of uprightness, ‖ For the sake of my beholders. **12** Do not give me to the will of my adversaries, ‖ For false witnesses have risen against me, ‖

And they breathe out violence to me. **13** I had not believed to look on the goodness of YHWH ‖ In the land of the living! **14** Look to YHWH—be strong, ‖ And He strengthens your heart, ‖ Indeed, look to YHWH!

28 BY DAVID. To You, O YHWH, I call, ‖ My rock, do not be silent to me! Lest You are silent to me, ‖ And I have been compared ‖ With those going down to the pit. **2** Hear the voice of my supplications, ‖ In my crying to You, ‖ In my lifting up my hands toward your holy oracle. **3** Do not draw me with the wicked, ‖ And with workers of iniquity, ‖ Speaking peace with their neighbors, ‖ And evil in their heart. **4** Give to them according to their acting, ‖ And according to the evil of their doings. Give to them according to the work of their hands. Return their deed to them. **5** For they do not attend to the doing of YHWH, ‖ And to the work of His hands. He throws them down, ‖ And does not build them up. **6** Blessed [is] YHWH, ‖ For He has heard the voice of my supplications. **7** YHWH [is] my strength, and my shield, ‖ In Him my heart trusted, and I have been helped. And my heart exults, ‖ And I thank Him with my song. **8** YHWH [is] strength to him, ‖ Indeed, the strength of the salvation of His anointed [is] He. **9** Save Your people, and bless Your inheritance, ‖ And feed them, and carry them for all time!

29 A PSALM OF DAVID. Ascribe to YHWH, you sons of the mighty, ‖ Ascribe to YHWH glory and strength. **2** Ascribe to YHWH the glory of His Name, ‖ Bow yourselves to YHWH, ‖ In the beauty of holiness. **3** The voice of YHWH [is] on the waters, ‖ The God of glory has thundered, ‖ YHWH [is] on many waters. **4** The voice of YHWH [is] with power, ‖ The voice of YHWH [is] with majesty, **5** The voice of YHWH [is] shattering cedars, ‖ Indeed, YHWH shatters the cedars of Lebanon. **6** And He causes them to skip as a calf, ‖ Lebanon and Sirion as a son of Reems, **7** The voice of YHWH is hewing fiery flames, **8** The voice of YHWH pains a wilderness, ‖ YHWH pains the wilderness of Kadesh. **9** The voice of YHWH pains the oaks, ‖ And makes bare the forests, ‖ And in His temple everyone says, "Glory!" **10** YHWH has sat on the flood, ‖ And YHWH sits [as] king for all time, **11** YHWH gives strength to His people, ‖ YHWH blesses His people with peace!

30 A PSALM. A SONG OF THE DEDICATION OF THE HOUSE OF DAVID. I exalt You, O YHWH, ‖ For You have drawn me up, ‖ And have not let my enemies rejoice over me. **2** My God YHWH, I have cried to You, ‖ And You heal me. **3** YHWH, You have brought up my soul from Sheol, ‖ You have kept me alive, ‖ From going down [to] the pit. **4** Sing praise to YHWH, you His saints, ‖ And give thanks at the remembrance of His holiness, **5** For—a moment [is] in His anger, ‖ Life [is] in His goodwill, ‖ At evening remains weeping, and at morning singing. **6** And I have said in my ease, "I am not moved for all time. **7** O YHWH, in Your good pleasure, ‖ You have caused strength to remain for my mountain," ‖ You have hidden Your face—I have been troubled. **8** To You, O YHWH, I call, ‖ And to YHWH I make supplication. **9** "What gain [is] in my blood? In my going down to corruption? Does dust thank You? Does it declare Your truth? **10** Hear, O YHWH, and favor me, O YHWH, be a helper to me." **11** You have turned my mourning to dancing for me, ‖ You have loosed my sackcloth, ‖ And gird me [with] joy. **12** So that glory praises You, and is not silent, ‖ O YHWH, my God, I thank You for all time!

31 TO THE OVERSEER. A PSALM OF DAVID. In You, O YHWH, I have trusted, ‖ Do not let me be ashamed for all time, ‖ In Your righteousness deliver me. **2** Incline Your ear to me quickly, deliver me, ‖ Be to me for a strong rock, ‖ For a house of bulwarks to save me. **3** For You [are] my rock and my bulwark, ‖ For Your Name's sake lead me and tend me. **4** Bring me out from the net that they hid for me, ‖ For You [are] my strength. **5** Into Your hand I commit my spirit, ‖ You have redeemed me, YHWH God of truth. **6** I have hated the observers of lying vanities, ‖ And I have been confident toward YHWH. **7** I rejoice, and am glad in Your kindness, ‖ In that You have seen my affliction, ‖ You have known my soul in adversities. **8** And You have not shut me up, ‖ Into the hand of an enemy, ‖ You have caused my feet to stand in a broad place. **9** Favor me, O YHWH, for distress [is] to me, ‖ My eye, my soul, and my body ‖ Have become old by provocation. **10** For my life has been consumed in sorrow ‖ And my years in sighing. My strength has been feeble because of my iniquity, ‖ And my bones have become old. **11** I have been a reproach among all my adversaries, ‖ And to my neighbors exceedingly, ‖ And a fear to my acquaintances, ‖ Those seeing me without—fled from me. **12** I have been forgotten as dead, out of mind, ‖ I have been as a perishing vessel. **13** For I have heard an evil account of many, ‖ Fear [is] all around. In their being united against me, ‖ They have devised to take my life, **14** And I have trusted on You, ‖ O YHWH, I have said, "You [are] my God." **15** In Your hand [are] my times, ‖ Deliver me from the hand of my enemies, ‖ And from my pursuers. **16** Cause Your face to shine on Your servant, ‖ Save me in Your kindness. **17** O YHWH, do not let me be ashamed, ‖ For I have called You, let the wicked be ashamed, ‖ Let them become silent to Sheol. **18** Let lips of falsehood become mute, ‖ That are speaking against the righteous, ‖ Ancient sayings, in pride and contempt. **19** How abundant is Your goodness, ‖ That You have laid up for those fearing You, ‖ You have worked for those trusting in You, ‖ Before sons of men. **20** You hide them in the secret place of Your presence, ‖ From schemes of man, ‖ You conceal them in a dwelling place, ‖ From the strife of tongues. **21** Blessed [is] YHWH, ‖ For He has made His kindness marvelous ‖ To me in a city of bulwarks. **22** And I have said in my haste, "I have been cut off from before Your eyes," ‖ But You have heard the voice of my supplications, ‖ In my crying to You. **23** Love YHWH, all you His saints, ‖ YHWH is keeping the faithful, ‖ And repaying a proud doer abundantly. **24** Be strong, and He strengthens your heart, ‖ All you who are waiting for YHWH!

32 AN INSTRUCTION OF DAVID. O the blessedness of him whose transgression [is] forgiven, ‖ Whose sin is covered. **2** O the blessedness of a man, ‖ To whom YHWH does not impute iniquity, ‖ And in whose spirit there is no deceit. **3** When I have kept silence, my bones have become old, ‖ Through my roaring all the day. **4** When by day and by night Your hand is heavy on me, ‖ My moisture has been changed ‖ Into the droughts of summer. Selah. **5** I cause You to know my sin, ‖ And I have not covered my iniquity. I have said, "I confess to YHWH concerning My transgressions," ‖ And You have taken away the iniquity of my sin. Selah. **6** For every saintly one prays this to You, ‖ In the time to find [You]. Surely at an overflowing of many waters, ‖ They do not come to him. **7** You [are] a hiding place for me, ‖ You keep me from distress, ‖ Surround me [with] songs of deliverance. Selah. **8** I cause you to act wisely, ‖ And direct you in the way that you go, ‖ I cause My eye to take counsel concerning you. **9** Do not be as a horse—as a mule, ‖ Without understanding, ‖ With bridle and bit, its ornaments, to curb, ‖ Not to come near to you. **10** Many [are] the pains of the wicked; As for him who is trusting in YHWH, ‖ Kindness surrounds him. **11** Be glad in YHWH, and rejoice, you righteous, ‖ And sing, all you upright of heart!

33 Sing, you righteous, in YHWH, ‖ [For] praise from upright ones [is] lovely. **2** Give thanks to YHWH with a harp, ‖ With stringed instrument of ten strings sing praise to Him, **3** Sing to Him a new song, ‖ Play skillfully with shouting. **4** For the word of YHWH [is] upright, ‖ And all His work [is] in faithfulness. **5** Loving righteousness and judgment, ‖ The earth is full of the kindness of YHWH. **6** By the word of YHWH ‖ The heavens have been made, ‖ And all their host by the breath of His mouth. **7** Gathering the waters of the sea as a heap, ‖ Putting the depths in treasuries. **8** All the earth is afraid of YHWH, ‖ All the inhabitants of the world are afraid of Him. **9** For He has spoken, and it is, ‖ He has commanded, and it stands. **10** YHWH made void the counsel of nations, ‖ He disallowed the thoughts of the peoples. **11** The counsel of YHWH stands for all time, ‖ The thoughts of His heart from generation to generation. **12** O the blessedness of the nation whose God [is] YHWH, ‖ Of the people He chose, ‖ For an inheritance to Him. **13** YHWH has looked from the heavens, ‖ He has seen all the sons of men. **14** From the fixed place of His dwelling, ‖ He looked to all inhabitants of the earth; **15** Who is forming their hearts together, ‖ Who is attending to all their works. **16** The king is not saved by the multitude of a force. A mighty man is not delivered, ‖ By abundance of power. **17** A false thing [is] the horse for safety, ‖ And he does not deliver ‖ By the abundance of his strength. **18** Behold, the eye of Y<small>HWH</small> [is] to those fearing Him, ‖ To those waiting for His kindness, **19** To deliver their soul from death, ‖ And to keep them alive in famine. **20** Our soul has waited for Y<small>HWH</small>, ‖ He [is] our help and our shield, **21** For our heart rejoices in Him, ‖ For we have trusted in His Holy Name. **22** Let Your kindness, O Y<small>HWH</small>, be on us, ‖ As we have waited for You!

34 B<small>Y</small> D<small>AVID</small>, <small>IN HIS CHANGING HIS BEHAVIOR BEFORE</small> A<small>BIMELECH, AND HE DRIVES HIM AWAY, AND HE GOES</small>. [A<small>LEPH</small>-B<small>ET</small>] I bless Y<small>HWH</small> at all times, ‖ His praise [is] continually in my mouth. **2** In Y<small>HWH</small> my soul boasts herself, ‖ The humble hear and rejoice. **3** Ascribe greatness to Y<small>HWH</small> with me, ‖ And we exalt His Name together. **4** I sought Y<small>HWH</small>, and He answered me, ‖ And delivered me from all my fears. **5** They looked expectantly to Him, ‖ And they became bright, ‖ And their faces are not ashamed. **6** This poor [one] called, and Y<small>HWH</small> heard, ‖ And saved him from all his distresses. **7** A messenger of Y<small>HWH</small> is encamping, ‖ Around those who fear Him, ‖ And He arms them. **8** Taste and see that Y<small>HWH</small> [is] good, ‖ O the blessedness of the man who trusts in Him. **9** Fear Y<small>HWH</small>, you His holy ones, ‖ For there is no lack to those fearing Him. **10** Young lions have lacked and been hungry, ‖ And those seeking Y<small>HWH</small> do not lack any good, **11** Come, children, listen to me, ‖ I teach you the fear of Y<small>HWH</small>. **12** Who [is] the man that is desiring life? Loving days to see good? **13** Keep your tongue from evil, ‖ And your lips from speaking deceit. **14** Turn aside from evil and do good, ‖ Seek peace and pursue it. **15** The eyes of Y<small>HWH</small> [are] to the righteous, ‖ And His ears to their cry. **16** (The face of Y<small>HWH</small> [is] on doers of evil, ‖ To cut off their memorial from earth.) **17** They cried, and Y<small>HWH</small> heard, ‖ And delivered them from all their distresses. **18** Y<small>HWH</small> [is] near to the broken of heart, ‖ And He saves the bruised of spirit. **19** Many [are] the afflictions of the righteous, ‖ Y<small>HWH</small> delivers him out of them all. **20** He is keeping all his bones, ‖ Not one of them has been broken. **21** Evil puts the wicked to death, ‖ And those hating the righteous are desolate. **22** Y<small>HWH</small> redeems the soul of His servants, ‖ And none trusting in Him are desolate!

35 B<small>Y</small> D<small>AVID</small>. Strive, Y<small>HWH</small>, with my strivers, fight with my fighters, **2** Take hold of shield and buckler, and rise for my help, **3** And draw out spear and lance, ‖ To meet my pursuers. Say to my soul, "I [am] your salvation." **4** They are ashamed and blush, those seeking my soul, ‖ Turned backward and confounded, ‖ Those devising my evil. **5** They are as chaff before wind, ‖ And a messenger of Y<small>HWH</small> driving away. **6** Their way is darkness and slipperiness, ‖ And a messenger of Y<small>HWH</small>—their pursuer. **7** For without cause they hid their net [in] a pit for me, ‖ Without cause they dug for my soul. **8** Desolation meets him—he does not know, ‖ And his net that he hid catches him, ‖ He falls into it for desolation. **9** And my soul is joyful in Y<small>HWH</small>, ‖ It rejoices in His salvation. **10** All my bones say, "Y<small>HWH</small>, who is like You, ‖ Delivering the poor from the [one] stronger than he, ‖ And the poor and needy from his plunderer." **11** Violent witnesses rise up, ‖ That which I have not known they ask me. **12** They pay me evil for good, bereaving my soul, **13** And I—in their sickness my clothing [is] sackcloth, ‖ I have humbled my soul with fastings, ‖ And my prayer returns to my bosom. **14** As [if] a friend, as [if] my brother, ‖ I habitually walked, ‖ As a mourner for a mother, ‖ I have bowed down mourning. **15** And they have rejoiced in my halting, ‖ And have been gathered together, ‖ The strikers were gathered against me, ‖ And I have not known, ‖ They have torn, and they have not ceased; **16** With profane ones, mockers in feasts, ‖ Gnashing their teeth against me. **17** Lord, how long do You behold? Keep my soul back from their desolations, ‖ My only one from young lions. **18** I thank You in a great assembly, ‖ I praise You among a mighty people. **19** Do not let my enemies rejoice over me [with] falsehood, ‖ Those hating me without cause wink the eye. **20** For they do not speak peace, ‖ And against the quiet of the land, ‖ They devise deceitful words, **21** And they enlarge their mouth against me, ‖ They said, "Aha, aha, our eye has seen." **22** You have seen, O Y<small>HWH</small>, ‖ Do not be silent, O Lord—do not be far from me, **23** Stir up, and wake to my judgment, ‖ My God, and my Lord, to my plea. **24** Judge me according to Your righteousness, O Y<small>HWH</small> my God, ‖ And they do not rejoice over me. **25** They do not say in their heart, "Aha, our desire." They do not say, "We swallowed him up." **26** They are ashamed and confounded together, ‖ Who are rejoicing at my evil. They put on shame and confusion, ‖ Who are magnifying themselves against me. **27** They sing and rejoice, who are desiring my righteousness, ‖ And they continually say, "YHWH is magnified, ‖ Who is desiring the peace of His servant." **28** And my tongue utters Your righteousness, ‖ All the day Your praise!

36 TO THE OVERSEER. BY A SERVANT OF YHWH, BY DAVID. The transgression of the wicked ‖ Is affirming within my heart, "Fear of God is not before his eyes, **2** For he made [it] smooth to himself in his eyes, ‖ To find his iniquity to be hated. **3** The words of his mouth [are] iniquity and deceit, ‖ He ceased to act prudently—to do good. **4** He devises iniquity on his bed, ‖ He stations himself on a way not good, ‖ He does not refuse evil." **5** O YHWH, Your kindness [is] in the heavens, ‖ Your faithfulness [is] to the clouds. **6** Your righteousness [is] as mountains of God, ‖ Your judgments [are] a great deep. You save man and beast, O YHWH. **7** How precious [is] Your kindness, O God, ‖ And the sons of men trust ‖ In the shadow of Your wings. **8** They are filled from the fatness of Your house, ‖ And You cause them to drink the stream of Your delights. **9** For a fountain of life [is] with You, ‖ In Your light we see light. **10** Draw out Your kindness to those knowing You, ‖ And Your righteousness to the upright of heart. **11** Do not let a foot of pride meet me, ‖ And do not let a hand of the wicked move me. **12** Workers of iniquity have fallen there, ‖ They have been overthrown, ‖ And have not been able to arise!

37 BY DAVID. [ALEPH-BET] Do not fret because of evildoers, ‖ Do not be envious against doers of iniquity, **2** For they are cut off speedily as grass, ‖ And fade as the greenness of the tender grass. **3** Trust in YHWH, and do good, ‖ Dwell [in] the land, and enjoy faithfulness, **4** And delight yourself on YHWH, ‖ And He gives to you the petitions of your heart. **5** Roll your way on YHWH, ‖ And trust on Him, and He works, **6** And has brought out your righteousness as light, ‖ And your judgment as noon-day. **7** Be silent for YHWH, and stay yourself for Him, ‖ Do not fret because of him ‖ Who is making his way prosperous, ‖ Because of a man doing wicked schemes. **8** Desist from anger, and forsake fury, ‖ Do not fret yourself to only do evil. **9** For evildoers are cut off, ‖ As for those waiting on YHWH, they possess the land. **10** And yet a little [while], and the wicked is not, ‖ And you have considered his place, and it is not. **11** And the humble possess the land, ‖ And they have delighted themselves ‖ In the abundance of peace. **12** The wicked is devising against the righteous, ‖ And gnashing his teeth against him. **13** The Lord laughs at him, ‖ For He has seen that his day comes. **14** The wicked have opened a sword, ‖ And they have bent their bow, ‖ To cause the poor and needy to fall, ‖ To slaughter the upright of the way. **15** Their sword enters into their own heart, ‖ And their bows are shattered. **16** Better [is] the little of the righteous, ‖ Than the store of many wicked. **17** For the arms of the wicked are shattered, ‖ And YHWH is sustaining the righteous. **18** YHWH knows the days of the perfect, ‖ And their inheritance is for all time. **19** They are not ashamed in a time of evil, ‖ And they are satisfied in days of famine. **20** But the wicked perish, and the enemies of YHWH, ‖ Have been consumed as the preciousness of lambs, ‖ They have been consumed in smoke. **21** The wicked is borrowing and does not repay, ‖ And the righteous is gracious and giving. **22** For His blessed ones possess the land, ‖ And His reviled ones are cut off. **23** The steps of a man [are] from YHWH, ‖ They have been prepared, ‖ And He desires his way. **24** When he falls, he is not cast down, ‖ For YHWH is sustaining his hand. **25** I have been young, ‖ I have also become old, ‖ And I have not seen the righteous forsaken, ‖ And his seed seeking bread. **26** All the day he is gracious and lending, ‖ And his seed [is] for a blessing. **27** Turn aside from evil, and do good, and dwell for all time. **28** For YHWH is loving judgment, ‖ And He does not forsake His saintly ones, ‖ They have been kept for all time, ‖ And the seed of the wicked is cut off. **29** The righteous possess the land, ‖ And they dwell on it forever. **30** The mouth of the righteous utters wisdom, ‖ And his tongue speaks judgment. **31** The law of his God [is] his heart, ‖ His steps do not slide. **32** The wicked is watching for the righteous, ‖ And is seeking to put him to death. **33** YHWH does not leave him in his hand, ‖ Nor

PSALMS

condemn him in his being judged. **34** Look to YHWH, and keep His way, ‖ And He exalts you to possess the land, ‖ In the wicked being cut off—you see! **35** I have seen the wicked terrible, ‖ And spreading as a green native plant, **36** And he passes away, and behold, he is not, ‖ And I seek him, and he is not found! **37** Observe the perfect, and see the upright, ‖ For the latter end of each [is] peace. **38** And transgressors were destroyed together, ‖ The latter end of the wicked was cut off. **39** And the salvation of the righteous [is] from YHWH, ‖ Their strong place in a time of adversity. **40** And YHWH helps them and delivers them, ‖ He delivers them from the wicked, ‖ And saves them, ‖ Because they trusted in Him!

38 A PSALM OF DAVID. "TO CAUSE TO REMEMBER." YHWH, do not reprove me in Your wrath, ‖ Nor discipline me in Your fury. **2** For Your arrows have come down on me, ‖ And You let down Your hand on me. **3** Soundness is not in my flesh, ‖ Because of Your indignation, ‖ Peace is not in my bones, ‖ Because of my sin. **4** For my iniquities have passed over my head, ‖ As a heavy burden—too heavy for me. **5** Stunk—my wounds have become corrupt, ‖ Because of my folly. **6** I have been bent down, ‖ I have been bowed down—to excess, ‖ I have gone mourning all the day. **7** For my flanks have been full of drought, ‖ And soundness is not in my flesh. **8** I have been feeble and struck—to excess, ‖ I have roared from disquietude of heart. **9** Lord, all my desire [is] before You, ‖ And my sighing has not been hid from You. **10** My heart [is] panting, my power has forsaken me, ‖ And the light of my eyes, ‖ Even they are not with me. **11** My lovers and my friends stand aloof from before my plague. And my neighbors have stood far off. **12** And those seeking my soul lay a snare, ‖ And those seeking my evil ‖ Have spoken mischievous things, ‖ And they meditate [on] deceits all the day. **13** And I, as deaf, do not hear. And as a mute one who does not open his mouth. **14** Indeed, I am as a man who does not hear, ‖ And in his mouth are no reproofs. **15** Because for You, O YHWH, I have waited, ‖ You answer, O Lord my God. **16** When I said, "Lest they rejoice over me, ‖ In the slipping of my foot they magnified themselves against me." **17** For I am ready to halt, ‖ And my pain [is] continually before me. **18** For I declare my iniquity, ‖ I am sorry for my sin. **19** And my enemies [are] lively, ‖ They have been strong, and those hating me without cause, ‖ Have been multiplied. **20** And those paying evil for good accuse me, ‖ Because of my pursuing good. **21** Do not forsake me, O YHWH, ‖ My God, do not be far from me, **22** Hurry to help me, O Lord, my salvation!

39 TO THE OVERSEER. FOR JEDUTHUN. A PSALM OF DAVID. I have said, "I observe my ways, ‖ Against sinning with my tongue, ‖ I keep a curb for my mouth, ‖ While the wicked [is] before me." **2** I was mute [with] silence, ‖ I kept silent from good, and my pain is excited. **3** My heart [is] hot within me, ‖ In my meditating the fire burns, ‖ I have spoken with my tongue. **4** "Cause me to know, O YHWH, my end, ‖ And the measure of my days—what it [is]," ‖ I know how frail I [am]. **5** Behold, You have made my days handbreadths, ‖ And my age [is] as nothing before You, ‖ Only, every man set up [is] all vanity. Selah. **6** Only, each habitually walks in an image, ‖ Only, [in] vain, they are disquieted, ‖ He heaps up and does not know who gathers them. **7** And now, what have I expected? O Lord, my hope—it [is] of You. **8** Deliver me from all my transgressions, ‖ Do not make me a reproach of the fool. **9** I have been mute, I do not open my mouth, ‖ Because You have done [it]. **10** Turn aside Your stroke from off me, ‖ From the striving of Your hand I have been consumed. **11** With reproofs against iniquity, ‖ You have corrected man, ‖ And dissolve his desirableness as a moth, ‖ Only, every man [is] vanity. Selah. **12** Hear my prayer, O YHWH, ‖ And give ear [to] my cry, ‖ Do not be silent to my tear, ‖ For I [am] a sojourner with You, ‖ A settler like all my fathers. **13** Look from me, and I brighten up before I go and am not!

40 TO THE OVERSEER. A PSALM OF DAVID. I have diligently expected YHWH, ‖ And He inclines to me, and hears my cry, **2** And He causes me to come up ‖ From a pit of desolation—from mire of mud, ‖ And He raises up my feet on a rock, ‖ He is establishing my steps. **3** And He puts a new song in my mouth, "Praise to our God." Many see and fear, and trust in YHWH. **4** O the blessedness of the man ‖

Who has made YHWH his trust, ‖ And has not turned to the proud, ‖ And those turning aside to lies. **5** You have done much, my God YHWH; Your wonders and Your thoughts toward us, ‖ There is none to arrange to You, ‖ I declare and speak: They have been more than to be numbered. **6** Sacrifice and present You have not desired, ‖ But a body You have prepared for me, ‖ Burnt and sin-offering You have not asked. **7** Then I said, "Behold, I have come, ‖ In the roll of the scroll it is written of me, **8** I have delighted to do Your pleasure, my God, ‖ And Your law [is] within my heart." **9** I have proclaimed tidings of righteousness ‖ In the great assembly, ‖ Behold, I do not restrain my lips, ‖ O YHWH, You have known. **10** I have not concealed Your righteousness ‖ In the midst of my heart, ‖ I have told of Your faithfulness and Your salvation, ‖ I have not hidden Your kindness and Your truth, ‖ To the great assembly. **11** You, O YHWH, do not restrain Your mercies from me, ‖ Your kindness and Your truth continually keep me. **12** For innumerable evils have surrounded me, ‖ My iniquities have overtaken me, ‖ And I have not been able to see; They have been more than the hairs of my head, ‖ And my heart has forsaken me. **13** Be pleased, O YHWH, to deliver me, ‖ O YHWH, make haste for my help. **14** They are ashamed and confounded together, ‖ Who are seeking my soul to destroy it, ‖ They are turned backward, ‖ And are ashamed, who are desiring my evil. **15** They are desolate because of their shame, ‖ Who are saying to me, "Aha, aha." **16** All seeking You rejoice and are glad in You, ‖ Those loving Your salvation continually say, "YHWH is magnified." **17** And I [am] poor and needy, ‖ The Lord devises for me. You [are] my help and my deliverer, O my God, do not linger.

41 TO THE OVERSEER. A PSALM OF DAVID. O the blessedness of him ‖ Who is acting wisely to the poor, ‖ In a day of evil YHWH delivers him. **2** YHWH preserves him and revives him, ‖ He is blessed in the land, ‖ And You do not give him into the will of his enemies. **3** YHWH supports [him] on a bed of sickness, ‖ You have turned his bed in his weakness. **4** I said, "O YHWH, favor me, ‖ Heal my soul, for I sinned against You," **5** My enemies say evil of me: When he dies—his name has perished! **6** And if he came to see—he speaks vanity, ‖ His heart gathers iniquity to itself, ‖ He goes out—at the street he speaks. **7** All hating me whisper together against me, ‖ Against me they devise evil to me: **8** A worthless thing is poured out on him, ‖ And because he lay down he does not rise again. **9** Even my ally, in whom I trusted, ‖ One eating my bread, ‖ Made the heel great against me, **10** And You, YHWH, favor me, ‖ And cause me to rise, ‖ And I give repayment to them. **11** By this I have known, ‖ That You have delighted in me, ‖ Because my enemy does not shout over me. **12** As for me, in my integrity, ‖ You have taken hold on me, ‖ And cause me to stand before You for all time. **13** Blessed [is] YHWH, God of Israel, ‖ From age to age. Amen and Amen.

42 TO THE OVERSEER. AN INSTRUCTION OF THE SONS OF KORAH. As a deer pants for streams of water, ‖ So my soul pants toward You, O God. **2** My soul thirsted for God, for the living God, ‖ When do I enter and see the face of God? **3** My tear has been bread day and night to me, ‖ In their saying to me all the day, "Where [is] your God?" **4** These I remember, and pour out my soul in me, ‖ For I pass over into the shelter, ‖ I go softly with them to the house of God, ‖ With the voice of singing and confession, ‖ The multitude keeping celebration! **5** Why bow yourself, O my soul? Indeed, are you troubled within me? Wait for God, for I still confess Him: The salvation of my countenance—my God! **6** My soul bows itself in me, ‖ Therefore I remember You from the land of Jordan, ‖ And of the Hermons, from Mount Mizar. **7** Deep is calling to deep ‖ At the noise of Your waterspouts, ‖ All Your breakers and Your billows passed over me. **8** By day YHWH commands His kindness, ‖ And by night a song [is] with me, ‖ A prayer to the God of my life. **9** I say to God my Rock, "Why have You forgotten me? Why do I go mourning in the oppression of an enemy?" **10** With a sword in my bones ‖ My adversaries have reproached me, ‖ In their saying to me all the day, "Where [is] your God?" **11** Why bow yourself, O my soul? And why are you troubled within me? Wait for God, for I still confess Him, ‖ The salvation of my countenance, and my God!

PSALMS

43 Judge me, O God, ‖ And plead my cause against a nation not pious, ‖ You deliver me from a man of deceit and perverseness, **2** For you [are] the God of my strength. Why have You cast me off? Why do I go up and down mourning, ‖ In the oppression of an enemy? **3** Send forth Your light and Your truth, ‖ They lead me, they bring me in, ‖ To Your holy hill, and to Your dwelling places. **4** And I go to the altar of God, ‖ To God, the joy of my rejoicing. And I thank You with a harp, O God, my God. **5** Why bow yourself, O my soul? And why are you troubled within me? Wait for God, for I still confess Him, ‖ The salvation of my countenance, and my God!

44 TO THE OVERSEER. AN INSTRUCTION OF THE SONS OF KORAH. O God, we have heard with our ears, ‖ Our fathers have recounted to us, ‖ The work You worked in their days, ‖ In the days of old. **2** You, [with] Your hand, have dispossessed nations. And You plant them. You afflict peoples, and send them away. **3** For they did not possess the land by their sword, ‖ And their arm did not give salvation to them, ‖ But Your right hand, and Your arm, ‖ And the light of Your countenance, ‖ Because You had accepted them. **4** You [are] He, my King, O God, ‖ Command the deliverances of Jacob. **5** By You we push our adversaries, ‖ By Your Name we tread down our withstanders, **6** For I do not trust in my bow, ‖ And my sword does not save me. **7** For You have saved us from our adversaries, ‖ And You have put to shame those hating us. **8** In God we have boasted all the day, ‖ And we thank Your Name for all time. Selah. **9** In anger You have cast off and cause us to blush, ‖ And do not go forth with our hosts. **10** You cause us to turn backward from an adversary, ‖ And those hating us, ‖ Have spoiled for themselves. **11** You make us food like sheep, ‖ And You have scattered us among nations. **12** You sell Your people—without wealth, ‖ And have not become great by their price. **13** You make us a reproach to our neighbors, ‖ A scorn and a reproach to our surrounders. **14** You make us an allegory among nations, ‖ A shaking of the head among peoples. **15** All the day my confusion [is] before me, ‖ And the shame of my face has covered me. **16** Because of the voice of a reproacher and reviler, ‖ Because of an enemy and a self-avenger. **17** All this met us, and we did not forget You, ‖ Nor have we dealt falsely in Your covenant. **18** We do not turn our heart backward, ‖ Nor turn aside our step from Your path. **19** But You have struck us in a place of dragons, ‖ And cover us over with death-shade. **20** If we have forgotten the Name of our God, ‖ And spread our hands to a strange God, **21** Does God not search this out? For He knows the secrets of the heart. **22** Surely, for Your sake we have been slain all the day, ‖ Reckoned as sheep of the slaughter. **23** Stir up—why do You sleep, O Lord? Awake, do not cast us off forever. **24** Why do You hide Your face? You forget our afflictions and our oppression, **25** For our soul has bowed to the dust, ‖ Our belly has cleaved to the earth. **26** Arise, a help to us, ‖ And ransom us for your kindness' sake.

45 TO THE OVERSEER. [SET] ON "LILIES." AN INSTRUCTION OF THE SONS OF KORAH. A SONG OF LOVES. My heart has stirred a good word, ‖ I am telling my works to the King, ‖ My tongue [is] the pen of a speedy writer. **2** You have been beautified above the sons of men, ‖ Grace has been poured into Your lips, ‖ Therefore God has blessed You for all time. **3** Gird Your sword on the thigh, O Mighty [One], ‖ Your splendor and Your majesty! **4** As for Your majesty—prosper [and] ride! Because of truth, meekness, [and] righteousness, ‖ And Your right hand shows You fearful things. **5** Your arrows [are] sharp—Peoples fall under You—In the heart of the enemies of the King. **6** Your throne, O God, [is for] all time and forever, ‖ A scepter of uprightness ‖ [Is] the scepter of Your kingdom. **7** You have loved righteousness and hate wickedness, ‖ Therefore God, Your God, has anointed You ‖ With oil of joy above Your companions. **8** Myrrh, and aloes, [and] cassia ‖ [Cover] all Your garments; Out of palaces of ivory, ‖ Stringed instruments have made You glad. **9** Daughters of kings [are] among Your precious ones, ‖ A queen has stood at Your right hand, ‖ In pure gold of Ophir. **10** Listen, O daughter, and see, incline your ear, ‖ And forget your people, and your father's house, **11** And the King desires your beauty, ‖ Because He [is] your Lord—bow yourself to Him, **12** And the daughter of Tyre with a present, ‖ The rich of the people appease your face. **13** All glory [is] the daughter of the king within, ‖

Her clothing [is] with filigrees of gold. **14** In various colors she is brought to the King; Afterward, virgins, her companions, ‖ Are brought to You. **15** They are brought with joy and gladness, ‖ They come into the palace of the King. **16** Instead of Your fathers are Your sons, ‖ You appoint them for princes in all the earth. **17** I make mention of Your Name in all generations, ‖ Therefore peoples praise You, ‖ For all time and forever!

46 TO THE OVERSEER. BY SONS OF KORAH. FOR GIRLS' [VOICES]. A SONG. God [is] our refuge and strength, ‖ A most sure help in adversities. **2** Therefore we do not fear in the changing of earth, ‖ And in the slipping of mountains ‖ Into the heart of the seas. **3** Roar—troubled are its waters, ‖ Mountains shake in its pride. Selah. **4** A river—its streams make glad the city of God, ‖ Your holy place of the dwelling places of the Most High. **5** God [is] in her midst—she is not moved, God helps her at the turn of the morning! **6** Nations have been troubled, ‖ Kingdoms have been moved, ‖ He has given forth with His voice—earth melts. **7** YHWH of Hosts [is] with us, ‖ The God of Jacob [is] a tower for us. Selah. **8** Come, see the works of YHWH, ‖ Who has done astonishing things in the earth, **9** Causing wars to cease, ‖ To the end of the earth, He shatters the bow, ‖ And He has cut apart the spear, ‖ He burns chariots with fire. **10** Desist, and know that I [am] God, ‖ I am exalted among nations, ‖ I am exalted in the earth. **11** YHWH of hosts [is] with us, ‖ The God of Jacob [is] a tower for us! Selah.

47 TO THE OVERSEER. A PSALM OF THE SONS OF KORAH. All you peoples, clap the hand, ‖ Shout to God with a voice of singing, **2** For YHWH Most High [is] fearful, ‖ A great King over all the earth. **3** He leads peoples under us, and nations under our feet. **4** He chooses for us our inheritance, ‖ The excellence of Jacob that He loves. Selah. **5** God has gone up with a shout, ‖ YHWH with the sound of a horn. **6** Praise God—praise—give praise to our king, praise. **7** For God [is] King of all the earth, ‖ Give praise, O understanding one. **8** God has reigned over nations, God has sat on His holy throne, **9** Nobles of peoples have been gathered, ‖ [With] the people of the God of Abraham, ‖ For the shields of earth [are] to God, ‖ Greatly has He been exalted!

48 A SONG. A PSALM OF THE SONS OF KORAH. Great [is] YHWH, and greatly praised, ‖ In the city of our God— His holy hill. **2** Beautiful [for] elevation, ‖ A joy of all the land, [is] Mount Zion, ‖ The sides of the north, the city of [the] great King. **3** God is known for a tower in her high places. **4** For behold, the kings met, they passed by together, **5** They have seen—so they have marveled, ‖ They have been troubled, they were hurried away. **6** Trembling has seized them there, ‖ Pain, as of a travailing woman. **7** By an east wind You shatter ships of Tarshish. **8** As we have heard, so we have seen, ‖ In the city of YHWH of hosts, ‖ In the city of our God, God establishes her for all time. Selah. **9** We have thought, O God, of Your kindness, ‖ In the midst of Your temple, **10** As [is] Your Name, O God, so [is] Your praise, ‖ Over the ends of the earth, ‖ Righteousness has filled Your right hand. **11** Mount Zion rejoices, ‖ The daughters of Judah are joyful, ‖ For the sake of Your judgments. **12** Surround Zion, and go around her, count her towers, **13** Set your heart to her bulwark, ‖ Consider her high places, ‖ So that you recount to a later generation, **14** That this God [is] our God— For all time and forever, ‖ He leads us over death!

49 TO THE OVERSEER. A PSALM OF THE SONS OF KORAH. Hear this, all you peoples, ‖ Give ear, all you inhabitants of the world. **2** Both low and high, together rich and needy. **3** My mouth speaks wise things, ‖ And the meditations of my heart [are] things of understanding. **4** I incline my ear to an allegory, ‖ I open my riddle with a harp: **5** Why do I fear in days of evil? The iniquity of my supplanters surrounds me. **6** Those trusting on their wealth, ‖ And in the multitude of their riches, ‖ Show themselves foolish. **7** A brother ransoms no one at all, ‖ He does not give to God his atonement. **8** And precious [is] the redemption of their soul, ‖ And it has ceased for all time. **9** And still he lives forever, ‖ He does not see the pit. **10** For he sees wise men die, ‖ Together the foolish and brutish perish, ‖ And have left their wealth to others. **11** Their heart [is that] their houses [are] for all time, ‖ Their dwelling places from generation to generation. They proclaimed their names over the lands. **12** And man does not remain in honor, ‖ He has been like the beasts, they have been cut off. **13** This their way [is] folly for them, ‖ And their posterity are pleased with their sayings. Selah. **14** They have set themselves as sheep for Sheol, ‖ Death afflicts them, ‖ And the upright rule over them in the morning, ‖ And their form [is] for consumption. Sheol [is] a dwelling for him. **15** Only, God ransoms my soul from the hand of Sheol, ‖ For He receives me. Selah. **16** Do not fear when one makes wealth, ‖ When the glory of his house is abundant, **17** For at his death he receives nothing, ‖ His glory does not go down after him. **18** For he blesses his soul in his life ‖ (And they praise you when you do well for yourself). **19** It comes to the generation of his fathers, ‖ They do not see the light forever. **20** Man in honor, who does not understand, ‖ Has been like the beasts, they have been cut off!

50 A Psalm of Asaph. The God of gods—YHWH—has spoken, ‖ And He calls to the earth ‖ From the rising of the sun to its going in. **2** From Zion, the perfection of beauty, God shone. **3** Our God comes, and is not silent, ‖ Fire devours before Him, ‖ And around Him it has been very tempestuous. **4** He calls to the heavens from above, ‖ And to the earth, to judge His people. **5** Gather My saints to Me, ‖ Making covenant with Me over a sacrifice. **6** And the heavens declare His righteousness, ‖ For God Himself is judging. Selah. **7** Hear, O My people, and I speak, ‖ O Israel, and I testify against you, ‖ God—I [am] your God. **8** I do not reprove you for your sacrifices, ‖ Indeed, your burnt-offerings ‖ [Are] continually before Me. **9** I do not take a bullock from your house, ‖ [Or] male goats from your folds. **10** For every beast of the forest [is] Mine, ‖ The livestock on the hills of oxen. **11** I have known every bird of the mountains, ‖ And the wild beast of the field [is] with Me. **12** If I am hungry I do not tell [it] to you, ‖ For the world and its fullness [is] Mine. **13** Do I eat the flesh of bulls, ‖ And drink the blood of male goats? **14** Sacrifice to God confession, ‖ And complete your vows to the Most High. **15** And call Me in a day of adversity, ‖ I deliver you, and you honor Me. **16** And to the wicked God has said: What to you—to recount My statutes? That you lift up My covenant on your mouth? **17** Indeed, you have hated instruction, ‖ And cast My words behind you. **18** If you have seen a thief, ‖ Then you are pleased with him, ‖ And your portion [is] with adulterers. **19** You have sent forth your mouth with evil, ‖ And your tongue joins deceit together, **20** You sit, you speak against your brother, ‖ You give slander against a son of your mother. **21** These you did, and I kept silent, ‖ You have thought that I am like you, ‖ I reprove you, and set in array before your eyes. **22** Now understand this, ‖ You who are forgetting God, ‖ Lest I tear, and there is no deliverer. **23** He who is sacrificing praise honors Me, ‖ As for him who makes a way, ‖ I cause him to look on the salvation of God!

51 To the Overseer. A Psalm of David, in the coming of Nathan the prophet to him when he has gone in to Bathsheba. Favor me, O God, according to Your kindness, ‖ According to the abundance of Your mercies, ‖ Blot out my transgressions. **2** Thoroughly wash me from my iniquity, ‖ And cleanse me from my sin, **3** For I know my transgressions, ‖ And my sin [is] continually before me. **4** Against You, You only, I have sinned, ‖ And done evil in Your eyes, ‖ So that You are righteous in Your words, ‖ You are pure in Your judging. **5** Behold, I have been brought forth in iniquity, ‖ And my mother conceives me in sin. **6** Behold, You have desired truth in the inward parts, ‖ And in the hidden part You cause me to know Wisdom. **7** You cleanse me with hyssop and I am clean, ‖ Wash me, and I am whiter than snow. **8** You cause me to hear joy and gladness, ‖ You make bones You have bruised joyful. **9** Hide Your face from my sin. And blot out all my iniquities. **10** Create for me a clean heart, O God, ‖ And renew a right spirit within me. **11** Do not cast me forth from Your presence, ‖ And do not take Your Holy Spirit from me. **12** Restore to me the joy of Your salvation, ‖ And a willing spirit sustains me. **13** I teach transgressors Your ways, ‖ And sinners return to You. **14** Deliver me from blood, O God, God of my salvation, ‖ My tongue sings of Your righteousness. **15** O Lord, you open my lips, ‖ And my mouth declares Your praise. **16** For You do not desire sacrifice, or I give [it], ‖ You do not accept burnt-offering. **17** The sacrifices of God [are] a broken spirit, ‖ A heart broken and bruised, O God, ‖ You do not despise. **18** Do good in Your good pleasure with Zion, ‖ You build the walls of Jerusalem. **19** Then You desire sacrifices of righteousness, ‖ Burnt-offering, and whole burnt-offering, ‖ Then they offer bullocks on your altar!

52 TO THE OVERSEER. AN INSTRUCTION OF DAVID, IN THE COMING IN OF DOEG THE EDOMITE, AND HE DECLARES TO SAUL AND SAYS TO HIM, "DAVID CAME TO THE HOUSE OF AHIMELECH." Why do you boast in evil, O mighty one? The kindness of God [is] all the day. **2** Your tongue devises mischiefs, ‖ Like a sharp razor, working deceit. **3** You have loved evil rather than good, ‖ Lying, than speaking righteousness. Selah. **4** You have loved all devouring words, ‖ O you deceitful tongue. **5** Also—God breaks you down forever, ‖ Takes you, and pulls you out of the tent, ‖ And He has uprooted you ‖ Out of the land of the living. Selah. **6** And the righteous see, ‖ And fear, and laugh at him. **7** "Behold, the man who does not make God his strong place, ‖ And trusts in the abundance of his riches, ‖ He is strong in his mischiefs." **8** And I, as a green olive in the house of God, ‖ I have trusted in the kindness of God, ‖ For all time and forever, **9** I thank You for all time, because You have done [it], ‖ And I wait [on] Your Name for [it is] good before Your saints!

53 TO THE OVERSEER. "ON A DISEASE." AN INSTRUCTION OF DAVID. A fool said in his heart, "There is no God." They have done corruptly, ‖ Indeed, they have done abominable iniquity, ‖ There is none doing good. **2** God looked on the sons of men from the heavens, ‖ To see if there is an understanding one, ‖ [One] seeking God. **3** Everyone went back, together they became filthy, ‖ There is none doing good—not even one. **4** Workers of iniquity have not known, ‖ Those eating my people have eaten bread, ‖ They have not called God. **5** There they feared a fear—there was no fear, ‖ For God has scattered the bones of him ‖ Who is encamping against you, ‖ You have put to shame, ‖ For God has despised them. **6** Who gives the salvation of Israel from Zion? When God turns back [to] a captivity of His people, ‖ Jacob rejoices—Israel is glad!

54 TO THE OVERSEER. WITH STRINGED INSTRUMENTS. AN INSTRUCTION OF DAVID, IN THE COMING IN OF THE ZIPHIM, AND THEY SAY TO SAUL, "IS DAVID NOT HIDING HIMSELF WITH US?" O God, save me by Your Name, and judge me by Your might. **2** O God, hear my prayer, ‖ Give ear to the sayings of my mouth, **3** For strangers have risen up against me ‖ And terrible ones have sought my soul, ‖ They have not set God before them. Selah. **4** Behold, God [is] a helper to me, ‖ The Lord [is] with those supporting my soul, **5** Turn back the evil to my enemies, ‖ Cut them off in Your truth. **6** I sacrifice to You with a free-will offering, ‖ I thank Your Name, O YHWH, for [it is] good, **7** For He delivered me from all adversity, ‖ And my eye has looked on my enemies!

55 TO THE OVERSEER. WITH STRINGED INSTRUMENTS. AN INSTRUCTION OF DAVID. Give ear, O God, [to] my prayer, ‖ And do not hide from my supplication. **2** Attend to me, and answer me, ‖ I mourn in my meditation, and make a noise, **3** Because of the voice of an enemy, ‖ Because of the oppression of the wicked, ‖ For they cause sorrow to move against me, ‖ And in anger they hate me. **4** My heart is pained within me, ‖ And terrors of death have fallen on me. **5** Fear and trembling come to me, ‖ And horror covers me. **6** And I say, "Who gives to me a pinion as a dove?" I fly away and rest, **7** Behold, I move far off, ‖ I lodge in a wilderness. Selah. **8** I hurry escape for myself, ‖ From a rushing wind, from a whirlwind. **9** Swallow up, O Lord, divide their tongue, ‖ For I saw violence and strife in a city. **10** By day and by night they go around it, on its walls. Both iniquity and perverseness [are] in its midst, **11** Mischiefs [are] in its midst. Fraud and deceit do not depart from its street. **12** For an enemy does not reproach me, or I bear [it], ‖ He who is hating me ‖ Has not magnified himself against me, ‖ Or I hide from him. **13** But you, a man—as my equal, ‖ My familiar friend, and my acquaintance. **14** When together we sweeten counsel, ‖ We walk into the house of God in company. **15** Desolations [are] on them, ‖ They go down [to] Sheol—alive, ‖ For wickedness

[is] in their dwelling, in their midst. **16** I call to God, and YHWH saves me. **17** Evening, and morning, and noon, ‖ I meditate, and make a noise, and He hears my voice, **18** He has ransomed my soul in peace ‖ From him who is near to me, ‖ For with the multitude they were with me. **19** God hears and afflicts them, ‖ And He sits of old. Selah. Because they have no changes, and do not fear God, **20** He has sent forth his hands against his well-wishers, ‖ He has defiled his covenant. **21** His mouth has been sweeter than honey, ‖ And his heart [is] war! His words have been softer than oil, ‖ And they [are] drawn [swords]. **22** Cast on YHWH that which He has given you, ‖ And He sustains you, ‖ He does not permit the moving of the righteous forever. **23** And You, O God, bring them down ‖ To a pit of destruction, ‖ Men of blood and deceit do not reach to half their days, ‖ And I trust in You!

56 TO THE OVERSEER. [SET] ON "A SILENT DOVE FAR OFF." A MIKTAM OF DAVID, IN THE PHILISTINES' TAKING HOLD OF HIM IN GATH. Favor me, O God, for man swallowed me up, ‖ All the day fighting he oppresses me, **2** My enemies have swallowed up all the day, ‖ For many [are] fighting against me, O Most High, **3** [In] the day I am afraid I am confident toward You. **4** In God I praise His word, in God I have trusted, ‖ I do not fear what flesh does to me. **5** All the day they wrest my words, ‖ All their thoughts [are] for evil concerning me, **6** They assemble, they hide, they watch my heels, ‖ When they have expected my soul. **7** They escape by iniquity, ‖ In anger put down the peoples, O God. **8** You have counted my wandering, ‖ You place my tear in Your bottle, ‖ Are they not in Your scroll? **9** Then turn back my enemies in the day I call. This I have known, that God [is] for me. **10** In God I praise the word, ‖ In YHWH I praise the word. **11** In God I trusted, ‖ I do not fear what man does to me, **12** On me, O God, [are] Your vows, ‖ I repay thank-offerings to You. **13** For You have delivered my soul from death, ‖ Do You not [keep] my feet from falling? To habitually walk before God in the light of the living!

57 TO THE OVERSEER. "DO NOT DESTROY." A MIKTAM OF DAVID, IN HIS FLEEING FROM THE FACE OF SAUL INTO A CAVE. Favor me, O God, favor me, ‖ For my soul is trusting in You, ‖ And I trust in the shadow of Your wings, ‖ Until the calamities pass over. **2** I call to God Most High, ‖ To God [who] is perfecting for me. **3** He sends from the heavens, and saves me, ‖ He reproached [the one] who is panting after me. Selah. God sends forth His kindness and His truth. **4** My soul [is] in the midst of lions, ‖ I lie down [among] flames—sons of men, ‖ Their teeth [are] a spear and arrows, ‖ And their tongue a sharp sword. **5** Be exalted above the heavens, O God, ‖ Your glory above all the earth. **6** They have prepared a net for my steps, ‖ My soul has bowed down, ‖ They have dug a pit before me, ‖ They have fallen into its midst. Selah. **7** My heart is prepared, O God, ‖ My heart is prepared, ‖ I sing and praise. **8** Awake, my glory, awake, stringed instrument and harp, ‖ I awake the morning dawn. **9** I thank You among the peoples, O Lord, ‖ I praise You among the nations. **10** For Your kindness [is] great to the heavens, ‖ And Your truth to the clouds. **11** Be exalted above the heavens, O God, Your glory above all the earth!

58 TO THE OVERSEER. "DO NOT DESTROY." A MIKTAM OF DAVID. Is it true, O silent one, that you speak righteously? Do you judge uprightly, O sons of men? **2** Even in heart you work iniquities, ‖ In the land you ponder the violence of your hands. **3** The wicked have been estranged from the womb, ‖ They have erred from the belly, speaking lies. **4** Their poison [is] as poison of a serpent, ‖ As a deaf cobra shutting its ear, **5** Which does not listen to the voice of whisperers, ‖ A charmer of most skillful charms. **6** O God, break their teeth in their mouth, ‖ Break down the jaw-teeth of young lions, O YHWH. **7** They are melted as waters, ‖ They go up and down for themselves, ‖ His arrow proceeds as they cut themselves off. **8** He goes on as a snail that melts, ‖ [As] an untimely birth of a woman, ‖ They have not seen the sun. **9** Before your pots discern the bramble, ‖ As living, He whirls away in His burning anger. **10** The righteous rejoices that he has seen vengeance, ‖ He washes his steps in the blood of the wicked. **11** And man says: "Surely fruit [is] for the righteous: Surely there is a God judging in the earth!"

PSALMS

59 To the Overseer. "Do Not Destroy." A Miktam of David, in Saul's sending, and they watch the house to put him to death. Deliver me from my enemies, O my God, ‖ Set me on high from my withstanders. **2** Deliver me from workers of iniquity, ‖ And save me from men of blood. **3** For behold, they laid wait for my soul, ‖ Strong ones are assembled against me, ‖ Not my transgression nor my sin, O YHWH. **4** Without punishment they run and prepare themselves, ‖ Stir up to meet me, and see. **5** And You, YHWH, God of Hosts, God of Israel, ‖ Awake to inspect all the nations. Do not favor any treacherous dealers of iniquity. Selah. **6** They return at evening, ‖ They make a noise like a dog, ‖ And go around the city. **7** Behold, they belch out with their mouths, ‖ Swords [are] in their lips, for "Who hears?" **8** And You, O YHWH, laugh at them, ‖ You mock at all the nations. **9** O my Strength, to You I take heed, ‖ For God [is] my tower—the God of my kindness. **10** God goes before me, ‖ He causes me to look on my enemies. **11** Do not slay them, lest my people forget, ‖ Shake them by Your strength, ‖ And bring them down, O Lord our shield. **12** The sin of their mouth [is] a word of their lips, ‖ And they are captured in their pride, ‖ And they recount from the curse and lying. **13** Consume in fury, consume and they are not, ‖ And they know that God is ruling in Jacob, ‖ To the ends of the earth. Selah. **14** And they return at evening, ‖ They make a noise like a dog, ‖ And they go around the city. **15** They wander for food, ‖ If they are not satisfied—then they murmur. **16** And I sing of Your strength, ‖ And at morning I sing of Your kindness, ‖ For You have been a tower to me, ‖ And a refuge for me in a day of adversity. **17** O my Strength, I sing praise to You, ‖ For God [is] my tower, the God of my kindness!

60 To the Overseer. [Set] on "Lily of Testimony." A Miktam of David, to teach, in his striving with Aram-Naharaim and with Aram-Zobah, when Joab turns back and strikes Edom in the Valley of Salt—twelve thousand. O God, You had cast us off, ‖ You had broken us—had been angry! You turn back to us. **2** You have caused the land to tremble, ‖ You have broken it, ‖ Heal its breaches, for it has moved. **3** You have shown Your people a hard thing, ‖ You have caused us to drink wine of trembling. **4** You have given an ensign to those fearing You, ‖ To be lifted up as an ensign ‖ Because of truth. Selah. **5** That Your beloved ones may be drawn out, ‖ Save [with] Your right hand, and answer us. **6** God has spoken in His holiness: I exult—I apportion Shechem, ‖ And I measure the Valley of Succoth, **7** Gilead [is] Mine, and Manasseh [is] Mine, ‖ And Ephraim [is] the strength of My head, ‖ Judah [is] My lawgiver, **8** Moab [is] My pot for washing, ‖ Over Edom I cast My shoe, ‖ Shout, concerning Me, O Philistia. **9** Who brings me [to] a city of bulwarks? Who has led me to Edom? **10** Is it not You, O God? Have You cast us off? And do You not go forth, O God, with our hosts? **11** Give to us help from adversity, ‖ And the deliverance of man [is] vain. **12** We do mightily in God, ‖ And He treads down our adversaries!

61 To the Overseer. On stringed instruments. By David. Hear, O God, my loud cry, attend to my prayer. **2** I call to You from the end of the land, ‖ In the feebleness of my heart, ‖ You lead me into a rock higher than I. **3** For You have been a refuge for me, ‖ A tower of strength because of the enemy. **4** I sojourn in Your tent for all ages, ‖ I trust in the secret place of Your wings. Selah. **5** For You, O God, have listened to my vows, ‖ You have appointed the inheritance ‖ Of those fearing Your Name. **6** You add days to the days of the king, ‖ His years as generation and generation. **7** He dwells before God for all time, ‖ Appoint kindness and truth—they keep him. **8** So I praise Your Name forever, ‖ When I pay my vows day by day!

62 To the Overseer. For Jeduthun. A Psalm of David. Toward God alone [is] my soul silent, ‖ My salvation [is] from Him. **2** He alone [is] my rock, and my salvation, ‖ My tower, I am not much moved. **3** Until when do you devise mischief against a man? All of you are destroyed, ‖ As a wall inclined, a hedge that is cast down. **4** Only—from his excellence ‖ They have consulted to drive away, ‖ They enjoy a lie, they bless with their mouth, ‖ And revile with their heart. Selah. **5** For God alone, be silent, O my soul, ‖ For my hope [is] from Him. **6** He alone [is] my rock and my salvation, ‖ My tower, I am not moved. **7** On God [is] my salvation, and my glory, ‖ The rock of my strength, my refuge [is] in God. **8** Trust in Him at all times, O people, ‖ Pour forth your heart before Him, ‖ God [is] a refuge for us. Selah. **9** Surely vanity the low, a lie the high. In balances to go up ‖ They [are] lighter than a breath. **10** Do not trust in oppression, ‖ And do not become vain in robbery, ‖ Do not set the heart [on] wealth when it increases. **11** Once has God spoken, twice I heard this, ‖ That "strength [is] with God." **12** And with You, O Lord, [is] kindness, ‖ For You repay to each, ‖ According to his work!

63 A PSALM OF DAVID, IN HIS BEING IN THE WILDERNESS OF JUDAH. O God, You [are] my God, earnestly I seek You, ‖ My soul has thirsted for You, ‖ My flesh has longed for You, ‖ In a dry and weary land, without waters. **2** So I have seen You in the sanctuary, ‖ To behold Your strength and Your glory. **3** Because better [is] Your kindness than life, ‖ My lips praise You. **4** So I bless You in my life, ‖ I lift up my hands in Your Name. **5** As [with] milk and fatness is my soul satisfied, ‖ And [with] singing lips my mouth praises. **6** If I have remembered You on my bed, ‖ I meditate on You in the watches. **7** For You have been a help to me, ‖ And I sing in the shadow of Your wings. **8** My soul has cleaved after You, ‖ Your right hand has taken hold on me. **9** And they who seek my soul for desolation, ‖ Go into the lower parts of the earth. **10** They cause him to run on the edge of the sword, ‖ They are a portion for foxes. **11** And the king rejoices in God, ‖ Everyone swearing by Him boasts, ‖ But the mouth of those speaking lies is stopped!

64 TO THE OVERSEER. A PSALM OF DAVID. Hear, O God, my voice, in my meditation, ‖ You keep my life from the fear of an enemy, **2** Hide me from the secret counsel of evildoers, ‖ From the tumult of workers of iniquity. **3** Who sharpened their tongue as a sword, ‖ They directed their arrow—a bitter word. **4** To shoot the perfect in secret places, ‖ Suddenly they shoot him, and do not fear. **5** They strengthen an evil thing for themselves, ‖ They recount of the hiding of snares, ‖ They have said, "Who looks at it?" **6** They search out perverse things, "We perfected a searching search," ‖ And the inward part of man, and the heart, [are] deep. **7** And God shoots them [with] an arrow, ‖ Their wounds have been sudden, **8** And they cause him to stumble, ‖ Their own tongue [is] against them, ‖ Every looker on them flees away. **9** And all men fear, and declare the work of God, ‖ And they have wisely considered His deed. **10** The righteous rejoice in YHWH, ‖ And have trusted in Him, ‖ And all the upright of heart boast!

65 TO THE OVERSEER. A PSALM OF DAVID. A SONG. To You, silence [and] praise, O God, in Zion, ‖ And to You a vow is completed. **2** Hearer of prayer, all flesh comes to You. **3** Matters of iniquities were mightier than I, ‖ Our transgressions—You cover them. **4** O the blessedness of [him whom] You choose, ‖ And draw near, he inhabits Your courts, ‖ We are satisfied with the goodness of Your house, ‖ Your holy temple. **5** By fearful things in righteousness You answer us, ‖ O God of our salvation, ‖ The confidence of all far off ‖ The ends of the earth and sea. **6** Establishing mountains by His power, ‖ He has been girded with might, **7** Restraining the noise of seas, the noise of their billows, ‖ And the multitude of the peoples. **8** And the inhabitants of the uttermost parts ‖ Are afraid from Your signs, ‖ You cause the outgoings of morning and evening to sing. **9** You have inspected the earth, and water it, ‖ You make it very rich, the stream of God [is] full of water, ‖ You prepare their grain, ‖ When thus You prepare it, **10** Its ridges have been filled, ‖ Its furrow has been deepened, ‖ You soften it with showers, ‖ Its springing up You bless. **11** You have crowned the year of Your goodness, ‖ And Your paths drop fatness. **12** The pastures of a wilderness drop, ‖ And You gird the hills with joy. **13** The meadows are clothed with the flock, ‖ And valleys are covered with grain, ‖ They shout—indeed, they sing!

66 TO THE OVERSEER. A SONG. A PSALM. Shout to God, all the earth. **2** Praise the glory of His Name, ‖ Make honorable His praise. **3** Say to God, "How fearful Your works—By the abundance of Your strength, ‖ Your enemies feign obedience to You. **4** All the earth bows to You, ‖ They sing praise to You, they praise Your Name." Selah. **5** Come, and see the

PSALMS

works of God, ‖ Fearful acts toward the sons of men. **6** He has turned a sea to dry land, ‖ Through a river they pass over on foot, ‖ There we rejoice in Him. **7** Ruling by His might for all time, ‖ His eyes watch among the nations, ‖ The stubborn do not exalt themselves. Selah. **8** Bless our God you peoples, ‖ And sound the voice of His praise, **9** Who has placed our soul in life, ‖ And has not permitted our feet to be moved. **10** For You have tried us, O God, ‖ You have refined us as the refining of silver. **11** You have brought us into a net, ‖ You have placed pressure on our loins. **12** You have caused man to ride at our head. We have entered into fire and into water, ‖ And You bring us out to a watered place. **13** I enter Your house with burnt-offerings, ‖ I complete my vows to You, **14** For my lips were opened, ‖ And my mouth spoke in my distress: **15** "I offer to You burnt-offerings of fatlings, ‖ With incense of rams, I prepare a bullock with male goats." Selah. **16** Come, hear, all you who fear God, ‖ And I recount what He did for my soul. **17** I have called to Him [with] my mouth, ‖ And exaltation [is] under my tongue. **18** Iniquity, if I have seen in my heart, ‖ The Lord does not hear. **19** But God has heard, ‖ He has attended to the voice of my prayer. **20** Blessed [is] God, ‖ Who has not turned aside my prayer, ‖ And His loving-kindness, from me!

67 TO THE OVERSEER. WITH STRINGED INSTRUMENTS. A PSALM. A SONG. God favors us and blesses us, ‖ [And] causes His face to shine with us. Selah. **2** For the knowledge of Your way in earth, ‖ Your salvation among all nations. **3** Peoples praise You, O God, ‖ Peoples praise You, all of them. **4** Nations rejoice and sing, ‖ For You judge peoples uprightly, ‖ And comfort peoples on earth. Selah. **5** Peoples confess You, O God, ‖ Peoples confess You—all of them. **6** Earth has given her increase, God blesses us—our God, **7** God blesses us, and all the ends of the earth fear Him!

68 TO THE OVERSEER. A PSALM. A SONG OF DAVID. God rises [and] His enemies are scattered! And those hating Him flee from His face. **2** You drive them away as the driving away of smoke, ‖ As the melting of wax before fire, ‖ The wicked perish at the presence of God. **3** And the righteous rejoice, they exult before God, ‖ And they rejoice with gladness. **4** Sing to God—praise His Name, ‖ Raise up a highway for Him who is riding in deserts, ‖ In YAH [is] His Name, and exult before Him. **5** Father of the fatherless, and judge of the widows, ‖ [Is] God in His holy habitation. **6** God—causing the lonely to dwell at home, ‖ Bringing out bound ones into prosperity, ‖ Only—the stubborn have inhabited a dry place. **7** O God, in Your going forth before Your people, ‖ In Your stepping through the wilderness, Selah. **8** The earth has shaken, ‖ Indeed, the heavens have dropped before God, ‖ This Sinai—before God, the God of Israel. **9** You shake out a shower of free-will gifts, O God. Your inheritance, when it has been weary, ‖ You have established it. **10** Your creature has dwelt in it, ‖ You prepare for the poor in Your goodness, O God. **11** The Lord gives the saying, ‖ The female proclaimers [are] a numerous host. **12** Kings of hosts utterly flee away, ‖ And a female inhabitant of the house apportions spoil. **13** Though you lie between two boundaries, ‖ Wings of a dove covered with silver, ‖ And her pinions with yellow gold. **14** When the Mighty spreads kings in it, it snows in Salmon. **15** A hill of God [is] the hill of Bashan, ‖ A hill of heights [is] the hill of Bashan. **16** Why do you envy, O high hills, ‖ The hill God has desired for His seat? YHWH also dwells forever. **17** The chariots of God [are] myriads, thousands of changes, ‖ The Lord [is] among them, in Sinai, in the sanctuary. **18** You have ascended on high, ‖ You have taken captivity captive, ‖ You have taken gifts for men, ‖ That even the stubborn may rest, O YAH God. **19** Blessed [is] the Lord, day by day He lays on us. God Himself [is] our salvation. Selah. **20** God Himself [is] to us a God for deliverances, ‖ And YHWH Lord has the outgoings of death. **21** Only—God strikes ‖ The head of His enemies, ‖ The hairy crown of a habitual walker in his guilt. **22** The Lord said: "From Bashan I bring back, ‖ I bring back from the depths of the sea. **23** So that you dash your foot ‖ In the blood of enemies—the tongue of Your dogs." **24** They have seen Your goings, O God, ‖ Goings of my God, my king, in the sanctuary. **25** Singers have been before, ‖ Behind [are] players on instruments, ‖ Virgins playing with timbrels in the midst. **26** In assemblies bless God, ‖ The Lord—

from the fountain of Israel. **27** There [is] little Benjamin, their ruler, ‖ Heads of Judah their defense, ‖ Heads of Zebulun—heads of Naphtali. **28** Your God has commanded your strength, ‖ Be strong, O God, You have worked this for us. **29** Because of Your temple at Jerusalem, ‖ Kings bring a present to You. **30** Rebuke a beast of the reeds, a herd of bulls, ‖ With calves of the peoples, ‖ Each humbling himself with pieces of silver, ‖ You scatter peoples delighting in conflicts. **31** Fat ones come out of Egypt, ‖ Cush causes her hands to run to God. **32** Kingdoms of the earth, sing to God, ‖ Praise the Lord! Selah. **33** To Him who is riding on the heavens of the heavens of old, ‖ Behold, He gives with His voice a strong voice. **34** Ascribe strength to God, ‖ His excellence [is] over Israel, and His strength in the clouds. **35** Fearful, O God, out of Your sanctuaries, ‖ The God of Israel Himself, ‖ Giving strength and might to the people. Blessed [is] God!

69 TO THE OVERSEER. [SET] ON "LILIES." BY DAVID. Save me, O God, for waters have come to the soul. **2** I have sunk in deep mire, ‖ And there is no standing, ‖ I have come into the depths of the waters, ‖ And a flood has overflown me. **3** I have been wearied with my calling, ‖ My throat has been burned, ‖ My eyes have been consumed, waiting for my God. **4** Those hating me without cause ‖ Have been more than the hairs of my head, ‖ Mighty have been my destroyers, ‖ My lying enemies, ‖ That which I did not take away—I bring back. **5** O God, You have known ‖ Concerning my overturn, ‖ And my desolations have not been hid from You. **6** Do not let those waiting on You be ashamed because of me, ‖ O Lord, YHWH of Hosts, ‖ Do not let those seeking You ‖ Blush because of me, ‖ O God of Israel. **7** For because of You I have borne reproach, ‖ Shame has covered my face. **8** I have been a stranger to my brother, ‖ And a foreigner to sons of my mother. **9** For [my] zeal for Your house has consumed me, ‖ And the reproaches of Your reproachers ‖ Have fallen on me. **10** And I weep in the fasting of my soul, ‖ And it is for a reproach to me. **11** And I make my clothing sackcloth, ‖ And I am for an allegory to them. **12** Those sitting at the gate meditate concerning me, ‖ And those drinking strong drink, ‖ Play on instruments. **13** And my prayer [is] to You, O YHWH, ‖ A time of good pleasure, O God, ‖ In the abundance of Your kindness, ‖ Answer me in the truth of Your salvation. **14** Deliver me from the mire, and do not let me sink, ‖ Let me be delivered from those hating me, ‖ And from deep places of waters. **15** Do not let a flood of waters overflow me, ‖ Nor let the deep swallow me up, ‖ Nor let the pit shut her mouth on me. **16** Answer me, O YHWH, for Your kindness [is] good, ‖ Turn to me according to the abundance of Your mercies, **17** And do not hide Your face from Your servant, ‖ For I am in distress—hurry, answer me. **18** Be near to my soul—redeem it, ‖ Ransom me because of my enemies. **19** You have known my reproach, ‖ And my shame, and my blushing, ‖ All my adversaries [are] before You. **20** Reproach has broken my heart, and I am sick, ‖ And I look for a bemoaner, and there is none, ‖ And for comforters, and I have found none. **21** And they give gall for my food, ‖ And cause me to drink vinegar for my thirst. **22** Their table before them is for a snare, ‖ And for a repayment—for a trap. **23** Their eyes are darkened from seeing, ‖ And their loins continually shake You. **24** Pour Your indignation on them, ‖ And the fierceness of Your anger seizes them. **25** Their tower is desolated, ‖ There is no dweller in their tents. **26** For they have pursued him [whom] You have struck, ‖ And recount of the pain of Your pierced ones. **27** Give punishment for their iniquity, ‖ And they do not enter into Your righteousness. **28** They are blotted out of the scroll of life, ‖ And are not written with the righteous. **29** And I [am] afflicted and pained, ‖ Your salvation, O God, sets me on high. **30** I praise the Name of God with a song, ‖ And I magnify Him with thanksgiving, **31** And it is better to YHWH than an ox, ‖ A bullock—horned [and] hoofed. **32** The humble have seen—they rejoice, ‖ You who seek God—and your heart lives. **33** For YHWH listens to the needy, ‖ And He has not despised His bound ones. **34** The heavens and earth praise Him, ‖ Seas, and every moving thing in them. **35** For God saves Zion, ‖ And builds the cities of Judah, ‖ And they have dwelt there, and possess it. **36** And the seed of His servants inherit it, ‖ And those loving His Name dwell in it!

70 TO THE OVERSEER. BY DAVID. "TO CAUSE TO REMEMBER." O God,

PSALMS

[hurry] to deliver me, ‖ O Y<small>HWH</small>, hurry to help me. **2** Let them be ashamed and confounded ‖ Who are seeking my soul, ‖ Let them be turned backward and blush ‖ Who are desiring my evil. **3** Let them turn back because of their shame, ‖ Who are saying, "Aha, aha." **4** Let all those seeking You rejoice and be glad in You, ‖ And let those loving Your salvation ‖ Continually say, "God is magnified." **5** And I [am] poor and needy, O God, hurry to me, ‖ You [are] my help and my deliverer, ‖ O Y<small>HWH</small>, do not linger!

71 In You, O Y<small>HWH</small>, I have trusted, ‖ Do not let me be disappointed for all time. **2** You deliver me in Your righteousness, ‖ And cause me to escape, ‖ Incline Your ear to me, and save me. **3** Be a rock to me—a habitation, ‖ To go in continually, ‖ You have given command to save me, ‖ For You [are] my rock and my bulwark. **4** O my God, cause me to escape ‖ From the hand of the wicked, ‖ From the hand of the perverse and violent. **5** For You [are] my hope, O Lord Y<small>HWH</small>, ‖ My trust from my youth. **6** I have been supported from the womb by You, ‖ You cut me out from my mother's bowels, ‖ My praise [is] continually in You. **7** I have been as a wonder to many, ‖ And You [are] my strong refuge. **8** My mouth is filled [with] Your praise, ‖ All the day [with] Your beauty. **9** Do not cast me off at the time of old age, ‖ Do not forsake me according to the consumption of my power. **10** For my enemies have spoken against me, ‖ And those watching my soul have taken counsel together, **11** Saying, "God has forsaken him, ‖ Pursue and catch him, for there is no deliverer." **12** O God, do not be far from me, ‖ O my God, make haste for my help. **13** They are ashamed, they are consumed, ‖ Who are opposing my soul, ‖ They are covered [with] reproach and blushing, ‖ Who are seeking my evil, **14** And I continually wait with hope, ‖ And have added to all Your praise. **15** My mouth recounts Your righteousness, ‖ All the day Your salvation, ‖ For I have not known the numbers. **16** I come in [the] might of Lord Y<small>HWH</small>, ‖ I mention Your righteousness— Yours alone. **17** God, You have taught me from my youth, ‖ And until now I declare Your wonders. **18** And also to old age and grey hairs, ‖ O God, do not forsake me, ‖ Until I declare Your strength to a generation, ‖ Your might to everyone that comes. **19** And Your righteousness, O God, [is] to the heights, ‖ Because You have done great things, ‖ O God, who [is] like You? **20** Because You have showed me many and sad distresses, ‖ You turn back—You revive me, ‖ And from the depths of the earth, ‖ You turn back—You bring me up. **21** You increase my greatness, ‖ And You surround—You comfort me, **22** I also thank You with a vessel of stringed instrument, ‖ Your truth, O my God, I sing to You with a harp, ‖ O Holy One of Israel, **23** My lips cry aloud when I sing praise to You, ‖ And my soul that You have redeemed, **24** My tongue also utters Your righteousness all the day, ‖ Because ashamed—because confounded, ‖ Have been those seeking my evil!

72 B<small>Y</small> S<small>OLOMON</small>. O God, give Your judgments to the king, ‖ And Your righteousness to the king's Son. **2** He judges Your people with righteousness, ‖ And Your poor with judgment. **3** The mountains bear peace to the people, ‖ And the heights by righteousness. **4** He judges the poor of the people, ‖ Gives deliverance to the sons of the needy, ‖ And bruises the oppressor. **5** They fear You with the sun, and before the moon, ‖ Generation— generations. **6** He comes down as rain on mown grass, ‖ As showers—sprinkling the earth. **7** The righteous flourish in His days, ‖ And abundance of peace until the moon is not. **8** And He rules from sea to sea, ‖ And from the river to the ends of the earth. **9** Desert-dwellers bow before Him, ‖ And His enemies lick the dust. **10** Kings of Tarshish and of the islands send back a present. Kings of Sheba and Seba bring a reward near. **11** And all kings bow themselves to Him, ‖ All nations serve Him, **12** For He delivers the needy who cries, ‖ And the poor when he has no helper, **13** He has pity on the poor and needy, ‖ And He saves the souls of the needy, **14** He redeems their soul from fraud and from violence, ‖ And their blood is precious in His eyes. **15** And He lives, and the gold of Sheba [is] given to Him, ‖ And prayer is continually made for Him, ‖ All day He is continually blessed. **16** There is a handful of grain in the earth, ‖ On the top of mountains, ‖ Its fruit shakes like Lebanon, ‖ And they flourish out of the city as the herb of the earth. **17** His Name is for all time, ‖

PSALMS

Before the sun is His Name continued, ‖ And they bless themselves in Him, ‖ All nations pronounce Him blessed. **18** Blessed is YHWH God, God of Israel, ‖ He alone is doing wonders, **19** And blessed [is] the Name of His glory for all time, ‖ And the whole earth is filled [with] His glory. Amen and amen! **20** The prayers of David son of Jesse have been ended.

73 A PSALM OF ASAPH. Surely God [is] good to Israel, to the clean of heart. And I—as a little thing, ‖ My feet have been turned aside, **2** As nothing, my steps have slipped, ‖ For I have been envious of the boastful, **3** I see the peace of the wicked, ‖ That there are no bands at their death, **4** And their might [is] firm. **5** They are not in the misery of mortals, ‖ And they are not plagued with common men. **6** Therefore pride has encircled them, ‖ Violence covers them as a dress. **7** Their eye has come out from fat. The imaginations of the heart transgressed; **8** They do corruptly, ‖ And they speak in the wickedness of oppression, ‖ They speak from on high. **9** They have set their mouth in the heavens, ‖ And their tongue walks in the earth. **10** Therefore His people return here, ‖ And waters of fullness are wrung out to them. **11** And they have said, "How has God known? And is there knowledge in the Most High?" **12** Behold, these [are] the wicked and easy ones of the age, ‖ They have increased strength. **13** Only—a vain thing! I have purified my heart, ‖ And I wash my hands in innocence, **14** And I am plagued all the day, ‖ And my reproof— every morning. **15** If I have said, "I recount thus," ‖ Behold, I have deceived a generation of Your sons. **16** And I think to know this, ‖ It [is] perverseness in my eyes, **17** Until I come into the sanctuaries of God, ‖ I attend to their latter end. **18** Surely You set them in slippery places, ‖ You have caused them to fall to desolations. **19** How they have become a desolation as in a moment, ‖ They have been ended— consumed from terrors. **20** As a dream from awakening, O Lord, ‖ In awaking, You despise their image. **21** For my heart shows itself violent, ‖ And my reins prick themselves, **22** And I am brutish, and do not know. I have been a beast with You. **23** And I [am] continually with You, ‖ You have laid hold on my right hand. **24** You lead me with Your counsel, ‖ And after, receive me [to] glory. **25** Whom do I have in the heavens? And none have I desired in earth [besides] You. **26** My flesh and my heart have been consumed, ‖ God [is] the rock of my heart and my portion for all time. **27** For behold, those far from You perish, ‖ You have cut off everyone, ‖ Who is going whoring from You. **28** And [the] nearness of God to me [is] good, ‖ I have placed my refuge in Lord YHWH, ‖ To recount all Your works!

74 AN INSTRUCTION OF ASAPH. Why, O God, have You cast off forever? Your anger smokes against the flock of Your pasture. **2** Remember Your congregation ‖ [That] You purchased of old, ‖ You redeemed the rod of Your inheritance, ‖ This Mount Zion—You dwelt in it. **3** Lift up Your steps to the continuous desolations, ‖ Everything the enemy did wickedly in the sanctuary. **4** Your adversaries have roared, ‖ In the midst of Your meeting-places, ‖ They have set their ensigns as ensigns. **5** He is known as one bringing in on high ‖ Against a thicket of wood—axes. **6** And now they break down its engravings, ‖ Together, with axe and hatchet, **7** They have sent Your sanctuary into fire, ‖ They defiled the Dwelling Place of Your Name to the earth, **8** They said in their hearts, "Let us oppress them together," ‖ They burned all the meeting-places of God in the land. **9** We have not seen our ensigns, ‖ There is no longer a prophet, ‖ Nor with us is one knowing how long. **10** Until when, O God, does an adversary reproach? Does an enemy despise Your Name forever? **11** Why do You turn back Your hand, ‖ Even Your right hand? Remove [it] from the midst of Your bosom. **12** And God [is] my king of old, ‖ Working salvation in the midst of the earth. **13** You have divided [the] sea by Your strength, ‖ You have shattered heads of dragons by the waters, **14** You have broken the heads of leviathan, ‖ You make him food for the people of desert-dwellers. **15** You have cleaved a fountain and a stream, ‖ You have dried up perennial flowings. **16** The day [is] Yours, ‖ The night [is] also Yours, ‖ You have prepared a light-giver—the sun. **17** You have set up all the borders of earth, ‖ Summer and winter—You have formed them. **18** Remember this—an enemy reproached YHWH, ‖ And a foolish people

PSALMS

have despised Your Name. **19** Do not give up to a [wild] creature, ‖ The soul of Your turtle-dove, ‖ Do not forget the life of Your poor ones forever. **20** Look attentively to the covenant, ‖ For the dark places of earth, ‖ Have been full of habitations of violence. **21** Do not let the oppressed turn back ashamed, ‖ Let the poor and needy praise Your Name, **22** Arise, O God, plead Your plea, ‖ Remember Your reproach from a fool all the day. **23** Do not forget the voice of Your adversaries, ‖ The noise of Your withstanders is going up continually!

75 To the Overseer. "Do not destroy." A Psalm of Asaph. A Song. We have given thanks to You, O God, ‖ We have given thanks, and Your Name [is] near, ‖ They have recounted Your wonders. **2** When I receive an appointment, I judge uprightly. **3** The earth and all its inhabitants are melted, ‖ I have pondered its pillars. Selah. **4** I have said to the boastful, "Do not be boastful," ‖ And to the wicked, "Do not raise up a horn." **5** Do not raise up your horn on high ‖ (You speak with a stiff neck). **6** For not from the east, or from the west, ‖ Nor from the wilderness—[is] elevation. **7** But God [is] judging, ‖ This He makes low—and this He lifts up. **8** For a cup [is] in the hand of YHWH, ‖ And the wine has foamed, ‖ It is full of mixture, and He pours out of it, ‖ Surely wring out its dregs, ‖ And all the wicked of the earth drink, **9** And I declare [it] for all time, ‖ I sing praise to the God of Jacob. **10** And I cut off all horns of the wicked, ‖ The horns of the righteous are exalted!

76 To the Overseer. With stringed instruments. A Psalm of Asaph. A Song. God [is] known in Judah, ‖ His Name [is] great in Israel. **2** And His dwelling place is in Salem, ‖ And His habitation in Zion. **3** There He has shattered arrows of a bow, ‖ Shield, and sword, and battle. Selah. **4** You [are] bright, majestic above hills of prey. **5** The mighty of heart have spoiled themselves, ‖ They have slept their sleep, ‖ And none of the men of might found their hands. **6** From Your rebuke, O God of Jacob, ‖ Both rider and horse have been fast asleep. **7** You, fearful [are] You, ‖ And who stands before You, ‖ Since You have been angry? **8** You have sounded judgment from the heavens, ‖ Earth has feared, and has been still, **9** In the rising of God to judgment, ‖ To save all the humble of earth. Selah. **10** For the fierceness of man praises You, ‖ You gird on the remnant of fierceness. **11** Vow and complete to your God YHWH, ‖ All you surrounding Him, ‖ They bring presents to the Fearful One. **12** He gathers the spirit of leaders, ‖ Fearful to the kings of earth!

77 To the Overseer. For Jeduthun. A Psalm of Asaph. My voice [is] to God, and I cry, ‖ My voice [is] to God, ‖ And He has given ear to me. **2** I sought the Lord in a day of my distress, ‖ My hand has been spread out by night, ‖ And it does not cease, ‖ My soul has refused to be comforted. **3** I remember God, and make a noise, ‖ I meditate, and my spirit is feeble. Selah. **4** You have taken hold of the watches of my eyes, ‖ I have been moved, and I do not speak. **5** I have reckoned the days of old, ‖ The years of the ages. **6** I remember my music in the night, ‖ I meditate with my heart, and my spirit searches diligently: **7** Does the Lord cast off for all ages? Does He add to be pleased no longer? **8** Has His kindness ceased forever? The saying failed from generation to generation? **9** Has God forgotten [His] favors? Has He shut up His mercies in anger? Selah. **10** And I say: "My weakness is, ‖ The changes of the right hand of the Most High." **11** I mention the doings of YAH, ‖ For I remember Your wonders of old, **12** And I have meditated on all Your working, ‖ And I talk concerning Your doings. **13** O God, Your way [is] in holiness, ‖ Who [is] a great god like God? **14** You [are] the God doing wonders. You have made Your strength known among the peoples, **15** You have redeemed Your people with strength, ‖ The sons of Jacob and Joseph. Selah. **16** The waters have seen You, O God, ‖ The waters have seen You, ‖ They are afraid—also depths are troubled. **17** Thick clouds have poured out waters, ‖ The skies have given forth a noise, ‖ Also— Your arrows go up and down. **18** The voice of Your thunder [is] in the spheres, ‖ Lightnings have lightened the world, ‖ The earth has trembled, indeed, it shakes. **19** Your way [is] in the sea, ‖ And Your paths in many waters, ‖ And Your tracks have not been known. **20** You have led Your people as a flock, ‖ By the hand of Moses and Aaron!

PSALMS

78 AN INSTRUCTION OF ASAPH. Give ear, O my people, to my law, ‖ Incline your ear to sayings of my mouth. **2** I open my mouth with an allegory, ‖ I bring forth hidden things of old, **3** That we have heard and know, ‖ And our fathers have recounted to us. **4** We do not hide from their sons, ‖ Recounting praises of YHWH to a later generation, ‖ And His strength, and His wonders that He has done. **5** And He raises up a testimony in Jacob, ‖ And has placed a law in Israel, ‖ That He commanded our fathers, ‖ To make them known to their sons. **6** So that a later generation knows, ‖ Sons who are born, rise and recount to their sons, **7** And place their confidence in God, ‖ And do not forget the doings of God, ‖ But keep His commands. **8** And they are not like their fathers, ‖ A generation apostatizing and being rebellious, ‖ A generation—it has not prepared its heart, ‖ Nor [is] its spirit steadfast with God. **9** Sons of Ephraim—armed bearers of bow, ‖ Have turned in a day of conflict. **10** They have not kept the covenant of God, ‖ And they have refused to walk in His law, **11** And they forget His doings, ‖ And His wonders that He showed them. **12** He has done wonders before their fathers, ‖ In the land of Egypt—the field of Zoan. **13** He cleft a sea, and causes them to pass over, ‖ Indeed, He causes waters to stand as a heap. **14** And leads them with a cloud by day, ‖ And with a light of fire all the night. **15** He cleaves rocks in a wilderness, ‖ And gives drink—as the great deep. **16** And brings out streams from a rock, ‖ And causes waters to come down as rivers. **17** And they still add to sin against Him, ‖ To provoke the Most High in the dry place. **18** And they try God in their heart, ‖ To ask food for their lust. **19** And they speak against God—they said: "Is God able to array a table in a wilderness?" **20** Behold, He has struck a rock, ‖ And waters flow, indeed, streams overflow. "Also, [is] He able to give bread? Does He prepare flesh for His people?" **21** Therefore YHWH has heard, ‖ And He shows Himself angry, ‖ And fire has been kindled against Jacob, ‖ And anger has also gone up against Israel, **22** For they have not believed in God, ‖ Nor have they trusted in His salvation. **23** And He commands clouds from above, ‖ Indeed, He has opened doors of the heavens. **24** And He rains manna on them to eat, ‖ Indeed, He has given grain of the heavens to them. **25** Each has eaten food of the mighty, ‖ He sent provision to them to satiety. **26** He causes an east wind to journey in the heavens, ‖ And leads a south wind by His strength, **27** And He rains on them flesh as dust, ‖ And as sand of the seas—winged bird, **28** And causes [it] to fall in the midst of His camp, ‖ Around His dwelling places. **29** And they eat, and are greatly satisfied, ‖ And He brings their desire to them. **30** They have not been estranged from their desire, ‖ Their food [is] yet in their mouth, **31** And the anger of God has gone up against them, ‖ And He slays among their fat ones, ‖ And He caused youths of Israel to bend. **32** With all this they have sinned again, ‖ And have not believed in His wonders. **33** And He consumes their days in vanity, ‖ And their years in trouble. **34** If He slew them, then they sought Him, ‖ And turned back, and earnestly sought God, **35** And they remember that God [is] their rock, ‖ And God Most High their redeemer. **36** And they deceive Him with their mouth, ‖ And lie to Him with their tongue, **37** And their heart has not been right with Him, ‖ And they have not been steadfast in His covenant. **38** And He, the Merciful One, pardons iniquity, and does not destroy, ‖ And has often turned back His anger, ‖ And does not awaken all His fury. **39** And He remembers that they [are] flesh, ‖ A wind going on—and it does not return. **40** How often do they provoke Him in the wilderness, ‖ Grieve Him in the desolate place? **41** Indeed, they turn back, and try God, ‖ And have limited the Holy One of Israel. **42** They have not remembered His hand ‖ The day He ransomed them from the adversary. **43** When He set His signs in Egypt, ‖ And His wonders in the field of Zoan, **44** And He turns their streams to blood, ‖ And they do not drink their floods. **45** He sends among them the beetle, and it consumes them, ‖ And the frog, and it destroys them, **46** And gives their increase to the caterpillar, ‖ And their labor to the locust. **47** He destroys their vine with hail, ‖ And their sycamores with frost, **48** And delivers their beasts up to the hail, ‖ And their livestock to the burning flames. **49** He sends on them the fury of His anger, ‖ Wrath, and indignation, and distress—A discharge of evil messengers. **50** He ponders a path for His anger, ‖ He did not keep back their soul from death, ‖ Indeed, He delivered up their life to the pestilence.

51 And He strikes every firstborn in Egypt, ‖ The first-fruit of the strong in tents of Ham. **52** And causes His people to journey as a flock, ‖ And guides them as a drove in a wilderness, **53** And He leads them confidently, ‖ And they have not been afraid, ‖ And the sea has covered their enemies. **54** And He brings them to the border of His sanctuary, ‖ This mountain His right hand had acquired, **55** And casts out nations from before them, ‖ And causes them to fall in the line of inheritance, ‖ And causes the tribes of Israel to dwell in their tents, **56** And they tempt and provoke God Most High, ‖ And have not kept His testimonies. **57** And they turn back, ‖ And deal treacherously like their fathers, ‖ They have been turned like a deceitful bow, **58** And make Him angry with their high places, ‖ And make Him zealous with their carved images, **59** God has heard, and shows Himself angry. And kicks exceedingly against Israel. **60** And He leaves the Dwelling Place of Shiloh, ‖ The tent He had placed among men, **61** And He gives His strength to captivity, ‖ And His beauty into the hand of an adversary, **62** And delivers His people up to the sword, ‖ And showed Himself angry with His inheritance. **63** Fire has consumed His young men, ‖ And His virgins have not been praised. **64** His priests have fallen by the sword, ‖ And their widows do not weep. **65** And the Lord wakes as a sleeper, ‖ As a mighty one crying aloud from wine. **66** And He strikes His adversaries backward, ‖ He has put a continuous reproach on them, **67** And He kicks against the tent of Joseph, ‖ And has not fixed on the tribe of Ephraim. **68** And He chooses the tribe of Judah, ‖ With Mount Zion that He loved, **69** And builds His sanctuary as a high place, ‖ Like the earth, He founded it for all time. **70** And He fixes on His servant David, ‖ And takes him from the folds of a flock, **71** He has brought him in from behind suckling ones, ‖ To rule over Jacob His people, ‖ And over Israel His inheritance. **72** And he rules them according to the integrity of his heart, ‖ And leads them by the skillfulness of his hands!

79 A Psalm of Asaph. O God, nations have come into Your inheritance, ‖ They have defiled Your holy temple, ‖ They made Jerusalem become heaps, **2** They gave the dead bodies of Your servants ‖ [As] food for the birds of the heavens, ‖ The flesh of Your saints ‖ For the wild beast of the earth. **3** They have shed their blood ‖ As water around Jerusalem, ‖ And there is none burying. **4** We have been a reproach to our neighbors, ‖ A scorn and a derision to our surrounders. **5** Until when, O YHWH? Are You angry forever? Your jealousy burns as fire. **6** Pour Your fury on the nations who have not known You, ‖ And on kingdoms that have not called on Your Name. **7** For [one] has devoured Jacob, ‖ And they have made his habitation desolate. **8** Do not remember for us the iniquities of forefathers, ‖ Hurry, let Your mercies go before us, ‖ For we have been very weak. **9** Help us, O God of our salvation, ‖ Because of the glory of Your Name, ‖ And deliver us, and cover over our sins, ‖ For Your Name's sake. **10** Why do the nations say, "Where [is] their God?" Let [it] be known among the nations before our eyes, ‖ The vengeance of the blood of Your servants that is shed. **11** Let the groaning of the prisoner come in before You, ‖ According to the greatness of Your arm, ‖ Leave the sons of death. **12** And return to our neighbors, ‖ Sevenfold to their bosom, their reproach, ‖ With which they reproached You, O Lord. **13** And we, Your people, and the flock of Your pasture, ‖ We give thanks to You for all time, ‖ We recount Your praise from generation to generation!

80 To the Overseer. [Set] to "Lilies of Testimony." A Psalm of Asaph. Shepherd of Israel, give ear, ‖ Leading Joseph as a flock, ‖ Inhabiting the cherubim—shine forth, **2** Before Ephraim, and Benjamin, and Manasseh, ‖ Wake up Your might, and come for our salvation. **3** O God, cause us to turn back, ‖ And cause Your face to shine, and we are saved. **4** YHWH, God of Hosts, until when? You have burned against the prayer of Your people. **5** You have caused them to eat bread of tears, ‖ And cause them to drink ‖ With tears a third time. **6** You make us a strife to our neighbors, ‖ And our enemies mock at it. **7** God of Hosts, turn us back, ‖ And cause Your face to shine, and we are saved. **8** You bring a vine out of Egypt, ‖ You cast out nations, and plant it. **9** You have looked before it, and root it, ‖ And it fills the land, **10** Hills have been covered [with] its shadow, ‖ And its boughs [are] cedars of God. **11** It sends forth its branches to the sea, ‖ And its shoots to the river. **12** Why have You broken down its hedges, ‖ And everyone passing by the way has plucked it? **13** A boar out of the forest tears it, ‖ And a wild beast of the fields grazes it. **14** God of Hosts, turn back, we implore You, ‖ Look from the heavens, and see, and inspect this vine, **15** And the root that Your right hand planted, ‖ And the branch You made strong for Yourself, **16** Burned with fire—cut down, ‖ They perish from the rebuke of Your face. **17** Let Your hand be on the man of Your right hand ‖ On the son of man You have strengthened for Yourself. **18** And we do not go back from You, ‖ You revive us, and in Your Name we call. **19** O Yhwh, God of Hosts, turn us back, ‖ Cause Your face to shine, and we are saved!

81 To the Overseer. On the Gittith. By Asaph. Cry aloud to God our strength, ‖ Shout to the God of Jacob. **2** Lift up a song, and give out a timbrel, ‖ A pleasant harp with stringed instrument. **3** Blow a horn in the month, ‖ In the new moon, at the day of our festival, **4** For it [is] a statute to Israel, ‖ An ordinance of the God of Jacob. **5** He has placed it—a testimony on Joseph, ‖ In his going forth over the land of Egypt. A lip, I have not known—I hear. **6** I turned aside his shoulder from the burden, ‖ His hands pass over from the basket. **7** In distress you have called and I deliver you, ‖ I answer you in the secret place of thunder, ‖ I try you by the waters of Meribah. Selah. **8** Hear, O My people, and I testify to you, ‖ O Israel, if you listen to me: **9** There is not in you a strange god, ‖ And you do not bow yourself to a strange god. **10** I [am] your God Yhwh, ‖ Who brings you up out of the land of Egypt. Enlarge your mouth, and I fill it. **11** But My people did not listen to My voice, ‖ And Israel has not consented to Me. **12** And I send them away in the enmity of their heart, ‖ They walk in their own counsels. **13** O that My people were listening to Me, ‖ Israel would walk in My ways. **14** As a little thing I cause their enemies to bow, ‖ And I turn back My hand against their adversaries, **15** Those hating Yhwh should have feigned [obedience] to Him, ‖ And their time would last for all time. **16** He causes him to eat of the fat of wheat, ‖ And I satisfy you [with] honey from a rock!

82 A Psalm of Asaph. God has stood in the congregation of God, ‖ He judges among the gods. **2** Until when do you judge perversely? And lift up the face of the wicked? Selah. **3** Judge the weak and fatherless, ‖ Declare the afflicted and the poor righteous. **4** Let the weak and needy escape, ‖ Deliver them from the hand of the wicked. **5** They did not know, nor do they understand, ‖ They habitually walk in darkness, ‖ All the foundations of earth are moved. **6** I have said, "You [are] gods, ‖ And sons of the Most High—all of you, **7** But you die as man, and you fall as one of the heads." **8** Rise, O God, judge the earth, ‖ For You have inheritance among all the nations!

83 A Song. A Psalm of Asaph. O God, let there be no silence to You, ‖ Do not be silent, nor be quiet, O God. **2** For behold, Your enemies roar, ‖ And those hating You have lifted up the head, **3** They take crafty counsel against Your people, ‖ And consult against Your hidden ones. **4** They have said, "Come, and we cut them off from [being] a nation, ‖ And the name of Israel is not remembered anymore." **5** For they consulted in heart together, ‖ They make a covenant against You, **6** Tents of Edom, and Ishmaelites, Moab, and the Hagarenes, **7** Gebal, and Ammon, and Amalek, Philistia with inhabitants of Tyre, **8** Asshur is also joined with them, ‖ They have been an arm to sons of Lot. Selah. **9** Do to them as Midian, ‖ As Sisera, as Jabin, at the Brook of Kishon. **10** They were destroyed at Endor, ‖ They were dung for the ground! **11** Make their nobles as Oreb and as Zeeb, ‖ And as Zebah and Zalmunna—all their princes, **12** Who have said, "Let us occupy the pastures of God for ourselves." **13** O my God, make them as a rolling thing, ‖ As stubble before wind. **14** As a fire burns a forest, ‖ And as a flame sets hills on fire, **15** So You pursue them with Your whirlwind, ‖ And trouble them with Your windstorm. **16** Fill their faces [with] shame, ‖ And they seek Your Name, O Yhwh. **17** They are ashamed and troubled forever, ‖ Indeed, they are confounded and lost. **18** And they know that You—Your Name [is] Yhwh—By

Yourself [are] the Most High over all the earth!

84 TO THE OVERSEER. ON THE GITTITH. A PSALM OF THE SONS OF KORAH. How beloved Your dwelling places, YHWH of Hosts! **2** My soul desired, indeed, it has also been consumed, ‖ For the courts of YHWH, ‖ My heart and my flesh cry aloud to the living God, **3** Even a sparrow has found a house, ‖ And a swallow a nest for herself, ‖ Where she has placed her brood— Your altars, O YHWH of Hosts, ‖ My king and my God. **4** O the blessedness of those inhabiting Your house, ‖ Yet they praise You. Selah. **5** O the blessedness of a man whose strength is in You, ‖ Highways [are] in their heart. **6** Those passing through a valley of weeping make it a spring, ‖ The early rain covers it with pools. **7** They go from strength to strength, ‖ He appears to God in Zion. **8** O YHWH, God of Hosts, hear my prayer, ‖ Give ear, O God of Jacob. Selah. **9** Our shield, see, O God, ‖ And behold the face of Your anointed, **10** For a day in Your courts [is] good, O Teacher! I have chosen rather to be at the threshold, ‖ In the house of my God, ‖ Than to dwell in tents of wickedness. **11** For YHWH God [is] a sun and a shield, ‖ YHWH gives grace and glory. He does not withhold good ‖ To those walking in uprightness. **12** YHWH of Hosts! O the blessedness of a man trusting in You.

85 TO THE OVERSEER. A PSALM OF THE SONS OF KORAH. You have accepted, O YHWH, Your land, ‖ You have turned [to] the captivity of Jacob. **2** You have carried away the iniquity of Your people, ‖ You have covered all their sin. Selah. **3** You have gathered up all Your wrath, ‖ You have turned back from the fierceness of Your anger. **4** Turn back [to] us, O God of our salvation, ‖ And make void Your anger with us. **5** Are You angry against us for all time? Do You draw out Your anger ‖ To generation and generation? **6** Do You not turn back? You revive us, ‖ And Your people rejoice in You. **7** Show us, O YHWH, your kindness, ‖ And You give to us Your salvation. **8** I hear what God, YHWH, speaks, ‖ For He speaks peace to His people, ‖ And to His saints, and they do not turn back to folly. **9** Surely His salvation [is] near to those fearing Him, ‖ That glory may dwell in our land. **10** Kindness and truth have met, ‖ Righteousness and peace have kissed, **11** Truth springs up from the earth, ‖ And righteousness looks out from the heavens, **12** YHWH also gives that which is good, ‖ And our land gives its increase. **13** Righteousness goes before Him, ‖ And makes a way for His footsteps!

86 A PRAYER OF DAVID. Incline, O YHWH, Your ear, ‖ Answer me, for I [am] poor and needy. **2** Keep my soul, for I [am] pious, ‖ Save Your servant who is trusting to You, O You, my God. **3** Favor me, O Lord, for I call to You all the day. **4** Make glad the soul of Your servant, ‖ For to You, O Lord, I lift up my soul. **5** For You, Lord, [are] good and forgiving, ‖ And abundant in kindness to all calling You. **6** Hear, O YHWH, my prayer, ‖ And attend to the voice of my supplications. **7** In a day of my distress I call You, ‖ For You answer me. **8** There is none like You among the gods, O Lord, ‖ And like Your works there are none. **9** All nations that You have made ‖ Come and bow themselves before You, O Lord, ‖ And give honor to Your Name. **10** For You [are] great, and doing wonders, ‖ You [are] God alone. **11** Show me, O YHWH, Your way, ‖ I walk in Your truth, ‖ My heart rejoices to fear Your Name. **12** I confess You, O Lord my God, with all my heart, ‖ And I honor Your Name for all time. **13** For Your kindness [is] great toward me, ‖ And You have delivered my soul from the lowest Sheol. **14** O God, the proud have risen up against me, ‖ And a company of the terrible sought my soul, ‖ And have not placed You before them, **15** And You, O Lord, [are] God, merciful and gracious, ‖ Slow to anger, and abundant in kindness and truth. **16** Look to me, and favor me, ‖ Give Your strength to Your servant, ‖ And give salvation to a son of Your handmaid. **17** Do with me a sign for good, ‖ And those hating me see and are ashamed, ‖ For You, O YHWH, have helped me, ‖ Indeed, You have comforted me!

87 A PSALM OF THE SONS OF KORAH. A SONG. His foundation [is] in holy mountains. **2** YHWH is loving the gates of Zion ‖ Above all the dwelling places of Jacob. **3** Honorable things are spoken in You, ‖ O city of God. Selah. **4** I mention Rahab and Babel to those knowing Me, ‖ Behold, Philistia, and Tyre, with Cush! This [one] was born there. **5** And of Zion it is said: Each one was born in her, ‖ And He, the Most High, establishes her. **6** YHWH recounts in the describing of the peoples, "This [one] was born there." Selah. **7** Also singers as players on instruments, ‖ All my fountains [are] in You!

88 A SONG. A PSALM OF THE SONS OF KORAH. TO THE OVERSEER. [SET] ON "SICKNESS TO AFFLICT." AN INSTRUCTION OF HEMAN THE EZRAHITE. O YHWH, God of my salvation, ‖ Daily I have cried, nightly before You, **2** My prayer comes in before You, ‖ Incline Your ear to my loud cry, **3** For my soul has been full of evils, ‖ And my life has come to Sheol. **4** I have been reckoned with those going down [to] the pit, ‖ I have been as a man without strength. **5** Among the dead—free, ‖ As pierced ones lying in the grave, ‖ Whom You have not remembered anymore, ‖ Indeed, they have been cut off by Your hand. **6** You have put me in the lowest pit, ‖ In dark places, in depths. **7** Your fury has lain on me, ‖ And You have afflicted [with] all Your breakers. Selah. **8** You have put my acquaintance far from me, ‖ You have made me an abomination to them, ‖ Shut up—I do not go forth. **9** My eye has grieved because of affliction, ‖ I called You, O YHWH, all the day, ‖ I have spread out my hands to You. **10** Do You do wonders to the dead? Does Rephaim rise? Do they thank You? Selah. **11** Is Your kindness recounted in the grave? Your faithfulness in destruction? **12** Are Your wonders known in the darkness? And Your righteousness in the land of forgetfulness? **13** And I, to You, O YHWH, I have cried, ‖ And in the morning my prayer comes before You. **14** Why, O YHWH, do You cast off my soul? You hide Your face from me. **15** I [am] afflicted, and expiring from youth, ‖ I have borne Your terrors—I pine away. **16** Your wrath has passed over me, ‖ Your terrors have cut me off, **17** They have surrounded me as waters all the day, ‖ They have gone around against me together, **18** You have put lover and friend far from me, ‖ My acquaintance [is] the place of darkness!

89 AN INSTRUCTION OF ETHAN THE EZRAHITE. Of the kind acts of YHWH, I sing for all time, ‖ From generation to generation I make known Your faithfulness with my mouth, **2** For I said, "Kindness is built for all time, ‖ The heavens! You establish Your faithfulness in them." **3** I have made a covenant for My chosen, ‖ I have sworn to My servant David: **4** "Even for all time I establish your seed, ‖ And have built your throne to generation and generation." Selah. **5** And the heavens confess Your wonders, O YHWH, ‖ Your faithfulness [is] also in an assembly of holy ones. **6** For who in the sky, compares himself to YHWH? [Who] is like to YHWH among sons of the mighty? **7** God is very terrible, ‖ In the secret counsel of His holy ones, ‖ And fearful over all surrounding Him. **8** O YHWH, God of Hosts, ‖ Who [is] like You—a strong YAH? And Your faithfulness [is] around You. **9** You [are] ruler over the pride of the sea, ‖ In the lifting up of its billows You restrain them. **10** You have bruised Rahab, as one wounded. You have scattered Your enemies with the arm of Your strength. **11** The heavens [are] Yours, ‖ The earth [is] also Yours, ‖ The habitable world and its fullness, ‖ You have founded them. **12** North and south You have appointed them, ‖ Tabor and Hermon sing in Your Name. **13** You have an arm with might, ‖ Strong is Your hand—high Your right hand. **14** Righteousness and judgment ‖ [Are] the fixed place of Your throne, ‖ Kindness and truth go before Your face. **15** O the blessedness of the people knowing the shout, ‖ O YHWH, they habitually walk in the light of Your face. **16** They rejoice in Your Name all the day, ‖ And they are exalted in Your righteousness, **17** For You [are] the beauty of their strength, ‖ And in Your good will is our horn exalted, **18** For our shield [is] of YHWH, ‖ And our king to the Holy One of Israel. **19** Then You have spoken in vision, ‖ To Your saint, indeed, ‖ You say, I have placed help on a mighty one, ‖ Exalted a chosen one out of the people, **20** I have found My servant David, ‖ With My holy oil I have anointed him. **21** With whom My hand is established, ‖ My arm also strengthens him. **22** An enemy does not exact on him, ‖ And a son of perverseness does not afflict him. **23** And I have beaten down his adversaries before him, ‖ And I plague those hating him, **24** And My faithfulness and kindness [are] with him, ‖ And in My Name is his horn exalted. **25** And I have set his hand on the sea, ‖ And his right hand on the rivers. **26** He proclaims to Me: "You [are] my Father, ‖ My God, and the rock of my

PSALMS

salvation." **27** I also appoint him firstborn, ‖ Highest of the kings of the earth. **28** For all time I keep for him My kindness, ‖ And My covenant [is] steadfast with him. **29** And I have set his seed forever, ‖ And his throne as the days of the heavens. **30** If his sons forsake My law, ‖ And do not walk in My judgments; **31** If they defile My statutes, ‖ And do not keep My commands, **32** I have looked after their transgression with a rod, ‖ And their iniquity with strokes, **33** And I do not break My kindness from him, ‖ Nor do I deal falsely in My faithfulness. **34** I do not profane My covenant, ‖ And I do not change that which is going forth from My lips. **35** Once I have sworn by My holiness, ‖ I do not lie to David, **36** His seed is for all time, ‖ And his throne [is] as the sun before Me, **37** It is established as the moon for all time, ‖ And the witness in the sky is steadfast. Selah. **38** And You, You have cast off, and reject, ‖ You have shown Yourself angry with Your anointed, **39** Have rejected the covenant of Your servant, ‖ You have defiled his crown to the earth, **40** You have broken down all his hedges, ‖ You have made his fortifications a ruin. **41** Everyone passing by the way has spoiled him, ‖ He has been a reproach to his neighbors, **42** You have exalted the right hand of his adversaries, ‖ You have caused all his enemies to rejoice. **43** Also—You turn back the sharpness of his sword, ‖ And have not established him in battle, **44** Have caused [him] to cease from his brightness, ‖ And have cast down his throne to the earth. **45** You have shortened the days of his youth, ‖ Have covered him over [with] shame. Selah. **46** Until when, O YHWH, are You hidden? Does Your fury burn as fire forever? **47** Remember how [short] my lifetime [is]. Why have You created in vain ‖ All the sons of men? **48** Who [is] the man that lives, and does not see death? He delivers his soul from the hand of Sheol. Selah. **49** Where [are] Your former kindnesses, O Lord, ‖ [Which] You have sworn to David in Your faithfulness? **50** Remember, O Lord, the reproach of Your servants, ‖ I have borne in my bosom all the strivings of the peoples, **51** With which Your enemies reproached, O YHWH, ‖ With which they have reproached ‖ The steps of Your anointed. **52** Blessed [is] YHWH for all time. Amen and amen!

90 A PRAYER OF MOSES, THE MAN OF GOD. Lord, You have been a habitation, ‖ To us—in generation and generation, **2** Before mountains were brought forth, ‖ And You form the earth and the world, ‖ Even from age to age You [are] God. **3** You turn man to a bruised thing, ‖ And say, Return, you sons of men. **4** For one thousand years in Your eyes [are] as yesterday, ‖ For it passes on, indeed, [as] a watch by night. **5** You have inundated them, they are asleep, ‖ In the morning he changes as grass. **6** In the morning it flourishes, and has changed, ‖ At evening it is cut down, and has withered. **7** For we were consumed in Your anger, ‖ And we have been troubled in Your fury. **8** You have set our iniquities before You, ‖ Our hidden things at the light of Your face, **9** For all our days pined away in Your wrath, ‖ We consumed our years as a meditation. **10** The days of our years, in them [are] seventy years, ‖ And if, by reason of might, eighty years, ‖ Yet their enlargement [is] labor and vanity, ‖ For it has been cut off quickly, and we fly away. **11** Who knows the power of Your anger? And according to Your fear—Your wrath? **12** Let [us] know to number our days correctly, ‖ And we bring the heart to wisdom. **13** Turn back, O YHWH, until when? And regret concerning Your servants. **14** Satisfy us at morning [with] Your kindness, ‖ And we sing and rejoice all our days. **15** Cause us to rejoice according to the days ‖ Wherein You have afflicted us, ‖ The years we have seen evil. **16** Let Your work appear to Your servants, ‖ And Your honor on their sons. **17** And let the pleasantness of our God YHWH be on us, ‖ And establish on us the work of our hands, ‖ Indeed, establish the work of our hands!

91 He who is dwelling ‖ In the secret place of the Most High, ‖ Habitually lodges in the shade of the Mighty, **2** He is saying of YHWH, "My refuge, and my bulwark, my God, I trust in Him," **3** For He delivers you from the snare of a fowler, ‖ From a calamitous pestilence. **4** He covers you over with His pinion, ‖ And under His wings you trust, ‖ His truth [is] a shield and buckler. **5** You are not afraid of fear by night, ‖ Of arrow that flies by day, **6** Of pestilence that walks in thick darkness, ‖ Of destruction that destroys at noon, **7** One thousand fall at your side, ‖ And a myriad at your right hand, ‖ [But] it does not come near to you. **8** But with your eyes you look, ‖ And you see the reward of the wicked, **9** (For You, O YHWH, [are] my refuge), ‖ You made the Most High your habitation. **10** Evil does not happen to you, ‖ And a plague does not come near your tent, **11** For He charges His messengers for you, ‖ To keep you in all your ways, **12** On the hands they bear you up, ‖ Lest you strike your foot against a stone. **13** You tread on lion and cobra, ‖ You trample young lion and dragon. **14** Because he has delighted in Me, ‖ I also deliver him—I set him on high, ‖ Because he has known My Name. **15** He calls Me, and I answer him, ‖ I [am] with him in distress, ‖ I deliver him, and honor him. **16** I satisfy him with [the] length of [his] days, ‖ And I cause him to look on My salvation!

92 A PSALM. A SONG FOR THE SABBATH DAY. [It is] good to give thanks to YHWH, ‖ And to sing praises to Your Name, O Most High, **2** To declare Your kindness in the morning, ‖ And Your faithfulness in the nights. **3** On ten strings and on stringed instrument, ‖ On higgaion, with harp. **4** For You have caused me to rejoice, O YHWH, in Your work, ‖ I sing concerning the works of Your hands. **5** How great Your works have been, O YHWH, ‖ Your thoughts have been very deep. **6** A brutish man does not know, ‖ And a fool does not understand this— **7** When the wicked flourish as an herb, ‖ And all workers of iniquity blossom—For their being destroyed forever and ever! **8** And You [are] high for all time, O YHWH. **9** For behold, Your enemies, O YHWH, ‖ For behold, Your enemies perish, ‖ All workers of iniquity separate themselves. **10** And You exalt my horn as a wild ox, ‖ I have been anointed with fresh oil. **11** And my eye looks on my enemies, ‖ Of those rising up against me, ‖ The evildoers, my ears hear. **12** The righteous flourish as a palm-tree, ‖ He grows as a cedar in Lebanon. **13** Those planted in the house of YHWH, ‖ In the courts of our God, flourish. **14** Still they bring forth in old age, ‖ They are fat and flourishing, **15** To declare that YHWH my Rock [is] upright, ‖ And there is no perverseness in Him!

93 YHWH has reigned, ‖ He has put on excellence, ‖ YHWH put on strength, He girded Himself, ‖ Also—the world is established, unmoved. **2** Your throne is established since then, ‖ You [are] from the age. **3** Floods have lifted up, O YHWH, ‖ Floods have lifted up their voice, ‖ Floods lift up their breakers. **4** Mightier than the voices of many mighty waters, breakers of a sea, ‖ [Is] YHWH on high, **5** Your testimonies have been very steadfast, ‖ Holiness befits Your house, O YHWH, for [the] length of [Your] days!

94 God of vengeance—YHWH! God of vengeance, shine forth. **2** Be lifted up, judging the earth, ‖ Send back a repayment on the proud. **3** Until when do the wicked, O YHWH—Until when do the wicked exult? **4** They utter—they speak arrogance, ‖ All working iniquity boast [about] themselves. **5** Your people, O YHWH, they bruise, ‖ And they afflict Your inheritance. **6** They slay widow and sojourner, ‖ And they murder fatherless ones. **7** And they say, "YAH does not see, ‖ And the God of Jacob does not consider." **8** Consider, you brutish among the people, ‖ And you foolish, when do you act wisely? **9** He who plants the ear, does He not hear? He who forms the eye, does He not see? **10** He who is instructing nations, does He not reprove? He who is teaching man knowledge [is] YHWH. **11** He knows the thoughts of man, that they [are] vanity. **12** O the blessedness of the man ‖ Whom You instruct, O YAH, ‖ And teach him out of Your law, **13** To give rest to him from days of evil, ‖ While a pit is dug for the wicked. **14** For YHWH does not leave His people, ‖ And does not forsake His inheritance. **15** For judgment turns back to righteousness, ‖ And after it all the upright of heart. **16** Who rises up for me with evildoers? Who stations himself for me with workers of iniquity? **17** Unless YHWH [were] a help to me, ‖ My soul had almost inhabited silence. **18** If I have said, "My foot has slipped," ‖ Your kindness, O YHWH, supports me. **19** In the abundance of my thoughts within me, ‖ Your comforts delight my soul. **20** Is a throne of mischief joined [with] You? A framer of perverseness by statute? **21** They decree against the soul of the righteous, ‖ And declare innocent blood wicked. **22** And YHWH is for a high place to me, ‖ And my

PSALMS

God [is] for a rock—my refuge, **23** And He turns back their iniquity on them, ‖ And in their wickedness cuts them off; Our God YHWH cuts them off!

95 Come, we sing to YHWH, ‖ We shout to the rock of our salvation. **2** We come before His face with thanksgiving, ‖ We shout to Him with psalms. **3** For YHWH [is] a great God, ‖ And a great King over all gods. **4** In whose hand [are] the deep places of earth, ‖ And the strong places of hills [are] His. **5** Whose is the sea, and He made it, ‖ And His hands formed the dry land. **6** Come in, we bow ourselves, and we bend, ‖ We kneel before YHWH our Maker. **7** For He [is] our God, and we the people of His pasture, ‖ And the flock of His hand, ‖ Today, if you listen to His voice, **8** Do not harden your heart as [in] Meribah, ‖ As [in] the day of Massah in the wilderness, **9** Where your fathers have tried Me, ‖ Have proved Me, indeed, have seen My work. **10** Forty years I am weary of the generation, ‖ And I say, "A people erring in heart—they! And they have not known My ways": **11** Where I swore in My anger, "If they come into My rest—!"

96 Sing to YHWH a new song, ‖ Sing to YHWH all the earth. **2** Sing to YHWH, bless His Name, ‖ Proclaim His salvation from day to day. **3** Declare His glory among nations, ‖ His wonders among all the peoples. **4** For YHWH [is] great, and greatly praised, ‖ He [is] fearful over all gods. **5** For all the gods of the peoples [are] nothing, ‖ And YHWH made the heavens. **6** Splendor and majesty [are] before Him, ‖ Strength and beauty are in His sanctuary. **7** Ascribe to YHWH, O families of the peoples, ‖ Ascribe to YHWH glory and strength. **8** Ascribe to YHWH the glory of His Name, ‖ Lift up a present and come into His courts. **9** Bow yourselves to YHWH, ‖ In the honor of holiness, ‖ Be afraid of His presence, all the earth. **10** Say among nations, "YHWH has reigned, ‖ Also—the world is established, unmoved, ‖ He judges the peoples in uprightness." **11** The heavens rejoice, and the earth is joyful, ‖ The sea and its fullness roar. **12** The field exults, and all that [is] in it, ‖ Then all trees of the forest sing, **13** Before YHWH, for He has come, ‖ For He has come to judge the earth. He judges the world in righteousness, ‖ And the peoples in His faithfulness!

97 YHWH has reigned, ‖ The earth is joyful, many islands rejoice. **2** Cloud and darkness [are] around Him, ‖ Righteousness and judgment the basis of His throne. **3** Fire goes before Him, ‖ And burns around His adversaries. **4** His lightnings have lightened the world, ‖ The earth has seen, and is pained. **5** Hills, like wax, melted before YHWH, ‖ Before the Lord of all the earth. **6** The heavens declared His righteousness, ‖ And all the peoples have seen His glory. **7** All servants of a carved image are ashamed, ‖ Those boasting themselves in idols, ‖ Bow yourselves to Him, all you gods. **8** Zion has heard and rejoices, ‖ And daughters of Judah are joyful, ‖ Because of Your judgments, O YHWH. **9** For You, YHWH, [are] Most High over all the earth, ‖ You have been exalted greatly over all gods. **10** You who love YHWH, hate evil, ‖ He is keeping the souls of His saints, ‖ He delivers them from the hand of the wicked. **11** Light [is] sown for the righteous, ‖ And joy for the upright of heart. **12** Rejoice, you righteous, in YHWH, ‖ And give thanks at the remembrance of His holiness!

98 A PSALM. Sing to YHWH a new song, ‖ For He has done wonders, ‖ His right hand and His holy arm have given salvation to Him. **2** YHWH has made His salvation known, ‖ Before the eyes of the nations, ‖ He has revealed His righteousness, **3** He has remembered His kindness, ‖ And His faithfulness to the house of Israel, ‖ All the ends of the earth have seen the salvation of our God. **4** Shout to YHWH, all the earth, ‖ Break forth, and cry aloud, and sing. **5** Sing to YHWH with harp, ‖ With harp, and voice of praise, **6** With trumpets, and voice of a horn, shout before the King, YHWH. **7** The sea and its fullness roar, ‖ The world and the inhabitants in it. **8** Floods clap hand, together hills cry aloud, **9** Before YHWH, ‖ For He has come to judge the earth, ‖ He judges the world in righteousness, ‖ And the people in uprightness!

99 YHWH has reigned, peoples tremble, ‖ The Inhabitant of the cherubim, the earth shakes. **2** YHWH [is] great in Zion, ‖ And He [is] high over all the peoples.

3 They praise Your Name, "Great, and fearful, [it] is holy!" **4** And the strength of the king ‖ Has loved judgment, ‖ You have established uprightness; Judgment and righteousness in Jacob, ‖ You have done. **5** Exalt our God YHWH, ‖ And bow yourselves at His footstool, He [is] holy. **6** Moses and Aaron among His priests, ‖ And Samuel among those proclaiming His Name. They are calling to YHWH, ‖ And He answers them. **7** He speaks to them in a pillar of cloud, ‖ They have kept His testimonies, ‖ And He has given the statute to them. **8** O YHWH, our God, ‖ You have afflicted them, ‖ You have been a forgiving God to them, ‖ And taking vengeance on their actions. **9** Exalt our God YHWH, ‖ And bow yourselves at His holy hill, ‖ For our God YHWH [is] holy!

100
A PSALM OF THANKSGIVING. Shout to YHWH, all the earth! **2** Serve YHWH with joy, come before Him with singing. **3** Know that YHWH [is] God, ‖ He made us, and we are His, ‖ His people—and the flock of His pasture. **4** Enter His gates with thanksgiving, ‖ His courts with praise, ‖ Give thanks to Him, bless His Name. **5** For YHWH [is] good, ‖ His kindness [is] for all time, ‖ And His faithfulness to generation and generation!

101
A PSALM OF DAVID. I sing kindness and judgment, ‖ To You, O YHWH, I sing praise. **2** I act wisely in a perfect way, ‖ When do You come to me? I habitually walk in the integrity of my heart, ‖ In the midst of my house. **3** I do not set a worthless thing before my eyes, ‖ I have hated the work of those turning aside, ‖ It does not adhere to me. **4** A perverse heart turns aside from me, ‖ I do not know wickedness. **5** Whoever slanders his neighbor in secret, ‖ Him I cut off, ‖ The high of eyes and proud of heart, ‖ Him I do not endure. **6** My eyes are on the faithful of the land, ‖ To dwell with me, ‖ Whoever is walking in a perfect way, he serves me. **7** He who is working deceit does not dwell in my house, ‖ Whoever is speaking lies is not established before my eyes. **8** At morning I cut off all the wicked of the land, ‖ To cut off from the city of YHWH ‖ All the workers of iniquity!

102
A PRAYER OF THE AFFLICTED WHEN HE IS FEEBLE, AND POURS OUT HIS COMPLAINT BEFORE YHWH. O YHWH, hear my prayer, indeed, my cry comes to You. **2** Do not hide Your face from me, ‖ In a day of my adversity, ‖ Incline Your ear to me, ‖ In the day I call, hurry, answer me. **3** For my days have been consumed in smoke, ‖ And my bones have burned as a firebrand. **4** Struck as the herb, and withered, is my heart, ‖ For I have forgotten to eat my bread. **5** From the voice of my sighing ‖ My bone has cleaved to my flesh. **6** I have been like to a pelican of the wilderness, ‖ I have been as an owl of the dry places. **7** I have watched, and I am ‖ As a bird alone on the roof. **8** All the day my enemies reproached me, ‖ Those mad at me have sworn against me. **9** Because I have eaten ashes as bread, ‖ And have mingled my drink with weeping, **10** From Your indignation and Your wrath, ‖ For You have lifted me up, ‖ And cast me down. **11** My days [are] stretched out as a shadow, ‖ And I am withered as the herb. **12** And You, O YHWH, abide for all time, ‖ And Your memorial from generation to generation. **13** You rise—You pity Zion, ‖ For the time to favor her, ‖ For the appointed time has come. **14** For Your servants have been pleased with her stones, ‖ And they favor her dust. **15** And nations fear the Name of YHWH, ‖ And all kings of the earth Your glory, **16** For YHWH has built Zion, ‖ He has been seen in His glory, **17** He turned to the prayer of the destitute, ‖ And He has not despised their prayer. **18** This is written for a later generation, ‖ And the people created praise YAH. **19** For He has looked ‖ From the high place of His sanctuary. YHWH looked attentively from the heavens to earth, **20** To hear the groan of the prisoner, ‖ To loose sons of death, **21** To declare in Zion the Name of YHWH, ‖ And His praise in Jerusalem, **22** In the peoples being gathered together, ‖ And the kingdoms—to serve YHWH. **23** He has humbled my power in the way, ‖ He has shortened my days. **24** I say, "My God, do not take me up in the midst of my days," Your years [are] through all generations. **25** You founded the earth before time, ‖ And the heavens [are] the work of Your hands. **26** They perish, and You remain, ‖ And all of them become old as a garment, ‖ You change them as clothing, ‖ And they are changed. **27** And You [are] the same, and Your years are not finished. **28** The

PSALMS

sons of Your servants continue, ‖ And their seed is established before You!

103 BY DAVID. Bless, O my soul, YHWH, ‖ And all my inward parts—His Holy Name. **2** Bless, O my soul, YHWH, ‖ And do not forget all His benefits, **3** Who is forgiving all your iniquities, ‖ Who is healing all your diseases, **4** Who is redeeming your life from destruction, ‖ Who is crowning you [with] kindness and mercies, **5** Who is satisfying your desire with good, ‖ Your youth renews itself as an eagle. **6** YHWH is doing righteousness and judgments ‖ For all the oppressed. **7** He makes His ways known to Moses, ‖ His acts to the sons of Israel. **8** YHWH [is] merciful and gracious, ‖ Slow to anger, and abundant in mercy. **9** He does not strive forever, ‖ Nor does He watch for all time. **10** He has not done to us according to our sins, ‖ Nor according to our iniquities ‖ Has He conferred benefits on us. **11** For as the height of the heavens [is] above the earth, ‖ His kindness has been mighty over those fearing Him. **12** He has put our transgressions far from us—as the distance of east from west. **13** As a father has mercy on sons, ‖ YHWH has mercy on those fearing Him. **14** For He has known our frame, ‖ Remembering that we [are] dust. **15** Mortal man! His days [are] as grass, ‖ He flourishes as a flower of the field; **16** For a wind has passed over it, and it is not, ‖ And its place does not discern it anymore. **17** And the kindness of YHWH ‖ [Is] from age even to age on those fearing Him, ‖ And His righteousness to sons' sons, **18** To those keeping His covenant, ‖ And to those remembering His precepts to do them. **19** YHWH has established His throne in the heavens, ‖ And His kingdom has ruled over all. **20** Bless YHWH, you His messengers, ‖ Mighty in power—doing His word, ‖ To listen to the voice of His word. **21** Bless YHWH, all you His hosts, ‖ His ministers—doing His pleasure. **22** Bless YHWH, all you His works, ‖ In all places of His dominion. Bless, O my soul, YHWH!

104 Bless, O my soul, YHWH! YHWH, my God, ‖ You have been very great, ‖ You have put on splendor and majesty. **2** Covering Himself [with] light as a garment, ‖ Stretching out the heavens as a curtain, **3** Who is laying the beam of His upper chambers in the waters, ‖ Who is making thick clouds His chariot, ‖ Who is walking on wings of wind, **4** Making His messengers—the winds, ‖ His ministers—the flaming fire. **5** He has founded earth on its bases, ‖ It is not moved for all time and forever. **6** The abyss! You have covered it as with clothing, ‖ Waters stand above hills. **7** They flee from Your rebuke, ‖ They hurry away from the voice of Your thunder. **8** They go up hills—they go down valleys, ‖ To a place You have founded for them. **9** You have set a border, they do not pass over, ‖ They do not turn back to cover the earth. **10** He is sending forth fountains in valleys, ‖ They go on between hills. **11** They water every beast of the field, ‖ Wild donkeys break their thirst. **12** The bird of the heavens dwells by them, ‖ From between the branches ‖ They give forth the voice. **13** Watering hills from His upper chambers, ‖ The earth is satisfied from the fruit of Your works. **14** Causing grass to spring up for livestock, ‖ And herb for the service of man, ‖ To bring forth bread from the earth, **15** And wine—it makes the heart of man glad, ‖ To cause the face to shine from oil, ‖ And bread—it supports the heart of man. **16** The trees of YHWH [are] satisfied, ‖ Cedars of Lebanon that He has planted, **17** Where birds make nests, ‖ The stork—the firs [are] her house. **18** The high hills [are] for wild goats, rocks [are] a refuge for hyraxes, **19** He made the moon for seasons, ‖ The sun has known his place of entrance. **20** You set darkness, and it is night, ‖ Every beast of the forest creeps in it. **21** The young lions are roaring for prey, ‖ And to seek their food from God. **22** The sun rises, they are gathered, ‖ And they crouch in their dens. **23** Man goes forth to his work, ‖ And to his service—until evening. **24** How many have been Your works, O YHWH, ‖ You have made all of them in wisdom, ‖ The earth is full of your possessions. **25** This, the sea, great and broad of sides, ‖ There [are] moving things—innumerable, ‖ Living creatures—small with great. **26** There ships go—[and] leviathan, ‖ That You have formed to play in it. **27** All of them look to You, ‖ To give their food in its season. **28** You give to them—they gather, ‖ You open Your hand—they [are] satisfied [with] good. **29** You hide Your face—they are troubled, ‖ You gather their spirit—they expire, ‖ And they return to their dust. **30** You send out Your Spirit, they are created, ‖ And You renew the face of the ground. **31** The glory of YHWH is for all time, ‖ YHWH rejoices in His works, **32** Who is looking to earth, and it trembles, ‖ He comes against hills, and they smoke. **33** I sing to YHWH during my life, ‖ I sing praise to my God while I exist. **34** My meditation on Him is sweet, ‖ I rejoice in YHWH. **35** Sinners are consumed from the earth, ‖ And the wicked are no more. Bless, O my soul, YHWH. Praise YAH!

105 Give thanks to YHWH—call on His Name, ‖ Make His acts known among the peoples. **2** Sing to Him—sing praise to Him, ‖ Meditate on all His wonders. **3** Boast yourselves in His Holy Name, ‖ The heart of those seeking YHWH rejoices. **4** Seek YHWH and His strength, ‖ Seek His face continually. **5** Remember His wonders that He did, ‖ His signs and the judgments of His mouth. **6** O seed of Abraham, His servant, ‖ O sons of Jacob, His chosen ones. **7** He [is] our God YHWH, ‖ His judgments [are] in all the earth. **8** He has remembered His covenant for all time, ‖ The word He commanded to one thousand generations, **9** That He has made with Abraham, ‖ And His oath to Isaac, **10** And establishes it to Jacob for a statute, ‖ To Israel—a perpetual covenant, **11** Saying, "I give the land of Canaan to you, ‖ The portion of your inheritance," **12** In their being few in number, ‖ But a few, and sojourners in it. **13** And they go up and down, from nation to nation, ‖ From a kingdom to another people. **14** He has not permitted any to oppress them ‖ And He reproves kings for their sakes. **15** "Do not strike against My anointed, ‖ And do no evil to My prophets." **16** And He calls a famine on the land, ‖ He has broken the whole staff of bread. **17** He has sent a man before them, ‖ Joseph has been sold for a servant. **18** They have afflicted his feet with chains, ‖ Iron has entered his soul, **19** Until the time of the coming of His word ‖ The saying of YHWH has tried him. **20** The king has sent, and looses him, ‖ The ruler of the peoples, and draws him out. **21** He has made him lord of his house, ‖ And ruler over all his possessions. **22** To bind his chiefs at his pleasure, ‖ And he makes his elderly wise. **23** And Israel comes into Egypt, ‖ And Jacob has sojourned in the land of Ham. **24** And He makes His people very fruitful, ‖ And makes it mightier than its adversaries. **25** He turned their heart to hate His people, ‖ To conspire against His servants. **26** He has sent His servant Moses, ‖ Aaron whom He had fixed on. **27** They have set among them the matters of His signs, ‖ And wonders in the land of Ham. **28** He has sent darkness, and it is dark, ‖ And they have not provoked His word. **29** He has turned their waters to blood, ‖ And puts their fish to death. **30** Their land has teemed [with] frogs, ‖ In the inner chambers of their kings. **31** He has commanded, and the beetle comes, ‖ Lice into all their border. **32** He has made their showers hail, ‖ A flaming fire [is] in their land. **33** And He strikes their vine and their fig, ‖ And shatters the trees of their border. **34** He has commanded, and the locust comes, ‖ And the cankerworm—innumerable, **35** And it consumes every herb in their land, ‖ And it consumes the fruit of their ground. **36** And He strikes every firstborn in their land, ‖ The first-fruit of all their strength, **37** And brings them out with silver and gold, ‖ And there is not a feeble one in its tribes. **38** Egypt has rejoiced in their going forth, ‖ For their fear had fallen on them. **39** He has spread a cloud for a covering, ‖ And fire to enlighten the night. **40** They have asked, and He brings quails, ‖ And satisfies them [with] bread of the heavens. **41** He has opened a rock, and waters flow, ‖ They have gone on in dry places—a river. **42** For He has remembered His holy word, ‖ With His servant Abraham, **43** And He brings forth His people with joy, ‖ His chosen ones with singing. **44** And He gives to them the lands of nations, ‖ And they possess the labor of peoples, **45** That they may observe His statutes, ‖ And may keep His laws. Praise YAH!

106 Praise YAH, give thanks to YHWH, for [He is] good, for His kindness [is] for all time! **2** Who utters the mighty acts of YHWH? Sounds all His praise? **3** O the blessedness of those keeping judgment, ‖ Doing righteousness at all times. **4** Remember me, O YHWH, ‖ With the favor of Your people, ‖ Look after me in Your salvation. **5** To look on the good of Your chosen ones, ‖ To rejoice in the joy of Your nation, ‖ To boast myself with Your inheritance. **6** We have sinned with our fathers, ‖ We have done perversely, we have done wickedly. **7** Our fathers in

Egypt, ‖ Have not considered wisely Your wonders, ‖ They have not remembered ‖ The abundance of Your kind acts, ‖ And provoke by the sea, at the Sea of Suph. **8** And He saves them for His Name's sake, ‖ To make His might known, **9** And rebukes the Sea of Suph, and it is dried up, ‖ And causes them to go ‖ Through depths as a wilderness. **10** And He saves them from the hand ‖ Of him who is hating, ‖ And redeems them from the hand of the enemy. **11** And waters cover their adversaries, ‖ One of them has not been left. **12** And they believe in His words, they sing His praise, **13** They have hurried—forgotten His works, ‖ They have not waited for His counsel. **14** And they lust greatly in a wilderness, ‖ And try God in a desert. **15** And He gives to them their request, ‖ And sends leanness into their soul. **16** And they are envious of Moses in the camp, ‖ Of Aaron, YHWH's holy one. **17** Earth opens, and swallows up Dathan, ‖ And covers over the company of Abiram. **18** And fire burns among their company, ‖ A flame sets the wicked on fire. **19** They make a calf in Horeb, ‖ And bow themselves to a molten image, **20** And change their glory ‖ Into the form of an ox eating herbs. **21** They have forgotten God their Savior, ‖ The doer of great things in Egypt, **22** Of wonderful things in the land of Ham, ‖ Of fearful things by the Sea of Suph. **23** And He commands to destroy them, ‖ Unless Moses, His chosen one, ‖ Had stood in the breach before Him, ‖ To turn back His wrath from destroying. **24** And they kick against the desirable land, ‖ They have not given credence to His word. **25** And they murmur in their tents, ‖ They have not listened to the voice of YHWH. **26** And He lifts up His hand to them, ‖ To cause them to fall in a wilderness, **27** And to cause their seed to fall among nations, ‖ And to scatter them through lands. **28** And they are coupled to Ba'al-Peor, ‖ And eat the sacrifices of the dead, **29** And they provoke to anger by their actions, ‖ And a plague breaks forth on them, **30** And Phinehas stands, and executes judgment, ‖ And the plague is restrained, **31** And it is reckoned to him for righteousness, ‖ From generation to generation—for all time. **32** And they cause wrath by the waters of Meribah, ‖ And it is evil to Moses for their sakes, **33** For they have provoked his spirit, ‖ And he speaks wrongfully with his lips. **34** They have not destroyed the peoples, ‖ As YHWH had commanded to them, **35** And mix themselves among nations, and learn their works, **36** And serve their idols, ‖ And they are for a snare to them. **37** And they sacrifice their sons and their daughters to the demons, **38** And they shed innocent blood—Blood of their sons and of their daughters, ‖ Whom they have sacrificed to idols of Canaan, ‖ And the land is profaned with blood. **39** And they are defiled with their works, ‖ And commit whoredom in their habitual doings. **40** And the anger of YHWH ‖ Is kindled against His people, ‖ And He detests His inheritance. **41** And gives them into the hand of nations, ‖ And those hating them rule over them, **42** And their enemies oppress them, ‖ And they are humbled under their hand. **43** He delivers them many times, ‖ And they rebel in their counsel, ‖ And they are brought low in their iniquity. **44** And He looks on their distress ‖ When He hears their cry, **45** And remembers His covenant for them, ‖ And is comforted, ‖ According to the abundance of His kindness. **46** And He appoints them for mercies ‖ Before all their captors. **47** Save us, O our God YHWH, and gather us from the nations, ‖ To give thanks to Your Holy Name, ‖ To glory in Your praise. **48** Blessed [is] YHWH, God of Israel, ‖ From age until age. And all the people said, "Amen, praise YAH!"

107 "Give thanks to YHWH, ‖ For [He is] good, for His kindness [is] for all time": **2** Let the redeemed of YHWH say [so], ‖ Whom He redeemed from the hand of an adversary. **3** And has gathered them from the lands, ‖ From east and from west, ‖ From north, and from the sea. **4** They wandered in a wilderness, in a desert by the way, ‖ They have not found a city of habitation. **5** Hungry—indeed—thirsty, ‖ Their soul becomes feeble in them, **6** And they cry to YHWH in their adversity, ‖ He delivers them from their distress, **7** And causes them to tread in a right way, ‖ To go to a city of habitation. **8** They confess to YHWH His kindness, ‖ And His wonders to the sons of men. **9** For He has satisfied a longing soul, ‖ And has filled a hungry soul [with] goodness. **10** Inhabitants of dark places and death-shade, ‖ Prisoners of affliction and of iron, **11** Because they changed the saying of God, ‖ And despised the counsel of the Most High. **12** And He humbles their heart with labor, ‖ They have been feeble, and there is no helper. **13** And they cry to YHWH in their adversity, ‖ He saves them from their distresses. **14** He brings them out from the dark place, ‖ And death-shade, ‖ And He draws away their bands. **15** They confess to YHWH His kindness, ‖ And His wonders to the sons of men. **16** For He has broken doors of bronze, ‖ And He has cut bars of iron. **17** Fools, by means of their transgression, ‖ And by their iniquities, afflict themselves. **18** Their soul detests all food, ‖ And they come near to the gates of death, **19** And cry to YHWH in their adversity, ‖ He saves them from their distresses, **20** He sends His word and heals them, ‖ And delivers [them] from their destructions. **21** They confess to YHWH His kindness, ‖ And His wonders to the sons of men, **22** And they sacrifice sacrifices of thanksgiving, ‖ And recount His works with singing. **23** Those going down [to] the sea in ships, ‖ Doing business in many waters, **24** They have seen the works of YHWH, ‖ And His wonders in the deep. **25** And He commands, and appoints a storm, ‖ And it lifts up its billows, **26** They go up [to] the heavens, they go down [to] the depths, ‖ Their soul is melted in evil. **27** They reel to and fro, and move as a drunkard, ‖ And all their wisdom is swallowed up. **28** And they cry to YHWH in their adversity, ‖ And He brings them out from their distresses. **29** He calms a whirlwind, ‖ And their billows are hushed. **30** And they rejoice because they are quiet, ‖ And He leads them to the haven of their desire. **31** They confess to YHWH His kindness, ‖ And His wonders to the sons of men, **32** And they exalt Him in [the] assembly of [the] people, ‖ And praise Him in [the] seat of [the] elderly. **33** He makes rivers become a wilderness, ‖ And fountains of waters become dry land. **34** A fruitful land becomes a barren place, ‖ For the wickedness of its inhabitants. **35** He makes a wilderness become a pool of water, ‖ And a dry land become fountains of waters. **36** And He causes the hungry to dwell there, ‖ And they prepare a city of habitation. **37** And they sow fields, and plant vineyards, ‖ And they make fruits of increase. **38** And He blesses them, and they multiply exceedingly, ‖ And He does not diminish their livestock. **39** And they are diminished, and bow down, ‖ By restraint, evil, and sorrow. **40** He is pouring contempt on nobles, ‖ And causes them to wander in vacancy—no way. **41** And sets the needy on high from affliction, ‖ And places families as a flock. **42** The upright see and rejoice, ‖ And all perversity has shut her mouth. **43** Who [is] wise, and observes these? They understand the kind acts of YHWH!

108

A SONG. A PSALM OF DAVID. My heart is prepared, O God, ‖ I sing, indeed, I sing praise, also my glory. **2** Awake, stringed instrument and harp, ‖ I awake the dawn. **3** I thank You among peoples, O YHWH, ‖ And I praise You among the nations. **4** For Your kindness [is] great above the heavens, ‖ And Your truth to the clouds. **5** Be exalted above the heavens, O God, ‖ And Your glory above all the earth. **6** That Your beloved ones may be delivered, ‖ Save [with] Your right hand, and answer us. **7** God has spoken in His holiness: I exult, I apportion Shechem, ‖ And I measure the Valley of Succoth, **8** Gilead [is] Mine, Manasseh [is] Mine, ‖ And Ephraim [is] the strength of My head, ‖ Judah [is] My lawgiver, **9** Moab [is] a pot for My washing, ‖ On Edom I cast My shoe, ‖ Over Philistia I habitually shout. **10** Who brings me [into] the fortified city? Who has led me to Edom? **11** Have You not, O God, cast us off? And You do not go out, O God, with our hosts! **12** Give to us help from adversity, ‖ And the salvation of man is vain. **13** We do mightily in God, ‖ And He treads down our adversaries!

109

TO THE OVERSEER. A PSALM OF DAVID. O God of my praise, do not be silent, **2** For the mouth of wickedness, and the mouth of deceit, ‖ They have opened against me, ‖ They have spoken with me—A tongue of falsehood, and words of hatred! **3** They have surrounded me about, ‖ And they fight me without cause. **4** For my love they oppose me, and I—prayer! **5** And they set against me evil for good, ‖ And hatred for my love. **6** Appoint the wicked over him, ‖ And an adversary stands at his right hand. **7** In his being judged, he goes forth wicked, ‖ And his prayer is for sin. **8** His days are few, another takes his oversight, **9** His sons are fatherless, and his wife a widow. **10** And his sons wander continually, ‖ Indeed, they have begged, ‖ And have sought out of their dry places. **11** An exactor lays a snare for

PSALMS

all that he has, ‖ And strangers spoil his labor. **12** He has none to extend kindness, ‖ Nor is there one showing favor to his orphans. **13** His posterity is for cutting off, ‖ Their name is blotted out in another generation. **14** The iniquity of his fathers ‖ Is remembered to YHWH, ‖ And the sin of his mother is not blotted out. **15** They are continually before YHWH, ‖ And He cuts off their memorial from earth. **16** Because that he has not remembered to do kindness, ‖ And pursues the poor man and needy, ‖ And the struck of heart—to slay, **17** And he loves reviling, and it meets him, ‖ And he has not delighted in blessing, ‖ And it is far from him. **18** And he puts on reviling as his robe, ‖ And it comes in as water into his midst, ‖ And as oil into his bones. **19** It is to him as apparel—he covers himself, ‖ And he girds it on for a continual girdle. **20** This [is] the wage of my accusers from YHWH, ‖ And of those speaking evil against my soul. **21** And You, O Lord YHWH, ‖ Deal with me for Your Name's sake, ‖ Because Your kindness [is] good, deliver me. **22** For I [am] poor and needy, ‖ And my heart has been pierced in my midst. **23** I have gone as a shadow when it is stretched out, ‖ I have been driven away as a locust. **24** My knees have been feeble from fasting, ‖ And my flesh has failed of fatness. **25** And I have been a reproach to them, ‖ They see me, they shake their head. **26** Help me, O YHWH my God, ‖ Save me, according to Your kindness. **27** And they know that this [is] Your hand, ‖ You, O YHWH, You have done it. **28** They revile, and You bless, ‖ They have risen, and are ashamed, ‖ And Your servant rejoices. **29** My accusers put on blushing, and are covered, ‖ Their shame [is] as an upper robe. **30** I thank YHWH greatly with my mouth, ‖ And I praise Him in the midst of many, **31** For He stands at the right hand of the needy, ‖ To save from those judging his soul.

110 A PSALM OF DAVID. A declaration of YHWH to my Lord: "Sit at My right hand, ‖ Until I make Your enemies Your footstool." **2** YHWH sends the rod of Your strength from Zion, ‖ Rule in the midst of Your enemies. **3** Your people [are] free-will gifts in the day of Your strength, in the honors of holiness, ‖ From the womb, from the morning, ‖ You have the dew of Your youth. **4** YHWH has sworn, and does not relent, "You [are] a priest for all time, ‖ According to the order of Melchizedek." **5** The Lord on Your right hand struck kings ‖ In the day of His anger. **6** He judges among the nations, ‖ He has completed the carcasses, ‖ Has struck the head over the mighty earth. **7** He drinks from a brook in the way, ‖ Therefore He lifts up the head!

111 Praise YAH! [ALEPH-BET] I thank YHWH with the whole heart, ‖ In the secret meeting of the upright, ‖ And of the congregation. **2** Great [are] the works of YHWH, ‖ Sought out by all desiring them. **3** Splendid and majestic is His work, ‖ And His righteousness is standing forever. **4** He has made a memorial of His wonders, ‖ YHWH [is] gracious and merciful. **5** He has given prey to those fearing Him, ‖ He remembers His covenant for all time. **6** He has declared the power of His works to His people, ‖ To give to them the inheritance of nations. **7** The works of His hands [are] true and just, ‖ All His appointments [are] steadfast. **8** They are sustained forever and for all time. They are made in truth and uprightness. **9** He has sent redemption to His people, ‖ He has appointed His covenant for all time, ‖ His Name [is] holy and fearful. **10** The fear of YHWH [is] the beginning of wisdom, ‖ Good understanding have all doing them, ‖ His praise [is] standing forever!

112 Praise YAH! [ALEPH-BET] O the blessedness of one fearing YHWH, ‖ He has greatly delighted in His commands. **2** His seed is mighty in the earth, ‖ The generation of the upright is blessed. **3** Wealth and riches [are] in his house, ‖ And his righteousness is standing forever. **4** Light has risen in darkness to the upright, ‖ Gracious, and merciful, and righteous. **5** The man—good, gracious, and lending, ‖ He sustains his matters in judgment. **6** For he is not moved for all time; For the righteous is a continuous memorial. **7** He is not afraid of an evil report, ‖ His heart is prepared [and] confident in YHWH. **8** His heart is sustained—he does not fear, ‖ Until he looks on his adversaries. **9** He has scattered—has given to the needy, ‖ His righteousness is standing forever, ‖ His horn is exalted with glory. **10** The wicked sees, and has been angry, ‖ He gnashes his teeth, and has melted, ‖ The desire of the wicked perishes!

113 Praise YAH! Praise, you servants of YHWH. Praise the Name of YHWH. **2** The Name of YHWH is blessed, ‖ From now on, and for all time. **3** From the rising of the sun to its going in, ‖ The Name of YHWH [is] praised. **4** YHWH [is] high above all nations, ‖ His glory [is] above the heavens. **5** Who [is] as our God YHWH, ‖ He is exalting [Himself] to sit? **6** He is humbling [Himself] to look ‖ On the heavens and on the earth. **7** He is raising up the poor from the dust, ‖ He exalts the needy from a dunghill. **8** To cause [them] to sit with princes, ‖ With the princes of His people. **9** Causing the barren one of the house to sit, ‖ A joyful mother of sons; praise YAH!

114 In the going out of Israel from Egypt, ‖ The house of Jacob from a strange people, **2** Judah became His sanctuary, ‖ Israel his dominion. **3** The sea has seen, and flees, ‖ The Jordan turns backward. **4** The mountains have skipped as rams, ‖ Heights as sons of a flock. **5** What is [ailing] you, O sea, that you flee? O Jordan, you turn back! **6** O mountains, you skip as rams! O heights, as sons of a flock! **7** From before the Lord be afraid, O earth, ‖ From before the God of Jacob, **8** He is turning the rock to a pool of waters, ‖ The flint to a fountain of waters!

115 Not to us, O YHWH, not to us, ‖ But to Your Name give glory, ‖ For Your kindness, for Your truth. **2** Why do the nations say, "Where, pray, [is] their God?" **3** And our God [is] in the heavens, ‖ All that He has pleased He has done. **4** Their idols [are] silver and gold, work of man's hands, **5** They have a mouth, and they do not speak, ‖ They have eyes, and they do not see, **6** They have ears, and they do not hear, ‖ They have a nose, and they do not smell, **7** Their hands, but they do not handle, ‖ Their feet, and they do not walk; **8** Nor do they mutter through their throat, ‖ Their makers are like them, ‖ Everyone who is trusting in them. **9** O Israel, trust in YHWH, "He [is] their help and their shield." **10** O house of Aaron, trust in YHWH, "He [is] their help and their shield." **11** You fearing YHWH, trust in YHWH, "He [is] their help and their shield." **12** YHWH has remembered us, He blesses, ‖ He blesses the house of Israel, ‖ He blesses the house of Aaron, **13** He blesses those fearing YHWH, ‖ The small with the great. **14** YHWH adds to you—to you and to your sons. **15** Blessed [are] you of YHWH, ‖ Maker of the heavens and earth, **16** The heavens—the heavens [are] YHWH's, ‖ And He has given the earth to sons of men; **17** The dead do not praise YAH, ‖ Nor any going down to silence. **18** And we, we bless YAH, ‖ From now on, and for all time. Praise YAH!

116 I have loved, because YHWH hears My voice, my supplication, **2** Because He has inclined His ear to me, ‖ And during my days I call. **3** Cords of death have surrounded me, ‖ And straits of Sheol have found me, ‖ I find distress and sorrow. **4** And in the Name of YHWH I call: Ah, now, O YHWH, deliver my soul, **5** YHWH [is] gracious, and righteous, ‖ Indeed, our God [is] merciful, **6** YHWH [is] a preserver of the simple, ‖ I was low, and He gives salvation to me. **7** Return, O my soul, to your rest, ‖ For YHWH has conferred benefits on you. **8** For You have delivered my soul from death, ‖ My eyes from tears, my feet from overthrowing. **9** I habitually walk before YHWH ‖ In the lands of the living. **10** I have believed, for I speak, ‖ I have been greatly afflicted. **11** I said in my haste, "Every man [is] a liar." **12** What do I return to YHWH? All His benefits [are] on me. **13** I lift up the cup of salvation, ‖ And in the Name of YHWH I call. **14** Let me complete my vows to YHWH, ‖ Now, before all His people. **15** Precious in the eyes of YHWH [is] the death of His saints. **16** Ah, now, O YHWH, for I [am] Your servant; I [am] Your servant, son of Your handmaid; You have opened my bonds. **17** I sacrifice a sacrifice of thanks to You, ‖ And in the Name of YHWH I call. **18** Let me complete my vows to YHWH, ‖ Now, before all His people, **19** In the courts of the house of YHWH, ‖ In your midst, O Jerusalem, praise YAH!

117 Praise YHWH, all you nations, ‖ Glorify Him, all you peoples! **2** For His kindness has been mighty to us, ‖ And the truth of YHWH [is] for all time. Praise YAH!

118 Give thanks to Y<small>HWH</small>, ‖ For [He is] good, for His kindness [is] for all time. **2** Now let Israel say, ‖ His kindness [is] for all time. **3** Now let the house of Aaron say, ‖ His kindness [is] for all time. **4** Now let those fearing Y<small>HWH</small> say, ‖ His kindness [is] for all time. **5** I called Y<small>AH</small> from the narrow place, ‖ Y<small>AH</small> answered me in a broad place. **6** Y<small>HWH</small> [is] for me, ‖ I do not fear what man does to me. **7** Y<small>HWH</small> [is] for me among my helpers, ‖ And I look on those hating me. **8** Better to take refuge in Y<small>HWH</small>, ‖ Than to trust in man, **9** Better to take refuge in Y<small>HWH</small>, ‖ Than to trust in princes. **10** All nations have surrounded me, ‖ In the Name of Y<small>HWH</small> I surely cut them off. **11** They have surrounded me, ‖ Indeed, they have surrounded me, ‖ In the Name of Y<small>HWH</small> I surely cut them off. **12** They surrounded me as bees, ‖ They have been extinguished as a fire of thorns, ‖ In the Name of Y<small>HWH</small> I surely cut them off. **13** You have severely thrust me to fall, ‖ And Y<small>HWH</small> has helped me. **14** Y<small>AH</small> is my strength and song, ‖ And He is to me for salvation. **15** A voice of singing and salvation, ‖ [Is] in the tents of the righteous, ‖ The right hand of Y<small>HWH</small> is doing valiantly. **16** The right hand of Y<small>HWH</small> is exalted, ‖ The right hand of Y<small>HWH</small> is doing valiantly. **17** I do not die, but live, ‖ And recount the works of Y<small>AH</small>, **18** Y<small>AH</small> has severely disciplined me, ‖ And has not given me up to death. **19** Open gates of righteousness to me, ‖ I enter into them—I thank Y<small>AH</small>. **20** This [is] the gate to Y<small>HWH</small>, ‖ The righteous enter into it. **21** I thank You, for You have answered me, ‖ And are to me for salvation. **22** A stone the builders refused ‖ Has become head of a corner. **23** This has been from Y<small>HWH</small>, ‖ It [is] wonderful in our eyes, **24** This [is] the day Y<small>HWH</small> has made, ‖ We rejoice and are glad in it. **25** Ah, now, O Y<small>HWH</small>, please save, ‖ Ah, now, O Y<small>HWH</small>, please prosper. **26** Blessed [is] He who is coming ‖ In the Name of Y<small>HWH</small>, ‖ We blessed you from the house of Y<small>HWH</small>, **27** God [is] Y<small>HWH</small>, and He gives light to us, ‖ Direct the festal-sacrifice with cords, ‖ To the horns of the altar. **28** You [are] my God, and I confess You, ‖ My God, I exalt You. **29** Give thanks to Y<small>HWH</small>, ‖ For [He is] good, for His kindness [is] for all time!

119 [A<small>LEPH</small>] O the blessedness of those perfect in the way, ‖ They are walking in the Law of Y<small>HWH</small>, **2** O the blessedness of those keeping His testimonies, ‖ They seek Him with the whole heart. **3** Indeed, they have not done iniquity, ‖ They have walked in His ways. **4** You have commanded us to diligently keep Your precepts, **5** O that my ways were prepared to keep Your statutes, **6** Then I am not ashamed ‖ In my looking to all Your commands. **7** I confess You with uprightness of heart, ‖ In my learning the judgments of Your righteousness. **8** I keep Your statutes, do not utterly leave me! **9** [B<small>ETH</small>] With what does a young man purify his path? To observe—according to Your word. **10** I have sought You with all my heart, ‖ Do not let me err from Your commands. **11** I have hid Your saying in my heart, ‖ That I do not sin before You. **12** Blessed [are] You, O Y<small>HWH</small>, teach me Your statutes. **13** With my lips I have recounted ‖ All the judgments of Your mouth. **14** I have rejoiced in the way of Your testimonies, ‖ As over all wealth. **15** I meditate on Your precepts, ‖ And I attentively behold Your paths. **16** I delight myself in Your statutes, ‖ I do not forget Your word. **17** [G<small>IMEL</small>] Confer benefits on Your servant, ‖ I live, and I keep Your word. **18** Uncover my eyes, and I behold wonders out of Your law. **19** I [am] a sojourner on earth, ‖ Do not hide Your commands from me. **20** My soul has broken for desire ‖ To Your judgments at all times. **21** You have rebuked the cursed proud, ‖ Who are erring from Your commands. **22** Remove reproach and contempt from me, ‖ For I have kept Your testimonies. **23** Princes also sat—they spoke against me, ‖ Your servant meditates on Your statutes, **24** Your testimonies [are] also my delight, ‖ The men of my counsel! **25** [D<small>ALETH</small>] My soul has cleaved to the dust, ‖ Quicken me according to Your word. **26** I have recounted my ways, ‖ And You answer me, teach me Your statutes, **27** Cause me to understand the way of Your precepts, ‖ And I meditate on Your wonders. **28** My soul has dropped from affliction, ‖ Establish me according to Your word. **29** Turn aside the way of falsehood from me ‖ And favor me with Your law. **30** I have chosen the way of faithfulness, ‖ I have compared Your judgments, **31** I have adhered to Your testimonies, ‖ O Y<small>HWH</small>, do not put me to shame. **32** I run the way of Your commands, ‖ For You enlarge my heart! **33** [HE] Show me, O YHWH, the way of Your statutes, ‖ And I keep it—[to] the end. **34** Cause me to understand, and I keep Your law, ‖ And observe it with the whole heart. **35** Cause me to tread in the path of Your commands, ‖ For I have delighted in it. **36** Incline my heart to Your testimonies, ‖ And not to dishonest gain. **37** Remove my eyes from seeing vanity, ‖ Quicken me in Your way. **38** Establish Your saying to Your servant, ‖ That [is] concerning Your fear. **39** Remove my reproach that I have feared, ‖ For Your judgments [are] good. **40** Behold, I have longed for Your precepts, ‖ Quicken me in Your righteousness, **41** [WAW] And Your kindness meets me, O YHWH, ‖ Your salvation according to Your saying. **42** And I answer him who is reproaching me a word, ‖ For I have trusted in Your word. **43** And You do not utterly take away ‖ The word of truth from my mouth, ‖ Because I have hoped for Your judgment. **44** And I keep Your law continually, ‖ For all time and forever. **45** And I habitually walk in a broad place, ‖ For I have sought Your precepts. **46** And I speak of Your testimonies before kings, ‖ And I am not ashamed. **47** And I delight myself in Your commands, ‖ That I have loved, **48** And I lift up my hands to Your commands, ‖ That I have loved, ‖ And I meditate on Your statutes! **49** [ZAYIN] Remember the word to Your servant, ‖ On which You have caused me to hope. **50** This [is] my comfort in my affliction, ‖ That Your saying has quickened me. **51** The proud have utterly scorned me, ‖ I have not turned aside from Your law. **52** I remembered Your judgments of old, O YHWH, ‖ And I comfort myself. **53** Horror has seized me, ‖ Because of the wicked forsaking Your law. **54** Your statutes have been songs to me, ‖ In the house of my sojournings. **55** I have remembered Your Name in the night, O YHWH, ‖ And I keep Your law. **56** This has been to me, ‖ That I have kept Your precepts! **57** [HETH] YHWH [is] my portion; I have said I would keep Your words, **58** I appeased Your face with the whole heart, ‖ Favor me according to Your saying. **59** I have reckoned my ways, ‖ And turn back my feet to Your testimonies. **60** I have made haste, ‖ And did not delay, to keep Your commands. **61** Cords of the wicked have surrounded me, ‖ I have not forgotten Your law. **62** At midnight I rise to give thanks to You, ‖ For the judgments of Your righteousness. **63** I [am] a companion to all who fear You, ‖ And to those keeping Your precepts. **64** Of Your kindness, O YHWH, the earth is full, ‖ Teach me Your statutes! **65** [TETH] You did good with Your servant, O YHWH, ‖ According to Your word. **66** Teach me the goodness of reason and knowledge, ‖ For I have believed in Your commands. **67** Before I am afflicted, I am erring, ‖ And now I have kept Your saying. **68** You [are] good, and doing good, ‖ Teach me Your statutes. **69** The proud have forged falsehood against me, ‖ I keep Your precepts with the whole heart. **70** Their heart has been thick as fat, ‖ I have delighted in Your law. **71** [It is] good for me that I have been afflicted, ‖ That I might learn Your statutes. **72** The Law of Your mouth [is] better to me ‖ Than thousands of gold and silver! **73** [YOD] Your hands made me and establish me, ‖ Cause me to understand, and I learn Your commands. **74** Those fearing You see me and rejoice, ‖ Because I have hoped for Your word. **75** I have known, O YHWH, ‖ That Your judgments [are] righteous, ‖ And [in] faithfulness You have afflicted me. **76** Please let Your kindness be to comfort me, ‖ According to Your saying to Your servant. **77** Your mercies meet me, and I live, ‖ For Your law [is] my delight. **78** The proud are ashamed, ‖ For [with] falsehood they dealt perversely with me. I meditate on Your precepts. **79** Those fearing You turn back to me, ‖ And those knowing Your testimonies. **80** My heart is perfect in Your statutes, ‖ So that I am not ashamed. **81** [KAPH] My soul has been consumed for Your salvation, ‖ I have hoped for Your word. **82** My eyes have been consumed for Your word, ‖ Saying, "When does it comfort me?" **83** For I have been as a bottle in smoke, ‖ I have not forgotten Your statutes. **84** How many [are] the days of Your servant? When do You execute judgment ‖ Against my pursuers? **85** The proud have dug pits for me, ‖ That [are] not according to Your law. **86** All Your commands [are] faithfulness, ‖ They have pursued me [with] falsehood, ‖ Help me. **87** They have almost consumed me on earth, ‖ And I have not forsaken Your precepts. **88** Quicken me according to Your kindness, ‖ And I keep the Testimony of Your mouth! **89** [LAMED] For all time, O YHWH, Your word is set up in the heavens.

PSALMS

90 Your faithfulness from generation to generation, ‖ You established earth, and it stands. **91** According to Your ordinances ‖ They have stood this day, for the whole— Your servants. **92** Unless Your law [were] my delights, ‖ Then had I perished in my affliction. **93** I do not forget Your precepts for all time, ‖ For You have quickened me by them. **94** I [am] Yours, save me, for I have sought Your precepts. **95** Your wicked waited for me to destroy me, ‖ I understand Your testimonies. **96** I have seen an end of all perfection, ‖ Your command [is] exceedingly broad! **97** [MEM] O how I have loved Your law! It [is] my meditation all the day. **98** Your command makes me wiser than my enemies, ‖ For it [is] before me for all time. **99** I have acted wisely above all my teachers. For Your testimonies [are] my meditation. **100** Above elderly—I understand more, ‖ For I have kept Your precepts. **101** I restrained my feet from every evil path, ‖ So that I keep Your word. **102** I did not turn aside from Your judgments, ‖ For You have directed me. **103** How sweet Your saying has been to my palate, ‖ Above honey to my mouth. **104** I have understanding from Your precepts, ‖ Therefore I have hated every false path! **105** [NUN] Your word [is] a lamp to my foot, ‖ And a light to my path. **106** I have sworn, and I confirm, ‖ To keep the judgments of Your righteousness. **107** I have been afflicted very much, ‖ O YHWH, quicken me, according to Your word. **108** Please accept [the] free-will offerings of my mouth, O YHWH, ‖ And teach me Your judgments. **109** My soul [is] in my hand continually, ‖ And I have not forgotten Your law. **110** The wicked have laid a snare for me, ‖ And I did not wander from your precepts. **111** I have inherited Your testimonies for all time, ‖ For they [are] the joy of my heart. **112** I have inclined my heart ‖ To do Your statutes, for all time—[to] the end! **113** [SAMEKH] I have hated doubting ones, ‖ And I have loved Your law. **114** You [are] my hiding place and my shield, ‖ I have hoped for Your word. **115** Turn aside from me, you evildoers, ‖ And I keep the commands of my God. **116** Sustain me according to Your saying, ‖ And I live, and You do not put me to shame because of my hope. **117** Support me, and I am saved, ‖ And I look on Your statutes continually. **118** You have trodden down ‖ All going astray from Your statutes, ‖ For their deceit [is] falsehood. **119** Dross! You have caused to cease ‖ All the wicked of the earth; Therefore I have loved Your testimonies. **120** My flesh has trembled from Your fear, ‖ And I have been afraid from Your judgments! **121** [AYIN] I have done judgment and righteousness, ‖ Do not leave me to my oppressors. **122** Make Your servant sure for good, ‖ Do not let the proud oppress me. **123** My eyes have been consumed for Your salvation. And for the saying of Your righteousness. **124** Do with Your servant according to Your kindness. And teach me Your statutes. **125** I [am] Your servant—cause me to understand, ‖ And I know Your testimonies. **126** Time for YHWH to work! They have made Your law void. **127** Therefore I have loved Your commands ‖ Above gold—even fine gold. **128** Therefore all my appointments I have declared wholly right, ‖ I have hated every path of falsehood! **129** [PE] Your testimonies [are] wonderful, ‖ Therefore my soul has kept them. **130** The opening of Your words enlightens, ‖ Instructing the simple. **131** I have opened my mouth, indeed, I pant, ‖ For I have longed for Your commands. **132** Look to me, and favor me, ‖ As customary to those loving Your Name. **133** Establish my steps by Your saying, ‖ And any iniquity does not rule over me. **134** Ransom me from the oppression of man, ‖ And I observe Your precepts, **135** Cause Your face to shine on Your servant, ‖ And teach me Your statutes. **136** Streams of waters have come down my eyes, ‖ Because they have not kept Your law! **137** [TSADE] You [are] righteous, O YHWH, ‖ And Your judgments [are] upright. **138** You have appointed Your testimonies, ‖ Righteous and exceedingly faithful, **139** My zeal has cut me off, ‖ For my adversaries forgot Your words. **140** Your saying [is] tried exceedingly, ‖ And Your servant has loved it. **141** I [am] small, and despised, ‖ I have not forgotten Your precepts. **142** Your righteousness [is] righteousness for all time, ‖ And Your law [is] truth. **143** Adversity and distress have found me, ‖ Your commands [are] my delights. **144** The righteousness of Your testimonies ‖ [Is] to cause me to understand, and I live! **145** [QOF] I have called with the whole heart, ‖ Answer me, O YHWH, I keep Your statutes, **146** I have called You, save me, ‖ And I keep Your testimonies. **147** I have gone forward in the dawn, and I cry, ‖

I have hoped for Your word. **148** My eyes have gone before the watches, ‖ To meditate on Your saying. **149** Hear my voice, according to Your kindness, ‖ YHWH, quicken me according to Your judgment. **150** My wicked pursuers have been near, ‖ They have been far off from Your law. **151** You [are] near, O YHWH, ‖ And all Your commands [are] truth. **152** I have known Your testimonies of old, ‖ That You have founded them for all time! **153** [RESH] See my affliction, and deliver me, ‖ For I have not forgotten Your law. **154** Plead my plea, and redeem me, ‖ Quicken me according to Your saying. **155** Salvation [is] far from the wicked, ‖ For they have not sought Your statutes. **156** Your mercies [are] many, O YHWH, ‖ Quicken me according to Your judgments. **157** My pursuers and adversaries are many, ‖ I have not turned aside from Your testimonies. **158** I have seen treacherous ones, ‖ And grieve myself, ‖ Because they have not kept Your saying. **159** See, for I have loved Your precepts, ‖ YHWH, quicken me according to Your kindness. **160** The sum of Your word [is] truth, ‖ And every judgment of Your righteousness [is] for all time! **161** [SHIN] Princes have pursued me without cause, ‖ And my heart was afraid because of Your words. **162** I rejoice concerning Your saying, ‖ As one finding abundant spoil. **163** I have hated falsehood, indeed I detest [it], ‖ I have loved Your law. **164** Seven [times] in a day I have praised You, ‖ Because of the judgments of Your righteousness. **165** Those loving Your law have abundant peace, ‖ And they have no stumbling-block. **166** I have waited for Your salvation, O YHWH, ‖ And I have done Your commands. **167** My soul has kept Your testimonies, ‖ And I love them exceedingly. **168** I have kept Your precepts and Your testimonies, ‖ For all my ways are before You! **169** [TAW] My loud cry comes near before You, O YHWH; Cause me to understand according to Your word. **170** My supplication comes in before You, ‖ Deliver me according to Your saying. **171** My lips utter praise, ‖ For You teach me Your statutes. **172** My tongue sings of Your saying, ‖ For all Your commands [are] righteous. **173** Your hand is for a help to me, ‖ For I have chosen Your commands. **174** I have longed for Your salvation, O YHWH, ‖ And Your law [is] my delight. **175** My soul lives, and it praises You, ‖ And Your judgments help me. **176** I wandered as a lost sheep, [so] seek Your servant, ‖ For I have not forgotten Your precepts!

120 A SONG OF THE ASCENTS. I have called to YHWH in my distress, ‖ And He answers me. **2** O YHWH, deliver my soul from a lying lip, ‖ From a deceitful tongue! **3** What does He give to you? And what does He add to you? O deceitful tongue! **4** Sharp arrows of a mighty one, with coals of broom trees. **5** Woe to me, for I have inhabited Mesech, ‖ I have dwelt with tents of Kedar. **6** My soul has dwelt too much with him who is hating peace. **7** I—peace, and when I speak they [are] for war!

121 A SONG OF THE ASCENTS. I lift up my eyes to the hills, ‖ From where does my help come? **2** My help [is] from YHWH, ‖ Maker of the heavens and earth, **3** He does not permit your foot to be moved, ‖ He who is preserving you does not slumber. **4** Behold, He does not slumber, nor sleep, ‖ He who is preserving Israel. **5** YHWH [is] He who is preserving you, ‖ YHWH [is] your shade on your right hand, **6** By day the sun does not strike you, ‖ Nor the moon by night. **7** YHWH preserves you from all evil, ‖ He preserves your soul. **8** YHWH preserves your going out and your coming in, ‖ From now on—even for all time!

122 A SONG OF THE ASCENTS. BY DAVID. I have rejoiced in those saying to me, "We go to the house of YHWH." **2** Our feet have been standing in your gates, O Jerusalem! **3** Jerusalem—the built one—[is] as a city that is joined to itself together. **4** For there tribes have gone up, ‖ Tribes of YAH, companies of Israel, ‖ To give thanks to the Name of YHWH. **5** For there thrones of judgment have sat, ‖ Thrones of the house of David. **6** Ask [for] the peace of Jerusalem, ‖ Those loving you are at rest. **7** Peace is in your bulwark, rest in your high places, **8** For the sake of my brothers and my companions, ‖ Please let me speak, "Peace [be] in you." **9** For the sake of the house of our God YHWH, ‖ I seek good for you!

123 A SONG OF THE ASCENTS. I have lifted up my eyes to You, ‖ O dweller in the heavens. **2** Behold, as eyes of menservants ‖ [Are] to the hand of their masters, ‖ As eyes of a maidservant ‖ [Are] to the hand of her mistress, ‖ So [are] our eyes to our God YHWH, ‖ Until He favors us. **3** Favor us, O YHWH, favor us, ‖ For we have been greatly filled with contempt, **4** Our soul has been greatly filled ‖ With the scorning of the easy ones, ‖ With the contempt of the arrogant!

124 A SONG OF THE ASCENTS. BY DAVID. If YHWH had not been for us ‖ (Pray, let Israel say), **2** If YHWH had not been for us, ‖ In the rising up of man against us, **3** Then they had swallowed us alive, ‖ In the burning of their anger against us, **4** Then the waters had overflowed us, ‖ The stream passed over our soul, **5** Then proud waters had passed over our soul. **6** Blessed [is] YHWH who has not given us, ‖ [As] prey to their teeth. **7** Our soul has escaped as a bird from a snare of fowlers, ‖ The snare was broken, and we have escaped. **8** Our help [is] in the Name of YHWH, ‖ Maker of the heavens and earth!

125 A SONG OF THE ASCENTS. Those trusting in YHWH [are] as Mount Zion, ‖ It is not moved—it abides for all time. **2** Jerusalem! Mountains [are] around her, ‖ And YHWH [is] around His people, ‖ From now on—even for all time. **3** For the rod of wickedness does not rest on the lot of the righteous, ‖ That the righteous do not put forth their hands on iniquity. **4** Do good, O YHWH, to the good, ‖ And to the upright in their hearts. **5** As for those turning [to] their crooked ways, ‖ YHWH causes them to go with workers of iniquity. Peace on Israel!

126 A SONG OF THE ASCENTS. In YHWH's turning back [to] the captivity of Zion, ‖ We have been as dreamers. **2** Then our mouth is filled [with] laughter, ‖ And our tongue [with] singing, ‖ Then they say among nations, "YHWH did great things with these." **3** YHWH did great things with us, ‖ We have been joyful. **4** Turn again, O YHWH, [to] our captivity, ‖ As streams in the south. **5** Those sowing in tears, reap with singing, **6** Whoever goes on and weeps, ‖ Carrying the basket of seed, ‖ Surely comes in with singing, carrying his sheaves!

127 A SONG OF THE ASCENTS. BY SOLOMON. If YHWH does not build the house, ‖ Its builders have labored at it in vain, ‖ If YHWH does not watch a city, ‖ A watchman has awoken in vain. **2** Vain for you who are rising early, ‖ Who delay sitting, eating the bread of griefs, ‖ So He gives sleep to His beloved one. **3** Behold, sons [are] an inheritance of YHWH, ‖ The fruit of the womb [is] a reward. **4** As arrows in the hand of a mighty one, ‖ So [are] the sons of the young men. **5** O the blessedness of the man ‖ Who has filled his quiver with them, ‖ They are not ashamed, ‖ For they speak with enemies in the gate!

128 A SONG OF THE ASCENTS. O the blessedness of everyone fearing YHWH, ‖ Who is walking in His ways. **2** You surely eat the labor of your hands, ‖ You [are] blessed, and good [is] to you. **3** Your wife [is] as a fruitful vine in the sides of your house, ‖ Your sons as olive plants around your table. **4** Behold, surely thus is the man blessed who is fearing YHWH. **5** YHWH blesses you out of Zion, ‖ Look, then, on the good of Jerusalem, ‖ All the days of your life, **6** And see the sons of your sons! Peace on Israel!

129 A SONG OF THE ASCENTS. Often they distressed me from my youth, ‖ Pray, let Israel say: **2** Often they distressed me from my youth, ‖ Yet they have not prevailed over me. **3** Plowers have plowed over my back, ‖ They have made their furrows long. **4** YHWH [is] righteous, ‖ He has cut apart cords of the wicked. **5** All hating Zion [are] confounded and turn backward. **6** They are as grass of the roofs, ‖ That withers before it was drawn out, **7** That has not filled the hand of a reaper, ‖ And the bosom of a binder of sheaves. **8** And the passers by have not said, "The blessing of YHWH [is] on you, ‖ We blessed you in the Name of YHWH!"

130 A SONG OF THE ASCENTS. I have called You from the depths, YHWH. **2** Lord, listen to my voice, ‖ Your ears are attentive to the voice of my supplications. **3** If You observe iniquities, Lord YAH, who stands? **4** But forgiveness [is] with You, that You may be feared. **5** I hoped [for] YHWH—my soul has hoped, ‖ And I have waited for His word. **6** My soul

[is] for the Lord, ‖ More than those watching for morning, ‖ Watching for morning! **7** Israel waits on YHWH, ‖ For kindness [is] with YHWH, ‖ And redemption [is] abundant with Him. **8** And He redeems Israel from all his iniquities!

131 A SONG OF THE ASCENTS. BY DAVID. YHWH, my heart has not been haughty, ‖ Nor have my eyes been high, ‖ Nor have I walked in great things, ‖ And in things too wonderful for me. **2** Have I not compared, and kept my soul silent, ‖ As a weaned one by its mother? As a weaned one by me [is] my soul. **3** Israel waits on YHWH, ‖ From now on, and for all time!

132 A SONG OF THE ASCENTS. Remember, YHWH, for David, all his afflictions; **2** Who has sworn to YHWH, ‖ He has vowed to the Mighty One of Jacob: **3** "If I enter into the tent of my house, ‖ If I go up on the couch of my bed, **4** If I give sleep to my eyes, ‖ To my eyelids—slumber, **5** Until I find a place for YHWH, dwelling places for the Mighty One of Jacob." **6** Behold, we have heard it in Ephratah, ‖ We have found it in the fields of the forest. **7** We come into His dwelling places, ‖ We bow ourselves at His footstool. **8** Arise, O YHWH, to Your rest, ‖ You, and the Ark of Your strength, **9** Your priests put on righteousness, ‖ And Your pious ones cry aloud. **10** For the sake of Your servant David, ‖ Do not turn back the face of Your anointed. **11** YHWH has sworn truth to David, ‖ He does not turn back from it: "Of the fruit of your body, ‖ I set on the throne for you. **12** If your sons keep My covenant, ‖ And My testimonies that I teach them, ‖ Their sons also forever and ever ‖ Sit on the throne for you." **13** For YHWH has fixed on Zion, ‖ He has desired [it] for a seat to Himself, **14** "This [is] My rest forever and ever, ‖ Here I sit, for I have desired it. **15** I greatly bless her provision, ‖ I satisfy her poor [with] bread, **16** And I clothe her priests [with] salvation, ‖ And her pious ones sing aloud. **17** There I cause a horn to spring up for David, ‖ I have arranged a lamp for My Anointed. **18** I clothe His enemies [with] shame, ‖ And His crown flourishes on Him!"

133 A SONG OF THE ASCENTS. BY DAVID. Behold, how good and how pleasant ‖ The dwelling of brothers—even together! **2** As the good oil on the head, ‖ Coming down on the beard, the beard of Aaron, ‖ That comes down on the skirt of his robes, **3** As dew of Hermon—That comes down on hills of Zion, ‖ For there YHWH commanded the blessing—Life for all time!

134 A SONG OF THE ASCENTS. Behold, bless YHWH, all servants of YHWH, ‖ Who are standing in the house of YHWH by night. **2** Lift up your hands [in] the sanctuary, ‖ And bless YHWH. **3** YHWH blesses you out of Zion, ‖ The Maker of the heavens and earth!

135 Praise YAH! Praise the Name of YHWH, ‖ Praise, you servants of YHWH, **2** Who are standing in the house of YHWH, ‖ In the courts of the house of our God. **3** Praise YAH! For YHWH [is] good, ‖ Sing praise to His Name, for [it is] pleasant. **4** For YAH has chosen Jacob for Himself, ‖ Israel for His peculiar treasure. **5** For I have known that YHWH [is] great, ‖ Indeed, our Lord [is] above all gods. **6** All that YHWH pleased He has done, ‖ In the heavens and in earth, ‖ In the seas and all deep places, **7** Causing vapors to ascend from the end of the earth, ‖ He has made lightnings for the rain, ‖ Bringing forth wind from His treasures. **8** Who struck the firstborn of Egypt, ‖ From man to beast. **9** He sent tokens and wonders into your midst, O Egypt, ‖ On Pharaoh and on all his servants. **10** Who struck many nations, and slew strong kings, **11** Even Sihon king of the Amorite, ‖ And Og king of Bashan, ‖ And all kingdoms of Canaan. **12** And He gave their land an inheritance, ‖ An inheritance to His people Israel, **13** O YHWH, Your Name [is] for all time, ‖ O YHWH, Your memorial from generation to generation. **14** For YHWH judges His people, ‖ And comforts Himself for His servants. **15** The idols of the nations [are] silver and gold, ‖ Work of the hands of man. **16** They have a mouth, and they do not speak, ‖ They have eyes, and they do not see, **17** They have ears, and they do not give ear, ‖ Nose—there is no breath in their mouth! **18** Their makers are like them, ‖ Everyone who is trusting in them. **19** O house of Israel, bless YHWH, ‖ O house of Aaron, bless YHWH, **20** O house of Levi, bless YHWH, ‖ Those fearing YHWH, bless YHWH. **21** Blessed [is]

YHWH from Zion, ‖ Inhabiting Jerusalem—praise YAH!

136 Give thanks to YHWH, ‖ For [He is] good, for His kindness [is] for all time. **2** Give thanks to the God of gods, ‖ For His kindness [is] for all time. **3** Give thanks to the Lord of lords, ‖ For His kindness [is] for all time. **4** To Him doing great wonders by Himself alone, ‖ For His kindness [is] for all time. **5** To Him making the heavens by understanding, ‖ For His kindness [is] for all time. **6** To Him spreading the earth over the waters, ‖ For His kindness [is] for all time. **7** To Him making great lights, ‖ For His kindness [is] for all time. **8** The sun to rule by day, ‖ For His kindness [is] for all time. **9** The moon and stars to rule by night, ‖ For His kindness [is] for all time. **10** To Him striking Egypt in their firstborn, ‖ For His kindness [is] for all time. **11** And bringing forth Israel from their midst, ‖ For His kindness [is] for all time. **12** By a strong hand and an outstretched-arm, ‖ For His kindness [is] for all time. **13** To Him cutting the Sea of Suph into parts, ‖ For His kindness [is] for all time, **14** And caused Israel to pass through its midst, ‖ For His kindness [is] for all time, **15** And shook out Pharaoh and his force in the Sea of Suph, ‖ For His kindness [is] for all time. **16** To Him leading His people in a wilderness, ‖ For His kindness [is] for all time. **17** To Him striking great kings, ‖ For His kindness [is] for all time. **18** Indeed, He slays majestic kings, ‖ For His kindness [is] for all time. **19** Even Sihon king of the Amorite, ‖ For His kindness [is] for all time. **20** And Og king of Bashan, ‖ For His kindness [is] for all time. **21** And He gave their land for inheritance, ‖ For His kindness [is] for all time. **22** An inheritance to Israel His servant, ‖ For His kindness [is] for all time. **23** Who has remembered us in our lowliness, ‖ For His kindness [is] for all time. **24** And He delivers us from our adversaries, ‖ For His kindness [is] for all time. **25** Giving food to all flesh, ‖ For His kindness [is] for all time. **26** Give thanks to the God of the heavens, ‖ For His kindness [is] for all time!

137 By rivers of Babylon—There we sat, ‖ Indeed, we wept when we remembered Zion. **2** We hung our harps on willows in its midst. **3** For there our captors asked us the words of a song, ‖ And our spoilers—joy: "Sing to us of a song of Zion." **4** How do we sing the song of YHWH, ‖ On the land of a stranger? **5** If I forget you, O Jerusalem, my right hand forgets! **6** My tongue cleaves to my palate, ‖ If I do not remember you, ‖ If I do not exalt Jerusalem above my chief joy. **7** Remember, YHWH, for the sons of Edom, ‖ The day of Jerusalem, ‖ Those saying, "Raze, raze to its foundation!" **8** O daughter of Babylon, O destroyed one, ‖ O the blessedness of him who repays to you your deed, ‖ That you have done to us. **9** O the blessedness of him who seizes, and has dashed your sucklings on the rock!

138 BY DAVID. I confess You with all my heart, ‖ I praise You before the gods. **2** I bow myself toward Your holy temple, ‖ And I confess Your Name, ‖ For Your kindness, and for Your truth, ‖ For You have made Your saying great above all Your Name. **3** In the day I called, when You answer me, ‖ You strengthen me in my soul [with] strength. **4** O YHWH, all kings of earth confess You, ‖ When they have heard the sayings of Your mouth. **5** And they sing in the ways of YHWH, ‖ For the glory of YHWH [is] great. **6** For YHWH [is] high, and He sees the lowly, ‖ And He knows the haughty from afar. **7** If I walk in the midst of distress You quicken me, ‖ You send forth Your hand against the anger of my enemies, ‖ And Your right hand saves me. **8** YHWH perfects for me, ‖ O YHWH, Your kindness [is] for all time, ‖ Do not let the works of Your hands fall!

139 TO THE OVERSEER. A PSALM OF DAVID. YHWH, You have searched me, and know. **2** You have known my sitting down, ‖ And my rising up, ‖ You have attended to my thoughts from afar. **3** You have fanned my path and my lying down, ‖ And have been acquainted [with] all my ways. **4** For there is not a word in my tongue, ‖ Behold, O YHWH, You have known it all! **5** You have besieged me behind and before, ‖ And You place Your hand on me. **6** Knowledge too wonderful for me, ‖ It has been set on high, ‖ I am not able for it. **7** To where do I go from Your Spirit? And to where do I flee from Your face? **8** If I ascend the heavens—You [are] there, ‖ And spread out a bed in Sheol, behold, You! **9** I take the wings of morning, ‖ I dwell in the uttermost part of the sea,

PSALMS

10 Also there Your hand leads me, ‖ And Your right hand holds me. **11** And I say, "Surely darkness bruises me," ‖ Then night [is] light to me. **12** Also darkness does not hide from You, ‖ And night shines as day, ‖ As [is] darkness so [is] light. **13** For You have possessed my reins, ‖ You cover me in my mother's belly. **14** I confess You, because I have been fearfully distinguished. Your works [are] wonderful, ‖ And my soul is knowing [it] well. **15** My substance was not hid from You, ‖ When I was made in secret, ‖ Curiously worked in the lower part of earth. **16** Your eyes saw my unformed substance, ‖ And all of them are written on Your scroll, ‖ The days they were formed—And not one among them. **17** And how precious Your thoughts have been to me, ‖ O God, how great has been their sum! **18** I recount them! They are more than the sand, ‖ I have awoken, and I am still with You. **19** Do You slay, O God, the wicked? Then, men of blood, turn aside from me! **20** Who exchange You for wickedness, ‖ Your enemies [are] lifted up to vanity. **21** Do I not hate, YHWH, those hating You? And grieve myself with Your withstanders? **22** I have hated them [with] perfect hatred, ‖ They have become enemies to me. **23** Search me, O God, and know my heart, ‖ Try me, and know my thoughts, **24** And see if a grievous way be in me, ‖ And lead me in a perpetual way!

140 TO THE OVERSEER. A PSALM OF DAVID. Deliver me, O YHWH, from an evil man, ‖ Keep me from one of violence. **2** Who have devised evils in the heart, ‖ All the day they assemble [for] wars. **3** They sharpened their tongue as a serpent, ‖ Poison of a viper [is] under their lips. Selah. **4** Preserve me, YHWH, from the hands of the wicked, ‖ Keep me from one of violence, ‖ Who have devised to overthrow my steps. **5** The proud hid a snare for me—and cords, ‖ They spread a net by the side of the path, ‖ They have set snares for me. Selah. **6** I have said to YHWH, "You [are] my God, ‖ Hear, YHWH, the voice of my supplications." **7** O YHWH, my Lord, strength of my salvation, ‖ You have covered my head in the day of armor. **8** Do not grant, O YHWH, the desires of the wicked, ‖ Do not bring forth his wicked scheme, ‖ They are high. Selah. **9** The chief of my surrounders, ‖ The perverseness of their lips covers them. **10** They cause burning coals to fall on themselves, ‖ He casts them into fire, ‖ Into deep pits—they do not arise. **11** A talkative man is not established in the earth, ‖ One of violence—evil hunts to overflowing. **12** I have known that YHWH executes ‖ The judgment of the afflicted, ‖ The judgment of the needy. **13** Surely the righteous give thanks to Your Name, ‖ The upright dwell with Your presence!

141 A PSALM OF DAVID. O YHWH, I have called You, hurry to me, ‖ Give ear [to] my voice when I call to You. **2** My prayer is prepared—incense before You, ‖ The lifting up of my hands—the evening present. **3** Set, O YHWH, a watch for my mouth, ‖ Watch over the door of my lips. **4** Do not incline my heart to an evil thing, ‖ To habitually do actions in wickedness, ‖ Working iniquity with men, ‖ Indeed, I do not eat of their pleasant things. **5** The righteous beat me [in] kindness. And reprove me, ‖ My head does not disallow oil of the head, ‖ For my prayer [is] still about their distress. **6** Their judges have been released by the sides of a rock, ‖ And they have heard my sayings, ‖ For they have been pleasant. **7** As one tilling and ripping up in the land, ‖ Have our bones been scattered at the command of Saul. **8** But to You, O YHWH, my Lord, [are] my eyes, ‖ In You I have trusted, ‖ Do not make my soul bare. **9** Keep me from the trap they laid for me, ‖ Even snares of workers of iniquity. **10** The wicked fall in their dragnets together, until I pass over!

142 AN INSTRUCTION OF DAVID. A PRAYER WHEN HE IS IN THE CAVE. My voice [is] to YHWH, I cry, ‖ My voice [is] to YHWH, I beg [for] grace. **2** I pour forth my meditation before Him, ‖ I declare my distress before Him. **3** When my spirit has been feeble in me, ‖ Then You have known my path; In the way [in] which I walk, ‖ They have hid a snare for me. **4** Looking on the right hand—and seeing, ‖ And I have none recognizing; Refuge has perished from me, ‖ There is none inquiring for my soul. **5** I have cried to you, O YHWH, ‖ I have said, "You [are] my refuge, ‖ My portion in the land of the living." **6** Attend to my loud cry, ‖ For I have become very low, ‖ Deliver me from my pursuers, ‖ For they have been stronger than I. **7** Bring forth my soul from prison to confess Your

Name, ‖ The righteous surround me about, ‖ When You confer benefits on me!

143 A PSALM OF DAVID. O YHWH, hear my prayer, ‖ Give ear to my supplications, ‖ Answer me in Your faithfulness—in Your righteousness. **2** And do not enter into judgment with Your servant, ‖ For no one living is justified before You. **3** For an enemy has pursued my soul, ‖ He has bruised my life to the earth, ‖ He has caused me to dwell in dark places, ‖ As the dead of old. **4** And my spirit has become feeble in me, ‖ My heart has become desolate within me. **5** I have remembered days of old, ‖ I have meditated on all Your acts, ‖ I muse on the work of Your hand. **6** I have spread forth my hands to You, ‖ My soul [is] as a weary land for You. Selah. **7** Hurry, answer me, O YHWH, ‖ My spirit has been consumed, ‖ Do not hide Your face from me, ‖ Or I have been compared with those going down [to] the pit. **8** Cause me to hear Your kindness in the morning, ‖ For I have trusted in You, ‖ Cause me to know the way that I go, ‖ For I have lifted up my soul to You. **9** Deliver me from my enemies, O YHWH, ‖ Near You I am covered. **10** Teach me to do Your good pleasure, ‖ For You [are] my God—Your Spirit [is] good, ‖ Lead me into a land of uprightness. **11** You quicken me for Your Name's sake, O YHWH, ‖ In Your righteousness, You bring out my soul from distress, **12** And in Your kindness cut off my enemies, ‖ And have destroyed all the adversaries of my soul, ‖ For I [am] Your servant!

144 BY DAVID. Blessed [is] YHWH my Rock, ‖ Who is teaching My hands for war, ‖ My fingers for battle. **2** My kind one, and my bulwark, ‖ My tower, and my deliverer, ‖ My shield, and in whom I have trusted, ‖ Who is subduing my people under me! **3** YHWH, what [is] man that You know him? The son of man, that You esteem him? **4** Man has been like a breath, ‖ His days [are] as a shadow passing by. **5** YHWH, incline Your heavens and come down, ‖ Strike against mountains, and they smoke. **6** Send forth lightning, and scatter them, ‖ Send forth Your arrows, and trouble them, **7** Send forth Your hand from on high, ‖ Free me, and deliver me from many waters, ‖ From the hand of sons of a stranger, **8** Because their mouth has spoken vanity, ‖ And their right hand [is] a right hand of falsehood. **9** O God, I sing to You a new song, ‖ I sing praise to You on a stringed instrument of ten strings. **10** Who is giving deliverance to kings, ‖ Who is freeing His servant David from the sword of evil. **11** Free me, and deliver me ‖ From the hand of sons of a stranger, ‖ Because their mouth has spoken vanity, ‖ And their right hand [is] a right hand of falsehood, **12** Because our sons [are] as plants, ‖ Becoming great in their youth, ‖ Our daughters as hewn stones, ‖ Polished—the likeness of a palace, **13** Our granaries [are] full, bringing out from kind to kind, ‖ Our flocks are bringing forth thousands, ‖ Ten thousands in our out-places, **14** Our oxen are carrying, there is no breach, ‖ And there is no outgoing, ‖ And there is no crying in our broad places. **15** O the blessedness of the people that is thus, ‖ O the blessedness of the people whose God [is] YHWH!

145 A PRAISE [SONG] OF DAVID. [ALEPH-BET] I exalt You, my God, O king, ‖ And bless Your Name for all time and forever. **2** Every day I bless You, ‖ And praise Your Name for all time and forever. **3** YHWH [is] great, and greatly praised, ‖ And there is no searching of His greatness. **4** Generation to generation praises Your works, ‖ And they declare Your mighty acts. **5** The majesty, the glory of Your splendor, ‖ And the matters of Your wonders, I declare. **6** And they tell of the strength of Your fearful acts, ‖ And I recount Your greatness. **7** They send forth the memorial of the abundance of Your goodness. And they sing of Your righteousness. **8** YHWH [is] gracious and merciful, ‖ Slow to anger, and great in kindness. **9** YHWH [is] good to all, ‖ And His mercies [are] over all His works. **10** O YHWH, all Your works confess You, ‖ And Your saints bless You. **11** They tell of the glory of Your kingdom, ‖ And they speak of Your might, **12** To make His mighty acts known to sons of men, ‖ The glory of the majesty of His kingdom. **13** Your kingdom [is] a kingdom of all ages, ‖ And Your dominion [is] in all generations. [[YHWH [is] faithful in all His words, ‖ And kind in all His works.]] **14** YHWH is supporting all who are falling, ‖ And raising up all who are bowed down. **15** The eyes of all look to You, ‖ And You are giving their food to them in its season, **16** Opening Your hand,

and satisfying ‖ The desire of every living thing. **17** YHWH [is] righteous in all His ways, ‖ And kind in all His works. **18** YHWH [is] near to all those calling Him, ‖ To all who call Him in truth. **19** He does the desire of those fearing Him, ‖ And He hears their cry, and saves them. **20** YHWH preserves all those loving Him, ‖ And He destroys all the wicked. **21** My mouth speaks the praise of YHWH, ‖ And all flesh blesses His Holy Name, ‖ For all time and forever!

146 Praise YAH! Praise, O my soul, YHWH. **2** I praise YHWH during my life, ‖ I sing praise to my God while I exist. **3** Do not trust in princes—in a son of man, ‖ For he has no deliverance. **4** His spirit goes forth, he returns to his earth, ‖ In that day his thoughts have perished. **5** O the blessedness of him ‖ Who has the God of Jacob for his help, ‖ His hope [is] on his God YHWH, **6** Making the heavens and earth, ‖ The sea and all that [is] in them, ‖ Who is keeping truth for all time, **7** Doing judgment for the oppressed, ‖ Giving bread to the hungry. **8** YHWH is loosing the prisoners, ‖ YHWH is opening (the eyes of) the blind, ‖ YHWH is raising the bowed down, ‖ YHWH is loving the righteous, **9** YHWH is preserving the strangers, ‖ He causes the fatherless and widow to stand, ‖ And He turns the way of the wicked upside down. **10** YHWH reigns for all time, ‖ Your God, O Zion, to generation and generation, ‖ Praise YAH!

147 Praise YAH! For [it is] good to praise our God, ‖ For pleasant—lovely [is] praise. **2** YHWH [is] building Jerusalem, ‖ He gathers the driven away of Israel. **3** Who is giving healing to the broken of heart, ‖ And is binding up their griefs. **4** Appointing the number of the stars, ‖ He gives names to all of them. **5** Our Lord [is] great, and abundant in power, ‖ There is no narration of His understanding. **6** YHWH is causing the meek to stand, ‖ Making the wicked low to the earth. **7** Answer to YHWH with thanksgiving, ‖ Sing to our God with a harp. **8** Who is covering the heavens with clouds, ‖ Who is preparing rain for the earth, ‖ Who is causing grass to spring up [on] mountains, **9** Giving to the beast its food, ‖ To the young of the ravens that call. **10** He does not delight in the might of the horse, ‖ He is not pleased in the legs of a man. **11** YHWH is pleased with those fearing Him, ‖ With those waiting for His kindness. **12** Glorify, O Jerusalem, YHWH, ‖ Praise your God, O Zion. **13** For He strengthened the bars of your gates, ‖ He has blessed your sons in your midst. **14** Who is making your border peace, ‖ He satisfies you [with] the fat of wheat. **15** Who is sending forth His saying [on] earth, ‖ His word runs very speedily. **16** Who is giving snow like wool, ‖ He scatters hoarfrost as ashes. **17** Casting forth His ice like morsels, ‖ Who stands before His cold? **18** He sends forth His word and melts them, ‖ He causes His wind to blow—the waters flow. **19** Declaring His words to Jacob, ‖ His statutes and His judgments to Israel. **20** He has not done so to any nation, ‖ As for judgments, they have not known them. Praise YAH!

148 Praise YAH! Praise YHWH from the heavens, ‖ Praise Him in high places. **2** Praise Him, all His messengers, ‖ Praise Him, all His hosts. **3** Praise Him, sun and moon, ‖ Praise Him, all stars of light. **4** Praise Him, heavens of heavens, ‖ And you waters that are above the heavens. **5** They praise the Name of YHWH, ‖ For He commanded, and they were created. **6** And He establishes them forever and for all time, ‖ He gave a statute, and they do not pass over. **7** Praise YHWH from the earth, ‖ Dragons and all deeps, **8** Fire and hail, snow and vapor, ‖ Whirlwind doing His word; **9** The mountains and all heights, ‖ Fruit tree, and all cedars, **10** The wild beast, and all livestock, ‖ Creeping thing, and winged bird, **11** Kings of earth, and all peoples, ‖ Chiefs, and all judges of earth, **12** Young men, and also maidens, ‖ Aged men, with youths, **13** They praise the Name of YHWH, ‖ For His Name alone has been set on high, ‖ His splendor [is] above earth and heavens. **14** And He exalts the horn of His people, ‖ The praise of all His saints, ‖ Of the sons of Israel, ‖ A people near Him. Praise YAH!

149 Praise YAH! Sing to YHWH a new song, ‖ His praise in an assembly of saints. **2** Israel rejoices in his Maker, ‖ Sons of Zion rejoice in their king. **3** They praise His Name in a dance, ‖ Sing praise to Him with timbrel and harp. **4** For YHWH is pleased with His people, ‖ He beautifies the humble with salvation. **5** Saints exult in glory, ‖ They sing aloud on their beds. **6** The exaltation of God [is] in their throat, ‖ And a two-edged sword in their hand. **7** To do vengeance among nations, ‖ Punishments among the peoples. **8** To bind their kings with chains, ‖ And their honored ones with chains of iron, **9** To do among them the judgment written, ‖ It [is] an honor for all his saints. Praise YAH!

150 Praise YAH! Praise God in His holy place, ‖ Praise Him in the expanse of His strength. **2** Praise Him in His mighty acts, ‖ Praise Him according to the abundance of His greatness. **3** Praise Him with blowing of horn, ‖ Praise Him with stringed instrument and harp. **4** Praise Him with timbrel and dance, ‖ Praise Him with stringed instruments and pipe. **5** Praise Him with cymbals of sounding, ‖ Praise Him with cymbals of shouting. **6** All that breathes praise YAH! Praise YAH!

PROVERBS

1 Proverbs of Solomon, son of David, king of Israel: **2** For knowing wisdom and instruction, ‖ For understanding sayings of intelligence, **3** For receiving the instruction of wisdom, ‖ Righteousness, judgment, and uprightness, **4** For giving to simple ones—prudence, ‖ To a youth—knowledge and discretion. **5** (The wise hear and increase learning, ‖ And the intelligent obtain counsels.) **6** For understanding a proverb and its sweetness, ‖ Words of the wise and their acute sayings. **7** Fear of YHWH [is the] beginning of knowledge, ‖ Fools have despised wisdom and instruction! **8** Hear, my son, the instruction of your father, ‖ And do not leave the law of your mother, **9** For they [are] a graceful wreath to your head, ‖ And chains to your neck. **10** My son, if sinners entice you, do not be willing. **11** If they say, "Come with us, we lay wait for blood, ‖ We watch secretly for the innocent without cause, **12** We swallow them as Sheol—alive, ‖ And whole—as those going down [to] the pit, **13** We find every precious substance, ‖ We fill our houses [with] spoil, **14** You cast your lot among us, ‖ One purse is—to all of us." **15** My son! Do not go in the way with them, ‖ Withhold your foot from their path, **16** For their feet run to evil, ‖ And they hurry to shed blood. **17** Surely in vain is the net spread out before the eyes of any bird. **18** And they lay wait for their own blood, ‖ They watch secretly for their own lives. **19** So [are] the paths of every gainer of dishonest gain, ‖ It takes the life of its owners. **20** Wisdom cries aloud in an outplace, ‖ She gives forth her voice in broad places, **21** She calls at the head of the multitudes, ‖ In the openings of the gates, ‖ In the city she says her sayings: **22** "Until when, you simple, do you love simplicity? And have scorners desired their scorning? And do fools hate knowledge? **23** Turn back at my reproof, behold, ‖ I pour forth my spirit to you, ‖ I make known my words with you. **24** Because I have called, and you refuse, ‖ I stretched out my hand, and none is attending, **25** And you slight all my counsel, ‖ And you have not desired my reproof. **26** I also laugh in your calamity, ‖ I deride when your fear comes, **27** When your fear comes as destruction, ‖ And your calamity comes as a windstorm, ‖ When adversity and distress come on you. **28** Then they call me, and I do not answer, ‖ They seek me earnestly, and do not find me. **29** Because that they have hated knowledge, ‖ And have not chosen the fear of YHWH. **30** They have not consented to my counsel, ‖ They have despised all my reproof, **31** And they eat of the fruit of their way, ‖ And they are filled from their own counsels. **32** For the turning of the simple slays them, ‖ And the security of the foolish destroys them. **33** And whoever is listening to me dwells confidently, ‖ And [is] quiet from fear of evil!"

2 My son, if you accept my sayings, ‖ And lay up my commands with you, **2** To cause your ear to attend to wisdom, ‖ You incline your heart to understanding, **3** For if you call for intelligence, ‖ [And] give forth your voice for intelligence, **4** If you seek her as silver, ‖ And search for her as hid treasures, **5** Then you understand the fear of YHWH, ‖ And you find the knowledge of God. **6** For YHWH gives wisdom, ‖ Knowledge and understanding from His mouth. **7** Even to lay up substance for the upright, ‖ A shield for those walking uprightly. **8** To keep the paths of judgment, ‖ And He preserves the way of His saints. **9** Then you understand righteousness, ‖ And judgment, and uprightness—every good path. **10** For wisdom comes into your heart, ‖ And knowledge is pleasant to your soul, **11** Thoughtfulness watches over you, ‖ Understanding keeps you, **12** To deliver you from an evil way, ‖ From any speaking contrary things, **13** Who are forsaking paths of uprightness, ‖ To walk in ways of darkness, **14** Who are rejoicing to do evil, ‖ They delight in [the] contrariness of the wicked, **15** Whose paths [are] crooked, ‖ Indeed, they are perverted in their ways. **16** To deliver you from the strange woman, ‖ From the stranger who has made her sayings smooth, **17** Who is forsaking the guide of her youth, ‖ And has forgotten the covenant of her God. **18** For her house has inclined to death, ‖ And her paths to Rephaim. **19** None going in to her return, ‖ Nor do they reach the paths of life. **20** That you go in the way of the good, ‖ And keep

PROVERBS

the paths of the righteous. **21** For the upright inhabit the earth, ‖ And the perfect are left in it, **22** And the wicked are cut off from the earth, ‖ And treacherous dealers plucked out of it!

3 My son! Do not forget my law, ‖ And let your heart keep my commands, **2** For [the] length of [your] days and years, ‖ Life and peace they add to you. **3** Do not let kindness and truth forsake you, ‖ Bind them on your neck, ‖ Write them on the tablet of your heart, **4** And find grace and good understanding ‖ In the eyes of God and man. **5** Trust to YHWH with all your heart, ‖ And do not lean to your own understanding. **6** In all your ways know Him, ‖ And He makes your paths straight. **7** Do not be wise in your own eyes, ‖ Fear YHWH, and turn aside from evil. **8** It is healing to your navel, ‖ And moistening to your bones. **9** Honor YHWH from your substance, ‖ And from the beginning of all your increase; **10** And your barns are filled [with] plenty, ‖ And your presses break forth [with] new wine. **11** Discipline of YHWH, my son, do not despise, ‖ And do not be distressed with His reproof, **12** For whom YHWH loves He reproves, ‖ Even as a father the son He is pleased with. **13** O the blessedness of a man [who] has found wisdom, ‖ And of a man [who] brings forth understanding. **14** For better [is] her merchandise ‖ Than the merchandise of silver, ‖ And than gold—her increase. **15** She [is] precious above rubies, ‖ And all your pleasures are not comparable to her. **16** Length of days [is] in her right hand, ‖ In her left [are] wealth and honor. **17** Her ways [are] ways of pleasantness, ‖ And all her paths [are] peace. **18** She [is] a tree of life to those laying hold on her, ‖ And whoever is retaining her [is] blessed. **19** YHWH founded the earth by wisdom, ‖ He prepared the heavens by understanding. **20** By His knowledge depths have been broken, ‖ And clouds drop dew. **21** My son! Do not let them turn from your eyes, ‖ Keep wisdom and thoughtfulness, **22** And they are life to your soul, and grace to your neck. **23** Then you go your way confidently, ‖ And your foot does not stumble. **24** If you lie down, you are not afraid, ‖ Indeed, you have lain down, ‖ And your sleep has been sweet. **25** Do not be afraid of sudden fear, ‖ And of the desolation of the wicked when it comes. **26** For YHWH is at your side, ‖ And He has kept your foot from capture. **27** Do not withhold good from its owners, ‖ When your hand [is] toward God to do [it]. **28** Do not say to your friend, ‖ "Go, and return, and tomorrow I give," ‖ When substance [is] with you. **29** Do not devise evil against your neighbor, ‖ And he sitting confidently with you. **30** Do not strive with a man without cause, ‖ If he has not done you evil. **31** Do not be envious of a man of violence, ‖ Nor fix on any of his ways. **32** For the perverted [is] an abomination to YHWH, ‖ And His secret counsel [is] with the upright. **33** The curse of YHWH [is] in the house of the wicked. And He blesses the habitation of the righteous. **34** If He scorns the scorners, ‖ Yet He gives grace to the humble. **35** The wise inherit glory, ‖ And fools are bearing away shame!

4 Hear, you sons, the instruction of a father, ‖ And give attention to know understanding. **2** For I have given to you good learning, do not forsake my law. **3** For I have been a son to my father—tender, ‖ And an only one before my mother. **4** And he directs me, and he says to me: "Let your heart retain my words, ‖ Keep my commands, and live. **5** Get wisdom, get understanding, ‖ Do not forget, nor turn away ‖ From the sayings of my mouth. **6** Do not forsake her, and she preserves you, ‖ Love her, and she keeps you. **7** The first thing [is] wisdom—get wisdom, ‖ And with all your getting get understanding. **8** Exalt her and she lifts you up, ‖ She honors you when you embrace her. **9** She gives a wreath of grace to your head, ‖ She gives you a crown of beauty freely." **10** Hear, my son, and receive my sayings, ‖ And years of life [are] multiplied to you. **11** I have directed you in a way of wisdom, ‖ I have caused you to tread in paths of uprightness. **12** In your walking your step is not restricted, ‖ And if you run, you do not stumble. **13** Lay hold on instruction, do not desist, ‖ Keep her, for she [is] your life. **14** Do not enter into the path of the wicked, ‖ And do not be blessed in a way of evildoers. **15** Avoid it, do not pass over into it, ‖ Turn aside from it, and pass on. **16** For they do not sleep if they do no evil, ‖ And their sleep has been taken away violently, ‖ If they do not cause [some] to stumble. **17** For they have eaten bread of wickedness, ‖ And they drink wine of violence. **18** And the path of the righteous

[is] as a shining light, ‖ Going and brightening until the day is established, **19** The way of the wicked [is] as darkness, ‖ They have not known at what they stumble. **20** My son, give attention to my words, ‖ Incline your ear to my sayings, **21** Do not let them turn aside from your eyes, ‖ Preserve them in the midst of your heart. **22** For they [are] life to those finding them, ‖ And healing to all their flesh. **23** Above every charge keep your heart, ‖ For out of it [are] the outgoings of life. **24** Turn aside a contrary mouth from you, ‖ And put perverse lips far from you, **25** Your eyes look straightforward, ‖ And your eyelids look straight before you. **26** Ponder the path of your feet, ‖ And all your ways [are] established. **27** Do not incline [to] the right or to the left, ‖ Turn aside your foot from evil!

5 My son! Give attention to my wisdom, ‖ Incline your ear to my understanding, **2** To observe thoughtfulness, ‖ And your lips keep knowledge. **3** For the lips of a strange woman drop honey, ‖ And her mouth [is] smoother than oil, **4** And her latter end [is] bitter as wormwood, ‖ Sharp as a sword [with] mouths. **5** Her feet are going down to death, ‖ Her steps take hold of Sheol. **6** The path of life—lest you ponder, ‖ Her paths have moved—you do not know. **7** And now, you sons, listen to me, ‖ And do not turn from sayings of my mouth. **8** Keep your way far from off her, ‖ And do not come near to the opening of her house, **9** Lest you give your splendor to others, ‖ And your years to the fierce, **10** Lest strangers be filled [with] your power, ‖ And your labors in the house of a stranger, **11** And you have howled in your latter end, ‖ In the consumption of your flesh and your food, **12** And have said, "How I have hated instruction, ‖ And my heart has despised reproof, **13** And I have not listened to the voice of my teachers, ‖ And have not inclined my ear to my teachers. **14** As a little thing I have been all evil, ‖ In the midst of an assembly and a congregation." **15** Drink waters out of your own cistern, ‖ Even flowing ones out of your own well. **16** Let your fountains be scattered abroad, ‖ In broad places streams of waters. **17** Let them be to you for yourself, ‖ And not to strangers with you. **18** Let your fountain be blessed, ‖ And rejoice because of the wife of your youth, **19** A doe of loves, and a roe of grace! Let her loves satisfy you at all times, ‖ Magnify yourself in her love continually. **20** And why do you magnify yourself, ‖ My son, with a stranger? And embrace the bosom of a strange woman? **21** For the ways of each are before the eyes of Y<small>HWH</small>, ‖ And He is pondering all his paths. **22** His own iniquities capture the wicked, ‖ And he is holden with the ropes of his sin. **23** He dies without instruction, ‖ And magnifies himself in the abundance of his folly!

6 My son! If you have been guarantor for your friend, ‖ Have struck your hand for a stranger, **2** Have been snared with sayings of your mouth, ‖ Have been captured with sayings of your mouth, **3** Do this now, my son, and be delivered, ‖ For you have come into the hand of your friend. Go, trample on yourself, and strengthen your friend, **4** Do not give sleep to your eyes, ‖ And slumber to your eyelids, **5** Be delivered as a roe from the hand, ‖ And as a bird from the hand of a fowler. **6** Go to the ant, O slothful one, ‖ See her ways and be wise; **7** Which has no captain, overseer, and ruler, **8** She prepares her bread in summer, ‖ She has gathered her food in harvest. **9** Until when, O slothful one, do you lie? When do you arise from your sleep? **10** A little sleep, a little slumber, ‖ A little clasping of the hands to rest, **11** And your poverty has come as a traveler, ‖ And your want as an armed man. **12** A man of worthlessness, a man of iniquity, ‖ Walking [with] perverseness of mouth, **13** Winking with his eyes, speaking with his feet, ‖ Directing with his fingers, **14** Contrariness [is] in his heart, devising evil at all times, ‖ He sends forth contentions. **15** Therefore his calamity comes suddenly, ‖ He is broken instantly—and no healing. **16** These six has Y<small>HWH</small> hated, ‖ Indeed, seven [are] abominations to His soul: **17** High eyes, ‖ False tongues, ‖ And hands shedding innocent blood, **18** A heart devising thoughts of vanity, ‖ Feet hastening to run to evil, **19** A false witness [who] breathes out lies, ‖ And one sending forth contentions between brothers. **20** Keep, my son, the command of your father, ‖ And do not leave the law of your mother. **21** Bind them on your heart continually, ‖ Tie them on your neck. **22** In your going up and down, it leads you, ‖ In your lying down, it watches over you, ‖

And you have awoken—it talks [with] you. **23** For the command [is] a lamp, ‖ And the Law a light, ‖ And a way of life [are] reproofs of instruction, **24** To preserve you from an evil woman, ‖ From the flattery of the tongue of a strange woman. **25** Do not desire her beauty in your heart, ‖ And do not let her take you with her eyelids. **26** For a harlot consumes to a cake of bread, ‖ And an adulteress hunts the precious soul. **27** Does a man take fire into his bosom, ‖ And are his garments not burned? **28** Does a man walk on the hot coals, ‖ And are his feet not scorched? **29** So [is] he who has gone in to the wife of his neighbor, ‖ None who touches her is innocent. **30** They do not despise the thief, ‖ When he steals to fill his soul when he is hungry, **31** And being found he repays sevenfold, ‖ He gives all the substance of his house. **32** He who commits adultery [with] a woman lacks heart, ‖ He who does it is destroying his soul. **33** He finds a stroke and shame, ‖ And his reproach is not wiped away, **34** For jealousy [is] the fury of a man, ‖ And he does not spare in a day of vengeance. **35** He does not accept the appearance of any atonement, ‖ Indeed, he does not consent, ‖ Though you multiply bribes!

7 My son! Keep my sayings, ‖ And lay up my commands with you. **2** Keep my commands, and live, ‖ And my law as the pupil of your eye. **3** Bind them on your fingers, ‖ Write them on the tablet of your heart. **4** Say to wisdom, "You [are] my sister." And cry to understanding, "Relative!" **5** To preserve you from a strange woman, ‖ From a stranger who has made her sayings smooth. **6** For at a window of my house, ‖ I have looked out through my casement, **7** And I see among the simple ones, ‖ I discern among the sons, ‖ A young man lacking understanding, **8** Passing on in the street, near her corner, ‖ And the way [to] her house he steps, **9** In the twilight—in the evening of day, ‖ In the darkness of night and blackness. **10** And behold, a woman to meet him—(A harlot's dress, and watchful of heart, **11** She [is] noisy, and stubborn, her feet do not rest in her house. **12** Now in an out-place, now in broad places, ‖ And she lies in wait near every corner)— **13** And she laid hold on him and kissed him, ‖ She has hardened her face and says to him, **14** "Sacrifices of peace-offerings [are] by me, ‖ Today I have completed my vows. **15** Therefore I have come forth to meet you, ‖ To earnestly seek your face, and I find you. **16** I decked my bed [with] ornamental coverings, ‖ Carved works—cotton of Egypt. **17** I sprinkled my bed [with] myrrh, aloes, and cinnamon. **18** Come, we are filled [with] love until the morning, ‖ We delight ourselves in loves. **19** For the man is not in his house, ‖ He has gone on a long journey. **20** He has taken a bag of money in his hand, ‖ At the day of the new moon he comes to his house." **21** She turns him aside with the abundance of her speech, ‖ She forces him with the flattery of her lips. **22** He is going after her straight away, he comes as an ox to the slaughter, ‖ And as a chain to the discipline of a fool, **23** Until an arrow splits his liver, ‖ As a bird has hurried to a snare, ‖ And has not known that it [is] for its life. **24** And now, you sons, listen to me, ‖ And give attention to sayings of my mouth. **25** Do not let your heart turn to her ways, ‖ Do not wander in her paths, **26** For many [are] the wounded she caused to fall, ‖ And mighty [are] all her slain ones. **27** The ways of Sheol—her house, ‖ Going down to inner chambers of death!

8 Does wisdom not call? And understanding give forth her voice? **2** At the head of high places by the way, ‖ She has stood between the paths, **3** At the side of the gates, at the mouth of the city, ‖ The entrance of the openings, she cries aloud, **4** "To you, O men, I call, ‖ And my voice [is] to the sons of men. **5** Understand, you simple ones, prudence, ‖ And you fools, understand the heart, **6** Listen, for I speak noble things, ‖ And the opening of my lips [is] uprightness. **7** For my mouth utters truth, ‖ And wickedness [is] an abomination to my lips. **8** All the sayings of my mouth [are] in righteousness, ‖ Nothing in them is contrary and perverse. **9** All of them [are] plain to the intelligent, ‖ And upright to those finding knowledge. **10** Receive my instruction, and not silver, ‖ And knowledge rather than choice gold. **11** For wisdom [is] better than rubies, ‖ Indeed, all delights are not comparable with it. **12** I, wisdom, have dwelt with prudence, ‖ And I find out a knowledge of purposes. **13** The fear of YHWH [is] to hate evil; Pride, and arrogance, and an evil way, ‖ And a contrary mouth, I have hated. **14** Counsel and substance [are] mine, ‖ I [am] understanding, I have might. **15** By me kings reign, and princes decree righteousness, **16** By me chiefs rule, and nobles, ‖ All judges of earth. **17** I love those loving me, ‖ And those seeking me earnestly find me. **18** Wealth and honor [are] with me, ‖ Lasting substance and righteousness. **19** My fruit [is] better than gold, even fine gold, ‖ And my increase than choice silver. **20** I cause to walk in a path of righteousness, ‖ In midst of paths of judgment, **21** To cause my lovers to inherit substance, ‖ Indeed, I fill their treasures. **22** YHWH possessed me—the beginning of His way, ‖ Before His works since then. **23** I was anointed from the age, from the first, ‖ From former states of the earth. **24** In there being no depths, I was brought forth, ‖ In there being no fountains heavy [with] waters, **25** Before mountains were sunk, ‖ Before heights, I was brought forth. **26** While He had not made the earth, and out-places, ‖ And the top of the dusts of the world. **27** In His preparing the heavens I [am] there, ‖ In His decreeing a circle on the face of the deep, **28** In His strengthening clouds above, ‖ In His making strong fountains of the deep, **29** In His setting for the sea its limit, ‖ And the waters do not transgress His command, ‖ In His decreeing the foundations of earth, **30** Then I am near Him, a workman, ‖ And I am a delight—day by day. Rejoicing before Him at all times, **31** Rejoicing in the habitable part of His earth, ‖ And my delights [are] with the sons of men. **32** And now, you sons, listen to me, ‖ Indeed, blessed are they who keep my ways. **33** Hear instruction, and be wise, and do not slight. **34** O the blessedness of the man listening to me, ‖ To watch at my doors day by day, ‖ To watch at the doorposts of my entrance. **35** For whoever is finding me, has found life, ‖ And brings out goodwill from YHWH. **36** And whoever is missing me, is wronging his soul, ‖ All hating me have loved death!"

9 Wisdom has built her house, ‖ She has hewn out her pillars—seven. **2** She has slaughtered her slaughter, ‖ She has mingled her wine, ‖ Indeed, she has arranged her table. **3** She has sent forth her girls, ‖ She cries on the tops of the high places of the city: **4** "Who [is] simple? Let him turn aside here." Whoever lacks heart: she has said to him, **5** "Come, eat of my bread, ‖ And drink of the wine I have mingled. **6** Forsake the simple and live, ‖ And be blessed in the way of understanding." **7** The instructor of a scorner ‖ Is receiving for it—shame, ‖ And a reprover of the wicked—his blemish. **8** Do not reprove a scorner, lest he hate you, ‖ Give reproof to the wise, and he loves you. **9** Give to the wise, and he is wiser still, ‖ Make known to the righteous, ‖ And he increases learning. **10** The commencement of wisdom [is] the fear of YHWH, ‖ And a knowledge of the Holy Ones [is] understanding. **11** For by me your days multiply, ‖ And years of life are added to you. **12** If you have been wise, you have been wise for yourself, ‖ And you have scorned—you bear [it] alone. **13** A foolish woman [is] noisy, ‖ Simple, and has not known what. **14** And she has sat at the opening of her house, ‖ On a throne—the high places of the city, **15** To call to those passing by the way, ‖ Who are going straight [on] their paths. **16** "Who [is] simple? Let him turn aside here." And whoever lacks heart—she said to him, **17** "Stolen waters are sweet, ‖ And hidden bread is pleasant." **18** And he has not known that Rephaim [are] there, ‖ Her invited ones in deep places of Sheol!

10 Proverbs of Solomon. A wise son causes a father to rejoice, ‖ And a foolish son [is] an affliction to his mother. **2** Treasures of wickedness do not profit, ‖ And righteousness delivers from death. **3** YHWH does not cause the soul of the righteous to hunger, ‖ And He thrusts away the desire of the wicked. **4** Poor [is] he who is working [with] a slothful hand, ‖ And the hand of the diligent makes rich. **5** Whoever is gathering in summer [is] a wise son, ‖ Whoever is sleeping in harvest [is] a son causing shame. **6** Blessings [are] for the head of the righteous, ‖ And the mouth of the wicked covers violence. **7** The remembrance of the righteous [is] for a blessing, ‖ And the name of the wicked rots. **8** The wise in heart accepts commands, ‖ And a talkative fool kicks. **9** Whoever is walking in integrity walks confidently, ‖ And whoever is perverting his ways is known. **10** Whoever is winking the eye gives grief, ‖ And a talkative fool kicks. **11** A fountain of life [is] the mouth of the righteous, ‖ And the mouth of the wicked covers violence. **12** Hatred awakens contentions, ‖ And love covers over all transgressions. **13** Wisdom is found in the lips of the intelligent, ‖ And a rod [is] for the back of him who is lacking understanding. **14** The wise lay up knowledge, and the mouth of a fool [is] near ruin. **15** The wealth of the rich [is] his strong city, ‖ The ruin of the poor [is] their poverty. **16** The wage of the righteous [is] for life, ‖ The increase of the wicked for sin. **17** A traveler to life [is] he who is keeping instruction, ‖ And whoever is forsaking rebuke is erring. **18** Whoever is covering hatred with lying lips, ‖ And whoever is bringing out an evil report is a fool. **19** In the abundance of words transgression does not cease, ‖ And whoever is restraining his lips [is] wise. **20** The tongue of the righteous [is] chosen silver, ‖ The heart of the wicked—as a little thing. **21** The lips of the righteous delight many, ‖ And fools die for lack of heart. **22** The blessing of YHWH—it makes rich, ‖ And He adds no grief with it. **23** To execute inventions [is] as play to a fool, ‖ And wisdom to a man of understanding. **24** The feared thing of the wicked meets him, ‖ And the desire of the righteous is given. **25** As the passing by of a windstorm, ‖ So the wicked is not, ‖ And the righteous is a perpetual foundation. **26** As vinegar to the teeth, ‖ And as smoke to the eyes, ‖ So [is] the slothful to those sending him. **27** The fear of YHWH adds days, ‖ And the years of the wicked are shortened. **28** The hope of the righteous [is] joyful, ‖ And the expectation of the wicked perishes. **29** The way of YHWH [is] strength to the perfect, ‖ And ruin to workers of iniquity. **30** The righteous is not moved for all time, ‖ And the wicked do not inhabit the earth. **31** The mouth of the righteous utters wisdom, ‖ And the tongue of contrariness is cut out. **32** The lips of the righteous know a pleasing thing, ‖ And the mouth of the wicked perverseness!

11 Balances of deceit [are] an abomination to YHWH, ‖ And a perfect weight [is] His delight. **2** Pride has come, and shame comes, ‖ And wisdom [is] with the lowly. **3** The integrity of the upright leads them, ‖ And the perverseness of the treacherous destroys them. **4** Wealth does not profit in a day of wrath, ‖ And righteousness delivers from death. **5** The righteousness of the perfect makes his way right, ‖ And by his wickedness the wicked fall. **6** The righteousness of the upright delivers them, ‖ And in mischief the treacherous are captured. **7** In the death of a wicked man, hope perishes, ‖ And the expectation of the iniquitous has been lost. **8** The righteous is drawn out from distress, ‖ And the wicked goes in instead of him. **9** A hypocrite corrupts his friend with the mouth, ‖ And the righteous are drawn out by knowledge. **10** A city exults in the good of the righteous, ‖ And in the destruction of the wicked [is] singing. **11** By the blessing of the upright is a city exalted, ‖ And by the mouth of the wicked thrown down. **12** Whoever is despising his neighbor lacks heart, ‖ And a man of understanding keeps silence. **13** A busybody is revealing secret counsel, ‖ And the faithful of spirit is covering the matter. **14** Without counsels a people falls, ‖ And deliverance [is] in a multitude of counselors. **15** An evil [one] suffers when he has been guarantor [for] a stranger, ‖ And whoever hates striking hands [in agreement] is confident. **16** A gracious woman retains honor, ‖ And terrible [men] retain riches. **17** A kind man is rewarding his own soul, ‖ And the fierce is troubling his own flesh. **18** The wicked is getting a lying wage, ‖ And whoever is sowing righteousness—a true reward. **19** Correctly [is] righteousness for life, ‖ And whoever is pursuing evil—for his own death. **20** The perverse of heart are an abomination to YHWH, ‖ And the perfect of the way [are] His delight. **21** Hand to hand, the wicked is not acquitted, ‖ And the seed of the righteous has escaped. **22** A ring of gold in the nose of a sow—A beautiful woman and stubborn of behavior. **23** The desire of the righteous [is] only good, ‖ The hope of the wicked [is] transgression. **24** There is [one] who is scattering, and yet is increased, ‖ And [one] who is keeping back from uprightness, only to want. **25** A liberal soul is made fat, ‖ And whoever is watering, he also is watered. **26** Whoever is withholding grain, the people execrate him, ‖ And a blessing [is] for the head of him who is selling. **27** Whoever is earnestly seeking good ‖ Seeks a pleasing thing, ‖ And whoever is seeking evil—it meets him. **28** Whoever is confident in his wealth falls, ‖ And as a leaf, the righteous flourish. **29** Whoever is troubling his own house inherits wind, ‖ And the fool [is] a servant to the wise of heart. **30** The fruit of the righteous [is] a tree of life, ‖ And whoever is taking souls [is] wise. **31** Behold, the righteous is repaid in the earth, ∥ Surely also the wicked and the sinner!

12 Whoever is loving instruction, is loving knowledge, ∥ And whoever is hating reproof [is] brutish. **2** The good brings forth favor from YHWH, ∥ And the man of wicked schemes He condemns. **3** A man is not established by wickedness, ∥ And the root of the righteous is not moved. **4** A virtuous woman [is] a crown to her husband, ∥ And as rottenness in his bones [is] one causing shame. **5** The thoughts of the righteous [are] justice, ∥ The counsels of the wicked—deceit. **6** The words of the wicked [are]: "Lay [in] wait for blood," ∥ And the mouth of the upright delivers them. **7** Overthrow the wicked, and they are not, ∥ And the house of the righteous stands. **8** A man is praised according to his wisdom, ∥ And the perverted of heart becomes despised. **9** Better [is] the lightly esteemed who has a servant, ∥ Than the self-honored who lacks bread. **10** The righteous knows the life of his beast, ∥ And the mercies of the wicked [are] cruel. **11** Whoever is tilling the ground is satisfied [with] bread, ∥ And whoever is pursuing vanities is lacking heart, **12** The wicked has desired the net of evildoers, ∥ And the root of the righteous gives. **13** The snare of the wicked [is] in transgression of the lips, ∥ And the righteous goes out from distress. **14** One [is] satisfied [with] good from the fruit of the mouth, ∥ And the deed of man's hands returns to him. **15** The way of a fool [is] right in his own eyes, ∥ And whoever is listening to counsel [is] wise. **16** The fool—his anger is known in a day, ∥ And the prudent is covering shame. **17** Whoever utters faithfulness declares righteousness, ∥ And a false witness—deceit. **18** A rash speaker is like piercings of a sword, ∥ And the tongue of the wise is healing. **19** The lip of truth is established forever, ∥ And a tongue of falsehood for a moment. **20** Deceit [is] in the heart of those devising evil, ∥ But for counselors of peace—joy. **21** No iniquity is desired by the righteous, ∥ And the wicked have been full of evil. **22** Lying lips [are] an abomination to YHWH, ∥ And steadfast doers [are] his delight. **23** A prudent man is concealing knowledge, ∥ And the heart of fools proclaims folly. **24** The hand of the diligent rules, ∥ And slothfulness becomes tributary. **25** Sorrow in the heart of a man bows down, ∥ And a good word makes him glad. **26** The righteous searches his companion, ∥ And the way of the wicked causes them to err. **27** The slothful does not roast his game, ∥ And the wealth of a diligent man is precious. **28** In the path of righteousness [is] life, ∥ And in the way of [that] path [is] no death!

13 A wise son—the instruction of a father, ∥ And a scorner—he has not heard rebuke. **2** A man eats good from the fruit of the mouth, ∥ And the soul of the treacherous—violence. **3** Whoever is keeping his mouth, is keeping his soul, ∥ Whoever is opening wide his lips—ruin to him! **4** The soul of the slothful is desiring, and does not have. And the soul of the diligent is made fat. **5** The righteous hates a false word, ∥ And the wicked causes abhorrence, and is confounded. **6** Righteousness keeps him who is perfect in the way, ∥ And wickedness overthrows a sin offering. **7** There is [he] who is making himself rich, and has nothing, ∥ Who is making himself poor, and wealth [is] abundant. **8** The ransom of a man's life [are] his riches, ∥ And the poor has not heard rebuke. **9** The light of the righteous rejoices, ∥ And the lamp of the wicked is extinguished. **10** A vain man causes debate through pride, ∥ And wisdom [is] with the counseled. **11** Wealth from vanity becomes little, ∥ And whoever is gathering by the hand becomes great. **12** Hope prolonged is making the heart sick, ∥ And a tree of life [is] the coming desire. **13** Whoever is despising the word is destroyed for it, ∥ And whoever is fearing the command is repaid. **14** The law of the wise [is] a fountain of life, ∥ To turn aside from snares of death. **15** Good understanding gives grace, ∥ And the way of the treacherous [is] hard. **16** Every prudent one deals with knowledge, ∥ And a fool spreads out folly. **17** A wicked messenger falls into evil, ∥ And a faithful ambassador is healing. **18** Whoever is refusing instruction—poverty and shame, ∥ And whoever is observing reproof is honored. **19** A desire accomplished is sweet to the soul, ∥ And an abomination to fools ∥ [Is] to turn from evil. **20** Whoever is walking with wise men is wise, ∥ And a companion of fools suffers evil. **21** Evil pursues sinners, ∥ And good repays the righteous. **22** A good man causes sons' sons to inherit, ∥ And the sinner's wealth [is] laid up for the righteous. **23** Abundance of food—the tillage of the poor, ‖ And substance is consumed without judgment. **24** Whoever is sparing his rod is hating his son, ‖ And whoever is loving him has hurried his discipline. **25** The righteous is eating to the satiety of his soul, ‖ And the belly of the wicked lacks!

14 Every wise woman has built her house, ‖ And the foolish breaks it down with her hands. **2** Whoever is walking in his uprightness is fearing YHWH, ‖ And the perverted is despising Him [in] his ways. **3** A rod of pride [is] in the mouth of a fool, ‖ And the lips of the wise preserve them. **4** Without oxen a stall [is] clean, ‖ And great [is] the increase by the power of the ox. **5** A faithful witness does not lie, ‖ And a false witness breathes out lies. **6** A scorner has sought wisdom, and it is not, ‖ And knowledge [is] easy to the intelligent. **7** Go from before a foolish man, ‖ Or you have not known the lips of knowledge. **8** The wisdom of the prudent [is] to understand his way, ‖ And the folly of fools [is] deceit. **9** Fools mock at a guilt-offering, ‖ And among the upright—a pleasing thing. **10** The heart knows its own bitterness, ‖ And a stranger does not interfere with its joy. **11** The house of the wicked is destroyed, ‖ And the tent of the upright flourishes. **12** There is a way—right before a man, ‖ And its latter end [are] ways of death. **13** Even in laughter is the heart pained, ‖ And the latter end of joy [is] affliction. **14** The backslider in heart is filled from his ways, ‖ And a good man—from his fruits. **15** The simple gives credence to everything, ‖ And the prudent attends to his step. **16** The wise is fearing and turning from evil, ‖ And a fool is transgressing and is confident. **17** Whoever is short of temper does folly, ‖ And a man of wicked schemes is hated. **18** The simple have inherited folly, ‖ And the prudent are crowned [with] knowledge. **19** The evil have bowed down before the good, ‖ And the wicked at the gates of the righteous. **20** The poor is hated even of his neighbor, ‖ And those loving the rich [are] many. **21** Whoever is despising his neighbor sins, ‖ Whoever is favoring the humble, ‖ O his blessedness. **22** Do they who are devising evil not err? And kindness and truth [are] to those devising good, **23** In all labor there is advantage, ‖ And a thing of the lips [is] only to want. **24** The crown of the wise is their wealth, ‖ The folly of fools [is] folly. **25** A true witness is delivering souls, ‖ And a deceitful one breathes out lies. **26** Strong confidence [is] in the fear of YHWH, ‖ And there is a refuge to His sons. **27** The fear of YHWH [is] a fountain of life, ‖ To turn aside from snares of death. **28** The honor of a king [is] in the multitude of a people, ‖ And the ruin of a prince in lack of people. **29** Whoever is slow to anger [is] of great understanding, ‖ And whoever is short in temper is exalting folly. **30** A healed heart [is] life to the flesh, ‖ And rottenness to the bones [is] envy. **31** An oppressor of the poor reproaches his Maker, ‖ And whoever is honoring Him ‖ Is favoring the needy. **32** The wicked is driven away in his wickedness, ‖ And the righteous [is] trustful in his death. **33** Wisdom rests in the heart of the intelligent. And it is known in the midst of fools. **34** Righteousness exalts a nation, ‖ And the righteousness of peoples [is] a sin-offering. **35** The favor of a king [is] to a wise servant, ‖ And one causing shame is an object of his wrath!

15 A soft answer turns back fury, ‖ And a grievous word raises up anger. **2** The tongue of the wise makes knowledge good, ‖ And the mouth of fools utters folly. **3** The eyes of YHWH are in every place, ‖ Watching the evil and the good. **4** A healed tongue [is] a tree of life, ‖ And perverseness in it—a breach in the spirit. **5** A fool despises the instruction of his father, ‖ And whoever is regarding reproof is prudent. **6** Abundant strength [is in] the house of the righteous, ‖ And in the increase of the wicked—trouble. **7** The lips of the wise scatter knowledge, ‖ And the heart of fools [is] not right. **8** The sacrifice of the wicked [is] an abomination to YHWH, ‖ And the prayer of the upright [is] His delight. **9** The way of the wicked [is] an abomination to YHWH, ‖ And He loves whoever is pursuing righteousness. **10** Discipline [is] grievous to him who is forsaking the path, ‖ Whoever is hating reproof dies. **11** Sheol and destruction [are] before YHWH, ‖ Surely also the hearts of the sons of men. **12** A scorner does not love his reprover, ‖ He does not go to the wise. **13** A joyful heart makes the face glad, ‖ And the spirit is struck by grief of heart. **14** The heart of the intelligent seeks knowledge, ‖ And the of fools enjoys folly. **15** All the days of the afflicted [are] evil, ‖ And gladness of heart [is] a perpetual banquet. **16** Better [is] a little with the fear of YHWH, ‖ Than much treasure, and tumult with it. **17** Better [is] an allowance of green herbs and love there, ‖ Than a fatted ox, and hatred with it. **18** A man of fury stirs up contention, ‖ And the slow to anger appeases strife. **19** The way of the slothful [is] as a hedge of briers, ‖ And the path of the upright is raised up. **20** A wise son makes a father glad. And a foolish man is despising his mother. **21** Folly is joy to one lacking heart, ‖ And a man of intelligence directs [his] going. **22** The making void of purposes [is] without counsel, ‖ And in a multitude of counselors it is established. **23** Joy [is] to a man in the answer of his mouth, ‖ And a word in its season—how good! **24** A path of life [is] on high for the wise, ‖ To turn aside from Sheol beneath. **25** YHWH pulls down the house of the proud, ‖ And He sets up the border of the widow. **26** Thoughts of wickedness [are] an abomination to YHWH, ‖ And sayings of pleasantness [are] pure. **27** A dishonest gainer is troubling his house, ‖ And whoever is hating gifts lives. **28** The heart of the righteous meditates to answer, ‖ And the mouth of the wicked utters evil things. **29** YHWH [is] far from the wicked, ‖ And He hears the prayer of the righteous. **30** The light of the eyes makes the heart glad, ‖ A good report makes the bone fat. **31** An ear that is hearing the reproof of life ‖ Lodges among the wise. **32** Whoever is refusing instruction is despising his soul, ‖ And whoever is hearing reproof ‖ Is getting understanding. **33** The fear of YHWH [is] the instruction of wisdom, ‖ And humility [is] before honor!

16 Arrangements of the heart [are] of man, ‖ An answer of the tongue from YHWH. **2** All the ways of a man are pure in his own eyes, ‖ And YHWH is pondering the spirits. **3** Roll your works to YHWH, ‖ And your purposes are established, **4** YHWH has worked all things for Himself, ‖ And also the wicked—for a day of evil. **5** Every proud one of heart [is] an abomination to YHWH, ‖ Hand to hand—he is not acquitted. **6** Iniquity is pardoned in kindness and truth, ‖ And in the fear of YHWH ‖ Turn aside from evil. **7** When a man's ways please YHWH, even his enemies, ‖ He causes to be at peace with him. **8** Better [is] a little with righteousness, ‖ Than abundance of increase without justice. **9** The heart of man devises his way, ‖ And YHWH establishes his step. **10** An oath [is] on the lips of a king, ‖ In judgment his mouth does not trespass. **11** A just beam and balances [are] YHWH's, ‖ All the stones of the bag [are] His work. **12** Doing wickedness [is] an abomination to kings, ‖ For a throne is established by righteousness. **13** Righteous lips [are] the delight of kings, ‖ And he loves whoever is speaking uprightly, **14** The fury of a king [is] messengers of death, ‖ And a wise man pacifies it. **15** In the light of a king's face [is] life, ‖ And his goodwill [is] as a cloud of the spring rain. **16** To get wisdom—how much better than gold, ‖ And to get understanding—to be chosen [more] than silver! **17** A highway of the upright [is] to turn from evil, ‖ Whoever is preserving his soul is watching his way. **18** Pride [is] before destruction, ‖ And before stumbling—a haughty spirit. **19** Better is humility of spirit with the poor, ‖ Than to apportion spoil with the proud. **20** The wise in any matter finds good, ‖ And whoever is trusting in YHWH, O his blessedness. **21** For the wise in heart is called intelligent, ‖ And sweetness of lips increases learning. **22** Understanding [is] a fountain of life to its possessors, ‖ The instruction of fools is folly. **23** The heart of the wise causes his mouth to act wisely, ‖ And he increases learning by his lips, **24** Sayings of pleasantness [are] a honeycomb, ‖ Sweet to the soul, and healing to the bone. **25** There is a way right before a man, ‖ And its latter end—ways of death. **26** A laboring man has labored for himself, ‖ For his mouth has caused [him] to bend over it. **27** A worthless man is preparing evil, ‖ And on his lips [is] as a burning fire. **28** A contrary man sends forth contention, ‖ A tale-bearer is separating a familiar friend. **29** A violent man entices his neighbor, ‖ And causes him to go in a way [that is] not good. **30** Consulting his eyes to devise contrary things, ‖ Moving his lips he has accomplished evil. **31** Grey hairs [are] a crown of beauty, ‖ It is found in the way of righteousness. **32** Better [is] the [one] slow to anger than the mighty, ‖ And the ruler over his spirit than he who is taking a city. **33** The lot is cast into the center, ‖ And all its judgment [is] from YHWH!

17 Better [is] a dry morsel, and rest with it, ‖ Than a house full of the sacrifices of strife. **2** A wise servant rules over a son causing shame, ‖ And he apportions an inheritance in the midst of brothers. **3** A refining pot [is] for silver, and a furnace for gold, ‖ And the trier of hearts [is] YHWH. **4** An evildoer is attentive to lips of vanity, ‖ Falsehood is giving ear to a mischievous tongue. **5** Whoever is mocking at the poor ‖ Has reproached his Maker, ‖ Whoever is rejoicing at calamity is not acquitted. **6** Sons' sons [are] the crown of old men, ‖ And the glory of sons [are] their fathers. **7** A lip of excellence is not fitting for a fool, much less a lip of falsehood for a noble. **8** A stone of grace [is] the bribe in the eyes of its possessors, ‖ Wherever it turns, it prospers. **9** Whoever is covering transgression is seeking love, ‖ And whoever is repeating a matter ‖ Is separating a familiar friend. **10** Rebuke comes down on the intelligent ‖ More than one hundred stripes on a fool. **11** An evil man seeks only rebellion, ‖ And a fierce messenger is sent against him. **12** The meeting of a bereaved bear by a man, ‖ And—not a fool in his folly. **13** Whoever is returning evil for good, ‖ Evil does not move from his house. **14** The beginning of contention [is] a letting out of waters, ‖ And leave the strife before it is meddled with. **15** Whoever is justifying the wicked, ‖ And condemning the righteous, ‖ Even both of these [are] an abomination to YHWH. **16** Why [is] this—a price in the hand of a fool to buy wisdom, ‖ And a heart—there is none? **17** The friend is loving at all times, ‖ And a brother is born for adversity. **18** A man lacking heart is striking hands, ‖ He becomes a guarantor before his friend. **19** Whoever is loving transgression is loving debate, ‖ Whoever is making his entrance high is seeking destruction. **20** The perverse of heart does not find good, ‖ And the [one] turned in his tongue falls into evil. **21** Whoever is begetting a fool has affliction for it, ‖ Indeed, the father of a fool does not rejoice. **22** A rejoicing heart does good to the body, ‖ And a struck spirit dries the bone. **23** The wicked takes a bribe from the bosom, ‖ To turn aside the paths of judgment. **24** The face of the intelligent [is] to wisdom, ‖ And the eyes of a fool—at the end of the earth. **25** A foolish son [is] a provocation to his father, ‖ And bitterness to her bearing him. **26** Also, [it] is not good to fine the righteous, ‖ To strike nobles for uprightness. **27** One acquainted with knowledge is sparing his words, ‖ And the cool of temper [is] a man of understanding. **28** Even a fool keeping silence is reckoned wise, ‖ He who is shutting his lips [seems] intelligent!

18 He who is separated seeks [his own] desire, ‖ He interferes with all wisdom. **2** A fool does not delight in understanding, ‖ But in uncovering his heart. **3** Contempt has also come with the coming of the wicked, ‖ And with shame—reproach. **4** The words of a man's mouth [are] deep waters, ‖ The fountain of wisdom [is] a flowing brook. **5** Favoring of the face of the wicked [is] not good, ‖ To turn aside the righteous in judgment. **6** The lips of a fool enter into strife, ‖ And his mouth calls for stripes. **7** The mouth of a fool [is] ruin to him, ‖ And his lips [are] the snare of his soul. **8** The words of a tale-bearer [are] as self-inflicted wounds, ‖ And they have gone down [to] the inner parts of the heart. **9** He also that is remiss in his work, ‖ He [is] a brother to a destroyer. **10** The Name of YHWH [is] a tower of strength, ‖ The righteous runs into it, and is set on high. **11** The wealth of the rich [is] the city of his strength, ‖ And as a wall set on high in his own imagination. **12** The heart of man is high before destruction, ‖ And humility [is] before honor. **13** Whoever is answering a matter before he hears, ‖ It is folly to him—and shame. **14** The spirit of a man sustains his sickness, ‖ And who bears a struck spirit? **15** The heart of the intelligent gets knowledge, ‖ And the ear of the wise seeks knowledge. **16** The gift of a man makes room for him, ‖ And it leads him before the great. **17** The first in his own cause [seems] righteous, ‖ [But] his neighbor comes and has searched him. **18** The lot causes contentions to cease, ‖ And it separates between the mighty. **19** A brother transgressed against is as a strong city, ‖ And contentions as the bar of a palace. **20** From the fruit of a man's mouth is his belly satisfied, ‖ [From the] increase of his lips he is satisfied. **21** Death and life [are] in the power of the tongue, ‖ And those loving it eat its fruit. **22** [Whoever] has found a wife has found good, ‖ And brings out goodwill from YHWH. **23** The poor speaks [with] supplications, ‖ And the rich answers fierce things. **24** A man with friends—to

PROVERBS

show himself friendly, ‖ And there is a lover adhering more than a brother!

19 Better [is] the poor walking in his integrity, ‖ Than the perverse [in] his lips—who [is] a fool. **2** Also, without knowledge the soul [is] not good, ‖ And the hasty in feet is sinning. **3** The folly of man perverts his way, ‖ And his heart is angry against YHWH. **4** Wealth adds many friends, ‖ And the poor is separated from his neighbor. **5** A false witness is not acquitted, ‖ Whoever breathes out lies is not delivered. **6** Many beg the face of the noble, ‖ And all have made friendship to a man of gifts. **7** All the brothers of the poor have hated him, ‖ Surely his friends have also been far from him, ‖ He is pursuing words—they are not! **8** Whoever is getting heart is loving his soul, ‖ He is keeping understanding to find good. **9** A false witness is not acquitted, ‖ And whoever breathes out lies perishes. **10** Luxury is not fitting for a fool, ‖ Much less for a servant to rule among princes. **11** The wisdom of a man has deferred his anger, ‖ And his glory [is] to pass over transgression. **12** The wrath of a king [is] a growl as of a young lion, ‖ And his goodwill as dew on the herb. **13** A foolish son [is] a calamity to his father, ‖ And the contentions of a wife [are] a continual dropping. **14** House and wealth [are] the inheritance of fathers, ‖ And an understanding wife [is] from YHWH. **15** Sloth causes deep sleep to fall, ‖ And an indolent soul hungers. **16** Whoever is keeping the command is keeping his soul, ‖ Whoever is despising His ways dies. **17** Whoever is lending [to] YHWH is favoring the poor, ‖ And He repays his deed to him. **18** Discipline your son, for there is hope, ‖ And do not lift up your soul to put him to death. **19** A man of great wrath is bearing punishment, ‖ For if you deliver, yet again you add. **20** Hear counsel and receive instruction, ‖ So that you are wise in your latter end. **21** The purposes in a man's heart [are] many, ‖ And the counsel of YHWH—it stands. **22** The desirableness of a man [is] his kindness, ‖ And the poor [is] better than a liar. **23** The fear of YHWH [is] to life, ‖ And he remains satisfied—he is not charged with evil. **24** The slothful has hidden his hand in a dish, ‖ Even to his mouth he does not bring it back. **25** Strike a scorner, and the simple acts prudently, ‖ And give reproof to the intelligent, ‖ He understands knowledge. **26** Whoever is spoiling a father causes a mother to flee, ‖ A son causing shame, and bringing confusion. **27** Cease, my son, to hear instruction—To err from sayings of knowledge. **28** A worthless witness scorns judgment, ‖ And the mouth of the wicked swallows iniquity. **29** Judgments have been prepared for scorners, ‖ And stripes for the back of fools!

20 Wine [is] a scorner—strong drink [is] noisy, ‖ And any going astray in it is not wise. **2** The fear of a king [is] a growl as of a young lion, ‖ He who is causing him to be angry is wronging his soul. **3** Cessation from strife is an honor to a man, ‖ And every fool interferes. **4** The slothful does not plow because of winter, ‖ He asks in harvest, and there is nothing. **5** Counsel in the heart of a man [is] deep water, ‖ And a man of understanding draws it up. **6** A multitude of men each proclaim his kindness, ‖ And a man of steadfastness who finds? **7** The righteous is habitually walking in his integrity, ‖ O the blessedness of his sons after him! **8** A king sitting on a throne of judgment, ‖ Is scattering all evil with his eyes, **9** Who says, "I have purified my heart, ‖ I have been cleansed from my sin?" **10** A stone and a stone, an ephah and an ephah, ‖ Even both of them [are] an abomination to YHWH. **11** Even by his actions a youth makes himself known, ‖ Whether his work is pure or upright. **12** A hearing ear, and a seeing eye—YHWH has even made both of them. **13** Do not love sleep, lest you become poor, ‖ Open your eyes—be satisfied [with] bread. **14** "Bad, bad," says the buyer, ‖ And then he boasts himself going his way. **15** Substance, gold, and a multitude of rubies, ‖ Indeed, a precious vessel, [are] lips of knowledge. **16** When a stranger has been guarantor, take his garment, ‖ And pledge it for strangers. **17** The bread of falsehood [is] sweet to a man, ‖ And afterward his mouth is filled [with] gravel. **18** You establish purposes by counsel, ‖ And with plans you make war. **19** The busybody is a revealer of secret counsels, ‖ And do not make yourself guarantor for a deceiver [with] his lips. **20** Whoever is vilifying his father and his mother, his lamp is extinguished in blackness of darkness. **21** An inheritance gotten wrongly at first, ‖ Even its latter end is not blessed. **22** Do not say, "I repay evil,"

‖ Wait for Y{HWH}, and He delivers you. **23** A stone and a stone [are] an abomination to Y{HWH}, ‖ And balances of deceit [are] not good. **24** The steps of a man [are] from Y{HWH}, ‖ And man—how does he understand his way? **25** A snare to a man [that] he has swallowed a holy thing, ‖ And to make inquiry after vows. **26** A wise king is scattering the wicked, ‖ And turns the wheel back on them. **27** The breath of man [is] a lamp of Y{HWH}, ‖ Searching all the inner parts of the heart. **28** Kindness and truth keep a king, ‖ And he has supported his throne by kindness. **29** The beauty of young men is their strength, ‖ And the honor of old men is grey hairs. **30** Blows that wound cleanse away evil, ‖ Also the scourges of the inner parts of the heart!

21 The heart of a king [is] streams of waters in the hand of Y{HWH}, ‖ He inclines it wherever He pleases. **2** Every way of a man [is] right in his own eyes, ‖ And Y{HWH} is pondering hearts. **3** To do righteousness and judgment, ‖ Is chosen of Y{HWH} rather than sacrifice. **4** Loftiness of eyes, and breadth of heart, ‖ Tillage of the wicked [is] sin. **5** The purposes of the diligent [are] only to advantage, ‖ And of every hasty one, only to want. **6** The making of treasures by a lying tongue, ‖ [Is] a vanity driven away of those seeking death. **7** The spoil of the wicked catches them, ‖ Because they have refused to do judgment. **8** The way of a man who is vile [is] contrary, ‖ And the pure—his work [is] upright. **9** Better to sit on a corner of the roof, ‖ Than [with] a woman of contentions and a house of company. **10** The soul of the wicked has desired evil, his neighbor is not gracious in his eyes. **11** When the scorner is punished, the simple becomes wise, ‖ And in giving understanding to the wise He receives knowledge. **12** The Righteous One is acting wisely ‖ Toward the house of the wicked, ‖ He is overthrowing the wicked for wickedness. **13** Whoever is shutting his ear from the cry of the poor, ‖ He also cries, and is not answered. **14** A gift in secret pacifies anger, ‖ And a bribe in the bosom—strong fury. **15** To do justice [is] joy to the righteous, ‖ But ruin to workers of iniquity. **16** A man who is wandering from the way of understanding, ‖ Rests in an assembly of Rephaim. **17** Whoever [is] loving mirth [is] a poor man, ‖ Whoever is loving wine and oil makes no wealth.

18 The wicked [is] an atonement for the righteous, ‖ And the treacherous dealer for the upright. **19** Better to dwell in a wilderness land, ‖ Than [with] a woman of contentions and anger. **20** A treasure to be desired, and oil, ‖ [Is] in the habitation of the wise, ‖ And a foolish man swallows it up. **21** Whoever is pursuing righteousness and kindness, ‖ Finds life, righteousness, and honor. **22** The wise has gone up a city of the mighty, ‖ And brings down the strength of its confidence. **23** Whoever is keeping his mouth and his tongue, ‖ Is keeping his soul from adversities. **24** Proud, haughty, scorner—his name, ‖ Who is working in the wrath of pride. **25** The desire of the slothful slays him, ‖ For his hands have refused to work. **26** All the day desiring he has desired, ‖ And the righteous gives and does not withhold. **27** The sacrifice of the wicked [is] abomination, ‖ Much more when he brings it in wickedness. **28** A false witness perishes, ‖ And an attentive man speaks forever. **29** A wicked man has hardened by his face, ‖ And the upright—he prepares his way. **30** There is no wisdom, nor understanding, ‖ Nor counsel against Y{HWH}. **31** A horse is prepared for a day of battle, ‖ And the deliverance [is] of Y{HWH}!

22 A name is chosen rather than much wealth, ‖ Than silver and than gold—good grace. **2** Rich and poor have met together, ‖ Y{HWH} [is] the Maker of them all. **3** The prudent has seen the evil, and is hidden, ‖ And the simple have passed on, and are punished. **4** The end of humility [is] the fear of Y{HWH}, riches, and honor, and life. **5** Thorns [and] snares [are] in the way of the perverse, ‖ Whoever is keeping his soul is far from them. **6** Give instruction to a youth about his way, ‖ Even when he is old he does not turn from it. **7** The rich rules over the poor, ‖ And a servant [is] the borrower to the lender. **8** Whoever is sowing perverseness reaps sorrow, ‖ And the rod of his anger wears out. **9** The good of eye—he is blessed, ‖ For he has given of his bread to the poor. **10** Cast out a scorner—and contention goes out, ‖ And strife and shame cease. **11** Whoever is loving cleanness of heart, ‖ His lips [are] grace, ‖ A king [is] his friend. **12** The eyes of Y{HWH} have kept knowledge, ‖ And He overthrows the words of the treacherous. **13** The slothful has said, "A lion [is] outside, ‖ I am slain in the midst of the broad places." **14** The mouth of strange women [is] a deep pit, ‖ The abhorred of YHWH falls there. **15** Folly is bound up in the heart of a youth, ‖ The rod of discipline puts it far from him. **16** He [who] is oppressing the poor to multiply his [riches], ‖ Is giving to the rich—only to want. **17** Incline your ear, and hear words of the wise, ‖ And set your heart to my knowledge, **18** For they are pleasant when you keep them in your heart, ‖ They are prepared together for your lips. **19** That your trust may be in YHWH, ‖ I caused you to know today, even you. **20** Have I not written to you three times ‖ With counsels and knowledge? **21** To cause you to know the certainty of sayings of truth, ‖ To return sayings of truth to those sending you. **22** Do not rob the poor because he [is] poor, ‖ And do not bruise the afflicted in the gate. **23** For YHWH pleads their cause, ‖ And has spoiled the soul of their spoilers. **24** Do not show yourself friendly with an angry man, ‖ And do not go in with a man of fury, **25** Lest you learn his paths, ‖ And have received a snare to your soul. **26** Do not be among those striking hands, ‖ Among sureties [for] burdens. **27** If you have nothing to pay, ‖ Why does he take your bed from under you? **28** Do not remove a border of ancient times, ‖ That your fathers have made. **29** Have you seen a man speedy in his business? He stations himself before kings, ‖ He does not station himself before obscure men!

23 When you sit to eat with a ruler, ‖ Diligently consider that which [is] before you, **2** And you have put a knife to your throat, ‖ If you [are] a man of appetite. **3** Have no desire to his delicacies, seeing it [is] lying food. **4** Do not labor to make wealth, ‖ Cease from your own understanding, ‖ Do you cause your eyes to fly on it? Then it is not. **5** For wealth makes wings to itself, ‖ It flies to the heavens as an eagle. **6** Do not eat the bread of an evil eye, ‖ And have no desire to his delicacies, **7** For as he has thought in his soul, so he [is]. "Eat and drink," he says to you, ‖ And his heart [is] not with you. **8** You vomit up your morsel you have eaten, ‖ And have marred your words that [are] sweet. **9** Do not speak in the ears of a fool, ‖ For he treads on the wisdom of your words. **10** Do not remove a border of ancient times, ‖ And do not enter into fields of the fatherless, **11** For their Redeemer [is] strong, ‖ He pleads their cause with you. **12** Bring your heart to instruction, ‖ And your ear to sayings of knowledge. **13** Do not withhold discipline from a youth, ‖ When you strike him with a rod he does not die. **14** You strike him with a rod, ‖ And you deliver his soul from Sheol. **15** My son, if your heart has been wise, ‖ My heart rejoices, even mine, **16** And my reins exult when your lips speak uprightly. **17** Do not let your heart be envious at sinners, ‖ But—in the fear of YHWH all the day. **18** For is there a posterity? Then your hope is not cut off. **19** Hear, my son, and be wise, ‖ And make your heart blessed in the way, **20** Do not become drunk with wine, ‖ Among gluttonous ones of flesh, **21** For the drunkard and glutton become poor, ‖ And drowsiness clothes with rags. **22** Listen to your father, who begot you, ‖ And do not despise your mother when she has become old. **23** Buy truth, and do not sell, ‖ Wisdom, and instruction, and understanding, **24** The father of the righteous rejoices greatly, ‖ The begetter of the wise rejoices in him. **25** Your father and your mother rejoice, ‖ Indeed, she bearing you is joyful. **26** Give, my son, your heart to me, ‖ And let your eyes watch my ways. **27** For a harlot [is] a deep ditch, ‖ And a strange woman [is] a narrow pit. **28** She also, as catching prey, lies in wait, ‖ And she increases the treacherous among men. **29** Who has woe? Who has sorrow? Who has contentions? Who has complaint? Who has wounds without cause? Who has redness of eyes? **30** Those lingering by the wine, ‖ Those going in to search out mixed wine. **31** Do not see wine when it shows itself red, ‖ When it gives its color in the cup, ‖ It goes up and down through the upright. **32** Its latter end—it bites as a serpent, ‖ And it stings as a viper. **33** Your eyes see strange women, ‖ And your heart speaks perverse things. **34** And you have been as one lying down in the heart of the sea, ‖ And as one lying down on the top of a mast. **35** "They struck me, I have not been sick, ‖ They beat me, I have not known. When I awake—I seek it yet again!"

24 Do not be envious of evil men, ‖ And do not desire to be with them. **2** For their heart meditates [on] destruction, ‖ And their lips speak perverseness. **3** A house is built by wisdom, ‖ And it establishes itself by understanding. **4** And the inner parts are filled by knowledge, ‖ [With] all precious and pleasant wealth. **5** The wise [is] mighty in strength, ‖ And a man of knowledge is strengthening power, **6** For you make war for yourself by plans, ‖ And deliverance [is] in a multitude of counselors. **7** Wisdom [is] high for a fool, he does not open his mouth in the gate. **8** Whoever is devising to do evil, ‖ They call him a master of wicked thoughts. **9** The thought of folly [is] sin, ‖ And a scorner [is] an abomination to man. **10** You have showed yourself weak in a day of adversity, ‖ Your power is restricted, **11** If [from] delivering those taken to death, ‖ And you take back those slipping to the slaughter. **12** When you say, "Behold, we did not know this." Is the Ponderer of hearts not He who understands? And the Keeper of your soul He who knows? And He has rendered to man according to his work. **13** My son, eat honey that [is] good, ‖ And the honeycomb [is] sweet to your palate. **14** So [is] the knowledge of wisdom to your soul, ‖ If you have found that there is a posterity ‖ And your hope is not cut off. **15** Do not lay wait, O wicked one, ‖ At the habitation of the righteous. Do not spoil his resting place. **16** For the righteous fall and rise seven [times], ‖ And the wicked stumble in evil. **17** Do not rejoice in the falling of your enemy, ‖ And do not let your heart be joyful in his stumbling, **18** Lest YHWH see, and [it be] evil in His eyes, ‖ And He has turned His anger from off him. **19** Do not fret yourself at evildoers, do not be envious at the wicked, **20** For there is not a posterity to the evil, ‖ The lamp of the wicked is extinguished. **21** Fear YHWH, my son, and the king, ‖ Do not mix yourself up with changers, **22** For their calamity rises suddenly, ‖ And the ruin of them both—who knows! **23** These are also for the wise: [It] is not good to discern faces in judgment. **24** Whoever is saying to the wicked, "You [are] righteous," ‖ Peoples execrate him—nations abhor him. **25** And it is pleasant to those reproving, ‖ And a good blessing comes on them. **26** He who is returning straightforward words kisses lips. **27** Prepare your work in an out-place, ‖ And make it ready in the field—go afterward, ‖ Then you have built your house. **28** Do not be a witness against your neighbor for nothing, ‖ Or you have enticed with your lips. **29** Do not say, "As he did to me, so I do to him, ‖ I render to each according to his work." **30** I passed by near the field of a slothful man, ‖ And near the vineyard of a man lacking heart. **31** And behold, it has gone up—all of it—thorns! Nettles have covered its face, ‖ And its stone wall has been broken down. **32** And I see—I set my heart, ‖ I have seen—I have received instruction, **33** A little sleep—a little slumber—A little folding of the hands to lie down. **34** And your poverty has come [as] a traveler, ‖ And your want as an armed man!

25 These are also proverbs of Solomon, that men of Hezekiah king of Judah transcribed: **2** The glory of God [is] to hide a thing, ‖ And the glory of kings [is] to search out a matter. **3** The heavens for height, and the earth for depth, ‖ And the heart of kings—[are] unsearchable. **4** Take away dross from silver, ‖ And a vessel goes forth for the refiner, **5** Take away the wicked before a king, ‖ And his throne is established in righteousness. **6** Do not honor yourself before a king, ‖ And do not stand in the place of the great. **7** For better [that] he has said to you, "Come up here," ‖ Than [that] he humbles you before a noble, ‖ Whom your eyes have seen. **8** Do not go forth to strive, hurry, turn, ‖ What do you do in its latter end, ‖ When your neighbor causes you to blush? **9** Plead your cause with your neighbor, ‖ And do not reveal the secret counsel of another, **10** Lest the hearer put you to shame, ‖ And your evil report not turn back. **11** Apples of gold in imagery of silver, ‖ [Is] the word spoken at its fit times. **12** A ring of gold, and an ornament of pure gold, ‖ [Is] the wise reprover to an attentive ear. **13** As a vessel of snow in a day of harvest, ‖ [So is] a faithful ambassador to those sending him, ‖ And he refreshes the soul of his masters. **14** Clouds and wind without rain, ‖ [Is] a man boasting himself in a false gift. **15** A ruler is persuaded by long-suffering, ‖ And a soft tongue breaks a bone. **16** You have found honey—eat your sufficiency, ‖ Lest you are satiated [with] it, and have vomited it. **17** Withdraw your foot from your neighbor's house, ‖ Lest he is satiated [with] you, and has hated you. **18** A maul, and a sword, and a sharp arrow, ‖ [Is] the man testifying a false testimony against his neighbor. **19** A bad tooth, and a tottering foot, ‖ [Is] the confidence of the treacherous in a day of adversity. **20** Whoever is taking away a garment in a cold day, ‖ [Is as] vinegar on natron, ‖ And a singer of songs on a sad heart. **21** If he who is hating you hungers, cause him to eat bread, ‖ And if he thirsts, cause him to drink water. **22** For you are putting coals on his head, ‖ And YHWH gives repayment to you. **23** A north wind brings forth rain, ‖ And a secret tongue—indignant faces. **24** Better to sit on a corner of a roof, ‖ Than [with] a woman of contentions, and a house of company. **25** [As] cold waters for a weary soul, ‖ So [is] a good report from a far country. **26** A spring troubled, and a fountain corrupt, ‖ [Is] the righteous falling before the wicked. **27** The eating of much honey is not good, ‖ Nor a searching out of one's own honor— honor. **28** A city broken down without walls, ‖ [Is] a man without restraint over his spirit!

26 As snow in summer, and as rain in harvest, ‖ So honor [is] not fitting for a fool. **2** As a bird by wandering, as a swallow by flying, ‖ So reviling without cause does not come. **3** A whip is for a horse, a bridle for a donkey, ‖ And a rod for the back of fools. **4** Do not answer a fool according to his folly, ‖ Lest you are like to him—even you. **5** Answer a fool according to his folly, ‖ Lest he is wise in his own eyes. **6** He is cutting off feet, he is drinking injury, ‖ Who is sending things by the hand of a fool. **7** The two legs of the lame have been weak, ‖ And an allegory in the mouth of fools. **8** As one who is binding a stone in a sling, ‖ So [is] he who is giving honor to a fool. **9** A thorn has gone up into the hand of a drunkard, ‖ And an allegory in the mouth of fools. **10** The Former of all [is] great, ‖ And He is rewarding a fool, ‖ And is rewarding transgressors. **11** As a dog has returned to its vomit, ‖ A fool is repeating his folly. **12** You have seen a man wise in his own eyes, ‖ More hope of a fool than of him! **13** The slothful has said, ‖ "A lion [is] in the way, ‖ A lion [is] in the broad places." **14** The door turns around on its hinge, ‖ And the on his bed. **15** The slothful n a dish, ‖ He is weary of his mouth. **16** Wiser [is] wn eyes, ‖ Than seven on. **17** Laying hold on a passer-by making [that is] not his own. be feeble, ‖ Who

is casting sparks, arrows, and death, **19** So has a man deceived his neighbor, ‖ And has said, "Am I not playing?" **20** Fire is going out without wood, ‖ And contention ceases without a tale-bearer, **21** Coal to burning coals, and wood to fire, ‖ And a man of contentions to kindle strife. **22** The words of a tale-bearer [are] as self-inflicted wounds, ‖ And they have gone down [to] the inner parts of the heart. **23** Silver of dross spread over potsherd, ‖ [Are] burning lips and an evil heart. **24** A hater pretends by his lips, ‖ And he places deceit in his heart, **25** When his voice is gracious do not trust in him, ‖ For seven abominations [are] in his heart. **26** Hatred is covered by deceit, ‖ Its wickedness is revealed in an assembly. **27** Whoever is digging a pit falls into it, ‖ And the roller of a stone, it turns to him. **28** A lying tongue hates its bruised ones, ‖ And a flattering mouth works an overthrow!

27 Do not boast about tomorrow, ‖ For you do not know what a day brings forth. **2** Let another praise you, and not your own mouth, ‖ A stranger, and not your own lips. **3** A stone [is] heavy, and the sand [is] heavy, ‖ And the anger of a fool ‖ Is heavier than them both. **4** Fury [is] fierce, and anger [is] overflowing, ‖ And who stands before jealousy? **5** Better [is] open reproof than hidden love. **6** The wounds of a lover are faithful, ‖ And the kisses of an enemy [are] abundant. **7** A satiated soul treads down a honeycomb, ‖ And every bitter thing [is] sweet [to] a hungry soul. **8** As a bird wandering from her nest, ‖ So [is] a man wandering from his place. **9** Perfume and incense make the heart glad, ‖ And the sweetness of one's friend—from counsel of the soul. **10** Do not forsake your own friend and the friend of your father, ‖ And do not enter the house of your brother in a day of your calamity, ‖ A near neighbor [is] better than a brother far off. **11** Be wise, my son, and make my heart glad, ‖ And I return a word [to] my reproacher. **12** The prudent has seen the evil, he is hidden, ‖ The simple have passed on, they are punished. **13** Take his garment when a stranger has been guarantor, ‖ And pledge it for a strange woman. **14** Whoever is greeting his friend with a loud voice, ‖ Rising early in the morning, ‖ It is reckoned a light thing to him. **15** A continual dropping in a day of rain, ‖ And a woman of contentions are alike, **16** Whoever is hiding her has hidden the wind, ‖ And the ointment of his right hand calls out. **17** Iron is sharpened by iron, ‖ And a man sharpens the face of his friend. **18** The keeper of a fig tree eats its fruit, ‖ And the preserver of his master is honored. **19** As [in] water the face [is] to face, ‖ So the heart of man to man. **20** Sheol and destruction are not satisfied, ‖ And the eyes of man are not satisfied. **21** A refining pot [is] for silver, and a furnace for gold, ‖ And a man according to his praise. **22** If you beat the foolish in a mortar, ‖ Among washed things—with a pestle, ‖ His folly does not turn aside from off him. **23** Know the face of your flock well, ‖ Set your heart to the droves, **24** For riches [are] not for all time, ‖ Nor a crown to generation and generation. **25** The hay was revealed, and the tender grass seen, ‖ And the herbs of mountains gathered. **26** Lambs [are] for your clothing, ‖ And the price of the field [are] male goats, **27** And a sufficiency of goats' milk [is] for your bread, ‖ For bread to your house, and life to your girls!

28 The wicked have fled and there is no pursuer, ‖ And the righteous is confident as a young lion. **2** By the transgression of a land its heads are many, ‖ And by an understanding man, ‖ Who knows right—it is prolonged. **3** A man—poor and oppressing the weak, ‖ [Is] a sweeping rain, and there is no bread. **4** Those forsaking the Law praise the wicked, ‖ Those keeping the Law plead against them. **5** Evil men do not understand judgment, ‖ And those seeking YHWH understand all. **6** Better [is] the poor walking in his integrity, ‖ Than the perverse of ways who is rich. **7** Whoever is keeping the Law is an intelligent son, ‖ And a friend of gluttons ‖ Causes his father to blush. **8** Whoever is multiplying his wealth by biting and usury, ‖ Gathers it for one favoring the poor. **9** Whoever is turning his ear from hearing the Law, ‖ Even his prayer [is] an abomination. **10** Whoever is causing the upright to err in an evil way, ‖ He falls into his own pit, ‖ And the perfect inherits good. **11** A rich man is wise in his own eyes, ‖ And the intelligent poor searches him. **12** In the exulting of the righteous the glory [is] abundant, ‖ And in the rising of the wicked man is apprehensive. **13** Whoever is covering his transgressions does not prosper, ‖ And he who is confessing and forsaking has mercy. **14** O the blessedness of a man fearing continually, ‖ And whoever is hardening his heart falls into evil. **15** A growling lion, and a ranging bear, ‖ [Is] the wicked ruler over a poor people. **16** A leader lacking understanding multiplies oppressions, ‖ Whoever is hating dishonest gain prolongs days. **17** A man oppressed with the blood of a soul, ‖ Flees to the pit, [and] none takes hold on him [to help]. **18** Whoever is walking uprightly is saved, ‖ And the perverted of ways falls at once. **19** Whoever is tilling his ground is satisfied [with] bread, ‖ And whoever is pursuing vanity, ‖ Is filled [with] poverty. **20** A steadfast man has multiplied blessings, ‖ And whoever is hastening to be rich is not acquitted. **21** [It] is not good to discern faces, ‖ And a man transgresses for a piece of bread. **22** The man [with] an evil eye [is] troubled for wealth, ‖ And he does not know that want meets him. **23** Whoever is reproving a man finds grace afterward, ‖ More than a flatterer with the tongue. **24** Whoever is robbing his father or his mother, ‖ And is saying, "It is not transgression," ‖ He is a companion to a destroyer. **25** Whoever is proud in soul stirs up contention, ‖ And whoever is trusting on YHWH is made fat. **26** Whoever is trusting in his heart is a fool, ‖ And whoever is walking in wisdom is delivered. **27** Whoever is giving to the poor has no lack, ‖ And whoever is hiding his eyes multiplied curses. **28** A man is hidden in the rising of the wicked, ‖ And the righteous multiply in their destruction!

29 A man often reproved, hardening the neck, ‖ Is suddenly broken, and there is no healing. **2** In the multiplying of the righteous the people rejoice, ‖ And in the ruling of the wicked the people sigh. **3** A man loving wisdom makes his father glad, ‖ And a friend of harlots destroys wealth. **4** A king establishes a land by judgment, ‖ And one receiving gifts throws it down. **5** A man taking a portion above his neighbor, ‖ Spreads a net for his own steps. **6** A snare [is] in the transgression of the evil, ‖ And the righteous sing and rejoice. **7** The righteous knows the plea of the poor, ‖ The wicked does not understand knowledge. **8** Men of scorning ensnare a city, ‖ And the wise turn back anger. wise man is judged by the fool

PROVERBS

And he has been angry, ‖ And he has laughed, and there is no rest. **10** Men of blood hate the perfect, ‖ And the upright seek his soul. **11** A fool brings out all his mind, ‖ And the wise restrains it until afterward. **12** A ruler who is attending to lying words, ‖ All his ministers [are] wicked. **13** The poor and the man of frauds have met together, ‖ YHWH is enlightening the eyes of them both. **14** A king that is judging the poor with truth, ‖ His throne is established forever. **15** A rod and reproof give wisdom, ‖ And a youth let away is shaming his mother. **16** In the multiplying of the wicked transgression multiplies, ‖ And the righteous look on their fall. **17** Discipline your son, and he gives you comfort, ‖ Indeed, he gives delights to your soul. **18** A people is made naked without a vision, ‖ And whoever is keeping the Law, O his blessedness! **19** By words a servant is not instructed though he understand, ‖ And there is nothing answering. **20** You have seen a man hasty in his words! More hope of a fool than of him. **21** Whoever is bringing up his servant delicately, from youth, ‖ [At] his latter end he is also continuator. **22** An angry man stirs up contention, ‖ And a furious man is multiplying transgression. **23** The pride of man humbles him, ‖ And humility of spirit upholds honor. **24** Whoever is sharing with a thief is hating his own soul, ‖ He hears execration, and does not tell. **25** Fear of man causes a snare, ‖ And the confident in YHWH is set on high. **26** Many are seeking the face of a ruler, ‖ And the judgment of each [is] from YHWH. **27** The perverse man [is] an abomination to the righteous, ‖ And the upright in the way [is] an abomination to the wicked!

30 Words of Agur, son of Jakeh, the burden, a declaration of the man to Ithiel—to Ithiel and Ucal: I have wearied myself [for] God, ‖ I have wearied myself [for] God, and am consumed. **2** For I am more brutish than anyone, ‖ And do not have the understanding of a man. **3** Nor have I learned wisdom, ‖ Yet I know the knowledge of the Holy Ones. **4** Who went up to the heavens, and comes down? Who has gathered the wind in His fists? Who has bound waters in a garment? Who established all ends of the earth? What [is] His Name? And what [is] His Son's Name? Surely you know! **5** Every saying of God [is] tried, ‖ He [is] a shield to those trusting in Him. **6** Do not add to His words, lest He reason with you, ‖ And you have been found false. **7** Two things I have asked from You, ‖ Do not withhold from me before I die. **8** Put vanity and a lying word far from me, ‖ Do not give poverty or wealth to me, ‖ Cause me to eat the bread of my portion, **9** Lest I become satiated, and have denied, ‖ And have said, "Who [is] YHWH?" And lest I am poor, and have stolen, ‖ And have laid hold of the Name of my God. **10** Do not accuse a servant to his lord, ‖ Lest he disapprove of you, and you are found guilty. **11** A generation lightly esteems their father, ‖ And does not bless their mother. **12** A generation—pure in their own eyes, ‖ But not washed from their own filth. **13** A generation—how high are their eyes, ‖ Indeed, their eyelids are lifted up. **14** A generation—their teeth [are] swords, ‖ And their jaw-teeth [are] knives, ‖ To consume the poor from earth, ‖ And the needy from [among] men. **15** To the leech [are] two daughters—Give! Give! Behold, three things are not satisfied, ‖ Four have not said "Sufficiency"; **16** Sheol, and a restrained womb, ‖ Earth—it [is] not satisfied [with] water, ‖ And fire—it has not said, "Sufficiency," **17** An eye that mocks at a father, ‖ And despises to obey a mother, ‖ Ravens of the valley dig it out, ‖ And young eagles eat it. **18** Three things have been too wonderful for me, ‖ Indeed, four that I have not known: **19** The way of the eagle in the heavens, ‖ The way of a serpent on a rock, ‖ The way of a ship in the heart of the sea, ‖ And the way of a man in youth. **20** So—the way of an adulterous woman, ‖ She has eaten and has wiped her mouth, ‖ And has said, "I have not done iniquity." **21** For three things has earth been troubled, ‖ And for four—it is not able to bear: **22** For a servant when he reigns, ‖ And a fool when he is satisfied with bread, **23** For a hated one when she rules, ‖ And a maidservant when she succeeds her mistress. **24** Four [are] little ones of earth, ‖ And they are made wiser than the wise: **25** The ants [are] a people not strong, ‖ And they prepare their food in summer, **26** hyraxes [are] a people not strong, ‖ And they place their house in a rock, **27** There is no king to the locust, ‖ And it goes out—each one shouting, **28** A spider with two hands takes hold, ‖ And is in the palaces of a king. **29** There are three going well, ‖ Indeed, four are good in going: **30** An old lion—mighty among beasts, ‖ That does not turn back from the face of any, **31** A girt one of the loins, ‖ Also a male goat, ‖ And a king—troops with him. **32** If you have been foolish in lifting yourself up, ‖ And if you have devised evil—hand to mouth! **33** For the churning of milk brings out butter, ‖ And the wringing of the nose brings out blood, ‖ And the forcing of anger brings out strife!

31 Words of Lemuel, a king, a declaration that his mother taught him: **2** "What, my son? And what, son of my womb? And what, son of my vows? **3** Do not give your strength to women, ‖ And your ways to wiping away of kings. **4** [It is] not for kings, O Lemuel, ‖ Not for kings, to drink wine, ‖ And for princes—a desire of strong drink. **5** Lest he drink, and forget the decree, ‖ And change the judgment of any of the sons of affliction. **6** Give strong drink to the perishing, ‖ And wine to the bitter in soul, **7** He drinks, and forgets his poverty, ‖ And he does not remember his misery again. **8** Open your mouth for the mute, ‖ For the right of all sons of change. **9** Open your mouth, judge righteously, ‖ Both the cause of the poor and needy!" **10** [ALEPH-BET] A woman of worth who finds? Indeed, her price [is] far above rubies. **11** The heart of her husband has trusted in her, ‖ And he does not lack spoil. **12** She has done him good, and not evil, ‖ All [the] days of her life. **13** She has sought wool and flax, ‖ And with delight she works [with] her hands. **14** She has been as ships of the merchant, ‖ She brings in her bread from afar. **15** Indeed, she rises while yet night, ‖ And gives food to her household, ‖ And a portion to her girls. **16** She has considered a field, and takes it, ‖ She has planted a vineyard from the fruit of her hands. **17** She has girded her loins with might, ‖ And strengthens her arms. **18** She has perceived when her merchandise [is] good, ‖ Her lamp is not extinguished in the night. **19** She has sent forth her hands on a spindle, ‖ And her hands have held a distaff. **20** She has spread forth her hand to the poor, ‖ Indeed, she sent forth her hands to the needy. **21** She is not afraid of her household from snow, ‖ For all her household are clothed [with] scarlet. **22** She has made ornamental coverings for herself, ‖ Silk and purple [are] her clothing. **23** Her husband is known in the gates, ‖ In his sitting with [the] elderly of [the] land. **24** She has made linen garments, and sells, ‖ And she has given a girdle to the merchant. **25** Strength and honor [are] her clothing, ‖ And she rejoices at a latter day. **26** She has opened her mouth in wisdom, ‖ And the law of kindness [is] on her tongue. **27** She [is] watching the ways of her household, ‖ And she does not eat bread of sloth. **28** Her sons have risen up, and pronounce her blessed, ‖ Her husband, and he praises her, **29** "The daughters who have done worthily [are] many, ‖ You have gone up above them all." **30** Favor [is] deceitful, and beauty [is] vain, ‖ A woman fearing Yhwh, she may boast herself. **31** Give to her of the fruit of her hands, ‖ And her works praise her in the gates!

ECCLESIASTES

1 Words of a preacher, son of David, king in Jerusalem: **2** Vanity of vanities, said the Preacher, vanity of vanities: the whole [is] vanity. **3** What advantage [is] to man by all his labor that he labors at under the sun? **4** A generation is going, and a generation is coming, and the earth is standing for all time. **5** Also, the sun has risen, and the sun has gone in, and to its place panting it is rising there. **6** Going to the south, and turning around to the north, turning around, turning around, the wind is going, and by its circuits the wind has returned. **7** All the streams are going to the sea, and the sea is not full; to a place to where the streams are going, there they are turning back to go. **8** All these things are wearying; a man is not able to speak, the eye is not satisfied by seeing, nor is the ear filled from hearing. **9** What [is] that which has been? It [is] that which is, and what [is] that which has been done? It [is] that which is done, and there is not an entirely new thing under the sun. **10** There is a thing of which [one] says: "See this, it [is] new!" Already it has been in the ages that were before us! **11** There is not a remembrance of former [generations]; and also of the latter that are, there is no remembrance of them with those that are at the last. **12** I, a preacher, have been king over Israel in Jerusalem. **13** And I have given my heart to seek and to search out by wisdom concerning all that has been done under the heavens. It [is] a sad travail God has given to the sons of man to be humbled by it. **14** I have seen all the works that have been done under the sun, and behold, the whole [is] vanity and distress of spirit! **15** A crooked thing [one] is not able to make straight, and a lacking thing is not able to be numbered. **16** I spoke with my heart, saying, "I, behold, have magnified and added wisdom above everyone who has been before me at Jerusalem, and my heart has seen wisdom and knowledge abundantly. **17** And I give my heart to know wisdom, and to know madness and folly: I have known that even this [is] distress of spirit; **18** for in abundance of wisdom [is] abundance of sadness, and he who adds knowledge adds pain."

2 I said in my heart, "Pray, come, I try you with mirth, and look on gladness"; and behold, even it [is] vanity. **2** Of laughter I said, "Foolish!" And of mirth, "What [is] this it is doing?" **3** I have sought in my heart to draw out with wine my appetite (and my heart leading in wisdom), and to take hold on folly until I see where this [is]—the good to the sons of man of that which they do under the heavens, the number of the days of their lives. **4** I made great my works, I built for myself houses, I planted for myself vineyards. **5** I made for myself gardens and paradises, and I planted in them trees of every fruit. **6** I made for myself pools of water, to water from them a forest shooting forth trees. **7** I acquired menservants, and maidservants, and sons of the house were to me; also, I had much substance—herd and flock—above all who had been before me in Jerusalem. **8** I also gathered for myself silver and gold, and the peculiar treasure of kings and of the provinces. I prepared for myself men-singers and women-singers, and the luxuries of the sons of man—a wife and wives. **9** And I became great, and increased above everyone who had been before me in Jerusalem; also, my wisdom stood with me. **10** And all that my eyes asked I did not keep back from them; I did not withhold my heart from any joy, for my heart rejoiced because of all my labor, and this has been my portion, from all my labor, **11** and I have looked on all my works that my hands have done, and on the labor that I have labored to do, and behold, the whole [is] vanity and distress of spirit, and there is no advantage under the sun! **12** And I turned to see wisdom, and madness, and folly, but what [is] the man who comes after the king? That which [is] already—they have done it! **13** And I saw that there is an advantage to wisdom above folly, like the advantage of the light above the darkness. **14** The wise—his eyes [are] in his head, and the fool is walking in darkness, and I also knew that one event happens with them all; **15** and I said in my heart, "As it happens with the fool, it happens also with me, and why am I then more wise?" And I spoke in my heart, that also this [is] vanity: **16** That there is no remembrance to the wise—with the fool—for all time, for that which [is] already, [in] the days that are coming is all forgotten, and how dies the wise? With the fool! **17** And I have hated life, for sad to me [is] the work that has been done under the sun, for the whole [is] vanity and distress of spirit. **18** And I have hated all my labor that I labor at under the sun, because I leave it to a man who is after me. **19** And who knows whether he is wise or foolish? Yet he rules over all my labor that I have labored at, and that I have done wisely under the sun! This [is] also vanity. **20** And I turned around to cause my heart to despair concerning all the labor that I labored at under the sun. **21** For there is a man whose labor [is] in wisdom, and in knowledge, and in equity, and to a man who has not labored therein he gives it—his portion! Even this [is] vanity and a great evil. **22** For what has been to a man by all his labor, and by the thought of his heart that he labored at under the sun? **23** For all his days are sorrows, and his travail sadness; even at night his heart has not lain down; this [is] also vanity. **24** There is nothing good in a man who eats, and has drunk, and has shown his soul good in his labor. This also I have seen that it [is] from the hand of God. **25** For who eats and who hurries out more than I? **26** For to a man who [is] good before Him, He has given wisdom, and knowledge, and joy; and to a sinner He has given travail, to gather and to heap up, to give to the good before God. Even this [is] vanity and distress of spirit.

3 To everything—a season, and a time to every delight under the heavens: **2** A time to bring forth, ‖ And a time to die. A time to plant, ‖ And a time to eradicate the planted. **3** A time to slay, ‖ And a time to heal, ‖ A time to break down, ‖ And a time to build up. **4** A time to weep, ‖ And a time to laugh. A time to mourn, ‖ And a time to skip. **5** A time to cast away stones, ‖ And a time to heap up stones. A time to embrace, ‖ And a time to be far from embracing. **6** A time to seek, ‖ And a time to destroy. A time to keep, ‖ And a time to cast away. **7** A time to tear, ‖ And a time to sew. A time to be silent, ‖ And a time to speak. **8** A time to love, ‖ And a time to hate. A time of war, ‖ And a time of peace. **9** What advantage does the doer have in that which he is laboring at? **10** I have seen the travail that God has given to the sons of man to be humbled by it. **11** The whole He has made beautiful in its season; also, that knowledge He has put in their heart without which man does not find out the work that God has done from the beginning even to the end. **12** I have known that there is no good for them except to rejoice and to do good during their life, **13** indeed, even every man who eats and has drunk and seen good by all his labor, it [is] a gift of God. **14** I have known that all that God does is for all time, to it nothing is to be added, and from it nothing is to be withdrawn; and God has worked that they fear before Him. **15** What is that which has been? Already it is, and that which [is] to be has already been, and God requires that which is pursued. **16** And again, I have seen under the sun the place of judgment—there [is] the wicked; and the place of righteousness—there [is] the wicked. **17** I said in my heart, "The righteous and the wicked God judges, for a time [is] to every matter and for every work there." **18** I said in my heart concerning the matter of the sons of man that God might cleanse them, so as to see that they themselves [are] beasts. **19** For an event [is to] the sons of man, and an event [is to] the beasts, even one event [is] to them; as the death of this, so [is] the death of that; and one spirit [is] to all, and the advantage of man above the beast is nothing, for the whole [is] vanity. **20** The whole are going to one place, the whole have been from the dust, and the whole are turning back to the dust. **21** Who knows the spirit of the sons of man that is going up on high, and the spirit of the beast that is going down below to the earth? **22** And I have seen that there is nothing better than that man rejoice in his works, for it [is] his portion; for who brings him to look on that which is after him?

4 And I have turned, and I see all the oppressions that are done under the sun, and behold, the tear of the oppressed, and they have no comforter; and at the hand of their oppressors [is] power, and they have no comforter. **2** And I am praising the dead who have already died above the living who are yet alive. **3** And better than both of them [is] he who has not yet been, in that he has not seen the evil work that has been done under the sun. **4** And I have seen all the labor, and all the benefit of the work, because for it a man is the envy of his

ECCLESIASTES

neighbor. Even this [is] vanity and distress of spirit. **5** The fool is clasping his hands, and eating his own flesh: **6** "Better [is] a handful [with] quietness, than two handfuls [with] labor and distress of spirit." **7** And I have turned, and I see a vain thing under the sun: **8** There is one, and there is not a second; even son or brother he has not, and there is no end to all his labor! His eye also is not satisfied with riches, and [he does not say], "For whom am I laboring and bereaving my soul of good?" This also is vanity, it is a sad travail. **9** The two [are] better than the one, in that they have a good reward by their labor. **10** For if they fall, the one raises up his companion, but woe to the one who falls and there is not a second to raise him up! **11** Also, if two lie down, then they have heat, but how has one heat? **12** And if the one strengthens himself, the two stand against him; and the threefold cord is not quickly broken. **13** Better is a poor and wise youth than an old and foolish king, who has not known to be warned anymore. **14** For from a house of prisoners he has come out to reign, for even in his own kingdom he has been poor. **15** I have seen all the living, who are walking under the sun, with the second youth who stands in his place; **16** there is no end to all the people, to all who were before them; also, the latter do not rejoice in him. Surely this also is vanity and distress of spirit.

5 Keep your feet when you go to a house of God, and draw near to hear rather than to give of fools the sacrifice, for they do not know they do evil. **2** Do not cause your mouth to hurry, and do not let your heart hurry to bring out a word before God, for God is in the heavens, and you on the earth, therefore let your words be few. **3** For the dream has come by abundance of business, and the voice of a fool by abundance of words. **4** When you vow a vow to God, do not delay to complete it, for there is no pleasure in fools; that which you vow—complete. **5** Better that you do not vow, than that you vow and do not complete. **6** Do not permit your mouth to cause your flesh to sin, nor say before the messenger that it [is] ignorance. Why is God angry because of your voice and has destroyed the work of your hands? **7** For in the abundance of dreams both vanities and words abound; but fear God. **8** If oppression of the poor, and violent taking away of judgment and righteousness you see in a province, do not marvel at the matter, for a higher than the high is observing, and high ones [are] over them. **9** And the abundance of a land is for all. A king for a field is served. **10** Whoever is loving silver is not satisfied [with] silver, nor he who is in love with stores [with] increase. Even this [is] vanity. **11** In the multiplying of good have its consumers been multiplied, and what benefit [is] to its possessor except the sight of his eyes? **12** Sweet [is] the sleep of the laborer whether he eat little or much; and the sufficiency of the wealthy is not permitting him to sleep. **13** There is a painful evil I have seen under the sun: wealth kept for its possessor, for his evil. **14** And that wealth has been lost in an evil business, and he has begotten a son and there is nothing in his hand! **15** As he came out from the belly of his mother, naked he turns back to go as he came, and he does not take away anything of his labor, that goes in his hand. **16** And this also [is] a painful evil, just as he came, so he goes, and what advantage [is] to him who labors for wind? **17** He also consumes all his days in darkness, and sadness, and wrath, and sickness abound. **18** Behold, that which I have seen: [It is] good, because beautiful, to eat, and to drink, and to see good in all one's labor that he labors at under the sun, the number of the days of his life that God has given to him, for it [is] his portion. **19** Every man also to whom God has given wealth and riches, and has given him power to eat of it, and to accept his portion, and to rejoice in his labor, this is a gift of God. **20** For he does not much remember the days of his life, for God is answering through the joy of his heart.

6 There is an evil that I have seen under the sun, and it [is] great on man: **2** A man to whom God gives wealth, and riches, and honor, and there is no lack to his soul of all that he desires, and God does not give him power to eat of it, but a stranger eats it; this [is] vanity, and it [is] an evil disease. **3** If a man begets one hundred, and lives many years, and is great, because they are the days of his years, and his soul is not satisfied from the goodness, and also he has not had a grave, I have said, "Better than he [is] the untimely birth." **4** For in vanity he came in, and in darkness he goes, and in darkness his name is covered, **5** even

ECCLESIASTES

the sun he has not seen nor known, more rest has this than that. **6** And though he had lived one thousand years twice over, yet he has not seen good; does not everyone go to the same place? **7** All the labor of man [is] for his mouth, ‖ And yet the soul is not filled. **8** For what advantage [is] to the wise above the fool? What to the poor who knows to walk before the living? **9** Better [is] the sight of the eyes than the going of the soul. This [is] also vanity and distress of spirit. **10** What [is] that which has been? Already is its name called, and it is known that it [is] man, ‖ And he is not able to contend with him who is stronger than he. **11** For there are many things multiplying vanity; What advantage [is] to man? **12** For who knows what [is] good for a man in life, the number of the days of the life of his vanity, and he makes them as a shadow? For who declares to man what is after him under the sun?

7 Better [is] a name than good perfume, ‖ And the day of death than the day of birth. **2** Better to go to a house of mourning, ‖ Than to go to a house of banqueting, ‖ For that is the end of all men, ‖ And the living lays [it] to his heart. **3** Better [is] sorrow than laughter, ‖ For by the sadness of the face the heart becomes better. **4** The heart of the wise [is] in a house of mourning, ‖ And the heart of fools in a house of mirth. **5** Better to hear a rebuke of a wise man, ‖ Than [for] a man to hear a song of fools, **6** For as the noise of thorns under the pot, ‖ So [is] the laughter of a fool, even this [is] vanity. **7** Surely oppression makes the wise mad, ‖ And a gift destroys the heart. **8** Better [is] the latter end of a thing than its beginning, ‖ Better [is] the patient of spirit, than the haughty of spirit. **9** Do not be hasty in your spirit to be angry, ‖ For anger in the bosom of fools rests. **10** Do not say, "What was it, ‖ That the former days were better than these?" For you have not asked wisely of this. **11** Wisdom [is] good with an inheritance, ‖ And an advantage [it is] to those beholding the sun. **12** For wisdom [is] a defense, money [is] a defense, ‖ And the advantage of the knowledge of wisdom [is], ‖ She revives her possessors. **13** See the work of God, ‖ For who is able to make straight that which He made crooked? **14** In a day of prosperity be in gladness, ‖ And in a day of calamity consider: God has also made this alongside of that, ‖ To the intent that man does not find anything after him. **15** The whole I have considered in the days of my vanity. There is a righteous one perishing in his righteousness, and there is a wrongdoer prolonging [himself] in his wrong. **16** Do not be over-righteous, nor show yourself too wise, why are you desolate? **17** Do not do much wrong, neither be a fool, why do you die within your time? **18** [It is] good that you lay hold on this, and also, do not withdraw your hand from that, for whoever is fearing God goes out with them all. **19** The wisdom gives strength to a wise man, more than wealth the rulers who have been in a city. **20** Because there is not a righteous man on earth that does good and does not sin. **21** Also to all the words that they speak do not give your heart, that you do not hear your servant reviling you. **22** For many times also has your heart known that you yourself have also reviled others. **23** All this I have tried by wisdom; I have said, "I am wise," and it [is] far from me. **24** Far off [is] that which has been, and deep, deep, who finds it? **25** I have turned around, also my heart, to know and to search, and to seek out wisdom, and reason, and to know the wrong of folly, and the madness of foolishness. **26** And I am finding more bitter than death, the woman whose heart [is] nets and snares, her hands [are] bands; the good before God escapes from her, but the sinner is captured by her. **27** See, this I have found, said the Preacher, one to one, to find out the reason **28** (that still my soul had sought, and I had not found), ‖ One man, a teacher, I have found, and a woman among all these I have not found. **29** See, this alone I have found, that God made man upright, and they have sought out many inventions.

8 Who [is] as the wise? And who knows the interpretation of a thing? The wisdom of man causes his face to shine, and the hardness of his face is changed. **2** I [counsel]: keep the command of a king, even for the sake of an oath [to] God. **3** Do not be troubled at his presence, you may go, do not stand in an evil thing, for all that he pleases he does. **4** Where the word of a king [is] power [is], and who says to him, "What do you do?" **5** Whoever is keeping a command knows no evil thing, and time and judgment the heart of the wise knows. **6** For to every delight there is a time and a

ECCLESIASTES

judgment, for the misfortune of man is great on him. **7** For he does not know that which will be, for when it will be who declares to him? **8** There is no man ruling over the spirit to restrain the spirit, and there is no authority over the day of death, and there is no discharge in battle, and wickedness does not deliver its possessors. **9** All this I have seen so as to give my heart to every work that has been done under the sun; a time that man has ruled over man to his own evil. **10** And so I have seen the wicked buried, and they went in, even from the Holy Place they go, and they are forgotten in the city whether they had so done. This [is] also vanity. **11** Because sentence has not been done [on] an evil work speedily, therefore the heart of the sons of man is full within them to do evil. **12** Though a sinner is doing evil one hundred [times], and prolonging [himself] for it, surely also I know that there is good to those fearing God, who fear before Him. **13** And good is not to the wicked, and he does not prolong days as a shadow, because he is not fearing before God. **14** There is a vanity that has been done on the earth, that there are righteous ones to whom it is coming according to the work of the wicked, and there are wicked ones to whom it is coming according to the work of the righteous. I have said that this [is] also vanity. **15** And I have praised mirth because there is no good to man under the sun except to eat and to drink, and to rejoice, and it remains with him of his labor the days of his life that God has given to him under the sun. **16** When I gave my heart to know wisdom and to see the business that has been done on the earth (for there is also a spectator in whose eyes sleep is not by day and by night), **17** then I considered all the work of God, that man is not able to find out the work that has been done under the sun, because though man labor to seek, yet he does not find; and even though the wise man speak of knowing he is not able to find.

9 But all this I have laid to my heart, so as to clear up the whole of this, that the righteous and the wise, and their works, [are] in the hand of God, neither love nor hatred does man know, the whole [is] before them. **2** The whole [is] as to the whole; one event is to the righteous and to the wicked, to the good, and to the clean, and to the unclean, and to him who is sacrificing, and to him who is not sacrificing; as [is] the good, so [is] the sinner, he who is swearing as he who is fearing an oath. **3** This [is] an evil among all that has been done under the sun, that one event [is] to all, and also the heart of the sons of man is full of evil, and madness [is] in their heart during their life, and after it—to the dead. **4** But [to] him who is joined to all the living there is confidence, for to a living dog it [is] better than to the dead lion. **5** For the living know that they die, and the dead do not know anything, and there is no more reward to them, for their remembrance has been forgotten. **6** Their love also, their hatred also, their envy also, has already perished, and they have no more portion for all time in all that has been done under the sun. **7** Go, eat your bread with joy, and drink your wine with a glad heart, for already has God been pleased with your works. **8** At all times let your garments be white, and do not let oil be lacking on your head. **9** See life with the wife whom you have loved, all the days of the life of your vanity, that He has given to you under the sun, all the days of your vanity, for it [is] your portion in life, even of your labor that you are laboring at under the sun. **10** All that your hand finds to do, with your power do, for there is no work, and plan, and knowledge, and wisdom in Sheol to where you are going. **11** I have turned so as to see under the sun, that not to the swift [is] the race, nor to the mighty the battle, nor even to the wise bread, nor even to the intelligent wealth, nor even to the skillful grace, for time and chance happen with them all. **12** For even man does not know his time; as fish that are taken hold of by an evil net, and as birds that are taken hold of by a snare, the sons of man are snared like these at an evil time when it falls on them suddenly. **13** This also I have seen: wisdom under the sun, and it is great to me. **14** A little city, and few men in it, and a great king has come to it, and has surrounded it, and has built against it great bulwarks; **15** and there has been found in it a poor wise man, and he has delivered the city by his wisdom, and men have not remembered that poor man! **16** And I said, "Better [is] wisdom than might, and the wisdom of the poor is despised, and his words are not heard." **17** The words of the wise are heard in quiet, ‖ More than the cry

ECCLESIASTES

of a ruler over fools. **18** Better [is] wisdom than weapons of conflict, ‖ And one sinner destroys much good!

10 Dead flies cause a perfumer's perfume ‖ To send forth a stink; The precious by reason of wisdom—By reason of honor—a little folly! **2** The heart of the wise [is] at his right hand, ‖ And the heart of a fool at his left. **3** And also, when he that is a fool ‖ Is walking in the way, his heart is lacking, ‖ And he has said to everyone, "He [is] a fool." **4** If the spirit of the ruler goes up against you, do not leave your place, ‖ For yielding quiets great sinners. **5** There is an evil I have seen under the sun, ‖ As ignorance that goes out from the ruler, **6** He has set the fool in many high places, ‖ And the rich sits in a low place. **7** I have seen servants on horses, ‖ And princes walking as servants on the earth. **8** Whoever is digging a pit falls into it, ‖ And whoever is breaking a hedge, a serpent bites him. **9** Whoever is removing stones is grieved by them, ‖ Whoever is cleaving trees endangered by them. **10** If the iron has been blunt, ‖ And he has not sharpened the face, ‖ Then he increases strength, ‖ And wisdom [is] advantageous to make right. **11** If the serpent bites without enchantment, ‖ Then there is no advantage to a master of the tongue. **12** Words of the mouth of the wise [are] gracious, ‖ And the lips of a fool swallow him up. **13** The beginning of the words of his mouth [is] folly, ‖ And the latter end of his mouth ‖ [Is] mischievous madness. **14** And the fool multiplies words: "Man does not know that which is—And that which is after him, who declares to him?" **15** The labor of the foolish wearies him, ‖ In that he has not known to go to the city. **16** Woe to you, O land, when your king [is] a youth, ‖ And your princes eat in the morning. **17** Blessed are you, O land, ‖ When your king [is] a son of nobles, ‖ And your princes eat in due season, ‖ For might, and not for drunkenness. **18** By slothfulness is the wall brought low, ‖ And by idleness of the hands the house drops. **19** For mirth they are making a feast, ‖ And wine makes life joyful, ‖ And the silver answers with all. **20** Even in your mind do not revile a king, ‖ And in the inner parts of your bed-chamber do not revile the rich: For a bird of the heavens causes the voice to go, ‖ And a possessor of wings declares the word.

11 Send forth your bread on the face of the waters, ‖ For in the multitude of the days you find it. **2** Give a portion to seven, and even to eight, ‖ For you do not know what evil is on the earth. **3** If the thick clouds are full of rain, ‖ On the earth they empty [themselves]; And if a tree falls in the south or to the north, ‖ The place where the tree falls, there it is. **4** Whoever is observing the wind does not sow, ‖ And whoever is looking on the thick clouds does not reap. **5** As you do not know what [is] the way of the spirit, ‖ How—bones in the womb of the full one, ‖ So you do not know the work of God who makes the whole. **6** In the morning sow your seed, ‖ And at evening do not withdraw your hand, ‖ For you do not know which is right, this or that, ‖ Or whether both of them alike [are] good. **7** Sweet also [is] the light, ‖ And good for the eyes to see the sun. **8** But if man lives many years, ‖ In all of them let him rejoice, ‖ And remember the days of darkness, ‖ For they are many! All that is coming [is] vanity. **9** Rejoice, O young man, in your childhood, ‖ And let your heart gladden you in days of your youth, ‖ And walk in the ways of your heart, ‖ And in the sight of your eyes, ‖ And know that for all these, God brings you into judgment. **10** And turn aside anger from your heart, ‖ And cause evil to pass from your flesh, ‖ For the childhood and the age [are] vanity!

12 Remember also your Creator in days of your youth, ‖ While that the evil days do not come, ‖ Nor the years have arrived, that you say, ‖ "I have no pleasure in them." **2** While that the sun is not darkened, and the light, ‖ And the moon, and the stars, ‖ And the thick clouds returned after the rain. **3** In the day that keepers of the house tremble, ‖ And men of strength have bowed themselves, ‖ And grinders have ceased, because they have become few. And those looking out at the windows have become dim, **4** And doors have been shut in the street. When the noise of the grinding is low, ‖ And [one] rises at the voice of the bird, ‖ And all daughters of song are bowed down. **5** Also of that which is high they are afraid, ‖ And of the low places in the way, ‖ And the almond-tree is despised, ‖ And the grasshopper has become a burden, ‖ And want is increased, ‖ For man is going to his perpetual home, ‖ And the mourners have gone around

ECCLESIASTES

through the street. **6** While that the silver cord is not removed, ‖ And the golden bowl broken, ‖ And the pitcher broken by the fountain, ‖ And the wheel broken at the well. **7** And the dust returns to the earth as it was, ‖ And the spirit returns to God who gave it. **8** Vanity of vanities, said the preacher, the whole [is] vanity. **9** And further, because the preacher was wise, he still taught the people knowledge, and gave ear, and sought out—he made right many allegories. **10** The preacher sought to find out pleasing words, and [that] written [by] the upright—words of truth. **11** Words of the wise [are] as the goads, and as nails planted [by] the masters of collections, they have been given by one Shepherd. **12** And further, from these, my son, be warned; the making of many scrolls has no end, and much study [is] a weariness of the flesh. **13** The end of the whole matter let us hear: "Fear God, and keep His commands, for this [is] the whole of man. **14** For every work God brings into judgment, with every hidden thing, whether good or bad."

SONG OF SONGS

1 The Song of Songs, that [is] of Solomon. **2** Let him kiss me with kisses of his mouth, ‖ For better [are] your loves than wine. **3** For fragrance [are] your good perfumes. Perfume emptied out—your name, ‖ Therefore have virgins loved you! **4** Draw me: we run after you, ‖ The king has brought me into his inner chambers, ‖ We delight and rejoice in you, ‖ We mention your loves more than wine, ‖ Uprightly they have loved you! **5** I [am] dark and lovely, daughters of Jerusalem, as tents of Kedar, as curtains of Solomon. **6** Do not fear me, because I [am] very dark, ‖ Because the sun has scorched me, ‖ The sons of my mother were angry with me, ‖ They made me keeper of the vineyards, ‖ My vineyard—my own—I have not kept. **7** Declare to me, you whom my soul has loved, ‖ Where you delight, ‖ Where you lie down at noon, ‖ For why am I as one veiled, ‖ By the ranks of your companions? **8** If you do not know, ‖ O beautiful among women, ‖ Go forth by the traces of the flock, ‖ And feed your kids by the shepherds' dwellings! **9** To my joyous one in chariots of Pharaoh, I have compared you, my friend, **10** Your cheeks have been lovely with garlands, your neck with chains. **11** We make garlands of gold for you, with studs of silver! **12** While the king [is] in his circle, ‖ My spikenard has given its fragrance. **13** A bundle of myrrh [is] my beloved to me, ‖ Between my breasts it lodges. **14** A cluster of cypress [is] my beloved to me, ‖ In the vineyards of En-Gedi! **15** Behold, you [are] beautiful, my friend, ‖ Behold, you [are] beautiful, your eyes [are] doves! **16** Behold, you [are] beautiful, my love, indeed, pleasant, ‖ Indeed, our bed [is] green, **17** The beams of our houses [are] cedars, ‖ Our rafters [are] firs, I [am] a rose of Sharon, a lily of the valleys!

2 As a lily among the thorns, **2** So [is] my friend among the daughters! **3** As a citron among trees of the forest, ‖ So [is] my beloved among the sons, ‖ In his shade I delighted, and sat down, ‖ And his fruit [is] sweet to my palate. **4** He has brought me to a house of wine, ‖ And his banner over me [is] love, **5** Sustain me with grape-cakes, ‖ Support me with citrons, for I [am] sick with love. **6** His left hand [is] under my head, ‖ And his right embraces me. **7** I have adjured you, daughters of Jerusalem, ‖ By the roes or by the does of the field, ‖ Do not stir up nor wake the love until she pleases! **8** The voice of my beloved! Behold, this— he is coming, ‖ Leaping on the mountains, skipping on the hills. **9** My beloved [is] like to a roe, ‖ Or to a young one of the harts. Behold, this—he is standing behind our wall, ‖ Looking from the windows, ‖ Blooming from the lattice. **10** My beloved has answered and said to me, ‖ "Rise up, my friend, my beautiful one, and come away, **11** For behold, the winter has passed by, ‖ The rain has passed away—it has gone. **12** The flowers have appeared in the earth, ‖ The time of the singing has come, ‖ And the voice of the turtle was heard in our land, **13** The fig tree has ripened her green figs, ‖ And the sweet-smelling vines have given forth fragrance, ‖ Rise, come, my friend, my beautiful one, indeed, come away. **14** My dove, in clefts of the rock, ‖ In a secret place of the ascent, ‖ Cause me to see your appearance, ‖ Cause me to hear your voice, ‖ For your voice [is] sweet, and your appearance lovely." **15** Seize for us foxes, ‖ Little foxes—destroyers of vineyards, ‖ Even our sweet-smelling vineyards. **16** My beloved [is] mine, and I [am] his, ‖ Who is delighting among the lilies, **17** Until the day breaks forth, ‖ And the shadows have fled away, ‖ Turn, be like, my beloved, ‖ To a roe, or to a young one of the harts, ‖ On the mountains of separation!

3 On my bed by night, I sought him whom my soul has loved; I sought him, and I did not find him! **2** Now let me rise, and go around the city, ‖ In the streets and in the broad places, ‖ I seek him whom my soul has loved! I sought him, and I did not find him. **3** The watchmen have found me ‖ (Who are going around the city), ‖ "Have you seen him whom my soul has loved?" **4** But I passed on a little from them, ‖ Until I found him whom my soul has loved! I seized him, and did not let him go, ‖ Until I brought him to the house of my mother— And the chamber of her that conceived me. **5** I have adjured you, daughters of

SONG OF SONGS

Jerusalem, ‖ By the roes or by the does of the field, ‖ Do not stir up nor wake the love until she pleases! **6** Who [is] this coming up from the wilderness, ‖ Like palm-trees of smoke, ‖ Perfumed [with] myrrh and frankincense, ‖ From every powder of the merchant? **7** Behold, his couch, that [is] of Solomon, ‖ Sixty mighty ones [are] around it, ‖ Of the mighty of Israel, **8** All of them holding sword, taught of battle, ‖ Each his sword by his thigh, for fear at night. **9** A palanquin King Solomon made for himself, ‖ Of the wood of Lebanon, **10** Its pillars he made of silver, ‖ Its bottom of gold, its seat of purple, ‖ Its midst lined [with] love, ‖ By the daughters of Jerusalem. **11** Go forth, and look, you daughters of Zion, ‖ On King Solomon, with the crown, ‖ With which his mother crowned him, ‖ In the day of his espousals, ‖ And in the day of the joy of his heart!

4 Behold, you [are] beautiful, my friend, behold, you [are] beautiful, ‖ Your eyes [are] doves behind your veil, ‖ Your hair as a row of the goats that have shone from Mount Gilead, **2** Your teeth as a row of the shorn ones that have come up from the washing, ‖ For all of them are forming twins, ‖ And a bereaved one is not among them. **3** As a thread of scarlet [are] your lips, ‖ And your speech [is] lovely, ‖ As the work of the pomegranate [is] your temple behind your veil, **4** As the Tower of David [is] your neck, built for an armory, ‖ The chief of the shields are hung on it, ‖ All shields of the mighty. **5** Your two breasts [are] as two fawns, ‖ Twins of a roe, that are feeding among lilies. **6** Until the day breaks forth, ‖ And the shadows have fled away, ‖ I go for myself to the mountain of myrrh, ‖ And to the hill of frankincense. **7** You [are] all beautiful, my friend, ‖ And there is not a blemish in you. Come from Lebanon, O spouse, **8** Come from Lebanon, come in. Look from the top of Amana, ‖ From the top of Shenir and Hermon, ‖ From the habitations of lions, ‖ From the mountains of leopards. **9** You have emboldened me, my sister-spouse, ‖ Emboldened me with one of your eyes, ‖ With one chain of your neck. **10** How beautiful have been your loves, my sister-spouse, ‖ How much better have been your loves than wine, ‖ And the fragrance of your perfumes than all spices. **11** Your lips drop honey, O spouse, ‖ Honey and milk [are] under your tongue, ‖ And the fragrance of your garments ‖ [Is] as the fragrance of Lebanon. **12** A garden shut up [is] my sister-spouse, ‖ A spring shut up—a fountain sealed. **13** Your shoots a paradise of pomegranates, ‖ With precious fruits, **14** Cypresses with nard—nard and saffron, ‖ Cane and cinnamon, ‖ With all trees of frankincense, ‖ Myrrh and aloes, with all chief spices. **15** A fount of gardens, a well of living waters, ‖ And flowings from Lebanon! **16** Awake, O north wind, and come, O south, ‖ Cause my garden to breathe forth, its spices let flow, ‖ Let my beloved come to his garden, ‖ And eat its pleasant fruits!

5 I have come to my garden, my sister-spouse, ‖ I have plucked my myrrh with my spice, ‖ I have eaten my comb with my honey, ‖ I have drunk my wine with my milk. Eat, O friends, drink, ‖ Indeed, drink abundantly, O beloved ones! **2** I am sleeping, but my heart wakes: The sound of my beloved knocking! "Open to me, my sister, my friend, ‖ My dove, my perfect one, ‖ For my head is filled [with] dew, ‖ My locks [with] drops of the night." **3** I have put off my coat, how do I put it on? I have washed my feet, how do I defile them? **4** My beloved sent his hand from the network, ‖ And my bowels were moved for him. **5** I rose to open to my beloved, ‖ And my hands dripped myrrh, ‖ Indeed, my fingers were flowing [with] myrrh, ‖ On the handles of the lock. **6** I opened to my beloved, ‖ But my beloved withdrew—he passed on, ‖ My soul went forth when he spoke, I sought him, and did not find him. I called him, and he did not answer me. **7** The watchmen who go around the city, ‖ Found me, struck me, wounded me, ‖ Keepers of the walls lifted up my veil from off me. **8** I have adjured you, daughters of Jerusalem, ‖ If you find my beloved—What do you tell him? That I [am] sick with love! **9** What [is] your beloved above [any] beloved, ‖ O beautiful among women? What [is] your beloved above [any] beloved, ‖ That thus you have adjured us? **10** My beloved [is] clear and ruddy, ‖ Conspicuous above a myriad! **11** His head [is] pure gold—fine gold, ‖ His locks flowing, dark as a raven, **12** His eyes as doves by streams of water, ‖ Washing in milk, sitting in fullness. **13** His cheeks [are] as a bed of the spice, towers of perfumes, ‖ His lips—lilies, dripping [and] flowing

[with] myrrh, **14** His hands rings of gold, set with beryl, ‖ His heart bright ivory, covered with sapphires, **15** His limbs pillars of marble, ‖ Founded on sockets of fine gold, ‖ His appearance as Lebanon, choice as the cedars. **16** His mouth is sweetness—and all of him desirable, ‖ This [is] my beloved, and this my friend, ‖ O daughters of Jerusalem!

6 To where has your beloved gone, ‖ O beautiful among women? To where has your beloved turned, ‖ And we seek him with you? **2** My beloved went down to his garden, ‖ To the beds of the spice, ‖ To delight himself in the gardens, and to gather lilies. **3** I [am] my beloved's, and my beloved [is] mine, ‖ Who is delighting himself among the lilies. **4** You [are] beautiful, my friend, as Tirzah, lovely as Jerusalem, ‖ Awe-inspiring as bannered hosts. **5** Turn around your eyes from before me, ‖ Because they have made me proud. Your hair [is] as a row of the goats, ‖ That have shone from Gilead, **6** Your teeth as a row of the lambs, ‖ That have come up from the washing, ‖ Because all of them are forming twins, ‖ And a bereaved one is not among them. **7** As the work of the pomegranate [is] your temple behind your veil. **8** Sixty are queens, and eighty concubines, ‖ And virgins without number. **9** One is my dove, my perfect one, ‖ She [is] one of her mother, ‖ She [is] the choice one of her that bore her, ‖ Daughters saw, and pronounce her blessed, ‖ Queens and concubines, and they praise her. **10** "Who [is] this that is looking forth as morning, ‖ Beautiful as the moon—clear as the sun, ‖ Awe-inspiring as bannered hosts?" **11** To a garden of nuts I went down, ‖ To look on the buds of the valley, ‖ To see to where the vine had flourished, ‖ The pomegranates had blossomed— **12** I did not know my soul, ‖ It made me—chariots of my people Nadib. **13** Return, return, O Shulammith! Return, return, and we look on you. What do you see in Shulammith?

7 As the chorus of "Mahanaim." How beautiful were your feet with sandals, O daughter of Nadib. The turnings of your sides [are] as ornaments, ‖ Work of the hands of a craftsman. **2** Your waist [is] a basin of roundness, ‖ It does not lack the mixture, ‖ Your body a heap of wheat, fenced with lilies, **3** Your two breasts as two young ones, twins of a roe, **4** Your neck as a tower of the ivory, ‖ Your eyes pools in Heshbon, near the Gate of Bath-Rabbim, ‖ Your face as a tower of Lebanon looking to Damascus, **5** Your head on you as Carmel, ‖ And the locks of your head as purple, ‖ The king is bound with the flowings! **6** How beautiful and how pleasant you have been, ‖ O love, in delights. **7** This your stature has been like to a palm, ‖ And your breasts to clusters. **8** I said, "Let me go up on the palm, ‖ Let me lay hold on its boughs," ‖ Indeed, let your breasts now be as clusters of the vine, ‖ And the fragrance of your face as citrons, **9** And your palate as the good wine—Flowing to my beloved in uprightness, ‖ Strengthening the lips of the aged! **10** I [am] my beloved's, and on me [is] his desire. **11** Come, my beloved, we go forth to the field, **12** We lodge in the villages, we go early to the vineyards, ‖ We see if the vine has flourished, ‖ The sweet smelling-flower has opened. The pomegranates have blossomed, ‖ There I give to you my loves; **13** The mandrakes have given fragrance, ‖ And at our openings all pleasant things, ‖ New, indeed, old, my beloved, I laid up for you!

8 Who makes you as a brother to me, ‖ Suckling the breasts of my mother? I find you outside, I kiss you, ‖ Indeed, they do not despise me, **2** I lead you, I bring you into my mother's house, ‖ She teaches me, I cause you to drink of the spiced wine, ‖ Of the juice of my pomegranate, **3** His left hand [is] under my head, ‖ And his right embraces me. **4** I have adjured you, daughters of Jerusalem, ‖ How you stir up, ‖ And how you wake the love until she pleases! **5** Who [is] this coming from the wilderness, ‖ Hastening herself for her beloved? Under the citron-tree I have awoken you, ‖ There your mother pledged you, ‖ There she [who] bore you gave a pledge. **6** Set me as a seal on your heart, as a seal on your arm, ‖ For strong as death is love, ‖ Sharp as Sheol is jealousy, ‖ Its burnings [are] burnings of fire, a flame of YAH! **7** Many waters are not able to quench the love, ‖ And floods do not wash it away. If one gives all the wealth of his house for love, ‖ Treading down—they tread on it. **8** We have a little sister, and she does not have breasts, ‖ What do we do for our sister, ‖ In the day that it is told of her? **9** If she is a wall, we build by her a palace of silver.

And if she is a door, ‖ We fashion by her board-work of cedar. **10** I [am] a wall, and my breasts as towers, ‖ Then I have been in his eyes as one finding peace. **11** Solomon has a vineyard in Baʻal-Hamon, ‖ He has given the vineyard to keepers, ‖ Each brings for its fruit one thousand pieces of silver; **12** My vineyard—my own—is before me, ‖ The one thousand [is] for you, O Solomon. And the two hundred for those keeping its fruit. O dweller in gardens! **13** The companions are attending to your voice, ‖ Cause me to hear. Flee, my beloved, and be like to a roe, **14** Or to a young one of the harts on mountains of spices!

ISAIAH

1 The visions of Isaiah son of Amoz, that he has seen concerning Judah and Jerusalem, in the days of Uzziah, Jotham, Ahaz, Hezekiah, kings of Judah. **2** Hear, O heavens, and give ear, O earth, ‖ For YHWH has spoken: "I have nourished and brought up sons, ‖ And they transgressed against Me. **3** An ox has known its owner, ‖ And a donkey the crib of its master, ‖ Israel has not known, ‖ My people have not understood." **4** Oh, sinning nation, a people heavy [with] iniquity, ‖ A seed of evildoers, sons—corrupters! They have forsaken YHWH, ‖ They have despised the Holy One of Israel, ‖ They have gone away backward. **5** Why are you struck anymore? You add apostasy! Every head has become diseased, and every heart [is] sick. **6** From the sole of the foot—to the head, ‖ There is no soundness in it, ‖ Wound, and bruise, and fresh striking! They have not been closed nor bound, ‖ Nor have they softened with ointment. **7** Your land [is] a desolation, your cities burned with fire, ‖ Your ground—strangers are consuming it before you, ‖ And a desolation as overthrown by strangers! **8** And the daughter of Zion has been left, ‖ As a shelter in a vineyard, ‖ As a lodge in a place of cucumbers—as a city besieged. **9** Unless YHWH of Hosts had left a remnant to us, ‖ Shortly—we had been as Sodom, ‖ We had been like to Gomorrah! **10** Hear the word of YHWH, you rulers of Sodom, ‖ Give ear to the Law of our God, you people of Gomorrah, **11** "Why the abundance of your sacrifices to Me?" says YHWH, ‖ "I have been satiated [with] burnt-offerings of rams, ‖ And fat of fatlings; And blood of bullocks, and lambs, ‖ And I have not desired male goats. **12** When you come to appear before Me, ‖ Who has required this of your hand, ‖ To trample My courts? **13** Do not add to bring in a vain present, ‖ Incense—it [is] an abomination to Me, ‖ New moon, and Sabbath, calling of convocation! Do not render iniquity—and a restraint! **14** My soul has hated your new moons and your set seasons, ‖ They have been on Me for a burden, ‖ I have been weary of bearing. **15** And in your spreading forth your hands, I hide My eyes from you, ‖ Also when you increase prayer, I do not hear, ‖ Your hands have been full of blood. **16** Wash yourselves, make yourselves pure, ‖ Turn aside the evil of your doings, from before My eyes, ‖ Cease to do evil, learn to do good. **17** Seek judgment, make the oppressed blessed, ‖ Judge the fatherless, strive [for] the widow. **18** Now come, and we settle this," says YHWH, "If your sins are as scarlet, they will be white as snow, ‖ If they are red as crimson, they will be as wool! **19** If you are willing, and have listened, ‖ The good of the land you consume, **20** And if you refuse, and have rebelled, ‖ You are consumed [by] the sword," ‖ For the mouth of YHWH has spoken. **21** How has a faithful city become a harlot? I have filled it [with] judgment, ‖ Righteousness lodges in it—now murderers. **22** Your silver has become dross, ‖ Your drink defiled with water. **23** Your princes [are] apostates, and companions of thieves, ‖ Everyone loving a bribe, and pursuing rewards, ‖ They do not judge the fatherless, ‖ And the plea of the widow does not come to them. **24** Therefore—a declaration of the Lord—YHWH of Hosts, the Mighty One of Israel: "Oh, I relieve Myself from My adversaries, ‖ And avenge Myself against My enemies, **25** And I turn back My hand on you, ‖ And I refine your dross as purity, ‖ And I turn aside all your tin, **26** And I give back your judges as at the first, ‖ And your counselors as in the beginning, ‖ After this you are called, A city of righteousness—a faithful city." **27** Zion is redeemed in judgment, ‖ And her captivity in righteousness. **28** And the destruction of transgressors and sinners [is] together, ‖ And those forsaking YHWH are consumed. **29** For [men] are ashamed because of the oaks ‖ That you have desired, ‖ And you are confounded because of the gardens ‖ That you have chosen. **30** For you are as an oak whose leaf is fading, ‖ And as a garden that has no water. **31** And the strong has been for tow, ‖ And his work for a spark, ‖ And both of them have burned together, ‖ And there is none quenching!

2 The thing that Isaiah son of Amoz has seen concerning Judah and Jerusalem: **2** And it has come to pass, ‖ In the latter end of the days, ‖ The mountain of YHWH's

ISAIAH

house is established, ‖ Above the top of the mountains, ‖ And it has been lifted up above the heights, ‖ And all the nations have flowed to it. 3 And many peoples have gone and said, "Come, and we go up to the mountain of YHWH, ‖ To the house of the God of Jacob, ‖ And He teaches us of His ways, ‖ And we walk in His paths, ‖ For a law goes forth from Zion, ‖ And a word of YHWH from Jerusalem. 4 And He has judged between the nations, ‖ And has given a decision to many peoples, ‖ And they have beat their swords to plowshares, ‖ And their spears to pruning-hooks, ‖ Nation does not lift up sword to nation, ‖ Nor do they learn anymore—war. 5 O house of Jacob, come, ‖ And we walk in the light of YHWH." 6 For You have left Your people, the house of Jacob. For they have been filled from the east, ‖ And [are] sorcerers like the Philistines, ‖ And strike hands with the children of strangers. 7 And its land is full of silver and gold, ‖ And there is no end to its treasures, ‖ And its land is full of horses, ‖ And there is no end to its chariots, 8 And its land is full of idols, ‖ It bows itself to the work of its hands, ‖ To that which its fingers have made, 9 And the low bows down, and the high is humbled, ‖ And You do not accept them. 10 Enter into a rock, and be hidden in dust, ‖ Because of the fear of YHWH, ‖ And because of the honor of His excellence. 11 The haughty eyes of man have been humbled, ‖ And the loftiness of men has been bowed down, ‖ And YHWH alone has been set on high in that day. 12 For a day [is] to YHWH of Hosts, ‖ For every proud and high one, ‖ And for every lifted up and low one, 13 And for all cedars of Lebanon, ‖ The high and the exalted ones, ‖ And for all oaks of Bashan, 14 And for all the high mountains, ‖ And for all the exalted heights, 15 And for every high tower, ‖ And for every fortified wall, 16 And for all ships of Tarshish, ‖ And for all desirable pictures. 17 And the haughtiness of man has been bowed down, ‖ And the loftiness of men humbled, ‖ And YHWH alone has been set on high in that day. 18 And the idols—they completely pass away. 19 And [men] have entered into caverns of rocks, ‖ And into caves of dust, ‖ Because of the fear of YHWH, ‖ And because of the honor of His excellence, ‖ In His rising to terrify the earth. 20 In that day man casts his idols of silver, ‖ And his idols of gold, ‖ That they have made for him to worship, ‖ To moles, and to bats, 21 To enter into cavities of the rocks, ‖ And into clefts of the high places, ‖ Because of the fear of YHWH, ‖ And because of the honor of His excellence, ‖ In His rising to terrify the earth. 22 Cease yourselves from man, ‖ Whose breath [is] in his nostrils, ‖ For—in what is he esteemed?

3 For behold, the Lord, YHWH of Hosts, ‖ Is turning aside from Jerusalem and from Judah ‖ [Both] stay and staff: Every stay of bread and every stay of water; 2 Mighty and man of war, judge and prophet, ‖ And diviner and elderly, 3 Head of fifty, and accepted of faces, ‖ And counselor, and wise craftsmen, ‖ And discerning charmer. 4 And I have made youths their heads, ‖ And sucklings rule over them. 5 And the people has exacted—man on man, ‖ Even a man on his neighbor, ‖ The youths enlarge themselves against the aged, ‖ And the lightly esteemed against the honored. 6 When one lays hold on his brother, ‖ Of the house of his father, [by] the garment, "Come, you are a ruler to us, ‖ And this ruin [is] under your hand." 7 He lifts up, in that day, saying, "I am not a binder up, ‖ And in my house is neither bread nor garment, ‖ You do not make me a ruler of the people." 8 For Jerusalem has stumbled, and Judah has fallen, ‖ For their tongue and their doings [are] against YHWH, ‖ To provoke the eyes of His glory. 9 The appearance of their faces witnessed against them, ‖ And their sin, as Sodom, they declared, ‖ They have not hidden! Woe to their soul, ‖ For they have done evil to themselves. 10 Say to the righteous that [it is] good, ‖ Because they eat the fruit of their doings. 11 Woe to the wicked—evil, ‖ Because the deed of his hand is done to him. 12 My people—its exactors [are] sucklings, ‖ And women have ruled over it. My people—your eulogists are causing to err, ‖ And the way of your paths swallowed up. 13 YHWH has stood up to plead, ‖ And He is standing to judge the peoples. 14 YHWH enters into judgment ‖ With [the] elderly of His people, and its heads: "And you, you have consumed the vineyard, ‖ Plunder of the poor [is] in your houses. 15 Why? Why do you [do this]? You bruise My people, ‖ And you grind the faces of the poor." A declaration of the Lord, YHWH of Hosts, ‖ And YHWH says: 16 "Because that daughters of Zion have been haughty, ‖

And they walk stretching out the neck, ‖ And deceiving [with] the eyes, ‖ They go walking and mincing, ‖ And they make a jingling with their feet, **17** The Lord has also scabbed ‖ The crown of the head of daughters of Zion, ‖ And YHWH exposes their simplicity. **18** In that day the Lord turns aside ‖ The beauty of the jingling ornaments, ‖ And of the embroidered works, ‖ And of the crescents, **19** Of the pendants, and the bracelets, and the veils, **20** Of the headdresses, and the ornaments of the legs, ‖ And of the bands, ‖ And of the perfume boxes, and the amulets, **21** Of the seals, and of the nose-rings, **22** Of the costly apparel, and of the mantles, ‖ And of the coverings, and of the purses, **23** Of the mirrors, and of the linen garments, ‖ And of the hoods, and of the veils, **24** And it has been, instead of spice is muck, ‖ And instead of a girdle, a rope, ‖ And instead of curled work, baldness, ‖ And instead of a stomacher a girdle of sackcloth. **25** For instead of glory, your men fall by sword, ‖ And your might in battle. **26** And her openings have lamented and mourned, ‖ Indeed, she has been emptied, she sits on the earth!"

4 And seven women have taken hold on one man, ‖ In that day, saying, "We eat our own bread, ‖ And we put on our own raiment, ‖ Only, let your name be called over us, ‖ Remove our reproach." **2** In that day is the Shoot of YHWH for desire and for glory, ‖ And the fruit of the earth ‖ For excellence and for beauty to the escaped of Israel. **3** And it has been, he who is left in Zion, ‖ And he who is remaining in Jerusalem, "Holy" is said of him, ‖ Of everyone who is written for life in Jerusalem. **4** If the Lord has washed away ‖ The filth of daughters of Zion, ‖ And purges the blood of Jerusalem from her midst, ‖ By the spirit of judgment, and by the spirit of burning. **5** Then YHWH has created ‖ Over every fixed place of Mount Zion, ‖ And over her convocations, ‖ A cloud by day, and smoke, ‖ And the shining of a flaming fire by night, ‖ That over all glory—a safeguard, **6** And a covering may be, ‖ For a shadow from drought by day, ‖ And for a refuge, and for a hiding place, ‖ From inundation and from rain!

5 Now let me sing for my Beloved, ‖ A song of my Beloved as to His vineyard: My beloved has a vineyard in a fruitful hill, **2** And He fences it, and casts out its stones, ‖ And plants it [with] a choice vine, ‖ And builds a tower in its midst, ‖ And has also hewn out a winepress in it, ‖ And He waits for the yielding of grapes, ‖ And it yields bad ones! **3** And now, O inhabitant of Jerusalem and man of Judah, ‖ Please judge between Me and My vineyard. **4** What [is there] to do still to My vineyard, ‖ That I have not done in it? For what reason have I waited for the yielding of grapes, ‖ And it yields [only] bad ones? **5** And now, pray, let Me cause you to know, ‖ That which I am doing to My vineyard, ‖ To turn its hedge aside, ‖ And it has been for consumption, ‖ To break down its wall, ‖ And it has been for a treading-place. **6** And I make it a waste, ‖ It is not pruned, nor arranged, ‖ And brier and thorn have gone up, ‖ And I lay a charge on the thick clouds, ‖ From raining on it rain. **7** Because the vineyard of YHWH of Hosts ‖ [Is] the house of Israel, ‖ And the man of Judah His pleasant plant, ‖ And He waits for judgment, and behold, oppression, ‖ For righteousness, and behold, a cry. **8** Woe [to] those joining house to house, ‖ They bring field near to field, ‖ Until there is no place, ‖ And you have been settled by yourselves ‖ In the midst of the land! **9** Do many houses not become a desolation by the weapons of YHWH of Hosts? Great and good without inhabitant! **10** For ten acres of vineyard yield one bath, ‖ And a homer of seed yields an ephah. **11** Woe [to] those rising early in the morning, ‖ They pursue strong drink! Lingering in twilight, wine inflames them! **12** And harp, and stringed instrument, tambourine, and pipe, ‖ And wine, have been their banquets, ‖ And they do not behold the work of YHWH, ‖ Indeed, they have not seen the work of His hands. **13** Therefore my people removed without knowledge, ‖ And its honorable ones are famished, ‖ And its multitude dried up of thirst. **14** Therefore Sheol has enlarged herself, ‖ And has opened her mouth without limit. And its honor has gone down, and its multitude, ‖ And its noise, and its exulting one—into her. **15** And the low is bowed down, and the high humbled, ‖ And the eyes of the haughty become low, **16** And YHWH of Hosts is high in judgment, ‖ And the Holy God sanctified in righteousness, **17** And lambs have fed according to their leading, ‖ And sojourners

ISAIAH

consume wastelands of the fat ones. **18** Woe [to] those drawing out iniquity with cords of vanity, ‖ And as [with] thick ropes of the cart—sin. **19** Who are saying, "Let Him hurry, ‖ Let Him hurry His work, that we may see, ‖ And let the counsel of the Holy One of Israel ‖ Draw near and come, and we know." **20** Woe [to] those saying to evil "good," and to good "evil," ‖ Putting darkness for light, and light for darkness, ‖ Putting bitter for sweet, and sweet for bitter. **21** Woe [to] the wise in their own eyes, ‖ And—before their own faces—intelligent! **22** Woe [to] the mighty to drink wine, ‖ And men of strength to mingle strong drink. **23** Declaring righteous the wicked for a bribe, ‖ And the righteousness of the righteous ‖ They turn aside from him. **24** Therefore, as a tongue of fire devours stubble, ‖ And flaming hay falls, ‖ Their root is as muck, ‖ And their flower goes up as dust. Because they have rejected the Law of YHWH of Hosts, ‖ And despised the saying of the Holy One of Israel. **25** Therefore the anger of YHWH has burned among His people, ‖ And He stretches out His hand against it, ‖ And strikes it, and the mountains tremble, ‖ And their carcass is as filth in the midst of the out-places. With all this His anger did not turn back, ‖ And still His hand is stretched out! **26** And He lifted up an ensign to the far-off nations, ‖ And hissed to it from the end of the earth, ‖ And behold, with haste, it comes swiftly. **27** There is none weary, nor stumbling in it, ‖ It does not slumber, nor sleep, ‖ Nor has the girdle of its loins been opened, ‖ Nor the strap of its sandals drawn away. **28** Whose arrows [are] sharp, and all its bows bent, ‖ Hooves of its horses have been reckoned as flint, ‖ And its wheels as a windstorm! **29** Its roaring [is] like a lioness, ‖ It roars like young lions, ‖ And it howls, and seizes prey, ‖ And carries away safely, and there is none delivering. **30** And it howls against it in that day as the howling of a sea, ‖ And it has looked attentively to the land, ‖ And behold, darkness—distress, ‖ And light has been darkened by its abundance!

6 In the year of the death of King Uzziah—I see the Lord, sitting on a throne, high and lifted up, and His train is filling the temple. **2** Seraphim are standing above it: each one has six wings; with two [each] covers its face, and with two [each] covers its feet, and with two [each] flies. **3** And this one has called to that, and has said: "HOLY, HOLY, HOLY, [is] YHWH of Hosts, ‖ The fullness of all the earth [is] His glory!" **4** And the posts of the thresholds are moved by the voice of him who is calling, and the house is full of smoke. **5** And I say, "Woe to me, for I have been silent, ‖ For I [am] a man of unclean lips, ‖ And I am dwelling in [the] midst of a people of unclean lips, ‖ Because the King, YHWH of Hosts, my eyes have seen." **6** And one of the seraphim flees to me, and in his hand—a burning coal (with tongs he has taken [it] from off the altar), **7** and he strikes against my mouth and says: "Behold, this has struck against your lips, ‖ And your iniquity is turned aside, ‖ And your sin is covered." **8** And I hear the voice of the Lord, saying, "Whom do I send? And who goes for Us?" And I say, "Here I [am], send me." **9** And He says, "Go, and you have said to this people, Hearing you hear, and you do not understand, ‖ And seeing you see, and you do not know. **10** Declare the heart of this people fat, ‖ And declare its ears heavy, ‖ And declare its eyes dazzled, ‖ Lest it see with its eyes, ‖ And hear with its ears, and consider with its heart, ‖ And it has turned back, and has health." **11** And I say, "Until when, O Lord?" And He says, "Surely until cities have been ruined without inhabitant, ‖ And houses without man, ‖ And the ground is ruined—a desolation, **12** And YHWH has put man far off, ‖ And the forsaken part [is] great in the heart of the land. **13** And yet a tenth in it, and it has turned, ‖ And has been for a burning, ‖ As a teil-tree, and as an oak, that in falling, ‖ Has substance in them, ‖ The holy seed [is] its substance!"

7 And it comes to pass in the days of Ahaz, son of Jotham, son of Uzziah, king of Judah, [that] Rezin king of Aram, and Pekah, son of Remaliah, king of Israel, have gone up to Jerusalem, to battle against it, and he is not able to fight against it. **2** And it is declared to the house of David, saying, "Aram has been led toward Ephraim," and his heart and the heart of his people is moved, like the moving of trees of a forest by the presence of wind. **3** And YHWH says to Isaiah, "Now go forth to meet Ahaz, you and your son Shear-Jashub, to the end of the conduit of the upper pool, to the highway of the fuller's

ISAIAH

field, **4** and you have said to him: Take heed, and be quiet, do not fear, ‖ And do not let your heart be timid, ‖ Because of these two tails of smoking brands, ‖ For the fierceness of the anger of Rezin and Aram, ‖ And the son of Remaliah. **5** Because that Aram counseled evil against you, Ephraim and the son of Remaliah, saying, **6** We go up into Judah, and we distress it, ‖ And we divide it to ourselves, ‖ And we cause a king to reign in its midst—The son of Tabeal. **7** Thus said Lord YHWH: It does not stand, nor will it be! **8** For the head of Aram [is] Damascus, ‖ And the head of Damascus [is] Rezin, ‖ And within sixty-five years ‖ Is Ephraim broken from [being] a people. **9** And the head of Ephraim [is] Samaria, ‖ And the head of Samaria [is] the son of Remaliah. If you do not give credence, ‖ Surely you are not steadfast." **10** And YHWH adds to speak to Ahaz, saying, **11** "Ask for a sign from your God YHWH, ‖ Make the request deep, or make [it] high upwards." **12** And Ahaz says, "I do not ask nor try YHWH." **13** And he says, "Now hear, O house of David, ‖ Is it a little thing for you to weary men, ‖ That you also weary my God? **14** Therefore the Lord Himself gives a sign to you, ‖ Behold, the virgin is conceiving, ‖ And is bringing forth a Son, ‖ And has called His Name Immanuel, **15** He eats butter and honey, ‖ When He knows to refuse evil, and to fix on good. **16** For before the youth knows ‖ To refuse evil, and to fix on good, ‖ The land you are distressed with is forsaken, because of her two kings. **17** YHWH brings on you, and on your people, ‖ And on the house of your father, ‖ Days that have not come, ‖ Even from the day of the turning aside of Ephraim from Judah, ‖ By the king of Asshur." **18** And it has come to pass in that day, ‖ YHWH hisses for a fly that [is] in the extremity of the brooks of Egypt, ‖ And for a bee that [is] in the land of Asshur. **19** And they have come, and all of them rested in the desolate valleys, ‖ And in holes of the rocks, and on all the thorns, ‖ And on all the commendable things. **20** In that day the Lord shaves, ‖ By a razor that is hired beyond the river, ‖ By the king of Asshur, ‖ The head, and the hair of the feet, ‖ Indeed, it also consumes the beard. **21** And it has come to pass in that day, ‖ A man keeps alive a heifer of the herd, ‖ And two of the flock, **22** And it has come to pass, ‖ He eats butter from the abundance of the yielding of milk, ‖ For everyone who is left in the heart of the land eats butter and honey. **23** And it has come to pass in that day, ‖ Every place where there are one thousand vines, ‖ At one thousand pieces of silver, ‖ Is for briers and for thorns. **24** He comes there with arrows and with bow, ‖ Because all the land is brier and thorn. **25** And all the hills that are kept in order with a mattock, ‖ There does not come [for] fear of brier and thorn, ‖ And it has been for the sending forth of ox, ‖ And for the treading of sheep!

8 And YHWH says to me, "Take a great tablet to yourself, and write on it with an engraving tool of man, ‖ To hurry spoil, enjoy prey." **2** And I cause faithful witnesses to testify to me, Uriah the priest, and Zechariah son of Jeberechiah. **3** And I draw near to the prophetess, and she conceives, and bears a son; and YHWH says to me, "Call his name Maher-shalal-hash-baz, **4** for before the youth knows to cry, My father, and, My mother, one takes away the wealth of Damascus and the spoil of Samaria, before the king of Asshur." **5** And YHWH adds to speak to me again, saying, **6** "Because that this people has refused ‖ The waters of Shiloah that go softly, ‖ And is rejoicing with Rezin and the son of Remaliah, **7** Therefore, behold, the Lord is bringing up on them, ‖ The waters of the river, the mighty and the great ‖ (The king of Asshur, and all his glory), ‖ And it has gone up over all its streams, ‖ And has gone on over all its banks. **8** And it has passed on into Judah, ‖ It has overflown and passed over, ‖ It comes to the neck, ‖ And the stretching out of its wings ‖ Has been the fullness of the breadth of your land, O Immanuel! **9** Be friends, O nations, and be broken, ‖ And give ear, all you far-off ones of earth, ‖ Gird yourselves, and be broken, ‖ Gird yourselves, and be broken. **10** Take counsel, and it is broken, ‖ Speak a word, and it does not stand, ‖ Because of Immanuel!" **11** For thus has YHWH spoken to me with strength of hand, and instructs me against walking in the way of this people, saying, **12** "You do not say, A confederacy, ‖ To all to whom this people says, A confederacy, ‖ And its fear you do not fear, ‖ Nor declare fearful. **13** YHWH of Hosts—Him you sanctify, ‖ And He [is] your Fear, and He your Dread, **14** And He has been for a sanctuary, ‖ And for a stone of stumbling, and for a rock of falling, ‖ To

ISAIAH

the two houses of Israel, ‖ For a trap and for a snare to the inhabitants of Jerusalem. **15** And many among them have stumbled and fallen, ‖ And been broken, and snared, and captured." **16** Bind up the testimony, ‖ Seal the Law among My disciples. **17** And I have waited for YHWH, ‖ Who is hiding His face from the house of Jacob, ‖ And I have looked for Him. **18** Behold, I, and the children whom YHWH has given to me, ‖ [Are] for signs and for wonders in Israel, ‖ From YHWH of Hosts, who is dwelling in Mount Zion. **19** And when they say to you, "Seek to those having familiar spirits, ‖ And to wizards, who chatter and mutter," ‖ Does a people not seek to its God? To the dead on behalf of the living? **20** To the Law and to the testimony! If not, let them say after this manner, "That there is no dawn to it." **21** And it has passed over into it, hardened and hungry, ‖ And it has come to pass, ‖ That it is hungry, and has been angry, ‖ And made light of its king, and of its God, ‖ And has looked upwards. **22** And it looks attentively to the land, ‖ And behold, adversity and darkness! Dimness, distress, and thick darkness are driven away, ‖ But not the dimness for which she is in distress!

9 For [there will be] no gloom on her who [is] distressed as at the former time. The land of Zebulun and the land of Naphtali, ‖ So the latter has honored the way of the sea, ‖ Beyond the Jordan, Galilee of the nations. **2** The people who are walking in darkness ‖ Have seen a great light, ‖ Dwellers in a land of death-shade, ‖ Light has shone on them. **3** You have multiplied the nation, ‖ You have made its joy great, ‖ They have rejoiced before You as the joy in harvest, ‖ As [men] rejoice in their apportioning spoil. **4** Because the yoke of its burden, ‖ And the staff of its shoulder, the rod of its exactor, ‖ You have broken as [in] the day of Midian. **5** For every battle of a warrior [is] with rushing, and raiment rolled in blood, ‖ And it has been for burning—fuel of fire. **6** For a Child has been born to us, ‖ A Son has been given to us, ‖ And the dominion is on His shoulder, ‖ And He calls His Name ‖ Wonderful, Counselor, Mighty God, ‖ Father of Eternity, Prince of Peace. **7** Of the increase of [His] dominion, ‖ And of peace, there is no end, ‖ On the throne of David, and on His kingdom, ‖ To establish it, and to support it, ‖ In judgment and in righteousness, ‖ From now on, even for all time, ‖ The zeal of YHWH of Hosts does this. **8** The Lord has sent a word into Jacob, ‖ And it has fallen in Israel. **9** And the people have known—all of it, Ephraim, and the inhabitant of Samaria, ‖ In pride and in greatness of heart, saying, **10** "Bricks have fallen, and we build hewn work, ‖ Sycamores have been cut down, and we renew cedars." **11** And YHWH sets the adversaries of Rezin on high above him, ‖ And he joins his enemies together, **12** Aram from before, and Philistia from behind, ‖ And they devour Israel with the whole mouth. With all this His anger has not turned back, ‖ And His hand is still stretched out. **13** And the people has not turned back to Him who is striking it, ‖ And they have not sought YHWH of Hosts. **14** And YHWH cuts off head and tail from Israel, ‖ Branch and reed—the same day. **15** Elderly and accepted of faces—he [is] the head, ‖ And prophet teaching falsehood—he [is] the tail. **16** And the eulogists of this people are causing to err, ‖ And its eulogized ones are consumed. **17** Therefore, the Lord does not rejoice over its young men, ‖ And He does not pity its orphans and its widows, ‖ For everyone [is] profane, and an evildoer, ‖ And every mouth is speaking folly. With all this His anger has not turned back, ‖ And His hand is still stretched out. **18** For wickedness has burned as a fire, ‖ It devours brier and thorn, ‖ And it kindles in thickets of the forest, ‖ And they lift themselves up, an exaltation of smoke! **19** In the wrath of YHWH of Hosts ‖ The land has been consumed, ‖ And the people is as fuel of fire; A man has no pity on his brother, **20** And cuts down on the right, and has been hungry, ‖ And he devours on the left, ‖ And they have not been satisfied, ‖ They each devour the flesh of his own arm. **21** Manasseh—Ephraim, and Ephraim—Manasseh, ‖ Together they [are] against Judah, ‖ With all this His anger has not turned back. And His hand is still stretched out!

10 "Woe [to] those decreeing decrees of iniquity, ‖ And writers who have prescribed perverseness, **2** Of My people, ‖ That widows may be their prey, ‖ That they may spoil the fatherless. **3** And what do you do at a day of inspection? And at desolation that comes from afar? Near whom do you flee for help? And where do

ISAIAH

you leave your glory? **4** It has bowed down without Me ‖ In the place of a bound one, ‖ And they fall in the place of the slain." With all this His anger has not turned back, ‖ And His hand is still stretched out. **5** "Woe [to] Asshur, a rod of My anger, ‖ And My indignation [is] a staff in their hand. **6** I send him against a profane nation, ‖ And concerning a people of My wrath ‖ I charge him, ‖ To spoil spoil, and to seize prey, ‖ And to make it a treading-place as the clay of out places. **7** And he does not think [it] so, ‖ And his heart does not reckon [it] so, ‖ For—to destroy [is] in his heart, ‖ And to cut off nations—not a few. **8** For he says, Are my princes not altogether kings? **9** Is not Calno as Carchemish? Is not Hamath as Arpad? Is not Samaria as Damascus? **10** As my hand has gotten to the kingdoms of a worthless thing, and their carved images, ‖ [Greater] than Jerusalem and than Samaria, **11** Do I not—as I have done to Samaria, ‖ And to her worthless things, ‖ So do to Jerusalem and to her grievous things?" **12** And it has come to pass, ‖ When the Lord fulfills all His work ‖ In Mount Zion and in Jerusalem, ‖ I see concerning the fruit of the greatness ‖ Of the heart of the king of Asshur, ‖ And concerning the glory of the height of his eyes. **13** For he has said, "I have worked by the power of my hand, ‖ And by my wisdom, for I have been intelligent, ‖ And I remove borders of the peoples, ‖ And I have spoiled their chief ones, ‖ And I put down the inhabitants as a mighty one, **14** And my hand gets to the wealth of the peoples as to a nest, ‖ And as a gathering of forsaken eggs ‖ I have gathered all the earth, ‖ And there has not been one moving wing, ‖ Or opening mouth, or whispering." **15** Does the axe glorify itself ‖ Against him who is hewing with it? Does the saw magnify itself ‖ Against him who is shaking it? As a rod waving those lifting it up! As a staff lifting up that which is not wood! **16** Therefore the Lord, the Lord of Hosts, ‖ Sends leanness among his fat ones, ‖ And under his glory ‖ He kindles a burning ‖ As the burning of a fire. **17** And the light of Israel has been for a fire, ‖ And his Holy One for a flame, ‖ And it has burned, and devoured his thorn ‖ And his brier in one day. **18** And the glory of his forest, and his fruitful field, ‖ He consumes from soul even to flesh, ‖ And it has been as the fainting of a standard-bearer. **19** And the rest of the trees of his forest [are] few, ‖ And a youth writes them. **20** And it has come to pass in that day, ‖ The remnant of Israel, ‖ And the escaped of the house of Jacob, ‖ Do not add anymore to lean on its striker, ‖ And have leaned on Y$_{HWH}$, ‖ The Holy One of Israel, in truth. **21** A remnant returns—a remnant of Jacob, ‖ To the Mighty God. **22** For though your people Israel be as the sand of the sea, ‖ A remnant of it returns, ‖ A consumption determined, ‖ Overflowing [with] righteousness. **23** For a consumption that is determined, ‖ The Lord, Y$_{HWH}$ of Hosts, ‖ Is making in the midst of all the land. **24** Therefore, thus said the Lord, Y$_{HWH}$ of Hosts: "Do not be afraid, My people, inhabiting Zion, because of Asshur, ‖ He strikes you with a rod, ‖ And his staff lifts up against you, in the way of Egypt. **25** For yet a very little [while], ‖ And the indignation has been completed, ‖ And My anger by their wearing out." **26** And Y$_{HWH}$ of Hosts is awaking for him, ‖ A scourge like the striking of Midian at the rock Oreb, ‖ And his rod [is] over the sea, ‖ And he has lifted it in the way of Egypt. **27** And it has come to pass in that day, ‖ His burden is turned from off your shoulder, ‖ And his yoke from off your neck, ‖ And the yoke has been destroyed, because of prosperity. **28** He has come in against Aiath, ‖ He has passed over into Migron, ‖ At Michmash he looks after his vessels. **29** They have gone over the passage, ‖ They have made Geba a lodging place, ‖ Rama has trembled, ‖ Gibeah of Saul fled. **30** Cry aloud [with] your voice, daughter of Gallim, ‖ Give attention, Laish! Answer her, Anathoth. **31** Madmenah has fled away, ‖ The inhabitants of the high places have hardened themselves. **32** Yet today to remain in Nob, ‖ The mountain of the daughter of Zion waves its hand, ‖ The hill of Jerusalem. **33** Behold, the Lord, Y$_{HWH}$ of Hosts, ‖ Is lopping a branch with violence, ‖ And the high of stature are cut down, ‖ And the lofty have become low, **34** And He has gone around the thickets of the forest with iron, ‖ And Lebanon falls by a mighty one!

11 And a Rod has come out from the stock of Jesse, ‖ And a Branch is fruitful from his roots. **2** The Spirit of Y$_{HWH}$ has rested on Him, ‖ The Spirit of wisdom and understanding, ‖ The Spirit of counsel and might, ‖ The Spirit of knowledge and fear of Y$_{HWH}$. **3** To refresh

ISAIAH

Him in the fear of Y<small>HWH</small>, ‖ And He does not judge by the sight of His eyes, ‖ Nor decides by the hearing of His ears. **4** And He has judged the poor in righteousness, ‖ And decided for the humble of earth in uprightness, ‖ And has struck earth with the rod of His mouth, ‖ And He puts the wicked to death with the breath of His lips. **5** And righteousness has been the girdle of His loins, ‖ And faithfulness—the girdle of His reins. **6** "And a wolf has sojourned with a lamb, ‖ And a leopard lies down with a kid, ‖ And calf, and young lion, and fatling [are] together, ‖ And a little youth is leader over them. **7** And cow and bear feed, ‖ Together their young ones lie down, ‖ And a lion eats straw as an ox. **8** And a suckling has played by the hole of a cobra, ‖ And on the den of a viper ‖ The weaned one has put his hand. **9** They do no evil, nor destroy in all My holy mountain, ‖ For the earth has been full with the knowledge of Y<small>HWH</small>, ‖ As the waters are covering the sea." **10** And there has been, in that day, ‖ A Root of Jesse that is standing for an ensign of peoples, ‖ Nations seek Him, ‖ And His rest has been glorious! **11** And it has come to pass in that day, ‖ The Lord adds His power a second time, ‖ To get the remnant of His people that is left, ‖ From Asshur, and from Egypt, ‖ And from Pathros, and from Cush, ‖ And from Elam, and from Shinar, ‖ And from Hamath, and from islands of the sea, **12** And He has lifted up an ensign to nations, ‖ And gathers the driven away of Israel, ‖ And He assembles the scattered of Judah, ‖ From the four wings of the earth. **13** And has turned aside the envy of Ephraim, ‖ And the adversaries of Judah are cut off, ‖ Ephraim does not envy Judah, ‖ And Judah does not distress Ephraim. **14** And they have flown on the shoulder of the Philistines westward, ‖ Together they spoil the sons of the east, ‖ Edom and Moab sending forth their hand, ‖ And sons of Ammon obeying them. **15** And Y<small>HWH</small> has devoted to destruction ‖ The tongue of the Sea of Egypt, ‖ And has waved His hand over the river, ‖ In the terror of His wind, ‖ And has struck it at the seven streams, ‖ And has caused [men] to tread [it] with shoes. **16** And there has been a highway, ‖ For the remnant of His people that is left, from Asshur, ‖ As there was for Israel in the day of his coming up out of the land of Egypt!

12 And you have said in that day: "I thank you, O Y<small>HWH</small>, ‖ Though You have been angry with me, ‖ Your anger turns back, ‖ And You comfort me. **2** Behold, God [is] my salvation, I trust, and do not fear, ‖ For my strength and song [is] Y<small>AH</small>—Y<small>HWH</small>, ‖ And He is to me for salvation. **3** And you have drawn waters with joy ‖ Out of the fountains of salvation, **4** And you have said in that day, ‖ Give praise to Y<small>HWH</small>, call on His Name. Make His acts known among the peoples. Make mention that His Name is set on high. **5** Praise Y<small>HWH</small>, for He has done excellence, ‖ This is known in all the earth. **6** Cry aloud, and sing, O inhabitant of Zion, ‖ For the Holy One of Israel [is] great in your midst!"

13 The burden of Babylon that Isaiah son of Amoz has seen: **2** "Lift up an ensign on a high mountain, ‖ Raise the voice to them, wave the hand, ‖ And they go into the openings of nobles. **3** I have given charge to My sanctified ones, ‖ Also I have called My mighty ones for My anger, ‖ Those rejoicing at My excellence." **4** A voice of a multitude in the mountains, ‖ A likeness of a numerous people, ‖ A voice of noise from the kingdoms of nations who are gathered, ‖ Y<small>HWH</small> of Hosts inspecting a host of battle! **5** They are coming in from a far-off land, ‖ From the end of the heavens, ‖ Y<small>HWH</small> and the instruments of His indignation, ‖ To destroy all the land. **6** Howl, for the Day of Y<small>HWH</small> [is] near, ‖ It comes as destruction from the Mighty. **7** Therefore, all hands fail, ‖ And every heart of man melts. **8** And they have been troubled, ‖ Pains and pangs take them, ‖ They are pained as a travailing woman, ‖ A man marvels at his friend, ‖ The appearance of flames—their faces! **9** Behold, the Day of Y<small>HWH</small> comes, ‖ Fierce, with wrath, and heat of anger, ‖ To make the land become a desolation, ‖ Indeed, He destroys its sinning ones from it. **10** For the stars of the heavens, and their constellations, ‖ Do not cause their light to shine, ‖ The sun has been darkened in its going out, ‖ And the moon does not cause its light to come forth. **11** "And I have appointed evil on the world, ‖ And on the wicked their iniquity, ‖ And have caused the excellence of the proud to cease, ‖ And I make the excellence of the terrible low. **12** I make man more rare than fine gold, ‖ And a common man than pure

ISAIAH

gold of Ophir. **13** Therefore I cause the heavens to tremble, ‖ And the earth shakes from its place, ‖ In the wrath of YHWH of Hosts, ‖ And in a day of the heat of His anger. **14** And it has been, as a roe driven away, ‖ And as a flock that has no gatherer, ‖ Each to his people—they turn, ‖ And each to his land—they flee. **15** Everyone who is found is thrust through, ‖ And everyone who is added falls by sword. **16** And their sucklings are dashed to pieces before their eyes, ‖ Their houses are spoiled, and their wives lain with. **17** Behold, I am stirring up the Medes against them, ‖ Who do not esteem silver, ‖ And gold—they do not delight in it. **18** And bows dash young men to pieces, ‖ And they do not pity the fruit of the womb, ‖ Their eye has no pity on sons. **19** And Babylon, the beauty of kingdoms, ‖ The glory, the excellence of the Chaldeans, ‖ Has been as overthrown by God, ‖ With Sodom and with Gomorrah. **20** She does not sit forever, ‖ Nor continue to many generations, ‖ Nor does Arab pitch tent there, ‖ And shepherds do not lie down there. **21** And desert-dwellers have lain down there, ‖ And their houses have been full of howlers, ‖ And daughters of an ostrich have dwelt there, ‖ And goats skip there. **22** And howlers—he has responded in his forsaken habitations, ‖ And dragons in palaces of delight, ‖ And her time [is] near to come, ‖ And her days are not drawn out!"

14 For YHWH loves Jacob, ‖ And has fixed again on Israel, ‖ And given them rest on their own land, ‖ And the sojourner has been joined to them, ‖ And they have been admitted to the house of Jacob. **2** And peoples have taken them, ‖ And have brought them to their place, ‖ And the house of Israel has inherited them, ‖ On the land of YHWH, ‖ For menservants and for maidservants, ‖ And they have been captors of their captors, ‖ And have ruled over their exactors. **3** And it has come to pass, ‖ In the day of YHWH's giving rest to you, ‖ From your grief, and from your trouble, ‖ And from the sharp bondage, ‖ That has been served on you, **4** That you have taken up this allegory ‖ Concerning the king of Babylon, and said, "How the exactor has ceased, **5** The golden one has ceased. YHWH has broken the staff of the wicked, ‖ The scepter of rulers. **6** He who is striking peoples in wrath, ‖ A striking without intermission, ‖ He who is ruling nations in anger, ‖ Pursuing without restraint! **7** At rest—all the earth has been quiet, ‖ They have broken forth [into] singing. **8** Even firs have rejoiced over you, ‖ Cedars of Lebanon, [saying], Since you have lain down, ‖ The hewer does not come up against us. **9** Sheol beneath has been troubled at you, ‖ To meet your coming in, ‖ It is waking up Rephaim for you, ‖ All chief ones of earth, ‖ It has raised up from their thrones ‖ All kings of nations. **10** All of them answer and say to you, Even you have become weak like us! You have become like to us! **11** Your excellence has been brought down to Sheol, ‖ The noise of your stringed instruments, ‖ The worm has been spread out under you, ‖ Indeed, the worm is covering you. **12** How you have fallen from the heavens, ‖ O shining one, son of the dawn! You have been cut down to earth, ‖ O weakener of nations. **13** And you said in your heart: I go up into the heavens, ‖ I raise my throne above the stars of God, ‖ And I sit on the mountain of meeting in the sides of the north. **14** I go up above the heights of a thick cloud, I am like to the Most High. **15** Only—you are brought down to Sheol, ‖ To the sides of the pit. **16** Your beholders look to you, they attend to you, ‖ Is this the man causing the earth to tremble, ‖ Shaking kingdoms? **17** He has made the world as a wilderness, ‖ And he has broken down his cities, ‖ He did not open the house of his bound ones. **18** All kings of nations—all of them, ‖ Have lain down in glory, each in his house, **19** And you have been cast out of your grave, ‖ As an abominable branch, raiment of the slain, ‖ Thrust through ones of the sword, ‖ Going down to the sons of the pit, ‖ As a carcass trodden down. **20** You are not united with them in burial, ‖ For you have destroyed your land, ‖ You have slain your people, ‖ The seed of evildoers is not named for all time. **21** Prepare slaughter for his sons; Because of the iniquity of their fathers, ‖ They do not rise, nor have possessed the land, ‖ Nor filled the face of the world [with] cities. **22** And I have risen up against them," ‖ A declaration of YHWH of Hosts, ‖ "And have cut off, in reference to Babylon, ‖ Name and remnant, and continuator and successor," ‖ A declaration of YHWH. **23** "And have made it for a possession of a hedgehog, ‖ And ponds of waters, ‖ And swept it with the broom of

ISAIAH

destruction." ‖ A declaration of YHWH of Hosts! **24** YHWH of Hosts has sworn, saying, "As I thought—so has it not been? And as I counseled—it stands; **25** To break Asshur in My land, ‖ And I tread him down on My mountain, ‖ And his yoke has turned from off them, ‖ Indeed, his burden turns aside from off their shoulder. **26** This [is] the counsel that is counseled for all the earth, ‖ And this [is] the hand that is stretched out for all the nations. **27** For YHWH of Hosts has purposed, ‖ And who makes void? And His hand that is stretched out, ‖ Who turns it back?" **28** In the year of the death of King Ahaz was this burden: **29** "Do not rejoice, Philistia, all of you, ‖ That the rod of your striker has been broken, ‖ For from the root of a serpent comes out a viper, ‖ And its fruit [is] a flying, burning serpent. **30** And the firstborn of the poor have delighted, ‖ And the needy lie down in confidence, ‖ And I have put to death your root with famine, ‖ And it slays your remnant. **31** Howl, O gate; cry, O city, ‖ You are melted, Philistia, all of you, ‖ For smoke has come from the north, ‖ And there is none alone in his set places." **32** And what does one answer the messengers of a nation? That YHWH has founded Zion, ‖ And the poor of His people take refuge in it!

15 The burden of Moab. Because in a night Ar of Moab was destroyed—It has been cut off, ‖ Because in a night Kir of Moab was destroyed—It has been cut off. **2** He has gone up to Bajith and Dibon, ‖ The high places—to weep, ‖ Moab howls on Nebo and on Medeba, ‖ Baldness [is] on all its heads, every beard cut off. **3** In its out-places they girded on sackcloth, ‖ On its pinnacles, and in its broad places, ‖ Everyone howls—going down with weeping. **4** And Heshbon and Elealeh cry, ‖ Their voice has been heard to Jahaz, ‖ Therefore the armed ones of Moab shout, ‖ His life has been grievous to him. **5** My heart [is] toward Moab, ‖ Her fugitives cry to Zoar, a heifer of the third [year], ‖ For—the ascent of Luhith—He goes up in it with weeping, ‖ For in the way of Horonaim, ‖ They wake up a cry of destruction. **6** For the waters of Nimrim are desolations, ‖ For the hay has been withered, ‖ The tender grass has been finished, ‖ There has not been a green thing. **7** Therefore the abundance he made, and their store, ‖ They carry to the Brook of the Willows. **8** For the cry has gone around the border of Moab, ‖ Its howling [is] to Eglaim, ‖ And its howling [is] to Beer-Elim. **9** For the waters of Dimon have been full of blood, ‖ For I set additions on Dimon, ‖ A lion for the escaped of Moab, ‖ And for the remnant of Adamah!

16 Send a lamb [to] the ruler of the land, ‖ From Selah in the wilderness, ‖ To the mountain of the daughter of Zion. **2** And it has come to pass, ‖ As a wandering bird, cast out of a nest, ‖ Are daughters of Moab, [at] fords of Arnon. **3** Bring in counsel, do judgment, ‖ Make your shadow as night in the midst of noon, ‖ Hide outcasts, do not reveal the wanderer. **4** My outcasts sojourn in you, O Moab, ‖ Be a secret hiding place for them, ‖ From the face of a destroyer, ‖ For the extortioner has ceased, ‖ Devastation has been finished, ‖ The tramplers are consumed out of the land. **5** And the throne is established in kindness, ‖ And [One] has sat on it in truth, in the tent of David, ‖ Judging and seeking judgment, and hastening righteousness. **6** We have heard of the pride of Moab—very proud, ‖ His pride, and his arrogance, and his wrath—his boastings [are] not right. **7** Therefore Moab howls for Moab, all of it howls, ‖ It meditates for the grape-cakes of Kir-Hareseth, ‖ They are surely struck. **8** Because fields of Heshbon languish, ‖ The vine of Sibmah, ‖ Lords of nations beat her choice vines, ‖ They have come to Jazer, ‖ They have wandered in a wilderness, ‖ Her plants have spread themselves, ‖ They have passed over a sea. **9** Therefore I weep with the weeping of Jazer, ‖ The vine of Sibmah, ‖ I water you [with] my tear, ‖ O Heshbon and Elealeh, ‖ For—for your summer fruits, and for your harvest, ‖ The shouting has fallen. **10** And gladness and joy have been removed from the fruitful field, ‖ And they do not sing in vineyards, nor shout, ‖ The treader does not tread wine in the presses, ‖ I have caused shouting to cease. **11** Therefore my bowels sound as a harp for Moab, ‖ And my inward parts for Kir-Haresh. **12** And it has come to pass, when it has been seen, ‖ That Moab has been weary on the high place, ‖ And he has come to his sanctuary to pray, ‖ And is not able. **13** This [is] the word that YHWH has spoken to Moab from that time, **14** And now YHWH has spoken, saying, "In three

ISAIAH

years, as years of a hired worker, ‖ The glory of Moab is lightly esteemed, ‖ With all the great multitude, ‖ And the remnant [is] little, small, not mighty!"

17 The burden of Damascus. Behold, Damascus is taken away from [being] a city, ‖ And it has been a heap—a ruin. **2** The cities of Aroer are forsaken, ‖ They are for droves, and they have lain down, ‖ And there is none troubling. **3** And the fortress has ceased from Ephraim, ‖ And the kingdom from Damascus, ‖ And the remnant of Aram are as the glory of the sons of Israel, ‖ A declaration of YHWH of Hosts! **4** And it has come to pass in that day, ‖ The glory of Jacob waxes poor, ‖ And the fatness of his flesh waxes lean. **5** And it has come to pass, ‖ As the gathering of the standing grain by the reaper, ‖ And his arm reaps the ears, ‖ And it has come to pass, ‖ As the gathering of the ears in the Valley of Rephaim, **6** And gleanings have been left in him, ‖ As the surrounding of an olive, ‖ Two—three berries on the top of a branch, ‖ Four—five on the fruitful boughs, ‖ A declaration of YHWH, God of Israel! **7** In that day man looks to His Maker, ‖ Indeed, his eyes look to the Holy One of Israel, **8** And he does not look to the altars. The work of his own hands, ‖ And that which his own fingers made, He does not see—the Asherim and the images. **9** In that day the cities of his strength are ‖ As the forsaken thing of the forest, ‖ And the branch that they have left, ‖ Because of the sons of Israel, ‖ It has also been a desolation. **10** Because you have forgotten the God of your salvation, ‖ And have not remembered the Rock of your strength, ‖ Therefore you plant plants of pleasantness, ‖ And sow it with a strange shoot, **11** You cause your plant to become great in the day, ‖ And make your seed to flourish in the morning, ‖ The harvest [is] a heap in a day of overflowing, ‖ And of mortal pain. **12** Woe [to] the multitude of many peoples, ‖ They sound as the sounding of seas; And the roaring of nations, ‖ As the roaring of mighty waters [that] make a crashing. **13** Nations crash as the roaring of many waters, ‖ And He rebuked them, ‖ And they fled far off, ‖ And were pursued as chaff of hills before wind, ‖ And as a rolling thing before a windstorm. **14** At evening, behold, terror, before morning it is not, ‖ This [is] the portion of our spoilers, ‖ And the lot of our plunderers!

18 Behold, land shadowed [with] wings, ‖ That [is] beyond the rivers of Cush, **2** That is sending ambassadors by sea, ‖ Even with implements of reed on the face of the waters—Go, swift messengers, ‖ To a nation drawn out and peeled, ‖ To a people fearful from its beginning and onward, ‖ A nation meeting out by line, and treading down, ‖ Whose land floods have spoiled. **3** All you inhabitants of the world, ‖ And you dwellers of earth, ‖ At the lifting up of an ensign on hills you look, ‖ And at the blowing of a horn you hear. **4** For thus said YHWH to me: "I rest, and I look on My settled place, ‖ As a clear heat on an herb. As a thick cloud of dew in the heat of harvest. **5** For before harvest, when the flower is perfect, ‖ And the blossom is producing unripe fruit, ‖ Then [One] has cut the sprigs with pruning hooks, ‖ And the branches He has turned aside, cut down. **6** They are left together to the ravenous bird of the mountains, ‖ And to the beast of the earth, ‖ And the ravenous bird has summered on them, ‖ And every beast of the earth winters on them. **7** At that time a present is brought to YHWH of Hosts, ‖ A nation drawn out and peeled. Even of a people fearful from the beginning until now, ‖ A nation meting out by line, and treading down, ‖ Whose land floods have spoiled, ‖ To the place of the Name of YHWH of Hosts—Mount Zion!"

19 The burden of Egypt. Behold, YHWH is riding on a swift thick cloud, ‖ And He has entered Egypt, ‖ And the idols of Egypt have been moved at His presence, ‖ And the heart of Egypt melts in its midst. **2** And I armed Egyptians against Egyptians, ‖ And they fought, each against his brother, ‖ And each against his neighbor, ‖ City against city, kingdom against kingdom. **3** And the spirit of Egypt has been emptied out in its midst. And I swallow up its counsel, ‖ And they have sought to the idols, ‖ And to the charmers, ‖ And to those having familiar spirits, ‖ And to the wizards. **4** And I have delivered the Egyptians ‖ Into the hand of a hard lord, ‖ And a strong king rules over them, ‖ A declaration of the Lord, YHWH of Hosts. **5** And waters have failed from the sea, ‖ And a river is desolated and dried up.

ISAIAH

6 And they have turned away the flowings, ‖ Brooks of the bulwark have been weak and dried up, ‖ Reed and flag have withered. **7** Exposed things by the brook, by the edge of the brook, ‖ And every sown thing of the brook, has withered, ‖ It has been driven away, and is not. **8** And the fishers have lamented, ‖ And all casting a hook into the brook have mourned, ‖ And those spreading dragnets on the face of the waters have languished. **9** And makers of fine flax have been ashamed, ‖ And weavers of networks. **10** And its foundations have been struck, ‖ All making wages [are] afflicted in soul. **11** Only, the princes of Zoan [are] fools, ‖ The counsel of the wise ones of the counselors of Pharaoh has become brutish. How do you say to Pharaoh, "I am a son of the wise, a son of kings of antiquity?" **12** Where [are] they now, your wise ones? Indeed, let them now tell [it] to you, ‖ And they know what YHWH of Hosts has counseled against Egypt! **13** Princes of Zoan have been foolish, ‖ Princes of Noph have been lifted up, ‖ And they have caused Egypt to err, ‖ The chief of her tribes. **14** YHWH has mingled in her midst ‖ A spirit of perverseness, ‖ And they have caused Egypt to err in all its work, ‖ As a drunkard errs in his vomit. **15** And there is no work to Egypt, ‖ That head or tail, branch or reed, may do. **16** In that day Egypt is like women, ‖ And it has mourned, and been afraid, ‖ Because of the waving of the hand of YHWH of Hosts, ‖ That He is waving over it. **17** And the land of Judah has been to Egypt for a cause of staggering, ‖ Everyone who mentions it, fears for himself, ‖ Because of the counsel of YHWH of Hosts, ‖ That He is counseling against it. **18** In that day there are five cities in the land of Egypt, ‖ Speaking the lip of Canaan, ‖ And swearing to YHWH of Hosts, ‖ "The city of destruction," is said of one. **19** In that day there is an altar to YHWH ‖ In the midst of the land of Egypt, ‖ And a standing pillar to YHWH near its border, **20** And it has been for a sign and for a testimony, ‖ To YHWH of Hosts in the land of Egypt, ‖ For they cry to YHWH from the face of oppressors, ‖ And He sends a Savior to them, ‖ Even a great one, and has delivered them. **21** And YHWH has been known to Egypt, ‖ And the Egyptians have known YHWH in that day, ‖ And done sacrifice and present, ‖ And vowed a vow to YHWH, and completed [it]. **22** And YHWH has struck Egypt, striking and healing, ‖ And they have turned back to YHWH, ‖ And He has accepted their plea, ‖ And has healed them. **23** In that day a highway is out of Egypt to Asshur, ‖ And the Assyrians have come into Egypt, ‖ And the Egyptians into Asshur, ‖ And the Egyptians have served with the Assyrians. **24** In that day Israel is third, ‖ With Egypt, and with Asshur, ‖ A blessing in the heart of the earth. **25** In that YHWH of Hosts blessed it, saying, "Blessed [is] My people—Egypt, ‖ And the work of My hands—Asshur, ‖ And My inheritance—Israel!"

20 In the year of the coming in of Tartan to Ashdod, when Sargon king of Asshur sends him, and he fights against Ashdod and captures it, **2** at that time YHWH spoke by the hand of Isaiah son of Amoz, saying, "Go, and you have loosed the sackcloth from off your loins, and you draw your sandal from off your foot," and he does so, going naked and barefoot. **3** And YHWH says, "As My servant Isaiah has gone naked and barefoot three years, a sign and a wonder for Egypt and for Cush, **4** so the king of Asshur leads the captivity of Egypt, and the expulsion of Cush, young and old, naked and barefoot, with seat uncovered—the nakedness of Egypt; **5** and they have been frightened and ashamed of Cush their confidence, and of Egypt their beauty, **6** and the inhabitant of this island has said in that day—Behold, thus [is] our trust, ‖ To where we have fled for help, ‖ To be delivered from the king of Asshur, ‖ And how do we escape—we?"

21 The burden of the wilderness of the sea. Like windstorms in the south for passing through, ‖ It has come from the wilderness, ‖ From a fearful land. **2** A hard vision has been declared to me, ‖ The treacherous dealer is dealing treacherously, ‖ And the destroyer is destroying. Go up, O Elam, besiege, O Media, ‖ I have caused all its sighing to cease. **3** Therefore my loins have been filled [with] great pain, ‖ Pangs have seized me as pangs of a travailing woman, ‖ I have been bent down by hearing, ‖ I have been troubled by seeing. **4** My heart has wandered, trembling has terrified me, ‖ He has made the twilight of my desire a fear to me, **5** Arrange the table, watch in the watchtower, ‖ Eat, drink, rise, you heads,

ISAIAH

anoint the shield, **6** For thus said the Lord to me: "Go, station the watchman, ‖ Let him declare that which he sees." **7** And he has seen a chariot—a couple of horsemen, ‖ The rider of a donkey, the rider of a camel, ‖ And he has given attention—He has increased attention! **8** And he cries, "A lion, my lord! I am continually standing on a watchtower by day, ‖ And I am stationed on my ward whole nights. **9** And behold, this, the chariot of a man is coming, ‖ A couple of horsemen." And he answers and says: "Fallen, fallen has Babylon, ‖ And He has broken all the carved images of her gods to the earth. **10** O my threshing, and the son of my floor, ‖ That which I heard from Y<small>HWH</small> of Hosts, God of Israel, ‖ I have declared to you!" **11** The burden of Dumah. [One] is calling to me from Seir, "Watchman, what of the night? Watchman, what of the night?" **12** The watchman has said, "Morning has come, and also night, ‖ If you inquire, inquire, return, come." **13** The burden on Arabia. You lodge in a forest in Arabia, ‖ O caravans of Dedanim. **14** Inhabitants of the land of Tema ‖ Have brought water to meet the thirsty, ‖ With his bread they came before a fugitive. **15** For they fled from the face of destructions, ‖ From the face of an outstretched sword, ‖ And from the face of a trodden bow, ‖ And from the face of the grievousness of battle. **16** For thus said the Lord to me: "Within a year, as years of a hired worker, ‖ All the glory of Kedar has been consumed. **17** And the remnant of the number of bow-men, ‖ The mighty of the sons of Kedar, are few, ‖ For Y<small>HWH</small>, God of Israel, has spoken!"

22 The burden of the Valley of Vision. What is [troubling] you now, that you have gone up, ‖ All of you—to the roofs? **2** Full of stirs—a noisy city—an exulting city, ‖ Your pierced are not pierced of the sword, ‖ Nor dead in battle. **3** All your rulers fled from the bow together, ‖ All found of you have been bound, ‖ They have been kept bound together, ‖ They have fled far off. **4** Therefore I said, "Look [away] from me, ‖ I am bitter in my weeping, do not hurry to comfort me, ‖ For the destruction of the daughter of my people." **5** For a day of noise, and of treading down, ‖ And of perplexity, [is] to the Lord, Y<small>HWH</small> of Hosts, ‖ In the Valley of Vision, digging down a wall, ‖ And crying to the mountain. **6** And Elam has carried a quiver, ‖ In a chariot of men—horsemen, ‖ And Kir has exposed a shield. **7** And it comes to pass, ‖ The choice of your valleys have been full of chariots, ‖ And the horsemen diligently place themselves at the gate. **8** And one removes the covering of Judah, ‖ And in that day you look ‖ To the armor of the house of the forest, **9** And you have seen the breaches of the City of David, ‖ For they have become many, ‖ And you gather the waters of the lower pool, **10** And you numbered the houses of Jerusalem, ‖ And you break down the houses to fortify the wall. **11** And you made a ditch between the two walls, ‖ For the waters of the old pool, ‖ And you have not looked to its Maker, ‖ And you have not seen its Framer of old. **12** And the Lord calls, Y<small>HWH</small> of Hosts, ‖ In that day, to weeping and to lamentation, ‖ And to baldness and to girding on of sackcloth, **13** And behold, joy and gladness, slaying of oxen, ‖ And slaughtering of sheep, ‖ Eating of flesh, and drinking of wine, ‖ Eat and drink, for tomorrow we die. **14** And it has been revealed in my ears, ‖ [By] Y<small>HWH</small> of Hosts: This iniquity is not pardoned to you, ‖ Until you die, said the Lord, Y<small>HWH</small> of Hosts. **15** Thus said the Lord, Y<small>HWH</small> of Hosts: "Go forth, go to this steward, ‖ To Shebna, who [is] over the house: **16** What are you [doing] here? And who has [allowed] you here? That you have hewn out a tomb for yourself here? Hewing his tomb on high, ‖ Carving a dwelling for himself in a rock. **17** Behold, Y<small>HWH</small> is casting you up and down, ‖ A casting up and down, O mighty one, **18** And your coverer covering, wrapping around, ‖ Wraps you around, O babbler, ‖ On a land of broad sides—there you die, ‖ And there the chariots of your glory [are] the shame of the house of your lord. **19** And I have thrust you from your station, ‖ And he throws you down from your office. **20** And it has come to pass in that day, ‖ That I have called to My servant, ‖ To Eliakim son of Hilkiah. **21** And I have clothed him with your coat, ‖ And I strengthen him with your girdle, ‖ And I give your garment into his hand, ‖ And he has been for a father to the inhabitant of Jerusalem, ‖ And to the house of Judah. **22** And I have placed the key ‖ Of the house of David on his shoulder, ‖ And he has opened, and none is shutting, ‖ And has shut, and none is opening. **23** And I have fixed him [as] a nail in a steadfast place, ‖

ISAIAH

And he has been for a throne of glory ‖ To the house of his father. **24** And they have hanged on him ‖ All the glory of the house of his father, ‖ The offspring and the issue, ‖ All vessels of small quality, ‖ From vessels of basins to all vessels of flagons. **25** In that day—a declaration of YHWH of Hosts, ‖ The nail that is fixed is moved ‖ In a steadfast place, ‖ Indeed, it has been cut down, and has fallen, ‖ And the burden that [is] on it has been cut off, ‖ For YHWH has spoken!"

23 The Burden of Tyre. Howl, you ships of Tarshish, ‖ For it has been destroyed, ‖ Without house, without entrance, ‖ From the land of Chittim it was revealed to them. **2** Be silent, you inhabitants of the island, ‖ Trader of Sidon, passing the sea, they filled you. **3** And the seed of Sihor [is] in many waters, ‖ Her increase [is] the harvest of the brook, ‖ And she is a market of nations. **4** Be ashamed, O Sidon; for the sea spoke, ‖ The strength of the sea, saying, "I have not been pained, nor have I brought forth, ‖ Nor have I nourished young men, [nor] brought up virgins." **5** As they are pained [at] the report of Egypt, ‖ So [at] the report of Tyre. **6** Pass over to Tarshish, howl, you inhabitants of the island, **7** Is this your exulting one? Her antiquity [is] from the days of old, ‖ Her own feet carry her far off to sojourn. **8** Who has counseled this against Tyre, ‖ The crowning one, whose traders [are] princes, ‖ Her merchants—the honored of earth? **9** YHWH of Hosts has counseled it, ‖ To defile the excellence of all beauty, ‖ To make light all the honored of earth. **10** Pass through your land as a brook, ‖ Daughter of Tarshish, ‖ There is no longer a girdle. **11** He has stretched out His hand over the sea, ‖ He has caused kingdoms to tremble, ‖ YHWH has charged concerning the merchant one, ‖ To destroy her strong places. **12** And He says, "You do not add to exult anymore, ‖ O oppressed one, virgin daughter of Sidon, ‖ To Chittim arise, pass over, ‖ Even there—there is no rest for you." **13** Behold, the land of the Chaldeans—this people was not, ‖ Asshur founded it for desert-dwellers, ‖ They raised its watchtowers, ‖ They lifted up her palaces—He has appointed her for a ruin! **14** Howl, you ships of Tarshish, ‖ For your strength has been destroyed. **15** And it has come to pass in that day, ‖ That Tyre is forgotten seventy years, ‖ According to the days of one king. At the end of seventy years there is to Tyre as the song of the harlot. **16** Take a harp, go around the city, O forgotten harlot, play well, ‖ Multiply song that you may be remembered. **17** And it has come to pass, ‖ At the end of seventy years YHWH inspects Tyre, ‖ And she has returned to her wage, ‖ And she committed fornication ‖ With all kingdoms of the earth on the face of the ground. **18** And her merchandise and her wage have been holy to YHWH, ‖ Not treasured up nor stored, ‖ For her merchandise is to those sitting before YHWH, ‖ To eat to satiety, and for a lasting covering!

24 Behold, YHWH is emptying the earth, ‖ And is making it desolate, ‖ And has overturned [it on] its face, ‖ And has scattered its inhabitants. **2** And it has been—as a people so a priest, ‖ As the servant so his master, ‖ As the maidservant so her mistress, ‖ As the buyer so the seller, ‖ As the lender so the borrower, ‖ As the usurer so he who is lifting [it] on himself. **3** The earth is utterly emptied, and utterly spoiled, ‖ For YHWH has spoken this word: **4** The earth has mourned, faded, ‖ The world has languished, faded, ‖ They have languished—the high place of the people of the earth. **5** And the earth has been defiled under its inhabitants, ‖ Because they have transgressed laws, ‖ They have changed a statute, ‖ They have made void a perpetual covenant. **6** Therefore a curse has consumed the earth, ‖ And the inhabitants in it become desolate, ‖ Therefore inhabitants of the earth have been consumed, ‖ And few men have been left. **7** The new wine has mourned, the vine languished, ‖ All the joyful of heart have sighed. **8** The joy of tambourines has ceased, ‖ The noise of exulting ones has ceased, ‖ The joy of a harp has ceased. **9** They do not drink wine with a song, ‖ Strong drink is bitter to those drinking it. **10** It was broken down—a city of emptiness, ‖ Every house has been shut from [its] entrance. **11** In out-places [is] a cry over the wine, ‖ All joy has been darkened, ‖ The joy of the land has been removed. **12** Desolation [is] left in the city, ‖ And the gate is struck [with] ruin. **13** When thus it is in the heart of the land, ‖ In the midst of the peoples, ‖ As the surrounding of the olive, ‖ As gleanings when harvest

ISAIAH

has been finished, **14** They lift up their voice, ‖ They sing of the excellence of YHWH, ‖ They have cried aloud from the sea. **15** Therefore honor YHWH in prosperity, ‖ In islands of the sea, the Name of YHWH, God of Israel. **16** From the skirt of the earth we heard songs, ‖ The desire of the righteous. And I say, "Leanness [is] to me, ‖ Leanness [is] to me, woe [is] to me." Treacherous dealers dealt treacherously, ‖ Indeed, treachery, treacherous dealers dealt treacherously. **17** Fear, and a snare, and a trap, ‖ [Are] on you, O inhabitant of the earth. **18** And it has come to pass, ‖ He who is fleeing from the noise of the fear falls into the snare, ‖ And he who is coming up from the midst of the snare, ‖ Is captured by the trap, ‖ For windows have been opened on high, ‖ And foundations of the earth are shaken. **19** The earth has been utterly broken down, ‖ The earth has been utterly broken, ‖ The earth has been utterly moved. **20** The earth staggers greatly as a drunkard, ‖ And it has been moved as a lodge, ‖ And its transgression has been heavy on it, ‖ And it has fallen, and does not add to rise. **21** And it has come to pass in that day, ‖ YHWH lays a charge on the host of the high place in the high place, ‖ And on the kings of the earth on the earth. **22** And they have been gathered—A gathering of bound ones in a pit, ‖ And they have been shut up in a prison, ‖ And after a multitude of days are inspected. **23** And the moon has been confounded, ‖ And the sun has been ashamed, ‖ For YHWH of Hosts has reigned ‖ In Mount Zion, and in Jerusalem, ‖ And before His elderly—glory!

25 O YHWH, You [are] my God, I exalt You, I confess Your Name, ‖ For You have done a wonderful thing, ‖ Counsels of old, steadfastness, O steadfast One. **2** For You made of a city a heap, ‖ Of a fortified city a ruin, ‖ A high place of strangers from [being] a city, ‖ It is not built for all time. **3** Therefore a strong people honors You, ‖ A city of the terrible nations fears You. **4** For You have been a stronghold for the poor, ‖ A stronghold for the needy in his distress, ‖ A refuge from storm, a shadow from heat, ‖ When the spirit of the terrible [is] as a storm—a wall. **5** As heat in a dry place, ‖ You humble the noise of strangers, ‖ [As] heat with the shadow of a thick cloud, ‖ The singing of the terrible is humbled. **6** And YHWH of Hosts has made, ‖ For all the peoples in this mountain, ‖ A banquet of fat things, ‖ A banquet of preserved things, ‖ Fat things full of marrow, ‖ Preserved things—refined. **7** And He has swallowed up in this mountain ‖ The face of the wrapping that is wrapped over all the peoples, ‖ And of the covering that is spread over all the nations. **8** He has swallowed up death in victory, ‖ And Lord YHWH has wiped [the] tear from off all faces, ‖ And He turns aside the reproach of His people from off all the earth, ‖ For YHWH has spoken. **9** And [one] has said in that day, "Behold, this [is] our God, ‖ We waited for Him, and He saves us, ‖ This [is] YHWH, we have waited for Him, ‖ We are glad and rejoice in His salvation!" **10** For the hand of YHWH rests on this mountain, ‖ And Moab is trodden down under Him, ‖ As straw is trodden down on a dunghill. **11** And He spread out His hands in its midst, ‖ As the swimmer spreads out to swim; And He has humbled his excellence ‖ With the machinations of his hands. **12** And the fortress of the high place of your walls ‖ He has bowed down—He has made low, ‖ He has caused [it] to come to the earth—to dust.

26 In that day this song is sung in the land of Judah: "We have a strong city, ‖ He makes salvation [for] walls and bulwark. **2** Open the gates, ‖ That a righteous nation may enter, ‖ Preserving steadfastness. **3** You keep [him] in peace [whose] imagination [is] stayed—peace! For he is confident in You. **4** Trust in YHWH forever, ‖ For in YAH—YHWH [is] a rock of ages, **5** For He bowed down the dwellers on high, ‖ A city set on high He makes low, ‖ He makes it low to the earth, ‖ He causes it to come to the dust, **6** A foot treads it down, ‖ Feet of the poor—steps of the weak. **7** The path for the righteous [is] uprightness, ‖ O upright One, ‖ You ponder the path of the righteous. **8** Also, [in] the path of Your judgments, ‖ O YHWH, we have waited [for] You, ‖ To Your Name and to Your remembrance ‖ [Is] the desire of the soul. **9** I desired You in the night [with] my soul, ‖ Also, I seek You earnestly [with] my spirit within me, ‖ For when Your judgments [are] on the earth, ‖ The inhabitants of the world have learned righteousness. **10** The wicked finds favor, ‖ He has not learned righteousness, ‖ He deals perversely in a land of

ISAIAH

straightforwardness, ‖ And does not see the excellence of YHWH. **11** O YHWH, Your hand [is] high—they do not see, ‖ They see the zeal of the people, and are ashamed, ‖ Also, the fire consumes Your adversaries. **12** O YHWH, You appoint peace to us, ‖ For You have also worked all our works for us. **13** O our God YHWH, lords have ruled us besides You, ‖ Only, by You we make mention of Your Name. **14** Dead—they do not live, ‖ Rephaim, they do not rise, ‖ Therefore You have inspected and destroy them, ‖ Indeed, you destroy all their memory. **15** You have added to the nation, O YHWH, ‖ You have added to the nation, ‖ You have been honored, ‖ You have put all the ends of the earth far off. **16** O YHWH, in distress they missed You, ‖ They have poured out a whisper, ‖ Your discipline [is] on them. **17** When a pregnant woman comes near to the birth, ‖ She is pained—she cries in her pangs, ‖ So we have been from Your face, O YHWH. **18** We have conceived, we have been pained. We have brought forth, as it were, wind, ‖ We do not work salvation in the earth, ‖ Nor do the inhabitants of the world fall. **19** Your dead live—My dead body, they rise. Awake and sing, you dwellers in the dust, ‖ For the dew of herbs [is] your dew, ‖ And you cause the land of Rephaim to fall. **20** Come, My people, enter into your inner chambers, ‖ And shut your doors behind you, ‖ Hide yourself shortly [for] a moment until the indignation passes over. **21** For behold, YHWH is coming out of His place, ‖ To charge the iniquity of the inhabitant of the earth on him, ‖ And the earth has revealed her blood, ‖ Nor does she cover her slain anymore!"

27 In that day YHWH lays a charge, ‖ With His sword—the sharp, and the great, and the strong, ‖ On leviathan—a fleeing serpent, ‖ And on leviathan—a crooked serpent, ‖ And He has slain the dragon that [is] in the sea. **2** In that day respond to her, "A desirable vineyard, **3** I, YHWH, am its keeper, ‖ I water it every moment, ‖ Lest any lay a charge against it, ‖ Night and day I keep it! **4** Fury is not in Me; Who gives Me a brier—a thorn in battle? I step into it, ‖ I burn it at once. **5** Or—he takes hold on My strength, ‖ [That] he makes peace with Me, ‖ [And] he makes peace with Me." **6** He causes those coming in to take root, ‖ Jacob blossoms, and Israel has flourished, ‖ And they have filled the face of the world [with] increase. **7** Has He struck him as the striking of his striker? Does He slay as the slaying of his slain? **8** In measure, in sending it forth, you strive with it, ‖ He has taken away by His sharp wind, ‖ In the day of an east wind, **9** Therefore the iniquity of Jacob is covered by this, ‖ And this [is] all the fruit—To take away his sin, ‖ In his setting all the stones of an altar, ‖ As chalkstones beaten in pieces, ‖ They do not rise—Asherim and images. **10** For the fortified city [is] alone, ‖ A habitation cast out and forsaken as a wilderness, ‖ There the calf delights, ‖ And there it lies down, ‖ And has consumed its branches. **11** In the withering of its branch it is broken off, ‖ Women are coming in [and] setting it on fire, ‖ For it [is] not a people of understanding, ‖ Therefore its Maker does not pity it, ‖ And its Former does not favor it. **12** And it has come to pass in that day, ‖ YHWH beats out from the branch of the river, ‖ To the stream of Egypt, ‖ And you are gathered one by one, O sons of Israel. **13** And it has come to pass in that day, ‖ It is blown with a great horn, ‖ And those perishing in the land of Asshur have come in, ‖ And those cast out in the land of Egypt, ‖ And have bowed themselves to YHWH, ‖ In the holy mountain—in Jerusalem!

28 Woe [to] the proud crown of the drunkards of Ephraim. And the fading flower of the beauty of his glory, ‖ That [is] on the head of the fat valley of the broken down of wine. **2** Behold, a mighty and strong one [is] to the Lord, ‖ As a storm of hail—a destructive shower, ‖ As an inundation of mighty waters overflowing, ‖ He cast down to the earth with the hand. **3** The proud crown of the drunkards of Ephraim is trodden down by feet, **4** And the fading flower of the beauty of his glory ‖ That [is] on the head of the fat valley, ‖ Has been as its first-fruit before summer, ‖ That its beholder sees; He swallows it while it [is] yet in his hand. **5** In that day YHWH of Hosts is ‖ For a crown of beauty, and for a circlet of glory, ‖ To the remnant of His people. **6** And for a spirit of judgment ‖ To him who is sitting in the judgment, ‖ And for might [to] those turning back the battle to the gate. **7** And even these have erred through wine, ‖ And have wandered through strong drink, ‖ Priest and prophet

ISAIAH

erred through strong drink, ‖ They have been swallowed up of the wine, ‖ They wandered because of the strong drink, ‖ They have erred in seeing, ‖ They have stumbled judicially. **8** For all tables have been full of vomit, ‖ Filth—without place! **9** By whom does He teach knowledge? And by whom does He cause to understand the report? The weaned from milk, the removed from breasts, **10** For rule on rule, rule on rule, ‖ Line on line, line on line, ‖ A little here, a little there, **11** For by scorned lip, and by another tongue, ‖ Does He speak to this people. **12** To whom He has said, "This [is] the rest, give rest to the weary, ‖ And this—the refreshing": And they have not been willing to hear, **13** And to whom a word of YHWH has been, ‖ Rule on rule, rule on rule, ‖ Line on line, line on line, ‖ A little here, a little there, ‖ So that they go and have stumbled backward, ‖ And been broken, and snared, and captured. **14** Therefore, hear a word of YHWH, you men of scorning, ‖ Ruling this people that [is] in Jerusalem. **15** Because you have said: "We have made a covenant with death, ‖ And we have made a provision with Sheol, ‖ An overflowing scourge, when it passes over, ‖ Does not meet us, ‖ Though we have made a lie our refuge, ‖ And have been hidden in falsehood." **16** Therefore, thus said Lord YHWH: "Behold, I am laying a foundation in Zion, ‖ A stone—a tried stone, a precious corner stone, a settled foundation, ‖ He who is believing does not make haste. **17** And I have put judgment for a line, ‖ And righteousness for a plummet, ‖ And hail sweeps away the refuge of lies, ‖ And waters overflow the secret hiding place. **18** And your covenant with death has been annulled, ‖ And your provision with Sheol does not stand, ‖ An overflowing scourge, when it passes over, ‖ Then you have been to it for a treading-place. **19** From the fullness of its passing over it takes you, ‖ For it passes over morning by morning, ‖ By day and by night, ‖ And it has been only a trembling to consider the report. **20** For the bed has been shorter ‖ Than to stretch one's self out in, ‖ And the covering has been narrower ‖ Than to wrap one's self up in. **21** For as YHWH rises [at] Mount Perazim, ‖ As He is troubled [at] the valley in Gibeon, ‖ To do His work—strange [is] His work, ‖ And to do His deed—strange [is] His deed." **22** And now, do not show yourselves scorners, ‖ Lest your bands are strong, ‖ For a consumption, that is determined, ‖ I have heard, by the Lord, YHWH of Hosts, ‖ [Is] for all the land. **23** Give ear, and hear my voice, ‖ Attend, and hear my saying: **24** Does the plowman plow the whole day to sow? He opens and harrows his ground! **25** Has he not, if he has made its face level, ‖ Then scattered fitches, and sprinkles cumin, ‖ And has placed the principal wheat, ‖ And the appointed barley, ‖ And the rye [in] its own border? **26** And his God instructs him for judgment, ‖ He directs him. **27** For fitches are not threshed with a sharp-pointed thing, ‖ And the wheel of a cart turned around on cumin, ‖ For fitches are beaten out with a staff, ‖ And cumin with a rod. **28** Bread-[grain] is beaten small, ‖ For he does not severely thresh it forever, ‖ Nor has a wheel of his cart crushed [it], ‖ Nor do his hooves beat it small. **29** Even this from YHWH of Hosts has gone out, ‖ He has made counsel wonderful, ‖ He has made wisdom great!

29 Woe [to] Ariel, Ariel, ‖ The city of the encampment of David! Add year to year, let festivals go around. **2** And I have sent distress to Ariel, ‖ And it has been lamentation and mourning, ‖ And it has been to me as Ariel. **3** And I encamped, O babbler, against you, ‖ And I laid siege against you—a camp. And I raised up bulwarks against you. **4** And you have been low, ‖ You speak from the earth, ‖ And make your saying low from the dust, ‖ And your voice has been from the earth, ‖ As one having a familiar spirit, ‖ And your saying whispers from the dust, **5** And as small dust has been ‖ The multitude of those scattering you, ‖ And as chaff passing on the multitude of the terrible, ‖ And it has been in an instant—suddenly. **6** You are inspected by YHWH of Hosts, ‖ With thunder, and with an earthquake, ‖ And great noise, windstorm, and whirlwind, ‖ And flame of devouring fire. **7** And as a dream, a vision of night, ‖ Has been the multitude of all the nations ‖ Who are warring against Ariel, ‖ And all its warriors, and its bulwark, ‖ Even of those distressing her. **8** And it has been, as when the hungry dreams, ‖ And behold, he is eating, ‖ And he has awoken, ‖ And his soul [is] empty, ‖ And as when the thirsty dreams, ‖ And behold, he is drinking, ‖ And he has awoken, ‖ And behold, he is weary, ‖ And his soul is

ISAIAH

longing, ‖ So is the multitude of all the nations ‖ Who are warring against Mount Zion. **9** Linger and wonder, look, indeed, look, ‖ Be drunk, and not with wine, ‖ Stagger, and not with strong drink. **10** For YHWH has poured out a spirit of deep sleep on you, ‖ And He closes your eyes—the prophets, ‖ And your heads—the seers—He covered. **11** And the vision of the whole is to you, ‖ As words of the sealed scroll, ‖ That they give to one knowing scrolls, ‖ Saying, "Please read this," ‖ And he has said, "I am not able, for it [is] sealed"; **12** And the scroll is given to him who has not known scrolls, ‖ Saying, "Please read this," ‖ And he has said, "I have not known scrolls." **13** And the Lord says: "Because this people has drawn near with its mouth, ‖ And they have honored Me with its lips, ‖ And it has put its heart far off from Me, ‖ And their fear of Me is a precept taught by men! **14** Therefore, behold, I am adding to do wonderfully with this people, ‖ A wonder, and a marvel, ‖ And the wisdom of its wise ones has perished, ‖ And the understanding of its intelligent ones hides itself." **15** Woe [to] those going deep from YHWH to hide counsel, ‖ And whose works have been in darkness. And they say, "Who is seeing us? And who is knowing us?" **16** Your perversion! Is the potter esteemed as clay, ‖ That the work says of its maker, "He has not made me?" And the framed thing said of its framer, "He did not understand?" **17** Is it not yet a very little [while], ‖ And Lebanon has turned into a fruitful field, ‖ And the fruitful field is reckoned for a forest? **18** And the deaf have heard the words of a scroll in that day, ‖ And out of thick darkness, and out of darkness, ‖ The eyes of the blind see. **19** And the humble have added joy in YHWH, ‖ And the poor among men ‖ Rejoice in the Holy One of Israel. **20** For the terrible one has ceased, ‖ And the scorner has been consumed, ‖ And all watching for iniquity have been cut off, **21** Who cause men to sin in word, ‖ And lay a snare for a reprover in the gate, ‖ And turn aside the righteous into emptiness. **22** Therefore, thus said YHWH, ‖ Who ransomed Abraham, ‖ Concerning the house of Jacob: "Jacob is not ashamed now, ‖ Nor does his face now become pale, **23** For in his seeing his children, ‖ The work of My hand, in his midst, ‖ They sanctify My Name, ‖ And have sanctified the Holy One of Jacob, ‖ And they declare the God of Israel fearful. **24** And the erring in spirit have known understanding, ‖ And murmurers learn doctrine!"

30 Woe [to] apostate sons, ‖ A declaration of YHWH! To do counsel, and not from Me, ‖ And to spread out a covering, and not of My Spirit, ‖ So as to add sin to sin. **2** Who are walking to go down to Egypt, ‖ And have not asked My mouth, ‖ To be strong in the strength of Pharaoh, ‖ And to trust in the shadow of Egypt. **3** And the strength of Pharaoh ‖ Has been to you for shame, ‖ And the trust in the shadow of Egypt confusion, **4** For his princes were in Zoan, ‖ And his messengers reach Hanes. **5** He made all ashamed of a people that do not profit, ‖ Not for help, and not for profit, ‖ But for shame, and also for reproach! **6** The burden of the beasts of the south. Into a land of adversity and distress, ‖ Of young lion and of old lion, ‖ From where [are] viper and flying, burning serpent, ‖ They carry their wealth on the shoulder of donkeys, ‖ And their treasures on the hump of camels, ‖ To a people not profitable. **7** Indeed, Egyptians [are] vanity, and help in vain, ‖ Therefore I have cried concerning this: "Their strength [is] to sit still." **8** No, go in, write it on a tablet with them, ‖ And inscribe it on a scroll, ‖ And it is for a latter day, for a witness for all time, **9** That this [is] a people of rebellion, sons—liars, ‖ Sons not willing to hear the Law of YHWH. **10** Who have said to seers, "Do not see," ‖ And to prophets, "Do not prophesy to us straightforward things, ‖ Speak to us smooth things, prophesy deceits, **11** Turn aside from the way, ‖ Decline from the path, ‖ Cause the Holy One of Israel ‖ To cease from before us." **12** Therefore, thus said the Holy One of Israel: "Because of your kicking against this word, ‖ And you trust in oppression, ‖ And perverseness, and rely on it, **13** Therefore this iniquity is to you as a breach falling, ‖ Swelled out in a wall set on high, ‖ Whose destruction comes suddenly, in an instant. **14** And He has broken it ‖ As the breaking of the potters' bottle, ‖ Beaten down—He does not spare, ‖ Nor is there found, in its beating down, ‖ A potsherd to take fire from the burning, ‖ And to draw out waters from a ditch." **15** For thus said Lord YHWH, ‖ The Holy One of Israel: "In returning and rest you are saved, ‖ In keeping quiet and in confidence is your might," ‖ And you have not been willing. **16** And you say, "No, for we flee on a horse," ‖ Therefore you flee, ‖ And, "We ride on the swift!" Therefore your pursuers are swift. **17** One thousand [flee] because of the rebuke of one, ‖ Because of the rebuke of five you flee, ‖ Until you have surely been left as a pole ‖ On the top of the mountain, ‖ And as an ensign on the height. **18** And therefore YHWH waits to favor you, ‖ And therefore He is exalted to pity you, ‖ For YHWH [is] a God of judgment, ‖ O the blessedness of all waiting for Him. **19** For the people in Zion dwell in Jerusalem, ‖ Do not weep—weeping, ‖ Pitying, He pities you at the voice of your cry, ‖ When He hears He answers you. **20** And the Lord has given to you bread of adversity, ‖ And water of oppression. And your teachers remove no longer, ‖ And your eyes have seen your teachers, **21** And your ear hears a word behind you, saying, "This [is] the way, go in it," ‖ When you turn to the right, ‖ And when you turn to the left. **22** And you have defiled the covering of Your carved images of silver, ‖ And the ephod of your molten image of gold, ‖ You scatter them as a sickening thing, "Go out," you say to it. **23** And He has given rain [for] your seed, ‖ With which you sow the ground, ‖ And bread, the increase of the ground, ‖ And it has been fat and plentiful, ‖ Your livestock enjoy an enlarged pasture in that day. **24** And the oxen and the young donkeys serving the ground, ‖ Eat fermented provender, ‖ That one is winnowing with shovel and fan. **25** And there has been on every high mountain, ‖ And on every exalted hill, ‖ Streams—conduits of waters, ‖ In a day of much slaughter, in the falling of towers. **26** And the light of the moon has been as the light of the sun, ‖ And the light of the sun is sevenfold, ‖ As the light of seven days, ‖ In the day of YHWH's binding up the breach of His people, ‖ When He heals the stroke of its wound. **27** Behold, the Name of YHWH is coming from far, ‖ His anger is burning, and the flame [is] great, ‖ His lips have been full of indignation, ‖ And His tongue [is] as a devouring fire. **28** And His breath [is] as an overflowing stream, ‖ It divides to the neck, ‖ To sift nations with a sieve of vanity, ‖ And a bridle causing to err, ‖ [Is] on the jaws of the peoples. **29** Singing is to you as in a night sanctified for a festival, ‖ And joy of heart as he who is going with a pipe, ‖ To go to the mountain of YHWH, ‖ To the rock of Israel. **30** And YHWH has caused ‖ The splendor of His voice to be heard, ‖ And the coming down of His arm ‖ He shows with the raging of anger, ‖ And the flame of a consuming fire, ‖ Scattering, and inundation, and hailstone. **31** For from the voice of YHWH Asshur [is] broken down, ‖ He strikes with a rod. **32** And every passage of the settled staff, ‖ That YHWH causes to rest on him, ‖ Has been with tambourines and with harps, ‖ And in battles of shaking He has fought with it. **33** For Tophet is arranged from former time, ‖ Even it is prepared for the king, ‖ He has made deep, ‖ He has made large, ‖ Its pile [is] fire and much wood, ‖ The breath of YHWH, ‖ As a stream of brimstone, is burning in it!

31 Woe [to] those going down to Egypt for help, ‖ And [who] lean on horses, ‖ And trust on chariots, because [they are] many, ‖ And on horsemen, because [they are] very strong, ‖ And have not looked on the Holy One of Israel, ‖ And have not sought YHWH. **2** And He [is] also wise, and brings in evil, ‖ And He has not turned aside His words, ‖ And He has risen against a house of evildoers, ‖ And against the help of workers of iniquity. **3** And the Egyptians [are men], and not God, ‖ And their horses [are] flesh, and not spirit, ‖ And YHWH stretches out His hand, ‖ And the helper has stumbled, ‖ And the helped one has fallen, ‖ And together all of them are consumed. **4** For thus said YHWH to me: "As the lion and the young lion growl over his prey, ‖ Against whom a multitude of shepherds is called, ‖ He is not frightened from their voice, ‖ And he is not humbled from their noise; So YHWH of Hosts comes down ‖ To war on Mount Zion, and on her height. **5** As birds flying, so does YHWH of Hosts ‖ Cover over Jerusalem, covering and delivering, ‖ Passing over, and causing to escape." **6** Turn back to Him from whom sons of Israel ‖ Have deepened apostasy. **7** For in that day each despises His idols of silver, and his idols of gold, ‖ That your hands made to you—a sin. **8** And Asshur has fallen by sword, not of the high, ‖ Indeed, a sword—not of the low, consumes him, ‖ And he has fled for himself from the face of a sword, ‖ And his young men become tributary. **9** And he passes on [to] his rock from fear, ‖ And his princes have been frightened by the ensign—a declaration of Y{HWH}, ‖ Who has a light in Zion, ‖ And who has a furnace in Jerusalem!

32 Behold, a king reigns for righteousness, ‖ As for princes, they rule for judgment. **2** And each has been as a hiding place [from] wind, ‖ And as a secret hiding place [from] inundation, ‖ As streams of waters in a dry place, ‖ As a shadow of a heavy rock in a weary land. **3** And the eyes of beholders are not dazzled, ‖ And the ears of hearers attend. **4** And the heart of those hurried understands to know, ‖ And the tongue of stammerers hurries to speak clearly. **5** A fool is no more called "noble," ‖ And to a miser it is not said, "rich"; **6** For a fool speaks folly, ‖ And his heart does iniquity, to do profanity, ‖ And to speak error concerning Y{HWH}, ‖ To empty the soul of the hungry, ‖ Indeed, he causes the thirsty to lack [their] drink. **7** And the miser—his instruments [are] evil, ‖ He has counseled wicked schemes, ‖ To corrupt the poor with lying sayings, ‖ Even when the needy speaks justly. **8** And the noble counseled noble things, ‖ And he rises up for noble things. **9** Women, easy ones, rise, hear my voice, ‖ Daughters, confident ones, give ear [to] my saying, **10** In days and a year ‖ You are troubled, O confident ones, ‖ For harvest has been consumed, ‖ The gathering does not come. **11** Tremble, you women, you easy ones, ‖ Be troubled, you confident ones, ‖ Strip and make bare, with a girdle on the loins, **12** They are lamenting for breasts, ‖ For fields of desire, for the fruitful vine. **13** Over the ground of my people thorn [and] brier go up, ‖ Surely over all houses of joy of the exulting city, **14** The palace has been left, ‖ The multitude of the city forsaken, ‖ Fort and watchtower have been for dens for all time, ‖ A joy of wild donkeys—a pasture of herds; **15** Until the Spirit is emptied out on us from on high, ‖ And a wilderness has become a fruitful field, ‖ And the fruitful field is reckoned for a forest. **16** And judgment has dwelt in the wilderness, ‖ And righteousness remains in the fruitful field. **17** And a work of the righteousness has been peace, ‖ And a service of the righteousness—Keeping quiet and confidence for all time. **18** And My people have dwelt in a peaceful habitation, ‖ And in steadfast dwelling places, ‖ And in quiet resting places. **19** And it has hailed in the going down of the forest, ‖ And the city is low in the valley. **20** Blessed [are] you sowing by all waters, ‖ Sending forth the foot of the ox and the donkey!

33 Woe, spoiler! And you not spoiled, ‖ And treacherous! And they did not deal treacherously with you, ‖ When you finish, O spoiler, you are spoiled, ‖ When you finish dealing treacherously, ‖ They deal treacherously with you. **2** O Y{HWH}, favor us, ‖ We have waited for You, ‖ Be their arm, in the mornings, ‖ Indeed, our salvation in time of adversity. **3** From the voice of a multitude peoples have fled, ‖ From Your exaltation nations have been scattered. **4** And Your spoil has been gathered, ‖ A gathering of the caterpillar, ‖ As a running to and fro of locusts ‖ He is running on it. **5** Y{HWH} is set on high, for He is dwelling on high, ‖ He filled Zion [with] judgment and righteousness, **6** And has been the steadfastness of your times, ‖ The strength of salvation, wisdom, and knowledge, ‖ Fear of Y{HWH}—it [is] His treasure. **7** Behold, "Their Ariel," they have cried outside, ‖ Messengers of peace weep bitterly. **8** Highways have been desolated, ‖ He who passes along the path has ceased, ‖ He has broken covenant, ‖ He has despised enemies, ‖ He has not esteemed a man. **9** The land has mourned, languished, ‖ Lebanon has been confounded, ‖ Sharon has been withered as a wilderness, ‖ And Bashan and Carmel are shaking. **10** Now I arise, says Y{HWH}, ‖ Now I am exalted, now I am lifted up. **11** You conceive chaff, you bear stubble; Your spirit—a fire [that] devours you. **12** And peoples have been [as] burnings of lime, ‖ Thorns, as sweepings, they burn with fire. **13** Hear, you far off, that which I have done, ‖ And know, you near ones, My might. **14** Sinners have been afraid in Zion, ‖ Trembling has seized the profane: Who dwells for us—consuming fire, ‖ Who dwells for us—burnings of the age? **15** Whoever is walking righteously, ‖ And is speaking uprightly, ‖ Kicking against gain of oppressions, ‖ Shaking his hands from taking hold on a bribe, ‖ Stopping his ear from hearing of blood, ‖ And shutting his eyes from looking on evil, **16** He inhabits high places, ‖ Strongholds of rock [are] his high tower, ‖ His bread has been given, his waters steadfast. **17** Your eyes see a king in his beauty, ‖ They see a far-off land. **18** Your heart meditates [on] terror, ‖ Where [is] he who is counting? Where [is] he who is weighing? Where [is] he who is counting the towers? **19** You do not see the strong people, ‖ A people deeper of lip than to be understood, ‖ Of a scorned tongue, there is no understanding. **20** See Zion, the city of our meetings, ‖ Your eyes see Jerusalem—a quiet habitation, ‖ A tent not taken down, its pins are not removed forever, ‖ And none of its cords are broken. **21** But YHWH [is] mighty for us there, ‖ A place of rivers—streams of broad sides, ‖ No ship with oars goes into it, ‖ And a mighty ship does not pass over it. **22** For YHWH, ours who is judging, ‖ YHWH our lawgiver, ‖ YHWH our King—He saves us. **23** Your ropes have been left, ‖ They do not correctly strengthen their mast, ‖ They have not spread out a sail, ‖ Then a prey of much spoil has been apportioned, ‖ The lame have taken spoil. **24** Nor does an inhabitant say, "I was sick"; The people dwelling in it [are] forgiven of [their] iniquity!

34 Come near, you nations, to hear, ‖ And you peoples, give attention, ‖ The earth and its fullness hear, ‖ The world, and all its productions. **2** For to YHWH [is] wrath against all the nations, ‖ And fury against all their host, ‖ He has devoted them to destruction, ‖ He has given them to slaughter. **3** And their wounded are cast out, ‖ And their carcasses cause their stench to ascend, ‖ And mountains have been melted from their blood. **4** And all the host of the heavens have been consumed, ‖ And the heavens have been rolled together as a scroll, ‖ And all their hosts fade, ‖ As the fading of a leaf of a vine, ‖ And as the fading one of a fig tree. **5** For My sword was soaked in the heavens, ‖ Behold, it comes down on Edom, ‖ On the people of My curse for judgment. **6** A sword [is] to YHWH—it has been full of blood, ‖ It has been made fat with fatness, ‖ With blood of lambs and male goats. With fat of kidneys of rams, ‖ For to YHWH [is] a sacrifice in Bozrah, ‖ And a great slaughter in the land of Edom. **7** And reems have come down with them, ‖ And bullocks with bulls, ‖ And their land has been soaked from blood, ‖ And their dust is made fat from fatness. **8** (For a day of vengeance [is] to YHWH, ‖ A year of recompenses for Zion's strife), **9** And her streams have been turned to pitch, ‖ And her dust to brimstone, ‖ And her land has become burning pitch. **10** She is not quenched by night and by day, ‖ Her smoke goes up for all time, ‖ She is desolate from generation to generation, ‖ Forever and ever, none is passing into her. **11** And pelican and hedgehog possess her, ‖ And owl and raven dwell in her, ‖ And He has stretched out over her ‖ A line of vacancy, and stones of emptiness. **12** They call her nobles [to] the kingdom, ‖ But there are none there, ‖ And all her princes are at an end. **13** And thorns have gone up her palaces, ‖ Nettle and bramble [are] in her fortresses, ‖ And it has been a habitation of dragons, ‖ A court for daughters of an ostrich. **14** And desert-dwellers have met with howlers, ‖ And the goat calls for its companion, ‖ Surely the night-owl has rested there, ‖ And has found a place of rest for herself. **15** The owl has made her nest there, ‖ Indeed, she lays, and has hatched, ‖ And has gathered under her shadow, ‖ Surely vultures have been gathered there, ‖ Each with its companion. **16** Seek out of the scroll of YHWH, and read, ‖ One of these has not been lacking, ‖ None has missed its companion, ‖ For My mouth—it has commanded, ‖ And His Spirit—He has gathered them. **17** And He has cast a lot for them, ‖ And His hand has apportioned [it] to them by line, ‖ They possess it for all time, ‖ They dwell in it from generation to generation!

35 They rejoice from the wilderness and dry place, ‖ And the desert rejoices, ‖ And flourishes as the rose, **2** Flourishing it flourishes, and rejoices, ‖ Indeed, [with] joy and singing, ‖ The glory of Lebanon has been given to it, ‖ The beauty of Carmel and Sharon, ‖ They see the glory of YHWH, ‖ The majesty of our God. **3** Strengthen the feeble hands, ‖ Indeed, strengthen the stumbling knees. **4** Say to the hurried of heart, "Be strong, ‖ Do not fear, behold, your God; vengeance comes, ‖ The repayment of God, ‖ He Himself comes and saves you." **5** Then eyes of the blind are opened, ‖ And ears of the deaf are unstopped, **6** Then the lame leap as a deer, ‖ And the tongue of the mute sings, ‖ For waters have been broken up in a wilderness, ‖ And streams in a desert. **7** And the mirage has become a pond, ‖ And the thirsty land—fountains of waters, ‖ In the habitation of dragons, ‖ Its place of lying down, ‖ A court for reed and rush. **8** And a highway has been there, and a way, ‖ And it is called the "Way of Holiness." The unclean do not pass over it, ‖ And He Himself [is] by them, ‖ Whoever is going in the way—even fools do not err. **9** No lion is there, ‖ Indeed, a destructive beast does not ascend it, ‖ It is not found there, ‖ And the redeemed have walked, **10** And the ransomed of YHWH return, ‖ And have entered Zion with singing, ‖ And [with] continuous joy on their head, ‖ They attain joy and gladness, ‖ And sorrow and sighing have fled away!

36 And it comes to pass, in the fourteenth year of King Hezekiah, Sennacherib king of Asshur has come up against all the fortified cities of Judah, and seizes them. **2** And the king of Asshur sends Rabshakeh from Lachish to Jerusalem, to King Hezekiah, with a heavy force, and he stands by the conduit of the upper pool, in the highway of the fuller's field, **3** and Eliakim son of Hilkiah goes forth to him, who [is] over the house, and Shebna the scribe, and Joah son of Asaph, the remembrancer. **4** And Rabshakeh says to them, "Now say to Hezekiah, Thus said the great king, the king of Asshur: What [is] this confidence in which you have confided? **5** I have said, Only a word of the lips! Counsel and might [are] for battle. Now, on whom have you trusted, that you have rebelled against me? **6** Behold, you have trusted on the staff of this broken reed—on Egypt—which a man leans on, and it has gone into his hand, and pierced it—so [is] Pharaoh king of Egypt to all those trusting on him. **7** And do you say to me, We have trusted in our God YHWH? Is it not He whose high places and whose altars Hezekiah has turned aside, and says to Judah and to Jerusalem, Bow yourselves before this altar? **8** And now, please negotiate with my lord the king of Asshur, and I give two thousand horses to you, if you are able to put riders on them for yourself. **9** And how do you turn back the face of one captain of the least of the servants of my lord, and trust on Egypt for yourself, for chariot and for horsemen? **10** And now, without YHWH have I come up against this land to destroy it? YHWH said to me, Go up to this land, and you have destroyed it." **11** And Eliakim says—and Shebna and Joah—to Rabshakeh, "Please speak to your servants [in] Aramaic, for we are understanding; and do not speak to us [in] Jewish, in the ears of the people who [are] on the wall." **12** And Rabshakeh says, "To your lord, and to you, has my lord sent me to speak these words? Is it not for the men—those sitting on the wall to eat their own dung and to drink their own water with you?" **13** And Rabshakeh stands and calls with a great voice [in] Jewish, and says, "Hear the words of the great king, the king of Asshur— **14** thus said the king: Do not let Hezekiah lift you up, for he is not able to deliver you; **15** and do not let Hezekiah make you trust to YHWH, saying, YHWH certainly delivers us, this city is not given into the hand of the king of Asshur. **16** Do not listen to Hezekiah, for thus said the king of Asshur: Make a blessing with me, and come out to me, and each of you eat of his vine, and each of his fig tree, and each drink the waters of his own well, **17** until my coming in, and I have taken you to a land like your own land, a land of grain and wine, a land of bread and vineyards; **18** lest Hezekiah persuades you, saying, YHWH delivers us. Have the gods of the nations each delivered his land out of the hand of the king of Asshur? **19** Where [are] the gods of Hamath and Arpad? Where [are] the gods of Sepharvaim, that they have delivered Samaria out of my hand? **20** Who among all the gods of these lands [are] they who have delivered their land out of my hand, that YHWH delivers Jerusalem out of my hand?" **21** And they keep silent, and have not answered him a word, for a command of the king is, saying, "Do not answer him." **22** And Eliakim son of Hilkiah, who [is] over the house, comes in, and Shebna the scribe, and Joah son of Asaph, the remembrancer, to Hezekiah, with torn garments, and they declare to him the words of Rabshakeh.

37 And it comes to pass, at King Hezekiah's hearing, that he tears his garments, and covers himself with sackcloth, and enters the house of YHWH, **2** and sends Eliakim, who [is] over the house, and Shebna the scribe, and [the] elderly of the priests, covering themselves with sackcloth, to Isaiah son of Amoz the prophet, **3** and they say to him, "Thus said Hezekiah: A day of distress, and rebuke, and despising, [is] this day; for sons have come to the birth, and there is not power to bear. **4** It may be your God YHWH hears the words of Rabshakeh with which the king of Asshur his lord has sent him to reproach the living God, and has decided concerning the words that your God YHWH has heard, and you have lifted up prayer for the remnant that is found." **5** And the servants of King Hezekiah come to Isaiah, **6** and Isaiah says to them, "Thus you say to your lord, Thus said YHWH: Do not be afraid because of the words that you have heard, with which the servants of the king of Asshur have reviled Me. **7** Behold, I am giving a spirit in him, and he has heard a report, and has turned back to his land, and I have caused him to fall by the sword in his land." **8** And Rabshakeh turns back and finds the king of Asshur fighting against Libnah, for he has heard that he has journeyed from Lachish. **9** And he hears concerning Tirhakah king of Cush, saying, "He has come out to fight with you"; and he hears, and sends messengers to Hezekiah, saying, **10** "Thus you speak to Hezekiah king of Judah, saying, Do not let your God in whom you are trusting lift you up, saying, Jerusalem is not given into the hand of the king of Asshur. **11** Behold, you have heard that which the kings of Asshur have done to all the lands—to devote them—and you are delivered! **12** Did the gods of the nations deliver them whom my fathers destroyed—Gozan, and Haran, and Rezeph, and the sons of Eden, who [are] in Telassar? **13** Where [is] the king of Hamath, and the king of Arpad, and the king of the city of Sepharvaim, Hena, and Ivvah?" **14** And Hezekiah takes the letters out of the hand of the messengers, and reads them, and Hezekiah goes up to the house of YHWH, and Hezekiah spreads it before YHWH. **15** And Hezekiah prays to YHWH, saying, **16** "YHWH of Hosts, God of Israel, inhabiting the cherubim, You [are] God Himself—You alone—to all kingdoms of the earth, You have made the heavens and the earth. **17** Incline, O YHWH, Your ear, and hear; open, O YHWH, Your eyes and see; and hear all the words of Sennacherib that he has sent to reproach the living God. **18** Truly, O YHWH, kings of Asshur have laid waste all the lands and their land, **19** so as to put their gods into fire—for they [are] no gods, but work of the hands of man, wood and stone—and they destroy them. **20** And now, our God YHWH, save us from his hand, and all kingdoms of the earth know that You [are] YHWH, You alone." **21** And Isaiah son of Amoz sends to Hezekiah, saying, "Thus said YHWH, God of Israel: That which you have prayed to Me concerning Sennacherib king of Asshur— **22** this [is] the word that YHWH spoke concerning him: Trampled on you, laughed at you, ‖ Has the virgin daughter of Zion, ‖ The daughter of Jerusalem has shaken the head behind you. **23** Whom have you reproached and reviled? And against whom—lifted up the voice? Indeed, you lift up your eyes on high ‖ Against the Holy One of Israel. **24** By the hand of your servants ‖ You have reviled the Lord, and say: In the multitude of my chariots ‖ I have come up to a high place of hills, ‖ The sides of Lebanon, ‖ And I cut down the height of its cedars, ‖ The choice of its firs, ‖ And I enter the high place of its extremity, ‖ The forest of its Carmel. **25** I have dug and drunk waters, ‖ And I dry up with the sole of my steps ‖ All floods of a bulwark. **26** Have you not heard from afar [that] I did it, ‖ From days of old—that I formed it? Now I have brought it in, ‖ And it is to make desolate, ‖ Ruinous heaps—fortified cities, **27** And their inhabitants are feeble-handed, ‖ They were broken down, and are dried up. They have been the herb of the field, ‖ And the greenness of the tender grass, ‖ Grass of the roofs, ‖ And blasted grain, before it has risen up. **28** And your sitting down, and your going out, ‖ And your coming in, I have known, ‖ And your anger toward Me. **29** Because of your anger toward Me, ‖ And your noise—it came up into My ears, ‖ I have put My hook in your nose, ‖ And My bridle in your lips, ‖ And I have caused you to turn back ‖ In the way in which you came. **30** And this [is] the sign to you, ‖ Self-sown grain [is] food of the year, ‖ And in the second year the spontaneous growth, ‖ And in the third year, sow and reap, ‖ And plant vineyards, and eat their fruit. **31** And it has continued—The escaped of the house of Judah that has been left—To take root beneath, ‖ And it has made fruit upward. **32** For a remnant goes forth from Jerusalem, ‖ And an escape from Mount Zion, ‖ The zeal of YHWH of Hosts does this. **33** Therefore, thus said YHWH, ‖ Concerning the king of Asshur: He does not come into this city, ‖ Nor does he shoot an arrow there, ‖ Nor does he come before

ISAIAH

it [with] shield, ‖ Nor does he pour out a mound against it. **34** In the way that he came, in it he turns back, ‖ And to this city he does not come in, ‖ A declaration of YHWH, **35** And I have covered over this city, ‖ To save it, for My own sake, ‖ And for the sake of My servant David." **36** And a messenger of YHWH goes out, and strikes in the camp of Asshur one hundred and eighty-five thousand; and [men] rise early in the morning, and behold, all of them [are] dead corpses. **37** And he journeys, and goes, and Sennacherib king of Asshur turns back, and dwells in Nineveh. **38** And it comes to pass, he is bowing himself in the house of his god Nisroch, and his sons Adrammelech and Sharezer have struck him with the sword, and they have escaped to the land of Ararat, and his son Esar-Haddon reigns in his stead.

38 In those days has Hezekiah been sick to death, and Isaiah son of Amoz, the prophet, comes to him and says to him, "Thus said YHWH: Give a charge to your house, for you [are] dying, and do not live." **2** And Hezekiah turns around his face to the wall, and prays to YHWH, **3** and says, "Ah, now, O YHWH, please remember how I have habitually walked before You in truth, and with a perfect heart, and I have done that which [is] good in your eyes"; and Hezekiah weeps [with] a great weeping. **4** And a word of YHWH is to Isaiah, saying, **5** "Go, and you have said to Hezekiah, Thus said YHWH, God of your father David: I have heard your prayer, I have seen your tear, behold, I am adding fifteen years to your days, **6** and out of the hand of the king of Asshur I deliver you and this city, and have covered over this city. **7** And this [is] to you the sign from YHWH, that YHWH does this thing that He has spoken. **8** Behold, I am bringing back the shadow of the degrees that it has gone down on the degrees of Ahaz, by the sun, backward ten degrees"; and the sun turns back ten degrees in the degrees that it had gone down. **9** A writing of Hezekiah king of Judah concerning his being sick when he revives from his sickness: **10** "I said in the cutting off of my days, ‖ I go to the gates of Sheol, ‖ I have numbered the remnant of my years. **11** I said, I do not see YAH—YAH! In the land of the living, ‖ I do not behold man anymore, ‖ With the inhabitants of the world. **12** My sojourning has departed, ‖ And been removed from me as a shepherd's tent, ‖ I have drawn together, as a weaver, my life, ‖ By weakness it cuts me off, ‖ From day to night You end me. **13** I have set [Him] as a lion until morning, ‖ So He breaks all my bones, ‖ From day to night You end me. **14** As a crane—a swallow—so I chatter, ‖ I mourn as a dove, ‖ My eyes have been drawn up on high, ‖ O YHWH, oppression [is] on me, be my guarantor. **15** What do I say? Seeing He spoke to me, ‖ And He Himself has worked, ‖ I go softly all my years for the bitterness of my soul. **16** Lord, [men] live by these, ‖ And by all in them [is] the life of my spirit, ‖ And You save me, make me to also live, **17** Behold, He changed bitterness to peace for me, ‖ And You have delighted in my soul without corruption, ‖ For You have cast all my sins behind Your back. **18** For Sheol does not confess You, ‖ Death does not praise You, ‖ Those going down to the pit do not hope for Your truth. **19** The living, the living, he confesses You, **20** Like myself today; A father makes known to [his] sons of Your faithfulness, ‖ O YHWH—to save me: And we sing my songs all [the] days of our lives ‖ In the house of YHWH." **21** And Isaiah says, "Let them take a bunch of figs, and plaster over the ulcer, and he lives." **22** And Hezekiah says, "What [is] the sign that I go up to the house of YHWH?"

39 At that time, Merodach-Baladan, son of Baladan, king of Babylon, has sent letters and a present to Hezekiah when he hears that he has been sick and has become strong. **2** And Hezekiah rejoices over them, and shows them the house of his spices, the silver, and the gold, and the spices, and the good ointment, and all the house of his vessels, and all that has been found in his treasures; there has not been a thing in his house, and in all his dominion, that Hezekiah has not showed them. **3** And Isaiah the prophet comes to King Hezekiah and says to him, "What did these men say? And from where do they come to you?" And Hezekiah says, "They have come to me from a far-off land—from Babylon." **4** And he says, "What did they see in your house?" And Hezekiah says, "They saw all that [is] in my house; there has not been a thing that I have not showed them among my treasures." **5** And Isaiah says to Hezekiah, "Hear a word of YHWH of

Hosts: **6** Behold, days are coming, and all that [is] in your house, and that your fathers have treasured up until this day, has been carried to Babylon; there is not a thing left, said YHWH; **7** and of your sons who come forth from you, whom you beget, they take, and they have been eunuchs in a palace of the king of Babylon." **8** And Hezekiah says to Isaiah, "The word of YHWH that you have spoken [is] good"; and he says, "Because there is peace and truth in my days."

40 "Comfort, comfort My people," says your God. **2** Speak to the heart of Jerusalem, and call to her, ‖ That her warfare has been completed, ‖ That her punishment has been accepted, ‖ That she has received from the hand of YHWH ‖ Double for all her sins. **3** A voice is crying in a wilderness: "Prepare the way of YHWH, ‖ Make straight in a desert a highway for our God. **4** Every valley is raised up, ‖ And every mountain and hill become low, ‖ And the crooked place has become a plain, ‖ And the entangled places a valley. **5** And the glory of YHWH has been revealed, ‖ And all flesh have seen [it] together, ‖ For the mouth of YHWH has spoken." **6** A voice is saying, "Call," ‖ And he said, "What do I call?" All flesh [is] grass, and all its goodness ‖ [Is] as a flower of the field: **7** Grass has withered, the flower faded, ‖ For the Spirit of YHWH blew on it, ‖ Surely the people [is] grass; **8** Grass has withered, the flower faded, ‖ But a word of our God rises forever. **9** Get up on a high mountain, O Zion, ‖ Proclaiming tidings, ‖ Lift up your voice with power, O Jerusalem, proclaiming tidings, ‖ Lift up, do not fear, say to cities of Judah, "Behold, your God." **10** Behold, Lord YHWH comes with strength, ‖ And His arm is ruling for Him, ‖ Behold, His hire [is] with Him, and His wage before Him. **11** He feeds His flock as a shepherd, ‖ He gathers lambs with His arm, ‖ And He carries [them] in His bosom: He leads suckling ones. **12** Who has measured the waters in the hollow of His hand, ‖ And has meted out the heavens by a span, ‖ And comprehended the dust of the earth in a measure, ‖ And has weighed the mountains in scales, ‖ And the hills in a balance? **13** Who has meted out the Spirit of YHWH, ‖ And [being] His counselor, teaches Him? **14** With whom [did] He consult, ‖ That he causes Him to understand? And teaches Him in the path of judgment, ‖ And teaches Him knowledge? And causes Him to know the way of understanding? **15** Behold, nations [are] as a drop from a bucket, ‖ And have been reckoned as small dust of the balance, ‖ Behold, He takes up islands as a small thing. **16** And Lebanon is not sufficient to burn, ‖ Nor its beasts sufficient for a burnt-offering. **17** All the nations [are] as nothing before Him, ‖ Less than nothing and emptiness, ‖ They have been reckoned to Him. **18** And to whom do you liken God, ‖ And what likeness do you compare to Him? **19** An artisan has poured out the carved image, ‖ And a refiner spreads it over with gold, ‖ And he is refining chains of silver. **20** He who is poor [by] raised-offerings, ‖ Chooses a tree [that is] not rotten, ‖ He seeks a skillful artisan for it, ‖ To establish a carved image—not moved. **21** Do you not know—do you not hear? Has it not been declared from the first to you? Have you not understood ‖ [From] the foundations of the earth? **22** He who is sitting on the circle of the earth, ‖ And its inhabitants [are] as grasshoppers, ‖ He who is stretching out the heavens as a thin thing, ‖ And spreads them as a tent to dwell in. **23** He who is making princes become nothing, ‖ Has made judges of earth formless; **24** Indeed, they have not been planted, ‖ Indeed, they have not been sown, ‖ Indeed, their stock is not taking root in the earth, ‖ And He has also blown on them, and they wither, ‖ And a whirlwind takes them away as stubble. **25** And to whom do you liken Me, ‖ And [to whom] I equal? Says the Holy One. **26** Lift up your eyes on high, ‖ And see—who has created these? He who is bringing out their host by number, ‖ He calls to all of them by name, ‖ By the abundance of His strength ‖ And mighty power, ‖ Not one is lacking. **27** Why say, O Jacob, and speak, O Israel, "My way has been hid from YHWH, ‖ And from my God my judgment passes over?" **28** Have you not known? Have you not heard? The God of the age—YHWH, ‖ Preparer of the ends of the earth, ‖ Is not wearied nor fatigued, ‖ There is no searching of His understanding. **29** He is giving power to the weary, ‖ And to those not strong He increases might. **30** Even youths are wearied and fatigued, ‖ And young men utterly stumble, **31** But those expecting YHWH pass [to] power, ‖ They raise up the pinion as eagles, ‖ They run and are not fatigued, ‖ They go on and do not faint!

41 Keep silent toward Me, O islands, ‖ And the peoples pass on [to] power, ‖ They come near, then they speak, "Together we draw near to judgment." **2** Who stirred up a righteous one from the east? He calls him to His foot, ‖ He gives nations before him, ‖ And He causes him to rule kings, ‖ He gives [them] as dust [to] his sword, ‖ As driven stubble [to] his bow. **3** He pursues them, he passes over in safety ‖ A path he does not enter with his feet. **4** Who has worked and done, ‖ Calling the generations from the first? I, YHWH, the first, and with the last I [am] He. **5** Islands have seen and fear, ‖ The ends of the earth tremble, ‖ They have drawn near, indeed, they come. **6** They each help his neighbor, ‖ And to his brother he says, "Be strong." **7** And an artisan strengthens the refiner, ‖ A smoother [with] a hammer, ‖ Him who is beating [on] an anvil, saying, "For joining it [is] good," ‖ And he strengthens it with nails, it is not moved! **8** And you, O Israel, My servant, ‖ Jacob, whom I have chosen, ‖ Seed of Abraham, My lover, **9** Whom I have taken hold of, from the ends of the earth, ‖ And from its near places I have called you, ‖ And I say to you, You [are] My servant, ‖ I have chosen you, and not rejected you. **10** Do not be afraid, for I [am] with you, do not look around, for I [am] your God, ‖ I have strengthened you, ‖ Indeed, I have helped you, indeed, I upheld you, ‖ With the right hand of My righteousness. **11** Behold, all those displeased with you, ‖ They are ashamed and blush, ‖ They are as nothing, indeed, ‖ The men who strive with you perish. **12** You seek them, and do not find them, ‖ The men who debate with you, ‖ They are as nothing, indeed, as nothing, ‖ The men who war with you. **13** For I, your God YHWH, ‖ Am strengthening your right hand, ‖ He who is saying to you, "Do not fear, I have helped you." **14** Do not fear, O worm Jacob, ‖ You men of Israel, ‖ I helped you, a declaration of YHWH, ‖ Even your redeemer, the Holy One of Israel. **15** Behold, I have set you for a new sharp threshing instrument, ‖ Possessing teeth, you thresh mountains, ‖ And beat small, and make hills as chaff. **16** You winnow them, and a wind lifts them up, ‖ And a whirlwind scatters them, ‖ And you rejoice in YHWH, ‖ [And] boast yourself in the Holy One of Israel. **17** The poor and the needy are seeking water, ‖ And there is none, ‖ Their tongue has failed with thirst, ‖ I, YHWH, answer them, ‖ The God of Israel— I do not forsake them. **18** I open rivers on high places, ‖ And fountains in midst of valleys, ‖ I make a wilderness become a pond of water, ‖ And a dry land becomes springs of water. **19** I give in a wilderness the cedar, ‖ Shittah, and myrtle, and oil-tree, ‖ I set in a desert the fir-pine and box-wood together. **20** So that they see, and know, ‖ And regard, and act wisely together, ‖ For the hand of YHWH has done this, ‖ And the Holy One of Israel has created it. **21** Bring your cause near, says YHWH, ‖ Bring your mighty ones near, says the King of Jacob. **22** They bring [them] near, and declare to us that which happens, ‖ Declare the first things—what they [are], ‖ And we set our heart, and know their latter end, ‖ Or cause us to hear the coming things. **23** Declare the things that are coming hereafter, ‖ And we know that you [are] gods, ‖ Indeed, you may do good or do evil, ‖ And we look around and see [it] together. **24** Behold, you [are] of nothing, and your work of nothing, ‖ An abomination—it fixes on you. **25** I have stirred up [one] from the north, ‖ And he comes, ‖ From the rising of the sun he calls in My Name, ‖ And he comes in [on] prefects as [on] clay, ‖ And as a potter treads down mire. **26** Who has declared from the first, and we know? And formerly, and we say, "Righteous?" Indeed, there is none declaring, ‖ Indeed, there is none proclaiming, ‖ Indeed, there is none hearing your sayings. **27** First to Zion, ‖ Behold, behold them, ‖ And to Jerusalem I give one proclaiming tidings, **28** And I see that there is no man, ‖ Indeed, of these that there is no counselor, ‖ And I ask them, and they return word: **29** "Behold, all of them [are] vanity, ‖ Their works [are] nothing, ‖ Their molten images [are] wind and emptiness!"

42 Behold, My servant, I take hold on Him, ‖ My Chosen One—My soul has accepted, I have put My Spirit on Him, ‖ He brings forth judgment to nations. **2** He does not cry, nor lift up, ‖ Nor cause His voice to be heard in the street. **3** A bruised reed He does not break, ‖ And faded flax He does not quench, ‖ He brings forth judgment to truth. **4** He does not become weak nor bruised, ‖ Until He sets judgment in the earth, ‖ And islands wait with hope for His law. **5** Thus said God, YHWH, ‖ Creating the heavens, and stretching them out, ‖ Spreading out the earth and its productions, ‖ Giving breath to the people on it, ‖ And spirit to those walking in it. **6** I, YHWH, called you in righteousness, ‖ And I lay hold on your hand, and keep you, ‖ And I give you for a covenant of a people, ‖ And a light of nations. **7** To open the eyes of the blind, ‖ To bring forth the bound one from prison, ‖ Those sitting in darkness from the house of restraint. **8** I [am] YHWH, this [is] My Name, ‖ And I do not give My glory to another, ‖ Nor My praise to carved images. **9** The former things, behold, have come, ‖ And I am declaring new things, ‖ Before they spring up I cause you to hear. **10** Sing a new song to YHWH, ‖ His praise from the end of the earth, ‖ You who are going down to the sea, and its fullness, ‖ Islands, and their inhabitants. **11** The wilderness and its cities lift up [their voice], ‖ Kedar inhabits the villages, ‖ The inhabitants of Sela sing, ‖ They cry from the top of mountains. **12** They ascribe to YHWH glory, ‖ And they declare His praise in the islands. **13** YHWH goes forth as a mighty one. He stirs up zeal as a man of war, ‖ He cries, indeed, He shrieks, ‖ He shows Himself mighty against His enemies. **14** I have kept silent from of old, ‖ I keep silent, I refrain Myself, ‖ I cry out as a travailing woman, ‖ I desolate and swallow up together. **15** I make desolate mountains and hills, ‖ And I dry up all their herbs, ‖ And I have made rivers become islands, ‖ And I dry up ponds. **16** And I have caused the blind to go, ‖ In a way they have not known, ‖ I cause them to tread in paths they have not known, ‖ I make a dark place become light before them, ‖ And unleveled places become a plain, ‖ These [are] the things I have done to them, ‖ And I have not forsaken them. **17** Removed backward—utterly ashamed, ‖ Are those trusting in a carved image, ‖ Those saying to a molten image, "You [are] our gods." **18** You deaf, hear; and you blind, look to see. **19** Who [is] blind but My servant? And deaf as My messenger I send? Who [is] blind as he who is at peace, ‖ Indeed, blind, as the servant of YHWH? **20** Seeing many things, and you do not observe, ‖ Opening ears, and he does not hear. **21** YHWH has delight for the sake of His righteousness, ‖ He magnifies law, and makes honorable. **22** And this [is] a people seized and spoiled, ‖ Snared in holes—all of them, ‖ And they were hidden in houses of restraint, ‖ They have been for a prey, ‖ And there is no deliverer, ‖ A spoil, and none is saying, "Restore." **23** Who among you gives ear [to] this? Attends, and hears afterward? **24** Who has given Jacob for a spoil, ‖ And Israel to the spoilers? Is it not YHWH—He against whom we sinned? Indeed, they have not been willing to walk in His ways, ‖ Nor have they listened to His law. **25** And He pours fury on him, ‖ His anger, and the strength of battle, ‖ And it sets him on fire all around, ‖ And he has not known, ‖ And it burns against him, and he does not lay it to heart!

43 And now, thus said YHWH, Your Creator, O Jacob, and your Fashioner, O Israel: Do not be afraid, for I have redeemed you, ‖ I have called on your name—you [are] Mine. **2** When you pass into waters, I [am] with you, ‖ And into floods, they do not overflow you, ‖ When you go into fire, you are not burned, ‖ And a flame does not burn against you. **3** For I—your God YHWH, ‖ The Holy One of Israel, your Savior, ‖ I have appointed Egypt your atonement, ‖ Cush and Seba in your stead. **4** Since you were precious in My eyes, ‖ You were honored, and I have loved you, ‖ And I appoint men in your stead, ‖ And peoples instead of your life. **5** Do not be afraid, for I [am] with you, ‖ I bring in your seed from the east, ‖ And I gather you from the west. **6** I am saying to the north, "Give up," ‖ And to the south, "Do not restrain." Bring in My sons from afar, ‖ And My daughters from the end of the earth. **7** Everyone who is called by My Name, ‖ Even for My glory I have created him, ‖ I have formed him, indeed, I have made him. **8** He brought out a blind people who have eyes, ‖ And deaf ones who have ears. **9** All the nations have been gathered together, ‖ And the peoples are assembled, ‖ Who among them declares this, ‖ And causes us to hear former things? They give their witnesses, ‖ And they are declared righteous, ‖ And they hear and say, "Truth." **10** You [are] My witnesses, a declaration of YHWH, ‖ And My servant whom I have chosen, ‖ So that you know and give credence to Me, ‖ And understand that I [am] He, ‖ Before Me there was no God formed, ‖ And after Me there is none. **11** I [am] YHWH, ‖ And besides Me there is no savior. **12** I declared, and saved, and proclaimed, ‖ And there is no stranger with you, ‖ And you [are] My witnesses, a declaration of YHWH, ‖ And I [am] God. **13** Even from the day I [am] He, ‖ And there is no deliverer from My hand, ‖ I work, and who turns it back? **14** Thus said YHWH, your Redeemer, ‖ The Holy One of Israel: "I have sent to Babylon for your sake, ‖ And caused bars to descend—all of them, ‖ And the Chaldeans, whose song [is] in the ships. **15** I [am] YHWH, your Holy One, ‖ Creator of Israel, your King." **16** Thus said YHWH, ‖ Who is giving a way in the sea, ‖ And a path in the strong waters. **17** Who is bringing forth chariot and horse, ‖ A force, even a strong one: "They lie down together—they do not rise, ‖ They have been extinguished, ‖ They have been quenched as flax." **18** Do not remember former things, ‖ And do not consider ancient things. **19** Behold, I am doing a new thing, now it springs up, ‖ Do you not know it? Indeed, I put a way in a wilderness, ‖ In a desolate place—floods. **20** The beast of the field honors Me, ‖ Dragons and daughters of an ostrich, ‖ For I have given waters in a wilderness, ‖ Floods in a desolate place, ‖ To give drink to My people—My chosen. **21** I have formed this people for Myself, ‖ They recount My praise. **22** And you have not called Me, O Jacob, ‖ For you have been wearied of Me, O Israel, **23** You have not brought to Me, ‖ The lamb of your burnt-offerings, ‖ And [with] your sacrifices you have not honored Me, ‖ I have not caused you to serve with a present, ‖ Nor wearied you with frankincense. **24** You have not bought Me sweet cane with money, ‖ And have not filled Me [with] the fat of your sacrifices, ‖ Only—you have caused Me to serve with your sins, ‖ You have wearied Me with your iniquities. **25** I [am] He who is blotting out Your transgressions for My own sake, ‖ And I do not remember your sins. **26** Cause Me to remember—we are judged together, ‖ Declare that you may be justified. **27** Your first father sinned, ‖ And your interpreters transgressed against Me, **28** And I defile princes of the sanctuary, ‖ And I give Jacob to destruction, and Israel to revilings!

44 "And now, hear, O Jacob, My servant, ‖ And Israel, whom I have fixed on— **2** Thus said YHWH, your Maker, and your Former, ‖ From the womb He helps you: Do not fear, My servant Jacob, ‖ And Yeshurun, whom I have fixed on. **3** For I pour waters on a thirsty one, ‖ And floods on a dry land, ‖ I pour My Spirit on your seed, ‖ And My blessing on your offspring. **4** And they have sprung up as among grass, ‖ As willows by conduits of water. **5** This [one] says, For I [am] YHWH's, ‖ And this calls [himself] by the name of Jacob, ‖ And this [one] writes [with] his hand, For YHWH, ‖ And surnames himself by the name of Israel." **6** Thus said YHWH, King of Israel, ‖ And his Redeemer, YHWH of Hosts: "I [am] the first, and I [am] the last, ‖ And besides Me there is no God. **7** And who [is] as I, call and declare it, ‖ And arrange it for Me, ‖ Since My placing the people of antiquity, ‖ And things that are coming, ‖ And those that come, they declare to them. **8** Do not fear, nor be afraid, ‖ Have I not caused you to hear from that time, and declared? And you [are] My witnesses, ‖ Is there a God besides Me? Indeed, there is none, ‖ I have not known another Rock." **9** Framers of a carved image, all of them [are] emptiness, ‖ And their desirable things do not profit, ‖ And they [are] their own witnesses, ‖ They do not see, nor know, that they may be ashamed. **10** Who has formed a god, ‖ And poured out a molten image—not profitable? **11** Behold, all his companions are ashamed, ‖ As for artisans—they [are] of men, ‖ All of them gather together, they stand up, ‖ They fear, they are ashamed together. **12** He has worked iron [with] an axe, ‖ And has worked with coals, ‖ And forms it with hammers, ‖ And works it by his powerful arm, ‖ Indeed, he is hungry, and there is no power, ‖ He does not drink water, and he is wearied. **13** He has worked [with] wood, ‖ He has stretched out a rule, ‖ He marks it out with a line, ‖ He makes it with carving tools, ‖ And he marks it out with a compass, ‖ And makes it according to the form of a man, ‖ According to the beauty of a man, ‖ To remain in the house. **14** Cutting down cedars for himself, ‖ He also takes a cypress, and an oak, ‖ And he strengthens [it] for himself ‖ Among the trees of a forest, ‖ He has planted an ash, and the shower nourishes [it]. **15** And it has been for man to burn, ‖ And he takes of them, and becomes warm, ‖ Indeed, he kindles [it], and has baked bread, ‖ Indeed, he makes a god, and bows himself, ‖ He has made it a carved image, ‖ And he falls down

ISAIAH

to it. **16** Half of it he has burned in the fire, ‖ By [this] half of it he eats flesh, ‖ He roasts a roasting and is satisfied, ‖ Indeed, he is warm and says: "Aha, I have become warm, I have enjoyed the light." **17** And he has made its remnant for a god—For his carved image, ‖ He falls down to it, and worships, ‖ And prays to it, and he says, "Deliver me, for you [are] my god." **18** They have not known, nor do they understand, ‖ For He has coated their eyes from seeing, ‖ Their heart from acting wisely. **19** And none turn [it] back to his heart, ‖ Nor has knowledge nor understanding to say, "I have burned half of it in the fire, ‖ Indeed, I have also baked bread over its coals, ‖ I roast flesh and I eat, ‖ And I make its remnant for an abomination, ‖ I fall down to the stock of a tree." **20** Feeding on ashes, the heart is deceived, ‖ It has turned him aside, ‖ And he does not deliver his soul, nor says: "Is there not a lie in my right hand?" **21** "Remember these, O Jacob, and Israel, ‖ For you [are] My servant, ‖ I formed you, you [are] a servant to Me, ‖ O Israel, you do not forget Me. **22** I have blotted out, as [by] a thick cloud, ‖ Your transgressions, ‖ And as [by] a cloud, your sins, ‖ Return to Me, for I have redeemed you." **23** Sing, O heavens, for YHWH has worked, ‖ Shout, O lower parts of earth, ‖ Break forth, O mountains, with singing, ‖ Forest, and every tree in it, ‖ For YHWH has redeemed Jacob, ‖ And He beautifies Himself in Israel. **24** Thus said YHWH, your Redeemer, ‖ And your Framer from the womb: "I [am] YHWH, doing all things, ‖ Stretching out the heavens by Myself, ‖ Spreading out the earth—who [is] with Me? **25** Making void the tokens of devisers, ‖ And makes diviners mad, ‖ Turning the wise backward, ‖ And makes their knowledge foolish. **26** Confirming the word of His servant, ‖ He perfects the counsel of His messengers, ‖ Who is saying of Jerusalem, ‖ She is inhabited, ‖ And of cities of Judah, ‖ They will be built, and her ruins I raise up, **27** Who is saying to the deep, ‖ Be dry, and your rivers I cause to dry up, **28** Who is saying of Cyrus, My shepherd, ‖ And he perfects all My delight, ‖ So as to say of Jerusalem, You are built, ‖ And of the temple, You are founded."

45 Thus said YHWH, ‖ To His anointed, to Cyrus, ‖ Whose right hand I have laid hold on, ‖ To subdue nations before him, ‖ Indeed, I loose loins of kings, ‖ To open double doors before him, ‖ Indeed, gates are not shut: **2** "I go before you, and make crooked places straight, ‖ I shatter doors of bronze, ‖ And I cut bars of iron apart, **3** And have given to you treasures of darkness, ‖ Even treasures of secret places, ‖ So that you know that I, YHWH, ‖ Who am calling on your name—[am] the God of Israel. **4** For the sake of My servant Jacob, ‖ And of Israel My chosen, ‖ I also call you by your name, I surname you, ‖ And you have not known Me. **5** I [am] YHWH, and there is none else, ‖ There is no God except Me, ‖ I gird you, and you have not known Me. **6** So that they know from the rising of the sun, ‖ And from the west, that there is none besides Me, ‖ I [am] YHWH, and there is none else, **7** Forming light, and creating darkness, ‖ Making peace, and creating calamity, ‖ I [am] YHWH, doing all these things. **8** Drop, you heavens, from above, ‖ And clouds cause righteousness to flow, ‖ Earth opens, and they are fruitful, ‖ Salvation and righteousness spring up together, ‖ I, YHWH, have created it. **9** Woe [to] him who is striving with his Former ‖ (A potsherd with potsherds of the ground!) Does clay say to its Framer, What [are] you doing? And your work, He has no hands? **10** Woe [to] him who is saying to a father, What do you beget? Or to a wife, What do you bring forth?" **11** Thus said YHWH, The Holy One of Israel, and his Former: "Ask Me of the things coming concerning My sons, ‖ Indeed, concerning the work of My hands, you command Me. **12** I made earth, and created man on it, ‖ My hands stretched out the heavens, ‖ And I have commanded all their host. **13** I have stirred him up in righteousness, ‖ And I make all his ways straight, ‖ He builds My city, and sends out My captivity, ‖ Not for price, nor for bribe," said YHWH of Hosts. **14** Thus said YHWH: "The labor of Egypt, ‖ And the merchandise of Cush, ‖ And of the Sebaim—men of measure, ‖ Pass over to you, and they are yours, ‖ They go after you, they pass over in chains, ‖ And they bow themselves to you, ‖ They pray to you: Surely God [is] in you, ‖ And there is none else, no [other] God." **15** Surely You [are] a God hiding Yourself, God of Israel—Savior! **16** They have been ashamed, ‖ And they have even blushed—all of them, ‖ Those carving images have gone together in confusion. **17** Israel has been saved in YHWH, ‖ A

ISAIAH

perpetual salvation! You are not ashamed nor confounded ‖ For all ages of eternity! **18** For thus said YHWH, Creator of the heavens, ‖ He is God, ‖ Former of earth, and its Maker, ‖ He established it—He did not create it empty, ‖ For He formed it to be inhabited: "I [am] YHWH, and there is none else. **19** I have not spoken in secret, in a dark place of the earth, ‖ I have not said to the seed of Jacob, ‖ Seek Me in vain, ‖ I [am] YHWH, speaking righteousness, ‖ Declaring uprightness. **20** Be gathered, and come in, ‖ Come near together, you escaped of the nations, ‖ They have not known, ‖ Who are lifting up the wood of their carved image, ‖ And praying to a god [that] does not save. **21** Declare, and bring near, ‖ Indeed, they take counsel together, ‖ Who has proclaimed this from of old? [Who] has declared it from that time? Is it not I—YHWH? And there is no other god besides Me, ‖ A God righteous and saving, there is none except Me. **22** Turn to Me, and be saved, all the ends of the earth, ‖ For I [am] God, and there is none else. **23** I have sworn by Myself, ‖ A word has gone out from My mouth in righteousness, ‖ And it does not return, ‖ That to Me, every knee bows, every tongue swears. **24** Only in YHWH, one has said, ‖ Do I have righteousness and strength, ‖ He comes to Him, ‖ And all those displeased with Him are ashamed. **25** In YHWH are all the seed of Israel justified, ‖ And they boast themselves."

46 Bel has bowed down, Nebo is stooping, ‖ Their idols have been for the beast and for livestock, ‖ Your burdens are loaded, a burden to the weary. **2** They have stooped, they have bowed together, ‖ They have not been able to deliver the burden, ‖ And have gone into captivity themselves. **3** "Listen to Me, O house of Jacob, ‖ And all the remnant of Israel, ‖ Who are borne from the belly, ‖ Who are carried from the womb, **4** Even to old age, I [am] He, and to grey hairs I carry, ‖ I made, and I bear, indeed, I carry and deliver. **5** To whom do you liken Me, and make equal? And compare Me, that we may be like? **6** They are pouring out gold from a bag, ‖ And they weigh silver on the beam, ‖ They hire a refiner, and he makes it a god, ‖ They fall down, indeed, they bow themselves. **7** They lift him up on the shoulder, ‖ They carry him, and cause him to rest in his place, ‖ And he stands, he does not move from his place, ‖ Indeed, one cries to him, and he does not answer, ‖ He does not save him from his adversity. **8** Remember this, and show yourselves men, ‖ Turn [it] back, O transgressors, to the heart. **9** Remember former things of old, ‖ For I [am] Mighty, and there is none else, ‖ God—and there is none like Me. **10** Declaring the latter end from the beginning, ‖ And from of old that which has not been done, ‖ Saying, My counsel stands, ‖ And all My delight I do. **11** Calling a ravenous bird from the east, ‖ The man of My counsel from a far land, ‖ Indeed, I have spoken, indeed, I bring it in, ‖ I have formed [it], indeed, I do it. **12** Listen to Me, you mighty in heart, ‖ Who are far from righteousness. **13** I have brought My righteousness near, ‖ It is not far off, ‖ And My salvation—it does not linger, ‖ And I have given salvation in Zion, ‖ For Israel My glory!"

47 "Come down, and sit on the dust, ‖ O virgin daughter of Babylon, ‖ Sit on the earth, there is no throne, ‖ O daughter of the Chaldeans, ‖ For they no longer cry to you, ‖ O tender and delicate one. **2** Take millstones, and grind flour, ‖ Remove your veil, draw up the skirt, ‖ Uncover the leg, pass over the floods. **3** Your nakedness is revealed, indeed, your reproach is seen, ‖ I take vengeance, and I do not meet a man." **4** Our redeemer [is] YHWH of Hosts, ‖ His Name [is] the Holy One of Israel. **5** "Sit silent, and go into darkness, ‖ O daughter of the Chaldeans, ‖ For they no longer cry to you, Mistress of kingdoms. **6** I have been angry against My people, I have defiled My inheritance ‖ And I give them into your hand, ‖ You have not appointed mercies for them, ‖ You have made your yoke very heavy on the aged, **7** And you say, I am mistress for all time, ‖ While you have not laid these things to your heart, ‖ You have not remembered the latter end of it. **8** And now, hear this, O luxurious one, ‖ Who is sitting confidently—Who is saying in her heart, I [am], and none else, ‖ I do not sit [as] a widow, nor know bereavement. **9** And these two things come to you, ‖ In a moment, in one day: childlessness and widowhood, ‖ They have come on you according to their perfection, ‖ In the multitude of your sorceries, ‖ In the exceeding might of your charms. **10** And you are confident in your wickedness, ‖ You have said, There is none seeing me, ‖

ISAIAH

Your wisdom and your knowledge, ‖ It is turning you back, ‖ And you say in your heart, I [am], and none else. **11** And evil has come in on you, ‖ You do not know its rising, ‖ And disaster falls on you, ‖ You are not able to pacify it, ‖ And desolation comes on you suddenly, ‖ You do not know. **12** Now stand in your charms, ‖ And in the multitude of your sorceries, ‖ In which you have labored from your youth, ‖ It may be you are able to profit, ‖ It may be you terrify! **13** You have been wearied in the multitude of your counsels, ‖ Now stand up and let them save you—The charmers of the heavens, ‖ Those looking on the stars, ‖ Those teaching concerning the months—From those things that come on you! **14** Behold, they have been as stubble! Fire has burned them, ‖ They do not deliver themselves from the power of the flame, ‖ There is not a coal to warm them, a light to sit before it. **15** So they have been to you with whom you have labored, ‖ Your merchants from your youth, ‖ They have each wandered to his passage, ‖ None is saving you!"

48 "Hear this, O house of Jacob, ‖ Who are called by the name of Israel, ‖ And from the waters of Judah came out, ‖ Who are swearing by the Name of Y<small>HWH</small>, ‖ And make mention of the God of Israel, ‖ Not in truth nor in righteousness. **2** For they have been called from the Holy City, ‖ And been supported on the God of Israel, ‖ Y<small>HWH</small> of Hosts [is] His Name. **3** I declared the former things from that time, ‖ And they have gone forth from My mouth, ‖ And I proclaim them, ‖ Suddenly I have done, and it comes. **4** From My knowing that you are obstinate, ‖ And your neck—a sinew of iron, ‖ And your forehead—bronze, **5** And from that time I declare [it] to you, ‖ Before it comes I have caused you to hear, ‖ Lest you say, My idol has done them, ‖ And my carved image, ‖ And my molten image commanded them. **6** You have heard, see the whole of it, ‖ And you, do you not declare? I have caused you to hear new things from this time, ‖ And things reserved that you did not know. **7** Now they have been produced and not from that time, ‖ Indeed, before the day, and you have not heard them, ‖ Lest you say, Behold, I have known them. **8** Indeed, you have not heard, ‖ Indeed, you have not known, ‖ Indeed, your ear has not opened from that time, ‖ For I have known you deal treacherously, ‖ And [are] a transgressor from the belly, ‖ One is crying to you. **9** I defer My anger for My Name's sake, ‖ And [for] My praise I restrain for you, ‖ So as not to cut you off. **10** Behold, I have refined you, and not with silver, ‖ I have chosen you in a furnace of affliction. **11** For My sake, for My own sake, I do [it], ‖ For how is it defiled? And I do not give My glory to another. **12** Listen to me, O Jacob, and Israel, My called one, ‖ I [am] He, ‖ I [am] first, and I [am] last; **13** Also, My hand has founded earth, ‖ And My right hand stretched out the heavens, ‖ I am calling to them, they stand together. **14** Be gathered, all of you, and hear, ‖ Who among them declared these things? Y<small>HWH</small> has loved him, ‖ He does His pleasure on Babylon, ‖ And His arm [is on] the Chaldeans. **15** I have spoken, indeed, I have called him, I have brought him in, ‖ And he has made his way prosperous. **16** Come near to Me, hear this, ‖ I have not spoken in secret from the beginning, ‖ From the time of its being, I [am] there, ‖ And now Lord Y<small>HWH</small> has sent Me, and His Spirit." **17** Thus said Y<small>HWH</small>, your Redeemer, ‖ The Holy One of Israel: "I [am] your God Y<small>HWH</small>, teaching you to profit, ‖ Causing you to tread in the way you go. **18** O that you had attended to My commands, ‖ Then your peace is as a river, ‖ And your righteousness as billows of the sea, **19** And your seed is as sand, ‖ And the offspring of your bowels as gravel, ‖ His name would not be cut off nor destroyed before Me." **20** Go out from Babylon, flee from the Chaldeans, ‖ Declare with a voice of singing, ‖ Cause this to be heard, ‖ Bring it forth to the end of the earth, ‖ Say, "Y<small>HWH</small> has redeemed His servant Jacob." **21** And they have not thirsted in wastelands, ‖ He has caused them to go on, ‖ He has caused waters from a rock to flow to them, ‖ Indeed, he cleaves a rock, and waters flow. **22** "There is no peace," said Y<small>HWH</small>, "for the wicked!"

49 Listen, O islands, to Me, ‖ And attend, O peoples, from afar, ‖ Y<small>HWH</small> has called Me from the womb, ‖ From the bowels of My mother ‖ He has made mention of My Name. **2** And He makes My mouth as a sharp sword, ‖ He has hid Me in the shadow of His hand, ‖ And He makes Me for a clear arrow, ‖ He has hid Me in His quiver. **3** And He says to me, "You are My

ISAIAH

servant, O Israel, ‖ In whom I beautify Myself." **4** And I said, "I labored in vain, ‖ I consumed my power for emptiness and vanity, ‖ But my judgment [is] with Yhwh, ‖ And my wage with my God." **5** "And now," said Yhwh, who is forming Me from the belly—His Servant, ‖ To bring Jacob back to Him ‖ (Though Israel is not gathered, ‖ Yet I am honored in the eyes of Yhwh, ‖ And My God has been My strength). **6** And He says, "It has been a light thing ‖ That You are My Servant ‖ To raise up the tribes of Jacob, ‖ And to bring back the preserved of Israel, ‖ And I have given You for a light to the nations, ‖ To be My salvation to the end of the earth." **7** Thus said Yhwh, Redeemer of Israel, His Holy One, ‖ To the despised in soul, ‖ To the detested of a nation, ‖ To the Servant of rulers: "Kings see, and have risen, princes, and worship, ‖ For the sake of Yhwh, who is faithful, ‖ The Holy of Israel, and He chooses You." **8** Thus said Yhwh: "In a time of good pleasure I answered You, ‖ And in a day of salvation I helped You, ‖ And I keep You, and give You, ‖ For a covenant of the people, ‖ To establish the earth, ‖ To cause to inherit desolate inheritances. **9** To say to the bound, Go out, ‖ To those in darkness, Be uncovered. They feed on the ways, ‖ And their pasture is in all high places. **10** They do not hunger, nor thirst, ‖ Nor do mirage and sun strike them, ‖ For He who is pitying them leads them, ‖ And tends them by fountains of waters. **11** And I have made all My mountains for a way, ‖ And My highways are lifted up. **12** Behold, these come in from afar, ‖ And behold, these from the north, and from the sea, ‖ And these from the land of Sinim." **13** Sing, O heavens, and rejoice, O earth, ‖ And break forth, O mountains, with singing, ‖ For Yhwh has comforted His people, ‖ And He pities His afflicted ones. **14** And Zion says, "Yhwh has forsaken me, ‖ And my Lord has forgotten me." **15** "Does a woman forget her suckling, ‖ The loved one—the son of her womb? Indeed, these forget—but I do not forget you. **16** Behold, I have carved you on the palms of the hand, ‖ Your walls [are] continually before Me. **17** Those building you have hurried, ‖ Those destroying you, and laying you waste, go out from you. **18** Lift up your eyes, [look] around and see, ‖ All of them have been gathered, ‖ They have come to you. [As] I live," a declaration of Yhwh! "Surely you put on all of them as an ornament, ‖ And you bind them on like a bride. **19** Because your ruins, and your desolate places, ‖ And the land of your ruins, ‖ Are now surely restricted because of inhabitants, ‖ And those consuming you have been far off. **20** Again the sons of your bereavement say in your ears: The place is too narrow for me, ‖ Come near to me—and I dwell. **21** And you have said in your heart: Who has begotten these for me? And I [am] bereaved and barren, ‖ A captive, and turned aside, ‖ And who has nourished these? Behold, I was left by myself, these—where [are] they from?" **22** Thus said Lord Yhwh: "Behold, I lift up My hand to nations, ‖ And I raise up My ensign to peoples, ‖ And they have brought your sons in the bosom, ‖ And your daughters are carried on the shoulder. **23** And kings have been your nursing fathers, ‖ And their princesses—your nursing mothers; Face to the earth—they bow down to you, ‖ And they lick up the dust of your feet, ‖ And you have known that I [am] Yhwh, ‖ That those expecting Me are not ashamed." **24** Is prey taken from the mighty? And the captive of the righteous delivered? **25** For thus said Yhwh: "Even the captive of the mighty is taken, ‖ And the prey of the terrible is delivered, ‖ And I strive with your striver, and I save your sons. **26** And I have caused your oppressors to eat their own flesh, ‖ And they drink their own blood as new wine, ‖ And all flesh has known that I, Yhwh, ‖ Your Savior, and your Redeemer, ‖ [Am] the Mighty One of Jacob!"

50 Thus said Yhwh: "Where [is] this—the bill of your mother's divorce, ‖ Whom I sent away? Or to which of My creditors have I sold you? Behold, you have been sold for your iniquities, ‖ And for your transgressions ‖ Your mother has been sent away. **2** Why have I come, and there is no one? I called, and there is none answering, ‖ Has My hand been at all short of redemption? And is there not power in Me to deliver? Behold, by My rebuke I dry up a sea, ‖ I make rivers a wilderness, ‖ Their fish stink, for there is no water, ‖ And die with thirst. **3** I clothe the heavens [with] blackness, ‖ And I make their covering sackcloth." **4** Lord Yhwh has given to Me ‖ The tongue of taught ones, ‖ To know to aid the weary [by] a word, ‖ He awakens [Me] morning by morning, ‖ He awakens

[My] ear to hear as taught ones. **5** Lord YHWH opened My ear, ‖ And I did not rebel—I did not move backward. **6** I have given My back to those striking, ‖ And My cheeks to those plucking out, ‖ I did not hide My face from shame and spitting. **7** And Lord YHWH gives help to Me, ‖ Therefore I have not been ashamed, ‖ Therefore I have set My face as a flint, ‖ And I know that I am not ashamed. **8** Near [is] He who is justifying Me, ‖ Who contends with Me? We stand together, who [is] My opponent? Let him come near to Me. **9** Behold, Lord YHWH gives help to Me, ‖ Who [is] he that declares Me wicked? Behold, all of them wear out as a garment, ‖ A moth eats them. **10** "Who [is] among you, fearing YHWH, ‖ Listening to the voice of His Servant, ‖ That has walked in dark places, ‖ And there is no brightness for him? Let him trust in the Name of YHWH, ‖ And lean on his God. **11** Behold, all you kindling a fire, girding on sparks, ‖ Walk in the light of your fire, ‖ And in the sparks you have caused to burn, ‖ This has been to you from My hand, ‖ You lie down in grief!"

51 "Listen to Me, you pursuing righteousness, ‖ Seeking YHWH, ‖ Look attentively to the rock—you have been hewn, ‖ And to the hole of the pit—you have been dug. **2** Look attentively to your father Abraham, ‖ And to Sarah—she brings you forth, ‖ For—one—I have called him, ‖ And I bless him, and multiply him." **3** For YHWH has comforted Zion, ‖ He has comforted all her ruins, ‖ And He sets her wilderness as Eden, ‖ And her desert as a garden of YHWH, ‖ Joy, indeed, gladness is found in her, ‖ Confession, and the voice of song. **4** "Attend to Me, O My people, ‖ And, O My nation, give ear to Me. For a law goes out from Me, ‖ And My judgment to the light, ‖ I cause peoples to rest. **5** My righteousness [is] near, ‖ My salvation has gone out, ‖ And My arms judge peoples, ‖ Islands wait on Me, ‖ Indeed, on My arm they wait with hope. **6** Lift up your eyes to the heavens, ‖ And look attentively to the earth beneath, ‖ For the heavens have vanished as smoke, ‖ And the earth wears out as a garment, ‖ And its inhabitants die as gnats, ‖ And My salvation is for all time, ‖ And My righteousness is not broken. **7** Listen to Me, you who know righteousness, ‖ A people in whose heart [is] My law, ‖ Do not fear the reproach of men, ‖ And do not be frightened of their reviling, **8** For a moth eats them as a garment, ‖ And a worm eats them as wool, ‖ And My righteousness is for all time, ‖ And My salvation from generation to generation." **9** Awake, awake, put on strength, O arm of YHWH, ‖ Awake, as [in] days of old, generations of the ages, ‖ Are You not it that is hewing down Rahab, ‖ Piercing a dragon? **10** Are You not it that is drying up a sea, ‖ Waters of a great deep? That has made deep places of a sea ‖ A way for the passing of the redeemed? **11** And the ransomed of YHWH return, ‖ And they have come to Zion with singing, ‖ And continuous joy [is] on their head, ‖ They attain gladness and joy, ‖ Sorrow and sighing have fled away, **12** "I [am] He who comforts you, ‖ Who [are] you—and you are afraid of man? He dies! And of the son of man—he is made [like] grass! **13** And you forget YHWH your Maker, ‖ Who is stretching out the heavens, and founding earth, ‖ And you continually fear all the day, ‖ Because of the fury of the oppressor, ‖ As he has prepared to destroy. And where [is] the fury of the oppressor? **14** A wanderer has hurried to be loosed, ‖ And he does not die in the pit, ‖ And his bread is not lacking. **15** And I [am] your God YHWH, ‖ Quieting the sea when its billows roar, ‖ YHWH of Hosts [is] His Name. **16** And I put My words in your mouth, ‖ And have covered you with the shadow of My hand, ‖ To plant the heavens, and to found earth, ‖ And to say to Zion, You [are] My people." **17** Stir yourself, stir yourself, rise, Jerusalem, ‖ You who have drunk from the hand of YHWH ‖ The cup of His fury, ‖ The goblet, the cup of trembling, you have drunk, ‖ You have wrung out. **18** There is not a leader to her ‖ Out of all the sons she has borne, ‖ And there is none laying hold on her hand ‖ Out of all the sons she has nourished. **19** These two are meeting you, ‖ Who is moved for you? Spoiling and destruction, famine and sword! By whom do I comfort you? **20** Your sons have been wrapped up, they have lain down, ‖ At the head of all out places, as an antelope [in] a dragnet, ‖ They are full of the fury of YHWH, ‖ The rebuke of Your God. **21** Therefore, please hear this, ‖ O afflicted and drunken one, and not with wine, **22** Thus said your Lord YHWH, and your God, ‖ He pleads [for] His people: "Behold,

ISAIAH

I have taken the cup of trembling out of your hand, ‖ The goblet, the cup of My fury, ‖ You do not add to drink it anymore. **23** And I have put it into the hand of those afflicting you, ‖ Who have said to your soul, ‖ Bow down, and we pass over, ‖ And you make your body as the earth, ‖ And as the street to those passing by!"

52 Awake, awake, put on your strength, O Zion, ‖ Put on the garments of your beauty, Jerusalem—the Holy City; For the uncircumcised and unclean no longer enter into you again. **2** Shake yourself from dust, arise, sit, O Jerusalem, ‖ Bands of your neck have loosed themselves, ‖ O captive daughter of Zion. **3** For thus said YHWH: "You have been sold for nothing, ‖ And you are redeemed without money." **4** For thus said Lord YHWH: "My people went down at first ‖ To Egypt to sojourn there, ‖ And Asshur—he has oppressed it for nothing. **5** And now, what [have] I here," ‖ A declaration of YHWH, ‖ "That My people are taken for nothing? Its rulers cause howling," ‖ A declaration of YHWH, ‖ "And My Name is continually despised all the day. **6** Therefore My people know My Name, ‖ Therefore, in that day, ‖ Surely I [am] He who is speaking, behold Me." **7** How lovely on the mountains, ‖ Have been the feet of one proclaiming tidings, ‖ Sounding peace, proclaiming good tidings, ‖ Sounding salvation, ‖ Saying to Zion, "Your God has reigned." **8** The voice of your watchmen! They have lifted up the voice, together they cry aloud, ‖ Because they see eye to eye, ‖ In YHWH's turning back [to] Zion. **9** Break forth, sing together, ‖ O ruins of Jerusalem, ‖ For YHWH has comforted His people, ‖ He has redeemed Jerusalem. **10** YHWH has made His holy arm bare ‖ Before the eyes of all the nations, ‖ And all the ends of the earth have seen ‖ The salvation of our God. **11** Turn aside, turn aside, go out from there, ‖ Do not touch the unclean, ‖ Go out from her midst, ‖ Be pure, who are carrying the weapons of YHWH. **12** For you do not go out in haste, ‖ Indeed, you do not go on with flight, ‖ For YHWH [is] going before you, ‖ And the God of Israel [is] gathering you! **13** "Behold, My Servant acts wisely, ‖ He is high, and has been lifted up, ‖ And has been very high." **14** As many have been astonished at You ‖ (His appearance so marred by man, ‖ And His form by sons of men), **15** So He sprinkles many nations. Kings shut their mouth concerning Him, ‖ For that which was not recounted to them they have seen, ‖ And that which they had not heard they have understood!

53 Who has given credence to that which we heard? And the arm of YHWH, ‖ On whom has it been revealed? **2** Indeed, He comes up as a tender plant before Him, ‖ And as a root out of dry land, ‖ He has no form or splendor when we observe Him, ‖ Nor appearance, that we desire Him. **3** He is despised, and left of men, ‖ A Man of pains, and acquainted with sickness, ‖ And as one hiding the face from us, ‖ He is despised, and we did not esteem Him. **4** Surely He has borne our sicknesses, ‖ And our pains—He has carried them, ‖ And we have esteemed Him [as] plagued, struck of God, and afflicted. **5** And He is pierced for our transgressions, bruised for our iniquities, ‖ The discipline of our peace [is] on Him, ‖ And by His scourging we are healed. **6** All of us, like sheep, have wandered, ‖ Man has turned to his own way, ‖ And YHWH has laid on Him the punishment of us all. **7** It has been exacted, and He has answered, ‖ And He does not open His mouth, ‖ He is brought as a lamb to the slaughter, ‖ And as a sheep before its shearers is silent, ‖ So He does not open His mouth. **8** By restraint and by judgment He has been taken, ‖ And of His generation who meditates, ‖ That He has been cut off from the land of the living? He is plagued by the transgression of My people, **9** And He appoints His grave with the wicked, ‖ And with the rich at His death, ‖ Because He has done no violence, ‖ Nor [is] deceit in His mouth. **10** And YHWH has delighted to crush Him, ‖ He has made Him sick; If His soul makes an offering for guilt, ‖ He sees [His] seed—He prolongs [His] days, ‖ And the pleasure of YHWH prospers in His hand. **11** Of the labor of His soul He sees—He is satisfied, ‖ Through His knowledge My Righteous Servant gives righteousness to many, ‖ And He bears their iniquities. **12** Therefore I give a portion to Him among the many, ‖ And He apportions spoil with the mighty, ‖ Because that He exposed His soul to death, ‖ And He was numbered with transgressors, ‖ And He has borne the sin of many, ‖ And He intercedes for transgressors.

ISAIAH

54 "Sing, O barren, she [who] has not borne! Break forth with singing, and cry aloud, ‖ She [who] has not brought forth! For more [are] the sons of the desolate, ‖ Than the sons of the married one," said YHWH. **2** "Enlarge the place of your tent, ‖ And they stretch out the curtains of your dwelling places, ‖ Do not restrain—lengthen your cords, ‖ And make your pins strong. **3** For you break forth right and left, ‖ And nations possess your seed, **4** And they cause desolate cities to be inhabited. Do not fear, for you are not ashamed, ‖ Nor blush, for you are not confounded, ‖ For you forget the shame of your youth, ‖ And the reproach of your widowhood ‖ You do not remember anymore. **5** For your Maker [is] your husband, ‖ YHWH of Hosts [is] His Name, ‖ And your Redeemer [is] the Holy One of Israel, ‖ He is called God of all the earth. **6** For as a woman forsaken and grieved in spirit, ‖ YHWH has called you, ‖ Even a youthful wife when she is refused," said your God. **7** "In a small moment I have forsaken you, ‖ And in great mercies I gather you, **8** In overflowing wrath I hid My face [for] a moment from you, ‖ And in perpetual kindness I have loved you, ‖ Said your Redeemer—YHWH! **9** For this [is as] the days of Noah to Me, ‖ In that I have sworn that the waters of Noah ‖ Do not pass over the earth again—So I have sworn, ‖ Wrath is not on you, ‖ Nor rebuke against you. **10** For the mountains depart, and the hills remove, ‖ And My kindness does not depart from you, ‖ And the covenant of My peace does not remove," ‖ Says YHWH, your loving one. **11** "O afflicted, storm-tossed, not comforted, ‖ Behold, I am laying your stones with cement, ‖ And have founded you with sapphires, **12** And have made your pinnacles of agate, ‖ And your gates of carbuncle stones, ‖ And all your border of stones of delight, **13** And all your sons are taught of YHWH, ‖ And the peace of your sons [is] abundant. **14** You establish yourself in righteousness, ‖ Be far from oppression, for you do not fear, ‖ And from ruin, for it does not come near to you. **15** Behold, he diligently assembles without My desire, ‖ Whoever has assembled near you falls by you! **16** Behold, I have created an artisan, ‖ Blowing on a fire of coals, ‖ And bringing out an instrument for his work, ‖ And I have created a destroyer to destroy. **17** No weapon formed against you prospers, ‖ And every tongue rising against you, ‖ You condemn in judgment. This [is] the inheritance of the servants of YHWH, ‖ And their righteousness from Me," a declaration of YHWH!

55 "Behold, every thirsty one, ‖ Come to the waters, ‖ And he who has no money, ‖ Come, buy and eat, ‖ Indeed, come, buy wine and milk ‖ Without money and without price. **2** Why do you weigh money for that which is not bread? And your labor for that which is not for satiety? Listen diligently to Me, and eat good, ‖ And your soul delights itself in fatness. **3** Incline your ear, and come to Me, ‖ Hear, and your soul lives, ‖ And I make a perpetual covenant for you, ‖ The kind blessings of David that are steadfast. **4** Behold, I have given him [as] a witness to peoples, ‖ A leader and commander to peoples. **5** Behold, a nation you do not know, you call, ‖ And a nation who does not know you runs to you, ‖ For the sake of your God YHWH, ‖ And for the Holy One of Israel, ‖ Because He has beautified you." **6** Seek YHWH while He may be found, ‖ Call Him while He is near, **7** Let the wicked forsake his way, ‖ And the man of iniquity his thoughts, ‖ And he returns to YHWH, ‖ And He pities him, ‖ And to our God, ‖ For He multiplies to pardon. **8** "For My thoughts [are] not your thoughts, ‖ Nor your ways My ways," ‖ A declaration of YHWH, **9** "For [as] high [as] the heavens have been above the earth, ‖ So high have been My ways above your ways, ‖ And My thoughts above your thoughts. **10** For as the shower comes down, ‖ And the snow from the heavens, ‖ And does not return there, ‖ But has watered the earth, ‖ And has caused it to yield, and to spring up, ‖ And has given seed to the sower, and bread to the eater, **11** So is My word that goes out of My mouth, ‖ It does not return to Me empty, ‖ But has done that which I desired, ‖ And prosperously effected that [for] which I sent it. **12** For you go forth with joy, ‖ And you are brought in with peace, ‖ The mountains and the hills ‖ Break forth before you [with] singing, ‖ And all trees of the field clap the hand. **13** Instead of the thorn comes up fir, ‖ Instead of the brier comes up myrtle, ‖ And it has been to YHWH for a name, ‖ For a perpetual sign—it is not cut off!"

56 Thus said YHWH: "Keep judgment, and do righteousness, ‖ For My

ISAIAH

salvation [is] near to come, ‖ And My righteousness to be revealed." **2** O the blessedness of a man who does this, ‖ And of a son of man who keeps hold on it, ‖ Keeping the Sabbath from defiling it, ‖ And keeping his hand from doing any evil. **3** Do not let a son of the stranger speak, ‖ Who is joined to YHWH, saying, "YHWH certainly separates me from His people." Nor let the eunuch say, "Behold, I am a dried up tree," **4** For thus said YHWH: "To the eunuchs who keep My Sabbaths, ‖ And have fixed on that which I desired, ‖ And are keeping hold on My covenant: **5** I have given to them in My house, ‖ And within My walls a station and a name, ‖ Better than sons and than daughters, ‖ I give a continuous name to him ‖ That is not cut off. **6** And sons of the stranger, who are joined to YHWH, ‖ To serve Him, and to love the Name of YHWH, ‖ To be for servants to Him, ‖ All keeping from defiling the Sabbath, ‖ And those keeping hold on My covenant, **7** I have brought them to My holy mountain, ‖ And caused them to rejoice in My house of prayer, ‖ Their burnt-offerings and their sacrifices ‖ [Are] for a pleasing thing on My altar, ‖ For My house is called a house of prayer for all the peoples." **8** A declaration of Lord YHWH, ‖ Who is gathering the outcasts of Israel: "Again I gather to him—to his gathered ones." **9** Every beast of the field, ‖ Come to devour, every beast in the forest. **10** His watchmen [are] blind—all of them, ‖ They have not known, ‖ All of them [are] mute dogs, they are not able to bark, ‖ Dozing, lying down, loving to slumber. **11** And the dogs [are] strong of desire, ‖ They have not known sufficiency, ‖ And they [are] shepherds! They have not known understanding, ‖ All of them turned to their own way, ‖ Each to his dishonest gain from his quarter: **12** "Come, I take wine, ‖ And we drink, gulp strong drink, ‖ And tomorrow has been as this day, ‖ Great—exceedingly abundant!"

57 The righteous has perished, ‖ And there is none laying [it] to heart, ‖ And men of kindness are gathered, ‖ Without any considering that from the face of evil ‖ The righteous one is gathered. **2** He enters into peace, they rest on their beds, ‖ [Each] is going straightforward. **3** "And you, come near here, ‖ O sons of a sorceress, seed of an adulterer, ‖ Even you commit whoredom. **4** Against whom do you sport yourselves? Against whom do you enlarge the mouth ‖ [And] prolong the tongue? Are you not children of transgression? A false seed? **5** Who are inflamed among oaks, under every green tree, ‖ Slaughtering the children in valleys, ‖ Under clefts of the rocks. **6** Your portion [is] among the smooth things of a brook, ‖ They [are] your lot, ‖ You have also poured out an oblation to them, ‖ You have caused a present to ascend, ‖ Am I comforted in these things? **7** On a mountain, high and exalted, ‖ You have set your bed, ‖ You have also gone up there to make a sacrifice. **8** And behind the door, and the post, ‖ You have set up your memorial, ‖ For you have removed from Me, and go up, ‖ You have enlarged your bed, ‖ And cut [a covenant] with them, ‖ You have loved their bed, the station you saw, **9** And go joyfully to the king in ointment, ‖ And multiply your perfumes, ‖ And send your ambassadors far off, ‖ And humble yourself to Sheol. **10** You have labored in the greatness of your way, ‖ You have not said, It is desperate. You have found the life of your hand, ‖ Therefore you have not been sick. **11** And of whom have you been afraid, and fear, ‖ That you lie, and have not remembered Me? You have not laid [it] to your heart, ‖ Am I not silent, even from of old? And you do not fear Me? **12** I declare your righteousness, and your works, ‖ And they do not profit you. **13** When you cry, let your gatherings deliver you, ‖ And wind carries all of them away, ‖ Vanity takes away, ‖ And whoever is trusting in Me inherits the land, ‖ And possesses My holy mountain." **14** And He has said, "Raise up, raise up, prepare a way, ‖ Lift a stumbling-block out of the way of My people." **15** For thus said the high and exalted One, ‖ Inhabiting eternity, and His Name [is] holy: "I dwell in the high and holy place, ‖ And with the bruised and humble of spirit, ‖ To revive the spirit of the humble, ‖ And to revive the heart of bruised ones, **16** For I do not strive for all time, nor am I angry forever, ‖ For the spirit is feeble before Me, ‖ And the souls I have made. **17** For the iniquity of his dishonest gain, ‖ I have been angry, and I strike him, ‖ Hiding—and am angry, ‖ And he goes on turning back in the way of his heart. **18** I have seen his ways, and I heal him, indeed, I lead him, ‖ And repay comforts to him and to his mourning ones. **19** Producing the fruit of the lips, ‖ Peace, peace, to the far off, and to the near,

ISAIAH

‖ And I have healed him," said YHWH. **20** And the wicked [are] as the driven out sea, ‖ For it is not able to rest, ‖ And its waters cast out filth and mire. **21** "There is no peace," said my God, "for the wicked!"

58 "Call with the throat, do not restrain, lift up your voice as a horn, ‖ And declare to My people their transgression, ‖ And to the house of Jacob their sins; **2** They seek Me day by day, ‖ And they desire the knowledge of My ways, ‖ As a nation that has done righteousness, ‖ And has not forsaken the judgment of its God, ‖ They ask of Me judgments of righteousness, ‖ They desire the drawing near of God: **3** Why have we fasted, and You have not seen? We have afflicted our soul, and You do not know. Behold, you find pleasure in the day of your fast, ‖ And exact all your laborers. **4** Behold, you fast for strife and debate, ‖ And to strike with the fist of wickedness, ‖ You do not fast as [this] day, ‖ To sound your voice in the high place. **5** Is this like the fast that I choose? The day of a man's afflicting his soul? To bow his head as a reed, ‖ And spread out sackcloth and ashes? Do you call this a fast, ‖ And a desirable day—to YHWH? **6** Is this not the fast that I chose—To loose the bands of wickedness, ‖ To shake off the burdens of the yoke, ‖ And to send out the oppressed free, ‖ And draw off every yoke? **7** Is it not to deal your bread to the hungry, ‖ And bring home the wandering poor, ‖ That you see the naked and cover him, ‖ And do not hide yourself from your own flesh? **8** Then your light breaks forth as the dawn, ‖ And your health springs up in haste, ‖ Your righteousness has gone before you, ‖ The glory of YHWH gathers you. **9** Then you call, and YHWH answers, ‖ You cry, and He says, Behold Me. If you turn aside the yoke from your midst, ‖ The sending forth of the finger, ‖ And the speaking of vanity, **10** And bring out your soul to the hungry, ‖ And satisfy the afflicted soul, ‖ Then your light has risen in the darkness, ‖ And your thick darkness [is] as noon. **11** And YHWH continually leads you, ‖ And has satisfied your soul in drought, ‖ And He arms your bones, ‖ And you have been as a watered garden, ‖ And as an outlet of waters, whose waters do not lie. **12** And they have built the ancient ruins from you, ‖ You raise up the foundations of many generations, ‖ And one calls you, Repairer of the breach, ‖ Restorer of paths to rest in. **13** If you turn your foot from the Sabbath, ‖ [From] doing your own pleasure on My holy day, ‖ And have cried to the Sabbath, A delight, ‖ To the holy of YHWH, Honored, ‖ And have honored it, without doing your own ways, ‖ Without finding your own pleasure, ‖ And speaking a word. **14** Then you delight yourself on YHWH, ‖ And I have caused you to ride on high places of earth, ‖ And have caused you to eat the inheritance of your father Jacob, ‖ For the mouth of YHWH has spoken!"

59 Behold, the hand of YHWH ‖ Has not been shortened from saving, ‖ Nor His ear heavy from hearing. **2** But your iniquities have been separating ‖ Between you and your God, ‖ And your sins have hidden ‖ The Presence from you—from hearing. **3** For your hands have been defiled with blood, ‖ And your fingers with iniquity, ‖ Your lips have spoken falsehood, ‖ Your tongue mutters perverseness. **4** There is none calling in righteousness, ‖ And there is none pleading in faithfulness, ‖ Trusting on emptiness, and speaking falsehood, ‖ Conceiving perverseness, and bearing iniquity. **5** They have hatched eggs of a viper, ‖ And weave webs of a spider, ‖ Whoever is eating their eggs dies, and the crushed hatches a viper. **6** Their webs do not become a garment, ‖ Nor do they cover themselves with their works, ‖ Their works [are] works of iniquity, ‖ And a deed of violence [is] in their hands. **7** Their feet run to evil, ‖ And they hurry to shed innocent blood, ‖ Their thoughts [are] thoughts of iniquity, ‖ Spoiling and destruction [are] in their highways. **8** They have not known a way of peace, ‖ And there is no judgment in their paths, ‖ They have made their paths perverse for themselves, ‖ None treading in it has known peace. **9** Therefore judgment has been far from us, ‖ And righteousness does not reach us, ‖ We wait for light, and behold, darkness, ‖ For brightness—in thick darkness we go, **10** We feel [for] the wall like the blind, ‖ Indeed, we feel as without eyes, ‖ We have stumbled at noon as at twilight, ‖ In desolate places as the dead. **11** We make a noise as bears—all of us, ‖ And we coo severely as doves; We wait for judgment, and there is none, ‖ For salvation—it has been far from us. **12** For our transgressions have been multiplied

ISAIAH

before You, ‖ And our sins have testified against us, ‖ For our transgressions [are] with us, ‖ And our iniquities—we have known them. **13** Transgressing, and lying against YHWH, ‖ And removing from after our God, ‖ Speaking oppression and apostasy, ‖ Conceiving and uttering from the heart ‖ Words of falsehood. **14** And judgment is removed backward, ‖ And righteousness stands far off, ‖ For truth has been feeble in the street, ‖ And straightforwardness is not able to enter, **15** And the truth is lacking, ‖ And whoever is turning aside from evil, ‖ Is making himself a spoil. And YHWH sees, and it is evil in His eyes, ‖ That there is no judgment. **16** And He sees that there is no man, ‖ And is astonished that there is no intercessor, ‖ And His own arm gives salvation to Him, ‖ And His righteousness—it sustained Him. **17** And He puts on righteousness as a breastplate, ‖ And a helmet of salvation on His head, ‖ And He puts on garments of vengeance [for] clothing, ‖ And is covered, as [with] an upper-robe, [with] zeal. **18** According to deeds—so He repays. Fury to His adversaries, [their] deed to His enemies, ‖ To the islands He repays [their] deed. **19** And from the west they fear the Name of YHWH, ‖ And from the rising of the sun—His glory, ‖ When an adversary comes in as a flood, ‖ The Spirit of YHWH has raised an ensign against him. **20** "And the Redeemer has come to Zion, ‖ Even to captives of transgression in Jacob," ‖ A declaration of YHWH. **21** "And I—this [is] My covenant with them," said YHWH, "My Spirit that [is] on you, ‖ And My words that I have put in your mouth, ‖ And from the mouth of your seed, ‖ And from the mouth of your seed's seed," said YHWH, "From now on, even for all time!"

60 Arise, shine, for your light has come, ‖ And the glory of YHWH has risen on you. **2** For behold, the darkness covers the earth, ‖ And thick darkness the peoples, ‖ And YHWH rises on you, ‖ And His glory is seen on you. **3** And nations have come to your light, ‖ And kings to the brightness of your rising. **4** "Lift up your eyes around and see, ‖ All of them have been gathered, they have come to you, ‖ Your sons come from afar, ‖ And your daughters are supported on the side. **5** Then you see, and have become bright, ‖ And your heart has been afraid and enlarged, ‖ For the multitude of the sea turn to you, ‖ The forces of nations come to you. **6** A multitude of camels covers you, ‖ Dromedaries of Midian and Ephah, ‖ All of them from Sheba come, ‖ They carry gold and frankincense, ‖ And they proclaim the praises of YHWH. **7** All the flock of Kedar are gathered to you, ‖ The rams of Nebaioth serve you, ‖ They ascend My altar for acceptance, ‖ And I beautify the house of My beauty. **8** Who [are] these—they fly as a thick cloud, ‖ And as doves to their windows? **9** Surely islands wait for Me, ‖ And ships of Tarshish first, ‖ To bring your sons from afar, ‖ Their silver and their gold with them, ‖ To the Name of your God YHWH, ‖ And to the Holy One of Israel, ‖ Because He has beautified you. **10** And sons of a stranger have built your walls, ‖ And their kings serve you, ‖ For in My wrath I have struck you, ‖ And in My good pleasure I have pitied you. **11** And your gates have continually opened, ‖ They are not shut by day and by night, ‖ To bring the force of nations to you, ‖ Even their kings are led. **12** For the nation and the kingdom that does not serve you perishes, ‖ Indeed, the nations are utterly desolated. **13** The glory of Lebanon comes to you, ‖ Fir, pine, and box together, ‖ To beautify the place of My sanctuary, ‖ And I make the place of My feet honorable. **14** And the sons of those afflicting you ‖ Have come to you, bowing down, ‖ And all despising you ‖ Have bowed themselves to the soles of your feet, ‖ And they have cried to you: The City of YHWH, ‖ Zion of the Holy One of Israel! **15** Instead of your being forsaken and hated, ‖ And none passing through, ‖ I have made you for a continuous excellence, ‖ A joy of generation and generation. **16** And you have sucked the milk of nations, ‖ Indeed, you suckle the breast of kings, ‖ And you have known that I, YHWH, ‖ Your Savior, and Your Redeemer, ‖ [Am] the Mighty One of Jacob. **17** Instead of the bronze I bring in gold, ‖ And instead of the iron I bring in silver, ‖ And instead of the wood bronze, ‖ And instead of the stone iron, ‖ And I have made your inspection peace, ‖ And your exactors righteousness. **18** Violence is not heard in your land anymore, ‖ Spoiling and destruction in your borders, ‖ And you have called your walls Salvation, ‖ And your gates Praise. **19** The sun is no longer your light by day, ‖ And for brightness the moon does not give light to you, ‖ And YHWH has become to you ‖ A continuous light, and your God your beauty. **20** Your sun goes in no more, ‖ And your moon is not removed, ‖ For YHWH becomes a continuous light to you. And the days of your mourning have been completed. **21** And all your people [are] righteous, ‖ They possess the earth for all time, ‖ A branch of My planting, ‖ A work of My hands, to be beautified. **22** The little one becomes a chief, ‖ And the small one a mighty nation, ‖ I, YHWH, hurry it in its own time!"

61 "[The] Spirit of Lord YHWH [is] on Me, ‖ Because YHWH anointed Me ‖ To proclaim tidings to the humble, ‖ He sent Me to bind the broken of heart, ‖ To proclaim liberty to the captives, ‖ And an opening of bands to [those] bound. **2** To proclaim the year of the favor of YHWH, ‖ And the day of vengeance of our God, ‖ To comfort all mourners. **3** To appoint to mourners in Zion, ‖ To give to them beauty instead of ashes, ‖ The oil of joy instead of mourning, ‖ A covering of praise for a faded spirit, ‖ And He is calling to them, Trees of righteousness, ‖ The planting of YHWH—to be beautified." **4** And they have built the ancient ruins, ‖ They raise up the desolations of the ancients, ‖ And they have renewed ruined cities, ‖ The desolations of generation and generation. **5** And strangers have stood and fed your flock, ‖ And the sons of a foreigner ‖ [Are] your farmers and your vinedressers. **6** And you are called priests of YHWH, ‖ It is said of you [that you are] ministers of our God, ‖ You consume the strength of nations, ‖ And you boast yourselves in their glory. **7** Instead of your shame—double [honor], ‖ And [instead of] confusion, ‖ They rejoice in their portion, ‖ Therefore they take possession in their land a second time, ‖ Continuous joy [is] for them. **8** "For I [am] YHWH, loving judgment, ‖ Hating plunder for a burnt-offering, ‖ And I have given their wage in truth, ‖ And I make a perpetual covenant for them. **9** And their seed has been known among the nations, ‖ And their offspring in the midst of the peoples, ‖ All their beholders acknowledge them, ‖ For they [are] a seed YHWH has blessed." **10** I greatly rejoice in YHWH, ‖ My soul rejoices in my God, ‖ For He clothed me with garments of salvation, ‖ [And] covered me with a robe of righteousness, ‖ As a bridegroom prepares ornaments, ‖ And as a bride puts on her jewels. **11** For as the earth brings forth her shoots, ‖ And as a garden causes its sown things to shoot up, ‖ So Lord YHWH causes righteousness and praise ‖ To shoot up before all the nations!

62 For Zion's sake I am not silent, ‖ And for Jerusalem's sake I do not rest, ‖ Until her righteousness goes out as brightness, ‖ And her salvation burns as a torch. **2** And nations have seen your righteousness, ‖ And all kings your glory, ‖ And He is giving a new name to you, ‖ That the mouth of YHWH defines. **3** And you have been a crown of beauty in the hand of YHWH, ‖ And a turban of royalty in the hand of your God, **4** It is not said of you anymore, "Forsaken!" And of your land it is not said anymore, "Desolate," ‖ For to you is cried, "My delight [is] in her," ‖ And to your land, "Married," ‖ For YHWH has delighted in you, ‖ And your land is married. **5** For a young man marries a virgin, ‖ Your builders marry you, ‖ With the joy of a bridegroom over a bride, ‖ Your God rejoices over you. **6** "On your walls, O Jerusalem, I have appointed watchmen, ‖ All the day and all the night, ‖ Continually, they are not silent." O you remembering YHWH, do not keep silence for yourselves, **7** And do not give silence to Him, ‖ Until He establishes, and until He makes Jerusalem a praise in the earth. **8** YHWH has sworn by His right hand, ‖ Even by the arm of His strength: "I do not give your grain anymore [as] food for your enemies, ‖ Nor do sons of a stranger drink your new wine, ‖ For which you have labored. **9** For those gathering it eat it, and have praised YHWH, ‖ And those collecting it drink it in My holy courts." **10** Pass on, pass on through the gates, ‖ Prepare the way of the people, ‖ Raise up, raise up the highway, clear it from stones, ‖ Lift up an ensign over the peoples. **11** Behold, YHWH has proclaimed to the end of the earth: "Say to the daughter of Zion, ‖ Behold, your salvation has come, ‖ Behold, His hire [is] with Him, ‖ And His wage before Him." **12** And they have cried to them, "The People of the Holy One! The Redeemed of YHWH!" Indeed, to you is called, "The sought out one, a city not forsaken!"

ISAIAH

63 Who [is] this coming from Edom? With dyed garments from Bozrah? This that is honorable in His clothing, ‖ Traveling in the abundance of His power? "I, speaking in righteousness, mighty to save." **2** Why [is] Your clothing red? And Your garments as treading in a winepress? **3** "I have trodden a wine vat by Myself, ‖ And of the peoples there is no one with Me, ‖ And I tread them in My anger, ‖ And I trample them in My fury, ‖ Their strength is sprinkled on My garments, ‖ And I have defiled all My clothing. **4** For the day of vengeance [is] in My heart, ‖ And the year of My redeemed has come. **5** And I look attentively, and there is none helping, ‖ And I am astonished that there is none supporting, ‖ And My own arm gives salvation to Me. And My wrath—it has supported Me. **6** And I tread down peoples in My anger, ‖ And I make them drunk in My fury, ‖ And I bring down their strength to earth." **7** I make mention of the kind acts of YHWH, ‖ The praises of YHWH, ‖ According to all that YHWH has done for us, ‖ And the abundance of the goodness to the house of Israel, ‖ That He has done for them, ‖ According to His mercies, ‖ And according to the abundance of His kind acts. **8** And He says, "Surely they [are] My people, ‖ Sons—they do not lie," and He is to them for a Savior. **9** In all their distress [He is] no adversary, ‖ And the Messenger of His Presence saved them, ‖ In His love and in His pity He redeemed them, ‖ And He lifts them up, ‖ And carries them all the days of old. **10** And they have been rebellious and have grieved His Holy Spirit, ‖ And He turns to them for an enemy, ‖ He Himself has fought against them. **11** And He remembers the days of old, ‖ Moses—his people. Where [is] He who is bringing them up from the sea, ‖ The shepherd of His flock? Where [is] He who is putting in its midst His Holy Spirit? **12** Leading by the right hand of Moses, the arm of His glory, ‖ Cleaving waters from before them, ‖ To make to Himself a continuous Name. **13** Leading them through the depths, ‖ They do not stumble as a horse in a plain. **14** As a beast goes down into a valley, ‖ The Spirit of YHWH causes him to rest, ‖ So You have led Your people, ‖ To make to Yourself a glorious Name. **15** Look attentively from the heavens, ‖ And see from Your holy and beautiful habitation, ‖ Where [is] Your zeal and Your might? The multitude of Your bowels and Your mercies—Are they restrained? **16** For You [are] our Father, ‖ For Abraham has not known us, ‖ And Israel does not acknowledge us, ‖ You, O YHWH, [are] our Father, ‖ Our Redeemer from the Age, [is] Your Name. **17** Why cause us to wander, O YHWH, from Your ways? You harden our heart from Your fear, ‖ Turn back for Your servants' sake, ‖ The tribes of Your inheritance. **18** For a little while Your holy people possessed, ‖ Our adversaries have trodden down Your sanctuary. **19** We have been from of old, ‖ You have not ruled over them, ‖ Your Name is not called on them!

64 Did You not tear the heavens? You came down, ‖ Mountains flowed from Your presence, **2** (As fire kindles stubble—Fire causes water to boil), ‖ To make Your Name known to Your adversaries, ‖ Nations tremble from Your presence. **3** In Your doing fearful things [that] we do not expect, ‖ You came down, ‖ Mountains flowed from Your presence. **4** Even from antiquity [men] have not heard, ‖ They have not given ear, ‖ Eye has not seen a God except You, ‖ He works for those waiting for Him. **5** You have met with the rejoicer ‖ And the doer of righteousness, ‖ In Your ways they remember You, ‖ Behold, You have been angry when we sin, ‖ By them [is] continuance, and we are saved. **6** And we are as unclean—all of us, ‖ And all our righteous acts [are] as garments of menstruation; And we fade as a leaf—all of us. And our iniquities take us away as wind. **7** And there is none calling on Your Name, ‖ Stirring himself up to lay hold on You, ‖ For You have hid Your face from us, ‖ And You melt us away by our iniquities. **8** And now, O YHWH, You [are] our Father, ‖ We [are] the clay, and You [are] our Framer, ‖ And the work of Your hand—all of us. **9** Do not be angry, O YHWH, very severely, ‖ Nor remember iniquity forever, ‖ Behold, look attentively, we implore You, ‖ We [are] all Your people. **10** Your holy cities have been a wilderness, ‖ Zion has been a wilderness, ‖ Jerusalem a desolation. **11** Our holy and our beautiful house, ‖ Where our fathers praised You, ‖ Has become burned with fire, ‖ And all our desirable things have become a ruin. **12** Do

ISAIAH

You refrain Yourself for these, YHWH? You are silent, and afflict us very severely!

65 "I have been inquired of by those who did not ask, ‖ I have been found by those who did not seek Me, ‖ I have said, Behold Me, behold Me, ‖ To a nation not calling on My Name. **2** I have spread out My hands all the day ‖ To an apostate people, ‖ Who are going in the way [that is] not good, ‖ After their own thoughts. **3** The people who are continually provoking Me to anger, ‖ To My face, ‖ Sacrificing in gardens, and making incense on the bricks: **4** Who are dwelling among tombs, ‖ And lodge in reserved places, ‖ Who are eating flesh of the sow, ‖ And a piece of abominations—their vessels. **5** Who are saying, Keep to yourself, do not come near to me, ‖ For I have declared you unholy. These [are] smoke in My anger, ‖ A fire burning all the day. **6** Behold, it is written before Me: I am not silent, but have repaid; And I have repaid into their bosom, **7** Your iniquities, and the iniquities of your fathers together," said YHWH, "Who have made incense on the mountains, ‖ And have reproached Me on the heights, ‖ And I have measured their former work into their bosom." **8** Thus said YHWH: "As the new wine is found in the cluster, ‖ And one has said, Do not destroy it for a blessing [is] in it, ‖ So I do for My servants' sake, ‖ Not to destroy the whole. **9** And I have brought out a Seed from Jacob, ‖ And from Judah a Possessor of My mountain, ‖ And My chosen ones possess it, ‖ And My servants dwell there. **10** And Sharon has been for the habitation of a flock, ‖ And the Valley of Achor for the lying down of a herd, ‖ For My people who have sought Me. **11** And you [are] those forsaking YHWH, ‖ Who are forgetting My holy mountain, ‖ Who are setting a table in array for Gad, ‖ And who are filling a mixture for Meni. **12** And I have numbered you for the sword, ‖ And all of you bow down for slaughter, ‖ Because I called, and you have not answered, ‖ I have spoken, and you have not listened, ‖ And you do evil in My eyes, ‖ And on that which I did not desire—fixed." **13** Therefore, thus said Lord YHWH: "Behold, My servants eat, and you hunger, ‖ Behold, My servants drink, and you thirst, ‖ Behold, My servants rejoice, and you are ashamed, **14** Behold, My servants sing from joy of heart, ‖ And you cry from pain of heart, ‖ And you howl from breaking of spirit. **15** And you have left your name ‖ For an oath for My chosen ones, ‖ And Lord YHWH has put you to death, ‖ And He gives another name to His servants; **16** So that he who is blessing himself in the earth, ‖ Blesses himself in the God of faithfulness, ‖ And he who is swearing in the earth, ‖ Swears by the God of faithfulness, ‖ Because the former distresses have been forgotten, ‖ And because they have been hid from My eyes. **17** For behold, I am creating new heavens and a new earth, ‖ And the former things are not remembered, ‖ Nor do they ascend on the heart. **18** But rejoice, and rejoice forever, that I [am] Creator, ‖ For behold, I am creating Jerusalem [to be] a rejoicing, ‖ And her people a joy. **19** And I have rejoiced in Jerusalem, ‖ And have rejoiced in My people, ‖ And the voice of weeping is not heard in her anymore, and the voice of crying. **20** There is not a suckling of [mere] days there anymore, ‖ And an aged man who does not complete his days, ‖ For the youth dies one hundred years old, ‖ And the sinner, one hundred years old, is lightly esteemed. **21** And they have built houses, and inhabited, ‖ And planted vineyards, and eaten their fruit. **22** They do not build, and another inhabit, ‖ They do not plant, and another eat, ‖ For as the days of a tree [are] the days of My people, ‖ And My chosen wear out the work of their hands. **23** They do not labor for a vain thing, ‖ Nor do they bring forth for trouble, ‖ For they [are] the seed of the blessed of YHWH, ‖ And their offspring with them. **24** And it has come to pass, ‖ They do not yet call, and I answer, ‖ They are yet speaking, and I hear. **25** Wolf and lamb feed as one, ‖ And a lion eats straw as an ox, ‖ As for the serpent—its food [is] dust, ‖ They do no evil, nor destroy, ‖ In all My holy mountain," said YHWH!

66 Thus said YHWH: "The heavens [are] My throne, ‖ And the earth My footstool, ‖ Where [is] this—the house that you build for Me? And where [is] this—the place—My rest? **2** And My hand has made all these, ‖ And all these things are," ‖ A declaration of YHWH! "And to this one I look attentively, ‖ To the humble and bruised in spirit, ‖ And who is trembling at My word. **3** Whoever slaughters the ox strikes a man, ‖ Whoever sacrifices the lamb beheads a dog, ‖ Whoever is bringing up a present—The blood of a sow, ‖ Whoever is making mention of frankincense, ‖ Is blessing iniquity. Indeed, they have fixed on their own ways, ‖ And their soul has delighted in their abominations. **4** I also—I fix on their distress, ‖ And I bring in their fears to them, ‖ Because I have called, and there is none answering, ‖ I spoke, and they have not listened, ‖ And they do evil in My eyes, ‖ And on that which I did not desire—fixed." **5** Hear a word of YHWH, ‖ You who are trembling at His word: "Your brothers who are hating you, ‖ Who are driving you out for My Name's sake, have said, ‖ YHWH is honored, and we look on your joy, ‖ But they are ashamed." **6** A voice of noise from the city, ‖ A voice from the temple, ‖ The voice of YHWH, ‖ Giving repayment to His enemies. **7** "Before she is pained she has brought forth, ‖ Before a pang comes to her, ‖ She has delivered a male. **8** Who has heard anything like this? Who has seen anything like these? Is earth caused to bring forth in one day? Is a nation born at once? For she has been pained, ‖ Zion has also borne her sons. **9** Do I bring to the birth, ‖ And not cause to bring forth?" says YHWH, ‖ "Am I not He who is causing to beget? I have also restrained," said your God. **10** "Rejoice with Jerusalem, ‖ And be glad in her, all you loving her, ‖ Rejoice with her for joy, ‖ All you who are mourning for her, **11** So that you suckle, and have been satisfied, ‖ From the breast of her consolations, ‖ So that you wring out, and have delighted yourselves ‖ From the abundance of her glory." **12** For thus said YHWH: "Behold, I am stretching out to her peace as a river, ‖ And the glory of nations as an overflowing stream, ‖ And you have sucked, ‖ You are carried on the side, ‖ And you are dandled on the knees. **13** As one whom his mother comforts, so do I comfort you, ‖ Indeed, you are comforted in Jerusalem." **14** And you have seen, and your heart has rejoiced, ‖ And your bones flourish as tender grass, ‖ And the hand of YHWH has been known to His servants, ‖ And He has been indignant with His enemies. **15** For behold, YHWH comes in fire, ‖ And His chariots as a windstorm, ‖ To refresh His anger in fury, ‖ And His rebuke in flames of fire. **16** For by fire and by His sword, ‖ YHWH does judgment with all flesh. And many have been YHWH's pierced ones. **17** "Those sanctifying and cleansing themselves [to go] to the gardens, ‖ One after another in the midst, ‖ Eating flesh of the sow, ‖ And of the abomination, and of the muroid, ‖ Are consumed together," ‖ A declaration of YHWH. **18** "And I—their works and their thoughts, ‖ I come to gather all the nations and tongues, ‖ And they have come and seen My glory. **19** And I have set a sign among them, ‖ And have sent out of them those escaping to the nations ‖ (Tarshish, Pul, and Lud, drawing bow, Tubal and Javan, the islands that are far off), ‖ Who have not heard My fame, nor seen My glory, ‖ And they have declared My glory among nations. **20** And they have brought all your brothers out of all the nations, ‖ A present to YHWH, ‖ On horses, and on chariot, and on litters, ‖ And on mules, and on dromedaries, ‖ To My holy mountain Jerusalem," said YHWH, "As the sons of Israel bring the present in a clean vessel, ‖ Into the house of YHWH. **21** And I also take of them for priests, ‖ For Levites," said YHWH. **22** "For as the new heavens and the new earth that I am making, ‖ Are standing before Me," ‖ A declaration of YHWH, ‖ "So your seed and your name remain. **23** And it has been from month to month, ‖ And from Sabbath to Sabbath, ‖ All flesh come to bow themselves before Me," said YHWH. **24** "And they have gone forth, ‖ And looked on the carcasses of the men ‖ Who are transgressing against Me, ‖ For their worm does not die, ‖ And their fire is not quenched, ‖ And they have been an abhorrence to all flesh!"

JEREMIAH

1 Words of Jeremiah son of Hilkiah, of the priests who [are] in Anathoth, in the land of Benjamin, **2** to whom the word of YHWH has been in the days of Josiah son of Amon, king of Judah, in the thirteenth year of his reign, **3** and it is in the days of Jehoiakim son of Josiah, king of Judah, until the completion of the eleventh year of Zedekiah son of Josiah, king of Judah, until the expulsion of Jerusalem in the fifth month. **4** And there is a word of YHWH to me, saying, **5** "Before I form you in the belly, I have known you; and before you come forth from the womb I have separated you; I have made you a prophet to the nations." **6** And I say, "Aah! Lord YHWH! Behold, I have not known—to speak, for I [am] a youth." **7** And YHWH says to me, "Do not say, I [am] a youth, for to all to whom I send you—go, and all that I command you—speak. **8** Do not be afraid of their faces, for I [am] with you to deliver you," a declaration of YHWH. **9** And YHWH puts forth His hand, and strikes against my mouth, and YHWH says to me, "Behold, I have put My words in your mouth. **10** See, I have charged you this day concerning the nations, and concerning the kingdoms, to pluck up, and to break down, and to destroy, and to throw down, to build, and to plant." **11** And there is a word of YHWH to me, saying, "What are you seeing, Jeremiah?" And I say, "I am seeing a rod of an almond tree." **12** And YHWH says to me, "You have seen well: for I am watching over My word to do it." **13** And there is a word of YHWH to me a second time, saying, "What are you seeing?" And I say, "I am seeing a blown pot, and its face [is] from the north." **14** And YHWH says to me, "From the north the evil is loosed against all inhabitants of the land. **15** For behold, I am calling for all families of the kingdoms of the north," a declaration of YHWH, "And they have come, and each put his throne at the opening of the gates of Jerusalem, and by its walls all around, and by all cities of Judah. **16** And I have spoken My judgments with them concerning all their evil, in that they have forsaken Me, and make incense to other gods, and bow themselves to the works of their own hands. **17** And you, you gird up your loins, and have arisen, and spoken to them all that I command you: do not be frightened because of them, lest I frighten you before them. **18** And I, behold, have given you this day for a fortified city, and for an iron pillar, and for bronze walls over all the land, to the kings of Judah, to its heads, to its priests, and to the people of the land; **19** and they have fought against you, and they do not prevail against you; for I [am] with you," a declaration of YHWH, "to deliver you."

2 And there is a word of YHWH to me, saying, **2** "Go, and you have called in the ears of Jerusalem, saying, Thus said YHWH: I have remembered for you ‖ The kindness of your youth, the love of your espousals, ‖ Your going after Me in a wilderness, in a land not sown. **3** Israel [is] holy to YHWH, ‖ The first-fruit of His increase, ‖ All consuming him are guilty, ‖ Calamity comes to them," ‖ A declaration of YHWH. **4** Hear a word of YHWH, O house of Jacob, ‖ And all you families of the house of Israel— **5** Thus said YHWH: "What perversity have your fathers found in Me, ‖ That they have gone far off from Me, ‖ And go after vanity, and become vain, **6** And have not said, Where [is] YHWH, ‖ Who brings us up out of the land of Egypt, ‖ Who leads us in a wilderness, ‖ In a land of deserts and pits, ‖ In a dry land, and of death-shade, ‖ In a land that none has passed through, ‖ Nor has man dwelt there? **7** Indeed, I bring you into a land of fruitful fields, ‖ To eat its fruit and its goodness, ‖ And you come in and defile My land, ‖ And have made My inheritance an abomination. **8** The priests have not said, Where [is] YHWH? And those handling the Law have not known Me. And the shepherds transgressed against Me, ‖ And the prophets have prophesied by Ba'al, ‖ And have gone after those who do not profit. **9** Therefore, I yet plead with you," ‖ A declaration of YHWH, ‖ "And I plead with your sons' sons. **10** For pass to the islands of Chittim and see, ‖ And send to Kedar and consider well, ‖ And see if there has been [anything] like this: **11** Has a nation changed gods? (And they [are] no gods!) And My people has changed its glory ‖ For

JEREMIAH

that which does not profit. **12** Be astonished, you heavens, at this, ‖ Indeed, be frightened, be greatly desolated," ‖ A declaration of YHWH. **13** "For My people have done two evils, ‖ They have forsaken Me, a fountain of living waters, ‖ To hew out for themselves wells—broken wells, ‖ That do not contain the waters. **14** [Is] Israel a servant? Is he a child of the house? Why has he been for a prey? **15** Young lions roar against him, ‖ They have given forth their voice, ‖ And make his land become a desolation, ‖ His cities have been burned without inhabitant. **16** Also sons of Noph and Tahapanes ‖ Consume you—the crown of the head! **17** Do you not do this to yourself? [By] your forsaking your God YHWH, ‖ At the time He is leading you in the way? **18** And now, why do you [go] in the way of Egypt, ‖ To drink the waters of Sihor? And why do you [go] in the way of Asshur, ‖ To drink the waters of the River? **19** Your wickedness instructs you, ‖ And your backslidings reprove you, ‖ Know and see that an evil and a bitter thing [is] your forsaking your God YHWH, ‖ And My fear not being on you," ‖ A declaration of Lord YHWH of Hosts. **20** "For from of old you have broken your yoke, ‖ Drawn away your bands, and say, I do not serve, ‖ For on every high height, and under every green tree, ‖ You are wandering—a harlot. **21** And I planted you [as] a choice vine, wholly of true seed, ‖ And how have you been turned ‖ Into the degenerate shoots of a strange vine to Me? **22** But though you wash with natron, ‖ And multiply soap to yourself, ‖ Your iniquity is marked before Me," ‖ A declaration of Lord YHWH. **23** "How can you say, I have not been defiled, ‖ I have not gone after the Ba'alim? See your way in a valley, know what you have done, ‖ A swift dromedary winding her ways, **24** A wild donkey accustomed to a wilderness, ‖ She has swallowed up wind in the desire of her soul, ‖ Her meeting—who turns her back? None seeking her weary themselves, ‖ In her month they find her. **25** Withhold your foot from being unshod, ‖ And your throat from thirst, ‖ And you say, It is incurable, ‖ No, for I have loved strangers, and I go after them. **26** As the shame of a thief when he is found, ‖ So has the house of Israel been put to shame, ‖ They, their kings, their heads, ‖ And their priests, and their prophets, **27** Saying to wood, You [are] my father! And to a stone, You have brought me forth, ‖ For they turned to me the back and not the face, ‖ And in the time of their distress, ‖ They say, Arise, and save us. **28** And where [are] your gods, that you have made to yourself? Let them arise, if they may save you, ‖ In the time of your distress, ‖ For—the number of your cities have been your gods, O Judah, **29** Why do you strive with Me? All of you have transgressed against Me," ‖ A declaration of YHWH. **30** "I have struck your sons in vain, ‖ They have not accepted instruction, ‖ Your sword has devoured your prophets, ‖ As a destroying lion. **31** O generation, see the word of YHWH: Have I been a wilderness to Israel? A land of thick darkness? Why have My people said, ‖ We wandered freely, ‖ We do not come to You again. **32** Does a virgin forget her ornaments? A bride her bands? And My people have forgotten Me [for] days without number. **33** Why do you make your ways pleasing to seek love? Therefore you have even taught the wicked your ways. **34** Also the blood of innocent needy souls ‖ Has been found on your skirts, ‖ I have not found them by digging, ‖ But on all these. **35** And you say, Because I have been innocent, ‖ Surely His anger has turned back from me? Behold, I have been judged with you, ‖ Because of your saying, I have not sinned. **36** What? You are very vile to repeat your way, ‖ You are even ashamed of Egypt, ‖ As you have been ashamed of Asshur, **37** Also you go out from this, ‖ And your hands on your head, ‖ For YHWH has kicked at your confidences, ‖ And you do not give prosperity to them!"

3 "Saying, Behold, one sends his wife away, ‖ And she has gone from him, ‖ And she has been to another man, ‖ Does he return to her again? Is that land not greatly defiled? And you have committed whoredom with many lovers, ‖ And turn to Me again," ‖ A declaration of YHWH. **2** "Lift your eyes to the high places, and see, ‖ Where have you not been lain with? You have sat for them on the ways, ‖ As an Arab in a wilderness, ‖ And you defile the land, ‖ By your fornications, and by your wickedness. **3** And showers are withheld, and there has been no spring rain. You have the forehead of a whorish woman, ‖ You have refused to be ashamed. **4** Have you not from now on called to Me, ‖ My Father, You [are] the leader of my youth? **5** Does

He keep for all time? Watch forever? Behold, you have spoken these things, ‖ And you do evil, and prevail." 6 And YHWH says to me, in the days of Josiah the king, "Have you seen that which backsliding Israel has done? She is going on every high mountain, and to the place of every green tree, and commits fornication there. 7 And I say, after her doing all these, Return to Me, and she has not returned, and her treacherous sister Judah sees it. 8 And I see that for all the causes whereby backsliding Israel committed adultery, I have sent her away, and I give the bill of her divorce to her; and her treacherous sister Judah has not feared, and goes and commits fornication—she also. 9 And it has come to pass, from the vileness of her fornication, that the land is defiled, and she commits fornication with stone and with wood. 10 And even in all this her treacherous sister Judah has not turned back to Me with all her heart, but with falsehood," a declaration of YHWH. 11 And YHWH says to me: "Backsliding Israel has justified herself, ‖ More than treacherous Judah. 12 Go, and you have proclaimed these words toward the north, and have said, Return, O backsliding Israel," ‖ A declaration of YHWH! "I do not cause My anger to fall on you, for I [am] kind," ‖ A declaration of YHWH, ‖ "I do not watch for all time. 13 Only, know your iniquity, ‖ For you have transgressed against your God YHWH, ‖ And you scatter your ways to strangers, ‖ Under every green tree, ‖ And you have not listened to My voice," ‖ A declaration of YHWH. 14 "Return, O backsliding sons," ‖ A declaration of YHWH. "For I have ruled over you, ‖ And taken you—one from a city, and two from a family, ‖ And have brought you to Zion, 15 And I have given shepherds to you ‖ According to My own heart, ‖ And they have fed you with knowledge and understanding. 16 And it has come to pass, when you are multiplied, ‖ And have been fruitful in the land, ‖ In those days," ‖ A declaration of YHWH, ‖ "They no longer say, The Ark of the Covenant of YHWH, ‖ Nor does it go up on the heart, ‖ Nor do they remember concerning it, ‖ Nor do they inspect, nor is it made again. 17 At that time they cry to Jerusalem, O throne of YHWH, ‖ And all the nations have been gathered to her, ‖ For the Name of YHWH, to Jerusalem, ‖ Nor do they go after the stubbornness of their evil heart anymore. 18 In those days the house of Judah ‖ Goes to the house of Israel, ‖ And they come together from the land of the south, ‖ To the land that I caused your fathers to inherit. 19 And I have said, How do I put you among the sons, ‖ And give a desirable land to you, ‖ A beautiful inheritance of the hosts of nations, ‖ And I say, You call Me—My Father, ‖ And you do not turn back from after Me. 20 But a woman has deceived her friend, ‖ So you have dealt treacherously with Me, ‖ O house of Israel," ‖ A declaration of YHWH. 21 A voice is heard on high places—weeping, ‖ Supplications of the sons of Israel, ‖ For they have made their way perverse, ‖ They have forgotten their God YHWH. 22 "Return, O backsliding sons, ‖ I cause your backslidings to cease." "Behold us, we have come to You, ‖ For You [are] our God YHWH. 23 Surely in vain—from the heights, ‖ The multitude of mountains—Surely the salvation of Israel [is] in our God YHWH. 24 And the shameful thing has devoured ‖ The labor of our fathers from our youth, ‖ Their flock and their herd, ‖ Their sons and their daughters. 25 We have lain down in our shame, and our confusion covers us, ‖ For we have sinned against our God YHWH, ‖ We, and our fathers, from our youth even to this day, ‖ Nor have we listened to the voice of our God YHWH!"

4 "If you return, O Israel," ‖ A declaration of YHWH, ‖ "Return to Me, ‖ And if you turn aside Your abominations from My face, ‖ Then you do not bemoan. 2 And you have sworn—YHWH lives, ‖ In truth, in judgment, and in righteousness, ‖ And nations have blessed themselves in Him, ‖ And they boast themselves in Him." 3 For thus said YHWH, ‖ To the man of Judah, and to Jerusalem: "Till for yourselves tillage, ‖ And do not sow to the thorns. 4 Be circumcised to YHWH, ‖ And turn aside the foreskins of your heart, ‖ O man of Judah, and you inhabitants of Jerusalem, ‖ Lest My fury goes out as fire, and has burned, ‖ And there is none quenching, ‖ Because of the evil of your doings." 5 Declare in Judah, and sound in Jerusalem, and say: "Blow a horn in the land, ‖ Call, Fill up together, ‖ And say, Assemble yourselves and let us go into the fortified cities. 6 Lift up an ensign toward Zion, ‖ Strengthen yourselves, do not stand still, ‖ For I am

JEREMIAH

bringing evil in from the north, ‖ And a great destruction." 7 A lion has gone up from his thicket, ‖ And a destroyer of nations has journeyed, ‖ He has come forth from his place ‖ To make your land become a desolation, ‖ Your cities are laid waste, without inhabitant. 8 For this, gird on sackcloth, lament and howl, ‖ For the fierce anger of YHWH has not turned back from us. 9 "And it has come to pass in that day," ‖ A declaration of YHWH, ‖ "The heart of the king perishes, ‖ And the heart of the princes, ‖ And the priests have been astonished, ‖ And the prophets wonder." 10 And I say, "Aah! Lord YHWH, ‖ Surely you have entirely forgotten this people and Jerusalem, ‖ Saying, Peace is for you, ‖ And a sword has struck to the soul!" 11 At that time it is said of this people, ‖ And of Jerusalem: "A dry wind of high places in the wilderness, ‖ The way of the daughter of My people ‖ (Not for winnowing, nor for cleansing), 12 A full wind from these comes for Me, ‖ Now also, I speak judgments with them." 13 "Behold, he comes up as clouds, ‖ And his chariots as a windstorm, ‖ His horses have been lighter than eagles, ‖ Woe to us, for we have been spoiled." 14 Wash evil from your heart, O Jerusalem, ‖ That you may be saved, ‖ Until when do you lodge in your heart ‖ Thoughts of your strength? 15 For a voice is declaring from Dan, ‖ And sounding sorrow from Mount Ephraim: 16 "Make mention to the nations, ‖ Behold, sound to Jerusalem, ‖ Besiegers are coming from the far-off land, ‖ And they give forth their voice against cities of Judah. 17 As the keepers of a field ‖ They have been against her all around, ‖ For she has been rebellious with Me," ‖ A declaration of YHWH. 18 "Your way and your doings have done these to you, ‖ This [is] your distress, for [it is] bitter, ‖ For it has struck to your heart." 19 My bowels, my bowels! I am pained [in] the walls of my heart, ‖ My heart makes a noise for me, I am not silent, ‖ For I have heard the voice of a horn, ‖ O my soul—a shout of battle! 20 Destruction on destruction is proclaimed, ‖ For all the land has been spoiled, ‖ My tents have suddenly been spoiled, ‖ In a moment—my curtains. 21 Until when do I see an ensign? Do I hear the voice of a horn? 22 "For My people [are] foolish, ‖ They have not known Me, ‖ They [are] foolish sons, ‖ Indeed, they [are] not intelligent, ‖ They [are] wise to do evil, ‖ And they have not known to do good." 23 I looked [to] the earth, and behold—formless and void, ‖ And to the heavens, and they [had] no light. 24 I have looked [to] the mountains, ‖ And behold, they are trembling. And all the hills moved themselves lightly. 25 I have looked, and behold, man is not, ‖ And all birds of the heavens have fled. 26 I have looked, and behold, ‖ The fruitful place [is] a wilderness, ‖ And all its cities have been broken down, ‖ Because of YHWH, ‖ Because of the fierceness of His anger. 27 For thus said YHWH: "All the land is a desolation, but I do not make a completion. 28 For this the earth mourns, ‖ And the heavens above have been black, ‖ Because I have spoken—I have purposed, ‖ And I have not relented, ‖ Nor do I turn back from it. 29 From the voice of the horseman, ‖ And of him shooting with the bow, ‖ All the city is fleeing, ‖ They have come into thickets, ‖ And they have gone up on cliffs, ‖ All the city is forsaken, ‖ And there is no one dwelling in them. 30 And you, O spoiled one, what do you do? For you put on scarlet, ‖ For you adorn yourself [with] ornaments of gold. For you tear your eyes with pain, ‖ In vain you make yourself beautiful, ‖ Unhealthy ones have kicked against you, ‖ They seek your life. 31 For I have heard a voice as of a travailing woman, ‖ Distress, as of one bringing forth a firstborn, ‖ The voice of the daughter of Zion, ‖ She laments herself, ‖ She spreads out her hands, ‖ Woe to me now, my soul is weary of slayers!"

5 "Go to and fro in streets of Jerusalem, ‖ And see now and know, ‖ And seek in her broad places, ‖ If you find a man, ‖ If there is one doing judgment, ‖ Seeking steadfastness—Then I am propitious to her. 2 And if they say, YHWH lives, ‖ Surely they swear to a falsehood." 3 YHWH, Your eyes, are they not on steadfastness? You have struck them, and they have not grieved, ‖ You have consumed them, ‖ They have refused to receive instruction, ‖ They made their faces harder than a rock, ‖ They have refused to turn back. 4 And I said, "Surely these [are] poor, ‖ They have been foolish, ‖ For they have not known the way of YHWH, ‖ The judgment of their God. 5 I go to the great, and I speak with them, ‖ For they have known the way of YHWH, ‖ The judgment of their God." Surely they have

JEREMIAH

broken the yoke together, ‖ They have drawn away the bands. **6** Therefore a lion out of the forest has struck them, ‖ A wolf of the deserts spoils them, ‖ A leopard is watching over their cities, ‖ Everyone who is going out of them is torn, ‖ For their transgressions have been many, ‖ Their backslidings have been mighty. **7** "I am not propitious to you for this, ‖ Your sons have forsaken Me, ‖ And are satisfied by [those who are] not gods, ‖ I satisfy them, and they commit adultery, ‖ And at the house of a harlot ‖ They gather themselves together. **8** Fed horses—they have been early risers, ‖ They each neigh to the wife of his neighbor. **9** Do I not lay a charge for these?" A declaration of YHWH, "And on a nation such as this, ‖ Does My soul not avenge itself? **10** Go up on her walls, and destroy, ‖ And I do not make a completion, ‖ Turn her branches aside, ‖ For they [are] not YHWH's, **11** For the house of Israel has dealt treacherously against Me, ‖ And the house of Judah," ‖ A declaration of YHWH. **12** They have lied against YHWH, ‖ And they say, "[It is] not He, ‖ Nor does evil come in against us, ‖ Indeed, we do not see sword and famine. **13** And the prophets become wind, ‖ And the word is not in them, ‖ Thus it is done to them." **14** Therefore, thus said YHWH, God of Hosts: "Because of your speaking this word, ‖ Behold, I am making My words become fire in your mouth, ‖ And this people wood, ‖ And it has devoured them. **15** Behold, I am bringing against you a nation from afar, ‖ O house of Israel," ‖ A declaration of YHWH, ‖ "It [is] a strong nation, ‖ It [is] an ancient nation, ‖ A nation whose tongue you do not know, ‖ Nor understand what it speaks. **16** Its quiver [is] as an open tomb, ‖ All of them—mighty ones. **17** And it has consumed your harvest and your bread, ‖ They consume your sons, and your daughters, ‖ It consumes your flock, and your herd, ‖ It consumes your vine and your fig tree, ‖ It makes your fortified cities poor, ‖ In which you are trusting—by the sword. **18** And even in those days," ‖ A declaration of YHWH, ‖ "I do not make you a completion. **19** And it has come to pass, when you say, Why has our God YHWH done all these [things] to us? That you have said to them, As you have forsaken Me, ‖ And serve the gods of a foreigner in your land, ‖ So you serve strangers in a land [that is] not yours.

20 Declare this in the house of Jacob, ‖ And sound it in Judah, saying, **21** Now hear this, ‖ O people, foolish and without heart, ‖ They have eyes, and they do not see, ‖ They have ears, and they do not hear. **22** Do you not fear Me?" A declaration of YHWH; "Are you not pained from My presence? Who has made sand the border of the sea, ‖ A perpetual limit, and it does not pass over it, ‖ They shake themselves, and they are not able, ‖ Indeed, its billows have sounded, and they do not pass over. **23** And this people has an apostatizing and rebelling heart, ‖ They have turned aside, and they go on. **24** And they have not said in their heart, ‖ Now let us fear our God YHWH, who is giving rain, ‖ The autumn rain and the spring rain, in its season, ‖ He keeps the appointed weeks of harvest for us. **25** Your iniquities have turned these away, ‖ And your sins have kept the good from you. **26** For the wicked have been found among My people. He watches like one who sets snares, ‖ They have set up a trap—they capture men. **27** As a cage full of birds, ‖ So their houses are full of deceit, ‖ Therefore they have been great, and are rich. **28** They have been fat, they have shone, ‖ Indeed, they have surpassed the acts of the evil, ‖ They have not judged judgment, ‖ The judgment of the fatherless—and they prosper, ‖ And they have not judged the judgment of the needy. **29** Do I not inspect for these," ‖ A declaration of YHWH, ‖ "On a nation such as this, ‖ Does My soul not avenge itself? **30** An astonishing and horrible thing has been in the land: **31** The prophets have prophesied falsely, ‖ And the priests bear rule by their means, ‖ And My people have loved [it] so, ‖ And what do they do at its latter end?"

6 "Strengthen yourselves, sons of Benjamin, ‖ From the midst of Jerusalem, ‖ And blow a horn in Tekoa, ‖ And lift up a flame over Beth-Haccerem, ‖ For evil has been seen from the north, ‖ And great destruction. **2** I have cut off the lovely and delicate one, ‖ The daughter of Zion. **3** Shepherds and their droves come to her, ‖ They have struck tents by her all around, ‖ They have each fed [in] his own station." **4** "Sanctify the battle against her, ‖ Rise, and we go up at noon. Woe to us, for the day has turned, ‖ For the shades of evening are stretched out, **5** Rise, and we go up by night, ‖ And we destroy her palaces." **6** For

JEREMIAH

thus said Yhwh of Hosts: "Cut down her wood, ‖ And pour out a mound against Jerusalem, ‖ She [is] the city to be inspected, ‖ She [is] full of oppression in her midst. **7** As the digging of a well, is [for] its waters, ‖ So she has dug [for] her wickedness, ‖ Violence and spoil is heard in her, ‖ Sickness and striking [are] continually before My face. **8** Be instructed, O Jerusalem, ‖ Lest My soul be alienated from you, ‖ Lest I make you a desolation, ‖ A land [that is] not inhabited." **9** Thus said Yhwh of Hosts: "They surely glean, as a vine, the remnant of Israel, ‖ Put your hand back, as a gatherer to the baskets." **10** To whom do I speak, and testify, and they hear? Behold, their ear [is] uncircumcised, ‖ And they are not able to attend. Behold, a word of Yhwh has been to them for a reproach, ‖ They do not delight in it. **11** And I have been filled with the fury of Yhwh ‖ (I have been weary of containing), "To pour [it] on the suckling in the street, ‖ And on the assembly of youths together, ‖ For even husband with wife are captured, ‖ [The] elderly with one full of days, **12** And their houses have been turned to others, ‖ Fields and wives together, ‖ For I stretch out My hand against the inhabitants of the land," ‖ A declaration of Yhwh. **13** "For from their least to their greatest, ‖ Everyone is gaining dishonest gain, ‖ And from prophet even to priest, ‖ Everyone is dealing falsely, **14** And they heal the breach of the daughter of My people slightly, ‖ Saying, Peace, peace! And there is no peace. **15** They were ashamed when they did abomination! Indeed, they are not at all ashamed, ‖ Indeed, they have not known blushing, ‖ Therefore they fall among those falling, ‖ In the time I have inspected them, ‖ They stumble," said Yhwh. **16** Thus said Yhwh: "Stand by the ways and see, and ask for paths of old, ‖ Where [is] this—the good way? And go in it, ‖ And find rest for yourselves. And they say, We do not go. **17** And I have raised up watchmen for you, ‖ Attend to the voice of the horn. And they say, We do not attend. **18** Therefore hear, O nations, and know, O congregation, ‖ That which [is] on them. **19** Hear, O earth, behold, I am bringing evil on this people, ‖ The fruit of their plans, ‖ For they gave no attention to My words, ‖ And My law—they kick against it. **20** Why [is] this to Me? Frankincense comes from Sheba, ‖ And the sweet cane from a far-off land, ‖ Your burnt-offerings [are] not for acceptance, ‖ And your sacrifices have not been sweet to Me." **21** Therefore, thus said Yhwh: "Behold, I give stumbling blocks to this people, ‖ And fathers and sons have stumbled against them together, ‖ The neighbor and his friend perish." **22** Thus said Yhwh: "Behold, a people has come from a north country, ‖ And a great nation is stirred up from the sides of the earth. **23** They take hold of bow and javelin, ‖ It [is] fierce, and they have no mercy, ‖ Their voice sounds as a sea, ‖ And they ride on horses, ‖ Set in array as a man of war, ‖ Against you, O daughter of Zion." **24** We have heard its sound, our hands have been feeble, ‖ Distress has seized us, pain as of a travailing woman. **25** Do not go forth to the field, ‖ And do not walk in the way, ‖ For the enemy has a sword, ‖ Fear [is] all around. **26** O daughter of my people, ‖ Gird on sackcloth, ‖ And roll yourself in ashes, ‖ Make mourning [as for] an only one, ‖ A most bitter lamentation, ‖ For the spoiler suddenly comes against us. **27** "I have given you a watchtower, ‖ A fortress among My people, ‖ And you know, and have tried their way. **28** All of them are turned aside by apostates, ‖ Walking slanderously—bronze and iron, ‖ All of them are corrupters. **29** The bellows have been burned, ‖ The lead has been consumed by fire, ‖ A refiner has refined in vain, ‖ And the wicked have not been drawn away. **30** They have called them rejected silver, ‖ For Yhwh has kicked against them!"

7 The word that has been to Jeremiah from Yhwh, saying, **2** "Stand in the gate of the house of Yhwh, and you have proclaimed this word there, and have said, Hear a word of Yhwh, all you of Judah, who are coming in at these gates, to bow before Yhwh." **3** Thus said Yhwh of Hosts, God of Israel: "Amend your ways, and your doings, ‖ And I cause you to dwell in this place. **4** Do not trust for yourselves ‖ To the words of falsehood, saying, ‖ The temple of Yhwh! The temple of Yhwh! These [are] the temple of Yhwh! **5** For if you thoroughly amend your ways and your doings, ‖ If you thoroughly do judgment ‖ Between a man and his neighbor, **6** You do not oppress sojourner, fatherless, and widow, ‖ And innocent blood is not shed in this place, ‖ And [you] do not walk after other gods, for evil to yourselves, **7** Then I have caused you to dwell in this place, ‖ In the land that I gave to your fathers, ‖ From age even to age. **8** Behold, you are trusting for yourselves ‖ On the words of falsehood, so as not to profit. **9** Stealing, murdering, and committing adultery, ‖ And swearing to falsehood, and giving incense to Ba'al, ‖ And going after other gods whom you did not know. **10** And you have come in and stood before Me, ‖ In this house on which My Name is called, ‖ And have said, We have been delivered, ‖ In order to do all these abominations. **11** Has this house, ‖ On which My Name is called, ‖ Been a den of burglars in your eyes? Even I, behold, have seen," ‖ A declaration of YHWH. **12** "But go now to My place that [is] in Shiloh, ‖ Where I caused My Name to dwell at first, ‖ And see that which I have done to it, ‖ For the wickedness of My people Israel. **13** And now, because of your doing all these works," ‖ A declaration of YHWH, ‖ "And I speak to you, rising early and speaking, ‖ And you have not listened, ‖ And I call you, and you have not answered, **14** I also have done to the house on which My Name is called, ‖ In which you are trusting, ‖ And to the place that I gave to you, and to your fathers, ‖ As I have done to Shiloh. **15** And I have cast you from before My face, ‖ As I have cast out all your brothers, ‖ The whole seed of Ephraim. **16** And you do not pray for this people, ‖ Nor lift up crying and prayer for them, ‖ Nor intercede with Me, for I do not hear you. **17** Are you not seeing what they are doing ‖ In cities of Judah, and in streets of Jerusalem? **18** The sons are gathering wood, ‖ And the fathers are causing the fire to burn, ‖ And the women are kneading dough, ‖ To make cakes to the queen of the heavens, ‖ And to pour out drink-offerings to other gods, ‖ So as to provoke Me to anger. **19** Are they provoking Me to anger?" A declaration of YHWH, "Is it not themselves, ‖ For the shame of their own faces?" **20** Therefore, thus said Lord YHWH: "Behold, My anger and My fury is poured out on this place, ‖ On man, and beast, and on tree of the field, ‖ And on fruit of the ground, ‖ And it has burned, and it is not quenched." **21** Thus said YHWH of Hosts, God of Israel: "Add your burnt-offerings to your sacrifices and eat flesh. **22** For I did not speak with your fathers, ‖ Nor did I command them in the day of My bringing them out of the land of Egypt, ‖ Concerning the matters of burnt-offering and sacrifice, **23** But this thing I commanded them, saying, ‖ Listen to My voice, ‖ And I have been to you for God, ‖ And you are to Me for a people, ‖ And have walked in all the way that I command you, ‖ So that it is well for you. **24** And they have not listened, nor inclined their ear, ‖ And they walk in the counsels, ‖ [And] in the stubbornness, of their evil hearts, ‖ And are backward and not forward. **25** Even from the day when your fathers ‖ Went out of the land of Egypt until this day, ‖ I send all My servants the prophets to you, ‖ Daily rising early and sending, **26** And they have not listened to Me, ‖ Nor inclined their ear— and they harden their neck, ‖ They have done evil above their fathers. **27** And you have spoken all these words to them, ‖ And they do not listen to you, ‖ And you have called to them, ‖ And they do not answer you. **28** And you have said to them: This [is] the nation that has not listened, ‖ To the voice of its God YHWH, ‖ Nor have they accepted instruction, ‖ Steadfastness has perished, ‖ Indeed, it has been cut off from their mouth. **29** Cut off your crown, and cast [it] away, ‖ And lift up lamentation on high places, ‖ For YHWH has rejected, ‖ And He leaves the generation of His wrath. **30** For the sons of Judah ‖ Have done evil in My eyes," ‖ A declaration of YHWH, ‖ "They have set their abominations in the house ‖ On which My Name is called—to defile it, **31** And have built the high places of Tophet, ‖ That [are] in the Valley of the Son of Hinnom, ‖ To burn their sons and their daughters with fire, ‖ Which I did not command, ‖ Nor did it come up on My heart. **32** Therefore, behold, days are coming," ‖ A declaration of YHWH, ‖ "And it is no longer said, The Tophet, ‖ And, Valley of the Son of Hinnom, ‖ But, Valley of the Slaughter, ‖ And they have buried in Tophet—without place. **33** And the carcass of this people has been for food ‖ To a bird of the heavens, and to a beast of the earth, ‖ And there is none troubling. **34** And I have caused to cease from cities of Judah, ‖ And from streets of Jerusalem, ‖ The voice of joy, and the voice of gladness, ‖ Voice of bridegroom, and voice of bride, ‖ For the land becomes a desolation!"

8 "At that time," ‖ A declaration of YHWH, ‖ "They bring the bones of the kings of Judah, ‖ And the bones of its princes, ‖ And

JEREMIAH

the bones of the priests, ‖ And the bones of the prophets, ‖ And the bones of inhabitants of Jerusalem, ‖ Out of their graves, **2** And have spread them to sun, and to moon, ‖ And to all the host of the heavens, that they have loved, ‖ And that they have served, ‖ And that they have walked after, ‖ And that they have sought, ‖ And to which they have bowed themselves, ‖ They are not gathered, nor buried, ‖ They are for dung on the face of the ground. **3** And death is chosen rather than life ‖ By all the remnant who are left of this evil family, ‖ In all the remaining places, to where I have driven them," ‖ A declaration of Y<small>HWH</small> of Hosts. **4** "And you have said to them, Thus said Y<small>HWH</small>: Do they fall, and not rise? Does he turn back, and not return? **5** Why has this people of Jerusalem ‖ Turned back—a continuous backsliding? They have kept hold on deceit, ‖ They have refused to turn back. **6** I have given attention, indeed, I listen, ‖ They do not speak right, ‖ No man has sighed over his wickedness, ‖ Saying, What have I done? Everyone has turned to his courses, ‖ As a horse is rushing into battle. **7** Even a stork in the heavens has known her seasons, ‖ And turtle, and swallow, and crane, ‖ Have watched the time of their coming, ‖ And—My people have not known the judgment of Y<small>HWH</small>. **8** How do you say, We [are] wise, ‖ And the Law of Y<small>HWH</small> [is] with us? Surely, behold, it has worked falsely, ‖ The false pen of scribes. **9** The wise have been ashamed, ‖ They have been frightened, and are captured, ‖ Behold, they kicked against a word of Y<small>HWH</small>, ‖ And what wisdom do they have? **10** Therefore, I give their wives to others, ‖ Their fields to dispossessors, ‖ For from the least even to the greatest, ‖ Everyone is gaining dishonest gain, ‖ From prophet even to priest, everyone is dealing falsely. **11** And they heal the breach of the daughter of My people slightly, ‖ Saying, Peace, peace! And there is no peace. **12** They were ashamed when they did abomination! Indeed, they are not ashamed at all, ‖ And they have not known blushing, ‖ Therefore, they fall among falling ones, ‖ They stumble in the time of their inspection, said Y<small>HWH</small>. **13** I utterly consume them," ‖ A declaration of Y<small>HWH</small>, ‖ "There are no grapes in the vine, ‖ Indeed, there are no figs in the fig tree, ‖ And the leaf has faded, ‖ And the strength they have passes from them. **14** Why are we sitting still? Be gathered, and we go into the fortified cities, ‖ And we are silent there, ‖ For our God Y<small>HWH</small> has made us silent, ‖ Indeed, He causes us to drink water of gall, ‖ For we have sinned against Y<small>HWH</small>. **15** Looking for peace—and there is no good, ‖ For a time of healing, and behold—terror. **16** The snorting of his horses has been heard from Dan, ‖ From the voice of the neighings of his mighty ones, ‖ All the land has trembled, ‖ And they come in and consume the land and its fullness, ‖ The city and the inhabitants in it. **17** For behold, I am sending serpents among you, ‖ Vipers that have no charmer, ‖ And they have bitten you," ‖ A declaration of Y<small>HWH</small>. **18** My sorrow [is] beyond comfort, ‖ My heart [is] sick in me. **19** Behold, the voice of a cry of the daughter of my people from a far-off land, ‖ Is Y<small>HWH</small> not in Zion? Is her King not in her? "Why have they provoked Me with their carved images, ‖ With the vanities of a foreigner?" **20** Harvest has passed, summer has ended, ‖ And we have not been saved. **21** For a breach of the daughter of my people I have been broken, ‖ I have been dark, ‖ Astonishment has seized me. **22** Is there no balm in Gilead? Is there no physician there? Why has the health of the daughter of my people not gone up?

9 Who makes my head waters, ‖ And my eye a fountain of tears? And I weep by day and by night, ‖ For the wounded of the daughter of my people. **2** Who gives me in a wilderness ‖ A lodging-place for travelers? And I leave my people, and go from them, ‖ For all of them [are] adulterers, ‖ An assembly of treacherous ones. **3** "And they bend their tongue, ‖ Their bow [is] a lie, ‖ And they have not been mighty for steadfastness in the land, ‖ For they have gone forth from evil to evil, ‖ And they have not known Me," ‖ A declaration of Y<small>HWH</small>! **4** "You each beware of his friend, ‖ And do not trust any brother, ‖ For every brother utterly supplants, ‖ For every friend slanderously walks, **5** And they each mock at his friend, ‖ And they do not speak truth, ‖ They taught their tongue to speak falsehood, ‖ They have labored to commit iniquity. **6** Your dwelling [is] in the midst of deceit, ‖ Through deceit they refused to know Me," ‖ A declaration of Y<small>HWH</small>. **7** Therefore, thus said Y<small>HWH</small> of Hosts: "Behold, I am refining them, and have tried them, ‖ For how do I deal with the daughter of My people? **8** Their tongue [is] a slaughtering arrow, ‖ It has spoken deceit in its mouth, ‖ It speaks peace with its neighbor, ‖ And in its heart it lays its ambush, **9** Do I not see after them for these things?" A declaration of YHWH, "Does My soul not avenge itself against a nation such as this?" **10** I lift up weeping and wailing for the mountains, ‖ And a lamentation for the habitations of the wilderness, ‖ For they have been burned up without any passing over, ‖ Nor have they heard the voice of livestock, ‖ From the bird of the heavens and to the beast—they have fled, ‖ They have gone. **11** "And I make Jerusalem become heaps, ‖ A habitation of dragons, ‖ And I make the cities of Judah a desolation, ‖ Without inhabitant." **12** Who [is] the wise man? And he understands this, ‖ And he to whom the mouth of YHWH spoke? And he declares it, ‖ For why has the land perished? It has been burned up as a wilderness, ‖ Without any passing through. **13** And YHWH says: "Because of their forsaking My law that I set before them, ‖ And they have not listened to My voice nor walked in it, **14** And they walk after the stubbornness of their heart, ‖ And after the Ba'alim, ‖ That their fathers taught them," **15** Therefore, thus said YHWH of Hosts, God of Israel: "Behold, I am causing them—this people—to eat wormwood, ‖ And I have caused them to drink water of gall, **16** And I have scattered them among nations ‖ Which they did not know, they and their fathers, ‖ And have sent the sword after them, ‖ Until I have consumed them." **17** Thus said YHWH of Hosts: "Consider, and call for mourning women, ‖ And they come, ‖ And send to the wise women, ‖ And they come, **18** And they hurry, and lift up a wailing for us. And tears run down our eyes, ‖ And waters flow from our eyelids. **19** For a voice of wailing is heard from Zion: How we have been spoiled! We have been greatly ashamed, ‖ Because we have forsaken the land, ‖ Because they have cast down our dwelling places." **20** But hear, you women, a word of YHWH, ‖ And your ear receives a word of His mouth, ‖ And teach your daughters wailing, ‖ And each her neighbor lamentation. **21** For death has come up into our windows, ‖ It has come into our palaces, ‖ To cut off the suckling from outside, ‖ Young men from the broad places. **22** Speak thus, "A declaration of YHWH, ‖ And the carcass of man has fallen, ‖ As dung on the face of the field, ‖ And as a handful after the reaper, ‖ And there is none gathering." **23** Thus said YHWH: "Do not let the wise boast himself in his wisdom, ‖ Nor let the mighty boast himself in his might, ‖ Do not let the rich boast himself in his riches, **24** But let the boaster boast himself in this, ‖ In understanding and knowing Me, ‖ For I [am] YHWH, doing kindness, ‖ Judgment, and righteousness, in the earth, ‖ For I have delighted in these," ‖ A declaration of YHWH. **25** "Behold, days are coming," ‖ A declaration of YHWH, ‖ "And I have laid a charge on all circumcised in the foreskin, **26** On Egypt, and on Judah, and on Edom, ‖ And on the sons of Ammon, and on Moab, ‖ And on all cutting the corner [of the beard], ‖ Who are dwelling in the wilderness, ‖ For all the nations [are] uncircumcised, ‖ And all the house of Israel [are] uncircumcised in heart!"

10 Hear the word, O house of Israel, ‖ That YHWH has spoken for you. **2** Thus said YHWH: "Do not accustom yourselves to the way of the nations, ‖ And do not be frightened by the signs of the heavens, ‖ For the nations are frightened by them. **3** For the statutes of the peoples are vanity, ‖ For one has cut a tree from a forest, ‖ Work of the hands of a craftsman, with an axe, **4** They beautify it with silver and with gold, ‖ They fix it with nails and with hammers, ‖ And it does not stumble. **5** They [are] stiff as a palm, and they do not speak, ‖ They are surely carried, for they do not step, ‖ Do not be afraid of them, for they do no evil, ‖ Indeed, to do good is also not in them." **6** Because there is none like You, O YHWH, ‖ You [are] great, and Your Name [is] great in might. **7** Who does not fear You, King of the nations? For it is befitting to You, ‖ For among all the wise of the nations, ‖ And in all their kingdom, there is none like You. **8** And as one they are brutish and foolish, ‖ An instruction of vanities [is] the tree itself. **9** Spread-out silver is brought from Tarshish, ‖ And gold from Uphaz, ‖ Work of an artisan, and of the hands of a refiner, ‖ Their clothing [is] blue and purple, ‖ Work of the skillful—all of them. **10** And YHWH [is] a God of truth, ‖ He [is] a living God, and a perpetual King, ‖ The earth shakes from His wrath, ‖ And nations do not endure His indignation. **11** Thus you say to them, "The gods who

JEREMIAH

have not made the heavens and earth, ‖ They perish from the earth, ‖ And from under these heavens." **12** The Maker of the earth by His power, ‖ The Establisher of the world by His wisdom, ‖ Who, by His understanding, stretched forth the heavens— **13** When He gives forth His voice, ‖ A multitude of waters [is] in the heavens, ‖ And He causes vapors to come up from the end of the earth, ‖ He has made lightnings for rain, ‖ And brings out wind from His treasures. **14** Every man is brutish by knowledge, ‖ Every refiner is put to shame by a carved image, ‖ For his molten image [is] false. And there is no breath in them. **15** They [are] vanity, work of erring ones, ‖ They perish in the time of their inspection. **16** The Portion of Jacob [is] not like these, ‖ For He [is] the Framer of all things, ‖ And Israel [is] the rod of His inheritance, ‖ YHWH of Hosts [is] His Name. **17** Gather your merchandise from the land, ‖ O dweller in the bulwark, **18** For thus said YHWH: "Behold, I am slinging out the inhabitants of the land at this time, ‖ And have been an adversary to them, ‖ So that they are found out." **19** Woe to me for my breaking, ‖ My striking has been grievous, ‖ And I said, "Surely this [is] my sickness, and I bear it." **20** My tent has been spoiled, ‖ And all my cords have been broken, ‖ My sons have gone out from me, and they are not, ‖ There is none stretching out my tent anymore, ‖ And raising up my curtains. **21** For the shepherds have become brutish, ‖ And they have not sought YHWH, ‖ Therefore they have not acted wisely, ‖ And all their flock is scattered. **22** A voice of a report, behold, it has come, ‖ Even a great shaking from the north country, ‖ To make the cities of Judah a desolation, ‖ A habitation of dragons. **23** I have known, O YHWH, that not of man [is] his way, ‖ Not of man [is] the going and establishing of his step. **24** Discipline me, O YHWH, only in judgment, ‖ Not in Your anger, lest You make me small. **25** Pour out Your fury on the nations that have not known You, ‖ And on the families that have not called on Your Name, ‖ For they have eaten up Jacob, ‖ Indeed, they have eaten him up, indeed, they consume him, ‖ And they have made his habitation desolate!

11 The word that has been to Jeremiah from YHWH, saying, **2** "Hear the words of this covenant, and you have spoken to the men of Judah, and to the inhabitants of Jerusalem, **3** and you have said to them, Thus said YHWH God of Israel: Cursed [is] the man who does not obey the words of this covenant, **4** That I commanded your fathers, ‖ In the day of My bringing them out from the land of Egypt, ‖ Out of the iron furnace, saying, Listen to My voice, and you have done them, ‖ According to all that I command you, ‖ And you have been to Me for a people, ‖ And I am to you for God, **5** In order to establish the oath that I have sworn to your fathers, ‖ To give to them a land flowing with milk and honey, as this day." And I answer and say, "Amen, O YHWH." **6** And YHWH says to me, "Proclaim all these words in the cities of Judah, and in the streets of Jerusalem, saying, ‖ Hear the words of this covenant, ‖ And you have done them. **7** For I certainly testified against your fathers, ‖ In the day of My bringing them up out of the land of Egypt—until this day, ‖ Rising early and testifying, saying, Listen to My voice, **8** And they have not listened nor inclined their ear, ‖ And they each walk in the stubbornness of their evil heart, ‖ And I bring on them all the words of this covenant, ‖ That I commanded to do, and they did not." **9** And YHWH says to me: "A conspiracy is found in the men of Judah, ‖ And in the inhabitants of Jerusalem. **10** They have turned back to the iniquities of their first fathers, ‖ Who refused to hear My words, ‖ And they have gone after other gods to serve them, ‖ The house of Israel and the house of Judah ‖ Have made void My covenant that I made with their fathers." **11** Therefore, thus said YHWH: "Behold, I am bringing calamity on them, ‖ That they are not able to go out from, ‖ And they have cried to Me, ‖ And I do not listen to them. **12** And the cities of Judah, and inhabitants of Jerusalem have gone, ‖ And they have cried to the gods, ‖ To whom they are making incense, ‖ And they give no deliverance at all to them, ‖ In the time of their distress. **13** For the number of your cities have been your gods, O Judah, ‖ And [for] the number of the streets of Jerusalem You have placed altars to a shameful thing, ‖ Altars to make incense to Ba'al. **14** And you, you do not pray for this people, ‖ Nor do you lift up cry and prayer for them, ‖ For I do not listen in the time of their calling to Me for their distress. **15** What has My

JEREMIAH

beloved to do in My house, ‖ Her doing wickedness with many, ‖ And does the holy flesh pass over from you? When you do evil, then you exult. **16** An olive, green, beautiful, of good fruit, ‖ Has YHWH called your name, ‖ At the noise of a great tumult He has kindled fire against it, ‖ And its thin branches have been broken. **17** And YHWH of Hosts, who is planting you, ‖ Has spoken calamity concerning you, ‖ For the evil of the house of Israel, and of the house of Judah, ‖ That they have done to themselves, ‖ To provoke Me to anger, to make incense to Ba'al." **18** And, O YHWH, cause me to know, and I know, ‖ Then You have showed me their doings. **19** And I [am] as a trained lamb brought to slaughter, ‖ And I have not known ‖ That they have devised schemes against me: "We destroy the tree with its food, ‖ And cut him off from the land of the living, ‖ And his name is not remembered again." **20** And O YHWH of Hosts, judging righteousness, ‖ Trying reins and heart, ‖ I see Your vengeance against them, ‖ For I have revealed my cause to You. **21** Therefore, thus said YHWH concerning the men of Anathoth, who are seeking your life, saying, "Do not prophesy in the Name of YHWH, and you do not die by our hands." **22** Therefore, thus said YHWH of Hosts: "Behold, I am seeing after them, ‖ The chosen ones die by sword, ‖ Their sons and their daughters die by famine, **23** And they have no remnant, ‖ For I bring calamity to the men of Anathoth, ‖ The year of their inspection!"

12 You [are] righteous, O YHWH, ‖ When I plead toward You, ‖ Only, let me speak judgments with You, ‖ Why did the way of the wicked prosper? All treacherous dealers have been at rest. **2** You have planted them, ‖ Indeed, they have taken root, ‖ They go on, indeed, they have made fruit, ‖ You [are] near in their mouth, ‖ And far off from their reins. **3** And You, O YHWH, You have known me, ‖ You see me, and have tried my heart with You, ‖ Draw them away as sheep to slaughter, ‖ And separate them for a day of slaughter. **4** Until when does the earth mourn, ‖ And the herb of the whole field wither? For the wickedness of those dwelling in it, ‖ Beast and bird have been consumed, ‖ Because they said, "He does not see our latter end." **5** "For you have run with footmen, ‖ And they weary you, ‖ And how you fret yourself with horses! Even in the land of peace, ‖ [In which] you are confident—And how will you do in the rising of Jordan? **6** For even your brothers and the house of your father, ‖ Even they dealt treacherously against you, ‖ Even they called after you fully, ‖ Do not trust in them when they speak good things to you. **7** I have forsaken My house, ‖ I have left My inheritance, ‖ I have given the beloved of My soul ‖ Into the hand of her enemies. **8** My inheritance has been to Me as a lion in a forest, ‖ She gave forth against Me with her voice, ‖ Therefore I have hated her. **9** [Is] My inheritance a speckled bird to Me? Is the bird around against her? Come, assemble, every beast of the field, ‖ Come for food. **10** Many shepherds destroyed My vineyard, ‖ They have trodden down My portion, ‖ They have made My desirable portion ‖ Become a wilderness—a desolation. **11** He has made it become a desolation, ‖ The desolation has mourned to Me, ‖ All the land has been desolated, ‖ But there is no one laying it to heart. **12** Spoilers have come in on all high places in the plain, ‖ For the sword of YHWH is consuming, ‖ From the end of the land even to the end of the land, ‖ There is no peace to any flesh. **13** They sowed wheat, and have reaped thorns, ‖ They have become sick—they do not profit, ‖ And they have been ashamed of your increases, ‖ Because of the fierceness of the anger of YHWH." **14** Thus said YHWH: "Concerning all My evil neighbors, who are striking against the inheritance that I caused My people—Israel—to inherit: Behold, I am plucking them from off their ground, ‖ And I pluck the house of Judah out of their midst. **15** And it has been, after My plucking them out, ‖ I turn back, and have pitied them, ‖ And I have brought them back, ‖ Each to his inheritance, and each to his land. **16** And it has come to pass, ‖ If they learn the ways of My people well, ‖ To swear by My Name, YHWH lives, ‖ As they taught My people to swear by Ba'al, ‖ Then they have been built up in the midst of My people. **17** And if they do not listen, ‖ Then I have plucked up that nation, ‖ Plucking up and destroying," ‖ A declaration of YHWH!

13 Thus said YHWH to me: "Go, and you have acquired a girdle of linen for yourself, and have placed it on your loins, and you do not cause it to enter into

JEREMIAH

water." **2** And I get the girdle, according to the word of YHWH, and I place [it] on my loins. **3** And there is a word of YHWH to me a second time, saying, **4** "Take the girdle that you have acquired, that [is] on your loins, and rise, go to the Euphrates, and hide it there in a hole of the rock"; **5** and I go and hide it by the Euphrates, as YHWH commanded me. **6** And it comes to pass, at the end of many days, that YHWH says to me, "Rise, go to the Euphrates, and take the girdle there, that I commanded you to hide there"; **7** and I go to the Euphrates, and dig, and take the girdle from the place where I had hid it; and behold, the girdle has been marred, it is not profitable for anything. **8** And there is a word of YHWH to me, saying, "Thus said YHWH: **9** Thus I mar the excellence of Judah, ‖ And the great excellence of Jerusalem. **10** This evil people, who refuse to hear My words, ‖ Who walk in the stubbornness of their heart, ‖ And go after other gods to serve them, ‖ And to bow themselves to them, ‖ Indeed it is—as this girdle, that is not profitable for anything. **11** For as the girdle cleaves to the loins of a man, ‖ So I caused to cleave to Me ‖ The whole house of Israel, ‖ And the whole house of Judah," ‖ A declaration of YHWH, ‖ "To be to Me for a people, and for a name, ‖ And for praise, and for beauty, ‖ And they have not listened. **12** And you have said this word to them, ‖ Thus said YHWH, God of Israel: Every bottle is full of wine, ‖ And they have said to you: Do we not certainly know that every bottle is full of wine? **13** And you have said to them, ‖ Thus said YHWH: Behold, I am filling all the inhabitants of this land, ‖ And the kings who sit for David on his throne, ‖ And the priests, and the prophets, ‖ And all the inhabitants of Jerusalem, ‖ [With] drunkenness, **14** And have dashed them against one another, ‖ And the fathers and the sons together," ‖ A declaration of YHWH, ‖ "I do not pity, nor spare, nor do I have mercy, ‖ So as not to destroy them." **15** Hear, and give ear—do not be haughty, ‖ For YHWH has spoken. **16** Give glory to your God YHWH, ‖ Before He causes darkness, ‖ And before your feet stumble on dark mountains, ‖ And you have waited for light, ‖ And He has made it for death-shade, ‖ And has appointed [it] for thick darkness. **17** And if you do not hear it, ‖ My soul weeps in secret places, because of pride, ‖ Indeed, it weeps and wails, ‖ And the tear comes down my eyes, ‖ For the flock of YHWH has been taken captive. **18** Say to the king and to the mistress: Make yourselves low—sit still, ‖ For your principalities have come down, ‖ The crown of your beauty. **19** The cities of the south have been shut up, ‖ And there is none opening, ‖ Judah has been removed—all of her, ‖ She has been completely removed— **20** Lift up your eyes, and see those coming in from the north, ‖ Where [is] the drove given to you, your beautiful flock? **21** What do you say when He looks after you? And you have taught them [to be] over you—leaders for head? Do pangs not seize you as a travailing woman? **22** And when you say in your heart, "Why have these met me?" For the abundance of your iniquity ‖ Have your skirts been uncovered, ‖ Have your heels suffered violence. **23** "Does a Cushite change his skin? And a leopard his spots? Can you also do good, who are accustomed to do evil? **24** And I scatter them as stubble, ‖ Passing away, by a wind of the wilderness. **25** This [is] your lot, the portion of your measures from Me," ‖ A declaration of YHWH, ‖ "Because you have forgotten Me, ‖ And trust in falsehood. **26** I have also made your skirts bare before your face, ‖ And your shame has been seen. **27** Your adulteries, and your neighings, ‖ The wickedness of your whoredom, on heights in a field, ‖ I have seen your abominations. Woe to you, O Jerusalem, ‖ You are not [yet] made clean—after when [will you be] again?"

14 That which has been the word of YHWH to Jeremiah concerning the matters of the scarcities: **2** "Judah has mourned, and her gates have languished, ‖ They have mourned to the earth, ‖ And the cry of Jerusalem has gone up. **3** And their majestic ones have sent their little ones to the water, ‖ They have come to ditches, ‖ They have not found water, ‖ They have turned back—their vessels empty! They have been ashamed, ‖ And have blushed and covered their head. **4** Because the ground has been broken, ‖ For there has been no rain in the land, ‖ Farmers have been ashamed, ‖ They have covered their head. **5** For even the doe in the field has brought forth—to forsake [it!] ‖ For there has been no grass. **6** And wild donkeys have stood on high places, ‖ They have swallowed up wind like dragons, ‖ Their

JEREMIAH

eyes have been consumed, for there is no herb." **7** Surely our iniquities have testified against us, ‖ O YHWH, work for Your Name's sake, ‖ For our backslidings have been many, ‖ We have sinned against You. **8** O Hope of Israel—its Savior in time of trouble, ‖ Why are You as a sojourner in the land? And as a traveler turned aside to lodge? **9** Why are You as one mute? As a mighty one not able to save? And You [are] in our midst, O YHWH, ‖ And Your Name is called over us, ‖ Do not leave us. **10** Thus said YHWH concerning this people: "They have loved to wander well, ‖ They have not restrained their feet, ‖ And YHWH has not accepted them, ‖ Now He remembers their iniquity, ‖ And inspects their sin." **11** And YHWH says to me: "You do not pray for this people for good. **12** When they fast, I do not listen to their cry, and when they cause burnt-offering and present to ascend, I do not accept them; for I am consuming them by sword, and by famine, and by pestilence." **13** And I say, "Aah! Lord YHWH, behold, the prophets are saying to them: You do not see a sword, indeed, famine is not [on] you, for I give true peace to you in this place." **14** And YHWH says to me: "The prophets are prophesying falsehood in My Name. I did not send them, nor command them, nor have I spoken to them. A false vision, and divination, and vanity—indeed, they are prophesying the deceit of their own heart to you. **15** Therefore, thus said YHWH concerning the prophets who are prophesying in My Name and I have not sent them, and they are saying, Sword and famine is not in this land: By sword and by famine are these prophets consumed. **16** And the people to whom they are prophesying are cast into out-places of Jerusalem, because of the famine and the sword, and they have none burying them—them, their wives, and their sons, and their daughters—and I have poured out their evil on them. **17** And you have said this word to them: Tears come down my eyes night and day, ‖ And they do not cease, ‖ For [with] a great breach, ‖ The virgin daughter of my people has been broken, ‖ A very grievous stroke. **18** If I have gone forth to the field, ‖ Then, behold, the pierced of the sword! And if I have entered the city, ‖ Then, behold, the diseased of famine! For both prophet and priest have gone up and down ‖ To a land that they did not know." **19** Have You utterly rejected Judah? Has Your soul loathed Zion? Why have You struck us, ‖ And there is no healing to us? Looking for peace, and there is no good, ‖ And for a time of healing, and behold, terror. **20** We have known, O YHWH, our wickedness, ‖ The iniquity of our fathers, ‖ For we have sinned against You. **21** Do not despise, for Your Name's sake, ‖ Do not dishonor the throne of Your glory, ‖ Remember, do not break Your covenant with us. **22** Are there any among the vanities of the nations causing rain? And do the heavens give showers? Are You not He, O our God YHWH? And we wait for you, for You have done all these!

15 And YHWH says to me: "Though Moses and Samuel should stand before Me, ‖ My soul is not toward this people, ‖ Send from before My face, and they go out. **2** And it has come to pass, when they say to you, ‖ To where do we go out? That you have said to them, ‖ Thus said YHWH: Those who [are] for death—to death, ‖ And those who are for the sword—to the sword, ‖ And those who are for famine—to famine, ‖ And those who are for captivity—to captivity. **3** And I have appointed four kinds over them," ‖ A declaration of YHWH, ‖ "The sword to slay, and the dogs to drag, ‖ And the bird of the heavens, ‖ And the beast of the earth, to consume and to devour. **4** And I have given them for a trembling ‖ To all kingdoms of the earth, ‖ Because of Manasseh son of Hezekiah king of Judah, ‖ For that which he did in Jerusalem. **5** For who has pity on you, O Jerusalem? And who bemoans for you? And who turns aside to ask of your welfare? **6** You have left Me," ‖ A declaration of YHWH, ‖ "You go backward, ‖ And I stretch out My hand against you, ‖ And I destroy you, ‖ I have been weary of relenting, **7** And I scatter them with a fan, ‖ In the gates of the land, ‖ I have bereaved [them], ‖ I have destroyed My people, ‖ They did not turn back from their ways. **8** Its widows have been more to Me than the sand of the seas, ‖ I brought on them—against the mother—A young man—a spoiler—at noon. I caused wrath and trouble to fall on her suddenly. **9** The bearer of seven has languished, ‖ She has breathed out her spirit, ‖ Her sun has gone in while yet day, ‖ It has been ashamed and confounded, ‖ And I give up their remnant

JEREMIAH

to the sword before their enemies," ‖ A declaration of YHWH. **10** Woe to me, my mother, ‖ For you have borne me, ‖ A man of strife and a man of contention to all the land, ‖ I have not lent on usury, ‖ Nor have they lent on usury to me—All of them are reviling me. **11** YHWH said, "Did I not direct you for good? Did I not intercede for you in a time of evil, ‖ And in a time of adversity, with the enemy? **12** Does one break iron, ‖ Northern iron and bronze? **13** I give your strength and your treasures for a prey—not for price, ‖ Even for all your sins, and in all your borders. **14** And I have caused your enemies ‖ To pass over into the land [that] You have not known, ‖ For a fire has been kindled in My anger, ‖ It burns against you." **15** You, You have known, O YHWH, ‖ Remember me, and inspect me, ‖ And take vengeance for me of my pursuers, ‖ In Your long-suffering do not take me away, ‖ Know [that] I have borne reproach for You. **16** Your words have been found, and I eat them, ‖ And Your word is to me for a joy, ‖ And for the rejoicing of my heart, ‖ For Your Name is called on me, O YHWH, God of Hosts. **17** I have not sat in an assembly of deriders, ‖ Nor do I exult, because of your hand—I have sat alone, ‖ For You have filled me [with] indignation. **18** Why has my pain been continuous? And my wound incurable? It has refused to be healed, ‖ You are surely as a failing stream to me, ‖ Waters [that are] not steadfast. **19** Therefore, thus said YHWH: "If you turn back, then I bring you back, ‖ You stand before Me, ‖ And if you bring out the precious from the vile, ‖ You are as My mouth! They return to you, ‖ And you do not return to them. **20** And I have made you to this people ‖ For a wall—bronze—fortified, ‖ And they have fought against you, ‖ And they do not prevail against you, ‖ For I [am] with you to save you, ‖ And to deliver you," ‖ A declaration of YHWH, **21** "And I have delivered you from the hand of evildoers, ‖ And I have ransomed you ‖ From the hand of the terrible!"

16 And there is a word of YHWH to me, saying, **2** "You do not take a wife to yourself, ‖ Nor do you have sons and daughters in this place." **3** For thus said YHWH, ‖ Of the sons and of the daughters who are born in this place, ‖ And of their mothers—those bearing them, ‖ And of their fathers—those begetting them in this land: **4** "They die painful deaths, ‖ They are not lamented, nor are they buried, ‖ For they are dung on the face of the ground, ‖ And are consumed by sword and by famine, ‖ And their carcass has been for food ‖ To the bird of the heavens, ‖ And to the beast of the earth." **5** For thus said YHWH: "Do not enter the house of a mourning-feast, ‖ Nor go to lament nor bemoan for them, ‖ For I have removed My peace from this people," ‖ A declaration of YHWH, ‖ "The kindness and the mercies. **6** And great and small have died in this land, ‖ They are not buried, and none lament for them, ‖ Nor does any cut himself, nor become bald for them. **7** Nor do they deal out to them for mourning, ‖ To comfort him concerning the dead, ‖ Nor cause them to drink a cup of consolations ‖ For his father and for his mother. **8** You do not enter a house of banqueting, ‖ To sit with them, to eat and to drink," **9** For thus said YHWH of Hosts, God of Israel: "Behold, I am causing to cease from this place, ‖ Before your eyes, and in your days, ‖ The voice of joy, and the voice of rejoicing, ‖ The voice of bridegroom and voice of bride. **10** And it has come to pass, ‖ When you declare all these words to this people, ‖ And they have said to you, ‖ Why has YHWH spoken all this great evil against us? Indeed, what [is] our iniquity, and what [is] our sin, ‖ That we have sinned against our God YHWH? **11** Then you have said to them: Because that your fathers have forsaken Me, ‖ A declaration of YHWH, ‖ And go after other gods, and serve them, ‖ And they bow themselves to them, ‖ And have forsaken Me, and not kept My law, **12** You also have done evil above your fathers, ‖ And behold, you are each walking after the stubbornness of his evil heart, ‖ So as not to listen to Me. **13** And I have cast you from off this land, ‖ On to a land that you have not known, ‖ You and your fathers, ‖ And you have served other gods there by day and by night, ‖ Where I do not give grace to you. **14** Therefore, behold, days are coming," ‖ A declaration of YHWH, ‖ "And it is not said anymore, ‖ YHWH lives, who brought up the sons of Israel out of the land of Egypt, **15** But, YHWH lives, who brought up the sons of Israel out of the land of the north, ‖ And out of all the lands to where He drove them, ‖ And I have brought them back to their land, ‖ That I gave to their fathers. **16** Behold, I am sending for many fishers," ‖ A declaration of YHWH, ‖ "And they have fished them, ‖ And after this I send for many hunters, ‖ And they have hunted them from off every mountain, ‖ And from off every hill, and from holes of the rocks. **17** For My eyes [are] on all their ways, ‖ They have not been hidden from My face, ‖ Nor has their iniquity been concealed from before My eyes. **18** And I have repaid a first—A second time—their iniquity and their sin, ‖ Because of their defiling My land, ‖ With the carcass of their detestable things, ‖ Indeed, their abominations have filled My inheritance." **19** O YHWH, my strength, and my fortress, ‖ And my refuge in a day of adversity, ‖ Nations come to You from the ends of the earth, ‖ And say, "Our fathers only inherited falsehood, ‖ Vanity, and none among them is profitable." **20** Does man make gods for himself, ‖ And they—no gods? **21** "Therefore, behold, I am causing them to know at this time, ‖ I cause them to know My hand and My might, ‖ And they have known that My Name [is] YHWH!"

17 "The sin of Judah is written with a pen of iron, ‖ With the point of a diamond, ‖ Engraved on the tablet of their heart, ‖ And on the horns of your altars, **2** As their sons remember their altars and their Asherim, ‖ By the green tree, by the high hills. **3** O My mountain in the field—your strength, ‖ All your treasures—I give for a prey, ‖ Your high places for sin in all your borders. **4** And you have let go—even through yourself, ‖ Of your inheritance that I gave to you, ‖ And I have caused you to serve your enemies, ‖ In a land that you have not known, ‖ For you have kindled a fire in My anger, ‖ It burns for all time." **5** Thus said YHWH: "Cursed [is] the man who trusts in man, ‖ And has made flesh his arm, ‖ And whose heart turns from YHWH. **6** And he has been as a naked thing in a desert, ‖ And does not see when good comes, ‖ And has inhabited parched places in a wilderness, ‖ A salt land, and not inhabited. **7** Blessed [is] the man who trusts in YHWH, ‖ And whose confidence has been YHWH. **8** And has been as a tree planted by waters, ‖ And he sends forth his roots by a stream, ‖ And he does not see when heat comes, ‖ And his leaf has been green, ‖ And he is not sorrowful in a year of scarcity, ‖ Nor does he cease from making fruit. **9** The heart [is] deceitful above all things, ‖ And it [is] incurable—who knows it? **10** I, YHWH, search the heart, try the reins, ‖ Even to give to each according to his way, ‖ According to the fruit of his doings. **11** A partridge hatching, and not bringing forth, ‖ [Is] one making wealth, and not by right, ‖ In the midst of his days he forsakes it, ‖ And in his latter end—he is a fool." **12** A throne of glory on high from the beginning, ‖ The place of our sanctuary, **13** The hope of Israel [is] YHWH, ‖ All forsaking You are ashamed. "And My apostates are written in the earth, ‖ For they have forsaken YHWH, ‖ A fountain of living waters." **14** Heal me, O YHWH, and I am healed, ‖ Save me, and I am saved, ‖ For You [are] my praise. **15** Behold, they are saying to me: "Where [is] the word of YHWH? Pray, let it come." **16** And I did not hurry from feeding after You, ‖ And I have not desired the desperate day, ‖ You have known the produce of my lips, ‖ It has been before Your face, **17** Do not be to me for a terror, ‖ You [are] my hope in a day of calamity. **18** Let my pursuers be ashamed, ‖ And do not let me be ashamed—me! Let them be frightened, ‖ And do not let me be frightened—me! Bring in on them a day of calamity, ‖ And destroy them a second time [with] destruction. **19** Thus said YHWH to me: "Go, and you have stood in the gate of the sons of the people, by which kings of Judah come in, and by which they go out, and in all gates of Jerusalem, **20** and you have said to them: Hear a word of YHWH, you kings of Judah, and all Judah, and all inhabitants of Jerusalem, who are coming in by these gates," **21** Thus said YHWH: "Take heed to yourselves, ‖ And you do not bear a burden on the day of rest, ‖ Nor have you brought [it] in by the gates of Jerusalem. **22** Nor do you take out a burden from your houses on the day of rest, ‖ Indeed, you do not do any work, ‖ And you have sanctified the day of rest, ‖ As I have commanded your fathers. **23** And they have not listened nor inclined their ear, ‖ And they stiffen their neck not to hear, ‖ And not to receive instruction. **24** And it has been, if you certainly listen to Me," ‖ A declaration of YHWH, ‖ "So as not to bring in a burden by the gates of this city on the day of rest, ‖ And to sanctify the day of rest, ‖ So as not to do any work in it— **25** Then kings and princes have entered by the gates of this city, ‖ Sitting on the throne of David,

JEREMIAH

‖ Riding in a chariot, and on horses, ‖ They, and their princes, the man of Judah, ‖ And inhabitants of Jerusalem, ‖ And this city has remained for all time. **26** And they have come in from cities of Judah, ‖ And from outskirts of Jerusalem, ‖ And from the land of Benjamin, ‖ And from the low country, ‖ And from the hill-country, ‖ And from the south, ‖ Bringing in burnt-offering, and sacrifice, ‖ And present, and frankincense, ‖ And bringing praise [to] the house of YHWH. **27** And if you do not listen to Me to sanctify the day of rest, ‖ And so as not to bear a burden, ‖ And to come in at the gates of Jerusalem on the day of rest, ‖ Then I have kindled a fire in its gates, ‖ And it has consumed the high places of Jerusalem, ‖ And it is not quenched!"

18 The word that has been to Jeremiah from YHWH, saying, **2** "Rise, and you have gone down [to] the potter's house, and there I cause you to hear My words"; **3** and I go down [to] the potter's house, and behold, he is doing a work on the stones, **4** and the vessel that he is making is marred, as clay in the hand of the potter, and he has turned and he makes it another vessel, as it was right in the eyes of the potter to make. **5** And there is a word of YHWH to me, saying, **6** "O house of Israel, am I not able to do to you as this potter?" A declaration of YHWH. "Behold, as clay in the hand of the potter, ‖ So [are] you in My hand, O house of Israel. **7** The moment I speak concerning a nation, ‖ And concerning a kingdom, ‖ To pluck up and to break down, and to destroy, **8** And that nation has turned from its evil, ‖ Because I have spoken against it, ‖ Then I have relented of the calamity that I thought to do to it. **9** And the moment I speak concerning a nation, ‖ And concerning a kingdom, to build, and to plant, **10** And it has done evil in My eyes, ‖ So as not to listen to My voice, ‖ Then I have relented of the good ‖ That I have spoken of doing to it. **11** And now, speak now to men of Judah, ‖ And against inhabitants of Jerusalem, saying, ‖ Thus said YHWH: Behold, I am framing calamity against you, ‖ And devising a scheme against you; Please turn back, each from his evil way, ‖ And amend your ways and your doings." **12** And they have said, "It is incurable, ‖ For we go after our own plans, ‖ And each of us does the stubbornness of his evil heart."

13 Therefore, thus said YHWH: "Now ask among the nations, ‖ Who has heard such things? The virgin of Israel has done a very horrible thing. **14** Does snow of Lebanon ‖ Cease from the rock of the field? Will the cold strange [waters] that are flowing be forsaken? **15** But My people have forgotten Me, they make incense to a vain thing, ‖ And they cause them to stumble in their ways—paths of old, ‖ To walk in paths—a way not raised up, **16** To make their land become a desolation, ‖ A continuous hissing, ‖ Everyone passing by it is astonished, ‖ And bemoans with his head. **17** I scatter them before an enemy as with an east wind, ‖ I show them the neck and not the face, ‖ In the day of their calamity."

18 And they say, "Come, ‖ And we devise schemes against Jeremiah, ‖ For law does not perish from the priest, ‖ Nor counsel from the wise, ‖ Nor the word from the prophet, ‖ Come, and we strike him with the tongue, ‖ And we do not attend to any of his words." **19** Give attention, O YHWH, to me, ‖ And listen to the voice of those contending with me. **20** Is evil repaid instead of good, ‖ That they have dug a pit for my soul? Remember my standing before You to speak good of them, ‖ To turn back Your wrath from them. **21** Therefore, give up their sons to famine, ‖ And cause them to run on the sides of the sword, ‖ And their wives are bereaved and widows, ‖ And their men are slain by death, ‖ Their young men [are] struck by sword in battle, **22** A cry is heard from their houses, ‖ For You suddenly bring a troop against them, ‖ For they dug a pit to capture me, ‖ And they have hidden snares for my feet. **23** And You, O YHWH, You have known, ‖ All their counsel against me [is] for death, ‖ You do not cover over their iniquity, ‖ Nor blot out their sin from before You, ‖ And they are made to stumble before You, ‖ Work against them in the time of Your anger!

19 Thus said YHWH: "Go, and you have acquired a potter's earthen vessel, and from [the] elderly of the people, and from [the] elderly of the priests, **2** and you have gone forth to the Valley of the Son of Hinnom, that [is] at the opening of the gate of the pottery, and have proclaimed there the words that I speak to you, **3** and have said, Hear a word of YHWH, you kings of Judah, and inhabitants of Jerusalem!" Thus said YHWH of Hosts, God of Israel:

JEREMIAH

"Behold, I am bringing in evil on this place, at which the ears of everyone who is hearing it tingles, **4** because that they have forsaken Me, and make known this place, and make incense in it to other gods, that they did not know, they and their fathers, and the kings of Judah, and they have filled this place [with] innocent blood, **5** and have built the high places of Ba'al to burn their sons with fire, burnt-offerings to Ba'al, that I did not command, nor spoke of, nor did it come up on My heart. **6** Therefore, behold, days are coming," a declaration of YHWH, "and this place is no longer called The Tophet and Valley of the Son of Hinnom, but Valley of the Slaughter. **7** And I have made void the counsel of Judah and Jerusalem in this place, and have caused them to fall by the sword before their enemies, and by the hand of those seeking their life, and I have given their carcass for food to the bird of the heavens, and to the beast of the earth, **8** and I have made this city for a desolation, and for a hissing, everyone passing by it is astonished, and hisses for all its plagues. **9** And I have caused them to eat the flesh of their sons, and the flesh of their daughters, and they each eat the flesh of his friend, in the siege and in the constriction with which their enemies constrict them, and those seeking their life." **10** "And you have broken the bottle before the eyes of the men who are going with you, **11** and have said to them, Thus said YHWH of Hosts: Thus I break this people and this city, as one breaks the potter's vessel, that is not able to be repaired again, and in Tophet they bury—without place to bury; **12** so I do to this place—a declaration of YHWH—and to its inhabitants, so as to make this city as Tophet; **13** and the houses of Jerusalem, and the houses of the kings of Judah, have been as the place of Tophet—defiled, even all the houses on whose roofs they have made incense to all the host of the heavens, so as to pour out oblations to other gods." **14** And Jeremiah comes in from Tophet, to where YHWH had sent him to prophesy, and he stands in the court of the house of YHWH, and he says to all the people: **15** "Thus said YHWH of Hosts, God of Israel: Behold, I am bringing to this city, and on all its cities, all the calamity that I have spoken against it, for they have hardened their neck to not hear My words!"

20 And Pashhur son of Immer the priest—who [is] also overseer, leader in the house of YHWH—hears Jeremiah prophesying these things, **2** and Pashhur strikes Jeremiah the prophet, and puts him in the stocks that [are] by the Upper Gate of Benjamin, that [is] by the house of YHWH. **3** And it comes to pass on the next day, that Pashhur brings Jeremiah out from the stocks, and Jeremiah says to him, "YHWH has not called your name Pashhur, but Terror on Every Side. **4** For thus said YHWH: Behold, I am making you for a fear to yourself, ‖ And to all loving you, ‖ And they have fallen by the sword of their enemies, and your eyes are beholding, ‖ And all Judah I give into the hand of the king of Babylon, ‖ And he has removed them to Babylon, ‖ And he has struck them with the sword. **5** And I have given all the strength of this city, ‖ And all its labor, and all its precious things, ‖ Indeed, I give all the treasures of the kings of Judah into the hand of their enemies, ‖ And they have spoiled them, and taken them, ‖ And have brought them into Babylon. **6** And you, Pashhur, and all dwelling in your house, ‖ Go into captivity. And you enter Babylon, ‖ And there you die, and there you are buried, ‖ You and all loving you, ‖ To whom you have prophesied falsely." **7** You have persuaded me, O YHWH, and I am persuaded; You have hardened me, and prevail, ‖ I have been for a laughter all the day, ‖ Everyone is mocking at me, **8** Because from the time I speak I cry out, I shout, "Violence and destruction!" ‖ For the word of YHWH has been to me ‖ For reproach and for derision all the day. **9** And I said, "I do not mention Him, ‖ Nor do I speak anymore in His Name," ‖ And it has been in my heart ‖ As a burning fire shut up in my bones, ‖ And I have been weary of containing, ‖ And I am not able. **10** For I have heard the evil report of many, "Fear [is] all around!" "Declare, and we declare it!" All my allies are watching [for] my halting, "Perhaps he is enticed, and we prevail over him, ‖ And we take our vengeance on him." **11** And YHWH [is] with me, as a mighty, awesome One, ‖ Therefore my persecutors stumble and do not prevail, ‖ They have been exceedingly ashamed, ‖ For they have not acted wisely, ‖ Continuous confusion is not forgotten. **12** And, O YHWH of Hosts, trier of the righteous, ‖ Beholder of reins and heart, ‖ I

JEREMIAH

see Your vengeance on them, ‖ For I have revealed my cause to you. **13** Sing to YHWH, praise YHWH, ‖ For He has delivered the soul of the needy ‖ From the hand of evildoers. **14** Cursed [is] the day in which I was born, ‖ The day that my mother bore me, ‖ Let it not be blessed! **15** Cursed [is] the man who bore tidings [to] my father, ‖ Saying, "A male child has been born to you," ‖ Making him very glad! **16** Then that man has been as the cities, ‖ That YHWH overthrew, and did not relent, ‖ And he has heard a cry in the morning, ‖ And a shout at noontime. **17** Because he has not put me to death from the womb, ‖ And my mother is to me—my grave, ‖ And her womb [is] a perpetual pregnancy. **18** Why [is] this? I have come out from the womb ‖ To see labor and sorrow, ‖ Indeed, my days are consumed in shame!

21 The word that has been to Jeremiah from YHWH, in King Zedekiah's sending to him Pashhur son of Malchiah and Zephaniah son of Maaseiah the priest, saying, **2** "Please inquire of YHWH for us, for Nebuchadnezzar king of Babylon has fought against us; perhaps YHWH deals with us according to all His wonders, and causes him to go up from off us." **3** And Jeremiah says to them, "Thus you say to Zedekiah, **4** Thus said YHWH, God of Israel: Behold, I am turning around the weapons of battle ‖ That [are] in your hand, ‖ With which you fight the king of Babylon, ‖ And the Chaldeans, who are laying siege against you, ‖ At the outside of the wall, ‖ And I have gathered them into the midst of this city, **5** And I have fought against you, ‖ With an outstretched hand, and with a strong arm, ‖ And in anger, and in fury, and in great wrath, **6** And I have struck the inhabitants of this city, ‖ Both man and beast, ‖ They die by a great pestilence. **7** And after this," ‖ A declaration of YHWH, ‖ "I give Zedekiah king of Judah, ‖ And his servants, and the people, ‖ And those left in this city, ‖ From the pestilence, from the sword, and from the famine, ‖ Into the hand of Nebuchadnezzar king of Babylon, ‖ And into the hand of their enemies, ‖ And into the hand of those seeking their life, ‖ And he has struck them by the mouth of the sword, ‖ He has no pity on them, ‖ Nor does he spare, nor does he have mercy." **8** "And you say to this people, Thus said YHWH: Behold, I am setting before you the way of life, ‖ And the way of death! **9** Whoever is abiding in this city—dies, ‖ By sword, and by famine, and by pestilence, ‖ And whoever is going forth, ‖ And has fallen to the Chaldeans, ‖ Who are laying siege against you—lives, ‖ And his life has been for a spoil to him. **10** For I have set My face against this city for calamity, ‖ And not for good," ‖ A declaration of YHWH. "It is given into the hand of the king of Babylon, ‖ And he has burned it with fire. **11** And as for the house of the king of Judah," ‖ Hear a word of YHWH; **12** O house of David, thus said YHWH: "Decide judgment in the morning, ‖ And deliver the plundered from the hand of the oppressor, ‖ Lest My fury go forth as fire, ‖ And has burned, and none is quenching, ‖ Because of the evil of your doings. **13** Behold, I [am] against you," ‖ A declaration of YHWH, ‖ "O inhabitant of the valley, rock of the plain, ‖ Who are saying, Who comes down against us? And who comes into our habitations? **14** And I have laid a charge against you, ‖ According to the fruit of your doings," ‖ A declaration of YHWH, ‖ "And I have kindled a fire in its forest, ‖ And it has consumed all its outskirts!"

22 Thus said YHWH: "Go down [to] the house of the king of Judah, and you have spoken this word there, and have said, **2** Hear a word of YHWH, O king of Judah, who are sitting on the throne of David, you, and your servants, and your people, who are coming in at these gates," **3** Thus said YHWH: "Do judgment and righteousness, ‖ And deliver the plundered from the hand of the oppressor, ‖ And sojourner, orphan, and widow, you do not oppress nor wrong, ‖ And innocent blood you do not shed in this place. **4** For if you certainly do this thing, ‖ Then kings sitting for David on his throne ‖ Have come in by the gates of this house, ‖ Riding on chariot, and on horses, ‖ He, and his servants, and his people. **5** And if you do not hear these words, ‖ I have sworn by Myself," ‖ A declaration of YHWH, ‖ "That this house is for a desolation." **6** For thus said YHWH concerning the house of the king of Judah: "You [are] Gilead to Me—head of Lebanon, ‖ If not—I make you a wilderness, ‖ Cities [that] are not inhabited. **7** And I have separated destroyers for you, ‖ Each with his weapons, ‖ And they have cut down the choice of your cedars, ‖ And have cast them on the fire." **8** And many

JEREMIAH

nations have passed by this city, ‖ And they have each said to his neighbor, "Why has YHWH done thus to this great city?" **9** And they have said, "Because that they have forsaken ‖ The covenant of their God YHWH, ‖ And bow themselves to other gods, and serve them." **10** You do not weep for the dead, nor bemoan for him, ‖ Weep severely for the traveler, ‖ For he does not return again, ‖ Nor has he seen the land of his birth. **11** For thus said YHWH concerning Shallum son of Josiah king of Judah, who is reigning instead of his father Josiah, who has gone forth from this place: "He does not return here again; **12** For he dies in the place to where they have removed him, ‖ And he does not see this land again. **13** Woe to him who is building his house by unrighteousness, ‖ And his upper chambers by injustice, ‖ He lays service on his neighbor for nothing, ‖ And he does not give his wage to him. **14** Who is saying, ‖ I build a large house for myself, ‖ And airy upper chambers, ‖ And he has cut out its windows for himself, ‖ Covered with cedar, and painted with vermillion. **15** Do you reign, because you are fretting yourself in cedar? Your father—did he not eat and drink? Indeed, he did judgment and righteousness, ‖ Then [it is] well with him. **16** He decided the cause of the poor and needy, ‖ Then [it is] well—is it not to know Me?" A declaration of YHWH. **17** "But your eyes and your heart are not, ‖ Except on your dishonest gain, ‖ And on shedding of innocent blood, ‖ And on oppression, and on doing of violence." **18** Therefore, thus said YHWH concerning Jehoiakim son of Josiah king of Judah: "They do not lament for him, ‖ Oh, my brother! And, Oh, my sister! They do not lament for him, ‖ Oh, lord! And, Oh, his splendor! **19** He is buried [with] the burial of a donkey, ‖ Dragged and cast out there to the gates of Jerusalem. **20** Go up to Lebanon, and cry, ‖ And give forth your voice in Bashan, ‖ And cry from Abarim, ‖ For all loving you have been destroyed. **21** I have spoken to you in your ease, ‖ You have said, I do not listen, ‖ This [is] your way from your youth, ‖ For you have not listened to My voice. **22** Wind consumes all your friends, ‖ And your lovers go into captivity, ‖ Surely then you are ashamed, ‖ And have blushed for all your wickedness. **23** O dweller in Lebanon, making a nest among cedars, ‖ How gracious have you been when pangs come to you, ‖ Pain—as of a travailing woman." **24** "[As] I live," ‖ A declaration of YHWH, ‖ "Though Coniah son of Jehoiakim king of Judah was a seal on My right hand, surely there I draw you away, **25** And I have given you into the hand of those seeking your life, ‖ And into hands of which you are afraid, ‖ Into the hand of Nebuchadnezzar king of Babylon, ‖ And into the hand of the Chaldeans. **26** And I have cast you, ‖ And your mother who bore you, to another country, ‖ Where you were not born, and you die there. **27** And to the land to where they are lifting up their soul to return, ‖ They do not return there." **28** A grief—a despised broken thing—is this man Coniah? A vessel in which there is no pleasure? Why have they been cast up and down, ‖ He and his seed, ‖ Indeed, were they cast on to a land that they did not know? **29** Earth, earth, earth, hear a word of YHWH! **30** Thus said YHWH: "Write this man down [as] childless, ‖ A man—he does not prosper in his days, ‖ For none of his seed prospers, ‖ Sitting on the throne of David, ‖ And ruling in Judah again!"

23 "Woe to shepherds destroying, ‖ And scattering the flock of My pasture," ‖ A declaration of YHWH. **2** Therefore, thus said YHWH, God of Israel, ‖ Against the shepherds who feed My people: "You have scattered My flock, and drive them away, ‖ And have not inspected them, ‖ Behold, I am charging on you the evil of your doings," ‖ A declaration of YHWH. **3** "And I gather the remnant of My flock ‖ Out of all the lands to where I drove them, ‖ And have brought them back to their fold, ‖ And they have been fruitful, and multiplied. **4** And I have raised shepherds for them, ‖ And they have fed them, ‖ And they no longer fear, nor are frightened, ‖ Nor are they lacking," ‖ A declaration of YHWH. **5** "Behold, days are coming," ‖ A declaration of YHWH, ‖ "And I have raised a righteous shoot to David, ‖ And a king has reigned and acted wisely, ‖ And done judgment and righteousness in the earth. **6** Judah is saved in His days, and Israel dwells confidently, ‖ And this [is] His Name that YHWH proclaims Him: Our Righteousness. **7** Therefore, behold, days are coming," ‖ A declaration of YHWH, ‖ "And they no longer say, YHWH lives who brought up ‖ The sons of Israel out of the land of Egypt, **8** But—YHWH lives, who

JEREMIAH

brought up, ‖ And who brought in, the seed of the house of Israel, ‖ From the land of the north, ‖ And from all the lands to where I drove them, ‖ And they have dwelt on their own ground!" 9 In reference to the prophets: My heart has been broken in my midst, ‖ All my bones have fluttered, ‖ I have been as a man—a drunkard, ‖ And as a man—wine has passed over him, ‖ Because of YHWH, and of His holy words. 10 For the land has been full of adulterers, ‖ For the land has mourned because of these, ‖ The pleasant places of the wilderness have dried up, ‖ And their course is evil, and their might—not right. 11 "For both prophet and priest have been profane, ‖ Indeed, I found their wickedness in My house," ‖ A declaration of YHWH. 12 "Therefore their way is as slippery places to them, ‖ They are driven into thick darkness, ‖ And they have fallen in it, ‖ For I bring in calamity against them, ‖ The year of their inspection," ‖ A declaration of YHWH. 13 "And I have seen folly in prophets of Samaria, ‖ They have prophesied by Ba'al, ‖ And cause My people—Israel—to err. 14 And I have seen a horrible thing in prophets of Jerusalem, ‖ Committing adultery, and walking falsely, ‖ Indeed, they strengthened the hands of evildoers, ‖ So that they have not turned back, ‖ Each from his wickedness, ‖ All of them have been as Sodom to me, ‖ And its inhabitants as Gomorrah." 15 Therefore, thus said YHWH of Hosts, concerning the prophets: "Behold, I am causing them to eat wormwood, ‖ And have caused them to drink water of gall, ‖ For from prophets of Jerusalem ‖ Profanity has gone forth to all the land." 16 Thus said YHWH of Hosts: "You do not listen to the words ‖ Of the prophets who are prophesying to you, ‖ They are making you vain things, ‖ They speak a vision of their own heart, ‖ Not from the mouth of YHWH. 17 Diligently saying to those despising, ‖ The word of YHWH: Peace is for you, ‖ And [to] everyone walking in the stubbornness of his heart, they have said: Evil does not come to you." 18 For who has stood in the counsel of YHWH, ‖ And sees and hears His word? Who has regarded My word, and listens? 19 Behold, a whirlwind of YHWH—Fury has gone out, even a piercing whirlwind, ‖ It stays on the head of the wicked. 20 The anger of YHWH does not turn back ‖ Until His doing, and until His establishing, ‖ The thoughts of His heart, ‖ In the latter end of the days ‖ You attend to it with understanding. 21 "I have not sent the prophets, and they have run, ‖ I have not spoken to them, and they have prophesied. 22 But if they stood in My counsel, ‖ Then they cause My people to hear My words, ‖ And they turn them back from their evil way, ‖ And from the evil of their doings. 23 [Am] I a God near," ‖ A declaration of YHWH, ‖ "And not a God far off? 24 Is anyone hidden in secret places, ‖ And I do not see him?" A declaration of YHWH, "Do I not fill the heavens and the earth?" A declaration of YHWH. 25 "I have heard that which the prophets said, ‖ Who prophesy falsehood in My Name, saying, ‖ I have dreamed, I have dreamed. 26 Until when is it in the heart of the prophets? The prophets of falsehood, ‖ Indeed, prophets of the deceit of their heart, 27 Who are devising to cause My people ‖ To forget My Name by their dreams, ‖ That they each recount to his neighbor, ‖ As their fathers forgot My Name for Ba'al. 28 The prophet with whom [is] a dream, ‖ Let him recount the dream, ‖ And he with whom [is] My word, ‖ Let him truly speak My word. What does the straw [have to do] with the grain?" A declaration of YHWH. 29 "Is it not thus? My word [is] as fire," ‖ A declaration of YHWH. "And as a hammer—it breaks a rock in pieces. 30 Therefore, behold, I [am] against the prophets," ‖ A declaration of YHWH, ‖ "Each stealing My words from his neighbor. 31 Behold, I [am] against the prophets," ‖ A declaration of YHWH, ‖ "Who are making their tongue smooth, ‖ And they affirm—an affirmation. 32 Behold, I [am] against the prophets of false dreams," ‖ A declaration of YHWH, ‖ "And they recount them, and cause My people to err, ‖ By their falsehoods, and by their instability, ‖ And I have not sent them, ‖ Nor have I commanded them, ‖ And they are not profitable to this people at all," ‖ A declaration of YHWH. 33 "And when this people, or the prophet, ‖ Or a priest, asks you, saying, What [is] the burden of YHWH? Then you have said to them: You [are] the burden, and I have left you," ‖ A declaration of YHWH. 34 "And the prophet, and the priest, and the people, ‖ That says, The burden of YHWH, ‖ I have seen after that man, and after his house. 35 Thus you each say to his neighbor, ‖ And each to his brother: What has YHWH answered? And what has YHWH spoken? **36** And you do not mention the burden of YHWH anymore, ‖ For the burden to each is His word, ‖ And you have overturned the words of the living God, YHWH of Hosts, our God. **37** Thus you say to the prophet, ‖ What has YHWH answered you? And what has YHWH spoken? **38** And if you say, The burden of YHWH, ‖ Therefore, thus said YHWH: Because of your saying this word, ‖ The burden of YHWH, ‖ And I send to you, saying, ‖ You do not say, The burden of YHWH. **39** Therefore, behold, I have utterly taken you away, ‖ And I have sent you out, ‖ And the city that I gave to you, ‖ And to your fathers, from before My face, **40** And I have put continuous reproach on you, ‖ And continuous shame that is not forgotten!"

24 YHWH has showed me, and behold, two baskets of figs, appointed before the temple of YHWH—after the removing by Nebuchadnezzar king of Babylon, of Jeconiah, son of Jehoiakim king of Judah, and the heads of Judah, and the artisan, and the smith, from Jerusalem, when he brings them into Babylon— **2** In one basket [are] very good figs, like the first-ripe figs, and in the other basket [are] very bad figs that are not eaten because of badness. **3** And YHWH says to me, "What are you seeing, Jeremiah?" And I say, "Figs, the good figs [are] very good, and the bad [are] very bad, that are not eaten because of badness." **4** And there is a word of YHWH to me, saying, **5** "Thus said YHWH, God of Israel: Like these good figs so I acknowledge ‖ The expulsion of Judah that I sent from this place, ‖ [To] the land of the Chaldeans—for good. **6** And I have set My eyes on them for good, ‖ And have brought them back to this land, ‖ And built them up, and I do not throw down, ‖ And have planted them, and do not pluck up. **7** And have given to them a heart to know Me, ‖ For I [am] YHWH, ‖ And they have been to Me for a people, ‖ And I am to them for God, ‖ For they turned back to Me with all their heart. **8** And like the bad figs that are not eaten for badness, ‖ Surely thus said YHWH: So I make Zedekiah king of Judah, ‖ And his heads, and the remnant of Jerusalem, ‖ Who are left in this land, ‖ And who are dwelling in the land of Egypt, **9** And I have given them for a trembling, ‖ For evil—to all kingdoms of the earth, ‖ For a reproach, and for an allegory, ‖ For a byword, and for a reviling, ‖ In all the places to where I drive them. **10** And I have sent the sword against them, ‖ The famine and the pestilence, ‖ Until their consumption from off the ground, ‖ That I gave to them and to their fathers!"

25 The word that has been to Jeremiah concerning all the people of Judah, in the fourth year of Jehoiakim son of Josiah king of Judah—it [is] the first year of Nebuchadnezzar king of Babylon— **2** Which Jeremiah the prophet has spoken concerning all the people of Judah, even to all the inhabitants of Jerusalem, saying, **3** "From the thirteenth year of Josiah son of Amon king of Judah, and to this day—this twenty-third year—the word of YHWH has been to me, and I speak to you, rising early and speaking, and you have not listened; **4** and YHWH has sent all His servants to you, the prophets, rising early and sending, and you have not listened, nor inclined your ear to hear, saying, **5** Please turn back, each from his evil way, and from the evil of your doings, and dwell on the ground that YHWH has given to you and to your fathers from age to age, **6** and you do not go after other gods to serve them, and to bow yourselves to them, nor do you provoke Me to anger with the work of your hands, and I do no evil to you; **7** and you have not listened to Me," a declaration of YHWH, "so as to provoke Me to anger with the work of your hands for evil to you. **8** Therefore, thus said YHWH of Hosts: Because that you have not obeyed My words, **9** behold, I am sending, and have taken all the families of the north—a declaration of YHWH—even to Nebuchadnezzar king of Babylon, My servant, and have brought them in against this land, and against its inhabitants, and against all these surrounding nations, and have devoted them, and appointed them for an astonishment, and for a hissing, and for continuous ruins. **10** And I have destroyed from them the voice of rejoicing, and the voice of joy, voice of bridegroom and voice of bride, noise of millstones, and the light of lamps. **11** And all this land has been for a desolation, for an astonishment, and these nations have served the king of Babylon seventy years. **12** And it has come to pass, at the fullness of seventy years, I charge against the king of Babylon, and against that nation," a declaration of

YHWH, "their iniquity, and against the land of the Chaldeans, and have appointed it for continuous desolations. **13** And I have brought in on that land all My words that I have spoken against it, all that is written in this scroll, that Jeremiah has prophesied concerning all the nations. **14** For laid service on them—also them—have many nations and great kings, and I have given repayment to them according to their doing, and according to the work of their hands." **15** For thus said YHWH, God of Israel, to me: "Take the wine cup of this fury out of My hand, and you have caused all the nations to drink it to whom I am sending you; **16** and they have drunk, and shaken themselves and shown themselves [to be] foolish, because of the sword that I am sending among them." **17** And I take the cup out of the hand of YHWH, and cause all the nations to drink to whom YHWH sent me: **18** Jerusalem, and the cities of Judah, ‖ And its kings, its heads, ‖ To give them to ruin, to astonishment, ‖ To hissing, and to reviling, as [at] this day; **19** Pharaoh king of Egypt, and his servants, ‖ And his heads, and all his people, **20** And all the mixed people, ‖ And all the kings of the land of Uz, ‖ And all the kings of the land of the Philistines, ‖ And Ashkelon, and Gaza, and Ekron, ‖ And the remnant of Ashdod, **21** Edom, and Moab, and the sons of Ammon, **22** And all the kings of Tyre, ‖ And all the kings of Sidon, ‖ And the kings of the island that [is] beyond the sea, **23** Dedan, and Tema, and Buz, ‖ And all cutting the corners [of the beard], **24** And all the kings of Arabia, ‖ And all the kings of the mixed people, ‖ Who are dwelling in the wilderness, **25** And all the kings of Zimri, ‖ And all the kings of Elam, ‖ And all the kings of Media, **26** And all the kings of the north, ‖ The near and the far off to one another, ‖ And all the kingdoms of the earth, ‖ That [are] on the face of the ground, ‖ And King Sheshach drinks after them. **27** "And you have said to them, Thus said YHWH of Hosts, God of Israel: Drink, indeed drink abundantly, ‖ And vomit, and fall, and do not rise, ‖ Because of the sword that I am sending among you. **28** And it has come to pass, ‖ When they refuse to receive the cup out of your hand to drink, ‖ That you have said to them, Thus said YHWH of Hosts: You certainly drink. **29** For behold, in the city over which My Name is called, ‖ I am beginning to bring ruin, ‖ And are you entirely acquitted? You are not acquitted, for I am proclaiming a sword, ‖ For all inhabitants of the land," ‖ A declaration of YHWH of Hosts. **30** "And you, you prophesy all these words to them, and have said to them: YHWH roars from the high place, ‖ And gives forth His voice from His holy habitation, ‖ He surely roars for His habitation, ‖ A shout as those treading [the grapes], ‖ God answers all the inhabitants of the land, **31** A rumbling has come to the end of the earth, ‖ For YHWH has a controversy with nations, ‖ He has executed judgment for all flesh, ‖ He has given the wicked to the sword," ‖ A declaration of YHWH. **32** Thus said YHWH of Hosts: "Behold, evil is going out from nation to nation, ‖ And a great whirlwind is stirred up from the sides of the earth. **33** And the pierced of YHWH have been in that day, ‖ From the end of the earth even to the end of the earth, ‖ They are not lamented, nor gathered, nor buried, ‖ For they are dung on the face of the ground. **34** Howl, you shepherds, and cry, ‖ And roll yourselves, you majestic of the flock, ‖ For your days have been full ‖ For slaughtering, and [for] your scatterings, ‖ And you have fallen as a desirable vessel. **35** And refuge has perished from the shepherds, ‖ And escape from the majestic of the flock. **36** A voice of the cry of the shepherds, ‖ And a howling of the majestic of the flock, ‖ For YHWH is spoiling their pasture. **37** And the peaceable habitations have been cut down, ‖ Because of the fierceness of the anger of YHWH. **38** He has forsaken His covert as a young lion, ‖ Surely their land has become a desolation, ‖ Because of the oppressing fierceness, ‖ And because of the fierceness of His anger!"

26 In the beginning of the reign of Jehoiakim son of Josiah, king of Judah, this word has been from YHWH, saying, **2** "Thus said YHWH: Stand in the court of the house of YHWH, and you have spoken to all [those of] the cities of Judah, who are coming to bow themselves in the house of YHWH, all the words that I have commanded you to speak to them—you do not diminish a word. **3** Perhaps they listen, and each turns back from his evil way; then I have relented concerning the evil that I am thinking of doing to them, because of the evil of their doings. **4** And you have said to them, Thus said YHWH: If you do

JEREMIAH

not listen to Me, to walk in My law that I set before you, **5** to listen to the words of My servants the prophets, whom I am sending to you, indeed, rising early and sending, and you have not listened, **6** then I have given up this house as Shiloh, and this city I give up for a reviling to all nations of the earth." **7** And the priests, and the prophets, and all the people, hear Jeremiah speaking these words in the house of YHWH, **8** and it comes to pass, at the completion of Jeremiah's speaking all that YHWH has commanded him to speak to all the people, that the priests, and the prophets, and all the people catch him, saying, "You surely die! **9** Why have you prophesied in the Name of YHWH, saying, This house will be as Shiloh, and this city is desolated, without inhabitant?" And all the people are assembled to Jeremiah in the house of YHWH. **10** And the heads of Judah hear these things, and they go up from the house of the king [to] the house of YHWH, and sit in the opening of the New Gate of YHWH. **11** And the priests and the prophets speak to the heads, and to all the people, saying, "Judgment of death [is] for this man, for he has prophesied against this city, as you have heard with your ears." **12** And Jeremiah speaks to all the heads, and to all the people, saying, "YHWH sent me to prophesy concerning this house, and concerning this city, all the words that you have heard. **13** And now, amend your ways, and your doings, and listen to the voice of your God YHWH, and YHWH relents concerning the evil that He has spoken against you. **14** And I, behold, I [am] in your hand, do to me as is good and as is right in your eyes; **15** only, certainly know that if you are putting me to death, you are surely putting innocent blood on yourselves, and on this city, and on its inhabitants; for YHWH has truly sent me to you to speak all these words in your ears." **16** And the heads and all the people say to the priests and to the prophets, "There is not a judgment of death for this man, for he has spoken to us in the Name of our God YHWH." **17** And men from [the] elderly of the land rise up and speak to all the assembly of the people, saying, **18** "Micah the Morashtite has been prophesying in the days of Hezekiah king of Judah, and he says to all the people of Judah, saying, Thus said YHWH of Hosts: Zion is a plowed field, and Jerusalem is heaps, || And the mountain of the house is for high places of a forest. **19** Did Hezekiah king of Judah and all Judah put him to death? Did he not fear YHWH? Indeed, he appeases the face of YHWH, and YHWH relents concerning the calamity that He spoke against them; and we are doing great evil against our souls." **20** And there has also been a man prophesying in the Name of YHWH, Urijah son of Shemaiah, of Kirjath-Jearim, and he prophesies against this city, and against this land according to all the words of Jeremiah, **21** and King Jehoiakim, and all his mighty ones, and all the heads, hear his words, and the king seeks to put him to death, and Urijah hears, and fears, and flees, and goes to Egypt. **22** And King Jehoiakim sends men to Egypt—Elnathan son of Achbor, and men with him to Egypt— **23** and they bring out Urijah from Egypt, and bring him to King Jehoiakim, and he strikes him with a sword, and casts his corpse to the graves of the sons of the people. **24** Only, the hand of Ahikam son of Shaphan has been with Jeremiah so as not to give him up into the hand of the people to put him to death.

27 In the beginning of the reign of Jehoiakim son of Josiah, king of Judah, this word has been to Jeremiah from YHWH, saying, **2** "Thus said YHWH to me: Make bands and yokes for yourself, **3** and you have put them on your neck, and have sent them to the king of Edom, and to the king of Moab, and to the king of the sons of Ammon, and to the king of Tyre, and to the king of Sidon, by the hand of messengers who are coming to Jerusalem, to Zedekiah king of Judah; **4** and you have commanded them for their lords, saying, Thus said YHWH of Hosts, God of Israel: **5** Thus you say to your lords, I have made the earth with man, and the livestock that [are] on the face of the earth, by My great power, and by My outstretched arm, and I have given it to whom it has been right in My eyes. **6** And now, I have given all these lands into the hand of Nebuchadnezzar king of Babylon, My servant, and I have also given the beast of the field to him to serve him; **7** and all the nations have served him, and his son, and his son's son, until the coming in of the time of his land, also it; and many nations and great kings have made him serve them. **8** And it has come to pass, the nation and the kingdom that does not serve

JEREMIAH

him—Nebuchadnezzar king of Babylon—and that which does not put its neck into the yoke of the king of Babylon, with sword, and with famine, and with pestilence, I lay a charge on that nation—a declaration of YHWH—until I consume them by his hand. **9** And you, you do not listen to your prophets, and to your diviners, and to your dreamers, and to your observers of clouds, and to your sorcerers who are speaking to you, saying, You do not serve the king of Babylon— **10** For they are prophesying falsehood to you, so as to remove you far from your ground, and I have driven you out, and you have perished. **11** And the nation that causes its neck to enter into the yoke of the king of Babylon, and has served him—I have left it on its ground—a declaration of YHWH—and it has tilled it, and dwelt in it." **12** And I have spoken to Zedekiah king of Judah according to all these words, saying, "Cause your necks to enter into the yoke of the king of Babylon, and serve him and his people, and live. **13** Why do you die, you and your people, by sword, by famine, and by pestilence, as YHWH has spoken concerning the nation that does not serve the king of Babylon? **14** And you do not listen to the words of the prophets who are speaking to you, saying, You do not serve the king of Babylon—for they are prophesying falsehood to you. **15** For I have not sent them—a declaration of YHWH—and they are prophesying falsely in My Name, so as to drive you out, and you have perished, you and the prophets who are prophesying to you." **16** And to the priests, and to all this people, I have spoken, saying, "Thus said YHWH: You do not listen to the words of your prophets, who are prophesying to you, saying, Behold, the vessels of the house of YHWH are now brought back from Babylon in haste, for they are prophesying falsehood to you. **17** You do not listen to them; serve the king of Babylon and live! Why is this city a ruin? **18** And if they are prophets, and if a word of YHWH is with them, let them now intercede with YHWH of Hosts, so that the vessels that are left in the house of YHWH, and [in] the house of the king of Judah, and in Jerusalem, have not gone into Babylon. **19** For thus said YHWH of Hosts concerning the pillars, and concerning the sea, and concerning the bases, and concerning the rest of the vessels that are left in this city, **20** that Nebuchadnezzar king of Babylon has not taken, in his removing Jeconiah son of Jehoiakim king of Judah from Jerusalem to Babylon with all the nobles of Judah and Jerusalem, **21** surely thus said YHWH of Hosts, God of Israel, concerning the vessels that are left of the house of YHWH, and of the house of the king of Judah, and [in] Jerusalem: **22** They are brought to Babylon, and there they are until the day of My inspecting them—a declaration of YHWH; then I have brought them up, and have brought them back to this place."

28 And it comes to pass, in that year, in the beginning of the reign of Zedekiah king of Judah, in the fourth year, in the fifth month, Hananiah son of Azur the prophet, who [is] of Gibeon, has spoken to me in the house of YHWH, before the eyes of the priests, and all the people, saying, **2** "Thus spoke YHWH of Hosts, God of Israel, saying, I have broken the yoke of the king of Babylon; **3** within two years of days I am bringing back to this place all the vessels of the house of YHWH that Nebuchadnezzar king of Babylon has taken from this place, and carries to Babylon, **4** and Jeconiah son of Jehoiakim, king of Judah, and all the expulsion of Judah, who are entering Babylon, I am bringing back to this place—a declaration of YHWH; for I break the yoke of the king of Babylon." **5** And Jeremiah the prophet says to Hananiah the prophet, before the eyes of the priests, and before the eyes of all the people who are standing in the house of YHWH, **6** indeed, Jeremiah the prophet says, "Amen! So may YHWH do; YHWH establish your words that you have prophesied, to bring back the vessels of the house of YHWH and all the expulsion from Babylon, to this place. **7** Only, please hear this word that I am speaking in your ears, and in the ears of all the people. **8** The prophets who have been before me, and before you, from of old, even they prophesy concerning many lands, and concerning great kingdoms, of battle, and of calamity, and of pestilence. **9** The prophet who prophesies of peace, by the word of the prophet coming to pass, the prophet is known [as] one whom YHWH has truly sent." **10** And Hananiah the prophet takes the yoke from off the neck of Jeremiah the prophet, and breaks it, **11** and Hananiah speaks before the eyes of all the people, saying, "Thus said YHWH: Thus I break the yoke of Nebuchadnezzar king of Babylon, within two years of days, from off the neck of all the nations"; and Jeremiah the prophet goes on his way. **12** And there is a word of YHWH to Jeremiah after the breaking, by Hananiah the prophet, of the yoke from off the neck of Jeremiah the prophet, saying, **13** "Go, and you have spoken to Hananiah, saying, Thus said YHWH: You have broken yokes of wood, and I have made yokes of iron instead of them. **14** For thus said YHWH of Hosts, God of Israel: I have put a yoke of iron on the neck of all these nations to serve Nebuchadnezzar king of Babylon, and they have served him, and I have also given the beast of the field to him." **15** And Jeremiah the prophet says to Hananiah the prophet, "Now hear, O Hananiah; YHWH has not sent you, and you have caused this people to trust on falsehood. **16** Therefore, thus said YHWH: Behold, I am casting you from off the face of the ground; you die this year, for you have spoken apostasy concerning YHWH." **17** And Hananiah the prophet dies in that year, in the seventh month.

29 And these [are] the words of the letter that Jeremiah the prophet sent from Jerusalem to the remnant of [the] elderly of the expulsion, and to the priests, and to the prophets, and to all the people—whom Nebuchadnezzar removed from Jerusalem to Babylon, **2** after the going forth of Jeconiah the king, and the mistress, and the officers, heads of Judah and Jerusalem, and the craftsman, and the smith, from Jerusalem— **3** by the hand of Eleasah son of Shaphan, and Gemariah son of Hilkiah, whom Zedekiah king of Judah sent to Babylon, to Nebuchadnezzar king of Babylon, saying, **4** "Thus said YHWH of Hosts, God of Israel, to all the expulsion that I removed from Jerusalem to Babylon: **5** Build houses and abide; and plant gardens and eat their fruit; **6** take wives and beget sons and daughters; and take wives for your sons, and give your daughters to husbands, and they bear sons and daughters; and multiply there, and you are not few; **7** and seek the peace of the city to where I have removed you, and pray to YHWH for it, for in its peace you have peace. **8** For thus said YHWH of Hosts, God of Israel: Do not let your prophets who [are] in your midst, and your diviners, lift you up, nor listen to their dreams, that you are causing [them] to dream; **9** for they are prophesying with falsehood to you in My Name; I have not sent them, a declaration of YHWH. **10** For thus said YHWH: Surely at the fullness of Babylon—seventy years—I inspect you, and have established My good word toward you, to bring you back to this place. **11** For I have known the thoughts that I am thinking toward you—a declaration of YHWH; thoughts of peace, and not of evil, to give posterity and hope to you. **12** And you have called Me, and have gone, and have prayed to Me, and I have listened to you, **13** and you have sought Me, and have found, for you seek Me with all your heart; **14** and I have been found by you—a declaration of YHWH; and I have turned back [to] your captivity, and have gathered you out of all the nations, and out of all the places to where I have driven you—a declaration of YHWH—and I have brought you back to the place from where I removed you. **15** Because you have said, YHWH has raised up prophets to us in Babylon, **16** surely thus said YHWH concerning the king who is sitting on the throne of David, and concerning all the people that are dwelling in this city, your brothers who did not go forth with you in the expulsion— **17** thus said YHWH of Hosts: Behold, I am sending the sword, the famine, and the pestilence among them, and I have given them up as figs that [are] vile, that are not eaten because of badness. **18** And I have pursued after them with sword, with famine, and with pestilence, and have given them for a trembling to all kingdoms of the earth, for a curse and for an astonishment, and for a hissing, and for a reproach among all the nations to where I have driven them, **19** because that they have not listened to My words—a declaration of YHWH—that I sent to them by My servants the prophets, rising early and sending, and you did not listen—a declaration of YHWH. **20** And you, hear a word of YHWH, all you of the captivity that I have sent from Jerusalem to Babylon— **21** thus said YHWH of Hosts, God of Israel, concerning Ahab son of Kolaiah, and concerning Zedekiah son of Maaseiah, who are prophesying falsehood to you in My Name: Behold, I am giving them into the hand of Nebuchadnezzar king of

JEREMIAH

Babylon, and he has struck them before your eyes, **22** and because of them a reviling has been taken by all the expulsion of Judah that [are] in Babylon, saying, YHWH sets you as Zedekiah, and as Ahab, whom the king of Babylon roasted with fire; **23** because that they have done folly in Israel, and commit adultery with the wives of their neighbors, and falsely speak a word in My Name that I have not commanded them, and I [am] He who knows and a witness—a declaration of YHWH. **24** And you speak to Shemaiah the Nehelamite, saying, **25** Thus said YHWH of Hosts, God of Israel, saying, Because that you have sent letters in your name to all the people who [are] in Jerusalem, and to Zephaniah son of Maaseiah the priest, and to all the priests, saying, **26** YHWH has made you priest instead of Jehoiada the priest, for there being inspectors of the house of YHWH over every man [who] is mad and making himself a prophet, and you have put him in the stocks and in the pillory. **27** And now, why have you not pushed against Jeremiah of Anathoth, who is making himself a prophet to you? **28** Because that he has sent to us [in] Babylon, saying, It [is] long, build houses and abide; and plant gardens and eat their fruit." **29** And Zephaniah the priest reads this letter in the ears of Jeremiah the prophet. **30** And there is a word of YHWH to Jeremiah, saying, **31** "Send to all the expulsion, saying, Thus said YHWH concerning Shemaiah the Nehelamite: Because that Shemaiah prophesied to you, and I have not sent him, and he causes you to trust on falsehood, **32** therefore, thus said YHWH: Behold, I am seeing after Shemaiah the Nehelamite, and after his seed, he has none dwelling in the midst of this people, nor does he look on the good that I am doing to My people," a declaration of YHWH, "for he has spoken apostasy against YHWH."

30 The word that has been to Jeremiah from YHWH, saying, **2** "Thus spoke YHWH, God of Israel, saying, Write for yourself all the words that I have spoken to you on a scroll. **3** For behold, days are coming—a declaration of YHWH—and I have turned back [to] the captivity of My people Israel and Judah, said YHWH, and I have caused them to return to the land that I gave to their fathers, and they possess it."

4 And these [are] the words that YHWH has spoken concerning Israel and concerning Judah: **5** Surely thus said YHWH: "We have heard a voice of trembling, ‖ Fear—and there is no peace. **6** Now ask and see, is a male bringing forth? Why have I seen every man ‖ [With] his hands on his loins, as a travailing woman, ‖ And all faces have been turned to paleness? **7** Woe! For that day [is] great, without any like it, ‖ Indeed, it [is] the time of Jacob's tribulation, ‖ Yet he is saved out of it. **8** And it has come to pass in that day, ‖ A declaration of YHWH of Hosts, ‖ I break his yoke from off your neck, ‖ And I draw away your bands, ‖ And strangers lay no more service on him. **9** And they have served their God YHWH, ‖ And David their king whom I raise up to them. **10** And you, do not be afraid, My servant Jacob, ‖ A declaration of YHWH, ‖ Nor be frightened, O Israel, ‖ For behold, I am saving you from afar, ‖ And your seed from the land of their captivity, ‖ And Jacob has turned back and rested, ‖ And is quiet, and there is none troubling. **11** For I [am] with you," ‖ A declaration of YHWH, ‖ "To save you, ‖ For I make an end of all the nations ‖ To where I have scattered you, ‖ Only, I do not make an end of you, ‖ And I have disciplined you in judgment, ‖ And do not entirely acquit you." **12** For thus said YHWH: "Your breach is incurable, your stroke grievous, **13** There is none judging your cause to bind up, ‖ There are no healing medicines for you. **14** All loving you have forgotten you, ‖ They do not seek you, ‖ For I struck you with the stroke of an enemy, ‖ The discipline of a fierce one, ‖ Because of the abundance of your iniquity, your sins have been mighty! **15** Why do you cry concerning your breach? Your pain [is] incurable, ‖ Because of the abundance of your iniquity, ‖ Your sins have been mighty! I have done these to you. **16** Therefore all consuming you are consumed, ‖ And all your adversaries—all of them—Go into captivity, ‖ And your spoilers have been for a spoil, ‖ And I give up all your plunderers to plunder. **17** For I increase health to you, ‖ And I heal you from your strokes," ‖ A declaration of YHWH, ‖ "For they have called you an outcast, [saying], ‖ It [is] Zion, ‖ There is none seeking for her." **18** Thus said YHWH: "Behold, I turn back [to] the captivity of the tents of Jacob, ‖ And I pity his dwelling places, ‖ And the city has been built on its heap, ‖ And the palace remains according to its ordinance. **19** And thanksgiving has gone forth from them, ‖ And the voice of playful ones, ‖ And I have multiplied them and they are not few, ‖ And made them honorable, and they are not small. **20** And his sons have been as before, ‖ And his congregation is established before Me, ‖ And I have seen after all his oppressors. **21** And his majestic one has been of himself, ‖ And his ruler goes forth from his midst, ‖ And I have caused him to draw near, ‖ And he has drawn near to Me, ‖ For who [is] he who has pledged his heart ‖ To draw near to Me?" A declaration of YHWH. **22** "And you have been to Me for a people, ‖ And I am to you for God." **23** Behold, a whirlwind of YHWH—Fury has gone forth—a cutting whirlwind, ‖ It stays on the head of the wicked. **24** The fierceness of the anger of YHWH ‖ Does not turn back until He has done [it], ‖ Indeed, until His establishing the purposes of His heart. In the latter end of the days you consider it!

31 "At that time," a declaration of YHWH, "I am the God of all families of Israel, ‖ And they are My people." **2** Thus said YHWH: "A people remaining from the sword ‖ Have found grace in the wilderness ‖ When Israel went to find rest." **3** YHWH has appeared to me from afar, "I have loved you with perpetual love, ‖ Therefore I have drawn you [with] kindness. **4** I build you again, ‖ And you have been built, ‖ O virgin of Israel, ‖ You put on your tambourines again, ‖ And have gone out in the chorus of the playful. **5** You plant vineyards in mountains of Samaria again, ‖ Planters have planted, and made common. **6** For there is a day, ‖ Watchmen have cried on Mount Ephraim, ‖ Rise, and we go up to Zion, to our God YHWH"; **7** For thus said YHWH: "Sing [with] joy for Jacob, ‖ And cry aloud at the head of the nations, ‖ Sound, praise, and say, ‖ Save, O YHWH, Your people, the remnant of Israel. **8** Behold, I am bringing them in from the north country, ‖ And have gathered them from the sides of the earth, ‖ Blind and lame [are] among them, ‖ Conceiving and travailing one—together, ‖ A great assembly—they return here. **9** They come in with weeping, ‖ And I bring them with supplications, ‖ I cause them to go to streams of waters, ‖ In a right way—they do not stumble in it, ‖ For I have been a Father to Israel, ‖ And Ephraim—he [is] My firstborn." **10** Hear a word of YHWH, O nations, ‖ And declare among the far off in the islands, and say: He who is scattering Israel gathers him, ‖ And has kept His flock as a shepherd, **11** For YHWH has ransomed Jacob, ‖ And redeemed him from a hand stronger than he. **12** And they have come in, ‖ And have sung in the high place of Zion, ‖ And flowed to the goodness of YHWH, ‖ For wheat, and for new wine, and for oil, ‖ And for the young of the flock and herd, ‖ And their soul has been as a watered garden, ‖ And they do not add to grieve anymore. **13** "Then a virgin rejoices in a chorus, ‖ Both young men and old men—together, ‖ And I have turned their mourning to joy, ‖ And have comforted them, ‖ And gladdened them above their sorrow, **14** And satisfied the soul of the priests [with] fatness, ‖ And My people are satisfied with My goodness," ‖ A declaration of YHWH. **15** Thus said YHWH: "A voice is heard in Ramah, ‖ Wailing [and] the weeping of bitterness, ‖ Rachel is weeping for her sons, ‖ She has refused to be comforted for her sons, because they are not." **16** Thus said YHWH: "Withhold your voice from weeping, and your eyes from tears, ‖ For there is a reward for your work," ‖ A declaration of YHWH, ‖ "And they have turned back from the land of the enemy. **17** And there is hope for your latter end," ‖ A declaration of YHWH, ‖ "And the sons have turned back [to] their border. **18** I have surely heard Ephraim bemoaning himself, ‖ You have disciplined me, ‖ And I am disciplined, as a heifer [that is] not taught, ‖ Turn me back, and I turn back, ‖ For You [are] my God YHWH. **19** For after my turning back I regretted, ‖ And after my being instructed I struck on the thigh, ‖ I have been ashamed, I have also blushed, ‖ For I have borne the reproach of my youth. **20** Is Ephraim a precious son to Me? A child of delights? For since My speaking against him, ‖ I still thoroughly remember him, ‖ Therefore My bowels have been moved for him, ‖ I love him greatly," ‖ A declaration of YHWH. **21** "Set up signs for yourself, ‖ Make heaps for yourself, ‖ Set your heart to the highway, the way you went, ‖ Turn back, O virgin of Israel, ‖ Turn back to these cities of yours. **22** Until when do you withdraw yourself, O backsliding daughter? For YHWH has prepared a new thing in the land, ‖ Woman surrounds

JEREMIAH

man." **23** Thus said YHWH of Hosts, God of Israel: "Still they say this word in the land of Judah, ‖ And in its cities, ‖ In My turning back [to] their captivity, ‖ YHWH blesses you, habitation of righteousness, ‖ Mountain of holiness. **24** And farmers have dwelt in Judah, ‖ And in all its cities together, ‖ And they have journeyed in order. **25** For I have satiated the weary soul, ‖ And I have filled every grieved soul." **26** On this I have awoken, and I behold, and my sleep has been sweet to me. **27** "Behold, days are coming," ‖ A declaration of YHWH, ‖ "And I have sown the house of Israel, ‖ And the house of Judah, ‖ With seed of man and seed of beast. **28** And it has been, as I watched over them to pluck up, ‖ And to break down, and to throw down, ‖ And to destroy, and to afflict; So I watch over them to build, and to plant," ‖ A declaration of YHWH. **29** "In those days they no longer say: Fathers have eaten unripe fruit, ‖ And the sons' teeth are blunted. **30** But—each dies for his own iniquity, ‖ Every man who is eating the unripe fruit, ‖ His teeth are blunted. **31** Behold, days are coming," ‖ A declaration of YHWH, ‖ "And I have made a new covenant ‖ With the house of Israel ‖ And with the house of Judah, **32** Not like the covenant that I made with their fathers, ‖ In the day of My laying hold on their hand, ‖ To bring them out of the land of Egypt, ‖ In that they made My covenant void, ‖ And I ruled over them," ‖ A declaration of YHWH. **33** "For this [is] the covenant that I make, ‖ With the house of Israel, after those days," ‖ A declaration of YHWH, ‖ "I have given My law in their inward part, ‖ And I write it on their heart, ‖ And I have been their God, ‖ And they are My people. **34** And they do not teach anymore ‖ Each his neighbor, and each his brother, ‖ Saying, Know YHWH, ‖ For they all know Me, from their least to their greatest," ‖ A declaration of YHWH; "For I pardon their iniquity, ‖ And I make no more mention of their sin." **35** Thus said YHWH, ‖ Who is giving the sun for a light by day, ‖ The statutes of moon and stars for a light by night, ‖ Quieting the sea when its billows roar, ‖ YHWH of Hosts [is] His Name: **36** "If these statutes depart from before Me," ‖ A declaration of YHWH, ‖ "Even the seed of Israel ceases ‖ From being a nation before Me [for] all the days." **37** Thus said YHWH: "If the heavens above can be measured, ‖ And the foundations of earth searched below, ‖ Even I kick against all the seed of Israel, ‖ For all that they have done," ‖ A declaration of YHWH. **38** "Behold, days [are coming]," ‖ A declaration of YHWH, ‖ "And the city has been built for YHWH, ‖ From the Tower of Hananeel to the Corner Gate. **39** And the measuring line has gone out again before it, over the height of Gareb, ‖ And it has gone around to Goah. **40** And all the valley of the carcasses and of the ashes, ‖ And all the fields to the Brook of Kidron, ‖ To the corner of the Horse Gate eastward, ‖ [Are] holy to YHWH, ‖ It is not plucked up, ‖ Nor is it thrown down anymore for all time!"

32 The word that has been to Jeremiah from YHWH in the tenth year of Zedekiah king of Judah—it [is] the eighteenth year of Nebuchadnezzar— **2** And then the forces of the king of Babylon are laying siege against Jerusalem, and Jeremiah the prophet has been shut up in the court of the prison that [is] in the house of the king of Judah, **3** where Zedekiah king of Judah has shut him up, saying, "Why are you prophesying, saying, Thus said YHWH: Behold, I am giving this city into the hand of the king of Babylon, and he has captured it; **4** and Zedekiah king of Judah does not escape out of the hand of the Chaldeans, but is certainly given into the hand of the king of Babylon, and his mouth has spoken with his mouth, and his eyes see his eyes, **5** and he leads Zedekiah [to] Babylon, and there he is until My inspecting him—a declaration of YHWH—because you fight with the Chaldeans, you do not prosper." **6** And Jeremiah says, "A word of YHWH has been to me, saying, **7** Behold, Hanameel son of Shallum, your uncle, is coming to you, saying, Buy my field that [is] in Anathoth for yourself, for the right of redemption [is] yours to buy." **8** And Hanameel, my uncle's son, comes to me, according to the word of YHWH, to the court of the prison, and says to me, "Please buy my field that [is] in Anathoth, that [is] in the land of Benjamin, for the right of possession [is] yours, and redemption yours—buy [it] for yourself." And I know that it [is] the word of YHWH, **9** and I buy the field that [is] in Anathoth from Hanameel, my uncle's son, and I weigh the money to him—seventeen shekels of

JEREMIAH

silver. **10** And I write in a scroll, and seal, and cause witnesses to testify, and weigh the silver in balances; **11** and I take the purchase scroll, the sealed one, according to law and custom, and the open one; **12** and I give the purchase scroll to Baruch son of Neriah, son of Maaseiah, before the eyes of Hanameel, my uncle's son, and before the eyes of the witnesses, those writing in the purchase scroll, before the eyes of all the Jews who are sitting in the court of the prison. **13** And I charge Baruch before their eyes, saying, **14** "Thus said YHWH of Hosts, God of Israel: Take these scrolls, this purchase scroll, both the sealed one and the open one, and you have put them in an earthen vessel, that they may remain many days. **15** For thus said YHWH of Hosts, God of Israel: Houses and fields and vineyards are bought in this land again." **16** And I pray to YHWH after my giving the purchase scroll to Baruch son of Neriah, saying, **17** "Aah! Lord YHWH, behold, You have made the heavens and the earth by Your great power, and by Your outstretched arm; there is nothing too wonderful for You: **18** doing kindness to thousands, and repaying iniquity of fathers into the bosom of their sons after them; God, the great, the mighty, YHWH of Hosts [is] His Name; **19** great in counsel, and mighty in act, in that Your eyes are open on all the ways of the sons of Adam, to give to each according to his ways, and according to the fruit of his doings; **20** in that you have done signs and wonders in the land of Egypt to this day, and in Israel, and among men, and You make for Yourself a name as [at] this day. **21** And You bring forth Your people Israel from the land of Egypt, with signs and with wonders, and by a strong hand, and by an outstretched arm, and by great fear, **22** and you give to them this land that you swore to their fathers to give to them, a land flowing with milk and honey, **23** and they come in, and possess it, and they have not listened to Your voice, and have not walked in Your law, all that which You laid a charge on them to do they have not done, and You proclaim all this calamity [to] them. **24** Behold, the [siege] mounds have come to the city to capture it, and the city has been given into the hand of the Chaldeans who are fighting against it, because of the sword, and the famine, and the pestilence; and that which You have spoken has come to pass, and behold, You are seeing. **25** Yet You have said to me, O Lord YHWH, Buy the field for yourself with money, and cause witnesses to testify—and the city has been given into the hand of the Chaldeans!" **26** And the word of YHWH is to Jeremiah, saying, **27** "Behold, I [am] YHWH, God of all flesh: is anything too wonderful for Me?" **28** Therefore, thus said YHWH: "Behold, I am giving this city into the hand of the Chaldeans, and into the hand of Nebuchadnezzar king of Babylon, and he has captured it. **29** And the Chaldeans who are fighting against this city have come in, and they have set this city on fire, and have burned it—and the houses on whose roofs they made incense to Ba'al, and poured out drink-offerings to other gods, so as to provoke Me to anger. **30** For the sons of Israel and the sons of Judah have been doing only evil in My eyes from their youth; for the sons of Israel are surely provoking Me with the work of their hands," a declaration of YHWH. **31** "For this city has been a cause of My anger and a cause of My fury, even from the day that they built it, and to this day—to turn it aside from before My face, **32** because of all the evil of the sons of Israel, and of the sons of Judah that they have done, so as to provoke Me—they, their kings, their heads, their priests, and their prophets, and the men of Judah, and the inhabitants of Jerusalem. **33** And they turn the neck to Me, and not the face, and teaching them, rising early and teaching, and they are not listening to accept instruction. **34** And they set their abominations in the house over which My Name is called, so as to defile it. **35** And they build the high places of Ba'al that [are] in the Valley of the Son of Hinnom, to cause their sons and their daughters to pass through to Molech, which I did not command them, nor did it come up on My heart to do this abomination, so as to cause Judah to sin. **36** And now, therefore, thus said YHWH, God of Israel, concerning this city, of which you are saying, It has been given into the hand of the king of Babylon by sword, and by famine, and by pestilence: **37** Behold, I am gathering them out of all the lands to where I have driven them in My anger, and in My fury, and in great wrath, and I have brought them back to this place, and have caused them to dwell confidently; **38** and they have been to Me for a people, and I am to them for God;

JEREMIAH

39 and I have given to them one heart and one way, to fear Me all the days, for the good of them and their sons after them: **40** and I have made a perpetual covenant for them, in that I do not turn back from after them for My doing them good, and I put My fear in their heart, so as not to turn aside from me; **41** and I have rejoiced over them to do them good, and have planted them in this land in truth, with all my heart, and with all My soul." **42** For thus said YHWH: "As I brought to this people all this great calamity, so I am bringing on them all the good that I am speaking concerning them; **43** and the field has been bought in this land of which you are saying, It [is] a desolation, without man and beast, it has been given into the hand of the Chaldeans. **44** They buy fields with money, so as to write in a scroll, and to seal, and to cause witnesses to testify, in the land of Benjamin, and in outskirts of Jerusalem, and in cities of Judah, and in cities of the hill-country, and in cities of the low country, and in cities of the south, for I return their captivity," a declaration of YHWH.

33 And there is a word of YHWH to Jeremiah a second time—and he [is] yet detained in the court of the prison—saying: **2** "Thus said YHWH who has made it, YHWH who has formed it, to establish it, YHWH [is] His Name: **3** Call to Me, and I answer you, indeed, I declare to you great and inaccessible things—you have not known them. **4** For thus said YHWH, God of Israel, concerning the houses of this city, and concerning the houses of the kings of Judah that are broken down for the [siege] mounds, and for the tool; **5** they are coming to fight with the Chaldeans, and to fill them with the carcasses of men, whom I have struck in My anger, and in My fury, and [for] whom I have hidden My face from this city, because of all their evil: **6** Behold, I am increasing health and cure to it, ‖ And have healed them, and revealed to them ‖ The abundance of peace and truth. **7** And I have turned back the captivity of Judah, ‖ And the captivity of Israel, ‖ And I have built them as at the first, **8** And cleansed them from all their iniquity ‖ That they have sinned against Me, ‖ And I have pardoned all their iniquities ‖ That they have sinned against Me, ‖ And that they transgressed against Me. **9** And it has been for a name of joy to Me, ‖ For praise, and for beauty, to all nations of the earth, ‖ Who hear of all the good that I am doing them, ‖ And they have feared, ‖ And they have trembled for all the good, ‖ And for all the peace, that I am doing to it." **10** Thus said YHWH: "Again is heard in this place—of which you are saying, It [is] dry, without man and without beast, ‖ In cities of Judah, and in streets of Jerusalem, ‖ That are desolated, without man, ‖ And without inhabitant, and without beast— **11** A voice of joy and a voice of gladness, ‖ Voice of bridegroom and voice of bride, ‖ The voice of those saying, ‖ Thank YHWH of Hosts, for YHWH [is] good, ‖ For His kindness [is] for all time, ‖ Who are bringing in thanksgiving to the house of YHWH, ‖ For I return the captivity of the land, ‖ As at the first," said YHWH. **12** Thus said YHWH of Hosts: "Again there is in this place—that is dry, ‖ Without man and beast, ‖ And in all its cities—a habitation of shepherds, ‖ Causing the flock to lie down. **13** In the cities of the hill-country, ‖ In the cities of the low country, ‖ And in the cities of the south, ‖ And in the land of Benjamin, ‖ And in the outskirts of Jerusalem, ‖ And in the cities of Judah, ‖ Again the flock passes by under the hands of the numberer," said YHWH. **14** "Behold, days are coming," a declaration of YHWH, "And I have established the good word ‖ That I spoke to the house of Israel, ‖ And concerning the house of Judah. **15** In those days, and at that time, ‖ I cause a Shoot of righteousness to shoot up to David, ‖ And He has done judgment and righteousness in the earth. **16** In those days Judah is saved, ‖ And Jerusalem dwells confidently, ‖ And this [is] what she is called: YHWH [is] Our Righteousness." **17** For thus said YHWH: "A man sitting on the throne of the house of Israel [is] never cut off from David, **18** And to the priests—the Levites, ‖ A man is not cut off from before My face, ‖ Causing a burnt-offering to ascend, ‖ And perfuming a present, and making sacrifice—all the days." **19** And there is a word of YHWH to Jeremiah, saying, **20** "Thus said YHWH: If you can break My covenant with the day, ‖ And My covenant with the night, ‖ So that they are not daily and nightly in their season, **21** My covenant is also broken with My servant David, ‖ So that he does not have a son reigning on his throne, ‖ And with the Levites the priests, My ministers. **22** As the host of the heavens is not numbered, ‖ Nor the sand of the sea measured, ‖ So I multiply the seed of My servant David, ‖ And My ministers the Levites." **23** And there is a word of YHWH to Jeremiah, saying, **24** "Have you not considered what this people have spoken, saying, ‖ The two families on which YHWH fixed, ‖ He rejects them? And they despise My people, so that they are no longer a people before them!" **25** Thus said YHWH: "If My covenant [is] not with day and night, ‖ [And if] I have not appointed the statutes of the heavens and earth— **26** I also reject the seed of Jacob, and My servant David, ‖ From taking rulers from his seed ‖ For the seed of Abraham, Isaac, and Jacob, ‖ For I return their captivity, and have pitied them."

34 The word that has been to Jeremiah from YHWH—and Nebuchadnezzar king of Babylon, and all his force, and all kingdoms of the land of the dominion of his hand, and all the peoples are fighting against Jerusalem, and against all its cities—saying: **2** "Thus said YHWH, God of Israel: Go, and you have spoken to Zedekiah king of Judah, and have said to him, Thus said YHWH: Behold, I am giving this city into the hand of the king of Babylon, and he has burned it with fire, **3** and you do not escape out of his hand, for you are certainly caught, and you are given into his hand, and your eyes see the eyes of the king of Babylon, and his mouth speaks with your mouth, and you enter Babylon. **4** Only, hear a word of YHWH, O Zedekiah king of Judah—thus said YHWH to you: You do not die by sword, **5** you die in peace, and with the burnings of your fathers, the former kings who have been before you, so they make a burning for you; and, Oh, lord, they lament for you, for the word I have spoken—a declaration of YHWH." **6** And Jeremiah the prophet speaks all these words to Zedekiah king of Judah in Jerusalem, **7** and the forces of the king of Babylon are fighting against Jerusalem, and against all the cities of Judah that are left—against Lachish, and against Azekah, for these have been left among the cities of Judah, cities of fortresses. **8** The word that has been to Jeremiah from YHWH, after the making of a covenant by King Zedekiah with all the people who [are] in Jerusalem, to proclaim liberty to them, **9** to each send out his manservant, and each his maidservant—the Hebrew and the Hebrewess—free, so as not to lay service on them—on any Jew, a brother, a man; **10** and all the heads listen, and all the people who have come into the covenant to each send forth his manservant and each his maidservant free, so as not to lay service on them anymore, indeed, they listen, and send them away; **11** and they turn afterward, and cause the menservants and the maidservants to return, whom they had sent forth free, and they subdue them for menservants and for maidservants. **12** And there is a word of YHWH to Jeremiah from YHWH, saying, **13** "Thus said YHWH, God of Israel: I made a covenant with your fathers in the day of My bringing them forth from the land of Egypt, from a house of servants, saying, **14** At the end of seven years you each send forth his brother, the Hebrew, who is sold to you, and has served you six years, indeed, you have sent him forth from you free: and your fathers did not listen to Me, nor inclined their ear. **15** And today you turn back and you do that which is right in My eyes, to each proclaim liberty to his neighbor, and you make a covenant before Me in the house over which My Name is called. **16** And you turn back, and defile My Name, and you each cause his manservant and each his maidservant, whom he had sent forth free (at their pleasure), to return, and you subdue them to be for menservants and for maidservants to you." **17** Therefore, thus said YHWH: "You have not listened to Me to proclaim freedom, each to his brother, and each to his neighbor; behold, I am proclaiming to you liberty," a declaration of YHWH, "to the sword, to the pestilence, and to the famine, and I have given you for a trembling to all kingdoms of the earth. **18** And I have given the men who are transgressing My covenant, who have not established the words of the covenant that they have made before Me, by the calf, that they have cut in two, and pass through between its pieces— **19** heads of Judah, and heads of Jerusalem, the officers, and the priests, and all the people of the land who had passed through between the pieces of the calf— **20** indeed, I have given them into the hand of their enemies, and into the hand of those seeking their soul, and their carcass has been for food to the bird of the heavens, and to the beast of the earth. **21** And I give Zedekiah king of Judah and his heads into the hand of their enemies, and into the hand of those seeking their soul, and into the hand of the forces of the king of Babylon that are going up from off you. **22** Behold, I am commanding," a declaration of YHWH, "and have brought them back to this city, and they have fought against it, and captured it, and burned it with fire, and I make the cities of Judah a desolation—without inhabitant."

35 The word that has been to Jeremiah from YHWH, in the days of Jehoiakim son of Josiah king of Judah, saying, **2** "Go to the house of the Rechabites, and you have spoken with them, and brought them into the house of YHWH, to one of the chambers, and caused them to drink wine." **3** And I take Jaazaniah son of Jeremiah, son of Habazziniah, and his brothers, and all his sons, and all the house of the Rechabites, **4** and bring them into the house of YHWH, to the chamber of the sons of Hanan son of Igdaliah, a man of God, that [is] near to the chamber of the princes, that [is] above the chamber of Maaseiah son of Shallum, keeper of the threshold; **5** and I put before the sons of the house of the Rechabites goblets full of wine, and cups, and I say to them, "Drink wine." **6** And they say, "We do not drink wine: for Jonadab son of Rechab, our father, charged us, saying, You do not drink wine, you and your sons—for all time; **7** and you do not build a house, and you do not sow seed, and you do not plant a vineyard, nor have of [these]; for you dwell in tents all your days, that you may live many days on the face of the ground to where you are sojourning. **8** And we listen to the voice of Jonadab son of Rechab, our father, to all that he commanded us, not to drink wine all our days, we, our wives, our sons, and our daughters; **9** nor to build houses to dwell in; and we have no vineyard, and field, and seed; **10** and we dwell in tents, and we listen, and we do according to all that Jonadab our father commanded us; **11** and it comes to pass, in the coming up of Nebuchadnezzar king of Babylon to the land, that we say, Come, and we enter Jerusalem, because of the force of the Chaldeans, and because of the force of Aram—and we dwell in Jerusalem." **12** And there is a word of YHWH to Jeremiah, saying, "Thus said YHWH of Hosts, God of Israel: **13** Go, and you have said to the men of Judah and to the inhabitants of Jerusalem: Do you not receive instruction to listen to My words? A declaration of YHWH. **14** The words of Jonadab son of Rechab, when he commanded his sons not to drink wine, have stood, and they have not drunk to this day, for they have obeyed the command of their father; and I have spoken to you, rising early and speaking, and you have not listened to Me. **15** And I send all My servants the prophets to you, rising early and sending, saying, Please turn back, each from his evil way, and amend your doings, indeed, you do not walk after other gods, to serve them; and dwell on the ground that I have given to you and to your fathers; and you have not inclined your ear, nor listened to Me. **16** Because the sons of Jonadab son of Rechab have stood by the command of their father that he commanded them, and this people have not listened to Me, **17** therefore, thus said YHWH, God of Hosts, God of Israel: Behold, I am bringing to Judah, and to all inhabitants of Jerusalem, all the calamity that I have spoken against them, because I have spoken to them, and they have not listened, indeed, I call to them, and they have not answered." **18** And Jeremiah said to the house of the Rechabites: "Thus said YHWH of Hosts, God of Israel: Because that you have listened to the command of your father Jonadab, and you observe all his commands, and do according to all that he commanded you; **19** therefore, thus said YHWH of Hosts, God of Israel: A man of Jonadab son of Rechab is not cut off [from] standing before Me all the days."

36 And it comes to pass, in the fourth year of Jehoiakim son of Josiah king of Judah, this word has been to Jeremiah from YHWH, saying, **2** "Take a roll of a scroll to yourself, and you have written on it all the words that I have spoken to you concerning Israel, and concerning Judah, and concerning all the nations, from the day I spoke to you, from the days of Josiah, even to this day; **3** perhaps the house of Israel so hears all the evil that I am thinking of doing to them, so that they each turn back from his evil way, and I have been propitious to their iniquity, and to their sin." **4** And Jeremiah calls Baruch son of

Neriah, and Baruch writes from the mouth of Jeremiah all the words of YHWH, that He has spoken to him, on a roll of a scroll. **5** And Jeremiah commands Baruch, saying, "I am restrained, I am not able to enter the house of YHWH; **6** but you have entered—and you have read in the scroll that you have written from my mouth, the words of YHWH, in the ears of the people, in the house of YHWH, in the day of the fast, and you also read them in the ears of all Judah who are coming in from their cities; **7** perhaps their supplication so falls before YHWH, and they each turn back from his evil way, for the anger and the fury that YHWH has spoken concerning this people [is] great." **8** And Baruch son of Neriah does according to all that Jeremiah the prophet commanded him, to read in the scroll the words of YHWH in the house of YHWH. **9** And it comes to pass, in the fifth year of Jehoiakim son of Josiah king of Judah, in the ninth month, they proclaimed a fast before YHWH to all the people in Jerusalem, and to all the people who are coming in from cities of Judah to Jerusalem; **10** and Baruch reads in the scroll the words of Jeremiah in the house of YHWH, in the chamber of Gemariah son of Shaphan the scribe, in the higher court, at the opening of the New Gate of the house of YHWH, in the ears of all the people. **11** And Michaiah son of Gemariah, son of Shaphan, hears all the words of YHWH from off the scroll, **12** and he goes down [to] the house of the king, to the chamber of the scribe, and behold, there all the heads are sitting: Elishama the scribe, and Delaiah son of Shemaiah, and Elnathan son of Acbor, and Gemariah son of Shaphan, and Zedekiah son of Hananiah, and all the heads. **13** And Micaiah declares to them all the words that he has heard when Baruch reads in the scroll in the ears of the people; **14** and all the heads send to Baruch, Jehudi son of Nethaniah, son of Shelemiah, son of Cushi, saying, "Take in your hand the scroll, which you have read in the ears of the people, and come." And Baruch son of Neriah takes the scroll in his hand and comes to them, **15** and they say to him, "Please sit down and read it in our ears," and Baruch reads [it] in their ears, **16** and it comes to pass, when they hear all the words, they have been afraid—one to another—and say to Baruch, "We surely declare all these words to the king." **17** And they asked Baruch, saying, "Please declare to us, how did you write all these words from his mouth?" **18** And Baruch says to them, "He pronounces from his mouth all these words to me, and I am writing on the scroll with ink." **19** And the heads say to Baruch, "Go, be hidden, you and Jeremiah, and let no one know where you [are]." **20** And they go to the king, to the court, and they have laid up the scroll in the chamber of Elishama the scribe, and they declare all the words in the ears of the king. **21** And the king sends Jehudi to take the scroll, and he takes it out of the chamber of Elishama the scribe, and Jehudi reads it in the ears of the king, and in the ears of all the heads who are standing by the king; **22** and the king is sitting in the winter-house, in the ninth month, and the stove is burning before him, **23** and it comes to pass, when Jehudi reads three or four leaves, he cuts it out with the scribe's knife, and has cast [it] into the fire that [is] on the stove, until the consumption of all the scroll by the fire that [is] on the stove. **24** And the king and all his servants who are hearing all these words have not been afraid, nor torn their garments. **25** And also Elnathan, and Delaiah, and Gemariah have interceded with the king not to burn the scroll, and he has not listened to them. **26** And the king commands Jerahmeel son of Hammelek, and Seraiah son of Azriel, and Shelemiah son of Abdeel, to take Baruch the scribe and Jeremiah the prophet, and YHWH hides them. **27** And there is a word of YHWH to Jeremiah—after the king's burning the scroll, even the words that Baruch has written from the mouth of Jeremiah—saying: **28** "Turn, take another scroll to yourself, and write on it all the former words that were on the first scroll that Jehoiakim king of Judah burned, **29** and say to Jehoiakim king of Judah, Thus said YHWH: You have burned this scroll, saying, Why have you written on it, saying, The king of Babylon surely comes in, and has destroyed this land, and caused man and beast to cease from it? **30** Therefore, thus said YHWH concerning Jehoiakim king of Judah: He has none sitting on the throne of David, and his carcass is cast out to heat by day, and to cold by night; **31** and I have charged on him, and on his seed, and on his servants, their iniquity; and I have brought in on them, and on the inhabitants of Jerusalem, and to the men of Judah, all the evil that I have spoken to them, and they did not listen." **32** And Jeremiah has taken another scroll, and gives it to Baruch son of Neriah the scribe, and he writes on it from the mouth of Jeremiah all the words of the scroll that Jehoiakim king of Judah has burned in the fire; and again there were added to them many words like these.

37 And King Zedekiah son of Josiah reigns instead of Coniah son of Jehoiakim whom Nebuchadnezzar king of Babylon had caused to reign in the land of Judah, **2** and he has not listened—he, and his servants, and the people of the land—to the words of YHWH that He spoke by the hand of Jeremiah the prophet. **3** And Zedekiah the king sends Jehucal son of Shelemiah, and Zephaniah son of Maaseiah the priest, to Jeremiah the prophet, saying, "Pray, we implore you, for us to our God YHWH." **4** And Jeremiah is coming in and going out in the midst of the people (and they have not put him in the prison-house), **5** and the force of Pharaoh has come out of Egypt, and the Chaldeans who are laying siege against Jerusalem hear their report, and go up from off Jerusalem. **6** And there is a word of YHWH to Jeremiah the prophet, saying, **7** "Thus said YHWH, God of Israel: Thus you say to the king of Judah who is sending you to Me, to seek Me: Behold, the force of Pharaoh that is coming out to you for help has turned back to its land, to Egypt, **8** and the Chaldeans have turned back and fought against this city, and captured it, and burned it with fire. **9** Thus said YHWH: Do not lift up your souls, saying, The Chaldeans surely go from off us, for they do not go; **10** for though you had struck all the force of the Chaldeans who are fighting with you, and there were left of them wounded men—they rise, each in his tent, and have burned this city with fire." **11** And it has come to pass, in the going up of the force of the Chaldeans from off Jerusalem, because of the force of Pharaoh, **12** that Jeremiah goes out from Jerusalem to go [to] the land of Benjamin, to receive a portion there in the midst of the people. **13** And it comes to pass, he is at the Gate of Benjamin, and there [is] a master of the ward, and his name is Irijah son of Shelemiah, son of Hananiah; and he catches Jeremiah the prophet, saying, "You are defecting to the Chaldeans!" **14** And Jeremiah says, "Falsehood! I am not defecting to the Chaldeans"; and he has not listened to him, and Irijah lays hold on Jeremiah, and brings him to the heads, **15** and the heads are angry against Jeremiah, and have struck him, and put him in the prison-house—the house of Jonathan the scribe, for they had made it for a prison-house. **16** When Jeremiah has entered into the house of the dungeon, and to the cells, then Jeremiah dwells there many days, **17** and King Zedekiah sends, and takes him, and the king asks him in his house in secret, and says, "Is there a word from YHWH?" And Jeremiah says, "There is," and he says, "You are given into the hand of the king of Babylon." **18** And Jeremiah says to King Zedekiah, "What have I sinned against you, and against your servants, and against this people, that you have put me into a prison-house? **19** And where [are] your prophets who prophesied to you, saying, The king of Babylon does not come in against you, and against this land? **20** And now, please listen, O my lord the king; please let my supplication fall before you, and do not cause me to return [to] the house of Jonathan the scribe, that I do not die there." **21** And King Zedekiah commands, and they commit Jeremiah into the court of the prison, also to give a cake of bread to him daily from the bakers' street, until the consumption of all the bread of the city, and Jeremiah dwells in the court of the prison.

38 And Shephatiah son of Mattan, and Gedaliah son of Pashhur, and Jucal son of Shelemiah, and Pashhur son of Malchiah, hear the words that Jeremiah is speaking to all the people, saying, **2** "Thus said YHWH: He who is remaining in this city dies, by sword, by famine, and by pestilence, and he who is going forth to the Chaldeans lives, and his soul has been to him for a prey, and he lives. **3** Thus said YHWH: This city is certainly given into the hand of the force of the king of Babylon, and he has captured it." **4** And the heads say to the king, "Now let this man be put to death, because that he is making feeble the hands of the men of war who are left in this city, and the hands of all the people, by speaking to them according to these words, for this man is not seeking for the peace of this people, but for its calamity." **5** And King Zedekiah says, "Behold, he [is] in

JEREMIAH

your hand: for the king is not able [to do] anything against you." **6** And they take Jeremiah, and cast him into the pit of Malchiah son of the king, that [is] in the court of the prison, and they send Jeremiah down with cords; and there is no water in the pit, but mire, and Jeremiah sinks in the mire. **7** And Ebed-Melech the Cushite, a eunuch who [is] in the king's house, hears that they have put Jeremiah into the pit; and the king is sitting at the Gate of Benjamin, **8** and Ebed-Melech goes forth from the king's house, and speaks to the king, saying, **9** "My lord, O king, these men have done evil [in] all that they have done to Jeremiah the prophet, whom they have cast into the pit, and he dies in his place because of the famine, for there is no more bread in the city." **10** And the king commands Ebed-Melech the Cushite, saying, "Take with you thirty men from here, and you have brought up Jeremiah the prophet from the pit, before he dies." **11** And Ebed-Melech takes the men with him, and enters the house of the king, to the place of the treasury, and takes there worn-out shreds of cloth, and worn-out rags, and sends them by cords into the pit to Jeremiah. **12** And Ebed-Melech the Cushite says to Jeremiah, "Now put the worn-out pieces of cloth and rags under your arms, at the place of the cords," and Jeremiah does so, **13** and they draw Jeremiah out with cords, and bring him up out of the pit, and Jeremiah dwells in the court of the prison. **14** And King Zedekiah sends, and takes Jeremiah the prophet to him, to the third entrance that [is] in the house of YHWH, and the king says to Jeremiah, "I am asking you something, do not hide anything from me." **15** And Jeremiah says to Zedekiah, "When I declare [it] to you, do you not surely put me to death? And when I counsel you, you do not listen to me." **16** And King Zedekiah swears to Jeremiah in secret, saying, "YHWH lives, He who made this soul for us, I do not put you to death, nor give you into the hand of these men who are seeking your soul." **17** And Jeremiah says to Zedekiah, "Thus said YHWH, God of Hosts, God of Israel: If you certainly go forth to the heads of the king of Babylon, then your soul has lived, and this city is not burned with fire, indeed, you have lived, you and your house. **18** And if you do not go forth to the heads of the king of Babylon, then this city has been given into the hand of the Chaldeans, and they have burned it with fire, and you do not escape from their hand." **19** And King Zedekiah says to Jeremiah, "I am fearing the Jews who have fallen to the Chaldeans, lest they give me into their hand, and they have insulted me." **20** And Jeremiah says, "They do not give you up; please listen to the voice of YHWH, to that which I am speaking to you, and it is well for you, and your soul lives. **21** And if you are refusing to go forth, this [is] the thing that YHWH has shown me: **22** That, behold, all the women who have been left in the house of the king of Judah are brought forth to the heads of the king of Babylon, and behold, they are saying: Persuaded you, and prevailed against you, ‖ Have your allies, ‖ Your feet have sunk into mire, ‖ They have been turned backward. **23** And all your wives and your sons are brought forth to the Chaldeans, and you do not escape from their hand, for you are caught by the hand of the king of Babylon, and this city is burned with fire." **24** And Zedekiah says to Jeremiah, "Let no man know of these words, and you do not die; **25** and when the heads hear that I have spoken with you, and they have come to you, and have said to you, Now declare to us what you spoke to the king, do not hide [it] from us, and we do not put you to death, and what the king spoke to you, **26** then you have said to them, I am causing my supplication to fall before the king, not to cause me to return to the house of Jonathan, to die there." **27** And all the heads come to Jeremiah, and ask him, and he declares to them according to all these words that the king commanded, and they keep silent from him, for the matter was not heard; **28** and Jeremiah dwells in the court of the prison until the day that Jerusalem has been captured, and he was [there] when Jerusalem was captured.

39 In the ninth year of Zedekiah king of Judah, in the tenth month, Nebuchadnezzar king of Babylon and all his force have come to Jerusalem, and they lay siege against it; **2** in the eleventh year of Zedekiah, in the fourth month, on the ninth of the month, the city has been broken up; **3** and all the heads of the king of Babylon come in, and they sit at the middle gate, Nergal-Sharezer, Samgar-

Nebo, Sarsechim, Rab-Saris, Nergal-Sharezer, chief magus, and all the rest of the heads of the king of Babylon. **4** And it comes to pass, when Zedekiah king of Judah and all the men of war have seen them, that they flee and go forth by night from the city, the way of the king's garden, through the gate between the two walls, and he goes forth the way of the plain. **5** And the forces of the Chaldeans pursue after them, and overtake Zedekiah in the plains of Jericho, and they take him, and bring him up to Nebuchadnezzar king of Babylon, to Riblah, in the land of Hamath, and he speaks with him—judgments. **6** And the king of Babylon slaughters the sons of Zedekiah, in Riblah, before his eyes, indeed, the king of Babylon has slaughtered all the nobles of Judah. **7** And he has blinded the eyes of Zedekiah, and he binds him with bronze chains to bring him to Babylon. **8** And the house of the king, and the house of the people, the Chaldeans have burned with fire, and they have broken down the walls of Jerusalem. **9** And the remnant of the people who are left in the city, and those defecting who have defected to him, and the remnant of the people who are left, Nebuzar-Adan, chief of the executioners, has removed [to] Babylon. **10** And Nebuzar-Adan, chief of the executioners, has left in the land of Judah the poor people who have nothing, and he gives vineyards and fields to them in that day. **11** And Nebuchadnezzar king of Babylon gives a charge concerning Jeremiah, by the hand of Nebuzar-Adan, chief of the executioners, saying, **12** "Take him, and place your eyes on him, and do no evil thing to him, but as he speaks to you, so do with him." **13** And Nebuzar-Adan, chief of the executioners, sends, and Nebushazban, chief of the eunuchs, and Nergal-Sharezer, chief magus, and all the chiefs of the king of Babylon, **14** indeed, they send and take Jeremiah out of the court of the prison, and give him to Gedaliah son of Ahikam, son of Shaphan, to carry him home, and he dwells in the midst of the people. **15** And a word of YHWH has been to Jeremiah—in his being detained in the court of the prison—saying: **16** "Go, and you have spoken to Ebed-Melech the Cushite, saying, Thus said YHWH of Hosts, God of Israel: Behold, I am bringing in My words to this city for calamity, and not for good, and they have been before you in that day. **17** And I have delivered you in that day—a declaration of YHWH—and you are not given into the hand of the men of whose face you are afraid, **18** for I certainly deliver you, and you do not fall by sword, and your life has been to you for a spoil, for you have trusted in Me—a declaration of YHWH."

40 The word that has been to Jeremiah from YHWH, after Nebuzar-Adan, chief of the executioners, has sent him from Ramah, in his taking him—and he a prisoner in chains—in the midst of all the expulsion of Jerusalem and of Judah, who are removed to Babylon. **2** And the chief of the executioners takes Jeremiah and says to him, "Your God YHWH has spoken this calamity concerning this place, **3** and YHWH brings [it] in, and does as He spoke, because you have sinned against YHWH, and have not listened to His voice, even this thing has been to you. **4** And now, behold, I have loosed you today from the chains that [are] on your hand; if [it is] good in your eyes to come with me [to] Babylon, come, and I keep my eye on you: and if [it is] evil in your eyes to come with me to Babylon, refrain; see, all the land [is] before you, to where [it is] good, and to where [it is] right in your eyes to go—go." **5** And while he does not reply—"Or turn back to Gedaliah son of Ahikam, son of Shaphan, whom the king of Babylon has appointed over the cities of Judah, and dwell with him in the midst of the people, or wherever it is right in your eyes to go—go." And the chief of the executioners gives a ration and gift to him, and sends him away, **6** and Jeremiah comes to Gedaliah son of Ahikam, to Mizpah, and dwells with him in the midst of the people who are left in the land. **7** And all the heads of the forces that [are] in the field hear, they and their men, that the king of Babylon has appointed Gedaliah son of Ahikam over the land, and that he has charged him [with] men, and women, and infants, and of the poor of the land, of those who have not been removed to Babylon; **8** and they come to Gedaliah at Mizpah, even Ishmael son of Nethaniah, and Johanan and Jonathan [the] sons of Kareah, and Seraiah son of Tanhumeth, and the sons of Ephai the Netophathite, and Jezaniah son of the Maachathite, they and their men. **9** And

Gedaliah son of Ahikam, son of Shaphan, swears to them and to their men, saying, "Do not be afraid of serving the Chaldeans, abide in the land, and serve the king of Babylon, and it is well for you; **10** and I, behold, I am dwelling in Mizpah to stand before the Chaldeans who have come to us, and you, gather wine, and summer fruit, and oil, and put [them] in your vessels, and dwell in your cities that you have taken." **11** And also all the Jews who [are] in Moab, and among the sons of Ammon, and in Edom, and who [are] in all the lands, have heard that the king of Babylon has given a remnant to Judah, and that he has appointed over them Gedaliah son of Ahikam, son of Shaphan, **12** and all the Jews from all the places to where they have been driven, return and enter the land of Judah, to Gedaliah, to Mizpah, and they gather wine and summer fruit—to multiply abundantly. **13** And Johanan son of Kareah, and all the heads of the forces that [are] in the field, have come to Gedaliah at Mizpah, **14** and they say to him, "Do you really know that Ba'alis king of the sons of Ammon has sent Ishmael son of Nethaniah to strike your soul?" And Gedaliah son of Ahikam has not given credence to them. **15** And Johanan son of Kareah has spoken to Gedaliah in secret, in Mizpah, saying, "Please let me go, and I strike Ishmael son of Nethaniah, and no one knows; why does he strike your soul? And all Judah who are gathered to you have been scattered, and the remnant of Judah has perished." **16** And Gedaliah son of Ahikam says to Johanan son of Kareah, "You do not do this thing, for you are speaking falsehood concerning Ishmael."

41 And it comes to pass, in the seventh month, Ishmael son of Nethaniah, son of Elishama, of the royal seed, and of the chiefs of the king, and ten men with him, have come to Gedaliah son of Ahikam, to Mizpah, and there they eat bread together in Mizpah. **2** And Ishmael son of Nethaniah rises, and the ten men who have been with him, and they strike Gedaliah son of Ahikam, son of Shaphan, with the sword, and he puts him to death whom the king of Babylon has appointed over the land. **3** And all the Jews who have been with him, with Gedaliah, in Mizpah, and the Chaldeans who have been found there—the men of war—Ishmael has struck. **4** And it comes to pass, on the second day of the putting of Gedaliah to death (and no one has known), **5** that men come in from Shechem, from Shiloh, and from Samaria—eighty men—with shaven beards, and torn garments, and cutting themselves, and [with] an offering and frankincense in their hand, to bring [them] to the house of YHWH. **6** And Ishmael son of Nethaniah goes forth to meet them, from Mizpah, going on and weeping, and it comes to pass, at meeting them, that he says to them, "Come to Gedaliah son of Ahikam." **7** And it comes to pass, at their coming into the midst of the city, that Ishmael son of Nethaniah slaughters them, at the midst of the pit, he and the men who [are] with him. **8** And ten men have been found among them, and they say to Ishmael, "Do not put us to death, for we have things hidden in the field—wheat, and barley, and oil, and honey." And he refrains, and has not put them to death in the midst of their brothers. **9** And the pit to where Ishmael has cast all the carcasses of the men whom he has struck along with Gedaliah, is that which King Asa made because of Baasha king of Israel—Ishmael son of Nethaniah has filled it with the pierced. **10** And Ishmael takes captive all the remnant of the people who [are] in Mizpah, the daughters of the king, and all the people who are left in Mizpah, whom Nebuzar-Adan, chief of the executioners, has committed [to] Gedaliah son of Ahikam, and Ishmael son of Nethaniah takes them captive, and goes to pass over to the sons of Ammon. **11** And Johanan son of Kareah, and all the heads of the forces that [are] with him, hear of all the evil that Ishmael son of Nethaniah has done, **12** and they take all the men, and go to fight with Ishmael son of Nethaniah, and they find him at the great waters that [are] in Gibeon. **13** And it comes to pass, when all the people who [are] with Ishmael see Johanan son of Kareah, and all the heads of the forces who [are] with him, that they rejoice. **14** And all the people whom Ishmael has taken captive from Mizpah turn around, indeed, they turn back, and go to Johanan son of Kareah. **15** And Ishmael son of Nethaniah has escaped, with eight men, from the presence of Johanan, and he goes to the sons of Ammon. **16** And Johanan son of Kareah, and all the heads of the forces who [are] with him, take all the remnant of the people whom he has brought back from Ishmael son of Nethaniah, from Mizpah—after he had struck Gedaliah son of Ahikam—mighty ones, men of war, and women, and infants, and eunuchs, whom he had brought back from Gibeon, **17** and they go and abide in the habitations of Chimham, that [are] near Beth-Lehem, to go to enter Egypt, **18** from the presence of the Chaldeans, for they have been afraid of them, for Ishmael son of Nethaniah had struck Gedaliah son of Ahikam, whom the king of Babylon had appointed over the land.

42 And they come near—all the heads of the forces, and Johanan son of Kareah, and Jezaniah son of Hoshaiah, and all the people from the least even to the greatest— **2** and they say to Jeremiah the prophet, "Please let our supplication fall before you, and pray for us to your God YHWH for all this remnant; for we have been left a few out of many, as your eyes see us; **3** and your God YHWH declares to us the way in which we walk, and the thing that we do." **4** And Jeremiah the prophet says to them, "I have heard: behold, I am praying to your God YHWH according to your words, and it has come to pass, the whole word that YHWH answers you, I declare to you—I do not withhold a word from you." **5** And they have said to Jeremiah, "YHWH is against us for a true and faithful witness, if—according to all the word with which your God YHWH sends you to us—we do not do so. **6** Whether [it is] good or evil, to the voice of our God YHWH, to whom we are sending you, we listen; because it is good for us when we listen to the voice of our God YHWH." **7** And it comes to pass, at the end of ten days, that there is a word of YHWH to Jeremiah, **8** and he calls to Johanan son of Kareah, and to all the heads of the forces that [are] with him, and to all the people, from the least even to the greatest, **9** and he says to them, "Thus said YHWH, God of Israel, to whom you sent me, to cause your supplication to fall before Him: **10** If you certainly dwell in this land, then I have built you up, and I do not throw down; and I have planted you, and I do not pluck up; for I have relented concerning the calamity that I have done to you. **11** Do not be afraid of the king of Babylon, whom you are afraid of; do not be afraid of him—a declaration of YHWH—for I [am] with you, to save you, and to deliver you from his hand. **12** And I give mercies to you, and he has pitied you, and caused you to return to your own ground. **13** And if you are saying, We do not dwell in this land—not to listen to the voice of your God YHWH, **14** saying, No; but we enter the land of Egypt, that we see no war, and do not hear the sound of a horn, and are not hungry for bread; and we dwell there— **15** And now, therefore, hear a word of YHWH, O remnant of Judah! Thus said YHWH of Hosts, God of Israel: If you really set your faces to enter Egypt, and have gone to sojourn there, **16** then it has come to pass, the sword that you are afraid of, overtakes you there, in the land of Egypt; and the hunger, because of which you are sorrowful, cleaves after you there in Egypt, and there you die. **17** Thus are all the men who have set their faces to enter Egypt to sojourn there; they die—by sword, by hunger, and by pestilence, and there is not a remnant and an escaped one to them, because of the calamity that I am bringing in on them; **18** for thus said YHWH of Hosts, God of Israel: As My anger and My fury have been poured out on the inhabitants of Jerusalem, so My fury is poured out on you in your entering Egypt, and you have been for an execration, and for an astonishment, and for a reviling, and for a reproach, and you do not see this place anymore. **19** YHWH has spoken against you, O remnant of Judah, do not enter Egypt: certainly know that I have testified against you today; **20** for you have showed yourselves perverse in your souls, for you sent me to your God YHWH, saying, Pray for us to our God YHWH, and according to all that our God YHWH says, so declare to us, and we have done [it]; **21** and I declare to you today, and you have not listened to the voice of your God YHWH, and to anything with which He has sent me to you. **22** And now, certainly know that by sword, by famine, and by pestilence you die, in the place that you have desired to go to sojourn there."

43 And it comes to pass, when Jeremiah finishes speaking to all the people all the words of their God YHWH, with which their God YHWH has sent him to them—all these words— **2** that Azariah son of Hoshaiah, and Johanan son of Kareah, and all the proud men, speak to Jeremiah, saying, "You are speaking falsehood; our God YHWH has not sent you to say, Do not enter Egypt to sojourn there; **3** for Baruch son of Neriah is moving you against us, in order to give us up into the hand of the Chaldeans, to put us to death, and to remove us to Babylon." **4** And Johanan son of Kareah, and all the heads of the forces, and all the people, have not listened to the voice of YHWH, to dwell in the land of Judah; **5** and Johanan son of Kareah, and all the heads of the forces, take all the remnant of Judah who have turned from all the nations to where they were driven to sojourn in the land of Judah, **6** the men, and the women, and the infant, and the daughters of the king, and every person that Nebuzar-Adan, chief of the executioners, had left with Gedaliah son of Ahikam, son of Shaphan, and Jeremiah the prophet, and Baruch son of Neriah, **7** and they enter the land of Egypt, for they have not listened to the voice of YHWH, and they come as far as Tahpanhes. **8** And there is a word of YHWH to Jeremiah in Tahpanhes, saying, **9** "Take great stones in your hand, and you have hidden them in the clay in the brick-kiln, that [is] at the opening of the house of Pharaoh in Tahpanhes, before the eyes of the men of Judah, **10** and you have said to them, Thus said YHWH of Hosts, God of Israel: Behold, I am sending, and I have taken Nebuchadnezzar king of Babylon, My servant, and I have set his throne above these stones that I have hid, and he has stretched out his pavilion over them, **11** and he has come, and struck the land of Egypt—those who [are] for death to death, and those who [are] for captivity to captivity, and those who [are] for the sword to the sword. **12** And I have kindled a fire in the houses of the gods of Egypt, and it has burned them, and he has taken them captive, and covered himself with the land of Egypt, as the shepherd covers himself with his garment, and he has gone forth there in peace; **13** and he has broken the standing pillars of the house of the sun, that [is] in the land of Egypt, and he burns the houses of the gods of Egypt with fire."

44 The word that has been to Jeremiah concerning all the Jews who are dwelling in the land of Egypt—who are dwelling in Migdol, and in Tahpanhes, and in Noph, and in the land of Pathros— saying, **2** "Thus said YHWH of Hosts, God of Israel: You have seen all the calamity that I have brought in on Jerusalem, and on all the cities of Judah, and behold, they [are] a desolation to this day, and there is none dwelling in them, **3** because of their wickedness that they have done, by provoking Me to anger, by going to make incense, by serving other gods, that they did not know, they, you, and your fathers. **4** And I send to you all My servants the prophets, rising early and sending, saying, Please do not do this abomination that I have hated— **5** and they have not listened nor inclined their ear to turn back from their wickedness, not to make incense to other gods, **6** and My fury is poured out, and My anger, and it burns in cities of Judah, and in streets of Jerusalem, and they are for a ruin, for a desolation, as [at] this day. **7** And now, thus said YHWH of Hosts, God of Israel: Why are you doing great evil to your own souls, to cut off man and woman, infant and suckling, from you, from the midst of Judah, so as not to leave a remnant to you: **8** by provoking Me to anger by the works of your hands, by making incense to other gods in the land of Egypt, to where you are going to sojourn, so as to cut yourselves off, and so as to your being for a reviling and for a reproach among all nations of the earth? **9** Have you forgotten the wickedness of your fathers, and the wickedness of the kings of Judah, and the wickedness of their wives, and your own wickedness, and the wickedness of your wives, that they have done in the land of Judah, and in streets of Jerusalem? **10** They have not been humbled to this day, nor have they been afraid, nor have they walked in My law, and in My statutes, that I have set before you and before your fathers. **11** Therefore, thus said YHWH of Hosts, God of Israel: Behold, I am setting My face against you for calamity, even to cut off all Judah, **12** and I have taken the remnant of Judah, who have set their faces to enter the land of Egypt to sojourn there, and they have all been consumed in the land of Egypt; they fall by sword [and] are consumed by famine, from the least even to the greatest, they die by sword and by famine, and they have been for an execration, for an astonishment, and for a reviling, and for a reproach. **13** And I have seen after those dwelling in the land of Egypt, as I saw after Jerusalem, with sword, with famine, and with pestilence,

JEREMIAH

14 and there is not an escaped and remaining one of the remnant of Judah, who are entering into the land of Egypt to sojourn there, even to turn back to the land of Judah, to where they are lifting up their soul to return to dwell, for they do not turn back, except those escaping." **15** And they answer Jeremiah—all the men who are knowing that their wives are making incense to other gods, and all the women who are remaining, a great assembly, even all the people who are dwelling in the land of Egypt, in Pathros—saying: **16** "The word that you have spoken to us in the Name of YHWH—we are not listening to you; **17** for we certainly do everything that has gone out of our mouth, to make incense to the queen of the heavens, and to pour out drink-offerings to her, as we have done, we, and our fathers, our kings, and our heads, in cities of Judah, and in streets of Jerusalem, and—we are satisfied with bread, and we are well, and we have not seen calamity. **18** And from the time we have ceased to make incense to the queen of the heavens, and to pour out drink-offerings to her, we have lacked all, and we have been consumed by sword and by famine, **19** and when we are making incense to the queen of the heavens, and pouring out drink-offerings to her—have we made cakes for her to idolize her, and to pour out drink-offerings to her, without our husbands?" **20** And Jeremiah says to all the people, concerning the men and concerning the women, and concerning all the people who are answering him, saying, **21** "The incense that you made in the cities of Judah, and in the streets of Jerusalem, you, and your fathers, your kings, and your heads, and the people of the land, has YHWH not remembered it? Indeed, it comes up on His heart. **22** And YHWH is not able to accept [you] anymore, because of the evil of your doings, because of the abominations that you have done, and your land is for a ruin, and for an astonishment, and for a reviling, without inhabitant, as [at] this day. **23** Because that you have made incense, and because you have sinned against YHWH, and have not listened to the voice of YHWH, and have not walked in His law, and in His statutes, and in His testimonies, therefore this calamity has met you as [at] this day." **24** And Jeremiah says to all the people, and to all the women, "Hear a word of YHWH, all Judah who [are] in the land of Egypt: **25** Thus spoke YHWH of Hosts, God of Israel, saying, You and your wives both speak with your mouth, and with your hands have fulfilled, saying, We certainly execute our vows that we have vowed, to make incense to the queen of the heavens, and to pour out drink-offerings to her. You certainly establish your vows, and certainly execute your vows. **26** Therefore, hear a word of YHWH, all Judah who are dwelling in the land of Egypt: Behold, I have sworn by My great Name, said YHWH, My Name is no longer proclaimed by the mouth of any man of Judah, saying, Lord YHWH lives—in all the land of Egypt. **27** Behold, I am watching over them for calamity, and not for good, and all the men of Judah who [are] in the land of Egypt have been consumed by sword and by famine, until their consumption. **28** And the escaped of the sword turn back out of the land of Egypt to the land of Judah, few in number, and all the remnant of Judah, who are coming into the land of Egypt to sojourn there, have known whose word is established, Mine or theirs. **29** And this [is] the sign to you—a declaration of YHWH—that I am seeing after you in this place, so that you know that My words are certainly established against you for calamity— **30** thus said YHWH: Behold, I am giving Pharaoh-Hophra king of Egypt into the hand of his enemies, and into the hand of those seeking his life, as I have given Zedekiah king of Judah into the hand of Nebuchadnezzar king of Babylon, his enemy, and who is seeking his life."

45 The word that Jeremiah the prophet has spoken to Baruch son of Neriah, in his writing these words on a scroll from the mouth of Jeremiah, in the fourth year of Jehoiakim son of Josiah king of Judah, saying, **2** "Thus said YHWH, God of Israel, concerning you, O Baruch: **3** You have said, Woe to me, now, for YHWH has added sorrow to my pain, I have been wearied with my sighing, and I have not found rest. **4** Thus you say to him, Thus said YHWH: Behold, that which I have built I am throwing down, and that which I have planted I am plucking up, even the whole land itself. **5** And you seek for great things—do not seek, for behold, I am bringing calamity on all flesh—a declaration of YHWH—and I have given your life to you for a spoil, in all places to where you go."

46 That which has been the word of YHWH to Jeremiah the prophet concerning the nations, **2** for Egypt, concerning the force of Pharaoh-Necho king of Egypt, that has been by the Euphrates River, in Carchemish, that Nebuchadnezzar king of Babylon has struck, in the fourth year of Jehoiakim son of Josiah king of Judah: **3** "Set shield and buckler in array, ‖ And draw near to battle. **4** Gird the horses, and go up, you horsemen, ‖ And station yourselves with helmets, ‖ Polish the javelins, put on the coats of mail. **5** Why have I seen them dismayed [and] turned backward? And their mighty ones are beaten down, ‖ And they have fled [to] a refuge, ‖ And did not turn their face, ‖ Fear [is] all around—a declaration of YHWH. **6** The swift do not flee, nor do the mighty escape, ‖ Northward, by the side of the Euphrates River, ‖ They have stumbled and fallen. **7** Who is this? He comes up as a flood, ‖ His waters shake themselves as rivers! **8** Egypt comes up as a flood, ‖ And the waters shake themselves as rivers. And he says, I go up; I cover the land, I destroy the city and the inhabitants in it. **9** Go up, you horses; and boast yourselves, you chariots, ‖ And go forth, you mighty, ‖ Cush and Phut handling the shield, ‖ And Lud handling—treading the bow. **10** And that day [is] to Lord YHWH of Hosts ‖ A day of vengeance, ‖ To be avenged of His adversaries, ‖ And the sword has devoured, and been satisfied, ‖ And it has been watered from their blood, ‖ For a sacrifice [is] to Lord YHWH of Hosts, ‖ In the land of the north, by the Euphrates River. **11** Go up to Gilead, and take balm, ‖ O virgin daughter of Egypt, ‖ You have multiplied medicines in vain, ‖ There is no healing for you. **12** Nations have heard of your shame, ‖ And your cry has filled the land, ‖ For the mighty stumbled on the mighty, ‖ Together they have fallen—both of them!" **13** The word that YHWH has spoken to Jeremiah the prophet concerning the coming in of Nebuchadnezzar king of Babylon, to strike the land of Egypt: **14** "Declare in Egypt, and sound in Migdol, ‖ And sound in Noph, and in Tahpanhes, say, ‖ Stand firm and prepare yourself, ‖ For a sword has devoured around you, **15** Why has your bull been swept away? He has not stood, because YHWH thrust him away. **16** He has multiplied the stumbling, ‖ Indeed, one has fallen on his neighbor, ‖ And they say: Rise, and we return to our people, ‖ And to the land of our birth, ‖ Because of the oppressing sword. **17** They have cried there: Pharaoh king of Egypt [is] a desolation, ‖ The appointed time has passed by. **18** [As] I live—an affirmation of the King, ‖ YHWH of Hosts [is] His Name, ‖ Surely as Tabor [is] among mountains, ‖ And as Carmel by the sea—he comes in, **19** Make goods for yourself for removal, ‖ O inhabitant, daughter of Egypt, ‖ For Noph becomes a desolation, ‖ And has been burned up, without inhabitant. **20** Egypt [is] a very beautiful heifer, ‖ Destruction comes into her from the north. **21** Even her hired ones in her midst [are] as calves of the stall, ‖ For even they have turned, ‖ They have fled together, they have not stood, ‖ For the day of their calamity has come on them, ‖ The time of their inspection. **22** Its voice goes on as a serpent, ‖ For they go with a force, ‖ And they have come in to her with axes, ‖ As hewers of trees. **23** They have cut down her forest, ‖ A declaration of YHWH, ‖ For it is not searched, ‖ For they have been more than the grasshopper, ‖ And they have no numbering. **24** The daughter of Egypt has been ashamed, ‖ She has been given into the hand of the people of the north. **25** YHWH of Hosts, God of Israel, has said: Behold, I am seeing after Amon of No, ‖ And after Pharaoh, and after Egypt, ‖ And after her gods, and after her kings, ‖ And after Pharaoh, and after those trusting in him, **26** And I have given them into the hand of those seeking their life, ‖ And into the hand of Nebuchadnezzar king of Babylon, ‖ And into the hand of his servants, ‖ And afterward it is inhabited, ‖ As [in] days of old—a declaration of YHWH. **27** And you, you do not fear, My servant Jacob, ‖ Nor [are] you dismayed, O Israel, ‖ For behold, I am saving you from afar—And your seed from the land of their captivity, ‖ And Jacob has turned back, ‖ And has been at rest, and been at ease, ‖ And there is none disturbing. **28** You do not fear, My servant Jacob, ‖ A declaration of YHWH, ‖ For I [am] with you, ‖ For I make an end of all the nations ‖ To where I have driven you, ‖ And I do not make an end of you, ‖ And I have reproved you in judgment, ‖ And do not entirely acquit you!"

JEREMIAH

47 That which has been the word of YHWH to Jeremiah concerning the Philistines, before Pharaoh strikes Gaza: **2** "Thus said YHWH: Behold, waters are going up from the north, ‖ And have been for an overflowing stream, ‖ And they overflow the land and its fullness, ‖ The city, and those dwelling in it, ‖ And men have cried out, ‖ And every inhabitant of the land has howled. **3** From the sound of the stamping of the hooves of his mighty ones, ‖ From the rushing of his chariot, ‖ The noise of his wheels, ‖ Fathers have not turned to sons, ‖ From feebleness of hands, **4** Because of the day that has come to spoil all the Philistines, ‖ To cut off every helping remnant from Tyre and from Sidon. For YHWH is spoiling the Philistines, ‖ The remnant of the island of Caphtor. **5** Baldness has come to Gaza, ‖ Ashkelon has been cut off, ‖ O remnant of their valley, ‖ Until when do you cut yourself? **6** Behold, sword of YHWH, until when are you not quiet? Be removed to your sheath, rest and cease. **7** How will it be quiet, ‖ And YHWH has given a charge to it, ‖ Against Ashkelon and against the seashore? He has appointed it there!"

48 Concerning Moab: "Thus said YHWH of Hosts, God of Israel: Woe to Nebo, for it is spoiled, ‖ Kiriathaim has been captured [and] put to shame, ‖ The high tower has been put to shame, ‖ Indeed, it has been broken down. **2** There is no longer praise of Moab, ‖ In Heshbon they devised evil against her: Come, and we cut it off from [being] a nation, ‖ Also, O Madmen, you are cut off, ‖ A sword goes after you. **3** A voice of a cry [is] from Horonaim, ‖ Spoiling and great destruction. **4** Moab has been destroyed, ‖ Her little ones have caused a cry to be heard. **5** For the ascent of Luhith with weeping, ‖ Weeping goes up, ‖ For in the descent of Horonaim ‖ Adversaries have heard a cry of desolation. **6** Flee, deliver yourselves, ‖ You are as a naked thing in a wilderness. **7** For because of your trusting in your works, ‖ And in your treasures, even you are captured, ‖ And Chemosh has gone out in a removal, ‖ His priests and his heads together. **8** And a spoiler comes to every city, ‖ And no city escapes, ‖ And the valley has perished, ‖ And the plain has been destroyed, as YHWH said. **9** Give wings to Moab, that she may go forth and flee away, ‖ And her cities are for a desolation, ‖ Without an inhabitant in them. **10** Cursed [is] he who is doing the work of YHWH slothfully, ‖ And cursed [is] he ‖ Who is withholding his sword from blood. **11** Moab is secure from his youth, ‖ And he [is] at rest for his preserved things, ‖ And he has not been emptied out from vessel to vessel, ‖ And he has not gone into captivity, ‖ Therefore his taste has remained in him, ‖ And his fragrance has not been changed. **12** Therefore, behold, days are coming, ‖ A declaration of YHWH, ‖ And I have sent wanderers to him, ‖ And they have caused him to wander, ‖ And they empty out his vessels, ‖ And they dash his bottles in pieces. **13** And Moab has been ashamed because of Chemosh, ‖ As the house of Israel has been ashamed ‖ Because of Beth-El, their confidence. **14** How do you say, We [are] mighty, ‖ And men of strength for battle? **15** Moab is spoiled, and has gone up [from] her cities, ‖ And the choice of its young men ‖ Have gone down to slaughter, ‖ An affirmation of the King, ‖ YHWH of Hosts [is] His Name. **16** The destruction of Moab is near to come, ‖ And his calamity has hurried exceedingly. **17** Bemoan for him, all you around him, ‖ And all knowing his name, say, ‖ How it has been broken, the staff of strength, ‖ The rod of beauty! **18** Come down from glory, sit in thirst, ‖ O inhabitant, daughter of Dibon, ‖ For a spoiler of Moab has come up to you, ‖ He has destroyed your fortifications. **19** Stand on the way, and watch, O inhabitant of Aroer, ‖ Ask the fugitive and escaped, ‖ Say, What has happened? **20** Moab has been put to shame, ‖ For it has been broken down, ‖ Howl and cry, declare in Arnon, ‖ For Moab is spoiled, **21** And judgment has come to the land of the plain—to Holon, ‖ And to Jahazah, and on Mephaath, **22** And on Dibon, and on Nebo, ‖ And on Beth-Diblathaim, and on Kirathaim, **23** And on Beth-Gamul, and on Beth-Meon, **24** And on Kerioth, and on Bozrah, ‖ And on all cities of the land of Moab, ‖ The far off and the near. **25** The horn of Moab has been cut down, ‖ And his arm has been broken, ‖ A declaration of YHWH. **26** Declare him drunk, ‖ For he made himself great against YHWH ‖ And Moab has struck in his vomit, ‖ And he has been for a derision—even he. **27** And was Israel not the derision to you? Was he found among thieves? For since your words concerning him, ‖ You bemoan yourself. **28** Forsake cities, and dwell in a rock, ‖ You inhabitants of Moab, ‖ And be as a dove making a nest in the passages of a pit's mouth. **29** We have heard of the arrogance of Moab, ‖ Exceedingly proud! His haughtiness, and his arrogance, ‖ And his pride, and the height of his heart, **30** I have known, a declaration of YHWH, ‖ His wrath, and [it is] not right, ‖ His boastings—they have done nothing right. **31** Therefore I howl for Moab, even for Moab—all of it, ‖ I cry for men of Kir-Heres, it mourns, **32** With the weeping of Jazer, I weep for you, O vine of Sibmah, ‖ Your branches have passed over a sea, ‖ They have come to the Sea of Jazer, ‖ On your summer fruits, and on your harvest, ‖ A spoiler has fallen. **33** And joy and gladness have been removed from the fruitful field, ‖ Even from the land of Moab, ‖ And I have caused wine to cease from winepresses, ‖ Shouting does not proceed, ‖ The shouting [is] not shouting! **34** Because of the cry of Heshbon to Elealeh, ‖ They have given their voice to Jahaz, ‖ From Zoar to Horonaim, ‖ A heifer of the third [year], ‖ For even [the] waters of Nimrim become desolations. **35** And I have caused to cease in Moab, ‖ A declaration of YHWH, ‖ Him who is offering in a high place, ‖ And him who is making incense to his god. **36** Therefore My heart sounds as pipes for Moab, ‖ And My heart sounds as pipes for men of Kir-Heres, ‖ Therefore the abundance he made perished. **37** For every head [is] bald, and every beard diminished, ‖ On all hands—cuttings, and on the loins—sackcloth. **38** On all roofs of Moab, and in her broad-places, ‖ All of it—lamentation, ‖ For I have broken Moab as a vessel in which there is no pleasure," ‖ A declaration of YHWH. **39** "How it has been broken down! They have howled, ‖ How Moab has turned the neck ashamed! And Moab has been for a derision ‖ And for a terror to all around her." **40** For thus said YHWH: "Behold, he flees as an eagle, ‖ And has spread his wings to Moab. **41** The cities have been captured, ‖ And the strongholds are caught, ‖ And the heart of the mighty of Moab ‖ Has been in that day as the heart of a distressed woman. **42** And Moab has been destroyed from [being] a people, ‖ For he exerted himself against YHWH. **43** Fear, and a snare, and a trap, [are] for you, ‖ O inhabitant of Moab—a declaration of YHWH, **44** Whoever is fleeing because of the fear falls into the snare, ‖ And whoever is coming up from the snare is captured by the trap, ‖ For I bring to her—to Moab—The year of their inspection, ‖ A declaration of YHWH. **45** In the shadow of Heshbon fugitives have stood powerless, ‖ For fire has gone forth from Heshbon, ‖ And a flame from within Sihon, ‖ And it consumes the corner of Moab, ‖ And the crown of the sons of Shaon. **46** Woe to you, O Moab, ‖ The people of Chemosh have perished, ‖ For your sons were taken with the captives, ‖ And your daughters with the captivity. **47** And I have turned back [to] the captivity of Moab, ‖ In the latter end of the days," ‖ A declaration of YHWH! "Until now [is] the judgment of Moab."

49 Concerning the sons of Ammon: "Thus said YHWH: Has Israel no sons? Has he no heir? Why has Malcam possessed Gad, ‖ And his people have dwelt in its cities? **2** Therefore, behold, days are coming, ‖ A declaration of YHWH, ‖ And I have sounded a shout of battle in Rabbah of the sons of Ammon, ‖ And it has been for a heap—a desolation, ‖ And her daughters are burned with fire, ‖ And Israel has succeeded its heirs, said YHWH. **3** Howl, Heshbon, for Ai is spoiled, ‖ Cry, daughters of Rabbah, gird on sackcloth, ‖ Lament, and go to and fro by the hedges, ‖ For Malcam goes into captivity, ‖ His priests and his princes together. **4** Why do you boast yourself in valleys? Your valley is flowing, ‖ O backsliding daughter, ‖ Who is trusting in her treasures: Who comes to me? **5** Behold, I am bringing fear in on you, ‖ A declaration of Lord YHWH of Hosts, ‖ From all around you, ‖ And you have each been driven out before it, ‖ And there is no gatherer of the wandering. **6** And after this I return the captivity of the sons of Ammon, ‖ A declaration of YHWH." **7** Concerning Edom: "Thus said YHWH of Hosts: Is wisdom no longer in Teman? Has counsel perished from the intelligent? Has their wisdom vanished? **8** Flee, turn, go deep to dwell, you inhabitants of Dedan, ‖ For I brought the calamity of Esau on him, ‖ The time I inspected him. **9** If gatherers have come to you, ‖ They do not leave gleanings, ‖ If thieves in the night, ‖ They have destroyed their sufficiency! **10** For I have made Esau bare, ‖ I have uncovered his secret places, ‖ And he is not able to be hidden, ‖ Spoiled [is] his seed, and his brothers, ‖ And his neighbors, and he is not.

JEREMIAH

11 Leave your orphans—I keep alive, ‖ And your widows—trust on Me, **12** For thus said Yhwh: They whose judgment is not to drink of the cup, ‖ Do certainly drink, ‖ And you [are] he that is entirely acquitted! You are not acquitted, for you certainly drink. **13** For I have sworn by Myself, ‖ A declaration of Yhwh, ‖ That for a desolation, for a reproach, ‖ For a dry place, and for a reviling—is Bozrah, ‖ And all her cities are for continuous ruins. **14** I have heard a report from Yhwh, ‖ And an ambassador is sent among nations, ‖ Gather yourselves and come in against her, ‖ And rise for battle. **15** For behold, I have made you little among nations, ‖ Despised among men. **16** Your terribleness has lifted you up, ‖ The pride of your heart, ‖ O dweller in clefts of the rock, ‖ Holding the high place of the height, ‖ For you make your nest high as an eagle, ‖ From there I bring you down, ‖ A declaration of Yhwh. **17** And Edom has been for a desolation, ‖ Everyone passing by her is astonished, ‖ And hisses because of all her plagues. **18** As the overthrow of Sodom and Gomorrah, ‖ And its neighbors, said Yhwh, ‖ No one dwells there, ‖ Nor does a son of man sojourn in her. **19** Behold, he comes up as a lion, ‖ Because of the rising of the Jordan, ‖ To the enduring habitation, ‖ But I cause to rest, ‖ I cause him to run from off her, ‖ And who is chosen? I lay a charge concerning her, ‖ For who is like Me? And who convenes Me? And who [is] this shepherd who stands before Me? **20** Therefore, hear the counsel of Yhwh, ‖ That He has counseled concerning Edom, ‖ And His plans that He has devised ‖ Concerning the inhabitants of Teman: Do little ones of the flock not drag them out, ‖ Does He not make their habitation desolate? **21** The earth has shaken from the noise of their fall, ‖ The cry—its voice is heard at the Sea of Suph. **22** Behold, He comes up as an eagle, and flies, ‖ And He spreads His wings over Bozrah, ‖ And the heart of the mighty of Edom has been in that day, ‖ As the heart of a travailing woman." **23** Concerning Damascus: "Hamath and Arpad have been ashamed, ‖ For they have heard an evil report, ‖ They have been melted, sorrow [is] in the sea, ‖ It is not able to be quiet. **24** Damascus has been feeble, ‖ She turned to flee, and fear strengthened her, ‖ Distress and pangs have seized her, as a travailing woman. **25** How it is not left—the city of praise, ‖ The city of My joy! **26** Therefore her young men fall in her broad places, ‖ And all the men of war are cut off in that day, ‖ A declaration of Yhwh of Hosts. **27** And I have kindled a fire against the wall of Damascus, ‖ And it consumed palaces of Ben-Hadad!" **28** Concerning Kedar, and concerning the kingdoms of Hazor that Nebuchadnezzar king of Babylon has struck: "Thus said Yhwh: Arise, go up to Kedar, ‖ And spoil the sons of the east. **29** They take their tents and their flock, ‖ Their curtains, and all their vessels, ‖ And they carry away their camels for themselves, ‖ And they called concerning them, ‖ Fear [is] all around. **30** Flee, bemoan mightily, go deep to dwell, ‖ You inhabitants of Hazor—a declaration of Yhwh, ‖ For Nebuchadnezzar king of Babylon has given counsel against you, ‖ Indeed, he devises a scheme against them. **31** Rise, go up to a nation at rest, ‖ Dwelling confidently, a declaration of Yhwh, ‖ It has no double gates nor bar, ‖ They dwell alone. **32** And their camels have been for a prey, ‖ And the multitude of their livestock for a spoil, ‖ And I have scattered them to every wind, ‖ Who cut off the corner [of the beard], ‖ And from all its passages I bring in their calamity, ‖ A declaration of Yhwh. **33** And Hazor has been for a habitation of dragons, ‖ A desolation for all time, ‖ No one dwells there, nor does a son of man sojourn in it!" **34** That which has been the word of Yhwh to Jeremiah the prophet concerning Elam, in the beginning of the reign of Zedekiah king of Judah, saying, **35** "Thus said Yhwh of Hosts: Behold, I am breaking the bow of Elam, ‖ The beginning of their might. **36** And I have brought four winds to Elam, ‖ From the four ends of the heavens, ‖ And have scattered them to all these winds, ‖ And there is no nation to where outcasts of Elam do not come in. **37** And I have frightened Elam before their enemies, ‖ And before those seeking their life, ‖ And I have brought calamity on them, ‖ The heat of My anger, ‖ A declaration of Yhwh, ‖ And I have sent the sword after them, ‖ Until I have consumed them; **38** And I have set My throne in Elam, ‖ And I have destroyed king and princes from there, ‖ A declaration of Yhwh. **39** And it has come to pass, in the latter end of the days, I return the captivity of Elam, ‖ A declaration of Yhwh!"

JEREMIAH

50 The word that Y<small>HWH</small> has spoken concerning Babylon, concerning the land of the Chaldeans, by the hand of Jeremiah the prophet: **2** "Declare among nations, and sound, ‖ And lift up an ensign, sound, do not hide, ‖ Say, Babylon has been captured, ‖ Bel has been put to shame, ‖ Merodach has been broken, ‖ Her grievous things have been put to shame, ‖ Her idols have been broken. **3** For a nation from the north has come up against her, ‖ It makes her land become a desolation, ‖ And there is not an inhabitant in it. From man even to beast, ‖ They have moved, they have gone. **4** In those days, and at that time," ‖ A declaration of Y<small>HWH</small>, ‖ "Sons of Israel come in, ‖ They and sons of Judah together, ‖ Going on and weeping they go, ‖ And they seek their God Y<small>HWH</small>. **5** They ask the way [to] Zion, ‖ Their faces [are] toward that place: Come in, and we are joined to Y<small>HWH</small>, ‖ A perpetual covenant—never forgotten. **6** My people have been a perishing flock, ‖ Their shepherds have caused them to err, ‖ Causing them to go back [on] the mountains, ‖ They have gone from mountain to hill, ‖ They have forgotten their crouching-place. **7** All finding them have devoured them, ‖ And their adversaries have said: We are not guilty, ‖ Because that they sinned against Y<small>HWH</small>, ‖ The habitation of righteousness, ‖ And the hope of their fathers—Y<small>HWH</small>. **8** Move from the midst of Babylon, ‖ And go out from the land of the Chaldeans; And be as male goats before a flock. **9** For behold, I am stirring up, ‖ And am causing to come up against Babylon, ‖ An assembly of great nations from [the] land of the north, ‖ And they have set in array against her, ‖ From there she is captured, ‖ Its arrow—as a skillful hero—does not return empty, **10** And Chaldea has been for a spoil, ‖ All her spoilers are satisfied," ‖ A declaration of Y<small>HWH</small>. **11** "Because you rejoice, because you exult, ‖ O spoilers of My inheritance, ‖ Because you increase as a heifer [at] the tender grass, ‖ And cry aloud as bulls, **12** Your mother has been greatly ashamed, ‖ She who bore you has been confounded, ‖ Behold, the last of nations [is] a wilderness, ‖ A dry land, and a desert. **13** Because of the wrath of Y<small>HWH</small> it is not inhabited, ‖ And it has been a desolation—all of it. Everyone passing by at Babylon is astonished, ‖ And hisses because of all her plagues. **14** Set yourselves in array against Babylon all around, ‖ All you treading a bow, ‖ Shoot at her, have no pity on the arrow, ‖ For she has sinned against Y<small>HWH</small>. **15** Shout against her all around, ‖ She has given forth her hand, ‖ Her foundations have fallen, ‖ Her walls have been thrown down, ‖ For it [is] the vengeance of Y<small>HWH</small>, ‖ Be avenged of her, as she did—do to her. **16** Cut off the sower from Babylon, ‖ And him handling the sickle in the time of harvest, ‖ Because of the oppressing sword, ‖ Each to his people—they turn, ‖ And each to his land—they flee. **17** Israel [is as] a scattered sheep, ‖ Lions have driven [him] away, ‖ At first, the king of Asshur devoured him, ‖ And now, at last, Nebuchadnezzar king of Babylon has broken his bone. **18** Therefore, thus said Y<small>HWH</small> of Hosts, God of Israel: Behold, I am seeing after the king of Babylon, ‖ And after his land, ‖ As I have seen after the king of Asshur; **19** And I have brought Israel back to his habitation, ‖ And he has fed on Carmel and on Bashan; And his soul is satisfied on Mount Ephraim and on Gilead. **20** In those days, and at that time," ‖ A declaration of Y<small>HWH</small>, ‖ "The iniquity of Israel is sought, and it is not, ‖ And the sin of Judah, and it is not found, ‖ For I am propitious to those whom I leave! **21** Against the land of Merathaim, go up against it, ‖ And to the inhabitants of Pekod, ‖ Dry up and devote their posterity," ‖ A declaration of Y<small>HWH</small>, ‖ "And do according to all that I have commanded you. **22** A noise of battle [is] in the land, ‖ And of great destruction. **23** How it has been cut and broken, ‖ The hammer of the whole earth! How Babylon has been for a desolation among nations! **24** I have laid a snare for you, ‖ And you are also captured, O Babylon, ‖ And you have known, ‖ You have been found, and are also caught, ‖ For you have stirred yourself up against Y<small>HWH</small>. **25** Y<small>HWH</small> has opened His treasury, ‖ And He brings out the weapons of His indignation, ‖ For a work [is] to Lord Y<small>HWH</small> of Hosts, ‖ In the land of the Chaldeans. **26** Come in to her from the extremity, ‖ Open her storehouses, ‖ Raise her up as heaps, and devote her, ‖ Let her have no remnant. **27** Slay all her cows, they go down to slaughter, ‖ Woe [is] on them, for their day has come, ‖ The time of their inspection. **28** A voice of fugitives and escaped ones ‖ [Is] from the land of Babylon, ‖ To declare in Zion the vengeance of our God YHWH, ‖ The vengeance of His temple. **29** Summon archers to Babylon, all treading the bow, ‖ Encamp against her all around, ‖ Let [her] have no escape; Repay to her according to her work, ‖ According to all that she did—do to her, ‖ For she has been proud against YHWH, ‖ Against the Holy One of Israel. **30** Therefore her young men fall in her broad places, ‖ And all her men of war are cut off in that day," ‖ A declaration of YHWH. **31** "Behold, I [am] against you, O pride," ‖ A declaration of Lord YHWH of Hosts, ‖ "For your day has come, the time of your inspection. **32** And pride has stumbled, ‖ And he has fallen, and has none raising up, ‖ And I have kindled a fire in his cities, ‖ And it has devoured all around him. **33** Thus said YHWH of Hosts: The sons of Israel are oppressed, ‖ And the sons of Judah together, ‖ And all their captors have kept hold on them, ‖ They have refused to send them away. **34** Their Redeemer [is] strong, ‖ YHWH of Hosts [is] His Name, ‖ He thoroughly pleads their cause, ‖ So as to cause the land to rest, ‖ And He has given trouble to the inhabitants of Babylon. **35** A sword [is] for the Chaldeans," ‖ A declaration of YHWH, ‖ "And it [is] on the inhabitants of Babylon, ‖ And on her heads, and on her wise men; **36** A sword [is] on the princes, ‖ And they have become foolish; A sword [is] on her mighty ones, ‖ And they have been broken down; **37** A sword [is] on his horses and on his chariot, ‖ And on all the rabble who [are] in her midst, ‖ And they have become women; A sword [is] on her treasuries, ‖ And they have been spoiled; **38** A sword [is] on her waters, and they have been dried up, ‖ For it [is] a land of carved images, ‖ And they boast themselves in idols. **39** Therefore desert-dwellers dwell with howlers, ‖ Indeed, daughters of the ostrich have dwelt in her, ‖ And it is not inhabited anymore forever, ‖ Nor dwelt in from generation to generation. **40** As the overthrow by God of Sodom, ‖ And of Gomorrah, and of its neighbors," ‖ A declaration of YHWH, ‖ "None dwell there, ‖ Nor does a son of man sojourn in her. **41** Behold, a people has come from the north, ‖ Even a great nation, ‖ And many kings are stirred up from the sides of the earth. **42** They seize bow and javelin, ‖ They [are] cruel, and they have no mercy, ‖ Their voice sounds as a sea, and they ride on horses, ‖ Set in array as a man for battle, ‖ Against you, O daughter of Babylon. **43** The king of Babylon has heard their report, ‖ And his hands have been feeble, ‖ Distress has seized him; pain as a travailing woman. **44** Behold, he comes up as a lion, ‖ Because of the rising of the Jordan, ‖ To the enduring habitation, ‖ But I cause to rest, I cause them to run from off her. And who is chosen? I lay a charge on her, ‖ For who [is] like Me? And who convenes Me? And who [is] this shepherd who stands before Me? **45** Therefore, hear the counsel of YHWH, ‖ That He counseled concerning Babylon, ‖ And His plans that He has devised ‖ Concerning the land of the Chaldeans; Do little ones of the flock not drag them out, ‖ Does He not make the habitation desolate over them? **46** From the sound of Babylon having been captured, ‖ The earth has been shaken, ‖ And a cry has been heard among nations!"

51 Thus said YHWH: "Behold, I am stirring up against Babylon, ‖ And the inhabitants of Leb, My withstanders, ‖ A destroying wind, **2** And I have sent fanners to Babylon, ‖ And they have fanned her, and they empty her land, ‖ For they have been against her, ‖ All around—in the day of evil. **3** Do not let the treader tread his bow, ‖ Nor lift himself up in his coat of mail, ‖ Nor have pity on her young men, ‖ Devote all her host to destruction. **4** And the wounded have fallen in the land of the Chaldeans, ‖ And the pierced-through in her streets. **5** For Israel and Judah are not forsaken ‖ By his God—by YHWH of Hosts, ‖ For their land has been full of guilt, ‖ Against the Holy One of Israel. **6** Flee from the midst of Babylon, ‖ And let each deliver his soul, ‖ Do not be cut off in her iniquity, ‖ For it [is] a time of vengeance for YHWH—His, ‖ He is rendering repayment to her. **7** Babylon [is] a golden cup in the hand of YHWH, ‖ Making all the earth drunk, ‖ Nations have drunk of her wine, ‖ Therefore nations boast themselves. **8** Babylon has suddenly fallen, ‖ Indeed, she is broken, howl for her, ‖ Take balm for her pain, perhaps she may be healed. **9** We healed Babylon, and she was not healed, ‖ Forsake her, and we go, each to his land, ‖ For her judgment has come to the heavens, ‖ And it has been lifted up to the clouds. **10** YHWH has brought forth our righteousnesses, ‖ Come, and we recount in Zion the work of our God YHWH.

JEREMIAH

11 Cleanse the arrows, fill the shields, ‖ YHWH has stirred up the spirit of the kings of Media, ‖ For His purpose [is] against Babylon to destroy her, ‖ For it [is] the vengeance of YHWH, ‖ The vengeance of His temple. **12** Lift up an ensign to the walls of Babylon, ‖ Strengthen the watch, ‖ Establish the watchers, prepare the ambush, ‖ For YHWH has both devised and done that which He spoke, ‖ Concerning the inhabitants of Babylon. **13** O dweller on many waters, abundant in treasures, ‖ Your end has come—the measure of your dishonest gain. **14** YHWH of Hosts has sworn by Himself, ‖ That, Surely I have filled you [with] men as the cankerworm, ‖ And they have cried against you—shouting. **15** Making [the] earth by His power, ‖ Establishing [the] world by His wisdom, ‖ Who by His understanding stretched out the heavens, **16** At the voice He gives forth, ‖ A multitude of waters [are] in the heavens, ‖ And He causes vapors to come up from the end of the earth, ‖ He has made lightnings for rain, ‖ And He brings out wind from His treasures. **17** Every man has been brutish by knowledge, ‖ Everyone has been put to shame—from refining a carved image, ‖ For his molten image [is] falsehood, ‖ And there is no breath in them. **18** They [are] vanity—a work of errors, ‖ They perish in the time of their inspection. **19** The Portion of Jacob [is] not like these, ‖ For He is forming the whole, ‖ And [Israel is] the tribe of His inheritance, ‖ YHWH of Hosts [is] His Name. **20** You [are] My shatterer—weapons of war, ‖ And I have broken in pieces nations by you, ‖ And I have destroyed kingdoms by you, **21** And I have broken in pieces horse and its rider by you, ‖ And I have broken in pieces chariot and its charioteer by you, **22** And I have broken in pieces man and woman by you, ‖ And I have broken in pieces old and young by you, ‖ And I have broken in pieces young man and virgin by you, **23** And I have broken in pieces shepherd and his drove by you, ‖ And I have broken in pieces farmer and his team by you, ‖ And I have broken in pieces governors and prefects by you. **24** And I have repaid to Babylon, ‖ And to all inhabitants of Chaldea, ‖ All the evil that they have done in Zion, ‖ Before your eyes," a declaration of YHWH. **25** "Behold, I [am] against you, O destroying mountain," ‖ A declaration of YHWH, ‖ "That is destroying all the earth, ‖ And I have stretched out My hand against you, ‖ And I have rolled you from the rocks, ‖ And given you for a burnt mountain. **26** And they do not take out of you a stone for a corner, ‖ And a stone for foundations, ‖ For you are continuous desolations," ‖ A declaration of YHWH. **27** "Lift up an ensign in the land, ‖ Blow a horn among nations, ‖ Sanctify nations against it, ‖ Summon against it the kingdoms of Ararat, Minni, and Ashkenaz, ‖ Appoint an infant head against it, ‖ Cause the horse to ascend as the rough cankerworm. **28** Sanctify against it the nations with the kings of Media, ‖ Its governors and all its prefects, ‖ And all the land of its dominion. **29** And the land shakes, and it is pained, ‖ For the purposes of YHWH have stood against Babylon, ‖ To make the land of Babylon a desolation without inhabitant. **30** The mighty of Babylon have ceased to fight, ‖ They have remained in strongholds, ‖ Their might has failed, they have become [as] women, ‖ They have burned her dwelling places, ‖ Her bars have been broken. **31** Runner runs to meet runner, ‖ And announcer to meet announcer, ‖ To announce to the king of Babylon, ‖ For his city has been captured—at the extremity. **32** And the passages have been captured, ‖ And they have burned the reeds with fire, ‖ And the men of war have been troubled. **33** For thus said YHWH of Hosts, God of Israel: The daughter of Babylon [is] as a threshing-floor, ‖ The time of her threshing—yet a little [while], ‖ And the time of her harvest has come. **34** Devoured us, crushed us, has Nebuchadnezzar king of Babylon, ‖ He has set us [as] an empty vessel, ‖ He has swallowed us as a dragon, ‖ He has filled his belly with my delicacies, ‖ He has driven us away. **35** My wrong, and [that of] my flesh, [is] on Babylon—The inhabitant of Zion says; And my blood [is] on the inhabitants of Chaldea—Jerusalem says. **36** Therefore, thus said YHWH: Behold, I am pleading your cause, ‖ And I have avenged your vengeance, ‖ And dried up her sea, and made her fountains dry. **37** And Babylon has been for heaps, ‖ A habitation of dragons, ‖ An astonishment, and a hissing, without inhabitant. **38** They roar together as young lions, ‖ They have shaken themselves as lions' whelps. **39** In their heat I make their banquets, ‖ And I have caused them to drink, so that they exult, ‖ And have slept a continuous sleep,

JEREMIAH

ǁ And do not awaken," a declaration of YHWH. **40** "I cause them to go down as lambs to slaughter, ǁ As rams with male goats. **41** How Sheshach has been captured, ǁ Indeed, the praise of the whole earth is caught, ǁ How Babylon has been for an astonishment among nations. **42** The sea has come up over Babylon, ǁ She has been covered with a multitude of its billows. **43** Her cities have been for a desolation, ǁ A dry land, and a wilderness, ǁ A land—none dwell in them, ǁ Nor does a son of man pass over into them. **44** And I have seen after Bel in Babylon, ǁ And I have brought forth that which he swallowed—from his mouth, ǁ And nations no longer flow to him, ǁ Also the wall of Babylon has fallen. **45** Go forth from her midst, O My people, ǁ And let each deliver his soul, ǁ Because of the fierceness of the anger of YHWH, **46** And lest your heart be tender, ǁ And you are afraid of the report that is heard in the land, ǁ And the report has come in [one] year, ǁ And after it [another] report in [another] year, ǁ And violence [is] in the land, ruler against ruler; **47** Therefore, behold, days are coming, ǁ And I have seen after the carved images of Babylon. And all its land is ashamed, ǁ And all its pierced ones fall in its midst. **48** And heavens and earth and all that [is] in them ǁ Have cried aloud against Babylon, ǁ For the spoilers come to her from the north," ǁ A declaration of YHWH. **49** "As Babylon [has caused the] pierced of Israel to fall, ǁ So they of Babylon have fallen, ǁ You pierced of all the earth. **50** You escaped of the sword, go on, do not stand, ǁ Remember YHWH from afar, ǁ And let Jerusalem come up on your heart. **51** We have been ashamed, for we heard reproach, ǁ Shame has covered our faces, ǁ For strangers have come in against the sanctuaries of the house of YHWH. **52** Therefore, behold, days are coming," ǁ A declaration of YHWH, ǁ "And I have seen after her carved images, ǁ And the wounded groan in all her land. **53** Because Babylon goes up to the heavens, ǁ And because she fortifies the high place of her strength, ǁ Spoilers come into her from Me," ǁ A declaration of YHWH. **54** "A voice of a cry [is] from Babylon, ǁ And of great destruction from the land of the Chaldean. **55** For YHWH is spoiling Babylon, ǁ And has destroyed her great voice, ǁ And her billows have sounded as many waters, ǁ Their voice has given forth a noise. **56** For a spoiler has come in against her—against Babylon, ǁ And her mighty ones have been captured, ǁ Their bows have been broken, ǁ For the God of recompenses—YHWH—certainly repays. **57** And I have caused her princes to drink, ǁ And her wise men, her governors, ǁ And her prefects, and her mighty ones, ǁ And they have slept a continuous sleep, ǁ And they do not awaken—an affirmation of the King, ǁ YHWH of Hosts [is] His Name. **58** Thus said YHWH of Hosts: The wall of Babylon—The broad one—is made utterly bare, ǁ And her high gates are burned with fire, ǁ And peoples labor in vain, ǁ And nations in fire, and have been weary!" **59** The word that Jeremiah the prophet has commanded Seraiah son of Neriah, son of Maaseiah, in his going with Zedekiah king of Judah to Babylon, in the fourth year of his reign—and Seraiah [is] a quiet prince; **60** and Jeremiah writes all the calamity that comes to Babylon on one scroll—all these words that are written concerning Babylon. **61** And Jeremiah says to Seraiah, "When you enter Babylon, then you have seen, and have read all these words, **62** and have said: YHWH, You have spoken concerning this place, to cut it off, that there is none dwelling in it, from man even to livestock, for it is a continuous desolation. **63** And it has come to pass, when you finish reading this scroll, you bind a stone to it, and have cast it into the midst of the Euphrates, **64** and said, Thus Babylon sinks, and she does not arise, because of the calamity that I am bringing in against it, and they have been weary." Until now [are the] words of Jeremiah.

52 Zedekiah [is] a son of twenty-one years in his reigning, and he has reigned eleven years in Jerusalem, and the name of his mother [is] Hamutal daughter of Jeremiah of Libnah. **2** And he does evil in the eyes of YHWH, according to all that Jehoiakim has done, **3** for because of the anger of YHWH, it has been in Jerusalem and Judah until He has cast them from before His face, and Zedekiah rebels against the king of Babylon. **4** And it comes to pass, in the ninth year of his reign, in the tenth month, on the tenth of the month, Nebuchadnezzar king of Babylon has come—he and all his force—against Jerusalem, and they encamp against it, and build against it a fortification all around;

JEREMIAH

5 and the city comes into siege until the eleventh year of King Zedekiah. **6** In the fourth month, on the ninth of the month, when the famine is severe in the city, and there has been no bread for the people of the land, **7** then the city is broken up, and all the men of war flee, and go forth from the city by night, the way of the gate between the two walls that [is] by the king's garden—and the Chaldeans [are] by the city all around—and they go the way of the plain. **8** And the forces of the Chaldeans pursue after the king, and overtake Zedekiah in the plains of Jericho, and all his forces have been scattered from him, **9** and they capture the king, and bring him up to the king of Babylon at Riblah, in the land of Hamath, and he speaks with him—judgments. **10** And the king of Babylon slaughters the sons of Zedekiah before his eyes, and he has also slaughtered all the princes of Judah in Riblah; **11** and he has blinded the eyes of Zedekiah, and he binds him in bronze chains, and the king of Babylon brings him to Babylon, and puts him in the house of inspection to the day of his death. **12** And in the fifth month, on the tenth of the month—it [is] the nineteenth year of King Nebuchadnezzar king of Babylon—Nebuzar-Adan, chief of the executioners, has come; he has stood before the king of Babylon in Jerusalem, **13** and he burns the house of YHWH, and the house of the king, and all the houses of Jerusalem—even every great house he has burned with fire, **14** and all the forces of the Chaldeans that [are] with the chief of the executioners have broken down all the walls of Jerusalem. **15** And of the poor of the people, and the remnant of the people who are left in the city, and those who are defecting, who have defected to the king of Babylon, and the remnant of the multitude, Nebuzar-Adan, chief of the executioners, has removed; **16** and of the poor of the land, Nebuzar-Adan, chief of the executioners, has left for vinedressers and for farmers. **17** And the pillars of bronze that [are] in the house of YHWH, and the bases, and the bronze sea that [is] in the house of YHWH, the Chaldeans have broken, and they carry away all the bronze of them to Babylon; **18** and the pots, and the shovels, and the snuffers, and the bowls, and the spoons, and all the vessels of bronze with which they minister, they have taken away; **19** and the basins, and the fire-pans, and the bowls, and the pots, and the lampstands, and the spoons, and the cups, the gold of that which [is] gold, and the silver of that which [is] silver, the chief of the executioners has taken. **20** The two pillars, the one sea, and the twelve bronze oxen that [are] beneath the bases, that King Solomon made for the house of YHWH, there was no weighing of the bronze of all these vessels. **21** As for the pillars, eighteen cubits [is] the height of the one pillar, and a cord of twelve cubits goes around it, and its thickness [is] four fingers hollow. **22** And the capital on it [is] of bronze, and the height of the one capital [is] five cubits, and network and pomegranates [are] on the capital all around, the whole [is] of bronze; and like these—the second pillar—and pomegranates. **23** And the pomegranates are ninety-six on a side, all the pomegranates [are] one hundred on the network all around. **24** And the chief of the executioners takes Seraiah the head priest, and Zephaniah the second priest, and the three keepers of the threshold, **25** and he has taken a certain eunuch out of the city, who has been inspector over the men of war, and seven men of those seeing the king's face, who have been found in the city, and the head scribe of the host, who musters the people of the land, and sixty men of the people of the land, who are found in the midst of the city; **26** and Nebuzar-Adan, chief of the executioners, takes them, and brings them to the king of Babylon at Riblah, **27** and the king of Babylon strikes them, and puts them to death in Riblah, in the land of Hamath, and he removes Judah from off its own ground. **28** This [is] the people whom Nebuchadnezzar has removed: in the seventh year, of Jews, three thousand and twenty-three; **29** in the eighteenth year of Nebuchadnezzar—from Jerusalem—eight hundred thirty-two souls; **30** in the twenty-third year of Nebuchadnezzar, Nebuzar-Adan, chief of the guard, has removed of Jewish souls, seven hundred forty-five; all the souls [are] four thousand and six hundred. **31** And it comes to pass, in the thirty-seventh year of the expulsion of Jehoiachin king of Judah, in the twelfth month, on the twenty-fifth of the month, Evil-Merodach king of Babylon has lifted up, in the year of his reign, the head of Jehoiachin king of Judah, and brings him out from the house of restraint, **32** and speaks good things with him, and sets his throne above the throne of the kings who [are] with him in Babylon, **33** and he has changed his prison garments, and he has continually eaten bread before him, all the days of his life. **34** And his allowance—a continual allowance—has been given to him by the king of Babylon, the matter of a day in its day, until [the] day of his death—all [the] days of his life.

LAMENTATIONS

1 [ALEPH-BET] How she has sat alone, ‖ The city abounding with people! She has been as a widow, ‖ The mighty among nations! Princes among provinces, ‖ She has become tributary! **2** She weeps severely in the night, ‖ And her tear [is] on her cheeks, ‖ There is no comforter for her out of all her lovers, ‖ All her friends dealt treacherously by her, ‖ They have been to her for enemies. **3** Removed has Judah because of affliction, ‖ And because of the abundance of her service; She has dwelt among nations, ‖ She has not found rest, ‖ All her pursuers have overtaken her between the straits. **4** The ways of Zion are mourning, ‖ Without any coming at the appointed time, ‖ All her gates are desolate, her priests sigh, ‖ Her virgins are afflicted—and she has bitterness. **5** Her adversaries have become chief, ‖ Her enemies have been at ease, ‖ For YHWH has afflicted her, ‖ For the abundance of her transgressions, ‖ Her infants have gone captive before the adversary. **6** And all her honor goes out from the daughter of Zion, ‖ Her princes have been as harts—They have not found pasture, ‖ And they go powerless before a pursuer. **7** Jerusalem has remembered ‖ [In] the days of her affliction and her mournings, all her desirable things that were from the days of old, ‖ In the falling of her people into the hand of an adversary, ‖ And she has no helper; Adversaries have seen her, ‖ They have laughed at her cessation. **8** A sin has Jerusalem sinned, ‖ Therefore she has become impure, ‖ All who honored her have esteemed her lightly, ‖ For they have seen her nakedness, ‖ Indeed, she herself has sighed and turns backward. **9** Her uncleanness [is] in her skirts, ‖ She has not remembered her latter end, ‖ And she comes down wonderfully, ‖ There is no comforter for her. See, O YHWH, my affliction, ‖ For an enemy has exerted himself. **10** His hand has spread out an adversary ‖ On all her desirable things, ‖ For she has seen—Nations have entered her sanctuary, ‖ Concerning which You commanded, ‖ "They do not come into the assembly to you." **11** All her people are sighing—seeking bread, ‖ They have given their desirable things ‖ For food to refresh the body; See, O YHWH, and behold attentively, ‖ For I have been lightly esteemed. **12** [Is it] nothing to you, all you passing by the way? Look attentively, and see, ‖ If there is any pain like my pain, ‖ That He is rolling to me? Whom YHWH has afflicted ‖ In the day of the fierceness of His anger. **13** From above He has sent fire into my bone, ‖ And it subdues it, He has spread a net for my feet, ‖ He has turned me backward, ‖ He has made me desolate—all the day sick. **14** Bound has been the yoke of my transgressions by His hand, ‖ They are wrapped together, ‖ They have gone up on my neck, ‖ He has caused my power to stumble, ‖ The Lord has given me into hands, ‖ I am not able to rise. **15** The Lord has trodden down all my mighty ones in my midst, ‖ He proclaimed an appointed time against me, ‖ To destroy my young men, ‖ The Lord has trodden a winepress, ‖ To the virgin daughter of Judah. **16** For these I am weeping, ‖ My eye, my eye, is running down with waters, ‖ For a comforter has been far from me, ‖ Refreshing my soul, ‖ My sons have been desolate, ‖ For mighty has been an enemy. **17** Zion has spread forth her hands, ‖ There is no comforter for her, ‖ YHWH has charged concerning Jacob, ‖ His neighbors [are] his adversaries, ‖ Jerusalem has become impure among them. **18** YHWH is righteous, ‖ For I have provoked His mouth. Now hear, all you peoples, and see my pain, ‖ My virgins and my young men have gone into captivity. **19** I called for my lovers, they have deceived me, ‖ My priests and my elderly have expired in the city; When they have sought food for themselves, ‖ Then they give back their soul. **20** See, O YHWH, for distress [is] to me, ‖ My bowels have been troubled, ‖ My heart has been turned in my midst, ‖ For I have greatly provoked, ‖ From outside the sword has bereaved, ‖ In the house [it is] as death. **21** They have heard that I have sighed, ‖ There is no comforter for me, ‖ All my enemies have heard of my calamity, ‖ They have rejoiced that You have done [it], ‖ You have brought in the day You have called, ‖ And they are like to me. **22** All their evil comes in before You, ‖ And one is doing to them as You have done

LAMENTATIONS

to me, ‖ For all my transgressions, ‖ For many [are] my sighs, and my heart [is] sick!

2 [ALEPH-BET] How the Lord clouds in His anger the daughter of Zion, ‖ He has cast from the heavens [to] earth the beauty of Israel, ‖ And has not remembered His footstool in the day of His anger. **2** The Lord has swallowed up, ‖ He has not pitied any of the pleasant places of Jacob, ‖ He has broken down in His wrath ‖ The fortresses of the daughter of Judah, ‖ He has caused to come to the earth, ‖ He defiled the kingdom and its princes. **3** He has cut off in the heat of anger every horn of Israel, ‖ He has turned backward His right hand ‖ From the face of the enemy, ‖ And He burns against Jacob as a flaming fire, ‖ It has devoured all around. **4** He has bent His bow as an enemy, ‖ His right hand has stood as an adversary, ‖ And He slays all the desirable ones of the eye, ‖ In the tent of the daughter of Zion, ‖ He has poured out as fire His fury. **5** The Lord has been as an enemy, ‖ He has swallowed up Israel, ‖ He has swallowed up all her palaces, ‖ He has destroyed His fortresses, ‖ And He multiplies in the daughter of Judah ‖ Mourning and moaning. **6** And He shakes as a garden His dwelling place, ‖ He has destroyed His appointed place, ‖ YHWH has forgotten in Zion the appointed time and Sabbath, ‖ And despises, in the indignation of His anger, king and priest. **7** The Lord has cast off His altar, ‖ He has rejected His sanctuary, ‖ He has shut up into the hand of the enemy ‖ The walls of her palaces, ‖ A noise they have made in the house of YHWH ‖ Like a day of appointment. **8** YHWH has devised to destroy the wall of the daughter of Zion, ‖ He has stretched out a line, ‖ He has not turned His hand from destroying, ‖ And He causes bulwark and wall to mourn, ‖ Together—they have been weak. **9** Sunk into the earth have her gates, ‖ He has destroyed and broken her bars, ‖ Her king and her princes [are] among the nations, ‖ There is no law, also her prophets ‖ Have not found vision from YHWH. **10** Sit on the earth—[the] elderly of Zion's daughter keep silent, ‖ They have caused dust to go up on their head, ‖ They have girded on sackcloth, ‖ The virgins of Jerusalem have ‖ Put their head down to the earth. **11** My eyes have been consumed by tears, ‖ My bowels have been troubled, ‖ My liver has been poured out to the earth, ‖ For the breach of the daughter of my people; In infant and suckling being feeble, ‖ In the broad places of the city, **12** To their mothers they say, ‖ "Where [are] grain and wine?" In their becoming feeble as a pierced one ‖ In the broad places of the city, ‖ In their soul pouring itself out into the bosom of their mothers. **13** What do I testify [to] you, what do I liken to you, ‖ O daughter of Jerusalem? What do I equal to you, and I comfort you, ‖ O virgin daughter of Zion? For great as a sea [is] your breach, ‖ Who gives healing to you? **14** Your prophets have seen for you a false and insipid thing, ‖ And have not revealed concerning your iniquity, ‖ To return your captivity, ‖ And they see for you false burdens and causes of expulsion. **15** Everyone passing by the way clapped hands at you, ‖ They have hissed—and they shake the head ‖ At the daughter of Jerusalem: "Is this the city of which they said: The perfection of beauty, a joy to all the land?" **16** Opened against you their mouth have all your enemies, ‖ They have hissed, indeed, they gnash the teeth, ‖ They have said: "We have swallowed [her] up, ‖ Surely this [is] the day that we looked for, ‖ We have found—we have seen." **17** YHWH has done that which He devised, ‖ He has fulfilled His saying ‖ That He commanded from the days of old, ‖ He has broken down and has not pitied, ‖ And causes an enemy to rejoice over you, ‖ He lifted up the horn of your adversaries. **18** Their heart has cried to the Lord; O wall of the daughter of Zion, ‖ Cause to go down tears as a stream daily and nightly, do not give rest to yourself, ‖ Do not let the daughter of your eye stand still. **19** Arise, cry aloud in the night, ‖ At the beginning of the watches. Pour out your heart as water, ‖ Before the face of the Lord, ‖ Lift up to Him your hands, for the soul of your infants, ‖ Who are feeble with hunger at the head of all out-places. **20** See, O YHWH, and look attentively, ‖ To whom You have acted thus, ‖ Do women eat their fruit, infants of a handbreadth? Slain in the sanctuary of the Lord are priest and prophet? **21** Lain on the earth [in] out-places have young and old, ‖ My virgins and my young men have fallen by the sword, ‖ You have slain in a day of Your anger, ‖ You have slaughtered—You have not pitied. **22** You call as [at] a day of appointment, ‖ My fears from all around, ‖ And there has not been in the day of the

LAMENTATIONS

anger of Y<small>HWH</small>, ‖ An escaped and remaining one, ‖ They whom I stretched out and nourished, ‖ My enemy has consumed!

3 [A<small>LEPH</small>-B<small>ET</small>] I [am] the man [who] has seen affliction ‖ By the rod of His wrath. **2** He has led me, and causes to go [in] darkness, and without light. **3** Surely against me He turns back, ‖ He turns His hand all the day. **4** He has worn out my flesh and my skin. He has broken my bones. **5** He has built up against me, ‖ And sets around poverty and weariness. **6** In dark places He has caused me to dwell, ‖ As the dead of old. **7** He has hedged me in, and I do not go out, ‖ He has made heavy my chain. **8** Also when I call and cry out, ‖ He has shut out my prayer. **9** He has hedged my ways with hewn work, ‖ My paths He has made crooked. **10** A bear lying in wait He [is] to me, ‖ A lion in secret hiding places. **11** My ways He is turning aside, and He pulls me in pieces, ‖ He has made me a desolation. **12** He has bent His bow, ‖ And sets me up as a mark for an arrow. **13** He has caused to enter into my reins ‖ The sons of His quiver. **14** I have been a derision to all my people, ‖ Their song all the day. **15** He has filled me with bitter things, ‖ He has filled me [with] wormwood. **16** And He breaks with gravel my teeth, ‖ He has covered me with ashes. **17** And You cast off my soul from peace, ‖ I have forgotten prosperity. **18** And I say, My strength and my hope have perished from Y<small>HWH</small>. **19** Remember my affliction and my mourning, ‖ Wormwood and gall! **20** Remember well, and my soul bows down in me. **21** This I turn to my heart—therefore I hope. **22** The kindnesses of Y<small>HWH</small>! For we have not been consumed, ‖ For His mercies have not ended. **23** New every morning, abundant [is] Your faithfulness. **24** My portion [is] Y<small>HWH</small>, my soul has said, ‖ Therefore I hope for Him. **25** Y<small>HWH</small> [is] good to those waiting for Him, ‖ To the soul [that] seeks Him. **26** [It is] good when one stays and stands still ‖ For the salvation of Y<small>HWH</small>. **27** [It is] good for a man that he bears a yoke in his youth. **28** He sits alone, and is silent, ‖ For He has laid [it] on him. **29** He puts his mouth in the dust, if so be, there is hope. **30** He gives to his striker the cheek, ‖ He is filled with reproach. **31** For the Lord does not cast off for all time. **32** For though He afflicted, yet He has pitied, ‖ According to the abundance of His kindness. **33** For He has not afflicted with His heart, ‖ Nor does He grieve the sons of men. **34** To bruise under one's feet any bound ones of earth, **35** To turn aside the judgment of a man, ‖ Before the face of the Most High, **36** To subvert a man in his cause, the Lord has not approved. **37** Who [is] this—he has spoken, and it is, ‖ [And] the Lord has not commanded [it]? **38** From the mouth of the Most High does not go forth the evils and the good. **39** Why does a living man sigh habitually, ‖ A man for his sin? **40** We search our ways, and investigate, ‖ And turn back to Y<small>HWH</small>. **41** We lift up our heart on the hands to God in the heavens. **42** We have transgressed and been rebellious, ‖ You have not forgiven. **43** You have covered Yourself with anger, ‖ And pursue us; You have slain—You have not pitied. **44** You have covered Yourself with a cloud, ‖ So that prayer does not pass through. **45** Outcast and refuse You make us ‖ In the midst of the peoples. **46** Opened against us their mouth have all our enemies. **47** Fear and a snare has been for us, ‖ Desolation and destruction. **48** Streams of water go down my eye, ‖ For the destruction of the daughter of my people. **49** My eye is poured out, ‖ And does not cease without intermission, **50** Until Y<small>HWH</small> looks and sees from the heavens, **51** My eye affects my soul, ‖ Because of all the daughters of my city. **52** Hunting—my enemies have hunted me without cause like the bird. **53** They have cut off my life in a pit, ‖ And they cast a stone against me. **54** Waters have flowed over my head, I have said, I have been cut off. **55** I called Your Name, O Y<small>HWH</small>, from the lower pit. **56** You have heard my voice, do not hide Your ear at my breathing—at my cry. **57** You have drawn near in the day I call You, You have said, Do not fear. **58** You have pleaded, O Lord, the pleadings of my soul, ‖ You have redeemed my life. **59** You have seen, O Y<small>HWH</small>, my overthrow, ‖ Judge my cause. **60** You have seen all their vengeance, ‖ All their thoughts of me. **61** You have heard their reproach, O Y<small>HWH</small>, ‖ All their thoughts against me, **62** The lips of my withstanders, ‖ Even their meditation against me all the day. **63** Their sitting down, and their rising up, ‖ Behold attentively, I [am] their song. **64** You return to them the deed, O Y<small>HWH</small>, ‖ According to the work of their hands. **65** You give to them a covered heart, ‖ Your curse to them. **66** You pursue in anger, and destroy them, ‖ From under the heavens of Y<small>HWH</small>!

4 [A<small>LEPH</small>-B<small>ET</small>] How the gold has become dim, ‖ Changed the best—the pure gold! Stones of the sanctuary are poured out ‖ At the head of all out-places. **2** The precious sons of Zion, ‖ Who are comparable with fine gold, ‖ How they have been reckoned earthen bottles, ‖ Work of the hands of a potter. **3** Even dragons have drawn out the breast, ‖ They have suckled their young ones, ‖ The daughter of my people has become cruel, ‖ Like the ostriches in a wilderness. **4** The tongue of a suckling has cleaved to his palate with thirst, ‖ Infants asked for bread, they have no dealer [of it] out. **5** Those eating of delicacies have been desolate in out-places, ‖ Those supported on scarlet have embraced dunghills. **6** And greater is the iniquity of the daughter of my people, ‖ Than the sin of Sodom, ‖ That was overturned as [in] a moment, ‖ And no hands were stayed on her. **7** Purer were her Nazarites than snow, ‖ Whiter than milk, ruddier of body than rubies, ‖ Of sapphire their form. **8** Their face has been darker than blackness, ‖ They have not been known in out-places, ‖ Their skin has cleaved to their bone, ‖ It has withered—it has been as wood. **9** Better have been the pierced of a sword ‖ Than the pierced of famine, ‖ For these flow away, pierced through, ‖ Without the increase of the field. **10** The hands of merciful women have boiled their own children, ‖ They have been for food to them, ‖ In the destruction of the daughter of my people. **11** Y<small>HWH</small> has completed His fury, ‖ He has poured out the fierceness of His anger, ‖ And He kindles a fire in Zion, ‖ And it devours her foundations. **12** The kings of earth did not believe, ‖ And any of the inhabitants of the world, ‖ That an adversary and enemy would come ‖ Into the gates of Jerusalem. **13** Because of the sins of her prophets, ‖ The iniquities of her priests, ‖ Who are shedding in her midst the blood of the righteous, **14** They have wandered naked in out-places, ‖ They have been defiled with blood, ‖ Without [any] being able to touch their clothing, **15** "Turn aside—unclean," they called to them, ‖ "Turn aside, turn aside, do not touch," ‖ For they fled—indeed, they have wandered, ‖ They have said among nations: "They do not add to sojourn." **16** The face of Y<small>HWH</small> has divided them, ‖ He does not add to behold them, ‖ They have not lifted up the face of priests, ‖ They have not favored [the] old and elderly. **17** While we exist—consumed are our eyes for our vain help, ‖ In our watchtower we have watched for a nation [that] does not save. **18** They have hunted our steps from going in our broad-places, ‖ Near has been our end, fulfilled our days, ‖ For our end has come. **19** Swifter have been our pursuers, ‖ Than the eagles of the heavens, ‖ On the mountains they have burned [after] us, ‖ In the wilderness they have laid wait for us. **20** The breath of our nostrils—the anointed of Y<small>HWH</small>, ‖ Has been captured in their pits, of whom we said: "We live among nations in his shadow." **21** Rejoice and be glad, O daughter of Edom, ‖ Dwelling in the land of Uz, ‖ Even to you a cup passes over, ‖ You are drunk, and make yourself naked. **22** Completed [is] your iniquity, daughter of Zion, ‖ He does not add to remove you, ‖ He has inspected your iniquity, O daughter of Edom, ‖ He has removed [you] because of your sins!

5 Remember, O Y<small>HWH</small>, what has befallen us, ‖ Look attentively, and see our reproach. **2** Our inheritance has been turned to strangers, ‖ Our houses to foreigners. **3** Orphans we have been—without a father, our mothers [are] as widows. **4** We have drunk our water for money, ‖ Our wood comes for a price. **5** For our neck we have been pursued, ‖ We have labored—there has been no rest for us. **6** [To] Egypt we have given a hand, ‖ [To] Asshur, to be satisfied with bread. **7** Our fathers have sinned—they are not, ‖ We have borne their iniquities. **8** Servants have ruled over us, ‖ There is no deliverer from their hand. **9** With our lives we bring in our bread, ‖ Because of the sword of the wilderness. **10** Our skin as an oven has been burning, ‖ Because of the raging of the famine. **11** Wives in Zion they have humbled, ‖ Virgins—in cities of Judah. **12** Princes have been hanged by their hand, ‖ Elderly faces have not been honored. **13** They have taken young men to grind, ‖ And youths have stumbled with wood. **14** Elderly have ceased from the gate, ‖ Young men from their song. **15** The joy of our heart has ceased, ‖ Our dancing has been turned to mourning. **16** The crown has fallen [from] our head, ‖ Woe [is] now to us, for we have sinned. **17** Our heart has been sick for this, ‖ Our eyes have been dim for these. **18** For the Mount of Zion—that is desolate, ‖ Foxes have gone up on it. **19** You, O Y<small>HWH</small>, remain for all time, ‖ Your throne to generation and generation. **20** Why do You forget us forever? You forsake us for [the] length of [our] days! **21** Turn us back, O Y<small>HWH</small>, to You, ‖ And we turn back, renew our days as of old. **22** For have You utterly rejected us? You have been angry against us—exceedingly?

EZEKIEL

1 And it comes to pass, in the thirtieth year, in the fourth [month], on the fifth of the month, and I [am] in the midst of the expulsion by the river Chebar, the heavens have been opened, and I see visions of God. **2** In the fifth of the month—it is the fifth year of the expulsion of King Jehoiachin— **3** the word of YHWH has certainly been to Ezekiel son of Buzi the priest, in the land of the Chaldeans, by the river Chebar, and there is on him there a hand of YHWH. **4** And I look, and behold, a turbulent wind is coming from the north, a great cloud, and fire catching itself, and brightness to it all around, and out of its midst as the color of electrum, out of the midst of the fire. **5** And out of its midst [is] a likeness of four living creatures, and this [is] their appearance; a likeness of man [is] to them, **6** and each had four faces and each of them had four wings, **7** and their feet [are] straight feet, and the sole of their feet [is] as a sole of a calf's foot, and they are sparkling as the color of bright bronze; **8** and on their four sides [each had] hands of man under their wings; and [each] of the four had their faces and their wings; **9** their wings [are] joining to one another, they do not turn around in their going, they each go straight forward. **10** As for the likeness of their faces, [each had] the face of a man, and toward the right the four had the face of a lion, and on the left the four had the face of an ox, and the four had the face of an eagle. **11** And their faces and their wings dividing from above, of each [are] two joining together, and two are covering their bodies. **12** And they each go straight forward, to where the Spirit is to go, they go, they do not turn around in their going. **13** As for the likeness of the living creatures, their appearances [are] as coals of fire—burning as the appearance of lamps; it is going up and down between the living creatures, and brightness [is] to the fire, and lightning is going forth out of the fire. **14** And the living creatures are running, and turning back, as the appearance of the flash. **15** And I see the living creatures, and behold, one wheel [is] in the earth, near the living creatures, at its four faces. **16** The appearance of the wheels and their works [is] as the color of beryl, and the four of them had one likeness, and their appearances and their works [are] as it were the wheel in the midst of the wheel. **17** On their four sides, in their going they go, they do not turn around in their going. **18** As for their rings, they are both high and fearful, and their rings, of the four of them, [are] full of eyes around them. **19** And in the going of the living creatures, the wheels go beside them, and in the living creatures being lifted up from off the earth, the wheels are lifted up. **20** To where the Spirit is to go, they go, there the Spirit [is] to go, and the wheels are lifted up alongside them, for a living spirit [is] in the wheels. **21** In their going, they go; and in their standing, they stand; and in their being lifted up from off the earth, the wheels are lifted up alongside them; for a living spirit [is] in the wheels. **22** And over the heads of the living creatures—a likeness of an expanse, as the color of the fearful ice, stretched out over their heads from above. **23** And under the expanse their wings [are] straight, one toward [its] sister; two [wings] of each are covering them, and two [wings] of each are covering their bodies. **24** And I hear the noise of their wings, as the noise of many waters, as the noise of the Mighty One, in their going—the noise of tumult, as the noise of a camp, in their standing they let their wings fall. **25** And there is a voice from above the expanse, that [is] above their head: in their standing they let their wings fall. **26** And above the expanse that [is] over their head, as an appearance of a sapphire stone, [is] the likeness of a throne, and on the likeness of the throne a likeness, as the appearance of man on it from above. **27** And I see as the color of electrum, as the appearance of fire all around within it, from the appearance of His loins and upward; and from the appearance of His loins and downward, I have seen as the appearance of fire, and brightness [is] all around Him. **28** As the appearance of the bow that is in a cloud in a day of rain, so [is] the appearance of the brightness all around.

2 His appearance [was] of the likeness of the glory of YHWH, and I see, and fall on my face, and I hear a voice speaking, and He says to me, "Son of man, stand on your feet, and I speak with you." **2** And [the]

EZEKIEL

Spirit comes into me when He has spoken to me, and causes me to stand on my feet, and I hear Him who is speaking to me. **3** And He says to me, "Son of man, I am sending you to the sons of Israel, to rebelling nations who have rebelled against Me; they and their fathers have transgressed against Me, to this very day. **4** And the sons [are] brazen-faced and hard-hearted to whom I am sending you, and you have said to them: Thus said Lord YHWH. **5** And they—whether they hear, or whether they refrain, for they [are] a house of rebellion—have known that a prophet has been in their midst. **6** And you, son of man, you are not afraid of them, indeed, you are not afraid of their words, for briers and thorns are with you, and you are dwelling near scorpions, you are not afraid of their words, and you are not frightened of their faces, for they [are] a house of rebellion, **7** and you have spoken My words to them, whether they hear or whether they refrain, for they [are] a rebellion. **8** And you, son of man, hear that which I am speaking to you; do not be of rebellion like the house of rebellion, open your mouth and eat that which I am giving to you." **9** And I look, and behold, a hand [is] sent forth to me, and behold, a roll of a scroll [is] in it, **10** and He spreads it before me, and it is written in front and behind, and written on it [are] lamentations, and mourning, and woe!

3 And He says to me, "Son of man, eat that which you find, eat this scroll, and go, speak to the house of Israel." **2** And I open my mouth, and He causes me to eat this scroll. **3** And He says to me, "Son of man, feed your belly, and fill your bowels with this scroll that I am giving to you"; and I eat it, and it is as honey for sweetness in my mouth. **4** And He says to me, "Son of man, go forth, go to the house of Israel, and you have spoken to them with My words. **5** For you [are] not sent to a people deep of lip and heavy of tongue—to the house of Israel; **6** not to many peoples, deep of lip and heavy of tongue, whose words you do not understand. If I had not sent you to them—they listen to you, **7** but the house of Israel are not willing to listen to you, for they are not willing to listen to Me, for all the house of Israel are brazen-faced and strong-hearted. **8** Behold, I have made your face strong against their face, and your forehead strong against their forehead.

9 As an adamant, harder than a rock, I have made your forehead; do not fear them, nor are you frightened before them, for they [are] a house of rebellion." **10** And He says to me, "Son of man, all My words that I speak to you, receive with your heart, and hear with your ears; **11** and go forth, go to the expulsion, to the sons of your people, and you have spoken to them, and have said to them: Thus said Lord YHWH; whether they hear, or whether they refrain." **12** And a spirit lifts me up, and I hear a noise behind me, a great rushing—"Blessed [is] the glory of YHWH from His place!" **13** Even a noise of the wings of the living creatures touching one another, and a noise of the wheels alongside them, even a noise of a great rushing. **14** And [the] Spirit has lifted me up, and takes me away, and I go bitterly, in the heat of my spirit, and the hand of YHWH [is] strong on me. **15** And I come to the expulsion, at Tel-Ahib, who are dwelling at the river Chebar, and where they are dwelling I also dwell [for] seven days, causing astonishment in their midst. **16** And it comes to pass, at the end of seven days, **17** that there is a word of YHWH to me, saying, "Son of man, I have given you [as] a watchman to the house of Israel, and you have heard a word from My mouth, and have warned them from Me. **18** In My saying to the wicked: You surely die; and you have not warned him, nor have spoken to warn the wicked from his wicked way, so that he lives; he—the wicked—dies in his iniquity, and I require his blood from your hand. **19** And you, because you have warned the wicked, and he has not turned back from his wickedness, and from his wicked way, he dies in his iniquity, and you have delivered your soul. **20** And in the turning back of the righteous from his righteousness, and he has done perversity, and I have put a stumbling-block before him, he dies; because you have not warned him, he dies in his sin, and his righteousness that he has done is not remembered, and I require his blood from your hand. **21** And you, because you have warned him—the righteous—that the righteous does not sin, and he has not sinned, he surely lives, because he has been warned; and you have delivered your soul." **22** And there is a hand of YHWH on me there, and He says to me, "Rise, go forth to the valley, and there I speak with you." **23** And I rise and go

EZEKIEL

forth to the valley, and behold, there the glory of YHWH is standing as the glory that I had seen by the river Chebar, and I fall on my face. **24** And [the] Spirit comes into me, and causes me to stand on my feet, and He speaks with me, and says to me, "Go in, be shut up in the midst of your house. **25** And you, son of man, behold, they have put thick bands on you, and have bound you with them, and you do not go forth in their midst; **26** and I cause your tongue to cleave to your palate, and you have been mute, and are not for a reprover to them, for they [are] a house of rebellion. **27** And in My speaking with you, I open your mouth, and you have said to them: Thus said Lord YHWH; the hearer hears, and the refrainer refrains; for they [are] a house of rebellion."

4 "And you, son of man, take a brick for yourself, and you have put it before you, and have carved a city on it—Jerusalem, **2** and have placed a siege against it, and built a fortification against it, and poured out a mound against it, and placed camps against it, indeed, set battering-rams against it all around. **3** And you, take an iron pan for yourself, and you have made it a wall of iron between you and the city; and you have prepared your face against it, and it has been in a siege, indeed, you have laid siege against it. It [is] a sign to the house of Israel. **4** And you, lie on your left side, and you have placed the iniquity of the house of Israel on it; the number of the days that you lie on it, you bear their iniquity. **5** And I have laid the years of their iniquity on you, the number of days, three hundred and ninety days; and you have borne the iniquity of the house of Israel. **6** And you have completed these, and have lain on your right side, a second time, and have borne the iniquity of the house of Judah forty days—a day for a year—a day for a year I have appointed to you. **7** And to the siege of Jerusalem you prepare your face, and your arm [is] uncovered, and you have prophesied concerning it. **8** And behold, I have put thick bands on you, and you do not turn from side to side until your completing the days of your siege. **9** And you, take for yourself wheat, and barley, and beans, and lentiles, and millet, and spelt, and you have put them in one vessel, and made them for bread for yourself; the number of the days that you are lying on your side—three hundred and ninety days—you eat it. **10** And your food that you eat [is] by weight, twenty shekels daily; from time to time you eat it. **11** And you drink water by measure, a sixth part of the hin; from time to time you drink [it]. **12** And you eat it [as] barley-cake, and it with dung—the filth of man—you bake before their eyes." **13** And YHWH says, "Thus the sons of Israel eat their defiled bread among the nations to where I drive them." **14** And I say, "Aah! Lord YHWH, behold, my soul is not defiled, and carcass, and torn thing, I have not eaten from my youth, even until now; nor has abominable flesh come into my mouth." **15** And He says to me, "See, I have given to you bullock's dung instead of man's dung, and you have made your bread by it." **16** And He says to me, "Son of man, behold, I am breaking the staff of bread in Jerusalem, and they have eaten bread by weight and with fear; and water by measure and with astonishment, they drink; **17** so that they lack bread and water, and have been astonished with one another, and been consumed in their iniquity."

5 "And you, son of man, take a sharp weapon for yourself, take the barber's razor for yourself, and you have caused [it] to pass over your head, and over your beard, and you have taken weighing scales for yourself, and apportioned them. **2** You burn a third part with fire in the midst of the city, at the fullness of the days of the siege; and you have taken the third part, you strike with a weapon around it; and the third part you scatter to the wind, and I draw out a weapon after them. **3** And you have taken there a few in number—and have bound them in your skirts; **4** and you take of them again, and have cast them into the midst of the fire, and have burned them in the fire—out of it comes forth a fire to all the house of Israel." **5** Thus said Lord YHWH: "This [is] Jerusalem, ‖ I have set her in the midst of the nations, ‖ And the lands [are] around her. **6** And she changes My judgments into wickedness more than the nations, ‖ And My statutes more than the lands that [are] around her, ‖ For they have kicked against My judgments, ‖ And My statutes—they have not walked in them." **7** Therefore, thus said Lord YHWH: "Because of your multiplying above the nations that [are] around you, ‖ You have not walked in My statutes, ‖ And you have not done My judgments, ‖ According to the judgments of the nations that [are] around you, you have not done." **8** Therefore, thus said Lord YHWH: "Behold, I [am] against you, even I, ‖ And I have done judgments in your midst, ‖ Before the eyes of the nations. **9** And I have done in you that which I have not done, ‖ And the like of which I do not do again, ‖ Because of all your abominations. **10** Therefore fathers eat sons in your midst, ‖ And sons eat their fathers, ‖ And I have done judgments in you, ‖ And have scattered all your remnant to every wind. **11** Therefore, [as] I live," a declaration of Lord YHWH, ‖ "Because you have defiled My sanctuary ‖ With all your detestable things, ‖ And with all your abominations, ‖ Therefore I also diminish you, ‖ And My eye does not pity, and I do not spare. **12** Your third part dies by pestilence, ‖ And are consumed by famine in your midst, ‖ And the third part fall by sword around you, ‖ And the third part I scatter to every wind, ‖ And I draw out a sword after them. **13** And My anger has been completed, ‖ And I have caused My fury to rest on them, ‖ And I have been comforted, ‖ And they have known that I, YHWH, have spoken in My zeal, ‖ In My completing My fury on them. **14** And I give you for a ruin, ‖ And for a reproach among nations that [are] around you, ‖ Before the eyes of everyone passing by. **15** And it has been a reproach and a reviling, ‖ An instruction and an astonishment, ‖ To nations that [are] around you, ‖ In My doing judgments in you, ‖ In anger and fury, and in furious reproofs, ‖ I, YHWH, have spoken. **16** In My sending the evil arrows of famine among them, ‖ That have been for destruction, ‖ That I send to destroy you, ‖ And I am adding famine on you, ‖ And I have broken your staff of bread. **17** And I have sent famine and evil beasts on you, ‖ And they have bereaved you, ‖ And pestilence and blood pass over on you, ‖ And I bring a sword in against you, ‖ I, YHWH, have spoken!"

6 And there is a word of YHWH to me, saying, **2** "Son of man, set your face toward mountains of Israel, and prophesy concerning them: **3** And you have said, Mountains of Israel, ‖ Hear a word of Lord YHWH! Thus said Lord YHWH, ‖ To the mountains, and to the hills, ‖ To the streams, and to the valleys: Behold, I am bringing in a sword against you, ‖ And I have destroyed your high places. **4** And your altars have been desolated, ‖ And your images have been broken, ‖ And I have caused your wounded to fall before your idols, **5** And I have put the carcasses of the sons of Israel before their idols, ‖ And I have scattered your bones around your altars. **6** In all your dwellings the cities are laid waste, ‖ And the high places are desolate, ‖ So that your altars are dry and desolate, ‖ Your idols have broken and ceased, ‖ And your images have been cut down, ‖ And your works have been blotted out. **7** And the wounded has fallen in your midst, ‖ And you have known that I [am] YHWH. **8** And I have caused [some] to remain, ‖ In their being for you the escaped of the sword among nations, ‖ In your being scattered through lands. **9** And your escaped have remembered Me among nations, ‖ To where they have been taken captive, ‖ Because I have been broken with their heart that is going whoring, ‖ That has turned aside from off Me, ‖ And with their eyes they are going whoring after their idols, ‖ And they have been loathsome in their own faces, ‖ For the evils that they have done—all their abominations. **10** And they have known that I [am] YHWH, ‖ I have not spoken to do this evil to them for nothing. **11** Thus said Lord YHWH: Strike with your palm, and stamp with your foot, ‖ And say: Aah! For all the evil abominations of the house of Israel, ‖ Which falls by sword, by famine, and by pestilence. **12** The far-off dies by pestilence, ‖ And the near falls by sword, ‖ And the left and the besieged dies by famine, ‖ And I have completed My fury on them. **13** And you have known that I [am] YHWH, ‖ In their wounded being in the midst of their idols, ‖ Around their altars, ‖ On every high hill, on all tops of mountains, ‖ And under every green tree, and under every thick oak, ‖ The place where they gave refreshing fragrance to all their idols. **14** And I have stretched out My hand against them, ‖ And have made the land a desolation, ‖ Even a desolation from the wilderness to Diblath, ‖ In all their dwellings, ‖ And they have known that I [am] YHWH!"

7 And there is a word of YHWH to me, saying, "And you, son of man, ‖ Thus said Lord YHWH to the ground of Israel: **2** An end, the end has come on the four corners of the land. **3** Now [is] the end for you, ‖ And I have sent My anger on you, ‖ And judged you according to your ways, ‖ And set all your abominations against you. **4** And My eye has no pity on you, nor do I spare, ‖ For I set your ways against you, ‖ And your abominations are in your midst, ‖ And you have known that I [am] YHWH. **5** Thus said Lord YHWH: Calamity, a single calamity, behold, it has come. **6** An end has come, the end has come, ‖ It has awoken for you, behold, it has come. **7** The circlet has come to you, O inhabitant of the land! The time has come, a day of trouble [is] near, ‖ And not the shouting of mountains. **8** Now shortly I pour out My fury on you, ‖ And have completed My anger against you, ‖ And judged you according to your ways, ‖ And set all your abominations against you. **9** And My eye does not pity, nor do I spare, ‖ I give to you according to your ways, ‖ And your abominations are in your midst, ‖ And you have known that [it is] I, YHWH, striking. **10** Behold, the day, behold, it has come, ‖ The circlet has gone forth, ‖ The rod has blossomed, the pride has flourished. **11** The violence has risen to a rod of wickedness, ‖ There is none of them, nor of their multitude, ‖ Nor of their noise, nor is there wailing for them. **12** The time has come, the day has arrived, ‖ The buyer does not rejoice, ‖ And the seller does not become a mourner, ‖ For wrath [is] to all its multitude. **13** For the seller does not turn to the sold thing, ‖ And yet their life [is] among the living, ‖ For the vision [is] to all its multitude, ‖ It does not turn back, ‖ And none strengthens his life by his iniquity. **14** They have blown with a horn to prepare the whole, ‖ And none is going to battle, ‖ For My wrath [is] to all its multitude. **15** The sword [is] outside, ‖ And the pestilence and the famine within, ‖ He who is in a field dies by sword, ‖ And he who is in a city—Famine and pestilence devour him. **16** And their fugitives have escaped away, ‖ And they have been on the mountains ‖ As doves of the valleys, ‖ All of them making a noise—each for his iniquity. **17** All the hands are feeble, and all knees go [as] waters. **18** And they have girded on sackcloth, ‖ And trembling has covered them, ‖ And shame [is] on all faces, ‖ And baldness on all their heads. **19** They cast their silver into out-places, ‖ And their gold becomes impurity. Their silver and gold are not able to deliver them, ‖ In a day of the wrath of YHWH, ‖ They do not satisfy their soul, ‖ And they do not fill their bowels, ‖ For it has been the stumbling-block of their iniquity. **20** As for the beauty of his ornament, ‖ He set it for excellence, ‖ And the images of their abominations, ‖ Their detestable things—they made in it, ‖ Therefore I have given it to them for impurity, **21** And I have given it into the hand of the strangers for a prey, ‖ And to the wicked of the land for a spoil, ‖ And they have defiled it. **22** And I have turned My face from them, ‖ And they have defiled My hidden place, ‖ Indeed, destroyers have come into it, and defiled it. **23** Make the chain; for the land ‖ Has been full of bloody judgments, ‖ And the city has been full of violence. **24** And I have brought in the wicked of the nations, ‖ And they have possessed their houses, ‖ And I have caused the excellence of the strong to cease, ‖ And those sanctifying them have been defiled. **25** Destruction has come, ‖ And they have sought peace, and there is none. **26** Disaster comes on disaster, and report is on report, ‖ And they have sought a vision from a prophet, ‖ And law perishes from [the] priest, ‖ And counsel from [the] elderly, **27** The king becomes a mourner, ‖ And a prince puts on desolation, ‖ And the hands of the people of the land are troubled, ‖ I deal with them from their own way, ‖ And I judge them with their own judgments, ‖ And they have known that I [am] YHWH!"

8 And it comes to pass, in the sixth year, in the sixth [month], on the fifth of the month, I am sitting in my house, and [the] elderly of Judah are sitting before me, and there a hand of Lord YHWH falls on me, **2** and I look, and behold, a likeness as the appearance of fire, from the appearance of His loins and downward—fire, and from His loins and upward, as the appearance of brightness, as the color of electrum. **3** And He puts forth a form of a hand, and takes me by a lock of my head, and [the] Spirit lifts me up between the earth and the heavens, and brings me to Jerusalem in visions of God, to the opening of the inner gate that is facing the north, where the seat of the figure of jealousy [is] that is making jealous, **4** and behold, there the glory of the God of Israel [is] as the appearance that I

EZEKIEL

saw in the valley. **5** And He says to me, "Son of man, now lift up your eyes [toward] the way of the north." And I lift up my eyes [toward] the way of the north, and behold, on the north of the gate of the altar [is] this figure of jealousy, at the entrance. **6** And He says to me, "Son of man, are you seeing what they are doing? The great abominations that the house of Israel is doing here, to keep far off from My sanctuary; and turn again, [and] see great abominations." **7** And He brings me to an opening of the court, and I look, and behold, a hole in the wall; **8** and He says to me, "Son of man, now dig through the wall"; and I dig through the wall, and behold, an opening. **9** And He says to me, "Go in, and see the evil abominations that they are doing here." **10** And I go in, and look, and behold, every form of creeping thing, and detestable beast—and all the idols of the house of Israel—carved on the wall, all around, **11** and seventy men from [the] elderly of the house of Israel—and Jaazaniah son of Shaphan standing in their midst—are standing before them, and each [with] his censer in his hand, and [the] abundance of [the] cloud of the incense is going up. **12** And He says to me, "Have you seen, son of man, that which elderly of the house of Israel are doing in the darkness, each in [the] inner chambers of his imagery, for they are saying, YHWH is not seeing us, YHWH has forsaken the land?" **13** And He says to me, "Turn again, [and] see [the] great abominations that they are doing." **14** And He brings me to the opening of the gate of the house of YHWH that [is] at the north, and behold, there the women are sitting, weeping for Tammuz. **15** And He says to me, "Have you seen, son of man? Turn again, [and] see greater abominations than these." **16** And He brings me into the inner court of the house of YHWH, and behold, at the opening of the temple of YHWH, between the porch and the altar, about twenty-five men, their backs toward the temple of YHWH, and their faces eastward, and they are bowing themselves eastward to the sun. **17** And He says to me, "Have you seen, son of man? Has it been a light thing to the house of Judah to do the abomination that they have done here, that they have filled the land with violence, and turn back to provoke Me to anger? And behold, they are putting forth the branch to their nose! **18** And I also deal in fury, My eye does not pity, nor do I spare, and they have cried [with] a loud voice in My ears and I do not hear them."

9 And He cries [with] a loud voice in my ears, saying, "Inspectors of the city have drawn near, and each [with] his destroying weapon in his hand." **2** And behold, six men are coming from the way of the upper gate, that is facing the north, and each [with] his slaughter-weapon in his hand, and one man in their midst is clothed with linen, and a scribe's inkhorn at his loins, and they come in, and stand near the bronze altar. **3** And the glory of the God of Israel has gone up from off the cherub, on which it has been, to the threshold of the house. **4** And He calls to the man who is clothed with linen, who has the scribe's inkhorn at his loins, and YHWH says to him, "Pass on into the midst of the city, into the midst of Jerusalem, and you have made a mark on the foreheads of the men who are sighing and who are groaning for all the abominations that are done in its midst." **5** And to the others he said in my ears, "Pass on into the city after him, and strike; your eye does not pity, nor do you spare; **6** aged, young man, and virgin, and infant, and women, you slay—to destruction; and against any man on whom [is] the mark you do not go near, and you begin from My sanctuary." **7** And they begin among the aged men who [are] before the house, and He says to them, "Defile the house, and fill the courts with the wounded, go forth." And they have gone forth and have struck in the city. **8** And it comes to pass, as they are striking, and I am left—that I fall on my face, and cry, and say, "Aah! Lord YHWH, are You destroying all the remnant of Israel, in Your pouring out Your wrath on Jerusalem?" **9** And He says to me, "The iniquity of the house of Israel and Judah [is] very, very great, and the land is full of blood, and the city has been full of perverseness, for they have said: YHWH has forsaken the land, and YHWH is not seeing. **10** And I also, My eye does not pity, nor do I spare; I have put their way on their own head." **11** And behold, the man clothed with linen, at whose loins [is] the inkhorn, is bringing back word, saying, "I have done as You have commanded me."

10 And I look, and behold, on the expanse that [is] above the head of

EZEKIEL

the cherubim, as a sapphire stone, as the appearance of the likeness of a throne, He has been seen over them. **2** And He speaks to the man clothed with linen and says, "Go into the midst of the wheel, to the place of the cherub, and fill your hands with coals of fire from between the cherubim, and scatter over the city." And he goes in before my eyes. **3** And the cherubim are standing on the right side of the house, at the going in of the man, and the cloud has filled the inner court, **4** and the glory of YHWH becomes high above the cherub, over the threshold of the house, and the house is filled with the cloud, and the court has been filled with the brightness of the glory of YHWH. **5** And a noise of the wings of the cherubim has been heard in the outer court, as the voice of God—the Mighty One—in His speaking. **6** And it comes to pass, in His commanding the man clothed with linen, saying, "Take fire from between the wheel, from between the cherubim," and he goes in and stands near the wheel, **7** that the [one] cherub puts forth his hand from between the cherubim to the fire that [is] between the cherubim, and lifts up, and gives [it] into the hands of him who is clothed with linen, and he receives, and comes forth. **8** And there appears in the cherubim the form of a hand of man under their wings, **9** and I look, and behold, four wheels near the cherubim, one wheel near one cherub, and another wheel near the other cherub, and the appearance of the wheels [is] as the color of a beryl stone. **10** And [as for] their appearances, [the] four had one likeness, as it were the wheel in the midst of the wheel. **11** In their going, they go on their four sides; they do not turn around in their going, for to the place to where the head turns, they go after it, they do not turn around in their going. **12** And all their flesh, and their backs, and their hands, and their wings, and the wheels, are full of eyes all around—[the] wheels [the] four had. **13** As for the wheels—they were called "Whirling Wheel" in my ears. **14** And four faces [are] to each; the face of the first [is] the face of the cherub, and the face of the second [is] the face of man, and of the third the face of a lion, and of the fourth the face of an eagle. **15** And the cherubim are lifted up, it [is] the living creature that I saw by the river Chebar. **16** And in the going of the cherubim, the wheels go beside them; and in the cherubim lifting up their wings to be high above the earth, the wheels do not turn around, even they, from being beside them. **17** In their standing they stand, and in their exaltation they are exalted with them: for [the] spirit of the living creature [is] in them. **18** And the glory of YHWH goes forth from off the threshold of the house, and stands over the cherubim, **19** and the cherubim lift up their wings, and are lifted up from the earth before my eyes; in their going forth, the wheels [are] also alongside them, and he stands at the opening of the east gate of the house of YHWH, and the glory of the God of Israel [is] over them from above. **20** It [is] the living creature that I saw under the God of Israel by the river Chebar, and I know that they are cherubim. **21** [The] four—each had four faces, and each had four wings, and the likeness of the hands of man [is] under their wings. **22** And the likeness of their faces, they [are] the faces that I saw by the river Chebar, their appearances and themselves; they each go straight forward.

11 And [the] Spirit lifts me up, and it brings me to the east gate of the house of YHWH, that is facing the east, and behold, at the opening of the gate [are] twenty-five men, and I see in their midst Jaazaniah son of Azzur, and Pelatiah son of Benaiah, heads of the people. **2** And He says to me, "Son of man, these [are] the men who are devising iniquity, and who are giving evil counsel in this city; **3** who are saying, It [is] not near—to build houses, it [is] the pot, and we [are] the flesh. **4** Therefore prophesy concerning them, prophesy, son of man." **5** And [the] Spirit of YHWH falls on me, and He says to me, "Say, Thus said YHWH: You have said correctly, O house of Israel, ‖ And I have known the steps of your spirit. **6** You multiplied your wounded in this city, ‖ And filled its out-places with the wounded. **7** Therefore, thus said Lord YHWH: Your wounded whom you placed in its midst, ‖ They [are] the flesh, and it [is] the pot, ‖ And He has brought you out from its midst. **8** You have feared a sword, ‖ And I bring in a sword against you, ‖ A declaration of Lord YHWH. **9** And I have brought you out of its midst, ‖ And given you into the hand of strangers, ‖ And I have done judgments among you. **10** You fall by the sword, ‖ I judge you on the border of Israel, ‖ And you

EZEKIEL

have known that I [am] YHWH. **11** It is not for a pot for you, ‖ Nor are you for flesh in its midst, ‖ I judge you at the border of Israel. **12** And you have known that I [am] YHWH, ‖ For you have not walked in My statutes, ‖ And you have not done My judgments, ‖ And according to the judgments of the nations ‖ Who are around you, you have done!" **13** And it comes to pass, at my prophesying, that Pelatiah son of Benaiah is dying, and I fall on my face, and cry—a loud voice—and say, "Aah! Lord YHWH, You are making an end of the remnant of Israel." **14** And there is a word of YHWH to me, saying, **15** "Son of man, your brothers, your brothers, men of your family, and all the house of Israel—all of it—[are] they to whom inhabitants of Jerusalem have said, Keep far off from YHWH; **16** it [is] ours, the land has been given for an inheritance; therefore say, Thus said Lord YHWH: Because I put them far off among nations, ‖ And because I scattered them through lands, I am also for a little sanctuary to them, ‖ In lands to where they have gone in. **17** Therefore say, Thus said Lord YHWH: And I have assembled you from the peoples, ‖ And I have gathered you from the lands, ‖ Into which you have been scattered, ‖ And I have given the ground of Israel to you. **18** And they have gone in there, ‖ And turned aside all its detestable things, ‖ And all its abominations—out of it. **19** And I have given one heart to them, ‖ And I give a new spirit in your midst, ‖ And I have turned the heart of stone out of their flesh, ‖ And I have given a heart of flesh to them. **20** So that they walk in My statutes, ‖ And keep My judgments, and have done them, ‖ And they have been to Me for a people, ‖ And I am to them for God. **21** As for those whose heart is going to the heart ‖ Of their detestable things and their abominations, ‖ I have put their way on their head, ‖ A declaration of Lord YHWH." **22** And the cherubim lift up their wings, and the wheels [are] alongside them, and the glory of the God of Israel [is] over them above. **23** And the glory of YHWH goes up from off the midst of the city, and stands on the mountain, that [is] on the east of the city. **24** And [the] Spirit has lifted me up, and brings me to Chaldea, to the expulsion, in a vision, by [the] Spirit of God, and the vision that I have seen goes up from off me; **25** and I speak to the expulsion all the matters of YHWH that He has showed me.

12 And there is a word of YHWH to me, saying, **2** "Son of man, you are dwelling in the midst of the house of rebellion, that have eyes to see, and they have not seen; they have ears to hear, and they have not heard; for they [are] a house of rebellion. **3** And you, son of man, make your vessels of removal, and remove by day before their eyes, and you have removed from your place to another place before their eyes, it may be they consider, for they [are] a house of rebellion. **4** And you have brought forth your vessels as vessels of removal by day before their eyes, and you go forth in the evening before their eyes, as the goings forth of a removal. **5** You dig through the wall before their eyes, and you have brought forth by it. **6** Carry on the shoulder before their eyes, bring forth in the darkness, cover your face, and you do not see the earth, for I have given you [as] a sign to the house of Israel." **7** And I do so, as I have been commanded; I have brought forth my vessels as vessels of removal by day, and I have dug through the wall with my hand in the evening; I have brought forth in the darkness, I have carried away on the shoulder, before their eyes. **8** And there is a word of YHWH to me, in the morning, saying, **9** "Son of man, have they not said to you—the house of Israel—the house of rebellion—What are you doing? **10** Say to them, Thus said Lord YHWH: This burden [concerns] the prince in Jerusalem, and all the house of Israel who are in their midst. **11** Say: I [am] your sign; as I have done so it is done to them, into a removal, into a captivity, they go. **12** As for the prince who [is] in their midst, he carries on the shoulder in the darkness, and he goes forth; they dig through the wall to bring forth by it; he covers his face that he may not look on the very surface of the land. **13** And I have spread My net for him, and he has been caught in My snare, and I have brought him to Babylon, the land of the Chaldeans, and he does not see it—and he dies there. **14** And all who are around him to help him, and all his bands, I scatter to every wind, and I draw out a sword after them. **15** And they have known that I [am] YHWH, in My scattering them among nations, and I have spread them through lands; **16** and I have left of them, a few in number, from the sword, from the famine, and from the pestilence, so that they recount all their abominations among the nations to where they have come, and they have known that I [am] YHWH." **17** And there is a word of YHWH to me, saying, **18** "Son of man, eat your bread in haste, and drink your water with trembling and with fear; **19** and you have said to the people of the land, Thus said Lord YHWH concerning the inhabitants of Jerusalem, concerning the land of Israel: They eat their bread with fear, and drink their water with astonishment, because its land is desolate, because of its fullness, because of the violence of all who are dwelling in it. **20** And the cities that are inhabited are laid waste, and the land is a desolation, and you have known that I [am] YHWH." **21** And there is a word of YHWH to me, saying, **22** "Son of man, what [is] this allegory to you, concerning the land of Israel, saying, The days are prolonged, and every vision has perished? **23** Therefore say to them, Thus said Lord YHWH: I have caused this allegory to cease, ‖ And they do not use it as an allegory in Israel again, ‖ But speak to them: The days have drawn near, ‖ And every vision has spoken. **24** For there is no longer any vain vision, and flattering divination, ‖ In the midst of the house of Israel. **25** For I, YHWH, speak, ‖ The word that I speak—it is done, ‖ It is not prolonged anymore, ‖ For in your days, O house of rebellion, I speak a word, and I have done it, ‖ A declaration of Lord YHWH." **26** And there is a word of YHWH to me, saying, **27** "Son of man, behold, the house of Israel is saying, The vision that he is seeing [is not] for many days, and he is prophesying of far-off times, **28** therefore say to them, Thus said Lord YHWH: None of My words are prolonged anymore, ‖ When I speak a word—it is done, ‖ A declaration of Lord YHWH!"

13 And there is a word of YHWH to me, saying, **2** "Son of man, prophesy concerning the prophets of Israel who are prophesying, and you have said to those prophesying from their own heart, Hear a word of YHWH! **3** Thus said Lord YHWH: Woe to the prophets who are foolish, ‖ Who are going after their own spirit, ‖ And they have seen nothing. **4** Your prophets have been ‖ As foxes in the wasteland, O Israel. **5** You have not gone up into breaches, ‖ Nor do you make a wall for the house of Israel, ‖ To stand in battle in a day of YHWH. **6** They have seen vanity, and lying divination, ‖ Who are saying: A declaration of YHWH, ‖ And YHWH has not sent them, ‖ And they have hoped to establish a word. **7** Have you not seen a vain vision, ‖ And spoken a lying divination, ‖ When you say, A declaration of YHWH, ‖ And I have not spoken? **8** Therefore, thus said Lord YHWH: Because you have spoken vanity, and seen a lie, ‖ Therefore, behold, I [am] against you, ‖ A declaration of Lord YHWH. **9** And My hand has been on the prophets, ‖ Who are seeing vanity, and who are divining a lie, ‖ They are not in the assembly of My people, ‖ And they are not written in the writing of the house of Israel, ‖ And they do not come to the ground of Israel, ‖ And you have known that I [am] Lord YHWH. **10** Because, even because, they caused My people to err, ‖ Saying, Peace! And there is no peace, ‖ And that one is building a wall, ‖ And behold, they are coating it with chalk. **11** Say to those coating with chalk—It falls, ‖ There has been an overflowing shower, ‖ And you, O hailstones, fall, ‖ And a turbulent wind breaks out, **12** And behold, the wall has fallen! Does one not say to you, Where [is] the coating that you coated? **13** Therefore, thus said Lord YHWH: I have broken with a turbulent wind in My fury, ‖ And an overflowing shower is in My anger, ‖ And hailstones in My fury—to consume. **14** And I have broken down the wall that you coated with chalk, ‖ And have caused it to come to the earth, ‖ And its foundation has been revealed, ‖ And it has fallen, ‖ And you have been consumed in its midst, ‖ And you have known that I [am] YHWH. **15** And I have completed My wrath on the wall, ‖ And on those coating it with chalk, ‖ And I say to you: The wall is not, ‖ And those coating it are not, **16** [These]—the prophets of Israel, who are prophesying concerning Jerusalem, ‖ And who are seeing a vision of peace for her, ‖ And there is no peace, ‖ A declaration of Lord YHWH. **17** And you, son of man, set your face against the daughters of your people, who are prophesying out of their own heart, and prophesy concerning them, **18** And you have said, Thus said Lord YHWH: Woe to those sowing [magic] bands for all joints of the arm, ‖ And to those making the veils ‖ For the head of every stature—to hunt

EZEKIEL

souls, ‖ Do you hunt the souls of My people? And do your souls that live remain alive? **19** Indeed, you pierce Me concerning My people, ‖ For handfuls of barley, ‖ And for pieces of bread, ‖ To put to death souls that should not die, ‖ And to keep alive souls that should not live, ‖ By your lying to My people—listening to lies. **20** Therefore, thus said Lord YHWH: Behold, I [am] against your [magic] bands, ‖ With which you are hunting there the souls of the flourishing, ‖ And I have torn them from off your arms, ‖ And have sent away the souls that you are hunting, ‖ The souls of the flourishing. **21** And I have torn your veils, ‖ And delivered My people out of your hand, ‖ And they are no longer for a prey in your hand, ‖ And you have known that I [am] YHWH. **22** Because of paining the heart of the righteous with falsehood, ‖ And I have not pained it, ‖ And strengthening the hands of the wicked, ‖ So as not to turn [him] back from his evil way, ‖ To keep him alive, **23** Therefore, you do not see vanity, ‖ And you do not divine divination again, ‖ And I have delivered My people out of your hand, ‖ And you have known that I [am] YHWH!"

14 And men from [the] elderly of Israel come to me, and sit before me. **2** And there is a word of YHWH to me, saying, **3** "Son of man, these men have caused their idols to go up on their heart, and they have put the stumbling-block of their iniquity before their faces; am I inquired of at all by them? **4** Therefore, speak with them, and you have said to them, Thus said Lord YHWH: Everyone of the house of Israel who causes his idols to go up to his heart, and sets the stumbling-block of his iniquity before his face, and has gone to the prophet—I, YHWH, have given an answer to him for this, for the abundance of his idols, **5** in order to catch the house of Israel by their heart, in that they have become estranged from off Me by their idols—all of them. **6** Therefore say to the house of Israel, Thus said Lord YHWH: Turn back, indeed, turn back from your idols, and turn back your faces from all your abominations, **7** for everyone of the house of Israel, and of the sojourners who sojourn in Israel, who is separated from after Me, and causes his idols to go up to his heart, and sets the stumbling-block of his iniquity before his face, and has come to the prophet to inquire of him concerning Me, I, YHWH, have answered him for Myself; **8** and I have set My face against that man, and made him for a sign, and for allegories, and I have cut him off from the midst of My people, and you have known that I [am] YHWH. **9** And the prophet, when he is enticed, and has spoken a word—I, YHWH, have enticed that prophet, and have stretched out My hand against him, and have destroyed him from the midst of My people Israel. **10** And they have borne their iniquity: as the iniquity of the inquirer, so is the iniquity of the prophet; **11** so that the house of Israel does not wander from after Me anymore, nor are they defiled with all their transgressions anymore, and they have been to Me for a people, and I am to them for God—a declaration of Lord YHWH." **12** And there is a word of YHWH to me, saying, **13** "Son of man, when the land sins against Me to commit a trespass, and I have stretched out My hand against it, and broken the staff of bread for it, and sent famine into it, and cut off man and beast from it— **14** and [despite] these three men [that] have been in its midst: Noah, Daniel, and Job—they [only] deliver their own soul by their righteousness," a declaration of Lord YHWH. **15** "If I cause an evil beast to pass through the land, and it has bereaved, and it has been a desolation, without any passing through because of the beast— **16** [despite] these three men in its midst— [as] I live," a declaration of Lord YHWH, "they deliver neither sons nor daughters; they alone are delivered, and the land is a desolation. **17** Or [if] I bring a sword in against that land, and I have said: Sword, pass over through the land, and I have cut off man and beast from it— **18** and [despite] these three men in its midst—[as] I live," a declaration of Lord YHWH, "they do not deliver sons and daughters, for they alone are delivered. **19** Or [if] I send pestilence to that land, and I have poured out My fury against it in blood, to cut off man and beast from it— **20** and [despite] Noah, Daniel, and Job, in its midst—[as] I live," a declaration of Lord YHWH, "they deliver neither son nor daughter; they, by their righteousness, [only] deliver their own soul." **21** For thus said Lord YHWH: "Although My four severe judgments— sword, and famine, and wild beast, and pestilence—I have sent to Jerusalem, to cut off man and beast from it, **22** yet, behold,

EZEKIEL

there has been left an escape in it, who are brought forth, sons and daughters, behold, they are coming forth to you, and you have seen their way, and their doings, and have been comforted concerning the calamity that I have brought in against Jerusalem, all that which I have brought in against it. **23** And they have comforted you, for you see their way and their doings, and you have known that I have not done all that which I have done in her for nothing," a declaration of Lord YHWH.

15 And there is a word of YHWH to me, saying, **2** "Son of man, ‖ What is the vine-tree more than any tree? The vine-branch that has been, ‖ Among trees of the forest? **3** Is wood taken from it to use for work? Do they take a pin of it to hang any vessel on it? **4** Behold, it has been given to the fire for fuel, ‖ The fire has eaten its two ends, ‖ And its midst has been scorched! Is it profitable for work? **5** Behold, in its being perfect it is not used for work, ‖ How much less when fire has eaten of it, ‖ And it is scorched, ‖ Has it been used yet for work?" **6** Therefore, thus said Lord YHWH: "As the vine-tree among trees of the forest, ‖ That I have given to the fire for fuel, ‖ So I have given the inhabitants of Jerusalem. **7** And I have set My face against them, ‖ They have gone forth from the fire, ‖ And the fire consumes them, ‖ And you have known that I [am] YHWH, ‖ In My setting My face against them. **8** And I have made the land a desolation, ‖ Because they have committed a trespass," ‖ A declaration of Lord YHWH!

16 And there is a word of YHWH to me, saying, **2** "Son of man, cause Jerusalem to know her abominations, and you have said, **3** Thus said Lord YHWH to Jerusalem: Your birth and your nativity ‖ [Are] of the land of the Canaanite, ‖ Your father the Amorite, and your mother a Hittite. **4** As for your nativity, in the day you were born, ‖ Your navel has not been cut, ‖ And you were not washed in water for ease, ‖ And you have not been salted at all, ‖ And you have not been swaddled at all. **5** No eye has had pity on you, to do any of these to you, ‖ To have compassion on you, ‖ And you are cast on the face of the field, ‖ With loathing of your soul ‖ In the day you were born! **6** And I pass over by you, ‖ And I see you trodden down in your blood, ‖ And I say to you in your blood, Live! Indeed, I say to you in your blood, Live! **7** I have made you a myriad as the shoot of the field, ‖ And you are multiplied, and are great, ‖ And come in with an excellent adornment, ‖ Breasts have been formed, and your hair has grown—And you, naked and bare! **8** And I pass over by you, and I see you, ‖ And behold, your time [is] a time of loves, ‖ And I spread My skirt over you, ‖ And I cover your nakedness, ‖ And I swear to you, and come into a covenant with you, ‖ A declaration of Lord YHWH, ‖ And you become Mine. **9** And I wash you with water, ‖ And I wash away your blood from off you, ‖ And I anoint you with oil. **10** And I clothe you with embroidery, ‖ And I shoe you with tachash [skin], ‖ And I gird you with fine linen, ‖ And I cover you with figured silk. **11** And I adorn you with adornments, ‖ And I give bracelets for your hands, ‖ And a chain for your neck. **12** And I give a ring for your nose, ‖ And rings for your ears, ‖ And a crown of beauty on your head. **13** And you put on gold and silver, ‖ And your clothing [is] fine linen, ‖ And figured silk and embroidery, ‖ You have eaten fine flour, and honey, and oil, ‖ And you are very, very beautiful, ‖ And go prosperously to the kingdom. **14** And your name goes forth among nations, ‖ Because of your beauty—for it [is] complete, ‖ In My honor that I have set on you, ‖ A declaration of Lord YHWH. **15** And you trust in your beauty, ‖ And go whoring because of your renown, ‖ And pour out your whoredoms on everyone passing by—to him [that would have] it. **16** And you take from your garments, ‖ And make spotted high-places for yourself, ‖ And go whoring on them, ‖ They are not coming in—nor will it be! **17** And you take your beautiful vessels ‖ Of My gold and My silver that I gave to you, ‖ And make images of a male for yourself, ‖ And go whoring with them, **18** And you take the garments of your embroidery, ‖ And cover them, ‖ And you have set My oil and My incense before them. **19** And My bread, that I gave to you, ‖ Fine flour, and oil, and honey, that I caused you to eat. You have even set it before them, ‖ For a refreshing fragrance—thus it is, ‖ A declaration of Lord YHWH. **20** And you take your sons and your daughters whom you have born to Me, ‖ And sacrifice them to them for food. Is it a little thing because of your whoredoms, **21** that you slaughter My sons, ‖ And give them up in causing them to pass over to them? **22** And with all your abominations and your whoredoms, ‖ You have not remembered the days of your youth, ‖ When you were naked and bare, ‖ You were trodden down in your blood! **23** And it comes to pass, after all your wickedness ‖ (Woe, woe, to you—a declaration of Lord YHWH), **24** That you build an arch for yourself, ‖ And make a high place for yourself in every broad place. **25** At every head of the way you have built your high place, ‖ And you make your beauty abominable, ‖ And open wide your feet to everyone passing by, ‖ And multiply your whoredoms, **26** And go whoring to sons of Egypt, ‖ Your neighbors—great of appetite! And you multiply your whoredoms, ‖ To provoke Me to anger. **27** And behold, I have stretched out My hand against you, ‖ And I diminish your portion, ‖ And give you to the desire of those hating you, ‖ The daughters of the Philistines, ‖ Who are ashamed of your wicked way. **28** And you go whoring to sons of Asshur, ‖ Without your being satisfied, ‖ And you go whoring with them, ‖ And also—you have not been satisfied. **29** And you multiply your whoredoms ‖ On the land of Canaan—toward Chaldea, ‖ And even with this you have not been satisfied. **30** How weak [is] your heart, ‖ A declaration of Lord YHWH, ‖ In your doing all these, ‖ The work of a domineering, whorish woman. **31** In your building your arch at the head of every way, ‖ You have made your high place in every broad place, ‖ And have not been as a whore deriding a wage. **32** The wife who commits adultery—Under her husband—receives strangers. **33** They give a gift to all whores, ‖ And you have given your gifts to all your lovers, ‖ And bribe them to come in to you, ‖ From all around—in your whoredoms. **34** And you are opposite from [other] women in your whoredoms, ‖ That none go whoring after you; And in your giving a wage, ‖ And a wage has not been given to you; Therefore you are the opposite. **35** Therefore, O whore, hear a word of YHWH! **36** Thus said Lord YHWH: Because of your bronze being poured forth, ‖ And your nakedness is revealed in your whoredoms near your lovers, ‖ And near all the idols of your abominations, ‖ And according to the blood of your sons, ‖ Whom you have given to them; **37** Therefore, behold, I am assembling all your lovers, ‖ To whom you have been sweet, ‖ And all whom you have loved, ‖ Besides all whom you have hated; And I have assembled them by you all around, ‖ And have revealed your nakedness to them, ‖ And they have seen all your nakedness. **38** And I have judged you—judgments of adulteresses, ‖ And of women shedding blood, ‖ And have given you blood, fury, and jealousy. **39** And I have given you into their hand, ‖ And they have thrown down your arch, ‖ And they have broken down your high places, ‖ And they have stripped you of your garments, ‖ And they have taken your beautiful vessels, ‖ And they have left you naked and bare. **40** And have caused an assembly to come up against you, ‖ And stoned you with stones, ‖ And thrust you through with their swords, **41** And burned your houses with fire, ‖ And done judgments in you before the eyes of many women, ‖ And I have caused you to cease from going whoring, ‖ And also, you no longer give a wage. **42** And I have caused My fury against you to rest, ‖ And My jealousy has turned aside from you, ‖ And I have been quiet, and I am not angry anymore. **43** Because you have not remembered the days of your youth, ‖ And give trouble to Me in all these, ‖ Therefore I also—behold—I put your way on [your own] head, ‖ A declaration of Lord YHWH, ‖ And you will not have done—have done this wickedness above all your abominations. **44** Behold, everyone using the allegory against you, ‖ Uses [this] allegory concerning [you], saying, ‖ As the mother—her daughter! **45** You [are] your mother's daughter, ‖ Loathing her husband and her sons, ‖ And you [are] your sisters' sister, ‖ Who loathed their husbands and their sons, ‖ Your mother [is] a Hittite, and your father an Amorite. **46** And your older sister [is] Samaria, she and her daughters, ‖ Who is dwelling at your left hand, ‖ And your younger sister, who is dwelling on your right hand, [is] Sodom and her daughters. **47** And you have not walked in their ways, ‖ And done according to their abominations, ‖ It has been loathed as a little thing, ‖ Indeed, you do more corruptly than they in all your ways. **48** [As] I live—a declaration of Lord YHWH, ‖ Your sister Sodom has not done—she and her daughters—As you have done—you and your daughters. **49** Behold, this has been the iniquity of your sister Sodom, ‖

EZEKIEL

Arrogancy, fullness of bread, and quiet ease, ‖ Have been to her and to her daughters, ‖ And the hand of the afflicted and needy ‖ She has not strengthened. **50** And they are haughty and do abomination before Me, ‖ And I turn them aside when I have seen. **51** And Samaria has not sinned even half of your sins, ‖ But you multiply your abominations more than they, ‖ And justify your sisters by all your abominations that you have done. **52** You also—bear your shame, ‖ That you have adjudged for your sisters, ‖ Because of your sins that you have done more abominably than they, ‖ They are more righteous than you, ‖ And you, also, be ashamed and bear your shame, ‖ In your justifying your sisters. **53** And I have turned back [to] their captivity, ‖ The captivity of Sodom and her daughters, ‖ And the captivity of Samaria and her daughters, ‖ And the captivity of your captives in their midst, **54** So that you bear your shame, ‖ And have been ashamed of all that you have done, ‖ In your comforting them. **55** And your sisters, Sodom and her daughters, ‖ Return to their former state, ‖ And Samaria and her daughters return to their former state, ‖ And you and your daughters return to your former state. **56** And your sister Sodom has not been for a report in your mouth, ‖ In the day of your arrogancy, **57** Before your wickedness is revealed, ‖ As [at] the time of the reproach of the daughters of Aram, ‖ And of all her neighbors, the daughters of the Philistines, ‖ Who are despising you all around. **58** Your wicked plans and your abominations, ‖ You have borne them, a declaration of Y<small>HWH</small>. **59** For thus said Lord Y<small>HWH</small>: I have dealt with you as you have done, ‖ In that you have despised an oath—to break covenant. **60** And I have remembered My covenant with you, ‖ In the days of your youth, ‖ And I have established a perpetual covenant for you. **61** And you have remembered your ways, ‖ And you have been ashamed, ‖ In your receiving your sisters—Your older with your younger, ‖ And I have given them to you for daughters, ‖ And not by your covenant. **62** And I have established My covenant with you, ‖ And you have known that I [am] Y<small>HWH</small>. **63** So that you remember, ‖ And you have been ashamed, ‖ And there is not an opening of the mouth to you anymore because of your shame, ‖ In My receiving atonement for you, ‖ For all that you have done, ‖ A declaration of Lord Y<small>HWH</small>!"

17 And there is a word of Y<small>HWH</small> to me, saying, **2** "Son of man, put forth a riddle, and use an allegory to the house of Israel, **3** and you have said, Thus said Lord Y<small>HWH</small>: The great eagle, great-winged, long-pinioned, ‖ Full of feathers, that has diverse colors, ‖ Has come to Lebanon, ‖ And he takes the foliage of the cedar, **4** He has cropped the top of its tender twigs, ‖ And he brings it to the land of Canaan. He has placed it in a city of merchants. **5** And he takes of the seed of the land, ‖ And puts it in a field of seed, ‖ He took [it] by many waters, ‖ He has set it in a conspicuous place. **6** And it springs up, and becomes a spreading vine, humble of stature, ‖ To turn its thin shoots toward itself, ‖ And its roots are under it, ‖ And it becomes a vine, and makes boughs, ‖ And sends forth beautiful branches. **7** And there is another great eagle, ‖ Great-winged, and abounding with feathers, ‖ And behold, this vine has bent its roots toward him, ‖ And it has sent out its thin shoots toward him, ‖ To water it from the furrows of its planting, **8** On a good field, by many waters, it is planted, to make branches, and to bear fruit, to be for a good vine. **9** Say, Thus said Lord Y<small>HWH</small>: It prospers—does he not draw out its roots, ‖ And cut off its fruit, and it is withered? [In] all the leaves of its springing it withers, ‖ And not by great strength, or by numerous people, ‖ To lift it up by its roots. **10** And behold, the planted thing—does it prosper? When the east wind comes against it, does it not utterly wither? On the furrows of its springing it withers." **11** And there is a word of Y<small>HWH</small> to me, saying, **12** "Now say to the house of rebellion, ‖ Have you not known what these [are]? Say, Behold, the king of Babylon has come to Jerusalem, ‖ And he takes its king, and its princes, ‖ And brings them to himself to Babylon. **13** And he takes of the seed of the kingdom, ‖ And makes a covenant with him, ‖ And brings him into an oath, ‖ And he has taken the mighty of the land, **14** That the kingdom may be humble, ‖ That it may not lift itself up, ‖ To keep his covenant—that it may stand. **15** And he rebels against him, ‖ To send his messengers to Egypt, ‖ To give to him horses, and many people, ‖ Does he prosper? Does he who is doing these things escape? And has he broken covenant and

EZEKIEL

escaped? **16** [As] I live—a declaration of Lord YHWH, ‖ Does he not—in the place of the king who is causing him to reign, ‖ Whose oath he has despised, ‖ And whose covenant he has broken—die with him in the midst of Babylon? **17** And not with a great force, and with a numerous assembly, ‖ Does Pharaoh maintain him in battle, ‖ By pouring out a mound, and in building a fortification, ‖ To cut off many souls. **18** And he despised the oath—to break covenant, ‖ And behold, he has given his hand, ‖ And all these he has done—he does not escape. **19** Therefore, thus said Lord YHWH: [As] I live—My oath that he has despised, ‖ And My covenant that he has broken, ‖ Have I not put it on his head? **20** And I have spread out My snare for him, ‖ And he has been caught in My net, ‖ And I have brought him to Babylon, ‖ And judged him there [for the] trespass ‖ That he has trespassed against Me. **21** And all his fugitives, with all his bands, ‖ Fall by sword, and those remaining, ‖ They are spread out to every wind, ‖ And you have known that I, YHWH, have spoken. **22** Thus said Lord YHWH: I have taken of the foliage of the high cedar, ‖ And I have set [it], ‖ I crop a tender one from the top of its tender shoots, ‖ And I have planted [it] on a high and lofty mountain. **23** In a mountain—the high place of Israel, I plant it, ‖ And it has borne boughs, and yielded fruit, ‖ And become a good cedar, ‖ And every bird of every [kind of] wing has dwelt under it, ‖ They dwell in the shade of its thin shoots. **24** And all trees of the field have known ‖ That I, YHWH, have made the high tree low, ‖ I have set the low tree on high, ‖ I have dried up the moist tree, ‖ And I have caused the dry tree to flourish, ‖ I, YHWH, have spoken, and have done [it]!"

18 And there is a word of YHWH to me, saying, **2** "What [is it] to you [that] you are using this allegory ‖ Concerning the ground of Israel, saying, ‖ Fathers eat unripe fruit, ‖ And the sons' teeth are blunted? **3** [As] I live," a declaration of Lord YHWH, "You no longer have the use of this allegory in Israel. **4** Behold, all the souls are Mine, ‖ As the soul of the father, ‖ So also the soul of the son—they are Mine, ‖ The soul that is sinning—it dies. **5** And a man, when he is righteous, ‖ And has done judgment and righteousness, **6** He has not eaten on the mountains, ‖ And has not lifted up his eyes ‖ To idols of the house of Israel, ‖ And did not defile his neighbor's wife, ‖ And did not come near to a separated woman, **7** He does not oppress a man, ‖ He returns his pledge to the debtor, ‖ He does not take away plunder, ‖ He gives his bread to the hungry, ‖ And covers the naked with a garment, **8** He does not give in usury, and does not take increase, ‖ He turns back his hand from perversity, ‖ He does true judgment between man and man. **9** He walks in My statutes, ‖ And he has kept My judgments—to deal truly, ‖ He [is] righteous—he surely lives," ‖ A declaration of Lord YHWH. **10** "And he has begotten a son, ‖ A burglar—a shedder of blood, ‖ And he has made a brother of one of these, **11** And he has not done all those, ‖ For he has even eaten on the mountains, ‖ And he has defiled his neighbor's wife, **12** He has oppressed the afflicted and needy, ‖ He has taken away plunder violently, ‖ He does not return a pledge, ‖ And he has lifted up his eyes to the idols, ‖ He has done abomination! **13** He has given in usury, and taken increase, ‖ And he lives? He does not live, ‖ He has done all these abominations, ‖ He surely dies, his blood is on him. **14** And—behold, he has begotten a son, ‖ And he sees all the sins of his father, ‖ That he has done, and he fears, ‖ And does not do like them, **15** He has not eaten on the mountains, ‖ And he has not lifted up his eyes ‖ To idols of the house of Israel, ‖ He has not defiled his neighbor's wife, **16** He has not oppressed a man, ‖ He has not bound a pledge, ‖ And he has not taken away plunder, ‖ He has given his bread to the hungry, ‖ And he covered the naked with a garment, **17** He has turned back his hand from the afflicted, ‖ He has not taken usury and increase, ‖ He has done My judgments, ‖ He has walked in My statutes, ‖ He does not die for the iniquity of his father, ‖ He surely lives. **18** His father—because he used oppression, ‖ Violently plundered a brother, ‖ And did that which [is] not good in the midst of his people, ‖ And behold, he is dying in his iniquity. **19** And you have said, Why has the son not borne of the iniquity of the father? And the son has done judgment and righteousness, ‖ He has kept all My statutes, ‖ And he does them, he surely lives. **20** The soul that sins—it dies. A son does not bear of the iniquity of the father, ‖ And a father does not bear of the iniquity of the son, ‖ The righteousness of the righteous is on him, ‖ And the wickedness of the wicked is on him. **21** And the wicked—when he turns back ‖ From all his sins that he has done, ‖ And he has kept all My statutes, ‖ And has done judgment and righteousness, ‖ He surely lives, he does not die. **22** All his transgressions that he has done ‖ Are not remembered to him, ‖ In his righteousness that he has done he lives. **23** Do I take pleasure [or] delight in the death of the wicked?" A declaration of Lord YHWH, "Is it not in his turning back from his way— And he has lived? **24** And in the turning back of the righteous from his righteousness, ‖ And he has done perversity, ‖ According to all the abominations ‖ That the wicked has done, ‖ Does he then live? All his righteous deeds that he has done are not remembered, ‖ For his trespass that he has trespassed, ‖ And for his sin that he has sinned, ‖ For them he dies. **25** And you have said, The way of the Lord is not pondered. Now hear, O house of Israel, ‖ My way—is it not pondered? Are not your ways unpondered? **26** In the turning back of the righteous from his righteousness, ‖ And he has done perversity, ‖ And he is dying by them, ‖ He dies for his perversity that he has done. **27** And in the turning back of the wicked ‖ From his wickedness that he has done, ‖ And he does judgment and righteousness, ‖ He keeps his soul alive. **28** And he sees and turns back, ‖ From all his transgressions that he has done, ‖ He surely lives, he does not die, **29** And the house of Israel has said, The way of the Lord is not pondered, ‖ My ways—are they not pondered? O house of Israel—are not your ways unpondered? **30** Therefore, I judge each according to his ways, ‖ O house of Israel," ‖ A declaration of Lord YHWH, ‖ "Turn back, indeed, turn yourselves back, ‖ From all your transgressions, ‖ And iniquity is not for a stumbling-block to you, **31** Cast away all your transgressions from over you, ‖ By which you have transgressed, ‖ And make a new heart and a new spirit for yourselves, ‖ And why do you die, ‖ O house of Israel? **32** For I have no pleasure in the death of the dying," ‖ A declaration of Lord YHWH, ‖ "Therefore turn back and live!"

19 "And you, lift up a lamentation to princes of Israel, **2** and you have said: What [is] your mother? A lioness, ‖ She has crouched down among lions, ‖ She has multiplied her whelps in the midst of young lions. **3** And she brings up one of her whelps, ‖ He has been a young lion, ‖ And he learns to tear prey, ‖ He has devoured man. **4** And nations hear of him, ‖ He has been caught in their pit, ‖ And they bring him to the land of Egypt in chains. **5** And as she waited she sees that her hope has perished, ‖ And she takes one of her whelps, ‖ She has made him a young lion. **6** And he goes up and down in the midst of lions, ‖ He has been a young lion, ‖ And he learns to tear prey, ‖ He has devoured man. **7** And he knows his forsaken habitations, ‖ And he has laid waste [to] their cities, ‖ And the land and its fullness is desolate, ‖ Because of the voice of his roaring. **8** And surrounding nations set against him from the provinces. And they spread out their net for him, ‖ He has been caught in their pit. **9** And they put him in prison—in chains, ‖ And they bring him to the king of Babylon, ‖ They bring him into bulwarks, ‖ So that his voice is not heard ‖ On mountains of Israel anymore. **10** Your mother, like the vine in your blood, ‖ Is being planted by waters, ‖ She was bearing fruit and full of boughs, ‖ Because of many waters. **11** And she has strong rods for scepters of rulers, ‖ And she is high in stature above—between thick branches, ‖ And it appears in its height ‖ In the multitude of its thin shoots. **12** And she is plucked up in fury, ‖ She has been cast to the earth, ‖ And the east wind has dried up her fruit, ‖ [The] rod of her strength has been broken and withered, ‖ Fire has consumed it. **13** And now she is planted in a wilderness, ‖ In a dry and thirsty land. **14** And fire goes forth from a rod of her boughs, ‖ It has devoured her fruit, ‖ And she has no rod of strength—a scepter to rule, ‖ A lamentation—and she has become for a lamentation!"

20 And it comes to pass, in the seventh year, in the fifth [month], on the tenth of the month, men from [the] elderly of Israel have come in to seek YHWH, and they sit before me; **2** and there is a word of YHWH to me, saying, **3** "Son of man, speak to the elderly of Israel, and you have said to them, Thus said Lord YHWH: Are you coming in to seek Me? [As] I live—I am not sought by you—a declaration of Lord YHWH. **4** Do you judge them? Do you judge, son of man? Cause them to know the

EZEKIEL

abominations of their fathers, **5** and you have said to them, Thus said Lord YHWH: In the day of My fixing on Israel, ‖ I lift up My hand, ‖ To the seed of the house of Jacob, ‖ And am known to them in the land of Egypt, ‖ And I lift up My hand to them, ‖ Saying, I [am] your God YHWH. **6** In that day I lifted up My hand to them, ‖ To bring them forth from the land of Egypt, ‖ To a land that I spied out for them, ‖ Flowing with milk and honey, ‖ It [is] a beauty to all the lands, **7** And I say to them, Let each cast away the detestable things of his eyes, ‖ And do not be defiled with the idols of Egypt, ‖ I [am] your God YHWH. **8** And they rebel against Me, ‖ And have not been willing to listen to Me, ‖ Each has not cast away the detestable things of their eyes, ‖ And have not forsaken the idols of Egypt, ‖ And I speak—to pour out My fury on them, ‖ To complete My anger against them, ‖ In the midst of the land of Egypt. **9** And I do [it] for My Name's sake, ‖ Not to defile [it] before the eyes of the nations, ‖ In whose midst they [are in], ‖ Before whose eyes I became known to them, ‖ To bring them out from the land of Egypt. **10** And I bring them out of the land of Egypt, ‖ And I bring them into the wilderness, **11** And I give My statutes to them, ‖ And I caused them to know My judgments, ‖ Which the man who does—lives by them. **12** And I have also given My Sabbaths to them, ‖ To be for a sign between Me and them, ‖ To know that I [am] YHWH who is sanctifying them. **13** And the house of Israel rebels against Me in the wilderness, ‖ They have not walked in My statutes, ‖ And they have despised My judgments, ‖ Which the man who does—lives by them. And they have greatly defiled My Sabbaths, ‖ And I speak—to pour out My fury on them in the wilderness, to consume them. **14** And I do [it] for My Name's sake, ‖ Not to defile [it] before the eyes of the nations, ‖ Before whose eyes I brought them forth. **15** And also, I have lifted up My hand to them in the wilderness, ‖ Not to bring them into the land that I had given, ‖ Flowing with milk and honey, ‖ It [is] a beauty to all the lands, **16** Because they kicked against My judgments, ‖ And they have not walked in My statutes, ‖ And they have defiled My Sabbaths, ‖ For their heart is going after their idols. **17** And My eye has pity on them—against destroying them, ‖ And I have not made an end of them in the wilderness. **18** And I say to their sons in the wilderness: Do not walk in the statutes of your fathers, ‖ And do not observe their judgments, ‖ And do not defile yourselves with their idols. **19** I [am] your God YHWH, walk in My statutes, ‖ And observe My judgments, and do them, **20** And sanctify My Sabbaths, ‖ And they have been for a sign between Me and you, ‖ To know that I [am] your God YHWH. **21** And the sons rebel against Me, ‖ They have not walked in My statutes, ‖ And they have not observed My judgments—to do them, ‖ Which the man who does—lives by them. They have defiled My Sabbaths, ‖ And I speak—to pour out My fury on them, ‖ To complete My anger against them in the wilderness. **22** And I have turned back My hand, ‖ And I do [it] for My Name's sake, ‖ Not to defile [it] before the eyes of the nations, ‖ Before whose eyes I brought them out. **23** I also, I have lifted up My hand to them in the wilderness, ‖ To scatter them among nations, ‖ And to spread them through lands. **24** Because they have not done My judgments, ‖ And they have despised My statutes, ‖ And they have defiled My Sabbaths, ‖ And their eyes have been after [the] idols of their fathers. **25** And I also, I have given statutes to them [that are] not good, ‖ And judgments by which they do not live. **26** And I defile them by their own gifts, ‖ By causing every opener of a womb to pass away, ‖ So that I make them desolate, ‖ So that they know that I [am] YHWH. **27** Therefore, speak to the house of Israel, son of man, and you have said to them, Thus said Lord YHWH: Still in this your fathers have reviled Me, ‖ In their committing a trespass against Me. **28** And I bring them into the land, ‖ That I lifted up My hand to give to them, ‖ And they see every high hill, and every thick tree, ‖ And they sacrifice their sacrifices there, ‖ And give the provocation of their offering there, ‖ And make their refreshing fragrance there, ‖ And they pour out their drink-offerings there. **29** And I say to them: What [is] the high place to where you are going in?" And its name is called "High Place" to this day. **30** "Therefore, say to the house of Israel, Thus said Lord YHWH: Are you defiling yourselves in the way of your fathers? And do you go whoring after their detestable things? **31** And in the offering of your gifts, ‖ In causing your sons to pass through fire, ‖ You are defiled by all your

EZEKIEL

idols to this day, ‖ And I am sought by you, O house of Israel? [As] I live—a declaration of Lord YHWH, I am not sought by you. **32** And that which is going up on your mind, ‖ It is not at all—in that you are saying: We will be as the nations, as the families of the lands, ‖ To serve wood and stone. **33** [As] I live—a declaration of Lord YHWH, ‖ Do I not, with a strong hand, ‖ And with an outstretched arm, ‖ And with poured out fury—rule over you? **34** And I have brought you forth from the peoples, ‖ And assembled you from the lands ‖ In which you have been scattered, ‖ With a strong hand and with an outstretched arm, ‖ And with poured out fury. **35** And I have brought you into the wilderness of the peoples, ‖ And have been judged with you there face to face. **36** As I was judged with your fathers, ‖ In the wilderness of the land of Egypt, ‖ So I am judged with you, ‖ A declaration of Lord YHWH. **37** And I have caused you to pass under the rod, ‖ And brought you into the bond of the covenant, **38** And cleared out the rebels from you, ‖ And those transgressing against Me, ‖ I bring them out from the land of their sojournings, ‖ And they do not come to the land of Israel, ‖ And you have known that I [am] YHWH. **39** And you, O house of Israel, thus said Lord YHWH: Each go, serve his idols, ‖ And afterward, if you are not listening to Me [anyway], ‖ But you do not defile My holy Name anymore by your gifts, and by your idols. **40** For on My holy mountain, ‖ On the mountain of the height of Israel, ‖ A declaration of Lord YHWH, ‖ All the house of Israel serves Me there, ‖ All of it, in the land—I accept them there, ‖ And I seek your raised-offerings there, ‖ And with the first-fruit of your gifts, ‖ With all your holy things. **41** With refreshing fragrance I accept you, ‖ In My bringing you out from the peoples, ‖ And I have assembled you from the lands ‖ In which you have been scattered, ‖ And I have been sanctified in you ‖ Before the eyes of the nations. **42** And you have known that I [am] YHWH, ‖ In My bringing you to the ground of Israel, ‖ To the land that I lifted up My hand ‖ To give it to your fathers, **43** And you have remembered your ways there, ‖ And all your doings, ‖ In which you have been defiled, ‖ And you have been loathsome in your own faces, ‖ For all your evils that you have done. **44** And you have known that I [am] YHWH, ‖ In My dealing with you for My Name's sake, ‖ Not according to your evil ways, ‖ And according to your corrupt doings, O house of Israel, ‖ A declaration of Lord YHWH." **45** And there is a word of YHWH to me, saying, **46** "Son of man, set your face the way of Teman, and prophesy to the south, and prophesy to the forest of the field—the south; **47** and you have said to the forest of the south, Hear a word of YHWH! Thus said Lord YHWH: Behold, I am kindling a fire in you, ‖ And it has devoured every moist tree in you, and every dry tree, ‖ The glowing flames are not quenched, ‖ And all faces from south to north have been burned by it. **48** And all flesh has seen, that I, YHWH, have kindled it—it is not quenched." **49** And I say, "Aah! Lord YHWH, ‖ They are saying of me, ‖ Is he not using allegories?"

21 And there is a word of YHWH to me, saying, **2** "Son of man, set your face toward Jerusalem, and prophesy to the holy places, and prophesy to the ground of Israel; **3** and you have said to the ground of Israel, Thus said YHWH: Behold, I [am] against you, ‖ And have brought out My sword from its scabbard, ‖ And have cut off righteous and wicked from you. **4** Because that I have cut off righteous and wicked from you, ‖ Therefore My sword goes out from its scabbard, ‖ To all flesh, from south to north. **5** And all flesh has known that I, YHWH, ‖ Have brought out My sword from its scabbard, ‖ It does not turn back anymore. **6** And you, son of man, sigh with breaking of loins, indeed, sigh before their eyes with bitterness, **7** and it has come to pass, when they say to you, Why are you sighing? That you have said: Because of the report, for it is coming, ‖ And every heart has melted, ‖ And all hands have been feeble, ‖ And every spirit is weak, ‖ And all knees go [as] waters, ‖ Behold, it is coming, indeed, it has been, ‖ A declaration of Lord YHWH." **8** And there is a word of YHWH to me, saying, **9** "Son of man, prophesy, and you have said, Thus said YHWH: Say, A sword, a sword is sharpened, and also polished. **10** It is sharpened so as to slaughter a slaughter. It is polished so as to have brightness, ‖ Or do we rejoice? It is despising the scepter of My son [as] every tree. **11** And He gives it for polishing, ‖ For laying hold of by the hand. It is sharpened—the sword—and polished, ‖ To

EZEKIEL

give it into the hand of a slayer. **12** Cry and howl, son of man, ‖ For it has been among My people, ‖ It [is] among all the princes of Israel, ‖ My people have been cast to the sword. Therefore strike on your thigh, **13** Because [it is] a trier, ‖ And what if it is even despising the scepter? It will not be, a declaration of Lord YHWH. **14** And you, son of man, prophesy, ‖ And strike hand on hand, ‖ And the sword is bent a third time, ‖ The sword of the wounded! It [is] the sword of the wounded—the great one, ‖ That is entering the inner chamber to them. **15** To melt the heart, and to multiply the ruins, ‖ I have set the point of a sword by all their gates. Aah! It is made for brightness, ‖ Wrapped up for slaughter. **16** Take possession of the right, place yourself at the left, ‖ To where your face is appointed. **17** And I also, I strike My hand on My hand, ‖ And have caused My fury to rest; I, YHWH, have spoken." **18** And there is a word of YHWH to me, saying, **19** "And you, son of man, appoint two ways for yourself, for the coming in of the sword of the king of Babylon; they come forth from one land, both of them. And create a station; create [it] at the top of the way of the city. **20** Appoint a way for the coming of the sword, ‖ To Rabbath of the sons of Ammon, ‖ And to Judah, in fortified Jerusalem. **21** For the king of Babylon has stood at the head of the way, ‖ At the top of the two ways, to use divination, ‖ He has moved lightly with the arrows, ‖ He has inquired of the teraphim, ‖ He has looked on the liver. **22** The divination [for] Jerusalem has been at his right, ‖ To place battering-rams, ‖ To open the mouth with slaughter, ‖ To lift up a voice with shouting, ‖ To place battering-rams against the gates, ‖ To pour out a mound, to build a fortification. **23** And it has been to them as a false divination in their eyes, ‖ Who have sworn oaths to them, ‖ But he is causing iniquity to be remembered [so they] are caught. **24** Therefore, thus said Lord YHWH: Because of your causing your iniquity to be remembered, ‖ In your transgressions being revealed, ‖ For your sins being seen, in all your doings, ‖ Because of your being remembered, ‖ You are caught by the hand. **25** And you, wounded, wicked one, ‖ Prince of Israel, whose day has come, ‖ In the time of the iniquity of the end, **26** Thus said Lord YHWH: Turn aside the turban, and carry away the crown, ‖ This—not this—make high the low, ‖ And make low the high. **27** An overturn, overturn, overturn, I make it, ‖ Also this has not been until the coming of Him, ‖ Whose [is] the judgment, and I have given it. **28** And you, son of man, prophesy, and you have said, Thus said Lord YHWH concerning the sons of Ammon, and concerning their reproach, and you have said: A sword, a sword, open for slaughter, ‖ Polished to the utmost for brightness! **29** In seeing a vain thing for you, ‖ In divining a lie for you, ‖ To put you on the necks of the wounded of the wicked, whose day has come, ‖ In the time of the iniquity of the end. **30** Turn [it] back to its scabbard; I judge you ‖ In the place where you were produced, ‖ In the land of your birth. **31** And I have poured My indignation on you, ‖ I blow against you with [the] fire of My wrath, ‖ And have given you into the hand of brutish men—craftsmen of destruction. **32** You are fuel for the fire, ‖ Your blood is in the midst of the land, ‖ You are not remembered, ‖ For I, YHWH, have spoken!"

22 And there is a word of YHWH to me, saying, **2** "And you, son of man, do you judge? Do you judge the city of blood? Then you have caused it to know all its abominations, **3** and you have said, Thus said Lord YHWH: The city is shedding blood in its midst, ‖ For the coming in of its time, ‖ And it has made idols on it for defilement. **4** You have been guilty by your blood that you have shed, ‖ And you have been defiled by your idols that you have made, ‖ And you cause your days to draw near, ‖ And have come to your years, ‖ Therefore I have given you [for] a reproach to nations, ‖ And a derision to all the lands. **5** The near and the far-off from you scoff at you, ‖ O defiled of name—abounding in trouble. **6** Behold, princes of Israel—each according to his arm ‖ Have been in you to shed blood. **7** They have made light of father and mother in you, ‖ They dealt oppressively to a sojourner in your midst, ‖ They oppressed fatherless and widow in you. **8** You have despised My holy things, ‖ And you have defiled My Sabbaths. **9** Men of slander have been in you to shed blood, ‖ And they have eaten on the mountains in you, ‖ They have done wickedness in your midst. **10** One has uncovered the nakedness of a father in you, ‖ They humbled the menstruous woman in you. **11** And each

EZEKIEL

has done abomination with the wife of his neighbor, ‖ And each has defiled his daughter-in-law through wickedness, ‖ And each has humbled his sister, his father's daughter, in you. **12** They have taken a bribe to shed blood in you, ‖ You have taken usury and increase, ‖ And cut off your neighbor by oppression, ‖ And you have forgotten Me, ‖ A declaration of Lord YHWH! **13** And behold, I have struck My hand, ‖ Because of your dishonest gain that you have gained, ‖ And for your blood that has been in your midst. **14** Does your heart stand—are your hands strong, ‖ For the days that I am dealing with you? I, YHWH, have spoken and have done [it]. **15** And I have scattered you among nations, ‖ And have spread you out among lands, ‖ And consumed your uncleanness out of you. **16** And you have been defiled in yourself ‖ Before the eyes of nations, ‖ And you have known that I [am] YHWH." **17** And there is a word of YHWH to me, saying, **18** "Son of man, the house of Israel has been for dross to Me, ‖ All of them [are] bronze, and tin, and iron, and lead, ‖ In the midst of a furnace—silver has been dross, **19** Therefore, thus said Lord YHWH: Because you have all become dross, ‖ Therefore, behold, I am gathering you into the midst of Jerusalem, **20** A gathering of silver, and bronze, and iron, and lead, and tin, ‖ Into the midst of a furnace—to blow fire on it, to melt it, ‖ So I gather in My anger and in My fury, ‖ And I have let rest, and have melted you. **21** And I have heaped you up, ‖ And blown on you in the fire of My wrath, ‖ And you have been melted in its midst. **22** As the melting of silver in the midst of a furnace, ‖ So you are melted in its midst, ‖ And you have known that I, YHWH, have poured out My fury on you." **23** And there is a word of YHWH to me, saying, **24** "Son of man, say to it, You [are] a land, ‖ It [is] not cleansed nor rained on in a day of indignation. **25** A conspiracy of its prophets [is] in its midst, ‖ As a roaring lion tearing prey; They have devoured the soul, ‖ They have taken wealth and glory, ‖ Its widows have multiplied in its midst. **26** Its priests have wronged My law, ‖ And they defile My holy things, ‖ They have not made separation between holy and common, ‖ And they have not made known [the difference] between the unclean and the clean, ‖ And they have hidden their eyes from My Sabbaths, ‖ And I am pierced in their midst. **27** Its princes [are] as wolves in its midst, ‖ Tearing prey, to shed blood, to destroy souls, ‖ For the sake of gaining dishonest gain. **28** And its prophets have coated with chalk for them, ‖ Seeing a vain thing, and divining a lie for them, ‖ Saying, Thus said Lord YHWH, ‖ And YHWH has not spoken. **29** The people of the land have used oppression, ‖ And have taken plunder away violently, ‖ And have oppressed humble and needy, ‖ And oppressed the sojourner without judgment. **30** And I seek from them a man making a wall, ‖ And standing in the breach before Me, ‖ In behalf of the land—not to destroy it, ‖ And I have found none. **31** And I pour out My indignation on them, ‖ I have consumed them by [the] fire of My wrath, ‖ I have put their way on their own head, ‖ A declaration of Lord YHWH!"

23 And there is a word of YHWH to me, saying, "Son of man, **2** Two women were daughters of one mother, **3** And they go whoring in Egypt, ‖ They have gone whoring in their youth, ‖ There they have bruised their breasts, ‖ And there they have dealt with the loves of their virginity. **4** And their names [are] Aholah the older, ‖ And Aholibah her sister, ‖ And they are Mine, and bear sons and daughters. As for their names—Samaria [is] Aholah, ‖ And Jerusalem [is] Aholibah. **5** And Aholah goes whoring under Me, and she lusts on her lovers, on the neighboring Assyrians, **6** Clothed with blue—governors and prefects, ‖ All of them desirable young men, ‖ Horsemen, riding on horses, **7** And she gives her whoredoms on them, ‖ The choice of the sons of Asshur, ‖ All of them—even all on whom she lusted, ‖ She has been defiled by all their idols. **8** And she has not forsaken her whoredoms out of Egypt, ‖ For with her they lay in her youth, ‖ And they dealt with the loves of her virginity, ‖ And they pour out their whoredoms on her. **9** Therefore I have given her into the hand of her lovers, ‖ Into the hand of sons of Asshur on whom she lusted. **10** They have uncovered her nakedness, ‖ They have taken her sons and her daughters, ‖ And they have slain her by sword, ‖ And she is a name for women, ‖ And they have done judgments with her. **11** And her sister Aholibah sees, ‖ And she makes her unhealthy love more corrupt than she, ‖ And her whoredoms than the whoredoms of her sister. **12** She has lusted on sons of Asshur, ‖ Governors and prefects, ‖ Neighboring ones—clothed in perfection, ‖ Horsemen, riding on horses, ‖ All of them desirable young men. **13** And I see that she has been defiled, ‖ One way [is] to them both. **14** And she adds to her whoredoms, ‖ And she sees men carved on the wall, ‖ Pictures of Chaldeans, carved with vermillion, **15** Girded with a girdle on their loins, ‖ Dyed attire spread out on their heads, ‖ The appearance of rulers—all of them, ‖ The likeness of sons of Babylon, ‖ Chaldea is the land of their birth. **16** And she lusts on them at the sight of her eyes, ‖ And sends messengers to them, to Chaldea. **17** And sons of Babylon come in to her, ‖ To the bed of loves, ‖ And they defile her with their whoredoms, ‖ And she is defiled with them, ‖ And her soul is alienated from them. **18** And she reveals her whoredoms, ‖ And she reveals her nakedness, ‖ And My soul is alienated from off her, ‖ As My soul was alienated from off her sister. **19** And she multiplies her whoredoms, ‖ To remember the days of her youth, ‖ When she went whoring in the land of Egypt. **20** And she lusts on their lovers, ‖ Whose flesh [is] the flesh of donkeys, ‖ And the emission of horses—their emission. **21** You look after the wickedness of your youth, ‖ In dealing out of Egypt your loves, ‖ For the sake of the breasts of your youth. **22** Therefore, O Aholibah, thus said Lord YHWH: Behold, I am stirring up your lovers against you, ‖ From whom your soul has been alienated, ‖ And have brought them in against you from all around. **23** Sons of Babylon, and of all Chaldea, Pekod, and Shoa, and Koa, ‖ All the sons of Asshur with them, ‖ Desirable young men, governors and prefects, ‖ All of them—rulers and proclaimed ones, ‖ All of them riding on horses. **24** And they have come in against you, ‖ With arms, rider, and wheel, ‖ And with an assembly of peoples; Buckler, and shield, and helmet, ‖ They set against you all around, ‖ And I have set judgment before them, ‖ They have judged you in their judgments. **25** And I have set My jealousy against you, ‖ And they have dealt with you in fury, ‖ They turn aside your nose and your ears, ‖ And your posterity falls by sword, ‖ They take away your sons and your daughters, ‖ And your posterity is devoured by fire. **26** And they have stripped you of your garments, ‖ And have taken your beautiful jewels. **27** And I have caused your wickedness to cease from you, ‖ And your whoredoms out of the land of Egypt, ‖ And you do not lift up your eyes to them, ‖ And you do not remember Egypt again. **28** For thus said Lord YHWH: Behold, I am giving you into a hand that you have hated, ‖ Into a hand from which you were alienated. **29** And they have dealt with you in hatred, ‖ And they have taken all your labor, ‖ And they have left you naked and bare, ‖ And the nakedness of your whoredoms has been revealed, ‖ And the wickedness of your whoredoms. **30** To do these things to you, ‖ In your going whoring after nations, ‖ Because you have been defiled with their idols, **31** You have walked in the way of your sister, ‖ And I have given her cup into your hand. **32** Thus said Lord YHWH: You drink the cup of your sister, ‖ The deep and the wide one ‖ (You are for laughter and for scorn), ‖ Abundant to contain. **33** You are filled with drunkenness and sorrow, ‖ A cup of astonishment and desolation, ‖ The cup of your sister Samaria. **34** And you have drunk it, and have drained [it], ‖ And you gnaw its earthen ware, ‖ And you pluck off your own breasts, ‖ For I have spoken, ‖ A declaration of Lord YHWH, **35** Therefore, thus said Lord YHWH: Because you have forgotten Me, ‖ And you cast Me behind your back, ‖ Even you also bear your wickedness and your whoredoms." **36** And YHWH says to me, "Son of man, ‖ Do you judge Aholah and Aholibah? Then declare their abominations to them. **37** For they have committed adultery, ‖ And blood [is] in their hands, ‖ They committed adultery with their idols, ‖ And also their sons whom they bore to Me, ‖ They caused to pass over to them for food. **38** Again, they have done this to Me, ‖ They defiled My sanctuary in that day, ‖ And they have defiled My Sabbaths. **39** And in their slaughtering their sons to their idols ‖ They also come into My sanctuary in that day to defile it, ‖ And behold, thus they have done in the midst of My house, **40** And also that they send to men coming from afar, ‖ To whom a messenger is sent, ‖ And behold, they have come in for whom you have washed, ‖ Painted your eyes, and put on adornment. **41** And you have sat on a couch of honor, ‖ And a table arrayed before it, ‖ And placed My incense and My oil on it. **42** And the voice of a multitude at ease [is] with her, ‖

EZEKIEL

And Sabeans from the wilderness are brought in to men of the common people, ‖ And they put bracelets on their hands, ‖ And a beautiful crown on their heads. **43** And I say of the worn-out one in adulteries, ‖ Now they commit her whoredoms—she also! **44** And they come in to her, ‖ As the coming in to a whorish woman, ‖ So they have come in to Aholah, ‖ And to Aholibah—the wicked women. **45** As for righteous men, they judge them with the judgment of adulteresses, ‖ And the judgment of women shedding blood, ‖ For they [are] adulteresses, ‖ And blood [is] in their hands. **46** For thus said Lord YHWH: Bring up an assembly against them, ‖ And give them to trembling and to spoiling. **47** And they have cast the stone of the assembly at them, ‖ And cut them with their swords, ‖ They slay their sons and their daughters, ‖ And they burn their houses with fire. **48** And I have caused wickedness to cease from the land, ‖ And all the women have been instructed, ‖ And they do not do according to your wickedness. **49** And they have put your wickedness on you, ‖ And you bear the sins of your idols, ‖ And you have known that I [am] Lord YHWH!"

24 And there is a word of YHWH to me, in the ninth year, in the tenth month, on the tenth of the month, saying, **2** "Son of man, write! Write the name of the day for yourself, this very day; the king of Babylon has leaned toward Jerusalem in this very day. **3** And use an allegory toward the house of rebellion, and you have said to them, Thus said Lord YHWH: To set on the pot, to set [it] on, and also to pour water into it, **4** To gather its pieces to it, every good piece, ‖ Thigh and shoulder, to fill in the choice of the bones. **5** To take the choice of the flock, ‖ And also to pile the bones under it, ‖ Boil it thoroughly, indeed, cook its bones in its midst. **6** Therefore, thus said Lord YHWH: Woe [to] the city of blood, ‖ A pot whose scum [is] in it, ‖ And its scum has not come out of it, ‖ By piece of it, by piece of it bring it out, a lot has not fallen on it. **7** For her blood has been in her midst, ‖ She has set it on a clear place of a rock, ‖ She has not poured it on the earth, ‖ To cover it over with dust. **8** To cause fury to come up to take vengeance, ‖ I have put her blood on a clear place of a rock—not to be covered. **9** Therefore, thus said Lord YHWH: Woe [to] the city of blood, indeed, I make the pile great. **10** Make the wood abundant, ‖ Kindle the fire, consume the flesh, ‖ And make the compound, ‖ And let the bones be burned. **11** And cause it to stand empty on its coals, ‖ So that its bronze is hot and burning, ‖ Its uncleanness has been melted in its midst, ‖ Its scum is consumed. **12** She has wearied herself [with] sorrows, ‖ And the abundance of her scum does not go out of her, ‖ Her scum [is] in the fire. **13** Wickedness [is] in your uncleanness, ‖ Because I have cleansed you, ‖ And you have not been cleansed, ‖ You are not cleansed from your uncleanness again, ‖ Until I have caused My fury to rest on you. **14** I, YHWH, have spoken, ‖ It has come, and I have done [it], ‖ I do not free, nor do I spare, nor do I regret, ‖ According to your ways, and according to your acts, ‖ They have judged you, ‖ A declaration of Lord YHWH." **15** And there is a word of YHWH to me, saying, **16** "Son of man, behold, I am taking the desire of your eyes from you by a stroke, and you do not mourn, nor weep, nor let your tear come. **17** Cease to groan [and] make no mourning [for] the dead, bind your headdress on yourself, and put your shoes on your feet, and you do not cover over the upper lip, and you do not eat [the] bread of men." **18** And I speak to the people in the morning, and my wife dies in the evening, and I do in the morning as I have been commanded. **19** And the people say to me, "Do you not declare to us what these [are] to us, that you are doing?" **20** And I say to them, "A word of YHWH has been to me, saying, **21** Say to the house of Israel, Thus said Lord YHWH: Behold, I am defiling My sanctuary, ‖ The excellence of your strength, ‖ The desire of your eyes, and the pitied of your soul, ‖ And your sons and your daughters whom you have left, fall by sword. **22** And you have done as I have done, ‖ You have not covered over the upper lip, ‖ And you do not eat [the] bread of men. **23** And your headdresses [are] on your heads, ‖ And your shoes [are] on your feet, ‖ You do not mourn nor do you weep, ‖ And you have wasted away for your iniquities, ‖ And you have howled to one another. **24** And Ezekiel has been for a type to you; according to all that he has done you do. In its coming in—you have known that I [am] Lord YHWH." **25** "And you, son of man, is it not in the day of My taking from them their strength, the joy of their beauty, the desire of their eyes, and the song of their soul—their sons and their daughters? **26** In that day the escaped one comes to you to cause the ears to hear. **27** In that day your mouth is opened with the escaped and you speak, and are not silent anymore, and you have been for a type to them, and they have known that I [am] YHWH."

25 And there is a word of YHWH to me, saying, **2** "Son of man, set your face toward the sons of Ammon, and prophesy against them; **3** and you have said to the sons of Ammon: Hear a word of Lord YHWH! Thus said Lord YHWH: Because of your saying, Aha, to My sanctuary, ‖ Because it has been defiled, ‖ And to the ground of Israel, ‖ Because it has been desolate, ‖ And to the house of Judah, ‖ Because they have gone into a removal: **4** Therefore, behold, I am giving you to sons of the east for a possession, ‖ And they set their towers in you, ‖ And have placed their dwelling places in you. They eat your fruit, and they drink your milk, **5** And I have given Rabbah for a habitation of camels, ‖ And the sons of Ammon for the crouching of a flock, ‖ And you have known that I [am] YHWH. **6** For thus said Lord YHWH: Because of your clapping the hand, ‖ And of your stamping with the foot, ‖ And you rejoice with all your despite in soul ‖ Against the ground of Israel, **7** Therefore, behold, I have stretched out My hand against you, ‖ And have given you for a portion to nations, ‖ And I have cut you off from the peoples, ‖ And caused you to perish from the lands; I destroy you, and you have known that I [am] YHWH. **8** Thus said Lord YHWH: Because of the saying of Moab and Seir: Behold, the house of Judah [is] as all the nations; **9** Therefore, behold, I am opening the shoulder of Moab—From the cities—from his cities—from his frontier, ‖ The beauty of the land, Beth-Jeshimoth, Ba'al-Meon, and Kiriathaim, **10** To the sons of the east, with the sons of Ammon, ‖ And I have given it for a possession, ‖ So that the sons of Ammon are not remembered among nations. **11** And I do judgments in Moab, ‖ And they have known that I [am] YHWH. **12** Thus said Lord YHWH: Because of the doings of Edom, ‖ In taking vengeance on the house of Judah, ‖ Indeed, they are very guilty, ‖ And they have taken vengeance on them.

13 Therefore, thus said Lord YHWH: I have stretched out My hand against Edom, ‖ And I have cut off man and beast from it, ‖ And given it up—a ruin, from Teman even to Dedan, ‖ They fall by sword. **14** And I have given My vengeance on Edom, ‖ By the hand of My people Israel, ‖ And they have done in Edom, ‖ According to My anger, and according to My fury, ‖ And they have known My vengeance, ‖ A declaration of Lord YHWH. **15** Thus said Lord YHWH: Because of the doings of the Philistines in vengeance, ‖ And they take vengeance with despite in soul, ‖ Destruction [with] continuous enmity, **16** Therefore, thus said Lord YHWH: Behold, I am stretching out My hand against the Philistines, ‖ And I have cut off the Cherethim, ‖ And destroyed the remnant of the haven of the sea, **17** And done great vengeance on them with furious reproofs, ‖ And they have known that I [am] YHWH, ‖ In My giving out My vengeance on them!"

26 And it comes to pass, in the eleventh year, on the first of the month, there has been a word of YHWH to me, saying, "Son of man, **2** Because that Tyre has said of Jerusalem: Aha, she has been broken, ‖ The doors of the peoples, ‖ She has turned around to me, ‖ I am filled—she has been laid waste, **3** Therefore, thus said Lord YHWH: Behold, I [am] against you, O Tyre, ‖ And have caused many nations to come up against you, ‖ As the sea causes its billows to come up. **4** And they have destroyed the walls of Tyre, ‖ And they have broken down her towers, ‖ And I have scraped her dust from her, ‖ And made her for a clear place of a rock. **5** She is a spreading place of nets in the midst of the sea, ‖ For I have spoken," ‖ A declaration of Lord YHWH, ‖ "And she has been for a spoil to nations. **6** And her daughters who [are] in the field, are slain by sword, ‖ And they have known that I [am] YHWH," **7** For thus said Lord YHWH: "Behold, I am bringing Nebuchadnezzar king of Babylon to Tyre, ‖ From the north—a king of kings, ‖ With horse, and with chariot, and with horsemen, ‖ Even an assembly, and a numerous people. **8** He slays your daughters in the field by sword, ‖ And he has made a fort against you, ‖ And has poured out a mound against you, ‖ And has raised a buckler against you. **9** And he places a battering-ram before him against

EZEKIEL

your walls, ‖ And he breaks your towers with his weapons. **10** From the abundance of his horses their dust cover you, ‖ From the noise of horseman, and wheel, and rider, ‖ Your walls shake, in his coming into your gates, ‖ As the coming into a city that has been broken-up. **11** He treads all your out-places with [the] hooves of his horses, ‖ He slays your people by sword, ‖ And the pillars of your strength come down to the earth. **12** And they have spoiled your wealth, ‖ And they have plundered your merchandise, ‖ And they have thrown down your walls, ‖ And they break down your desirable houses, ‖ And your stones, and your wood, and your dust, ‖ They place in the midst of the waters. **13** And I have caused the noise of your songs to cease, ‖ And the voice of your harps is heard no more. **14** And I have given you up for a clear place of a rock, ‖ You are a spreading-place of nets, ‖ You are not built up anymore, ‖ For I, YHWH, have spoken," ‖ A declaration of Lord YHWH. **15** Thus said Lord YHWH to Tyre: "Do not—from the noise of your fall, ‖ In the groaning of the wounded, ‖ In the slaying of the slaughter in your midst—The islands shake? **16** And all princes of the sea have come down from off their thrones, ‖ And they have turned their robes aside, ‖ And strip off their embroidered garments, ‖ They put on trembling, ‖ They sit on the earth, ‖ And they have trembled every moment, ‖ And they have been astonished at you, **17** And have lifted up a lamentation for you, ‖ And said to you: How you have perished, ‖ That are inhabited from the seas, ‖ The praised city, that was strong in the sea, ‖ She and her inhabitants, ‖ Who put their terror on all her inhabitants! **18** Now the islands tremble [on the] day of your fall; The islands that [are] in the sea have been troubled at your outgoing." **19** For thus said Lord YHWH: "In My making you a city dried up, ‖ Like cities that have not been inhabited, ‖ In bringing up the deep against you, ‖ Then the great waters have covered you. **20** And I have caused you to go down, ‖ With those going down to the pit, ‖ To the people of old, ‖ And I have caused you to dwell ‖ In the lower parts of the earth—in ancient ruins, ‖ With those going down to the pit, ‖ So that you are not inhabited, ‖ And I have given beauty in the land of the living. **21** I make you a terror, and you are not, ‖ And you are sought, and are not found anymore—for all time," ‖ A declaration of Lord YHWH!

27 And there is a word of YHWH to me, saying, **2** "And you, son of man, lift up a lamentation concerning Tyre, and you have said to Tyre: **3** O dweller on the entrances of the sea, ‖ Merchant of the peoples to many islands, Thus said Lord YHWH: O Tyre, you have said, ‖ I [am] the perfection of beauty. **4** Your borders [are] in the heart of the seas, ‖ Your builders have perfected your beauty. **5** They have built of firs from Senir all your double-boarded ships for you, ‖ They have taken of cedars from Lebanon to make a mast for you, **6** They made your oars of oaks from Bashan, ‖ They have made your bench of ivory, ‖ A branch of Ashurim from islands of Chittim. **7** Your sail has been of fine linen with embroidery from Egypt, ‖ To be for your ensign, ‖ Your covering has been of blue and purple from islands of Elishah. **8** Inhabitants of Sidon and Arvad have been rowers for you, ‖ Your wise men, O Tyre, have been in you, ‖ They [are] your pilots. **9** The elderly of Gebal and its wise men have been in you, ‖ Strengthening your breach; All ships of the sea and their mariners, ‖ Have been in you, to trade your merchandise. **10** Persia and Lud and Phut ‖ Have been in your forces—your men of war. They hung up shield and helmet in you, ‖ They have given out your honor. **11** The sons of Arvad, and your force, ‖ [Are] on your walls all around, ‖ And short swordsmen have been in your towers, ‖ They have hung up their shields on your walls all around, ‖ They have perfected your beauty. **12** Tarshish [is] your merchant, ‖ Because of the abundance of all wealth, ‖ They have given silver, iron, tin, and lead [for] your wares. **13** Javan, Tubal, and Meshech—they [are] your merchants, ‖ They have given [the] soul of man, and vessels of bronze, [for] your merchandise. **14** Those of the house of Togarmah, ‖ They have given horses, and riding steeds, and mules [for] your wares. **15** Sons of Dedan [are] your merchants, ‖ Many islands [are] the market of your hand, ‖ They sent back horns of ivory and ebony [for] your reward. **16** Aram [is] your merchant, ‖ Because of the abundance of your works, ‖ They have given emerald, purple, and embroidery, ‖ And fine linen, and coral, and agate for your wares. **17** Judah and the land of

EZEKIEL

Israel—they [are] your merchants, ‖ They have given wheat of Minnith, and Pannag, ‖ And honey, and oil, and balm [for] your merchandise. **18** Damascus [is] your merchant, ‖ For the abundance of your works, ‖ Because of the abundance of all wealth, ‖ For wine of Helbon, and white wool. **19** Dan and Javan go about with your wares, ‖ They have given shining iron, cassia, and cane, ‖ It has been in your merchandise. **20** Dedan [is] your merchant, ‖ For clothes of freedom for riding. **21** Arabia, and all princes of Kedar, ‖ They [are] the traders of your hand, ‖ For lambs, and rams, and male goats, ‖ In these your merchants. **22** Merchants of Sheba and Raamah—they [are] your merchants, ‖ They have given the chief of all spices, ‖ And every precious stone, and gold [for] your wares. **23** Haran, and Canneh, and Eden, merchants of Sheba, Asshur—Chilmad—[are] your merchants, **24** They [are] your merchants for perfect things, ‖ For wrappings of blue, and embroidery, ‖ And for treasuries of rich apparel, ‖ With cords bound and girded, for your merchandise, **25** Ships of Tarshish are journeying [with] your merchandise for you, ‖ And you are filled and honored greatly, ‖ In the heart of the seas. **26** Those rowing you have brought you into great waters, ‖ The east wind has broken you in the heart of the seas. **27** Your wealth and your wares, ‖ Your merchandise, your mariners, ‖ And your pilots, strengtheners of your breach, ‖ And the traders of your merchandise, ‖ And all your men of war, who [are] in you, ‖ And in all your assembly that [is] in your midst, ‖ Fall into the heart of the seas in the day of your fall, **28** At the voice of the cry of your pilots the outskirts shake. **29** And all handling an oar come down from their ships, ‖ Mariners [and] all the pilots of the sea stand on the land, **30** And have sounded with their voice for you, ‖ And cry bitterly, and cause dust to go up on their heads, ‖ They roll themselves in ashes; **31** And they have made themselves bald for you, ‖ And they have girded on sackcloth, ‖ And they have wept for you, ‖ In bitterness of soul—a bitter mourning. **32** And their sons have lifted up a lamentation for you, ‖ And they have lamented over you, Who [is] as Tyre? As the cut-off one in the midst of the sea? **33** With the outgoing of your wares from the seas, ‖ You have filled many peoples, ‖ With the abundance of your riches, and your merchandise, ‖ You have enriched [the] kings of earth. **34** At the time of [your] being broken by the seas in the depths of the waters, ‖ Your merchandise and all your assembly have fallen in your midst. **35** All inhabitants of the islands have been astonished at you, ‖ And their kings have been severely afraid, ‖ They have been troubled in countenance. **36** Merchants among the peoples have shrieked for you, ‖ You have been terrors, and you are not—for all time!"

28 And there is a word of Y<small>HWH</small> to me, saying, **2** "Son of man, say to the leader of Tyre, Thus said Lord Y<small>HWH</small>: Because your heart has been high, ‖ And you say: I [am] a god, ‖ I have inhabited the habitation of God, ‖ In the heart of the seas, ‖ And you [are] man, and not God, ‖ And you give out your heart as the heart of God, **3** Behold, you [are] wiser than Daniel, ‖ No hidden thing have they concealed from you. **4** By your wisdom and by your understanding ‖ You have made wealth for yourself, ‖ And make gold and silver in your treasuries. **5** By the abundance of your wisdom, ‖ Through your merchandise, ‖ You have multiplied your wealth, ‖ And your heart is high through your wealth. **6** Therefore, thus said Lord Y<small>HWH</small>: Because of your giving out your heart as the heart of God, **7** Therefore, behold, I am bringing in strangers against you, ‖ The terrible of the nations, ‖ And they have drawn out their swords ‖ Against the beauty of your wisdom, ‖ And they have pierced your brightness. **8** They bring you down to destruction, ‖ You die by the deaths of the wounded, in the heart of the seas. **9** Do you really say, I [am] God, ‖ Before him who is slaying you? And you [are] man, and not God, ‖ In the hand of him who is piercing you. **10** You die the deaths of the uncircumcised, ‖ By the hand of strangers, for I have spoken," ‖ A declaration of Lord Y<small>HWH</small>. **11** And there is a word of Y<small>HWH</small> to me, saying, **12** "Son of man, lift up a lamentation for the king of Tyre, ‖ And you have said to him, Thus said Lord Y<small>HWH</small>: You are sealing up a measurement, ‖ Full of wisdom, and perfect in beauty. **13** You have been in Eden, the garden of God, ‖ Every precious stone [was] your covering, ‖ Ruby, topaz, and diamond, beryl, onyx, and jasper, ‖ Sapphire, emerald, and

EZEKIEL

carbuncle, and gold, ‖ The workmanship of your tambourines and of your pipes, ‖ In you in the day of your being produced, have been created; **14** And I established you as the anointed, covering cherub, ‖ You have been in [the] holy mountain of God, ‖ You have walked up and down in [the] midst of [the] stones of fire. **15** You [were] perfect in your ways, ‖ From [the] day of your being created, ‖ Until perversity was found in you. **16** By [the] abundance of your merchandise ‖ They have filled your midst with violence, ‖ And you sin, ‖ And I thrust you from [the] mountain of God, ‖ And I destroy you, O covering cherub, ‖ From [the] midst of [the] stones of fire. **17** Your heart has been high because of your beauty, ‖ You have corrupted your wisdom because of your brightness, ‖ I have cast you to earth, ‖ I have set you before kings, to look on you, **18** From [the] abundance of your iniquity, ‖ By [the] perversity of your merchandise, ‖ You have defiled your sanctuaries, ‖ And I bring forth fire from your midst, ‖ It has devoured you, ‖ And I make you become ashes on the earth, ‖ In [the] eyes of all beholding you. **19** All knowing you among the peoples ‖ Have been astonished at you, ‖ You have been terrors, and you are not—for all time." **20** And there is a word of YHWH to me, saying, **21** "Son of man, set your face toward Sidon, and prophesy concerning it; **22** and you have said, Thus said Lord YHWH: Behold, I [am] against you, O Sidon, ‖ And I have been honored in your midst, ‖ And they have known that I [am] YHWH, ‖ In My doing judgments in her, ‖ And I have been sanctified in her. **23** And I have sent pestilence into her, ‖ And blood into her out-places, ‖ The wounded has been judged in her midst, ‖ By the sword on her all around, ‖ And they have known that I [am] YHWH. **24** And there is no more pricking brier and paining thorn ‖ For the house of Israel, ‖ Of all around them—despising them, ‖ And they have known that I [am] Lord YHWH. **25** Thus said Lord YHWH: In My gathering the house of Israel, ‖ Out of the peoples among whom they were scattered, ‖ I have been sanctified in them, ‖ Before the eyes of the nations, ‖ And they have dwelt on their ground, ‖ That I gave to My servant, to Jacob, **26** And they have dwelt confidently on it, ‖ And built houses, and planted vineyards, ‖ And dwelt confidently—in My doing judgments, ‖ On all those despising them all around, ‖ And they have known that I [am] their God YHWH!"

29 In the tenth year, in the tenth [month], on the twelfth of the month, a word of YHWH has been to me, saying, **2** "Son of man, set your face against Pharaoh king of Egypt, and prophesy concerning him, and concerning Egypt—all of it. **3** Speak, and you have said, Thus said Lord YHWH: Behold, I [am] against you, ‖ Pharaoh king of Egypt! The great dragon that is crouching in the midst of his floods, ‖ Who has said, My flood [is] my own, ‖ And I have made it [for] myself. **4** And I have put hooks in your jaws, ‖ And I have caused the fish of your floods to cleave to your scales, ‖ And I have caused you to come up from the midst of your floods, ‖ And every fish of your floods cleaves to your scales. **5** And I have left you in the wilderness, ‖ You and every fish of your floods, ‖ You fall on the face of the field, ‖ You are not gathered nor assembled, ‖ I have given you for food to the beast of the earth and to the bird of the heavens. **6** And all inhabitants of Egypt have known ‖ That I [am] YHWH, ‖ Because of their being a staff of reed to the house of Israel. **7** In their taking hold of you by your hand, ‖ You crush and have torn every shoulder of theirs, ‖ And in their leaning on you you are broken, ‖ And have caused all their thighs to stand. **8** Therefore, thus said Lord YHWH: Behold, I am bringing in a sword against you, ‖ And have cut off man and beast from you. **9** And the land of Egypt has been for a desolation and a ruin, ‖ And they have known that I [am] YHWH, ‖ Because he said: The flood [is] mine, and I made [it]. **10** Therefore, behold, I [am] against you, and against your floods, ‖ And have given the land of Egypt for ruins, ‖ A dry place, a desolation, from Migdol to Syene, ‖ And to the border of Cush. **11** A foot of man does not pass over into it, ‖ Indeed, the foot of beast does not pass into it, ‖ Nor is it inhabited forty years. **12** And I have made the land of Egypt a desolation, ‖ In the midst of desolate lands, ‖ And its cities, in the midst of cities [that are] laid waste, ‖ Are a desolation [for] forty years, ‖ And I have scattered the Egyptians among nations, ‖ And I have dispersed them through lands. **13** But thus said Lord YHWH: At the end of forty years I gather the Egyptians ‖ Out of the peoples to where

EZEKIEL

they have been scattered, **14** And I have turned back [to] the captivity of Egypt, ‖ And I have brought them back ‖ [To] the land of Pathros, to the land of their birth, ‖ And they have been a low kingdom there. **15** It is lowest of the kingdoms, ‖ And it does not lift itself up above the nations anymore, ‖ And I have made them few, ‖ So as not to rule among nations. **16** And it is no longer for confidence to the house of Israel, ‖ Bringing iniquity to remembrance, ‖ By their turning after them, ‖ And they have known that I [am] Lord YHWH." **17** And it comes to pass, in the twenty-seventh year, in the first [month], on the first of the month, a word of YHWH has been to me, saying, **18** "Son of man, Nebuchadnezzar king of Babylon, ‖ Has caused his force to serve a great service against Tyre, ‖ Every head [is] bald—every shoulder peeled, ‖ And neither he, nor his force, had reward out of Tyre, ‖ For the service that he served against it. **19** Therefore, thus said Lord YHWH: Behold, I am giving the land of Egypt to Nebuchadnezzar king of Babylon, ‖ And he has taken away its store, ‖ And has taken its spoil, and taken its prey, ‖ And it has been a reward to his force. **20** I have given to him his wage for which he labored—The land of Egypt, in that they worked for Me, ‖ A declaration of Lord YHWH. **21** In that day I cause a horn to shoot up for the house of Israel, ‖ And I give an opening to your mouth in their midst, ‖ And they have known that I [am] YHWH!"

30 And there is a word of YHWH to me, saying, **2** "Son of man, prophesy, and you have said, Thus said Lord YHWH: Howl, Aah! For the day! **3** For a day [is] near, a day [is] near to YHWH! It is a time of cloud [over] the nations. **4** And a sword has come into Egypt, ‖ And there has been great pain in Cush, ‖ In the falling of the wounded in Egypt, ‖ And they have taken its store, ‖ And its foundations have been broken down. **5** Cush, and Phut, and Lud, and all the mixture, and Chub, ‖ And the sons of the land of the covenant fall by sword with them, **6** Thus said YHWH: And those supporting Egypt have fallen, ‖ And the arrogance of her strength has come down, ‖ From Migdol to Syene, they fall by sword in her, ‖ A declaration of Lord YHWH. **7** And they have been desolated in the midst of desolate lands, ‖ And its cities are in the midst of cities [that are] laid waste.

8 And they have known that I [am] YHWH, ‖ In My giving fire against Egypt, ‖ And all her helpers have been broken. **9** In that day messengers go forth from before Me in ships, ‖ To trouble confident Cush, ‖ And there has been great pain among them, ‖ As the day of Egypt, for behold, it has come. **10** Thus said Lord YHWH: I have caused the multitude of Egypt to cease, ‖ By the hand of Nebuchadnezzar king of Babylon, **11** He and his people with him—the terrible of nations, ‖ Are brought in to destroy the land, ‖ And they have drawn their swords against Egypt, ‖ And have filled the land [with] the wounded. **12** And I have made floods a dry place, ‖ And I have sold the land into the hand of evildoers, ‖ And I have made the land desolate, ‖ And its fullness, by the hand of strangers, ‖ I, YHWH, have spoken. **13** Thus said Lord YHWH: And I have destroyed idols, ‖ And caused vain things to cease from Noph, ‖ And there is no longer a prince of the land of Egypt, ‖ And I give fear in the land of Egypt. **14** And I have made Pathros desolate, ‖ And I have given fire against Zoan, ‖ And I have done judgments in No, **15** And I have poured out My fury on Sin, the stronghold of Egypt, ‖ And I have cut off the multitude of No. **16** And I have given fire against Egypt, ‖ Sin is greatly pained, and No is to be broken, ‖ And Noph has daily distresses. **17** The youths of Aven and Pi-Beseth fall by sword, ‖ And these go into captivity. **18** And the day has been dark in Tehaphnehes, ‖ In My breaking the yokes of Egypt there, ‖ And the excellence of her strength has ceased in her, ‖ Her! A cloud covers her, ‖ And her daughters go into captivity. **19** And I have done judgments in Egypt, ‖ And they have known that I [am] YHWH." **20** And it comes to pass, in the eleventh year, in the first [month], on the seventh of the month, a word of YHWH has been to me, saying, "Son of man, **21** I have broken the arm of Pharaoh, king of Egypt, ‖ And behold, it has not been bound up to give healing, ‖ To put a bandage to bind it, ‖ To strengthen it—to lay hold on the sword. **22** Therefore, thus said Lord YHWH: Behold, I [am] against Pharaoh, king of Egypt, ‖ And I have broken his arms, ‖ The strong one and the broken one, ‖ And have caused the sword to fall out of his hand, **23** And I have scattered the Egyptians among nations, ‖ And have spread them through lands, **24** And I have strengthened the arms of the king of Babylon, ‖ And have given My sword into his hand, ‖ And I have broken the arms of Pharaoh, ‖ And he has groaned the groans of a pierced one—before him. **25** And I have strengthened the arms of the king of Babylon, ‖ And the arms of Pharaoh fall down, ‖ And they have known that I [am] YHWH, ‖ In My giving My sword into the hand of the king of Babylon, ‖ And he has stretched it out toward the land of Egypt. **26** And I have scattered the Egyptians among nations, ‖ And I have spread them through lands, ‖ And they have known that I [am] YHWH!"

31 And it comes to pass, in the eleventh year, in the third [month], on the first of the month, a word of YHWH has been to me, saying, **2** "Son of man, say to Pharaoh king of Egypt, and to his multitude: To whom have you been like in your greatness? **3** Behold, Asshur, a cedar in Lebanon, ‖ Beautiful in branch, and shading bough, and high in stature, ‖ And its foliage has been between thickets. **4** Waters have made it great, ‖ The deep has exalted him with its flowings, ‖ Going around its planting, ‖ And it has sent forth its conduits to all trees of the field. **5** Therefore his stature has been higher than all trees of the field, ‖ And his boughs are multiplied, and his branches are long, ‖ Because of many waters in his shooting forth. **6** Every bird of the heavens has made a nest in his boughs, ‖ And every beast of the field has brought forth under his branches, ‖ And all great nations dwell in his shade. **7** And he is beautiful in his greatness, ‖ In the length of his thin shoots, ‖ For his root has been by great waters. **8** Cedars have not hid him in the garden of God, ‖ Firs have not been like to his boughs, ‖ And plane-trees have not been as his branches, ‖ No tree in the garden of God has been like to him in his beauty, **9** I have made him beautiful in the multitude of his thin shoots, ‖ And all trees of Eden that [are] in the garden of God envy him. **10** Therefore, thus said Lord YHWH: Because that you have been high in stature, ‖ And he yields his foliage between thickets, ‖ And his heart is high in his haughtiness, **11** I give him into the hand of a god of nations, ‖ He deals severely with him, ‖ In his wickedness I have cast him out. **12** And strangers cut him off, ‖ The terrible of nations, and they leave him, ‖ His thin shoots have fallen on the mountains and in all valleys, ‖ And his boughs are broken at all streams of the land, ‖ And all peoples of the land go down from his shade, and they leave him. **13** Every bird of the heavens dwells on his ruin, ‖ And all beasts of the field have been on his boughs, **14** In order that none of the trees of the waters ‖ May become haughty because of their stature, ‖ Nor give their foliage between thickets, ‖ Nor any drinking waters stand up to them in their haughtiness, ‖ For all of them are given up to death, ‖ To the lower earth, ‖ In the midst of the sons of men, ‖ To those going down to the pit. **15** Thus said Lord YHWH: I have caused mourning in the day of his going down to Sheol, ‖ I have covered the deep over him, and diminish its flowings, ‖ And many waters are restrained, ‖ And I make Lebanon black for him, ‖ And all trees of the field [have been] a covering for him. **16** I have caused nations to shake at the sound of his fall, ‖ In My causing him to go down to Sheol, ‖ With those going down to the pit, ‖ And all trees of Eden are comforted in the lower earth, ‖ The choice and good of Lebanon—All drinking waters. **17** Those with him have also gone down to Sheol, ‖ To the pierced of the sword, ‖ And—his arm—they dwelt in his shade in the midst of nations. **18** To whom have you been thus like, ‖ In glory and in greatness among the trees of Eden? And you have been brought down with the trees of Eden, ‖ To the lower earth, ‖ You lie in the midst of the uncircumcised, ‖ With the pierced of the sword. This [is] Pharaoh, and all his multitude, ‖ A declaration of Lord YHWH!"

32 And it comes to pass, in the twelfth year, in the twelfth month, on the first of the month, a word of YHWH has been to me, saying, **2** "Son of man, lift up a lamentation for Pharaoh king of Egypt, and you have said to him: You have been like a young lion of nations, ‖ And you [are] as a dragon in the seas, ‖ And you come forth with your flowings, ‖ And trouble the waters with your feet, ‖ And you foul their flowings. **3** Thus said Lord YHWH: And I have spread out My net for you, ‖ With an assembly of many peoples, ‖ And they have brought you up in My net. **4** And I have left you in the land, ‖ I cast you out on the face of the field, ‖ And I have caused every bird of the heavens to dwell on you, ‖ And have satisfied every beast of the earth with you. **5** And I have put your flesh on the mountains, ‖ And filled the valleys [with] your heap, **6** And watered the land with your flowing, ‖ From your blood—to the mountains, ‖ And streams are filled with you. **7** And in quenching you I have covered the heavens, ‖ And have made their stars black, ‖ I cover the sun with a cloud, ‖ And the moon does not cause its light to shine. **8** I make all luminaries of light in the heavens black over you, ‖ And I have given darkness over your land, ‖ A declaration of Lord YHWH, **9** And I have distressed the heart of many peoples, ‖ In My bringing in your destruction among nations, ‖ To lands that you have not known. **10** And I have made many peoples astonished at you, ‖ And their kings are afraid because of you with trembling, ‖ In My brandishing My sword before their faces, ‖ And they have trembled every moment, ‖ Each for his life—in the day of your fall. **11** For thus said Lord YHWH: A sword of the king of Babylon enters you, **12** I cause your multitude to fall by swords of the mighty, ‖ The terrible of nations—all of them, ‖ And they have spoiled the excellence of Egypt, ‖ And all her multitude has been destroyed. **13** And I have destroyed all her beasts, ‖ From beside many waters, ‖ And a foot of man does not trouble them anymore, ‖ Indeed, the hooves of beasts do not trouble them. **14** Then I cause their waters to sink, ‖ And I cause their rivers to go as oil, ‖ A declaration of Lord YHWH. **15** In My making the land of Egypt a desolation, ‖ And the land has been desolated of its fullness, ‖ In My striking all the inhabitants in it, ‖ Then they have known that I [am] YHWH. **16** It [is] a lamentation, and they have lamented her, ‖ Daughters of the nations lament her, ‖ For Egypt, and for all her multitude, they lament her, ‖ A declaration of Lord YHWH." **17** And it comes to pass, in the twelfth year, on the fifteenth of the month, a word of YHWH has been to me, saying, **18** "Son of man, ‖ Wail for the multitude of Egypt, ‖ And cause it to go down, ‖ It, and the daughters of majestic nations, ‖ To the lower parts of the earth, ‖ With those going down to the pit. **19** Whom have you surpassed in beauty? Go down, and be laid with [the] uncircumcised. **20** They fall in the midst of the pierced of the sword, ‖ She has been given [to] the sword, ‖ They drew her out, and all her multitude. **21** The gods of the mighty speak to him out of the midst of Sheol, ‖ With his helpers—they have gone down, ‖ They have lain with the uncircumcised, ‖ The pierced of the sword. **22** There [is] Asshur, and all her assembly, ‖ His graves [are] around him, ‖ All of them [are] wounded, who are falling by sword, **23** Whose graves are appointed in the sides of the pit, ‖ And her assembly is around her grave, ‖ All of them wounded, falling by sword, ‖ Because they gave terror in the land of the living. **24** There [is] Elam, and all her multitude, ‖ Around her grave, ‖ All of them wounded, who are falling by sword, ‖ Who have gone down uncircumcised to the lower parts of the earth, ‖ Because they gave their terror in the land of the living, ‖ And they bear their shame with those going down to the pit. **25** They have appointed a bed for her in the midst of the wounded, ‖ With all her multitude, ‖ Her graves [are] around them, ‖ All of them uncircumcised, pierced of the sword, ‖ For their terror was given in the land of the living, ‖ And they bear their shame with those going down to the pit, ‖ He has been set in the midst of the pierced. **26** There [is] Meshech, Tubal, and all her multitude, ‖ Her graves [are] around them, ‖ All of them uncircumcised, pierced by the sword, ‖ For they gave their terror in the land of the living, **27** And they do not lie with the mighty, ‖ Who are falling of the uncircumcised, ‖ Who have gone down to Sheol with their weapons of war, ‖ And they put their swords under their heads, ‖ And their iniquities are on their bones, ‖ For the terror of the mighty [is] in the land of the living. **28** And you are broken in the midst of the uncircumcised, ‖ And lie with the pierced of the sword. **29** There [is] Edom, her kings, and all her princes, ‖ Who have been given up in their might, ‖ With the pierced of the sword, ‖ They lie with the uncircumcised, ‖ And with those going down to the pit. **30** There [are] princes of the north, ‖ All of them, and every Zidonian, ‖ Who have gone down with the pierced in their terror, ‖ They are ashamed of their might, ‖ And they lie uncircumcised with the pierced of the sword, ‖ And they bear their shame with those going down to the pit. **31** Then Pharaoh sees, ‖ And he has been comforted for all his multitude, ‖ The pierced of the sword—Pharaoh and all his force, ‖ A declaration of Lord YHWH. **32** For I have given his terror in the land of the living, ‖ And he has been laid down in [the] midst of [the] uncircumcised, ‖ With [the] pierced of [the] sword—Pharaoh, and all his multitude, ‖ A declaration of Lord YHWH!"

33 And there is a word of YHWH to me, saying, **2** "Son of man, speak to the sons of your people, and you have said to them: When I bring a sword on a land, ‖ And the people of the land have taken one man out of their borders, ‖ And made him their watchman, **3** And he has seen the sword coming against the land, ‖ And has blown with a horn, and has warned the people, **4** And the hearer has heard the voice of the horn, and he has not taken warning, ‖ And the sword comes in, and takes him away, ‖ His blood is on his [own] head. **5** The voice of the horn he heard, ‖ And he has not taken warning, his blood is on him, ‖ And he who took warning has delivered his soul. **6** And the watchman, when he sees the sword coming in, ‖ And he has not blown with a horn, ‖ And the people have not been warned, ‖ And a sword comes in, ‖ And takes away a soul from them, ‖ He is taken away in his iniquity, ‖ And I require his blood from the hand of the watchman. **7** And you, son of man, ‖ I gave you [as] a watchman for the house of Israel, ‖ And you have heard a word from My mouth, ‖ And you have warned them from Me. **8** In My saying to the wicked, O wicked one—you surely die, ‖ And you have not spoken to warn the wicked from his way, ‖ He—the wicked—dies in his iniquity, ‖ And I require his blood from your hand. **9** And you, when you have warned the wicked of his way, to turn back from it, ‖ And he has not turned back from his way, ‖ He dies in his iniquity, ‖ And you have delivered your soul. **10** And you, son of man, say to the house of Israel: You have spoken correctly, saying, ‖ Surely our transgressions and our sins [are] on us, ‖ And we are wasting away in them, ‖ How, then, do we live? **11** Say to them, [As] I live—a declaration of Lord YHWH, ‖ I do not delight in the death of the wicked, ‖ But in the turning of the wicked from his way, and he has lived. Turn back, turn back, from your evil ways! Indeed, why do you die, O house of Israel? **12** And you, son of man, say to the sons of your people: The righteousness of the righteous does not deliver him in the day of his transgression, ‖ And the wickedness of the wicked, ‖ He does not stumble for it in the day of his turning from his wickedness, ‖ And the righteous is not able to live in it in the day of his sinning. **13** In My saying of the righteous: He surely lives, ‖ And—he has trusted on his righteousness, ‖ And he has done perversity, ‖ All his righteous acts are not remembered, ‖ And for his perversity that he has done, ‖ He dies for it. **14** And in My saying to the wicked: You surely die, ‖ And—he has turned back from his sin, ‖ And has done judgment and righteousness, **15** (The wicked restores a pledge, he repays [for] plunder), ‖ He has walked in the statutes of life, ‖ So as not to do perversity, ‖ He surely lives—he does not die. **16** All his sin—his sins that he has sinned—are not remembered against him, ‖ He has done judgment and righteousness, ‖ He surely lives. **17** And the sons of your people have said: The way of the Lord is not pondered, ‖ As for them—their way is not pondered. **18** In the turning back of the righteous from his righteousness, ‖ And he has done perversity—he dies for it. **19** And in the turning back of the wicked from his wickedness, ‖ And he has done judgment and righteousness—he lives by them. **20** And you have said, The way of the Lord is not pondered; I judge each of you according to his ways, O house of Israel." **21** And it comes to pass, in the twelfth year—in the tenth [month], in the fifth of the month—of our removal, one who is escaped from Jerusalem comes to me, saying, "The city has been struck." **22** And the hand of YHWH has been to me in the evening, before the coming in of the escaped one, and He opens my mouth until [his] coming to me in the morning, and my mouth is opened, and I have not been silent again. **23** And there is a word of YHWH to me, saying, **24** "Son of man, the inhabitants of these ruins on the ground of Israel are speaking, saying, Abraham has been alone—and he possesses the land, and we [are] many—the land has been given to us for a possession. **25** Therefore say to them, Thus said Lord YHWH: You eat with the blood, ‖ And you lift up your eyes to your idols, ‖ And you shed blood, ‖ Should you then inherit the land? **26** You have stood on your sword, ‖ You have done abomination, ‖ You have each defiled the wife of his

EZEKIEL

neighbor, ‖ Should you then possess the land? **27** Thus you say to them, Thus said Lord YHWH: [As] I live—do they who [are] in the ruins not fall by the sword? And they who [are] on the face of the field, ‖ I have given for food to the beast, ‖ And they who are in strongholds and in caves die by pestilence. **28** And I have made the land a desolation and an astonishment, ‖ And the excellence of its strength has ceased, ‖ And mountains of Israel have been desolated, ‖ Without anyone passing through. **29** And they have known that I [am] YHWH, ‖ In My making the land a desolation and an astonishment, ‖ For all their abominations that they have done. **30** And you, son of man, ‖ The sons of your people who are speaking about you, ‖ By the walls, and in openings of the houses, ‖ Have spoken with one another, each with his brother, ‖ Saying, Please come in, ‖ And hear what the word [is] that comes out from YHWH. **31** And they come in to you as the coming in of a people, ‖ And they sit before you— My people, ‖ And have heard your words, and they do not do them, ‖ For they are making unhealthy loves with their mouth, ‖ Their heart is going after their dishonest gain. **32** And behold, you [are] as a singer of unhealthy loves to them, ‖ A beautiful voice, and playing well on an instrument, ‖ And they have heard your words, and they are not doing them. **33** And in its coming in—behold, it has come, ‖ And they have known that a prophet has been in their midst!"

34 And there is a word of YHWH to me, saying, **2** "Son of man, prophesy concerning shepherds of Israel, prophesy, and you have said to them, Thus said Lord YHWH to the shepherds: Woe [to] the shepherds of Israel, ‖ Who have been feeding themselves! Do the shepherds not feed the flock? **3** You eat the fat, and you put on the wool, ‖ You slaughter the fed one, ‖ You do not feed the flock. **4** You have not strengthened the weak, ‖ And you have not healed the sick one, ‖ And you have not bound up the broken, ‖ And have not brought back the driven away, ‖ And you have not sought the lost, ‖ And you have ruled them with might and with rigor. **5** And they are scattered from want of a shepherd, ‖ And are for food to every beast of the field, ‖ Indeed, they are scattered. **6** My flock goes astray on all the mountains, ‖ And on every high hill, ‖ And My flock has been scattered on [the] whole face of the earth, ‖ And there is none inquiring, and none seeking. **7** Therefore, shepherds, hear a word of YHWH: **8** [As] I live—a declaration of Lord YHWH, ‖ If not, because of My flock being for a prey, ‖ Indeed, My flock is for food to every beast of the field, ‖ Because there is no shepherd, ‖ And My shepherds have not sought My flock, ‖ And the shepherds feed themselves, ‖ And they have not fed My flock. **9** Therefore, O shepherds, hear a word of YHWH! **10** Thus said Lord YHWH: Behold, I [am] against the shepherds, ‖ And have required My flock from their hand, ‖ And caused them to cease from feeding the flock, ‖ And the shepherds feed themselves no more, ‖ And I have delivered My flock from their mouth, ‖ And they are not for food to them. **11** For thus said Lord YHWH: Behold, I—even I, have required My flock, ‖ And I have sought it out. **12** As a shepherd's searching of his drove, ‖ In the day of his being in the midst of his scattered flock, so I seek My flock, ‖ And have delivered them out of all places, ‖ To where they have been scattered, ‖ In a day of cloud and thick darkness. **13** And I have brought them out from the peoples, ‖ And have gathered them from the lands, ‖ And brought them to their own ground, ‖ And have fed them on mountains of Israel, ‖ By streams, and by all dwellings of the land. **14** I feed them with good pasture, ‖ And their habitation is on mountains of the high place of Israel, ‖ There they lie down in a good habitation, ‖ And they enjoy fat pastures on mountains of Israel. **15** I feed My flock, and cause them to lie down, ‖ A declaration of Lord YHWH. **16** I seek the lost, and bring back the driven away, ‖ And I bind up the broken, and I strengthen the sick, ‖ And I destroy the fat and the strong, ‖ I feed it with judgment. **17** And you, My flock, thus said Lord YHWH: Behold, I am judging between sheep and sheep, ‖ Between rams and male goats. **18** Is it a little thing for you—[that] you enjoy the good pasture, ‖ And tread down the remnant of your pasture with your feet, ‖ And drink a depth of waters, ‖ And trample the remainder with your feet, **19** And My flock consumes the trodden thing of your feet, ‖ And drinks the trampled thing of your feet? **20** Therefore, thus said Lord YHWH to them: Behold, I—even I, have

EZEKIEL

judged between fat sheep and lean sheep. **21** Because you thrust away with side and with shoulder, ‖ And push all the diseased with your horns, ‖ Until you have scattered them to the out-place, **22** Therefore I have given safety to My flock, ‖ And they are not for prey anymore, ‖ And I have judged between sheep and sheep. **23** And have raised up one shepherd over them, ‖ And he has fed them—My servant David, ‖ He feeds them, and he is their shepherd, **24** And I, YHWH, I am their God, ‖ And My servant David [is] prince in their midst, ‖ I, YHWH, have spoken. **25** And I have made a covenant of peace with them, ‖ And caused evil beasts to cease out of the land, ‖ And they have dwelt confidently in a wilderness, ‖ And they have slept in forests. **26** And I have given them, and the outskirts of My hill, a blessing, ‖ And caused the shower to come down in its season, ‖ They are showers of blessing. **27** And the tree of the field has given its fruit, ‖ And the land gives her increase, ‖ And they have been confident on their land, ‖ And they have known that I [am] YHWH, ‖ In My breaking the bands of their yoke, ‖ And I have delivered them from the hand of those laying service on them. **28** And they are no longer a prey to nations, ‖ And the beast of the earth does not devour them, ‖ And they have dwelt confidently, ‖ And there is none troubling. **29** And I have raised a plantation of renown for them, ‖ And they are no longer consumed by hunger in the land, ‖ And they no longer bear the shame of the nations. **30** And they have known that I, YHWH, their God, [am] with them, ‖ And they—the house of Israel—My people, ‖ A declaration of Lord YHWH. **31** And you, My flock, the flock of My pasture, ‖ You [are] men [and] I [am] your God, ‖ A declaration of Lord YHWH!"

35 And there is a word of YHWH to me, saying, **2** "Son of man, set your face against Mount Seir, and prophesy against it, **3** and you have said to it, Thus said Lord YHWH: Behold, I [am] against you, O Mount Seir, ‖ And have stretched out My hand against you, ‖ And made you a desolation and an astonishment. **4** I make your cities a ruin, and you are a desolation, ‖ And you have known that I [am] YHWH. **5** Because of your having continuous enmity, ‖ And you saw the sons of Israel, ‖ By the hands of the sword, ‖ In the time of their calamity, ‖ In the time of the iniquity of the end: **6** Therefore, [as] I live—a declaration of Lord YHWH, ‖ Surely I appoint you for blood, ‖ And blood pursues you, ‖ If you have not hated blood, ‖ Blood also pursues you. **7** And I have given Mount Seir for a desolation and an astonishment, ‖ And have cut off from it him who is passing over and him who is returning, **8** And filled his mountains with his wounded, ‖ Your hills, and your valleys, and all your streams, ‖ The pierced of the sword fall into them. **9** I make you continuous desolations, ‖ And your cities do not return, ‖ And you have known that I [am] YHWH. **10** Because of your saying: The two nations and the two lands are mine, and we have possessed it, ‖ And YHWH has been there; **11** Therefore, [as] I live—a declaration of Lord YHWH, ‖ And I have done according to your anger, ‖ And according to your envy, ‖ With which you have worked, ‖ Because of your hatred against them, ‖ And I have been known among them when I judge you. **12** And you have known that I [am] YHWH, ‖ I have heard all your despisings that you have spoken ‖ Against mountains of Israel, saying, ‖ A desolation—they were given to us for food. **13** And you magnify yourselves against Me with your mouth, ‖ And have made your words abundant against Me; I have heard. **14** Thus said Lord YHWH: According to the rejoicing of the whole land, ‖ I make a desolation of you. **15** According to your joy at the inheritance of the house of Israel because of desolation, ‖ So I do to you—you are a desolation, ‖ O Mount Seir, and all Edom—all of it, ‖ And they have known that I [am] YHWH!"

36 "And you, son of man, prophesy to mountains of Israel, and you have said, O mountains of Israel, hear a word of YHWH! **2** Thus said Lord YHWH: Because the enemy said against you, Aha! The high places of old have also become our possession, **3** therefore, prophesy, and you have said, Thus said Lord YHWH: Because, even because, of desolating, ‖ And of swallowing you up from all around, ‖ For your being a possession to the remnant of the nations, ‖ And you are taken up on the tip of the tongue, ‖ And [are] an evil report to the people. **4** Therefore, O mountains of Israel, ‖ Hear a word of Lord YHWH! Thus said Lord YHWH, to mountains, and to hills, ‖ To streams, and to valleys, ‖ And to ruins that [are] desolate, ‖ And to cities that are forsaken, ‖ That have been for a prey, ‖ And for a scorn, to the remnant of the surrounding nations, **5** Therefore, thus said Lord YHWH: Have I not, in the fire of My jealousy, ‖ Spoken against the remnant of the nations, ‖ And against Edom—all of it, ‖ Who gave My land to themselves for a possession, ‖ With the joy of the whole heart—with despite of soul, ‖ For the sake of casting it out for a prey? **6** Therefore, prophesy concerning the ground of Israel, ‖ And you have said to mountains, and to hills, ‖ To streams, and to valleys, ‖ Thus said Lord YHWH: Behold, I, in My jealousy and in My fury, have spoken, ‖ Because you have borne the shame of nations. **7** Therefore, thus said Lord YHWH: I have lifted up My hand, ‖ Do the nations who [are] surrounding you not bear their own shame? **8** And you, O mountains of Israel, ‖ You give out your branch, ‖ And you bear your fruits for My people Israel, ‖ For they have drawn near to come. **9** For behold, I [am] for you, and have turned to you, ‖ And you have been tilled and sown. **10** And I have multiplied men on you, ‖ All the house of Israel—all of it, ‖ And the cities have been inhabited, ‖ And the ruins are built. **11** And I have multiplied man and beast on you, ‖ And they have multiplied and been fruitful, ‖ And I have caused you to dwell according to your former states, ‖ And I have done better than at your beginnings, ‖ And you have known that I [am] YHWH. **12** And I have caused man to walk over you—My people Israel, ‖ And they possess you, and you have been their inheritance, ‖ And you no longer add to bereave them. **13** Thus said Lord YHWH: Because they are saying to you, You [are] a devourer of men, ‖ And you have been a bereaver of your nations, **14** Therefore, you no longer devour man, ‖ And you do not cause your nations to stumble anymore, ‖ A declaration of Lord YHWH. **15** And I do not proclaim the shame of the nations to you anymore, ‖ And you no longer bear the reproach of peoples, ‖ And your nations do not stumble anymore, ‖ A declaration of Lord YHWH." **16** And there is a word of YHWH to me, saying, **17** "Son of man, ‖ The house of Israel are dwelling on their land, ‖ And they defile it by their way and by their doings, ‖ Their way has been as the uncleanness of a separated one before Me. **18** And I pour out My fury on them ‖ For the blood that they shed on the land, ‖ And they have defiled it with their idols. **19** And I scatter them among nations, ‖ And they are spread through lands, ‖ According to their way, and according to their doings, ‖ I have judged them. **20** And one goes to the nations to where they have gone, ‖ And they defile My holy Name by saying to them, ‖ These [are] the people of YHWH, ‖ And they have gone forth from His land. **21** And I have pity on My holy Name, ‖ That the house of Israel has defiled ‖ Among the nations to where they have gone in. **22** Therefore, say to the house of Israel, Thus said Lord YHWH: I am not working for your sake, ‖ O house of Israel, but for My holy Name ‖ That you have defiled ‖ Among the nations to where you have gone in. **23** And I have sanctified My great Name, ‖ That is profaned among the nations, ‖ That you have defiled in your midst, ‖ And the nations have known that I [am] YHWH, ‖ A declaration of Lord YHWH, ‖ In My being sanctified in you before your eyes. **24** And I have taken you out of the nations, ‖ And have gathered you out of all the lands, ‖ And I have brought you into your land, **25** And I have sprinkled clean water over you, ‖ And you have been clean; I cleanse you from all your uncleannesses, ‖ And from all your idols. **26** And I have given a new heart to you, ‖ And I give a new spirit in your midst, ‖ And I have turned aside the heart of stone out of your flesh, ‖ And I have given a heart of flesh to you. **27** And I give My Spirit in your midst, ‖ And I have done this, so that you walk in My statutes, ‖ And you keep My judgments, and have done them. **28** And you have dwelt in the land that I have given to your fathers, ‖ And you have been to Me for a people, ‖ And I am to you for God. **29** And I have saved you from all your uncleannesses, ‖ And I have called to the grain, and multiplied it, ‖ And I have put no famine on you. **30** And I have multiplied the fruit of the tree, ‖ And the increase of the field, ‖ So that you do not receive a reproach of famine among nations anymore. **31** And you have remembered your ways that [are] evil, ‖ And your doings that [are] not good, ‖ And have been loathsome in your own faces, ‖ For your iniquities, and for your abominations. **32** I am not working for your sake, ‖ A

EZEKIEL

declaration of Lord YHWH, ‖ Be it known to you, ‖ Be ashamed and confounded, because of your ways, ‖ O house of Israel. **33** Thus said Lord YHWH: In the day of My cleansing you from all your iniquities, ‖ I have caused the cities to be inhabited, ‖ And the ruins have been built, **34** And the desolate land is tilled, ‖ Instead of which it was a desolation before the eyes of everyone passing by, **35** And they have said: This land, that was desolated, ‖ Has been as the Garden of Eden, ‖ And the cities—the dried up, ‖ And the desolated, and the broken down, ‖ [And the] fortified have remained. **36** And the nations who are left around you have known ‖ That I, YHWH, have built the thrown down, ‖ I have planted the desolated: I, YHWH, have spoken, and I have done [it]. **37** Thus said Lord YHWH: Yet this I am inquired of by the house of Israel to do for them: I multiply them as a flock of men, **38** As a flock of holy ones, as a flock of Jerusalem, ‖ In her appointed times, ‖ So the dried up cities are full of flocks of man, ‖ And they have known that I [am] YHWH!"

37 There has been a hand of YHWH on me, and He takes me forth in [the] Spirit of YHWH, and places me in the midst of the valley, and it is full of bones, **2** and He causes me to pass over by them, all around, and behold, very many [are] on the face of the valley, and behold—very dry. **3** And He says to me, "Son of man, do these bones live?" And I say, "O Lord YHWH, You have known." **4** And He says to me, "Prophesy concerning these bones, and you have said to them, O dry bones, hear a word of YHWH! **5** Thus said Lord YHWH to these bones: Behold, I am bringing a spirit into you, and you have lived, **6** and I have given sinews on you, and cause flesh to come up on you, and covered you over with skin, and given a spirit in you, and you have lived, and you have known that I [am] YHWH." **7** And I have prophesied as I have been commanded, and there is a noise as I am prophesying, and behold, a rushing, and the bones draw near, bone to its bone. **8** And I beheld, and behold, sinews [are] on them, and flesh has come up, and skin covers them over above—and there is no spirit in them. **9** And He says to me: "Prophesy to the Spirit, prophesy, son of man, and you have said to the Spirit, Thus said Lord YHWH: Come in from the four winds, O Spirit, and breathe on these slain, and they live." **10** And I have prophesied as He commanded me, and the Spirit comes into them, and they live, and stand on their feet—a very, very great force. **11** And He says to me, "Son of man, these bones are the whole house of Israel; behold, they are saying, Our bones have dried up, ‖ And our hope has perished, ‖ We have been cut off by ourselves. **12** Therefore, prophesy, and you have said to them, Thus said Lord YHWH: Behold, I am opening your graves, ‖ And have brought you up out of your graves, O My people, ‖ And brought you into the land of Israel. **13** And you have known that I [am] YHWH, ‖ In My opening your graves, ‖ And in My bringing you up out of your graves, O My people. **14** And I have given My Spirit in you, and you have lived, ‖ And I have caused you to rest on your land, ‖ And you have known that I, YHWH, have spoken, and I have done [it], ‖ A declaration of YHWH." **15** And there is a word of YHWH to me, saying, **16** "And you, son of man, take one stick for yourself, and write on it, ‖ For Judah, and for the sons of Israel, his companions; and take another stick, and write on it, ‖ For Joseph, the stick of Ephraim, and all the house of Israel, his companions, **17** and bring them near to one another, to you, for one stick, and they have become one in your hand. **18** And when sons of your people speak to you, saying, Do you not declare to us what these [are] to you? **19** Speak to them, Thus said Lord YHWH: Behold, I am taking the stick of Joseph, that [is] in the hand of Ephraim, and the tribes of Israel his companions, and have given them to him, with the stick of Judah, and have made them become one stick, and they have been one in My hand. **20** And the sticks on which you write have been in your hand before your eyes, **21** and speak to them, Thus said Lord YHWH: Behold, I am taking the sons of Israel, ‖ From among the nations to where they have gone, ‖ And have gathered them from all around, ‖ And I have brought them into their land. **22** And I have made them become one nation in the land, on mountains of Israel, ‖ And one king is to them all for king, ‖ And they are no longer as two nations, ‖ Nor are they divided anymore into two kingdoms again. **23** Nor are they defiled anymore with their idols, ‖ And with their abominations, ‖ And with any of their transgressions, ‖ And I have

EZEKIEL

saved them out of all their dwellings, ‖ In which they have sinned, ‖ And I have cleansed them, ‖ And they have been to Me for a people, ‖ And I am to them for God. **24** And My servant David [is] king over them, ‖ And they all have one shepherd, ‖ And they go in My judgments, ‖ And they keep My statutes, and have done them. **25** And they have dwelt on the land that I gave to My servant, to Jacob, ‖ In which your fathers have dwelt, ‖ And they have dwelt on it, they and their sons, ‖ And their son's sons—for all time, ‖ And My servant David [is] their prince for all time. **26** And I have made a covenant of peace with them, ‖ It is a perpetual covenant with them, ‖ And I have placed them, and multiplied them, ‖ And placed My sanctuary in their midst for all time. **27** And My dwelling place has been over them, ‖ And I have been to them for God, ‖ And they have been to Me for a people. **28** And the nations have known that I, YHWH, am sanctifying Israel, ‖ In My sanctuary being in their midst for all time!"

38 And there is a word of YHWH to me, saying, **2** "Son of man, set your face toward Gog, of the land of Magog, chief prince of [[*or* prince of Rosh,]] Meshech and Tubal, and prophesy concerning him, **3** and you have said, Thus says Lord YHWH: Behold, I [am] against you, O Gog, ‖ Chief prince of [[*or* prince of Rosh,]] Meshech and Tubal, **4** And I have turned you back, ‖ And I have put hooks in your jaws, ‖ And have brought you out, and all your force, ‖ Horses and horsemen, ‖ All of them clothed in perfection, ‖ A numerous assembly, [with] buckler and shield, ‖ All of them handling swords. **5** Persia, Cush, and Phut, with them, ‖ All of them [with] shield and helmet. **6** Gomer and all its bands, ‖ The house of Togarmah [from] the sides of the north, ‖ And all its bands, many peoples with you, **7** Be prepared, indeed, prepare yourself, ‖ You and all your assemblies who are assembled to you, ‖ And you have been for a watch for them. **8** After many days you are appointed, ‖ In the latter end of the years you come into a land brought back from sword—Gathered out of many peoples, ‖ On mountains of Israel, ‖ That have been for a continuous ruin, ‖ And it has been brought out from the peoples, ‖ And all of them have dwelt safely. **9** And you have gone up—you come in as desolation, ‖ You are as a cloud to cover the land, ‖ You and all your bands, and many peoples with you. **10** Thus said Lord YHWH: And it has come to pass in that day, ‖ Things come up on your heart, ‖ And you have thought an evil thought, **11** And you have said: I go up over a land of open places, ‖ I go to those at rest, dwelling confidently, ‖ All of them are dwelling without walls, ‖ And they have no bar and doors— **12** To take a spoil, and to take a prey, ‖ To turn back your hand on inhabited ruins, ‖ And on a people gathered out of nations, ‖ Making livestock and substance, ‖ Dwelling on a high part of the land. **13** Sheba, and Dedan, and merchants of Tarshish, ‖ And all its young lions say to you, ‖ Are you coming to take spoil? Have you assembled your assembly to take prey? To carry away silver and gold? To take away livestock and substance? To take a great spoil? **14** Therefore, prophesy, son of man, and you have said to Gog, Thus said Lord YHWH: In that day, in the dwelling of My people Israel safely, ‖ Do you not know? **15** And you have come in out of your place, ‖ From the sides of the north, ‖ You and many peoples with you, ‖ Riding on horses—all of them, ‖ A great assembly, and a numerous force. **16** And you have come up against My people Israel, ‖ As a cloud to cover the land, ‖ It is in the latter end of the days, ‖ And I have brought you in against My land, ‖ In order that the nations may know Me, ‖ In My being sanctified in you before their eyes, O Gog. **17** Thus said Lord YHWH: Are you he of whom I spoke in former days, ‖ By the hand of My servants, prophets of Israel, ‖ Who were prophesying [for] years in those days, ‖ To bring you in against them? **18** And it has come to pass in that day, ‖ In the day of the coming in of Gog against the land of Israel, ‖ A declaration of Lord YHWH, ‖ My fury comes up in My face, **19** And in My zeal, in the fire of My wrath, ‖ I have spoken: Is there not a great rushing on the land of Israel in that day? **20** And rushed from My presence have fishes of the sea, ‖ And the bird of the heavens, ‖ And the beast of the field, ‖ And every creeping thing that is creeping on the ground, ‖ And all men who [are] on the face of the ground, ‖ And the mountains have been thrown down, ‖ And the ascents have fallen, ‖ And every wall falls to the earth. **21** And I have called for a sword against him throughout all My mountains, ‖ A declaration of Lord YHWH,

‖ The sword of each is against his brother. **22** And I have judged him with pestilence and with blood, ‖ And an overflowing rain and hailstones, ‖ I rain fire and brimstone on him, and on his bands, ‖ And on many peoples who [are] with him. **23** And I have magnified Myself, and sanctified Myself, ‖ And I have been known before the eyes of many nations, ‖ And they have known that I [am] YHWH!"

39 "And you, son of man, prophesy concerning Gog, and you have said, Thus said Lord YHWH: Behold, I [am] against you, O Gog, ‖ Chief prince of [[*or* prince of Rosh,]] Meshech and Tubal, **2** And have turned you back, and enticed you, ‖ And caused you to come up from the sides of the north, ‖ And brought you in against mountains of Israel, **3** And have struck your bow out of your left hand, ‖ Indeed, I cause your arrows to fall out of your right. **4** You fall on mountains of Israel, ‖ You, and all your bands, and the peoples who [are] with you, ‖ To ravenous bird—a bird of every wing, ‖ And [to] a beast of the field, I have given you for food. **5** You fall on the face of the field, for I have spoken, ‖ A declaration of Lord YHWH. **6** And I have sent a fire against Magog, ‖ And against the confident inhabitants of the islands, ‖ And they have known that I [am] YHWH. **7** And I make My holy Name known in the midst of My people Israel, ‖ And I do not defile My holy Name anymore, ‖ And the nations have known that I, YHWH, the Holy One, [am] in Israel. **8** Behold, it has come, and it has been done, ‖ A declaration of Lord YHWH, ‖ It [is] the day of which I spoke. **9** And those dwelling [in the] cities of Israel have gone out, ‖ And they have burned and kindled [a fire], ‖ With armor, and shield, and buckler, ‖ With bow, and with arrows, ‖ And with hand weapon, and with javelin, ‖ And they have caused a fire to burn seven years with them, **10** And they do not take wood out of the field, ‖ Nor do they hew out of the forests, ‖ For they cause the fire to burn with armor, ‖ And they have spoiled their spoilers, ‖ And they have plundered their plunderers, ‖ A declaration of Lord YHWH. **11** And it has come to pass in that day, I give a place to Gog there—a grave in Israel, the valley of those passing by, east of the sea, and it is stopping those passing by, and they have buried there Gog, and all his multitude, and have cried, O valley of the multitude of Gog! **12** And the house of Israel has buried them—in order to cleanse the land—seven months. **13** Indeed, all the people of the land have buried them, and it has been to them for a name—the day of My being honored—a declaration of Lord YHWH. **14** And they separate men for continual employment, with those passing through, passing on through the land, burying those who are left on the face of the earth, to cleanse it. At the end of seven months they search. **15** And those passing by have passed through the land, and seen a bone of man, and one has constructed a sign near it until those burying have buried it in the valley of the multitude of Gog. **16** And also the name of the city [is] The Multitude; and they have cleansed the land. **17** And you, son of man, thus said Lord YHWH: Say to the bird—every wing, and to every beast of the field: Be assembled and come in, ‖ Be gathered from all around, ‖ For My sacrifice that I am sacrificing for you, ‖ A great sacrifice on mountains of Israel, ‖ And you have eaten flesh, and drunk blood. **18** You eat [the] flesh of [the] mighty, ‖ And you drink [the] blood of [the] princes of the earth, ‖ Of rams, of lambs, and of male goats, ‖ Of calves, fatlings of Bashan—all of them. **19** And you have eaten fat to satiety, ‖ And you have drunk blood—to drunkenness, ‖ Of My sacrifice that I sacrificed for you. **20** And you have been satisfied at My table with horse and rider, ‖ Mighty man, and every man of war, ‖ A declaration of Lord YHWH. **21** And I have given My glory among nations, ‖ And all the nations have seen My judgment that I have done, ‖ And My hand that I have laid on them. **22** And the house of Israel has known that I [am] their God YHWH, ‖ From that day and from now on. **23** And the nations have known ‖ That the house of Israel was removed for their iniquity, ‖ Because they have trespassed against Me, ‖ And I hide My face from them, ‖ And give them into the hand of their adversaries, ‖ And they fall by sword—all of them. **24** According to their uncleanness, ‖ And according to their transgressions, I have done with them, ‖ And I hide My face from them. **25** Therefore, thus said Lord YHWH: Now I bring back the captivity of Jacob, ‖ And I have pitied all the house of Israel, ‖ And have been zealous for My holy Name. **26** And they have forgotten their shame, ‖

And all their trespass that they trespassed against Me, ‖ In their dwelling on their land confidently and none troubling. **27** In My bringing them back from the peoples, ‖ I have assembled them from the lands of their enemies, ‖ And I have been sanctified in them before the eyes of the many nations, **28** And they have known that I [am] their God YHWH, ‖ In My removing them to the nations, ‖ And I have gathered them to their land, ‖ And I leave none of them there anymore. **29** And I do not hide My face from them anymore, ‖ In that I have poured out My Spirit on the house of Israel, ‖ A declaration of Lord YHWH!"

40 In the twenty-fifth year of our removal, in the beginning of the year, on the tenth of the month, in the fourteenth year after which the city was struck, on this very same day a hand of YHWH has been on me, and He brings me in there; **2** in visions of God He has brought me into the land of Israel, and causes me to rest on a very high mountain, and on it [is] as the frame of a city from the south. **3** And He brings me in there, and behold, a man, his appearance as the appearance of bronze, and a thread of flax in his hand, and a measuring-reed, and he is standing at the gate, **4** and the man speaks to me: "Son of man, see with your eyes, ‖ And hear with your ears, ‖ And set your heart to all that I am showing you, ‖ For in order to show [it] you, ‖ You have been brought in here, ‖ Declare all that you are seeing to the house of Israel." **5** And behold, a wall all around on the outside of the house, and a measuring-reed in the hand of the man, six cubits by a cubit and a handbreadth, and he measures the breadth of the building—one reed, and the height—one reed. **6** And he comes to the gate whose front [is] eastward, and he goes up by its steps, and he measures the threshold of the gate—one reed broad, even one threshold—one reed broad, **7** and the little chamber—one reed long and one reed broad, and between the little chambers—five cubits, and the threshold of the gate, from the side of the porch of the gate from within—one reed. **8** And he measures the porch of the gate from within—one reed, **9** and he measures the porch of the gate—eight cubits, and its posts—two cubits, and the porch of the gates from within, **10** and the little chambers of the gate eastward, three on this side and three on that side; the three of them—one measure, and the posts—one measure, on this side and on that side. **11** And he measures the breadth of the opening of the gate—ten cubits, the length of the gate—thirteen cubits; **12** and a border before the little chambers—one cubit, and one cubit [is] the border on this side, and the little chamber—six cubits on this side, and six cubits on that side. **13** And he measures the gate from the roof of the [one] little chamber to the roof of another; the breadth—twenty-five cubits, opening opposite opening. **14** And he makes the posts of sixty cubits, even to the post of the court, the gate all around; **15** and by the front of the gate of the entrance, by the front of the porch of the inner gate—fifty cubits; **16** and narrow windows [are] in the little chambers, and in their posts on the inside of the gate all around—and so to the arches—and windows all around on the inside, and palm-trees [are] on the post. **17** And he brings me into the outer court, and behold, chambers and a pavement made for the court all around—thirty chambers on the pavement— **18** and the pavement to the side of the gates, corresponding to the length of the gates, [is] the lower pavement; **19** and he measures the breadth from before the lower gate, to the front of the inner court, on the outside—one hundred cubits, eastward and northward. **20** As for the gate of the outer court whose front [is] northward, he has measured its length and its breadth; **21** and its little chambers, three on this side and three on that side, and its posts and its arches have been according to the measure of the first gate, its length [is] fifty cubits, and breadth [is] twenty-five by the cubit; **22** and its windows, and its arches, and its palm-trees [are] according to the measure of the gate whose face [is] eastward, and they go up on it by seven steps, and its arches [are] before them. **23** And the gate of the inner court [is] opposite the gate at the north and at the east; and he measures from gate to gate—one hundred cubits. **24** And he causes me to go southward, and behold, a gate southward, and he has measured its posts and its arches according to these measurements; **25** and windows [are] in it and in its arches all around, like these windows, the length—fifty cubits, and the breadth—twenty-five cubits; **26** and seven steps [are] its ascent, and its arches [are]

EZEKIEL

before them, and palm-trees [are] in it, one on this side and one on that side, on its posts; **27** and the gate of the inner court [is] southward, and he measures from gate to gate southward, one hundred cubits. **28** And he brings me into the inner court by the south gate, and he measures the south gate according to these measurements; **29** and its little chambers, and its posts, and its arches [are] according to these measurements, and windows [are] in it and in its arches all around; the length—fifty cubits, and the breadth—twenty-five cubits. **30** As for the arches all around, the length—twenty-five cubits, and the breadth—five cubits; **31** and its arches [are] toward the outer court, and palm-trees [are] on its posts, and eight steps [are] its ascent. **32** And he brings me into the inner court eastward, and he measures the gate according to these measurements; **33** and its little chambers, and its posts, and its arches [are] according to these measurements: and windows [are] in it and in its arches all around, the length—fifty cubits, and the breadth—twenty-five cubits; **34** and its arches [are] toward the outer court, and palm-trees [are] toward its posts, on this side and on that side, and eight steps [are] its ascent. **35** And he brings me into the north gate, and has measured according to these measurements; **36** its little chambers, its posts, and its arches; and windows [are] in it all around: the length—fifty cubits, and the breadth—twenty-five cubits; **37** and its posts [are] toward the outer court, and palm-trees [are] on its posts, on this side and on that side, and eight steps [are] its ascent. **38** And the chamber and its opening [is] by the posts of the gates, there they purge the burnt-offering. **39** And in the porch of the gate [are] two tables on this side and two tables on that side, to slaughter on them the burnt-offering, and the sin-offering, and the guilt-offering; **40** and at the side without, at the going up to the opening of the north gate, [are] two tables; and at the other side that [is] at the porch of the gate, [are] two tables; **41** four tables [are] on this side and four tables on that side, at the side of the gate, eight tables on which they slaughter. **42** And the four tables for burnt-offering [are] of hewn stone: the length—one cubit and a half, and the breadth—one cubit and a half, and the height—one cubit; they place on them the instruments with which they slaughter the burnt-offering and the sacrifice. **43** And the boundaries [are] one handbreadth, prepared within all around: and the flesh of the offering [is] on the tables. **44** And on the outside of the inner gate [are] chambers of the singers, in the inner court, that [are] at the side of the north gate, and their fronts [are] southward, one at the side of the east gate [with] front northward. **45** And he speaks to me: "This chamber, whose front [is] southward, [is] for priests keeping charge of the house; **46** and the chamber, whose front [is] northward, [is] for priests keeping charge of the altar: they [are] sons of Zadok, who are drawing near of the sons of Levi to YHWH, to serve Him." **47** And he measures the court: the length—one hundred cubits, and the breadth—one hundred cubits, square, and the altar [is] before the house. **48** And he brings me to the porch of the house, and he measures the post of the porch—five cubits on this side and five cubits on that side, and the breadth of the gate—three cubits on this side and three cubits on that side; **49** the length of the porch—twenty cubits, and the breadth—eleven [[*or* twelve]] cubits; and they go up to it by the [[ten]] steps. And pillars [are] by the posts, one on this side and one on that side.

41 And he brings me into the temple, and he measures the posts, six cubits the breadth on this side and six cubits the breadth on that side—the breadth of the tent. **2** And the breadth of the opening [is] ten cubits; and the sides of the opening [are] five cubits on this side and five cubits on that side; and he measures its length—forty cubits, and the breadth—twenty cubits. **3** And he has gone inward, and measures the post of the opening—two cubits, and the opening—six cubits, and the breadth of the opening—seven cubits. **4** And he measures its length—twenty cubits, and the breadth—twenty cubits, to the front of the temple, and he says to me, "This [is] the Holy of Holies." **5** And he measures the wall of the house—six cubits, and the breadth of the side-chamber—four cubits, all around the house. **6** And the side-chambers [are] side-chamber by side-chamber, thirty-three times; and they are entering into the wall—which the house has for the side-chambers all around—to be taken hold of, and they are not taken hold of by the wall of the house. **7** And it has become wider when one has turned even higher toward the side-chambers, for the encompassment of the house [is] even higher all around the house: therefore the breadth of the house [goes] upwards, and so the lower [story] goes up to the higher by the middle. **8** And I have looked at the height all around the house: the foundations of the side-chambers [are] the fullness of the reed, six cubits by the joining. **9** The breadth of that wall, of the side-chamber, at the outside, [is] five cubits; and the space remaining of the side-chambers—that of the house, **10** and between the chambers—[is] a breadth of twenty cubits around the house, all around. **11** And the opening of the side-chamber [is] to the remaining [space], one opening northward and one opening southward, and the breadth of the remaining space [is] five cubits all around. **12** As for the building that [is] at the front of the separate place [at] the corner westward, the breadth [is] seventy cubits, and the wall of the building [is] five cubits broad all around, and its length—ninety cubits. **13** And he has measured the house, the length [is] one hundred cubits; and the separate place, and the building, and its walls, the length [is] one hundred cubits; **14** and the breadth of the front of the house, and of the separate place eastward—one hundred cubits. **15** And he has measured the length of the building to the front of the separate place that [is] at its back part, and its galleries on this side and on that side—one hundred cubits. And the inner temple and the porches of the court, **16** the thresholds, and the narrow windows, and the galleries around the three of them, opposite the threshold, [were] paneled with wood all around—and the ground to the windows, and the windows were covered, **17** over above the opening, and to the inner-house, and at the outside, and by all the wall all around inside and outside [by] measurements. **18** And it is made [with] cherubim and palm-trees, and a palm-tree [is] between cherub and cherub, and two faces [are] on the cherub; **19** and the face of a man toward the palm-tree on this side and the face of a young lion toward the palm-tree on that side; it is made to all the house all around. **20** From the earth to above the opening the cherubim and the palm-trees [were] made, and [on] the wall of the temple. **21** The doorpost of the temple [is] square, and of the front of the sanctuary, the appearance [is] as that appearance. **22** Of the altar, the wood [is] three cubits in height, and its length—two cubits; and its corners [are] to it, and its length, and its walls [are] of wood, and he speaks to me, "This [is] the table that [is] before Y<small>HWH</small>." **23** And the temple and the sanctuary had two doors; **24** and the doors had two panels, two turning panels: two on one door, and two panels on the other. **25** And made on them, on the doors of the temple, [are] cherubim and palm-trees as are made on the walls, and a thickness of wood [is] at the front of the porch on the outside. **26** And narrow windows and palm-trees [are] on this side and on that side, at the sides of the porch, and the side-chambers of the house, and the thick places.

42 And he brings me forth to the outer court, the way northward, and he brings me into the chamber that [is] opposite the separate place, and that [is] opposite the building at the north. **2** At the front of the length [is] one hundred cubits [at] the north opening, and the breadth—fifty cubits. **3** Opposite the twenty [cubits] that are of the inner court, and opposite the pavement that [is] of the outer court, [is] gallery [with] face toward gallery, in the three [stories]. **4** And at the front of the chambers [is] a walk of ten cubits in breadth to the inner part, a way of one cubit, and their openings [are] at the north. **5** And the upper chambers [are] short, for the galleries contain more than these, than the lower, and than the middle one, of the building; **6** for they [are] threefold, and they have no pillars as the pillars of the court, therefore it has been kept back—more than the lower and than the middle one—from the ground. **7** As for the wall that [is] at the outside, alongside the chambers, the way of the outer-court at the front of the chambers, its length [is] fifty cubits; **8** for the length of the chambers that [are] in the outer court [is] fifty cubits, and of those on the front of the temple—one hundred cubits. **9** And under these chambers [is] the entrance from the east, in one's going into them from the outer court. **10** In the breadth of the wall of the court eastward, to the front of the separate place, and to the front of the building, [are] chambers. **11** And the way before them [is] as the appearance of the

EZEKIEL

chambers that [are] northward, according to their length so [is] their breadth, and all their outlets, and according to their fashions, and according to their openings. **12** And according to the openings of the chambers that [are] southward [is] an opening at the head of the way, the way directly in the front of the wall eastward in entering them. **13** And he says to me, "The north chambers, the south chambers, that [are] at the front of the separate place, they [are] holy chambers, where the priests (who [are] near to YHWH) eat the most holy things, there they place the most holy things, and the present, and the sin-offering, and the guilt-offering, for the place [is] holy. **14** In the priests' going in, they do not come out from the sanctuary to the outer court, and there they place their garments with which they minister, for they [are] holy, and have put on other garments, and have drawn near to that which [is] for the people." **15** And he has finished the measurements of the inner house, and has brought me forth the way of the gate whose front [is] eastward, and he has measured it all around. **16** He has measured the east side with the measuring-reed, five hundred reeds, with the measuring-reed all around. **17** He has measured the north side, five hundred reeds, with the measuring reed all around. **18** The south side he has measured, five hundred reeds, with the measuring-reed. **19** He has turned around to the west side, he has measured five hundred reeds with the measuring-reed. **20** At the four sides he has measured it; it had a wall all around, the length—five hundred, and the breadth—five hundred, to separate between the holy and the profane place.

43 And he causes me to go to the gate, the gate that is looking eastward. **2** And behold, the glory of the God of Israel has come from the way of the east, and His voice [is] as the noise of many waters, and the earth has shone from His glory. **3** And according to the appearance [is] the appearance that I saw, as the appearance that I saw in my coming in to destroy the city, and the appearances [are] as the appearance that I saw at the river Chebar, and I fall on my face. **4** And the glory of YHWH has come into the house, the way of the gate whose face [is] eastward. **5** And [the] Spirit takes me up, and brings me into the inner court, and behold, the glory of YHWH has filled the house. **6** And I hear one speaking to me from the house, and a man has been standing near me, **7** and He says to me: "Son of man, the place of My throne, ‖ And the place of the soles of My feet, ‖ Where I dwell in the midst of the sons of Israel for all time, ‖ The house of Israel defiles My holy Name no longer, ‖ They, and their kings, by their whoredom, ‖ And by the carcasses of their kings—their high places. **8** In their putting their threshold with My threshold, ‖ And their doorpost near My doorpost, ‖ And the wall between Me and them, ‖ And they have defiled My holy Name, ‖ By their abominations that they have done, ‖ And I consume them in My anger. **9** Now they put their whoredom far off, ‖ And the carcasses of their kings—from Me, ‖ And I have dwelt in their midst for all time. **10** You, son of man, ‖ Show the house of Israel the house, ‖ And they are ashamed of their iniquities, ‖ And they have measured the measurement. **11** And since they have been ashamed of all that they have done, ‖ The form of the house, and its measurement, ‖ And its outlets, and its inlets, and all its forms, ‖ And all its statutes, even all its forms, ‖ And all its laws—cause them to know, ‖ And write [it] before their eyes, ‖ And they observe all its forms, ‖ And all its statutes, and have done them. **12** This [is] a law of the house: on the top of the mountain, all its border all around [is] most holy; behold, this [is] a law of the house. **13** And these [are] measurements of the altar by cubits: the cubit [is] a cubit and a handbreadth, and the center [is] a cubit, and the breadth a cubit; and its border on its edge around [is] one span, and this [is] the upper part of the altar. **14** And from the center of the ground to the lower border [is] two cubits, and the breadth—one cubit, and from the lesser border to the greater border—four cubits, and the breadth a cubit. **15** And the altar [is] four cubits, and from the altar and upward [are] four horns. **16** And the altar [is] twelve long by twelve broad, square in its four sides. **17** And the border [is] fourteen long by fourteen broad, at its four sides, and the border around it [is] half a cubit, and the center of it [is] a cubit around, and its steps are looking eastward." **18** And He says to me, "Son of man, thus said Lord YHWH: These [are] statutes of the altar in the day of its being made to cause burnt-offering to go

EZEKIEL

up on it, and to sprinkle blood on it. **19** And you have given to the priests, the Levites—who [are] of the seed of Zadok, who are near to Me, a declaration of Lord YHWH, to serve Me—a calf from the herd, for a sin-offering. **20** And you have taken of its blood, and have put it on its four horns, and on the four corners of its border, and on the border all around, and have cleansed it, and purified it. **21** And you have taken the bullock of the sin-offering, and have burned it in the appointed place of the house at the outside of the sanctuary. **22** And on the second day you bring a kid of the goats near, a perfect one, for a sin-offering, and they have cleansed the altar, as they cleansed [it] for the bullock. **23** In your finishing cleansing, you bring a calf near, a son of the herd, a perfect one, and a ram out of the flock, a perfect one. **24** And you have brought them near before YHWH, and the priests have cast salt on them, and have caused them to go up, a burnt-offering to YHWH. **25** [For] seven days you prepare a goat daily for a sin-offering; and they also prepare a bullock, a son of the herd, and a ram out of the flock—perfect ones. **26** [For] seven days they purify the altar, and have cleansed it, and filled their hand. **27** And the days are completed, and it has come to pass on the eighth day, and from now on, the priests prepare your burnt-offerings and your peace-offerings on the altar, and I have accepted you—a declaration of Lord YHWH."

44 And he causes me to turn back the way of the gate of the outer sanctuary that is looking eastward, and it is shut. **2** And YHWH says to me, "This gate is shut, it is not opened, and none go in by it, for YHWH, God of Israel, has come in by it, and it has been shut. **3** The prince, who [is] prince, he sits by it to eat bread before YHWH, he comes in by the way of the porch of the gate, and by its way he goes out." **4** And he brings me in the way of the north gate to the front of the house, and I look, and behold, the glory of YHWH has filled the house of YHWH, and I fall on my face. **5** And YHWH says to me, "Son of man, set your heart, and see with your eyes, and hear with your ears, all that I am speaking with you, all of the statutes of the house of YHWH, and all of its laws; and you have set your heart to the entrance of the house, with all the outlets of the sanctuary, **6** and have said to [the] rebellion, to the house of Israel, Thus said Lord YHWH: Enough from you—of all your abominations, O house of Israel. **7** In your bringing in sons of a stranger, uncircumcised of heart, and uncircumcised of flesh, to be in My sanctuary, to defile it, even My house, in your bringing near My bread, fat, and blood, and they break My covenant by all your abominations, **8** and you have not kept [the] charge of My holy things, and you set [others] for keeping My charge in My sanctuary for you. **9** Thus said Lord YHWH: No son of a stranger, uncircumcised of heart, and uncircumcised of flesh, comes into My sanctuary, even any son of a stranger, who [is] in the midst of the sons of Israel. **10** And the Levites who have gone far off from Me, in the wandering of Israel when they went astray from Me after their idols, and they have borne their iniquity. **11** And they have been servants in My sanctuary, overseers at the gates of the house, and servants at the house; they slay the burnt-offering and the sacrifice for the people, and they stand before them to serve them. **12** Because that they serve them before their idols, and have been for a stumbling-block of iniquity to the house of Israel, therefore I have lifted up My hand against them—a declaration of Lord YHWH—and they have borne their iniquity. **13** And they do not draw near to Me to act as My priest, and to draw near to any of My holy things, to the Holy of Holies, and they have borne their shame and their abominations that they have done, **14** and I made them keepers of the charge of the house, for all its service and for all that is done in it. **15** And the priests, the Levites, sons of Zadok, who have kept the charge of My sanctuary in the wandering of the sons of Israel from off Me, they draw near to Me to serve Me, and have stood before Me, to bring fat and blood near to Me—a declaration of Lord YHWH: **16** they come into My sanctuary, and they draw near to My table to serve Me, and they have kept My charge. **17** And it has come to pass, in their going into the gates of the inner court, they put on linen garments; and no wool comes up on them in their ministering in the gates of the inner court and within. **18** Linen headdresses are on their head, and linen trousers are on their loins, they are not restrained with sweat. **19** And in their going forth to the

EZEKIEL

outer court—to the outer court to the people—they strip off their garments, in which they are ministering, and have placed them in the holy chambers, and have put on other garments; and they do not sanctify the people in their own garments. **20** And they do not shave their head, and they do not send forth the lock; they certainly trim their heads. **21** And no priest drinks wine in their coming into the inner court. **22** And they do not take a widow or divorced woman to themselves for wives, but they take virgins of the seed of the house of Israel, and the widow who is widow of a priest. **23** And they direct My people between holy and common, and they cause them to discern between unclean and clean. **24** And concerning controversy, they stand up for judgment; they judge it with My judgments; and they keep My law and My statutes in all My appointed places; and they sanctify My Sabbaths. **25** And he does not come near to any dead man to be defiled, but if for father, and for mother, and for son, and for daughter, for brother, for sister who has not been to a man, they may defile themselves. **26** And after his cleansing, they number seven days to him. **27** And in the day of his coming into the sanctuary, into the inner court, to minister in the sanctuary, he brings his sin-offering near—a declaration of Lord YHWH. **28** And it has been for an inheritance to them; I [am] their inheritance, and you do not give a possession to them in Israel; I [am] their possession. **29** The present, and the sin-offering, and the guilt-offering, they eat, and every devoted thing in Israel is theirs. **30** And the first of all the first-fruits of all, and every raised-offering of all, of all your raised-offerings, are the priests'; and you give the first of your dough to the priest, to cause a blessing to rest on your house. **31** The priests do not eat any carcass or torn thing, from the bird or from the beast."

45 "And in your causing the land to fall into inheritance, you lift up a raised-offering to YHWH, a holy [portion] of the land: the length—twenty-five thousand [is] the length, and the breadth—ten thousand; it [is] holy in all its surrounding border. **2** There is of this for the sanctuary five hundred by five hundred, square, around; and fifty cubits of outskirt [is] around it. **3** And by this measure you measure: the length—twenty-five thousand, and the breadth—ten thousand: and the sanctuary is in it, the Holy of Holies. **4** It [is] the holy [portion] of the land; it is for priests, servants of the sanctuary, who are drawing near to serve YHWH; and it has been a place for their houses, and a holy place for the sanctuary. **5** And of the twenty-five thousand of length, and of the ten thousand of breadth, there is to the Levites, servants of the house, for them—for a possession—twenty chambers. **6** And of the possession of the city you set [an area] of five thousand breadth, and twenty-five thousand length, alongside the raised-offering of the holy [portion]; it is for all the house of Israel. **7** And for the prince: on this side and on that side of the raised-offering of the holy place, and of the possession of the city, at the front of the raised-offering of the holy place, and at the front of the possession of the city, from the west corner westward, and from the east corner eastward—and the length [is] corresponding to one of the portions from the west border to the east border— **8** of the land there is for a possession to him in Israel, and My princes do not oppress My people anymore, and they give the land to the house of Israel according to their tribes." **9** Thus said Lord YHWH: "Enough from you—princes of Israel; turn violence and spoil aside, and do judgment and righteousness; lift up your exactions from off My people—a declaration of Lord YHWH. **10** You must have just balances, and a just ephah, and a just bath. **11** The ephah and the bath is of one measure, for the bath to carry a tenth of the homer, and the ephah a tenth of the homer: its measurement is according to the homer. **12** And the shekel [is] twenty gerah: twenty shekels, twenty-five shekels, fifteen shekels—is your maneh. **13** This [is] the raised-offering that you lift up; a sixth part of the ephah of a homer of wheat, also you have given a sixth part of the ephah of a homer of barley, **14** and the portion of oil, the bath of oil, a tenth part of the bath out of the cor, a homer of ten baths—for ten baths [are] a homer; **15** and one lamb out of the flock, out of two hundred, out of the watered country of Israel, for a present, and for a burnt-offering, and for peace-offerings, to make atonement by them—a declaration of Lord YHWH. **16** All the people of the land are at this raised-offering for the prince in Israel. **17** And on the prince are the burnt-offerings, and the present, and the drink-offering, in celebrations, and in new moons, and in Sabbaths, in all appointed times of the house of Israel: he makes the sin-offering, and the present, and the burnt-offering, and the peace-offerings, to make atonement for the house of Israel." **18** Thus said Lord YHWH: "In the first [month], on the first of the month, you take a bullock, a son of the herd, a perfect one, and have cleansed the sanctuary: **19** and the priest has taken from the blood of the sin offering, and has put [it] on the doorpost of the house, and on the four corners of the border of the altar, and on the post of the gate of the inner court. **20** And so you do on the seventh of the month, because of each erring one, and because of the simple one—and you have purified the house. **21** In the first [month], on the fourteenth day of the month, you have the Passover, a celebration of seven days, unleavened bread is eaten. **22** And the prince has prepared on that day, for himself, and for all the people of the land, a bullock, a sin-offering. **23** And [on] the seven days of the celebration he prepares a burnt-offering to YHWH, seven bullocks, and seven rams, perfect ones, daily [for] seven days, and a sin-offering, a kid of the goats, daily. **24** And he prepares a present of an ephah for a bullock, and an ephah for a ram, and a hin of oil for an ephah. **25** In the seventh [month], on the fifteenth day of the month, in the celebration, he does according to these things [for] seven days; as the sin-offering so the burnt-offering, and as the present so also the oil."

46 Thus said Lord YHWH: "The gate of the inner court that is looking eastward is shut [during] the six days of work, and on the day of rest it is opened, and in the day of the new moon it is opened; **2** and the prince has come in the way of the porch of the gate from the outside, and he has stood by the post of the gate, and the priests have made his burnt-offering, and his peace-offerings, and he has bowed himself by the opening of the gate, and has gone forth, and the gate is not shut until the evening. **3** And the people of the land have bowed themselves at the opening of that gate, on Sabbaths, and on new moons, before YHWH. **4** And the burnt-offering that the prince brings near to YHWH on the day of rest [is] six lambs, perfect ones, and a ram, a perfect one. **5** And the present [is] an ephah for a ram, and for the lambs a present, the gift of his hand, and a hin of oil for an ephah. **6** And on the day of the new moon—a bullock, a son of the herd, a perfect one, and six lambs and a ram; they are perfect. **7** And with an ephah for a bullock, and an ephah for a ram, he prepares a present, and for the lambs as his hand attains, and a hin of oil for an ephah. **8** And in the coming in of the prince, he comes in the way of the porch of the gate, and by its way he goes out. **9** And in the coming in of the people of the land before YHWH at appointed times, he who has come in the way of the north gate to bow himself, goes out the way of the south gate, and he who has come in the way of the south gate, goes out by the way of the north gate: he does not turn back the way of the gate by which he came in, but he goes out opposite it. **10** And in their coming in the prince in their midst comes in, and in their going out he goes out. **11** And in celebrations, and in appointed times, the present is an ephah for a bullock, and an ephah for a ram, and for lambs the gift of his hand, and a hin of oil for an ephah. **12** And when the prince makes a free-will burnt-offering, or free-will peace-offerings, to YHWH, then he has opened the gate that is looking eastward for himself, and has made his burnt-offering and his peace-offerings as he does in the day of rest, and he has gone out, and has shut the gate after his going out. **13** And you make a daily burnt-offering of a lamb, son of a year, a perfect one, to YHWH; you make it morning by morning. **14** And you make a present with it morning by morning, a sixth part of the ephah, and a third part of the hin of oil, to temper with the fine flour, a present to YHWH, by a continuous statute—continually; **15** and they prepare the lamb, and the present, and the oil, morning by morning—a continual burnt-offering." **16** Thus said Lord YHWH: "When the prince gives a gift to any of his sons, it [is] his inheritance, it [is] for his sons; it [is] their possession by inheritance. **17** And when he gives a gift out of his inheritance to one of his servants, then it has been his until the year of freedom, and it has turned back to the prince, only the inheritance of his sons is theirs. **18** And the prince does not take from the people's inheritance to oppress them—from their

EZEKIEL

possession; he causes his sons to inherit out of his own possession, so that My people are not each scattered from his possession." **19** And he brings me in through the entrance that [is] by the side of the gate, to the holy chambers, to the priests, that are looking northward, and behold, there [is] a place in their two sides westward. **20** And he says to me, "This [is] the place where the priests boil the guilt-offering and the sin-offering, where they bake the present, so as not to bring [it] out to the outer court, to sanctify the people." **21** And he brings me out to the outer court, and causes me to pass over to the four corners of the court, and behold, a court in a corner of the court, [moreover] a court in [every] corner of the corner. **22** In the four corners of the court [are] enclosed courts, forty long and thirty broad, [with] one measure for the four corners. **23** And a row [is] all around in them—around the four of them—and made with boilers under the rows all around. **24** And he says to me, "These [are] the houses of those boiling where the servants of the house boil the sacrifice of the people."

47 And he causes me to turn back to the opening of the house; and behold, water is coming forth from under the threshold of the house eastward, for the front of the house [is] eastward, and the water is coming down from beneath, from the right side of the house, from south of the altar. **2** And he causes me to go out the way of the gate northward, and causes me to turn around the way outside, to the gate that [is] outside, the way that is looking eastward, and behold, water is coming forth from the right side. **3** In the going out of the man eastward—and a line in his hand—then he measures one thousand by the cubit, and he causes me to pass over into the waters—waters [to my] ankles. **4** And he measures one thousand, and causes me to pass over into the waters—waters [to my] knees. And he measures one thousand, and causes me to pass over—waters [to my] loins. **5** And he measures one thousand—a stream that I am not able to pass over; for the waters have risen—waters to swim in—a stream that is not passed over. **6** And he says to me, "Have you seen, son of man?" And he leads me, and brings me back to the edge of the stream. **7** In my turning back, then, behold, at the edge of the stream [are] very many trees, on this side and on that side. **8** And he says to me, "These waters are going forth to the east circuit, and have gone down to the desert, and have entered the sea; they are brought forth to the sea, and the waters have been healed. **9** And it has come to pass, every living creature that teems, wherever the streams come, lives: and there has been great abundance of fish, for these waters have come there, and they are healed; and everything to where the stream comes has lived. **10** And it has come to pass, fishers stand by it, from En-Gedi even to En-Eglaim; they are a spreading place for the nets; their fish are of the same kind as the fish of the Great Sea—very many. **11** Its miry and its marshy places—they are not healed; they have been given up to salt. **12** And there comes up by the stream, on its edge, on this side and on that side, every [kind of] fruit-tree whose leaf does not fade, and its fruit is not consumed, it yields first-fruits according to its months, because its waters are coming forth from the sanctuary; and its fruits have been for food, and its leaf for medicine." **13** Thus said Lord YHWH: "This [is] the border whereby you inherit the land, according to the twelve tribes of Israel; Joseph [has two] portions. **14** And you have inherited it, one as well as another, in that I have lifted up My hand to give it to your fathers; and this land has fallen to you in inheritance. **15** And this [is] the border of the land at the north quarter; from the Great Sea, the way of Hethlon, at the coming in to Zedad: **16** Hamath, Berothah, Sibraim, that [is] between the border of Damascus and the border of Hamath; Hazar-Hatticon, that [is] at the coast of Havran. **17** And the border from the sea has been Hazar-Enan, the border of Damascus, and Zaphon at the north, and the border of Hamath: and [this is] the north quarter. **18** And the east quarter [is] from between Havran, and Damascus, and Gilead, and the land of Israel, [to] the Jordan; you measure from the border on the Eastern Sea: and [this is] the east quarter. **19** And the south quarter southward [is] from Tamar to the waters of Meriboth-Kadesh, the stream to the Great Sea: and [this is] the south quarter southward. **20** And the west quarter [is] the Great Sea, from the border until opposite the coming in to Hamath: this [is] the west quarter. **21** And you have divided this land

EZEKIEL

to yourselves, according to the tribes of Israel; **22** and it has come to pass, you separate it for an inheritance to yourselves, and to the sojourners who are sojourning in your midst, who have begotten sons in your midst, and they have been to you as native, with the sons of Israel; they are separated with you for an inheritance in the midst of the tribes of Israel. **23** And it has come to pass, in the tribe with which the sojourner sojourns, there you give his inheritance," a declaration of Lord Y<small>HWH</small>.

48 "And these [are] the names of the tribes: from the north end to the side of the way of Hethlon, at the coming in to Hamath, Hazar-Enan, the border of Damascus northward, in the direction of Hamath, and they have been his—east side to west, Dan, one [portion]; **2** and by the border of Dan, from the east side to the west side, Asher, one [portion]; **3** and by the border of Asher, from the east side even to the west side, Naphtali, one [portion]; **4** and by the border of Naphtali, from the east side to the west side, Manasseh, one [portion]; **5** and by the border of Manasseh, from the east side to the west side, Ephraim, one [portion]; **6** and by the border of Ephraim, from the east side even to the west side, Reuben, one [portion]; **7** and by the border of Reuben, from the east side to the west side, Judah, one [portion]; **8** and by the border of Judah, from the east side to the west side is the raised-offering that you lift up, twenty-five thousand [cubits] broad and long, as one of the parts, from the east side to the west side: and the sanctuary has been in its midst. **9** The raised-offering that you lift up to Y<small>HWH</small> [is] twenty-five thousand long and ten thousand broad. **10** And of these is the holy raised-offering for the priests, northward twenty-five thousand, and westward ten thousand [in] breadth, and eastward ten thousand [in] breadth, and southward twenty-five thousand [in] length: and the sanctuary of Y<small>HWH</small> has been in its midst. **11** For the priests who are sanctified of the sons of Zadok, who have kept My charge, who did not err in the erring of the sons of Israel, as the Levites erred, **12** even the raised-offering has been for them, out of the raised-offering of the land, most holy, by the border of the Levites. **13** And [to] the Levites alongside the border of the priests [are] twenty-five thousand [in] length, and ten thousand [in] breadth, all the length [is] twenty-five thousand, and the breadth ten thousand. **14** And they do not sell of it, nor exchange, nor cause the first-fruit of the land to pass away: for [it is] holy to Y<small>HWH</small>. **15** And the five thousand that is left in the breadth, on the front of the twenty-five thousand, is common—for the city, for dwelling, and for outskirt, and the city has been in its midst. **16** And these [are] its measurements: the north side—four thousand and five hundred, and the south side—four thousand and five hundred, and on the east side—four thousand and five hundred, and the west side—four thousand and five hundred. **17** And the outskirt of the city has been northward—two hundred and fifty, and southward—two hundred and fifty, and eastward—two hundred and fifty, and westward—two hundred and fifty. **18** And the remainder in length alongside the raised-offering of the holy [portion is] ten thousand eastward, and ten thousand westward, and it has been alongside the raised-offering of the holy [portion], and its increase has been for food for those serving the city, **19** even [to] him who is serving the city, they serve it out of all the tribes of Israel. **20** All the raised-offering [is] twenty-five thousand by twenty-five thousand square—you lift up the raised-offering of the holy [portion] with the possession of the city. **21** And the remainder [is] for the prince, on this side and on that side of the raised-offering of the holy [portion], and of the possession of the city, on the front of the twenty-five thousand of the raised-offering to the east border, and westward, on the front of the twenty-five thousand on the west border, alongside the portions of the prince; and the raised-offering of the holy [portion], and the sanctuary of the house, has been in its midst. **22** And from the possession of the Levites, from the possession of the city, in the midst of that which is for the prince, between the border of Judah and the border of Benjamin, there is for the prince. **23** As for the rest of the tribes, from the east side to the west side, Benjamin, one [portion]; **24** and by the border of Benjamin, from the east side to the west side, Simeon, one [portion]; **25** and by the border of Simeon, from the east side to the west side, Issachar, one [portion]; **26** and by the border of Issachar, from the east side to the west side, Zebulun, one [portion]; **27** and by the border of Zebulun, from the east side to the west side, Gad, one [portion]; **28** and by the border of Gad, at the south side southward, the border has been from Tamar [to] the waters of Meriboth-Kadesh, the stream by the Great Sea. **29** This [is] the land that you separate by inheritance to the tribes of Israel, and these [are] their divisions," a declaration of Lord Y{HWH}. **30** "And these [are] the outgoings of the city: on the north side, four thousand and five hundred measures; **31** and the gates of the city [are] according to the names of the tribes of Israel; three gates northward—one gate of Reuben, one gate of Judah, one gate of Levi. **32** And on the east side, four thousand and five hundred, and three gates—one gate of Joseph, one gate of Benjamin, one gate of Dan. **33** And the south side, four thousand and five hundred, and three gates—one gate of Simeon, one gate of Issachar, one gate of Zebulun. **34** The west side, four thousand and five hundred, [with] their three gates—one gate of Gad, one gate of Asher, one gate of Naphtali. **35** [It is] eighteen thousand around, and the renown of the city [is] from the day Y{HWH} [is] there."

DANIEL

1 In the third year of the reign of Jehoiakim king of Judah, Nebuchadnezzar king of Babylon has come to Jerusalem, and lays siege against it; **2** and the Lord gives into his hand Jehoiakim king of Judah, and some of the vessels of the house of God, and he brings them in [to] the land of Shinar, [to] the house of his god, and the vessels he has brought in [to] the treasure-house of his god. **3** And the king says, to Ashpenaz master of his eunuchs, to bring in out of the sons of Israel (even of the royal seed, and of the chiefs), **4** boys in whom there is no blemish, and of good appearance, and skillful in all wisdom, and possessing knowledge, and teaching thought, and who have ability to stand in the palace of the king, and to teach them the literature and language of the Chaldeans. **5** And the king appoints for them a rate, day by day, of the king's portion of food, and of the wine of his drinking, so as to nourish them three years, that at the end thereof they may stand before the king. **6** And there are among them out of the sons of Judah, Daniel, Hananiah, Mishael, and Azariah, **7** and the chief of the eunuchs sets names on them, and he sets on Daniel, Belteshazzar; and on Hananiah, Shadrach; and on Mishael, Meshach; and on Azariah, Abed-Nego. **8** And Daniel purposes in his heart that he will not defile himself with the king's portion of food, and with the wine of his drinking, and he seeks of the chief of the eunuchs that he may not defile himself. **9** And God gives Daniel for kindness and for mercies before the chief of the eunuchs; **10** and the chief of the eunuchs says to Daniel, "I am fearing my lord the king, who has appointed your food and your drink, for why does he see your faces sadder than [those of] the boys which [are] of your circle? Then you have made my head indebted to the king," **11** And Daniel says to the Meltzar, whom the chief of the eunuchs has appointed over Daniel, Hananiah, Mishael, and Azariah, **12** "Please try your servants [for] ten days; and they give to us from the vegetables and we eat, and water, and we drink; **13** and our appearance is seen before you, and the appearance of the boys who are eating the king's portion of food, and as you see— deal with your servants." **14** And he listens to them, to this word, and tries them ten days: **15** and at the end of ten days their appearance has appeared better and fatter in flesh then any of the boys who are eating the king's portion of food. **16** And the Meltzar is taking away their portion of food, and the wine of their drink, and is giving to them vegetables. **17** As for these four boys, God has given to them knowledge and understanding in every [kind of] literature, and wisdom; and Daniel has given instruction about every [kind of] vision and dreams. **18** And at the end of the days that the king had said to bring them in, the chief of the eunuchs brings them in before Nebuchadnezzar. **19** And the king speaks with them, and there has not been found among them all like Daniel, Hananiah, Mishael, and Azariah, and they stand before the king; **20** and [in] any matter of wisdom [and] understanding that the king has sought of them, he finds them ten hands above all the enchanters, the conjurers, who [are] in all his kingdom. **21** And Daniel is to the first year of Cyrus the king.

2 And in the second year of the reign of Nebuchadnezzar, Nebuchadnezzar has dreamed dreams, and his spirit moves itself, and his sleep has been against him; **2** and the king says to call for enchanters, and for conjurers, and for sorcerers, and for Chaldeans, to declare to the king his dreams. And they come in and stand before the king; **3** and the king says to them, "I have dreamed a dream, and my spirit is moved to know the dream." **4** And the Chaldeans speak to the king [in] Aramaic, "O king, live for all ages, tell the dream to your servants, and we show the interpretation." **5** The king has answered and said to the Chaldeans, "The thing is gone from me; if you do not cause me to know the dream and its interpretation, you are made pieces, and your houses are made dunghills; **6** and if the dream and its interpretation you show, gifts, and fee, and great glory you receive from before me, therefore the dream and its interpretation you show me." **7** They have answered a second time, and are saying, "Let the king tell the dream to his servants, and we show the interpretation." **8** The king has answered and said, "Of a truth I know that you are gaining time, because that you have seen that the thing is gone from me, **9** [so] that, if you do not cause me to know the dream—one is your sentence, seeing a lying and corrupt word you have prepared to speak before me, until the time is changed, therefore tell the dream to me, then I know that you show me its interpretation." **10** The Chaldeans have answered before the king, and are saying, "There is not a man on the earth who is able to show the king's matter; therefore, no king, chief, and ruler, has asked such a thing as this of any scribe, and enchanter, and Chaldean; **11** and the thing that the king is asking [is] precious, and there are no others that show it before the king, except the gods, whose dwelling is not with flesh." **12** Therefore the king has been furious and very angry, and has said to destroy all the wise men of Babylon. **13** And the sentence has gone forth, and the wise men are being slain, and they have sought Daniel and his companions to be slain. **14** Then Daniel has replied [with] counsel and discretion to Arioch chief of the executioners of the king, who has gone forth to slay the wise men of Babylon. **15** He has answered and said to Arioch the king's captain, "Why [is] the sentence so urgent from before the king?" Then Arioch has made the thing known to Daniel, **16** and Daniel has gone up, and sought of the king that he would give him time to show the interpretation to the king. **17** Then Daniel has gone to his house, and to Hananiah, Mishael, and Azariah, his companions, he has made the thing known, **18** and to seek mercies from before the God of the heavens concerning this secret, that they do not destroy Daniel and his companions with the rest of the wise men of Babylon. **19** Then to Daniel, in a vision of the night, the secret has been revealed. Then Daniel has blessed the God of the heavens. **20** Daniel has answered and said, "Let the Name of God be blessed from age even to age, for wisdom and might—for they are His. **21** And He is changing times and seasons, He is causing kings to pass away, and He is raising up kings; He is giving wisdom to the wise, and knowledge to those possessing understanding. **22** He is revealing deep and hidden things; He has known what [is] in darkness, and light has dwelt with Him. **23** You, O God of my fathers, I am thanking and praising, for wisdom and might You have given to me; and now, You have caused me to know that which we have sought from You, for the king's matter You have caused us to know." **24** Therefore Daniel has gone up to Arioch, whom the king has appointed to destroy the wise men of Babylon; he has gone, and thus has said to him, "You do not destroy the wise men of Babylon, bring me up before the king, and I show the interpretation to the king." **25** Then Arioch in haste has brought up Daniel before the king, and thus has said to him, "I have found a man of the sons of the expulsion of Judah, who makes known the interpretation to the king." **26** The king has answered and said to Daniel, whose name [is] Belteshazzar, "Are you able to cause me to know the dream that I have seen, and its interpretation?" **27** Daniel has answered before the king and said, "The secret that the king is asking, the wise men, the enchanters, the scribes, the soothsayers, are not able to show to the king; **28** but there is a God in the heavens, a revealer of secrets, and He has made known to King Nebuchadnezzar that which [is] to be in the latter end of the days. Your dream and the visions of your head on your bed are these: **29** You, O king, your thoughts on your bed have come up [concerning] that which [is] to be after this, and the Revealer of secrets has caused you to know that which [is] to be. **30** As for me—not for [any] wisdom that is in me above any living has this secret been revealed to me; but for the intent that the interpretation to the king they make known, and the thoughts of your heart you know. **31** You, O king, were looking, and behold, a certain great image. This image [is] mighty, and its brightness excellent; it is standing before you, and its appearance [is] terrible. **32** This image! Its head [is] of fine gold, its breasts and its arms of silver, its belly and its thighs of bronze; **33** its legs of iron, its feet, part of them of iron, and part of them of clay. **34** You were looking until a stone has been cut out without hands, and it has struck the image on its feet, that [are] of iron and of clay, and it has broken them small; **35** then broken small together have been the iron, the clay, the bronze, the silver, and the gold, and they

DANIEL

have been as chaff from the summer threshing-floor, and the wind has carried them away, and no place has been found for them: and the stone that struck the image has become a great mountain, and has filled all the land. **36** This [is] the dream, and its interpretation we tell before the king. **37** You, O king, are a king of kings, for the God of the heavens a kingdom, strength, and might, and glory, has given to you; **38** and wherever sons of men are dwelling, the beast of the field, and the bird of the heavens, He has given into your hand, and has caused you to rule over them all; you [are] this head of gold. **39** And after you another kingdom arises lower than those, and another third kingdom of bronze, that rules over all the earth. **40** And the fourth kingdom is strong as iron, because that iron is breaking small, and making feeble, all [things], even as iron that is breaking all these, it beats small and breaks. **41** As for that which you have seen: the feet and toes, part of them potter's clay, and part of them iron, the kingdom is divided: and some of the standing of the iron [is] to be in it, because that you have seen the iron mixed with miry clay. **42** As for the toes of the feet, part of them iron, and part of them clay: some part of the kingdom is strong, and some part of it is brittle. **43** Because you have seen iron mixed with miry clay, they are mixing themselves with the seed of men: and they are not adhering with one another, even as iron is not mixed with clay. **44** And in the days of these kings the God of the heavens raises up a kingdom that is not destroyed for all time, and its kingdom is not left to another people: it beats small and ends all these kingdoms, and it stands for all time. **45** Because that you have seen that out of the mountain a stone has been cut without hands, and it has beaten the iron small, the bronze, the clay, the silver, and the gold; the great God has made known to the king that which [is] to be after this; and the dream [is] true, and its interpretation steadfast." **46** Then King Nebuchadnezzar has fallen on his face, and to Daniel he has done homage, and present, and sweet things, he has said to pour out to him. **47** The king has answered Daniel and said, "Of a truth [it is] that your God is a God of gods, and a Lord of kings, and a revealer of secrets, since you have been able to reveal this secret." **48** Then the king has made Daniel great, and many great gifts he has given to him, and has caused him to rule over all the province of Babylon, and chief of the prefects over all the wise men of Babylon. **49** And Daniel has sought from the king, and he has appointed over the work of the province of Babylon, Shadrach, Meshach, and Abed-Nego, and Daniel [is] in the gate of the king.

3 Nebuchadnezzar the king has made an image of gold, its height sixty cubits, its breadth six cubits; he has raised it up in the Valley of Dura, in the province of Babylon; **2** and Nebuchadnezzar the king has sent to gather the satraps, the prefects, and the governors, the counselors, the treasurers, the judges, the magistrates, and all the rulers of the province, to come to the dedication of the image that Nebuchadnezzar the king has raised up. **3** Then are gathered the satraps, the prefects, and the governors, the counselors, the treasurers, the judges, the magistrates, and all the rulers of the province, to the dedication of the image that Nebuchadnezzar the king has raised up: and they are standing before the image that Nebuchadnezzar has raised up. **4** And a crier is calling mightily: "They are saying to you: O peoples, nations, and languages! **5** At the time that you hear the voice of the horn, the flute, the harp, the lyre, the stringed instrument, the symphony, and all kinds of music, you fall down and pay respect to the golden image that Nebuchadnezzar the king has raised up: **6** and whoever does not fall down and pay respect, in that hour he is cast into the midst of a burning fiery furnace." **7** Therefore at that time, when all the peoples are hearing the voice of the horn, the flute, the harp, the lyre, the stringed instrument, and all kinds of music, falling down are all the peoples, nations and languages, worshiping the golden image that Nebuchadnezzar the king has raised up. **8** Therefore at that time certain Chaldeans have drawn near, and accused the Jews; **9** they have answered, indeed, they are saying to Nebuchadnezzar the king, "O king, live for all ages! **10** You, O king, have made a decree that every man who hears the voice of the horn, the flute, the harp, the lyre, the stringed instrument, and the symphony, and all kinds of music, falls down and pays respect to the golden image; **11** and whoever does not fall down and pay respect, is cast into the midst of a burning fiery furnace. **12** There are certain Jews whom you have appointed over the work of the province of Babylon—Shadrach, Meshach, and Abed-Nego, these men have not made of you, O king, [any] regard; your gods they are not serving, and to the golden image you have raised up—are not making worship." **13** Then Nebuchadnezzar, in anger and fury, has said to bring in Shadrach, Meshach, and Abed-Nego. Then these men have been brought in before the king. **14** Nebuchadnezzar has answered and said to them, "Is [it] a laid plan, O Shadrach, Meshach, and Abed-Nego—my gods you are not serving, and to the golden image that I have raised up you are not worshiping? **15** Now behold, you are ready, so that at the time that you hear the voice of the horn, the flute, the harp, the lyre, the stringed instrument, and the symphony, and all kinds of music, you fall down and pay respect to the image that I have made! But if you do not worship—in that hour you are cast into the midst of a burning fiery furnace; who is that God who delivers you out of my hands?" **16** Shadrach, Meshach, and Abed-Nego have answered, indeed, they are saying to King Nebuchadnezzar, "We have no need concerning this matter to answer you. **17** Behold, it is; our God whom we are serving, is able to deliver us from a burning fiery furnace; and from your hand, O king, He delivers. **18** And behold—not! Be it known to you, O king, that we are not serving your gods, and we do not worship the golden image you have raised up." **19** Then Nebuchadnezzar has been full of fury, and the expression of his face has been changed concerning Shadrach, Meshach, and Abed-Nego; he answered and said to heat the furnace seven times above that which it is seen to be heated; **20** and to certain mighty men who [are] in his force he has said to bind Shadrach, Meshach, and Abed-Nego, to cast into the burning fiery furnace. **21** Then these men have been bound in their coats, their tunics, and their turbans, and their clothing, and have been cast into the midst of the burning fiery furnace. **22** Therefore, because that the word of the king is urgent, and the furnace heated exceedingly, those men who have taken up Shadrach, Meshach, and Abed-Nego—the spark of the fire has killed them. **23** And these three men, Shadrach, Meshach, and Abed-Nego, have fallen down in the midst of the burning fiery furnace—bound. **24** Then Nebuchadnezzar the king has been astonished, and has risen in haste; he has answered and said to his counselors, "Have we not cast three men into the midst of the fire—bound?" They have answered and are saying to the king, "Certainly, O king." **25** He answered and has said, "Behold, I am seeing four men loose, walking in the midst of the fire, and they have no hurt; and the appearance of the fourth [is] like to a son of the gods." **26** Then Nebuchadnezzar has drawn near to the gate of the burning fiery furnace; he has answered and said, "Shadrach, Meshach, and Abed-Nego, servants of God Most High come forth, indeed, come"; then Shadrach, Meshach, and Abed-Nego come forth, from the midst of the fire; **27** and gathered together, the satraps, the prefects, and the governors, and the counselors of the king, are seeing these men, that the fire has no power over their bodies, and the hair of their head has not been singed, and their coats have not changed, and the smell of fire has not passed on them. **28** Nebuchadnezzar has answered and has said, "Blessed [is] the God of Shadrach, Meshach, and Abed-Nego, who has sent His messenger, and has delivered His servants who trusted on Him." And the word of the king changed, and gave up their bodies that they might not serve nor pay respect to any god except to their own God. **29** "And by me a decree is made, that any people, nation, and language, that speaks erroneously concerning the God of Shadrach, Meshach, and Abed-Nego, he is made pieces, and its house is made a dunghill, because that there is no other god who is able thus to deliver." **30** Then the king has caused Shadrach, Meshach, and Abed-Nego, to prosper in the province of Babylon.

4 "Nebuchadnezzar the king to all peoples, nations, and languages, who are dwelling in all the earth: Your peace be great! **2** The signs and wonders that God Most High has done with me, it is good before me to show. **3** How great His signs! And how mighty His wonders! His kingdom [is] a continuous kingdom, and His rule [is] with generation and generation. **4** I, Nebuchadnezzar, have been at rest in my house, and flourishing in my palace: **5** a dream I have seen, and it makes me afraid, and the conceptions on my bed, and the visions of my head, trouble me. **6** And by me a decree is made, to cause all the wise men of Babylon to come up before me, that the interpretation of the dream they may cause me to know. **7** Then coming up are the scribes, the enchanters, the Chaldeans, and the soothsayers, and the dream I have told before them, and its interpretation they are not making known to me. **8** And at last Daniel has come up before me, whose name [is] Belteshazzar—according to the name of my god—and in whom [is] the spirit of the holy gods, and the dream before him I have told: **9** O Belteshazzar, master of the scribes, as I have known that the spirit of the holy gods [is] in you, and no secret presses you, the visions of my dream that I have seen, and its interpretation, tell. **10** As for the visions of my head on my bed, I was looking, and behold, a tree in the midst of the earth, and its height [is] great: **11** the tree has become great, indeed, strong, and its height reaches to the heavens, and its vision to the end of the whole land; **12** its leaves [are] beautiful, and its budding great, and food for all [is] in it: under it the beast of the field takes shade, and in its boughs dwell the birds of the heavens, and of it are all flesh fed. **13** I was looking, in the visions of my head on my bed, and behold, a sifter, even a holy one, from the heavens is coming down. **14** He is calling mightily, and thus has said, Cut down the tree, and cut off its branches, shake off its leaves, and scatter its budding, move away let the beast from under it, and the birds from off its branches; **15** but the stump of its roots leave in the earth, even with a band of iron and bronze, in the tender grass of the field, and with the dew of the heavens is it wet, and with the beasts [is] his portion in the herb of the earth; **16** his heart from man's is changed, and the heart of a beast is given to him, and seven times pass over him; **17** by the decree of the sifters [is] the sentence, and by the saying of the holy ones the requirement, to the intent that the living may know that the Most High is ruler in the kingdom of men, and to whom He wills He gives it, and the lowest of men He raises up over it. **18** This dream I have seen, I King Nebuchadnezzar; and you, O Belteshazzar, tell the interpretation, because that all the wise men of my kingdom are not able to cause me to know the interpretation, and you [are] able, for the spirit of the holy gods [is] in you." **19** Then Daniel, whose name [is] Belteshazzar, has been astonished about one hour, and his thoughts trouble him; the king has answered and said, "O Belteshazzar, do not let the dream and its interpretation trouble you." Belteshazzar has answered and said, "My lord, the dream—to those hating you, and its interpretation—to your enemies! **20** The tree that you have seen, that has become great and strong, and its height reaches to the heavens, and its vision to all the land, **21** and its leaves [are] beautiful, and its budding great, and food for all [is] in it, under it the beast of the field dwells, and on its boughs the birds of the heavens sit. **22** It [is] you, O king, for you have become great and mighty, and your greatness has become great, and has reached to the heavens, and your dominion to the end of the earth; **23** and that which the king has seen—a sifter, even a holy one, coming down from the heavens, and he has said, Cut down the tree, and destroy it; but the stump of its roots leave in the earth, even with a band of iron and bronze, in the tender grass of the field, and with the dew of the heavens it is wet, and with the beast of the field [is] his portion, until seven times pass over him. **24** This [is] the interpretation, O king, and it [is] the decree of the Most High that has come against my lord the king: **25** and they are driving you away from men, and your dwelling is with the beast of the field, and they cause you to eat the herb as oxen, and they are wetting you by the dew of the heavens, and pass over you seven times, until you know that the Most High is ruler in the kingdom of men, and to whom He wills He gives it. **26** And that which they said—to leave the stump of the roots of the tree; your kingdom abides for you, after that you know that the heavens are ruling. **27** Therefore, O king, let my counsel be acceptable to you, and your sins by righteousness break off, and your perversity by pitying the poor, behold, it is a lengthening of your ease." **28** All—has come on Nebuchadnezzar the king. **29** At the end of twelve months, on the palace of the kingdom of Babylon he has been walking; **30** the king has answered and

DANIEL

said, "Is this not that great Babylon that I have built, for the house of the kingdom, in the might of my strength, and for the glory of my honor?" **31** While the word is [in] the king's mouth a voice from the heavens has fallen: "They are saying to you: O Nebuchadnezzar the king, the kingdom has passed from you, **32** and from men they are driving you away, and your dwelling [is] with the beast of the field, they cause you to eat the herb as oxen, and pass over you seven times, until you know that the Most High is ruler in the kingdom of men, and to whom He wills He gives it." **33** In that hour the thing has been fulfilled on Nebuchadnezzar, and from men he is driven, and he eats the herb as oxen, and his body is wet by the dew of the heavens, until his hair has become great as eagles, and his nails as birds. **34** "And at the end of the days I, Nebuchadnezzar, have lifted up my eyes to the heavens, and my understanding returns to me, and I have blessed the Most High, and the Perpetual Living One I have praised and honored, whose dominion [is] a continuous dominion, and His kingdom with generation and generation; **35** and all who are dwelling on the earth are reckoned as nothing, and according to His will He is doing among the forces of the heavens and those dwelling on the earth, and there is none that claps with his hand and says to Him, What have You done? **36** At that time my understanding returns to me, and for the glory of my kingdom, my honor and my brightness return to me, and to me my counselors and my great men seek, and over my kingdom I have been made right, and abundant greatness has been added to me. **37** Now I, Nebuchadnezzar, am praising and exalting and honoring the King of the heavens, for all His works [are] truth, and His paths judgment, and those walking in pride He is able to humble."

5 Belshazzar the king has made a great feast to one thousand of his great men, and before the one thousand he is drinking wine; **2** Belshazzar has said—while tasting the wine—to bring in the vessels of gold and of silver that his father Nebuchadnezzar had taken from the temple that [is] in Jerusalem, that the king may drink with them, and his great men, his wives, and his concubines. **3** Then they have brought in the vessels of gold that had been taken out of the temple of the house of God that [is] in Jerusalem, and the king and his great men, his wives and his concubines, have drunk with them; **4** they have drunk wine, and have praised the gods of gold, and of silver, of bronze, of iron, of wood, and of stone. **5** In that hour fingers of a man's hand have come forth, and they are writing in front of the lampstand, on the plaster of the wall of the king's palace: and the king is seeing the extremity of the hand that is writing; **6** then the king's countenance has changed, and his thoughts trouble him, and the joints of his loins are loosed, and his knees are striking against one another. **7** The king calls mightily, to bring up the enchanters, the Chaldeans, and the soothsayers. The king has answered and said to the wise men of Babylon, that, "Any man who reads this writing, and shows me its interpretation, he puts on purple, and a bracelet of gold [is] on his neck, and he rules third in the kingdom." **8** Then all the wise men of the king are coming up, and they are not able to read the writing, and to make known the interpretation to the king; **9** then King Belshazzar is greatly troubled, and his countenance is changing in him, and his great men are perplexed. **10** The queen, on account of the words of the king and his great men, has come up to the banquet-house. The queen has answered and said, "O king, live for all ages; do not let your thoughts trouble you, nor your countenance be changed: **11** there is a man in your kingdom in whom [is] the spirit of the holy gods: and in the days of your father, light, and understanding, and wisdom—as the wisdom of the gods—was found in him; and your father King Nebuchadnezzar, chief of the scribes, enchanters, Chaldeans, soothsayers, established him—your father, O king— **12** because that an excellent spirit, and knowledge, and understanding, interpreting of dreams, and showing of enigmas, and loosing of knots was found in him, in Daniel, whose name the king made Belteshazzar: now let Daniel be called, and the interpretation he shows." **13** Then Daniel has been caused to come up before the king; the king has answered and said to Daniel, "You are that Daniel who [is] of the sons of the expulsion of Judah, whom my father the king brought in out of Judah? **14** And I have heard of you, that the spirit of the gods [is] in you, and light, and

DANIEL

understanding, and excellent wisdom have been found in you. **15** And now, caused to come up before me have been the wise men, the enchanters, that they may read this writing, and its interpretation to cause me to know: and they are not able to show the interpretation of the thing: **16** and I have heard of you, that you are able to give interpretations, and to loose knots: now, behold—you are able to read the writing, and its interpretation to cause me to know—purple you put on, and a bracelet of gold [is] on your neck, and you rule third in the kingdom." **17** Then Daniel has answered and said before the king, "Your gifts be to yourself, and give your fee to another; nevertheless, the writing I read to the king, and the interpretation I cause him to know; **18** you, O king, God Most High, a kingdom, and greatness, and glory, and honor, gave to your father Nebuchadnezzar: **19** and because of the greatness that He gave to him, all peoples, nations, and languages were trembling and fearing before him: whom he willed he was slaying, and whom he willed he was keeping alive, and whom he willed he was raising up, and whom he willed he was making low; **20** and when his heart was high, and his spirit was strong to act proudly, he has been caused to come down from the throne of his kingdom, and his glory they have caused to pass away from him, **21** and he is driven from the sons of men, and his heart has been like with the beasts, and with the wild donkeys [is] his dwelling; they cause him to eat the herb like oxen, and by the dew of the heavens is his body wet, until he has known that God Most High is ruler in the kingdom of men, and whom He wills He raises up over it. **22** And you, his son, Belshazzar, have not humbled your heart, though all this you have known; **23** and against the Lord of the heavens you have lifted up yourself; and the vessels of His house they have brought in before you, and you, and your great men, your wives, and your concubines, are drinking wine with them, and gods of silver, and of gold, of bronze, of iron, of wood, and of stone, that are not seeing, nor hearing, nor knowing, you have praised: and the God in whose hand [is] your breath, and all your ways, Him you have not honored. **24** Then from before Him is the extremity of the hand sent, and the writing is noted down; **25** and this [is] the writing that is noted down: Numbered, Numbered, Weighed, and Divided. **26** This [is] the interpretation of the thing: Numbered—God has numbered your kingdom, and has finished it. **27** Weighed—You are weighed in the balances, and have been found lacking. **28** Divided—Your kingdom is divided, and it has been given to the Medes and Persians." **29** Then Belshazzar has spoken, and they have clothed Daniel with purple, and a bracelet of gold [is] on his neck, and they have proclaimed concerning him that he is the third ruler in the kingdom. **30** In that night Belshazzar king of the Chaldeans is slain, **31** and Darius the Mede has received the kingdom when a son of sixty-two years.

6 It has been good before Darius, and he has established over the kingdom satraps—one hundred and twenty—that they may be throughout the whole kingdom, **2** and three presidents higher than they, of whom Daniel [is] first, that these satraps may give to them an account, and the king have no loss. **3** Then this Daniel has been overseer over the presidents and satraps, because that an excellent spirit [is] in him, and the king has thought to establish him over the whole kingdom. **4** Then the presidents and satraps have been seeking to find a cause of complaint against Daniel concerning the kingdom, and any cause of complaint and corruption they are not able to find, because that he [is] faithful, and any error and corruption have not been found in him. **5** Then these men are saying, "We do not find against this Daniel any cause of complaint, except we have found [it] against him in the Law of his God." **6** Then these presidents and satraps have assembled near the king, and thus they are saying to him: "O King Darius, live for all ages! **7** Taken counsel have all the presidents of the kingdom, the prefects, and the satraps, the counselors, and the governors, to establish a royal statute, and to strengthen an interdict, that any who seeks a petition from any god and man until thirty days, except of you, O king, is cast into a den of lions. **8** Now, O king, you establish the interdict, and sign the writing, that it is not to be changed, as a law of Media and Persia, that does not pass away." **9** Therefore King Darius has signed the writing and interdict. **10** And Daniel,

DANIEL

when he has known that the writing is signed, has gone up to his house, and the window being opened for him, in his upper chamber, toward Jerusalem, three times in a day he is kneeling on his knees, and praying, and confessing before his God, because that he was doing [it] before this. **11** Then these men have assembled, and found Daniel praying and pleading grace before his God; **12** then they have come near, indeed, they are saying before the king concerning the king's interdict: "Have you not signed an interdict, that any man who seeks from any god and man until thirty days, except of you, O king, is cast into a den of lions?" The king has answered and said, "The thing [is] certain as a law of Media and Persia, that does not pass away." **13** Then they have answered, indeed, they are saying before the king, that, "Daniel, who [is] of the sons of the expulsion of Judah, has not placed on you, O king, [any] regard, nor on the interdict that you have signed, and three times in a day he is seeking his petition." **14** Then the king, when he has heard the matter, is greatly displeased at himself, and on Daniel he has set the heart to deliver him, and until the going up of the sun he was arranging to deliver him. **15** Then these men have assembled near the king, and are saying to the king, "Know, O king, that the law of Media and Persia [is] that any interdict and statute that the king establishes is not to be changed." **16** Then the king has spoken, and they have brought Daniel, and have cast [him] into a den of lions. The king has answered and said to Daniel, "Your God, whom you are serving continually, delivers you Himself." **17** And a stone has been brought and placed at the mouth of the den, and the king has sealed it with his signet, and with the signet of his great men, that the purpose is not changed concerning Daniel. **18** Then the king has gone to his palace, and he has passed the night fasting, and dahavan have not been brought up before him, and his sleep has fled [from] off him. **19** Then the king rises in the early morning, at the light, and he has gone in haste to the den of lions; **20** and at his coming near to the den, to Daniel, with a grieved voice, he cries. The king has answered and said to Daniel, "O Daniel, servant of the living God, your God, whom you are serving continually, is He able to deliver you from the lions?" **21** Then Daniel has spoken with the king: "O king, live for all ages: **22** my God has sent His messenger, and has shut the lions' mouths, and they have not injured me: because that before Him purity has been found in me; and also before you, O king, injury I have not done." **23** Then was the king very glad for him, and he has commanded Daniel to be taken up out of the den, and Daniel has been taken up out of the den, and no injury has been found in him, because he has believed in his God. **24** And the king has spoken, and they have brought those men who had accused Daniel, and to the den of lions they have cast them, they, their sons, and their wives; and they have not come to the lower part of the den until the lions have power over them, and all their bones they have broken small. **25** Then Darius the king has written to all the peoples, nations, and languages, who are dwelling in all the land: "Your peace be great! **26** From before me a decree is made, that in every dominion of my kingdom they are trembling and fearing before the God of Daniel, for He [is] the living God, and abiding for all ages, and His kingdom that which [is] not destroyed, and His dominion [is] to the end. **27** A deliverer, and rescuer, and doer of signs and wonders in the heavens and in earth [is] He who has delivered Daniel from the paw of the lions." **28** And this Daniel has prospered in the reign of Darius, and in the reign of Cyrus the Persian.

7 In the first year of Belshazzar king of Babylon, Daniel has seen a dream, and the visions of his head on his bed, then he has written the dream, the chief of the things he has said. **2** Daniel has answered and said, "I was seeing in my vision by night, and behold, the four winds of the heavens are coming forth to the Great Sea; **3** and four great beasts are coming up from the sea, diverse from one another. **4** The first [is] like a lion, and it has an eagle's wings. I was seeing until its wings have been plucked, and it has been lifted up from the earth, and on feet as a man it has been caused to stand, and a heart of man is given to it. **5** And behold, another beast, a second, like to a bear, and to the same authority it has been raised, and three ribs [are] in its mouth, between its teeth, and thus they are saying to it, Rise, consume much flesh. **6** After this I was seeing, and behold, another like a leopard, and it has four wings of a bird on its back, and the beast has four heads, and dominion is given to it. **7** After this I was seeing in the visions of the night, and behold, a fourth beast, terrible and fearful, and exceedingly strong; and it has very great iron teeth, it has consumed, indeed, it breaks small, and it has trampled the remnant with its feet; and it [is] diverse from all the beasts that [are] before it; and it has ten horns. **8** I was considering about the horns, and behold, another horn, a little one, has come up between them, and three of the first horns have been eradicated from before it, and behold, eyes as the eyes of man [are] in this horn, and a mouth speaking great things. **9** I was seeing until thrones have been thrown down, and the Ancient of Days is seated, His garment [is] white as snow, and the hair of His head [is] as pure wool, His throne flames of fire, its wheels burning fire. **10** A flood of fire is proceeding and coming forth from before Him, one million serve Him and one hundred million rise up before Him, judgment has been set, and the scrolls have been opened. **11** I was seeing, then, because of the voice of the great words that the horn is speaking, I was seeing until the beast is slain, and his body has been destroyed, and given to the burning fire; **12** and the rest of the beasts have caused their dominion to pass away, and a prolongation in life is given to them, until a season and a time. **13** I was seeing in the visions of the night, and behold, [One] like a Son of Man was coming with the clouds of the heavens, and to the Ancient of Days He has come, and before Him they have brought Him near. **14** And to Him is given dominion, and glory, and a kingdom, and all peoples, nations, and languages serve Him, His dominion [is] a continuous dominion, that does not pass away, and His kingdom that which is not destroyed. **15** My spirit has been pierced—I, Daniel—in the midst of the sheath, and the visions of my head trouble me; **16** I have drawn near to one of those standing, and the certainty I seek from him of all this; and he has spoken to me, indeed, the interpretation of the things he has caused me to know: **17** These great beasts, that [are] four, [are] four kings, they rise up from the earth; **18** and the saints of the Most High receive the kingdom, and they strengthen the kingdom for all time, even for all time and all ages. **19** Then I wished for certainty concerning the fourth beast, that was diverse from them all, exceedingly fearful; its teeth of iron, and its nails of bronze, it has devoured, it breaks small, and it has trampled the remnant with its feet; **20** and concerning the ten horns that [are] in its heads, and of the other that came up, and before which three have fallen, even of that horn that has eyes, and a mouth speaking great things, and whose appearance [is] great above its companions. **21** I was seeing, and this horn is making war with the saints, and has prevailed over them, **22** until the Ancient of Days has come, and judgment is given to the saints of the Most High, and the time has come, and the saints have strengthened the kingdom. **23** Thus he said: The fourth beast is the fourth kingdom in the earth, that is diverse from all kingdoms, and it consumes all the earth, and treads it down, and breaks it small. **24** And the ten horns out of the kingdom [are] ten kings, they rise, and another rises after them, and it is diverse from the former, and it humbles three kings; **25** and it speaks words as an adversary of the Most High, and it wears out the saints of the Most High, and it hopes to change seasons and law; and they are given into its hand, until a time, and times, and a division of a time. **26** And judgment is set, and they cause his dominion to pass away, to perish, and to be destroyed—to the end; **27** and the kingdom, and the dominion, even the greatness of the kingdom under the whole heavens, is given to the people—the saints of the Most High, His kingdom [is] a continuous kingdom, and all dominions serve and obey Him. **28** Here [is] the end of the matter. I, Daniel, [am] greatly troubled [by] my thoughts, and my countenance is changed on me, and I have kept the matter in my heart."

8 "In the third year of the reign of Belshazzar the king, a vision has appeared to me—I Daniel—after that which had appeared to me at the beginning. **2** And I see in a vision, and it comes to pass, in my seeing, and I [am] in Shushan the palace that [is] in Elam the province, and I see in a vision, and I have been by the stream Ulai. **3** And I lift up my eyes, and look, and behold, a certain ram is standing before the stream, and it has two horns, and the two horns [are] high; and one [is] higher

DANIEL

than the other, and the high one is coming up last. **4** I have seen the ram pushing westward, and northward, and southward, and no living creatures stand before it, and there is none delivering out of its hand, and it has done according to its pleasure, and has exerted itself. **5** And I have been considering, and behold, a young male goat has come from the west, over the face of the whole earth, whom none is touching in the earth; as for the young male goat, a conspicuous horn [is] between its eyes. **6** And it comes to the ram possessing the two horns, that I had seen standing before the stream, and runs to it in the fury of its power. **7** And I have seen it coming near the ram, and it becomes embittered at it, and strikes the ram, and breaks its two horns, and there has been no power in the ram to stand before it, and it casts it to the earth, and tramples it down, and there has been no deliverer to the ram out of its power. **8** And the young male goat has exerted itself very much, and when it is strong, the great horn has been broken; and a vision of four comes up in its place, at the four winds of the heavens. **9** And from one of them has come forth a little horn, and it exerts itself greatly toward the south, and toward the east, and toward the beautiful [land]; **10** indeed, it exerts to the host of the heavens, and causes to fall to the earth of the host, and of the stars, and tramples them down. **11** And to the prince of the host it exerts itself, and the continual [sacrifice] has been taken away by it, and thrown down the base of his sanctuary. **12** And the host is given up, with the continual [sacrifice], through transgression, and it throws down truth to the earth, and it has worked, and prospered. **13** And I hear a certain holy one speaking, and a certain holy one says to the wonderful numberer who is speaking: Until when [is] the vision of the continual [sacrifice], and of the transgression, an astonishment, to make a treading down of both sanctuary and host? **14** And he says to me, Until evening—morning two thousand and three hundred, then is the holy place declared right. **15** And it comes to pass in my seeing—I, Daniel—the vision, that I require understanding, and behold, standing before me [is] as the appearance of a mighty one. **16** And I hear a voice of man between [the banks of] Ulai, and he calls and says: Gabriel, cause this [one] to understand the appearance. **17** And he comes in near my station, and at his coming in I have been afraid, and I fall on my face, and he says to me: Understand, son of man, for at the time of the end [is] the vision. **18** And in his speaking with me, I have been in a trance on my face, on the earth; and he comes against me, and causes me to stand on my station, **19** and says: Behold, I am causing you to know that which is in the latter end of the indignation; for at the appointed time [is] the end. **20** The ram that you have seen possessing two horns, [are] the kings of Media and Persia. **21** And the young male goat, the hairy one, [is] the king of Javan; and the great horn that [is] between its eyes is the first king; **22** and that being broken, four stand up in its place, four kingdoms stand up from the nation, and not in its power. **23** And in the latter end of their kingdom, about the perfecting of the transgressors, a king stands up, fierce of face, and understanding hidden things; **24** and his power has been mighty, and not by his own power; and he destroys wonderful things, and he has prospered, and worked, and destroyed mighty ones, and the people of the Holy Ones. **25** And by his understanding he has also caused deceit to prosper in his hand, and in his heart he exerts himself, and by ease he destroys many; and he stands against the Prince of princes—and he is broken without hand. **26** And the appearance of the evening and of the morning, that is told, is true; and you, hide the vision, for [it is] after many days. **27** And I, Daniel, have been, indeed, I became sick [for] days, and I rise, and do the king's work, and am astonished at the appearance, and there is none understanding."

9 "In the first year of Darius, son of Ahasuerus, of the seed of the Medes, who has been made king over the kingdom of the Chaldeans, **2** in the first year of his reign, I, Daniel, have understood by scrolls the number of the years (in that a word of YHWH has been to Jeremiah the prophet), concerning the fulfilling of the desolations of Jerusalem—seventy years; **3** and I set my face toward the Lord God, to seek [by] prayer and supplications, with fasting, and sackcloth, and ashes. **4** And I pray to my God YHWH, and confess, and say: Ah, now, O Lord God, the great and the fearful, keeping the covenant and the kindness to those loving Him and to those keeping His commands; **5** we have sinned, and done perversely, and done wickedly, and rebelled, to turn aside from Your commands, and from Your judgments: **6** and we have not listened to Your servants, the prophets, who have spoken in Your Name to our kings, our heads, and our fathers, and to all the people of the land. **7** To You, O Lord, [is] the righteousness, and to us the shame of face, as [at] this day, to the men of Judah, and to the inhabitants of Jerusalem, and to all Israel, who are near, and who are far off, in all the lands to where You have driven them, in their trespass that they have trespassed against You. **8** O Lord, to us [is] the shame of face, to our kings, to our heads, and to our fathers, in that we have sinned against You. **9** To the Lord our God [are] the mercies and the forgivenesses, for we have rebelled against Him, **10** and have not listened to the voice of our God YHWH, to walk in His laws, that He has set before us by the hand of His servants the prophets; **11** and all Israel has transgressed Your law, to turn aside so as not to listen to Your voice; and poured on us is the execration, and the oath, that is written in the Law of Moses, servant of God, because we have sinned against Him. **12** And He confirms His words that He has spoken against us, and against our judges who have judged us, to bring great calamity on us, in that it has not been done under the whole heavens as it has been done in Jerusalem, **13** as it is written in the Law of Moses, all this evil has come on us, and we have not appeased the face of our God YHWH to turn back from our iniquities, and to act wisely in Your truth. **14** And YHWH watches for the evil, and brings it on us, for our God YHWH is righteous concerning all His works that He has done, and we have not listened to His voice. **15** And now, O Lord our God, who has brought forth Your people from the land of Egypt by a strong hand, and makes for Yourself a name as at this day, we have sinned, we have done wickedly. **16** O Lord, according to all Your righteous acts, please let Your anger and Your fury turn back from Your city Jerusalem, Your holy mountain, for by our sins, and by the iniquities of our fathers, Jerusalem and Your people [are] for a reproach to all our neighbors; **17** and now, listen, O our God, to the prayer of Your servant, and to his supplication, and cause Your face to shine on Your sanctuary that [is] desolate, for the Lord's sake. **18** Incline, O my God, Your ear, and hear, open Your eyes and see our desolations, and the city on which Your Name is called; for not for our righteous acts are we causing our supplications to fall before You, but for Your mercies that [are] many. **19** O Lord, hear, O Lord, forgive; O Lord, attend and do; do not delay, for Your own sake, O my God, for Your Name is called on Your city, and on Your people. **20** And while I am speaking, and praying, and confessing my sin, and the sin of my people Israel, and causing my supplication to fall before my God YHWH, for the holy mountain of my God, **21** indeed, while I am speaking in prayer, then that one Gabriel, whom I had seen in vision at the commencement, being caused to fly swiftly, is coming to me at the time of the evening present. **22** And he gives understanding, and speaks with me, and says, O Daniel, now I have come forth to cause you to consider understanding wisely; **23** at the commencement of your supplications the word has come forth, and I have come to declare [it], for you [are] greatly desired, and understand concerning the matter, and consider concerning the appearance. **24** Seventy periods of seven are determined for your people and for your holy city, to shut up the transgression, and to seal up sins, and to cover iniquity, and to bring in continuous righteousness, and to seal up vision and prophet, and to anoint the Holy of Holies. **25** And you know, and consider wisely, from the going forth of the word to restore and to build Jerusalem until Messiah the Leader [is] seven periods of seven, and sixty-two periods of seven: the broad place has been built again, and the rampart, even in the distress of the times. **26** And after the sixty-two periods of seven, Messiah is cut off, but not for Himself, and the people of the leader who is coming destroy the city and the holy place; and its end [is] with a flood, and until the end [is] war, [and] desolations [are] determined. **27** And he has strengthened a covenant with many [for] one period of seven, and [in] the midst of the period of seven he causes sacrifice and present to cease, and by the wing of abominations he is making desolate, even until the consummation, and that which is determined is poured on the desolate one."

DANIEL

10 In the third year of Cyrus king of Persia, a thing is revealed to Daniel, whose name is called Belteshazzar, and the thing [is] true, and the warfare [is] great: and he has understood the thing, and has understanding about the appearance. **2** "In those days, I, Daniel, have been mourning three weeks of days; **3** I have not eaten desirable bread, and no flesh and wine came into my mouth, and I have not anointed myself at all, until the completion of three weeks of days. **4** And in the twenty-fourth day of the first month, I have been by the side of the great river, that [is] Hiddekel: **5** and I lift up my eyes, and look, and behold, a certain one clothed in linen, and his loins girt with pure gold of Uphaz, **6** and his body as a beryl, and his face as the appearance of lightning, and his eyes as lamps of fire, and his arms and his feet as the aspect of bright bronze, and the voice of his words as the voice of a multitude. **7** And I, Daniel, have seen the vision by myself, and the men who have been with me have not seen the vision, but a great trembling has fallen on them, and they flee to be hidden; **8** and I have been left by myself, and I see this great vision, and there has been no power left in me, and my splendor has been turned in me to corruption, indeed, I have not retained power. **9** And I hear the voice of his words, and when I hear the voice of his words, then I have been in a trance on my face, and my face [is] to the earth; **10** and behold, a hand has come against me, and shakes me on my knees and the palms of my hands. **11** And he says to me: Daniel, man greatly desired, attend to the words that I am speaking to you, and stand on your station, for now I have been sent to you. And when he speaks with me this word, I have stood trembling. **12** And he says to me: Do not fear, Daniel, for from the first day that you gave your heart to understand, and to humble yourself before your God, your words have been heard, and I have come because of your words. **13** And the head of the kingdom of Persia is standing in opposition in front of me [for] twenty-one days, and behold, Michael, first of the chief heads, has come to help me, and I have remained there near the kings of Persia; **14** and I have come to cause you to understand that which happens to your people in the latter end of the days, for yet the vision [is] after days. **15** And when he speaks with me about these things, I have set my face toward the earth, and have been silent; **16** and behold, as the manner of the sons of men, he is striking against my lips, and I open my mouth, and I speak, and say to him who is standing in opposition in front of me: My lord, by the vision my pangs have been turned against me, and I have retained no power. **17** And how is the servant of this my lord able to speak with this my lord? As for me, from now on there remains in me no power, indeed, breath has not been left in me. **18** And he adds, and strikes against me, as the appearance of a man, and strengthens me, **19** and he says: Do not fear, O man greatly desired, peace to you, be strong, indeed, be strong; and when he speaks with me, I have strengthened myself, and I say, Let my lord speak, for you have strengthened me. **20** And he says, Have you known why I have come to you? And now I return to fight with the head of Persia; indeed, I am going forth, and behold, the head of Javan has come; **21** but I declare to you that which is noted down in the Writing of Truth, and there is not one strengthening himself with me, concerning these, except Michael your head."

11 "And I, in the first year of Darius the Mede, my standing [is] for a strengthener, and for a stronghold to him; **2** and now, I declare to you truth: Behold, yet three kings are standing for Persia, and the fourth becomes far richer than all, and according to his strength by his riches he stirs up the whole, with the kingdom of Javan. **3** And a mighty king has stood, and he has ruled a great dominion, and has done according to his will; **4** and according to his standing is his kingdom broken, and divided to the four winds of the heavens, and not to his posterity, nor according to his dominion that he ruled, for his kingdom is plucked up—and for others apart from these. **5** And a king of the south—even of his princes—becomes strong, and prevails against him, and has ruled; a great dominion [is] his dominion. **6** And at the end of years they join themselves together, and a daughter of the king of the south comes to the king of the north to do upright things; and she does not retain the power of the arm; and he does not stand, nor his arm; and she is given up, she, and those bringing her in, and her child, and he who is strengthening her in [these] times. **7** And [one] has stood up from a branch of her roots, [in] his station, and he comes to the bulwark, indeed, he comes into a stronghold of the king of the north, and has worked against them, and has done mightily; **8** and also their gods, with their princes, with their desirable vessels of silver and gold, he brings in captivity [to] Egypt; and he stands more years than the king of the north. **9** And the king of the south has come into the kingdom, and turned back to his own land; **10** and his sons stir themselves up, and have gathered a multitude of great forces, and he has certainly come in, and overflowed, and passed through, and he turns back, and they stir themselves up to his stronghold. **11** And the king of the south becomes embittered, and has gone forth and fought with him, with the king of the north, and has caused a great multitude to stand, and the multitude has been given into his hand, **12** and he has carried away the multitude, his heart is high, and he has caused myriads to fall, and he does not become strong. **13** And the king of the north has turned back, and has caused a multitude to stand, greater than the first, and at the end of the times a second time he certainly comes in with a great force, and with much substance; **14** and in those times many stand up against the king of the south, and sons of the destroyers of your people lift themselves up to establish the vision—and they have stumbled. **15** And the king of the north comes in, and pours out a mound, and has captured fortified cities; and the arms of the south do not stand, nor the people of his choice, indeed, there is no power to stand. **16** And he who is coming to him does according to his will, and there is none standing before him; and he stands in the desirable land, and [it is] wholly in his hand. **17** And he sets his face to go in with the strength of his whole kingdom, and upright ones with him; and he has worked, and the daughter of women he gives to him, to corrupt her; and she does not stand, nor is for him. **18** And he turns back his face to the islands, and has captured many; and a prince has caused his reproach of himself to cease; without his reproach he turns [it] back to him. **19** And he turns back his face to the strongholds of his land, and has stumbled and fallen, and is not found. **20** And stood up on his station has [one] causing an exactor to pass over the honor of the kingdom, and in a few days he is destroyed, and not in anger, nor in battle. **21** And a despicable one has stood up on his station, and they have not given to him the splendor of the kingdom, and he has come in quietly, and has strengthened the kingdom by flatteries. **22** And the arms of the flood are overflowed from before him, and are broken; and also the leader of the covenant. **23** And after they join themselves to him, he works deceit, and has increased, and has been strong by a few of the nation. **24** Peaceably even into the fertile places of the province He comes, and he has done that which his fathers did not, nor his fathers' fathers; prey, and spoil, and substance, he scatters to them, and against fortifications he devises his plans, even for a time. **25** And he stirs up his power and his heart against the king of the south with a great force, and the king of the south stirs himself up to battle with a very great and mighty force, and does not stand, for they devise plans against him, **26** and those eating his portion of food destroy him, and his force overflows, and many wounded have fallen. **27** And both of the kings' hearts [are] to do evil, and at one table they speak lies, and it does not prosper, for yet the end [is] at a time appointed. **28** And he turns back [to] his land with great substance, and his heart [is] against the holy covenant, and he has worked, and turned back to his land. **29** At the appointed time he turns back, and has come against the south, and it is not as the former, and as the latter. **30** And ships of Chittim have come in against him, and he has been pained, and has turned back, and has been insolent toward the holy covenant, and has worked, and turned back, and he understands concerning those forsaking the holy covenant. **31** And strong ones stand up out of him, and have defiled the sanctuary, the stronghold, and have turned aside the continual [sacrifice], and appointed the desolating abomination. **32** And those acting wickedly [against] the covenant, he defiles by flatteries; and the people knowing their God are strong, and have worked. **33** And the teachers of the people give understanding to many; and they have stumbled by sword, and by flame, by captivity, and by spoil—days. **34** And in their stumbling, they are helped—a little help, and joined to them have been many with flatteries. **35** And some of the teachers stumble for refining by them, and for purifying, and for making white—until the end of the time, for [it is] yet for a time appointed. **36** And the king has done according to his will, and exalts himself, and magnifies himself against every god, and he speaks wonderful things against the God of gods, and has prospered until the indignation has been completed, for that which is determined has been done. **37** And to the God of his fathers he does not attend, nor to the desire of women, indeed, he does not attend to any god, for he magnifies himself against all. **38** And to the god of strongholds, on his station, he gives honor; indeed, to a god whom his fathers did not know he gives honor, with gold, and with silver, and with precious stone, and with desirable things. **39** And he has dealt in the fortresses of the strongholds with a strange god whom he has acknowledged; he multiplies honor, and has caused them to rule over many, and the ground he apportions at a price. **40** And at the time of the end, a king of the south pushes himself forward with him, and a king of the north storms against him, with chariot, and with horsemen, and with many ships; and he has come into the lands, and has overflowed, and passed over, **41** and has come into the desirable land, and many stumble, and these escape from his hand: Edom, and Moab, and the chief of the sons of Ammon. **42** And he sends forth his hand on the lands, and the land of Egypt is not for an escape; **43** and he has ruled over treasures of gold and of silver, and over all the desirable things of Egypt, and Lubim and Cushim [are] at his steps. **44** And reports trouble him out of the east and out of the north, and he has gone forth in great fury to destroy, and to devote many to destruction; **45** and he plants the tents of his palace between the seas and the holy desirable mountain, and has come to his end, and there is no helper to him."

12 "And at that time Michael stands up, the great head, who is standing up for the sons of your people, and there has been a time of distress, such as has not been since there has been a nation until that time, and at that time your people escape, everyone who is found written in the scroll. **2** And the multitude of those sleeping in the dust of the ground awake, some to continuous life, and some to reproaches—to continuous abhorrence. **3** And those teaching shine as the brightness of the expanse, and those justifying the multitude as stars for all time and forever." **4** "And you, O Daniel, hide the things, and seal the scroll until the time of the end, many go to and fro, and knowledge is multiplied." **5** "And I have looked—I, Daniel—and behold, two others are standing, one here at the edge of the flood and one there at the edge of the flood, **6** and he says to the one clothed in linen, who [is] on the waters of the flood, Until when [is] the end of these wonders? **7** And I hear the one clothed in linen, who [is] on the waters of the flood, and he lifts up his right hand and his left to the heavens, and swears by Him who is living for all time, that, After a time, times, and a half, and at the completion of the scattering of the power of the holy people, all these are finished. **8** And I have heard, and I do not understand, and I say, O my lord, what [is] the latter end of these? **9** And he says, Go, Daniel; for hidden and sealed [are] the things until the time of the end. **10** Purify themselves, indeed, make themselves white, indeed, many are refined: and the wicked have done wickedly, and none of the wicked understand, and those acting wisely understand; **11** and from the time of the turning aside of the continuous [sacrifice], and to the giving out of the desolating abomination, [are] one thousand, two hundred, and ninety days. **12** O the blessedness of him who is waiting earnestly, and comes to the one thousand, three hundred, thirty-five days. **13** And you, go on to the end, then you rest, and stand in your lot at the end of the days."

HOSEA

1 A word of YHWH that has been to Hosea, son of Beeri, in the days of Uzziah, Jotham, Ahaz, Hezekiah, kings of Judah, and in the days of Jeroboam son of Joash, king of Israel: **2** The commencement of YHWH's speaking by Hosea. And YHWH says to Hosea, "Go, take a woman of whoredoms for yourself, and children of whoredoms, for the land goes utterly whoring from after YHWH." **3** And he goes and takes Gomer daughter of Diblaim, and she conceives and bears a son to him; **4** and YHWH says to him, "Call his name Jezreel, for yet a little, and I have charged the blood of Jezreel on the house of Jehu, and have caused the kingdom of the house of Israel to cease; **5** and it has come to pass in that day that I have broken the bow of Israel in the Valley of Jezreel." **6** And she conceives again, and bears a daughter, and He says to him, "Call her name Lo-Ruhamah [(Not Loved)], for I no longer pity the house of Israel, for I utterly take them away; **7** and I pity the house of Judah, and have saved them by their God YHWH, and do not save them by bow, and by sword, and by battle, by horses, and by horsemen." **8** And she weans Lo-Ruhamah, and conceives, and bears a son; **9** and He says, "Call his name Lo-Ammi [(Not My People)], for you [are] not My people, and I am not for you; **10** and the number of the sons of Israel has been as the sand of the sea that is not measured nor numbered, and it has come to pass in the place where it is said to them, You [are] not My people, it is said to them, Sons of the Living God; **11** and the sons of Judah and the sons of Israel have been gathered together, and they have appointed one head for themselves, and have gone up from the land, for great [is] the day of Jezreel."

2 "Say to your brothers—Ammi, ‖ And to your sisters—Ruhamah. **2** Plead with your mother—plead ‖ (For she [is] not My wife, and I [am] not her husband), ‖ And she turns her whoredoms from before her, ‖ And her adulteries from between her breasts, **3** Lest I strip her naked. And have set her up as [in] the day of her birth, ‖ And have made her as a wilderness, ‖ And have set her as a dry land, ‖ And have put her to death with thirst. **4** And her sons I do not pity, ‖ For they [are] sons of whoredoms, **5** For their mother has gone whoring, ‖ Their conceiver has acted shamefully, ‖ For she has said, I go after my lovers, ‖ Those giving my bread and my water, ‖ My wool and my flax, my oil and my drink. **6** Therefore, behold, I am hedging up your way with thorns, ‖ And I have made a wall for her, ‖ And her paths she does not find. **7** And she has pursued her lovers, ‖ And she does not overtake them, ‖ And has sought them, and does not find [them], ‖ And she has said: I go, and I return to my first husband, ‖ For—better to me then than now. **8** And she did not know that I had given to her ‖ The grain, and the new wine, and the oil. Indeed, I multiplied silver to her, ‖ And the gold they prepared for Ba'al. **9** Therefore I return, ‖ And I have taken My grain in its season, ‖ And My new wine in its appointed time, ‖ And I have taken away My wool and My flax, covering her nakedness. **10** And now I reveal her dishonor before the eyes of her lovers, ‖ And none deliver her out of My hand. **11** And I have caused all her joy to cease, ‖ Her festival, her new moon, and her Sabbath, ‖ Even all her appointed times, **12** And made desolate her vine and her fig tree, ‖ Of which she said, They [are] a wage to me, ‖ That my lovers have given to me, ‖ And I have made them for a forest, ‖ And a beast of the field has consumed them. **13** And I have charged on her the days of the Ba'alim, ‖ To whom she makes incense, ‖ And puts on her ring and her ornament, ‖ And goes after her lovers, ‖ And forgot Me," a declaration of YHWH. **14** "Therefore, behold, I am enticing her, ‖ And have caused her to go to the wilderness, ‖ And I have spoken to her heart, **15** And given to her her vineyards from there, ‖ And the Valley of Achor for an opening of hope, ‖ And she has responded there as in the days of her youth, ‖ And as in the day of her coming up out of the land of Egypt. **16** And it has come to pass in that day," ‖ A declaration of YHWH, ‖ "You call Me: My husband, ‖ And do not call Me anymore: My lord. **17** And I have turned aside the names of the lords from her mouth, ‖ And they are not remembered anymore by their name. **18** And I have made a covenant for them in that day, ‖ With the beast of the field, ‖ And with the bird of the heavens, ‖ And the creeping thing of the ground, ‖ And bow, and sword, and war I break from off the land, ‖ And have caused them to lie down confidently. **19** And I have betrothed you to Me for all time, ‖ And betrothed you to Me in righteousness, ‖ And in judgment, and kindness, and mercies, **20** And betrothed you to Me in faithfulness, ‖ And you have known YHWH. **21** And it has come to pass in that day, I answer," ‖ A declaration of YHWH, ‖ "I answer the heavens, and they answer the earth. **22** And the earth answers the grain, ‖ And the new wine, and the oil, ‖ And they answer Jezreel. **23** And I have sowed her to Me in the land, ‖ And I have pitied Lo-Ruhamah, ‖ And I have said to Lo-Ammi, You [are] My people, ‖ And he says, My God!"

3 And YHWH says to me: "Again, go, love a woman, loved of a friend, and an adulteress, like the loved of YHWH, the sons of Israel, and they are turning to other gods, and are lovers of grape-cakes." **2** And I buy her for myself for fifteen pieces of silver, and a homer and a lethech of barley; **3** and I say to her, "You remain many days for Me, you do not go whoring, nor become anyone's; and I also [am] for you." **4** For the sons of Israel remain without a king for many days, and there is no prince, and there is no sacrifice, and there is no standing pillar, and there is no ephod and teraphim. **5** Afterward the sons of Israel have turned back, and sought their God YHWH, and David their king, and have hurried to YHWH, and to His goodness, in the latter end of the days.

4 "Hear a word of YHWH, sons of Israel, ‖ For a strife [is] to YHWH with inhabitants of the land, ‖ For there is no truth, nor kindness, ‖ Nor knowledge of God in the land; **2** Swearing, and lying, and murdering, ‖ And stealing, and committing adultery—have increased, ‖ And blood has touched against blood. **3** Therefore the land mourns, ‖ And every dweller is weak in it, ‖ With the beast of the field, ‖ And with the bird of the heavens, ‖ And the fishes of the sea—they are removed. **4** Only, let no one strive, nor reprove a man, ‖ And your people [are] as those striving with a priest.

5 And you have stumbled in the day, ‖ And a prophet has also stumbled with you in the night, ‖ And I have cut off your mother. **6** My people have been cut off for lack of knowledge, ‖ Because you have rejected knowledge, ‖ I reject you from being priest to Me, ‖ And you forget the Law of your God—I forget your sons, I also! **7** According to their abundance so they sinned against Me, ‖ I change their glory into shame. **8** The sin of My people they eat, ‖ And to their iniquity lift up their soul. **9** And it has been, like people, like priest, ‖ And I have charged on it its ways, ‖ And its habitual doings I return to it. **10** And they have eaten, and are not satisfied, ‖ They have gone whoring, and do not increase, ‖ For they have left off taking heed to YHWH. **11** Whoredom, and wine, and new wine, take the heart, **12** My people at its staff asks and its rod declares to it, ‖ For a spirit of whoredoms has caused to err, ‖ And they go whoring from under their God. **13** On tops of the mountains they sacrifice, ‖ And on the hills they make incense, ‖ Under oak, and poplar, and terebinth, ‖ For good [is] its shade. **14** Therefore your daughters commit whoredom, ‖ And your spouses commit adultery, ‖ I do not see after your daughters when they commit whoredom, ‖ And after your spouses when they commit adultery, ‖ For they with the harlots are separated, ‖ And with the whores they sacrifice, ‖ A people that does not understand kicks. **15** Though you [are] a harlot, O Israel, ‖ Do not let Judah become guilty, ‖ And do not come to Gilgal, nor go up to Beth-Aven, ‖ Nor swear, YHWH lives. **16** For Israel has turned aside as a stubborn heifer, ‖ Now YHWH feeds them as a lamb in a large place. **17** Ephraim is joined to idols, leave him alone. **18** Sour [is] their drink, ‖ They have gone whoring diligently, ‖ Her protectors have thoroughly loved shame. **19** Wind has distressed her with its wings, ‖ And they are ashamed of their sacrifices!"

5 "Hear this, O priests, and attend, O house of Israel, ‖ And, O house of the king, give ear, ‖ For the judgment [is] for you, ‖ For you have been a snare on Mizpah, ‖ And a net spread out on Tabor. **2** And to slaughter sinners have gone deep, ‖ And I [am] a chain to them all. **3** I have known Ephraim, ‖ And Israel has not been hid from Me, ‖ For now you have gone whoring, Ephraim, ‖ Israel is defiled. **4** They do not give up their habitual doings, ‖ To turn back to their God, ‖ For a spirit of whoredoms [is] in their midst, ‖ And YHWH they have not known. **5** And humbled has been the excellence of Israel to his face, ‖ And Israel and Ephraim stumble by their iniquity, ‖ Judah has also stumbled with them. **6** With their flock and with their herd, ‖ They go to seek YHWH, and do not find, ‖ He has withdrawn from them. **7** Against YHWH they dealt treacherously, ‖ For they have begotten strange sons, ‖ Now a month consumes them [with] their portions. **8** Blow a horn in Gibeah, a trumpet in Ramah, ‖ Shout, O Beth-Aven, after you, O Benjamin. **9** Ephraim is for a desolation in a day of reproof, ‖ I have made known a sure thing among the tribes of Israel. **10** Princes of Judah have been as those removing a border, ‖ I pour out My wrath as water on them. **11** Ephraim is oppressed, broken in judgment, ‖ When he pleased he went after the command. **12** And I [am] as a moth to Ephraim, ‖ And as a rotten thing to the house of Judah. **13** And Ephraim sees his sickness, and Judah his wound, ‖ And Ephraim goes to Asshur, ‖ And sends to a warlike king, ‖ And he is not able to give healing to you, ‖ Nor does he remove a scar from you. **14** For I [am] as a lion to Ephraim, ‖ And as a young lion to the house of Judah, I tear and go, ‖ I carry away, and there is no deliverer. **15** I go—I return to My place, ‖ Until they are desolate, and have sought My face. In their distress they seek Me speedily!"

6 "Come, and we turn back to YHWH, ‖ For He has torn, and He heals us, ‖ He strikes, and He binds us up. **2** He revives us after two days, ‖ In the third day He raises us up, ‖ And we live before Him. **3** And we know—we pursue to know YHWH, ‖ His going forth is prepared as the dawn, ‖ And He comes in as a shower to us, ‖ As spring rain [and] autumn rain to the earth." **4** "What do I do to you, O Ephraim? What do I do to you, O Judah? Your goodness [is] as a cloud of the morning, ‖ And as dew rising early—going. **5** Therefore I have hewed by prophets, ‖ I have slain them by sayings of My mouth, ‖ And My judgments go forth to the light. **6** For kindness I desired, and not sacrifice, ‖ And a knowledge of God above burnt-offerings. **7** And they, as Adam, transgressed a covenant, ‖ There they dealt treacherously against Me. **8** Gilead [is] a city of workers of iniquity, ‖ Slippery from blood. **9** And as bands wait for a man, ‖ A company of priests murder—the way to Shechem, ‖ For they have done wickedness. **10** In the house of Israel I have seen a horrible thing, ‖ There [is] the whoredom of Ephraim—Israel is defiled. **11** Also, O Judah, a harvest is appointed to you, ‖ In My turning back [to] the captivity of My people!"

7 "When I give healing to Israel, ‖ Then the iniquity of Ephraim is revealed, ‖ And the wickedness of Samaria, ‖ For they have worked falsehood, ‖ And a thief comes in, ‖ A troop has stripped off in the street, **2** And they do not say to their heart, ‖ [That] I have remembered all their evil, ‖ Now their doings have surrounded them, ‖ They have been before My face. **3** With their wickedness they make a king glad, ‖ And with their lies—princes. **4** All of them [are] adulterers, ‖ Like a burning oven of a baker, ‖ He ceases from stirring up after kneading the dough, until its leavening. **5** A day of our king! Princes have defiled themselves [with] the poison of wine, ‖ He has drawn out his hand with scorners. **6** For they have drawn near, ‖ Their heart [is] as an oven ‖ In their lying in wait—their baker sleeps all night, ‖ Morning! He is burning as a flaming fire. **7** All of them are warm as an oven, ‖ And they have devoured their judges, ‖ All their kings have fallen, ‖ There is none calling to Me among them. **8** Ephraim! He mixes himself among peoples, ‖ Ephraim has been an unturned cake. **9** Strangers have devoured his power, ‖ And he has not known, ‖ Also old age has sprinkled [itself] on him, ‖ And he has not known. **10** And the excellence of Israel has been humbled to his face, ‖ And they have not turned back to their God YHWH, ‖ Nor have they sought Him for all this. **11** And Ephraim is as a simple dove without heart, ‖ Egypt they called on—[to] Asshur they have gone. **12** When they go I spread over them My net, ‖ As the bird of the heavens I bring them down, ‖ I discipline them as their congregation has heard. **13** Woe to them, for they wandered from Me, ‖ Destruction to them, for they transgressed against Me, ‖ And I ransom them, and they have spoken lies against Me, **14** And have not cried to Me with their heart, but howl on their beds; They assemble themselves for grain and new wine, ‖ They turn aside against Me. **15** And I instructed—I strengthened their arms, ‖ And concerning Me they think evil! **16** They turn back—not to the Most High, ‖ They have been as a deceitful bow, ‖ Their princes fall by sword, ‖ From the insolence of their tongue, ‖ This [is] their derision in the land of Egypt!"

8 "To your mouth—a horn, ‖ As an eagle against the house of YHWH, ‖ Because they transgressed My covenant, ‖ And against My law they have rebelled. **2** To Me they cry, My God, we—Israel—have known You. **3** Israel has cast off good, an enemy pursues him. **4** They have made kings, and not by Me, ‖ They have made princes, and I have not known, ‖ Their silver and their gold they have made to them idols, ‖ So that they are cut off. **5** Your calf has cast off, O Samaria, ‖ My anger has burned against them; Until when are they not capable of purity? **6** For even it [is] of Israel; a craftsman made it, ‖ And it [is] not God, ‖ For the calf of Samaria is fragments! **7** For wind they sow, and a windstorm they reap, ‖ Stalk it has none—a shoot not yielding grain, ‖ If so be it yield—strangers swallow it up. **8** Israel has been swallowed up, ‖ Now they have been among nations, ‖ As a vessel in which is no delight. **9** For they have gone up [to] Asshur, ‖ A wild donkey alone by himself [is] Ephraim, ‖ They have hired lovers! **10** Also though they hire among nations, ‖ Now I gather them, and they are pained a little, ‖ From the burden of a king of princes. **11** Because Ephraim multiplied altars to sin, ‖ They have been to him altars to sin. **12** I write for him numerous things of My law, ‖ As a strange thing they have been reckoned. **13** The sacrifices of My offerings! They sacrifice flesh, and they eat, ‖ YHWH has not accepted them, ‖ Now He remembers their iniquity, ‖ And inspects their sin, ‖ They return [to] Egypt. **14** And Israel forgets his Maker, and builds temples, ‖ And Judah has multiplied cities of defense, ‖ And I have sent a fire into his cities, ‖ And it has consumed their palaces!"

9 "Do not rejoice, O Israel, do not be joyful like the peoples, ‖ For you have gone whoring from your God, ‖ You have loved a wage near all floors of grain. **2** Floor and winepress do not feed them, ‖ And new wine fails in her, **3** They do not abide in the land of YHWH, ‖ And Ephraim has turned back [to] Egypt, ‖ And they eat an unclean thing in Asshur. **4** They do not pour out wine to YHWH, ‖ Nor are they sweet to Him, ‖ Their sacrifices [are] as bread of mourners to them, ‖ All eating it are unclean: For their bread [is] for themselves, ‖ It does not come into the house of YHWH. **5** What do you do at the day appointed? And at the day of YHWH's festival? **6** For behold, they have gone because of destruction, ‖ Egypt gathers them, Moph buries them, ‖ The desirable things of their silver, ‖ Nettles possess them—a thorn [is] in their tents. **7** The days of inspection have come in, ‖ The days of repayment have come in, Israel knows! The prophet [is] a fool, ‖ Mad [is] the man of the spirit, ‖ Because of the abundance of your iniquity, ‖ And great [is] the hatred. **8** Ephraim is looking [away] from My God, ‖ The prophet! A snare of a fowler [is] over all his ways, ‖ Hatred [is] in the house of his God. **9** They have gone deep—have done corruptly, ‖ As [in] the days of Gibeah, ‖ He remembers their iniquity, He inspects their sins. **10** As grapes in a wilderness I found Israel, ‖ As the first-fruit in a fig tree, at its beginning, I have seen your fathers, ‖ They have gone in [to] Ba'al-Peor, ‖ And are separated to a shameful thing, ‖ And have become abominable like their love. **11** Ephraim [is] as a bird, their glory flies away, without birth, and without womb, and without conception. **12** For though they nourish their sons, I have made them childless—without man, ‖ Surely also, woe to them when I turn aside from them. **13** Ephraim! When I have looked to the rock, ‖ Is planted in comeliness, ‖ And Ephraim [is] to bring out his sons to a slayer. **14** Give to them, YHWH—what do You give? Give to them miscarrying womb, and dry breasts. **15** All their evil [is] in Gilgal, ‖ Surely there I have hated them, ‖ Because of the evil of their doings, ‖ Out of My house I drive them, ‖ I no longer love them, ‖ All their heads [are] apostates. **16** Ephraim has been struck, ‖ Their root has dried up, they do not yield fruit, ‖ Indeed, though they bring forth, ‖ I have put to death the desired of their womb. **17** My God rejects them, ‖ Because they have not listened to Him, ‖ And they are wanderers among nations!"

HOSEA

10 "Israel [is] an empty vine, ‖ He makes fruit like to himself, ‖ According to the abundance of his fruit, ‖ He has multiplied for the altars, ‖ According to the goodness of his land, ‖ They have made good standing-pillars. **2** Their heart has been divided, now they are guilty, ‖ He breaks down their altars, ‖ He destroys their standing-pillars. **3** For now they say: We have no king, ‖ Because we have not feared YHWH, ‖ And the king—what does he do for us? **4** They have spoken words, ‖ To swear falsehood in making a covenant, ‖ And flourished as a poisonous herb has judgment, on the furrows of a field. **5** For the inhabitants of Samaria fear the calves of Beth-Aven, ‖ Surely its people have mourned on account of it, ‖ And its priests leap about on account of it, ‖ Because of its glory, for it has removed from it, **6** Also, it is carried to Asshur, a present to a warlike king, ‖ Ephraim receives shame, ‖ And Israel is ashamed of its own counsel. **7** Samaria is cut off! Its king [is] as wrath on the face of the waters. **8** And high places of Aven have been destroyed, the sin of Israel. Thorn and bramble go up on their altars, ‖ And they have said to hills, Cover us, ‖ And to heights, Fall on us. **9** From the days of Gibeah you have sinned, O Israel, ‖ There they have stood, ‖ Battle does not overtake them in Gibeah, ‖ Because of sons of perverseness. **10** When I desire, then I bind them, ‖ And peoples have gathered against them, ‖ When they bind themselves to their two iniquities. **11** And Ephraim [is] a trained heifer—loving to thresh, ‖ And I have passed over on the goodness of its neck, ‖ I cause [one] to ride Ephraim, ‖ Judah plows, Jacob harrows for him. **12** Sow for yourselves in righteousness, ‖ Reap according to loving-kindness, ‖ Till for yourselves tillage of knowledge, ‖ To seek YHWH, ‖ Until He comes and shows righteousness to you. **13** You have plowed wickedness, ‖ Perversity you have reaped, ‖ You have eaten the fruit of lying, ‖ For you have trusted in your way, ‖ In the abundance of your might. **14** And a tumult rises among your people, ‖ And all your fortresses are spoiled, ‖ As the spoiling of Shalman of Beth-Arbel, ‖ In a day of battle, ‖ Mother against sons dashed in pieces. **15** Thus has Beth-El done to you, ‖ Because of the evil of your wickedness, ‖ In the dawn a king of Israel is utterly cut off!"

11 "Because Israel [is] a youth, and I love him, ‖ Out of Egypt I have called for My Son. **2** They have called to them correctly, ‖ They have gone from before them, ‖ They sacrifice to lords, ‖ And make incense to carved images. **3** And I have caused Ephraim to go on foot, ‖ Taking them by their arms, ‖ And they have not known that I strengthened them. **4** I draw them with cords of man, ‖ With thick cords of love, ‖ And I am to them as a raiser up of a yoke on their jaws, ‖ And I incline to him—I feed [him]. **5** He does not return to the land of Egypt, ‖ And Asshur—he [is] his king, ‖ For they have refused to return. **6** The sword has been grievous in his cities, ‖ And it has ended his bars, and consumed—from their own counsels. **7** And My people are hanging in suspense about My returning, ‖ And to the Most High they call, ‖ Together they do not exalt. **8** How do I give you up, O Ephraim? Do I deliver you up, O Israel? How do I make you as Admah? Do I set you as Zeboim? My heart is turned in Me, ‖ My sympathy has been kindled together. **9** I do not do the fierceness of My anger, ‖ I do not turn back to destroy Ephraim, ‖ For I [am] God, and not a man—The Holy One in your midst, and I do not enter in enmity. **10** They go after YHWH—He roars as a lion, ‖ When He roars, then the sons from the west tremble. **11** They tremble as a sparrow out of Egypt, ‖ And as a dove out of the land of Asshur, ‖ And I have caused them to dwell in their own houses," ‖ A declaration of YHWH. **12** "Ephraim has surrounded Me with feigning, ‖ And the house of Israel with deceit. And Judah is again ruling with God, ‖ And [is] faithful with the Holy Ones!"

12 "Ephraim is enjoying wind, ‖ And is pursuing an east wind, ‖ All the day he multiplies lying and spoiling, ‖ And they make a covenant with Asshur, ‖ And oil is carried to Egypt. **2** And YHWH has a controversy with Judah, ‖ To lay a charge on Jacob according to his ways, ‖ He returns to him according to his doings. **3** In the womb he took his brother by the heel, ‖ And by his strength he was a prince with God, **4** Indeed, he is a prince to the Messenger, ‖ And he overcomes [by] weeping, ‖ And he makes supplication to Him, ‖ At Bethel He finds him, ‖ And there He speaks with us, **5** Even YHWH, God of the Hosts, YHWH [is] His memorial. **6** And you, through your God, turn, ‖ Keep kindness and judgment, ‖ And wait on your God continually. **7** Canaan! In his hand [are] balances of deceit! He has loved to oppress. **8** And Ephraim says, ‖ Surely I have become rich, I have found wealth for myself, ‖ All my labors—they do not find against me iniquity that [is] sin. **9** And I—your God YHWH from the land of Egypt, ‖ Again I turn you back into tents, ‖ As in the days of the appointed time. **10** And I have spoken to the prophets, ‖ And I have multiplied vision, ‖ And by the hand of the prophets I use allegories. **11** Surely Gilead [is] iniquity, ‖ They have been only vanity, ‖ In Gilead they have sacrificed bullocks, ‖ Also their altars [are] as heaps, on the furrows of a field. **12** And Jacob flees to the country of Aram, ‖ And Israel serves for a wife, ‖ Indeed, he has kept watch for a wife. **13** And by a prophet has YHWH brought up Israel out of Egypt, ‖ And by a prophet it has been watched. **14** Ephraim has most bitterly provoked, ‖ And he leaves his blood on himself, ‖ And his Lord turns his reproach back to him!"

13 "When Ephraim speaks tremblingly, ‖ He has been lifted up in Israel, ‖ When he becomes guilty in Baʻal he dies. **2** And now they sin, ‖ And make for themselves a molten image of their silver, ‖ By their own understanding—idols, ‖ A work of artisans—all of it, ‖ Of them they say, who [are] sacrificers among men, The calves let them kiss. **3** Therefore they are as a cloud of the morning, ‖ And as dew, rising early, going away, ‖ As chaff tossed about out of a floor, ‖ And as smoke out of a window. **4** And I [am] your God YHWH from the land of Egypt, ‖ And you do not know a God besides Me, ‖ And a Savior—there is none except Me. **5** I have known you in a wilderness, ‖ In a land of droughts. **6** They are satiated according to their feedings, ‖ They have been satiated, ‖ And their heart is lifted up, ‖ Therefore they have forgotten Me, **7** And I am to them as a lion, ‖ I look out as a leopard by the way. **8** I meet them as a bereaved bear, ‖ And I tear the enclosure of their heart, ‖ And I consume them there as a lioness, ‖ A beast of the field tears them. **9** You have destroyed yourself, O Israel, ‖ But in Me [is] your help; **10** Where [is] your king now—And he saves you in all your cities? And your judges of whom you said, ‖ Give a king and heads to me? **11** I give to you a king in My anger, ‖ And I take away in My wrath. **12** Bound up [is] the iniquity of Ephraim, ‖ Hidden [is] his sin, **13** Pangs of a travailing woman come to him, ‖ He [is] not a wise son, ‖ For he does not remain [at] the time for the breaking forth of sons. **14** Will I ransom them from the hand of Sheol? Will I redeem them from death? Where [is] your plague, O death? Where your destruction, O Sheol? Comfort is hid from My eyes. **15** Though he produces fruit among brothers, ‖ An east wind comes in, a wind of YHWH, ‖ From a wilderness it is coming up, ‖ And it dries up his fountain, ‖ And his spring becomes dry, ‖ It—it spoils a treasure—every desirable vessel. **16** Samaria becomes desolate, ‖ Because she has been rebellious against her God, ‖ They fall by sword, ‖ Their sucklings are dashed in pieces, ‖ And its pregnant ones are ripped up!"

14 "Turn back, O Israel, to your God YHWH, ‖ For you have stumbled by your iniquity. **2** Take words with you, and turn to YHWH, ‖ Say to Him, Take away all iniquity, and give good, ‖ And we render the fruit of our lips. **3** Asshur does not save us, we do not ride on a horse, ‖ Nor do we say anymore, Our god, to the work of our hands, ‖ For in You the fatherless find mercy. **4** I heal their backsliding, I love them freely, ‖ For My anger has turned back from him. **5** I am as dew to Israel, he flourishes as a lily, ‖ And he strikes forth his roots as Lebanon. **6** His shoots go on, ‖ And his splendor is as an olive, ‖ And he has fragrance as Lebanon. **7** The dwellers return under his shadow, ‖ They revive [as] grain, and flourish as a vine, ‖ His memorial [is] as wine of Lebanon. **8** O Ephraim, what have I anymore to do with idols? I have answered, and I look after him: I [am] as a green fir-tree, ‖ Your fruit is found from Me. **9** Who [is] wise, and understands these? Prudent, and knows them? For upright are the ways of YHWH, ‖ And the righteous go on in them, ‖ And the transgressors stumble therein!"

JOEL

1 A word of YHWH that has been to Joel, son of Pethuel: **2** Hear this, you aged ones, ‖ And give ear, all you inhabitants of the land, ‖ Has this been in your days? Or in the days of your fathers? **3** Concerning it talk to your sons, ‖ And your sons to their sons, ‖ And their sons to another generation. **4** What is left of the palmer-worm, the locust has eaten, ‖ And what is left of the locust, ‖ The cankerworm has eaten, ‖ And what is left of the cankerworm, ‖ The caterpillar has eaten. **5** Awake, you drunkards, and weep, ‖ And howl all drinking wine, because of the juice, ‖ For it has been cut off from your mouth. **6** For a nation has come up on My land, ‖ Strong, and there is no number, ‖ Its teeth [are] the teeth of a lion, ‖ And it has the jaw-teeth of a lioness. **7** It has made My vine become a desolation, ‖ And My fig tree become a splinter, ‖ It has made it thoroughly bare, and has cast down, ‖ Its branches have been made white. **8** Wail, as a virgin girds with sackcloth, ‖ For the husband of her youth. **9** Present and drink-offering have been cut off from the house of YHWH, ‖ The priests have mourned, servants of YHWH. **10** The field is spoiled, ‖ The ground has mourned, ‖ For the grain is spoiled, ‖ New wine has been dried up, oil languishes. **11** Be ashamed, you farmers, ‖ Howl, vinedressers, for wheat and for barley, ‖ For the harvest of the field has perished. **12** The vine has been dried up, ‖ And the fig tree languishes, ‖ Pomegranate, also palm, and apple-tree, ‖ All trees of the field have withered, ‖ For joy has been dried up from the sons of men. **13** Gird, and lament, you priests, ‖ Howl, you servants of the altar, ‖ Come in, lodge in sackcloth, servants of my God, ‖ For present and drink-offering have been withheld from the house of your God. **14** Sanctify a fast, proclaim a restraint, ‖ Gather [the] elderly [and] all those inhabiting the land, ‖ [Into the] house of your God YHWH, **15** And cry to YHWH, "Aah! For the day! For [the] Day of YHWH [is] near, ‖ And it comes as destruction from [the] Almighty. **16** Is food not cut off before our eyes? Joy and rejoicing from the house of our God? **17** Scattered things have rotted under their clods, ‖ Storehouses have been desolated, ‖ Granaries have been broken down, ‖ For the grain has withered. **18** How livestock have sighed! Perplexed have been droves of oxen, ‖ For there is no pasture for them, ‖ Also droves of sheep have been desolated. **19** To You, O YHWH, I call, ‖ For fire has consumed lovely places of a wilderness, ‖ And a flame has set on fire all trees of the field. **20** Also the livestock of the field long for You, ‖ For dried up have been streams of water, ‖ And fire has consumed lovely places of a wilderness!"

2 Blow a horn in Zion, ‖ And shout in My holy hill, ‖ All inhabitants of the earth tremble, ‖ For the Day of YHWH is coming, for [it is] near! **2** A day of darkness and thick darkness, ‖ A day of cloud and thick darkness, ‖ As darkness spread on the mountains, ‖ A people numerous and mighty, ‖ Like there has not been from of old, ‖ And after it there is not again—Until the years of generation and generation. **3** Before it fire has consumed, ‖ And after it a flame burns, ‖ As the Garden of Eden [is] the land before it, ‖ And after it a wilderness—a desolation! And also there has not been to it an escape, **4** As the appearance of horses [is] its appearance, ‖ And as horsemen, so they run. **5** As the noise of chariots, they skip on the tops of the mountains, ‖ As the noise of a flame of fire devouring stubble, ‖ As a mighty people set in array for battle. **6** Pained are peoples from its face, ‖ All faces have gathered paleness. **7** They run as mighty ones, ‖ As men of war they go up a wall, ‖ And they each go in his own ways, ‖ And they do not change their paths. **8** And each does not press his brother, ‖ They each go on in his way, ‖ If they fall by the missile, they are not cut off. **9** In the city they run to and fro, ‖ On the wall they run, ‖ Into houses they go up by the windows, ‖ They go in as a thief. **10** At their face the earth has trembled, ‖ The heavens have shaken, ‖ Sun and moon have been black, ‖ And stars have gathered up their shining. **11** And YHWH has given forth His voice before His force, ‖ For His camp [is] very great, ‖ For mighty [is] the doer of His word, ‖ For great [is] the Day of YHWH—very fearful, ‖ And who bears it? **12** "And also now," a declaration of YHWH, ‖ "Turn back to Me with all your heart, ‖ And with fasting, and with weeping, ‖ And with lamentation." **13** And tear your heart, and not your garments, ‖ And turn back to your God YHWH, ‖ For He [is] gracious and merciful, ‖ Slow to anger, and abundant in kindness, ‖ And relenting from evil. **14** Who knows—He turns back, ‖ Indeed—He has relented, ‖ And He has left behind Him a blessing, ‖ A present and drink-offering of your God YHWH? **15** Blow a horn in Zion, ‖ Sanctify a fast—proclaim a restraint. **16** Gather the people, sanctify an assembly, ‖ Assemble the aged, ‖ Gather infants and sucklings of the breasts, ‖ Let a bridegroom go out from his inner chamber, ‖ And a bride out of her closet. **17** Let the priests weep between the porch and the altar, servants of YHWH, ‖ And let them say: "Have pity, O YHWH, on Your people, ‖ And do not give Your inheritance to reproach, ‖ To the ruling over them of nations, ‖ Why do they say among peoples, Where [is] their God?" **18** And let YHWH be zealous for His land, ‖ And have pity on His people. **19** Let YHWH answer and say to His people, ‖ "Behold, I am sending to you the grain, ‖ And the new wine, and the oil, ‖ And you have been satisfied with it, ‖ And I make you no longer a reproach among nations, **20** And the northern I put far off from you, ‖ And have driven him to a land dry and desolate, ‖ With his face toward the Eastern Sea, ‖ And his rear to the Western Sea, ‖ And his stink has come up, ‖ And his stench comes up, ‖ For he has exerted himself to work." **21** Do not fear, O land! Be glad and rejoice, ‖ For YHWH has exerted Himself to work. **22** Do not fear, O livestock of the field! For pastures of a wilderness have sprung up, ‖ For the tree has borne its fruit, ‖ Fig tree and vine have given their strength! **23** And you sons of Zion, ‖ Be glad and rejoice in your God YHWH, ‖ For He has given to you the Teacher for righteousness, ‖ And causes a shower to come down to you, ‖ Early rain and spring rain [as] in the beginning. **24** And the floors have been full [with] pure grain, ‖ And the presses have overflown [with] new wine and oil. **25** "And I have repaid to you the years that the locust consumed, ‖ The cankerworm, and the caterpillar, and the palmer-worm, ‖ My great force that I sent against you. **26** And you have eaten, eating and being satisfied, ‖ And have praised the Name of your God YHWH, ‖ Who has dealt with you wonderfully, ‖ And My people are not ashamed for all time. **27** And you have known that I [am] in the midst of Israel, ‖ And I [am] your God YHWH, and there is none else, ‖ And My people are not ashamed for all time. **28** And it has come to pass afterward, ‖ I pour out My Spirit on all flesh, ‖ And your sons and your daughters have prophesied, ‖ Your old men dream dreams, ‖ Your young men see visions. **29** And also on the menservants and on the maidservants, ‖ In those days I pour out My Spirit. **30** And I have given wonders in the heavens and in the earth: Blood, and fire, and columns of smoke. **31** The sun is turned to darkness, and the moon to blood, ‖ Before the coming of the Day of YHWH, ‖ The great and the fearful. **32** And it has come to pass, ‖ Everyone who calls on the Name of YHWH is delivered, ‖ For in Mount Zion and in Jerusalem there is an escape, ‖ As YHWH has said, ‖ And among the remnants whom YHWH is calling!"

3 "For behold, in those days, and in that time, ‖ When I turn back [to] the captivity of Judah and Jerusalem, **2** Then I have gathered all the nations, ‖ And caused them to go down to the Valley of Jehoshaphat, ‖ And I have been in judgment with them there, ‖ Concerning My people and My inheritance—Israel, ‖ Whom they scattered among nations, ‖ And My land they have apportioned. **3** And for My people they cast a lot, ‖ And they give the young man for a harlot, ‖ And have sold the young woman for wine, ‖ That they may drink. **4** And also, what [are] you to Me, O Tyre and Sidon, ‖ And all circuits of Philistia? Are you rendering repayment to Me? And if you are giving repayment to Me, ‖ Swiftly, quickly, I return your repayment on your head. **5** In that My silver and My gold you took, ‖ And My desirable things that are good, ‖ You have brought into your temples. **6** And sons of Judah, and sons of Jerusalem, ‖ You have sold to the sons of Javan, ‖ To put them far off from their border. **7** Behold, I am stirring them up out of the place ‖ To where you have sold them, ‖ And I have turned back your repayment on your head, **8** And have sold your sons and your daughters ‖ Into the hand of the sons of Judah, ‖ And they have sold them to Sabeans, ‖ To a nation far off, for YHWH has spoken."

9 Proclaim this among nations, ‖ Sanctify a war, stir up the mighty ones, ‖ Come near, come up, let all the men of war. **10** Beat your plowshares to swords, ‖ And your pruning-hooks to javelins, ‖ Let the weak say, "I [am] mighty." **11** Hurry, and come in, all you nations around, ‖ And be gathered together, ‖ There cause to come down, O YHWH, ‖ Your mighty ones. **12** "Let the nations wake and come up to the Valley of Jehoshaphat, ‖ For there I sit to judge all the nations around. **13** Send forth a sickle, ‖ For harvest has ripened, ‖ Come in, come down, for the press has been filled, ‖ Winepresses have overflowed, ‖ For great [is] their wickedness." **14** Multitudes, multitudes [are] in the Valley of Decision, ‖ For near [is] the Day of YHWH in the Valley of Decision. **15** Sun and moon have been black, ‖ And stars have gathered up their shining. **16** And YHWH roars from Zion, ‖ And gives forth His voice from Jerusalem, ‖ And the heavens and earth have shaken, ‖ And YHWH [is] a refuge to His people, ‖ And a stronghold to sons of Israel. **17** "And you have known that I [am] your God YHWH, ‖ Dwelling in Zion, My holy mountain, ‖ And Jerusalem has been holy, ‖ And strangers do not pass over into it again." **18** And it has come to pass in that day, ‖ The mountains drop down juice, ‖ And the hills flow [with] milk, ‖ And all streams of Judah go [with] water, ‖ And a fountain from the house of YHWH goes forth, ‖ And has watered the Valley of Shittim. **19** "Egypt becomes a desolation, ‖ And Edom becomes a desolation, a wilderness, ‖ For violence [to] sons of Judah, ‖ Whose innocent blood they shed in their land. **20** And Judah dwells for all time, ‖ And Jerusalem to generation and generation. **21** And I have declared their blood innocent, ‖ [That] I did not declare innocent, ‖ And YHWH is dwelling in Zion!"

AMOS

1 Words of Amos—who has been among herdsmen of Tekoa—that he has seen concerning Israel, in the days of Uzziah king of Judah, and in the days of Jeroboam son of Joash king of Israel, two years before the shaking; **2** and he says, "YHWH roars from Zion, ‖ And gives forth His voice from Jerusalem, ‖ And pastures of the shepherds have mourned, ‖ And the top of Carmel has withered!" **3** And thus said YHWH: "For three transgressions of Damascus, ‖ And for four, I do not reverse it, ‖ Because of their threshing Gilead with sharp-pointed irons, **4** And I have sent a fire against the house of Hazael, ‖ And it has consumed the palaces of Ben-Hadad. **5** And I have broken the bar of Damascus, ‖ And cut off the inhabitant from Bikat-Aven, ‖ And a holder of a scepter from Beth-Eden, ‖ And the people of Aram have been removed to Kir," said YHWH. **6** Thus said YHWH: "For three transgressions of Gaza, ‖ And for four, I do not reverse it, ‖ Because of their removing a complete captivity, ‖ To deliver up to Edom, **7** And I have sent a fire against the wall of Gaza, ‖ And it has consumed her palaces; **8** And I have cut off the inhabitant from Ashdod, ‖ And a holder of a scepter from Ashkelon, ‖ And have turned back My hand against Ekron, ‖ And the remnant of the Philistines have perished," said Lord YHWH. **9** Thus said YHWH: "For three transgressions of Tyre, ‖ And for four, I do not reverse it, ‖ Because of their delivering up a complete captivity to Edom, ‖ And they did not remember the brotherly covenant, **10** And I have sent a fire against the wall of Tyre, ‖ And it has consumed her palaces." **11** Thus said YHWH: "For three transgressions of Edom, ‖ And for four, I do not reverse it, ‖ Because of his pursuing his brother with a sword, ‖ And he has destroyed his mercies, ‖ And his anger tears continuously, ‖ And his wrath—he has kept it forever, **12** And I have sent a fire against Teman, ‖ And it has consumed palaces of Bozrah." **13** Thus said YHWH: "For three transgressions of the sons of Ammon, ‖ And for four, I do not reverse it, ‖ Because of their ripping up the pregnant ones of Gilead, ‖ To enlarge their border, **14** And I have kindled a fire against the wall of Rabbah, ‖ And it has consumed her palaces, ‖ With a shout in a day of battle, ‖ With a whirlwind in a day of windstorm, **15** And their king has gone in a removal, ‖ He and his heads together," said YHWH!

2 Thus said YHWH: "For three transgressions of Moab, ‖ And for four, I do not reverse it, ‖ Because of his burning the bones of the king of Edom to lime, **2** And I have sent a fire against Moab, ‖ And it has consumed the palaces of Kerioth, ‖ And Moab is dying with noise, ‖ With shouting, with voice of a horn. **3** And I have cut off judge from her midst, ‖ And I slay all its heads with him," said YHWH. **4** Thus said YHWH: "For three transgressions of Judah, ‖ And for four, I do not reverse it, ‖ Because of their loathing the Law of YHWH, ‖ And His statutes they have not kept, ‖ And their lies cause them to err, ‖ After which their fathers walked, **5** And I have sent a fire against Judah, ‖ And it has consumed palaces of Jerusalem." **6** Thus said YHWH: "For three transgressions of Israel, ‖ And for four, I do not reverse it, ‖ Because of their selling the righteous for silver, ‖ And the needy for a pair of sandals. **7** Who are panting for the dust of the earth on the head of the poor, ‖ And the way of the humble they turn aside, ‖ And a man and his father go to the girl, ‖ So as to defile My holy Name. **8** And they stretch themselves on pledged garments near every altar, ‖ And the wine of fined ones they drink [in] the house of their gods. **9** And I have destroyed the Amorite from before them, ‖ Whose height [is] as the height of cedars, ‖ And he [is] strong as the oaks, ‖ And I destroy his fruit from above, ‖ And his roots from beneath. **10** And I have brought you up from the land of Egypt, ‖ And cause you to go in a wilderness forty years, ‖ To possess the land of the Amorite. **11** And I raise of your sons for prophets, ‖ And of your choice ones for Nazarites, ‖ Is this not true, O sons of Israel?" A declaration of YHWH. **12** "And you cause the Nazarites to drink wine, ‖ And on the prophets you have laid a charge, ‖ Saying, Do not prophesy! **13** Behold, I am pressing you under, ‖ As the full cart presses a sheaf for itself. **14** And refuge has perished from the swift,

‖ And the strong does not strengthens his power, ‖ And the mighty does not deliver his soul. **15** And the handler of the bow does not stand, ‖ And the swift does not deliver [himself] with his feet, ‖ And the rider of the horse does not deliver his soul. **16** And the courageous of heart among the mighty, ‖ Flees naked in that day," ‖ A declaration of YHWH!

3 Hear this word that YHWH has spoken concerning you, O sons of Israel, concerning all the family that I brought up from the land of Egypt, saying, **2** "Only you have I known of all families of the earth, ‖ Therefore I charge on you all your iniquities." **3** Do two walk together if they have not met? **4** Does a lion roar in a forest and he has no prey? Does a young lion give out his voice from his habitation, ‖ If he has not caught? **5** Does a bird fall into a snare of the earth, ‖ And there is no trap for it? Does a snare go up from the ground, ‖ And it does not capture prey? **6** Is a horn blown in a city, ‖ And do people not tremble? Is there affliction in a city, ‖ And YHWH has not done [it]? **7** For Lord YHWH does nothing, ‖ Except He has revealed His counsel to His servants the prophets. **8** A lion has roared—who does not fear? Lord YHWH has spoken—who does not prophesy? **9** "Sound to palaces in Ashdod, ‖ And to palaces in the land of Egypt, and say: Be gathered on mountains of Samaria, ‖ And see many troubles within her, ‖ And oppressed ones in her midst. **10** And they have not known to act straightforwardly," ‖ A declaration of YHWH, ‖ "Who are treasuring up violence and spoil in their palaces." **11** Therefore, thus said Lord YHWH: "An adversary—and surrounding the land, ‖ And he has brought down your strength from you, ‖ And your palaces have been spoiled." **12** Thus said YHWH: "As the shepherd delivers from the lion's mouth ‖ Two legs, or a piece of an ear, ‖ So the sons of Israel are delivered, ‖ Who are sitting in Samaria on the corner of a bed, ‖ And in Damascus [on that of] a couch. **13** Hear and testify to the house of Jacob," ‖ A declaration of Lord YHWH, God of Hosts. **14** "For in the day of My charging the transgressions of Israel on him, I have laid a charge on the altars of Beth-El, ‖ And the horns of the altar have been cut off, ‖ And they have fallen to the earth. **15** And I have struck the winter-house with the summer-house, ‖ And houses of ivory have perished, ‖ And many houses have been consumed," ‖ A declaration of YHWH!

4 Hear this word, you cows of Bashan, ‖ Who [are] on the mountain of Samaria, ‖ Who are oppressing the poor, ‖ Who are bruising the needy, ‖ Who are saying to their lords: "Bring in, and we drink." **2** Lord YHWH has sworn by His holiness, ‖ "Behold, days are coming on you, ‖ And He has taken you away with hooks, ‖ And your posterity with fish-hooks. **3** And [by] breaches you go forth, ‖ A woman before her, ‖ And you have cast down the high place," ‖ A declaration of YHWH. **4** "Enter Beth-El, and transgress, ‖ At Gilgal multiply transgression, ‖ And bring in your sacrifices every morning, ‖ Your tithes every third year. **5** And burn a thank-offering with leaven as incense, ‖ And proclaim willing gifts, sound! For so you have loved, O sons of Israel," ‖ A declaration of Lord YHWH. **6** "And I also—I have given to you cleanness of teeth in all your cities, ‖ And lack of bread in all your places, ‖ And you have not turned back to Me," ‖ A declaration of YHWH. **7** "And I also—I have withheld from you the rain, ‖ While yet three months to harvest, ‖ And I have sent rain on one city, ‖ And on another city I do not send rain, ‖ One portion is rained on, ‖ And the portion on which it does not rain withers. **8** And two or three cities have wandered, ‖ To the same city to drink water, ‖ And they are not satisfied, ‖ And you have not turned back to Me," ‖ A declaration of YHWH. **9** "I have struck you with blasting and with mildew, ‖ The abundance of your gardens and of your vineyards, ‖ And of your figs, and of your olives, ‖ The palmer-worm eats, ‖ And you have not turned back to Me," ‖ A declaration of YHWH. **10** "I have sent among you pestilence by the way of Egypt, ‖ I have slain your choice ones by sword, ‖ With your captive horses, ‖ And I cause the stink of your camps to come up—Even into your nostrils, ‖ And you have not turned back to Me," ‖ A declaration of YHWH. **11** "I have overturned among you, ‖ Like the overturn by God of Sodom and Gomorrah, ‖ And you are as a brand delivered from a burning, ‖ And you have not turned back to Me," ‖ A declaration of YHWH. **12** "Therefore, thus I do to you, O Israel, at last, ‖ Because this I do to you, ‖

AMOS

Prepare to meet your God, O Israel." **13** For behold, the Former of mountains, and Creator of wind, ‖ And the Declarer to man what [is] His thought, ‖ He is making dawn obscurity, ‖ And is treading on high places of earth, ‖ YHWH, God of Hosts, [is] His Name!

5 Hear this word that I am bearing to you, ‖ A lamentation, O house of Israel: **2** "Fallen, not to rise again, has the virgin of Israel, ‖ Left on her land—she has none [to] raise [her] up." **3** For thus said Lord YHWH: "The city that is going out one thousand, ‖ Leaves one hundred, ‖ And that which is going out one hundred, ‖ Leaves ten to the house of Israel." **4** For thus said YHWH to the house of Israel: "Seek Me, and live, **5** And do not seek Beth-El, and do not enter Gilgal, ‖ And do not pass through Beer-Sheba, ‖ For Gilgal utterly removes, ‖ And Beth-El becomes vanity. **6** Seek YHWH, and live, ‖ Lest He prosper as fire [against] the house of Joseph, ‖ And it has consumed, ‖ And there is no quencher for Beth-El— **7** You who are turning judgment to wormwood, ‖ And have put down righteousness to the earth!" **8** The Maker of the Pleiades and Orion, ‖ And He who is turning death-shade to the morning—And He has made day [as] dark [as] night—Who is calling to the waters of the sea, ‖ And pours them on the face of the earth, ‖ YHWH [is] His Name; **9** Who is brightening up the spoiled against the strong, ‖ And the spoiled comes against a fortress. **10** They have hated a reprover in the gate, ‖ And they detest a plain speaker. **11** Therefore, because of your trampling on the poor, ‖ And the tribute of grain you take from him, ‖ Houses of hewn work you have built, ‖ And you do not dwell in them, ‖ Desirable vineyards you have planted, ‖ And you do not drink their wine. **12** For I have known—many [are] your transgressions, ‖ And mighty your sins, ‖ Adversaries of the righteous, taking ransoms, ‖ And you turned aside the needy in the gate. **13** Therefore the wise is silent at that time, ‖ For it [is] an evil time. **14** Seek good, and not evil, that you may live, and it is so; YHWH, God of Hosts, [is] with you, as you said. **15** Hate evil, and love good, ‖ And set up judgment in the gate, ‖ It may be YHWH, God of Hosts, pities the remnant of Joseph. **16** Therefore, thus said YHWH, God of Hosts, the Lord: "Lamentation is in all broad places, ‖ And in all out-places they say, Oh! Oh! And called the farmer to mourning, ‖ And the skillful of wailing to lamentation. **17** And in all vineyards [is] lamentation, ‖ For I pass into your midst," said YHWH. **18** Behold, you who are desiring the Day of YHWH, ‖ Why [is] this to you—the Day of YHWH? It is darkness, and not light, **19** As [when] one flees from the face of the lion, ‖ And the bear has met him, ‖ And he has come into the house, ‖ And has leaned his hand on the wall, ‖ And the serpent has bitten him. **20** Is not the Day of YHWH darkness and not light, ‖ Even thick darkness that has no brightness? **21** "I have hated—I have loathed your festivals, ‖ And I am not refreshed by your restraints. **22** For though you cause burnt-offerings and your presents to ascend to Me, ‖ I am not pleased, ‖ And I do not behold the peace-offering of your fatlings. **23** Turn the noise of your songs aside from Me, ‖ Indeed, I do not hear the praise of your stringed instruments. **24** And judgment rolls on as waters, ‖ And righteousness as a perennial stream. **25** Did you bring sacrifices and offerings near to Me, ‖ In a wilderness forty years, O house of Israel? **26** And you bore Succoth your king, and Chiun your images, ‖ The star of your god, that you made for yourselves. **27** And I removed you beyond Damascus," said YHWH—God of Hosts [is] His Name.

6 Woe [to] those secure in Zion, ‖ And those confident on the mountain of Samaria, ‖ The marked of the chief of the nations, ‖ And the house of Israel has come to them. **2** Pass over [to] Calneh and see, ‖ And go there [to] Hamath the great, ‖ And go down [to] Gath of the Philistines, ‖ Are [they] better than these kingdoms? [Is] their border greater than your border? **3** Who are putting away the day of evil, ‖ And you bring the seat of violence near, **4** Who are lying down on beds of ivory, ‖ And are spread out on their couches, ‖ And are eating lambs from the flock, ‖ And calves from the midst of the stall, **5** Who are taking part according to the stringed instrument, ‖ Like David they invented for themselves instruments of music; **6** Who are drinking with bowls of wine, ‖ And anoint themselves [with] chief perfumes, ‖ And have not been pained for the breach of Joseph. **7** Therefore they now go at the head of the captives, ‖ And the mourning-feast of stretched-out ones is turned aside. **8** Lord YHWH has sworn by Himself, ‖ A declaration of YHWH, God of Hosts: "I am abominating the excellence of Jacob, ‖ And his high places I have hated, ‖ And I have delivered up the city and its fullness." **9** And if there are left ten persons in one house, ‖ It has come to pass—that they have died. **10** And his loved one has lifted him up, even his burner, ‖ To bring forth the bones from the house, ‖ And he said to him who [is] in the sides of the house, ‖ "Is there [any] yet with you?" And he said, "None," ‖ Then he said, "Hush! We must not make mention of the Name of YHWH." **11** For behold, YHWH is commanding, ‖ And He has struck the great house [with] breaches, ‖ And the little house [with] clefts. **12** Do horses run on a rock? Does one plow [it] with oxen? For you have turned judgment to gall, ‖ And the fruit of righteousness to wormwood. **13** O you who are rejoicing at nothing, ‖ Who are saying, "Have we not taken to ourselves horns by our strength?" **14** "Surely, behold, I am raising a nation against you, O house of Israel," ‖ A declaration of YHWH, God of Hosts, ‖ "And they have oppressed you from the coming in to Hamath, ‖ To the stream of the desert."

7 Thus Lord YHWH has showed me, and behold, He is forming locusts at the beginning of the ascending of the latter growth, and behold, the latter growth [is] after the mowings of the king [[*or* King Gog]]; **2** and it has come to pass, when it has finished to consume the herb of the land, that I say, "Lord YHWH, please forgive, ‖ How does Jacob arise—for he [is] small?" **3** YHWH has relented of this, "It will not be," said YHWH. **4** Thus has Lord YHWH showed me, and behold, Lord YHWH is calling to contend by the fire, and it consumes the great deep, indeed, it has consumed the portion, and I say, **5** "Lord YHWH, please cease, ‖ How does Jacob arise—for he [is] small?" **6** YHWH has relented of this, "It also will not be," said Lord YHWH. **7** Thus has He showed me, and behold, the Lord is standing by a wall [made according to] a plumb-line, and in His hand a plumb-line; **8** and YHWH says to me, "What are you seeing, Amos?" And I say, "A plumb-line"; and the Lord says: "Behold, I am setting a plumb-line in the midst of My people Israel, I no longer pass over to it. **9** And high places of Isaac have been desolated, ‖ And sanctuaries of Israel are dried up, ‖ And I have risen against the house of Jeroboam with a sword." **10** And Amaziah priest of Beth-El sends to Jeroboam king of Israel, saying, "Amos has conspired against you in the midst of the house of Israel; the land is not able to bear all his words, **11** for thus said Amos: Jeroboam dies by sword, ‖ And Israel certainly removes from off its land." **12** And Amaziah says to Amos, "Seer, go, flee to the land of Judah for yourself, and eat bread there, and there you prophesy; **13** and no longer prophesy [at] Beth-El anymore, for it [is] the king's sanctuary, and it [is] the royal house." **14** And Amos answers and says to Amaziah, "I [am] no prophet, nor [am] I a prophet's son, but I [am] a herdsman, and a cultivator of sycamores, **15** and YHWH takes me from after the flock, and YHWH says to me, Go, prophesy to My people Israel. **16** And now, hear a word of YHWH: You are saying, Do not prophesy against Israel, nor drop [anything] against the house of Isaac, **17** therefore, thus said YHWH: Your wife goes whoring in the city, ‖ And your sons and your daughters fall by sword, ‖ And your land is apportioned by line, ‖ And you die on an unclean land, ‖ And Israel certainly removes from off its land."

8 Thus has Lord YHWH showed me, and behold, a basket of summer-fruit. **2** And He says, "What are you seeing, Amos?" And I say, "A basket of summer-fruit." And YHWH says to me: "The end has come to My people Israel, ‖ I no longer pass over to it anymore. **3** And female singers have howled of a palace in that day," ‖ A declaration of Lord YHWH, ‖ "Many [are] the carcasses, into any place throw—hush!" **4** Hear this, you who are swallowing up the needy, ‖ To cause the poor of the land to cease, **5** Saying, "When does the new moon pass, ‖ And we sell ground grain? And the Sabbath, and we open out pure grain? To make little the ephah, ‖ And to make great the shekel, ‖ And to use balances of deceit perversely. **6** To purchase the poor with money, ‖ And the needy for a pair of sandals, ‖ Indeed, the refuse of the pure grain we sell." **7** YHWH has sworn by the excellence of Jacob: "I do not forget any of their works forever. **8** Does the land not tremble for this, ‖ And every dweller in it has mourned? And all of

AMOS

it has come up as a flood. And it has been cast out, and has sunk, ‖ Like the flood of Egypt. **9** And it has come to pass in that day," ‖ A declaration of Lord YHWH, ‖ "I have caused the sun to go in at noon, ‖ And caused darkness on the land in a day of light, **10** And have turned your festivals to mourning, ‖ And all your songs to lamentation, ‖ And caused sackcloth to come up on all loins, ‖ And on every head—baldness, ‖ And made it as a mourning of an only one, ‖ And its latter end as a day of bitterness. **11** Behold, days are coming," ‖ A declaration of Lord YHWH, ‖ "And I have sent a famine into the land, ‖ Not a famine of bread, nor a thirst of water, ‖ But of hearing the words of YHWH. **12** And they have wandered from sea to sea, ‖ And from north even to east, ‖ They go to and fro to seek the word of YHWH, ‖ And they do not find [it]. **13** In that day the beautiful virgins, ‖ And the young men, faint with thirst. **14** Those swearing by the guilt of Samaria, ‖ And who have said, Your god lives, O Dan, ‖ And, The way of Beer-Sheba lives, ‖ Indeed, they have fallen and do not rise again!"

9 I have seen the Lord standing by the altar, and He says, ‖ "Strike the knob, and the thresholds shake, ‖ And cut them off by the head—all of them, ‖ And I slay their posterity with a sword, ‖ None that flee of them flee away, ‖ Nor a fugitive of them escape. **2** If they dig through into Sheol, ‖ From there My hand takes them, ‖ And if they go up [to] the heavens, ‖ From there I cause them to come down. **3** And if they are hid in the top of Carmel, ‖ From there I search out, and have taken them, ‖ And if they are hid from My eyes in the bottom of the sea, ‖ From there I command the serpent, ‖ And it has bitten them. **4** And if they go into captivity before their enemies, ‖ From there I command the sword, ‖ And it has slain them, ‖ And I have set My eye on them for evil, ‖ And not for good." **5** And [it is] the Lord, YHWH of Hosts, ‖ Who is striking against the land, and it melts, ‖ And mourned have all the inhabitants in it, ‖ And all of it has come up as a flood, ‖ And it has sunk—like the flood of Egypt. **6** Who is building His upper chambers in the heavens; As for His troop, ‖ On earth He has founded it, ‖ Who is calling for the waters of the sea, ‖ And pours them out on the face of the land, ‖ YHWH [is] His Name. **7** "Are you not as sons of Cushim to Me, O sons of Israel?" A declaration of YHWH. "Did I not bring Israel up out of the land of Egypt? And the Philistines from Caphtor, and Aram from Kir? **8** Behold, [the] eyes of Lord YHWH [are] on the sinful kingdom, ‖ And I have destroyed it from off the face of the ground, ‖ Only, I do not utterly destroy the house of Jacob," ‖ A declaration of YHWH. **9** "For behold, I am commanding, ‖ And I have shaken among all the nations the house of Israel, ‖ As [one] shakes with a sieve, ‖ And there does not fall a grain [to] the earth. **10** By sword all sinners of My people die, ‖ Who are saying, ‖ Evil does not overtake, or go before, ‖ For our sakes. **11** In that day I raise the dwelling place of David that is fallen, ‖ And I have repaired their breaches, ‖ And I raise up its ruins, ‖ And I have built it up as in days of old, **12** So that they possess the remnant of Edom, ‖ And all the nations on whom My Name is called," ‖ A declaration of YHWH—the doer of this. **13** "Behold, days are coming," ‖ A declaration of YHWH, ‖ "And the plowman has come near to the reaper, ‖ And the treader of grapes to the scatterer of seed, ‖ And the mountains have dropped juice, ‖ And all the hills melt. **14** And I have turned back [to] the captivity of My people Israel, ‖ And they have built desolate cities, and inhabited, ‖ And have planted vineyards, and drunk their wine, ‖ And made gardens, and eaten their fruit. **15** And I have planted them on their own ground, ‖ And they are not plucked up anymore from off their own ground, ‖ That I have given to them," said your God YHWH!

OBADIAH

1 Thus said Lord YHWH to Edom ‖ (We have heard a report from YHWH, ‖ And an ambassador among nations was sent, ‖ "Rise, indeed, let us rise against her for battle"): **2** "Behold, I have made you little among nations, ‖ You [are] despised exceedingly. **3** The pride of your heart has lifted you up, ‖ O dweller in clefts of a rock ‖ (A high place [is] his habitation, ‖ He is saying in his heart: Who brings me down [to] earth?) **4** If you go up high as an eagle, ‖ And if you set your nest between stars, ‖ From there I bring you down," ‖ A declaration of YHWH. **5** "If thieves have come in to you, ‖ If spoilers of the night, ‖ How have you been cut off! Do they not steal their sufficiency? If gatherers have come in to you, ‖ Do they not leave gleanings? **6** How has Esau been searched out! His hidden things have flowed out, **7** All your allies have sent you to the border, ‖ Forgotten you, prevailed over you, have your friends, ‖ They make your bread a snare under you, ‖ There is no understanding in him! **8** Is it not in that day," a declaration of YHWH, ‖ "That I have destroyed the wise out of Edom, ‖ And understanding out of the mountain of Esau? **9** And your mighty ones have been broken down, O Teman, ‖ So that everyone of the mountain of Esau is cut off. **10** For slaughter, for violence [to] your brother Jacob, ‖ Shame covers you, ‖ And you have been cut off for all time. **11** In the day of your standing aloof from the opposite [side], ‖ In the day of strangers taking his force captive, ‖ And foreigners have entered his gates, ‖ And have cast a lot for Jerusalem, ‖ Even you [are] as one of them! **12** And—you do not look on the day of your brother, ‖ On the day of his alienation, ‖ Nor do you rejoice over sons of Judah, ‖ In the day of their destruction, ‖ Nor make your mouth great in a day of distress. **13** Nor come into a gate of My people in a day of their calamity, ‖ Nor look, even you, on its misfortune in a day of its calamity, ‖ Nor send forth against its force in a day of its calamity, **14** Nor stand by the breach to cut off its escaped, ‖ Nor deliver up its remnant in a day of distress. **15** For near [is] the Day of YHWH, on all the nations, ‖ As you have done, it is done to you, ‖ Your deed turns back on your own head. **16** For—as you have drunk on My holy mountain, ‖ All the nations drink continually, ‖ And they have drunk and have swallowed, ‖ And they have been as [if] they have not been. **17** And in Mount Zion there is an escape, ‖ And it has been holy, ‖ And the house of Jacob has possessed their possessions. **18** And the house of Jacob has been a fire, ‖ And the house of Joseph a flame, ‖ And the house of Esau for stubble, ‖ And they have burned among them, ‖ And they have consumed them, ‖ And there is not a remnant to the house of Esau," ‖ For YHWH has spoken. **19** And they have possessed the south with the mountain of Esau, ‖ And the low country with the Philistines, ‖ And they have possessed the field of Ephraim, ‖ And the field of Samaria, ‖ And Benjamin with Gilead. **20** And the expulsion of this force of the sons of Israel, ‖ That [is with] the Canaanites to Zarephat, ‖ And the expulsion of Jerusalem that [is] with the Sepharad, ‖ Possess the cities of the south. **21** And saviors have gone up on Mount Zion, ‖ To judge the mountain of Esau, ‖ And the kingdom has been to YHWH!

JONAH

1 And there is a word of Yhwh to Jonah son of Amittai, saying, **2** "Rise, go to Nineveh, the great city, and proclaim against it that their wickedness has come up before Me." **3** And Jonah rises to flee to Tarshish from the face of Yhwh, and goes down [to] Joppa, and finds a ship going [to] Tarshish, and he gives its fare, and goes down into it, to go with them to Tarshish from the face of Yhwh. **4** And Yhwh has cast a great wind on the sea, and there is a great storm in the sea, and the ship has reckoned to be broken; **5** and the mariners are afraid, and they each cry to his god, and cast the goods that [are] in the ship into the sea, to make [it] light of them; and Jonah has gone down to the sides of the vessel, and he lies down, and is fast asleep. **6** And the chief of the company draws near to him and says to him, "What are you [doing], O sleeper? Rise, call to your God, it may be God considers Himself of us, and we do not perish." **7** And they each say to his neighbor, "Come, and we cast lots, and we know on whose account this evil [is] on us." And they cast lots, and the lot falls on Jonah. **8** And they say to him, "Now declare to us, on whose account [is] this evil on us? What [is] your occupation, and where do you come from? What [is] your country, seeing you are not of this people?" **9** And he says to them, "I—a Hebrew, and I fear Yhwh, God of the heavens, who made the sea and the dry land." **10** And the men fear a great fear, and say to him, "What [is] this you have done!" For the men have known that he is fleeing from the face of Yhwh, for he has told them. **11** And they say to him, "What do we do to you that the sea may cease from us, for the sea is more and more turbulent?" **12** And he says to them, "Lift me up, and cast me into the sea, and the sea ceases from you; for I know that on my account this great storm [is] on you." **13** And the men row to turn back to the dry land, and are not able, for the sea is more and more turbulent against them. **14** And they cry to Yhwh, and say, "Ah, now, O Yhwh, please do not let us perish for this man's life, and do not lay innocent blood on us! For You, Yhwh, as You have pleased, You have done." **15** And they lift up Jonah, and cast him into the sea, and the sea ceases from its raging; **16** and the men fear Yhwh [with] a great fear, and sacrifice a sacrifice to Yhwh, and vow vows. **17** And Yhwh appoints a great fish to swallow up Jonah, and Jonah is in the bowels of the fish three days and three nights.

2 And Jonah prays to his God Yhwh from the bowels of the fish. **2** And he says: "I called, because of my distress, to Yhwh, ‖ And He answers me, ‖ From the belly of Sheol I have cried, ‖ You have heard my voice. **3** When You cast me [into] the deep, ‖ Into the heart of the seas, ‖ Then the flood surrounds me, ‖ All Your breakers and Your billows have passed over me. **4** And I said: I have been cast out from before Your eyes ‖ (Yet I add to look to Your holy temple!) **5** Waters have surrounded me to the soul, ‖ The deep surrounds me, ‖ The weed is bound to my head. **6** To the cuttings of mountains I have come down, ‖ The earth, her bars [are] behind me for all time. And You bring my life up from the pit, O Yhwh my God. **7** In the feebleness of my soul within me, ‖ I have remembered Yhwh, ‖ And my prayer comes to You, ‖ Into Your holy temple. **8** Those observing lying vanities forsake their own mercy. **9** And I—with a voice of thanksgiving—I sacrifice to You, ‖ That which I have vowed I complete, ‖ Salvation [is] of Yhwh." **10** And Yhwh speaks to the fish, and it vomits Jonah out on the dry land.

3 And there is a word of Yhwh to Jonah a second time, saying, **2** "Rise, go to Nineveh, the great city, and proclaim to it the proclamation that I am speaking to you"; **3** and Jonah rises, and he goes to Nineveh, according to the word of Yhwh. And Nineveh has been a great city before God, a journey of three days. **4** And Jonah begins to go into the city—a journey of one day—and proclaims and says, "Yet forty days and Nineveh is overturned!" **5** And the men of Nineveh believe in God, and proclaim a fast, and put on sackcloth, from their greatest even to their least, **6** seeing the word comes to the king of Nineveh, and he rises from his throne, and removes his honorable robe from off him, and spreads

JONAH

out sackcloth, and sits on the ashes, **7** and he cries and says in Nineveh by a decree of the king and his great ones, saying, "Man and beast, herd and flock—do not let them taste anything, do not let them feed, do not even let them drink water; **8** and let man and beast cover themselves [with] sackcloth, and let them call to God mightily, and let them each turn back from his evil way, and from the violence that [is] in their hands. **9** Who knows? He turns back, and God has relented, and has turned back from the heat of His anger, and we do not perish." **10** And God sees their works, that they have turned back from their evil way, and God relents of the evil that He spoke of doing to them, and He has not done [it].

4 And it is grievous to Jonah—a great evil—and he is displeased at it; **2** and he prays to YHWH, and he says, "Ah, now, O YHWH, is this not my word while I was in my own land—therefore I was beforehand [going] to flee to Tarshish—that I have known that You [are] a God, gracious and merciful, slow to anger, and abundant in kindness, and relenting of evil? **3** And now, O YHWH, please take my soul from me, for better [is] my death than my life." **4** And YHWH says, "Is doing good displeasing to you?" **5** And Jonah goes forth from the city, and sits on the east of the city, and makes a shelter for himself there, and sits under it in the shade, until he sees what is in the city. **6** And YHWH God appoints a gourd, and causes it to come up over Jonah, to be a shade over his head, to give deliverance to him from his affliction, and Jonah rejoices because of the gourd [with] great joy. **7** And God appoints a worm at the going up of the dawn on the next day, and it strikes the gourd, and it dries up. **8** And it comes to pass, about the rising of the sun, that God appoints a cutting east wind, and the sun strikes on the head of Jonah, and he wraps himself up, and asks for his soul to die, and says, "Better [is] my death than my life." **9** And God says to Jonah: "Is doing good displeasing to you, because of the gourd?" And he says, "To do good is displeasing to me—to death." **10** And YHWH says, "You have had pity on the gourd, for which you did not labor, neither did you nourish it, which came up [as] a son of night, and perished [as] a son of night, **11** and I—do I not have pity on Nineveh, the great city, in which there are more than one hundred twenty thousand of mankind, who have not known between their right hand and their left—and much livestock?"

MICAH

1 A word of Y{\sc hwh} that has been to Micah the Morashite in the days of Jotham, Ahaz, Hezekiah, kings of Judah, that he has seen concerning Samaria and Jerusalem: **2** Hear, O peoples, all of them! Attend, O earth, and its fullness, ‖ And Lord Y{\sc hwh} is against you for a witness, ‖ The Lord from His holy temple. **3** For behold, Y{\sc hwh} is going out from His place, ‖ And He has come down, ‖ And has trodden on high places of earth. **4** The mountains have been melted under Him, ‖ And the valleys split themselves, ‖ As wax from the presence of fire, ‖ As waters cast down by a slope. **5** For the transgression of Jacob [is] all this, ‖ And for the sins of the house of Israel. What [is] the transgression of Jacob? Is it not Samaria? And what the high places of Judah? Is it not Jerusalem? **6** "And I have set Samaria for a heap of the field, ‖ For plantations of a vineyard, ‖ And poured out into a valley her stones, ‖ And her foundations I uncover. **7** And all her carved images are beaten down, ‖ And all her wages are burned with fire, ‖ And all her idols I make a desolation, ‖ For from the wage of a harlot she gathered, and to the wage of a harlot they return." **8** For this I lament and howl, ‖ I go spoiled and naked, ‖ I make a lamentation like dragons, ‖ And a mourning like daughters of an ostrich. **9** For mortal [are] her wounds, ‖ For it has come to Judah, ‖ It has come to a gate of My people—to Jerusalem. **10** In Gath do not tell—in Acco do not weep, ‖ In Beth-Aphrah, roll yourself in dust. **11** Pass over for you, O inhabitant of Shaphir, ‖ Naked one of shame. The inhabitant of Zaanan has not gone out, ‖ The lamentation of Beth-Ezel takes from you its standing. **12** For the inhabitant of Maroth has stayed for good, ‖ For calamity has come down from Y{\sc hwh} to the gate of Jerusalem. **13** Bind the chariot to a swift beast, O inhabitant of Lachish, ‖ The beginning of sin [is] she to the daughter of Zion, ‖ For in you have been found the transgressions of Israel. **14** Therefore you give presents to Moresheth-Gath, ‖ The houses of Achzib become a lying thing to the kings of Israel. **15** Yet I bring the possessor to you, O inhabitant of Mareshah, ‖ The glory of Israel comes to Adullam. **16** Make bald and shave, for your delightful sons, ‖ Enlarge your baldness as an eagle, ‖ For they have removed from you!

2 Woe [to] those devising iniquity, ‖ And working evil on their beds, ‖ In the morning light they do it, ‖ For their hand is—to God. **2** And they have desired fields, ‖ And they have taken violently, ‖ And houses, and they have taken away, ‖ And have oppressed a man and his house, ‖ Even a man and his inheritance. **3** Therefore, thus said Y{\sc hwh}: "Behold, I am devising against this family calamity, ‖ From which you do not remove your necks, ‖ Nor walk loftily, for it [is] a time of evil. **4** In that day [one] takes up for you an allegory, ‖ And he has wailed a wailing of woe, ‖ He has said, We have been utterly spoiled, ‖ The portion of my people He changes, ‖ How He moves toward me! To the backslider our fields He apportions." **5** Therefore, you have no caster of a line by lot ‖ In the assembly of Y{\sc hwh}. **6** You do not prophesy—they prophesy, ‖ They do not prophesy to these, ‖ It does not remove shame. **7** [Those] named the house of Jacob: "Has the Spirit of Y{\sc hwh} been shortened? Are these His doings? Do My words not benefit the people that are walking uprightly? **8** And recently My people raise up as an enemy, ‖ You strip off the honorable ornament from the outer garment, ‖ From the confident passers by, ‖ You who are turning back from war. **9** The women of My people you cast out from its delightful house, ‖ From its sucklings you take away My honor for all time. **10** Rise and go, for this [is] not the rest, ‖ Because of uncleanness it corrupts, ‖ And corruption is powerful. **11** If one is going [with] the wind, ‖ And [with] falsehood has lied: I prophesy to you of wine, and of strong drink, ‖ He has been the prophet of this people! **12** I surely gather you, O Jacob, all of you, ‖ I surely bring together the remnant of Israel, ‖ Together I set it as the flock of Bozrah, ‖ As a drove in the midst of its pasture, ‖ It makes a noise because of man. **13** The breaker has gone up before them, ‖ They have broken through, ‖ Indeed, they pass through the gate, ‖ Indeed, they go out through it, ‖ And

MICAH

their king passes on before them, ‖ And YHWH at their head!"

3 And I say, "Now hear, O heads of Jacob, ‖ And you judges of the house of Israel, ‖ Is it not for you to know the judgment? **2** You who are hating good, and loving evil, ‖ Taking violently their skin from off them, ‖ And their flesh from off their bones, **3** And who have eaten the flesh of My people, ‖ And their skin from off them have stripped, ‖ And their bones they have broken, ‖ And they have spread [them] out as in a pot, ‖ And as flesh in the midst of a cauldron." **4** Then they cry to YHWH, ‖ And He does not answer them, ‖ And hides His face from them at that time, ‖ As they have made evil their doings. **5** Thus said YHWH concerning the prophets ‖ Who are causing My people to err, ‖ Who are biting with their teeth, ‖ And have cried "Peace," ‖ And he who does not give to their mouth, ‖ They have sanctified against him war: **6** "Therefore you have a night without vision, ‖ And you have darkness without divination, ‖ And the sun has gone in on the prophets, ‖ And the day has been black over them. **7** And the seers have been ashamed, ‖ And the diviners have been confounded, ‖ And all of them have covered their lip, ‖ For there is no answer, O God." **8** And yet I have been full of power by the Spirit of YHWH, ‖ And of judgment, and of might, ‖ To declare to Jacob his transgression, ‖ And to Israel his sin. **9** Now hear this, O heads of the house of Jacob, ‖ And you judges of the house of Israel, ‖ Who are making judgment abominable, ‖ And pervert all uprightness. **10** Building up Zion with blood, ‖ And Jerusalem with iniquity. **11** Her heads judge for a bribe, ‖ And her priests teach for hire, ‖ And her prophets divine for silver, ‖ And on YHWH they lean, saying, ‖ "Is not YHWH in our midst? Evil does not come in on us." **12** Therefore, for your sake, Zion is plowed a field, and Jerusalem is heaps, ‖ And the mountain of the house [is] for high places of a forest!

4 And it has come to pass, ‖ In the latter end of the days, ‖ The mountain of the house of YHWH ‖ Is established above the top of the mountains, ‖ And it has been lifted up above the hills, ‖ And flowed to it have peoples. **2** And gone have many nations and said, ‖ "Come and we go up to the mountain of YHWH, ‖ And to the house of the God of Jacob, ‖ And He teaches us of His ways, ‖ And we walk in His paths," ‖ For a law goes forth from Zion, ‖ And a word of YHWH from Jerusalem. **3** And He has judged between many peoples, ‖ And given a decision to mighty nations far off, ‖ They have beaten their swords to plowshares, ‖ And their spears to pruning-hooks, ‖ Nation does not lift up sword to nation, ‖ Nor do they learn war anymore. **4** And they have sat each under his vine, ‖ And under his fig tree, ‖ And there is none troubling, ‖ For the mouth of YHWH of Hosts has spoken. **5** For all the peoples walk, ‖ Each in the name of its god—and we, ‖ We walk in the Name of our God YHWH, ‖ For all time and forever. **6** "In that day," a declaration of YHWH, ‖ "I gather the halting one, ‖ And the driven away one I bring together, ‖ And she whom I have afflicted. **7** And I have set the halting for a remnant, ‖ And the far-off for a mighty nation, ‖ And YHWH has reigned over them in Mount Zion, ‖ From now on, and for all time. **8** And you, O Tower of Eder, ‖ Fort of the daughter of Zion, to you it comes, ‖ Indeed, the former rule has come in, ‖ The kingdom to the daughter of Jerusalem." **9** Now why do you shout aloud? Is there no king in you? Has your counselor perished, ‖ That pain as of a travailing woman has taken hold of you? **10** Be pained, and bring forth, O daughter of Zion, ‖ As a travailing woman, ‖ For now you go forth from the city, ‖ And you have dwelt in the field, ‖ And you have gone to Babylon, ‖ There you are delivered, ‖ There YHWH redeems you from the hand of your enemies. **11** And now, many nations have gathered against you, who are saying: "Let her be defiled, and our eyes look on Zion." **12** They have not known the thoughts of YHWH, ‖ Nor have they understood His counsel, ‖ For He has gathered them as a sheaf [into] a threshing-floor. **13** Arise, and thresh, O daughter of Zion, ‖ For I make your horn iron, ‖ And I make your hooves bronze, ‖ And you have beaten small many peoples, ‖ And I have devoted to YHWH their gain, ‖ And their wealth to the Lord of the whole earth!

5 Now gather yourself together, O daughter of troops, ‖ He has laid a siege against us, ‖ They strike [the] judge of Israel on the cheek with a rod. **2** "And you, Beth-Lehem Ephratah, ‖ Little to be among the

MICAH

chiefs of Judah! From you He comes forth to Me—to be ruler in Israel, ‖ And His comings forth [are] of old, ‖ From the days of antiquity." **3** Therefore He gives them up until the time she who brings forth has brought forth, ‖ And the remnant of His brothers return to the sons of Israel. **4** And He has stood and delighted in the strength of YHWH, ‖ In the excellence of the Name of His God YHWH, ‖ And they have remained, ‖ For now He is great to the ends of the earth. **5** And this [One] has been peace. Asshur, when he comes into our land, ‖ And when he treads in our palaces, ‖ We have raised against him seven shepherds, ‖ And eight anointed of man. **6** And they have afflicted the land of Asshur with the sword, ‖ And the land of Nimrod at its openings, ‖ And He has delivered from Asshur when he comes into our land, ‖ And when he treads in our borders. **7** And the remnant of Jacob has been in the midst of many peoples, ‖ As dew from YHWH—as showers on the herb, ‖ That does not wait for man, nor stays for the sons of men. **8** Indeed, the remnant of Jacob has been among nations, ‖ In the midst of many peoples, ‖ As a lion among beasts of a forest, ‖ As a young lion among ranks of a flock, ‖ Which if it has passed through, ‖ Has both trodden down and has torn, ‖ And there is no deliverer. **9** High is your hand above your adversaries, ‖ And all your enemies are cut off. **10** "And it has come to pass in that day," ‖ A declaration of YHWH, ‖ "I have cut off your horses from your midst, ‖ And I have destroyed your chariots, **11** And I have cut off the cities of your land, ‖ And I have thrown down all your fortresses, **12** And have cut off sorcerers out of your hand, ‖ And observers of clouds—you have none. **13** And I have cut off your carved images, ‖ And your standing-pillars out of your midst, ‖ And you do not bow yourself anymore ‖ To the work of your hands. **14** And I have plucked up your Asherim out of your midst, ‖ And I have destroyed your enemies. **15** And I have done vengeance in anger and in fury, ‖ With the nations who have not listened!"

6 Now hear that which YHWH is saying: "Rise—strive with the mountains, ‖ And cause the hills to hear your voice. **2** Hear, O mountains, the strife of YHWH, ‖ You strong ones—foundations of earth! For a strife [is] to YHWH, with His people, ‖ And with Israel He reasons. **3** O My people, what have I done to you? And how have I wearied you? Testify against Me. **4** For I brought you up from the land of Egypt, ‖ And I have ransomed you from the house of servants, ‖ And I send Moses, Aaron, and Miriam before you. **5** O My people, please remember ‖ What Balak king of Moab counseled, ‖ What Balaam son of Beor answered him ‖ (From Shittim to Gilgal), ‖ In order to know the righteous acts of YHWH." **6** With what do I come before YHWH? Do I bow to God Most High? Do I come before Him with burnt-offerings? With calves—sons of a year? **7** Is YHWH pleased with thousands of rams? With myriads of streams of oil? Do I give my firstborn [for] my transgression? The fruit of my body [for] the sin of my soul? **8** He has declared to you, O man, what [is] good; Indeed, what is YHWH requiring of you, ‖ Except—to do judgment, and love kindness, ‖ And to walk lowly with your God? **9** A voice of YHWH calls to the city, ‖ And wisdom fears Your Name, ‖ "Hear the rod, and Him who appointed it. **10** Are there yet [in] the house of the wicked ‖ Treasures of wickedness, ‖ And the abhorred meager ephah? **11** Do I reckon [it] pure with balances of wickedness? And with a bag of deceitful stones? **12** Whose rich ones have been full of violence, ‖ And its inhabitants have spoken falsehood, ‖ And their tongue [is] deceitful in their mouth. **13** And I also, I have begun to strike you, ‖ To make desolate, because of your sins. **14** You eat, and you are not satisfied, ‖ And your pit [is] in your midst, ‖ And you remove, and do not deliver, ‖ And that which you deliver, I give to a sword. **15** You sow, and you do not reap, ‖ You tread the olive, ‖ And you do not pour out oil, ‖ And new wine—and you do not drink wine. **16** And the statutes of Omri are kept habitually, ‖ And all the work of the house of Ahab, ‖ And you walk in their counsels, ‖ For My giving you for a desolation, ‖ And its inhabitants for a hissing, ‖ And you bear the reproach of My people!"

7 My woe [is] to me, ‖ For I have been as gatherings of summer-fruit, ‖ As gleanings of harvest, ‖ There is no cluster to eat, ‖ The first-ripe fruit has my soul desired. **2** The kind have perished out of the land, ‖ And upright among men—there are none, ‖ All of them lie in wait for blood, ‖

They each hunt his brother [with] a net. **3** On the evil [are] both hands to do [it] well, ‖ The prince is asking—also the judge—for repayment, ‖ And the great—he is speaking the mischief of his soul, ‖ And they wrap it up. **4** Their best one [is] as a brier, ‖ The upright one—than a thorn-hedge, ‖ The day of your watchmen—Your visitation—has come. Now is their perplexity. **5** Do not believe in a friend, ‖ Do not trust in a leader, ‖ From her who is lying in your bosom keep the openings of your mouth. **6** For a son is dishonoring a father, ‖ A daughter has stood against her mother, ‖ A daughter-in-law against her mother-in-law, ‖ The enemies of each [are] the men of his house. **7** And I—in YHWH I watch, ‖ I wait for the God of my salvation, ‖ My God hears me. **8** You do not rejoice over me, O my enemy, ‖ When I have fallen, I have risen, ‖ When I sit in darkness YHWH is a light to me. **9** I bear the indignation of YHWH, ‖ For I have sinned against Him, ‖ Until He pleads my cause, ‖ And has executed my judgment, ‖ He brings me forth to the light, ‖ I look on His righteousness. **10** And my enemy sees, ‖ And shame covers her, ‖ Who says to me, "Where [is] your God YHWH?" My eyes look on her, ‖ Now she is for a treading-place, ‖ As mire of the out-places. **11** The day to build your walls! That day—removed is the limit. **12** That day—even to you it comes in, ‖ From Asshur and the cities of the fortress, ‖ And from the fortress even to the river, ‖ And from sea to sea, and mountain to mountain. **13** And the land has been for a desolation, ‖ Because of its inhabitants, ‖ Because of the fruit of their doings. **14** Rule Your people with Your rod, ‖ The flock of Your inheritance, ‖ Dwelling alone [in] a forest in the midst of Carmel, ‖ They enjoy Bashan and Gilead as in days of old. **15** "According to the days of your coming forth out of the land of Egypt, ‖ I show it wonderful things." **16** Nations see, and they are ashamed of all their might, ‖ They lay a hand on the mouth, their ears are deaf. **17** They lick dust as a serpent, as fearful things of earth, ‖ They tremble from their enclosures, ‖ They are afraid of our God YHWH, ‖ Indeed, they are afraid of You. **18** Who [is] a God like You? Taking away iniquity, ‖ And passing by the transgression of the remnant of His inheritance, ‖ He has not retained His anger forever, ‖ Because He delights [in] kindness. **19** He turns back, He pities us, ‖ He subdues our iniquities, ‖ And You cast all their sins into the depths of the sea. **20** You give truth to Jacob, kindness to Abraham, ‖ That You have sworn to our fathers, from the days of antiquity!

NAHUM

1 Burden of Nineveh. The Scroll of the Vision of Nahum the Elkoshite. **2** A God zealous and avenging [is] YHWH, ‖ An avenger [is] YHWH, and possessing fury. An avenger [is] YHWH on His adversaries, ‖ And He is watching for His enemies. **3** YHWH [is] slow to anger, and great in power, ‖ And YHWH does not entirely acquit, ‖ In a windstorm and in a storm [is] His way, ‖ And a cloud [is] the dust of His feet. **4** He is pushing against a sea, and dries it up, ‖ Indeed, He has made all the floods dry, ‖ Bashan and Carmel [are] languishing, ‖ Indeed, the flower of Lebanon [is] languishing. **5** Mountains have shaken because of Him, ‖ And the hills have been melted; And the earth [is] lifted up at His presence, ‖ And the world and all dwelling in it. **6** Who stands before His indignation? And who rises up in the heat of His anger? His fury has been poured out like fire, ‖ And the rocks have been broken by Him. **7** Good [is] YHWH for a strong place in a day of distress. And He knows those trusting in Him. **8** And with a flood passing over, ‖ An end He makes of its place, ‖ And darkness pursues His enemies. **9** What do we devise against YHWH? He is making an end, distress does not arise twice. **10** For while princes [are] perplexed, ‖ And with their drink are drunken, ‖ They have been consumed as stubble fully dried. **11** From you has come forth a deviser of evil ‖ Against YHWH—a worthless counselor. **12** Thus said YHWH: "Though complete, and thus many, ‖ Yet thus they have been cut off, ‖ And he has passed away. Though I afflicted you, I afflict you no longer. **13** And now I break his rod from off you, ‖ And your bands I draw away." **14** And YHWH has commanded concerning you, ‖ "No more of your name spreads abroad, ‖ I cut off carved and molten image from the house of your gods, ‖ I appoint your grave, for you have been vile." **15** Behold, on the mountains the feet of one proclaiming tidings, sounding peace! Celebrate, O Judah, your festivals, complete your vows, ‖ For the worthless no longer pass over into you, ‖ He has been completely cut off!

2 A scatterer has come up to your face, ‖ Keep the bulwark, watch the way, ‖ Strengthen the loins, strengthen power mightily. **2** For YHWH has turned back to the excellence of Jacob, ‖ As [to] the excellence of Israel, ‖ For emptiers have emptied them out, ‖ And they have marred their branches. **3** The shield of his mighty ones has become red, ‖ Men of might [are in] scarlet, ‖ With fiery torches [is] the chariot in a day of his preparation, ‖ And the firs have been caused to tremble. **4** In outplaces the chariots shine, ‖ They go to and fro in broad places, ‖ Their appearances [are] like torches, ‖ As lightnings they run. **5** He remembers his majestic ones, ‖ They stumble in their goings, ‖ They hurry [to] its wall, ‖ And the covering is prepared. **6** Gates of the rivers have been opened, ‖ And the palace is dissolved. **7** And it is established—she has removed, ‖ She has been brought up, ‖ And her handmaids are leading as the voice of doves, ‖ Tabering on their hearts. **8** And Nineveh [is] as a pool of waters, ‖ From of old it [is]—and they are fleeing! "Stand, stand"; and none is turning! **9** Seize silver, seize gold, ‖ And there is no end to the prepared things, ‖ [To] the abundance of all desirable vessels. **10** She is empty, indeed, emptiness and waste, ‖ And the heart has melted, ‖ And the knees have struck together, ‖ And great pain [is] in all loins, ‖ And the faces of all of them have gathered paleness. **11** Where [is] the habitation of lionesses? And a feeding-place it [is] for young lions ‖ Where a lion has walked, an old lion, ‖ A lion's whelp, and there is none troubling. **12** The lion is tearing parts [for] his whelps, ‖ And is strangling for his lionesses, ‖ And he fills his holes [with] prey, ‖ And his habitations [with] torn flesh. **13** "Behold, I [am] against you," ‖ A declaration of YHWH of Hosts, ‖ "And I have burned its chariot in smoke, ‖ And a sword consumes your young lions, ‖ And I have cut off your prey from the land, ‖ And the voice of your messengers is not heard anymore!"

3 Woe [to] the city of blood, ‖ She is all full with lies [and] burglary, ‖ Prey does not depart. **2** The sound of a whip, ‖ And the sound of the rattling of a wheel, ‖ And of a prancing horse, and of a bounding chariot, ‖ Of a horseman mounting. **3** And the flame of a sword, and the lightning of a spear, ‖ And the abundance of the wounded, ‖ And the weight of carcasses, ‖ Indeed, there is no end to the bodies, ‖ They stumble over their bodies. **4** Because of the abundance of the fornications of a harlot, ‖ The goodness of the grace of the lady of witchcrafts, ‖ Who is selling nations by her fornications, ‖ And families by her witchcrafts. **5** "Behold, I [am] against you," ‖ A declaration of Y<small>HWH</small> of Hosts, ‖ "And have removed your skirts before your face, ‖ And have showed nations your nakedness, ‖ And kingdoms your shame, **6** And I have cast on you abominations, ‖ And dishonored you, and made you as a sight. **7** And it has come to pass, ‖ Each of your beholders flees from you, ‖ And has said: Nineveh is spoiled, ‖ Who bemoans for her? From where do I seek comforters for you?" **8** Are you better than No-Ammon, ‖ That is dwelling among brooks? Waters she has around her, ‖ Whose bulwark [is] the sea, waters her wall. **9** Cush her might, and Egypt, and there is no end. Put and Lubim have been for your help. **10** Even she becomes an exile, ‖ She has gone into captivity, ‖ Even her sucklings are dashed to pieces ‖ At the top of all out-places, ‖ And for her honored ones they cast a lot, ‖ And all her great ones have been bound in chains. **11** Even you are drunken, you are hidden, ‖ Even you seek a strong place, because of an enemy. **12** All your fortresses [are] fig trees with first-fruits, ‖ If they are shaken, ‖ They have fallen into the mouth of the eater. **13** Behold, your people [are] women in your midst, ‖ To your enemies thoroughly opened ‖ Have been the gates of your land, ‖ Fire has consumed your bars. **14** Waters of a siege draw for yourself, ‖ Strengthen your fortresses, ‖ Enter into mire, and tread on clay, ‖ Make strong a brick-kiln. **15** There a fire consumes you, ‖ A sword cuts you off, ‖ It consumes you as a cankerworm! Make yourself heavy as the cankerworm, ‖ Make yourself heavy as the locust. **16** Multiply your merchants above the stars of the heavens, ‖ The cankerworm has stripped off, and flees away. **17** Your crowned ones [are] as a locust, ‖ And your princes as great grasshoppers, ‖ That encamp in hedges in a day of cold, ‖ The sun has risen, and it flees away, ‖ And its place where they are is not known. **18** Your friends have slumbered, king of Asshur, ‖ Your majestic ones rest, ‖ Your people have been scattered on the mountains, ‖ And there is none gathering. **19** There is no weakening of your destruction, ‖ Your striking [is] grievous, ‖ All hearing your fame have clapped the hand at you, ‖ For over whom did your wickedness not pass continually?

HABAKKUK

1 The burden that Habakkuk the prophet has seen: **2** Until when, O YHWH, have I cried, ‖ And You do not hear? I cry to You, "Violence!" And You do not save. **3** Why do You show me iniquity, ‖ And cause [me] to behold perversity? And spoiling and violence [are] before me, ‖ And there is strife, and contention lifts [itself] up, **4** Therefore law ceases, ‖ And judgment does not go forth forever, ‖ For the wicked is surrounding the righteous, ‖ Therefore wrong judgment goes forth. **5** "Look on nations, and behold and marvel greatly. For a work He is working in your days, ‖ You do not believe though it is declared. **6** For behold, I am raising up the Chaldeans, ‖ The bitter and hasty nation, ‖ That is going to the broad places of earth, ‖ To occupy dwelling places not his own. **7** He [is] terrible and fearful, ‖ His judgment and his excellence go forth from him. **8** His horses have been swifter than leopards, ‖ And sharper than evening wolves, ‖ And his horsemen have increased, ‖ Even his horsemen from afar come in, ‖ They fly as an eagle, hastening to consume. **9** All for violence—he comes in, ‖ Their faces swallowing up the east wind, ‖ And he gathers a captivity as the sand. **10** And he scoffs at kings, ‖ And princes [are] a laughter to him, ‖ He laughs at every fortification, ‖ And he heaps up dust, and captures it. **11** Then the spirit has passed on, ‖ Indeed, he transgresses, ‖ And [ascribes] this—his power—to his god." **12** Are You not of old, O YHWH, my God, my Holy One? We do not die, O YHWH, ‖ You have appointed him for judgment, ‖ And, O Rock, You have founded him for reproof. **13** Purer of eyes than to behold evil, ‖ You are not able to look on perverseness, ‖ Why do You behold the treacherous? You keep silent when the wicked ‖ Swallow the more righteous than he, **14** And You make man as fishes of the sea, ‖ As a creeping thing [with] none ruling over him. **15** He has brought up each of them with a hook, ‖ He catches it in his net, and gathers it in his dragnet, ‖ Therefore he delights and rejoices. **16** Therefore he sacrifices to his net, ‖ And makes incense to his dragnet, ‖ For by them [is] his portion fertile, and his food fat. **17** Does he therefore empty his net, ‖ And continually not spare to slay nations?

2 On my charge I stand, and I station myself on a bulwark, and I watch to see what He speaks against me, and what I reply to my reproof. **2** And YHWH answers me and says: "Write a vision, and explain on the tablets, ‖ That he may run who is reading it. **3** For yet the vision [is] for a season, ‖ And it breathes for the end, and does not lie, ‖ If it lingers, wait for it, ‖ For surely it comes, it is not late. **4** Behold, a presumptuous one! His soul is not upright within him, ‖ And the righteous lives by his faith. **5** And also, because the wine [is] treacherous, ‖ A man is haughty, and does not remain at home, ‖ Who has enlarged his soul as Sheol, ‖ And is as death that is not satisfied, ‖ And gathers to itself all the nations, ‖ And assembles to itself all the peoples, **6** Are these not—all of them—an allegory taken up against him, ‖ And a moral of acute sayings for him, ‖ And say, Woe [to] him who is multiplying [what is] not his? Until when also is he multiplying to himself heavy pledges? **7** Do your usurers not instantly rise up, ‖ And those shaking you awake, ‖ And you have been a spoil to them? **8** Because you have spoiled many nations, ‖ All the remnant of the peoples spoil you, ‖ Because of man's blood, and of violence [to] the land, ‖ [To] the city, and [to] all dwelling in it. **9** Woe [to] him who is gaining evil gain for his house, ‖ To set his nest on high, ‖ To be delivered from the hand of evil, **10** You have counseled a shameful thing to your house, ‖ To cut off many peoples, and your soul [is] sinful. **11** For a stone cries out from the wall, ‖ And a beam from the wood answers it. **12** Woe [to] him who is building a city by blood, ‖ And establishing a city by iniquity. **13** Behold, is it not from YHWH of Hosts ‖ And peoples are fatigued for fire, ‖ And nations for vanity are weary? **14** For the earth is full of the knowledge of the glory of YHWH, ‖ As the waters cover over a sea. **15** Woe [to] him who is giving drink to his neighbor, ‖ Pouring out your bottle, and also making drunk, ‖ In order to look on their nakedness. **16** You have been filled—shame without honor, ‖ Drink also, and be uncircumcised, ‖ Turn around to you does the cup of the right hand of YHWH, ‖ And shameful spewing [is] on your glory. **17** For violence [done to] Lebanon covers you, ‖ And spoil of beasts frightens them, ‖ Because of man's blood, and of violence [to] the land, ‖ [To] the city, and [to] all dwelling in it. **18** What profit has a carved image given ‖ That its former has hewn it? A molten image and teacher of falsehood, ‖ That the former has trusted on his own formation—to make mute idols? **19** Woe [to] him who is saying to wood, Awake, ‖ To a mute stone, Stir up, ‖ It [is] a teacher! Behold, it is overlaid—gold and silver, ‖ And there is no spirit in its midst. **20** And YHWH [is] in His holy temple, ‖ Be silent before Him, all the earth!"

3 A prayer of Habakkuk the prophet, [set] on shigionoth: **2** O YHWH, I heard your report, ‖ I have been afraid, O YHWH, ‖ Your work! In midst of years revive it, ‖ In the midst of years You make known, ‖ In anger You remember mercy. **3** God comes from Teman, ‖ The Holy One from Mount Paran. Pause! His splendor has covered the heavens, ‖ And His praise has filled the earth. **4** And the brightness is as the light, ‖ He has rays out of His hand, ‖ And there— the hiding of His strength. **5** Before Him goes pestilence, ‖ And a burning flame goes forth at His feet. **6** He has stood, and He measures earth, ‖ He has seen, and He shakes off nations, ‖ And mountains of antiquity scatter themselves, ‖ The hills of old have bowed, ‖ The ways of old [are] His. **7** Under sorrow I have seen tents of Cushan, ‖ Curtains of the land of Midian tremble. **8** Has YHWH been angry against rivers? Against rivers [is] Your anger? [Is] Your wrath against the sea? For You ride on Your horses—Your chariots of salvation. **9** You make Your bow utterly naked, ‖ The tribes have sworn, saying, "Pause!" You cleave the earth [with] rivers. **10** Seen You—pained are mountains, ‖ An inundation of waters has passed over, ‖ The deep has given forth its voice, ‖ It has lifted up its hands high. **11** Sun—moon—has stood—a habitation, ‖ Your arrows go on at the light, ‖ At the brightness, the glittering of Your spear. **12** In indignation You tread earth, ‖ In anger You thresh nations. **13** You have gone forth for the salvation of Your people, ‖ For salvation with Your Anointed, ‖ You have struck the head of the house of the wicked, ‖ Laying bare the foundation to the neck. Pause! **14** You have pierced the head of his leaders with his own rods, ‖ They are tempestuous to scatter me, ‖ Their exultation [is] as to consume the poor in secret. **15** You have proceeded through the sea with Your horses—the clay of many waters. **16** I have heard, and my belly trembles, ‖ At the noise have my lips quivered, ‖ Rottenness comes into my bones, ‖ And in my place I tremble, ‖ That I rest for a day of distress, ‖ At the coming up of the people, he overcomes it. **17** Though the fig tree does not flourish, ‖ And there is no produce among vines, ‖ The work of the olive has failed, ‖ And fields have not yielded food, ‖ The flock has been cut off from the fold, ‖ And there is no herd in the stalls, **18** Yet I, in YHWH I exult, ‖ I am joyful in the God of my salvation. **19** YHWH the Lord [is] my strength, ‖ And He makes my feet like does, ‖ And causes me to tread on my high-places. To the overseer with my stringed instruments!

ZEPHANIAH

1 A word of YHWH that has been to Zephaniah son of Cushi, son of Gedaliah, son of Amariah, son of Hezikiah, in the days of Josiah son of Amoz, king of Judah: **2** "I utterly consume all from off the face of the ground," ‖ A declaration of YHWH. **3** "I consume man and beast, ‖ I consume bird of the heavens, and fishes of the sea, ‖ And the stumbling-blocks—the wicked, ‖ And I have cut off man from the face of the ground," ‖ A declaration of YHWH, **4** "And I have stretched out My hand against Judah, ‖ And against all inhabiting Jerusalem, ‖ And cut off from this place the remnant of Ba'al, ‖ The name of the idolatrous priests, with the priests, **5** And those bowing themselves ‖ On the roofs to the host of the heavens, ‖ And those bowing themselves, ‖ Swearing to YHWH, and swearing by Malcham, **6** And those removing from after YHWH, ‖ And who have not sought YHWH, nor implored Him." **7** Hush! Because of Lord YHWH, ‖ For near [is the] Day of YHWH, ‖ For YHWH has prepared a sacrifice, ‖ He has sanctified His invited ones. **8** "And it has come to pass, ‖ In the day of the sacrifice of YHWH, ‖ That I have laid a charge on the heads, ‖ And on sons of the king, ‖ And on all putting on strange clothing. **9** And I have laid a charge on everyone ‖ Who is leaping over the threshold in that day, ‖ Who are filling the house of their masters ‖ [With] violence and deceit. **10** And there has been in that day," ‖ A declaration of YHWH, ‖ "The noise of a cry from the Fish Gate, ‖ And of a howling from the Second [Quarter], ‖ And of great destruction from the hills. **11** Howl, you inhabitants of the hollow place, ‖ For all the merchant people have been cut off, ‖ All carrying silver have been cut off. **12** And it has come to pass at that time, ‖ I search Jerusalem with lights, ‖ And I have laid a charge on the men ‖ Who are hardened on their preserved things, ‖ Who are saying in their heart: YHWH does no good, nor does He do evil. **13** And their wealth has been for a spoil, ‖ And their houses for desolation, ‖ And they have built houses, and do not inhabit, ‖ And they have planted vineyards, ‖ And they do not drink their wine." **14** Near [is] the Great Day of YHWH, ‖ Near, and hastening exceedingly, ‖ The noise of the Day of YHWH, ‖ There a mighty one bitterly shrieks. **15** A day of wrath [is] that day, ‖ A day of adversity and distress, ‖ A day of devastation and desolation, ‖ A day of darkness and gloominess, ‖ A day of cloud and thick darkness, **16** A day of horn and shouting against the fortified cities, ‖ And against the high corners. **17** "And I have sent distress to men, ‖ And they have walked as the blind, ‖ For against YHWH they have sinned, ‖ And poured out is their blood as dust, ‖ And their flesh [is] as dung." **18** Even their silver, even their gold, is not able to deliver them in a day of the wrath of YHWH, and in the fire of His jealousy is the whole land consumed, for He makes only a hurried end of all the inhabitants of the land!

2 Bend yourselves, indeed, bend, ‖ O nation not desired, **2** Before the bringing forth of a statute, ‖ The day has passed on as chaff, ‖ While the heat of the anger of YHWH has not yet come in on you, ‖ While [the] Day of the anger of YHWH has not yet come in on you, **3** Seek YHWH, all you humble of the land, ‖ Who have done His judgment, ‖ Seek righteousness, seek humility, ‖ It may be you are hidden in the Day of the anger of YHWH. **4** For Gaza is forsaken, ‖ And Ashkelon [is] for a desolation, ‖ Ashdod! At noon they cast her forth, ‖ And Ekron is rooted up. **5** Behold! O inhabitants of the seacoast, ‖ Nation of the Cherethites, ‖ A word of YHWH [is] against you, ‖ Canaan, land of the Philistines, ‖ "And I have destroyed you without an inhabitant." **6** And the seacoast has been habitations, ‖ Cottages [for] shepherds, and folds [for] a flock. **7** And the coast has been for the remnant of the house of Judah, ‖ By them they have pleasure, ‖ In houses of Ashkelon they lie down at evening, ‖ For their God YHWH inspects them, ‖ And He has turned back [to] their captivity. **8** "I have heard the reproach of Moab, ‖ And the revilings of the sons of Ammon, ‖ With which they reproached My people, ‖ And magnify [themselves] against their border. **9** Therefore, [as] I live," ‖ A declaration of YHWH of Hosts, God of Israel, ‖ "Surely Moab is as Sodom, ‖ And the sons of Ammon as Gomorrah, ‖ An overrunning of nettles and salt-pits, ‖ And a desolation for all time. A remnant of My people seizes them, ‖ And a remnant of My nation inherits them." **10** This [is] to them for their arrogancy, ‖ Because they have reproached, ‖ And they magnify [themselves] against the people of Y H W H of Hosts. **11** Fearful [is] Y H W H against them, ‖ For He made all gods of the land bare, ‖ And all islanders of the nations bow themselves to Him, ‖ Each from his place. **12** "Also you, O Cushim, they [are] pierced of My sword." **13** And He stretches His hand against the north, ‖ And destroys Asshur, ‖ And He sets Nineveh for a desolation, ‖ A dry land like a wilderness. **14** And droves have crouched in her midst, ‖ Every beast of the nation, ‖ Both pelican and hedgehog lodge in her knobs, ‖ A voice sings at the window, ‖ "Destruction [is] at the threshold, ‖ For the cedar-work is exposed." **15** This [is] the exulting city that is dwelling confidently, ‖ That is saying in her heart, ‖ "I [am], and there is none beside me," ‖ How she has been for a desolation, ‖ A crouching-place for beasts, ‖ Everyone passing by her hisses, ‖ He shakes his hand!

3 Woe [to] the rebelling and defiling, ‖ The oppressing city! **2** She has not listened to the voice, ‖ She has not accepted instruction, ‖ In Y H W H she has not trusted, ‖ She has not drawn near to her God. **3** Her heads in her midst [are] roaring lions, ‖ Her judges [are] wolves [as in] evening, ‖ They have not gnawn the bone in the morning. **4** Her prophets unstable—men of treachery, ‖ Her priests have defiled the sanctuary, ‖ They have violated the Law. **5** Y H W H [is] righteous in her midst, ‖ He does not do perverseness, ‖ Morning by morning His judgment He gives to the light, ‖ It has not been lacking, ‖ And the perverse do not know shame. **6** "I have cut off nations, ‖ Desolated have been their chief ones, ‖ I have laid waste their out-places without any passing by, ‖ Destroyed have been their cities, ‖ Without man, without inhabitant. **7** I have said: Only, you fear Me, ‖ You accept instruction, ‖ And her habitation is not cut off, ‖ All that I have appointed for her, ‖ But they have risen early, ‖ They have corrupted all their doings. **8** Therefore, wait for Me," ‖ A declaration of Y H W H, ‖ "For the day of My rising for prey, ‖ For My judgment [is] to gather nations, ‖ To assemble kingdoms, ‖ To pour out on them My indignation, ‖ All the heat of My anger, ‖ For by the fire of My jealousy all the earth is consumed. **9** For then I turn a pure lip to peoples, ‖ To call all of them by the Name of Y H W H, ‖ To serve Him [with] one shoulder. **10** From beyond the rivers of Cush, My supplicants, ‖ The daughter of My scattered ones, ‖ Bring My present. **11** In that day you are not ashamed because of any of your actions, ‖ With which you have transgressed against Me, ‖ For then I turn aside from your midst ‖ The exulting ones of your excellence, ‖ And you are to be haughty no longer, ‖ In My holy mountain. **12** And I have left in your midst a people humble and poor, ‖ And they have trusted in the Name of Y H W H. **13** The remnant of Israel does no perversity, nor speaks lies, ‖ Nor is a deceitful tongue found in their mouth, ‖ For they have delight, and have lain down, ‖ And there is none troubling." **14** Cry aloud, O daughter of Zion, shout, O Israel, ‖ Rejoice and exult with the whole heart, O daughter of Jerusalem. **15** Y H W H has turned aside your judgments, ‖ He has faced your enemy, ‖ The King of Israel, Y H W H, [is] in your midst, ‖ You see evil no more. **16** In that day it is said to Jerusalem, ‖ "Do not fear, O Zion, ‖ Do not let your hands be feeble. **17** Your God Y H W H [is] in your midst, ‖ A mighty one [to] save, ‖ He rejoices over you with joy, ‖ He works in His love, ‖ He delights over you with singing." **18** "I have gathered My afflicted from the appointed place, ‖ They have been bearing reproach from you for her sake. **19** Behold, I am dealing with all afflicting you at that time, ‖ And I have saved the halting one, ‖ And I gather the ones driven out, ‖ And have set them for a praise and for a name, ‖ In all the land of their shame. **20** At that time I bring you in, ‖ Even at the time of My assembling you, ‖ For I give you for a name, and for a praise, ‖ Among all peoples of the land, ‖ In My turning back [to] your captivity before your eyes," said Y H W H!

HAGGAI

1 In the second year of Darius the king, in the sixth month, on the first day of the month, a word of YHWH has been by the hand of Haggai the prophet, to Zerubbabel son of Shealtiel, governor of Judah, and to Joshua son of Josedech, the high priest, saying, **2** "Thus spoke YHWH of Hosts, saying, This people—they have said, ‖ The time has not come, ‖ The time the house of YHWH [is] to be built." **3** And there is a word of YHWH by the hand of Haggai the prophet, saying, **4** "Is it time for you to dwell in your covered houses, ‖ And this house to lie waste?" **5** And now, thus said YHWH of Hosts: "Set your heart to your ways. **6** You have sown much, and brought in little, ‖ To eat, and not to satiety, ‖ To drink, and not to drunkenness, ‖ To clothe, and none has heat, ‖ And he who is hiring himself out, ‖ Is hiring himself for a bag pierced through." **7** Thus said YHWH of Hosts: "Set your heart to your ways. **8** Go up the mountain, and you have brought in wood, ‖ And build the house, and I am pleased with it. And I am honored," said YHWH. **9** "Looking for much, and behold, little, ‖ And you brought [it] home, and I blew on it—why?" A declaration of YHWH of Hosts, ‖ "Because of My house that is desolate, ‖ And you are running—each to his house, **10** Therefore, over you the heavens have refrained from dew, ‖ And the land has refrained its increase. **11** And I proclaim drought on the land, ‖ And on the mountains, and on the grain, ‖ And on the new wine, and on the oil, ‖ And on what the ground brings forth, ‖ And on man, and on beast, ‖ And on all labor of the hands." **12** And Zerubbabel son of Shealtiel, and Joshua son of Josedech, the high priest, and all the remnant of the people, listen to the voice of their God YHWH, and to the words of Haggai the prophet, as their God YHWH had sent him, and the people are afraid of the face of YHWH. **13** And Haggai, messenger of YHWH, in messages of YHWH, speaks to the people, saying, "I [am] with you, a declaration of YHWH." **14** And YHWH stirs up the spirit of Zerubbabel son of Shealtiel, governor of Judah, and the spirit of Joshua son of Josedech, the high priest, and the spirit of all the remnant of the people, and they come in, and work in the house of YHWH of Hosts their God, **15** in the twenty-fourth day of the sixth month, in the second year of Darius the king.

2 In the seventh [month], on the twenty-first of the month, a word of YHWH has been by the hand of Haggai the prophet, saying, **2** "Now speak to Zerubbabel son of Shealtiel, governor of Judah, and to Joshua son of Josedech, the high priest, and to the remnant of the people, saying, **3** Who among you has been left that saw this house in its former glory? And what are you seeing it now? Is it not, compared with it, as nothing in your eyes? **4** And now, be strong, O Zerubbabel," ‖ A declaration of YHWH, ‖ "And be strong, O Joshua, son of Josedech, the high priest, ‖ And be strong, all you people of the land," ‖ A declaration of YHWH, ‖ "And do, for I [am] with you," ‖ A declaration of YHWH of Hosts. **5** "The thing that I covenanted with you, ‖ In your coming forth from Egypt, ‖ And My Spirit is remaining in your midst, do not fear." **6** For thus said YHWH of Hosts: "Yet once more—it [is] a little, ‖ And I am shaking the heavens and the earth, ‖ And the sea, and the dry land, **7** And I have shaken all the nations, ‖ And they have come [to] the desire of all the nations, ‖ And I have filled this house [with] glory," said YHWH of Hosts. **8** "The silver [is] Mine, and the gold [is] Mine," ‖ A declaration of YHWH of Hosts. **9** "Greater is the glory of this latter house, ‖ Than of the former," said YHWH of Hosts, ‖ "And I give peace in this place," ‖ A declaration of YHWH of Hosts. **10** On the twenty-fourth of the ninth [month], in the second year of Darius, a word of YHWH has been by the hand of Haggai the prophet, saying, **11** Thus said YHWH of Hosts: "Now ask the priests of the Law, saying, **12** Behold, [when] one carries holy flesh in the skirt of his garment, and he has come with his skirt against the bread, or against the stew, or against the wine, or against the oil, or against any food—is it holy?" And the priests answer and say, "No." **13** And Haggai says, "If the unclean of body comes against any of these, is it unclean?" And the priests answer and say, "It is unclean." **14** And Haggai answers and says, "So [is] this people, and so [is] this nation before Me," a declaration of YHWH, "and so [is] every work of their hands, and that which they bring near there—it is unclean. **15** And now, please lay [it] to your heart, ‖ From this day and onward, ‖ Before the laying of stone to stone in the temple of YHWH. **16** From that time [one] has come to a heap of twenty, ‖ And it has been ten, ‖ He has come to the wine vat to draw out fifty measures, ‖ And it has been twenty. **17** I have struck you with blasting, ‖ And with mildew, and with hail—All the work of your hands, ‖ And there is none of you with Me," ‖ A declaration of YHWH. **18** "Now set [it] to your heart, from this day and onward, from the twenty-fourth day of the ninth [month], even from the day that the temple of YHWH has been founded, set [it] to your heart. **19** Is the seed yet in the barn? And until now the vine and the fig, ‖ And the pomegranate, and the olive-tree, ‖ Have not borne—from this day I bless." **20** And there is a word of YHWH a second time to Haggai, on the twenty-fourth of the month, saying, **21** "Speak to Zerubbabel governor of Judah, saying, I am shaking the heavens and the earth, **22** And have overturned the throne of kingdoms, ‖ And I have destroyed the strength of kingdoms of the nations, ‖ And overturned chariot and its charioteers, ‖ And horses and their riders have come down, ‖ Each by the sword of his brother. **23** In that day," a declaration of YHWH of Hosts, ‖ "I take you, Zerubbabel, son of Shealtiel, My servant," ‖ A declaration of YHWH, ‖ "And have set you as a signet, ‖ For I have fixed on you," ‖ A declaration of YHWH of Hosts!

ZECHARIAH

1 In the eighth month, in the second year of Darius, a word of YHWH has been to Zechariah, son of Berechiah, son of Iddo the prophet, saying, **2** "YHWH was angry against your fathers—wrath! **3** And you have said to them, Thus said YHWH of Hosts: Return to Me, ‖ A declaration of YHWH of Hosts, ‖ And I return to you, said YHWH of Hosts. **4** You will not be as your fathers, ‖ To whom the former prophets called, ‖ Saying, Thus said YHWH of Hosts: Please turn back from your evil ways and from your evil doings, ‖ And they did not listen, ‖ Nor attend to Me—a declaration of YHWH. **5** Your fathers—where [are] they? And the prophets—do they live for all time? **6** Only, My words and My statutes, ‖ That I commanded My servants the prophets, ‖ Have they not overtaken your fathers? And they turn back and say: As YHWH of Hosts designed to do to us, ‖ According to our ways, and according to our doings, ‖ So He has done to us." **7** On the twenty-fourth day of the eleventh month (it [is] the month of Sebat), in the second year of Darius, a word of YHWH has been to Zechariah, son of Berechiah, son of Iddo the prophet. [He was] saying: **8** I have seen by night, and behold, one riding on a red horse, and he is standing between the myrtles that [are] in the shade, and behind him [are] horses, red, bay, and white. **9** And I say, "What [are] these, my lord?" And the messenger who is speaking with me says to me, "I show you what these [are]." **10** And the one who is standing between the myrtles answers and says, "These [are] they whom YHWH has sent to walk up and down in the land." **11** And they answer the Messenger of YHWH who is standing between the myrtles, and say, "We have walked up and down in the land, and behold, all the land is sitting still, and at rest." **12** And the Messenger of YHWH answers and says, "YHWH of Hosts! Until when do You not pity Jerusalem, and the cities of Judah, that You have abhorred these seventy years?" **13** And YHWH answers the messenger, who is speaking with me, good words, comfortable words. **14** And the messenger who is speaking with me, says to me, "Call, saying, Thus said YHWH of Hosts: I have been zealous for Jerusalem, ‖ And for Zion [with] great zeal. **15** And [with] great wrath I am angry against the nations who are at ease, ‖ For I was a little angry, and they assisted—for evil. **16** Therefore, thus said YHWH: I have turned to Jerusalem with mercies, ‖ My house is built in it, ‖ A declaration of YHWH of Hosts, ‖ And a line is stretched over Jerusalem. **17** Again call, saying, ‖ Thus said YHWH of Hosts: Again My cities overflow from good, ‖ And YHWH has again comforted Zion, ‖ And He has fixed again on Jerusalem." **18** And I lift up my eyes, and look, and behold, four horns. **19** And I say to the messenger who is speaking with me, "What [are] these?" And he says to me, "These [are] the horns that have scattered Judah, Israel, and Jerusalem." **20** And YHWH shows me four artisans. **21** And I say, "What [are] these coming to do?" And He speaks, saying, "These [are] the horns that have scattered Judah, so that no one has lifted up his head, and these come to trouble them, to cast down the horns of the nations who are lifting up a horn against the land of Judah—to scatter it."

2 And I lift up my eyes, and look, and behold, a man, and in his hand a measuring line. **2** And I say, "To where are you going?" And he says to me, "To measure Jerusalem, to see how much [is] its breadth and how much its length." **3** And behold, the messenger who is speaking with me is going out, and another messenger is going out to meet him, **4** and he says to him, "Run, speak to this young man, saying, ‖ Jerusalem is inhabited [as] open places, ‖ From the abundance of man and beast in her midst. **5** And I am to her— a declaration of YHWH—A wall of fire all around, ‖ And I am for glory in her midst. **6** Behold, and flee from the land of the north, ‖ A declaration of YHWH, ‖ For as the four winds of the heavens, ‖ I have spread you abroad, ‖ A declaration of YHWH. **7** Behold, Zion, be delivered who are dwelling [with] the daughter of Babylon. **8** For thus said YHWH of Hosts: He has sent Me after glory to the nations who are spoiling you, ‖ For he who is coming against you, ‖ Is coming against the pupil of

ZECHARIAH

His eye. **9** For behold, I am waving My hand against them, ‖ And they have been a spoil to their servants. And you have known that YHWH of Hosts has sent Me. **10** Sing, and rejoice, O daughter of Zion, ‖ For behold, I am coming, and have dwelt in your midst, ‖ A declaration of YHWH. **11** And many nations have been joined to YHWH in that day, ‖ And they have been to Me for a people, ‖ And I have dwelt in your midst, ‖ And you have known that YHWH of Hosts has sent Me to you. **12** And YHWH has inherited Judah, ‖ His portion on the holy ground, ‖ And He has fixed again on Jerusalem. **13** Hush, all flesh, because of YHWH, ‖ For He has been roused up from His holy habitation!"

3 And he shows me Joshua the high priest standing before the Messenger of YHWH, and Satan standing at his right hand, to be an adversary to him. **2** And YHWH says to Satan: "YHWH pushes against you, O Satan; ‖ Indeed, YHWH pushes against you, ‖ Who is fixing on Jerusalem, ‖ Is this not a brand delivered from fire?" **3** And Joshua was clothed with filthy garments, and is standing before the Messenger. **4** And He answers and speaks to those standing before Him, saying, "Turn aside the filthy garments from off him." And He says to him, "See, I have caused your iniquity to pass away from off you, so as to clothe you with costly apparel." **5** He also said, "Let them set a pure turban on his head." And they set the pure turban on his head, and clothe him with garments. And the Messenger of YHWH is standing, **6** and the Messenger of YHWH protests to Joshua, saying, **7** "Thus said YHWH of Hosts: If you walk in My ways, ‖ And if you keep My charge, ‖ Then also you judge My house, ‖ And also you keep My courts, ‖ And I have given to you conductors among these standing by. **8** Now hear, O Joshua the high priest, ‖ You and your companions sitting before you ‖ (For men of type [are] they), ‖ For behold, I am bringing in My servant—a Shoot. **9** For behold, the stone that I put before Joshua, ‖ On one stone [are] seven eyes, ‖ Behold, I am engraving its engraving, ‖ A declaration of YHWH of Hosts, ‖ And I have removed the iniquity of that land in one day. **10** In that day—a declaration of YHWH of Hosts, ‖ You call, each to his neighbor, ‖ To the place of the vine, ‖ And to the place of the fig tree!"

4 And the messenger who is speaking with me turns back, and stirs me up as one who is stirred up out of his sleep, **2** and he says to me, "What are you seeing?" And I say, "I have looked, and behold, a lampstand of gold—all of it, and its bowl [is] on its top, and its seven lamps [are] on it, and twice seven pipes [are] to the lights that [are] on its top, **3** and two olive-trees [are] by it, one on the right of the bowl and one on its left." **4** And I answer and speak to the messenger who is speaking with me, saying, "What [are] these, my lord?" **5** And the messenger who is speaking with me answers and says to me, "Have you not known what these [are]?" And I say, "No, my lord." **6** And he answers and speaks to me, saying, "This [is] a word of YHWH to Zerubbabel, saying, ‖ Not by a force, nor by power, ‖ But—by My Spirit, said YHWH of Hosts. **7** Who [are] you, O great mountain ‖ Before Zerubbabel—for a plain! And he has brought forth the top-stone, ‖ Cries of Grace, grace—[are] to it." **8** And there is a word of YHWH to me, saying, **9** "Hands of Zerubbabel founded this house, ‖ And his hands finish it, ‖ And you have known that YHWH of Hosts ‖ Has sent Me to you. **10** For who trampled on the day of small things, ‖ They have rejoiced, ‖ And seen the tin weight in the hand of Zerubbabel, ‖ These seven [are] the eyes of YHWH, ‖ They are going to and fro in all the land." **11** And I answer and say to him, "What [are] these two olive-trees, on the right of the lampstand, and on its left?" **12** And I answer a second time, and say to him, "What [are] the two branches of the olive trees that, by means of the two golden pipes, are emptying out of themselves the oil?" **13** And he speaks to me, saying, "Have you not known what these [are]?" And I say, "No, my lord." **14** And he says, "These [are] the two sons of the oil, who are standing by the Lord of the whole earth."

5 And I turn back, and lift up my eyes, and look, and behold, a flying scroll. **2** And he says to me, "What are you seeing?" And I say, "I am seeing a flying scroll, its length [is] twenty by the cubit, and its breadth [is] ten by the cubit." **3** And he says to me, "This [is] the execration that is going forth over the face of all the land, for everyone

ZECHARIAH

who is stealing, on the one side, according to it, has been declared innocent, and everyone who has sworn, on the other side, according to it, has been declared innocent." **4** "I have brought it out," a declaration of YHWH of Hosts, "and it has come into the house of the thief, and into the house of him who has sworn in My Name with a falsehood, and it has remained in the midst of his house, and has consumed it, both its wood and its stones."

5 And the messenger who is speaking with me goes forth and says to me, "Now lift up your eyes, and [do you] see what this [is] that is coming forth?" **6** And I say, "What [is] it?" And he says, "This—the ephah that is coming forth." And he says, "This [is] their aspect in all the land. **7** And behold, a disc of lead lifted up; and this [is] a woman sitting in the midst of the ephah." **8** And he says, "This [is] the wicked woman." And he casts her into the midst of the ephah, and casts the weight of lead on its mouth. **9** And I lift up my eyes, and see, and behold, two women are coming forth, and wind [is] in their wings; and they have wings like wings of the stork, and they lift up the ephah between the earth and the heavens. **10** And I say to the messenger who is speaking with me, "To where [are] they causing the ephah to go?" **11** And he says to me, "To build a house for it in the land of Shinar." And it has been prepared and has been placed there on its base.

6 And I turn back, and lift up my eyes, and look, and behold, four chariots are coming forth from between two of the mountains, and the mountains [are] mountains of bronze. **2** In the first chariot [are] red horses, and in the second chariot brown horses, **3** and in the third chariot white horses, and in the fourth chariot strong spotted horses. **4** And I answer and say to the messenger who is speaking with me, "What [are] these, my lord?" **5** And the messenger answers and says to me, "These [are] four spirits of the heavens coming forth from presenting themselves before the Lord of the whole earth. **6** The brown horses that [are] therein, are coming forth to the land of the north; and the white have come forth to their back part; and the spotted have come forth to the land of the south; **7** and the strong ones have come forth, and they seek to go to walk up and down in the earth"; and he says, "Go, walk up and down in the earth"; and they walk up and down in the earth. **8** And he calls me, and speaks to me, saying, "See, those coming forth to the land of the north have caused My Spirit to rest in the land of the north." **9** And there is a word of YHWH to me, saying, **10** "Take of the captivity (who came from Babylon) from Heldai, from Tobijah, and from Jedaiah, and you have come in—you, in that day, indeed, you have come into the house of Josiah son of Zephaniah, **11** and you have taken silver and gold, and have made a crown, and have placed [it] on the head of Joshua son of Josedech, the high priest, **12** and have spoken to him, saying, ‖ Thus spoke YHWH of Hosts, saying, ‖ Behold, the Man! A Shoot—[is] His Name, ‖ And from His place He shoots up, ‖ And He has built the temple of YHWH. **13** Indeed, He builds the temple of YHWH, ‖ And He carries away splendor, ‖ And He has sat and ruled on His throne, ‖ And has been a priest on His throne, ‖ And a counsel of peace is between both. **14** And the crown is to Helem, and to Tobijah, and to Jedaiah, and to Hen son of Zephaniah, for a memorial in the temple of YHWH. **15** And the far-off come in, and they have built in the temple of YHWH, and you have known that YHWH of Hosts has sent me to you, indeed, it has come to pass, if you certainly listen to the voice of your God YHWH."

7 And it comes to pass, in the fourth year of Darius the king, a word of YHWH has been to Zechariah, in the fourth of the ninth month, in Chisleu. **2** And Beth-El sends Sherezer and Regem-Melech, and its men, to appease the face of YHWH, **3** speaking to the priests who [are] at the house of YHWH of Hosts, and to the prophets, saying, "Do I weep in the fifth month—being separated—as I have done these so many years?" **4** And there is a word of YHWH of Hosts to me, saying, **5** "Speak to all the people of the land, and to the priests, saying, **6** When you fasted with mourning in the fifth and in the seventh [months]— even these seventy years—did you keep the fast [to] Me? And when you eat, and when you drink, is it not you who are eating, and you who are drinking? **7** Are [these] not the words that YHWH proclaimed by the hand of the former prophets, in Jerusalem's being inhabited, and [in] safety, and its cities around it, and

ZECHARIAH

the south and the plain—abiding?" **8** And there is a word of YHWH to Zechariah, saying, **9** "Thus spoke YHWH of Hosts, saying, ‖ Judge [with] true judgment, ‖ And do kindness and mercy with one another. **10** And do not oppress widow, and fatherless, ‖ Sojourner, and poor, ‖ And you do not devise the calamity of one another in your heart. **11** And they refuse to attend, ‖ And they give a stubborn shoulder, ‖ And their ears are made heavy against hearing. **12** And their heart they have made adamant, ‖ Against hearing the Law, and the words, ‖ That YHWH of Hosts sent by His Spirit, ‖ By the hand of the former prophets, ‖ And there is great wrath from YHWH of Hosts. **13** And it comes to pass, as He called, ‖ And they have not listened, ‖ So they call, and I do not listen," said YHWH of Hosts. **14** "And I toss them on all the nations, ‖ That they have not known, ‖ The land has been desolate behind them, ‖ Of any passing by and turning back, ‖ And they set a desirable land for a desolation!"

8 And there is a word of YHWH of Hosts, saying, **2** "Thus said YHWH of Hosts: I have been zealous for Zion with great zeal, ‖ With great heat I have been zealous for her. **3** Thus said YHWH: I have turned back to Zion, ‖ And I have dwelt in the midst of Jerusalem, ‖ And Jerusalem has been called The City of Truth, ‖ And The Mountain of YHWH of Hosts, ‖ The Holy Mountain. **4** Thus said YHWH of Hosts: Again old men and old women dwell ‖ In broad places of Jerusalem, ‖ And each his staff in his hand, ‖ Because of abundance of days. **5** And broad places of the city are full of boys and girls, ‖ Playing in its broad places. **6** Thus said YHWH of Hosts: Surely it is wonderful in the eyes of the remnant of this people in those days, ‖ Also in My eyes it is wonderful, ‖ A declaration of YHWH of Hosts. **7** Thus said YHWH of Hosts: Behold, I am saving My people from the land of the rising, ‖ And from the land of the going in, of the sun, **8** And I have brought them in, ‖ They have dwelt in the midst of Jerusalem, ‖ And they have been to Me for a people, ‖ And I am to them for God, ‖ In truth and in righteousness. **9** Thus said YHWH of Hosts: Let your hands be strong, ‖ You who are hearing in these days these words from the mouth of the prophets, ‖ That in the day the house of YHWH of Hosts has been founded, ‖ The temple [is] to be built. **10** For before those days there has been no hiring of man, ‖ Indeed, a hiring of beasts there is none; And to him who is going out, ‖ And to him who is coming in, ‖ There is no peace because of the adversary, ‖ And I send all men—each against his neighbor. **11** And now, not as [in] the former days [am] I to the remnant of this people, ‖ A declaration of YHWH of Hosts. **12** Because of the sowing of peace, ‖ The vine gives her fruit, ‖ And the earth gives her increase, ‖ And the heavens give their dew, ‖ And I have caused the remnant of this people ‖ To inherit all these. **13** And it has come to pass, ‖ As you have been a reviling among nations, ‖ O house of Judah, and house of Israel, ‖ So I save you, and you have been a blessing, ‖ Do not fear, let your hands be strong. **14** For thus said YHWH of Hosts: As I purposed to do evil to you, ‖ When your fathers made Me angry—said YHWH of Hosts—And I did not relent, **15** So I have turned back, I have purposed, in these days, ‖ To do good with Jerusalem, ‖ And with the house of Judah—do not fear! **16** These [are] the things that you do: Each speak truth with his neighbor, ‖ Judge [with] truth and peaceful judgment in your gates, **17** And do not devise the evil of his neighbor in your heart, ‖ And do not love a false oath, ‖ For all these [are] things that I have hated, ‖ A declaration of YHWH." **18** And there is a word of YHWH of Hosts to me, saying, **19** "Thus said YHWH of Hosts: The fast of the fourth, and the fast of the fifth, and the fast of the seventh, and the fast of the tenth [months], are to the house of Judah for joy and for rejoicing, and for pleasant appointed times, and the truth and the peace they have loved. **20** Thus said YHWH of Hosts: Yet peoples come, and inhabitants of many cities, **21** Indeed, inhabitants of one ‖ Have gone to another, saying, ‖ We go diligently, ‖ To appease the face of YHWH, ‖ To seek YHWH of Hosts—I go, even I. **22** Indeed, many peoples have come in, and mighty nations, ‖ To seek YHWH of Hosts in Jerusalem, ‖ And to appease the face of YHWH. **23** Thus said YHWH of Hosts: In those days ten men of all languages of the nations take hold, ‖ Indeed, they have taken hold on the skirt of a man, a Jew, saying, ‖ We go with you, for we heard God [is] with you!"

9 The burden of a word of YHWH against the land of Hadrach, and Demmeseh—

ZECHARIAH

his place of rest: (When to YHWH [is] the eye of man, ‖ And of all the tribes of Israel). **2** And also Hamath borders thereon, ‖ Tyre and Sidon, for—very wise! **3** And Tyre builds a bulwark for herself, ‖ And heaps silver as dust, ‖ And gold as mire of outplaces. **4** Behold, the Lord dispossesses her, ‖ And He has struck her force in the sea, ‖ And she is consumed with fire. **5** Ashkelon sees and fears, ‖ Also Gaza, and she is exceedingly pained, ‖ Also Ekron— for her expectation dried up, ‖ And a king has perished from Gaza, ‖ And Ashkelon does not remain, **6** "And a foreigner has dwelt in Ashdod, ‖ And I have cut off the excellence of the Philistines. **7** And turned aside his blood from his mouth, ‖ His abominations from between his teeth, ‖ And he has remained, even he, to our God, ‖ And he has been as a leader in Judah, ‖ And Ekron as a Jebusite. **8** And I have pitched a camp for My house, ‖ Because of the passer through, and of the returner, ‖ And an exactor does not pass through against them again, ‖ For now, I have seen with My eyes. **9** Rejoice exceedingly, O daughter of Zion, ‖ Shout, O daughter of Jerusalem, ‖ Behold, your King comes to you, ‖ Righteous and having salvation, ‖ Afflicted—and riding on a donkey, ‖ And on a colt—a son of female donkeys. **10** And I have cut off the chariot from Ephraim, ‖ And the horse from Jerusalem, ‖ Indeed, the bow of battle has been cut off, ‖ And He has spoken peace to nations, ‖ And His rule [is] from sea to sea, ‖ And from the river to the ends of the earth. **11** Also You—by the blood of Your covenant, ‖ I have sent Your prisoners out of the pit, ‖ There is no water in it. **12** Return to a stronghold, ‖ You prisoners of the hope, ‖ Even today a second announcer I restore to you. **13** For I have trodden for Myself with Judah, ‖ I have filled a bow [with] Ephraim, ‖ And I have stirred up your sons, O Zion, ‖ Against your sons, O Javan, ‖ And I have set you as the sword of a hero." **14** And YHWH appears for them, ‖ And His arrow has gone forth as lightning, ‖ And Lord YHWH blows with a horn, ‖ And He has gone with whirlwinds of the south. **15** YHWH of Hosts covers them over, ‖ And they consumed, and subdued sling-stones, ‖ Indeed, they have drunk, ‖ They have made a noise as wine, ‖ And they have been full as a bowl, ‖ As corners of an altar. **16** And their God YHWH has saved them in that day, ‖ As a flock of His people, ‖ For stones of a crown are displaying themselves over His ground. **17** For what His goodness! And what His beauty! Grain the young men, ‖ And new wine the virgins—make fruitful!

10 They asked of YHWH rain ‖ In a time of spring rain, ‖ YHWH is making lightnings, ‖ And He gives to them rain [in] showers. To each—the herb in the field. **2** Because the teraphim spoke iniquity, ‖ And the diviners have seen a falsehood, ‖ And dreams of the vanity they speak, ‖ [With] vanity they give comfort, ‖ Therefore they have journeyed as a flock, ‖ They are afflicted, for there is no shepherd. **3** "My anger burned against the shepherds, ‖ And I lay a charge against the male goats, ‖ For YHWH of Hosts has inspected His flock, the house of Judah, ‖ And set them as His splendid horse in battle. **4** From him [is] a cornerstone, ‖ From him a nail, from him a battle-bow, ‖ From him goes forth every exactor together. **5** And they have been as heroes, ‖ Treading in mire of out-places in battle, ‖ And they have fought, for YHWH [is] with them, ‖ And have put to shame riders of horses. **6** And I have made the house of Judah mighty, ‖ And I save the house of Joseph, ‖ And I have caused them to dwell, for I have loved them, ‖ And they have been as [if] I had not cast them off, ‖ For I [am] their God YHWH, ‖ And I answer them. **7** And Ephraim has been as a hero, ‖ And their heart has rejoiced as wine, ‖ And their sons see, and they have rejoiced, ‖ Their heart rejoices in YHWH. **8** I hiss for them, and I gather them, ‖ For I have redeemed them, ‖ And they have multiplied as they multiplied. **9** And I sow them among peoples, ‖ And in far-off places they remember Me, ‖ And they have lived with their sons, ‖ And they have turned back. **10** And I have brought them back from the land of Egypt, ‖ And I gather them from Asshur, ‖ And I bring them into the land of Gilead and Lebanon, ‖ And [space] is not found for them there. **11** And He has passed over through the sea, ‖ And has pressed and struck billows in the sea, ‖ And all depths of a flood have been dried up, ‖ And the excellence of Asshur has been brought down, ‖ And the rod of Egypt turns aside. **12** And I have made them mighty in YHWH, ‖ And in His Name they walk up and down," ‖ A declaration of YHWH!

ZECHARIAH

11 Open, O Lebanon, your doors, ‖ And fire devours among your cedars. **2** Howl, O fir, for the cedar has fallen, ‖ For their majestic ones were destroyed, ‖ Howl, you oaks of Bashan, ‖ For the enclosed forest has come down, **3** A voice of the howling of the shepherds! For their robe of honor was destroyed, ‖ A voice of the roaring of young lions! For the excellence of Jordan was destroyed. **4** Thus said my God YHWH: "Feed the flock of the slaughter, **5** Whose buyers slay them, and are not guilty, ‖ And their sellers say, Blessed [is] YHWH, ‖ And I am rich, ‖ And their shepherds have no pity on them. **6** For I no longer have pity on inhabitants of the land, ‖ A declaration of YHWH, ‖ And behold, I am causing man to come forth, ‖ Each into the hand of his neighbor, ‖ And into the hand of his king, ‖ And they have beaten down the land, ‖ And I do not deliver out of their hand." **7** And I feed the flock of slaughter, even you, you afflicted of the flock; and I take two staffs to myself; I have called one Pleasantness, and I have called the other Bands, and I feed the flock. **8** And I cut off the three shepherds in one month, and my soul is grieved with them, and also their soul has abhorred me. **9** And I say, "I do not feed you, the dying, let die; and the cut off, let be cut off; and the remaining ones, let each eat the flesh of its neighbor." **10** And I take my staff Pleasantness, and cut it apart, to make void my covenant that I had made with all the peoples: **11** and it is broken in that day, and the afflicted of the flock who are observing me know well, that it [is] a word of YHWH. **12** And I say to them: "If good in your eyes, give my hire, and if not, refrain"; and they weigh out my hire—thirty pieces of silver. **13** And YHWH says to me, "Cast it to the potter"; the good price that I have been prized at by them, and I take the thirty pieces of silver, and cast them [into] the house of YHWH, to the potter. **14** And I cut apart my second staff, Bands, ‖ To break the unity between Judah and Israel. **15** And YHWH says to me, "Again take to yourself the instrument of a foolish shepherd. **16** For behold, I am raising up a shepherd in the land, ‖ The cut off he does not inspect, ‖ The shaken off he does not seek, ‖ And the broken he does not heal, ‖ The standing he does not sustain, ‖ And the flesh of the fat he eats, ‖ And their hooves he breaks off. **17** Woe [to] the worthless shepherd, forsaking the flock, ‖ A sword [is] on his arm, and on his right eye, ‖ His arm is utterly dried up, ‖ And his right eye is very dim!"

12 The burden of a word of YHWH on Israel. A declaration of YHWH, ‖ Stretching out the heavens, and founding earth, ‖ And forming the spirit of man in his midst: **2** "Behold, I am making Jerusalem a cup of reeling ‖ To all the surrounding peoples, ‖ And it is also against Judah, ‖ In the siege against Jerusalem. **3** And it has come to pass in that day, ‖ I make Jerusalem a burdensome stone to all the peoples, ‖ All loading it are completely pressed down, ‖ And gathered against it have been all nations of the earth. **4** In that day," a declaration of YHWH, ‖ "I strike every horse with astonishment, ‖ And its rider with madness, ‖ And on the house of Judah I open My eyes, ‖ And every horse of the peoples I strike with blindness, **5** And leaders of Judah have said in their heart, ‖ The inhabitants of Jerusalem [are] strength to me, ‖ In YHWH of Hosts their God. **6** In that day I make the leaders of Judah ‖ As a hearth of fire among trees, ‖ And as a torch of fire in a sheaf, ‖ And they have consumed—on the right and on the left— all the surrounding peoples, ‖ And Jerusalem has again inhabited her place in Jerusalem. **7** And YHWH has saved the tents of Judah first, ‖ So that the beauty of the house of David does not become great against Judah, ‖ And the beauty of the inhabitant of Jerusalem. **8** In that day YHWH covers over the inhabitant of Jerusalem, ‖ And the stumbling among them has been in that day as David, ‖ And the house of David as God—As the Messenger of YHWH—before them. **9** And it has come to pass in that day, ‖ I seek to destroy all the nations ‖ Who are coming in against Jerusalem, **10** And I have poured on the house of David, ‖ And on the inhabitant of Jerusalem, ‖ The Spirit of grace and supplications, ‖ And they have looked to Me whom they pierced, ‖ And they have mourned over Him, ‖ Like a mourning over the only one, ‖ And they have been in bitterness for Him, ‖ Like a bitterness over the firstborn. **11** In that day, great is the mourning of Jerusalem, ‖ As the mourning of Hadadrimmon in the Valley of Megiddon, **12** And the land has mourned— every family apart, ‖ The family of the

ZECHARIAH

house of David apart, ‖ And their women apart; The family of the house of Nathan apart, ‖ And their women apart; **13** The family of the house of Levi apart, ‖ And their women apart; The family of Shimei apart, ‖ And their women apart, **14** All the families that are left, ‖ Every family apart, and their women apart!"

13 "In that day there is a fountain opened ‖ To the house of David ‖ And to the inhabitants of Jerusalem, ‖ For sin and for impurity. **2** And it has come to pass in that day," ‖ A declaration of YHWH of Hosts, ‖ "I cut off the names of the idols from the land, ‖ And they are not remembered anymore, ‖ And also the prophets and the spirit of uncleanness ‖ I cause to pass away from the land. **3** And it has been, when one prophesies again, ‖ That his parents, his father and his mother, ‖ Have said to him, You do not live, ‖ For you have spoken falsehood in the Name of YHWH, ‖ And his father and his mother, his parents, ‖ Have pierced him through in his prophesying. **4** And it has come to pass in that day, ‖ The prophets are ashamed, each of his vision, in his prophesying, ‖ And they do not put on a hairy robe to deceive. **5** And [one] has said, I am not a prophet, ‖ A man—I am a tiller of ground, ‖ For ground [is] my possession from my youth. **6** And [one] has said to him, ‖ What [are] these wounds in your hands? And he has said, Because I was struck [at] home by my lovers. **7** Sword, awake against My Shepherd, ‖ And against a hero—My Fellow," ‖ A declaration of YHWH of Hosts. "Strike the Shepherd, and the flock is scattered, ‖ And I have put back My hand on the little ones. **8** And it has come to pass, ‖ In all the land," a declaration of YHWH, ‖ "Two parts in it are cut off—they expire, ‖ And the third is left in it. **9** And I have brought the third into fire, ‖ And refined them like a refining of silver, ‖ And have tried them like a trying of gold, ‖ It calls in My Name, and I answer it, ‖ I have said, It [is] My people, ‖ And it says, YHWH [is] my God!"

14 Behold, a day has come to YHWH, ‖ And your spoil has been divided in your midst. **2** And I have gathered all the nations to Jerusalem to battle, ‖ And the city has been captured, ‖ And the houses have been spoiled, ‖ And the women are lain with, ‖ Half the city has gone forth in a removal, ‖ And the remnant of the people are not cut off from the city. **3** And YHWH has gone forth, ‖ And He has fought against those nations, ‖ As in the day of His fighting in a day of conflict. **4** And His feet have stood, in that day, ‖ On the Mount of Olives, ‖ That [is] eastward before Jerusalem, ‖ And the Mount of Olives has been cleft at its midst, ‖ To the east, and to the west, a very great valley, ‖ And half of the mountain is removed toward the north, ‖ And half toward the south. **5** And you have fled [to] the valley of My mountains, ‖ For the valley of the mountains joins to Azal, ‖ And you have fled as you fled before the shaking, ‖ In the days of Uzziah king of Judah, ‖ And my God YHWH has come in, ‖ All holy ones [are] with You. **6** And it has come to pass in that day, ‖ The precious light is not, it is dense darkness, **7** And there has been one day, ‖ It is known to YHWH, not day nor night, ‖ And it has been at evening-time—there is light. **8** And it has come to pass in that day, ‖ Living waters go forth from Jerusalem, ‖ Half of them to the Eastern Sea, ‖ And half of them to the Western Sea, ‖ It is in summer and in winter. **9** And YHWH has become King over all the earth, ‖ In that day YHWH is one, and His Name one. **10** All the land is changed as a plain, ‖ From Geba to Rimmon, south of Jerusalem, ‖ And she has been high, and has dwelt in her place, ‖ Even from the Gate of Benjamin ‖ To the place of the first gate, to the front gate, ‖ And from the Tower of Hananeel, ‖ To the wine-vats of the king. **11** And they have dwelt in her, ‖ And destruction is no more, ‖ And Jerusalem has dwelt confidently. **12** And this is the plague with which YHWH plagues all the peoples who have warred against Jerusalem: He has consumed away its flesh, ‖ And it is standing on its feet, ‖ And its eyes are consumed in their holes, ‖ And its tongue is consumed in their mouth. **13** And it has come to pass in that day, ‖ A great destruction [from] YHWH is among them, ‖ And they have each seized the hand of his neighbor, ‖ And his hand has gone up against the hand of his neighbor. **14** And also Judah is fought with in Jerusalem, ‖ And the force of all the surrounding nations has been gathered, ‖ Gold, and silver, and apparel, in great abundance. **15** And so is the plague of the horse, of the mule, ‖ Of the camel, and of the donkey, ‖ And of all the

ZECHARIAH

livestock that are in these camps, ‖ As this plague. **16** And it has come to pass, ‖ Everyone who has been left of all the nations, ‖ Who are coming in against Jerusalem, ‖ They have also gone up from year to year, ‖ To bow themselves to the King, YHWH of Hosts, ‖ And to celebrate the Celebration of the Shelters. **17** And it has come to pass, ‖ That he who does not go up of the families of the land to Jerusalem, ‖ To bow himself to the King, YHWH of Hosts, ‖ Even on them there is no shower. **18** And if the family of Egypt does not go up, nor come in, ‖ Then on them is the plague ‖ With which YHWH plagues the nations ‖ That do not go up to celebrate the Celebration of Shelters. **19** This is the punishment of the sin of Egypt, ‖ And the punishment of the sin of all the nations, ‖ That do not go up to celebrate the Celebration of Shelters. **20** In that day "Holy to YHWH" is [engraved] on bells of the horse, ‖ And the pots in the house of YHWH ‖ Have been as bowls before the altar. **21** And every pot in Jerusalem and in Judah, ‖ Have been holy to YHWH of Hosts, ‖ And all those sacrificing have come in, ‖ And have taken of them, and boiled in them, ‖ And in that day there is no merchant anymore in the house of YHWH of Hosts!

MALACHI

1 The burden of a word of YHWH to Israel by the hand of Malachi: **2** "I have loved you, said YHWH, ‖ And you have said, ‖ In what have You loved us? **3** Is not Esau Jacob's brother?" A declaration of YHWH, ‖ "And I love Jacob, and Esau I have hated, ‖ And I make his mountains a desolation, ‖ And his inheritance for dragons of a wilderness. **4** Because Edom says, We have been made poor, ‖ And we return and we build the ruins, ‖ Thus said YHWH of Hosts: They build, and I destroy, ‖ And [men] have called to them, ‖ O region of wickedness, ‖ O people whom YHWH defied for all time. **5** And your eyes see, and you say, ‖ YHWH is magnified beyond the border of Israel, **6** A son honors a father, and a servant his master. And if I [am] a father, where [is] My glory? And if I [am] a master, where [is] My fear? Said YHWH of Hosts to you, ‖ O priests, despising My Name! And you have said, In what have we despised Your Name? **7** You are bringing defiled bread near on My altar, ‖ And you have said, In what have we defiled You? In your saying, The table of YHWH—it [is] despicable, **8** And when you bring the blind near for sacrifice, [saying], ‖ There is no evil, ‖ And when you bring the lame and sick near, [saying], ‖ There is no evil; Now bring it near to your governor—Does he accept you? Or does he lift up your face?" said YHWH of Hosts. **9** "And now, please appease the face of God, ‖ And He favors us; This has been from your own hand, ‖ Does He accept your faces?" said YHWH of Hosts. **10** "Who [is] even among you, ‖ And he shuts the double doors? Indeed, you do not kindle My altar for nothing, ‖ I have no pleasure in you," said YHWH of Hosts, ‖ "And I do not accept a present of your hand. **11** For from the rising of the sun to its going in, ‖ Great [is] My Name among nations, ‖ And in every place incense is brought near for My Name, and a pure present, ‖ For great [is] My Name among nations," said YHWH of Hosts. **12** "And you are defiling it in your saying, ‖ The table of YHWH—it is defiled, ‖ As for its fruit—its food is despicable. **13** And you have said, Behold, what a weariness, ‖ And you have puffed at it," said YHWH of Hosts, ‖ "And you have brought in plunder, ‖ And the lame and the sick, ‖ And you have brought in the present! Do I accept it from your hand?" said YHWH. **14** "And a deceiver [is] cursed, who has in his drove a male, ‖ And is vowing, and is sacrificing a marred thing to the Lord, ‖ For I [am] a great King," said YHWH of Hosts, ‖ "And My Name [is] revered among nations!"

2 "And now, to you [is] this charge, O priests, **2** If you do not listen, and if you do not lay [it] to heart, ‖ To give glory to My Name," said YHWH of Hosts, ‖ "I have sent the curse against you, ‖ And I have cursed your blessings, ‖ Indeed, I have also cursed it, ‖ Because you are not laying [it] to heart. **3** Behold, I am pushing away the seed before you, ‖ And have scattered dung before your faces, ‖ Dung of your festivals, ‖ And it has taken you away with it. **4** And you have known that I have sent this charge to you, ‖ For My covenant being with Levi," said YHWH of Hosts. **5** "My covenant has been of life and of peace with him, ‖ And I make them a fear to him, and he fears Me, ‖ And because of My Name he has been frightened. **6** The law of truth has been in his mouth, ‖ And perverseness has not been found in his lips, ‖ In peace and in uprightness he walked with Me, ‖ And he brought back many from iniquity. **7** For the lips of a priest preserve knowledge, ‖ And they seek law from his mouth, ‖ For he [is] a messenger of YHWH of Hosts. **8** And you, you have turned from the way, ‖ You have caused many to stumble in the Law, ‖ You have corrupted the covenant of Levi," said YHWH of Hosts. **9** "And I also, I have made you despised and low before all the people, ‖ Because you are not keeping My ways, ‖ And are accepting by superficial things in the Law." **10** Have we not all one Father? Has not our God created us? Why do we deal treacherously, ‖ Each against his brother, ‖ To defile the covenant of our fathers? **11** Judah has dealt treacherously, ‖ And abomination has been done in Israel and in Jerusalem, ‖ For Judah has defiled the holy thing of YHWH that He has loved, ‖ And has married the daughter of a strange god. **12** YHWH cuts off the man who does it, ‖ Tempter and tempted—from the tents of Jacob, ‖ Even he who is bringing a present near to YHWH of Hosts. **13** And you do this a second time, ‖ Covering the altar of YHWH with tears, ‖ With weeping and groaning, ‖ Because there is no more turning to the present, ‖ Or receiving of a pleasing thing from your hand. **14** And you have said, "Why?" Because YHWH has testified between you ‖ And the wife of your youth, ‖ That you have dealt treacherously against her, ‖ And she [is] your companion, and your covenant-wife. **15** And He did not make one [only], ‖ And a remnant of the Spirit [is] for him. And what [is] the one [alone]! He is seeking a godly seed. And you have been watchful over your spirit, ‖ And with the wife of your youth, ‖ None deal treacherously. **16** "For He hates sending away," said YHWH, God of Israel, ‖ "And he [who] has covered violence with his clothing," said YHWH of Hosts, ‖ "And you have been watchful over your spirit, ‖ And you do not deal treacherously." **17** You have wearied YHWH with your words, ‖ And you have said, "In what have we wearied Him?" In your saying, "Every evildoer [is] good in the eyes of YHWH, ‖ And He is delighting in them," ‖ Or, "Where [is] the God of judgment?"

3 "Behold, I am sending My messenger, ‖ And he has prepared a way before Me, ‖ And suddenly the Lord whom you are seeking comes into His temple, ‖ Even the Messenger of the Covenant, ‖ Whom you are desiring, ‖ Behold, He is coming," said YHWH of Hosts. **2** "And who is bearing the day of His coming? And who is standing in His appearing? For He [is] as fire of a refiner, ‖ And as soap of a fuller. **3** And He has sat, a refiner and purifier of silver, ‖ And He has purified the sons of Levi, ‖ And has refined them as gold and as silver, ‖ And they have been bringing a present near to YHWH in righteousness. **4** And the present of Judah and Jerusalem has been sweet to YHWH, ‖ As in days of old, and as in former years. **5** And I have drawn near to you for judgment, ‖ And I have been a witness, ‖ Making haste against sorcerers, and against adulterers, ‖ And against swearers to a falsehood, ‖ And against oppressors of the hire of a hired worker, ‖ Of a widow, and of a fatherless one, ‖ And those turning aside a sojourner, ‖ And who do not fear Me," said YHWH of Hosts. **6** "For I, YHWH, have not changed, ‖ And you, the sons of Jacob, ‖ You have not been consumed. **7** Even from the days of your fathers You have turned aside from My statutes, ‖ And you have not taken heed. Return to Me, and I return to you," said YHWH of Hosts. "And you have said, ‖ In what do we turn back? **8** Does man deceive God? But you are deceiving Me, ‖ And you have said, ‖ In what have we deceived You? The tithe and the raised-offering! **9** You are cursed with a curse! And you are deceiving Me—this nation—all of it. **10** Bring in all the tithe to the treasure-house, ‖ And there is food in My house; When you have tried Me, now, with this," said YHWH of Hosts, ‖ "Do I not open the windows of the heavens to you? Indeed, I have emptied on you a blessing until there is no space. **11** And I have pushed against the consumer for you, ‖ And He does not destroy the fruit of your ground, ‖ Nor does the vine in the field miscarry to you," said YHWH of Hosts. **12** "And all the nations have declared you blessed, ‖ For you are a delightful land," said YHWH of Hosts. **13** "Your words have been hard against Me," said YHWH, ‖ "And you have said, What have we spoken against You? **14** You have said, A vain thing to serve God! And what gain when we kept His charge? And when we have gone in black, ‖ Because of YHWH of Hosts? **15** And now, we are declaring the proud blessed, ‖ Indeed, those doing wickedness have been built up, ‖ Indeed, they have tempted God, and escape. **16** Then have those fearing YHWH spoken to one another, ‖ And YHWH attends and hears, ‖ And a scroll of memorial is written before Him ‖ Of those fearing YHWH, ‖ And of those esteeming His Name. **17** And they have been to Me," said YHWH of Hosts, ‖ "In the day that I am appointing—a peculiar treasure, ‖ And I have had pity on them, ‖ As one has pity on his son who is serving him. **18** And you have turned back and considered, ‖ Between the righteous and the wicked, ‖ Between the servant of God and him who is not His servant."

4 "For behold, the day has come, burning as a furnace, ‖ When all the proud and all those doing wickedness have been stubble, ‖ And the day that came has burned them," said YHWH of Hosts, ‖ "That there is not left to them root or branch, **2** But for you fearing My Name, ‖ The Sun of Righteousness has risen with healing in His wings, ‖ And you have gone forth, ‖ And have bounded as calves of a stall. **3** And you have trodden down the wicked, ‖ For they are ashes under the soles of your feet, ‖ In the day that I am appointing," said YHWH of Hosts. **4** "Remember the Law of My servant Moses, ‖ That I commanded him in Horeb, ‖ For all Israel—statutes and judgments. **5** Behold, I am sending Elijah the prophet to you, ‖ Before the coming of the great and fearful Day of YHWH. **6** And he has turned back the heart of fathers to sons, ‖ And the heart of sons to their fathers, ‖ Before I come and have utterly struck the land!"

~ THE END OF THE OLD TESTAMENT ~

THE NEW TESTAMENT
OF OUR LORD AND SAVIOR JESUS CHRIST

MATTHEW

1 [The] scroll of the birth of Jesus Christ, Son of David, Son of Abraham. **2** Abraham begot Isaac, and Isaac begot Jacob, and Jacob begot Judah and his brothers, **3** and Judah begot Perez and Zerah of Tamar, and Perez begot Hezron, and Hezron begot Ram, **4** and Ram begot Amminadab, and Amminadab begot Nahshon, and Nahshon begot Salmon, **5** and Salmon begot Boaz of Rahab, and Boaz begot Obed of Ruth, and Obed begot Jesse, **6** and Jesse begot David the king. And David the king begot Solomon, of her [who had been] Uriah's, **7** and Solomon begot Rehoboam, and Rehoboam begot Abijah, and Abijah begot Asa, **8** and Asa begot Jehoshaphat, and Jehoshaphat begot Joram, and Joram begot Uzziah, **9** and Uzziah begot Jotham, and Jotham begot Ahaz, and Ahaz begot Hezekiah, **10** and Hezekiah begot Manasseh, and Manasseh begot Amon, and Amon begot Josiah, **11** and Josiah begot Jeconiah and his brothers, at the Babylonian removal. **12** And after the Babylonian removal, Jeconiah begot Shealtiel, and Shealtiel begot Zerubbabel, **13** and Zerubbabel begot Abiud, and Abiud begot Eliakim, and Eliakim begot Azor, **14** and Azor begot Sadok, and Sadok begot Achim, and Achim begot Eliud, **15** and Eliud begot Eleazar, and Eleazar begot Matthan, and Matthan begot Jacob, **16** and Jacob begot Joseph, the husband of Mary, of whom was begotten Jesus, who is named Christ. **17** All the generations, therefore, from Abraham to David [are] fourteen generations, and from David to the Babylonian removal fourteen generations, and from the Babylonian removal to the Christ, fourteen generations. **18** And of Jesus Christ, the birth was thus: for His mother Mary having been betrothed to Joseph, before their coming together she was found to have conceived from the Holy Spirit, **19** and her husband Joseph being righteous, and not willing to make her an example, resolved to send her away privately. **20** And on his thinking of these things, behold, a messenger of the LORD appeared to him in a dream, saying, "Joseph, son of David, you may not fear to receive your wife Mary, for that which was begotten in her is of [the] Holy Spirit, **21** and she will bring forth a Son, and you will call His Name Jesus, for He will save His people from their sins." **22** And all this has come to pass, that it may be fulfilled that was spoken by the LORD through the prophet, saying, **23** "Behold, the virgin will conceive, and she will bring forth a Son, and they will call His Name Emmanuel," which is, being interpreted, "God with us." **24** And Joseph, having risen from sleep, did as the messenger of the LORD directed him, and received his wife, **25** and did not know her until she brought forth her Son—the firstborn, and he called His Name Jesus.

2 And Jesus having been born in Beth-Lehem of Judea, in the days of Herod the king, behold, magi from the east came to Jerusalem, **2** saying, "Where is He who was born King of the Jews? For we saw His star in the east, and we came to worship Him." **3** And Herod the king having heard, was stirred, and all Jerusalem with him, **4** and having gathered all the chief priests and scribes of the people, he was inquiring from them where the Christ is born. **5** And they said to him, "In Beth-Lehem of Judea, for thus it has been written through the prophet: **6** And you, Beth-Lehem, the land of Judah, you are by no means the least among the leaders of Judah, for out of you will come One leading, who will feed My people Israel." **7** Then Herod, having called the magi privately, inquired exactly from them the time of the appearing star, **8** and having sent them to Beth-Lehem, he said, "Having gone—inquire exactly for the Child, and whenever you may have found, bring me back word, that I also having come may worship Him." **9** And they, having heard the king, departed, and behold, the star, that they saw in the east, went before them, until, having come, it stood over where the Child was. **10** And having seen the star, they rejoiced with exceedingly great joy, **11** and having come into the house, they found the Child with His mother Mary, and having fallen down they worshiped Him, and having opened their treasures, they presented to Him gifts, gold, and frankincense, and myrrh, **12** and having been divinely warned in a dream

MATTHEW

not to return to Herod, through another way they withdrew to their own region. **13** And on their having withdrawn, behold, a messenger of the LORD appears in a dream to Joseph, saying, "Having risen, take the Child and His mother, and flee to Egypt, and be there until I may speak to you, for Herod is about to seek the Child to destroy Him." **14** And he, having risen, took the Child and His mother by night, and withdrew to Egypt, **15** and he was there until the death of Herod, that it might be fulfilled that was spoken by the LORD through the prophet, saying, "Out of Egypt I called My Son." **16** Then Herod, having seen that he was deceived by the magi, was very angry, and having sent forth, he slew all the male children in Beth-Lehem, and in all its borders, from two years and under, according to the time that he inquired exactly from the magi. **17** Then was fulfilled that which was spoken by Jeremiah the prophet, saying, **18** "A voice in Ramah was heard—weeping and much mourning—Rachel weeping [for] her children, and she would not be comforted because they are not." **19** And Herod having died, behold, a messenger of the LORD appears in a dream to Joseph in Egypt, **20** saying, "Having risen, take the Child and His mother, and be going to the land of Israel, for they have died—those seeking the life of the Child." **21** And he, having risen, took the Child and His mother, and came to the land of Israel, **22** and having heard that Archelaus reigns over Judea instead of his father Herod, he was afraid to go there, and having been divinely warned in a dream, he withdrew to the parts of Galilee, **23** and coming, he dwelt in a city named Nazareth, that it might be fulfilled that was spoken through the Prophets, that "He will be called a Nazarene."

3 And in those days John the Immerser comes, proclaiming in the wilderness of Judea, **2** and saying, "Convert, for the kingdom of the heavens has come near," **3** for this is he having been spoken of by Isaiah the prophet, saying, "A voice of one crying in the wilderness: Prepare the way of the LORD, ‖ Make His paths straight." **4** And this John had his clothing of camel's hair, and a girdle of skin around his loins, and his nourishment was locusts and honey of the field. **5** Then were going forth to him Jerusalem, and all Judea, and all the region around the Jordan, **6** and they were immersed in the Jordan by him, confessing their sins. **7** And having seen many of the Pharisees and Sadducees coming about his immersion, he said to them, "Brood of vipers! Who showed you to flee from the coming wrath? **8** Bear, therefore, fruits worthy of conversion, **9** and do not think to say in yourselves, We have a father—Abraham, for I say to you that God is able to raise children to Abraham out of these stones, **10** and now also, the axe is laid to the root of the trees, therefore, every tree not bearing good fruit is cut down, and is cast into fire. **11** I indeed immerse you in water for conversion, but He who is coming after me is mightier than I, of whom I am not worthy to carry the sandals, He will immerse you in the Holy Spirit and fire, **12** whose fan [is] in His hand, and He will thoroughly cleanse His floor, and will gather His wheat into the storehouse, but He will burn the chaff with unquenchable fire." **13** Then Jesus comes from Galilee to John at the Jordan, to be immersed by him, **14** but John was forbidding Him, saying, "I have need to be immersed by You—and You come to me?" **15** But Jesus answering said to him, "Permit [it] now, for thus it is fitting to us to fulfill all righteousness," then he permits Him. **16** And having been immersed, Jesus immediately went up from the water, and behold, the heavens were opened to Him, and He saw the Spirit of God descending as a dove, and coming on Him, **17** and behold, a voice out of the heavens, saying, "This is My Son, the Beloved, in whom I delighted."

4 Then Jesus was led up to the wilderness by the Spirit, to be tempted by the Devil, **2** and having fasted forty days and forty nights, afterward He hungered. **3** And the tempting [one], having come to Him, said, "If You are the Son of God—speak that these stones may become loaves." **4** But He answering said, "It has been written: Man does not live on bread alone, but on every word coming forth from the mouth of God." **5** Then the Devil takes Him to the [holy] city, and sets Him on the pinnacle of the temple, **6** and says to Him, "If You are the Son of God—cast Yourself down, for it has been written that, His messengers He will charge concerning you, and on hands they will bear you up, that you may not

MATTHEW

dash your foot on a stone." **7** Jesus said to him again, "It has been written: You will not tempt the LORD your God." **8** Again the Devil takes Him to a very high mountain, and shows to Him all the kingdoms of the world and their glory, **9** and says to Him, "All these I will give to You, if falling down You may worship me." **10** Then Jesus says to him, "Go—Satan, for it has been written: You will worship the LORD your God, and Him only will you serve." **11** Then the Devil leaves Him, and behold, messengers came and were ministering to Him. **12** And Jesus, having heard that John was delivered up, withdrew to Galilee, **13** and having left Nazareth, having come, He dwelt at Capernaum that is by the sea, in the borders of Zebulun and Naphtali, **14** that it might be fulfilled that was spoken through Isaiah the prophet, saying, **15** "Land of Zebulun and land of Naphtali, way of the sea, beyond the Jordan, Galilee of the nations! **16** The people that is sitting in darkness saw a great light, and to those sitting in a region and shadow of death—light arose to them." **17** From that time Jesus began to proclaim and to say, "Convert, for the kingdom of the heavens has come near." **18** And Jesus, walking by the Sea of Galilee, saw two brothers, Simon named Peter and his brother Andrew, casting a drag into the sea—for they were fishers— **19** and He says to them, "Come after Me, and I will make you fishers of men," **20** and they, immediately, having left the nets, followed Him. **21** And having advanced from there, He saw two other brothers, James of Zebedee, and his brother John, in the boat with their father Zebedee, refitting their nets, and He called them, **22** and they, immediately, having left the boat and their father, followed Him. **23** And Jesus was going in all of Galilee teaching in their synagogues, and proclaiming the good news of the kingdom, and healing every disease and every sickness among the people, **24** and His fame went forth to all Syria, and they brought to Him all the ill having manifold oppressing diseases and torments—and demoniacs, and lunatics, and paralytics—and He healed them. **25** And there followed Him many multitudes from Galilee, and Decapolis, and Jerusalem, and Judea, and beyond the Jordan.

5 And having seen the multitudes, He went up to the mountain, and He having sat down, His disciples came to Him, **2** and having opened His mouth, He was teaching them, saying, **3** "Blessed the poor in spirit—because theirs is the kingdom of the heavens. **4** Blessed the mourning—because they will be comforted. **5** Blessed the meek—because they will inherit the land. **6** Blessed those hungering and thirsting for righteousness—because they will be filled. **7** Blessed the kind—because they will find kindness. **8** Blessed the clean in heart—because they will see God. **9** Blessed the peacemakers—because they will be called sons of God. **10** Blessed those persecuted for righteousness' sake—because theirs is the kingdom of the heavens. **11** Blessed are you whenever they may reproach you, and may persecute, and may say any evil thing against you falsely for My sake— **12** rejoice and be glad, because your reward [is] great in the heavens, for thus they persecuted the prophets who were before you. **13** You are the salt of the earth, but if the salt may lose savor, in what will it be salted? It is good for nothing from now on, except to be cast outside, and to be trodden down by men. **14** You are the light of the world, a city set on a mountain is not able to be hid; **15** nor do they light a lamp and put it under the measure, but on the lampstand, and it shines to all those in the house; **16** so let your light shine before men, that they may see your good works, and may glorify your Father who [is] in the heavens. **17** Do not suppose that I came to throw down the Law or the Prophets—I did not come to throw down, but to fulfill; **18** for truly I say to you, until the heaven and the earth may pass away, one iota or one tittle may not pass away from the Law, until all may come to pass. **19** Therefore whoever may loose one of these commands—the least—and may teach men so, he will be called least in the kingdom of the heavens, but whoever may do and may teach [them], he will be called great in the kingdom of the heavens. **20** For I say to you that if your righteousness may not abound above that of the scribes and Pharisees, you may not enter into the kingdom of the heavens. **21** You heard that it was said to the ancients: You will not murder, and whoever may murder will be in danger of the judgment; **22** but I say to you that

MATTHEW

everyone who is angry at his brother without cause will be in danger of the judgment, and whoever may say to his brother, Stupid, will be in danger of the Sanhedrin, and whoever may say, Moron, will be in danger of the Gehenna of fire. **23** If, therefore, you may bring your gift to the altar, and there may remember that your brother has anything against you, **24** leave there your gift before the altar, and go—first be reconciled to your brother, and then having come, bring your gift. **25** Be agreeing with your opponent quickly, while you are in the way with him, that the opponent may not deliver you to the judge, and the judge may deliver you to the officer, and you may be cast into prison; **26** truly I say to you, you may not come forth from there until you may pay the last penny. **27** You heard that it was said to the ancients: You will not commit adultery; **28** but I say to you that everyone who is looking on a woman to desire her, already committed adultery with her in his heart. **29** But if your right eye causes you to stumble, pluck it out and cast from you, for it is good to you that one of your members may perish, and not your whole body be cast into Gehenna. **30** And if your right hand causes you to stumble, cut it off, and cast from you, for it is good to you that one of your members may perish, and not your whole body be cast into Gehenna. **31** And it was said that, Whoever may put away his wife, let him give to her a writing of divorce; **32** but I say to you that whoever may put away his wife, except for the matter of whoredom, makes her to commit adultery; and whoever may marry her who has been put away commits adultery. **33** Again, you heard that it was said to the ancients: You will not swear falsely, but you will pay to the LORD your oaths; **34** but I say to you not to swear at all; neither by Heaven, because it is the throne of God, **35** nor by the earth, because it is His footstool, nor by Jerusalem, because it is [the] city of [the] great King, **36** nor may you swear by your head, because you are not able to make one hair white or black; **37** but let your word be, Yes, Yes, No, No, and that which is more than these is of the evil [one]. **38** You heard that it was said: Eye for eye, and tooth for tooth; **39** but I say to you not to resist the evil, but whoever will slap you on your right cheek, turn to him also the other; **40** and whoever is willing to take you to law, and to take your coat—also permit to him the cloak. **41** And whoever will impress you one mile, go with him two; **42** to him who is asking of you be giving, and him who is willing to borrow from you, you may not turn away. **43** You heard that it was said: You will love your neighbor, and will hate your enemy; **44** but I say to you, love your enemies, bless those cursing you, do good to those hating you, and pray for those accusing you falsely, and persecuting you, **45** that you may be sons of your Father in the heavens, because He causes His sun to rise on evil and good, and He sends rain on righteous and unrighteous. **46** For if you may love those loving you, what reward do you have? Do the tax collectors not also do the same? **47** And if you may greet your brothers only, what do you do abundant? Do the nations not also do so? **48** You will therefore be perfect, as your Father who [is] in the heavens is perfect."

6 "Take heed not to do your kindness before men, to be seen by them, and if not—you have no reward from your Father who [is] in the heavens; **2** whenever, therefore, you may do kindness, you may not sound a trumpet before you as the hypocrites do, in the synagogues, and in the streets, that they may have glory from men; truly I say to you, they have their reward! **3** But you, doing kindness, do not let your left hand know what your right hand does, **4** that your kindness may be in secret, and your Father who is seeing in secret will reward you Himself. **5** And when you may pray, you will not be as the hypocrites, because they cherish to pray standing in the synagogues and in the corners of the broad places, that they may be seen of men; truly I say to you that they have their reward. **6** But you, when you may pray, go into your chamber, and having shut your door, pray to your Father who [is] in secret, and your Father who is seeing in secret will reward you. **7** And—praying—you may not use vain repetitions like the nations, for they think that in their speaking much they will be heard, **8** therefore do not be like them, for your Father knows those things that you have need of before your asking Him; **9** therefore pray thus: Our Father who [is] in the heavens, hallowed be Your Name. **10** Your kingdom come, Your will come to

MATTHEW

pass, as in Heaven also on the earth. **11** Give us today our appointed bread. **12** And forgive us our debts, as we also forgive our debtors. **13** And may You not lead us into temptation, but deliver us from the evil [one], because Yours is the kingdom, and the power, and the glory—for all ages. Amen. **14** For if you may forgive men their trespasses He also will forgive you—your Father who [is] in the heavens; **15** but if you may not forgive men their trespasses, neither will your Father forgive your trespasses. **16** And when you may fast, do not be as the hypocrites, of sour countenances, for they disfigure their faces, that they may appear to men fasting; truly I say to you that they have their reward. **17** But you, fasting, anoint your head, and wash your face, **18** that you may not appear to men fasting, but to your Father who [is] in secret, and your Father, who is seeing in secret, will reward you. **19** Do not treasure up to yourselves treasures on the earth, where moth and rust disfigure, and where thieves break through and steal, **20** but treasure up to yourselves treasures in Heaven, where neither moth nor rust disfigure, and where thieves do not break through nor steal, **21** for where your treasure is, there will your heart be also. **22** The lamp of the body is the eye, if, therefore, your eye may be perfect, all your body will be enlightened, **23** but if your eye may be evil, all your body will be dark; if, therefore, the light that [is] in you is darkness—the darkness, how great! **24** None is able to serve two lords, for either he will hate the one and love the other, or he will hold to the one, and despise the other; you are not able to serve God and wealth. **25** Because of this I say to you, do not be anxious for your life, what you may eat, and what you may drink, nor for your body, what you may put on. Is not life more than nourishment, and the body than clothing? **26** Look to the birds of the sky, for they do not sow, nor reap, nor gather into storehouses, and your heavenly Father nourishes them; are you not much better than they? **27** And who of you, being anxious, is able to add to his age one cubit? **28** And why are you anxious about clothing? Consider well the lilies of the field; how do they grow? They do not labor, nor do they spin; **29** and I say to you that not even Solomon in all his glory was clothed as one of these. **30** And if the herb of the field, that today is, and tomorrow is cast into the furnace, God so clothes—not much more you, O you of little faith? **31** Therefore you may not be anxious, saying, What may we eat? Or, What may we drink? Or, [With] what may we be clothed? **32** For the nations seek for all these, for your heavenly Father knows that you have need of all these; **33** but seek first the Kingdom of God and His righteousness, and all these will be added to you. **34** Therefore do not be anxious for tomorrow, for tomorrow will be anxious for its own things; sufficient for the day [is] the evil of it."

7 "Do not judge, that you may not be judged, **2** for in what judgment you judge, you will be judged, and in what measure you measure, it will be measured to you. **3** And why do you behold the speck that [is] in your brother's eye, and do not consider the beam that [is] in your own eye? **4** Or, how will you say to your brother, Permit [that] I may cast out the speck from your eye, and behold, the beam [is] in your own eye? **5** Hypocrite, first cast out the beam out of your own eye, and then you will see clearly to cast out the speck out of your brother's eye. **6** You may not give that which is [holy] to the dogs, nor cast your pearls before the pigs, that they may not trample them among their feet, and having turned—may tear you apart. **7** Ask, and it will be given to you; seek, and you will find; knock, and it will be opened to you; **8** for everyone who is asking receives, and he who is seeking finds, and to him who is knocking it will be opened. **9** Or what man is of you, of whom, if his son may ask [for] a loaf—a stone will he present to him? **10** And if he may ask [for] a fish—a serpent will he present to him? **11** If, therefore, you being evil, have known to give good gifts to your children, how much more will your Father who [is] in the heavens give good things to those asking Him? **12** All things, therefore, whatever you may will that men may be doing to you, so also do to them, for this is the Law and the Prophets. **13** Go in through the narrow gate, because wide [is] the gate and broad the way that is leading to the destruction, and many are those going in through it; **14** how narrow [is] the gate and compressed the way that is leading to life, and few are those finding it! **15** But take heed of the false prophets who

MATTHEW

come to you in sheep's clothing, and inwardly are ravenous wolves. **16** From their fruits you will know them; do [men] gather grapes from thorns? Or figs from thistles? **17** So every good tree yields good fruits, but the bad tree yields evil fruits. **18** A good tree is not able to yield evil fruits, nor a bad tree to yield good fruits. **19** Every tree not yielding good fruit is cut down and is cast into fire: **20** therefore from their fruits you will know them. **21** Not everyone who is saying to Me, Lord, Lord, will come into the kingdom of the heavens, but he who is doing the will of My Father who is in the heavens. **22** Many will say to Me in that day, Lord, Lord, have we not prophesied in Your Name? And in Your Name cast out demons? And in Your Name done many mighty things? **23** And then I will acknowledge to them, that—I never knew you, depart from Me you who are working lawlessness. **24** Therefore, everyone who hears these words of Mine, and does them, I will liken him to a wise man who built his house on the rock; **25** and the rain descended, and the streams came, and the winds blew, and they beat on that house, and it did not fall, for it had been founded on the rock. **26** And everyone who is hearing these words of Mine, and is not doing them, will be likened to a foolish man who built his house on the sand; **27** and the rain descended, and the streams came, and the winds blew, and they beat on that house, and it fell, and its fall was great." **28** And it came to pass, when Jesus finished these words, the multitudes were astonished at His teaching, **29** for He was teaching them as having authority, and not as the scribes.

8 And when He came down from the mountain, great multitudes followed Him, **2** and behold, a leper having come, was prostrating to Him, saying, "Lord, if You are willing, You are able to cleanse me"; **3** and having stretched forth the hand, Jesus touched him, saying, "I will, be cleansed," and immediately his leprosy was cleansed. **4** And Jesus says to him, "See, you may tell no one, but go, show yourself to the priest, and bring the gift that Moses commanded for a testimony to them." **5** And Jesus having entered into Capernaum, there came to Him a centurion calling on Him, **6** and saying, "Lord, my young man has been laid in the house a paralytic, fearfully afflicted," **7** and Jesus says to him, "I, having come, will heal him." **8** And the centurion answering said, "Lord, I am not worthy that You may enter under my roof, but only say a word, and my servant will be healed; **9** for I also am a man under authority, having under myself soldiers, and I say to this one, Go, and he goes, and to another, Be coming, and he comes, and to my servant, Do this, and he does [it]." **10** And Jesus having heard, wondered, and said to those following, "Truly I say to you, not even in Israel have I found such great faith; **11** and I say to you that many from east and west will come and recline with Abraham, and Isaac, and Jacob, in the kingdom of the heavens, **12** but the sons of the kingdom will be cast forth into the outer darkness—there will be the weeping and the gnashing of the teeth." **13** And Jesus said to the centurion, "Go, and as you believed let it be to you"; and his young man was healed in that hour. **14** And Jesus having come into the house of Peter, saw his mother-in-law laid, and fevered, **15** and He touched her hand, and the fever left her, and she arose, and was ministering to them. **16** And evening having come, they brought to Him many demoniacs, and He cast out the spirits with a word, and healed all who were ill, **17** that it might be fulfilled that was spoken through Isaiah the prophet, saying, "He took our sicknesses Himself, and bore the diseases." **18** And Jesus having seen great multitudes around Him, commanded to depart to the other side; **19** and a certain scribe having come, said to Him, "Teacher, I will follow You wherever You may go"; **20** and Jesus says to him, "The foxes have holes, and the birds of the sky places of rest, but the Son of Man has nowhere He may lay the head." **21** And another of His disciples said to Him, "Lord, permit me first to depart and to bury my father"; **22** and Jesus said to him, "Follow Me, and permit the dead to bury their own dead." **23** And when He entered into the boat His disciples followed Him, **24** and behold, a great storm arose in the sea, so that the boat was being covered by the waves, but He was sleeping, **25** and His disciples having come to Him, awoke Him, saying, "Lord, save us! We are perishing!" **26** And He says to them, "Why are you fearful, O you of little faith?" Then having risen, He rebuked the winds and the sea, and there was a great

MATTHEW

calm; **27** and the men wondered, saying, "What kind—is this, that even the wind and the sea obey Him?" **28** And He having come to the other side, to the region of the Gergesenes, there met Him two demoniacs, coming forth out of the tombs, very fierce, so that no one was able to pass over by that way, **29** and behold, they cried out, saying, "What [regards] us and You, [[Jesus,]] Son of God? Did You come here to afflict us before the time?" **30** And there was a herd of many pigs feeding far off from them, **31** and the demons were calling on Him, saying, "If You cast us forth, permit us to go away into the herd of the pigs"; **32** and He says to them, "Go." And having come forth, they went into the herd of the pigs, and behold, the whole herd of the pigs rushed down the steep, into the sea, and died in the waters, **33** and those feeding fled, and having gone into the city, they declared all, and the matter of the demoniacs. **34** And behold, all the city came forth to meet Jesus, and having seen Him, they called on [Him] that He might depart from their borders.

9 And having gone into the boat, He passed over, and came to His own city, **2** and behold, they were bringing to Him a paralytic, laid on a bed, and Jesus having seen their faith, said to the paralytic, "Take courage, child, your sins have been forgiven." **3** And behold, certain of the scribes said within themselves, "This One speaks evil." **4** And Jesus, having known their thoughts, said, "Why think evil in your hearts? **5** For which is easier? To say, Your sins are forgiven; or to say, Rise and walk? **6** But that you may know that the Son of Man has power on the earth to forgive sins—(then He says to the paralytic)—Having risen, take up your bed, and go to your house." **7** And he, having risen, went to his house, **8** and the multitudes having seen, wondered, and glorified God, who gave such power to men. **9** And Jesus passing on from there saw a man sitting at the tax office named Matthew, and says to him, "Follow Me," and he, having risen, followed Him. **10** And it came to pass, He reclining in the house, that behold, many tax collectors and sinners having come, were dining with Jesus and His disciples, **11** and the Pharisees having seen, said to His disciples, "Why does your teacher eat with the tax collectors and sinners?" **12** And Jesus having heard, said to them, "They who are whole have no need of a physician, but they who are ill; **13** but having gone, learn what [this] is: Kindness I will, and not sacrifice; for I did not come to call righteous men, but sinners." **14** Then the disciples of John come to Him, saying, "Why do we and the Pharisees fast much, and Your disciples do not fast?" **15** And Jesus said to them, "Can the sons of the bride-chamber mourn, so long as the bridegroom is with them? But days will come when the bridegroom may be taken from them, and then they will fast. **16** And no one puts a patch of undressed cloth on an old garment, for its filling up takes from the garment, and a worse split is made. **17** Nor do they put new wine into old skins, and if not—the skins burst, and the wine runs out, and the skins are destroyed, but they put new wine into new skins, and both are preserved together." **18** While He is speaking these things to them, behold, a ruler having come, was prostrating to Him, saying that "My daughter just now died, but having come, lay Your hand on her, and she will live." **19** And Jesus having risen, followed him, also His disciples, **20** and behold, a woman having a flow of blood [for] twelve years, having come to Him behind, touched the fringe of His garments, **21** for she said within herself, "If only I may touch His garment, I will be saved." **22** And Jesus having turned, and having seen her, said, "Take courage, daughter, your faith has saved you," and the woman was saved from that hour. **23** And Jesus having come into the house of the ruler, and having seen the pipers and the multitude making tumult, **24** He says to them, "Withdraw, for the girl did not die, but sleeps," and they were deriding Him; **25** but when the multitude was put forth, having gone in, He took hold of her hand, and the girl arose, **26** and the fame of this went forth to all the land. **27** And Jesus passing on from there, two blind men followed Him, calling and saying, "Deal kindly with us, Son of David!" **28** And He having come into the house, the blind men came to Him, and Jesus says to them, "Do you believe that I am able to do this?" They say to Him, "Yes, Lord." **29** Then He touched their eyes, saying, "According to your faith let it be to you," **30** and their eyes were opened, and Jesus strictly charged them, saying, "See, let no one know"; **31** but they, having gone forth, spread His fame in all that land. **32** And as they are coming forth, behold, they brought to Him a man mute, a demoniac, **33** and the demon having been cast out, the mute spoke, and the multitude wondered, saying that "It was never so seen in Israel," **34** but the Pharisees said, "By the ruler of the demons He casts out the demons." **35** And Jesus was going up and down all the cities and the villages, teaching in their synagogues, and proclaiming the good news of the kingdom, and healing every disease and every sickness among the people. **36** And having seen the multitudes, He was moved with compassion for them, that they were faint and cast aside, as sheep not having a shepherd; **37** then He says to His disciples, "The harvest indeed [is] abundant, but the workmen few; **38** therefore implore the Lord of the harvest that He may put forth workmen to His harvest."

10 And having called His twelve disciples to Himself, He gave to them power over unclean spirits, so as to be casting them out, and to be healing every disease and every sickness. **2** And of the twelve apostles the names are these: first, Simon, who is called Peter, and his brother Andrew; James of Zebedee, and his brother John; **3** Philip, and Bartholomew; Thomas, and Matthew the tax collector; James of Alpheus, and Lebbeus who was surnamed Thaddeus; **4** Simon the Zealot, and Judas Iscariot, who also delivered Him up. **5** These twelve Jesus sent forth, having given command to them, saying, "Do not go away to the way of the nations, and do not go into a city of the Samaritans, **6** and be going rather to the lost sheep of the house of Israel. **7** And going on, proclaim, saying that the kingdom of the heavens has come near; **8** be healing [those] ailing, raising the dead, cleansing lepers, casting out demons—freely you received, freely give. **9** Do not provide gold, nor silver, nor brass in your girdles, **10** nor leather pouch for the way, nor two coats, nor sandals, nor staff—for the workman is worthy of his nourishment. **11** And into whatever city or village you may enter, inquire who in it is worthy, and abide there, until you may go forth. **12** And coming into the house greet it, **13** and if indeed the house is worthy, let your peace come on it; and if it is not worthy, let your peace return to you. **14** And whoever may not receive you nor hear your words, coming forth from that house or city, shake off the dust of your feet, **15** truly I say to you, it will be more tolerable for the land of Sodom and Gomorrah in the day of judgment than for that city. **16** Behold, I send you forth as sheep in the midst of wolves, therefore be wise as the serpents, and pure as the doves. **17** And take heed of men, for they will give you up to Sanhedrins, and in their synagogues they will scourge you, **18** and before governors and kings you will be brought for My sake, for a testimony to them and to the nations. **19** And whenever they may deliver you up, do not be anxious how or what you may speak, for it will be given you in that hour what you will speak; **20** for you are not the speakers, but the Spirit of your Father that is speaking in you. **21** And brother will deliver up brother to death, and father child, and children will rise up against parents, and will put them to death, **22** and you will be hated by all because of My Name, but he who has endured to the end, he will be saved. **23** And whenever they may persecute you in this city, flee to the other, for truly I say to you, you may not have finished [going through] the cities of Israel until the Son of Man may come. **24** A disciple is not above the teacher, nor a servant above his lord; **25** sufficient to the disciple that he may be as his teacher, and the servant as his lord; if the master of the house they called Beelzebul, how much more those of his household? **26** You may not, therefore, fear them, for there is nothing covered that will not be revealed, and hid that will not be known; **27** that which I tell you in the darkness, speak in the light, and that which you hear at the ear, proclaim on the housetops. **28** And do not be afraid of those killing the body, and are not able to kill the soul, but rather fear Him who is able to destroy both soul and body in Gehenna. **29** Are not two sparrows sold for an assarion? And one of them will not fall on the ground without your Father; **30** and of you—even the hairs of the head are all numbered; **31** therefore, do not be afraid, you are better than many sparrows. **32** Everyone, therefore, who will confess in Me before men, I also will confess in him before My Father who is in the heavens; **33** and whoever will deny Me before men,

I also will deny him before My Father who is in the heavens. **34** You may not suppose that I came to put peace on the earth; I did not come to put peace, but a sword; **35** for I came to set a man at variance against his father, and a daughter against her mother, and a daughter-in-law against her mother-in-law, **36** and the enemies of a man are those of his household. **37** He who is cherishing father or mother above Me, is not worthy of Me, and he who is cherishing son or daughter above Me, is not worthy of Me, **38** and whoever does not receive his cross and follow after Me, is not worthy of Me. **39** He who found his life will lose it, and he who lost his life for My sake will find it. **40** He who is receiving you receives Me, and he who is receiving Me receives Him who sent Me; **41** he who is receiving a prophet in the name of a prophet, will receive a prophet's reward, and he who is receiving a righteous man in the name of a righteous man, will receive a righteous man's reward, **42** and whoever may give to drink to one of these little ones a cup of cold water only in the name of a disciple, truly I say to you, he may not lose his reward."

11 And it came to pass, when Jesus finished directing His twelve disciples, He departed from there to teach and to preach in their cities. **2** And John having heard in the prison the works of the Christ, having sent two of his disciples, **3** said to Him, "Are You He who is coming, or do we look for another?" **4** And Jesus answering said to them, "Having gone, declare to John the things that you hear and see, **5** blind receive sight, and lame walk, lepers are cleansed, and deaf hear, dead are raised, and poor have good news proclaimed, **6** and blessed is he who may not be stumbled in Me." **7** And as they are going, Jesus began to say to the multitudes concerning John, "What did you go out to the wilderness to view? A reed shaken by the wind? **8** But what did you go out to see? A man clothed in soft garments? Behold, those wearing the soft things are in the kings' houses. **9** But what did you go out to see? A prophet? Yes, I say to you, and more than a prophet, **10** for this is he of whom it has been written: Behold, I send My messenger before Your face, who will prepare Your way before You. **11** Truly I say to you, there has not risen, among those born of women, [one] greater than John the Immerser, but he who is least in the kingdom of the heavens is greater than he. **12** And from the days of John the Immerser until now, the kingdom of the heavens suffers violence, and violent men seize it by force, **13** for all the Prophets and the Law prophesied until John, **14** and if you are willing to receive [it], he is Elijah who was about to come; **15** he who is having ears to hear—let him hear. **16** And to what will I liken this generation? It is like little children in marketplaces, sitting and calling to others, **17** and saying, We piped to you, and you did not dance, we lamented to you, and you did not strike the breast. **18** For John came neither eating nor drinking, and they say, He has a demon; **19** the Son of Man came eating and drinking, and they say, Behold, a man, a glutton, and a wine-drinker, a friend of tax collectors and sinners; and wisdom was justified of her children." **20** Then He began to reproach the cities in which were done most of His mighty works, because they did not convert. **21** "Woe to you, Chorazin! Woe to you, Bethsaida! Because, if in Tyre and Sidon had been done the mighty works that were done in you, long ago in sackcloth and ashes they had converted; **22** but I say to you, to Tyre and Sidon it will be more tolerable in [the] day of judgment than for you. **23** And you, Capernaum, which were exalted to Heaven, will be brought down to Hades, because if the mighty works that were done in you had been done in Sodom, it had remained to this day; **24** but I say to you, to the land of Sodom it will be more tolerable in [the] day of judgment than to you." **25** At that time Jesus answering said, "I confess to You, Father, Lord of the heavens and of the earth, that You hid these things from wise and understanding ones, and revealed them to babies. **26** Yes, Father, because so it was good pleasure before You. **27** All things were delivered to Me by My Father, and none know the Son, except the Father, nor does any know the Father, except the Son, and he to whom the Son may resolve to reveal [Him]. **28** Come to Me, all you laboring and burdened ones, and I will give you rest; **29** take up My yoke on you, and learn from Me, because I am meek and humble in heart, and you will find rest to your souls, **30** for My yoke [is] easy, and My burden is light."

MATTHEW

12 At that time Jesus went on the Sabbaths through the grainfields, and His disciples were hungry, and they began to pluck ears, and to eat, **2** and the Pharisees having seen, said to Him, "Behold, Your disciples do that which it is not lawful to do on a Sabbath." **3** And He said to them, "Did you not read what David did when he was hungry, himself and those with him— **4** how he went into the house of God, and ate the Bread of the Presentation, which it is not lawful to him to eat, nor to those with him, except to the priests alone? **5** Or did you not read in the Law that on the Sabbaths the priests in the temple profane the Sabbath and are blameless? **6** And I say to you that [One] greater than the temple is here; **7** and if you had known what [this] is: Kindness I will, and not sacrifice—you had not condemned the blameless, **8** for the Son of Man is Lord even of the Sabbath." **9** And having departed from there, He went to their synagogue, **10** and behold, there was a man having the hand withered, and they questioned Him, saying, "Is it lawful to heal on the Sabbaths?" That they might accuse Him. **11** And He said to them, "What man will be of you who will have one sheep, and if this may fall on the Sabbaths into a ditch, will not lay hold on it and raise [it]? **12** How much better, therefore, is a man than a sheep? So that it is lawful on the Sabbaths to do good." **13** Then He says to the man, "Stretch forth your hand," and he stretched [it] forth, and it was restored whole as the other. **14** And the Pharisees having gone forth, held a consultation against Him, how they might destroy Him, **15** and Jesus having known, withdrew from there, and there followed Him great multitudes, and He healed them all, **16** and charged them that they might not make Him apparent, **17** that it might be fulfilled that was spoken through Isaiah the prophet, saying, **18** "Behold, My Servant, whom I chose, ‖ My Beloved, in whom My soul delighted, ‖ I will put My Spirit on Him, ‖ And He will declare judgment to the nations; **19** He will not strive nor cry, ‖ Nor will any hear His voice in the broad places; **20** A bruised reed He will not break, ‖ And smoking flax He will not quench, ‖ Until He may put forth judgment to victory, **21** And in His Name will nations hope." **22** Then was brought to Him a demoniac, blind and mute, and He healed him, so that the blind and mute both spoke and saw. **23** And all the multitudes were amazed and said, "Is this the Son of David?" **24** But the Pharisees having heard, said, "This One does not cast out demons, except by Beelzebul, ruler of the demons." **25** And Jesus, knowing their thoughts, said to them, "Every kingdom having been divided against itself is desolated, and no city or house having been divided against itself stands, **26** and if Satan casts out Satan, against himself he was divided, how then does his kingdom stand? **27** And if I, by Beelzebul, cast out the demons, your sons—by whom do they cast out? Because of this they will be your judges. **28** But if I, by the Spirit of God, cast out the demons, then the Kingdom of God has already come to you. **29** Or how is one able to go into the house of the strong man, and to snatch his goods, if first he may not bind the strong man? And then his house he will plunder. **30** He who is not with Me is against Me, and he who is not gathering with Me, scatters. **31** Because of this I say to you, all sin and slander will be forgiven to men, but the slander of the Spirit will not be forgiven to men. **32** And whoever may speak a word against the Son of Man it will be forgiven to him, but whoever may speak against the Holy Spirit, it will not be forgiven him, neither in this age, nor in that which is coming. **33** Either make the tree good, and its fruit good, or make the tree bad, and its fruit bad, for from the fruit is the tree known. **34** Brood of vipers! How are you able to speak good things—being evil? For out of the abundance of the heart the mouth speaks. **35** The good man out of the good treasure of the heart puts forth the good things, and the evil man out of the evil treasure puts forth evil things. **36** And I say to you that every idle word that men may speak, they will give for it a reckoning in [the] day of judgment; **37** for from your words you will be declared righteous, and from your words you will be declared unrighteous." **38** Then certain of the scribes and Pharisees answered, saying, "Teacher, we will to see a sign from You." **39** And He answering said to them, "A generation, evil and adulterous, seeks a sign, and a sign will not be given to it, except the sign of Jonah the prophet; **40** for as Jonah was in the belly of the fish three days and three nights, so will the Son of Man be in the heart of the earth three days and three nights. **41** Men of Nineveh will stand up in the judgment with this generation, and will condemn it, for they converted at the proclamation of Jonah, and behold, [One] greater than Jonah [is] here! **42** A queen of the south will rise up in the judgment with this generation, and will condemn it, for she came from the ends of the earth to hear the wisdom of Solomon, and behold, [One] greater than Solomon [is] here! **43** And when the unclean spirit may go forth from the man, it walks through dry places seeking rest and does not find; **44** then it says, I will return to my house from where I came forth; and having come, it finds [it] unoccupied, swept, and adorned: **45** then it goes, and takes with itself seven other spirits more evil than itself, and having gone in they dwell there, and the last of that man becomes worse than the first; so will it also be to this evil generation." **46** And while He was yet speaking to the multitudes, behold, His mother and brothers had stood outside, seeking to speak to Him, **47** and one said to Him, "Behold, Your mother and Your brothers stand outside, seeking to speak to You." **48** And He answering said to him who spoke to Him, "Who is My mother? And who are My brothers?" **49** And having stretched forth His hand toward His disciples, He said, "Behold, My mother and My brothers! **50** For whoever may do the will of My Father who is in the heavens, He is My brother, and sister, and mother."

13 And in that day Jesus, having gone forth from the house, was sitting by the sea, **2** and gathered together to Him were many multitudes, so that He having gone into the boat sat down, and all the multitude on the beach stood, **3** and He spoke to them many things in allegories, saying, "Behold, the sower went forth to sow, **4** and in his sowing, some indeed fell by the way, and the birds having come, devoured them, **5** and others fell on the rocky places where they did not have much earth, and immediately they sprang forth, through having no depth of earth, **6** and the sun having risen they were scorched, and through having no root, they withered, **7** and others fell on the thorns, and the thorns came up and choked them, **8** and others fell on the good ground, and were giving fruit, some indeed a hundredfold, and some sixty, and some thirty. **9** He who is having ears to hear—let him hear."

10 And the disciples having come near, said to Him, "Why do You speak to them in allegories?" **11** And He answering said to them that, "To you it has been given to know the secrets of the kingdom of the heavens, and to these it has not been given, **12** for whoever has, it will be given to him, and he will have overabundance, and whoever has not, even that which he has will be taken from him. **13** Because of this, in allegories I speak to them, because seeing they do not see, and hearing they do not hear, nor understand, **14** and fulfilled on them is the prophecy of Isaiah that says, With hearing you will hear, and you will not understand, and seeing you will see, and you will not perceive, **15** for the heart of this people was made obtuse, and with the ears they barely heard, and they closed their eyes, lest they might see with the eyes, and might hear with the ears, and understand with the heart, and turn back, and I might heal them. **16** And blessed are your eyes because they see, and your ears because they hear, **17** for truly I say to you that many prophets and righteous men desired to see that which you look on, and they did not see, and to hear that which you hear, and they did not hear. **18** You, therefore, hear the allegory of the sower: **19** Everyone hearing the word of the kingdom, and not understanding—the evil one comes, and snatches that which has been sown in his heart; this is that sown by the way. **20** And that sown on the rocky places, this is he who is hearing the word, and immediately with joy is receiving it, **21** and he has no root in himself, but is temporary, and persecution or tribulation having happened because of the word, immediately he is stumbled. **22** And that sown toward the thorns, this is he who is hearing the word, and the anxiety of this age, and the deceitfulness of the riches, chokes the word, and it becomes unfruitful. **23** And that sown on the good ground: this is he who is hearing the word, and is understanding, who indeed bears fruit, and makes, some indeed a hundredfold, and some sixty, and some thirty." **24** Another allegory He set before them, saying, "The kingdom of the heavens was likened to a man sowing good seed in his field, **25** and while men are sleeping, his enemy came and sowed darnel in the midst of the wheat, and went away, **26** and when the herb sprang up, and yielded fruit, then appeared

MATTHEW

also the darnel. **27** And the servants of the householder, having come near, said to him, Lord, did you not sow good seed in your field? From where then does it have the darnel? **28** And he says to them, A man, an enemy, did this; and the servants said to him, Will you, then, [that] having gone away we may gather it up? **29** And he said, No, lest—gathering up the darnel—you root up with it the wheat; **30** permit both to grow together until the harvest, and in the time of the harvest I will say to the reapers, Gather up first the darnel, and bind it in bundles, to burn it, and the wheat gather up into my storehouse." **31** Another allegory He set before them, saying, "The kingdom of the heavens is like to a grain of mustard, which a man having taken, sowed in his field, **32** which less, indeed, is than all the seeds, but when it may be grown, is greatest of the herbs, and becomes a tree, so that the birds of the sky come and rest in its branches." **33** Another allegory He spoke to them: "The kingdom of the heavens is like to leaven, which a woman having taken, hid in three measures of meal, until the whole was leavened." **34** All these things Jesus spoke in allegories to the multitudes, and without an allegory He was not speaking to them, **35** that it might be fulfilled that was spoken through the prophet, saying, "I will open in allegories My mouth, ‖ I will utter things having been hidden from the foundation of the world." **36** Then having let away the multitudes, Jesus came into the house, and His disciples came near to Him, saying, "Explain to us the allegory of the darnel of the field." **37** And He answering said to them, "He who is sowing the good seed is the Son of Man, **38** and the field is the world, and the good seed, these are the sons of the kingdom, and the darnel are the sons of the evil one, **39** and the enemy who sowed them is the Devil, and the harvest is [the] full end of the age, and the reapers are messengers. **40** As, then, the darnel is gathered up, and is burned with fire, so will it be in the full end of this age; **41** the Son of Man will send forth His messengers, and they will gather up out of His kingdom all the stumbling-blocks, and those doing the lawlessness, **42** and will cast them into the furnace of the fire; there will be the weeping and the gnashing of the teeth. **43** Then will the righteous shine forth as the sun in the kingdom of their Father. He who is having ears to hear—let him hear. **44** Again, the kingdom of the heavens is like to treasure hid in the field, which a man having found, hid, and from his joy goes, and all, as much as he has, he sells, and buys that field. **45** Again, the kingdom of the heavens is like to a man, a merchant, seeking good pearls, **46** who having found one pearl of great price, having gone away, has sold all, as much as he had, and bought it. **47** Again, the kingdom of the heavens is like to a net that was cast into the sea, and gathered together of every kind, **48** which, when it was filled, having drawn up again on the beach, and having sat down, they gathered the good into vessels, and the bad they cast out, **49** so will it be in the full end of the age, the messengers will come forth and separate the evil out of the midst of the righteous, **50** and will cast them into the furnace of the fire; there will be the weeping and the gnashing of the teeth." **51** Jesus says to them, "Did you understand all these?" They say to Him, "Yes, Lord." **52** And He said to them, "Because of this, every scribe having been discipled in regard to the kingdom of the heavens is like to a man, a householder, who brings forth out of his treasure things new and old." **53** And it came to pass, when Jesus finished these allegories, He removed from there, **54** and having come to His own country, He was teaching them in their synagogue, so that they were astonished, and were saying, "From where to this One this wisdom and the mighty works? **55** Is this not the carpenter's Son? Is His mother not called Mary, and His brothers James, and Joses, and Simon, and Judas? **56** And His sisters—are they not all with us? From where, then, to this One all these?" **57** And they were stumbled at Him. And Jesus said to them, "A prophet is not without honor except in his own country, and in his own house": **58** and He did not do many mighty works there, because of their unbelief.

14 At that time Herod the tetrarch heard the fame of Jesus, **2** and said to his servants, "This is John the Immerser, he rose from the dead, and because of this the mighty energies are working in him." **3** For Herod having laid hold on John, bound him, and put him in prison, because of Herodias, his brother Philip's wife, **4** for John was saying to him, "It is not lawful to you to have her," **5** and willing to kill him,

MATTHEW

he feared the multitude, because as a prophet they were holding him. **6** But the birthday of Herod being kept, the daughter of Herodias danced in the midst, and pleased Herod, **7** after which with an oath he professed to give her whatever she might ask. **8** And she, having been instigated by her mother, says, "Give me here on a plate the head of John the Immerser"; **9** and the king was grieved, but because of the oaths and of those dining with him, he commanded [it] to be given; **10** and having sent, he beheaded John in the prison, **11** and his head was brought on a plate, and was given to the girl, and she brought [it] near to her mother. **12** And his disciples having come, took up the body, and buried it, and having come, they told Jesus, **13** and Jesus having heard, withdrew from there in a boat to a desolate place by Himself, and the multitudes having heard followed Him on land from the cities. **14** And Jesus having come forth, saw a great multitude, and was moved with compassion on them, and healed their sick; **15** and evening having come, His disciples came to Him, saying, "The place is desolate, and the hour has now past, let away the multitudes that, having gone into the villages, they may buy food for themselves." **16** And Jesus said to them, "They have no need to go away—you give them to eat." **17** And they say to Him, "We have nothing here except five loaves and two fishes." **18** And He said, "Bring them to Me here." **19** And having commanded the multitudes to recline on the grass, and having taken the five loaves and the two fishes, having looked up to the sky, He blessed, and having broken, He gave the loaves to the disciples, and the disciples [gave] to the multitudes, **20** and they all ate, and were filled, and they took up what was over of the broken pieces twelve handbaskets full; **21** and those eating were about five thousand men, apart from women and children. **22** And immediately Jesus constrained His disciples to go into the boat, and to go before Him to the other side, until He might let away the multitudes; **23** and having let away the multitudes, He went up to the mountain by Himself to pray, and evening having come, He was there alone, **24** and the boat was now in the midst of the sea, distressed by the waves, for the wind was contrary. **25** And in the fourth watch of the night Jesus went away to them, walking on the sea, **26** and the disciples having seen Him walking on the sea, were troubled, saying, "It is an apparition," and from the fear they cried out; **27** and immediately Jesus spoke to them, saying, "Take courage! I AM; do not be afraid." **28** And Peter answering Him said, "Lord, if it is You, command me to come to You on the waters"; **29** and He said, "Come"; and having gone down from the boat, Peter walked on the waters to come to Jesus, **30** but seeing the vehement wind, he was afraid, and having begun to sink, he cried out, saying, "Lord, save me!" **31** And immediately Jesus, having stretched forth the hand, laid hold of him and says to him, "Little faith! For why did you waver?" **32** And they having gone into the boat, the wind stilled, **33** and those in the boat having come, worshiped Him, saying, "You are truly God's Son." **34** And having passed over, they came into the land of Gennesaret, **35** and having recognized Him, the men of that place sent forth to all that surrounding region, and they brought to Him all who were ill, **36** and were calling on Him that they might only touch the fringe of His garment, and as many as touched were saved.

15 Then they come to Jesus from Jerusalem—scribes and Pharisees—saying, **2** "Why do Your disciples transgress the tradition of the elders? For they do not wash their hands when they may eat bread." **3** And He answering said to them, "Why also do you transgress the command of God because of your tradition? **4** For God commanded, saying, Honor your father and mother; and, He who is speaking evil of father or mother—let him die the death; **5** but you say, Whoever may say to father or mother, An offering [is] whatever you may be profited by me— **6** and he may not honor his father or his mother, and you set aside the command of God because of your tradition. **7** Hypocrites, Isaiah prophesied well of you, saying, **8** This people draws near to Me with their mouth, and with the lips it honors Me, but their heart is far off from Me; **9** and in vain they worship Me, teaching teachings—commands of men." **10** And having called near the multitude, He said to them, "Hear and understand: **11** [it is] not that which is coming into the mouth [that] defiles the man, but that which

MATTHEW

is coming forth from the mouth, this defiles the man." **12** Then His disciples having come near, said to Him, "Have You known that the Pharisees, having heard the word, were stumbled?" **13** And He answering said, "Every plant that My heavenly Father did not plant will be rooted up; **14** leave them alone, they are guides—blind of blind; and if blind may guide blind, both will fall into a ditch." **15** And Peter answering said to Him, "Explain to us this allegory." **16** And Jesus said, "Are you also yet without understanding? **17** Do you not understand that all that is going into the mouth passes into the belly, and is cast forth into the drain? **18** But the things coming forth from the mouth come forth from the heart, and these defile the man; **19** for out of the heart come forth evil thoughts, murders, adulteries, whoredoms, thefts, false witnessings, slanders: **20** these are the things defiling the man; but to eat with unwashed hands does not defile the man." **21** And Jesus having come forth from there, withdrew to the parts of Tyre and Sidon, **22** and behold, a woman, a Canaanite, having come forth from those borders, called to Him, saying, "Deal kindly with me, Lord, Son of David; my daughter is miserably demonized." **23** And He did not answer her a word; and His disciples having come to Him, were asking Him, saying, "Let her away, because she cries after us"; **24** and He answering said, "I was not sent except to the lost sheep of the house of Israel." **25** And having come, she was worshiping Him, saying, "Lord, help me"; **26** and He answering said, "It is not good to take the children's bread, and to cast to the little dogs." **27** And she said, "Yes, Lord, for even the little dogs eat of the crumbs that are falling from their lords' table"; **28** then answering, Jesus said to her, "O woman, great [is] your faith, let it be to you as you will"; and her daughter was healed from that hour. **29** And having departed from there, Jesus came near to the Sea of Galilee, and having gone up to the mountain, He was sitting there, **30** and there came to Him great multitudes, having with them lame, blind, mute, maimed, and many others, and they cast them at the feet of Jesus, and He healed them, **31** so that the multitudes wondered, seeing mute ones speaking, maimed whole, lame walking, and blind seeing; and they glorified the God of Israel. **32** And Jesus having called near His disciples, said, "I have compassion on the multitude, because now three days they continue with Me, and they do not have what they may eat; and to let them away fasting I will not, lest they faint in the way." **33** And His disciples say to Him, "From where to us in a wilderness [will we get] so many loaves, as to fill so great a multitude?" **34** And Jesus says to them, "How many loaves do you have?" And they said, "Seven, and a few little fishes." **35** And He commanded the multitudes to sit down on the ground, **36** and having taken the seven loaves and the fishes, having given thanks, He broke, and gave to His disciples, and the disciples [gave] to the multitude. **37** And they all ate, and were filled, and they took up what was over of the broken pieces seven baskets full, **38** and those eating were four thousand men, apart from women and children. **39** And having let away the multitudes, He went into the boat, and came to the borders of Magdala.

16 And the Pharisees and Sadducees having come, tempting, questioned Him, to show to them a sign from Heaven, **2** and He answering said to them, "Evening having come, you say, Fair weather, for the sky is red, **3** and at morning, Foul weather today, for the sky is red—gloomy; hypocrites, you indeed know to discern the face of the sky, but the signs of the times you are not able! **4** An evil and adulterous generation seeks a sign, and a sign will not be given to it, except the sign of Jonah the prophet"; and having left them He went away. **5** And His disciples having come to the other side, forgot to take loaves, **6** and Jesus said to them, "Beware, and take heed of the leaven of the Pharisees and Sadducees"; **7** and they were reasoning in themselves, saying, "Because we took no loaves." **8** And Jesus having known, said to them, "Why reason you in yourselves, you of little faith, because you took no loaves? **9** Do you not yet understand, nor remember the five loaves of the five thousand, and how many hand-baskets you took up? **10** Nor the seven loaves of the four thousand, and how many baskets you took up? **11** How do you not understand that I did not speak to you of bread—to take heed of the leaven of the Pharisees and Sadducees?" **12** Then they understood that He did not say to take heed of the leaven of

MATTHEW

the bread, but of the teaching of the Pharisees and Sadducees. **13** And Jesus, having come to the parts of Caesarea Philippi, was asking His disciples, saying, "Who do men say I am—the Son of Man?" **14** And they said, "Some, John the Immerser, and others, Elijah, and others, Jeremiah, or one of the prophets." **15** He says to them, "And you—who do you say I am?" **16** And Simon Peter answering said, "You are the Christ, the Son of the living God." **17** And Jesus answering said to him, "Blessed are you, Simon Bar-Jona, because flesh and blood did not reveal [it] to you, but My Father who is in the heavens. **18** And I also say to you that you are Peter, and on this rock I will build My Assembly, and [the] gates of Hades will not prevail against it; **19** and I will give to you the keys of the kingdom of the heavens, and whatever you may bind on the earth will be having been bound in the heavens, and whatever you may loose on the earth will be having been loosed in the heavens." **20** Then He charged His disciples that they may say to no one that He is Jesus the Christ. **21** From that time Jesus began to show to His disciples that it is necessary for Him to go away to Jerusalem, and to suffer many things from the elders, and chief priests, and scribes, and to be put to death, and the third day to rise. **22** And having taken Him aside, Peter began to rebuke Him, saying, "Be kind to Yourself, Lord; this will not be to You"; **23** and He having turned, said to Peter, "Get behind Me, Satan! You are a stumbling-block to Me, for you do not mind the things of God, but the things of men." **24** Then Jesus said to His disciples, "If anyone wills to come after Me, let him disown himself, and take up his cross, and follow Me, **25** for whoever may will to save his life will lose it, and whoever may lose his life for My sake will find it; **26** for what is a man profited if he may gain the whole world, but of his life suffer loss? Or what will a man give as an exchange for his life? **27** For the Son of Man is about to come in the glory of His Father, with His messengers, and then He will reward each according to his work. **28** Truly I say to you, there are certain of those standing here who will not taste of death until they may see the Son of Man coming in His kingdom."

17 And after six days Jesus takes Peter, and James, and his brother John, and brings them up to a high mountain by themselves, **2** and He was transfigured before them, and His face shone as the sun, and His garments became white as the light, **3** and behold, Moses and Elijah appeared to them, talking together with Him. **4** And Peter answering said to Jesus, "Lord, it is good to us to be here; if You will, we may make three shelters here: one for You, and one for Moses, and one for Elijah." **5** While he is yet speaking, behold, a bright cloud overshadowed them, and behold, a voice out of the cloud, saying, "This is My Son, the Beloved, in whom I delighted; hear Him." **6** And the disciples having heard, fell on their face, and were exceedingly afraid, **7** and Jesus having come near, touched them, and said, "Rise, do not be afraid," **8** and having lifted up their eyes, they saw no one, except Jesus only. **9** And as they are coming down from the mountain, Jesus charged them, saying, "Say to no one the vision, until the Son of Man may rise out of the dead." **10** And His disciples questioned Him, saying, "Why then do the scribes say that Elijah must come first?" **11** And Jesus answering said to them, "Elijah does indeed come first, and will restore all things, **12** and I say to you, Elijah already came, and they did not know him, but did with him whatever they would, so also the Son of Man is about to suffer by them." **13** Then the disciples understood that He spoke to them concerning John the Immerser. **14** And when they came to the multitude, there came to Him a man, kneeling down to Him, **15** and saying, "Lord, deal kindly with my son, for he is [a] lunatic, and suffers miserably, for he often falls into the fire, and often into the water, **16** and I brought him near to Your disciples, and they were not able to heal him." **17** And Jesus answering said, "O generation, unsteadfast and perverse, until when will I be with you? Until when will I bear you? Bring him to Me here"; **18** and Jesus rebuked him, and the demon went out of him, and the boy was healed from that hour. **19** Then the disciples having come to Jesus by Himself, said, "Why were we not able to cast him out?" **20** And Jesus said to them, "Through your want of faith; for truly I say to you, if you may have faith as a grain of mustard, you will say to this mountain, Move from here to there, and it will move, and nothing will be impossible to you, **21** [[and this kind does not go forth except in prayer and fasting."]] **22** And while they are living in Galilee, Jesus said to them, "The Son of Man is about to be delivered up into the hands of men, **23** and they will kill Him, and the third day He will rise," and they were exceedingly sorry. **24** And they having come to Capernaum, those receiving the didrachmas came near to Peter and said, "Your teacher—does He not pay the didrachmas?" He says, "Yes." **25** And when he came into the house, Jesus anticipated him, saying, "What do you think, Simon? The kings of the earth—from whom do they receive custom or poll-tax? From their sons or from the strangers?" **26** Peter says to Him, "From the strangers." Jesus said to him, "Then the sons are free; **27** but that we may not cause them to stumble, having gone to the sea, cast a hook, and the fish that has come up first take up, and having opened its mouth, you will find a stater, that having taken, give to them for Me and you."

18 At that hour the disciples came near to Jesus, saying, "Who, now, is greater in the kingdom of the heavens?" **2** And Jesus having called near a child, set him in the midst of them, **3** and said, "Truly I say to you, if you may not be turned and become as the children, you may not enter into the kingdom of the heavens; **4** whoever then may humble himself as this child, he is the greater in the kingdom of the heavens. **5** And he who may receive one such child in My Name, receives Me, **6** and whoever may cause to stumble one of those little ones who are believing in Me, it is better for him that a weighty millstone may be hanged on his neck, and he may be sunk in the depth of the sea. **7** Woe to the world from the stumbling-blocks! For there is necessity for the stumbling-blocks to come, but woe to that man through whom the stumbling-block comes! **8** And if your hand or your foot causes you to stumble, cut them off and cast [them] from you; it is good for you to enter into life lame or maimed, rather than having two hands or two feet, to be cast into the continuous fire. **9** And if your eye causes you to stumble, pluck it out and cast from you; it is good for you to enter into life one-eyed, rather than having two eyes to be cast into the Gehenna of fire. **10** Beware! You may not despise one of these little ones, for I say to you that their messengers in the heavens always behold the face of My Father who is in the heavens, **11** [[for the Son of Man came to save the lost.]] **12** What do you think? If a man may have one hundred sheep, and there may go astray one of them, does he not—having left the ninety-nine, having gone on the mountains—seek that which is gone astray? **13** And if it may come to pass that he finds it, truly I say to you that he rejoices over it more than over the ninety-nine that have not gone astray; **14** so it is not [the] will in [the] presence of your Father who is in the heavens that one of these little ones may perish. **15** And if your brother may sin against you, go and show him his fault between you and him alone, if he may hear you, you gained your brother; **16** and if he may not hear, take with you yet one or two, that by the mouth of two witnesses or three every word may stand. **17** And if he may not hear them, say [it] to the assembly, and if also the assembly he may not hear, let him be to you as the heathen man and the tax collector. **18** Truly I say to you, whatever things you may bind on the earth will be having been bound in the heavens, and whatever things you may loose on the earth will be having been loosed in the heavens. **19** Again, I say to you that if two of you may agree on the earth concerning anything, whatever they may ask—it will be done to them from My Father who is in the heavens, **20** for where there are two or three gathered together—to My Name, there am I in the midst of them." **21** Then Peter having come near to Him, said, "Lord, how often will my brother sin against me, and I forgive him—until seven times?" **22** Jesus says to him, "I do not say to you until seven times, but until seventy times seven. **23** Because of this was the kingdom of the heavens likened to a man, a king, who willed to take reckoning with his servants, **24** and he having begun to take account, there was brought near to him one debtor of a myriad of talents, **25** and he having nothing to pay, his lord commanded him to be sold, and his wife, and the children, and all, whatever he had, and payment to be made. **26** The servant then, having fallen down, was prostrating to him, saying, Lord, have patience with me, and I will pay you all; **27** and the lord of that servant having been moved with compassion released him, and the debt he forgave him. **28** And that servant having come forth, found one of his fellow-servants who was owing him one hundred denarii, and having laid hold, he took him by the throat, saying, Pay me that which you owe. **29** His fellow-servant then, having fallen down at his feet, was calling on him, saying, Have patience with me, and I will pay you all; **30** and he would not, but having gone away, he cast him into prison, until he might pay that which was owing. **31** And his fellow-servants having seen the things that were done, were grieved exceedingly, and having come, showed fully to their lord all the things that were done; **32** then having called him, his lord says to him, Evil servant! All that debt I forgave you, seeing you called on me; **33** did it not seem necessary to you to have dealt kindly with your fellow servant, as I also dealt kindly with you? **34** And having been angry, his lord delivered him to the inquisitors, until he might pay all that was owing to him; **35** so also My heavenly Father will do to you, if you may not forgive each one his brother from your hearts their trespasses."

19 And it came to pass, when Jesus finished these words, He removed from Galilee, and came to the borders of Judea, beyond the Jordan, **2** and great multitudes followed Him, and He healed them there. **3** And the Pharisees came near to Him, tempting Him, and saying to Him, "Is it lawful for a man to put away his wife for every cause?" **4** And He answering said to them, "Did you not read that He who made [them] from the beginning, made them a male and a female, **5** and said, For this cause will a man leave father and mother, and cleave to his wife, and they will be—the two—for one flesh? **6** So that they are no longer two, but one flesh; what therefore God joined together, let no man separate." **7** They say to Him, "Why then did Moses command to give a roll of divorce, and to put her away?" **8** He says to them, "Moses for your stiffness of heart permitted you to put away your wives, but from the beginning it has not been so. **9** And I say to you that whoever may put away his wife, if not for whoredom, and may marry another, commits adultery; and he who married her that has been put away, commits adultery." **10** His disciples say to Him, "If the case of the man with the woman is so, it is not good to marry." **11** And He said to them, "All do not receive this word, but those to whom it has been given; **12** for there are eunuchs who from the mother's womb were so born; and there are eunuchs who were made eunuchs by men; and there are eunuchs who kept themselves eunuchs because of the kingdom of the heavens: he who is able to receive [it]—let him receive." **13** Then were brought near to Him children that He might put hands on them and pray, and the disciples rebuked them. **14** But Jesus said, "Permit the children, and do not forbid them to come to Me, for of such is the kingdom of the heavens"; **15** and having laid [His] hands on them, He departed from there. **16** And behold, one having come near, said to Him, "Good Teacher, what good thing will I do that I may have continuous life?" **17** And He said to him, "Why do you call Me good? No one [is] good except one—God; but if you will to enter into life, keep the commands." **18** He says to Him, "What kind?" And Jesus said, "You will not murder, You will not commit adultery, You will not steal, You will not bear false witness, **19** Honor your father and mother, and, You will love your neighbor as yourself." **20** The young man says to Him, "All these I kept from my youth; what yet do I lack?" **21** Jesus said to him, "If you will to be perfect, go away, sell what you have, and give to the poor, and you will have treasure in Heaven, and come, follow Me." **22** And the young man, having heard the word, went away sorrowful, for he had many possessions; **23** and Jesus said to His disciples, "Truly I say to you that hardly will a rich man enter into the kingdom of the heavens; **24** and again I say to you, it is easier for a camel to go through the eye of a needle, than for a rich man to enter into the Kingdom of God." **25** And His disciples having heard, were exceedingly amazed, saying, "Who, then, is able to be saved?" **26** And Jesus having earnestly beheld, said to them, "With men this is impossible, but with God all things are possible." **27** Then Peter answering said to Him, "Behold, we left all, and followed You, what then will we have?" **28** And Jesus said to them, "Truly I say to you that you who followed Me, in the regeneration, when the Son of Man

MATTHEW

may sit on a throne of His glory, will sit—you also—on twelve thrones, judging the twelve tribes of Israel; **29** and everyone who left houses, or brothers, or sisters, or father, or mother, or wife, or children, or fields, for My Name's sake, will receive a hundredfold, and will inherit continuous life; **30** and many first will be last, and last first."

20 "For the kingdom of the heavens is like to a man, a householder, who went forth with the morning to hire workmen for his vineyard, **2** and having agreed with the workmen for a denarius a day, he sent them into his vineyard. **3** And having gone forth about the third hour, he saw others standing in the marketplace idle, **4** and to these he said, Go—also you—to the vineyard, and whatever may be righteous I will give you; **5** and they went away. Again, having gone forth about the sixth and the ninth hour, he did in like manner. **6** And about the eleventh hour, having gone forth, he found others standing idle and says to them, Why have you stood here idle all day? **7** They say to him, Because no one hired us; he says to them, Go—you also—to the vineyard, and whatever may be righteous you will receive. **8** And evening having come, the lord of the vineyard says to his steward, Call the workmen, and pay them the reward, having begun from the last—to the first. **9** And they of about the eleventh hour having come, each received a denarius. **10** And the first having come, supposed that they will receive more, and they received, they also, each a denarius, **11** and having received [it], they were murmuring against the householder, saying, **12** that, These, the last, worked one hour, and you made them equal to us, who were bearing the burden of the day—and the heat. **13** And he answering said to one of them, Friend, I do no unrighteousness to you; did you not agree with me for a denarius? **14** Take that which is yours, and go; and I will to give to this, the last, also as to you; **15** is it not lawful to me to do what I will in my own? Is your eye evil because I am good? **16** So the last will be first, and the first last, for many are called, and few chosen." **17** And Jesus going up to Jerusalem, took the twelve disciples by themselves in the way and said to them, **18** "Behold, we go up to Jerusalem, and the Son of Man will be delivered to the chief priests and scribes, **19** and they will condemn Him to death, and will deliver Him to the nations to mock, and to scourge, and to crucify, and the third day He will rise again." **20** Then came near to Him the mother of the sons of Zebedee, with her sons, prostrating and asking something from Him, **21** and He said to her, "What do you will?" She says to Him, "Say that they may sit—these two sons of mine—one on Your right hand and one on the left, in Your kingdom." **22** And Jesus answering said, "You have not known what you ask for yourselves; are you able to drink of the cup that I am about to drink? And with the immersion that I am immersed with, to be immersed?" They say to Him, "We are able." **23** And He says to them, "Of My cup indeed you will drink, and with the immersion that I am immersed with you will be immersed; but to sit on My right hand and on My left is not Mine to give, but—to those for whom it has been prepared by My Father." **24** And the ten having heard, were much displeased with the two brothers, **25** and Jesus having called them near, said, "You have known that the rulers of the nations exercise lordship over them, and those [who are] great exercise authority over them, **26** but not so will it be among you, but whoever may will among you to become great, let him be your servant; **27** and whoever may will among you to be first, let him be your servant; **28** even as the Son of Man did not come to be ministered to, but to minister, and to give His life [as] a ransom for many." **29** And they going forth from Jericho, there followed Him a great multitude, **30** and behold, two blind men sitting by the way, having heard that Jesus passes by, cried, saying, "Deal kindly with us, Lord—Son of David." **31** And the multitude charged them that they might be silent, and they cried out the more, saying, "Deal kindly with us Lord—Son of David." **32** And having stood, Jesus called them and said, "What do you will [that] I may do to you?" **33** They say to Him, "Lord, that our eyes may be opened"; **34** and having been moved with compassion, Jesus touched their eyes, and immediately their eyes received sight, and they followed Him.

MATTHEW

21 And when they came near to Jerusalem, and came to Bethphage, to the Mount of Olives, then Jesus sent two disciples, **2** saying to them, "Go on into the village in front of you, and immediately you will find a donkey bound, and a colt with her—having loosed, you bring to Me; **3** and if anyone may say anything to you, you will say that the LORD has need of them, and immediately He will send them." **4** And all this came to pass, that it might be fulfilled that was spoken through the prophet, saying, **5** "Tell the daughter of Zion, Behold, your King comes to you, meek, and mounted on a donkey, and a colt, a foal of a beast of burden." **6** And the disciples having gone and having done as Jesus commanded them, **7** brought the donkey and the colt, and put on them their garments, and set [Him] on them; **8** and the very great multitude spread their own garments in the way, and others were cutting branches from the trees, and were strewing in the way, **9** and the multitudes who were going before, and who were following, were crying, saying, "Hosanna to the Son of David, blessed is He who is coming in the Name of the LORD; Hosanna in the highest!" **10** And He having entered into Jerusalem, all the city was moved, saying, "Who is this?" **11** And the multitudes said, "This is Jesus the prophet, who [is] from Nazareth of Galilee." **12** And Jesus entered into the temple of God, and cast forth all those selling and buying in the temple, and the tables of the money-changers He overturned, and the seats of those selling the doves, **13** and He says to them, "It has been written: My house will be called a house of prayer; but you made it a den of robbers." **14** And there came to Him blind and lame men in the temple, and He healed them, **15** and the chief priests and the scribes having seen the wonderful things that He did, and the children crying in the temple, and saying, "Hosanna to the Son of David," were much displeased; **16** and they said to Him, "Do You hear what these say?" And Jesus says to them, "Yes, did you never read, that, Out of the mouth of babies and sucklings You prepared praise?" **17** And having left them, He went forth out of the city to Bethany, and lodged there, **18** and in the morning turning back to the city, He hungered, **19** and having seen a certain fig tree on the way, He came to it, and found nothing in it except leaves only, and He says to it, "No more fruit may be from you—throughout the age"; and instantly the fig tree withered. **20** And the disciples having seen, wondered, saying, "How did the fig tree instantly wither?" **21** And Jesus answering said to them, "Truly I say to you, if you may have faith, and may not doubt, not only this of the fig tree will you do, but even if to this mountain you may say, Be lifted up and be cast into the sea, it will come to pass; **22** and all—as much as you may ask in the prayer, believing, you will receive." **23** And He having come into the temple, there came to Him when teaching the chief priests and the elders of the people, saying, "By what authority do You do these things? And who gave You this authority?" **24** And Jesus answering said to them, "I will ask you—I also—one word, which if you may tell Me, I also will tell you by what authority I do these things; **25** the immersion of John, from where was it? From Heaven, or from men?" And they were reasoning with themselves, saying, "If we should say, From Heaven, He will say to us, Why, then, did you not believe him? **26** And if we should say, From men, we fear the multitude, for all hold John as a prophet." **27** And answering Jesus they said, "We have not known." He said to them—He also, "Neither do I tell you by what authority I do these things. **28** And what do you think? A man had two children, and having come to the first, he said, Child, go, today be working in my vineyard. **29** And he answering said, I will not, but at last, having regretted, he went. **30** And having come to the second, he said in the same manner, and he answering said, I [go], lord, and did not go; **31** which of the two did the will of the father?" They say to Him, "The first." Jesus says to them, "Truly I say to you that the tax collectors and the prostitutes go before you into the Kingdom of God, **32** for John came to you in the way of righteousness, and you did not believe him, and the tax collectors and the prostitutes believed him, and you, having seen, did not regret at last—to believe him. **33** Hear another allegory: There was a certain man, a householder, who planted a vineyard, and put a hedge around it, and dug in it a winepress, and built a tower, and gave it out to farmers, and went abroad. **34** And when the season of the fruits came near, he sent his servants

MATTHEW

to the farmers, to receive the fruits of it, **35** and the farmers having taken his servants, one they scourged, and one they killed, and one they stoned. **36** Again he sent other servants more than the first, and they did to them in the same manner. **37** And at last he sent to them his son, saying, They will respect my son; **38** and the farmers having seen the son, said among themselves, This is the heir, come, we may kill him, and may possess his inheritance; **39** and having taken him, they cast [him] out of the vineyard, and killed him; **40** whenever therefore the lord of the vineyard may come, what will he do to these farmers?" **41** They say to Him, "Evil men—he will grievously destroy them, and will give out the vineyard to other farmers who will give back to him the fruits in their seasons." **42** Jesus says to them, "Did you never read in the Writings: A stone that the builders disallowed, it became head of a corner; from the LORD has this come to pass, and it is wonderful in our eyes? **43** Because of this I say to you that the Kingdom of God will be taken from you, and given to a nation bringing forth its fruit; **44** and he who is falling on this stone will be broken, and on whomsoever it may fall it will crush him to pieces." **45** And the chief priests and the Pharisees having heard His allegories, knew that He speaks of them, **46** and seeking to lay hold on Him, they feared the multitudes, seeing they were holding Him as a prophet.

22 And Jesus answering, again spoke to them in allegories, saying, **2** "The kingdom of the heavens was likened to a man, a king, who made wedding feasts for his son, **3** and he sent forth his servants to call those having been called to the wedding feasts, and they were not willing to come. **4** Again he sent forth other servants, saying, Say to those who have been called: Behold, I prepared my early meal, my oxen and the fatlings have been killed, and all things [are] ready, come to the wedding feasts; **5** and they, having disregarded [it], went away, one to his own field, and the other to his merchandise; **6** and the rest, having laid hold on his servants, mistreated and slew [them]. **7** And the king having heard, was angry, and having sent forth his soldiers, he destroyed those murderers, and their city he set on fire; **8** then he says to his servants, The wedding feast indeed is ready, and those called were not worthy, **9** be going, then, on to the cross-ways, and as many as you may find, call to the wedding feasts. **10** And those servants, having gone forth to the ways, gathered all, as many as they found, both bad and good, and the wedding was filled with those reclining. **11** And the king having come in to view those reclining, saw there a man not clothed with wedding clothes, **12** and he says to him, Friend, how did you come in here, not having wedding clothes? And he was speechless. **13** Then the king said to the servants, Having bound his feet and hands, take him up and cast forth into the outer darkness, there will be the weeping and the gnashing of the teeth; **14** for many are called, and few chosen." **15** Then the Pharisees having gone, took counsel how they might ensnare Him in words, **16** and they send to Him their disciples with the Herodians, saying, "Teacher, we have known that You are true, and the way of God in truth You teach, and You are not caring for anyone, for You do not look to the face of men; **17** tell us, therefore, what do You think? Is it lawful to give tribute to Caesar or not?" **18** And Jesus having known their wickedness, said, "Why do you tempt Me, hypocrites? **19** Show Me the tribute-coin." And they brought to Him a denarius; **20** and He says to them, "Whose [is] this image and the inscription?" **21** They say to Him, "Caesar's"; then He says to them, "Render therefore the things of Caesar to Caesar, and the things of God to God"; **22** and having heard they wondered, and having left Him they went away. **23** In that day there came near to Him Sadducees who are saying there is not a resurrection, and they questioned Him, saying, **24** "Teacher, Moses said if anyone may die having no children, his brother will marry his wife, and will raise up seed to his brother. **25** And there were with us seven brothers, and the first having married died, and having no seed, he left his wife to his brother; **26** in like manner also the second, and the third, to the seventh, **27** and last of all the woman also died; **28** therefore in the resurrection, of which of the seven will she be wife—for all had her?" **29** And Jesus answering said to them, "You go astray, not knowing the Writings, nor the power of God; **30** for in the resurrection they do not marry, nor are they given in marriage, but are as messengers of God in Heaven. **31** And concerning the resurrection of the dead, did you not read that which was spoken to you by God, saying, **32** I am the God of Abraham, and the God of Isaac, and the God of Jacob? God is not a God of dead men, but of living." **33** And having heard, the multitudes were astonished at His teaching; **34** and the Pharisees, having heard that He silenced the Sadducees, were gathered together to Him; **35** and one of them, a lawyer, questioned, tempting Him, and saying, **36** "Teacher, which [is] the great command in the Law?" **37** And Jesus said to him, "You will love the LORD your God with all your heart, and with all your soul, and with all your understanding— **38** this is a first and great command; **39** and the second [is] like to it: You will love your neighbor as yourself; **40** on these—the two commands—all the Law and the Prophets hang." **41** And the Pharisees having been gathered together, Jesus questioned them, **42** saying, "What do you think concerning the Christ? Of whom is He Son?" They say to Him, "Of David." **43** He says to them, "How then does David in the Spirit call Him Lord, saying, **44** The LORD said to my Lord, ‖ Sit at My right hand, ‖ Until I may make Your enemies Your footstool? **45** If then David calls Him Lord, how is He his son?" **46** And no one was able to answer Him a word, nor did any dare question Him from that day [on].

23 Then Jesus spoke to the multitudes, and to His disciples, **2** saying, "On the seat of Moses sat down the scribes and the Pharisees; **3** all, then, as much as they may say to you to observe, observe and do, but according to their works do not do, for they say, and do not do; **4** for they bind together burdens [too] heavy and grievous to bear, and lay [them] on the shoulders of men, but with their finger they will not move them. **5** And all their works they do to be seen by men, and they make broad their phylacteries, and enlarge the fringes of their garments, **6** they also cherish the first couches at the banquets, and the first seats in the synagogues, **7** and the salutations in the marketplaces, and to be called by men, Rabbi, Rabbi. **8** And you may not be called Rabbi, for one is your teacher—the Christ, and you are all brothers; **9** and you may not call [any] your father on the earth, for one is your Father, who is in the heavens, **10** nor may you be called teachers, for one is your teacher—the Christ. **11** And the greater of you will be your servant, **12** and whoever will exalt himself will be humbled, and whoever will humble himself will be exalted. **13** Woe to you, scribes and Pharisees, hypocrites! Because you shut up the kingdom of the heavens before men, for you do not go in, nor do you permit those going in to enter. **14** [[Woe to you, scribes and Pharisees, hypocrites! Because you eat up the houses of the widows, and for a pretense make long prayers, because of this you will receive more abundant judgment.]] **15** Woe to you, scribes and Pharisees, hypocrites! Because you go around the sea and the dry land to make one proselyte, and whenever it may happen—you make him a son of Gehenna twofold more than yourselves. **16** Woe to you, blind guides, who are saying, Whoever may swear by the temple, it is nothing, but whoever may swear by the gold of the temple—is debtor! **17** Fools and blind! For which [is] greater, the gold, or the temple that is sanctifying the gold? **18** And, Whoever may swear by the altar, it is nothing, but whoever may swear by the gift that is on it—is debtor! **19** Fools and blind! For which [is] greater, the gift, or the altar that is sanctifying the gift? **20** He therefore who swore by the altar, swears by it, and by all things on it; **21** and he who swore by the temple, swears by it, and by Him who is dwelling in it; **22** and he who swore by Heaven, swears by the throne of God, and by Him who is sitting on it. **23** Woe to you, scribes and Pharisees, hypocrites! Because you give tithe of the mint, and the dill, and the cumin, and neglected the weightier things of the Law—judgment, and kindness, and faith; these it was necessary to do, and those not to neglect. **24** Blind guides! Who are straining out the gnat, and are swallowing the camel. **25** Woe to you, scribes and Pharisees, hypocrites! Because you make clean the outside of the cup and the plate, and within they are full of robbery and self-indulgence. **26** Blind Pharisee! First cleanse the inside of the cup and the plate, that the outside of them may also become clean. **27** Woe to you, scribes and Pharisees, hypocrites! Because you are like to whitewashed graves, which outwardly indeed appear beautiful, and within are full

MATTHEW

of bones of dead men, and of all uncleanness; **28** so also you outwardly indeed appear to men righteous, and within you are full of hypocrisy and lawlessness. **29** Woe to you, scribes and Pharisees, hypocrites! Because you build the graves of the prophets, and adorn the tombs of the righteous, **30** and say, If we had been in the days of our fathers, we would not have been partakers with them in the blood of the prophets. **31** So that you testify to yourselves that you are sons of them who murdered the prophets; **32** and you fill up the measure of your fathers. **33** Serpents! Brood of vipers! How may you escape from the judgment of Gehenna? **34** Because of this, behold, I send to you prophets, and wise men, and scribes, and of them you will kill and crucify, and of them you will scourge in your synagogues, and will pursue from city to city, **35** that on you may come all the righteous blood being poured out on the earth from the blood of Abel the righteous, to the blood of Zacharias son of Barachias, whom you murdered between the temple and the altar: **36** truly I say to you, all these things will come on this generation. **37** Jerusalem, Jerusalem, that are killing the prophets, and stoning those sent to you, how often I willed to gather your children together, as a hen gathers her own chickens under the wings, and you did not will. **38** Behold, your house is left to you desolate; **39** for I say to you, you may not see Me from now on, until you may say, Blessed [is] He who is coming in the Name of the LORD."

24 And having gone forth, Jesus departed from the temple, and His disciples came near to show Him the buildings of the temple, **2** and Jesus said to them, "Do you not see all these? Truly I say to you, there may not be left here a stone on a stone that will not be thrown down." **3** And when He is sitting on the Mount of Olives, the disciples came near to Him by Himself, saying, "Tell us, when will these be? And what [is] the sign of Your coming, and of the full end of the age?" **4** And Jesus answering said to them, "Take heed that no one may lead you astray, **5** for many will come in My Name, saying, I am the Christ, and they will lead many astray, **6** and you will begin to hear of wars, and reports of wars; see, do not be troubled, for it is necessary for all [these] to come to pass, but the end is not yet. **7** For nation will rise against nation, and kingdom against kingdom, and there will be famines, and pestilences, and earthquakes, in various places; **8** and all these [are the] beginning of travails; **9** then they will deliver you up to tribulation, and will kill you, and you will be hated by all the nations because of My Name; **10** and then will many be stumbled, and they will deliver up one another, and will hate one another. **11** And many false prophets will arise, and will lead many astray; **12** and because of the abounding of the lawlessness, the love of the many will become cold; **13** but he who endured to the end, he will be saved; **14** and this good news of the kingdom will be proclaimed in all the world, for a testimony to all the nations, and then will the end arrive. **15** Whenever, therefore, you may see the abomination of the desolation, that was spoken of through Daniel the prophet, standing in the holy place (whoever is reading let him observe) **16** then those in Judea—let them flee to the mountains; **17** he on the housetop—do not let him come down to take up anything out of his house; **18** and he in the field—do not let him turn back to take his garments. **19** And woe to those with child, and to those giving suck in those days; **20** and pray that your flight may not be in winter, nor on a Sabbath; **21** for there will then be great tribulation, such as was not from the beginning of the world until now, no, nor may be. **22** And if those days were not shortened, no flesh would have been saved; but because of the chosen will those days be shortened. **23** Then if anyone may say to you, Behold, here [is] the Christ! Or, Here! You may not believe; **24** for there will arise false Christs, and false prophets, and they will give great signs and wonders, so as to lead astray, if possible, also the chosen. **25** Behold, I told you beforehand. **26** If therefore they may say to you, Behold, He is in the wilderness, you may not go forth; Behold, in the inner chambers, you may not believe; **27** for as the lightning comes forth from the east, and appears to the west, so will also be the coming of the Son of Man; **28** for wherever the carcass may be, there the eagles will be gathered together. **29** And immediately after the tribulation of those days, the sun will be darkened, and the moon will not give her light, and the stars will fall from the sky, and the powers of the heavens will be shaken; **30** and then will appear the sign of the Son of Man in the sky; and then will all the tribes of the earth strike the breast, and they will see the Son of Man coming on the clouds of Heaven, with power and much glory; **31** and He will send His messengers with a great sound of a trumpet, and they will gather together His chosen from the four winds, from the ends of the heavens to the ends thereof. **32** And from the fig tree learn the allegory: when its branch may have already become tender, and it may put forth the leaves, you know that summer [is] near, **33** so also you, when you may see all these, you know that it is near—at the doors. **34** Truly I say to you, this generation may not pass away until all these may come to pass. **35** The heaven and the earth will pass away, but My words will not pass away. **36** And concerning that day and the hour no one has known—not even the messengers of the heavens—except My Father only; **37** and as the days of Noah—so will also be the coming of the Son of Man; **38** for as they were, in the days before the flood, eating, and drinking, marrying, and giving in marriage, until the day Noah entered into the Ark, **39** and they did not know until the flood came and took all away, so will also be the coming of the Son of Man. **40** Then two [men] will be in the field: one is received, and one is left; **41** two [women] will be grinding in the mill: one is received, and one is left. **42** Watch therefore, because you have not known in what hour your Lord comes; **43** and know this, that if the master of the house had known in what watch the thief comes, he had watched, and did not permit his house to be broken through; **44** because of this also you, become ready, because in what hour you do not think, the Son of Man comes. **45** Who, then, is the servant, faithful and wise, whom his lord set over his household, to give them the nourishment in season? **46** Blessed that servant, whom his lord, having come, will find doing so; **47** truly I say to you that he will set him over all his substance. **48** And if that evil servant may say in his heart, My lord delays to come, **49** and may begin to beat the fellow-servants, and to eat and to drink with the drunken, **50** the lord of that servant will arrive in a day when he does not expect, and in an hour of which he does not know, **51** and will cut him off, and will appoint his portion with the hypocrites; there will be the weeping and the gnashing of the teeth."

25 "Then will the kingdom of the heavens be likened to ten virgins, who, having taken their lamps, went forth to meet the bridegroom; **2** and five of them were prudent, and five foolish; **3** they who were foolish having taken their lamps, did not take with themselves oil; **4** and the prudent took oil in their vessels, with their lamps. **5** And the bridegroom lingering, they all nodded and were sleeping, **6** and in the middle of the night a cry was made, Behold, the bridegroom comes; go forth to meet him! **7** Then all those virgins rose, and trimmed their lamps, **8** and the foolish said to the prudent, Give us of your oil, because our lamps are going out; **9** and the prudent answered, saying, Lest there may not be sufficient for us and you, go rather to those selling, and buy for yourselves. **10** And while they are going away to buy, the bridegroom came, and those ready went in with him to the wedding feasts, and the door was shut; **11** and afterward come also the rest of the virgins, saying, Lord, lord, open to us; **12** and he answering said, Truly I say to you, I have not known you. **13** Watch therefore, for you have not known the day nor the hour in which the Son of Man comes. **14** For—as a man going abroad called his own servants, and delivered to them his substance, **15** and to one he gave five talents, and to another two, and to another one, to each according to his several ability, went abroad immediately. **16** And he who received the five talents, having gone, worked with them, and made five other talents; **17** in like manner also he who [received] the two, he gained, also he, other two; **18** and he who received the one, having gone away, dug in the earth, and hid his lord's money. **19** And after a long time comes the lord of those servants, and takes reckoning with them; **20** and he who received the five talents, having come, brought five other talents, saying, Lord, you delivered five talents to me; behold, I gained five other talents besides them. **21** And his lord said to him, Well done, good and faithful servant, you were faithful over a few things, I will set you over many things; enter into the joy of your lord. **22** And he

MATTHEW

also, who received the two talents, having come, said, Lord, you delivered to me two talents; behold, I gained two other talents besides them. **23** His lord said to him, Well done, good and faithful servant, you were faithful over a few things, I will set you over many things; enter into the joy of your lord. **24** And he also who has received the one talent, having come, said, Lord, I knew you, that you are a hard man, reaping where you did not sow, and gathering from where you did not scatter; **25** and having been afraid, having gone away, I hid your talent in the earth; behold, you have your own! **26** And his lord answering said to him, Evil servant, and slothful, you had known that I reap where I did not sow, and I gather from where I did not scatter! **27** It was necessary [for] you then to put my money to the money-lenders, and having come I had received my own with increase. **28** Take therefore from him the talent, and give to him having the ten talents, **29** for to everyone having will be given, and he will have overabundance, and from him who is not having, even that which he has will be taken from him; **30** and cast forth the unprofitable servant into the outer darkness; there will be the weeping and the gnashing of the teeth. **31** And whenever the Son of Man may come in His glory, and all the holy messengers with Him, then He will sit on a throne of His glory; **32** and all the nations will be gathered together before Him, and He will separate them from one another, as the shepherd separates the sheep from the goats, **33** and He will set the sheep indeed on His right hand, and the goats on the left. **34** Then the King will say to those on His right hand, Come, the blessed of My Father, inherit the kingdom that has been prepared for you from the foundation of the world; **35** for I hungered, and you gave Me to eat; I thirsted, and you gave Me to drink; I was a stranger, and you received Me; **36** naked, and you clothed Me; I was sick, and you looked after Me; I was in prison, and you came to Me. **37** Then will the righteous answer Him, saying, Lord, when did we see You hungering, and we nourished? Or thirsting, and we gave to drink? **38** And when did we see You a stranger, and we received? Or naked, and we clothed? **39** And when did we see You ailing or in prison, and we came to You? **40** And the King answering, will say to them, Truly I say to you, inasmuch as you did [it] to one of these My brothers—the least—you did [it] to Me. **41** Then will He say also to those on the left hand, Go from Me, the cursed, into the continuous fire that has been prepared for the Devil and his messengers; **42** for I hungered, and you gave Me nothing to eat; I thirsted, and you gave Me nothing to drink; **43** I was a stranger, and you did not receive Me; naked, and you did not clothe Me; sick and in prison, and you did not look after Me. **44** Then they will answer, they also, saying, Lord, when did we see You hungering, or thirsting, or a stranger, or naked, or sick, or in prison, and we did not minister to You? **45** Then will He answer them, saying, Truly I say to you, inasmuch as you did [it] not to one of these, the least, you did [it] not to Me. **46** And these will go away into continuous punishment, but the righteous into continuous life."

26 And it came to pass, when Jesus finished all these words, He said to His disciples, **2** "You have known that after two days the Passover comes, and the Son of Man is delivered up to be crucified." **3** Then were gathered together the chief priests, and the scribes, and the elders of the people, into the court of the chief priest who was called Caiaphas; **4** and they consulted together that they might take Jesus by guile, and kill [Him], **5** and they said, "Not in the celebration, that there may not be a tumult among the people." **6** And Jesus having been in Bethany, in the house of Simon the leper, **7** there came to Him a woman having an alabaster box of ointment, very precious, and she poured on His head as He is reclining. **8** And having seen [it], His disciples were much displeased, saying, "To what purpose [is] this waste? **9** For this ointment could have been sold for much, and given to the poor." **10** And Jesus having known, said to them, "Why do you give trouble to the woman? For a good work she worked for Me; **11** for you always have the poor with you, and you do not always have Me; **12** for she having put this ointment on My body—for My burial she did [it]. **13** Truly I say to you, wherever this good news may be proclaimed in the whole world, what this [one] did will also be spoken of—for a memorial of her." **14** Then one of the Twelve, who is called Judas Iscariot,

MATTHEW

having gone to the chief priests, said, **15** "What are you willing to give me, and I will deliver Him up to you?" And they weighed out to him thirty pieces of silver, **16** and from that time he was seeking a convenient season to deliver Him up. **17** And on the first [day] of the Unleavened [Bread] the disciples came near to Jesus, saying to Him, "Where will You [that] we may prepare for You to eat the Passover?" **18** And He said, "Go away into the city, to such a one, and say to him, The Teacher says, My time is near; near you I keep the Passover with My disciples"; **19** and the disciples did as Jesus appointed them, and prepared the Passover. **20** And evening having come, He was reclining with the Twelve, **21** and while they are eating, He said, "Truly I say to you that one of you will deliver Me up." **22** And being grieved exceedingly, they began to say to Him, each of them, "Is it I, Lord?" **23** And He answering said, "He who dipped with Me the hand in the dish, he will deliver Me up; **24** the Son of Man indeed goes, as it has been written concerning Him, but woe to that man through whom the Son of Man is delivered up! It were good for him if that man had not been born." **25** And Judas—he who delivered Him up—answering said, "Is it I, Rabbi?" He says to him, "You have said." **26** And while they were eating, Jesus having taken the bread, and having blessed, broke, and was giving [it] to the disciples, and said, "Take, eat, this is My body"; **27** and having taken the cup, and having given thanks, He gave to them, saying, "Drink of it—all; **28** for this is My blood of the New Covenant, that is being poured out for many, for forgiveness of sins; **29** and I say to you that I may not drink from now on this produce of the vine, until that day when I may drink it with you new in the kingdom of My Father." **30** And having sung a hymn, they went forth to the Mount of Olives; **31** then Jesus says to them, "All you will be stumbled at Me this night; for it has been written: I will strike the Shepherd, and the sheep of the flock will be scattered abroad; **32** but after My having risen, I will go before you to Galilee." **33** And Peter answering said to Him, "Even if all will be stumbled at You, I will never be stumbled." **34** Jesus said to him, "Truly I say to you that this night, before rooster-crowing, three times you will deny Me." **35** Peter says to Him, "Even if it may be necessary for me to die with You, I will not deny You"; in like manner also said all the disciples. **36** Then Jesus comes with them to a place called Gethsemane, and He says to the disciples, "Sit here, until having gone away, I will pray over there." **37** And having taken Peter and the two sons of Zebedee, He began to be sorrowful, and to be very heavy; **38** then He says to them, "Exceedingly sorrowful is My soul—to death; abide here, and watch with Me." **39** And having gone forward a little, He fell on His face, praying, and saying, "My Father, if it be possible, let this cup pass from Me; nevertheless, not as I will, but as You." **40** And He comes to the disciples, and finds them sleeping, and He says to Peter, "So! You were not able to watch with Me one hour! **41** Watch, and pray, that you may not enter into temptation: the spirit indeed is forward, but the flesh weak." **42** Again, a second time, having gone away, He prayed, saying, "My Father, if this cup cannot pass away from Me except I drink it, Your will be done"; **43** and having come, He finds them again sleeping, for their eyes were heavy. **44** And having left them, having gone away again, He prayed a third time, saying the same word; **45** then He comes to His disciples and says to them, "Sleep on from now on, and rest! Behold, the hour has come near, and the Son of Man is delivered up into the hands of sinners. **46** Rise, let us go; behold, he who is delivering Me up has come near." **47** And while He is yet speaking, behold, Judas, one of the Twelve came, and with him a great multitude, with swords and sticks, from the chief priests and elders of the people. **48** And he who delivered Him up gave them a sign, saying, "Whomsoever I will kiss, it is He, lay hold on Him"; **49** and immediately, having come to Jesus, he said, "Greetings, Rabbi," and kissed Him; **50** and Jesus said to him, "Friend, for what are you present?" Then having come near, they laid hands on Jesus, and took hold on Him. **51** And behold, one of those with Jesus, having stretched forth the hand, drew his sword, and having struck the servant of the chief priest, he took off his ear. **52** Then Jesus says to him, "Turn back your sword to its place; for all who took the sword will perish by the sword; **53** do you think that I am not able now to call on My Father, and He will place beside Me more than twelve legions of messengers? **54** How then may the Writings be fulfilled, that thus it must happen?" **55** In that hour Jesus said to the multitudes, "Did you come forth as against a robber, with swords and sticks, to take Me? Daily I was with you sitting, teaching in the temple, and you did not lay hold on Me; **56** but all this has come to pass, that the Writings of the prophets may be fulfilled"; then all the disciples, having left Him, fled. **57** And those laying hold on Jesus led [Him] away to Caiaphas the chief priest, where the scribes and the elders were gathered together, **58** and Peter was following Him far off, to the court of the chief priest, and having gone in within, he was sitting with the officers, to see the end. **59** And the chief priests, and the elders, and all the council, were seeking false witness against Jesus, that they might put Him to death, **60** and they did not find; and many false witnesses having come near, they did not find; and at last two false witnesses having come near, **61** said, "This One said, I am able to throw down the temple of God, and after three days to build it." **62** And the chief priest having stood up, said to Him, "Nothing You answer? What do these witness against You?" **63** And Jesus was silent. And the chief priest answering said to Him, "I adjure You, by the living God, that You may say to us if You are the Christ—the Son of God." **64** Jesus says to him, "You have said; nevertheless I say to you, hereafter you will see the Son of Man sitting on the right hand of the Power and coming on the clouds of Heaven." **65** Then the chief priest tore his garments, saying, "He has slandered; what need have we yet of witnesses? Behold, now you heard His slander; **66** what do you think?" And they answering said, "He is worthy of death." **67** Then they spit in His face and punched Him, and others slapped, **68** saying, "Declare to us, O Christ, who he is that struck You?" **69** And Peter was sitting in the court outside, and there came near to him a certain maid, saying, "And you were with Jesus of Galilee!" **70** And he denied before all, saying, "I have not known what you say." **71** And he having gone forth to the porch, another female saw him, and says to those there, "And this one was with Jesus of Nazareth"; **72** and again he denied with an oath, "I have not known the Man." **73** And after a while those standing near having come, said to Peter, "Truly you also are of them, for even your speech makes you evident." **74** Then he began to curse, and to swear, "I have not known the Man"; and immediately a rooster crowed, **75** and Peter remembered the saying of Jesus, He having said to him, "Before rooster-crowing, you will deny Me three times"; and having gone outside, he wept bitterly.

27 And morning having come, all the chief priests and the elders of the people took counsel against Jesus, so as to put Him to death; **2** and having bound Him, they led [Him] away, and delivered Him up to Pontius Pilate, the governor. **3** Then Judas—he who delivered Him up—having seen that He was condemned, having regretted, brought back the thirty pieces of silver to the chief priests and to the elders, saying, **4** "I sinned, having delivered up innocent blood"; and they said, "What [is that] to us? You will see!" **5** And having cast down the pieces of silver in the temple, he departed, and having gone away, he strangled himself. **6** And the chief priests having taken the pieces of silver, said, "It is not lawful to put them into the treasury, seeing it is the price of blood"; **7** and having taken counsel, they bought the potter's field with them, for the burial of strangers; **8** therefore that field was called, "Field of Blood," to this day. **9** Then was fulfilled that spoken through Jeremiah the prophet, saying, "And I took the thirty pieces of silver, the price of Him who has been priced, whom they of the sons of Israel priced, **10** and gave them for the potter's field, as the LORD appointed to me." **11** And Jesus stood before the governor, and the governor questioned Him, saying, "Are You the King of the Jews?" And Jesus said to him, "You say [it]." **12** And in His being accused by the chief priests and the elders, He did not answer anything; **13** then Pilate says to Him, "Do You not hear how many things they witness against You?" **14** And He did not answer him, not even to one word, so that the governor wondered greatly. **15** And at the celebration the governor had been accustomed to release one to the multitude, a prisoner, whom they willed, **16** and they had a noted prisoner then, called Barabbas, **17** therefore they having been gathered together, Pilate said to them, "Whom do you will [that] I may release to you? Barabbas or Jesus who is called

Christ?" **18** For he had known that they had delivered Him up because of envy. **19** And as he is sitting on the judgment seat, his wife sent to him, saying, "Nothing—to you and to that Righteous One, for I suffered many things today in a dream because of Him." **20** And the chief priests and the elders persuaded the multitudes that they might ask for themselves Barabbas, and might destroy Jesus; **21** and the governor answering said to them, "Which of the two will you [that] I may release to you?" And they said, "Barabbas." **22** Pilate says to them, "What then will I do with Jesus who is called Christ?" They all say to him, "Let [Him] be crucified!" **23** And the governor said, "Why, what evil did He do?" And they were crying out the more, saying, "Let [Him] be crucified!" **24** And Pilate having seen that it profits nothing, but rather a tumult is made, having taken water, he washed the hands before the multitude, saying, "I am innocent from the blood of this Righteous One; you will see [to it] yourselves"; **25** and all the people answering said, "His blood [is] on us, and on our children!" **26** Then he released Barabbas to them, and having scourged Jesus, he delivered [Him] up that He may be crucified; **27** then the soldiers of the governor having taken Jesus to the Praetorium, gathered to Him all the band; **28** and having unclothed Him, they put a crimson cloak around Him, **29** and having plaited Him a garland out of thorns they put [it] on His head, and [put] a reed in His right hand, and having kneeled before Him, they were mocking Him, saying, "Hail, the King of the Jews!" **30** And having spit on Him, they took the reed, and were striking on His head; **31** and when they had mocked Him, they took off the cloak from Him, and put His own garments on Him, and led Him away to crucify [Him]. **32** And coming forth, they found a man, a Cyrenian, by name Simon: they impressed him that he might carry His cross; **33** and having come to a place called Golgotha, which is called "Place of [the] Skull," **34** they gave Him vinegar mixed with gall to drink, and having tasted, He would not drink. **35** And having crucified Him, they divided His garments, casting a lot, [[that it might be fulfilled which was spoken by the prophet: "They divided My garments to themselves, and they cast a lot over My clothing";]] **36** and sitting down, they were watching Him there, **37** and they put up over His head, His accusation written: "THIS IS JESUS, THE KING OF THE JEWS." **38** Then two robbers are crucified with Him, one on the right hand and one on the left, **39** and those passing by kept slandering Him, wagging their heads, **40** and saying, "You that are throwing down the temple, and in three days building [it], save Yourself; if You are the Son of God, come down from the cross." **41** And in like manner also the chief priests mocking, with the scribes and elders, said, **42** "He saved others; He is not able to save Himself! If He is King of Israel, let Him come down now from the cross, and we will believe Him; **43** He has trusted on God, let Him now deliver Him if He wants Him, because He said, I am [the] Son of God"; **44** with the same also the robbers, who were crucified with Him, were reproaching Him. **45** And from the sixth hour darkness came over all the land to the ninth hour, **46** and about the ninth hour Jesus cried out with a great voice, saying, "Eli, Eli, lama sabachthani?" That is, "My God, My God, why did You forsake Me?" **47** And certain of those standing there having heard, said, "He calls Elijah"; **48** and immediately, one of them having run, and having taken a sponge, having filled [it] with vinegar, and having put [it] on a reed, was giving Him to drink, **49** but the rest said, "Let alone, let us see if Elijah comes—about to save Him." **50** And Jesus having again cried with a great voice, yielded the spirit; **51** and behold, the veil of the temple was torn in two from top to bottom, and the earth quaked, and the rocks were split, **52** and the tombs were opened, and many bodies of the holy ones who have fallen asleep, arose, **53** and having come forth out of the tombs after His rising, they went into the holy city, and appeared to many. **54** And the centurion, and those with him watching Jesus, having seen the earthquake, and the things that were done, were exceedingly afraid, saying, "Truly this was God's Son." **55** And there were there many women beholding from afar, who followed Jesus from Galilee, ministering to Him, **56** among whom was Mary the Magdalene, and Mary the mother of James and of Joses, and the mother of the sons of Zebedee. **57** And evening having come, there came a rich man from Arimathea named Joseph, who also himself was discipled to Jesus, **58** he having gone near to Pilate, asked for himself the body of Jesus; then Pilate commanded the body to be given back. **59** And having taken the body, Joseph wrapped it in clean linen, **60** and laid it in his new tomb that he hewed in the rock, and having rolled a great stone to the door of the tomb, he went away; **61** now Mary the Magdalene was there, and the other Mary, sitting opposite the grave. **62** And on the next day that is after the Preparation, the chief priests and the Pharisees were gathered together to Pilate, **63** saying, "Lord, we have remembered that this deceiver said while yet living, After three days I rise; **64** command, then, the grave to be made secure until the third day, lest His disciples, having come by night, may steal Him away, and may say to the people, He rose from the dead, and the last deceit will be worse than the first." **65** And Pilate said to them, "You have a guard, go away, make [it] secure—as you have known"; **66** and they, having gone, made the grave secure, having sealed the stone, together with the guard.

28 Now after [the] Sabbaths, it being dawn, toward the first [day] of the weeks, Mary the Magdalene came, and the other Mary, to see the grave, **2** and behold, there came a great earthquake, for a messenger of the LORD, having come down out of Heaven, having come, rolled away the stone from the door, and was sitting on it, **3** and his countenance was as lightning, and his clothing white as snow, **4** and from the fear of him the keepers shook, and they became as dead men. **5** And the messenger answering said to the women, "Do not fear, for I have known that you seek Jesus who has been crucified; **6** He is not here, for He rose, as He said; come, see the place where the LORD was lying; **7** and having gone quickly, say to His disciples that He rose from the dead; and behold, He goes before you to Galilee, there you will see Him; behold, I have told you." **8** And having gone forth quickly from the tomb, with fear and great joy, they ran to tell His disciples; **9** and as they were going to tell His disciples, then behold, Jesus met them, saying, "Greetings!" And having come near, they laid hold of His feet, and worshiped Him. **10** Then Jesus says to them, "Do not fear, go away, tell My brothers that they may go away to Galilee, and there they will see Me." **11** And while they are going on, behold, certain of the guard having come into the city, reported to the chief priests all the things that happened, **12** and having been gathered together with the elders, having also taken counsel, they gave much money to the soldiers, **13** saying, "Say that His disciples having come by night, stole Him—we being asleep; **14** and if this is heard by the governor, we will persuade him, and you keep free from anxiety." **15** And they, having received the money, did as they were taught, and this account was spread abroad among Jews until this day. **16** And the eleven disciples went to Galilee, to the mountain where Jesus appointed them, **17** and having seen Him, they worshiped Him, but some wavered. **18** And having come near, Jesus spoke to them, saying, "All authority in Heaven and on earth was given to Me; **19** having gone, then, disciple all the nations, immersing them into the Name of the Father, and of the Son, and of the Holy Spirit, **20** teaching them to observe all, whatever I commanded you, and behold, I am with you all the days—until the full end of the age."

MARK

1 A beginning of the good news of Jesus Christ, Son of God. **2** As it has been written in the Prophets: "Behold, I send My messenger before Your face, ‖ Who will prepare Your way before You. **3** A voice of one calling in the wilderness: Prepare the way of the LORD, ‖ Make His paths straight." **4** John came immersing in the wilderness, and proclaiming an immersion of conversion for forgiveness of sins, **5** and there were going forth to him all the region of Judea, and they of Jerusalem, and they were all immersed by him in the river Jordan, confessing their sins. **6** And John was clothed with camel's hair, and a girdle of skin around his loins, and eating locusts and honey of the field, **7** and he proclaimed, saying, "He comes—who is mightier than I—after me, of whom I am not worthy—having stooped down—to loose the strap of His sandals; **8** I indeed immersed you in water, but He will immerse you in the Holy Spirit." **9** And it came to pass in those days, Jesus came from Nazareth of Galilee, and was immersed by John in the Jordan; **10** and immediately coming up from the water, He saw the heavens dividing, and the Spirit coming down on Him as a dove; **11** and a voice came out of the heavens, "You are My Son, the Beloved, in whom I delighted." **12** And immediately the Spirit puts Him forth into the wilderness, **13** and He was there in the wilderness forty days, being tempted by Satan, and He was with the beasts, and the messengers were ministering to Him. **14** And after the delivering up of John, Jesus came to Galilee, proclaiming the good news of the Kingdom of God, **15** and saying, "The time has been fulfilled, and the Kingdom of God has come near, convert and believe in the good news." **16** And walking by the Sea of Galilee, He saw Simon, and his brother Andrew, casting a drag into the sea, for they were fishers, **17** and Jesus said to them, "Come after Me, and I will make you to become fishers of men"; **18** and immediately, having left their nets, they followed Him. **19** And having gone on there a little, He saw James of Zebedee, and his brother John, and they were in the boat refitting the nets, **20** and immediately He called them, and having left their father Zebedee in the boat with the hired servants, they went away after Him. **21** And they go on to Capernaum, and immediately, on the Sabbaths, having gone into the synagogue, He was teaching, **22** and they were astonished at His teaching, for He was teaching them as having authority, and not as the scribes. **23** And there was in their synagogue a man with an unclean spirit, and he cried out, **24** saying, "What [regards] us and You, Jesus the Nazarene? You came to destroy us; I have known You, who You are—the Holy One of God." **25** And Jesus rebuked him, saying, "Be silenced, and come forth out of him," **26** and the unclean spirit having convulsed him, and having cried with a great voice, came forth out of him, **27** and they were all amazed, so as to reason among themselves, saying, "What is this? What new teaching [is] this? That with authority He also commands the unclean spirits, and they obey Him!" **28** And the fame of Him went forth immediately to all the region of Galilee. **29** And immediately, having come forth out of the synagogue, they went into the house of Simon and Andrew, with James and John, **30** and the mother-in-law of Simon was lying fevered, and immediately they tell Him about her, **31** and having come near, He raised her up, having laid hold of her hand, and the fever left her immediately, and she was ministering to them. **32** And evening having come, when the sun set, they brought to Him all who were ill and who were demoniacs, **33** and the whole city was gathered together near the door, **34** and He healed many who were ill of manifold diseases, and He cast forth many demons, and was not permitting the demons to speak, because they knew Him. **35** And very early, it being yet night, having risen, He went forth, and went away to a desolate place, and was praying there; **36** and Simon and those with him went in quest of Him, **37** and having found Him, they say to Him, "All seek You"; **38** and He says to them, "We may go into the next towns, that there also I may preach, for—for this I came forth." **39** And He was preaching in their synagogues, in all Galilee, and is casting out the demons,

MARK

40 and there comes to Him a leper, calling on Him, and kneeling to Him, and saying to Him, "If You may will, You are able to cleanse me." 41 And Jesus having been moved with compassion, having stretched forth the hand, touched him and says to him, "I will, be cleansed"; 42 and He having spoken, immediately the leprosy went away from him, and he was cleansed. 43 And having sternly charged him, immediately He put him forth, 44 and says to him, "See [that] you may say nothing to anyone, but go away, show yourself to the priest, and bring near for your cleansing the things Moses directed, for a testimony to them." 45 And he, having gone forth, began to proclaim much, and to spread the thing abroad, so that He was no longer able to openly enter into the city, but He was outside in desolate places, and they were coming to Him from every quarter.

2 And again He entered into Capernaum, after [some] days, and it was heard that He is in the house, 2 and immediately many were gathered together, so that there was no more room, not even at the door, and He was speaking to them the word. 3 And they come to Him, bringing a paralytic, carried by four, 4 and not being able to come near to Him because of the multitude, they uncovered the roof where He was, and having broken [it] up, they let down the pallet on which the paralytic was lying, 5 and Jesus having seen their faith, says to the paralytic, "Child, your sins have been forgiven you." 6 And there were certain of the scribes sitting there, and reasoning in their hearts, 7 "Why does this One thus speak evil words? Who is able to forgive sins except one—God?" 8 And immediately Jesus, having known in His spirit that they thus reason in themselves, said to them, "Why do you reason these things in your hearts? 9 Which is easier? To say to the paralytic, Your sins are forgiven; or to say, Rise, and take up your pallet, and walk? 10 And that you may know that the Son of Man has authority on the earth to forgive sins—(He says to the paralytic)— 11 I say to you, rise, and take up your pallet, and go away to your house"; 12 and he rose immediately, and having taken up the pallet, he went forth before all, so that all were astonished, and glorify God, saying, "Never thus did we see." 13 And He went forth again by the sea, and all the multitude was coming to Him, and He was teaching them, 14 and passing by, He saw Levi of Alpheus sitting at the tax office, and says to him, "Follow Me," and he, having risen, followed Him. 15 And it came to pass, in His reclining in his house, that many tax collectors and sinners were dining with Jesus and His disciples, for there were many, and they followed Him. 16 And the scribes and the Pharisees, having seen Him eating with the tax collectors and sinners, said to His disciples, "Why—that with the tax collectors and sinners He eats and drinks?" 17 And Jesus, having heard, says to them, "They who are strong have no need of a physician, but they who are ill; I did not come to call righteous men, but sinners." 18 And the disciples of John and those of the Pharisees were fasting, and they come and say to Him, "Why do the disciples of John and those of the Pharisees fast, and Your disciples do not fast?" 19 And Jesus said to them, "Are the sons of the bride-chamber able, while the bridegroom is with them, to fast? As long a time [as] they have the bridegroom with them they are not able to fast; 20 but days will come when the bridegroom may be taken from them, and then they will fast— in those days. 21 And no one sews a patch of undressed cloth on an old garment, and if not—the new, filling it up, takes from the old and the split becomes worse; 22 and no one puts new wine into old skins, and if not—the new wine bursts the skins, and the wine is poured out, and the skins will be destroyed; but new wine is to be put into new skins." 23 And it came to pass—He is going along on the Sabbaths through the grainfields—and His disciples began to make a way, plucking the ears, 24 and the Pharisees said to Him, "Behold, why do they do on the Sabbaths that which is not lawful?" 25 And He said to them, "Did you never read what David did when he had need and was hungry, he and those with him? 26 How he went into the house of God, in [the days of] Abiathar the chief priest, and ate the Bread of the Presentation, which it is not lawful to eat, except to the priests, and he also gave to those who were with him?" 27 And He said to them, "The Sabbath was made for man, not man for the Sabbath, 28 so that the Son of Man is also Lord of the Sabbath."

MARK

3 And He entered again into the synagogue, and there was there a man having the hand withered, **2** and they were watching Him, whether on the Sabbaths He will heal him, that they might accuse Him. **3** And He says to the man having the hand withered, "Rise up in the midst." **4** And He says to them, "Is it lawful on the Sabbaths to do good, or to do evil? To save life, or to kill?" But they were silent. **5** And having looked around on them with anger, being grieved for the hardness of their heart, He says to the man, "Stretch forth your hand"; and he stretched forth, and his hand was restored whole as the other; **6** and the Pharisees having gone forth, immediately, with the Herodians, were taking counsel against Him how they might destroy Him. **7** And Jesus withdrew with His disciples to the sea, and a great multitude from Galilee followed Him, and from Judea, **8** and from Jerusalem, and from Idumea and beyond the Jordan; and they around Tyre and Sidon—a great multitude—having heard how He was doing great things, came to Him. **9** And He said to His disciples that a little boat may wait on Him, because of the multitude, that they may not press on Him, **10** for He healed many, so that they threw themselves on Him, in order to touch Him—as many as had plagues; **11** and the unclean spirits, when they were seeing Him, were falling down before Him, and were crying, saying, "You are the Son of God"; **12** and many times He was charging them that they might not make Him apparent. **13** And He goes up to the mountain, and calls near whom He willed, and they went away to Him; **14** and He appointed twelve, that they may be with Him, and that He may send them forth to preach, **15** and to have power to heal the sicknesses, and to cast out the demons. **16** And He put on Simon the name Peter; **17** and James of Zebedee, and John the brother of James, and He put on them names—Boanerges, that is, "Sons of thunder"; **18** and Andrew, and Philip, and Bartholomew, and Matthew, and Thomas, and James of Alpheus, and Thaddeus, and Simon the Zealot, **19** and Judas Iscariot, who also delivered Him up; and they come into a house. **20** And a multitude comes together again, so that they are not even able to eat bread; **21** and those alongside Him having heard, went forth to lay hold on Him, for they said that He was beside Himself, **22** and the scribes who [are] from Jerusalem having come down, said, "He has Beelzebul," and, "By the ruler of the demons He casts out the demons." **23** And having called them near, He said to them in allegories, "How is Satan able to cast out Satan? **24** And if a kingdom is divided against itself, that kingdom cannot be made to stand; **25** and if a house is divided against itself, that house cannot be made to stand; **26** and if Satan rose against himself, and has been divided, he cannot be made to stand, but has an end. **27** No one is able to spoil the vessels of the strong man, having entered into his house, if first he may not bind the strong man, and then he will spoil his house. **28** Truly I say to you that all sins will be forgiven to the sons of men, and slanders with which they might have slandered, **29** but whoever may slander in regard to the Holy Spirit has no forgiveness—throughout the age, but is in danger of continuous judgment; **30** because they said, He has an unclean spirit." **31** Then His brothers and mother come, and standing outside, they sent to Him, calling Him, **32** and a multitude was sitting around Him, and they said to Him, "Behold, Your mother and Your brothers seek You outside." **33** And He answered them, saying, "Who is My mother, or My brothers?" **34** And having looked around in a circle to those sitting around Him, He says, "Behold, My mother and My brothers! **35** For whoever may do the will of God, he is My brother, and My sister, and mother."

4 And again He began to teach by the sea, and there was gathered to Him a great multitude, so that He, having gone into the boat, sat in the sea, and all the multitude was near the sea, on the land, **2** and He taught them many things in allegories, and He said to them in His teaching: **3** "Listen, behold, the sower went forth to sow; **4** and it came to pass, in the sowing, some fell by the way, and the birds of the sky came and devoured it; **5** and other fell on the rocky ground, where it did not have much earth, and immediately it sprang forth, because of having no depth of earth, **6** and the sun having risen, it was scorched, and because of having no root it withered; **7** and other fell toward the thorns, and the thorns came up and choked it, and it gave no fruit; **8** and other fell to the good ground, and was giving fruit, coming up and increasing, and it was bearing, one thirty-fold, and one sixty, and one a hundred." **9** And He said to them, "He who is having ears to hear—let him hear." **10** And when He was alone, those around Him, with the Twelve, asked Him of the allegory, **11** and He said to them, "To you it has been given to know the secret of the Kingdom of God, but to those who are outside, in allegories are all the things done, **12** that seeing they may see and not perceive, and hearing they may hear and not understand, lest they may turn, and the sins may be forgiven them." **13** And He says to them, "Have you not known this allegory? And how will you know all the allegories? **14** He who is sowing sows the word; **15** and these are they by the way where the word is sown: and whenever they may hear, Satan immediately comes, and he takes away the word that has been sown in their hearts. **16** And these are they, in like manner, who are sown on the rocky ground: who, whenever they may hear the word, immediately receive it with joy, **17** and have no root in themselves, but are temporary; afterward tribulation or persecution having come because of the word, immediately they are stumbled. **18** And these are they who are sown toward the thorns: these are they who are hearing the word, **19** and the anxieties of this age, and the deceitfulness of the riches, and the desires concerning the other things, entering in, choke the word, and it becomes unfruitful. **20** And these are they who on the good ground have been sown: who hear the word, and receive, and bear fruit, one thirty-fold, and one sixty, and one a hundred." **21** And He said to them, "Does the lamp come that it may be put under the measure, or under the bed—not that it may be put on the lampstand? **22** For there is not anything hid that may not be revealed, nor was anything kept hid but that it may come to light. **23** If any has ears to hear—let him hear." **24** And He said to them, "Take heed what you hear; in what measure you measure, it will be measured to you; and to you who hear it will be added; **25** for whoever may have, there will be given to him, and whoever has not, also that which he has will be taken from him." **26** And He said, "Thus is the Kingdom of God: as if a man may cast the seed on the earth, **27** and may sleep, and may rise night and day, and the seed springs up and grows, he has not known how; **28** for of itself the earth bears fruit, first a blade, afterward an ear, afterward full grain in the ear; **29** and whenever the fruit may yield itself, immediately he sends forth the sickle, because the harvest has come." **30** And He said, "To what may we liken the Kingdom of God, or in what allegory may we compare it? **31** As a grain of mustard, which, whenever it may be sown on the earth, is less than any of the seeds that are on the earth; **32** and whenever it may be sown, it comes up, and becomes greater than any of the herbs, and makes great branches, so that under its shade the birds of the sky are able to rest." **33** And with many such allegories He was speaking to them the word, as they were able to hear, **34** and without an allegory He was not speaking to them, and by themselves, to His disciples He was expounding all. **35** And He says to them on that day, evening having come, "We may pass over to the other side"; **36** and having let away the multitude, they take Him up as He was in the boat, and other little boats were also with Him. **37** And there comes a great storm of wind, and the waves were beating on the boat, so that it is now being filled, **38** and He Himself was on the stern, sleeping on the pillow, and they wake Him up, and say to Him, "Teacher, are You not caring that we perish?" **39** And having awoken, He rebuked the wind and said to the sea, "Peace, be stilled"; and the wind stilled, and there was a great calm, **40** and He said to them, "Why are you so fearful? How have you no faith?" **41** And they feared a great fear and said to one another, "Who, then, is this, that even the wind and the sea obey Him?"

5 And they came to the other side of the sea, to the region of the Gadarenes, **2** and He having come forth out of the boat, immediately there met Him out of the tombs a man with an unclean spirit, **3** who had his dwelling in the tombs, and not even with chains was anyone able to bind him, **4** because that many times he had been bound with shackles and chains, and the chains had been pulled in pieces by him, and the shackles broken in pieces, and none was able to tame him, **5** and always, night and day, he was in the mountains, and in the tombs, crying and cutting himself with stones. **6** And having seen Jesus from afar, he ran and prostrated to Him, **7** and having called with a loud voice, he said, "What [regards] me and You, Jesus, Son of God the Most High? I adjure You by God, may You not afflict me!" **8** For He said to him, "Come forth, unclean spirit, out of the man!" **9** And He was questioning him, "What [is] your name?" And he answered, saying, "Legion [is] my name, because we are many"; **10** and he was calling on Him much, that He may not send them out of the region. **11** And there was there, near the mountains, a great herd of pigs feeding, **12** and all the demons called on Him, saying, "Send us to the pigs, that into them we may enter"; **13** and immediately Jesus gave them leave, and having come forth, the unclean spirits entered into the pigs, and the herd rushed down the steep place to the sea—and they were about two thousand—and they were choked in the sea. **14** And those feeding the pigs fled, and told in the city, and in the fields, and they came forth to see what it is that has been done; **15** and they come to Jesus, and see the demoniac, sitting, and clothed, and right-minded—him having had the legion—and they were afraid; **16** and those having seen [it], declared to them how it had come to pass to the demoniac, and about the pigs; **17** and they began to call on Him to go away from their borders. **18** And He having gone into the boat, the demoniac was calling on Him that he may be with Him, **19** and Jesus did not permit him, but says to him, "Go away to your house, to your own [friends], and tell them how the LORD did great things to you, and dealt kindly with you"; **20** and he went away, and began to proclaim in the Decapolis how Jesus did great things to him, and all were wondering. **21** And Jesus having passed over in the boat again to the other side, there was gathered a great multitude to Him, and He was near the sea, **22** and behold, there comes one of the chiefs of the synagogue, by name Jairus, and having seen Him, he falls at His feet, **23** and he was calling on Him much, saying, "My little daughter is at the last extremity—that having come, You may lay on her [Your] hands, so that she may be saved, and she will live"; **24** and He went away with him. And there was following Him a great multitude, and they were thronging Him, **25** and a certain woman, being with a flow of blood [for] twelve years, **26** and having suffered many things under many physicians, and having spent all that she had, and having profited nothing, but rather having come to the worse, **27** having heard about Jesus, having come in the multitude behind, she touched His garment, **28** for she said, "If I may even touch His garments, I will be saved"; **29** and immediately the fountain of her blood was dried up, and she knew in the body that she has been healed of the plague. **30** And immediately Jesus having known in Himself that power had gone forth out of Him, having turned in the multitude, said, "Who touched My garments?" **31** And His disciples said to Him, "You see the multitude thronging You, and You say, Who touched Me!" **32** And He was looking around to see her who did this, **33** and the woman, having been afraid, and trembling, knowing what was done on her, came, and fell down before Him, and told Him all the truth, **34** and He said to her, "Daughter, your faith has saved you; go away in peace, and be whole from your plague." **35** As He is yet speaking, there come from the chief of the synagogue's [house, certain], saying, "Your daughter died, why do you still harass the Teacher?" **36** And Jesus immediately, having heard the word that is spoken, says to the chief of the synagogue, "Do not be afraid, only believe." **37** And He did not permit anyone to follow with Him, except Peter, and James, and John the brother of James; **38** and He comes into the house of the chief of the synagogue, and sees a tumult, much weeping and wailing; **39** and having gone in He says to them, "Why do you make a tumult, and weep? The child did not die, but sleeps"; **40** and they were laughing at Him. And He, having put all forth, takes the father of the child, and the mother, and those with Him, and goes in where the child is lying, **41** and having taken the hand of the child, He says to her, "Talitha cumi"; which is, being interpreted, "Girl (I say to you), arise." **42** And immediately the girl arose, and was walking, for she was twelve years [old]; and they were amazed with a great amazement, **43** and He charged them much, that no one may know this thing, and He said that there be given to her to eat.

6 And He went forth from there, and came to His own country, and His disciples follow Him, **2** and Sabbath having come, He began to teach in the synagogue, and many hearing were astonished, saying, "From where [did] this One [hear] these things? And what [is] the wisdom that was given to Him, that also such mighty works are done through His hands? **3** Is this not the carpenter, the Son of Mary, and brother of James, and Joses, and Judas, and Simon? And are His sisters not here with us?" And they were being stumbled at Him. **4** And Jesus said to them, "A prophet is not without honor, except in his own country, and among his relatives, and in his own house"; **5** and He was not able to do any mighty work there, except having put hands on a few sick, He healed [them]; **6** and He wondered because of their unbelief. And He was going around the villages, in a circle, teaching, **7** and He calls near the Twelve, and He began to send them forth two by two, and He was giving them power over the unclean spirits, **8** and He commanded them that they may take nothing for the way, except a staff only—no leather pouch, no bread, no brass in the girdle, **9** but having been shod with sandals, and you may not put on two coats. **10** And He said to them, "Whenever you may enter into a house, remain there until you may depart from there, **11** and as many as may not receive you nor hear you, going out from there, shake off the dust that is under your feet for a testimony to them; [[truly I say to you, it will be more tolerable for Sodom or Gomorrah in [the] day of judgment than for that city."]] **12** And having gone forth they were preaching that [men] might convert, **13** and they were casting out many demons, and they were anointing many sick with oil, and they were healing [them]. **14** And King Herod heard (for His Name became public), and he said, "John the Immerser was raised out of the dead, and because of this the mighty powers are working in him." **15** Others said, "It is Elijah," and others said, "It is a prophet, or as one of the prophets." **16** And Herod having heard, said, "He whom I beheaded—John—this is he; he was raised out of the dead." **17** For Herod himself, having sent forth, laid hold on John, and bound him in the prison, because of Herodias, the wife of his brother Philip, because he married her, **18** for John said to Herod, "It is not lawful for you to have the wife of your brother"; **19** and Herodias was having a quarrel with him, and was willing to kill him, and was not able, **20** for Herod was fearing John, knowing him [to be] a righteous and holy man, and was keeping watch over him, and having heard him, was doing many things, and hearing him gladly. **21** And a seasonable day having come when Herod on his birthday was making a banquet to his great men, and to the chiefs of thousands, and to the first men of Galilee, **22** and the daughter of that Herodias having come in, and having danced, and having pleased Herod and those dining with him, the king said to the girl, "Ask of me whatever you will, and I will give to you," **23** and he swore to her, "Whatever you may ask me, I will give to you—to the half of my kingdom." **24** And she, having gone forth, said to her mother, "What will I ask for myself?" And she said, "The head of John the Immerser"; **25** and having come in immediately with haste to the king, she asked, saying, "I will that you may immediately give me the head of John the Immerser on a plate." **26** And the king, made very sorrowful because of the oaths and of those reclining with him, would not put her away, **27** and immediately the king having sent a guardsman, commanded his head to be brought, **28** and he having gone, beheaded him in the prison, and brought his head on a plate, and gave it to the girl, and the girl gave it to her mother; **29** and having heard, his disciples came and took up his corpse, and laid it in the tomb. **30** And the apostles are gathered together to Jesus, and they told Him all, and how many things they did, and how many things they taught, **31** and He said to them, "Come yourselves apart to a desolate place, and rest a little," for those coming and those going were many, and not even to eat had they opportunity, **32** and they went away to a desolate place, in the boat, by themselves. **33** And the multitudes saw them going away, and many recognized Him, and they ran there by land from all the cities, and went before them, and came together to Him, **34** and having come forth, Jesus saw a great multitude, and was moved with compassion on them, that they were as sheep not having a shepherd, and He began to teach many things. **35** And now the hour being advanced, His disciples having come near to Him, say, "The place is desolate, and the hour is now advanced, **36** let them away, that having gone away into the surrounding fields and villages, they may buy loaves for themselves, for they do not have what they may eat." **37** And He answering said to them, "You give them to eat," and they say to Him, "Having gone away, may we buy two hundred denarii worth of loaves, and give to them to eat?" **38** And He says to them, "How many loaves do you have? Go and see"; and having known, they say, "Five, and two fishes." **39** And He commanded them to make all recline in companies on the green grass, **40** and they sat down in squares, by hundreds, and by fifties. **41** And having taken the five loaves and the two fishes, having looked up to the sky, He blessed, and broke the loaves, and was giving [them] to His disciples, that they may set [them] before them, and the two fishes He divided to all, **42** and they all ate, and were filled, **43** and they took up of broken pieces twelve hand-baskets full, and of the fishes, **44** and those eating of the loaves were about five thousand men. **45** And immediately He constrained His disciples to go into the boat, and to go before [Him] to the other side, to Bethsaida, until He may let the multitude away, **46** and having taken leave of them, He went away to the mountain to pray. **47** And evening having come, the boat was in the midst of the sea, and He alone on the land; **48** and He saw them harassed in the rowing, for the wind was against them, and about the fourth watch of the night He comes to them walking on the sea, and wished to pass by them. **49** And they having seen Him walking on the sea, thought [it] to be an apparition, and cried out, **50** for they all saw Him, and were troubled, and immediately He spoke with them, and says to them, "Take courage! I AM; do not be afraid." **51** And He went up to them into the boat, and the wind stilled, and greatly out of measure they were amazed in themselves, and were wondering, **52** for they did not understand concerning the loaves, for their heart has been hard. **53** And having passed over, they came on the land of Gennesaret, and drew to the shore, **54** and they having come forth out of the boat, immediately having recognized Him, **55** they ran around through all that surrounding region, and they began to carry around on the pallets those being ill, where they were hearing that He is, **56** and wherever He was going, to villages, or cities, or fields, in the marketplaces they were laying the ailing, and were calling on Him, that they may touch if it were but the fringe of His garment, and as many as were touching Him were saved.

7 And gathered together to Him are the Pharisees, and certain of the scribes, having come from Jerusalem, **2** and having seen certain of His disciples with defiled hands—that is, unwashed—eating bread, they found fault; **3** for the Pharisees, and all the Jews, if they do not wash the hands to the wrist, do not eat, holding the tradition of the elders, **4** and [coming] from the marketplace, if they do not immerse themselves, they do not eat; and many other things there are that they received to hold, immersions of cups, and pots, and bronze vessels, and couches. **5** Then the Pharisees and the scribes question Him, "Why do Your disciples not walk according to the tradition of the elders, but eat the bread with unwashed hands?" **6** And He answering said to them, "Well did Isaiah prophesy concerning you, hypocrites, as it has been written: This people honors Me with the lips, and their heart is far from Me; **7** and in vain they worship Me, teaching teachings, commands of men; **8** for having put away the command of God, you hold the tradition of men, immersions of pots and cups; and many other such like things you do." **9** And He said to them, "Well do you put away the command of God that you may keep your tradition; **10** for Moses said, Honor your father and your mother; and, He who is speaking evil of father or mother—let him die the death; **11** and you say, If a man may say to father or to mother, Korban (that is, a gift), [is] whatever you may be profited out of mine, **12** and you no longer permit him to do anything for his father or for his mother, **13** setting aside the word of God for your tradition that you delivered; and many such like things you do." **14** And having called near all the multitude, He said to them, "Listen to Me, you all, and understand; **15** there is nothing from outside the man entering into him that is able to defile him, but the things coming out from him, those are the things defiling the man. **16** [[If any has ears to hear—let him hear."]] **17** And when He entered into a house from the multitude, His disciples were questioning Him about the allegory,

MARK

18 and He says to them, "So also you are without understanding! Do you not perceive that nothing from outside entering into the man is able to defile him? **19** Because it does not enter into his heart, but into the belly, and into the drain it goes out, purifying all the meats." **20** And He said, "That which is coming out from the man, that defiles the man; **21** for from within, out of the heart of men, the evil reasonings come forth, adulteries, whoredoms, murders, **22** thefts, covetous desires, wickedness, deceit, arrogance, an evil eye, slander, pride, foolishness; **23** all these evils come forth from within, and they defile the man." **24** And from there having risen, He went away to the borders of Tyre and Sidon, and having entered into the house, He wished none to know, and He was not able to be hid, **25** for a woman having heard about Him, whose little daughter had an unclean spirit, having come, fell at His feet— **26** and the woman was a Greek, a Syro-Phoenician by nation—and was asking Him that He may cast forth the demon out of her daughter. **27** And Jesus said to her, "First permit the children to be filled, for it is not good to take the children's bread, and to cast [it] to the little dogs." **28** And she answered and says to Him, "Yes, Lord; for the little dogs under the table also eat of the children's crumbs." **29** And He said to her, "Because of this word, go; the demon has gone forth out of your daughter"; **30** and having come away to her house, she found the demon gone forth, and the daughter laid on the bed. **31** And again, having gone forth from the coasts of Tyre and Sidon, He came to the Sea of Galilee, through the midst of the coasts of Decapolis, **32** and they bring to Him a deaf, stuttering man, and they call on Him that He may put the hand on him. **33** And having taken him away from the multitude by Himself, He put His fingers to his ears, and having spit, He touched his tongue, **34** and having looked to the sky, He sighed, and says to him, "Ephphatha," that is, "Be opened"; **35** and immediately his ears were opened, and the string of his tongue was loosed, and he was speaking plain. **36** He charged them that they may tell no one, but the more He was charging them, the more abundantly they were proclaiming [it], **37** and they were being astonished beyond measure, saying, "He has done all things well; He makes both the deaf to hear, and the mute to speak."

8 In those days the multitude being very great, and not having what they may eat, Jesus having called near His disciples, says to them, **2** "I have compassion on the multitude, because now three days they continue with Me, and they have not what they may eat; **3** and if I will let them away fasting to their home, they will faint in the way, for certain of them are come from far." **4** And His disciples answered Him, "From where will anyone be able to feed these here in a wilderness with bread?" **5** And He was questioning them, "How many loaves do you have?" And they said, "Seven." **6** And He commanded the multitude to sit down on the ground, and having taken the seven loaves, having given thanks, He broke, and was giving to His disciples that they may set before [them]; and they set before the multitude. **7** And they had a few small fishes, and having blessed, He said to set them also before [them]; **8** and they ate and were filled, and they took up that which was over of broken pieces—seven baskets; **9** and those eating were about four thousand. And He let them away, **10** and immediately having entered into the boat with His disciples, He came to the parts of Dalmanutha, **11** and the Pharisees came forth, and began to dispute with Him, seeking from Him a sign from Heaven, tempting Him; **12** and having sighed deeply in His spirit, He says, "Why does this generation seek after a sign? Truly I say to you, no sign will be given to this generation." **13** And having left them, having entered again into the boat, He went away to the other side; **14** and they forgot to take loaves, and except one loaf they had nothing with them in the boat, **15** and He was charging them, saying, "Take heed, beware of the leaven of the Pharisees, and of the leaven of Herod," **16** and they were reasoning with one another, saying, "Because we have no loaves." **17** And Jesus having known, says to them, "Why do you reason, because you have no loaves? Do you not yet perceive, nor understand, yet have you hardened your heart? **18** Having eyes, do you not see? And having ears, do you not hear? And do you not remember? **19** When I broke the five loaves to the five thousand, how many

MARK

hand-baskets full of broken pieces did you take up?" They say to Him, "Twelve." **20** "And when the seven to the four thousand, how many hand-baskets full of broken pieces did you take up?" And they said, "Seven." **21** And He said to them, "How do you not understand?" **22** And He comes to Bethsaida, and they bring to Him one blind, and call on Him that He may touch him, **23** and having taken the hand of the blind man, He led him forth outside the village, and having spit on his eyes, having put [His] hands on him, He was questioning him if he beholds anything: **24** and he, having looked up, said, "I behold men, as I see trees, walking." **25** Afterward again He put [His] hands on his eyes, and made him look up, and he was restored, and discerned all things clearly, **26** and He sent him away to his house, saying, "Neither may you go into the village, nor tell [it] to any in the village." **27** And Jesus went forth, and His disciples, into the villages of Caesarea Philippi, and in the way He was questioning His disciples, saying to them, "Who do men say I am?" **28** And they answered, "John the Immerser, and others Elijah, but others one of the prophets." **29** And He says to them, "And you—who do you say I am?" And Peter answering says to him, "You are the Christ." **30** And He strictly charged them that they may tell no one about it, **31** and began to teach them that it is necessary for the Son of Man to suffer many things, and to be rejected by the elders, and chief priests, and scribes, and to be killed, and to rise again after three days; **32** and openly He was speaking the word. And Peter having taken Him aside, began to rebuke Him, **33** and He, having turned, and having looked on His disciples, rebuked Peter, saying, "Get behind Me, Satan, because you do not mind the things of God, but the things of men." **34** And having called near the multitude, with His disciples, He said to them, "Whoever wills to come after Me—let him disown himself, and take up his cross, and follow Me; **35** for whoever may will to save his life will lose it; and whoever may lose his life for My sake and for the good news' sake, he will save it; **36** for what will it profit a man, if he may gain the whole world, and forfeit his life? **37** Or what will a man give as an exchange for his life? **38** For whoever may be ashamed of Me, and of My words, in this adulterous and sinful generation, the Son of Man will also be ashamed of him when He may come in the glory of His Father with the holy messengers."

9 And He said to them, "Truly I say to you that there are certain of those standing here, who may not taste of death until they see the Kingdom of God having come in power." **2** And after six days Jesus takes Peter, and James, and John, and brings them up to a high mountain by themselves, alone, and He was transfigured before them, **3** and His garments became glittering, exceedingly white, as snow, so as a launderer on the earth is not able to whiten [them]. **4** And there appeared to them Elijah with Moses, and they were talking with Jesus. **5** And Peter answering says to Jesus, "Rabbi, it is good to us to be here; and we may make three shelters, for You one, and for Moses one, and for Elijah one": **6** for he was not knowing what he might say, for they were greatly afraid. **7** And there came a cloud overshadowing them, and there came a voice out of the cloud, saying, "This is My Son, the Beloved, hear Him"; **8** and suddenly, having looked around, they saw no one anymore, but Jesus only with themselves. **9** And as they are coming down from the mountain, He charged them that they may declare to no one the things that they saw, except when the Son of Man may rise out of the dead; **10** and the thing they kept to themselves, questioning together what the rising out of the dead is. **11** And they were questioning Him, saying that the scribes say that Elijah must come first. **12** And He answering said to them, "Elijah indeed, having come first, restores all things; and how has it been written concerning the Son of Man, that He may suffer many things, and be set at nothing? **13** But I say to you that also Elijah has come, and they did to him what they willed, as it has been written of him." **14** And having come to the disciples, He saw a great multitude around them, and scribes questioning with them, **15** and immediately, all the multitude having seen Him, were amazed, and running near, were greeting Him. **16** And He questioned the scribes, "What do you dispute with them?" **17** And one out of the multitude answering said, "Teacher, I brought my son to You, having a mute spirit; **18** and wherever it seizes him, it tears him, and he foams, and gnashes his teeth, and pines away; and I spoke to Your disciples that they may cast it out, and they were not able." **19** And He answering him, said, "O generation unbelieving, until when will I be with you? Until when will I suffer you? Bring him to Me"; **20** and they brought him to Him, and he having seen Him, immediately the spirit convulsed him, and he, having fallen on the earth, was wallowing—foaming. **21** And He questioned his father, "How much time is it since this came to him?" And he said, "From childhood, **22** and many times it also cast him into fire, and into water, that it might destroy him; but if You are able to do anything, help us, having compassion on us." **23** And Jesus said to him, "If you are able to believe! All things are possible to the one that is believing"; **24** and immediately the father of the child, having cried out with tears, said, "I believe, Lord; be helping my unbelief." **25** Jesus having seen that a multitude runs together, rebuked the unclean spirit, saying to it, "Spirit—mute and deaf—I charge you, come forth out of him, and you may no longer enter into him"; **26** and having cried, and convulsed him much, it came forth, and he became as dead, so that many said that he was dead, **27** but Jesus, having taken him by the hand, lifted him up, and he arose. **28** And He having come into the house, His disciples were questioning Him by Himself, "Why were we not able to cast it forth?" **29** And He said to them, "This kind is able to come forth with nothing except with prayer and fasting." **30** And having gone forth there, they were passing through Galilee, and He did not wish that any may know, **31** for He was teaching His disciples, and He said to them, "The Son of Man is being delivered into the hands of men, and they will kill Him, and having been killed, the third day He will rise," **32** but they were not understanding the saying, and they were afraid to question Him. **33** And He came to Capernaum, and being in the house, He was questioning them, "What were you reasoning in the way among yourselves?" **34** And they were silent, for they reasoned with one another in the way who is greater; **35** and having sat down He called the Twelve, and He says to them, "If any wills to be first, he will be last of all, and minister of all." **36** And having taken a child, He set him in the midst of them, and having taken him in His arms, said to them, **37** "Whoever may receive one of such children in My Name, receives Me, and whoever may receive Me, does not receive Me, but Him who sent Me." **38** And John answered Him, saying, "Teacher, we saw a certain one casting out demons in Your Name, who does not follow us, and we forbade him, because he does not follow us." **39** And Jesus said, "Do not forbid him, for there is no one who will do a mighty work in My Name, and will be readily able to speak evil of Me: **40** for he who is not against us is for us; **41** for whoever may give you to drink a cup of water in My Name, because you are Christ's, truly I say to you, he may not lose his reward; **42** and whoever may cause to stumble one of the little ones believing in Me, better is it for him if a millstone is hanged around his neck, and he has been cast into the sea. **43** And if your hand may cause you to stumble, cut it off; it is better for you to enter into life maimed, than having the two hands, to go away into Gehenna, into the fire—the unquenchable— **44** [[where their worm is not dying, and the fire is not being quenched.]] **45** And if your foot may cause you to stumble, cut it off; it is better for you to enter into life lame, than having the two feet to be cast into Gehenna, into the fire—the unquenchable— **46** [[where their worm is not dying, and the fire is not being quenched.]] **47** And if your eye may cause you to stumble, cast it out; it is better for you to enter into the Kingdom of God one-eyed, than having two eyes, to be cast into the Gehenna of fire— **48** where their worm is not dying, and the fire is not being quenched; **49** for everyone will be salted with fire, and every sacrifice will be salted with salt. **50** The salt [is] good, but if the salt may become saltless, in what will you season [it]? Have in yourselves salt, and have peace in one another."

10 And having risen from there, He comes to the coasts of Judea, through the other side of the Jordan, and again multitudes come together to Him, and as He had been accustomed, again He was teaching them. **2** And the Pharisees, having come near, questioned Him if it is lawful for a husband to put away a wife, tempting Him, **3** and He answering said to them, "What did Moses command you?" **4** And they said, "Moses permitted to write a bill of divorce, and to put away." **5** And Jesus answering said to them, "For the stiffness of your heart he wrote you this command, **6** but from the beginning of the creation God made them a male and a female; **7** on this account will a man leave his father and mother, and will cleave to his wife, **8** and they will be—the two—for one flesh, so that they are no longer two, but one flesh; **9** what God therefore joined together, do not let man separate." **10** And in the house His disciples again questioned Him of the same thing, **11** and He says to them, "Whoever may put away his wife, and may marry another, commits adultery against her; **12** and if a woman may put away her husband, and is married to another, she commits adultery." **13** And they were bringing to Him children that He might touch them, and the disciples were rebuking those bringing them, **14** and Jesus having seen, was much displeased, and He said to them, "Permit the children to come to Me, and do not forbid them, for of such is the Kingdom of God; **15** truly I say to you, whoever may not receive the Kingdom of God as a child—he may not enter into it"; **16** and having taken them in His arms, having put [His] hands on them, He was blessing them. **17** And as He is going forth into the way, one having run and having kneeled to Him, was questioning Him, "Good Teacher, what may I do that I may inherit continuous life?" **18** And Jesus said to him, "Why do you call Me good? No one [is] good except one—God; **19** you have known the commands: You may not commit adultery, You may not murder, You may not steal, You may not bear false witness, You may not defraud, Honor your father and mother." **20** And he answering said to Him, "Teacher, all these I have kept from my youth." **21** And Jesus having looked on him, loved him, and said to him, "One thing you lack: go away, whatever you have—sell, and give to the poor, and you will have treasure in Heaven, and come, follow Me, having taken up the cross." **22** And he—gloomy at the word—went away sorrowing, for he was having many possessions. **23** And Jesus having looked around, says to His disciples, "How hardly will they who have riches enter into the Kingdom of God!" **24** And the disciples were astonished at His words, and Jesus again answering says to them, "Children, how hard it is to those trusting on riches to enter into the Kingdom of God! **25** It is easier for a camel to enter through the eye of the needle, than for a rich man to enter into the Kingdom of God." **26** And they were astonished beyond measure, saying to themselves, "And who is able to be saved?" **27** And Jesus, having looked on them, says, "With men it is impossible, but not with God; for all things are possible with God." **28** And Peter began to say to Him, "Behold, we left all, and we followed You." **29** And Jesus answering said, "Truly I say to you, there is no one who left house, or brothers, or sisters, or father, or mother, or wife, or children, or fields, for My sake, and for the good news', **30** who may not receive a hundredfold now in this time, houses, and brothers, and sisters, and mothers, and children, and fields, with persecutions, and in the age that is coming, continuous life; **31** and many first will be last, and the last first." **32** And they were in the way going up to Jerusalem, and Jesus was going before them, and they were amazed, and following they were afraid. And having again taken the Twelve, He began to tell them the things about to happen to Him: **33** "Behold, we go up to Jerusalem, and the Son of Man will be delivered to the chief priests, and to the scribes, and they will condemn Him to death, and will deliver Him to the nations, **34** and they will mock Him, and scourge Him, and spit on Him, and kill Him, and the third day He will rise again." **35** And there come near to Him James and John, the sons of Zebedee, saying, "Teacher, we wish that whatever we may ask for ourselves, You may do for us"; **36** and He said to them, "What do you wish Me to do for you?" **37** And they said to Him, "Grant to us that, one on Your right hand and one on Your left, we may sit in Your glory"; **38** and Jesus said to them, "You have not known what you ask; are you able to drink of the cup that I drink of, and with the immersion that I am immersed with—to be immersed?" **39** And they said to Him, "We are able"; and Jesus said to them, "Of the cup indeed that I drink of, you will drink, and with the immersion that I am immersed with, you will be immersed; **40** but to sit on My right and on My left is not Mine to give, but—to those for whom it has been prepared." **41** And the ten having heard, began to be much displeased at James and John, **42** but Jesus having called them near, says to them, "You have known that they who are considered to rule the nations exercise lordship over them, and their great ones exercise authority on them; **43** but not so will it be among you; but whoever may will to become great among you, he will be your minister, **44** and whoever of you may will to become first, he will be servant of all; **45** for even the Son of Man did not come to be ministered to, but to minister, and to give His life [as] a ransom for many." **46** And they come to Jericho, and as He is going forth from Jericho with His disciples and a great multitude, a son of Timaeus—Bartimaeus the blind—was sitting beside the way begging, **47** and having heard that it is Jesus the Nazarene, he began to cry out, and to say, "The Son of David—Jesus! Deal kindly with me"; **48** and many were rebuking him that he might keep silent, but the more abundantly he cried out, "Son of David, deal kindly with me." **49** And Jesus having stood, He commanded him to be called, and they call the blind man, saying to him, "Take courage, rise, He calls you"; **50** and he, having cast away his garment, having risen, came to Jesus. **51** And answering, Jesus says to him, "What do you will I may do to you?" And the blind man said to Him, "Rabboni, that I may see again"; **52** and Jesus said to him, "Go, your faith has saved you": and immediately he saw again, and was following Jesus in the way.

11 And when they come near to Jerusalem, to Bethphage, and Bethany, to the Mount of Olives, He sends forth two of His disciples, **2** and says to them, "Go away into the village that is in front of you, and immediately, entering into it, you will find a colt tied, on which no one of men has sat, having loosed it, bring [it]: **3** and if anyone may say to you, Why do you do this? Say that the LORD has need of it, and immediately He will send it here." **4** And they went away, and found the colt tied at the door outside, by the two ways, and they loose it, **5** and certain of those standing there said to them, "What do you—loosing the colt?" **6** And they said to them as Jesus commanded, and they permitted them. **7** And they brought the colt to Jesus, and cast their garments on it, and He sat on it, **8** and many spread their garments in the way, and others were cutting down branches from the trees, and were strewing in the way. **9** And those going before and those following were crying out, saying, "Hosanna! Blessed [is] He who is coming in the Name of the LORD; **10** blessed is the coming kingdom, in the Name of the LORD, of our father David; Hosanna in the highest!" **11** And Jesus entered into Jerusalem, and into the temple, and having looked around on all things, it being now evening, He went forth to Bethany with the Twelve. **12** And on the next day, they having come forth from Bethany, He hungered, **13** and having seen a fig tree far off having leaves, He came, if perhaps He will find anything in it, and having come to it, He found nothing except leaves, for it was not a time of figs, **14** and Jesus answering said to it, "No longer from you—throughout the age—may any eat fruit"; and His disciples were hearing. **15** And they come to Jerusalem, and Jesus having gone into the temple, began to cast forth those selling and buying in the temple, and He overthrew the tables of the money-changers and the seats of those selling the doves, **16** and He did not permit that any might carry a vessel through the temple, **17** and He was teaching, saying to them, "Has it not been written: My house will be called a house of prayer for all the nations? And you made it a den of robbers!" **18** And the scribes and the chief priests heard, and they were seeking how they will destroy Him, for they were afraid of Him, because all the multitude was astonished at His teaching; **19** and when evening came, He was going forth outside the city. **20** And in the morning, passing by, they saw the fig tree having been dried up from the roots, **21** and Peter having remembered says to Him, "Rabbi, behold, the fig tree that You cursed is dried up." **22** And Jesus answering says to them, "Have faith from God; **23** for truly I say to you that whoever may say to this mountain, Be taken up, and be cast into the sea, and may not doubt in his heart, but may believe that the things that he says come to pass, it will be to him whatever he may say. **24** Because of this I say to you, all whatever—praying—you ask, believe that you receive, and it will be to you. **25** And whenever you may stand praying, forgive, if you have anything against anyone, that your Father who is in the heavens may also forgive you your trespasses; **26** [[and, if

MARK

you do not forgive, neither will your Father who is in the heavens forgive your trespasses."]] **27** And they come again to Jerusalem, and in the temple, as He is walking, there come to Him the chief priests, and the scribes, and the elders, **28** and they say to Him, "By what authority do You do these things? And who gave You this authority that You may do these things?" **29** And Jesus answering said to them, "I will question you—I also—one word; and answer Me, and I will tell you by what authority I do these things; **30** the immersion of John—was it from Heaven or from men? Answer Me." **31** And they were reasoning with themselves, saying, "If we may say, From Heaven, He will say, Why then did you not believe him? **32** But if we may say, From men…" They were fearing the people, for all were holding that John was indeed a prophet; **33** and answering they say to Jesus, "We have not known"; and Jesus answering says to them, "Neither do I tell you by what authority I do these things."

12 And He began to speak to them in allegories: "A man planted a vineyard, and put a hedge around, and dug a wine vat, and built a tower, and gave it out to farmers, and went abroad; **2** and he sent to the farmers at the due time a servant, that from the farmers he may receive from the fruit of the vineyard; **3** and they, having taken him, severely beat [him], and sent him away empty. **4** And again he sent to them another servant, and having cast stones at that one, they wounded [him] in the head, and sent [him] away—dishonored. **5** And again he sent another, and that one they killed; and many others, some beating, and some killing. **6** Having yet therefore one son—his beloved—he also sent him to them last, saying, They will respect my son; **7** and those farmers said among themselves, This is the heir, come, we may kill him, and the inheritance will be ours; **8** and having taken him, they killed, and cast [him] forth outside the vineyard. **9** What therefore will the lord of the vineyard do? He will come and destroy the farmers, and will give the vineyard to others. **10** And this Writing you did not read: A stone that the builders rejected, it became the head of a corner; **11** this was from the LORD, and it is wonderful in our eyes." **12** And they were seeking to lay hold on Him, and they feared the multitude, for they knew that He spoke the allegory against them, and having left Him, they went away; **13** and they send to Him certain of the Pharisees and of the Herodians, that they may ensnare Him in discourse, **14** and they having come, say to Him, "Teacher, we have known that You are true, and You are not caring for anyone, for You do not look to the face of men, but in truth teach the way of God; is it lawful to give tribute to Caesar or not? May we give, or may we not give?" **15** And He, knowing their hypocrisy, said to them, "Why do you tempt Me? Bring Me a denarius, that I may see"; **16** and they brought, and He says to them, "Whose [is] this image, and the inscription?" And they said to Him, "Caesar's"; **17** and Jesus answering said to them, "Give back the things of Caesar to Caesar, and the things of God to God"; and they wondered at Him. **18** And the Sadducees come to Him, who say there is not a resurrection, and they questioned Him, saying, **19** "Teacher, Moses wrote to us that if anyone's brother may die, and may leave a wife, and may leave no children, that his brother may take his wife, and raise up seed to his brother. **20** There were then seven brothers, and the first took a wife, and dying, he left no seed; **21** and the second took her, and died, not having left seed, and the third in like manner, **22** and the seven took her, and left no seed, last of all the woman also died; **23** in the resurrection, then, whenever they may rise, of which of them will she be wife—for the seven had her as wife?" **24** And Jesus answering said to them, "Do you not go astray because of this, not knowing the Writings, nor the power of God? **25** For when they may rise out of the dead, they neither marry nor are they given in marriage, but are as messengers who are in the heavens. **26** And concerning the dead, that they rise: have you not read in the Scroll of Moses (at the bush), how God spoke to him, saying, I [am] the God of Abraham, and the God of Isaac, and the God of Jacob; **27** He is not the God of dead men, but a God of living men; you then go greatly astray." **28** And one of the scribes having come near, having heard them disputing, knowing that He answered them well, questioned Him, "Which is the first command of all?" **29** And Jesus answered him, "The first of all the commands—

Hear, O Israel: The LORD is our God, the LORD is one; **30** and you will love the LORD your God out of all your heart, and out of all your soul, and out of all your understanding, and out of all your strength—this [is] the first command; **31** and the second [is] like [it], this, You will love your neighbor as yourself—there is no other command greater than these." **32** And the scribe said to Him, "Well, Teacher, in truth You have spoken that there is one God, and there is none other but He; **33** and to love Him out of all the heart, and out of all the understanding, and out of all the soul, and out of all the strength, and to love one's neighbor as one's self, is more than all the whole burnt-offerings and the sacrifices." **34** And Jesus, having seen him that he answered with understanding, said to him, "You are not far from the Kingdom of God"; and no one dared question Him anymore. **35** And Jesus answering said, teaching in the temple, "How do the scribes say that the Christ is son of David? **36** For David himself said in the Holy Spirit, The LORD said to my Lord, ‖ Sit on My right hand, ‖ Until I place Your enemies—Your footstool; **37** therefore David himself calls Him Lord, and from where is He his son?" And the great multitude were hearing Him gladly, **38** and He was saying to them in His teaching, "Beware of the scribes who will to walk in long robes, and love salutations in the marketplaces, **39** and first seats in the synagogues, and first couches at the banquets, **40** who are devouring the widows' houses, and for a pretense are making long prayers; these will receive more abundant judgment." **41** And Jesus having sat down opposite the treasury, was beholding how the multitude puts brass into the treasury, and many rich were putting in much, **42** and having come, a poor widow put in two mites, which are a penny. **43** And having called near His disciples, He says to them, "Truly I say to you that this poor widow has put in more than all those putting into the treasury; **44** for all, out of their abundance, put in, but she, out of her want, put in all that she had—all her living."

13 And as He is going forth out of the temple, one of His disciples says to Him, "Teacher, see! What stones! And what buildings!" **2** And Jesus answering said to him, "See these great buildings? There may not be left a stone on a stone that may not be thrown down." **3** And as He is sitting at the Mount of Olives, opposite the temple, Peter, and James, and John, and Andrew, were questioning Him by Himself, **4** "Tell us when these things will be? And what [is] the sign when all these may be about to be fulfilled?" **5** And Jesus answering them, began to say, "Take heed lest anyone may lead you astray, **6** for many will come in My Name, saying, I am [He], and many they will lead astray; **7** and when you may hear of wars and reports of wars, do not be troubled, for these ought to be, but the end [is] not yet; **8** for nation will rise against nation, and kingdom against kingdom, and there will be earthquakes in various places, and there will be famines and troubles; these [are the] beginning of travails. **9** And take heed to yourselves, for they will deliver you up to Sanhedrins, and to synagogues, you will be beaten, and before governors and kings you will be set for My sake, for a testimony to them; **10** and to all the nations it is first necessary that the good news be proclaimed. **11** And when they may lead you, delivering up, do not be anxious beforehand what you may speak, nor premeditate, but whatever may be given to you in that hour, that speak, for it is not you who are speaking, but the Holy Spirit. **12** And brother will deliver up brother to death, and father child, and children will rise up against parents, and will put them to death, **13** and you will be hated by all because of My Name, but he who has endured to the end—he will be saved. **14** And when you may see the abomination of the desolation, that was spoken of by Daniel the prophet, standing where it should not (whoever is reading let him understand), then those in Judea, let them flee to the mountains; **15** and he on the housetop, do not let him come down into the house, nor come in to take anything out of his house; **16** and he who is in the field, do not let him turn to the things behind, to take up his garment. **17** And woe to those with child, and to those giving suck, in those days; **18** and pray that your flight may not be in winter, **19** for those days will be tribulation, such as has not been from the beginning of the creation that God created, until now, and may not be [again]; **20** and if the LORD did not shorten the days, no flesh had been saved; but because of the chosen, whom He chose to

Himself, He shortened the days. **21** And then, if any may say to you, Behold, here [is] the Christ, or, Behold, there, you may not believe; **22** for there will rise false Christs and false prophets, and they will give signs and wonders, to seduce, if possible, also the chosen; **23** and you, take heed; behold, I have foretold you all things. **24** But in those days, after that tribulation, the sun will be darkened, and the moon will not give her light, **25** and the stars of the sky will be falling, and the powers that are in the heavens will be shaken. **26** And then they will see the Son of Man coming in clouds with much power and glory, **27** and then He will send His messengers, and gather together His chosen from the four winds, from the end of the earth to the end of heaven. **28** And from the fig tree learn the allegory: when the branch may already become tender, and may put forth the leaves, you know that the summer is near; **29** so you, also, when you may see these coming to pass, you know that it is near, at the doors. **30** Truly I say to you that this generation may not pass away until all these things may come to pass; **31** the heaven and the earth will pass away, but My words will not pass away. **32** And concerning that day and the hour no one has known—not even the messengers who are in Heaven, not even the Son—except the Father. **33** Take heed, watch and pray, for you have not known when the time is; **34** as a man who is gone abroad, having left his house, and given to his servants the authority, and to each one his work, also commanded the doorkeeper that he may watch; **35** watch, therefore, for you have not known when the lord of the house comes, at evening, or at midnight, or at rooster-crowing, or at the morning; **36** lest, having come suddenly, he may find you sleeping; **37** and what I say to you, I say to all, Watch!"

14 And the Passover and the Unleavened [Bread] were after two days, and the chief priests and the scribes were seeking how, by guile, having taken hold of Him, they might kill Him; **2** and they said, "Not in the celebration, lest there will be a tumult of the people." **3** And He, being in Bethany, in the house of Simon the leper, at His reclining, there came a woman having an alabaster box of ointment, of spikenard, very precious, and having broken the alabaster box, poured [it] on His head; **4** and there were certain much displeased within themselves, and saying, "For what has this waste of the ointment been made? **5** For this could have been sold for more than three hundred denarii, and given to the poor"; and they were murmuring at her. **6** And Jesus said, "Leave her alone; why are you giving her trouble? She worked a good work on Me; **7** for you always have the poor with you, and whenever you may will you are able to do them good, but you do not always have Me; **8** she did what she could, she anticipated to anoint My body for the embalming. **9** Truly I say to you, wherever this good news may be proclaimed in the whole world, what this woman did will also be spoken of—for a memorial of her." **10** And Judas the Iscariot, one of the Twelve, went away to the chief priests that he might deliver Him up to them, **11** and having heard, they were glad, and promised to give him money, and he was seeking how, conveniently, he might deliver Him up. **12** And the first day of the Unleavened [Bread], when they were killing the Passover, His disciples say to Him, "Where will You, [that] having gone, we may prepare, that You may eat the Passover?" **13** And He sends forth two of His disciples and says to them, "Go away into the city, and there a man carrying a pitcher of water will meet you, follow him; **14** and wherever he may go in, say to the master of the house: The Teacher says, Where is the guest-chamber, where the Passover, with My disciples, I may eat? **15** And he will show you a large upper room, furnished, prepared—make ready for us there." **16** And His disciples went forth, and came into the city, and found as He said to them, and they made ready the Passover. **17** And evening having come, He comes with the Twelve, **18** and as they are reclining, and eating, Jesus said, "Truly I say to you that one of you who is eating with Me will deliver Me up." **19** And they began to be sorrowful, and to say to Him one by one, "Is it I?" And another, "Is it I?" **20** And He answering said to them, "One of the Twelve who is dipping with Me in the dish; **21** the Son of Man indeed goes, as it has been written concerning Him, but woe to that man through whom the Son of Man is delivered up; it were good to him if that man had not been born." **22** And as they are eating, Jesus having taken bread, having blessed, broke, and gave to them, and said, "Take, eat; this is My body." **23** And having taken the cup, having given thanks, He gave to them, and they drank of it—all; **24** and He said to them, "This is My blood of the New Covenant, which is being poured out for many; **25** truly I say to you that I may drink no more of the produce of the vine until that day when I may drink it new in the Kingdom of God." **26** And having sung a hymn, they went forth to the Mount of Olives, **27** and Jesus says to them, "All of you will be stumbled at Me this night, because it has been written: I will strike the Shepherd, and the sheep will be scattered abroad; **28** but after My having risen I will go before you to Galilee." **29** And Peter said to Him, "And if all will be stumbled, yet not I." **30** And Jesus said to him, "Truly I say to you that today, this night, before a rooster will crow twice, three times you will deny Me." **31** And he spoke the more vehemently, "If it may be necessary for me to die with You—I will in no way deny You"; and in like manner also said they all. **32** And they come to a spot, the name of which [is] Gethsemane, and He says to His disciples, "Sit here until I may pray"; **33** and He takes Peter, and James, and John with Him, and began to be amazed, and to be very heavy, **34** and He says to them, "My soul is exceedingly sorrowful—to death; remain here, and watch." **35** And having gone forward a little, He fell on the earth, and was praying that, if it be possible, the hour may pass from Him, **36** and He said, "Abba, Father; all things are possible to You; make this cup pass from Me; but not what I will, but what You [will]." **37** And He comes, and finds them sleeping, and says to Peter, "Simon, you sleep! You were not able to watch one hour! **38** Watch and pray, that you may not enter into temptation; the spirit indeed is forward, but the flesh weak." **39** And again having gone away, He prayed, saying the same word; **40** and having returned, He found them sleeping again, for their eyes were heavy, and they had not known what they might answer Him. **41** And He comes the third time and says to them, "Sleep on from now on, and rest—it is over; the hour came; behold, the Son of Man is delivered up into the hands of the sinful; **42** rise, we may go, behold, he who is delivering Me up has come near."

43 And immediately—while He is yet speaking—Judas comes near, one of the Twelve, and with him a great multitude with swords and sticks, from the chief priests, and the scribes, and the elders; **44** and he who is delivering Him up had given a token to them, saying, "Whomsoever I will kiss, it is He, lay hold on Him, and lead Him away safely," **45** and having come, immediately, having gone near Him, he says, "Rabbi, Rabbi," and kissed Him. **46** And they laid on Him their hands, and kept hold on Him; **47** and a certain one of those standing by, having drawn the sword, struck the servant of the chief priest, and took off his ear. **48** And Jesus answering said to them, "As against a robber you came out, with swords and sticks, to take Me! **49** Daily I was with you teaching in the temple, and you did not lay hold on Me—but that the Writings may be fulfilled." **50** And having left Him they all fled; **51** and a certain young man was following Him, having cast a linen cloth on [his] naked [body], and the young men lay hold on him, **52** and he, having left the linen cloth, fled from them naked. **53** And they led Jesus away to the chief priest, and all the chief priests, and the elders, and the scribes come together; **54** and Peter followed Him far off, to the inside of the hall of the chief priest, and he was sitting with the officers, and warming himself near the fire. **55** And the chief priests and all the Sanhedrin were seeking testimony against Jesus—to put Him to death, and they were not finding, **56** for many were bearing false testimony against Him, and their testimonies were not alike. **57** And certain having risen up, were bearing false testimony against Him, saying, **58** "We heard Him saying, I will throw down this temple made with hands, and by three days, I will build another made without hands"; **59** and neither so was their testimony alike. **60** And the chief priest, having risen up in the midst, questioned Jesus, saying, "You do not answer anything! Why do these testify against You?" **61** And He was keeping silent and did not answer anything. Again the chief priest was questioning Him and says to Him, "Are You the Christ—the Son of the Blessed?" **62** And Jesus said, "I AM; and you will see the Son of Man sitting on the right hand of the Power and coming with the clouds of Heaven." **63** And the chief priest, having torn his garments, says,

"What need have we yet of witnesses? **64** You heard the slander, what appears to you?" And they all condemned Him to be worthy of death, **65** and certain began to spit on Him, and to cover His face, and to punch Him, and to say to Him, "Prophesy"; and the officers were striking Him with their palms. **66** And Peter being in the hall beneath, there comes one of the maids of the chief priest, **67** and having seen Peter warming himself, having looked on him, she said, "And you were with Jesus of Nazareth!" **68** And he denied, saying, "I have not known [Him], neither do I understand what you say"; and he went forth outside to the porch, and a rooster crowed. **69** And the maid having seen him again, began to say to those standing near, "This is of them"; **70** and he was again denying. And after a while again, those standing near said to Peter, "Truly you are of them, for you also are a Galilean, and your speech is alike"; **71** and he began to curse, and to swear, "I have not known this Man of whom you speak"; **72** and a second time a rooster crowed, and Peter remembered the saying that Jesus said to him, "Before a rooster crows twice, you may deny Me three times"; and having thought thereon—he was weeping.

15 And immediately, in the morning, the chief priests having made a consultation with the elders, and scribes, and the whole Sanhedrin, having bound Jesus, led [Him] away, and delivered [Him] to Pilate; **2** and Pilate questioned Him, "Are You the King of the Jews?" And He answering said to him, "You say [it]." **3** And the chief priests were accusing Him of many things, [but He answered nothing.] **4** And Pilate again questioned Him, saying, "You do not answer anything? Behold, how many things they testify against You!" **5** And Jesus no longer answered anything, so that Pilate wondered. **6** And at every celebration he was releasing to them one prisoner, whomsoever they were asking for; **7** and there was [one] named Barabbas, bound with those making insurrection with him, who had committed murder in the insurrection. **8** And the multitude having cried out, began to ask for themselves as he was always doing to them, **9** and Pilate answered them, saying, "Will you [that] I will release to you the King of the Jews?" **10** For he knew that the chief priests had delivered Him up because of envy; **11** and the chief priests moved the multitude that he might rather release Barabbas to them. **12** And Pilate answering, again said to them, "What, then, will you [that] I will do to Him whom you call King of the Jews?" **13** And they again cried out, "Crucify Him!" **14** And Pilate said to them, "Why—what evil did He do?" And they cried out the more vehemently, "Crucify Him!" **15** And Pilate, resolving to do that which [was] satisfactory to the multitude, released Barabbas to them, and delivered up Jesus—having scourged [Him]—that He might be crucified. **16** And the soldiers led Him away into the hall, which is [the] Praetorium, and call together the whole band, **17** and clothe Him with purple, and having plaited a garland of thorns, they put [it] on Him, **18** and began to greet Him, "Hail, King of the Jews!" **19** And they were striking Him on the head with a reed, and were spitting on Him, and having bent the knee, were prostrating to Him, **20** and when they [had] mocked Him, they took the purple from off Him, and clothed Him in His own garments, and they led Him forth, that they may crucify Him. **21** And they impress a certain one passing by—Simon, a Cyrenian, coming from the field, the father of Alexander and Rufus—that he may carry His cross, **22** and they bring Him to the place [called] Golgotha, which is, being interpreted, "Place of [the] Skull"; **23** and they were giving Him wine mingled with myrrh to drink, and He did not receive [it]. **24** And having crucified Him, they were dividing His garments, casting a lot on them, what each may take; **25** and it was the third hour, and they crucified Him; **26** and the inscription of His accusation was written above: "THE KING OF THE JEWS." **27** And they crucify two robbers with Him, one on the right hand and one on His left, **28** [[and the Writing was fulfilled that is saying, "And He was numbered with lawless ones."]] **29** And those passing by were slandering Him, shaking their heads, and saying, "Ha! The [One] throwing down the temple, and building [it] in three days! **30** Save Yourself, and come down from the cross!" **31** And in like manner also the chief priests, mocking with one another, with the scribes, said, "He saved others; He is not able to save Himself. **32** The Christ! The King of Israel—let Him come down now from the cross, that we may see and believe"; and those crucified with Him were reproaching Him. **33** And the sixth hour having come, darkness came over the whole land until the ninth hour, **34** and at the ninth hour Jesus cried with a great voice, saying, "Eloi, Eloi, lamma sabachthani?" Which is, being interpreted, "My God, My God, why did You forsake Me?" **35** And certain of those standing by, having heard, said, "Behold, He calls Elijah"; **36** and one having run, and having filled a sponge with vinegar, having also put [it] on a reed, was giving Him to drink, saying, "Let alone, let us see if Elijah comes to take Him down." **37** And Jesus having uttered a loud cry, yielded the spirit, **38** and the veil of the temple was torn in two from top to bottom, **39** and the centurion who was standing opposite Him, having seen that, having so cried out, He yielded the spirit, said, "Truly this Man was [the] Son of God." **40** And there were also women beholding far off, among whom was also Mary the Magdalene, and Mary of James the less, and of Joses, and Salome, **41** who also, when He was in Galilee, were following Him and were ministering to Him, and many other women who came up with Him to Jerusalem. **42** And now evening having come, seeing it was the Preparation, that is, before Sabbath, **43** Joseph of Arimathea, an honorable counselor, who also himself was waiting for the Kingdom of God, came, boldly entered in to Pilate, and asked for the body of Jesus. **44** And Pilate wondered if He were already dead, and having called near the centurion, questioned him if He were long dead, **45** and having known [it] from the centurion, he granted the body to Joseph. **46** And he, having brought fine linen, and having taken Him down, wrapped Him in the linen, and laid Him in a tomb that had been hewn out of a rock, and he rolled a stone to the door of the tomb, **47** and Mary the Magdalene, and Mary of Joses, were beholding where He is laid.

16 And the Sabbath having past, Mary the Magdalene, and Mary of James, and Salome, bought spices, that having come, they may anoint Him, **2** and early in the morning of the first [day] of the weeks, they come to the tomb, at the rising of the sun, **3** and they said among themselves, "Who will roll away the stone out of the door of the tomb for us?" **4** And having looked, they see that the stone has been rolled away—for it was very great, **5** and having entered into the tomb, they saw a young man sitting on the right hand, clothed in a long white robe, and they were amazed. **6** And he says to them, "Do not be amazed, you seek Jesus the Nazarene, the crucified [One]: He rose—He is not here; behold the place where they laid Him! **7** And go, say to His disciples and Peter that He goes before you to Galilee; there you will see Him, as He said to you." **8** And having come forth quickly, they fled from the tomb, and trembling and amazement had seized them, and they said to no one anything, for they were afraid. [[**9** And He, having risen in the morning of the first of the week, appeared first to Mary the Magdalene, out of whom He had cast seven demons; **10** she having gone, told those who had been with Him, mourning and weeping; **11** and they, having heard that He is alive, and was seen by her, did not believe. **12** And after these things, to two of them, as they are going into a field, walking, He appeared in another form, **13** and they having gone, told [it] to the rest; not even them did they believe. **14** Afterward, as they are reclining, He appeared to the Eleven, and reproached their unbelief and stiffness of heart, because they did not believe those having seen Him being raised; **15** and He said to them, "Having gone into all the world, proclaim the good news to all the creation; **16** he who has believed and has been immersed will be saved; and he who has not believed will be condemned. **17** And signs will accompany those believing these things: they will cast out demons in My Name; they will speak with new tongues; **18** they will take up serpents; and if they may drink any deadly thing, it will not hurt them; they will lay hands on the ailing, and they will be well." **19** The LORD, then, indeed, after speaking to them, was received up to Heaven, and sat on the right hand of God; **20** and they, having gone forth, preached everywhere, the LORD working with [them], and confirming the word, through the signs following. Amen.]]

LUKE

1 Seeing that many took in hand to set in order a narration of the matters that have been fully assured among us, **2** as they delivered to us, who from the beginning became eyewitnesses, and officers of the word, **3** it seemed good also to me, having followed from the first after all things exactly, to write to you in order, most noble Theophilus, **4** that you may know the certainty of the things wherein you were instructed. **5** There was in the days of Herod, the king of Judea, a certain priest, by name Zacharias, of the division of Abijah, and his wife of the daughters of Aaron, and her name Elizabeth; **6** and they were both righteous before God, going on in all the commands and righteousnesses of the LORD blameless, **7** and they had no child, because that Elizabeth was barren, and both were advanced in their days. **8** And it came to pass, in his acting as priest, in the order of his division before God, **9** according to the custom of the priesthood, his lot was to make incense, having gone into the temple of the LORD, **10** and all the multitude of the people were praying outside, at the hour of the incense. **11** And there appeared to him a messenger of the LORD standing on the right side of the altar of the incense, **12** and Zacharias, having seen, was troubled, and fear fell on him; **13** and the messenger said to him, "Do not fear, Zacharias, for your supplication was heard, and your wife Elizabeth will bear a son to you, and you will call his name John, **14** and there will be joy to you, and gladness, and many will rejoice at his birth, **15** for he will be great before the LORD, and wine and strong drink he may not drink, and he will be full of the Holy Spirit, even from his mother's womb; **16** and he will turn many of the sons of Israel to the LORD their God, **17** and he will go before Him, in the spirit and power of Elijah, to turn hearts of fathers to children, and disobedient ones to the wisdom of righteous ones, to make ready for the LORD, a people prepared." **18** And Zacharias said to the messenger, "Whereby will I know this? For I am aged, and my wife is advanced in her days?" **19** And the messenger answering said to him, "I am Gabriel, who has been standing near before God, and I was sent to speak to you, and to proclaim this good news to you, **20** and behold, you will be silent, and not able to speak, until the day that these things will come to pass, because you did not believe my words that will be fulfilled in their season." **21** And the people were waiting for Zacharias, and wondering at his lingering in the temple, **22** and having come out, he was not able to speak to them, and they perceived that he had seen a vision in the temple, and he was beckoning to them, and remained mute. **23** And it came to pass, when the days of his service were fulfilled, he went away to his house, **24** and after those days, his wife Elizabeth conceived, and hid herself five months, saying, **25** "Thus the LORD has done to me, in days in which He looked on [me], to take away my reproach among men." **26** And in the sixth month the messenger Gabriel was sent by God, to a city of Galilee, the name of which [is] Nazareth, **27** to a virgin, betrothed to a man, whose name [is] Joseph, of the house of David, and the name of the virgin [is] Mary. **28** And the messenger having come in to her, said, "Greetings, favored one, the LORD [is] with you; blessed [are] you among women"; **29** and she, having seen, was troubled at his word, and was reasoning of what kind this salutation may be. **30** And the messenger said to her, "Do not fear, Mary, for you have found favor with God; **31** and behold, you will conceive in the womb, and will bring forth a Son, and call His Name Jesus; **32** He will be great, and He will be called Son of the Highest, and the LORD God will give Him the throne of His father David, **33** and He will reign over the house of Jacob for all ages; and of His kingdom there will be no end." **34** And Mary said to the messenger, "How will this be, seeing I do not know a husband?" **35** And the messenger answering said to her, "The Holy Spirit will come on you, and the power of the Highest will overshadow you, therefore also the holy-begotten thing will be called Son of God; **36** and behold, Elizabeth, your relative, she also has conceived a son in her old age, and this is the sixth month to her who was called barren; **37** because nothing will be impossible with God." **38** And Mary said, "Behold, the maidservant of the LORD; let it be to me according to your saying," and the messenger went away from her. **39** And Mary having arisen in those days, went into the hill-country, with haste, to a city of Judea, **40** and entered into the house of Zacharias, and greeted Elizabeth. **41** And it came to pass, when Elizabeth heard the salutation of Mary, the baby leapt in her womb; and Elizabeth was filled with the Holy Spirit, **42** and spoke out with a loud voice and said, "Blessed [are] you among women, and blessed [is] the Fruit of your womb; **43** and from where [is] this to me, that the mother of my Lord might come to me? **44** For behold, when the voice of your salutation came to my ears, the baby in my womb leapt in gladness; **45** and blessed [is] she who believed, for there will be a completion to the things spoken to her from the LORD." **46** And Mary said, "My soul magnifies the LORD, **47** And my spirit was glad on God my Savior, **48** Because He looked on the lowliness of His maidservant, ‖ For behold, from now on all the generations will call me blessed, **49** For He who is mighty did great things to me, ‖ And holy [is] His Name, **50** And His kindness [is] to generations of generations, ‖ To those fearing Him; **51** He did powerfully with His arm, ‖ He scattered abroad the proud in the thought of their heart, **52** He brought down the mighty from thrones, ‖ And He exalted the lowly, **53** He filled the hungry with good, ‖ And the rich He sent away empty; **54** He has taken hold of His servant Israel, ‖ To remember kindness, **55** As He spoke to our fathers, ‖ To Abraham and to his seed—throughout the age." **56** And Mary remained with her about three months, and turned back to her house. **57** And to Elizabeth was the time fulfilled for her bringing forth, and she bore a son, **58** and the neighbors and her relatives heard that the LORD was making His kindness great with her, and they were rejoicing with her. **59** And it came to pass, on the eighth day, they came to circumcise the child, and they were calling him by the name of his father, Zacharias, **60** and his mother answering said, "No, but he will be called John." **61** And they said to her, "There is none among your relatives who is called by this name," **62** and they were making signs to his father, what he would wish him to be called, **63** and having asked for a tablet, he wrote, saying, "John is his name"; and they all wondered; **64** and his mouth was opened immediately, and his tongue, and he was speaking, praising God. **65** And fear came on all those dwelling around them, and in all the hill-country of Judea were all these sayings spoken of, **66** and all who heard laid them up in their hearts, saying, "What then will this child be?" And the hand of the LORD was with him. **67** And his father Zacharias was filled with the Holy Spirit, and prophesied, saying, **68** "Blessed [is] the LORD, the God of Israel, ‖ Because He looked on, ‖ And worked redemption for His people, **69** And raised a horn of salvation to us, ‖ In the house of His servant David, **70** As He spoke by the mouth of His holy prophets, ‖ Which have been from the age; **71** Salvation from our enemies, ‖ And out of the hand of all hating us, **72** To do kindness with our fathers, ‖ And to be mindful of His holy covenant, **73** An oath that He swore to Abraham our father, **74** To give to us, without fear, ‖ Having been delivered out of the hand of our enemies, **75** To serve Him, in holiness and righteousness ‖ Before Him, all the days of our life. **76** And you, child, ‖ Prophet of the Highest will you be called; For you will go before the face of the LORD, ‖ To prepare His ways. **77** To give knowledge of salvation to His people ‖ In forgiveness of their sins, **78** Through the yearnings of our God, ‖ In which the rising from on high looked on us, **79** To give light to those sitting in darkness and death-shade, ‖ To guide our feet to a way of peace." **80** And the child grew, and was strengthened in spirit, and he was in the deserts until the day of his showing to Israel.

2 And it came to pass in those days, there went forth a decree from Caesar Augustus that all the world be registered— **2** this census first came to pass when Quirinius was governor of Syria— **3** and all were going to be registered, each to his proper city, **4** and Joseph also went up from Galilee, out of the city of Nazareth, to Judea, to the city of David, that is called Beth-Lehem, because of his being of the house and family of David, **5** to register himself with Mary his betrothed wife, being with Child. **6** And it came to pass, in their being there, the days were fulfilled for her bringing forth, **7** and she brought forth her Son—the firstborn, and wrapped Him up, and laid Him down in the manger, because there was not a place for them in the guest-chamber. **8** And there were shepherds in the same region, lodging in the field and keeping the night-watches over their flock, **9** and behold, a messenger of the LORD stood over them, and the glory of the LORD shone around them, and they feared [with] a great fear. **10** And the messenger said to them, "Do not fear, for behold, I bring you good news of great joy that will be to all the people, **11** because today in the city of David a Savior was born to you, who is Christ the LORD! **12** And this [is] the sign to you: you will find a Baby wrapped up, lying in the manger." **13** And suddenly there came with the messenger a multitude of the heavenly host, praising God, and saying, **14** "Glory in the highest to God, and on earth peace, among men—good will!" **15** And it came to pass, when the messengers were gone away from them to the heavens, that the men, the shepherds, said to one another, "We may indeed go over to Beth-Lehem and see this thing that has come to pass, that the LORD made known to us!" **16** And they came, having hurried, and found both Mary, and Joseph, and the Baby lying in the manger, **17** and having seen, they made known abroad concerning the saying spoken to them concerning the Child. **18** And all who heard [it] wondered concerning the things spoken to them by the shepherds; **19** and Mary was preserving all these things, pondering [them] in her heart; **20** and the shepherds turned back, glorifying and praising God for all those things they heard and saw, as it was spoken to them. **21** And when eight days were fulfilled to circumcise the Child, then was His Name called Jesus, having been so called by the messenger before His being conceived in the womb. **22** And when the days of their purification were fulfilled, according to the Law of Moses, they brought Him up to Jerusalem, to present to the LORD, **23** as it has been written in the Law of the LORD: "Every male opening a womb will be called holy to the LORD," **24** and to give a sacrifice, according to that said in the Law of the LORD: "A pair of turtle-doves, or two young pigeons." **25** And behold, there was a man in Jerusalem whose name [is] Simeon, and this man is righteous and devout, looking for the comforting of Israel, and the Holy Spirit was on him, **26** and it has been divinely told him by the Holy Spirit—not to see death before he may see the Christ of the LORD. **27** And he came in the Spirit into the temple, and in the parents bringing in the child Jesus, for their doing according to the custom of the Law regarding Him, **28** then he took Him in his arms, and blessed God, and he said, **29** "Now You send Your servant away, O LORD, according to Your word, in peace, **30** because my eyes saw Your salvation, **31** which You prepared before the face of all the peoples, **32** a light to the uncovering of nations, and the glory of Your people Israel." **33** And Joseph and His mother were wondering at the things spoken concerning Him, **34** and Simeon blessed them and said to His mother Mary, "Behold, this [One] is set for the falling and rising again of many in Israel, and for a sign spoken against— **35** (and also a sword will pass through your own soul)—that the reasonings of many hearts may be revealed." **36** And there was Anna, a prophetess, daughter of Phanuel, of the tribe of Asher, she was much advanced in days, having lived with a husband seven years from her virginity, **37** and she [is] a widow of about eighty-four years, who did not depart from the temple, serving with fasts and supplications, night and day, **38** and she, at that hour, having come in, was confessing, likewise, to the LORD, and was speaking concerning Him to all those looking for redemption in Jerusalem. **39** And when they completed all things according to the Law of the LORD, they turned back to Galilee, to their city of Nazareth; **40** and the Child grew and was strengthened in spirit, being filled with wisdom, and the grace of God was on Him. **41** And His parents were going yearly to Jerusalem, at the Celebration of the Passover, **42** and when He became twelve years old, they having gone up to Jerusalem according to the custom of the celebration, **43** and having finished the days, in their returning the child Jesus remained behind in Jerusalem, and Joseph and His mother did not know, **44** and having supposed Him to be in the company, they went a day's journey, and were seeking Him among the relatives and among the acquaintances, **45** and having not found Him, they turned back to Jerusalem seeking Him. **46** And it came to

LUKE

pass, after three days they found Him in the temple, sitting in the midst of the teachers, both hearing them and questioning them, **47** and all those hearing Him were astonished at His understanding and answers. **48** And having seen Him, they were amazed, and His mother said to Him, "Child, why did You do this to us? Behold, Your father and I, sorrowing, were seeking You." **49** And He said to them, "Why [is it] that you were seeking Me? Did you not know that it is necessary for Me to be in the things of My Father?" **50** And they did not understand the saying that He spoke to them, **51** and He went down with them, and came to Nazareth, and He was subject to them, and His mother was keeping all these sayings in her heart, **52** and Jesus was advancing in wisdom, and in stature, and in favor with God and men.

3 And in the fifteenth year of the government of Tiberius Caesar—Pontius Pilate being governor of Judea, and Herod tetrarch of Galilee, and his brother Philip, tetrarch of Ituraea and of the region of Trachonitis, and Lysanias tetrarch of Abilene, **2** [and] Annas and Caiaphas being chief priests—there came a word of God to John the son of Zacharias, in the wilderness, **3** and he came to all the region around the Jordan, proclaiming an immersion of conversion for forgiveness of sins, **4** as it has been written in the scroll of the words of Isaiah the prophet: "A voice of one crying in the wilderness: Prepare the way of the LORD, ‖ Make His paths straight; **5** Every valley will be filled, ‖ And every mountain and hill will be made low, ‖ And the crooked will become straightness, ‖ And the rough become smooth ways; **6** And all flesh will see the salvation of God." **7** Then he said to the multitudes coming forth to be immersed by him, "Brood of vipers! Who prompted you to flee from the coming wrath? **8** Make, therefore, fruits worthy of conversion, and do not begin to say within yourselves, We have a father—Abraham; for I say to you that God is able to raise children to Abraham out of these stones; **9** and also the axe is already laid to the root of the trees, every tree, therefore, not making good fruit is cut down, and it is cast into fire." **10** And the multitudes were questioning him, saying, "What, then, will we do?" **11** And he answering says to them, "He having two coats, let him impart to him having none; and he having food, let him do in like manner." **12** And there also came tax collectors to be immersed, and they said to him, "Teacher, what will we do?" **13** And he said to them, "Exact no more than that directed you." **14** And also questioning him were those warring, saying, "And we, what will we do?" And he said to them, "Do violence to no one, nor accuse falsely, and be content with your wages." **15** And the people are looking forward, and all are reasoning in their hearts concerning John, whether or not he may be the Christ; **16** John answered, saying to all, "I indeed immerse you in water, but He comes who is mightier than I, of whom I am not worthy to loose the strap of His sandals—He will immerse you in the Holy Spirit and fire; **17** whose winnowing shovel [is] in His hand, and He will thoroughly cleanse His floor, and will gather the wheat into His storehouse, and He will burn the chaff with unquenchable fire." **18** And therefore, indeed, with many other things, exhorting, he was proclaiming good news to the people, **19** and Herod the tetrarch, being reproved by him concerning Herodias, the wife of his brother Philip, and concerning all the evils that Herod did, **20** added also this to all, that he shut up John in the prison. **21** And it came to pass, in all the people being immersed, Jesus also being immersed, and praying, Heaven was opened, **22** and the Holy Spirit came down in a bodily appearance, as if a dove, on Him, and a voice came out of Heaven, saying, "You are My Son, the Beloved, in You I delighted." **23** And Jesus Himself was beginning to be about thirty years of age, being, as was supposed, Son of Joseph, **24** the [son] of Eli, the [son] of Matthat, the [son] of Levi, the [son] of Melchi, the [son] of Janna, the [son] of Joseph, **25** the [son] of Mattathias, the [son] of Amos, the [son] of Nahum, the [son] of Esli, **26** the [son] of Naggai, the [son] of Maath, the [son] of Mattathias, the [son] of Semei, the [son] of Joseph, the [son] of Judah, **27** the [son] of Joanna, the [son] of Rhesa, the [son] of Zerubbabel, the [son] of Shealtiel, **28** the [son] of Neri, the [son] of Melchi, the [son] of Addi, the [son] of Cosam, the [son] of Elmodam, the [son] of Er, **29** the [son] of Jose, the [son] of Eliezer, the [son] of Jorim, the [son] of Matthat, **30** the [son] of Levi, the [son] of Simeon, the

LUKE

[son] of Judah, the [son] of Joseph, the [son] of Jonan, the [son] of Eliakim, **31** the [son] of Melea, the [son] of Mainan, the [son] of Mattatha, the [son] of Nathan, **32** the [son] of David, the [son] of Jesse, the [son] of Obed, the [son] of Boaz, the [son] of Salmon, the [son] of Nahshon, **33** the [son] of Amminadab, the [son] of Aram, the [son] of Esrom, the [son] of Perez, **34** the [son] of Judah, the [son] of Jacob, the [son] of Isaac, the [son] of Abraham, the [son] of Terah, the [son] of Nahor, **35** the [son] of Serug, the [son] of Reu, the [son] of Peleg, the [son] of Eber, **36** the [son] of Salah, the [son] of Cainan, the [son] of Arphaxad, the [son] of Shem, the [son] of Noah, the [son] of Lamech, **37** the [son] of Methuselah, the [son] of Enoch, the [son] of Jared, the [son] of Mahalaleel, **38** the [son] of Cainan, the [son] of Enos, the [son] of Seth, the [son] of Adam, the [son] of God.

4 And Jesus, full of the Holy Spirit, turned back from the Jordan, and was brought in the Spirit into the wilderness, **2** being tempted by the Devil forty days, and He did not eat anything in those days, and they having been ended, He afterward hungered, **3** and the Devil said to Him, "If You are [the] Son of God, speak to this stone that it may become bread." **4** And Jesus answered him, saying, "It has been written, that, Not on bread only will man live, but on every saying of God." **5** And the Devil having brought Him up to a high mountain, showed to Him all the kingdoms of the world in a moment of time, **6** and the Devil said to Him, "To You I will give all this authority, and their glory, because to me it has been delivered, and to whomsoever I will, I give it; **7** You, then, if You may worship me—all will be Yours." **8** And Jesus answering him said, "[[Get behind Me, Satan, for]] it has been written: You will worship the LORD your God, and Him only you will serve." **9** And he brought Him to Jerusalem, and set Him on the pinnacle of the temple, and said to Him, "If You are the Son of God, cast Yourself down from here, **10** for it has been written: To His messengers He will give charge concerning you, to guard over you; **11** and: On hands they will bear you up, lest at any time you may dash your foot against a stone." **12** And Jesus answering said to him, "It has been said, You will not tempt the LORD your God." **13** And having ended all temptation, the Devil departed from Him until a convenient season. **14** And Jesus turned back in the power of the Spirit to Galilee, and a fame went forth through all the surrounding region concerning Him, **15** and He was teaching in their synagogues, being glorified by all. **16** And He came to Nazareth, where He has been brought up, and He went in, according to His custom, on the day of the Sabbaths, into the synagogue, and stood up to read; **17** and there was given over to Him a scroll of Isaiah the prophet, and having unfolded the scroll, He found the place where it has been written: **18** "The Spirit of the LORD [is] on Me, ‖ Because He anointed Me ‖ To proclaim good news to the poor, ‖ Sent Me to heal the broken of heart, ‖ To proclaim to captives deliverance, ‖ And to blind receiving of sight, ‖ To send the bruised away with deliverance, **19** To proclaim the acceptable year of the LORD." **20** And having folded the scroll, having given [it] back to the officer, He sat down, and the eyes of all in the synagogue were gazing on Him. **21** And He began to say to them, "Today this writing has been fulfilled in your ears"; **22** and all were bearing testimony to Him, and were wondering at the gracious words that are coming forth out of His mouth, and they said, "Is this not the Son of Joseph?" **23** And He said to them, "Certainly you will say to Me this allegory, Physician, heal yourself; as great things as we heard done in Capernaum, do also here in Your country"; **24** and He said, "Truly I say to you, no prophet is accepted in his own country; **25** and of a truth I say to you, many widows were in the days of Elijah, in Israel, when the sky was shut for three years and six months, when great famine came on all the land, **26** and to none of them was Elijah sent, but—to Sarepta of Sidon, to a woman, a widow; **27** and many lepers were in the time of Elisha the prophet, in Israel, and none of them was cleansed, but—Naaman the Syrian." **28** And all in the synagogue were filled with wrath, hearing these things, **29** and having risen, they put Him forth outside the city, and brought Him to the brow of the hill on which their city had been built—to cast Him down headlong, **30** and He, having gone through the midst of them, went away. **31** And He came down to Capernaum, a city of Galilee, and was teaching them on the Sabbaths, **32** and they

LUKE

were astonished at His teaching, because His word was with authority. **33** And in the synagogue was a man having a spirit of an unclean demon, and he cried out with a great voice, **34** "Aah! What [regards] us and You, Jesus, O Nazarene? You came to destroy us; I have known who You are—the Holy One of God!" **35** And Jesus rebuked him, saying, "Be silenced, and come forth out of him"; and the demon having cast him into the midst, came forth from him, having hurt him nothing; **36** and amazement came on all, and they were speaking together with one another, saying, "What [is] this word, that with authority and power He commands the unclean spirits, and they come forth?" **37** And there was going forth a fame concerning Him to every place of the surrounding region. **38** And having risen out of the synagogue, He entered into the house of Simon, and the mother-in-law of Simon was pressed with a great fever, and they asked Him about her, **39** and having stood over her, He rebuked the fever, and it left her, and immediately, having risen, she was ministering to them. **40** And at the setting of the sun, all, as many as had any ailing with manifold diseases, brought them to Him, and He, having put hands on each one of them, healed them. **41** And demons were also coming forth from many, crying out and saying, "You are the Christ, the Son of God"; and rebuking, He did not permit them to speak, because they knew Him to be the Christ. **42** And day having come, having gone forth, He went on to a desolate place, and the multitudes were seeking Him, and they came to Him, and were restraining Him—not to go on from them, **43** and He said to them, "Also to the other cities it is necessary for Me to proclaim good news of the Kingdom of God, because for this I have been sent"; **44** and He was preaching in the synagogues of Galilee.

5 And it came to pass, in the multitude pressing on Him to hear the word of God, that He was standing beside the Lake of Gennesaret, **2** and He saw two boats standing beside the lake, and the fishers, having gone away from them, were washing the nets, **3** and having entered into one of the boats, that was Simon's, He asked him to put back a little from the land, and having sat down, was teaching the multitudes out of the boat. **4** And when He left off speaking, He said to Simon, "Put back into the deep, and let down your nets for a catch"; **5** and Simon answering said to Him, "Master, through the whole night, having labored, we have taken nothing, but at Your saying I will let down the net." **6** And having done this, they enclosed a great multitude of fishes, and their net was breaking, **7** and they beckoned to the partners who [are] in the other boat, having come, to help them; and they came, and filled both the boats, so that they were sinking. **8** And Simon Peter having seen, fell down at the knees of Jesus, saying, "Depart from me, because I am a sinful man, O Lord"; **9** for astonishment seized him, and all those with him, at the catch of the fishes that they took, **10** and in like manner also James and John, sons of Zebedee, who were partners with Simon; and Jesus said to Simon, "Do not fear, from now on you will be catching men"; **11** and they, having brought the boats to the land, having left all, followed Him. **12** And it came to pass, in His being in one of the cities, that behold, a man full of leprosy, and having seen Jesus, having fallen on [his] face, he implored Him, saying, "Lord, if You may will, You are able to cleanse me"; **13** and having stretched forth [His] hand, He touched him, having said, "I will, be cleansed"; and immediately the leprosy went away from him. **14** And He charged him to tell no one, "But having gone away, show yourself to the priest, and bring near for your cleansing according as Moses directed, for a testimony to them"; **15** but the more was the report going abroad concerning Him, and great multitudes were coming together to hear, and to be healed by Him of their sicknesses, **16** and He was withdrawing Himself in the desolate places and was praying. **17** And it came to pass, on one of the days, that He was teaching, and there were sitting by Pharisees and teachers of the Law, who were come out of every village of Galilee, and Judea, and Jerusalem, and the power of the LORD was—to heal them. **18** And behold, men carrying a man on a bed, who has been struck with palsy, and they were seeking to bring him in, and to place before Him, **19** and having not found by what way they may bring him in because of the multitude, having gone up on the housetop, through the tiles they let him down with the little bed, into the midst before Jesus, **20** and He having seen their faith, said to him, "Man, your sins have been forgiven you." **21** And the scribes and the Pharisees began to reason, saying, "Who is this that speaks evil words? Who is able to forgive sins, except God only?" **22** And Jesus having known their reasonings, answering, said to them, "What reason you in your hearts? **23** Which is easier—to say, Your sins have been forgiven you? Or to say, Arise, and walk? **24** And that you may know that the Son of Man has authority on the earth to forgive sins—(He said to the one struck with palsy)—I say to you, arise, and having taken up your little bed, be going on to your house." **25** And immediately having risen before them, having taken up [that] on which he was lying, he went away to his house, glorifying God, **26** and astonishment took all, and they were glorifying God, and were filled with fear, saying, "We saw strange things today." **27** And after these things He went forth, and beheld a tax collector, by name Levi, sitting at the tax office, and said to him, "Follow Me"; **28** and he, having left all, having arisen, followed Him. **29** And Levi made a great entertainment to Him in his house, and there was a great multitude of tax collectors and others who were with them reclining, **30** and the scribes and the Pharisees among them were murmuring at His disciples, saying, "Why do You eat and drink with tax collectors and sinners?" **31** And Jesus answering said to them, "They who are well have no need of a physician, but they that are ill: **32** I did not come to call righteous men, but sinners, to conversion." **33** And they said to Him, "Why do the disciples of John fast often, and make supplications—in like manner also those of the Pharisees—but Yours eat and drink?" **34** And He said to them, "Are you able to make the sons of the bridechamber—in the Bridegroom being with them—to fast? **35** But days will come, and when the Bridegroom may be taken away from them, then they will fast in those days." **36** And He spoke also an allegory to them: "No one puts a patch of new clothing on old clothing, and if otherwise, the new also makes a split, and with the old the patch does not agree, that [is] from the new. **37** And no one puts new wine into old skins, and if otherwise, the new wine will burst the skins, and itself will be poured out, and the skins will be destroyed; **38** but new wine is to be put into new skins, and both are preserved together; **39** and no one having drunk old, immediately wishes new, for he says, The old is better."

6 And it came to pass, on a Sabbath, as He is going through the grainfields, that His disciples were plucking the ears, and were eating, rubbing with the hands, **2** and certain of the Pharisees said to them, "Why do you do that which is not lawful to do on the Sabbaths?" **3** And Jesus answering said to them, "Did you not read even this that David did when he hungered, himself and those who are with him, **4** how he went into the house of God, and took the Bread of the Presentation, and ate, and gave also to those with him, which it is not lawful to eat, except only to the priests?" **5** And He said to them, "The Son of Man is Lord also of the Sabbath." **6** And it came to pass also, on another Sabbath, that He goes into the synagogue, and teaches, and there was there a man, and his right hand was withered, **7** and the scribes and the Pharisees were watching Him, if on the Sabbath He will heal, that they might find an accusation against Him. **8** And He Himself had known their reasonings and said to the man having the withered hand, "Rise, and stand in the midst"; and he having risen, stood. **9** Then Jesus said to them, "I will question you something: is it lawful on the Sabbaths to do good, or to do evil? To save life or to kill?" **10** And having looked around on them all, He said to the man, "Stretch forth your hand"; and he did so, and his hand was restored whole as the other; **11** and they were filled with madness, and were speaking with one another what they might do to Jesus. **12** And it came to pass in those days, He went forth to the mountain to pray, and was passing the night in the prayer of God, **13** and when it became day, He called near His disciples, also having chosen twelve from them, whom He also named apostles: **14** Simon, whom He also named Peter, and his brother Andrew, James and John, Philip and Bartholomew, **15** Matthew and Thomas, James of Alphaeus, and Simon called Zealot, **16** Judas of James, and Judas Iscariot, who also became betrayer. **17** And having come down with them, He stood on a level spot; and a crowd of His disciples, and a great multitude of the people from all

LUKE

Judea, and Jerusalem, and the seacoast of Tyre and Sidon, **18** who came to hear Him and to be healed of their diseases, [gathered]. And those harassed by unclean spirits [also gathered] and were healed. **19** And all the multitude were seeking to touch Him, because power was going forth from Him, and He was healing all. **20** And He, having lifted up His eyes to His disciples, said: "Blessed the poor— because yours is the Kingdom of God. **21** Blessed those hungering now—because you will be filled. Blessed those weeping now—because you will laugh. **22** Blessed are you when men will hate you, and when they will separate you, and will reproach, and will cast forth your name as evil, for the Son of Man's sake— **23** rejoice in that day, and leap, for behold, your reward [is] great in Heaven, for according to these things were their fathers doing to the prophets. **24** But woe to you—the rich, because you have gotten your comfort. **25** Woe to you who have been filled— because you will hunger. Woe to you who are laughing now—because you will mourn and weep. **26** Woe to you when all men will speak well of you—for according to these things were their fathers doing to false prophets. **27** But I say to you who are hearing, love your enemies, do good to those hating you, **28** bless those cursing you, pray for those maligning you; **29** and to him striking you on the cheek, give also the other, and from him taking away from you the mantle, also the coat you may not keep back. **30** And to everyone who is asking of you, be giving; and from him who is taking away your goods, do not be asking again; **31** and as you wish that men may do to you, do also to them in like manner; **32** and—if you love those loving you, what grace is it to you? For also the sinful love those loving them; **33** and if you do good to those doing good to you, what grace is it to you? For also the sinful do the same; **34** and if you lend [to those] of whom you hope to receive back, what grace is it to you? For also the sinful lend to sinners— that they may receive again as much. **35** But love your enemies, and do good, and lend, hoping for nothing again, and your reward will be great, and you will be sons of the Highest, because He is kind to the ungracious and evil; **36** be therefore merciful, as also your Father is merciful. **37** And do not judge, and you may not be judged; do not condemn, and you may not be condemned; release, and you will be released. **38** Give, and it will be given to you; good measure, pressed, and shaken, and running over, they will give into your bosom; for with that measure with which you measure, it will be measured to you again." **39** And He spoke an allegory to them, "Is blind able to lead blind? Will they not both fall into a pit? **40** A disciple is not above his teacher, but everyone perfected will be as his teacher. **41** And why do you behold the speck that is in your brother's eye, and do not consider the beam that [is] in your own eye? **42** Or how are you able to say to your brother, Brother, permit, I may take out the speck that [is] in your eye— yourself not beholding the beam in your own eye? Hypocrite, first take the beam out of your own eye, and then you will see clearly to take out the speck that [is] in your brother's eye. **43** For there is not a good tree making bad fruit, nor a bad tree making good fruit; **44** for each tree is known from its own fruit, for they do not gather figs from thorns, nor do they crop a grape from a bramble. **45** The good man out of the good treasure of his heart brings forth that which [is] good; and the evil man out of the evil treasure of his heart brings forth that which [is] evil; for out of the abounding of the heart his mouth speaks. **46** And why do you call Me, Lord, Lord, and do not do what I say? **47** Everyone who is coming to Me, and is hearing My words, and is doing them, I will show you to whom he is like: **48** he is like to a man building a house, who dug and deepened, and laid a foundation on the rock, and a flood having come, the stream broke forth on that house, and was not able to shake it, for it had been founded on the rock. **49** And he who heard and did not, is like to a man having built a house on the earth, without a foundation, against which the stream broke forth, and immediately it fell, and the ruin of that house became great."

7 And when He completed all His sayings in the ears of the people, He went into Capernaum; **2** and a certain centurion's servant being ill, was about to die, who was much valued by him, **3** and having heard about Jesus, he sent to Him elders of the Jews, imploring Him, that having come He might thoroughly save his servant. **4** And they, having come near to Jesus, were

LUKE

calling on Him earnestly, saying, "He is worthy to whom You will do this, **5** for he loves our nation, and he built to us the synagogue." **6** And Jesus was going on with them, and now when He is not far distant from the house the centurion sent to Him friends, saying to Him, "Lord, do not be troubled, for I am not worthy that You may enter under my roof; **7** for this reason I did not consider myself worthy to come to You, but say in a word, and my boy will be healed; **8** for I also am a man placed under authority, having under myself soldiers, and I say to this [one], Go, and he goes; and to another, Be coming, and he comes; and to my servant, Do this, and he does [it]." **9** And having heard these things Jesus wondered at him, and having turned to the multitude following Him, He said, "I say to you, not even in Israel did I find so much faith"; **10** and those sent, having turned back to the house, found the ailing servant in health. **11** And it came to pass, on the next day, He was going on to a city called Nain, and there were going with Him many of His disciples, and a great multitude, **12** and as He came near to the gate of the city, then, behold, one dead was being carried forth, an only son of his mother, and she a widow, and a great multitude of the city was with her. **13** And the LORD having seen her, was moved with compassion toward her and said to her, "Do not be weeping"; **14** and having come near, He touched the bier, and those carrying [it] stood still, and He said, "Young man, to you I say, Arise"; **15** and the dead sat up, and began to speak, and He gave him to his mother; **16** and fear took hold of all, and they were glorifying God, saying, "A great prophet has risen among us," and, "God looked on His people." **17** And the account of this went forth in all Judea about Him, and in all the region around. **18** And the disciples of John told him about all these things, **19** and John having called near a certain two of his disciples, sent to Jesus, saying, "Are You He who is coming, or do we look for another?" **20** And having come near to Him, the men said, "John the Immerser sent us to You, saying, Are You He who is coming, or do we look for another?" **21** And in that hour He cured many from diseases, and plagues, and evil spirits, and He granted sight to many blind. **22** And Jesus answering said to them, "Having gone on, report to John what you saw and heard, that blind men see again, lame walk, lepers are cleansed, deaf hear, dead are raised, poor have good news proclaimed; **23** and blessed is he whoever may not be stumbled in Me." **24** And the messengers of John having gone away, He began to say to the multitudes concerning John: "What have you gone forth into the wilderness to look on? A reed shaken by the wind? **25** But what have you gone forth to see? A man clothed in soft garments? Behold, they in splendid clothing, and living in luxury, are in the houses of kings! **26** But what have you gone forth to see? A prophet? Yes, I say to you, and much more than a prophet: **27** this is he concerning whom it has been written: Behold, I send My messenger before Your face, who will prepare Your way before You; **28** for I say to you, there is not a greater prophet, among those born of women, than John the Immerser; but the least in the Kingdom of God is greater than he." **29** And all the people having heard, and the tax collectors, declared God righteous, having been immersed with the immersion of John, **30** but the Pharisees and the lawyers put away the counsel of God for themselves, having not been immersed by him. **31** And the LORD said, "To what, then, will I liken the men of this generation? And to what are they like? **32** They are like to children, to those sitting in a marketplace, and calling to one another, and saying, We piped to you, and you did not dance, we mourned to you, and you did not weep! **33** For John the Immerser came neither eating bread nor drinking wine, and you say, He has a demon; **34** the Son of Man came eating and drinking, and you say, Behold, a man, a glutton, and a wine drinker, a friend of tax collectors and sinners; **35** and the wisdom was justified from all her children." **36** And a certain one of the Pharisees was asking Him that He might eat with him, and having gone into the house of the Pharisee He reclined, **37** and behold, a woman in the city, who was a sinner, having known that He reclines in the house of the Pharisee, having provided an alabaster box of ointment, **38** and having stood behind, beside His feet, weeping, she began to wet His feet with the tears, and with the hairs of her head she was wiping, and was kissing His feet, and was anointing with the ointment. **39** And the Pharisee who called

Him, having seen, spoke within himself, saying, "This One, if He were a prophet, would have known who and of what kind [is] the woman who touches Him, that she is a sinner." **40** And Jesus answering said to him, "Simon, I have something to say to you"; and he says, "Teacher, say on." **41** "Two debtors were to a certain creditor; one was owing five hundred denarii, and the other fifty; **42** and they not having [with which] to give back, he forgave both; which of them then, do you say, will love him more?" **43** And Simon answering said, "I suppose that to whom he forgave the more"; and He said to him, "You judged correctly." **44** And having turned to the woman, He said to Simon, "See this woman? I entered into your house; you did not give water for My feet, but this woman wet My feet with tears, and wiped with the hairs of her head; **45** you did not give a kiss to Me, but this woman, from what [time] I came in, did not cease kissing My feet; **46** you did not anoint My head with oil, but this woman anointed My feet with oil; **47** therefore I say to you, her many sins have been forgiven, because she loved much; but to whom is forgiven little, loves little." **48** And He said to her, "Your sins have been forgiven"; **49** and those dining with Him began to say within themselves, "Who is this, who also forgives sins?" **50** And He said to the woman, "Your faith has saved you, be going on to peace."

8 And it came to pass thereafter, that He was going through every city and village, preaching and proclaiming good news of the Kingdom of God, and the Twelve [are] with Him, **2** and certain women who were healed of evil spirits and sicknesses, Mary who is called Magdalene, from whom seven demons had gone forth, **3** and Joanna wife of Chuza, steward of Herod, and Susanna, and many others, who were ministering to Him from their substance. **4** And a great multitude having gathered, and those who from city and city were coming to Him, He spoke by an allegory: **5** "The sower went forth to sow his seed, and in his sowing some indeed fell beside the way, and it was trodden down, and the birds of the sky devoured it. **6** And other fell on the rock, and having sprung up, it withered, through having no moisture. **7** And other fell amidst the thorns, and the thorns having sprung up with it, choked it. **8** And other fell on the good ground, and having sprung up, it made fruit a hundredfold." Saying these things, He was calling, "He having ears to hear—let him hear." **9** And His disciples were questioning Him, saying, "What may this allegory be?" **10** And He said, "To you it has been given to know the secrets of the Kingdom of God, but to the rest in allegories, that seeing they may not see, and hearing they may not understand. **11** And this is the allegory: the seed is the word of God, **12** and those beside the way are those hearing, then comes the Devil, and takes up the word from their heart, lest having believed, they may be saved. **13** And those on the rock: they who, when they may hear, receive the word with joy, and these have no root, who for a time believe, and in time of temptation fall away. **14** And that which fell to the thorns: these are they who have heard, and going forth, through anxieties, and riches, and pleasures of life, are choked, and do not bear to completion. **15** And that in the good ground: these are they who in an upright and good heart, having heard the word, retain [it], and bear fruit in continuance. **16** And no one having lighted a lamp covers it with a vessel, or puts [it] under a bed; but he puts [it] on a lampstand, that those coming in may see the light, **17** for nothing is secret, that will not become visible, nor hid, that will not be known and become visible. **18** See, therefore, how you hear, for whoever may have, there will be given to him, and whoever may not have, also what he seems to have will be taken from him." **19** And there came to Him His mother and brothers, and they were not able to get to Him because of the multitude, **20** and it was told Him, saying, "Your mother and Your brothers stand outside, wishing to see You"; **21** and He answering said to them, "My mother and My brothers! They are those who are hearing the word of God, and doing." **22** And it came to pass, on one of the days, that He Himself went into a boat with His disciples, and He said to them, "We may go over to the other side of the lake"; and they set forth, **23** and as they are sailing He fell deeply asleep, and there came down a storm of wind to the lake, and they were filling, and were in peril. **24** And having come near, they awoke Him, saying, "Master, Master, we perish!" And He, having arisen, rebuked

LUKE

the wind and the raging of the water, and they ceased, and there came a calm, **25** and He said to them, "Where is your faith?" And they being afraid wondered, saying to one another, "Who, then, is this, that He even commands the winds and the water, and they obey Him?" **26** And they sailed down to the region of the Gadarenes that is opposite Galilee, **27** and He having gone forth on the land, there met Him a certain man, out of the city, who had demons for a long time, and was not clothed with a garment, and was not abiding in a house, but in the tombs, **28** and having seen Jesus, and having cried out, he fell before Him, and with a loud voice, said, "What [regards] me and You, Jesus, Son of God Most High? I implore You, may You not afflict me!" **29** For He commanded the unclean spirit to come forth from the man, for many times it had caught him, and he was being bound with chains and shackles—guarded, and breaking apart the bonds he was driven by the demons into the deserts. **30** And Jesus questioned him, saying, "What is your name?" And he said, "Legion," because many demons were entered into him, **31** and he was calling on Him that He may not command them to go away into the abyss, **32** and there was there a herd of many pigs feeding on the mountain, and they were calling on Him that He might permit them to enter into these, and He permitted them, **33** and the demons having gone forth from the man, entered into the pigs, and the herd rushed down the steep into the lake, and were drowned. **34** And those feeding [them], having seen what was come to pass, fled, and having gone, told [it] to the city, and to the fields; **35** and they came forth to see what was come to pass, and they came to Jesus, and found the man sitting, out of whom the demons had gone forth, clothed, and right-minded, at the feet of Jesus, and they were afraid; **36** and those also having seen [it], told them how the demoniac was saved. **37** And the whole multitude of the region of the Gadarenes asked Him to go away from them, because they were pressed with great fear, and He having entered into the boat, turned back. **38** And the man from whom the demons had gone forth was imploring of Him to be with Him, and Jesus sent him away, saying, **39** "Return to your house, and tell how God did great things to you"; and he went away through all the city proclaiming how Jesus did great things to him. **40** And it came to pass, in the turning back of Jesus, the multitude received Him, for they were all looking for Him, **41** and behold, there came a man whose name [is] Jairus, and he was a chief of the synagogue, and having fallen at the feet of Jesus, was calling on Him to come to his house, **42** because he had an only daughter about twelve years [old], and she was dying. And in His going away, the multitudes were thronging Him, **43** and a woman, being with a flow of blood for twelve years, who, having spent all her living on physicians, was not able to be healed by any, **44** having come near behind, touched the fringe of His garment, and immediately the flow of her blood stood still. **45** And Jesus said, "Who [is] it that touched Me?" And all denying, Peter and those with him said, "Master, the multitudes press You, and throng [You], and You say, Who [is] it that touched Me?" **46** And Jesus said, "Someone touched Me, for I knew power having gone forth from Me." **47** And the woman, having seen that she was not hid, trembling, came, and having fallen before Him, for what cause she touched Him declared to Him before all the people, and how she was healed instantly; **48** and He said to her, "Take courage, daughter, your faith has saved you, be going on to peace." **49** While He is yet speaking, there comes a certain one from the chief of the synagogue's [house], saying to him, "Your daughter has died, do not harass the Teacher"; **50** and Jesus having heard, answered him, saying, "Do not be afraid, only believe, and she will be saved." **51** And having come into the house, He permitted no one to go in, except Peter, and James, and John, and the father of the child, and the mother; **52** and they were all weeping, and beating themselves for her, and He said, "Do not weep, she did not die, but sleeps"; **53** and they were deriding Him, knowing that she died; **54** and He having put all forth outside, and having taken hold of her hand, called, saying, "Child, arise"; **55** and her spirit came back, and she arose immediately, and He directed that there be given to her to eat; **56** and her parents were amazed, but He charged them to say to no one what had come to pass.

9 And having called together His twelve disciples, He gave them power and

LUKE

authority over all the demons, and to cure diseases, **2** and He sent them to proclaim the Kingdom of God, and to heal the ailing. **3** And He said to them, "Take nothing for the way, neither staff, nor leather pouch, nor bread, nor money; neither have two coats each; **4** and into whatever house you may enter, remain there, and depart from there; **5** and as many as may not receive you, going forth from that city, even the dust from your feet shake off, for a testimony against them." **6** And going forth they were going through the several villages, proclaiming good news, and healing everywhere. **7** And Herod the tetrarch heard of all the things being done by Him, and was perplexed, because it was said by some that John has been raised out of the dead, **8** and by some that Elijah appeared, and by others, that a prophet, one of the ancients, was risen; **9** and Herod said, "I beheaded John, but who is this concerning whom I hear such things?" And he was seeking to see Him. **10** And the apostles having turned back, declared to Him how they did great things, and having taken them, He withdrew by Himself into a city called Bethsaida, **11** and the multitudes having known followed Him, and having received them, He was speaking to them concerning the Kingdom of God, and He cured those having need of service. **12** And the day began to decline, and the Twelve having come near, said to Him, "Let away the multitude, that having gone into the surrounding villages and the fields, they may lodge and may find provision, because here we are in a desolate place." **13** And He said to them, "You give them to eat"; and they said, "We have no more than five loaves and two fishes: except, having gone, we may buy food for all this people"; **14** for they were about five thousand men. And He said to His disciples, "Cause them to recline in companies, in each fifty"; **15** and they did so, and made all to recline; **16** and having taken the five loaves and the two fishes, having looked up to the sky, He blessed them, and broke, and was giving to the disciples to set before the multitude; **17** and they ate, and were all filled, and there was taken up what was over to them of broken pieces, twelve baskets. **18** And it came to pass, as He is praying alone, the disciples were with Him, and He questioned them, saying, "Who do the multitudes say I am?" **19** And they answering said, "John the Immerser; and others, Elijah; and others, that a prophet, one of the ancients, was risen"; **20** and He said to them, "And you—who do you say I am?" And Peter answering said, "The Christ of God." **21** And having charged them, He commanded [them] to say this to no one, **22** saying, "It is necessary for the Son of Man to suffer many things, and to be rejected by the elders, and chief priests, and scribes, and to be killed, and to be raised the third day." **23** And He said to all, "If anyone wills to come after Me, let him disown himself, and take up his cross daily, and follow Me; **24** for whoever may will to save his life will lose it, and whoever may lose his life for My sake, he will save it; **25** for what is a man profited, having gained the whole world, and having lost or having forfeited himself? **26** For whoever may be ashamed of Me and of My words, of this one will the Son of Man be ashamed when He may come in His glory, and the Father's, and the holy messengers'; **27** and I say to you, truly, there are certain of those standing here who will not taste of death until they may see the Kingdom of God." **28** And it came to pass, after these words, as it were eight days, that having taken Peter, and John, and James, He went up to the mountain to pray, **29** and it came to pass, in His praying, the appearance of His face became altered, and His clothing became flashing white. **30** And behold, two men were speaking together with Him, who were Moses and Elijah, **31** who having appeared in glory, spoke of His outgoing that He was about to fulfill in Jerusalem, **32** but Peter and those with him were heavy with sleep, and having awoken, they saw His glory, and the two men standing with Him. **33** And it came to pass, in their parting from Him, Peter said to Jesus, "Master, it is good to us to be here; and we may make three shelters: one for You, and one for Moses, and one for Elijah," not knowing what he says: **34** and as he was speaking these things, there came a cloud, and overshadowed them, and they feared in their entering into the cloud, **35** and a voice came out of the cloud, saying, "This is My Son, the Beloved; hear Him"; **36** and when the voice was past, Jesus was found alone; and they were silent, and declared to no one in those days anything of what they have seen. **37** And it came to pass on the next day, they having come down from the mountain, a great multitude met Him there, **38** and behold, a man from the multitude cried out, saying, "Teacher, I implore You, look on my son, because he is my only begotten; **39** and behold, a spirit takes him, and suddenly he cries out, and it convulses him, with foaming, and it hardly departs from him, bruising him, **40** and I implored Your disciples that they might cast it out, and they were not able." **41** And Jesus answering said, "O generation, unsteadfast and perverse, until when will I be with you, and endure you? Bring your son near here"; **42** and as he is yet coming near, the demon threw him down, and convulsed [him], and Jesus rebuked the unclean spirit, and healed the youth, and gave him back to his father. **43** And they were all amazed at the greatness of God, and while all are wondering at all things that Jesus did, He said to His disciples, **44** "Lay to your ears these words, for the Son of Man is about to be delivered up into the hands of men." **45** And they were not knowing this saying, and it was veiled from them, that they might not perceive it, and they were afraid to ask Him about this saying. **46** And there entered a reasoning among them, this— who may be greater of them. **47** And Jesus having seen the reasoning of their heart, having taken hold of a child, set him beside Him, **48** and said to them, "Whoever may receive this child in My Name, receives Me, and whoever may receive Me, receives Him who sent Me, for he who is least among you all—he will be great." **49** And John answering said, "Master, we saw a certain one casting forth the demons in Your Name, and we forbade him, because he does not follow with us"; **50** and Jesus said to him, "Do not forbid, for he who is not against us, is for us." **51** And it came to pass, in the completing of the days of His being taken up, that He fixed His face to go on to Jerusalem, **52** and He sent messengers before His face, and having gone on, they went into a village of Samaritans, to make ready for Him, **53** and they did not receive Him, because His face was going on to Jerusalem. **54** And His disciples James and John having seen, said, "Lord, will You [that] we may command fire to come down from Heaven, and to consume them, as Elijah also did?" **55** And having turned, He rebuked them and said, "You have not known of what spirit you are, **56** for the Son of Man did not come to destroy men's lives, but to save"; and they went on to another village. **57** And it came to pass, as they are going on in the way, a certain one said to Him, "I will follow You wherever You may go, Lord"; **58** and Jesus said to him, "The foxes have holes, and the birds of the sky places of rest, but the Son of Man has nowhere He may recline the head." **59** And He said to another, "Follow Me"; and he said, "Lord, permit me, having gone away, to first bury my father"; **60** and Jesus said to him, "Permit the dead to bury their own dead, and you, having gone away, publish the Kingdom of God." **61** And another also said, "I will follow You, Lord, but first permit me to take leave of those in my house"; **62** and Jesus said to him, "No one having put his hand on a plow, and looking back, is fit for the Kingdom of God."

10 And after these things, the LORD also appointed seventy others, and sent them by twos before His face, to every city and place to where He Himself was about to come, **2** then He said to them, "The harvest [is] indeed abundant, but the workmen few; implore then the Lord of the harvest, that He may put forth workmen to His harvest. **3** Go away; behold, I send you forth as lambs in the midst of wolves; **4** carry no bag, no leather pouch, nor sandals; and greet no one on the way; **5** and into whatever house you enter, first say, Peace to this house; **6** and if indeed there may be there the son of peace, your peace will rest on it; and if not so, it will turn back on you. **7** And remain in that house, eating and drinking the things they have, for worthy [is] the workman of his hire; do not go from house to house, **8** and into whatever city you enter, and they may receive you, eat the things set before you, **9** and heal the ailing in it, and say to them, The Kingdom of God has come near to you. **10** And into whatever city you enter, and they may not receive you, having gone forth to its broad places, say, **11** And the dust that has cleaved to us from your city, we wipe off against you, but know this, that the Kingdom of God has come near to you; **12** and I say to you that it will be more tolerable for Sodom in that day than for that city. **13** Woe to you, Chorazin; woe to you, Bethsaida; for if the mighty works that were done in you had been done in Tyre and Sidon, they had converted long ago, sitting in sackcloth and ashes; **14** but it will be more tolerable for Tyre and Sidon in the judgment than for you. **15** And you, Capernaum, which were exalted to Heaven, you will be brought down to Hades. **16** He who is hearing you, hears Me; and he who is putting you away, puts Me away; and he who is putting Me away, puts away Him who sent Me." **17** And the seventy turned back with joy, saying, "Lord, and the demons are being subjected to us in Your Name"; **18** and He said to them, "I was beholding Satan having fallen as lightning from Heaven; **19** behold, I give to you the authority to tread on serpents and scorpions, and on all the power of the enemy, and nothing by any means will hurt you; **20** but do not rejoice in this, that the spirits are subjected to you, but rejoice rather that your names were written in the heavens." **21** In that hour Jesus was glad in the Spirit and said, "I confess to You, Father, Lord of Heaven and of earth, that You hid these things from wise men and understanding, and revealed them to babies; yes, Father, because so it became good pleasure before You. **22** All things were delivered up to Me by My Father, and no one knows who the Son is, except the Father, and who the Father is, except the Son, and he to whom the Son may resolve to reveal [Him]." **23** And having turned to the disciples, He said, by themselves, "Blessed the eyes that are perceiving what you perceive; **24** for I say to you that many prophets and kings wished to see what you perceive, and did not see, and to hear what you hear, and did not hear." **25** And behold, a certain lawyer stood up, trying Him, and saying, "Teacher, what having done, will I inherit continuous life?" **26** And He said to him, "In the Law what has been written? How do you read [it]?" **27** And he answering said, "You will love the LORD your God out of all your heart, and out of all your soul, and out of all your strength, and out of all your understanding, and your neighbor as yourself." **28** And He said to him, "You answered correctly; do this, and you will live." **29** And he, willing to declare himself righteous, said to Jesus, "And who is my neighbor?" **30** And Jesus having taken up [the word], said, "A certain man was going down from Jerusalem to Jericho, and fell among robbers, and having stripped him and inflicted blows, they went away, leaving [him] half dead. **31** And by a coincidence a certain priest was going down in that way, and having seen him, he passed over on the opposite side; **32** and in like manner also, a Levite, having been around the place, having come and seen, passed over on the opposite side. **33** But a certain Samaritan, journeying, came along him, and having seen him, he was moved with compassion, **34** and having come near, he bound up his wounds, pouring on oil and wine, and having lifted him up on his own beast, he brought him to an inn, and was careful of him; **35** and on the next day, going forth, taking out two denarii, he gave to the innkeeper and said to him, Be careful of him, and whatever you may spend more, I, in my coming again, will give back to you. **36** Who, then, of these three, seems to you to have become neighbor of him who fell among the robbers?" **37** And he said, "He who did the kindness with him," then Jesus said to him, "Be going on, and you be doing in like manner." **38** And it came to pass, in their going on, that He entered into a certain village, and a certain woman, by name Martha, received Him into her house, **39** and she also had a sister, called Mary, who also, having seated herself beside the feet of Jesus, was hearing the word, **40** and Martha was distracted about much serving, and having stood by Him, she said, "Lord, do You not care that my sister left me alone to serve? Say then to her that she may partake along with me." **41** And Jesus answering said to her, "Martha, Martha, you are anxious and disquieted about many things, **42** but of one thing there is need, and Mary chose the good part; that will not be taken away from her."

11 And it came to pass, in His being in a certain place praying, as He ceased, a certain one of His disciples said to Him, "Lord, teach us to pray, as also John taught his disciples." **2** And He said to them, "When you may pray, say: Our Father who is in the heavens, hallowed be Your Name; Your kingdom come, Your will come to pass, as in Heaven also on earth; **3** be giving us daily our appointed bread; **4** and forgive us our sins, for we also ourselves forgive everyone indebted to us; and may You not bring us into temptation, but deliver us from the evil [one]." **5** And He said to them, "Who of you will have a friend, and will go on to him at midnight, and may say to him, Friend, lend me three loaves, **6** seeing a friend of mine came out of the way to me, and I have not what I will set before him, **7** and he from within answering may say, Do not give me trouble, the door has already been shut, and my children are with me in the bed, I am not able, having risen, to give to you. **8** I say to you, even if he will not give to him, having risen, because of his being his friend, yet because of his persistence, having risen, he will give him as many as he needs; **9** and I say to you, ask, and it will be given to you; seek, and you will find; knock, and it will be opened to you; **10** for everyone who is asking receives; and he who is seeking finds; and to him who is knocking it will be opened. **11** And of which of you—the father—[if] the son will ask [for] a loaf, will present to him a stone? And [if] a fish, instead of a fish, will present to him a serpent? **12** And [if] he may ask [for] an egg, will present to him a scorpion? **13** If, then, you, being evil, have known to be giving good gifts to your children, how much more will the Father who is from Heaven give the Holy Spirit to those asking Him!" **14** And He was casting forth a demon, and it was mute, and it came to pass, the demon having gone forth, the mute man spoke, and the multitudes wondered, **15** and certain of them said, "By Beelzebul, ruler of the demons, He casts forth the demons"; **16** and others, tempting, were asking [for] a sign out of Heaven from Him. **17** And He, knowing their thoughts, said to them, "Every kingdom having been divided against itself is desolated; and house against house falls; **18** and if Satan was also divided against himself, how will his kingdom be made to stand? For you say by Beelzebul is My casting forth the demons, **19** but if I, by Beelzebul, cast forth the demons—your sons, by whom do they cast forth? Because of this they will be your judges; **20** but if by the finger of God I cast forth the demons, then the Kingdom of God came unaware on you. **21** When the strong man may keep his hall armed, his goods are in peace; **22** but when the stronger than he, having come on [him], may overcome him, he takes away his whole armor in which he had trusted, and he distributes his spoils; **23** he who is not with Me is against Me, and he who is not gathering with Me scatters. **24** When the unclean spirit may go forth from the man, it walks through waterless places seeking rest, and not finding, it says, I will return to my house from where I came forth; **25** and having come, it finds [it] swept and adorned; **26** then it goes, and takes to it seven other spirits more evil than itself, and having entered, they dwell there, and the last of that man becomes worse than the first." **27** And it came to pass, in His saying these things, a certain woman having lifted up the voice out of the multitude, said to Him, "Blessed the womb that carried You, and the breasts that You sucked!" **28** And He said, "Indeed, rather, blessed those hearing the word of God, and keeping [it]!" **29** And the multitudes crowding together on Him, He began to say, "This generation is evil, it seeks after a sign, and a sign will not be given to it, except the sign of Jonah the prophet, **30** for as Jonah became a sign to the Ninevites, so also will the Son of Man be to this generation. **31** A queen of the south will rise up in the judgment with the men of this generation, and will condemn them, because she came from the ends of the earth to hear the wisdom of Solomon; and behold, [One] greater than Solomon [is] here! **32** Men of Nineveh will stand up in the judgment with this generation, and will condemn it, because they converted at the proclamation of Jonah; and behold, [One] greater than Jonah [is] here! **33** And no one having lighted a lamp, puts [it] in a secret place, nor under the measure, but on the lampstand, that those coming in may behold the light. **34** The lamp of the body is the eye, when then your eye may be simple, your whole body is also lightened; and when it may be evil, your body is also darkened; **35** take heed, then, lest the light that [is] in you is darkness; **36** if then your whole body is lightened, not having any part darkened, the whole will be lightened, as when the lamp by the brightness may give you light." **37** And in [His] speaking, a certain Pharisee was asking Him that He might dine with him, and having gone in, He reclined, **38** and the Pharisee having seen, wondered that He did not first immerse Himself before the early meal. **39** And the LORD said to him, "Now you, the Pharisees, make the outside of the cup and of the plate clean, but your inward part is full of robbery and wickedness. **40** Unthinking [ones]! Did He who made the outside not also make the inside? **41** But what you have given [as] alms, and behold, all things are clean to you. **42** But woe to you, the Pharisees, because you tithe the mint, and the rue, and every herb, and you pass by the judgment and the love of God; these things [you] should do, and those not to be neglecting. **43** Woe to you, the Pharisees, because you love the first seats in the synagogues and the salutations in the marketplaces. **44** Woe to you, scribes and Pharisees, hypocrites, because you are as the unseen tombs, and the men walking above have not known." **45** And one of the lawyers answering, says to Him, "Teacher, saying these things, You also insult us"; **46** and He said, "And to you, the lawyers, woe! Because you burden men with burdens [too] grievous to bear, and you yourselves do not touch the burdens with one of your fingers. **47** Woe to you, because you build the tombs of the prophets, and your fathers killed them. **48** Then you testify, and are well pleased with the works of your fathers, because they indeed killed them, and you build their tombs; **49** because of this also the wisdom of God said: I will send to them prophets, and apostles, and some of them they will kill and persecute, **50** that the blood of all the prophets, that is being poured forth from the foundation of the world, may be required from this generation— **51** from the blood of Abel to the blood of Zacharias, who perished between the altar and the house; yes, I say to you, it will be required from this generation. **52** Woe to you, the lawyers, because you took away the key of the knowledge; you yourselves did not enter; and you hindered those coming in." **53** And in His speaking these things to them, the scribes and the Pharisees began fearfully to urge and to press Him to speak about many things, **54** laying wait for Him, and seeking to catch something out of His mouth, that they might accuse Him.

12 At which time the myriads of the multitude having been gathered together, so as to tread on one another, He began to say to His disciples, first, "Take heed to yourselves of the leaven of the Pharisees, which is hypocrisy; **2** and there is nothing covered that will not be revealed, and hid that will not be known; **3** because whatever you said in the darkness will be heard in the light, and what you spoke to the ear in the innerchambers will be proclaimed on the housetops. **4** And I say to you, my friends, do not be afraid of those killing the body, and after these things are not having anything more to do; **5** but I will show to you whom you may fear: fear Him who, after the killing, is having authority to cast into Gehenna; yes, I say to you, fear Him. **6** Are not five sparrows sold for two assaria? And one of them is not forgotten before God, **7** but even the hairs of your head have all been numbered; therefore do not fear, you are of more value than many sparrows. **8** And I say to you, everyone who may confess in Me before men, the Son of Man will also confess in him before the messengers of God, **9** and he who has denied Me before men, will be denied before the messengers of God, **10** and everyone who will say a word to the Son of Man, it will be forgiven to him, but the [one] having slandered to the Holy Spirit will not be forgiven. **11** And when they bring you before the synagogues, and the rulers, and the authorities, do not be anxious how or what you may reply, or what you may say, **12** for the Holy Spirit will teach you in that hour what [you] should say." **13** And a certain one out of the multitude said to Him, "Teacher, say to my brother to divide with me the inheritance." **14** And He said to him, "Man, who set Me a judge or a divider over you?" **15** And He said to them, "Observe, and beware of the covetousness, because his life is not in the abundance of one's goods." **16** And He spoke an allegory to them, saying, "Of a certain rich man the field brought forth well; **17** and he was reasoning within himself, saying, What will I do, because I have nowhere I will gather together my fruits? **18** And he said, This I will do, I will take down my storehouses, and I will build greater ones, and I will gather together there all my products and my good things, **19** and I will say to my soul, Soul, you have many good things laid up for many years, be resting, eat, drink, be merry. **20** And God said to him, Unthinking [one]! This night your life is required of you, and what things you prepared—to whom will they be [given]? **21** So [is] he who is treasuring up to himself, and is not rich toward God." **22** And He said to His disciples, "Because of this, to you I say, do not be anxious for your life, what you may eat; nor for the body, what you may put on; **23** life is more than nourishment, and the body than clothing. **24** Consider the ravens, that they do not sow, nor reap, to which there is no barn nor storehouse, and God nourishes them; how much better are you than the birds? **25** And who of you, being anxious, is able to add to his age one cubit? **26** If, then, you are not able for the least—why are you anxious for the rest? **27** Consider the lilies, how do they grow? They do not labor, nor do they spin, and I say to you, not even Solomon in all his glory was clothed as one of these; **28** and if the herbage in the field, that today is, and tomorrow is cast into an oven, God so clothes, how much more you of little faith? **29** And you—do not seek what you may eat, or what you may drink, and do not be in suspense, **30** for the nations of the world seek after all these things, and your Father has known that you have need of these things; **31** but seek the Kingdom of God, and all these things will be added to you. **32** Do not fear, little flock, because your Father delighted to give you the kingdom; **33** sell your goods, and give alms, make to yourselves bags that do not become old, a treasure unfailing in the heavens, where thief does not come near, nor moth destroy; **34** for where your treasure is, there your heart will be also. **35** Let your loins be girded, and the lamps burning, **36** and you [be] like to men waiting for their lord when he will return out of the wedding feasts, that he having come and knocked, immediately they may open to him. **37** Blessed those servants, whom the lord, having come, will find watching; truly I say to you that he will gird himself, and will cause them to recline, and having come near, will minister to them; **38** and if he may come in the second watch, and in the third watch he may come, and may find [it] so, blessed are those servants. **39** And know this, that if the master of the house had known what hour the thief comes, he would have watched, and would not have permitted his house to be broken through; **40** and you, then, become ready, because at the hour you do not think, the Son of Man comes." **41** And Peter said to Him, "Lord, do You speak this allegory to us, or also to all?" **42** And the LORD said, "Who, then, is the faithful and prudent steward whom the lord will set over his household, to give in season the wheat measure? **43** Blessed that servant, whom his lord, having come, will find doing so; **44** truly I say to you that he will set him over all his goods. **45** And if that servant may say in his heart, My lord delays to come, and may begin to beat the menservants and the maidservants, to eat also, and to drink, and to be drunken, **46** the lord of that servant will come in a day in which he does not look for [him], and in an hour that he does not know, and will cut him off, and he will appoint his portion with the unfaithful. **47** And that servant, who having known his lord's will, and having not prepared, nor having gone according to his will, will be beaten with many stripes, **48** and he who, not having known, and having done things worthy of stripes, will be beaten with few; and to everyone to whom much was given, much will be required from him; and to whom they committed much, more abundantly they will ask of him. **49** I came to cast fire to the earth, and what I wish [is] if it were already kindled! **50** But I have an immersion to be immersed with, and how I am pressed until it may be accomplished! **51** Do you think that I came to give peace in the earth? No, I say to you, but rather division; **52** for there will be from now on five in one house divided—three against two, and two against three; **53** a father will be divided against a son, and a son against a father, a mother against a daughter, and a daughter against a mother, a mother-in-law against her daughter-in-law, and a daughter-in-law against her mother-in-law." **54** And He also said to the multitudes, "When you may see the cloud rising from the west, immediately you say, A shower comes, and it is so; **55** and when a south wind is blowing, you say that there will be heat, and it is; **56** hypocrites! You have known to discern the face of the earth and of the sky, but how do you not discern this time? **57** And why, also, of yourselves, do you not judge what is righteous? **58** For as you are going away with your opponent to the ruler, in the way give diligence to be released from him, lest he may drag you to the judge, and the judge may deliver you to the officer, and the officer may cast you into prison; **59** I say to you, you may not come forth from there until even the last mite you may give back."

13 And there were some present at that time, telling Him about the

LUKE

Galileans, whose blood Pilate mingled with their sacrifices; **2** and Jesus answering said to them, "Do you think that these Galileans became sinners beyond all the Galileans, because they have suffered such things? **3** No—I say to you, but if you may not convert, even so will all you perish. **4** Or those eighteen on whom the tower in Siloam fell, and killed them, do you think that these became debtors beyond all men who are dwelling in Jerusalem? **5** No—I say to you, but if you may not convert, all you will perish in like manner." **6** And He spoke this allegory: "A certain one had a fig tree planted in his vineyard, and he came seeking fruit in it, and he did not find; **7** and he said to the vinedresser, Behold, three years I come seeking fruit in this fig tree, and do not find [it], cut it off, why does it also render the ground useless? **8** And he answering says to him, Lord, permit it also this year, until I may dig around it, and cast in dung; **9** and if indeed it may bear fruit—and if not so, thereafter you will cut it off." **10** And He was teaching in one of the synagogues on the Sabbath, **11** and behold, there was a woman having a spirit of disability [for] eighteen years, and she was bent together, and not able to bend back at all, **12** and Jesus having seen her, called [her] near and said to her, "Woman, you have been loosed from your disability"; **13** and He laid on her [His] hands, and immediately she was set upright, and was glorifying God. **14** And the chief of the synagogue answering—much displeased that on the Sabbath Jesus healed—said to the multitude, "Six days there are in which it is necessary to be working; in these, then, coming, be healed, and not on the day of the Sabbath." **15** Then the LORD answered him and said, "Hypocrite, do not each of you loose his ox or donkey from the stall on the Sabbath, and having led [it] away, water [it]? **16** And this one, being a daughter of Abraham, whom Satan bound eighteen years, behold, did [she] not ought to be loosed from this bond on the day of the Sabbath?" **17** And He saying these things, all who were opposed to Him were being ashamed, and all the multitude were rejoicing over all the glorious things that are being done by Him. **18** And He said, "To what is the Kingdom of God like? And to what will I liken it? **19** It is like to a grain of mustard, which a man having taken, cast into his garden, and it increased, and came to a great tree, and the birds of the heavens rested in its branches." **20** And again He said, "To what will I liken the Kingdom of God? **21** It is like leaven, which a woman, having taken, hid in three measures of meal, until all was leavened." **22** And He was going through cities and villages, teaching, and making progress toward Jerusalem; **23** and a certain one said to Him, "Lord, are those saved few?" And He said to them, **24** "Be striving to go in through the straight gate, because many, I say to you, will seek to go in, and will not be able; **25** from the time the Master of the house may have risen up, and may have shut the door, and you may begin to stand outside, and to knock at the door, saying, Lord, Lord, open to us, and He answering will say to you, I have not known you from where you are, **26** then you may begin to say, We ate before You, and drank, and You taught in our broad places; **27** and He will say, I say to you, I have not known you from where you are; depart from Me, all you workers of the unrighteousness. **28** There will be there the weeping and the gnashing of the teeth when you may see Abraham, and Isaac, and Jacob, and all the prophets, in the Kingdom of God, and yourselves being cast outside; **29** and they will come from east and west, and from north and south, and will recline in the Kingdom of God, **30** and behold, there are last who will be first, and there are first who will be last." **31** On that day there came near certain Pharisees, saying to Him, "Go forth, and be going on from here, for Herod wishes to kill You"; **32** and He said to them, "Having gone, say to that fox, Behold, I cast forth demons, and perfect cures today and tomorrow, and the third [day] I am being perfected; **33** but it is necessary for Me today, and tomorrow, and the [day] following, to go on, because it is not possible for a prophet to perish out of Jerusalem. **34** Jerusalem, Jerusalem, that is killing the prophets, and stoning those sent to her, how often I willed to gather together your children, as a hen [gathers] her brood under the wings, and you did not will. **35** Behold, your house is being left to you desolate, and truly I say to you, you may not see Me, until it may come when you may say, Blessed [is] He who is coming in the Name of the LORD."

LUKE

14 And it came to pass, on His going into the house of a certain one of the chiefs of the Pharisees, on a Sabbath, to eat bread, that they were watching Him; **2** and behold, there was a certain dropsical man before Him; **3** and Jesus answering spoke to the lawyers and Pharisees, saying, "Is it lawful to heal on the Sabbath?" **4** And they were silent, and having taken hold of [him], He healed him, and let [him] go; **5** and answering them He said, "Of which of you will a donkey or ox fall into a pit, and he will not immediately draw it up on the Sabbath day?" **6** And they were not able to answer Him again to these things. **7** And He spoke an allegory to those called, marking how they were choosing out the first couches, saying to them, **8** "When you may be called by anyone to wedding feasts, you may not recline on the first couch, lest [one] more honorable than you may have been called by him, **9** and he who called you and him having come will say to you, Give to this one [your] place, and then you may begin to occupy the last place with shame. **10** But when you may be called, having gone on, recline in the last place, that when he who called you may come, he may say to you, Friend, come up higher; then you will have glory before those dining with you; **11** because everyone who is exalting himself will be humbled, and he who is humbling himself will be exalted." **12** And He also said to him who called Him, "When you may make an early meal or a dinner, do not be calling your friends, nor your brothers, nor your relatives, nor rich neighbors, lest they may also call you again, and a repayment may come to you; **13** but when you may make a feast, be calling poor, maimed, lame, blind, **14** and you will be blessed, because they have nothing to repay you, for it will be repaid to you in the resurrection of the righteous." **15** And one of those dining with Him, having heard these things, said to Him, "Blessed [is] he who will eat bread in the Kingdom of God"; **16** and He said to him, "A certain man made a great dinner, and called many, **17** and he sent his servant at the hour of the dinner to say to those having been called, Be coming, because now all things are ready. **18** And all began with one [voice] to excuse themselves. The first said to him, I bought a field, and I have need to go forth and see it; I beg of you, have me excused. **19** And another said, I bought five yoke of oxen, and I go on to prove them; I beg of you, have me excused. **20** And another said, I married a wife, and because of this I am not able to come. **21** And that servant having come, told these things to his lord, then the master of the house, having been angry, said to his servant, Go forth quickly into the broad places and lanes of the city, and the poor, and maimed, and lame, and blind, bring in here. **22** And the servant said, Lord, it has been done as you commanded, and still there is room. **23** And the lord said to the servant, Go forth into the ways and hedges, and constrain to come in, that my house may be filled; **24** for I say to you that none of those men who have been called will taste of my dinner." **25** And there were going on with Him great multitudes, and having turned, He said to them, **26** "If anyone comes to Me, and does not hate his own father, and mother, and wife, and children, and brothers, and sisters, and yet even his own life, he is not able to be My disciple; **27** and whoever does not carry his cross, and come after Me, is not able to be My disciple. **28** For who of you, willing to build a tower, does not first, having sat down, count the expense, whether he has the things for completing? **29** Lest that he having laid a foundation, and not being able to finish, all who are beholding may begin to mock him, **30** saying, This man began to build, and was not able to finish. **31** Or what king going on to engage with another king in war, does not, having sat down, first consult if he with ten thousand is able to meet him who is coming against him with twenty thousand? **32** And if not so—he being yet a long way off—having sent a delegation, he asks the things for peace. **33** So, then, everyone of you who does not take leave of all that he himself has, is not able to be My disciple. **34** The salt [is] good, but if the salt becomes tasteless, with what will it be seasoned? **35** It is neither fit for land nor for manure—they cast it outside. He who is having ears to hear—let him hear."

15 And all the tax collectors and sinners were coming near to Him, to hear Him, **2** and the Pharisees and the scribes were murmuring, saying, "This One receives sinners, and eats with them." **3** And He spoke to them this allegory, saying, **4** "What man of you having one

LUKE

hundred sheep, and having lost one out of them, does not leave behind the ninety-nine in the wilderness, and go on after the lost one, until he may find it? **5** And having found, he lays [it] on his shoulders rejoicing, **6** and having come into the house, he calls together the friends and the neighbors, saying to them, Rejoice with me, because I found my sheep—the lost one. **7** I say to you that [more] joy will be in Heaven over one sinner converting, rather than over ninety-nine righteous men who have no need of conversion. **8** Or what woman having ten drachmas, if she may lose one drachma, does not light a lamp, and sweep the house, and seek carefully until she may find? **9** And having found, she calls together the female friends and the neighbors, saying, Rejoice with me, for I found the drachma that I lost. **10** So I say to you, joy comes before the messengers of God over one sinner converting." **11** And He said, "A certain man had two sons, **12** and the younger of them said to the father, Father, give me the portion of the substance falling to [me], and he divided to them the living. **13** And not many days after, having gathered all together, the younger son went abroad to a far country, and there he scattered his substance, living riotously; **14** and he having spent all, there came a mighty famine on that country, and himself began to be in want; **15** and having gone on, he joined himself to one of the citizens of that country, and he sent him into the fields to feed pigs, **16** and he was desirous to fill his belly from the husks that the pigs were eating, and no one was giving to him. **17** And having come to himself, he said, How many hired workers of my father have a superabundance of bread, and I am perishing here with hunger! **18** Having risen, I will go on to my father, and will say to him, Father, I sinned—to Heaven, and before you, **19** and I am no longer worthy to be called your son; make me as one of your hired workers. **20** And having risen, he went to his own father, and he being yet far distant, his father saw him, and was moved with compassion, and having ran he fell on his neck and kissed him; **21** and the son said to him, Father, I sinned—to Heaven, and before you, and I am no longer worthy to be called your son. **22** And the father said to his servants, Bring forth the foremost robe, and clothe him, and give a ring for his hand, and sandals for the feet; **23** and having brought the fatted calf, kill [it], and having eaten, we may be merry, **24** because this son of mine was dead, and lived again, and he was lost, and was found; and they began to be merry. **25** And his elder son was in a field, and as, coming, he drew near to the house, he heard music and dancing, **26** and having called near one of the young men, he was inquiring what these things might be, **27** and he said to him, Your brother has arrived, and your father killed the fatted calf, because he received him back in health. **28** And he was angry, and would not go in, therefore his father, having come forth, was pleading him; **29** and he answering said to the father, Behold, so many years I serve you, and never did I transgress your command, and you never gave to me a kid that I might make merry with my friends; **30** but when your son—this one who devoured your living with prostitutes—came, you killed to him the fatted calf. **31** And he said to him, Child, you are always with me, and all my things are yours; **32** but to be merry, and to be glad, it was necessary, because this your brother was dead, and lived again, he was lost, and was found."

16 And He also said to His disciples, "A certain man was rich, who had a steward, and he was accused to him as scattering his goods; **2** and having called him, he said to him, What [is] this I hear about you? Render the account of your stewardship, for you may not be steward any longer. **3** And the steward said in himself, What will I do, because my lord takes away the stewardship from me? I am not able to dig, I am ashamed to beg— **4** I have known what I will do, that, when I may be removed from the stewardship, they may receive me to their houses. **5** And having called near each one of his lord's debtors, he said to the first, How much do you owe to my lord? **6** And he said, One hundred baths of oil; and he said to him, Take your bill, and having sat down write fifty. **7** Afterward to another he said, And you, how much do you owe? And he said, One hundred cors of wheat; and he says to him, Take your bill, and write eighty. **8** And the lord commended the unrighteous steward that he did prudently, because the sons of this age are more prudent than the sons of the light in respect to their generation. **9** And I say to you, make to

LUKE

yourselves friends out of the wealth of unrighteousness, that when you may fail, they may receive you into the continuous dwelling places. **10** He who is faithful in the least, [is] also faithful in much; and he who in the least [is] unrighteous, is also unrighteous in much; **11** if, then, in the unrighteous wealth you did not become faithful—who will entrust to you the true? **12** And if in the other's you did not become faithful—who will give to you your own? **13** No servant is able to serve two lords, for either he will hate the one, and he will love the other; or one he will hold to, and of the other he will be heedless; you are not able to serve God and wealth." **14** And also the Pharisees, being lovers of money, were hearing all these things, and were deriding Him, **15** and He said to them, "You are those declaring yourselves righteous before men, but God knows your hearts; because that which is high among men [is] abomination before God; **16** the Law and the Prophets [are] until John; since then the good news of the Kingdom of God is proclaimed, and everyone presses into it; **17** and it is easier for the heaven and the earth to pass away, than one tittle to fall of the Law. **18** Everyone who is sending his wife away, and marrying another, commits adultery; and everyone who is marrying her sent away from a husband commits adultery. **19** And—a certain man was rich, and was clothed in purple and fine linen, making merry sumptuously every day, **20** and there was a certain poor man, by name Lazarus, who was laid at his porch, full of sores, **21** and desiring to be filled from the crumbs that are falling from the table of the rich man; indeed, also the dogs, coming, were licking his sores. **22** And it came to pass, that the poor man died, and that he was carried away by the messengers into the bosom of Abraham—and the rich man also died, and was buried; **23** and having lifted up his eyes in Hades, being in torments, he sees Abraham far off, and Lazarus in his bosom, **24** and having cried, he said, Father Abraham, deal kindly with me, and send Lazarus, that he may dip the tip of his finger in water, and may cool my tongue, because I am distressed in this flame. **25** And Abraham said, Child, remember that you received your good things in your life, and Lazarus in like manner the evil things, and now he is comforted, and you are distressed; **26** and besides all these things, between us and you a great chasm is fixed, so that they who are willing to go over from here to you are not able, nor do they pass through from there to us. **27** And he said, I ask, then, father, that you may send him to the house of my father, **28** for I have five brothers, so that he may thoroughly testify to them, that they also may not come to this place of torment. **29** Abraham says to him, They have Moses and the prophets, let them hear them; **30** and he said, No, father Abraham, but if anyone from the dead may go to them, they will convert. **31** And he said to him, If they do not hear Moses and the prophets, neither will they be persuaded if one may rise out of the dead."

17 And He said to the disciples, "It is impossible for the stumbling blocks not to come, but woe [to him] through whom they come; **2** it is more profitable to him if a weighty millstone is put around his neck, and he has been cast into the sea, than that he may cause one of these little ones to stumble. **3** Take heed to yourselves, and if your brother may sin in regard to you, rebuke him, and if he may change his mind, forgive him, **4** and if seven times in the day he may sin against you, and seven times in the day may return to you, saying, I change my mind, you will forgive him." **5** And the apostles said to the LORD, "Add to us faith"; **6** and the LORD said, "If you had faith as a grain of mustard, you would have said to this sycamine, Be uprooted, and be planted in the sea, and it would have obeyed you. **7** But who is he of you—having a servant plowing or feeding—who, to him having come in out of the field, will say, Having come, recline at once? **8** But will not [rather] say to him, Prepare what I may dine, and having girded yourself around, minister to me, until I eat and drink, and after these things you will eat and drink? **9** Does he have favor to that servant because he did the things directed? I think not. **10** So also you, when you may have done all the things directed you, say, We are unprofitable servants, because that which we owed to do we have done." **11** And it came to pass, in His going on to Jerusalem, that He passed through the midst of Samaria and Galilee, **12** and He entering into a certain village, there ten leprous men met Him, who stood far off, **13** and they lifted up the voice, saying,

"Jesus, Master, deal kindly with us"; **14** and having seen [them], He said to them, "Having gone on, show yourselves to the priests"; and it came to pass, in their going, they were cleansed, **15** and one of them having seen that he was healed turned back, glorifying God with a loud voice, **16** and he fell on [his] face at His feet, giving thanks to Him, and he was a Samaritan. **17** And Jesus answering said, "Were not the ten cleansed, and the nine—where? **18** There were none found who turned back to give glory to God, except this foreigner"; **19** and He said to him, "Having risen, be going on, your faith has saved you." **20** And having been questioned by the Pharisees when the Kingdom of God comes, He answered them and said, "The Kingdom of God does not come with observation; **21** nor will they say, Behold, here; or, Behold, there; for behold, the Kingdom of God is within you." **22** And He said to His disciples, "Days will come when you will desire to see one of the days of the Son of Man and you will not behold [it]; **23** and they will say to you, Behold, here; or, Behold, there; you may not go away, nor follow; **24** for as the lightning is flashing out of one [part] under the sky [and] shines to the other [part] under the sky, so will the Son of Man also be in His day; **25** and first it is necessary for Him to suffer many things, and to be rejected by this generation. **26** And as it came to pass in the days of Noah, so will it also be in the days of the Son of Man; **27** they were eating, they were drinking, they were marrying, they were given in marriage, until the day that Noah entered into the Ark, and the flood came, and destroyed all; **28** in like manner also, as it came to pass in the days of Lot; they were eating, they were drinking, they were buying, they were selling, they were planting, they were building; **29** and on the day Lot went forth from Sodom, He rained fire and brimstone from the sky, and destroyed all. **30** According to these things it will be, in the day the Son of Man is revealed; **31** in that day, he who will be on the housetop, and his vessels in the house, do not let him come down to take them away; and he in the field, in like manner, do not let him turn backward; **32** remember the wife of Lot. **33** Whoever may seek to save his life, will lose it; and whoever may lose it, will preserve it. **34** I say to you, in that night there will be two [men] on one bed: one will be taken, and the other will be left; **35** two [women] will be grinding at the same place together: one will be taken, and the other will be left; **36** [[two [men] will be in the field: one will be taken, and the other left."]] **37** And they answering say to Him, "Where, Lord?" And He said to them, "Where the body [is], there the eagles will be gathered together."

18 And He also spoke an allegory to them, that it is always necessary to pray and not to faint, **2** saying, "A certain judge was in a certain city—he is not fearing God, and he is not regarding man— **3** and a widow was in that city, and she was coming to him, saying, Do me justice on my opponent, **4** and he would not for a time, but after these things he said in himself, Even if I do not fear God, and do not regard man, **5** yet because this widow gives me trouble, I will do her justice, lest, continuously coming, she may bruise me." **6** And the LORD said, "Hear what the unrighteous judge says: **7** and will God not execute justice to His chosen ones, who are crying to Him day and night—bearing long in regard to them? **8** I say to you that He will execute justice to them quickly; but the Son of Man having come, will He find faith on the earth?" **9** And He also spoke to some who have been trusting in themselves that they were righteous, and have been despising the rest, this allegory: **10** "Two men went up to the temple to pray, one a Pharisee, and the other a tax collector; **11** the Pharisee having stood by himself, thus prayed: God, I thank You that I am not as the rest of men, rapacious, unrighteous, adulterers, or even as this tax collector; **12** I fast twice in the week, I give tithes of all things—as many as I possess. **13** And the tax collector, having stood far off, would not even lift up the eyes to the sky, but was striking on his breast, saying, God be propitious to me—the sinner! **14** I say to you, this one went down declared righteous, to his house, rather than that one: for everyone who is exalting himself will be humbled, and he who is humbling himself will be exalted." **15** And they were also bringing the babies near, that He may touch them, and the disciples having seen, rebuked them, **16** and Jesus having called them near, said, "Permit the little children to come to Me, and do not forbid them, for of such is the Kingdom of God; **17** truly I say to you, whoever may not receive the Kingdom of God as a little child, may not enter into it." **18** And a certain ruler questioned Him, saying, "Good Teacher, what having done—will I inherit continuous life?" **19** And Jesus said to him, "Why do you call Me good? No one [is] good, except one—God; **20** you have known the commands: You may not commit adultery, You may not murder, You may not steal, You may not bear false witness, Honor your father and your mother." **21** And he said, "All these I kept from my youth"; **22** and having heard these things, Jesus said to him, "Yet one thing to you is lacking: all things—as many as you have—sell, and distribute to the poor, and you will have treasure in Heaven, and come, follow Me"; **23** and he, having heard these things, became very sorrowful, for he was exceedingly rich. **24** And Jesus having seen him become very sorrowful, said, "How hardly will those having riches enter into the Kingdom of God! **25** For it is easier for a camel to enter through the eye of a needle, than for a rich man to enter into the Kingdom of God." **26** And those who heard, said, "And who is able to be saved?" **27** And He said, "The things impossible with men are possible with God." **28** And Peter said, "Behold, we left all, and followed You"; **29** and He said to them, "Truly I say to you that there is not one who left house, or parents, or brothers, or wife, or children, for the sake of the Kingdom of God, **30** who may not receive back manifold more in this time, and in the coming age, continuous life." **31** And having taken the Twelve aside, He said to them, "Behold, we go up to Jerusalem, and all things will be accomplished that have been written through the prophets to the Son of Man, **32** for He will be delivered up to the nations, and will be mocked, and insulted, and spit on, **33** and having scourged they will put Him to death, and on the third day He will rise again." **34** And they understood none of these things, and this saying was hid from them, and they were not knowing the things said. **35** And it came to pass, in His coming near to Jericho, a certain blind man was sitting beside the way begging, **36** and having heard a multitude going by, he was inquiring what this may be, **37** and they brought him word that Jesus the Nazarene passes by, **38** and he cried out, saying, "Jesus, Son of David, deal kindly with me"; **39** and those going before were rebuking him, that he might be silent, but he was crying out much more, "Son of David, deal kindly with me!" **40** And Jesus having stood, commanded him to be brought to Him, and he having come near, He questioned him, **41** saying, "What do you will I will do to you?" And he said, "Lord, that I may receive sight." **42** And Jesus said to him, "Receive your sight; your faith has saved you"; **43** and instantly he received sight, and was following Him, glorifying God; and all the people, having seen, gave praise to God.

19 And having entered, He was passing through Jericho, **2** and behold, a man, by name called Zaccheus, and he was a chief tax collector, and he was rich, **3** and he was seeking to see Jesus, who He is, and was not able for the multitude, because he was small in stature, **4** and having run forward before, he went up on a sycamore, that he may see Him, because through that [way] He was about to pass by. **5** And as Jesus came up to the place, having looked up, He saw him and said to him, "Zaccheus, having hurried, come down, for it is necessary for Me to remain in your house today"; **6** and he having hurried came down, and received Him rejoicing; **7** and having seen [it], they were all murmuring, saying, "He went in to lodge with a sinful man!" **8** And Zaccheus having stood, said to the LORD, "Behold, half of my goods, Lord, I give to the poor, and if I took by false accusation anything of anyone, I give back fourfold." **9** And Jesus said to him, "Today salvation came to this house, inasmuch as he also is a son of Abraham; **10** for the Son of Man came to seek and to save the lost." **11** And while they are hearing these things, having added He spoke an allegory, because of His being near to Jerusalem, and of their thinking that the Kingdom of God is immediately about to appear. **12** He therefore said, "A certain man of birth went on to a far country, to take to himself a kingdom, and to return, **13** and having called ten servants of his own, he gave ten minas to them and said to them, Do business—until I come; **14** and his citizens were hating him, and sent a delegation after him, saying, We do not wish this one to reign over us. **15** And it came to pass, on his coming back, having taken the kingdom, that he commanded these servants to be called to him, to whom he gave the money, that he might know what anyone had done in business. **16** And the first came near, saying, Lord, your mina gained ten minas; **17** and he said to him, Well done, good servant, because you became faithful in a very little, be having authority over ten cities. **18** And the second came, saying, Lord, your mina made five minas; **19** and he also said to this one, And you, become [ruler] over five cities. **20** And another came, saying, Lord, behold, your mina, that I had lying away in a napkin; **21** for I was afraid of you, because you are an austere man; you take up what you did not lay down, and reap what you did not sow. **22** And he says to him, Out of your mouth I will judge you, evil servant: you knew that I am an austere man, taking up what I did not lay down, and reaping what I did not sow! **23** And why did you not give my money to the bank, and I, having come, might have received it with interest? **24** And to those standing by he said, Take the mina from him, and give to him having the ten minas— **25** (and they said to him, Lord, he has ten minas)— **26** for I say to you that to everyone having will be given, and from him not having, also what he has will be taken from him, **27** but those my enemies, who did not wish me to reign over them, bring here and slay before me." **28** And having said these things, He went on before, going up to Jerusalem. **29** And it came to pass, as He came near to Bethphage and Bethany, to that called the Mount of Olives, He sent two of His disciples, **30** having said, "Go away into the village in front of [you], in which, entering in, you will find a colt bound, on which no one of men ever sat, having loosed it, bring [it]; **31** and if anyone questions you, Why do you loose [it]? Thus you will say to him: The LORD has need of it." **32** And those sent, having gone away, found according as He said to them, **33** and while they are loosing the colt, its owners said to them, "Why do you loose the colt?" **34** And they said, "The LORD has need of it"; **35** and they brought it to Jesus, and having cast their garments on the colt, they sat Jesus on it. **36** And as He is going, they were spreading their garments in the way, **37** and as He is coming near now, at the descent of the Mount of Olives, the whole multitude of the disciples began rejoicing to praise God with a great voice for all the mighty works they had seen, **38** saying, "Blessed [is] the King coming in the Name of the LORD; peace in Heaven, and glory in the highest!" **39** And certain of the Pharisees from the multitude said to Him, "Teacher, rebuke Your disciples"; **40** and He answering said to them, "I say to you that if these will be silent, the stones will cry out!" **41** And when He came near, having seen the city, He wept over it, **42** saying, "If you knew, even you, at least in this your day, the things for your peace; but now they were hid from your eyes. **43** Because days will come on you, and your enemies will cast a rampart around you, and surround you around, and press you on every side, **44** and lay you low, and your children within you, and they will not leave in you a stone on a stone, because you did not know the time of your inspection." **45** And having entered into the temple, He began to cast forth those selling in it, and those buying, **46** saying to them, "It has been written, My house is a house of prayer—but you made it a den of robbers." **47** And He was teaching daily in the temple, but the chief priests and the scribes were seeking to destroy Him—also the chiefs of the people— **48** and they were not finding what they will do, for all the people were hanging on Him, hearing Him.

20 And it came to pass, on one of those days, as He is teaching the people in the temple, and proclaiming good news, the chief priests and the scribes, with the elders, came on [Him], **2** and spoke to Him, saying, "Tell us by what authority You do these things? Or who is he that gave to You this authority?" **3** And He answering said to them, "I will question you—I also—one thing, and tell Me: **4** the immersion of John, was it from Heaven, or from men?" **5** And they reasoned with themselves, saying, "If we may say, From Heaven, He will say, Why, then, did you not believe him? **6** And if we may say, From men, all the people will stone us, for they are having been persuaded John to be a prophet." **7** And they answered that they did not know from where [it was], **8** and Jesus said to them, "Neither do I say to you by what authority I do these things." **9** And He began to speak to the people this allegory: "A certain man planted a vineyard, and gave it out to farmers, and went abroad for a long time, 10 and at the season he sent a servant to the farmers, that they may give to him from the fruit of the vineyard, but the farmers having beat him, sent [him] away empty. 11 And he added to send another servant, and they also having beaten and dishonored that one, sent [him] away empty; 12 and he added to send a third, and this one also, having wounded, they cast out. 13 And the owner of the vineyard said, What will I do? I will send my son, the beloved, perhaps having seen this one, they will respect [him]; 14 and having seen him, the farmers reasoned among themselves, saying, This is the heir; come, we may kill him, that the inheritance may become ours; 15 and having cast him outside of the vineyard, they killed [him]; what, then, will the owner of the vineyard do to them? 16 He will come, and destroy these farmers, and will give the vineyard to others." And having heard, they said, "Let it not be!" 17 And He, having looked on them, said, "What, then, is this that has been written: A stone that the builders rejected—this became head of a corner? 18 Everyone who has fallen on that stone will be broken, and on whom it may fall, it will crush him to pieces." 19 And the chief priests and the scribes sought to lay hands on Him in that hour, and they feared the people, for they knew that He spoke this allegory against them. 20 And having watched [Him], they sent forth ones lying in wait, feigning themselves to be righteous, that they might take hold of His word, to deliver Him up to the rule and to the authority of the governor, 21 and they questioned Him, saying, "Teacher, we have known that You say and teach correctly, and do not receive a person, but in truth teach the way of God. 22 Is it lawful to us to give tribute to Caesar or not?" 23 And He, having perceived their craftiness, said to them, "Why do you tempt Me? 24 Show Me a denarius; of whom does it have an image and inscription?" And they answering said, "Of Caesar": 25 and He said to them, "Give back, therefore, the things of Caesar to Caesar, and the things of God to God"; 26 and they were not able to take hold on His saying before the people, and having wondered at His answer, they were silent. 27 And certain of the Sadducees, who are denying that there is a resurrection, having come near, questioned Him, 28 saying, "Teacher, Moses wrote to us if anyone's brother may die, having a wife, and he may die childless—that his brother may take the wife, and may raise up seed to his brother. 29 There were, then, seven brothers, and the first having taken a wife, died childless, 30 and the second took the wife, and he died childless, 31 and the third took her, and in like manner also the seven—they left no children, and they died; 32 and last of all the woman also died: 33 in the resurrection, then, of which of them does she become wife? For the seven had her as wife." 34 And Jesus answering said to them, "The sons of this age marry and are given in marriage, 35 but those accounted worthy to obtain that age, and the resurrection that is out of the dead, neither marry, nor are they given in marriage; 36 for neither are they able to die anymore—for they are like messengers—and they are sons of God, being sons of the resurrection. 37 And that the dead are raised, even Moses showed at the Bush, since he calls the LORD the God of Abraham, and the God of Isaac, and the God of Jacob; 38 and He is not a God of dead men, but of living, for all live to Him." 39 And certain of the scribes answering said, "Teacher, You said well"; 40 and they no longer dared question Him anything. 41 And He said to them, "How do they say the Christ is [the] son of David, 42 and David himself says in [the] Scroll of Psalms, The LORD said to my Lord, ‖ Sit on My right hand, 43 Until I will make Your enemies Your footstool; 44 David, then, calls Him Lord, and how is He his son?" 45 And all the people hearing, He said to His disciples, 46 "Take heed of the scribes, who are wishing to walk in long robes, and are cherishing salutations in the markets, and first seats in the synagogues, and first couches at the banquets, 47 who devour the houses of the widows, and make long prayers for a pretense, these will receive more abundant judgment."

21 And having looked up, He saw those who cast their gifts into the treasury—rich men, 2 and He also saw a certain poor widow casting two mites there, 3 and He said, "Truly I say to you that this poor widow cast in more than all; 4 for all these out of their superabundance cast into the gifts to God, but this one out

LUKE

of her want, all the living that she had, cast in." **5** And [as] some were speaking about the temple, that it has been adorned with good stones and devoted things, He said, **6** "These things that you behold—days will come in which there will not be left a stone on a stone that will not be thrown down." **7** And they questioned Him, saying, "Teacher, when, then, will these things be? And what [is] the sign when these things may be about to happen?" **8** And He said, "See—you may not be led astray, for many will come in My Name, saying, I am [He], and the time has come near; do not then go on after them; **9** and when you may hear of wars and uprisings, do not be terrified, for it is necessary for these things to happen first, but the end [is] not immediately." **10** Then He said to them, "Nation will rise against nation, and kingdom against kingdom, **11** also great shakings, and there will be famines and pestilences in every place; also there will be fearful things and great signs from the sky; **12** and before all these, they will lay on you their hands, and persecute, delivering up to synagogues and prisons, being brought before kings and governors for My Name's sake; **13** and it will become to you for a testimony. **14** Settle, then, to your hearts, not to meditate beforehand to reply, **15** for I will give to you a mouth and wisdom that all your opposers will not be able to refute or resist. **16** And you will be delivered up also by parents, and brothers, and relatives, and friends, and they will put [some] of you to death; **17** and you will be hated by all because of My Name— **18** and a hair out of your head will not perish; **19** in your patience possess your souls. **20** And when you may see Jerusalem surrounded by encampments, then know that her desolation has come near; **21** then those in Judea, let them flee to the mountains; and those in her midst, let them depart out; and those in the countries, do not let them come in to her; **22** because these are days of vengeance, to fulfill all things that have been written. **23** And woe to those with child, and to those giving suck, in those days; for there will be great distress on the land, and wrath on this people; **24** and they will fall by the mouth of the sword, and will be led captive to all the nations, and Jerusalem will be trodden down by nations, until the times of nations be fulfilled. **25** And there will be signs in sun, and moon, and stars, and on the earth distress of nations with perplexity, sea and wave roaring; **26** men fainting at heart from fear, and expectation of the things coming on the world, for the powers of the heavens will be shaken. **27** And then they will see the Son of Man coming in a cloud, with power and much glory; **28** and these things beginning to happen, bend yourselves back, and lift up your heads, because your redemption draws near." **29** And He spoke an allegory to them: "See the fig tree, and all the trees, **30** when they may now cast forth, having seen, of yourselves you know that now the summer is near; **31** so also you, when you may see these things happening, you know that the Kingdom of God is near; **32** truly I say to you, this generation may not pass away until all may have come to pass; **33** the sky and the earth will pass away, but My words may not pass away. **34** And take heed to yourselves lest your hearts may be weighed down with carousing, and drunkenness, and anxieties of life, and suddenly that day may come on you, **35** for it will come as a snare on all those dwelling on the face of all the earth, **36** watch, then, in every season, praying that you may be accounted worthy to escape all these things that are about to come to pass, and to stand before the Son of Man." **37** And He was teaching in the temple during the days, and during the nights, going forth, He was lodging at [that] called the Mount of Olives; **38** and all the people were coming early to Him in the temple to hear Him.

22 And the Celebration of the Unleavened [Bread] was coming near, that is called Passover, **2** and the chief priests and the scribes were seeking how they may take Him up, for they were afraid of the people. **3** And Satan entered into Judas, who is surnamed Iscariot, being of the number of the Twelve, **4** and he, having gone away, spoke with the chief priests and the magistrates, how he might deliver Him up to them, **5** and they rejoiced, and covenanted to give him money, **6** and he agreed, and was seeking a favorable season to deliver Him up to them without tumult. **7** And the day of the Unleavened [Bread] came, in which it was necessary [for] the Passover to be sacrificed, **8** and He sent Peter and John, saying, "Having gone on, prepare to us the Passover, that we may

LUKE

eat"; **9** and they said to Him, "Where do You will that we might prepare?" **10** And He said to them, "Behold, in your entering into the city, a man will meet you there, carrying a pitcher of water, follow him into the house where he goes in, **11** and you will say to the master of the house, The Teacher says to you, Where is the guest-chamber where I may eat the Passover with My disciples? **12** And he will show you a large upper room furnished, make ready there"; **13** and they, having gone away, found as He has said to them, and they made the Passover ready. **14** And when the hour was come, He reclined, and the twelve apostles with Him, **15** and He said to them, "With desire I desired to eat this Passover with you before My suffering, **16** for I say to you that I may eat of it no longer until it may be fulfilled in the Kingdom of God." **17** And having taken a cup, having given thanks, He said, "Take this and divide to yourselves, **18** for I say to you that I may not drink of the produce of the vine until the Kingdom of God may come." **19** And having taken bread, having given thanks, He broke and gave to them, saying, "This is My body, that is being given for you, do this in remembrance of Me." **20** In like manner, also, the cup after the dining, saying, "This cup [is] the New Covenant in My blood, that is being poured forth for you. **21** But behold, the hand of him delivering Me up [is] with Me on the table, **22** and, indeed, the Son of Man goes according to what has been determined; but woe to that man through whom He is being delivered up." **23** And they began to reason among themselves who then of them it may be who is about to do this thing. **24** And there happened also a strife among them—who of them is accounted to be greater. **25** And He said to them, "The kings of the nations exercise lordship over them, and those exercising authority on them are called benefactors; **26** but you [are] not so, but he who is greater among you—let him be as the younger; and he who is leading, as he who is ministering; **27** for who is greater? He who is reclining, or he who is ministering? Is it not he who is reclining? And I am in your midst as He who is ministering. **28** And you are those who have remained with Me in My temptations, **29** and I appoint to you a kingdom, as My Father appointed to Me, **30** that you may eat and may drink at My table, in My kingdom, and may sit on thrones, judging the twelve tribes of Israel." **31** And the LORD said, "Simon, Simon, behold, Satan asked for himself to sift you as the wheat, **32** and I implored for you that your faith may not fail; and you, when you turned, strengthen your brothers." **33** And he said to Him, "Lord, I am ready to go with You both to prison and to death"; **34** and He said, "I say to you, Peter, a rooster will not crow today, before you may disown knowing Me three times." **35** And He said to them, "When I sent you without bag, and leather pouch, and sandals, did you lack anything?" And they said, "Nothing." **36** Then He said to them, "But now, he who is having a bag, let him take [it] up, and in like manner also a leather pouch; and he who is not having, let him sell his garment, and buy a sword, **37** for I say to you that this which has been written is necessary to be accomplished in Me: And He was reckoned with lawless ones; for also the things concerning Me have an end." **38** And they said, "Lord, behold, here [are] two swords"; and He said to them, "It is sufficient." **39** And having gone forth, He went on, according to custom, to the Mount of Olives, and His disciples also followed Him, **40** and having come to the place, He said to them, "Pray to not enter into temptation." **41** And He was withdrawn from them, as it were a stone's cast, and having fallen on the knees He was praying, **42** saying, "Father, if You are willing, remove this cup from Me, but not My will, but Yours be done." **43** And there appeared to Him a messenger from Heaven strengthening Him; **44** and having been in agony, He was more earnestly praying, and His sweat became, as it were, great drops of blood falling on the ground. **45** And having risen up from the prayer, having come to the disciples, He found them sleeping from the sorrow, **46** and He said to them, "Why do you sleep? Having risen, pray that you may not enter into temptation." **47** And while He is speaking, behold, a multitude, and he who is called Judas, one of the Twelve, was coming before them, and he came near to Jesus to kiss Him, **48** and Jesus said to him, "Judas, do you deliver up the Son of Man with a kiss?" **49** And those around Him, having seen what was about to be, said to Him, "Lord, will we strike with a sword?" **50** And a certain one of them struck the servant of the chief priest, and took off his right ear, **51** and Jesus answering said, "Permit thus far," and having touched his ear, He healed him. **52** And Jesus said to those having come on Him—chief priests, and magistrates of the temple, and elders, "Have you come forth with swords and sticks as on a robber? **53** While daily I was with you in the temple, you stretched forth no hands against Me; but this is your hour and the power of the darkness." **54** And having taken Him, they led and brought Him into the house of the chief priest. And Peter was following far off, **55** and they having kindled a fire in the midst of the court, and having sat down together, Peter was sitting in the midst of them, **56** and a certain maid having seen him sitting at the light, and having earnestly looked at him, she said, "And this one was with Him!" **57** And he disowned Him, saying, "Woman, I have not known Him." **58** And after a while, another having seen him, said, "And you are of them!" And Peter said, "Man, I am not." **59** And one hour, as it were, having intervened, a certain other was confidently affirming, saying, "Of a truth this one also was with Him, for he is also a Galilean"; **60** and Peter said, "Man, I have not known what you say"; and immediately, while he is speaking, a rooster crowed. **61** And the LORD, having turned, looked on Peter, and Peter remembered the word of the LORD, how He said to him, "Before a rooster will crow, you may disown Me three times"; **62** and Peter having gone outside, wept bitterly. **63** And the men who were holding Jesus were mocking Him, beating [Him]; **64** and having blindfolded Him, they were striking Him on the face, and were questioning Him, saying, "Prophesy who he is who struck You?" **65** And many other things, slandering, they spoke in regard to Him. **66** And when it became day there was gathered together the eldership of the people, chief priests also, and scribes, and they led Him up to their own Sanhedrin, **67** saying, "If You are the Christ, tell us." And He said to them, "If I may tell you, you will not believe; **68** and if I also question [you], you will not answer Me or send Me away; **69** from now on, there will be the Son of Man sitting on the right hand of the power of God." **70** And they all said, "You, then, are the Son of God?" And He said to them, "You say [it], because I AM"; **71** and they said, "What need do we have yet of testimony? For we ourselves heard [it] from His mouth."

23 And having risen, the whole multitude of them led Him to Pilate, **2** and began to accuse Him, saying, "We found this One perverting the nation, and forbidding to give tribute to Caesar, saying Himself to be Christ, a king." **3** And Pilate questioned Him, saying, "You are the King of the Jews?" And He answering him, said, "You say [it]." **4** And Pilate said to the chief priests and the multitude, "I find no fault in this Man"; **5** and they were the more urgent, saying, "He stirs up the people, teaching throughout the whole of Judea—having begun from Galilee—to this place." **6** And Pilate having heard of Galilee, questioned if the Man is a Galilean, **7** and having known that He is from the jurisdiction of Herod, he sent Him back to Herod, he also being in Jerusalem in those days. **8** And Herod rejoiced exceedingly having seen Jesus, for he was wishing to see Him for a long [time], because of hearing many things about Him, and he was hoping to see some sign done by Him, **9** and was questioning Him in many words, and He answered him nothing. **10** And the chief priests and the scribes stood vehemently accusing Him, **11** and Herod with his soldiers having set Him at nothing, and having mocked, having cast radiant apparel around Him, sent Him back to Pilate, **12** and both Pilate and Herod became friends with one another on that day, for they were previously at enmity between themselves. **13** And Pilate having called together the chief priests, and the rulers, and the people, **14** said to them, "You brought this Man to me as perverting the people, and behold, I having examined [Him] before you, found no fault in this Man in those things you bring forward against Him; **15** no, neither Herod, for he sent Him back to us, and behold, nothing worthy of death is having been done by Him; **16** having corrected, therefore, I will release Him," **17** [[for it was necessary for him to release to them one at every celebration,]] **18** and they cried out—the whole multitude—saying, "Away with this One, and release Barabbas to us," **19** who had been cast into prison, because of a certain sedition made in the city, and murder. **20** Pilate again then—wishing to release Jesus—called to them, **21** but they were calling out, saying, "Crucify! Crucify Him!" **22** And he said to them a third time, "Why, what evil did He do? I found no cause of death in Him; having corrected Him, then, I will release [Him]." **23** And they were pressing with loud voices asking Him to be crucified, and their voices, and those of the chief priests, were prevailing, **24** and Pilate gave judgment for their request being done, **25** and he released him who because of sedition and murder has been cast into the prison, whom they were asking for, and he gave up Jesus to their will. **26** And as they led Him away, having taken hold on Simon, a certain Cyrenian, coming from the field, they put the cross on him to carry [it] behind Jesus. **27** And a great multitude of the people were following Him, and of women, who also were beating themselves and lamenting Him, **28** and Jesus having turned to them, said, "Daughters of Jerusalem, do not weep for Me, but weep for yourselves and for your children; **29** for behold, days come in which they will say, Blessed the barren, and wombs that did not bear, and breasts that did not give suck; **30** then they will begin to say to the mountains, Fall on us, and to the hills, Cover us; **31** for if they do these things in the green tree, what may happen in the dry?" **32** And there were also others—two evildoers—with Him, to be put to death; **33** and when they came to the place that is called "[Place] of [the] Skull," there they crucified Him and the evildoers, one on the right hand and one on the left. **34** And Jesus said, "Father, forgive them, for they have not known what they do"; and parting His garments they cast a lot. **35** And the people were standing, looking on, and the rulers were also sneering with them, saying, "He saved others, let Him save Himself, if this be the Christ, the Chosen One of God." **36** And the soldiers were also mocking Him, coming near and offering vinegar to Him, **37** and saying, "If You are the King of the Jews, save Yourself." **38** And there was also an inscription written over Him [[in letters of Greek, and Latin, and Hebrew]]: "THIS IS THE KING OF THE JEWS." **39** And one of the evildoers who were hanged was slandering Him, saying, "If You are the Christ, save Yourself and us." **40** And the other answering, was rebuking him, saying, "Do you not even fear God, that you are in the same judgment? **41** And we indeed justly, for we are receiving back [things] worthy of what we did, but this One did nothing out of place"; **42** and he said to Jesus, "Remember me, Lord, when You may come in Your kingdom"; **43** and Jesus said to him, "Truly I say to you, today you will be with Me in Paradise." **44** And it was, as it were, the sixth hour, and darkness came over all the land until the ninth hour, **45** and the sun was darkened, and the veil of the temple was torn in the middle, **46** and having cried with a loud voice, Jesus said, "Father, into Your hands I commit My spirit"; now having said this, He breathed His last. **47** And the centurion having seen what was done, glorified God, saying, "Truly this Man was righteous"; **48** and all the multitudes having come together to this sight, beholding the things that came to pass, turned back striking their breasts; **49** and all His acquaintances stood far off, and women who followed Him from Galilee, beholding these things. **50** And behold, a man, by name Joseph, being a counselor, a man good and righteous, **51** from Arimathea, a city of the Jews, who also himself was expecting the Kingdom of God, he was not consenting to their counsel and deed, **52** he having gone near to Pilate, asked for the body of Jesus, **53** and having taken it down, he wrapped it in fine linen, and placed it in a hewn out tomb, where no one was yet laid. **54** And it was [the] Day of Preparation, and Sabbath was approaching, **55** and the women who also have come with Him out of Galilee having followed after, beheld the tomb, and how His body was placed, **56** and having turned back, they made ready spices and ointments, and on the Sabbath, indeed, they rested, according to the command.

24 And on the first [day] of the weeks, at early dawn, they came to the tomb, carrying the spices they made ready, and certain [others] with them, **2** and they found the stone having been rolled away from the tomb, **3** and having gone in, they did not find the body of the Lord Jesus. **4** And it came to pass, while they are perplexed about this, that behold, two men stood by them in clothing—flashing [with light]; **5** and on their having become afraid, and having inclined the face to the earth, they said to them, "Why do you seek the living with the dead? **6** He is not here, but was

LUKE

raised; remember how He spoke to you, being yet in Galilee, **7** saying, It is necessary for the Son of Man to be delivered up into the hands of sinful men, and to be crucified, and to rise again [on] the third day." **8** And they remembered His sayings, **9** and having turned back from the tomb, told all these things to the Eleven, and to all the rest. **10** And it was Mary the Magdalene, and Joanna, and Mary of James, and the other women with them, who told these things to the apostles, **11** and their sayings appeared before them as idle talk, and they were not believing them. **12** And Peter having risen, ran to the tomb, and having stooped down he sees the linen clothes lying alone, and he went away to his own home, wondering at that having come to pass. **13** And behold, two of them were going on during that day to a village, being sixty stadia distant from Jerusalem, the name of which [is] Emmaus, **14** and they were conversing with one another about all these things that have happened. **15** And it came to pass in their conversing and reasoning together, that Jesus Himself, having come near, was going on with them, **16** and their eyes were restrained so as not to know Him, **17** and He said to them, "What [are] these words that you exchange with one another, walking, and you are sad?" **18** And one, whose name was Cleopas, answering, said to Him, "Are You alone visiting Jerusalem and have not known the things having come to pass in it in these days?" **19** And He said to them, "What things?" And they said to Him, "The things about Jesus of Nazareth, who became a man—a prophet—powerful in deed and word, before God and all the people, **20** how also the chief priests and our rulers delivered Him up to a judgment of death, and crucified Him; **21** and we were hoping that it is He who is about to redeem Israel, and also with all these things, this third day is passing today since these things happened. **22** And certain of our women also astonished us, coming early to the tomb, **23** and having not found His body, they came, saying to have also seen an apparition of messengers who say He is alive, **24** and certain of those with us went away to the tomb, and found [it] so, even as the women said, and they did not see Him." **25** And He said to them, "O inconsiderate and slow in heart to believe on all that the prophets spoke! **26** Was it not necessary [for] the Christ to suffer these things, and to enter into His glory?" **27** And having begun from Moses, and from all the Prophets, He was expounding to them in all the Writings the things about Himself. **28** And they came near to the village to where they were going, and He made an appearance of going on further, **29** and they constrained Him, saying, "Remain with us, for it is toward evening," and the day declined, and He went in to remain with them. **30** And it came to pass, in His reclining with them, having taken the bread, He blessed, and having broken, He was giving to them, **31** and their eyes were opened, and they recognized Him, and He became unseen by them. **32** And they said to one another, "Was our heart not burning within us as He was speaking to us in the way, and as He was opening the Writings up to us?" **33** And they, having risen up the same hour, turned back to Jerusalem, and found the Eleven gathered together, and those with them, **34** saying, "The Lord was indeed raised, and was seen by Simon"; **35** and they were expounding the things in the way, and how He was made known to them in the breaking of the bread, **36** and as they are speaking these things, Jesus Himself stood in the midst of them, and says to them, "Peace to you"; **37** and being amazed, and becoming frightened, they were thinking themselves to see a spirit. **38** And He said to them, "Why are you troubled? And why do reasonings come up in your hearts? **39** See My hands and My feet, that I am He; handle Me and see, because a spirit does not have flesh and bones as you see Me having." **40** And having said this, He showed the hands and the feet to them, **41** and while they are not believing from the joy, and wondering, He said to them, "Do you have anything here to eat?" **42** And they gave to Him part of a broiled fish, and of a honeycomb, **43** and having taken, He ate before them, **44** and He said to them, "These [are] the words that I spoke to you, being yet with you, that it is necessary to be fulfilled all the things that are written in the Law of Moses, and the Prophets, and the Psalms, about Me." **45** Then He opened up their understanding to understand the Writings, **46** and He said to them, "Thus it has been written, and thus it was necessary [for] the Christ to suffer, and to rise out of the dead [on] the third day, **47** and conversion and forgiveness of sins is to be proclaimed in His Name to all the nations, beginning from Jerusalem: **48** and you are witnesses of these things. **49** And behold, I send the promise of My Father on you, but you—abide in the city of Jerusalem until you are clothed with power from on high." **50** And He led them forth outside—to Bethany, and having lifted up His hands He blessed them, **51** and it came to pass, in His blessing them, He was parted from them, and was carried up into Heaven; **52** and they, having worshiped Him, turned back to Jerusalem with great joy, **53** and were continually in the temple, praising and blessing God. Amen.

JOHN

1 In the beginning was the Word, and the Word was with God, and the Word was God; **2** this One was in the beginning with God; **3** all things happened through Him, and without Him not even one thing happened that has happened. **4** In Him was life, and the life was the light of men, **5** and the light shined in the darkness, and the darkness did not perceive it. **6** There came a man—having been sent from God—whose name [is] John, **7** this one came for testimony, that he might testify about the Light, that all might believe through him; **8** that one was not the Light, but—that he might testify about the Light. **9** He was the true Light, which enlightens every man, coming into the world; **10** He was in the world, and the world was made through Him, and the world did not know Him; **11** He came to [His] own, and [His] own did not receive Him; **12** but as many as received Him, to them He gave authority to become sons of God—to those believing in His Name, **13** who were begotten, not of blood, nor of will of flesh, nor of will of man, but of God. **14** And the Word became flesh, and dwelt among us, and we beheld His glory, glory as of [the] only begotten of [the] Father, full of grace and truth. **15** John testifies concerning Him, and has cried, saying, "This was He of whom I said, He who is coming after me has come before me, for He was before me." **16** And we all received out of His fullness, and grace for grace; **17** for the Law was given through Moses, the grace and the truth came through Jesus Christ. **18** No one has ever seen God; the only begotten God who is on the bosom of the Father—He has expounded [Him]. **19** And this is the testimony of John when the Jews sent priests and Levites out of Jerusalem, that they might question him, "Who are you?" **20** And he confessed and did not deny, and confessed, "I am not the Christ." **21** And they questioned him, "What then? Are you Elijah?" And he says, "I am not." "Are you the prophet?" And he answered, "No." **22** Then they said to him, "Who are you, that we may give an answer to those sending us? What do you say concerning yourself?" **23** He said, "I [am] a voice of one crying in the wilderness: Make straight the way of the LORD, as Isaiah the prophet said." **24** And those sent were of the Pharisees, **25** and they questioned him and said to him, "Why, then, do you immerse, if you are not the Christ, nor Elijah, nor the prophet?" **26** John answered them, saying, "I immerse in water, but in the midst of you has stood He whom you have not known, it is this One who is coming after me, who has been before me, **27** of whom I am not worthy that I may loose the strap of His sandal." **28** These things came to pass in Bethabara, beyond the Jordan, where John was immersing. **29** On the next day John sees Jesus coming to him and says, "Behold, the Lamb of God, who is taking away the sin of the world; **30** this is He concerning whom I said, After me comes a Man who has come before me, because He was before me; **31** and I did not know Him, but that He might be revealed to Israel, because of this I came immersing in water." **32** And John testified, saying, "I have seen the Spirit coming down out of Heaven as a dove, and [that] One remained on Him; **33** and I did not know Him, but He who sent me to immerse in water, He said to me, On whomsoever you may see the Spirit coming down, and remaining on Him, this is He who is immersing in the Holy Spirit; **34** and I have seen, and have testified, that this is the Son of God." **35** On the next day, again, John was standing, and two of his disciples, **36** and having looked on Jesus walking, he says, "Behold, the Lamb of God"; **37** and the two disciples heard him speaking, and they followed Jesus. **38** And Jesus having turned, and having beheld them following, says to them, "What do you seek?" And they said to Him, "Rabbi" (which is, being interpreted, Teacher), "where do You remain?" **39** He says to them, "Come and see"; they came and saw where He remains, and they remained with Him that day and the hour was about the tenth. **40** Andrew, the brother of Simon Peter, was one of the two who heard from John, and followed Him; **41** this one first finds his own brother Simon and says to him, "We have found the Messiah," (which is, being interpreted, Anointed One), **42** and he brought him to Jesus: and having looked

JOHN

on him, Jesus says, "You are Simon, the son of Jonas, you will be called Cephas," (which is interpreted, A rock). **43** On the next day He willed to go forth to Galilee, and He finds Philip and says to him, "Follow Me." **44** And Philip was from Bethsaida, of the city of Andrew and Peter; **45** Philip finds Nathanael and says to him, "Him of whom Moses wrote in the Law, and the Prophets, we have found, Jesus the Son of Joseph, who [is] from Nazareth!" **46** And Nathanael said to him, "Is any good thing able to be out of Nazareth?" Philip said to him, "Come and see." **47** Jesus saw Nathanael coming to Him, and He says concerning him, "Behold, truly an Israelite, in whom is no guile"; **48** Nathanael says to Him, "From where do You know me?" Jesus answered and said to him, "Before Philip's calling you, being under the fig tree, I saw you." **49** Nathanael answered and says to Him, "Rabbi, You are the Son of God, You are the King of Israel." **50** Jesus answered and said to him, "Because I said to you, I saw you under the fig tree, you believe; you will see greater things than these"; **51** and He says to him, "Truly, truly, I say to you, from now on you will see Heaven opened, and the messengers of God going up and coming down on the Son of Man."

2 And [on] the third day a wedding happened in Cana of Galilee, and the mother of Jesus was there, **2** and also Jesus was called, and His disciples, to the wedding; **3** and wine having failed, the mother of Jesus says to Him, "They have no wine"; **4** Jesus says to her, "What [is that] to Me and to you, woman? My hour is not yet come." **5** His mother says to the servants, "Whatever He may say to you—do." **6** And there were six water-jugs of stone there, placed according to the purifying of the Jews, holding each two or three measures. **7** Jesus says to them, "Fill the water-jugs with water"; and they filled them—to the brim; **8** and He says to them, "Draw out, now, and carry to the headwaiter"; and they bore. **9** And as the headwaiter tasted the water become wine, and did not know where it is from (but the servants knew, who have drawn the water), the headwaiter calls the bridegroom, **10** and says to him, "Every man, at first, sets forth the good wine; and when they may have drunk freely, then the inferior; you kept the good wine until now." **11** This [is the] beginning of the signs Jesus did in Cana of Galilee, and revealed His glory, and His disciples believed in Him; **12** after this He went down to Capernaum, He, and His mother, and His brothers, and His disciples; and they did not remain there many days. **13** And the Passover of the Jews was near, and Jesus went up to Jerusalem, **14** and He found in the temple those selling oxen, and sheep, and doves, and the money-changers sitting, **15** and having made a whip of small cords, He put all forth out of the temple, also the sheep, and the oxen; and He poured out the coins of the money-changers, and He overthrew the tables, **16** and He said to those selling the doves, "Take these things from here; do not make the house of My Father a house of merchandise." **17** And His disciples remembered that it is written: "The zeal of Your house ate Me up"; **18** the Jews then answered and said to Him, "What sign do You show to us—that You do these things?" **19** Jesus answered and said to them, "Destroy this temple, and in three days I will raise it up." **20** The Jews, therefore, said, "This temple was built [in] forty-six years, and will You raise it up in three days?" **21** But He spoke concerning the temple of His body; **22** when, then, He was raised out of the dead, His disciples remembered that He said this to them, and they believed the Writing, and the word that Jesus said. **23** And as He was in Jerusalem, in the Passover, in the celebration, many believed in His Name, beholding His signs that He was doing; **24** and Jesus Himself was not trusting Himself to them, because of His knowing all [men], **25** and because He had no need that any should testify concerning man, for He Himself was knowing what was in man.

3 And there was a man of the Pharisees, his name Nicodemus, a ruler of the Jews; **2** this one came to Him by night and said to Him, "Rabbi, we have known that You have come from God—a teacher, for no one is able to do these signs that You do, if God may not be with him." **3** Jesus answered and said to him, "Truly, truly, I say to you, if anyone may not be born from above, he is not able to see the Kingdom of God"; **4** Nicodemus says to Him, "How is a man able to be born, being old? Is he able to enter into the womb of his mother a

JOHN

second time, and to be born?" **5** Jesus answered, "Truly, truly, I say to you, if anyone may not be born of water and the Spirit, he is not able to enter into the Kingdom of God; **6** that which has been born of the flesh is flesh, and that which has been born of the Spirit is spirit. **7** You may not wonder that I said to you, It is required for you to be born from above; **8** the Spirit blows where [that] One wills, and you hear [that] One's voice, but you have not known from where [that] One comes, and to where [that] One goes; thus is everyone who has been born of the Spirit." **9** Nicodemus answered and said to Him, "How are these things able to happen?" **10** Jesus answered and said to him, "You are the teacher of Israel and you do not know these things? **11** Truly, truly, I say to you, what We have known We speak, and what We have seen We testify, and you do not receive Our testimony; **12** if I spoke to you of the earthly things, and you do not believe, how, if I will speak to you of the heavenly things, will you believe? **13** And no one has gone up to Heaven, except He who came down out of Heaven—the Son of Man who is in Heaven. **14** And as Moses lifted up the serpent in the wilderness, so it is necessary for the Son of Man to be lifted up, **15** that everyone who is believing in Him may not perish, but may have continuous life, **16** for God so loved the world that He gave the only begotten Son, that everyone who is believing in Him may not perish, but may have continuous life. **17** For God did not send His Son into the world that He may judge the world, but that the world may be saved through Him; **18** he who is believing in Him is not judged, but he who is not believing has been judged already, because he has not believed in the Name of the only begotten Son of God. **19** And this is the judgment, that the light has come into the world, and men loved the darkness rather than the light, for their works were evil; **20** for everyone who is doing wicked things hates the light, and does not come into the light, that his works may not be detected; **21** but he who is doing the truth comes into the light, that his works may be revealed, that in God they are having been worked." **22** After these things Jesus and His disciples came into the land of Judea, and there He tarried with them, and was immersing; **23** and John was also immersing in Aenon, near to Salem, because there were many waters there, and they were coming and were being immersed— **24** for John was not yet cast into the prison— **25** there arose then a question from the disciples of John with [some] Jews about purifying, **26** and they came to John and said to him, "Rabbi, He who was with you beyond the Jordan, to whom you testified, behold, this One is immersing, and all are coming to Him." **27** John answered and said, "A man is not able to receive anything if it may not have been given him from Heaven; **28** you yourselves testify to me that I said, I am not the Christ, but that I am having been sent before Him; **29** He who is having the bride is bridegroom, and the friend of the bridegroom, who is standing and hearing Him, rejoices with joy because of the voice of the bridegroom; this, then, my joy has been fulfilled. **30** It is necessary [for] Him to increase, and me to become less; **31** He who is coming from above is above all; he who is from the earth, from the earth he is, and from the earth he speaks; He who is coming from Heaven is above all. **32** And what He has seen and heard—this He testifies, and none receives His testimony; **33** he who is receiving His testimony sealed that God is true; **34** for He whom God sent, He speaks the sayings of God; for God does not give the Spirit by measure; **35** the Father loves the Son, and has given all things into His hand; **36** he who is believing in the Son has continuous life; and he who is not believing the Son will not see life, but the wrath of God remains on him."

4 When therefore the LORD knew that the Pharisees heard that Jesus makes and immerses more disciples than John, **2** (though indeed Jesus Himself was not immersing, but His disciples), **3** He left Judea and went away again to Galilee, **4** and it was necessary [for] Him to go through Samaria. **5** He comes, therefore, to a city of Samaria, called Sychar, near to the place that Jacob gave to his son Joseph; **6** and there was there a well of Jacob. Jesus therefore having been weary from the journeying, was thus sitting on the well; it was as it were the sixth hour; **7** there comes a woman out of Samaria to draw water. Jesus says to her, "Give Me to drink"; **8** for His disciples were gone away into the city that they may buy food; **9** the Samaritan

JOHN

woman therefore says to Him, "How do You, being a Jew, ask drink from me, being a Samaritan woman?" For Jews have no dealing with Samaritans. **10** Jesus answered and said to her, "If you had known the gift of God, and who it is who is saying to you, Give Me to drink, you would have asked Him, and He would have given you living water." **11** The woman says to Him, "Lord, You do not even have a vessel to draw with, and the well is deep; from where, then, have You the living water? **12** Are You greater than our father Jacob, who gave us the well, and himself drank out of it, and his sons, and his livestock?" **13** Jesus answered and said to her, "Everyone who is drinking of this water will thirst again; **14** but whoever may drink of the water that I will give him, may not thirst—throughout the age; and the water that I will give him will become in him a well of water, springing up to continuous life." **15** The woman says to Him, "Lord, give me this water, that I may not thirst, nor come here to draw." **16** Jesus says to her, "Go, call your husband, and come here"; **17** the woman answered and said, "I do not have a husband." Jesus says to her, "Well did you say—I do not have a husband; **18** for you have had five husbands, and now, he whom you have is not your husband; you have said this correctly." **19** The woman says to Him, "Lord, I perceive that You are a prophet; **20** our fathers worshiped in this mountain, and You say that in Jerusalem is the place where it is required to worship." **21** Jesus says to her, "Woman, believe Me, that there comes an hour when neither in this mountain, nor in Jerusalem, will you worship the Father; **22** you worship what you have not known; we worship what we have known, because salvation is of the Jews; **23** but there comes an hour, and it now is, when the true worshipers will worship the Father in spirit and truth, for the Father also seeks such to worship Him; **24** God [is] Spirit, and those worshiping Him should worship in spirit and truth." **25** The woman says to Him, "I have known that Messiah comes, who is called Christ, when that One may come, He will tell us all things"; **26** Jesus says to her, "I who am speaking to you am [He]." **27** And on this came His disciples, and were wondering that He was speaking with a woman, no one, however, said, "What do You seek?" Or "Why do You speak with her?" **28** The woman then left her water-jug and went away into the city, and says to the men, **29** "Come, see a Man who told me all things—as many as I did; is this the Christ?" **30** They went forth therefore out of the city, and were coming to Him. **31** And in the meanwhile His disciples were asking Him, saying, "Rabbi, eat"; **32** and He said to them, "I have food to eat that you have not known." **33** The disciples then said to one another, "Did anyone bring Him anything to eat?" **34** Jesus says to them, "My food is that I may do the will of Him who sent Me, and may finish His work; **35** do not say that it is yet four months, and the harvest comes; behold, I say to you, lift up your eyes, and see the fields, that they are white to harvest already. **36** And he who is reaping receives a reward, and gathers fruit to continuous life, that both he who is sowing and he who is reaping may rejoice together; **37** for in this the saying is the true one, that one is the sower and another the reaper. **38** I sent you to reap on that which you have not labored; others labored, and you have entered into their labor." **39** And many from that city believed in Him, of the Samaritans, because of the word of the woman testifying, "He told me all things—as many as I did." **40** When, then, the Samaritans came to Him, they were asking Him to remain with them, and He remained there two days; **41** and many more believed because of His word, **42** and said to the woman, "We no longer believe because of your speaking; for we ourselves have heard and known that this is truly the Savior of the world—the Christ." **43** And after the two days He went forth from there, and went away to Galilee, **44** for Jesus Himself testified that a prophet will not have honor in his own country; **45** when then, He came to Galilee, the Galileans received Him, having seen all things that He did in Jerusalem in the celebration—for they also went to the celebration. **46** Jesus came, therefore, again to Cana of Galilee, where He made the water wine, and there was a certain attendant, whose son was ailing in Capernaum, **47** he, having heard that Jesus comes out of Judea to Galilee, went away to Him, and was asking Him that He may come down and may heal his son, for he was about to die. **48** Jesus then said to him,

JOHN

"If you may not see signs and wonders, you will not believe." **49** The attendant says to Him, "Lord, come down before my child dies"; **50** Jesus says to him, "Be going on; your son lives." And the man believed the word that Jesus said to him, and was going on, **51** and he now going down, his servants met him, and told, saying, "Your child lives"; **52** he inquired then of them the hour in which he became better, and they said to him, "Yesterday at the seventh hour the fever left him"; **53** then the father knew that [it was] in that hour in which Jesus said to him, "Your son lives," and he himself believed, and his whole house; **54** this again [was] a second sign Jesus did, having come out of Judea to Galilee.

5 After these things there was a celebration of the Jews, and Jesus went up to Jerusalem, **2** and there is in Jerusalem by the sheep-[gate] a pool that is called in Hebrew Bethesda, having five porches, **3** in these were lying a great multitude of the ailing, blind, lame, withered, [[waiting for the moving of the water, **4** for a messenger at a set time was going down in the pool, and was troubling the water, the first then having gone in after the troubling of the water, became whole of whatever sickness he was held.]] **5** And there was a certain man there being in ailment thirty-eight years, **6** him Jesus having seen lying, and having known that he is already a long time, He says to him, "Do you wish to become whole?" **7** The ailing man answered Him, "Lord, I have no man, that, when the water may be troubled, he may put me into the pool, and while I am coming, another goes down before me." **8** Jesus says to him, "Rise, take up your pallet, and be walking"; **9** and immediately the man became whole, and he took up his pallet, and was walking, and it was a Sabbath on that day, **10** the Jews then said to him that has been healed, "It is a Sabbath; it is not lawful to you to take up the pallet." **11** He answered them, "He who made me whole—that One said to me, Take up your pallet, and be walking"; **12** they questioned him, then, "Who is the Man who is saying to you, Take up your bed and be walking?" **13** But he that was healed had not known who He is, for Jesus moved away, a multitude being in the place. **14** After these things, Jesus finds him in the temple and said to him, "Behold, you have become whole; sin no more, lest something worse may happen to you." **15** The man went away, and told the Jews that it is Jesus who made him whole, **16** and because of this were the Jews persecuting Jesus, and seeking to kill Him, because these things He was doing on a Sabbath. **17** And Jesus answered them, "My Father works until now, and I work"; **18** because of this, then, were the Jews seeking the more to kill Him, because not only was He breaking the Sabbath, but He also called God His own Father, making Himself equal to God. **19** Jesus therefore responded and said to them, "Truly, truly, I say to you, the Son is not able to do anything of Himself, if He may not see the Father doing anything; for whatever things He may do, these also the Son does in like manner; **20** for the Father cherishes the Son, and shows to Him all things that He Himself does; and greater works than these He will show Him, that you may wonder. **21** For as the Father raises the dead, and makes alive, so also the Son makes alive whom He wills; **22** for neither does the Father judge anyone, but all the judgment He has given to the Son, **23** that all may honor the Son according as they honor the Father; he who is not honoring the Son, does not honor the Father who sent Him. **24** Truly, truly, I say to you, he who is hearing My word, and is believing Him who sent Me, has continuous life, and he does not come into judgment, but has passed out of death into life. **25** Truly, truly, I say to you, [that] there comes an hour, and it now is, when the dead will hear the voice of the Son of God, and those having heard will live; **26** for as the Father has life in Himself, so He gave also to the Son to have life in Himself, **27** and authority He gave Him also to do judgment, because He is Son of Man. **28** Do not wonder at this, because there comes an hour in which all those in the tombs will hear His voice, **29** and they will come forth; those who did good things to a resurrection of life, and those who practiced evil things to a resurrection of judgment. **30** I am not able of Myself to do anything; according as I hear I judge, and My judgment is righteous, because I do not seek My own will, but the will of the Father who sent Me. **31** If I testify concerning Myself, My testimony is not true; **32** there is another who is testifying concerning Me, and I have known that the testimony that

He testifies concerning Me is true; **33** you have sent to John, and he has testified to the truth. **34** But I do not receive testimony from man, but these things I say that you may be saved; **35** he was the burning and shining lamp, and you willed to be glad, for an hour, in his light. **36** But I have the testimony greater than John's, for the works that the Father gave Me, that I might finish them, the works themselves that I do, they testify concerning Me, that the Father has sent Me. **37** And the Father who sent Me has testified Himself concerning Me; you have neither heard His voice at any time, nor have you seen His appearance; **38** and you do not have His word remaining in you, because you do not believe Him whom He sent. **39** You search the Writings, because you think in them to have continuous life, and these are they that are testifying concerning Me; **40** and you do not will to come to Me, that you may have life; **41** I do not receive glory from man, **42** but I have known you, that you do not have the love of God in yourselves. **43** I have come in the Name of My Father, and you do not receive Me; if another may come in his own name, him you will receive; **44** how are you able—you—to believe, receiving glory from one another, and the glory that [is] from God alone you do not seek? **45** Do not think that I will accuse you to the Father; there is [one] who is accusing you, Moses—in whom you have hoped; **46** for if you were believing Moses, you would have been believing Me, for he wrote concerning Me; **47** but if you do not believe his writings, how will you believe My sayings?"

6 After these things Jesus went away beyond the Sea of Galilee (of Tiberias), **2** and there was following Him a great multitude, because they were seeing His signs that He was doing on the ailing; **3** and Jesus went up to the mountain, and He was sitting with His disciples there, **4** and the Passover was near, the celebration of the Jews. **5** Jesus then having lifted up [His] eyes and having seen that a great multitude comes to Him, says to Philip, "From where will we buy loaves, that these may eat?" **6** And this He said, trying him, for He Himself had known what He was about to do. **7** Philip answered Him, "Two hundred denarii worth of loaves are not sufficient to them, that each of them may receive some little"; **8** one of His disciples—Andrew, the brother of Simon Peter—says to Him, **9** "There is one little boy here who has five barley loaves and two fishes, but these—what are they to so many?" **10** And Jesus said, "Make the men to sit down"; and there was much grass in the place, the men then sat down, in number, as it were, five thousand, **11** and Jesus took the loaves, and having given thanks He distributed [them] to the disciples, and the disciples to those reclining, in like manner, also of the little fishes as much as they wished. **12** And when they were filled, He says to His disciples, "Gather together the broken pieces that are left over, that nothing may be lost"; **13** they gathered together, therefore, and filled twelve hand-baskets with broken pieces, from the five barley loaves that were over to those having eaten. **14** The men, then, having seen the sign that Jesus did, said, "This is truly the Prophet who is coming into the world"; **15** Jesus, therefore, having known that they are about to come, and to seize Him by force that they may make Him king, retired again to the mountain Himself alone. **16** And when evening came, His disciples went down to the sea, **17** and having entered into the boat, they were going over the sea to Capernaum, and darkness had already come, and Jesus had not come to them, **18** the sea also—a great wind blowing—was being raised, **19** having pushed onward, therefore, about twenty-five or thirty stadia, they behold Jesus walking on the sea, and coming near to the boat, and they were afraid; **20** and He says to them, "I AM; do not be afraid"; **21** they were willing then to receive Him into the boat, and immediately the boat came to the land to which they were going. **22** On the next day, the multitude that was standing on the other side of the sea, having seen that there was no other little boat there except one—that into which His disciples entered—and that Jesus did not go in with His disciples into the little boat, but His disciples went away alone **23** (and other little boats came from Tiberias, near the place where they ate the bread, the LORD having given thanks), **24** when therefore the multitude saw that Jesus is not there, nor His disciples, they also entered into the boats themselves, and came to Capernaum seeking Jesus; **25** and having found Him on the other side of the sea, they said to Him,

"Rabbi, when have You come here?" **26** Jesus answered them and said, "Truly, truly, I say to you, you seek Me, not because you saw signs, but because you ate of the loaves, and were satisfied; **27** do not work for the food that is perishing, but for the food that is remaining to continuous life, which the Son of Man will give to you, for the Father sealed Him—[even] God." **28** Therefore they said to Him, "What may we do that we may work the works of God?" **29** Jesus answered and said to them, "This is the work of God, that you may believe in Him whom He sent." **30** Therefore they said to Him, "What sign, then, do You do, that we may see and may believe You? What do You work? **31** Our fathers ate the manna in the wilderness, according as it is having been written: He gave them bread out of Heaven to eat." **32** Jesus, therefore, said to them, "Truly, truly, I say to you, Moses did not give you the bread out of Heaven, but My Father gives you the true bread out of Heaven; **33** for the bread of God is Him coming down out of Heaven, and giving life to the world." **34** Therefore they said to Him, "Lord, always give us this bread." **35** And Jesus said to them, "I AM the bread of life; he who is coming to Me may not hunger, and he who is believing in Me may not thirst—at any time; **36** but I said to you that you also have seen Me, and you do not believe; **37** all that the Father gives to Me will come to Me; and him who is coming to Me, I will never cast outside, **38** because I have come down out of Heaven, not that I may do My will, but the will of Him who sent Me. **39** And this is the will of the Father who sent Me, that all that He has given to Me, I may lose none of it, but may raise it up in the last day; **40** and this is the will of Him who sent Me, that everyone who is beholding the Son, and is believing in Him, may have continuous life, and I will raise him up in the last day." **41** The Jews, therefore, were murmuring at Him, because He said, "I AM the bread that came down out of Heaven"; **42** and they said, "Is this not Jesus, the Son of Joseph, whose father and mother we have known? How then does this One say, I have come down out of Heaven?" **43** Jesus answered, therefore, and said to them, "Do not murmur with one another; **44** no one is able to come to Me if the Father who sent Me may not draw him, and I will raise him up in the last day; **45** it is having been written in the Prophets: And they will all be taught of God; everyone, therefore, who heard from the Father, and learned, comes to Me; **46** not that anyone has seen the Father, except He who is from God, He has seen the Father. **47** Truly, truly, I say to you, he who is believing in Me has continuous life; **48** I AM the bread of life; **49** your fathers ate the manna in the wilderness and they died; **50** this is the bread that is coming down out of Heaven, that anyone may eat of it, and not die. **51** I AM the living bread that came down out of Heaven; if anyone may eat of this bread he will live—throughout the age; and the bread also that I will give is My flesh, that I will give for the life of the world." **52** The Jews, therefore, were striving with one another, saying, "How is this One able to give us [His] flesh to eat?" **53** Jesus, therefore, said to them, "Truly, truly, I say to you, if you may not eat the flesh of the Son of Man, and may not drink His blood, you have no life in yourselves; **54** he who is eating My flesh, and is drinking My blood, has continuous life, and I will raise him up in the last day; **55** for My flesh is truly food, and My blood is truly drink; **56** he who is eating My flesh, and is drinking My blood, remains in Me, and I in him. **57** According as the living Father sent Me, and I live because of the Father, he also who is eating Me, even that one will live because of Me; **58** this is the bread that came down out of Heaven; not as your fathers ate the manna, and died; he who is eating this bread will live—throughout the age." **59** He said these things in a synagogue, teaching in Capernaum; **60** many, therefore, of His disciples having heard, said, "This word is hard; who is able to hear it?" **61** And Jesus having known in Himself that His disciples are murmuring about this, said to them, "Does this stumble you? **62** If then you may behold the Son of Man going up where He was before? **63** It is the Spirit that is giving life; the flesh does not profit anything; the sayings that I speak to you are spirit, and they are life; **64** but there are certain of you who do not believe"; for Jesus had known from the beginning who they are who are not believing, and who is he who will deliver Him up, **65** and He said, "Because of this I have said to you, No one is able to come to Me if it may not have been given him from My Father." **66** From this [time]

JOHN

many of His disciples went away backward, and were no longer walking with Him, **67** Jesus, therefore, said to the Twelve, "Do you also wish to go away?" **68** Simon Peter, therefore, answered Him, "Lord, to whom will we go? You have sayings of continuous life; **69** and we have believed, and we have known, that You are the Christ, the Son of the living God." **70** Jesus answered them, "Did I not choose you—the Twelve? And of you—one is a devil." **71** And He spoke of Judas, [son] of Simon Iscariot, for he was about to deliver Him up, being one of the Twelve.

7 And Jesus was walking after these things in Galilee, for He did not wish to walk in Judea, because the Jews were seeking to kill Him, **2** and the celebration of the Jews was near—that of Shelters— **3** His brothers, therefore, said to Him, "Depart from here, and go away to Judea, that Your disciples may also behold Your works that You do; **4** for no one does anything in secret, and himself seeks to be in public; if you do these things—reveal Yourself to the world"; **5** for not even His brothers were believing in Him. **6** Jesus, therefore, says to them, "My time is not yet present, but your time is always ready; **7** the world is not able to hate you, but it hates Me, because I testify concerning it that its works are evil. **8** You—go up to this celebration; I do not yet go up to this celebration, because My time has not yet been fulfilled"; **9** and saying these things to them, He remained in Galilee. **10** And when His brothers went up, then also He Himself went up to the celebration, not openly, but as in secret; **11** the Jews, therefore, were seeking Him in the celebration, and said, "Where is that One?" **12** And there was much murmuring about Him among the multitudes, some indeed said, "He is good"; and others said, "No, but He leads the multitude astray"; **13** no one, however, was speaking freely about Him, through fear of the Jews. **14** And it being now the middle of the celebration, Jesus went up to the temple, and He was teaching, **15** and the Jews were wondering, saying, "How has this One known letters—having not learned?" **16** Jesus answered them and said, "My teaching is not Mine, but His who sent Me; **17** if anyone may will to do His will, he will know concerning the teaching, whether it is of God, or—[if] I speak from Myself. **18** He who is speaking from himself seeks his own glory, but he who is seeking the glory of him who sent him, this one is true, and unrighteousness is not in him; **19** has not Moses given you the Law? And none of you does the Law; why do you seek to kill Me?" **20** The multitude answered and said, "You have a demon, who seeks to kill You?" **21** Jesus answered and said to them, "I did one work, and you all wonder, **22** because of this, Moses has given you the circumcision—not that it is of Moses, but of the fathers—and on a Sabbath you circumcise a man; **23** if a man receives circumcision on a Sabbath that the Law of Moses may not be broken, are you angry with Me that I made a man all whole on a Sabbath? **24** Do not judge according to appearance, but the righteous judgment judge." **25** Certain, therefore, of the Jerusalemites said, "Is this not He whom they are seeking to kill? **26** And behold, He speaks freely, and they say nothing to Him; did the rulers truly know that this is the Christ? **27** But this One—we have known where He is from; and the Christ, when He comes, no one knows where He is from." **28** Jesus cried, therefore, in the temple, teaching and saying, "You have both known Me, and you have known from where I am; and I have not come of Myself, but He who sent Me is true, whom you have not known; **29** and I have known Him, because I am from Him, and He sent Me." **30** They were seeking, therefore, to seize Him, and no one laid the hand on Him, because His hour had not yet come, **31** and many out of the multitude believed in Him and said, "The Christ—when He may come—will He do more signs than these that this One did?" **32** The Pharisees heard the multitude murmuring these things concerning Him, and the Pharisees and the chief priests sent officers that they may take Him; **33** Jesus, therefore, said to them, "Yet a short time I am with you, and I go away to Him who sent Me; **34** you will seek Me, and you will not find; and where I am, you are not able to come." **35** The Jews, therefore, said among themselves, "To where is this One about to go that we will not find Him? Is He about to go to the dispersion of the Greeks, and to teach the Greeks? **36** What is this word that He said, You will seek Me, and you will not find? And, Where I am, you are not able to come?" **37** And in the last, the great day of the celebration, Jesus stood and cried, saying, "If anyone thirsts, let him come to Me and drink; **38** he who is believing in Me, according as the Writing said, Rivers of living water will flow out of his belly"; **39** and this He said of the Spirit, which those believing in Him were about to receive; for not yet was the Holy Spirit, because Jesus was not yet glorified. **40** Many, therefore, out of the multitude, having heard the word, said, "This is truly the Prophet"; **41** others said, "This is the Christ"; and others said, "Why, does the Christ come out of Galilee? **42** Did the Writing not say that out of the seed of David, and from Beth-Lehem—the village where David was—the Christ comes?" **43** A division, therefore, arose among the multitude because of Him. **44** And certain of them were willing to seize Him, but no one laid hands on Him; **45** the officers came, therefore, to the chief priests and Pharisees, and they said to them, "Why did you not bring Him?" **46** The officers answered, "Never so spoke man—as this Man." **47** The Pharisees, therefore, answered them, "Have you also been led astray? **48** Did anyone out of the rulers believe in Him? Or out of the Pharisees? **49** But this multitude, that is not knowing the Law, is accursed." **50** Nicodemus says to them—he who came by night to Him—being one of them, **51** "Does our law judge the Man, if it may not hear from Him first, and know what He does?" **52** They answered and said to him, "Are you also out of Galilee? Search and see that a prophet has not risen out of Galilee"; [[**53** and each one went on to his house, but Jesus went on to the Mount of Olives.

8 And at dawn He came again to the temple [courts], **2** and all the people were coming to Him, and having sat down, He was teaching them; **3** and the scribes and the Pharisees bring to Him a woman having been taken in adultery, and having set her in the midst, **4** they say to Him, "Teacher, this woman was taken in the very crime [of] committing adultery, **5** and in the Law, Moses commanded us that such be stoned; You, therefore, what do You say?" **6** And this they said, trying Him, that they might have to accuse Him. And Jesus, having stooped down, with the finger He was writing on the ground, **7** and when they continued asking Him, having bent Himself back, He said to them, "The sinless of you—let him cast the first stone at her"; **8** and again having stooped down, He was writing on the ground, **9** and they having heard, and being convicted by the conscience, were going forth one by one, having begun from the elders—to the last; and Jesus was left alone, and the woman standing in the midst. **10** And Jesus having bent Himself back, and having seen no one but the woman, said to her, "Woman, where are those—your accusers? Did no one pass sentence on you?" **11** And she said, "No one, Lord"; and Jesus said to her, "Neither do I pass sentence on you; be going on, and sin no more."]] **12** Again, therefore, Jesus spoke to them, saying, "I AM the light of the world; he who is following Me will not walk in the darkness, but he will have the light of life." **13** The Pharisees, therefore, said to Him, "You testify of Yourself, Your testimony is not true"; **14** Jesus answered and said to them, "And if I testify of Myself—My testimony is true, because I have known from where I came, and to where I go, and you have not known from where I come, or to where I go. **15** You judge according to the flesh; I do not judge anyone, **16** and even if I do judge My judgment is true, because I am not alone, but I and the Father who sent Me; **17** and also in your law it has been written that the testimony of two men is true; **18** I am [One] who is testifying of Myself, and the Father who sent Me testifies of Me." **19** They said, therefore, to Him, "Where is Your father?" Jesus answered, "You have neither known Me nor My Father: if you had known Me, you had also known My Father." **20** Jesus spoke these sayings in the treasury, teaching in the temple, and no one seized Him, because His hour had not yet come; **21** therefore Jesus said again to them, "I go away, and you will seek Me, and you will die in your sin; to where I go away, you are not able to come." **22** The Jews, therefore, said, "Will He kill Himself, because He says, To where I go away, you are not able to come?" **23** And He said to them, "You are from beneath, I am from above; you are of this world, I am not of this world; **24** I said, therefore, to you, that you will die in your sins, for if you may not believe that I AM, you will die in your sins." **25** They said, therefore, to Him, "You—who are You?" And Jesus said to them, "Even what

JOHN

I spoke of to you at the beginning; **26** many things I have to speak concerning you and to judge, but He who sent Me is true, and I—what things I heard from Him—these I say to the world." **27** They did not know that He spoke to them of the Father; **28** Jesus, therefore, said to them, "When you may lift up the Son of Man then you will know that I AM; and I do nothing of Myself, but according as My Father taught Me, these things I speak; **29** and He who sent Me is with Me; the Father did not leave Me alone, because I always do the things pleasing to Him." **30** As He is speaking these things, many believed in Him; **31** Jesus, therefore, said to the Jews who believed in Him, "If you may remain in My word, you are truly My disciples, **32** and you will know the truth, and the truth will make you free." **33** They answered Him, "We are seed of Abraham; and we have been servants to no one at any time; how do You say—You will become free?" **34** Jesus answered them, "Truly, truly, I say to you, everyone who is committing sin, is a servant of sin; **35** and the servant does not remain in the house—throughout the age, the Son remains—throughout the age; **36** if then the Son may make you free, in reality you will be free. **37** I have known that you are seed of Abraham, but you seek to kill Me, because My word has no place in you; **38** I speak that which I have seen with My Father, and you, therefore, do that which you have seen with your father." **39** They answered and said to Him, "Our father is Abraham"; Jesus says to them, "If you were children of Abraham, the works of Abraham you were doing; **40** and now, you seek to kill Me—a Man who has spoken to you the truth I heard from God; Abraham did not do this; **41** you do the works of your father." They said, therefore, to Him, "We have not been born of whoredom; we have one Father—God"; **42** Jesus then said to them, "If God were your father, you were loving Me, for I came forth from God, and am come; for neither have I come of Myself, but He sent Me; **43** why do you not know My speech? Because you are not able to hear My word. **44** You are of a father—the Devil, and the desires of your father you will to do; he was a manslayer from the beginning, and he has not stood in the truth, because there is no truth in him; when one may speak the falsehood, he speaks of his own, because he is a liar—also his father. **45** And because I say the truth, you do not believe Me. **46** Who of you convicts Me of sin? And if I speak truth, why do you not believe Me? **47** He who is of God, he hears the sayings of God; because of this you do not hear, because you are not of God." **48** The Jews, therefore, answered and said to Him, "Do we not say well, that You are a Samaritan, and have a demon?" **49** Jesus answered, "I do not have a demon, but I honor My Father, and you dishonor Me; **50** and I do not seek My own glory; there is [One] who is seeking and is judging; **51** truly, truly, I say to you, if anyone may keep My word, he may not see death—throughout the age." **52** The Jews, therefore, said to Him, "Now we have known that You have a demon; Abraham died, and the prophets, and You say, If anyone may keep My word, he will not taste of death—throughout the age! **53** Are You greater than our father Abraham, who died? And the prophets died; whom do You make Yourself?" **54** Jesus answered, "If I glorify Myself, My glory is nothing; it is My Father who is glorifying Me, of whom you say that He is your God; **55** and you have not known Him, and I have known Him, and if I say that I have not known Him, I will be like you—speaking falsely; but I have known Him, and I keep His word; **56** your father Abraham was glad that he might see My day; and he saw, and rejoiced." **57** The Jews, therefore, said to Him, "You are not yet fifty years old, and You have seen Abraham?" **58** Jesus said to them, "Truly, truly, I say to you, before Abraham's coming—I AM"; **59** they took up, therefore, stones that they may cast at Him, but Jesus hid Himself, and went forth out of the temple, going through the midst of them, and so passed by.

9 And passing by, He saw a man blind from birth, **2** and His disciples asked Him, saying, "Rabbi, who sinned, this one or his parents, that he should be born blind?" **3** Jesus answered, "Neither this one sinned nor his parents, but that the works of God may be revealed in him; **4** it is necessary for Me to be working the works of Him who sent Me while it is day; night comes when no one is able to work: **5** when I am in the world, I AM [the] light of the world." **6** Saying these things, He spat on the ground, and made clay of the spittle, and rubbed the clay on the eyes of the blind man, and said to him, **7** "Go away, wash at the pool of Siloam," which is, interpreted, Sent. He went away, therefore, and washed, and came seeing; **8** the neighbors, therefore, and those seeing him before, that he was blind, said, "Is this not he who is sitting and begging?" **9** Others said, "This is he"; and others, "He is like to him"; he himself said, "I am [he]." **10** They said, therefore, to him, "How were your eyes opened?" **11** He answered and said, "A man called Jesus made clay, and rubbed my eyes, and said to me, Go away to the pool of Siloam, and wash; and having gone away and having washed, I received sight"; **12** they said, therefore, to him, "Where is that One?" He says, "I have not known." **13** They bring him who once [was] blind to the Pharisees, **14** and it was a Sabbath when Jesus made the clay, and opened his eyes. **15** Again, therefore, the Pharisees also were asking him how he received sight, and he said to them, "He put clay on my eyes, and I washed—and I see." **16** Certain of the Pharisees therefore said, "This Man is not from God, because He does not keep the Sabbath"; others said, "How is a man—a sinful one—able to do such signs?" And there was a division among them. **17** They said to the blind man again, "You—what do you say of Him—that He opened your eyes?" **18** And he said, "He is a prophet." The Jews, therefore, did not believe concerning him that he was blind and received sight, until they called the parents of him who received sight, **19** and they asked them, saying, "Is [this] your son, of whom you say that he was born blind? How then does he now see?" **20** His parents answered them and said, "We have known that this is our son, and that he was born blind; **21** and how he now sees, we have not known; or who opened his eyes, we have not known; he is of age, ask him; he himself will speak concerning himself." **22** His parents said these things, because they were afraid of the Jews, for the Jews had already agreed together, that if anyone may confess Him—Christ, he may be put out of the synagogue; **23** because of this his parents said, "He is of age, ask him." **24** They called, therefore, the man who was blind a second time, and they said to him, "Give glory to God, we have known that this Man is a sinner"; **25** he answered, therefore, and said, "If He is a sinner—I have not known, one thing I have known, that, being blind, now I see." **26** And they said to him again, "What did He do to you? How did He open your eyes?" **27** He answered them, "I told you already, and you did not hear; why do you wish to hear [it] again? Do you also wish to become His disciples?" **28** They reviled him, therefore, and said, "You are His disciple, and we are Moses' disciples; **29** we have known that God has spoken to Moses, but this One—we have not known where He is from." **30** The man answered and said to them, "Why, in this is a wonderful thing, that you have not known where He is from, and He opened my eyes! **31** And we have known that God does not hear sinners, but if anyone may be a worshiper of God, and may do His will, He hears him; **32** from the age it was not heard that anyone opened eyes of one who has been born blind; **33** if this One were not from God, He were not able to do anything." **34** They answered and said to him, "In sins you were born altogether, and you teach us?" And they cast him forth outside. **35** Jesus heard that they cast him forth outside, and having found him, He said to him, "Do you believe in the Son of God?" **36** He answered and said, "Who is He, Lord, that I may believe in Him?" **37** And Jesus said to him, "You have both seen Him, and He who is speaking with you is He"; **38** and he said, "I believe, Lord," and worshiped Him. **39** And Jesus said, "I came to this world for judgment, that those not seeing may see, and those seeing may become blind." **40** And those of the Pharisees who were with Him heard these things, and they said to Him, "Are we also blind?" **41** Jesus said to them, "If you were blind, you were not having had sin, but now you say—We see, therefore your sin remains."

10 "Truly, truly, I say to you, he who is not entering through the door to the fold of the sheep, but is going up from another side, that one is a thief and a robber; **2** and he who is entering through the door is shepherd of the sheep; **3** the doorkeeper opens to this one, and the sheep hear his voice, and his own sheep he calls by name, and leads them forth; **4** and when he may put forth his own sheep, he goes on before them, and the sheep follow him, because they have known his voice; **5** and

JOHN

they will not follow a stranger, but will flee from him, because they have not known the voice of strangers." **6** Jesus spoke this allegory to them, and they did not know what the things were that He was speaking to them; **7** Jesus therefore said again to them, "Truly, truly, I say to you, I AM the door of the sheep; **8** all, as many as came before Me, are thieves and robbers, but the sheep did not hear them; **9** I AM the door, if anyone may come in through Me, he will be saved, and he will come in, and go out, and find pasture. **10** The thief does not come, except that he may steal, and kill, and destroy; I came that they may have life, and may have [it] abundantly. **11** I AM the good shepherd; the good shepherd lays His life down for the sheep; **12** and the hired worker, and not being a shepherd, whose own the sheep are not, beholds the wolf coming, and leaves the sheep, and flees; and the wolf snatches them, and scatters the sheep; **13** and the hired worker flees because he is a hired worker, and is not caring for the sheep. **14** I AM the good shepherd, and I know My [sheep], and am known by Mine, **15** according as the Father knows Me, and I know the Father, and My life I lay down for the sheep, **16** and other sheep I have that are not of this fold, these also it is necessary for Me to bring, and My voice they will hear, and there will become one flock—one shepherd. **17** Because of this the Father loves Me, because I lay down My life, that again I may take it; **18** no one takes it from Me, but I lay it down of Myself; authority I have to lay it down, and authority I have again to take it; this command I received from My Father." **19** Therefore, again, there came a division among the Jews, because of these words, **20** and many of them said, "He has a demon, and is mad, why do you hear Him?" **21** Others said, "These sayings are not those of a demoniac; is a demon able to open blind men's eyes?" **22** And the Dedication in Jerusalem came, and it was winter, **23** and Jesus was walking in the temple, in the porch of Solomon, **24** the Jews, therefore, came around Him and said to Him, "Until when do You hold our soul in suspense? If You are the Christ, tell us freely." **25** Jesus answered them, "I told you, and you do not believe; the works that I do in the Name of My Father, these testify concerning Me; **26** but you do not believe, for you are not of My sheep, **27** according as I said to you: My sheep hear My voice, and I know them, and they follow Me, **28** and I give continuous life to them, and they will not perish—throughout the age, and no one will snatch them out of My hand; **29** My Father, who has given to Me, is greater than all, and no one is able to snatch out of the hand of My Father; **30** I and the Father are one." **31** Therefore, again, the Jews took up stones that they may stone Him; **32** Jesus answered them, "I showed you many good works from My Father; because of which work of them do you stone Me?" **33** The Jews answered Him, saying, "We do not stone You for a good work, but for slander, and because You, being a man, make Yourself God." **34** Jesus answered them, "Is it not having been written in your law: I said, you are gods? **35** If He called them gods to whom the word of God came (and the Writing is not able to be broken), **36** of Him whom the Father sanctified and sent into the world, do you say—You slander, because I said, I am [the] Son of God? **37** If I do not do the works of My Father, do not believe Me; **38** and if I do, even if you may not believe Me, believe the works, that you may know and may believe that the Father [is] in Me, and I in Him." **39** Therefore they were seeking again to seize Him, and He went forth out of their hand, **40** and went away again to the other side of the Jordan, to the place where John was at first immersing, and remained there, **41** and many came to Him and said, "John, indeed, did no sign, and all things, as many as John said about this One were true"; **42** and many believed in Him there.

11 And there was a certain one ailing, Lazarus, from Bethany, of the village of Mary and Martha her sister— **2** and it was Mary who anointed the LORD with ointment, and wiped His feet with her hair, whose brother Lazarus was ailing— **3** therefore the sisters sent to Him, saying, "Lord, behold, he whom You cherish is ailing"; **4** and Jesus having heard, said, "This ailment is not to death, but for the glory of God, that the Son of God may be glorified through it." **5** And Jesus was loving Martha, and her sister, and Lazarus, **6** when, therefore, He heard that he is ailing, then indeed He remained in the place in which He was two days, **7** then after this, He says to the disciples, "We may go to Judea again"; **8** the disciples say to Him, "Rabbi, the Jews were just seeking to stone You, and again You go there?" **9** Jesus answered, "Are there not twelve hours in the day? If anyone may walk in the day, he does not stumble, because he sees the light of this world; **10** and if anyone may walk in the night, he stumbles, because the light is not in him." **11** He said these things, and after this He says to them, "Our friend Lazarus has fallen asleep, but I go on that I may awake him"; **12** therefore His disciples said, "Lord, if he has fallen asleep, he will be saved"; **13** but Jesus had spoken about his death, but they thought that He speaks about the repose of sleep. **14** Then, therefore, Jesus said to them freely, "Lazarus has died; **15** and I rejoice, for your sake (that you may believe), that I was not there; but we may go to him"; **16** therefore Thomas, who is called Didymus, said to the fellow-disciples, "We may go—we also, that we may die with Him." **17** Jesus, therefore, having come, found him having already been four days in the tomb. **18** And Bethany was near to Jerusalem, about fifteen stadia off, **19** and many of the Jews had come to Martha and Mary, that they might comfort them concerning their brother; **20** Martha, therefore, when she heard that Jesus comes, met Him, and Mary kept sitting in the house. **21** Martha, therefore, said to Jesus, "Lord, if You had been here, my brother had not died; **22** but even now, I have known that whatever You may ask of God, God will give to You"; **23** Jesus says to her, "Your brother will rise again." **24** Martha says to Him, "I have known that he will rise again in the resurrection in the last day"; **25** Jesus said to her, "I AM the resurrection, and the life; he who is believing in Me, even if he may die, will live; **26** and everyone who is living and believing in Me will not die—throughout the age; **27** do you believe this?" She says to Him, "Yes, Lord, I have believed that You are the Christ, the Son of God, who is coming into the world." **28** And having said these things, she went away, and called Mary her sister privately, saying, "The Teacher is present, and calls you"; **29** she, when she heard, rises up quickly, and comes to Him; **30** and Jesus had not yet come into the village, but was in the place where Martha met Him; **31** the Jews, therefore, who were with her in the house, and were comforting her, having seen Mary that she rose up quickly and went forth, followed her, saying, "She goes away to the tomb, that she may weep there." **32** Mary, therefore, when she came where Jesus was, having seen Him, fell at His feet, saying to Him, "Lord, if You had been here, my brother had not died"; **33** Jesus, therefore, when He saw her weeping, and the Jews who came with her weeping, groaned in the spirit, and troubled Himself, and He said, **34** "Where have you laid him?" They say to Him, "Lord, come and see"; **35** Jesus wept. **36** The Jews, therefore, said, "Behold, how He was cherishing him!" **37** And certain of them said, "Was not this One, who opened the eyes of the blind man, also able to cause that this one might not have died?" **38** Jesus, therefore, again groaning in Himself, comes to the tomb, and it was a cave, and a stone was lying on it, **39** Jesus says, "Take away the stone"; the sister of him who has died—Martha—says to Him, "Lord, he already stinks, for he is four days dead"; **40** Jesus says to her, "Did I not say to you that if you may believe, you will see the glory of God?" **41** Therefore they took away the stone where the dead was laid, and Jesus lifted His eyes upwards, and said, "Father, I thank You that You heard Me; **42** and I knew that You always hear Me, but because of the multitude that is standing by, I said [it], that they may believe that You sent Me." **43** And saying these things, He cried out with a loud voice, "Lazarus, come forth!" **44** And he who died came forth, feet and hands being bound with grave-clothes, and his face was bound around with a napkin; Jesus says to them, "Loose him, and permit to go." **45** Many, therefore, of the Jews who came to Mary, and beheld what Jesus did, believed in Him; **46** but certain of them went away to the Pharisees, and told them what Jesus did; **47** the chief priests, therefore, and the Pharisees, gathered together [the] Sanhedrin and said, "What may we do? Because this Man does many signs? **48** If we may leave Him alone thus, all will believe in Him; and the Romans will come, and will take away both our place and nation." **49** And a certain one of them, Caiaphas, being chief priest of that year, said to them, "You have not known anything, **50** nor reason that it is good for us that one man may die for the people, and

JOHN

not the whole nation perish." **51** And he did not say this of himself, but being chief priest of that year, he prophesied that Jesus was about to die for the nation, **52** and not for the nation only, but that also the children of God, who have been scattered abroad, He may gather together into one. **53** From that day, therefore, they took counsel together that they may kill Him; **54** Jesus, therefore, was no longer freely walking among the Jews, but went away from there into the region near the wilderness, to a city called Ephraim, and there He tarried with His disciples. **55** And the Passover of the Jews was near, and many went up to Jerusalem out of the country before the Passover, that they might purify themselves; **56** therefore they were seeking Jesus and said with one another, standing in the temple, "What appears to you—that He may not come to the celebration?" **57** And both the chief priests and the Pharisees had given a command, that if anyone may know where He is, he may show [it], so that they may seize Him.

12 Jesus, therefore, six days before the Passover, came to Bethany, where Lazarus was, who had died, whom He raised out of the dead; **2** they made, therefore, a dinner to Him there, and Martha was ministering, and Lazarus was one of those reclining together with Him; **3** Mary, therefore, having taken a pound of ointment of spikenard, of great price, anointed the feet of Jesus and wiped His feet with her hair, and the house was filled from the fragrance of the ointment. **4** Therefore one of His disciples—Judas Iscariot, of Simon, who is about to deliver Him up—says, **5** "Why was this ointment not sold for three hundred denarii, and given to the poor?" **6** And he said this, not because he was caring for the poor, but because he was a thief, and had the bag, and what things were put in he was carrying. **7** Jesus, therefore, said, "Permit her; she has kept it for the day of My embalming, **8** for you always have the poor with yourselves, and you do not always have Me." **9** Therefore, a great multitude of the Jews knew that He is there, and they came, not only because of Jesus, but that they may also see Lazarus, whom He raised out of the dead; **10** and the chief priests took counsel, that they may also kill Lazarus, **11** because on account of him many of the Jews were going away, and were believing in Jesus. **12** On the next day, a great multitude that came to the celebration, having heard that Jesus comes to Jerusalem, **13** took the branches of the palms, and went forth to meet Him, and were crying, "Hosanna! Blessed [is] He who is coming in the Name of the LORD—the King of Israel"; **14** and Jesus having found a young donkey sat on it, according as it is written, **15** "Do not fear, daughter of Zion, behold, your King comes, sitting on a colt of a donkey." **16** And His disciples did not know these things at first, but when Jesus was glorified, then they remembered that these things were having been written about Him, and these things they did to Him. **17** The multitude, therefore, who are with Him, were testifying that He called Lazarus out of the tomb, and raised him out of the dead; **18** because of this the multitude also met Him, because they heard of His having done this sign, **19** therefore the Pharisees said among themselves, "You see that you do not gain anything, behold, the world went after Him." **20** And there were certain Greeks out of those coming up that they may worship in the celebration, **21** these then came near to Philip, who [is] from Bethsaida of Galilee, and were asking him, saying, "Lord, we wish to see Jesus"; **22** Philip comes and tells Andrew, and again Andrew and Philip tell Jesus. **23** And Jesus responded to them, saying, "The hour has come that the Son of Man may be glorified; **24** truly, truly, I say to you, if the grain of the wheat, having fallen to the earth, may not die, itself remains alone; and if it may die, it bears much fruit; **25** he who is cherishing his life will lose it, and he who is hating his life in this world will keep it to continuous life; **26** if anyone may minister to Me, let him follow Me, and where I am, there My servant will be also; and if anyone may minister to Me—the Father will honor him. **27** Now My soul has been troubled; and what will I say—Father, save Me from this hour? But because of this I came to this hour; **28** Father, glorify Your Name." Therefore there came a voice out of Heaven, "I both glorified, and again I will glorify [it]"; **29** the multitude, therefore, having stood and heard, were saying that there has been thunder; others said, "A messenger has spoken to Him." **30** Jesus answered and said, "This voice has not come because of Me, but because of you; **31** now is a judgment of this world, now will the ruler of this world be cast forth; **32** and I, if I may be lifted up from the earth, will draw all men to Myself." **33** And this He said signifying by what death He was about to die; **34** the multitude answered Him, "We heard that the Christ remains out of the Law—throughout the age; and how do You say that it is required that the Son of Man be lifted up? Who is this—the Son of Man?" **35** Therefore Jesus said to them, "Yet a short time is the light with you; walk while you have the light, that darkness may not overtake you; and he who is walking in the darkness has not known where he goes; **36** while you have the light, believe in the light, that you may become sons of light." Jesus spoke these things, and having gone away, He was hid from them, **37** yet He, having done so many signs before them, they were not believing in Him, **38** that the word of Isaiah the prophet might be fulfilled, which he said, "LORD, who gave credence to our report? And the arm of the LORD—to whom was it revealed?" **39** Because of this they were not able to believe, that again Isaiah said, **40** "He has blinded their eyes, and hardened their heart, that they might not see with the eyes, and understand with the heart, and turn, and I might heal them"; **41** Isaiah said these things when he saw His glory, and spoke of Him. **42** Still, however, out of the rulers many also believed in Him, but because of the Pharisees they were not confessing, that they might not be put out of the synagogue, **43** for they loved the glory of men more than the glory of God. **44** And Jesus cried and said, "He who is believing in Me, does not believe in Me, but in Him who sent Me; **45** and He who is beholding Me, beholds Him who sent Me; **46** I—light to the world—have come, that everyone who is believing in Me may not remain in the darkness; **47** and if anyone may hear My sayings, and not believe, I do not judge him, for I did not come that I might judge the world, but that I might save the world. **48** He who is rejecting Me, and not receiving My sayings, has one who is judging him, the word that I spoke, that will judge him in the last day, **49** because I did not speak from Myself, but the Father who sent Me, He gave Me a command, what I may say, and what I may speak, **50** and I have known that His command is continuous life; what, therefore, I speak, according as the Father has said to Me, so I speak."

13 And before the Celebration of the Passover, Jesus knowing that His hour has come, that He may depart out of this world to the Father, having loved His own who [are] in the world—to the end He loved them. **2** And dinner having come, the Devil already having put [it] into the heart of Judas of Simon, Iscariot, that he may deliver Him up, **3** Jesus knowing that all things the Father has given to Him—into [His] hands, and that He came forth from God, and He goes to God, **4** rises from the dinner, and lays down His garments, and having taken a towel, He girded Himself; **5** afterward He puts water into the basin, and began to wash the feet of His disciples, and to wipe with the towel with which He was being girded. **6** He comes, therefore, to Simon Peter, and that one says to Him, "Lord, You—do You wash my feet?" **7** Jesus answered and said to him, "That which I do you have not known now, but you will know after these things"; **8** Peter says to Him, "You may not wash my feet—throughout the age." Jesus answered him, "If I may not wash you, you have no part with Me"; **9** Simon Peter says to Him, "Lord, not my feet only, but also the hands and the head." **10** Jesus says to him, "He who has been bathed has no need except to wash his feet, but he is clean altogether; and you are clean, but not all"; **11** for He knew him who is delivering Him up; because of this He said, "You are not all clean." **12** When, therefore, He washed their feet, and took His garments, having reclined again, He said to them, "Do you know what I have done to you? **13** You call Me the Teacher and the LORD, and you say well, for I am; **14** if then I washed your feet—the LORD and the Teacher—you also ought to wash one another's feet. **15** For I gave to you an example, that, according as I did to you, you also may do; **16** truly, truly, I say to you, a servant is not greater than his lord, nor an apostle greater than he who sent him; **17** if you have known these things, you are blessed if you may do them; **18** I do not speak concerning you all; I have known whom I chose for Myself; but that the Writing may be fulfilled: He who is

JOHN

eating the bread with Me, lifted up his heel against Me. **19** From this time I tell you, before its coming to pass, that, when it may come to pass, you may believe that I AM; **20** truly, truly, I say to you, he who is receiving whomsoever I may send, receives Me; and he who is receiving Me, receives Him who sent Me." **21** Having said these things, Jesus was troubled in the spirit, and testified and said, "Truly, truly, I say to you that one of you will deliver Me up"; **22** the disciples were looking, therefore, at one another, doubting concerning of whom He speaks. **23** And there was one of His disciples reclining in the bosom of Jesus, whom Jesus was loving; **24** Simon Peter, then, beckons to this one, to inquire who he may be concerning whom He speaks, **25** and that one having leaned back on the breast of Jesus, responds to Him, "Lord, who is it?" **26** Jesus answers, "It is that one to whom I, having dipped the morsel, will give it"; and having dipped the morsel, He gives [it] to Judas of Simon, Iscariot. **27** And after the morsel, then Satan entered into that one. Jesus, therefore, says to him, "What you do—do quickly"; **28** and none of those reclining to eat knew for what intent He said this to him, **29** for certain [of them] were thinking, since Judas had the bag, that Jesus says to him, "Buy what we have need of for the celebration"; or that he may give something to the poor; **30** having received, therefore, the morsel, that one immediately went forth, and it was night. **31** When, therefore, he went forth, Jesus says, "Now was the Son of Man glorified, and God was glorified in Him; **32** if God was glorified in Him, God will also glorify Him in Himself; indeed, He will immediately glorify Him. **33** Little children, yet a little [while] am I with you; you will seek Me, and according as I said to the Jews, I also say to you now: To where I go away, you are not able to come. **34** A new command I give to you, that you love one another; according as I loved you, that you also love one another; **35** in this will all know that you are My disciples, if you may have love one to another." **36** Simon Peter says to Him, "Lord, to where do You go away?" Jesus answered him, "To where I go away, you are not able now to follow Me, but afterward you will follow Me." **37** Peter says to Him, "Lord, why am I not able to follow You now? I will lay down my life for You"; **38** Jesus answered him, "You will lay down your life for Me? Truly, truly, I say to you, a rooster will not crow until you may deny Me three times."

14 "Do not let your heart be troubled, believe in God, believe also in Me; **2** in the house of My Father are many rooms; and if not, I would have told you; I go on to prepare a place for you; **3** and if I go on and prepare a place for you, I come again, and will receive you to Myself, that where I am you also may be; **4** and to where I go away you have known, and the way you have known." **5** Thomas says to Him, "Lord, we have not known to where You go away, and how are we able to know the way?" **6** Jesus says to him, "I AM the way, and the truth, and the life, no one comes to the Father, if not through Me; **7** if you had known Me, you would also have known My Father, and from this time you have known Him, and have seen Him." **8** Philip says to Him, "Lord, show to us the Father, and it is enough for us"; **9** Jesus says to him, "Such [a] long time am I with you, and you have not known Me, Philip? He who has seen Me has seen the Father; and how do you say, Show to us the Father? **10** Do you not believe that I [am] in the Father, and the Father is in Me? The sayings that I speak to you, I do not speak from Myself, and the Father who is abiding in Me does the works Himself; **11** believe Me, that I [am] in the Father, and the Father in Me; and if not, because of the works themselves, believe Me. **12** Truly, truly, I say to you, he who is believing in Me, the works that I do—that one will also do, and greater than these he will do, because I go on to My Father; **13** and whatever you may ask in My Name, I will do, that the Father may be glorified in the Son; **14** if you ask anything in My Name I will do [it]. **15** If you love Me, keep My commands, **16** and I will ask the Father, and He will give to you another Comforter, that He may remain with you throughout the age: **17** the Spirit of truth, whom the world is not able to receive, because it does not see nor know [this] One, and you know [this] One, because [this] One remains with you, and will be in you. **18** I will not leave you bereaved, I come to you; **19** yet a little [while] and the world beholds Me no more, and you behold Me, because I live, and you will live; **20** in that day you will know that

JOHN

I [am] in My Father, and you in Me, and I in you; **21** he who is having My commands, and is keeping them, that one it is who is loving Me, and he who is loving Me will be loved by My Father, and I will love him, and will manifest Myself to him." **22** Judas says to Him (not the Iscariot), "Lord, what has come to pass, that You are about to manifest Yourself to us, and not to the world?" **23** Jesus answered and said to him, "If anyone may love Me, he will keep My word, and My Father will love him, and We will come to him, and We will make [an] abode with him; **24** he who is not loving Me does not keep My words; and the word that you hear is not Mine, but the Father's who sent Me. **25** These things I have spoken to you, remaining with you, **26** and the Comforter, the Holy Spirit, whom the Father will send in My Name, He will teach you all things, and remind you of all things that I said to you. **27** Peace I leave to you; My peace I give to you. Not according as the world gives do I give to you. Do not let your heart be troubled, nor let it be afraid. **28** You heard that I said to you, I go away, and I come to you. If you loved Me, you would have rejoiced that I said, I go on to the Father, because My Father is greater than I. **29** And now I have said [it] to you before it comes to pass, that when it may come to pass, you may believe. **30** I will no longer talk much with you, for the ruler of this world comes, and he has nothing in Me; **31** but that the world may know that I love the Father, and according as the Father gave Me command, so I do; arise, we may go from here."

15 "I AM the true vine, and My Father is the vinedresser; **2** every branch not bearing fruit in Me, He takes it away, and everyone bearing fruit, He cleanses by pruning it, that it may bear more fruit; **3** you are already clean, because of the word that I have spoken to you; **4** remain in Me, and I in you, as the branch is not able to bear fruit of itself, if it may not remain in the vine, so neither you, if you may not remain in Me. **5** I AM the vine, you the branches; he who is remaining in Me, and I in him, this one bears much fruit, because apart from Me you are not able to do anything; **6** if anyone may not remain in Me, he was cast forth outside as the branch, and was withered, and they gather them, and cast into fire, and they are burned; **7** if you may remain in Me, and My sayings may remain in you, whatever you may wish you will ask, and it will be done to you. **8** In this was My Father glorified, that you may bear much fruit, and you will become My disciples. **9** According as the Father loved Me, I also loved you, remain in My love; **10** if you may keep My commands, you will remain in My love, according as I have kept the commands of My Father, and remain in His love; **11** these things I have spoken to you, that My joy in you may remain, and your joy may be full. **12** This is My command, that you love one another, according as I loved you; **13** greater love has no one than this, that anyone may lay down his life for his friends; **14** you are My friends if you may do whatever I command you; **15** I no longer call you servants, because the servant has not known what his lord does, and I have called you friends, because all things that I heard from My Father, I made known to you. **16** You did not choose Me, but I chose you, and appointed you, that you might go away, and might bear fruit, and your fruit might remain, that whatever you may ask of the Father in My Name, He may give you. **17** These things I command you, that you love one another; **18** if the world hates you, you know that it has hated Me before you; **19** if you were of the world, the world would have been cherishing its own, but because you are not of the world, but I chose [you] out of the world—because of this the world hates you. **20** Remember the word that I said to you: A servant is not greater than his lord; if they persecuted Me, they will also persecute you; if they kept My word, they will also keep yours; **21** but all these things will they do to you, because of My Name, because they have not known Him who sent Me; **22** if I had not come and spoken to them, they were not having sin; but now they have no pretext for their sin. **23** He who is hating Me, hates My Father also; **24** if I did not do among them the works that no other has done, they were not having sin, and now they have both seen and hated both Me and My Father; **25** but—that the word may be fulfilled that was written in their law— They hated Me without a cause. **26** And when the Comforter may come, whom I will send to you from the Father—the Spirit of truth, who comes forth from the

Father, He will testify of Me; **27** and you also testify, because you are with Me from the beginning."

16 "These things I have spoken to you, that you may not be stumbled. **2** They will put you out of the synagogues, but an hour comes that everyone who has killed you may think to offer service to God; **3** and these things they will do to you, because they did not know the Father, nor Me. **4** But these things I have spoken to you, that when the hour may come, you may remember them, that I said [them] to you, and I did not say these things to you from the beginning, because I was with you; **5** and now I go away to Him who sent Me, and none of you asks Me, To where do you go? **6** But because I have said to you these things, the sorrow has filled your heart. **7** But I tell you the truth; it is better for you that I go away, for if I may not go away, the Comforter will not come to you, and if I go on, I will send Him to you; **8** and having come, He will convict the world concerning sin, and concerning righteousness, and concerning judgment; **9** concerning sin indeed, because they do not believe in Me; **10** and concerning righteousness, because I go away to My Father, and you behold Me no more; **11** and concerning judgment, because the ruler of this world has been judged. **12** I have yet many things to say to you, but you are not able to bear [them] now; **13** and when He may come—the Spirit of truth—He will guide you to all the truth, for He will not speak from Himself, but as many things as He will hear He will speak, and the coming things He will tell you; **14** He will glorify Me, because He will take of Mine, and will tell to you. **15** All things, as many as the Father has, are Mine; because of this I said that He will take of Mine, and will tell to you; **16** a little while, and you do not behold Me, and again a little while, and you will see Me, because I go away to the Father." **17** Therefore [some] of His disciples said to one another, "What is this that He says to us, A little while, and you do not behold Me, and again a little while, and you will see Me, and, Because I go away to the Father?" **18** They said then, "What is this He says—the little while? We have not known what He says." **19** Jesus, therefore, knew that they were wishing to ask Him, and He said to them, "Concerning this do you seek with one another, because I said, A little while, and you do not behold Me, and again a little while, and you will see Me? **20** Truly, truly, I say to you that you will weep and lament, and the world will rejoice; and you will be sorrowful, but your sorrow will become joy. **21** The woman, when she may bear, has sorrow, because her hour came, and when she may bear the child, she no longer remembers the anguish, because of the joy that a man was born into the world. **22** And you, therefore, now indeed have sorrow; and again I will see you, and your heart will rejoice, and no one takes your joy from you, **23** and in that day you will question nothing of Me; truly, truly, I say to you, as many things as you may ask of the Father in My Name, He will give you; **24** until now you asked nothing in My Name; ask, and you will receive, that your joy may be full. **25** I have spoken these things in allegories to you, but there comes an hour when I will no longer speak to you in allegories, but will tell you freely of the Father. **26** In that day you will make request in My Name, and I do not say to you that I will ask the Father for you, **27** for the Father Himself cherishes you, because you have cherished Me, and you have believed that I came forth from God; **28** I came forth from the Father, and have come into the world; again I leave the world, and go on to the Father." **29** His disciples say to Him, "Behold, now You speak freely, and You do not speak allegory; **30** now we have known that You have known all things, and have no need that anyone questions You; in this we believe that You came forth from God." **31** Jesus answered them, "Now do you believe? Behold, there comes an hour, **32** and now it has come, that you may be scattered, each to his own things, and you may leave Me alone, and I am not alone, because the Father is with Me; **33** these things I have spoken to you, that in Me you may have peace, in the world you will have tribulation, but take courage—I have overcome the world."

17 These things Jesus spoke, and lifted up His eyes to the sky, and said, "Father, the hour has come, glorify Your Son, that Your Son may also glorify You, **2** according as You gave to Him authority over all flesh, that—all that You have given to Him—He may give to them continuous life; **3** and this is the continuous life, that they may know You, the only true God, and Him whom You sent—Jesus Christ; **4** I glorified You on the earth, having completed the work that You have given Me, that I should do. **5** And now, glorify Me, You Father, with Yourself, with the glory that I had with You before the world was; **6** I revealed Your Name to the men whom You have given to Me out of the world; they were Yours, and You have given them to Me, and they have kept Your word; **7** now they have known that all things, as many as You have given to Me, are from You, **8** because the sayings that You have given to Me, I have given to them, and they themselves received, and have known truly, that I came forth from You, and they believed that You sent Me. **9** I ask in regard to them; I do not ask in regard to the world, but in regard to those whom You have given to Me, because they are Yours, **10** and all Mine are Yours, and Yours [are] Mine, and I have been glorified in them; **11** and I am no longer in the world, and these are in the world, and I come to You. Holy Father, keep them in Your Name, whom You have given to Me, that they may be one as We [are one]; **12** when I was with them in the world, I was keeping them in Your Name; I guarded those whom You have given to Me, and none of them were destroyed, except the son of the destruction, that the Writing may be fulfilled. **13** And now I come to You, and these things I speak in the world, that they may have My joy fulfilled in themselves; **14** I have given Your word to them, and the world hated them, because they are not of the world, as I am not of the world; **15** I do not ask that You may take them out of the world, but that You may keep them out of the evil. **16** They are not of the world, as I am not of the world; **17** sanctify them in Your truth, Your word is truth; **18** as You sent Me into the world, I also sent them into the world; **19** and I sanctify Myself for them, that they also may be sanctified in truth themselves. **20** And I do not ask in regard to these alone, but also in regard to those who will be believing in Me through their word, **21** that they all may be one, as You Father [are] in Me, and I in You, that they also may be one in Us, that the world may believe that You sent Me. **22** And I have given to them the glory that You have given to Me, that they may be one as We are one— **23** I in them, and You in Me, that they may be perfected into one, and that the world may know that You sent Me, and loved them as You loved Me. **24** Father, those whom You have given to Me, I will that where I am they also may be with Me, that they may behold My glory that You gave to Me, because You loved Me before the foundation of the world. **25** Righteous Father, also the world did not know You, and I knew You, and these have known that You sent Me, **26** and I made known to them Your Name, and will make known, that the love with which You loved Me may be in them, and I in them."

18 Having said these things, Jesus went forth with His disciples beyond the Brook of Kidron, where [there] was a garden, into which He entered, Himself and His disciples, **2** and Judas also, who delivered Him up, had known the place, because Jesus assembled there with His disciples many times. **3** Judas, therefore, having taken the band and officers out of the chief priests and Pharisees, comes there with torches and lamps, and weapons; **4** Jesus, therefore, knowing all things that are coming on Him, having gone forth, said to them, "Whom do you seek?" **5** They answered Him, "Jesus the Nazarene"; Jesus says to them, "I AM"; and Judas who delivered Him up was standing with them. **6** When, therefore, He said to them, "I AM," they went away backward, and fell to the ground. **7** Again, therefore, He questioned them, "Whom do you seek?" And they said, "Jesus the Nazarene"; **8** Jesus answered, "I said to you that I AM; if, then, you seek Me, permit these to go away"; **9** that the word might be fulfilled that He said, "Those whom You have given to Me, I did not lose even one of them." **10** Simon Peter, therefore, having a sword, drew it, and struck the chief priest's servant, and cut off his right ear—and the name of the servant was Malchus— **11** Jesus, therefore, said to Peter, "Put the sword into the sheath; the cup that the Father has given to Me, may I not drink it?" **12** The band, therefore, and the captain, and the officers of the Jews, took hold on Jesus, and bound Him, **13** and they led Him away to Annas first, for he was father-in-law of Caiaphas, who was chief priest of that year, **14** and Caiaphas was he who gave counsel to the Jews that it is good for one man to perish for the people. **15** And following Jesus was

JOHN

Simon Peter, and the other disciple, and that disciple was known to the chief priest, and he entered with Jesus into the hall of the chief priest, **16** and Peter was standing at the door outside, therefore the other disciple who was known to the chief priest went forth, and he spoke to the doorkeeper, and he brought in Peter. **17** Then the maid, the doorkeeper, says to Peter, "Are you also of the disciples of this Man?" He says, "I am not"; **18** and the servants and the officers were standing, having made a fire of coals, because it was cold, and they were warming themselves, and Peter was standing with them, and warming himself. **19** The chief priests, therefore, questioned Jesus concerning His disciples, and concerning His teaching; **20** Jesus answered him, "I spoke freely to the world, I always taught in a synagogue, and in the temple, where the Jews always come together; and I spoke nothing in secret; **21** why do you question Me? Question those having heard what I spoke to them; behold, these have known what I said." **22** And He having said these things, one of the officers standing by gave Jesus a slap, saying, "Thus do You answer the chief priest?" **23** Jesus answered him, "If I spoke ill, testify concerning the ill; and if well, why do you strike Me?" **24** Annas then sent Him bound to Caiaphas the chief priest. **25** And Simon Peter was standing and warming himself, then they said to him, "Are you also of His disciples?" He denied and said, "I am not." **26** One of the servants of the chief priest, being a relative of him whose ear Peter cut off, says, "Did I not see you in the garden with Him?" **27** Again, therefore, Peter denied, and immediately a rooster crowed. **28** They led, therefore, Jesus from Caiaphas into the Praetorium, and it was early, and they themselves did not enter into the Praetorium, that they might not be defiled, but that they might eat the Passover; **29** Pilate, therefore, went forth to them and said, "What accusation do you bring against this Man?" **30** They answered and said to him, "If He were not doing evil, we had not delivered Him to you." **31** Pilate, therefore, said to them, "Take Him—you—and judge Him according to your law"; the Jews, therefore, said to him, "It is not lawful to us to put anyone to death"; **32** that the word of Jesus might be fulfilled which He said, signifying by what death He was about to die. **33** Pilate, therefore, entered into the Praetorium again, and called Jesus, and said to Him, "You are the King of the Jews?" **34** Jesus answered him, "Do you say this from yourself? Or did others say it to you about Me?" **35** Pilate answered, "Am I a Jew? Your nation and the chief priests delivered You up to me; what did You do?" **36** Jesus answered, "My kingdom is not of this world; if My kingdom were of this world, My officers had struggled that I might not be delivered up to Jews; but now My kingdom is not from here." **37** Pilate, therefore, said to Him, "Are You then a king?" Jesus answered, "You say [it], because I am a king; I have been born for this, and I have come into the world for this, that I may testify to the truth; everyone who is of the truth, hears My voice." **38** Pilate says to Him, "What is truth?" And having said this, again he went forth to the Jews and says to them, "I find no fault in Him; **39** and you have a custom that I will release to you one in the Passover; do you determine, therefore, [that] I will release to you the King of the Jews?" **40** Therefore they all cried out again, saying, "Not this One—but Barabbas"; and Barabbas was a robber.

19 Then, therefore, Pilate took Jesus and scourged [Him], **2** and the soldiers having plaited a garland of thorns, placed [it] on His head, and they cast a purple garment around Him, **3** and said, "Hail! The King of the Jews"; and they were giving Him slaps. **4** Pilate, therefore, again went forth outside and says to them, "Behold, I bring Him to you outside, that you may know that I find no fault in Him"; **5** Jesus, therefore, came forth outside, bearing the thorny garland and the purple garment; and he says to them, "Behold, the Man!" **6** When, therefore, the chief priests and the officers saw Him, they cried out, saying, "Crucify! Crucify!" Pilate says to them, "Take Him yourselves and crucify, for I find no fault in Him"; **7** the Jews answered him, "We have a law, and according to our law He ought to die, for He made Himself Son of God." **8** When, therefore, Pilate heard this word, he was more afraid, **9** and entered again into the Praetorium and says to Jesus, "Where are You from?" And Jesus gave him no answer. **10** Pilate, therefore, says to Him, "Do You not speak to me? Have You not known that I have authority to crucify You, and I have authority to release You?" **11** Jesus answered, "You would have no authority against Me if it were not having been given you from above; because of this, he who is delivering Me up to you has greater sin." **12** From this [time] Pilate was seeking to release Him, and the Jews were crying out, saying, "If you may release this One, you are not a friend of Caesar; everyone making himself a king speaks against Caesar." **13** Pilate, therefore, having heard this word, brought Jesus outside—and he sat down on the judgment seat—to a place called, "Pavement," and in Hebrew, Gabbatha; **14** and it was the Preparation of the Passover, and as it were the sixth hour, and he says to the Jews, "Behold, your King!" **15** And they cried out, "Take away! Take away! Crucify Him!" Pilate says to them, "Will I crucify your King?" The chief priests answered, "We have no king except Caesar." **16** Then, therefore, he delivered Him up to them, that He may be crucified, and they took Jesus and led [Him] away, **17** and carrying His cross, He went forth to the [place] called "Place of [the] Skull," which is called in Hebrew, Golgotha— **18** where they crucified Him, and with Him two others, on this side and on that side, but Jesus in the middle. **19** And Pilate also wrote a title, and put [it] on the cross, and it was written: "Jesus the Nazarene, the King of the Jews"; **20** therefore many of the Jews read this title, because the place was near to the city where Jesus was crucified, and it was having been written in Hebrew, in Greek, in Latin. **21** The chief priests of the Jews therefore said to Pilate, "Do not write, The King of the Jews, but that this One said, I am King of the Jews"; **22** Pilate answered, "What I have written, I have written." **23** The soldiers, therefore, when they crucified Jesus, took His garments, and made four parts, to each soldier a part, also the coat, and the coat was seamless, from the top woven throughout; **24** they said, therefore, to one another, "We may not tear it, but cast a lot for it, whose it will be"; that the Writing might be fulfilled, that is saying, "They divided My garments to themselves, and they cast a lot for My clothing"; the soldiers, therefore, indeed, did these things. **25** And there stood by the cross of Jesus His mother, and His mother's sister, Mary of Cleopas, and Mary the Magdalene; **26** Jesus, therefore, having seen [His] mother, and the disciple standing by, whom He was loving, He says to His mother, "Woman, behold, your son"; **27** afterward He says to the disciple, "Behold, your mother"; and from that hour the disciple took her to his own [home]. **28** After this, Jesus knowing that all things have now been accomplished, that the Writing may be fulfilled, says, "I thirst"; **29** a vessel, therefore, was placed full of vinegar, and having filled a sponge with vinegar, and having put [it] around a hyssop stalk, they put [it] to His mouth; **30** when, therefore, Jesus received the vinegar, He said, "It has been accomplished." And having bowed the head, gave up the spirit. **31** The Jews, therefore, that the bodies might not remain on the cross on the Sabbath, since it was the Preparation (for that Sabbath day was a great one), asked of Pilate that their legs may be broken, and they [are] taken away. **32** The soldiers, therefore, came, and they indeed broke the legs of the first and of the other who was crucified with Him, **33** and having come to Jesus, when they saw Him already having been dead, they did not break His legs; **34** but one of the soldiers pierced His side with a spear, and immediately there came forth blood and water; **35** and he who has seen has testified, and his testimony is true, and that one has known that he speaks true things, that you also may believe. **36** For these things came to pass, that the Writing may be fulfilled, "A bone of Him will not be broken"; **37** and again another Writing says, "They will look to Him whom they pierced." **38** And after these things, Joseph of Arimathea—being a disciple of Jesus, but concealed, through the fear of the Jews—asked of Pilate, that he may take away the body of Jesus, and Pilate gave leave; he came, therefore, and took away the body of Jesus, **39** and Nicodemus also came—who came to Jesus by night at the first—carrying a mixture of myrrh and aloes, as it were, one hundred pounds. **40** Therefore they took the body of Jesus, and bound it with linen clothes with the spices, according as it was the custom of the Jews to prepare for burial; **41** and there was a garden in the place where He was crucified, and a new tomb in the garden, in which no one was yet laid; **42** therefore, because the tomb was near, there they laid

Jesus because of the Preparation of the Jews.

20 And on the first [day] of the weeks, Mary the Magdalene comes early (there being yet darkness) to the tomb, and she sees the stone having been taken away out of the tomb; **2** she runs, therefore, and comes to Simon Peter, and to the other disciple whom Jesus was cherishing, and says to them, "They took away the Lord out of the tomb, and we have not known where they laid Him." **3** Peter, therefore, went forth, and the other disciple, and they were coming to the tomb, **4** and the two were running together, and the other disciple ran forward more quickly than Peter, and came first to the tomb, **5** and having stooped down, sees the linen clothes lying, yet, indeed, he did not enter. **6** Simon Peter, therefore, comes, following him, and he entered into the tomb, and beholds the linen clothes lying [there], **7** and the napkin that was on His head not lying with the linen clothes, but apart, having been folded up, in one place; **8** then, therefore, the other disciple who came first to the tomb entered also, and he saw and believed; **9** for they did not yet know the Writing, that it was necessary for Him to rise again out of the dead. **10** The disciples therefore went away again to their own friends, **11** and Mary was standing near the tomb, weeping outside; as she was weeping, then, she stooped down into the tomb, and beholds two messengers in white, sitting, **12** one at the head and one at the feet, where the body of Jesus had been laid. **13** And they say to her, "Woman, why do you weep?" She says to them, "Because they took away my Lord, and I have not known where they laid Him"; **14** and having said these things, she turned backward, and sees Jesus standing, and she had not known that it is Jesus. **15** Jesus says to her, "Woman, why do you weep? Whom do you seek?" She, supposing that He is the gardener, says to Him, "Lord, if You carried Him away, tell me where You laid Him, and I will take Him away"; **16** Jesus says to her, "Mary!" Having turned, she says to Him, "Rabboni!" That is to say, "Teacher." **17** Jesus says to her, "Do not be touching Me, for I have not yet ascended to My Father; and be going on to My brothers, and say to them, I ascend to My Father and your Father, and [to] My God and your God." **18** Mary the Magdalene comes, reporting to the disciples that she has seen the LORD, and [that] He said these things to her. **19** It being, therefore, evening, on that day, the first [day] of the weeks, and the doors having been shut where the disciples were assembled through fear of the Jews, Jesus came and stood in the midst, and says to them, "Peace to you"; **20** and having said this, He showed them His hands and side; the disciples, therefore, rejoiced, having seen the LORD. **21** Jesus, therefore, said to them again, "Peace to you; according as the Father has sent Me, I also send you"; **22** having said this, He breathed on [them], and says to them, "Receive the Holy Spirit; **23** if you may forgive the sins of any, they are forgiven them; if you may retain of any, they have been retained." **24** And Thomas, one of the Twelve, who is called Didymus, was not with them when Jesus came; **25** the other disciples, therefore, said to him, "We have seen the Lord!" And he said to them, "If I may not see the mark of the nails in His hands, and may [not] put my finger into the mark of the nails, and may [not] put my hand into His side, I will not believe." **26** And after eight days, again His disciples were within, and Thomas [was] with them; Jesus comes, the doors having been shut, and He stood in the midst and said, "Peace to you!" **27** Then He says to Thomas, "Bring your finger here, and see My hands, and bring your hand, and put [it] into My side, and do not become unbelieving, but believing." **28** And Thomas answered and said to Him, "My Lord and my God!" **29** Jesus says to him, "Because you have seen Me, Thomas, you have believed; blessed [are] those having not seen, and having believed." **30** Many indeed, therefore, other signs Jesus also did before His disciples that are not written in this scroll; **31** and these have been written that you may believe that Jesus is the Christ, the Son of God, and that believing, you may have life in His Name.

21 After these things Jesus Himself again appeared to the disciples on the Sea of Tiberias, and He revealed Himself thus: **2** Simon Peter, and Thomas who is called Didymus, and Nathanael from Cana of Galilee, and the [sons] of Zebedee, and two of His other disciples were together. **3** Simon Peter says to them, "I go away to fish"; they say to him, "We go—we also—

JOHN

with you"; they went forth and immediately entered into the boat, and on that night they caught nothing. 4 And morning having now come, Jesus stood at the shore, yet indeed the disciples did not know that it is Jesus; 5 Jesus, therefore, says to them, "Boys, do you have any meat?" 6 They answered Him, "No"; and He said to them, "Cast the net at the right side of the boat, and you will find [some]"; they cast, therefore, and no longer were they able to draw it, from the multitude of the fishes. 7 That disciple, therefore, whom Jesus was loving says to Peter, "It is the Lord!" Simon Peter, therefore, having heard that it is the LORD, girded on the outer coat (for he was naked), and cast himself into the sea; 8 and the other disciples came by the little boat, for they were not far from the land, but about two hundred cubits away, dragging the net of the fishes; 9 when, therefore, they came to the land, they behold a fire of coals lying [there], and a fish lying on it, and bread. 10 Jesus says to them, "Bring from the fishes that you caught now"; 11 Simon Peter went up, and drew the net up on the land, full of great fishes—one hundred fifty-three; and though they were so many, the net was not split. 12 Jesus says to them, "Come, dine"; and none of the disciples were venturing to inquire of Him, "Who are You?" Knowing that it is the LORD; 13 Jesus, therefore, comes and takes the bread and gives [it] to them, and the fish in like manner; 14 this [is] now a third time Jesus was revealed to His disciples, having been raised from the dead. 15 When, therefore, they dined, Jesus says to Simon Peter, "Simon, [son] of Jonas, do you love Me more than these?" He says to Him, "Yes, Lord; You have known that I cherish You"; He says to him, "Feed My lambs." 16 He says to him again, a second time, "Simon, [son] of Jonas, do you love Me?" He says to Him, "Yes, Lord; You have known that I cherish You"; He says to him, "Tend My sheep." 17 He says to him the third time, "Simon, [son] of Jonas, do you cherish Me?" Peter was grieved that He said to him the third time, "Do you cherish Me?" And he said to Him, "Lord, You have known all things; You know that I cherish You." Jesus says to him, "Feed My sheep; 18 truly, truly, I say to you, when you were younger, you were girding yourself and were walking to where you willed, but when you may be old, you will stretch forth your hands, and another will gird you, and will carry [you] to where you do not will"; 19 and this He said, signifying by what death he will glorify God; and having said this, He says to him, "Follow Me." 20 And having turned, Peter sees the disciple whom Jesus was loving following (who also reclined in the dinner on His breast and said, "Lord, who is he who is delivering You up?") 21 Having seen this one, Peter says to Jesus, "Lord, and what of this one?" 22 Jesus says to him, "If I will him to remain until I come, what [is that] to you? Follow Me." 23 This word, therefore, went forth to the brothers that this disciple does not die, yet Jesus did not say to him that he does not die, but, "If I will him to remain until I come, what [is that] to you?" 24 This is the disciple who is testifying concerning these things, and he wrote these things, and we have known that his testimony is true. 25 And there are also many other things—as many as Jesus did—which, if they may be written one by one, I think the world itself does not even have place for the scrolls written. Amen.

ACTS

1 The former account, indeed, I made concerning all things, O Theophilus, that Jesus began both to do and to teach, **2** until the day in which, having given command through the Holy Spirit to the apostles whom He chose out, He was taken up, **3** to whom He also presented Himself alive after His suffering, in many certain proofs, being seen by them through forty days, and speaking the things concerning the Kingdom of God. **4** And being assembled together with them, He commanded them not to depart from Jerusalem, but to wait for the promise of the Father, "Which you heard from Me; **5** because John, indeed, immersed in water, but you will be immersed in the Holy Spirit not many days after these." **6** They, therefore, indeed, having come together, were questioning Him, saying, "Lord, do You at this time restore the kingdom to Israel?" **7** And He said to them, "It is not yours to know times or seasons that the Father appointed in His own authority; **8** but you will receive power at the coming of the Holy Spirit on you, and you will be witnesses for Me both in Jerusalem, and in all Judea and Samaria, and to the end of the earth." **9** And having said these things—they beholding—He was taken up, and a cloud received Him up from their sight; **10** and as they were looking steadfastly to the sky in His going on, then, behold, two men stood by them in white clothing, **11** who also said, "Men, Galileans, why do you stand gazing into the sky? This Jesus who was received up from you into Heaven, will so come in what manner you saw Him going on to Heaven." **12** Then they returned to Jerusalem from [that] called the Mount of Olives, that is near Jerusalem, a Sabbath's journey; **13** and when they came in, they went up into the upper room, where were abiding both Peter, and James, and John, and Andrew, Philip, and Thomas, Bartholomew, and Matthew, James, of Alphaeus, and Simon the Zealot, and Judas, of James; **14** these were all continuing with one accord in prayer and supplication, with women, and Mary the mother of Jesus, and with His brothers. **15** And in these days, Peter having risen up in the midst of the disciples, said (also the multitude of the names at the same place was, as it were, one hundred and twenty), **16** "Men, brothers, it was necessary [for] this Writing to be fulfilled that the Holy Spirit spoke beforehand through the mouth of David, concerning Judas, who became guide to those who took Jesus, **17** because he was numbered among us, and received the share in this ministry. **18** (This one, indeed, then, purchased a field out of the reward of unrighteousness, and falling headlong, burst apart in the midst, and all his bowels gushed forth, **19** and it became known to all those dwelling in Jerusalem, insomuch that this place is called, in their proper dialect, Aceldama, that is, Field of Blood.) **20** For it has been written in [the] Scroll of Psalms: Let his lodging-place become desolate, and let no one be dwelling in it, and let another take his oversight. **21** It is necessary, therefore, of the men who went with us during all the time in which the Lord Jesus went in and went out among us, **22** beginning from the immersion of John, to the day in which He was received up from us, one of these to become with us a witness of His resurrection." **23** And they set two, Joseph called Barsabas, who was surnamed Justus, and Matthias, **24** and having prayed, they said, "You, LORD, who are knowing the heart of all, show which one You chose of these two, **25** to receive the share of this ministry and apostleship, from which Judas, by transgression, fell, to go on to his proper place"; **26** and they gave their lots, and the lot fell on Matthias, and he was numbered with the eleven apostles.

2 And in the day of the Pentecost being fulfilled, they were all with one accord at the same place, **2** and there came suddenly out of the sky a sound as of a violent rushing wind, and it filled all the house where they were sitting, **3** and there appeared to them divided tongues, as it were of fire; it also sat on each one of them, **4** and they were all filled with the Holy Spirit, and began to speak with other tongues, according as the Spirit was giving them to declare. **5** And there were Jews dwelling in Jerusalem, devout men from every nation of those under the heaven, 6 and the rumor of this having come, the multitude came together, and was confounded, because they were, each one, hearing them speaking in his proper dialect, 7 and they were all amazed, and wondered, saying to one another, "Behold, are not all these who are speaking Galileans? 8 And how do we hear, each in our proper dialect, in which we were born? 9 Parthians, and Medes, and Elamites, and those dwelling in Mesopotamia, in Judea also, and Cappadocia, Pontus, and Asia, 10 Phrygia also, and Pamphylia, Egypt, and the parts of Libya that [are] along Cyrene, and the strangers of Rome, both Jews and proselytes, 11 Cretes and Arabians, we heard them speaking the great things of God in our tongues." 12 And they were all amazed, and were in doubt, saying to one another, "What would this wish to be?" 13 And others mocking said, "They are full of sweet wine"; 14 and Peter having stood up with the Eleven, lifted up his voice and declared to them: "Men—Jews, and all those dwelling in Jerusalem! Let this be known to you, and listen to my sayings, 15 for these are not drunken, as you take it up, for it is the third hour of the day. 16 But this is that which has been spoken through the prophet Joel: 17 And it will be in the last days, says God, ‖ I will pour out of My Spirit on all flesh, ‖ And your sons and your daughters will prophesy, ‖ And your young men will see visions, ‖ And your old men will dream dreams; 18 And also on My menservants, and on My maidservants, ‖ In those days, I will pour out of My Spirit, ‖ And they will prophesy; 19 And I will give wonders in the sky above, ‖ And signs on the earth beneath—Blood, and fire, and vapor of smoke, 20 The sun will be turned to darkness, ‖ And the moon to blood, ‖ Before the coming of the Day of the LORD—the great and conspicuous; 21 And it will be, everyone who, if he may have called on the Name of the LORD, will be saved. 22 Men, Israelites! Hear these words: Jesus the Nazarene, a man approved of God among you by mighty works, and wonders, and signs, that God did through Him in the midst of you, according as also you yourselves have known, 23 this One, by the determinate counsel and foreknowledge of God, being given out, having been taken by lawless hands, having been crucified—you slew, 24 whom God raised up, having loosed the travails of death, because it was not possible for Him to be held by it; 25 for David says in regard to Him: I foresaw the LORD always before me—Because He is on my right hand—That I may not be moved; 26 Because of this was my heart cheered, ‖ And my tongue was glad, ‖ And yet—my flesh will also rest on hope, 27 Because You will not leave my soul to Hades, ‖ Nor will You give Your Holy One to see corruption; 28 You made known to me ways of life, ‖ You will fill me with joy with Your countenance. 29 Men, brothers! It is permitted to speak with freedom to you concerning the patriarch David, that he both died and was buried, and his tomb is among us to this day; 30 therefore, being a prophet, and knowing that God swore to him with an oath, out of the fruit of his loins, according to the flesh, to raise up the Christ, to sit on his throne, 31 having foreseen, he spoke concerning the resurrection of the Christ, that His soul was not left to Hades, nor did His flesh see corruption. 32 God raised up this Jesus, of which we are all witnesses; 33 then having been exalted at the right hand of God—also having received the promise of the Holy Spirit from the Father—He poured forth this which you now see and hear; 34 for David did not go up into the heavens, and he says himself: The LORD says to my Lord, ‖ Sit at My right hand, 35 Until I make Your enemies Your footstool; 36 assuredly, therefore, let all the house of Israel know that God made Him both Lord and Christ—this Jesus whom you crucified." 37 And having heard, they were pricked to the heart; they also say to Peter and to the rest of the apostles, "What will we do, men, brothers?" 38 And Peter said to them, "Convert, and each of you be immersed on the Name of Jesus Christ, for forgiveness of sins, and you will receive the gift of the Holy Spirit, 39 for the promise is to you and to your children, and to all those far off, as many as the LORD our God will call." 40 Also with many more other words he was testifying and exhorting, saying, "Be saved from this perverse generation"; 41 then those, indeed, who gladly received his word were immersed, and there were added on that day, as it were, three thousand souls, 42 and they were continuing steadfastly in the teaching of the apostles, and the fellowship, and the breaking of the bread, and the prayers. **43** And fear came on every soul, also many wonders and signs were being done through the apostles, **44** and all those believing were at the same place, and had all things common, **45** and they were selling the possessions and the goods, and were parting them to all, according as anyone had need. **46** Also continuing daily with one accord in the temple, also breaking bread at every house, they were partaking of food in gladness and simplicity of heart, **47** praising God, and having favor with all the people, and the LORD was adding those being saved every day to the Assembly.

3 And Peter and John were going up at the same time into the temple, at the hour of the prayer, the ninth [hour], **2** and a certain man, being lame from the womb of his mother, was being carried, whom they were laying every day at the gate of the temple, called Beautiful, to ask a kindness from those entering into the temple, **3** who, having seen Peter and John about to go into the temple, was begging to receive a kindness. **4** And Peter, having looked steadfastly toward him with John, said, "Look toward us"; **5** and he was giving heed to them, looking to receive something from them; **6** and Peter said, "I have no silver and gold, but what I have, that I give to you; in the Name of Jesus Christ of Nazareth, rise up and be walking." **7** And having seized him by the right hand, he raised [him] up, and instantly his feet and ankles were strengthened, **8** and springing up, he stood, and was walking, and entered with them into the temple, walking and springing, and praising God; **9** and all the people saw him walking and praising God, **10** and they knew him, that this it was who for a kindness was sitting at the Beautiful Gate of the temple, and they were filled with wonder and amazement at what has happened to him. **11** And at the lame man who was healed holding Peter and John, all the people ran together to them in the porch called Solomon's—greatly amazed, **12** and Peter having seen, answered to the people, "Men, Israelites! Why do you wonder at this? Or why do you look on us so earnestly, as if by our own power or piety we have made him to walk? **13** The God of Abraham, and of Isaac, and of Jacob, the God of our fathers, glorified His child Jesus, whom you delivered up, and denied Him in the presence of Pilate, he having given judgment to release [Him], **14** and you denied the Holy and Righteous One, and desired a man—a murderer—to be granted to you, **15** and the Prince of life you killed, whom God raised out of the dead, of which we are witnesses; **16** and on the faith of His Name, this one whom you see and have known, His Name made strong, even the faith that [is] through Him gave to him this perfect soundness before you all. **17** And now, brothers, I have known that through ignorance you did [it], as also your rulers; **18** and God, what things He had declared before through the mouth of all His prophets, that the Christ should suffer, He thus fulfilled; **19** convert, therefore, and turn back, for your sins being blotted out, that times of refreshing may come from the presence of the LORD, **20** and He may send Jesus Christ who before has been preached to you, **21** whom Heaven required, indeed, to receive until times of a restitution of all things, of which God spoke through the mouth of all His holy prophets from the age. **22** For Moses, indeed, said to the fathers—The LORD your God will raise up a Prophet to you out of your brothers, like to me; you will hear Him in all things, as many as He may speak to you; **23** and it will be, every soul that may not hear that Prophet will be utterly destroyed out of the people; **24** and also all the prophets from Samuel and those following in order, as many as spoke, also foretold of these days. **25** You are sons of the prophets, and of the covenant that God made to our fathers, saying to Abraham: And in your Seed will all the families of the earth be blessed; **26** to you first, God, having raised up His child Jesus, sent Him, blessing you, in the turning away of each one from your evil ways."

4 And as they are speaking to the people, there came to them the priests, and the magistrate of the temple, and the Sadducees— **2** being grieved because of their teaching the people, and preaching in Jesus the resurrection out of the dead— **3** and they laid hands on them, and put them in custody until the next day, for it was evening already; **4** and many of those hearing the word believed, and the number of the men became, as it were, five thousand. **5** And it came to pass the next day, there were gathered together of them the rulers, and elders, and scribes, to Jerusalem, **6** and Annas the chief priest, and Caiaphas, and John, and Alexander, and as many as were of the family of the chief priest, **7** and having set them in the midst, they were inquiring, "In what power, or in what name did you do this?" **8** Then Peter, having been filled with the Holy Spirit, said to them: "Rulers of the people, and elders of Israel, **9** if we are examined today concerning the good deed to the ailing man, by whom he has been saved, **10** be it known to all of you, and to all the people of Israel, that in the Name of Jesus Christ of Nazareth, whom you crucified, whom God raised out of the dead, in Him has this one stood by before you whole. **11** This is the stone that was set at nothing by you—the builders, that became head of a corner; **12** and there is not salvation in any other, for there is no other name under Heaven that has been given among men, in which it is required of us to be saved." **13** And beholding the openness of Peter and John, and having perceived that they are illiterate men and commoners, they were wondering—they were also taking knowledge of them that they had been with Jesus— **14** and seeing the man standing with them who has been healed, they had nothing to say against [it], **15** and having commanded them to go away out of the Sanhedrin, they took counsel with one another, **16** saying, "What will we do to these men? Because that, indeed, a notable sign has been done through them [is] apparent to all those dwelling in Jerusalem, and we are not able to deny [it]; **17** but that it may spread no further toward the people, let us strictly threaten them to no longer speak in this Name to any man." **18** And having called them, they charged them not to speak at all, nor to teach, in the Name of Jesus, **19** and Peter and John answering to them said, "Whether it is righteous before God to listen to you rather than to God, judge; **20** for we cannot but speak what we saw and heard." **21** And they having further threatened [them], let them go, finding no way how they may punish them, because of the people, because all were glorifying God for that which has been done, **22** for above forty years of age was the man on whom had been done this sign of the healing. **23** And being let go, they went to their own friends, and declared whatever the chief priests and the elders said to them, **24** and they having heard, lifted up the voice to God with one accord and said, "LORD, You [are] God, who made the heaven, and the earth, and the sea, and all that [are] in them, **25** who, through the mouth of Your servant David, said, Why did nations rage, and peoples meditate vain things? **26** The kings of the earth stood up, and the rulers were gathered together against the LORD and against His Christ; **27** for gathered together of a truth against Your holy child Jesus, whom You anointed, were both Herod and Pontius Pilate, with nations and peoples of Israel, **28** to do whatever Your hand and Your counsel determined before to come to pass. **29** And now, LORD, look on their threatenings, and grant to Your servants to speak Your word with all freedom, **30** in the stretching forth of Your hand, for healing, and signs, and wonders, to come to pass through the Name of Your holy child Jesus." **31** And they having prayed, the place was shaken in which they were gathered together, and they were all filled with the Holy Spirit, and were speaking the word of God with freedom, **32** and of the multitude of those who believed, the heart and the soul were one, and not one was saying that anything of the things he had was his own, but all things were in common to them. **33** And with great power the apostles were giving the testimony to the resurrection of the Lord Jesus, great grace was also on them all, **34** for there was not anyone among them who lacked, for as many as were possessors of fields, or houses, selling [them], were bringing the prices of the thing sold, **35** and were laying them at the feet of the apostles, and distribution was being made to each according as anyone had need. **36** And Joses, who was surnamed by the apostles Barnabas—which is, having been interpreted, Son of Comfort—a Levite, of Cyprus by birth, **37** a field being his, having sold [it], brought the money and laid [it] at the feet of the apostles.

5 And a certain man, Ananias by name, with his wife Sapphira, sold a possession, **2** and kept back of the price—his wife also knowing—and having brought a certain part, he laid [it] at the feet of the apostles. **3** And Peter said, "Ananias, why did Satan fill your heart, for you to lie to the Holy Spirit, and to keep back of the price of the place? **4** While it remained, did it not remain yours? And having been sold, was it not in your authority? Why [is] it that you put this thing in your heart? You did not lie to men, but to God"; **5** and Ananias hearing these words, having fallen down, expired, and great fear came on all who heard these things, **6** and having risen, the younger men wound him up, and having carried forth, they buried [him]. **7** And it came to pass, about three hours after, that his wife, not knowing what has happened, came in, **8** and Peter answered her, "Tell me if for so much you sold the place"; and she said, "Yes, for so much." **9** And Peter said to her, "How was it agreed by you to tempt the Spirit of the LORD? Behold, the feet of those who buried your husband [are] at the door, and they will carry you forth"; **10** and immediately she fell down at his feet, and expired, and the young men having come in, found her dead, and having carried forth, they buried [her] by her husband; **11** and great fear came on all the Assembly, and on all who heard these things. **12** And through the hands of the apostles came many signs and wonders among the people, and they were all with one accord in the porch of Solomon; **13** and of the rest no one was daring to join himself to them, but the people were magnifying them, **14** (and the more were believers added to the LORD, multitudes of both men and women), **15** so as to bring forth the ailing into the broad places, and to lay [them] on beds and pallets, that at the coming of Peter, even [his] shadow might overshadow someone of them; **16** and there were also coming together the people of the surrounding cities to Jerusalem, carrying ailing persons, and those harassed by unclean spirits—who were all healed. **17** And having risen, the chief priest, and all those with him—being the sect of the Sadducees—were filled with zeal, **18** and laid their hands on the apostles, and put them in a public prison; **19** but through the night a messenger of the LORD opened the doors of the prison, having also brought them forth, he said, **20** "Go on, and standing, speak in the temple to the people all the sayings of this life"; **21** and having heard, they entered into the temple at the dawn, and were teaching. And the chief priest having come, and those with him, they called together the Sanhedrin and all the Senate of the sons of Israel, and they sent to the prison to have them brought, **22** and the officers having come, did not find them in the prison, and having turned back, they told, **23** saying, "We indeed found the prison shut in all safety, and the keepers standing outside before the doors, and having opened—we found no one within." **24** And as the priest, and the magistrate of the temple, and the chief priests, heard these words, they were doubting concerning them to what this would come; **25** and coming near, a certain one told them, saying, "Behold, the men whom you put in the prison are in the temple standing and teaching the people"; **26** then the magistrate having gone away with officers, brought them without violence, for they were fearing the people, lest they should be stoned; **27** and having brought them, they set [them] in the Sanhedrin, and the chief priest questioned them, **28** saying, "Did we not strictly command you not to teach in this Name? And behold, you have filled Jerusalem with your teaching, and you intend to bring on us the blood of this Man." **29** And Peter and the apostles answering, said, "It is required to obey God, rather than men; **30** and the God of our fathers raised up Jesus, whom you slew, having hanged on a tree; **31** this One, God, a Prince and a Savior, has exalted with His right hand, to give conversion to Israel, and forgiveness of sins; **32** and we are His witnesses of these sayings, and the Holy Spirit also, whom God gave to those obeying Him." **33** And they having heard, were cut [to the heart], and were intending to slay them, **34** but a certain one, having risen up in the Sanhedrin—a Pharisee, by name Gamaliel, a teacher of law honored by all the people—commanded to put the apostles forth a little, **35** and said to them, "Men, Israelites, take heed to yourselves about these men, what you are about to do, **36** for before these days Theudas rose up, saying that he was someone, to whom a number of men joined themselves, as it were four hundred, who was slain, and all, as many as were obeying him, were scattered, and came to nothing. **37** After this one, Judas the Galilean rose up, in the days of the census, and drew away people after him, and that one perished, and all, as many as were obeying him, were scattered; **38** and now I say to you, refrain from these men, and leave them alone, because if this counsel or this work may be of men, it will be overthrown, **39** and if it be of God, you are not able to overthrow it, lest perhaps you are also found fighting against God." **40** And to him they agreed, and having called near the apostles, having beaten [them], they commanded [them] not to speak in the Name of Jesus, and let them go; **41** they, indeed, then, departed from the presence of the Sanhedrin, rejoicing that for His Name they were counted worthy to suffer dishonor, **42** also every day in the temple, and in every house, they were not ceasing teaching and proclaiming good news—Jesus the Christ.

6 And in these days, the disciples multiplying, there came a murmuring of the Hellenists at the Hebrews, because their widows were being overlooked in the daily ministry, **2** and the Twelve, having called near the multitude of the disciples, said, "It is not pleasing that we, having left the word of God, minister at tables; **3** look out, therefore, brothers, seven men of you who are testified well of, full of the Holy Spirit and wisdom, whom we may set over this necessity, **4** and we to prayer, and to the ministry of the word, will give ourselves continually." **5** And the thing was pleasing before all the multitude, and they chose Stephen, a man full of faith and the Holy Spirit, and Philip, and Prochorus, and Nicanor, and Timon, and Parmenas, and Nicolaus, a proselyte of Antioch, **6** whom they set before the apostles, and they, having prayed, laid [their] hands on them. **7** And the word of God increased, and the number of the disciples multiplied in Jerusalem exceedingly; a great multitude of the priests were also obedient to the faith. **8** And Stephen, full of faith and power, was doing great wonders and signs among the people, **9** and there arose certain of those of the synagogue, the [one] called Libertines (and Cyrenians, and Alexandrians, and of those from Cilicia, and Asia), disputing with Stephen, **10** and they were not able to resist the wisdom and the Spirit with which he was speaking; **11** then they suborned men, saying, "We have heard him speaking slanderous sayings in regard to Moses and God." **12** They also stirred up the people, and the elders, and the scribes, and having come on [him], they caught him, and brought [him] to the Sanhedrin; **13** they also set up false witnesses, saying, "This one does not cease to speak evil sayings against this holy place and the Law, **14** for we have heard him saying that this Jesus the Nazarean will overthrow this place, and will change the customs that Moses delivered to us"; **15** and gazing at him, all those sitting in the Sanhedrin saw his face as it were the face of a messenger.

7 And the chief priest said, "Are then these things so?" **2** And he said, "Men, brothers, and fathers, listen! The God of glory appeared to our father Abraham, being in Mesopotamia, before his dwelling in Haran, **3** and He said to him, Go forth out of your land, and out of your relatives, and come to a land that I will show you. **4** Then having come forth out of the land of the Chaldeans, he dwelt in Haran, and from there, after the death of his father, He removed him to this land wherein you now dwell, **5** and He gave him no inheritance in it, not even a footstep, and promised to give it to him for a possession, and to his seed after him—he having no child. **6** And God spoke thus, that his seed will be sojourning in a strange land, and they will cause it to serve, and will do it evil [for] four hundred years. **7** And the nation whom they will serve I will judge, said God; And after these things they will come forth and will do Me service in this place. **8** And He gave to him a covenant of circumcision, and so he begot Isaac, and circumcised him on the eighth day, and Isaac [begot] Jacob, and Jacob—the twelve patriarchs; **9** and the patriarchs, having been moved with jealousy, sold Joseph to Egypt, and God was with him, **10** and delivered him out of all his tribulations, and gave him favor and wisdom before Pharaoh king of Egypt, and he set him—governor over Egypt and all his house. **11** And there came a scarcity on all the land of Egypt and Canaan, and great tribulation, and our fathers were not finding sustenance, **12** and Jacob having heard that there was grain in Egypt, sent forth our fathers a first time; **13** and at the second time was Joseph made known to his brothers, and Joseph's family became disclosed to Pharaoh, **14** and Joseph having sent, called for his father Jacob, and all his relatives—with seventy-five souls— **15** and Jacob went down to Egypt, and died, himself and our fathers, **16** and they were carried over into Shechem, and were laid in the tomb that Abraham bought for a price in money from the sons of Emmor, of Shechem. **17** And according as the time of the promise was drawing near, which God swore to Abraham, the people increased and multiplied in Egypt, **18** until another king rose, who had not known Joseph; **19** this one, having dealt subtly with our family, did evil to our fathers, causing to expose their babies, that they might not live; **20** in which time Moses was born, and he was fair to God, and he was brought up [for] three months in the house of his father; **21** and he having been set outside, the daughter of Pharaoh took him up, and reared him to herself for a son; **22** and Moses was taught in all wisdom of the Egyptians, and he was powerful in words and in works. **23** And when forty years were fulfilled to him, it came on his heart to look after his brothers, the sons of Israel; **24** and having seen a certain one suffering injustice, he defended, and did justice to the oppressed, having struck the Egyptian; **25** and he was supposing his brothers to understand that God gives salvation through his hand; and they did not understand. **26** On the succeeding day, also, he showed himself to them as they are striving, and urged them to peace, saying, Men, you are brothers, why do you do injustice to one another? **27** And he who is doing injustice to the neighbor, thrusted him away, saying, Who set you a ruler and a judge over us? **28** Do you wish to kill me, as you killed the Egyptian yesterday? **29** And Moses fled at this word, and became a sojourner in the land of Midian, where he begot two sons, **30** and forty years having been fulfilled, there appeared to him in the wilderness of Mount Sinai [the] Messenger of the LORD, in a flame of fire of a bush, **31** and Moses having seen, wondered at the sight; and he drawing near to behold, there came a voice of the LORD to him, **32** I [am] the God of your fathers; the God of Abraham, and the God of Isaac, and the God of Jacob. And Moses having become terrified, did not dare behold, **33** and the LORD said to him, Loose the sandal of your feet, for the place in which you have stood is holy ground; **34** seeing I have seen the affliction of My people that [is] in Egypt, and I heard their groaning, and came down to deliver them; and now come, I will send you to Egypt. **35** This Moses, whom they refused, saying, Who set you a ruler and a judge? This one God sent [as] a ruler and a redeemer, by the hand of [the] Messenger who appeared to him in the bush; **36** this one brought them forth, having done wonders and signs in the land of Egypt, and in the Red Sea, and in the wilderness forty years; **37** this is the Moses who said to the sons of Israel: The LORD your God will raise up to you a Prophet out of your brothers, like to me, Him will you hear. **38** This is he who was in the assembly in the wilderness, with the Messenger who is speaking to him in Mount Sinai, and with our fathers who received the living oracles to give to us; **39** to whom our fathers did not wish to become obedient, but thrusted away, and turned back in their hearts to Egypt, **40** saying to Aaron, Make to us gods who will go on before us, for this Moses, who brought us forth out of the land of Egypt, we have not known what has happened to him. **41** And they made a calf in those days, and brought a sacrifice to the idol, and were rejoicing in the works of their hands, **42** and God turned, and gave them up to do service to the host of Heaven, according as it has been written in the scroll of the Prophets: Did you offer slain beasts and sacrifices to Me forty years in the wilderness, O house of Israel? **43** And you took up the dwelling place of Moloch, and the star of your god Remphan—the figures that you made to worship them, and I will remove your dwelling beyond Babylon. **44** The Dwelling Place of the Testimony was among our fathers in the wilderness, according as He directed, who is speaking to Moses, to make it according to the figure that he had seen; **45** which also our fathers having in succession received, brought in with Joshua, into the possession of the nations whom God drove out from the presence of our fathers, until the days of David, **46** who found favor before God, and requested to find a dwelling place for the God of Jacob; **47** and Solomon built Him a house. **48** But the Most High does not dwell in sanctuaries made with hands, according as the prophet says: **49** Heaven [is] My throne, ‖ And the earth My footstool, ‖ What house will you build to Me? Says the LORD; Or what [is] the place of My rest? **50** Has My hand not made all these things? **51** You stiff-necked and uncircumcised in heart and in ears! You always resist the

Holy Spirit; as your fathers—also you; **52** which of the prophets did your fathers not persecute? And they killed those who declared before about the coming of the Righteous One, of whom you have now become betrayers and murderers, **53** who received the Law by arrangement of messengers, and did not keep [it]." **54** And hearing these things, they were cut to the hearts, and gnashed the teeth at him; **55** and being full of the Holy Spirit, having looked steadfastly to the sky, he saw the glory of God, and Jesus standing on the right hand of God, **56** and he said, "Behold, I see the heavens having been opened, and the Son of Man standing on the right hand of God." **57** And they, having cried out with a loud voice, stopped their ears, and rushed with one accord on him, **58** and having cast him forth outside of the city, they were stoning [him]—and the witnesses put down their garments at the feet of a young man called Saul— **59** and they were stoning Stephen, [as he was] calling and saying, "Lord Jesus, receive my spirit"; **60** and having bowed the knees, he cried with a loud voice, "LORD, may You not lay to them this sin"; and having said this, he fell asleep.

8 And Saul was assenting to his death, and there came in that day a great persecution on the Assembly in Jerusalem, all were also scattered abroad in the regions of Judea and Samaria, except the apostles; **2** and devout men carried Stephen away, and made great lamentation over him; **3** and Saul was making havoc of the Assembly, entering into every house, and dragging away men and women, giving them up to prison; **4** they then indeed, having been scattered, went abroad proclaiming good news—the word. **5** And Philip having gone down to a city of Samaria, was preaching the Christ to them; **6** the multitudes were also giving heed to the things spoken by Philip, with one accord, in their hearing and seeing the signs that he was doing, **7** for unclean spirits came forth from many who were possessed, crying with a loud voice, and many who have been paralytic and lame were healed, **8** and there was great joy in that city. **9** And a certain man, by name Simon, was previously in the city using magic, and amazing the nation of Samaria, saying himself to be a certain great one, **10** to whom they were all giving heed, from small to great, saying, "This one is the great power of God"; **11** and they were giving heed to him, because of his having amazed them for a long time with deeds of magic. **12** And when they believed Philip, proclaiming good news, the things concerning the Kingdom of God and the Name of Jesus Christ, they were immersed—both men and women; **13** and Simon himself also believed, and having been immersed, he was continuing with Philip, beholding also signs and mighty acts being done, he was amazed. **14** And the apostles in Jerusalem having heard that Samaria has received the word of God, sent Peter and John to them, **15** who having come down prayed concerning them, that they may receive the Holy Spirit— **16** for as yet He was fallen on none of them, and only they have been immersed—into the Name of the Lord Jesus; **17** then they were laying hands on them, and they received the Holy Spirit. **18** And Simon, having beheld that through the laying on of the hands of the apostles the Holy Spirit is given, brought money before them, **19** saying, "Give also to me this authority, that on whomsoever I may lay the hands, he may receive the Holy Spirit." **20** And Peter said to him, "Your silver with you— may it be to destruction! Because you thought to possess the gift of God through money; **21** you have neither part nor lot in this thing, for your heart is not right before God; **22** convert, therefore, from this your wickedness, and implore God, if then the purpose of your heart may be forgiven you, **23** for in the gall of bitterness, and bond of unrighteousness, I perceive you being." **24** And Simon answering, said, "Implore for me to the LORD, that nothing may come on me of the things you have spoken." **25** They indeed, therefore, having testified fully, and spoken the word of the LORD, turned back to Jerusalem; they also proclaimed good news in many villages of the Samaritans. **26** And a messenger of the LORD spoke to Philip, saying, "Arise, and go on toward the south, on the way that is going down from Jerusalem to Gaza." (This is desolate.) **27** And having arisen, he went on, and behold, a man of Ethiopia, a eunuch, a man of rank, of Candace the queen of the Ethiopians, who was over all her treasure, who had come to Jerusalem to worship; **28** he was also returning, and is sitting on his chariot, and he was reading the prophet Isaiah. **29** And the Spirit said to Philip, "Go near, and be joined to this chariot"; **30** and Philip having run near, heard him reading the prophet Isaiah and said, "Do you then know what you read?" **31** And he said, "Why, how am I able, if someone may not guide me?" He called Philip also, having come up, to sit with him. **32** And the passage of the Writing that he was reading was this: "He was led as a sheep to slaughter, ‖ And as a lamb before his shearer is silent, ‖ So He does not open His mouth; **33** In His humiliation His judgment was taken away, ‖ And His generation—who will declare? Because His life is taken from the earth." **34** And the eunuch answering Philip said, "I beg you, about whom does the prophet say this? About himself, or about some other one?" **35** And Philip having opened his mouth, and having begun from this Writing, proclaimed good news to him—Jesus. **36** And as they were going on the way, they came on some water, and the eunuch said, "Behold, water; what hinders me to be immersed?" **37** [[And Philip said, "If you believe out of all the heart, it is lawful"; and he answering said, "I believe Jesus Christ to be the Son of God";]] **38** and he commanded the chariot to stand still, and they both went down to the water, both Philip and the eunuch, and he immersed him; **39** and when they came up out of the water, the Spirit of the LORD snatched up Philip, and the eunuch saw him no more, for he was going on his way rejoicing; **40** and Philip was found at Azotus, and passing through, he was proclaiming good news to all the cities, until his coming to Caesarea.

9 And Saul, yet breathing of threatening and slaughter to the disciples of the LORD, having gone to the chief priest, **2** asked from him letters to Damascus, to the synagogues, that if he may find any being of The Way, both men and women, he may bring them bound to Jerusalem. **3** And in the going, he came near to Damascus, and suddenly there shone around him a light from Heaven, **4** and having fallen on the earth, he heard a voice saying to him, "Saul, Saul, why do you persecute Me?" **5** And he said, "Who are You, Lord?" And the LORD said, "I am Jesus whom you persecute; [[hard for you to kick at the goads"; **6** trembling also, and astonished, he said, "Lord, what do You wish me to do?" And the LORD [said] to him,]] "Arise, and enter into the city, and it will be told [to] you what you must do." **7** And the men who are journeying with him stood speechless, indeed hearing the voice but seeing no one, **8** and Saul arose from the earth, and his eyes having been opened, he beheld no one, and leading him by the hand they brought him to Damascus, **9** and he was three days without seeing, and he neither ate nor drank. **10** And there was a certain disciple in Damascus, by name Ananias, and the LORD said to him in a vision, "Ananias"; and he said, "Behold me, Lord"; **11** and the LORD [says] to him, "Having risen, go on to the street that is called Straight, and seek in the house of Judas, [one] by name Saul of Tarsus, for behold, he prays, **12** and he saw in a vision a man, by name Ananias, coming in, and putting a hand on him, that he may see again." **13** And Ananias answered, "LORD, I have heard from many about this man, how many evils he did to Your holy ones in Jerusalem, **14** and here he has authority from the chief priests, to bind all those calling on Your Name." **15** And the LORD said to him, "Go, because this one is a chosen vessel to Me, to carry My Name before nations and kings—also the sons of Israel; **16** for I will show him how many things he must suffer for My Name." **17** And Ananias went away, and entered into the house, and having put on him [his] hands, said, "Saul, brother, the LORD has sent me—Jesus who appeared to you in the way in which you were coming—that you may see again, and may be filled with the Holy Spirit." **18** And immediately there fell from his eyes as it were scales, he also saw again instantly, and having risen, was immersed, **19** and having received nourishment, was strengthened, and Saul was with the disciples in Damascus certain days, **20** and immediately he was preaching the Christ in the synagogues, that He is the Son of God. **21** And all those hearing were amazed and said, "Is this not he who laid waste in Jerusalem those calling on this Name, and here to this intent had come, that he might bring them bound to the chief priests?" **22** And Saul was still more strengthened, and he was confounding the Jews dwelling in Damascus, proving that this is the Christ. **23** And when many days were fulfilled, the Jews took counsel together to kill him, **24** and their counsel against [him] was known to Saul; they were also watching the gates both day and night, that they may kill him, **25** and the disciples having taken him, by night let him down by the wall, letting down in a basket. **26** And Saul, having come to Jerusalem, tried to join himself to the disciples, and they were all afraid of him, not believing that he is a disciple, **27** and Barnabas having taken him, brought [him] to the apostles, and declared to them how he saw the LORD in the way, and that He spoke to him, and how in Damascus he was speaking boldly in the Name of Jesus. **28** And he was with them, coming in and going out in Jerusalem, **29** and speaking boldly in the Name of the Lord Jesus; he was both speaking and disputing with the Hellenists, and they were taking in hand to kill him, **30** and the brothers having known, brought him down to Caesarea, and sent him forth to Tarsus. **31** Then, indeed, the assemblies throughout all Judea, and Galilee, and Samaria, had peace, being built up, and going on in the fear of the LORD, and in the comfort of the Holy Spirit, they were multiplied. **32** And it came to pass that Peter, passing throughout all [quarters], also came down to the holy ones who were dwelling at Lydda, **33** and he found there a certain man, Aeneas by name—for eight years laid on a pallet—who was paralytic, **34** and Peter said to him, "Aeneas, Jesus the Christ heals you; arise and spread for yourself"; and immediately he rose, **35** and all those dwelling at Lydda and Saron saw him, and turned to the LORD. **36** And in Joppa there was a certain female disciple, by name Tabitha (which interpreted, is called Dorcas); this woman was full of good works and kind acts that she was doing; **37** and it came to pass in those days she, having ailed, died, and having bathed her, they laid her in an upper chamber, **38** and Lydda being near to Joppa, the disciples having heard that Peter is in that [place], sent two men to him, calling on him not to delay to come through to them. **39** And Peter having risen, went with them, whom having come, they brought into the upper chamber, and all the widows stood by him weeping, and showing coats and garments, as many as Dorcas was making while she was with them. **40** And Peter having put them all forth outside, having bowed the knees, prayed, and having turned to the body, said, "Tabitha, arise"; and she opened her eyes, and having seen Peter, she sat up, **41** and having given her [his] hand, he lifted her up, and having called the holy ones and the widows, he presented her alive, **42** and it became known throughout all Joppa, and many believed on the LORD; **43** and it came to pass, that he remained many days in Joppa, with a certain one, Simon a tanner.

10 And there was a certain man in Caesarea, by name Cornelius, a centurion from a cohort that is called Italian, **2** pious, and fearing God with all his house, also doing many kind acts to the people, and always imploring God; **3** he saw in a vision openly, as it were the ninth hour of the day, a messenger of God coming in to him, and saying to him, "Cornelius"; **4** and he having looked earnestly on him, and becoming afraid, said, "What is it, Lord?" And he said to him, "Your prayers and your kind acts came up for a memorial before God, **5** and now send men to Joppa, and send for a certain one Simon, who is surnamed Peter; **6** this one lodges with a certain Simon a tanner, whose house is by the sea; this one will speak to you what you must do." **7** And when the messenger who is speaking to Cornelius went away, having called two of his servants, and a pious soldier of those waiting on him continually, **8** and having expounded all things to them, he sent them to Joppa. **9** And on the next day, as these are proceeding on the way, and are drawing near to the city, Peter went up on the housetop to pray, about the sixth hour, **10** and he became very hungry, and wished to eat; and they making ready, there fell on him a trance, **11** and he beholds Heaven opened, and a certain vessel descending to him, as a great sheet, bound at the four corners, and let down on the earth, **12** in which were all the four-footed beasts of the earth, and the wild beasts, and the creeping things, and the birds of the sky, **13** and there came a voice to him: "Having risen, Peter, slay and eat." **14** And Peter said, "Not so, Lord; because at no time did I eat anything common or unclean"; **15** and [there is] a voice again a second time to him: "What God cleansed, you do not declare common"; **16** and this was done three times, and again was the vessel received up to Heaven. **17** And as Peter was perplexed in himself what the vision that he saw might be, then, behold, the men who have been sent from Cornelius, having made inquiry for the house of Simon, stood at the gate, **18** and having called, they were asking if Simon, who is surnamed Peter, lodges here. **19** And Peter thinking about the vision, the Spirit said to him, "Behold, three men seek you; **20** but having risen, go down and go on with them, doubting nothing, because I have sent them"; **21** and Peter having come down to the men who have been sent from Cornelius to him, said, "Behold, I am he whom you seek, what [is] the cause for which you are present?" **22** And they said, "Cornelius, a centurion, a man righteous and fearing God, well testified to, also, by all the nation of the Jews, was divinely warned by a holy messenger to send for you, to his house, and to hear sayings from you." **23** Having called them in, therefore, he lodged them, and on the next day Peter went forth with them, and certain of the brothers from Joppa went with him, **24** and on the next day they entered into Caesarea; and Cornelius was waiting for them, having called together his relatives and near friends, **25** and as it came that Peter entered in, Cornelius having met him, having fallen at [his] feet, worshiped [him]; **26** and Peter raised him, saying, "Stand up; I am also a man myself"; **27** and talking with him he went in, and finds many having come together. **28** And he said to them, "You know how it is unlawful for a man, a Jew, to keep company with, or to come to, one of another race, but God showed to me to call no man common or unclean; **29** therefore also without contradicting I came, having been sent for; I ask, therefore, for what matter you sent for me?" **30** And Cornelius said, "Four days ago until this hour, I was fasting, and [at] the ninth hour praying in my house, and behold, a man stood before me in radiant clothing, **31** and he said, Cornelius, your prayer was heard, and your kind acts were remembered before God; **32** send, therefore, to Joppa, and call for Simon, who is surnamed Peter; this one lodges in the house of Simon a tanner, by the sea, who having come, will speak to you; **33** at once, therefore, I sent to you; you also did well, having come; now, therefore, we are all present before God to hear all things that have been commanded you by God."

34 And Peter having opened his mouth, said, "Of a truth, I perceive that God is not favoring by appearance, **35** but in every nation he who is fearing Him, and is working righteousness, is acceptable to Him; **36** the word that He sent to the sons of Israel, proclaiming good news—peace through Jesus Christ (this One is Lord of all), **37** you have known the word that came throughout all Judea, having begun from Galilee, after the immersion that John preached; **38** Jesus who [is] from Nazareth—how God anointed Him with the Holy Spirit and power; who went through, doing good, and healing all those oppressed by the Devil, because God was with Him; **39** and we are witnesses of all things that He did, both in the country of the Jews, and in Jerusalem—whom they slew, having hanged [Him] on a tree. **40** This One God raised up [on] the third day, and gave Him to become visible, **41** not to all the people, but to witnesses, to those having been chosen before by God— to us who ate with [Him], and drank with Him, after His rising out of the dead; **42** and He commanded us to preach to the people, and to fully testify that it is He who has been ordained judge of living and dead by God— **43** to this One do all the Prophets testify, that through His Name everyone that is believing in Him receives forgiveness of sins." **44** While Peter is yet speaking these sayings, the Holy Spirit fell on all those hearing the word, **45** and those of circumcision [who were] believing were astonished—as many as came with Peter— because the gift of the Holy Spirit has also been poured out on the nations, **46** for they were hearing them speaking with tongues and magnifying God. **47** Then Peter answered, "Is anyone able to forbid the water, that these may not be immersed, who received the Holy Spirit—even as us also?" **48** He commanded them to also be immersed in the Name of the LORD; then they implored him to remain certain days.

11 And the apostles and the brothers who are in Judea heard that the nations also received the word of God, **2** and when Peter came up to Jerusalem, those of circumcision were contending with him, **3** saying, "You went in to uncircumcised men, and ate with them!" **4** And Peter having begun, set [it] forth to them in order, saying, **5** "I was in the city of

Joppa praying, and I saw in a trance a vision, a certain vessel coming down, as a great sheet by four corners being let down out of Heaven, and it came to me; **6** at which having looked steadfastly, I was considering, and I saw the four-footed beasts of the earth, and the wild beasts, and the creeping things, and the birds of the sky; **7** and I heard a voice saying to me, Having risen, Peter, slay and eat; **8** and I said, Not so, Lord, because anything common or unclean has at no time entered into my mouth; **9** and a voice answered me a second time out of Heaven, What God cleansed, you do not declare common. **10** And this happened three times, and again was all drawn up to Heaven, **11** and behold, immediately, three men stood at the house in which I was, having been sent from Caesarea to me, **12** and the Spirit said to me to go with them, doubting nothing, and these six brothers also went with me, and we entered into the house of the man, **13** he also declared to us how he saw the messenger standing in his house, and saying to him, Send men to Joppa, and call for Simon, who is surnamed Peter, **14** who will speak sayings by which you will be saved, you and all your house. **15** And in my beginning to speak, the Holy Spirit fell on them, even as also on us in the beginning, **16** and I remembered the saying of the LORD, how He said, John indeed immersed in water, but you will be immersed in the Holy Spirit; **17** if then God gave to them the equal gift as also to us, having believed on the Lord Jesus Christ, I—how was I able to withstand God?" **18** And they, having heard these things, were silent, and were glorifying God, saying, "Then, indeed, God also gave conversion to life to the nations." **19** Those, indeed, therefore, having been scattered abroad, from the tribulation that came after Stephen, went through to Phoenicia, and Cyprus, and Antioch, speaking the word to none except to Jews only; **20** and there were certain of them, men of Cyprus and Cyrene, who having entered into Antioch, were speaking to the Hellenists, proclaiming good news—the Lord Jesus, **21** and the hand of the LORD was with them, a great number also, having believed, turned to the LORD. **22** And the account was heard in the ears of the assembly that [is] in Jerusalem concerning them, and they sent forth Barnabas to go through to Antioch, **23** who, having come, and having seen the grace of God, was glad, and was exhorting all with purpose of heart to cleave to the LORD, **24** because he was a good man, and full of the Holy Spirit, and of faith, and a great multitude was added to the LORD. **25** And Barnabas went forth to Tarsus, to seek for Saul, **26** and having found him, he brought him to Antioch, and it came to pass that they assembled together a whole year in the assembly, and taught a great multitude, and the disciples were first called Christians in Antioch. **27** And in those days there came from Jerusalem prophets to Antioch, **28** and one of them, by name Agabus, having stood up, signified through the Spirit a great scarcity is about to be throughout all the world—which also came to pass in the time of Claudius Caesar— **29** and the disciples, according as anyone was prospering, determined each of them to send for ministry to the brothers dwelling in Judea, **30** which also they did, having sent to the elders by the hand of Barnabas and Saul.

12 And about that time, Herod the king put forth his hands to do evil to certain of those of the Assembly, **2** and he killed James, the brother of John, with the sword, **3** and having seen that it is pleasing to the Jews, he added to lay hold of Peter also—and they were the days of the Unleavened [Bread]— **4** whom also having seized, he put in prison, having delivered [him] to four squads of four soldiers to guard him, intending to bring him forth to the people after the Passover. **5** Peter, therefore, indeed, was kept in the prison, and fervent prayer was being made by the Assembly to God for him, **6** and when Herod was about to bring him forth, the same night was Peter sleeping between two soldiers, having been bound with two chains, guards were also keeping the prison before the door, **7** and behold, a messenger of the LORD stood by, and a light shone in the buildings, and having struck Peter on the side, he raised him up, saying, "Rise in haste," and his chains fell from off [his] hands. **8** The messenger also said to him, "Gird yourself, and bind on your sandals"; and he did so; and he says to him, "Cast your garment around and follow me"; **9** and having gone forth, he was following him, and he did not know that it is true that which is done through the messenger, and was thinking he saw a vision, **10** and having passed through a first ward, and a second, they came to the iron gate that is leading into the city, which opened to them of its own accord, and having gone forth, they went on through one street, and immediately the messenger departed from him. **11** And Peter having come to himself, said, "Now I have known of a truth that the LORD sent forth His messenger, and delivered me out of the hand of Herod, and all the expectation of the people of the Jews"; **12** also, having considered, he came to the house of Mary, the mother of John, who is surnamed Mark, where there were many thronged together and praying. **13** And Peter having knocked at the door of the porch, there came a girl to listen, by name Rhoda, **14** and having known the voice of Peter, from the joy she did not open the porch, but having run in, told of the standing of Peter before the porch, **15** and they said to her, "You are mad"; and she was confidently affirming [it] to be so, and they said, "It is his messenger"; **16** and Peter was continuing knocking, and having opened, they saw him, and were astonished, **17** and having beckoned to them with the hand to be silent, he declared to them how the LORD brought him out of the prison, and he said, "Declare these things to James and to the brothers"; and having gone forth, he went on to another place. **18** And day having come, there was not a little stir among the soldiers what then was become of Peter, **19** and Herod having sought for him, and having not found, having examined the guards, commanded [them] to be led away to punishment, and having gone down from Judea to Caesarea, he was abiding [there]. **20** And Herod was highly displeased with the Tyrians and Sidonians, and with one accord they came to him, and having made a friend of Blastus, who [is] over the bed-chambers of the king, they were asking peace, because of their country being nourished from the king's; **21** and on a set day, Herod having clothed himself in kingly clothing, and having sat down on the judgment seat, was making an oration to them, **22** and the populace were shouting, "The voice of a god, and not of a man!" **23** And immediately a messenger of the LORD struck him in return for that he did not give the glory to God, and having been eaten of worms, he expired. **24** And the word of God grew and multiplied, **25** and Barnabas and Saul turned back out of Jerusalem, having fulfilled the ministry, having also taken John with [them], who was surnamed Mark.

13 And there were certain in Antioch, in the assembly there, prophets and teachers: both Barnabas, and Simeon who is called Niger, and Lucius the Cyrenian, Manaen also—Herod the tetrarch's foster-brother—and Saul; **2** and in their ministering to the LORD and fasting, the Holy Spirit said, "Separate to Me both Barnabas and Saul to the work to which I have called them," **3** then having fasted, and having prayed, and having laid the hands on them, they sent [them] away. **4** These, indeed, then, having been sent forth by the Holy Spirit, went down to Seleucia, and from there they sailed to Cyprus, **5** and having come to Salamis, they declared the word of God in the synagogues of the Jews, and they also had John [as] a servant; **6** and having gone through the island to Paphos, they found a certain magus, a false prophet, a Jew, whose name [is] Bar-Jesus; **7** who was with the proconsul Sergius Paulus, an intelligent man; this one having called for Barnabas and Saul, desired to hear the word of God, **8** and there withstood them Elymas the magus—for so is his name interpreted—seeking to pervert the proconsul from the faith. **9** And Saul—who also [is] Paul—having been filled with the Holy Spirit, and having looked steadfastly on him, **10** said, "O full of all guile, and all recklessness, son of a devil, enemy of all righteousness, will you not cease perverting the right ways of the LORD? **11** And now, behold, a hand of the LORD [is] on you, and you will be blind, not seeing the sun for a season"; and instantly there fell on him a mist and darkness, and he, going around, was seeking some to lead [him] by the hand; **12** then the proconsul having seen what has come to pass, believed, being astonished at the teaching of the LORD. **13** And those around Paul having set sail from Paphos, came to Perga of Pamphylia, and John having departed from them, turned back to Jerusalem, **14** and they having gone through from Perga, came to Antioch of Pisidia, and having gone into the synagogue on the day of the Sabbaths, they

ACTS

sat down, **15** and after the reading of the Law and of the Prophets, the chief men of the synagogue sent to them, saying, "Men, brothers, if there be a word in you of exhortation to the people—say on." **16** And Paul having risen, and having beckoned with the hand, said, "Men, Israelites, and those fearing God, listen: **17** the God of this people Israel chose our fathers, and He exalted the people in their sojourning in the land of Egypt, and He brought them out of it with a high arm; **18** and about a period of forty years He endured their conduct in the wilderness, **19** and having destroyed seven nations in the land of Canaan, He divided their land to them by lot. **20** And after these things, about four hundred and fifty years, He gave judges—until Samuel the prophet; **21** and thereafter they asked for a king, and God gave to them Saul, son of Kish, a man of the tribe of Benjamin, for forty years; **22** and having removed him, He raised up to them David for king, to whom also having testified, He said, I found David, the [son] of Jesse, a man according to My heart, who will do all My will. **23** Of this one's seed, God, according to promise, raised to Israel a Savior—Jesus, **24** John having first preached, before His coming, an immersion of conversion to all the people of Israel; **25** and as John was fulfilling the course, he said, Whom do you suppose I am? I am not [He], but behold, He comes after me, of whom I am not worthy to loose the sandal of [His] feet. **26** Men, brothers, sons of the race of Abraham, and those among you fearing God, to you was the word of this salvation sent, **27** for those dwelling in Jerusalem, and their chiefs, having not known this One, also the voices of the Prophets, which are being read every Sabbath—having judged [Him]—fulfilled, **28** and having found no cause of death, they asked of Pilate that He should be slain, **29** and when they fulfilled all the things written about Him, having taken [Him] down from the tree, they laid Him in a tomb; **30** and God raised Him out of the dead, **31** and He was seen for many days of those who came up with Him from Galilee to Jerusalem, who are His witnesses to the people. **32** And we proclaim good news to you—that the promise made to the fathers, **33** God has completed this in full to us their children, having raised up Jesus, as also in the second Psalm it has been written: You are My Son—I have begotten You today.

34 And that He raised Him up out of the dead, to no longer return to corruption, He has said this: I will give to You the holy [blessings] of David [that are] faithful; **35** for what reason He also says in another [place]: You will not give Your Holy One to see corruption; **36** for David, indeed, having served his own generation by the will of God, fell asleep, and was added to his fathers, and saw corruption, **37** but He whom God raised up, did not see corruption. **38** Let it therefore be known to you, men, brothers, that the forgiveness of sins is declared to you through this One, **39** and from all things in the Law of Moses from which you were not able to be declared righteous, everyone who is believing in this One is declared righteous; **40** see, therefore, it may not come on you that has been spoken in the Prophets: **41** See, you despisers, and wonder, and perish, because I work a work in your days, a work in which you may not believe, though anyone may declare [it] to you." **42** And having gone forth out of the synagogue of the Jews, the nations were calling on [them] that on the next Sabbath these sayings may be spoken to them, **43** and the synagogue having been dismissed, many of the Jews and of the devout proselytes followed Paul and Barnabas, who, speaking to them, were persuading them to remain in the grace of God. **44** And on the coming Sabbath, almost all the city was gathered together to hear the word of God, **45** and the Jews having seen the multitudes, were filled with zeal, and contradicted the things spoken by Paul—contradicting and slandering. **46** And speaking boldly, Paul and Barnabas said, "It was necessary that the word of God be first spoken to you, and seeing you thrust it away, and do not judge yourselves worthy of the continuous life, behold, we turn to the nations; **47** for so the LORD has commanded us: I have set you for a light of nations—for your being for salvation to the end of the earth." **48** And the nations hearing were glad, and were glorifying the word of the LORD, and believed—as many as were appointed to continuous life; **49** and the word of the LORD was spread abroad through all the region. **50** And the Jews stirred up the devout and honorable women, and the first men of the city, and raised persecution against Paul and Barnabas, and put them out from their borders; **51** and having shaken off the dust of their feet against them, they came to Iconium, **52** and the disciples were filled with joy and the Holy Spirit.

14 And it came to pass in Iconium, that they entered together into the synagogue of the Jews, and spoke, so that there believed a great multitude of both Jews and Greeks; **2** and the unbelieving Jews stirred up and made the souls of the nations evil against the brothers; **3** [for a] long time, indeed, therefore, they abided speaking boldly in the LORD, who is testifying to the word of His grace, and granting signs and wonders to come to pass through their hands. **4** And the multitude of the city was divided, and some were with the Jews, and some with the apostles, **5** and when there was a purpose both of the nations and of the Jews with their rulers to mistreat [them], and to stone them, **6** they having become aware, fled to the cities of Lycaonia, Lystra, and Derbe, and the surrounding region, **7** and there they were proclaiming good news. **8** And a certain man in Lystra, impotent in the feet, was sitting, being lame from the womb of his mother—who never had walked; **9** this one was hearing Paul speaking, who, having steadfastly beheld him, and having seen that he has faith to be saved, **10** said with a loud voice, "Stand up on your feet upright"; and he was springing and walking, **11** and the multitudes having seen what Paul did, lifted up their voice in the speech of Lycaonia, saying, "The gods, having become like men, came down to us"; **12** they were also calling Barnabas Zeus, and Paul Hermes, since he was the leader in speaking. **13** And the priest of the Zeus that is before their city, having brought oxen and garlands to the porches, wished to sacrifice with the multitudes, **14** and having heard, the apostles Barnabas and Paul, having torn their garments, sprung into the multitude, crying **15** and saying, "Men, why do you do these things? And we are similar-feeling men with you, proclaiming good news to you, to turn to the living God from these vanities, who made the heaven, and the earth, and the sea, and all the things in them; **16** who in the past generations permitted all the nations to go on in their ways, **17** though, indeed, He did not leave Himself without witness, doing good—giving rains to us from Heaven, and fruitful seasons, filling our hearts with food and gladness"; **18** and saying these things, they scarcely restrained the multitudes from sacrificing to them. **19** And there came there, from Antioch and Iconium, Jews, and they having persuaded the multitudes, and having stoned Paul, drew him outside of the city, having supposed him to be dead; **20** and the disciples having surrounded him, having risen he entered into the city, and on the next day he went forth with Barnabas to Derbe. **21** Having also proclaimed good news to that city, and having discipled many, they turned back to Lystra, and Iconium, and Antioch, **22** confirming the souls of the disciples, exhorting to remain in the faith, and that it is required of us to enter into the Kingdom of God through many tribulations, **23** and having appointed to them elders in every assembly by vote, having prayed with fastings, they commended them to the LORD in whom they had believed. **24** And having passed through Pisidia, they came to Pamphylia, **25** and having spoken the word in Perga, they went down to Attalia, **26** and [from] there sailed to Antioch, from where they had been given by the grace of God for the work that they fulfilled; **27** and having come and gathered the assembly together, they declared as many things as God did with them, and that He opened a door of faith to the nations; **28** and they abided there with the disciples [for] not a short time.

15 And certain having come down from Judea, were teaching the brothers, "If you are not circumcised after the custom of Moses, you are not able to be saved"; **2** there having been, therefore, not a little dissension and debate to Paul and Barnabas with them, they arranged for Paul and Barnabas, and certain others of them, to go up to the apostles and elders to Jerusalem about this question; **3** they indeed, then, having been sent forward by the assembly, were passing through Phoenicia and Samaria, declaring the conversion of the nations, and they were causing great joy to all the brothers. **4** And having come to Jerusalem, they were received by the assembly, and the apostles, and the elders; they also declared as many things as God did with them; **5** and there rose up certain of those of the sect of the Pharisees who believed, saying, "It is required to circumcise them, to command them also to keep the Law of Moses." 6 And there were gathered together the apostles and the elders, to see about this matter, 7 and there having been much disputing, Peter having risen up said to them, "Men, brothers, you know that from former days God made choice among us, through my mouth, for the nations to hear the word of the good news, and to believe; 8 and the heart-knowing God bore them testimony, having given to them the Holy Spirit, even as also to us, 9 and also put no difference between us and them, having purified their hearts by faith; 10 now, therefore, why do you tempt God, to put a yoke on the neck of the disciples, which neither our fathers nor we were able to bear? 11 But through the grace of the Lord Jesus Christ, we believe to be saved, even as also they." 12 And all the multitude kept silence and were listening to Barnabas and Paul expounding as many signs and wonders as God did among the nations through them; 13 and after they were silent, James answered, saying, "Men, brothers, listen to me: 14 Simeon expounded how at first God looked on [us] to take a people out of [the] nations for His Name, 15 and to this the words of the Prophets agree, as it has been written: 16 After these things I will return, ‖ And I will rebuild the dwelling place of David that has fallen down, ‖ And I will rebuild its ruins, ‖ And I will set it upright— 17 That the remnant of men may seek after the LORD, ‖ And all the nations on whom My Name has been called, ‖ Says the LORD, who is doing all these things. 18 Known from the ages to God are all His works. 19 For this reason I judge: not to trouble those who turn back to God from the nations, 20 but to write to them to abstain from the defilements of the idols, and the whoredom, and the strangled thing, and the blood; 21 for Moses has those preaching him from former generations in every city—being read every Sabbath in the synagogues." 22 Then it seemed good to the apostles and the elders, with the whole assembly, to send to Antioch with Paul and Barnabas chosen men out of themselves—Judas surnamed Barsabas, and Silas, leading men among the brothers— 23 having written through their hand thus: "The apostles, and the elders, and the brothers, to those in Antioch, and Syria, and Cilicia, brothers, who [are] of the nations, greeting; 24 seeing we have heard that some having gone forth from us troubled you with words, subverting your souls, saying to be circumcised and to keep the Law, to whom we gave no charge, 25 it seemed good to us, having come together with one accord, to send to you chosen men, with our beloved Barnabas and Paul— 26 men who have given up their lives for the Name of our Lord Jesus Christ— 27 we have sent, therefore, Judas and Silas, and they are telling the same things by word. 28 For it seemed good to the Holy Spirit, and to us, to lay no more burden on you, except these necessary things: 29 to abstain from things offered to idols, and blood, and a strangled thing, and whoredom; keeping yourselves from which, you will do well; be strong!" 30 They then, indeed, having been let go, went to Antioch, and having brought the multitude together, delivered the letter, 31 and having read [it] they rejoiced for the consolation; 32 Judas also and Silas, also being prophets themselves, through much discourse exhorted the brothers, and confirmed, 33 and having passed some time, they were let go with peace from the brothers to the apostles; 34 [[and it seemed good to Silas to remain there still.]] 35 And Paul and Barnabas continued in Antioch, teaching and proclaiming good news— with many others also—the word of the LORD; 36 and after certain days, Paul said to Barnabas, "Having turned back again, we may look after our brothers, in every city in which we have preached the word of the LORD—how they are." 37 And Barnabas resolved to take with [them] John called Mark, 38 and Paul was not thinking it good to take him with them who withdrew from them from Pamphylia, and did not go with them to the work; 39 there came, therefore, a sharp contention, so that they were parted from one another, and Barnabas having taken Mark, sailed to Cyprus, 40 and Paul having chosen Silas, went forth, having been given up to the grace of God by the brothers; 41 and he went through Syria and Cilicia, confirming the assemblies.

16 And he came to Derbe and Lystra, and behold, a certain disciple was there, by name Timotheus, son of a certain woman, a believing Jewess, but of a father, a Greek, **2** who was well testified to by the brothers in Lystra and Iconium; **3** Paul wished this one to go forth with him, and having taken [him], he circumcised him, because of the Jews who are in those places, for they all knew his father—that he was a Greek. **4** And as they were going on through the cities, they were delivering to them the decrees to keep, that have been judged by the apostles and the elders who [are] in Jerusalem, **5** then, indeed, were the assemblies established in the faith, and were abounding in number every day; **6** and having gone through Phrygia and the region of Galatia, having been forbidden by the Holy Spirit to speak the word in Asia, **7** having gone toward Mysia, they were trying to go on toward Bithynia, and the Spirit did not permit them, **8** and having passed by Mysia, they came down to Troas. **9** And a vision through the night appeared to Paul—a certain man of Macedonia was standing, calling on him, and saying, "Having passed through to Macedonia, help us." **10** And when he saw the vision, immediately we endeavored to go forth to Macedonia, assuredly gathering that the LORD has called us to preach good news to them, **11** having set sail, therefore, from Troas, we came with a straight course to Samothracia, on the next day also to Neapolis, **12** there also to Philippi, which is a principal city of the part of Macedonia—a colony. And we were abiding in this city some days; **13** on the day of the Sabbaths we also went forth outside of the city, by a river, where there used to be prayer, and having sat down, we were speaking to the women who came together, **14** and a certain woman, by name Lydia, a seller of purple, of the city of Thyatira, worshiping God, was hearing, whose heart the LORD opened to attend to the things spoken by Paul; **15** and when she was immersed, and her household, she called on us, saying, "If you have judged me to be faithful to the LORD, having entered into my house, remain"; and she constrained us. **16** And it came to pass in our going on to prayer, a certain maid, having a spirit of Python, met us, who brought much employment to her masters by soothsaying; **17** she having followed Paul and us, was crying, saying, "These men are servants of the Most High God, who declare to us [the] way of salvation!" **18** And this she was doing for many days, but Paul having been grieved, and having turned, said to the spirit, "I command you, in the Name of Jesus Christ, to come forth from her"; and it came forth the same hour. **19** And her masters having seen that the hope of their employment was gone, having caught Paul and Silas, drew [them] into the marketplace, to the rulers, **20** and having brought them to the magistrates, they said, "These men being Jews exceedingly trouble our city; **21** and they proclaim customs that are not lawful for us to receive nor to do, being Romans." **22** And the multitude rose up together against them, and the magistrates having torn their garments from them, were commanding to beat [them] with rods, **23** having also laid on them many blows, they cast them into prison, having given charge to the jailor to keep them safely, **24** who having received such a charge, put them into the inner prison, and fastened their feet in the stocks. **25** And at midnight Paul and Silas praying, were singing hymns to God, and the prisoners were hearing them, **26** and suddenly a great earthquake came, so that the foundations of the prison were shaken, also all the doors were immediately opened, and of all—the bands were loosed; **27** and the jailor having come out of sleep, and having seen the doors of the prison open, having drawn a sword, was about to kill himself, supposing the prisoners to have fled, **28** and Paul cried out with a loud voice, saying, "You may not do yourself any harm, for we are all here!" **29** And having asked for a light, he sprang in, and he fell down before Paul and Silas trembling, **30** and having brought them forth, said, "Lords, what must I do that I may be saved?" **31** And they said, "Believe on the Lord Jesus Christ, and you will be saved—you and your household." **32** And they spoke to him the word of the LORD, and to all those in his household; **33** and having taken them, in that hour of the night, he bathed [them] from the blows, and immediately he and all of his were immersed, **34** having also brought them into his house, he set food before [them], and was glad with all the household, he having believed in God. **35** And day having come, the magistrates sent the rod-bearers, saying, "Let those men go"; **36** and the jailor told these words to Paul, "The magistrates have sent, that you may be let go; now, therefore, having gone forth go on in peace"; **37** and Paul said to them,

"Having beaten us publicly uncondemned—men, being Romans—they cast [us] to prison, and now privately they cast us forth! Why no! But having come themselves, let them bring us forth." **38** And the rod-bearers told these sayings to the magistrates, and they were afraid, having heard that they are Romans, **39** and having come, they implored them, and having brought [them] forth, they were asking [them] to go forth from the city; **40** and they, having gone forth out of the prison, entered into [the house of] Lydia, and having seen the brothers, they comforted them, and went forth.

17 And having passed through Amphipolis, and Apollonia, they came to Thessalonica, where the synagogue of the Jews was, **2** and according to the custom of Paul, he went in to them, and for three Sabbaths he was reasoning with them from the Writings, **3** opening and alleging that it was necessary [for] the Christ to suffer, and to rise again out of the dead, and that "this is the Christ—Jesus whom I proclaim to you." **4** And certain of them believed, and attached themselves to Paul and to Silas, also a great multitude of the worshiping Greeks, also not a few of the principal women. **5** And the Jews, having been moved with envy, and having taken to themselves certain evil men of the agitators, and having made a crowd, were setting the city in an uproar; having also assailed the house of Jason, they were seeking them to bring [them] to the populace, **6** and having not found them, they drew Jason and certain brothers to the city rulers, calling aloud, "These, having put the world in commotion, are also present here, **7** whom Jason has received; and all these do contrary to the decrees of Caesar, saying another to be king—Jesus." **8** And they troubled the multitude and the city rulers, hearing these things, **9** and having taken security from Jason and the rest, they let them go. **10** And the brothers immediately, through the night, sent forth both Paul and Silas to Berea, who having come, went into the synagogue of the Jews; **11** and these were more noble than those in Thessalonica; they received the word with all readiness of mind, examining the Writings every day [to see] whether those things were so; **12** therefore, many of them, indeed, believed, and not a few of the honorable Greek women and men. **13** And when the Jews from Thessalonica knew that also in Berea was the word of God declared by Paul, they came there also, agitating the multitudes; **14** and then immediately the brothers sent forth Paul, to go on as it were to the sea, but both Silas and Timotheus were remaining there. **15** And those conducting Paul, brought him to Athens, and having received a command to Silas and Timotheus that with all speed they may come to him, they departed; **16** and Paul waiting for them in Athens, his spirit was stirred in him, beholding the city wholly given to idolatry, **17** therefore, indeed, he was reasoning in the synagogue with the Jews, and with the worshiping persons, and in the marketplace every day with those who met with him. **18** And certain of the Epicurean and of the Stoic philosophers, were meeting together to see him, and some were saying, "What would this seed picker wish to say?" And others, "He seems to be an announcer of strange demons"; because he proclaimed to them Jesus and the resurrection as good news, **19** having also taken him, they brought [him] to the Areopagus, saying, "Are we able to know what this new teaching [is] that is spoken by you, **20** for you bring certain strange things to our ears? We resolve, then, to know what these things would wish to be"; **21** and all Athenians, and the strangers sojourning, for nothing else were at leisure but to say something, and to hear some newer thing. **22** And Paul, having stood in the midst of the Areopagus, said, "Men, Athenians, in all things I perceive you as over-religious; **23** for passing through and contemplating your objects of worship, I also found an altar on which had been inscribed: To God—unknown; whom, therefore—not knowing—you worship, this One I announce to you. **24** God, who made the world, and all things in it, this One, being Lord of Heaven and of earth, does not dwell in temples made with hands, **25** neither is He served by the hands of men—needing anything, He giving life to all, and breath, and all things; **26** He also made every nation of man of one blood, to dwell on all the face of the earth—having ordained times before appointed, and the bounds of their dwellings— **27** to seek the LORD, if perhaps they felt after Him and found, though, indeed, He is not far from each one of us, **28** for in Him we live, and move, and are; as certain of your poets have also said: For we are also His offspring. **29** Being, therefore, offspring of God, we ought not to think the Godhead to be like to gold, or silver, or stone, [an] engraving of art and imagination of man; **30** therefore indeed God, having overlooked the times of ignorance, now commands all men everywhere to convert, **31** because He set a day in which He is about to judge the world in righteousness, by a Man whom He ordained, having given assurance to all, having raised Him out of the dead." **32** And having heard of a resurrection of the dead, some, indeed, were mocking, but others said, "We will hear you again concerning this"; **33** and so Paul went forth from the midst of them, **34** and certain men having cleaved to him, believed, among whom [is] also Dionysius the Areopagite, and a woman, by name Damaris, and others with them.

18 And after these things, Paul having departed out of Athens, came to Corinth, **2** and having found a certain Jew, by name Aquilas, of Pontus by birth, lately come from Italy, and his wife Priscilla—because of Claudius having directed all the Jews to depart out of Rome—he came to them, **3** and because of being of the same craft, he remained with them, and was working, for they were tentmakers as to craft; **4** and he was reasoning in the synagogue every Sabbath, persuading both Jews and Greeks. **5** And when both Silas and Timotheus came down from Macedonia, Paul was pressed in the Spirit, testifying fully to the Jews Jesus the Christ; **6** and on their resisting and slandering, having shaken [his] garments, he said to them, "Your blood [is] on your head—I am clean; from now on I will go on to the nations." **7** And having departed from there, he went to the house of a certain one, by name Justus, a worshiper of God, whose house was adjoining the synagogue, **8** and Crispus, the ruler of the synagogue believed in the LORD with all his house, and many of the Corinthians hearing were believing, and they were being immersed. **9** And the LORD said through a vision in the night to Paul, "Do not be afraid, but be speaking and you may not be silent; **10** because I am with you, and no one will set on you to do evil [to] you, because I have many people in this city"; **11** and he continued a year and six months, teaching the word of God among them. **12** And Gallio being proconsul of Achaia, the Jews made a rush with one accord on Paul, and brought him to the judgment seat, **13** saying, "This one persuades men to worship God against the Law"; **14** and Paul being about to open [his] mouth, Gallio said to the Jews, "If, indeed, then, it was anything unrighteous, or an act of wicked recklessness, O Jews, according to reason I had borne with you, **15** but if it is a question concerning words and names, and of your law, look [to it] yourselves, for I do not intend to be a judge of these things," **16** and he drives them from the judgment seat; **17** and all the Greeks having taken Sosthenes, the chief man of the synagogue, were beating [him] before the judgment seat, and Gallio was not even caring for these things. **18** And Paul having remained yet a good many days, having taken leave of the brothers, was sailing to Syria—and with him [are] Priscilla and Aquilas—having shorn [his] head in Cenchera, for he had a vow; **19** and he came down to Ephesus, and left them there, and he himself having entered into the synagogue reasoned with the Jews: **20** and they having requested [him] to remain a longer time with them, he did not consent, **21** but took leave of them, saying, "It is necessary for me by all means to keep the coming celebration at Jerusalem, and again I will return to you—God willing." And he sailed from Ephesus, **22** and having come down to Caesarea, having gone up, and having greeted the assembly, he went down to Antioch. **23** And having stayed some time, he went forth, going successively through the region of Galatia and Phrygia, strengthening all the disciples. **24** And a certain Jew, Apollos by name, an Alexandrian by birth, a man of eloquence, being mighty in the Writings, came to Ephesus; **25** this one was instructed in the way of the LORD, and being fervent in the Spirit, was speaking and teaching exactly the things about the LORD, knowing only the immersion of John; **26** this one also began to speak boldly in the synagogue, and Aquilas and Priscilla having heard of him, took him to [them], and more exactly set forth to him The Way of God, **27** and he resolving to go through into Achaia, the brothers wrote to the disciples, having exhorted them to receive him, who having come, helped them much who have believed through grace, **28** for he was powerfully refuting the Jews publicly, showing through the Writings Jesus to be the Christ.

19 And it came to pass, in Apollos being in Corinth, Paul having gone through the upper parts, came to Ephesus, and having found certain disciples, **2** he said to them, "Having believed, did you receive the Holy Spirit?" And they said to him, "But we did not even hear whether there is any Holy Spirit"; **3** and he said to them, "Into what, then, were you immersed?" And they said, "Into John's immersion." **4** And Paul said, "John, indeed, immersed with an immersion of conversion, saying to the people that they should believe in Him who is coming after him—that is, in the Christ—Jesus"; **5** and they, having heard, were immersed into the Name of the Lord Jesus, **6** and Paul having laid [his] hands on them, the Holy Spirit came on them, they were also speaking with tongues, and prophesying, **7** and all the men were, as it were, twelve. **8** And having gone into the synagogue, he was speaking boldly for three months, reasoning and persuading the things concerning the Kingdom of God, **9** and when certain were hardened and were disbelieving, speaking evil of The Way before the multitude, having departed from them, he separated the disciples, reasoning every day in the school of a certain Tyrannus. **10** And this happened for two years so that all those dwelling in Asia heard the word of the Lord Jesus, both Jews and Greeks, **11** also mighty works—not common—God was working through the hands of Paul, **12** so that even to the ailing were brought from his body handkerchiefs or aprons, and the diseases departed from them; the evil spirits also went forth from them. **13** And certain of the wandering exorcist Jews, took on [them] to name over those having the evil spirits the Name of the Lord Jesus, saying, "We adjure you by Jesus, whom Paul preaches"; **14** and there were certain—seven sons of Sceva, a Jew, a chief priest—who are doing this thing; **15** and the evil spirit, answering, said, "I know Jesus, and I am acquainted with Paul; and you—who are you?" **16** And the man, in whom was the evil spirit, leaping on them, and having overcome them, prevailed against them, so that they fled naked and wounded out of that house, **17** and this became known to all, both Jews and Greeks, who are dwelling at Ephesus, and fear fell on them all, and the Name of the Lord Jesus was being magnified; **18** many also of those who believed were coming, confessing and declaring their acts, **19** and many of those who had practiced the superfluous arts, having brought the scrolls together, were burning [them] before all; and they reckoned together the prices of them, and found [it] fifty thousand pieces of silver, **20** so powerfully was the word of God increasing and prevailing. **21** And when these things were fulfilled, Paul purposed in the Spirit, having gone through Macedonia and Achaia, to go on to Jerusalem, saying, "After my being there, it is also necessary for me to see Rome"; **22** and having sent to Macedonia two of those ministering to him—Timotheus and Erastus—he himself stayed a time in Asia. **23** And there came, at that time, not a little stir about The Way, **24** for a certain one, Demetrius by name, a worker in silver, making silver sanctuaries of Artemis, was bringing to the craftsmen not a little gain, **25** whom, having brought in a crowd together, and those who worked around such things, he said, "Men, you know that by this work we have our wealth; **26** and you see and hear, that not only at Ephesus, but almost in all Asia, this Paul, having persuaded, turned away a great multitude, saying that they who are made by hands are not gods; **27** and not only is this department in danger for us of coming into disregard, but also, that of the great goddess Artemis, the temple is to be reckoned for nothing, and also her greatness is about to be brought down, whom all Asia and the world worships." **28** And having heard, and having become full of wrath, they were crying out, saying, "Great [is] the Artemis of the Ephesians!" **29** And the whole city was filled with confusion; they rushed also with one accord into the theater, having caught Gaius and Aristarchus, Macedonians, Paul's fellow-travelers. **30** And on Paul's resolving to enter in to the populace, the disciples were not permitting him, **31** and also some of the chief men of Asia, being his friends, having sent to him, were pleading [with] him not to venture into the theater himself. **32** Some indeed, therefore, were calling out one thing, and some another, for the assembly was confused, and the greater part did not know for what they had come together; **33** and out of the multitude they put forward Alexander—the Jews thrusting him forward—and Alexander having beckoned with the hand, wished to make defense to the populace, **34** and having known that he is a Jew, one voice came out of all, for about two hours, crying, "Great [is] the Artemis of the Ephesians!" **35** And the public clerk having quieted the multitude, says, "Men, Ephesians, why, who is the man that does not know that the city of the Ephesians is temple-keeper of the great goddess Artemis, and of that which fell down from Zeus? **36** These things, then, being undeniable, it is necessary for you to be quiet, and to do nothing rashly. **37** For you brought these men, who are neither temple-robbers nor slandering of your goddess; **38** if indeed, therefore, Demetrius and the craftsmen with him have a matter with anyone, court [days] are held, and there are proconsuls; let them accuse one another. **39** And if you seek after anything concerning other matters, it will be determined in the legal assembly; **40** for we are also in peril of being accused of insurrection in regard to this day, there being no occasion by which we will be able to give an account of this concourse"; **41** and having said these things, he dismissed the assembly.

20 And after the ceasing of the tumult, Paul having called near the disciples, and having embraced [them], went forth to go on to Macedonia; **2** and having gone through those parts, and having exhorted them with many words, he came to Greece; **3** and having continued three months—a counsel of the Jews having been against him—being about to set forth to Syria, there came [to him] a resolution of returning through Macedonia. **4** And there were accompanying him to Asia, Sopater of Pyrrhus from Berea, and of Thessalonians Aristarchus and Secundus, and Gaius of Derbe, and Timotheus, and of Asians Tychicus and Trophimus; **5** these, having gone before, remained for us in Troas, **6** and we sailed, after the days of the Unleavened [Bread], from Philippi, and came to them to Troas in five days, where we abided seven days. **7** And on the first [day] of the weeks, the disciples having been gathered together to break bread, Paul was discoursing to them, about to depart on the next day, he was also continuing the discourse until midnight, **8** and there were many lamps in the upper chamber where they were gathered together, **9** and there a certain youth was sitting, by name Eutychus, on the window—being borne down by a deep sleep, Paul discoursing long—he having sunk down from the sleep, fell down from the third story, and was lifted up dead. **10** And Paul, having gone down, fell on him, and having embraced [him], said, "Make no tumult, for his life is in him"; **11** and having come up, and having broken bread, and having tasted, for a long time also having talked—until daylight, so he went forth, **12** and they brought up the boy alive, and were comforted in no ordinary measure. **13** And we having gone before to the ship, sailed to Assos, there intending to take in Paul, for so he had arranged, intending himself to go on foot; **14** and when he met with us at Assos, having taken him up, we came to Mitylene, **15** and there having sailed, on the next day we came opposite Chios, and the next day we arrived at Samos, and having remained in Trogyllium, on the following day we came to Miletus, **16** for Paul decided to sail past Ephesus, that there may not be to him a loss of time in Asia, for he was hurrying, if it were possible for him, to be at Jerusalem on the day of the Pentecost. **17** And from Miletus, having sent to Ephesus, he called for the elders of the assembly, **18** and when they were come to him, he said to them, "You know from the first day in which I came to Asia, how I was with you at all times; **19** serving the LORD with all humility, and many tears, and temptations, that befell me in the counsels of the Jews against [me]; **20** how I kept back nothing of what things are profitable, not to declare to you, and to teach you publicly, and in every house, **21** testifying fully both to Jews and Greeks, conversion toward God, and faith toward our Lord Jesus Christ. **22** And now, behold, I—bound in the Spirit—go on to Jerusalem, not knowing the things that will befall me in it, **23** except that the Holy Spirit fully testifies in every city, saying that bonds and tribulations remain for me; **24** but I make account of none of these, neither do I count my life precious to myself, so that I finish my course with joy, and the ministry that I received from the Lord Jesus, to fully testify [to] the good news of the grace of God. **25** And now, behold, I have known that you will no longer see my face, among all you [to] whom I went preaching the Kingdom of God; **26** for this reason I take you to witness this day, that I [am] clear from the blood of all, **27** for I did not keep back from declaring to you all the counsel of God. **28** Take heed, therefore, to yourselves, and to all the flock, among which the Holy Spirit made you overseers, to feed the Assembly of God that He acquired through His own blood, **29** for I have known this, that there will enter in, after my departing, grievous wolves to you, not sparing the flock, **30** and there will arise men of your own selves, speaking perverse things, to draw away the disciples after them. **31** Therefore, watch, remembering that three years, night and day, I did not cease with tears warning each one; **32** and now, I commend you, brothers, to God, and to the word of His grace, that is able to build up, and to give you an inheritance among all those sanctified. **33** I coveted the silver or gold or clothing of no one; **34** and you yourselves know that to my necessities, and to those who were with me, these hands ministered; **35** I showed you all things, that, thus laboring, it is necessary to partake with the ailing, to also be mindful of the words of the Lord Jesus, that He Himself said: It is more blessed to give than to receive." **36** And having said these things, having bowed his knees, with them all, he prayed, **37** and there came a great weeping to all, and having fallen on the neck of Paul, they were kissing him, **38** sorrowing most of all for the word that he had said—that they are about to see his face no longer; and they were accompanying him to the ship.

21 And it came to pass, at our sailing, having been parted from them, having run direct, we came to Coos, and the succeeding [day] to Rhodes, and there to Patara, **2** and having found a ship passing over to Phoenicia, having gone on board, we sailed, **3** and having discovered Cyprus, and having left it on the left, we were sailing to Syria, and landed at Tyre, for there was the ship discharging the cargo. **4** And having found out the disciples, we tarried there seven days, and they said to Paul, through the Spirit, not to go up to Jerusalem; **5** but when it came that we completed the days, having gone forth, we went on, all bringing us on the way, with women and children, to the outside of the city, and having bowed the knees on the shore, we prayed, **6** and having embraced one another, we embarked in the ship, and they returned to their own friends. **7** And we, having finished the course, from Tyre came down to Ptolemais, and having greeted the brothers, we remained one day with them; **8** and on the next day Paul and his company having gone forth, we came to Caesarea, and having entered into the house of Philip the evangelist—who is of the seven—we remained with him, **9** and this one had four daughters, virgins, prophesying. **10** And we remaining many more days, there came down a certain one from Judea, a prophet, by name Agabus, **11** and he having come to us, and having taken up the girdle of Paul, having also bound his own hands and feet, said, "Thus says the Holy Spirit: The man whose is this girdle—so will the Jews in Jerusalem bind, and they will deliver [him] up into the hands of nations." **12** And when we heard these things, we called on [him]—both we, and those of that place—not to go up to Jerusalem, **13** and Paul answered, "Why are you weeping, and crushing my heart? For I am ready, not only to be bound, but also to die at Jerusalem for the Name of the Lord Jesus"; **14** and he not being persuaded, we were silent, saying, "The will of the LORD be done." **15** And after these days, having taken [our] vessels, we were going up to Jerusalem, **16** and there went also of the disciples from Caesarea with us, bringing with them him with whom we may lodge, a certain Mnason of Cyprus, an aged disciple. **17** And we having come to Jerusalem, the brothers gladly received us, **18** and on the next day Paul was going in with us to James, all the elders also came, **19** and having greeted them, he was expounding, one by one, each of the things God did among the nations through his ministry, **20** and they having heard, were glorifying the LORD. They also said to him, "You see, brother, how many myriads there are of Jews who have believed, and all are zealous of the Law, **21** and they are instructed concerning you, that you teach departure from Moses to all

Jews among the nations, saying not to circumcise the children, nor to walk after the customs; **22** what then is it? Certainly the multitude must come together, for they will hear that you have come. **23** This, therefore, that we say to you, do. We have four men having a vow on themselves, **24** having taken these, be purified with them, and be at expense with them, that they may shave the head, and all may know that the things of which they have been instructed concerning you are nothing, but you walk—yourself also—keeping the Law. **25** And concerning those of the nations who have believed, we have written, having given judgment, that they observe no such thing, except to keep themselves both from idol-sacrifices, and blood, and a strangled thing, and whoredom." **26** Then Paul, having taken the men, on the following day, having purified himself with them, was entering into the temple, announcing the fulfilment of the days of the purification, until the offering was offered for each one of them. **27** And as the seven days were about to be fully ended, the Jews from Asia having beheld him in the temple, were stirring up all the multitude, and they laid hands on him, **28** crying out, "Men, Israelites! help! This is the man who, against the people, and the Law, and this place, is teaching all everywhere; and further, also, he brought Greeks into the temple, and has defiled this holy place"; **29** for they had seen before Trophimus, the Ephesian, in the city with him, whom they were supposing that Paul brought into the temple. **30** All the city was also moved and there was a running together of the people, and having laid hold on Paul, they were drawing him out of the temple, and immediately were the doors shut, **31** and they seeking to kill him, a rumor came to the chief captain of the band that all Jerusalem has been thrown into confusion, **32** who, at once, having taken soldiers and centurions, ran down on them, and they having seen the chief captain and the soldiers, left off beating Paul. **33** Then the chief captain, having come near, took him, and commanded [him] to be bound with two chains, and was inquiring who he may be, and what it is he has been doing, **34** and some were crying out one thing, and some another, among the multitude, and not being able to know the certainty because of the tumult, he commanded him to be carried into the stronghold, **35** and when he came on the steps, it happened he was carried by the soldiers, because of the violence of the multitude, **36** for the crowd of the people was following after, crying, "Away with him." **37** And Paul being about to be led into the stronghold, says to the chief captain, "Is it permitted to me to say anything to you?" And he said, "Do you know Greek? **38** Are you not, then, the Egyptian who made an uprising before these days, and led the four thousand men of the assassins into the desert?" **39** And Paul said, "I, indeed, am a man, a Jew, of Tarsus of Cilicia, a citizen of no insignificant city; and I implore you, permit me to speak to the people." **40** And he having given him leave, Paul having stood on the stairs, beckoned with the hand to the people, and there having been a great silence, he spoke to them in the Hebrew dialect, saying:

22 "Men, brothers, and fathers, hear my defense now to you." **2** and they having heard that he was speaking to them in the Hebrew dialect, they became even more silent, and he says, **3** "I, indeed, am a man, a Jew, having been born in Tarsus of Cilicia, and brought up in this city at the feet of Gamaliel, having been taught according to the exactness of a law of the fathers, being zealous of God, as all you are today. **4** And this Way I persecuted to death, binding and delivering up to prisons both men and women, **5** as also the chief priest testifies to me, and all the eldership; from whom also having received letters to the brothers, to Damascus, I was going on, to bring also those there bound to Jerusalem that they might be punished, **6** and it came to pass, in my going on and coming near to Damascus, about noon, suddenly out of Heaven there shone a great light around me; **7** I also fell to the ground, and I heard a voice saying to me, Saul, Saul, why do you persecute Me? **8** And I answered, Who are You, Lord? And He said to me, I am Jesus the Nazarene whom you persecute— **9** and they who are with me saw the light, and became afraid, and they did not hear the voice of Him who is speaking to me— **10** and I said, What will I do, Lord? And the LORD said to me, Having risen, go on to Damascus, and there it will be told you concerning all things that have been appointed for you to do. **11** And when

I did not see from the glory of that light, being led by the hand by those who are with me, I came to Damascus, **12** and a certain one, Ananias, a pious man according to the Law, being testified to by all the Jews dwelling [there], **13** having come to me and stood by [me], said to me, Saul, brother, look up; and the same hour I looked up to him; **14** and he said, The God of our fathers chose you beforehand to know His will, and to see the Righteous One, and to hear a voice out of His mouth, **15** because you will be His witness to all men of what you have seen and heard; **16** and now, why do you linger? Having risen, immerse yourself, and wash away your sins, calling on the Name of the LORD. **17** And it came to pass, when I returned to Jerusalem, and while I was praying in the temple, I came into a trance, **18** and I saw Him saying to me, Hurry and go forth in haste out of Jerusalem, because they will not receive your testimony concerning Me; **19** and I said, LORD, they know that I was imprisoning and was scourging those believing on You in every synagogue; **20** and when the blood of your witness Stephen was being poured forth, I was also standing by and assenting to his death, and keeping the garments of those putting him to death; **21** and He said to me, Go, because I will send you to far-off nations." **22** And they were hearing him to this word, and they lifted up their voice, saying, "Away from the earth with such a one; for it is not fit for him to live." **23** And they crying out and casting up their garments, and throwing dust into the air, **24** the chief captain commanded him to be brought into the stronghold, saying, "Let him be examined by scourges," that he might know for what cause they were crying so against him. **25** And as he was stretching him with the straps, Paul said to the centurion who was standing by, "Is it lawful to you to scourge a man, a Roman, uncondemned?" **26** And the centurion having heard, having gone near to the chief captain, told, saying, "Take heed what you are about to do, for this man is a Roman"; **27** and the chief captain having come near, said to him, "Tell me, are you a Roman?" And he said, "Yes"; **28** and the chief captain answered, "I, with a great sum, obtained this citizenship"; but Paul said, "But I have even been born [so]." **29** Immediately, therefore, they departed from him, those being about to examine him, and the chief captain was also afraid, having learned that he is a Roman, and because he had bound him, **30** and the next day, intending to know the certainty for what reason he is accused by the Jews, he loosed him from the bonds, and commanded the chief priests and all their Sanhedrin to come, and having brought down Paul, he set [him] before them.

23 And Paul having earnestly beheld the Sanhedrin, said, "Men, brothers, I have lived to God in all good conscience to this day"; **2** and the chief priest Ananias commanded those standing by him to strike him on the mouth, **3** then Paul said to him, "God is about to strike you, you whitewashed wall, and you sit judging me according to the Law, and violating law, order me to be struck!" **4** And those who stood by said, "Do you revile the chief priest of God?" **5** And Paul said, "I did not know, brothers, that he is chief priest, for it has been written: You will not speak evil of the ruler of your people"; **6** and Paul having known that one part are Sadducees, and the other Pharisees, cried out in the Sanhedrin, "Men, brothers, I am a Pharisee—son of a Pharisee—concerning [the] hope and resurrection of [the] dead I am judged." **7** And he having spoken this, there came a dissension of the Pharisees and of the Sadducees, and the crowd was divided, **8** for Sadducees, indeed, say there is no resurrection, nor messenger, nor spirit, but Pharisees confess both. **9** And there came a great cry, and the scribes of the Pharisees' part having arisen, were striving, saying, "We find no evil in this man; and if a spirit spoke to him, or a messenger, we may not fight against God"; **10** and a great dissension having come, the chief captain having been afraid lest Paul may be pulled to pieces by them, commanded the army, having gone down, to seize him out of their midst, and to bring [him] into the stronghold. **11** And on the following night, the LORD having stood by him, said, "Take courage, Paul, for as you fully testified [to] the things concerning Me at Jerusalem, so you must also testify at Rome." **12** And day having come, certain of the Jews having made a concourse, cursed themselves, saying neither to eat nor to drink until they may kill Paul; **13** and they were more than forty who made this conspiracy by oath, **14** who having come near to the chief priests and to the elders said, "With a curse we accursed ourselves—to taste nothing until we have killed Paul; **15** now, therefore, you, signify to the chief captain, with the Sanhedrin, that tomorrow he may bring him down to you, as being about to know more exactly the things concerning him; and we, before his coming near, are ready to put him to death." **16** And the son of Paul's sister having heard of the lying in wait, having gone and entered into the stronghold, told Paul, **17** and Paul having called near one of the centurions, said, "Lead this young man to the chief captain, for he has something to tell him." **18** He indeed, then, having taken him, brought him to the chief captain and says, "The prisoner Paul, having called me near, asked [me] to bring to you this young man, having something to say to you." **19** And the chief captain having taken him by the hand, and having withdrawn by themselves, inquired, "What is that which you have to tell me?" **20** And he said, "The Jews agreed to request you, that tomorrow you may bring down Paul to the Sanhedrin, as being about to inquire something more exactly concerning him; **21** you, therefore, may you not yield to them, for there more than forty men of them lie in wait for him, who cursed themselves—not to eat nor to drink until they kill him, and now they are ready, waiting for the promise from you." **22** The chief captain, then, indeed, let the young man go, having charged [him], "Tell no one that you have shown these things to me"; **23** and having called a certain two of the centurions near, he said, "Make ready two hundred soldiers, that they may go on to Caesarea, and seventy horsemen, and two hundred spearmen, from the third hour of the night; **24** also provide beasts, that, having set Paul on, they may bring him safe to Felix the governor"; **25** he having written a letter after this description: **26** "Claudius Lysias, to the most noble governor Felix, greetings: **27** This man having been taken by the Jews, and being about to be killed by them—having come with the army, I rescued him, having learned that he is a Roman; **28** and intending to know the cause for which they were accusing him, I brought him down to their Sanhedrin, **29** whom I found accused concerning questions of their law, and having no accusation worthy of death or bonds; **30** and a plot having been intimated to me against this man—about to be of the Jews—I sent to you at once, having also given command to the accusers to say the things against him before you; be strong." **31** Then, indeed, the soldiers according to that directed them, having taken up Paul, brought him through the night to Antipatris, **32** and on the next day, having permitted the horsemen to go on with him, they returned to the stronghold; **33** those having entered into Caesarea, and delivered the letter to the governor, also presented Paul to him. **34** And the governor having read [it], and inquired of what province he is, and understood that [he is] from Cilicia; **35** "I will hear you," he said, "when your accusers may also have come"; he also commanded him to be kept in the Praetorium of Herod.

24 And after five days the chief priest Ananias came down, with the elders, and a certain orator—Tertullus, and they disclosed to the governor [the things] against Paul; **2** and he having been called, Tertullus began to accuse [him], saying, "Enjoying much peace through you, and worthy deeds being done to this nation through your forethought, **3** always, also, and everywhere we receive it, most noble Felix, with all thankfulness; **4** and that I may not be further tedious to you, I exhort you to hear us concisely in your gentleness; **5** for having found this man a pestilence, and moving a dissension to all the Jews through the world—also a ringleader of the sect of the Nazarenes— **6** who also tried to profane the temple, whom we also took, [[and wished to judge according to our law, **7** and Lysias the chief captain having come near, took away out of our hands with much violence, **8** having commanded his accusers to come to you,]] from whom you may be able, yourself having examined, to know concerning all these things of which we accuse him"; **9** and the Jews also agreed, professing these things to be so. **10** And Paul—the governor having beckoned to him to speak—answered, "Knowing [that] for many years you have been a judge to this nation, I answer more cheerfully the things concerning myself; **11** you being able to know that it is not more than twelve days to me since I went up to worship in Jerusalem, **12** and neither did they find me reasoning

ACTS

with anyone in the temple, or making a dissension of the multitude, nor in the synagogues, nor in the city; **13** nor are they able to prove against me the things concerning which they now accuse me. **14** And I confess this to you, that, according to The Way that they call a sect, so I serve the God of the fathers, believing all things that have been written in the Law and the Prophets, **15** having hope toward God, which they themselves also wait for, [that] there is about to be a resurrection of the dead, both of righteous and unrighteous; **16** and in this I exercise myself, to always have a conscience void of offense toward God and men. **17** And after many years I came, about to do kind acts to my nation, and offerings, **18** in which certain Jews from Asia found me purified in the temple, not with multitude, nor with tumult, **19** whom it is necessary to be present before you, and to accuse, if they had anything against me, **20** or let these same say if they found any unrighteousness in me in my standing before the Sanhedrin, **21** except concerning this one voice, in which I cried, standing among them—Concerning a resurrection of the dead I am judged by you today." **22** And having heard these things, Felix delayed them—having known more exactly of the things concerning The Way—saying, "When Lysias the chief captain may come down, I will know fully the things concerning you"; **23** having also given a direction to the centurion to keep Paul, to let [him] also have liberty, and to forbid none of his own friends to minister or to come near to him. **24** And after certain days, Felix having come with his wife Drusilla, being a Jewess, he sent for Paul, and heard him concerning faith toward Christ, **25** and he reasoning concerning righteousness, and self-control, and the judgment that is about to be, Felix, having become afraid, answered, "For the present be going, and having time, I will call for you"; **26** and at the same time also hoping that money will be given to him by Paul, that he may release him, therefore, also sending for him often, he was conversing with him; **27** and two years having been fulfilled, Felix received a successor, Porcius Festus; Felix also willing to lay a favor on the Jews, left Paul bound.

25 Festus, therefore, having come into the province, after three days went up to Jerusalem from Caesarea, **2** and the chief priest and the principal men of the Jews disclosed to him [the things] against Paul, and were calling on him, **3** asking favor against him, that he may send for him to Jerusalem, making an ambush to put him to death in the way. **4** Then, indeed, Festus answered that Paul is kept in Caesarea, and is himself about to go forth speedily, **5** "Therefore those able among you," he says, "having come down together, if there be anything in this man—let them accuse him"; **6** and having tarried among them more than ten days, having gone down to Caesarea, on the next day having sat on the judgment seat, he commanded Paul to be brought; **7** and he having come, there stood around the Jews who have come down from Jerusalem—many and weighty charges they are bringing against Paul, which they were not able to prove, **8** he making defense, [said,] "Neither in regard to the Law of the Jews, nor in regard to the temple, nor in regard to Caesar—did I commit any sin." **9** And Festus willing to lay on the Jews a favor, answering Paul, said, "Are you willing, having gone up to Jerusalem, to be judged before me there concerning these things?" **10** And Paul said, "At the judgment seat of Caesar I am standing, where it is necessary for me to be judged; I did no unrighteousness to Jews, as you also very well know; **11** for if I am indeed unrighteous, and have done anything worthy of death, I do not deprecate to die; and if there is none of the things of which these accuse me, no one is able to make a favor of me to them; I appeal to Caesar!" **12** Then Festus, having communed with the council, answered, "To Caesar you have appealed; to Caesar you will go." **13** And certain days having passed, Agrippa the king, and Bernice, came down to Caesarea greeting Festus, **14** and as they were continuing there more days, Festus submitted to the king the things concerning Paul, saying, "There is a certain man, left by Felix, a prisoner, **15** about whom, in my being at Jerusalem, the chief priests and the elders of the Jews laid information, asking a decision against him, **16** to whom I answered, that it is not a custom of Romans to make a favor of any man to die, before that he who is accused may have the accusers face to face, and may receive place of defense in regard to the charge laid against [him]. **17** They, therefore, having come together—I, making no delay, on the succeeding [day] having sat on the judgment seat, commanded the man to be brought, **18** concerning whom the accusers, having stood up, were bringing against [him] no accusation of the things I was thinking of, **19** but certain questions concerning their own religion they had against him, and concerning a certain Jesus who was dead, whom Paul affirmed to be alive; **20** and I, doubting in regard to the question concerning this, asked if he was willing to go on to Jerusalem, and to be judged there concerning these things— **21** but Paul having appealed to be kept to the hearing of Sebastus, I commanded him to be kept until I might send him to Caesar." **22** And Agrippa said to Festus, "I was also intending to hear the man myself"; and he said, "Tomorrow you will hear him"; **23** on the next day, therefore—on the coming of Agrippa and Bernice with much display, and they having entered into the audience chamber, with the chief captains also, and the principal men of the city, and Festus having ordered—Paul was brought forth. **24** And Festus said, "King Agrippa, and all men who are present with us, you see this one, about whom all the multitude of the Jews dealt with me, both in Jerusalem and here, crying out, He ought not to live any longer; **25** and I, having found him to have done nothing worthy of death, and he also himself having appealed to Sebastus, I decided to send him, **26** concerning whom I have no certain thing to write to [my] lord, for what reason I brought him forth before you, and especially before you, King Agrippa, that the examination having been made, I may have something to write; **27** for it seems to me irrational, sending a prisoner, not to also signify the charges against him."

26 And Agrippa said to Paul, "It is permitted to you to speak for yourself"; then Paul having stretched forth the hand, was making a defense: **2** "Concerning all things of which I am accused by Jews, King Agrippa, I have thought myself blessed, being about to make a defense before you today, **3** especially knowing you to be acquainted with all things—both customs and questions—among Jews; for this reason, I implore you to hear me patiently. **4** The manner of my life then, indeed, from youth—which from the beginning was among my nation, in Jerusalem—all the Jews know, **5** knowing me before from the first (if they may be willing to testify), that after the most exact sect of our worship, I lived a Pharisee; **6** and now for the hope of the promise made to the fathers by God, I have stood judged, **7** to which our twelve tribes, intently serving night and day, hope to come, concerning which hope I am accused, King Agrippa, by the Jews; **8** why is it judged incredible with you if God raises the dead? **9** I indeed, therefore, thought with myself that it was necessary [for me] to do many things against the Name of Jesus of Nazareth, **10** which I also did in Jerusalem, and I shut up many of the holy ones in prison, having received the authority from the chief priests; they also being put to death, I gave my vote against them, **11** and in every synagogue, often punishing them, I was constraining [them] to speak evil, being also exceedingly mad against them, I was also persecuting [them] even to strange cities. **12** In which things, also, going on to Damascus—with authority and commission from the chief priests— **13** at midday, I saw in the way, O king, out of Heaven, above the brightness of the sun, shining around me a light—and those going on with me; **14** and we all having fallen to the earth, I heard a voice speaking to me, and saying in the Hebrew dialect, Saul, Saul, why do you persecute Me? [It is] hard for you to kick against goads! **15** And I said, Who are You, Lord? And He said, I am Jesus whom you persecute; **16** but rise, and stand on your feet, for this I appeared to you, to appoint you an officer and a witness both of the things you saw, and of the things [in which] I will appear to you, **17** delivering you from the people, and the nations, to whom I now send you, **18** to open their eyes, to turn [them] from darkness to light, and [from] the authority of Satan to God, for their receiving forgiveness of sins, and a lot among those having been sanctified by faith that [is] toward Me. **19** After which, King Agrippa, I was not disobedient to the heavenly vision, **20** but to those in Damascus first, and to those in Jerusalem, also to all the region of Judea, and to the nations, I was preaching to convert, and to turn back to God, doing works worthy of conversion; **21** because of these things the Jews—having caught me in the temple—were endeavoring to kill [me]. **22** Having obtained, therefore, help from God, until this day, I have stood witnessing both to small and to great, saying nothing besides the things that both the prophets and Moses spoke of as about to come, **23** that the Christ is to suffer, whether first by a resurrection from the dead, He is about to proclaim light to the people and to the nations." **24** And he thus making a defense, Festus said with a loud voice, "You are mad, Paul; much learning turns you mad!" **25** And he says, "I am not mad, most noble Festus, but of truth and soberness I speak forth the sayings; **26** for the king knows concerning these things, before whom I also speak boldly, for none of these things, I am persuaded, are hidden from him; for this thing has not been done in a corner; **27** do you believe, King Agrippa, the prophets? I have known that you believe!" **28** And Agrippa said to Paul, "In [so] little you persuade me to become a Christian?" **29** And Paul said, "I would have wished to God, both in a little, and in much, not only you, but also all those hearing me today, to become such as I also am—except these bonds." **30** And he having spoken these things, the king rose up, and the governor, Bernice also, and those sitting with them, **31** and having withdrawn, they were speaking to one another, saying, "This man does nothing worthy of death or of bonds"; **32** and Agrippa said to Festus, "This man might have been released if he had not appealed to Caesar."

27 And when our sailing to Italy was determined, they were delivering up both Paul and certain others, prisoners, to a centurion, by name Julius, of the band of Sebastus, **2** and having embarked in a ship of Adramyttium, we, being about to sail by the coasts of Asia, set sail, there being with us Aristarchus, a Macedonian of Thessalonica, **3** on the next [day] also we touched at Sidon, and Julius, courteously treating Paul, permitted [him], having gone on to friends, to receive [their] care. **4** And there, having set sail, we sailed under Cyprus, because of the winds being contrary, **5** and having sailed over the sea down by Cilicia and Pamphylia, we came to Myria of Lycia, **6** and there the centurion having found a ship of Alexandria, sailing to Italy, put us into it, **7** and having sailed slowly many days, and with difficulty coming down by Cnidus, the wind not permitting us, we sailed under Crete, down by Salmone, **8** and hardly passing it, we came to a certain place called Fair Havens, near to which was the city of Lasaea. **9** And much time being spent, and the sailing now being dangerous—because of the fast also being already past—Paul was admonishing, **10** saying to them, "Men, I perceive that with hurt, and much damage, not only of the load and of the ship, but also of our lives—the voyage is about to be"; **11** but the centurion gave more credence to the pilot and to the shipowner than to the things spoken by Paul; **12** and the haven being not well placed to winter in, the greater part gave counsel to sail from there, if somehow they might be able, having attained to Phoenix, to winter [there], [which is] a haven of Crete, looking to the southwest and northwest, **13** and a south wind blowing softly, having thought they had obtained [their] purpose, having lifted anchor, they sailed close by Crete, **14** and not long after, there came down from it a turbulent wind [that] is called the Euroclydon, **15** and the ship being caught, and not being able to bear up against the wind, having given [her] up, we were carried on, **16** and having run under a certain little island called Clauda, we were hardly able to become masters of the boat, **17** which having taken up, they were using helps, undergirding the ship, and fearing lest they may fall into the [sandbars of] Syrtis, having let down the mast—so were carried on. **18** And we, being exceedingly storm-tossed, the succeeding [day] they were making a clearing, **19** and on the third [day] we cast out the tackling of the ship with our own hands, **20** and neither sun nor stars appearing for more days, and not a little storm lying on us, from then on all hope was taken away of our being saved. **21** And there having been long fasting, then Paul having stood in the midst of them, said, "It was necessary, indeed, O men—having listened to me—not to set sail from Crete, and to save this hurt and damage; **22** and now I exhort you to be of good cheer, for there will be no loss of life among you—but of the ship; **23** for this night there stood by me a messenger of God—whose I am, and whom I serve—

24 saying, Do not be afraid Paul; it is necessary for you to stand before Caesar; and behold, God has granted to you all those sailing with you; 25 for this reason be of good cheer, men! For I believe God, that so it will be, even as it has been spoken to me, 26 and on a certain island it is necessary for us to be cast." 27 And when the fourteenth night came—we being carried up and down in the Adria—toward the middle of the night the sailors were supposing that some country drew near to them; 28 and having sounded they found twenty fathoms, and having gone a little farther, and again having sounded, they found fifteen fathoms, 29 and fearing lest we may fall on rough places, having cast four anchors out of the stern, they were wishing day to come. 30 And the sailors seeking to flee out of the ship, and having let down the boat to the sea, in pretense as [if] out of the prow they are about to cast anchors, 31 Paul said to the centurion and to the soldiers, "If these do not remain in the ship—you are not able to be saved"; 32 then the soldiers cut off the ropes of the boat, and permitted it to fall off. 33 And until the day was about to be, Paul was calling on all to partake of nourishment, saying, "Fourteen days today, waiting, you continue fasting, having taken nothing, 34 for this reason I call on you to take nourishment, for this is for your safety, for of not one of you will a hair fall from the head"; 35 and having said these things, and having taken bread, he gave thanks to God before all, and having broken [it], he began to eat; 36 and all having become of good cheer, also took food themselves, 37 (and we were—all the souls in the ship—two hundred, seventy-six), 38 and having eaten sufficient nourishment, they were lightening the ship, casting forth the wheat into the sea. 39 And when the day came, they were not discerning the land, but were perceiving a certain bay having a beach, into which they took counsel, if possible, to thrust forward the ship, 40 and having taken up the anchors, they were committing [it] to the sea, at the same time—having loosed the bands of the rudders, and having hoisted up the foresail to the wind—they were making for the shore, 41 and having fallen into a place of two seas, they ran the ship aground, and the prow, indeed, having stuck fast, remained immoveable, but the stern was broken by the violence of the waves. 42 And the soldiers' counsel was that they should kill the prisoners, lest anyone having swam out should escape, 43 but the centurion, resolving to save Paul, hindered them from the counsel, and commanded those able to swim, having cast themselves out first—to get to the land, 44 and the rest, some indeed on boards, and some on certain things of the ship; and thus it came to pass that all came safe to the land.

28

And having been saved, then they knew that the island is called Malta, 2 and the foreigners were showing us no ordinary kindness, for having kindled a fire, they received us all, because of the pressing rain, and because of the cold; 3 but Paul having gathered together a quantity of sticks, and having laid [them] on the fire, a viper—having come out of the heat—fastened on his hand. 4 And when the foreigners saw the beast hanging from his hand, they said to one another, "Certainly this man is a murderer, whom, having been saved out of the sea, the justice did not permit to live"; 5 he then, indeed, having shaken off the beast into the fire, suffered no evil, 6 and they were expecting him to be about to be inflamed, or to suddenly fall down dead, and they, expecting [it] a long time, and seeing nothing uncommon happening to him, changing [their] minds, said he was a god. 7 And in the neighborhood of that place were lands of the principal man of the island, by name Publius, who, having received us, courteously lodged [us for] three days; 8 and it came to pass, the father of Publius was lying, oppressed with fevers and dysentery, to whom Paul, having entered and having prayed, having laid [his] hands on him, healed him; 9 this, therefore, being done, also the others in the island having sicknesses were coming and were healed; 10 who also honored us with many honors, and we setting sail—they were loading [us] with the things that were necessary. 11 And after three months, we set sail in a ship (that had wintered in the island) of Alexandria, with the sign Dioscuri, 12 and having landed at Syracuse, we remained three days, 13 there having gone around, we came to Rhegium, and after one day, a south wind having sprung up, the second [day] we came to Puteoli, 14 where, having found brothers, we were called on to remain with them seven days, and thus we came to Rome; **15** and there, the brothers having heard the things concerning us, came forth to meet us, as far as [the] Forum of Appius, and Three Taverns—whom Paul having seen, having given thanks to God, took courage. **16** And when we came to Rome, the centurion delivered up the prisoners to the captain of the barracks, but Paul was permitted to remain by himself, with the soldier guarding him. **17** And it came to pass after three days, Paul called together those who are the principal men of the Jews, and they having come together, he said to them: "Men, brothers, I—having done nothing contrary to the people, or to the customs of the fathers—a prisoner from Jerusalem, was delivered up into the hands of the Romans; **18** who having examined me, were willing to release [me], because of their being no cause of death in me, **19** and the Jews having spoken against [it], I was constrained to appeal to Caesar—not as having anything to accuse my nation of; **20** for this cause, therefore, I called for you to see and to speak with [you], for because of the hope of Israel I am bound with this chain." **21** And they said to him, "We neither received letters concerning you from Judea, nor did anyone who came of the brothers declare or speak any evil concerning you, **22** and we think it good from you to hear what you think, for indeed, concerning this sect it is known to us that it is spoken against everywhere"; **23** and having appointed him a day, more of them came to him, to the lodging, to whom he was setting [it] forth, testifying fully the Kingdom of God, persuading them also of the things concerning Jesus, both from the Law of Moses, and the Prophets, from morning until evening, **24** and some, indeed, were believing the things spoken, and some were not believing. **25** And not being agreed with one another, they were going away, Paul having spoken one word, "The Holy Spirit spoke well through Isaiah the prophet to our fathers, **26** saying, Go on to this people and say, With hearing you will hear, and you will not understand, and seeing you will see, and you will not perceive, **27** for the heart of this people was made obtuse, and with the ears they barely heard, and they closed their eyes, lest they may see with the eyes, and may understand with the heart, and should turn, and I may heal them. **28** Be it known, therefore, to you, that the salvation of God was sent to the nations, these also will hear it"; **29** [[and he having said these things, the Jews went away, having much debate among themselves;]] **30** and Paul remained an entire two years in his own hired [house], and was receiving all those coming in to him, **31** preaching the Kingdom of God, and teaching the things concerning the Lord Jesus Christ with all boldness—unforbidden.

ROMANS

1 Paul, a servant of Jesus Christ, a called apostle, having been separated to the good news of God, **2** which He announced before through His prophets in holy writings, **3** concerning His Son—who has come of the seed of David according to the flesh, **4** who is marked out [as the] Son of God in power, according to the Spirit of sanctification, by the resurrection from the dead—Jesus Christ our Lord; **5** through whom we received grace and apostleship, for obedience of faith among all the nations, in behalf of His Name; **6** among whom are also you, the called of Jesus Christ; **7** to all who are in Rome, beloved of God, called holy ones: Grace to you and peace from God our Father and the Lord Jesus Christ! **8** First, indeed, I thank my God through Jesus Christ for you all, that your faith is proclaimed in the whole world; **9** for God is my witness, whom I serve in my spirit in the good news of His Son, how unceasingly I make mention of you, **10** always in my prayers imploring, if by any means now at length I will have a prosperous journey, by the will of God, to come to you, **11** for I long to see you, that I may impart to you some spiritual gift, that you may be established; **12** and that is, that I may be comforted together among you, through faith in one another, both yours and mine. **13** And I do not wish you to be ignorant, brothers, that many times I purposed to come to you—and was hindered until the present time—that some fruit I might have also among you, even as also among the other nations. **14** Both to Greeks and to foreigners, both to wise and to thoughtless, I am a debtor, **15** so, as much as in me is, I am ready also to you who [are] in Rome to proclaim good news, **16** for I am not ashamed of the good news of the Christ, for it is the power of God to salvation to everyone who is believing, both to Jew first, and to Greek. **17** For the righteousness of God in it is revealed from faith to faith, according as it has been written: "And the righteous one will live by faith," **18** for the wrath of God is revealed from Heaven on all impiety and unrighteousness of men, holding down the truth in unrighteousness. **19** Because that which is known of God is revealed among them, for God revealed [it] to them, **20** for the invisible things of Him from the creation of the world, by the things made being understood, are plainly seen, both His eternal power and Godhead—to their being inexcusable; **21** because, having known God they did not glorify [Him] as God, nor gave thanks, but were made vain in their reasonings, and their unintelligent heart was darkened, **22** professing to be wise, they were made fools, **23** and changed the glory of the incorruptible God into the likeness of an image of corruptible man, and of birds, and of quadrupeds, and of reptiles. **24** For this reason also God gave them up, in the desires of their hearts, to uncleanness, to dishonor their bodies among themselves; **25** who changed the truth of God into the lie, and honored and served the creature rather than the Creator, who is blessed for all ages. Amen. **26** Because of this God gave them up to dishonorable affections, for even their females changed the natural use into that against nature; **27** and in like manner also the males having left the natural use of the female, burned in their longing toward one another; males with males working shame, and the repayment of their error that was fit, in themselves receiving. **28** And according as they did not approve of having God in knowledge, God gave them up to a disapproved mind, to do the things not seemly; **29** having been filled with all unrighteousness, whoredom, wickedness, covetousness, malice; full of envy, murder, strife, deceit, evil dispositions; whisperers, **30** evil-speakers, God-haters, insulting, proud, boasters, inventors of evil things, disobedient to parents, **31** unintelligent, faithless, without natural affection, implacable, unmerciful; **32** who the righteous judgment of God having known—that those practicing such things are worthy of death—not only do them, but also have delight with those practicing them.

2 Therefore, you are inexcusable, O man—everyone who is judging—for in that in which you judge the other, yourself you condemn, for the same things you practice who are judging, **2** and we have known that the judgment of God is according to truth, on those practicing such things. **3** And do you think this, O man, who are judging those who such things are practicing, and are doing them, that you will escape the judgment of God? **4** Or the riches of His goodness, and forbearance, and long-suffering, do you despise, not knowing that the goodness of God leads you to conversion? **5** But according to your hardness and impenitent heart, you treasure up wrath to yourself in [the] day of wrath and of the revelation of the righteous judgment of God, **6** who will render to each according to his works; **7** to those, indeed, who in continuance of a good work, seek glory, and honor, and incorruptibility—continuous life; **8** and to those contentious, and disobedient, indeed, to the truth, and obeying the unrighteousness—indignation and wrath, **9** tribulation and distress, on every soul of man that is working the evil, both of Jew first, and of Greek; **10** and glory, and honor, and peace, to everyone who is working the good, both to Jew first, and to Greek. **11** For there is no favor by appearance with God, **12** for as many as sinned without law, will also perish without law, and as many as sinned in law, through law will be judged, **13** for not the hearers of the Law [are] righteous before God, but the doers of the Law will be declared righteous. **14** For when nations that have no law, by nature may do the things of the Law, these not having a law—to themselves are a law, **15** who show the work of the Law written in their hearts, their conscience also witnessing with them, and between one another the thoughts accusing or else defending, **16** in the day when God will judge the secrets of men, according to my good news, through Jesus Christ. **17** Behold, you are named a Jew, and rest on the Law, and boast in God, **18** and know the will, and approve the distinctions, being instructed out of the Law, **19** and have confidence that you yourself are a leader of blind ones, a light of those in darkness, **20** a corrector of foolish ones, a teacher of babies, having the form of the knowledge and of the truth in the Law. **21** You, then, who are teaching another, do you not teach yourself? **22** You who are preaching not to steal, do you steal? You who are saying not to commit adultery, do you commit adultery? You who are abhorring the idols, do you rob temples? **23** You who boast in the Law, through the transgression of the Law do you dishonor God? **24** For evil is spoken of the Name of God among the nations because of you, according as it has been written. **25** For circumcision, indeed, profits, if you may practice law, but if you may be a transgressor of law, your circumcision has become uncircumcision. **26** If, therefore, the uncircumcision may keep the righteousness of the Law, will not his uncircumcision be reckoned for circumcision? **27** And the uncircumcision, by nature, fulfilling the Law, will judge you who, through letter and circumcision, [are] a transgressor of law. **28** For he is not a Jew who is [so] outwardly, neither [is] circumcision that which is outward in flesh; **29** but a Jew [is] he who is [so] inwardly, and circumcision [is] of the heart, in spirit, not in letter, of which the praise is not of men, but of God.

3 What, then, [is] the superiority of the Jew? Or what the profit of the circumcision? **2** Much in every way; for first, indeed, that they were entrusted with the oracles of God; **3** for what, if certain were faithless? Will their faithlessness make the faithfulness of God useless? **4** Let it not be! And let God become true, and every man false, according as it has been written: "That You may be declared righteous in Your words, and may overcome in Your being judged." **5** And if our unrighteousness establishes God's righteousness, what will we say? Is God unrighteous who is inflicting the wrath? (I speak after the manner of a man.) **6** Let it not be! Since how will God judge the world? **7** For if the truth of God in my falsehood abounded more to His glory, why am I also yet judged as a sinner? **8** And not, as we are spoken evil of, and as certain affirm us to say, "We may do the evil things, that the good ones may come?" Whose judgment is righteous. **9** What, then? Are we better? Not at all! For we charged before both Jews and Greeks with being all under sin, **10** according as it has been written: "There is none righteous, not even one; **11** there is none who is understanding, there is none who is seeking after God. **12** All went out of the way, together they became unprofitable, there is none doing good, there is not even one. **13** Their throat [is] an opened grave;

with their tongues they used deceit; poison of cobras [is] under their lips— **14** whose mouth is full of cursing and bitterness. **15** Their feet [are] swift to shed blood. **16** Ruin and misery [are] in their ways. **17** And a way of peace they did not know. **18** There is no fear of God before their eyes." **19** And we have known that as many things as the Law says, to those in the Law it speaks, that every mouth may be stopped, and all the world may come under judgment to God; **20** for this reason by works of law will no flesh be declared righteous before Him, for through law is a knowledge of sin. **21** And now apart from law the righteousness of God has been revealed, testified to by the Law and the Prophets, **22** and the righteousness of God [is] through the faith of Jesus Christ to all, and on all those believing—for there is no difference, **23** for all have sinned and fall short of the glory of God— **24** being declared righteous freely by His grace through the redemption that [is] in Christ Jesus, **25** whom God set forth [as] a propitiatory covering, through faith in His blood, for the showing forth of His righteousness, because of the passing over of the former sins in the forbearance of God— **26** for the showing forth of His righteousness in the present time, for His being righteous, and declaring him righteous who [is] of the faith of Jesus. **27** Where then [is] the boasting? It was excluded; by what law? Of works? No, but by a law of faith: **28** therefore we reckon a man to be declared righteous by faith, apart from works of law. **29** [Is He] only the God of Jews, and not also of nations? **30** Yes, also of nations; since [there is] one God who will declare righteous circumcision by faith, and uncircumcision through faith. **31** Do we then make law useless through faith? Let it not be! Indeed, we establish law.

4 What, then, will we say Abraham our father to have found, according to flesh? **2** For if Abraham was declared righteous by works, he has to boast—but not before God; **3** for what does the writing say? "And Abraham believed God, and it was reckoned to him for righteousness"; **4** and to him who is working, the reward is not reckoned of grace, but of debt; **5** and to him who is not working, and is believing on Him who is declaring righteous the impious, his faith is reckoned for righteousness— **6** even as David also speaks of the blessedness of the man to whom God reckons righteousness apart from works: **7** "Blessed [are] they whose lawless acts were forgiven, ‖ And whose sins were covered; **8** Blessed [is] the man ‖ To whom the LORD may not reckon sin." **9** [Is] this blessedness, then, on the circumcision, or also on the uncircumcision—for we say that faith was reckoned to Abraham for righteousness? **10** How then was it reckoned? He being in circumcision, or in uncircumcision? Not in circumcision, but in uncircumcision; **11** and he received a sign of circumcision, a seal of the righteousness of faith in the uncircumcision, for his being father of all those believing through uncircumcision, for the righteousness also being reckoned to them, **12** and father of circumcision to those not of circumcision only, but who also walk in the steps of faith, that [is] in the uncircumcision of our father Abraham. **13** For not through law [is] the promise to Abraham, or to his seed, of his being heir of the world, but through the righteousness of faith; **14** for if they who are of law [are] heirs, faith has been made void, and the promise has been made useless; **15** for the Law works wrath; for where law is not, neither [is] transgression. **16** Because of this [it is] of faith, that [it may be] according to grace, for the promise being sure to all the seed, not to that which [is] of the Law only, but also to that which [is] of the faith of Abraham, **17** who is father of us all (according as it has been written: "A father of many nations I have set you,") before Him whom he believed—God, who is quickening the dead, and is calling the things that are not as being. **18** Who, against hope, believed in hope, for his becoming father of many nations according to that spoken: "So will your seed be"; **19** and having not been weak in faith, he did not consider his own body, already become dead (being about one hundred years old), and the deadness of Sarah's womb, **20** and at the promise of God did not stagger in unbelief, but was strengthened in faith, having given glory to God, **21** and having been fully persuaded that what He has promised He is also able to do: **22** for this reason also it was reckoned to him for righteousness. **23** And it was not written on his account alone that

ROMANS

it was reckoned to him, **24** but also on ours, to whom it is about to be reckoned—to us believing on Him who raised up Jesus our Lord out of the dead, **25** who was delivered up because of our offenses, and was raised up because of our being declared righteous.

5 Having been declared righteous, then, by faith, we have peace toward God through our Lord Jesus Christ, **2** through whom also we have the access by faith into this grace in which we have stood, and we boast on the hope of the glory of God. **3** And not only [so], but we also boast in the tribulations, knowing that the tribulation works endurance; **4** and the endurance, experience; and the experience, hope; **5** and the hope does not make ashamed, because the love of God has been poured forth in our hearts through the Holy Spirit that has been given to us. **6** For in our being still ailing, Christ in due time died for the impious; **7** for scarcely for a righteous man will anyone die, for the good man perhaps someone also dares to die; **8** and God commends His own love to us, that, in our being still sinners, Christ died for us; **9** much more, then, having been declared righteous now in His blood, we will be saved through Him from the wrath; **10** for if, being enemies, we have been reconciled to God through the death of His Son, much more, having been reconciled, we will be saved in His life. **11** And not only [so], but we are also boasting in God, through our Lord Jesus Christ, through whom we now received the reconciliation; **12** because of this, even as through one man sin entered into the world, and through sin—death; and thus to all men death passed through, for that all sinned; **13** for until law sin was in the world: and sin is not reckoned when there is not law; **14** but death reigned from Adam until Moses, even on those having not sinned in the likeness of Adam's transgression, who is a type of Him who is coming. **15** But not as the offense so also [is] the free gift; for if by the offense of the one the many died, much more the grace of God, and the free gift in grace of the one man Jesus Christ, abound to the many; **16** and not as through one who sinned [is] the free gift, for the judgment indeed [is] of one to condemnation, but the gift [is] of many offenses to a declaration of "Righteous," **17** for if by the offense of the one death reigned through the one, much more those who are receiving the abundance of grace and of the free gift of righteousness, in life will reign through the one—Jesus Christ. **18** So, then, as through one offense to all men [it is] to condemnation, so also through one declaration of "Righteous" [it is] to all men to justification of life; **19** for as through the disobedience of the one man, the many were constituted sinners: so also through the obedience of the One, will the many be constituted righteous. **20** And law came in, that the offense might abound, and where sin abounded, grace hyper-abounded, **21** that even as sin reigned in death, so also grace may reign, through righteousness, to continuous life, through Jesus Christ our Lord.

6 What, then, will we say? Will we continue in sin that grace may abound? **2** Let it not be! We who died to sin—how will we still live in it? **3** Are you ignorant that we, as many as were immersed into Christ Jesus, were immersed into His death? **4** We were buried together, then, with Him through the immersion into death, that even as Christ was raised up out of the dead through the glory of the Father, so we also might walk in newness of life. **5** For if we have become planted together to the likeness of His death, [so] we also will be of the resurrection; **6** knowing this, that our old man was crucified with [Him], that the body of sin may be made useless, for our no longer serving sin; **7** for he who has died has been set free from sin. **8** And if we died with Christ, we believe that we also will live with Him, **9** knowing that Christ, having been raised up out of the dead, dies no more; death has no more lordship over Him; **10** for in that He died, He died to sin once, and in that He lives, He lives to God; **11** so also you, reckon yourselves to be dead indeed to sin, and living to God in Jesus Christ our Lord. **12** Do not let then sin reign in your mortal body, to obey it in its desires; **13** neither present your members instruments of unrighteousness to sin, but present yourselves to God as living out of the dead, and your members instruments of righteousness to God; **14** for sin will not have lordship over you, for you are not under law, but under grace. **15** What then? Will we sin because we are not under law but under grace? Let it not be! **16** Have you not known that to whom you present yourselves servants for obedience, servants you are to him to whom you obey, whether of sin to death, or of obedience to righteousness? **17** And thanks to God, that you were servants of sin, and—were obedient from the heart to the form of teaching to which you were delivered up; **18** and having been freed from sin, you became servants to righteousness. **19** I speak in a human [way], because of the weakness of your flesh, for even as you presented your members servants to the uncleanness and to the lawlessness—to the lawlessness, so now present your members servants to righteousness—to sanctification, **20** for when you were servants of sin, you were free from righteousness. **21** What fruit, therefore, were you having then, in the things of which you are now ashamed? For the end of those [is] death. **22** And now, having been freed from sin, and having become servants to God, you have your fruit—to sanctification, and the end continuous life; **23** for the wages of sin [is] death, and the gift of God [is] continuous life in Christ Jesus our Lord.

7 Are you ignorant, brothers—for to those knowing law I speak—that the law has lordship over the man as long as he lives? **2** For the married woman to the living husband has been bound by law, and if the husband may die, she has been free from the law of the husband; **3** so then, the husband being alive, she will be called an adulteress if she may become another man's; and if the husband may die, she is free from the law, so as not to be an adulteress, having become another man's. **4** So that, my brothers, you also were made dead to the law through the body of the Christ, for your becoming another's, who was raised up out of the dead, that we might bear fruit to God; **5** for when we were in the flesh, the passions of sins, that [are] through the Law, were working in our members, to bear fruit to death; **6** and now we have ceased from the Law, that being dead in which we were held, so that we may serve in newness of spirit, and not in oldness of letter. **7** What, then, will we say? The Law [is] sin? Let it not be! But I did not know sin except through law, for also the covetousness I had not known if the Law had not said: **8** "You will not covet"; and sin having received an opportunity, through the command, worked in me all covetousness—for apart from law sin is dead. **9** And I was alive apart from law once, and the command having come, sin revived, and I died; **10** and the command that [is] for life, this was found by me for death; **11** for sin, having received an opportunity, through the command, deceived me, and through it, slew [me], **12** so that the Law, indeed, [is] holy, and the command holy, and righteous, and good. **13** That which is good then, has it become death to me? Let it not be! But sin, that it might appear sin, through the good, working death to me, that sin might become exceedingly sinful through the command. **14** For we have known that the Law is spiritual, and I am fleshly, sold by sin; **15** for that which I work, I do not acknowledge; for not what I will, this I practice, but what I hate, this I do. **16** And if what I do not will, this I do, I consent to the Law that [it is] good, **17** and now it is no longer I that work it, but sin dwelling in me, **18** for I have known that there does not dwell in me, that is, in my flesh, good: for to will is present with me, and I do not find to work that which is right, **19** for the good that I will, I do not do; but the evil that I do not will, this I practice. **20** And if what I do not will, this I do, it is no longer I that work it, but sin that is dwelling in me. **21** I find, then, the law, that when I desire to do what is right, the evil is present with me, **22** for I delight in the Law of God according to the inward man, **23** and I behold another law in my members, warring against the law of my mind, and bringing me into captivity to the law of sin that [is] in my members. **24** A wretched man I [am]! Who will deliver me out of the body of this death? **25** I thank God—through Jesus Christ our Lord; so then, I myself indeed serve the Law of God with the mind, and with the flesh, the law of sin.

8 There is, then, now no condemnation to those in Christ Jesus, who walk not according to the flesh, but according to the Spirit; **2** for the law of the Spirit of life in Christ Jesus set me free from the law of sin and of death; **3** for what the Law was not able to do, in that it was weak through the flesh, God, His own Son having sent in the likeness of sinful flesh, and for sin, condemned sin in the flesh, **4** that the righteousness of the Law may be fulfilled in us, who do not walk according to the flesh, but according to the Spirit. **5** For those who are according to the flesh, mind the things of the flesh; and those according to the Spirit, the things of the Spirit; **6** for the mind of the flesh [is] death, and the mind of the Spirit—life and peace; **7** because the mind of the flesh [is] enmity to God, for to the Law of God it does not subject itself, **8** for neither is it able; and those who are in the flesh are not able to please God. **9** And you are not in the flesh, but in the Spirit, if indeed the Spirit of God dwells in you; and if anyone does not have the Spirit of Christ—this one is not His; **10** and if Christ [is] in you, the body, indeed, [is] dead because of sin, and the Spirit [is] life because of righteousness, **11** and if the Spirit of Him who raised up Jesus out of the dead dwells in you, He who raised up the Christ out of the dead will also quicken your dying bodies, through His Spirit dwelling in you. **12** So, then, brothers, we are debtors, not to the flesh, to live according to the flesh; **13** for if according to the flesh you live, you are about to die; and if, by the Spirit, the deeds of the body you put to death, you will live; **14** for as many as are led by the Spirit of God, these are the sons of God; **15** for you did not receive a spirit of bondage again for fear, but you received [the] Spirit of adoption in which we cry, "Abba! Father!" **16** [This] One—the Spirit—testifies with our spirit, that we are children of God; **17** and if children, also heirs, heirs, indeed, of God, and heirs together of Christ—if, indeed, we suffer together, that we may also be glorified together. **18** For I reckon that the sufferings of the present time [are] not worthy [to be compared] with the glory about to be revealed in us; **19** for the earnest looking out of the creation expects the revelation of the sons of God; **20** for to vanity was the creation made subject—not of its will, but because of Him who subjected [it]—in hope, **21** that also the creation itself will be set free from the servitude of the corruption to the liberty of the glory of the children of God; **22** for we have known that all the creation groans together, and travails in pain together until now. **23** And not only [so], but also we ourselves, having the first-fruit of the Spirit, we also ourselves groan in ourselves, expecting adoption—the redemption of our body; **24** for in hope we were saved, and hope beheld is not hope; for what anyone beholds, why does he also hope for [it]? **25** And if what we do not behold we hope for, through continuance we expect [it]. **26** And in like manner also, the Spirit helps our weaknesses; for what we may pray for, as it is necessary, we have not known, but [this] One—the Spirit—makes intercession for us with unutterable groanings, **27** and He who is searching the hearts has known what [is] the mind of the Spirit, because according to God He intercedes for holy ones. **28** And we have known that to those loving God all things work together for good, to those who are called according to purpose; **29** because whom He foreknew, He also foreordained, conformed to the image of His Son, that He might be firstborn among many brothers; **30** and whom He foreordained, these also He called; and whom He called, these also He declared righteous; and whom He declared righteous, these also He glorified. **31** What, then, will we say to these things? If God [is] for us, who [is] against us? **32** He who indeed did not spare His own Son, but delivered Him up for us all, how will He not also with Him grant to us all things? **33** Who will lay a charge against the chosen ones of God? God [is] He that is declaring righteous; **34** who [is] he that is condemning? Christ [is] He that died, indeed, rather also, was raised up; who is also on the right hand of God—who also interceded for us. **35** Who will separate us from the love of the Christ? Tribulation, or distress, or persecution, or famine, or nakedness, or peril, or sword? **36** According as it has been written: "For Your sake we are put to death all the day long; we were reckoned as sheep of slaughter." **37** But in all these we more than conquer, through Him who loved us; **38** for I am persuaded that neither death, nor life, nor messengers, nor principalities, nor powers, nor things present, **39** nor things about to be, nor height, nor depth, nor any other created thing, will be able to separate us from the love of God that [is] in Christ Jesus our Lord.

9 Truth I say in Christ, I do not lie, my conscience bearing testimony with me in the Holy Spirit, **2** that I have great grief and unceasing pain in my heart— **3** for I was wishing, I myself, to be accursed from

ROMANS

the Christ—for my brothers, my relatives, according to the flesh, **4** who are Israelites, whose [is] the adoption, and the glory, and the covenants, and the lawgiving, and the service, and the promises, **5** whose [are] the fathers, and of whom [is] the Christ, according to the flesh, who is God over all, blessed for all ages. Amen. **6** And it is not possible that the word of God has failed; for not all who [are] of Israel are these of Israel; **7** nor because they are seed of Abraham [are] all children, but, "in Isaac will a seed be called to you"; **8** that is, the children of the flesh—these [are] not children of God; but the children of the promise are reckoned for seed; **9** for the word of promise [is] this: "According to this time I will come, and there will be to Sarah a son." **10** And not only [so], but also Rebecca, having conceived by one—our father Isaac **11** (for they being not yet born, neither having done anything good or evil, that the purpose of God, according to [divine] selection, might remain; not of works, but of Him who is calling), **12** it was said to her, "The greater will serve the less"; **13** according as it has been written: "Jacob I loved, and Esau I hated." **14** What, then, will we say? Unrighteousness [is] with God? Let it not be! **15** For to Moses He says, "I will do kindness to whom I do kindness, and I will have compassion on whom I have compassion"; **16** so then—not of him who is willing, nor of him who is running, but of God who is doing kindness; **17** for the Writing says to Pharaoh, "For this very thing I raised you up, that I might show in you My power, and that My Name might be declared in all the land"; **18** so then, to whom He wills, He does kindness, and to whom He wills, He hardens. **19** You will say, then, to me, "Why does He yet find fault? For who has resisted His counsel?" **20** No, but, O man, who are you that are answering again to God? Will the thing formed say to Him who formed [it], Why did you make me thus? **21** Does the potter not have authority over the clay, out of the same lump to make one vessel to honor and one to dishonor? **22** And if God, willing to show the wrath and to make known His power, endured, in much long suffering, vessels of wrath fitted for destruction, **23** and that He might make known the riches of His glory on vessels of kindness, that He before prepared for glory, whom also He called—us— **24** not only out of Jews, but also out of nations, **25** as also in Hosea He says, "I will call what [is] not My people—My people; and her not beloved—Beloved, **26** and it will be—in the place where it was said to them, You [are] not My people; there they will be called sons of the living God." **27** And Isaiah cries concerning Israel, "If the number of the sons of Israel may be as the sand of the sea, the remnant will be saved; **28** for a matter He is finishing, and is cutting short in righteousness, because a matter cut short will the LORD do on the land." **29** And according as Isaiah says before, "Except the LORD of Hosts left to us a seed, we had become as Sodom, and we had been made like Gomorrah." **30** What, then, will we say? That nations who are not pursuing righteousness attained to righteousness, and righteousness that [is] of faith, **31** and Israel, pursuing a law of righteousness, did not arrive at a law of righteousness; **32** why? Because—not by faith, but as by works of law; for they stumbled at the stone of stumbling, **33** according as it has been written: "Behold, I place in Zion a stone of stumbling and a rock of offense; and everyone who is believing thereon will not be ashamed."

10 Brothers, the pleasure indeed of my heart, and my supplication that [is] to God for Israel, is—for salvation; **2** for I bear them testimony that they have a zeal of God, but not according to knowledge, **3** for not knowing the righteousness of God, and seeking to establish their own righteousness, they did not submit to the righteousness of God. **4** For Christ is an end of law for righteousness to everyone who is believing, **5** for Moses describes the righteousness that [is] of the Law, that, "The man who did them will live in them," **6** and the righteousness of faith thus speaks: "You may not say in your heart, Who will go up to Heaven?" (that is, to bring Christ down) **7** or, "Who will go down to the abyss?" (that is, to bring up Christ out of the dead). **8** But what does it say? "The saying is near you—in your mouth, and in your heart": that is, the saying of the faith that we preach; **9** that if you may confess with your mouth that Jesus [is] LORD, and may believe in your heart that God raised Him out of the dead, you will be saved, **10** for with the heart

[one] believes to righteousness, and with the mouth is confession made to salvation; **11** for the Writing says, "Everyone who is believing on Him will not be ashamed," **12** for there is no difference between Jew and Greek, for the same Lord of all [is] rich to all those calling on Him, **13** for "Everyone who, if he may have called on the Name of the LORD, will be saved." **14** How then will they call on [Him] in whom they did not believe? And how will they believe [on Him] of whom they did not hear? And how will they hear apart from one preaching? **15** And how will they preach, if they may not be sent? According as it has been written: "How beautiful the feet of those proclaiming good tidings of peace, of those proclaiming good tidings of the good things!" **16** But they were not all obedient to the good tidings, for Isaiah says, "LORD, who gave credence to our report?" **17** So then faith [is] by a report, and the report through a saying of God, **18** but I say, did they not hear? Yes, indeed, "their voice went forth to all the earth, and their sayings to the ends of the habitable world." **19** But I say, did Israel not know? First Moses says, "I will provoke you to jealousy by [that which is] not a nation, ‖ By an unintelligent nation I will anger you," **20** and Isaiah is very bold and says, "I was found by those not seeking Me; I became visible to those not inquiring after Me"; **21** and to Israel He says, "All the day I stretched out My hands to a people unbelieving and contradicting."

11 I say then, did God cast away His people? Let it not be! For I am also an Israelite, of the seed of Abraham, of the tribe of Benjamin: **2** God did not cast away His people whom He knew before; have you not known—in Elijah—what the Writing says? How he pleads with God concerning Israel, saying, **3** "LORD, they killed Your prophets, and they dug down Your altars, and I was left alone, and they seek my life"; **4** but what does the divine answer say to him? "I left to Myself seven thousand men who did not bow a knee to Ba'al." **5** So then also in the present time there has been a remnant according to the [divine] selection of grace; **6** and if by grace, no longer of works, otherwise grace becomes no longer grace; and if of works, it is no longer grace, otherwise work is no longer work. **7** What then? What Israel seeks after, this it did not obtain, and the chosen obtained, and the rest were hardened, **8** according as it has been written: "God gave to them a spirit of deep sleep, eyes not to see, and ears not to hear, to this very day," **9** and David says, "Let their table become for a snare, and for a trap, and for a stumbling-block, and for a repayment to them; **10** let their eyes be darkened—not to behold, and You always bow down their back." **11** I say then, did they stumble that they might fall? Let it not be! But by their fall the salvation [is] to the nations, to arouse them to jealousy; **12** and if their fall [is] the riches of [the] world, and their diminishment the riches of nations, how much more their fullness? **13** For to you I speak—to the nations—inasmuch as I am indeed an apostle of nations, I glorify my ministry; **14** if I will arouse my own flesh to jealousy by any means, and will save some of them, **15** for if the casting away of them [is] a reconciliation of the world, what the reception—if not life out of the dead? **16** And if the first-fruit [is] holy, the lump also; and if the root [is] holy, the branches also. **17** And if certain of the branches were broken off, and you, being a wild olive tree, were grafted in among them, and became a fellow-partaker of the root and of the fatness of the olive tree— **18** do not boast against the branches; and if you boast, you do not bear the root, but the root you! **19** You will say, then, "The branches were broken off, that I might be grafted in"; right! **20** By unbelief they were broken off, and you have stood by faith; do not be high-minded, but be fearing; **21** for if God did not spare the natural branches— lest perhaps He also will not spare you. **22** Behold, then, goodness and severity of God—on those indeed who fell, severity; and on you, goodness, if you may remain in the goodness, otherwise, you also will be cut off. **23** And those also, if they may not remain in unbelief, will be grafted in, for God is able to graft them in again; **24** for if you, out of the olive tree, wild by nature, were cut out, and contrary to nature, were grafted into a good olive tree, how much rather will they, who [are] according to nature, be grafted into their own olive tree? **25** For I do not wish you to be ignorant, brothers, of this secret—that you may not be wise in your own conceits—that hardness in part to Israel has happened until the fullness of the nations may come in; **26** and so all Israel will be saved, according as it has been written: "There will come forth out of Zion He who is delivering, and He will turn away impiety from Jacob, **27** and this to them [is] the covenant from Me when I may take away their sins." **28** As regards, indeed, the good tidings, [they are] enemies on your account; and as regards the [divine] selection—beloved on account of the fathers; **29** for the gifts and the calling of God are irrevocable; **30** for as you also once did not believe in God, and now found kindness by the unbelief of these, **31** so also these now did not believe, that in your kindness they also may find kindness; **32** for God shut up together the whole to unbelief, that to the whole He might do kindness. **33** O depth of riches, and wisdom and knowledge of God! How unsearchable His judgments, and untraceable His ways! **34** For who knew the mind of the LORD? Or who became His counselor? **35** Or who first gave to Him, and it will be given back to him again? **36** Because of Him, and through Him, and to Him [are] all things; to Him [is] the glory—for all ages. Amen.

12 I call on you, therefore, brothers, through the compassions of God, to present your bodies [as] a sacrifice—living, sanctified, acceptable to God—your intelligent service; **2** and do not be conformed to this age, but be transformed by the renewing of your mind, for your proving what [is] the will of God—the good, and acceptable, and perfect. **3** For I say, through the grace that was given to me, to everyone who is among you, not to think above what it ought to think; but to think so as to think wisely, as to each God dealt a measure of faith, **4** for as in one body we have many members, and all the members do not have the same office, **5** so we, the many, are one body in Christ, and members of one another—each one. **6** And having gifts, different according to the grace that was given to us: whether prophecy, according to the proportion of faith; **7** or ministry, in the ministry; or he who is teaching, in the teaching; **8** or he who is exhorting, in the exhortation; he who is sharing, in simplicity; he who is leading, in diligence; he who is doing kindness, in cheerfulness. **9** The love unhypocritical: abhorring the evil; cleaving to the good; **10** in the love of brothers, to one another kindly affectioned: in the honor going before one another; **11** in the diligence not slothful; in the spirit fervent; serving the LORD; **12** in the hope rejoicing; in the tribulation enduring; in the prayer persevering; **13** to the necessities of the holy ones communicating; the hospitality pursuing. **14** Bless those persecuting you; bless, and do not curse; **15** to rejoice with the rejoicing, and to weep with the weeping, **16** of the same mind toward one another, not minding the high things, but with the lowly going along; do not become wise in your own conceit; **17** giving back to no one evil for evil; providing right things before all men. **18** If possible—so far as in you—with all men being in peace; **19** not avenging yourselves, beloved, but give place to the wrath, for it has been written: "Vengeance [is] Mine, **20** I will repay again, says the LORD"; if, then, your enemy hungers, feed him; if he thirsts, give him drink; for doing this, you will heap coals of fire on his head. **21** Do not be overcome by the evil, but overcome, in the good, the evil.

13 Let every soul be subject to the higher authorities, for there is no authority except from God, and the authorities existing are appointed by God, **2** so that he who is setting himself against the authority, has resisted against God's ordinance; and those resisting will receive judgment to themselves. **3** For those ruling are not a terror to the good works, but to the evil; and do you wish to not be afraid of the authority? Be doing that which is good, and you will have praise from it, **4** for it is a servant of God to you for good; and if you may do that which is evil, be fearing, for it does not bear the sword in vain; for it is a servant of God, an avenger for wrath to him who is doing that which is evil. **5** For this reason it is necessary to be subject, not only because of the wrath, but also because of the conscience, **6** for because of this you also pay tribute; for they are servants of God, on this very thing attending continually; **7** render, therefore, to all [their] dues; to whom tribute, the tribute; to whom custom, the custom; to whom fear, the fear; to whom honor, the honor. **8** To no one owe anything, except to love one another; for he who is loving the other—he has fulfilled law, **9** for, "You will not commit adultery, You will not murder,

You will not steal, You will not bear false testimony, You will not covet"; and if there is any other command, in this word it is summed up, in this: "You will love your neighbor as yourself"; **10** the love to the neighbor works no ill; the love, therefore, [is] the fullness of law. **11** And this, knowing the time, that for us, the hour already [is] to be aroused out of sleep, for now our salvation [is] nearer than when we believed; **12** the night advanced, and the day came near; let us lay aside, therefore, the works of the darkness, and let us put on the armor of the light; **13** as in daytime, let us walk properly; not in reveling and drunkenness, not in promiscuity and licentiousness, not in strife and jealousy; **14** but put on the Lord Jesus Christ, and take no forethought for the flesh—for desires.

14 And receive him who is weak in the faith—not to determinations of reasonings; **2** one believes that he may eat all things—and he who is weak eats herbs; **3** do not let him who is eating despise him who is not eating: and do not let him who is not eating judge him who is eating, for God received him. **4** You—who are you that are judging another's domestic [affairs]? To his own master he stands or falls; and he will be made to stand, for God is able to make him stand. **5** One judges one day above another, and another judges every day [alike]; let each be fully assured in his own mind. **6** He who is regarding the day, he regards [it] to the LORD, and he who is not regarding the day, he does not regard [it] to the LORD. He who is eating, he eats to the LORD, for he gives thanks to God; and he who is not eating, he does not eat to the LORD, and gives thanks to God. **7** For none of us lives to himself, and none dies to himself; **8** for both, if we may live, we live to the LORD; if also we may die, we die to the LORD; both then if we may live, also if we may die, we are the LORD's; **9** for because of this Christ both died and rose again, and lived again, that He may be Lord both of dead and of living. **10** And you, why do you judge your brother? Or again, you, why do you set at nothing your brother? For we will all stand at the judgment seat of the Christ; **11** for it has been written: "I live! Says the LORD—Every knee will bow to Me, and every tongue will confess to God"; **12** so, then, each of us will give reckoning to God concerning himself; **13** therefore, may we judge one another no longer, but rather judge this, not to put a stumbling-stone before the brother, or an offense. **14** I have known, and am persuaded, in the Lord Jesus, that nothing [is] unclean of itself, except to him who is reckoning anything to be unclean—to that one [it is] unclean; **15** and if your brother is grieved through food, you no longer walk according to love; do not destroy with your food that one for whom Christ died. **16** Do not let, then, evil be spoken of your good, **17** for the Kingdom of God is not eating and drinking, but righteousness, and peace, and joy in the Holy Spirit; **18** for he who in these things is serving the Christ, [is] acceptable to God and approved of men. **19** So, then, may we pursue the things of peace, and the things of building up one another. **20** Do not cast down the work of God for the sake of food; all things, indeed, [are] pure, but evil [is] to the man who is eating through stumbling. **21** [It is] not right to eat flesh, nor to drink wine, nor to [do anything] in which your brother stumbles, or is made to fall, or is weak. **22** You have faith! Have [it] to yourself before God; blessed is he who is not judging himself in what he approves, **23** and he who is making a difference, if he may eat, has been condemned, because [it is] not of faith; and all that [is] not of faith is sin.

15 And we ought—we who are strong—to bear the weaknesses of the powerless, and not to please ourselves; **2** for let each one of us please the neighbor for good, for edification, **3** for even the Christ did not please Himself, but according as it has been written: "The reproaches of those reproaching You fell on Me"; **4** for as many things as were written before, for our instruction were written before, that through the endurance, and the exhortation of the Writings, we might have the hope. **5** And may the God of the endurance, and of the exhortation, give to you to have the same mind toward one another, according to Christ Jesus, **6** that with one accord—with one mouth—you may glorify the God and Father of our Lord Jesus Christ; **7** for this reason receive one another, according as also the Christ received us, to the glory of God. **8** And I say Jesus Christ to have become a servant of circumcision for the truth of God, to confirm the promises to the fathers, **9** and the nations for kindness to glorify God, according as it has been written: "Because of this I will confess to You among nations, and to Your Name I will sing praise"; **10** and again it says, "Rejoice you nations, with His people"; **11** and again, "Praise the LORD, all you nations; and laud Him, all you peoples"; **12** and again, Isaiah says, "There will be the root of Jesse, and He who is rising to rule nations—on Him will nations hope"; **13** and the God of the hope will fill you with all joy and peace in the believing, for your abounding in the hope in power of the Holy Spirit. **14** And I am persuaded, my brothers—I myself also—concerning you, that you yourselves also are full of goodness, having been filled with all knowledge, also able to admonish one another; **15** and the more boldly I wrote to you, brothers, in part, as putting you in mind, because of the grace that is given to me by God, **16** for my being a servant of Jesus Christ to the nations, acting as priest in the good news of God, that the offering up of the nations may become acceptable, sanctified by the Holy Spirit. **17** I have, then, a boasting in Christ Jesus, in the things pertaining to God, **18** for I will not dare to speak anything of the things that Christ did not work through me, to obedience of nations, by word and deed, **19** in power of signs and wonders, in power of the Spirit of God; so that I, from Jerusalem, and in a circle as far as Illyricum, have fully preached the good news of the Christ; **20** and so counting it honor to proclaim good news, not where Christ was named—that on another's foundation I might not build— **21** but according as it has been written: "To whom it was not told concerning Him, they will see; and they who have not heard, will understand." **22** For this reason, also, I was hindered many times from coming to you, **23** and now, no longer having place in these parts, and having a longing to come to you for many years, **24** when I may go on to Spain I will come to you, for I hope in going through, to see you, and by you to be set forward there, if of you first, in part, I will be filled. **25** And now, I go on to Jerusalem, ministering to the holy ones; **26** for it pleased Macedonia and Achaia well to make a certain contribution for the poor of the holy ones who [are] in Jerusalem; **27** for it pleased well, and their debtors they are, for if the nations participated in their spiritual things, they ought also, in the fleshly things, to minister to them. **28** This, then, having finished, and having sealed to them this fruit, I will return through you, to Spain; **29** and I have known that coming to you—in the fullness of the blessing of the good news of Christ I will come. **30** And I call on you, brothers, through our Lord Jesus Christ, and through the love of the Spirit, to strive together with me in the prayers for me to God, **31** that I may be delivered from those not believing in Judea, and that my ministry, that [is] for Jerusalem, may become acceptable to the holy ones; **32** that in joy I may come to you, through the will of God, and may be refreshed with you, **33** and the God of peace [be] with you all. Amen.

16 And I commend you to Phoebe our sister—being a servant of the assembly that [is] in Cenchrea— **2** that you may receive her in the LORD, worthily of the holy ones, and may assist her in whatever matter she may have need of you, for she also became a leader of many, and of myself. **3** Greet Priscilla and Aquilas, my fellow-workmen in Christ Jesus— **4** who laid down their own neck for my life, to whom not only I give thanks, but also all the assemblies of the nations— **5** and the assembly at their house; greet Epaenetus, my beloved, who is first-fruit of Achaia to Christ. **6** Greet Mary, who labored much for us; **7** greet Andronicus and Junias, my relatives, and my fellow-captives, who are of note among the apostles, who also have been in Christ before me. **8** Greet Amplias, my beloved in the LORD; **9** greet Arbanus, our fellow-workman in Christ, and Stachys, my beloved; **10** greet Apelles, the approved in Christ; greet those of the [household] of Aristobulus; **11** greet Herodion, my relative; greet those of the [household] of Narcissus, who are in the LORD; **12** greet Tryphaena, and Tryphosa, who are laboring in the LORD; greet Persis, the beloved, who labored much in the LORD. **13** Greet Rufus, the chosen one in the LORD, and his mother and mine, **14** greet Asyncritus, Phlegon, Hermas, Patrobas, Hermes, and the brothers with them; **15** greet Philologus, and Julias, Nereus, and his sister, and Olympas, and all the holy ones with them; **16** greet one another in a holy kiss; the assemblies of Christ greet you. **17** And I call on you, brothers, to mark those who are causing the divisions and the stumbling-blocks, contrary to the teaching that you learned, and turn away from them; **18** for such do not serve our Lord Jesus Christ, but their own belly; and through the good word and fair speech they deceive the hearts of the harmless. **19** For your obedience reached to all; I rejoice, therefore, as regards you, and I wish you to be wise, indeed, as to the good, and pure as to the evil; **20** and the God of peace will bruise Satan under your feet quickly; the grace of our Lord Jesus Christ [be] with you. Amen! **21** Timotheus greets you, my fellow-workman, and Lucius, and Jason, and Sosipater, my relatives; **22** I, Tertius, greet you (who wrote the letter) in the LORD; **23** Gaius greets you, my host, and of the whole Assembly; Erastus greets you, the steward of the city, and Quartus the brother. **24** [[The grace of our Lord Jesus Christ [be] with you all! Amen.]] **25** And to Him who is able to establish you, according to my good news, and the preaching of Jesus Christ, according to the revelation of the secret, having been kept secret in the times of the ages, **26** and now having been revealed, also, through prophetic writings, according to a command of the perpetual God, having been made known to all the nations for obedience of faith— **27** to the only wise God, through Jesus Christ, to Him [be] glory for all ages. Amen.

1 CORINTHIANS

1 Paul, a called apostle of Jesus Christ, through the will of God, and Sosthenes the brother, **2** to the Assembly of God that is in Corinth, to those sanctified in Christ Jesus, called holy ones, with all those calling on the Name of our Lord Jesus Christ in every place—both theirs and ours; **3** Grace to you and peace from God our Father and the Lord Jesus Christ! **4** I give thanks to my God always concerning you for the grace of God that was given to you in Christ Jesus, **5** that in everything you were enriched in Him, in all discourse and all knowledge, **6** according as the testimony of the Christ was confirmed in you, **7** so that you are not behind in any gift, waiting for the revelation of our Lord Jesus Christ, **8** who also will confirm you to the end—unblamable in the day of our Lord Jesus Christ; **9** faithful [is] God, through whom you were called into the fellowship of His Son Jesus Christ our Lord. **10** And I call on you, brothers, through the Name of our Lord Jesus Christ, that the same thing you may all say, and there may not be divisions among you, and you may be perfected in the same mind, and in the same judgment, **11** for it was signified to me concerning you, my brothers, by those of Chloe, that contentions are among you; **12** and I say this, that each one of you says, "I, indeed, am of Paul," and "I of Apollos," and "I of Cephas," and "I of Christ." **13** Has the Christ been divided? Was Paul crucified for you? Or were you immersed into the name of Paul? **14** I give thanks to God that I immersed no one of you, except Crispus and Gaius— **15** that no one may say that to my own name I immersed; **16** and I also immersed Stephanas' household—further, I have not known if I immersed any other. **17** For Christ did not send me to immerse, but to proclaim good news, not in wisdom of discourse, that the Cross of the Christ may not be made of no effect; **18** for the word of the Cross to those indeed perishing is foolishness, and to us—those being saved—it is the power of God, **19** for it has been written: "I will destroy the wisdom of the wise, and the intelligence of the intelligent I will bring to nothing"; **20** where [is] the wise? Where the scribe? Where a disputer of this age? Did God not make foolish the wisdom of this world? **21** For seeing in the wisdom of God the world through the wisdom did not know God, it pleased God through the foolishness of the preaching to save those believing. **22** Since also Jews ask a sign, and Greeks seek wisdom, **23** also we preach Christ crucified, to Jews, indeed, a stumbling-block, and to Greeks foolishness, **24** and to those called—both Jews and Greeks—Christ the power of God, and the wisdom of God, **25** because the foolishness of God is wiser than men, and the weakness of God is stronger than men; **26** for see your calling, brothers, that not many [are] wise according to the flesh, not many mighty, not many noble; **27** but God chose the foolish things of the world that He may put the wise to shame; and God chose the weak things of the world that He may put the strong to shame; **28** and God chose the base things of the world, and the things despised, and the things that are not, that He may make useless the things that are— **29** that no flesh may glory before Him; **30** but out of Him you are in Christ Jesus, who became to us from God wisdom, righteousness also, and sanctification, and redemption, **31** that, according as it has been written: "He who is glorying—let him glory in the LORD."

2 And I, having come to you, brothers, came—not in superiority of discourse or wisdom—declaring to you the testimony of God, **2** for I decided not to know anything among you, except Jesus Christ, and Him crucified; **3** and I, in weakness, and in fear, and in much trembling, was with you; **4** and my word and my preaching was not in persuasive words of wisdom, but in demonstration of the Spirit and of power— **5** that your faith may not be in the wisdom of men, but in the power of God. **6** And wisdom we speak among the perfect, and wisdom not of this age, nor of the rulers of this age—of those becoming useless, **7** but we speak the hidden wisdom of God in a secret, that God foreordained before the ages to our glory, **8** which no one of the rulers of this age knew, for if they had known, they would not have crucified the Lord of Glory; **9** but

1 CORINTHIANS

according as it has been written: "What eye did not see, and ear did not hear, and on the heart of man did not come up, what God prepared for those loving Him"; **10** but God revealed [them] to us through His Spirit, for the Spirit searches all things, even the depths of God, **11** for who of men has known the things of the man, except the spirit of the man that [is] in him? So also the things of God no one has known, except the Spirit of God. **12** And we did not receive the spirit of the world, but the Spirit that [is] of God, that we may know the things conferred by God on us, **13** which things we also speak, not in words taught by human wisdom, but in those taught by the Holy Spirit, comparing spiritual things with spiritual things, **14** and the natural man does not receive the things of the Spirit of God, for they are foolishness to him, and he is not able to know [them], because they are discerned spiritually; **15** and he who is spiritual, indeed discerns all things, and he himself is discerned by no one; **16** for who knew the mind of the LORD that he will instruct Him? And we have the mind of Christ.

3 And I, brothers, was not able to speak to you as to spiritual, but as to fleshly—as to babies in Christ; **2** with milk I fed you, and not with meat, for you were not yet able, but not even yet are you now able, **3** for yet you are fleshly, for where [there is] among you envying, and strife, and divisions, are you not fleshly, and walk in the manner of men? **4** For when one may say, "I, indeed, am of Paul," and another, "I—of Apollos," are you not fleshly? **5** Who, then, is Paul, and who Apollos, but servants through whom you believed, and to each as the LORD gave? **6** I planted, Apollos watered, but God was giving growth; **7** so that neither is he who is planting anything, nor he who is watering, but He who is giving growth—God; **8** and he who is planting and he who is watering are one, and each will receive his own reward according to his own labor, **9** for we are fellow-workmen of God; you are God's tillage, God's building. **10** According to the grace of God that was given to me, as a wise master-builder, I have laid a foundation, and another builds on [it], **11** for no one is able to lay another foundation except that which is laid, which is Jesus the Christ; **12** and if anyone builds on this foundation gold, silver, precious stones, wood, hay, straw— **13** the work will become visible of each, for the day will declare [it], because it is revealed in fire, and the work of each, what kind it is, the fire will prove; **14** if the work of anyone remains that he built on [it], he will receive a wage; **15** if the work of any is burned up, he will suffer loss, but himself will be saved, but so as through fire. **16** Have you not known that you are a temple of God, and the Spirit of God dwells in you? **17** If anyone ruins the temple of God, God will ruin him; for the temple of God is holy, which you are. **18** Let no one deceive himself; if anyone seems to be wise among you in this age—let him become a fool, that he may become wise, **19** for the wisdom of this world is foolishness with God, for it has been written: "Who is taking the wise in their craftiness"; **20** and again, "The LORD knows the reasonings of the wise, that they are vain." **21** So then, let no one glory in men, for all things are yours, **22** whether Paul, or Apollos, or Cephas, or the world, or life, or death, or things present, or things about to be—all are yours, **23** and you [are] Christ's, and Christ [is] God's.

4 Let a man so reckon us as officers of Christ, and stewards of the secrets of God, **2** and as to the rest, it is required in the stewards that one may be found faithful, **3** and to me it is for a very little thing that by you I may be judged, or by man's Day, but I do not even judge myself, **4** for I have been conscious of nothing for myself, but I have not been declared right in this—and He who is discerning me is the LORD: **5** so, then, judge nothing before the time, until the LORD may come, who will both bring to light the hidden things of the darkness, and will reveal the counsels of the hearts, and then the praise will come to each from God. **6** And these things, brothers, I transferred to myself and to Apollos because of you, that in us you may learn not to think above that which has been written, that you may not be puffed up one for one against the other, **7** for who makes you to differ? And what do you have, that you did not receive? And if you also received, why do you glory as not having received? **8** Already you are having been filled, already you were rich, apart from us you reigned, and I also wish you reigned, that we also may reign together with you, **9** for I think that God set forth us the apostles last—as appointed to death, because we became a spectacle to the world, and messengers, and men; **10** we [are] fools because of Christ, and you wise in Christ; we [are] ailing, and you strong; you glorious, and we dishonored; **11** to the present hour we both hunger, and thirst, and are naked, and are battered, and wander, **12** and labor, working with [our] own hands; being reviled, we bless; being persecuted, we endure; **13** being spoken evil of, we plead; we became as filth of the world—of all things an outcast—until now. **14** Not [as] putting you to shame do I write these things, but I admonish as my beloved children, **15** for if a myriad of child-conductors you may have in Christ, yet not many fathers; for in Christ Jesus, through the good news, I begot you; **16** I call on you, therefore, become followers of me; **17** because of this I sent to you Timotheus, who is my child, beloved and faithful in the LORD, who will remind you of my ways in Christ, according as everywhere in every assembly I teach. **18** And some were puffed up as if I were not coming to you; **19** but I will come quickly to you, if the LORD may will, and I will not know the word of those puffed up, but the power; **20** for not in word is the Kingdom of God, but in power. **21** What do you wish? Will I come to you with a rod, or in love, also with a spirit of meekness?

5 Whoredom is actually heard of among you, and such whoredom as is not even named among the nations—as that one has the wife of the father! **2** And you are having been puffed up, and did not rather mourn, that he may be removed out of the midst of you who did this work, **3** for I indeed, as being absent as to the body, and present as to the spirit, have already judged, as being present, him who so worked this thing: **4** in the Name of our Lord Jesus Christ—you being gathered together, also my spirit—with the power of our Lord Jesus Christ, **5** to deliver up such a one to Satan for the destruction of the flesh, that the spirit may be saved in the Day of the Lord Jesus. **6** Your glorying [is] not good; have you not known that a little leaven leavens the whole lump? **7** Cleanse out, therefore, the old leaven, that you may be a new lump, according as you are unleavened, for our Passover was sacrificed for us also—Christ, **8** so that we may keep the celebration, not with old leaven, nor with the leaven of evil and wickedness, but with unleavened [bread] of sincerity and truth. **9** I wrote to you in the letter, not to keep company with whoremongers— **10** and certainly not with the whoremongers of this world, or with the covetous, or extortioners, or idolaters, seeing you ought then to go forth out of the world— **11** and now, I wrote to you not to keep company with [him], if anyone, being named a brother, may be a whoremonger, or covetous, or an idolater, or a railer, or a drunkard, or an extortioner—do not even eat together with such a one; **12** for what have I also to judge those outside? Do you not judge those within? **13** And judge those without God; and put away the evil from among yourselves.

6 Dare anyone of you, having a matter with the other, go to be judged before the unrighteous, and not before the holy ones? **2** Have you not known that the holy ones will judge the world? And if the world is judged by you, are you unworthy of the smaller judgments? **3** Have you not known that we will judge messengers? Why not then the things of life? **4** Of the things of life, indeed, then, if you may have judgment, those despised in the Assembly—these you cause to sit; **5** I speak to your shame: so there is not among you one wise man, not even one, who will be able to discern in the midst of his brothers! **6** But brother with brother goes to be judged, and this before unbelievers! **7** Already, indeed, then, there is altogether a fault among you, that you have judgments with one another; why do you not rather suffer injustice? Why not be defrauded? **8** But you do injustice, and you defraud, and these—brothers! **9** Have you not known that the unrighteous will not inherit the Kingdom of God? Do not be led astray; neither whoremongers, nor idolaters, nor adulterers, nor effeminate, nor sodomites, **10** nor thieves, nor covetous, nor drunkards, nor revilers, nor extortioners, will inherit the Kingdom of God. **11** And certain of you were these! But you were washed, but you were sanctified, but you were declared righteous, in the Name of the Lord Jesus, and in the Spirit of our God. **12** All things are lawful to me, but

1 CORINTHIANS

all things are not profitable; all things are lawful to me, but I will not be under authority by any; **13** the meats [are] for the belly, and the belly for the meats. And God will make useless both this and these; and the body [is] not for whoredom, but for the LORD, and the LORD for the body; **14** and God raised both the LORD, and will raise us up through His power. **15** Have you not known that your bodies are members of Christ? Having taken, then, the members of the Christ, will I make [them] members of a prostitute? Let it not be! **16** Have you not known that he who is joined to the prostitute is one body? For it says, "The two will be into one flesh." **17** And he who is joined to the LORD is one spirit; **18** flee the whoredom; every sin—whatever a man may commit—is outside the body, and he who is committing whoredom sins against his own body. **19** Have you not known that your body is a temple of the Holy Spirit in you, which you have from God? And you are not your own, **20** for you were bought with a price; glorify, then, God in your body and in your spirit, which are God's.

7 And concerning the things of which you wrote to me: [it is] good for a man not to touch a woman, **2** and because of the whoredom let each man have his own wife, and let each woman have her proper husband; **3** to the wife let the husband render the due benevolence, and in like manner also the wife to the husband; **4** the wife does not have authority over her own body, but the husband; and in like manner also, the husband does not have authority over his own body, but the wife. **5** Do not defraud one another, except by consent for a time, that you may be free for fasting and prayer, and again may come together, that Satan may not tempt you because of your self-indulgence; **6** and this I say by way of concurrence—not of command, **7** for I wish all men to be even as I myself [am]; but each has his own gift of God, one indeed thus and one thus. **8** And I say to the unmarried and to the widows: it is good for them if they may remain even as I [am]; **9** and if they do not have continence—let them marry, for it is better to marry than to burn; **10** and to the married I announce—not I, but the LORD—do not let a wife separate from a husband: **11** but, and if she may separate, let her remain unmarried, or let her be reconciled to the husband, and do not let a husband send a wife away. **12** And to the rest I speak—not the LORD—if any brother has an unbelieving wife, and she is pleased to dwell with him, do not let him send her away; **13** and a woman who has an unbelieving husband, and he is pleased to dwell with her, do not let her send him away; **14** for the unbelieving husband has been sanctified in the wife, and the unbelieving wife has been sanctified in the husband; otherwise your children are unclean, but now they are holy. **15** And if the unbelieving separates himself—let him separate himself: the brother or the sister is not under servitude in such [cases], and in peace has God called us; **16** for what, have you known, O wife, whether you will save the husband? Or what, have you known, O husband, whether you will save the wife? **17** If not, as God distributed to each, as the LORD has called each—so let him walk; and thus I direct in all the assemblies: **18** being circumcised—was anyone called? Do not let him become uncircumcised; in uncircumcision was anyone called? Do not let him be circumcised; **19** the circumcision is nothing, and the uncircumcision is nothing—but a keeping of the commands of God. **20** Each in the calling in which he was called—in this let him remain; **21** a servant—were you called? Do not be anxious; but if also you are able to become free—use [it] rather; **22** for he who [is] in the LORD—having been called a servant—is the LORD's freedman: in like manner also he the freeman, having been called, is servant of Christ: **23** you were bought with a price, do not become servants of men; **24** each, in that in which he was called, brothers, in this let him remain with God. **25** And concerning the virgins, I do not have a command of the LORD; and I give judgment as having obtained kindness from the LORD to be faithful. **26** I suppose, therefore, this to be good because of the present necessity, that [it is] good for a man that the matter be thus: **27** Have you been bound to a wife? Do not seek to be loosed; have you been loosed from a wife? Do not seek a wife. **28** But, and if you may marry, you did not sin; and if the virgin may marry, she did not sin; and such will have tribulation in the flesh: and I spare you. **29** And this I say, brothers, the time from now on is having been shortened—that both those having wives may be as not

1 CORINTHIANS

having; **30** and those weeping, as not weeping; and those rejoicing, as not rejoicing; and those buying, as not possessing; **31** and those using this world, as not using [it] up; for the [present] form of this world is passing away. **32** And I wish you to be without anxiety; the unmarried is anxious for the things of the LORD, how he will please the LORD; **33** and the married is anxious for the things of the world, how he will please the wife. **34** The wife and the virgin have been distinguished: the unmarried is anxious for the things of the LORD, that she may be holy both in body and in spirit, and the married is anxious for the things of the world, how she will please the husband. **35** And this I say for your own profit: not that I may cast a noose on you, but for the seemliness and devotedness to the LORD, undistractedly, **36** and if anyone thinks [it] to be unseemly to his virgin, if she may be beyond the bloom of age, and it ought to be so, what he wills let him do; he does not sin—let him marry. **37** And he does well who has stood steadfast in the heart—not having necessity—and has authority over his own will, and he has determined this in his heart—to keep his own virgin; **38** so that both he who is giving in marriage does well, and he who is not giving in marriage does better. **39** A wife has been bound by law [for] as long [a] time as her husband may live, and if her husband may sleep, she is free to be married to whom she will—only in the LORD; **40** and she is happier if she may so remain—according to my judgment; and I think I also have the Spirit of God.

8 And concerning the things sacrificed to idols, we have known that we all have knowledge: knowledge puffs up, but love builds up; **2** and if anyone thinks to know anything, he has not yet known anything according as it is required to know; **3** and if anyone loves God, this one has been known by Him. **4** Concerning the eating then of the things sacrificed to idols, we have known that an idol [is] nothing in the world, and that there is no other God except one; **5** for even if there are those called gods, whether in Heaven, whether on earth—as there are many gods and many lords— **6** yet to us [is] one God, the Father, of whom [are] all things, and we to Him; and one Lord, Jesus Christ, through whom [are] all things, and we through Him; **7** but not in all men [is] the knowledge, and certain with conscience of the idol, until now, eat [it] as a thing sacrificed to an idol, and their conscience, being weak, is defiled. **8** But food does not commend us to God, for neither if we may eat are we in advance; nor if we may not eat, are we behind; **9** but see, lest this privilege of yours may become a stumbling-block to the weak, **10** for if anyone may see you that have knowledge in an idol's temple reclining to eat, will not his conscience—he being weak—be emboldened to eat the things sacrificed to idols? **11** For the [one] being weak—the brother for whom Christ died—will perish by your knowledge. **12** And thus sinning in regard to the brothers, and striking their weak conscience—you sin in regard to Christ; **13** for this reason, if food causes my brother to stumble, I may not eat flesh—throughout the age—that I may not cause my brother to stumble.

9 Am I not an apostle? Am I not free? Have I not seen Jesus Christ our Lord? Are you not my work in the LORD? **2** If I am not an apostle to others—yet doubtless I am to you; for you are the seal of my apostleship in the LORD. **3** My defense to those who examine me in this: **4** do we not have authority to eat and to drink? **5** Do we not have authority to lead about a sister—a wife—as also the other apostles, and the brothers of the LORD, and Cephas? **6** Or do only Barnabas and I have no authority not to work? **7** Who serves as a soldier at his own expense at any time? Who plants a vineyard and does not eat of its fruit? Or who feeds a flock and does not eat of the milk of the flock? **8** Do I speak these things according to man? Or does the Law not also say these things? **9** For in the Law of Moses it has been written: "you will not muzzle an ox treading out grain"; does God care for the oxen? **10** Or by all means does He say [it] because of us? Yes, because of us it was written, because in hope ought the plower to plow, and he who is treading [ought] of his hope to partake in hope. **11** If we sowed to you the spiritual things—[is it] great if we reap your fleshly things? **12** If others partake of the authority over you—[do] we not more? But we did not use this authority, but we bear all things, that we may give no hindrance to the good news of the Christ. **13** Have you not known that those working

1 CORINTHIANS

about the things of the temple eat of the temple, and those waiting at the altar are partakers with the altar? **14** So also the LORD directed to those proclaiming the good news to live of the good news. **15** And I have used none of these things; neither did I write these things that it may be so done in my case, for [it is] good for me rather to die, than that anyone may make my glorying void; **16** for if I may proclaim good news, it is no glorying for me, for necessity is laid on me, and woe is to me if I may not proclaim good news; **17** for if I do this willingly, I have a reward; and if unwillingly—I have been entrusted with a stewardship! **18** What, then, is my reward? That proclaiming good news, without charge I will make the good news of the Christ, not to abuse my authority in the good news; **19** for being free from all men, I made myself servant to all men, that the more I might gain; **20** and to the Jews I became like a Jew, that I might gain Jews; to those under law as under law, that I might gain those under law; **21** to those without law, as without law—(not being without law to God, but within law to Christ)—that I might gain those without law; **22** to the weak I became weak, that I might gain the weak; to all men I have become all things, that by all means I may save some. **23** And I do this because of the good news, that I may become a fellow-partaker of it; **24** have you not known that those running in a race—all indeed run, but one receives the prize? So run that you may obtain; **25** and everyone who is striving is temperate in all things; these, indeed, then, that they may receive a corruptible garland, but we an incorruptible. **26** I, therefore, thus run, not as uncertainly, thus I fight, as not beating air; **27** but I bruise my body, and bring [it] into servitude, lest by any means, having preached to others—I myself may become disapproved.

10 And I do not wish you to be ignorant, brothers, that all our fathers were under the cloud, and all passed through the sea, **2** and all were immersed into Moses in the cloud, and in the sea; **3** and all ate the same spiritual food, **4** and all drank the same spiritual drink, for they were drinking of a spiritual rock following them, and the rock was the Christ; **5** but in the most of them God was not well pleased, for they were strewn in the wilderness, **6** and those things became types of us, for our not passionately desiring evil things, as also these desired. **7** Neither become idolaters, as certain of them, as it has been written: "The people sat down to eat and to drink, and stood up to play"; **8** neither may we commit whoredom, as certain of them committed whoredom, and there fell in one day twenty-three thousand; **9** neither may we tempt the Christ, as also certain of them tempted, and perished by the serpents; **10** neither murmur, as also some of them murmured, and perished by the destroyer. **11** And all these things happened to those persons as types, and they were written for our admonition, to whom the end of the ages came, **12** so that he who is thinking to stand—let him observe, lest he fall. **13** No temptation has taken you—except that of man; and God is faithful, who will not permit you to be tempted above what you are able, but He will make, with the temptation, also the outlet, for your being able to bear [it]. **14** For this reason, my beloved, flee from the idolatry; **15** as to wise men I speak—judge what I say. **16** The cup of the blessing that we bless—is it not the fellowship of the blood of the Christ? The bread that we break—is it not the fellowship of the body of the Christ? **17** Because one bread, one body, are we the many—for we all partake of the one bread. **18** See Israel according to the flesh! Are those not eating the sacrifices in the fellowship of the altar? **19** What do I say then? That an idol is anything? Or that a sacrifice offered to an idol is anything? **20** [No,] but that the things that the nations sacrifice—they sacrifice to demons and not to God; and I do not wish you to come into the fellowship of the demons. **21** You are not able to drink the cup of the LORD and the cup of demons; you are not able to partake of the table of the LORD and of the table of demons; **22** do we arouse the LORD to jealousy? Are we stronger than He? **23** All things are lawful to me, but not all things are profitable; all things are lawful to me, but not all things build up; **24** let no one seek his own—but each another's. **25** Eat whatever is sold in the meat-market, not inquiring, because of the conscience, **26** for the earth and its fullness [are] the LORD's; **27** and if anyone of the unbelieving calls you, and you wish to go, eat all that is set before you, inquiring nothing, because of the conscience; **28** and if anyone may say to you, "This is a thing sacrificed to an idol," do not eat, because of that one who showed [it], and of the conscience, for the LORD's [is] the earth and its fullness: 29 and conscience, I say, not of yourself, but of the other, for why [is it] that my liberty is judged by another's conscience? 30 And if I partake thankfully, why am I spoken of [as] evil, for that for which I give thanks? 31 Whether, then, you eat, or drink, or do anything, do all to the glory of God; 32 become offenseless, both to Jews and Greeks, and to the Assembly of God; 33 as I also please all in all things, not seeking my own profit, but that of many—that they may be saved.

11 Become followers of me, as I also [am] of Christ. 2 And I praise you, brothers, that in all things you remember me, and according as I delivered to you, you keep the deliverances, 3 and I wish you to know that the Christ is the head of every man, and the head of a woman is the husband, and the head of Christ is God. 4 Every man praying or prophesying, having the head covered, dishonors his head, 5 and every woman praying or prophesying with the head uncovered, dishonors her own head, for it is one and the same thing with her being shaven, 6 for if a woman is not covered—then let her be shorn, and if [it is] a shame for a woman to be shorn or shaven—let her be covered; 7 for a man, indeed, ought not to cover the head, being the image and glory of God, and a woman is the glory of a man, 8 for a man is not of a woman, but a woman [is] of a man, 9 for also was a man not created because of the woman, but a woman because of the man; 10 because of this the woman ought to have [a token of] authority on the head, because of the messengers; 11 but neither [is] a man apart from a woman, nor a woman apart from a man, in the LORD, 12 for as the woman [is] of the man, so also the man [is] through the woman, and all the things [are] of God. 13 Judge in your own selves: is it seemly for a woman to pray to God uncovered? 14 Does not even nature itself teach you, that if a man indeed has long hair, it is a dishonor to him? 15 And a woman, if she has long hair, it is a glory to her, because the hair has been given to her instead of a covering; 16 and if anyone thinks to be contentious, we have no such custom, neither the assemblies of God. 17 And declaring this, I give no praise, because you do not come together for the better, but for the worse; 18 for first, indeed, coming together in an assembly, I hear of divisions being among you, and I partly believe [it], 19 for it is also necessary for sects to be among you, that those approved may become visible among you; 20 you, then, coming together at the same place—it is not to eat the LORD's Dinner; 21 for each takes his own dinner before in the eating, and one is hungry, and another is drunk; 22 why, do you not have houses to eat and to drink in? Or do you despise the Assembly of God, and shame those not having? What may I say to you? Will I praise you in this? I do not praise! 23 For I received from the LORD that which I also delivered to you, that the Lord Jesus in the night in which He was delivered up, took bread, 24 and having given thanks, He broke, and said, "Take, eat, this is My body that is being broken for you; do this—to the remembrance of Me." 25 In like manner also the cup after the supping, saying, "This cup is the New Covenant in My blood; do this, as often as you may drink [it]—to the remembrance of Me"; 26 for as often as you may eat this bread, and may drink this cup, you show forth the death of the LORD—until He may come; 27 so that whoever may eat this bread or may drink the cup of the LORD unworthily, he will be guilty of the body and blood of the LORD: 28 and let a man be proving himself, and so let him eat of the bread, and let him drink of the cup; 29 for he who is eating and drinking unworthily, he eats and drinks judgment to himself—not discerning the body of the LORD. 30 Because of this many [are] weak and sickly among you, and many sleep; 31 for if we were discerning ourselves, we would not be being judged, 32 and being judged by the LORD, we are disciplined, that we may not be condemned with the world; 33 so then, my brothers, coming together to eat, wait for one another; 34 and if anyone is hungry, let him eat at home, that you may not come together to judgment; and the rest, whenever I may come, I will arrange.

12 And concerning the spiritual things, brothers, I do not wish you to be ignorant; 2 you have known that you were nations, being carried away as you were led to the mute idols; **3** for this reason, I give you to understand that no one, speaking in the Spirit of God, says Jesus [is] accursed, and no one is able to say Jesus [is] LORD, except in the Holy Spirit. **4** And there are diversities of gifts, and the same Spirit; **5** and there are diversities of ministries, and the same Lord; **6** and there are diversities of workings, and it is the same God—who is working all in all. **7** And to each has been given the manifestation of the Spirit for profit; **8** for to one through the Spirit has been given a word of wisdom, and to another a word of knowledge, according to the same Spirit; **9** and to another faith in the same Spirit, and to another gifts of healings in the same Spirit; **10** and to another in-workings of mighty deeds; and to another prophecy; and to another discernings of spirits; and to another [various] kinds of tongues; and to another interpretation of tongues: **11** and the one and the same Spirit works all these, dividing to each individually as He intends. **12** For even as the body is one, and has many members, and all the members of the one body, being many, are one body, so also [is] the Christ, **13** for also in one Spirit we were all immersed into one body, whether Jews or Greeks, whether servants or freemen, and all were made to drink one Spirit, **14** for also the body is not one member, but many. **15** If the foot may say, "Because I am not a hand, I am not of the body," is it not, because of this, not of the body? **16** And if the ear may say, "Because I am not an eye, I am not of the body," is it not, because of this, not of the body? **17** If the whole body [were] an eye, where the hearing? If the whole hearing, where the smelling? **18** And now, God set the members, each one of them in the body, according as He willed, **19** and if all were one member, where [is] the body? **20** And now, indeed, [are] many members, but one body; **21** and an eye is not able to say to the hand, "I have no need of you"; nor again the head to the feet, "I have no need of you." **22** But much more the members of the body seeming to be weaker are necessary, **23** and those that we think to be less honorable of the body, around these we put more abundant honor, and our unseemly things have more abundant seemliness, **24** and our seemly things have no need; but God tempered the body together, having given more abundant honor to the lacking part, **25** that there may be no division in the body, but that the members may have the same anxiety for one another, **26** and whether one member suffers, all the members suffer with [it], or one member is glorified, all the members rejoice with [it]; **27** and you are the body of Christ, and members in particular. **28** And some, indeed, God set in the Assembly: first apostles, secondly prophets, thirdly teachers, afterward powers, afterward gifts of healings, helpings, governings, various kinds of tongues. **29** [Are] all apostles? [Are] all prophets? [Are] all teachers? [Are] all powers? **30** [Do] all have gifts of healings? Do all speak with tongues? Do all interpret? **31** And earnestly desire the better gifts; and yet I show to you a far [more] excelling way:

13 If I speak with the tongues of men and of messengers, and do not have love, I have become sounding brass, or a clanging cymbal; **2** and if I have prophecy, and know all the secrets, and all the knowledge, and if I have all faith, so as to remove mountains, and do not have love, I am nothing; **3** and if I give away all my goods to feed others, and if I give up my body that I may be burned, and do not have love, I am profited nothing. **4** Love is long-suffering, it is kind, love does not envy, love does not vaunt itself, is not puffed up, **5** does not act unseemly, does not seek its own things, is not provoked, does not impute evil, **6** [does] not rejoice over unrighteousness, and rejoices with the truth; **7** it bears all things, it believes all, it hopes all, it endures all. **8** Love never fails; and whether [there be] prophecies, they will become useless; whether tongues, they will cease; whether knowledge, it will become useless; **9** for we know in part, and we prophesy in part; **10** and when that which is perfect may come, then that which [is] in part will become useless. **11** When I was a child, I was speaking as a child, I was thinking as a child, I was reasoning as a child, and when I have become a man, I have made useless the things of the child; **12** for we now see obscurely through a mirror, and then face to face; now I know in part, and then I will fully know, as I was also known; **13** and now there remains faith, hope, love—these three; and the greatest of these [is] love.

1 CORINTHIANS

14 Pursue love, and earnestly seek the spiritual things, and rather that you may prophesy, **2** for he who is speaking in an [unknown] tongue—he does not speak to men, but to God, for no one listens, and he speaks secrets in spirit; **3** and he who is prophesying to men speaks edification, and exhortation, and comfort; **4** he who is speaking in an [unknown] tongue, edifies himself, and he who is prophesying, edifies the Assembly; **5** and I wish you all to speak with tongues, and more that you may prophesy, for greater is he who is prophesying than he who is speaking with tongues, except one may interpret, that the Assembly may receive edification. **6** And now, brothers, if I may come to you speaking tongues, what will I profit you, except I will speak to you either in revelation, or in knowledge, or in prophesying, or in teaching? **7** Yet the things without life giving sound—whether pipe or harp—if they may not give a difference in the sounds, how will be known that which is piped or that which is harped? **8** For also, if a trumpet may give an uncertain sound, who will prepare himself for battle? **9** So also you, if you may not give speech easily understood through the tongue—how will that which is spoken be known? For you will be speaking to air. **10** There are, it may be, so many kinds of voices in the world, and none of them is unmeaning. **11** If, then, I do not know the power of the voice, I will be a foreigner to him who is speaking, and he who is speaking is a foreigner to me; **12** so you also, since you are earnestly desirous of spiritual gifts, seek for the building up of the Assembly that you may abound; **13** for this reason he who is speaking in an [unknown] tongue—let him pray that he may interpret; **14** for if I pray in an [unknown] tongue, my spirit prays, and my understanding is unfruitful. **15** What then is it? I will pray [in] the spirit, and I will also pray [with] understanding; I will sing psalms [in] the spirit, and I will also sing psalms [with] understanding; **16** since, if you may bless in spirit, he who is filling the place of the commoner, how will he say the Amen at your giving of thanks, since he has not known what you say? **17** For you, indeed, give thanks well, but the other is not built up! **18** I give thanks to my God—more than you all with tongues speaking—**19** but I wish to speak five words in an assembly through my understanding, that I also may instruct others, rather than myriads of words in an [unknown] tongue. **20** Brothers, do not become children in the understanding, but in the evil be children, and in the understanding become perfect; **21** in the Law it has been written, that, "With other tongues and with other lips I will speak to this people, and even so they will not hear Me, says the LORD"; **22** so that the tongues are for a sign, not to the believing, but to the unbelieving; and the prophecy [is] not for the unbelieving, but for the believing. **23** If, therefore, the whole assembly may come together to the same place, and all may speak with tongues, and there may come in commoners or unbelievers, will they not say that you are mad? **24** And if all may prophesy, and anyone may come in, an unbeliever or commoner, he is convicted by all, he is discerned by all, **25** and so the secrets of his heart become visible, and so having fallen on [his] face, he will worship God, declaring that God really is among you. **26** What then is it, brothers? Whenever you may come together, each of you has a psalm, has a teaching, has a tongue, has a revelation, has an interpretation. Let all things be for building up; **27** if anyone speaks an [unknown] tongue, by two, or at the most, by three, and in turn, and let one interpret; **28** and if there may be no interpreter, let him be silent in an assembly, and let him speak to himself, and to God. **29** And prophets—let two or three speak, and let the others discern, **30** and if [anything] may be revealed to another [who is] sitting, let the first be silent; **31** for you are able, one by one, all to prophesy, that all may learn, and all may be exhorted, **32** and the spiritual gift of prophets are subject to prophets, **33** for God is not [a God] of tumult, but of peace, as in all the assemblies of the holy ones. **34** Your women, let them be silent in the assemblies, for it has not been permitted to them to speak, but to be subject, as the Law also says; **35** and if they wish to learn anything, let them question their own husbands at home, for it is a shame to women to speak in an assembly. **36** Did the word of God come forth from you? Or did it come to you alone? **37** If anyone thinks to be a prophet, or spiritual, let him acknowledge the things that I write to you—that they are commands of the

LORD; **38** and if anyone is ignorant—let him be ignorant; **39** so that, brothers, earnestly desire to prophesy, and do not forbid to speak with tongues; **40** let all things be done decently and in order.

15 And I make known to you, brothers, the good news that I proclaimed to you, which you also received, in which you also have stood, **2** through which you are also being saved, if you hold fast [to] the word—what I proclaimed as good news to you—unless you believed in vain. **3** For I delivered to you as most important what I also received: that Christ died for our sins according to the Writings, **4** and that He was buried, and that He has risen on the third day according to the Writings, **5** and that He appeared to Cephas, then to the Twelve, **6** afterward He appeared to above five hundred brothers at once, of whom the greater part remain until now, and some also fell asleep; **7** afterward He appeared to James, then to all the apostles. **8** And last of all—as to the untimely birth—He also appeared to me, **9** for I am the least of the apostles, who am not worthy to be called an apostle, because I persecuted the Assembly of God, **10** and by the grace of God I am what I am, and His grace that [is] toward me did not come in vain, but I labored more abundantly than they all, yet not I, but the grace of God that [is] with me; **11** whether, then, I or they, so we preach, and so you believed. **12** And if Christ is preached, that He has risen out of the dead, how [do] certain among you say that there is no resurrection of [the] dead? **13** And if there is no resurrection of [the] dead, neither has Christ risen; **14** and if Christ has not risen, then our preaching [is] void, and your faith [is] also void, **15** and we are also found [to be] false witnesses of God, because we testified of God that He raised up the Christ, whom He did not raise if then dead persons do not rise; **16** for if dead persons do not rise, neither has Christ risen, **17** and if Christ has not risen, your faith is vain, you are yet in your sins; **18** then, also, those having fallen asleep in Christ perished; **19** if we only have hope in Christ in this life, we are to be most pitied of all men. **20** And now, Christ has risen out of the dead—He became the first-fruits of those sleeping, **21** for since through man [is] death, also through Man [is] a resurrection of the dead, **22** for even as in Adam all die, so also in the Christ all will be made alive, **23** and each in his proper order: Christ, a first-fruit, afterward those who are the Christ's in His coming, **24** then—the end, when He may deliver up the kingdom to God, even the Father, when He may have made all rule useless, and all authority and power. **25** For it is necessary for Him to reign until He may have put all the enemies under His feet. **26** The last enemy is done away with—death. **27** For He put all things under His feet, and when one may say that all things have been subjected, [it is] evident that He is excepted who subjected all things to Him, **28** and when all things may be subjected to Him, then also the Son Himself will be subject to Him, who subjected to Him all things, that God may be the all in all. **29** Seeing what will they do who are immersed for the dead, if the dead do not rise at all? Why are they also immersed for the dead? **30** Why do we also stand in peril every hour? **31** I die every day, by the glorying of you that I have in Christ Jesus our Lord. **32** If I fought with wild beasts in Ephesus after the manner of a man, what [is] the advantage to me if the dead do not rise? Let us eat and drink, for tomorrow we die! **33** Do not be led astray; evil communications corrupt good manners; **34** wake up, as is right, and do not sin; for some have an ignorance of God; I say [it] to you for shame. **35** But someone will say, "How do the dead rise?" **36** Unwise! You—what you sow is not quickened except it may die; **37** and that which you sow, you do not sow the body that will be, but a bare grain, it may be of wheat, or of someone of the others, **38** and God gives a body to it according as He willed, and its proper body to each of the seeds. **39** All flesh [is] not the same flesh, but there is one flesh of men, and another flesh of beasts, and another of fishes, and another of birds; **40** and [there are] heavenly bodies and earthly bodies; but one [is] the glory of the heavenly, and another that of the earthly; **41** one glory of sun, and another glory of moon, and another glory of stars, for star differs from star in glory. **42** So also [is] the resurrection of the dead: it is sown in corruption, it is raised in incorruption; **43** it is sown in dishonor, it is raised in glory; it is sown in weakness, it is raised in power; **44** it is sown a natural body, it is raised a spiritual body; there is a natural body, and there is a spiritual body; **45** so also it has been written: "The first man Adam became a living creature," the last Adam [is] for a life-giving spirit, **46** but that which is spiritual [is] not first, but that which [was] natural, afterward that which [is] spiritual. **47** The first man [is] out of the earth—earthly; the second Man [is] the LORD out of Heaven; **48** as [is] the earthly, such [are] also the earthly; and as [is] the heavenly, such [are] also the heavenly; **49** and according as we bore the image of the earthly, we will also bear the image of the heavenly. **50** And this I say, brothers, that flesh and blood are not able to inherit the Kingdom of God, nor does the corruption inherit the incorruption. **51** Behold, I tell you a secret: we indeed will not all sleep, but we will all be changed; **52** in a moment, in the twinkling of an eye, in the last trumpet, for it will sound, and the dead will be raised incorruptible, and we will be changed; **53** for it is necessary for this corruptible to put on incorruption, and this mortal to put on immortality; **54** and when this corruptible may have put on incorruption, and this mortal may have put on immortality, then will be brought to pass the word that has been written: "Death was swallowed up—to victory; **55** Where, O Death, your sting? Where, O Death [[*or* Hades]], your victory?" **56** And the sting of death [is] sin, and the power of sin the Law; **57** and to God—thanks, to Him who is giving us the victory through our Lord Jesus Christ; **58** so that, my beloved brothers, become steadfast, unmovable, abounding in the work of the LORD at all times, knowing that your labor in the LORD is not vain.

16 And concerning the collection that [is] for the holy ones, as I directed to the assemblies of Galatia, so also you—do; **2** on every first [day] of the week, let each one of you lay by him, treasuring up whatever he may have prospered, that when I may come then collections may not be made; **3** and whenever I may come, whomsoever you may approve, through letters, these I will send to carry your favor to Jerusalem; **4** and if it be worthy for me also to go, with me they will go. **5** And I will come to you when I pass through Macedonia—for I pass through Macedonia— **6** and with you, it may be, I will abide, or even winter, that you may send me forward wherever I go, **7** for I do not wish to see you now in the passing, but I hope to remain a certain time with you, if the LORD may permit; **8** and I will remain in Ephesus until the Pentecost, **9** for a door has been opened to me—great and effectual—and withstanders [are] many. **10** And if Timotheus may come, see that he may become without fear with you, for he works the work of the LORD, even as I, **11** no one, then, may despise him; and send him forward in peace, that he may come to me, for I expect him with the brothers; **12** and concerning Apollos our brother, I begged him much that he may come to you with the brothers, and it was not at all [his] will that he may come now, and he will come when he may find convenient. **13** Watch, stand in the faith; be men, be strong; **14** let all your things be done in love. **15** And I beg you, brothers, you have known the household of Stephanas, that it is the first-fruit of Achaia, and they set themselves to the ministry to the holy ones— **16** that you also be subject to such, and to everyone who is working with [us] and laboring; **17** and I rejoice over the coming of Stephanas, and Fortunatus, and Achaicus, because these filled up the lack of you; **18** for they refreshed my spirit and yours; acknowledge, therefore, those who [are] such. **19** The assemblies of Asia greet you; Aquilas and Priscilla greet you much in the LORD, with the assembly in their house; **20** all the brothers greet you; greet one another in a holy kiss. **21** The salutation of [me], Paul, with my hand; **22** if anyone does not cherish the Lord Jesus Christ—let him be accursed! The LORD has come! **23** The grace of the Lord Jesus Christ [is] with you; **24** my love [is] with you all in Christ Jesus! Amen.

2 CORINTHIANS

1 Paul, an apostle of Jesus Christ, through the will of God, and Timotheus the brother, to the Assembly of God that is in Corinth, with all the holy ones who are in all Achaia: **2** Grace to you and peace from God our Father and the Lord Jesus Christ! **3** Blessed [is] God, even the Father of our Lord Jesus Christ, the Father of mercies, and God of all comfort, **4** who is comforting us in all our tribulation, for our being able to comfort those in any tribulation through the comfort with which we are comforted ourselves by God; **5** because, as the sufferings of the Christ abound to us, so through the Christ our comfort also abounds; **6** and whether we be in tribulation, [it is] for your comfort and salvation, that is worked in the enduring of the same sufferings that we also suffer; whether we are comforted, [it is] for your comfort and salvation; **7** and our hope [is] steadfast for you, knowing that even as you are partakers of the sufferings—so also of the comfort. **8** For we do not wish you to be ignorant, brothers, of our tribulation that happened to us in Asia, that we were exceedingly burdened above [our] power, so that we even despaired of life; **9** but we ourselves have had the sentence of death in ourselves, that we may not be trusting on ourselves, but on God, who is raising the dead, **10** who delivered us out of so great a death, and delivers, in whom we have hoped that even yet He will deliver; **11** you also working together for us by your supplication, that the gift through many persons to us, through many, may be thankfully acknowledged for us. **12** For our glorying is this: the testimony of our conscience, that in simplicity and sincerity of God, not in fleshly wisdom, but in the grace of God, we conducted ourselves in the world, and more abundantly toward you; **13** for no other things do we write to you, but what you either read or also acknowledge, and I hope that you will also acknowledge to the end, **14** according as you also acknowledged us in part, that we are your glory, even as also you [are] ours, in the Day of the Lord Jesus; **15** and in this confidence I was intending to come to you before, that you might have a second favor, **16** and to pass to Macedonia through you, and to come to you again from Macedonia, and to be sent forward by you to Judea. **17** This, therefore, intending, did I then use the lightness; or the things that I counsel, [did] I counsel according to the flesh, that it may be with me Yes, yes, and No, no? **18** And God [is] faithful, that our word to you did not become Yes and No, **19** for the Son of God, Jesus Christ, having been preached through us among you—through me and Silvanus and Timotheus—did not become Yes and No, but in Him it has become Yes; **20** for as many as [are] promises of God, in Him [are] the Yes, and in Him the Amen, for glory to God through us; **21** and He who is confirming you with us into Christ, and anointed us, [is] God, **22** who also sealed us, and gave the deposit of the Spirit in our hearts. **23** And I call on God for a witness on my soul, that sparing you, I did not come to Corinth yet; **24** not that we are lords over your faith, but we are workers together with your joy, for by faith you stand.

2 And I decided this to myself, not to come again to you in sorrow, **2** for if I make you sorry, then who is he who is making me glad, except he who is made sorry by me? **3** And I wrote to you this same thing, that having come, I may not have sorrow from them of whom it was necessary [for] me to have joy, having confidence in you all, that my joy is of you all, **4** for out of much tribulation and pressure of heart I wrote to you through many tears, not that you might be made sorry, but that you might know the love that I have more abundantly toward you. **5** And if anyone has caused sorrow, he has not caused sorrow to me, but in part, that I may not burden you all; **6** sufficient to such a one is this punishment, that [is] by the greater part, **7** so that, on the contrary, [it is] rather for you to forgive and to comfort, lest by over abundant sorrow such a one may be swallowed up; **8** for this reason, I call on you to confirm love to him, **9** for this also I wrote, that I might know your proof, whether you are obedient in regard to all things. **10** And to whom you forgive anything—I also; for I also, if I have forgiven anything, to whom I have forgiven [it], because of you—in the person of Christ—[I forgive it,] **11** that we may not be over-reached by Satan, for we are not ignorant of his schemes. **12** And having come to Troas for the good news of the Christ, and a door having been opened to me in the LORD, **13** I have not had rest to my spirit, on my not finding my brother Titus, but having taken leave of them, I went forth to Macedonia; **14** and to God [is] thanks, who at all times is leading us in triumph in the Christ, and the fragrance of His knowledge He is revealing through us in every place; **15** we are a refreshing fragrance to God because of Christ, in those being saved, and in those being lost; **16** to one, indeed, a fragrance of death to death, and to the other, a fragrance of life to life; and who is sufficient for these things? **17** For we are not as the many, adulterating the word of God, but as of sincerity—but as of God; in the presence of God, in Christ we speak.

3 Do we begin again to recommend ourselves, except we need, as some, letters of recommendation to you, or from you? **2** You are our letter, having been written in our hearts, known and read by all men, **3** revealed that you are a letter of Christ ministered by us, not written with ink, but with the Spirit of the living God, not in the tablets of stone, but in fleshy tablets of the heart, **4** and such trust we have through the Christ toward God, **5** not that we are sufficient of ourselves to think anything, as of ourselves, but our sufficiency [is] of God, **6** who also made us sufficient [to be] servants of the New Covenant, not of letter, but of the Spirit; for the letter kills, and the Spirit makes alive. **7** And if the ministry of death, in letters, engraved in stones, came in glory, so that the sons of Israel were not able to look steadfastly into the face of Moses, because of the glory of his face—which was being made useless, **8** how will the ministry of the Spirit not be more in glory? **9** For if the ministry of the condemnation [is] glory, much more does the ministry of righteousness abound in glory; **10** for also even that which has been glorious, has not been glorious—in this respect, because of the superior glory; **11** for if that which is being made useless [is] through glory, much more that which is remaining [is] in glory. **12** Having, then, such hope, we use much freedom of speech, **13** and [are] not as Moses, who was putting a veil on his own face, for the sons of Israel not to look steadfastly into the end of that which is being made useless, **14** but their minds were hardened, for to this day the same veil at the reading of the Old Covenant remains unwithdrawn—which in Christ is being made useless— **15** but until today, when Moses is read, a veil lies on their heart, **16** and whenever they may turn to the LORD, the veil is taken away. **17** And the LORD is the Spirit; and where the Spirit of the LORD [is], there [is] liberty; **18** and we all, with unveiled face, beholding the glory of the LORD in a mirror, are being transformed into the same image, from glory to glory, even as by the Spirit of the LORD.

4 Because of this, having this ministry, according as we received kindness, we do not faint, **2** but renounced for ourselves the hidden things of shame, not walking in craftiness, nor deceitfully using the word of God, but by the manifestation of the truth recommending ourselves to every conscience of men, before God; **3** and if our good news is also veiled, it is veiled in those perishing, **4** in whom the god of this age blinded the minds of the unbelieving, that there does not shine forth to them the enlightening of the good news of the glory of the Christ, who is the image of God; **5** for we do not preach ourselves, but Christ Jesus—LORD, and [we are] ourselves your servants because of Jesus; **6** because [it is] God who said, "Light will shine out of darkness," who shined in our hearts, for the enlightening of the knowledge of the glory of God in the face of Jesus Christ. **7** And we have this treasure in earthen vessels, that the excellence of the power may be of God, and not of us, **8** being in tribulation in every [way], but not crushed; perplexed, but not despairing; **9** persecuted, but not forsaken; cast down, but not destroyed; **10** at all times carrying around in the body the dying of the Lord Jesus, that the life of Jesus may also be revealed in our body, **11** for we who are living are always delivered up to death because of Jesus, that the life of Jesus may also be revealed in our dying flesh, **12** so that, death indeed works in us, and life in you. **13** And having the same spirit of faith, according to that which has been written: "I believed, therefore I spoke"; we also believe, therefore we also speak; **14** knowing that He who raised up the Lord Jesus, will also raise us up through Jesus, and will present [us] with you, **15** for all things [are] because of you, that the grace having been multiplied, because of the thanksgiving of the more, may abound to the glory of God; **16** for this reason, we do not faint, but if our outward man also decays, yet the inward is renewed day by day; **17** for the momentary light matter of our tribulation works out for us more and more an exceedingly continuous weight of glory— **18** we [are] not looking to the things seen, but to the things not seen; for the things seen [are] temporary, but the things not seen [are] continuous.

5 For we have known that if the tent of our earthly house may be thrown down, we have a building from God, a house not made with hands—perpetual—in the heavens, **2** for also in this we groan, earnestly desiring to clothe ourselves with our dwelling that is from Heaven, **3** if so be that, having clothed ourselves, we will not be found naked, **4** for we also who are in the tent groan, being burdened, seeing we do not wish to unclothe ourselves, but to clothe ourselves, that the mortal may be swallowed up of life. **5** And He who worked us to this very thing [is] God, who also gave to us the deposit of the Spirit; **6** having courage, then, at all times, and knowing that being at home in the body, we are away from home from the LORD— **7** for we walk through faith, not through sight— **8** we have courage, and are well pleased, rather, to be away from the home of the body, and to be at home with the LORD. **9** We are also ambitious for this reason, whether at home or away from home, to be well pleasing to Him, **10** for it is necessary for all of us to have appeared before the judgment seat of the Christ, that each one may receive the things [done] through the body, in reference to the things that he did, whether good or evil; **11** having known, therefore, the fear of the LORD, we persuade men, and we are revealed to God, and I also hope to have been revealed in your consciences; **12** for we do not again recommend ourselves to you, but we are giving occasion to you of glorifying in our behalf, that you may have [something] in reference to those glorifying in face and not in heart; **13** for whether we were beside ourselves, [it was] to God; whether we be of sound mind, [it is] to you, **14** for the love of the Christ constrains us, having judged thus: that if one died for all, then the whole died, **15** and He died for all, that those living may no longer live to themselves, but to Him who died for them, and was raised again. **16** So that we, from now on, have known no one according to the flesh, and even if we have known Christ according to the flesh, yet now we know Him [thus] no longer; **17** so that if anyone [is] in Christ—[he is] a new creature; the old things passed away, behold, all things have become new. **18** And all things [are] of God, who reconciled us to Himself through Jesus Christ, and gave to us the ministry of the reconciliation, **19** how that God was in Christ—reconciling the world to Himself, not reckoning to them their trespasses; and having put in us the word of the reconciliation, **20** in behalf of Christ, then, we are ambassadors, as if God were calling through us, we implore, in behalf of Christ, "Be reconciled to God"; **21** He made Him having not known sin [to be] sin in our behalf, that we may become the righteousness of God in Him.

6 And also working together we call on [you] that you do not receive the grace of God in vain— **2** for He says, "In an acceptable time I heard you, and in a day of salvation I helped you, behold, now [is] a well-accepted time; behold, now, a day of salvation." **3** In nothing giving any cause of offense, that the ministry may not be blamed, **4** but in everything recommending ourselves as God's servants; in much patience, in tribulations, in necessities, in distresses, **5** in stripes, in imprisonments, in insurrections, in labors, in watchings, in fastings, **6** in pureness, in knowledge, in long-suffering, in kindness, in the Holy Spirit, in unhypocritical love, **7** in the word of truth, in the power of God, through the armor of righteousness, on the right and on the left, **8** through glory and dishonor, through evil report and good report, as leading astray, and true; **9** as unknown, and recognized; as dying, and behold, we live; as disciplined, and not put to death; **10** as sorrowful, and always rejoicing; as poor, and making many rich; as having nothing, and possessing all things. **11** Our mouth has been open to you, O Corinthians, our heart has been enlarged! **12** You are not restricted in us, and you are restricted in your [own] yearnings, **13** and [as] a repayment of the same kind (as to children I say [it]), be enlarged—also you! **14** Do not become yoked with others—unbelievers, for what partaking [is there] to righteousness and lawlessness? **15** And what fellowship to light with darkness? And what concord to Christ with Belial? Or what part to a believer with an unbeliever? **16** And what agreement to the temple of God with idols? For you are a temple of the living God, according as God said, "I will dwell in them, and will walk among [them], and I will be their God, and they will be My people, **17** for this reason, come forth out of the midst of them, and be separated, says the LORD, and do not touch an unclean thing, and I will receive you, **18** and I will be for a Father to you, and you will be sons and daughters to Me, says the LORD Almighty."

7 Having, then, these promises, beloved, may we cleanse ourselves from every defilement of flesh and spirit, perfecting sanctification in the fear of God; **2** receive us; no one did we wrong; no one did we ruin; no one did we defraud; **3** I do not say [it] to condemn you, for I have said before that you are in our hearts to die together and to live together; **4** great [is] my freedom of speech to you, great my glory on your behalf; I have been filled with the comfort, I hyper-abound with the joy on all our tribulation, **5** for we also, having come to Macedonia, our flesh has had no relaxation, but on every side we are in tribulation: fightings outside, fears within; **6** but He who is comforting the cast-down—God—He comforted us in the coming of Titus; **7** and not only in his coming, but also in the comfort with which he was comforted over you, declaring to us your longing desire, your lamentation, your zeal for me, so that I rejoiced the more, **8** because even if I made you sorry in the letter, I do not regret—if even I regretted—for I perceive that the letter, even if for an hour, made you sorry. **9** I now rejoice, not that you were made sorry, but that you were made sorry to conversion, for you were made sorry toward God, that you might receive damage from us in nothing; **10** for sorrow toward God works conversion to salvation without regret, and the sorrow of the world works death, **11** for behold, this same thing—your being made sorry toward God—how much diligence it works in you! But defense, but displeasure, but fear, but longing desire, but zeal, but revenge; in everything you approved yourselves to be pure in the matter. **12** If, then, I also wrote to you—not for his cause who did wrong, nor for his cause who suffered wrong, but for our diligence in your behalf being revealed to you before God— **13** because of this we have been comforted in your comfort, and more abundantly the more we rejoiced in the joy of Titus, that his spirit has been refreshed from you all; **14** because if I have boasted anything to him in your behalf, I was not put to shame; but as we spoke to you all things in truth, so also our boasting before Titus became truth, **15** and his yearnings are more abundantly toward you, remembering the obedience of you all, how you received him with fear and trembling; **16** I rejoice, therefore, that in everything I have courage in you.

8 And we make known to you, brothers, the grace of God, that has been given in the assemblies of Macedonia, **2** because in much trial of tribulation the abundance of their joy, and their deep poverty, abounded to the riches of their liberality; **3** because, according to [their] power, I testify, and above [their] power, they were willing of themselves, **4** with much plea calling on us to receive the favor and the fellowship of the ministry to the holy ones, **5** and not according as we expected, but they gave themselves first to the LORD, and to us, through the will of God, **6** so that we exhorted Titus, that, according as he began before, so also he may also finish this favor to you, **7** but even as in everything you abound, in faith, and word, and knowledge, and all diligence, and in your love to us, that also in this grace you may abound; **8** I do not speak according to command, but because of the diligence of others, and proving the genuineness of your love, **9** for you know the grace of our Lord Jesus Christ, that because of you He became poor—being rich, that you may become rich by that poverty. **10** And I give an opinion in this: for this [is] expedient to you, who not only to do, but also to will, began before—a year ago, **11** and now also finish doing [it], that even as [there is] the readiness of the will, so also the finishing, out of that which you have, **12** for if the willing mind is present, it is well-accepted according to that which anyone may have, not according to that which he does not have; **13** for I do not speak that for others [to be] released, and you pressured, **14** but by equality, at the present time your abundance—for their want, that also their abundance may be for your want, that there may be equality, **15** according as it has been written: "He who [gathered] much, had nothing over; and he who [gathered] little, had no lack." **16** And thanks to God, who is putting the same diligence for you in the heart of Titus, **17** because he indeed accepted the exhortation, and being more diligent, he went forth to you of his own accord, **18** and we sent with him the brother, whose praise in the good news [is] through all the assemblies, **19** and not only so, but who was also appointed by vote by the assemblies, our fellow-traveler, with this favor that is ministered by us, to the glory of the same Lord, and your willing mind; **20** avoiding this, lest anyone may blame us in this abundance that is ministered by us, **21** providing right things, not only before the LORD, but also before men; **22** and we sent our brother with them, whom we proved being diligent many times in many things, and now much more diligent, by the great confidence that is toward you, **23** whether—about Titus—my partner and fellow-worker toward you, whether—our brothers, apostles of assemblies—glory of Christ; **24** the showing therefore of your love, and of our boasting on your behalf, show to them, even in the face of the assemblies.

9 For indeed, concerning the ministry that [is] for the holy ones, it is superfluous for me to write to you, **2** for I have known your readiness of mind, which in your behalf I boast of to Macedonians, that Achaia has been prepared a year ago, and your zeal stirred up the greater part, **3** and I sent the brothers, that our boasting on your behalf may not be made vain in this respect; that, according as I said, you may be ready, **4** lest if Macedonians may come with me, and find you unprepared, we may be put to shame (that we do not say—you) in this same confidence of boasting. **5** Therefore I thought [it] necessary to exhort the brothers, that they may go before to you, and may make up before your formerly announced blessing, that this be ready, as a blessing, and not as covetousness. **6** And [remember] this: he who is sowing sparingly, will also reap sparingly; and he who is sowing in blessings, will also reap in blessings; **7** each one, according as he purposes in heart, not out of sorrow or out of necessity, for God loves a cheerful giver, **8** and God [is] able to cause all grace to abound to you, that in everything always having all sufficiency, you may abound to every good work, **9** according as it has been written: "He dispersed abroad, He gave to the poor, His righteousness remains throughout the age," **10** and may He who is supplying seed to the sower, and bread for food, supply and multiply your seed sown, and increase the fruits of your righteousness, **11** being enriched to all liberality in everything, which works thanksgiving through us to God, **12** because the ministry of this service not only is supplying the wants of the holy ones, but is also abounding through many thanksgivings to God, **13** through the proof of this ministry glorifying God for the subjection of your confession to the good news of the Christ, and [for] the liberality of the fellowship to them and to all, **14** and by their supplication in your behalf, longing after you because of the exceeding grace of God on you; **15** thanks also to God for His unspeakable gift!

10 And I, Paul, myself, call on you—through the meekness and gentleness of the Christ—who in presence [am] indeed humble among you, and being absent, have courage toward you, **2** and I implore [you], that, being present, I may not have courage, with the confidence with which I reckon to be bold against certain reckoning us as walking according to the flesh; **3** for walking in the flesh, we do not war according to the flesh, **4** for the weapons of our warfare [are] not fleshly, but powerful to God for bringing down of strongholds, **5** bringing down reasonings, and every high thing lifted up against the knowledge of God, and bringing into captivity every thought to the obedience of the Christ, **6** and being in readiness to avenge every disobedience whenever your obedience may be fulfilled. **7** You see the outward appearance. If anyone has trusted in himself to be Christ's, let him reckon this again from himself, that according as he is

Christ's, so also we [are] Christ's; **8** for even if I will also boast anything more abundantly concerning our authority, that the LORD gave us for building up, and not for casting you down, I will not be ashamed, **9** that I may not seem as if I would terrify you through the letters, **10** "because the letters indeed," says one, "[are] weighty and strong, and the bodily presence weak, and the speech despicable." **11** This one—let him reckon thus: that such as we are in word, through letters, being absent, such also, being present, [we are] in deed. **12** For we do not make bold to rank or to compare ourselves with certain of those commending themselves, but they, measuring themselves among themselves, and comparing themselves with themselves, are not wise, **13** and we will not boast ourselves in regard to the unmeasured things, but after the measure of the line that the God of measure appointed to us—to reach even to you; **14** for we do not stretch ourselves too much, as not reaching to you, for even to you we came in the good news of the Christ, **15** not boasting of the things not measured, in other men's labors, and having hope—your faith increasing—in you to be enlarged, according to our line—into abundance, **16** to proclaim good news in the [places] beyond you, not in another's line in regard to the things made ready, to boast; **17** and he who is boasting—let him boast in the LORD; **18** for he who is commending himself is not approved, but he whom the LORD commends.

11 O that you were bearing with me a little of the folly, but you also bear with me: **2** for I am zealous for you with zeal of God, for I betrothed you to one Husband, a pure virgin, to present to Christ, **3** and I fear, lest, as the serpent deceived Eve in his subtlety, so your minds may be corrupted from the simplicity that [is] in the Christ; **4** for if, indeed, he who is coming preaches another Jesus whom we did not preach, or you receive another spirit which you did not receive, or other good news which you did not accept—well were you bearing [it], **5** for I reckon that I have been nothing behind the very chiefest apostles, **6** and even if a commoner in speech—yet not in knowledge, but in everything we were made evident in all things to you. **7** Did I do sin—humbling myself that you might be exalted, because I freely proclaimed the good news of God to you? **8** I robbed other assemblies, having taken wages, for your ministry; **9** and being present with you, and having been in want, I was chargeable to no one, for the brothers supplied my lack—having come from Macedonia—and I kept myself burdenless to you in everything, and will keep. **10** The truth of Christ is in me, because this boasting will not be stopped in regard to me in the regions of Achaia; **11** for what reason? Because I do not love you? God has known! **12** And what I do, I also will do, that I may cut off the occasion of those wishing an occasion, that in that which they boast they may be found according as we also; **13** for those such [are] false apostles, deceitful workers, transforming themselves into apostles of Christ, **14** and no wonder—for even Satan transforms himself into a messenger of light; **15** [it is] no great thing, then, if his servants also transform themselves as servants of righteousness—whose end will be according to their works. **16** Again I say, may no one think me to be a fool; and if otherwise, receive me even as a fool, that I also may boast a little. **17** That which I speak, I do not speak according to the LORD, but as in foolishness, in this the confidence of boasting; **18** since many boast according to the flesh, I also will boast: **19** for you gladly bear with the fools—being wise, **20** for you bear, if anyone is bringing you under bondage, if anyone devours, if anyone takes away, if anyone exalts himself, if anyone strikes you on the face; **21** I speak in reference to dishonor, how that we were weak, and in whatever anyone is bold—in foolishness I say [it]—I also am bold. **22** Are they Hebrews? I also! Are they Israelites? I also! Are they seed of Abraham? I also! **23** Are they servants of Christ? As [if] beside myself I speak—I [am] more; in labors more abundantly, in stripes above measure, in prisons more frequently, in deaths many times. **24** Five times I received from Jews forty [stripes] except one; **25** three times I was beaten with rods, once I was stoned, three times I was shipwrecked, I have passed a night and a day in the deep; **26** journeys many times, perils of rivers, perils of robbers, perils from [my own] race, perils from nations, perils in city, perils in wilderness, perils in sea, perils

2 CORINTHIANS

among false brothers; **27** in laboriousness and painfulness, many times in watchings, in hunger and thirst, many times in fastings, in cold and nakedness; **28** apart from the things without—the crowding on me that is daily—the care of all the assemblies. **29** Who is weak, and I am not weak? Who is stumbled, and I am not burned? **30** If it is necessary to boast, I will boast of the things of my weakness; **31** the God and Father of our Lord Jesus Christ—who is blessed for all ages—has known that I do not lie! **32** In Damascus the governor [under] Aretas the king was watching the city of the Damascenes, wishing to seize me, **33** and I was let down through a window in a rope basket, through the wall, and fled out of his hands.

12 To boast, really, is not profitable for me, for I will come to visions and revelations of the LORD. **2** I have known a man in Christ, fourteen years ago—whether in the body I have not known, whether out of the body I have not known, God has known—such a one being snatched up to the third heaven; **3** and I have known such a man—whether in the body, whether out of the body, I have not known, God has known— **4** that he was snatched up to the paradise, and heard unutterable sayings, that it is not possible for man to speak. **5** Of such a one I will boast, and of myself I will not boast, except in my weaknesses, **6** for if I may wish to boast, I will not be a fool, for I will say truth; but I refrain, lest in regard to me anyone may think anything above what he sees me, or hears anything of me; **7** and that by the exceeding greatness of the revelations I might not be exalted too much, there was given to me a thorn in the flesh, a messenger of Satan, that he might batter me, that I might not be exalted too much. **8** I called on the LORD three times concerning this thing, that it might depart from me, **9** and He said to me, "My grace is sufficient for you, for My power is perfected in weakness"; most gladly, therefore, will I rather boast in my weaknesses, that the power of the Christ may rest on me: **10** for this reason I am well pleased in weaknesses, in damages, in necessities, in persecutions, in distresses—for Christ; for whenever I may be weak, then I am powerful; **11** I have become a fool—boasting; you compelled me; for I ought to have been commended by you, for I was behind the very chiefest apostles in nothing—even if I am nothing. **12** The signs, indeed, of the apostle were worked among you in all patience, in signs, and wonders, and mighty deeds, **13** for what is there in which you were inferior to the rest of the assemblies, except that I myself was not a burden to you? Forgive me this injustice! **14** Behold, a third time I am ready to come to you, and I will not be a burden to you, for I do not seek yours, but you, for the children ought not to lay up for the parents, but the parents for the children, **15** and I will most gladly spend and be entirely spent for your souls, even if, loving you more abundantly, I am loved less. **16** And be it [so], I did not burden you, but being crafty, I took you with guile; **17** anyone of those whom I have sent to you—did I take advantage of you by him? **18** I begged Titus, and sent with [him] the brother; did Titus take advantage of you? Did we not walk in the same Spirit? Did we not [walk] in the same steps? **19** Again, [do] you think that we are making defense to you? We speak before God in Christ; and all things, beloved, [are] for your up-building, **20** for I fear lest, having come, I may not find you such as I wish, and I may be found by you such as you do not wish, lest there be strifes, envyings, wraths, revelries, slanders, whisperings, puffings up, insurrections, **21** lest again having come, my God may humble me in regard to you, and I may mourn many of those having sinned before, and having not changed their mind concerning the uncleanness, and whoredom, and licentiousness, that they practiced.

13 I come to you this third time; on the mouth of two or three witnesses will every saying be established; **2** I have said before, and I say [it] before, as being present, the second time, and being absent, now, I write to those having sinned before, and to all the rest, that if I come again, I will not spare, **3** since you seek a proof of the Christ speaking in me, who is not weak to you, but is powerful in you, **4** for even if He was crucified from weakness, yet He lives from the power of God; for we also are weak in Him, but we will live with Him from the power of God toward you. **5** Try yourselves, if you are in the faith; prove yourselves; do you not know yourselves,

2 CORINTHIANS

that Jesus Christ is in you, if you are not disapproved of in some respect? **6** And I hope that you will know that we are not disapproved of; **7** and I pray before God that you do no evil, not that we may appear approved, but that you may do that which is right, and we may be as disapproved; **8** for we are not able to do anything against the truth, but for the truth; **9** for we rejoice when we may be weak, but you may be powerful; and we also pray for this—your perfection! **10** Because of this, these things—being absent—I write, that being present, I may not treat [any] sharply, according to the authority that the LORD gave me for building up, and not for casting down. **11** From now on, brothers, rejoice; be made perfect, be comforted, be of the same mind, be at peace, and the God of love and peace will be with you. **12** Greet one another in a holy kiss. **13** All the holy ones greet you. **14** The grace of the Lord Jesus Christ, and the love of God, and the fellowship of the Holy Spirit, [is] with you all! Amen.

GALATIANS

1 Paul, an apostle—not from men, nor through man, but through Jesus Christ, and God the Father, who raised Him out of the dead— **2** and all the brothers with me, to the assemblies of Galatia: **3** Grace to you and peace from God the Father and our Lord Jesus Christ, **4** who gave Himself for our sins, that He might deliver us out of the present evil age, according to the will of our God and Father, **5** to whom [is] the glory through the ages of the ages. Amen. **6** I wonder that you are so quickly removed from Him who called you in the grace of Christ to another good news— **7** not that there is another, except there are certain who are troubling you, and wishing to pervert the good news of the Christ; **8** but even if we or a messenger out of Heaven may proclaim good news to you different from what we proclaimed to you—let him be accursed! **9** As we have said before, and now say again: if anyone may proclaim to you good news different from what you received—let him be accursed! **10** For do I now persuade men, or God? Or do I seek to please men? For if I yet pleased men—I should not be Christ's servant. **11** And I make known to you, brothers, the good news that was proclaimed by me, that it is not according to man, **12** for neither did I receive it from man, nor was I taught [it], but through a revelation of Jesus Christ, **13** for you heard of my behavior once in Judaism, that I was exceedingly persecuting the Assembly of God, and destroying it, **14** and I was advancing in Judaism above many equals in age in my own race, being more abundantly zealous of my fathers' deliverances, **15** and when God was well pleased—having separated me from the womb of my mother, and having called [me] through His grace— **16** to reveal His Son in me, that I might proclaim Him as good news among the nations, I did not immediately confer with flesh and blood, **17** nor did I go up to Jerusalem to those who were apostles before me, but I went away to Arabia, and again returned to Damascus; **18** then, after three years I went up to Jerusalem to inquire about Peter, and remained with him fifteen days, **19** and I did not see [any] other of the apostles, except James, the brother of the LORD. **20** And the things that I write to you, behold, before God—I do not lie; **21** then I came into the regions of Syria and of Cilicia, **22** and was unknown by face to the assemblies of Judea, that [are] in Christ, **23** and they were only hearing that "he who is persecuting us then, now proclaims good news—the faith that he was then destroying"; **24** and they were glorifying God in me.

2 Then after fourteen years again I went up to Jerusalem with Barnabas, having also taken Titus with me; **2** and I went up by revelation, and submitted the good news to them that I preach among the nations, and privately to those esteemed, lest I ran or might run in vain; **3** but not even Titus, who [is] with me, being a Greek, was compelled to be circumcised— **4** and [that] because of the false brothers brought in unaware, who came in secretly to spy out our liberty that we have in Christ Jesus, that they might bring us under bondage, **5** to whom not even for an hour we gave place by subjection, that the truth of the good news might remain to you. **6** And from those who were esteemed to be something—whatever they were then, it makes no difference to me. God does not accept the face of man, for to me those esteemed added nothing, **7** but on the contrary, having seen that I have been entrusted with the good news of the uncircumcision, as Peter with [that] of the circumcision, **8** for He who worked with Peter to the apostleship of the circumcision, worked also in me in regard to the nations, **9** and having known the grace that was given to me, James, and Cephas, and John, who were esteemed to be pillars, they gave to me a right hand of fellowship, and to Barnabas, that we may go to the nations, and they to the circumcision, **10** only, that we should be mindful of the poor, which I also was diligent—this very thing—to do. **11** And when Peter came to Antioch, I stood up against him to the face, because he was blameworthy, **12** for before the coming of some from James, he was eating with the nations, and when they came, he was withdrawing and separating himself, fearing those of circumcision, **13** and the other Jews acted hypocritically with him, so that Barnabas was also carried away by their hypocrisy. **14** But when I saw that they are not walking uprightly to the truth of the good news, I said to Peter before all, "If you, being a Jew, live in the manner of the nations, and not in the manner of the Jews, how do you compel the nations to live like Jews? **15** We by nature Jews, and not sinners of the nations, **16** having also known that a man is not declared righteous by works of law, but through faith from Jesus Christ, we also believed in Christ Jesus, that we might be declared righteous by faith from Christ, and not by works of law, because no flesh will be declared righteous by works of law." **17** And if, seeking to be declared righteous in Christ, we were also ourselves found sinners, [is] Christ then a servant of sin? Let it not be! **18** For if the things I threw down, these again I build up, I set myself forth [as] a transgressor; **19** for I died through law that I may live to God; **20** I have been crucified with Christ, and I no longer live, but Christ lives in me; and that which I now live in the flesh—I live in the faith of the Son of God, who loved me and gave Himself for me; **21** I do not make the grace of God void, for if righteousness [is] through law—then Christ died in vain.

3 O thoughtless Galatians, who bewitched you, not to obey the truth—before whose eyes [it] was previously written [about] Jesus Christ having been crucified? **2** I only wish to learn this from you: did you receive the Spirit by works of the Law, or by the hearing of faith? **3** Are you so thoughtless? Having begun in the Spirit, do you now end in the flesh? **4** So many things you suffered in vain! If, indeed, even in vain. **5** He, therefore, who is supplying the Spirit to you and working mighty acts among you—[is it] by works of law or by the hearing of faith? **6** According as Abraham believed God, and it was reckoned to him for righteousness; **7** know, then, that those of faith—these are sons of Abraham, **8** and the Writing, having foreseen that God declares righteous the nations by faith, foretold the good news to Abraham: **9** "All the nations will be blessed in you"; so that those of faith are blessed with the believing Abraham, **10** for as many as are of works of law are under a curse, for it has been written: "Cursed [is] everyone who is not remaining in all things that have been written in the Scroll of the Law—to do them," **11** and [it] is evident that in law no one is declared righteous with God, because "The righteous will live by faith"; **12** and the Law is not by faith, rather, "The man who did them will live in them." **13** Christ redeemed us from the curse of the Law, having become a curse for us, for it has been written: "Cursed is everyone who is hanging on a tree," **14** that the blessing of Abraham may come to the nations in Christ Jesus, that we may receive the promise of the Spirit through faith. **15** Brothers, I say [it] as a man, no one even makes void or adds to a confirmed covenant of man, **16** and to Abraham were the promises spoken, and to his Seed; He does not say, "And to seeds," as of many, but as of one, "And to your Seed," which is Christ; **17** and this I say, a covenant confirmed before by God to Christ, the Law, that came four hundred and thirty years after, does not set aside, to make void the promise, **18** for if the inheritance [is] by law, [it is] no longer by promise, but God granted [it] to Abraham through promise. **19** Why, then, the Law? It was added on account of the transgressions, until the Seed might come to which the promise has been made, having been set in order through messengers in the hand of a mediator—**20** and the mediator is not of one, but God is one. **21** [Is] the Law, then, against the promises of God? Let it not be! For if a law was given that was able to make alive, truly there would have been righteousness by law, **22** but the Writing shut up the whole under sin, that the promise by faith of Jesus Christ may be given to those believing. **23** And before the coming of faith, we were being kept under law, shut up to the faith about to be revealed, **24** so that the Law became our tutor—to Christ, that we may be declared righteous by faith, **25** and faith having come, we are no longer under a tutor, **26** for you are all sons of God through faith in Christ Jesus, **27** for as many as were immersed into Christ put on Christ; **28** there is neither Jew nor Greek, there is neither servant nor freeman, there is neither male and female, for you are all one in Christ Jesus; **29** and if you [are] of Christ then you are seed of Abraham, and heirs according to promise.

GALATIANS

4 And I say, now as much time as the heir is a child, he differs nothing from a servant, [though] being lord of all, **2** but is under tutors and stewards until the time appointed of the father, **3** so we also, when we were children, were in servitude under the elements of the world, **4** and when the fullness of time came, God sent forth His Son, come of a woman, come under law, **5** that He may redeem those under law, that we may receive the adoption as sons; **6** and because you are sons, God sent forth the Spirit of His Son into your hearts, crying, "Abba! Father!" **7** So that you are no longer a servant, but a son, and if a son, also an heir of God through Christ. **8** But then, indeed, having not known God, you were in servitude to those [that are] not by nature gods, **9** and now, having known God—and rather being known by God—how [do] you turn again to the weak and poor elements to which you desire anew to be in servitude? **10** You observe days, and months, and times, and years! **11** I am afraid for you, lest I labored in vain for you. **12** I implore you, brothers, become as I [am]—because I also [am] as you; you did not hurt me; **13** and you have known that through weakness of the flesh I proclaimed good news to you at the first, **14** and you did not despise nor reject my trial that [is] in my flesh, but you received me as a messenger of God—as Christ Jesus; **15** what then was your blessedness? For I testify to you, that if possible, having plucked out your eyes, you would have given [them] to me; **16** so have I become your enemy, being true to you? **17** They are zealous for you—[yet] not well, but they wish to shut us out, that you may be zealous for them; **18** and [it is] good to be zealously regarded, in what is good, at all times, and not only in my being present with you; **19** my little children, of whom I travail in birth again until Christ may be formed in you, **20** indeed I was wishing to be present with you now, and to change my voice, because I am in doubt about you. **21** Tell me, you who are willing to be under law, do you not hear the Law? **22** For it has been written that Abraham had two sons, one by the maidservant and one by the free [woman], **23** but he who [is] of the maidservant has been according to flesh, but he who [is] of the free [woman], through the promise, **24** which things are allegorized, for these are the two covenants: one, indeed, from Mount Sinai, bringing forth to servitude, which is Hagar; **25** for this Hagar is Mount Sinai in Arabia, and corresponds to the Jerusalem that now [is], and is in servitude with her children, **26** and the Jerusalem above is the free [woman], which is mother of us all, **27** for it has been written: "Rejoice, O barren, who is not bearing; break forth and cry, you who are not travailing, because many [are] the children of the desolate—more than of her having the husband." **28** And we, brothers, as Isaac, are children of promise, **29** but as he then who was born according to the flesh persecuted him [born] according to the Spirit, so also now; **30** but what does the Writing say? "Cast forth the maidservant and her son, for the son of the maidservant may not be heir with the son of the free [woman]"; **31** then, brothers, we are not a maidservant's children, but the free [woman's].

5 In the freedom, then, with which Christ made you free—stand, and do not be held fast again by a yoke of servitude. **2** Behold! I, Paul, say to you, that if you are [to be] circumcised, Christ will profit you nothing; **3** and I testify again to every man circumcised, that he is a debtor to do the whole law; **4** you were voided from the Christ, you who are declared righteous in law; you fell away from grace; **5** for we by the Spirit, by faith, wait for a hope of righteousness, **6** for in Christ Jesus neither circumcision avails anything, nor uncircumcision, but faith working through love. **7** You were running well; who hindered you [so as] not to obey the truth? **8** The persuasion [is] not of Him who is calling you! **9** A little leaven leavens the whole lump; **10** I have confidence in regard to you in the LORD that you will not be otherwise minded; and he who is troubling you will bear the judgment, whoever he may be. **11** And I, brothers, if I still preach circumcision, why am I still persecuted? Then the stumbling-block of the Cross has been done away [with]; **12** O that even they would cut themselves off who are unsettling you! **13** For you were called to freedom, brothers, only the freedom [is] not for an occasion to the flesh, but serve one another through the love, **14** for all the Law is fulfilled in one word—in this: "You will love your neighbor as yourself"; **15** and if you bite and devour one another, see that you may not be consumed by one another.

GALATIANS

16 And I say, walk in the Spirit, and you may not fulfill the desire of the flesh; **17** for the flesh desires contrary to the Spirit, and the Spirit contrary to the flesh, and these are opposed to one another, that the things that you may will—these you may not do; **18** and if you are led by the Spirit, you are not under law. **19** And the works of the flesh are also evident, which are: adultery, whoredom, uncleanness, licentiousness, **20** idolatry, witchcraft, enmities, strife, jealousy, wraths, rivalries, dissensions, sects, **21** envyings, murders, drunkenness, reveling, and such like, of which I tell you before, as I also said before, that those doing such things will not inherit the Kingdom of God. **22** And the fruit of the Spirit is: love, joy, peace, long-suffering, kindness, goodness, faith, **23** meekness, [and] self-control. Against such there is no law; **24** and those who are of Christ Jesus have crucified the flesh with the affections and the desires; **25** if we may live in the Spirit, we may also walk in the Spirit; **26** let us not become vainglorious—provoking one another, envying one another!

6 Brothers, even if a man may be overtaken in any trespass, you who [are] spiritual restore such a one in a spirit of meekness, considering yourself—lest you also may be tempted. **2** Bear the burdens of one another, and so fill up the law of the Christ, **3** for if anyone thinks [himself] to be something—being nothing—he deceives himself; **4** and let each one prove his own work, and then he will have the glorying in regard to himself alone, and not in regard to the other, **5** for each one will bear his own burden. **6** And let him who is instructed in the word share with him who is instructing in all good things. **7** Do not be led astray: God is not mocked; for what a man may sow—that he will also reap, **8** because he who is sowing to his own flesh, of the flesh will reap corruption; and he who is sowing to the Spirit, of the Spirit will reap continuous life; **9** and in doing good we should not be weary, for at the proper time we will reap—not desponding; **10** therefore, then, as we have opportunity, may we work the good to all, and especially to those of the household of faith. **11** You see in how large letters I have written to you with my own hand; **12** as many as are willing to make a good appearance in the flesh, these constrain you to be circumcised—only that they may not be persecuted for the Cross of the Christ, **13** for neither do those circumcised keep the Law themselves, but they wish you to be circumcised, that they may glory in your flesh. **14** And for me, let it not be—to glory, except in the Cross of our Lord Jesus Christ, through which the world has been crucified to me, and I to the world; **15** for in Christ Jesus neither circumcision avails anything, nor uncircumcision, but a new creation; **16** and as many as walk by this rule—peace on them, and kindness, and on the Israel of God! **17** From now on, let no one give me trouble, for I carry the scars of the Lord Jesus in my body. **18** The grace of our Lord Jesus Christ [is] with your spirit, brothers! Amen.

EPHESIANS

1 Paul, an apostle of Jesus Christ through the will of God, to the holy ones who are in Ephesus, and to the faithful in Christ Jesus: **2** Grace to you and peace from God our Father and the Lord Jesus Christ! **3** Blessed [is] the God and Father of our Lord Jesus Christ, who blessed us in every spiritual blessing in the heavenly [places] in Christ, **4** according as He chose us in Him before the foundation of the world, for our being holy and unblemished before Him, in love, **5** having foreordained us to the adoption of sons through Jesus Christ to Himself, according to the good pleasure of His will, **6** to the praise of the glory of His grace, in which He made us accepted in the beloved, **7** in whom we have the redemption through His blood, the forgiveness of the trespasses, according to the riches of His grace, **8** in which He abounded toward us in all wisdom and prudence, **9** having made known to us the secret of His will, according to His good pleasure, that He purposed in Himself, **10** in regard to the dispensation of the fullness of the times, to bring into one the whole in the Christ, both the things in the heavens, and the things on the earth—in Him; **11** in whom also we obtained an inheritance, being foreordained according to the purpose of Him who is working all things according to the counsel of His will, **12** for our being to the praise of His glory, [even] those who first hoped in the Christ, **13** in whom you also, having heard the word of the truth—the good news of your salvation—in whom also having believed, you were sealed with the Holy Spirit of the promise, **14** which is a deposit of our inheritance, to the redemption of the acquired possession, to the praise of His glory. **15** Because of this I also, having heard of your faith in the Lord Jesus, and the love to all the holy ones, **16** do not cease giving thanks for you, making mention of you in my prayers, **17** that the God of our Lord Jesus Christ, the Father of the glory, may give to you a spirit of wisdom and revelation in the recognition of Him, **18** the eyes of your understanding being enlightened, for your knowing what is the hope of His calling, and what the riches of the glory of His inheritance in the holy ones, **19** and what the exceeding greatness of His power to us who are believing, according to the working of the power of His might, **20** which He worked in the Christ, having raised Him out of the dead, and sat [Him] at His right hand in the heavenly [places], **21** far above all principality, and authority, and might, and lordship, and every name named, not only in this age, but also in the coming one; **22** and He put all things under His feet, and gave Him—head over all things to the Assembly, **23** which is His body, the fullness of Him who is filling all in all.

2 Also you—being dead in trespasses and sins, **2** in which you once walked according to the age of this world, according to the ruler of the authority of the air, of the spirit that is now working in the sons of disobedience, **3** among whom we also all walked once in the desires of our flesh, doing the wishes of the flesh and of the thoughts, and were by nature children of wrath—as also the others, **4** but God, being rich in kindness, because of His great love with which He loved us, **5** even being dead in the trespasses, made us alive together with the Christ (by grace you are saved), **6** and raised [us] up together, and sat [us] together in the heavenly [places] in Christ Jesus, **7** that He might show, in the ages that are coming, the exceeding riches of His grace in kindness toward us in Christ Jesus, **8** for by grace you are saved, through faith, and this [is] not of yourselves—[it is] the gift of God, **9** not of works, that no one may boast; **10** for we are His workmanship, created in Christ Jesus on good works, which God prepared before, that we may walk in them. **11** For this reason, remember, that you [were] once the nations in the flesh, who are called Uncircumcision by that called Circumcision in the flesh made by hands, **12** that you were at that time apart from Christ, having been alienated from the commonwealth of Israel, and strangers to the covenants of the promise, having no hope, and without God in the world; **13** but now, in Christ Jesus, you being once far off became near in the blood of the Christ, **14** for He is our peace, who made both one,

EPHESIANS

and broke down the middle wall of the partition of hostility, **15** the enmity in His flesh, having done away [with] the Law of the commands in ordinances, that He might create the two into one new man in Himself, making peace, **16** and might reconcile both in one body to God through the Cross, having slain the enmity by it, **17** and having come, He proclaimed good news—peace to you—the far-off and the near, **18** because through Him we have the access—we both—in one Spirit to the Father. **19** Then, therefore, you are no longer strangers and foreigners, but fellow-citizens of the holy ones, and of the household of God, **20** being built on the foundation of the apostles and prophets, Jesus Christ Himself being chief corner-[stone], **21** in whom all the building fitly framed together increases to a holy temple in the LORD, **22** in whom you also are built together, for a habitation of God in the Spirit.

3 For this cause, I Paul, the prisoner of Christ Jesus for you the nations, **2** if, indeed, you heard of the dispensation of the grace of God that was given to me in regard to you, **3** that by revelation He made known to me the secret, according as I wrote before in few [words]— **4** in regard to which you are able, reading [it], to understand my knowledge in the secret of the Christ, **5** which in other generations was not made known to the sons of men, as it was now revealed to His holy apostles and prophets in the Spirit— **6** that the nations are fellow-heirs, and of the same body, and partakers of His promise in the Christ, through the good news, **7** of which I became a servant, according to the gift of the grace of God that was given to me, according to the working of His power; **8** to me—the less than the least of all the holy ones—was given this grace, among the nations to proclaim good news—the untraceable riches of the Christ, **9** and to cause all to see what [is] the fellowship of the secret that has been hid from the ages in God, who created all things by Jesus Christ, **10** that there might be made known now to the principalities and the authorities in the heavenly [places], through the Assembly, the manifold wisdom of God, **11** according to a purpose of the ages, which He made in Christ Jesus our Lord, **12** in whom we have the freedom and the access in confidence through the faith of Him, **13** for this reason, I ask [you] not to faint in my tribulations for you, which is your glory. **14** For this cause I bow my knees to the Father of our Lord Jesus Christ, **15** of whom the whole family in the heavens and on earth is named, **16** that He may give to you, according to the riches of His glory, to be strengthened through His Spirit with might, in regard to the inner man, **17** that the Christ may dwell through the faith in your hearts, having been rooted and founded in love, **18** that you may be in strength to comprehend, with all the holy ones, what [is] the breadth, and length, and depth, and height, **19** to know also the love of the Christ that is exceeding the knowledge, that you may be filled—to all the fullness of God; **20** and to Him who is able to do exceedingly [and] abundantly above all things that we ask or think, according to the power that is working in us, **21** to Him [is] the glory in the Assembly in Christ Jesus, to all the generations of the age of the ages. Amen.

4 I, the prisoner of the LORD, then call on you to walk worthily of the calling with which you were called, **2** with all lowliness and meekness, with long-suffering, bearing with one another in love, **3** being diligent to keep the unity of the Spirit in the bond of peace; **4** one body and one Spirit, according as you were also called in one hope of your calling; **5** one Lord, one faith, one immersion, **6** one God and Father of all, who [is] over all, and through all, and in you all, **7** and to each one of you was given grace, according to the measure of the gift of Christ, **8** for this reason, it says, "Having gone up on high He led captive captivity, and gave gifts to men." **9** And that, He went up, what is it except that He also went down first into the lower parts of the earth? **10** He who went down is the same who also went up far above all the heavens, that He may fill all things— **11** and He gave some [as] apostles, and some [as] prophets, and some [as] proclaimers of good news, and some [as] shepherds and teachers, **12** to the perfecting of the holy ones, for a work of ministry, for a building up of the body of the Christ, **13** until we may all come to the unity of faith and of the recognition of the Son of God, to a perfect man, to a measure of stature of the fullness of the Christ, **14** that we may no longer be children, being tossed by waves and being carried around by every wind of the teaching, in the cunning of men, in craftiness, to the scheming of leading astray, **15** and [speaking] truth in love, we may increase to Him [in] all things, who is the head—the Christ; **16** from whom the whole body, being fitly joined together and united, through the supply of every joint, according to the working in the measure of each single part, the increase of the body makes for the building up of itself in love. **17** This, then, I say, and I testify in the LORD: you are no longer to walk, as also the other nations walk, in the vanity of their mind, **18** being darkened in the understanding, being alienated from the life of God, because of the ignorance that is in them, because of the hardness of their heart, **19** who, having ceased to feel, gave themselves up to the licentiousness, for the working of all uncleanness in greediness; **20** and you did not so learn the Christ, **21** if [it] so be [that] you heard Him, and were taught in Him, as truth is in Jesus; **22** concerning the former behavior you are to put off the old man, that is corrupt according to the desires of the deceit, **23** and to be renewed in the spirit of your mind, **24** and to put on the new man, which, according to God, was created in righteousness and kindness of the truth. **25** For this reason, putting away the lying, each speak truth with his neighbor, because we are members of one another; **26** be angry and do not sin; do not let the sun go down on your wrath, **27** neither give place to the Devil; **28** whoever is stealing let him no longer steal, but rather let him labor, working the thing that is good with the hands, that he may have to impart to him having need. **29** Let no corrupt word go forth out of your mouth, but what is good to the necessary building up, that it may give grace to the hearers; **30** and do not make the Holy Spirit of God sorrowful, in which you were sealed to [the] day of redemption. **31** Let all bitterness, and wrath, and anger, and clamor, and slander, be put away from you, with all malice, **32** and become kind to one another, tenderhearted, forgiving one another, according as God also forgave you in Christ.

5 Become, then, followers of God, as beloved children, **2** and walk in love, as the Christ also loved us, and gave Himself for us, an offering and a sacrifice to God for an odor of a refreshing fragrance, **3** and whoredom, and all uncleanness, or covetousness, do not let it even be named among you, as is proper to holy ones; **4** also filthiness, and foolish talking, or jesting—the things not fit—but rather thanksgiving; **5** for you know this, that every whoremonger, or unclean, or covetous person, who is an idolater, has no inheritance in the kingdom of the Christ and God. **6** Let no one deceive you with vain words, for because of these things comes the anger of God on the sons of the disobedience; **7** do not become, then, partakers with them, **8** for you were once darkness, and now light in the LORD; walk as children of light, **9** for the fruit of the light [is] in all goodness, and righteousness, and truth, **10** proving what is well-pleasing to the LORD; **11** and have no fellowship with the unfruitful works of the darkness and rather even convict, **12** for it is a shame even to speak of the things done by them in secret, **13** and all the things reproved by the light are revealed, for everything that is revealed is light; **14** for this reason it says, "Arouse yourself, you who are sleeping, and arise out of the dead, and the Christ will shine on you." **15** See, then, how exactly you walk, not as unwise, but as wise, **16** redeeming the time, because the days are evil; **17** do not become fools because of this, but—understanding what [is] the will of the LORD, **18** and do not be drunk with wine, in which is wastefulness, but be filled in the Spirit, **19** speaking to yourselves in psalms and hymns and spiritual songs, singing and making melody in your heart to the LORD, **20** always giving thanks for all things, in the Name of our Lord Jesus Christ, to the God and Father, **21** subjecting yourselves to one another in the fear of Christ. **22** The wives: [subject yourselves] to your own husbands, as to the LORD, **23** because the husband is head of the wife, as also the Christ [is] head of the Assembly, and He is Savior of the body, **24** but even as the Assembly is subject to Christ, so also [are] the wives [subject] to their own husbands in everything. **25** The husbands: love your own wives, as the Christ also loved the Assembly, and gave Himself for it, **26** that He might sanctify it, having cleansed [it] with the bathing of the water in the saying, **27** that He might present the Assembly to

Himself in glory, having no spot or wrinkle, or any of such things, but that it may be holy and unblemished; **28** so ought the husbands to love their own wives as their own bodies: he who is loving his own wife—he loves himself; **29** for no one ever hated his own flesh, but nourishes and nurtures it, as also the LORD—the Assembly, **30** because we are members of His body, [[of His flesh, and of His bones.]] **31** "For this cause will a man leave his father and mother, and will be joined to his wife, and the two will be into one flesh"; **32** this secret is great, and I speak in regard to Christ and to the Assembly; **33** but you also, everyone in particular—let each so love his own wife as himself, and the wife—that she may revere the husband.

6 The children: obey your parents in the LORD, for this is right; **2** honor your father and mother, **3** which is the first command with a promise, "That it may be well with you, and you may live a long time on the land." **4** And the fathers: do not provoke your children, but nourish them in the instruction and admonition of the LORD. **5** The servants: obey the masters according to the flesh with fear and trembling, in the simplicity of your heart, as to the Christ; **6** not with eye-service as men-pleasers, but as servants of the Christ, doing the will of God out of [your] soul, **7** serving with goodwill, as to the LORD, and not to men, **8** having known that whatever good thing each one may do, this he will receive from the LORD, whether servant or freeman. **9** And the masters! Do the same things to them, letting threatening alone, having also known that your Master is in the heavens, and favor by appearance is not with Him. **10** As to the rest, my brothers, be strong in the LORD, and in the power of His might; **11** put on the whole armor of God, so you are able to stand against the schemes of the Devil, **12** because our wrestling is not with flesh and blood, but with the principalities, with the authorities, with the world-rulers of the darkness of this age, with the spiritual [forces] of evil in the heavenly [places]; **13** because of this take up the whole armor of God, that you may be able to resist in the day of the evil, and having done all things—to stand. **14** Stand, therefore, having your loins girded around in truth, and having put on the breastplate of righteousness, **15** and having the feet shod in the preparation of the good news of peace; **16** in all, having taken up the shield of faith, in which you will be able to quench all the fiery darts of the evil one, **17** and receive the helmet of the salvation, and the sword of the Spirit, which is the word of God, **18** through all prayer and supplication praying at all times in the Spirit, and in this, watching in all perseverance and supplication for all the holy ones— **19** and in behalf of me, that to me may be given a word in the opening of my mouth, in freedom, to make known the secret of the good news, **20** for which I am an ambassador in a chain, that in it I may speak freely—as it is necessary for me to speak. **21** And that you may know—you also—the things concerning me—what I do, Tychicus will make all things known to you, the beloved brother and faithful servant in the LORD, **22** whom I sent to you for this very thing, that you might know the things concerning us, and that he might comfort your hearts. **23** Peace to the brothers, and love, with faith, from God the Father, and the Lord Jesus Christ! **24** The grace with all those loving our Lord Jesus Christ—undecayingly! Amen.

PHILIPPIANS

1 Paul and Timotheus, servants of Jesus Christ, to all the holy ones in Christ Jesus who are in Philippi, with overseers and servants: **2** Grace to you and peace from God our Father and the Lord Jesus Christ! **3** I give thanks to my God on all the remembrance of you, **4** always, in every supplication of mine for you all, with joy making the supplication, **5** for your contribution to the good news from the first day until now, **6** having been confident of this very thing, that He who began a good work in you, will complete [it] until [the] day of Jesus Christ, **7** according as it is righteous for me to think this in behalf of you all, because of my having you in the heart, both in my bonds, and [in] the defense and confirmation of the good news, all of you being fellow-partakers with me of grace. **8** For God is my witness, how I long for you all with [the] yearnings of Jesus Christ, **9** and this I pray, that your love may abound yet more and more in full knowledge, and all discernment, **10** for your proving the things that differ, that you may be pure and offenseless—to [the] Day of Christ, **11** being filled with the fruit of righteousness, that [is] through Jesus Christ, to the glory and praise of God. **12** And I intend you to know, brothers, that the things concerning me, rather have come to an advancement of the good news, **13** so that my bonds have become evident in Christ in the whole Praetorium, and to all the other places, **14** and the greater part of the brothers in the LORD, having confidence by my bonds, are more abundantly bold to fearlessly speak the word. **15** Certain, indeed, even through envy and contention, and certain also through goodwill, preach the Christ; **16** one, indeed, of rivalry proclaims the Christ, not purely, supposing to add affliction to my bonds, **17** and the other out of love, having known that I am set for defense of the good news: **18** what then? In every way, whether in pretense or in truth, Christ is proclaimed—and I rejoice in this, indeed, and will rejoice. **19** For I have known that this will turn out to me for salvation, through your supplication, and the supply of the Spirit of Christ Jesus, **20** according to my earnest expectation and hope, that I will be ashamed in nothing, and in all freedom, as always, also Christ will now be magnified in my body, whether through life or through death, **21** for to me to live [is] Christ, and to die [is] gain. **22** And if to live in the flesh [is] to me a fruit of work, then what will I choose? I do not know; **23** for I am pressed by the two, having the desire to depart, and to be with Christ, for it is far better, **24** and to remain in the flesh is more necessary on your account, **25** and being persuaded of this, I have known that I will remain and continue with you all, to your advancement and joy of the faith, **26** that your boasting may abound in Christ Jesus in me through my coming again to you. **27** Only conduct yourselves worthily of the good news of the Christ, that, whether having come and seen you, whether being absent I may hear of the things concerning you, that you stand fast in one spirit, with one soul, striving together for the faith of the good news, **28** and not be terrified in anything by those opposing, which is indeed a token of destruction to them, and to you of salvation, and that from God; **29** because to you it was granted, on behalf of Christ, not only to believe in Him, but also to suffer on behalf of Him; **30** having the same conflict, such as you saw in me, and now hear of in me.

2 If, then, any exhortation [is] in Christ, if any comfort of love, if any fellowship of [the] Spirit, if any yearnings and mercies, **2** fulfill my joy, that you may mind the same thing—having the same love—of one soul—minding the one thing, **3** nothing in rivalry or vainglory, but in humility of mind counting one another more excellent than yourselves— **4** do not each look to your own, but each also to the things of others. **5** For let this mind be in you that [is] also in Christ Jesus, **6** who, being in the form of God, thought [it] not something to be seized to be equal to God, **7** but emptied Himself, having taken the form of a servant, having been made in the likeness of men, **8** and having been found in appearance as a man, He humbled Himself, having become obedient to death—even death of a cross, **9** for this reason, also, God highly exalted Him, and gave to Him a Name that [is] above every name, **10** that in the Name of Jesus every knee may bow—of heavenlies, and earthlies, and what are under the earth— **11** and every tongue may confess that Jesus Christ [is] LORD, to the glory of God the Father. **12** So that, my beloved, as you always obey, not as in my presence only, but now much more in my absence, work out your own salvation with fear and trembling, **13** for it is God who is working in you both to will and to work for His good pleasure. **14** Do all things without murmurings and deliberations, **15** that you may become blameless and pure children of God, unblemished in the midst of a crooked and perverse generation, among whom you appear as luminaries in the world, **16** holding forth the word of life, for rejoicing to me in regard to [the] Day of Christ, that I did not run in vain, nor did I labor in vain; **17** but if I also am poured forth on the sacrifice and service of your faith, I rejoice and am glad with you all, **18** because of this you also rejoice and are glad with me. **19** And I hope, in the Lord Jesus, to send Timotheus to you quickly, that I also may be of good spirit, having known the things concerning you, **20** for I have no one like-minded, who will sincerely care for the things concerning you, **21** for the whole seek their own things, not the things of Christ Jesus, **22** and you know his proof, that as a child [serves] a father, he served with me in regard to the good news; **23** I indeed hope to send him, when I may see through the things concerning me—immediately; **24** and I trust in the LORD that I will also come quickly myself. **25** And I thought [it] necessary to send to you Epaphroditus—my brother and fellow-workman and fellow-soldier, and your apostle and servant to my need, **26** seeing he was longing after you all, and in heaviness, because you heard that he ailed, **27** for he also ailed near to death, but God dealt kindly with him, and not with him only, but also with me, that I might not have sorrow on sorrow. **28** The more eagerly, therefore, I sent him, that having seen him again you may rejoice, and I may be less sorrowful; **29** receive him, therefore, in the LORD, with all joy, and hold such in honor, **30** because on account of the work of the Christ he drew near to death, having hazarded life that he might fill up your deficiency of service to me.

3 As to the rest, my brothers, rejoice in the LORD; indeed, [it] is not tiresome to me to write to you the same things, and for you [is] sure. **2** Look out for the dogs! Look out for the evil-workers! Look out for the mutilation! **3** For we are the circumcision, who are serving God by the Spirit, and glorying in Christ Jesus, and having no trust in flesh, **4** though I also have [cause of] trust in flesh. If any other one thinks to have trust in flesh, I more: **5** circumcision on the eighth day! Of the race of Israel! Of the tribe of Benjamin! A Hebrew of Hebrews! According to law—a Pharisee! **6** According to zeal—persecuting the Assembly! According to righteousness that is in law—becoming blameless! **7** But what things were gains to me, these I have counted loss, because of the Christ; **8** yes, indeed, and I count all things to be loss, because of the excellence of the knowledge of Christ Jesus my Lord, because of whom I suffered loss of all things, and count them to be refuse, that I may gain Christ, and be found in Him, **9** not having my righteousness, which [is] of law, but that which [is] through faith from Christ—the righteousness that is of God by faith, **10** to know Him, and the power of His resurrection, and the fellowship of His sufferings, being conformed to His death, **11** if anyhow I may attain to the resurrection of the dead. **12** Not that I already obtained, or have already been perfected, but I pursue, if I also may lay hold of that for which I was also laid hold of by Christ Jesus; **13** brothers, I do not reckon myself to have laid hold [of it], but one thing [I do]—indeed forgetting the things behind, and stretching forth to the things before— **14** I pursue to the mark for the prize of the high calling of God in Christ Jesus. **15** As many, therefore, as [are] perfect—let us think this, and if [in] anything you think otherwise, this also will God reveal to you, **16** but to what we have attained—walk by the same rule, think the same thing; **17** together become my followers, brothers, and observe those thus walking, according as you have us—a pattern; **18** for many walk of whom I told you [about] many times—and now also weeping tell—[they are] the enemies of the Cross of the Christ, **19** whose end [is] destruction, whose god [is] the belly, and whose glory [is] in their shame, who are minding the things on earth. **20** For our citizenship is in the heavens, from where we also await a Savior—the Lord Jesus Christ— **21** who will transform the body of our humiliation to its becoming conformed to the body of His glory, according to the working of His power, even to subject all things to Himself.

4 So then, my brothers, beloved and longed for, my joy and garland, so stand in the LORD, beloved. **2** I exhort Euodia, and I exhort Syntyche, to be of the same mind in the LORD; **3** and I also ask you, genuine yoke-fellow, be assisting those women who strove along with me in the good news, with Clement also, and the others, my fellow-workers, whose names [are] in [the] Scroll of Life. **4** Rejoice in the LORD always; again I will say, rejoice! **5** Let your reasonableness be known to all men; the LORD [is] near; **6** be anxious for nothing, but in everything by prayer, and by supplication, with thanksgiving, let your requests be made known to God; **7** and the peace of God, that is surpassing all understanding, will guard your hearts and your thoughts in Christ Jesus. **8** As to the rest, brothers, as many things as are true, as many as [are] revered, as many as [are] righteous, as many as [are] pure, as many as [are] lovely, as many as [are] of good report, if any worthiness, and if any praise, think on these things; **9** the things that you also learned, and receive, and hear, and saw in me, do those, and the God of peace will be with you. **10** And I rejoiced in the LORD greatly, that now at length you flourished again in caring for me, for which also you were caring, and lacked opportunity; **11** I do not say that in respect of want, for I learned in the things in which I am—to be content; **12** I have known both to be abased, and I have known to abound; in everything and in all things I have been initiated, both to be full and to be hungry, both to abound and to be in want. **13** I have strength for all things, in Christ's strengthening me; **14** but you did well, having shared in my tribulation; **15** and you have known, even you Philippians, that in the beginning of the good news when I went forth from Macedonia, no assembly communicated with me in regard to giving and receiving except you only; **16** because in Thessalonica also, both once and again you sent to my need; **17** not that I seek after the gift, but I seek after the fruit that is overflowing to your account; **18** and I have all things, and abound; I am filled, having received from Epaphroditus the things from you—an odor of a refreshing fragrance—a sacrifice acceptable, well-pleasing to God: **19** and my God will supply all your need, according to His riches in glory in Christ Jesus; **20** and to God, even our Father, [is] the glory through the ages of the ages. Amen. **21** Every holy one in Christ Jesus greets you; the brothers with me greet you; **22** all the holy ones greet you, and especially those of Caesar's house. **23** The grace of our Lord Jesus Christ [is] with you all! Amen.

COLOSSIANS

1 Paul, an apostle of Jesus Christ through the will of God, and Timotheus the brother, **2** to the holy ones in Colossae, and to the faithful brothers in Christ: Grace to you and peace from God our Father and the Lord Jesus Christ! **3** We give thanks to the God and Father of our Lord Jesus Christ, always praying for you, **4** having heard of your faith in Christ Jesus, and of the love that [is] to all the holy ones, **5** because of the hope that is laid up for you in the heavens, which you heard of beforehand by the word of the truth of the good news, **6** which has come to you, as also in all the world, and is bearing fruit, as also in you, from the day in which you heard, and knew the grace of God in truth, **7** as you also learned from Epaphras, our beloved fellow-servant, who is a faithful servant of the Christ for you, **8** who also declared to us your love in the Spirit. **9** Because of this, we also, from the day in which we heard, do not cease praying for you, and asking that you may be filled with the full knowledge of His will in all wisdom and spiritual understanding, **10** to walk worthily of the LORD, pleasing in all, being fruitful in every good work, and increasing in the knowledge of God, **11** in all might being made mighty according to the power of His glory, to all endurance and long-suffering with joy. **12** Giving thanks to the Father who has qualified us for the participation of the inheritance of the holy ones in the light, **13** who rescued us out of the authority of the darkness, and translated [us] into the kingdom of the Son of His love, **14** in whom we have the redemption [[through His blood]], the forgiveness of sins, **15** who is the image of the invisible God, firstborn of all creation, **16** because all things were created in Him, those in the heavens, and those on the earth, those visible, and those invisible, whether thrones, whether lordships, whether principalities, whether authorities; all things have been created through Him and for Him, **17** and He is before all, and all things have consisted in Him. **18** And He is the head of the body—the Assembly—who is a beginning, a firstborn out of the dead, that He might become first in all [things] Himself, **19** because all the fullness was pleased to dwell in Him, **20** and through Him to reconcile all things to Himself—having made peace through the blood of His Cross—through Him, whether the things on the earth, whether the things in the heavens. **21** And you—once being alienated, and enemies in the mind, in the evil works, yet now He reconciled, **22** in the body of His flesh through death, to present you holy, and unblemished, and unblameable before Himself, **23** if you also remain in the faith, being founded and settled, and not moved away from the hope of the good news, which you heard, which was preached in all the creation that [is] under Heaven, of which I, Paul, became a servant. **24** I now rejoice in my sufferings for you, and fill up the things lacking of the tribulations of the Christ in my flesh for His body, which is the Assembly, **25** of which I became a servant according to the dispensation of God, that was given to me for you, to fulfill the word of God, **26** the secret that has been hid from the ages and from the generations, but now was revealed to His holy ones, **27** to whom God willed to make known what [is] the riches of the glory of this secret among the nations—which is Christ in you, the hope of the glory, **28** whom we proclaim, warning every man, and teaching every man, in all wisdom, that we may present every man perfect in Christ Jesus, **29** for which I also labor, striving according to His working that is working in me in power.

2 For I wish you to know how great a conflict I have for you and those in Laodicea, and as many as have not seen my face in the flesh, **2** that their hearts may be comforted, being united in love, and to all riches of the full assurance of the understanding, to the full knowledge of the secret of the God and Father, and of the Christ, **3** in whom are all the treasures of the wisdom and the knowledge hid, **4** and this I say, that no one may deceive you with enticing words, **5** for if even in the flesh I am absent—yet in the spirit I am with you, rejoicing and beholding your order, and the steadfastness of your faith in regard to Christ; **6** as, then, you received Christ

Jesus the LORD, walk in Him, **7** being rooted and built up in Him, and confirmed in the faith, as you were taught—abounding in it in thanksgiving. **8** See that no one will be carrying you away as spoil through philosophy and vain deceit, according to the tradition of men, according to the rudiments of the world, and not according to Christ, **9** because in Him dwells all the fullness of the Godhead bodily, **10** and you are made full in Him, who is the head of all principality and authority, **11** in whom you also were circumcised with a circumcision not made with hands, in the putting off of the body of sins of the flesh by the circumcision of the Christ, **12** being buried with Him in the immersion, in which you also rose with [Him] through the faith of the working of God, who raised Him out of the dead. **13** And you—being dead in the trespasses and the uncircumcision of your flesh—He made alive together with Him, having forgiven you all the trespasses, **14** having blotted out the handwriting in the ordinances that is against us, that was contrary to us, and He has taken it out of the way, having nailed it to the Cross; **15** having stripped the principalities and the authorities, He made a show of them openly—having triumphed over them by it. **16** Let no one, then, judge you in eating or in drinking, or in respect of a celebration, or of a new moon, or of Sabbaths, **17** which are a shadow of the coming things, but the body [is] of the Christ; **18** let no one deceive you of your prize, delighting in humble-mindedness and [in] worship of the messengers, intruding into the things he has not seen, being vainly puffed up by the mind of his flesh, **19** and not holding the Head, from which all the body—gathering supply through the joints and bands, and being knit together—may increase with the increase of God. **20** If, then, you died with the Christ from the rudiments of the world, why, as living in the world, are you subject to ordinances— **21** you may not touch, nor taste, nor handle— **22** which are all for destruction with the using, after the commands and teachings of men, **23** which are, indeed, having a matter of wisdom in self-willed religion, and humble-mindedness, and neglecting of body—not of any value to satisfying the flesh.

3 If, then, you were raised with the Christ, seek the things above, where the Christ is, seated on the right hand of God; **2** mind the things above, not the things on the earth, **3** for you died, and your life has been hid with the Christ in God; **4** when the Christ—our life—may have appeared, then we will also appear with Him in glory. **5** Put to death, then, your members that [are] on the earth—whoredom, uncleanness, passion, evil desire, and the covetousness, which is idolatry— **6** because of which things comes the anger of God on the sons of the disobedience, **7** in which you also—you once walked, when you lived in them; **8** but now put off, even you, the whole—anger, wrath, malice, slander, filthy talking—out of your mouth. **9** Do not lie to one another, having put off the old man with his practices, **10** and having put on the new, which is renewed in regard to knowledge, after the image of Him who created him, **11** where there is not Greek and Jew, circumcision and uncircumcision, foreigner, Scythian, servant, freeman, but Christ [is] all and in all. **12** Put on, therefore, as chosen ones of God, holy and beloved, yearnings of mercies, kindness, humble-mindedness, meekness, long-suffering, **13** bearing with one another, and forgiving each other, if anyone may have a quarrel with anyone, as the Christ also forgave you—so also you; **14** and above all these things, [have] love, which is a bond of the perfection, **15** and let the peace of God rule in your hearts, to which you were also called in one body, and become thankful. **16** Let the word of Christ dwell in you richly, in all wisdom, teaching and admonishing each other, in psalms, and hymns, and spiritual songs, in grace singing in your hearts to the LORD; **17** and all, whatever you may do in word or in work, [do] all things in the Name of the Lord Jesus—giving thanks to the God and Father, through Him. **18** The wives: be subject to your own husbands, as is fit in the LORD; **19** the husbands: love your wives, and do not be bitter with them; **20** the children: obey the parents in all things, for this is well-pleasing to the LORD; **21** the fathers: do not distress your children, lest they be discouraged; **22** the servants: obey those who are masters in all things according to the flesh, not in eye-service as men-pleasers, but in simplicity of heart, fearing God; **23** and all, whatever you may do—out of soul work—as to the LORD, and not to men, **24** having known that you will receive the repayment of the inheritance from the LORD—for you serve the LORD Christ; **25** and he who is doing unrighteously will receive what he did unrighteously, and there is no favor by appearance.

4 The masters: give that which is righteous and equal to the servants, having known that you also have a Master in the heavens. **2** Continue in the prayer, watching in it in thanksgiving, **3** also praying for us at the same time, that God may open to us a door for the word, to speak the secret of the Christ, because of which I have also been bound, **4** that I may reveal it, as it is necessary for me to speak. **5** Walk in wisdom toward those outside, redeeming the time, **6** your word always being seasoned with salt in grace—to know how it is necessary for you to answer each one. **7** Tychicus will make known to you all the things concerning me—the beloved brother, and faithful servant, and fellow-servant in the LORD— **8** whom I sent to you for this very thing, that he might know the things concerning you, and might comfort your hearts, **9** with Onesimus the faithful and beloved brother, who is of you; they will make known to you all things that [are] here. **10** Aristarchus greets you, my fellow-captive, and Marcus, the nephew of Barnabas (concerning whom you received commands—if he may come to you, receive him), **11** and Jesus who is called Justus, who are of circumcision: these [are the] only fellow-workers for the Kingdom of God who become a comfort to me. **12** Epaphras greets you, who [is] of you, a servant of Christ, always striving for you in the prayers, that you may stand perfect and made full in all the will of God, **13** for I testify to him that he has much zeal for you, and those in Laodicea, and those in Hierapolis. **14** Lucas greets you, the beloved physician, and Demas; **15** those in Laodicea greet you—brothers, and Nymphas, and the assembly in his house; **16** and when the letter may be read with you, cause that it may also be read in the assembly of the Laodiceans, and the [letter] from Laodicea that you also may read; **17** and say to Archippus, "See to the ministry that you received in the LORD, that you may fulfill it." **18** The salutation [is] by my hand, Paul. Remember my bonds. The grace [is] with you! Amen.

1 THESSALONIANS

1 Paul, and Silvanus, and Timotheus, to the assembly of Thessalonians in God the Father and the Lord Jesus Christ: Grace to you and peace from God our Father and the Lord Jesus Christ! **2** We always give thanks to God for you all, making mention of you in our prayers, **3** unceasingly remembering your work of faith, and the labor of the love, and the endurance of the hope, of our Lord Jesus Christ, in the presence of our God and Father, **4** having known, beloved brothers, by God, your [divine] selection, **5** because our good news did not come to you in word only, but also in power, and in the Holy Spirit, and in much assurance, even as you have known of what sort we became among you for your sake, **6** and you became imitators of us and of the LORD, having received the word in much tribulation with joy of the Holy Spirit, **7** so that you became patterns to all those believing in Macedonia and Achaia, **8** for from you has sounded forth the word of the LORD, not only in Macedonia and Achaia, but also in every place your faith toward God went forth, so that we have no need to say anything, **9** for they themselves declare concerning us what entrance we had to you, and how you turned to God from the idols, to serve a living and true God, **10** and to wait for His Son from the heavens, whom He raised out of the dead—Jesus, who is rescuing us from the anger that is coming.

2 For you have known, brothers, that our entrance to you has not been in vain, **2** but having both suffered before, and having been mistreated (as you have known) in Philippi, we were bold in our God to speak to you the good news of God in much conflict, **3** for our exhortation [is] not out of deceit, nor out of uncleanness, nor in guile, **4** but as we have been approved by God to be entrusted with the good news, so we speak, not as pleasing men, but God, who is proving our hearts, **5** for at no time did we come with speech of flattery (as you have known), nor in a pretext for covetousness (God [is] witness), **6** nor seeking glory from men, neither from you nor from others, being able to be burdensome, as Christ's apostles. **7** But we became gentle in your midst, as a nurse may nurture her own children, **8** so being desirous of you, we are well-pleased to impart to you not only the good news of God, but also our own souls, because you have become beloved to us, **9** for you remember, brothers, our labor and travail, for working night and day not to be a burden on any of you, we preached the good news of God to you; **10** you [are] witnesses—God also—how piously and righteously and blamelessly we became to you who believe, **11** even as you have known how we are exhorting each one of you, as a father his own children, and comforting, and testifying, **12** for your walking worthily of God, who is calling you to His own kingdom and glory. **13** And because of this we also continually give thanks to God, that, having received the word of God [by] your hearing from us, you accepted, not the word of men, but as it truly is, the word of God, who also works in you who believe; **14** for you became imitators, brothers, of the assemblies of God that are in Judea in Christ Jesus, because you suffered such things, even you, from your own countrymen, as they also from the Jews, **15** who put to death both the Lord Jesus and their own prophets, and persecuted us, and they are not pleasing God, and [are] contrary to all men, **16** forbidding us to speak to the nations that they might be saved, so as to always fill up their sins, but [God's] anger came on them—to the end! **17** And we, brothers, having been taken from you for the space of an hour—in presence, not in heart—hurried more abundantly to see your face in much desire; **18** for this reason we wished to come to you (I, indeed, Paul), both once and again, and Satan hindered us; **19** for what [is] our hope, or joy, or garland of rejoicing? Are not even you before our Lord Jesus Christ at His coming? **20** For you are our glory and joy.

3 For this reason, enduring no longer, we thought good to be left in Athens alone, **2** and sent Timotheus—our brother, and a servant of God, and our fellow-workman in the good news of the Christ—to establish you, and to comfort you concerning your

1 THESSALONIANS

faith, **3** that no one be moved in these tribulations, for you have known that we are set for this, **4** for even when we were with you, we said to you beforehand that we are about to suffer tribulation, as it also came to pass, and you have known [it]; **5** because of this also, I, no longer enduring, sent to know your faith, lest he who is tempting tempted you, and our labor might be in vain. **6** And Timotheus now having come to us from you, and having declared good news to us of your faith and love, and that you always have a good remembrance of us, desiring much to see us, as we also [to see] you, **7** because of this we were comforted, brothers, over you, in all our tribulation and necessity, through your faith, **8** because now we live, if you may stand fast in the LORD. **9** For what thanks are we able to repay to God for you, for all the joy with which we delight because of you in the presence of our God, **10** exceedingly imploring night and day, that we might see your face, and perfect the things lacking in your faith? **11** And our God and Father Himself, and our Lord Jesus Christ, direct our way to you, **12** and the LORD cause you to increase and to abound in the love to one another, and to all, even as we also to you, **13** in order to have established your hearts, blameless in sanctification before our God and Father, at the coming of our Lord Jesus Christ with all His holy ones.

4 As to the rest, then, brothers, we request, and call on you in the Lord Jesus, as you received from us how it is necessary for you to walk and to please God, that you may abound the more, **2** for you have known what commands we gave you through the Lord Jesus; **3** for this is the will of God—your sanctification: that you abstain from the whoredom, **4** that each of you know to possess his own vessel in sanctification and honor, **5** not in the affection of desire, as also the nations that were not knowing God, **6** that no one goes beyond and defrauds his brother in the matter, because the LORD [is] an avenger of all these, as we also spoke to you before and testified, **7** for God did not call us to uncleanness, but in sanctification. **8** He, therefore, who is despising, does not despise man, but God, who also gave His Holy Spirit to us. **9** And concerning the brotherly love, you have no need of [my] writing to you, for you yourselves are God-taught to love one another, **10** for you do it also to all the brothers who [are] in all Macedonia; and we call on you, brothers, to abound still more, **11** and to study to be quiet, and to do your own business, and to work with your own hands, as we commanded you, **12** that you may walk properly to those outside, and may have lack of nothing. **13** And I do not wish you to be ignorant, brothers, concerning those who have fallen asleep, that you may not sorrow, as also the rest who have no hope, **14** for if we believe that Jesus died and rose again, so also God will bring with Him those asleep through Jesus, **15** for we say this to you in the word of the LORD, that we who are living—who remain over to the coming of the LORD—may not precede those asleep, **16** because the LORD Himself, with a shout, with the voice of a chief-messenger, and with the trumpet of God, will come down from Heaven, and the dead in Christ will rise first; **17** then we who are living, who are remaining over, will be snatched up together with them in [the] clouds to meet the LORD in [the] air, and so we will always be with the LORD; **18** so, then, comfort one another with these words.

5 And concerning the times and the seasons, brothers, you have no need of my writing to you, **2** for you have thoroughly known that the Day of the LORD so comes as a thief in the night, **3** for when they may say, "Peace and security," then sudden destruction comes [on] them, as the travail [on] her who is with child, and they will not escape; **4** but you, brothers, are not in darkness, that the Day may catch you as a thief; **5** you are all sons of light, and sons of day; we are not of night, nor of darkness, **6** so, then, we may not sleep as also the others, but watch and be sober, **7** for those sleeping, sleep by night, and those making themselves drunk, are drunken by night, **8** and we, being of the day—let us be sober, putting on a breastplate of faith and love, and a helmet—a hope of salvation, **9** because God did not appoint us to anger, but to the acquiring of salvation through our Lord Jesus Christ, **10** who died for us, that whether we wake—whether we sleep—we may live together with Him; **11** for this reason, comfort one another, and build up one another, as also you do. **12** And we ask you, brothers, to know those laboring among you and leading you in the LORD and admonishing you, **13** and to esteem them very abundantly in love, because of their work; be at peace among yourselves; **14** and we exhort you, brothers, admonish the disorderly, comfort the feeble-minded, support the weak, be patient to all; **15** see [that] no one may render evil for evil to anyone, but always pursue that which is good, both to one another and to all; **16** always rejoice; **17** continually pray; **18** give thanks in everything, for this [is] the will of God in Christ Jesus in regard to you. **19** Do not quench the Spirit; **20** do not despise prophesyings; **21** prove all things; hold fast [to] that which is good; **22** abstain from all appearance of evil; **23** and may the God of peace Himself sanctify you wholly, and may your whole spirit and soul and body be preserved, unblameably at the coming of our Lord Jesus Christ; **24** He who is calling you is steadfast, who also will do [it]. **25** Brothers, pray for us. **26** Greet all the brothers with a holy kiss. **27** I charge you [by] the LORD, that the letter be read to all the holy brothers. **28** The grace of our Lord Jesus Christ [is] with you! Amen.

2 THESSALONIANS

1 Paul, and Silvanus, and Timotheus, to the assembly of Thessalonians in God our Father, and the Lord Jesus Christ: **2** Grace to you and peace from God our Father and the Lord Jesus Christ! **3** We always ought to give thanks to God for you, brothers, as it is fitting, because your faith increases greatly, and the love of each one of you all abounds to one another, **4** so that we ourselves glory in you in the assemblies of God, for your endurance and faith in all your persecutions and tribulations that you bear— **5** a token of the righteous judgment of God, for your being counted worthy of the Kingdom of God, for which you also suffer, **6** since [it is] a righteous thing with God to give back to those troubling you—tribulation, **7** and to you who are troubled—rest with us in the revelation of the Lord Jesus from Heaven, with messengers of His power, **8** in flaming fire, giving vengeance to those not knowing God, and to those not obeying the good news of our Lord Jesus Christ, **9** who will suffer justice—continuous destruction—from the face of the LORD, and from the glory of His strength, **10** when He may come to be glorified in His holy ones, and to be wondered at by all those believing—because our testimony was believed among you—in that day; **11** for which we also always pray for you, that our God may count you worthy of the calling, and may fulfill all the good pleasure of goodness, and the work of faith in power, **12** that the Name of our Lord Jesus Christ may be glorified in you, and you in Him, according to the grace of our God and Lord Jesus Christ.

2 And we ask you, brothers, in regard to the coming of our Lord Jesus Christ, and of our gathering together to Him, **2** that you are not quickly shaken in mind, nor be troubled, neither through spirit, neither through word, neither through letters as through us, as that the Day of the LORD has arrived; **3** do not let anyone deceive you in any way, because if the departure may not come first, the man of lawlessness may [not] be revealed—the son of destruction, **4** who is opposing and is raising himself up above all called god or worshiped, so as for him to have sat down in the temple of God, proclaiming that he is God. **5** Do you not remember that, yet being with you, I said these things to you? **6** And now, you have known what is restraining, for his being revealed in his own time, **7** for the secret of lawlessness already works, only the [One] now restraining [will do so] until He may come out of [the] midst, **8** and then the lawless one will be revealed, whom the LORD will consume with the Spirit of His mouth, and will nullify at the appearance of His coming, **9** whose coming is according to the working of Satan, in all power, and signs, and lying wonders, **10** and in all deceitfulness of the unrighteousness in those perishing, because they did not receive the love of the truth for their being saved, **11** and because of this God will send to them a working of delusion, for their believing the lie, **12** that they may be judged—all who did not believe the truth, but were well pleased in the unrighteousness. **13** And we ought to give thanks to God always for you, brothers, beloved by the LORD, that God chose you from the beginning to salvation, in sanctification of the Spirit, and belief of the truth, **14** to which He called you through our good news, to the acquiring of the glory of our Lord Jesus Christ; **15** so, then, brothers, stand fast, and hold the traditions that you were taught, whether through word, whether through our letter; **16** and may our Lord Jesus Christ Himself, and our God and Father, who loved us, and gave continuous comfort, and good hope in grace, **17** comfort your hearts, and establish you in every good word and work.

3 As to the rest, pray, brothers, concerning us, that the word of the LORD may run and may be glorified, as also with you, **2** and that we may be delivered from the unreasonable and evil men, for not all [are] of the faith; **3** but faithful is the LORD who will establish you, and will guard [you] from the evil [one]; **4** and we now have confidence in the LORD, that which we command you both do and will do; **5** and the LORD direct your hearts to the love of God, and to the endurance of the Christ. **6** And we command you, brothers, in the Name of our Lord Jesus Christ, to withdraw yourselves from every brother walking disorderly, and not after the tradition that you received from us, **7** for you have known how it is necessary to imitate us, because we did not act disorderly among you; **8** nor did we eat bread of anyone for nothing, but in labor and in travail, working night and day, not to be chargeable to any of you; **9** not because we have no authority, but that we might give ourselves to you [as] a pattern, to imitate us; **10** for even when we were with you, this we commanded you, that if anyone is not willing to work, neither let him eat, **11** for we hear of some walking disorderly among you, working nothing, but being busybodies, **12** and such we command and exhort through our Lord Jesus Christ, that working with quietness, they may eat their own bread; **13** and you, brothers, may you not be weary doing well, **14** and if anyone does not obey our word through the letter, note this one, and have no company with him, that he may be ashamed, **15** and do not count as an enemy, but admonish as a brother; **16** and may the LORD of peace Himself always give to you peace in every way; the LORD [is] with you all! **17** The salutation by the hand of me, Paul, which is a sign in every letter; thus I write. **18** The grace of our Lord Jesus Christ [is] with you all! Amen.

1 TIMOTHY

1 Paul, an apostle of Jesus Christ, according to a command of God our Savior, and of the Lord Jesus Christ our hope, **2** to Timotheus—genuine child in faith: Grace, kindness, peace, from God our Father and Christ Jesus our Lord! **3** According as I exhorted you to remain in Ephesus—I going on to Macedonia—that you might charge certain [ones] not to teach any other thing, **4** nor to give heed to fables and endless genealogies, that cause questions rather than [the] stewardship of God which [is] in faith. **5** And the end of the charge is love out of a pure heart, and of a good conscience, and of unhypocritical faith, **6** from which certain [men], having swerved, turned aside to vain discourse, **7** willing to be teachers of law, not understanding either the things they say, nor concerning what they confidently assert, **8** and we have known that the Law [is] good, if anyone may use it lawfully; **9** having known this, that law is not set for a righteous man, but for lawless and insubordinate persons, ungodly and sinners, impious and profane, murderers of fathers and murderers of mothers, manslayers, **10** whoremongers, homosexuals, enslavers, liars, perjured persons, and if there be any other thing that is adverse to sound doctrine, **11** according to the good news of the glory of the blessed God, with which I was entrusted. **12** And I give thanks to Him who enabled me— Christ Jesus our Lord—that He reckoned me steadfast, having put [me] to the ministry, **13** who before was speaking slander, and persecuting, and insulting, but I found kindness, because, being ignorant, I did [it] in unbelief, **14** and the grace of our Lord exceedingly abounded, with faith and love that [is] in Christ Jesus. **15** The word [is] steadfast, and worthy of all acceptance, that Christ Jesus came into the world to save sinners—of whom I am first; **16** but because of this I found kindness, that Jesus Christ might first show forth all long-suffering in me, for a pattern of those about to believe on Him to continuous life. **17** And to the King of the ages, the incorruptible, invisible, only wise God, [is] honor and glory through the ages of the ages! Amen. **18** I commit to you this charge, child Timotheus, according to the prophecies that went before on you, that you may war in them the good warfare, **19** having faith and a good conscience, which some having thrust away, made shipwreck concerning the faith, **20** of whom are Hymenaeus and Alexander, whom I delivered to Satan, that they might be instructed not to speak evil.

2 I exhort, then, first of all, there be made supplications, prayers, intercessions, thanksgivings, for all men— **2** for kings, and all who are in authority, that we may lead a quiet and peaceable life in all piety and gravity, **3** for this [is] right and acceptable before God our Savior, **4** who wills all men to be saved, and to come to the full knowledge of the truth; **5** for [there is] one God, also one mediator of God and of men—the man Christ Jesus, **6** who gave Himself [as] a ransom for all—the testimony in its own times— **7** in regard to which I was set a preacher and apostle— truth I say in Christ, I do not lie—a teacher of nations, in faith and truth. **8** I intend, therefore, that men pray in every place, lifting up holy hands, apart from anger and deliberation; **9** also the women in like manner, in orderly apparel, to adorn themselves with modesty and sobriety, not in braided hair, or gold, or pearls, or clothing of great price, **10** but—which becomes women professing godly piety— through good works. **11** Let a woman learn in quietness in all subjection, **12** and I do not allow a woman to teach, nor to rule a husband, but to be in quietness, **13** for Adam was formed first, then Eve, **14** and Adam was not deceived, but the woman, having been deceived, came into transgression, **15** and she will be saved through the childbearing, if they remain in faith, and love, and sanctification, with sobriety.

3 The word [is] steadfast: If anyone longs for overseership, he desires a right work; **2** it is required, therefore, the overseer to be blameless, a husband of one wife, vigilant, sober, respectable, a friend of strangers, apt to teach, **3** not given to wine, not a striker, but gentle, not

1 TIMOTHY

contentious, not a lover of money, **4** leading his own house well, having children in subjection with all dignity, **5** (and if anyone has not known [how] to lead his own house, how will he take care of an assembly of God?) **6** not a new convert, lest having been puffed up he may fall to a judgment of the Devil; **7** and it is required of him also to have a good testimony from those outside, that he may not fall into reproach and a snare of the Devil. **8** Servants, in like manner, dignified, not double-tongued, not given to much wine, not given to shameful gain, **9** having the secret of the faith in a pure conscience, **10** and let these also first be proved, then let them minister, being unblameable. **11** Women, in like manner, dignified, not false accusers, vigilant, faithful in all things. **12** Servants—let them be husbands of one wife, leading the children well, and their own houses, **13** for those who ministered well acquire a good step to themselves, and much boldness in faith that [is] in Christ Jesus. **14** I write to you these things, hoping to come to you soon, **15** and if I delay, that you may know how it is required to conduct yourself in the house of God, which is an assembly of the living God—a pillar and foundation of the truth, **16** and confessedly, great is the secret of piety: who was revealed in flesh, declared righteous in [the] Spirit, seen by messengers, preached among nations, believed on in the world, taken up in glory!

4 And the Spirit expressly says that in latter times some will depart from the faith, giving heed to seducing spirits and teachings of demons, **2** speaking lies in hypocrisy, being seared in their own conscience, **3** forbidding to marry—to abstain from meats that God created to be received with thanksgiving by those believing and acknowledging the truth, **4** because every creature of God [is] good, and nothing [is] to be rejected, with thanksgiving being received, **5** for it is sanctified through the word of God and intercession. **6** Placing these things before the brothers, you will be a good servant of Jesus Christ, being nourished by the words of the faith, and of the good teaching, which you followed after, **7** but reject the profane and old women's fables, and exercise yourself to piety, **8** for bodily exercise is to little profit, but piety is profitable to all things, having promise of the life that now is, and of that which is coming; **9** the word [is] steadfast, and worthy of all acceptance; **10** for this we both labor and are reproached, because we hope on the living God, who is Savior of all men—especially of those believing. **11** Charge these things, and teach; **12** let no one despise your youth, but become a pattern of those believing in word, in behavior, in love, in spirit, in faith, in purity; **13** until I come, give heed to the reading, to the exhortation, to the teaching; **14** do not be careless of the gift in you, that was given you through prophecy, with laying on of the hands of the eldership; **15** be careful of these things; be in these things, that your advancement may be evident in all things; **16** take heed to yourself and to the teaching; remain in them, for doing this thing, you will save both yourself and those hearing you.

5 You may not rebuke an elder, but exhort [him] as a father, younger persons as brothers, **2** aged women as mothers, younger ones as sisters—in all purity; **3** honor widows who are really widows; **4** and if any widow has children or grandchildren, let them first learn to show piety to their own house, and to give back a repayment to the parents, for this is right and acceptable before God. **5** And she who is really a widow and desolate, has hoped on God, and remains in the supplications and in the prayers night and day, **6** but she given to luxury [while] living has died; **7** and charge these things, that they may be blameless; **8** and if anyone does not provide for his own, and especially for those of the household, he has denied the faith, and he is worse than an unbeliever. **9** A widow—do not let her be enrolled under sixty years of age, having been a wife of one husband, **10** being testified to in good works: if she brought up children, if she entertained strangers, if she washed holy ones' feet, if she relieved those in tribulation, if she followed after every good work; **11** and be refusing younger widows, for when they may revel against the Christ, they wish to marry, **12** having judgment, because they cast away the first faith, **13** and also at the same time, they learn [to be] idle, going around the houses; and not only idle, but also tattlers and busybodies, speaking things they should not; **14** I intend, therefore, younger ones to marry, to bear children, to be mistress of the house, to give no occasion to the opposer of reviling; **15** for some already turned aside after Satan. **16** If any believing man or believing woman has widows, let them relieve them, and do not let the assembly be burdened, that it may relieve those [who are] really widows. **17** Let them, the well-leading elders, be counted worthy of double honor, especially those laboring in word and teaching, **18** for the Writing says, "You will not muzzle an ox treading out," and, "Worthy [is] the workman of his reward." **19** Do not receive an accusation against an elder, except on two or three witnesses. **20** Reprove those sinning before all, that the others may also have fear; **21** I fully testify, before God and the Lord Jesus Christ, and the chosen messengers, that you may keep these things, without prejudging, doing nothing by partiality. **22** Be quickly laying hands on no one, nor be having fellowship with [the] sins of others; be keeping yourself pure; **23** no longer be drinking water, but be using a little wine, because of your stomach and of your frequent sicknesses; **24** the sins of certain men are evident beforehand, leading before to judgment, but some also they follow after; **25** in like manner the right works are also evident beforehand, and those that are otherwise are not able to be hid.

6 As many as are servants under a yoke, let them reckon their own masters worthy of all honor, that evil may not be spoken of the Name of God and the teaching; **2** and those having believing masters, do not let them slight [them], because they are brothers, but rather let them serve, because they are steadfast and beloved, who are partaking of the benefit. Be teaching and exhorting these things; **3** if anyone be teaching otherwise, and does not consent to sound words—those of our Lord Jesus Christ—and to the teaching according to piety, **4** he is proud, knowing nothing, but unhealthy about questions and word-striving, out of which come envy, strife, slanders, evil-surmisings, **5** wranglings of men wholly corrupted in mind, and destitute of the truth, supposing the piety to be gain; depart from such; **6** but it is great gain—the piety with contentment; **7** for we brought nothing into the world—because neither are we able to carry out anything; **8** but having food and raiment—with these we will suffice ourselves; **9** and those intending to be rich fall into temptation and a snare, and many desires, foolish and hurtful, that sink men into ruin and destruction, **10** for the love of money is a root of all the evils, which certain [ones] longing for went astray from the faith, and pierced themselves through with many sorrows; **11** and you, O man of God, flee these things, and pursue righteousness, piety, faith, love, endurance, meekness. **12** Be striving the good strife of the faith; be laying hold on the continuous life to which you also were called, and did profess the right profession before many witnesses. **13** I charge you, before God, who is making all things alive, and of Christ Jesus, who testified the right profession before Pontius Pilate, **14** that you keep the command unspotted, unblameable, until the appearing of our Lord Jesus Christ, **15** which He will show in His own times—the blessed and only sovereign, the King of the kings and Lord of the lords, **16** having immortality alone, dwelling in unapproachable light, whom no one of men saw, nor is able to see, to whom [is] honor and perpetual might! Amen. **17** Charge those rich in the present age not to be high-minded, nor to hope in the uncertainty of riches, but in the living God, who is giving to us all things richly for enjoyment— **18** to do good, to be rich in good works, to be ready to impart, willing to communicate, **19** treasuring up to themselves a right foundation for the time to come, that they may lay hold on [that which is] truly life. **20** O Timotheus, guard the thing entrusted, avoiding the profane vain-words and opposition of the falsely-named knowledge, **21** which certain [ones] professing—swerved concerning the faith. The grace [is] with you! Amen.

2 TIMOTHY

1 Paul, an apostle of Jesus Christ, through the will of God, according to a promise of life that [is] in Christ Jesus, **2** to Timotheus, beloved child: Grace, kindness, peace, from God the Father and Christ Jesus our Lord! **3** I am thankful to God, whom I serve from progenitors in a pure conscience, that I unceasingly have remembrance concerning you in my supplications night and day, **4** desiring to see you greatly, being mindful of your tears, that I may be filled with joy, **5** taking remembrance of the unhypocritical faith that is in you, that first dwelt in your grandmother Lois, and your mother Eunice, and I am persuaded that also in you. **6** For which cause I remind you to stir up the gift of God that is in you through the putting on of my hands, **7** for God did not give us a spirit of fear, but of power, and of love, and of a sound mind; **8** therefore you may not be ashamed of the testimony of our Lord, nor of me His prisoner, but you suffer evil along with the good news according to the power of God, **9** who saved us, and called with a holy calling, not according to our works, but according to His own purpose and grace, that was given to us in Christ Jesus, before the times of the ages, **10** and was made visible now through the appearing of our Savior Jesus Christ, who indeed abolished death, and enlightened life and immortality through the good news, **11** to which I was placed a preacher and an apostle, and a teacher of nations, **12** for which cause these things I also suffer, but I am not ashamed, for I have known in whom I have believed, and have been persuaded that He is able to guard that which I have committed to Him—to that day. **13** Hold the pattern of sound words, which you heard from me, in faith and love that [is] in Christ Jesus; **14** guard the good thing committed through the Holy Spirit that is dwelling in us; **15** you have known this, that they turned from me—all those in Asia, of whom are Phygellus and Hermogenes; **16** may the LORD give kindness to the house of Onesiphorus, because he refreshed me many times, and was not ashamed of my chain, **17** but being in Rome, he sought me very diligently and found [me]; **18** may the LORD give to him to find kindness from the LORD in that day; and you very well know how much he ministered in Ephesus.

2 You, therefore, my child, be strong in the grace that [is] in Christ Jesus, **2** and the things that you heard from me through many witnesses, be committing these things to steadfast men, who will also be sufficient to teach others; **3** you, therefore, suffer evil as a good soldier of Jesus Christ; **4** no one serving as a soldier entangles himself with the affairs of life, that he may please him who enlisted him; **5** and if anyone also may strive, he is not crowned, except he may strive lawfully; **6** it is first necessary [for] the laboring farmer to partake of the fruits; **7** be considering what things I say, for the LORD gives to you understanding in all things. **8** Remember Jesus Christ, raised out of the dead, of the seed of David, according to my good news, **9** in which I suffer evil—to bonds, as an evildoer, but the word of God has not been bound; **10** because of this I endure all things, because of the chosen ones, that they also may obtain salvation that [is] in Christ Jesus, with perpetual glory. **11** The word [is] steadfast: For if we died together—we will also live together; **12** if we endure together—we will also reign together; if we deny [Him], He will also deny us; **13** if we are not steadfast, He remains steadfast; He is not able to deny Himself. **14** Remind [them] of these things, testifying fully before the LORD—not to strive about words to nothing profitable, but to the subversion of those hearing; **15** be diligent to present yourself approved to God—a workman not ashamed, straightly cutting the word of truth; **16** and stand aloof from the profane vain talkings, for they will advance to more impiety, **17** and their word will have pasture as a gangrene, of whom is Hymenaeus and Philetus, **18** who swerved concerning the truth, saying the resurrection to have already been, and overthrows the faith of some; **19** sure, nevertheless, the foundation of God has stood, having this seal: "The LORD has known those who are His," and, "Let him depart from unrighteousness—everyone who is naming the Name of

Christ." **20** And in a great house there are not only vessels of gold and of silver, but also of wood and of earth, and some to honor, and some to dishonor: **21** if, then, anyone may cleanse himself from these, he will be a vessel to honor, sanctified and profitable to the master—having been prepared to every good work; **22** and flee the youthful lusts, and pursue righteousness, faith, love, peace, with those calling on the LORD out of a pure heart; **23** and be avoiding the foolish and uninstructed questions, having known that they beget strife, **24** and a servant of the LORD must not quarrel, but to be gentle to all, apt to teach, patient under evil, **25** instructing those opposing in meekness—if perhaps God may give to them conversion to an acknowledging of the truth, **26** and they may awake out of the Devil's snare, having been caught by him at his will.

3 And know this, that in the last days there will come perilous times, **2** for men will be lovers of themselves, lovers of money, boasters, proud, slanderous, disobedient to parents, unthankful, unkind, **3** without natural affection, implacable, false accusers, without control, barbaric, not lovers of those who are good, **4** traitors, reckless, lofty, lovers of pleasure more than lovers of God, **5** having a form of piety, but having denied its power; and be turning away from these, **6** for of these there are those coming into the houses and leading captive the weak women, loaded with sins, led away with manifold desires, **7** always learning, and never able to come to a knowledge of truth, **8** and even as Jannes and Jambres stood against Moses, so these also stand against the truth, men corrupted in mind, disapproved concerning the faith; **9** but they will not advance any further, for their folly will be evident to all, as theirs also became. **10** And you have followed after my teaching, manner of life, purpose, faith, long-suffering, love, endurance, **11** the persecutions, the afflictions, that befell me in Antioch, in Iconium, in Lystra; what persecutions I endured! And the LORD delivered me out of all. **12** And all who will to live piously in Christ Jesus will also be persecuted, **13** and evil men and impostors will advance to the worse, leading astray and being led astray. **14** And you—remain in the things which you learned and were entrusted with, having known from whom you learned, **15** and because you have known the Holy Writings from infancy, which are able to make you wise—to salvation, through faith that [is] in Christ Jesus. **16** Every Writing [is] God-breathed, and profitable for teaching, for conviction, for correction, for instruction that [is] in righteousness, **17** that the man of God may be fitted—having been completed for every good work.

4 I fully testify, then, before God, and the Lord Jesus Christ, who is about to judge [the] living and dead at His appearing and His Kingdom— **2** preach the word; be earnest in season, out of season; convict, rebuke, exhort, in all long-suffering and teaching, **3** for there will be a season when they will not endure the sound teaching, but they will heap up teachers according to their own desires—having an itching ear, **4** and, indeed, they will turn away from hearing the truth, and they will be turned aside to the fables. **5** But you—watch in all things; suffer evil; do the work of one proclaiming good news; make full assurance of your ministry, **6** for I am already being poured out, and the time of my release has arrived; **7** I have striven the good strife, I have finished the course, I have kept the faith; **8** from now on there is laid up for me the garland of righteousness that the LORD—the Righteous Judge—will give to me in that day, and not only to me, but also to all those loving His appearing. **9** Be diligent to come to me quickly, **10** for Demas forsook me, having loved the present age, and went on to Thessalonica, Crescens to Galatia, Titus to Dalmatia; **11** only Lucas is with me; having taken Mark, bring [him] with you, for he is profitable to me for ministry; **12** and I sent Tychicus to Ephesus; **13** coming, bring the cloak that I left in Troas with Carpus and the scrolls—especially the parchments. **14** Alexander the coppersmith did me much evil; may the LORD repay to him according to his works, **15** of whom you also beware, for he has greatly stood against our words; **16** no one stood with me in my first defense, but all forsook me (may it not be reckoned to them), **17** but the LORD stood by me, and strengthened me, that the preaching might be fully assured through me, and all the nations might hear, and I was freed out of the mouth of a lion, **18** and the LORD will free me from every evil work, and will save [me]—to His heavenly kingdom; to whom [is] the glory through the ages of the ages! Amen. **19** Greet Prisca and Aquilas, and Onesiphorus' household; **20** Erastus remained in Corinth, and I left Trophimus ailing in Miletus; **21** be diligent to come before winter. Eubulus greets you, and Pudens, and Linus, and Claudia, and all the brothers. **22** The Lord Jesus Christ [is] with your spirit. The grace [is] with you! Amen.

TITUS

1 Paul, a servant of God, and an apostle of Jesus Christ, according to the faith of the chosen ones of God, and an acknowledgment of truth that [is] according to piety, **2** on hope of continuous life, which God, who does not lie, promised before times of ages **3** (and He revealed His word in [His] own times), in preaching, which I was entrusted with, according to a charge of God our Savior, **4** to Titus—true child according to a common faith: Grace, [[kindness,]] peace, from God the Father and the Lord Jesus Christ our Savior! **5** For this cause I left you in Crete, that you may arrange the things lacking, and may set elders down in every city, as I appointed to you, **6** if anyone is blameless, a husband of one wife, having believing children, not under accusation of riotous living or insubordinate— **7** for it is required of the overseer to be blameless, as God's steward, not self-pleased, nor prone to anger, not given to wine, not an abuser, not given to shameful gain, **8** but a lover of strangers, a lover of [the] good, sober-minded, righteous, holy, self-controlled, **9** holding—according to the teaching—to the steadfast word, that he may also be able to exhort in the sound teaching, and to convict the deniers; **10** for there are many both insubordinate, vain-talkers, and mind-deceivers—especially those of the circumcision— **11** whose mouths must be covered, who overturn whole households, teaching what things it should not, for [the] sake of shameful gain. **12** A certain one of them, a prophet of their own, said, "Cretans! Always liars, evil beasts, lazy bellies!" **13** This testimony is true; for which cause convict them sharply, that they may be sound in the faith, **14** not giving heed to Jewish fables and commands of men, turning themselves away from the truth. **15** All things, indeed, [are] pure to the pure, and nothing [is] pure to the defiled and unsteadfast, but even the mind and the conscience of them [is] defiled. **16** They profess to know God, but they deny [Him] by their works, being abominable, and disobedient, and disapproved to every good work.

2 But you—speak what is suitable [according] to the sound teaching. **2** Elders [are] to be temperate, dignified, sober, sound in faith, in the love, in the endurance. **3** Aged women, in like manner, in behavior as becomes sacred persons, not false accusers, not enslaved to much wine, teachers of good things, **4** that they may make the young women sober-minded, to be lovers of [their] husbands, lovers of [their] children, **5** sober, pure, keepers of [their own] houses, good, subject to their own husbands, that evil may not be spoken of the word of God. **6** The younger men, in like manner, exhort [them] to be sober-minded. **7** Concerning all things, present yourself [as] a pattern of good works—in the teaching [with] uncorruptedness, dignity, **8** sound discourse [that is] blameless, so that he who is of the contrary may be ashamed, having nothing evil to say concerning you. **9** Servants [are] to be subject to their own masters, to be well-pleasing in all things, not contradicting, **10** not stealing, but showing all good steadfastness, that the teaching of God our Savior they may adorn in all things. **11** For the saving grace of God has appeared to all men, **12** teaching us, that denying the impiety and the worldly desires, we may live soberly, and righteously, and piously in the present age, **13** waiting for the blessed hope and appearing of the glory of our great God and Savior Jesus Christ, **14** who gave Himself for us, that He might ransom us from all lawlessness, and might purify to Himself a special people, zealous of good works. **15** Speak these things, and exhort and convict with all authority; let no one despise you!

3 Remind them to be subject to principalities and authorities, to obey rule, to be ready to every good work, **2** to speak evil of no one, not to be quarrelsome—gentle, showing all meekness to all men, **3** for we, also, were once thoughtless, disobedient, led astray, serving manifold desires and pleasures, living in malice and envy, odious—hating one another; **4** and when the kindness and the love to men of God our Savior appeared **5** (not by works that [are] in righteousness that we did but according to His kindness), He saved us, through a bathing of regeneration, and a renewing of the Holy Spirit, **6** which He poured on us richly, through Jesus Christ our Savior, **7** that having been declared righteous by His grace, we may become heirs according to the hope of continuous life. **8** The word [is] steadfast; and concerning these things I intend you to affirm fully, that they may be thoughtful, to be leading in good works—who have believed God; these are the good and profitable things to men, **9** but stand away from foolish questions, and genealogies, and contentions, and strivings about law—for they are unprofitable and vain. **10** Reject a heretical man, after a first and second admonition, **11** having known that he has been subverted who [is] such, and sins, being self-condemned. **12** When I will send Artemas to you, or Tychicus, be diligent to come to me to Nicopolis, for I have determined to winter there. **13** Diligently send forth Zenas the lawyer and Apollos on their way, that nothing to them may be lacking, **14** and let them learn—ours also—to be leading in good works to the necessary uses, that they may not be unfruitful. **15** All those with me greet you. Greet those cherishing us in faith. The grace [is] with you all!

PHILEMON

1 Paul, a prisoner of Christ Jesus, and Timotheus the brother, to Philemon our beloved and fellow-worker, **2** and Apphia the beloved, and Archippus our fellow-soldier, and the assembly in your house: **3** Grace to you and peace from God our Father and the Lord Jesus Christ! **4** I give thanks to my God, always making mention of you in my prayers, **5** hearing of your love and faith that you have to the Lord Jesus and toward all the holy ones, **6** that the fellowship of your faith may become working in the full knowledge of every good thing that [is] in you toward Christ Jesus; **7** for we have much joy and comfort in your love, because the yearnings of the holy ones have been refreshed through you, brother. **8** For this reason, having in Christ much boldness to command you that which is fit— **9** because of the love I rather plead, being such a one as Paul the aged, and now also a prisoner of Jesus Christ; **10** I beg you concerning my child—whom I begot in my bonds—Onesimus, **11** who once was to you unprofitable, and now is profitable to me and to you, **12** whom I sent again to you—he who is my own heart, **13** whom I intended to retain to myself, that in your behalf he might minister to me in the bonds of the good news, **14** but apart from your mind I willed to do nothing, so that your good deed may not be as of necessity, but of willingness, **15** for perhaps because of this he departed for an hour, that you may have him continuously, **16** no longer as a servant, but above a servant—a beloved brother, especially to me, and how much more to you, both in the flesh and in the LORD! **17** If, then, you have fellowship with me, receive him as me, **18** and if he did hurt to you, or owes anything, charge this to me; **19** I, Paul, wrote with my hand, I will repay; besides, that I may not say that you also owe to me yourself. **20** Yes, brother, may I have profit of you in the LORD; refresh my yearnings in the LORD; **21** I wrote to you having been confident in your obedience, having known that you will also do above what I may say; **22** and at the same time also prepare for me a lodging, for I hope that through your prayers I will be granted to you. **23** Epaphras greets you (my fellow-captive in Christ Jesus), **24** Marcus, Aristarchus, Demas, Lucas, my fellow-workmen! **25** The grace of our Lord Jesus Christ [is] with your spirit! Amen.

HEBREWS

1 In many parts and many ways, God, having spoken long ago to the fathers by the prophets, **2** in these last days speaks to us in [His] Son, whom He appointed heir of all things, through whom He also made the ages; **3** who being the brightness of the glory, and the impress of His subsistence, bearing up also all things by the saying of His might—having made a cleansing of our sins through Himself, sat down at the right hand of the Greatness in the highest, **4** having become so much better than the messengers, as He inherited a more excellent name than them. **5** For to which of the messengers did He ever say, "You are My Son—today I have begotten You?" And again, "I will be to Him for a Father, and He will be to Me for a Son?" **6** And when again He may bring the firstborn into the world, He says, "And let them worship Him—all messengers of God"; **7** and to the messengers, indeed, He says, "The [One] who is making His messengers spirits, and His ministers a flame of fire"; **8** but to the Son: "Your throne, O God, [is] throughout the age of the age; The scepter of righteousness [is the] scepter of Your kingdom; **9** You loved righteousness, and hated lawlessness; Because of this He anointed You—God, Your God—With oil of gladness above Your partners"; **10** and, "You, LORD, founded the earth at the beginning, ‖ And the heavens are a work of Your hands. **11** These will perish, but You remain, ‖ And all will become old as a garment, **12** And You will roll them together as a mantle, and they will be changed, ‖ But You are the same, and Your years will not fail." **13** And to which of the messengers did He ever say, "Sit at My right hand, ‖ Until I may make Your enemies Your footstool?" **14** Are they not all spirits of service—being sent forth for ministry because of those about to inherit salvation?

2 Because of this it is more abundantly necessary to take heed to the things heard, lest we may drift away, **2** for if the word being spoken through messengers became steadfast, and every transgression and disobedience received a just repayment, **3** how will we escape, having neglected such great salvation? Which having received [that] spoken through the LORD [from] the beginning, was confirmed to us by those having heard, **4** God also bearing joint-witness both with signs and wonders, and manifold powers, and distributions of the Holy Spirit, according to His will. **5** For He did not subject the coming world to messengers, concerning which we speak, **6** and one in a certain place testified fully, saying, "What is man, that You are mindful of him, ‖ Or a son of man, that You look after him? **7** You made him [a] little less than messengers, ‖ You crowned him with glory and honor, ‖ And set him over the works of Your hands, **8** You put all things in subjection under his feet," for in the subjecting to Him all things, He left nothing to Him unsubjected, but now we do not yet see all things subjected to Him, **9** and we see Him who was made [a] little less than messengers—Jesus—because of the suffering of death, having been crowned with glory and honor, that by the grace of God He might taste of death for everyone. **10** For it was fitting to Him, because of whom [are] all things, and through whom [are] all things, bringing many sons to glory, to make the author of their salvation perfect through sufferings, **11** for both He who is sanctifying and those sanctified [are] all of one, for which cause He is not ashamed to call them brothers, **12** saying, "I will declare Your Name to My brothers, ‖ In the midst of an assembly I will sing praise to You"; and again, "I will be trusting on Him"; **13** and again, "Behold, I and the children that God gave to Me." **14** Seeing, then, the children have partaken of flesh and blood, He Himself also took part of the same in like manner, that through death He might destroy him having the power of death—that is, the Devil— **15** and might deliver those, whoever, with fear of death, throughout all their life, were subjects of bondage, **16** for doubtless, He does not lay hold of messengers, but He lays hold of [the] seed of Abraham, **17** for this reason it seemed necessary to Him to be made like the brothers in all things, that He might become a kind and faithful Chief Priest in the things related to God, to make

HEBREWS

propitiation for the sins of the people, **18** for in that He suffered, Himself being tempted, He is able to help those who are tempted.

3 For this reason, holy brothers, partakers of a heavenly calling, consider the Apostle and Chief Priest of our profession, Christ Jesus, **2** being faithful to Him who appointed Him, as also Moses [was] in all His house. **3** For this One has been counted worthy of more glory than Moses, inasmuch as He who builds it has more honor than the house. **4** For every house is built by someone, and He who built all things [is] God, **5** and Moses [was] indeed steadfast in all His house, as an attendant, for a testimony of those things that were to be spoken— **6** but Christ, as a Son over His house, whose house we are, if we hold fast the boldness and the rejoicing of the hope to the end. **7** For this reason, as the Holy Spirit says, "Today, if you may hear His voice— **8** you may not harden your hearts, as in the provocation, in the day of the temptation in the wilderness, **9** in which your fathers tempted Me; they proved Me, and saw My works [for] forty years; **10** for this reason I was grieved with that generation and said, They always go astray in [their] heart, and these have not known My ways; **11** so I swore in My anger, They will [not] enter into My rest." **12** Watch out, brothers, lest there will be in any of you an evil heart of unbelief in the falling away from the living God, **13** but exhort one another every day, while [it] is called "Today," that none of you may be hardened by the deceitfulness of sin, **14** for we have become partakers of the Christ, if we may hold fast the confidence [we had] at the beginning to the end, **15** as it is said, "Today, if you may hear His voice, you may not harden your hearts, as in the provocation." **16** For who [were those], having heard, [that] provoked, but not all those having come out of Egypt through Moses? **17** But with whom was He grieved forty years? Was it not with those who sinned, whose carcasses fell in the wilderness? **18** And to whom did He swear that they will not enter into His rest, except to those who did not believe? **19** And we see that they were not able to enter in because of unbelief.

4 We may fear, then, lest a promise being left of entering into His rest, anyone of you may seem to have come short, **2** for we also are having good news proclaimed, even as they, but the word heard did not profit them, not being mixed with faith in those who heard, **3** for we enter into the rest—we who believed, as He said, "So I swore in My anger, They will [not] enter into My rest"; and yet the works were done from the foundation of the world, **4** for He spoke in a certain place concerning the seventh [day] thus: "And God rested in the seventh day from all His works"; **5** and in this [place] again, "They will [not] enter into My rest"; **6** since then, it remains for some to enter into it, and those who first heard good news did not enter in because of unbelief— **7** again He limits a certain day, "Today," in David saying, after so long a time, as it has been said, "Today, if you may hear His voice, you may not harden your hearts," **8** for if Joshua had given them rest, He would not have spoken after these things concerning another day; **9** there remains, then, a Sabbath rest to the people of God, **10** for he who entered into His rest, he also rested from his works, as God from His own. **11** May we be diligent, then, to enter into that rest, that no one may fall in the same example of the unbelief, **12** for the Word of God is living, and working, and sharper—beyond every two-edged sword—and piercing as far as [the] division of soul and spirit, of joints and also marrows, and a discerner of thoughts and intents of the heart; **13** and there is not a created thing hidden before Him, but all things [are] naked and open to His eyes—with whom is our reckoning. **14** Having, then, a great Chief Priest having passed through the heavens—Jesus the Son of God—may we hold fast the profession, **15** for we do not have a Chief Priest unable to sympathize with our weaknesses, but [One] tempted in all things in like manner, [yet] without sin; **16** we may come near, then, with freedom, to the throne of grace, that we may receive kindness, and find grace—for seasonable help.

5 For every chief priest taken out of men is set in things [pertaining] to God in behalf of men, that he may offer both gifts and sacrifices for sins, **2** being able to be gentle to those being ignorant and going astray, since he is also surrounded with weakness; **3** and because of this [weakness] he ought, just as for the people, so also for himself, to bring forward [sacrifices] for sins; **4** and no one takes the honor to himself, but he who is called by God, as also Aaron. **5** So also the Christ did not glorify Himself to become Chief Priest, but He who spoke to Him: "You are My Son, today I have begotten You"; **6** just as He also says in another [place], "You [are] a priest throughout the age, according to the order of Melchizedek"; **7** who in the days of His flesh having offered up both prayers and supplications with strong crying and tears to Him who was able to save Him from death, and having been heard in respect to that which He feared, **8** though being a Son, [He] learned obedience by the things which He suffered, **9** and having been made perfect, He became the cause of continuous salvation to all those obeying Him, **10** having been called by God a Chief Priest according to the order of Melchizedek, **11** concerning the Word, of whom we have much [to speak], and of hard explanation to say, since you have become dull of hearing, **12** for even owing to be teachers, because of the time, again you have need that one teach you what [are] the elements of the beginning of the oracles of God, and you have become having need of milk, and not of strong food, **13** for everyone who is partaking of milk [is] unskilled in the word of righteousness— for he is an infant, **14** and the strong food is of perfect men, who because of the use are having the senses exercised, to both the discernment of good and of evil.

6 For this reason, having left the word of the beginning of the Christ, we may advance to perfection, not laying again a foundation of conversion from dead works, and of faith on God, **2** of the teaching of immersions, also of laying on of hands, also of [the] resurrection of the dead, and of continuous judgment, **3** and this we will do, if God may permit, **4** for [it is] impossible for those once enlightened, having also tasted of the heavenly gift, and having become partakers of the Holy Spirit, **5** and tasted the good saying of God, also the powers of the coming age, **6** and having fallen away, to renew [them] again to conversion, having crucified to themselves the Son of God again, and exposed to public shame. **7** For the earth, having drunk in the rain coming on it many times, and is bringing forth herbs fit for those because of whom it is also dressed, partakes of blessing from God, **8** but that which is bearing thorns and briers [is] disapproved of, and near to cursing, whose end [is] for burning; **9** but we are persuaded, concerning you, beloved, the things that are better, and accompanying salvation, though even thus we speak, **10** for God is not unrighteous to forget your work, and the labor of love that you showed to His Name, having ministered to the holy ones and ministering; **11** and we desire each one of you to show the same diligence, to the full assurance of the hope to the end, **12** that you may not become slothful, but followers of those who through faith and patient endurance are inheriting the promises. **13** For God, having made promise to Abraham, seeing He was not able to swear by [any] greater, swore by Himself, **14** saying, "Blessing I will indeed bless you, and multiplying I will multiply you"; **15** and so, having patiently endured, he obtained the promise; **16** for men swear by the greater, and the oath [is] for confirmation of the end of all their controversy, **17** in which God, more abundantly willing to show to the heirs of the promise the immutability of His counsel, interposed by an oath, **18** that through two immutable things, in which [it is] impossible for God to lie, we may have a strong comfort, having fled for refuge, to lay hold on the hope being set before [us], **19** which we have, as an anchor of the soul, both sure and steadfast, and entering into that within the veil, **20** to where a forerunner entered for us—Jesus, having become Chief Priest throughout the age after the order of Melchizedek.

7 For this Melchizedek, king of Salem, priest of God Most High, who met Abraham turning back from the striking of the kings, and blessed him, **2** to whom also Abraham divided a tenth of all (first, indeed, being interpreted, "King of righteousness," and then also, "King of Salem," which is, King of Peace), **3** without father, without mother, without genealogy, having neither beginning of days nor end of life, and having been like the Son of God, remains a priest continually. **4** And see how great this one [is], to whom Abraham the patriarch also gave a tenth out of the

HEBREWS

best of the spoils, **5** and those, indeed, out of the sons of Levi receiving the priesthood, have a command to take tithes from the people according to the Law, that is, their brothers, even though they came forth out of the loins of Abraham; **6** and he who was not reckoned by genealogy of them, received tithes from Abraham, and he has blessed him having the promises, **7** and apart from all controversy, the less is blessed by the better— **8** and here, indeed, men who die receive tithes, and there [he] who is testified to that he was living, **9** and so to speak, through Abraham even Levi who is receiving tithes, has paid tithes, **10** for he was yet in the loins of the father when Melchizedek met him. **11** If indeed, then, perfection were through the Levitical priesthood—for the people under it had received law—what further need, according to the order of Melchizedek, for another priest to arise, and not to be called according to the order of Aaron? **12** For the priesthood being changed, of necessity also, a change comes of the Law, **13** for He of whom these things are said in another tribe has had part, of whom no one gave attendance at the altar, **14** for [it is] evident that out of Judah has arisen our Lord, in regard to which tribe Moses spoke nothing concerning priesthood. **15** And it is yet more abundantly most evident, if according to the likeness of Melchizedek there arises another priest, **16** who did not come according to the law of a fleshly command, but according to the power of an endless life, **17** for He testifies, "You [are] a priest—throughout the age, according to the order of Melchizedek"; **18** for an annulling indeed comes of the command going before because of its weakness, and unprofitableness **19** (for nothing did the Law perfect), and the bringing in of a better hope, through which we draw near to God. **20** And inasmuch as [it is] not apart from oath **21** (for those indeed apart from oath have become priests, and He [became priest] with an oath through Him who is saying to Him, "The LORD swore, and will not regret, You [are] a priest throughout the age, according to the order of Melchizedek"), **22** by so much also has Jesus become guarantee of a better covenant, **23** and those indeed are many who have become priests, because by death they are hindered from remaining; **24** and He, because of His remaining throughout the age, has the inviolable priesthood, **25** from where also He is able to save to the very end, those coming through Him to God—ever living to make intercession for them. **26** For also such a Chief Priest was fitting for us—holy, innocent, undefiled, separate from the sinners, and having become higher than the heavens, **27** who has no daily necessity, as the chief priests, to first offer up sacrifice for His own sins, then for those of the people; for this He did once, having offered up Himself; **28** for the Law appoints men [as] chief priests, having weakness, but the word of the oath that [is] after the Law [appoints] the Son having been perfected throughout the age.

8 And the sum concerning the things spoken of [is]: we have such a Chief Priest, who sat down at the right hand of the throne of the Greatness in the heavens, **2** a servant of the holy places, and of the true dwelling place, which the LORD set up, and not man, **3** for every chief priest is appointed to offer both gifts and sacrifices, from where [it is] necessary for this One to also have something that He may offer; **4** for if, indeed, He were on earth, He would not be a priest (there being the priests who are offering the gifts according to the Law, **5** who to an example and shadow serve of the heavenly things, as Moses has been divinely warned, being about to construct the Dwelling Place, for, "See," He says, "[that] you will make all things according to the pattern that was shown to you on the mountain"), **6** but now He has obtained a more excellent service, how much He is also mediator of a better covenant, which has been sanctioned on better promises, **7** for if that first were faultless, a place would not have been sought for a second. **8** For finding fault, He says to them, "Behold, days come, says the LORD, and I will complete with the house of Israel, and with the house of Judah, a new covenant, **9** not according to the covenant that I made with their fathers, in the day of My taking [them] by their hand, to bring them out of the land of Egypt—because they did not remain in My covenant, and I did not regard them, says the LORD— **10** because this [is] the covenant that I will make with the house of Israel, after those days, says the LORD, giving My laws into their mind, and I will write them on their hearts, and I will be to them for a God, and they will be to Me for a people; **11** and they will not each teach his neighbor, and each his brother, saying, Know the LORD, because they will all know Me—from the small one of them to the great one of them, **12** because I will be merciful to their unrighteousness, and I will remember their sins and their lawlessnesses no more." **13** In the saying "new," He has made the first obsolete, and what is becoming obsolete and growing old [is] near disappearing.

9 It had, indeed, then (even the first dwelling place) ordinances of service, also a worldly sanctuary, **2** for a dwelling place was prepared, the first, in which was both the lampstand, and the table, and the Bread of the Presentation—which is called "Holy"; **3** and after the second veil a dwelling place that is called "Holy of Holies," **4** having a golden censer, and the Ark of the Covenant overlaid all over with gold, in which [is] the golden pot having the manna, and the rod of Aaron that budded, and the tablets of the covenant, **5** and over it cherubim of the glory, overshadowing the propitiatory covering, concerning which we are not to particularly speak now. **6** And these things having been thus prepared, into the first dwelling place, indeed, the priests go in at all times, performing the services, **7** and into the second, once in the year, only the chief priest, not apart from blood, which he offers for himself and the errors of the people. **8** By this the Holy Spirit was making evident that the way of the holy [places] has not yet been revealed, the first dwelling place yet having a standing, **9** which [is] an allegory in regard to the present time, in which both gifts and sacrifices are offered, which are not able, in regard to conscience, to make perfect him who is serving, **10** only on the basis of food, and drinks, and different immersions, and fleshly ordinances—until the time of reformation imposed on [them]. **11** But Christ having come, Chief Priest of the coming good things, through the greater and more perfect dwelling place not made with hands—that is, not of this creation— **12** neither through blood of goats and calves, but through His own blood, entered in once into the holy places, having obtained continuous redemption; **13** for if the blood of bulls, and goats, and ashes of a heifer, sprinkling those defiled, sanctifies to the purifying of the flesh, **14** how much more will the blood of the Christ (who through the perpetual Spirit offered Himself unblemished to God) purify your conscience from dead works to serve the living God? **15** And because of this, He is mediator of a new covenant, that [His] death having come for redemption of the transgressions under the first covenant, those called may receive the promise of the continuous inheritance, **16** for where a covenant [is], [it is] necessary to establish the death of the [one] having made [it], **17** for a covenant is affirmed at death, since it is not in force at all when the [one] having made [it] lives, **18** for which reason, not even the first has been initiated apart from blood, **19** for every command having been spoken, according to law, by Moses, to all the people, having taken the blood of the calves and goats, with water, and scarlet wool, and hyssop, he sprinkled both the scroll itself and all the people, **20** saying, "This [is] the blood of the covenant that God enjoined to you," **21** and he sprinkled both the Dwelling Place and all the vessels of the service with blood in like manner, **22** and with blood almost all things are purified according to the Law, and forgiveness does not come apart from blood-shedding. **23** [It is] necessary, therefore, the pattern indeed of the things in the heavens to be purified with these, and the heavenly things themselves with better sacrifices than these; **24** for the Christ did not enter into holy places made with hands—figures of the true—but into Heaven itself, now to be manifested in the presence of God for us; **25** nor that He may offer Himself many times, even as the chief priest enters into the holy places every year with blood of others, **26** otherwise it was necessary for Him to suffer many times from the foundation of the world, but now He has been revealed once, at the full end of the ages, for [the] annulling of sin through His sacrifice; **27** and as it is reserved for men to die once, and after this—judgment, **28** so also the Christ, having been offered once to bear the sins of many, will appear a second time, apart from a sin-offering, for salvation to those waiting for Him!

10 For the Law having a shadow of the good things coming—not the very image of the matters, every year, by the

HEBREWS

same sacrifices that they offer continually, is never able to make perfect those coming near, 2 since, would they not have ceased to be offered, because of those serving having no more conscience of sins, having been purified once? 3 But in those [sacrifices] is a remembrance of sins every year, 4 for it is impossible for blood of bulls and goats to take away sins. 5 For this reason, coming into the world, He says, "Sacrifice and offering You did not will, and a body You prepared for Me; 6 in burnt-offerings, and concerning sin-offerings, You did not delight. 7 Then I said, Behold, I come (in a volume of the scroll it has been written concerning Me), to do, O God, Your will"; 8 saying above, "Sacrifice, and offering, and burnt-offerings, and concerning sin-offering You did not will, nor delight in" (which are offered according to the Law), 9 then He said, "Behold, I come to do, O God, Your will"; He takes away the first that He may establish the second; 10 in which will, we have been sanctified through the offering of the body of Jesus Christ once for all, 11 and every priest, indeed, has daily stood serving, and offering the same sacrifices many times, that are never able to take away sins. 12 But He, having offered one sacrifice for sin—to the end, sat down at the right hand of God— 13 as to the rest, expecting until He may place His enemies [as] His footstool, 14 for by one offering He has perfected to the end those being sanctified; 15 and the Holy Spirit also testifies to us, for after that He has said before, 16 "This [is] the covenant that I will make with them after those days, says the LORD, giving My laws on their hearts, and I will write them on their minds," 17 and, "I will remember their sins and their lawlessness no more"; 18 and where [there is] forgiveness of these, there is no longer offering for sin. 19 Having, therefore, brothers, boldness for the entrance into the holy places, by the blood of Jesus, 20 which [is] the way He initiated for us—new and living, through the veil, that is, His flesh— 21 and a Great Priest over the house of God, 22 may we draw near with a true heart, in full assurance of faith, having the hearts sprinkled from an evil conscience, and having the body bathed with pure water; 23 may we hold fast the unwavering profession of the hope (for He who promised [is] faithful), 24 and may we consider to provoke one another to love and to good works, 25 not forsaking the assembling of ourselves together, as [is] a custom of some, but exhorting, and so much the more as you see the Day coming near. 26 For [if] we are sinning willingly after receiving the full knowledge of the truth—there remains no more sacrifice for sins, 27 but a certain fearful looking for of judgment, and fiery zeal, about to devour the opposers; 28 anyone having set aside a law of Moses dies without mercies on the basis of two or three witnesses. 29 Of how much worse punishment will he be counted worthy who trampled on the Son of God, and counted the blood of the covenant a common thing, by which he was sanctified, and having insulted the Spirit of grace? 30 For we have known Him who is saying, "Vengeance [is] Mine, I will repay, says the LORD"; and again, "The LORD will judge His people." 31 [It is] fearful to fall into [the] hands of [the] living God. 32 But call to your remembrance the former days, in which, having been enlightened, you endured much conflict of sufferings; 33 this indeed, being made spectacles with both insults and afflictions, now this, having become partners of those so living, 34 for you also sympathized with my bonds, and the robbery of your goods you received with joy, knowing that you have in yourselves a better substance in the heavens, and an enduring one. 35 You may not cast away, then, your boldness, which has great repayment of reward, 36 for you have need of patience, that having done the will of God, you may receive the promise. 37 "For yet [in] a very, very little [while], He who is coming will come, and will not linger," 38 but, "The righteous will live by faith; and if he may draw back, My soul has no pleasure in him." 39 But we are not of those drawing back to destruction, but of those believing to a preserving of soul.

11 Now faith is [the] substance of things hoped for, [the] proof of matters not being seen, 2 for by this, the elders were well-attested. 3 By faith we understand the ages to have been prepared by a saying of God, in regard to the things seen having not come out of things appearing. 4 By faith Abel offered a better sacrifice to God than Cain, through which he was testified to be righteous, God testifying of his gifts, and through it, he being dead, yet speaks. 5 By

faith Enoch was translated—not to see death, and was not found, because God translated him; for before his translation he had been testified to—that he had pleased God well, 6 and apart from faith it is impossible to please [Him], for it is required of him who is coming to God to believe that He exists and [that] He becomes a rewarder to those seeking Him. 7 By faith Noah, having been divinely warned concerning the things not yet seen, having feared, prepared an ark to the salvation of his house, through which he condemned the world, and he became heir of the righteousness according to faith. 8 By faith Abraham, being called, obeyed, to go forth into the place that he was about to receive for an inheritance, and he went forth, not knowing to where he goes. 9 By faith he sojourned in the land of the promise as a strange country, having dwelt in dwelling places with Isaac and Jacob, fellow-heirs of the same promise, 10 for he was looking for the city having the foundations, whose craftsman and constructor [is] God. 11 And by faith Sarah, herself barren, received power to conceive seed even after the time of life, seeing she judged Him who promised faithful; 12 for this reason, also, from one—and that of one who had become dead—were begotten as the stars of the sky in multitude, and innumerable as the sand that [is] by the seashore. 13 All these died in faith, having not received the promises, but having seen them from afar, and having been persuaded, and having greeted [them], and having confessed that they are strangers and sojourners on the earth, 14 for those saying such things make apparent that they seek a country; 15 and if, indeed, they had been mindful of that from which they came forth, they might have had an opportunity to return, 16 but now they long for better, that is, heavenly, for this reason God is not ashamed of them, to be called their God, for He prepared a city for them. 17 By faith Abraham has offered up Isaac, being tried, even the [one] having received the promises offered up his only begotten, 18 of whom it was said, "In Isaac will your Seed be called," 19 reckoning that God is even able to raise up out of the dead, from where also in a figurative sense he received [him]. 20 By faith, concerning coming things, Isaac blessed Jacob and Esau. 21 By faith Jacob, dying, blessed each of the sons of Joseph and worshiped on the top of his staff. 22 By faith Joseph, dying, made mention concerning the outgoing of the sons of Israel, and gave command concerning his bones. 23 By faith Moses, having been born, was hid three months by his parents, because they saw the child beautiful, and were not afraid of the decree of the king. 24 By faith Moses, having become great, refused to be called a son of the daughter of Pharaoh, 25 having chosen rather to be afflicted with the people of God, than to have sin's pleasure for a season, 26 having reckoned the reproach of the Christ greater wealth than the treasures in Egypt, for he looked to the repayment of reward. 27 By faith he left Egypt behind, having not been afraid of the wrath of the king, for as seeing the Invisible One—he endured. 28 By faith he kept the Passover, and the sprinkling of the blood, so that He who is destroying the firstborn might not touch them. 29 By faith they passed through the Red Sea as through dry land, which having made an attempt [to cross], the Egyptians were swallowed up. 30 By faith the walls of Jericho fell, having been surrounded for seven days. 31 By faith Rahab the prostitute did not perish with those who disbelieved, having received the spies with peace. 32 And what yet will I say? For the time will fail me recounting about Gideon, also Barak, and Samson, and Jephthah, also David, and Samuel, and the prophets, 33 who through faith subdued kingdoms, worked righteousness, obtained promises, stopped mouths of lions, 34 quenched the power of fire, escaped the mouth of the sword, were made powerful out of weakness, became strong in battle, caused armies of the foreigners to give way; 35 women received their dead by a resurrection, and others were tortured, not accepting the redemption, that they might receive a better resurrection, 36 and others received trial of mockings and scourgings, and yet of bonds and imprisonment; 37 they were stoned, they were sawn apart, they were tried; they died in the killing of the sword; they went around in sheepskins, in goatskins—being destitute, afflicted, injuriously treated, 38 of whom the world was not worthy; wandering in deserts, and mountains, and caves, and the holes of the earth; 39 and all these, having been testified to through faith, did not receive the promise, 40 God, having provided something better for us, that apart from us they might not be made perfect.

12 Therefore, we also having so great a cloud of witnesses set around us, having put off every weight, and the closely besetting sin, may we run the contest that is set before us through endurance, **2** looking to the Author and Perfecter of the faith—Jesus, who, for the joy set before Him, endured a cross, having despised shame, and sat down at the right hand of the throne of God; **3** for again consider Him who endured such contradiction from the sinners to Himself, that you may not be wearied in your souls—being faint. **4** You did not yet resist to blood—striving with sin; **5** and you have forgotten the exhortation that speaks fully to you as to sons, "My son, do not despise [the] discipline of [the] LORD, nor be faint, being reproved by Him, **6** for whom the LORD loves He disciplines, and He scourges every son whom He receives"; **7** if you endure discipline, God bears Himself to you as to sons, for who is a son whom a father does not discipline? **8** And if you are apart from discipline, of which all have become partakers, then you are bastards, and not sons. **9** Then, indeed, we have had fathers of our flesh, correctors, and we respected [them]; will we not much rather be subject to the Father of the spirits, and live? **10** For they, indeed, for a few days, according to what seemed good to them, were disciplining, but He for profit, to be partakers of His separation; **11** and all discipline for the present, indeed, does not seem to be of joy, but of sorrow, yet afterward it yields the peaceable fruit of righteousness to those exercised through it. **12** For this reason, lift up the hanging-down hands and the loosened knees; **13** and make straight paths for your feet, so that which is lame may not be turned aside, but rather be healed; **14** pursue peace with all, and the separation, apart from which no one will see the LORD, **15** observing lest anyone be failing of the grace of God, lest any root of bitterness springing up may give trouble, and through this many may be defiled; **16** lest anyone be a fornicator, or a profane person, as Esau, who in exchange for one morsel of food sold his birthright, **17** for you know that also afterward, wishing to inherit the blessing, he was disapproved of, for he did not find a place of conversion, though having sought it with tears. **18** For you did not come near to the mountain touched and scorched with fire, and to blackness, and darkness, and storm, **19** and a sound of a trumpet, and a voice of sayings, which those having heard begged that a word might not be added to them, **20** for they were not bearing that which is commanded, "And if a beast may touch the mountain, it will be stoned, or shot through with an arrow," **21** and (so terrible was the sight), Moses said, "I am exceedingly fearful, and trembling." **22** But you came to Mount Zion, and to [the] city of the living God, to the heavenly Jerusalem, and to myriads of messengers, **23** to the assembly-place and Assembly of the Firstborn registered in Heaven, and to God the judge of all, and to spirits of righteous men made perfect, **24** and to a mediator of a new covenant—Jesus, and to blood of sprinkling, speaking better things than that of Abel! **25** Watch out lest you refuse Him who is speaking, for if those did not escape who refused him who was divinely speaking on earth—much less we who turn away from Him who [speaks] from Heaven, **26** whose voice shook the earth then, and now He has promised, saying, "Yet once [more]—I shake not only the earth, but also Heaven"; **27** and this, "Yet once [more]," makes evident the removal of the things shaken, as of things having been made, that the things not shaken may remain; **28** for this reason, receiving a kingdom that cannot be shaken, may we have grace, through which we may serve God well-pleasingly, with reverence and fear, **29** for our God [is] also a consuming fire.

13 Let brotherly love remain. **2** Do not be forgetful of hospitality, for through this some entertained messengers unaware. **3** Be mindful of those in bonds, as having been bound with them, of those maltreated, as yourselves also being in the body. **4** The marriage [is to be] honored by all, and the bed undefiled, for God will judge whoremongers and adulterers. **5** [Be] without covetous behavior, being content with the things present, for He has said, "No, I will not leave, no, nor forsake you," **6** so that we boldly say, "The LORD [is] to me a helper, and I will not fear what man will do to me." **7** Be mindful of those leading you, who spoke to you the word of

God, who, considering the outcome of [their] behavior, imitate [their] faith: **8** Jesus Christ—the same yesterday and today and for all ages. **9** Do not be carried away with strange and manifold teachings, for [it is] good that by grace the heart is confirmed, not with meats, in which they who were occupied were not profited; **10** we have an altar from which they who are serving the Dwelling Place have no authority to eat, **11** for of those beasts whose blood is brought for sin into the holy places through the chief priest—of these the bodies are burned outside the camp. **12** For this reason, also Jesus—that He might sanctify the people through [His] own blood—suffered outside the gate; **13** now then, may we go forth to Him outside the camp, bearing His reproach; **14** for we have no abiding city here, but we seek the coming one. **15** Through Him, then, we may always offer up a sacrifice of praise to God, that is, the fruit of lips, giving thanks to His Name. **16** And do not be forgetful of doing good and of fellowship, for God is well-pleased with such sacrifices. **17** Be obedient to those leading you, and be subject, for these watch for your souls, as about to give account, that they may do this with joy, and not sighing, for this [is] unprofitable to you. **18** Pray for us, for we trust that we have a good conscience, willing to behave well in all things, **19** and I call on [you] to do this more abundantly, that I may be restored to you more quickly. **20** And the God of peace, who brought up the Great Shepherd of the sheep out of the dead—by the blood of a perpetual covenant—our Lord Jesus, **21** make you perfect in every good work to do His will, doing in you that which is well-pleasing before Him, through Jesus Christ, to whom [is] the glory through the ages of the ages! Amen. **22** And I beg you, brothers, endure the word of the exhortation, for I have also written to you through few words. **23** Know that the brother Timotheus is released, with whom I will see you, if he may come more shortly. **24** Greet all those leading you, and all the holy ones. Those from Italy greet you. **25** The grace [is] with you all! Amen.

JAMES

1 James, a servant of God and of the Lord Jesus Christ, to the twelve tribes who are in the dispersion: Greetings! **2** Count [it] all joy, my brothers, when you may fall into manifold temptations, **3** knowing that the proof of your faith works endurance, **4** and let the endurance have a perfect work, that you may be perfect and complete, lacking in nothing. **5** And if any of you lacks wisdom, let him ask from God, who is giving to all generously, and not reproaching, and it will be given to him; **6** but let him ask in faith, doubting nothing, for he who is doubting has been like a wave of the sea, driven by wind and tossed; **7** for do not let that man suppose that he will receive anything from the LORD— **8** a soul-split man [is] unstable in all his ways. **9** And let the brother who is low rejoice in his exaltation, **10** but the rich in his becoming low, because he will pass away as a flower of grass; **11** for the sun rose with the burning heat, and withered the grass, and the flower of it fell, and the beauty of its appearance perished, so also the rich in his way will fade away! **12** Blessed [is] the man who endures temptation, because, becoming approved, he will receive the garland of life, which the LORD promised to those loving Him. **13** Let no one who is being tempted say, "I am tempted from God," for God is not tempted by evils, and Himself tempts no one, **14** but each one is tempted, being led away and enticed by his own desires; **15** afterward the desire having conceived, gives birth to sin, and sin having been perfected, brings forth death. **16** Do not be led astray, my beloved brothers. **17** Every good giving, and every perfect gift, is from above, coming down from the Father of lights, with whom is no variation, or shadow of turning; **18** having willed [it], He begot us with a word of truth, for our being a certain first-fruit of His creatures. **19** So then, my beloved brothers, let every man be swift to hear, slow to speak, slow to anger, **20** for the wrath of a man does not work the righteousness of God; **21** for this reason, having put aside all filthiness and superabundance of evil, receive the implanted word in meekness, that is able to save your souls; **22** and become doers of the word, and not hearers only, deceiving yourselves, **23** because, if anyone is a hearer of the word and not a doer, this one has been like to a man viewing his natural face in a mirror, **24** for he viewed himself, and has gone away, and immediately he forgot what kind of [man] he was; **25** but he who looked into [the] perfect law—that of liberty, and continued there, not becoming a forgetful hearer, but a doer of work—this one will be blessed in his doing. **26** If anyone thinks to be religious among you, not bridling his tongue, but deceiving his heart, the religion of this one [is] vain; **27** religion pure and undefiled with the God and Father is this: to look after orphans and widows in their tribulation—to keep himself unspotted from the world.

2 My brothers, do not hold the faith of the glory of our Lord Jesus Christ in favor by appearance, **2** for if there may come into your synagogue a man with gold ring, in radiant clothing, and there may also come in a poor man in vile clothing, **3** and you may look on him bearing the radiant clothing, and may say to him, "You—sit here well," and may say to the poor man, "You—stand there," or, "Sit here under my footstool," **4** you did not judge fully in yourselves, and became ill-reasoning judges. **5** Listen, my beloved brothers, did God not choose the poor of this world, rich in faith, and heirs of the kingdom that He promised to those loving Him? **6** But you dishonored the poor one. Do the rich not oppress you and themselves draw you to judgment-seats? **7** Do they not themselves speak evil of the good Name having been called on you? **8** If, indeed, you fulfill royal law, according to the Writing: "You will love your neighbor as yourself," you do well; **9** but if you favor by appearance, you work sin, being convicted by the Law as transgressors; **10** for whoever will keep the whole Law, but will stumble in one [point], he has become guilty of all; **11** for He who is saying, "You may not commit adultery," also said, "You may not murder"; but if you will not commit adultery, but will commit murder, you have become a transgressor of law; **12** thus, speak and so act as [one] about to be judged by a law of liberty, **13** for the judgment without mercy [is] to him having not done mercy, and mercy exults over judgment. **14** What [is] the profit, my brothers, if anyone may speak of having faith, but he may not have works? Is that faith able to save him? **15** And if a brother or sister may be naked, and may be destitute of daily food, **16** and anyone of you may say to them, "Depart in peace, be warmed, and be filled," but may not give to them the things necessary for the body, what [is] the profit? **17** So also faith, if it may not have works, is dead by itself. **18** But someone may say, "You have faith, and I have works." Show me your faith without works, and I will show you my faith out of works. **19** You believe that God is one; you do well! The demons also believe—and shudder! **20** And do you wish to know, O vain man, that faith apart from works is dead? **21** Was not our father Abraham considered righteous out of works, having brought up his son Isaac on the altar? **22** Do you see that faith was working with his works, and faith was perfected out of the works? **23** And the Writing was fulfilled that is saying, "And Abraham believed God, and it was reckoned to him for righteousness"; and, "Friend of God" he was called. **24** You see, then, that man is considered righteous out of works, and not out of faith only; **25** and in like manner also Rahab the prostitute—was she not considered righteous out of works, having received the messengers, and having sent [them] forth by another way? **26** For as the body apart from [the] spirit is dead, so also the faith apart from works is dead.

3 Do not let many be teachers, my brothers, having known that we will receive greater judgment, **2** for we all make many stumbles; if anyone does not stumble in word, this one [is] a perfect man, able to also bridle the whole body; **3** behold, the bits we put into the mouths of the horses for their obeying us, and we direct their whole body; **4** behold, also the ships, being so great, and being driven by fierce winds, are directed by a very small rudder, wherever the impulse of the [one] steering wills, **5** so also the tongue is a little member, and boasts greatly; behold, how much forest a little fire kindles! **6** And the tongue [is] a fire, the world of the unrighteousness, so the tongue is set in our members, which is spotting our whole body, and is setting on fire the course of nature, and is set on fire by Gehenna. **7** For every nature, both of beasts and of birds, both of creeping things and things of the sea, is subdued, and has been subdued, by the human nature, **8** but no one of men is able to subdue the tongue—[it is] an unruly evil, full of deadly poison; **9** with it we bless the God and Father, and with it we curse the men made according to [the] likeness of God; **10** out of the same mouth comes forth blessing and cursing; it does not need, my brothers, these things to so happen; **11** does the fountain out of the same opening pour forth the sweet and the bitter? **12** Is a fig tree able, my brothers, to make olives? Or a vine figs? Neither is salty [water able] to have made sweet water. **13** Who [is] wise and intelligent among you? Let him show his works out of good behavior in meekness of wisdom, **14** yet, if you have bitter zeal, and rivalry in your heart, do not glory, nor lie against the truth; **15** this wisdom is not descending from above, but earthly, physical, demon-like, **16** for where zeal and rivalry [are], there is insurrection and every evil matter; **17** but the wisdom from above, first, indeed, is pure, then peaceable, gentle, well-convinced, full of kindness and good fruits, uncontentious, and unhypocritical— **18** and the fruit of righteousness in peace is sown to those making peace.

4 From where [are] wars and fightings among you? [Is it] not from here, out of your passions warring in your members? **2** You desire, and do not have, [so] you murder; and you are zealous, and are not able to attain, [so] you fight and war; and you do not have, because of your not asking; **3** you ask, and you do not receive, because you ask badly, that you may spend [it] in your pleasures. **4** Adulterers and adulteresses! Have you not known that friendship of the world is enmity with God? Whoever, then, may intend to be a friend of the world, he is designated [as] an enemy of God. **5** Or, do you think that the Writing says emptily, "The Spirit that has dwelt in us yearns with envy," **6** but [God] gives greater grace, for this reason it says, "God sets Himself up against proud ones, and He gives grace to lowly ones." **7** Be subject, then, to God; stand up against the Devil, and he will flee from you; **8** draw near to

God, and He will draw near to you; cleanse hands, you sinners! And purify hearts, you split-souled! **9** Be exceedingly afflicted, and mourn, and weep, let your laughter be turned to mourning, and the joy to heaviness; **10** be made low before the LORD, and He will exalt you. **11** Do not speak against one another, brothers; he who is speaking against a brother, and is judging his brother, speaks against law, and judges law, and if you judge law, you are not a doer of law but a judge. **12** One is the lawgiver, who is able to save and to destroy; you—who are you that judges the other? **13** Go, now, you who are saying, "Today and tomorrow we will go on to such a city, and will pass there one year, and traffic, and make gain," **14** who does not know the thing of tomorrow; for what is your life? For it is a vapor that is appearing for a little [while], and then is vanishing; **15** instead, you [ought] to say, "If the LORD may will, we will live, and do this or that"; **16** but now you glory in your pride; all such glorying is evil; **17** to him, then, knowing to do good, and not doing [it], it is sin to him.

5 Go, now, you rich! Weep, howling over your miseries that are coming on [you]; **2** your riches have rotted, and your garments have become moth-eaten; **3** your gold and silver have rotted, and the rust of them will be to you for a testimony, and will eat your flesh as fire. You have stored up treasure in the last days! **4** Behold, the reward of the workmen cries out, of those who in-gathered your fields, which has been fraudulently kept back by you, and the exclamations of those who reaped have entered into the ears of the LORD of Hosts; **5** you lived in luxury on the earth, and were wanton; you nourished your hearts, as in a day of slaughter; **6** you condemned—you murdered the righteous; he does not resist you. **7** Be patient, then, brothers, until the coming of the LORD; behold, the farmer expects the precious fruit of the earth, being patient for it, until he may receive rain—early and latter; **8** you also be patient; establish your hearts, because the coming of the LORD has drawn near; **9** do not murmur against one another, brothers, that you may not be condemned; behold, the Judge has stood before the door. **10** Brothers, [as] an example of the suffering of evil and of patience, take the prophets who spoke in the Name of the LORD; **11** behold, we call those who are enduring blessed; you heard of the endurance of Job, and you have seen the end from the LORD, that the LORD is very compassionate, and pitying. **12** And before all things, my brothers, do not swear, neither by Heaven, neither by the earth, neither by any other oath, but let your "Yes" be yes, and the "No," no, that you may not fall under judgment. **13** Does anyone suffer evil among you? Let him pray; is anyone of good cheer? Let him sing psalms; **14** is anyone sick among you? Let him call for the elders of the assembly, and let them pray over him, having anointed him with oil, in the Name of the LORD, **15** and the prayer of faith will save the distressed one, and the LORD will raise him up, and if he may have committed sins, they will be forgiven to him. **16** Be confessing to one another the trespasses, and be praying for one another, that you may be healed; very strong is a working supplication of a righteous man; **17** Elijah was a similar-feeling man as us, and with prayer he prayed—not to rain, and it did not rain on the land three years and six months; **18** and again he prayed, and the sky gave rain, and the land brought forth her fruit. **19** Brothers, if anyone among you may go astray from the truth, and anyone may turn him back, **20** let him know that he who turned back a sinner from the straying of his way will save a soul from death, and will cover a multitude of sins.

1 PETER

1 Peter, an apostle of Jesus Christ, to the chosen sojourners of the dispersion of Pontus, Galatia, Cappadocia, Asia, and Bithynia, **2** according to [the] foreknowledge of God the Father, by [the] sanctification of the Spirit, to [the] obedience and sprinkling of the blood of Jesus Christ: Grace and peace be multiplied to you! **3** Blessed [is] the God and Father of our Lord Jesus Christ, who, according to the abundance of His kindness begot us again to a living hope, through the resurrection of Jesus Christ out of the dead, **4** to an incorruptible inheritance, and undefiled, and unfading, reserved for you in the heavens, **5** who, in the power of God are being guarded, through faith, to salvation, ready to be revealed in the last time, **6** in which you are glad, a little now, if it be necessary, being made to sorrow in various trials, **7** so that the proof of your faith—much more precious than gold that is perishing, and being approved through fire—may be found to [result in] praise, and honor, and glory, at the revelation of Jesus Christ, **8** whom, having not seen, you love, in whom, now believing [although] not seeing, you are glad with unspeakable joy and have been filled with glory, **9** receiving the outcome of the faith—salvation of your souls; **10** concerning which salvation [the] prophets sought out and searched out, who prophesied concerning the grace toward you, **11** searching in regard to what or what manner of time the Spirit of Christ that was in them was signifying, testifying beforehand of the sufferings of Christ and the glory after these, **12** to whom it was revealed, that not to themselves, but to us they were ministering these, which now were told to you (through those who proclaimed good news to you), by the Holy Spirit sent from Heaven, to which things messengers desire to look into intently. **13** For this reason, having girded up the loins of your mind, being sober, hope perfectly on the grace that is being brought to you in the revelation of Jesus Christ, **14** as obedient children, not fashioning yourselves to the former desires in your ignorance, **15** but according as He who called you [is] holy, you also, become holy in all behavior, **16** because it has been written: "Become holy, because I am holy"; **17** and if you call on the Father, who is judging without favoritism according to the work of each, pass the time of your sojourn in fear, **18** having known that, not with corruptible things—silver or gold—were you redeemed from your foolish behavior inherited from our forefathers, **19** but with precious blood, as of a lamb unblemished and unspotted—Christ's— **20** foreknown, indeed, before the foundation of the world, and revealed in the last times because of you, **21** who through Him believe in God who raised [Him] out of the dead, and gave glory to Him, so that your faith and hope may be in God. **22** Having purified your souls in the obedience of the truth through the Spirit to unhypocritical brotherly love, love one another earnestly out of a pure heart, **23** being begotten again, not out of corruptible seed, but incorruptible, through a word of God—living and remaining—throughout the age; **24** because all flesh [is] as grass, and all glory of man as flower of grass; the grass withered, and the flower of it fell away, **25** but the saying of the LORD remains—throughout the age; and this is the saying of good news that was proclaimed to you.

2 Having put aside, then, all evil, and all guile, and hypocrisies, and envyings, and all evil speakings, **2** as newborn babies, desire the reasonable, unspoiled milk, so that you may grow up to salvation, **3** if [it] so be [that] you tasted that the LORD [is] good, **4** to whom coming—a living stone—having indeed been disapproved of by men, but with God—choice [and] precious, **5** and you yourselves are built up as living stones [into] a spiritual house, a holy priesthood, to offer up spiritual sacrifices acceptable to God through Jesus Christ. **6** For this reason, also, it is contained in the Writing: "Behold, I lay in Zion a chief cornerstone, choice, precious, and he who is believing on Him may not be put to shame"; **7** to you, then, who are believing—the preciousness; but to the unbelieving, [the] stone that the builders disapproved of—this One has become the head of [the] corner, **8** and a stone of

1 PETER

stumbling and a rock of offense—who are stumbling at the word, being unbelieving—to which they were also set. **9** But you [are] a chosen race, a royal priesthood, a holy nation, a people acquired, that you may show forth the excellencies of Him who called you out of darkness into His wonderful light, **10** who [were] once not a people, but [are] now the people of God; who had not found mercy, but now have found mercy. **11** Beloved, I call on [you], as strangers and sojourners, to keep from the fleshly desires that war against the soul, **12** having your behavior right among the nations, so that whenever they speak against you as evildoers, seeing [your] good works, they may glorify God in [the] day of inspection. **13** Be subject, then, to every human creation, because of the Lord, whether to a king, as the highest, **14** whether to governors, as to those sent through him, for punishment, indeed, of evildoers, and a praise of those doing good; **15** because, so is the will of God, doing good, to put to silence the ignorance of the foolish men— **16** as free, and not having freedom as the cloak of evil, but as servants of God; **17** give honor to all; love the brotherhood; fear God; honor the king. **18** Servants, be subject in all fear to the masters, not only to the good and gentle, but also to the crooked; **19** for this [is] grace: if anyone endures sorrows because of conscience toward God, suffering unrighteously; **20** for what renown [is it], if sinning and being battered, you endure [it]? But if, doing good and suffering [for it], you endure, this [is] grace with God, **21** for to this you were called, because Christ also suffered for you, leaving to you an example, that you may follow His steps, **22** who did not commit sin, nor was guile found in His mouth, **23** who being reviled—was not reviling again, suffering—was not threatening, and was committing Himself to Him who is judging righteously, **24** who Himself bore our sins in His body on the tree, that having died to sins, we may live to righteousness, by whose stripes you were healed; **25** for you were as sheep going astray, but now you turned back to the Shepherd and Overseer of your souls.

3 Wives, be subject to your own husbands in like manner, that even if some are disobedient to the word, they may be won through the behavior of the wives without the word, **2** having beheld your pure behavior in fear, **3** whose adorning—let it not be that which is outward, of braiding of hair, and of putting around of things of gold, or of putting on of garments, **4** but— the hidden man of the heart, by the incorruptible [thing] of the meek and quiet spirit, which is of great value before God, **5** for thus once also the holy women who hoped on God were adorning themselves, being subject to their own husbands, **6** as Sarah was obedient to Abraham, calling him "lord," of whom you became daughters, doing good, and not fearing any terror. **7** Husbands, in like manner, dwelling with [them], according to knowledge, as to a weaker vessel—to the wife—imparting honor, as also being heirs together of the grace of life, that your prayers are not hindered. **8** And finally, be all of one mind, having fellow-feeling, loving as brothers, compassionate, courteous, **9** not giving back evil for evil, or reviling for reviling, but on the contrary, blessing, having known that you were called to this, that you may inherit a blessing; **10** for "he who is willing to love life, and to see good days, let him guard his tongue from evil, and his lips—not to speak guile; **11** let him turn aside from evil, and do good, let him seek peace and pursue it; **12** because the eyes of the Lord [are] on the righteous, and His ears—to their supplication, but the face of the Lord [is] against those doing evil"; **13** and who [is] he who will be doing you evil, if you may become imitators of Him who is good? **14** But if you also should suffer because of righteousness, [you are] blessed! And do not be afraid of their fear, nor be troubled, **15** but sanctify the Lord God in your hearts. And always [be] ready for defense to everyone who is asking of you an account concerning the hope that [is] in you, with meekness and fear, **16** having a good conscience, so that whenever they speak against you as evildoers, they may be ashamed—[those] who are maligning your good behavior in Christ; **17** for if the will of God wills it, [it is] better to suffer doing good, than doing evil; **18** also because Christ suffered once for sin—righteous for unrighteous—that He might lead us to God, indeed having been put to death in the flesh, but having been made alive in the Spirit, **19** by which, having gone, He also

1 PETER

preached to the spirits in prison, **20** who sometime [ago] disobeyed when once the long-suffering of God waited, in [the] days of Noah—an ark being prepared—in which few, that is, eight souls, were saved through water, **21** also an antitype to immersion which now saves you—not a putting away of the filth of flesh, but the question of a good conscience in regard to God, through the resurrection of Jesus Christ, **22** who is at the right hand of God, having gone on to Heaven—messengers, and authorities, and powers, having been subjected to Him.

4 Christ, then, having suffered for us in the flesh, you also arm yourselves with the same mind, because he who suffered in the flesh has finished [with] sin, **2** no longer in the desires of men, but in the will of God, to live the rest of the time in the flesh; **3** for the time has sufficiently passed to have carried out the will of the nations, having walked in licentiousness, lusts, excesses of wines, revelings, drinking-bouts, and unlawful idolatries, **4** in which they think it strange—your not running with them to the same excess of wastefulness, slandering [you]— **5** who will give an account to Him who is ready to judge [the] living and [the] dead, **6** for this also was good news proclaimed to dead men, that they may be judged, indeed, according to men in the flesh, but may live according to God in the Spirit. **7** Now the end of all things has come near; be sober-minded, then, and be sober in [your] prayers. **8** Before all things, having earnest love among yourselves, because love covers a multitude of sins; **9** [be] hospitable to one another, without murmuring; **10** each [one], according as he received a gift, ministering it to one another, as good stewards of the manifold grace of God; **11** if anyone speaks, [speak] as oracles of God; if anyone ministers, [minister] as of the strength which God supplies, so that in all things God may be glorified through Jesus Christ, to whom is the glory and the power through the ages of the ages. Amen. **12** Beloved, do not think it strange at the fiery suffering among you that is coming to try you, as if a strange thing were happening to you, **13** but according as you have fellowship with the sufferings of the Christ, rejoice, that you may also rejoice in the revelation of His glory—exulting; **14** if you are reproached in the Name of Christ—[you are] blessed, because the Spirit of glory and of God rests on you; in regard, indeed, to them, is evil spoken of Him, and in regard to you, He is glorified; **15** for let none of you suffer as a murderer, or thief, or evildoer, or as a meddler into other men's matters; **16** and if as a Christian, do not let him be ashamed, but let him glorify God in this respect; **17** because it is the time of the judgment to have begun from the house of God, and if first from us, what [is] the end of those disobedient to the good news of God? **18** And if the righteous man is scarcely saved, where will the ungodly and sinner appear? **19** So that those also suffering according to the will of God, as to a steadfast Creator, let them commit their own souls in doing good.

5 Elders who [are] among you, I exhort [you], [as] a fellow-elder, and a witness of the sufferings of the Christ, and a partaker of the glory about to be revealed, **2** feed the flock of God that [is] among you, overseeing not by compulsion, but willingly, neither for shameful gain, but eagerly, **3** neither as exercising lordship over the heritages, but becoming patterns for the flock, **4** and the Chief Shepherd having appeared, you will receive the unfading garland of glory. **5** In like manner, you young [ones], be subject to elders, and all subjecting yourselves to one another; clothe yourselves with humble-mindedness, because God resists the proud, but He gives grace to the humble; **6** be humbled, then, under the powerful hand of God, that He may exalt you in good time, **7** having cast all your care on Him, because He cares for you. **8** Be sober, vigilant, because your opponent the Devil walks around as a roaring lion, seeking whom he may swallow up, **9** whom you must resist, steadfast in the faith, having known the same sufferings of your brotherhood to be accomplished in the world. **10** And the God of all grace, who called you to His perpetual glory in Christ Jesus, having suffered a little, Himself make you perfect, establish, strengthen, settle [you]; **11** to Him [is] the glory and the power through the ages and the ages! Amen. **12** Through Silvanus, the faithful brother as I reckon, I wrote through few [words] to you, exhorting and testifying this to be the true grace of God in which you have stood. **13** She in Babylon chosen with you greets you, and my son Marcus. **14** Greet one another in a kiss of love. Peace to you all who [are] in Christ Jesus! Amen.

2 PETER

1 Simeon Peter, a servant and an apostle of Jesus Christ, to those who obtained an equally precious faith with us in the righteousness of our God and Savior Jesus Christ: **2** Grace and peace be multiplied to you in the acknowledgment of God and of Jesus our Lord! **3** As His divine power has given to us all things pertaining to life and piety, through the acknowledgment of Him who called us through glory and virtue, **4** through which the most great and precious promises have been given to us, that through these you may become partakers of a divine nature, having escaped from the corruption [and] lust in the world. **5** And [for] this same [reason] also, having brought in all diligence, supplement your faith with virtue, and with virtue—knowledge, **6** and with knowledge—self-control, and with self-control—endurance, and with endurance—piety, **7** and with piety—brotherly kindness, and with brotherly kindness—love; **8** for these things being in you and abounding, make [you] neither inert nor unfruitful in regard to the knowledge of our Lord Jesus Christ, **9** for he with whom these things are not present is blind, dim-sighted, having become forgetful of the cleansing of his old sins; **10** therefore, rather, brothers, be diligent to make steadfast your calling and [divine] selection, for doing these things you may never stumble; **11** in this way the entrance into the continuous kingdom of our Lord and Savior Jesus Christ will be richly supplemented to you. **12** Therefore, I will always be ready to remind you about these things, although you have known [them] and have been established in the present truth, **13** and I think right, so long as I am in this tent, to stir you up in reminding [you], **14** having known that the laying aside of my tent is soon, even as our Lord Jesus Christ also showed to me. **15** And I will also be diligent [to ensure] that you always have a remembrance to make of these things after my departure. **16** For having not followed out skillfully devised fables, we made known to you the power and coming of our Lord Jesus Christ, but having become eyewitnesses of His majesty— **17** for having received honor and glory from God the Father, such a voice being borne to Him by the Excellent Glory: "This is My Son, the Beloved, in whom I delighted"; **18** and we heard this voice borne out of Heaven, being with Him at the holy mountain. **19** And we have a more firm prophetic word, to which we do well giving heed, as to a lamp shining in a dark place, until day may dawn, and [the] morning star may arise in your hearts; **20** knowing this first, that no prophecy of the Writing comes of private exposition, **21** for prophecy never came by [the] will of man, but men spoke from God, being brought by the Holy Spirit.

2 But there also came false prophets among the people, as there will also be false teachers among you, who will stealthily bring in destructive sects, even denying the Master who bought them, bringing quick destruction to themselves, **2** and many will follow out their destructive ways, because of whom the way of the truth will be spoken of [as] evil, **3** and in covetousness, with forged words, they will make merchandise of you, whose judgment of old is not idle, and their destruction does not slumber. **4** For if God did not spare messengers having sinned, but having cast [them] down to Tartarus with chains of deepest gloom, delivered [them], having been reserved to judgment, **5** and did not spare the old world, but kept the eighth person, Noah, a preacher of righteousness, having brought a flood on the world of the impious, **6** and having turned the cities of Sodom and Gomorrah to ashes, condemned with an overthrow, having set [them as] an example to those about to be impious, **7** and He rescued righteous Lot, worn down by the conduct of the lawless in licentiousness, **8** for the righteous [man] dwelling among them was tormented in [his] righteous soul, day by day, in seeing and hearing unlawful works— **9** the LORD has known to rescue [the] pious out of temptation, and to keep [the] unrighteous being punished to [the] day of judgment, **10** and chiefly those following after the flesh in lust [and] defilement, and despising lordship. Bold, self-pleased, they are not afraid to speak evil of glorious ones, 11 whereas messengers, being greater in strength and power, do not bear a slanderous judgment against them before the LORD; 12 and these, as irrational natural beasts, made to be caught and destroyed—in what things they are ignorant of, slandering—in their destruction will be destroyed; 13 doing unjustly, [they will receive] a reward of unrighteousness, esteeming pleasure in the day, [and] luxury—[they are] spots and blemishes, reveling in their deceits, feasting with you, 14 having eyes full of adultery, and unable to cease from sin, enticing unstable souls, having a heart exercised in covetousnesses, children of a curse, 15 having forsaken a right way, they went astray, having followed in the way of Balaam the [son] of Bosor, who loved a reward of unrighteousness, 16 and had a rebuke of his own iniquity—a mute donkey, having spoken in man's voice, forbid the madness of the prophet. 17 These are wells without water, and clouds driven by a storm, to whom the deepest gloom of darkness has been kept throughout the age; 18 for speaking swollen words of vanity, they entice in desires of the flesh—licentiousness, those who had truly escaped from those conducting themselves in error, 19 promising liberty to them, themselves being servants of corruption, for by whom anyone has been overcome, he has been brought to servitude to this one also; 20 for if having escaped from the defilements of the world, in the acknowledging of the LORD and Savior Jesus Christ, and again being entangled by these things, they have been overcome, the last things have become worse to them than the first, 21 for it were better to them not to have acknowledged the way of righteousness, than having acknowledged [it], to turn back from the holy command delivered to them, 22 and that of the true proverb has happened to them: "A dog turned back on his own vomit," and, "A sow having bathed herself—to rolling in mire."

3 This [is] now, beloved, a second letter I write to you, in both which I stir up your pure mind in reminding [you] 2 to be mindful of the sayings said before by the holy prophets, and of the command of us the apostles of the LORD and Savior, 3 knowing this first, that there will come scoffers in the last days, going on according to their own desires, 4 and saying, "Where is the promise of His coming? For since the fathers fell asleep, all things so remain from the beginning of the creation"; 5 for this they willingly conceal, that the heavens existed long ago, and the earth having been established by the word of God out of water and through water, 6 through which the world then, having been flooded by water, was destroyed; 7 and by the same word, the present heavens and earth, having been stored up for fire, are being preserved until [the] day of judgment and destruction of impious men. 8 And do not let this one thing be concealed from you, beloved, that one day with the LORD [is] as one thousand years and one thousand years as one day; 9 the LORD is not slow in regard to the promise, as some count slowness, but is long-suffering to us, not intending any to be lost, but all to come to conversion, 10 and it will come—the Day of the LORD—as a thief in the night, in which the heavens will pass away with a rushing noise, and the elements will be dissolved with burning heat, and [the] earth and the works in it will not be found. 11 All these, then, being dissolved, what kind of persons ought you to be in holy behaviors and pious acts, 12 waiting for and hurrying the coming of the Day of God, by which the heavens, being on fire, will be dissolved, and the elements will melt with burning heat? 13 And we wait for new heavens and a new earth according to His promise, in which righteousness dwells; 14 for this reason, beloved, waiting for these things, be diligent, spotless and unblameable, to be found by Him in peace, 15 and count the long-suffering of our Lord [as] salvation, according as also our beloved brother Paul—according to the wisdom given to him—wrote to you, 16 as also in all the letters, speaking in them concerning these things, among which are some things [that are] hard to be understood, which the untaught and unstable twist, as also the other Writings, to their own destruction. 17 You, then, beloved, knowing before, take heed, lest, together with the error of the impious being led away, you may fall from your own steadfastness, 18 and increase in grace, and in the knowledge of our Lord and Savior Jesus Christ; to Him

[is] the glory both now, and to the day of the age! Amen.

1 JOHN

1 That which was from the beginning, that which we have heard, that which we have seen with our eyes, that which we beheld, and our hands handled, concerning the Word of Life— **2** and the Life appeared, and we have seen, and testify, and declare to you the continuous Life, which was with the Father, and was revealed to us— **3** we declare to you that which we have seen and heard, that you also may have fellowship with us, and our fellowship [is] with the Father, and with His Son Jesus Christ; **4** and these things we write to you, that your joy may be full. **5** And this is the message that we have heard from Him, and announce to you, that God is light, and darkness is not in Him at all; **6** if we may say, "We have fellowship with Him," and may walk in the darkness—we lie, and do not [speak] the truth; **7** and if we may walk in the light, as He is in the light—we have fellowship with one another, and the blood of His Son Jesus Christ cleanses us from every sin; **8** if we may say, "We have no sin," we lead ourselves astray, and the truth is not in us; **9** if we may confess our sins, He is steadfast and righteous that He may forgive us the sins, and may cleanse us from every unrighteousness; **10** if we may say, "We have not sinned," we make Him a liar, and His word is not in us.

2 My little children, these things I write to you that you may not sin: and if anyone may sin, we have an Advocate with the Father, Jesus Christ, [the] Righteous One, **2** and He is [the] propitiation for our sins, and not only for ours, but also for the whole world, **3** and in this we know that we have known Him, if we may keep His commands; **4** he who is saying, "I have known Him," and is not keeping His commands, is a liar, and the truth is not in him; **5** and whoever may keep His word, truly the love of God has been perfected in him; in this we know that we are in Him. **6** He who is saying he remains in Him, himself ought to also walk according as He walked. **7** Beloved, I do not write a new command to you, but an old command, that you had from the beginning—the old command is the word that you heard from the beginning; **8** again, a new command I write to you, which is true in Him and in you, because the darkness is passing away, and the true light now shines; **9** he who is saying he is in the light, and is hating his brother, he is in the darkness until now; **10** he who is loving his brother, he remains in the light, and there is not a stumbling-block in him; **11** but he who is hating his brother, he is in the darkness, and he walks in the darkness, and he has not known where he goes, because the darkness blinded his eyes. **12** I write to you, little children, because sins have been forgiven you through His Name; **13** I write to you, fathers, because you have known Him who [is] from the beginning; I write to you, young men, because you have overcome the evil [one]; I write to you, little youths, because you have known the Father; **14** I wrote to you, fathers, because you have known Him who [is] from the beginning; I wrote to you, young men, because you are strong, and the word of God remains in you, and you have overcome the evil [one]. **15** Do not love the world, nor the things in the world; if anyone loves the world, the love of the Father is not in him, **16** because all that [is] in the world—the desire of the flesh, and the desire of the eyes, and the ostentation of [one's] life—is not of the Father, but of the world, **17** and the world is passing away, and the desire of it, but he who is doing the will of God, he remains—throughout the age. **18** Little youths, it is the last hour; and even as you heard that the antichrist comes, even now antichrists have become many—whereby we know that it is [the] last hour; **19** they went forth out of us, but they were not of us, for if they had been of us, they would have remained with us; but [they went out] so that they might be revealed that they are not all of us. **20** And you have an anointing from the Holy One, and have known all things; **21** I did not write to you because you have not known the truth, but because you have known it, and because no lie is of the truth. **22** Who is the liar, except he who is denying that Jesus is the Christ? This one is the antichrist who is denying the Father and the Son; **23** everyone who is denying the Son, neither has the Father; he who is

1 JOHN

confessing the Son has the Father also. **24** You, then, that which you heard from the beginning, let it remain in you; if that which you heard from the beginning may remain in you, you also will remain in the Son and in the Father, **25** and this is the promise that He promised us—the continuous life. **26** These things I wrote to you concerning those leading you astray; **27** and you, the anointing that you received from Him, it remains in you, and you have no need that anyone may teach you, but as the same anointing teaches you concerning all, and is true, and is not a lie, and even as was taught you, you will remain in Him. **28** And now, little children, remain in Him, so that when He may have appeared, we may have boldness, and may not be ashamed before Him, at His coming; **29** if you know that He is righteous, know that everyone doing righteousness, has been begotten of Him.

3 See what love the Father has given to us, that we may be called children of God; because of this the world does not know us, because it did not know Him. **2** Beloved, now, we are children of God, and it was not yet revealed what we will be. We have known that if He may have appeared, we will be like Him, because we will see Him as He is; **3** and everyone who is having this hope on Him, purifies himself, even as He is pure. **4** Everyone who is doing sin, he also does lawlessness, and sin is lawlessness, **5** and you have known that He appeared that He may take away our sins, and sin is not in Him; **6** everyone who is remaining in Him does not sin; everyone who is sinning, has not seen Him, nor known Him. **7** Little children, let no one lead you astray; he who is doing righteousness is righteous, even as He is righteous, **8** he who is doing sin, he is of the Devil, because the Devil sins from the beginning; for this [reason] the Son of God appeared, that He may undo the works of the Devil; **9** everyone who has been begotten of God, he does not sin, because His seed remains in him, and he is not able to sin, because he has been begotten of God. **10** In this are revealed the children of God, and the children of the Devil; everyone who is not doing righteousness, is not of God, and he who is not loving his brother, **11** because this is the message that you heard from the beginning, that we may love one another, **12** not as Cain—he was of the evil one, and he slew his brother. And for [what] reason did he slay him? Because his works were evil, and those of his brother [were] righteous. **13** Do not wonder, my brothers, if the world hates you; **14** we have known that we have passed out of death into life, because we love the brothers; he who is not loving [his] brother remains in death. **15** Everyone who is hating his brother is a manslayer, and you have known that no manslayer has continuous life remaining in him; **16** in this we have known love, because He laid down His life for us, and we ought to lay down [our] lives for the brothers; **17** and whoever may have the goods of the world, and may view his brother having need, and may shut up his yearnings from him—how does the love of God remain in him? **18** My little children, may we not love in word nor in tongue, but in work and in truth! **19** And in this we know that we are of the truth, and before Him we will assure our hearts, **20** because if our heart may condemn—because greater is God than our heart, and He knows all things. **21** Beloved, if our heart may not condemn us, we have boldness toward God, **22** and whatever we may ask, we receive from Him, because we keep His commands, and we do the things pleasing before Him, **23** and this is His command, that we may believe in the Name of His Son Jesus Christ, and may love one another, even as He gave command to us, **24** and he who is keeping His commands, remains in Him, and He in him; and in this we know that He remains in us, from the Spirit that He gave us.

4 Beloved, do not believe every spirit, but prove the spirits, if they are of God, because many false prophets have gone forth into the world. **2** In this you know the Spirit of God: every spirit that confesses Jesus Christ having come in the flesh, it is of God, **3** and every spirit that does not confess Jesus Christ having come in the flesh, it is not of God; and this is that of the antichrist, which you heard that it comes, and now it is already in the world. **4** You are of God, little children, and you have overcome them; because greater is He who [is] in you, than he who is in the world. **5** They are of the world, because they speak of this from the world, and the world hears them; **6** we are of God; he who is knowing

1 JOHN

God hears us; he who is not of God, does not hear us; from this we know the Spirit of truth and the spirit of error. **7** Beloved, may we love one another, because love is of God, and everyone loving has been begotten of God, and knows God; **8** he who is not loving did not know God, because God is love. **9** In this was revealed the love of God in us, because God has sent His only begotten Son into the world, that we may live through Him; **10** in this is love, not that we loved God, but that He loved us, and sent His Son [as] the propitiation for our sins. **11** Beloved, if God so loved us, we also ought to love one another; **12** no one has ever seen God; if we may love one another, God remains in us, and His love is having been perfected in us; **13** in this we know that we remain in Him, and He in us, because of His Spirit He has given us. **14** And we have seen and testify that the Father has sent the Son [as] Savior of the world; **15** whoever may confess that Jesus is the Son of God, God remains in him, and he in God; **16** and we have known and believed the love that God has in us; God is love, and he who is remaining in love, remains in God, and God in him. **17** In this, love has been perfected with us, that we may have boldness in the day of judgment, because even as He is, we also are in this world. **18** There is no fear in love, but perfect love casts out fear, because fear involves punishment, and he who is fearing has not been made perfect in love; **19** we love Him, because He first loved us; **20** if anyone may say, "I love God," and may hate his brother, he is a liar; for he who is not loving his brother whom he has seen, how is he able to love God whom he has not seen? **21** And this [is] the command we have from Him, that he who is loving God, may also love his brother.

5 Everyone who is believing that Jesus is the Christ has been begotten of God, and everyone who is loving Him who begot, also loves him who is begotten of Him. **2** In this we know that we love the children of God, when we may love God and may keep His commands; **3** for this is the love of God, that we may keep His commands, and His commands are not burdensome; **4** because everyone who is begotten of God overcomes the world, and this is the victory that overcame the world—our faith. **5** Who is he who is overcoming the world, if not he who is believing that Jesus is the Son of God? **6** This One is He who came through water and blood—Jesus the Christ, not in water only, but in the water and the blood; and the Spirit is the [One] testifying, because the Spirit is the truth, **7** because [there] are three who are testifying [[in Heaven: the Father, the Word, and the Holy Spirit, and these three are one; **8** and [there] are three who are testifying in the earth]]: the Spirit, and the water, and the blood, and the three are into the one. **9** If we receive the testimony of men, the testimony of God is greater, because this is the testimony of God that He has testified concerning His Son. **10** He who is believing in the Son of God has the testimony in himself; he who is not believing God has made Him a liar, because he has not believed in the testimony that God has testified concerning His Son; **11** and this is the testimony, that God gave continuous life to us, and this life is in His Son; **12** he who is having the Son has life; he who is not having the Son of God does not have life. **13** I wrote these things to you who are believing in the Name of the Son of God, that you may know that you have continuous life, and that you may believe in the Name of the Son of God. **14** And this is the boldness that we have toward Him, that if we may ask anything according to His will, He hears us, **15** and if we have known that He hears us, whatever we may ask, we have known that we have the requests that we have requested from Him. **16** If anyone may see his brother sinning a sin [that is] not to death, he will ask, and He will give life to him—to those not sinning to death; there is sin to death—I do not say that he may ask concerning it; **17** all unrighteousness is sin, and there is sin [that is] not to death. **18** We have known that everyone who has been begotten of God does not sin, but He who was begotten of God keeps him, and the evil one does not touch him; **19** we have known that we are of God, and the whole world lies [under the power] of the evil [one]; **20** but we have known that the Son of God has come, and has given us a mind that we may know Him who is true, and we are in Him who is true, in His Son Jesus Christ; this One is the true God and the continuous Life! **21** Little children, guard yourselves from idols! Amen.

2 JOHN

1 The elder to the chosen lady, and to her children, whom I love in truth, and not only I, but also all those having known the truth, **2** because of the truth that is remaining in us, and will be with us throughout the age, **3** there will be with you grace, mercy, [and] peace from God the Father, and from the Lord Jesus Christ, the Son of the Father, in truth and love. **4** I rejoiced exceedingly that I have found of your children walking in truth, even as we received a command from the Father; **5** and now I implore you, lady, not as writing to you a new command, but which we had from the beginning, that we may love one another, **6** and this is love, that we may walk according to His commands; this is the command, even as you heard from the beginning, that you may walk in it, **7** because many deceivers entered into the world, who are not confessing Jesus Christ coming in flesh; this one is he who is leading astray, and the antichrist. **8** See to yourselves that you may not lose the things that we worked for, but may receive a full reward; **9** everyone who is transgressing, and is not remaining in the teaching of the Christ, does not have God; he who is remaining in the teaching of the Christ, this one has both the Father and the Son; **10** if anyone comes to you, and does not bear this teaching, do not receive him into the house, and do not say to him, "Greetings!" **11** For he who is saying to him, "Greetings," has fellowship with his evil works. **12** Having many things to write to you, I did not intend [it] with paper and ink, but I hope to come to you, and speak mouth to mouth, that our joy may be full. **13** The children of your chosen sister greet you. Amen.

3 JOHN

1 The elder to Gaius the beloved, whom I love in truth! **2** Beloved, I desire you to prosper concerning all things, and to be in health, even as your soul prospers, **3** for I rejoiced exceedingly, brothers coming and testifying of the truth in you, even as you walk in truth; **4** I have no joy greater than these things, that I may hear of my children walking in truth. **5** Beloved, you act faithfully in whatever you may do toward the brothers and the one [among] strangers, **6** who testified of your love before an assembly, whom you will do well, having sent forward worthily of God, **7** because they went forth for [His] Name, receiving nothing from the nations; **8** we, then, ought to receive such, that we may become fellow-workers to the truth. **9** I wrote to the assembly, but he who is loving to be first among them—Diotrephes—does not receive us; **10** because of this, if I may come, I will cause him to remember his works that he does, talking nonsense against us with evil words; and not content with these, neither does he himself receive the brothers, and he forbids those intending [to receive them], and he casts [them] out of the assembly. **11** Beloved, do not be following that which is evil, but that which is good; he who is doing good, he is of God, [but] he who is doing evil has not seen God; **12** testimony has been given to Demetrius by all, and by the truth itself, and we also—we testify, and you have known that our testimony is true. **13** Many things I had to write, but I do not wish to write to you through ink and pen, **14** and I hope to see you soon, and we will speak mouth to mouth. Peace to you! The friends greet you. Be greeting the friends by name.

JUDE

1 Judas, a servant of Jesus Christ, and brother of James, to those called, having been loved in God [the] Father, and having been kept in Jesus Christ, 2 mercy and peace and love be multiplied to you! 3 Beloved, using all diligence to write to you concerning our common salvation, I had necessity to write to you, exhorting [you] to fight for the faith once delivered to the holy ones, 4 for there came in certain men stealthily, having been written beforehand to this judgment long ago, impious, perverting the grace of our God to licentiousness, and denying our only Master and Lord—Jesus Christ. 5 Now I intend to remind you, you once having known all this, that Jesus, having saved a people out of the land of Egypt, He secondly destroyed those not having believed; 6 messengers also, those who did not keep their own principality, but left their proper dwelling, He has kept in eternal bonds under darkness until [the] judgment of [the] great day, 7 as Sodom and Gomorrah, and the cities around them, in like manner to these [messengers], having given themselves to whoredom, and having gone after other flesh, have been set before [as] an example, undergoing the justice of continuous fire. 8 In like manner, nevertheless, those dreaming indeed defile the flesh, and they disregard lordship, and they speak evil of glorious [ones], 9 yet Michael, the chief messenger, when disputing with the Devil, reasoning about the body of Moses, did not dare to bring against [him] a judgment of slander, but said, "The LORD rebuke you!" 10 But these, indeed, whatever [things] they have not known, they speak evil of; and whatever [they know], like the irrational beasts, they understand naturally—in these they are corrupted; 11 woe to them! Because they went on in the way of Cain, and they rushed to the deceit of Balaam for reward, and in the controversy of Korah they perished. 12 These are stains at your love-feasts, feasting together with you without fear, shepherding themselves; waterless clouds, being carried away by winds; autumnal trees without fruit, having died twice, having been uprooted; 13 wild waves of a sea, foaming up their own shameful [deeds]; stars going astray, for whom the gloom of the darkness throughout the age has been kept. 14 And Enoch, the seventh from Adam, also prophesied to these, saying, "Behold, the LORD has come with myriads of His holy ones, 15 to do judgment against all, and to convict all their impious ones, concerning all their works of impiety that they did impiously, and concerning all the harsh [words] that impious sinners spoke against Him." 16 These are discontented grumblers, walking according to their own lusts; and their mouth speaks swollen words, giving admiration to persons for the sake of profit; 17 but you, beloved, remember the sayings spoken before by the apostles of our Lord Jesus Christ, 18 that they said to you, that in the last time there will be scoffers, following after their own lusts of impieties, 19 these are those causing divisions, natural men, not having the Spirit. 20 But you, beloved, building yourselves up on your most holy faith, praying in the Holy Spirit, 21 keep yourselves in the love of God, waiting for the mercy of our Lord Jesus Christ [resulting] in continuous life; 22 and, indeed, show mercy to those who are doubting, 23 and rescue others by snatching [them] out of fire; but show mercy to others in fear, hating even the coat having been stained from the flesh. 24 And to Him who is able to guard you without stumbling, and to set [you] in the presence of His glory unblemished, in gladness, 25 to the only wise God our Savior, [is] glory and greatness, power and authority, both now and forever! Amen.

REVELATION

1 A revelation of Jesus Christ that God gave to Him to show to His servants what things must quickly come to pass; and He signified [it], having sent through His messenger to His servant John, **2** who testified [to] the word of God, and the testimony of Jesus Christ, as many things as he also saw. **3** Blessed is he who is reading, and those hearing the words of the prophecy, and keeping the things written in it, for the time is near! **4** John, to the seven assemblies that [are] in Asia: Grace to you, and peace, from Him who is, and who was, and who is coming, and from the Seven Spirits that are before His throne, **5** and from Jesus Christ, the faithful witness, the firstborn out of the dead, and the ruler of the kings of the earth; to Him loving us and having released us from our sins in His blood, **6** [He] has also made us kings and priests to His God and Father, to Him—the glory and the power through the ages of the ages! Amen. **7** Behold, He comes with the clouds, and every eye will see Him, even those who pierced Him, and all the tribes of the land will wail because of Him. Yes! Amen! **8** "I am the Alpha and the Omega, beginning and end, says the LORD, who is, and who was, and who is coming—the Almighty." **9** I, John, who [am] also your brother, and fellow-partner in the tribulation, and in the kingdom and endurance of Jesus Christ, was in the island that is called Patmos, because of the word of God, and because of the testimony of Jesus Christ; **10** I was in the Spirit on the LORD's Day, and I heard a great voice behind me, as of a trumpet, saying, **11** "I am the Alpha and the Omega, the First and the Last," and, "Write what you see in a scroll, and send [it] to the seven assemblies that [are] in Asia: to Ephesus, and to Smyrna, and to Pergamos, and to Thyatira, and to Sardis, and to Philadelphia, and to Laodicea." **12** And I turned to see the voice that spoke with me, and having turned, I saw seven golden lampstands, **13** and in the midst of the seven lampstands, [One] like a Son of Man, clothed to the foot, and having been girded around at the breasts with a golden girdle, **14** and His head and hairs [were] white, as if white wool—as snow, and His eyes as a flame of fire; **15** and His feet like to frankincense-colored brass, as having been fired in a furnace, and His voice as a sound of many waters; **16** and having seven stars in His right hand, and out of His mouth a sharp two-edged sword is proceeding, and His countenance—as the sun shining in its might. **17** And when I saw Him, I fell at His feet as dead, and He placed His right hand on me, saying to me, "Do not be afraid; I am the First and the Last, **18** and He who is living, and I became dead, and behold, I am living through the ages of the ages. Amen! And I have the keys of Hades and of death. **19** Write the things that you have seen, and the things that are, and the things that are about to come after these things; **20** the secret of the seven stars that you have seen on My right hand, and the seven golden lampstands: the seven stars are messengers of the seven assemblies, and the seven lampstands that you have seen are seven assemblies."

2 "To the messenger of the Ephesian assembly write: These things says He who is holding the seven stars in His right hand, who is walking in the midst of the seven golden lampstands: **2** I have known your works, and your labor, and your endurance, and that you are not able to bear evil ones, and that you have tried those saying themselves to be apostles and are not, and have found them liars, **3** and you bore, and have endurance, and have toiled because of My Name, and have not been weary. **4** But I have against you that you left your first love! **5** Remember, then, from where you have fallen, and convert, and do the first works; and if not, I come to you quickly, and will remove your lampstand from its place—if you may not convert; **6** but this you have, that you hate the works of the Nicolaitans, that I also hate. **7** He who is having an ear—let him hear what the Spirit says to the assemblies: To him who is overcoming—I will give to him to eat of the Tree of Life that is in the midst of the paradise of God. **8** And to the messenger of the assembly of the Smyrneans write: These things says the First and the Last, who became dead and lived: **9** I have known your works, and tribulation, and poverty—yet you are rich—and the slander of those saying themselves to be Jews, and are not, but [are] a synagogue of Satan. **10** Do not be afraid of the things that you are about to suffer; behold, the Devil is about to cast [some] of you into prison, that you may be tried, and you will have tribulation ten days; become faithful to death, and I will give to you the garland of life. **11** He who is having an ear—let him hear what the Spirit says to the assemblies: He who is overcoming may not be injured of the second death. **12** And to the messenger of the assembly in Pergamos write: These things says He who is having the sharp two-edged sword: **13** I have known your works, and where you dwell—where the throne of Satan [is]—and you hold fast My Name, and you did not deny My faith, even in the days in which Antipas [was] My faithful witness, who was put to death beside you, where Satan dwells. **14** But I have a few things against you: that you have there those holding the teaching of Balaam, who taught Balak to cast a stumbling-block before the sons of Israel, to eat idol-sacrifices, and to commit whoredom; **15** so have you, even you, those holding the teaching of the Nicolaitans—which thing I hate. **16** Convert! And if not, I come to you quickly, and will fight against them with the sword of My mouth. **17** He who is having an ear—let him hear what the Spirit says to the assemblies: To him who is overcoming, I will give to him to eat from the hidden manna, and will give to him a white stone, and on the stone a new name written, that no one knew except him who is receiving [it]. **18** And to the messenger of the assembly of Thyatira write: These things says the Son of God, who is having His eyes as a flame of fire, and His feet like to frankincense-colored brass: **19** I have known your works, and love, and ministry, and faith, and your endurance, and your works—and the last [are] more than the first. **20** But I have a few things against you: that you allow the woman Jezebel, who is calling herself a prophetess, to teach, and to lead astray, My servants to commit whoredom, and to eat idol-sacrifices; **21** and I gave to her a time that she might convert from her whoredom, and she did not convert; **22** behold, I will cast her into a bed, and those committing adultery with her into great tribulation—if they may not convert from her works, **23** and I will kill her children in death, and all the assemblies will know that I am He who is searching affections and hearts; and I will give to you—to each—according to your works. **24** And to you I say, and to the rest who are in Thyatira, as many as do not have this teaching, and who did not know the depths of Satan, as they say—I will not put on you another burden, **25** but hold that which you have, until I may come; **26** and he who is overcoming, and who is keeping My works to the end, I will give to him authority over the nations, **27** and he will rule them with a rod of iron—they will be broken as the vessels of the potter—as I have also received from My Father; **28** and I will give to him the morning star. **29** He who is having an ear—let him hear what the Spirit says to the assemblies."

3 "And to the messenger of the assembly in Sardis write: These things says He who is having the Seven Spirits of God, and the seven stars: I have known your works, and that you have the name that you live, and you are dead; **2** be watching, and strengthen the rest of the things that are about to die, for I have not found your works fulfilled before God. **3** Remember, then, what you have received and heard, and keep [it] and convert: if, then, you may not watch, I will come on you as a thief, and you may not know what hour I will come on you. **4** You have a few names even in Sardis who did not defile their garments, and they will walk with Me in white, because they are worthy. **5** The [one] thus overcoming will be clothed in white garments, and I will not blot out his name from the Scroll of Life, and I will confess his name before My Father, and before His messengers. **6** He who is having an ear—let him hear what the Spirit says to the assemblies. **7** And to the messenger of the assembly in Philadelphia write: These things says the Holy [One], the True [One], having the key of David, the [One] opening and no one will shut, and shutting and no one opens: **8** I have known your works; behold, I have set before you a door having been opened, which no one is able to shut it, because you have little power, and yet have kept My word, and have not denied My Name; **9** behold, I give from the synagogue of Satan—those saying themselves to be Jews, and are not, but lie—behold, I will make them that they may come and prostrate before your feet, and may know that I loved you. **10** Because you kept the word of My endurance, I also will keep you from the hour of the trial that is about to come on all the world, to try those dwelling on the earth. **11** Behold, I come quickly, be holding fast that which you have, that no one may receive your garland. **12** He who is overcoming—I will make him a pillar in the temple of My God, and he may not go outside anymore, and I will write on him the Name of My God, and the name of the city of My God, the New Jerusalem, that comes down out of Heaven from My God—also My new Name. **13** He who is having an ear—let him hear what the Spirit says to the assemblies. **14** And to the messenger of the assembly of the Laodiceans write: These things says the Amen, the Witness—the Faithful and True—the Chief of the creation of God: **15** I have known your works, that you are neither cold nor hot; I wish you were cold or hot. **16** So—because you are lukewarm, and neither cold nor hot, I am about to vomit you out of My mouth; **17** because you say—I am rich, and have grown rich, and have need of nothing, and have not known that you are the wretched, and miserable, and poor, and blind, and naked; **18** I counsel you to buy from Me gold fired by fire, that you may be rich, and white garments that you may be clothed, and the shame of your nakedness may not be revealed, and with eye-salve anoint your eyes, that you may see. **19** As many as I cherish, I convict and discipline; be zealous, then, and convert; **20** behold, I have stood at the door, and I knock; if anyone may hear My voice, and may open the door, I will come in to him, and will dine with him, and he with Me. **21** He who is overcoming—I will give to him to sit with Me in My throne, as I also overcame and sat down with My Father in His throne. **22** He who is having an ear—let him hear what the Spirit says to the assemblies."

4 After these things I saw, and behold, a door opened in the sky, and the first voice that I heard—as of a trumpet speaking with me, saying, "Come up here, and I will show you what must come to pass after these things"; **2** and immediately I was in [the] Spirit, and behold, a throne was set in Heaven, and on the throne is [One] sitting, **3** and He who is sitting was in appearance like a stone, jasper and sardine: and a rainbow was around the throne in appearance like an emerald. **4** And around the throne [are] twenty-four thrones, and sitting on the thrones I saw twenty-four elders, having been clothed in white garments, and on their heads golden garlands; **5** and out of the throne proceed lightnings, and thunders, and voices; and seven lamps of fire are burning before the throne, which are the Seven Spirits of God, **6** and before the throne—a sea of glass like to crystal, and in the midst of the throne, and around the throne—four living creatures, full of eyes before and behind; **7** and the first living creature—like a lion; and the second living creature—like a calf; and the third living creature has the face as a man; and the fourth living creature—like an eagle flying. **8** And the four living creatures, one by one of them had six wings respectively, around and within [are] full of eyes, and they have no rest day and night, saying, "HOLY, HOLY, HOLY, the LORD God, the Almighty, who was, and who is, and who is coming"; **9** and when the living creatures give glory, and honor, and thanksgiving, to the [One] sitting on the throne, the [One] living through the ages of the ages, **10** the twenty-four elders will fall down before the [One] sitting on the throne, and worship the [One] living through the ages of the ages, and they will cast their garlands before the throne, saying, **11** "Worthy are You, our Lord and God, to receive the glory, and the honor, and the power, because You created all things, and because of Your will they existed and were created."

5 And I saw a scroll on the right hand of Him who is sitting on the throne, written within and on the back, sealed with seven seals; **2** and I saw a strong messenger crying with a great voice, "Who is worthy to open the scroll and to loose its seals?" **3** And no one was able in Heaven, nor on the earth, nor under the earth, to open the scroll, nor to behold it. **4** And I was weeping much, because no one was found worthy to open and to read the scroll, nor to behold it, **5** and one of the elders says to me, "Do not weep; behold, the Lion of the tribe of Judah, the root of David, has overcome to open the scroll, and to loose its seven seals"; **6** and I saw, and behold, in the midst of the throne, and of the four living creatures, and in the midst of the elders, a Lamb standing as having been slain, having seven horns and seven eyes, which are the Seven Spirits of God, which are sent to all the earth, **7** and He came and took the scroll out of the right hand of Him who is sitting on the throne. **8** And when He took the scroll, the four living creatures and the twenty-four elders fell before the Lamb, each one having harps and golden bowls full of incenses, which are the prayers of the holy ones, **9** and they sing a new song, saying, "Worthy are You to take the scroll, and to open its seals, because You were slain, and You purchased us to God in Your blood, out of every tribe, and tongue, and people, and nation, **10** and made them [to be] to our God kings and priests, and they will reign on the earth." **11** And I saw, and I heard the voice of many messengers around the throne, and the living creatures, and the elders—and the number of them was myriads of myriads, and thousands of thousands— **12** saying with a great voice, "Worthy is the Lamb that was slain to receive the power, and riches, and wisdom, and strength, and honor, and glory, and blessing!" **13** And every creature that is in Heaven, and on the earth, and under the earth, and the things that are on the sea, and all things in them, I heard saying, "To Him who is sitting on the throne and to the Lamb—the blessing, and the honor, and the glory, and the might— through the ages of the ages!" **14** And the four living creatures said, "Amen!" And the twenty-four elders fell down and they worship Him who is living through the ages of the ages.

6 And I saw when the Lamb opened one of the seals, and I heard one of the four living creatures saying, as it were a voice of thunder, "Come and behold!" **2** And I saw, and behold, a white horse, and he who is sitting on it is having a bow, and there was given to him a garland, and he went forth overcoming, and that he may overcome. **3** And when He opened the second seal, I heard the second living creature saying, "Come and behold!" **4** And there went forth another horse— fire-colored, and to him who is sitting on it, there was given to him to take peace from the earth, and that they may slay one another, and there was given to him a great sword. **5** And when He opened the third seal, I heard the third living creature saying, "Come and behold!" And I saw, and behold, a black horse, and he who is sitting on it is having a balance in his hand, **6** and I heard a voice in the midst of the four living creatures saying, "A measure of wheat for a denarius, and three measures of barley for a denarius, and you may not injure the oil and the wine." **7** And when He opened the fourth seal, I heard the voice of the fourth living creature saying, "Come and behold!" **8** And I saw, and behold, a pale horse, and he who is sitting on him— his name is Death, and Hades follows with him, and there was given to them authority to kill over the fourth part of the earth with sword, and with hunger, and with death, and by the beasts of the earth. **9** And when He opened the fifth seal, I saw under the altar the souls of those slain because of the word of God, and because of the testimony that they held, **10** and they were crying with a great voice, saying, "Until when, O Master, the Holy and the True, do You not judge and take vengeance of our blood from those dwelling on the earth?" **11** And there was given to each one a white robe, and it was said to them that they may rest themselves yet a short time, until may also be fulfilled their fellow-servants and their brothers, who are about to be killed—even as they. **12** And I saw when He opened the sixth seal, and behold, a great earthquake came, and the sun became black as sackcloth of hair, and the moon became as blood, **13** and the stars of Heaven fell to the earth—as a fig tree casts her unripe figs, being shaken by a great wind— **14** and the sky departed as a scroll rolled up, and every mountain and island were moved out of their places; **15** and the kings of the earth, and the great men, and the rich, and the chiefs of thousands, and the mighty, and every servant, and every freeman, hid themselves in the dens, and in the rocks of the mountains, **16** and they say to the mountains and to the rocks, "Fall on us, and hide us from the face of Him who is sitting on the throne, and from the anger of the Lamb," **17** because the great day of His anger has come, and who is able to stand?

7 And after these things I saw four messengers, standing on the four corners of the earth, holding the four winds of the earth, that the wind may not blow on the earth, nor on the sea, nor on any tree;

REVELATION

2 and I saw another messenger going up from the rising of the sun, having a seal of the living God, and he cried with a great voice to the four messengers, to whom it was given to injure the land and the sea, saying, **3** "Do not injure the land, nor the sea, nor the trees, until we may seal the servants of our God on their foreheads." **4** And I heard the number of those sealed—one hundred forty-four thousand, having been sealed out of every tribe of the sons of Israel: **5** of the tribe of Judah twelve thousand were sealed; of the tribe of Reuben twelve thousand were sealed; of the tribe of Gad twelve thousand were sealed; **6** of the tribe of Asher twelve thousand were sealed; of the tribe of Naphtali twelve thousand were sealed; of the tribe of Manasseh twelve thousand were sealed; **7** of the tribe of Simeon twelve thousand were sealed; of the tribe of Levi twelve thousand were sealed; of the tribe of Issachar twelve thousand were sealed; **8** of the tribe of Zebulun twelve thousand were sealed; of the tribe of Joseph twelve thousand were sealed; of the tribe of Benjamin twelve thousand were sealed. **9** After these things I saw, and behold, a great multitude, which no one was able to number, out of all nations, and tribes, and peoples, and tongues, standing before the throne, and before the Lamb, having been clothed [in] white robes, and palms in their hands, **10** and crying with a great voice, saying, "Salvation to our God, the [One] sitting on the throne, and to the Lamb!" **11** And all the messengers stood around the throne, and the elders and the four living creatures, and they fell on their faces and worshiped God, **12** saying, "Amen! The blessing, and the glory, and the wisdom, and the thanksgiving, and the honor, and the power, and the strength, [are] to our God through the ages of the ages! Amen!" **13** And one of the elders answered, saying to me, "These having been clothed with the white robes, who are they, and from where have they come?" **14** And I have said to him, "Lord, you have known"; and he said to me, "These are those who are coming out of the Great Tribulation, and they washed their robes, and they made their robes white in the blood of the Lamb; **15** because of this they are before the throne of God, and they do service to Him day and night in His temple, and He who is sitting on the throne will dwell over them; **16** they will not hunger anymore, nor may the sun fall on them, nor any heat, **17** because the Lamb that [is] in the midst of the throne will feed them, and will lead them to living fountains of waters, and God will wipe away every tear from their eyes."

8 And when He opens the seventh seal, there came silence in Heaven about half an hour, **2** and I saw the seven messengers who have stood before God, and there were given to them seven trumpets, **3** and another messenger came, and he stood at the altar, having a golden censer, and there was given to him much incense, that he may give [it] to the prayers of all the holy ones on the golden altar that [is] before the throne, **4** and the smoke of the incenses, with the prayers of the holy ones, went up before God out of the hand of the messenger; **5** and the messenger took the censer, and filled it out of the fire of the altar, and cast [it] to the earth, and there came voices, and thunders, and lightnings, and an earthquake. **6** And the seven messengers who are having the seven trumpets prepared themselves that they may sound the trumpets; **7** and the first messenger sounded the trumpet, and there came hail and fire, mingled with blood, and it was cast to the earth, and the third of the trees were burned up, and all the green grass was burned up. **8** And the second messenger sounded the trumpet, and [something] like a great mountain burning with fire was cast into the sea, and the third of the sea became blood, **9** and the third of the creatures that [are] in the sea died, those having life, and the third of the ships were destroyed. **10** And the third messenger sounded the trumpet, and there fell out of the sky a great star, burning as a lamp, and it fell on the third of the rivers, and on the fountains of waters, **11** and the name of the star is called Wormwood, and the third of the waters become wormwood, and many of the men died [because] of the waters, because they were made bitter. **12** And the fourth messenger sounded the trumpet, and the third of the sun was struck, and the third of the moon, and the third of the stars, that the third of them may be darkened, and that the day may not shine—the third of it, and the night in like manner. **13** And I saw, and I heard one messenger, flying in midair, saying with a great voice, "Woe, woe, woe, to those dwelling on the earth because of the rest of the voices of the trumpet of the three messengers being about to sound trumpets."

9 And the fifth messenger sounded the trumpet, and I saw a star having fallen to the earth out of Heaven, and there was given to him the key of the pit of the abyss, **2** and [he] opened the pit of the abyss, and there came up a smoke out of the pit as smoke of a great furnace, and the sun and the air were darkened from the smoke of the pit. **3** And out of the smoke came forth locusts to the earth, and there was given to them authority, as scorpions of the earth have authority, **4** and it was said to them that they may not injure the grass of the earth, nor any green thing, nor any tree, but only the men who do not have the seal of God on their foreheads, **5** and it was given to them that they may not kill them, but that they may be tormented five months, and their torment—as the torment of a scorpion—when it may strike a man; **6** and in those days men will seek death and they will not find it, and they will desire to die, and death will flee from them. **7** And the likenesses of the locusts—like to horses made ready to battle, and on their heads [something] as garlands like gold, and their faces as faces of men, **8** and they had hair as hair of women, and their teeth were as [those] of lions, **9** and they had breastplates as breastplates of iron, and the noise of their wings—as the noise of chariots of many horses running to battle; **10** and they have tails like to scorpions, and stings were in their tails; and their authority [is] to injure men five months; **11** and they have over them a king—the messenger of the abyss—a name [is] to him in Hebrew, Abaddon, and in the Greek he has a name, Apollyon. **12** The first woe went forth, behold, there yet come two woes after these things. **13** And the sixth messenger sounded the trumpet, and I heard a voice out of the four horns of the altar of gold that is before God, **14** saying to the sixth messenger who had the trumpet, "Loose the four messengers who are bound at the great river Euphrates"; **15** and the four messengers were loosed, who have been made ready for the hour, and day, and month, and year, that they may kill the third of mankind; **16** and the number of the forces of the horsemen—twice ten thousand ten thousands, and I heard the number of them. **17** And thus I saw the horses in the vision, and those sitting on them, having breastplates of fire, and jacinth, and brimstone; and the heads of the horses [are] as heads of lions, and out of their mouths proceed fire, and smoke, and brimstone; **18** by these three plagues the third of mankind was killed, from the fire, and from the smoke, and from the brimstone, that is proceeding out of their mouths, **19** for the power of the horses are in their mouth, and in their tails, for their tails [are] like serpents, having heads, and they injure with them. **20** And the rest of mankind, who were not killed in these plagues, neither converted from the works of their hands, that they may not worship the demons, and idols, those of gold, and those of silver, and those of brass, and those of stone, and those of wood, that are neither able to see, nor to hear, nor to walk, **21** and they did not convert from their murders, nor from their sorceries, nor from their whoredoms, nor from their thefts.

10 And I saw another strong messenger coming down out of Heaven, clothed with a cloud, and a rainbow on the head, and his face as the sun, and his feet as pillars of fire, **2** and he had in his hand a little scroll opened, and he placed his right foot on the sea, and the left on the land, **3** and he cried with a great voice, as a lion roars, and when he cried, the seven thunders spoke out their voices; **4** and when the seven thunders spoke their voices, I was about to write, and I heard a voice out of Heaven saying to me, "Seal the things that the seven thunders spoke," and, "You may not write these things." **5** And the messenger whom I saw standing on the sea, and on the land, lifted up his hand to the sky, **6** and swore by Him who lives through the ages of the ages, who created the sky and the things in it, and the land and the things in it, and the sea and the things in it—that time will not be yet, **7** but in the days of the voice of the seventh messenger, when he may be about to sound the trumpet, and the secret of God may be accomplished, as He declared to His own servants, to the prophets. **8** And the voice that I heard out of Heaven is again speaking with me, and saying, "Go, take the little scroll that is open in the hand of the messenger who has been standing on the sea, and on the land": **9** and I went away to the messenger, saying to him, "Give me the little scroll"; and he says to me, "Take, and eat it up, and it will make your belly bitter, but in your mouth it will be sweet as honey." **10** And I took the little scroll out of the hand of the messenger, and ate it up, and it was in my mouth sweet as honey, and when I ate it my belly was made bitter; **11** and he says to me, "You must again prophesy about many peoples, and nations, and tongues, and kings."

11 And there was given to me a reed like to a rod, [[and the messenger stood,]] saying, "Rise, and measure the temple of God, and the altar, and those worshiping in it; **2** and leave out the court that is outside the temple, and you may not measure it, because it was given to the nations, and they will tread down the holy city forty-two months; **3** and I will give to My two witnesses, and they will prophesy one thousand, two hundred, sixty days, clothed with sackcloth"; **4** these are the two olive [trees], and the two lampstands that stand before the God of the earth; **5** and if anyone may will to injure them, fire proceeds out of their mouth, and devours their enemies, and if anyone may will to injure them, thus it is required of him to be killed. **6** These have authority to shut the sky, that rain may not rain in the days of their prophecy, and they have authority over the waters to turn them to blood, and to strike the land with every plague, as often as they may will. **7** And when they may finish their testimony, the beast that is coming up out of the abyss will make war with them, and overcome them, and kill them, **8** and their body [is] on the street of the great city that is called spiritually Sodom and Egypt, where also their Lord was crucified, **9** and they gaze—[those] of the peoples, and tribes, and tongues, and nations—on their dead bodies three and a half days, and they will not allow their dead bodies to be put into tombs, **10** and those dwelling on the earth will rejoice over them, and will make merry, and they will send gifts to one another, because these—the two prophets—tormented those dwelling on the earth. **11** And after the three and a half days, [the] Spirit of life from God entered into them, and they stood on their feet, and great fear fell on those beholding them, **12** and they heard a great voice out of Heaven saying to them, "Come up here"; and they went up to Heaven in the cloud, and their enemies beheld them; **13** and in that hour a great earthquake came, and the tenth of the city fell, and seven thousand names of men were killed in the earthquake, and the rest became frightened, and they gave glory to the God of Heaven. **14** The second woe went forth, behold, the third woe comes quickly. **15** And the seventh messenger sounded the trumpet, and there came great voices in Heaven, saying, "The kingdoms of the world became [those] of our Lord and of His Christ, and He will reign through the ages of the ages!" **16** And the twenty-four elders, who are sitting on their thrones before God, fell on their faces and worshiped God, **17** saying, "We give thanks to You, O LORD God, the Almighty, who is, and who was, and who is coming, because You have taken Your great power and reigned; **18** and the nations were angry, and Your anger came, and the time of the dead to be judged, and to give the reward to Your servants, to the prophets, and to the holy ones, and to those fearing Your Name, to the small and to the great, and to destroy those who are destroying the earth." **19** And the temple of God was opened in Heaven, and the Ark of His Covenant was seen in His temple, and there came lightnings, and voices, and thunders, and an earthquake, and great hail.

12 And a great sign was seen in the sky: a woman clothed with the sun, and the moon under her feet, and on her head a garland of twelve stars, **2** and having [a child] in [her] womb she cries out, travailing and being in pain to bring forth. **3** And there was seen another sign in the sky, and behold, a great fire-colored dragon, having seven heads and ten horns, and seven crowns on his heads, **4** and his tail draws the third of the stars of the sky, and he cast them to the earth; and the dragon stood before the woman who is about to bring forth, that when she may bring forth, he may devour her child; **5** and she brought forth a male son, who is about to rule all the nations with a rod of iron, and her child was snatched up to God and to His throne, **6** and the woman fled into the wilderness, where she has a place made ready from God, that there they may nourish her—one thousand, two hundred, sixty days. **7** And there came war in Heaven: Michael and his messengers warred against the dragon, and the dragon and his messengers warred, **8** and they did not prevail, nor was their place found anymore in Heaven; **9** and the great dragon was cast forth—the old serpent, who is called "Devil," and "Satan," who is leading the whole world astray—he was cast forth to the earth, and his messengers were cast forth with him. **10** And I heard a great voice saying in Heaven, "Now came the salvation, and the power, and the kingdom, of our God, and the authority of His Christ, because the accuser of our brothers was cast down, who is accusing them before our God day and night; **11** and they overcame him because of the blood of the Lamb, and because of the word of their testimony, and they did not love their life—to death; **12** because of this be glad, you heavens, and those who dwell in them; woe to those inhabiting the earth and the sea, because the Devil went down to you, having great wrath, having known that he has [a] short time." **13** And when the dragon saw that he was cast forth to the earth, he pursued the woman who brought forth the male, **14** and there were given to the woman two wings of the great eagle, that she may fly into the wilderness, to her place, where she is nourished a time, and times, and half a time, from the face of the serpent; **15** and the serpent cast forth out of his mouth water as a river after the woman, that he may cause her to be carried away by the river, **16** and the earth helped the woman, and the earth opened its mouth and swallowed up the river that the dragon cast forth out of his mouth; **17** and the dragon was angry against the woman, and went away to make war with the rest of her seed, those keeping the commands of God, and having the testimony of Jesus.

13 And I stood on the sand of the sea, and I saw a beast coming up out of the sea, having seven heads and ten horns, and ten crowns on its horns, and on its heads names of slander, **2** and the beast that I saw was like to a leopard, and its feet as of a bear, and its mouth as the mouth of a lion, and the dragon gave to it his power, and his throne, and great authority. **3** And I saw one of its heads as slain to death, and its deadly wound was healed, and all the earth wondered after the beast, **4** and they worshiped the dragon who gave authority to the beast, and they worshiped the beast, saying, "Who [is] like to the beast? Who is able to war with it?" **5** And there was given to it a mouth speaking great things, and slanders, and there was given to it authority to make war forty-two months, **6** and it opened its mouth for slander toward God, to slander His Name, and of His dwelling place, and of those who dwell in Heaven, **7** and there was given to it to make war with the holy ones, and to overcome them, and there was given to it authority over every tribe, and tongue, and nation. **8** And all who are dwelling on the earth will worship him, whose names have not been written in the Scroll of Life of the Lamb slain from the foundation of the world; **9** if anyone has an ear—let him hear: **10** if anyone [goes] into captivity, into captivity he goes; if anyone is to be killed with sword, it is necessary of him by sword to be killed; here is the endurance and the faith of the holy ones. **11** And I saw another beast coming up out of the earth, and it had two horns like a lamb, and it was speaking as a dragon, **12** and all the authority of the first beast does it do before it, and it makes the earth and those dwelling in it that they will worship the first beast, whose deadly wound was healed, **13** and it does great signs, that fire also it may make to come down from the sky to the earth before men, **14** and it leads astray those dwelling on the earth, because of the signs that were given it to do before the beast, saying to those dwelling on the earth to make an image to the beast that has the wound of the sword and lived, **15** and there was given to it to give a spirit to the image of the beast, that also the image of the beast may speak, and it may cause as many as will not worship the image of the beast, that they may be killed. **16** And it makes all, the small, and the great, and the rich, and the poor, and the freemen, and the servants, that it may give to them a mark on their right hand or on their foreheads, **17** and that no one may be able to buy, or to sell, except he who is having the mark, or the name of the beast, or the number of his name. **18** Here is the wisdom! He who is having the understanding, let him count the number of the beast, for it is the number of a man, and its number: six hundred sixty-six.

REVELATION

14 And I saw, and behold, a Lamb was standing on Mount Zion, and with Him one hundred forty-four thousand, having the Name of His Father written on their foreheads; **2** and I heard a voice out of Heaven, as a voice of many waters, and as a voice of great thunder, and I heard a voice of harpists harping with their harps, **3** and they sing, as it were, a new song before the throne, and before the four living creatures, and the elders, and no one was able to learn the song except the one hundred forty-four thousand who have been bought from the earth; **4** these are they who were not defiled with women, for they are virgin; these are they who are following the Lamb wherever He may go; these were bought from among men—a first-fruit to God and to the Lamb— **5** and in their mouth there was not found guile, for they are unblemished before the throne of God. **6** And I saw another messenger flying in midair, having continuous good news to proclaim to those dwelling on the earth, and to every nation, and tribe, and tongue, and people, **7** saying in a great voice, "Fear God, and give to Him glory, because the hour of His judgment came, and worship Him who made the sky, and the land, and sea, and fountains of waters." **8** And another messenger followed, saying, "Fallen, fallen is Babylon the great, because of the wine of the wrath of her whoredom she has given to all nations to drink." **9** And a third messenger followed them, saying in a great voice, "If anyone worships the beast and his image, and receives a mark on his forehead or on his hand, **10** he also will drink of the wine of the wrath of God that has been mingled unmixed in the cup of His anger, and he will be tormented in fire and brimstone before the holy messengers, and before the Lamb, **11** and the smoke of their torment goes up through ages of ages; and they have no rest day and night, who are worshiping the beast and his image, also if any receive the mark of his name. **12** Here is endurance of the holy ones; here [are] those keeping the commands of God, and the faith of Jesus." **13** And I heard a voice out of Heaven saying to me, "Write: Blessed are the dead who are dying in the LORD from this time!" "Yes," says the Spirit, "That they may rest from their labors—and their works follow them!" **14** And I saw, and behold, a white cloud, and on the cloud [One] sitting like [a] Son of Man, having on His head a golden garland, and in His hand a sharp sickle; **15** and another messenger came forth out of the temple crying in a great voice to Him who is sitting on the cloud, "Send forth Your sickle and reap, because the hour of reaping has come to You, because the harvest of the earth has been ripe"; **16** and He who is sitting on the cloud put forth His sickle on the earth, and the earth was reaped. **17** And another messenger came forth out of the temple that [is] in Heaven, having—he also—a sharp sickle, **18** and another messenger came forth out from the altar, having authority over the fire, and he called with a great cry to him having the sharp sickle, saying, "Send forth your sharp sickle, and gather the clusters of the vine of the earth, because her grapes have come to perfection"; **19** and the messenger put forth his sickle to the earth, and gathered the vine of the earth, and cast [it] into the great winepress of the wrath of God; **20** and the winepress was trodden outside of the city, and blood came forth out of the winepress—to the bridles of the horses, one thousand six hundred stadia.

15 And I saw another sign in the sky, great and wonderful: seven messengers having the seven last plagues, because in these the wrath of God was completed, **2** and I saw as a sea of glass mingled with fire, and those who gain the victory over the beast, and his image, and his mark, [and] the number of his name, standing by the sea of the glass, having harps of God, **3** and they sing the song of Moses, servant of God, and the song of the Lamb, saying, "Great and wonderful [are] Your works, O LORD God, the Almighty, righteous and true [are] Your ways, O King of holy ones! **4** Who may not fear You, O LORD, and glorify Your Name? Because You alone [are] holy, because all the nations will come and worship before You, because Your righteous acts were revealed." **5** And after these things I saw, and behold, the temple of the Dwelling Place of the Testimony was opened in Heaven; **6** and the seven messengers having the seven plagues came forth out of the temple, clothed in linen, pure and radiant, and girded around the breasts with golden girdles: **7** and one of the four living creatures gave to the seven messengers seven golden bowls, full of the wrath of

God, who is living through the ages of the ages; **8** and the temple was filled with smoke from the glory of God, and from His power, and no one was able to enter into the temple until the seven plagues of the seven messengers may be completed.

16 And I heard a great voice out of the temple saying to the seven messengers, "Go away, and pour out the bowls of the wrath of God into the earth"; **2** and the first went away, and poured out his bowl into the earth, and there came a sore—bad and grievous—to men, those having the mark of the beast, and those worshiping his image. **3** And the second messenger poured out his bowl into the sea, and it became blood as of [one] dead, and every living soul in the sea died. **4** And the third messenger poured out his bowl into the rivers, and into the fountains of the waters, and there came blood, **5** and I heard the messenger of the waters, saying, "Righteous, O LORD, are You, who is, and who was, [[and who will be,]] the Holy [One], because You judged these things, **6** because they poured out [the] blood of holy ones and prophets, and You gave to them blood to drink, for they are worthy"; **7** and I heard another out of the altar, saying, "Yes, LORD God, the Almighty, true and righteous [are] Your judgments." **8** And the fourth messenger poured out his bowl on the sun, and there was given to him to scorch men with fire, **9** and men were scorched with great heat, and they slandered the Name of God, who has authority over these plagues, and they did not convert—to give to Him glory. **10** And the fifth messenger poured out his bowl on the throne of the beast, and his kingdom became darkened, and they were gnawing their tongues from the pain, **11** and they slandered the God of Heaven, from their pains, and from their sores, and they did not convert from their works. **12** And the sixth messenger poured out his bowl on the great river, the Euphrates, and its water was dried up, that the way of the kings who are from the rising of the sun may be made ready; **13** and I saw [come] out of the mouth of the dragon, and out of the mouth of the beast, and out of the mouth of the false prophet, three unclean spirits like frogs— **14** for they are spirits of demons, doing signs—which go forth to the kings of the earth, and of the whole world, to bring them together to the battle of that great day of God the Almighty. **15** ("Behold, I come as a thief; blessed [is] he who is watching, and keeping his garments, that he may not walk naked, and they may see his unseemliness.") **16** And they brought them together to the place that is called in Hebrew Armageddon. **17** And the seventh messenger poured out his bowl on the air, and there came forth a great voice from the temple of Heaven, from the throne, saying, "It is done!" **18** And there came voices, and thunders, and lightnings; and a great earthquake came, such as has not come since men came on the earth, so mighty an earthquake—so great! **19** And it came—the great city—into three parts, and the cities of the nations fell, and Babylon the great was remembered before God, to give to her the cup of the wine of the wrath of His anger, **20** and every island fled away, and mountains were not found, **21** and great hail (as of talent weight) comes down out of the sky on men, and men slandered God because of the plague of the hail, because its plague is very great.

17 And there came one of the seven messengers, who were having the seven bowls, and he spoke with me, saying to me, "Come, I will show to you the judgment of the great whore, who is sitting on the many waters, **2** with whom the kings of the earth committed whoredom; and those inhabiting the earth were made drunk from the wine of her whoredom"; **3** and he carried me away to a wilderness in the Spirit, and I saw a woman sitting on a scarlet-colored beast, full of names of slander, having seven heads and ten horns, **4** and the woman was clothed with purple and scarlet-color, and gilded with gold, and precious stone, and pearls, having a golden cup in her hand full of abominations and uncleanness of her whoredom, **5** and on her forehead was a name written: "SECRET, BABYLON THE GREAT, THE MOTHER OF THE WHORES, AND THE ABOMINATIONS OF THE EARTH." **6** And I saw the woman drunken from the blood of the holy ones, and from the blood of the witnesses of Jesus, and I wondered—having seen her—with great wonder; **7** and the messenger said to me, "For this reason did you wonder? I will tell you the secret of the woman and of the beast that [is] carrying her, which has the seven heads and the ten

REVELATION

horns. **8** The beast that you saw: it was, and it is not, and it is about to come up out of the abyss, and to go away to destruction, and those dwelling on the earth will wonder, whose names have not been written on the Scroll of Life from the foundation of the world, beholding the beast that was, and is not, although it is. **9** Here [is] the mind that is having wisdom: the seven heads are seven mountains on which the woman sits, **10** and there are seven kings, the five fell, and the one is, the other did not yet come, and when he may come, it is necessary for him to remain a short time; **11** and the beast that was, and is not, he also is eighth, and he is out of the seven, and he goes away to destruction. **12** And the ten horns that you saw are ten kings who did not yet receive a kingdom, but receive authority as kings one hour with the beast; **13** these have one mind, and they will give over their own power and authority to the beast; **14** these will make war with the Lamb, and the Lamb will overcome them, because He is Lord of lords, and King of kings, and those with Him are called, and chosen, and steadfast." **15** And he says to me, "The waters that you saw, where the whore sits, are peoples, and multitudes, and nations, and tongues; **16** and the ten horns that you saw, and the beast, these will hate the whore, and will make her desolate and naked, and will eat her flesh, and will burn her in fire, **17** for God gave into their hearts to do His purpose, and to make one purpose, and to give their kingdom to the beast until the sayings of God may be fulfilled, **18** and the woman that you saw is the great city that is having reign over the kings of the earth."

18 And after these things I saw another messenger coming down out of Heaven, having great authority, and the earth was lightened from his glory, **2** and he cried in might [with] a great voice, saying, "Fallen, fallen is Babylon the great! And she became a habitation of demons, and a hold of every unclean spirit, and a hold of every unclean and hateful bird, **3** because all the nations have drunk of the wine of the wrath of her whoredom, and the kings of the earth committed whoredom with her, and merchants of the earth were made rich from the power of her indulgence." **4** And I heard another voice out of Heaven, saying, "Come forth out of her, My people, that you may not partake with her sins, and that you may not receive of her plagues, **5** because her sins have reached up to Heaven, and God remembered her unrighteousness. **6** Render to her as she also rendered to you, and double to her twofold according to her works; in the cup that she mingled mingle to her double. **7** As much as she glorified herself and indulged, so much torment and sorrow give to her, because in her heart she says, I sit [as] queen, and I am not a widow, and I will not see sorrow; **8** because of this, in one day, will come her plagues: death, and sorrow, and famine; and she will be utterly burned in fire, because strong [is] the LORD God who is judging her; **9** and the kings of the earth will weep over her and strike themselves for her, who committed whoredom and indulged with her, when they may see the smoke of her burning, **10** having stood from afar because of the fear of her torment, saying, Woe, woe, the great city! Babylon, the strong city! Because in one hour your judgment came. **11** And the merchants of the earth will weep and mourn over her, because no one buys their cargo anymore; **12** cargo of gold, and silver, and precious stone, and pearls, and fine linen, and purple, and silk, and scarlet, and all fragrant wood, and every vessel of ivory, and every vessel of most precious wood, and brass, and iron, and marble, **13** and cinnamon, and amomum, and incense, and ointment, and frankincense, and wine, and oil, and fine flour, and wheat, and cattle, and sheep, and of horses, and of chariots, and of bodies and souls of men. **14** And the fruits of the desire of your soul went away from you, and all things—the sumptuous and the radiant—went away from you, and no more at all may you find them. **15** The merchants of these things, who were made rich by her, will stand far off because of the fear of her torment, weeping, and mourning, **16** and saying, Woe, woe, the great city, that was clothed with fine linen, and purple, and scarlet, and gilded in gold, and precious stone, and pearls— **17** because in one hour so much riches were made desolate! And every shipmaster, and all the company on the ships, and sailors, and as many as work the sea, stood far off, **18** and were crying, seeing the smoke of her burning, saying, What [city is] like to the great city? **19** And they cast dust on their heads, and were crying out, weeping and mourning, saying, Woe, woe, the great city! In which were made rich all having ships in the sea, out of her costliness—for in one hour was she made desolate. **20** Be glad over her, O Heaven, and you holy apostles and prophets, because God judged your judgment of her!" **21** And one strong messenger took up a stone as a great millstone, and cast [it] into the sea, saying, "Thus with violence will Babylon be cast, the great city, and may not be found anymore at all; **22** and voice of harpists, and musicians, and pipers, and trumpeters, may not be heard at all in you anymore; and any craftsman of any craft may not be found at all in you anymore; and noise of a millstone may not be heard at all in you anymore; **23** and light of a lamp may not shine at all in you anymore; and voice of bridegroom and of bride may not be heard at all in you anymore; because your merchants were the great ones of the earth, because all the nations were led astray in your sorcery, **24** and in her blood of prophets and of holy ones was found, and of all those who have been slain on the earth."

19 And after these things I heard a great voice of a great multitude in Heaven, saying, "Hallelujah! The salvation, and the glory, and the power [belong] to the LORD our God; **2** because true and righteous [are] His judgments, because He judged the great whore who corrupted the earth in her whoredom, and He avenged the blood of His servants at her hand"; **3** and a second time they said, "Hallelujah"; and her smoke comes up through the ages of the ages! **4** And the twenty-four elders and the four living creatures fell down and they worshiped God who is sitting on the throne, saying, "Amen! Hallelujah!" **5** And a voice out of the throne came forth, saying, "Praise our God, all you His servants, and those fearing Him, both the small and the great"; **6** and I heard as the voice of a great multitude, and as the voice of many waters, and as the voice of mighty thunderings, saying, "Hallelujah! Because our Lord, the God, the Almighty, has reigned! **7** May we rejoice and exult, and give the glory to Him, because the marriage of the Lamb has come, and His wife has made herself ready; **8** and there was given to her that she may be clothed with fine linen, pure and radiant, for the fine linen is the righteous acts of the holy ones." **9** And he says to me, "Write: Blessed [are] they who have been called to the banquet of the marriage of the Lamb"; and he says to me, "These [are] the true words of God"; **10** and I fell before his feet to worship him, and he says to me, "Behold—No! I am your fellow servant, and of your brothers, those having the testimony of Jesus; worship God, for the testimony of Jesus is the spirit of the prophecy." **11** And I saw Heaven having been opened, and behold, a white horse, and He who is sitting on it is called Faithful and True, and in righteousness He judges and makes war, **12** and His eyes [are] as a flame of fire, and on His head [are] many crowns—having a Name written that no one has known, except Himself, **13** and He is clothed with a garment covered with blood, and His Name is called, The Word of God. **14** And the armies in Heaven were following Him on white horses, clothed in fine linen—white and pure; **15** and out of His mouth proceeds a sharp sword, that with it He may strike the nations, and He will rule them with a rod of iron, and He treads the press of the wine of the wrath and the anger of God the Almighty, **16** and He has on the garment and on His thigh the name written: "KING OF KINGS, AND LORD OF LORDS." **17** And I saw one messenger standing in the sun, and he cried [with] a great voice, saying to all the birds that are flying in midair, "Come and be gathered together to the banquet of the great God [[*or* the great banquet of God]], **18** that you may eat flesh of kings, and flesh of chiefs of thousands, and flesh of strong men, and flesh of horses, and of those sitting on them, and the flesh of all—freemen and servants—both small and great." **19** And I saw the beast, and the kings of the earth, and their armies, having been gathered together to make war with Him who is sitting on the horse, and with His army; **20** and the beast was taken, and with him the false prophet who did the signs before him, in which he led astray those who received the mark of the beast, and those who worshiped his image; the two were cast living into the lake of the fire that is burning with brimstone; **21** and the rest were killed with the sword of Him who is sitting on the horse, which is proceeding out of His mouth, and all the birds were filled with their flesh.

20 And I saw a messenger coming down out of Heaven, having the key of the abyss, and a great chain over his hand, **2** and he laid hold on the dragon, the ancient serpent, who is [the] Devil and Satan, and bound him one thousand years, **3** and he cast him into the abyss, and shut him up, and put a seal on him, that he may no longer lead the nations astray, until the one thousand years may be completed; and after these it is necessary for him to be loosed a short time. **4** And I saw thrones, and they [that] sat on them, and judgment was given to them, and the souls of those who have been beheaded because of the testimony of Jesus, and because of the word of God, and who did not worship the beast, nor his image, and did not receive the mark on their forehead and on their hand, and they lived and reigned with the Christ one thousand years; **5** and the rest of the dead did not live again until the one thousand years may be completed; this [is] the first resurrection. **6** Blessed and holy— he who is having part in the first resurrection; the second death has no authority over these, but they will be priests of God and of the Christ, and will reign with Him one thousand years. **7** And when the one thousand years may be completed, Satan will be loosed out of his prison, **8** and he will go forth to lead the nations astray, that are in the four corners of the earth—Gog and Magog—to gather them together to war, of whom the number—as the sand of the sea; **9** and they went up over the breadth of the land, and surrounded the camp of the holy ones, and the beloved city, and there came down fire from God out of Heaven, and devoured them; **10** and the Devil, who is leading them astray, was cast into the lake of fire and brimstone where the beast and the false prophet [are], and they will be tormented day and night through the ages of the ages. **11** And I saw a great white throne, and Him who is sitting on it, from whose face the earth and the sky fled away, and no place was found for them; **12** and I saw the dead, small and great, standing before God, and scrolls were opened, and another scroll was opened, which is that of the life, and the dead were judged out of the things written in the scrolls—according to their works; **13** and the sea gave up those dead in it, and death and Hades gave up the dead in them, and they were judged, each one according to their works; **14** and death and Hades were cast into the lake of the fire—this [is] the second death; **15** and if anyone was not found written in the Scroll of Life, he was cast into the lake of the fire.

21 And I saw a new heaven and a new earth, for the first heaven and the first earth passed away, and the sea is no more; **2** and I saw the holy city, New Jerusalem, coming down from God out of Heaven, made ready as a bride adorned for her husband; **3** and I heard a great voice out of Heaven, saying, "Behold, the dwelling place of God [is] with men, and He will dwell with them, and they will be His peoples, and God Himself will be with them [as] their God, **4** and God will wipe away every tear from their eyes, and there will be no more death, nor sorrow, nor crying, nor will there be anymore pain, because the first things passed away." **5** And He who is sitting on the throne said, "Behold, I make all things new"; and He says to me, "Write, because these words are true and steadfast"; **6** and He said to me, "It is done! I am the Alpha and the Omega, the Beginning and the End. To him who is thirsting, I will give of the fountain of the water of life freely. **7** The [one] who is overcoming will inherit all things, and I will be his God, and he will be My son. **8** But to fearful, and unsteadfast, and abominable, and murderers, and whoremongers, and sorcerers, and idolaters, and all the liars, their part [is] in the lake that is burning with fire and brimstone, which is the second death." **9** And one of the seven messengers, having the seven bowls that are full of the seven last plagues, came and spoke with me, saying, "Come, I will show you the bride, the wife of the Lamb," **10** and he carried me away in the Spirit to a mountain great and high, and showed me the great city, the holy Jerusalem, coming down out of Heaven from God, **11** having the glory of God, and her light—like a most precious stone, as a jasper stone clear as crystal, **12** also having a great and high wall, having twelve gates, and at the gates twelve messengers, and names written thereon, which are [those] of the twelve tribes of the sons of Israel— **13** at the east three gates, at the north three gates, at the south three gates, at the west three gates; **14** and the wall of the city had twelve foundations, and on them names of the twelve apostles of the Lamb. **15** And he who is speaking with me had a golden reed, that he may measure the city, and its gates, and its wall; **16** and the city lies square, and the length of it is as great as the breadth; and he measured the city with the reed—twelve thousand stadia; the length, and the breadth, and the height of it are equal. **17** And he measured its wall—one hundred forty-four cubits, the measure of a man, that is, of the messenger; **18** and the building of its wall was jasper, and the city [is] pure gold—like to pure glass. **19** And the foundations of the wall of the city have been adorned with every precious stone: the first foundation jasper, the second sapphire, the third chalcedony, the fourth emerald, **20** the fifth sardonyx, the sixth sardius, the seventh chrysolite, the eighth beryl, the ninth topaz, the tenth chrysoprase, the eleventh jacinth, the twelfth amethyst. **21** And the twelve gates [are] twelve pearls, each one of the gates respectively was of one pearl; and the street of the city [is] pure gold—as transparent glass. **22** And I did not see a temple in it, for the LORD God, the Almighty, and the Lamb, are its temple. **23** And the city has no need of the sun, nor of the moon, that they may shine in it; for the glory of God lightens it, and the lamp of it—the Lamb; **24** and the nations will walk by its light, and the kings of the earth bring their glory and honor into it, **25** and its gates will never be shut by day, for night will not be there; **26** and they will bring the glory and the honor of the nations into it; **27** and there may never enter into it anything defiling and doing abomination, and a lie, if not those written in the Lamb's Scroll of Life.

22 And he showed me [the] river of [the] water of life, radiant as crystal, going forth out of the throne of God and of the Lamb **2** in the midst of its street, and of the river on this side and on that—[the] Tree of Life, producing twelve fruits, yielding its fruit according to each month, and the leaves of the tree [are] for the healing of the nations; **3** and there will no longer be any curse, and the throne of God and of the Lamb will be in it, and His servants will serve Him, **4** and they will see His face, and His Name [is] on their foreheads, **5** and there will be no night there, and they have no need of [the] light of a lamp and of [the] light of [the] sun, because the LORD God gives them light, and they will reign through the ages of the ages. **6** And he said to me, "These words [are] steadfast and true, and the LORD God of the holy prophets sent His messenger to show to His servants the things that must come quickly. **7** Behold, I come quickly; blessed [is] he who is keeping the words of the prophecy of this scroll." **8** And I, John, am he who is seeing these things and hearing, and when I heard and beheld, I fell down to worship before the feet of the messenger who is showing me these things; **9** and he says to me, "Behold—No! For I am your fellow servant, and of your brothers the prophets, and of those keeping the words of this scroll; worship God." **10** And He says to me, "You may not seal the words of the prophecy of this scroll, because the time is near. **11** The [one] being unrighteous—let him be unrighteous still; and the filthy—let him be filthy still; and the righteous—let him do righteousness still; and the holy—let him be holy still. **12** Behold, I come quickly, and My reward [is] with Me, to render to each as his work will be; **13** I am the Alpha and the Omega—the Beginning and End—the First and the Last. **14** Blessed are those washing their robes that the authority will be theirs to the Tree of Life, and they may enter into the city by the gates; **15** and outside [are] the dogs, and the sorcerers, and the whoremongers, and the murderers, and the idolaters, and everyone cherishing and doing falsehood. **16** I, Jesus, sent My messenger to testify to you these things concerning the assemblies; I am the root and the offspring of David, the radiant morning star! **17** And the Spirit and the bride say, Come! And he who is hearing—let him say, Come! And he who is thirsting—let him come; and he who is willing—let him take the water of life freely. **18** For I testify to everyone hearing the words of the prophecy of this scroll, if anyone may add to these, God will add to him the plagues that have been written in this scroll, **19** and if anyone may take away from the words of the scroll of this prophecy, God will take away his part from the Scroll of Life, and out of the holy city, and the things that have been written in this scroll." **20** The [One] testifying [to]

REVELATION

these things says, "Yes, I come quickly!" Amen. Come, Lord Jesus! **21** The grace of our Lord Jesus Christ [is] with all [[the holy ones. Amen.]]

~ THE END OF THE NEW TESTAMENT ~

COVENANT OF THE CCC

WE BELIEVE in One God, revealed to the world as YHWH of Israel,
Uncreated, self-existent, eternal, all-powerful, and unchanging.
He knows all things and there is nowhere where He is not.
He is good, His word is inerrant, and His nature is love.

WE BELIEVE God subsists as the mutual indwelling of three persons:
The Father, the Son, and the Holy Spirit, in eternal communion.
God the Son and God the Holy Spirit come from God the Father,
And throughout eternity they have always existed with the Father.

WE BELIEVE God created time, space, matter, and all things,
Accomplishing His initial act of creation in only six days.
On the sixth day God created Man in His own image out of dust,
Adam the first male and Eve the first female.

WE BELIEVE God said the man should be joined to his wife,
And in so doing the two would become one flesh in marriage.
In diversity He created the marital union sacred, monogamous,
And dissoluble only by death or unfaithfulness.

WE BELIEVE God gave Man the choice of obedience or rebellion,
And Adam and Eve willfully rebelled by eating the forbidden fruit,
Which came from the Tree of the Knowledge of Good and Evil.
They suffered spiritual death and passed their sin nature on to us.

WE BELIEVE that God justly judged the world with a flood,
Sparing Noah and his family through whom came the nations.
And from Noah's son Shem came Abraham, Isaac, and Jacob,
And from Jacob the twelve tribes of Israel and the prophets.

WE BELIEVE that in the fullness of time God gave us His Son,
Born under the law to redeem those condemned by the law.
He was born in the town of Bethlehem to a virgin named Mary,
And in accordance with God's command was named Jesus.

WE BELIEVE Jesus was chosen before the creation of the world,
To live a sinless human life in perfect obedience to the Father,
That He might die a substitutionary death in place of sinners,
Giving forgiveness of sins and eternal life to all who trust in Him.

WE BELIEVE Jesus freely gave His life in obedience to the Father,
And at the order of Pontius Pilate was flogged and crucified.
At the ninth hour He declared His purpose in death was finished,
And He died and was buried in the tomb of Joseph of Arimathea.

WE BELIEVE that death had no power over God's perfect Son,
And on the third day He conquered death by rising to life again.
This was literal, physical, and attested to by over 500 witnesses,
And is the event that gives power and validation to our faith.

WE BELIEVE men are only reconciled to God through Jesus Christ,
And receive salvation by grace through faith apart from works.
By the Spirit all believers are baptized into one body, the Church.
Christians baptize, share communion, and love one another.

WE BELIEVE the Church is a universal priesthood of believers.
Membership is not obtained by belonging to a denomination,
But is received by trusting in Jesus for the forgiveness of sins.
The Church awaits Jesus' soon return when He will call us home.

CONVICTIONS OF THE CCC

1. THERE IS ONE GOD WHO IS ETERNAL, SELF-EXISTENT, ALL-POWERFUL, ALL-KNOWING, EVERYWHERE-PRESENT, COMPLETELY GOOD, AND NEVER CHANGING. GOD IS PERFECT IN MORAL CHARACTER AND HIS NATURE IS LOVE. GOD ALONE CAN DECLARE WHETHER CONDUCT IS RIGHT OR WRONG.

Scripture References: Deuteronomy 6:4; Isaiah 44:8; Psalm 90:2; Isaiah 40:28; Exodus 3:14; Revelation 19:6; Psalm 147:5; 1 John 3:20; Psalm 139:7–8; Jeremiah 23:24; Psalm 119:68; James 1:17; Hebrews 13:8; 1 John 4:8; Judges 21:25; Isaiah 45:19

---

2. GOD SUBSISTS ETERNALLY IN THREE PERSONS: THE FATHER, THE SON, AND THE HOLY SPIRIT. THESE THREE ARE NEITHER PARTS NOR MODES.

Scripture References: Matthew 28:19; Luke 1:35; 3:21–22; John 1:1–2; 10:30; 14:16; 2 Corinthians 13:14; 1 Peter 1:2; see also Genesis 1:26; 3:22; 11:7

---

3. THE BIBLE IS A COMPILATION OF GOD'S WORDS AND IN ITS ORIGINAL HEBREW, GREEK, AND ARAMAIC FORM IS INERRANT AND SUFFICIENT IN ITSELF FOR TEACHING CHRISTIAN BELIEF AND PRACTICE. IT SHOULD BE INTERPRETED LITERALLY, HISTORICALLY, AND AT FACE VALUE UNLESS THE TEXT ITSELF ALLOWS FOR A DIFFERENT INTERPRETATION IN A SPECIFIC PASSAGE.

Scripture References: Exodus 20:11; Matthew 5:18; 19:4–6; 24:37–39; John 10:35; Acts 1:16; Romans 15:4; 2 Timothy 3:16; 2 Peter 1:20–21; 3:15–16; 2 Thessalonians 2:14–15; Revelation 22:18–19; see also Genesis 41:25–27; Matthew 13:18–23; 13:36–43; Revelation 1:20

---

4. MANKIND WAS GIVEN THE FREE CHOICE TO OBEY GOD OR REBEL AGAINST HIM IN THE GARDEN OF EDEN AND FREELY CHOSE TO REBEL BY EATING THE FORBIDDEN FRUIT FROM THE TREE OF THE KNOWLEDGE OF GOOD AND EVIL. THIS CHOICE BROUGHT DEATH, SEPARATION FROM GOD, AND A SINFUL NATURE TO THE ENTIRE HUMAN RACE.

Scripture References: Genesis 2:16–17; 3; 6:5; Isaiah 59:1–2; Romans 3:23; 5:12–18; 6:23; 1 Corinthians 15:22

5. GOD PLANNED IN ADVANCE TO SEND HIS SON INTO THE WORLD TO DIE FOR THE SINS OF MANKIND. THIS PLAN INCLUDED THE COVENANT OF BLESSING WITH ABRAHAM AND THE INSTITUTION OF THE NATION OF ISRAEL AND WAS FORESHADOWED BY THE SYSTEM OF ATONING SACRIFICES IN THE LEVITICAL LAW.

Scripture References: Genesis 22:17–18; Isaiah 53; Jeremiah 1:5; Luke 24:27; John 5:39; Acts 8:30–35; Colossians 2:17; Hebrews 10:1–23; Revelation 13:8

---

6. GOD BECAME MAN IN THE PERSON OF JESUS CHRIST. JESUS LIVED A SINLESS AND MORALLY PERFECT LIFE. HE WAS CRUCIFIED AT THE HANDS OF THE ROMANS AND THROUGH DEATH HE ATONED FOR THE SINS OF MANKIND. HE WAS BURIED AND ON THE THIRD DAY ROSE PHYSICALLY FROM THE DEAD, CONQUERING DEATH AND SIN. SALVATION IS FOUND IN CHRIST ALONE BY GRACE ALONE THROUGH FAITH ALONE AND NOT BY WORKS.

Scripture References: Isaiah 7:14; 9:6; Matthew 1:22–23; Luke 1:35; John 1:14; Philippians 2:6–8; Colossians 1:15; 1 John 4:2; Isaiah 53:9; John 19:4; 2 Corinthians 5:21; 1 Peter 1:18–19; 2:22; Hebrews 4:15; 1 John 3:5; Mark 15:43–47; Matthew 28:1–15; Romans 6:4; 8:11; 1 Corinthians 15:1–32; 1 Peter 1:3; Ephesians 2:8–9

---

7. JESUS PROMISED THAT IN ACCORDANCE WITH THE SCRIPTURES HE WOULD PHYSICALLY RETURN TO EARTH TO RESCUE HIS CHURCH, PUT AN END TO SIN, AND REIGN AS KING OVER ISRAEL AND THE WHOLE EARTH. BY HIM THE LIVING AND THE DEAD WILL BE JUDGED, SOME INHERITING ETERNAL LIFE AND OTHERS RECEIVING ETERNAL PUNISHMENT. CHRISTIANS MUST BE WATCHFUL AND READY FOR THESE EVENTS.

Scripture References: Psalms 72:8–11; Daniel 2:44; 7:13–14; Ezekiel 33:1–6; Zechariah 14:1–9; Matthew 16:27; 24:37–44; 25:1–13, 46; Luke 12:37–40; 17:28–30; 18:8; 21:34–36; John 5:22; 14:3; Romans 2:16; 1 Corinthians 15:52; 1 Thessalonians 4:13–18; Revelation 1:7; 11:15; 20:4–6

POSITIONS OF THE CCC

While agreement with the **Covenant** and **Convictions** is all that is necessary for fellowship, the CCC maintains immutable, biblically-defined positions on moral issues regardless of what an individual member may believe or an associated denomination may teach. All believers and associated denominations are strongly exhorted to hold fast to these positions regardless of familial, cultural, or political pressure, recognizing that believing in and practicing biblical morality is strong evidence of one's saving faith.

Abortion is without question the murder of a child made in God's image. It should not be permitted even in the case of rape or incest as the child is innocent of any perpetrator's crime. The commission of the terrible evil of rape or incest can never justify the terrible evil of murder. In exceptional cases a mother's life may be jeopardized by pregnancy and only in this exceptional case does the CCC not take an absolute position. However, the mark of a Christian is love and sacrifice and the exemplary mother will put her child's life before her own, trusting that God will be faithful in the midst of tragic circumstances.

Adultery is intrinsically evil and never permissible under any circumstances, not only the physical act of adultery (Ex. 20:14), but also adulterous thoughts (Mt. 5:27–28).

Alcohol consumption is permissible and is in fact encouraged in some Scriptures (1 Tim. 5:23; Eccl. 9:7), but moderation is necessary. Intoxication and drunkenness are not permissible (Eph. 5:18; 1 Cor. 6:10). The Christian should never drink so much that he or she loses cognitive control and the ability to maintain a Christlike demeanor (Prov. 20:1; 23:29–35).

Anti-Semitism, a form of racism, should never be found in the thoughts, words, writings, or actions of a believer. Gentile believers have not replaced Jewish believers and in fact salvation has come from the Jews. The Apostle Paul likens the entirety of the people of God to an olive tree, which is Israel. Unbelieving Jews have been cut off from the tree and believing Gentiles have been grafted in (Rom. 11:17–24), but the roots of the tree remain Jewish through Abraham, Isaac, Jacob, and the King of the Jews—Jesus. In fact, the Bible promises that one day the Jews will return to God and all Israel will be saved (Rom. 11:25–28; Isa. 45:17; Jer. 31:1). God gave to the descendants of Abraham through Isaac and Jacob a specific area of land that they still have yet to take full possession of according to the promise. Since God is the ultimate sovereign of the earth and His word is true and the land deed still stands, Christians cannot support efforts such as the two-state solution. The Bible proclaims that judgment will befall those who divide God's covenant land (Jl. 3:1–2).

Contraception is not mentioned in Scripture except in the case of Onan who sinned by preventing his wife from becoming pregnant in order to withhold from her dead husband an heir (Gen. 38:8–10). For this reason only contraception that may result in the death of an embryo or done against the will of one's spouse is forbidden. Christians should be wise about this and research diligently before engaging in intercourse with one's spouse. Drugs such as Plan B are never permissible, but even typical hormonal contraception drugs may result in abortion and their use is thus discouraged. Natural family planning is encouraged and in all cases the husband and wife should be one in heart and mind.

Divorce is inherently evil (Mk. 10:11–12), except in the case of marital unfaithfulness (Mt. 5:32). However, even in the case of adultery it is exemplary and most commendable to extend grace and forgiveness and ultimately reconcile with one's spouse recognizing that Christ died for us while we were yet sinners (Rom. 5:8) and God has reconciled us by the death of His Son (Rom. 5:10).

Embryonic stem cell research is never permissible because the embryos are in fact children in their earliest stage of development and therefore those who destroy embryos are murdering children made in the image of God. The Bible is clear that human life begins in the womb (Job 31:15; Ps. 22:10; 139:13; Jer. 1:5; Ex. 21:22–23) and science is clear that an organism's life begins at conception.

Eugenics in most forms should be understood as evil—especially historic eugenics programs that aimed at eradicating minority populations, killing the mentally handicapped, and murdering the terminally ill. Eugenics continues today in many forms including sex-selective abortions, minority-focused placement of abortion facilities, abortion of babies with trisomy disorders, and many instances of euthanasia. These are all intrinsically evil and Christians should themselves avoid these things while preaching forcefully against them.

Euthanasia, which is the intentional killing of a man or woman by both the perpetrator and the one being killed, is unquestionably murder and must not be committed or advocated by any believer.

Fornication, which is sexual activity outside of marriage, is always sinful (Mt. 15:19; 1 Cor. 6:9). God created sex to be enjoyed within the boundaries of marriage and within those boundaries there is great freedom for husband and wife. God created sex for building unity between husband and wife (Gen. 2:24; Mk. 10:8), for pleasure (1 Cor. 7:3–9; Prov. 5:18–19; Song 4:1–16), and for producing offspring (Gen. 1:28; 9:7; Mal. 2:15) and it is only in the context of marriage that these three purposes find their ultimate fulfillment. Men and women in a romantic relationship should not cohabitate before marriage, so that they avoid fornication and the appearance of evil (1 Thess. 5:22).

Gender roles are biblical and must be upheld in the Christian community. Men and women are equal before God in regards to intrinsic value and salvation (Gen. 1:27; Gal. 3:28), but nevertheless have been given by God specific callings. The man is the head of his family—not as a coercive force, but as a servant leader (1 Cor. 11:3). The man is called by God to protect and manage his family well (1 Tim. 3:4), love his wife, and even lay his life down for her (Eph. 5:25). In regards to church leadership, men are called to exercise authority over the congregation, both in teaching to the collective assembly (1 Cor. 14:34–35) and in shepherding (1 Tim. 2:8–3:13). Women are called to respect their husbands out of willful humility (1 Pet. 3:1) and to help and encourage them (Gen. 2:18). In the Christian community women are uniquely called to teach and disciple other women (Tit. 2:3–5).

Genetic manipulation of plants and animals without combining genes from different species is permissible although the Bible does not appear to speak to this issue. Wisdom should be exercised in regards to this issue. However, the creation of hybrid species is unadvisable since God created plants and animals after their own kind (Gen. 1:11, 24). The creation of human/animal hybrids, three-parent babies, or babies resulting from the genetic material of two men or two women are intrinsically evil acts and Christian geneticists should seriously and prayerfully consider the spiritual implications of these creations.

Homosexuality is repeatedly condemned in the Bible as a sin and an abomination (1 Tim. 1:9–10; 1 Cor. 6:9–10; Lev. 18:22; 20:13), as well as unnatural (Rom. 1:26–28). God created sexuality for the purpose of intimacy and pleasure between a husband and wife and ultimately for bringing children into the world. Christians who struggle with homosexuality should flee temptation by any means necessary and should not define themselves by their struggle (1 Cor. 6:11).

Homosexual marriage is intrinsically evil for two reasons: first, because homosexual acts are sinful and unnatural, and second, because it is diametrically opposed to God's design for marriage, which is repeatedly defined in the Bible as the union of one man and one woman (Gen. 2:24; Mt. 19:5; Mk. 10:7; Eph. 5:31).

In Vitro Fertilization is not permissible for the same reason embryonic stem cell research is not permissible: embryos are necessarily destroyed thus the act of murder is committed.

Marrying unbelievers is not permissible for the committed Christian (2 Cor. 6:14), though having already been married before coming to faith is a common occurrence. In such a case the believer must remain committed to their unbelieving spouse and through love and faithfulness attempt to win them over with the Gospel (1 Cor. 7:12–16; 1 Pet. 3:1).

Media must be monitored and controlled in the Christian life. There is no justification, artistic or otherwise, for Christians to watch or listen to sinful things for the purpose of entertainment. There is much media a believer can enjoy, but that which is full of cursing, wonton violence, or sexuality is never permissible. The martyr Telemachus stands as an eternal symbol of this truth.

Narcotic use for the express purpose of treating an injury or disease is permissible, but narcotic use for the purpose of intoxication is a great and destructive evil to oneself, to one's family, and to one's society. There is evidence that drug intoxication is partly what was intended when the Bible speaks of the sin of sorcery.

Pornography is never permissible in any form as it is a form of adultery, or in the case of the unmarried, fornication. Pornography also promotes the objectification and abuse of women and children, is by some measures more addictive than heroine, causes permanent emotional and physical desensitization, and even induces early puberty in children exposed from a young age.

Racism is not in accord with the character of Christ who has made all believers one (Gal. 3:28; Rom. 3:29) for God does not show partiality (Acts 10:34; Rom. 2:11). Believers must not favor the rich over the poor (Jas. 2:1–9), but must show equal favor to all in regards to wealth, station, fame, or race. However, culture has greatly twisted and abused the word *racism* by extending it to include areas where believers in fact should lovingly discriminate between right and wrong: regarding religion, culture, and sinful behaviors.

Slavery, including and especially sexual slavery and trafficking, is never tolerable. Modern slavery differs greatly from biblical indentured servitude, which in certain times and cultures was lawful, in that modern slavery is illegal, always abusive, and routinely violent and coercive. With more people enslaved today than at any time in history, Christians should advocate zealously for their freedom and protection.

Speech should be Christlike in every way and "seasoned with salt" (Col. 4:6). Lies, curses, crude joking, and malicious gossip should never proceed from the mouth of a believer (Mt. 12:36; Prov. 19:5; Tit. 3:2; Eph. 5:4; 1 Tim. 5:13).

Theft is an obvious and unquestionable sin and is not dependent on circumstance (Ex. 20:15). The poor may not steal from the rich even though the rich have more and the poor have less. Instead, the believer struggling with poverty should work diligently (2 Thess. 3:10), trusting in God to provide (Mt. 6:25–34), and making his or her needs known openly to the Christian community (Acts 2:44–45). Believers should not take anything unlawfully, including intellectual property, music, or media. Believers selling products or services that they know are scams or falsely advertised are committing theft as well as lying and should cease immediately (Prov. 11:1; 20:23), returning the money that was stolen.

Transgenderism is both sinful and a great deceit. Sinful in that it defies God's created order of male and female and deceitful in that it convinces a person that they can be something that they are not nor could ever be. Christians must refer to a man in masculine terms and a female in feminine terms regardless of how that person may define himself—even if this results in physical, emotional, or legal consequences for the believer. Men should strive for masculinity and women for femininity (1 Cor. 6:9; 16:13), fully embracing God's design.

ABOUT THE BIBLE

The Bible is a written record of God's revelations to mankind. As originally transcribed by the Spirit-led men who recorded these revelations, it is completely inerrant—a perfect record of history, science, and spiritual truth. The theme of the Bible regards the fall of human beings into spiritual death in the Garden of Eden and God's plan to redeem them through a substitutionary sacrifice. This promised "Seed," born of woman, would crush the head of the serpent—the Devil—and free those who trust in God from death and the penalty and power of sin. In the Hebrew Bible, which Christians call the *Old Testament*, the Seed is prophesied to be the Messiah, or "Anointed One" of God, who would inherit the throne of His ancestor David and save believers from their sins. In the Greek portion of the Bible, called the *New Testament*, the Messiah is revealed to be God's only begotten Son, the Lord Jesus Christ. Jesus the Messiah lived a sinless life and took upon Himself the sins of all on the Cross. He was crucified, buried in a tomb, and on the third day He came back to life. Hundreds of His disciples witnessed Him risen from the dead and many went on to give their lives in martyrdom, testifying to the truth of forgiveness of sins in Christ alone, and the promise that all who trust in Him will be resurrected to inherit eternal life in union with God. In accordance with the Scriptures, the Lord Jesus will return to earth one day to restore the Kingdom to Israel and to reign over all the nations of the world. Preceding this event, believers are promised to be transformed into immortal bodies, being taken to Heaven to escape the coming wrath.

Languages of the Bible:	Hebrew, Aramaic, and Greek	Most of the Old Testament was originally composed in Hebrew, although some scholars argue a nearly equal portion was composed in Aramaic. At minimum, large portions of Daniel and Ezra were written in Aramaic. It is thought that all of the New Testament was written in Greek with strong Hebrew and Aramaic influences.
Date of composition:	Circa 15th century BC through the end of the 1st century AD	It is traditionally thought that Moses transcribed the first five books, called the *Torah* or *Pentateuch*. The Apostle John is believed to be the author of some of the latest books of the New Testament, including the Gospel of John and Revelation, which were written toward the end of the 1st century.
Number of books:	66	There have been varying schools of thought as to what constitutes the full canon of Scripture, but among Christian scholars there is widespread consensus that the 66 books found in most versions constitute the unquestionable Protocanon. Other books, called the Deuterocanon, are sometimes included.

The Covenant Christian Coalition is an international, evangelical, post-denominational coalition of churches still faithful to Christ and the Gospel.

You can learn more at www.ccc.one.

SOLA FIDE · SOLA GRATIA · SOLUS CHRISTUS · SOLA SCRIPTURA · SOLI DEO GLORIA

www.ingramcontent.com/pod-product-compliance
Lightning Source LLC
Chambersburg PA
CBHW031353160426
42811CB00092B/105